I0820889

AMERICA'S
TEST KITCHEN

# ALSO BY AMERICA'S TEST KITCHEN

Umma
When Southern Women Cook
Food Gifts
America's Test Kitchen 25th Anniversary Cookbook
A Very Chinese Cookbook
Boards
Gatherings

The Sheet Pan
The Skillet
Cook It in Your Dutch Oven
Cook It in Cast Iron
Ultimate Air Fryer Perfection
Kitchen Gear

Baking for Two
Everyday Bread
The Perfect Cookie
The Perfect Pie
The Perfect Cake
The Cook's Illustrated Baking Book

The Science of Good Cooking
Cook's Science
The New Cooking School Cookbook: Fundamentals
The New Cooking School Cookbook:
Advanced Fundamentals

Mostly Meatless
Vegan for Everybody
Vegan Cooking for Two
Cooking with Plant-Based Meat
Vegetables Illustrated
How Can It Be Gluten Free Cookbook Collection

The Complete Plant-Based Cookbook
The Complete Beans and Grains Cookbook
The Complete Mediterranean Cookbook
The Complete Cooking for Two Cookbook
The Complete Diabetes Cookbook
The Complete Vegetarian Cookbook
The Complete One Pot
The Complete Autumn and Winter Cookbook
The Complete Summer Cookbook
The Complete Modern Pantry
The Complete Salad Cookbook

The Complete Cook's Country TV Show Cookbook

For a full listing of all our books:
CooksIllustrated.com
AmericasTestKitchen.com

# PRAISE FOR AMERICA'S TEST KITCHEN TITLES

A Best Cookbook of 2024

*LA TIMES* ON *WHEN SOUTHERN WOMEN COOK*

"This 'very' Chinese cookbook from a father-son duo is a keeper. The book—ATK's first devoted to Chinese cooking—proves that you can teach and entertain in the same volume . . . All in all, it's one of the most charming works I've seen in years, and I already want to get a second copy."

*WASHINGTON POST* ON *A VERY CHINESE COOKBOOK*

"An exhaustive but approachable primer for those looking for a 'flexible' diet. Chock-full of tips, you can dive into the science of plant-based cooking or just sit back and enjoy the 500 recipes."

*MINNEAPOLIS STAR TRIBUNE* ON *THE COMPLETE PLANT-BASED COOKBOOK*

"Here are the words just about any vegan would be happy to read: 'Why This Recipe Works.' Fans of America's Test Kitchen are used to seeing the phrase, and now it applies to the growing collection of plant-based creations in *Vegan for Everybody*."

*WASHINGTON POST* ON *VEGAN FOR EVERYBODY*

"This comprehensive guide is packed with delicious recipes and fun menu ideas but its unique draw is the personal narrative and knowledge-sharing of each ATK chef, which will make this a hit."

*BOOKLIST* ON *GATHERINGS*

"True to its name, this smart and endlessly enlightening cookbook is about as definitive as it's possible to get in the modern vegetarian realm."

*MEN'S JOURNAL* ON *THE COMPLETE VEGETARIAN COOKBOOK*

"A mood board for one's food board is served up in this excellent guide . . . This has instant classic written all over it."

*PUBLISHERS WEEKLY* (STARRED REVIEW) ON *BOARDS: STYLISH SPREADS FOR CASUAL GATHERINGS*

"Reassuringly hefty and comprehensive, *The Complete Autumn and Winter Cookbook* by America's Test Kitchen has you covered with a seemingly endless array of seasonal fare . . . This overstuffed compendium is guaranteed to warm you from the inside out."

NPR ON *THE COMPLETE AUTUMN AND WINTER COOKBOOK*

"If you're one of the 30 million Americans with diabetes, *The Complete Diabetes Cookbook* by America's Test Kitchen belongs on your kitchen shelf."

PARADE.COM ON *THE COMPLETE DIABETES COOKBOOK*

"Another flawless entry in the America's Test Kitchen canon, *Bowls* guides readers of all culinary skill levels in composing one-bowl meals from a variety of cuisines."

BUZZFEED BOOKS ON *BOWLS*

"*The Perfect Cookie* . . . is, in a word, perfect. This is an important and substantial cookbook . . . If you love cookies, but have been a tad shy to bake on your own, all your fears will be dissipated. This is one book you can use for years with magnificently happy results."

HUFFPOST ON *THE PERFECT COOKIE*

"The book offers an impressive education for curious cake makers, new and experienced alike. A summation of 25 years of cake making at ATK, there are cakes for every taste."

*WALL STREET JOURNAL* ON *THE PERFECT CAKE*

"The go-to gift book for newlyweds, small families, or empty nesters."

*ORLANDO SENTINEL* ON *THE COMPLETE COOKING FOR TWO COOKBOOK*

"*Five-Ingredient Dinners* is as close to a sure thing to an easy meal as you'll find . . . If you want to get cooking, cut down on takeout, and deliver a ton of flavor, you can't lose with these recipes."

*PROVIDENCE JOURNAL* ON *FIVE-INGREDIENT DINNERS*

Domino
AMERICA'S
TEST KITCHEN

TEST KITCHEN

AMERICA'S
TEST KITCHEN

# THE COMPLETE AMERICA'S TEST KITCHEN TV SHOW COOKBOOK 2001–2026

AMERICA'S TEST KITCHEN

AMERICA'S TEST KITCHEN
21 Drydock Avenue, Boston, MA 02210

THE COMPLETE AMERICA'S TEST KITCHEN TV SHOW COOKBOOK:
Every recipe and product rating from the most-watched cooking show on public TV

Revised Edition

ISBN: 978-1-954210-46-2
ISSN: 2162-6944

Printed in China

10 9 8 7 6 5 4

Distributed by: Penguin Random House Publisher Services, tel: 800-733-3000

EDITORIAL DIRECTOR, BOOKS: Adam Kowit
EXECUTIVE MANAGING EDITOR: Debra Hudak
CONTRIBUTING EDITOR: Elizabeth Carduff
ASSISTANT EDITOR: Julia Arwine
EDITORIAL SUPPORT: Amelia Freidline
DESIGN DIRECTOR: Lindsey Timko Chandler
ART DIRECTOR: Katie Barranger
DESIGNER: Jen Kanavos Hoffman
PHOTOGRAPHY DIRECTOR: Julie Bozzo Cote
SENIOR PHOTOGRAPHY PRODUCER: Meredith Mulcahy
SENIOR STAFF PHOTOGRAPHERS: Steve Klise and Daniel J. van Ackere
STAFF PHOTOGRAPHER: Kritsada Panichgul
ADDITIONAL PHOTOGRAPHY: Beth Fuller, Joseph Keller, and Carl Tremblay
FOOD STYLING: Sheila Jarnes, Catrine Kelty, Chantal Lambeth, Kendra McKnight, Ashley Moore, Marie Piraino,
Mary Jane Sawyer, Elle Simone Scott, Kendra Smith, and Sally Staub
PROJECT MANAGER, BOOKS: Kelly Gauthier
SENIOR PRINT PRODUCTION SPECIALIST: Lauren Robbins
PRODUCTION AND IMAGING COORDINATOR: Amanda Yong
PRODUCTION AND IMAGING SPECIALIST: Tricia Neumyer
PRODUCTION AND IMAGING ASSISTANT: Chloe Petraske
COPYEDITOR: Cheryl Redmond
PROOFREADER: Vicki Rowland
INDEXER: Elizabeth Parson

CHIEF EXECUTIVE OFFICER: Dan Suratt
CHIEF CONTENT OFFICER: Dan Souza
SENIOR CONTENT ADVISER: Jack Bishop
EXECUTIVE EDITORIAL DIRECTORS: Julia Collin Davison and Bridget Lancaster
SENIOR DIRECTOR, BOOK SALES: Emily Logan

SUPPORT FOR THE AMERICA'S TEST KITCHEN TELEVISION SERIES HAS BEEN PROVIDED BY OUR SPONSORS:

AMERICAN CRUISE LINES

Breville

PLUGRÀ
PREMIUM EUROPEAN STYLE

# Contents

# WELCOME TO AMERICA'S TEST KITCHEN

This book has been tested, written, and edited by the folks at America's Test Kitchen, where curious cooks become confident cooks. Located in Boston's Seaport District in the historic Innovation and Design Building, it features 15,000 square feet of kitchen space including multiple photography and video studios. It is the home of *Cook's Illustrated* magazine and *Cook's Country* magazine and is the workday destination for more than 60 test cooks, editors, and cookware specialists. Our mission is to empower and inspire confidence, community, and creativity in the kitchen.

Our television show captivates culinary enthusiasts with our unique, scientific approach to cooking. We showcase the best recipes developed in the test kitchen alongside our most exhaustive equipment tests and our most interesting food tastings from the past year.

Julia Collin Davison and Bridget Lancaster co-host the show and ask the questions you might ask. It's the job of our chefs, Sam Block, Keith Dresser, Joe Gitter, Aran Goyoaga, Becky Hays, Alex Heugel, Antoinette Johnson, Lan Lam, Vallery Lomas, Erin McMurrer, Ben Mims, Elle Simone Scott, Nik Sharma, Dan Souza, Erica Turner, and Maggie Zhu to demonstrate our recipes. The chefs show Julia and Bridget what works and what doesn't, and explain why. In the process, they discuss (and show you) the best examples from our development process, as well as the worst.

Adam Ried, Lisa McManus, and Hannah Crowley, our equipment experts, share highlights from our rigorous testing process in the Equipment and Gear Heads segments. They reveal their recommended tools and offer helpful tips on how best to use and care for your equipment. Jack Bishop is our ingredient expert and shares his advice on how to shop for, store, and get the most out of your ingredients. Dan Souza explains the science behind certain ingredients and recipes, and Lan Lam delves into everyday kitchen techniques.

Although just 22 cooks and editors appear on the television show, nearly 100 others work behind the scenes. Executive Producer Kaitlin Keleher conceived and developed each episode with help from Supervising Producer Caroline Rickert, Senior Producer Alex Curran-Cardarelli, Associate Producer Angelica Quintanilla, and Director of Production Diane Knox. Special thanks to Director Herb Sevush and Director of Photography Dan Anderson.

Along with the on-air crew, Director of Culinary Production Erin McMurrer, Culinary Producer Alli Berkey, and Managing

Culinary Producer Meri Lesogor helped plan and organize the 26 television episodes filmed in September 2024 and May 2025 and ran the "back kitchen," where all the food that appeared on camera originated. Culinary Production Coordinator Heather Tolmie supported these efforts. Chase Brightwell, Sawyer Phillips, Valerie Sizhe Li, Sarah Sandler, and Crispin Lopez organized the ingredients and equipment segments. Additional editorial support came from Steve Dunn and Andrea Geary.

Senior Science Editor Paul Adams researched the science behind the recipes and wrote the science animations. Additional support was provided by our Production and Equipment Coordinator Mitchell Farias.

During filming, Assistant Culinary Producers Mel Velasco and Brooke Calhoun, along with chefs Graciel Caces, Rob Chalmers, Leslie Garetto, Lee Tan, and Christine Tobin prepped and cooked all the food needed on set. Ashley Moore and Kendra Smith provided food styling. Manager of Procurement and Kitchen Facilities Rachel Applebaum and Ingredient Receiving Specialist Christopher Miller were charged with making sure all the ingredients we needed were on hand. Special thanks to Kitchen Facilities and Video Equipment Associate Ethan Rogers, Assistant Culinary Producer Wes Lane, and Culinary Assistant Malcolm Jackson, who helped coordinate the kitchen with the television set by readying props, equipment, and food. Deva Djaafar and Octavia Pidoux assisted with facilities management.

We also appreciate the hard work of the production team, including Mick Bell, Ian Bishop, Jock Blaney, Mikaela Bloomberg, Fletcher Burns, Mike Duca, Kerry Haymann, Eric Fisher, Rose Fortuna, Eric Goddard, Lee Holloway, Brian Henderson, Harlem Logan, Keith McManus, Jay Maurer, Justin Perro, Brad Price, Taylor Steele, and Jennifer Tawa. Jennifer Cuciti, Ryan Doris, and Will Rogan supported our remote shoots.

Additional thanks to our Senior Director of Post Production Chen Margolis and editors Steven Huffaker and Herb Sevush; Senior Online Editor and Colorist Will Rogan; and Assistant Editors Caroline Barry, Ruthie LaMay, and Ben Mushinski. Motion graphics were provided by Neoscape.

We also would like to thank Hope Hennessey for managing station relations, Dani Cook at WETA Station Relations, and the team at American Public Television that presents the show: Judy Barlow, Tom Davison, and Reina Roberts.

American Cruise Lines, Breville, Plugrà, and Smithey sponsored the show, and we thank them for their support.

# CHAPTER 1 Appetizers and Drinks

Photos (left to right): Lumpiang Shanghai with Seasoned Vinegar; ATK 25; Zaalouk; Albóndigas en Chipotle; Spanish Tortilla with Roasted Red Peppers and Peas; Fresh Margaritas; Cōngyóubǐng

## Classic Guacamole

**MAKES** 2 cups

**WHY THIS RECIPE WORKS** Guacamole is traditionally made in a molcajete, a three-legged Mexican mortar made of volcanic rock. To simulate the molcajete's coarse surface, we minced the onion and chile by hand with kosher salt; the coarse crystals broke down the aromatics, releasing their juices and flavors and transforming them into a paste that was easy to combine with the avocado and other ingredients. (The salt will also help the aromatics break down in a regular mortar and pestle.) A bit of lime zest added further brightness without acidity. We used a whisk to mix and mash the avocado into the paste, creating a creamy but still chunky dip. Chopped tomato and cilantro added fruity flavor and freshness. For a spicier version, mince and add the serrano ribs and seeds to the onion mixture. A mortar and pestle can be used to process the onion mixture. Be sure to use Hass avocados here; Florida, or "skinny," avocados are too watery for dips.

- 2 tablespoons finely chopped onion
- 1 serrano chile, stemmed, seeded, and minced
- 1 teaspoon kosher salt
- ¼ teaspoon grated lime zest plus 1½–2 tablespoons juice
- 3 ripe avocados, halved, pitted, and cut into ½-inch pieces
- 1 plum tomato, cored, seeded, and cut into ⅛-inch dice
- 2 tablespoons chopped fresh cilantro

Place onion, serrano, salt, and lime zest on cutting board and chop until very finely minced. Transfer onion mixture to medium bowl and stir in 1½ tablespoons lime juice. Add avocados and, using sturdy whisk, mash and stir mixture until well combined with some ¼- to ½-inch chunks of avocado remaining. Stir in tomato and cilantro. Season with salt and up to additional 1½ teaspoons lime juice to taste. Serve.

## Chunky Guacamole

**MAKES** 2½ to 3 cups

**WHY THIS RECIPE WORKS** Not only eaten as a party dip, guacamole is also the traditional accompaniment to several Mexican dishes. But since avocado has a delicate flavor, it's easy for the secondary ingredients in guacamole to overshadow the primary one. We wanted to get back to the basics of this dish, emphasizing the avocado. Hass avocados, the dark, pebbly-skinned type, worked best, and they needed to be perfectly ripe; they should yield slightly to a gentle squeeze. We wanted a chunky texture in our guacamole, so instead of mashing or pureeing the avocados we diced two of them and mashed one lightly. Combining the avocados gave the guacamole a chunky, cohesive texture. As for flavorings, just a bit of finely minced onion provided some bite but not overwhelming onion flavor. Lime juice was essential for its bright citrus flavor. Cumin, a jalapeño, and fresh cilantro rounded out the dip's flavors. Cool and creamy, our guacamole makes a perfect partner to a bowl of tortilla chips or a garnish to a variety of Mexican dishes. To minimize the risk of discoloration, prepare the minced ingredients first so they are ready to mix with the avocados as soon as they are cut. Ripe avocados are essential here. To test for ripeness, try to flick the small stem off the end of the avocado. If it comes off easily and you can see green underneath it, the avocado is ripe. If it does not come off or if you see brown underneath after prying it off, the avocado is not ripe. If you like, garnish the guacamole with diced tomatoes and chopped cilantro just before serving. Guacamole can be covered with plastic wrap, pressed directly onto the surface of the mixture, and refrigerated for up to 1 day. Return the guacamole to room temperature, removing the plastic wrap at the last moment, before serving.

- 3 medium, ripe avocados
- ¼ cup minced fresh cilantro leaves
- 2 tablespoons minced onion
- 1 small jalapeño chile, stemmed, seeded, and minced
- 1 medium garlic clove, minced or pressed through a garlic press (about 1 teaspoon)
- ½ teaspoon ground cumin (optional)
- Table salt
- 2 tablespoons juice from 1 lime

**1.** Halve 1 avocado, remove the pit, and scoop the flesh into a medium bowl. Mash the flesh lightly with the cilantro, onion, jalapeño, garlic, cumin (if using), and ¼ teaspoon salt with the tines of a fork until just combined.

**2.** Halve, pit, and cube the remaining 2 avocados. Add the cubes to the bowl with the mashed avocado mixture.

**3.** Sprinkle the lime juice over the diced avocado and mix the entire contents of the bowl lightly with a fork until combined but still chunky. Season with salt, if necessary, and serve.

## Creamy Herbed Spinach Dip

**MAKES** about 1½ cups

**WHY THIS RECIPE WORKS** Spinach dip made with sour cream and soup mixes are flat and stale tasting. We ditched the mix to create a creamy spinach dip brimming with big, bold flavors. We were surprised to discover that frozen spinach actually made a better-tasting dip with a vibrant, more intense flavor than one made with fresh spinach. We used a food processor to chop the spinach and then enriched it with sour cream, mayonnaise, and a mixture of fresh herbs and seasonings. The only problem was that our dip, which took just about 15 minutes to make, took almost two hours to chill. Fortunately the solution turned out to be a simple one. Instead of thawing the spinach completely, we only partially thawed it, allowing the chunks of icy spinach to thoroughly cool the dip as they broke down in the food processor. This produces a cold dip that can be served without further chilling. Instead of microwaving, the frozen spinach can also be thawed at room temperature for 1½ hours, then squeezed of excess liquid. The garlic must be minced or pressed before going into the food processor; otherwise, the dip will contain large chunks of garlic. The dip can be covered with plastic wrap and refrigerated for up to 2 days.

- 1 (10-ounce) box frozen chopped spinach
- ½ cup sour cream
- ½ cup mayonnaise
- 3 scallions, white parts only, sliced thin
- ½ cup packed fresh parsley leaves
- 1 tablespoon minced fresh dill
- 1 small garlic clove, minced or pressed through a garlic press (about ½ teaspoon)
- ½ teaspoon table salt
- ¼ teaspoon ground black pepper
- ¼ teaspoon hot sauce
- ½ red bell pepper, chopped fine

**1.** Thaw the spinach in a microwave for 3 minutes at 40 percent power. (The edges should be thawed but not warm; the center should be soft enough to be broken into icy chunks.) Squeeze the partially frozen spinach to remove excess water.

**2.** Process the spinach, sour cream, mayonnaise, scallions, parsley, dill, garlic, salt, pepper, and hot sauce in a food processor until smooth and creamy, about 30 seconds. Transfer the mixture to a bowl and stir in the bell pepper; serve.

## Ultracreamy Hummus

**MAKES** 3 cups

**WHY THIS RECIPE WORKS** This hummus is velvety-smooth and creamy, with a satisfyingly rich, balanced flavor. To achieve a perfectly smooth texture, we simmered canned chickpeas with water and baking soda for 20 minutes and then quickly removed their grainy skins by gently swishing them under a few changes of water. Tahini is a major source of richness and flavor in hummus. To avoid the bitter flavors that can come from tahini made with heavily roasted sesame seeds, we chose a light-colored tahini, which indicated that the seeds were only gently roasted. For balanced garlic flavor, we steeped the garlic in lemon juice and salt to extract its flavor and deactivate alliinase, the enzyme that gives this allium its harsh bite. Finally, we added ample fresh lemon juice to give the hummus a bright flavor. The hummus will thicken slightly over time; add warm water, 1 tablespoon at a time, as needed to restore its creamy consistency. Serve with crudités and pita bread or crackers. If desired, you can omit the parsley, reserved chickpeas, and extra cumin in step 5 and top with our Baharat-Spiced Beef Topping for Hummus or Spiced Walnut Topping for Hummus (page 4). Hummus can be refrigerated in airtight container for up to 5 days. Let sit, covered, at room temperature for 30 minutes before serving.

- 2 (15-ounce) cans chickpeas, rinsed
- ½ teaspoon baking soda
- 4 garlic cloves, peeled
- ⅓ cup lemon juice (2 lemons), plus extra for seasoning
- 1 teaspoon table salt
- ¼ teaspoon ground cumin, plus extra for garnish
- ½ cup tahini, stirred well
- 2 tablespoons extra-virgin olive oil, plus extra for drizzling
- 1 tablespoon minced fresh parsley

**1.** Combine chickpeas, baking soda, and 6 cups water in medium saucepan and bring to boil over high heat. Reduce heat and simmer, stirring occasionally, until chickpea skins begin to float to surface and chickpeas are creamy and very soft, 20 to 25 minutes.

**2.** While chickpeas cook, mince garlic using garlic press or rasp-style grater. Measure out 1 tablespoon garlic and set aside; discard remaining garlic. Whisk lemon juice, salt, and reserved garlic together in small bowl and let sit for 10 minutes. Strain garlic-lemon mixture through fine-mesh strainer set over bowl, pressing on solids to extract as much liquid as possible; discard solids.

**3.** Drain chickpeas in colander and return to saucepan. Fill saucepan with cold water and gently swish chickpeas with your fingers to release skins. Pour off most of water into colander to collect skins, leaving chickpeas behind in saucepan. Repeat filling, swishing, and draining 3 or 4 times until most skins have been removed (this should yield about ¾ cup skins); discard skins. Transfer chickpeas to colander to drain.

**4.** Set aside 2 tablespoons whole chickpeas for garnish. Process garlic-lemon mixture, ¼ cup water, cumin, and remaining chickpeas in food processor until smooth, about 1 minute, scraping down sides of bowl as needed. Add tahini and oil and process until hummus is smooth, creamy, and light, about 1 minute, scraping down sides of bowl as needed. (Hummus should have pourable consistency similar to yogurt. If too thick, loosen with water, adding 1 teaspoon at a time.) Season with salt and extra lemon juice to taste.

**5.** Transfer to serving bowl and sprinkle with parsley, reserved chickpeas, and extra cumin. Drizzle with extra oil and serve.

## Baharat-Spiced Beef Topping for Hummus

**MAKES** 2 cups

Baharat is a warm, savory Middle Eastern spice blend. Ground lamb can be used in place of the beef, if desired. Toast the pine nuts in a dry skillet over medium-high heat until fragrant, 3 to 5 minutes. Serve the topping over hummus, garnishing with additional pine nuts and chopped fresh parsley.

- 2 teaspoons water
- ½ teaspoon table salt
- ¼ teaspoon baking soda
- 8 ounces 85 percent lean ground beef
- 1 tablespoon extra-virgin olive oil
- ¼ cup finely chopped onion
- 2 garlic cloves, minced
- 1 teaspoon hot smoked paprika
- 1 teaspoon ground cumin
- ¼ teaspoon pepper
- ¼ teaspoon ground coriander
- ⅛ teaspoon ground cloves
- ⅛ teaspoon ground cinnamon
- ¼ cup pine nuts, toasted
- 2 teaspoons lemon juice

**1.** Combine water, salt, and baking soda in large bowl. Add beef and toss to combine. Let sit for 5 minutes.

**2.** Heat oil in 12-inch nonstick skillet over medium heat until shimmering. Add onion and garlic and cook, stirring occasionally, until onion is softened, 3 to 4 minutes. Add paprika, cumin, pepper, coriander, cloves, and cinnamon and cook, stirring constantly, until fragrant, about 30 seconds. Add beef and cook, breaking up meat with wooden spoon, until beef is no longer pink, about 5 minutes. Add pine nuts and lemon juice and toss to combine.

## Spiced Walnut Topping for Hummus

**MAKES** ¾ cup

Do not overprocess; the topping should remain coarse-textured. Serve the topping over hummus. Topping can be refrigerated for up to 5 days.

- ¾ cup extra-virgin olive oil
- ⅓ cup walnuts
- ¼ cup paprika
- ¼ cup tomato paste
- 2 garlic cloves, peeled
- 1 teaspoon ground turmeric
- ½ teaspoon ground cumin
- ½ teaspoon ground allspice
- ½ teaspoon table salt
- ¼ teaspoon cayenne pepper

Process all ingredients in food processor until uniform coarse puree forms, about 30 seconds, scraping down sides of bowl halfway through processing.

# Curry Deviled Eggs with Easy-Peel Hard-Cooked Eggs

**MAKES** 12 eggs

**WHY THIS RECIPE WORKS** Getting the shells off all the eggs for deviled eggs can be a real hassle. If you start boiled eggs in cold water, the proteins in the egg white set slowly, giving them time to fuse to the surrounding membrane, so when you remove the shell, parts of the white come with it. For frustration-free peeling, we placed cold eggs directly into hot steam (in a steamer basket set over boiling water in a saucepan), which rapidly denatured the outermost egg white proteins, causing them to form a solid gel that shrank and pulled away from the membrane. The shells slipped off easily to reveal smooth, unblemished hard-cooked eggs. Using steam to cook the eggs also helped us avoid chalky or green-tinged yolks. Because the eggs never touched the water, they didn't lower the water temperature, making it easy to determine the optimum cooking time for consistently perfect results. To slice, lay the egg on its side and sweep the blade cleanly down the center. Wipe the knife after each egg. You may use either regular or reduced-fat mayonnaise. If preferred, use a pastry bag fitted with a large plain or star tip to fill egg halves.

- 1 recipe Easy-Peel Hard-Cooked Eggs
- 3 tablespoons mayonnaise
- 1 tablespoon minced fresh parsley, plus 12 small whole parsley leaves for garnishing
- 1½ teaspoons lemon juice
- 1 teaspoon Dijon mustard
- 1 teaspoon curry powder
- Pinch cayenne pepper

**1.** Slice each egg in half lengthwise with paring knife. Transfer yolks to bowl; arrange whites on serving platter. Mash yolks with fork until no large lumps remain. Add mayonnaise and use rubber spatula to smear mixture against side of bowl until thick, smooth paste forms, 1 to 2 minutes. Add minced parsley, lemon juice, mustard, curry powder, and cayenne and mix until fully incorporated.

**2.** Transfer yolk mixture to small heavy-duty plastic bag. Press mixture into 1 corner and twist top of bag. Using scissors, snip ½ inch off filled corner. Squeezing bag, distribute yolk mixture evenly among egg white halves. Garnish each egg half with parsley leaf and serve.

## Bacon and Chive Deviled Eggs

Cook 2 slices bacon, chopped fine, in 10-inch skillet over medium heat until crisp, 5 to 7 minutes. Using slotted spoon, transfer bacon to paper towel–lined plate. Reserve 1 tablespoon fat. To thick, smooth yolk paste add reserved bacon fat, 1 tablespoon minced fresh chives, 2 teaspoons distilled white vinegar, ⅛ teaspoon salt, and pinch cayenne and mix until fully incorporated. Stir in three-quarters of bacon. Distribute yolk mixture evenly among egg white halves. Omit parsley leaf garnish. Sprinkle each egg half with remaining bacon and serve.

## Easy-Peel Hard-Cooked Eggs

**MAKES** 6 eggs

Be sure to use large, cold eggs that have no cracks. You can cook fewer than six eggs without altering the timing, or more eggs as long as your pot and steamer basket can hold them in a single layer. If you don't have a steamer basket, use a spoon or tongs to gently place the eggs in the water; it does not matter if the eggs are above the water or partially submerged. Unpeeled cooked eggs can be stored in the refrigerator for up to three days.

- 6 large eggs

**1.** Bring 1 inch water to rolling boil in medium saucepan over high heat. Place eggs in steamer basket. Transfer basket to saucepan. Cover, reduce heat to medium-low, and cook eggs for 13 minutes.

**2.** When eggs are almost finished cooking, combine 2 cups ice cubes and 2 cups cold water in medium bowl. Using tongs or spoon, transfer eggs to ice bath; let sit for 15 minutes. Peel before using.

## Spanish Tortilla with Roasted Red Peppers and Peas

**SERVES** 4 to 6

**WHY THIS RECIPE WORKS** This classic Spanish omelet is immensely appealing, but can be greasy and heavy if prepared incorrectly. Typical recipes call for up to 4 cups of extra-virgin olive oil to cook the potatoes, which can lead to an overly oily tortilla. We wanted an intensely rich, velvety egg-and-potato omelet that didn't require using a quart of oil. We first stuck with the traditional volume of olive oil until we could determine the proper ratio of ingredients. We chose starchy russet potatoes, thinly sliced, and standard yellow onions. We also settled on a ratio of eggs to potatoes that allowed the tortilla to set firm and tender, with the eggs and potatoes melding into one another. Unfortunately, when we reduced the amount of oil in the pan, half the potatoes were frying while the other half were steaming. We started over with slightly firmer, less starchy Yukon Golds. With a fraction of the oil in the skillet, they were starchy enough to become meltingly tender as they cooked, but sturdy enough to stir and flip halfway through cooking. To flip the omelet we simply slid the tortilla out of the pan and onto one plate. Then, placing another plate upside down over the tortilla, we easily flipped the whole thing and slid the tortilla back in the pan. Spanish tortillas are often served warm or at room temperature with olives, pickles, and Garlic Mayonnaise as an appetizer. They may also be served with a salad as a light entrée. For the most traditional tortilla, omit the roasted red peppers and peas.

- 6 tablespoons plus 1 teaspoon extra-virgin olive oil, divided
- 1½ pounds (3 to 4 medium) Yukon Gold potatoes, peeled, quartered, and cut into ⅛-inch-thick slices
- 1 small onion, halved and sliced thin
- 1 teaspoon table salt, divided
- ¼ teaspoon pepper
- 8 large eggs
- ½ cup jarred roasted red peppers, rinsed, dried, and cut into ½-inch pieces
- ½ cup frozen peas, thawed
- Garlic Mayonnaise (optional; recipe follows)

**1.** Toss ¼ cup oil, potatoes, onion, ½ teaspoon salt, and pepper in large bowl until potato slices are thoroughly separated and coated in oil. Heat 2 tablespoons oil in 10-inch nonstick skillet over medium-high heat until shimmering. Reduce heat to medium-low, add potato mixture to skillet, and set bowl aside (do not rinse). Cover and cook, stirring occasionally with heat-resistant rubber spatula, until potatoes offer no resistance when poked with paring knife, 22 to 28 minutes (some potato slices may break into smaller pieces).

**2.** Meanwhile, whisk eggs and remaining ½ teaspoon salt in reserved bowl until just combined. Using heat-resistant rubber spatula, fold hot potato mixture, red peppers, and peas into eggs until combined, making sure to scrape all of potato mixture out of skillet. Return skillet to medium-high heat, add remaining 1 teaspoon oil, and heat until just beginning to smoke. Add egg-potato mixture and cook, shaking pan and folding mixture constantly for 15 seconds; smooth top of mixture with heat-resistant rubber spatula. Reduce heat to medium, cover, and cook, gently shaking pan every 30 seconds, until bottom is golden brown and top is lightly set, about 2 minutes.

**3.** Using heat-resistant rubber spatula, loosen tortilla from pan, shaking it back and forth until tortilla slides around. Slide tortilla onto large plate. Invert tortilla onto second large plate and slide it, browned side up, back into skillet. Tuck edges of tortilla into skillet. Return pan to medium heat and continue to cook, gently shaking pan every 30 seconds, until second side is golden brown, about 2 minutes longer. Slide tortilla onto cutting board; let cool for at least 15 minutes. Cut tortilla into cubes or wedges and serve with garlic mayonnaise, if using.

### Garlic Mayonnaise

**MAKES** 1¼ cups

Mayonnaise can be refrigerated in airtight container for up to 4 days.

- 2 large egg yolks
- 2 teaspoons Dijon mustard
- 2 teaspoons lemon juice
- 1 garlic clove, minced
- ¾ cup vegetable oil
- 1 tablespoon water
- ¼ cup extra-virgin olive oil
- ½ teaspoon table salt
- ¼ teaspoon pepper

Process yolks, mustard, lemon juice, and garlic in food processor until combined, about 10 seconds. With machine running, slowly drizzle in vegetable oil, about 1 minute. Transfer mixture to medium bowl and whisk in water. Whisking constantly, slowly drizzle in olive oil, about 30 seconds. Whisk in salt and pepper.

## Cheesy Nachos with Guacamole and Salsa

**SERVES** 4 to 6

**WHY THIS RECIPE WORKS** Prepackaged cheese and guacamole and jarred salsa can transform nachos into bland fast food. We wanted nachos with hot, crisp tortilla chips, plentiful cheese and toppings, and the right amount of spicy heat. To ensure that all of the chips would be cheesy and spicy, we layered tortilla chips with a full pound of shredded cheddar and sliced jalapeños. Layering the jalapeños with the cheese also helped the chiles stick to the chips. We prepared a quick homemade salsa and chunky guacamole to spoon around the edges of the hot nachos. Spoonfuls of sour cream and chopped fresh scallions provided the final touches. Served with lime wedges, this fresh take on nachos is light-years beyond any fast-food version.

- 8 ounces tortilla chips
- 1 pound cheddar cheese, shredded (about 4 cups)
- 2 large jalapeño chiles, sliced thin (about ¼ cup)
- 2 scallions, sliced thin
- ½ cup sour cream
- 1 recipe One-Minute Salsa
- 1 recipe Classic Guacamole (page 2)
- Lime wedges

Adjust oven rack to middle position and heat oven to 400 degrees. Spread half of chips in even layer in 13 by 9-inch baking dish. Sprinkle chips evenly with 2 cups cheddar and half of jalapeño slices. Repeat with remaining chips, cheddar, and jalapeños. Bake until cheese is melted, 7 to 10 minutes. Remove nachos from oven and sprinkle with scallions. Along edge of the baking dish, drop scoops of sour cream, salsa, and guacamole. Serve immediately, passing lime wedges separately.

### One-Minute Salsa

**MAKES 1 CUP**

This quick salsa can be made with either fresh or canned tomatoes. If you like, replace the jalapeño with ½ chipotle chile in adobo sauce, minced.

- 2 tablespoons chopped red onion
- 2 tablespoons fresh cilantro leaves
- 2 teaspoons lime juice
- ½ small jalapeño chile, stemmed and seeded (about 1½ teaspoons)
- 1 small garlic clove, minced (about ½ teaspoon)
- ¼ teaspoon table salt
- Pinch pepper
- 2 small ripe tomatoes, each cored and cut into eighths, or one (14.5-ounce) can diced tomatoes, drained

Pulse onion, cilantro, lime juice, jalapeño, garlic, salt, and pepper in food processor until minced, about 5 pulses, scraping down sides of work bowl as necessary. Add tomatoes and pulse until coarsely chopped, about 2 pulses.

## Buffalo Cauliflower Bites

**SERVES** 4 to 6

**WHY THIS RECIPE WORKS** Deemed "better than wings" by anyone who tries them, these crunchy, tangy, spicy cauliflower bites will be the new star of your game day table. The key was to come up with a crunchy coating that would hold up under the buffalo sauce. A mixture of cornstarch and cornmeal gave us an ultracrisp exterior. Because cauliflower is not naturally moist, the mixture didn't adhere; so we dunked the florets in canned coconut milk, which had the right viscosity. Frying helped to achieve an unbelievably crackly crust and tender interior. Since these cauliflower bites are vegan, we developed a ranch dressing that uses a homemade vegan mayonnaise (recipes follow). We used Frank's RedHot Original Cayenne Pepper Sauce, but other hot sauces can be used. Use a Dutch oven that holds 6 quarts or more for this recipe.

**BUFFALO SAUCE**

- ¼ cup coconut oil
- ½ cup hot sauce
- 1 tablespoon packed dark brown sugar
- 2 teaspoons cider vinegar

**CAULIFLOWER**

- 1-2 quarts peanut or vegetable oil for frying
- ¾ cup cornstarch
- ¼ cup cornmeal
- ½ teaspoon table salt
- ¼ teaspoon pepper
- ⅔ cup canned coconut milk
- 1 tablespoon hot sauce
- 1 pound cauliflower florets, cut into 1½-inch pieces
- 1 recipe Vegan Ranch Dressing

**1. FOR THE BUFFALO SAUCE:** Melt coconut oil in small saucepan over low heat. Whisk in hot sauce, brown sugar, and vinegar until combined. Remove from heat and cover to keep warm; set aside.

**2. FOR THE CAULIFLOWER:** Line platter with triple layer of paper towels. Add oil to large Dutch oven until it measures about 1½ inches deep and heat over medium-high heat to 400 degrees. While oil heats, combine cornstarch, cornmeal, salt, and pepper in small bowl. Whisk coconut milk and hot sauce together in large bowl. Add cauliflower and toss to coat well. Sprinkle cornstarch mixture over cauliflower; fold with rubber spatula until thoroughly coated.

**3.** Fry half of cauliflower, adding 1 or 2 pieces to oil at a time, until golden and crisp, gently stirring as needed to prevent pieces from sticking together, about 3 minutes. Using slotted spoon, transfer fried cauliflower to prepared platter.

**4.** Return oil to 400 degrees and repeat with remaining cauliflower. Transfer ½ cup sauce to clean large bowl, add fried cauliflower, and toss gently to coat. Serve immediately with dressing and remaining sauce.

## Vegan Ranch Dressing

**MAKES** ½ cup

We strongly prefer our homemade Vegan Mayonnaise (recipe follows) but you can use store-bought.

- ½ cup vegan mayonnaise
- 2 tablespoons unsweetened plain coconut milk yogurt
- 1 teaspoon white wine vinegar
- 1½ teaspoons minced fresh chives
- 1½ teaspoons minced fresh dill
- ¼ teaspoon garlic powder
- ⅛ teaspoon table salt
- ⅛ teaspoon pepper

Whisk all ingredients in bowl until smooth. (Dressing can be refrigerated for up to 4 days.)

## Vegan Mayonnaise

**MAKES** 1 cup

Aquafaba, the liquid found in a can of chickpeas, gives our mayo volume and emulsified body without any off-flavors or off-textures.

- ⅓ cup aquafaba
- 1½ teaspoons lemon juice
- ½ teaspoon table salt
- ½ teaspoon sugar
- ½ teaspoon Dijon mustard
- 1¼ cups vegetable oil
- 3 tablespoons extra-virgin olive oil

**1.** Process aquafaba, lemon juice, salt, sugar, and mustard in food processor for 10 seconds. With processor running, gradually add vegetable oil in slow, steady stream until mixture is thick and creamy, scraping down sides of bowl as needed, about 3 minutes.

**2.** Transfer mixture to bowl. Whisking constantly, slowly add olive oil until emulsified. If pools of oil form on surface, stop addition of oil and whisk mixture until well combined, then resume adding oil. Mayonnaise should be thick and glossy with no oil pools on surface. (Mayonnaise can be refrigerated for up to 1 week.)

## Albóndigas en Salsa de Almendras (Spanish-Style Meatballs in Almond Sauce)

**MAKES** 24 meatballs

**WHY THIS RECIPE WORKS** These tender, bite-size meatballs cloaked in a rich, almond-based sauce appear on tapas menus in Spain. To make them at home, we started by pulsing ground pork, garlic, parsley, egg, and a panade of bread and water in a food processor. After shaping the mixture into 1-inch balls, we skipped browning, instead cooking the meatballs in a mixture of white wine, chicken broth, and softened onion flavored with paprika and saffron. This gentler method quickly cooked the meatballs through. For the picada, which thickens and flavors the sauce, we ground blanched almonds and bread until fine and then fried them in oil. We then mixed in minced garlic and parsley before stirring the picada into the sauce. A splash of sherry vinegar and a sprinkling of fresh parsley at the end added brightness to balance the flavors. Sometimes fully cooked ground pork retains a slightly pink hue; trust your thermometer. These meatballs can be served as an appetizer with toothpicks or as a main course alongside a vegetable and potatoes or rice.

**PICADA**

- ¼ cup slivered almonds
- 1 slice hearty white sandwich bread, torn into 1-inch pieces
- 2 tablespoons extra-virgin olive oil
- 3 tablespoons minced fresh parsley
- 2 garlic cloves, minced

**MEATBALLS**

- 1 slice hearty white sandwich bread, torn into 1-inch pieces
- 1 large egg
- 2 tablespoons water
- 2 tablespoons chopped fresh parsley, divided
- 2 garlic cloves, minced
- 1 teaspoon table salt
- ½ teaspoon pepper
- 1 pound ground pork
- 1 tablespoon extra-virgin olive oil
- ½ cup finely chopped onion
- ½ teaspoon paprika
- 1 cup chicken broth
- ½ cup dry white wine
- ¼ teaspoon saffron threads, crumbled
- 1 teaspoon sherry vinegar

**1. FOR THE PICADA:** Process almonds in food processor until finely ground, about 20 seconds. Add bread and process until bread is finely ground, about 15 seconds. Transfer almond-bread mixture to 12-inch nonstick skillet. Add oil and cook over medium heat, stirring often, until mixture is golden brown, 3 to 5 minutes. Transfer to bowl. Stir in parsley and garlic and set aside. Wipe skillet clean with paper towels.

**2. FOR THE MEATBALLS:** Process bread in now-empty processor until finely ground, about 15 seconds. Add egg, water, 1 tablespoon parsley, garlic, salt, and pepper and process until smooth paste forms, about 20 seconds, scraping down sides of bowl as necessary. Add pork and pulse until combined, about 5 pulses.

**3.** Remove processor blade. Using your moistened hands, form generous 1 tablespoon pork mixture into 1-inch round meatball and transfer to plate; repeat with remaining pork mixture to form 24 meatballs.

**4.** Heat oil in now-empty skillet over medium heat until shimmering. Add onion and cook, stirring occasionally, until softened, 4 to 6 minutes. Add paprika and cook until fragrant, about 30 seconds. Add broth and wine and bring to simmer. Stir in saffron. Add meatballs and adjust heat to maintain simmer. Cover and cook until meatballs register 160 degrees, 6 to 8 minutes, flipping meatballs once.

**5.** Stir in picada and continue to cook, uncovered, until sauce has thickened slightly, 1 to 2 minutes longer. Off heat, stir in vinegar. Season with salt and pepper to taste. Transfer to platter, sprinkle with remaining 1 tablespoon parsley, and serve.

## Albondigas en Chipotle (Meatballs in Chipotle Sauce)

**SERVES** 4 to 6

**WHY THIS RECIPE WORKS** Meatballs in chipotle sauce is a classic Mexican dish that features a smoky, spicy, chipotle chile–infused tomato sauce and tender, rice-packed meatballs. For our recipe, we parcooked the rice to ensure that it became fully tender by the time the meatballs finished cooking. Instead of using a laundry list of ingredients to flavor our meatballs, we looked to a common Mexican ingredient with plenty of its own seasoning: chorizo. By substituting chorizo for a portion of the ground beef in the meatballs, we were able to quickly infuse them with spicy, rich flavor. A panade, a mixture of milk and bread, kept the meatballs tender. To develop a rich sauce, we used canned fire-roasted tomatoes, which echoed the deep smoky flavors of the chipotle chile. The addition of red wine vinegar and brown sugar helped balance the sauce with tart and sweet notes. Canned chipotle chile in adobo sauce was easy to use and provided heat, smokiness, and a bit of acidity. Serve with rice or tortillas.

- ½ cup long-grain white rice
- ½ teaspoon table salt, plus salt for cooking rice
- 2 tablespoons extra-virgin olive oil
- 1 onion, chopped fine
- 3 garlic cloves, minced
- 1 tablespoon minced fresh oregano or 1 teaspoon dried
- ¼ teaspoon ground cumin
- 1 (14.5-ounce) can crushed fire-roasted tomatoes
- 1 cup chicken broth
- 2 tablespoons red wine vinegar
- 1 tablespoon minced canned chipotle chile in adobo sauce
- 1 tablespoon packed brown sugar
- 1 bay leaf
- 2 slices hearty white sandwich bread, torn into 1-inch pieces
- ½ cup whole milk
- 12 ounces Mexican-style chorizo sausage, casings removed
- 12 ounces 90 percent lean ground beef
- 1 teaspoon pepper
- 2 tablespoons chopped fresh cilantro

**1.** Adjust oven rack to middle position and heat oven to 350 degrees. Bring 4 cups water to boil in medium saucepan. Add rice and 1 teaspoon salt and cook, stirring occasionally, for 8 minutes. Drain rice in fine-mesh strainer, rinse with cold water, and drain again; set aside.

**2.** Heat oil in now-empty saucepan over medium heat until shimmering. Add onion and cook until softened, about 5 minutes. Stir in garlic, oregano, and cumin and cook until fragrant, about 30 seconds. Stir in tomatoes, broth, vinegar, chipotle, sugar, and bay leaf and bring to simmer; transfer sauce to 13 by 9-inch baking dish.

**3.** Mash bread and milk to paste with fork in large bowl. Add parcooked rice, chorizo, beef, pepper, and salt and mix with your hands until thoroughly combined.

**4.** Pinch off and roll mixture into 16 meatballs (¼ cup each) and nestle into sauce. Spoon some sauce over meatballs, cover tightly with aluminum foil, and bake until meatballs are cooked through, about 1 hour.

**5.** Remove dish from oven and let meatballs rest in sauce, covered, for 15 minutes. Transfer meatballs to serving platter. Discard bay leaf, skim any fat off surface of sauce, and season with salt and pepper to taste. Pour sauce over meatballs, sprinkle with cilantro, and serve.

## Zaalouk (Moroccan Eggplant Meze)

**SERVES** 4 **SEASON 26**

**WHY THIS RECIPE WORKS** To make zaalouk, Morocco's ubiquitous meze, cooks slow-cook a whole eggplant until its skin lightly chars and its flesh softens. Then they mash and sauté it with tomatoes; garlic; spices such as cumin, paprika, and cayenne; cilantro; lemon juice; and plenty of olive oil. Leaving the skin on the eggplant as it cooked not only protected the flesh from drying out but also encouraged the fruit's pectin and hemicellulose to dissolve and create its plush texture. Peeling the tomatoes ensured that no chewy bits of skin distracted from the eggplant's silkiness. Mashing the mixture as it simmered helped any large pieces break down. Even though it was peeled away after charring, the eggplant skin contributed smoky, pleasantly bitter char flavor to the porous eggplant flesh, giving the finished dish complexity and depth. Using 1 pound of tomatoes per 1½ pounds of eggplant added fruity vibrancy without overpowering the eggplant's flavor. Lemon juice and cilantro added more freshness, and plenty of minced garlic as well as some cumin, paprika, salt, and sugar contributed savory, earthy depth and a touch of sweetness. You can broil the eggplant or grill it over gas or charcoal. For the best results, use in-season, round tomatoes or vine-ripened tomatoes; do not use plum tomatoes. To peel the tomatoes, use a serrated peeler or blanch and shock them. Serve warm or at room temperature with crusty bread or alongside a protein such as chicken or fish for a meal. Zaalouk can be refrigerated for up to 24 hours. Let sit at room temperature for 20 minutes and garnish with remaining olive oil and cilantro before serving.

- 1½ pounds eggplant
- ¼ cup extra-virgin olive oil, divided
- 7 garlic cloves, minced
- 1 teaspoon ground cumin
- 1 teaspoon paprika
- 1 teaspoon table salt
- ½ teaspoon sugar
- ⅛ teaspoon cayenne pepper
- 1 pound tomatoes, cored, peeled, and chopped
- 2 tablespoons minced fresh cilantro, divided
- 1 tablespoon lemon juice, plus extra for serving

**1.** Poke eggplant about 6 times with paring knife.

**2A. TO BROIL:** Adjust oven rack 12 inches from broiler element and heat broiler. Line rimmed baking sheet with aluminum foil and place eggplant on prepared sheet. Broil until skin is shriveled and slightly darkened and eggplant yields to gentle pressure, about 25 minutes, flipping eggplant halfway through cooking. Let eggplant cool on sheet, about 10 minutes.

**2B. TO GRILL:** Place eggplant on grill over medium-high heat and cook until skin is shriveled and slightly darkened and eggplant yields to gentle pressure, about 25 minutes, flipping eggplant halfway through cooking. Transfer eggplant to foil-lined baking sheet and let cool, about 10 minutes.

**3.** When eggplant has cooled, peel and discard skin. Chop eggplant flesh coarse and transfer to bowl. (Eggplant can be refrigerated for up to 24 hours.)

**4.** Heat 2 tablespoons oil in 12-inch nonstick or carbon-steel skillet over medium heat until shimmering. Add garlic, cumin, paprika, salt, sugar, and cayenne and cook until fragrant, 30 to 60 seconds. Stir in tomatoes and cook, mashing and stirring occasionally with wooden spoon, until tomatoes have softened and most liquid has evaporated, 12 to 15 minutes. Stir in eggplant and 1½ tablespoons cilantro and continue to cook, mashing and stirring occasionally, until eggplant has broken down and mixture is dry, 12 to 15 minutes longer.

**5.** Off heat, stir in lemon juice. Season with salt and extra lemon juice to taste. Transfer to shallow bowl and garnish with remaining 2 tablespoons oil and remaining 1½ teaspoons cilantro. Serve.

## Frico

**MAKES** 8 large wafers

**WHY THIS RECIPE WORKS** As an accompaniment to cocktails or eaten just as a snack, frico is a simple, crisp wafer of flavorful cheese, usually Montasio, that has been melted and browned. We wanted to find the secret behind great frico, and then determine the best substitute for Montasio cheese, which isn't available in many supermarkets. Cheese simply grated into a hot pan could turn into a sticky mess, but we found that using a nonstick skillet allowed us to cook the frico without adding butter or oil. We discovered that it was easy to turn the frico to the other side once the first side was browned if we first took the skillet off the heat; the slightly cooled cheese didn't stretch or tear when we flipped it. Turning the heat down to cook the second side gave the best results; a pan that was too hot turned the cheese bitter. Many recipes suggest Parmesan as a substitute for Montasio, but we found Asiago cheese to be a better stand-in—though the real thing is even better. Serve frico with drinks and a bowl of marinated olives or marinated sun-dried tomatoes. Frico is also good crumbled into a salad, crouton-style.

- 1 pound Montasio or aged Asiago cheese, grated fine (about 8 cups)

**1.** Sprinkle 2 ounces (about 1 cup) of grated cheese over bottom of 10-inch nonstick skillet set over medium-high heat. Use heat-resistant rubber spatula or wooden spoon to tidy lacy outer edges of cheese. Cook, shaking pan occasionally to ensure even distribution of cheese over pan bottom, until edges are lacy and toasted, about 4 minutes. Remove pan from heat and allow cheese to set for about 30 seconds.

**2.** Using fork on top and heat-resistant spatula underneath, carefully flip cheese wafer and return pan to medium heat. Cook until second side is golden brown, about 2 minutes. Slide cheese wafer out of pan and transfer to plate. Repeat with remaining cheese. Serve within 1 hour.

## Crispy Cacio e Pepe Bites

**MAKES** 49 croquettes

**WHY THIS RECIPE WORKS** We picked up the technique for these fried squares of tapioca deliciousness from John and Beverly Clark at Parachute Restaurant in Chicago. At the restaurant they were served as a snack: four bites of Pecorino-heavy fried tapioca, dusted in nori powder. They're cheesy and gooey like good arancini, but the tapioca creates an appealing lighter, stretchier texture. They are a nod to the classic Roman dish cacio e pepe. We upped the amount of Pecorino and folded in a lot of black pepper. The result, which we dubbed tapiocacio e pepe, is a dead-simple, gluten-free, cheesy party bite. Tapioca pearls are the same pearls used for tapioca pudding. Do not use minute tapioca. This recipe is heavy on black pepper—if you generally prefer less pepper, reduce to 1 tablespoon. All-purpose flour may be substituted for the tapioca starch. In step 1, constant stirring guarantees that the tapioca pearls do not stick to the bottom of the saucepan. The mixture will become more difficult to stir the longer it cooks. Don't be alarmed. Keep calm and stir on.

- 1 quart whole milk
- 2 cups small tapioca pearls
- 3½ ounces Pecorino Romano, grated fine (1¾ cups), plus extra for serving
- 5 teaspoons pepper
- 2½ teaspoons kosher salt
- ½ cup tapioca starch, plus extra as needed
- 1 quart vegetable oil, for frying

**1.** Grease 8-inch square baking pan with vegetable oil spray. Bring milk to boil in large saucepan over medium-high heat. Add tapioca pearls and cook, stirring occasionally, until milk returns to boil, 30 to 60 seconds. Reduce heat to medium and simmer, stirring constantly, until tapioca plumps and exterior turns translucent (very center will remain white) and mixture is thickened, 6 to 8 minutes.

**2.** Off heat, fold in Pecorino, pepper, and salt. Working quickly, using rubber spatula, transfer tapioca mixture to prepared pan and spread into even layer. Let cool for 20 minutes. Cover and refrigerate until firm, at least 2 hours or up to 24 hours.

**3.** Place ½ cup tapioca starch in shallow dish; lightly dust cutting board with extra tapioca starch. Invert tapioca square onto cutting board. Cut tapioca into 49 squares (7 rows by 7 rows), wiping knife with damp dish towel as needed to prevent sticking. Roll cubes in tapioca starch, shaking off excess, and transfer to baking sheet. (Cut, dusted cubes can be refrigerated in airtight container for up to 3 days.)

**4.** Heat oil in large saucepan over high heat to 375 degrees. Add one-third of cubes and fry, stirring frequently, until golden brown, 2 to 4 minutes, adjusting heat as necessary to maintain oil between 350 and 375 degrees. Transfer to paper towel–lined baking sheet or plate and blot to remove excess oil; season lightly with salt. Repeat with remaining cubes in 2 batches. Transfer croquettes to serving platter, dust generously with Pecorino, and serve.

## Baked Brie en Croûte

**SERVES** 8 to 10

**WHY THIS RECIPE WORKS** The combination of warm, creamy Brie encased in a flaky puff pastry crust with sweet fruit topping sets a rich, refined tone for this appetizer. And while this cheese plate centerpiece is impressive, it could hardly be easier to prepare. Working with a firm wheel of cheese promised gooey cheese that still held its shape. Freezing the pastry-wrapped Brie for 20 minutes kept it from melting too much during baking. Adding the preserves after baking kept the flavor bright. To thaw frozen puff pastry, let it stand either in the refrigerator for 24 hours or on the counter for 30 minutes to 1 hour. The Brie can be prepared through step 1 (but do not freeze) and refrigerated, wrapped tightly in plastic wrap, for up to 24 hours. Freeze for 20 minutes before continuing with step 2. Serve with sliced baguette or crackers.

- 1 (9 by 9½-inch) sheet frozen puff pastry, thawed
- 1 large egg, lightly beaten
- 1 (8-ounce) wheel firm Brie cheese
- ¼ cup apricot preserves or hot pepper jelly

**1.** Roll puff pastry into 12-inch square on lightly floured counter. Using pie plate or other round guide, trim pastry to 9-inch circle with paring knife. Brush edges lightly with beaten egg. Place Brie in center of pastry circle and wrap it in pastry. Brush exterior of pastry with beaten egg and transfer it to parchment paper–lined baking sheet. Freeze for 20 minutes.

**2.** Adjust oven rack to middle position and heat oven to 425 degrees. Bake cheese until exterior is deep golden brown, 20 to 25 minutes.

**3.** Transfer to wire rack. Spoon preserves into exposed center of Brie. Let cool for about 30 minutes. Serve with crackers or bread.

## Bouyourdi (Spicy Greek Baked Feta)

**SERVES** 4 to 6

**WHY THIS RECIPE WORKS** Warm, creamy feta quells the blaze of chiles in this crowd-pleasing taverna classic. To make this beloved Thessalonian meze, we started with Greek sheep's milk feta; ripe in-season tomatoes; and grassy, mild bell pepper. To double down on spiciness, we added both fresh chiles and dried chile flakes to create just enough heat to balance the creamy dairy. A hearty dose of extra-virgin olive oil enhanced the dish's overall richness and unified its components. We served the bouyourdi out of its earthenware baking dish with crusty bread alongside. Use feta made from sheep's milk. If possible, purchase feta sold in brine, which will be more moist. Do not use precrumbled feta; it will become tough and dry in the oven. If your block of feta is thicker than 1 inch, slice it into 1-inch slabs before using. This dish is meant to be spicy. Bukovo pepper flakes are traditional, but any red pepper flakes can be used. Use an 8-inch square broiler-safe baking dish or a shallow earthenware dish or cazuela to mimic the clay vessel traditionally used for this dish. Serve with thick slices of crusty or toasted bread.

- 1 large tomato, cored
- 1 longhorn chile or ½ jalapeño chile, stemmed
- ¼ green bell pepper, cut into ¼-inch pieces
- 3 tablespoons extra-virgin olive oil, divided
- 1½ teaspoons dried oregano, divided
- 1 (7-ounce) block feta cheese
- ½ teaspoon bukovo or red pepper flakes

**1.** Adjust oven rack to upper-middle position and heat oven to 350 degrees.

**2.** Slice two ¼-inch rounds from tomato and set aside. Chop remaining tomato into ½-inch pieces and place in small bowl. Cut longhorn chile in half crosswise (reserve 1 half for other use). Slice two ¼-inch rings from longhorn chile half and set aside. Mince remaining longhorn chile and add to chopped tomatoes along with bell pepper, 2 tablespoons oil, and 1 teaspoon oregano. Stir to combine, pour into baking dish, and smooth into even layer.

**3.** Center feta block on top of vegetables. Arrange tomato slices and longhorn chile rings in single layer on top of feta. Drizzle with remaining 1 tablespoon oil and sprinkle with remaining ½ teaspoon oregano. Cover dish tightly with aluminum foil and bake until diced vegetables have softened and tomato slices are beginning to soften at edges, about 25 minutes.

**4.** Remove foil and return dish to oven. Turn on broiler. Broil until edges of tomato and longhorn chile slices are browned, 4 to 7 minutes. Remove dish from oven, sprinkle with bukovo, and serve.

## Gougères

**MAKES** 24 puffs **SEASON 26**

**WHY THIS RECIPE WORKS** Cheesy, crisp, airy, and delicate, gougères are a great choice for entertaining since they can be thrown together quickly before a party or prepared in advance and recrisped. They begin with a traditional choux paste, which we made by cooking water, butter, and flour until a dough formed. Then we used the food processor to beat in two eggs plus an extra egg white. The added white improves crispness and provides more water, which turns to steam and helps the gougères puff even more, and its proteins provide better structure for more airiness. Most gougères lack cheese flavor, but we packed an extra ounce of Gruyère into our puffs. Use a Gruyère that has been aged for about one year. The doubled baking sheets prevent the undersides of the puffs from overbrowning. Alternatively, loosely roll up an 18 by 12-inch piece of aluminum foil, unroll it, and set it in a rimmed baking sheet. Cover the foil with a sheet of parchment paper and proceed with the recipe. In step 4, the dough can be piped using a pastry bag fitted with a ½-inch plain tip. Cooled gougères can be stored in an airtight container at room temperature for up to 24 hours or frozen in a zipper-lock bag for up to 1 month. To serve, crisp gougères in a 300-degree oven for about 7 minutes.

- 2 large eggs plus 1 large white
- ¼ teaspoon salt
- ½ cup water
- 2 tablespoons unsalted butter, cut into 4 pieces
- Pinch cayenne pepper
- ½ cup (2½ ounces) all-purpose flour
- 4 ounces Gruyère cheese, shredded (1 cup)

**1.** Adjust oven rack to upper-middle position and heat oven to 425 degrees. Line rimmed baking sheet with parchment paper and nest it in second rimmed baking sheet. In 2-cup liquid measuring cup, beat eggs and white and salt until well combined. (You should have about ½ cup egg mixture. Discard excess.) Set aside.

**2.** Heat water, butter, and cayenne in small saucepan over medium heat. When mixture begins to simmer, reduce heat to low and immediately stir in flour using wooden spoon. Cook, stirring constantly, using smearing motion, until mixture is very thick, forms ball, and pulls away from sides of saucepan, about 30 seconds.

**3.** Immediately transfer mixture to food processor and process with feed tube open for 5 seconds to cool slightly. With processor running, gradually add reserved egg mixture in steady stream, then scrape down sides of bowl and add Gruyère. Process until paste is very glossy and flecked with coarse cornmeal–size pieces of cheese, 30 to 40 seconds. (If not using immediately, transfer paste to bowl, press sheet of greased parchment directly on surface, and store at room temperature for up to 2 hours.)

**4.** Scoop 1 level tablespoon of dough. Using second small spoon, scrape dough onto prepared sheet into 1½-inch-wide, 1-inch-tall mound. Repeat, spacing mounds 1 to 1¼ inches apart. (You should have 24 mounds.) Using back of spoon lightly coated with vegetable oil spray, smooth away any creases and large peaks on each mound.

**5.** Bake until gougères are puffed and upper two-thirds of each are light golden brown (bottom third will still be pale), 14 to 20 minutes. Turn off oven; leave gougères in oven until uniformly golden brown, 10 to 15 minutes (do not open oven for at least 8 minutes). Transfer gougères to wire rack and let cool for 15 minutes. Serve warm.

## Pa amb Tomàquet (Catalan Tomato Bread)

**SERVES** 4 to 6

**WHY THIS RECIPE WORKS** Pa amb tomàquet—Catalan bread with tomato—is as simple as cooking gets, but the crunchy yet tender toasted bread and ripe tomato pulp make for an unbeatable combination, especially when seasoned with coarse salt and lavished with fruity olive oil. Ciabatta mimicked the airy structure of traditional pan de cristal. Halving the loaf laterally and cutting the halves into slices maximized its surface area for optimal toastiness. Toasted dry under the broiler, the bread charred lightly and quickly, so its interior crumb remained tender—a textural contrast that was just right for both supporting and absorbing the tomatoes' liquid. Rubbing a garlic clove over the toasts infused them with subtle savoriness. Halving and grating ripe round tomatoes on a box grater yielded loads of sweet, skin-free pulp that could be uniformly seasoned and spooned onto the toasts. If possible, use ripe local tomatoes here. Avoid plum tomatoes; they're not juicy enough. If ciabatta is unavailable, substitute a crusty baguette, cut into 4-inch pieces. Use a fresh, robust, high-quality olive oil here. Serve as an appetizer or as an accompaniment to any meal.

- 2 large ripe tomatoes, halved through equator
- ½ teaspoon table salt
- 1 loaf ciabatta, halved horizontally and sliced crosswise 2 inches thick
- 1 large garlic clove, peeled and halved crosswise
- 3 tablespoons extra-virgin olive oil, plus extra for serving
- Flake sea salt

**1.** Place box grater in medium bowl. Rub cut side of tomatoes against large holes of grater until tomato flesh is reduced to pulp (skins should remain intact). Discard skins. (You should have about 1½ cups pulp.) Stir in table salt.

**2.** Adjust oven rack 6 inches from broiler element and heat broiler. Set wire rack in rimmed baking sheet and arrange bread slices cut side up on rack. Broil until browned, crisp, and starting to char at edges, 2 to 4 minutes. Rub toasts with cut side of garlic (apply more pressure for more-potent flavor; rub lightly for delicate flavor).

**3.** Arrange toasts on serving plate. Distribute tomato pulp evenly among toasts and spread to edges. Drizzle with oil and season lightly with flake sea salt. Serve immediately, passing extra oil and sea salt separately.

## Red Pepper Coques

**MAKES** 4 coques **SEASON 26**

**WHY THIS RECIPE WORKS** Coques are thin and crunchy Catalan flatbreads served in many tapas bars. Some are sweet, featuring a topping of candied fruit and nuts, but we set our sights on an intensely savory version topped with bold Spanish flavors. To get the perfect crust for our coques, we started with our thin-crust pizza dough since it produced a thin, flavorful crust that was appropriate for this dish. But to set our crust apart from pizza and get an extra-crisp base, we increased the amount of oil in the dough from 1 to 3 tablespoons and brushed each coca with more oil before baking. Parbaking the dough before topping it helped prevent a soggy crust and created a sturdy base. For a deeply flavorful topping, we started with onions and roasted red peppers. Garlic, red pepper flakes, and sherry vinegar brought depth, heat, and rounded acidity. We cooked the topping before spreading it on the parbaked dough to intensify the flavors. It is important to use ice water in the dough to prevent it from overheating in the food processor. We recommend King Arthur brand bread flour. If you cannot fit two coques on a single baking sheet, bake them in two batches.

**DOUGH**

- 3 cups (16½ ounces) bread flour
- 2 teaspoons sugar
- ½ teaspoon instant or rapid-rise yeast
- 1⅓ cups ice water
- 3 tablespoons extra-virgin olive oil
- 1½ teaspoons salt

**TOPPING**

- ½ cup extra-virgin olive oil, divided
- 2 large onions, halved and sliced thin
- 2 cups jarred roasted red peppers, patted dry and sliced thin
- 3 tablespoons sugar
- 3 garlic cloves, minced
- 1½ teaspoons salt
- ¼ teaspoon red pepper flakes
- 2 bay leaves
- 3 tablespoons sherry vinegar
- ¼ cup pine nuts (optional)
- 1 tablespoon minced fresh parsley

**1. FOR THE DOUGH:** Pulse flour, sugar, and yeast in food processor until combined, about 5 pulses. With processor running, slowly add ice water and process until dough is just combined and no dry flour remains, about 10 seconds. Let dough rest for 10 minutes.

**2.** Add oil and salt to dough and process until dough forms satiny, sticky ball that clears sides of bowl, 30 to 60 seconds. Transfer dough to lightly floured counter and knead by hand to form smooth, round ball, about 30 seconds. Place dough seam side down in lightly greased large bowl or container, cover tightly with plastic wrap, and refrigerate for at least 24 hours or up to 3 days.

**3. FOR THE TOPPING:** Heat 3 tablespoons oil in 12-inch nonstick skillet over medium heat until shimmering. Stir in onions, red peppers, sugar, garlic, salt, pepper flakes, and bay leaves. Cover and cook, stirring occasionally, until onions are softened and have released their juice, about 10 minutes. Remove lid and continue to cook, stirring often, until onions are golden brown, 10 to 15 minutes. Off heat, discard bay leaves. Transfer onion mixture to bowl, stir in vinegar, and let cool completely before using.

**4.** Press down on dough to deflate. Transfer dough to clean counter, divide into quarters, and cover loosely with greased plastic. Working with 1 piece of dough at a time (keep remaining pieces covered), form into rough ball by stretching dough around your thumbs and pinching edges together so that top is smooth.

**5.** Place ball seam side down on counter and, using your cupped hands, drag in small circles until dough feels taut and round. Space dough balls 3 inches apart, cover loosely with greased plastic, and let rest for 1 hour.

**6.** Adjust oven racks to upper-middle and lower-middle positions and heat oven to 500 degrees. Coat 2 rimmed baking sheets with 2 tablespoons oil each. Generously coat 1 dough ball with flour and place on well-floured counter. Press and roll into 14 by 5-inch oval. Arrange oval on prepared sheet, with long edge fitted snugly against 1 long side of sheet, and reshape as needed. (If dough resists stretching, let it relax for 10 to 20 minutes before trying to stretch it again.) Repeat with remaining dough balls, arranging 2 ovals on each sheet, spaced ½ inch apart. Using fork, poke surface of dough 10 to 15 times.

**7.** Brush dough ovals with remaining 1 tablespoon oil and bake until puffed, 6 to 8 minutes, switching and rotating sheets halfway through baking.

**8.** Scatter onion mixture evenly over flatbreads, from edge to edge, then sprinkle with pine nuts, if using. Bake until topping is heated through and edges of flatbreads are deep golden brown and crisp, about 15 minutes, switching and rotating sheets halfway through baking. Let flatbreads cool on sheets for 10 minutes, then transfer to cutting board using metal spatula. Sprinkle with parsley, slice, and serve.

## Bruschetta with Artichoke Hearts and Parmesan

**SERVES** 8 to 10

**WHY THIS RECIPE WORKS** Bruschetta can be anything from a simple piece of crispy, garlicky bread drizzled with olive oil to an elaborately topped toast. We strove for a middle ground, pairing year-round, pantry-ready ingredients such as canned artichoke hearts with a sharp cheese such as Parmesan to create the punchy, concentrated flavors we wanted for a standout bruschetta recipe. We pulsed some of the bruschetta topping ingredients in the food processor until they formed a rough paste, which provided a stable base for the other toppings and allowed us to easily pick up our bruschetta and eat it neatly.

- 1 (14-ounce) can artichoke hearts, rinsed and patted dry with paper towels
- 2 teaspoons juice from 1 lemon
- 1 garlic clove, minced or pressed through garlic press
- 2 tablespoons extra-virgin olive oil, plus extra for serving
- 2 tablespoons finely shredded fresh basil leaves
- ¼ teaspoon table salt
- ¼ teaspoon pepper
- 2 ounces Parmesan cheese, 1 ounce finely grated (about ½ cup), 1 ounce shaved into strips with vegetable peeler
- 1 recipe Toasted Bread for Bruschetta

Pulse artichoke hearts, lemon juice, garlic, olive oil, basil, salt, and pepper in food processor until coarse puree forms, about six 1-second pulses, scraping down bowl with rubber spatula once during processing. Add grated Parmesan and pulse to combine, about two 1-second pulses. Divide artichoke mixture among toasts and spread to edges. Top with shaved Parmesan. Sprinkle with black pepper to taste, drizzle with olive oil, and serve.

### Toasted Bread for Bruschetta

**SERVES** 8 to 10

Toast the bread just before assembling the bruschetta.

- 1 (10 by 5-inch) loaf country bread with thick crust, ends discarded, sliced crosswise into ¾-inch-thick pieces
- 1 garlic clove, peeled
- ¼ cup extra-virgin olive oil

Adjust oven rack 4 inches from broiler element and heat broiler. Arrange bread in single layer on aluminum foil–lined baking sheet. Broil until bread is deep golden and toasted on both sides, 1 to 2 minutes per side. Lightly rub 1 side of each toast with garlic (you will not use all of garlic). Brush with oil and season with salt to taste.

## Caramelized Onion, Pear, and Bacon Tart

**MAKES** 2 tarts, Serves 8 to 10

**WHY THIS RECIPE WORKS** Sweet, salty, and savory, this cast-iron tart has it all. A topping of caramelized onion, sweet sliced pear, and bits of bacon balanced the flavor profile; creamy goat cheese added both tang and richness. You can use ready-made pizza dough instead of making it from scratch.

- 8 slices bacon, chopped fine
- 2 pounds onions, halved and sliced ¼ inch thick
- 1 teaspoon minced fresh thyme or ¼ teaspoon dried
- 1½ teaspoons packed brown sugar
- ¾ teaspoon table salt
- 2 tablespoons balsamic vinegar
- 1 pound pizza dough
- 1 Bosc pear, quartered, cored, and sliced ¼ inch thick, divided
- 4 ounces goat cheese, crumbled (1 cup), divided
- 2 tablespoons minced fresh chives

**1.** Adjust oven rack to upper-middle position and heat oven to 500 degrees. Cook bacon in 12-inch cast-iron skillet over medium heat until crispy, 7 to 9 minutes. Using slotted spoon, transfer bacon to bowl. Measure out and reserve ¼ cup fat; discard remaining fat.

**2.** Add 2 tablespoons reserved fat, onions, thyme, sugar, and salt to now-empty skillet. Cover and cook, stirring occasionally, until onions are softened, 8 to 10 minutes. Uncover and continue to cook, stirring occasionally, until onions are deep golden brown, about 10 minutes. Stir in vinegar and cook until almost completely evaporated, about 2 minutes; transfer to bowl.

**3.** Wipe skillet clean with paper towels, then grease with 1 tablespoon reserved fat. Place dough on lightly floured counter, divide in half, and cover with greased plastic wrap. Press and roll 1 piece of dough (keeping remaining dough covered) into 11-inch round. Transfer dough to prepared skillet and gently push it to corners of pan. Spread half of onion mixture over dough, leaving ½-inch border around edge. Scatter half of pear, half of bacon, and ½ cup goat cheese evenly over top.

**4.** Set skillet over medium-high heat and cook until outside edge of dough is set, tart is lightly pulled, and bottom crust is spotty brown when gently lifted with spatula, 2 to 4 minutes. Transfer skillet to oven and bake until edge of tart is golden brown, 7 to 10 minutes.

**5.** Using potholders, remove skillet from oven and slide tart onto wire rack; let cool slightly. Being careful of hot skillet handle, repeat with remaining 1 tablespoon reserved fat, dough, and toppings. Sprinkle tarts with chives and cut into wedges. Serve.

### Classic Pizza Dough

**MAKES** 1 pound

- 2 cups plus 2 tablespoons bread flour (11½ ounces)
- 1⅛ teaspoons instant or rapid-rise yeast
- ¾ teaspoon table salt
- 1 tablespoon olive oil
- ¾ cup warm water (110 degrees)

**1.** Pulse flour, yeast, and salt together in food processor to combine, about 5 pulses. With processor running, add oil, then water, and process until rough ball forms, 30 to 40 seconds. Let dough rest for 2 minutes, then process for 30 seconds longer. (If after 30 seconds dough is very sticky and clings to blade, add extra flour as needed.)

**2.** Transfer dough to lightly floured counter and knead by hand to form smooth, round ball, about 1 minute. Place dough in large, lightly greased bowl, cover tightly with greased plastic wrap, and let rise until doubled in size, 1 to 1½ hours. (Alternatively, dough can be refrigerated for at least 8 hours or up to 16 hours.)

## French Onion and Bacon Tart

**SERVES** 6 to 8

**WHY THIS RECIPE WORKS** French onion tart is similar to quiche but delivers more onions than custard. We simplified the crust and found we could shorten the overall preparation time if we left the lid on the skillet throughout cooking. The bacon acted as a crisp foil to the creamy filling, but we found a traditional custard with the bacon to be too rich. So we reduced the number of eggs and switched out the cream for half-and-half. As for the bacon, we sprinkled it on top of the custard. A simple pat-in-the-pan crust eliminated lots of work, and it could be made in a food processor. Either yellow or white onions work well in this recipe, but do not use sweet onions, such as Vidalias, which will make the tart watery. This tart can be served hot or at room temperature.

**CRUST**

- 1¼ cups (6¼ ounces) unbleached all-purpose flour
- 1 tablespoon sugar
- ½ teaspoon table salt
- 8 tablespoons (1 stick) unsalted butter, cut into ½-inch cubes and chilled
- 2-3 tablespoons ice water

FILLING

- 4 ounces bacon (about 4 slices), halved lengthwise and cut crosswise into ¼-inch pieces
- Vegetable oil, as needed
- 1½ pounds onions (about 3 medium), halved pole to pole and cut crosswise into ¼-inch slices (about 6 cups)
- ¾ teaspoon table salt
- 1 sprig fresh thyme
- 2 large eggs
- ½ cup half-and-half
- ¼ teaspoon ground black pepper

**1. FOR THE CRUST:** Spray a 9-inch tart pan with a removable bottom with vegetable oil spray; set aside. Pulse the flour, sugar, and salt together in a food processor until combined, about 4 pulses. Scatter the butter pieces over the flour mixture and pulse until the mixture resembles coarse sand, about 15 pulses. Add 2 tablespoons of the ice water and continue to process until large clumps of dough form and no powdery bits remain, about 5 seconds. If the dough doesn't clump, add the remaining 1 tablespoon water and pulse to incorporate, about 4 pulses. Transfer the dough to the greased tart pan and, working outward from the center, pat the dough into an even layer, sealing any cracks. Working around the edge, press the dough firmly into the corners of the pan and up the sides, using your thumb to level off the top edge. Lay plastic wrap over the dough and smooth out any bumps or shallow areas. Place the tart shell on a plate and freeze for 30 minutes.

**2.** Adjust an oven rack to the middle position and heat the oven to 375 degrees. Place the frozen tart shell (still in the tart pan) on a rimmed baking sheet. Gently press a piece of extra-wide heavy-duty foil that has been sprayed with vegetable oil spray against the dough and over the edges of the tart pan. Fill the shell with pie weights and bake until the top edge of the dough just starts to color and the surface of dough under the foil no longer looks wet, about 30 minutes. Remove the tart shell from the oven and carefully remove the weights and foil. Return the baking sheet with the tart shell to the oven and continue to bake, uncovered, until golden brown, 5 to 10 minutes. Set the baking sheet with the tart shell on a wire rack to cool while making the filling. (Do not turn off the oven.)

**3.** For the filling: While the crust is baking, cook the bacon in a 12-inch nonstick skillet over medium heat until browned and crisp, 8 to 10 minutes. Using a slotted spoon, transfer the bacon to a paper towel–lined plate; set aside. Pour off all but 2 tablespoons bacon fat from the skillet (or add vegetable oil if needed to make this amount).

**4.** Add the onions, salt, and thyme to the skillet. Cover and cook until the onions release their liquid and start to wilt, about 10 minutes. Reduce the heat to low and continue to cook, covered, until the onions are very soft, about 20 minutes, stirring once or twice (if after 15 minutes the onions look wet, remove the lid and continue to cook for another 5 minutes). Remove the pan from the heat and cool for 5 minutes.

**5.** Whisk the eggs, half-and-half, and pepper together in a large bowl. Remove the thyme from the onions; discard. Stir the onions into the egg mixture until just incorporated. Spread the onion mixture over the bottom of the baked crust and sprinkle the reserved bacon evenly on top.

**6.** Bake the tart on the baking sheet until the center of the tart feels firm to the touch, 20 to 25 minutes. Set the baking sheet with the tart on a wire rack and cool for at least 10 minutes. Remove the tart pan ring, gently slide a thin-bladed spatula between the pan bottom and crust to loosen, and slide the tart onto a serving plate. Cut into wedges and serve.

## Erbazzone (Swiss Chard Pie)

SERVES 12

**WHY THIS RECIPE WORKS** Hailing from central Italy, this savory winter pie packs several pounds of hearty greens between layers of flaky pie crust, with additional flavor provided by pancetta and Parmigiano Reggiano cheese. After we browned the pancetta we cooked the aromatics and wilted the chard in its rendered fat. Ricotta is a controversial ingredient in erbazzone; many recipes don't include it, though some sources claim it's not erbazzone without it. We preferred the earthier taste of the erbazzone without the ricotta; we've provided the option to include it. This dough will be moister than most pie doughs; as the dough chills, it will absorb any excess moisture, leaving it supple and workable.

CRUST

- 20 tablespoons (2½ sticks) unsalted butter, chilled
- 2½ cups (12½ ounces) all-purpose flour, divided
- 1 teaspoon table salt
- ½ cup ice water, divided

FILLING

- 1 tablespoon extra-virgin olive oil
- 3 ounces pancetta, chopped fine, divided
- 1 onion, chopped fine
- 4 garlic cloves, minced
- 3 pounds Swiss chard, stemmed and cut into 1-inch pieces
- 4 ounces Parmesan cheese, grated (2 cups)
- 6 ounces (¾ cup) whole-milk ricotta cheese (optional)
- 1 large egg, lightly beaten

**1. FOR THE CRUST:** Grate half stick butter using coarse holes on box grater and place in freezer. Cut remaining 2 sticks butter into ½-inch pieces.

**2.** Pulse 1½ cups flour and salt in food processor until combined, about 4 pulses. Add butter pieces and process until homogeneous dough forms, about 30 seconds. Using your hands, carefully break dough into 2-inch pieces and redistribute evenly around processor blade. Add remaining 1 cup flour and pulse until mixture is broken into pieces no larger than 1 inch (most pieces will be much smaller), 4 or 5 pulses. Empty mixture into medium bowl. Add grated butter and toss until butter pieces are separated and coated with flour.

**3.** Sprinkle ¼ cup ice water over mixture. Toss with rubber spatula until mixture is evenly moistened. Sprinkle remaining ¼ cup ice water over mixture and toss to combine. Press dough with spatula until dough sticks together. Divide dough in half and transfer to sheets of plastic wrap. Draw edges of plastic wrap over first dough half and press firmly on sides and top to form compact, fissure-free mass. Flatten to form 5-inch square. Repeat with second dough half. Refrigerate for at least 2 hours or up to 2 days. Let chilled dough sit on counter to soften slightly, about 10 minutes, before rolling.

**4. FOR THE FILLING:** Adjust oven rack to lower-middle position and heat oven to 400 degrees. Cook oil and ⅓ cup pancetta in Dutch oven over medium-low heat until pancetta is browned and fat is rendered, 5 to 7 minutes. Using slotted spoon, transfer pancetta to bowl. Pour out all but 1 tablespoon fat from pot.

**5.** Add onion to fat left in pot and cook over medium heat until softened, about 5 minutes. Stir in garlic and cook until fragrant, about 30 seconds. Increase heat to high. Add chard, 1 handful at a time, and cook until beginning to wilt, about 1 minute. Cover and continue to cook, stirring occasionally, until chard is wilted but still bright green, 2 to 4 minutes. Uncover and continue to cook until liquid evaporates, about 5 minutes. Transfer chard to large bowl and let cool completely, about 30 minutes.

**6.** Grease rimmed baking sheet. Stir Parmesan; ricotta, if using; and cooked pancetta into chard. Roll 1 dough square into 14 by 10-inch rectangle on well-floured counter. Roll dough loosely around rolling pin and unroll it onto prepared sheet. Spread chard mixture evenly over crust, leaving 1-inch border around edges. Brush edges of crust with egg.

**7.** Roll remaining dough square into 14 by 10-inch rectangle on well-floured counter. Roll dough loosely around rolling pin and unroll it over filling. Press edges of crusts together to seal. Roll edges inward and use your fingers to crimp. Using sharp knife, cut through top crust into 12 equal squares (do not cut through filling). Brush with remaining egg and sprinkle with remaining pancetta.

**8.** Bake until pie is golden brown and pancetta is crispy, 30 to 35 minutes, rotating sheet halfway through baking. Transfer sheet to wire rack and let pie cool completely, about 30 minutes. Transfer pie to cutting board, cut into squares, and serve.

## Cōngyóubǐng (Scallion Pancakes)

**SERVES** 4 to 6

**WHY THIS RECIPE WORKS** The best cōngyóubǐng are crispy and browned on the outside and flaky and chewy inside. For our version, we opted for a boiling-water dough that stretched easily but did not spring back. Next we rolled the dough into a large, thin round; brushed it with a mixture of oil and flour; and sprinkled it with salt and scallions before rolling it into a cylinder. We coiled the cylinder into a spiral and then rolled it out into a round again. Making a small slit in the center of the pancake prevented steam from building up, so it laid flat and cooked evenly. A dipping sauce complemented the richness of the pancakes. We prefer the steady, even heat of a cast-iron skillet; a heavy stainless-steel skillet may be used, but you may have to increase the heat slightly. To make the pancakes ahead of time, stack the uncooked pancakes between layers of parchment paper, wrap tightly in plastic wrap, and refrigerate for up to 24 hours or freeze for up to 1 month. If frozen, thaw in a single layer for 15 minutes before cooking.

**DIPPING SAUCE**

- 2 tablespoons soy sauce
- 1 scallion, sliced thin
- 1 tablespoon water
- 2 teaspoons rice vinegar
- 1 teaspoon honey
- 1 teaspoon toasted sesame oil
- Pinch red pepper flakes

**PANCAKES**

- 1½ cups (7½ ounces) plus 1 tablespoon all-purpose flour, divided
- ¾ cup boiling water
- 7 tablespoons vegetable oil, divided
- 1 tablespoon toasted sesame oil
- 1 teaspoon kosher salt, divided
- 4 scallions, sliced thin, divided

**1. FOR THE DIPPING SAUCE:** Whisk all ingredients together in small bowl; set aside.

**2. FOR THE PANCAKES:** Using wooden spoon, mix 1½ cups flour and boiling water in bowl to form rough dough. When cool enough to handle, transfer dough to lightly floured counter and knead until tacky (but not sticky) ball forms, about 4 minutes (dough will not be perfectly smooth). Cover loosely with plastic wrap and let rest for 30 minutes.

**3.** While dough is resting, stir together 1 tablespoon vegetable oil, sesame oil, and remaining 1 tablespoon flour. Set aside.

**4.** Place 10-inch cast-iron skillet over low heat to preheat. Divide dough in half. Cover 1 half of dough with plastic wrap and set aside. Roll remaining dough into 12-inch round on lightly floured counter. Drizzle with 1 tablespoon oil-flour mixture and use pastry brush to spread evenly over entire surface. Sprinkle with ½ teaspoon salt and half of scallions. Roll dough into cylinder. Coil cylinder into spiral, tuck end underneath, and flatten spiral with your palm. Cover with plastic and repeat with remaining dough, oil-flour mixture, salt, and scallions.

**5.** Roll first spiral into 9-inch round. Cut ½-inch slit in center of pancake. Place 2 tablespoons vegetable oil in skillet and increase heat to medium-low. Place 1 pancake in skillet (oil should sizzle). Cover and cook, shaking skillet occasionally, until pancake is slightly puffy and golden brown on underside, 1 to 1½ minutes. (If underside is not browned after 1 minute, turn heat up slightly. If it is browning too quickly, turn heat down slightly.) Drizzle 1 tablespoon vegetable oil over pancake. Use pastry brush to distribute over entire surface. Carefully flip pancake. Cover and cook, shaking skillet occasionally, until second side is golden brown, 1 to 1½ minutes. Uncover skillet and continue to cook until bottom is deep golden brown and crispy, 30 to 60 seconds longer. Flip and cook until deep golden brown and crispy, 30 to 60 seconds. Transfer to wire rack. Repeat with remaining 3 tablespoons vegetable oil and remaining pancake. Cut each pancake into 8 wedges and serve, passing dipping sauce separately.

### SHAPING CŌNGYÓUBǏNG

**1.** Roll dough into 12-inch round on lightly floured counter. Drizzle round with 1 tablespoon oil-flour mixture and use pastry brush to distribute evenly; sprinkle with salt and half of scallions.

**2.** Roll up dough round into cylinder.

**3.** Coil cylinder, tucking end underneath, then flatten with your palm. Repeat with remaining dough and cover with plastic.

**4.** Roll out first flattened spiral into 9-inch round; cut ½-inch slit in center of pancake.

## Sesame Balls

**MAKES** 8 balls

**WHY THIS RECIPE WORKS** The Cantonese always make fried sesame balls around Chinese New Year because they are thought to bring good luck and good fortune. We cannot promise gold or silver if you make these, but what we can promise are irresistibly crisp and chewy fried balls with a sweet bean paste center and a coating of sesame seeds all the way around. These delicious fried treats are easy to make and other than the oil for frying, there are just six ingredients. To make the dough, we whisked together the flour, baking powder, and salt and then added a hot sugar syrup and kneaded the dough briefly. After resting for 30 minutes, the dough was ready to be rolled into balls. Then we flattened the balls (no rolling pin required), and added the portioned red bean paste. Now we were ready for some simple shaping, sealing, and rolling (in sesame seeds). The frying instructions must be carefully followed; if the oil gets too hot, the balls will burst. Glutinous rice flour is also sold as sweet rice flour. We developed this recipe using Mochiko brand rice flour. Lotus seed paste, black sesame seed paste, or mung bean paste can be used in place of the red bean paste. This recipe can be easily doubled; fry the sesame balls in two batches.

- 1½ cups (8¼ ounces) glutinous rice flour
- ½ teaspoon baking powder
- ⅛ teaspoon table salt
- ⅓ cup (2⅓ ounces) sugar
- 8 teaspoons smooth sweetened red bean paste
- ½ cup sesame seeds
- 2 quarts peanut or vegetable oil for frying

**1.** Whisk flour, baking powder, and salt together in large bowl. Bring ¾ cup water and sugar to boil in small saucepan over high heat until sugar has dissolved. Using rubber spatula, stir hot syrup into flour mixture until combined and no dry flour remains. Transfer dough to clean counter and knead with hands until smooth, about 3 minutes. Return dough to bowl, cover tightly with plastic wrap, and let rest for 30 minutes.

**2.** Meanwhile, divide bean paste into 1 teaspoon portions. Using lightly moistened hands, roll each portion into ball and transfer to plate. Cover loosely with plastic and refrigerate until ready to use.

**3.** Divide dough into 8 equal pieces (about 2 ounces each). Cover with damp towel. Working with 1 piece of dough at a time, use hands to roll into ball. Place ball on counter and flatten with palm of hand into 2-inch-wide circle. Place 1 portion of bean paste in center of circle. Gather sides of dough around paste, pushing out air pockets, and pinch top to seal, enclosing paste in center. Remoisten hands and roll ball, smoothing any cracks with your fingertips. Cover with damp towel.

**4.** Place ½ cup water in small bowl. Place sesame seeds in shallow plate. Working with 1 ball at a time, roll in water, letting excess drip off, then coat with sesame seeds, pressing gently to adhere. Transfer to plate.

**5.** Line rimmed baking sheet with triple layer of paper towels. Add oil to 14-inch flat-bottomed wok or large Dutch oven until it measures about 1½ inches deep and heat over medium-high heat to 325 degrees. Using spider skimmer or slotted spoon, carefully add balls, 1 at a time, to hot oil. Cook, stirring constantly, until balls begin to float, about 4 minutes. Adjust burner, if necessary, to maintain oil temperature between 300 and 325 degrees.

**6.** Using spider skimmer, fully submerge each ball, gently pressing it against side or bottom of wok to deflate by about ½ inch, then release. Continuously submerge, press, and release balls until puffy and light golden brown, about 4 minutes. Using spider skimmer, transfer sesame balls to prepared sheet. Let cool for 5 minutes. Serve.

### SHAPING SESAME BALLS

**1.** Place 1 portion of bean paste on dough circle, then gather sides of dough around paste, pushing out air pockets.

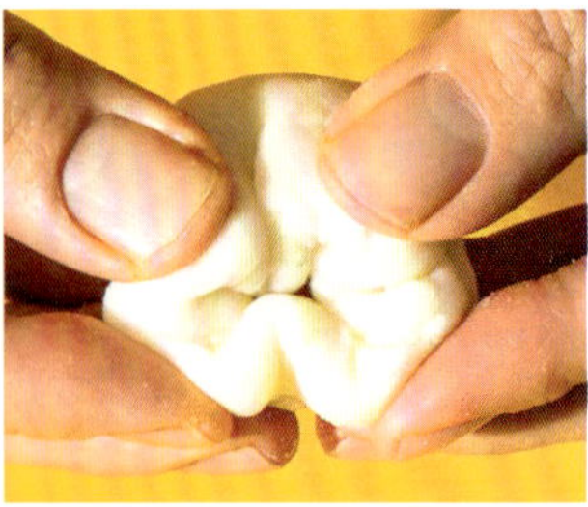

**2.** Pinch top of dough to seal, enclosing paste in center.

**3.** Working with 1 ball at a time, roll in water, letting excess drip off, then coat with sesame seeds, pressing gently to adhere.

## Pakoras (South Asian Spiced Vegetable Fritters)

**MAKES** 15 pakoras

**WHY THIS RECIPE WORKS** Pakoras are spiced vegetable fritters from the Indian subcontinent that are made with a thick batter of besan (flour milled from skinned and split brown chickpeas) and water. These crispy fritters make a satisfying snack. For vegetable-forward pakoras, a 4:1 ratio of chopped and shredded vegetables plus a colorful trio of spinach, potato, and red onion added to the batter worked nicely. For the spices we used liberal doses of cumin, coriander, turmeric, Kashmiri chile powder, fenugreek, and ajwain (an ingredient frequently added as a digestive aid). Baking powder kept the pakoras light and fluffy on the inside, and frying just five at a time created evenly cooked interiors that weren't greasy. For the best texture, we recommend measuring the prepped onion and potato by weight. Besan (also known as gram flour) is made from brown chickpeas. To substitute standard chickpea flour (made from white chickpeas), add an additional 2 tablespoons of water to the batter. Besan, ajwain, and Kashmiri chile powder can be found in South Asian markets. If ajwain is unavailable, substitute dried thyme. If fenugreek is unavailable, it can be omitted. Use a Dutch oven that holds 6 quarts or more. Serve with Carrot-Tamarind Chutney (recipe follows).

- 1 large red onion, halved and sliced thin (1½ cups/5 ounces)
- 1 large russet potato, peeled and shredded (1½ cups/6½ ounces)
- 1 cup baby spinach, chopped
- 1 serrano chile, stemmed and minced
- 1 teaspoon ground cumin
- 1 teaspoon ground coriander
- 1 teaspoon ajwain
- ½ teaspoon table salt
- ½ teaspoon Kashmiri chile powder
- ¼ teaspoon ground fenugreek
- ¾ cup besan
- 1 teaspoon baking powder
- ½ teaspoon ground turmeric
- ¼ cup water
- 2 quarts canola oil for frying

**1.** In large bowl, combine onion, potato, spinach, serrano, cumin, coriander, ajwain, salt, chile powder, and fenugreek. Toss vegetables until coated with spices. Using your hands, squeeze mixture until vegetables are softened and release some liquid, about 45 seconds (do not drain).

**2.** In small bowl, mix together besan, baking powder, and turmeric. Sprinkle over vegetable mixture and stir until besan is no longer visible and mixture forms sticky mass. Add water and stir vigorously until water is well incorporated.

**3.** Adjust oven rack to middle position and heat oven to 200 degrees. Set wire rack in rimmed baking sheet. Add oil to large Dutch oven until it measures about 1½ inches deep and heat over medium-low heat to 375 degrees.

**4.** Transfer heaping tablespoonful of batter to oil, using second spoon to ease batter out of spoon. Stir batter briefly and repeat portioning until there are 5 pakoras in oil. Fry, adjusting burner, if necessary, to maintain oil temperature of 370 to 380 degrees, until pakoras are deep golden brown, 1½ to 2 minutes per side. Using spider skimmer or slotted spoon, transfer pakoras to prepared rack and place in oven. Return oil to 375 degrees and repeat with remaining batter in 2 batches. Serve immediately.

### Carrot-Tamarind Chutney

**MAKES** 1 cup

Tamarind juice concentrate can usually be found in South Asian markets but is also readily available online.

½ cup chopped peeled carrot
¼ cup chopped red onion
3 tablespoons tamarind juice concentrate
2 tablespoons water
1 tablespoon lemon juice
2 teaspoons sugar
½ teaspoon ground cumin
½ teaspoon ground coriander
½ teaspoon table salt

Process carrot and onion in food processor until finely chopped, about 20 seconds, scraping down sides of bowl halfway through processing. Add tamarind concentrate, water, lemon juice, sugar, cumin, coriander, and salt and process until combined, about 20 seconds, scraping down sides of bowl halfway through processing (mixture will not be completely smooth). Transfer to bowl. (Chutney can be refrigerated for up to 3 days.)

## Gỏi Cuốn (Vietnamese Summer Rolls)

**SERVES 4**

**WHY THIS RECIPE WORKS** Springy noodles, crisp lettuce, fresh herbs, and a bit of protein for heft make traditional gỏi cuốn a pleasure to eat. For the shrimp, we used indirect rather than direct heat to ensure they stayed tender. We found that briefly dunking the rice paper wrappers in cold water and transferring them to the counter while still stiff left them with enough surface moisture, hydrated them perfectly, and made them easier to work with and elastic enough to contain a generous amount of filling. If Thai basil is unavailable, increase the mint and cilantro to 1½ cups each. A wooden surface will draw moisture away from the wrappers, so assemble the rolls directly on your counter or on a plastic cutting board. If part of the wrapper starts to dry out while you are forming the rolls, moisten it with your dampened fingers. If you like, serve with Nước Chấm (recipe follows).

**PEANUT-HOISIN SAUCE**

1 Thai chile, sliced thin
1 garlic clove, minced
1 teaspoon kosher salt
⅔ cup water
⅓ cup creamy peanut butter
3 tablespoons hoisin sauce
2 tablespoons tomato paste
1 tablespoon distilled white vinegar

**SUMMER ROLLS**

6 ounces rice vermicelli
10 ounces boneless country-style pork ribs, trimmed
2 teaspoons kosher salt
18 medium-large shrimp (31 to 40 per pound), peeled, deveined, and tails removed (see page 523)
1 cup fresh mint leaves
1 cup fresh cilantro leaves and thin stems
1 cup Thai basil leaves
12 (8½-inch) round rice paper wrappers
12 leaves red or green leaf lettuce, thick ribs removed
2 scallions, sliced thin on bias

**1. FOR THE PEANUT-HOISIN SAUCE:** Using mortar and pestle (or on cutting board using flat side of chef's knife), mash Thai chile, garlic, and salt to fine paste. Transfer to medium bowl. Add water, peanut butter, hoisin, tomato paste, and vinegar and whisk until smooth.

**2. FOR THE SUMMER ROLLS:** Bring 2 quarts water to boil in medium saucepan. Stir in noodles. Cook until noodles are tender but not mushy, 3 to 4 minutes. Drain noodles and rinse with cold water until cool. Drain noodles again, then spread on large plate to dry.

**3.** Bring 2 quarts water to boil in now-empty saucepan. Add pork and salt. Reduce heat, cover, and simmer until thickest part of pork registers 150 degrees, 8 to 12 minutes. Transfer pork to cutting board, reserving water.

**4.** Return water to boil. Add shrimp and cover. Let stand off heat until shrimp are opaque throughout, about 3 minutes. Drain shrimp and rinse with cold water until cool. Transfer to cutting board. Pat shrimp dry and halve lengthwise. Transfer to second plate.

**5.** When pork is cool enough to handle, cut each rib crosswise into 2-inch lengths. Slice each 2-inch piece lengthwise ⅛ inch thick (you should have at least 24 slices) and transfer to plate with shrimp. Tear mint, cilantro, and Thai basil into 1-inch pieces and combine in bowl.

**6.** Fill large bowl with cold water. Submerge 1 wrapper in water until wet on both sides, no longer than 2 seconds. Shake gently over bowl to remove excess water, then lay wrapper flat on work surface (wrapper will be fairly stiff but will continue to soften as you assemble roll). Repeat with second wrapper and place next to first wrapper. Fold 1 lettuce leaf and place on lower third of first wrapper, leaving about ½-inch margin on each side. Spread ⅓ cup noodles on top of lettuce, then sprinkle with 1 teaspoon scallions. Top scallions with 2 slices pork. Spread ¼ cup herb mixture over pork.

7. Bring lower edge of wrapper up and over herbs. Roll snugly but gently until long sides of greens and noodles are enclosed. Fold in sides to enclose ends. Arrange 3 shrimp halves, cut side up, on remaining section of wrapper. Continue to roll until filling is completely enclosed in neat cylinder. Transfer roll to serving platter, shrimp side up, and cover with plastic wrap. Repeat with second moistened wrapper. Repeat with remaining wrappers and filling, keeping completed rolls covered with plastic. Uncover and serve with sauces as desired. (Leftovers can be wrapped tightly and refrigerated for up to 24 hours, but wrappers will become chewier and may break in places.)

### ROLLING A SUMMER ROLL

**1.** Bring lower edge of wrapper up and over herbs.

**2.** Roll snugly but gently until greens and noodles are enclosed.

**3.** Fold in sides to enclose ends.

**4.** Arrange 3 shrimp halves, cut side up, on remaining wrapper.

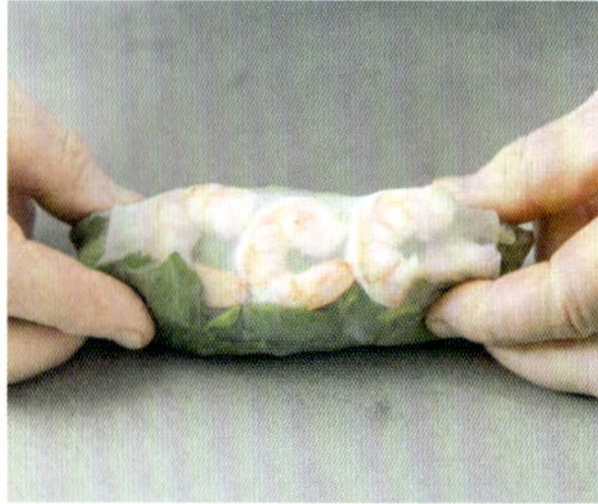

**5.** Continue to roll until filling is completely enclosed in neat cylinder.

## Nước Chấm (Vietnamese Dipping Sauce)

**MAKES** 1 cup

Hot water helps the sugar dissolve into the sauce.

- 3 tablespoons sugar, divided
- 1 small Thai chile, stemmed and minced
- 1 garlic clove, minced
- ⅔ cup hot water
- 5 tablespoons fish sauce
- ¼ cup lime juice (2 limes)

Using mortar and pestle (or on cutting board using flat side of chef's knife), mash 1 tablespoon sugar, Thai chile, and garlic to fine paste. Transfer to medium bowl and add hot water and remaining 2 tablespoons sugar. Stir until sugar is dissolved. Stir in fish sauce and lime juice.

## Lumpiang Shanghai with Seasoned Vinegar

**MAKES** 18 to 20 lumpia

**WHY THIS RECIPE WORKS** Lumpiang Shanghai (often referred to as "lumpia") are relatives of Chinese egg rolls, a staple at Filipino holidays and celebrations. Our lumpiang Shanghai feature a savory pork and vegetable filling flavored with soy sauce, pepper, garlic, and ginger. We pulsed the vegetables and aromatics in a food processor until they were finely chopped before pulsing in the pork along with 2 tablespoons of beaten egg. We sealed the lumpia with beaten egg and then fried them in 350-degree oil until their exteriors were golden brown and crispy. We paired the rolls with white cane vinegar seasoned with garlic, pepper, and soy sauce. Sukang maasim is a Filipino vinegar made from sugarcane. It boasts a balanced, versatile tart-sweetness but you can substitute distilled white vinegar. Look for spring roll wrappers or lumpia wrappers in the frozen foods section of an Asian market. Use a Dutch oven that holds 6 quarts or more. Crisp leftover lumpia by baking them in a 425-degree oven for 8 to 10 minutes. When removed from the oven, the rolls will be soft; they will crisp as they cool. Serve warm or at room temperature. Instead of the dipping sauce, you can serve the lumpia with a store-bought sweet chili sauce if desired.

**DIPPING SAUCE**

- ⅔ cup sukang maasim
- 1 tablespoon soy sauce
- 1½ teaspoons pepper
- 1 teaspoon sugar
- 1 garlic clove, minced
- Pinch table salt

**LUMPIA**

- ½ cup chopped onion
- ⅓ cup chopped carrot
- ⅓ cup chopped celery
- 4 garlic cloves, peeled
- 1 (½-inch) piece ginger, peeled

- 1 large egg
- 1 pound ground pork
- 1 tablespoon soy sauce
- 1 teaspoon pepper
- ¼ teaspoon table salt
- 18–20 (8-inch) square lumpia wrappers or spring roll wrappers
- 1½ quarts vegetable oil for frying

**1. FOR THE DIPPING SAUCE:** Stir all ingredients together in bowl. Let stand at room temperature for at least 30 minutes to let flavors meld or refrigerate for up to 4 days.

**2. FOR THE LUMPIA:** Process onion, carrot, celery, garlic, and ginger in food processor until finely chopped, scraping down sides of bowl as needed, about 20 seconds. Beat egg in small bowl until homogeneous. Add 2 tablespoons beaten egg to food processor, reserving remainder. Add pork, soy sauce, pepper, and salt and process until combined, scraping down sides of bowl as needed, 10 to 15 seconds. Transfer mixture to large heavy-duty zipper-lock bag and snip 1 corner to create 1-inch opening. Peel wrappers apart to separate; stack neatly and cover with very lightly dampened dish towel.

### ROLLING LUMPIA

**1.** Pipe even 5 by ¾-inch strip of filling just below center of wrapper.

**2.** Apply light layer of egg wash onto top corner of wrapper with pastry brush, making sure to brush all the way to edges.

**3.** Fold bottom corner of wrapper over filling and gently press along length of filling to remove air pockets.

**4.** Fold side corners over to enclose filling and gently roll to form tight cylinder.

**3.** Place 1 wrapper on counter so 1 corner points to edge of counter. Pipe 5 by ¾-inch strip of filling parallel to counter, just below center of wrapper. Using pastry brush, apply light layer of egg wash onto upper 1½ inches of top corner of wrapper, making sure to brush all the way to edges. Fold bottom corner of wrapper over filling and press gently along length of filling to remove air pockets. Fold side corners over to enclose filling snugly and gently roll to form tight cylinder. Transfer, egg-washed corner down, to rimmed baking sheet or large platter. (Do not stack.) Wipe any excess egg from counter and repeat with remaining wrappers and filling, filling two at a time if you feel comfortable with it. (Lumpia can be refrigerated in single layer in airtight container for up to 24 hours. Alternatively, freeze in single layer and then stack in airtight container and freeze for up to 1 month. Do not thaw before frying.)

**4.** Heat oil in Dutch oven over medium heat to 350 degrees. Set wire rack in rimmed baking sheet. Line rack with paper towels. Using tongs, transfer 6 lumpia to oil and fry, adjusting burner, if necessary, to maintain oil temperature of 340 to 360 degrees, until lumpia are golden brown, 5 to 7 minutes (frozen lumpia will take 1 to 2 minutes longer). Transfer to prepared rack. Repeat with remaining lumpia in 2 batches. Let cool for at least 5 minutes before serving with dipping sauce.

## Shrimp Cocktail

**SERVES 8** **SEASON 26**

**WHY THIS RECIPE WORKS** Shrimp cocktail should feel like luxury: plump, snappy, well-chilled meat with clean, oceanic sweetness. Nailing that profile is all about poaching the shrimp just right. Brining the shrimp seasoned them deeply, evenly, and quickly. Poaching them in the brine along with additional lightly seasoned water enhanced their flavor even more. Heating a measured amount of shrimp and water together allowed the shrimp to cook gradually so that there was little risk of overshooting the mark of 140 degrees. Calibrating the recipe so that the shrimp reached 140 degrees when the water reached 160 allowed us to monitor the temperature of the water instead of the temperature of the shrimp. For some fresh takes on the dipping sauce, see Chipotle-Lime Cocktail Sauce, Creole Rémoulade, and Creamy Chermoula (recipes follow). Serve with any or all of the sauces. Sauces can be refrigerated for up to 24 hours. See page 22 for instructions on substituting other shrimp sizes.

- 3 tablespoons table salt, divided
- 2 tablespoons sugar
- 2 pounds shell-on jumbo shrimp (16 to 20 per pound), peeled and deveined, tails left on (see page 523)
- 8 cups ice

**1.** Dissolve 2 tablespoons salt and sugar in 1 quart cold (65- to 70-degree) water in large Dutch oven. Submerge shrimp in brine for 15 minutes. Meanwhile, combine ice and 1 quart water in large bowl and set aside.

**2.** Add additional 1 quart cold water and remaining 1 tablespoon salt to Dutch oven and gently stir until salt dissolves. Set pot over medium heat and cook, stirring frequently, until water registers 160 degrees and shrimp are firm and have turned pink, about 12 minutes.

**3.** Using spider skimmer or slotted spoon, immediately transfer shrimp to prepared ice bath and let shrimp cool completely, about 10 minutes. Drain shrimp and transfer to bowl. Cover and refrigerate until ready to use.

## Chipotle-Lime Cocktail Sauce

**SERVES** 8 (Makes about 1 cup)

For a vibrantly fruity and smoky riff on the ketchup-horseradish profile of classic cocktail sauce, we seasoned that same base with chipotle chile in adobo, lime zest and juice, and cilantro.

- 1 cup ketchup
- ¼ cup prepared horseradish
- 2 tablespoons minced fresh cilantro
- 2 teaspoons minced canned chipotle chile in adobo sauce
- 1 teaspoon grated lime zest plus 2 teaspoons juice
- 1 teaspoon Worcestershire sauce

Whisk all ingredients in bowl until combined.

## Creamy Chermoula Sauce

**SERVES** 8 (Makes about 1 cup)

Garlicky, lemony, herby, spiced chermoula sauce, the oil-based condiment that's a staple for fish and seafood throughout North Africa, took on rich, lush body when we paired it with Greek yogurt, making it a particularly nice cocktail sauce alternative for poached shrimp.

- ¼ cup lemon juice (2 lemons)
- 1 tablespoon honey
- ½ cup canola oil
- 3 tablespoons extra-virgin olive oil
- 2 garlic cloves, minced
- ½ teaspoon smoked paprika
- ½ teaspoon ground cumin
- ½ teaspoon ground coriander
- ½ teaspoon table salt
- ⅛ teaspoon pepper
- ¼ cup plus 2 tablespoons plain Greek yogurt
- 4 teaspoons minced fresh mint
- 4 teaspoons minced fresh cilantro

Combine lemon juice and honey in blender. With blender running on medium-high speed, slowly add canola oil and olive oil until incorporated. Continue to process until mixture is smooth and creamy, 1½ to 2 minutes. Add garlic, smoked paprika, cumin, coriander, salt, and pepper and blend until combined, about 10 seconds. Add yogurt and blend until thickened to dipping sauce consistency, about 10 seconds. Transfer sauce to bowl and stir in mint and cilantro. Season with salt to taste.

## Creole Rémoulade

**SERVES** 8 (makes about 1 cup)

In addition to mustard and minced garlic, we added Louisiana-style hot sauce and a dash of Old Bay to give this classic mayonnaise-based sauce a tinge of heat and savory tang.

- 1 cup mayonnaise
- 2 tablespoons whole-grain mustard
- 1 tablespoon Louisiana-style hot sauce
- 1 tablespoon minced fresh parsley
- 2 teaspoons capers, minced
- 2 teaspoons Worcestershire sauce
- 1 teaspoon grated lemon zest plus 1 tablespoon juice
- 1 garlic clove, minced
- ½ teaspoon Old Bay Seasoning
- ¼ teaspoon pepper

Whisk all ingredients in bowl until combined.

## Customizing Shrimp Cocktail

If you want to scale up or down the yield on your shrimp cocktail or use a larger size shrimp, here's how:

To halve the yield, simply follow the original recipe as written. To double the recipe, instead of cooking 4 pounds in one pot, make two separate batches. To use extra-large shrimp (21–25), heat the water to 155 degrees. For extra-jumbo shrimp (13–15), heat the water to 163 degrees.

# Herb-Poached Shrimp with Cocktail Sauce

**SERVES** 4

---

**WHY THIS RECIPE WORKS** Nothing is more basic than shrimp cocktail and, given its simplicity, few dishes are more difficult to improve. Yet we set out to do just that; we wanted to work on the shrimp's flavor, the cooking method, and the cocktail sauce. Shrimp cook quickly, so there's little time to add flavor in the pan. We based our cooking liquid on shrimp stock, and added wine, lemon juice, herbs, and spices. To keep the shrimp in contact with this flavorful liquid as long as possible, we brought the mixture to a boil, turned off the heat, and then added the shrimp; the hot liquid cooked the shrimp slowly while they absorbed the stock's flavor. We determined that the classic sauce base, ketchup, was best. We added horseradish, which is the usual ingredient for spicing up the sauce, but we also included chili powder, cayenne, and lemon juice for extra spiciness. When using larger or smaller shrimp, increase or decrease, respectively, the cooking times for the shrimp by one to two minutes. When using such large shrimp, we find it wise to remove the large black vein. Use horseradish from a freshly opened bottle and mild chili powder for the best flavor in the sauce.

**SHRIMP**

- 1 pound jumbo shrimp (16 to 20 per pound; see note), peeled, deveined (see page 523), and shells reserved
- 1 teaspoon table salt
- 1 cup dry white wine
- 4 peppercorns
- 5 coriander seeds
- ½ bay leaf
- 5 sprigs fresh parsley
- 1 sprig fresh tarragon
- 1 teaspoon juice from 1 lemon

**COCKTAIL SAUCE**

- 1 cup ketchup
- 1 tablespoon juice from 1 small lemon
- 2½ teaspoons prepared horseradish
- 1 teaspoon ancho or other mild chili powder
- Pinch cayenne pepper
- Table salt and ground black pepper

**1. FOR THE SHRIMP:** Bring the reserved shells, 3 cups water, and salt to a boil in a medium saucepan over medium-high heat; reduce the heat to low, cover, and simmer until fragrant, about 20 minutes. Strain the stock through a fine-mesh strainer, pressing on the shells to extract all the liquid.

**2.** Bring the stock and remaining ingredients except the shrimp to a boil in a 3- or 4-quart saucepan over high heat; boil for 2 minutes. Turn off the heat and stir in the shrimp; cover and let stand until the shrimp are firm and pink, 8 to 10 minutes. Meanwhile, fill a large bowl with ice water. Drain the shrimp, reserving the stock for another use. Immediately transfer the shrimp to the ice water to stop cooking and chill thoroughly, about 3 minutes. Remove the shrimp from the ice water and pat dry with paper towels.

**3. FOR THE SAUCE:** Stir all the ingredients together in a small bowl; season with salt and pepper to taste. Serve the chilled shrimp with the cocktail sauce.

## Cóctel de Camarón (Mexican Shrimp Cocktail)

**SERVES** 4 to 6

**WHY THIS RECIPE WORKS** This popular Mexican dish consists of cooked shrimp tossed with chopped vegetables in a bright tomato sauce. For shrimp that were tender, not rubbery, we cooked them using residual heat. Bringing the cooking water to a full boil before adding the shrimp ensured that there was enough heat in the saucepan to cook them through. Cutting the shrimp into bite-size pieces made them easier to eat. For a sauce that wasn't too sweet, we used a combination of savory V8 juice and ketchup plus lime juice and hot sauce. V8's slightly viscous consistency, along with the ketchup, gave the sauce body to nicely coat the shrimp. Cucumber and red onion added crunch, avocado added creaminess, and cilantro

added freshness. We prefer untreated shrimp, but if your shrimp are treated with salt or additives such as sodium tripolyphosphate, do not add the salt in step 1. The balanced flavor of Valentina, Cholula, or Tapatío hot sauce works best here. If using a spicier, vinegary hot sauce such as Tabasco, start with half the amount called for and adjust to your taste after mixing. Saltines are a traditional accompaniment, but tortilla chips or thick-cut potato chips are also good.

- 1¼ pounds large shrimp (26 to 30 per pound), peeled, deveined, and tails removed (see page 523)
- ¼ teaspoon table salt, plus salt for cooking shrimp
- 1 cup V8 juice, chilled
- ½ cup ketchup
- 3 tablespoons lime juice (2 limes), plus lime wedges for serving
- 2 teaspoons hot sauce, plus extra for serving
- ½ English cucumber, cut into ½-inch pieces
- 1 cup finely chopped red onion
- 1 avocado, halved, pitted, and cut into ½-inch pieces
- ¼ cup chopped fresh cilantro
- Saltines

**1.** Bring 3 cups water to boil in large saucepan over high heat. Stir in shrimp and 1 tablespoon salt. Cover and let stand off heat until shrimp are opaque, about 5 minutes, shaking saucepan halfway through. Fill large bowl halfway with ice and water. Transfer shrimp to ice bath and let cool for 3 to 5 minutes. Once cool, cut each shrimp crosswise into 3 pieces.

**2.** Combine V8 juice, ketchup, lime juice, hot sauce, and salt in medium bowl. Add cucumber, onion, and shrimp and stir until evenly coated. Stir in avocado and cilantro. Portion cocktail into individual bowls or glasses and serve immediately, passing saltines, lime wedges, and extra hot sauce separately.

## Gravlax

**MAKES** 1 pound salmon

**WHY THIS RECIPE WORKS** Gravlax is a terrific make-ahead appetizer. Compared with smoked salmon, lox, and nova, which are all usually brined and then smoked, gravlax relies on a one-step process. The name, derived from "gravad lax" (Swedish for "buried salmon"), alludes to covering the fish with a salt-and-sugar cure (and typically dill). We used skin-on salmon because it made slicing the cured fish easier. A splash of brandy added flavor, helped the cure adhere, and assisted in the preserving process. Instead of granulated sugar we opted for brown sugar as its more complex flavor complemented the salmon. Pressing the salmon under a few cans helped it release moisture and gave the fillet a firmer, more sliceable texture. We basted the salmon with the released liquid once a day to help speed up the curing process and to keep it from drying out. Serve on crackers or rye bread topped with crème fraîche, shallot, and herbs (or other garnishes).

- ⅓ cup packed light brown sugar
- ¼ cup kosher salt
- 1 (1-pound) skin-on salmon fillet
- 3 tablespoons brandy
- 1 cup coarsely chopped fresh dill

**1.** Combine sugar and salt in bowl. Place salmon, skin side down, in 13 by 9-inch baking dish. Drizzle entire surface with brandy. Rub salmon evenly with sugar mixture, pressing firmly to adhere. Cover with dill, pressing firmly to adhere.

**2.** Cover salmon loosely with plastic wrap; top with square baking dish or pie plate; and weight with several large, heavy cans. Refrigerate until salmon feels firm, about 3 days, basting salmon with liquid released into dish once a day.

**3.** Scrape off dill. Remove salmon from dish and pat dry with paper towels. Slice thin and serve. (Gravlax can be wrapped tightly in plastic and refrigerated for up to 1 week. Don't slice until ready to serve.)

## Roasted Oysters on the Half Shell with Mustard Butter

**SERVES** 4 to 6

**WHY THIS RECIPE WORKS** Roasting is a great option if you're nervous about shucking or eating raw oysters or if you simply want a new way to serve them on the half shell. Warming the oysters in a hot oven made them easier to shuck; we placed them on a baking sheet covered in a layer of crumpled aluminum foil to steady them and ensure that they didn't tip over and spill their flavorful liquor. After shucking them, we dolloped the oysters with mustard butter and returned them to the oven to cook through. After just a few minutes, they emerged plump, tender, and dressed with a punchy sauce. You'll need an oyster knife and a large serving platter for this recipe. Using oysters that are 2½ to 3 inches long ensures that they will cook evenly.

- 5 tablespoons unsalted butter, softened
- 3 tablespoons minced fresh parsley, divided
- 1 tablespoon whole-grain mustard
- 24 oysters, 2½ to 3 inches long, well scrubbed
- Lemon wedges

**1.** Adjust oven rack to middle position and heat oven to 450 degrees. Stir butter, 2 tablespoons parsley, and mustard in bowl until well combined. Gently crumple and uncrumple two 24-inch lengths of aluminum foil. Place 1 piece in 18 by 13-inch rimmed baking sheet and second piece on large serving platter; cover foil on platter with dish towel for presentation, if desired. Nestle oysters, cupped side down, into foil on prepared sheet and bake until oysters open slightly, about 5 minutes. (It's OK to eat oysters that don't open.) Let oysters rest until cool enough to handle, about 5 minutes.

**2.** Shuck 1 oyster and discard top shell. Return oyster to foil, being careful not to spill much liquid. Repeat with remaining oysters.

**3.** Distribute mustard butter evenly among oysters, about ¾ teaspoon per oyster. Bake until thickest part of largest oyster registers 160 to 165 degrees, 5 to 8 minutes. Let rest for 5 minutes. Using tongs, carefully transfer oysters to prepared platter, nestling them into foil or towel to hold them level. Sprinkle remaining 1 tablespoon parsley over oysters. Serve, passing lemon wedges separately.

## Rhode Island–Style Fried Calamari

**SERVES** 4

**WHY THIS RECIPE WORKS** This version of fried calamari features tender squid and sliced banana peppers encased in a crispy, lacy, golden-brown crust. Dipping the squid in milk helped the dredge adhere while proteins in the milk encouraged browning. We added baking powder to the dredging mixture to lighten the texture of the coating. If desired, serve the calamari with Spicy Mayonnaise (page 321) or marinara sauce. Use a Dutch oven that holds 6 quarts or more for this recipe.

- ½ cup milk
- 1 teaspoon table salt
- 1½ cups all-purpose flour
- 1 tablespoon baking powder
- ½ teaspoon pepper
- 1 pound squid, bodies sliced crosswise ¾ inch thick, any extra-long tentacles trimmed to match length of shorter ones
- 1½ cups jarred sliced banana peppers
- 2 quarts vegetable oil for frying
- Lemon wedges

**1.** Set wire rack in rimmed baking sheet. Set second rack in second sheet and line with triple layer of paper towels. Heat oven to 200 degrees.

**2.** Whisk milk and salt together in medium bowl. Combine flour, baking powder, and pepper in second medium bowl. Add squid to milk mixture and toss to coat. Using your hands or slotted spoon, remove half of squid, allowing excess milk mixture to drip back into bowl, and add to bowl with flour mixture. Using your hands, toss to coat evenly. Gently shake off excess flour and place coated squid in single layer on unlined rack. Repeat with remaining squid. Add 1 cup banana peppers to flour mixture and toss with your hands to coat evenly. Gently shake off excess flour mixture and sprinkle peppers evenly among squid. Let sit for 10 minutes.

**3.** While squid and peppers rest, heat oil in large Dutch oven over high heat to 350 degrees. Carefully add half of squid and peppers and fry for exactly 3 minutes (squid will be golden brown). Using slotted spoon or spider skimmer, transfer calamari and peppers to paper towel–lined rack and place in oven to keep warm. Return oil to 350 degrees and repeat with remaining squid and peppers. Transfer calamari and peppers to platter, top with remaining peppers, and serve immediately with lemon wedges.

### FRYING CALAMARI

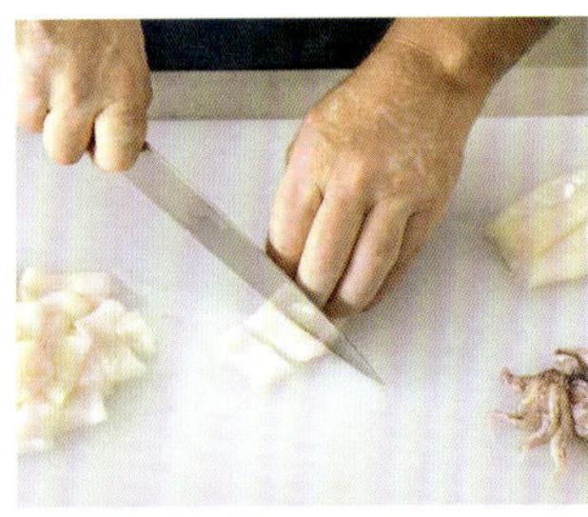

**1.** Slice squid bodies into ¾-inch-thick rings. Cut any long tentacles to match size of shorter ones. Dredge in flourbaking powder mixture and rest on wire rack.

**2.** Fry squid in 2 batches to prevent oil temperature from dropping too much so that pieces brown and crisp quickly. Use spider skimmer or slotted spoon to transfer first batch of calamari to paper towel–lined rack and transfer to oven to keep warm.

## Warm-Spiced Pecans with Rum Glaze

**MAKES** 2 cups

**WHY THIS RECIPE WORKS** Most spiced nuts are made with a heavily sugared syrup that causes the nuts to clump awkwardly and leaves your hands in a sticky mess. We wanted to get maximum flavor and balanced sweetness with minimum mess. We tried two popular methods—boiling the nuts in syrup and tossing them in butter—and eliminated both straight off. The former made the nuts sticky, and the latter dulled their flavor. A third method, coating the nuts with an egg white mixture, pretty much overwhelmed them with a candy-like coating. What finally worked was a light glaze made from very small amounts of liquid (we like either rum or water), sugar, and butter, which left the nuts just tacky enough to pick up an even, light coating of dry spices. The spiced nuts can be stored in an airtight container at room temperature for up to five days.

- 2 cups raw pecan halves

**SPICE MIX**

- 2 tablespoons sugar
- ¾ teaspoon table salt
- ½ teaspoon ground cinnamon
- ⅛ teaspoon ground cloves
- ⅛ teaspoon ground allspice

**RUM GLAZE**

- 1 tablespoon rum, preferably dark, or water
- 1 tablespoon unsalted butter
- 2 teaspoons vanilla extract
- 1 teaspoon light or dark brown sugar

**1.** Adjust oven rack to middle position and heat oven to 350 degrees. Line rimmed baking sheet with parchment paper and spread pecans on it in even layer; toast until fragrant and color deepens slightly, about 8 minutes, rotating sheet halfway through baking. Transfer sheet with the nuts to wire rack.

**2. FOR THE SPICE MIX:** While nuts are toasting, combine all ingredients in medium bowl; set aside.

**3. FOR THE RUM GLAZE:** Bring all ingredients to boil in medium saucepan over medium-high heat, whisking constantly. Stir in pecans and cook, stirring constantly with wooden spoon, until almost all of liquid has evaporated, about 1½ minutes.

**4.** Transfer glazed pecans to bowl with spice mix; toss well to coat. Return glazed spiced pecans to parchment-lined baking sheet to cool before serving.

## ATK 25

**MAKES** 2 cocktails

**WHY THIS RECIPE WORKS** Bridget developed this recipe for our 25th anniversary TV show. The elegant French 75 cocktail, which is simply gin, simple syrup, lemon juice, and Champagne, became the starting point. Ruby-red grenadine added tart and sweet notes and reflected our signature red color. We strongly prefer Champagne for this cocktail, but you can use another sparkling wine as long as it is labeled extra brut. Use a channel knife to make the lemon twist.

**GRENADINE**

- ¾ cup sugar
- 5 ounces unsweetened 100 percent pomegranate juice
- 8 allspice berries, lightly crushed
- ½ teaspoon pomegranate molasses (optional)

**COCKTAIL**

- 2 ounces London Dry gin
- 1¼ ounces unsweetened 100 percent pomegranate juice
- 1 ounce lemon juice, plus lemon twist for garnishing
- 1 ounce grenadine
- 4 ounces extra-dry Champagne, chilled

**1. FOR THE GRENADINE:** Heat sugar; pomegranate juice; allspice berries; and pomegranate molasses, if using, in small saucepan over medium-low heat, whisking often, until sugar has dissolved, 2 to 4 minutes; do not boil. Let cool completely, about 30 minutes, then strain through fine-mesh strainer into airtight container. (Grenadine can be refrigerated for up to 1 month. Shake gently before using.)

**2. FOR THE COCKTAIL:** Add gin, pomegranate juice, lemon juice, and grenadine to cocktail shaker, then fill with ice. Shake mixture until fully combined and well chilled, about 15 seconds. Double-strain cocktail into 2 chilled flute glasses. Add 2 ounces Champagne to each glass and garnish with lemon twist. Serve.

## Champagne Cocktail

**MAKES** 1 cocktail

**WHY THIS RECIPE WORKS** Sparkling wine cocktails are one of the easiest ways to make a party feel festive. We crafted three classic bubbly cocktails that come together quickly. The first was a Champagne cocktail: We placed an Angostura bitters–soaked sugar cube in the bottom of a chilled flute and then filled the glass with Champagne and garnished it with a lemon twist. These four ingredients interacted to form a cocktail that evolved from sip to sip. Bursting bubbles aromatized lemon oils from the twist to make the first sip bright and citrusy. Then the Champagne's flavors and aromas took over, with whispers of warm spices and orange hinting at what was to come. As the sugar cube dissolved, it created a bitters-infused syrup. Because this syrup was denser than the wine, it stayed at the bottom of the flute. The final sips delivered the flavors of the Angostura and balanced the bitters with the wine's acidity and the sugar's sweetness. For our second cocktail, a mimosa, we fortified strained and chilled orange juice with orange liqueur and then topped it off with sparkling wine. And finally, we fortified peach juice with peach schnapps and then topped it off with sparkling wine to make a Bellini. We strongly prefer Champagne here, but you can use another quality sparkling wine as long as it's brut or extra brut. Tilt the glass to a 45-degree angle and pour the wine down the side of the glass to minimize foaming. Use a channel knife to make the lemon twist.

- 1 sugar cube
- ¼ teaspoon Angostura bitters
- 5½ fluid ounces (½ cup plus 3 tablespoons) Champagne, chilled
- 1 lemon twist

Place sugar cube in small bowl. Add bitters to sugar cube. Transfer soaked sugar cube to chilled champagne flute. Add champagne and garnish with lemon twist. Serve.

### Mimosa

**MAKES** 1 cocktail

Use strained fresh-squeezed orange juice here. We like Cointreau, but any orange liqueur will work here. Tilt the glass to a 45-degree angle and pour the wine down the side of the glass to minimize foaming.

- 2½ fluid ounces (¼ cup plus 1 tablespoon) orange juice, strained and chilled
- ¼ fluid ounce (1½ teaspoons) orange liqueur
- 3 fluid ounces (¼ cup plus 2 tablespoons) sparkling wine, chilled
- 1 orange twist

Add orange juice and orange liqueur to chilled champagne flute; stir with spoon to combine. Add wine. Using spoon, gently lift juice mixture from bottom to top of glass to combine. Garnish with orange twist. Serve.

### Bellini

**MAKES** 1 cocktail

Either peach juice or nectar works well here. Tilt the glass to a 45-degree angle and pour the wine down the side of the glass to minimize foaming.

- 2½ fluid ounces (¼ cup plus 1 tablespoon) peach juice or nectar, chilled
- ¼ fluid ounce (1½ teaspoons) peach schnapps
- 3 fluid ounces (¼ cup plus 2 tablespoons) sparkling wine, chilled
- 1 thin slice peach (optional)

Add peach juice and peach schnapps to chilled champagne flute; stir with spoon to combine. Add wine. Using spoon, gently lift juice mixture from bottom to top of glass to combine. Garnish with peach slice, if using. Serve.

## Fireside

**MAKES** 1 cocktail

**WHY THIS RECIPE WORKS** We love to serve—and sip—this cocktail during the autumn months. The drink is, essentially, a warmly spiced version of a brandy old-fashioned, a gentler version of the traditional whiskey-based cocktail. To make our Fireside, we first replace the bourbon in a standard old-fashioned recipe with brandy (for a luxe version, you could even use cognac). The cinnamon, clove, and allspice in our Spiced Syrup emphasizes the brandy's dried-fruit and subtle warm spice notes. Citrus bitters provide zingy brightness—think of it as not unlike the lemon juice that's added to the very best spiced apple pie fillings. The optional Pumpkin Pie Spice Rim Sugar will further bump up the spiced elements and add a little sweetness. If you like, garnish each drink with a strip of orange peel instead of (or in addition to) the apple slice.

- ¼ cup Pumpkin Pie Spice Rim Sugar (optional; recipe follows)
- Orange wedge (optional, if using sugar)
- 2 ounces brandy or cognac
- 1 teaspoon Spiced Syrup (recipe follows)
- ⅛ teaspoon citrus bitters
- 1 apple slice

**1.** Spread sugar, if using, into even layer on small saucer. Moisten about ½ inch of chilled old-fashioned glass rim by running orange wedge around outer edge; dry any excess juice with paper towel. Roll moistened rim in sugar to coat. Remove any excess sugar that falls into glass; set aside.

**2.** Add brandy, spiced syrup, and bitters to mixing glass, then fill three-quarters full with ice. Stir until mixture is fully combined and well chilled, about 30 seconds. Fill prepared glass halfway with ice. Strain cocktail into glass. Garnish with apple slice and serve.

### Make-Ahead Firesides for Four

Combine 8 ounces brandy, 2 ounces water, 4 teaspoons Spiced Syrup, and ¼ teaspoon citrus bitters in serving pitcher or large container. Cover and refrigerate until flavors meld and mixture is well chilled, at least 2 hours or up to 24 hours. Stir to recombine. Serve as above. Makes 4 cocktails.

### Pumpkin Pie Spice Rim Sugar

**MAKES** about ½ cup

This recipe can easily be doubled.

- ½ cup sugar
- 2 teaspoons ground cinnamon
- 1 teaspoon ground ginger
- ½ teaspoon ground nutmeg
- ½ teaspoon ground allspice

Whisk all ingredients in bowl until combined. (Sugar can be stored in an airtight container for up to 1 month. Occasionally sugar can clump together during storage; break up any clumps before using.)

### Spiced Syrup

**MAKES** about 8 ounces

- ¾ cup sugar
- 5 ounces water
- 1 cinnamon stick
- 8 allspice berries, lightly crushed
- 4 whole cloves

Heat sugar, water, cinnamon stick, allspice berries, and cloves in small saucepan over medium heat, whisking often, until sugar has dissolved, about 5 minutes; do not boil. Let cool completely, about 30 minutes. Strain syrup through fine-mesh strainer into airtight container; discard solids (Syrup can be refrigerated for up to 1 month. Shake well before using.)

## Fresh Margaritas

**MAKES** 1 quart

**WHY THIS RECIPE WORKS** Poorly crafted margaritas tend to be slushy concoctions made with little more than ice, tequila, and corn syrup. For a great margarita, we found that the key was using equal parts alcohol and citrus juice. For a mellow flavor, we preferred reposado tequila, made from 100 percent blue agave, which is aged about 12 months. Unaged tequilas gave our margaritas a harsh flavor. And those made with superpremium tequilas, which are aged up to 6 years, tasted smooth, but their distinct tannic taste dominated the cocktail. For balanced citrus flavors, orange-flavored triple sec worked best. We steeped lemon and lime zest in their own juice which provided a burst of fresh flavor. The longer the zest and juice mixture is allowed to steep, the more developed the citrus flavors will be in the finished margaritas. We recommend steeping for the full 24 hours, although the margaritas will still be great if the mixture is steeped for only the minimum 4 hours. If you can't find superfine sugar, process an equal amount of regular sugar in a food processor for 30 seconds.

4 teaspoons grated lime zest plus ½ cup juice (4 limes)
4 teaspoons grated lemon zest plus ½ cup juice (3 lemons)
¼ cup superfine sugar
Pinch table salt
2 cups crushed ice, divided
1 cup 100 percent agave tequila, preferably reposado
1 cup triple sec

**1.** Combine lime zest and juice, lemon zest and juice, sugar, and salt in large liquid measuring cup; cover with plastic wrap and refrigerate until flavors meld, 4 to 24 hours.

**2.** Divide 1 cup crushed ice among 4 or 6 margarita or double old-fashioned glasses. Strain juice mixture into 1-quart pitcher or cocktail shaker. Add tequila, triple sec, and remaining 1 cup crushed ice; stir or shake until thoroughly combined and chilled, 20 to 60 seconds. Strain into ice-filled glasses and serve immediately.

## The Best Sangria

**SERVES 4**

**WHY THIS RECIPE WORKS** Many people mistake sangria for an unruly collection of fruit awash in a sea of overly sweetened red wine. We experimented with untold varieties of fruit to put in our sangria and concluded that simpler is better. We preferred the straightforward tang of citrus in the form of oranges and lemons. And we discovered that the zest and pith as well as the fruit itself make an important contribution to flavor. Orange liqueur is standard in recipes for sangria, and after experimenting we found that here, as with the wine, cheaper was just fine, this time in the form of triple sec. The longer sangria sits before drinking, the more smooth and mellow it will taste. A full day is best, but if that's impossible, give it a minimum of two hours to sit. Use large, heavy, juicy oranges and lemons for the best flavor. If you can't find superfine sugar, process an equal amount of regular sugar in a food processor for 30 seconds. Doubling or tripling the recipe is fine, but you'll have to switch to a large punch bowl in place of the pitcher. An inexpensive Merlot is the best choice for this recipe.

2 large juice oranges, washed (1 sliced, 1 juiced)
1 large lemon, washed and sliced
¼ cup superfine sugar
1 (750-milliliter) bottle inexpensive, fruity, medium-bodied red wine, chilled
¼ cup triple sec

**1.** Add sliced orange, lemon, and sugar to large pitcher. Mash fruit gently with wooden spoon until fruit releases some juice, but is not totally crushed, and sugar dissolves, about 1 minute. Stir in orange juice, wine, and triple sec; refrigerate for at least 2 hours or up to 8 hours.

**2.** Before serving, add 6 to 8 ice cubes and stir briskly to distribute settled fruit and pulp; serve immediately.

## Rosé Sangria

**MAKES** 12 cocktails

**WHY THIS RECIPE WORKS** From its humble—and ancient—roots in Spain, sangria's popularity has spread worldwide. While sangria is traditionally made with red wine, other types can be used; here we opted for pretty pink rosé and updated the mix-ins to match its lighter flavor profile for a refreshing twist on the classic that really allowed the rosé's flavor to shine. This meant choosing our mix-ins judiciously, so after some experimentation we stuck to adding only a couple cups of mixed berries. A few ounces of delicately floral elderflower liqueur highlighted these fresh flavors, and pomegranate juice deepened the color of the sangria and complemented the berries. A splash of simple syrup rounded out the drink with a subtle sweetness. The longer sangria rests before serving, the smoother and mellower it will taste. Give it an absolute minimum of 2 hours and up to 8 hours if possible.

2 (750-ml) bottles rosé wine
2 cups mixed berries
8 ounces pomegranate juice
4 ounces elderflower liqueur
4 ounces Simple Syrup

**1.** Combine all ingredients in serving pitcher or large container. Cover and refrigerate until flavors meld and mixture is well chilled, at least 2 hours or up to 8 hours.

**2.** Stir sangria to recombine, then serve in chilled wine glasses half-filled with ice, garnishing individual portions with macerated berries.

### Simple Syrup

**MAKES 8 OUNCES**

¾ cup sugar
5 ounces warm tap water

Whisk sugar and warm water in bowl until sugar has dissolved. Let cool completely, about 10 minutes, before transferring to airtight container. (Syrup can be refrigerated for up to 1 month. Shake well before using.)

## New Englander

**MAKES** 1 nonalcoholic cocktail

**WHY THIS RECIPE WORKS** A tart, vivid red New Englander is the perfect thing to serve alongside the rich fare so many of us gravitate toward in wintertime: It's elegant, festive, and sure to perk up your taste buds. The star of the drink is our cranberry shrub syrup. Cranberries are the ideal fruit to receive the sweet-tart shrub treatment; the syrup's luscious flavor shines when mixed with seltzer and a bit of lime juice. We found that the syrup had just the right sweetness. This recipe makes enough shrub syrup for up to four cocktails. To make additional cocktails, increase the lime juice and seltzer accordingly and repeat step 3.

**CRANBERRY SHRUB SYRUP**

- 2 cups fresh or frozen cranberries
- 1 cup sugar
- 6 ounces water
- 1 ounce white wine vinegar

**NEW ENGLANDER**

- ¼ ounce lime juice, plus lime twist for garnishing
- 6 ounces seltzer, chilled

**1. FOR THE CRANBERRY SHRUB SYRUP:** Bring cranberries, sugar, and water to boil in large saucepan over high heat. Reduce heat to medium-low, cover, and simmer until cranberries are beginning to break down, about 5 minutes.

**2.** Remove saucepan from heat and use potato masher to crush cranberries. Set fine-mesh strainer over medium bowl and line with triple layer of cheesecloth that overhangs edges. Transfer cranberry mixture to prepared strainer and let drain until liquid no longer runs freely and mixture is cool enough to touch, about 30 minutes. Pull edges of cheesecloth together to form pouch, then gently squeeze pouch to extract as much syrup as possible; discard solids. Whisk in vinegar. (Shrub syrup can be stored in airtight container for up to 1 month. Shake well before using.)

**3. FOR THE NEW ENGLANDER:** Fill chilled collins glass halfway with ice. Add 2 ounces shrub syrup and lime juice and stir to combine using bar spoon. Add seltzer and, using spoon, gently lift shrub mixture from bottom of glass to top to combine. Top with additional ice and garnish with lime twist. Serve.

### New Englander with Vodka

Add 1 ounce vodka to glass with shrub syrup.

## Holiday Eggnog

**SERVES** 12 to 16

**WHY THIS RECIPE WORKS** The rich creamy flavor of a really fine eggnog is too good to pass up. It's well worth knowing how to make this indulgent treat; the homemade version beats store-bought by a mile. We started by tinkering with a standard custard recipe (six eggs to 4 cups milk to ½ cup sugar). To enhance the custard's flavor and richness, we added two extra egg yolks, a little more sugar, and a bit of salt. Many eggnog recipes call for the milk to be added to the beaten eggs very gradually; we found that this did indeed make for a smoother texture. Last, but not least, were the flavorings. Call us traditionalists, but in the end we felt that nothing beat vanilla extract and nutmeg for true holiday eggnog flavor. Adding the milk to the eggs in small increments and blending after each addition helps ensure a smooth custard. To prevent curdling, do not heat the custard beyond 165 degrees. If it does begin to curdle, remove it from the heat immediately, pour it into a bowl set over a larger bowl of ice water to stop the cooking, and proceed with the recipe. You can omit the brandy to make a nonalcoholic eggnog, but you should also decrease the cream to ¼ cup to keep the right consistency. For the same reason, increase the cream to ¾ cup if you add another ½ cup alcohol for a high-test eggnog.

- 6 large eggs plus 2 large yolks
- ½ cup plus 2 tablespoons sugar
- 4 cups whole milk
- ¼ teaspoon table salt
- ½ cup brandy, bourbon, or dark rum
- 1 tablespoon vanilla extract
- ½ teaspoon freshly grated nutmeg, plus extra for serving
- ½ cup heavy cream

**1.** Whisk eggs, yolks, and sugar in medium bowl until thoroughly combined, about 30 seconds; set aside. Bring milk and salt to simmer in large saucepan over medium-high heat, stirring occasionally.

**2.** When milk mixture comes to simmer, remove from heat and, whisking constantly, slowly pour into yolk mixture to temper. Return milk-yolk mixture to saucepan. Place over medium-low heat and cook, stirring constantly, until mixture reaches 160 to 165 degrees, 2 to 5 minutes.

**3.** Immediately pour custard through fine-mesh strainer into large bowl; stir in liquor, vanilla, and nutmeg. Cover with plastic wrap and refrigerate until well chilled, at least 3 hours or up to 3 days.

**4.** Just before serving, using stand mixer fitted with whisk attachment, whip cream on medium-low speed until foamy, about 1 minute. Increase speed to high and whip until soft peaks form, 1 to 3 minutes. Whisk whipped cream into chilled eggnog. Serve, garnished with extra nutmeg.

CHAPTER 2 # Eggs and Breakfast

Photos (left to right):German Pancake; Çılbır; Breakfast Tacos; Liège Waffles; Congee; Classic Strawberry Jam; Crepes with Berries and Apricot Beurre Monté

# Perfect Scrambled Eggs

**SERVES 4**

**WHY THIS RECIPE WORKS** For foolproof rich scrambled eggs with moist curds that were creamy and light, we used a combination of high and low heat. The first step was to add salt to the uncooked eggs; salt dissolved some of the egg proteins so they were unable to bond when cooked, creating more tender curds. Beating the eggs until just combined, using the gentle action of a fork rather than a whisk, ensured that our scramble didn't turn tough. For intense creaminess, we chose half-and-half over milk; it produced rich, clean-tasting curds that were both fluffy and stable. To replicate the richer flavor of farm-fresh eggs, we added extra yolks. Finally, we started the eggs on medium-high heat to create puffy curds and then finished them over low heat so that they wouldn't overcook. A 10-inch skillet kept the eggs in a thicker layer, trapping more steam and producing heartier curds. It's important to follow the visual cues in this recipe, as pan thickness will affect cooking times. If using an electric stove, heat one burner on low heat and a second on medium-high heat; move the skillet between burners when it's time to adjust the heat. To dress up the dish, add 2 tablespoons of chopped parsley, chives, basil, or cilantro or 1 tablespoon of dill or tarragon to the eggs after reducing the heat to low.

- 8 large whole eggs
- 2 large yolks
- ¼ cup half-and-half
- ⅜ teaspoon table salt
- ¼ teaspoon pepper
- 1 tablespoon unsalted butter, chilled

**1.** Beat eggs, yolks, half-and-half, salt, and pepper with fork until eggs are thoroughly combined and color is pure yellow; do not overbeat.

**2.** Heat butter in 10-inch nonstick skillet over medium-high heat until fully melted (butter should not brown), swirling to coat pan. Add egg mixture and, using heatproof rubber spatula, constantly and firmly scrape along bottom and sides of skillet until eggs begin to clump and spatula just leaves trail on bottom of pan, 1½ to 2½ minutes. Reduce heat to low and gently but constantly fold eggs until clumped and just slightly wet, 30 to 60 seconds. Immediately transfer eggs to warmed plates and season with salt to taste. Serve immediately.

### TIMING SCRAMBLED EGGS

When spatula just leaves trail through eggs, turn the dial from medium-high to low.

# Fluffy Scrambled Eggs

**SERVES 4**

**WHY THIS RECIPE WORKS** Sometimes the simplest things can be the hardest to get right. And this is true when it comes to fluffy scrambled eggs. Seemingly easy to make, they can easily go wrong, and overcooking is probably the most common problem. We wanted scrambled eggs that turn out of the pan into a mound of large, soft curds—cooked enough to hold their shape but soft enough to eat with a spoon. We learned that beating the eggs too much before cooking them can result in toughness, so we whisked our eggs just until they were combined. Milk was better than water as an addition to scrambled eggs; the sugar, proteins, and fat in milk helped create large curds, which trapped steam for that pillowy texture we were after. A nonstick skillet was a must to prevent sticking, and pan size mattered as well; if the skillet was too large, the eggs spread out in too thin a layer and overcooked. Getting the pan hot was crucial for moist, puffy curds, and constant gentle stirring—really more like pushing and folding—prevented overcooking. Cooked on the stove until they were almost done, which took only a couple minutes, these eggs finished cooking on the way to the table, remaining moist and meltingly soft. These eggs cook very quickly, so it's important to be ready to eat before you start to cook them.

- 8 large eggs
- ½ cup milk
- ½ teaspoon table salt
- Pinch ground black pepper
- 1 tablespoon unsalted butter

**1.** Whisk the eggs, milk, salt, and pepper together in a medium bowl until any streaks are gone and the color is pure yellow.

**2.** Melt the butter in a 10-inch nonstick skillet over high heat, swirling to coat the pan. Add the eggs and, using a heatproof rubber spatula, cook while gently pushing, lifting, and folding them from one side of the pan to the other as they form curds. Continue until the eggs are nicely clumped into a single mound but remain shiny and wet, 1½ to 2 minutes. Serve.

# Creamy French-Style Scrambled Eggs

**SERVES 4**

**WHY THIS RECIPE WORKS** American-style scrambled eggs are the speediest of home-cooked breakfasts, but French cooks (and often British ones) employ a more leisurely approach, cooking their eggs slowly over low heat. This technique can take five times as long as the American version, but the reward is eggs that are extravagantly creamy and rich. The velvety texture of traditional French-style scrambled eggs is believed to be the combined result of slow cooking and the addition of plenty of cream and butter, but we found a way to make them without all the added fat. We used steaming water, rather than melted butter, to indicate when our nonstick skillet was hot enough to begin cooking the eggs. Stirring constantly controlled the coagulation of the proteins so that some formed delicate curds while the rest thickened into a saucy consistency. Adding a tablespoon of water at the end of cooking diluted the proteins, giving our eggs the perfect texture. Finally, a sprinkle of fresh minced herbs complemented their richness. For the creamiest, richest-tasting result, be sure to cook these eggs slowly, following the visual cue provided. It should take 12 to 14 minutes total. Though the eggs will be rather loose, their extended cooking time ensures that they reach a safe temperature. You can prepare two servings by halving the amounts of all the ingredients and using an 8-inch skillet. Chives or tarragon can be substituted for the parsley, if desired. Serve with buttered toast.

- 8 large eggs
- ½ teaspoon table salt
- 3 tablespoons water
- 1 teaspoon minced fresh parsley

**1.** Using fork, beat eggs and salt until blended. Heat 2 tablespoons water in 10-inch nonstick skillet over low heat until steaming. Add egg mixture and immediately stir with rubber spatula. Cook, stirring slowly and constantly, scraping edges and bottom of skillet, for 4 minutes. (If egg mixture is not steaming after 4 minutes, increase heat slightly.)

**2.** Continue to stir slowly until eggs begin to thicken and small curds begin to form, about 4 minutes longer (if curds have not begun to form, increase heat slightly). If any large curds form, mash with spatula. As curds start to form, stir vigorously, scraping edges and bottom of skillet, until eggs are thick enough to hold their shape when pushed to 1 side of skillet, 4 to 6 minutes. Remove skillet from heat. Add remaining 1 tablespoon water and parsley and stir vigorously until incorporated, about 30 seconds. Serve.

## Xīhóngshì Chǎo Jīdàn (Chinese Stir-Fried Tomatoes and Eggs)

**SERVES 4**

**WHY THIS RECIPE WORKS** This classic Chinese stir-fry featuring pillowy egg curds enrobed in a chunky, savory-sweet tomato sauce is often the first thing Chinese children learn how to make. Typically served with plenty of steamed white rice, it's soothing, homey comfort food. We started by beating eggs with a little Shaoxing wine and toasted sesame oil to add savory notes as well as tenderness—the liquid and oil diluted the egg proteins and kept them from bonding too closely and turning tough. Quickly cooking the eggs over medium-high heat promoted airier curds. For the tomato base, garlic, ginger, and scallions provided savoriness while canned tomatoes gave us year-round consistency. Simmering the tomatoes with a measured amount of sugar made the base taste concentrated and rich before we combined it with the eggs. Serve with rice.

- 4 scallions, white parts sliced thin, green parts cut into 1-inch lengths
- 3 tablespoons vegetable oil, divided
- 3 garlic cloves, sliced thin
- 2 teaspoons grated fresh ginger
- 8 large eggs
- 2 tablespoons Shaoxing wine or dry sherry
- 1 teaspoon toasted sesame oil
- 1 teaspoon table salt, divided
- 1 (28-ounce) can whole peeled tomatoes, drained with juice reserved, cut into 1-inch pieces
- 2 teaspoons sugar

**1.** Combine scallion whites, 1 tablespoon vegetable oil, garlic, and ginger in small bowl; set aside. Whisk eggs, Shaoxing wine, sesame oil, and ½ teaspoon salt together in separate bowl.

**2.** Heat remaining 2 tablespoons vegetable oil in 12-inch nonstick or carbon-steel skillet or 14-inch flat-bottomed wok over medium-high heat until shimmering. Add egg mixture. Using rubber spatula, slowly but constantly scrape along bottom and sides of pan until eggs just form cohesive mass, 1 to 2 minutes (eggs will not be completely dry); transfer to clean bowl.

**3.** Add garlic mixture to now-empty pan and cook over medium heat, mashing mixture into pan, until fragrant, about 30 seconds. Add tomatoes and their juice, sugar, and remaining ½ teaspoon salt and simmer until almost completely dry, 5 to 7 minutes. Stir in egg mixture and scallion greens and cook, breaking up any large curds, until heated through, about 1 minute. Serve.

## Scrambled Eggs with Asparagus, Smoked Salmon, and Chives

**SERVES 4**

**WHY THIS RECIPE WORKS** When you want a heartier take on scrambled eggs, it's tempting to round up leftover cooked vegetables, toss them in a hot skillet with beaten eggs, and stir until curds form. But we wanted hearty scrambled eggs that were foolproof. We nixed spinach and Swiss chard: They tended to weep after cooking, making the eggs watery. Superdelicate greens were also out: They liked to clump, which made them difficult to disperse evenly. We settled on fresh asparagus, chives, and luxurious smoked salmon. But for this fresher take on scrambled eggs, we wanted to use extra-virgin olive oil for its grassy savoriness. Using oil would also reduce the amount of moisture we were adding to the eggs, ensuring that the asparagus would not get soggy. We beat some oil into the eggs, along with chives, salt, and pepper, and also used the oil, instead of butter, to cook the eggs. Just before they were fully cooked we added the asparagus, which we rendered crisp-tender first in a skillet. We then transferred our dish to a serving platter, draped it with glossy pieces of smoked salmon, and added more fresh chives. If you can't find thin asparagus, peel the bottom halves of the spears until the white flesh is exposed and then halve each spear lengthwise before cutting it into ½-inch pieces. This recipe can be easily halved if desired; use a 10-inch skillet.

- 8 large eggs
- 3 tablespoons extra-virgin olive oil, divided
- 2 tablespoons minced fresh chives, divided
- ¼ teaspoon table salt
- ¼ teaspoon pepper
- 1 garlic clove, minced
- 8 ounces thin asparagus, trimmed and cut into ½-inch lengths
- 2 tablespoons water
- 2 ounces smoked salmon, torn into ½-inch strips

**1.** In medium bowl, beat eggs, 2 tablespoons oil, 1 tablespoon chives, salt, and pepper with fork until no streaks of white remain. Heat 1 teaspoon oil and garlic in 12-inch nonstick skillet over medium heat until fragrant, about 1 minute. Add asparagus and water, cover, and cook, stirring occasionally, until asparagus is crisp-tender, 3 to 4 minutes. Uncover and continue to cook until moisture has evaporated, about 1 minute longer. Transfer asparagus mixture to small bowl and set aside. Wipe skillet clean with paper towels.

**2.** Heat remaining 2 teaspoons oil in now-empty skillet over medium-high heat until shimmering. Add egg mixture and, using rubber spatula, constantly and firmly scrape along bottom and sides of skillet until eggs begin to clump and spatula just leaves trail on bottom of skillet, 30 to 60 seconds. Reduce heat to low and gently but constantly fold eggs until clumped and just slightly wet, 30 to 60 seconds. Fold in asparagus mixture. Transfer to serving dish, top with salmon, sprinkle with remaining 1 tablespoon chives, and serve.

### Scrambled Eggs with Pinto Beans and Cotija Cheese

**SERVES 4**

If cotija cheese is unavailable, you can substitute feta cheese. We like to serve these eggs with warm tortillas and hot sauce. This recipe can easily be halved if desired; use a 10-inch skillet.

- 8 large eggs
- 3 tablespoons extra-virgin olive oil, divided
- ¼ teaspoon table salt
- ¼ cup jarred sliced jalapeños, chopped coarse
- 2 garlic cloves, minced
- 1 (15-ounce) can pinto beans, rinsed
- ¼ cup chopped fresh cilantro, divided
- 1 ounce cotija cheese, crumbled (¼ cup)

**1.** In medium bowl, beat eggs, 2 tablespoons oil, and salt with fork until no streaks of white remain. Heat 1 teaspoon olive oil, jalapeños, and garlic in 12-inch nonstick skillet over medium heat until fragrant, about 1 minute. Add beans and 3 tablespoons cilantro and cook, stirring frequently, until moisture has evaporated, about 1 minute. Transfer bean mixture to small bowl and set aside. Wipe skillet clean with paper towels.

**2.** Heat remaining 2 teaspoons oil in now-empty skillet over medium-high heat until shimmering. Add egg mixture and, using rubber spatula, constantly and firmly scrape along bottom and sides of skillet until eggs begin to clump and spatula just leaves trail on bottom of skillet, 30 to 60 seconds. Reduce heat to low and gently but constantly fold eggs until clumped and just slightly wet, 30 to 60 seconds. Fold in bean mixture. Transfer to serving dish, sprinkle with cotija and remaining 1 tablespoon cilantro, and serve.

### Scrambled Eggs with Shiitake Mushrooms and Feta Cheese

**SERVES 4**

This recipe can be easily halved, if desired; use a 10-inch skillet. Oyster or cremini mushrooms can be substituted for the shiitake mushrooms, if desired; to prepare the oyster or cremini mushrooms, trim the stems but do not remove them. Precrumbled feta is often coated with cellulose to keep it from caking. For the best results, buy a block of feta and crumble it yourself.

- 8 large eggs
- 3 tablespoons extra-virgin olive oil, divided
- ¼ teaspoon table salt, divided
- ¼ teaspoon pepper
- 1 shallot, minced
- 1 teaspoon minced fresh thyme
- 8 ounces shiitake mushrooms, stemmed and sliced thin
- ¼ cup water
- 1 ounce feta cheese, crumbled (¼ cup)

**1.** In medium bowl, beat eggs, 2 tablespoons oil, ⅛ teaspoon salt, and pepper with fork until no streaks of white remain. Heat 1 teaspoon oil, shallot, thyme, and remaining ⅛ teaspoon salt in 12-inch nonstick skillet over medium heat, stirring occasionally, until shallot is softened and beginning to brown, 2 to 3 minutes. Add mushrooms and water, cover, and cook, stirring frequently, until mushrooms are softened, 5 to 8 minutes. Uncover and continue to cook until moisture has evaporated, 2 to 3 minutes longer. Transfer mushroom mixture to small bowl and set aside. Wipe skillet clean with paper towels.

**2.** Heat remaining 2 teaspoons oil in now-empty skillet over medium-high heat until shimmering. Add egg mixture and, using rubber spatula, constantly and firmly scrape along bottom and sides of skillet until eggs begin to clump and spatula just leaves trail on bottom of skillet, 30 to 60 seconds. Reduce heat to low and gently but constantly fold eggs until clumped and just slightly wet, 30 to 60 seconds. Fold in mushroom mixture. Transfer to serving dish, sprinkle with feta, and serve.

## Scrambled Eggs with Sausage, Sweet Pepper, and Cheddar Cheese

**SERVES** 4 to 6

**WHY THIS RECIPE WORKS** For a superhearty breakfast, we wanted to pair scrambled eggs with sausage, peppers, and cheese. But even a sprinkling of sausage or vegetables discolored the eggs and made them watery. We found that cooking in stages—sautéing our aromatics and removing them, cooking the eggs, then folding in all the other ingredients off the heat—prevented discoloration and helped with the wateriness. We were able to get rid of the last bit of wateriness by substituting a smaller amount of half-and-half—with its higher fat content and lower water content—for milk. Breakfast meats, crunchy vegetables, and dry leafy greens were successful additions to our eggs, so long as we avoided any that were moisture-laden. These eggs were not as fluffy as plain eggs, but the difference was imperceptible once we added meats and vegetables. We prefer sweet Italian sausage here, especially for breakfast, but you can certainly use spicy sausage, if desired.

- 12 large eggs
- 6 tablespoons half-and-half
- ¾ teaspoon table salt
- ¼ teaspoon ground black pepper
- 1 teaspoon vegetable oil
- 8 ounces sweet Italian sausage, casings removed, sausage crumbled into ½-inch pieces
- 1 red bell pepper, stemmed, seeded, and cut into ½-inch cubes
- 3 scallions, white and green parts separated, both sliced thin on the bias
- 1 tablespoon unsalted butter
- 1½ ounces sharp cheddar cheese, shredded (about ⅓ cup)

**1.** Whisk the eggs, half-and-half, salt, and pepper together in a medium bowl.

**2.** Heat the oil in a 12-inch nonstick skillet over medium heat until shimmering. Add the sausage and cook until beginning to brown but still pink in the center, about 2 minutes. Add the bell pepper and scallion whites; continue to cook, stirring occasionally, until the sausage is cooked through and the pepper is beginning to brown, about 3 minutes. Spread the mixture in a single layer on a medium plate; set aside.

**3.** Thoroughly wipe out the skillet with paper towels, add the butter, and melt over medium heat, swirling to coat the pan. Add the eggs and, using a heatproof rubber spatula, cook while gently pushing, lifting, and folding them from one side of the pan to the other as they form curds. Cook the eggs until large curds form but the eggs are still very moist, 2 to 3 minutes. Off the heat, gently fold in the sausage mixture and cheddar until evenly distributed; if the eggs are still underdone, return the skillet to medium heat for no longer than 30 seconds. Divide the eggs among individual plates, sprinkle with the scallion greens, and serve.

## Eggs Pipérade

**SERVES** 4

**WHY THIS RECIPE WORKS** When serving up eggs pipérade for breakfast, one thing is for certain: All diners are in for a healthy serving of flavor-packed vegetables. This Basque dish serves up scrambled eggs in a vibrant sauté of tender bell peppers, onions, and tomatoes—the winning combination we love in ratatouille. We wanted our vegetables to soften but retain their structure, so we kept a close eye on our skillet. We started with the onions; as soon as the pieces began to brown in the hot oil, we brought in the aromatics: minced garlic, minced fresh thyme, paprika, and red pepper flakes. After allowing them to bloom, we introduced the peppers. Using both cubanelle and red bell peppers contributed great color and subtle sweetness. Once the peppers were just softened, coarsely chopped canned tomatoes brought in bright acidity and their juice helped meld the vegetables' flavors as the liquid reduced. Some minced fresh parsley and a touch of sherry vinegar tied the vegetables together before we turned our attention to the eggs. With the peppers and onions waiting on our serving platter, we prepared some lightly seasoned scrambled eggs, folding them in a hot oiled pan until cooked but still slightly wet. We served our sautéed vegetables and perfectly moist eggs with a final sprinkling of parsley. We prefer to make this dish with cubanelle peppers, but green peppers can be substituted in a pinch. When serving, the eggs and pepper mixture can be served separately or the eggs can be gently folded into the pepper mixture, which is more traditional.

- 6 tablespoons extra-virgin olive oil
- 1 large onion, cut into ½-inch pieces
- 1 large bay leaf
- Table salt and pepper
- 4 garlic cloves, minced
- 1 teaspoon minced fresh thyme
- 2 teaspoons paprika
- ¾ teaspoon red pepper flakes
- 3 red bell peppers (7 to 8 ounces each), stemmed, seeded, and cut into ⅜-inch strips
- 3 cubanelle peppers (3 to 4 ounces each), stemmed, seeded, and cut into ⅜-inch strips
- 1 (14-ounce) can whole peeled tomatoes, drained with ¼ cup juice reserved, chopped coarse
- 3 tablespoons minced fresh parsley
- 2 teaspoons sherry vinegar
- 8 large eggs

**1.** Heat 3 tablespoons oil in 12-inch nonstick skillet over medium heat until shimmering. Add onion, bay leaf, and ½ teaspoon salt and cook, stirring occasionally, until softened and just starting to brown, about 6 minutes. Add garlic, thyme, paprika, and pepper flakes and cook, stirring occasionally, until fragrant, about 1 minute. Add bell peppers, cubanelle peppers, and 1 teaspoon salt; cover; and cook, stirring occasionally, until peppers begin to soften, about 10 minutes.

**2.** Remove cover and stir in tomatoes and juice. Reduce heat to medium-low and cook, uncovered, stirring occasionally, until mixture appears dry and peppers are tender but not mushy, 10 to 12 minutes. Discard bay leaf; stir in 2 tablespoons parsley and vinegar. Season with salt and pepper to taste. Transfer pepper mixture to serving dish. Wipe out skillet with paper towels.

**3.** While pepper mixture cooks, beat eggs, 2 tablespoons oil, ½ teaspoon salt, and ¼ teaspoon pepper with fork until eggs are thoroughly combined and color is pure yellow.

**4.** Return now-empty skillet to medium-high heat, add remaining 1 tablespoon oil and heat until shimmering. Add egg mixture and, using rubber spatula, constantly and firmly scrape along bottom and sides of skillet until eggs begin to clump and spatula just leaves trail on bottom of pan, 30 to 60 seconds. Reduce heat to low and gently but constantly fold eggs until clumped and just slightly wet, 30 to 60 seconds. Immediately transfer eggs to serving dish with pepper mixture, sprinkle with remaining 1 tablespoon parsley, and serve.

## Matzo Brei

**SERVES 2**

**WHY THIS RECIPE WORKS** Matzo brei (Yiddish for "fried matzo") is an Ashkenazi dish of eggs, matzo (unleavened flatbread made from flour and water), and fat that's eaten during Passover. It's a quick, comforting, and transformative way to use up just a handful of ingredients. To make a scrambled version with hearty egg presence, we used three eggs for two sheets of matzo; that way, the cooked dish was cohesive and boasted plenty of tender, rich pockets of egg. Soaking the broken matzo pieces in the whisked eggs cut out the usual separate step of soaking them in water or milk before cooking. Frying the egg-matzo mixture, as well as plenty of chopped onion, in flavorful fat such as butter or schmaltz suffused the dish with rich flavor that worked well as a backdrop for a range of toppings and seasonings. The brittleness of matzo makes it challenging to break into uniform pieces; don't worry if yours are slightly irregular. Different brands of matzo hydrate at slightly different rates; start checking for softness at the beginning of the time range in step 2. Matzo brei can be served with condiments such as sour cream, crème fraîche, yogurt, hot sauce, applesauce, or ketchup.

- 2½ tablespoons unsalted butter or schmaltz
- ⅔ cup chopped onion
- ½ teaspoon pepper, divided
- ¼ teaspoon table salt, divided
- 3 large eggs
- 2 sheets plain, unsalted matzo (about 2 ounces), broken into approximate 1½-inch pieces

**1.** Melt butter in 10-inch nonstick skillet over medium heat. Add onion, ¼ teaspoon pepper, and ⅛ teaspoon salt and cook, stirring occasionally, until onion has softened and started to brown, 6 to 8 minutes.

**2.** While onion cooks, whisk eggs, remaining ¼ teaspoon pepper, and remaining ⅛ teaspoon salt in medium bowl until no streaks of white remain. Add matzo pieces to egg mixture. Stir and fold until matzo is thoroughly coated with egg and pieces have softened (they should maintain their shape, but you should be able to break them easily with spatula), 2 to 4 minutes.

**3.** Add matzo mixture to skillet and gently but constantly stir and fold mixture onto itself, scraping along bottom and sides of skillet as needed until eggs are soft and just set, about 2 minutes. Serve immediately, seasoning with salt and pepper to taste.

### Matzo Brei with Smoked Salmon and Dill

Transfer to serving dish; top with 1 ounce smoked salmon, torn into ½-inch strips; sprinkle with 1 tablespoon chopped fresh dill; and pass crème fraîche separately.

### Matzo Brei with Mushrooms and Chives

Substitute ⅔ cup chopped white mushrooms for onion. Transfer to serving dish and sprinkle with 2 tablespoons minced fresh chives; pass crème fraîche separately.

### Matzo Brei with Cinnamon and Sugar

Omit onion and pepper. Add 1 teaspoon ground cinnamon and 1 teaspoon sugar to eggs. Cook in butter. Serve with maple syrup.

## Breakfast Tacos: Scrambled Eggs, Migas, and Charred Tortillas

**SERVES** 4 to 6

**WHY THIS RECIPE WORKS** A breakfast taco spread, with creamy scrambled eggs wrapped in softly charred tortillas and showered with flavorful toppings, makes a fun way to cook breakfast for a crowd. We used a really long serving board for an assembly-line presentation, with tortillas and eggs first, followed by toppings and, finally, sauces. Because nothing is worse than cold eggs, we saved the scrambling for last. First, we got the toppings set up; we liked scallions, avocados, salsa roja (recipe follows), pickled jalapeños, Monterey Jack cheese, hot sauce, and lime wedges. Next, we charred the tortillas and wrapped them up to keep them warm. Finally we scrambled the eggs, called everyone to the table, and served the scramble right from the skillet. If you like, level up your board by adding a mixture of sautéed poblanos, beans, and corn as well as browned chorizo.

### Scrambled Eggs

Be sure to follow the visual cues when making the eggs, as your pan's thickness will affect the cooking time. If you're using an electric stovetop, heat a second burner on low and move the skillet to it when it's time to adjust the heat.

- 12 large eggs
- ½ teaspoon table salt
- ¼ teaspoon pepper
- 2 tablespoons unsalted butter

**CHARRING TORTILLAS**

**1.** If you have a gas stove, hold 1 tortilla with tongs over flame, turning every few seconds to get even char. If you have an electric stove, heat a little oil in a skillet and warm tortilla over medium-high heat, turning every few seconds.

**2.** Wrap tortillas in clean dish towel to keep warm. Or, use a tortilla warmer.

**1.** Whisk eggs, salt, and pepper in bowl until thoroughly combined and mixture is pure yellow, about 1 minute. Melt butter in 12-inch nonstick skillet over medium heat. Add egg mixture and, using heat-resistant rubber spatula, constantly and firmly scrape along bottom and sides of skillet until eggs begin to clump and spatula leaves trail on bottom of skillet, 1½ to 2½ minutes.

**2.** Reduce heat to low. Gently but constantly fold egg mixture until clumped and slightly wet, 30 to 60 seconds. Season with salt and pepper to taste. Serve immediately.

### Migas

Omit butter. Heat 3 tablespoons vegetable oil in 12-inch nonstick skillet over medium-high heat until shimmering. Cut six 6-inch corn tortillas into 1 by ½-inch strips, then add to pan and cook, stirring occasionally, until golden brown, 4 to 6 minutes. Add 1 finely chopped onion, 1 finely chopped bell pepper, and 1 tablespoon minced jalapeño and cook until vegetables are softened, 5 to 7 minutes. Add egg mixture to tortilla mixture and proceed with recipe as directed. Before serving, gently fold in ⅓ cup shredded Monterey Jack and 1 tablespoon chopped fresh cilantro.

### Sautéed Poblanos, Beans, and Corn

**MAKES** 3 cups

Perfect for adding heft to your taco or even replacing eggs for vegan guests, this bean sauté comes together quickly and without a whole lot of planning thanks to canned beans and frozen corn.

- 1 tablespoon vegetable oil
- 2 poblano chiles, stemmed, seeded, and chopped
- 1 (15-ounce) can pinto beans, rinsed
- 1 cup frozen corn
- ½ cup chopped onion
- 2 teaspoons chili powder
- ¼ teaspoon table salt

Heat oil in 12-inch nonstick skillet over medium heat until shimmering. Add poblanos, beans, corn, onion, chili powder, and salt and cook until softened, 6 to 8 minutes.

### Salsa Roja

**MAKES 1½ cups**

This drizzle-able, slightly spicy, tomatoey sauce—meant to be served warm—brings breakfast tacos to life. To make the salsa spicier, reserve and add the jalapeño seeds to the blender before processing. Make sure to drain the tomatoes after microwaving them so that the salsa does not become too watery.

- 1 pound plum tomatoes, cored and chopped
- 2 garlic cloves, chopped
- 1 jalapeño chile, stemmed, seeded, and chopped
- 2 tablespoons chopped fresh cilantro
- 1 tablespoon lime juice
- 1 teaspoon table salt
- ¼ teaspoon red pepper flakes

**1.** Combine tomatoes and garlic in bowl and microwave, uncovered, until steaming and liquid begins to pool in bottom of bowl, about 4 minutes. Transfer tomato mixture to fine-mesh strainer set over bowl and let drain for 5 minutes.

**2.** Combine jalapeño, cilantro, lime juice, salt, pepper flakes, and drained tomato mixture in blender. Process until smooth, about 45 seconds. Season with salt to taste. Serve warm. (Salsa can be refrigerated for up to 3 days; cover and microwave briefly to rewarm before serving.)

## Fluffy Omelets

**SERVES 2**

**WHY THIS RECIPE WORKS** A different breed than French-style rolled omelets or diner-style omelets folded into half-moons, fluffy omelets are made by baking whipped eggs in a skillet until they rise above the lip of the pan. We love their impressive height and delicate texture. But most recipes result in oozing soufflés or dry, bouncy rounds—or eggs that barely puff up at all. To give our omelet lofty height without making it tough, we folded butter-enriched yolks into stiffly whipped whites stabilized with cream of tartar. The whipped whites gave the omelet great lift while the yolks and butter kept it tender and rich-tasting. We chose light but flavorful fillings that satisfied without weighing down the omelet. A teaspoon of white vinegar or lemon juice can be used in place of the cream of tartar, and a hand mixer or a whisk can be used in place of a stand mixer. We recommend using the filling that accompanies this recipe; it is designed not to interfere with the cooking of the omelet.

- 4 large eggs, separated
- 1 tablespoon unsalted butter, melted, plus 1 tablespoon unsalted butter
- ¼ teaspoon table salt
- ¼ teaspoon cream of tartar
- 1 recipe mushroom filling
- 1 ounce Parmesan cheese, grated (½ cup)

**1.** Adjust oven rack to middle position and heat oven to 375 degrees. Whisk egg yolks, melted butter, and salt together in bowl. Place egg whites in bowl of stand mixer and sprinkle cream of tartar over surface. Fit stand mixer with whisk and whip egg whites on medium-low speed until foamy, 2 to 2½ minutes. Increase speed to medium-high and whip until stiff peaks just start to form, 2 to 3 minutes. Fold egg yolk mixture into egg whites until no white streaks remain.

**2.** Heat remaining 1 tablespoon butter in 12-inch ovensafe nonstick skillet over medium-high heat, swirling to coat bottom of pan. When butter foams, quickly add egg mixture, spreading into even layer with spatula. Remove pan from heat and gently sprinkle filling and Parmesan evenly over top of omelet. Transfer to oven and cook until center of omelet springs back when lightly pressed, 4½ minutes for slightly wet omelet and 5 minutes for dry omelet.

**3.** Run spatula around edges of omelet to loosen, shaking gently to release. Slide omelet onto cutting board and let stand for 30 seconds. Using spatula, fold omelet in half. Cut omelet in half crosswise and serve immediately.

### Mushroom Filling

**MAKES ¾ cup**

- 1 teaspoon olive oil
- 1 shallot, sliced thin
- 4 ounces white or cremini mushrooms, trimmed and chopped
- ⅛ teaspoon table salt
- 1 teaspoon balsamic vinegar

Heat oil in 12-inch nonstick skillet over medium-high heat until shimmering. Add shallot and cook until softened and starting to brown, about 2 minutes. Add mushrooms and salt and season with pepper to taste. Cook until liquid has evaporated and mushrooms begin to brown, 6 to 8 minutes. Transfer mixture to bowl and stir in vinegar.

## Family-Size Tomato, Bacon, and Garlic Omelet

**SERVES 4**

**WHY THIS RECIPE WORKS** Cooking omelets one at a time for more than a couple of people just isn't practical. We wanted to find a way to make an omelet that was big enough to serve four people. We wanted it to have tender, not rubbery, eggs and a hearty flavorful filling. Flipping a huge eight-egg omelet was clearly not going to work, so we had to find a way to cook the top of the omelet as well as the bottom. Cooking the eggs longer over lower heat resulted in an unpleasant texture. Broiling to cook the top of the eggs worked, but it dried out the omelet, and we wanted it to be creamy. Then we had the idea of covering the pan after the bottom of the eggs was set

but the top was still runny, which worked like a charm. The lid trapped the heat and moisture to steam the top of the omelet, and it partially melted the cheese as well. Now we had a perfectly cooked omelet for four, with tender eggs and bits of melted cheese in every bite. Assemble the filling ingredients before making the omelet.

**FILLING**

- 8 slices bacon (about 8 ounces), minced
- 1 large ripe tomato, cored, seeded, and chopped fine
- ½ green bell pepper, stemmed, seeded, and chopped fine
- 4 medium cloves garlic, minced (about 4 teaspoons)

**OMELET**

- 8 large eggs
- ½ teaspoon table salt
- ⅛ teaspoon pepper
- 2 tablespoons unsalted butter
- 3 ounces shredded pepper Jack cheese (about ¾ cup)

**1. FOR THE FILLING:** Fry the bacon in a 12-inch nonstick skillet over medium-high heat until crisp, about 8 minutes. Stir in the tomato and bell pepper and cook until the vegetables are softened, about 6 minutes. Stir in the garlic and cook until fragrant, about 30 seconds. Transfer the mixture to a paper towel–lined plate. Wipe the skillet clean with paper towels.

**2. FOR THE OMELET:** Whisk the eggs, salt, and pepper together. Melt the butter in a 12-inch nonstick skillet over medium heat, swirling to coat the skillet, until the foaming subsides.

**3.** Add the eggs and bacon mixture and cook, stirring gently in a circular motion, until the mixture is slightly thickened, about 1 minute. Use a heatproof rubber spatula to pull the cooked edges of the egg toward the center of the pan, tilting the pan so the uncooked egg runs to the cleared edge of the pan. Repeat until the bottom of the omelet is just set but the top is still runny, about 1 minute. Cover the skillet, reduce the heat to low, and cook until the top of the omelet begins to set but is still moist, about 5 minutes.

**4.** Remove the pan from the heat. Sprinkle the cheese evenly over the eggs, cover, and let sit until the cheese partially melts, about 1 minute. Slide half of the omelet onto a serving platter using the spatula, then tilt the skillet so the remaining omelet flips over onto itself, forming a half-moon shape. Cut into wedges and serve immediately.

## Omelet with Cheddar and Chives

**MAKES** 1 omelet

**WHY THIS RECIPE WORKS** For an elegant and easy cheese omelet, we started by cooking three beaten eggs in an 8-inch nonstick skillet. Stirring constantly as the eggs cooked broke up the curds so that the texture of the finished omelet was even and fine. Once only a small amount of liquid egg remained, we cut the heat and smoothed this "glue" over the curds so that they held together. The filling must be at serving temperature before being rolled into the omelet; microwaving the cheese melted it just enough. Shaping the cheese filling into a strip and centering it in the omelet perpendicular to the handle made it easy to roll the eggs around the filling and out of the skillet. Covering the skillet after adding the filling trapped steam which helped the bottom of the eggs set enough to withstand rolling. Using a rubber spatula to slide the eggs to the far side of the skillet and folding them partway over the filling started the rolling process. Switching our grip and tilting the skillet forward allowed us to fully invert the omelet onto a plate below. Read the recipe carefully and have your ingredients and equipment ready before you begin. To ensure success, work at a steady pace. For the best results, cook the omelet in a nonstick skillet that's in good condition (not scratched or worn). To serve two, make two three-egg omelets instead of a single six-egg omelet. Omelets can be held for 10 minutes in an oven set to the lowest temperature.

- 3 large eggs
- Pinch table salt
- 1 ounce extra-sharp cheddar cheese, shredded (¼ cup)
- 1½ teaspoons unsalted butter
- 1½ teaspoons chopped fresh chives

**1.** Beat eggs and salt in bowl until few streaks of white remain.

**2.** Sprinkle cheese in even layer on small plate. Microwave at 50 percent power until cheese is just melted, 30 to 60 seconds. Set aside.

**3.** Melt butter in 8-inch nonstick skillet over medium heat, swirling skillet to distribute butter across skillet bottom. When butter sizzles evenly across skillet bottom, add eggs. Cook, stirring constantly with rubber spatula and breaking up large curds, until eggs are mass of small to medium curds surrounded by small amount of liquid egg. Immediately remove skillet from heat.

**4.** Working quickly, scrape eggs from sides of skillet, then smooth into even layer. Using fork, fold cheese into 2-inch-wide strip and transfer to center of eggs perpendicular to handle. Cover for 1 minute. Remove lid and run spatula underneath perimeter of eggs to loosen omelet. Gently ease spatula under eggs and slide omelet toward edge of skillet opposite handle until edge of omelet is even with lip of skillet. Using spatula, fold egg on handle side of skillet over filling. With your nondominant hand, grasp handle with underhand grip and hold skillet at 45-degree angle over top half of plate. Slowly tilt skillet toward yourself while using spatula to gently roll omelet onto plate. Sprinkle chives over omelet and serve.

### FORMING AN OMELET

**1.** Cook, stirring constantly and scraping bits of egg from sides of skillet into middle. Remove from heat; scrape eggs from sides and smooth into even layer.

**2.** Place cheese filling in center of eggs perpendicular to skillet handle. Cover for 1 minute.

**3.** Loosen omelet and slide to rim opposite handle. Fold eggs partway over filling.

**4.** Grasp handle with nondominant hand; hold skillet over plate at 45-degree angle. Slowly tilt skillet toward yourself while using spatula to roll omelet onto plate.

## French Omelets

**SERVES 2**

**WHY THIS RECIPE WORKS** The French omelet is a pristine rolled affair. Our perfect French omelet recipe had to give us golden yellow eggs with an ultracreamy texture rolled around minimal filling. Instead of a classic black carbon-steel omelet pan and a fork, a nonstick skillet and bamboo skewers or wooden chopsticks gave us small and silky curds. Preheating the pan eliminated any hot spots. For a creamy texture, we added very cold butter to the beaten eggs. To keep the omelet light, we avoided excessive beating. The omelet cooked so quickly it was hard to judge when it was done, so we turned off the heat when the eggs were still runny and covered the pan to finish cooking them. For an easy rolling method, we slid the omelet onto a paper towel and used the towel to roll the omelet into the a cylinder. If you don't have skewers or chopsticks to stir the eggs in step 3, use the handle of a wooden spoon. Warm the plates in a 200-degree oven.

- 2 tablespoons unsalted butter, cut into 2 pieces
- ½ teaspoon vegetable oil
- 4 large eggs plus 2 large egg yolks, cold, divided
- ¼ teaspoon table salt, divided
- ⅛ teaspoon black pepper, divided
- 2 tablespoons shredded Gruyère cheese, divided
- 4 teaspoons minced fresh chives, divided

**1.** Cut 1 tablespoon butter in half. Cut remaining 1 tablespoon butter into small pieces, transfer to small bowl, and place in freezer while preparing eggs and skillet, at least 10 minutes. Meanwhile, heat oil in 8-inch nonstick skillet over low heat for 10 minutes.

**2.** Crack 2 eggs into medium bowl and separate third egg; reserve white for another use and add yolk to bowl. Add ⅛ teaspoon salt and pinch pepper. Break yolks with fork, then beat eggs at moderate pace, about 80 strokes, until yolks and whites are well combined. Stir in half of frozen butter cubes.

**3.** When skillet is fully heated, use paper towels to wipe out oil, leaving thin film on bottom and sides of skillet. Add half of reserved 1 tablespoon butter to skillet and heat until melted. Swirl butter to coat skillet, add egg mixture, and increase heat to medium-high. Use 2 chopsticks or wooden skewers to scramble eggs using quick circular motion to move around skillet, scraping cooked egg from side of skillet as you go, until eggs are almost cooked but still slightly runny, 45 to 90 seconds. Turn off heat (remove skillet from heat if using electric burner) and smooth eggs into even layer using heat-proof rubber spatula. Sprinkle omelet with 1 tablespoon Gruyère and 2 teaspoons chives. Cover skillet with tight-fitting lid and let sit, 1 minute for runnier omelet and 2 minutes for firmer omelet.

**4.** Heat skillet over low heat for 20 seconds, uncover, and, using heatproof rubber spatula, loosen edges of omelet from skillet. Place folded square of paper towel onto warmed plate and slide omelet out of skillet onto paper towel so that omelet lies flat on plate and hangs about 1 inch off paper towel. Roll omelet into neat cylinder and set aside. Return skillet to low heat and heat for 2 minutes before repeating instructions for second omelet starting with step 2. Serve.

### ROLLING A FRENCH OMELET

Slide finished omelet onto paper towel–lined plate. Use paper towel to lift omelet and roll it up.

## Denver Omelets

**SERVES** 2

**WHY THIS RECIPE WORKS** A substantial Denver omelet has become a breakfast feature in American restaurants and diners. Filled with ham and lots of vegetables in addition to cheese, it's a meal in itself. But it's hard to get the vegetables cooked without overcooking the eggs. Cooking the filling separately, before the eggs, seemed to be the best way to avoid undercooked vegetables. In addition to the standard onion and green bell pepper, we also included red bell pepper, which made for a more colorful filling. Instead of julienning the vegetables, we finely chopped them; this made our filling easier to eat, and the peppers' skin was less intrusive. Ham steak was the easiest kind of ham to dice; it also imparted a welcome smoky flavor to the rest of the filling. For more complexity of flavor, we included garlic and parsley, which are unusual in a Denver omelet, and a dash of hot sauce livened things up without adding too much spiciness. We cooked the eggs according to our tried-and-true method, with some dairy (we used a little heavy cream, but milk worked as well) to keep the eggs from drying out, and added the warm filling just before folding the omelet onto a plate. Both components—eggs and filling—were perfectly cooked. You can make one omelet after another in the same pan, although you may need to reduce the heat.

- 6 large eggs
- 2 tablespoons heavy cream or milk
- ½ teaspoon table salt
- ¼ teaspoon ground black pepper
- 2 tablespoons unsalted butter
- 4 ounces Monterey Jack cheese, shredded (about 1 cup)
- 1 recipe Filling for Denver Omelets (recipe follows)

**1.** Whisk together 3 of the eggs, 1 tablespoon of the cream, ¼ teaspoon of the salt, and ⅛ teaspoon of the pepper in a small bowl until thoroughly combined.

**2.** Melt 1 tablespoon of the butter in a 10-inch nonstick skillet over medium-high heat until it just begins to brown, swirling to coat the pan. Add the eggs to the skillet and cook until the edges begin to set, 2 to 3 seconds, then, with a heatproof rubber spatula, stir in a circular motion until slightly thickened, about 10 seconds. Use the spatula to pull the cooked edges into the center, then tilt the pan to one side so that the uncooked egg runs to the edge of the pan. Repeat until the omelet is just set but still moist on the surface, 1 to 2 minutes.

**3.** Sprinkle ½ cup of the cheese evenly over the eggs and allow to partially melt, 15 to 20 seconds. With the handle of the pan facing you, spoon half the filling over the left side of the omelet. Slide the filling-topped half of the omelet onto a warmed plate using the spatula, then tilt the skillet so the remaining omelet folds over the filling in a half-moon shape; set aside. Repeat the instructions for the second omelet. Serve.

### Filling for Denver Omelets

**MAKES** enough to fill 2 omelets

A ham steak is our top choice for this recipe, although canned ham and sliced deli ham will work. (If using sliced deli ham, add it with the garlic, parsley, and hot sauce.)

- 1 tablespoon unsalted butter
- ½ red bell pepper, stemmed, seeded, and chopped fine
- ½ green bell pepper, stemmed, seeded, and chopped fine
- 1 small onion, minced
- ¼ teaspoon table salt
- 4 ounces ham steak, diced (about 1 cup)
- 1 tablespoon minced fresh parsley leaves
- 1 garlic clove, minced or pressed through a garlic press (about 1 teaspoon)
- ½ teaspoon hot sauce

Melt the butter in a 10-inch nonstick skillet over medium-high heat. Add the peppers, onion, and salt and cook, stirring occasionally, until the onion begins to soften, 5 to 7 minutes. Add the ham and cook until the peppers begin to brown, about 2 minutes. Add the parsley, garlic, and hot sauce and cook for 30 seconds. Transfer to a small bowl and cover to keep warm.

## Bauernfrühstück (German Farmer's Breakfast)

**SERVES 4** SEASON 26

**WHY THIS RECIPE WORKS** Bauernfrühstück, literally "farmer's breakfast" in German, is a by-product of the classic and comforting German side dish of Bratkartoffeln (pan-fried potatoes, bacon, onions, and herbs). Whisked, seasoned eggs are poured on top of the Bratkartoffeln and fried like an omelet. We wanted tender, golden-brown potatoes with slightly crisp edges infused with smoky flavor from the bacon and slight oniony sweetness. While the dish is typically made with leftover boiled potatoes, we wanted a recipe that started with raw, so we cooked the potatoes in a covered skillet, allowing them to steam and absorb flavor. When we removed the lid, the potatoes were allowed to brown and crisp around the edges. Covering the frying pan after adding the eggs allowed the eggs to fully set and slide out easily from the pan and created one big piece perfect for slicing to serve. For the most traditional flavor, use a hickory-smoked bacon. If the bacon is difficult to chop, place it in the freezer for 10 to 15 minutes to firm it up.

- 3 slices bacon, chopped fine
- ½ cup finely chopped onion
- 3 tablespoons unsalted butter, divided
- 2 pounds Yukon Gold potatoes, peeled and sliced crosswise ½ inch thick
- ¾ teaspoon table salt, divided
- 6 large eggs
- ¼ teaspoon pepper
- 1 tablespoon chopped fresh parsley

**1.** Cook bacon in 12-inch nonstick or carbon-steel skillet over medium-high heat until golden brown at edges and just starting to render, 3 to 5 minutes. Add onion and continue to cook until onion is soft and golden brown, 3 to 5 minutes. Using slotted spoon, transfer bacon and onion to bowl, leaving fat in skillet (you should have about 1 teaspoon).

**2.** Add 2 tablespoons butter to bacon fat and melt over medium heat. Add potatoes and ½ teaspoon salt and stir to coat potatoes evenly with fat. Cover and cook, shaking pan occasionally, for 9 minutes. After 9 minutes, potatoes should be bubbling at edges; if there is no moisture around potatoes, lower heat slightly; if there is no or little sizzling around potatoes, increase heat slightly. Cover and continue to cook until potatoes can be easily pierced with tip of paring knife, 6 to 9 minutes.

**3.** Remove lid and gently stir potatoes (it is OK if some potatoes break). Continue to cook, uncovered, gently stirring every 2 to 3 minutes until potatoes are golden brown (not all surfaces will be brown), about 10 minutes. Meanwhile, whisk eggs in bowl and add pepper and remaining ¼ teaspoon salt; set aside.

**4.** Add bacon and onion to skillet and stir gently to combine. Add remaining 1 tablespoon butter and swirl skillet so butter melts in between potatoes. Pour eggs over potatoes and cook, without stirring, until eggs begin to set, 45 seconds to 1 minute. Using rubber spatula, lift edge of cooked egg, then tilt pan to 1 side, so uncooked egg runs underneath. Repeat process, working around pan edge, using spatula to gently scrape uncooked egg toward rim of skillet, until top is just slightly wet, 1½ to 2 minutes.

**5.** Cover and cook until eggs are set and no longer appear runny, 2 to 3 minutes. Using rubber spatula, loosen from skillet and transfer to serving platter. Season with salt and pepper to taste and garnish with parsley. Slice and serve.

## Broccoli and Feta Frittata

**SERVES 4 to 6**

**WHY THIS RECIPE WORKS** Sometimes called a lazy cook's omelet, a frittata contains the same ingredients but doesn't require folding the eggs around the filling, which takes practice. We wanted to uncover the keys to a tender, evenly cooked, cohesive frittata, and we wanted it to be big and hearty enough to serve at least four for dinner. We started with a well-seasoned filling made with bold ingredients and combined it with a dozen eggs to make a substantial dinner. To ensure that the frittata was cohesive, we chopped the filling ingredients small so that they could be surrounded and held in place by the eggs. To help the eggs stay tender even when cooked to a relatively high temperature, we added milk and salt. The liquid diluted the proteins, making it harder for them to coagulate and turn the eggs rubbery, and salt weakened the interactions between proteins, producing a softer curd. Finally, for eggs that were cooked fully and evenly, we started the frittata on the stovetop, stirring until a spatula left a trail in the curds, and then transferred the skillet to the oven to gently finish. A 12-inch ovensafe skillet is necessary for this recipe. This frittata can be served warm or at room temperature.

- 12 large eggs
- ⅓ cup whole milk
- ¾ teaspoon table salt, divided
- 1 tablespoon extra-virgin olive oil
- 12 ounces broccoli florets, cut into ½-inch pieces (4 cups)
- Pinch red pepper flakes
- 3 tablespoons water
- ½ teaspoon grated lemon zest plus ½ teaspoon juice
- 4 ounces feta cheese, crumbled into ½-inch pieces (1 cup)

**1.** Adjust oven rack to middle position and heat oven to 350 degrees. Whisk eggs, milk, and ½ teaspoon salt in bowl until well combined.

**2.** Heat oil in 12-inch ovensafe nonstick skillet over medium-high heat until shimmering. Add broccoli, pepper flakes, and remaining ¼ teaspoon salt; cook, stirring frequently, until broccoli is crisp-tender and spotty brown, 7 to 9 minutes. Add water and lemon zest and juice; continue to cook, stirring constantly, until broccoli is just tender and no water remains in skillet, about 1 minute longer.

3. Add feta and egg mixture and cook, using rubber spatula to stir and scrape bottom of skillet until large curds form and spatula leaves trail through eggs but eggs are still very wet, about 30 seconds. Smooth curds into even layer and cook, without stirring, for 30 seconds. Transfer skillet to oven and bake until frittata is slightly puffy and surface bounces back when lightly pressed, 6 to 9 minutes. Using rubber spatula, loosen frittata from skillet and transfer to cutting board. Let stand for 5 minutes before slicing and serving.

## Asparagus, Ham, and Gruyère Frittata

**SERVES** 6 to 8

**WHY THIS RECIPE WORKS** A frittata loaded with meat and vegetables often ends up dry, overstuffed, and overcooked. We wanted a frittata big enough to make a substantial meal for 6 to 8 people—with a pleasing balance of egg to filling, firm yet moist eggs, and a lightly browned crust. We started with a dozen eggs, which we found required 3 cups of cooked vegetables and meat for balance. Most any vegetable or meat can be added to a frittata, with two caveats: The food must be cut into small pieces, and it must be precooked to drive off excess moisture and fat. A little half-and-half added a touch of creaminess. Given the large number of eggs, we had to shorten the time the frittata spent on the stovetop so that the bottom wouldn't scorch. We started the eggs on medium heat and stirred them so they could cook quickly yet evenly. With the eggs still on the wet side, we slid the skillet under the broiler until the top had puffed and browned but removed it while the eggs in the center were still slightly wet and runny, allowing the residual heat to finish the cooking. A 12-inch ovensafe nonstick skillet is necessary for this recipe. Because broilers vary so much in intensity, watch the frittata carefully as it cooks.

- 12 large eggs
- 3 tablespoons half-and-half
- ½ teaspoon table salt
- ¼ teaspoon pepper
- 2 teaspoons olive oil
- 8 ounces asparagus, tough ends trimmed, spears cut on the bias into ¼-inch pieces
- 4 ounces ¼-inch-thick deli ham, cut into ½-inch cubes (about ¾ cup)
- 1 medium shallot, minced (about 3 tablespoons)
- 3 ounces Gruyère cheese, cut into ¼-inch cubes (about ¾ cup)

1. Adjust an oven rack about 5 inches from the broiler element and heat the broiler. Whisk the eggs, half-and-half, salt, and pepper together in a medium bowl. Set aside.

2. Heat the oil in a 12-inch ovensafe nonstick skillet over medium heat until shimmering; add the asparagus and cook, stirring occasionally, until lightly browned and almost tender, about 3 minutes. Add the ham and shallot and cook until the shallot softens, about 2 minutes.

3. Stir the Gruyère into the eggs; add the egg mixture to the skillet and cook, using a heatproof rubber spatula to stir and scrape the bottom of the skillet, until large curds form and the spatula begins to leave a wake but the eggs are still very wet, about 2 minutes. Shake the skillet to distribute the eggs evenly and cook without stirring to let the bottom set, about 30 seconds.

4. Slide the skillet under the broiler and cook until the surface is puffed and spotty brown, yet the center remains slightly wet and runny when cut into with a paring knife, 3 to 4 minutes. Using a potholder (the skillet handle will be hot), remove the skillet from the oven and let stand for 5 minutes to finish cooking; using the spatula, loosen the frittata from the skillet and slide it onto a platter or cutting board. Cut into wedges and serve.

## Perfect Poached Eggs

**MAKES** 4

**WHY THIS RECIPE WORKS** Poached eggs can be tricky to get right; they should should be a neat pouch of tender egg, evenly cooked all the way through, with a yolk that is barely runny. But boiling water can agitate the eggs until they are a ragged mess. So we first examined the type of pan used. Most recipes require a deep saucepan, but we found that a skillet worked better: The water boiled faster, and the egg hit bottom sooner, and thus more gently, so that it could solidify before becoming stringy. Vinegar lowered the boiling point of the water, so we could cook the eggs over more gentle heat. The critical discovery, however, was cooking eggs in still, not bubbling, water—as long as it was hot enough. So we covered the skillet and turned off the heat after adding the eggs to the boiling water, and the residual heat cooked the eggs. Without bubbling water to tear them apart, our eggs were perfectly shaped, with no feathery whites in sight. To get four eggs into boiling water at the same time, crack each into a small cup with a handle. Holding two cups in each hand, lower the lip of each cup just into the water and tip the eggs into the pan.

Table salt
2 tablespoons distilled white vinegar
4 large eggs, each cracked into a small handled cup
Ground black pepper

**1.** Fill an 8- to 10-inch nonstick skillet nearly to the rim with water, add 1 teaspoon salt and the vinegar, and bring the mixture to a boil over high heat.

**2.** Lower the lip of each cup just into the water; tip the eggs into the boiling water, cover, and immediately remove the pan from the heat. Poach the eggs for 4 minutes for medium-firm yolks. (For firmer yolks, poach for 4½ minutes; for looser yolks, poach for 3 minutes.)

**3.** With a slotted spoon, carefully lift and drain each egg over the skillet. Season with salt and pepper to taste and serve.

## Sous Vide Soft-Poached Eggs

**MAKES** 1 to 16 eggs

**WHY THIS RECIPE WORKS** Eggs are perhaps the poster child for sous vide cooking: The technique can produce eggs with unique texture; the method is hands-off; and the recipe is easily scalable. Typically, sous vide eggs are cooked at a low temperature (around 145°F/63°C) for at least an hour. This provides a yolk that is slightly thickened but still runny and a barely set white. We found the white to be too loose when cooked in this temperature range, but some recipes call for cracking "63-degree eggs" into simmering water to better set the whites. We wanted to ditch that extra step, so we opted to cook at a higher temperature for a shorter time to set more of the white. This method produced a traditional poached egg—right out of the shell. And with the ability to make these eggs ahead of time—just reheat them in a 140-degree water bath—this recipe is perfect for the brunch crowd. Be sure to use large eggs that have no cracks and are cold from the refrigerator. Fresher eggs have tighter egg whites and are better suited for this recipe. Serve with crusty bread or toast.

1–16 large eggs, chilled

**1.** Using sous vide circulator, bring water to 167 degrees in 7-quart container. Using slotted spoon, gently lower eggs into prepared water bath, cover, and cook for 12 minutes.

**2.** Meanwhile, fill large bowl halfway with ice and water. Using slotted spoon, transfer eggs to ice bath and let sit until cool enough to touch, about 1 minute. To serve, crack eggs into individual bowls and season with salt and pepper to taste.

**TO MAKE AHEAD:** Eggs can be rapidly chilled in ice bath for 10 minutes and then refrigerated for up to 5 days. To reheat, lower eggs into water bath set to 140 degrees and cook until heated through, at least 15 minutes or up to 60 minutes. Crack into bowls as directed.

## Soft-Cooked Eggs

**MAKES** 4

**WHY THIS RECIPE WORKS** Traditional methods for making soft-cooked eggs are hit or miss. First, we found that fridge-cold eggs and boiling water reduced temperature variables, which makes the recipe more foolproof, and it provides the steepest temperature gradient, which ensures that the yolk at the center stays fluid while the white cooks through. Using only ½ inch of boiling water instead of several cups to cook the eggs means that the recipe takes less time and energy from start to finish. Because of the curved shape of the eggs, they actually have very little contact with the water, so they do not lower the water temperature when they go into the saucepan. This means that you can use the same timing for anywhere from one to six eggs. Because precise timing is vital to the success of this recipe, we strongly recommend using a digital timer. If you have one, a steamer basket makes lowering the eggs into the boiling water easier. We recommend serving these eggs in eggcups and with buttered toast for dipping, or you may simply use the dull side of a butter knife to crack the egg along the equator, break the egg in half, and scoop out the insides with a teaspoon.

4 large eggs

**1.** Bring ½ inch water to boil in medium saucepan over medium-high heat. Using tongs, gently place eggs in boiling water (eggs will not be submerged). Cover saucepan and cook eggs for 6½ minutes.

**2.** Remove cover, transfer saucepan to sink, and place under cold running water for 30 seconds. Remove eggs from pan and serve, seasoning with salt and pepper to taste.

## Eggs Benedict with Perfect Poached Eggs and Foolproof Hollandaise

**SERVES** 4

**WHY THIS RECIPE WORKS** To produce poached eggs with tender, tidy whites, we drained the eggs in a colander. We also deposited them into the boiling water one by one to prevent them from being jostled. Salted water with vinegar helped the whites set up quickly. Using a Dutch oven filled with 6 cups of water left plenty of headspace so that steam fully cooked the gooey portion of the white. Our unconventional technique for hollandaise required whisking softened butter and egg yolks in a double boiler, creating an emulsion stable enough to be chilled and reheated. We served our perfect eggs atop toasted English muffins and bacon, topped with our velvety hollandaise. For the best results, be sure to use the freshest eggs possible. The hollandaise can be refrigerated in an airtight container for three days. Reheat in the microwave on 50 percent power, stirring every 10 seconds, about 1 minute.

HOLLANDAISE

- 8 tablespoons unsalted butter, cut into 8 pieces and softened
- 4 large egg yolks
- ⅓ cup boiling water
- 2 teaspoons lemon juice
- Pinch cayenne pepper

EGGS

- 1 tablespoon distilled white vinegar
- Table salt, for cooking eggs
- 8 large eggs

- 4 English muffins, split
- 8 slices Canadian bacon

**1. FOR THE HOLLANDAISE:** Whisk butter and egg yolks in large heat-resistant bowl set over medium saucepan filled with ½ inch of barely simmering water (don't let bowl touch water). Slowly add boiling water and cook, whisking constantly, until thickened and sauce registers 160 to 165 degrees, 7 to 10 minutes.

**2.** Off heat, stir in lemon juice and cayenne; season with salt. Cover and set aside in warm place until serving time.

**3. FOR THE EGGS:** Bring 6 cups water to boil in Dutch oven over high heat, and add vinegar and 1 teaspoon salt. Fill second Dutch oven halfway with water and heat over high heat until water registers 150 degrees; adjust heat as needed to maintain 150 degrees.

**4.** Crack 4 eggs, one at a time, into colander. Let stand until loose, watery whites drain away from eggs, 20 to 30 seconds. Gently transfer eggs to 2-cup liquid measuring cup. Remove first pot with added vinegar from heat. With lip of measuring cup just above surface of water, gently tip eggs into water, one at a time, leaving space between them. Cover pot and let stand until whites closest to yolks are just set and opaque, about 3 minutes. If after 3 minutes whites are not set, let stand in water, checking every 30 seconds, until eggs reach desired doneness. (For medium-cooked yolks, let eggs sit in pot, covered, for 4 minutes, then begin checking for doneness.)

**5.** Using slotted spoon, carefully lift and drain each egg over Dutch oven, then transfer to pot filled with 150-degree water and cover. Return Dutch oven used for cooking eggs to boil and repeat steps 4 and 5 with remaining 4 eggs.

**6.** Adjust oven rack 6 inches from broiler element and heat broiler. Arrange English muffins, split side up, on baking sheet and broil until golden brown, 2 to 4 minutes. Place 1 slice bacon on each English muffin and broil until beginning to brown, about 1 minute. Remove muffins from oven and transfer to serving plates. Using slotted spoon, carefully lift and drain each egg and lay on top of each English muffin. Spoon hollandaise over top and serve.

## Çılbır (Turkish Poached Eggs with Yogurt and Spiced Butter)

SERVES 4

**WHY THIS RECIPE WORKS** Çılbır, a hot meze and light meal cooked in homes all over Turkey, consists of a just-set egg, garlicky yogurt, and swirls of spiced butter. To make it, we started with a base of strained yogurt, which provided a plush, creamy bed for the poached egg. Grated garlic mixed seamlessly with the yogurt. For perfect poached eggs, we drained the loose whites before dropping the eggs into water seasoned with salt and vinegar. This helped the whites set up quickly, ensuring that the yolks would still be liquid, as did gently cooking the eggs off the heat. For the finishing touch, we melted butter until it started to sizzle and turn nutty before adding fruity red pepper flakes, which turned the butter bright red. Strained yogurt has had some of the whey removed so that it's thicker than regular yogurt. Turkish strained yogurt is ideal for çılbır, but if you can't find it, Greek yogurt works well, too; do not use labneh, which is too thick for this recipe. A rasp-style grater makes quick work of turning the garlic into a paste. We strongly recommend seeking out the mild Turkish red pepper flakes pul biber or Aleppo pepper; however, ½ teaspoon of paprika can be substituted. For the tidiest presentation, use the freshest eggs possible. Çılbır can be eaten at any time of day; we like to pair it with a salad when serving it for lunch or dinner.

- 1 cup plain whole-milk strained yogurt
- ½ teaspoon garlic, minced to paste
- ⅛ teaspoon table salt, plus salt for cooking eggs
- 4 large eggs
- 1 tablespoon distilled white vinegar
- 2 tablespoons unsalted butter
- 1 teaspoon pul biber or ground dried Aleppo pepper
- ¼ teaspoon dried mint (optional)
- Pita, flatbread, or crusty bread

**1.** Stir yogurt, garlic, and salt in medium bowl until just combined. Divide yogurt mixture evenly among 4 serving plates or shallow bowls, spreading each portion with small spatula or back of spoon to make flat bed large enough to hold 1 poached egg. Set aside plates and allow yogurt to warm up while you prepare eggs.

**2.** Bring 1½ quarts water to boil in Dutch oven over high heat. Meanwhile, crack eggs, one at a time, into colander. Let stand until loose, watery parts of whites drain away from eggs, 20 to 30 seconds. Gently transfer eggs to 2-cup liquid measuring cup.

**3.** Add vinegar and 1 teaspoon salt to boiling water. Remove pot from heat. With lip of measuring cup just above surface of water, gently tip eggs into water, one at a time, leaving space between them. Cover pot and let stand until whites closest to yolks are just set and opaque, about 3 minutes. If after 3 minutes whites are not set, let stand in water, checking every 30 seconds, until eggs reach desired doneness.

**4.** While eggs cook, heat butter in small saucepan over medium heat until it sputters, 2 to 3 minutes. Stir in pepper flakes (butter will foam) and remove from heat.

**5.** Using slotted spoon, carefully lift and drain 1 egg over pot. Pat bottom of spoon dry with paper towel and gently place egg on yogurt bed. Repeat with remaining eggs. Drizzle butter evenly over eggs. Sprinkle each serving with pinch dried mint, if using, and season with salt and pepper to taste. Serve immediately, passing pita separately.

## Huevos Rancheros

**SERVES** 2 to 4

**WHY THIS RECIPE WORKS** Roughly translated as "rancher's eggs" or "country eggs," this Mexican egg dish was devised to use up leftover salsa and tortillas for a quick but filling breakfast. Over the years it's become a popular brunch dish in the United States. For our version, we examined each component of the dish to produce a satisfying meal. The salsa is a crucial element, and we know from experience that jarred salsa can't compare to freshly made, so we looked for ways to maximize the flavor of our supermarket tomatoes. We found that roasting plum tomatoes turned them more flavorful, and we thought roasting the onion and jalapeños improved their flavor as well. It was difficult to get fried eggs from the skillet onto the tortillas neatly (and without breaking the yolks), so we turned to poaching the eggs for a tidier presentation. We made things even easier by poaching them right in the simmering salsa, saving ourselves a pot to clean in the bargain. To pep up the supermarket tortillas, we brushed them with a little oil, sprinkled them with salt, and toasted them in the oven. Crisp tortillas, creamy eggs, and fiery salsa combined for a great version of this Mexican classic. To save time, make the salsa the day before and store it in the refrigerator. If you like, serve with Refried Beans (recipe follows).

- 3 jalapeño chiles, halved, seeds and ribs removed, divided
- 1½ pounds ripe plum tomatoes (about 6 medium), cored and halved
- ½ onion, cut into ½-inch wedges
- 3 tablespoons vegetable oil, divided
- 1 tablespoon tomato paste
- 2 garlic cloves, peeled
- 1 teaspoon table salt
- ½ teaspoon ground cumin
- ⅛ teaspoon cayenne pepper
- 3 tablespoons minced fresh cilantro, divided
- 1–2 tablespoons lime juice, plus lime wedges for serving
- 4 (6-inch) corn tortillas
- 4 large eggs

**1.** Adjust oven rack to middle position and heat oven to 375 degrees. Mince 1 jalapeño and set aside. In medium bowl, combine tomatoes, remaining 2 jalapeños, onion, 2 tablespoons oil, tomato paste, garlic, 1 teaspoon salt, cumin, and cayenne; toss to mix thoroughly. Place vegetables, cut side down, on rimmed baking sheet. Roast until tomatoes are tender and skins begin to shrivel and brown, 35 to 45 minutes; cool on baking sheet for 10 minutes. Increase oven temperature to 450 degrees. Using tongs, transfer roasted onion, garlic, and jalapeños to food processor. Process until almost completely broken down, about 10 seconds, pausing halfway through to scrape down sides of workbowl with rubber spatula. Add tomatoes and process until salsa is slightly chunky, about 15 seconds more. Add 2 tablespoons cilantro and reserved minced jalapeño and season with salt, pepper, and lime juice to taste.

**2.** Brush both sides of each tortilla lightly with remaining 1 tablespoon oil, sprinkle both sides with salt, and place on clean baking sheet. Bake until tops just begin to color, 5 to 7 minutes; flip tortillas and continue to bake until golden brown, 2 to 3 minutes more.

**3.** Meanwhile, bring salsa to gentle simmer in 12-inch nonstick skillet over medium heat. Remove from heat and make 4 shallow wells in salsa with back of large spoon. Break 1 egg into cup, then carefully pour egg into well in salsa; repeat with remaining 3 eggs. Season each egg with salt and pepper, then cover skillet and place over medium-low heat. Cook to desired doneness: 4 to 5 minutes for runny yolks, 6 to 7 minutes for set yolks.

**4.** Place tortillas on serving plates; gently scoop 1 egg onto each tortilla. Spoon salsa around each egg, covering tortillas but leaving portion of eggs exposed. Sprinkle with remaining 1 tablespoon cilantro and serve with lime wedges.

### Refried Beans

**MAKES** 3 cups

- 2 (15-ounce) cans pinto beans, rinsed, divided
- ¾ cup chicken broth
- ½ teaspoon table salt
- 3 slices bacon, chopped fine
- 1 small onion, chopped fine
- 1 large jalapeño chile, stemmed, seeded, and minced

½ teaspoon ground cumin
2 garlic cloves, minced
2 tablespoons minced fresh cilantro
2 teaspoons lime juice

**1.** Process all but 1 cup of beans with broth and salt in food processor until smooth, about 15 seconds, scraping down sides of workbowl with rubber spatula if necessary. Add remaining beans and pulse until slightly chunky, about 10 pulses.

**2.** Cook bacon in 12-inch nonstick skillet over medium heat until bacon just begins to brown and most of fat has rendered, about 4 minutes. Transfer to small bowl lined with strainer; discard bacon and add 1 tablespoon fat back to skillet. Increase heat to medium-high; add onion, jalapeño, and cumin; and cook until softened and just starting to brown, 3 to 5 minutes. Stir in garlic and cook until fragrant, about 30 seconds. Reduce heat to medium, stir in pureed beans, and cook until thick and creamy, 4 to 6 minutes. Off heat, stir in cilantro and lime juice.

## Shakshuka (Eggs in Spicy Tomato and Roasted Red Pepper Sauce)

**SERVES 4**

**WHY THIS RECIPE WORKS** Shakshuka is a Tunisian one-pan dish great for a savory breakfast or when you're looking to dress up some eggs for dinner. For the sauce, we blended whole peeled tomatoes and jarred roasted red peppers for a mix of sweetness, smokiness, and acidity. Adding pita bread helped prevent the silky-smooth sauce from weeping. A combination of garlic, tomato paste, and ground spices created the distinct flavor profile we were after. To ensure that the eggs cooked just right, we added them to the skillet off the heat and covered the whites with sauce to help speed their cooking. Chopped fresh cilantro, crumbled feta, and sliced kalamata olives on top provided texture and bright contrasting flavor. Served with a green salad, this dish makes a satisfying brunch, lunch, or dinner. Use a glass lid if you have it. If not, feel free to peek at the eggs frequently as they cook. Top with Zhoug (Spicy Cilantro Sauce) (recipe follows), if desired.

4 (8-inch) pita breads, divided
1 (28-ounce) can whole peeled tomatoes, drained
3 cups jarred roasted red peppers, divided
¼ cup extra-virgin olive oil
4 garlic cloves, sliced thin
1 tablespoon tomato paste
2 teaspoons ground coriander
2 teaspoons smoked paprika
1 teaspoon ground cumin
½ teaspoon table salt
¼ teaspoon pepper
¼ teaspoon cayenne pepper
8 large eggs
½ cup coarsely chopped fresh cilantro leaves and stems
1 ounce feta cheese, crumbled (¼ cup)
¼ cup pitted kalamata olives, sliced

**1.** Cut enough pita bread into ½-inch pieces to equal ½ cup (about one-third of 1 pita). Cut remaining pitas into wedges for serving. Process pita pieces, tomatoes, and half of red peppers in blender until smooth, 1 to 2 minutes. Chop remaining red peppers into ¼-inch pieces and set aside.

**2.** Heat oil in 12-inch skillet over medium heat until shimmering. Add garlic and cook, stirring occasionally, until golden, 1 to 2 minutes. Add tomato paste, coriander, paprika, cumin, salt, pepper, and cayenne, and cook, stirring constantly, until rust-colored and fragrant, 1 to 2 minutes. Stir in tomato–red pepper puree and reserved red peppers (mixture may sputter) and bring to simmer. Reduce heat to maintain simmer; cook, stirring occasionally, until slightly thickened (spatula will leave trail that slowly fills in behind it, but sauce will still slosh when skillet is shaken), 10 to 12 minutes.

**3.** Remove skillet from heat. Using back of spoon, make 8 dime-size indentations in sauce (7 around perimeter and 1 in center). Crack 1 egg into small bowl and pour into 1 indentation (it will hold yolk in place but not fully contain egg). Repeat with remaining 7 eggs. Spoon sauce over edges of egg whites so that whites are partially covered and yolks are exposed.

**4.** Bring to simmer over medium heat (there should be small bubbles across entire surface). Reduce heat to maintain simmer. Cover and cook until yolks film over, 4 to 5 minutes. Continue to cook, covered, until whites are softly but uniformly set (if skillet is shaken lightly, each egg should jiggle as a single unit), 1 to 2 minutes longer. Off heat, sprinkle with cilantro, feta, and olives. Serve immediately, passing pita wedges.

### Zhoug (Spicy Cilantro Sauce)

**MAKES 1 cup**

This Yemenite hot sauce is often served as an accompaniment to shakshuka or falafel but also adds a kick to roasted or grilled meats, fish, and vegetables or stirred into dips like hummus.

- 2 cups fresh cilantro leaves and stems
- 4 Thai chiles, stemmed
- 3 garlic cloves, peeled
- ½ teaspoon ground coriander
- ½ teaspoon ground cumin
- ½ teaspoon table salt
- ½ cup extra-virgin olive oil

Pulse cilantro, Thai chiles, garlic, coriander, cumin, and salt in food processor until coarsely chopped, 8 to 10 pulses. Transfer to small bowl. Add oil and stir until sauce has consistency of loose paste. Season with salt to taste. (Sauce can be refrigerated in airtight container for up to 2 weeks. Let come to room temperature before serving).

## Green Shakshuka

**SERVES 4**

**WHY THIS RECIPE WORKS** For a vibrant, earthy green shakshuka, we replaced the robust tomato and pepper sauce from red shakshuka with a mix of leafy greens and herbs: savory, mineral-y Swiss chard; tender baby spinach; and a bunch of fresh parsley. We started by softening the thinly sliced stems of the chard with onion and garlic in olive oil and then added cumin and coriander before wilting the chard leaves, parsley, and spinach. Next, we pureed a portion of the cooked greens with water and bread. The bread helped bind some of the water so that the puree was thick and homogeneous. The puree provided a smooth consistency for evenly transferring heat to the eggs, which helped them cook at the same rate, while the portion of unblended greens provided a sturdy bed for the eggs. Cooking the eggs covered allowed them to be heated from above and below. If sumac, which adds brightness, is unavailable, omit it in the steps and serve with lemon wedges (lemon juice may dull the color of the greens). Use a glass lid if you have one. If not, peek at the eggs frequently as they cook. Serve with hot sauce and garnish with Microwave-Fried Garlic (recipe follows).

- 6 tablespoons extra-virgin olive oil
- 1 pound Swiss chard, stems sliced ¼ inch thick (2 cups), leaves cut into 1½- to 2-inch pieces (8 cups)
- 1 onion, chopped fine
- 8 garlic cloves, sliced thin
- 1 teaspoon table salt, divided
- 2 teaspoons ground coriander
- 2 teaspoons ground cumin
- 2 cups plus 2 tablespoons chopped fresh parsley leaves and stems, divided
- 1 pound (16 cups) baby spinach
- 1 ounce country-style bread, cut into ½-inch pieces (½ cup), plus bread for serving
- 1¼ cups water
- 1½ teaspoons ground sumac, divided
- 8 large eggs
- 1 ounce goat cheese or feta cheese, crumbled (¼ cup)

**1.** Heat oil in 12-inch nonstick skillet over medium heat until shimmering. Add chard stems, onion, garlic, and ½ teaspoon salt. Cook, stirring occasionally, until vegetables are soft and lightly browned, 8 to 10 minutes.

**2.** Add coriander and cumin and cook until fragrant, about 1 minute. Add chard leaves and 2 cups parsley. Adjust heat to medium-low and cook, covered, stirring occasionally, until greens are just wilted but still bright green, 2 to 3 minutes.

**3.** Add half of spinach, cover, and cook until just wilted. Add remaining spinach and cook, covered, stirring occasionally, until all spinach is wilted but still bright green, 3 to 5 minutes. Off heat, transfer 1½ cups greens mixture to blender. Add bread, water, 1 teaspoon sumac, and remaining ½ teaspoon salt. Process until smooth puree forms, about 1 minute, scraping sides of blender jar as needed. Stir puree into skillet and smooth into even layer.

**4.** Using back of spoon, make 8 shallow indentations (about 1 inch wide) in surface of greens (seven around perimeter and one in center). Crack 1 egg into each indentation (which will hold yolk in place but not fully contain egg). Spoon greens over edges of egg whites so whites are partially covered and yolks are exposed.

**5.** Bring to simmer over medium heat. Cover and cook until yolks film over, 3 to 5 minutes, adjusting heat to maintain gentle simmer. Continue to cook, covered, until whites are softly but uniformly set (if skillet is shaken lightly, each egg should jiggle as single unit), 1 to 2 minutes longer. Off heat, sprinkle with goat cheese, remaining 2 tablespoons parsley, and remaining ½ teaspoon sumac. Season with salt to taste and serve, passing bread separately.

### Microwave-Fried Garlic

**MAKES** ½ cup

- ½ cup thinly sliced garlic
- ½ cup vegetable oil
- 1 teaspoon confectioners' sugar

1. Stir garlic into oil in medium bowl.

2. Microwave for 3 minutes. If garlic hasn't begun to brown, stir and microwave 90 seconds longer.

3. Repeat stirring and microwaving in 30-second increments until slices are golden brown, keeping in mind that garlic will continue to darken and crisp as it cools.

4. Using slotted spoon, transfer garlic to paper towel–lined plate. Dust garlic with sugar (to offset any bitterness) and season it with salt to taste. (Fried garlic can be stored in airtight container at room temperature for up to 2 days.)

## Baked Eggs Florentine

**SERVES 6**

**WHY THIS RECIPE WORKS** Baked eggs can be hard to get right. We wanted a creamy, slightly runny yolk and a tender white—in the same ramekin. The answer turned out to be insulation—that is, adding a spinach cream sauce to provide a barrier between the egg and the very hot sides of the ramekin. We also found that pulling the eggs from the oven before they were done and allowing carryover cooking to finish the job delivered first-rate baked eggs. For the eggs to cook properly, it is imperative to add them to the hot, filling-lined ramekins quickly. Prepare by cracking eggs into separate bowls or teacups while the filled ramekins are heating. Use 6-ounce ramekins with 3¼-inch diameters, measured from the inner lip. We developed this recipe using a glass baking dish; if using a metal baking pan, reduce the oven temperature to 425 degrees. This recipe can be doubled and baked in two 13 by 9-inch dishes. If doubling, increase the baking times in steps 3 and 4 by 1 minute.

- 2 tablespoons unsalted butter
- 1 large shallot, minced
- 1 tablespoon all-purpose flour
- ¾ cup half-and-half
- 10 ounces frozen spinach, thawed and squeezed dry
- 2 ounces Parmesan cheese, grated (1 cup)
- Table salt and pepper
- ⅛ teaspoon dry mustard
- ⅛ teaspoon ground nutmeg
- Pinch cayenne pepper
- Vegetable oil spray
- 6 large eggs

1. Adjust oven rack to middle position and heat oven to 500 degrees.

2. Melt butter in medium saucepan over medium heat. Add shallot and cook, stirring occasionally, until softened, about 3 minutes. Stir in flour and cook, stirring constantly, for 1 minute. Gradually whisk in half-and-half; bring mixture to boil, whisking constantly. Simmer, whisking frequently, until thickened, 2 to 3 minutes. Remove pan from heat and stir in spinach, Parmesan, ¾ teaspoon salt, ½ teaspoon pepper, mustard, nutmeg, and cayenne.

3. Lightly spray six 6-ounce ramekins with oil spray. Evenly divide spinach filling among ramekins. Using back of spoon, push filling 1 inch up sides of ramekins, making shallow indentation in center of filling large enough to hold egg. Place filled ramekins in 13 by 9-inch glass baking dish. Bake ramekins until filling just starts to brown, about 7 minutes, rotating dish halfway through baking.

4. While filling is heating, crack eggs (taking care not to break yolks) into individual cups or bowls. Remove baking dish with ramekins from oven and place on wire rack. Gently pour eggs from cups into hot ramekins, centering yolk in filling. Lightly spray surface of each egg with oil spray and sprinkle each with pinch of salt. Return baking dish to oven and bake until whites are just opaque but still tremble, 6 to 8 minutes, rotating dish halfway through baking.

5. Remove dish from oven and, using tongs, transfer ramekins to wire rack. Let stand until whites are firm and set (yolks should still be runny), about 10 minutes. Serve immediately.

**TO MAKE AHEAD:** Follow recipe through step 3, skipping step of baking lined ramekins. Wrap ramekins with plastic wrap and refrigerate for up to 3 days. To serve, heat lined ramekins, directly from refrigerator, for additional 3 to 4 minutes (10 to 11 minutes total) before proceeding with recipe.

## Galettes Complètes (Buckwheat Crepes with Ham, Egg, and Cheese)

**SERVES 4**

**WHY THIS RECIPE WORKS** Brittany, France, is famous for buckwheat crepes filled with savory ingredients. Because buckwheat flour is gluten-free, the pancakes can easily turn out brittle and inflexible. Using a combination of buckwheat flour and gluten-forming all-purpose flour produced crepes that were pliable yet resilient. Increasing the salt and butter rounded out the bitter edge of the buckwheat, so the crepes were nutty, rich, and well seasoned. For a classic Breton dish, we paired the buckwheat crepes with salty ham, nutty Gruyère cheese, and a runny egg. The crepes will give off steam as they cook, but if at any point the skillet begins to smoke, remove it from the burner and turn down the heat. Stacking the crepes on a wire rack allows excess steam to escape so that they won't stick together. Assembling four filled crepes on a rimmed baking sheet and baking them in a hot oven streamlined the usual approach of cooking them individually on the stovetop. This recipe yields 10 crepes, but only four are needed; extra crepes can be wrapped tightly in plastic wrap and refrigerated for up to three days or stacked between sheets of parchment paper and frozen for up to one month. Allow frozen crepes to thaw completely in refrigerator before using. Salted butter is traditional, though unsalted butter can be substituted. If using unsalted butter, add an additional ¼ teaspoon of salt to the batter. Serve with salad for a light brunch or lunch.

**CREPES**

- ½ teaspoon vegetable oil
- ¾ cup (3⅜ ounces) buckwheat flour
- ¼ cup (1¼ ounces) all-purpose flour
- ½ teaspoon table salt
- 2 cups milk
- 3 large eggs
- 4 tablespoons salted butter, melted and cooled

**FILLING**

- 4 thin slices deli ham (2 ounces)
- 5½ ounces Gruyère cheese, shredded (1⅓ cups)
- 4 large eggs
- 1 tablespoon salted butter, melted
- 4 teaspoons chopped fresh chives

**1. FOR THE CREPES:** Adjust oven rack to middle position and heat oven to 450 degrees. Heat oil in 12-inch nonstick skillet over low heat for at least 5 minutes.

**2.** While skillet heats, whisk buckwheat flour, all-purpose flour, and salt together in medium bowl. In second bowl, whisk together milk and eggs. Add half of milk mixture to flour mixture and whisk until smooth. Add melted butter and whisk until incorporated. Whisk in remaining milk mixture until smooth.

**3.** Using paper towel, wipe out skillet, leaving thin film of oil on bottom and sides. Increase heat to medium and let skillet heat for 1 minute. Test heat of skillet by placing 1 teaspoon batter in center and cooking for 20 seconds. If mini crepe is golden brown on bottom, skillet is properly heated; if it is too light or too dark, adjust heat accordingly and retest.

**4.** Lift skillet off heat and pour ⅓ cup batter into far side of skillet; swirl gently in clockwise direction until batter evenly covers bottom of skillet. Return skillet to heat and cook crepe, without moving it, until surface is dry and crepe starts to brown at edges, loosening crepe from sides of skillet with rubber spatula, about 35 seconds. Gently slide spatula underneath edge of crepe, grasp edge with your fingertips, and flip crepe. Cook until second side is lightly spotted, about 20 seconds. Transfer crepe to wire rack. Return skillet to heat for 10 seconds before repeating with remaining batter. As crepes are done, stack on rack.

**5. FOR THE FILLING:** Line rimmed baking sheet with parchment paper and spray with vegetable oil spray. Arrange 4 crepes spotty side down on prepared sheet (they will hang over edge). (Reserve remaining crepes for another use.) Working with 1 crepe at a time, place 1 slice of ham in center of crepe, followed by ⅓ cup Gruyère, covering ham evenly. Make small well in center of cheese. Crack 1 egg into well. Fold in 4 sides, pressing to adhere.

**6.** Brush crepe edges with melted butter and transfer sheet to oven. Bake until egg whites are uniformly set and yolks have filmed over but are still runny, 8 to 10 minutes. Using thin metal spatula, transfer each crepe to plate and sprinkle with 1 teaspoon chives. Serve immediately.

## Perfect Fried Eggs

**SERVES 2**

**WHY THIS RECIPE WORKS** There are two common problems when it comes to fried eggs: undercooked whites and an overcooked yolks. A hot nonstick skillet, a touch of butter, and a lid combine to produce perfectly cooked fried eggs—with crisp edges, tender whites, and runny yolks—in just a few minutes. When checking the eggs for doneness, lift the lid just a crack to prevent loss of steam should they need further cooking. When cooked, the thin layer of white surrounding the yolk will turn opaque, but the yolk should remain runny. To cook two eggs, use an 8- or 9-inch nonstick skillet and halve the amounts of oil and butter. You can use this method with extra-large or jumbo eggs without altering the timing.

- 2 teaspoons vegetable oil
- 4 large eggs
- Table salt and pepper
- 2 teaspoons unsalted butter, cut into 4 pieces and chilled

**1.** Heat oil in 12- or 14-inch nonstick skillet over low heat for 5 minutes. Meanwhile, crack 2 eggs into small bowl and season with salt and pepper. Repeat with remaining 2 eggs and second small bowl.

**2.** Increase heat to medium-high and heat until oil is shimmering. Add butter to skillet and quickly swirl to coat pan. Working quickly, pour 1 bowl of eggs in 1 side of pan and second bowl of eggs in other side. Cover and cook for 1 minute. Remove skillet from burner and let stand, covered, 15 to 45 seconds for runny yolks (white around edge of yolk will be barely opaque), 45 to 60 seconds for soft but set yolks, and about 2 minutes for medium-set yolks. Slide eggs onto plates and serve.

## MAKING PERFECT FRIED EGGS

1. Heat oil in nonstick skillet over low heat for 5 minutes.

2. While skillet heats, crack 2 eggs into small bowl. Repeat with remaining eggs and second small bowl.

3. Increase heat. Add butter and swirl to coat pan. Working quickly, position bowls on either side of skillet and add eggs simultaneously.

4. Cover and cook 1 minute. Remove skillet from burner and let stand, covered, until eggs achieve desired doneness.

## Spanish Migas with Fried Eggs

**SERVES** 4 to 6

**WHY THIS RECIPE WORKS** Spanish migas is a rich, satisfying hash made by frying bread crumbs (and larger pieces of bread) in pork fat. For our version we started by kneading water seasoned with salt and smoked paprika into the bread, adding extra water as needed, until the bread was softened. Frying a mixture of chorizo, bacon, and garlic created meaty, savory flavor and rendered the pork fat, which we used to fry the bread until the smallest pieces were browned and crisped throughout and larger pieces were crisped on the outside and moist within. Blistered Cubanelle and red bell peppers added vegetal notes and pops of color. We topped the dish with a sprinkling of parsley and sunny-side up fried eggs. Fresh or stale bread can be used here. Buy fully cooked Spanish-style chorizo that is somewhat soft; if you can't find it, substitute linguica. Anaheim chiles can be used in place of the Cubanelles. Serve as a hearty breakfast or brunch or with a salad for dinner.

- ⅓ cup water, plus extra as needed
- 1 teaspoon table salt, divided
- 1 teaspoon smoked paprika, divided
- 5 (¾-inch-thick) slices rustic, crusty bread (9 ounces), bottom crust removed, cut into ½- to ¾-inch cubes (5 cups)
- 6 large eggs
- ¼ cup extra-virgin olive oil
- 6 ounces Spanish-style chorizo sausage, halved lengthwise and sliced ¼ inch thick
- 2 slices thick-cut bacon, cut into ½-inch pieces
- 4 garlic cloves, smashed and peeled
- 2 Cubanelle peppers, stemmed, seeded, and cut into ½-inch pieces
- 1 red bell pepper, stemmed, seeded, and cut into ½-inch pieces
- ½ teaspoon sherry vinegar
- 1 tablespoon minced fresh parsley, divided

**1.** Whisk water, ½ teaspoon salt, and ½ teaspoon paprika in large bowl until salt is dissolved. Add bread and knead gently with your hands until liquid is absorbed and half of bread has broken down into smaller pieces. If bread does not break down, add extra water, 1 tablespoon at a time, and continue to knead until you have mix of bigger and smaller pieces interspersed with a few crumbs. Set aside. Crack 3 eggs into small bowl. Repeat with remaining 3 eggs and second small bowl. Set aside eggs.

**2.** Heat oil, chorizo, bacon, and garlic in 12-inch nonstick or carbon-steel skillet over medium heat, stirring frequently, until bacon fat is rendered and bacon is just beginning to crisp at edges, 6 to 8 minutes. Using slotted spoon, transfer chorizo and bacon to medium bowl; discard garlic. Reserve 2 tablespoons fat. Pour remaining fat over bread mixture and toss to combine. Add bread to now-empty skillet and cook over medium-high heat, stirring frequently, until smallest pieces are browned and crisp throughout and larger pieces are crisp on exterior and moist within, 12 to 15 minutes. Return bread mixture to now-empty bowl.

**3.** Add 1 tablespoon reserved fat, Cubanelle and bell peppers, remaining ½ teaspoon salt, and remaining ½ teaspoon paprika to now-empty skillet. Cook over high heat until peppers are softened and slightly blistered, 3 to 5 minutes. Return chorizo mixture to skillet with peppers and cook, stirring frequently, until heated through, about 30 seconds. Sprinkle with vinegar and 2 teaspoons parsley and toss to combine. Transfer to bowl with bread and toss to combine. Transfer to wide serving bowl.

**4.** Heat remaining 1 tablespoon reserved fat in now-empty skillet over medium-high heat until shimmering. Swirl to coat skillet. Working quickly, pour 1 bowl of eggs in 1 side of skillet and second bowl of eggs in other side. Cover and cook for 1 minute. Remove skillet from heat and let sit, covered, for 15 to 45 seconds for runny yolks (white around edge of yolk will be barely opaque), 45 to 60 seconds for soft but set yolks, and about 2 minutes for medium-set yolks. Transfer eggs to top of migas, sprinkle with remaining 1 teaspoon parsley, and serve.

## Baked Eggs for Sandwiches

SERVES 4

**WHY THIS RECIPE WORK** These egg sandwiches feature tender, creamy eggs that stay put inside the bread. Inspired by a recipe from restaurateur and cookbook author Joanne Chang, we whisked water into the eggs, seasoned them lightly, and then gently baked them in a water bath. We then tucked squares of the baked eggs into lightly toasted rolls along with a zippy ingredient such as kimchi or pepperoncini; a creamy element such as mayo or avocado as well as cheese and deli meat or smoked salmon. This recipe requires an 8-inch square metal baking pan. Avoid using a ceramic or glass dish, which will increase the cooking time and could cause the eggs to overcook during cooling. For maximum efficiency, prepare your sandwich fillings while the eggs cook, and toast the bread while the eggs cool. Alternatively, let the eggs cool completely after cutting them, stack them in an airtight container, and refrigerate them for up to three days. To reheat, arrange the egg squares on a large plate and microwave at 50 percent power until they're warm (about 45 seconds for a single square or 2 to 3 minutes for four squares).

- 8 large eggs
- ¼ teaspoon table salt

**1.** Adjust oven rack to middle position and heat oven to 300 degrees. Whisk eggs and salt in large bowl until well combined. Whisk in ⅔ cup water. Spray 8-inch square baking pan with vegetable oil spray. Pour egg mixture into prepared pan and set pan on rimmed baking sheet. Add 1½ cups water to sheet. Transfer sheet to oven and bake until eggs are fully set, 35 to 40 minutes, rotating pan halfway through baking. Remove pan from sheet, transfer to wire rack, and let cool for 10 minutes.

**2.** Run knife around edges of pan and, using dish towel or oven mitts, invert eggs onto cutting board (if eggs stick to pan, tap bottom of pan firmly to dislodge). Cut into 4 equal squares.

### Egg, Kimchi, and Avocado Sandwiches

We like the flavor and texture of kaiser rolls for these sandwiches. Blot the kimchi dry while the eggs bake.

- ¼ cup mayonnaise
- 4 kaiser rolls, halved and lightly toasted
- ¼ cup chopped fresh cilantro
- 1 recipe Baked Eggs for Sandwiches
- 1 ripe avocado, halved, pitted, and sliced thin
- ¾ cup cabbage kimchi, drained, chopped coarse, and blotted dry with paper towels

Spread mayonnaise on roll bottoms. Sprinkle cilantro over mayonnaise. Using spatula, transfer 1 egg square to each sandwich. Top each egg square with avocado and then kimchi. Set roll tops over kimchi and serve.

### Egg, Smoked Salmon, and Dill Sandwiches

We like the flavor and texture of rye bread for these sandwiches. Soak the onion while the eggs bake.

- ½ small red onion, sliced thin
- ¼ cup plain Greek yogurt
- 8 slices hearty rye sandwich bread, lightly toasted
- 2 tablespoons chopped fresh dill
- 1 recipe Baked Eggs for Sandwiches
- 4 ounces smoked salmon

**1.** Place onion in bowl, cover with ice water, and let sit for 15 minutes. Drain onion well and pat dry.

**2.** Spread yogurt on 4 slices of toast. Sprinkle dill over yogurt. Using spatula, transfer 1 egg square to each sandwich. Top each egg square with smoked salmon and then onion. Set remaining 4 slices of toast over onion and serve.

### Egg, Ham, and Pepperoncini Sandwiches

We like the flavor and texture of English muffins for these sandwiches.

- ¼ cup apricot jam
- 4 English muffins, split and lightly toasted
- 1 recipe Baked Eggs for Sandwiches
- 4 slices deli cheddar cheese (4 ounces)
- 4 slices deli ham (4 ounces)
- ¼ cup pepperoncini, sliced and blotted dry

Spread jam on muffin bottoms. Using spatula, transfer 1 egg square to each sandwich. Top each egg square with cheddar, then ham, and then pepperoncini. Set muffin tops over pepperoncini and serve.

### Egg, Salami, and Tomato Sandwiches

We like the flavor and texture of bulkie rolls for these sandwiches.

- ¼ cup mayonnaise
- 4 bulkie rolls, halved and lightly toasted
- ¼ cup chopped fresh basil
- 1 recipe Baked Eggs for Sandwiches
- 12–16 thin slices salami (4 ounces)
- 4 thin tomato slices

Spread mayonnaise on roll bottoms. Sprinkle basil over mayonnaise. Using spatula, transfer 1 egg square to each sandwich. Top each egg square with salami and then 1 tomato slice. Set roll tops over tomato and serve.

## Biscuit Breakfast Sandwiches

SERVES 6 SEASON 26

**WHY THIS RECIPE WORKS** Biscuits are often almost as tall as they are wide, but filling such a biscuit makes it too tall to eat comfortably, so we designed biscuits with a low profile for these breakfast sandwiches. Since the biscuits were only part of the recipe, we wanted them to be as simple as possible. Instead of rubbing cold butter into the flour to distribute it throughout the dough, we stirred melted butter into the cold buttermilk, where it formed tiny curds that were easily incorporated into the dry ingredients. Rather than forming individual biscuits, we patted the dough into a pan and cut it into six portions before baking. To ensure that we got a bit of sausage in every bite (but not enough to overwhelm the sandwich), we butterflied breakfast links and pressed them into 4 by 2-inch rectangles. Making a couple of thin omelets and folding and cutting them to the size of our biscuits made our sandwiches neater and more cohesive than scrambled or fried eggs, and melty cheese reinforced that cohesion. These sandwiches are delicious when fresh, but they can also be made ahead and reheated for a quick breakfast on the go. We like pepper Jack cheese here, but you can substitute another good melter such as American or Muenster, if preferred.

**BISCUITS**

- 1⅔ cups (8⅓ ounces) all-purpose flour
- 1½ teaspoons sugar
- 1¼ teaspoons baking powder
- ¼ teaspoon baking soda
- 1 teaspoon table salt
- 5 tablespoons unsalted butter, melted and cooled slightly
- 1 cup buttermilk, chilled

**FILLINGS**

- 6 (3½- to 4-inch) breakfast sausage links
- 6 large eggs, divided
- ¼ teaspoon table salt, divided
- 2 teaspoons unsalted butter, divided
- 6 slices pepper Jack cheese (2¼ ounces), halved

**1. FOR THE BISCUITS:** Adjust oven rack to middle position and heat oven to 450 degrees. Generously grease 8-inch square baking pan. Whisk flour, sugar, baking powder, baking soda, and salt together in bowl.

**2.** Add melted butter to buttermilk and stir until small clumps form. Add buttermilk mixture to flour mixture and stir well until fully combined. Transfer dough to prepared pan. Using your lightly greased hands, pat dough into even layer and into corners of pan (dough will be thin). Using bench scraper sprayed with vegetable oil spray, cut dough in half. Turn pan 90 degrees and make 2 equidistant parallel cuts to create 6 rectangles. Bake until golden brown, about 20 minutes. Let biscuits cool in pan for 5 minutes. Transfer biscuits to wire rack. Turn off oven.

**3. FOR THE FILLINGS:** While biscuits bake, line half of large plate with paper towels. Slice 1 sausage lengthwise, stopping just short of slicing all the way through. Open sausage up like book; invert onto cold 12-inch nonstick skillet; press to flatten into rectangle; and remove casing, if desired. Repeat with remaining sausages. Cook over medium-high heat until firm to touch, about 2 minutes per side. Transfer sausages to paper towel–lined side of prepared plate. Wipe out skillet with paper towels.

**4.** Beat 3 eggs with ⅛ teaspoon salt until whites and yolks are thoroughly combined. Melt 1 teaspoon butter in now-empty skillet over medium-high heat. Swirl butter over surface of pan. Add eggs and tilt pan to evenly coat bottom. Cover, reduce heat to low, and cook for 45 seconds. Uncover and tilt to swirl uncooked egg to edges of omelet. Cover and continue to cook until top is just set, 45 to 60 seconds. Slide skillet off heat. Run spatula around edges to loosen.

**5.** Fold 4 sides of egg toward middle to create 8-inch square. Fold square in half to create 8 by 4-inch rectangle. Use edge of spatula to cut rectangle crosswise into 3 rectangles. Transfer to unlined side of plate. Repeat with remaining 3 eggs, ⅛ teaspoon salt, and 1 teaspoon butter. After cooking and portioning second batch of eggs, return first batch of eggs and all sausages to skillet. Cover to keep warm.

**6.** Separate biscuits into 6 portions. Stand 1 biscuit on side and gently saw in half with serrated knife. Repeat with remaining biscuits. Arrange biscuit bottoms on now-empty plate and top each with ½ slice cheese, 1 egg portion, 1 sausage, and remaining ½ slice cheese. Arrange biscuit tops over cheese. Place sandwiches in still-warm oven until cheese is melted, at least 5 minutes or up to 20 minutes. Serve (plate will be hot). (Refrigerate leftover sandwiches for up to 3 days. To reheat, place sandwich on plate and cover with bowl. Microwave for 1 minute. Uncover and let sit for 1 minute before serving. Crusts of reheated biscuits will be softer.)

## Cachapas con Queso de Mano (Venezuelan Cheese-Filled Corn Cakes)

SERVES 4 SEASON 26

**WHY THIS RECIPE WORKS** When made in Venezuela with indigenous corn, cachapas comprise little more than corn, salt, and butter. We needed to adapt the recipe to work with American corn varieties. We made ours with modest amounts of masarepa, egg, and Mexican crema to create structurally sound cakes that hewed closely to the flavor and texture of those made in Venezuela. Cooking the cakes in butter until they were deeply browned yielded lightly crisp cakes that paired beautifully with thick slices of queso de mano, a fresh cow's-milk cheese. Once the corn cakes and cheese were married, a brief stint in a warm oven encouraged the cheese to relax and become pliable. Frozen (thawed) or—in a pinch—drained canned corn will also work in this recipe (allowing cachapas to be enjoyed year-round). Masarepa is instant corn flour; common brands include P.A.N., Goya, and Areparina. Queso de mano is a mild Venezuelan cheese sold in large disks. Depending on the brand of cheese you use, you might have to piece scraps together to create all four discs of cheese. If queso de mano is unavailable, one 8-ounce ball of fresh mozzarella can be used instead. Slice the mozzarella into six ½-inch-thick slices, leaving four slices whole and cutting two in half; use one whole plus one half-slice per cachapa. In step 4, warm the cachapas for 5 to 7 minutes.

- 8 ounces queso de mano
- 4 ears corn, kernels cut from cobs (3 cups), divided
- ¼ cup masarepa
- 3 tablespoons Mexican crema or sour cream
- 1 large egg
- 1 tablespoon sugar
- ¾ teaspoon table salt
- 2 tablespoons plus 4 teaspoons unsalted butter, divided

**1.** Adjust oven rack to middle position and heat oven to 200 degrees. Line rimmed baking sheet with parchment. Using 3½-inch round cutter, cut queso de mano into 4 rounds; set aside. (Save cheese scraps for dishes such as omelets, nachos, tacos, or burritos.)

**2.** Process 2¼ cups corn, masarepa, crema, egg, sugar, and salt in blender on medium speed until thick batter forms, 20 to 30 seconds. Add remaining ¾ cup corn and pulse until kernels are evenly incorporated, about 3 pulses. Transfer batter to bowl and let rest for 10 minutes.

**3.** Melt 1 tablespoon butter in 12-inch nonstick skillet over low heat. Using ¼-cup dry measuring cup, portion batter into skillet in 4 places, leaving about ½ inch between portions. Gently spread batter into 4-inch rounds. Increase heat to medium and cook until corn cakes smell of caramelized sugar and bottom sides are well browned, 4 to 5 minutes (if cachapas are not well browned, increase heat slightly and continue to cook until well browned before flipping). Using thin, wide spatula, flip corn cakes and continue to cook until second sides are well browned, 3 to 4 minutes longer. Transfer corn cakes to prepared sheet and place in oven. Wipe out skillet with paper towel and repeat with second tablespoon of butter and remaining batter.

**4.** Top half of corn cakes with 1 piece of cheese each; place remaining corn cakes on top of cheese. Return cachapas to oven and bake until cheese is warm and soft, 3 to 4 minutes. Top each cachapa with 1 teaspoon butter and serve immediately.

## Simple Cheese Quiche

SERVES 6 to 8

**WHY THIS RECIPE WORKS** Our ideal quiche has a tender, buttery pastry case embracing a velvety-smooth custard that is neither too rich nor too lean. We tested numerous combinations of dairy and eggs to find the perfect combination. The baking temperature was equally important; 350 degrees was low enough to set the custard gently and hot enough to brown the top before the filling dried out and became rubbery. To keep the crust from becoming soggy, we parbaked it before adding the filling. To avoid spilling the custard, we set the parbaked crust in the oven before pouring the custard into the pastry shell. For perfectly baked quiche every time, we pulled it out of the oven when it was still slightly soft and allowed it to set up as it cooled. Be sure to add the custard to the pie shell while the crust is still warm so that the quiche will bake evenly. You can substitute other fresh herbs, such as thyme, tarragon, marjoram, or parsley, for the chives.

- 1 recipe single-crust pie dough (pages 944–945), rolled into 12-inch round
- 5 large eggs
- 2 cups half-and-half
- ¼ teaspoon table salt
- ¼ teaspoon pepper
- 4 ounces cheddar cheese, shredded (1 cup)
- 1 tablespoon minced fresh chives

**1.** Adjust oven rack to middle position and heat oven to 375 degrees. Grease 10-inch cast-iron skillet. Roll crust loosely around rolling pin and gently unroll it onto prepared skillet. Ease crust into skillet by gently lifting and supporting edge of dough with your hand while pressing into skillet bottom and corners with your other hand. Tuck ½ inch of dough underneath itself to form tidy, even edge that lies against sides of skillet. Press tucked edge against sides of skillet using index finger to create attractive fluted rim. Wrap skillet loosely in plastic wrap and freeze until dough is firm, about 30 minutes.

**2.** Line pie crust with double layer of aluminum foil, covering edges, and fill with pie weights. Transfer skillet to oven and bake until pie dough looks dry and is pale in color, 25 to 30 minutes. Using pot holders, transfer skillet to wire rack and remove weights and foil. Reduce oven temperature to 350 degrees.

**3.** Beat eggs, half-and-half, salt, and pepper with fork in 4-cup liquid measuring cup. Stir in cheddar. Being careful of hot skillet handle, return skillet to oven. Carefully pour egg mixture into shell until it reaches about ½ inch from top edge of crust (you may have extra egg mixture).

**4.** Bake quiche until center is set and knife inserted 1-inch from edge comes out clean, about 30 minutes. Let quiche cool for at least 1 hour before sprinkling with chives and serving.

## Quiche Lorraine

**SERVES 8**

**WHY THIS RECIPE WORKS** Quiche Lorraine, one might argue, is the king of all quiches with its smoky bacon, pungent Gruyère cheese and creamy custard. We experimented with multiple combinations of egg and dairy to find the one that would provide just the right balance of richness and lightness. Eggs alone were not rich enough; whole eggs plus yolks provided the degree of richness we wanted. For the dairy component, we found that equal parts of milk and heavy cream worked best. This custard was creamy and smooth. After layering bacon and Gruyère over the bottom of the pie shell—for a classic quiche Lorraine—we poured the custard on top and baked the quiche until it was puffed and set around the edges but still jiggled in the center; the residual heat finished cooking the center without turning the top into a rubbery skin. Before serving the quiche, we let it cool on a wire rack, which is a small but important step; this allows air to circulate under the crust and prevents it from becoming soggy. The center of the quiche will be surprisingly soft when it comes out of the oven, but the filling will continue to set (and sink somewhat) as it cools. If the pie shell has been previously baked and cooled, place it in the heating oven for about five minutes to warm it, making sure that it does not burn.

- 1 recipe single-crust pie dough (pages 944–945), fitted into a 9-inch pie plate and chilled
- 8 ounces bacon (about 8 slices), cut into ½-inch pieces
- 2 large whole eggs plus 2 large egg yolks
- 1 cup whole milk
- 1 cup heavy cream
- ½ teaspoon table salt
- ½ teaspoon ground white pepper
- Pinch freshly grated nutmeg
- 4 ounces Gruyère cheese, shredded (about 1 cup)

**1.** Adjust an oven rack to the middle position and heat the oven to 375 degrees. Line the chilled crust with a double layer of foil and fill with pie weights. Bake until the pie dough looks dry and is light in color, 25 to 30 minutes. Transfer the pie plate to a wire rack and remove the weights and foil.

**2.** Cook the bacon in a 12-inch nonstick skillet over medium heat until crisp, about 5 minutes. Using a slotted spoon, transfer the bacon to a paper towel–lined plate. Whisk the remaining ingredients except the Gruyère together in a medium bowl.

**3.** Spread the Gruyère and bacon evenly over the bottom of the warm pie shell and set the shell on the oven rack. Pour the custard mixture into the pie shell (it should come to about ½ inch below the crust's rim). Bake until light golden brown and a knife blade inserted about 1 inch from the edge comes out clean and the center feels set but still soft, 32 to 35 minutes. Transfer the quiche to a wire rack and cool. Serve warm or at room temperature.

## Breakfast Strata with Spinach and Gruyère

**SERVES 6**

**WHY THIS RECIPE WORKS** A classic breakfast dish, strata is easy to prepare, presents a variety of flavors, can feed a crowd and, perhaps best of all, can (and indeed should) be made ahead of time. Too often, though, it is overloaded with fillings; we wanted a savory bread pudding with a balanced, well-seasoned filling. Recipes recommend all kinds of bread to use; we liked supermarket French or Italian loaves, which were neutral in flavor but had a sturdy texture. Rather than cubing the bread, which is often recommended, we sliced it to retain the layered quality of the dish and let the slices dry slightly (stale bread held up better than fresh). We used whole eggs and half-and-half for the custard, with a tad more dairy than eggs, and increased the amount of custard to saturate the bread more fully. A surprisingly successful addition to the custard was white wine, which we reduced to evaporate the alcohol; it brightened all the flavors. A key to ensuring cohesiveness in the strata was weighting it while it rested for at least 1 hour; this way, every piece of bread absorbed some custard. We kept our fillings minimal so they wouldn't overwhelm the bread and custard, and we sautéed the filling ingredients before adding them to the casserole to keep moisture from turning the dish watery. To weigh down the assembled strata, use two 1-pound boxes of sugar, laid side by side over the plastic-covered surface. To double this recipe, use a 13 by 9-inch baking dish greased with 1½ tablespoons butter and increase the baking time in step 5 to 1 hour and 20 minutes.

- 8–10 (½-inch-thick) slices supermarket French or Italian bread
- 5 tablespoons unsalted butter, softened, divided
- 4 shallots, minced (about ½ cup)
- 1 (10-ounce) package frozen chopped spinach, thawed and squeezed dry
- ½ cup dry white wine
- 6 ounces Gruyère cheese, shredded (1½ cups), divided
- 6 large eggs
- 1¾ cups half-and-half
- 1 teaspoon table salt
- Pinch pepper

**1.** Adjust oven rack to middle position and heat oven to 225 degrees. Arrange bread in single layer on rimmed baking sheet and bake until dry and crisp, about 40 minutes, turning slices over halfway through baking time. (Alternatively, leave slices out overnight to dry.) Let bread cool completely, then spread butter evenly over 1 side of each bread slice, using 2 tablespoons butter; set aside.

**2.** Heat 2 tablespoons butter in 10-inch nonstick skillet over medium heat. Add shallots and cook until softened, about 3 minutes. Add spinach and season with salt and pepper; cook until spinach is warm, about 2 minutes. Transfer to medium bowl and set aside. Add wine to skillet, increase heat to medium-high, and simmer until reduced to ¼ cup, 2 to 3 minutes; set aside.

**3.** Butter 8-inch square baking dish with remaining 1 tablespoon butter; arrange half of bread slices, buttered side up, in single layer in dish. Sprinkle half of spinach mixture, then ½ cup Gruyère, evenly over bread slices. Arrange remaining bread slices in single layer over cheese; sprinkle remaining spinach mixture and ½ cup Gruyère evenly over bread. Whisk eggs in medium bowl until combined; whisk in reduced wine, half-and-half, salt, and pepper. Pour egg mixture evenly over bread layers.

**4.** Wrap strata tightly with plastic wrap, pressing wrap against surface of strata. Weigh strata down and refrigerate for at least 1 hour or up to 24 hours.

**5.** Remove dish from refrigerator and let stand at room temperature for 20 minutes. Meanwhile, adjust oven rack to middle position and heat oven to 325 degrees. Uncover strata and sprinkle remaining ½ cup Gruyère evenly over surface; bake until both edges and center are puffed and edges have pulled away slightly from sides of dish, 50 to 55 minutes. Let cool on wire rack for 5 minutes and serve.

## French Toast

**SERVES 4**

**WHY THIS RECIPE WORKS** When it comes to French toast, the results can be hardly worth the trouble. We wanted French toast that was crisp on the outside and soft on the inside, with rich, custard-like flavor. We first focused on determining which type of bread fared best in a typical milk-egg batter. French and Italian breads were just too chewy. We then turned to white sandwich bread, which comes in two kinds: regular and hearty. Regular turned gloppy; hearty bread crisped up nicely on the outside, but still had mushiness. Drying out the bread in a low oven, however, produced French toast that was crisp on the outside and velvety on the inside. As for flavor, tasters thought the French toast tasted overly eggy. We recalled a recipe that required bread dipped in milk mixed with just yolks, versus whole eggs. The yolks-only soaking liquid made a huge difference, turning the taste rich and custard-like. For flavorings, we settled on cinnamon, vanilla, and brown sugar. For nutty butter flavor, we incorporated melted butter into the soaking liquid, warming the milk first to prevent the butter from solidifying. For best results, choose a firm sandwich bread, such as Arnold Country White or Pepperidge Farm Farmhouse Hearty White, or a good challah. To prevent the butter from clumping during mixing, warm the milk in a microwave or small saucepan until warm to the touch (about 80 degrees). The French toast can be cooked all at once on an electric griddle, but may take an extra 2 to 3 minutes per side. Set the griddle temperature to 350 degrees and use the entire amount of butter for cooking. Serve with warm maple syrup.

- 8 large slices high-quality hearty white sandwich bread or challah
- 1½ cups whole milk, warmed
- 3 large egg yolks
- 3 tablespoons light brown sugar
- 2 tablespoons unsalted butter, melted, plus 2 tablespoons for cooking
- 1 tablespoon vanilla extract
- ½ teaspoon ground cinnamon
- ¼ teaspoon table salt

**1.** Adjust oven rack to middle position and heat oven to 300 degrees. Place bread on wire rack set over rimmed baking sheet. Bake bread until almost dry throughout (center should remain slightly moist), about 16 minutes, flipping slices halfway through cooking. Remove bread from rack and let cool for 5 minutes. Return baking sheet with wire rack to oven and reduce temperature to 200 degrees.

2. Whisk milk, egg yolks, sugar, 2 tablespoons melted butter, vanilla, cinnamon, and salt in large bowl until well blended. Transfer mixture to 13 by 9-inch baking pan.

3. Soak bread in milk mixture until saturated but not falling apart, 20 seconds per side. Using firm slotted spatula, pick up 1 bread slice and allow excess milk mixture to drip off; repeat with remaining slices. Place soaked bread on another baking sheet or platter.

4. Melt ½ tablespoon of butter in 12-inch skillet over medium-low heat. Use slotted spatula to transfer 2 slices of soaked bread to skillet and cook until golden brown, 3 to 4 minutes. Flip and continue to cook until second side is golden brown, 3 to 4 minutes longer. (If toast is cooking too quickly, reduce heat slightly.) Transfer to baking sheet in oven. Wipe out skillet with paper towels. Repeat cooking with remaining bread, 2 pieces at a time, adding ½ tablespoon more butter for each batch. Serve warm.

## Everyday French Toast

**SERVES 4**

**WHY THIS RECIPE WORKS** A good version of French toast turns ordinary bread into a luxurious morning treat. We wanted a way to keep all its endearing qualities and make it a snap to make. To start, we learned that staggering the order of ingredients added to the eggs made it easier to whisk them together and made the mixture more cohesive. But after our first batch, we wanted more richness and depth. Melted butter made it more luxurious. Next we moved on to how long to soak the bread—too little time and the custard didn't penetrate the bread enough, but too long and the bread was too delicate. Then in true test kitchen fashion we measured the exact soaking depth for best results: ¼ inch. This led us to our breakthrough discovery: pouring the custard onto a rimmed baking sheet, adding the bread and then baking and then broiling it made things better and easier all around. We developed this recipe to work with presliced supermarket bread that measures 4 by 6 inches and is ¾ inch thick. Top with butter and maple syrup or confectioners' sugar, if desired.

- 3 large eggs
- 1 tablespoon vanilla extract
- 2 teaspoons packed brown sugar
- ½ teaspoon ground cinnamon
- ¼ teaspoon table salt
- 2 tablespoons unsalted butter, melted
- 1 cup milk
- 8 slices hearty white sandwich bread

1. Adjust 1 oven rack to lowest position and second rack 5 to 6 inches from broiler element. Heat oven to 425 degrees. Generously spray bottom and sides of 18 by 13-inch rimmed baking sheet with vegetable oil spray. Whisk eggs, vanilla, sugar, cinnamon, and salt in large bowl until sugar is dissolved and no streaks of egg remain. Whisking constantly, drizzle in melted butter. Whisk in milk.

2. Pour egg mixture into prepared sheet. Arrange bread in single layer in egg mixture, leaving small gaps between slices. Working quickly, use your fingers to flip slices in same order you placed them in sheet. Let sit until slices absorb remaining custard, about 1 minute. Bake on lower rack until bottoms of slices are golden brown, 10 to 15 minutes. Transfer sheet to upper rack and heat broiler. (Leave sheet in oven while broiler heats.) Broil until tops of slices are golden brown, watching carefully and rotating sheet if necessary to prevent burning, 1 to 4 minutes.

3. Using thin metal spatula, carefully flip each slice. Serve.

## French Toast Casserole

**SERVES 4 to 6**

**WHY THIS RECIPE WORKS** French toast is a delicious, easy-to-make breakfast favorite, but we made it even easier—and more crowd friendly—by translating the concept of French toast into a casserole that takes advantage of the cast-iron skillet's heat-retaining ability to replicate the crisp-crusted texture of conventional French toast in a family-size dish. Potato bread, with its sturdy slices, was the perfect choice for the base of our casserole. To ensure that the bread would fit easily in a skillet, we halved the slices and layered them in the pan with a brown sugar–cinnamon mixture and butter. Repeating this process to create a double stack, we then poured egg custard over the top so it could soak through the layers of bread. For a satisfying crunch, we topped the casserole with sliced almonds before putting it into the oven and finished the baked casserole with a light dusting of confectioners' sugar. We developed this recipe using Martin's Potato Bread, which has 16 slices per loaf, so you'll need to buy two loaves. With other brands, it may also be necessary to trim the slices to fit six in a single layer.

- 1 tablespoon unsalted butter, softened, plus 4 tablespoons melted, divided
- 6 tablespoons packed (2⅔ ounces) brown sugar
- 1½ teaspoons ground cinnamon
- ¼ teaspoon ground nutmeg
- Pinch table salt
- 10 slices potato sandwich bread, halved diagonally
- 1⅔ cups whole milk
- 4 large eggs
- 3 tablespoons sliced almonds, toasted
- Confectioners' sugar

1. Adjust oven rack to middle position and heat oven to 350 degrees. Grease 12-inch cast-iron skillet with softened butter. Mix brown sugar, cinnamon, nutmeg, and salt together in bowl.

2. Sprinkle 2 tablespoons brown sugar mixture over bottom of prepared skillet. Arrange half of bread pieces in even layer in skillet. Drizzle with 1½ tablespoons melted butter and sprinkle with 2 tablespoons brown sugar mixture. Repeat layering with remaining bread pieces, 1½ tablespoons melted butter, and 2 tablespoons brown sugar mixture.

**3.** Whisk milk and eggs together until well combined, then pour mixture over bread and press gently to help bread soak up egg mixture. Sprinkle with almonds and remaining brown sugar mixture.

**4.** Transfer skillet to oven and bake until casserole is slightly puffed and golden brown and bubbling around edges, about 30 minutes, rotating skillet halfway through baking.

**5.** Using potholders, transfer skillet to wire rack, brush casserole with remaining 1 tablespoon melted butter, and let cool for 15 minutes. Sprinkle with confectioners' sugar and serve.

## Easy Pancakes

**MAKES** sixteen 4-inch pancakes

**WHY THIS RECIPE WORKS** Everyone loves sitting down to a plate of fluffy, golden pancakes, but making them is another matter. Nobody wants to run out for buttermilk before the first meal of the day, never mind haul out their stand mixer to whip egg whites. That's where box mixes come in, but their convenience is hardly worth the results: rubbery pancakes with a Styrofoam-like flavor. We wanted tender, fluffy, flavorful pancakes that were simple to make using pantry-friendly ingredients and basic kitchen tools. To make them tall and fluffy, we prepared a thick batter by using a relatively small amount of liquid and lots of baking powder. We also mixed the batter minimally to ensure that lumpy pockets of flour remained, and we let the batter rest briefly, allowing the flour pockets to hydrate slightly. Sugar, vanilla, and baking soda provided sweetness, depth, and tang. The pancakes can be cooked on an electric griddle set to 350 degrees. They can be held in a preheated 200-degree oven on a wire rack set in a rimmed baking sheet. Serve with salted butter and maple syrup or with a flavored butter (recipe follows).

- 2 cups (10 ounces) all-purpose flour
- 3 tablespoons sugar
- 4 teaspoons baking powder
- ½ teaspoon baking soda
- 1 teaspoon table salt
- 2 large eggs
- ¼ cup plus 1 teaspoon vegetable oil, divided
- 1½ cups milk
- ½ teaspoon vanilla extract

**1.** Whisk flour, sugar, baking powder, baking soda, and salt together in large bowl. Whisk eggs and ¼ cup oil in second medium bowl until well combined. Whisk milk and vanilla into egg mixture. Add egg mixture to flour mixture and stir gently until just combined (batter should remain lumpy with few streaks of flour). Let batter sit for 10 minutes before cooking.

**2.** Heat ½ teaspoon oil in 12-inch nonstick skillet over medium-low heat until shimmering. Using paper towels, carefully wipe out oil, leaving thin film on bottom and sides of skillet. Drop 1 tablespoon batter in center of skillet. If pancake is pale golden brown after 1 minute, skillet is ready. If it is too light or too dark, adjust heat accordingly.

**3.** Using ¼-cup dry measuring cup, portion batter into skillet in 3 places, leaving 2 inches between portions. If necessary, gently spread batter into 4-inch round. Cook until edges are set, first sides are golden brown, and bubbles on surface are just beginning to break, 2 to 3 minutes. Using thin, wide spatula, flip pancakes and continue to cook until second sides are golden brown, 1 to 2 minutes longer. Serve. Repeat with remaining batter, using remaining ½ teaspoon oil as necessary.

### Orange-Almond Butter

**MAKES** ½ cup

Do not use buckwheat honey; its intense flavor will overwhelm the other flavors.

- 8 tablespoons unsalted butter, cut into ¼-inch pieces, divided
- 2 teaspoons grated orange zest
- 2 teaspoons honey
- ¼ teaspoon almond extract
- ⅛ teaspoon table salt

Microwave 2 tablespoons butter in medium bowl until melted, about 1 minute. Stir in orange zest, honey, almond extract, salt, and remaining 6 tablespoons butter. Let mixture stand for 2 minutes. Whisk until smooth. (Butter can be refrigerated for up to 3 days.)

## Blueberry Pancakes

**MAKES** about sixteen 4-inch pancakes

**WHY THIS RECIPE WORKS** Blueberry pancakes sound appetizing, but they are often rubbery or dense and they inevitably take on an unappealing blue-gray hue. Starting with the pancakes themselves, we determined that unbleached flour, sugar, a little salt, and both baking powder and baking soda were essential for the dry ingredients. One egg added just enough structure and richness without making the pancakes overly eggy. Buttermilk was the preferred dairy component, but we searched for a substitute. Lemon juice thickens milk almost to the consistency of buttermilk and adds a similar tang that tasters actually preferred. Mixing the batter too strenuously leads to tough pancakes; it's time to stop mixing when there are still a few lumps and streaks of flour. Once we had great-tasting pancakes, we turned to the blueberries. Stirring them into the batter can lead to smashing and those blue-gray streaks, so we simply dropped some onto the batter after we'd ladled it into the skillet. If using frozen berries, rinse them under cool water in a mesh strainer until the water runs clear, and then spread them on a paper towel–lined plate to dry. If you have buttermilk on hand, use 2 cups instead of the milk and lemon juice. To keep pancakes warm while cooking the remaining batter, hold them in a 200-degree oven on a greased wire rack set over a baking sheet.

- 2 cups milk
- 1 tablespoon juice from 1 lemon
- 2 cups (10 ounces) unbleached all-purpose flour

2 tablespoons sugar
2 teaspoons baking powder
½ teaspoon baking soda
½ teaspoon table salt
1 large egg
3 tablespoons unsalted butter, melted and cooled slightly
1–2 teaspoons vegetable oil
1 cup fresh or frozen blueberries, preferably wild, rinsed and dried

**1.** Whisk the milk and lemon juice together in a medium bowl or large measuring cup; set aside to thicken while preparing the other ingredients. Whisk the flour, sugar, baking powder, baking soda, and salt together in a medium bowl.

**2.** Whisk the egg and melted butter into the milk until combined. Make a well in the center of the dry ingredients in the bowl; pour in the milk mixture and whisk very gently until just combined (a few lumps should remain). Do not overmix.

**3.** Heat a 12-inch nonstick skillet over medium heat for 3 to 5 minutes; add 1 teaspoon of the oil and brush to coat the skillet bottom evenly. Pour ¼ cup batter onto three spots on the skillet; sprinkle 1 tablespoon of the blueberries over each pancake. Cook the pancakes until large bubbles begin to appear, 1½ to 2 minutes. Using a thin-bladed spatula, flip the pancakes and cook until golden brown on the second side, 1 to 1½ minutes longer. Serve and repeat with the remaining batter, using the remaining 1 teaspoon vegetable oil if necessary.

## Deluxe Blueberry Pancakes

**MAKES** 12 pancakes

**WHY THIS RECIPE WORKS** This special take on blueberry pancakes is a result of infusing the batter with a combination of buttermilk and malted milk powder. The former added tang and interacted with the baking soda to provide better lift; the latter boosted the lactic sweetness and contributed a faint roasty note that complemented the bursts of punchy, tart berries. Stirring melted butter (rather than vegetable oil) into the batter and frying the pancakes in more butter made for rich-tasting pancakes with lightly crispy edges. Folding the berries into the batter ensured that they were encased in the crumb instead of sitting on the surface, where they might burn when the pancakes were flipped. This recipe requires the viscosity of buttermilk. You can substitute ⅔ cup of plain Greek yogurt (any fat level) and 1⅓ cups of water for the buttermilk; do not use buttermilk powder or a mixture of milk and lemon juice. For the best results, weigh the flour. An electric griddle set at 325 degrees can be used in place of a skillet; if using a large griddle, cook six pancakes at a time in 1 tablespoon of butter. We like serving these pancakes with salted butter and maple syrup.

2 tablespoons unsalted butter, plus 3 tablespoons melted and cooled slightly
2 cups (10 ounces) all-purpose flour
3 tablespoons malted milk powder

2 tablespoons sugar
2 teaspoons baking powder
½ teaspoon baking soda
½ teaspoon table salt
2 cups buttermilk
1 large egg
7½ ounces (1½ cups) blueberries
½ teaspoon vegetable oil

**1.** If planning on serving all pancakes at once, set wire rack in rimmed baking sheet and heat oven to 200 degrees. Cut 2 tablespoons butter into ½-tablespoon pieces and set aside. Whisk flour, milk powder, sugar, baking powder, baking soda, and salt together in medium bowl. Whisk buttermilk, egg, and melted butter together in second medium bowl (it's OK if butter forms clumps). Make well in center of flour mixture and add buttermilk mixture; whisk until just combined (a few lumps should remain). Fold in blueberries.

**2.** Heat oil in 12-inch nonstick skillet over medium-low heat until shimmering. Using paper towels, carefully wipe out oil, leaving thin film on bottom and sides of skillet. Drop 1 tablespoon batter in center of skillet. If pancake is pale golden brown after 1 minute, skillet is ready. If it is too light or too dark, adjust heat accordingly. Discard pancake.

**3.** Melt ½ tablespoon butter in now-empty skillet and use spatula to spread over surface. When butter is sizzling, use ⅓-cup dry measuring cup or slightly mounded 2-ounce (#16) portion scoop to portion batter into skillet in 3 places. Using back of cup or scoop, gently spread each portion into 4½-inch round. Cook until edges are set and first side is deep golden brown (coloring will not be even), 2 to 3 minutes. Using thin, wide spatula, flip pancakes and continue to cook until bottoms are just set, about 1 minute longer. Gently slide pancakes around skillet to collect butter. Cook until second sides are deep golden brown, 1 to 1½ minutes. Serve pancakes immediately, or transfer to prepared wire rack and place in oven to keep warm. Repeat with remaining butter and batter in 3 batches.

## Lemon Ricotta Pancakes

**MAKES** 12 (4-inch) pancakes

**WHY THIS RECIPE WORKS** Light, fluffy ricotta pancakes are sophisticated enough for special occasions, but getting the balance of ingredients just right is essential for pancakes that are puffy and tender, not dense and wet. To compensate for the extra weight of the ricotta, we decreased the amount of flour and stirred four whipped egg whites into the batter. Baking soda provided extra rise and aided with browning. Bright, tangy lemon juice complemented the rich, creamy ricotta, and lemon zest enhanced the citrus flavor without watering down the batter. A touch of vanilla extract brought depth and subtle sweetness. For a company-worthy finishing touch, we draped the pancakes with a warm fruit compote. An electric griddle set at 325 degrees can also be used to cook the pancakes. We prefer the flavor of whole-milk ricotta, but part-skim will work, too; avoid nonfat ricotta. Serve with confectioners' sugar or a fruit topping (recipe follows).

- ⅔ cup (3⅓ ounces) all-purpose flour
- ½ teaspoon baking soda
- ½ teaspoon table salt
- 8 ounces (1 cup) whole-milk ricotta cheese
- 2 large eggs, separated, plus 2 large whites
- ⅓ cup whole milk
- 1 teaspoon grated lemon zest plus 4 teaspoons juice
- ½ teaspoon vanilla extract
- 2 tablespoons unsalted butter, melted
- ¼ cup (1¾ ounces) sugar
- 1–2 teaspoons vegetable oil

**1.** Adjust oven rack to middle position and heat oven to 200 degrees. Spray wire rack set inside rimmed baking sheet with vegetable oil spray; place in oven. Whisk flour, baking soda, and salt together in medium bowl and make well in center. Add ricotta, egg yolks, milk, lemon zest and juice, and vanilla and whisk until just combined. Gently stir in butter.

**2.** Using stand mixer fitted with whisk, whip egg whites on medium-low speed until foamy, about 1 minute. Increase speed to medium-high and whip whites to soft, billowy mounds, about 1 minute. Gradually add sugar and whip until glossy, soft peaks form, 1 to 2 minutes. Transfer one-third of whipped egg whites to batter and whisk gently until mixture is lightened. Using rubber spatula, gently fold remaining egg whites into batter.

**3.** Heat 1 teaspoon oil in 12-inch nonstick skillet over medium heat until shimmering. Using paper towels, wipe out oil, leaving thin film on bottom and sides of pan. Using ¼-cup measure or 2-ounce ladle, portion batter into pan in 3 places, leaving 2 inches between portions. Gently spread each portion into a 4-inch round. Cook until edges are set and first side is deep golden brown, 2 to 3 minutes. Using thin, wide spatula, flip pancakes and continue to cook until second side is golden brown, 2 to 3 minutes longer. Serve pancakes immediately or transfer to wire rack in preheated oven. Repeat with remaining batter, using remaining oil as needed.

### Apple-Cranberry Topping

**MAKES** 2½ cups

- 3 Golden Delicious apples, peeled, cored, halved, and cut into ¼-inch pieces
- ¼ cup dried cranberries
- 1 tablespoon sugar
- 1 teaspoon cornstarch
- Pinch table salt
- Pinch ground nutmeg

Combine all ingredients in bowl and microwave until apples are softened but not mushy and juices are slightly thickened, 4 to 6 minutes, stirring once halfway through microwaving. Stir and serve.

## 100 Percent Whole-Wheat Pancakes

**MAKES** 15 pancakes

**WHY THIS RECIPE WORKS** Most recipes for whole-wheat pancakes call for a mix of white and whole-wheat flours, and a host of extra flavorings. Why not just whole-wheat flour? We discovered that using all whole-wheat flour actually delivers light, fluffy, and tender pancakes—not the dense cakes you'd imagine—because whole-wheat flour contains slightly less gluten-forming protein than white flour and because the bran in whole-wheat flour cuts through any gluten strands that do form. Recipes for pancakes made with white flour advise undermixing to avoid dense, tough pancakes, but with whole-wheat flour we were guaranteed light and tender cakes even as we whisked our batter to a smooth consistency. We saw no need to cover up whole wheat's natural flavor with other add-ins; its earthy, nutty taste proved to be the perfect complement to maple syrup. An electric griddle set at 350 degrees can be used in place of a skillet. If substituting buttermilk powder and water for fresh buttermilk, use only 2 cups of water to prevent the pancakes from being too wet. To ensure the best flavor, use either recently purchased whole-wheat flour or flour that has been stored in the freezer for less than 12 months. Serve with maple syrup and butter.

- 2 cups (11 ounces) whole-wheat flour
- 2 tablespoons sugar
- 1½ teaspoons baking powder
- ½ teaspoon baking soda
- ¾ teaspoon table salt
- 2¼ cups buttermilk
- 5 tablespoons plus 2 teaspoons vegetable oil, divided
- 2 large eggs

**1.** Adjust oven rack to middle position and heat oven to 200 degrees. Spray wire rack set in rimmed baking sheet with vegetable oil spray; place in oven.

**2.** Whisk flour, sugar, baking powder, baking soda, and salt together in medium bowl. Whisk buttermilk, 5 tablespoons oil, and eggs together in second medium bowl. Make well in center of flour mixture and pour in buttermilk mixture; whisk until smooth. (Mixture will be thick; do not add more buttermilk.)

**3.** Heat 1 teaspoon oil in 12-inch nonstick skillet over medium heat until shimmering. Using paper towels, carefully wipe out oil, leaving thin film on bottom and sides of pan. Using ¼-cup dry measuring cup or 2-ounce ladle, portion batter into pan in 3 places. Gently spread each portion into 4½-inch round. Cook until edges are set, first side is golden brown, and bubbles on surface are just beginning to break, 2 to 3 minutes. Using thin, wide spatula, flip pancakes and continue to cook until second side is golden brown, 1 to 2 minutes longer. Serve pancakes immediately or transfer to wire rack in oven. Repeat with remaining batter, using remaining 1 teaspoon oil as necessary.

## Spiced Pear, Buckwheat, and Almond Pancakes

**MAKES** twelve 3-inch pancakes **SEASON 26**

**WHY THIS RECIPE WORKS** These pancakes are naturally gluten-free, featuring both buckwheat and almond flours. They are earthy and tender with a delicate crust. It was essential—and very quick—to make our own homemade buckwheat flour from buckwheat groats in a blender. A combination of warm spices complemented the pear in the batter. To keep the pancakes light and tender, we separated the eggs, whipped the whites, and gently folded them in. A topping of caramelized pear wedges added an extra dose of sweetness and looked beautiful. Darker store-bought buckwheat flour has extra hull added to it, which makes it a bit denser, darker, and bitter-tasting; we don't recommend using it here. Comice pears are lovely in this recipe, but any variety will work. Use the large holes of a box grater to grate the pear.

**PANCAKES**

- 1 cup (5¾ ounces) buckwheat groats
- 1 cup (4 ounces) blanched, finely ground almond flour
- 1 tablespoon baking powder
- 1½ teaspoons table salt
- 1 teaspoon ground cinnamon
- ¾ teaspoon ground ginger
- ½ teaspoon ground cardamom
- 1 ripe but firm pear, peeled and grated (¾ cup)
- 2 large eggs, separated
- ⅔ cup milk
- ¼ cup maple syrup
- 2 teaspoons vanilla extract
- 2 tablespoons unsalted butter, divided

**TOPPING**

- 2 tablespoons unsalted butter
- 2 tablespoons maple syrup, plus extra for serving
- ⅛ teaspoon table salt
- 2 ripe but firm pears, peeled, cored, and cut into ¾-inch-thick wedges
- ½ cup sliced almonds, toasted

**1. FOR THE PANCAKES:** Adjust oven rack to middle position and heat oven to 200 degrees. Set wire rack in rimmed baking sheet. Process buckwheat groats in blender on high speed until as fine as possible, about 1 minute. Transfer to large bowl.

**2.** Add almond flour, baking powder, salt, cinnamon, ginger, and cardamom to bowl with buckwheat flour and whisk to combine. Whisk together grated pear, egg yolks, milk, maple syrup, and vanilla in second bowl, then add to flour mixture, stirring to combine; set aside.

**3.** Whisk egg whites by hand in medium bowl until they are airy and hold very soft peaks, about 1 minute. Using rubber spatula, gently fold whipped whites into pancake batter until no white streaks remain.

**4.** Melt ½ tablespoon butter in 12-inch nonstick skillet over medium heat. Drop 1 tablespoon batter in center of skillet. If pancake is pale golden brown after 1 minute, skillet is ready. If it is too light or too dark, adjust heat accordingly.

**5.** Use ¼-cup dry measuring cup to portion batter into skillet in 3 places. If necessary, gently spread batter into 3-inch round. Cook until bubbles on surface form, edges are set, and first sides of pancakes are golden brown, about 2 minutes, and batter will dry out slightly.) Using thin, wide spatula, flip pancakes and cook until second side is golden brown, about 2 minutes. (You may need to adjust heat if pancakes are getting too dark.) Transfer to prepared rack and place in oven to keep warm. Wipe skillet clean then repeat with remaining butter and batter in 3 more batches, wiping out skillet between each batch.

**6. FOR THE TOPPING:** Wipe out now-empty skillet with paper towels, then add butter, maple syrup, and salt and cook over medium-high heat until butter is melted. Add pear wedges and cook until lightly caramelized on both cut sides, about 3 to 4 minutes, flipping halfway through.

**7.** Top pancakes with sautéed pears, toasted almonds, and extra maple syrup. Serve immediately.

## Crepes with Berries and Apricot Beurre Monté

**SERVES** 4

**WHY THIS RECIPE WORKS** Beurre monté, emulsified melted butter, is a classic French preparation that gilds everything it's drizzled over, adding richness and a glossy appearance. It can also be used as a creamy sauce base for a range of savory or sweet seasonings. Vigorously whisking cold butter into simmering water broke up the butterfat into droplets that dispersed throughout the water, establishing a thick, creamy emulsion. Whisking apricot preserves, peach schnapps, and lemon juice into the beurre monté produced a rich sauce that paired well with crepes and berries. Preheating the pan over a low flame ensured that it was thoroughly heated. We poured the batter into the pan and used a tilt-and-shake method to distribute it evenly. To allow for practice, this recipe yields

10 crepes; only eight are needed for serving. Remove the berries from the fridge at least 1 hour before serving. The beurre monté can be covered and kept warm over your stove's lowest setting for up to 1 hour; it will break if simmered for an extended period of time; it cannot be cooled and reheated.

**CREPES**

- ½ teaspoon vegetable oil
- 1 cup (5 ounces) all-purpose flour
- 1 teaspoon sugar
- ½ teaspoon kosher salt
- 1½ cups milk
- 3 large eggs
- 2 tablespoons unsalted butter, melted and cooled

**BEURRE MONTÉ**

- 3 tablespoons water
- 8 tablespoons unsalted butter, cut into 8 pieces and chilled
- 1½ tablespoons apricot preserves
- 1½ teaspoons peach schnapps
- 1 teaspoon lemon juice
- ⅛ teaspoon kosher salt

- 4 ounces (1 cup) fresh raspberries, blackberries, or blueberries, room temperature

**1. FOR THE CREPES:** Place oil in 12-inch nonstick skillet and heat over low heat for at least 10 minutes. While skillet is heating, whisk flour, sugar, and salt together in medium bowl. In separate bowl, whisk together milk and eggs. Add half of milk mixture to dry ingredients and whisk until smooth. Whisk in melted butter. Whisk in remaining milk mixture until smooth.

**2.** Using paper towel, wipe out skillet, leaving thin film of oil on bottom and sides. Increase heat to medium and let skillet heat for 1 minute. After 1 minute, test heat of skillet by placing 1 teaspoon batter in center and cook for 20 seconds. If mini crepe is golden brown on bottom, skillet is properly heated. If it is too light or too dark, adjust heat accordingly and retest.

**3.** Pour ¼ cup batter into pan and tilt and shake gently until batter evenly covers bottom of pan. Cook crepe without moving it until top surface is dry and crepe starts to brown at edges, loosening crepe from side of pan with rubber spatula, about 25 seconds. Gently slide spatula underneath edge of crepe, grasp edge with your fingertips, and flip crêpe. Cook until second side is lightly spotted, about 20 seconds. Transfer cooked crepe to wire rack. Return pan to heat and heat for 10 seconds before repeating with remaining batter. As crepes are done, stack on wire rack. (Crepes can be covered and refrigerated for up to 2 days.)

**4. FOR THE BEURRE MONTÉ:** Bring water to simmer in small saucepan over medium-high heat; reduce heat to maintain very gentle simmer. Add 1 piece butter and cook, whisking constantly, until butter is melted, 20 to 30 seconds. Continue to cook, whisking in butter 1 piece at a time until all butter is incorporated and sauce has consistency of thin gravy, 3 to 4 minutes. Whisk in preserves, schnapps, lemon juice, and salt. Reduce heat to lowest possible setting and cover to keep warm.

**5. TO SERVE:** Transfer crepes to large plate and cover with second plate. Microwave until crepes are warm, 30 to 45 seconds. Arrange crepes on serving plates. Scatter berries over crepes. Whisk sauce vigorously to blend in any butterfat that has collected on surface. Spoon sauce over crepes and serve immediately.

## German Pancake

**SERVES 4**

**WHY THIS RECIPE WORKS** The German pancake, sometimes called a Dutch baby, is a study in contrasts: The edge of the skillet-size breakfast specialty puffs dramatically to form a tall, crispy rim with a texture similar to that of a popover while the base remains flat, custardy, and tender, like a thick crepe. Our German pancake achieves its dramatic appearance and contrasting textures thanks to a few test kitchen tricks. First, we mixed up a simple batter containing just the right amounts of eggs, flour, and milk to produce a pancake with crispy yet tender edges and a custardy center. To produce a tall, puffy rim and an even, substantial center, we started the pancake in a cold oven and then turned the heat to 375 degrees. This allowed the center of the pancake to begin to set up before the rim got hot enough to puff up. Finally, we put fruit on as a topping rather than baking it into the pancake. Without fruit to weigh things down, the pancake puffed dramatically and its texture remained delicate. A traditional 12-inch skillet can be used in place of the nonstick skillet; coat it lightly with vegetable oil spray before using. As an alternative to sugar and lemon juice, serve the pancake with maple syrup or our Brown Sugar–Apple Topping (recipe follows).

- 1¾ cups (8¾ ounces) all-purpose flour
- ¼ cup (1¾ ounces) sugar, divided
- 1 tablespoon grated lemon zest plus 1 tablespoon juice
- ½ teaspoon table salt
- ⅛ teaspoon ground nutmeg
- 1½ cups milk
- 6 large eggs
- 1½ teaspoons vanilla extract
- 3 tablespoons unsalted butter

**1.** Whisk flour, 3 tablespoons sugar, lemon zest, salt, and nutmeg together in large bowl. Whisk milk, eggs, and vanilla together in second bowl. Whisk two-thirds of milk mixture into flour mixture until no lumps remain, then slowly whisk in remaining milk mixture until smooth.

**2.** Adjust oven rack to lower-middle position. Melt butter in 12-inch ovensafe nonstick skillet over medium-low heat. Add batter to skillet, immediately transfer to oven, and set oven to 375 degrees. Bake until edges are deep golden brown and center is beginning to brown, 30 to 35 minutes.

**3.** Transfer skillet to wire rack and sprinkle pancake with lemon juice and remaining 1 tablespoon sugar. Gently transfer pancake to cutting board, cut into wedges, and serve.

### Brown Sugar–Apple Topping

**MAKES** 2 cups

You can substitute Honeycrisp or Fuji apples for the Braeburn apples, if desired.

- 2 tablespoons unsalted butter
- ⅓ cup water
- ¼ cup packed (1¾ ounces) brown sugar
- ¼ teaspoon ground cinnamon
- ⅛ teaspoon table salt
- 1¼ pounds Braeburn apples (3 to 4 apples), peeled, cored, halved, and cut into ½-inch-thick wedges, wedges halved crosswise

Melt butter in 12-inch skillet over medium heat. Add water, sugar, cinnamon, and salt and whisk until sugar dissolves. Add apples, increase heat to medium-high, and bring to simmer. Cover and cook, stirring occasionally, for 5 minutes. Uncover and continue to cook until apples are translucent and just tender and sauce is thickened, 5 to 7 minutes longer. Transfer to bowl and serve. (Topping can be refrigerated for up to 2 days.)

## German Apple Pancake

**SERVES** 4

**WHY THIS RECIPE WORKS** More akin to popovers than American pancakes, German apple pancakes are golden and puffed outside, custardy inside, with apples baked right in. And the dish can suffer from many of the same problems as popovers, too: not enough rise, dense texture, and a too-eggy flavor. We wanted to get this pancake just right. Flour and eggs are the basis of the batter; half-and-half for the dairy component imparted richness and a light texture. Sugar, salt, and vanilla completed the batter. Steam, not leavening, is what puffs the pancake, so to get the maximum rise we needed to find the right oven temperature. A very hot oven burned the exterior of the pancake; preheating the oven to a high temperature as well as preheating the pan, then lowering the temperature when the pancake went in, proved the ideal method. Granny Smith apples were our top pick if you like a little tartness; otherwise Braeburns are a good choice for their sweetness. We cooked apples with brown sugar for a deeper flavor, along with butter, cinnamon, and a bright touch of lemon juice. To keep the apples from being pushed out of the pan when the pancake rose, we first poured the batter around the edge of the skillet, then over the apples. Our pancake puffed spectacularly, and every bite contained tender apples. A 10-inch ovensafe skillet is necessary for this recipe; we highly recommend using a nonstick skillet for the sake of easy cleanup, but a regular skillet will work. If you prefer tart apples, use Granny Smiths; if you prefer sweet ones, use Braeburns.

- ½ cup (2½ ounces) unbleached all-purpose flour
- 1 tablespoon granulated sugar
- ½ teaspoon table salt
- 2 large eggs
- ⅔ cup half-and-half
- 1 teaspoon vanilla extract
- 2 tablespoons unsalted butter
- 1¼ pounds Granny Smith or Braeburn apples (3 to 4 large apples), peeled, quartered, cored, and cut into ½-inch-thick slices
- ¼ cup packed (1¾ ounces) light or dark brown sugar
- ¼ teaspoon ground cinnamon
- 1 teaspoon juice from 1 lemon
- Confectioners' sugar, for dusting
- Maple syrup or Caramel Sauce (recipe follows), for serving

**1.** Adjust an oven rack to the upper-middle position and heat the oven to 500 degrees.

**2.** Whisk the flour, granulated sugar, and salt together in a medium bowl. In a second medium bowl, whisk the eggs, half-and-half, and vanilla together until combined. Add the liquid ingredients to the dry ingredients and whisk until no lumps remain, about 20 seconds; set the batter aside.

**3.** Melt the butter in a 10-inch ovensafe nonstick skillet over medium-high heat. Add the apples, brown sugar, and cinnamon; cook, stirring frequently with a heatproof rubber spatula, until the apples are golden brown, about 10 minutes. Off the heat, stir in the lemon juice.

**4.** Working quickly, pour the batter around the edge of the pan and then over the apples. Place the skillet in the oven and immediately reduce the oven temperature to 425 degrees. Bake until the pancake edges are brown and puffy and have risen above the edges of the skillet, about 18 minutes.

**5.** Using a potholder (the skillet handle will be hot), remove the skillet from the oven and loosen the pancake edges with a heatproof rubber spatula; invert the pancake onto a platter. Dust with confectioners' sugar, cut into wedges, and serve with maple syrup or Caramel Sauce.

## Caramel Sauce

**MAKES** about 1½ cups

Cooking the sugar with some water in a covered pot helps trap moisture and ensures that the sugar will dissolve. When the hot cream mixture is added in step 3, the hot sugar syrup will bubble vigorously (and dangerously), so don't use a smaller saucepan. If you make the caramel sauce ahead, reheat it in the microwave or a small saucepan over low heat until warm and fluid.

- ½ cup water
- 1 cup (7 ounces) sugar
- 1 cup heavy cream
- ⅛ teaspoon table salt
- ½ teaspoon vanilla extract
- ½ teaspoon juice from 1 lemon

**1.** Place the water in a 2-quart saucepan; pour the sugar into the center of the pan, taking care not to let the sugar crystals stick to the sides of the pan. Cover and bring the mixture to a boil over high heat; once the mixture is boiling, uncover the pan and continue to boil until the sugar syrup is thick and straw-colored and registers 300 degrees on an instant-read thermometer, about 7 minutes. Reduce the heat to medium and continue to cook until the syrup is deep amber and registers 350 degrees, 1 to 2 minutes.

**2.** Meanwhile, bring the cream and salt to a simmer in a small saucepan over high heat (if the cream boils before the sugar syrup reaches a deep amber color, remove the cream from the heat and cover to keep warm).

**3.** Remove the pan with the sugar syrup from the heat; very carefully pour about one-quarter of the hot cream into it (the mixture will bubble vigorously), and let the bubbling subside. Add the remaining cream, the vanilla, and lemon juice; whisk until the sauce is smooth. (The sauce can be cooled and refrigerated in an airtight container for up to 2 weeks.)

## Classic Buttermilk Waffles

**MAKES** 3 to 4 waffles, depending on the size of the iron

**WHY THIS RECIPE WORKS** Waffles should be moist and fluffy inside and crisp and brown outside—more like a soufflé with a crust than a pancake. We wanted to find the way to achieve this archetypal waffle. Thick batter is the secret of the crisp exterior and custardy interior of a waffle, so we used a higher proportion of flour to liquid than that of standard recipes. With buttermilk (and buttermilk makes the best-tasting waffles) there's no need for baking powder, and we found that eliminating it also helped crisp up the waffles. A small amount of cornmeal added a pleasing crunch. Separating the egg and folding the whipped white into the batter was a definite improvement; we could see the pockets of air when we cut into a waffle made this way. Like pancakes, waffles turn tough when the batter is over mixed, so we used a light hand, adding the liquid gradually and using more of a folding motion to mix. Cooked to a medium toasty brown, these waffles were everything we wanted them to be. The secret to great waffles is a thick batter, so don't expect a pourable batter. The optional dash of cornmeal adds a pleasant crunch to the finished waffle. This recipe can be doubled or tripled. Make toaster waffles out of leftover batter—undercook the waffles a bit, cool them on a wire rack, wrap them in plastic wrap, and freeze. Pop them in the toaster for a quick breakfast. The waffles are best served fresh from the iron but can be held in an oven until all of the batter is used. As you make the waffles, place them on a wire rack set in a rimmed baking sheet, cover them with a clean dish towel, and place the baking sheet in a 200-degree oven.

- 1 cup (5 ounces) unbleached all-purpose flour
- 1 tablespoon cornmeal (optional)
- ½ teaspoon table salt
- ¼ teaspoon baking soda
- ⅞ cup buttermilk
- 1 large egg, separated
- 2 tablespoons unsalted butter, melted and cooled

**1.** Following the manufacturer's instructions, heat a waffle iron. Whisk the flour, cornmeal (if using), salt, and baking soda together in a medium bowl. In a separate medium bowl, whisk the buttermilk, egg yolk, and melted butter together.

**2.** Beat the egg white with an electric mixer on medium-low speed until foamy, about 1 minute. Increase the speed to medium-high and whip the whites to stiff peaks, 2 to 4 minutes.

**3.** Add the liquid ingredients to the dry ingredients in a thin, steady stream while mixing gently with a rubber spatula. (Do not add the liquid faster than you can incorporate it into the batter.) Toward the end of mixing, use a folding motion to incorporate the ingredients. Gently fold the egg white into the batter.

**4.** Spread an appropriate amount of batter onto the waffle iron. Following the manufacturer's instructions, cook the waffle until golden brown, 2 to 5 minutes. Serve.

## Best Buttermilk Waffles

**MAKES** eight 7-inch round waffles

**WHY THIS RECIPE WORKS** Waffles are generally not something you can make on busy mornings, but we wanted superior waffles that required little more than measuring out some flour and cracking an egg; and we were not willing to sacrifice quality to get there. To get crisp, the exterior of a waffle must first become dry, but moist steam racing past the crisping waffle as it cooks slows down the process. We needed a drier batter with plenty of leavening oomph. To do this, we took a cue from Japanese tempura batters, which often use seltzer or club soda in place of still water. The tiny bubbles of carbon dioxide released from the water inflate the batter the same way as a chemical leavener—minus the metallic taste that baking soda and powder sometimes impart. We replaced the buttermilk in our pancake recipe with a mixture of seltzer and powdered buttermilk. These waffles were incredibly light, but not as crisp as we wanted. Because butter contains water, the melted butter in our batter was imparting moisture to the waffles, preventing them from crisping. When we replaced the melted butter with oil, the result was a crisp texture along with excellent flavor. While the waffles can be eaten directly from the waffle iron, they will have a crispier exterior if rested in a warm oven for 10 minutes. Buttermilk powder is available in most supermarkets and is generally located near the dried milk products or in the baking aisle (leftover powder can be kept in the refrigerator for up to a year). Seltzer or club soda gives these waffles their light texture; use a freshly opened container for maximum lift. Avoid Perrier, which is not bubbly enough. Serve with butter and warm maple syrup.

- 2 cups (10 ounces) unbleached all-purpose flour
- ½ cup dried buttermilk powder
- 1 tablespoon sugar
- ¾ teaspoon table salt
- ½ teaspoon baking soda
- ½ cup sour cream
- 2 large eggs
- ¼ cup vegetable oil
- ¼ teaspoon vanilla extract
- 1¼ cups unflavored seltzer water or club soda

**1.** Adjust oven rack to middle position and heat oven to 250 degrees. Set wire rack over rimmed baking sheet and place baking sheet in oven. Whisk flour, buttermilk powder, sugar, salt, and baking soda in large bowl to combine. Whisk sour cream, eggs, oil, and vanilla in medium bowl to combine. Gently stir seltzer into wet ingredients. Make well in center of dry ingredients and pour in wet ingredients. Gently stir until just combined. Batter should remain slightly lumpy with streaks of flour.

**2.** Heat waffle iron and bake waffles according to manufacturer's instructions (use about ⅓ cup for 7-inch round iron). Transfer waffles to rack in warm oven and hold for up to 10 minutes before serving.

## Yeasted Waffles

**MAKES** six 7-inch round waffles or four 9-inch square waffles

**WHY THIS RECIPE WORKS** Raised waffles sound old-fashioned and require advance preparation, but they are crisp, tasty, and easy to prepare. A tiny bit of planning makes our recipe easy to have ready in the morning. We wanted yeasted waffles that were creamy and airy, tangy, and refined and complex. We settled on all-purpose flour, found the right amount of yeast to provide pleasant tang, and added a full stick of melted butter for rich flavor. Refrigerating the batter overnight kept the growth of the yeast under control and produced waffles with superior flavor. All we had to do in the morning was heat up the waffle iron. The batter must be made 12 to 24 hours in advance. We prefer the texture of the waffles made in a classic waffle iron, but a Belgian waffle iron will work, though it will make fewer waffles. The waffles are best served fresh from the iron but can be held in an oven until all of the batter is used. As you make the waffles, place them on a wire rack set in a baking sheet, cover them with a clean dish towel, and place the baking sheet in a 200-degree oven. When the final waffle is in the iron, remove the towel to allow the waffles to crisp for a few minutes. These waffles are quite rich; buttering them before eating may be superfluous.

- 1¾ cups milk
- 8 tablespoons unsalted butter, cut into 8 pieces
- 2 cups (10 ounces) all-purpose flour
- 1 tablespoon sugar
- 1½ teaspoons instant or rapid-rise yeast
- 1 teaspoon table salt
- 2 large eggs
- 1 teaspoon vanilla extract

**1.** Heat milk and butter in small saucepan over medium-low heat until butter is melted, 3 to 5 minutes. Let mixture cool until warm to touch.

**2.** Whisk flour, sugar, yeast, and salt together in large bowl. In small bowl, whisk eggs and vanilla together. Gradually whisk warm milk mixture into flour mixture until smooth, then whisk in egg mixture. Scrape down bowl with rubber spatula, cover tightly with plastic wrap, and refrigerate for at least 12 hours or up to 24 hours.

**3.** Adjust oven rack to middle position and heat oven to 200 degrees. Set wire rack in rimmed baking sheet and place in oven. Heat waffle iron according to manufacturer's instructions. Remove batter from refrigerator when waffle iron is hot (batter will be foamy and doubled in size). Whisk batter to recombine (batter will deflate).

**4.** Cook waffles according to manufacturer's instructions (use about ½ cup batter for 7-inch round iron and about 1 cup batter for 9-inch square iron). Serve immediately or transfer to wire rack in oven to keep warm while cooking remaining waffles.

## Liège Waffles

**MAKES** 8 waffles

**WHY THIS RECIPE WORKS** Unlike Brussels or American waffles, made from batter and typically eaten for breakfast, the Liège kind traditionally are handheld treats for eating any time of day. They're made from yeasted dough that's scented with vanilla, enriched with plenty of fat (usually butter), and studded with chunks of pearl sugar. As the waffle bakes, sugar near the surface melts and then caramelizes against the hot iron, forming a satisfyingly crunchy crust. Using minimal liquid in the dough ensured that the waffles stayed crisp, and resting the dough overnight encouraged gluten development that rendered the crumb properly feathery, with subtle elastic chew. Dredging the risen dough portions in granulated sugar helped the waffles caramelize all over as they baked, and calibrating the iron temperature to 360 to 365 degrees ensured that the dough cooked through and browned simultaneously. You'll need a Belgian waffle iron for this recipe. Belgian pearl sugar is available at some supermarkets or online; do not use smaller Swedish pearl sugar. Unlike American waffles, these are meant to be served warm as a snack or a dessert, not as breakfast. To serve them all at once, hold the waffles on a wire rack set in a rimmed baking sheet in a 200-degree oven while the others finish cooking.

- 2 cups (11 ounces) bread flour
- 1½ tablespoons granulated sugar plus ⅓ cup for coating dough
- 2 teaspoons instant or rapid-rise yeast
- 1 teaspoon table salt
- 12 tablespoons unsalted butter, cut into 12 pieces and softened
- ½ cup warm milk (110 degrees)
- 1 large egg
- 1 tablespoon vanilla extract
- 1 cup (5½ ounces) Belgian pearl sugar

**1.** Whisk flour, 1½ tablespoons granulated sugar, yeast, and salt together in bowl of stand mixer. Add butter, milk, egg, and vanilla. Fit stand mixer with dough hook and mix on low speed until all flour is moistened, about 1 minute. Increase speed to medium-low and continue to mix until dough is smooth and elastic, 12 to 15 minutes, scraping down bowl halfway through mixing (dough will be very soft and will stick to sides and bottom of bowl). Transfer to medium bowl. Cover and refrigerate for at least 8 hours or up to 48 hours.

**2.** Line rimmed baking sheet with parchment paper and spray lightly with vegetable oil spray. Transfer dough to counter and flatten to about 1 inch thickness (dough will be firm). Spread pearl sugar over dough and press into dough. Beginning with edge nearest you, roll dough into cylinder, enclosing sugar. Knead dough until sugar is evenly incorporated (a bench scraper is helpful for releasing dough from counter; if pieces of sugar pop out of dough, press them back in).

**3.** Divide dough into 8 equal portions (each should weigh just over 3½ ounces). Roll 1 portion between your hands to form 4-inch-long sausage shape. Pat into rough 4 by 2-inch oval. Transfer to prepared baking sheet. Repeat with remaining portions. Cover and let rise until puffy and room temperature, 1½ to 2 hours.

**4.** Heat Belgian waffle iron to 360 degrees (drop of water on iron will skitter across surface and take 4 to 5 seconds to evaporate). As iron heats, spread remaining ⅓ cup granulated sugar in small dish. Place 1 dough portion in sugar and turn to coat on all sides. Transfer to center of waffle iron and close lid so it rests on dough but do not press down or lock. Cook until waffle is deep golden brown and surface sugar is beginning to caramelize, about 2½ minutes. Using 2 forks, spear waffle on left and right sides; lift, and transfer to wire rack to cool (surface sugar will be hot; do not handle for at least 90 seconds). Repeat with remaining dough and serve.

## Ten-Minute Steel-Cut Oatmeal

**SERVES** 4

**WHY THIS RECIPE WORKS** Most oatmeal fans agree that the steel-cut version of the grain offers the best flavor and texture, but many balk at the 40-minute cooking time. We decreased the cooking time to only 10 minutes by stirring the oats into boiling water the night before; the grains hydrated and softened overnight. In the morning, we added more water (or fruit juice or milk) and simmered the mixture for 4 to 6 minutes, until thick and creamy. A brief resting period off the heat ensured the perfect consistency. The oatmeal will continue to thicken as it cools. If you prefer a looser consistency, thin the oatmeal with boiling water. Customize your oatmeal with toppings such as brown sugar, toasted nuts, maple syrup, or dried fruit.

- 4 cups water, divided
- 1 cup steel-cut oats
- ¼ teaspoon table salt

**1.** Bring 3 cups water to boil in large saucepan over high heat. Remove pan from heat; stir in oats and salt. Cover pan and let stand overnight.

**2.** Stir remaining 1 cup water into oats and bring to boil over medium-high heat. Reduce heat to medium and cook, stirring occasionally, until oats are softened but still retain some chew and mixture thickens and resembles warm pudding, 4 to 6 minutes. Remove pan from heat and let stand for 5 minutes. Stir and serve, passing desired toppings separately.

### Apple-Cinnamon Steel-Cut Oatmeal

Increase salt to ½ teaspoon. Substitute ½ cup apple cider and ½ cup whole milk for water in step 2. Stir ½ cup peeled, grated sweet apple, 2 tablespoons packed dark brown sugar, and ½ teaspoon ground cinnamon into oatmeal with cider and milk. Sprinkle each serving with 2 tablespoons coarsely chopped toasted walnuts.

### Carrot-Spice Steel-Cut Oatmeal

Increase salt to ¾ teaspoon. Substitute ½ cup carrot juice and ½ cup whole milk for water in step 2. Stir ½ cup finely grated carrot, ¼ cup packed dark brown sugar, ⅓ cup dried currants, and ½ teaspoon ground cinnamon into oatmeal with carrot juice and milk. Sprinkle each serving with 2 tablespoons coarsely chopped toasted pecans.

### Banana-Coconut Steel-Cut Oatmeal

Increase salt to ½ teaspoon. Substitute 1 cup canned coconut milk for water in step 2. Stir ½ cup toasted shredded coconut, 2 diced bananas, and ½ teaspoon vanilla extract into oatmeal before serving.

## Congee (Chinese Rice Porridge)

**SERVES** 4 to 6

**WHY THIS RECIPE WORKS** Great congee features soft, barely intact grains gently bound by their silky, viscous cooking liquid. Our formula started with a 13:1 ratio of liquid to long-grain white rice, which produced an appropriately loose porridge (we cut the water with a little chicken broth to give our congee clean flavor with a savory backbone). Then we simmered the rice vigorously to encourage the grains to break down in about 45 minutes (instead of a more typical 90-minute gentle simmer), partially covering the pot to help the contents cook quickly while minimizing evaporation. To prevent the congee from boiling over, we rinsed excess starch from the raw rice and wedged a wooden spoon between the lid and the side of the pot, giving the water bubbles a chance to escape. For vegetarian congee, substitute water for the chicken broth. Jasmine rice can be substituted for conventional long-grain white rice; do not use basmati. We prefer the distinctive flavor of Chinese black vinegar here; look for it in Asian supermarkets. Congee provides a subtle savory background for toppings like jammy eggs and fried shallots.

- ¾ cup long-grain white rice
- 1 cup chicken broth
- ¾ teaspoon table salt
- Scallions, sliced thin on bias
- Fresh cilantro leaves
- Dry-roasted peanuts, chopped coarse
- Chili oil
- Soy sauce
- Chinese black vinegar

**1.** Place rice in fine-mesh strainer and rinse under cold running water until water runs clear. Drain well and transfer to Dutch oven. Add broth, salt, and 9 cups water and bring to boil over high heat. Reduce heat to maintain vigorous simmer. Cover pot, tucking wooden spoon horizontally between pot and lid to hold lid ajar. Cook, stirring occasionally, until mixture is thickened, glossy, and reduced by half, 45 to 50 minutes.

**2.** Serve congee in bowls, passing scallions, cilantro, peanuts, oil, soy sauce, and vinegar separately.

### Easy-Peel Jammy Eggs

**MAKES** 1 to 6 eggs

This method will yield eggs with runny yolks and fully set whites. Be sure to use large eggs that have no cracks and are cold from the refrigerator and to use a pot that is large enough to hold the eggs in a single layer.

- 1–6 large eggs

Bring ½ inch water to boil in medium saucepan over medium-high heat. Using tongs, gently place up to 6 eggs in boiling water (eggs will not be submerged). Cover and cook for 8 minutes. Transfer saucepan to sink and run cold water over eggs for 30 seconds to stop cooking. Peel before using.

### Microwave-Fried Shallots

**MAKES** ½ cup

Fried shallots deliver bursts of crunch and savory flavor to Congee but they're easy to overcook and require constant stirring. The microwave solves all that.

- 3 shallots, sliced thin
- ½ cup vegetable oil

Combine shallots and oil in medium bowl. Microwave for 5 minutes. Stir and continue to microwave 2 minutes longer. Repeat stirring and microwaving in 2-minute increments until beginning to brown, 4 to 6 minutes. Repeat stirring and microwaving in 30-second increments until deep golden brown, 30 seconds to 2 minutes. Using slotted spoon, transfer shallots to paper towel–lined plate; season with salt to taste. Let drain and crisp, about 5 minutes.

## Almond Granola with Dried Fruit

**MAKES** 9 cups

**WHY THIS RECIPE WORKS** Store-bought granola suffers from many shortcomings. It's often loose and gravelly and/or infuriatingly expensive. We wanted to make our own granola at home, with big, satisfying clusters and crisp texture. The secret was to firmly pack the granola mixture into a rimmed baking sheet before baking. Once baked, we had a granola "bark" that we could break into crunchy lumps of any size. Chopping the almonds by hand is our first choice for superior texture and crunch as a food process does a lousy job of chopping nuts evenly. Use a single type of your favorite dried fruit or a combination. Do not use quick oats.

- ⅓ cup maple syrup
- ⅓ cup packed (2⅓ ounces) light brown sugar
- 4 teaspoons vanilla extract
- ½ teaspoon table salt
- ½ cup vegetable oil
- 5 cups (15 ounces) old-fashioned rolled oats
- 2 cups (10 ounces) raw almonds, chopped coarse
- 2 cups raisins or other dried fruit, chopped

**1.** Adjust oven rack to upper-middle position and heat oven to 325 degrees. Line rimmed baking sheet with parchment paper.

**2.** Whisk maple syrup, brown sugar, vanilla, and salt in large bowl. Whisk in oil. Fold in oats and almonds until thoroughly coated.

**3.** Transfer oat mixture to prepared baking sheet and spread across sheet into thin, even layer (about ⅜ inch thick). Using stiff metal spatula, compress oat mixture until very compact. Bake until lightly browned, 40 to 45 minutes, rotating pan once halfway through baking. Let cool on wire rack to room temperature, about 1 hour. Break cooled granola into pieces of desired size. Stir in dried fruit. (Granola can be stored in airtight container for up to 2 weeks.)

## Diner-Style Home Fries

**SERVES** 2 to 3

**WHY THIS RECIPE WORKS** Whether made at home or eaten out, home fries frequently suffer from the same problems: greasy or undercooked potatoes, and bland or unbalanced flavors. We wanted a recipe that produced potatoes with a crisp crust and a tender interior. We found that medium-starch Yukon Golds remained moist even when crisped on the outside. Attempts to cook raw diced potato in the skillet ended in failure; precooking was the way to go. We tried baking, boiling, and dicing the potatoes before frying them, but they overcooked. What finally worked was parcooking the potatoes—placing them in water and bringing them just to a boil, then immediately draining them before frying. This gave the interior of the potatoes a head start in the cooking process, but they weren't in the water long enough to absorb much liquid. The result: firm cubes with crisp, browned exteriors. A combination of butter and oil worked best for frying. Onion was the perfect foil for these potatoes; we cooked it in the skillet before adding the potatoes. If doubling this recipe, cook two batches of home fries separately. While making the second batch, keep the first batch hot and crisp by spreading the fries on a baking sheet placed in a 300-degree oven.

- 2½ tablespoons corn oil or peanut oil
- 1 medium onion, minced
- 1 pound (2 medium) Yukon Gold potatoes, scrubbed and cut into ½-inch cubes
- Table salt
- 1 tablespoon unsalted butter
- 1 teaspoon paprika (optional)
- 1 tablespoon minced fresh parsley leaves (optional)
- Ground black pepper

**1.** Heat 1 tablespoon of the oil in a 12-inch skillet over medium-high heat until shimmering. Add the onion and cook, stirring frequently, until browned, 8 to 10 minutes. Transfer the onion to a small bowl and set aside.

**2.** Meanwhile, place the potatoes in a large saucepan, cover with ½ inch of water, add 1 teaspoon salt, and bring to a boil over high heat. As soon as the water begins to boil, drain the potatoes thoroughly in a colander.

**3.** Heat the butter and the remaining 1½ tablespoons oil in the now-empty skillet over medium-high heat. Add the potatoes and shake the skillet to evenly distribute the potatoes in a single layer, making sure that one side of each piece is touching the surface of the skillet. Cook without stirring until one side of the potatoes is golden brown, 4 to 5 minutes, then carefully turn the potatoes, making sure the potatoes remain in a single layer. Repeat the process until the potatoes are tender and browned on most sides, turning three or four times, 10 to 15 minutes longer. Add the onions, paprika (if using), parsley (if using), ¼ teaspoon salt, and pepper to taste; serve.

## Home Fries for a Crowd

**SERVES** 6 to 8

**WHY THIS RECIPE WORKS** Making home fries the traditional way requires constant monitoring while standing over a hot skillet, after which you get only three servings at most. We wanted a quicker, more hands-off method for making a larger amount. To speed things up, we developed a hybrid cooking technique: First, we parboiled diced russet potatoes, and then we coated them in oil and cooked them in a very hot oven. We discovered that boiling the potatoes with baking soda quickly broke down their exterior while leaving their insides nearly raw, ensuring home fries with a crisp, brown crust and a moist, fluffy interior. We added diced onions in the last 20 minutes of oven time and finished the home fries with chives to reinforce the onion flavor. Don't skip the baking soda in this recipe. It's critical for home fries with just the right crisp texture.

3½ pounds russet potatoes, peeled and cut into ¾-inch dice
½ teaspoon baking soda
3 tablespoons unsalted butter, cut into 12 pieces
Kosher salt and pepper
Pinch cayenne pepper
3 tablespoons vegetable oil
2 onions, cut into ½-inch dice
3 tablespoons minced chives

1. Adjust oven rack to lowest position, place rimmed baking sheet on rack, and heat oven to 500 degrees.

2. Bring 10 cups water to boil in Dutch oven over high heat. Add potatoes and baking soda. Return to boil and cook for 1 minute. Drain potatoes. Return potatoes to Dutch oven and place over low heat. Cook, shaking pot occasionally, until any surface moisture has evaporated, about 2 minutes. Remove from heat. Add butter, 1½ teaspoons salt, and cayenne; mix with rubber spatula until potatoes are coated with thick, starchy paste, about 30 seconds.

3. Remove baking sheet from oven and drizzle with 2 tablespoons oil. Transfer potatoes to baking sheet and spread into even layer. Roast for 15 minutes. While potatoes roast, combine onions, remaining 1 tablespoon oil, and ½ teaspoon salt in bowl.

4. Remove baking sheet from oven. Using thin, sharp metal spatula, scrape and turn potatoes. Clear about 8 by 5-inch space in center of baking sheet and add onion mixture. Roast for 15 minutes.

5. Scrape and turn again, mixing onions into potatoes. Continue to roast until potatoes are well browned and onions are softened and beginning to brown, 5 to 10 minutes. Stir in chives and season with salt and pepper to taste. Serve immediately.

## Oven-Fried Bacon

**SERVES** 4 to 6

**WHY THIS RECIPE WORKS** A couple strips of crispy bacon are always a welcome accompaniment to a plate of eggs, but bacon requires frequent monitoring when cooked on the stovetop. The microwave produces unevenly cooked and flavorless strips, so we looked to the oven for an easier way. Bacon renders its fat while cooking, so it was important to choose a pan that would contain it; a rimmed baking sheet worked just fine, and it enabled us to cook more strips at the same time. We didn't have to turn the bacon because the heat of the oven cooked it evenly, though rotating the sheet front to back halfway through ensured even cooking. Compared to stovetop frying, bacon cooked in the oven wasn't quite as crispy, but it was crispy enough, and it had the same great meaty flavor. A large rimmed baking sheet is important here to contain the rendered bacon fat. If cooking more than one tray of bacon, switch their oven positions once about halfway through cooking. You can use thin- or thick-cut bacon here, though the cooking times will vary.

12 slices bacon

Adjust an oven rack to the middle position and heat the oven to 400 degrees. Arrange the bacon slices on a rimmed baking sheet. Cook until the fat begins to render, 5 to 6 minutes; rotate the pan. Continue cooking until the bacon is crispy and browned, 5 to 6 minutes longer for thin-cut bacon, 8 to 10 minutes for thick-cut. Transfer the bacon to a paper towel–lined plate, drain, and serve.

## Breakfast Sausage Patties

**MAKES** 16 patties

**WHY THIS RECIPE WORKS** You need a reliable formula to make a good batch of fresh bulk sausage. We started by weighing the trimmed pork (a well-marbled butt roast) in grams; this allowed us to calculate the precise amount of salt to add (1.5 percent of the weight of the trimmed meat). Curing the meat with the salt (and seasonings) for at least 8 hours before grinding ensured proper salinity and juiciness; plus, the salt dissolved the meat proteins (myosin), which acted as a glue that bound up the meat mixture and gave the sausage its snap. Kneading the pork mixture further developed its myosin. Briefly freezing the cured pork before grinding firmed it up so that it contained distinct pieces of meat and fat. This prevented the pork fat from overheating and melting away during grinding and from leaking out when the sausage was cooked. Once made, the sausage could be used right away, seasoned and cooked into breakfast patties, or refrigerated or frozen for later use. Because sausage requires a precise ratio of salt to trimmed meat, you'll need a scale that measures in grams, and you'll need to do some simple math. This recipe requires at least 8 hours of salting. Because you'll be measuring the salt by weight instead of volume, you can use either table salt or kosher salt. Pork butt roast is often labeled Boston butt. For the best texture, buy a well-marbled roast that has a defined fat cap. This recipe can easily be halved or doubled and freezes well.

- 2 pounds boneless pork butt roast with at least ¼-inch-thick fat cap
- Table salt
- 1 recipe Breakfast Sausage Seasoning

**1.** Leaving fat cap intact, cut pork into ¾-inch pieces, trimming and discarding all sinew and connective tissue. Weigh trimmed pork and note weight in grams. Multiply weight of pork by 0.015 to determine salt amount (round to nearest gram). Weigh out salt.

**2.** Toss pork, salt, and seasoning in bowl until well combined. Cover and refrigerate for at least 8 hours or up to 2 days.

**3.** Transfer pork to rimmed baking sheet and spread in single layer, leaving space around each chunk. Freeze until pork is very firm and starting to harden around edges but still pliable, 35 to 55 minutes.

**4A. FOR A GRINDER:** Place meat grinder attachments, including coarse die (3/16 or ¼ inch), in freezer for at least 1 hour before using. Set medium bowl in large bowl filled with ice. Grind pork at medium speed into prepared medium bowl.

**4B. FOR A FOOD PROCESSOR:** Place one-quarter of pork in food processor and pulse until ground into ⅛- to 1/16-inch pieces, 14 to 16 pulses, stopping to redistribute pork around bowl as necessary to ensure meat is evenly ground. Transfer ground pork to large bowl. Repeat with remaining 3 batches of pork.

**5.** Inspect ground pork carefully, discarding any strands of gristle or silver skin. Using your hands or stiff rubber spatula, knead pork vigorously, smearing against sides and bottom of bowl, until pork begins to tighten, feels tacky, and sticks to bottom of bowl and palm of your hand, 1½ to 2 minutes. Use immediately or wrap bowl tightly in plastic wrap and refrigerate for up to 24 hours (or transfer sausage to zipper-lock bag and freeze for up to 1 month).

**6. TO MAKE PATTIES:** Using your damp hands, divide meat into 16 pieces (about 2 ounces each) and form into 2½-inch patties about ½ inch thick. Heat 2 teaspoons vegetable oil in 12-inch nonstick skillet over medium heat. Cook half of patties until well browned on both sides and meat registers 145 to 150 degrees, 3 to 5 minutes per side. Transfer to serving platter and tent with aluminum foil. Repeat with remaining patties. Serve. (Raw sausage patties can be refrigerated, covered, for up to 24 hours or frozen for up to 1 month. Cook frozen patties for 7 to 9 minutes per side.)

## Breakfast Sausage Seasoning

**MAKES** about 2 tablespoons

- 1 tablespoon packed light brown sugar
- 2 teaspoons rubbed sage
- 1 teaspoon pepper
- ¼ teaspoon cayenne pepper

Combine all ingredients in small bowl.

## Classic Strawberry Jam

**MAKES** four 1-cup jars

**WHY THIS RECIPE WORKS** Strawberry jam is a universal favorite. Naturally low in pectin, strawberries are often cooked too long, causing the fruit to lose its bright flavor. We shortened the cooking time by cutting the strawberries into smaller pieces and then mashing them to release their juices and jump-start the cooking process. Shredded apple added natural pectin and fresh flavor to the mix. Lemon juice added acidity to balance the sugar's sweetness and helped the natural pectin to gel. Small, fragrant berries produce the best jam. For safety reasons, be sure to use bottled lemon juice, not fresh-squeezed juice, in this recipe.

- 3 pounds strawberries, hulled and cut into ½-inch pieces (10 cups)
- 3 cups sugar
- 1¼ cups peeled and shredded Granny Smith apple (1 large apple)
- 2 tablespoons bottled lemon juice

**1.** Place 2 small plates in freezer to chill. Set canning rack in large pot, place four 1-cup jars in rack, and add water to cover by 1 inch. Bring to simmer over medium heat, then turn off heat and cover to keep hot.

**2.** In Dutch oven, crush strawberries with potato masher until fruit is mostly broken down. Stir in sugar, apple, and lemon juice and bring to boil, stirring often, over medium-high heat. Once sugar is completely dissolved, boil mixture, stirring and adjusting heat as needed, until thickened and registers 217 to 220 degrees, 20 to 25 minutes. (Temperature will be lower at higher elevations.) Remove pot from heat.

**3.** To test consistency, place 1 teaspoon jam on chilled plate and freeze for 2 minutes. Drag your finger through jam on plate; jam has correct consistency when your finger leaves distinct trail. If runny, return pot to heat and simmer for 1 to 3 minutes longer before retesting. Skim any foam from surface of jam using spoon.

**4.** Place dish towel flat on counter. Using jar lifter, remove jars from pot, draining water back into pot. Place jars upside down on towel and let dry for 1 minute. Using funnel and ladle, portion hot jam into hot jars, leaving ¼ inch headspace. Slide wooden skewer along inside edge of jar and drag upward to remove air bubbles.

**5A. FOR SHORT-TERM STORAGE:** Let jam cool to room temperature, cover, and refrigerate until jam is set, 12 to 24 hours. (Jam can be refrigerated for up to 2 months.)

**5B. FOR LONG-TERM STORAGE:** While jars are hot, wipe rims clean, add lids, and screw on rings until fingertip-tight; do not overtighten. Return pot of water with canning rack to boil. Lower jars into water, cover, bring water back to boil, then start timer. Cooking time will depend on your altitude: Boil 10 minutes for up to 1,000 feet, 15 minutes for 1,001 to 3,000 feet, 20 minutes for 3,001 to 6,000 feet, or 25 minutes for 6,001 to 8,000 feet. Turn off heat and let jars sit in pot for 5 minutes. Remove jars from pot and let cool for 24 hours. Remove rings, check seal, and clean rims. (Sealed jars can be stored for up to 1 year.)

## Chocolate Hazelnut Spread

**MAKES** 1½ cups

**WHY THIS RECIPE WORKS** Much as we love Nutella, we couldn't resist making our own homemade version of the chocolate-hazelnut spread without the additives and palm oil. We wanted a texture closer to natural peanut butter with a deeply nutty, chocolaty punch. After blanching raw hazelnuts in water and baking soda, we transferred them to ice water. Their skin was easily removed by rubbing with a dish towel. Roasting the hazelnuts on a baking sheet brought out their buttery fragrance and nutty flavor. The final step was pulling out our food processor and whirling the nuts into a smooth paste before adding in sugar, cocoa, oil, vanilla, and salt. Hazelnut oil works best to reinforce the spread's flavors, but walnut and vegetable oils are also passable.

- 2 cups hazelnuts
- 6 tablespoons baking soda
- 1 cup (4 ounces) confectioners' sugar
- ⅓ cup (1 ounce) unsweetened cocoa powder
- 2 tablespoons hazelnut oil
- 1 teaspoon vanilla extract
- ⅛ teaspoon table salt

**1.** Fill large bowl halfway with ice and water. Bring 4 cups water to boil. Add hazelnuts and baking soda and boil for 3 minutes. Transfer nuts to ice bath with slotted spoon, drain, and slip skins off with dish towel.

**2.** Adjust oven rack to middle position and heat oven to 375 degrees. Place hazelnuts in single layer on rimmed baking sheet and roast until fragrant and golden brown, 12 to 15 minutes, rotating sheet halfway through roasting.

**3.** Process hazelnuts in food processor until oil is released and smooth, loose paste forms, about 5 minutes, scraping down sides of bowl often.

**4.** Add sugar, cocoa, oil, vanilla, and salt and process until fully incorporated and mixture begins to loosen slightly and becomes glossy, about 2 minutes, scraping down sides of bowl as needed.

**5.** Transfer spread to jar with tight-fitting lid. Chocolate hazelnut spread can be stored at room temperature or refrigerated for up to 1 month.

## Cold-Brew Coffee Concentrate

**MAKES** about 1½ cups; enough for 3 cups iced coffee

**WHY THIS RECIPE WORKS** Coffee brewed between 195 and 205 degrees will contain more aroma compounds, dissolved solids, and flavor than coffee brewed at 72 degrees, but heat also extracts the bitterness and astringency found in coffee beans. The appeal of cold brew lies in its milder acidity and bitterness, which lets more of the dark chocolate, caramel, ripe black fruit, and vanilla flavors come to the fore. To make the best cold brew, we tried a number of out-there techniques, including near-continuous agitation and five-day-long

extractions in the refrigerator. But in the end, a simple steep in a French press was the best method. Using a high ratio of ground beans to water produced a concentrate that was easy to store and could be diluted as desired. After trying various brew times we found that a 24-hour steep delivered the best flavor. Pouring the concentrate through a coffee filter–lined fine-mesh strainer ensured that it was free of sediment. Our finishing touch? A pinch of kosher salt, which rounded out the cold brew's flavors and further masked it's already minimal bitterness. This concentrated coffee needs to be diluted before drinking. We recommend a 1:1 ratio of concentrate to water, but you can dilute it more if you like.

- 9 ounces medium-roast coffee beans, ground coarse (3½ cups)
- 3½ cups filtered water, room temperature
- Kosher salt (optional)

**1.** Stir coffee and water together in large (about 2-quart) glass French press. Allow raft of ground coffee to form, about 10 minutes, then stir again to recombine. Cover with plastic wrap and let sit at room temperature for 24 hours.

**2.** Line fine-mesh strainer with coffee filter and set over large liquid measuring cup. Place lid on press and slowly and evenly press plunger down on grounds to separate them from coffee concentrate. Pour concentrate into prepared strainer. Line large bowl with triple layer of cheesecloth, with cheesecloth overhanging edge of bowl. Transfer grounds to cheesecloth. Gather edges of cheesecloth together and twist; then, holding pouch over strainer, firmly squeeze grounds until liquid no longer runs freely from pouch; discard grounds.

**3.** Using back of ladle or rubber spatula, gently stir concentrate to help filter it through strainer. Concentrate can be refrigerated in jar with tight-fitting lid for up to 1 week.

### Iced Coffee

Combine equal parts coffee concentrate and cold water. Add pinch kosher salt, if using, and pour into glass with ice.

CHAPTER 3 # Soup and Stews

Photos (left to right): Cataplana; Hong Kong-Style Wonton Noodle Soup; Chraime; Silky Butternut Squash Soup; Multicooker Hawaiian Oxtail Soup; Fresh Corn Chowder; Zarzuela

## Classic Chicken Noodle Soup

**SERVES** 6 to 8

**WHY THIS RECIPE WORKS** For chicken noodle soup made the old-fashioned way you must start with a whole chicken. We began by cutting the chicken, minus the breast, into small pieces, cutting through bones to expose the marrow which added body and flavor to the soup. For additional flavor, we sweated the browned pieces in a covered pot with an onion, then simmered them briefly. We reserved some of the skimmed fat from the broth to sauté aromatics and carrots for the soup, and we added in tender chicken breast pieces that had already been poached in the broth. The egg noodles cooked right in the pot absorbing meaty flavor from the broth. Using a cleaver will allow you to cut up the chicken parts quickly, but a chef's knife or kitchen shears will also work.

**STOCK**

- 1 tablespoon vegetable oil
- 1 (4-pound) whole chicken, breast removed, split, and reserved; remaining chicken cut into 2-inch pieces
- 1 onion, chopped
- 2 quarts boiling water
- 2 teaspoons table salt
- 2 bay leaves

**SOUP**

- 2 tablespoons chicken fat, reserved from making stock, or vegetable oil
- 1 onion, chopped
- 1 large carrot, peeled and sliced ¼ inch thick
- 1 celery rib, sliced ¼ inch thick
- ½ teaspoon dried thyme
- 3 ounces egg noodles (about 2 cups)
- ¼ cup minced fresh parsley leaves

**1. FOR THE STOCK:** Heat oil in Dutch oven over medium-high heat until shimmering. Add half of chicken pieces and cook until lightly browned, about 5 minutes per side. Transfer cooked chicken to bowl and repeat with remaining chicken pieces; transfer to bowl with first batch. Add onion and cook, stirring frequently, until onion is translucent, 3 to 5 minutes. Return chicken pieces to pot. Reduce heat to low, cover, and cook until chicken releases its juices, about 20 minutes.

**2.** Increase heat to high; add boiling water, reserved chicken breast pieces, salt, and bay leaves. Reduce heat to medium-low and simmer until flavors have blended, about 20 minutes.

**3.** Remove breast pieces from pot. When cool, remove skin and bones from breast pieces and discard. Shred meat with your fingers or 2 forks and set aside. Strain stock through fine-mesh strainer into container, pressing on solids to extract as much liquid as possible; discard solids. Allow liquid to settle for about 5 minutes and skim off fat; reserve 2 tablespoons, if desired. (Shredded chicken, strained stock, and fat can be refrigerated in separate airtight containers for up to 2 days.)

**4. FOR THE SOUP:** Heat reserved chicken fat in large Dutch oven over medium-high heat. Add onion, carrot, and celery and cook until softened, about 5 minutes. Add thyme and reserved stock and simmer until vegetables are tender, 10 to 15 minutes.

**5.** Add noodles and reserved shredded chicken and cook until just tender, 5 to 8 minutes. Stir in parsley, season with salt and pepper to taste, and serve.

## Hearty Chicken Noodle Soup

**SERVES** 4 to 6

**WHY THIS RECIPE WORKS** This is a crave-worthy version of chicken noodle soup chock-full of chicken, noodles, and vegetables—a true meal in a bowl. We began by jump-starting the flavor of our soup with a mixture of store-bought chicken broth and water, but the broth-and-water base had a distinctly flat flavor. A few pounds of chicken parts created a rich stock, but browning the parts and then simmering them was just too fussy for what we wanted. Instead, we turned to a somewhat unlikely but more convenient substitute—store-bought ground chicken. Ground chicken offers more surface area and exponentially more flavor, providing a great-tasting stock when sautéed with aromatics and then simmered with the broth and water. A little cornstarch thickened the rich stock. Next we added the chicken (breasts that had been poached in the stock and then shredded), vegetables, and noodles. Along with onion, celery, and carrots, we further enriched the soup with potato and Swiss chard. When skimming the fat off the stock, leave a little bit on the surface to enhance the soup's flavor.

**STOCK**

- 1 tablespoon vegetable oil
- 1 pound ground chicken
- 1 small onion, chopped medium
- 1 medium carrot, peeled and chopped medium

- 1 celery rib, chopped medium
- 2 quarts low-sodium chicken broth
- 4 cups water
- 2 bay leaves
- 2 teaspoons table salt
- 2 (12-ounce) bone-in, skin-on chicken breast halves, cut in half crosswise

**SOUP**

- ¼ cup cold water
- 3 tablespoons cornstarch
- 1 small onion, halved and sliced thin
- 2 medium carrots, peeled, halved lengthwise, and cut crosswise into ¾-inch pieces
- 1 medium celery rib, halved lengthwise and cut crosswise into ½-inch pieces
- 1 medium russet potato (about 8 ounces), peeled and cut into ¾-inch cubes
- 1½ ounces egg noodles (about 1 cup)
- 4–6 Swiss chard leaves, ribs removed, torn into 1-inch pieces (about 2 cups; optional)
- 1 tablespoon minced fresh parsley leaves
- Table salt and ground black pepper

**1. FOR THE STOCK:** Heat the oil in a large Dutch oven over medium-high heat until shimmering. Add the ground chicken, onion, carrot, and celery. Cook, stirring frequently, until the chicken is no longer pink, 5 to 10 minutes (do not brown the chicken).

**2.** Reduce the heat to medium-low. Add the broth, water, bay leaves, salt, and chicken breasts; cover and cook for 30 minutes. Remove the lid, increase the heat to high, and bring to a boil. (If the liquid is already boiling when the lid is removed, remove the chicken breasts immediately and continue with the recipe.) Transfer the chicken breasts to a large plate and set aside. Continue to cook the stock for 20 minutes, adjusting the heat to maintain a gentle boil. Strain the stock through a fine-mesh strainer into a container, pressing on the solids to extract as much liquid as possible; discard the solids. Allow the liquid to settle about 5 minutes and skim off the fat. (The strained stock can be refrigerated in an airtight container for up to 2 days or frozen for up to 3 months. The chicken breasts can be stored in a zipper-lock bag with the air squeezed out.)

**3. FOR THE SOUP:** Return the stock to a Dutch oven set over medium-high heat. In a small bowl, combine the water and cornstarch until a smooth slurry forms; stir into the stock and bring to a gentle boil. Add the onion, carrots, celery, and potato and cook until the potato pieces are almost tender, 10 to 15 minutes, adjusting the heat as necessary to maintain a gentle boil. Add the egg noodles and continue to cook until all the vegetables and noodles are tender, about 5 minutes longer.

**4.** Meanwhile, remove the skin and bones from the reserved cooked chicken and discard. Shred the meat with your fingers or two forks. Add the shredded chicken, Swiss chard (if using), and parsley to the soup and cook until heated through, about 2 minutes. Season with salt and pepper to taste and serve.

## Slow-Cooker Old-Fashioned Chicken Noodle Soup

**SERVES** 6 to 8

**WHY THIS RECIPE WORKS** Making chicken noodle soup with a deep flavor requires a few tricks when using a slow cooker. First, we used a combination of bone-in chicken thighs and breasts; cooked and shredded breast meat was the perfect choice for the final soup, but bone-in thighs (which we browned first) were key for giving the broth its deep flavor during the long cooking time. To prevent the breast meat from overcooking we wrapped the chicken breast inside a foil packet. Since we were already dirtying a skillet to brown the chicken thighs,we browned and softened the vegetables and aromatics as well, which added even more flavor. Tomato paste, gave the soup body and brought out the savory, umami notes of our soup. We cooked the noodles separately to ensure perfect texture and added them in at the end, along with frozen peas that we simply let sit in the soup to heat through.

- 1½ pounds bone-in, skin-on chicken thighs, trimmed
- Table salt and ground black pepper
- 1 tablespoon vegetable oil
- 3 medium carrots, peeled and chopped medium
- 2 celery ribs, chopped medium
- 1 medium onion, minced
- 3 medium garlic cloves, minced or pressed through a garlic press (about 1 tablespoon)
- 1 tablespoon tomato paste
- 2 teaspoons minced fresh thyme or ½ teaspoon dried
- ⅛ teaspoon red pepper flakes
- 8 cups low-sodium chicken broth
- 2 bay leaves
- 1 (12-ounce) bone-in, skin-on split chicken breast, trimmed
- 1½ ounces wide egg noodles (about 1 cup)
- ½ cup frozen peas
- 2 tablespoons minced fresh parsley leaves

**1.** Dry the chicken thighs with paper towels and season with salt and pepper. Heat the oil in a 12-inch skillet over medium-high heat until just smoking. Brown the chicken thighs well on both sides, 6 to 8 minutes. Transfer to a plate, let cool slightly, and discard the skin.

**2.** Pour off all but 1 tablespoon fat left in the skillet. Add the carrots, celery, and onion and cook over medium heat until the vegetables are softened, 7 to 10 minutes. Stir in the garlic, tomato paste, thyme, and red pepper flakes and cook until fragrant, about 30 seconds. Stir in 1 cup of the chicken broth, scraping up any browned bits; transfer to the slow cooker.

**3.** Stir the remaining 7 cups broth and the bay leaves into the slow cooker. Nestle the browned chicken thighs with any accumulated juice into the slow cooker. Season the chicken breast with salt and pepper and place on one side of a large piece of aluminum foil. Fold the foil over the chicken and crimp to seal the edges. Place the foil packet on top of the soup, pressing gently as needed to fit. Cover and cook until the chicken is tender, 4 to 6 hours on low.

**4.** Remove the foil packet, open it carefully (watch for steam), and transfer the chicken breast to a cutting board. Transfer the chicken thighs to a cutting board. Let all of the chicken cool slightly, then shred it into bite-size pieces with two forks, discarding the skin and bones. Let the soup settle for 5 minutes, then skim the fat from the surface using a large spoon. Discard the bay leaves.

**5.** Bring 4 quarts water to a boil in a large pot. Add 1 tablespoon salt and the noodles to the boiling water and cook until tender, then drain. Stir the cooked noodles, shredded chicken, and peas into the soup and let sit until heated through, about 5 minutes. Stir in the parsley, season with salt and pepper to taste, and serve.

## Pressure-Cooker Chicken Noodle Soup

**SERVES 8**

**WHY THIS RECIPE WORKS** With its velvety broth and deep flavor, old-fashioned chicken noodle soup is an ideal pressure-cooker candidate since the pressure cooker can extract flavor from the meat, skin, and bones of a whole chicken in just 20 minutes. We started by putting the chicken into the pot with some aromatics, carrots, celery, and water. Placing the chicken in the pot breast side up allowed the thighs and more delicate breast meat to cook through at the same time since the thighs were in contact with the pot's bottom. After 20 minutes, the meat practically fell off the bones, making it easy to shred and stir back in. Soy sauce gave the broth even deeper, richer meaty flavor.

- 1 tablespoon vegetable oil
- 1 onion, chopped fine
- 3 garlic cloves, minced (about 1 teaspoon)
- 1 minced fresh thyme or ¼ teaspoon dried
- 8 cups water
- 4 carrots, peeled and sliced
- 2 celery ribs, sliced ½ inch thick
- 2 tablespoons soy sauce
- 1 (4-pound) whole chicken, giblets discarded
- Table salt and pepper
- 4 ounces (2⅔ cups) wide egg noodles
- ¼ cup minced fresh parsley

**1.** Heat oil in pressure-cooker pot over medium heat until shimmering. Add onion and cook until softened, about 5 minutes. Stir in garlic and thyme and cook until fragrant, about 30 seconds. Stir in water, carrots, celery, and soy sauce, scraping up any browned bits. Season chicken with salt and pepper and place, breast side up, in pot.

**2.** Lock pressure-cooker lid in place and bring to high pressure over medium-high heat. As soon as pot reaches high pressure, reduce heat to medium-low and cook for 20 minutes, adjusting heat as needed to maintain high pressure.

**3.** Remove pot from heat. Quick release pressure, then carefully remove lid, allowing steam to escape away from you.

**4.** Transfer chicken to cutting board, let cool slightly, then shred meat into bite-size pieces, discarding skin and bones. Meanwhile, using large spoon, skim excess fat from surface of soup. Bring soup to boil, stir in noodles, and cook until tender, about 5 minutes. Stir in shredded chicken and parsley, season with salt and pepper to taste, and serve.

## Avgolemono (Greek Chicken and Rice Soup with Egg and Lemon)

**SERVES 4 to 6**

**WHY THIS RECIPE WORKS** Avgolemono gets its name from the egg-lemon mixture that thickens and flavors it. Our version contains tender shreds of chicken that are poached to perfection by sitting off the heat in hot broth. We flavored the broth with citrusy coriander and lemon zest, which gave it savory depth and enhanced the soup's lemon flavor. Processing eggs, yolks, and a portion of the cooked rice in a blender and then stirring this puree into the hot broth gave our avgolemono a velvety consistency. If you have homemade chicken broth, we recommend using it in this recipe, as it gives the soup the best flavor and body. Our preferred commercial chicken broth is Swanson Chicken Stock. Use a vegetable peeler to remove strips of zest from the lemons.

- 1½ pounds boneless, skinless chicken breasts, trimmed
- 1¾ teaspoons table salt
- 12 (3-inch) strips lemon zest plus 6 tablespoons juice, plus extra juice for seasoning (3 lemons)
- 2 sprigs fresh dill, plus 2 teaspoons chopped
- 2 teaspoons coriander seeds
- 1 teaspoon black peppercorns
- 1 garlic clove, peeled and smashed
- 8 cups chicken broth
- 1 cup long-grain rice
- 2 large eggs plus 2 large yolks

**1.** Cut each chicken breast in half lengthwise. Toss with salt and let sit at room temperature for at least 15 minutes or up to 30 minutes. Cut 8-inch square of triple-thickness cheesecloth. Place lemon zest, dill sprigs, coriander seeds, peppercorns, and garlic in center of cheesecloth and tie into bundle with kitchen twine.

**2.** Bring broth, rice, and spice bundle to boil in large saucepan over high heat. Reduce heat to low, cover, and cook for 5 minutes. Turn off heat, add chicken, cover, and let sit for 15 minutes.

**3.** Transfer chicken to large plate and discard spice bundle. Using 2 forks, shred chicken into bite-size pieces. Using ladle, transfer 1 cup cooked rice to blender (leave any liquid in pot). Add lemon juice and eggs and yolks to blender and process until smooth, about 1 minute.

**4.** Return chicken and any accumulated juices to pot. Return soup to simmer over high heat. Remove pot from heat and stir in egg mixture until fully incorporated. Stir in chopped dill and season with salt, pepper, and extra lemon juice to taste. Serve.

## Italian Chicken Soup with Parmesan Dumplings

**SERVES** 4 to 6

**WHY THIS RECIPE WORKS** This rustic northern Italian specialty features tender dumplings deeply flavored with Parmesan and served in a light chicken broth. We modernized the classic recipe a bit, making it more hearty and a bit easier by adding flavor to store-bought chicken broth using browned chicken thighs. The dumplings traditionally comprise bread crumbs, egg, and Parmesan cheese. In our recipe, egg whites kept the texture light and airy and bound the bread-and-cheese dumplings, and chicken fat added richness. We shaped the dumplings into balls before poaching them in our enriched broth. Fennel, carrots, and escarole complement the shredded chicken and the flavorful dumplings. Use the large holes of a box grater to shred the Parmesan. To ensure that the dumplings remain intact during cooking, roll them until the surfaces are smooth and no cracks remain.

- 1½ pounds bone-in chicken thighs, trimmed
- Table salt and pepper
- 1 teaspoon vegetable oil
- 1 fennel bulb, 1 tablespoon fronds minced, stalks discarded, bulb halved, cored, and cut into ½-inch pieces
- 1 onion, chopped fine
- 2 carrots, peeled and cut into ¾-inch pieces
- ½ cup dry white wine
- 8 cups chicken broth
- 1 Parmesan cheese rind, plus 3 ounces Parmesan, shredded (1 cup)
- 2 slices hearty white sandwich bread, torn into 1-inch pieces
- 2 large egg whites
- ¼ teaspoon grated lemon zest
- Pinch ground nutmeg
- ½ small head escarole (6 ounces), trimmed and cut into ½-inch pieces

**1.** Pat chicken dry with paper towels and season with salt and pepper. Heat oil in Dutch oven over medium-high heat until just smoking. Add chicken, skin side down, and cook until well browned, 6 to 8 minutes. Transfer chicken to plate. Discard skin.

**2.** Drain off all but 1 teaspoon fat from pot and reserve 1 tablespoon fat for dumplings. Return pot to medium heat. Add fennel bulb, onion, carrots, and ½ teaspoon salt and cook, stirring occasionally, until vegetables soften and begin to brown, about 5 minutes. Add wine and cook, scraping up any browned bits, until almost dry, about 2 minutes. Return chicken to pot; add broth and Parmesan rind and bring to boil. Reduce heat to low, cover, and simmer until chicken is tender and registers 175 degrees, about 30 minutes. Transfer chicken to plate. Discard Parmesan rind. Cover broth and remove from heat. When cool enough to handle, use 2 forks to shred chicken into bite-size pieces. Discard bones.

**3.** While broth is simmering, adjust oven rack to middle position and heat oven to 350 degrees. Pulse bread in food processor until finely ground, 10 to 15 pulses. Measure out

1 cup bread crumbs and transfer to parchment paper–lined rimmed baking sheet (set aside remainder for another use). Toast until light brown, about 5 minutes. Transfer to medium bowl, reserving sheet and parchment, and let bread crumbs cool completely.

**4.** Pulse shredded Parmesan in now-empty food processor until finely ground, 10 to 15 pulses. Transfer Parmesan to bowl with cooled bread crumbs and add reserved 1 tablespoon fat, egg whites, lemon zest, ⅛ teaspoon pepper, and nutmeg. Mix until thoroughly combined. Refrigerate dough for 15 minutes.

**5.** Working with 1 teaspoon dough at a time, roll into smooth balls and place on parchment-lined sheet (you should have about 28 dumplings).

**6.** Return broth to simmer over medium-high heat. Add escarole and chicken and return to simmer. Add dumplings and cook, adjusting heat to maintain gentle simmer, until dumplings float to surface and are cooked through, 3 to 5 minutes. Stir in fennel fronds. Season with salt and pepper to taste, and serve.

**TO MAKE AHEAD:** Prepare recipe through step 5. Refrigerate broth, shredded chicken, and dumplings separately for up to 24 hours. To serve, proceed with step 6 as directed.

## Hong Kong–Style Wonton Noodle Soup

**SERVES** 4 to 6

**WHY THIS RECIPE WORKS** The wontons in Hong Kong–style noodle soup are characterized by square yellow wrappers, juicy pork, and large pieces of shrimp. To achieve a cohesive filling, we agitated ground pork to release its sticky myosin proteins before seasoning it with scallion, Shaoxing wine, sesame oil, oyster sauce, and soy sauce and combining it with a piece of halved shrimp in each wrapper. For a flavorful seafood broth, we used the shells reserved from the shrimp as well as pungent flounder powder—a crucial part of this soup's Hong Kong identity. Dried flounder powder contributed savoriness and concentrated fish flavor. A splash of soy sauce and a pinch of white pepper rounded out the broth. Bright green bok choy and thin, fresh wonton noodles perfectly complemented the bouncy wontons and the savory seafood broth. To make the wontons, the filling is divided among 24 wonton wrappers and the shrimp pieces are pressed on top. Be sure to leave the ends of wontons open. Look for freshly ground pork, which is typically sold in bulk at the butcher's counter, where it has a higher percentage of fat and a coarser texture than prepackaged pork. We prefer homemade chicken broth; however, store-bought broth can be substituted. If flounder powder is unavailable, it can be omitted, though the soup will not be as full-bodied. Do not substitute flounder fish seasoning (which contains added salt and flavorings) or powders made from other varieties of fish. Serve with Chinese red vinegar, a finishing vinegar with a hint of sweetness.

- 1 teaspoon vegetable oil
- 12 large shrimp (26 to 30 per pound), peeled, deveined, tails removed, and shells reserved (see page 523)
- 4 cups Chicken Broth (page 140)
- 2 cups water
- ¼ teaspoon plus ⅛ teaspoon table salt, divided
- 1 teaspoon dried flounder fish powder, divided
- 1 tablespoon soy sauce, divided
- ¼ teaspoon white pepper, divided
- 4 ounces ground pork
- 1 scallion, minced
- 1 tablespoon Shaoxing wine
- 2 teaspoons oyster sauce
- ½ teaspoon toasted sesame oil, plus extra for serving
- 24 (3-inch) square Hong Kong–style wonton wrappers
- 2 heads baby bok choy (4 ounces each), greens separated
- 6 ounces fresh thin wonton noodles

**1.** Heat vegetable oil in large saucepan over high heat until shimmering. Add reserved shrimp shells and cook, stirring frequently, until shells begin to turn spotty brown, about 2 minutes. Add broth, water, and ¼ teaspoon salt and bring to boil. Off heat, stir in ½ teaspoon flounder powder and let steep for 15 minutes. Strain broth through fine-mesh strainer and return to now-empty saucepan. Stir in 2 teaspoons soy sauce and ⅛ teaspoon pepper. Cover and keep warm.

**2.** Halve each shrimp crosswise; set aside. Using wooden spoon or 4 bundled chopsticks, vigorously stir pork in medium bowl until it has stiffened and started to pull away from sides of bowl and has slightly lightened in color, about 5 minutes. Stir in scallion, Shaoxing wine, oyster sauce, sesame oil, remaining ⅛ teaspoon salt, remaining ½ teaspoon flounder powder, remaining 1 teaspoon soy sauce, and remaining ⅛ teaspoon pepper until well combined.

**3.** Lightly dust parchment paper–lined rimmed baking sheet with flour. Place 6 wrappers on sheet, place heaping ½ teaspoon pork filling in center of each wrapper, then top with 1 piece of shrimp and gently press into filling. Form wontons by gathering corners of wrapper around filling and pinching dough tightly just above filling to seal; leave ends of wrapper unsealed. Transfer wontons to prepared sheet, cover with damp dish towel, and repeat with remaining wrappers and filling in 3 batches. (Wontons can be refrigerated for up to 24 hours or frozen on sheet until solid, then transferred to zipper-lock bag and stored in freezer for up to 1 month. Do not thaw frozen dumplings before cooking; increase simmer time to about 6 minutes.)

**4.** Meanwhile, bring 4 quarts water to boil in Dutch oven. Add bok choy and cook until tender, about 1 minute. Using spider skimmer or slotted spoon, transfer bok choy to plate. Return water to boil, add wonton noodles, and cook until just tender. Using spider skimmer, transfer noodles to colander and rinse thoroughly; divide noodles among serving bowls. Return water to boil, add wontons, and cook until wontons turn translucent and tender and float to the top, about 4 minutes. Using spider skimmer, divide wontons among bowls and top with bok choy.

**5.** Return broth to boil over high heat, then ladle over bok choy, noodles, and dumplings. Serve, passing extra sesame oil separately.

### MAKING WONTONS

**1.** Place heaping ½ teaspoon pork filling in center of each wrapper, then top with 1 piece of shrimp and gently press into filling.

**2.** Form wontons by gathering corners of wrapper around filling.

**3.** Pinch dough tightly just above filling to seal; leave ends of wrapper unsealed.

## Tortilla Soup

**SERVES 6**

**WHY THIS RECIPE WORKS** This intensely flavored tortilla soup is our quicker version of the traditional dish. We broke the soup down to its three classic components—the flavor base, the chicken stock, and the garnishes—and devised techniques and substitute ingredients that streamlined the recipe. We achieved maximum flavor by composing a puree made from chipotles, tomatoes, onions, garlic, jalapeños, and epazote, and then frying the puree in oil. We then added the puree to canned chicken broth after poaching chicken in it. We easily oven-toasted lightly oiled tortilla strips instead of frying them and served the soup over them topped with a range of traditional garnishes. Despite its somewhat lengthy ingredient list, this recipe is very easy to prepare. To make ahead, complete the soup short of adding the shredded chicken to the pot at the end of step 3. Return the soup to a simmer over medium-high heat before proceeding. The tortilla strips and the garnishes are best prepared the day of serving.

**TORTILLA STRIPS**

- 8 (6-inch) corn tortillas, cut into ½-inch-wide strips
- 1 tablespoon vegetable oil

**SOUP**

- 2 bone-in, skin-on split chicken breasts (about 1½ pounds) or 4 bone-in, skin-on chicken thighs (about 1¼ pounds), skin removed and trimmed
- 8 cups chicken broth
- 1 very large white onion (about 1 pound), peeled and quartered, divided
- 4 garlic cloves, peeled, divided
- 2 sprigs fresh epazote or 8 to 10 sprigs fresh cilantro plus 1 sprig fresh oregano
- ½ teaspoon plus ⅛ teaspoon table salt, divided
- 2 tomatoes, cored and quartered
- ½ jalapeño chile
- 1 chipotle chile in adobo sauce, plus up to 1 tablespoon adobo sauce
- 1 tablespoon vegetable oil

**GARNISHES**

- Lime wedges
- Avocado, peeled, pitted, and diced fine
- Cotija cheese, crumbled, or Monterey Jack cheese, diced fine
- Fresh cilantro leaves
- Jalapeño chile, minced
- Crema Mexicana or sour cream

1. **FOR THE TORTILLA STRIPS:** Adjust oven rack to middle position and heat oven to 425 degrees. Spread tortilla strips on rimmed baking sheet; drizzle with oil and toss until evenly coated. Bake until strips are deep golden brown and crisped, about 14 minutes, rotating pan and shaking strips (to redistribute) halfway through baking. Season strips lightly with salt; transfer to plate lined with several layers of paper towels.

2. **FOR THE SOUP:** While tortilla strips bake, bring chicken, broth, 2 onion quarters, 2 garlic cloves, epazote, and ½ teaspoon salt to boil over medium-high heat in large saucepan; reduce the heat to low, cover, and simmer until chicken is just cooked through, about 20 minutes. Using tongs, transfer chicken to large plate. Pour broth through fine-mesh strainer; discard solids in strainer. When cool enough to handle, shred chicken into bite-size pieces; discard bones.

3. Puree tomatoes, jalapeño, chipotle chile, 1 teaspoon adobo sauce, remaining 2 onion quarters, and remaining 2 garlic cloves in food processor until smooth, about 20 seconds. Heat oil in Dutch oven over high heat until shimmering; add tomato-onion puree and remaining ⅛ teaspoon salt and cook, stirring frequently, until mixture has darkened in color, about 10 minutes. Stir strained broth into tomato mixture, bring to boil, then reduce heat to low and simmer to blend flavors, about 15 minutes. Taste soup; if desired, add up to 2 teaspoons more adobo sauce. Add shredded chicken and simmer until heated through, about 5 minutes. To serve, place portions of tortilla strips in bottom of individual bowls and ladle soup into the bowls; pass garnishes separately.

## Thai Chicken Soup

**SERVES 6 to 8**

**WHY THIS RECIPE WORKS** Tom kha gai is a Thai chicken and coconut soup flavored with galangal, makrut lime leaves, lemongrass, and bird's eye chiles. We wanted to create a chicken soup inspired by these bright flavors. We developed a rich chicken-flavored broth by using equal parts chicken broth and coconut milk (adding the coconut milk in two stages: at the beginning and just before serving). Lemongrass added floral and citrusy flavors. We substituted some of the other traditional ingredients with jarred red curry paste, which included all the flavors we were missing. Just adding a dollop at the very end of cooking and whisking it with pungent fish sauce and tart lime juice allowed all the flavors to come through loud and clear. To make slicing the chicken easier, freeze it for 15 minutes. Although we prefer the richer, more complex flavor of regular coconut milk, light coconut milk can be substituted for one or both cans. For a spicier soup, add additional red curry paste to taste.

**SOUP**

- 1 teaspoon peanut or vegetable oil
- 3 stalks lemongrass, bottom 5 inches only, trimmed and sliced thin
- 3 large shallots, chopped coarse (about ¾ cup)
- 8 sprigs fresh cilantro, chopped coarse
- 3 tablespoons fish sauce
- 4 cups low-sodium chicken broth
- 2 (14-ounce) cans coconut milk
- 1 tablespoon sugar
- 8 ounces white mushrooms, wiped clean and sliced ¼ inch thick
- 1 pound boneless, skinless chicken breasts, trimmed, halved lengthwise, and cut on the bias into ⅛-inch pieces
- 3 tablespoons juice from 2 limes
- 2 teaspoons Thai red curry paste

**GARNISH**

- ½ cup loosely packed fresh cilantro leaves
- 2 Thai, serrano, or jalapeño chiles, seeds and ribs removed, chiles sliced thin
- 2 scallions, sliced thin on the bias
- Lime wedges, for serving

**1.** Heat the oil in a large saucepan over medium heat until just shimmering. Add the lemongrass, shallots, cilantro sprigs, and 1 tablespoon of the fish sauce and cook, stirring frequently, until just softened but not browned, 2 to 5 minutes.

**2.** Stir in the broth and 1 can of the coconut milk and bring to a simmer over high heat. Cover, reduce the heat to low, and simmer until the flavors have blended, about 10 minutes. Pour the broth through a fine-mesh strainer, discarding the solids in the strainer. (At this point, the soup can be refrigerated in an airtight container for up to 1 day.)

**3.** Return the strained soup to a clean saucepan and bring to a simmer over medium-high heat. Stir in the remaining can of coconut milk and the sugar and bring to a simmer. Reduce the heat to medium, add the mushrooms, and cook until just tender, 2 to 3 minutes. Add the chicken and cook, stirring constantly, until no longer pink, 1 to 3 minutes. Remove the soup from the heat.

**4.** Whisk the remaining 2 tablespoons fish sauce, the lime juice, and curry paste together, then stir into the soup. Ladle the soup into individual bowls and garnish with the cilantro, chiles, and scallions. Serve with the lime wedges.

## Chicken and Sausage Gumbo

**SERVES 6**

**WHY THIS RECIPE WORKS** Most recipes for the beloved Louisiana soup, gumbo, start with a wet roux, a cooked paste of flour and fat that can take an hour or more to make. We streamlined this process by using a dry roux of oven-toasted flour, which gave the same effect as a wet roux but without the oil. To flavor our gumbo we used easy-to-work-with boneless, skinless chicken thighs and andouille sausage, rounding out the dish with garlic, thyme, bay leaves, and spices. We stirred in white vinegar rather than hot sauce at the end for acidity without adding heat to an already well-seasoned dish. We strongly recommend using andouille, but in a pinch, kielbasa can be substituted. The salt level of the final dish may vary depending on the brand of sausage, so liberal seasoning with additional salt at the end may be necessary. Serve over white rice.

- 1 cup all-purpose flour
- 1 tablespoon vegetable oil
- 1 onion, chopped fine
- 1 green bell pepper, chopped fine
- 2 celery ribs, chopped fine
- 3 garlic cloves, minced
- 2 bay leaves
- 1 tablespoon minced fresh thyme
- 1 teaspoon paprika
- ½ teaspoon cayenne pepper
- ¼ teaspoon table salt
- ¼ teaspoon pepper
- 4 cups chicken broth, divided
- 2 pounds boneless, skinless chicken thighs, trimmed
- 8 ounces andouille sausage, sliced into ¼-inch-thick half-moons
- 6 scallions, sliced thin
- 1 teaspoon distilled white vinegar
- Hot sauce

**1.** Adjust oven rack to middle position and heat oven to 425 degrees. Place flour in 12-inch ovensafe skillet and bake, stirring occasionally, until color of ground cinnamon or dark brown sugar, 40 to 55 minutes. (As flour approaches desired color it will take on a very nutty aroma that will smell faintly of burnt popcorn and it will need to be stirred more frequently.) Transfer flour to medium bowl and cool. (Toasted flour can be stored in airtight container for up to 1 week.)

**2.** Heat oil in Dutch oven over medium heat until shimmering. Add onion, pepper, and celery and cook, stirring frequently, until softened, 5 to 7 minutes. Stir in garlic, bay leaves, thyme, paprika, cayenne, salt, and pepper and cook until fragrant, about 1 minute. Stir in 2 cups broth. Add chicken thighs in single layer (they will not be completely submerged by liquid) and bring to simmer. Reduce heat to medium-low, cover, and simmer until chicken is fork tender, 15 to 17 minutes. Transfer chicken to plate.

**3.** Slowly whisk remaining 2 cups broth into toasted flour until thick, batter-like paste forms. (Add broth in small increments to prevent clumps from forming.) Return pot to medium heat and slowly whisk flour paste into gumbo, making sure each addition is incorporated before adding next. Stir sausage into gumbo. Simmer, uncovered, until gumbo thickens slightly, 20 to 25 minutes.

**4.** Once cool enough to handle, shred chicken into bite-size pieces. Stir chicken and scallions into gumbo. Remove pot from heat and stir in vinegar and season with salt to taste. Discard bay leaves. Serve, passing hot sauce at table. (Gumbo can be refrigerated in airtight container for up to 24 hours).

## Best Chicken Stew

**SERVES** 6 to 8

**WHY THIS RECIPE WORKS** While recipes for chicken stew are few and far between, the ones we've come across are either too fussy, or seem more soup than stew. We wanted to develop a chicken stew recipe with succulent bites of chicken, tender vegetables, and a truly robust gravy. To start, we created an ultraflavorful gravy using chicken wings, which we later discarded. Browning the wings lent deep chicken flavor to the stew and browning them in rendered bacon fat lent porky depth and just a hint of smoke. Soy sauce and anchovy paste, though unusual for chicken stew, lent more savory depth (without making the stew taste salty or fishy). To finish our stew, we added white wine for brightness and a sprinkle of parsley for freshness. Mashed anchovy fillets (rinsed and dried before mashing) can be used instead of anchovy paste. Use small red potatoes measuring 1½ inches in diameter.

- 2 pounds boneless, skinless chicken thighs, halved crosswise and trimmed
- 3 slices bacon, chopped
- 1 pound chicken wings, halved at joint
- 1 onion, chopped fine
- 1 celery rib, minced
- 2 garlic cloves, minced
- 2 teaspoons anchovy paste
- 1 teaspoon minced fresh thyme
- 5 cups chicken broth, divided
- 1 cup dry white wine, plus extra for seasoning
- 1 tablespoon soy sauce
- 3 tablespoons unsalted butter, cut into 3 pieces
- ⅓ cup all-purpose flour
- 1 pound small red potatoes, unpeeled, quartered
- 4 carrots, peeled and cut into ½-inch pieces
- 2 tablespoons chopped fresh parsley

**1.** Adjust oven rack to lower-middle position and heat oven to 325 degrees. Arrange chicken thighs on baking sheet and lightly season both sides with salt and pepper; cover with plastic wrap and set aside.

**2.** Cook bacon in Dutch oven over medium-low heat, stirring occasionally, until crispy, 6 to 8 minutes. Using slotted spoon, transfer bacon to medium bowl. Add chicken wings to pot, increase heat to medium, and cook until well browned on both sides, 10 to 12 minutes; transfer wings to bowl with bacon.

**3.** Add onion, celery, garlic, anchovy paste, and thyme to fat in pot; cook, stirring occasionally, until dark fond forms on pan bottom, 2 to 4 minutes. Increase heat to high; stir in 1 cup broth, wine, and soy sauce, scraping up any browned bits; and bring to boil. Cook, stirring occasionally, until liquid evaporates and vegetables begin to sizzle again, 12 to 15 minutes. Add butter and stir to melt; sprinkle flour over vegetables and stir to combine. Gradually whisk in remaining 4 cups broth until smooth. Stir in wings and bacon, potatoes, and carrots; bring to simmer. Transfer to oven and cook, uncovered, for 30 minutes, stirring once halfway through cooking.

**4.** Remove pot from oven. Use wooden spoon to draw gravy up sides of pot and scrape browned fond into stew. Place over high heat, add thighs, and bring to simmer. Return pot to oven, uncovered, and continue to cook, stirring occasionally, until chicken offers no resistance when poked with fork and vegetables are tender, about 45 minutes longer. (Stew can be refrigerated for up to 2 days.)

**5.** Discard wings and season stew with up to 2 tablespoons extra wine. Season with salt and pepper to taste, sprinkle with parsley, and serve.

## Chicken Bouillabaisse

**SERVES** 4 to 6

**WHY THIS RECIPE WORKS** Bouillabaisse is a traditional French stew bursting with fish and shellfish and the flavors of Provence. For this version featuring chicken, we substituted canned chicken broth for fish stock and added flour and tomato paste to the saffron and cayenne before adding the broth for extra body. White wine and orange zest brought complexity to the broth, and adding the pastis, an anise-flavored liqueur, early on gave the alcohol time to cook off and leave behind a hint of sweetness. To help the chicken skin stay crisp after browning, we switched from stovetop to oven cooking. We rested the chicken on the potatoes as the bouillabaisse cooked in the oven so that

the skin stayed out of the liquid and remained crisp. A finishing blast from the broiler before serving further enhanced the crispness. The rouille and croutons (steps 4 and 5) can be prepared either as the chicken cooks or up to 2 days in advance.

BOUILLABAISSE

- 3 pounds split bone-in chicken breast (or thighs or drumsticks), skin-on, trimmed of excess fat
- Table salt and pepper
- 2 tablespoons extra-virgin olive oil
- 1 large leek (white and light green parts only), halved lengthwise, rinsed, and sliced thin (about 1 cup) (see page 545)
- 1 small fennel bulb, halved lengthwise, cored, and sliced thin (about 2 cups)
- ¼ teaspoon saffron threads
- ¼ teaspoon cayenne pepper
- 1 tablespoon all-purpose flour
- 4 garlic cloves, minced (about 4 teaspoons)
- 1 tablespoon tomato paste
- 1 (14.5-ounce) can diced tomatoes, drained
- ½ cup dry white wine
- 3 cups chicken broth
- 1 strip orange zest (from 1 orange), about 3 inches long, cleaned of white pith
- ¼ cup pastis or Pernod
- ¾ pound Yukon Gold potatoes (1 large or 2 small), cut into ¾-inch cubes
- 1 tablespoon chopped fresh tarragon leaves or parsley leaves

ROUILLE AND CROUTONS

- 3 tablespoons water
- ¼ teaspoon saffron threads
- 1 baguette
- 4 teaspoons lemon juice
- 2 teaspoons Dijon mustard
- 1 large egg yolk
- ¼ teaspoon cayenne pepper
- 2 small garlic cloves, minced (about 1½ teaspoons)
- ½ cup vegetable oil
- ½ cup plus 2 tablespoons extra-virgin olive oil
- Table salt and pepper

**1. FOR THE BOUILLABAISSE:** Adjust oven racks to middle and lower positions and heat oven to 375 degrees. Pat chicken dry with paper towels and season with salt and pepper. Heat oil in large Dutch oven over medium-high heat until just smoking. Add chicken pieces, skin side down, and cook without moving until well browned, 5 to 8 minutes. Using tongs, flip chicken and brown other side, about 3 minutes. Transfer chicken to large plate.

**2.** Add leek and fennel; cook, stirring often, until vegetables begin to soften and turn translucent, about 4 minutes. Add saffron, cayenne, flour, garlic, and tomato paste and cook until fragrant, about 30 seconds. Add tomatoes, wine, broth, orange zest, pastis, and potatoes; bring to simmer. Reduce heat to medium-low and simmer for 10 minutes.

**3.** Nestle chicken thighs and drumsticks into simmering liquid with skin above surface of liquid; cook, uncovered, for 5 minutes. Nestle breast pieces into simmering liquid, adjusting pieces as necessary to ensure skin stays above surface of liquid. Bake on middle rack, uncovered, until thickest part of chicken registers 145 degrees for breasts and 160 degrees for drumsticks and thighs, 10 to 20 minutes.

**4. FOR THE ROUILLE:** While chicken cooks, microwave water and saffron in medium microwave-safe bowl until water is steaming, 10 to 20 seconds. Allow to sit for 5 minutes. Cut 3-inch piece off of baguette; remove and discard crust. Tear crustless bread into 1-inch chunks (you should have about 1 cup). Stir bread pieces and lemon juice into saffron-infused water; soak for 5 minutes. Using whisk, mash soaked bread mixture until uniform paste forms, 1 to 2 minutes. Whisk in mustard, egg yolk, cayenne, and garlic until smooth, about 15 seconds. Whisking constantly, slowly drizzle in vegetable oil in steady stream until smooth mayonnaise-like consistency is reached, scraping down bowl as necessary. Slowly whisk in ½ cup olive oil in steady stream until smooth. Season to taste with salt and pepper.

**5. FOR THE CROUTONS:** Cut remaining baguette into ¾-inch-thick slices. Arrange slices in single layer on rimmed baking sheet. Drizzle with remaining 2 tablespoons olive oil and season with salt and pepper. Bake on lower rack until light golden brown (bread can be toasted while bouillabaisse is in oven), 10 to 15 minutes.

**6.** Remove bouillabaisse and croutons from oven and set oven to broil. Once heated, return bouillabaisse to oven and cook until chicken skin is crisp and thickest part of chicken registers 160 degrees for breasts and 175 degrees for drumsticks and thighs, 5 to 10 minutes (smaller pieces may cook faster than larger pieces; remove individual pieces as they reach temperature).

**7.** Transfer chicken pieces to large plate. Skim excess fat from broth. Stir tarragon into broth and season with salt and pepper. Transfer broth and potatoes to large shallow serving bowls and top with chicken pieces. Drizzle 1 tablespoon rouille over each portion and spread 1 teaspoon rouille on each crouton. Serve, floating 2 croutons in each bowl and passing remaining croutons and rouille separately.

## White Chicken Chili

**SERVES** 6 to 8

**WHY THIS RECIPE WORKS** Chili made with chicken has become popular as a lighter, fresher alternative to the red kind. Though many recipes produce something more akin to chicken and bean soup, we thought there was potential to develop a rich stew-like chili with moist chicken, tender beans, and a complex flavor profile. We chose bone-in, skin-on breasts, later shredding the meat and discarding the skin and bones; we used the fat rendered from searing them to cook the aromatics. A combination of chiles—jalapeño, Anaheim, and poblano chiles—which have distinct characteristics that complemented one another, lent depth of flavor. Using canned cannellini beans circumvented the hassle of dried beans and tasted just as good. We tried thickening the chili with masa harina, which we had used as a thickener in other chili recipes, but the texture and flavor didn't work well here. Instead, we pureed some of the chili mixture, beans, and broth, which made the chili thicker without compromising its flavor. To finish, a minced raw jalapeño stirred in before serving provided a shot of fresh chile flavor. If Anaheim chiles cannot be found, add an additional poblano and jalapeño to the chili. To use chicken thighs, increase the cooking time in step 4 to about 40 minutes or until the chicken registers 175 degrees on an instant-read thermometer. Serve the chili with sour cream, tortilla chips, and lime wedges.

- 3 pounds bone-in, skin-on chicken breast halves, trimmed
- ¾ teaspoon table salt, divided
- ½ teaspoon pepper
- 1 tablespoon vegetable oil
- 3 jalapeño chiles
- 3 poblano chiles, stemmed, seeded, and cut into large pieces
- 3 Anaheim chiles, stemmed, seeded, and cut into large pieces
- 2 onions, cut into large pieces
- 6 garlic cloves, minced
- 1 tablespoon ground cumin
- 1½ teaspoons ground coriander
- 2 (15-ounce) cans cannellini beans, rinsed, divided
- 3 cups chicken broth, divided
- ¼ cup minced fresh cilantro leaves
- 3 tablespoons lime juice (2 limes)
- 4 scallions, white and light green parts sliced thin

**1.** Sprinkle chicken evenly with ½ teaspoon salt and pepper. Heat oil in Dutch oven over medium-high heat until just smoking. Add chicken, skin side down, and cook without moving until the skin is golden brown, about 4 minutes. Using tongs, turn chicken and lightly brown other side, about 2 minutes. Transfer chicken to plate; remove and discard skin.

**2.** While chicken is browning, remove and discard ribs and seeds from 2 jalapeños; mince flesh. In food processor, pulse half of poblanos, Anaheims, and onions until consistency of chunky salsa, 10 to 12 pulses, scraping down sides of workbowl halfway through. Transfer mixture to medium bowl. Repeat with remaining poblanos, Anaheims, and onions; combine with first batch (do not wash food processor blade or workbowl).

**3.** Pour off all but 1 tablespoon fat from Dutch oven (adding more vegetable oil if necessary) and reduce heat to medium. Add minced jalapeños, chile-onion mixture, garlic, cumin, coriander, and remaining ¼ teaspoon salt. Cover and cook, stirring occasionally, until vegetables soften, about 10 minutes. Remove pot from heat.

**4.** Transfer 1 cup cooked vegetable mixture to now-empty food processor workbowl. Add 1 cup beans and 1 cup broth and process until smooth, about 20 seconds. Add vegetable-bean mixture, remaining 2 cups broth, and chicken breasts to Dutch oven and bring to boil over medium-high heat. Reduce heat to medium-low and simmer, covered, stirring occasionally, until chicken registers 160 degrees (175 degrees if using thighs), 15 to 20 minutes (40 minutes if using thighs).

**5.** Using tongs, transfer chicken to large plate. Stir in remaining beans and continue to simmer, uncovered, until beans are heated through and chili has thickened slightly, about 10 minutes.

**6.** Mince remaining jalapeño, reserving and mincing ribs and seeds, and set aside. When cool enough to handle, shred chicken into bite-size pieces, discarding bones. Stir shredded chicken, cilantro, lime juice, scallions, and minced jalapeño (with seeds if desired) into chili and return to simmer. Season with salt and pepper to taste, and serve.

## Vietnamese Beef Pho

**SERVES** 4 to 6

**WHY THIS RECIPE WORKS** Traditional versions of this beef and noodle soup call for simmering beef bones for hours to make a deeply flavorful broth. For a quicker version, we simmered ground beef in spiced store-bought broth, which gave us complexity and depth in a fraction of the time. To serve the soup, we poured our broth over thinly sliced strip steak and gathered a variety of garnishes, such as lime wedges, hoisin and chile sauces, and bean sprouts. Our favorite store-bought beef broth is Better Than Bouillon Roasted Beef Base. An equal weight of tri-tip steak or blade steak can be substituted for the strip steak; make sure to trim all connective tissue and excess fat. One 14- or 16-ounce package of rice noodles will serve four to six. Look for noodles that are about ⅛ inch wide; these are often labeled "small."

- 1 pound 85 percent lean ground beef
- 2 onions, quartered through root end
- 12 cups beef broth
- ¼ cup fish sauce, plus extra for seasoning
- 1 (4-inch) piece ginger, sliced into thin rounds
- 1 cinnamon stick
- 2 tablespoons sugar, plus extra for seasoning
- 6 star anise pods
- 6 whole cloves
- 2 teaspoons table salt, plus extra for seasoning
- 1 teaspoon black peppercorns
- 1 (1-pound) boneless strip steak, trimmed and halved
- 14–16 ounces (⅛-inch-wide) rice noodles
- ⅓ cup chopped fresh cilantro
- 3 scallions, sliced thin (optional)

Bean sprouts
Sprigs fresh Thai or Italian basil
Lime wedges
Hoisin sauce
Sriracha sauce

1. Break ground beef into rough 1-inch chunks and drop in Dutch oven. Add water to cover by 1 inch. Bring mixture to boil over high heat. Boil for 2 minutes, stirring once or twice. Drain ground beef in colander and rinse well under running water. Wash out pot and return ground beef to pot.

2. Place 6 onion quarters in pot with ground beef. Slice remaining 2 onion quarters as thin as possible and set aside for garnish. Add broth, 2 cups water, fish sauce, ginger, cinnamon, sugar, star anise, cloves, salt, and peppercorns to pot and bring to boil over high heat. Reduce heat to medium-low and simmer, partially covered, for 45 minutes.

3. Pour broth through colander set in large bowl. Discard solids. Strain broth through fine-mesh strainer lined with triple thickness of cheesecloth; add water as needed to equal 11 cups. Return broth to pot and season with extra sugar and salt (broth should taste overseasoned). Cover and keep warm over low heat.

4. While broth simmers, place steak on large plate and freeze until very firm, 35 to 45 minutes. Once firm, cut against grain into ⅛-inch-thick slices. Return steak to plate and refrigerate until needed.

5. Place noodles in large container and cover with hot tap water. Soak until noodles are pliable, 10 to 15 minutes; drain noodles. Meanwhile, bring 4 quarts water to boil in large pot. Add drained noodles and cook until almost tender, 30 to 60 seconds. Drain immediately and divide noodles among individual bowls.

6. Bring broth to rolling boil over high heat. Divide steak among individual bowls, shingling slices on top of noodles. Pile reserved onion slices on top of steak slices and sprinkle with cilantro and scallions, if using. Ladle hot broth into each bowl. Serve immediately, passing bean sprouts, basil sprigs, lime wedges, hoisin, sriracha, and extra fish sauce separately.

## Beef and Vegetable Soup

**SERVES** 4 to 6

**WHY THIS RECIPE WORKS** Rich and hearty beef and vegetable soup with old-fashioned flavor usually takes hours to make, but this version develops the same flavors and textures in under an hour. Sirloin tip steaks were the best choice here—when cut into small pieces, the meat was tender and offered the illusion of being cooked for hours; plus, its meaty flavor imparted richness to the soup. In place of labor-intensive homemade beef broth, we doctored store-bought beef broth with aromatics and lightened its flavor profile with chicken broth. To further boost the flavor of the beef, we added cremini mushrooms, tomato paste, soy sauce, and red wine, ingredients that are rich in glutamates, naturally occurring compounds that accentuate the meat's hearty flavor. To mimic the rich body of a homemade meat stock (made rich through the gelatin released by the meat bones' collagen during the long simmering process), we relied on powdered gelatin. Choose whole sirloin tip steaks over ones that have been cut into small pieces for stir-fries. If sirloin tip steaks are unavailable, substitute blade or flank steak, removing any hard gristle or excess fat. White mushrooms can be used in place of the cremini mushrooms, with some trade-off in flavor. If you like, add 1 cup of frozen peas, frozen corn, or frozen cut green beans during the last 5 minutes of cooking. For a heartier soup, add 10 ounces of red potatoes, cut into ½-inch pieces (2 cups), during the last 15 minutes of cooking.

- 1 pound sirloin tip steaks, trimmed and cut into ½-inch pieces
- 2 tablespoons soy sauce
- 1 teaspoon vegetable oil
- 1 pound cremini mushrooms, trimmed and quartered
- 1 large onion, chopped
- 2 tablespoons tomato paste
- 1 garlic clove, minced

½ cup red wine
4 cups beef broth
1¾ cups chicken broth
4 carrots, peeled and cut into ½-inch pieces
2 celery ribs, cut into ½-inch pieces
1 bay leaf
1 tablespoon unflavored gelatin
½ cup cold water
2 tablespoons minced fresh parsley leaves

**1.** Combine beef and soy sauce in medium bowl; set aside for 15 minutes.

**2.** Heat oil in Dutch oven over medium-high heat until just smoking. Add mushrooms and onion; cook, stirring frequently, until onion is browned and dark bits form on pan bottom, 8 to 12 minutes. Transfer vegetables to bowl.

**3.** Add beef and cook, stirring occasionally, until liquid evaporates and meat starts to brown, 6 to 10 minutes. Add tomato paste and garlic; cook, stirring constantly, until fragrant, about 30 seconds. Add red wine, scraping bottom of the pot with wooden spoon to loosen any browned bits, and cook until syrupy, 1 to 2 minutes.

**4.** Add beef broth, chicken broth, carrots, celery, bay leaf, and browned mushrooms and onion; bring to boil. Reduce heat to low, cover, and simmer until vegetables and meat are tender, 25 to 30 minutes. While soup is simmering, sprinkle gelatin over cold water in small bowl and let sit until gelatin softens, about 5 minutes.

**5.** When soup is finished, turn off heat. Discard bay leaf. Add gelatin mixture and stir until completely dissolved. Stir in parsley, season with salt and pepper to taste, and serve.

## Italian Wedding Soup

**SERVES** 6 to 8

**WHY THIS RECIPE WORKS** Traditional recipes for this hearty soup featuring meatballs, tender greens, and pasta require an afternoon-long stint on the stovetop, which starts with building the brodo, a long-cooked broth made from the bones of meat and poultry. Wanting a quicker path to this richly flavored soup, we created a speedy yet ultrasavory broth by simmering ground beef and pork in a mixture of chicken and beef broth. Dried porcini mushrooms and Worcestershire sauce further boosted the meaty flavor. For the meatballs, we nixed the hard-to-find ground veal and stuck with ground beef and ground pork. To make up for the loss in texture from omitting the veal, we added baking powder and whipped the pork in a stand mixer to ensure the meatballs remained light, juicy, and supple. Chopped kale and ditalini, stirred in toward the end of the cooking time, became perfectly tender in a matter of minutes. Use a rasp-style grater to process the onion and garlic for the meatballs. Tubettini or orzo can be used in place of the ditalini.

**BROTH**

1 onion, chopped
1 fennel bulb, stalks discarded, bulb halved, cored, and chopped
4 garlic cloves, peeled and smashed
¼ ounce dried porcini mushrooms, rinsed
4 ounces ground pork
4 ounces 85 percent lean ground beef
1 bay leaf
½ cup dry white wine
1 tablespoon Worcestershire sauce
4 cups chicken broth
2 cups beef broth
2 cups water

**MEATBALLS**

1 slice hearty white sandwich bread, crusts removed, torn into 1-inch pieces
5 tablespoons heavy cream
¼ cup grated Parmesan cheese
4 teaspoons finely grated onion
½ teaspoon finely grated garlic
Table salt and pepper
6 ounces ground pork
1 teaspoon baking powder
6 ounces 85 percent lean ground beef
2 teaspoons minced fresh oregano
1 cup ditalini pasta
12 ounces kale, stemmed and cut into ½-inch pieces (6 cups)

**1. FOR THE BROTH:** Heat onion, fennel, garlic, porcini, pork, beef, and bay leaf in Dutch oven over medium-high heat; cook, stirring frequently, until meats are no longer pink, about 5 minutes. Add wine and Worcestershire; cook for 1 minute. Add chicken broth, beef broth, and water; bring to simmer. Reduce heat to low, cover, and simmer for 30 minutes.

**2. FOR THE MEATBALLS:** While broth simmers, combine bread, cream, Parmesan, onion, garlic, and pepper to taste in bowl; using fork, mash mixture to uniform paste. Using stand mixer fitted with paddle, beat pork, baking powder, and ½ teaspoon salt on high speed until smooth and pale, 1 to 2 minutes, scraping down bowl as needed. Add bread mixture, beef, and oregano; mix on medium-low speed until just incorporated, 1 to 2 minutes, scraping down bowl as needed. Using moistened hands, form heaping teaspoons of meat mixture into smooth, round meatballs; you should have 30 to 35 meatballs. Cover and refrigerate for up to 1 day.

**3.** Strain broth through fine-mesh strainer set over large bowl or container, pressing on solids to extract as much liquid as possible. Wipe out Dutch oven and return broth to pot. (Broth can be refrigerated for up to 3 days. Skim off fat before reheating.)

**4.** Return broth to simmer over medium-high heat. Add pasta and kale; cook, stirring occasionally, for 5 minutes. Add meatballs; return to simmer and cook, stirring occasionally, until meatballs are cooked through and pasta is tender, 3 to 5 minutes. Season with salt and pepper to taste and serve.

## Best Beef Stew

**SERVES** 6 to 8

**WHY THIS RECIPE WORKS** We wanted a rich-tasting but approachable beef stew with tender meat, flavorful vegetables, and a rich brown gravy that justified the time it took to prepare. After browning the beef (chuck-eye is our preferred cut for stew), we caramelized the usual choices of onions and carrots, rather than just adding them raw to the broth. To mimic the luxurious, mouth-coating texture of beef stews made with homemade stock (provided by the collagen in bones that is transformed into gelatin when simmered), we included powdered gelatin and flour. Frozen pearl onions added a touch of elegance to this stew and are added toward the end of cooking along with some frozen peas. Use a good-quality medium-bodied wine, such as a Côtes du Rhône or Pinot Noir, for this stew. Try to find beef that is well marbled with white veins of fat. While the blade steak will yield slightly thinner pieces after trimming, it should still be cut into 1½-inch pieces. Look for salt pork that looks meaty and is roughly 75 percent lean.

- 2 garlic cloves, minced
- 4 anchovy fillets, minced fine (about 2 teaspoons)
- 1 tablespoon tomato paste
- 1 (4-pound) boneless chuck-eye roast, trimmed and cut into 1½-inch pieces
- 2 tablespoons vegetable oil, divided
- 1 large onion, halved and sliced ⅛ inch thick
- 4 carrots, peeled and cut into 1-inch pieces
- ¼ cup unbleached all-purpose flour
- 2 cups red wine
- 2 cups chicken broth
- 4 ounces salt pork, rinsed of excess salt
- 2 bay leaves
- 4 sprigs fresh thyme
- 1 pound Yukon Gold potatoes, unpeeled, cut into 1-inch pieces
- 1½ cups frozen pearl onions, thawed
- 2 teaspoons unflavored gelatin
- ½ cup water
- 1 cup frozen peas, thawed
- Table salt and ground black pepper

**1.** Adjust oven rack to lower-middle position and heat oven to 300 degrees. Combine garlic and anchovies in small bowl and press mixture with back of fork to form paste. Stir in tomato paste and set mixture aside.

**2.** Pat meat dry with paper towels (do not season meat). Heat 1 tablespoon vegetable oil in Dutch oven over high heat until just starting to smoke. Add half of beef and cook until well browned on all sides, about 8 minutes total, reducing heat if oil begins to smoke or fond begins to burn. Transfer beef to large plate. Repeat with remaining 1 tablespoon vegetable oil and remaining beef, leaving second batch of meat in pot after browning.

**3.** Reduce heat to medium and return first batch of beef to pot. Add onion and carrots to pot and stir to combine with beef. Cook, scraping bottom of pan to loosen any browned bits, until onion is softened, 1 to 2 minutes. Add garlic mixture and cook, stirring constantly, until fragrant, about 30 seconds. Add flour and cook, stirring constantly, until no dry flour remains, about 30 seconds.

**4.** Slowly add wine, scraping bottom of pan to loosen any browned bits. Increase heat to high and allow wine to simmer until thickened and slightly reduced, about 2 minutes. Stir in broth, salt pork, bay leaves, and thyme. Bring to simmer, cover, transfer to oven, and cook for 1½ hours.

## Hearty Beef and Vegetable Stew

**SERVES** 4 to 6

**WHY THIS RECIPE WORKS** This healthy take on beef stew uses less meat and is packed with hearty winter vegetables. To start we browned the beef to get a good base on which to build layers of flavor. We then cooked portobello mushrooms in the fat left behind, infusing them with meaty flavor. We didn't skimp on aromatics, and flour and tomato paste helped thicken the stew. For more complexity, we used a mixture of wine, chicken broth, and beef broth. We then returned the browned meat to the pot, along with the root vegetables. Kale, peas, and parsley came last, as they required less time to cook through.

- 2 pounds boneless beef chuck-eye roast, trimmed and cut into 1½-inch pieces
- Table salt and pepper
- 5 teaspoons canola oil
- 1 large portobello mushroom cap, cut into ½-inch pieces
- 2 onions, chopped fine
- 3 garlic cloves, minced
- 1 tablespoon minced fresh thyme or 1 teaspoon dried
- 3 tablespoons all-purpose flour
- 1 tablespoon tomato paste
- 1½ cups dry red wine
- 2 cups chicken broth
- 2 cups beef broth
- 2 bay leaves
- 12 ounces red potatoes, unpeeled, cut into 1-inch pieces
- 4 carrots, peeled, halved lengthwise, and sliced 1 inch thick
- 4 parsnips, peeled, halved lengthwise, and sliced 1 inch thick
- 8 ounces kale, stemmed and sliced into ½-inch-wide strips
- ½ cup frozen peas
- ¼ cup minced fresh parsley

**1.** Adjust oven rack to lower-middle position and heat oven to 300 degrees. Pat beef dry with paper towels and season with salt and pepper. Heat 1 teaspoon oil in Dutch oven over medium-high heat until just smoking. Brown half of meat on all sides, 5 to 10 minutes; transfer to bowl. Repeat with 1 teaspoon oil and remaining beef; transfer to bowl.

**2.** Add mushroom pieces to fat left in pot, cover, and cook over medium heat until softened and wet, about 5 minutes. Uncover and continue to cook until mushroom pieces are dry and browned, 5 to 10 minutes.

**3.** Stir in remaining 1 tablespoon oil and onions and cook until softened, 5 to 7 minutes. Stir in garlic and thyme and cook until fragrant, about 30 seconds. Stir in flour and tomato paste and cook until flour is lightly browned, about 1 minute.

**4.** Slowly whisk in wine, scraping up any browned bits. Slowly whisk in chicken broth and beef broth until smooth. Stir in bay leaves and browned meat and bring to simmer. Cover, transfer pot to oven, and cook for 1½ hours.

**5.** Stir in potatoes, carrots, and parsnips and continue to cook in oven until meat and vegetables are tender, about 1 hour. Stir in kale and continue to cook in oven until tender, about 10 minutes. Remove stew from oven and remove bay leaves. Stir in peas and parsley and let stew sit for 5 to 10 minutes. Season with salt and pepper to taste. Serve.

## Tuscan-Style Beef Stew

**SERVES** 6 to 8

**WHY THIS RECIPE WORKS** Tuscany's rich beef stew, peposo, is meant to be a simple dish of slow-cooked beef shin, Chianti, garlic, and peppercorns, but many recipes yield bland beef. To give our stew plenty of body, we salted chunks of short ribs and browned half of the meat to kickstart the sauce with flavorful fond. We deglazed the pot with red wine and stirred in the sauce's building blocks: water, shallots, carrots, garlic, rosemary, bay leaves, and peppercorns. Gelatin, tomato paste, and anchovy paste created a smooth texture and rich taste. We added in the uncooked beef chunks and brought the stew to a simmer before transferring it to the oven for a long, slow braise. Before serving, we removed the tender beef, strained and defatted the liquid, and returned the liquid to the pot. Adding more wine reinforced and freshened its impact before we reduced it to a thick, lush sauce. Just before spooning the sauce over the beef, we poured in one more hit of Chianti, this time mixed with a couple teaspoons of cornstarch for a final thickening boost. We prefer boneless short ribs in this recipe because they require very little trimming. If you cannot find them, substitute a 5-pound chuck roast trimmed and cut into 2-inch pieces. Serve with polenta or crusty bread.

- 4 pounds boneless beef short ribs, trimmed and cut into 2-inch pieces
- Table salt
- 1 tablespoon vegetable oil
- 1 (750-ml) bottle Chianti
- 1 cup water
- 4 shallots, halved lengthwise
- 2 carrots, peeled and halved lengthwise
- 1 garlic head, cloves separated, unpeeled, and crushed
- 4 sprigs fresh rosemary
- 2 bay leaves
- 1 tablespoon cracked black peppercorns, plus extra for serving
- 1 tablespoon unflavored gelatin
- 1 tablespoon tomato paste
- 1 teaspoon anchovy paste
- 2 teaspoons pepper
- 2 teaspoons cornstarch

**1.** Toss beef and 1½ teaspoons salt together in bowl and let stand at room temperature for 30 minutes. Adjust oven rack to lower-middle position and heat oven to 300 degrees.

**2.** Heat oil in large Dutch oven over medium-high heat until just smoking. Pat beef dry with paper towels. Add half of beef in single layer and cook until well browned on all sides, about 8 minutes total, reducing heat if fond begins to burn. Stir in 2 cups wine, water, shallots, carrots, garlic, rosemary, bay leaves, cracked peppercorns, gelatin, tomato paste, anchovy paste, and remaining beef. Bring to simmer and cover tightly with sheet of heavy-duty aluminum foil, then lid. Transfer to oven and cook until beef is tender, 2 to 2¼ hours, stirring halfway through cooking.

**3.** Using slotted spoon, transfer beef to bowl; cover tightly with foil and set aside. Strain sauce through fine-mesh strainer into fat separator. Wipe out pot with paper towels. Let liquid settle for 5 minutes, then return defatted liquid to pot.

**4.** Add 1 cup wine and pepper and bring mixture to boil over medium-high heat. Simmer briskly, stirring occasionally, until sauce is thickened to consistency of heavy cream, 12 to 15 minutes.

**5.** Combine remaining wine and cornstarch in small bowl. Reduce heat to medium-low, return beef to pot, and stir in cornstarch-wine mixture. Cover and simmer until just heated through, 5 to 8 minutes. Season with salt to taste. Serve, passing extra cracked peppercorns separately. (Stew can be refrigerated for up to 3 days.)

## Daube Provençal

**SERVES** 4 to 6

**WHY THIS RECIPE WORKS** Daube Provençal is the king of beef stews due to its classic Provencal ingredients. We wanted to create a bold version that could be re-created in an American home kitchen, a stew that would garner raves at any dinner party. We followed the basic formula for building a meat stew that starts on the stove but is braised long and slow in the oven. To give it a Provencal spin, we concentrated on selecting and managing the complex blend of ingredients that defines this dish. We chose briny niçoise olives, bright tomatoes, floral orange peel, and the regional flavors of thyme and bay leaf. A few anchovies added complexity without a fishy taste, and salt pork contributed rich body. A whole bottle of wine added bold flavor and needed just a little cooking to tame its raw bite. Serve with egg noodles or boiled potatoes. Cabernet Sauvignon is our favorite wine for this recipe, but Côtes du Rhône and Zinfandel also work. Because the tomatoes are added just before serving, it is preferable to use canned whole tomatoes and dice them yourself—uncooked, they are more tender than canned diced tomatoes. Once the salt pork, thyme, and bay leaves are removed in step 4, the daube can be cooled and refrigerated in an airtight container for up to 4 days. Before reheating, skim the hardened fat from the surface, then continue with the recipe.

- ¾ ounce dried porcini mushrooms, rinsed
- 1 (3½-pound) boneless beef chuck-eye roast, trimmed and cut into 2-inch chunks
- 1½ teaspoons table salt
- 1 teaspoon ground black pepper
- 4 tablespoons olive oil
- 5 ounces salt pork, rind removed
- 2 medium onions, halved pole to pole and cut into ⅛-inch-thick slices (about 4 cups)
- 4 large carrots, peeled and cut into 1-inch-thick rounds (about 2 cups)
- 2 tablespoons tomato paste
- 4 medium garlic cloves, peeled and sliced thin
- ⅓ cup unbleached all-purpose flour
- 1 (750-milliliter) bottle bold red wine
- 1 cup low-sodium chicken broth
- 1 cup water
- 1 cup pitted niçoise olives, drained well
- 4 strips zest from 1 orange, each strip about 3 inches long, removed with a vegetable peeler, cleaned of white pith, and cut lengthwise into thin strips
- 2 anchovy fillets, minced (about 1 teaspoon)
- 5 sprigs fresh thyme, tied together with kitchen twine
- 2 bay leaves
- 1 (14.5-ounce) can whole tomatoes, drained and cut into ½-inch cubes
- 2 tablespoons minced fresh parsley leaves

**1.** Combine the mushrooms and 1 cup water in a small microwave-safe bowl; cover with plastic wrap, cut three vents for steam with a knife, and microwave on high power for 30 seconds. Let stand until the mushrooms soften, about 5 minutes. Lift the mushrooms from the liquid with a fork and chop into ½-inch pieces (you should have about 4 tablespoons). Strain the liquid through a fine-mesh strainer lined with a paper towel into a medium bowl. Set the mushrooms and liquid aside.

**2.** Adjust an oven rack to the lower-middle position and heat the oven to 325 degrees. Dry the beef thoroughly with paper towels, then season with the salt and pepper. Heat 2 tablespoons of the oil in a large heavy-bottomed Dutch oven over medium-high heat until just smoking; add half of the beef. Cook without moving the pieces until well browned, about 2 minutes on each side, for a total of 8 to 10 minutes, reducing the heat if the fat begins to smoke. Transfer the meat to a medium bowl. Repeat with the remaining 2 tablespoons oil and the remaining beef.

**3.** Reduce the heat to medium and add the salt pork, onions, carrots, tomato paste, and garlic to the now-empty pot; cook, stirring occasionally, until light brown, about 2 minutes. Stir in the flour and cook, stirring constantly, about 1 minute. Slowly add the wine, gently scraping up any browned bits. Add the broth, water, and beef with any accumulated juices. Increase the heat to medium-high and bring to a simmer. Add the mushrooms and their liquid, ½ cup of the olives, the orange zest, anchovies, thyme, and bay leaves, distributing evenly and arranging the beef so it is completely covered by the liquid; partially cover the pot and place in the oven. Cook until a fork inserted in the beef meets little resistance (the meat should not be falling apart), 2½ to 3 hours.

**4.** Discard the salt pork, thyme, and bay leaves. Add the tomatoes and the remaining ½ cup olives; warm over medium-high heat until heated through, about 1 minute. Cover the pot and allow the stew to settle, about 5 minutes. Using a spoon, skim the excess fat from the surface of the stew. Stir in the parsley and serve.

## Beef Burgundy

SERVES 6

**WHY THIS RECIPE WORKS** Leave it to the French to make beef stew into an elegant affair. Unfortunately, when translated to the home kitchen, classic, intensely flavorful beef burgundy, also known as boeuf bourguignon, can lose its appeal. We wanted to bring this dish to its earthy, robust, warm potential: satisfyingly large chunks of tender meat draped with a velvety sauce brimming with the flavor of good Burgundy wine and studded with caramelized mushrooms and pearl onions. We started by rendering salt pork until crisp, then browned large chunks of beef chuck roast in the rendered fat. For the braising liquid, a combination of chicken broth and water, enhanced with a small amount of dried porcini mushrooms and tomato paste, provided balanced, well-rounded flavor. We deglazed the pan twice, used a roux to thicken the sauce, and then added the wine. Wrapping the aromatic vegetables in cheesecloth made it easy to remove them from the braising liquid. Thick-cut bacon can be substituted for the salt pork; cut the bacon crosswise into ¼-inch pieces and treat it just as you would the salt pork, but note that you will have no rind to include in the vegetable and herb pouch. Boiled potatoes are the traditional accompaniment, but mashed potatoes or buttered noodles are nice as well.

**STEW**

- 6 ounces salt pork, trimmed of rind and rind reserved, salt pork cut into ¼-inch pieces
- 2 medium onions, chopped coarse
- 2 medium carrots, chopped coarse
- 1 medium head garlic, cloves separated and crushed but unpeeled
- 10 sprigs fresh parsley, torn into pieces
- 6 sprigs fresh thyme
- 2 bay leaves, crumbled
- ½ teaspoon black peppercorns
- ½ ounce dried porcini mushrooms, rinsed (optional)
- 1 (4- to 4½-pound) boneless beef chuck-eye roast, trimmed and cut into 2-inch chunks
- Table salt and ground black pepper
- 2½ cups water
- 4 tablespoons (½ stick) unsalted butter, cut into 4 pieces
- ⅓ cup unbleached all-purpose flour
- 1¾ cups low-sodium chicken broth
- 1 (750-milliliter) bottle red Burgundy or Pinot Noir
- 1 teaspoon tomato paste
- 2 tablespoons brandy
- 3 tablespoons minced fresh parsley leaves

**ONION AND MUSHROOM GARNISH**

- 7 ounces (about 1¾ cups) frozen pearl onions
- ¾ cup water
- 1 tablespoon unsalted butter
- 1 tablespoon sugar
- ½ teaspoon table salt
- 10 ounces medium white mushrooms, wiped clean and halved

**1. FOR THE STEW:** Bring the salt pork, reserved salt pork rind, and 3 cups water to a boil in a medium saucepan over high heat. Boil for 2 minutes, then drain well.

**2.** Lay a double layer of cheesecloth (each piece should measure 22 by 8 inches) in a medium bowl, placing the sheets perpendicular to each other. Place the onions, carrots, garlic, parsley pieces, thyme, bay leaves, peppercorns, porcini mushrooms (if using), and salt pork rind in the cheesecloth-lined bowl. Gather together the edges of the cheesecloth and fasten them securely with kitchen twine; trim the excess cheesecloth with scissors if necessary. Set the pouch in a large ovensafe Dutch oven. Adjust the oven rack to the lower-middle position and heat the oven to 300 degrees.

**3.** Cook the salt pork in a 12-inch skillet over medium heat until lightly browned and crisp, about 12 minutes. With a slotted spoon, transfer the salt pork to the pot. Pour off and reserve all but 2 teaspoons of the fat from the skillet. Pat the beef dry with paper towels and season with salt and pepper. Add half of the beef to the skillet, increase the heat to high, and brown in a single layer, turning once or twice, until deep brown, about 7 minutes; transfer the browned beef to the pot. Add ½ cup of the water to the skillet and scrape the pan with a wooden spoon to loosen the browned bits; add the liquid to the pot.

**4.** Heat 2 teaspoons of the reserved pork fat in the skillet over high heat until smoking. Add the remaining beef in a single layer, turning once or twice, until deep brown, about 7 minutes; transfer the browned beef to the pot. Add ½ cup more water to the skillet and scrape the pan with a wooden spoon to loosen the browned bits; add the liquid to the pot.

**5.** Melt the butter in the skillet over medium heat. Whisk in the flour and cook, stirring constantly, until light brown, about 5 minutes. Gradually whisk in the chicken broth and the remaining 1½ cups water. Increase the heat to medium-high and bring to a simmer, stirring frequently, until thickened; add the mixture to the pot. Add 3 cups of the wine and the tomato paste to the pot and season with salt and pepper to taste; stir to combine. Set the pot over high heat and bring to a boil; cover and place in the oven. Cook until the meat is tender, 2½ to 3 hours.

**6.** Remove the pot from the oven and transfer the vegetable and herb pouch to a mesh strainer; set the strainer over the pot. Using the back of a spoon, press the liquid from the pouch into the pot; discard the pouch. With a slotted spoon, transfer the beef to a medium bowl; set aside. Let the pot contents settle for about 15 minutes, then skim off and discard the fat.

**7.** Bring the liquid in the pot to a boil over medium-high heat. Simmer, stirring occasionally, until thickened and reduced to about 3 cups, 15 to 25 minutes.

**8. FOR THE ONION AND MUSHROOM GARNISH:** Meanwhile, bring the pearl onions, ½ cup of the water, the butter, sugar, and ¼ teaspoon of the salt to a boil in a 10-inch skillet over high heat. Cover, reduce the heat to medium-low, and simmer, shaking the pan occasionally, until the onions are tender, about 5 minutes. Uncover, increase the heat to high, and simmer until all the liquid evaporates, about 3 minutes. Add the mushrooms and the remaining ¼ teaspoon salt. Cook, stirring occasionally, until the liquid released by the mushrooms evaporates and the vegetables are browned, about 5 minutes. Transfer the vegetables to a bowl and set aside. Add the remaining ¼ cup water to the skillet and scrape the pan with a wooden spoon to loosen the browned bits; add the liquid to the pot with the reducing sauce.

**9.** When the sauce has reduced, reduce the heat to medium-low and stir in the beef, the remaining 2 tablespoons wine, the brandy, and the mushrooms and onions (and any accumulated juices). Cover the pot and cook until heated through, 5 to 8 minutes. Season with salt and pepper to taste and serve, sprinkling individual servings with the parsley.

## Slow-Cooker Beef Burgundy

**SERVES** 6 to 8

---

**WHY THIS RECIPE WORKS** Given the amount of simmering time required for classic Beef Burgundy (page 89), we thought this stew could be easily morphed into a slow-cooker version that would have the same tender beef chunks and rich, earthy sauce as the original. For a long braise, chuck roast cut into pieces is the best choice. The usual first step in making a stew is to brown the meat, but we found that we could get the same meaty flavor base from browning only half the beef. We used rendered bacon fat instead of oil; the bacon would go back into the stew at the end, lending a smoky note. Sautéed carrots and onions went into the slow-cooker insert next, with plenty of garlic, thyme, and tomato paste. As our braising liquid, beef broth tasted tinny but chicken broth worked well. We mixed it with red wine and a surprising ingredient, soy sauce, which intensified the savory flavors in the stew as well as deepened its color. To enrich the sauce, we stirred in a small amount of tapioca, a common thickening agent, in place of flour. We prepared the traditional onion and mushroom garnish separately, when the stew was almost finished cooking, and folded it in. The final touch was more red wine, which we reduced first so that it wouldn't impart a sour alcoholic taste. This slow-cooker beef burgundy had everything we would expect from the refined French original. Make sure to use the low setting on your slow cooker; the stew will burn on the high setting. Don't spend a lot of money for the wine in this recipe—in our testing, we found that California Pinot Noir wines in the $6 to $20 price range worked just fine. Boiled potatoes are the traditional accompaniment, but mashed potatoes or buttered noodles are nice as well.

**STEW**

- 8 ounces (about 8 slices) bacon, cut into ¼-inch pieces
- 1 (4-pound) boneless beef chuck-eye roast, trimmed and cut into 1½-inch chunks
- Table salt and ground black pepper
- 1 large onion, minced
- 2 carrots, peeled and minced
- 8 medium garlic cloves, minced or pressed through a garlic press (about 2 tablespoons plus 2 teaspoons)
- 2 teaspoons chopped fresh thyme leaves
- 4 tablespoons tomato paste
- 2½ cups Pinot Noir
- 1½ cups low-sodium chicken broth
- ⅓ cup soy sauce
- 3 bay leaves
- 3 tablespoons Minute tapioca
- 3 tablespoons minced fresh parsley leaves

**ONION AND MUSHROOM GARNISH**

- 8 ounces (about 2 cups) frozen pearl onions
- ½ cup water
- 5 tablespoons unsalted butter
- 1 tablespoon sugar
- 10 ounces white mushrooms, wiped clean and quartered
- Table salt

**1. FOR THE STEW:** Cook the bacon in a 12-inch skillet over medium-high heat until crisp. Using a slotted spoon, transfer the bacon to a paper towel–lined plate and refrigerate. Pour half of the bacon fat into a small bowl; set the skillet with the remaining bacon fat aside.

**2.** Pat the beef dry with paper towels and season with salt and pepper; place half of the beef in a slow-cooker insert. Heat the skillet with the remaining bacon fat over medium-high heat until smoking. Cook the remaining beef in a single layer until deep brown on all sides, about 8 minutes. Transfer the browned beef to the slow-cooker insert.

**3.** Add the reserved bacon fat to the now-empty skillet and heat over medium-high heat until shimmering. Add the onion, carrots, and ¼ teaspoon salt and cook until the vegetables begin to brown, about 5 minutes. Add the garlic and thyme and cook until fragrant, about 30 seconds. Add the tomato paste and stir until beginning to brown, about 45 seconds. Transfer the mixture to the slow-cooker insert.

**4.** Return the now-empty skillet to high heat and add 1½ cups of the wine, the chicken broth, and soy sauce. Simmer, scraping up any browned bits, for about 1 minute. Transfer the wine mixture to the slow-cooker insert.

**5.** Stir the bay leaves and tapioca into the slow-cooker insert. Set the slow cooker on low, cover, and cook until the meat is fork-tender, about 9 hours.

**6. FOR THE ONION AND MUSHROOM GARNISH:** Bring the pearl onions, water, butter, and sugar to a boil in a 12-inch skillet over high heat. Cover and simmer over medium-low heat until the onions are tender, about 5 minutes. Uncover, increase the heat to high, and cook until the liquid evaporates, about 3 minutes. Add the mushrooms and ¼ teaspoon salt and cook until the vegetables are browned and glazed, about 5 minutes.

**7.** When ready to serve, discard the bay leaves and stir in the onion and mushroom garnish and the reserved bacon. Bring the remaining 1 cup wine to a boil in a 12-inch skillet over high heat and simmer until reduced by half, about 5 minutes. Stir the reduced wine and parsley into the stew and season with salt and pepper to taste. Serve.

## Modern Beef Burgundy

**SERVES** 6 to 8

**WHY THIS RECIPE WORKS** This modern take on boeuf bourguinon hews closely to what makes that stew so appealing, namely beef braised in an ultrarich sauce with a savory garnish of mushrooms and pearl onions. To eliminate the time-consuming step of searing the beef, we cooked the stew uncovered in a roasting pan in the oven so that the exposed meat browned as it braised. This method worked so well that we also used the oven, rather than the stovetop, to render the salt pork and to caramelize the traditional mushroom and pearl onion garnish. Salting the beef before cooking and adding some anchovy paste and porcini mushrooms enhanced the meaty savoriness of the dish. If the pearl onions have a papery outer coating, remove it by rinsing them in warm water and gently squeezing individual onions between your fingertips. Two minced anchovy fillets can be used in place of the anchovy paste. Serve with mashed potatoes or buttered noodles.

- 1 (4-pound) boneless beef chuck-eye roast, trimmed and cut into 1½- to 2-inch pieces, scraps reserved
- Table salt and pepper
- 6 ounces salt pork, cut into ¼-inch pieces
- 3 tablespoons unsalted butter
- 1 pound cremini mushrooms, trimmed, halved if medium or quartered if large
- 1½ cups frozen pearl onions, thawed
- 1 tablespoon sugar
- ⅓ cup all-purpose flour
- 4 cups beef broth
- 1 (750-ml) bottle red Burgundy or Pinot Noir
- 5 teaspoons unflavored gelatin
- 1 tablespoon tomato paste
- 1 teaspoon anchovy paste
- 2 onions, chopped coarse
- 2 carrots, peeled and cut into 2-inch lengths
- 1 garlic head, cloves separated, unpeeled, and crushed
- 2 bay leaves
- ½ teaspoon black peppercorns
- ½ ounce dried porcini mushrooms, rinsed
- 10 sprigs fresh parsley, plus 3 tablespoons minced
- 6 sprigs fresh thyme

**1.** Toss beef and 1½ teaspoons salt together in bowl and let stand at room temperature for 30 minutes.

**2.** Adjust oven racks to lower-middle and lowest positions and heat oven to 500 degrees. Place salt pork, beef scraps, and 2 tablespoons butter in large roasting pan. Roast on lower-middle rack until well browned and fat has rendered, 15 to 20 minutes.

**3.** While salt pork and beef scraps roast, toss cremini mushrooms, pearl onions, remaining 1 tablespoon butter, and sugar together on rimmed baking sheet. Roast on lowest rack, stirring occasionally, until moisture released by mushrooms evaporates and vegetables are lightly glazed, 15 to 20 minutes. Transfer vegetables to large bowl, cover, and refrigerate.

**4.** Remove roasting pan from oven and reduce temperature to 325 degrees. Sprinkle flour over rendered fat and whisk until no dry flour remains. Whisk in broth, 2 cups wine, gelatin, tomato paste, and anchovy paste until combined. Add onions, carrots, garlic, bay leaves, peppercorns, porcini mushrooms, parsley sprigs, and thyme sprigs to pan. Arrange beef in single layer on top of vegetables. Add water as needed to come three-quarters up side of beef (beef should not be submerged). Return roasting pan to oven and cook until meat is tender, 3 to 3½ hours, stirring after 90 minutes and adding water to keep meat at least half-submerged.

**5.** Using slotted spoon, transfer beef to bowl with cremini mushrooms and pearl onions; cover and set aside. Strain braising liquid through fine-mesh strainer set over large bowl, pressing on solids to extract as much liquid as possible; discard solids. Stir in remaining wine and let cooking liquid settle, 10 minutes. Using wide shallow spoon, skim fat off surface and discard.

**6.** Transfer liquid to Dutch oven and bring mixture to boil over medium-high heat. Simmer briskly, stirring occasionally, until sauce is thickened to consistency of heavy cream, 15 to 20 minutes. Reduce heat to medium-low, stir in beef and mushroom-onion garnish, cover, and cook until just heated through, 5 to 8 minutes. Season with salt and pepper to taste. Stir in minced parsley and serve. (Stew can be made up to 3 days in advance.)

## Nikujaga (Beef and Potato Stew)

SERVES 4

**WHY THIS RECIPE WORKS** Nikujaga (Japanese for "meat and potatoes") is a simple but flavorful beef stew with thin slices of meat and a generous portion of potatoes in a thin, sweet-savory dashi or broth. To start, we made the dashi by infusing water with kombu (kelp) and katsuobushi (bonito flakes). Next, we browned thinly sliced well-marbled beef short rib to achieve rich, meaty flavor. Rather than add the onion to the broth raw, we caramelized it in the beef fat to enhance its flavor. Mirin and sugar added to the dish's signature sweetness and balanced the heartiness of the beef and the brightness of the sake. Simmering the meat, broth, and potatoes for just 30 minutes allowed the potatoes and meat to tenderize without overcooking. The potatoes released their natural starches into the stew, thickening it slightly. Look for lean ribs cut from the chuck. If you need to buy bone-in English-style ribs, slice off the bones, cartilage, and excess fat. If your short ribs are a single slab, cut them into 2- to 3-inch-wide strips.

- 4 cups water
- 1 (4-inch) square piece kombu
- 1 cup katsuobushi (bonito flakes)
- 1 pound boneless beef short ribs, trimmed
- 1 tablespoon vegetable oil
- 1 onion, halved and sliced thin
- ¼ cup sake or dry vermouth
- 1½ pounds Yukon Gold potatoes, unpeeled, cut into 1½-inch pieces
- ⅓ cup soy sauce
- ¼ cup mirin
- 2 tablespoons sugar
- 2 scallions, sliced thin on bias

**1.** Bring water and kombu to simmer in large saucepan over medium heat. Once water reaches simmer, discard kombu and remove saucepan from heat. Stir in katsuobushi and let sit for 5 minutes. Strain dashi through fine-mesh strainer into large bowl; discard solids. Set aside.

**2.** Cut each short rib with grain into 2- to 2½-inch-wide strips and place on large plate; freeze until firm, about 15 minutes. Slice each piece against grain ¼ inch thick. Heat oil in Dutch oven over medium-high heat until just smoking. Brown meat on all sides, 5 to 10 minutes; transfer to bowl.

**3.** Pour off all but 2 tablespoons fat from pot. Add onion to fat left in pot and cook until softened and well browned, 7 to 10 minutes. Stir in sake, scraping up any browned bits. Stir in reserved dashi, potatoes, soy sauce, mirin, sugar, and beef and any accumulated juices and bring to simmer. Reduce heat to medium-low; partially cover; and cook until potatoes are tender, 25 to 30 minutes. Sprinkle individual portions with scallions before serving.

## Alcatra (Portuguese-Style Beef Stew)

SERVES 6

**WHY THIS RECIPE WORKS** Alcatra, a simple and meaty Portuguese beef stew, features tender chunks of beef braised in wine with onions, garlic, and spices. Unlike beef stews that require searing the beef to build savory flavor or adding flavor boosters like tomato paste and anchovies, this recipe skips those steps and ingredients, highlighting the warm and bright flavors of the spices and wine as much as the meatiness of the beef. We used beef shank because it is lean (which means the cooking liquid doesn't need to be skimmed) and full of collagen, which broke down into gelatin and gave the sauce full body. Submerging the sliced onions completely in the liquid under the meat caused them to form a meaty-tasting compound that amped up the savory flavor of the broth. Slices of smoky-sweet Spanish chorizo sausage matched up perfectly with the other flavors in the stew. Beef shank is sold both crosscut and long-cut (with and without bones). We prefer long-cut since it has more collagen. You can substitute 4 pounds of bone-in crosscut shank if that's all you can find. Remove the bones before cooking and save them for another use. Crosscut shank cooks more quickly, so check the stew for doneness in step 2 after 3 hours. A 3½- to 4-pound chuck roast, trimmed of fat and cut into 2½-inch pieces, can be substituted for the shank. Serve this dish with crusty bread or boiled potatoes.

- 3 pounds boneless long-cut beef shanks
- 1 teaspoon table salt
- 5 garlic cloves, peeled and smashed
- 5 allspice berries
- 4 bay leaves
- 1½ teaspoons peppercorns
- 2 large onions, halved and sliced thin
- 2¼ cups dry white wine
- ¼ teaspoon ground cinnamon
- 8 ounces Spanish-style chorizo sausage, cut into ¼-inch-thick rounds

**1.** Adjust oven rack to middle position and heat oven to 325 degrees. Trim away any fat or large pieces of connective tissue from exterior of shanks (silverskin can be left on meat). Cut each shank crosswise into 2½-inch pieces. Sprinkle meat with salt.

**2.** Cut 8-inch square of triple-thickness cheesecloth. Place garlic, allspice berries, bay leaves, and peppercorns in center of cheesecloth and tie into bundle with kitchen twine. Arrange onions and spice bundle in Dutch oven in even layer. Add wine and cinnamon. Arrange shank pieces in single layer on top of onions. Cover and cook until beef is tender, about 3½ hours.

**3.** Remove pot from oven and add chorizo. Using tongs, flip each piece of beef over, making sure that chorizo is submerged. Cover and let stand until chorizo is warmed through, about 20 minutes. Discard spice bundle. Season with salt and pepper to taste. Serve.

## Catalan-Style Beef Stew with Mushrooms

**SERVES** 4 to 6

**WHY THIS RECIPE WORKS** Supremely meaty and complexly flavored, Spanish beef stew is a little different than its American counterpart. It starts with a sofrito, a slow-cooked jam-like mixture of onions, spices, and herbs that builds a flavor-packed base. We normally use chuck-eye for stew but swapped it out for boneless beef short ribs, determining that they gave us a beefier-tasting stew. We finished the stew with a mixture of toasted bread, toasted almonds, garlic, and parsley. This mixture, called a picada, brightened the stew's flavor and thickened the broth. While we developed this recipe with Albariño, a dry Spanish white wine, you can also use a Sauvignon Blanc. Remove the woody base of the oyster mushroom stems before cooking. An equal amount of quartered button mushrooms may be substituted for the oyster mushrooms. Serve the stew with boiled or mashed potatoes or rice.

**STEW**

- 2 tablespoons olive oil
- 2 large onions, chopped fine
- ½ teaspoon sugar
- Kosher salt and pepper
- 2 plum tomatoes, halved lengthwise, pulp grated on large holes of box grater, and skins discarded
- 1 teaspoon smoked paprika
- 1 bay leaf
- 1½ cups dry white wine
- 1½ cups water
- 1 large sprig fresh thyme
- ¼ teaspoon ground cinnamon
- 2½ pounds boneless beef short ribs, trimmed and cut into 2-inch cubes

**PICADA**

- ¼ cup whole blanched almonds
- 2 tablespoons olive oil
- 1 slice hearty white sandwich bread, crusts removed, torn into 1-inch pieces
- 2 garlic cloves, peeled
- 3 tablespoons minced fresh parsley

- 8 ounces oyster mushrooms, trimmed
- 1 teaspoon sherry vinegar

**1. FOR THE STEW:** Adjust oven rack to middle position and heat oven to 300 degrees. Heat oil in Dutch oven over medium-low heat until shimmering. Add onions, sugar, and ½ teaspoon salt; cook, stirring often, until onions are deeply caramelized, 30 to 40 minutes. Add tomatoes, smoked paprika, and bay leaf; cook, stirring often, until darkened and thick, 5 to 10 minutes.

**2.** Add wine, water, thyme sprig, and cinnamon to pot, scraping up any browned bits. Season beef with 1½ teaspoons salt and ½ teaspoon pepper and add to pot. Increase heat to high and bring to simmer. Transfer to oven and cook, uncovered. After 1 hour stir stew to redistribute meat, return to oven, and continue to cook, uncovered, until meat is tender, 1½ to 2 hours longer.

**3. FOR THE PICADA:** While stew is in oven, heat almonds and 1 tablespoon oil in 10-inch skillet over medium heat; cook, stirring often, until almonds are golden brown, 3 to 6 minutes. Using slotted spoon, transfer almonds to food processor. Return now-empty skillet to medium heat, add bread, and cook, stirring often, until toasted, 2 to 4 minutes; transfer to food processor with almonds. Add garlic and process until mixture is finely ground, about 20 seconds, scraping down bowl as needed. Transfer mixture to bowl, stir in parsley, and set aside.

**4.** Return again-empty skillet to medium heat. Heat remaining 1 tablespoon oil until shimmering. Add mushrooms and ½ teaspoon salt; cook, stirring often, until tender, 5 to 7 minutes. Transfer to bowl and set aside.

**5.** Remove bay leaf and thyme sprig. Stir picada, mushrooms, and vinegar into stew. Season with salt and pepper to taste and serve.

## Carbonnade à la Flamande

**SERVES** 6

**WHY THIS RECIPE WORKS** In Belgian carbonnade, the heartiness of beef melds with the sweetness of sliced onions in a broth that is rich, and satisfying, with the malty flavor of beer. Top blade steak, which has a fair amount of marbling, provided the best texture and a "buttery" flavor that worked well alongside the onions and beer. Because overcaramelization caused the onions to disintegrate, we made sure just to brown them lightly. Fresh thyme and bay leaves provided seasoning, and a splash of cider vinegar added the right level of acidity. The light lagers we tried resulted in pale, watery stews; better were dark ales and stouts. But beer alone often made for bitter-tasting stew, so we included some broth; a combination of chicken and beef broth gave us more solid and complex

flavor. Top blade steaks (also called blade or flat-iron steaks) are our first choice, but any boneless roast from the chuck will work. Buttered egg noodles or mashed potatoes make excellent accompaniments to carbonnade.

- 3½ pounds top blade steaks, 1 inch thick, trimmed of gristle and fat and cut into 1-inch pieces
- 1¼ teaspoons table salt, divided
- ¾ teaspoon pepper
- 3 tablespoons vegetable oil, divided
- 2 pounds yellow onions, halved and sliced ¼ inch thick
- 1 tablespoon tomato paste
- 2 garlic cloves, minced
- 3 tablespoons unbleached all-purpose flour
- ¾ cup chicken broth
- ¾ cup beef broth
- 1½ cups (12-ounce bottle or can) dark beer or stout
- 4 sprigs fresh thyme, tied with kitchen twine
- 2 bay leaves
- 1 tablespoon cider vinegar

**1.** Adjust oven rack to the lower-middle position and heat oven to 300 degrees. Dry beef thoroughly with paper towels, then sprinkle with ¾ teaspoon salt and pepper. Heat 2 teaspoons oil in Dutch oven over medium-high heat until beginning to smoke; add one-third of beef to pot. Cook without moving until well browned, 2 to 3 minutes; using tongs, turn each piece and continue cooking until second side is well browned, about 5 minutes longer. Transfer browned beef to medium bowl. Repeat with 2 teaspoons oil and half of remaining beef. (If drippings in bottom of pot are very dark, add ½ cup chicken or beef broth and scrape pan bottom with wooden spoon to loosen browned bits; pour liquid into bowl with browned beef, then proceed.) Repeat once more with 2 teaspoons oil and remaining beef.

**2.** Add remaining 1 tablespoon oil to now-empty Dutch oven; reduce heat to medium-low. Add onions, tomato paste, and remaining ½ teaspoon salt; cook, scraping the bottom of pot with wooden spoon to loosen browned bits, until onions have released some moisture, about 5 minutes. Increase heat to medium and continue to cook, stirring occasionally, until onions are lightly browned, 12 to 14 minutes. Stir in garlic and cook until fragrant, about 30 seconds. Add flour and stir until onions are evenly coated and flour is lightly browned, about 2 minutes. Stir in broths, scraping pan bottom to loosen any browned bits; stir in beer, thyme, bay leaves, vinegar, browned beef with any accumulated juices, and salt and pepper to taste. Increase heat to medium-high and bring to full simmer, stirring occasionally; cover partially, then place pot in oven. Cook until fork inserted into beef meets little resistance, 2 to 2½ hours.

**3.** Discard thyme and bay leaves. Season with salt and pepper to taste, and serve. (Stew can be cooled and refrigerated in airtight container for up to 4 days; reheat over medium-low heat.)

### TRIMMING BLADE STEAKS

To trim blade steaks, halve each steak lengthwise, leaving gristle on 1 half. Then simply cut gristle away.

## Hungarian Beef Stew

**SERVES 6**

**WHY THIS RECIPE WORKS** Some versions of Hungarian goulash served in the United States bear little resemblance to the traditional dish. We wanted the real deal—a simple dish of tender braised beef packed with paprika flavor. To achieve the desired spicy intensity, some recipes call for as much as half a cup of paprika per three pounds of meat, but that much fine spice gave the dish a gritty, dusty texture. The chefs at a few Hungarian restaurants introduced us to paprika cream, a condiment as common in Hungarian cooking as the dried spice. We created our own quick version by pureeing dried paprika with roasted red peppers and a little tomato paste and vinegar. This mixture imparted vibrant paprika flavor without any grittiness. As for the meat, after settling on chuck-eye roast, we bought a whole roast and cut it into uniform, large pieces to ensure even cooking. Since searing the meat first—normally standard stew protocol—competed with the paprika's brightness, we referred back to a trend we noticed in the goulash recipes we researched: skipping the sear. We tried this, softening the onions in the pot first, adding paprika paste, carrots, and then meat before placing the covered pot in the oven. Sure enough, the onions and meat provided enough liquid to stew the meat, and the bits of beef that cooked above the liquid line browned in the hot air. Do not substitute hot, half-sharp, or smoked Spanish paprika for the sweet paprika in the stew. Since paprika is vital to this recipe, it is best to use a fresh container. We prefer chuck-eye roast, but any boneless roast from the chuck will work. Serve the stew over boiled potatoes or egg noodles.

- 1 boneless chuck-eye roast (about 3½ pounds), trimmed of excess fat and cut into 1½-inch cubes
- Table salt
- 1 (12-ounce) jar roasted red peppers, drained and rinsed (about 1 cup)
- ⅓ cup sweet paprika
- 2 tablespoons tomato paste
- 1 tablespoon white vinegar
- 2 tablespoons vegetable oil
- 6 medium onions, minced (about 6 cups)
- 4 large carrots, peeled and cut into 1-inch-thick rounds (about 2 cups)
- 1 bay leaf
- 1 cup beef broth, warmed
- ¼ cup sour cream (optional)
- Ground black pepper

**1.** Adjust an oven rack to the lower-middle position and heat the oven to 325 degrees. Sprinkle the meat evenly with 1 teaspoon salt and let stand for 15 minutes. Process the roasted peppers, paprika, tomato paste, and 2 teaspoons of the vinegar in a food processor until smooth, 1 to 2 minutes, scraping down the sides as needed.

**2.** Combine the oil, onions, and 1 teaspoon salt in a large Dutch oven; cover and set over medium heat. Cook, stirring occasionally, until the onions have softened but have not yet begun to brown, 8 to 10 minutes. (If the onions begin to brown, reduce the heat to medium-low and stir in 1 tablespoon water.)

**3.** Stir in the paprika mixture; cook, stirring occasionally, until the onions stick to the bottom of the pan, about 2 minutes. Add the beef, carrots, and bay leaf; stir until the beef is well coated. Using a rubber spatula, scrape down the sides of the pot. Cover the pot and transfer to the oven. Cook until the meat is almost tender and the surface of the liquid is ½ inch below the top of the meat, 2 to 2½ hours, stirring every 30 minutes. Remove the pot from the oven and add enough beef broth that the surface of the liquid is ¼ inch from the top of the meat (the beef should not be fully submerged). Return the covered pot to the oven and continue to cook until a fork slips easily in and out of the beef, about 30 minutes longer.

**4.** Skim the fat off the surface using a wide spoon; stir in the remaining 1 teaspoon vinegar and the sour cream (if using). Remove the bay leaf, season with salt and pepper to taste, and serve. (The stew can be cooled, covered tightly, and refrigerated in an airtight container for up to 2 days; wait to add the optional sour cream until after reheating. Before reheating, skim the hardened fat from the surface and add enough water to the stew to thin it slightly.)

## Multicooker Hawaiian Oxtail Soup

**SERVES** 4 to 6

**WHY THIS RECIPE WORKS** In Hawaii, Chinese-influenced oxtail soup is a local favorite dating from the mid-to late 19th century, when scores of Chinese immigrants arrived on Hawaii's shores as laborers. Star anise, the aged Mandarin orange peel known as chen pi, and ginger perfume the broth. Collagen-rich oxtail typically takes 3 to 4 hours of simmering to turn tender, but we dramatically cut down on the cooking time by using the multicooker with an hour under pressure and a 30-minute natural pressure release. We added the aromatics and other classic ingredients—peanuts, dried jujubes, and dried shiitakes—at the same time as the oxtails. We strained the broth, reheated it on the highest sauté function, and then wilted the gai choy in the stock off the heat. Look for oxtails that are approximately 2 inches thick; thaw them if they're frozen. If necessary, you can substitute dry-roasted peanuts for the raw peanuts, four Medjool dates for the jujubes, 1½ tablespoons of dried orange peel or three strips of fresh orange zest for the chen pi, and 1 pound of stemmed American mustard greens for the gai choy. For a complete Hawaiian-style meal, serve with white rice.

- 8 ounces fresh ginger, sliced thin, plus 4 tablespoons peeled and grated for serving
- 5 star anise pods
- ¼ ounce chen pi
- 3 pounds oxtails, fat trimmed to ¼ inch or less
- 8 cups water
- ½ cup raw peanuts
- 8 dried jujubes
- 1 ounce dried whole shiitake mushrooms, stemmed and rinsed
- ¼ cup soy sauce, plus extra for serving
- ½ teaspoon table salt
- 1 pound gai choy, trimmed and cut into 2-inch pieces
- 1 cup fresh cilantro leaves
- 4 scallions, sliced thin on bias

**1.** Bundle sliced ginger, star anise, and chen pi in single layer of cheesecloth and secure with kitchen twine. Add cheesecloth bundle, oxtails, water, peanuts, jujubes, mushrooms, soy sauce, and salt to multicooker.

**2.** Lock lid into place and close pressure-release valve. Select high pressure-cook function and cook for 1 hour. Turn off multicooker and let pressure release naturally for 30 minutes. Quick-release any remaining pressure, then carefully remove lid, allowing steam to escape away from you.

**3.** Discard cheesecloth bundle. Using slotted spoon, transfer oxtails, peanuts, and mushrooms to large bowl; tent with aluminum foil; and let rest while finishing soup. Strain broth through fine-mesh strainer into large bowl or container, pressing on solids to extract as much liquid as possible; discard solids. Let broth settle for 5 minutes. Using wide, shallow spoon or ladle, skim excess fat from surface. (Broth can be refrigerated overnight before defatting to allow for easier skimming. Reheat oxtails, peanuts, and mushrooms in simmering broth before adding gai choy in step 4.)

**4.** Return defatted broth to now-empty pot. Using highest sauté function, bring broth to simmer, then turn off multicooker. Stir in gai choy and cook, using residual heat, until wilted, about 3 minutes. Season with extra soy sauce to taste.

**5.** Slice mushrooms thin, if desired. Divide oxtails, peanuts, and mushrooms among bowls, then ladle hot broth and gai choy over oxtails. Sprinkle each bowl with cilantro and scallions. Serve, passing grated ginger and extra soy sauce separately.

## Our Favorite Chili

**SERVES** 6 to 8

**WHY THIS RECIPE WORKS** Our goal in creating an "ultimate" beef chili was to determine which of the "secret ingredients" recommended by chili experts around the world were spot-on—and which were expendable. We started with the beef. Most recipes call for ground beef, but we preferred meaty blade steaks, which don't require much trimming and stayed in big chunks in our finished chili. For complex chile flavor, we traded in the commercial chili powder in favor of ground dried ancho and arbol chiles; for a grassy heat, we added fresh jalapeños. Dried beans, brined before cooking, stayed creamy for the duration of cooking. Beer and chicken broth outperformed red wine, coffee, and beef broth as the liquid components. For balancing sweetness, light molasses beat out other offbeat ingredients (including prunes and Coca-Cola). And finally, for the right level of thickness, flour and peanut butter didn't perform as promised; instead, a small amount of ordinary cornmeal sealed the deal, providing just the right consistency in our ultimate beef chili. A 4-pound chuck-eye roast, well trimmed of fat, can be substituted for the steak. Because much of the chili flavor is held in the fat of this dish, refrain from skimming fat from the surface. Dried New Mexican or guajillo chiles make a good substitute for the anchos; each dried arbol may be replaced with 1/8 teaspoon cayenne pepper. If you prefer not to work with any whole dried chiles, the anchos and arbols can be replaced with 1/2 cup commercial chili powder and 1/4 to 1/2 teaspoon cayenne pepper, though the texture of the chili will be slightly compromised. Good choices for condiments include diced avocado, finely chopped red onion, chopped cilantro leaves, lime wedges, sour cream, and shredded Monterey Jack or cheddar cheese.

- Table salt
- 8 ounces dried pinto beans (1¼ cups), picked over and rinsed
- 6 dried ancho chiles, stemmed, seeded, and torn into 1-inch pieces
- 2–4 dried arbol chiles, stemmed, seeded, and split into 2 pieces
- 3 tablespoons cornmeal
- 2 teaspoons dried oregano
- 2 teaspoons ground cumin
- 2 teaspoons cocoa powder
- 2½ cups low-sodium chicken broth
- 2 medium onions, cut into ¾-inch pieces
- 3 small jalapeño chiles, stemmed, seeded, and cut into ½-inch pieces
- 3 tablespoons vegetable oil
- 4 medium garlic cloves, minced or pressed through a garlic press (about 4 teaspoons)
- 1 (14.5-ounce) can diced tomatoes
- 2 teaspoons light molasses
- 3½ pounds blade steak, ¾ inch thick, trimmed and cut into ¾-inch pieces (see page 94)
- 1 (12-ounce) bottle mild lager, such as Budweiser

**1.** Combine 3 tablespoons salt, 4 quarts water, and the beans in a Dutch oven and bring to a boil over high heat. Remove the pot from the heat, cover, and let sit for 1 hour. Drain and rinse well.

**2.** Adjust an oven rack to the lower-middle position and heat the oven to 300 degrees. Place the ancho chiles in a 12-inch skillet set over medium-high heat; toast, stirring frequently, until the flesh is fragrant, 4 to 6 minutes, reducing the heat if the chiles begin to smoke. Transfer to a food processor and cool. Do not wash out the skillet.

**3.** Add the arbol chiles, cornmeal, oregano, cumin, cocoa, and ½ teaspoon salt to the food processor with the toasted ancho chiles; process until finely ground, about 2 minutes. With the processor running, slowly add ½ cup chicken broth until a smooth paste forms, about 45 seconds, scraping down the sides of the bowl as necessary. Transfer the paste to a small bowl. Place the onions in the now-empty processor and pulse until roughly chopped, about 4 pulses. Add the jalapeños and pulse until the consistency of chunky salsa, about 4 pulses, scraping down the bowl as necessary.

**4.** Heat 1 tablespoon oil in the Dutch oven over medium-high heat. Add the onion mixture and cook, stirring occasionally, until the moisture has evaporated and the vegetables are softened, 7 to 9 minutes. Add the garlic and cook until fragrant, about 1 minute. Add the chile paste, tomatoes, and molasses; stir until the chile paste is thoroughly combined. Add the remaining 2 cups chicken broth and the drained beans; bring to a boil, then reduce the heat to a simmer.

**5.** Meanwhile, heat 1 tablespoon more oil in the 12-inch skillet over medium-high heat until shimmering. Pat the beef dry with paper towels and sprinkle with 1 teaspoon salt. Add half of the beef and cook until browned on all sides, about 10 minutes. Transfer the meat to the Dutch oven. Add half of the beer to the skillet, scraping up any browned bits from the bottom of the skillet, and bring to a simmer. Transfer the beer to the Dutch oven. Repeat with the remaining 1 tablespoon oil, the remaining steak, and the remaining beer. Stir to combine and return the mixture to a simmer.

**6.** Cover the pot and transfer to the oven. Cook until the meat and beans are fully tender, 1½ to 2 hours. Let the chili stand, uncovered, for 10 minutes. Stir well, season with salt to taste, and serve. (The chili can be refrigerated for up to 3 days.)

## Chili con Carne

SERVES 6

**WHY THIS RECIPE WORKS** Real Texas chili, made with dried chiles rather than chili powder, should have exceptional chile flavor but not overpowering heat; a smooth, rich sauce; and hearty chunks of meat. We wanted to develop the ultimate version. There are many types of dried chiles, and we chose a combination of ancho and New Mexican for a balance of earthy, fruity sweetness and crisp acidity. We got the best flavor by toasting and grinding chiles ourselves. Chuck-eye is our favored cut of beef for stews, and it seemed right for our chili. We browned the meat in fat rendered from bacon, which added a smoky depth to the dish. Although many traditional recipes include neither tomatoes nor onions, we found both to be valuable additions. Masa harina helped thicken the chili while adding a subtle corn flavor. We recommend toasting whole dried chiles and grinding them in a minichopper or spice-dedicated coffee grinder. Dried chiles should be moist and pliant. To toast and grind dried chiles: Place the chiles on a baking sheet in a 350-degree oven until fragrant and puffed, about 6 minutes. Cool, stem, and seed the pods and tear them into pieces. Place the in a spice grinder and process until powdery, 30 to 45 seconds. For hotter chili, add a pinch of cayenne pepper or a dash of hot sauce. Serve with your favorite chili garnishes.

- 3 medium ancho pods (about ½ ounce), toasted and ground, or 3 tablespoons ancho chile powder
- 3 medium New Mexican pods (about ¾ ounce), toasted and ground, or 3 tablespoons New Mexican chile powder
- 2 tablespoons cumin seeds, toasted in a dry skillet over medium heat until fragrant, about 4 minutes, and ground
- 2 teaspoons dried oregano, preferably Mexican
- 7½ cups water, plus extra for the masa harina or cornstarch
- 4 pounds beef chuck-eye roast, trimmed of excess fat and cut into 1-inch cubes
- Table salt
- 8 ounces bacon (about 8 slices), cut into ¼-inch pieces
- 1 medium onion, minced
- 5 medium garlic cloves, minced or pressed through a garlic press (about 5 teaspoons)
- 4–5 small jalapeño chiles, stemmed, seeded, and minced
- 1 cup canned crushed tomatoes or plain tomato sauce
- 2 tablespoons juice from 1 lime
- 5 tablespoons masa harina or 3 tablespoons cornstarch
- Ground black pepper

**1.** Mix the chili powders, cumin, and oregano in a small bowl and stir in ½ cup of the water to form a thick paste; set aside. Toss the beef cubes with 2 teaspoons salt in a large bowl; set aside.

**2.** Fry the bacon in a large Dutch oven over medium-low heat until the fat renders and the bacon crisps, about 10 minutes. Remove the bacon with a slotted spoon to a paper towel–lined plate; pour all but 2 teaspoons fat from the pot into a small

bowl; set aside. Increase the heat to medium-high; sauté the meat in four batches until well browned on all sides, about 5 minutes per batch, adding 2 teaspoons more bacon fat to the pot each time as necessary. Set the browned meat aside in a large bowl.

**3.** Reduce the heat to medium and add 3 tablespoons more bacon fat to the now-empty pan. Add the onion and sauté until softened, 5 to 6 minutes. Add the garlic and jalapeños and sauté until fragrant, about 1 minute. Add the chili powder mixture and sauté until fragrant, 2 to 3 minutes. Add the reserved bacon and browned beef, the remaining 7 cups water, the crushed tomatoes, and lime juice. Bring to a simmer. Continue to cook at a steady simmer (lowering the heat as necessary) until the meat is tender and the juices are dark and rich and starting to thicken, about 2 hours.

**4.** Mix the masa harina with ⅔ cup water (or cornstarch with 3 tablespoons water) in a small bowl to form a smooth paste. Increase the heat to medium, stir in the paste, and simmer until thickened, 5 to 10 minutes. Season generously with salt and pepper to taste. Serve immediately or, for best flavor, cool slightly, cover, and refrigerate overnight or for up to 5 days. Reheat before serving.

## Best Ground Beef Chili

SERVES 8 to 10

**WHY THIS RECIPE WORKS** Our ground beef chili can hold its own against the traditional chunky beef kind. We used 85 percent lean ground beef for flavor and tenderness. To protect the meat from dryness, we treated it with salt and baking soda. Both ingredients helped the meat hold on to moisture so that the whole 2 pounds of beef could be browned in one batch. Simmering the meat for 90 minutes gave its collagen enough time to break down. We made a homemade chili powder for potent spicy flavor, and we used tortilla chips to add both bulk and corn flavor. Shortly before serving, we stirred any flavorful orange fat collected on the top back into the chili. Diced avocado, sour cream, and shredded Monterey Jack or cheddar cheese are also good options for garnishing. This chili is intensely flavored and should be served with tortilla chips and/or plenty of steamed white rice.

- 2 pounds 85 percent lean ground beef
- 2 tablespoons plus 2 cups water, divided
- 1½ teaspoons table salt
- ¾ teaspoon baking soda
- 6 dried ancho chiles, stemmed, seeded, and torn into 1-inch pieces
- 1 ounce tortilla chips, crushed (¼ cup)
- 2 tablespoons ground cumin
- 1 tablespoon paprika
- 1 tablespoon garlic powder
- 1 tablespoon ground coriander
- 2 teaspoons dried oregano
- 2 teaspoons pepper
- ½ teaspoon dried thyme
- 1 (14.5-ounce) can whole peeled tomatoes
- 1 tablespoon vegetable oil
- 1 onion, chopped fine
- 3 garlic cloves, minced
- 1–2 teaspoons minced canned chipotle chile in adobo sauce
- 1 (15-ounce) can pinto beans, undrained
- 2 teaspoons sugar
- 2 tablespoons cider vinegar
- Lime wedges
- Coarsely chopped cilantro
- Chopped red onion

**1.** Adjust oven rack to lower-middle position and heat oven to 275 degrees. Toss beef with 2 tablespoons water, salt, and baking soda in bowl until thoroughly combined. Set aside for 20 minutes.

**2.** Meanwhile, place anchos in Dutch oven set over medium-high heat; toast, stirring frequently, until fragrant, 4 to 6 minutes, reducing heat if anchos begin to smoke. Transfer to food processor and let cool.

**3.** Add tortilla chips, cumin, paprika, garlic powder, coriander, oregano, pepper, and thyme to food processor with anchos and process until finely ground, about 2 minutes. Transfer mixture to bowl. Process tomatoes and their juice in now-empty workbowl until smooth, about 30 seconds.

**4.** Heat oil in now-empty pot over medium-high heat until shimmering. Add onion and cook, stirring occasionally, until softened, 4 to 6 minutes. Add garlic and cook until fragrant, about 1 minute. Add beef and cook, stirring with wooden spoon to break meat up into ¼-inch pieces, until beef is browned and fond begins to form on pot bottom, 12 to 14 minutes. Add ancho mixture and chipotle; cook, stirring frequently, until fragrant, 1 to 2 minutes.

**5.** Add beans and their liquid, sugar, tomato puree, and remaining 2 cups water. Bring to boil, scraping bottom of pot to loosen any browned bits. Cover, transfer to oven, and cook until meat is tender and chili is slightly thickened, 1½ to 2 hours, stirring occasionally to prevent sticking.

**6.** Remove chili from oven and let stand, uncovered, for 10 minutes. Stir in any fat that has risen to top of chili, then add vinegar and season with salt to taste. Serve, passing lime wedges, cilantro, and chopped onion separately. (Chili can be refrigerated for up to 3 days.)

## Simple Beef Chili with Kidney Beans

**SERVES** 8 to 10

**WHY THIS RECIPE WORKS** Everyone should have a supersimple chili to make on a busy weeknight (or a lazy weekend). To start, we added the spices with the aromatics to get the most flavor, and used commercial chili powder with a boost from more cumin, oregano, cayenne, and coriander. For the meat, 85 percent lean ground beef gave us full flavor. A combination of diced tomatoes and tomato puree gave our chili a well-balanced saucy backbone. We added canned red kidney beans with the tomatoes so that they absorbed flavor. For a rich, thick consistency, we cooked the chili with the lid on for half of the cooking time. Good choices for condiments include diced fresh tomatoes, diced avocado, sliced scallions, chopped red onion, chopped cilantro leaves, sour cream, and shredded Monterey Jack or cheddar cheese. If you are a fan of spicy food, consider using a little more of the red pepper flakes or cayenne—or both. The flavor of the chili improves with age; if possible, make it a day or up to three days in advance and reheat before serving. Leftovers can be frozen for up to one month.

- 2 tablespoons vegetable oil
- 2 onions, chopped fine
- 1 red bell pepper, stemmed, seeded, and chopped
- 6 garlic cloves, minced
- ¼ cup chili powder
- 1 tablespoon ground cumin
- 2 teaspoons ground coriander
- 1 teaspoon red pepper flakes
- 1 teaspoon dried oregano
- ½ teaspoon cayenne pepper
- 2 pounds 85 percent lean ground beef
- 2 (15-ounce) cans dark red kidney beans, rinsed
- 1 (28-ounce) can diced tomatoes
- 1 (28-ounce) can tomato puree
- ½ teaspoon table salt
- Lime wedges

**1.** Heat oil in Dutch oven over medium heat until shimmering but not smoking. Add onions, bell pepper, garlic, chili powder, cumin, coriander, red pepper flakes, oregano, and cayenne and cook, stirring occasionally, until the vegetables are softened and beginning to brown, about 10 minutes. Increase heat to medium-high and add half of beef. Cook, breaking up pieces with wooden spoon, until no longer pink and just beginning to brown, 3 to 4 minutes. Add remaining beef and cook, breaking up pieces with wooden spoon, until no longer pink, 3 to 4 minutes.

**2.** Add beans, tomatoes with juice, tomato puree, and ½ teaspoon salt. Bring to boil, then reduce heat to low and simmer, covered, stirring occasionally, for 1 hour. Remove lid and continue to simmer for 1 hour longer, stirring occasionally (if chili begins to stick to bottom of the pot, stir in ½ cup water and continue to simmer), until beef is tender and chili is dark, rich, and slightly thickened. Season with salt to taste. Serve with lime wedges.

## Hot and Sour Soup

**SERVES** 6 to 8

**WHY THIS RECIPE WORKS** True to its name, hot and sour soup features spicy, bracing, and pungent elements. We created the "hot" side of the soup with two heat sources—distinctive, penetrating white pepper and a little chili oil. For the "sour" component, we preferred the traditional Chinese black vinegar, but found that a tablespoon each of balsamic and red wine vinegar made a suitable substitution. Cornstarch turned out to be a key ingredient: A cornstarch-based slurry thickened the soup; adding cornstarch to the pork marinade gave the pork a protective sheath that kept it tender; and beating the egg with cornstarch before drizzling it into the thickened soup kept the egg light, wispy, and cohesive. Pork and tofu are the usual additions to the broth, and we included substitutes for a few other classic ingredients, settling on fresh shiitakes in lieu of wood ear mushrooms and canned bamboo shoots instead of lily buds. Spicy, bracing, rich, and complex, our version of this soup stayed true to its name. To make slicing the pork chop easier, freeze it for 15 minutes. We prefer the distinctive flavor of Chinese black vinegar; look for it in Asian supermarkets. If you can't find it, use 1 tablespoon red wine vinegar and 1 tablespoon balsamic vinegar. This soup is very spicy. For a less spicy soup, omit the chili oil altogether or add only 1 teaspoon.

- 7 ounces (½ block) extra-firm tofu
- ¼ cup soy sauce
- 3 tablespoons plus 1½ teaspoons cornstarch
- 1 teaspoon toasted sesame oil
- 1 (6-ounce) boneless center-cut pork chop (about ½ inch thick), trimmed and cut into 1-inch-long matchsticks
- 3 tablespoons plus 1 teaspoon water
- 1 large egg
- 6 cups low-sodium chicken broth
- 1 (5-ounce) can bamboo shoots, sliced into matchsticks (about 1 cup)
- 4 ounces shiitake mushrooms, stemmed, wiped clean, caps sliced ¼ inch thick
- 5 tablespoons Chinese black vinegar
- 2 teaspoons chili oil
- 1 teaspoon ground white pepper
- 3 scallions, sliced thin

**1.** Place the tofu in a pie plate, top with a heavy plate, and weigh down with two heavy cans. Set the tofu aside until it has released about ½ cup liquid, about 15 minutes. When drained, cut the tofu into ½-inch cubes and set aside.

**2.** Meanwhile, whisk 1 tablespoon of the soy sauce, 1 teaspoon of the cornstarch, and the sesame oil together in a medium bowl. Stir in the pork, cover, and let marinate for at least 10 minutes or up to 30 minutes.

**3.** Combine 3 tablespoons more cornstarch with 3 tablespoons of the water in a small bowl. Mix the remaining ½ teaspoon cornstarch with the remaining 1 teaspoon water in a second small bowl, then add the egg and beat with a fork until combined.

**4.** Bring the broth to a simmer in a large saucepan over medium-low heat. Add the bamboo shoots and mushrooms and simmer until the mushrooms are just tender, 2 to 3 minutes. Stir in the diced tofu and pork with its marinade and continue to simmer, stirring to separate any pieces of pork that stick together, until the pork is no longer pink, about 2 minutes.

**5.** Stir the cornstarch mixture to recombine, then add it to the soup, increase the heat to medium-high, and cook, stirring occasionally, until the soup thickens and turns translucent, about 1 minute. Stir in the remaining 3 tablespoons soy sauce, the vinegar, chili oil, and pepper and turn off the heat.

**6.** Without stirring the soup, use a soup spoon to slowly drizzle very thin streams of the egg mixture into the pot in a circular motion. Let the soup sit off the heat for 1 minute. Briefly return the soup to a simmer over medium-high heat, then remove from the heat immediately. Gently stir the soup once to evenly distribute the egg; ladle into individual bowls, sprinkle with the scallions, and serve.

## Caldo Verde

**SERVES** 6 to 8

**WHY THIS RECIPE WORKS** This soup of sausage, potatoes, and hearty greens is a staple in many Portuguese households. While the flavors are rich, it's not a heavy soup. Without changing the soup's essentially light character, we wanted to create a slightly heartier result—something that could function as a main course. To start, we replaced the Portuguese linguica sausage with widely available Spanish-style chorizo, which boasts a similar garlicky profile. We sautéed the sausage right in the Dutch oven in just 1 tablespoon of olive oil, eliminating the need to dirty an extra skillet. For deeper flavor, we split the water with an equal amount of chicken broth. Collard greens offered a more delicate sweetness and a meatier bite than kale, and chopping the leaves into bite-size pieces made them more spoon-friendly. Finally, we swapped out starchy russet potatoes for sturdy Yukon Golds, which held their shape during cooking. Pureeing some of the potatoes and a few tablespoons of olive oil into our soup base made a creamier, heartier dish. A bit of white wine vinegar brightened the pot. We prefer collard greens, but kale can be substituted. Serve this soup with hearty bread and, for added richness, a final drizzle of extra-virgin olive oil.

- ¼ cup extra-virgin olive oil, divided
- 12 ounces Spanish-style chorizo sausage, cut into ½-inch pieces
- 1 onion, chopped fine
- 4 garlic cloves, minced
- 1¼ teaspoons table salt
- ¼ teaspoon red pepper flakes
- 2 pounds Yukon Gold potatoes, peeled and cut into ¾-inch pieces
- 4 cups chicken broth
- 4 cups water
- 1 pound collard greens, stemmed and cut into 1-inch pieces
- 2 teaspoons white wine vinegar

**1.** Heat 1 tablespoon oil in Dutch oven over medium-high heat until shimmering. Add chorizo and cook, stirring occasionally, until lightly browned, 4 to 5 minutes. Transfer chorizo to bowl and set aside. Reduce heat to medium and add onion, garlic, salt, and pepper flakes and season with pepper to taste. Cook, stirring frequently, until onion is translucent, 2 to 3 minutes. Add potatoes, broth, and water; increase heat to high and bring to boil. Reduce heat to medium-low and simmer, uncovered, until potatoes are just tender, 8 to 10 minutes.

**2.** Transfer ¾ cup solids and ¾ cup broth to blender jar. Add collard greens to pot and simmer for 10 minutes. Stir in chorizo and continue to simmer until greens are tender, 8 to 10 minutes longer.

**3.** Add remaining 3 tablespoons oil to soup in blender and process until very smooth and homogeneous, about 1 minute. Remove pot from heat and stir pureed soup mixture and vinegar into soup. Season with salt and pepper to taste, and serve. (Soup can be refrigerated for up to 2 days.)

## French-Style Pork Stew

**SERVES** 8 to 10

**WHY THIS RECIPE WORKS** In the boiled dinner known as potée, multiple cuts of pork, sausages, and vegetables are simmered until tender, then served with their flavorful cooking liquid. We set out to turn this dish into a fork-friendly stew that was robust but not heavy. Pork butt, cut into chunks, became succulent and tender with the long cooking time. A smoked ham shank and kielbasa gave our stew the delicate smokiness and intense porky notes found in traditional versions, plus it provided such meaty flavor and complexity that we could skip the extra step of browning the pork. Chicken broth cut with water provided a subtle flavor base; simmering it with aromatics and seasonings added depth. For ease, we limited the traditional roster of vegetables to carrots, potatoes, and cabbage which we added toward the end of cooking so they would retain their texture. Serve with crusty bread.

- 6 sprigs fresh parsley
- 3 large sprigs fresh thyme
- 5 garlic cloves, unpeeled
- 2 bay leaves
- 1 tablespoon black peppercorns
- 2 whole cloves
- 5 cups water
- 4 cups chicken broth
- 3 pounds boneless pork butt roast, trimmed and cut into 1- to 1½-inch pieces
- 1 meaty smoked ham shank or 2–3 smoked ham hocks (1¼ pounds)
- 2 onions, halved through root end, root end left intact
- 4 carrots, peeled, narrow end cut crosswise into ½-inch pieces, wide end halved lengthwise and cut into ½-inch pieces

1 pound Yukon Gold potatoes, unpeeled, cut into ¾-inch pieces
12 ounces kielbasa sausage, halved lengthwise and sliced ½ inch thick
8 cups shredded savoy cabbage
Table salt and pepper
¼ cup chopped fresh parsley

**1.** Adjust oven rack to middle position and heat oven to 325 degrees. Cut 10-inch square of triple-thickness cheesecloth. Place parsley sprigs (fold or break to fit), thyme sprigs, garlic, bay leaves, peppercorns, and cloves in center of cheesecloth and tie into bundle with kitchen twine.

**2.** Bring water, chicken broth, pork butt, ham shank, onions, and herb bundle to simmer in large Dutch oven over medium-high heat, skimming off scum that rises to surface. Cover pot and place in oven. Cook until pork chunks are tender and skewer inserted into meat meets little resistance, 1¼ to 1½ hours.

**3.** Using slotted spoon, discard cheesecloth bundle and onion halves. Transfer shank to plate. Add carrots and potatoes to pot and stir to combine. Cover pot and return to oven. Cook until vegetables are almost tender, 20 to 25 minutes. When cool enough to handle, using two forks, remove meat from shank and shred into bite-size pieces; discard skin and bones.

**4.** Add shredded shank meat, kielbasa, and cabbage to pot. Stir to combine, cover, and return to oven. Cook until kielbasa is heated through and cabbage is wilted and tender, 15 to 20 minutes. Season with salt and pepper to taste, then stir in parsley. Ladle into bowls and serve.

## Hot Ukrainian Borscht

**SERVES** 6 to 8

**WHY THIS RECIPE WORKS** The markers of classic Ukrainian borscht include beets for their earthy sweetness and vivid color, as well as green cabbage, carrots, onions, and potatoes—staple crops that grow abundantly in Ukrainian soil. Pork, the cuisine's default protein, builds up a meaty backbone, and a souring agent such as vinegar, lemon juice, or tomatoes invigorates the broth. We cooked collagen-rich pork butt slowly to yield a full-bodied broth with succulent meat for the soup. Shredding the beets and carrots helped the hard roots cook efficiently and varied their texture from the chunkier potatoes. We also separately sautéed the beets and carrots before simmering them; the high heat helped them soften quickly and intensified their savory sweetness. Loads of tomato paste, briefly sautéed with the beets to deepen its flavor, plus a last-minute shot of lemon juice, brightened the earthy, meaty broth. Pork butt roast is often labeled Boston butt in the supermarket. In step 2, the chilled fat hardens on the surface of the broth and is easy to remove with a spoon. This soup benefits from being made in advance—at least a few hours before eating and up to three days. Serve with bread. Garnish with sour cream, if desired.

**BROTH**

10 cups water
1 (2-pound) boneless pork butt roast, well trimmed and cut in half
1 onion, halved
1 large carrot, sliced 1 inch thick
2 bay leaves
½ teaspoon table salt

**SOUP**

1 pound Yukon Gold potatoes, peeled and cut into 1-inch pieces
½ small head green cabbage, halved, cored, and sliced thin crosswise (5 cups)
1½ teaspoons table salt, divided
¼ cup vegetable oil
1 onion, chopped fine
8 ounces beets, trimmed, peeled, and shredded (2 cups)
2 carrots, peeled and shredded (1½ cups)
1 (6-ounce) can tomato paste
⅓ cup chopped fresh dill, plus more for garnish
1 tablespoon lemon juice, plus more for serving

**1. FOR THE BROTH:** Combine all ingredients in Dutch oven and bring to boil over high heat. Adjust heat to simmer and cook, covered, until pork is tender, about 2 hours, occasionally skimming foam off surface.

**2.** Transfer pork to large plate or cutting board. Discard onion, carrot, and bay leaves. When pork is cool enough to handle, cut into bite-size pieces (it's OK if meat starts to shred). Skim fat from surface of broth. (Alternatively, let broth cool completely and refrigerate overnight. Refrigerate pork separately.)

**3. FOR THE SOUP:** Reserve ½ cup broth. In Dutch oven, bring remaining broth to boil over high heat. Add potatoes, cabbage, and ½ teaspoon salt. Adjust heat to maintain gentle simmer and cook, covered, until potatoes are just tender, 8 to 10 minutes.

**4.** Meanwhile, heat oil in 12-inch skillet over medium heat until shimmering. Add onion and cook, stirring frequently, until softened, about 5 minutes. Add beets, carrots, and ½ teaspoon salt and cook, stirring frequently, until softened, 3 to 5 minutes. Stir in tomato paste (mixture will be thick) and cook until fragrant and tomato paste is slightly darkened in color, 1 to 2 minutes. Slowly add reserved broth, scraping bottom of pan to loosen any browned bits.

**5.** Add beet mixture to Dutch oven and stir gently to combine. Cover and simmer for 5 minutes. Stir in pork, dill, lemon juice, and remaining ½ teaspoon salt. Season with salt, pepper, and lemon juice to taste. Portion borscht into bowls and garnish each serving with more dill. Serve. (Borscht can be refrigerated for up to 3 days or frozen for up to 4 months.)

## Chile Verde con Cerdo (Green Chili with Pork)

**SERVES** 6 to 8

**WHY THIS RECIPE WORKS** To make a vibrant chile verde, we started by salting chunks of pork butt roast for an hour, which ensured that the meat cooked up well seasoned and juicy. Gently braising the pork in the oven allowed the meat's fat and collagen to break down, making it supple. We browned the pork trimmings instead of the chunks which built a savory fond without drying out the meat. To concentrate the flavors of the tomatillos, poblanos, jalapeño, and garlic we broiled them. Warm spices and sugar softened the chile's acidity and heat. Omitting broth and/or water minimized the amount of liquid in the pot, so that the salsa—the only source of liquid—reduced to a tight, flavorful sauce that clung nicely to the meat. Pork butt roast is often labeled Boston butt in the supermarket. If your jalapeño is shorter than 3 inches long, you may wish to use two. If fresh tomatillos are unavailable, substitute three 11-ounce cans of tomatillos, drained, rinsed, and patted dry; broil as directed. Serve with white rice and/or warm corn tortillas.

- 1 (3½- to 4-pound) boneless pork butt roast, trimmed and cut into 1½-inch pieces, trimmings reserved
- 1 tablespoon plus 1 teaspoon kosher salt, divided
- 1 cup water
- 1½ pounds tomatillos, husks and stems removed, rinsed well and dried
- 5 poblano chiles, stemmed, halved, and seeded
- 1 large onion, peeled, cut into 8 wedges through root end
- 5 garlic cloves, unpeeled
- 1 jalapeño chile, stemmed and halved
- 1 tablespoon vegetable oil
- 1 teaspoon dried oregano
- 1 teaspoon ground cumin
- ⅛ teaspoon ground cinnamon
- Pinch ground cloves
- 2 bay leaves
- 2 teaspoons sugar
- 1 teaspoon pepper
- ½ cup minced fresh cilantro, plus extra for serving
- Lime wedges

**1.** Toss pork pieces with 1 tablespoon salt in large bowl. Cover and refrigerate for 1 hour. Meanwhile, chop pork trimmings coarse. Transfer to Dutch oven. Add water and bring to simmer over high heat. Cook, adjusting heat to maintain vigorous simmer and stirring occasionally, until all liquid evaporates and trimmings begin to sizzle, about 12 minutes. Continue to cook, stirring frequently, until dark fond forms on bottom of pot and trimmings have browned and crisped, about 6 minutes longer. Using slotted spoon, discard trimmings. Pour off all but 2 tablespoons fat; set aside pot.

**2.** Adjust 1 oven rack to lower-middle position and second rack 6 inches from broiler element and heat broiler. Line rimmed baking sheet with aluminum foil. Place tomatillos, poblanos, onion, garlic, and jalapeño on prepared sheet and drizzle with oil. Arrange chiles skin side up. Broil until chile skins are blackened and vegetables begin to soften, 10 to 13 minutes, rotating sheet halfway through broiling. Transfer poblanos, jalapeño, and garlic to cutting board.

**3.** Turn off broiler and heat oven to 325 degrees. Transfer tomatillos, onion, and any accumulated juices to food processor. When poblanos, jalapeño, and garlic are cool enough to handle, remove and discard skins (it's OK if some small bits of chile skin remain). Remove seeds from jalapeño and reserve. Add poblanos, jalapeño, and garlic to processor. Pulse until mixture is roughly pureed, about 10 pulses, scraping down sides of bowl as needed. If spicier chili is desired, add reserved jalapeño seeds and pulse 3 times.

**4.** Heat reserved fat in Dutch oven over medium heat until just shimmering. Add oregano, cumin, cinnamon, and cloves and cook, stirring constantly, until fragrant, about 30 seconds. Stir in tomatillo mixture, bay leaves, sugar, pepper, and remaining 1 teaspoon salt, scraping up any browned bits. Stir in pork and bring to simmer. Cover, transfer to oven, and cook until pork is tender, about 1½ hours, stirring halfway through cooking.

**5.** Remove pot from oven and let sit, covered, for 10 minutes. Discard bay leaves. Using heatproof rubber spatula, scrape browned bits from sides of pot. Stir in any fat that has risen to top of chili. Stir in cilantro; season with salt and pepper to taste. Serve, passing lime wedges and extra cilantro separately.

## Irish Stew with Carrots and Turnips

**SERVES** 6

**WHY THIS RECIPE WORKS** At its most traditional, Irish stew is made with just lamb, onions, potatoes, and water. There's no browning or precooking to develop flavor; the raw ingredients are simply layered in a pot and cooked until tender. While this technique may yield a meal that's nutritious, sustaining, and warm, the stew can often be bland. We wanted a rich, deeply flavored stew as delicious as it was filling. For a version with real flavor, finding the right cut of meat was half the battle. We found that slicing the meat from a lamb shoulder chop off the bone, browning it, and then adding the bones and meat to the stewing liquid gave us a rich-tasting broth and the velvety texture that only marrow-rich bones can contribute. Thoroughly browned onions contributed much more flavor than onions added raw, and starchy turnips provided a bit of thickening power and a welcome buttery richness. Chopped parsley added a finishing flourish of color and freshness for an Irish stew that was anything but bland. Try to buy shoulder chops from the butcher. In most supermarkets, lamb shoulder chops are thin, often about ½ inch thick. At this thickness, the stew meat is too insubstantial. Ideally, we liked chops cut 1½ inches thick, but 1-inch chops will suffice.

- 4½ pounds lamb shoulder chops, each 1 to 1½ inches thick
- 3 tablespoons vegetable oil
- 3 medium-large onions, chopped coarse (about 5 cups)
- ¼ teaspoon table salt
- 4 tablespoons unbleached all-purpose flour
- 3 cups water
- 1 teaspoon dried thyme
- ½ pound carrots, peeled and sliced ¼ inch thick
- ½ pound turnips, peeled and cut into 1-inch cubes
- ¼ cup minced fresh parsley leaves

**1.** Adjust oven rack to lower-middle position and heat oven to 300 degrees. Cut meat from bones and reserve bones. Trim meat of excess fat and cut into 1½-inch cubes. Season meat generously with salt and pepper.

**2.** Heat 1 tablespoon oil in large ovenproof Dutch oven over medium-high heat until shimmering, about 2 minutes. Add half of meat to pot so that individual pieces are close together but not touching. Cook, without moving, until sides touching pot are well-browned, 2 to 3 minutes. Using tongs, turn each piece and continue cooking until most sides are well-browned, about 5 minutes longer. Transfer meat to medium bowl, add another 1 tablespoon oil to pot, and swirl to coat pan bottom. Brown remaining lamb; transfer meat to bowl and set aside.

**3.** Reduce heat to medium, add remaining tablespoon oil, and swirl to coat pan bottom. Add onions and ¼ teaspoon salt and cook, stirring frequently and vigorously, scraping bottom of pot with wooden spoon to loosen browned bits, until onions have browned, about 8 minutes. Add flour and stir until onions are evenly coated, 1 to 2 minutes.

**4.** Stir in 1½ cups of water, scraping pan bottom and edges with wooden spoon to loosen remaining browned bits. Gradually remaining 1½ cups water, stirring constantly and scraping pan edges to dissolve flour. Add thyme and 1 teaspoon salt and bring to simmer. Add bones and then meat and accumulated juices. Return to simmer, cover, and place in oven. Cook for 1 hour.

**5.** Remove pot from oven and place carrots and turnips on top of meat and bones. Cover and return pot to oven and cook until meat is tender, about 1 hour. If serving immediately, stir carrots and turnips into liquid, wait 5 minutes, and spoon off any fat that rises to top. (Stew can be covered and refrigerated for up to 3 days. Spoon off congealed fat and bring back to simmer over medium-low heat.)

**6.** Stir in parsley and adjust seasoning with salt and pepper. Remove bones if desired. Serve immediately.

## New England Clam Chowder

**SERVES 6**

**WHY THIS RECIPE WORKS** Good traditional chowder can be daunting for the home cook. The biggest hurdle is a finicky ingredient that most people don't know how to work with—clams. We wanted to come up with a clam chowder that was economical, could be prepared quickly, and provided a simple method for working with the star ingredient. We tested a variety of clams and found that medium-size hard-shell clams guaranteed the most clam flavor. Rather than shucking the raw clams and adding them to the pot, we easily steamed the clams to open them, then used the steaming liquid as our broth. The steamed clams had to be pulled from the pot when they had just opened; allowing them to open completely meant they would overcook quickly when returned to the soup to heat through. Waxy red potatoes were the best choice for our creamy chowder and bacon added great smoky flavor. As for the creaminess factor, using a modest amount of heavy cream instead of milk meant that we could use less dairy for a rich chowder that tasted distinctly of clams. Don't skip the step of scrubbing the clams; many clams have bits of sand embedded in their shells that can ruin a pot of chowder. To remove the sand, simply scrub them under cold, running water using a soft brush.

- 7 pounds medium-size hard-shell clams, such as cherrystones, washed and scrubbed clean
- 3 slices thick-cut bacon, cut into ¼-inch pieces
- 1 large onion, chopped
- 2 tablespoons all-purpose flour
- 1½ pounds red potatoes, unpeeled, cut into ½-inch chunks
- 1 bay leaf
- 1 teaspoon fresh thyme or ¼ teaspoon dried thyme
- 1 cup heavy cream
- 2 tablespoons minced fresh parsley leaves

**1.** Bring 3 cups water to boil in Dutch oven. Add clams and cover with tight-fitting lid. Cook for 5 minutes, uncover, and stir with wooden spoon. Quickly cover pot and steam until clams just open, 2 to 4 minutes. (Don't let clams open completely.) Transfer clams to large bowl and let cool slightly; reserve broth. Open clams with paring knife, holding clams over bowl to catch any juices. With knife, sever muscle that attaches clam to bottom shell and transfer meat to cutting board; discard shells. Mince clams and set aside. Pour clam broth into large bowl, holding back last few tablespoons of broth in case of sediment; set clam broth aside. (You should have about 5 cups. If not, add bottled clam juice or water to make this amount.) Rinse and dry pot, then return pot to burner.

**2.** Cook bacon in pot over medium heat until crispy, 5 to 7 minutes. Add onion and cook, stirring occasionally, until softened, about 5 minutes. Add flour and stir until lightly colored, about 1 minute. Gradually whisk in reserved clam broth. Add potatoes, bay leaf, and thyme and simmer until potatoes are tender, about 10 minutes. Add clams, cream, parsley, and salt and pepper to taste; bring to simmer. Discard bay leaf, and serve.

## New England Fish Chowder

**SERVES** 6 to 8

**WHY THIS RECIPE WORKS** New England fish chowder got its start on the fishing vessels that plied the Newfoundland coast in the 18th century; sailors would throw a piece of their catch into a pot with water, salt pork, and hardtack. Today, this chowder is typically bulked up with potatoes and given a glug of milk or cream for added richness. For a chowder with a delicate, clean-tasting broth that was creamy but not so rich that you couldn't taste the fish, we started by gently poaching flaky cod in water flavored with salt pork and onions and perfumed with bay leaf and thyme. To this stock we introduced milk, as opposed to other rich dairy additives like half-and-half and heavy cream, to keep the chowder light and fresh-tasting. The starch from the potatoes plus a tablespoon of cornstarch worked together to help thicken the chowder and prevent the milk from curdling as it simmered. Haddock, or another flaky white fish, can be substituted for the cod. Garnish the chowder with minced fresh chives, crispy bacon bits, or oyster crackers.

- 2 tablespoons unsalted butter
- 2 onions, cut into ½-inch dice
- 4 ounces salt pork, rind removed, rinsed, and cut into 2 pieces
- 1½ teaspoons minced fresh thyme
- ¾ teaspoon table salt
- 1 bay leaf
- 5 cups water
- 2 pounds skinless cod fillets, sliced crosswise into 6 equal pieces
- 1½ pounds Yukon Gold potatoes, peeled and cut into ½-inch dice
- 2 cups whole milk
- 1 tablespoon cornstarch
- ½ teaspoon pepper

**1.** Melt butter in Dutch oven over medium heat. Add onions, salt pork, thyme, salt, and bay leaf; cook, stirring occasionally, until onions are softened but not browned, 3 to 5 minutes. Add water and bring to simmer. Remove pot from heat; gently place cod in water; cover; and let cod stand until opaque and nearly cooked through, about 5 minutes. Using metal spatula, transfer cod to bowl.

**2.** Return pot to medium-high heat, add potatoes, and bring to simmer. Cook until potatoes are tender and beginning to break apart, about 20 minutes.

**3.** Meanwhile, whisk milk, cornstarch, and pepper together in bowl. Stir milk mixture into chowder and return to simmer. Return cod and any accumulated juices to pot. Remove pot from heat, cover, and let stand for 5 minutes. Remove and discard salt pork and bay leaf. Stir gently with wooden spoon to break cod into large pieces. Season with salt and pepper to taste. Serve immediately.

## Cioppino

**SERVES** 4 to 6

**WHY THIS RECIPE WORKS** Brought to San Francisco by Italian immigrants, the earliest versions of cioppino were uncomplicated affairs made by fishermen with the day's catch. We wanted a restaurant-worthy cioppino in which every component was perfectly cooked but which could be on the table quickly and with minimal fuss. First, we scaled down the seafood. For the fish, halibut fillets worked perfectly—they were tender and had just enough heft. As for the shellfish, a combination of briny littleneck clams and savory-sweet mussels had the flavors we were looking for. The only way to perfectly cook three varieties of seafood was to cook each one separately and bring them all together in the hot broth to serve. We poached the halibut in the broth while the clams and mussels steamed in a separate pan. Removing them as they opened ensured ideal doneness for each one. We used white wine to steam the mussels and clams, and then added the briny cooking liquid to the stew for a boost of intense seafood flavor. Replacing the water in the broth with bottled clam juice improved the broth even further. Any firm-fleshed, ¾- to 1-inch-thick whitefish (such as cod or sea bass) can be substituted for halibut. Discard clams or mussels with unpleasant odors, cracked shells, or shells that won't close. If littlenecks are not available, substitute Manila or mahogany clams, or use 2 pounds of mussels. If using only mussels, skip step 3 and cook them all at once with the butter and wine for 3 to 5 minutes.

- ¼ cup vegetable oil
- 2 large onions, chopped fine
- ½ teaspoon table salt
- ½ teaspoon pepper
- ¼ cup water
- 4 garlic cloves, minced
- 2 bay leaves
- 1 teaspoon dried oregano
- ⅛–¼ teaspoon red pepper flakes
- 1 (28-ounce) can whole peeled tomatoes, drained with juice reserved, chopped coarse
- 1 (8-ounce) bottle clam juice
- 1 (1½-pound) skinless halibut fillet, ¾ to 1 inch thick, cut into 6 pieces
- 1 pound littleneck clams, scrubbed (see page 106)

- 1¼ cups dry white wine
- 4 tablespoons unsalted butter
- 1 pound mussels, scrubbed and debearded (see page 543)
- ¼ cup chopped fresh parsley
- Extra-virgin olive oil

**1.** Heat vegetable oil in Dutch oven over medium-high heat until shimmering. Add onions, salt, and pepper; cook, stirring frequently, until onions begin to brown, 7 to 9 minutes. Add water and cook, stirring frequently, until onions are soft, 2 to 4 minutes. Stir in garlic, bay leaves, oregano, and pepper flakes and cook for 1 minute. Stir in tomatoes and reserved juice and clam juice and bring to simmer. Reduce heat to low, cover, and simmer for 5 minutes.

**2.** Submerge halibut in broth, cover, and simmer gently until fish is cooked through, 12 to 15 minutes. Remove pot from heat and, using slotted spoon, transfer halibut to plate; cover with aluminum foil and set aside.

**3.** Bring clams, wine, and butter to boil in covered 12-inch skillet over high heat. Steam until clams just open, 5 to 8 minutes, transferring them to pot with tomato broth as they open.

**4.** Once all clams have been transferred to pot, add mussels to skillet; cover; and cook over high heat until mussels have opened, 2 to 4 minutes, transferring them to pot with tomato broth as they open. Pour cooking liquid from skillet into pot, being careful not to pour any grit from skillet into pot. Return broth to simmer.

**5.** Stir parsley into broth and season with salt and pepper to taste. Divide halibut among serving bowls. Ladle broth over halibut, making sure each portion contains both clams and mussels. Drizzle with olive oil and serve immediately.

## Cataplana (Portuguese Seafood Stew)

**SERVES** 4 to 6

**WHY THIS RECIPE WORKS** This stunning one-pot stew is named after the clamshell-shaped copper pot in which it's traditionally cooked. Our recipe takes inspiration from the classic dish amêijoas na cataplana (clams in a cataplana). To mimic the steamy cooking environment of a cataplana, we cooked our version in a Dutch oven with a tight-fitting lid. We added clams and shrimp at the very end of cooking, preserving their delicate textures and rendering them plump, juicy, and tender. Clam juice boosted the seafood flavor of the dish but also ensured that there was enough delicious broth for soaking up crusty bread. We prefer untreated shrimp, but if your shrimp are treated with salt or additives such as sodium tripolyphosphate (STPP), do not add the salt in step 1. Look for small littleneck or Manila clams that are all about 2 inches across so that they cook at the same rate. If you've had past problems with gritty clams or this is your first time cooking clams, you may wish to purge them before cooking. We call for linguica sausage, but if it's unavailable, you can substitute chouriço or Spanish chorizo. Serve with crusty bread.

- 12 ounces extra-large shrimp (21 to 25 per pound), peeled, deveined, and cut in half crosswise (see page 523)
- ¾ teaspoon table salt, divided
- 2 tablespoons extra-virgin olive oil
- 12 ounces linguica sausage, quartered lengthwise and sliced ¼ inch thick
- 2 garlic cloves, minced
- ¾ teaspoon smoked paprika
- ½ teaspoon red pepper flakes
- 1 large onion, halved and sliced thin
- 1 fennel bulb, stalks discarded, bulb halved, cored, and sliced thin lengthwise
- 1 red bell pepper, stemmed, seeded, and cut into ¼-inch-wide strips
- 1 (28-ounce) can whole peeled tomatoes, drained and chopped coarse
- 1 (8-ounce) bottle clam juice
- ½ cup dry white wine
- 3 pounds littleneck or Manila clams, scrubbed
- ½ cup chopped fresh parsley
- Lemon wedges

**1.** Combine shrimp and ¼ teaspoon salt in bowl; refrigerate until needed. Heat oil in large Dutch oven over medium-high heat until shimmering. Add linguica and cook, stirring occasionally, until browned and fat is slightly rendered, about 4 minutes. Stir in garlic, paprika, and pepper flakes and cook until fragrant, about 30 seconds.

**2.** Add onion, fennel, bell pepper, and remaining ½ teaspoon salt and cook, stirring occasionally, until vegetables are softened, 8 to 10 minutes. Stir in tomatoes, clam juice, and wine. Bring to simmer and cook, stirring occasionally, until thickened slightly, about 5 minutes.

**3.** Increase heat to high and bring mixture to boil. Stir in clams; cover and cook until clams have opened, 5 to 7 minutes, stirring halfway through cooking. Off heat, stir in shrimp. Cover and let stand off heat until shrimp are opaque and just cooked through, about 5 minutes. Discard any unopened clams. Stir in parsley and season with salt to taste. Transfer to serving bowl, if desired, and serve, passing lemon wedges separately.

### SCRUBBING CLAMS

Before cooking clams, use a soft brush to scrub them well to remove any sand and grit.

## Zarzuela (Spanish Seafood Stew)

SERVES 6 to 8 SEASON 26

**WHY THIS RECIPE WORKS** Zarzuela is a classic Catalan seafood stew in a ruddy, spiced tomato broth. We made it our goal to allow the flavors of the stew's fish, shrimp, squid, and mussels to take center stage. We used spices such as saffron and paprika sparingly so as not to overwhelm the delicate flavor of the seafood. Wine and brandy cooked down so that their alcohol didn't impart any harsh flavor. We used a hybrid cooking method for the seafood in which we cooked the mussels, covered, in the rapidly simmering broth for 4 minutes before the more delicate seafood—cod, shrimp, and squid—were added to poach off the heat until just cooked through. Haddock or other firm-fleshed, flaky white fish can be substituted for cod. If using prepeeled shrimp, reduce the amount to 8 ounces. Do not use shrimp that are larger than what's called for here, as they may not cook through by the time the other seafood is done. If desired, substitute the contents of one 14.5-ounce can of whole peeled tomatoes that have been drained (reserve the juice) and chopped coarse for the fresh tomatoes. Serve with crusty bread and a crisp green salad.

- 1 pound skinless cod fillets, 1 to 1½ inches thick and cut into ¾- to 1-inch pieces
- 12 ounces extra-large shrimp (21 to 25 per pound), peeled, deveined, and tails removed (see page 523)
- 8 ounces squid, bodies sliced crosswise into ½-inch-thick rings, tentacles left whole
- 1 teaspoon table salt, divided
- 1 cup dry white wine
- 2 tablespoons brandy
- 2 tablespoons lemon juice, divided, plus lemon wedges for serving
- ¼ teaspoon saffron threads, crumbled
- ⅓ cup slivered almonds
- ½ cup minced fresh parsley, divided
- 2 large tomatoes, halved through equator
- ⅓ cup extra-virgin olive oil
- 1 large onion, chopped fine
- 1 red bell pepper, stemmed, seeded, and cut into ¼-inch pieces
- 2 garlic cloves, minced
- ½ teaspoon paprika
- ½ teaspoon smoked paprika
- ¼ teaspoon red pepper flakes
- 2 (8-ounce) bottles clam juice
- ½ cup pitted green Manzanilla olives, chopped
- 1 pound mussels, scrubbed and debearded

**1.** Combine cod, shrimp, squid, and ¾ teaspoon salt in medium bowl; refrigerate until needed. Combine wine, brandy, 1 tablespoon lemon juice, and saffron in 1-cup liquid measuring cup and set aside. Pulse almonds in food processor until finely ground, about 20 pulses. Add ⅓ cup parsley and process until finely ground, about 10 pulses; set aside.

**2.** Place box grater in medium bowl. Rub cut side of tomatoes against large holes of grater until tomato flesh is reduced to pulp (skins should remain intact). Discard skins. (You should have about 1½ cups pulp.)

**3.** Heat oil in Dutch oven over medium-high heat until shimmering. Add onion, bell pepper, and remaining ¼ teaspoon salt, and cook, stirring frequently, until softened, 7 to 8 minutes. Stir in garlic, paprika, smoked paprika, and pepper flakes and cook for 1 minute. Add wine mixture and cook, stirring occasionally, until liquid has mostly evaporated, 4 to 6 minutes. Add clam juice, olives, ground almond mixture, and tomato pulp and stir to combine. Adjust heat to maintain vigorous simmer and cook, uncovered, until liquid has reduced and thickened slightly, 6 to 8 minutes.

**4.** Add mussels, cover, and cook for 4 minutes. Add seafood mixture and stir to evenly distribute, making sure all pieces are submerged in liquid. Cover and remove pot from heat. Let stand for 15 minutes, until shrimp, cod, and squid are opaque and just cooked through, gently stirring once halfway through resting.

**5.** Add remaining 1 tablespoon lemon juice and season with salt and pepper to taste. Garnish with remaining parsley and serve immediately, passing lemon wedges separately.

## Chraime

SERVES 4

**WHY THIS RECIPE WORKS** This spicy, garlicky, and aromatic tomato-based fish stew was brought to Israel by Libyan and Moroccan Jewish immigrants and commonly appears on Shabbat, Rosh Hashanah, and Passover tables. Our take paid homage to both Libyan and Moroccan versions: Grassy fresh jalapeños and bright Aleppo pepper brought varied heat, and tomato paste and bell pepper provided balancing sweetness. Cherry tomatoes, tossed in almost at the end of cooking, added fresh pops of sweet acidity. Using a spice blend was an easy way to incorporate the dish's varied spices; 1 tablespoon of the Tunisian spice blend tabil added a range of flavors from earthy muskiness to bright citrus notes. Black sea bass, cod, hake, or pollock can be substituted for the haddock. Thin, tail-end fillets can be folded to achieve proper thickness. This dish is typically spicy; for a milder dish, reduce the amount of Aleppo pepper to 1 or 2 teaspoons. Serve with challah, if desired.

- 3 tablespoons extra virgin olive oil, plus extra for drizzling
- 1 onion, chopped fine
- 1 red bell pepper, stemmed, seeded, and chopped
- 1 jalapeño chile, stemmed, seeded, and minced
- ¾ teaspoon table salt
- ¼ cup tomato paste
- 6 garlic cloves, minced
- 1 tablespoon tabil (recipe follows)
- 1 tablespoon ground dried Aleppo pepper
- 2 teaspoons paprika
- ¼ teaspoon pepper
- 1½ cups water
- 1½ pounds skinless haddock fillets, ½ to ¾ inch thick, cut into 3-inch pieces
- 10 ounces cherry tomatoes
- ½ cup chopped fresh cilantro
- Lemon wedges

**1.** Heat oil in 12-inch skillet over medium heat until shimmering. Add onion, bell pepper, jalapeño, and salt and cook until vegetables are softened, 5 to 7 minutes. Stir in tomato paste, garlic, tabil, Aleppo pepper, paprika, and pepper and cook until fragrant, about 30 seconds. Stir in water, scraping up any browned bits, and bring to simmer. Reduce heat to low; cover; and cook until flavors meld, about 15 minutes.

**2.** Nestle haddock into sauce and spoon some of sauce over fish. Sprinkle tomatoes around haddock and return to simmer. Reduce heat to low; cover; and cook until fish flakes apart when gently prodded with paring knife and registers 135 degrees, 5 to 7 minutes. Season with salt and pepper to taste. Sprinkle with cilantro and drizzle with extra oil. Serve with lemon wedges.

### Tabil

**MAKES** ½ cup

The word "tabil" is sometimes translated as "coriander," so it's no surprise that coriander is the most prominent ingredient in this Tunisian spice blend. The blend lends dishes a beautiful, complex aroma.

- 3½ tablespoons coriander seeds
- 2 tablespoons plus 2 teaspoons caraway seeds
- 5 teaspoons cumin seeds

Combine all ingredients in bowl. (Tabil can be stored in airtight container at room temperature for up to 1 month.)

## Caldo de Siete Mares (Soup of the Seven Seas)

**SERVES** 6 to 8

**WHY THIS RECIPE WORKS** Prepared by Mexican fisherman, caldo de siete mares combines the catch of the day with a few vegetables in a spicy seafood broth. For our version, we settled on a combination of mussels, catfish, and shrimp, all native to the Gulf of Mexico. To create a seafood stock, we cooked shrimp shells with an aromatic spice mixture then simmered them in clam juice and chicken broth. Smoky ancho chiles and onion and garlic provided the classic flavor base. For the vegetables, we opted for corn and tomatoes, which we simmered along with the mussels in the fragrant broth just until tender; then, to guard against overcooking, we removed them before adding the shrimp and catfish to the pot. Sole is a good substitute for catfish.

- 3 dried ancho chiles, stemmed, seeded, and torn into ½-inch pieces (¾ cup)
- 1 onion, quartered
- 3 garlic cloves, peeled
- 1 tablespoon dried oregano
- 2 teaspoons ground cumin
- 2 teaspoons sugar
- 2 bay leaves
- 1 teaspoon pepper
- 3 tablespoons vegetable oil
- 1 pound large shrimp (26 to 30 per pound), peeled, deveined, tails removed, and shells reserved (see page 523)
- ½ teaspoon table salt
- 5 cups chicken broth
- 2 (8-ounce) bottles clam juice
- 2 ears corn, husks and silk removed, cut into 1-inch rounds
- 1 pound russet potatoes, peeled and cut into ½-inch pieces
- 1 pound mussels, scrubbed and debearded
- 1½ pounds skinless catfish fillets, cut into 2-inch pieces
- 2 tablespoons minced fresh cilantro
- Lime wedges

**1.** Toast anchos in Dutch oven over medium-high heat, stirring frequently, until fragrant, 2 to 6 minutes; transfer to food processor. Add onion, garlic, oregano, cumin, sugar, bay leaves, and pepper to processor and pulse until coarsely chopped, about 15 pulses.

**2.** Heat oil in now-empty pot over medium-high heat until shimmering. Add ancho mixture, shrimp shells, and salt and cook, stirring frequently, until mixture has darkened in color and shrimp shells have turned bright pink, 2 to 3 minutes. Stir in broth and clam juice, scraping up any browned bits, and bring to simmer. Cook until flavors meld, about 10 minutes. Strain broth through fine-mesh strainer; discard solids. Return strained broth to again-empty pot and bring to simmer.

**3.** Stir in corn and potatoes and simmer until potatoes are tender, 8 to 10 minutes. Increase heat to medium-high, stir in mussels, cover, and simmer briskly until most mussels have opened, 3 to 4 minutes (discard any unopened mussels). Using slotted spoon, divide mussels, potatoes, and corn among individual bowls.

**4.** Return broth to gentle simmer over low heat. Add catfish and shrimp to pot, cover, and cook until catfish and shrimp are opaque throughout, about 3 minutes. Off heat, gently stir in cilantro and season with salt and pepper to taste. Ladle broth, shrimp, and catfish over mussels and vegetables. Serve with lime wedges.

## Guay Tiew Tom Yum Goong (Thai Hot and Sour Noodle Soup with Shrimp)

**SERVES** 4 to 6

**WHY THIS RECIPE WORKS** This Thai soup known as tom yum contains generous amounts of shrimp and rice noodles—along with oyster mushrooms and cherry tomatoes—in a highly aromatic broth bursting with hot, sour, salty, and sweet flavors. We created vibrancy by smashing galangal, scallions, lemongrass, makrut lime leaves, and Thai chiles to release their flavorful oils and then simmering them in store-bought chicken broth. Then we rounded out the classic flavor profile with fish sauce, lime juice, cilantro, and Thai basil. Finally, we added a dollop of homemade nam prik pao, a Thai chili jam with robust sweet, savory, and slightly spicy notes. If galangal is unavailable, substitute fresh ginger. Makrut lime leaves add a lot to this soup. If you can't find them, substitute three 3-inch strips each of lemon zest and lime zest. We prefer vermicelli made from 100 percent rice flour to varieties that include a secondary starch such as cornstarch. If you can find only the latter, soak them longer—up to 15 minutes.

- 4 ounces rice vermicelli
- 2 lemongrass stalks, trimmed to bottom 6 inches
- 4 scallions, trimmed, white parts left whole, green parts cut into 1-inch lengths
- 6 makrut lime leaves, torn if large
- 2 Thai chiles, stemmed (1 left whole, 1 sliced thin), divided, plus 2 Thai chiles, stemmed and sliced thin, for serving (optional)
- 1 (2-inch) piece fresh galangal, peeled and sliced into ¼-inch-thick rounds
- 8 cups chicken broth
- 1 tablespoon sugar, plus extra for seasoning
- 8 ounces oyster mushrooms, trimmed and torn into 1-inch pieces
- 3 tablespoons fish sauce, plus extra for seasoning
- 1 pound extra-large shrimp (21 to 25 per pound), peeled, deveined, and tails removed (see page 523)
- 12 ounces cherry tomatoes, halved
- 2 tablespoons lime juice, plus extra for seasoning, plus lime wedges for serving
- ½ cup fresh cilantro leaves
- ¼ cup fresh Thai basil leaves, torn if large (optional)
- 1 recipe Nam Prik Pao (optional)(recipe follows)

**1.** Bring 4 quarts water to boil in large pot. Remove from heat, add vermicelli, and let sit, stirring occasionally, until vermicelli are fully tender, 10 to 15 minutes. Drain, rinse with cold water, drain again, and distribute evenly among large soup bowls.

**2.** Place lemongrass, scallion whites, lime leaves, whole Thai chile, and galangal on cutting board and lightly smash with meat pounder or bottom of small skillet until mixture is moist and very fragrant. Transfer lemongrass mixture to Dutch oven. Add broth and sugar and bring to boil over high heat. Reduce heat and simmer for 15 minutes. Using slotted spoon, remove solids from pot and discard.

**3.** Add mushrooms, fish sauce, scallion greens, and sliced Thai chile and simmer for 3 to 4 minutes. Stir in shrimp. Cover and let sit off heat until shrimp are opaque and cooked through, 4 to 5 minutes. Stir in tomatoes and lime juice. Season with extra sugar, extra fish sauce, and extra lime juice to taste.

**4.** Ladle soup into bowls of noodles; sprinkle with cilantro and Thai basil, if using. Serve, drizzled with nam prik pao, if using, and passing lime wedges and extra sliced Thai chiles, if using, separately.

## Nam Prik Pao (Thai Chili Jam)

MAKES ¾ cup

This sweet, savory, and spicy condiment is the classic garnish for guay tiew tom yum goong, but it's too good to be relegated to a single use. Thai cooks also use it on fried eggs, noodles, and white rice; in stir-fries; or even as a sandwich spread. Slice the shallots to a consistent thickness to ensure even cooking. For a spicier jam, add more chile seeds.

- ½ cup vegetable oil
- 2 large shallots, sliced thin
- 4 large garlic cloves, sliced thin
- 10 dried arbol chiles, stemmed, halved lengthwise, and seeds reserved
- 2 tablespoons packed brown sugar
- 3 tablespoons lime juice, plus extra for seasoning (2 limes)
- 2 tablespoons fish sauce, plus extra for seasoning

**1.** Set fine-mesh strainer over heatproof bowl. Heat oil and shallots in medium saucepan over medium-high heat, stirring frequently, until shallots are deep golden brown, 10 to 14 minutes. Using slotted spoon, transfer shallots to second bowl. Add garlic to hot oil and cook, stirring constantly, until golden brown, 2 to 3 minutes. Using slotted spoon, transfer garlic to bowl with shallots. Add arbols and half of reserved seeds to hot oil and cook, stirring constantly, until arbols turn deep red, 1 to 2 minutes. Strain oil through prepared strainer into bowl; reserve oil and transfer arbols to bowl with shallots and garlic. Do not wash saucepan.

**2.** Process shallot mixture, sugar, and lime juice in food processor until thick paste forms, 15 to 30 seconds, scraping down sides of bowl as needed.

**3.** Return paste to now-empty saucepan and add fish sauce and 2 tablespoons reserved oil. Bring to simmer over medium-low heat. Cook, stirring frequently, until mixture is thickened and has jam-like consistency, 4 to 5 minutes. Off heat, season with extra lime juice, extra fish sauce, and salt to taste. (Jam can be refrigerated for up to 1 month.)

## Moqueca (Brazilian Shrimp and Fish Stew)

SERVES 6

**WHY THIS RECIPE WORKS** For a bright, fresh, and filling version of this traditional Brazilian stew, we started with the seafood. Cod and shrimp made for a nice balance of flavor and texture, and both were easy to find. After tossing the seafood with garlic, salt, and pepper, we looked to the other components of the stew. To balance the richness and sweetness of the coconut milk with the flavorful aromatics, we blended the onion, tomatoes, and a portion of the cilantro in the food processor until they had the texture of a slightly chunky salsa, which added body to the stew. We kept the bell peppers diced for contrasting texture and bite. To properly cook the seafood, we brought the broth to a boil to make sure the pot was superhot, added the seafood and lime juice, covered the pot, and removed it from the heat, allowing the seafood to gently cook in the residual heat. To finish our moqueca, we added more cilantro and a couple of tablespoons of homemade pepper sauce, which elevated the stew with its bright, vinegary tang. Pickled hot cherry peppers are usually sold jarred, next to the pickles or jarred roasted red peppers at the supermarket. Haddock or other firm-fleshed, flaky whitefish may be substituted for cod. We prefer untreated shrimp, but if your shrimp are treated with sodium, do not add salt to the shrimp in step 2. Our favorite coconut milk is made by Aroy-D. Serve with steamed white rice.

PEPPER SAUCE

- 4 pickled hot cherry peppers (3 ounces)
- ½ onion, chopped coarse
- ¼ cup extra-virgin olive oil
- ⅛ teaspoon sugar

STEW

- 1 pound large shrimp (26 to 30 per pound), peeled, deveined, and tails removed (see page 523)
- 1 pound skinless cod fillets (¾ to 1 inch thick), cut into 1½-inch pieces
- 3 garlic cloves, minced
- 1½ teaspoons table salt, divided
- ¼ teaspoon pepper
- 1 onion, chopped coarse
- 1 (14.5-ounce) can whole peeled tomatoes
- ¾ cup chopped fresh cilantro, divided
- 2 tablespoons extra-virgin olive oil
- 1 red bell pepper, stemmed, seeded, and cut into ½-inch pieces
- 1 green bell pepper, stemmed, seeded, and cut into ½-inch pieces
- 1 (14-ounce) can coconut milk
- 2 tablespoons lime juice

**1. FOR THE PEPPER SAUCE:** Process all ingredients in food processor until smooth, about 30 seconds, scraping down sides of bowl as needed. Season with salt to taste and transfer to separate bowl. Rinse out processor bowl.

**2. FOR THE STEW:** Toss shrimp and cod with garlic, ½ teaspoon salt, and pepper in bowl and set aside. Process onion, tomatoes and their juice, and ¼ cup cilantro in food processor until finely chopped and mixture has texture of pureed salsa, about 30 seconds.

**3.** Heat oil in large Dutch oven over medium-high heat until shimmering. Add red and green bell peppers and ½ teaspoon salt and cook, stirring frequently, until softened, 5 to 7 minutes. Add onion-tomato mixture and remaining ½ teaspoon salt. Reduce heat to medium and cook, stirring frequently, until puree has reduced and thickened slightly, 3 to 5 minutes (pot should not be dry).

**4.** Increase heat to high, stir in coconut milk, and bring to boil (mixture should be bubbling across entire surface). Add seafood mixture and lime juice and stir to evenly distribute seafood, making sure all pieces are submerged in liquid. Cover pot and remove from heat. Let stand until shrimp and cod are opaque and just cooked through, 15 minutes.

**5.** Gently stir in 2 tablespoons pepper sauce and remaining ½ cup cilantro, being careful not to break up cod too much. Season with salt and pepper to taste. Serve, passing remaining pepper sauce separately.

## Creole-Style Shrimp and Sausage Gumbo

**SERVES** 6 to 8

**WHY THIS RECIPE WORKS** With shrimp, sausage, and vegetables in a deeply flavored, rich brown sauce with a touch of heat, gumbo is a unique one-pot meal. The basis of gumbo is the roux, which is flour cooked in fat. For a deep, dark roux in half the time, we heated the oil before adding the flour. We also added the roux to room-temperature shrimp stock (supplemented with clam juice) to prevent separating. For flavor, we used plenty of garlic, dried thyme and bay leaves but just ¼ teaspoon cayenne pepper. We added spicy andouille sausage and simmered everything for half an hour, tossing in the shrimp only during the last few minutes of cooking. You can add filé powder if you like, but our gumbo is delicious even without it. Making a dark roux can be dangerous, as the mixture reaches temperatures in excess of 400 degrees. Therefore, use a deep pot for cooking the roux and long-handled utensils for stirring it, and be careful not to splash it on yourself. One secret to smooth gumbo is adding shrimp stock that is neither too hot nor too cold to the roux. For a stock that is at the right temperature when the roux is done, start preparing it before you tend to the vegetables and other ingredients, strain it, and then give it a head start on cooling by immediately adding the ice water and clam juice. Start the roux only after you've made the stock. Alternatively, you can also make the stock ahead of time and bring it to room temperature before using. Serve over white rice.

- 1½ pounds small shrimp (51 to 60 per pound), shells removed and reserved (see page 523)
- 3½ cups ice water
- 1 (8-ounce) bottle clam juice
- ½ cup vegetable oil
- ½ cup all-purpose flour, preferably bleached
- 2 medium onions, minced
- 1 medium red bell pepper, stemmed, seeded, and chopped fine
- 1 medium celery rib, chopped fine
- 6 medium garlic cloves, minced (about 2 tablespoons)
- 1 teaspoon dried thyme
- Table salt
- Cayenne pepper
- 2 bay leaves
- 1 pound smoked sausage, such as andouille or kielbasa, sliced ¼ inch thick
- ½ cup minced fresh parsley leaves
- 4 medium scallions, white and green parts, sliced thin
- Ground black pepper

**1.** Bring the reserved shrimp shells and 4½ cups water to a boil in a stockpot or large saucepan over medium-high heat. Reduce the heat to medium-low and simmer for 20 minutes. Strain the stock and add the ice water and clam juice (you should have about 2 quarts of tepid stock, 100 to 110 degrees); discard the shells. Set the stock aside.

**2.** Heat the oil in a Dutch oven or large, heavy-bottomed saucepan over medium-high heat until it registers 200 degrees on an instant-read thermometer, 1½ to 2 minutes. Reduce the heat to medium and gradually stir in the flour with a wooden spatula or spoon, making sure to work out any lumps that may form. Continue stirring constantly, reaching into the corners of the pan, until the mixture has a toasty aroma and is deep reddish brown, about 20 minutes. (The roux will thin as it cooks; if it begins to smoke, remove the pan from the heat and stir the roux constantly to cool slightly.)

**3.** Add the onions, bell pepper, celery, garlic, thyme, 1 teaspoon salt, and ¼ teaspoon cayenne to the roux and cook, stirring frequently, until the vegetables soften, 8 to 10 minutes. Add 4 cups of the reserved stock in a slow, steady stream while stirring vigorously. Stir in the remaining 4 cups of stock. Increase the heat to high and bring to a boil. Reduce the heat to medium-low, skim the foam from the surface with a wide spoon, add the bay leaves, and simmer, uncovered, skimming the foam as it rises to the surface, about 30 minutes. (The mixture can be covered and set aside for several hours. Reheat when ready to proceed.)

**4.** Stir in the sausage and continue simmering to blend the flavors, about 30 minutes. Stir in the shrimp and simmer until cooked through, about 5 minutes. Off the heat, stir in the parsley and scallions and season with salt, black pepper, and cayenne to taste.

## Garlicky Shrimp, Tomato, and White Bean Stew

**SERVES** 4 to 6

**WHY THIS RECIPE WORKS** To give this riff on white bean stew fuller seafood flavor, we made a quick concentrated stock with the shrimp shells and used it to simmer the beans. We also cooked the shrimp with the beans rather than separately and sautéed minced anchovies with the aromatics. To season the shrimp and keep them plump and juicy, we brined them briefly, added them late in the cooking process, and reduced the heat so they cooked gently. Canned beans and canned tomatoes made this dish fast and doable at any time of year; plus, the liquid from one of the cans of beans lent good body to the stew. Plenty of fresh basil and lemon juice and zest provide freshness and nice acidity. We prefer untreated shrimp, but if your shrimp are treated with added salt or preservatives like sodium tripolyphosphate, skip brining in step 1 and increase the salt to ½ teaspoon in step 3. Serve with crusty bread.

- 2 tablespoons sugar
- Table salt and pepper
- 1 pound large shell-on shrimp (26 to 30 per pound), peeled, deveined (see page 523), and tails removed, shells reserved
- ¼ cup extra-virgin olive oil
- 1 onion, chopped fine
- 4 garlic cloves, peeled, halved lengthwise, and sliced thin
- 2 anchovy fillets, rinsed, patted dry, and minced
- ¼ teaspoon red pepper flakes
- 2 (15-ounce) cans cannellini beans (1 can drained and rinsed, 1 can left undrained)
- 1 (14.5-ounce) can diced tomatoes, drained
- ¼ cup shredded fresh basil
- ½ teaspoon grated lemon zest plus 1 tablespoon juice

**1.** Dissolve sugar and 1 tablespoon salt in 1 quart cold water in large container. Submerge shrimp in brine, cover, and refrigerate for 15 minutes. Remove shrimp from brine and pat dry with paper towels.

**2.** Heat 1 tablespoon oil in 12-inch skillet over medium heat until shimmering. Add shrimp shells and cook, stirring frequently, until they begin to turn spotty brown and skillet starts to brown, 5 to 6 minutes. Remove skillet from heat and carefully add 1 cup water. When bubbling subsides, return skillet to medium heat and simmer gently, stirring occasionally, for 5 minutes. Strain mixture through colander set over large bowl. Discard shells and reserve liquid (you should have about ¼ cup). Wipe skillet clean with paper towels.

**3.** Heat 2 tablespoons oil, onion, garlic, anchovies, pepper flakes, ¼ teaspoon salt, and ⅛ teaspoon pepper in now-empty skillet over medium-low heat. Cook, stirring occasionally, until onion is softened, about 5 minutes. Add 1 can drained beans, 1 can beans and their liquid, tomatoes, and shrimp stock and bring to simmer. Simmer, stirring occasionally, for 15 minutes.

**4.** Reduce heat to low, add shrimp, cover, and cook, stirring once during cooking, until shrimp are just opaque, 5 to 7 minutes. Remove skillet from heat and stir in basil and lemon zest and juice. Season with salt and pepper to taste. Transfer to serving dish, drizzle with remaining 1 tablespoon oil, and serve.

## Crab and Shrimp Stew

**SERVES** 4 **SEASON 26**

**WHY THIS RECIPE WORKS** This hearty, warming stew is chock-full of sweet crab and tender shrimp, making it a weeknight meal that feels extra special. A quick roux provided body and richness, and a slew of pantry ingredients—including tomato paste, smoked paprika, and Old Bay Seasoning—made the broth pop. Cooking the shrimp gently in the last few minutes ensured it stayed tender. Salt amounts in seafood stock vary brand to brand so be sure to season the stew with salt and pepper to taste before serving. Serve over rice or with crusty bread, if desired.

- 4 tablespoons unsalted butter
- ¼ cup all purpose flour
- 1 small onion, chopped fine
- 2 celery ribs, thinly sliced
- 1 small green bell pepper, chopped fine
- 1 teaspoon table salt, divided
- 2 tablespoons tomato paste
- 4 garlic cloves, minced
- 1 teaspoon smoked paprika
- 1 teaspoon Old Bay Seasoning
- 1 teaspoon dried thyme
- ¼ teaspoon cayenne pepper
- 2 bay leaves
- 4 cups seafood stock
- 1 (14.5-ounce) can diced tomatoes
- 8 ounces large shrimp (26 to 30 per pound), peeled and deveined (see page 523)
- 8 ounces lump crabmeat, picked over for shells
- 2 tablespoons chopped fresh parsley
- 1 tablespoon lemon juice, plus lemon wedges for serving
- 1 tablespoon Worcestershire sauce
- Hot sauce

**1.** Melt butter in Dutch oven over medium heat. Sprinkle flour over top, reduce heat to medium-low, and cook, stirring constantly until flour is color of cinnamon, about 10 minutes.

**2.** Stir in onion, celery, bell pepper, and ½ teaspoon salt and increase heat to medium. Cook, stirring often, until vegetables are softened, about 8 minutes. Stir in tomato paste, garlic, paprika, Old Bay, thyme, cayenne and bay leaves. Cook until fragrant, about 2 minutes. Stir in seafood stock, tomatoes and their juice, and remaining ½ teaspoon salt. Bring to vigorous simmer, then reduce heat to medium-low and simmer until thickened slightly, about 20 minutes.

**3.** Stir in shrimp and crab, increase heat to medium-high and return to brief simmer, then remove from heat and let sit until shrimp are opaque throughout, about 5 minutes. Remove bay leaves. Stir in parsley, lemon juice and Worcestershire and season with salt and pepper to taste. Serve with lemon wedges and hot sauce.

## Broccoli-Cheese Soup

**SERVES** 6 to 8

**WHY THIS RECIPES WORKS** We were after a soup with pure broccoli flavor that wasn't hiding behind the cream or the cheese. Overcooked broccoli has a sulfurous flavor, but we discovered when we cooked our broccoli beyond the point of just overcooked—for a full hour—those sulfur-containing compounds broke down, leaving behind intense, nutty broccoli. Its texture was fairly soft, but that was perfect for use in a soup. Adding baking soda to the pot sped up the process, shortening the broccoli's cooking time to a mere 20 minutes. A little spinach lent bright green color to the soup without taking over the flavor. After adding cheddar and Parmesan, we had a soup so full of flavor and richness that it didn't even need the typical cream. Serve with Buttery Croutons (page 114), if desired. To make a vegetarian version of this soup, substitute vegetable broth for the chicken broth.

- 2 tablespoons unsalted butter
- 2 pounds broccoli, florets chopped into 1-inch pieces, stems peeled and sliced ¼ inch thick
- 1 onion, chopped coarse
- 2 garlic cloves, minced
- 1½ teaspoons dry mustard
- 1 teaspoon table salt
- Pinch cayenne pepper
- 3–4 cups water, divided
- ¼ teaspoon baking soda
- 2 cups chicken broth
- 2 ounces baby spinach (about 2 cups)
- 3 ounces sharp cheddar cheese, shredded (¾ cup)
- 1½ ounces Parmesan cheese, grated fine (¾ cup), plus extra for serving

**1.** Melt butter in Dutch oven over medium-high heat. Add broccoli, onion, garlic, mustard, salt, and cayenne and cook, stirring frequently, until fragrant, about 6 minutes. Add 1 cup water and baking soda. Bring to simmer, cover, and cook until broccoli is very soft, about 20 minutes, stirring once during cooking.

**2.** Add broth and 2 cups water and increase heat to medium-high. When mixture begins to simmer, stir in spinach and cook until wilted, about 1 minute. Transfer half of soup to blender, add cheddar and Parmesan, and process until smooth, about 1 minute. Transfer soup to medium bowl and repeat with remaining soup. Return soup to Dutch oven, place over medium heat and bring to simmer. Adjust consistency of soup with up to 1 cup water. Season with salt and pepper to taste. Serve, passing extra Parmesan.

## Silky Butternut Squash Soup

**SERVES** 4 to 6

**WHY THIS RECIPE WORKS** The best butternut squash soup strikes a perfect balance between nuttiness and sweetness. Getting that balance right depends on selecting just a few key ingredients so the sweet squash flavor can take center stage. We found our answer to intense squash flavor in the squash's seeds and fibers. We sautéed them with shallots and butter, simmered them in water, and then used the liquid to steam the unpeeled quartered squash. Once the squash had cooled, we scooped out the flesh and pureed it with the steaming liquid for a perfectly smooth texture. Dark brown sugar intensified the sweetness of the squash. Finally, we enriched the soup with heavy cream and a pinch of nutmeg to round out the rich flavors. Lightly toasted pumpkin seeds, croutons, drizzles of balsamic vinegar, or sprinklings of paprika or cracked black pepper make appealing accompaniments to this soup.

- 4 tablespoons unsalted butter
- 1 large shallot, minced (about ¼ cup)
- 3 pounds butternut squash (about 1 large squash), cut in half lengthwise, each half cut in half widthwise; seeds and fibers scraped out and reserved
- 6 cups water
- 1½ teaspoons table salt
- ½ cup heavy cream
- 1 teaspoon dark brown sugar
- Pinch grated nutmeg

**1.** Melt butter in Dutch oven over medium-low heat. Add shallot and cook, stirring frequently, until translucent, about 3 minutes. Add seeds and fibers from squash and cook, stirring occasionally, until butter turns saffron color, about 4 minutes.

**2.** Add water and salt to pot and bring to boil over high heat. Reduce heat to medium-low, place squash, cut side down, in steamer basket, and lower basket into pot. Cover and steam until squash is completely tender, about 30 minutes. Take pot off heat and use tongs to transfer squash to rimmed baking sheet. When cool enough to handle, use large spoon to scrape flesh from skin. Reserve squash flesh in bowl and discard skin.

**3.** Strain steaming liquid through fine-mesh strainer into second bowl; discard solids in strainer. (You should have 2½ to 3 cups liquid.) Rinse and dry pot.

**4.** Working in batches and filling blender jar only halfway for each batch, puree squash, adding enough reserved steaming liquid to obtain smooth consistency. Transfer puree to clean pot and stir in remaining steaming liquid, cream, and brown sugar. Warm soup over medium-low heat until hot, about 3 minutes. Stir in nutmeg, season with salt to taste, and serve. (Soup can be refrigerated in airtight container for up to 2 days. Warm over low heat until hot; do not boil.)

## Soeupa alla Valpellinentze (Savoy Cabbage Soup with Ham, Rye Bread, and Fontina)

**SERVES** 6 to 8

**WHY THIS RECIPE WORKS** High in the Italian Alps, the dish known as soeupa alla valpellinentze features a decadent combination of rich beef broth, pancetta, cabbage, rye bread, and nutty fontina cheese. Savoy cabbage is the regional favorite, and its subtly sweet flavor worked beautifully with the earthy rye bread, which we dried in the oven. We built flavor and tenderized the cabbage by braising it with pancetta, onion, bay leaf, and beef broth before layering it in a casserole dish with the stale bread. The topping of cheese turned appealingly bubbly under the broiler. Any type of hearty rye bread will work well here. You will need a 13 by 9-inch broiler-safe baking dish for this recipe.

- 12 ounces hearty rye bread, cut into 1½-inch pieces
- 2 tablespoons extra-virgin olive oil
- 1 tablespoon unsalted butter
- 4 ounces pancetta, chopped fine
- 1 onion, halved and sliced thin
- ½ teaspoon table salt
- 3 garlic cloves, minced
- 1 head savoy cabbage (1½ pounds), cored and cut into 1-inch pieces
- 4 cups beef broth
- 2 bay leaves
- 4 ounces fontina cheese, shredded (1 cup)
- 1 tablespoon chopped fresh parsley

**1.** Adjust oven rack to middle position and heat oven to 250 degrees. Spread bread in even layer on rimmed baking sheet and bake, stirring occasionally, until dried and crispy throughout, about 45 minutes; let croutons cool completely.

2. Heat oil and butter in Dutch oven over medium-low heat until butter is melted. Add pancetta and cook until browned and fat is rendered, about 8 minutes. Stir in onion and salt and cook over medium heat until softened and lightly browned, 5 to 7 minutes. Stir in garlic and cook until fragrant, about 30 seconds.

3. Stir in cabbage, broth, and bay leaves and bring to boil. Reduce heat to low, cover, and simmer until cabbage is tender, about 45 minutes.

4. Adjust oven rack 6 inches from broiler element and heat broiler. Discard bay leaves. Spread half of cabbage mixture evenly in bottom of 13 by 9-inch broiler-safe baking dish, then top with half of croutons. Repeat with remaining cabbage mixture and croutons. Gently press down on croutons with rubber spatula until thoroughly saturated. Sprinkle fontina over top and broil until melted and spotty brown, about 4 minutes. Sprinkle with parsley and serve.

## Carrot-Ginger Soup

**SERVES** 6

---

**WHY THIS RECIPE WORKS** The coupling of sweet carrots and pungent ginger has the potential to produce an elegant, flavorful soup. But in most versions, the hapless addition of other vegetables, fruits, or dairy makes it difficult to truly taste the starring flavors. We wanted to bring this soup to its full potential and produce a version with a smooth, silken texture and pure, clean flavors. For unadulterated carrot flavor, we used water in place of vegetable broth. Swapping ¾ cup of carrot juice for some of the water and stirring in another ¾ cup right before serving gave us intense carrot flavor. We also used peeled and sliced carrots; the earthy, sweet cooked carrots and the bright, raw carrot juice provided a well-balanced depth of flavor. To amp up ginger flavor, we used a combination of fresh and crystallized ginger. For a silky consistency, we added just ½ teaspoon baking soda, which helped to break down the cell walls of the carrots for a soup that was downright velvety. As finishing touches, a sprinkle of fresh chives and a swirl of sour cream provided subtle onion flavor and mild tang while crisp, Buttery Croutons (recipe follows) provided textural contrast.

- 2 tablespoons unsalted butter
- 2 onions, chopped fine
- ¼ cup minced crystallized ginger
- 1 tablespoon grated fresh ginger
- 2 garlic cloves, peeled and smashed
- Table salt and pepper
- 1 teaspoon sugar
- 2 pounds carrots, peeled and sliced ¼ inch thick
- 4 cups water
- 1½ cups carrot juice
- 2 sprigs fresh thyme
- ½ teaspoon baking soda
- 1 tablespoon cider vinegar
- Chopped chives
- Sour cream

1. Melt butter in large saucepan over medium heat. Add onions, crystallized ginger, fresh ginger, garlic, 2 teaspoons salt, and sugar; cook, stirring frequently, until onions are softened but not browned, 5 to 7 minutes.

2. Increase heat to high; add carrots, water, ¾ cup carrot juice, thyme sprigs, and baking soda and bring to simmer. Reduce heat to medium-low and simmer, covered, until carrots are very tender, 20 to 25 minutes.

3. Discard thyme sprigs. Working in batches, process soup in blender until smooth, 1 to 2 minutes. Return soup to clean pot and stir in vinegar and remaining ¾ cup carrot juice. (Soup can be refrigerated for up to 4 days.) Return to simmer over medium heat and season with salt and pepper to taste. Serve with sprinkle of chives and dollop of sour cream.

### Buttery Croutons

**MAKES** about 2 cups

- 3 tablespoons unsalted butter
- 1 tablespoon olive oil
- 3 large slices high-quality sandwich bread, cut into ½-inch cubes (about 2 cups)
- Table salt

Heat the butter and oil in a 12-inch skillet over medium heat. When the foaming subsides, add the bread cubes and cook, stirring frequently, until golden brown, about 10 minutes. Transfer the croutons to a paper towel–lined plate and season with salt to taste.

## Cauliflower Soup

**SERVES** 4 to 6

---

**WHY THIS RECIPE WORKS** For a creamy cauliflower soup that tasted first and foremost of cauliflower, we did away with the distractions—no cream, flour, or overpowering seasonings. Cauliflower, simmered until tender, produced a creamy, velvety smooth puree, without the aid of any cream, due to its low insoluble fiber content. For the purest flavor, we cooked it in salted water (instead of broth), skipped the spice rack entirely, and bolstered it with sautéed onion and leek. We added the cauliflower to the simmering water in two stages so our soup offered the grassy flavor of just-cooked cauliflower and the sweeter, nuttier flavor of long-cooked cauliflower. Finally, for a rich garnish, we fried a portion of the florets in butter until both the cauliflower and butter were golden brown and used each as a separate garnish. White wine vinegar may be substituted for the sherry vinegar.

- 1 head cauliflower (2 pounds)
- 8 tablespoons unsalted butter, cut into 1-tablespoon pieces, divided
- 1 leek, white and light green parts only, halved lengthwise, sliced thin, and washed thoroughly (see page 545)
- 1 small onion, halved and sliced thin

1½ teaspoons table salt
4½ cups water
½ teaspoon sherry vinegar
3 tablespoons minced fresh chives

**1.** Pull off outer leaves of cauliflower and trim stem. Using paring knife, cut around core to remove; thinly slice core and reserve. Cut heaping 1 cup of ½-inch florets from head of cauliflower; set aside. Cut remaining cauliflower crosswise into ½-inch-thick slices.

**2.** Melt 3 tablespoons butter in large saucepan over medium-low heat. Add leek, onion, and salt; cook, stirring frequently, until onion is softened but not browned, about 7 minutes.

**3.** Increase heat to medium-high; add water, sliced core, and half of sliced cauliflower; and bring to simmer. Reduce heat to medium-low and simmer gently for 15 minutes. Add remaining sliced cauliflower, return to simmer, and continue to cook until cauliflower is tender and crumbles easily, 15 to 20 minutes longer.

**4.** While soup simmers, melt remaining 5 tablespoons butter in 8-inch skillet over medium heat. Add reserved florets and cook, stirring frequently, until florets are golden brown and butter is browned, 6 to 8 minutes. Remove skillet from heat and use slotted spoon to transfer florets to small bowl. Toss florets with vinegar and season with salt to taste. Pour browned butter in skillet into small bowl and reserve for garnishing.

**5.** Process soup in blender until smooth, about 45 seconds. Rinse out pan. Return pureed soup to pan and return to simmer over medium heat, adjusting consistency with up to ½ cup water as needed (soup should have thick, velvety texture, but should be thin enough to settle with a flat surface after being stirred) and seasoning with salt to taste. Serve, garnishing individual bowls with browned florets, drizzles of browned butter, and chives and seasoning with pepper to taste.

## Fresh Corn Chowder

**SERVES 6** SEASON 26

**WHY THIS RECIPE WORKS** This thick and lush chowder is bursting with fresh corn flavor. While developing our recipe we discovered that a combination of rendered salt pork and butter gave us a better-tasting soup. To pump up the corn flavor, we added grated corn and corn milk (which comes from scraping the cobs with the back of a knife). The grated corn also acted as a thickener. Using chicken broth rather than water as the base gave our chowder better body. And adding the corn kernels at the very end prevented overcooking. Be sure to use salt pork, not fatback, for the chowder. Streaks of lean meat distinguish salt pork from fatback; fatback is pure fat. We prefer Spanish onions for their sweet, mild flavor, but all-purpose yellow onions will work fine too. Use a variety of yellow corn for this soup.

10 ears corn, husks and silks removed
3 ounces salt pork, rind removed, cut into two 1-inch cubes
1 tablespoon unsalted butter
1 large onion, chopped fine
1 teaspoon table salt
2 garlic cloves, minced
3 tablespoons all-purpose flour
3 cups chicken broth
2 cups whole milk
12 ounces red potatoes, unpeeled, cut into ¼-inch cubes
1 teaspoon minced fresh thyme leaves or ¼ teaspoon dried
1 bay leaf
1 cup heavy cream
2 tablespoons minced fresh parsley

**1.** Using chef's knife, cut kernels from 4 ears corn (you should have about 3 cups). Grate kernels from remaining 6 ears on large holes of box grater into bowl, then firmly scrape any pulp remaining on cobs with back of butter knife or vegetable peeler (you should have 2 generous cups kernels and pulp).

**2.** Cook salt pork in Dutch oven over medium-high heat, turning with tongs and pressing down on pieces to render fat, until cubes are crisp and golden brown, about 10 minutes. Reduce heat to low, stir in butter, onion, and 1 teaspoon salt, cover, and cook until onion is softened, about 12 minutes. Remove salt pork and reserve. Add garlic and cook until fragrant, about 1 minute. Whisk in flour and cook, stirring constantly, about 2 minutes. Whisking constantly, gradually add broth. Add milk, potatoes, thyme, bay leaf, grated corn and pulp, and reserved salt pork and bring to boil. Reduce heat to medium-low and simmer until potatoes are almost tender, 8 to 10 minutes. Add reserved corn kernels and heavy cream and return to simmer. Simmer until corn kernels are tender yet still slightly crunchy, about 5 minutes. Discard bay leaf and salt pork. Stir in parsley, season with salt and pepper to taste, and serve immediately.

## Lighter Corn Chowder

SERVES 6

**WHY THIS RECIPE WORKS** We were looking for a corn chowder recipe that was a bit less heavy, but would pack corn flavor in every spoonful. Inspired by a recipe that juiced corn kernels, a trick that delivered pronounced corn flavor, we strained the scrapings and pulp from several cobs through a dish towel to get unadulterated corn juice (when we added the unstrained pulp to the pot, the soup curdled). This delivered the intense corn flavor we were after. We lightened things up by using water as our primary liquid; just 1 cup of half-and-half gave our chowder the right richness. When removing the kernels from the cob make sure to remove only the part of the kernel sticking out of the cob. Cutting deeper will result in too much fibrous material coming off the corn. Yukon Gold potatoes can be substituted for the red potatoes. Minced chives can be used in place of the basil.

- 8 ears corn, husks and silk removed
- 3 tablespoons unsalted butter
- 1 medium onion, chopped fine
- 4 ounces (about 4 slices) bacon, halved lengthwise, then cut crosswise into ¼-inch pieces
- 2 teaspoons minced fresh thyme leaves
- Table salt and ground black pepper
- ¼ cup unbleached all-purpose flour
- 5 cups water
- 12 ounces red potatoes, cut into ½-inch cubes
- 1 cup half-and-half
- Sugar
- 3 tablespoons chopped fresh basil leaves

**1.** Using a chef's knife, cut the kernels from the ears of corn; transfer to a bowl and set aside (you should have 5 to 6 cups). Holding the cobs over a second bowl, use the back of a butter knife to firmly scrape any pulp remaining on the cobs into the bowl (you should have 2 to 2½ cups of pulp). Transfer the pulp to the center of a clean dish towel set in a medium bowl. Wrap the towel tightly around the pulp and squeeze until dry. Discard the pulp in the towel and set the corn juice aside (you should have about ⅔ cup of juice).

**2.** Melt the butter in a Dutch oven over medium heat. Add the onion, bacon, thyme, 2 teaspoons salt, and 1 teaspoon pepper and cook, stirring frequently, until the onion is softened and beginning to brown, 8 to 10 minutes. Stir in the flour and cook, stirring constantly, for 2 minutes. Whisking constantly, gradually add the water and then bring to a boil. Add the corn kernels and the potatoes. Return to a simmer, reduce the heat to medium-low, and cook until the potatoes have softened, 15 to 18 minutes.

**3.** Transfer 2 cups of the chowder to a blender and process until smooth, 1 to 2 minutes. Return the puree to the pot, stir in the half-and-half, and return to a simmer. Remove the pot from the heat and stir in the reserved corn juice. Season with salt, pepper, and up to 1 tablespoon sugar to taste. Sprinkle with the basil and serve.

## Leek, Fennel, and Squash Soup with Sausage

SERVES 4 TO 6 **SEASON 26**

**WHY THIS RECIPE WORKS** The traditional Basque soup called porrusalda, which translates to leek broth, is usually made with lots of leeks, garlic, and winter squash (sometimes even carrot). It is mostly made without any meat, but to enrich it a bit more, many cooks add a couple of pieces of pork rib bones or even chorizo. For our superflavorful interpretation, we added hot Italian sausage to boost the flavor and spiciness of the soup and added white beans to make it a hearty and satisfying one-pot meal. Sweet, earthy kabocha squash added creaminess and body to the soup along with a lovely orange hue. The final texture of the soup relies on the starchiness of the kabocha, but in a pinch you can use butternut squash. You can skip peeling the kabocha squash if you prefer.

- 1 pound hot Italian sausage, casings removed
- 1½ pounds leeks, white and light green parts only, halved lengthwise, cut into ½-inch pieces, and washed thoroughly
- 1 fennel bulb, halved, cored, and cut into ¼-inch pieces
- 4 garlic cloves, peeled and sliced thin
- 1 tablespoon extra-virgin olive oil
- ¼ teaspoon table salt
- 1 bay leaf
- 4 sprigs fresh thyme
- 1½ pounds kabocha squash, peeled, seeded, and cut into 1-inch pieces
- 6 cups chicken broth
- 1 (15-ounce) can cannellini beans, rinsed
- ½ cup finely chopped fresh parsley

**1.** Cook sausage in Dutch oven over medium-high heat until browned, 5 to 7 minutes, breaking up meat with wooden spoon. Use slotted spoon to transfer sausage to plate, leaving fat behind in pot; set sausage aside.

**2.** Add leeks, fennel, garlic, oil, salt, bay leaf, and thyme sprigs to pot. Reduce heat to medium and cook, stirring occasionally, until vegetables are tender and just beginning to brown, about 7 minutes.

**3.** Stir in squash, broth, beans, and sausage, scraping up any browned bits. Cover pot, increase heat to high, and bring soup to vigorous simmer. Reduce heat to medium and simmer vigorously until squash is tender, 20 to 25 minutes, adjusting heat as needed. Remove pot from heat, discard bay leaf and thyme sprigs, and stir in parsley. Season with salt and pepper to taste. Serve.

## Creamy Mushroom Soup

**SERVES** 6 to 8

**WHY THIS RECIPE WORKS** Mushroom soups have great potential, but they often disappoint with their lackluster taste and less-than-stellar texture. We chose to use readily available white mushrooms, which are often underestimated. To bring out their flavor we had to slice them by hand (processing made for uneven and bruised pieces) and then sweat them in a covered pot with butter and shallots; roasted mushrooms were nixed because the juices released during roasting had browned on the pan and were lost, making for flavorless soup. Chicken broth proved a better addition than water for the liquid base, and dried porcini mushrooms amplified the mushroom flavor. After pureeing the soup, we added cream and a splash of Madeira for body. A garnish of sautéed mushrooms adds great appeal to this creamy soup.

- 6 tablespoons (¾ stick) unsalted butter
- 3 large shallots, minced (about ¾ cup)
- 1 medium garlic clove, minced or pressed through a garlic press (about 1 teaspoon)
- ½ teaspoon freshly grated nutmeg
- 2 pounds white mushrooms, wiped clean and sliced ¼ inch thick
- 4 cups hot water
- 3½ cups low-sodium chicken broth
- ½ ounce dried porcini mushrooms, rinsed well
- ⅓ cup Madeira or dry sherry
- 1 cup heavy cream
- 2 teaspoons juice from 1 lemon
- Table salt and ground black pepper
- 1 recipe Sautéed Wild Mushrooms, for garnish

**1.** Melt the butter in a large Dutch oven over medium-low heat. Add the shallots and sauté, stirring frequently, until softened, about 4 minutes. Stir in the garlic and nutmeg and cook until fragrant, about 30 seconds. Increase the heat to medium, add the white mushrooms, and stir to coat with the butter. Cook, stirring occasionally, until the mushrooms release some liquid, about 7 minutes. Reduce the heat to medium-low, cover the pot, and cook, stirring occasionally, until the mushrooms have released all their liquid, about 20 minutes.

**2.** Add the water, chicken broth, and porcini mushrooms. Cover, bring to a simmer, then reduce the heat to low and simmer until the mushrooms are fully tender, about 20 minutes.

**3.** Working in batches, puree the soup in a blender until smooth, filling the blender jar only halfway for each batch. Rinse and dry the pot; return the soup to the pot. Stir in the Madeira and cream and bring to a simmer over low heat. Add the lemon juice and season with salt and pepper to taste. Ladle the soup into bowls, garnish with sautéed wild mushrooms, and serve. (The soup, minus the garnish, can be refrigerated in an airtight container for up to 2 days. Warm over low heat until hot; do not boil.)

### Sautéed Wild Mushrooms

**MAKES** enough to garnish 6 to 8 bowls of soup

- 2 tablespoons unsalted butter
- 8 ounces shiitake, chanterelle, oyster, or cremini mushrooms, stems trimmed and discarded, mushrooms wiped clean and sliced thin
- Table salt and ground black pepper

**1.** Melt the butter in a medium skillet over low heat. Add the mushrooms and season with salt and pepper to taste. Cover and cook, stirring occasionally, until the mushrooms release their liquid, about 10 minutes for shiitakes and chanterelles, about 5 minutes for oysters, and about 9 minutes for cremini.

**2.** Uncover and continue to cook, stirring occasionally, until the liquid released by the mushrooms has evaporated and the mushrooms are browned, about 2 minutes for shiitakes, oysters, and cremini and about 3 minutes for chanterelles. Serve immediately as garnish for the soup.

## Mushroom Bisque

**SERVES** 6 to 10

**WHY THIS RECIPE WORKS** Mushroom bisque should be luxuriously creamy but packed with distinct earthy flavor, so we started with the mushrooms. A combination of white, cremini, and shiitake mushrooms promised the perfect balance of buttery and earthy notes, and microwaving them concentrated their intensity by expelling the excess moisture. We saved the flavorful liquid for later and browned the mushrooms in oil in a Dutch oven. Adding a chopped onion, fresh thyme, and pepper boosted the base's flavors and a splash of sherry elevated the mushrooms' meaty profile. Stirring in the reserved mushroom juices at this point reinforced the fungi's impact. After adding water and broth, we brought the pot to a

simmer, removed the thyme sprig, and blended the mushroom mixture into a creamy bisque with a blender. Taking a tip from Julia Child's recipe, we whisked together cream and egg yolks to form a classic French thickener called a liaison. The yolks contributed the same silkening effect of heavy cream but without dulling or diluting the bisque. A touch of lemon juice at the very end sharpened the flavor to perfection. Tying the thyme sprig with twine makes it easier to remove from the pot. For the smoothest result, use a conventional blender rather than an immersion blender. Our Fried Shallots can replace the garnish of cream and chopped chives.

- 1 pound white mushrooms, trimmed
- 8 ounces cremini mushrooms, trimmed
- 8 ounces shiitake mushrooms, stemmed
- Kosher salt and pepper
- 2 tablespoons vegetable oil
- 1 small onion, chopped fine
- 1 sprig fresh thyme, tied with kitchen twine
- 2 tablespoons dry sherry
- 4 cups water
- 3½ cups chicken broth
- ⅔ cup heavy cream, plus extra for serving
- 2 large egg yolks
- 1 teaspoon lemon juice
- Chopped fresh chives

**1.** Toss white mushrooms, cremini mushrooms, shiitake mushrooms, and 1 tablespoon salt together in large bowl. Cover with large plate and microwave, stirring every 4 minutes, until mushrooms have released their liquid and reduced to about one-third their original volume, about 12 minutes. Transfer mushrooms to colander set in second large bowl and drain well. Reserve liquid.

**2.** Heat oil in Dutch oven over medium heat until shimmering. Add mushrooms and cook, stirring occasionally, until mushrooms are browned and fond has formed on bottom of pot, about 8 minutes. Add onion, thyme sprig, and ¼ teaspoon pepper and cook, stirring occasionally, until onion is just softened, about 2 minutes. Add sherry and cook until evaporated. Stir in reserved mushroom liquid and cook, scraping up any browned bits. Stir in water and broth and bring to simmer. Reduce heat to low and simmer for 20 minutes.

**3.** Discard thyme sprig. Working in batches, process soup in blender until very smooth, 1½ to 2 minutes per batch. Return soup to now-empty pot and bring to simmer over low heat. (Soup can be refrigerated for up to 2 days. Warm to 150 degrees before proceeding with recipe.)

**4.** Whisk cream and egg yolks together in medium bowl. Stirring slowly and constantly, add 2 cups soup to cream mixture. Stirring constantly, slowly pour cream mixture into simmering soup. Heat gently, stirring constantly, until soup registers 165 degrees (do not overheat). Stir in lemon juice and season with salt and pepper to taste. Serve immediately, garnishing each serving with 1 teaspoon extra cream and sprinkle of chives.

### Fried Shallots

MAKES 1 CUP

Once cooled, you can store the shallots in an airtight container at room temperature for up to 3 days. You can strain the oil after cooking the shallots and reserve it for another use.

- ½ cup vegetable oil
- 3 shallots, sliced thin
- Table salt

Cook oil and shallots in medium saucepan over high heat, stirring constantly, until shallots are deep golden, 11 to 13 minutes (they will still be soft; do not overcook). Using slotted spoon, transfer shallots to paper towel–lined plate, season with salt, and let drain and turn crisp, about 5 minutes, before serving.

## Best French Onion Soup

SERVES 6

**WHY THIS RECIPE WORKS** The ideal French onion soup combines a broth redolent of sweet caramelized onions with a slice of toasted baguette and melted cheese. The secret to a rich broth was to caramelize the onions fully. Caramelizing the onions, deglazing the pot, and then repeating this process dozens of times kept ratcheting up the flavor. But this is a laborious process. Fortunately, we found that if we first cooked the onions, covered, in a hot oven, we only needed to deglaze the onions on the stovetop three or four times. Just one type of onion (yellow) was sufficient, but a combination of three different liquids (water, chicken broth, and beef broth) added maximum flavor. For the topping, we toasted the bread before floating it on the soup and added only a modest sprinkling of nutty Gruyère so the broth wasn't overpowered. Sweet onions, such as Vidalia or Walla Walla, will make this dish overly

sweet. Note that the process of caramelizing the onions in step 2 takes 45 to 60 minutes. Use broiler-safe crocks and keep the rims of the bowls 4 to 5 inches from the heating element to obtain a proper gratinée of melted cheese. If using ordinary soup bowls, sprinkle the toasted bread slices with Gruyère and return them to the broiler until the cheese melts, then float them on top of the soup. For the best flavor, make the soup a day or two in advance. Alternatively, prepare the onions through step 1, let cool in the pot, and refrigerate for up to three days before proceeding with the recipe.

**SOUP**

- 3 tablespoons unsalted butter, cut into 3 pieces
- 4 pounds onions, halved and sliced through root end ¼ inch thick
- 1½ teaspoons table salt, divided
- 2 cups water, divided, plus extra for deglazing
- ½ cup dry sherry
- 4 cups chicken broth
- 2 cups beef broth
- 6 sprigs fresh thyme, tied together with kitchen twine
- 1 bay leaf

**CHEESE CROUTONS**

- 1 small baguette, cut on bias into ½-inch slices
- 8 ounces Gruyère cheese, shredded (2 cups)

**1. FOR THE SOUP:** Adjust oven rack to lower-middle position and heat oven to 400 degrees. Generously spray inside of large (at least 7-quart) Dutch oven with vegetable oil spray. Add butter, onions, and 1 teaspoon salt to pot. Cook, covered, for 1 hour (onions will be moist and slightly reduced in volume). Remove pot from oven and stir onions, scraping bottom and sides of pot. Return pot to oven with lid slightly ajar and continue to cook until onions are very soft and golden brown, 1½ to 1¾ hours longer, stirring onions and scraping bottom and sides of pot after 1 hour.

**2.** Carefully remove pot from oven and place over medium-high heat. Cook onions, stirring frequently and scraping bottom and sides of pot, until liquid evaporates and onions brown, 15 to 20 minutes, reducing heat to medium if onions are browning too quickly. Continue to cook, stirring frequently, until pot bottom is coated with dark crust, 6 to 8 minutes, adjusting heat as necessary. (Scrape any browned bits that collect on spoon back into onions.) Stir in ¼ cup water, scraping pot bottom to loosen crust, and cook until water evaporates and pot bottom has formed another dark crust, 6 to 8 minutes. Repeat process of deglazing 2 or 3 more times, until onions are very dark brown. Stir in sherry and cook, stirring frequently, until sherry evaporates, about 5 minutes.

**3.** Stir in 2 cups water, chicken broth, beef broth, thyme sprigs, bay leaf, and remaining ½ teaspoon salt, scraping up any final bits of browned crust on bottom and sides of pot. Increase heat to high and bring to simmer. Reduce heat to low, cover, and simmer for 30 minutes. Discard thyme sprigs and bay leaf, then season with salt and pepper to taste.

**4. FOR THE CROUTONS:** While soup simmers, heat oven to 400 degrees. Arrange baguette slices in single layer on rimmed baking sheet and bake until dry, crisp, and golden at edges, about 10 minutes. Set aside.

**5.** Adjust oven rack 6 inches from broiler element and heat broiler. Set individual broiler-safe crocks on baking sheet and fill each with about 1¾ cups of soup. Top each bowl with 1 or 2 baguette slices (do not overlap slices) and sprinkle evenly with Gruyère. Broil until cheese is melted and bubbly around edges, 3 to 5 minutes. Let cool for 5 minutes; serve.

## Streamlined French Onion Soup

**SERVES 6**

**WHY THIS RECIPE WORKS** Streamlined versions of onion soup often amount to a sad crock of flavorless onions floating in supersalty beef bouillon topped with an oily blob of cheese. We wanted to make a better onion soup but in record time. We cheated from the get-go and created a simple broth with store-bought beef and chicken broths and wine. Red onions were chosen for their subtle complexity and nuance, and for the maximum flavor they offered when caramelized. To prevent the toasted bread slices from getting too soggy, we placed them atop the soup, so only the bottom was submerged. For the cheese, we liked a combination of pungent Swiss cheese topped with subdued Asiago. Tie the parsley and thyme sprigs together with kitchen twine so they will be easy to retrieve from the soup pot. Use broiler-safe crocks and keep the rims of the bowls 4 to 5 inches from the heating element to obtain a proper gratinée of melted, bubbly cheese. If using ordinary soup bowls, top the toasted bread slices with the cheeses as directed in step 3 and return them to the broiler until the cheese melts, then float them on top of the soup.

**SOUP**

- 2 tablespoons unsalted butter
- 3 pounds red onions (about 6 medium), halved pole to pole and sliced crosswise ⅛ inch thick
- Table salt
- 6 cups low-sodium chicken broth
- 1¾ cups beef broth
- ¼ cup dry red wine
- 2 sprigs fresh parsley
- 1 sprig fresh thyme
- 1 bay leaf
- 1 tablespoon balsamic vinegar
- Ground black pepper

**CHEESE CROUTONS**

- 1 small baguette, cut on the bias into ½-inch slices
- 4½ ounces thinly sliced Swiss cheese
- 1½ ounces Asiago cheese, grated (about ¾ cup)

**1. FOR THE SOUP:** Melt the butter in a large Dutch oven over medium-high heat. Add the onions and ½ teaspoon salt and cook, stirring frequently, until the onions are reduced and syrupy and the inside of the pot is coated with a deep brown crust, 30 to 35 minutes. Add the chicken and beef broths, red wine, parsley, thyme, and bay leaf, scraping the pot bottom with a wooden spoon to loosen the browned bits, and bring to a simmer. Simmer to blend the flavors, about 20 minutes; discard the herbs. Stir in the balsamic vinegar and season with salt and pepper to taste. (The cooled soup can be refrigerated in an airtight container for up to 2 days; return to a simmer before finishing the soup with the croutons and cheese.)

**2. FOR THE CROUTONS:** Adjust an oven rack to the upper-middle position and heat the oven to 350 degrees. Arrange the baguette slices on a rimmed baking sheet and bake, turning once, until lightly browned, about 15 minutes. Remove the bread from the oven, carefully adjust an oven rack 6 inches from the broiler element, and heat the broiler.

**3.** Set individual broiler-safe crocks on the baking sheet and fill each with about 1½ cups of the soup. Top each bowl with two baguette slices and divide the Swiss cheese slices, placing them in a single layer, if possible, on the bread; sprinkle with 2 tablespoons of the grated Asiago and broil until the cheese is browned and bubbly around the edges, 7 to 10 minutes. Cool for 5 minutes; serve.

## Creamy Pea Soup

**SERVES** 4 to 6

**WHY THIS RECIPE WORKS** Sweet pea soup is a labor of love—fresh peas are shelled, blanched, cooked with other vegetables, then passed through a sieve. We were after a fuss-free but still elegant version of this special soup. Our goal was a streamlined approach that would produce a soup with silky texture and real pea flavor. Both garden and grocery store peas can be disappointing; fresh pods often reveal tough, starchy pellets that require a significant amount of time spent shelling. Instead, we decided to use frozen peas. For maximum pea flavor, we ground the frozen peas in a food processor before adding them to our simple soup base of chicken broth and shallots. Adding some Boston lettuce leaves gave the soup a wonderfully frothy texture. And a small dose of heavy cream added richness. A few classic croutons are the perfect embellishment to this smooth soup.

- 4 tablespoons (½ stick) unsalted butter
- 4 large shallots, minced (about 1 cup), or 2 medium leeks, white and light green parts chopped fine and rinsed thoroughly (about 1⅓ cups)
- 2 tablespoons unbleached all-purpose flour
- 3½ cups low-sodium chicken broth
- 1½ pounds frozen peas (about 4½ cups), partially thawed at room temperature for 10 minutes
- 12 small leaves Boston lettuce (about 3 ounces), washed and dried
- ½ cup heavy cream
- Table salt and ground black pepper

**1.** Melt the butter in a large saucepan over low heat. Add the shallots and cook, covered, until softened, 8 to 10 minutes, stirring occasionally. Add the flour and cook, stirring constantly, until thoroughly combined, about 30 seconds. Whisking constantly, gradually add the chicken broth. Increase the heat to high and bring to a boil. Reduce the heat to medium-low and simmer for 3 to 5 minutes.

**2.** Meanwhile, process the peas in a food processor until coarsely chopped, about 20 seconds. Add the peas and lettuce to the saucepan. Increase the heat to medium-high, cover, and return to a simmer; cook for 3 minutes. Uncover, reduce the heat to medium-low, and continue to simmer 2 minutes longer.

**3.** Working in batches, puree the soup in a blender until smooth, filling the blender jar only halfway for each batch. Strain the soup through a fine-mesh strainer into a large bowl; discard the solids in the strainer. Rinse and dry the saucepan; return the pureed mixture to the saucepan and stir in the cream. Warm the soup over low heat until hot, about 3 minutes. Season with salt and pepper to taste and serve. (The soup can be refrigerated in an airtight container for up to 2 days. Warm over low heat until hot; do not boil.)

## Rustic Potato-Leek Soup

**SERVES** 6

**WHY THIS RECIPE WORKS** Rustic potato-leek soup often disappoints with soft, mealy potatoes and overcooked leeks. We wanted to perfect this soup so both ingredients would be at their best and the dish would retain its textural integrity and bright flavor. We quickly eliminated potatoes with high or medium starch levels because they broke down too quickly in the chicken broth. Waxy, low-starch red potatoes were perfect—they kept their shape and didn't become waterlogged during cooking. To pump up the flavor we used a substantial amount of leeks and sautéed both the white and light green parts in butter. Leeks and potatoes require different cooking times, so we staggered the cooking—leeks first, then potatoes, and then we removed the pot from the stove so the potatoes could gently cook through in the hot broth without becoming mushy. A bit of flour added with the sautéed leeks gave the broth body. Leeks can vary in size; if your leeks have large white and light green parts, use the smaller amount of leeks.

- 6 tablespoons (¾ stick) unsalted butter
- 4–5 pounds leeks, white and light green parts only, halved lengthwise, sliced crosswise 1 inch thick, and rinsed thoroughly (about 11 cups); (see page 545)
- 1 tablespoon unbleached all-purpose flour
- 5¼ cups low-sodium chicken broth
- 1¾ pounds red potatoes (about 5 medium), peeled and cut into ¾-inch chunks
- 1 bay leaf
- Table salt and ground black pepper

**1.** Melt the butter in a large Dutch oven over medium-low heat. Add the leeks, increase the heat to medium, cover, and cook, stirring occasionally, until the leeks are tender but not mushy, 15 to 20 minutes; do not brown them. Add the flour and cook, stirring constantly, until thoroughly combined, about 2 minutes.

**2.** Increase the heat to high; whisking constantly, gradually add the broth. Add the potatoes and bay leaf, cover, and bring to a boil. Reduce the heat to medium-low and simmer, covered, until the potatoes are almost tender, 5 to 7 minutes. Remove the pot from the heat and let stand, covered, until the potatoes are tender, 10 to 15 minutes. Discard the bay leaf, season with salt and pepper to taste, and serve. (The soup can be refrigerated in an airtight container for up to 2 days. Warm over low heat until hot; do not boil.)

## Ultimate Cream of Tomato Soup

**SERVES** 3 to 4

**WHY THIS RECIPES WORKS** Canned cream of tomato soup is a childhood favorite. We wanted a version for grown-ups, a well-balanced cream of tomato soup, one with rich color, great tomato flavor, and a silky texture. Right away, we turned to canned tomatoes; fresh tomatoes are at their best just a few months out of the year and we didn't want to restrict our soup-making to just one season. To coax the most flavor from our canned whole tomatoes, we roasted them. The intense dry heat concentrated the flavor, and a sprinkling of brown sugar encouraged caramelization. We cooked our roasted tomatoes with shallots, chicken broth, and reserved tomato juice to develop robust flavor, then pureed the tomatoes (with broth) to keep the deep flavor of the tomato broth intact. Finished with heavy cream and a splash of brandy, this soup will satisfy everyone at the table. Make sure to use canned whole tomatoes that are not packed in puree; you will need some of the juice to make the soup.

- 2 (28-ounce) cans whole tomatoes (not packed in puree), drained, 3 cups juice reserved, tomatoes seeded
- 1½ tablespoons dark brown sugar
- 4 tablespoons unsalted butter
- 4 large shallots, minced
- 1 tablespoon tomato paste
- Pinch ground allspice
- 2 tablespoons unbleached all-purpose flour
- 1¾ cups chicken broth
- ½ cup heavy cream
- 2 tablespoons brandy or dry sherry
- Cayenne pepper

**1.** Adjust oven rack to upper-middle position and heat oven to 450 degrees; line rimmed baking sheet with aluminum foil. Spread tomatoes in single layer on foil, and sprinkle evenly with brown sugar. Bake until all liquid has evaporated and tomatoes begin to color, about 30 minutes. Let tomatoes cool slightly, then peel them off foil; transfer to small bowl and set aside.

**2.** Heat butter over medium heat in medium nonreactive saucepan until foaming; add shallots, tomato paste, and allspice. Reduce heat to low, cover, and cook, stirring occasionally, until shallots are softened, 7 to 10 minutes. Add flour and cook, stirring constantly, until thoroughly combined, about 30 seconds. Whisking constantly, gradually add broth; stir in reserved tomato juice and roasted tomatoes. Cover, increase heat to medium, and bring to boil; reduce heat to low and simmer, stirring occasionally, to blend flavors, about 10 minutes.

**3.** Strain mixture through fine-mesh strainer set over medium bowl. Process solids from strainer and 1 cup strained liquid in blender until smooth, 1 to 2 minutes. (Soup can be refrigerated for up to 3 days or frozen for up to 2 months. Reheat over low heat before proceeding with step 4.)

**4.** Return pureed mixture and remaining strained liquid to clean saucepan. Stir in cream and heat over low heat until hot, about 3 minutes. Off heat, stir in brandy. Season with salt and cayenne to taste, and serve.

## Creamless Creamy Tomato Soup

**SERVES 6**

**WHY THIS RECIPE WORKS** Creamy tomato soup boasts a bright, sweet tomato flavor when done right, but not everyone is a fan of rich cream soups. Our first step was to choose canned tomatoes over fresh tomatoes—canned are simply more consistent in flavor than your average supermarket tomato. We mashed whole tomatoes (preferred over diced or crushed for their concentrated flavor) with a potato masher, then combined them with aromatics sautéed in extra-virgin olive oil, not butter, which guaranteed bright, clean flavor. Stirring in some olive oil before pureeing our soup added back vital flavor that was lost when we cooked the oil. To combat the acid in the tomatoes, we added full-flavored brown sugar. And for an ultra-creamy texture without the cream, we pureed sandwich bread into the soup. For a final touch, we stirred chicken broth into the pot and simmered the soup briefly to give our the soup a velvety feel. If half of the soup fills your blender more than halfway, process the soup in three batches, but do not add more olive oil for the third batch. You can also use a hand-held blender to process the soup directly in the pot. Serve this soup topped with Buttery Croutons (page 114), if desired. For an even smoother soup, strain the pureed mixture through a fine-mesh strainer before stirring in the chicken broth in step 2.

- ¼ cup extra-virgin olive oil, plus extra for drizzling
- 1 medium onion, chopped medium
- 3 medium garlic cloves, minced or pressed through a garlic press (about 1 tablespoon)
- Pinch red pepper flakes (optional)
- 1 bay leaf
- 2 (28-ounce) cans whole tomatoes
- 3 slices high-quality white sandwich bread, crusts removed, torn into 1-inch pieces
- 1 tablespoon brown sugar
- 2 cups low-sodium chicken broth
- 2 tablespoons brandy (optional)
- Table salt and ground black pepper
- ¼ cup chopped fresh chives

**1.** Heat 2 tablespoons of the oil in a large Dutch oven over medium-high heat until shimmering. Add the onion, garlic, red pepper flakes (if using), and bay leaf. Cook, stirring frequently, until the onion is translucent, 3 to 5 minutes. Stir in the tomatoes with their juice. Using a potato masher, mash until no pieces bigger than 2 inches remain. Stir in the bread and sugar and bring the soup to a boil. Reduce the heat to medium and cook, stirring occasionally, until the bread is completely saturated and starts to break down, about 5 minutes. Remove and discard the bay leaf.

**2.** Transfer half of the soup to a blender. Add 1 tablespoon more oil and process until the soup is smooth and creamy, 2 to 3 minutes. Transfer to a large bowl and repeat with the remaining soup and the remaining 1 tablespoon oil. Rinse and dry the Dutch oven and return the soup to the pot. Stir in the

chicken broth and brandy (if using). Return the soup to a boil and season with salt and pepper to taste. Ladle the soup into bowls, sprinkle with the chopped chives, drizzle with olive oil, and serve. (The soup, minus the garnish, can be refrigerated in an airtight container for up to 2 days. Warm over low heat until hot; do not boil. Garnish with Candied Bacon Bits or Maple Sour Cream.

## Sweet Potato Soup

**SERVES** 4 to 6 as a main dish or 8 as a starter

**WHY THIS RECIPE WORKS** The secrets to a creamy sweet potato soup are to use the peels and turn off the heat. Most recipes call for so many other ingredients that the sweet potato flavor ends up muted and overpowered. By cutting back to shallot, thyme, and butter and using water instead of broth, we put the focus on the main ingredient. For extra earthiness, we also pureed some of the potato skins into the soup. However, the real key to intensifying the sweet potato flavor was to use only a minimal amount of flavor-diluting water. To do so, we let the sweet potatoes sit in hot water off heat to make use of an enzyme that converts their starch content to sugar. Less starch meant we could create a soup with less water, keeping the sweet potato flavor in the forefront. To highlight the earthiness of the sweet potatoes, we incorporate a quarter of the skins into the soup. In addition to the chives, serve the soup with Candied Bacon Bits and Maple Sour Cream (recipes follow). The garnishes can be prepared during step 1 while the sweet potatoes stand in the water.

- 4 tablespoons unsalted butter
- 1 shallot, sliced thin
- 4 sprigs fresh thyme
- 4¼ cups water, plus extra as needed
- 2 pounds sweet potatoes, peeled, halved lengthwise, and sliced ¼ inch thick, ¼ of peels reserved

1 tablespoon packed brown sugar
½ teaspoon cider vinegar
Table salt and pepper
Minced fresh chives

**1.** Melt butter in large saucepan over medium-low heat. Add shallot and thyme sprigs and cook until shallot is softened but not browned, about 5 minutes. Add water, increase heat to high, and bring to simmer. Remove pot from heat, add sweet potatoes and reserved peels, and let stand uncovered for 20 minutes.

**2.** Add sugar, vinegar, 1½ teaspoons salt, and ¼ teaspoon pepper. Bring to simmer over high heat. Reduce heat to medium-low, cover, and cook until potatoes are very soft, about 10 minutes.

**3.** Discard thyme sprigs. Working in batches, process soup in blender until smooth, 45 to 60 seconds. Return soup to clean pot. Bring to simmer over medium heat, adjusting consistency with extra water if desired. Season with salt and pepper to taste. Serve, topping each portion with sprinkle of chives.

### Candied Bacon Bits

**MAKES** about ¼ cup

Break up any large chunks before serving.

4 slices bacon, cut into ½-inch pieces
2 teaspoons packed dark brown sugar
½ teaspoon cider vinegar

Cook bacon in 10-inch nonstick skillet over medium heat until crisp and well rendered, 6 to 8 minutes. Using slotted spoon, remove bacon from skillet and discard fat. Return bacon to skillet and add brown sugar and vinegar. Cook over low heat, stirring constantly, until bacon is evenly coated. Transfer to plate in single layer. Let bacon cool completely.

### Maple Sour Cream

**MAKES** ⅓ cup

Maple balances the sweet potatoes' earthiness.

⅓ cup sour cream
1 tablespoon maple syrup

Combine ingredients in bowl.

#### PUTTING PEELS TO WORK

Instead of discarding the sweet potato peels, we add a small quantity of them into our soup before blending to take advantage of an earthy-tasting compound they contain called methoxypyrazine.

## Super Greens Soup with Lemon-Tarragon Cream

**SERVES** 4 to 6

**WHY THIS RECIPE WORKS** We wanted a deceptively delicious, silky-smooth soup that delivered a big dose of healthy greens. First, we built a flavorful foundation of sweet caramelized onions and earthy sautéed mushrooms. We added broth, water, and lots of leafy greens (we liked a mix of chard, kale, arugula, and parsley), and simmered until the greens became tender before blending them smooth. We were happy with the soup's depth of flavor, but it was watery and too thin. Many recipes we found used potatoes as a thickener, but they lent an overwhelmingly earthy flavor. Instead, we used Arborio rice: The rice's high starch content thickened the soup to a velvety, lush consistency without clouding its bright, vegetal flavors. For a vibrant finish, we whisked together heavy cream, sour cream, lemon zest, lemon juice, and tarragon and drizzled it over the top. Our favorite brand of Arborio rice is RiceSelect.

¼ cup heavy cream
3 tablespoons sour cream
½ teaspoon plus 2 tablespoons extra-virgin olive oil, divided
1¼ teaspoons table salt, divided
½ teaspoon minced fresh tarragon
¼ teaspoon finely grated lemon zest plus ½ teaspoon juice
1 onion, halved through root end and sliced thin
¾ teaspoon light brown sugar
3 ounces white mushrooms, trimmed and sliced thin
2 garlic cloves, minced
Pinch cayenne pepper
3 cups water
3 cups vegetable broth
⅓ cup Arborio rice
12 ounces Swiss chard, stemmed and chopped coarse
9 ounces kale, stemmed and chopped coarse
¼ cup fresh parsley leaves
2 ounces (2 cups) baby arugula

1. Combine cream, sour cream, ½ teaspoon oil, ¼ teaspoon salt, tarragon, and lemon zest and juice in bowl. Cover and refrigerate until ready to serve.

2. Heat remaining 2 tablespoons oil in Dutch oven over medium-high heat until shimmering. Stir in onion, sugar, and remaining 1 teaspoon salt and cook, stirring occasionally, until onion releases some moisture, about 5 minutes. Reduce heat to low and cook, stirring often and scraping up any browned bits, until onion is deeply browned and slightly sticky, about 30 minutes. (If onion is sizzling or scorching, reduce heat. If onion is not browning after 15 to 20 minutes, increase heat.)

3. Stir in mushrooms and cook until they have released their moisture, about 5 minutes. Stir in garlic and cayenne and cook until fragrant, about 30 seconds. Stir in water, broth, and rice, scraping up any browned bits, and bring to boil. Reduce heat to low, cover, and simmer for 15 minutes.

4. Stir in chard, kale, and parsley, 1 handful at a time, until wilted and submerged in liquid. Return to simmer, cover, and cook until greens are tender, about 10 minutes.

5. Off heat, stir in arugula until wilted. Working in batches, process soup in blender until smooth, about 1 minute per batch. Return pureed soup to clean pot and season with salt and pepper to taste. Drizzle individual portions with lemon-tarragon cream and serve.

## Classic Gazpacho

**SERVES** 8 to 10

**WHY THIS RECIPE WORKS** Spain's famous chilled soup, gazpacho, boasts bright flavors, distinct pieces of vegetables, and a bracing tomato broth. But gazpacho can be grainy with the addition of too much bread (a common thickener) or watery from an abundance of macerated vegetables. We were after a chunky gazpacho that was well seasoned with vibrant tomato flavor. We had to figure out the best method for preparing the vegetables. Although it was a breeze to use, the blender broke down our vegetables beyond recognition. Next, we tried the food processor, but even this machine pulverized some of our tomatoes, and the resulting soup was closer to a slushie than a good gazpacho. For the best texture, we had to chop the vegetables by hand. Tomatoes are the star player in this dish, and early on we decided that full, ripe beefsteaks were the best option. As for peppers, we preferred red over green for their sweeter flavor. Onion and garlic are usually too overpowering in gazpacho, so we kept to modest levels. A combination of tomato juice and ice cubes—to help chill the soup—provided the right amount of liquid for our broth. And instead of using bread as a thickener, we saved it to make croutons. Now our gazpacho was nice and chunky, and brightly flavored. This recipe makes a large quantity, but it can be easily halved if you prefer. Traditionally, the same vegetables used in the soup are also used as garnish. If that appeals to you, cut additional vegetables while you prepare those called for in the recipe. Other garnish possibilities include Garlic Croutons (recipe follows), chopped pitted black olives, chopped Foolproof Hard-Cooked Eggs (page 147), and finely diced avocado.

- 3 medium ripe beefsteak tomatoes (about 1½ pounds), cored and cut into ¼-inch cubes (about 4 cups)
- 2 medium red bell peppers (about 1 pound), stemmed, seeded, and cut into ¼-inch cubes (about 2 cups)
- 2 small cucumbers (about 1 pound), one peeled and the other with skin on, both seeded and cut into ¼-inch cubes (about 2 cups)
- ½ small sweet onion (such as Vidalia, Maui, or Walla Walla) or 2 large shallots, minced (about ½ cup)
- 2 medium garlic cloves, minced or pressed through a garlic press (about 2 teaspoons)
- ⅓ cup sherry vinegar
- Table salt and ground black pepper
- 5 cups tomato juice
- 8 ice cubes
- 1 teaspoon hot pepper sauce (optional)
- Extra-virgin olive oil, for serving

1. Combine the tomatoes, peppers, cucumbers, onion, garlic, vinegar, 2 teaspoons salt, and pepper to taste in a large (at least 4-quart) nonreactive bowl. Let stand until the vegetables just begin to release their juices, about 5 minutes. Stir in the tomato juice, ice cubes, and hot pepper sauce (if using). Cover tightly and refrigerate to blend flavors, at least 4 hours and up to 2 days.

2. Season with salt and pepper to taste and remove and discard any unmelted ice cubes. Serve cold, drizzling each portion with about 1 teaspoon olive oil and topping with the desired garnishes.

### Garlic Croutons

**MAKES** about 3 cups

- 3 tablespoons extra-virgin olive oil
- 3 medium garlic cloves, minced or pressed through a garlic press (about 1 tablespoon)
- ¼ teaspoon table salt
- 6 slices high-quality white sandwich bread, cut into ½-inch cubes (about 3 cups)

1. Adjust an oven rack to the middle position and heat the oven to 350 degrees. Combine the oil, garlic, and salt in a small bowl; let stand 20 minutes, then pour through a fine-mesh strainer into a medium bowl. Discard the garlic. Add the bread cubes to the bowl with the oil and toss to coat.

2. Spread the bread cubes in an even layer on a rimmed baking sheet and bake, stirring occasionally, until golden, about 15 minutes. Cool on the baking sheet to room temperature. (The croutons can be stored in an airtight container or a plastic bag for up to 1 day.)

## Creamy Gazpacho Andaluz

**SERVES** 4 to 6

**WHY THIS RECIPE WORKS** In the States, the classic "liquid salsa" style of gazpacho reigns supreme. But in Spain, the birthplace of gazpacho, a variety of styles abound. The most popular type by far comes from Andalusia, the southernmost region of the country. It starts with the same vegetables as its chunky cousin, but is blended with bread to give it some body. The result is a creamy, complex soup. But unless you have fresh, flavorful vegetables, in particular fresh, ripe tomatoes, this soup can be unremarkable and bland. So how could we ensure a flavorful gazpacho using supermarket tomatoes? In a word, salt. Salting gave even mid-winter tomatoes a deep, full flavor. Figuring the same process could improve the cucumbers, onions, and bell peppers, we salted them as well. To maximize the flavor of our soup even more, we soaked the bread in the vegetables' exuded liquid. With a garnish of chopped vegetables, fresh herbs, and drizzles of extra-virgin olive oil and sherry vinegar, this Spanish classic can be enjoyed any time of the year. For ideal flavor, allow the gazpacho to sit in the refrigerator overnight. Serve the soup with additional extra-virgin olive oil, sherry vinegar, ground black pepper, and the reserved diced vegetables. Red wine vinegar can be substituted for the sherry vinegar. Although we prefer kosher salt in this soup, half the amount of table salt can be used.

- 3 pounds (about 6 medium) ripe tomatoes, cored
- 1 small cucumber, peeled, halved, and seeded
- 1 medium green bell pepper, halved, cored, and seeded
- 1 small red onion, peeled and halved
- 2 medium garlic cloves, peeled and quartered
- 1 small serrano chile, stemmed and halved lengthwise
- Kosher salt
- 1 slice high-quality white sandwich bread, crust removed, torn into 1-inch pieces
- ½ cup extra-virgin olive oil, plus extra for serving
- 2 tablespoons sherry vinegar, plus extra for serving
- 2 tablespoons finely minced parsley, chives, or basil leaves
- Ground black pepper

1. Roughly chop 2 pounds of the tomatoes, half of the cucumber, half of the bell pepper, and half of the onion and place in a large bowl. Add the garlic, chile, and 1½ teaspoons salt; toss until well combined. Set aside.

2. Cut the remaining tomatoes, cucumber, and pepper into ¼-inch dice; place the vegetables in a medium bowl. Mince the remaining onion and add to the diced vegetables. Toss with ½ teaspoon salt and transfer to a fine-mesh strainer set over a medium bowl. Set aside for 1 hour.

3. Transfer the drained diced vegetables to a medium bowl and set aside. Add the bread pieces to the exuded liquid (there should be about ¼ cup) and soak for 1 minute. Add the soaked bread and any remaining liquid to the roughly chopped vegetables and toss thoroughly to combine.

4. Transfer half of the vegetable-bread mixture to a blender and process for 30 seconds. With the blender running, slowly drizzle in ¼ cup of the oil and continue to blend until completely smooth, about 2 minutes. Strain the soup through a fine-mesh strainer into a large bowl, using the back of a ladle or rubber spatula to press the soup through the strainer. Repeat with the remaining vegetable-bread mixture and ¼ cup more olive oil.

5. Stir the vinegar, parsley, and half of the diced vegetables into the soup and season with salt and pepper to taste. Cover and refrigerate overnight or for at least 2 hours to chill completely and develop the flavors. Serve, passing the remaining diced vegetables, olive oil, vinegar, and pepper separately.

## Mulligatawny Soup

**SERVES** 6 to 8

**WHY THIS RECIPE WORKS** Originating in India and adapted to suit British tastes, mulligatawny soup is mildly spicy and richly flavored, with a number of spices in its lineup. We wanted an elegant, but potent, rendition of this classic soup—nothing thin or raw-tasting. Chicken broth proved to be the best base for this pureed vegetable-laden soup; beef broth was too strong and vegetable broth gave us an overly vegetal soup. For the spices, good-quality curry powder is a must, and a little cumin and cayenne pepper made for the perfect spice mix. Garlic, ginger, and coconut were a given—essentials in mulligatawny—but the best way to incorporate them wasn't immediately clear. We ended up adopting a technique common in Indian cooking—we pureed the raw garlic and ginger with water so that they could be mixed into the soup for fresh bites of garlic and ginger. The best source for true coconut flavor turned out to be shredded unsweetened coconut. Finally, to give the finished soup the right amount of body, we made a roux with our aromatics and pureed the soup with a banana, which imparted a rich, sweet flavor to the dish (a potato worked fine, too). A swirl of yogurt and sprinkling of cilantro were the crowning touches on our richly spiced, velvety mulligatawny. Leave the garlic and ginger puree from step 1 in the blender while making the soup; when the finished soup is pureed in the same blender, it will pick up a hit of spicy raw garlic and ginger. For a heartier soup, stir in cooked white rice.

- 4 medium garlic cloves, 2 peeled and 2 minced or pressed through a garlic press
- 1½ tablespoons minced or grated fresh ginger
- ¼ cup water
- 3 tablespoons unsalted butter
- 2 medium onions, chopped medium
- 1 teaspoon tomato paste
- ½ cup shredded unsweetened coconut
- ¼ cup unbleached all-purpose flour
- 1½ tablespoons curry powder
- 1 teaspoon ground cumin
- ¼ teaspoon cayenne pepper
- 7 cups low-sodium chicken broth
- 2 medium carrots, peeled and chopped medium
- 1 celery rib, chopped medium
- 1 medium very ripe banana (about 5 ounces), peeled, or 1 medium red potato (about 5 ounces), peeled and cut into 1-inch chunks
- Table salt and ground black pepper
- Plain yogurt
- 2 tablespoons minced fresh cilantro leaves

**1.** Puree the 2 peeled whole garlic cloves, 2 teaspoons of the ginger, and the water in a blender until smooth; leave the mixture in the blender and set aside.

**2.** Melt the butter in a large Dutch oven over medium heat. Add the onions and tomato paste and cook, stirring frequently, until the onions are softened and beginning to brown, about 3 minutes. Stir in the coconut and cook until fragrant, about 1 minute. Add the minced garlic, the remaining 2½ teaspoons ginger, the flour, curry powder, cumin, and cayenne; stir until evenly combined, about 1 minute. Whisking constantly, gradually add the chicken broth.

**3.** Add the carrots, celery, and banana to the pot. Increase the heat to medium-high and bring to a boil. Cover, reduce the heat to low, and simmer until the vegetables are tender, about 20 minutes.

**4.** Working in batches, puree the soup in the blender with the garlic and ginger until smooth, filling the blender jar only halfway for each batch. Wash and dry the pot. Return the pureed soup to the pot and season with salt and pepper to taste. Warm the soup over medium heat until hot, about 1 minute. Ladle the soup into bowls, spoon a dollop of yogurt into each bowl, sprinkle with the cilantro, and serve. (The soup, minus the garnishes, can be refrigerated in an airtight container for up to 3 days. Warm over low heat until hot; do not boil.)

## Soupe au Pistou (Provençal Vegetable Soup)

**SERVES 6**

**WHY THIS RECIPES WORKS** Provençal vegetable soup is a classic French summer soup with a delicate broth that is intensified by a dollop of pistou, the French equivalent of Italy's pesto. We wanted a simple version that focused on fresh seasonal vegetables. Leeks, green beans, and zucchini all made the cut; we like their summery flavors, different shapes, and varying shades of green. We added canned white beans (which were far more convenient than dried in this quick-cooking soup) and orecchiette for its easy-to-spoon shape. Using the liquid from the canned beans added much-needed body to the broth. For the pistou, we just whirred basil, Parmesan, olive oil, and garlic together in our food processor. For the best flavor, we prefer broth prepared from our Vegetable Broth Base (page 141), but you can use store-bought broth.

**PISTOU**

- ¾ cup fresh basil leaves
- 1 ounce Parmesan cheese, grated (½ cup)
- ⅓ cup extra-virgin olive oil
- 1 garlic clove, minced

**SOUP**

- 1 tablespoon extra-virgin olive oil
- 1 leek, white and light green parts only, halved lengthwise, sliced ½ inch thick, and washed thoroughly
- 1 celery rib, cut into ½-inch pieces
- 1 carrot, peeled and sliced ¼ inch thick
- ½ teaspoon table salt
- 2 garlic cloves, minced
- 3 cups vegetable broth
- 3 cups water
- ½ cup orecchiette or other short pasta
- 8 ounces haricots verts or green beans, trimmed and cut into ½-inch lengths
- 1 (15-ounce) can cannellini or navy beans, undrained
- 1 small zucchini, halved lengthwise, seeded, and cut into ¼-inch pieces
- 1 large tomato, cored, seeded, and cut into ¼-inch pieces

**1. FOR THE PISTOU:** Process all ingredients in food processor until smooth, scraping down sides of bowl as needed, about 15 seconds. (Pistou can be refrigerated for up to 4 hours.)

**2. FOR THE SOUP:** Heat oil in Dutch oven over medium heat until shimmering. Add leek, celery, carrot, and salt and cook until vegetables are softened, 8 to 10 minutes. Stir in garlic and cook until fragrant, about 30 seconds. Stir in broth and water and bring to simmer.

**3.** Stir in pasta and simmer until slightly softened, about 5 minutes. Stir in haricots verts and simmer until bright green but still crunchy, 3 to 5 minutes. Stir in cannellini beans and their liquid, zucchini, and tomato and simmer until pasta and vegetables are tender, about 3 minutes. Season with salt and pepper to taste. Serve, topping individual portions with generous tablespoon pistou.

## Hearty Minestrone

**SERVES** 6 to 8

---

**WHY THIS RECIPE WORKS** Excellent minestrone soup relies on perfectly ripe vegetables. But we're often stuck with lackluster supermarket offerings. We wanted a soup that squeezed every ounce of flavor out of supermarket vegetables and was as satisfying as minestrone served in Italy. To start, we limited our vegetables to a manageable six: onions, celery, carrots, cabbage, zucchini, and tomato. We began our soup by sautéing some finely diced pancetta in a Dutch oven, then browned the vegetables in the rendered fat, which helped develop sweetness and lent a rich flavor. We decided to use cannellini beans (a favorite for their creamy texture and buttery flavor), which we soaked overnight in salted water to ensure they cooked evenly and turned out well seasoned. We added the soaked beans along with the cooking liquid (and a Parmesan rind) and simmered them together vigorously—this helped the beans release their starch to thicken the soup. Once the beans were tender, we returned the vegetables to the pot and simmered everything together. Rather than using all water, we replaced a portion with chicken broth. But it wasn't until we landed on an unusual addition—V8 juice, rather than canned tomatoes—that our soup boasted consistent tomato flavor in every spoonful. If you are pressed for time you can "quick-brine" your beans. In step 1, combine the salt, water, and beans in a large Dutch oven and bring to a boil over high heat. Remove the pot from the heat, cover, and let stand 1 hour. Drain and rinse the beans and proceed with the recipe. We prefer cannellini beans, but navy or great Northern beans can be used. We prefer pancetta, but bacon can be used in its place. A Parmesan rind is added for flavor, but can be replaced with a 2-inch chunk of the cheese. In order for the starch from the beans to thicken the soup, it is important to maintain a vigorous simmer in step 3.

- Table salt
- ½ pound dried cannellini beans (about 1 cup), rinsed and picked over
- 1 tablespoon extra-virgin olive oil, plus extra for serving
- 3 ounces pancetta, cut into ¼-inch pieces
- 2 medium celery ribs, cut into ½-inch pieces (about ¾ cup)
- 1 medium carrot, peeled and cut into ½-inch pieces (about ¾ cup)
- 2 small onions, peeled and cut into ½-inch pieces (about 1½ cups)
- 1 medium zucchini, trimmed and cut into ½-inch pieces (about 1 cup)
- ½ small head green cabbage, halved, cored, and cut into ½-inch pieces (about 2 cups)
- 2 medium garlic cloves, minced or pressed through a garlic press (about 2 teaspoons)
- ⅛–¼ teaspoon red pepper flakes
- 8 cups water
- 2 cups low-sodium chicken broth
- 1 piece Parmesan cheese rind, about 5 by 2 inches
- 1 bay leaf
- 1½ cups V8 juice
- ½ cup chopped fresh basil leaves
- Ground black pepper
- Grated Parmesan cheese, for serving

**1.** Dissolve 1½ tablespoons salt in 2 quarts cold water in a large bowl or container. Add the beans and soak at room temperature for at least 8 hours and up to 24 hours. Drain the beans and rinse well.

**2.** Heat the oil and pancetta in a large Dutch oven over medium-high heat. Cook, stirring occasionally, until the pancetta is lightly browned and the fat has rendered, 3 to 5 minutes. Add the celery, carrot, onions, and zucchini; cook, stirring frequently, until the vegetables are softened and lightly browned, 5 to 9 minutes. Stir in the cabbage, garlic, ½ teaspoon salt, and red pepper flakes; continue to cook until the cabbage starts to wilt, 1 to 2 minutes longer. Transfer the vegetables to a rimmed baking sheet and set aside.

**3.** Add the soaked beans, water, broth, Parmesan rind, and bay leaf to the now-empty Dutch oven and bring to a boil over high heat. Reduce the heat and vigorously simmer, stirring occasionally, until the beans are fully tender and the liquid begins to thicken, 45 to 60 minutes.

**4.** Add the reserved vegetables and V8 juice to the pot; cook until the vegetables are soft, about 15 minutes. Discard the bay leaf and Parmesan rind, stir in the basil, and season with salt and pepper to taste. Serve with olive oil and grated Parmesan.

## Ciambotta (Italian Vegetable Stew)

**SERVES** 6 to 8

---

**WHY THIS RECIPE WORKS** Italy's ciambotta is a ratatouille-like stew chock-full of veggies that makes for a hearty one-bowl meal with nary a trace of meat. We wanted to avoid the sad fate of some recipes, which end in mushy vegetables drowning in a weak broth. To optimize the texture of the zucchini and peppers, we employed the dry heat of a skillet. To address the broth, we embraced eggplant's natural tendency to fall apart and cooked it until it completely assimilated into a thickened tomato-enriched sauce. Finally, we found that a traditional pestata of garlic and herbs provided the biggest flavor punch when added near the end of cooking. Serve this hearty vegetable stew with crusty bread.

PESTATA

- ⅓ cup chopped fresh basil
- ⅓ cup fresh oregano leaves
- 6 garlic cloves, minced
- 2 tablespoons extra-virgin olive oil
- ¼ teaspoon red pepper flakes

STEW

- 12 ounces eggplant, peeled and cut into ½-inch pieces
  Table salt
- ¼ cup extra-virgin olive oil
- 1 large onion, chopped
- 1 pound russet potatoes, peeled and cut into ½-inch pieces
- 2 tablespoons tomato paste
- 2¼ cups water
- 1 (28-ounce) can whole peeled tomatoes, drained with juice reserved, chopped coarse
- 2 zucchini (8 ounces each), halved lengthwise, seeded, and cut into ½-inch pieces
- 2 red or yellow bell peppers, stemmed, seeded, and cut into ½-inch pieces
- 1 cup shredded fresh basil

**1. FOR THE PESTATA:** Process all ingredients in food processor until finely ground, about 1 minute, scraping down sides as needed. Set aside.

**2. FOR THE STEW:** Toss eggplant with 1½ teaspoons salt in bowl. Line surface of large plate with double layer of coffee filters and lightly spray with vegetable oil spray. Spread eggplant in even layer over coffee filters. Microwave eggplant, uncovered, until dry to touch and slightly shriveled, 8 to 12 minutes, tossing once halfway through to ensure that eggplant cooks evenly.

**3.** Heat 2 tablespoons oil in Dutch oven over high heat until shimmering. Add eggplant, onion, and potatoes; cook, stirring frequently, until eggplant browns and surface of potatoes becomes translucent, about 2 minutes. Push vegetables to sides of pot; add 1 tablespoon oil and tomato paste to clearing. Cook paste, stirring frequently, until brown fond develops on bottom of pot, about 2 minutes. Add 2 cups water and chopped tomatoes and juice, scraping up any browned bits, and bring to boil. Reduce heat to medium, cover, and simmer gently until eggplant is completely broken down and potatoes are tender, 20 to 25 minutes.

**4.** Meanwhile, heat remaining 1 tablespoon oil in 12-inch skillet over high heat until smoking. Add zucchini, bell peppers, and ½ teaspoon salt; cook, stirring occasionally, until vegetables are browned and tender, 10 to 12 minutes. Push vegetables to sides of skillet; add pestata and cook until fragrant, about 1 minute. Stir pestata into vegetables and transfer vegetables to bowl. Add remaining ¼ cup water to skillet off heat, scraping up browned bits.

**5.** Remove Dutch oven from heat and stir reserved vegetables and water from skillet into vegetables in Dutch oven. Cover pot and let stand for 20 minutes to allow flavors to meld. Stir in basil and season with salt to taste; serve.

## Black Bean Soup

SERVES 6

**WHY THIS RECIPE WORKS** Black bean soup is full of robust earthy flavor. Our easy-to-make recipe results in a soup rich with sweet, spicy, smoky flavors and brightened with fresh garnishes. Dried beans imparted good flavor to the broth as they simmered, and we didn't have to soak them first. A touch of baking soda in the cooking water kept the beans from turning gray. Ham steak provided the smoky pork flavor of a ham hock and more meat as well. We spiced up the aromatics with lots of cumin and some red pepper flakes. For a chunky texture in our soup, we pureed it only partially, thickening it further with a slurry of cornstarch and water. Dried beans tend to cook unevenly, so be sure to taste several beans to determine their doneness in step 1. Though you do not need to offer all of the garnishes listed, do choose at least a couple; garnishes are essential for this soup, as they add not only flavor but texture and color as well. Leftover soup can be refrigerated in an airtight container for up to three days; reheat it in a saucepan over medium heat until hot, stirring in additional chicken broth if it has thickened beyond your liking.

BEANS

- 1 pound (2 cups) dried black beans, rinsed and picked over
- 4 ounces ham steak, trimmed of rind
- 2 bay leaves
- 5 cups water
- ⅛ teaspoon baking soda
- 1 teaspoon table salt

SOUP

- 3 tablespoons olive oil
- 2 large onions, minced
- 3 celery ribs, chopped fine
- 1 large carrot, chopped
- ½ teaspoon table salt

- 5–6 garlic cloves, minced (about 2 tablespoons)
- 1½ tablespoons ground cumin
- ½ teaspoon red pepper flakes
- 6 cups chicken broth
- 2 tablespoons cornstarch
- 2 tablespoons water
- 2 tablespoons lime juice

Lime wedges
Minced fresh cilantro leaves
Red onion, diced fine
Avocado, peeled, pitted, and diced medium
Sour cream

1. **FOR THE BEANS:** Place beans, ham, bay leaves, water, and baking soda in large saucepan with tight-fitting lid. Bring to boil over medium-high heat; using large spoon, skim foam as it rises to surface. Stir in salt, reduce heat to low, cover, and simmer briskly until beans are tender, 1¼ to 1½ hours (if necessary, add 1 cup more water and continue to simmer until beans are tender); do not drain beans. Discard bay leaves. Remove ham steak (ham steak darkens to color of beans), cut it into ¼-inch cubes, and set aside.

2. **FOR THE SOUP:** Heat oil in large Dutch oven over medium-high heat until shimmering but not smoking; add onions, celery, carrot, and salt and cook, stirring occasionally, until vegetables are soft and lightly browned, 12 to 15 minutes. Reduce heat to medium-low and add garlic, cumin, and red pepper flakes; cook, stirring constantly, until fragrant, about 3 minutes. Stir in beans, bean cooking liquid, and chicken broth. Increase heat to medium-high and bring to boil, then reduce heat to low and simmer, uncovered, stirring occasionally, to blend flavors, about 30 minutes.

3. **TO FINISH THE SOUP:** Ladle 1½ cups beans and 2 cups liquid into food processor or blender, process until smooth, and return to pot. Stir cornstarch and water in small bowl until combined, then gradually stir half of cornstarch mixture into soup; bring to boil over medium-high heat, stirring occasionally, to fully thicken. If soup is still thinner than desired once boiling, stir remaining cornstarch mixture to recombine and gradually stir mixture into soup; return to boil to fully thicken. Off heat, stir in lime juice and reserved ham; ladle soup into bowls and serve immediately, passing garnishes separately.

## Pasta e Fagioli (Italian Pasta and Bean Soup)

**SERVES** 8 to 10

**WHY THIS RECIPE WORKS** The American version of this hearty Italian bean-and-vegetable stew can easily turn out bland, with mushy beans and pasta and too much tomato. And it can take hours to prepare. We wanted rich broth, perfectly cooked beans and pasta, and complex flavors—and we wanted to prepare it in a reasonable amount of time. Substituting canned beans for dried would saved the most preparation time, and we found cannellini beans to be the closest to the dried cranberry beans used in traditional recipes. We built deep flavor by sautéing pancetta and, for aromatics, onion, garlic, and celery. Diced tomatoes went in next. A small amount of minced anchovies was unidentifiable but added complexity. Chicken broth diluted with water was our cooking liquid; chicken broth alone made the dish taste too much like chicken soup. A Parmesan rind added another layer of flavor, and the pasta went in last. The flavors of our thick, hearty soup harmonized perfectly and, best of all, we spent less than an hour at the stove. This soup does not hold well because the pasta absorbs the liquid, becomes mushy, and leaves the soup dry. You can, however, make the soup in two stages. Once the beans are simmered with the tomatoes, before the broth and water are added, the mixture can be cooled and refrigerated for up to 3 days. When ready to complete the soup, discard the Parmesan rind (otherwise it will become stringy), add the liquid, bring the soup to a boil, and proceed with the recipe.

- 1 tablespoon extra-virgin olive oil, plus extra for drizzling
- 3 ounces pancetta or bacon (about 3 slices), chopped fine
- 1 medium onion, minced
- 1 celery rib, chopped fine
- 4 medium garlic cloves, minced or pressed through a garlic press (about 4 teaspoons)
- 1 teaspoon dried oregano
- ¼ teaspoon red pepper flakes
- 3 anchovy fillets, minced to a paste (about 1½ teaspoons)
- 1 (28-ounce) can diced tomatoes
- 1 piece Parmesan cheese rind, about 5 inches by 2 inches
- 2 (15.5-ounce) cans cannellini beans, drained and rinsed
- 3½ cups low-sodium chicken broth
- 2½ cups water
- Table salt
- 8 ounces small pasta such as ditalini, tubetini, conchiglietti, or orzo
- 4 tablespoons chopped fresh parsley leaves
- Ground black pepper
- Grated Parmesan cheese, for serving

1. Heat the oil in a large Dutch oven over medium-high heat until shimmering. Add the pancetta and cook, stirring occasionally, until it begins to brown, 3 to 5 minutes. Add the onion and celery and cook, stirring occasionally, until the vegetables are softened, 5 to 7 minutes. Add the garlic, oregano, red pepper flakes, and anchovies and cook, stirring constantly, until fragrant, about 30 seconds. Add the tomatoes with their juice, scraping up any browned bits. Add the cheese rind and beans; bring to a boil, then reduce the heat to low and simmer to blend the flavors, 10 minutes. Add the chicken broth, water, and 1 teaspoon salt; increase the heat to high and bring to a boil. Add the pasta and cook until tender, about 10 minutes.

2. Discard the cheese rind. Off the heat, stir in 3 tablespoons of the parsley; season with salt and pepper to taste. Ladle the soup into individual bowls; drizzle each serving with olive oil and sprinkle with a portion of the remaining 1 tablespoon parsley. Serve immediately, passing the grated Parmesan separately.

## Pasta e Ceci (Pasta with Chickpeas)

**SERVES** 4 to 6

**WHY THIS RECIPE WORKS** Pasta e ceci, a sibling of pasta e fagioli, is a hearty and fast one-pot meal that's simple to prepare, yet packed full of satisfying flavor. To keep the cooking time to under an hour, we used canned chickpeas—along with their starchy liquid—to add even more body and flavor to the dish. Cooking the chickpeas and ditalini in the same pot blended the dish, and the additional starch released by the pasta created a silky texture. We simmered the chickpeas before adding the pasta, in order to achieve the perfect creamy softness. Using a food processor produced a finely minced soffritto of onions, garlic, carrot, celery, and pancetta that gave the dish a meaty backbone. And we achieved depth of flavor by adding anchovy, tomatoes, and Parmesan. Parsley and lemon juice provided a bright contrast just before serving. Another short pasta, such as orzo, can be substituted for the ditalini, but make sure to substitute by weight and not by volume.

- 2 ounces pancetta, cut into ½-inch pieces
- 1 small carrot, peeled and cut into ½-inch pieces
- 1 small celery rib, cut into ½-inch pieces
- 4 garlic cloves, peeled
- 1 onion, halved and cut into 1-inch pieces
- 1 (14-ounce) can whole peeled tomatoes, drained
- ¼ cup extra-virgin olive oil, plus extra for serving
- 2 teaspoons minced fresh rosemary
- 1 anchovy fillet, rinsed, patted dry, and minced
- ¼ teaspoon red pepper flakes
- 2 (15-ounce) cans chickpeas, undrained
- 2 cups water
- 1 teaspoon table salt
- 8 ounces (1½ cups) ditalini
- 1 tablespoon lemon juice
- 1 tablespoon minced fresh parsley
- 1 ounce Parmesan cheese, grated (½ cup)

**1.** Process pancetta in food processor until ground to paste, about 30 seconds, scraping down sides of bowl as needed. Add carrot, celery, and garlic and pulse until finely chopped, 8 to 10 pulses. Add onion and pulse until onion is cut into ⅛- to ¼-inch pieces, 8 to 10 pulses. Transfer pancetta mixture to large Dutch oven. Pulse tomatoes in now-empty food processor until coarsely chopped, 8 to 10 pulses. Set aside.

**2.** Add oil to pancetta mixture in Dutch oven and cook over medium heat, stirring frequently, until fond begins to form on bottom of pot, about 5 minutes. Add rosemary, anchovy, and pepper flakes and cook until fragrant, about 1 minute. Stir in tomatoes, chickpeas and their liquid, water, and salt and bring to boil, scraping up any browned bits. Reduce heat to medium-low and simmer for 10 minutes. Add pasta and cook, stirring frequently, until tender, 10 to 12 minutes. Stir in lemon juice and parsley and season with salt and pepper to taste. Serve, passing Parmesan and extra oil separately.

## Pasta e Piselli (Pasta and Peas)

**SERVES** 4

**WHY THIS RECIPE WORKS** Like its better-known cousins pasta e fagioli and pasta e ceci, the traditional Italian dish pasta e piselli combines a legume, peas, with small pasta to form a hearty soup. For a one-pot meal, we cooked the pasta in a broth flavored with sautéed onion and savory pancetta, simultaneously infusing the pasta with savoriness and thickening the rich, silky broth. Then we added the peas (we used frozen petite peas) and immediately took the pot off the heat to preserve their tenderness and color. A sprinkle of Pecorino Romano contributed richness and tangy depth. Last-minute additions of minced herbs and extra-virgin olive oil punched up the aroma and flavors of the dish. If you'd prefer to substitute small pasta such as tubetti, ditalini, elbow macaroni, or small shells for the ditalini, do so by weight, not by volume. We prefer frozen petite peas (also labeled as petits pois or baby sweet peas) because they are sweeter and less starchy than fresh peas or regular frozen peas, but you can substitute regular frozen peas. Do not defrost the peas before using them. For a vegetarian version, omit the pancetta, substitute vegetable broth for the chicken broth, and add an extra 2 tablespoons of grated cheese. Pecorino Romano adds a welcome sharpness; do not substitute Parmesan.

- 2 tablespoons extra-virgin olive oil, plus extra for drizzling
- 1 onion, chopped fine
- 2 ounces pancetta, chopped fine
- ½ teaspoon table salt
- ½ teaspoon pepper
- 2½ cups chicken broth
- 2½ cups water
- 7½ ounces (1½ cups) ditalini
- 1½ cups frozen petite peas
- ⅓ cup minced fresh parsley
- ¼ cup grated Pecorino Romano cheese, plus extra for serving
- 2 tablespoons minced fresh mint

**1.** Heat oil in large saucepan over medium heat until shimmering. Add onion, pancetta, salt, and pepper and cook, stirring frequently, until onion is softened, 7 to 10 minutes.

**2.** Add broth and water and bring to boil over high heat. Stir in pasta and cook, stirring frequently, until liquid returns to boil. Reduce heat to maintain simmer; cover; and cook until pasta is al dente, 8 to 10 minutes.

**3.** Stir in peas and remove saucepan from heat. Stir in parsley, Pecorino, and mint. Season with salt and pepper to taste. Serve, drizzling with extra oil and passing extra Pecorino separately.

## Acquacotta (Tuscan White Bean and Escarole Soup)

**SERVES** 8 to 10

**WHY THIS RECIPE WORKS** In this Tuscan soup, water, vegetables, beans, and fresh herbs are transformed into a supremely satisfying meal when egg yolks are whisked into the broth before it's ladled over toasted bread. We used chicken broth and amped up the flavor with a soffritto, a mixture of sautéed onion, celery, and garlic. A food processor made quick work of finely chopping these ingredients as well as the canned tomatoes that flavor the broth. Aromatic parsley, oregano, and fennel fronds gave our soup its distinctive taste. Finally, we thickened the broth with a mixture of the bean canning liquid and egg yolks before serving our finished soup over toasted slices of crusty bread. If escarole is unavailable, you can substitute 8 ounces of kale. We prefer Pecorino Romano's salty flavor, but Parmesan can be substituted, if desired. If your cheese has a rind, slice it off the wedge and add it to the pot with the broth in step 3 (remove it before serving). We like to serve this soup the traditional way, with a poached or soft-cooked egg spooned on top of the toast before the broth is ladled into the bowl.

**SOUP**

- 1 large onion, chopped coarse
- 2 celery ribs, chopped coarse
- 4 garlic cloves, peeled
- 1 (28-ounce) can whole peeled tomatoes
- ½ cup extra-virgin olive oil
- ¾ teaspoon table salt
- ⅛ teaspoon red pepper flakes
- 8 cups chicken broth
- 1 fennel bulb, 2 tablespoons fronds minced, stalks discarded, bulb halved, cored, and cut into ½-inch pieces
- 2 (15-ounce) cans cannellini beans, drained with liquid reserved, rinsed
- 1 small head escarole (10 ounces), trimmed and cut into ½-inch pieces (8 cups)
- 2 large egg yolks
- ½ cup chopped fresh parsley
- 1 tablespoon minced fresh oregano
- Grated Pecorino Romano cheese
- Lemon wedges

**TOAST**

- 10 (½-inch-thick) slices thick-crusted country bread
- ¼ cup extra-virgin olive oil

**1. FOR THE SOUP:** Pulse onion, celery, and garlic in food processor until very finely chopped, 15 to 20 pulses, scraping down sides of bowl as needed. Transfer onion mixture to Dutch oven. Add tomatoes and their juice to now-empty processor and pulse until tomatoes are finely chopped, 10 to 12 pulses; set aside.

**2.** Stir oil, ¾ teaspoon salt, and pepper flakes into onion mixture. Cook over medium-high heat, stirring occasionally, until light brown fond begins to form on bottom of pot, 12 to 15 minutes. Stir in tomato mixture, increase heat to high, and cook, stirring frequently, until mixture is very thick and rubber spatula leaves distinct trail when dragged across bottom of pot, 9 to 12 minutes.

**3.** Add broth and fennel bulb to pot and bring to simmer. Reduce heat to medium-low and simmer until fennel begins to soften, 5 to 7 minutes. Stir in beans and escarole and cook until fennel is fully tender, about 10 minutes.

**4.** Whisk egg yolks and reserved bean liquid together in bowl, then stir into soup. Stir in parsley, oregano, and fennel fronds. Season with salt and pepper to taste.

**5. FOR THE TOAST:** Adjust oven rack about 5 inches from broiler element and heat broiler. Place bread on aluminum foil–lined rimmed baking sheet, drizzle with oil, and season with salt and pepper. Broil until bread is deep golden brown.

**6.** Place 1 slice bread in bottom of each individual bowl. Ladle soup over toasted bread. Serve, passing Pecorino and lemon wedges separately.

## Hearty Tuscan Bean Stew

**SERVES** 8

**WHY THIS RECIPE WORKS** Unlike pasta e fagioli, where beans and pasta share the spotlight, Tuscan bean soup boasts creamy, buttery cannellini beans in the starring role. Ideally, the beans should have a uniformly tender texture, but too often the skins are tough and the insides mealy—or the beans turn mushy. We wanted to fix the bean problem and convert this Italian classic into a hearty, rustic stew for a deeply flavorful one-pot meal. Since the beans are the centerpiece of this stew, we concentrated on cooking them perfectly. After testing soaking times, we settled on soaking the beans overnight, a method that consistently produced the most tender and evenly cooked beans. But none of the methods we tested properly softened the skins. The answer was to soak the beans in salted water. Brining the beans, rather than the conventional approach of soaking them in plain water and then cooking them in salt water, allowed the salt to soften the skins but kept it from penetrating inside, where it could make the beans mealy. Gently cooking the beans in a 250-degree oven produced perfectly cooked beans that stayed intact. The final trick was to add the tomatoes toward the end of cooking, since their acid interfered with the softening process. To complete our stew, we looked

to other Tuscan flavors, including pancetta, kale, lots of garlic, and rosemary. To make it even more substantial, we served the stew on toasted country bread, drizzled with fruity extra-virgin olive oil. We prefer the creamier texture of beans soaked overnight for this recipe. If you're short on time, quick-soak them: Place the rinsed beans in a large heat-resistant bowl. Bring 2 quarts water and 3 tablespoons salt to a boil. Pour the water over the beans and let them sit for 1 hour. Drain and rinse the beans well before proceeding with step 2. If pancetta is unavailable, substitute 4 ounces bacon (about 4 slices).

- Table salt
- 1 pound (about 2 cups) dried cannellini beans, picked over and rinsed
- 1 tablespoon extra-virgin olive oil, plus extra for drizzling
- 6 ounces pancetta or bacon, cut into ¼-inch pieces (see note)
- 1 large onion, chopped medium (about 1½ cups)
- 2 medium celery ribs, cut into ½-inch pieces (about ¾ cup)
- 2 medium carrots, peeled and cut into ½-inch pieces (about 1 cup)
- 8 medium garlic cloves, peeled and crushed
- 4 cups low-sodium chicken broth
- 3 cups water
- 2 bay leaves
- 1 bunch kale or collard greens (about 1 pound), stems trimmed and leaves chopped into 1-inch pieces (about 8 cups loosely packed)
- 1 (14.5-ounce) can diced tomatoes, drained
- 1 sprig fresh rosemary
- Ground black pepper
- 8 slices country white bread, each 1¼ inches thick, broiled until golden brown on both sides and rubbed with a garlic clove (optional)

**1.** Dissolve 3 tablespoons salt in 4 quarts cold water in a large bowl or container. Add the beans and soak at room temperature for at least 8 hours or up to 24 hours. Drain the beans and rinse well.

**2.** Adjust an oven rack to the lower-middle position and heat the oven to 250 degrees. Heat the oil and pancetta in a large Dutch oven over medium heat. Cook, stirring occasionally, until the pancetta is lightly browned and the fat has rendered, 6 to 10 minutes. Add the onion, celery, and carrots. Cook, stirring occasionally, until the vegetables are softened and lightly browned, 10 to 16 minutes. Stir in the garlic and cook until fragrant, about 1 minute. Stir in the broth, water, bay leaves, and soaked beans. Increase the heat to high and bring the mixture to a simmer. Cover the pot, transfer it to the oven, and cook until the beans are almost tender (the very center of the beans will still be firm), 45 minutes to 1 hour.

**3.** Remove the pot from the oven and stir in the kale and tomatoes. Return the pot to the oven and continue to cook until the beans and greens are fully tender, 30 to 40 minutes longer.

**4.** Remove the pot from the oven and submerge the rosemary sprig in the stew. Cover and let stand for 15 minutes. Discard the bay leaves and rosemary sprig and season the stew with salt and pepper to taste. If desired, use the back of a spoon to press some beans against the side of the pot to thicken the stew. Serve over the toasted bread (if using) and drizzle with olive oil.

## Jamaican Stew Peas with Spinners

**SERVES** 6 to 8

**WHY THIS RECIPE WORKS** In order to replicate this homey Jamaican stew using ingredients easily found in American supermarkets, we made some simple substitutions. We started by swapping in dried small red beans for the Jamaican dried red peas, which can be difficult to source in the United States. Instead of salted pig tails or salted beef, we used smoked ham hocks, which, though not traditional, was not a huge leap since some cooks make stew peas using the leftover bone from a Christmas ham. Fine-tuning the spices and aromatics—allspice berries, garlic, garlic powder, celery, thyme, and a Scotch bonnet chile—gave the stew rich, nuanced flavor, and a combination of chicken broth and coconut milk added savoriness and sweet creaminess. To make the dish even more satisfying, we finished by adding the rustic flour-and-water dumplings known as spinners. Small dried dark-red beans (usually labeled "small red beans") are similar to the dried red peas used in Jamaica and have a creamy texture when cooked, but you can substitute dried red kidney beans, if desired. If you don't have any coconut oil on hand, you can substitute vegetable oil. If you can't find a Scotch bonnet chile, use a habanero. For the best results, use full-fat coconut milk. Serve with white rice.

- 1 pound (about 2 cups) small dried red beans, picked over and rinsed
- 6 cups plus 3 tablespoons water, divided
- 4 sprigs fresh thyme, plus 1 tablespoon chopped, divided
- 1 Scotch bonnet chile, pierced once with tip of paring knife
- 1 bay leaf
- 1 teaspoon whole allspice berries
- 1 tablespoon unrefined coconut oil

- 1 onion, chopped
- 1 green bell pepper, stemmed, seeded, and chopped
- 1 large celery rib, chopped (¾ cup)
- 3 tablespoons minced garlic
- 2 teaspoons garlic powder
- 1¼ teaspoons table salt, divided
- ½ teaspoon pepper
- 2 (12-ounce) smoked ham hocks
- 2 cups chicken broth
- 1 (14-ounce) can coconut milk
- ½ cup all-purpose flour
- 6 scallions, chopped

**1.** Combine beans and 6 cups water in large container and soak at room temperature for at least 8 hours or up to 24 hours.

**2.** Bundle thyme sprigs, Scotch bonnet, bay leaf, and allspice in cheesecloth; secure with kitchen twine; and set aside. Heat oil in large Dutch oven over medium heat until shimmering. Add onion, bell pepper, celery, garlic, garlic powder, ½ teaspoon salt, and pepper and cook, stirring occasionally, until onion is translucent, 6 to 8 minutes.

**3.** Add beans and their soaking liquid, ham hocks, chicken broth, cheesecloth bundle, and ½ teaspoon salt. Increase heat to high and bring to boil. Lower heat to maintain vigorous simmer. Cook uncovered, stirring occasionally, until beans start to soften and liquid is slightly reduced, about 1½ hours. Stir in coconut milk and continue to cook until beans are completely soft (it's OK if some skins crack) and sauce thickens, about 30 minutes longer.

**4.** While stew simmers, combine flour and remaining ¼ teaspoon salt in bowl. Make well in mixture. Gradually add remaining 3 tablespoons water, stirring until shaggy mass forms. Knead in bowl until dough clears sides of bowl and forms tight ball (if dough seems too dry to shape, add up to 2 teaspoons water, ½ teaspoon at a time). Pinch off about 1 teaspoon dough and roll between your palms to form 3-inch-long dumpling with tapered ends. Transfer to plate and repeat with remaining dough (you should have 14 to 16 dumplings).

**5.** Taste stew; adjust spiciness, if desired, by pressing cheesecloth bundle against side of pot with back of spoon to release juice of Scotch bonnet. Discard bundle and transfer ham hocks to plate to cool slightly. Gently drop dumplings into stew. Simmer, without stirring, until dumplings are set, about 5 minutes. While dumplings cook, debone ham hocks and cut meat into ½-inch pieces (you'll have ½ to ⅔ cup meat); discard bones, skin, and fat. Stir meat, scallions, and chopped thyme into stew. Season with salt and pepper to taste. Simmer until flavors have melded and scallions have softened slightly, 10 to 15 minutes. Serve.

**MAKING SPINNERS**

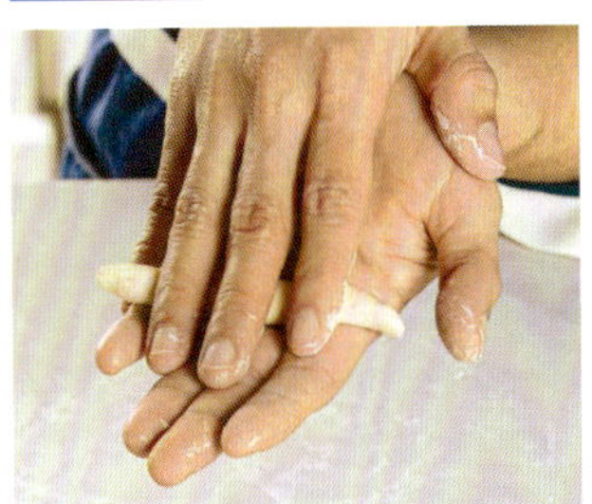

These dumplings are an essential component of stew peas. As they poach, some of the flour sloughs off, giving the broth body. To make one, pinch off about 1 teaspoon of dough and roll it between your palms to form 3-inch-long dumpling with tapered ends.

## Modern Ham and Split Pea Soup

**SERVES** 6 to 8

**WHY THIS RECIPE WORKS** We wanted a spoon-coating, richly flavorful broth studded with tender shreds of sweet-smoky meat. To avoid having to bake a ham beforehand, we needed a substitute for the traditional ham bone. Ham hock made the soup greasy and was skimpy on the meat. Ham steak, however, was plenty meaty and infused the soup with a fuller pork flavor—and we could get away with using just 1 pound. Our soup still needed richness and smokiness, and adding a few strips of raw bacon to the pot did the job. Unsoaked peas broke down just as well as soaked and were better at absorbing the flavor of the soup, so we skipped the traditional soaking step. To dress up our recipe, we garnished it with a handful of fresh peas; their sweetness popped against the hearty, smoky broth. Fresh chopped mint leaves and a drizzle of good balsamic vinegar added visual appeal and punched up the flavors even more. Floating gently fried croutons on the surface rounded off our updated version of this classic soup. Four ounces of regular sliced bacon can be used, but the thinner slices are a little harder to remove from the soup. Depending on the age and brand of split peas, the consistency of the soup may vary slightly. If the soup is too thin at the end of step 3, increase the heat and simmer, uncovered, until the desired consistency is reached. If it is too thick, thin it with a little water. In addition to sprinkling the soup with Buttery Croutons (page 114), we also like to garnish it with fresh peas, chopped mint, and a drizzle of aged balsamic vinegar.

- 2 tablespoons unsalted butter
- 1 large onion, chopped fine
- Table salt and ground black pepper
- 2 medium garlic cloves, minced or pressed through a garlic press (about 2 teaspoons)
- 7 cups water
- 1 ham steak (about 1 pound), skin removed, cut into quarters
- 3 slices thick-cut bacon
- 1 pound (2 cups) green split peas, picked over and rinsed
- 2 sprigs fresh thyme
- 2 bay leaves
- 2 medium carrots, peeled and cut into ½-inch pieces
- 1 medium celery rib, cut into ½-inch pieces

**1.** Heat the butter in a Dutch oven over medium-high heat. Add the onion and ½ teaspoon salt and cook, stirring frequently, until the onion is softened, about 3 to 4 minutes. Add the garlic and cook until fragrant, about 30 seconds. Add the water, ham steak, bacon, peas, thyme, and bay leaves. Increase the heat to high and bring to a simmer, stirring frequently to keep the peas from sticking to the bottom. Reduce the heat to low, cover, and simmer until the peas are tender but not falling apart, about 45 minutes.

**2.** Remove the ham steak, cover with aluminum foil or plastic wrap to prevent drying out, and set aside. Stir in the carrots and celery and continue to simmer, covered, until the vegetables are tender and the peas have almost completely broken down, about 30 minutes longer.

**3.** When cool enough to handle, shred the ham into small bite-size pieces. Remove and discard the thyme, bay leaves, and bacon slices. Stir the ham back into the soup and return to a simmer. Season with salt and pepper to taste and serve. (The soup can be refrigerated for up to 3 days. If necessary, thin it with water when reheating.)

## Hearty Ham and Split Pea Soup with Potatoes

**SERVES 6**

**WHY THIS RECIPE WORKS** Split pea soup is a great comfort food, especially in the winter months, We wanted a recipe for an old-fashioned ham and split pea soup that could be made anytime, with a readily available cut of ham that would also provide enough meat for really hearty soup. We found that we could get good, meaty ham stock with a picnic shoulder, a small, inexpensive cut that adds great flavor and provides plenty of meat for the soup (and some leftovers too). While it was easy enough to cook the peas in the ham stock, our vegetables benefited from a sauté in a separate pan. We found that caramelized vegetables gave this straightforward soup a richness and depth of flavor that had been missing—it was well worth the time spent washing an extra pan. Adding a few red potatoes with the carrots, celery, and onions turned our soup into a truly satisfying meal. Use an entire small 2½-pound smoked picnic portion ham if you can find one. Otherwise, buy a half-picnic ham and remove some meat, which you can

roast and use in sandwiches, salads, or omelets. To remove the meat, loosen the large comma-shaped muscles on top of the ham with your fingers, then use a knife to cut the membrane separating the comma-shaped muscles from the rest of the ham.

- 2½ pounds smoked ham, bone-in
- 4 bay leaves
- 12 cups water
- 1 pound (2 cups) green split peas, picked over and rinsed
- 1 teaspoon dried thyme
- 2 tablespoons extra-virgin olive oil
- 2 onions, chopped
- 2 carrots, peeled and chopped
- 2 celery ribs, chopped
- 1 tablespoon unsalted butter
- 2 garlic cloves, minced
- Pinch sugar
- 3 small red potatoes (about 8 ounces), unpeeled, cut into ½-inch chunks
- Minced red onion (optional)
- Balsamic vinegar

**1.** Place ham in large Dutch oven, add bay leaves and water, cover, and bring to boil over medium-high heat. Reduce heat to low and simmer until meat is tender and pulls away from bone, 2 to 2½ hours. Remove ham meat and bone from pot and set aside.

**2.** Add split peas and thyme and simmer, uncovered, until peas are tender but not dissolved, about 45 minutes. Meanwhile, shred meat into bite-size pieces and set aside. Discard rind and bone.

**3.** Heat oil in large skillet over medium-high heat until shimmering. Add onions, carrots, and celery and sauté, stirring frequently, until most of liquid evaporates and vegetables begin to brown, 5 to 6 minutes. Reduce heat to medium-low and add butter, garlic, and sugar. Cook vegetables, stirring frequently, until deeply browned, 30 to 35 minutes; set aside.

4. Add sautéed vegetables, potatoes, and shredded ham to pot with split peas. Simmer until potatoes are tender, peas dissolve, and soup thickens to consistency of light cream, about 20 minutes. Season with pepper to taste. Discard bay leaves and ladle soup into bowls. Sprinkle with red onion, if using, and serve, passing balsamic vinegar separately. (Soup, minus garnishes, can be refrigerated in airtight container for up to 2 days. Warm over low heat until hot; do not boil.)

## Hearty Lentil Soup

**SERVES** 4 to 6

**WHY THIS RECIPE WORKS** A hot bowl of lentil soup provides warm comfort on a cold day and, when properly prepared, tastes great—maybe even better—the next day. We wanted a hearty lentil soup worthy of a second bowl, not the tasteless variety we have so often encountered. While lentilles du Puy are our top choice for lentil soup, we found that almost any lentil (other than red lentils) can be used. To keep the lentils from losing their shape as they cooked, we sweated them with sautéed aromatic vegetables before adding chicken broth to the soup pot. These lentils stayed intact in our final soup, but their flavor was weak. Revisiting this step, we added canned tomatoes and crisp bacon, which gave our lentils a huge flavor boost. And because we cooked the bacon first, we could then use the rendered fat to sauté our vegetables and aromatics, which brought a nice smoky flavor to the soup. For a texture that was neither too smooth nor too thick, we pureed a few cups of the soup and added it back to the pot to warm through. Lentil soup needs plenty of acidity, so we used white wine as part of the broth and finished the soup with balsamic vinegar. Lentilles du Puy, also called French green lentils, are our first choice for this recipe, but brown, black, or regular green lentils are fine, too. Note that cooking times will vary depending on the type of lentils used. Be sure to rinse and then carefully sort through the lentils to remove any small stones.

- 3 ounces (3 slices) bacon, cut into ¼-inch pieces
- 1 large onion, minced
- 2 medium carrots, peeled and chopped medium
- 3 medium garlic cloves, minced or pressed through a garlic press (about 1 tablespoon)
- 1 (14.5-ounce) can diced tomatoes, drained
- 1 bay leaf
- 1 teaspoon minced fresh thyme leaves
- 1 cup (7 ounces) lentils, rinsed and picked over
- 1 teaspoon table salt
- Ground black pepper
- ½ cup dry white wine
- 4½ cups low-sodium chicken broth
- 1½ cups water
- 1½ teaspoons balsamic vinegar
- 3 tablespoons minced fresh parsley leaves

1. Fry the bacon in a large Dutch oven over medium-high heat, stirring occasionally, until the fat is rendered and the bacon is crisp, 3 to 4 minutes. Add the onion and carrots; cook, stirring occasionally, until the vegetables begin to soften, about 2 minutes. Add the garlic and cook until fragrant, about 30 seconds. Stir in the tomatoes, bay leaf, and thyme; cook until fragrant, about 30 seconds. Stir in the lentils, salt, and pepper to taste; cover, reduce the heat to medium-low, and cook until the vegetables are softened and the lentils have darkened, 8 to 10 minutes.

2. Uncover, increase the heat to high, add the wine, and bring to a simmer. Add the chicken broth and water; bring to a boil, cover partially, and reduce the heat to low. Simmer until the lentils are tender but still hold their shape, 30 to 35 minutes; discard the bay leaf.

3. Puree 3 cups of the soup in a blender until smooth, then return to the pot. Stir in the vinegar and heat the soup over medium-low heat until hot, about 5 minutes. Stir in 2 tablespoons of the parsley. Ladle the soup into bowls, garnish with the remaining parsley, and serve. (The soup, minus the garnish, can be refrigerated in an airtight container for up to 2 days. Warm over low heat until hot; do not boil.)

## Hearty Spanish-Style Lentil and Chorizo Soup

**SERVES** 6 to 8

**WHY THIS RECIPE WORKS** For our own version of Spain's thick and smoky lentil soup, we started with the lentils. Soaking them in a warm brine for 30 minutes before cooking prevented blowouts and ensured they were well seasoned. Browning links of Spanish chorizo and then simmering them in the soup ensured a juicy texture. Slowly sweating finely chopped aromatics in the chorizo's fat gave our soup incredible depth of flavor. For more intensity, we finished the soup with an Indian preparation called a tadka, which is a mixture of spices (smoked paprika ramped up the smoky notes) and

sometimes finely minced aromatics (we used onion and garlic) bloomed in oil. Adding a little flour helped thicken the soup and some sherry vinegar brightened its flavors. We prefer French green lentils, or lentilles du Puy, for this recipe, but it will work with any type of lentil except red or yellow. Grate the onion on the large holes of a box grater. If Spanish-style chorizo is not available, kielbasa sausage can be substituted. Red wine vinegar can be substituted for the sherry vinegar. Smoked paprika comes in three varieties: sweet (dulce), bittersweet or medium hot (agridulce), and hot (picante). For this recipe, we prefer the sweet kind.

- 1 pound (2¼ cups) lentils, picked over and rinsed
- Table salt and pepper
- 1 large onion
- 5 tablespoons extra-virgin olive oil
- 1½ pounds Spanish-style chorizo sausage, pricked with fork several times
- 3 carrots, peeled and cut into ¼-inch pieces
- 3 tablespoons minced fresh parsley
- 3 tablespoons sherry vinegar, plus extra for seasoning
- 7 cups water, plus extra as needed
- 2 bay leaves
- ⅛ teaspoon ground cloves
- 2 tablespoons sweet smoked paprika
- 3 garlic cloves, minced
- 1 tablespoon all-purpose flour

**1.** Place lentils and 2 teaspoons salt in heatproof container. Cover with 4 cups boiling water and let soak for 30 minutes. Drain well.

**2.** Meanwhile, finely chop three-quarters of onion (you should have about 1 cup) and grate remaining quarter (you should have about 3 tablespoons). Heat 2 tablespoons oil in Dutch oven over medium heat until shimmering. Add chorizo and cook until browned on all sides, 6 to 8 minutes. Transfer chorizo to large plate. Reduce heat to low and add chopped onion, carrots, 1 tablespoon parsley, and 1 teaspoon salt. Cover and cook, stirring occasionally, until vegetables are very soft but not brown, 25 to 30 minutes. If vegetables begin to brown, add 1 tablespoon water to pot.

**3.** Add lentils and sherry vinegar to vegetables; increase heat to medium-high; and cook, stirring frequently, until vinegar starts to evaporate, 3 to 4 minutes. Add 7 cups water, chorizo, bay leaves, and cloves; bring to simmer. Reduce heat to low, cover, and cook until lentils are tender, about 30 minutes.

**4.** Heat remaining 3 tablespoons oil in small saucepan over medium heat until shimmering. Add paprika, grated onion, garlic, and ½ teaspoon pepper; cook, stirring constantly, until fragrant, 2 minutes. Add flour and cook, stirring constantly, 1 minute longer. Remove chorizo and bay leaves from lentils. Stir paprika mixture into lentils and continue to cook until flavors have blended and soup has thickened, 10 to 15 minutes. When chorizo is cool enough to handle, cut in half lengthwise, then cut each half into ¼-inch-thick slices. Return chorizo to soup along with remaining 2 tablespoons parsley and heat through, about 1 minute. Season with salt, pepper, and up to 2 teaspoons sherry vinegar to taste, and serve. (Soup can be made up to 3 days in advance.)

## Harira (Moroccan Lentil and Chickpea Soup)

**SERVES** 6 to 8

**WHY THIS RECIPES WORKS** A popular Moroccan soup, harira features a hearty mix of legumes flavored with warm spices and fresh herbs. Like countless other regional dishes, harira's exact ingredients vary from region to region and even from family to family. For our version, we carefully reduced the ingredient list and altered the technique to deliver harira's flavors in less time. We decided to omit the meat (lamb, chicken, or beef is common) in this soup—with all the other robust flavors and textures in the mix, the meat wasn't missed. To save time, we opted for convenient canned chickpeas rather than dried beans, plus quick-cooking lentils. We pared down the number of spices to a key five available in most supermarkets. For more depth of flavor, we also replaced half the water with chicken broth. Using large amounts of just two herbs made for quicker prep and a more efficient use of fresh ingredients. Finishing the dish with fresh lemon juice helped focus all the flavors. This wonderfully complex-tasting, spice-filled soup, made almost entirely from pantry ingredients, brought humble lentils to a whole other level. For a vegetarian version, substitute vegetable broth for the chicken broth and water. We like to garnish this soup with a small amount of harissa, a fiery North African chili paste.

- ⅓ cup extra-virgin olive oil
- 1 large onion, chopped fine
- 2 celery ribs, chopped fine
- 5 garlic cloves, minced
- 1 tablespoon grated fresh ginger

- 2 teaspoons ground coriander
- 2 teaspoons smoked paprika
- 1 teaspoon ground cumin
- ½ teaspoon ground cinnamon
- ⅛ teaspoon red pepper flakes
- ¾ cup minced fresh cilantro, divided
- ½ cup minced fresh parsley, divided
- 4 cups chicken broth
- 4 cups water
- 1 (15-ounce) can chickpeas, rinsed
- 1 cup brown lentils, picked over and rinsed
- 1 (28-ounce) can crushed tomatoes
- ½ cup orzo
- 4 ounces Swiss chard, stemmed and cut into ½-inch pieces
- 2 tablespoons lemon juice, plus lemon wedges for serving

**1.** Heat oil in large Dutch oven over medium-high heat until shimmering. Add onion and celery and cook, stirring frequently, until translucent and starting to brown, 7 to 8 minutes. Reduce heat to medium, add garlic and ginger, and cook until fragrant, 1 minute. Stir in coriander, paprika, cumin, cinnamon, and pepper flakes and cook for 1 minute. Stir in ½ cup cilantro and ¼ cup parsley and cook for 1 minute.

**2.** Stir in broth, water, chickpeas, and lentils; increase heat to high and bring to simmer. Reduce heat to medium-low, partially cover, and simmer gently until lentils are just tender, about 20 minutes.

**3.** Stir in tomatoes and pasta and simmer, partially covered, for 7 minutes, stirring occasionally. Stir in chard and continue to cook, partially covered, until pasta is tender, about 5 minutes longer. Off heat, stir in lemon juice, remaining ¼ cup cilantro, and remaining ¼ cup parsley. Season with salt and pepper to taste. Serve, passing lemon wedges separately.

## Red Lentil Soup with Warm Spices

**SERVES** 4 to 6

**WHY THIS RECIPE WORKS** Red lentils are one of our favorite legumes. They cook quickly and don't require any presoaking or brining like other beans. One of their best qualities, however, is that they disintegrate when cooked, forming a creamy, thick puree—perfect for a satisfying soup. Their mild flavor does require a bit of embellishment, so we started by sautéing onions in butter and used the warm mixture to bloom some fragrant spices found in North African cooking. Tomato paste and garlic completed the base before the addition of the lentils, and a mix of chicken broth and water gave the soup a full, rounded character. After only 15 minutes of cooking, the lentils were soft enough to be pureed with a whisk. A generous dose of lemon juice brought the flavors into focus, and a drizzle of spice-infused butter and a sprinkle of fresh cilantro completed the transformation of commonplace ingredients into a comforting soup. Pair this soup with a salad and bread for lunch or a light supper.

- 4 tablespoons unsalted butter, divided
- 1 large onion, chopped fine
- 1 teaspoon table salt
- ¾ teaspoon ground coriander
- ½ teaspoon ground cumin
- ¼ teaspoon ground ginger
- ¼ teaspoon pepper
- ⅛ teaspoon ground cinnamon
- Pinch cayenne pepper
- 1 tablespoon tomato paste
- 1 garlic clove, minced
- 4 cups chicken broth
- 2 cups water
- 10½ ounces (1½ cups) red lentils, picked over and rinsed
- 2 tablespoons lemon juice, plus extra for seasoning
- 1½ teaspoons dried mint, crumbled
- 1 teaspoon paprika
- ¼ cup chopped fresh cilantro

**1.** Melt 2 tablespoons butter in large saucepan over medium heat. Add onion and salt and cook, stirring occasionally, until softened but not browned, about 5 minutes. Add coriander, cumin, ginger, pepper, cinnamon, and cayenne and cook until fragrant, about 2 minutes. Stir in tomato paste and garlic and cook for 1 minute. Stir in broth, water, and lentils and bring to simmer. Simmer vigorously, stirring occasionally, until lentils are soft and about half are broken down, about 15 minutes.

**2.** Whisk soup vigorously until it is coarsely pureed, about 30 seconds. Stir in lemon juice and season with salt and extra lemon juice to taste. Cover and keep warm. (Soup can be refrigerated for up to 3 days. Thin soup with water, if desired, when reheating.)

**3.** Melt remaining 2 tablespoons butter in small skillet over medium-low heat. Remove from heat and stir in mint and paprika. Ladle soup into individual bowls, drizzle each portion with 1 teaspoon spiced butter, sprinkle with cilantro, and serve.

## Farmhouse Vegetable and Barley Soup

**SERVES** 6 to 8

**WHY THIS RECIPE WORKS** Most recipes for hearty winter vegetable soups, it turns out, are neither quick nor easy. For a satisfying soup that doesn't take the better part of a day to make, we started with canned chicken broth. To this we added soy sauce and ground dried porcini mushrooms. These ingredients added a savory, almost meaty flavor to the soup base. To make the soup more filling, we added barley to the hearty combination of carrots, potatoes, leeks, cabbage, and turnips. We prefer an acidic, unoaked white wine such as Sauvignon Blanc for this recipe. We love the richness added by the Lemon-Thyme Butter and Herbed Croutons, but the soup can also be garnished with crisp bacon or crumbled cheddar cheese. You will need at least a 6-quart Dutch oven for this recipe.

- ⅛ ounce dried porcini mushrooms, rinsed
- 8 sprigs fresh parsley plus 3 tablespoons minced
- 4 sprigs fresh thyme
- 1 bay leaf
- 2 tablespoons unsalted butter
- 1½ pounds leeks, white and light green parts sliced ½ inch thick and washed thoroughly
- 2 carrots, peeled and cut into ½-inch pieces
- 2 celery ribs, cut into ¼-inch pieces
- ⅓ cup dry white wine
- 2 teaspoons soy sauce
- Table salt and pepper
- 6 cups water
- 4 cups low-sodium chicken broth or vegetable broth
- ½ cup pearl barley
- 1 garlic clove, peeled and smashed
- 1½ pounds Yukon Gold potatoes, peeled and cut into ½-inch pieces
- 1 turnip, peeled and cut into ¾-inch pieces
- 1½ cups chopped green cabbage
- 1 cup frozen peas
- 1 teaspoon lemon juice

**1.** Grind mushrooms with spice grinder until they resemble fine meal, 10 to 30 seconds. Measure out 2 teaspoons porcini powder; reserve remainder for another use. Using kitchen twine, tie together parsley sprigs, thyme sprigs, and bay leaf.

**2.** Melt butter in large Dutch oven over medium heat. Add leeks, carrots, celery, wine, soy sauce, and 2 teaspoons salt. Cook, stirring occasionally, until liquid has evaporated and celery is softened, about 10 minutes.

**3.** Add water, chicken broth, barley, porcini powder, herb bundle, and garlic; increase heat to high and bring to boil. Reduce heat to medium-low and simmer, partially covered, for 25 minutes.

**4.** Add potatoes, turnip, and cabbage; return to simmer and cook until barley, potatoes, turnip, and cabbage are tender, 18 to 20 minutes.

**5.** Remove pot from heat and remove herb bundle. Stir in peas, lemon juice, and minced parsley; season with salt and pepper to taste. Serve, passing Lemon-Thyme Butter and Herbed Croutons separately.

### Lemon-Thyme Butter

**MAKES** 6 tablespoons

- 6 tablespoons unsalted butter, softened
- 1 tablespoon minced fresh thyme
- ¾ teaspoon finely grated lemon zest plus ¼ teaspoon juice
- Pinch table salt

Combine all ingredients in bowl.

### Herbed Croutons

**MAKES** about 2½ cups

Our favorite brand of sandwich bread is Arnold Country White Bread.

- 1 tablespoon unsalted butter
- 1 teaspoon minced fresh parsley
- ½ teaspoon minced fresh thyme
- 4 slices hearty white sandwich bread, cut into ½-inch pieces
- Table salt and pepper

Melt butter in 10-inch skillet over medium heat. Add parsley and thyme; cook, stirring constantly, for 20 seconds. Add bread and cook, stirring frequently, until light golden brown, 5 to 10 minutes. Season with salt and pepper to taste.

## Quinoa and Vegetable Stew

**SERVES** 6 to 8

**WHY THIS RECIPE WORKS** Quinoa stews are common in many South American regions. Traditional recipes call for annatto powder and Andean varieties of potatoes and corn. We found that paprika has a similar flavor profile to annatto powder; we rounded it out with cumin and coriander. Red bell pepper, tomatoes, red potatoes, sweet corn, and frozen peas were a nice mix of vegetables. We added the quinoa after the potatoes had softened and cooked it until it released starch to help give body to the stew. Finally, we added the traditional garnishes: queso fresco, avocado, and cilantro. We like the convenience of prewashed quinoa. If you buy unwashed quinoa (or are unsure whether it's washed), be sure to rinse it before cooking to remove its bitter protective coating (called saponin). This stew tends to thicken as it sits; add additional warm vegetable broth to loosen. Do not omit the garnishes; they are important to the flavor of the stew.

- 2 tablespoons vegetable oil
- 1 onion, chopped
- 1 red bell pepper, stemmed, seeded, and cut into ½-inch pieces
- 5 garlic cloves, minced
- 1 tablespoon paprika
- 2 teaspoons ground coriander
- 1½ teaspoons ground cumin
- 6 cups vegetable broth
- 1 pound red potatoes, unpeeled, cut into ½-inch pieces
- 1 cup prewashed white quinoa
- 1 cup fresh or frozen corn
- 2 tomatoes, cored and chopped coarse
- 1 cup frozen peas
- 8 ounces queso fresco or feta cheese, crumbled (2 cups)
- 1 avocado, halved, pitted, and diced
- ½ cup minced fresh cilantro

**1.** Heat oil in Dutch oven over medium heat until shimmering. Add onion and bell pepper and cook until softened, 5 to 7 minutes. Stir in garlic, paprika, coriander, and cumin and cook until fragrant, about 30 seconds. Stir in broth and potatoes and bring to boil over high heat. Reduce heat to medium-low and simmer gently for 10 minutes.

**2.** Stir in quinoa and simmer for 8 minutes. Stir in corn and simmer until potatoes and quinoa are just tender, 5 to 7 minutes. Stir in tomatoes and peas and let heat through, about 2 minutes.

**3.** Off heat, season with salt and pepper to taste. Sprinkle individual portions with queso fresco, avocado, and cilantro before serving.

## Wild Rice and Mushroom Soup

**SERVES** 6 to 8

**WHY THIS RECIPE WORKS** For a rich, earthy, nutty-tasting soup, we had to figure out how to make wild rice and mushrooms do more than just add bulk. Fresh cremini mushrooms provided a meaty texture, and dried shiitakes, ground into a powder and added to the broth, ensured full-bodied mushroom flavor. Simmering the wild rice with baking soda decreased the cooking time and brought out its complex flavor. Cooking the rice in the oven, instead of on the stovetop, made it tender with a pleasant chew. To infuse the entire soup with wild rice flavor, we replaced some of the water in the soup with the rice's leftover cooking liquid. Including tomato paste and soy sauce amplified the nutty, earthy flavor profile. A final addition of cornstarch helped suspend the rice in the broth to give our soup a velvety texture. White mushrooms can be substituted for the cremini mushrooms. We use a spice grinder to process the dried shiitake mushrooms, but a blender also works.

- ¼ ounce dried shiitake mushrooms, rinsed
- 4¼ cups water, divided
- 1 sprig fresh thyme
- 1 bay leaf
- 5 garlic cloves, peeled (1 whole, 4 minced)
- 1½ teaspoons table salt
- ¼ teaspoon baking soda
- 1 cup wild rice
- 4 tablespoons unsalted butter
- 1 pound cremini mushrooms, trimmed and sliced ¼ inch thick
- 1 onion, chopped fine
- 1 teaspoon tomato paste
- 1 teaspoon pepper
- ⅔ cup dry sherry
- 4 cups chicken broth
- 1 tablespoon soy sauce
- ¼ cup cornstarch
- ½ cup heavy cream
- ¼ cup minced fresh chives
- ¼ teaspoon finely grated lemon zest

**1.** Adjust oven rack to middle position and heat oven to 375 degrees. Grind shiitake mushrooms in spice grinder until finely ground (you should have about 3 tablespoons).

**2.** Bring 4 cups water, thyme sprig, bay leaf, whole garlic clove, ¾ teaspoon salt, and baking soda to boil in medium saucepan over high heat. Add rice and return to boil. Cover saucepan, transfer to oven, and bake until rice is tender, 35 to 50 minutes. Strain rice through fine-mesh strainer set in 4-cup liquid measuring cup; discard thyme sprig, bay leaf, and garlic clove. Add enough water to reserved cooking liquid to measure 3 cups.

**3.** Melt butter in Dutch oven over high heat. Add cremini mushrooms, onion, tomato paste, pepper, minced garlic, and remaining 3/4 teaspoon salt. Cook, stirring occasionally, until vegetables are browned and dark fond develops on bottom of pot, 15 minutes. Add sherry, scraping up any browned bits, and cook until reduced and pot is almost dry, about 2 minutes. Add ground shiitake mushrooms, reserved rice cooking liquid, broth, and soy sauce and bring to boil. Reduce heat to low and simmer, covered, until onion and mushrooms are tender, about 20 minutes.

**4.** Whisk cornstarch and remaining 1/4 cup water together in small bowl. Stir cornstarch slurry into soup; return to simmer; and cook until thickened, about 2 minutes. Remove pot from heat and stir in cooked rice, cream, chives, and lemon zest. Cover and let stand for 20 minutes. Season with salt and pepper to taste, and serve.

## Ajo Blanco (Spanish Chilled Almond and Garlic Soup)

**SERVES** 6 to 8

**WHY THIS RECIPE WORKS** Spanish white gazpacho, or ajo blanco, predates the red version. It is a silky soup that requires only a handful of ingredients: almonds, garlic, bread, vinegar, and water. It's served ice-cold and garnished with almonds, sliced grapes, or even peppery olive oil. At its best, it is a study in contrasts: Some bites offer a nutty crunch, while others are sharply fruity and floral. But the first batches we whipped up were far from impressive. Some were watery and bland; others were grainy and salad dressing-esque. We wanted to nail down a foolproof way to make this chilled soup. When it came to technique, we found that the order in which we added ingredients to the blender made all the difference. First, we buzzed the almonds until they were powdery, then added bread (which had been soaked in water), a clove of garlic, a splash of sherry vinegar, and salt and pepper. Once these ingredients were pureed, we drizzled in the olive oil and finally thinned the soup with more water. We liked the fruity, peppery pop that we got from premium olive oil. The sherry vinegar and a pinch of cayenne added brightness and bite. For just a hint of flowery bitter almond flavor, we mixed a tablespoon of the pureed soup with 1/8 teaspoon almond extract, then stirred a teaspoon of the mixture back into the soup. For garnishes, we thinly sliced green grapes and toasted a few almonds in oil to add crunch. An extra drizzle of olive oil made for a rich finish and a beautiful presentation. This rich soup is best when served in small portions (about 6 ounces). Use a good-quality extra-virgin olive oil. Our favorite supermarket brands include Carapelli Original Extra Virgin Olive Oil. Too much almond extract can ruin the soup, hence the unusual mixing technique in step 4.

- 6 slices hearty white sandwich bread, crusts removed
- 4 cups water
- 2½ cups (8¾ ounces) plus ⅓ cup sliced blanched almonds
- 1 garlic clove, peeled
- 3 tablespoons sherry vinegar
- Kosher salt and pepper
- Pinch cayenne pepper
- ½ cup extra-virgin olive oil, plus extra for drizzling
- ⅛ teaspoon almond extract
- 2 teaspoons vegetable oil
- 6 ounces seedless green grapes, sliced thin (1 cup)

**1.** Combine bread and water in bowl and let soak for 5 minutes. Process 2½ cups almonds in blender until finely ground, about 30 seconds, scraping down sides of blender jar as needed.

**2.** Using your hands, remove bread from water, squeeze it lightly, and transfer to blender with almonds. Measure 3 cups soaking water and set aside; transfer remaining soaking water to blender.

**3.** Add garlic, vinegar, 1¼ teaspoons salt, and cayenne to blender and process until mixture has consistency of cake batter, 30 to 45 seconds. With blender running, add olive oil in thin, steady stream, about 30 seconds. Add reserved soaking water and process for 1 minute. Season with salt and pepper to taste. Strain soup through fine-mesh strainer set in bowl, pressing on solids to extract liquid.

**4.** Measure 1 tablespoon of soup into second bowl and stir in almond extract. Return 1 teaspoon of extract mixture to soup; discard remainder. Chill for at least 3 hours or up to 24 hours.

**5.** Heat vegetable oil in 8-inch skillet over medium-high heat until oil begins to shimmer. Add remaining ⅓ cup almonds and cook, stirring constantly, until golden brown, 3 to 4 minutes. Immediately transfer to bowl and stir in ¼ teaspoon salt.

**6.** Ladle soup into shallow bowls. Mound an equal amount of grapes in center of each bowl. Sprinkle cooled almonds over soup and drizzle with extra-virgin olive oil. Serve immediately.

## Chicken Broth

**MAKES** 8 cups

**WHY THIS RECIPE WORKS** Good homemade chicken broth is liquid gold. In this recipe we coaxed out rich flavor and full body by using chicken wings, which are convenient as well as gelatin-rich, giving the broth a luscious consistency. Minimal additions ensure the broth tastes as chicken-y as possible. Chicken wings are readily available but we also like to think ahead and put other resources to good use. We like to hold on to leftover trimmings and carcasses from roasted or poached poultry in our freezer. Once we have about a pound or more, we substitute them for an equal amount of wings. If you have a large pot (at least 12 quarts), you can easily double this recipe to make 1 gallon.

- 4 pounds chicken wings
- 3½ quarts water
- 1 (1-inch) piece ginger, sliced into ¼-inch-thick rounds
- 2 scallions, cut into 2-inch lengths
- 1½ teaspoons table salt

**1.** Bring chicken and water to boil in large stockpot or Dutch oven over medium-high heat, skimming off any scum that comes to surface. Reduce heat to low and simmer gently for 3 hours.

**2.** Add ginger, scallions, and salt and continue to simmer for 2 hours. Strain broth through fine-mesh strainer into large pot or container, pressing on solids to extract as much liquid as possible; discard solids. Let broth settle for about 5 minutes, then, using wide, shallow spoon, skim excess fat from surface. (Cooled broth can be refrigerated for up to 4 days or frozen for up to 1 month.)

### Pressure-Cooker Chicken Broth

**TOTAL TIME** 1½ hours

Add all ingredients to 6- or 8-quart electric pressure cooker. Lock lid in place and close pressure release valve. Select high pressure cook function and cook for 1 hour. Turn off pressure cooker and let pressure release naturally for 15 minutes. Quick-release any remaining pressure, then carefully remove lid, allowing steam to escape away from you. Strain broth as directed. (If using stovetop pressure cooker, bring cooker to high pressure over medium-high heat. As soon as indicator signals that pot has reached high pressure, reduce heat to medium-low and cook, adjusting heat as needed to maintain high pressure. Remove cooker from heat before allowing pressure to release.)

### Enriched Chicken and Pork Broth

Substitute 2 pounds pork necks for 2 pounds of chicken wings.

## Vegetable Broth Base

**MAKES** 1¾ cups base; enough for 7 quarts broth

**WHY THIS RECIPE WORKS** Homemade broth enlivens any dish, but for vegetarian cooking, an overpowering broth can be ruinous. For our base, we focused on mild but impactful vegetables. Mirepoix, a mix of chopped onions, celery, and carrots, is a classic combination; we started there, swapping in leeks for their mild onion flavor and minimal moisture content. Celery root had a creamier, more complex celery taste than celery ribs. Dried minced onions reinforced the leeks, and carrots contributed pleasant sweetness. Tomato paste and soy sauce bolstered the savory qualities, and parsley added brightness. Kosher salt seasoned the broth while keeping it convenient: Salt lowers water's freezing point, so the concentrate would remain easy to scoop. Even better, our base had less salt than most store-bought broths. Creating the base was easy: We pulsed the ingredients in a food processor and froze the paste. For the best balance of flavors, measure the prepped vegetables by weight. Kosher salt aids in grinding the vegetables. The broth base contains enough salt to keep it from freezing solid, making it easy to remove 1 tablespoon at a time. To make 1 cup of broth, stir 1 tablespoon of fresh or frozen broth base into 1 cup of boiling water. If particle-free broth is desired, let the broth steep for 5 minutes and then strain it through a fine-mesh strainer.

- 2 leeks, white and light green parts only, chopped and washed thoroughly (2½ cups or 5 ounces); (see page 545)
- 2 carrots, peeled and cut into ½-inch pieces (⅔ cup or 3 ounces)
- ½ small celery root, peeled and cut into ½-inch pieces (¾ cup or 3 ounces)
- ½ cup (½ ounce) parsley leaves and thin stems
- 3 tablespoons dried minced onions
- 2 tablespoons kosher salt
- 1½ tablespoons tomato paste
- 3 tablespoons soy sauce

Process leeks, carrots, celery root, parsley, minced onions, and salt in food processor, scraping down sides of bowl frequently, until paste is as fine as possible, 3 to 4 minutes. Add tomato paste and process for 1 minute, scraping down sides of bowl every 20 seconds. Add soy sauce and continue to process 1 minute longer. Transfer mixture to airtight container and tap firmly on counter to remove air bubbles. Press small piece of parchment paper flush against surface of mixture and cover. Freeze for up to 6 months.

# CHAPTER 4 Salads

Photos (left to right): Shaved Celery Salad with Pomegranate-Honey Vinaigrette; Chopped Carrot Salad with Fennel, Orange, and Hazelnuts; Classic Caesar Salad for Two; Shrimp Salad; Salade Lyonnaise; Pai Huang Gua (Smashed Cucumbers); Classic Tuna Salad

## Foolproof Vinaigrette

**MAKES** ¼ cup, enough to dress 8 to 10 cups lightly packed greens

**WHY THIS RECIPE WORKS** Vinaigrettes often seem a little slipshod—harsh and bristling in one bite, dull and oily in the next. We were determined to nail down a formula for the perfect vinaigrette, one that would consistently yield a harmonious blend of bright vinegar and rich oil in every forkful. First, top-notch ingredients make a big difference here. We liked fruity extra-virgin olive oil as an all-purpose oil option, and walnut oil for nuttier vinaigrettes. As for mixing methods, whisking together the ingredients only gets you so far. We used a key ingredient—mayonnaise—to emulsify oil and vinegar for a stabilized, smooth dressing. Red wine, white wine, or champagne vinegar will work in this recipe. This vinaigrette works with nearly any type of greens. For a hint of garlic flavor, rub the inside of the salad bowl with a cut clove of garlic before adding the lettuce.

- 1 tablespoon wine vinegar
- 1½ teaspoons very finely minced shallot
- ½ teaspoon mayonnaise
- ½ teaspoon Dijon mustard
- ⅛ teaspoon table salt
- 3 tablespoons extra-virgin olive oil

**1.** Combine vinegar, shallot, mayonnaise, mustard, salt, and pepper to taste in small nonreactive bowl. Whisk until mixture is milky in appearance and no lumps of mayonnaise remain.

**2.** Place oil in small measuring cup so that it is easy to pour. Whisking constantly, very slowly drizzle oil into vinegar mixture. If pools of oil are gathering on surface as you whisk, stop adding oil and whisk mixture well to combine, then resume whisking in oil in a slow stream. Vinaigrette should be glossy and lightly thickened, with no pools of oil on its surface.

## Leafy Green Salad with Red Wine Vinaigrette

**SERVES** 4 to 6

**WHY THIS RECIPE WORKS** We wanted to develop a recipe for this basic salad—a mix of well-chosen greens tossed with a light vinaigrette that was neither harsh nor oily. We went back to the basics and revisited standard vinaigrette proportions. In most cases, 4 parts oil to 1 part vinegar produces the best balance of flavors in a vinaigrette, so that's where we started. Red wine vinegar was the foundation of our vinaigrette. Before whisking the vinaigrette ingredients together, we added salt and pepper to the vinegar. This step mutes these seasonings a bit and prevents them from becoming too overpowering. With the right mix of salad greens—we like a combination of mild, delicate greens and peppery greens—this leafy salad makes the perfect complement to any main dish. For the best results, use at least two kinds of greens. A blend of mild, delicate greens, such as Boston and leaf lettuces, and peppery greens, such as arugula and watercress, is ideal. Romaine adds crunch and texture. If you like, add mild fresh herbs, such as chives, tarragon, or basil, in small amounts.

- 2¼ teaspoons red wine vinegar
- ⅛ teaspoon table salt
- Pinch ground black pepper
- 3 tablespoons extra-virgin olive oil
- 8 cups mixed salad greens, washed, dried, and torn into bite-sized pieces

Combine the vinegar, salt, and pepper in a bowl; add the oil and whisk until combined. Place the greens in a large bowl, drizzle the vinaigrette over the greens, and toss to coat evenly. Serve.

## Leafy Green Salad with Rich and Creamy Blue Cheese Dressing

**SERVES** 4 to 6

**WHY THIS RECIPE WORKS** Cool and crunchy salad greens coated with creamy blue cheese dressing are simply irresistible. But getting the right proportion of dressing to greens can be tricky. We wanted lettuce lightly napped with a creamy, tangy dressing. Starting with the dressing, we found perfection using the right creamy components. Three creamy ingredients were essential: mayonnaise for body, sour cream to supply tang, and buttermilk to thin out and further reinforce the dressing's bold flavors. A bit of sugar brought some much-needed sweetness, and white wine vinegar gave our dressing some zing. As for the main ingredient, we ruled out really pungent blue cheeses as too overpowering; a mild blue cheese works best. For the right chunky consistency, we mixed the crumbled blue cheese with the buttermilk before adding any other ingredients. Sturdy romaine and curly leaf lettuce hold up well to this thick dressing. In a pinch, whole milk can be used in place of the buttermilk; the dressing will be a bit lighter and milder in flavor, but will still taste good.

- 2½ ounces blue cheese, crumbled (about ½ cup)
- 3 tablespoons buttermilk
- 3 tablespoons sour cream
- 2 tablespoons mayonnaise
- 2 teaspoons white wine vinegar
- ¼ teaspoon sugar
- ⅛ teaspoon garlic powder
- Table salt and ground black pepper
- 10 cups loosely packed sturdy salad greens, such as romaine or curly leaf lettuce, washed, dried, and torn into bite size pieces

**1.** Mash the blue cheese and buttermilk in a small bowl with a fork until the mixture resembles cottage cheese with small curds. Stir in the sour cream, mayonnaise, vinegar, sugar, and garlic powder and season with salt and pepper to taste. (The dressing can be refrigerated in an airtight container for up to 2 weeks.)

**2.** Place the greens in a large bowl. Pour the dressing over the greens and toss to coat evenly. Serve.

## Salad with Herbed Baked Goat Cheese and Vinaigrette

**SERVES 6**

**WHY THIS RECIPE WORKS** Warm goat cheese salad has been a fixture on restaurant menus for years, featuring artisanal cheeses, organic greens, barrel-aged vinegars, and imported oils. But too often what arrives is unremarkable. We wanted to bring this restaurant favorite home with creamy cheese rounds infused with the flavor of fresh herbs and surrounded by crisp, golden breading, all cradled by lightly dressed greens. Ground Melba toasts (those ultra-dry and crispy crackers) made the crispiest crust for the goat cheese. After dipping the cheese rounds in beaten egg and herbs, we coated them with the crumbs, shaped them into attractive disks, and froze them to set the cheese and the crust. With the oven super hot and the cheese very cold, the cheese developed a crispy crust (with no oozing) and kept its shape, and a quick brush of olive oil on the outside of the disks lent flavor to the crumbs without turning them oily. A mix of greens paired well with the tangy flavor of the goat cheese, and a simple, light vinaigrette was all that was needed to finish this elegant salad. The baked goat cheese should be served warm. Prepare the salad components while the cheese is in the freezer, then toss the greens and vinaigrette while the cheese cools a bit after baking.

**GOAT CHEESE**

- 3 ounces white Melba toasts (about 2 cups)
- 1 teaspoon ground black pepper
- 3 large eggs
- 2 tablespoons Dijon mustard
- 1 tablespoon chopped fresh thyme leaves
- 1 tablespoon chopped fresh chives
- 12 ounces goat cheese
- Extra-virgin olive oil

**SALAD**

- 6 tablespoons extra-virgin olive oil
- 2 tablespoons red wine vinegar
- 1 tablespoon Dijon mustard
- 1 teaspoon minced shallot
- ¼ teaspoon table salt
- Ground black pepper
- 14 cups mixed delicate and spicy salad greens, such as arugula, baby spinach, and frisée, washed and dried

**1. FOR THE CHEESE:** In a food processor, process the Melba toasts to fine, even crumbs, about 1½ minutes; transfer the crumbs to a medium bowl and stir in the pepper. Whisk the eggs and mustard in a second medium bowl until combined. Combine the thyme and chives in a small bowl.

**2.** Using dental floss or kitchen twine, divide the cheese into 12 equal pieces by slicing the log lengthwise through the middle and each half into six even pieces. Roll each piece of cheese into a ball; roll each ball in the combined fresh herbs to coat lightly. Transfer 6 pieces to the egg mixture and turn each piece to coat; transfer to the Melba crumbs and turn each piece to coat, pressing the crumbs into the cheese. Flatten each ball gently with your fingertips into a disk about 1½ inches wide and 1 inch thick and set on a baking sheet. Repeat with the remaining 6 pieces of cheese. Transfer the baking sheet to the freezer and freeze the disks until firm, about 30 minutes. Adjust an oven rack to the top position and heat the oven to 475 degrees.

**3. FOR THE SALAD:** Meanwhile, whisk the oil, vinegar, mustard, shallot, and salt in a small bowl until combined; season with pepper to taste. Set aside.

**4.** Remove the cheese from the freezer and brush the tops and sides evenly with olive oil. Bake until the crumbs are golden brown and the cheese is slightly soft, 7 to 9 minutes (or 9 to 12 minutes if the cheese is completely frozen). Using a thin metal spatula, transfer the cheese to a paper towel–lined plate and cool for 3 minutes.

**5.** Place the greens in a large bowl, drizzle the vinaigrette over them, and toss to coat. Divide the greens among individual plates; place two rounds of goat cheese on each salad and serve.

## Hearty Green Salad with Chickpeas, Pickled Cauliflower, and Seared Halloumi for Two

**SERVES 2**

**WHY THIS RECIPE WORKS** For a dynamic vegetarian salad, we riffed on classic chef's salad. First we made quick pickled cauliflower florets and then turned part of the acidic brine into the vinaigrette; the rest we mixed into a thicker, creamier dressing with Greek yogurt and tahini to coat the other components. Pan-seared slabs of salty halloumi, canned chickpeas, and juicy grapes rounded out the salad's profile. Whole-milk, 2 percent, and 0 percent Greek yogurt will all work here. If Aleppo pepper is unavailable, substitute ⅜ teaspoon of paprika and ⅛ teaspoon of cayenne pepper. This recipe can easily be doubled.

- ¼ cup cider vinegar
- 2 teaspoons honey
- 1 teaspoon table salt, divided
- 2 cups (1-inch) cauliflower florets
- ½ teaspoon plus 2 tablespoons extra-virgin olive oil, divided
- 4 ounces halloumi cheese, cut into 4 slices
- ½ small head green leaf lettuce (4 ounces), torn into bite-size pieces
- ½ small head radicchio (3 ounces), cored and sliced thin
- ⅔ cup canned chickpeas, rinsed
- 3 tablespoons plain Greek yogurt
- 2 tablespoons tahini
- 1 small garlic clove, minced
- ½ teaspoon ground dried Aleppo pepper
- 6 ounces seedless red grapes, halved (1 cup)

**1.** Whisk vinegar, honey, and 3/4 teaspoon salt together in medium bowl. Add cauliflower and stir to coat. Microwave until simmering, 1½ to 2 minutes. Stir, then cover and let sit, stirring occasionally, until cauliflower is crisp-tender, about 5 minutes. Using slotted spoon, transfer cauliflower to small plate, leaving liquid in bowl.

**2.** Heat ½ teaspoon oil in 8-inch nonstick skillet over medium-high heat until shimmering. Add halloumi and cook until brown on both sides, 60 to 90 seconds per side. Remove from heat and cover to keep warm.

**3.** Transfer 2 tablespoons pickling liquid to large bowl. Add remaining 2 tablespoons oil and whisk to combine. Add lettuce and radicchio, season with salt and pepper to taste, and toss to combine. Distribute greens evenly between 2 shallow serving bowls. Place chickpeas in now-empty bowl.

**4.** Add yogurt, tahini, garlic, Aleppo pepper, and remaining 1/4 teaspoon salt to remaining pickling liquid and whisk until combined. Add 1/4 cup yogurt mixture to chickpeas and toss to combine. Arrange cauliflower, halloumi, and grapes in piles atop greens. Drizzle remaining yogurt mixture over cauliflower, grapes, and halloumi in each bowl. Divide chickpea mixture evenly between bowls and serve.

## Spicy Salad with Mustard and Balsamic Vinaigrette

**SERVES** 8 to 10

**WHY THIS RECIPE WORKS** We had a craving for a bold salad, one using spicy and bitter greens dressed in a pungent, mustardy vinaigrette. We started by focusing on peppery arugula and watercress. And for a salad that could hold its own with rich dishes, we used both balsamic vinegar and Dijon mustard as the acidic components. Minced shallot provided another strong flavor and added a bit of texture to our vinaigrette. We mixed the greens and vinaigrette together a little at a time to ensure that all the greens were well covered. Boldly flavored, this spicy salad with mustard and balsamic vinaigrette will wake up any dulled palate. This salad makes a perfect partner to rich main dishes, like lasagna, because its bitter greens and zesty vinaigrette help to cut the richness.

- 6 tablespoons extra-virgin olive oil
- 4 teaspoons balsamic vinegar
- 1 tablespoon Dijon mustard
- 1 teaspoon finely minced shallot
- ¼ teaspoon table salt
- ⅛ teaspoon ground black pepper
- 16 cups spicy greens, such as arugula, watercress, mizuna, and baby mustard greens, washed and dried

Whisk the oil, vinegar, mustard, shallot, salt, and pepper together in a bowl until combined. Place the greens in a large bowl, drizzle the dressing over the greens a little at a time, and toss to coat evenly, adding more vinaigrette if the greens seem dry. Serve.

## Arugula Salad with Figs, Prosciutto, Walnuts, and Parmesan

**SERVES** 6

**WHY THIS RECIPE WORKS** Unlike everyday iceberg lettuce, spicy arugula is more than just a leafy backdrop for salad garnishes. But arugula's complex, peppery flavor also makes it something of a challenge to pair with other ingredients. We wanted a truly outstanding arugula-based salad with co-starring ingredients that would stand up to these spicy greens. Salad combinations with harsh, one-dimensional flavor profiles (adding radishes and lemon-buttermilk dressing to arugula, for example) struck out, with too much abrasive flavor. What we did like were the salads containing fruit and cheese, so we decided to pair our arugula with sweet and salty ingredients. Fried prosciutto strips and shaved Parmesan fit the bill when it came to upping the saltiness of our salad. A spoonful of jam added to the vinaigrette helped to emulsify the dressing and provided a sweet contrast to arugula's peppery bite. For additional sweetness, dried figs worked well and toasted walnuts delivered just the right amount of crunch. Honey can be substituted for the jam.

- 4 tablespoons extra-virgin olive oil
- 2 ounces thinly sliced prosciutto, cut into ¼-inch strips
- 3 tablespoons balsamic vinegar
- 1 tablespoon raspberry jam
- ½ cup dried figs, stems removed, fruit chopped into ¼-inch pieces
- 1 small shallot, minced (about 1 tablespoon)
- Table salt and ground black pepper
- 5 ounces loosely packed baby arugula (about 5 cups), washed and dried
- ½ cup walnuts, toasted and chopped
- 2 ounces Parmesan cheese, shaved into thin strips with a vegetable peeler

**1.** Heat 1 tablespoon of the oil in a 10-inch nonstick skillet over medium heat; add the prosciutto and fry until crisp, stirring frequently, about 7 minutes. Using a slotted spoon, transfer to a paper towel–lined plate and set aside to cool.

2. Whisk the vinegar and jam together in a medium microwave-safe bowl until combined; stir in the figs. Cover with plastic wrap, cut several steam vents in the plastic, and microwave on high until the figs are plump, 30 seconds to 1 minute. Whisk in the remaining 3 tablespoons oil, the shallot, ¼ teaspoon salt, and ⅛ teaspoon pepper until combined. Cool to room temperature.

3. Toss the arugula with the vinaigrette in a large bowl; season with salt and pepper to taste. Divide the salad among individual plates; top each with a portion of the prosciutto, walnuts, and Parmesan. Serve.

## Wilted Spinach Salad with Warm Bacon Dressing

**SERVES** 4 to 6

**WHY THIS RECIPE WORKS** Traditional wilted spinach salad, tossed with warm bacon dressing, makes for an appealing and elegant salad. But too often, this salad is a soggy mess of slimy spinach, bogged down from too much oil and too much heat. We wanted perfectly wilted spinach, a balanced dressing, and crisp pieces of meaty bacon throughout. Baby spinach was preferred for its tender, sweet qualities. Thick-cut bacon provided more textural interest than regular sliced bacon. And using the bacon fat to cook the onion and garlic gave our salad a smoky flavor. For the vinaigrette, a generous amount of cider vinegar, enhanced with sugar, cut the richness of the bacon fat. Pouring the hot vinaigrette right over the baby spinach provided enough heat to wilt it without saturating it. Wedges of hard-cooked egg added heartiness. This salad comes together quickly, so have the ingredients ready before you begin cooking. When adding the vinegar mixture to the skillet, step back from the stovetop—the aroma is quite potent.

- 6 ounces baby spinach (about 6 cups), washed and dried
- 3 tablespoons cider vinegar
- ½ teaspoon sugar
- ¼ teaspoon ground black pepper
- Pinch table salt
- 10 ounces (about 8 slices) thick-cut bacon, cut into ½-inch pieces
- ½ medium red onion, chopped medium
- 1 small garlic clove, minced or pressed through a garlic press (about ½ teaspoon)
- 3 hard-cooked eggs (recipe follows), peeled and quartered

1. Place the spinach in a large bowl. Whisk the vinegar, sugar, pepper, and salt in a small bowl until the sugar dissolves; set aside.

2. Fry the bacon in a medium skillet over medium-high heat, stirring occasionally, until crisp, about 10 minutes. Using a slotted spoon, transfer the bacon to a paper towel–lined plate. Pour off all but 3 tablespoons of the bacon fat left in the pan. Add the onion to the skillet and cook over medium heat, stirring frequently, until softened, about 3 minutes. Stir in the garlic and cook until fragrant, about 15 seconds. Add the vinegar mixture, then remove the skillet from the heat. Working quickly, scrape the bottom of the skillet with a wooden spoon to loosen the browned bits. Pour the hot dressing over the spinach, add the bacon, and toss gently until the spinach is slightly wilted. Divide the salad among individual plates, arrange the egg quarters over each, and serve.

### Foolproof Hard-Cooked Eggs

**MAKES** 3

You can double or triple this recipe as long as you use a pot large enough to hold the eggs in a single layer, covered by an inch of water.

- 3 large eggs

1. Place the eggs in a medium saucepan, cover with 1 inch of water, and bring to a boil over high heat. Remove the pan from the heat, cover, and let sit for 10 minutes. Meanwhile, fill a medium bowl with 1 quart water and one tray of ice cubes.

2. Transfer the eggs to the ice bath with a slotted spoon and let sit for 5 minutes. Peel the eggs.

## Classic Caesar Salad for Two

**SERVES** 2

**WHY THIS RECIPE WORKS** Every component counts when making a great Caesar salad: crisp-tender romaine lettuce, a creamy dressing, and crunchy, garlicky croutons strewn throughout. We used both extra-virgin olive oil and vegetable oil in the dressing to give it a mellower flavor, and an egg yolk delivered richness. For robust but not aggressive garlic flavor, we grated a small garlic clove into a paste and steeped it in lemon juice. Adding Parmesan to the dressing and sprinkling more on top before serving provided a double layer of cheese flavor. Chewy ciabatta bread pieces tossed with garlic, olive oil, and Parmesan made perfect croutons when pan-fried. You will need one small ciabatta roll for this recipe. You can substitute 2 tablespoons Egg Beaters for the egg yolk.

**CROUTONS**

- 2 tablespoons extra-virgin olive oil, divided
- 1 small garlic clove, minced to paste
- 2 ounces ciabatta bread, cut into ¾-inch pieces (1½ cups)
- 1 tablespoon water
- Pinch table salt
- 2 teaspoons grated Parmesan cheese

**SALAD**

- 1½ teaspoons lemon juice, plus extra for seasoning
- 1 small garlic clove, minced to paste
- 1 large egg yolk
- 2 anchovy fillets, rinsed, patted dry, and mashed to fine paste
- ⅛ teaspoon Worcestershire sauce
- 2½ tablespoons vegetable oil
- 2½ teaspoons extra-virgin olive oil
- ⅓ cup grated Parmesan cheese, divided
- 1 small romaine lettuce heart (4½ ounces), torn into bite-size pieces

**1. FOR THE CROUTONS:** Combine 1 tablespoon oil and garlic in small bowl; set aside. Place bread pieces in separate bowl and sprinkle with water and salt. Toss, squeezing gently until bread absorbs water. Heat remaining 1 tablespoon oil in 10-inch nonstick skillet over medium-high heat until shimmering. Add bread and cook, stirring frequently, until browned and crispy, 7 to 10 minutes.

**2.** Off heat, clear center of skillet, add oil-garlic mixture, and cook until fragrant, about 10 seconds. Stir mixture into croutons, sprinkle with Parmesan, and toss to coat. Transfer croutons to bowl and let cool while finishing salad.

**3. FOR THE SALAD:** Whisk lemon juice and garlic together in large bowl and let sit for 10 minutes.

**4.** Whisk egg yolk, anchovies, and Worcestershire into lemon-garlic mixture. Whisking constantly, drizzle vegetable oil and olive oil into bowl in slow, steady stream until fully emulsified. Whisk in 3 tablespoons Parmesan and season with pepper to taste.

**5.** Add lettuce and croutons to dressing and toss gently to coat. Season with extra lemon juice, salt, and pepper to taste. Sprinkle with remaining Parmesan and serve immediately.

## Kale Caesar Salad

**SERVES 4**

**WHY THIS RECIPE WORKS** Here earthy kale takes the place of romaine for a great aesar salad. In experimenting with dressings, we found that the heartier kale really needed a thicker mayonnaise base to stand up to it. Using that as a starting point, we cut out half the mayonnaise, replacing it with low-fat yogurt. We found we needed only a half cup of Parmesan to get the satisfying, nutty flavor so essential to Caesar dressing. The addition of anchovy fillets provided rich umami notes. A 10-minute soak in warm water tenderized the kale. We swapped the usual white bread croutons for croutons made from whole-grain bread, as the hearty greens paired well with the more rustic croutons.

- 12 ounces curly kale, stemmed and cut into 1-inch pieces (16 cups)
- 3 ounces rustic whole-grain bread, cut into ½-inch cubes (1½ cups)
- 2 tablespoons extra-virgin olive oil, divided
- ⅛ teaspoon plus ½ teaspoon table salt, divided
- ⅛ teaspoon plus ½ teaspoon pepper, divided
- 3 tablespoons mayonnaise
- 3 tablespoons plain low-fat yogurt
- 1 ounce Parmesan cheese, grated (½ cup), divided
- 1 tablespoon lemon juice
- 2 teaspoons white wine vinegar
- 2 teaspoons Worcestershire sauce
- 2 teaspoons Dijon mustard
- 3 anchovy fillets, rinsed and minced
- 1 garlic clove, minced

**1.** Adjust oven rack to middle position and heat oven to 350 degrees. Place kale in large bowl and cover with warm tap water (110 to 115 degrees). Swish kale around to remove grit. Let kale sit in warm water bath for 10 minutes. Remove kale from water and spin dry in salad spinner in multiple batches. Pat leaves dry with paper towels if still wet.

**2.** Toss bread, 1 tablespoon oil, ⅛ teaspoon salt, and ⅛ teaspoon pepper together in bowl. Spread on rimmed baking sheet and bake until golden and crisp, about 15 minutes. Let croutons cool completely on sheet. (Cooled croutons can be stored in airtight container at room temperature for up to 24 hours.)

**3.** In large bowl whisk mayonnaise, yogurt, ¼ cup Parmesan, lemon juice, vinegar, Worcestershire sauce, mustard, anchovies, garlic, remaining ½ teaspoon salt, and remaining ½ teaspoon pepper until well combined. Whisking constantly, drizzle in remaining 1 tablespoon oil until combined.

**4.** Toss kale with dressing and refrigerate for at least 20 minutes or up to 6 hours. Toss dressed kale with croutons and remaining ¼ cup Parmesan. Serve.

## Kale Salad with Radishes, Grapefruit, and Candied Pepitas

**SERVES 6 to 8** SEASON 26

**WHY THIS RECIPE WORKS** We wanted to create a make-ahead holiday salad that would complement and enhance the traditional spread. Accompanied by pops of bright citrus, a zingy dressing, crisp raw vegetables, and candied nuts, kale can be downright festive. Using kale as the hearty base meant the dish could be dressed and ready to go hours ahead of time without compromising taste, texture, or appearance. Adding raw radishes meant minimal preparation with maximum crunch. Taking advantage of seasonal fruit, we incorporated grapefruit to add a bright burst of color and refreshing, juicy, and sweet-tart flavor. To tie the salad together, we infused cardamom into both a punchy vinaigrette and crunchy pepitas. Use flat-leaf parsley for this salad. The candied nuts will be moist and slightly soft out of the oven but will be very crisp once cool. This vibrant salad makes a versatile side to any number of dishes.

- 1 large egg white
- 1 tablespoon unsalted butter, melted
- 2 tablespoons granulated sugar
- 2 tablespoons packed brown sugar
- 1½ teaspoons ground cardamom, divided
- 1½ teaspoons table salt, divided
- Pinch cayenne pepper
- 1 cup raw pepitas
- ¼ cup extra-virgin olive oil, divided
- 3 tablespoons white wine vinegar
- ¼ teaspoon pepper
- 1 red grapefruit
- 12 ounces curly kale, stemmed and chopped (10 cups)
- 1½ cup fresh parsley leaves, chopped coarse
- 6 radishes, trimmed, halved, and sliced into thin half-moons

**1.** Adjust oven rack to middle rack position and heat oven to 350 degrees. Line rimmed baking sheet with parchment paper. Whisk egg white in bowl until frothy. Add melted butter, both sugars, ½ teaspoon cardamom, ½ teaspoon salt, and cayenne and whisk until combined. Add pepitas and stir to evenly coat.

**2.** Spread pepitas on prepared sheet in single layer and bake until seeds are deeply browned and fragrant, 15 to 17 minutes, stirring halfway through cooking. Transfer sheet to wire rack and let seeds cool completely, about 20 minutes. Break into ½-inch clusters. (Pepitas can be stored at room temperature for up to 1 week.)

**3.** Meanwhile, whisk 3 tablespoons oil, vinegar, pepper, remaining 1 teaspoon cardamom and remaining 1 teaspoon salt together in small bowl. Cut away peel and pith from grapefruit. Cut grapefruit into sixths from pole to pole, then cut crosswise into ¼-inch-thick pieces.

**4.** Combine kale and remaining 1 tablespoon oil in large bowl. Gently knead and squeeze kale until leaves are evenly coated, have started to soften, and are slightly wilted, about 1 minute. Add grapefruit, candied pepitas, parsley, radishes, and vinaigrette, and toss until well combined. Transfer salad to platter and serve. Salad can be stored at room temperature for up to 3 hours or refrigerated for up to 2 days (if refrigerating, add seeds just before serving).

## Salade Lyonnaise

**SERVES 4**

**WHY THIS RECIPE WORKS** With an Italian assist, our version of this iconic salad of crisp bitter greens, poached egg, and salted cured pork would be at home in any French bistro. Choosing a mix of bitter greens—frisée and chicory—gave this classic French salad enough volume, structure, and flavor to stand up to the richer elements of bacon and egg. To keep the flavor true to the French original, we called for pancetta rather than American bacon since it is unsmoked, salt cured, and rolled just like ventreche (also known as French pancetta). Making a bold, warm vinaigrette in the skillet not only infused the salad with richer bacon flavor but also allowed us to gently tenderize the frisée. Poached eggs delivered both runny yolks and tender whites that easily melded into the salad, which was critical to the success of the dish. Order a ½-inch-thick slice of pancetta at the deli counter; presliced or diced pancetta is likely to dry out or become tough. If you can't find chicory or escarole, dandelion greens make a good substitute. If using escarole, strip away the first four or five outer leaves and reserve them for another use. Serve this salad with crusty bread as a light lunch or dinner.

- 1 (½-inch-thick) slice pancetta (about 5 ounces)
- 2 tablespoons extra-virgin olive oil
- 1 tablespoon minced shallot
- 2 tablespoons red wine vinegar
- 4 teaspoons Dijon mustard
- 1 head frisée (6 ounces), torn into bite-size pieces
- 5 ounces chicory or escarole, torn into bite-size pieces (5 cups)
- 1 recipe Perfect Poached Eggs (recipe follows)

**1.** Cut pancetta vertically into thirds, then cut each third crosswise into ¼-inch-wide pieces. Combine pancetta and 2 cups water in 10-inch nonstick or carbon-steel skillet and bring to boil over medium-high heat. Boil for 5 minutes, then drain. Return pancetta to now-empty skillet. Add oil and cook over medium-low heat, stirring occasionally, until lightly browned but still chewy, 4 to 6 minutes.

**2.** Pour off all but 2 tablespoons fat from skillet, leaving pancetta in skillet. Add shallot and cook, stirring frequently, until slightly softened, about 30 seconds. Off heat, add vinegar and mustard and stir to combine.

**3.** Drizzle vinaigrette over frisée in large bowl and toss thoroughly to coat. Add chicory and toss again. Season with salt and pepper to taste. Divide salad among 4 plates. Gently place 1 egg on top of each salad, then season with salt and pepper to taste. Serve immediately.

## Perfect Poached Eggs

**MAKES** 4 eggs

Use the freshest eggs possible for this recipe.

- 4 large eggs
- 1 tablespoon distilled white vinegar
- Table salt for poaching eggs

**1.** Bring 6 cups water to boil in Dutch oven over high heat. Meanwhile, crack eggs, one at a time, into colander. Let stand until loose, watery whites drain away from eggs, 20 to 30 seconds. Gently transfer eggs to 2-cup liquid measuring cup.

**2.** Add vinegar and 1 teaspoon salt to boiling water. Remove pot from heat. With lip of measuring cup just above surface of water, gently tip eggs into water, one at a time, leaving space between them. Cover pot and let stand until whites closest to yolks are just set and opaque, about 3 minutes. If after 3 minutes whites are not set, let stand in water, checking every 30 seconds, until whites are set.

**3.** Using slotted spoon, carefully lift and drain each egg over Dutch oven. Season with salt and pepper to taste, and serve.

## Salade Niçoise for Two

**SERVES** 2

**WHY THIS RECIPE WORKS** Cooking the potatoes for our salade Niçoise in heavily salted water ensured that they were well seasoned; using that same water for the green beans was not only efficient but also meant that some of the calcium ions in the beans' cell walls were displaced by plentiful sodium ions, breaking the links between the pectin molecules in the beans. This effect caused the beans to soften quickly while remaining a brilliant green. Breaking with tradition, we flattened the cooked potatoes and crisped their exteriors in a hot skillet while our eggs cooked to a jammy, not hard-cooked, consistency. The mixture of hot and cold and crisp and creamy elements made the salad more interesting to eat, and the punchy, lemon-heavy vinaigrette, spiked with anchovies to enhance its savoriness, complemented the hearty components perfectly. A final sprinkling of briny capers and olives gave our salad traditional Mediterranean flair. This recipe moves quickly, so be sure to have all your ingredients in place before starting. You can substitute 1 teaspoon of anchovy paste for the anchovies. A high-quality oil-packed tuna such as Tonnino Tuna Fillets in Olive Oil works well here. If Niçoise olives are unavailable, substitute chopped pitted kalamatas. We like jammy eggs, with a consistency halfway between soft- and hard-cooked, in this salad. If you prefer soft-cooked eggs, cook them for 7 minutes; if you prefer hard-cooked eggs, cook them for 12 minutes.

**VINAIGRETTE**

- 3 tablespoons extra-virgin olive oil
- 2 tablespoons lemon juice
- 1 tablespoon minced shallot
- 1 teaspoon minced fresh thyme
- 1 teaspoon Dijon mustard
- 2 anchovies, rinsed and minced
- ¼ teaspoon table salt
- ⅛ teaspoon pepper

**SALAD**

- 5 ounces grape tomatoes, halved lengthwise
- ¼ teaspoon sugar
- ⅛ teaspoon table salt, plus salt for cooking vegetables
- 12 ounces small red potatoes, 1 to 2 inches in diameter
- 6 ounces green beans, trimmed
- 3 tablespoons extra-virgin olive oil
- 3 large eggs
- 1 (5- to 7-ounce) jar/can olive oil-packed tuna, drained and broken into bite-size pieces with fork
- 2 tablespoons chopped pitted Niçoise olives
- 1 tablespoon capers

**1. FOR THE VINAIGRETTE:** Whisk all ingredients together in small bowl.

**2. FOR THE SALAD:** Stir together tomatoes, sugar, and salt in small bowl. Bring 6 cups water to boil in medium saucepan over medium-high heat. Add potatoes and 3 tablespoons salt and cook until potatoes are easily pierced with paring knife, 12 to 15 minutes. Using tongs, transfer potatoes to cutting board, leaving water in saucepan.

**3.** Return water to boil. Add green beans and cook until just tender, 4 to 5 minutes. While green beans cook, fill medium bowl halfway with ice and water. Using tongs, transfer green beans to ice water, leaving water in saucepan. Let beans cool, about 5 minutes. While green beans cool, gently flatten each potato with side of chef's knife to ½- to ¾-inch thickness (it's OK if some potatoes crumble).

**4.** Heat oil in 10-inch nonstick skillet over medium-high heat until shimmering. Add potatoes and cook until brown and lightly crisped on both sides, 2 to 3 minutes per side. Meanwhile, return water to boil over medium-high heat. Add eggs, cover, and cook for 8 minutes (eggs needn't be submerged).

**5.** Line cutting board with double layer of paper towels. Transfer crisped potatoes to half of paper towel and season with salt to taste. Transfer green beans to remaining half of paper towel to drain, leaving cold water in bowl.

**6.** Divide tomatoes, tuna, and beans between 2 plates, piling them in separate mounds. Transfer cooked eggs to cold water to chill for 30 seconds. Peel and halve eggs and place 3 halves on each plate. Divide potatoes between plates. Drizzle each salad with 2 tablespoons vinaigrette. Sprinkle salads with olives and capers and serve, passing extra vinaigrette.

### Salad Niçoise for Four

You'll need a large cutting board for draining the potatoes and beans; alternatively, use a large rimmed baking sheet.

To serve four, double all ingredients except water and salt used for cooking the potatoes, eggs, and beans. Fry potatoes in 12-inch skillet.

## Classic Tuna Salad

**MAKES** 2 cups, enough for 4 sandwiches

**WHY THIS RECIPE WORKS** Tuna salads have been given a bad name by their typically mushy, watery, and bland condition. We wanted a tuna salad that was evenly textured, moist, and well seasoned. We learned that there are three keys to a great tuna salad. The first is to drain the tuna thoroughly in a colander; don't just tip the water out of the can. Next, break up the tuna with your fingers for a finer, more even texture. Finally, season the tuna before adding the mayonnaise for maximum flavor. Some additions to tuna salad are a matter of taste, but we thought that small amounts of garlic and mustard added another dimension, and minced pickle was a piquant touch. Our favorite canned tuna in water is American Tuna Pole Caught Wild Albacore.

- 2 (6-ounce) cans solid white tuna in water
- 1 small celery rib, minced (about ¼ cup)
- 2 tablespoons lemon juice
- 2 tablespoons minced red onion
- 2 tablespoons minced dill or sweet pickles
- 2 tablespoons minced fresh parsley
- ½ small garlic clove, minced
- ½ teaspoon table salt
- ¼ teaspoon ground black pepper
- ½ cup mayonnaise
- ¼ teaspoon Dijon mustard

Drain tuna in colander and shred with your fingers until no clumps remain and texture is fine and even. Transfer tuna to medium bowl and mix in celery, lemon juice, onion, pickles, parsley, garlic, salt, and pepper until evenly blended. Fold in mayonnaise and mustard until tuna is evenly moistened. (Tuna salad can be refrigerated in airtight container for up to 3 days.)

## Pan Bagnat (Provençal Tuna Sandwich)

**SERVES** 4 to 6

**WHY THIS RECIPE WORKS** Pan bagnat features a crusty baguette packed with high-quality jarred tuna, olives, capers, tomatoes, hard-cooked eggs, fresh herbs, and a mustardy vinaigrette. We used a large baguette, which offered enough surface area to accommodate the filling, and removed the inner crumb from the bottom half of the loaf to create a trough that provided more space. Processing the olives, capers, anchovies, and herbs into a coarse "salad" helped those components hold together, and applying the salad in two layers in the sandwich distributed its assertive flavors. Stirring the vinaigrette into the olive salad thickened the dressing so that it didn't oversaturate the crumb, and we also thoroughly drained the tuna and tomato slices to remove much of their liquid. We wrapped the sandwich halves with plastic wrap and pressed them for at least an hour under a heavy Dutch oven, which tamped down the filling, making for a compact sandwich. We developed this recipe with Tonnino Tuna Fillets in Olive Oil, but you can substitute three 5-ounce cans of another oil-packed tuna. To accommodate the filling, the baguette should be approximately 18 inches long, 3 inches wide, and at least 2 inches tall. A ciabatta of similar size will work, as will individual ciabatta rolls. You can substitute 1 tablespoon of oregano for the marjoram and kalamata olives for the niçoise. See page 147 for our recipe for Foolproof Hard-Cooked Eggs.

- 1 vine-ripened tomato, cored and sliced thin
- 1 small red onion, sliced thin
- 3 tablespoons red wine vinegar
- 1 garlic clove, minced
- ¼ teaspoon table salt
- 1 large baguette, halved horizontally
- ¾ cup niçoise olives, pitted
- ½ cup fresh parsley leaves and tender stems
- 3 tablespoons capers, rinsed
- 2 tablespoons fresh marjoram leaves
- 3 anchovy fillets, rinsed and patted dry
- ½ cup extra-virgin olive oil, divided
- 2 tablespoons Dijon mustard
- ¼ teaspoon pepper
- 2 (6½-ounce) jars oil-packed tuna, drained
- 3 hard-cooked eggs, sliced thin (see page 5)

**1.** Adjust oven rack to middle position and heat oven to 350 degrees. Lay tomato slices on paper towel–lined plate and set aside. Place onion, vinegar, garlic, and salt in bowl and toss to combine. Using your hands or metal spoon, remove inner crumb from baguette bottom to create trough, leaving ¼-inch border on sides and bottom. Place baguette halves cut side up on baking sheet and bake until very lightly toasted, 5 minutes.

**2.** Pulse olives, parsley, capers, marjoram, and anchovies in food processor until coarsely but evenly chopped, 10 to 12 pulses. Transfer olive mixture to bowl with onion mixture. Add ¼ cup oil, mustard, and pepper and toss to combine.

**3.** Brush inside of each baguette half with 1 tablespoon oil. Place two-thirds of olive mixture in hollow of baguette bottom and spread evenly. Distribute tuna evenly over olive mixture and drizzle with remaining 2 tablespoons oil. Shingle tomato slices over tuna. Shingle egg slices over tomato. Top eggs with remaining olive mixture and cap with baguette top (sandwich will be very full).

**4.** Press gently on sandwich and slice in half crosswise on bias. Wrap each half tightly in plastic wrap. Place rimmed baking sheet on top of sandwiches and weight with heavy Dutch oven or two 5-pound bags of flour or sugar for 1 hour, flipping sandwiches halfway through weighting. (Wrapped sandwiches can be refrigerated for up to 24 hours. Let come to room temperature before serving.)

**5.** Unwrap sandwiches, slice each sandwich in half (or in thirds to serve 6) on bias, and serve.

## Classic Chicken Salad

**SERVES** 4 to 6

**WHY THIS RECIPE WORKS** Recipes for chicken salad are only as good as the chicken itself. If the chicken is dry or flavorless, no amount of dressing or add-ins will camouflage it. To ensure juicy and flavorful chicken, we used a method based on sous vide cooking (submerging vacuum-sealed foods in a temperature-controlled water bath). Our ideal formula was four chicken breasts and 6 cups of cold water heated to 170 degrees and then removed from the heat, covered, and left to stand for about 15 minutes. This yielded incomparably moist chicken that was perfect for chicken salad. To ensure that the chicken cooks through, don't use breasts that weigh more than 8 ounces or are thicker than 1 inch. Make sure to start with cold water in step 1. We like the combination of parsley and tarragon, but 2 tablespoons of one or the other is fine. This salad can be served in a sandwich or spooned over leafy greens.

- Table salt for cooking chicken
- 4 (6- to 8-ounce) boneless, skinless chicken breasts, no more than 1 inch thick, trimmed
- ½ cup mayonnaise
- 2 tablespoons lemon juice
- 1 teaspoon Dijon mustard
- ¼ teaspoon pepper
- 2 celery ribs, minced
- 1 shallot, minced
- 1 tablespoon minced fresh parsley
- 1 tablespoon minced fresh tarragon

**1.** Dissolve 2 tablespoons salt in 6 cups cold water in Dutch oven. Submerge chicken in water. Heat pot over medium heat until water registers 170 degrees. Turn off heat, cover pot, and let stand until chicken registers 165 degrees, 15 to 17 minutes.

**2.** Transfer chicken to paper towel–lined baking sheet. Refrigerate until chicken is cool, about 30 minutes. While chicken cools, whisk mayonnaise, lemon juice, mustard, and pepper together in large bowl.

**3.** Pat chicken dry with paper towels and cut into ½-inch pieces. Transfer chicken to bowl with mayonnaise mixture. Add celery, shallot, parsley, and tarragon; toss to combine. Season with salt and pepper to taste. Serve. (Salad can be refrigerated for up to 2 days.)

### Waldorf Chicken Salad

Add ½ teaspoon ground fennel seeds to mayonnaise mixture in step 2. Substitute 1 teaspoon minced fresh thyme for parsley and add 1 peeled Granny Smith apple, cut into ¼-inch pieces, and ½ cup coarsely chopped toasted walnuts to salad with celery.

## Shrimp Salad

**SERVES** 4

**WHY THIS RECIPE WORKS** Most shrimp salads drown in a sea of mayonnaise, in part to hide the rubbery, flavorless shrimp. For perfectly cooked shrimp without the extra work of grilling, roasting, or sautéing. We found that starting them in cold water (with lemon, herbs, pepper, sugar, and salt) and then cooking them over gentle heat resulted in tender shrimp. The longer cooking time infused the shrimp with the flavors of the poaching liquid. We didn't want to mask these tender, flavorful shrimp with too much dressing, so we scaled back the mayonnaise to a modest amount. Celery added a nice crunch, and shallot, herbs, and lemon juice perked up and rounded out the flavors. This recipe can also be prepared with large shrimp (31 to 40 per pound); the cooking time will be 1 to 2 minutes shorter. The shrimp can be cooked up to 24 hours in advance, but hold off on dressing the salad until ready to serve. The recipe can be easily doubled; cook the shrimp in a 7-quart Dutch oven and increase the cooking time to 12 to 14 minutes. Serve the salad spooned over salad greens or on buttered and grilled buns.

- 1 pound extra-large shrimp (21 to 25 per pound), peeled and deveined (see page 523)
- 5 tablespoons lemon juice (2 to 3 lemons), spent halves reserved
- 5 sprigs fresh parsley plus 1 teaspoon minced fresh parsley
- 3 sprigs fresh tarragon plus 1 teaspoon minced fresh tarragon
- 1 teaspoon whole black peppercorns
- 1 tablespoon sugar for cooking shrimp
- 1 teaspoon table salt for cooking shrimp
- ¼ cup mayonnaise
- 1 small celery rib, minced (about ⅓ cup)
- 1 small shallot, minced (about 1 tablespoon)

**1.** Combine shrimp, ¼ cup lemon juice, reserved lemon halves, parsley sprigs, tarragon sprigs, whole peppercorns, sugar, and 1 teaspoon salt with 2 cups cold water in medium saucepan. Place saucepan over medium heat and cook shrimp, stirring several times, until pink, firm to touch, and centers are no longer translucent, 8 to 10 minutes (water should be just bubbling around edge of pan and register 165 degrees). Remove pan from heat, cover, and let shrimp sit in broth for 2 minutes.

**2.** Meanwhile, fill medium bowl with ice water. Drain shrimp into colander and discard lemon halves, herbs, and spices. Immediately transfer shrimp to ice water to stop cooking and chill thoroughly, about 3 minutes. Remove shrimp from ice water and pat dry with paper towels.

**3.** Whisk together mayonnaise, celery, shallot, remaining 1 tablespoon lemon juice, minced parsley, and minced tarragon in medium bowl. Cut shrimp in half lengthwise and then each half into thirds; add shrimp to mayonnaise mixture and toss to combine. Season with salt and pepper to taste, and serve.

## Panzanella (Italian Bread Salad)

SERVES 4

**WHY THIS RECIPE WORKS** In the best Italian bread salad panzanella, the sweet juice of tomatoes mixes with a bright vinaigrette, moistening chunks of crusty bread until they're soft and just a little chewy. We toasted fresh bread in the oven, rather than using the traditional day-old bread. The bread lost enough moisture to absorb the dressing without getting waterlogged. A 10-minute soak in the dressing yielded perfectly moistened, nutty-tasting bread ready to be tossed with the tomatoes, which we salted to intensify their flavor. Cucumber and shallot for crunch and bite plus plenty of chopped fresh basil perfected our salad. The success of this recipe depends on high-quality ingredients, including ripe, in-season tomatoes and fruity olive oil. Fresh basil is also a must. Your bread may vary in density, so you may not need the entire loaf for this recipe.

- 1 (1-pound) loaf rustic Italian or French bread, cut or torn into 1-inch pieces (about 6 cups)
- ½ cup extra-virgin olive oil, divided
- ¾ teaspoon table salt, divided
- 1½ pounds tomatoes, cored, seeded, and cut into 1-inch pieces
- 3 tablespoons red wine vinegar
- ¼ teaspoon pepper
- 1 cucumber, peeled, halved lengthwise, seeded, and sliced thin
- 1 shallot, sliced thin
- ¼ cup chopped fresh basil

**1.** Adjust oven rack to middle position and heat oven to 400 degrees. Toss bread pieces with 2 tablespoons oil and ¼ teaspoon salt; arrange bread in single layer on rimmed baking sheet. Toast bread pieces until just starting to turn light golden, 15 to 20 minutes, stirring halfway through baking. Set aside and let cool to room temperature.

**2.** Gently toss tomatoes and remaining ½ teaspoon salt in large bowl. Transfer to colander set over bowl; set aside to drain for 15 minutes, tossing occasionally.

**3.** Whisk vinegar, pepper, and remaining 6 tablespoons oil into tomato juices. Add bread pieces, toss to coat, and let stand for 10 minutes, tossing occasionally.

**4.** Add tomatoes, cucumber, shallot, and basil to bowl with bread pieces and toss to coat. Season with salt and pepper to taste, and serve immediately.

## Fattoush (Pita Bread Salad with Tomatoes and Cucumber)

SERVES 4

**WHY THIS RECIPE WORKS** The Levantine salad, fattoush, combines fresh, flavorful produce with crisp pita and bright herbs. We skipped seeding and salting the cucumbers and tomatoes, favoring the crisp texture of an English cucumber (which has fewer seeds) and the flavorful seeds and jelly of the tomato. We fended off soggy bread by brushing the craggy sides of the pita with plenty of olive oil before baking. The oil prevented the pita from absorbing the salad's moisture while still allowing them to take on some of its flavor. A summery blend of mint, cilantro, and arugula comprised the salad's greenery, and a lemony vinaigrette lent it a bright finish. The success of this recipe depends on ripe, in-season tomatoes. A rasp-style grater makes quick work of turning the garlic into a paste.

- 2 (8-inch) pita breads
- 3 tablespoons plus ¼ cup extra-virgin olive oil, divided
- 3 tablespoons lemon juice
- ¼ teaspoon garlic, minced to paste
- ¼ teaspoon table salt
- 1 pound tomatoes, cored and cut into ¾-inch pieces
- 1 English cucumber, peeled and sliced ⅛ inch thick
- 1 cup arugula, chopped coarse
- ½ cup chopped fresh cilantro
- ½ cup chopped fresh mint
- 4 scallions, sliced thin

**1.** Adjust oven rack to middle position and heat oven to 375 degrees. Using kitchen shears, cut around perimeter of each pita and separate into 2 thin rounds. Cut each round in half. Place pita bread, smooth side down, on wire rack set in rimmed baking sheet. Brush 3 tablespoons oil over surface of pita. (Pita does not need to be uniformly coated. Oil will absorb and spread as it bakes.) Season with salt and pepper to taste. Bake until pita is crisp and pale golden brown, 10 to 14 minutes.

2. While pita toasts, whisk lemon juice, garlic, and ¼ teaspoon salt together in small bowl. Let stand for 10 minutes.

3. Place tomatoes, cucumber, arugula, cilantro, mint, and scallions in large bowl. Break pita into ½-inch pieces and place in bowl with vegetables. Add lemon-garlic mixture and remaining ¼ cup oil and toss to coat. Season with salt and pepper to taste. Serve immediately.

## Horiatiki Salata (Hearty Greek Salad)

**SERVES** 4 to 6

**WHY THIS RECIPE WORKS** Imagine bites of sweet tomatoes, briny olives, savory onion, crunchy cucumber, and tangy feta—without any lettuce filler—and you've got horiatiki salata, the real Greek salad. Ripe tomatoes are loaded with juice that can flood the salad, so we tossed halved wedges (perfect for chunky but manageable bites) with salt and let them drain in a colander for 30 minutes. Soaking the onion slices in ice water lessened their hot bite while maintaining their fresh, crisp texture. A creamy Greek feta, which must be made with at least 70 percent fatty sheep's milk, brought richness to the vegetables. When we tried subbing in fresh oregano for the traditional dried, we understood why the dried herb is preferred: Its more delicate flavor complemented—but didn't upstage—the vegetables. Vinaigrette isn't traditionally used to dress horiatiki salata, but we did tweak the custom of drizzling the salad separately with oil and vinegar by tossing the vegetables with each component, ensuring that the mixture was lightly but evenly dressed. Soaking the sliced onion in ice water tempers its heat and bite. Use only large, round tomatoes here, not Roma or cherry varieties, and use the ripest in-season tomatoes you can find. A fresh, fruity, peppery olive oil works well here if you have it. We prefer to use feta by Real Greek Feta or Dodoni in this recipe. The salad can be served with crusty bread as a light meal for four.

- 1¾ pounds tomatoes, cored
- ¾ teaspoon table salt, plus salt for salting tomatoes
- ½ red onion, sliced thin
- 2 tablespoons red wine vinegar
- 1 teaspoon dried oregano, plus extra for seasoning
- ½ teaspoon pepper
- 1 English cucumber, quartered lengthwise and cut into ¾-inch chunks
- 1 green bell pepper, stemmed, seeded, and cut into 2 by ½-inch strips
- 1 cup pitted kalamata olives
- 2 tablespoons capers, rinsed
- 5 tablespoons extra-virgin olive oil, divided
- 1 (8-ounce) block feta cheese, sliced into ½-inch-thick triangles

1. Cut tomatoes into ½-inch-thick wedges. Cut wedges in half crosswise. Toss tomatoes and ½ teaspoon salt together in colander set in large bowl. Let drain for 30 minutes. Place onion in small bowl, cover with ice water, and let sit for 15 minutes. Whisk vinegar, oregano, pepper, and salt together in second small bowl.

2. Discard tomato juice and transfer tomatoes to now-empty bowl. Drain onion and add to bowl with tomatoes. Add vinegar mixture, cucumber, bell pepper, olives, and capers and toss to combine. Drizzle with ¼ cup oil and toss gently to coat. Season with salt and pepper to taste. Transfer to serving platter and top with feta. Season each slice of feta with extra oregano to taste. Drizzle feta with remaining 1 tablespoon oil. Serve.

## Greek Salad

**SERVES** 6 to 8

**WHY THIS RECIPE WORKS** Many versions of Greek salad consist of iceberg lettuce, chunks of green pepper, and a few pale wedges of tomato, sparsely dotted with cubes of feta and garnished with one or two olives. We wanted a salad with crisp ingredients and bold flavors. A combination of lemon juice, red wine vinegar, garlic, and olive oil made a zesty vinaigrette. We marinated onion and cucumber slices in the vinaigrette which helped mute the sting of raw onion in the salad. We swapped in crisp, flavorful romaine for the iceberg. And along with sliced tomatoes, we added jarred roasted red peppers for a bit of sweetness. A handful of kalamata olives and tangy feta cheese lent the traditional touches, and torn mint and parsley leaves gave our salad a fresh finish. For efficiency, prepare the other salad ingredients while the onion and cucumber marinate.

**VINAIGRETTE**

- 6 tablespoons extra-virgin olive oil
- 3 tablespoons red wine vinegar
- 2 teaspoons minced fresh oregano leaves
- 1½ teaspoons juice from 1 lemon
- 1 medium garlic clove, minced or pressed through a garlic press (about 1 teaspoon)
- ½ teaspoon table salt
- ⅛ teaspoon ground black pepper

SALAD

- ½ medium red onion, sliced thin (about ¾ cup)
- 1 medium cucumber, peeled, halved lengthwise, seeded, and sliced ⅛ inch thick
- 2 romaine hearts, washed, dried, and torn into 1½-inch pieces (about 8 cups)
- 2 medium, firm, ripe tomatoes (6 ounces each), cored, seeded, and each tomato cut into 12 wedges
- 6 ounces jarred roasted red bell peppers, cut into 2 by ½-inch strips (about 1 cup)
- ¼ cup loosely packed fresh parsley leaves, torn
- ¼ cup loosely packed fresh mint leaves, torn
- 20 large pitted kalamata olives, quartered
- 5 ounces feta cheese, crumbled (about 1¼ cups)

**1. FOR THE VINAIGRETTE:** Whisk the oil, vinegar, oregano, lemon juice, garlic, salt, and pepper in a large bowl until combined.

**2.** Add the onion and cucumber to the vinaigrette and toss; let stand to blend the flavors, about 20 minutes.

**3. FOR THE SALAD:** Add the romaine, tomatoes, peppers, parsley, and mint to the bowl with the onions and cucumbers; toss to coat with the vinaigrette.

**4.** Transfer the salad to a serving bowl or platter; sprinkle the olives and feta over the salad and serve.

## Mediterranean Chopped Salad

SERVES 4 to 6

**WHY THIS RECIPE WORKS** Chopped salads are often little better than a random collection of cut-up produce from the crisper drawer exuding moisture that turns the salad watery and bland. We wanted a lively, thoughtfully chosen composition of lettuce and vegetables—cut into bite-size pieces—with supporting players like beans and cheese contributing hearty flavors and chunky textures. Salting the cucumber and tomatoes to remove excess moisture was an important first step. As for the dressing, we found that an assertive blend of equal parts oil and vinegar delivered the bright, acidic kick this salad needed. We also found that marinating the bell peppers and onions in the dressing for 5 minutes before adding the cheese and other tender components brought a welcome flavor boost.

- 1 cucumber, peeled, halved lengthwise, seeded, and cut into ½-inch dice (about 1¼ cups)
- 1 pint grape tomatoes, quartered (about 1½ cups)
- Table salt for salting vegetables
- 3 tablespoons extra-virgin olive oil
- 3 tablespoons red wine vinegar
- 1 garlic clove, minced
- 1 (15-ounce) can chickpeas, drained and rinsed
- ½ cup pitted kalamata olives, chopped
- ½ small red onion, minced (about ¼ cup)
- ½ cup chopped fresh parsley
- 1 romaine lettuce heart, cut into ½-inch pieces (about 3 cups)
- 4 ounces feta cheese, crumbled (1 cup)

**1.** Combine cucumber, tomatoes, and 1 teaspoon salt in colander set over bowl and drain for 15 minutes.

**2.** Whisk oil, vinegar, and garlic together in large bowl. Add drained cucumber and tomatoes, chickpeas, olives, onion, and parsley. Toss and let stand at room temperature to blend flavors, 5 minutes.

**3.** Add romaine and feta and toss to combine. Season with salt and pepper to taste, and serve.

## Beet Salad with Spiced Yogurt and Watercress

SERVES 6

**WHY THIS RECIPES WORKS** For a stunning beet salad we used a yogurt-lime dressing as an ultracreamy landing pad for beets and watercress. Beets are very dense, so roasting whole ones can take up to 2 hours. Instead, we peeled and cut the beets into small chunks and microwaved them in a covered bowl with a small amount of water. Peeling them before cooking cut out the wait time for them to cool. Cutting them into pieces exposed much more surface area so they cooked faster, and cooking them in the microwave (as opposed to on the stovetop) caused water molecules inside the beets to boil rapidly and intensely, so they cooked through in less than 30 minutes. Instead of tossing the components together, we used the yogurt as an anchor for the other ingredients by thinning it with lime juice and water, spreading it on a platter, and topping it with lightly dressed beets and greens as well as toasted pistachios for crunch. Be sure to wear gloves when peeling and dicing the beets to prevent your hands from becoming stained. The moisture content of Greek yogurt varies, so add the water slowly in step 2. We like to make this salad with watercress, but baby arugula can be substituted, if desired. For the best presentation, use red beets here, not golden or Chioggia beets.

- 2 pounds beets, trimmed, peeled, and cut into ¾-inch pieces
- 1 teaspoon plus 2 pinches table salt, divided
- 1¼ cups plain Greek yogurt
- ¼ cup minced fresh cilantro, divided
- 3 tablespoons extra-virgin olive oil, divided
- 2 teaspoons grated fresh ginger
- 1 teaspoon grated lime zest plus 2 tablespoons juice, divided, plus extra juice for seasoning (2 limes)
- 1 garlic clove, minced
- ½ teaspoon ground cumin
- ½ teaspoon ground coriander
- ¼ teaspoon pepper
- 5 ounces (5 cups) watercress, torn into bite-size pieces
- ¼ cup shelled pistachios, toasted and chopped, divided

**1.** In largest bowl your microwave will accommodate, stir together beets, ⅓ cup water, and ½ teaspoon salt. Cover with plate and microwave until beets can be easily pierced with paring knife, 25 to 30 minutes, stirring halfway through microwaving. Drain beets in colander and let cool.

2. In medium bowl, whisk together yogurt, 3 tablespoons cilantro, 2 tablespoons oil, ginger, lime zest and 1 tablespoon juice, garlic, cumin, coriander, pepper, and ½ teaspoon salt. Slowly stir in up to 3 tablespoons water until mixture has consistency of regular yogurt. Season with salt, pepper, and extra lime juice to taste. Spread yogurt mixture over serving platter.

3. In large bowl, combine watercress, 2 tablespoons pistachios, 2 teaspoons oil, 1 teaspoon lime juice, and pinch salt and toss to coat. Arrange watercress mixture on top of yogurt mixture, leaving 1-inch border of yogurt mixture. Add beets to now-empty bowl and toss with remaining 1 teaspoon oil, remaining 2 teaspoons lime juice, and remaining pinch salt. Place beet mixture on top of watercress mixture. Sprinkle salad with remaining 2 tablespoons pistachios and remaining 1 tablespoon cilantro and serve.

## Broccoli Salad with Creamy Avocado Dressing

**SERVES** 4 to 6

**WHY THIS RECIPE WORKS** This dynamic salad combines crisp broccoli, dried fruit, nuts, and a creamy dressing. We made a lush but light dressing by replacing the mayonnaise with avocado and olive oil, buzzing them in a food processor with garlic and lemon for a bright and savory flavor. We balanced the sweet tang of dried fruit and rich toasty flavors of the nuts by adding shallot and tarragon. Blanching and shocking the broccoli softened its raw edge and brightened its color. To ensure that the florets and stems cooked evenly, we layered them strategically in the pot. Be sure to use a fully ripe Hass avocado here.

- 1 cup water
- ¾ teaspoon table salt, plus salt for cooking broccoli
- 1½ pounds broccoli, florets cut into 1-inch pieces, stalks peeled, halved lengthwise, and sliced ¼ inch thick
- 1 avocado, halved, pitted, and cut into ½-inch pieces
- 2 tablespoons extra-virgin olive oil
- 1 teaspoon grated lemon zest, plus 3 tablespoons juice
- 1 garlic clove, minced
- ¼ teaspoon pepper
- ½ cup dried cranberries
- ½ cup sliced almonds, toasted
- 1 shallot, sliced thin
- 1 tablespoon minced fresh tarragon

1. Bring water and ½ teaspoon salt to boil in large saucepan over high heat. Add broccoli stalks, then place florets on top of stalks so that they sit just above water. Cover and cook until broccoli is bright green and crisp-tender, about 3 minutes. Meanwhile, fill large bowl halfway with ice and water. Drain broccoli well, transfer to ice water, and let sit until just cool, about 2 minutes. Transfer broccoli to triple layer of paper towels and dry well. Dry bowl and set aside.

2. Process avocado, oil, lemon zest and juice, garlic, salt, and pepper in food processor until smooth, about 30 seconds, scraping down sides of bowl as needed. Season with salt and pepper to taste.

3. Combine broccoli, dressing, cranberries, almonds, shallot, and tarragon in now-empty large bowl until evenly coated. Season with salt and pepper to taste. Serve.

## Brussels Sprout Salad with Warm Mustard Vinaigrette

**SERVES** 6

**WHY THIS RECIPE WORKS** Though most often sautéed or roasted, raw brussels sprouts make a great salad green and here they play a starring role. We dressed our brussels sprout salad in a warm mustard vinaigrette that gently tenderized the sprouts while letting them retain their fresh flavor. Bites of quick pickled shallot and dried apricots added pop to this elegant salad, while ricotta salata cheese, chopped toasted pistachios, and watercress added richness, flavor, and a touch of bitterness. We dressed the salad in the skillet before transferring it to a serving bowl. A food processor's slicing blade can be used to slice the brussels sprouts, but the salad will be less tender.

- 5 tablespoons white wine vinegar
- 1 tablespoon whole-grain mustard
- 1 teaspoon sugar
- ¼ teaspoon table salt
- 1 shallot, halved through root end and sliced thin crosswise
- ¼ cup dried apricots, chopped
- 5 tablespoons vegetable oil
- ⅓ cup shelled pistachios, chopped
- 1½ pounds brussels sprouts, trimmed, halved, and sliced thin
- 1½ ounces (1½ cups) watercress, chopped
- 4 ounces ricotta salata, shaved into thin strips using vegetable peeler

1. Whisk vinegar, mustard, sugar, and salt together in bowl. Add shallot and apricots, cover tightly with plastic wrap, and microwave until steaming, 30 to 60 seconds. Stir briefly to submerge shallot. Let cool to room temperature, about 15 minutes.

2. Heat oil in 12-inch skillet over medium heat until shimmering. Add pistachios and cook, stirring frequently, until pistachios are golden brown, 1 to 2 minutes. Off heat, whisk in shallot mixture. Add brussels sprouts and toss with tongs until dressing is evenly distributed and sprouts darken slightly, 1 to 2 minutes. Transfer to serving bowl. Add watercress and ricotta salata and toss to combine. Season with salt and pepper to taste, and serve immediately.

## Chopped Carrot Salad with Fennel, Orange, and Hazelnuts

**SERVES** 4 to 6

**WHY THIS RECIPE WORKS** We were inspired by a recipe by Joan Nathan to create a finely chopped carrot salad that delivered the vegetable's juicy, earthy sweetness but offered a texture that's more like grains, with a pleasant crunch. Finely chopping carrots in the food processor, instead of grating them by hand, produced the delicately crunchy, light-textured base we were after. The food processor broke down the carrots in seconds, and we saved even more time by not peeling the carrots; scrubbing them was sufficient, and the skins contributed a subtle but pleasant bitterness. We added bulk and contrasting flavor to the carrots with lots of fresh chives (chopped by hand to avoid overprocessing the leaves in the food processor), toasted hazelnuts, and chopped fennel. A bright dressing bound it all together. We prefer the convenience and the hint of bitterness that leaving the carrots unpeeled lends to this salad; just be sure to scrub the carrots well before using them.

- ¾ cup hazelnuts, toasted and skinned
- ¼ cup extra-virgin olive oil
- 2 tablespoons white wine vinegar
- 1 teaspoon table salt
- ½ teaspoon pepper
- ¼ teaspoon orange zest plus ⅓ cup juice
- 1 fennel bulb, stalks discarded, bulb halved, cored, and cut into 1-inch pieces
- 1 pound carrots, trimmed and cut into 1-inch pieces
- ½ cup finely chopped fresh chives, divided

Pulse hazelnuts in food processor until coarsely chopped, 10 to 12 pulses; transfer to small bowl. Whisk oil, vinegar, salt, pepper, and orange zest and juice in large bowl until combined. Pulse fennel in now-empty processor until coarsely chopped, 10 to 12 pulses; transfer to bowl with dressing. Process carrots in again-empty processor until finely chopped, 10 to 20 seconds, scraping down sides of bowl as needed. Transfer carrots to bowl with fennel mixture. Add ¼ cup chives and half of hazelnuts and toss to combine. Season with salt to taste. Transfer to serving platter, sprinkle with remaining ¼ cup chives and remaining hazelnuts, and serve.

## Lao Hu Cai (Tiger Salad)

**SERVES** 4

**WHY THIS RECIPE WORKS** This vibrant Chinese salad, called tiger salad for its bold flavors and textures, is traditionally served to stimulate the appetite at the beginning of a meal or to reset the palate between courses. We balanced the bracing vinaigrette (a combination of unseasoned rice vinegar, sugar, salt, soy sauce, and sesame oil), piquant scallions, and hot chiles with the herbal freshness of cilantro and the juicy crunch of sliced celery, which together made up the salad's vegetable base. The earthy sweetness of chopped roasted peanuts and toasted sesame seeds and the rich sesame oil added further layers of texture and flavor to the dish. For a spicier salad, include the chile seeds. For less spice, substitute half of a small green bell pepper (cut into 2-inch-long matchsticks) for the serrano.

- 1 tablespoon unseasoned rice vinegar
- 1 teaspoon sugar
- ½ teaspoon table salt
- ½ teaspoon soy sauce
- ¾ teaspoon toasted sesame oil
- 1 Thai chile, stemmed, halved, seeded, and sliced thin
- 3½ cups fresh cilantro leaves and tender stems, chopped into 2-inch lengths
- 4 celery ribs, sliced on bias ¼ inch thick
- 3 scallions, white and green parts sliced thin on bias
- 1 serrano chile, stemmed, quartered, seeded, and sliced thin
- 2 teaspoons sesame seeds, toasted
- 2 tablespoons chopped salted dry-roasted peanuts

1. In small bowl, stir vinegar, sugar, salt, and soy sauce until sugar and salt are completely dissolved. Add oil and Thai chile and stir to combine.

2. In large bowl, combine cilantro, celery, scallions, and serrano. Sprinkle with sesame seeds and dressing and toss to combine.

3. Transfer salad to platter, sprinkle with peanuts, and serve immediately.

## Shaved Celery Salad with Pomegranate-Honey Vinaigrette

**SERVES** 4 to 6 **SEASON 26**

**WHY THIS RECIPE WORKS** This fresh, light salad employs both celery ribs and celery root. Our tasters especially loved how the combination of sweet-tart pomegranate seeds and rich, salty Pecorino Romano cheese boosted the flavors and textures of the celery parts. Shaving the celery root thin with a vegetable peeler eliminated any need to cook the root. Chopped frisée gave the salad more substance, and toasted walnuts added more crunch. For the dressing, we echoed the flavor of the pomegranate seeds by whisking pomegranate molasses with red wine vinegar, honey, shallot, and olive oil. Use the large holes of a box grater to shred the Pecorino Romano. A mandoline can also be used to shave the celery root in step 2.

2 tablespoons pomegranate molasses
1 tablespoon red wine vinegar
1 small shallot, minced
2 teaspoons honey
¼ teaspoon table salt
Pinch pepper
2 tablespoons extra-virgin olive oil
14 ounces celery root, trimmed, peeled, and quartered
4 celery ribs, sliced thin on bias, plus ½ cup celery leaves
1 head frisée (6 ounces), trimmed and cut into 1-inch pieces
1½ ounces Pecorino Romano cheese, shredded (½ cup)
¼ cup pomegranate seeds, divided
½ cup walnuts, toasted and chopped coarse

**1.** Whisk pomegranate molasses, vinegar, shallot, honey, salt, and pepper together in large bowl. While whisking constantly, slowly drizzle in oil until combined.

**2.** Using sharp vegetable peeler, shave celery root into thin ribbons. Add celery root, celery ribs and leaves, frisée, Pecorino, and 2 tablespoons pomegranate seeds to bowl with dressing and toss gently to coat. Season with salt and pepper to taste. Sprinkle with walnuts and remaining 2 tablespoons pomegranate seeds. Serve.

## Esquites (Mexican-Style Corn Salad)

**SERVES** 6 to 8

**WHY THIS RECIPE WORKS** This recipe provides a simpler route to enjoying elote (Mexican street corn) in salad form (esquites) that doesn't require firing up the grill. First, we cooked the kernels in two batches in a little oil in a covered skillet on the stovetop. The kernels browned and charred while the lid prevented the kernels from popping out of the hot skillet. It also trapped steam, which helped to cook the corn. Once all the corn was perfectly toasted, we used the hot skillet to bloom chili powder and cook minced garlic, which tempered its bite. To tie everything together, we made a simple crema, which we tossed with the charred corn and spices before adding crumbled cotija, chopped cilantro, and sliced scallions. If desired, substitute plain Greek yogurt for the sour cream. We like serrano chiles here, but you can substitute a jalapeño chile that has been halved lengthwise and sliced into ⅛-inch-thick half-moons. Adjust the amount of chiles to suit your taste. If cotija cheese is unavailable, substitute feta cheese.

3 tablespoons lime juice, plus extra for seasoning (2 limes)
3 tablespoons sour cream
1 tablespoon mayonnaise
1–2 serrano chiles, stemmed and cut into ⅛-inch-thick rings
¾ teaspoon table salt, divided
2 tablespoons plus 1 teaspoon vegetable oil, divided
6 ears corn, kernels cut from cobs (6 cups)
2 garlic cloves, minced
½ teaspoon chili powder
4 ounces cotija cheese, crumbled (1 cup)
¾ cup coarsely chopped fresh cilantro
3 scallions, sliced thin

**1.** Combine lime juice, sour cream, mayonnaise, serrano(s), and ¼ teaspoon salt in large bowl. Set aside.

**2.** Heat 1 tablespoon oil in 12-inch nonstick skillet over high heat until shimmering. Add half of corn and spread into even layer. Sprinkle with ¼ teaspoon salt. Cover and cook, without stirring, until corn touching skillet is charred, about 3 minutes. Remove skillet from heat and let stand, covered, for 15 seconds, until any popping subsides. Transfer corn to bowl with sour cream mixture. Repeat with 1 tablespoon oil, remaining ¼ teaspoon salt, and remaining corn.

**3.** Return now-empty skillet to medium heat and add remaining 1 teaspoon oil, garlic, and chili powder. Cook, stirring constantly, until fragrant, about 30 seconds. Transfer garlic mixture to bowl with corn mixture and toss to combine. Let cool for at least 15 minutes.

**4.** Add cotija, cilantro, and scallions and toss to combine. Season salad with salt and up to 1 tablespoon extra lime juice to taste. Serve.

## Sesame Lemon Cucumber Salad

**SERVES** 4

**WHY THIS RECIPE WORKS** More often than not, cucumbers in cucumber salad turn soft and watery, having lost their crunchy texture and released enough liquid to dilute the dressing. This phenomenon made the primary goal of our cucumber salad easy to identify: Maximize the crunch. Because water makes cucumbers lose their texture, we had to salt and weight the cucumbers to draw off excess moisture. We also rinsed them and patted them dry before tossing the cucumbers with a rice vinegar, lemon juice, and sesame oil vinaigrette, a flavorful combination. Toasted sesame seeds added even more textural interest. Mild rice vinegar works well in this sesame dressing.

3 medium cucumbers (about 2 pounds), peeled, halved lengthwise, seeded, and sliced ¼ inch thick
1 tablespoon table salt

¼ cup rice vinegar
2 tablespoons toasted sesame oil
1 tablespoon juice from 1 lemon
1 tablespoon sesame seeds, toasted
2 teaspoons sugar
⅛ teaspoon red pepper flakes

**1.** Toss the cucumbers with the salt in a colander set over a large bowl. Weight the cucumbers with a gallon-sized zipper-lock bag filled with water; drain for 1 to 3 hours. Rinse and pat dry.

**2.** Whisk the remaining ingredients together in a medium bowl. Add the cucumbers; toss to coat. Serve chilled or at room temperature.

## Pai Huang Gua (Smashed Cucumbers)

**SERVES** 4

**WHY THIS RECIPE WORKS** Pai huang gua, smashed cucumbers, is a Sichuan dish that is typically served with rich, spicy food. We started with English cucumbers, which are nearly seedless and have a thin, crisp skin. Placing them in a zipper-lock bag and smashing them into large, irregular pieces sped up a salting step that helped to expel excess water. The craggy pieces also did a better job of holding on to the dressing. Using black vinegar, an aged rice-based vinegar, added a mellow complexity to the soy sauce and sesame dressing. We recommend using Chinese Chinkiang (or Zhenjiang) black vinegar in this dish because of its complex flavor. If you can't find it, you can substitute 2 teaspoons of rice vinegar and 1 teaspoon of balsamic vinegar. A rasp-style grater makes quick work of turning the garlic into a paste.

2 (14-ounce) English cucumbers
Kosher salt for salting cucumbers
4 teaspoons Chinese black vinegar
1 teaspoon garlic, minced to paste
1 tablespoon soy sauce
2 teaspoons toasted sesame oil
1 teaspoon sugar
1 teaspoon sesame seeds, toasted

**1.** Trim and discard ends from cucumbers. Cut cucumbers crosswise into 3 equal lengths. Place pieces in large zipper-lock bag and seal bag. Using small skillet or rolling pin, firmly but gently smash cucumbers until flattened and split lengthwise into 3 or 4 spears. Tear spears into rough 1- to 1½-inch pieces and transfer to colander set in large bowl. Toss pieces with 1½ teaspoons salt and let stand for at least 15 minutes or up to 30 minutes.

**2.** While cucumber sits, whisk vinegar and garlic together in small bowl; let stand at least 5 minutes or up to 15 minutes.

**3.** Whisk soy sauce, sesame oil, and sugar into vinegar mixture until sugar has dissolved. Transfer cucumber pieces to medium bowl and discard any extracted liquid. Add dressing and sesame seeds to cucumbers and toss to combine. Serve immediately.

## Crispy Eggplant Salad with Tomatoes, Herbs, and Fried Shallots

**SERVES** 2 to 3

**WHY THIS RECIPE WORKS** For this salad, we took elements from Sicilian caponata—eggplant, tomatoes, herbs, and vinegary notes—and married them with intense Thai flavors. We first dehydrated the eggplant and then shallow-fried it before marinating it in nam prik, a bright Thai condiment made with lime juice, fish sauce, rice vinegar, ginger, garlic, and chile. We tossed in juicy cherry tomatoes, a healthy amount of fresh herbs, and crispy fried shallots for a dish that delivered all of the five tastes and as many different textures. Japanese eggplant was our unanimous favorite, but globe or Italian eggplant can be substituted. Palm sugar yields the best results, but an equal amount of light brown sugar can be used. Genovese basil is a fine substitute for the Thai basil. Chopped roasted peanuts make a crunchy substitute for the fried shallots. Depending on the size of your microwave, you may need to microwave the eggplant in two batches. Be sure to remove the eggplant from the microwave immediately so that the steam can escape. Serve this salad with sticky rice, grilled steak, or both.

2 tablespoons fish sauce
2 tablespoons unseasoned rice vinegar
2 tablespoons lime juice
2 tablespoons (⅞ ounce) palm sugar
1 (1-inch piece) ginger, peeled and chopped coarse
2 garlic cloves, chopped coarse
½ red Thai chile, seeded and sliced thin
1 cup cherry tomatoes, halved
2 large Japanese eggplants (1½ pounds), sliced in half lengthwise, then cut crosswise into 1½-inch pieces
1 teaspoon kosher salt
2 cups vegetable oil
½ cup fresh cilantro leaves
½ cup fresh mint leaves
½ cup fresh Thai basil leaves
½ cup Fried Shallots (recipe follows)

**1.** Process fish sauce, vinegar, lime juice, palm sugar, ginger, garlic, and chile in blender on high until ginger, garlic, and palm sugar are broken down and dressing is mostly smooth, about 1 minute. Transfer to medium serving bowl and stir in tomatoes. Set aside while preparing eggplant.

**2.** Toss eggplant and salt together in medium bowl. Line entire surface of large microwave-safe dish with double layer of coffee filters and lightly spray with nonstick cooking spray. Spread eggplant in even layer over coffee filters. Microwave until eggplant feels dry and pieces shrink to about 1 inch, about 10 minutes, flipping halfway through to dry sides evenly. Remove eggplant from microwave and immediately transfer to paper towel–lined plate.

**3.** Heat oil in Dutch oven over high heat to 375 degrees. Fry eggplant, stirring occasionally, until flesh is deep golden brown and edges are crispy, 5 to 7 minutes. Transfer to paper towel–lined baking sheet or plate and blot to remove excess oil. Transfer to bowl with nam prik (fish sauce mixture) and toss to evenly dress.

4. Toss cilantro, mint, and basil together in small bowl. Thoroughly fold half of herb mixture into eggplant. Top eggplant mixture with remaining herb mixture and sprinkle with fried shallots. Serve.

## Fried Shallots and Fried Shallot Oil

**MAKES** about 1½ cups fried shallots and about 1¾ cups fried shallot oil

Crispy fried shallots are one of our all-time favorite garnishes. Once you get used to having them on hand, they start to infiltrate your cooking in many delicious ways—try them in sandwiches, on salads, and on top of pureed soups, just to start. But this recipe is for Fried Shallot Oil as much as it is for Fried Shallots. Most oil used for home frying is destined for the trash, but this golden oil is infused with rich fried shallot flavor and is great in stir-fries and curries or as a garnish for soups and stews. If the shallots are not sliced to a consistent thickness, they will cook and brown unevenly. We tested slicing the shallots by hand and using the disk blade on a food processor, but only a mandoline provided the consistent thickness required for this recipe. It is crucial to strain the shallots from the oil while they are still deep golden—not brown—to prevent them from turning bitter. Finishing the shallots in a low oven removes their excess moisture without the risk of overbrowning. This recipe can be halved and cooked in a small saucepan.

- 1 pound shallots, peeled
- 2 cups vegetable oil
- ½ teaspoon kosher salt

1. Adjust oven rack to middle position and heat oven to 200 degrees. Using mandoline, slice shallots 1⁄16 inch thick. Set fine-mesh strainer over heatproof bowl. Line baking sheet with double layer of paper towels.

2. Combine shallots and oil in medium saucepan and heat over high heat, stirring frequently, until shallots wilt and lose bright pink color and oil is bubbling vigorously over entire surface of pot, about 4 minutes. Continue to cook over high heat, stirring frequently, until few shallots turn golden, 8 to 11 minutes. Reduce heat to medium-low so that oil is bubbling gently, and continue to cook, stirring frequently, until shallots are deep golden, 2 to 4 minutes.

3. Immediately strain oil into prepared bowl. Quickly spread shallots onto prepared sheet and sprinkle evenly with salt; stir shallots to incorporate salt and blot oil on paper towel. Slide shallots off paper towel directly onto sheet; discard paper towel. Bake until shallots are dry and firm to touch, 15 to 25 minutes. Let shallots and oil cool completely and store separately in airtight containers. (Shallots can be stored at room temperature for up to 1 month; shallot oil can be stored in refrigerator for up to 1 month.)

## Green Bean Salad with Cherry Tomatoes and Feta

**SERVES** 4 to 6

**WHY THIS RECIPE WORKS** Cooking vegetables until they're soft enough to be speared with a fork generally means you've got to boil the living color out of them—not to mention all their fresh, grassy flavor. To make the beans in this salad tender, bright green, and deeply flavored, we blanched them in heavily salted water (¼ cup of salt to 2 quarts of water). This quickly softened the pectin in the beans' skins, so they became tender before losing their vibrant color; it also seasoned them inside and out and gave them a meaty, highly seasoned, and intensely green-beany flavor—without making them overly salty. We made these flavorful green beans the star ingredient in a Mediterranean composition using cherry tomatoes, briny feta cheese, mint, and parsley and also created a French-style version with capers and tarragon and one inspired by Southeast Asian flavors. If you don't own a salad spinner, lay the green beans on a clean dish towel to dry in step 2. The blanched, shocked, and dried green beans can be refrigerated in a zipper-lock bag for up to two days.

- 1½ pounds green beans, trimmed and cut into 1- to 2-inch lengths
- ¼ teaspoon table salt, plus salt for blanching
- 12 ounces cherry tomatoes, halved
- ¼ cup extra-virgin olive oil
- 2 tablespoons chopped fresh mint
- 2 tablespoons chopped fresh parsley
- 1 tablespoon lemon juice
- ¼ teaspoon pepper
- 2 ounces feta cheese, crumbled (½ cup)

1. Bring 2 quarts water to boil in large saucepan over high heat. Add green beans and ¼ cup salt, return to boil, and cook until green beans are bright green and tender, 5 to 8 minutes.

2. While green beans cook, fill large bowl halfway with ice and water. Drain green beans in colander and immediately transfer to ice bath. When green beans are no longer warm to touch, drain in colander and dry thoroughly in salad spinner.

3. Place green beans, tomatoes, oil, mint, parsley, lemon juice, pepper, and salt in bowl and toss to combine. Transfer to platter, sprinkle with feta, and serve.

### Green Bean Salad with Shallot, Mustard, and Tarragon

1 shallot, sliced thin
1 tablespoon white wine vinegar
¼ teaspoon table salt, plus salt for blanching
1½ pounds green beans, trimmed and cut into 1- to 2-inch lengths
3 tablespoons extra-virgin olive oil
1 tablespoon Dijon mustard
1 tablespoon capers, rinsed and minced
2 teaspoons minced fresh tarragon
¼ teaspoon pepper

**1.** Place shallot, vinegar, and salt in large bowl and toss to combine; set aside. Bring 2 quarts water to boil in large saucepan over high heat. Add green beans and ¼ cup salt, return to boil, and cook until green beans are bright green and tender, 5 to 8 minutes.

**2.** While green beans cook, fill large bowl halfway with ice and water. Drain green beans in colander and immediately transfer to ice bath. When green beans are no longer warm to touch, drain in colander and dry thoroughly in salad spinner.

**3.** Add green beans, oil, mustard, capers, tarragon, and pepper to bowl with shallot mixture and toss to combine. Transfer to platter and serve.

### Green Bean Salad with Carrots, Cilantro, Fried Shallots, and Peanuts

⅓ cup vegetable oil
2 shallots, sliced thin
1½ pounds green beans, trimmed and cut into 1- to 2-inch lengths
Table salt for blanching
3 tablespoons lime juice (2 limes)
2 tablespoons fish sauce
1½ teaspoons sugar
1 teaspoon paprika
½ teaspoon cayenne pepper
2 carrots, peeled and shredded
¼ cup chopped fresh cilantro
¼ cup dry-roasted peanuts, chopped

**1.** Add oil and shallots to 8-inch nonstick skillet and cook over medium-high heat, stirring frequently, until shallots are deep golden brown, 10 to 14 minutes. Using slotted spoon, transfer shallots to paper towel–lined plate; season with salt to taste. Pour 3 tablespoons shallot oil into large bowl and set aside (reserve remaining oil for another use).

**2.** Bring 2 quarts water to boil in large saucepan over high heat. Add green beans and ¼ cup salt, return to boil, and cook until green beans are bright green and tender, 5 to 8 minutes.

**3.** While green beans cook, fill large bowl halfway with ice and water. Drain green beans in colander and immediately transfer to ice bath. When green beans are no longer warm to touch, drain in colander and dry thoroughly in salad spinner.

**4.** Add lime juice, fish sauce, 1 tablespoon water, sugar, paprika, and cayenne to bowl with reserved shallot oil and whisk until sugar is dissolved. Add green beans, carrots, and 2 tablespoons cilantro and toss to combine. Transfer to platter; sprinkle with peanuts, fried shallots, and remaining 2 tablespoons cilantro; and serve.

## Greek Cherry Tomato Salad

**SERVES** 4 to 6

**WHY THIS RECIPE WORKS** Cherry tomatoes are sweet, juicy, and available year-round—and especially tempting during the cold winter months when summer seems eons away. We wanted an easy recipe that would make the most of their sweetness. Simply slicing cherry tomatoes in half and sprucing them up with vinaigrette resulted in a waterlogged salad with no flavor. So we quartered and salted them, and then took them for a spin in a salad spinner to remove as much of the jelly and seeds as possible. Reducing the jelly with red wine vinegar concentrated its flavor, and olive oil brought the tomato flavor to the forefront of the dressing. Cucumber contributed welcome crunch, while chopped olives and crumbled feta added a briny touch. If in-season cherry tomatoes are unavailable, substitute vine-ripened cherry tomatoes or grape tomatoes from the supermarket. Cut grape tomatoes in half along the equator (rather than quartering them). If you don't have a salad spinner, after the salted tomatoes have stood for 30 minutes, wrap the bowl tightly with plastic wrap and gently shake to remove seeds and excess liquid. Strain the liquid and proceed with the recipe as directed. The amount of liquid given off by the tomatoes will depend on their ripeness. If you have less than ½ cup juice after spinning, proceed with the recipe using the entire amount of juice and reduce it to 3 tablespoons as directed (the cooking time will be shorter).

2 pints ripe cherry tomatoes, quartered (about 4 cups)
½ teaspoon sugar
Table salt
1 medium shallot, minced (about 3 tablespoons)
1 tablespoon red wine vinegar
2 medium garlic cloves, minced or pressed through a garlic press (about 2 teaspoons)
½ teaspoon dried oregano
2 tablespoons extra-virgin olive oil
Ground black pepper
1 small cucumber, peeled, halved lengthwise, seeded, and cut into ½-inch pieces
½ cup chopped pitted kalamata olives
4 ounces feta cheese, crumbled (about 1 cup)
3 tablespoons chopped fresh parsley leaves

**1.** Toss the tomatoes, sugar, and ¼ teaspoon salt in a medium bowl; let stand for 30 minutes. Transfer the tomatoes to a salad spinner and spin until the seeds and excess liquid have been removed, 45 to 60 seconds, stirring to redistribute the tomatoes several times during spinning. Return the tomatoes to the bowl and set aside. Strain the tomato liquid through a fine-mesh strainer into a liquid measuring cup, pressing on the solids to extract as much liquid as possible.

**2.** Bring ½ cup of the tomato liquid (discard any extra), the shallot, vinegar, garlic, and oregano to a simmer in a small saucepan over medium heat. Simmer until reduced to 3 tablespoons, 6 to 8 minutes. Transfer the mixture to a small bowl and cool to room temperature, about 5 minutes. Whisk in the oil until combined and season with salt and pepper to taste.

**3.** Add the cucumber, olives, feta, parsley, and dressing to the bowl with the tomatoes; toss gently and serve.

## All-American Potato Salad

**SERVES** 4 to 6

**WHY THIS RECIPE WORKS** For an extra-flavorful potato salad, we took advantage of our discovery that seasoning the potatoes while they're hot maximizes flavor. We tossed hot potatoes with white vinegar and found russet potatoes to be more flavorful than other potato varieties treated the same way. Russets do crumble a bit when mixed, but we found this quality charming, not alarming. Just ½ cup of mayonnaise dressed 2 pounds of potatoes perfectly. Note that this recipe calls for celery seeds, not celery salt; if only celery salt is available, use the same amount but omit the addition of salt in the dressing. When testing the potatoes for doneness, simply taste a piece; do not overcook the potatoes or they will become mealy and will break apart. The potatoes must be just warm, or even fully cooled, when you add the dressing. If you find the potato salad a little dry for your liking, add up to 2 tablespoons more mayonnaise.

- 2 pounds russet potatoes (3 to 4 medium), peeled and cut into ¾-inch cubes
- ½ teaspoon table salt, plus salt for cooking potatoes
- 2 tablespoons distilled white vinegar
- ½ cup mayonnaise
- 1 celery rib, chopped fine
- 3 tablespoons sweet pickle relish
- 2 tablespoons minced red onion
- 2 tablespoons minced fresh parsley
- ¾ teaspoon dry mustard
- ¾ teaspoon celery seeds
- ¼ teaspoon pepper
- 2 Easy-Peel Hard-Cooked Eggs (page 5), peeled and cut into ¼-inch cubes (optional)

**1.** Place potatoes in large saucepan and add water to cover by 1 inch. Bring to boil over medium-high heat; add 1 tablespoon salt, reduce heat to medium, and simmer, stirring once or twice, until potatoes are tender, about 8 minutes.

**2.** Drain potatoes and transfer to large bowl. Add vinegar and, using rubber spatula, toss gently to combine. Let stand until potatoes are just warm, about 20 minutes.

**3.** Meanwhile, in small bowl, stir together mayonnaise, celery, relish, onion, parsley, dry mustard, celery seeds, pepper, and salt. Using rubber spatula, gently fold dressing and eggs, if using, into potatoes. Cover with plastic wrap and refrigerate until chilled, about 1 hour; serve. (Potato salad can be covered and refrigerated for up to 1 day.)

## American Potato Salad with Eggs and Sweet Pickles

**SERVES** 4 to 6

**WHY THIS RECIPE WORKS** Few salads make a splash at potlucks or picnics the way potato salad does—this classic, all-American side always seems to disappear first. We wanted a recipe for a traditional, creamy (read: mayonnaise-based) potato salad that looked good—no mushy, sloppy spuds—and tasted even better. We began by choosing red potatoes. The skin adds color to a typically monochromatic salad. We boiled them whole for best flavor and then used a serrated knife to cut the potatoes into fork-friendly chunks—the serrated edge helps prevent the skins from tearing for a nicer presentation. While the potatoes were still warm, we drizzled them with vinegar and added a sprinkle of salt and pepper; this preseasoning gave the finished salad more flavor. When the potatoes were cool, we folded in the final traditional touches—mayonnaise, pickles, and red onion—for a perfect potluck potato salad, with a creamy dressing and firm bites of potato. Use sweet pickles, not relish, for the best results. For potatoes that cook through at the same rate, buy potatoes that are roughly the same size.

- 2 pounds red potatoes (about 6 medium), scrubbed
- ¼ cup red wine vinegar
- Table salt and ground black pepper
- ½ cup mayonnaise
- ¼ cup sweet pickles, chopped fine
- 3 Easy-Peel Hard-Cooked Eggs (page 5), peeled and cut into ½-inch pieces
- 1 celery rib, chopped fine
- 2 tablespoons minced red onion
- 2 tablespoons minced fresh parsley leaves
- 2 teaspoons Dijon mustard

**1.** Place the potatoes in a large saucepan, cover with 1 inch of water, and bring to a boil over medium-high heat. Reduce the heat to medium and simmer, stirring occasionally, until the potatoes are tender (a paring knife can be slipped in and out of the potatoes with little resistance), 25 to 30 minutes.

**2.** Drain the potatoes and cool slightly; peel if desired. Cut the potatoes into ¾-inch pieces, using a serrated knife, while still warm, rinsing the knife occasionally in warm water to remove starch.

**3.** Combine the potatoes, vinegar, ½ teaspoon salt, and ¼ teaspoon pepper in a large bowl and toss gently. Cover and refrigerate until cool, about 20 minutes.

**4.** Meanwhile, combine the remaining ingredients and salt and pepper to taste. Add the potatoes, stir gently to combine, and serve. (The salad can be refrigerated in an airtight container for up to 1 day.)

## French Potato Salad with Dijon Mustard and Fines Herbes

SERVES 6

**WHY THIS RECIPE WORKS** French potato salad, served warm or at room temperature, is composed of sliced potatoes glistening with olive oil, white wine vinegar, and plenty of fresh herbs. The potatoes should be tender but not mushy, and the flavor of the vinaigrette should penetrate the relatively bland potatoes but not be oily or dull. To prevent torn skins and broken slices, we had to slice the potatoes before boiling them. To tone down the flavor of harsh garlic, we blanched it before mixing the vinaigrette. A little extra vinegar added a pleasing sharpness, while some reserved potato water added just the right amount of moisture and saltiness to the salad. Dijon mustard combined with strong herbs also perked things up. Pouring the vinaigrette over the warm potatoes on a sheet pan, then folding in the other ingredients, kept the slices intact. If fresh chervil isn't available, substitute an additional ½ tablespoon minced parsley and an additional ½ teaspoon minced tarragon. For best flavor, serve the salad warm, but to make ahead, follow the recipe through step 2, cover with plastic wrap, and refrigerate. Before serving, bring the salad to room temperature, then add the shallot and herbs.

- 2 pounds red potatoes (about 6 medium or 18 small), unpeeled, sliced ¼ inch thick
- Table salt for cooking potatoes
- 1 medium garlic clove, peeled and threaded on skewer
- ¼ cup extra-virgin olive oil
- 1½ tablespoons champagne vinegar or white wine vinegar
- 2 teaspoons Dijon mustard
- ½ teaspoon pepper
- 1 small shallot, minced (about 1 tablespoon)
- 1 tablespoon minced fresh chervil
- 1 tablespoon minced fresh parsley
- 1 tablespoon minced fresh chives
- 1 teaspoon minced fresh tarragon

**1.** Place potatoes, 6 cups cold water, and 2 tablespoons salt in a large saucepan. Bring to boil over high heat, then reduce heat to medium. Lower skewered garlic into simmering water and blanch, about 45 seconds. Immediately run garlic under cold tap water to stop cooking process; remove garlic from skewer and set aside. Simmer potatoes, uncovered, until tender but still firm (paring knife can be slipped into and out of center of potato slice with no resistance), about 5 minutes. Drain potatoes, reserving ¼ cup cooking water. Arrange hot potatoes close together in single layer on rimmed baking sheet.

**2.** Press garlic through garlic press or mince by hand. Whisk garlic, reserved potato cooking water, oil, vinegar, mustard, and pepper in small bowl until combined. Drizzle dressing evenly over warm potato slices; let stand for 10 minutes.

**3.** Meanwhile, toss shallot, chervil, parsley, chives, and tarragon gently together in small bowl. Transfer potatoes to large serving bowl. Add shallot-herb mixture and mix lightly with rubber spatula to combine. Serve immediately.

## Austrian-Style Potato Salad

SERVES 4 to 6

**WHY THIS RECIPE WORKS** Austrian-style potato salad, which features sliced potatoes and a tangy vinaigrette, is an elegant change from a creamy potato salad. This style of potato salad calls on the starch from the potatoes along with an unexpected ingredient, chicken broth, to create the dressing. After cooking the sliced potatoes in broth, which we cut with an equal amount of water, we reduced the cooking liquid and mixed it with vinegar, mustard, chives, and cornichons for flavor. To give the dressing more body, and impart a rustic texture, we mashed in a small amount of our cooked potatoes. After mixing the rest of the sliced potatoes with the thick vinaigrette, we had a luxurious, rich, and very different kind of potato salad. To maintain its consistency, don't refrigerate the salad; it should be served within a few hours of preparation.

- 2 pounds Yukon Gold potatoes (about 4 medium), peeled, quartered, and sliced ½ inch thick
- 1 cup low-sodium chicken broth
- 2 tablespoons white wine vinegar
- 1 tablespoon sugar
- Table salt
- ¼ cup vegetable oil
- 1 small red onion, minced
- 6 cornichons, minced (about 2 tablespoons)
- 2 tablespoons minced fresh chives
- 1 tablespoon Dijon mustard
- Ground black pepper

**1.** Bring 1 cup water, the potatoes, broth, 1 tablespoon of the vinegar, the sugar, and 1 teaspoon salt to a boil in a 12-inch skillet over high heat. Reduce the heat to medium-low, cover, and cook until the potatoes are tender (a paring knife can be slipped in and out of the potatoes with little resistance), 15 to 17 minutes. Remove the cover, increase the heat to high, and cook until the liquid has reduced, about 2 minutes.

**2.** Drain the potatoes in a colander set over a large bowl, reserving the cooking liquid. Set the potatoes aside. Pour off all but ½ cup cooking liquid (if ½ cup liquid does not remain, add water to make this amount). Whisk the cooking liquid, the remaining 1 tablespoon vinegar, the oil, onion, cornichons, chives, and mustard together in a large bowl.

**3.** Add ½ cup of the cooked potatoes to the bowl with the cooking liquid mixture and mash with a potato masher until a thick vinaigrette forms (the mixture will be slightly chunky). Add the remaining potatoes, stirring gently to combine. Season with salt and pepper to taste. Serve warm or at room temperature.

## Creamy Coleslaw

**SERVES 4**

---

**WHY THIS RECIPE WORKS** No other food embodies an outdoor grillfest quite like coleslaw. This summery salad offers a crunch and creaminess that contrasts well with sweet and savory barbecued meats and vegetables. But, despite its simplicity, coleslaw can be tough to get just right. Usually, the coleslaw ends up limp and sitting in a pool of water. We wanted a crisp salad and a creamy dressing that wouldn't be waterlogged. To prevent the salad from getting watery, we salted the cabbage until it wilted, then rinsed and dried it. Removing the excess water helped to keep our dressing thick and creamy, and ensured the cabbage stayed crunchy. For the dressing, we used mayonnaise and rice vinegar; these made a creamy dressing that was flavorful but not too harsh. All our coleslaw needed now was black pepper and some shredded carrot for color, further crunch, and a little sweetness. If you like caraway or celery seeds, add ¼ teaspoon of either with the mayonnaise and vinegar. If you like a tangier slaw, replace some or all of the mayonnaise with an equal amount of sour cream. To serve the coleslaw immediately, rinse the salted cabbage and carrot in a large bowl of ice water, drain them in a colander, pick out any ice cubes, then pat the vegetables dry before dressing.

- 1 pound red or green cabbage (about ½ medium head), shredded (about 6 cups)
- 1 large carrot, peeled and shredded
- 1 teaspoon table salt
- ½ small onion, minced
- ½ cup mayonnaise
- 2 tablespoons rice vinegar
- Ground black pepper

**1.** Toss the cabbage and carrot with the salt in a colander set over a medium bowl. Let stand until the cabbage wilts, at least 1 hour or up to 4 hours. Rinse the cabbage and carrot under cold running water (or in a large bowl of ice water if serving immediately). Press, but do not squeeze, to drain; pat dry with paper towels.

**2.** Combine the cabbage, carrot, onion, mayonnaise, and vinegar in a medium bowl; toss to coat and season with pepper to taste. Serve chilled or at room temperature. (The coleslaw can be refrigerated in an airtight container for up to 2 days.)

## Creamy Buttermilk Coleslaw

**SERVES 4**

---

**WHY THIS RECIPE WORKS** Order barbecue down South and you'll likely get buttermilk coleslaw on the side. Unlike all-mayonnaise coleslaw, buttermilk coleslaw is coated in a creamy and refreshingly tart dressing. This recipe showcases the best attributes of this slaw: a pickle-crisp texture and a tangy dressing that clings to it. To prevent watery coleslaw, we salted, rinsed, and dried the shredded cabbage. As the salted cabbage sat, moisture was pulled out of it, wilting it to the right crispy texture. For a tangy dressing that clung to the cabbage, we supplemented the buttermilk with mayonnaise and sour cream. Adding shredded carrot contributed color and sweetness while the mild flavor of shallot was a welcome addition. Sugar, mustard, and cider vinegar amped up the slaw's tanginess. To serve the coleslaw immediately, rinse the salted cabbage in a large bowl of ice water, drain it in a colander, pick out any ice cubes, then pat the cabbage dry before dressing.

- 1 pound red or green cabbage (about ½ medium head), shredded (about 6 cups)
- ¼ teaspoon table salt, plus salt for salting cabbage
- 1 medium carrot, peeled and shredded
- ½ cup buttermilk
- 2 tablespoons mayonnaise
- 2 tablespoons sour cream
- 1 small shallot, minced (about 1 tablespoon)
- 2 tablespoons minced fresh parsley
- ½ teaspoon cider vinegar
- ½ teaspoon sugar
- ¼ teaspoon Dijon mustard
- ⅛ teaspoon pepper

**1.** Toss cabbage with 1 teaspoon salt in colander set over medium bowl. Let stand until cabbage wilts, at least 1 hour or up to 4 hours. Rinse cabbage under cold running water (or in large bowl of ice water if serving immediately). Press, but do not squeeze, to drain; pat dry with paper towels. Transfer cabbage to large bowl; add carrot.

**2.** Combine buttermilk, mayonnaise, sour cream, shallot, parsley, vinegar, sugar, mustard, pepper, and salt in small bowl. Pour buttermilk dressing over cabbage and carrot and toss to coat. Serve chilled or at room temperature. (Coleslaw can be refrigerated in airtight container for up to 2 days.)

## Cabbage and Red Pepper Salad with Lime-Cumin Vinaigrette

**SERVES 6 to 8**

---

**WHY THIS RECIPE WORKS** Salting ahead of time creates pickle-crisp cabbage that is perfect for combining with bold flavors. Cabbage salads are diluted by the cabbage itself. Its cells are full of water that leaches out once a salad is allowed to sit. One way to solve this problem in our coleslaw recipe, we figured, was to get rid of some of this water before making the salad, and the easiest way to do that was to salt the cabbage to draw out the liquid. While this method does take just a bit of the crunch out of the cabbage, the cabbage salad recipes made with it had a nice pickle-crisp texture, and no one could call them watery.

- 1 pound green cabbage (about ½ medium head), shredded fine
- 1 teaspoon table salt
- 2 tablespoons lime juice
- 1 teaspoon grated lime zest from 1 lime
- 2 tablespoons olive oil
- 1 tablespoon rice vinegar or sherry vinegar
- 1 tablespoon honey
- 1 teaspoon ground cumin
- Pinch cayenne pepper
- 1 red bell pepper, seeded and cut into thin strips

**1.** Toss shredded cabbage and 1 teaspoon salt in colander or large mesh strainer set over medium bowl. Let stand until cabbage wilts, at least 1 hour or up to 4 hours. Rinse cabbage under cold running water (or in large bowl of ice water if serving immediately). Press, but do not squeeze, to drain; pat dry with paper towels. (Can be stored in zipper-lock bag and refrigerated overnight.)

**2.** Stir together lime juice, zest, oil, vinegar, honey, cumin, and cayenne in medium bowl. Toss cabbage and red pepper in dressing. Season to taste with salt; cover and refrigerate until ready to serve.

## Cool and Creamy Macaroni Salad

**SERVES** 8 to 10

**WHY THIS RECIPE WORKS** Macaroni salad seems simple enough—toss elbow macaroni and seasonings with a mayo-based dressing. So why does this salad often fall short? We set out to make a picnic-worthy macaroni salad with tender pasta and a creamy, well-seasoned dressing. First we had to get the pasta texture just right. To do this, we didn't drain the macaroni as thoroughly as we could have; any excess water was absorbed by the pasta as it sat, which prevented the finished salad from drying out. We also cooked the macaroni to a point where it still had some bite so the pasta wouldn't get too soft when mixed with the mayonnaise. For the most flavor, we seasoned the pasta first—before adding the mayo—so that the seasonings could penetrate and flavor the macaroni. Garlic powder added flavor (fresh garlic was too harsh), and lemon juice and Dijon mustard enlivened the creamy dressing. Don't drain the macaroni too well before adding the other ingredients—a little extra moisture will keep the salad from drying out. If you've made the salad ahead of time, simply stir in a little warm water to loosen the texture before serving.

- Table salt for cooking pasta
- 1 pound elbow macaroni
- ½ small red onion, minced
- 1 celery rib, chopped fine
- ¼ cup minced fresh parsley

- 2 tablespoons lemon juice
- 1 tablespoon Dijon mustard
- ⅛ teaspoon garlic powder
- Pinch cayenne pepper
- 1½ cups mayonnaise

**1.** Bring 4 quarts water to boil in large pot. Stir 1 tablespoon salt and pasta into boiling water and cook, stirring often, until nearly tender, about 5 minutes. Drain pasta and rinse with cold water until cool, then drain briefly so that macaroni remains moist. Transfer to large bowl.

**2.** Stir in onion, celery, parsley, lemon juice, mustard, garlic powder, and cayenne and let sit until flavors are absorbed, about 2 minutes. Add mayonnaise and let sit until salad is no longer watery, 5 to 10 minutes. Season with salt and pepper to taste, and serve. (Salad can be refrigerated in airtight container for up to 2 days.)

## Pasta Salad with Pesto

**SERVES** 8 to 10

**WHY THIS RECIPE WORKS** Pasta salad with pesto should be light and refreshing, not dry and dull. We decided to perfect this salad—and keep it fresh, green, garlicky, and full of herbal flavor. To ensure that the pesto coated the pasta, we didn't rinse it after cooking. Instead, we spread the pasta to cool in a single layer on a baking sheet; a splash of oil helped prevent it from sticking. For the pesto, we blanched the garlic to tame its harsh bite. To keep the vivid green color of the basil from fading, we added baby spinach. For a creamy, pesto, we enriched it with mayonnaise. We folded extra pine nuts into the salad for an appealing crunch. Using a pasta shape with a textured surface, like farfalle, guaranteed that the pesto wouldn't slide off. This salad is best served the day it is made; if it's been refrigerated, bring it to room temperature before serving. The pesto can be made a day ahead—just cook the garlic in a small saucepan of boiling water for 1 minute.

- 2 medium garlic cloves, unpeeled
- Table salt
- 1 pound farfalle
- ¼ cup plus 1 tablespoon extra-virgin olive oil
- 3 cups packed fresh basil leaves (about 4 ounces)
- 1 cup packed baby spinach (about 1 ounce)
- ¾ cup pine nuts (3¾ ounces), toasted
- 2 tablespoons juice from 1 lemon
- ½ teaspoon ground black pepper
- 1½ ounces Parmesan cheese, finely grated (about ¾ cup), plus extra for serving
- 6 tablespoons mayonnaise
- 1 pint cherry tomatoes, quartered, or grape tomatoes, halved (optional)

**1.** Bring 4 quarts water to a boil in a large pot. Add the garlic to the boiling water and let cook for 1 minute. Remove the garlic with a slotted spoon and rinse under cold water; set aside to cool. Stir 1 tablespoon salt and the pasta into the boiling water and cook, stirring often, until the pasta is just past al dente. Reserve ¼ cup of the pasta cooking water, drain the pasta, toss with 1 tablespoon of the oil, spread in a single layer on a rimmed baking sheet, and cool to room temperature, about 30 minutes.

**2.** Peel and mince the garlic or press it through a garlic press. Process the garlic, basil, spinach, ¼ cup of the nuts, lemon juice, pepper, remaining ¼ cup oil, and 1 teaspoon salt in a food processor until smooth, scraping down the sides of the work bowl as necessary. Add the Parmesan and mayonnaise and process until thoroughly combined. Transfer the mixture to a large serving bowl. Cover and refrigerate until ready to assemble the salad.

**3.** Toss the pasta with the pesto, adding the reserved pasta water, 1 tablespoon at a time, until the pesto evenly coats the pasta. Fold in the remaining ½ cup nuts and the tomatoes (if using). Serve, passing extra Parmesan separately.

## Antipasto Pasta Salad

**SERVES** 6 to 8

**WHY THIS RECIPE WORKS** We love a traditional antipasto platter, chock-full of cured meats, cheese, and pickled vegetables, and we thought it would translate well to a hearty pasta salad. We quickly decided that short, curly pasta was the best shape to use, as its curves held on to the salad's other components, making for a more cohesive dish. Quickly rendering the fat from the meats in the microwave helped to keep this salad from becoming greasy. We used an increased ratio of vinegar to oil in the dressing—the sharp, acidic flavor cut the richness of the meats and cheese for a brighter-tasting salad. For well-seasoned pasta, we tossed the hot pasta with the dressing—hot pasta absorbs dressing better than cold pasta. Slicing the meat into thick strips meant that its hearty flavor wasn't lost among the other ingredients. And grating the cheese, rather than cubing it, made for evenly distributed sharp flavor throughout the salad. We also liked the addition of 1 cup chopped pitted kalamata olives or 1 cup jarred artichokes, drained and quartered, to this salad.

- 8 ounces sliced pepperoni, cut into ¼-inch strips
- 8 ounces thick-sliced soppressata or salami, halved and cut into ¼-inch strips
- 10 tablespoons red wine vinegar
- 6 tablespoons extra-virgin olive oil
- 3 tablespoons mayonnaise
- 1 (12-ounce) jar pepperoncini, drained (2 tablespoons liquid reserved), stemmed, and chopped coarse
- 4 garlic cloves, minced
- ½ teaspoon table salt, plus salt for cooking pasta
- ½ teaspoon pepper
- ¼ teaspoon red pepper flakes
- 1 pound short, curly pasta, such as fusilli or campanelle
- 1 pound white mushrooms, trimmed and quartered
- 4 ounces aged provolone cheese, grated (1 cup)
- 1 (12-ounce) jar roasted red peppers, drained, patted dry, and chopped coarse
- 1 cup chopped fresh basil

**1.** Bring 4 quarts water to boil in large pot. Place pepperoni on large paper towel–lined plate. Cover with second paper towel and place soppressata on top. Cover with another paper towel and microwave on high power for 1 minute. Discard paper towels and set pepperoni and soppressata aside.

**2.** Whisk 5 tablespoons vinegar, oil, mayonnaise, pepperoncini liquid, garlic, salt, pepper, and pepper flakes together in medium bowl.

**3.** Stir 1 tablespoon salt and pasta into boiling water and cook, stirring often, until pasta is just past al dente. Drain pasta and return it to pot. Pour ½ cup of dressing and remaining 5 tablespoons vinegar over pasta and toss to combine; season with salt and pepper to taste. Spread pasta in single layer on rimmed baking sheet and let cool to room temperature, about 30 minutes.

**4.** Meanwhile, bring remaining dressing to simmer in large skillet over medium-high heat. Add mushrooms and cook until lightly browned, about 8 minutes. Transfer to large bowl and cool to room temperature.

**5.** Add meat, provolone, peppers, basil, and pasta to mushrooms and toss to combine. Season with salt and pepper to taste, and serve.

## Italian Pasta Salad

**SERVES** 8 to 10

**WHY THIS RECIPE WORKS** We wanted to give this summertime staple a makeover, which would involve improving the texture of the noodles, picking the perfect mix-ins, and creating a flavorful dressing that would cling well. First, we opted for corkscrew-shaped fusilli pasta, as the shape has plenty of nooks and crannies for capturing dressing and is easy to spear with a fork. We purposefully cooked the pasta until it was a little too soft so that as it cooled and firmed up, it would have just the right tender texture. Rather than toss raw vegetables into the mix, we took inspiration from Italian antipasto platters and used intensely flavored jarred ingredients like sun-dried tomatoes, kalamata olives, and pepperoncini—a mix of

textures that didn't overshadow the pasta. For heartiness, we included salami, and to balance the salt and tang, we add chunks of creamy mozzarella, fresh basil, and peppery arugula. To ensure the pasta itself was just as flavorful as the rest of the dish, we made a thick, punchy dressing by processing some of the salad ingredients themselves—capers and pepperoncini plus their tangy liquid—with olive oil infused with garlic, red pepper flakes, and anchovies. The pasta firms as it cools, so overcooking is key to ensuring the proper texture. We prefer a small, individually packaged, dry Italian-style salami such as Genoa or soppressata, but unsliced deli salami can be used. If the salad is not being eaten right away, don't add the arugula and basil until right before serving.

- 1 pound fusilli
- Table salt and pepper
- ¼ cup extra-virgin olive oil
- 3 anchovy fillets, rinsed, patted dry, and minced
- 3 garlic cloves, minced
- ¼ teaspoon red pepper flakes
- 1 cup pepperoncini, stemmed, plus 2 tablespoons reserved liquid
- 2 tablespoons capers, rinsed
- ½ cup oil-packed sun-dried tomatoes, sliced thin
- ½ cup pitted kalamata olives, quartered
- 8 ounces salami, cut into ⅜-inch dice
- 8 ounces fresh mozzarella cheese, cut into ⅜-inch dice and patted dry with paper towels
- 2 cups (2 ounces) baby arugula
- 1 cup chopped fresh basil

**1.** Bring 4 quarts water to boil in large pot. Add pasta and 1 tablespoon salt and cook, stirring often, until pasta is tender throughout, 2 to 3 minutes past al dente. Drain pasta and rinse under cold water until chilled. Drain well and transfer to large bowl.

**2.** Meanwhile, combine oil, anchovies, garlic, and pepper flakes in 1-cup liquid measuring cup. Cover and microwave until oil is bubbling and fragrant, 30 to 60 seconds. Set aside.

**3.** Slice half of pepperoncini into thin rings and set aside. Transfer remaining pepperoncini to food processor. Add capers and pulse until finely chopped, 8 to 10 pulses, scraping down sides of bowl as necessary. Add 2 tablespoons reserved pepperoncini liquid and warm oil mixture and process until combined, about 20 seconds.

**4.** Add dressing to pasta and toss to combine. Add sun-dried tomatoes, olives, salami, mozzarella, arugula, basil, and reserved pepperoncini rings and toss well. Season to taste with salt and pepper. Serve. (Salad can be refrigerated for up to 3 days. Bring to room temperature before serving.)

## Rice Salad with Oranges, Olives, and Almonds

**SERVES** 6 to 8

**WHY THIS RECIPE WORKS** Rice makes a light, refreshing salad when dressed properly and studded with vegetables—and it makes a nice change from pasta salad. But unlike pasta, rice can't stand up to assertive flavors or be bogged down by a heavy vinaigrette. To get rice salad just right, we would have to include a few bright, tangy ingredients and use a light hand when making the dressing. To start out with as much flavor as possible, we toasted the rice to intensify its flavor and then boiled it in a large amount of water, as we would pasta. This method kept the rice tender when cool. To dry the rice, we spread it out on a large baking sheet—this guaranteed that the rice didn't clump or become waterlogged. As for the vinaigrette, restraint was key. We used small amounts of oil, vinegar, and seasonings to complement, but not overshadow, the grains of rice. Orange segments, slivered almonds, and chopped olives gave the salad character and textural interest. And a brief rest to blend the flavors yielded a rice salad that was bright and balanced. Taste the rice as it nears the end of its cooking time; it should be cooked through and firm, but not crunchy. Be careful not to overcook the rice or the grains will be blown out.

- 1½ cups long-grain or basmati rice
- Table salt
- 2 tablespoons extra-virgin olive oil
- ¼ teaspoon grated zest plus 1 tablespoon juice from 1 orange
- 2 teaspoons sherry vinegar
- 1 small garlic clove, minced or pressed through a garlic press (about ½ teaspoon)
- ½ teaspoon ground black pepper
- 2 medium oranges, peel and pith removed, and cut into segments
- ⅓ cup chopped pitted green olives
- ⅓ cup slivered almonds, toasted
- 2 tablespoons fresh oregano leaves, minced

**1.** Bring 4 quarts water to a boil in a large pot. Heat a medium skillet over medium heat until hot, about 3 minutes; add the rice and toast, stirring frequently, until faintly fragrant and some grains turn opaque, about 5 minutes.

**2.** Stir 1½ teaspoons salt and the rice into the boiling water. Cook, uncovered, until the rice is tender but not soft, 8 to 10 minutes for long-grain rice or about 15 minutes for basmati. Line a rimmed baking sheet with foil or parchment paper. Drain the rice in a colander and spread on the prepared baking sheet. Cool while preparing the salad ingredients.

**3.** Whisk the oil, orange zest and juice, vinegar, garlic, 1 teaspoon salt, and pepper together in a small bowl. Combine the rice, oranges, olives, almonds, and oregano in a large bowl; drizzle the dressing over the salad and toss to combine. Let stand for 20 minutes to blend the flavors, and serve.

## Barley Salad with Pomegranate, Pistachios, and Feta

SERVES 6 to 8

**WHY THIS RECIPE WORKS** We set out to develop a recipe for a vibrantly spiced pearl barley salad with the right balance of sweetness, tang, and nuttiness. Before we could focus on building these exciting flavors, we had to find a consistent cooking method for our barley. We wanted the grains to remain distinct, rather than cohesive as in a pilaf. We turned to what we call the "pasta method," in which we simply boil the grains until tender. With our perfectly cooked barley set aside, we turned our attention back to flavor. Inspired by the flavors of Egypt, we incorporated toasty pistachios, tangy pomegranate molasses, and bright, vegetal cilantro, all balanced by warm, earthy spices and sweet golden raisins. Salty feta cheese, pungent scallions, and pomegranate seeds adorned the top of the dish for a colorful composed salad with dynamic flavors and textures. Do not substitute hulled barley or hull-less barley in this recipe. If using quick-cooking or presteamed barley (read the ingredient list on the package to determine this), you will need to decrease the barley cooking time in step 1.

- 1½ cups pearl barley
- Table salt and pepper
- 3 tablespoons extra-virgin olive oil, plus extra for serving
- 2 tablespoons pomegranate molasses
- ½ teaspoon ground cinnamon
- ¼ teaspoon ground cumin
- ⅓ cup golden raisins
- ½ cup coarsely chopped cilantro
- ¼ cup shelled pistachios, toasted and chopped coarse
- 3 ounces feta cheese, cut into ½-inch cubes (¾ cup)
- 6 scallions, green parts only, sliced thin
- ½ cup pomegranate seeds

**1.** Bring 4 quarts water to boil in Dutch oven. Add barley and 1 tablespoon salt, return to boil, and cook until tender, 20 to 40 minutes. Drain barley, spread onto rimmed baking sheet, and let cool completely, about 15 minutes.

**2.** Whisk oil, molasses, cinnamon, cumin, and ½ teaspoon salt together in large bowl. Add barley, raisins, cilantro, and pistachios and toss gently to combine. Season with salt and pepper to taste. Spread barley salad evenly on serving platter and arrange feta, scallions, and pomegranate seeds in separate diagonal rows on top. Drizzle with extra oil and serve.

## Tabbouleh

SERVES 4

**WHY THIS RECIPE WORKS** Tabbouleh has long been a meze staple in the Middle East, but these days it can be found in the refrigerated section of virtually every American supermarket. Its brief (and healthful) ingredient list explains its popularity: Chopped fresh parsley and mint, tomatoes, onion, and bits of nutty bulgur are tossed with lemon and olive oil for a refreshing appetizer or side dish. It all sounds simple enough, but it's easy to create a version that's hopelessly soggy, with flavor that is either too bold or too bland. We wanted a flavorful dish that would feature a hefty amount of parsley as well as a decent amount of bulgur. A high ratio of chopped parsley to chopped mint put the emphasis on the bright, peppery parsley but didn't overpower the other ingredients. Bulgur is made by boiling, drying, and grinding wheat kernels, so it needs only to be soaked, not cooked. We soaked it in lemon juice to infuse it with flavor. Extra-virgin olive oil tempered the tart lemon juice. To avoid soggy tabbouleh, we salted the tomatoes, and then, rather than throw out the exuded liquid, we added it to the bulgur-soaking liquid. Two sliced scallions (preferred over red or white onion) rounded out the mix. Serve the salad with the crisp inner leaves of romaine lettuce and wedges of pita.

- 3 medium round tomatoes, cored and cut into ½-inch pieces
- Table salt and pepper
- ½ cup medium-grind bulgur
- ¼ cup lemon juice (2 lemons)
- 6 tablespoons extra-virgin olive oil

- 1/8 teaspoon cayenne pepper
- 1½ cups chopped fresh parsley
- ½ cup chopped fresh mint
- 2 scallions, sliced thin

**1.** Toss tomatoes and 1/4 teaspoon salt in large bowl. Transfer to fine-mesh strainer, set strainer in bowl, and let stand for 30 minutes, tossing occasionally.

**2.** Rinse bulgur in fine-mesh strainer under cold running water. Drain well and transfer to second bowl. Stir in 2 tablespoons lemon juice and 2 tablespoons juice from draining tomatoes. Let stand until grains are beginning to soften, 30 to 40 minutes.

**3.** Whisk remaining 2 tablespoons lemon juice, oil, cayenne, and 1/4 teaspoon salt together in large bowl. Add drained tomatoes, soaked bulgur, parsley, mint, and scallions; toss gently to combine. Cover and let stand at room temperature until flavors have blended and bulgur is tender, about 1 hour. Toss to recombine, season with salt and pepper to taste, and serve immediately.

## Farro Salad with Asparagus, Sugar Snap Peas, and Tomatoes

**SERVES** 6

**WHY THIS RECIPE WORKS** Farro comes in a few different forms, but our favorite is minimally processed whole farro, in which the germ and bran have been retained. It has a nutty flavor and chewy texture and cooks in 20 minutes, making it one of the fastest-cooking whole grains. We found that the simplest cooking method was best: Boil in salted water for about 20 minutes until tender and drain well. Its versatility makes it ideal for salads, soups, and side dishes. Extra cooked farro can be stored in the refrigerator for up to five days.

- 6 ounces asparagus, trimmed and cut into 1-inch lengths
- 6 ounces sugar snap peas, strings removed, cut into 1-inch lengths
- Table salt and pepper
- 3 tablespoons extra-virgin olive oil
- 2 tablespoons lemon juice
- 2 tablespoons minced shallot
- 1 teaspoon Dijon mustard
- 1 recipe Simple Farro, room temperature
- 6 ounces cherry tomatoes, halved
- 3 tablespoons chopped fresh dill
- 2 ounces feta cheese, crumbled (½ cup)

**1.** Bring 2 quarts water to boil in large saucepan. Add asparagus, snap peas, and 1 tablespoon salt. Cook until vegetables are crisp-tender, 2 to 3 minutes. Using slotted spoon, transfer vegetables to rimmed baking sheet and let cool for 15 minutes.

**2.** Whisk oil, lemon juice, shallot, mustard, 1/4 teaspoon salt, and 1/4 teaspoon pepper together in large bowl. Add cooled vegetables, farro, tomatoes, dill, and 1/4 cup feta to dressing and toss to combine. Season with salt and pepper to taste and transfer to serving bowl. Sprinkle salad with remaining 1/4 cup feta and serve.

### Simple Farro

**MAKES** 2½ cups

We prefer the flavor and texture of whole-grain farro. Pearled farro can be used, but cooking times vary, so start checking for doneness after 10 minutes. Do not use quick-cooking farro in this recipe. Warm farro can be tossed with butter or olive oil and salt and pepper for a simple yet hearty side dish. It can also be added to soups or, when cooled, added to salads.

- 1½ cups whole farro, rinsed
- 1 tablespoon table salt

Bring 2 quarts water to boil in large saucepan. Add farro and salt. Return to boil, reduce heat, and simmer until grains are tender with slight chew, 15 to 20 minutes. Drain well. (Farro can be refrigerated for up to 5 days.)

## Wheat Berry Salad with Radicchio, Dried Cherries, and Pecans

**SERVES** 4 to 6

**WHY THIS RECIPE WORKS** The earthy, nutty flavor and firm chew of whole grains make them an ideal choice for a hearty side dish or light main course. Though many recipes call for cooking whole grains in a measured amount of water until all the liquid is absorbed, we found that cooking the wheat berries like pasta—simply simmering them in an abundance of water until they were tender but still chewy—yielded faster and more consistent results. Soaking the wheat berries overnight, while optional, helped to further shorten the cooking time and prevented the grains from blowing out. Parsley and radicchio added color and fresh bite to the salad, and chewy, sweet dried cherries; crunchy toasted pecans; and creamy, pungent blue cheese crumbles contributed welcome textural interest. If using refrigerated grains, let them come to room temperature before making the salad. Any whole grain can be substituted for the wheat berries. Any variety of radicchio can be used.

- 3 tablespoons extra-virgin olive oil
- 2 tablespoons red wine vinegar
- 1 small shallot, minced
- ½ teaspoon table salt
- ½ teaspoon pepper
- 2¾ cups cooked wheat berries
- 1 cup chopped Chioggia radicchio
- 1 cup fresh parsley leaves
- ½ cup pecans, toasted and chopped coarse, divided
- ¼ cup dried cherries
- 1 ounce blue cheese, crumbled (¼ cup)

Whisk oil, vinegar, shallot, salt, and pepper together in large bowl. Add wheat berries, radicchio, parsley, half of pecans, and cherries to dressing and toss to combine. Season with salt and pepper to taste. Transfer to serving bowl and sprinkle with blue cheese and remaining pecans. Serve.

## Lentil Salad with Olives, Mint, and Feta

**SERVES** 4 to 6

**WHY THIS RECIPE WORKS** The most important step in making a lentil salad is cooking the lentils so they maintain their shape and firm-tender bite. We found two keys to ensuring the ideal texture. First, we brined the lentils in warm salt water. With brining, the lentils' skins softened, which led to fewer blowouts. Second, we cooked the lentils in the oven, which heated them gently and uniformly. We paired our perfectly cooked lentils with a tart vinaigrette and bold mix-ins. French green lentils, or lentilles du Puy, are our preferred choice for this recipe, but it works with any type of lentil except red or yellow. Brining helps keep the lentils intact, but if you don't have time, they'll still taste good without it. The salad can be served warm or at room temperature.

- 1 cup lentils, picked over and rinsed
- ½ teaspoon table salt, plus salt for soaking lentils
- 6 cups water
- 2 cups chicken broth
- 5 garlic cloves, lightly crushed and peeled
- 1 bay leaf
- 5 tablespoons extra-virgin olive oil
- 3 tablespoons white wine vinegar
- ½ cup pitted kalamata olives, chopped coarse
- ½ cup minced fresh mint
- 1 large shallot, minced
- 1 ounce feta cheese, crumbled (¼ cup)

**1.** Place lentils and 1 teaspoon salt in bowl. Cover with 4 cups warm water (about 110 degrees) and soak for 1 hour. Drain well. (Drained lentils can be refrigerated for up to 2 days before cooking.)

**2.** Adjust oven rack to middle position and heat oven to 325 degrees. Combine drained lentils, remaining 2 cups water, broth, garlic, bay leaf, and salt in ovensafe medium saucepan. Cover and bake until lentils are tender but remain intact, 40 minutes to 1 hour. Meanwhile, whisk oil and vinegar together in large bowl.

**3.** Drain lentils well; discard garlic and bay leaf. Add drained lentils, olives, mint, and shallot to dressing and toss to combine. Season with salt and pepper to taste. Transfer to serving dish, sprinkle with feta, and serve.

### Lentil Salad with Pomegranate and Walnuts

Substitute lemon juice for white wine vinegar. Omit olives, mint, and feta cheese. Add drained lentils, shallot, and ¼ cup chopped fresh cilantro to dressing and toss to combine. Season with salt and pepper to taste. Sprinkle with ⅓ cup coarsely chopped toasted walnuts and ⅓ cup pomegranate seeds before serving.

## Mango, Orange, and Jicama Salad

**SERVES** 4 to 6

**WHY THIS RECIPE WORKS** It doesn't require much to put together a stunning fruit salad in the summer but come winter, the task requires more creativity. Working with the citrus and tropical fruits available in colder months, we set our sights on a nuanced salad. A pairing of 1 part citrus fruit to 4 parts tropical fruit produced a juicy—not waterlogged—salad. We started with oranges and mangos and then created a simple bright dressing by heating sugar, lime juice and zest, red pepper flakes, and a pinch of salt to form a tangy-sweet syrup infused with a touch of spicy heat. The mild sweetness and supercrisp texture of jicama, softened slightly in the hot syrup, contributed just enough crunch to finish off the salad.

- 3 tablespoons sugar
- ¼ teaspoon grated lime zest plus 3 tablespoons juice (2 limes)
- ¼ teaspoon red pepper flakes
- Pinch salt
- 12 ounces jicama, peeled and cut into ¼-inch dice (1½ cups)
- 2 oranges
- 2 mangos, peeled, pitted, and cut into ½-inch dice

**1.** Bring sugar, lime zest and juice, pepper flakes, and salt to simmer in small saucepan over medium heat, stirring constantly, until sugar is dissolved, 1 to 2 minutes. Remove pan from heat, stir in jicama, and let syrup cool for 20 minutes.

**2.** Meanwhile, cut away peel and pith from oranges. Slice into ½-inch-thick rounds, then cut rounds into ½-inch pieces. Place oranges and mangos in large bowl.

**3.** When syrup is cool, pour over oranges and mangos and toss to combine. Refrigerate for 15 minutes before serving.

### Papaya, Clementine, and Chayote Salad

Chayote, also called mirliton, is often sold with other tropical fruits and vegetables. If you can't find chayote, substitute an equal amount of jicama.

Substitute 2 teaspoons grated fresh ginger for red pepper flakes; 1 chayote, peeled, halved, pitted, and cut into ¼-inch dice, for jicama; 3 clementines, peeled and each segment cut into 3 pieces, for oranges; and 2 large papayas, peeled, seeded, and cut into ½-inch dice, for mangos.

### Pineapple, Grapefruit, and Cucumber Salad

Substitute ground cardamom for red pepper flakes; 1 cucumber, peeled, halved lengthwise, seeded, and cut into ¼-inch dice, for jicama; 1 grapefruit for oranges; and 1 pineapple, peeled, cored, and cut into ½-inch dice, for mangos.

## Watermelon Salad with Cotija and Serrano Chiles

**SERVES** 4 to 6

**WHY THIS RECIPE WORKS** Melon salads are prone to some common pitfalls: namely, watered-down dressings and garnishes that slide to the bottom of the salad bowl. Because watermelons vary in sweetness, we started by tasting our watermelon to determine how much sugar to incorporate into our dressing. To counter the abundant water contributed by the watermelon, we made an intense dressing with assertive ingredients such as lime juice, scallions, serrano chiles, and fresh cilantro, but we skipped the oil, which would only be repelled by the water on the surface of the watermelon. Instead we added richness with chopped roasted pepitas and cotija cheese, which adhered to the surface of the watermelon pieces and held on to the dressing. To avoid watering down the dressing, we left the watermelon in large chunks, which freed less juice and accentuated the contrast between the well-seasoned exterior and the sweet, juicy interior. Taste your melon as you cut it up: If it's very sweet, omit the sugar; if it's less sweet, add the sugar to the dressing. Jalapeños can be substituted for the serranos. If cotija cheese is unavailable, substitute feta cheese. This salad makes a light and refreshing accompaniment to grilled meat or fish.

- ⅓ cup lime juice (3 limes)
- 2 scallions, white and green parts separated and sliced thin
- 2 serrano chiles, stemmed, halved, seeded, and sliced thin crosswise
- 1–2 tablespoons sugar (optional)
- ¾ teaspoon table salt
- 6 cups 1½-inch seedless watermelon pieces
- 3 ounces cotija cheese, crumbled (¾ cup), divided
- 5 tablespoons chopped fresh cilantro, divided
- 5 tablespoons chopped roasted, salted pepitas, divided

Combine lime juice, scallion whites, and serranos in large bowl and let sit for 5 minutes. Stir in sugar, if using, and salt. Add watermelon, ½ cup cotija, ¼ cup cilantro, ¼ cup pepitas, and scallion greens and stir to combine. Transfer to shallow serving bowl. Sprinkle with remaining ¼ cup cotija, remaining 1 tablespoon cilantro, and remaining 1 tablespoon pepitas and serve.

### Cantaloupe Salad with Olives and Red Onion

**SERVES** 4 to 6

Taste your melon as you cut it up: If it's very sweet, omit the honey; if it's less sweet, add the honey to the dressing. We like the gentle heat and raisiny sweetness of ground dried Aleppo pepper here, but if it's unavailable, substitute ¾ teaspoon of paprika and ¼ teaspoon of cayenne pepper. This salad makes a light and refreshing accompaniment to grilled meat or fish and couscous or steamed white rice.

- ½ red onion, sliced thin
- ⅓ cup lemon juice (2 lemons)
- 1–3 teaspoons honey (optional)
- 1 teaspoon ground dried Aleppo pepper
- ½ teaspoon table salt
- 1 cantaloupe, peeled, halved, seeded, and cut into 1½-inch chunks (6 cups)
- 5 tablespoons chopped fresh parsley, divided
- 5 tablespoons chopped fresh mint, divided
- ¼ cup finely chopped pitted oil-cured olives, divided

Combine onion and lemon juice in large bowl and let sit for 5 minutes. Stir in honey, if using; Aleppo pepper; and salt. Add cantaloupe, ¼ cup parsley, ¼ cup mint, and 3 tablespoons olives and stir to combine. Transfer to shallow serving bowl. Sprinkle with remaining 1 tablespoon parsley, remaining 1 tablespoon mint, and remaining 1 tablespoon olives and serve.

### Honeydew Salad with Peanuts and Lime

**SERVES 4 TO 6**

Taste your melon as you cut it up: If it's very sweet, omit the sugar; if it's less sweet, add the sugar to the dressing. This salad makes a light and refreshing accompaniment to grilled meat or fish and steamed white rice.

- ⅓ cup lime juice (3 limes)
- 1 shallot, sliced thin
- 2 Thai chiles, stemmed, seeded, and minced
- 1 garlic clove, minced
- ½ teaspoon table salt
- 1–2 tablespoons sugar (optional)
- 1 tablespoon fish sauce
- 1 honeydew melon, peeled, halved, seeded, and cut into 1½-inch chunks (6 cups)
- 5 tablespoons chopped fresh cilantro, divided
- 5 tablespoons chopped fresh mint, divided
- 5 tablespoons salted dry-roasted peanuts, chopped fine, divided

**1.** Combine lime juice and shallot in large bowl. Using mortar and pestle (or on cutting board using flat side of chef's knife), mash Thai chiles, garlic, and salt to fine paste. Add chile paste; sugar, if using; and fish sauce to lime juice mixture and stir to combine.

**2.** Add honeydew, ¼ cup cilantro, ¼ cup mint, and ¼ cup peanuts and toss to combine. Transfer to shallow serving bowl. Sprinkle with remaining 1 tablespoon cilantro, remaining 1 tablespoon mint, and remaining 1 tablespoon peanuts and serve.

# CHAPTER 5 Pasta, Noodles, and Dumplings

Photos (left to right): Pasta with Rustic Slow-Simmered Tomato Sauce with Meat; Baked Manicotti; Pork, Fennel, and Lemon Ragu with Pappardelle; Japchae; Har Gow; Pasta alla Norma; Gnocchi à la Parisienne with Arugula, Tomatoes, and Olives

## Fresh Pasta Without a Machine

**MAKES** 1 pound

**WHY THIS RECIPE WORKS** Not everyone has a pasta machine, and rolling out pasta dough by hand is no easy task. For an easy-to-roll pasta dough (that would still cook up into delicate, springy noodles), we added six extra egg yolks and a couple of tablespoons of olive oil to our dough. In addition, we incorporated an extended resting period to allow the gluten network to relax. To roll and cut the pasta, we first divided the pasta into smaller manageable pieces, then used a rolling pin to roll the dough and a sharp knife to cut the dough into noodles. If using a high-protein all-purpose flour like King Arthur brand, increase the number of egg yolks to seven. The longer the dough rests in step 2, the easier it will be to roll out. When rolling out the dough, avoid adding too much flour, which may result in excessive snapback. Serve with Olive Oil Sauce with Anchovies and Parsley or a sauce of your choice.

- 2 cups (10 ounces) all-purpose flour, plus extra as needed
- 2 large eggs, plus 6 large yolks
- 2 tablespoons extra-virgin olive oil
- Table salt for cooking pasta

**1.** Process flour, eggs and yolks, and oil in food processor until mixture forms cohesive dough that feels soft and is barely tacky to touch, about 45 seconds. (If dough sticks to your fingers, add up to ¼ cup flour, 1 tablespoon at a time, until barely tacky. If dough doesn't become cohesive, add up to 1 tablespoon water, 1 teaspoon at a time, until it just comes together; process 30 seconds longer.)

**2.** Transfer dough to clean surface and knead by hand to form smooth, uniform ball, 1 to 2 minutes. Shape dough into 6-inch-long cylinder. Wrap with plastic wrap and set aside at room temperature to rest for at least 1 hour or up to 4 hours.

**3.** Cut cylinder crosswise into 6 equal pieces. Working with 1 piece of dough (rewrap remaining dough), dust both sides with flour, place cut side down on clean counter, and press into 3-inch square. Using heavy rolling pin, roll into 6-inch square. Dust both sides of dough lightly with flour.

**4A. FOR STRAND PASTA:** Starting at center of square, roll dough away from you in 1 motion. Return rolling pin to center of dough and roll toward you in 1 motion. Repeat steps of rolling until dough sticks to counter and measures roughly 12 inches long. Lightly dust both sides of dough with flour and continue rolling dough until it measures roughly 20 inches long and 6 inches wide, lifting dough frequently to release it from counter. (You should be able to easily see outline of your fingers through dough.) If dough firmly sticks to counter and wrinkles when rolled out, dust dough lightly with flour. Transfer pasta sheet to clean dish towel and let sit, uncovered, until firm around edges, about 15 minutes; meanwhile, roll out remaining dough. Starting with 1 short end, gently fold pasta sheet at 2-inch intervals until sheet has been folded into flat, rectangular roll. With sharp chef's knife, slice crosswise into 3⁄16-inch-wide strands. Use your fingers to unfurl pasta and transfer to baking sheet. Repeat folding and cutting remaining sheets of dough. Cook pasta within 1 hour.

**4B. FOR GARGANELLI:** Starting at center of square, roll dough away from you in 1 motion. Return rolling pin to center of dough and roll toward you in 1 motion. Repeat steps of rolling until dough sticks to counter and measures roughly 12 inches long. Lightly dust both sides of dough with flour and continue rolling dough until it measures roughly 15 inches long and 6 inches wide, lifting dough frequently to release it from counter. If dough firmly sticks to counter and wrinkles when rolled out, dust dough lightly with flour. Transfer pasta sheet to clean dish towel and let sit, uncovered, until firm around edges, about 15 minutes; meanwhile, roll out remaining dough. Using sharp knife or pizza cutter, cut 1 air-dried pasta sheet into 1½-inch squares; discard scraps. Lay 1 square of pasta diagonally on counter or, to create ridges in pasta, on top of garganelli or gnocchi board, inverted fork, or wire rack. Wrap 1 corner of pasta square around ⅜-inch dowel (or pencil), and with gentle pressure roll away from you until pasta is completely wrapped around dowel and seam is sealed. Slide shaped pasta off dowel onto lightly floured rimmed baking sheet and repeat with remaining pasta squares and sheets.

**5.** Bring 4 quarts water to boil in large pot. Add pasta and 1 tablespoon salt and cook until tender but still al dente, about 3 minutes. Reserve 1 cup cooking water. Drain pasta and toss with sauce; serve immediately.

**TO MAKE AHEAD:** Follow recipes through step 4, transfer baking sheet of pasta to freezer, and freeze until pasta is firm. Transfer to zipper-lock bag and store for up to 2 weeks. Cook frozen pasta straight from freezer as directed in step 5.

### Olive Oil Sauce with Anchovies and Parsley

**MAKES** 1 cup; enough for 1 pound pasta

Mincing the anchovies ensures that their flavor gets evenly distributed. Use a high-quality extra-virgin olive oil in this recipe.

- ⅓ cup extra-virgin olive oil
- 2 garlic cloves, minced
- 2 anchovy fillets, rinsed, patted dry, and minced
- ⅛ teaspoon table salt
- ½ teaspoon pepper
- 4 teaspoons lemon juice
- 2 tablespoons chopped fresh parsley

**1.** Heat oil in 12-inch skillet over medium-low heat until shimmering. Add garlic, anchovies, ⅛ teaspoon salt, and ½ teaspoon pepper; cook until fragrant, about 30 seconds. Remove pan from heat and cover to keep warm.

**2.** To serve, return pan to medium heat. Add pasta, ½ cup reserved cooking water, lemon juice, and parsley; toss to combine, adding remaining cooking water as needed to adjust consistency. Season with salt and pepper to taste; serve immediately.

### ROLLING, CUTTING, AND SHAPING PASTA DOUGH BY HAND

**1.** Shape dough into 6-inch cylinder; wrap in plastic wrap and let rest for at least 1 hour. Divide into 6 equal pieces. Reserve 1 piece; rewrap remaining 5.

**2.** Working with reserved piece, dust both sides with flour, then press cut side down into 3-inch square. With rolling pin, roll into 6-inch square, then dust both sides again with flour.

**3.** Roll dough to 12 by 6 inches, rolling from center of dough 1 way at a time, then dust with flour. Continue rolling to desired size, lifting frequently to release from counter. Transfer dough to clean dish towel and air-dry for about 15 minutes.

**4.** Using sharp knife or pizza cutter, cut dried pasta sheet into 1½-inch squares. Lay 1 square diagonally on counter or, to create ridges in pasta, on top of a garganelli or gnocchi board, inverted fork or wire rack.

**5.** Wrap 1 corner of pasta square around ⅜-inch dowel (or pencil), and with gentle pressure roll away from you until pasta is completely wrapped around dowel and seam is sealed.

**6.** Slide shaped pasta off dowel onto lightly floured rimmed baking sheet and repeat with remaining pasta squares and sheets.

# Pasta Aglio e Olio (Pasta with Garlic and Oil)

**SERVES** 4 to 6

**WHY THIS RECIPE WORKS** Nothing sounds easier than pasta with olive oil and garlic, but too often this dish turns out oily or rife with burnt garlic. We were after a flawless version of this quick classic, with bright, deep garlic flavor and no trace of bitterness or harshness. For a mellow flavor, we cooked most of the garlic over low heat until sticky and straw-colored; a modest amount of raw garlic added at the end brought in some potent fresh garlic flavor. Extra-virgin olive oil and reserved pasta cooking water helped to keep our garlic and pasta saucy. A splash of lemon juice and sprinkling of red pepper flakes added some spice and brightness to this simple, yet complex-flavored recipe. For a twist on pasta with garlic and oil, try sprinkling toasted fresh bread crumbs over individual bowls, but prepare them in advance. Simply pulse two slices of high-quality white sandwich bread, torn into quarters, in a food processor to coarse crumbs. Combine with 2 tablespoons extra-virgin olive oil; season with salt and pepper; and bake on a rimmed baking sheet at 375 degrees until golden brown, 8 to 10 minutes.

- 1 pound spaghetti
- 1¼ teaspoons table salt, divided, plus salt for cooking pasta
- 6 tablespoons extra-virgin olive oil, divided
- 12 garlic cloves, minced, divided
- 3 tablespoons chopped fresh parsley
- 2 teaspoons lemon juice
- ¾ teaspoon red pepper flakes
- ½ cup grated Parmesan cheese (optional)

**1.** Bring 4 quarts water to boil in large pot. Add pasta and 1 tablespoon salt and cook, stirring often, until al dente; reserve ⅓ cup cooking water, then drain pasta and return it to pot.

**2.** Meanwhile, heat 3 tablespoons oil, 3 tablespoons garlic, and ½ teaspoon salt over low heat in 10-inch nonstick skillet. Cook, stirring constantly, until garlic is sticky and straw-colored, 10 to 12 minutes. Off heat, stir in parsley, lemon juice, pepper flakes, 2 tablespoons reserved pasta cooking water, and remaining garlic.

**3.** Transfer drained pasta to warm serving bowl; add remaining 3 tablespoons oil and remaining reserved pasta cooking water and toss to combine. Add garlic mixture and remaining ¾ teaspoon salt; toss to combine. Serve, sprinkling individual bowls with Parmesan, if desired.

# Spaghetti al Limone (Spaghetti with Lemon and Olive Oil)

**SERVES** 4

**WHY THIS RECIPE WORKS** Making lemon the star of a pasta dish is not as easy as it might seem and requires the right co-stars and the perfect balance of lemon juice and zest. We wanted a dish bursting with bright, bracing lemon flavor and

moistened with just enough fruity olive oil to coat each delicate strand. Starting with lemon flavor, we found that the right amount of juice per pound of pasta was extremely small, and if we leaned more to either side, the lemon flavor became either too tart or barely noticeable. We added some grated zest to the sauce which boosted the power of the lemon without making the sauce overly acidic. Equal amounts of cream and olive oil formed the base of the sauce; the cream neutralized some of the acids in the juice while the oil added fruity, floral notes.

- Table salt and ground black pepper
- 1 pound spaghetti
- ¼ cup extra-virgin olive oil, plus extra for drizzling
- 1 medium shallot, minced (about 3 tablespoons)
- ¼ cup heavy cream
- 1 ounce Parmesan cheese, grated (about ½ cup), plus extra for serving
- 2 teaspoons grated zest plus ¼ cup juice from 2 lemons
- 2 tablespoons chopped fresh basil leaves

**1.** Bring 4 quarts water to a boil in a large pot. Add 1 tablespoon salt and the pasta to the boiling water and cook until al dente. Reserve 1¾ cups of the cooking water, then drain the pasta.

**2.** Heat 1 tablespoon of the oil in the now-empty pot over medium heat until shimmering. Add the shallot and ½ teaspoon salt and cook until softened, about 2 minutes. Stir in 1½ cups of the reserved cooking water and the cream, bring to a simmer, and cook for 2 minutes. Off the heat, add the drained pasta, remaining 3 tablespoons oil, Parmesan, lemon zest, lemon juice, and ½ teaspoon pepper, and toss to combine.

**3.** Cover and let the pasta rest for 2 minutes, tossing frequently and adding the remaining cooking water as needed to adjust the consistency. Stir in the basil and season with salt and pepper to taste. Drizzle individual portions with oil and serve, passing the additional Parmesan separately.

## Spaghetti Cacio e Pepe (Spaghetti with Pecorino Romano and Black Pepper)

**SERVES** 4 to 6

**WHY THIS RECIPE WORKS** This Roman spaghetti makes a delicious and quick pantry supper. But in some versions, the creamy sauce can turn into clumps of solidified cheese. We wanted a sauce that was intensely cheesy but also creamy and smooth. Our science editor explained why the cheese clumps in this dish. Cheese consists mainly of three basic substances: fat, protein, and water. When a hard cheese like Pecorino is heated, its fat begins to melt and its proteins soften. The fat acts as a sort of glue, fusing the proteins together. In order to coat the cheese and prevent the proteins from sticking together, we needed to introduce a starch into the mix. It occurred to us that as pasta cooks, it releases starch into the water so we reduced the amount of water to concentrate the starch and whisked some of the cooking liquid into the cheese. This helped, but we found we also needed an emulsifier—something to bind together the sauce. By switching the butter for cream, we created a light, perfectly smooth sauce that had all the cheese flavor we wanted—no clumps in sight. High-quality ingredients are essential in this dish, most importantly, imported Pecorino Romano. For a slightly less rich dish, substitute half-and-half for the heavy cream. Do not adjust the amount of water for cooking the pasta; the amount used is critical to the success of the recipe. Make sure to stir the pasta frequently while cooking so that it doesn't stick to the pot. Draining the pasta water into the serving bowl warms the bowl and helps keeps the dish hot until it is served. Letting the dish rest briefly before serving allows the flavors to develop and the sauce to thicken.

- 4 ounces Pecorino Romano, grated fine (about 2 cups), plus 2 ounces grated coarse (about 1 cup), for serving
- 1 pound spaghetti
- Table salt
- 2 tablespoons heavy cream
- 2 teaspoons extra-virgin olive oil
- 1½ teaspoons ground black pepper

**1.** Place the finely grated Pecorino in a medium bowl. Set a colander in a large bowl.

**2.** Bring 2 quarts water to a boil in a large Dutch oven. Add the pasta and 1½ teaspoons salt and cook, stirring frequently, until the pasta is al dente. Drain the pasta into the colander set in the bowl, reserving the cooking water. Pour 1½ cups of the cooking water into a liquid measuring cup and discard the remainder and then place the pasta in the empty bowl.

**3.** Slowly whisk 1 cup of the reserved pasta water into the finely grated Pecorino until smooth. Whisk in the cream, oil, and pepper. Gradually pour the cheese mixture over the pasta, tossing to coat. Let the pasta rest for 1 to 2 minutes, tossing frequently, adjusting the consistency with the remaining ½ cup reserved pasta cooking water as needed. Serve, passing the coarsely grated Pecorino separately.

## Pasta Cacio e Uova (Pasta with Cheese and Eggs)

**SERVES** 4

**WHY THIS RECIPE WORKS** This cheese and egg pasta, called cas' e ova in its native Naples, makes its way to the table in a flash. The method is simple: Mix beaten eggs and cheese with garlic-infused lard, hot pasta, and some of its starchy cooking water. While we liked this with olive oil, cacio e uova made with lard not only tasted fuller and richer, it also heightened the cheese flavor and felt cleaner on the palate. To keep our sauce from scrambling, we mixed the sauce and pasta together off the heat. This melted the cheese and brought the eggs up to temperature gently. Tubetti is traditionally used for this dish, but you can substitute 8 ounces (2 cups) of elbow macaroni. Lard contributes an incomparably rich, savory flavor to the sauce. Look for it in the meat section, or near the shortening, or near the butter. Our favorites are U.S. Dreams Lard and John Morrell Snow Cap Lard. Because this dish is very rich, we recommend serving it in small portions.

- 3 tablespoons lard or extra-virgin olive oil
- 2 garlic cloves, lightly crushed and peeled
- 2 large eggs
- 1 ounce Parmesan cheese, grated (½ cup)
- 1 ounce Pecorino Romano cheese, grated (½ cup)
- 2 tablespoons minced fresh parsley
- ¼ teaspoon table salt, plus salt for cooking pasta
- ¼ teaspoon pepper
- 8 ounces (1½ cups) tubetti

**1.** Melt lard in 8-inch skillet over medium-low heat. Add garlic and cook, swirling skillet and flipping garlic occasionally, until garlic is pale golden brown, 7 to 10 minutes. (Tiny bubbles will surround garlic, but garlic should not actively fry. Reduce heat if necessary.) Turn off heat, but leave skillet on burner. Discard garlic.

**2.** While garlic cooks, bring 2 quarts water to boil in large saucepan. Beat eggs in medium bowl until very few streaks of white remain. Stir in Parmesan, Pecorino, parsley, salt, and pepper and set aside.

**3.** Stir pasta and 1½ teaspoons salt into boiling water and cook, stirring often, until pasta is tender (slightly past al dente). Reserve ¼ cup cooking water, then drain pasta and return it to saucepan. Immediately add lard, egg mixture, and 1 tablespoon reserved cooking water to pasta and stir until cheese is fully melted. Adjust consistency with remaining reserved cooking water, 1 tablespoon at a time, as needed. Serve immediately.

## Pasta with Creamy Lemon–Sichuan Peppercorn Sauce

**SERVES** 4 to 6 **SEASON 26**

**WHY THIS RECIPE WORKS** This vibrant creamy pasta dish features bright lemon, fragrant miso, and crème fraîche. But its real star is Sichuan peppercorns. They create a unique numbing and tingling sensation due to a compound that interacts with our nerve endings, triggering a phenomenon known as chemesthesis, which is responsible for the distinctive sensation. To get even flavor distribution and a pronounced (but not overwhelming) level of that buzzing sensation, we toasted and ground 4 teaspoons of Sichuan peppercorns and incorporated them in two ways: gently heated in some oil to release their flavorful compounds that formed the base of the creamy sauce, and stirred into the pasta right before serving. Use high-quality Sichuan peppercorns in this recipe, and pick through them to remove any debris. We call for a mortar and pestle to grind the peppercorns, but you can also use a spice grinder. Serve with extra lemon juice if you like a very punchy sauce.

- 1 pound spaghetti
- Table salt for cooking pasta
- 4 teaspoons red Sichuan peppercorns
- 3 tablespoons extra-virgin olive oil
- 2 garlic cloves, minced
- 1 cup chicken broth
- 1 cup crème fraîche
- 3 tablespoons white miso
- 2 teaspoons grated lemon zest plus 2 tablespoons juice
- 1 teaspoon pepper
- 2 tablespoons chopped fresh parsley
- Parmesan cheese (optional)

**1.** Bring 4 quarts water to boil in large pot. Add pasta and 1 tablespoon salt and cook, stirring often, until al dente. Reserve 1 cup cooking water, then drain pasta and return it to pot.

**2.** Meanwhile, heat dry medium saucepan over medium heat for 1 minute. Add Sichuan peppercorns and toast until fragrant, about 1 minute, stirring frequently. Transfer to mortar and pestle and let cool to room temperature then grind until coarsely ground; set aside.

**3.** Cook oil, garlic, and half of ground Sichuan peppercorns over medium heat in now-empty saucepan until fragrant, about 1 minute. Stir in broth and bring to boil. Reduce heat to medium-low and simmer until reduced by half, 4 to 5 minutes.

**4.** Whisk in crème fraîche, miso, lemon zest and juice, and pepper; increase heat to medium-high, and return to brief simmer. Season with salt and pepper to taste.

**5.** Add sauce and ½ cup reserved cooking water to pasta in pot and toss to combine. Adjust consistency with remaining reserved cooking water as needed. Stir in remaining ground Sichuan peppercorns, then season with salt and pepper to taste. Sprinkle with parsley and serve with Parmesan, if using.

## Pasta and Fresh Tomato Sauce with Garlic and Basil

**SERVES 4 TO 6**

**WHY THIS RECIPE WORKS** The best fresh tomato sauces capture the contrasting sweet and tart flavors of ripe tomatoes. But often, these sauces get waterlogged from the tomato juice. We wanted a cooked sauce that allowed the flavors of the traditional players—tomatoes, basil, garlic, and oil—to meld, but not become watered down. Quick cooking was the key to preserving fresh tomato flavor and creating a sauce that was both hearty and brightly flavored. To prevent unattractive pieces of curled-up tomato skin floating in our finished sauce, we simply peeled the tomatoes by boiling them and pulling off their skins. Seeded tomatoes made for a less watery start to the sauce, and cooking them down for a brief period facilitated the evaporation of any remaining liquid. Chopped fresh basil rounded out the flavors of the sauce, and a last-minute drizzle of olive oil brought a richness that complemented the sweetness of the tomatoes. To peel the tomatoes, dunk the cored tomatoes in a pot of boiling water until the skins split and begin to curl around the cored area, 15 to 30 seconds; transfer the tomatoes to a bowl of ice water, then peel off the skins with your fingers. This chunky sauce works best with tubular pasta shapes, such as penne or fusilli. If you'd like to serve it with spaghetti or linguine, puree the sauce in a blender or food processor before adding the basil. This recipe can be doubled and prepared in a 12-inch skillet.

- 3 tablespoons extra-virgin olive oil
- 2 medium garlic cloves, minced or pressed through a garlic press (about 2 teaspoons)
- 2 pounds ripe tomatoes (about 4 large), cored, peeled, seeded, and cut into ½-inch pieces
- 2 tablespoons chopped fresh basil leaves
- Table salt
- 1 pound penne, fusilli, or other short tubular pasta (see note)

**1.** Cook 2 tablespoons of the oil and the garlic in a 10-inch skillet over medium heat until fragrant, about 30 seconds. Stir in the tomatoes and cook over medium-high heat until the liquid released by the tomatoes evaporates and the tomato pieces form a chunky sauce, about 10 minutes. Stir in the basil and salt to taste; cover.

**2.** Meanwhile, bring 4 quarts water to a boil in a large pot. Add 1 tablespoon salt and the pasta to the boiling water and cook, stirring often, until al dente. Reserve ½ cup of the cooking water then drain the pasta and return it to the pot. Add ¼ cup of the reserved cooking water, the sauce, and the remaining 1 tablespoon oil and toss to combine. Adjust the consistency of the sauce with the remaining reserved pasta cooking water as needed. Serve.

## Pasta Caprese

**SERVES 4 TO 6**

**WHY THIS RECIPE WORKS** The summer salad composed of creamy mozzarella, fresh basil, and sweet tomatoes has become so popular that we wanted to translate it to a simple-yet-elegant pasta dish. Specifically, we wanted creamy pockets of milky mozzarella throughout the dish, rather than the chewy wads that can occur when cheese hits hot pasta. Supermarket mozzarella worked well in this dish; the trick was to dice and freeze it for just 10 minutes before tossing it with the hot pasta to keep the cheese soft and creamy (instead of dry and clumpy). Otherwise, handmade mozzarella (minus the freezing step) worked well. To boost the flavor of supermarket tomatoes, we added a little sugar for sweetness and fresh lemon juice for brightness. Marinating the tomatoes and mozzarella with olive oil, minced shallot, salt, and a pinch of black pepper while the pasta was cooking added even more flavor. This dish will be very warm, not hot. The success of this recipe depends on high-quality ingredients, including ripe, in-season tomatoes and a fruity olive oil. Don't skip the step of freezing the mozzarella, as freezing prevents it from turning chewy when it comes in contact with the hot pasta. Additional lemon juice or up to 1 teaspoon sugar can be added at the end to taste, depending on the ripeness of the tomatoes.

- ¼ cup extra-virgin olive oil
- 2–4 teaspoons juice from 1 lemon
- 1 small garlic clove, minced or pressed through a garlic press (about ½ teaspoon)
- 1 small shallot, minced (about 1 tablespoon)
- Table salt and ground black pepper
- 1½ pounds ripe tomatoes (about 3 large), cored, seeded, and cut into ½-inch dice
- 12 ounces fresh mozzarella cheese, cut into ½-inch cubes
- 1 pound penne, fusilli, or campanelle
- ¼ cup chopped fresh basil leaves
- 1 teaspoon sugar (optional)

**1.** Whisk the oil, 2 teaspoons of the lemon juice, the garlic, shallot, ½ teaspoon salt, and ¼ teaspoon pepper together in a large bowl. Add the tomatoes and toss gently to combine; set aside. Do not marinate the tomatoes for longer than 45 minutes.

**2.** While the tomatoes are marinating, place the mozzarella on a plate and freeze until slightly firm, about 10 minutes. Bring 4 quarts water to a boil in a large pot. Add 1 tablespoon salt and the pasta to the boiling water and cook, stirring often, until al dente. Drain well.

**3.** Add the pasta and mozzarella to the tomato mixture and toss gently to combine. Let stand for 5 minutes. Stir in the basil, season with salt and pepper to taste, and add additional lemon juice or sugar, if desired. Serve immediately.

## Pasta with Burst Cherry Tomato Sauce and Fried Caper Crumbs

**SERVES** 4 to 6

**WHY THIS RECIPE WORKS** Cherry tomatoes are the perfect choice for a quick fresh tomato sauce. You can toss them directly into the pan without any prep, and they don't need lengthy cooking to concentrate their flavor or thicken into a sauce. That's because they're naturally more flavorful than the bigger varieties used in sauce, and they're full of soluble pectin that breaks down readily to a saucy consistency. To ensure that some of the cherry tomatoes remained intact and would pop in the mouth, we cooked them for 10 minutes in a covered saucepan, where only the tomatoes in contact with the bottom of the pan burst and those on top steamed more gently. To keep the sauce bright and tomato-focused, we sautéed the tomatoes with garlic, pepper flakes, and a touch of sugar, along with anchovies that melded into the mix without fishiness. Butter tossed with the pasta brought a light, creamy richness to the dish. We finished it with fresh basil and a topping of fried bread crumbs and capers. Be sure to use cherry tomatoes; grape tomatoes won't break down as much and will produce a drier sauce. If desired, you can substitute 1 cup (2 ounces) of grated Parmesan cheese.

**TOPPING**

- 2 tablespoons extra-virgin olive oil
- ¼ cup capers, rinsed and patted dry
- 1 anchovy fillet, rinsed, patted dry, and minced
- ½ cup panko bread crumbs
- ⅛ teaspoon table salt
- ⅛ teaspoon pepper
- ¼ cup minced fresh parsley
- 1 teaspoon grated lemon zest

**PASTA**

- ¼ cup extra-virgin olive oil
- 2 garlic cloves, sliced thin
- 2 anchovy fillets, rinsed and patted dry
- 2 pounds cherry tomatoes
- 1½ teaspoons table salt, plus salt for cooking pasta
- ¼ teaspoon sugar
- ⅛–¼ teaspoon red pepper flakes
- 12 ounces penne rigate, orecchiette, campanelle, or other short pasta
- 2 tablespoons unsalted butter, cut into 2 pieces and chilled
- 1 cup fresh basil leaves, torn if large

**1. FOR THE TOPPING:** Heat oil in 10-inch skillet over medium heat until shimmering. Add capers and anchovy and cook, stirring frequently, until capers have darkened and shrunk, 3 to 4 minutes. Using slotted spoon, transfer caper mixture to paper towel–lined plate; set aside. Leave oil in skillet and return skillet to medium heat. Add panko, salt, and pepper to skillet and cook, stirring constantly, until panko is golden brown, 4 to 5 minutes. Transfer panko to medium bowl. Stir in parsley, lemon zest, and reserved caper mixture.

**2. FOR THE PASTA:** Bring 4 quarts water to boil in large pot. While water is coming to boil, heat oil, garlic, and anchovies in large saucepan over medium heat. Cook, stirring occasionally, until anchovies break down and garlic is lightly browned, 4 to 5 minutes. Add tomatoes, salt, sugar, and pepper flakes to saucepan and stir to combine. Cover and increase heat to medium-high. Cook, without stirring, for 10 minutes.

**3.** Meanwhile, add pasta and 1 tablespoon salt to boiling water. Cook, stirring often, until al dente. Reserve ½ cup cooking water, then drain pasta and return it to pot. Off heat, add butter and tomato mixture to pasta and stir gently until oil, butter, and tomato juices combine to form light sauce, about 15 seconds. Adjust consistency with reserved cooking water as needed, adding 2 tablespoons at a time. Stir in basil and season with salt to taste. Serve, passing topping separately.

## Farfalle with Tomatoes, Olives, and Feta

**SERVES** 4 to 6

**WHY THIS RECIPE WORKS** When tomatoes are in season, there's no better time to make a simple, fresh tomato sauce. We like the classic pairing of tomatoes and olives, so we set out to make an easy, not too watery, sauce with Mediterranean flavors. Seeding the tomatoes rid them of excess moisture and prevented a watery sauce. Instead of peeling the tomato skins, we decided to leave them on so that the chopped tomatoes would have some structural integrity and not disintegrate. By making a no-cook sauce—the other components were fresh mint, chopped kalamata olives, and feta—we were able to prepare it quickly while the drained pasta waited on the sidelines. The potent olives and feta added a bright zestiness to our pasta, and the mint amplified the sauce's freshness. To prevent the feta from melting into the pasta, add it only after the tomatoes have been tossed with the pasta, which gives the mixture the opportunity to cool slightly.

- Table salt
- 1 pound farfalle
- 1½ pounds ripe tomatoes (about 3 large), cored, seeded, and cut into ½-inch pieces
- ½ cup pitted kalamata olives, chopped coarse
- ¼ cup extra-virgin olive oil
- 1 tablespoon chopped fresh mint leaves
- Ground black pepper
- 6 ounces feta cheese, crumbled (about 1½ cups)

**1.** Bring 4 quarts water to a boil in a large pot. Add 1 tablespoon salt and the pasta to the boiling water and cook, stirring often, until al dente. Reserve ½ cup of the cooking water then drain the pasta and return it to the pot.

**2.** Meanwhile, combine the tomatoes, olives, oil, mint, ½ teaspoon salt, and ¼ teaspoon pepper in a medium bowl. Add the sauce to the pasta and adjust the consistency of the sauce with the reserved pasta cooking water as needed. Add the feta and toss to combine. Season with salt and pepper to taste and serve.

## Pasta with Creamy Tomato Sauce

**SERVES** 4 to 6

**WHY THIS RECIPE WORKS** In a great creamy tomato sauce, the acidity of the tomatoes is balanced with the richness of dairy. Readily available, canned crushed tomatoes trumped canned whole and diced tomatoes. Before adding the tomatoes, we cooked a few tablespoons of tomato paste with some onion, garlic, and sun-dried tomatoes. A pinch of red pepper flakes, a splash of wine, and a little minced prosciutto added depth and tamed the sauce's sweetness; a bit of reserved uncooked crushed tomatoes and another splash of wine stirred in before serving brought the sauce's ingredients together. We added cream to the finished sauce to enrich it without dulling the tomato flavor. Use high-quality crushed tomatoes; our favorite brand is San Merican.

- 3 tablespoons unsalted butter
- 1 small onion, minced
- 1 ounce prosciutto, minced (about 2 tablespoons)
- 1 bay leaf
- Pinch red pepper flakes
- Table salt
- 3 medium garlic cloves, minced or pressed through a garlic press (about 1 tablespoon)
- 2 ounces oil-packed sun-dried tomatoes, drained, rinsed, patted dry, and chopped coarse (about 3 tablespoons)
- 2 tablespoons tomato paste
- ¼ cup plus 2 tablespoons dry white wine
- 2 cups plus 2 tablespoons crushed tomatoes (from one 28-ounce can)
- 1 pound ziti, penne, or other short tubular pasta
- ½ cup heavy cream
- Ground black pepper
- ¼ cup chopped fresh basil leaves
- Grated Parmesan cheese, for serving

**1.** Melt the butter in a medium saucepan over medium heat. Add the onion, prosciutto, bay leaf, red pepper flakes, and ¼ teaspoon salt; cook, stirring occasionally, until the onion is very soft and beginning to turn light gold, 8 to 12 minutes. Increase the heat to medium-high, add the garlic, and cook until fragrant, about 30 seconds. Stir in the sun-dried tomatoes and tomato paste and cook, stirring constantly, until slightly darkened, 1 to 2 minutes. Add ¼ cup of the wine and cook, stirring frequently, until the liquid has evaporated, 1 to 2 minutes.

**2.** Add 2 cups of the crushed tomatoes and bring to a simmer. Reduce the heat to low, partially cover, and cook, stirring occasionally, until the sauce is thickened, 25 to 30 minutes.

**3.** Meanwhile, bring 4 quarts water to a boil in a large pot. Add 1 tablespoon salt and the pasta to the boiling water and cook, stirring often, until al dente. Reserve ½ cup of the cooking water then drain the pasta and return it to the pot.

**4.** Remove the bay leaf from the sauce and discard. Stir the cream, remaining 2 tablespoons crushed tomatoes, and remaining 2 tablespoons wine into the sauce; season with salt and pepper to taste. Add the sauce to the pasta and adjust the consistency of the sauce with the reserved pasta cooking water as needed. Stir in the basil and serve, passing the Parmesan separately.

## Penne alla Vodka (Penne with Vodka Sauce)

**SERVES** 4 to 6

**WHY THIS RECIPE WORKS** Splashes of vodka and cream can turn run-of-the-mill tomato sauce into luxurious restaurant fare—or a heavy, boozy mistake. Despite the simple ingredients, we found recipes for penne alla vodka gave us results that varied widely. Many were absurdly rich (with more cream than tomatoes) and others were too harsh from a heavy hand with the vodka. We wanted to fine-tune this modern classic to strike the right balance of sweet, tangy, spicy, and creamy. To achieve a sauce with the right consistency, we pureed half the tomatoes (which helped the sauce cling nicely to the pasta) and cut the rest into chunks. For sweetness, we added sautéed minced onions; for depth of flavor, we used a bit of tomato paste. We found we needed a liberal amount of vodka to cut through the richness and add "zinginess" to the sauce, but we needed to add it to the tomatoes early on to allow the alcohol to mostly (but not completely) cook off and prevent a boozy flavor. Adding a little heavy cream to the sauce gave it a nice consistency, and we finished cooking the penne in the sauce to encourage cohesiveness. So that the sauce and pasta finish cooking at the same time, drop the pasta into the boiling water just after adding the vodka to the sauce.

- 1 (28-ounce) can whole tomatoes, drained, juice reserved
- 2 tablespoons olive oil
- ½ small onion, minced

1 tablespoon tomato paste
2 medium garlic cloves, minced or pressed through a garlic press (about 2 teaspoons)
¼ teaspoon red pepper flakes
Table salt
⅓ cup vodka
½ cup heavy cream
1 pound penne
2 tablespoons minced fresh basil leaves
Grated Parmesan cheese, for serving

**1.** Puree half of the tomatoes in a food processor until smooth. Dice the remaining tomatoes into ½-inch pieces, discarding the cores. Combine the pureed and diced tomatoes in a liquid measuring cup (you should have about 1⅔ cups). Add the reserved juice to equal 2 cups.

**2.** Heat the oil in a large saucepan over medium heat until shimmering. Add the onion and tomato paste and cook, stirring occasionally, until the onion is light golden around the edges, about 3 minutes. Add the garlic and red pepper flakes; cook, stirring constantly, until fragrant, about 30 seconds.

**3.** Stir in the tomatoes and ½ teaspoon salt. Remove the pan from the heat and add the vodka. Return the pan to medium-high heat and simmer briskly until the alcohol flavor is cooked off, 8 to 10 minutes; stir frequently and lower the heat to medium if the simmering becomes too vigorous. Stir in the cream and cook until hot, about 1 minute.

**4.** Meanwhile, bring 4 quarts water to a boil in a large pot. Add 1 tablespoon salt and the pasta to the boiling water. Cook, stirring often, until just shy of al dente. Reserve ½ cup of the cooking water then drain the pasta and return it to the pot. Add the sauce to the pasta and toss over medium heat until the pasta absorbs some of the sauce, 1 to 2 minutes. Adjust the consistency of the sauce with the reserved pasta cooking water as needed. Stir in the basil and season with salt to taste. Serve immediately, passing the Parmesan separately.

## Quick Tomato Sauce

**MAKES** about 3 cups

**WHY THIS RECIPE WORKS** In a perfect world, garden-ripe tomatoes make the best quick tomato sauce. But that isn't realistic for most of the year. We wanted to create a complex, brightly flavored sauce with the next best alternative—canned tomatoes—that tasted of full, fruity tomatoes, in the time it took to boil pasta. Choosing the right can of tomatoes was a critical first step. Crushed tomatoes were the best choice because they would save us the step of pureeing. We also shredded a small amount of onion on a box grater before sautéing; the shredded pieces cooked faster and became sweeter more quickly. We sautéed the onion in butter, which caramelized when heated, and added garlic, sugar, and the crushed tomatoes, then simmered the sauce briefly. To make up for the lost fragrance of fresh tomatoes, we added chopped fresh basil and extra-virgin olive oil. This recipe makes enough to sauce a pound of pasta. High-quality canned tomatoes will make a big difference in this sauce; our preferred brand of crushed tomatoes is San Merican. Grate the onion on the large holes of a box grater.

2 tablespoons unsalted butter
¼ cup grated onion
¼ teaspoon dried oregano
Table salt
2 medium garlic cloves, minced or pressed through a garlic press (about 2 teaspoons)
1 (28-ounce) can crushed tomatoes
¼ teaspoon sugar
2 tablespoons chopped fresh basil leaves
1 tablespoon extra-virgin olive oil
Ground black pepper

Melt the butter in a medium saucepan over medium heat. Add the onion, oregano, and ½ teaspoon salt; cook, stirring occasionally, until the liquid has evaporated and the onion is golden brown, about 5 minutes. Add the garlic and cook until fragrant, about 30 seconds. Stir in the tomatoes and sugar; bring to a simmer over high heat. Lower the heat to medium-low and simmer until slightly thickened, about 10 minutes. Off the heat, stir in the basil and oil; season with salt and pepper to taste.

## Marinara Sauce

**MAKES** 4 cups

**WHY THIS RECIPE WORKS** Making a tomato sauce with deep, complex flavor usually requires hours of simmering. We wanted to produce a multidimensional marinara sauce in under an hour, perfect for any night of the week. Our first challenge was picking the right tomatoes. We found canned whole tomatoes, which we hand-crushed to remove the hard core, to be the best choice in terms of both flavor and texture. We boosted tomato flavor by sautéing the tomato pieces until they glazed the bottom of the pan, after which we added their liquid. We shortened the simmering time by using a skillet instead of a saucepan (the greater surface area of a skillet encourages faster evaporation and flavor concentration). Finally, we added just the right amount of sugar, red wine (we especially liked Chianti and Merlot), and, just before serving, a few uncooked canned tomatoes for texture, fresh basil for fresh herbal flavor, and olive oil for richness. You can figure on about 3 cups of sauce per pound of pasta. Chianti or Merlot works well for the dry red wine. Because canned tomatoes vary in acidity and saltiness, it's best to add salt, pepper, and sugar to taste just before serving. If you prefer a chunkier sauce, give it just three or four pulses in the food processor in step 4.

- 2 (28-ounce) cans whole tomatoes
- 3 tablespoons extra-virgin olive oil, divided
- 1 onion, chopped fine
- 2 garlic cloves, minced
- ½ teaspoon dried oregano
- ⅓ cup dry red wine
- 3 tablespoons chopped fresh basil
- Sugar

**1.** Pour tomatoes into strainer set over large bowl. Open tomatoes with your hands and remove and discard fibrous cores; let tomatoes drain excess liquid, about 5 minutes. Remove ¾ cup tomatoes from strainer and set aside. Reserve 2½ cups tomato juice and discard remainder.

**2.** Heat 2 tablespoons oil in 12-inch skillet over medium heat until shimmering. Add onion and cook, stirring occasionally, until softened and golden around edges, 6 to 8 minutes. Add garlic and oregano and cook, stirring constantly, until garlic is fragrant, about 30 seconds.

**3.** Add tomatoes from strainer and increase heat to medium-high. Cook, stirring every minute, until liquid has evaporated and tomatoes begin to stick to bottom of pan and browned bits form around pan edges, 10 to 12 minutes. Add wine and cook until thick and syrupy, about 1 minute. Add reserved tomato juice and bring to simmer; reduce heat to medium and cook, stirring occasionally and scraping up any browned bits, until sauce is thickened, 8 to 10 minutes.

**4.** Transfer sauce to food processor and add reserved tomatoes; pulse until slightly chunky, about 8 pulses. Return sauce to skillet; add basil and remaining 1 tablespoon oil; and season with salt, pepper, and sugar to taste. Serve. (Sauce can be refrigerated in airtight container for up to 3 days or frozen for up to 1 month.)

## Spaghetti all'Assassina

SERVES 4 **SEASON 26**

**WHY THIS RECIPE WORKS** The defining aspects of this hyper-local dish from Bari, Italy, are spaghetti strands with textures that run from soft to al dente to crisp (even within a single strand) and a spicy, concentrated tomato sauce that clings tightly to the pasta. To achieve these hallmarks, we started by including a generous amount of extra-virgin olive oil in a simple sauce of garlic, red pepper flakes, and passata di pomodoro (uncooked tomato puree). We then added raw spaghetti to the sauce in a skillet, followed periodically by cupfuls of a simple tomato broth (tomato paste diluted with water). Each time the pan threatened to dry out, we added more broth. We made sure not to stir the pasta too much as it turned tender and started to crisp and char in spots. To finish the delicious, deeply satisfying dish, we turned the heat to full blast so that some of the strands could develop a smoky char. This recipe was developed with our winning spaghetti, De Cecco Spaghetti No. 12. Other brands of spaghetti may vary in thickness, which will affect the cooking time and the amount of broth required. Fish spatulas work well for flipping the pasta in step 4. Passata is an uncooked tomato puree; we used Pomì brand. If you cannot find it, tomato puree can be used. For a spicier dish, use ¾ teaspoon of red pepper flakes. The sauce will splatter as it cooks, which is why we call for using a long-handled spatula in step 2. A splatter screen helps contain the splattering.

### MAKING SPAGHETTI ALL'ASSASSINA

**1.** Lay pasta on top of simmered tomato sauce and add 1 cup tomato broth. When broth is mostly absorbed, add another cup broth and cook, shaking skillet occasionally until sauce thickens and begins to sizzle.

**2.** Using two thin spatulas, flip half of pasta so bottom is on top and spread into even layer. Repeat with remaining pasta. Add 1 cup broth and repeat cooking until sauce sizzles. Add another cup broth and cook until sauce sizzles. Repeat dividing and flipping.

**3.** Add 1 cup broth and repeat cooking until sauce sizzles. Pasta should be firm and cooked through. If not, add remaining 1 cup broth ½ cup at a time and cook, checking frequently until pasta is cooked through.

**4.** Increase heat to high and cook pasta without moving until underside is deeply browned and crisp and some strands are beginning to char 3 to 5 minutes. Remove skillet from heat an drizzle with remaining 2 tablespoons oil.

6 cups water
¼ cup tomato paste
1 teaspoon sugar
⅓ cup plus 2 tablespoons extra-virgin olive oil, divided
2 garlic cloves, minced
½–¾ teaspoon red pepper flakes
1 cup tomato passata
1¾ teaspoons table salt
12 ounces spaghetti

**1.** Whisk water, tomato paste, and sugar together in medium saucepan. Bring to simmer over medium-high heat, then reduce heat to low to keep tomato broth warm.

**2.** Heat ⅓ cup oil, garlic, and pepper flakes in 12-inch nonstick skillet over medium heat. Cook, stirring frequently with long-handled rubber spatula, until garlic is golden brown, about 2 minutes. Stir in passata and salt. Cook, stirring frequently, until sauce thickens and oil around edges of skillet begins to sizzle, about 4 minutes.

**3.** Add pasta in even layer and increase heat to medium-high. Add 1 cup tomato broth and cook, pushing between pasta strands frequently with edge of spatula to prevent clumping, until broth has been mostly absorbed by pasta and sauce around edges of skillet begins to sizzle, 4 to 5 minutes. Add 1 cup broth and cook, shaking skillet occasionally and continuing to prod pasta strands with spatula, until broth has been mostly absorbed and sauce begins to sizzle, 5 to 7 minutes.

**4.** Using 2 thin spatulas, gently flip half of pasta so bottom is on top and spread into even layer. Repeat with remaining half of pasta. Add 1 cup broth and cook, continuing to shake skillet and prod pasta, until broth has been mostly absorbed and sauce begins to sizzle, 5 to 7 minutes. Add 1 cup broth and repeat cooking until sauce begins to sizzle, 5 to 7 minutes. Repeat dividing and flipping pasta.

**5.** Add 1 cup broth and repeat cooking until sauce begins to sizzle, 5 to 7 minutes. Pasta should be firm but cooked through. If not, add remaining 1 cup broth, ½ cup at a time, and continue to cook, checking frequently, until pasta is cooked through.

**6.** Increase heat to high and cook pasta, without moving it, until underside is deeply browned and crisp and some strands are beginning to char, 3 to 5 minutes. Remove skillet from heat, drizzle with remaining 2 tablespoons oil, and serve immediately.

## Spaghetti Puttanesca

**SERVE 4 to 6**

**WHY THIS RECIPE WORKS** Puttanesca is a gutsy tomato sauce punctuated by the brash, zesty flavors of garlic, anchovies, olives, and capers. But if the ingredients aren't well-balanced, the sauce comes off as too fishy, too garlicky, too briny, or just plain too salty. We wanted to harmonize the bold flavors in this Neapolitan dish and not let any one preside over the others. For a sauce with the best tomato flavor and a slightly clingy consistency, we used canned diced tomatoes and kept the cooking time to a minimum to retain their fresh flavor and their meaty texture. To tame the garlic and prevent it from burning, we soaked minced garlic in a bit of water before sautéing it. Cooking the garlic and anchovies with red pepper flakes (before adding the tomatoes) helped their flavors bloom and added a subtle heat. We chose to add the olives and capers when the sauce was finished—this prevented them from disintegrating in the sauce. Reserved tomato juice from the canned tomatoes moistened the pasta, and a last-minute addition of minced parsley preserved the fresh flavors of the sauce. The pasta and sauce cook in about the same amount of time, so begin the sauce just after you add the pasta to the boiling water in step 1.

3 medium garlic cloves, minced or pressed through a garlic press (about 1 tablespoon)
Table salt
1 pound spaghetti
1 (28-ounce) can diced tomatoes, drained and ½ cup juice reserved
2 tablespoons extra-virgin olive oil, plus extra for drizzling
4 teaspoons minced anchovy fillets (about 8 fillets)
1 teaspoon red pepper flakes
½ cup pitted kalamata olives, chopped coarse
¼ cup minced fresh parsley leaves
3 tablespoons capers, rinsed

**1.** Combine the garlic with 1 tablespoon water in a small bowl; set aside. Bring 4 quarts water to a boil in a large pot. Add 1 tablespoon salt and the pasta to the boiling water and cook, stirring often, until al dente. Reserve ½ cup of the cooking water then drain the pasta and return it to the pot. Add ¼ cup of the reserved tomato juice and toss to combine.

**2.** Meanwhile, heat the oil, anchovies, garlic mixture, and red pepper flakes in a 12-inch skillet over medium heat. Cook, stirring frequently, until the garlic is fragrant, 2 to 3 minutes. Add the tomatoes and simmer until slightly thickened, about 8 minutes.

**3.** Stir the olives, parsley, and capers into the sauce. Pour the sauce over the pasta and toss to combine; adjust the consistency of the sauce with the remaining reserved tomato juice or reserved pasta cooking water as needed. Season with salt to taste, drizzle with 1 tablespoon oil, if desired, and serve immediately.

## Summer Pasta Puttanesca

**SERVES 4**

**WHY THIS RECIPE WORK** When we make pasta puttanesca with fresh tomatoes, we want the tomatoes to share equal billing with the pungently flavorful olives and anchovies typical of this robust sauce. For a puttanesca that would make the most of fresh tomatoes, we opted to use grape or cherry tomatoes, which are both excellent in summer and among the best varieties of tomatoes available year-round. To retain the fresh tomato flavor, we pureed the tomatoes and strained the juices, which we cooked down briefly to thicken the sauce. We added the tomato pulp back in at the end of cooking so we wouldn't lose the fresh tomato flavor. We traded the traditional long pasta for frilly campanelle, which held on to the coarse sauce and gave our dish a summery flair. We prefer to make this dish with campanelle, but fusilli and orecchiette also work. Very finely mashed anchovy fillets (rinsed and dried before mashing) can be used instead of anchovy paste. Buy a good-quality black olive, such as kalamata, Gaeta, or Alfonso.

- 3 tablespoons extra-virgin olive oil
- 4 garlic cloves, minced
- 1 tablespoon anchovy paste
- ¼ teaspoon red pepper flakes
- ¼ teaspoon dried oregano
- 1½ pounds grape or cherry tomatoes
- 1 pound campanelle
- Table salt
- ½ cup pitted kalamata olives, chopped coarse
- 3 tablespoons capers, rinsed and minced
- ½ cup minced fresh parsley

**1.** Combine oil, garlic, anchovy paste, pepper flakes, and oregano in bowl. Process tomatoes in blender until finely chopped but not pureed, 15 to 45 seconds. Transfer to fine-mesh strainer set in large bowl and let drain for 5 minutes, occasionally pressing gently on solids with rubber spatula to extract liquid (this should yield about ¾ cup). Reserve tomato liquid in bowl and tomato pulp in strainer.

**2.** Bring 4 quarts water to boil in large pot. Add campanelle and 1 tablespoon salt and cook, stirring often, until al dente. Reserve 1 cup cooking water, then drain campanelle and return it to pot.

**3.** While campanelle is cooking, cook garlic-anchovy mixture in 12-inch skillet over medium heat, stirring frequently, until garlic is fragrant but not brown, 2 to 3 minutes. Add tomato liquid and simmer until reduced to ⅓ cup, 2 to 3 minutes. Add tomato pulp, olives, and capers; cook until just heated through, 2 to 3 minutes. Stir in parsley.

**4.** Pour sauce over campanelle and toss to combine, adding reserved cooking water as needed to adjust consistency. Season with salt to taste. Serve immediately.

## Penne Arrabbiata

**SERVES 6**

**WHY THIS RECIPE WORKS** Arrabbiata means "angry" in Italian, and one bite of this peasant-style pasta sauce will confirm that it was aptly named. To deliver an arrabbiata with complex flavor and not just searing heat, we crafted a recipe that included three different types of pepper. By supplementing pepper flakes with paprika and pickled pepperoncini, we built deep flavor while keeping the spiciness in check. Pecorino Romano, tomato paste, and anchovies, added umami notes and richness to this traditionally simple sauce. Finally, using canned tomatoes helped bring the sauce to the table quickly and means the dish can be enjoyed year-round. This recipe will work with other short tubular pastas like ziti or rigatoni.

- 1 (28-ounce) can whole peeled tomatoes
- ¼ cup extra-virgin olive oil
- ¼ cup stemmed, patted dry, and minced pepperoncini
- 2 tablespoons tomato paste
- 1 garlic clove, minced
- 1 teaspoon red pepper flakes
- 4 anchovy fillets, rinsed, patted dry, and minced to paste
- ½ teaspoon paprika
- Table salt and pepper
- ¼ cup grated Pecorino Romano, plus extra for serving
- 1 pound penne

**1.** Pulse tomatoes and their juice in food processor until finely chopped, about 10 pulses.

**2.** Heat oil, pepperoncini, tomato paste, garlic, pepper flakes, anchovies, paprika, ½ teaspoon salt, and ½ teaspoon pepper in medium saucepan over medium-low heat, stirring occasionally, until deep red in color, 7 to 8 minutes.

**3.** Add tomatoes and Pecorino and bring to simmer. Cook, stirring occasionally, until thickened, about 20 minutes.

**4.** Bring 4 quarts water to boil in large pot. Add pasta and 1 tablespoon salt and cook, stirring often, until al dente. Reserve ½ cup cooking water, then drain pasta and return it to pot. Add sauce and toss to combine, adjusting consistency with reserved cooking water as needed. Season with salt and pepper to taste. Serve, passing extra Pecorino separately.

## Pasta alla Zozzona

**SERVES 4**

**WHY THIS RECIPE WORKS** Pasta alla zozzona is a fusion of two Roman classics, amatriciana and carbonara, with pork sausage and onions taking this dish over the top. "Zozzona," a Roman dialect word for "dirty," references the dish's rich flavor and the unusual mash-up of ingredients. To create a meaty, creamy, and decadent pasta that reflects the true tradition of pasta alla zozzona, we used equal parts guanciale and Italian sausage both for pork flavor and to create pork fat that emulsified into the passata and created a creamy, not greasy, sauce. Egg yolks and Pecorino Romano imparted further creaminess to the sauce. Guanciale (cured pork jowl) adds savory depth and richness to this dish. If unavailable, use the high-quality pancetta; be sure to buy a 5-ounce chunk. Do not use bacon; its smoky flavor will overpower the dish. Passata is an uncooked tomato puree; if you're buying the Pomì brand it may be labeled "strained tomatoes." If you cannot find it, you can use tomato puree instead.

- 5 ounces guanciale
- 1 tablespoon extra-virgin olive oil
- 5 ounces sweet Italian sausage, casings removed, broken into 1-inch pieces
- ½ cup finely chopped onion
- ¾ cup passata
- 8 ounces rigatoni
- Table salt for cooking pasta

1 ounce Pecorino Romano cheese, grated fine (½ cup), plus extra for serving
2 large egg yolks
¼ teaspoon pepper

**1.** Slice guanciale into ¼-inch-thick strips, then cut each strip crosswise into ¼-inch pieces. Heat guanciale and oil in 10-inch nonstick skillet over medium heat, stirring frequently, until fat is rendered and guanciale is starting to brown, 4 to 6 minutes.

**2.** Add sausage and onion and cook, using wooden spoon to break meat into pieces no larger than ½ inch, until sausage is no longer pink, 8 to 10 minutes. Stir in passata; reduce heat to medium-low; and simmer, covered, stirring occasionally, until fat is fully incorporated, 2 to 4 minutes.

**3.** Meanwhile, bring 2 quarts water to boil in large pot. Add pasta and 1 teaspoon salt and cook, stirring often, until al dente. Reserve 1 cup cooking water, then drain pasta and return it to pot. Add tomato-meat sauce to pasta. Set pot over medium-low heat and stir until pasta is well coated, about 1 minute.

**4.** Whisk Pecorino, egg yolks, and pepper in medium bowl until combined. Slowly whisk ½ cup of reserved cooking water into egg yolk mixture (mixture will not be smooth). Off heat, stir egg yolk mixture into pasta until sauce looks glossy and is slightly thickened, about 1 minute. Adjust sauce consistency with remaining reserved cooking water as needed. Transfer pasta to platter and serve immediately, passing extra Pecorino separately.

## Pasta alla Trapanese (Pasta with Tomato and Almond Pesto)

**SERVES** 4 to 6

**WHY THIS RECIPE WORKS** In the Sicilian village of Trapani, there's a very different kind of pesto—it's basically pesto crossed with tomato sauce. Almonds replace pine nuts, but the big difference is the appearance of fresh tomatoes as a fruity, sweet accent. Cherry and grape tomatoes proved equal contenders, sharing a similar brightness and juiciness that was far more reliable than that of their larger cousins. We processed the tomatoes with a handful of basil, garlic, and toasted almonds. The almonds contributed body and thickened the sauce while retaining just enough crunch to offset the tomatoes' pulpiness; using blanched, slivered almonds avoided the muddy flavor often contributed by papery skins. We added a scant amount of hot vinegar peppers for zing, then drizzled in olive oil in a slow, steady stream to emulsify the pesto. While we prefer linguine or spaghetti, any pasta shape will work here. You may substitute ½ teaspoon of red wine vinegar and ¼ teaspoon of red pepper flakes for the pepperoncini.

1 pound linguine or spaghetti
1 teaspoon table salt, plus salt for cooking pasta
¼ cup slivered almonds, toasted
12 ounces cherry or grape tomatoes

½ cup packed fresh basil leaves
1 garlic clove, minced
1 small pepperoncini, stemmed, seeded, and minced (about ½ teaspoon)
Pinch red pepper flakes (optional)
⅓ cup extra-virgin olive oil
1 ounce Parmesan cheese, grated (½ cup), plus extra for serving

**1.** Bring 4 quarts water to boil in large pot. Add pasta and 1 tablespoon salt and cook, stirring often, until al dente. Reserve ½ cup cooking water, then drain pasta and return it to pot.

**2.** Meanwhile, process almonds; tomatoes; basil; garlic; pepperoncini; salt; and pepper flakes, if using, in food processor until smooth, about 1 minute, scraping down sides of bowl as needed. With machine running, slowly drizzle in oil, about 30 seconds.

**3.** Add pesto and Parmesan to pasta and adjust consistency of sauce with reserved pasta cooking water as needed. Serve immediately, passing extra Parmesan separately.

## Pasta all'Amatriciana

**SERVES** 4 to 6

**WHY THIS RECIPE WORKS** Although the Roman version of this pasta dish is popular, there is another, slightly different version that hails from Amatrice, a town northeast of Rome. Rather than minced onions, the Amatrician version calls for wine in the sauce. To create a flavor profile similar to that of the traditional dish, we needed an alternative to guanciale, or cured pork jowl. Humble salt pork, though an unlikely solution, provided the rich, clean meatiness we were after and proved to be a perfect foil for the acidity of the wine and tomatoes. To ensure tender bites of pork throughout, we simmered it in water to gently cook it and render fat, which allowed the meat to turn golden once the water evaporated. Finally, to ensure the grated Pecorino Romano didn't clump in the hot sauce, we mixed it with a little cooled rendered pork fat. Now the flavor of pork, tomato, chili flakes, and Pecorino shone through. Look for salt pork that is roughly 70 percent fat and 30 percent lean meat; leaner salt pork may not render enough fat. If difficult to slice, the salt pork can be put in the freezer for 15 minutes to firm up. In this dish, it is essential to use high-quality imported cheese labeled "Romano."

- 8 ounces salt pork, rind removed, rinsed thoroughly, and patted dry
- ½ cup water
- ½ teaspoon red pepper flakes
- 2 tablespoons tomato paste
- ¼ cup red wine
- 1 (28-ounce) can diced tomatoes
- 2 ounces Pecorino Romano, grated fine (1 cup)
- 1 pound spaghetti
- 1 tablespoon table salt

**1.** Slice salt pork into ¼-inch-thick strips, then cut each strip crosswise into ¼-inch pieces. Bring pork and water to simmer in 10-inch nonstick skillet over medium heat; cook until water evaporates and pork begins to sizzle, 5 to 8 minutes. Reduce heat to medium-low and continue to cook, stirring frequently, until fat renders and pork turns golden, 5 to 8 minutes longer. Using slotted spoon, transfer salt pork to bowl. Pour off all but 1 tablespoon fat from skillet. Reserve remaining fat.

**2.** Return skillet to medium heat and add tomato paste and pepper flakes; cook, stirring constantly, for 20 seconds. Stir in wine and cook for 30 seconds. Stir in tomatoes and their juice and rendered pork and bring to simmer. Cook, stirring frequently, until thickened, 12 to 16 minutes. While sauce simmers, stir 2 tablespoons reserved fat and ½ cup Pecorino together in bowl to form paste.

**3.** Meanwhile, bring 4 quarts water to boil in large Dutch oven. Add pasta and salt and cook, stirring often, until al dente. Reserve 1 cup cooking water, then drain pasta and return it to pot.

**4.** Add sauce, ⅓ cup cooking water, and Pecorino mixture to pasta and toss well to coat, adding cooking water as needed to adjust consistency. Serve, passing remaining ½ cup Pecorino separately.

## Pasta with Tomato, Bacon, and Onion

**SERVES** 4 to 6

**WHY THIS RECIPE WORKS** There are two versions of the classic Italian pasta dish pasta all'amatriciana: one from Amatrice, and one from Rome. The Roman version boasts a rich sauce containing tomatoes, bacon, onion, and Pecorino Romano cheese and generally calls for a long, tubular pasta. (The version from Amatrice adds wine, leaves out the onions, and often calls for spaghetti.) We decided to re-create the rich, hearty Roman version in our kitchen. In Rome, the dish traditionally uses a type of bacon called guanciale (made from pork jowls), which is easy to find in central Italy but not so easy to locate in the United States. Thickly sliced pancetta proved a good substitute for guanciale. Canned diced tomatoes, minced onion, and red pepper flakes made a flavorful, aromatic backbone to our sauce. Finally, we tossed the crisp pancetta in with the tomato sauce and pasta and sprinkled grated Pecorino Romano cheese on top. This dish is traditionally made with bucatini, also called perciatelli, which appear to be thick, round strands but are actually thin, extra-long tubes. Linguine works fine, too. When buying pancetta, ask the butcher to slice it ¼ inch thick; if using bacon, buy slab bacon and cut it into ¼-inch-thick slices yourself. If the pancetta that you're using is very lean, it's unlikely that you will need to drain off any fat before adding the onion.

- 2 tablespoons extra-virgin olive oil
- 6 ounces pancetta or bacon, sliced ¼ inch thick and cut into strips 1 inch long and ¼ inch wide
- 1 medium onion, minced
- ½ teaspoon red pepper flakes, or to taste
- 1 (28-ounce) can diced tomatoes, drained and juice reserved
- Table salt
- 1 pound bucatini, perciatelli, or linguine
- ⅓ cup grated Pecorino Romano cheese

**1.** Bring 4 quarts water to a boil in a large pot.

**2.** Meanwhile, heat the oil in a 12-inch skillet over medium heat until shimmering. Add the pancetta and cook, stirring occasionally, until lightly browned and crisp, about 8 minutes. Using a slotted spoon, transfer the pancetta to a paper towel–lined plate; set aside. Pour off all but 2 tablespoons of fat from the skillet. Add the onion and cook over medium heat until softened, about 5 minutes. Add the pepper flakes and cook, about 30 seconds. Stir in the tomatoes and reserved juice and simmer until slightly thickened, about 10 minutes.

**3.** While the sauce is simmering, add 1 tablespoon salt and the pasta to the boiling water and cook, stirring often, until al dente. Reserve ½ cup of the cooking water then drain the pasta and return it to the pot.

**4.** Add the pancetta to the sauce and season with salt to taste. Add the sauce to the pasta and toss over low heat to combine, about 30 seconds. Add the Pecorino and toss again. Adjust the consistency of the sauce with the reserved pasta cooking water as needed and serve immediately.

## Rigatoni with Tomatoes, Bacon, and Fennel

**SERVES** 4 to 6

**WHY THIS RECIPE WORKS** Often, making even a simple pasta requires at least two large pots: one to boil the pasta, and another to make the sauce. We wanted to streamline prep for an easy, one-pot pasta dinner with a tomato sauce bolstered with smoky bacon and fragrant fennel seeds. We used the rendered the fat from chopped bacon to soften some onion and garlic. A couple of minced anchovies—an umami powerhouse—dramatically amped up the sauce's savoriness. We browned

the canned tomatoes to deepen their flavor, reserving the juice to use as part of the pasta cooking liquid. A bit of broth and water made up the rest of the liquid; we added the pasta straight to the pot and used the absorption method to cook it to al dente perfection. You can substitute 1 pound of ziti or penne for the rigatoni, if desired.

- 6 slices bacon, cut into ½-inch pieces
- 1 onion, chopped fine
- ¼ teaspoon table salt
- 3 garlic cloves, minced
- 2 anchovy fillets, rinsed, patted dry, and minced
- 2 teaspoons fennel seeds, lightly cracked
- ¼ teaspoon red pepper fakes
- 1 (28-ounce) can diced tomatoes, drained with juice reserved
- 2½ cups chicken broth
- 2 cups water, plus extra as needed
- 1 pound rigatoni
- ¼ cup grated Pecorino Romano cheese, plus extra for serving
- 2 tablespoons minced fresh parsley

**1.** Cook bacon in Dutch oven over medium-high heat until crispy, about 5 minutes. Using slotted spoon, transfer bacon to paper towel–lined plate; set aside for serving. Pour all but 2 tablespoons of fat from pot.

**2.** Add onion and salt to fat left in pot and cook over medium heat until onion is softened, about 5 minutes. Stir in garlic, anchovies, fennel seeds, and pepper flakes and cook until fragrant, about 1 minute. Stir in tomatoes and cook until dry and slightly darkened, about 5 minutes.

**3.** Stir in broth, water, and reserved tomato juice, scraping up any browned bits, and bring to boil. Stir in pasta, return to vigorous simmer, and cook, stirring often, until pasta is tender, 15 to 20 minutes. Off heat, stir in Pecorino and parsley and adjust sauce consistency with extra hot water as needed. Season with salt and pepper to taste. Serve, sprinkling individual portions with reserved bacon and extra Pecorino.

## Simple Italian-Style Meat Sauce

**MAKES** about 6 cups

**WHY THIS RECIPE WORKS** Old-fashioned Italian-style meat sauces require hours of simmering. We wanted a quick, weeknight meat sauce with long-simmered concentrated flavor and tender meat. Browned chopped onions and mushrooms gave the sauce a rich flavor base; browning the mushrooms made them so soft and supple they practically disappeared into the finished sauce. Deglazing the pan with tomato paste and tomato juice further boosted flavor. To tenderize the meat, we incorporated a panade—a paste of bread and milk—into the meat before cooking; we combined the panade and the meat in a food processor to avoid chili-like chunks. We cooked the meat mixture just until it lost its raw color; any longer, and the meat turned dry and mealy. Finishing the meat in a combination of canned diced and crushed tomatoes gave us the best mix of textures. A handful of grated Parmesan, added just before serving, lent the sauce a tangy, complex character. You can figure on about 3 cups of sauce per pound of pasta. Except for ground round, this recipe will work with most types of ground beef, as long as it is 85 percent lean. Our preferred brand of crushed tomatoes is San Merican.

- 4 ounces white mushrooms, wiped clean and broken into rough pieces
- 1 large slice high-quality white sandwich bread, torn into quarters
- 2 tablespoons whole milk
- Table salt and ground black pepper
- 1 pound 85 percent lean ground beef
- 1 tablespoon olive oil
- 1 medium onion, minced
- 6 medium garlic cloves, minced or pressed through a garlic press (about 2 tablespoons)
- 1 tablespoon tomato paste
- ¼ teaspoon red pepper flakes
- 1 (14.5-ounce) can diced tomatoes, drained, ¼ cup juice reserved
- 1 tablespoon minced fresh oregano leaves or 1 teaspoon dried oregano
- 1 (28-ounce) can crushed tomatoes
- ¼ cup grated Parmesan cheese

**1.** Pulse the mushrooms in a food processor until finely chopped, about 8 pulses, scraping down the sides of the workbowl as needed; transfer to a medium bowl. Add the bread, milk, ½ teaspoon salt, and ½ teaspoon black pepper to the food processor and pulse until a paste forms, about 8 pulses. Add the beef and pulse until the mixture is well combined, about 6 pulses.

**2.** Heat the oil in a large saucepan over medium-high heat until just smoking. Add the onion and mushrooms; cook, stirring frequently, until the vegetables are browned and dark bits form on the pan bottom, 6 to 12 minutes. Stir in the garlic, tomato paste, and red pepper flakes; cook until fragrant and the tomato paste starts to brown, about 1 minute. Add the

¼ cup reserved tomato juice and the oregano scraping the bottom of the pan with a wooden spoon to loosen the browned bits. Add the meat mixture and cook, breaking the meat into small pieces with a wooden spoon, until no longer pink, 2 to 4 minutes, making sure that the meat does not brown.

**3.** Stir in the diced and crushed tomatoes and bring to a simmer; reduce the heat to low and simmer gently until the sauce has thickened and the flavors have blended, about 30 minutes. Stir in the cheese and the remaining 1 teaspoon fresh oregano; season with salt and pepper to taste. (The sauce can be refrigerated in an airtight container for up to 3 days or frozen for up to 1 month.)

## Pasta with Hearty Italian Meat Sauce (Sunday Gravy)

**SERVES** 8 to 10

**WHY THIS RECIPE WORKS** Traditional "Sunday gravy" is a labor of love, an all-day kitchen affair, involving six or seven types of meat and a bunch of tomatoes. To honor this meaty extravaganza but shortcut the cooking, we limited the dish to just one kind of sausage and one pork cut—plus meatballs. Hot Italian links gave the sauce a mild kick while we chose baby back ribs because they weren't too fatty and turned moist and tender in just a few hours. Meatloaf mix, a combination of ground beef, pork, and veal, produced tender meatballs. To help the meatballs retain their shape we browned them first. Canned crushed tomatoes led to a thick sauce with bright tomato flavor and cooking the tomato paste until it nearly blackened concentrated its sweetness. The best beefy booster for the sauce turned out to be beef broth. Six tablespoons of plain yogurt thinned with 2 tablespoons of milk can be substituted for the buttermilk. This recipe can be prepared through step 4 and then cooled and refrigerated in the Dutch oven for up to 2 days. To reheat, drizzle ½ cup water over the sauce (do not stir in) and warm on the lower-middle rack of a 325-degree oven for 1 hour before proceeding with the recipe.

**SAUCE**

- 2 tablespoons olive oil
- 1 (2¼-pound) rack baby back ribs, cut into 2-rib sections
- Table salt and ground black pepper
- 1 pound hot Italian sausage links
- 2 medium onions, minced
- 1¼ teaspoons dried oregano
- 3 tablespoons tomato paste
- 4 medium garlic cloves, minced or pressed through a garlic press (about 4 teaspoons)
- 2 (28-ounce) cans crushed tomatoes
- ⅔ cup low-sodium beef broth

**MEATBALLS AND PASTA**

- 2 slices high-quality white sandwich bread, crusts removed and bread cut into ½-inch cubes
- ½ cup buttermilk
- ¼ cup chopped fresh parsley leaves
- 2 garlic cloves, minced (about 2 teaspoons)
- 1 large egg yolk
- Table salt
- ¼ teaspoon red pepper flakes
- 1 pound meatloaf mix
- 2 ounces thinly sliced prosciutto, minced
- 1 ounce Pecorino Romano cheese, grated (about ½ cup)
- ½ cup olive oil
- 1½ pounds spaghetti or linguine
- ¼ cup chopped fresh basil leaves
- Grated Parmesan cheese, for serving

**1. FOR THE SAUCE:** Adjust an oven rack to the lower-middle position and heat the oven to 325 degrees. Heat the oil in a large Dutch oven over medium-high heat until just smoking. Pat the ribs dry with paper towels and season with salt and pepper. Add half of the ribs to the pot and brown on both sides, 5 to 7 minutes total. Transfer the ribs to a large plate and repeat with the remaining ribs. After transferring the second batch of ribs to the plate, brown the sausages on all four sides, 5 to 7 minutes total. Transfer the sausages to the plate with the ribs.

**2.** Reduce the heat to medium, add the onions and oregano; cook, stirring occasionally, until beginning to brown, about 5 minutes. Add the tomato paste and cook, stirring constantly, until very dark, about 3 minutes. Stir in the garlic and cook until fragrant, about 30 seconds. Add the crushed tomatoes and broth, scraping up any browned bits. Return the ribs and sausage to the pot; bring to a simmer, cover, and transfer to the oven. Cook until the ribs are tender, about 2½ hours.

**3. FOR THE MEATBALLS:** Meanwhile, combine the bread cubes, buttermilk, parsley, garlic, egg yolk, ½ teaspoon salt, and the red pepper flakes in a medium bowl and mash with a fork until no bread chunks remain. Add the meatloaf mix, prosciutto, and Pecorino Romano to the bread mixture; mix with your hands until thoroughly combined. Divide the mixture into 12 pieces; roll into balls, transfer to a plate, cover with plastic wrap, and refrigerate until ready to use.

**4.** When the sauce is 30 minutes from being done, heat the oil in a large nonstick skillet over medium-high heat until shimmering. Add the meatballs and cook until well browned all over, 5 to 7 minutes. Transfer the meatballs to a paper towel–lined plate to drain briefly. Remove the sauce from the oven and skim the fat from the top with a large spoon. Transfer the browned meatballs to the sauce and gently submerge. Return the pot to the oven and continue cooking until the meatballs are just cooked through, about 15 minutes.

**5.** Meanwhile, bring 6 quarts water to a boil in a large pot. Add 2 tablespoons salt and the pasta to the boiling water and cook, stirring often, until al dente. Reserve ½ cup of the cooking water then drain the pasta and return it to the pot.

**6.** Using tongs, transfer the meatballs, ribs, and sausage to a serving platter and cut the sausages in half. Stir the basil into the sauce and season with salt and pepper to taste. Add 1 cup of the sauce and the reserved pasta cooking water to the pasta; toss to coat. Serve, passing the remaining sauce, meat platter, and Parmesan separately.

# Pasta with Rustic Slow-Simmered Tomato Sauce with Meat

**SERVES** 4

**WHY THIS RECIPE WORKS** Slow-simmered Italian meat sauce—the kind without meatballs—relies on pork for rich flavor. But pork today is so lean, we needed an option that could provide enough fat and flavor to create a robust meat sauce with tender meat. We used fattier boneless pork butt roast, which turned meltingly tender when cooked for a long time and added meaty flavor. Boneless beef short ribs can also be used, but they need to cook a little longer. Red wine accentuated the meatiness of the sauce, which was built on a simple combination of sautéed onion and canned whole tomatoes. Pork butt roast is often labeled Boston butt in the supermarket. To prevent the sauce from becoming greasy, trim the meat well and drain off most of the fat from the skillet after browning. This thick, rich sauce is best with tubular pasta, such as ziti or penne. Pass grated Pecorino Romano (especially nice with pork) or Parmesan cheese at the table.

- 1 tablespoon extra-virgin olive oil
- 1½ pounds boneless pork butt roast or boneless beef short ribs, trimmed and cut into 1½-inch pieces
- ¾ teaspoon table salt, divided, plus salt for cooking pasta
- ½ teaspoon pepper
- 1 onion, chopped fine
- ½ cup red wine
- 1 (28-ounce) can whole peeled tomatoes, drained with juice reserved, chopped fine
- 1 pound short tubular pasta

**1.** Heat oil in 12-inch skillet over medium-high heat until shimmering. Sprinkle meat with ½ teaspoon salt and pepper and brown on all sides, turning occasionally with tongs, 5 to 7 minutes. Transfer meat to large plate; pour off all but 1 teaspoon fat from skillet. Add onion and remaining ¼ teaspoon salt and cook until softened, 2 to 3 minutes. Add wine and simmer briskly, scraping up any browned bits, until wine reduces by half, about 2 minutes.

**2.** Return meat and any accumulated juices to skillet; add tomatoes and reserved juice. Bring to boil, then reduce heat to low; cover; and simmer gently, turning meat several times, until meat is very tender, 1½ to 2 hours for pork and 2 to 2½ hours for beef. (If beef isn't tender after 2 hours, add ¼ cup water and continue to cook until tender.)

**3.** Transfer meat to clean plate. Using 2 forks, shred meat into bite-size pieces, discarding any large pieces of fat or connective tissue. Return meat to skillet. Return sauce to simmer over medium heat and cook, uncovered, until slightly thickened, about 5 minutes. Season with salt and pepper to taste.

**4.** Bring 4 quarts water to boil in large pot. Add pasta and 1 tablespoon salt and cook, stirring often, until al dente. Reserve ½ cup cooking water, then drain pasta and return to pot. Add sauce to pasta and toss to combine, adjusting consistency with reserved cooking water as needed. Serve. (Sauce can be refrigerated for up to 4 days or frozen for up to 2 months.)

# Ragu alla Bolognese

**MAKES** about 6 cups

**WHY THIS RECIPE WORKS** Unlike meat sauces in which tomatoes dominate, Bolognese sauce is about the meat, with the tomatoes in a supporting role. We wanted a traditional recipe for this complexly flavored sauce, with rich meatiness up front and a good balance of sweet, salty, and acidic flavors. We also wanted a velvety texture that would lightly cling to the noodles. For an ultrameaty version, we used six different types of meat: ground beef, pork, and veal; pancetta; mortadella; and chicken livers. These meats and the combination of red wine and tomato paste gave us a rich, complex sauce with balanced acidity. The addition of gelatin lent the sauce a silky texture. This recipe makes enough sauce for 2 pounds of pasta. Eight teaspoons of gelatin is equivalent to one (1-ounce) box of gelatin. If you can't find ground veal, use an additional 12 ounces of ground beef.

- 1 cup chicken broth
- 1 cup beef broth
- 8 teaspoons unflavored gelatin
- 1 onion, chopped coarse
- 1 large carrot, peeled and chopped coarse
- 1 celery rib, chopped coarse
- 4 ounces pancetta, chopped
- 4 ounces mortadella, chopped
- 6 ounces chicken livers, trimmed
- 3 tablespoons extra-virgin olive oil
- ¾ pound 85 percent lean ground beef
- ¾ pound ground veal
- ¾ pound ground pork
- 3 tablespoons minced fresh sage
- 1 (6-ounce) can tomato paste
- 2 cups dry red wine
- 1 pound pappardelle or tagliatelle
- Table salt for cooking pasta
- Grated Parmesan cheese

**1.** Combine chicken broth and beef broth in bowl; sprinkle gelatin over top and set aside. Pulse onion, carrot, and celery in food processor until finely chopped, about 10 pulses, scraping down bowl as needed; transfer to separate bowl. Pulse pancetta and mortadella in now-empty food processor until finely chopped, about 25 pulses, scraping down bowl as needed; transfer to second bowl. Process chicken livers in now-empty food processor until pureed, about 5 seconds; transfer to third bowl.

**2.** Heat oil in Dutch oven over medium-high heat until shimmering. Add beef, veal, and pork; cook, breaking up pieces with wooden spoon, until all liquid has evaporated and meat begins to sizzle, 10 to 15 minutes. Add pancetta mixture and sage; cook, stirring frequently, until pancetta is translucent, 5 to 7 minutes, adjusting heat as needed to keep fond from burning. Add chopped vegetables and cook, stirring frequently, until softened, 5 to 7 minutes. Add tomato paste and cook, stirring constantly, until rust-colored and fragrant, about 3 minutes.

**3.** Stir in wine, scraping up any browned bits. Simmer until sauce has thickened, about 5 minutes. Stir in broth mixture and return to simmer. Reduce heat to low and cook at bare simmer until thickened (wooden spoon should leave trail when dragged through sauce), about 1½ hours.

**4.** Stir in pureed chicken livers, bring to boil, and remove from heat. Season with salt and pepper to taste; cover and keep warm.

**5.** Bring 4 quarts water to boil in large pot. Add pasta and 1 tablespoon salt and cook, stirring often, until al dente. Reserve ¾ cup cooking water, then drain pasta and return it to pot. Add half of sauce and reserved cooking water to pasta and toss to combine. Transfer to serving bowl and serve, passing Parmesan separately. (Leftover sauce can be refrigerated for up to 3 days or frozen for up to 1 month.)

## Fettuccine with Bolognese Sauce

**SERVES 4**

**WHY THIS RECIPE WORKS** There are many ways to interpret what "real" Bolognese sauce is. But no matter the ingredients, the sauce should be hearty and rich, with plenty of meaty character. We started simple—with just onions, carrots, and celery, sautéed in butter. Meatloaf mix provided the right amount of meatiness. For dairy, which tenderizes the meat and gives the sauce a rich flavor, we used milk. Once the milk had reduced, we added white wine, which added a delicate brightness. After adding the canned tomatoes. We simmered the sauce at the lowest possible heat for about three hours. Don't drain the pasta too meticulously; a little water left clinging to the noodles will help distribute the sauce evenly, as will the addition of 2 tablespoons of butter. If doubling this recipe, increase the simmering times for the milk and the wine to 30 minutes each, and increase the simmering time once the tomatoes are added to 4 hours. You can substitute equal amounts of 80 percent lean ground beef, ground veal, and ground pork for the meatloaf mix (the total amount of meat should be ¾ pound).

- 5 tablespoons unsalted butter
- 2 tablespoons minced onion
- 2 tablespoons minced carrot
- 2 tablespoons minced celery
- ¾ pound meatloaf mix
- Table salt
- 1 cup whole milk
- 1 cup dry white wine
- 1 (28-ounce) can diced tomatoes
- 1 pound fresh or dried fettuccine
- Grated Parmesan cheese, for serving

**1.** Melt 3 tablespoons of the butter in a large Dutch oven over medium heat. Add the onion, carrot, and celery and cook until softened but not browned, about 6 minutes. Add the meat and ½ teaspoon salt; crumble the meat into tiny pieces with a wooden spoon. Cook, continuing to crumble the meat, just until it loses its raw color but has not yet browned, about 3 minutes.

**2.** Add the milk and simmer until the milk evaporates and only rendered fat remains, 10 to 15 minutes. Add the wine and simmer until the wine evaporates, 10 to 15 minutes longer. Add the tomatoes with their juice and bring to a simmer. Reduce the heat to low so that the sauce continues to simmer just barely, with an occasional bubble or two at the surface, until the liquid has evaporated, about 3 hours. Season with salt to taste. (The sauce can be refrigerated in an airtight container for up to 3 days or frozen for up to 1 month.)

**3.** Bring 4 quarts water to a boil in a large pot. Add 1 tablespoon salt and the pasta to the boiling water and cook, stirring often, until al dente. Reserve ½ cup of the cooking water then drain the pasta and return it to the pot. Add the sauce and remaining 2 tablespoons butter; toss to combine. Adjust the consistency of the sauce with the reserved pasta cooking water as needed. Serve, passing the Parmesan separately.

## Weeknight Pasta Bolognese

**SERVES 4 to 6**

**WHY THIS RECIPE WORKS** The first step in streamlining Bolognese was using a food processor to chop the vegetables, including the canned tomatoes and their juice. To develop sweetness in the sauce without the day-long simmering, we reduced white wine in a separate pan and added it to the sauce at the end; a little bit of sugar, stirred in with the garlic to help it caramelize, amplified the sweetness. Instead of browning the ground meat, we cooked it with milk, which helped to soften it in a short amount of time. To amp up the sauce's meaty flavor, we added chopped pancetta, dried porcini mushrooms, and the flavorful liquid left behind from rehydrating them. In about an hour, our sauce had all the rich meatiness of a long-simmered Bolognese. Sweet white wines such as Gewürztraminer, Riesling, and even white Zinfandel work well in this sauce. You can substitute equal amounts of 80 percent lean ground beef, ground veal, and ground pork for the meatloaf mix (the total amount of meat should be 1¼ pounds).

- ½ ounce dried porcini mushrooms
- 1¼ cups sweet white wine
- ½ small carrot, peeled and chopped coarse (about ½ cup)
- ½ small onion, chopped coarse (about ¼ cup)
- 3 ounces pancetta, cut into 1-inch chunks
- 1 (28-ounce) can whole tomatoes
- 1½ tablespoons unsalted butter
- 1 teaspoon sugar
- 1 small garlic clove, minced or pressed through a garlic press (about ½ teaspoon)
- 1¼ pounds meatloaf mix
- 1½ cups whole milk
- 2 tablespoons tomato paste
- Table salt
- ⅛ teaspoon ground black pepper
- 1 pound pasta
- Grated Parmesan cheese, for serving

1. Combine the porcini and ½ cup water in a small microwave-safe bowl; cover the bowl with plastic wrap, cut three vents for steam with a knife, and microwave on high power for 30 seconds. Let stand until the mushrooms have softened, about 5 minutes. Transfer the mushrooms to a second small bowl and reserve the liquid; pour the liquid through a paper towel–lined mesh strainer. Set the mushrooms and the strained liquid aside.

2. Bring the wine to a simmer in a 10-inch nonstick skillet over medium heat; reduce the heat to low and continue to simmer until the wine is reduced to 2 tablespoons, about 20 minutes. Set aside.

3. Meanwhile, pulse the carrot in a food processor until broken down into ¼-inch pieces, about 10 pulses. Add the onion and pulse until the vegetables are broken down into ⅛-inch pieces, about 10 pulses. Transfer the vegetables to a small bowl. Process the reserved mushrooms until well ground, about 15 seconds, scraping down the sides of the workbowl as needed. Transfer the mushrooms to the bowl with the vegetables. Process the pancetta until the pieces are no larger than ¼ inch, 30 to 35 seconds, scraping down the sides of the workbowl as needed; transfer to a small bowl. Pulse the tomatoes with their juice until chopped fine, about 8 pulses.

4. Melt the butter in a 12-inch skillet over medium-high heat. Cook the pancetta, stirring frequently, until well browned, about 2 minutes. Add the carrot, onion, and mushrooms and cook, stirring frequently, until the vegetables are softened but not browned, about 4 minutes. Add the sugar and garlic and cook until fragrant, about 30 seconds. Add the meat, breaking it into 1-inch pieces with a wooden spoon, and cook for about 1 minute. Add the milk and stir to break the meat into ½-inch pieces; bring to a simmer, reduce the heat to medium, and cook, stirring to break the meat into smaller pieces, until most of the liquid has evaporated and the meat begins to sizzle, 18 to 20 minutes. Stir in the tomato paste and cook until combined, about 1 minute. Add the tomatoes, reserved mushroom soaking liquid, ¼ teaspoon salt, and the pepper; bring to a simmer over medium-high heat, then reduce the heat to medium and simmer until the liquid is reduced and the sauce is thickened, 12 to 15 minutes. Stir in the reduced wine and simmer to blend the flavors, about 5 minutes.

5. Meanwhile, bring 4 quarts water to a boil in a large pot. Add 1 tablespoon salt and the pasta to the boiling water and cook, stirring often, until al dente. Reserve ½ cup of the cooking water then drain the pasta and return it to the pot. Add 2 cups of the sauce and 2 tablespoons of the reserved pasta cooking water to the pasta; toss to combine and adjust the consistency of the sauce with the remaining reserved pasta cooking water as needed. Serve immediately, topping individual bowls with ¼ cup sauce and passing the Parmesan separately.

## Weeknight Tagliatelle with Bolognese Sauce

**SERVES** 4 to 6

**WHY THIS RECIPE WORKS** To create a Bolognese sauce that could come together quickly on a busy weeknight but rival the richness of a long-cooked version, we started by browning the aromatic vegetables to develop a flavorful fond; we also treated the ground beef with a baking soda solution to ensure that it stayed tender. Adding pancetta, which we ground and browned deeply with the aromatic vegetables, boosted the sauce's meaty flavor, and tomato paste added depth and brightness. We also added Parmesan cheese, directly to the sauce as it cooked for its umami richness. To develop concentrated flavor and a consistency that nicely coated the pasta, we boiled beef broth until it was reduced by half and added it to the sauce, which then needed to simmer only 30 minutes longer. If you use our recommended beef broth, Better Than Bouillon Roasted Beef Base, you can skip step 2 and make a concentrated broth by adding 4 teaspoons paste to 2 cups water. The cooked sauce will look thin but will thicken once tossed with the pasta. If you can't find tagliatelle, you can substitute pappardelle. Substituting other pasta may result in a too-wet sauce.

- 1 pound 93 percent lean ground beef
- ½ teaspoon pepper, divided
- ¼ teaspoon baking soda
- 4 cups beef broth
- 6 ounces pancetta, chopped coarse
- 1 onion, chopped coarse
- 1 large carrot, peeled and chopped coarse
- 1 celery rib, chopped coarse
- 1 tablespoon unsalted butter
- 1 tablespoon extra-virgin olive oil
- 3 tablespoons tomato paste
- 1 cup dry red wine
- 1 ounce Parmesan cheese, grated (½ cup), plus extra for serving
- 1 pound tagliatelle
- Table salt for cooking pasta

1. Toss beef with 2 tablespoons water, 1/4 teaspoon pepper, and baking soda in bowl until thoroughly combined. Set aside.

2. While beef sits, bring broth to boil over high heat in large pot (this pot will be used to cook pasta in step 6) and cook until reduced to 2 cups, about 15 minutes; set aside.

3. Pulse pancetta in food processor until finely chopped, 15 to 20 pulses. Add onion, carrot, and celery and pulse until vegetables are finely chopped and mixture has paste-like consistency, 12 to 15 pulses, scraping down sides of bowl as needed.

4. Heat butter and oil in large Dutch oven over medium-high heat until shimmering. Add pancetta-vegetable mixture and remaining 1/4 teaspoon pepper and cook, stirring occasionally, until liquid has evaporated, about 8 minutes. Spread mixture in even layer in bottom of pot and continue to cook, stirring every couple of minutes, until very dark browned bits form on bottom of pot, 7 to 12 minutes longer. Stir in tomato paste and cook until paste is rust-colored and bottom of pot is dark brown, 1 to 2 minutes.

5. Reduce heat to medium, add beef, and cook, using wooden spoon to break meat into pieces no larger than 1/4 inch, until beef has just lost its raw pink color, 4 to 7 minutes. Stir in wine, scraping up any browned bits, and bring to simmer. Cook until wine has evaporated and sauce has thickened, about 5 minutes. Stir in broth and Parmesan. Return sauce to simmer; cover, reduce heat to low, and simmer for 30 minutes (sauce will look thin). Remove from heat and season with salt and pepper to taste.

6. Rinse pot that held broth. While sauce simmers, bring 4 quarts water to boil in now-empty pot. Add pasta and 1 tablespoon salt and cook, stirring occasionally, until al dente. Reserve 1/4 cup cooking water, then drain pasta. Add pasta to pot with sauce and toss to combine. Adjust sauce consistency with reserved cooking water as needed. Transfer to platter or individual bowls and serve, passing extra Parmesan separately.

## Beef Short Rib Ragu

**MAKES** 5 cups; enough for 1 pound pasta

**WHY THIS RECIPE WORKS** A typical Sunday gravy is an all-day affair calling for several different kinds of meats. For a simplified version we could make in about 2 hours, we chose rich, beefy boneless short ribs. Umami-rich porcini mushrooms, tomato paste, and anchovies added great depth of flavor. To prevent scorching, we moved the braising operation to the oven. Removing the lid partway through cooking thickened the sauce and browned the meat, deepening its flavor and eliminating the messy step of browning it before braising. A touch of five-spice powder underscored the savory taste of the beef and mushrooms. If you can't find boneless short ribs, use a 2½-pound chuck-eye roast, trimmed and cut into 1-inch chunks. This recipe can be doubled, and the sauce can be frozen. Better Than Bouillon Roasted Beef Base is our taste test winner.

- 1½ cups beef broth, divided
- ½ ounce dried porcini mushrooms, rinsed
- 1 tablespoon extra-virgin olive oil
- 1 onion, chopped fine
- 2 garlic cloves, minced
- 1 tablespoon tomato paste
- 3 anchovy fillets, rinsed, patted dry, and minced
- ½ teaspoon five-spice powder
- ½ cup dry red wine
- 1 (14.5-ounce) can whole peeled tomatoes, drained with juice reserved, chopped fine
- 2 pounds boneless beef short ribs, trimmed
- Table salt and pepper

1. Adjust oven rack to middle position and heat oven to 350 degrees. Microwave ½ cup broth and mushrooms in covered bowl until steaming, about 1 minute. Let sit until softened, about 5 minutes. Drain mushrooms in fine-mesh strainer lined with coffee filter, pressing to extract all liquid; reserve liquid and chop mushrooms fine.

2. Heat oil in Dutch oven over medium heat until shimmering. Add onion and cook, stirring occasionally, until softened, about 5 minutes. Add garlic and cook until fragrant, about 1 minute. Add tomato paste, anchovies, and five-spice powder and cook, stirring frequently, until mixture has darkened and fond forms on pot bottom, 3 to 4 minutes. Add wine, increase heat to medium-high, and bring to simmer, scraping up any browned bits. Continue to cook, stirring frequently, until wine is reduced and pot is almost dry, 2 to 4 minutes. Add tomatoes and reserved juice, remaining 1 cup broth, reserved mushroom soaking liquid, and mushrooms and bring to simmer.

3. Toss beef with 3/4 teaspoon salt and season with pepper. Add beef to pot, cover, and transfer to oven. Cook for 1 hour.

4. Uncover and continue to cook until beef is tender, 1 to 1¼ hours longer.

5. Remove pot from oven; using slotted spoon, transfer beef to cutting board and let cool for 5 minutes. Using 2 forks, shred beef into bite-size pieces, discarding any large pieces of fat or

connective tissue. Using large spoon, skim off any excess fat that has risen to surface of sauce. Return beef to sauce and season with salt and pepper to taste. (Sauce can be refrigerated for up to 3 days or frozen for up to 2 months.)

## Rigatoni with Beef and Onion Ragu

**SERVES** 6 to 8

**WHY THIS RECIPE WORKS** This thrifty yet supremely satisfying meat sauce, known as alla genovese, was born in 16th-century Naples. It began as a combination of beef and aromatic vegetables that were cooked down to make two meals: a savory sauce for pasta and another, separate meal of cooked beef. Later, most of the vegetables took a back seat to onions, which became the foundation of this deeply flavorful sauce. To make the ultrasavory recipe work in a modern context, we turned all the elements into one substantial sauce by shredding the meat into the sauce. To eliminate the need for stirring and monitoring during cooking, we moved the process from the stovetop to the even heat of the oven. A surprising ingredient—water—proved essential to extracting maximum flavor from the onions. We also added tomato paste for extra flavor and color. To encourage the sauce to cling to the pasta, we vigorously stirred them together so that the starch from the pasta added body to the sauce. A bit of grated Pecorino brought the flavors together. If marjoram is unavailable, substitute an equal amount of oregano. Pair this dish with a lightly dressed salad of assertively flavored greens.

- 1 (1- to 1¼-pound) boneless beef chuck-eye roast, cut into 4 pieces and trimmed of large pieces of fat
- 1 teaspoon kosher salt, plus salt for cooking pasta
- ½ teaspoon pepper
- 2 ounces pancetta, cut into ½-inch pieces
- 2 ounces salami, cut into ½-inch pieces
- 1 small carrot, peeled and cut into ½-inch pieces
- 1 small celery rib, cut into ½-inch pieces
- 2½ pounds onions, halved and cut into 1-inch pieces
- 2 tablespoons tomato paste
- 1 cup dry white wine, divided
- 2 tablespoons minced fresh marjoram, divided
- 1 pound rigatoni
- 1 ounce Pecorino Romano cheese, grated (½ cup), plus extra for serving

**1.** Sprinkle beef with salt and pepper and set aside. Adjust oven rack to lower-middle position and heat oven to 300 degrees.

**2.** Process pancetta and salami in food processor until ground to paste, about 30 seconds, scraping down sides of bowl as needed. Add carrot and celery and process 30 seconds longer, scraping down sides of bowl as needed. Transfer paste to Dutch oven and set aside. Pulse onions in processor in 2 batches, until ⅛- to ¼-inch pieces form, 8 to 10 pulses per batch.

**3.** Cook pancetta mixture over medium heat, stirring frequently, until fat is rendered and fond begins to form on bottom of pot, about 5 minutes. Add tomato paste and cook, stirring constantly, until browned, about 90 seconds. Stir in 2 cups water, scraping up any browned bits. Stir in onions and bring to boil. Stir in ½ cup wine and 1 tablespoon marjoram. Add beef and push into onions to ensure that it is submerged. Transfer to oven and cook, uncovered, until beef is fully tender, 2 to 2½ hours.

**4.** Transfer beef to carving board. Place pot over medium heat and cook, stirring frequently, until mixture is almost completely dry. Stir in remaining ½ cup wine and cook for 2 minutes, stirring occasionally. Using 2 forks, shred beef into bite-size pieces. Stir beef and remaining 1 tablespoon marjoram into sauce and season with salt and pepper to taste. Remove from heat, cover, and keep warm.

**5.** Bring 4 quarts water to boil in large pot. Add pasta and 2 tablespoons salt and cook, stirring often, until just al dente. Drain pasta and add to warm sauce. Add Pecorino and stir vigorously over low heat until sauce is slightly thickened and rigatoni is fully tender, 1 to 2 minutes. Serve, passing extra Pecorino separately.

## Spaghetti and Meatballs

**SERVES** 4 to 6

**WHY THIS RECIPE WORKS** After all the work of making meatballs, it is a huge disappointment when they turn out dense and flavorless. What we were after was nothing short of great meatballs: crusty and dark brown on the outside and soft and moist on the inside. A binder of white bread soaked in buttermilk gave the meatballs a creamy texture and an appealing tang. An egg yolk was also important as its fats and emulsifiers added moistness and richness. Adding some ground pork to the usual ground beef enhanced the flavor. Broiling dried out the meatballs; pan-frying was the best way to brown the meatballs and kept the interior moist. Finally, building the tomato sauce on top of the browned bits left in the pan after frying the meatballs made for a hearty, robust-tasting sauce. The shaped meatballs can be covered with plastic wrap and refrigerated for several hours ahead of serving time; fry the meatballs and make the sauce at the last minute. If you don't have buttermilk, you can substitute 6 tablespoons of plain yogurt thinned with 2 tablespoons of milk.

**MEATBALLS**

- 2 slices hearty white sandwich bread, crusts removed, torn into small pieces
- ½ cup buttermilk
- 12 ounces 85 percent lean ground beef
- 4 ounces ground pork
- ¼ cup grated Parmesan cheese
- 2 tablespoons minced fresh parsley
- 1 large egg yolk
- 1 garlic clove, minced
- ¾ teaspoon table salt
- ⅛ teaspoon pepper
- Vegetable oil for pan-frying

TOMATO SAUCE AND PASTA

- 2 tablespoons extra-virgin olive oil
- 1 garlic clove, minced
- 1 (28-ounce) can crushed tomatoes
- 1 tablespoon chopped fresh basil
- 1 pound spaghetti
- Table salt for cooking pasta
- Grated Parmesan cheese

**1. FOR THE MEATBALLS:** Mash bread and buttermilk to smooth paste in large bowl. Let stand for 10 minutes.

**2.** Add beef, pork, Parmesan, parsley, egg yolk, garlic, salt, and pepper to mashed bread; stir gently until uniform. Gently form into 1½-inch round meatballs (about 14 meatballs). (When forming meatballs use light touch; if you compact meatballs too much, they can become dense and hard.)

**3.** Pour oil into 12-inch skillet until it measures depth of ¼ inch. Heat over medium-high heat until shimmering. Add meatballs in single layer and cook until well browned on all sides, about 10 minutes. Transfer meatballs to paper towel–lined plate and discard oil left in skillet.

**4.** For the sauce: Add oil and garlic to now-empty skillet and cook over medium heat, scraping up any browned bits, until fragrant, about 30 seconds. Add tomatoes with their juice; bring to simmer; and cook until sauce thickens, about 10 minutes. Stir in basil and season with salt and pepper to taste. Add meatballs and simmer, turning them occasionally, until heated through, about 5 minutes.

### MAKING MEATBALLS

**1.** Use fork to mash bread and buttermilk into smooth paste.

**2.** Working with 3 tablespoons meatball mixture at a time, form mixture into 1½-inch ball by gently rolling it between your palms.

**3.** Fry meatballs, turning every so often, until crusty golden brown all over.

**5. FOR THE PASTA:** Meanwhile, bring 4 quarts water to boil in large pot. Add pasta and 1 tablespoon salt and cook, stirring often, until al dente. Reserve ½ cup cooking water, then drain pasta and return it to pot. Add several large spoonfuls of tomato sauce (without meatballs) to pasta and toss to coat. Adjust consistency of sauce with reserved pasta cooking water as needed. Serve immediately, topping individual bowls with more tomato sauce and several meatballs and passing Parmesan separately.

## Classic Spaghetti and Meatballs for a Crowd

SERVES 12

**WHY THIS RECIPE WORKS** Making spaghetti and meatballs for a crowd can try the patience of even an Italian grandmother. For an easier way, we roast them on a wire rack. Adding powdered gelatin to a mix of ground chuck and pork plumped the meatballs and lent them a soft richness. Prosciutto gave the meatballs extra meatiness, and a panade using panko kept the meat moist and tender. To create a rich sauce, we braised the meatballs in marinara sauce for about an hour. To make sure the sauce didn't overreduce, we swapped half the crushed tomatoes in our marinara recipe for an equal portion of tomato juice. If you don't have buttermilk, substitute 1 cup whole-milk plain yogurt thinned with ½ cup whole milk. You can cook the pasta in two separate pots if you do not have a large enough pot to cook all of the pasta together. Once cooked, the sauce and the meatballs can be cooled and refrigerated for up to 2 days. To reheat, drizzle ½ cup of water over the sauce, without stirring, and reheat on the lower-middle rack of a 325-degree oven for 1 hour.

MEATBALLS

- 2¼ cups panko bread crumbs
- 1½ cups buttermilk
- 1½ teaspoons unflavored gelatin
- 3 tablespoons water
- 2 pounds 85 percent lean ground beef
- 1 pound ground pork
- 6 ounces thinly sliced prosciutto, chopped fine
- 3 large eggs
- 3 ounces Parmesan cheese, grated (about 1½ cups)
- 6 tablespoons minced fresh parsley leaves
- 3 medium garlic cloves, minced or pressed through a garlic press (about 1 tablespoon)
- 1½ teaspoons table salt
- ½ teaspoon ground black pepper

SAUCE

- 3 tablespoons extra-virgin olive oil
- 1 large onion, grated
- 6 medium garlic cloves, minced or pressed through a garlic press (about 2 tablespoons)
- 1 teaspoon dried oregano
- ½ teaspoon red pepper flakes

- 3 (28-ounce) cans crushed tomatoes
- 6 cups tomato juice
- 6 tablespoons dry white wine
- Table salt and ground black pepper
- ½ cup minced fresh basil leaves
- 3 tablespoons minced fresh parsley leaves
- Sugar

- 3 pounds spaghetti
- 2 tablespoons table salt
- Grated Parmesan cheese, for serving

**1. FOR THE MEATBALLS:** Adjust the oven racks to the lower-middle and upper-middle positions and heat the oven to 450 degrees. Set 2 wire racks in 2 aluminum foil–lined rimmed baking sheets and spray the racks with vegetable oil spray.

**2.** Combine the bread crumbs and buttermilk in a large bowl and let sit, mashing occasionally with a fork, until a smooth paste forms, about 10 minutes. Meanwhile, sprinkle the gelatin over the water in a small bowl and allow to soften for 5 minutes.

**3.** Mix the ground beef, ground pork, prosciutto, eggs, Parmesan, parsley, garlic, salt, pepper, and gelatin mixture into the bread-crumb mixture using your hands. Pinch off and roll the mixture into 2-inch meatballs (about 40 meatballs total) and arrange on the prepared sheets. Bake until well browned, about 30 minutes, switching and rotating the sheets halfway through baking.

**4. FOR THE SAUCE:** While the meatballs bake, heat the oil in a Dutch oven over medium heat until shimmering. Add the onion and cook until softened and lightly browned, 5 to 7 minutes. Stir in the garlic, oregano, and red pepper flakes and cook until fragrant, about 30 seconds. Stir in the crushed tomatoes, tomato juice, wine, 1½ teaspoons salt, and ¼ teaspoon pepper, bring to a simmer, and cook until thickened slightly, about 15 minutes.

**5.** Remove the meatballs from the oven and reduce the oven temperature to 300 degrees. Gently nestle the meatballs into the sauce. Cover, transfer to the oven, and cook until the meatballs are firm and the sauce has thickened, about 1 hour.

**6.** Meanwhile, bring 10 quarts water to boil in a 12-quart pot. Add the pasta and salt and cook, stirring often, until al dente. Reserve ½ cup of the cooking water, then drain the pasta and return it to the pot.

**7.** Gently stir the basil and parsley into the sauce and season with sugar, salt, and pepper to taste. Add 2 cups of the sauce (without meatballs) to the pasta and toss to combine, adding the reserved cooking water to adjust the consistency as needed. Serve, topping individual portions with more tomato sauce and several meatballs and passing the Parmesan separately.

## Sausage Meatballs and Spaghetti

**SERVES** 4 to 6

**WHY THIS RECIPE WORKS** For a change of pace, enter meatballs made with Italian sausage. To temper sausage's springy texture, we added ground pork, brined with baking soda and salt to impart tenderness and help the meat retain juices. A panade made with heavy cream brought more fat into the mix. We pulsed the meat mixture in a food processor, which cut the panade into the meat evenly, and processed the meat in stages, which kept it from turning tough. To highlight the flavors of Italian sausage, we added ground fennel seeds, oregano, black pepper, and red pepper flakes. We baked the meatballs in a hot oven to brown them in a single batch. A simple tomato sauce complemented the spiced-up meatballs. After a quick simmer, we added fresh basil and the meatballs to the pot to finish cooking. The fennel seeds can be coarsely ground in a spice grinder or using the bottom of a heavy skillet. A #30 scoop, loosely filled, works well for portioning the meatballs.

**MEATBALLS**

- ½ teaspoon table salt
- ¼ teaspoon baking soda
- 4 teaspoons water
- 12 ounces ground pork
- 2 slices hearty white sandwich bread, crusts removed, cut into ½-inch pieces
- ⅓ cup heavy cream
- ⅓ cup grated Parmesan cheese, plus extra for serving
- 2 large egg yolks
- 2 garlic cloves, minced
- 1 teaspoon fennel seeds, coarsely ground
- 1 teaspoon dried oregano
- 1 teaspoon pepper
- ½ teaspoon red pepper flakes
- 12 ounces sweet Italian sausage, casings removed and broken into 1-inch pieces

**TOMATO SAUCE**

- 2 tablespoons extra-virgin olive oil
- 1 garlic clove, minced
- 1 (28-ounce) can crushed tomatoes
- 1 (15-ounce) can tomato sauce
- Table salt
- 1 tablespoon chopped fresh basil

- 1 pound spaghetti

**1. FOR THE MEATBALLS:** Adjust oven rack to upper middle position and heat oven to 500 degrees. Place wire rack in aluminum foil–lined rimmed baking sheet. Spray wire rack with vegetable oil spray.

**2.** Dissolve salt and baking soda in water in large bowl. Add pork and fold gently to combine; let stand for 10 minutes.

**3.** Pulse bread, cream, Parmesan, egg yolks, garlic, fennel seeds, oregano, pepper, and pepper flakes in food processor until smooth paste forms, about 10 pulses, scraping down sides of bowl as needed. Add pork mixture (do not wash out bowl) and pulse until mixture is well combined, about 5 pulses.

**4.** Transfer half of pork mixture to now-empty large bowl. Add sausage to food processor and pulse until just combined, 4 to 5 pulses. Transfer sausage-pork mixture to large bowl with pork mixture. Using your hands, gently fold together until mixture is just combined.

**5.** With your wet hands, lightly shape mixture into 1¾-inch round meatballs (about 1 ounce each); you should have about 24 meatballs. Arrange meatballs, evenly spaced, on prepared rack and bake until browned, about 15 minutes, rotating sheet halfway through baking.

**6. FOR THE TOMATO SAUCE:** While meatballs bake, heat oil in Dutch oven over medium heat until shimmering. Add garlic and cook, stirring frequently, until fragrant, about 30 seconds. Stir in crushed tomatoes, tomato sauce, and ¼ teaspoon salt and bring to boil. Reduce heat and simmer gently until slightly thickened, about 10 minutes. Stir in basil and season with salt to taste.

**7.** Add meatballs to sauce and simmer gently, turning them occasionally, until cooked through, 5 to 10 minutes. Cover and keep warm over low heat.

**8.** Bring 4 quarts water to boil in large pot. Add pasta and 1 tablespoon salt and cook, stirring often, until al dente. Reserve ½ cup cooking water, then drain pasta and return it to pot.

**9.** Add ½ cup sauce and ¼ cup reserved cooking water to pasta and toss to combine. Transfer pasta to large serving platter and top with meatballs and remaining sauce, adjusting consistency with remaining reserved cooking water as needed. Serve, passing extra Parmesan separately.

## Pappardelle with Duck and Chestnut Ragu

**SERVES 4**

**WHY THIS RECIPE WORKS** We found inspiration in the Veneto area of Italy for our robust ragu that pairs duck with sweet, creamy chestnuts. Slowly browning duck legs produced plenty of flavorful fat for cooking aromatics. Assertive rosemary and acidic red wine cut through the duck's richness to make a flavorful, lustrous sauce that clung beautifully to wide noodles such as pappardelle. Chestnuts not only thickened the sauce but also appeared in the crispy bread crumb topping. You can find fresh chestnuts seasonally in markets, but they must be roasted before use and are difficult to peel. We prefer to purchase the roasted peeled chestnuts that are sold jarred or vacuum-packed in many supermarkets near other nuts. Don't substitute water chestnuts, which belong to an entirely different plant family.

- 2 cups (9 ounces) peeled cooked chestnuts, divided
- 1 large onion, chopped coarse
- 1 carrot, peeled and chopped coarse
- 1 celery rib, chopped coarse
- 2 (12- to 14-ounce) duck leg quarters, trimmed
- 1 teaspoon table salt, plus salt for cooking pasta
- 1½ teaspoons minced fresh rosemary, divided
- 1 cup dry red wine
- 2½ cups chicken broth
- ¼ cup panko bread crumbs
- 1 teaspoon red wine vinegar
- 1 pound fresh pappardelle (recipe follows)

**1.** Adjust oven rack to middle position and heat oven to 300 degrees. Pulse chestnuts in food processor until finely chopped, 10 to 12 pulses, scraping down sides of bowl as needed; transfer to bowl. Pulse onion, carrot, and celery in now-empty processor until finely chopped, 10 to 12 pulses; set aside.

**2.** Using metal skewer, poke 15 to 20 holes in skin of each duck leg quarter, then pat dry with paper towels. Place duck skin side down in Dutch oven and cook over medium heat until well browned on first side and fat has rendered, 15 to 20 minutes. Flip duck and continue to cook until well browned on second side, about 3 minutes; transfer to plate. Pour off and reserve all but 2 tablespoons fat from pot.

**3.** Add vegetable mixture and salt to fat left in pot and cook over medium heat until vegetables are softened, 5 to 7 minutes. Stir in 1 teaspoon rosemary and cook until fragrant, about 30 seconds. Stir in wine, scraping up any browned bits, and cook until reduced slightly, about 1 minute.

**4.** Stir in broth and half of chestnuts. Nestle duck into pot with any accumulated juices and bring to simmer. Cover, transfer pot to oven, and cook until duck is very tender and falling off bones, about 2 hours.

**5.** While duck cooks, heat 1 tablespoon reserved fat in 10-inch skillet over medium heat until shimmering (discard remaining fat or reserve for another use). Add panko and cook, stirring frequently, until light golden brown, 2 to 3 minutes. Stir in remaining chestnuts and remaining ½ teaspoon rosemary and cook until fragrant and deep golden brown, about 2 minutes; set aside.

**6.** Remove pot from oven. Transfer duck to cutting board, let cool slightly, then shred meat into bite-size pieces using 2 forks; discard skin and bones. Bring sauce to simmer over medium-high heat and cook until thickened slightly, 3 to 5 minutes. Stir in shredded meat and vinegar and season with salt and pepper to taste.

**7.** Meanwhile, bring 4 quarts water to boil in large pot. Add pasta and 1 tablespoon salt and cook, stirring often, until al dente. Reserve ½ cup cooking water, then drain pasta and return it to pot. Add sauce and toss to combine. Adjust consistency with reserved cooking water as needed. Season with salt and pepper to taste. Sprinkle individual portions with chestnut-panko mixture before serving.

## Fresh Pappardelle

**MAKES** 1 pound

Use this tender, easy-to-roll dough for strand pasta. Six egg yolks, in addition to two whole eggs and a couple tablespoons of olive oil, make the dough incredibly supple while also adding great flavor. The addition of olive oil is a debated topic in Italy, but we find that it makes the dough easier to roll while still keeping it springy and delicate. You can roll this dough with a manual pasta machine or by hand. Resting the dough for at least 30 minutes before rolling allows the gluten—the protein network that forms when flour and liquid interact and that makes doughs chewy—time to relax and minimizes contraction. If using a high-protein all-purpose flour, such as King Arthur, increase the number of egg yolks to seven.

- 2 cups (10 ounces) all-purpose flour, plus extra as needed
- 2 large eggs plus 6 large yolks
- 2 tablespoons extra-virgin olive oil

**1A. FOR MIXING AND KNEADING WITH A MACHINE:** Process flour, eggs and yolks, and oil in food processor until mixture forms cohesive dough that feels soft and is barely tacky to touch, about 45 seconds. (If dough sticks to your fingers, add up to ¼ cup flour, 1 tablespoon at a time, until barely tacky. If dough doesn't become cohesive, add up to 1 tablespoon water, 1 teaspoon at a time, until it just comes together; process 30 seconds longer.)

**1B. FOR MIXING AND KNEADING BY HAND:** Place flour in large bowl. Using fork, mix eggs, egg yolks, and oil together in separate bowl, then stir into flour. Using your hands, knead dough in bowl until mixture forms cohesive dough that feels soft and is barely tacky to touch, about 3 minutes. (If dough sticks to your fingers after 3 minutes, add up to ¼ cup flour, 1 tablespoon at a time, until barely tacky. If dough doesn't become cohesive, add up to 1 tablespoon water, 1 teaspoon at a time, until it just comes together; knead 1 minute longer.)

**2.** Transfer dough to clean surface and knead by hand to form smooth, uniform ball, 1 to 2 minutes. Shape dough into 6-inch-long cylinder. Wrap with plastic wrap and set aside at room temperature to rest for at least 30 minutes or up to 4 hours.

**3.** Transfer dough to clean counter, divide into 3 pieces, and cover with plastic wrap. Flatten 1 piece of dough into ½-inch-thick disk. Using pasta machine with rollers set to widest position, feed dough through rollers twice. Bring tapered ends of dough toward middle and press to seal. Feed dough seam side first through rollers again. Repeat feeding dough tapered ends first through rollers set at widest position, without folding, until dough is smooth and barely tacky.

**4.** Narrow rollers to next setting and feed dough through rollers twice. Continue to progressively narrow rollers, feeding dough through each setting twice, until dough is thin and semitransparent. Transfer sheet of pasta to liberally floured sheet of parchment paper. Cover with second sheet of parchment, followed by damp dish towel to keep pasta from drying out. Repeat rolling with remaining 2 pieces of dough, stacking pasta sheets between floured layers of parchment.

**5.** Cut 1 air-dried pasta sheet in half crosswise. Starting with short end, gently fold each half-sheet at 2-inch intervals to create flat, rectangular roll.

**6.** Using sharp knife, slice pasta rolls crosswise into 1-inch-wide sections. Use your fingers to unfurl pasta strands, then liberally dust strands with flour and transfer them to lightly floured rimmed baking sheet. Repeat with remaining pasta sheets.

### CUTTING PAPPARDELLE BY HAND

**1.** Cut 1 air-dried pasta sheet in half crosswise. Starting with short end, gently fold each half-sheet at 2-inch intervals to create flat, rectangular roll.

**2.** Using sharp knife, slice pasta rolls crosswise 1 inch wide. Use your fingers to unfurl pasta, then liberally dust strands with flour and transfer them to lightly floured rimmed baking sheet. Repeat with remaining pasta sheets.

## Pork, Fennel, and Lemon Ragu with Pappardelle

**SERVES** 4 to 6

**WHY THIS RECIPE WORKS** This white ragu, known as ragù bianco, skips tomatoes in favor of bright lemon and rich cream. This version features shreds of meltingly tender braised pork punctuated by tart lemon, licorice-y fennel, and salty Pecorino Romano cheese. We ensured plenty of savoriness in the ragu by creating fond twice. We first browned finely chopped pancetta, onion, and fennel in a Dutch oven and then added water and a touch of cream to create a braising liquid. A pork shoulder, which we halved crosswise to make cooking faster and shredding easier, simmered in this liquid in the oven, where a second fond formed on the sides of the pot. After scraping this second fond into the sauce, we brightened its flavor with plenty of lemon juice before adding the pasta. Pork butt roast is often labeled Boston butt in the supermarket. To ensure that the sauce isn't greasy, be sure to trim the roast of all excess surface fat. You can substitute tagliatelle for the pappardelle, if desired.

- 4 ounces pancetta, chopped
- 1 large onion, chopped fine
- 1 large fennel bulb, 2 tablespoons fronds chopped, stalks discarded, bulb halved, cored, and chopped fine
- 4 garlic cloves, minced
- 2 teaspoons finely chopped fresh thyme
- 1½ teaspoons table salt, plus salt for cooking pasta
- 1 teaspoon pepper
- ⅓ cup heavy cream
- 1 (1½-pound) boneless pork butt roast, well trimmed and cut in half across grain
- 1½ teaspoons grated lemon zest plus ¼ cup juice (2 lemons)
- 12 ounces pappardelle
- 2 ounces Pecorino Romano cheese, grated (1 cup), plus extra for serving

**1.** Adjust oven rack to middle position and heat oven to 350 degrees. Cook pancetta and ⅔ cup water in Dutch oven over medium-high heat, stirring occasionally, until water has evaporated and dark fond forms on bottom of pot, 8 to 10 minutes. Add onion and fennel bulb and cook, stirring occasionally, until vegetables soften and start to brown, 5 to 7 minutes. Stir in garlic, thyme, salt, and pepper and cook until fragrant, about 30 seconds.

**2.** Stir in cream and 2 cups water, scraping up any browned bits. Add pork and bring to boil over high heat. Cover, transfer to oven, and cook until pork is tender, about 1½ hours.

**3.** Transfer pork to large plate and let cool for 15 minutes. Cover pot so fond will steam and soften. Using spatula, scrape browned bits from sides of pot and stir into sauce. Stir in lemon zest and juice.

**4.** While pork cools, bring 4 quarts water to boil in large pot. Using 2 forks, shred pork into bite-size pieces, discarding any large pieces of fat or connective tissue. Return pork and any juices to Dutch oven. Cover and keep warm.

**5.** Add pasta and 1 tablespoon salt to boiling water and cook, stirring occasionally, until al dente. Reserve 2 cups cooking water, then drain pasta and add it to Dutch oven. Add Pecorino and ¾ cup reserved cooking water and stir until sauce is slightly thickened and cheese is fully melted, 2 to 3 minutes. If desired, stir in remaining reserved cooking water, ¼ cup at a time, to adjust sauce consistency. Season with salt and pepper to taste and sprinkle with fennel fronds. Serve immediately, passing extra Pecorino separately.

## Pasta alla Norcina

**SERVES 6**

**WHY THIS RECIPE WORKS** Pasta alla norcina, from an Italian village in Umbria, features tender pasta and richly flavored pork sausage in a light cream sauce. For our version we bypassed store-bought Italian sausage—the size of the grind and the fat levels varied too much, and the seasonings were out of place in this dish—and made our own. Brining ground pork and mixing it briefly with a spatula ensured it had a sausage-like snappy texture; rosemary, nutmeg, and garlic offered robust flavor. Adding baking soda and searing our sausage in patty form before chopping it into small pieces helped it stay juicy and tender when it finished cooking in the cream sauce. Finely chopped mushrooms provided earthy background notes, and a splash of wine balanced the richness of the dish. For the pasta, we preferred orecchiette, which cradled the chunky sauce nicely. White mushrooms may be substituted for the cremini mushrooms. Short tubular or molded pastas such as mezze rigatoni or shells may be substituted for the orecchiette.

- Kosher salt and pepper
- ¼ teaspoon baking soda
- 4 teaspoons water
- 8 ounces ground pork
- 3 garlic cloves, minced
- 1¼ teaspoons minced fresh rosemary
- ⅛ teaspoon ground nutmeg
- 8 ounces cremini mushrooms, trimmed
- 7 teaspoons vegetable oil
- ¾ cup heavy cream
- 1 pound orecchiette
- ½ cup dry white wine
- 1½ ounces Pecorino Romano, grated (¾ cup)
- 3 tablespoons minced fresh parsley
- 1 tablespoon lemon juice

**1.** Spray large dinner plate with vegetable oil spray. Dissolve 1⅛ teaspoons salt and baking soda in water in medium bowl. Add pork and fold gently to combine; let stand for 10 minutes.

**2.** Add 1 teaspoon garlic, ¾ teaspoon rosemary, nutmeg, and ¾ teaspoon pepper to pork and stir and smear with rubber spatula until well combined and tacky, 10 to 15 seconds. Transfer pork mixture to greased plate and form into rough 6-inch patty. Pulse mushrooms in food processor until finely chopped, 10 to 12 pulses.

**3.** Heat 2 teaspoons oil in 12-inch skillet over medium-high heat until just smoking. Add patty and cook without moving it until bottom is well browned, 2 to 3 minutes. Flip patty and continue to cook until second side is well browned, 2 to 3 minutes longer (very center of patty will be raw). Remove pan from heat and transfer patty to cutting board. Using tongs to steady patty, roughly chop into ⅛- to ¼-inch pieces. Transfer meat to bowl and add cream; set aside.

**4.** Bring 4 quarts water to boil in large Dutch oven. Stir in orecchiette and 2 tablespoons salt and cook, stirring often, until al dente. Reserve 1½ cups cooking water, then drain orecchiette and return it to pot.

**5.** While orecchiette cooks, return now-empty skillet to medium heat. Add 1 tablespoon oil, mushrooms, and ⅛ teaspoon salt; cook, stirring frequently, until mushrooms are browned, 5 to 7 minutes. Stir in remaining 2 teaspoons oil, remaining 2 teaspoons garlic, remaining ½ teaspoon rosemary, and ½ teaspoon pepper; cook until fragrant, about 30 seconds. Stir in wine, scraping up any browned bits, and cook until completely evaporated, 1 to 2 minutes. Stir in meat-cream mixture and ¾ cup reserved cooking water and simmer until meat is no longer pink, 1 to 3 minutes. Remove pan from heat and stir in Pecorino until smooth.

**6.** Add sauce, parsley, and lemon juice to orecchiette and toss well to coat, adjusting consistency with remaining cooking water as needed. Season with salt and pepper to taste, and serve.

## Orecchiette with Broccoli Rabe and Sausage

**SERVES** 6 to 8

**WHY THIS RECIPE WORKS** In southern Italy, broccoli rabe and orecchiette is a popular combination. Sausage is a common addition, as the pork's richness mingles well with the bitter green. The trick to this dish is cooking the broccoli rabe just right and limiting the number of ingredients so that at the end, you have a moist and flavorful pasta dish. We started by browning the sausage in a skillet; while the sausage cooked, we blanched broccoli rabe in a separate pot. We then added the broccoli rabe to the sausage in the skillet to absorb the rich, meaty flavors. For easier cleanup, we cooked the orecchiette in the pot used to blanch the broccoli rabe. Once the pasta was cooked through, we drained it, returned it to the pot, and tossed it with the broccoli rabe–sausage mixture. A combination of Pecorino Romano cheese and some of the pasta cooking water created a creamy sauce that clung lightly to the pasta, sausage, and broccoli rabe. We prefer the flavor and texture of fresh pasta here, but dried can be used as well.

- 2 tablespoons extra-virgin olive oil
- 8 ounces hot or sweet Italian sausage, casings removed
- 6 garlic cloves, minced
- ¼ teaspoon red pepper flakes
- 1 pound broccoli rabe, trimmed and cut into 1½-inch pieces
- Table salt for cooking broccoli rabe and pasta
- 1 pound fresh or dried orecchiette
- 2 ounces Pecorino Romano, grated (1 cup)

**1.** Heat oil in 12-inch nonstick skillet over medium-high heat until just smoking. Add sausage and cook, breaking up meat into rough ½-inch pieces with wooden spoon, until lightly browned, about 5 minutes. Stir in garlic and pepper flakes and cook until fragrant, about 30 seconds; set aside.

**2.** Meanwhile, bring 4 quarts water to boil in large pot. Add broccoli rabe and 1 tablespoon salt and cook, stirring often, until crisp-tender, about 2 minutes. Using slotted spoon, transfer broccoli rabe to skillet with sausage mixture.

**3.** Return water to boil; add pasta; and cook, stirring often, until al dente. Reserve 1 cup cooking water, then drain pasta and return it to pot. Add sausage–broccoli rabe mixture, Pecorino, and ⅓ cup reserved cooking water and toss to combine. Adjust consistency with remaining ⅔ cup reserved cooking water as needed. Season with salt and pepper to taste. Serve.

## Pici alla Boscaiola (Handmade Pasta with Mushrooms and Sausage)

**SERVES** 4 **SEASON 26**

**WHY THIS RECIPE WORKS** Making pici, long hearty strands of hand-rolled pasta, is rewarding and produces a quality of pasta that's unlike anything dried. Combining nearly equal parts all-purpose and semolina flours with just enough water and a bit of olive oil made for a firm, silky, beautifully extensible dough. Kneading the mass strengthened its gluten, the network of proteins that give the noodles their chew; after a 30-minute rest, we cut it into small pieces and rolled each into a long, thin rope, coating each strand in a dusting of semolina to prevent it from sticking to the others. A brief boil in heavily salted water produced a satisfying, resilient texture while also seasoning the pici. Dried porcini and fresh cremini mushrooms, paired with sweet Italian sausage and a bit of cream, is our take on the traditional "woodsman's" sauce, the heartiness of which perfectly befits the noodles' robust chew. We developed this recipe using Bob's Red Mill No. 1 Durum Wheat Semolina Flour. If using finer semolina, such as Caputo Semola, add 1½ tablespoons more water. We strongly recommend weighing the semolina and all-purpose flours. Semolina that's left over from dusting the pasta can be sifted and saved for later use. A clean work surface provides friction for rolling the strands. If your work surface becomes covered with semolina or oil, wipe it before proceeding; if the pasta still slides, moisten your hands. Because this dish is quite hearty, we like to pair it with a crisp, light salad.

**PICI**

- 1¼ cups (6¼ ounces) all-purpose flour
- 1 cup (5¾ ounces) semolina flour, plus 1 cup for coating pasta
- ⅔ cup water, room temperature
- 2 tablespoons extra-virgin olive oil, plus 1 tablespoon for brushing dough
- Table salt for cooking pasta

SAUCE

- ½ ounce dried porcini mushrooms, rinsed and chopped fine
- ½ cup boiling water
- 2 tablespoons extra-virgin olive oil
- ½ onion, chopped fine
- ¾ teaspoon table salt
- Pinch red pepper flakes
- 4 ounces cremini mushrooms, trimmed and chopped
- ½ cup water
- ½ cup dry white wine
- 8 ounces sweet Italian sausage, casings removed, meat mashed with fork
- ½ cup heavy cream
- ¼ cup chopped fresh parsley, divided

**1. FOR THE PICI:** Whisk all-purpose flour and 1 cup semolina flour together in medium bowl and make well in center. Add water and 2 tablespoons oil and stir with fork until shaggy dough forms. Transfer dough to counter and knead until smooth and elastic, 6 to 8 minutes (dough will be firm). Wrap in damp dish towel and let rest on counter for 30 minutes. While dough rests, make sauce.

**2. FOR THE SAUCE:** Place porcini mushrooms in small bowl. Stir in boiling water. Cover and let sit until fully softened, about 20 minutes. Drain, reserving liquid. Heat oil in 12-inch skillet over medium heat until shimmering. Stir in onion, salt, and pepper flakes. Cover and cook, stirring frequently, until onions are translucent, 6 to 8 minutes. Stir in cremini mushrooms, water, wine, and porcini mushrooms and increase heat to medium-high. Cook, stirring occasionally, until liquid has mostly evaporated, about 8 minutes. Add sausage and cook, breaking up meat with back of fork, until just cooked through, about 5 minutes. Stir in cream. Cover and set aside.

**3.** Sprinkle rimmed baking sheet with ¼ cup semolina flour. Repeat with second baking sheet. Place remaining ½ cup semolina flour in wide, shallow bowl. Divide dough into 4 equal portions. Shape portions into balls. Place 3 balls under damp dish towel. Pat remaining ball into 3-inch disk and brush both sides with oil. Pat and stretch into 6-inch square of even thickness. Cut dough into 12 strips. Separate strips and place under damp dish towel.

**4.** Starting at center of 1 strip, roll dough into strand about ⅛ inch wide and at least 24 inches long (consistent width is more important than consistent length; if strand breaks, simply pinch pieces back together). Transfer to bowl of semolina and toss to coat. Gather strand loosely in your hand over bowl and shake gently to remove excess semolina. Transfer to prepared baking sheet, bending strand to fit. Dust your hands over sheet to remove excess semolina. Repeat with remaining strips (strands can touch as long as they're well dusted with semolina). Repeat with remaining dough portions and oil, placing half of pici on each baking sheet.

**5.** Bring 4 quarts water to boil in large pot. Lift pici and gently shake over baking sheet to remove excess semolina. Add all pici and 1 tablespoon salt to water and bring to boil. Cook until noodles are tender but still springy, about 3 minutes (start timer when water returns to boil). As pasta cooks, bring sauce to simmer over medium heat. Reserve 1 cup pasta water and drain pasta.

**6.** Add pici and reserved porcini water to sauce and cook, stirring constantly until pasta is well coated, about 1 minute, loosening consistency with reserved pasta water, if desired. Stir in 3 tablespoons parsley. Transfer to 4 bowls and sprinkle with remaining 1 tablespoon parsley. Serve.

### SHAPING PICI

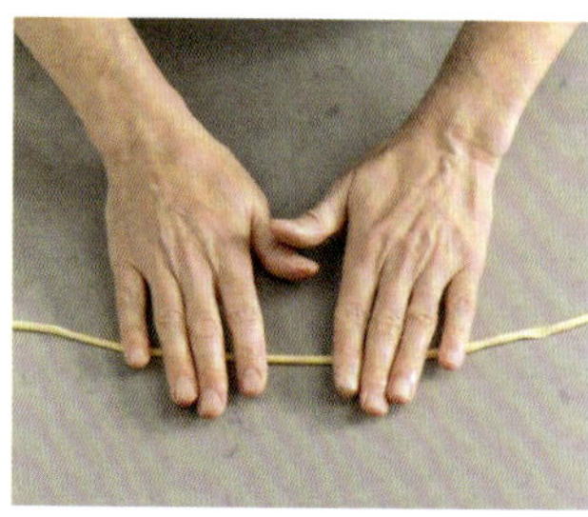

**1.** Start at center of strand, moving your hands outward as you roll.

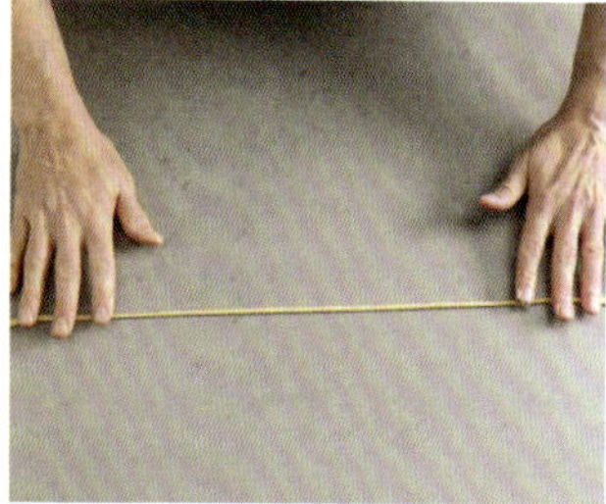

**2.** When center of strand is about ⅛ inch wide, roll your hands back and forth to evenly thin ends.

## Meatless "Meat" Sauce with Chickpeas and Mushrooms

**MAKES** 6 cups; enough for 2 pounds pasta

**WHY THIS RECIPE WORKS** This vegetarian version of tomato-meat sauce boasts a rich, savory flavor, and hearty, unctuous body—the qualities we wanted most in a quick meat sauce. We started with cremini mushrooms and tomato paste—both rich sources of savory flavor. We let the food processor do the work for us, using it to chop up our mushrooms, onions, and chickpeas, which added hearty texture. Extra-virgin olive oil did double duty, cooking the mushrooms and the classic Italian aromatics of garlic, dried oregano, and red pepper flakes and enriching the sauce. To loosen the sauce without diluting its flavor, we added vegetable broth. Chopped fresh basil added a bright finish. Make sure to rinse the chickpeas after pulsing them in the food processor or the sauce will be too thick. Our favorite canned chickpeas are from Goya, our favorite crushed tomatoes are from San Merican, and our favorite tomato paste is from Cento.

- 10 ounces cremini mushrooms, trimmed
- 6 tablespoons extra-virgin olive oil, divided
- 1 teaspoon table salt
- 1 onion, chopped
- 5 garlic cloves, minced
- 1¼ teaspoons dried oregano

- ¼ teaspoon red pepper flakes
- ¼ cup tomato paste
- 1 (28-ounce) can crushed tomatoes
- 2 cups vegetable broth
- 1 (15-ounce) can chickpeas, rinsed
- 2 tablespoons chopped fresh basil

**1.** Pulse mushrooms in 2 batches in food processor until chopped into ⅛- to ¼-inch pieces, 7 to 10 pulses, scraping down sides of bowl as needed. (Do not clean workbowl.)

**2.** Heat 5 tablespoons oil in Dutch oven over medium-high heat until shimmering. Add mushrooms and salt and cook, stirring occasionally, until mushrooms are browned and fond has formed on bottom of pot, about 8 minutes.

**3.** While mushrooms cook, pulse onion in food processor until finely chopped, 7 to 10 pulses, scraping down sides of bowl as needed. (Do not clean workbowl.) Transfer onion to pot with mushrooms and cook, stirring occasionally, until onion is soft and translucent, about 5 minutes. Combine garlic, oregano, pepper flakes, and remaining 1 tablespoon oil in bowl.

**4.** Add tomato paste to pot and cook, stirring constantly, until mixture is rust-colored, 1 to 2 minutes. Reduce heat to medium and push vegetables to sides of pot. Add garlic mixture to center and cook, stirring constantly, until fragrant, about 30 seconds. Stir in tomatoes and broth; bring to simmer over high heat. Reduce heat to low and simmer sauce for 5 minutes, stirring occasionally.

**5.** While sauce simmers, pulse chickpeas in food processor until chopped into ¼-inch pieces, 7 to 10 pulses. Transfer chickpeas to fine-mesh strainer and rinse under cold running water until water runs clear; drain well. Add chickpeas to pot and simmer until sauce is slightly thickened, about 15 minutes. Stir in basil and season with salt and pepper to taste. (Sauce can be refrigerated for up to 2 days or frozen for up to 1 month.)

## Spaghetti with Mushroom and Tomato Sauce (Quick Mushroom Ragu)

SERVES 4

**WHY THIS RECIPE WORKS** We wanted a mushroom ragu that combined the naturally hearty texture of fresh mushrooms with the concentrated flavor of dried ones—and that could be on the table in about 30 minutes. Using pancetta and its fat compensated for the lean nature of the mushrooms and made our mushroom ragu meatier. Portobello mushrooms gave our dish bulk, while smoky porcini gave it concentrated flavor. Adding tomato paste and fresh crushed tomatoes to our mushrooms after they'd browned sweetened our sauce but also let the mushrooms shine through. Finally, fresh rosemary finished our dish with brightness. Use a spoon to scrape the dark brown gills from the portobellos.

- 1 cup low-sodium chicken broth
- 1 ounce dried porcini mushrooms, rinsed
- 4 ounces pancetta, cut into ½-inch pieces
- 8 ounces portobello mushroom caps, gills removed, caps cut into ½-inch pieces (about 1½ cups)
- 3 tablespoons extra-virgin olive oil
- 4 medium garlic cloves, peeled and sliced thin
- 1 tablespoon tomato paste
- 2 teaspoons minced fresh rosemary leaves
- 1 (14.5-ounce) can whole peeled tomatoes, roughly crushed by hand
- Table salt and pepper
- 1 pound spaghetti
- Grated Pecorino Romano cheese

**1.** Microwave broth and porcini in covered bowl until steaming, about 1 minute. Let sit until softened, about 10 minutes. Drain mushrooms through fine-mesh strainer lined with coffee filter into medium bowl, reserve broth, and chop mushrooms fine.

**2.** Heat pancetta in 12-inch skillet over medium heat; cook, stirring occasionally, until rendered and crisp, 7 to 10 minutes. Add portobellos, chopped porcini, oil, garlic, tomato paste, and rosemary; cook, stirring occasionally, until all liquid has evaporated and tomato paste starts to brown, 5 to 7 minutes. Add reserved broth and crushed tomatoes and their juice; increase heat to high and bring to simmer. Reduce heat to medium-low and simmer until thickened, 15 to 20 minutes. Season with salt and pepper to taste.

**3.** While sauce simmers, bring 4 quarts water to boil in large Dutch oven. Add pasta and 1 tablespoon salt; cook, stirring often, until al dente. Reserve ½ cup cooking water, then drain pasta and return it to pot. Add sauce to pasta and toss to combine. Add reserved cooking water as needed to adjust consistency and season with salt and pepper to taste. Serve, passing Pecorino separately.

## Triple Mushroom Pasta

**SERVES** 4 to 6 **SEASON 26**

**WHY THIS RECIPE WORKS** For a pasta dish that's packed with earthy mushroom flavor, we used a trio of mushrooms: white mushrooms, maitakes, and dried porcini. To start, we made a double-mushroom duxelles by grinding affordable white mushrooms and dried porcini in a food processor with aromatics and cooking it all together. A touch of cream finished the dark, savory duxelles. To cook the pasta, we used an unconventional method: We boiled a full pound of campanelle in just 5 cups of water to create a superstarchy liquid. We didn't drain the pasta when it was just shy of al dente. Instead, we stirred in the creamy duxelles to build an ultrarich, creamy sauce that coated the frilly campanelle. Torn maitakes seared in extra-virgin olive oil created a beautiful crisp, brown topping for the dish. If you can't find maitake (hen-of-the-woods) mushrooms, substitute oyster or cremini mushrooms. We prefer campanelle here, but rigatoni or medium shells can be used; the pasta cooking time may differ. To achieve the proper consistency, boil the pasta after you've made the crispy mushrooms and duxelles.

**CRISPY MUSHROOMS**

- 2 tablespoons extra-virgin olive oil
- 8 ounces maitake mushrooms, trimmed and torn into ½-inch pieces

**DUXELLES**

- ¼ ounce dried porcini mushrooms, rinsed
- 1 shallot, peeled
- 3 garlic cloves, peeled
- 1 pound white mushrooms, quartered
- 2 tablespoons unsalted butter
- ½ teaspoon table salt
- ½ cup heavy cream
- ⅛ teaspoon pepper
- 1 tablespoon lemon juice

**PASTA**

- 5 cups water
- 1 pound campanelle
- 1 teaspoon table salt
- 1 ounce Pecorino Romano cheese, grated (½ cup)
- 2 tablespoons chopped fresh parsley

**1.** For the crispy mushrooms: Heat oil in 12-inch skillet over medium heat until shimmering. Add maitakes and cook, without stirring, until mushrooms begin to wilt at edges, 2 to 3 minutes. Gently stir and continue to cook, stirring occasionally, until mushrooms are well browned and crisp, 7 to 9 minutes longer. Remove from heat. Season mushrooms with salt and pepper to taste, transfer to bowl, and set aside until serving (do not wash skillet).

**2. FOR THE DUXELLES:** Add porcini mushrooms, shallot, and garlic to food processor and process until finely chopped, 10 to 15 seconds, scraping down sides of bowl halfway through processing. Add white mushrooms and process until very finely chopped, 40 to 55 seconds, scraping down sides of bowl halfway through processing.

**3.** Add butter to now-empty skillet and heat over medium heat until butter is foaming, 1 to 2 minutes. Add mushroom mixture and salt and cook, stirring occasionally, until mushroom liquid has evaporated and mushrooms have darkened in color, 10 to 12 minutes. Remove from heat. Stir in heavy cream, pepper, and lemon juice. Set aside.

**4. FOR THE PASTA:** Bring water to boil in large Dutch oven. Stir in pasta and salt. Adjust heat to medium so water is at gentle boil and cook partially covered, stirring occasionally, until pasta is just shy of al dente, 6 to 8 minutes (there will be about ½ inch cooking water in bottom of pot). Do not drain pasta.

**5.** Remove pot from heat. Add duxelles and Pecorino and stir vigorously until pasta is coated in lightly thickened sauce, 1 to 2 minutes (sauce will thicken as it cools). Transfer pasta to serving bowl. Top with crispy mushrooms and parsley. Serve immediately.

## Pasta with Sautéed Mushrooms and Thyme

**SERVES** 4 to 6

**WHY THIS RECIPE WORKS** Pasta with mushrooms can be watery and tasteless. But when done right, this dish transforms an ordinary box of pasta and a package of mushrooms into something special. We wanted to combine the intense flavor of sautéed mushrooms with a light cream sauce to create a woodsy, full-flavored pasta dish. For optimum flavor and texture, we used a combination of shiitake and cremini mushrooms; cremini mushrooms provided richness and meatiness, and the shiitakes contributed hearty flavor and a pleasant, chewy texture. Cooking the mushrooms in a skillet (not in the sauce) improved their flavor; adding salt to the pan helped the mushrooms release their juices and enhanced browning. We then added chicken broth and cream to the browned bits left in the skillet after the mushrooms were removed. Garlic, shallots, and thyme rounded out the flavors of our simple sauce, and lemon juice added brightness. We added the browned mushrooms back in for a chunky sauce that paired nicely with short pasta with lots of crevices—we liked either campanelle or farfalle. Vegetable broth can be substituted for the chicken broth to make this dish vegetarian. If you add the pasta to the boiling water at the same time the cremini go into the skillet, the pasta and sauce will finish at the same time.

- Table salt
- 1 pound campanelle or farfalle
- 2 tablespoons unsalted butter
- 2 tablespoons extra-virgin olive oil
- 4 large shallots, minced (about 1 cup)
- 3 medium garlic cloves, minced or pressed through a garlic press (about 1 tablespoon)
- 10 ounces shiitake mushrooms, stems discarded, caps wiped clean and sliced ¼ inch thick
- 10 ounces cremini mushrooms, wiped clean and sliced ¼ inch thick
- 1 tablespoon plus 1 teaspoon minced fresh thyme leaves
- 1¼ cups low-sodium chicken broth
- ½ cup heavy cream
- 1 tablespoon juice from 1 lemon
- Ground black pepper
- 2 ounces Parmesan cheese, grated (about 1 cup)
- 2 tablespoons minced fresh parsley leaves

**1.** Bring 4 quarts water to a boil in a large pot. Add 1 tablespoon salt and the pasta to the boiling water and cook, stirring often, until al dente. Reserve ½ cup of the cooking water then drain the pasta and return it to the pot.

**2.** Meanwhile, melt the butter with the oil over medium heat in a 12-inch skillet. Add the shallots and cook, stirring occasionally, until softened and translucent, about 4 minutes. Add the garlic and cook until fragrant, about 30 seconds. Increase the heat to medium-high; add the shiitakes and cook, stirring occasionally, for 2 minutes. Add the cremini and ½ teaspoon salt; cook, stirring occasionally, until the moisture released by the mushrooms has evaporated and the mushrooms are golden brown, about 8 minutes. Add the thyme and cook until fragrant, about 30 seconds. Transfer the mushrooms to a bowl and set aside.

**3.** Add the chicken broth to the skillet and bring to a boil, scraping up the browned bits. Off the heat, stir in the cream and lemon juice and season with salt and pepper to taste.

**4.** Add the mushrooms, chicken broth mixture, cheese, and parsley to the pasta. Toss over medium-low heat until the cheese melts and the pasta absorbs most of the liquid, about 2 minutes. Adjust the consistency of the sauce with the reserved pasta cooking water as needed and serve immediately.

## Fusilli with Ricotta and Spinach

**SERVES** 4 to 6

**WHY THIS RECIPE WORKS** There are many recipes that pair simple boiled pasta with spinach and ricotta as a simplified, "deconstructed" version of stuffed shells, manicotti, or ravioli. But the versions we tried lacked complexity and suffered from a gritty texture. To boost the flavor of the ricotta, we mixed in some extra-virgin olive oil, salt, and pepper. Then we set out to tackle the sauce's gritty, chalky texture. Heat caused the ricotta curds to release water and coagulate, rendering the sauce grainy. To minimize this effect, we dolloped most of the ricotta on top of the pasta so that tasters got concentrated hits of cheese here and there, much as they would when eating filled pasta. We mixed the rest of the ricotta with cream (to stabilize the milk proteins), along with sautéed garlic, cayenne, and nutmeg for warmth, and used this mixture to dress the warm pasta. As for the spinach, simply tossing the coarsely chopped leaves into the pot with the pasta at the end of cooking gave us slightly wilted but still brilliant green spinach. Letting the pasta sit dressed for a few minutes before serving drew out some of the pasta's starches for a creamy, velvety texture. We like fusilli for this recipe since its shape traps the sauce, but penne and campanelle also work well.

- 11 ounces (1⅓ cups) whole-milk ricotta cheese
- 3 tablespoons extra-virgin olive oil
- Table salt and pepper
- 1 pound fusilli
- 1 pound (16 cups) baby spinach, chopped coarse
- 4 garlic cloves, minced
- ¼ teaspoon ground nutmeg
- ⅛ teaspoon cayenne pepper
- ¼ cup heavy cream
- 1 teaspoon grated lemon zest plus 2 teaspoons juice
- 1 ounce Parmesan cheese, grated (½ cup), plus extra for serving

**1.** Whisk 1 cup ricotta, 1 tablespoon oil, ¼ teaspoon pepper, and ⅛ teaspoon salt in medium bowl until smooth; set aside.

**2.** Bring 4 quarts water to boil in large pot. Add pasta and 1 tablespoon salt and cook, stirring often, until al dente. Reserve 1 cup cooking water. Stir spinach into pot with pasta and cook until wilted, about 30 seconds. Drain pasta and spinach and return them to pot.

**3.** While pasta cooks, heat remaining 2 tablespoons oil, garlic, nutmeg, and cayenne in saucepan over medium heat until fragrant, about 1 minute. Remove pan from heat and whisk in remaining ⅓ cup ricotta, cream, lemon zest and juice, and ¾ teaspoon salt until smooth.

**4.** Add ricotta-cream mixture and Parmesan to pasta and toss to combine. Let pasta rest, tossing frequently, until sauce has thickened slightly and coats pasta, 2 to 4 minutes, adjusting consistency with reserved cooking water as needed. Transfer pasta to serving platter, dot evenly with reserved ricotta mixture, and serve, passing extra Parmesan separately.

## Foolproof Spaghetti Carbonara

**SERVES 4**

**WHY THIS RECIPE WORKS** This quintessential Roman pasta dish is made with simple ingredients, but the results can be disappointing. We wanted to make a classic carbonara that was foolproof but not so rich that eating a full serving was impossible. We started by replacing the guanciale, or cured pork jowl, with readily available bacon. To approximate the meaty chew of guanciale, we cooked the bacon with a little water, which produced tender-chewy pieces. We used just a touch of the rendered fat in our sauce for consistent bacon flavor in every bite. To make a richly eggy sauce that wouldn't become dry and clumpy when mixed with the pasta, we used three eggs and an extra yolk for richness. Boiling the pasta in half the usual amount of water gave us extra starchy water to coat the proteins and fats in the cheese, preventing them from separating or clumping, and making for a perfectly velvety sauce. Tossing the spaghetti with the sauce in a warm serving bowl allowed the warm pasta to gently "cook" the carbonara sauce without overcooking the eggs. The heat from the cooking water and the hot spaghetti will "cook" the sauce only if used immediately. Warming the mixing and serving bowls helps the sauce stay creamy. Our favorite bacon is Vande Rose Applewood Smoked Artisan Dry Cured Bacon.

- 8 slices bacon, cut into ½-inch pieces
- ½ cup water
- 3 garlic cloves, minced
- 2½ ounces Pecorino Romano, grated (1¼ cups)
- 3 large eggs plus 1 large yolk
- 1 teaspoon pepper
- 1 pound spaghetti
- Table salt for cooking pasta

**1.** Bring bacon and water to simmer in 10-inch nonstick skillet over medium heat; cook until water evaporates and bacon begins to sizzle, about 8 minutes. Reduce heat to medium-low and continue to cook until fat is rendered and bacon browns, 5 to 8 minutes longer. Add garlic and cook, stirring constantly, until fragrant, about 30 seconds. Strain bacon mixture through fine-mesh strainer set in bowl. Set aside bacon mixture. Measure out 1 tablespoon fat and place in medium bowl. Whisk Pecorino, eggs and yolk, and pepper into fat until combined.

**2.** Meanwhile, bring 2 quarts water to boil in Dutch oven. Set colander in large bowl. Add pasta and 1 teaspoon salt to pot; cook, stirring frequently, until al dente. Drain pasta in colander set in bowl, reserving cooking water. Pour 1 cup cooking water into liquid measuring cup and discard remainder. Return pasta to now-empty bowl.

**3.** Slowly whisk ½ cup reserved cooking water into Pecorino mixture. Gradually pour Pecorino mixture over pasta, tossing to coat. Add bacon mixture and toss to combine. Let pasta rest, tossing frequently, until sauce has thickened slightly and coats pasta, 2 to 4 minutes, adjusting consistency with remaining reserved cooking water if needed. Serve immediately.

## Spaghetti alla Carbonara

**SERVES 4 TO 6**

**WHY THIS RECIPE WORKS** Spaghetti carbonara is a mainstay on Italian restaurant menus, but the velvety, bacon-laced sauce can be elusive for the home cook. Three eggs, mixed with a combination of Pecorino Romano and Parmesan cheeses, made a silky sauce that could cling to the spaghetti. Raw garlic gave the sauce a bit of zing without being overpowering, but we deemed heavy cream an unnecessary addition, since it weighed down the dish and dulled the cheese flavor. In place of the traditional guanciale (salt-cured pork jowl), we used American bacon, which we sautéed to give our dish the perfect crunch and a hint of sweetness and smoke. For added brightness, white wine was just the thing. The acidity of the wine cut through the richness of the bacon for a lighter, brighter sauce. We found that the mixing method was key to this dish; mixing the hot spaghetti with the egg and cheese mixture before gently tossing in the crispy pieces of bacon ensured that every bite was perfect. Although we call for spaghetti in this recipe, you can substitute linguine or fettuccine.

- ¼ cup extra-virgin olive oil
- 8 ounces (about 8 slices) bacon, halved lengthwise and cut into ¼-inch pieces
- ½ cup dry white wine
- 3 large eggs
- 1½ ounces Parmesan cheese, grated (about ¾ cup)
- ¼ cup grated Pecorino Romano cheese
- 1 large garlic clove, minced or pressed through a garlic press (about 1½ teaspoons)
- 1 pound spaghetti
- Table salt and ground black pepper

**1.** Adjust an oven rack to the lower-middle position, set an ovensafe serving bowl on the rack, and heat the oven to 200 degrees. Bring 4 quarts water to a boil in a large pot.

**2.** While the water is heating, heat the oil in a large skillet over medium heat until shimmering. Add the bacon and cook, stirring occasionally, until crisp, about 8 minutes. Add the wine and simmer until it is slightly reduced, 6 to 8 minutes. Remove from the heat and cover. Whisk the eggs, cheeses, and garlic together in a small bowl; set aside.

**3.** When the water comes to a boil, add 1 tablespoon salt and the pasta. Cook, stirring often, until al dente. Reserve ½ cup of the cooking water; drain the pasta. Remove the warm bowl from the oven and add the pasta. Immediately pour the egg and bacon mixtures over the pasta, season with salt and pepper to taste, and toss to coat; adjust the consistency of the sauce with the reserved pasta cooking water as needed. Serve immediately.

## Pasta alla Gricia (Rigatoni with Pancetta and Pecorino Romano)

**SERVES 6**

**WHY THIS RECIPE WORKS** One of Rome's little-known but iconic pasta dishes, pasta alla gricia is a simple dish based on cured pork, black pepper, and Pecorino Romano. The fat from the pork (guanciale is traditional, but easier-to-find pancetta works well) combines with starchy pasta cooking water and cheese to create a creamy sauce for the pasta. Traditionally the parcooked pasta finishes cooking in the sauce, but the technique can be finicky. For consistent results, we cooked the pasta to al dente in half the usual amount of water and then added the extra-starchy pasta cooking water to the rendered pork fat and reduced the mixture to a specific volume. This further concentrated the starches in the water and emulsified the mixture before we added the pasta. Because this pasta is quite rich, serve it in slightly smaller portions with a green vegetable or salad. For the best results, use the highest-quality pancetta you can find. If you can find guanciale, we recommend using it and increasing the browning time in step 2 to 10 to 12 minutes. Because we call for cutting the pancetta to a specified thickness, we recommend having it cut to order at the deli counter; avoid presliced or prediced products.

- 8 ounces pancetta, sliced ¼ inch thick
- 1 tablespoon extra-virgin olive oil
- 1 pound rigatoni
- 1 teaspoon coarsely ground pepper, plus extra for serving
- 2 ounces Pecorino Romano cheese, grated fine (1 cup), plus extra for serving

**1.** Slice each round of pancetta into rectangular pieces that measure about ½ inch by 1 inch.

**2.** Heat pancetta and oil in Dutch oven over medium-low heat, stirring frequently, until fat is rendered and pancetta is deep golden brown but still has slight pinkish hue, 8 to 10 minutes, adjusting heat as necessary to keep pancetta from browning too quickly. Using slotted spoon, transfer pancetta to bowl; set aside. Pour fat from pot into liquid measuring cup (you should have ¼ to ⅓ cup fat; discard any extra). Return fat to Dutch oven.

**3.** While pancetta cooks, set colander in large bowl. Bring 2 quarts water to boil in large pot. Add pasta and cook, stirring often, until al dente. Drain pasta in prepared colander, reserving cooking water.

**4.** Add pepper and 2 cups reserved cooking water to Dutch oven with fat and bring to boil over high heat. Boil mixture rapidly, scraping up any browned bits, until emulsified and reduced to 1½ cups, about 5 minutes. (If you've reduced it too far, add more reserved cooking water to equal 1½ cups.)

**5.** Reduce heat to low, add pasta and pancetta, and stir to evenly coat. Add Pecorino and stir until cheese is melted and sauce is slightly thickened, about 1 minute. Off heat, adjust sauce consistency with remaining reserved cooking water as needed. Transfer pasta to platter and serve immediately, passing extra pepper and Pecorino separately.

## Tagliatelle with Prosciutto and Peas

**SERVES 4 to 6**

**WHY THIS RECIPE WORKS** Prosciutto and Parmesan are packed with complementary flavors, so when combining them in a pasta dish, we aimed to maximize their impact. Adding prosciutto in two stages created complex, porky flavor. Mincing an ounce of prosciutto and simmering it with softened shallots and cream created a meaty sauce. We opted for tagliatelle, its long ribbons of dried egg pasta a fitting substitute for fresh pasta. We stirred together the pasta, reserved water, and the prosciutto-cream mixture, adding in strips of raw prosciutto for the meat's fruity, nutty fragrance. Grated Parmesan plus Gruyère (another nutty, aromatic cheese) worked perfectly. We used frozen peas as a sweet, bright foil to the rich sauce. We prefer imported prosciutto di Parma sliced 1/16 inch thick or domestically made prepackaged Volpi Traditional Prosciutto. Look for a hard Gruyère that is aged for at least 10 months. Pappardelle can be substituted for the tagliatelle.

- 6 ounces thinly sliced prosciutto
- 1 tablespoon unsalted butter
- 1 shallot, minced
- Table salt and pepper
- 1 cup heavy cream
- 1 pound tagliatelle
- 1½ cups frozen petite peas, thawed
- 1 ounce Parmesan cheese, grated (½ cup)
- 1 ounce Gruyère cheese, grated (½ cup)

**1.** Slice 5 ounces prosciutto crosswise into ¼-inch-wide strips; set aside. Mince remaining 1 ounce prosciutto. Melt butter in 10-inch skillet over medium-low heat. Add shallot and ¼ teaspoon salt and cook until softened, about 2 minutes. Stir in cream and minced prosciutto and bring to simmer. Cook, stirring occasionally, until cream mixture measures 1 cup, 5 to 7 minutes. Remove pan from heat and cover to keep warm.

**2.** Meanwhile, bring 4 quarts water to boil in large pot. Add pasta and 1 tablespoon salt and cook, stirring often, until al dente. Reserve 2 cups cooking water, then drain pasta and return it to pot.

**3.** Add 1 cup reserved cooking water, cream mixture, prosciutto strips, peas, Parmesan, Gruyère, and 1 teaspoon pepper to pasta. Toss gently until pasta is well coated. Transfer pasta to serving bowl and serve immediately, adjusting consistency with remaining reserved cooking water as needed.

## Fettuccine Alfredo

**SERVES** 4 to 6

**WHY THIS RECIPE WORKS** Fettuccine Alfredo—tender pasta bathed in a silky, creamy cheese sauce—always sounds so tempting. But too often, restaurant-style fettuccine Alfredo means gargantuan portions, overcooked pasta, and a sauce that quickly congeals in the bowl. We were after a better Alfredo, with a luxurious sauce that remained supple and velvety from the first bite of pasta to the last. We first discovered that fresh pasta was essential as a base—dried noodles didn't hold on to the sauce, and the delicate nature of fresh pasta brought a more sophisticated tone to the dish. Turning our attention to the sauce, we found that a light hand was necessary when adding two of the richer ingredients: the cheese and the butter. To manage the heavy cream, we reduced a portion of it, then added the remaining amount uncooked. This technique produced not only a luxurious texture but also a fresher flavor. A pinch of freshly grated nutmeg added a spicy, sweet undertone to this elegant dish. Fresh pasta is the best choice for this dish; supermarkets sell 9-ounce containers of fresh pasta in the refrigerated section. When boiling the pasta, undercook it slightly (just shy of al dente) because the pasta cooks an additional minute or two in the sauce just before serving. Note that fettuccine Alfredo must be served immediately; it does not hold or reheat well.

- 1½ cups heavy cream
- 2 tablespoons unsalted butter
- Table salt
- ¼ teaspoon ground black pepper
- 9 ounces fresh fettuccine
- 1½ ounces Parmesan cheese, grated (about ¾ cup)
- ⅛ teaspoon grated nutmeg

**1.** Bring 1 cup of the heavy cream and the butter to a simmer in a medium saucepan over medium heat; reduce the heat to low and simmer gently until the mixture reduces to ⅔ cup, 12 to 15 minutes. Off the heat, stir in the remaining ½ cup cream, ½ teaspoon salt, and the pepper.

**2.** While the cream reduces, bring 4 quarts water to a boil in a large pot. Add 1 tablespoon salt and the pasta to the boiling water and cook, stirring often, until just shy of al dente. Reserve ¼ cup of the cooking water then drain the pasta and return it to the pot.

**3.** Meanwhile, return the cream mixture to a simmer over medium-high heat; reduce the heat to low and add the pasta, cheese, and nutmeg to the cream mixture. Cook over low heat, tossing the pasta to combine, until the cheese is melted, the sauce coats the pasta, and the pasta is just al dente, 1 to 2 minutes. Stir in the reserved pasta cooking water and toss to coat; the sauce may look thin but will gradually thicken as the pasta is served. Serve immediately.

## Classic Macaroni and Cheese

**SERVES** 6 to 8

**WHY THIS RECIPE WORKS** Old-fashioned macaroni and cheese takes no shortcuts. This family favorite should boast tender pasta in a smooth, creamy sauce with great cheese flavor. Too often, the dish, which is baked in the oven, dries out or curdles. We aimed to create a foolproof version. We cooked the pasta until just past al dente and then combined it with a béchamel-based cheese sauce. For the best flavor and a creamy texture, we used a combination of sharp cheddar and Monterey Jack. We combined the cooked pasta with the sauce and heated it through on the stovetop, rather than in the oven. This step helped ensure the dish didn't dry out, but remained smooth and creamy. And to give the dish a browned topping, we sprinkled it with bread crumbs and ran it briefly under the broiler. It's crucial to cook the pasta until tender—that is, just past the al dente stage. Whole, low-fat, and skim milk all work well in this recipe. The recipe may be halved and baked in an 8-inch square, broiler-safe baking dish. If desired, offer celery salt or hot sauce for sprinkling at the table.

**BREAD CRUMB TOPPING**

- 6 slices high-quality white sandwich bread, torn into quarters
- 3 tablespoons cold unsalted butter, cut into 6 pieces

MACARONI AND CHEESE

- 1 tablespoon plus 1 teaspoon table salt
- 1 pound elbow macaroni
- 5 tablespoons unsalted butter
- 6 tablespoons unbleached all-purpose flour
- 1½ teaspoons dry mustard
- ¼ teaspoon cayenne pepper (optional)
- 5 cups milk
- 8 ounces Monterey Jack cheese, shredded (about 2 cups)
- 8 ounces sharp cheddar cheese, shredded (about 2 cups)

1. FOR THE BREAD CRUMB TOPPING: Pulse the bread and butter in a food processor until coarsely ground, 10 to 15 pulses. Set aside.

2. FOR THE MACARONI AND CHEESE: Adjust an oven rack to the lower-middle position and heat the broiler. Bring 4 quarts water to a rolling boil in a large pot. Add 1 tablespoon of the salt and the macaroni and stir to separate the noodles. Cook until tender, drain, and set aside.

3. In the now-empty pot, melt the butter over medium-high heat. Add the flour, mustard, cayenne (if using), and remaining 1 teaspoon salt and whisk well to combine. Continue whisking until the mixture becomes fragrant and deepens in color, about 1 minute. Whisking constantly, gradually add the milk; bring the mixture to a boil, whisking constantly (the mixture must reach a full boil to fully thicken), then reduce the heat to medium and simmer, whisking occasionally, until thickened to the consistency of heavy cream, about 5 minutes. Off the heat, whisk in the cheeses until fully melted. Add the pasta and cook over medium-low heat, stirring constantly, until the mixture is steaming and heated through, about 6 minutes.

4. Transfer the mixture to a broiler-safe 13 by 9-inch baking dish and sprinkle with the bread crumbs. Broil until deep golden brown, 3 to 5 minutes. Cool for 5 minutes, then serve.

## Grown-Up Stovetop Macaroni and Cheese

SERVES 4

WHY THIS RECIPE WORKS We turned to science to help make our mac and cheese creamy and smooth. We were inspired by an innovative recipe calling for adding sodium citrate, an emulsifier, to cheese to keep it smooth when heated (instead of adding flour to make a béchamel). American cheese, which contains a similar stabilizing ingredient, was the solution. But because it tastes so plain, we combined it with Gruyère and blue cheese, as well as mustard and cayenne for more sophisticated flavor. We cooked the macaroni in a smaller-than-usual amount of water, so we didn't have to drain it; the liquid that was left after the elbows were hydrated was just enough to form the base of the sauce. Rather than bake the mac and cheese, we sprinkled toasted panko bread crumbs on top to keep things simple. Creamette makes our favorite elbow macaroni. Because the macaroni is cooked in a measured amount of liquid, we don't recommend using different shapes or sizes of pasta. Use a 4-ounce block of American cheese from the deli counter rather than presliced cheese.

- 1¾ cups water
- 1 cup milk
- 8 ounces elbow macaroni
- 4 ounces American cheese, shredded (1 cup)
- ½ teaspoon Dijon mustard
- Small pinch cayenne pepper
- 3½ ounces Gruyère cheese, shredded (¾ cup)
- 2 tablespoons crumbled blue cheese
- ⅓ cup panko bread crumbs
- 1 tablespoon extra-virgin olive oil
- Table salt and pepper
- 2 tablespoons grated Parmesan cheese

1. Bring water and milk to boil in medium saucepan over high heat. Stir in macaroni and reduce heat to medium-low. Cook, stirring frequently, until macaroni is soft (slightly past al dente), 6 to 8 minutes. Add American cheese, mustard, and cayenne and cook, stirring constantly, until cheese is completely melted, about 1 minute. Off heat, stir in Gruyère and blue cheese until evenly distributed but not melted. Cover saucepan and let stand for 5 minutes.

2. Meanwhile, combine panko, oil, ⅛ teaspoon salt, and ⅛ teaspoon pepper in 8-inch nonstick skillet until panko is evenly moistened. Cook over medium heat, stirring frequently, until evenly browned, 3 to 4 minutes. Off heat, sprinkle Parmesan over panko mixture and stir to combine. Transfer panko mixture to small bowl.

3. Stir macaroni until sauce is smooth (sauce may look loose but will thicken as it cools). Season with salt and pepper to taste. Transfer to warm serving dish and sprinkle panko mixture over top. Serve immediately.

## Everyday Lighter Macaroni and Cheese

SERVES 4 to 6

WHY THIS RECIPE WORKS Weighing in at about 650 calories and 40 grams of fat per serving, a bowl of homemade mac and cheese is a welcome treat every once in a while, like a slice of cake. But many of us want to enjoy this family favorite a little more often. We aimed to develop a lighter version of mac and cheese—macaroni in a creamy (not rubbery or grainy), cheesy sauce—with a fraction of the calories. We slashed both fat and calories by replacing full-fat cheddar with low-fat—its flavor and texture are vastly superior to nonfat cheddar. We also swapped in 2 percent milk for the whole milk and added 2 percent evaporated milk to ensure a creamy consistency. And we found that we could eliminate butter entirely by thickening the sauce with cornstarch instead of a classic roux. In the end, we cut the calories by almost half and the fat grams by 75 percent, turning full-fat macaroni and cheese into a dish we could eat every day. Don't be tempted to use either preshredded or nonfat cheddar cheese in this dish—the texture and flavor of the macaroni and cheese will suffer substantially. For best results, choose a low-fat cheddar cheese that is sold in block form and has roughly 50 percent of the fat and calories of regular cheese (we like Cracker Barrel brand).

- Table salt
- 8 ounces elbow macaroni (about 2 cups)
- 1 (12-ounce) can 2 percent reduced-fat evaporated milk
- ¾ cup 2 percent milk
- ¼ teaspoon dry mustard
- ⅛ teaspoon garlic powder or celery salt (optional)
- Pinch cayenne pepper
- 2 teaspoons cornstarch
- 8 ounces 50 percent light cheddar cheese, shredded (about 2 cups)

**1.** Bring 2½ quarts water to a boil in a large saucepan. Stir in 2 teaspoons salt and the macaroni; cook until the pasta is completely cooked and tender, about 5 minutes. Drain the pasta and leave it in the colander; set aside.

**2.** Add the evaporated milk, ½ cup of the 2 percent milk, the mustard, garlic powder (if using), cayenne, and ½ teaspoon salt to the now-empty saucepan. Bring the mixture to a boil, then reduce to a simmer. Whisk the cornstarch and remaining ¼ cup milk together, then whisk it into the simmering mixture. Continue to simmer, whisking constantly, until the sauce has thickened and is smooth, about 2 minutes.

**3.** Off the heat, gradually whisk in the cheddar until melted and smooth. Stir in the macaroni and let the macaroni and cheese sit off the heat until the sauce has thickened slightly, 2 to 5 minutes, before serving.

## Bow Tie Pasta with Pesto

**SERVES** 4 to 6

**WHY THIS RECIPE WORKS** Pasta with pesto makes for a satisfying, summery meal. But getting pesto right isn't always so easy; the sauce can be anywhere from too thin and watery to too thick and overpoweringly garlicky. Our goal was to heighten the basil and subdue the garlic flavors in pesto so that each major element balanced the next. We started by briefly blanching whole unpeeled garlic cloves to tame their flavor and prevent them from taking over the sauce. Then we bruised the basil in a plastic bag with a meat pounder (you could also use a rolling pin) to unlock its flavor; we found that this method released the most herbal flavors from the basil. With the basil flavor boosted and the garlic toned down, it was time to process the ingredients with toasted nuts and stir in the Parmesan. Finally, we reserved some of the pasta cooking water, which was essential to thin out the pesto once it had been added to the pasta. The water also softened and blended the flavors a bit, and highlighted the creaminess of the cheese and nuts. Basil usually darkens in homemade pesto, but you can preserve the green color by adding the optional parsley. For sharper flavor, substitute 1 tablespoon finely grated Pecorino Romano cheese for 1 tablespoon of the Parmesan. For a change from farfalle, try curly shapes, such as fusilli, which can trap bits of the pesto.

- 3 medium garlic cloves, threaded on a skewer
- 2 cups packed fresh basil leaves
- 2 tablespoons fresh flat-leaf parsley leaves (optional)
- ¼ cup pine nuts, walnuts, or almonds, toasted
- 7 tablespoons extra-virgin olive oil
- Table salt
- ¼ cup grated Parmesan
- 1 pound farfalle

**1.** Bring 4 quarts water to a boil in a large pot. Lower the skewered garlic into the water and boil for 45 seconds. Immediately run the garlic under cold water. Remove the garlic from the skewer, peel, and mince.

**2.** Place the basil and parsley (if using) in a zipper-lock bag and pound with the flat side of a meat pounder or a rolling pin until all the leaves are bruised.

**3.** Process the nuts, garlic, basil, oil, and ½ teaspoon salt in a food processor until smooth, scraping down the sides of the workbowl as necessary. Transfer the mixture to a small bowl, stir in the cheese, and season with salt to taste. (The pesto can be covered with a sheet of plastic wrap pressed against the surface and refrigerated for up to 5 days.)

**4.** Add 1 tablespoon salt and the pasta to the boiling water and cook, stirring often, until al dente. Reserve ½ cup of the cooking water then drain the pasta and return it to the pot. Stir in ¼ cup reserved cooking water and the pesto; adjust the consistency of the sauce with the remaining reserved pasta cooking water as needed. Serve immediately.

## Nontraditional Pestos

**SERVES** 4 to 6

**WHY THIS RECIPE WORKS** Pesto doesn't always mean basil, pine nuts, and Parmesan. We wanted to make quick pestos with a variety of other potent ingredients, like sun-dried tomatoes, goat cheese, and kalamata olives. For pestos that were flavorful but not harsh, we tamed the garlic by toasting unpeeled cloves in a hot skillet or replaced most of it with sun-dried tomatoes. Then we processed the garlic or sun-dried tomatoes with olive oil, nuts, cheese, and olives, among other ingredients, to create smooth sauces that cling well to pasta. And to keep the pasta moist, we made sure to reserve some of the pasta cooking water to thin the pesto.

## Cavatappi with Arugula, Goat Cheese, and Sun-Dried Tomato Pesto

**SERVES** 4 to 6

Make sure to rinse the herbs and seasonings from the sun-dried tomatoes. Farfalle can be substituted for the campanelle.

- 1 cup oil-packed sun-dried tomatoes (one 8½-ounce jar), drained, rinsed, patted dry, and chopped coarse
- 1 ounce Parmesan cheese, grated (about ½ cup)
- 6 tablespoons extra-virgin olive oil
- ¼ cup walnuts, toasted
- 1 small garlic clove, minced or pressed through a garlic press (about ½ teaspoon)
- Table salt and ground black pepper
- 1 pound campanelle
- 1 medium bunch arugula, washed, dried, stemmed, and torn into bite-size pieces (about 6 cups)
- 3 ounces goat cheese, crumbled (about ¾ cup)

**1.** Process the sun-dried tomatoes, Parmesan, oil, walnuts, garlic, ½ teaspoon salt, and ⅛ teaspoon pepper in a food processor until smooth, scraping down the sides of the workbowl as necessary. Transfer the mixture to a small bowl and set aside.

**2.** Bring 4 quarts water to a boil in a large pot. Add 1 tablespoon salt and the pasta to the boiling water and cook, stirring often, until al dente. Reserve ¾ cup of the cooking water then drain the pasta and return it to the pot. Immediately stir in the arugula until wilted. Stir ½ cup of the reserved pasta cooking water into the pesto and add the pesto to the pasta. Toss to combine, adjusting the consistency of the sauce with the remaining reserved pasta cooking water as needed. Serve immediately, sprinkling the cheese over individual bowls.

## Penne with Toasted Nut and Parsley Pesto

**SERVES** 4 to 6

Toasting the unpeeled garlic in a skillet reduces its harshness and gives it a mellow flavor that works well in pesto.

- 3 medium garlic cloves, unpeeled
- 1 cup pecans, walnuts, whole blanched almonds, skinned hazelnuts, unsalted pistachios, or pine nuts, or any combination thereof, toasted
- ½ cup packed fresh parsley leaves
- 7 tablespoons extra-virgin olive oil
- 1 ounce Parmesan cheese, grated (about ½ cup)
- Table salt and ground black pepper
- 1 pound penne

**1.** Toast the garlic in a small skillet over medium heat, shaking the pan occasionally, until softened and spotty brown, about 8 minutes; when cool, remove and discard the skins.

**2.** Process the garlic, nuts, parsley, and oil in a food processor until smooth, scraping down the sides of the workbowl as necessary. Transfer the mixture to a small bowl and stir in the Parmesan; season with salt and pepper to taste.

**3.** Bring 4 quarts water to a boil in a large pot. Add 1 tablespoon salt and the pasta to the boiling water and cook, stirring often, until al dente. Reserve ½ cup of the cooking water then drain the pasta and return it to the pot. Stir ¼ cup of the reserved pasta cooking water into the pesto and add the pesto to the pasta. Toss to combine, adjusting the consistency of the sauce with the remaining reserved pasta cooking water as needed. Serve immediately.

## Spaghetti with Olive Pesto

**SERVES 4 TO 6**

This black pesto is called olivada in Italy. Make sure to use high-quality olives in this recipe. The anchovy adds flavor but not fishiness to the pesto and we recommend its inclusion.

- 3 medium garlic cloves, unpeeled
- 1½ cups pitted kalamata olives
- 1 ounce Parmesan cheese, grated (about ½ cup), plus extra for serving
- 6 tablespoons extra-virgin olive oil
- ¼ cup packed fresh parsley leaves
- 1 medium shallot, chopped coarse (about 3 tablespoons)
- 8 large basil leaves
- 1 tablespoon juice from 1 lemon
- 1 anchovy fillet, rinsed (optional)
- Table salt and ground black pepper
- 1 pound spaghetti
- Lemon wedges, for serving

**1.** Toast the garlic in a small skillet over medium heat, shaking the pan occasionally, until the garlic is softened and spotty brown, about 8 minutes; when cool, remove and discard the skins.

**2.** Process the garlic, olives, ½ cup of the Parmesan, oil, parsley, shallot, basil, lemon juice, and anchovy (if using) in a food processor, scraping down the sides of the workbowl as necessary. Transfer the mixture to a small bowl and season with salt and pepper to taste.

**3.** Bring 4 quarts water to a boil in a large pot. Add 1 tablespoon salt and the pasta to the boiling water and cook, stirring often, until al dente. Reserve ½ cup of the cooking water then drain the pasta and return it to the pot. Stir ¼ cup of the reserved pasta cooking water into the pesto and add the pesto to the pasta. Toss to combine, adjusting the consistency of the sauce with the remaining reserved pasta cooking water as needed. Serve immediately, passing the lemon wedges and extra Parmesan separately.

## Spring Vegetable Pasta

**SERVES** 4 to 6

**WHY THIS RECIPE WORKS** In pasta primavera, the vegetables and pasta are tossed together in a sauce made with broth and heavy cream. We love this classic, but sometimes we want a lighter, brighter version. As for the vegetables, we wanted true spring vegetables. To start, we chose asparagus and green peas, adding chives for bite and garlic and leeks for depth and sweetness. For a deeply flavored sauce that would unify the pasta and vegetables, we borrowed a technique from risotto, lightly toasting the pasta in olive oil before cooking it in broth and white wine. The sauce flavored the pasta as it cooked while the pasta added starch to the sauce, thickening it without the need for heavy cream. This nontraditional approach gave us a light but creamy sauce with sweet, grassy flavors that paired perfectly with the vegetables. This was a dish that truly tasted like spring. Campanelle is our pasta of choice in this dish, but farfalle and penne are good substitutes.

- 1½ pounds leeks, white and light green parts halved lengthwise, sliced ½ inch thick, and washed; 3 cups coarsely chopped dark green parts, washed
- 1 pound asparagus, tough ends trimmed, chopped coarse, and reserved, spears cut on bias into ½-inch lengths
- 2 cups frozen peas, thawed
- 4 medium garlic cloves, minced or pressed through a garlic press (about 4 teaspoons)
- 4 cups vegetable broth
- 1 cup water
- 2 tablespoons minced fresh mint leaves
- 2 tablespoons minced fresh chives
- ½ teaspoon grated zest plus 2 tablespoons juice from 1 lemon
- 6 tablespoons extra-virgin olive oil
- Table salt and ground black pepper
- ¼ teaspoon red pepper flakes
- 1 pound campanelle
- 1 cup dry white wine
- 1 ounce grated Parmesan cheese (about ½ cup), plus extra for serving

**1.** Bring the leek greens, asparagus trimmings, 1 cup of the peas, half of the garlic, the broth, and water to simmer in a large saucepan. Reduce the heat to medium-low and simmer gently for 10 minutes. While the broth simmers, combine the mint, chives, and lemon zest in a bowl; set aside.

**2.** Strain the broth through a fine-mesh strainer into a large liquid measuring cup, pressing on the solids to extract as much liquid as possible (you should have 5 cups broth; add water as needed to measure 5 cups). Discard the solids and return the broth to the saucepan. Cover and keep warm.

**3.** Heat 2 tablespoons of the oil in a Dutch oven over medium heat until shimmering. Add the leeks and a pinch salt and cook, covered, stirring occasionally, until the leeks begin to brown, about 5 minutes. Add the asparagus spears and cook until the asparagus is crisp-tender, 4 to 6 minutes. Add the remaining garlic and the red pepper flakes and cook until fragrant, about 30 seconds. Add the remaining 1 cup peas and continue to cook for 1 minute longer. Transfer the vegetables to a plate and set aside. Wipe out the pot.

**4.** Heat the remaining ¼ cup oil in the now-empty pot over medium heat until shimmering. Add the pasta and cook, stirring often, until just beginning to brown, about 5 minutes. Add the wine and cook, stirring constantly, until absorbed, about 2 minutes.

**5.** When the wine is fully absorbed, add the warm broth and bring to a boil. Cook, stirring frequently, until most of the liquid is absorbed and the pasta is al dente, 8 to 10 minutes. Off the heat, stir in half of the herb mixture, the vegetables, lemon juice, and ½ cup of the Parmesan. Season with salt and pepper to taste and serve immediately, passing the additional Parmesan and the remaining herb mixture separately.

## Campanelle with Asparagus, Basil, and Balsamic Glaze

**SERVES** 4 to 6

**WHY THIS RECIPE WORKS** Asparagus is a natural starting point when trying to make a tomato-free vegetarian pasta sauce. Its sweet, vegetable flavor and quick-cooking nature is a terrific match to pasta. But more often than not, asparagus sauces are bland and boring. We wanted to keep it simple but make this dish livelier. First, we focused on how to cook the asparagus. Boiling and steaming diluted the vegetable's grassy flavor, so they were out. Instead, we browned the asparagus in a hot skillet, after cutting it into bite-size pieces, for a sauce that was both quick and flavorful. The asparagus caramelized just a bit, and the heat brought out the flavors of the other ingredients, such as onions, walnuts, and garlic. To finish off the dish, we paired the asparagus with a balance of salty, sweet, and sour ingredients—balsamic vinegar, basil, and pecorino worked well. Campanelle is a frilly trumpet-shaped pasta that pairs nicely with this sauce. If you cannot find it, fusilli works well too. Use a vegetable peeler to shave the cheese.

- Table salt
- 1 pound campanelle
- ¾ cup balsamic vinegar
- 5 tablespoons extra-virgin olive oil
- 1 pound asparagus, tough ends trimmed, thick spears halved lengthwise and cut into 1-inch lengths
- 1 medium red onion, halved and sliced thin (about 1½ cups)
- ½ teaspoon ground black pepper
- ¼ teaspoon red pepper flakes
- 1 cup chopped fresh basil leaves
- 2 ounces Pecorino Romano cheese, shaved (about 1 cup)
- 1 tablespoon juice from 1 lemon

**1.** Bring 4 quarts water to a boil in a large pot. Add 1 tablespoon salt and the pasta to the boiling water and cook, stirring often, until al dente. Reserve ½ cup of the cooking water then drain the pasta and return it to the pot.

**2.** While the pasta is cooking, bring the balsamic vinegar to a boil in an 8-inch skillet over medium-high heat; reduce the heat to medium and simmer gently until reduced to ¼ cup, 15 to 20 minutes.

**3.** Meanwhile, heat 2 tablespoons of the oil in a 12-inch nonstick skillet over high heat until smoking. Add the asparagus, onion, black pepper, red pepper flakes, and ½ teaspoon salt and stir to combine. Cook, without stirring, until the asparagus begins to brown, about 1 minute, then stir and continue to cook, stirring occasionally, until the asparagus is crisp-tender, about 4 minutes longer.

**4.** Add the asparagus mixture, basil, ½ cup of the Pecorino, the lemon juice, and the remaining 3 tablespoons oil to the pasta and toss to combine. Adjust the consistency of the sauce with the reserved pasta cooking water as needed. Serve immediately, drizzling 1 to 2 teaspoons balsamic glaze over individual servings and passing the remaining ½ cup Pecorino separately.

## Pasta with Cauliflower, Bacon, and Bread Crumbs

**SERVES** 4 to 6

**WHY THIS RECIPE WORKS** For an at-home version of pasta with cauliflower, a restaurant favorite, without the mountain of dirty pots and pans, we set out to streamline this recipe. We piled cauliflower florets into an oiled skillet and cooked them just enough to ensure a crisp-tender texture to contrast with the al dente pasta. Cooking the campanelle as we would a risotto—allowing the liquid to slowly absorb into the pasta—meant any of the starches we would otherwise lose after draining would stay in the pot, creating a creamy sauce. Chopped onion and minced fresh thyme established the flavorful base to which we added the uncooked campanelle and just enough chicken broth and white wine to cook the pasta, contributing complex flavor and lush texture. Once the liquid had absorbed, we stirred in the nutty cauliflower florets, plus parsley and lemon for liveliness. A sprinkling of crunchy panko crumbs cooked with salty bacon pieces offered a perfect crispy finish. Farfalle, orecchiette, or gemelli can be substituted for the campanelle. If the pasta seems too dry, stir in up to ¼ cup of hot water.

- 3 slices bacon, cut into ¼-inch pieces
- ½ cup panko bread crumbs
- Table salt and pepper
- 2 tablespoons vegetable oil
- 1 large head cauliflower (3 pounds), cored and cut into 1-inch florets
- 1 onion, chopped fine
- ½ teaspoon minced fresh thyme
- 1 pound campanelle
- 5½ cups chicken broth
- ½ cup dry white wine
- 3 tablespoons minced fresh parsley
- 1 teaspoon lemon juice, plus lemon wedges for serving

**1.** Cook bacon in 12-inch skillet over medium-high heat until crispy, 5 to 7 minutes. Add panko and ¼ teaspoon pepper and cook, stirring frequently, until panko is well browned, 2 to 4 minutes. Transfer panko mixture to bowl and wipe out skillet.

**2.** Heat 5 teaspoons oil in now-empty skillet over medium-high heat until shimmering. Add cauliflower and 1 teaspoon salt; cook, stirring occasionally, until cauliflower is crisp-tender and browned in spots, 10 to 12 minutes. Remove pan from heat and cover to keep warm.

**3.** Heat remaining 1 teaspoon oil in Dutch oven over medium heat until shimmering. Add onion, thyme, and ½ teaspoon salt; cook, stirring frequently, until onion has softened, 4 to 7 minutes. Increase heat to high, add pasta, broth, and wine, and bring to simmer. Cook pasta, stirring frequently, until most of liquid is absorbed and pasta is al dente, 8 to 10 minutes.

**4.** Remove pot from heat; stir in parsley, lemon juice, and cauliflower; and season with salt and pepper to taste. Serve, passing panko mixture and lemon wedges separately.

## Pasta alla Norma

**SERVES** 6 to 8

**WHY THIS RECIPE WORKS** Pasta alla norma is Sicily's most iconic pasta dish. It consists of a lively combination of tender eggplant and robust tomato sauce, which is seasoned with herbs, mixed with al dente pasta, and finished with shreds of salty, milky ricotta salata. The dish gets its name from the epic opera *Norma*; just as the opera is associated with perfection, so too is the hearty pasta. We salted and microwaved the eggplant to quickly draw out its moisture so that it wouldn't absorb too much oil, and we added a secret ingredient, anchovies, to our tomato sauce to give it a deep, savory flavor without any fishiness. We waited until the last minute to combine the eggplant and sauce; this prevented the eggplant from becoming soggy. If coffee filters are not available, food-safe, undyed paper towels can be substituted when microwaving the eggplant. Be sure to remove the eggplant from the microwave immediately so that the steam can escape. For a spicier dish, use the larger amount of pepper flakes.

- 1½ pounds eggplant, cut into ½-inch pieces
- ½ teaspoon table salt, plus salt for cooking pasta
- ¼ cup extra-virgin olive oil, divided
- 4 garlic cloves, minced
- 2 anchovy fillets, rinsed, patted dry, and minced
- ¼–½ teaspoon red pepper flakes
- 1 (28-ounce) can crushed tomatoes
- 6 tablespoons chopped fresh basil
- 1 pound ziti, rigatoni, or penne
- 3 ounces ricotta salata, shredded (1 cup)

**1.** Toss eggplant with salt in bowl. Line entire surface of plate with double layer of coffee filters and lightly spray with vegetable oil spray. Spread eggplant in even layer on coffee filters; wipe out and reserve bowl. Microwave until eggplant is dry and shriveled to one-third of its original size, 8 to 15 minutes (eggplant should not brown). Transfer eggplant immediately to paper towel–lined plate. Let cool slightly.

**2.** Transfer eggplant to now-empty bowl, drizzle with 1 tablespoon oil, and toss gently to coat; discard coffee filters and reserve plate. Heat 1 tablespoon oil in 12-inch nonstick skillet over medium-high heat until shimmering. Add eggplant and cook, stirring occasionally, until well browned and fully tender, about 10 minutes. Remove skillet from heat and transfer eggplant to now-empty plate.

**3.** Add 1 tablespoon oil, garlic, anchovies, and pepper flakes to now-empty skillet and cook using residual heat, stirring constantly, until fragrant and garlic becomes pale golden, about 1 minute (if skillet is too cool to cook mixture, set it over medium heat). Add tomatoes and bring to simmer over medium-high heat. Cook, stirring occasionally, until slightly thickened, 8 to 10 minutes.

**4.** Gently stir in eggplant and cook until heated through and flavors meld, 3 to 5 minutes. Stir in basil and remaining 1 tablespoon oil. Season with salt to taste.

**5.** Meanwhile, bring 4 quarts water to boil in large pot. Add pasta and 1 tablespoon salt and cook, stirring often, until al dente. Reserve ½ cup cooking water, then drain pasta and return it to pot. Add sauce and toss to combine. Adjust consistency with reserved cooking water as needed. Serve, passing ricotta salata separately.

## Pasta with Pesto, Potatoes, and Green Beans

**SERVES 6**

**WHY THIS RECIPE WORKS** We hadn't thought of putting pasta and potatoes in the same dish until we learned that it's the preferred way to serve pesto in Liguria, Italy—the birthplace of the basil sauce. But our initial attempts at the dish needed work. The sauce was slightly grainy and the sharp, raw garlic dominated. Timing was another issue: When everything was cooked together, the green beans could be jarringly crisp and the pasta way too soft—or vice versa. How could we get all the elements of this dish to cook perfectly? The traditional method called for cutting the potatoes into chunks and then, once cooked, vigorously mixing them with the pesto, pasta, and green beans. The agitation sloughed off their corners, which dissolved into the dish, pulling the pesto and cooking water together to form a simple sauce. Simply trading out starchy russets for creamy, waxy red potatoes eliminated graininess and made our sauce smooth. We cooked the potatoes fully, then used the starchy water to cook the pasta. As for the pesto, we toasted the garlic and pine nuts for warm, mellow flavor (then used the same skillet to quickly steam the green beans). We used plenty of pasta water to bring the sauce together. Two tablespoons of butter made it even silkier, and a splash of lemon juice brought all the flavors into focus. If gemelli is unavailable, penne or rigatoni make good substitutes. Use large red potatoes measuring 3 inches or more in diameter.

- ¼ cup pine nuts
- 3 garlic cloves, unpeeled
- 1 pound large red potatoes, peeled and cut into ½-inch pieces
- ½ teaspoon table salt, plus salt for cooking vegetables
- 12 ounces green beans, trimmed and cut into 1½-inch lengths
- 2 cups fresh basil leaves
- 1 ounce Parmesan cheese, grated (½ cup)
- 7 tablespoons extra-virgin olive oil
- 1 pound gemelli
- 2 tablespoons unsalted butter, cut into ½-inch pieces and chilled
- 1 tablespoon lemon juice
- ½ teaspoon pepper

**1.** Toast pine nuts and garlic in 10-inch skillet over medium heat, stirring frequently, until pine nuts are golden and fragrant and garlic darkens slightly, 3 to 5 minutes. Transfer to bowl and let cool. Peel garlic and chop coarse.

**2.** Bring 3 quarts water to boil in large pot. Add potatoes and 1 tablespoon salt and cook until potatoes are tender but still hold their shape, 9 to 12 minutes. Using slotted spoon, transfer potatoes to rimmed baking sheet. (Do not discard water.)

**3.** Meanwhile, bring ½ cup water and ¼ teaspoon salt to boil in now-empty skillet over medium heat. Add green beans, cover, and cook until tender, 5 to 8 minutes. Drain green beans and transfer to sheet with potatoes.

**4.** Process basil, Parmesan, oil, pine nuts, garlic, and salt in food processor until smooth, about 1 minute.

**5.** Add pasta to water in large pot and cook, stirring often, until al dente. Set colander in large bowl. Drain pasta in colander, reserving cooking water in bowl. Return pasta to pot. Add butter, lemon juice, pepper, potatoes and green beans, pesto, and 1¼ cups reserved cooking water and stir vigorously with rubber spatula until sauce takes on creamy appearance. Add additional cooking water as needed to adjust consistency and season with salt and pepper to taste. Serve immediately.

## Linguine allo Scoglio (Linguini with Seafood)

SERVES 6

**WHY THIS RECIPE WORKS** To create a seafood pasta dish with rich, savory seafood flavor in every bite (not just in the pieces of shellfish), we made a sauce with clam juice and four minced anchovies, which fortified the juices shed by the shellfish. Cooking the shellfish in a careful sequence—precooking hardier clams and mussels first and then adding the shrimp and squid during the final few minutes of cooking—ensured that every piece was plump and tender. We parboiled the linguine and then finished cooking it directly in the sauce; the noodles soaked up flavor while shedding starches that thickened the sauce so that it clung well to the pasta. Fresh cherry tomatoes, lots of garlic, fresh herbs, and lemon made for a bright, clean, complex-tasting sauce. For a simpler version of this dish, you can omit the clams and squid and increase the amounts of mussels and shrimp to 1½ pounds each; you'll also need to increase the amount of salt in step 2 to ¾ teaspoon. If you can't find fresh squid, it's available frozen at many supermarkets and typically has the benefit of being precleaned. Bar Harbor makes our favorite clam juice.

- 6 tablespoons extra-virgin olive oil, divided
- 12 garlic cloves, minced
- ¼ teaspoon red pepper flakes
- 1 pound littleneck clams, scrubbed
- 1 pound mussels, scrubbed and debearded
- 1¼ pounds cherry tomatoes (half of tomatoes halved, remaining left whole)
- 1 (8-ounce) bottle clam juice
- 1 cup dry white wine
- 1 cup minced fresh parsley, divided
- 1 tablespoon tomato paste
- 4 anchovy fillets, rinsed, patted dry, and minced
- 1 teaspoon minced fresh thyme
- ½ teaspoon table salt, plus salt for cooking pasta
- 1 pound linguine
- 1 pound extra-large shrimp (21 to 25 per pound), peeled and deveined (see page 523)
- 8 ounces squid, sliced crosswise into ½-inch-thick rings
- 2 teaspoons grated lemon zest, plus lemon wedges for serving

**1.** Heat ¼ cup oil in large Dutch oven over medium-high heat until shimmering. Add garlic and pepper flakes and cook until fragrant, about 1 minute. Add clams, cover, and cook, shaking pan occasionally, for 4 minutes. Add mussels, cover, and continue to cook, shaking pan occasionally, until clams and mussels have opened, 3 to 4 minutes longer. Transfer clams and mussels to bowl, discarding any that haven't opened, and cover to keep warm; leave any broth in pot.

**2.** Add whole tomatoes, clam juice, wine, ½ cup parsley, tomato paste, anchovies, thyme, and salt to pot and bring to simmer over medium-high heat. Reduce heat to medium and cook, stirring occasionally, until tomatoes have started to break down and sauce is reduced by one-third, about 10 minutes.

**3.** Meanwhile, bring 4 quarts water to boil in large pot. Add pasta and 1 tablespoon salt and cook, stirring often, for 7 minutes. Reserve ½ cup cooking water, then drain pasta.

**4.** Add pasta to sauce in Dutch oven and cook over medium heat, stirring gently, for 2 minutes. Reduce heat to medium-low, stir in shrimp, cover, and cook for 4 minutes. Stir in squid, lemon zest, halved tomatoes, and remaining ½ cup parsley; cover and continue to cook until shrimp and squid are just cooked through, about 2 minutes longer. Gently stir in clams and mussels. Remove pot from heat, cover, and let stand until clams and mussels are warmed through, about 2 minutes. Season with salt and pepper to taste, and adjust consistency with reserved cooking water as needed. Transfer to large serving dish, drizzle with remaining 2 tablespoons oil, and serve, passing lemon wedges separately.

## Spanish-Style Toasted Pasta with Shrimp

SERVES 4

**WHY THIS RECIPE WORKS** Paella may be one of the biggest stars of Spanish cooking, but there's another related dish equally deserving of raves: fideuà. This richly flavored dish swaps the rice for thin noodles that are typically toasted until nut-brown before being cooked in a garlicky, tomatoey stock loaded with seafood. Traditional recipes for fideuà can take several hours to prepare. We wanted to speed up the process but keep the deep flavors of the classic recipes. To replace the slow-cooked fish stock of the classics, we made a quick shrimp stock using the shrimp's shells, a combination of chicken broth and water, and a bay leaf. To boost the flavor of the shrimp we marinated it in olive oil, garlic, salt, and pepper. In step 5, if your skillet is not broiler-safe, once the pasta is tender transfer the mixture to a broiler-safe 13 by 9-inch baking dish lightly coated with olive oil; scatter the shrimp over the pasta and stir them in to partially submerge. Broil and serve as directed.

- 3 tablespoons plus 2 teaspoons extra-virgin olive oil, divided
- 3 garlic cloves, minced, divided
- ¾ teaspoon table salt, divided
- ⅛ plus ½ teaspoon pepper, divided
- 1½ pounds extra-large shrimp (21 to 25 per pound), peeled and deveined, shells reserved (see page 523)
- 2¾ cups water
- 1 cup chicken broth
- 1 bay leaf
- 8 ounces spaghettini or thin spaghetti, broken into 1- to 2-inch lengths
- 1 onion, chopped fine
- 1 (14.5-ounce) can diced tomatoes, drained and chopped fine
- 1 teaspoon paprika
- 1 teaspoon smoked paprika
- ½ teaspoon anchovy paste
- ¼ cup dry white wine
- 1 tablespoon chopped fresh parsley
- Lemon wedges
- 1 recipe Aioli (optional) (recipe follows)

**1.** Combine 1 tablespoon oil, 1 teaspoon garlic, ¼ teaspoon salt, and ⅛ teaspoon pepper in medium bowl. Add shrimp, toss to coat, and refrigerate until ready to use.

**2.** Place reserved shrimp shells, water, broth, and bay leaf in medium bowl. Cover and microwave until liquid is hot and shells have turned pink, about 6 minutes. Set aside until ready to use.

**3.** Toss spaghettini and 2 teaspoons oil in broiler-safe 12-inch skillet until spaghettini is evenly coated. Toast spaghettini over medium-high heat, stirring frequently, until browned and nutty in aroma (spaghettini should be color of peanut butter), 6 to 10 minutes. Transfer spaghettini to bowl. Wipe out skillet with paper towel.

**4.** Heat remaining 2 tablespoons oil in now-empty skillet over medium-high heat until shimmering. Add onion and ¼ teaspoon salt; cook, stirring frequently, until onion is softened and beginning to brown around edges, 4 to 6 minutes. Add tomatoes and cook, stirring occasionally, until mixture is thick, dry, and slightly darkened in color, 4 to 6 minutes. Reduce heat to medium and add paprika, smoked paprika, anchovy paste, and remaining garlic. Cook until fragrant, about 1½ minutes. Add spaghettini and stir to combine. Adjust oven rack 5 to 6 inches from broiler element and heat broiler.

**5.** Pour shrimp broth through fine-mesh strainer into skillet. Add wine, remaining ¼ teaspoon salt, and remaining ½ teaspoon pepper and stir well. Increase heat to medium-high and bring to simmer. Cook uncovered, stirring occasionally, until liquid is slightly thickened and spaghettini is just tender, 8 to 10 minutes. Scatter shrimp over spaghettini and stir shrimp into spaghettini to partially submerge. Transfer skillet to oven and broil until shrimp are opaque and surface of spaghettini is dry with crisped, browned spots, 5 to 7 minutes. Remove from oven and let stand, uncovered, for 5 minutes. Sprinkle with parsley and serve immediately, passing lemon wedges and aioli, if using, separately.

### Aioli

**MAKES** ¾ cup

- 2 large egg yolks
- 4 teaspoons lemon juice
- 1 garlic clove, minced to paste
- ¼ teaspoon table salt
- ⅛ teaspoon sugar
- ½ cup vegetable oil
- ¼ cup extra-virgin olive oil

In large bowl, combine egg yolks, lemon juice, garlic, ¼ teaspoon salt, and sugar. Whisking constantly, very slowly drizzle oils into egg mixture until thick and creamy. Season with salt and white pepper to taste.

## Garlicky Shrimp Pasta

**SERVES** 4 to 6

**WHY THIS RECIPE WORKS** In theory, garlic shrimp pasta has all the makings of an ideal weeknight meal—just toss a few quick-cooking ingredients with boiled pasta. In reality, delicate shrimp cooks fast, which translates to overcooked in a matter of seconds. Meanwhile, garlic can become bitter, depending on how it's treated. Add to that the challenge of getting a brothy sauce to coat the pasta, and this simple recipe turns into a precarious balancing act. We wanted al dente pasta and moist shrimp bound by a sauce infused with a deep garlic flavor. For the best flavor and texture, we used quick-frozen, extra-large shrimp and marinated them with minced garlic before a quick sauté in garlic oil. We also cut each shrimp into thirds before cooking to ensure that every bite of pasta had a tasty morsel of shrimp. With sweet low notes from the infused oil and brasher high notes from the garlic, we finally had a balanced garlic flavor. As for the sauce, to deglaze the pan, we preferred the clean taste of vermouth or white wine; bottled clam broth added complexity. Using a chunky tubular pasta instead of traditional linguine made it easy to find the shrimp. To get the sauce to cling to the pasta, we stirred flour into the oil just before adding the vermouth and clam juice and tossed in some cold butter to finish. Marinate the shrimp while you prepare the remaining ingredients. Any short tubular or curly pasta works well here.

- 1 pound extra-large shrimp (21 to 25 per pound), peeled, deveined (see page 523), and each shrimp cut into 3 pieces
- 3 tablespoons olive oil
- 5 medium garlic cloves, minced or pressed through a garlic press (about 5 teaspoons), plus 4 medium garlic cloves, smashed
- Table salt
- 1 pound mezze rigatoni, fusilli, or campanelle
- ¼–½ teaspoon red pepper flakes
- 2 teaspoons unbleached all-purpose flour
- ½ cup dry vermouth or white wine
- ¾ cup clam juice
- ½ cup chopped fresh parsley leaves
- 3 tablespoons unsalted butter, cut into 3 pieces
- 1 teaspoon lemon juice, plus lemon wedges for serving
- Ground black pepper

**1.** Toss the shrimp, 1 tablespoon of the oil, 2 teaspoons of the minced garlic, and ¼ teaspoon salt in a medium bowl. Let the shrimp marinate at room temperature 20 minutes.

**2.** Heat the 4 smashed garlic cloves and the remaining 2 tablespoons oil in a 12-inch skillet over medium-low heat, stirring occasionally, until the garlic is light golden brown, 4 to 7 minutes. Remove the skillet from the heat and use a slotted spoon to remove the garlic from the skillet; discard the garlic. Set the skillet aside.

**3.** Bring 4 quarts water to a boil in a large pot. Add 1 tablespoon salt and the pasta to the boiling water and cook, stirring often, until al dente. Reserve ½ cup of the cooking water then drain the pasta and return it to the pot.

**4.** While the pasta cooks, return the skillet with the oil to medium heat; add the shrimp with the marinade to the skillet in a single layer. Cook the shrimp, undisturbed, until the oil starts to bubble gently, 1 to 2 minutes. Stir the shrimp and continue to cook until almost cooked through, about 1 minute longer. Using a slotted spoon, transfer the shrimp to a medium bowl. Add the remaining 3 teaspoons minced garlic and the red pepper flakes to the skillet and cook until fragrant, about 1 minute. Add the flour and cook, stirring constantly, for 1 minute; stir in the vermouth and cook for 1 minute. Add the clam juice and parsley; cook until the mixture starts to thicken, 1 to 2 minutes. Off the heat, whisk in the butter and lemon juice. Add the shrimp and sauce to the pasta and adjust the consistency of the sauce with the reserved pasta cooking water as needed. Season with black pepper to taste. Serve immediately, passing the lemon wedges separately.

## Shrimp Fra Diavolo with Linguine

**SERVES** 4 to 6

**WHY THIS RECIPE WORKS** Some recipes for shrimp fra diavolo ("brother devil" in Italian) lack depth of flavor, with the star ingredients, shrimp and garlic, contributing little to an acidic, unbalanced tomato sauce. We wanted a classic shrimp fra diavolo with a seriously garlicky, spicy tomato sauce studded with sweet, firm shrimp. For a streamlined procedure that would produce deep flavor, we seared the shrimp first to help them caramelize and enrich their sweetness. Following a brief sear with olive oil, salt, and red pepper flakes—the pepper flakes also benefited from the sear, as they took on toasty, earthy notes—we flambéed the shrimp with cognac. The combined forces of cognac and flame brought out the shrimp's sweet, tender notes and imbued our fra diavolo with the cognac's richness and complexity. We then sautéed the garlic slowly for a mellow nutty flavor and reserved some raw garlic for a last-minute punch of heat and spice. Simmered diced tomatoes and a splash of white wine (balanced by a bit of sugar) completed our perfect fra diavolo in less than 30 minutes. One teaspoon of red pepper flakes will give the sauce a little kick, but you may want to add more depending on your taste.

- Table salt
- 1 pound linguine or spaghetti
- 1 pound large shrimp (31 to 40 per pound), peeled and deveined (see page 523)
- 6 tablespoons extra-virgin olive oil
- 1 teaspoon red pepper flakes, plus more to taste
- ¼ cup cognac or brandy
- 12 medium garlic cloves, minced or pressed through a garlic press (about ¼ cup)
- 1 (28-ounce) can diced tomatoes, drained
- 1 cup dry white wine
- ½ teaspoon sugar
- ¼ cup minced fresh parsley leaves

**1.** Bring 4 quarts water to a boil in a large pot. Add 1 tablespoon salt and the pasta to the boiling water and cook, stirring often, until al dente. Reserve ½ cup of the cooking water then drain the pasta and return it to the pot.

**2.** Meanwhile, toss the shrimp with 2 tablespoons of the oil, ½ teaspoon of the red pepper flakes, and ¾ teaspoon salt. Heat a 12-inch skillet over high heat. Add the shrimp to the skillet in a single layer and cook, without stirring, until the bottoms of the shrimp turn spotty brown, about 30 seconds. Remove the skillet from the heat, flip the shrimp, and add the cognac; wait until the cognac has warmed slightly, about 5 seconds, and return the skillet to high heat. Wave a lit match over the skillet until the cognac ignites, shaking the pan to distribute the flame over the entire pan. When the flames subside (this will take 15 to 30 seconds), transfer the shrimp to a medium bowl and set aside. Let the skillet cool, off the heat, about 2 minutes.

**3.** Add 3 tablespoons more oil and 3 tablespoons of the garlic to the cooled skillet and cook over low heat, stirring constantly, until the garlic becomes sticky and straw colored, 7 to 10 minutes. Add the remaining red pepper flakes, ¾ teaspoon salt, the tomatoes, wine, and sugar, increase the heat to medium-high, and simmer until thickened, about 8 minutes.

**4.** Stir the shrimp with accumulated juices, the remaining 1 tablespoon garlic, and the parsley into the tomato sauce. Simmer until the shrimp have heated through, about 1 minute. Off the heat, stir in the remaining 1 tablespoon oil. Add ½ cup of the tomato sauce (no shrimp) to the pasta; toss to coat and adjust the consistency of the sauce with the reserved pasta cooking water as needed. Serve immediately, topping individual bowls with the sauce and shrimp.

## Shrimp Fra Diavolo

**SERVES 4**

**WHY THIS RECIPE WORKS** Shrimp fra diavolo is a classic Italian American combo of shrimp, tomatoes, garlic, and hot pepper, often served over spaghetti or with crusty bread. But the spices can be so heavy-handed that they completely overwhelm the other flavors, and the fragile shrimp can be overcooked and flavorless, identifiable only by their shape. We wanted to preserve the fiery character of fra diavolo but also heighten the other flavors—particularly the brininess of the shrimp—so that they could stand up to the heat. To build a rich, briny seafood base, we borrowed a technique from shrimp bisque: sautéing the shrimp shells in a little oil until they and the surface of the pan were spotty brown and then deglazing the pan with wine to pick up the flavorful fond. Some canned tomato liquid rounded out our shrimp "stock." To bloom the flavors of our aromatics, we sautéed some garlic, red pepper flakes, oregano, and a couple anchovy fillets for extra-savory (but not fishy) seafood flavor. We added our stock back to the aromatics and used this flavorful sauce to gently poach the shrimp. At the end of cooking, we stirred in some minced pepperoncini and their brine for a boost of tangy heat. Handfuls of chopped basil and parsley added freshness, and a drizzle of fruity extra-virgin olive oil made for a rich finish. If the shrimp you are using have been treated with salt (check the bag's ingredient list), skip the salting in step 1 and add ¼ teaspoon of salt to the sauce in step 3. Adjust the amount of pepper flakes depending on how spicy you want the dish. Serve the shrimp with a salad and crusty bread or over spaghetti. If serving with spaghetti, adjust the consistency of the sauce with some reserved pasta cooking water.

- 1½ pounds large shrimp (26 to 30 per pound), peeled and deveined (see page 523), shells reserved
- Table salt
- 1 (28-ounce) can whole peeled tomatoes
- 3 tablespoons vegetable oil
- 1 cup dry white wine
- 4 garlic cloves, minced
- ½–1 teaspoon red pepper flakes
- ½ teaspoon dried oregano
- 2 anchovy fillets, rinsed, patted dry, and minced
- ¼ cup chopped fresh basil
- ¼ cup chopped fresh parsley
- 1½ teaspoons minced pepperoncini, plus 1 teaspoon brine
- 2 tablespoons extra-virgin olive oil

**1.** Toss shrimp with ½ teaspoon salt and set aside. Pour tomatoes into colander set over large bowl. Pierce tomatoes with edge of rubber spatula and stir briefly to release juice. Transfer drained tomatoes to small bowl and reserve juice. Do not wash colander.

**2.** Heat 1 tablespoon vegetable oil in 12-inch skillet over high heat until shimmering. Add shrimp shells and cook, stirring frequently, until they begin to turn spotty brown and skillet starts to brown, 2 to 4 minutes. Remove skillet from heat and carefully add wine. When bubbling subsides, return skillet to heat and simmer until wine is reduced to about 2 tablespoons, 2 to 4 minutes. Add reserved tomato juice and simmer to meld flavors, 5 minutes. Pour contents of skillet into colander set over bowl. Discard shells and reserve liquid. Wipe out skillet with paper towels.

**3.** Heat remaining 2 tablespoons vegetable oil, garlic, pepper flakes, and oregano in now-empty skillet over medium heat, stirring occasionally, until garlic is straw-colored and fragrant, 1 to 2 minutes. Add anchovies and stir until fragrant, about 30 seconds. Remove from heat. Add drained tomatoes and mash with potato masher until coarsely pureed. Return to heat and stir in reserved tomato juice mixture. Increase heat to medium-high and simmer until mixture has thickened, about 5 minutes.

4. Add shrimp to skillet and simmer gently, stirring and turning shrimp frequently, until they are just cooked through, 4 to 5 minutes. Remove pan from heat. Stir in basil, parsley, and pepperoncini and brine and season with salt to taste. Drizzle with olive oil and serve.

## Creamy Baked Four-Cheese Pasta

**SERVES** 4 to 6

**WHY THIS RECIPE WORKS** We love macaroni and cheese (who doesn't?), but sometimes we want a more sophisticated version. Enter the classic Italian iteration, pasta ai quattro formaggi, made with four cheeses and heavy cream. We set out to make a cheesy, creamy casserole with great flavor, properly cooked pasta, and a crisp bread crumb topping. For the best flavor and texture, we used fontina, Gorgonzola, Pecorino Romano, and Parmesan cheeses. Heating the cheese and cream together made a curdled mess, so instead we built a basic white sauce (a béchamel) by cooking butter with flour and then adding cream. Combining the hot sauce and pasta with the cheese—and not cooking the cheese in the sauce—preserved the flavor of the cheeses. Knowing the pasta would spend time in the oven, we drained it before it was al dente so it wouldn't turn to mush when baked. Topped with bread crumbs and more Parmesan, and baked in a very hot oven, our pasta dinner was silky smooth and rich but not heavy.

- 2 slices high-quality white sandwich bread, torn into quarters
- 1 ounce Parmesan cheese, grated (about ½ cup)
- Table salt and ground black pepper
- 4 ounces Italian fontina cheese, rind removed, shredded (about 1 cup)
- 3 ounces Gorgonzola cheese, crumbled (about ¾ cup)
- 1 ounce Pecorino Romano cheese, grated (about ½ cup)
- 1 pound penne
- 2 teaspoons unsalted butter
- 2 teaspoons unbleached all-purpose flour
- 1½ cups heavy cream

1. Pulse the bread in a food processor to coarse crumbs, about 10 to 15 pulses. Transfer to a small bowl. Stir in ¼ cup of the Parmesan, ¼ teaspoon salt, and ⅛ teaspoon pepper; set aside.

2. Adjust an oven rack to the middle position and heat the oven to 500 degrees.

3. Bring 4 quarts water to a boil in a large pot. Combine the remaining ¼ cup Parmesan and the fontina, Gorgonzola, and Pecorino Romano cheeses in a large bowl; set aside. Add 1 tablespoon salt and the pasta to the boiling water and cook, stirring often.

4. While the pasta is cooking, melt the butter in a small saucepan over medium-low heat. Whisk in the flour until no lumps remain, about 30 seconds. Gradually whisk in the cream, increase the heat to medium, and bring to a boil, stirring occasionally; reduce the heat to medium-low and simmer for 1 minute longer. Stir in ¼ teaspoon salt and ¼ teaspoon pepper; cover and set aside.

5. When the pasta is just shy of al dente, drain it, leaving it slightly wet. Add the pasta to the bowl with the cheeses; immediately pour the cream mixture over, then cover the bowl and let stand for 3 minutes. Uncover the bowl and stir with a rubber spatula, scraping the bottom of the bowl, until the cheeses are melted and the mixture is thoroughly combined.

6. Transfer the pasta to a 13 by 9-inch baking dish, then sprinkle evenly with the reserved bread crumbs, pressing down lightly. Bake until the topping is golden brown, about 7 minutes. Serve immediately.

## Baked Ziti

**SERVES** 8 to 10

**WHY THIS RECIPE WORKS** Baked ziti is the ultimate comfort food, but there are so many ways it can go wrong. First we tackled the sauce by cooking sautéed garlic with canned diced tomatoes and tomato sauce. Fresh basil and dried oregano added aromatic flavor. Then we added ricotta. Rather than baking up creamy and rich as we expected, the it was grainy and dulled the sauce. Cottage cheese proved to be a great replacement—its curds are similar to ricotta, but are creamier and tangier. For more flavor, we combined the cottage cheese with eggs, Parmesan, and heavy cream thickened with cornstarch. When it came to the pasta, we undercooked it and then baked it with a generous amount of sauce for perfectly al dente pasta and plenty of sauce left to keep our baked ziti moist. As for the mozzarella, we cubed it, so that the finished casserole had gooey bits of cheese. We prefer baked ziti made with heavy cream, but whole milk can be substituted by increasing the amount of cornstarch to 2 teaspoons and increasing the cooking time in step 3 by 1 to 2 minutes. Our preferred brand of mozzarella is Polly-O. Part-skim mozzarella can also be used.

- 1 pound (2 cups) whole-milk or 1 percent cottage cheese
- 2 large eggs, lightly beaten
- 3 ounces Parmesan cheese, grated (1½ cups), divided
- 1 pound ziti or other short tubular pasta
- Table salt for cooking pasta
- 2 tablespoons extra-virgin olive oil
- 5 garlic cloves, minced
- 1 (28-ounce) can tomato sauce
- 1 (14.5-ounce) can diced tomatoes
- 1 teaspoon dried oregano
- ½ cup plus 2 tablespoons chopped fresh basil, divided
- 1 teaspoon sugar
- 1 cup heavy cream
- ¾ teaspoon cornstarch
- 8 ounces whole-milk mozzarella cheese, cut into ¼-inch pieces (1½ cups), divided

1. Adjust oven rack to middle position and heat oven to 350 degrees. Whisk cottage cheese, eggs, and 1 cup Parmesan together in medium bowl; set aside. Bring 4 quarts water to boil in large pot. Add pasta and 1 tablespoon salt and cook, stirring occasionally, until pasta begins to soften but is not yet cooked through, 5 to 7 minutes. Drain pasta and leave in colander (do not wash pot).

2. Meanwhile, heat oil and garlic in 12-inch skillet over medium heat until garlic is fragrant but not brown, about 2 minutes. Stir in tomato sauce, diced tomatoes, and oregano; simmer until thickened, about 10 minutes. Off heat, stir in ½ cup basil and sugar; season with salt and pepper to taste.

3. Stir cream and cornstarch together in small bowl; transfer mixture to now-empty pasta pot set over medium heat. Bring to simmer and cook until thickened, 3 to 4 minutes. Remove pot from heat and add cottage cheese mixture, 1 cup tomato sauce, and ¾ cup mozzarella; stir to combine. Add pasta and stir to coat thoroughly with sauce.

4. Transfer pasta to 13 by 9-inch baking dish and spread remaining tomato sauce evenly over pasta. Sprinkle remaining ¾ cup mozzarella and remaining ½ cup Parmesan over top. Cover baking dish tightly with aluminum foil and bake for 30 minutes.

5. Remove foil and continue to cook until cheese is bubbling and beginning to brown, about 30 minutes longer. Let cool for 20 minutes. Sprinkle with remaining 2 tablespoons basil and serve.

## Skillet Baked Ziti

**SERVES 4**

**WHY THIS RECIPE WORKS** Baked ziti, a hearty combination of pasta, tomato sauce, and gooey cheese, can be time-consuming and fussy, between making the sauce, boiling the pasta, and then assembling and baking the dish. We were looking for a method that would give us the same delicious results but in less time and without watching over, or dirtying, a multitude of pots. Instead of preparing the components of the dish separately, we found we could get all our cooking done in a skillet—including the pasta. How? We thinned the sauce with water so that the pasta cooked through in the sauce without drying out. (And the thin sauce reduced to a nicely thick consistency.) To start building the sauce, we sautéed lots of garlic with red pepper flakes, then added crushed tomatoes, water, and the ziti. When the pasta was almost tender (it would finish cooking in the oven), we added some heavy cream, for richness and body, and shredded mozzarella cheese. Parmesan boosted the cheesy flavor, and fresh basil and pepper were all the seasonings we needed to finish our skillet baked ziti. To complete this recipe in 30 minutes, preheat your oven before assembling the ingredients. If your skillet is not ovensafe, transfer the pasta mixture to a shallow 2-quart casserole dish before sprinkling with the cheese and baking. Packaged preshredded mozzarella is a real time-saver here. Penne can be used in place of the ziti.

- 1 tablespoon olive oil
- 6 medium garlic cloves, minced or pressed through a garlic press (about 2 tablespoons)
- ¼ teaspoon red pepper flakes
- Table salt
- 1 (28-ounce) can crushed tomatoes
- 3 cups water
- 12 ounces ziti (3¾ cups)
- ½ cup heavy cream
- 1 ounce Parmesan cheese, grated (about ½ cup)
- ¼ cup minced fresh basil leaves
- Ground black pepper
- 4 ounces whole milk mozzarella cheese, shredded (about 1 cup)

1. Adjust an oven rack to the middle position and heat the oven to 475 degrees.

2. Heat the oil in a 12-inch ovensafe nonstick skillet over medium-high heat until hot. Add the garlic, red pepper flakes, and ½ teaspoon salt and sauté until fragrant, about 1 minute. Add the crushed tomatoes, water, ziti, and ½ teaspoon salt. Cover and cook, stirring often and adjusting the heat as needed to maintain a vigorous simmer, until the ziti is almost tender, 15 to 18 minutes.

3. Stir in the cream, Parmesan, and basil. Season with salt and pepper to taste. Sprinkle the mozzarella evenly over the ziti. Transfer the skillet to the oven and bake until the cheese has melted and browned, about 10 minutes. Using potholders (the skillet handle will be hot), remove the skillet from the oven. Serve.

## Cast Iron Baked Ziti with Charred Tomatoes

**SERVES 4**

**WHY THIS RECIPE WORKS** This skillet-baked ziti puts a new spin on the traditional version by cooking the pasta right in the sauce, streamlining the whole process, and also by using grape tomatoes. The hot cast-iron skillet allowed us to get a nice blistery char on the grape tomatoes, bringing a deep, caramelized flavor to the sauce. We further bolstered the sauce by sautéing garlic, red pepper flakes, and tomato paste with the charred tomatoes. We then mashed everything to a coarse consistency and diluted it with water so that we could cook the ziti right in the sauce. Cooking the ziti in the skillet with the sauce saved us from using an extra pot, and the starch released from the pasta during cooking helped thicken the sauce nicely. We finished the sauce by stirring in basil and Parmesan. We then sprinkled the whole dish with mozzarella and broiled it in the oven. Being able to go from the stovetop to the broiler was another perk of the cast-iron pan, and the dish needed only 5 minutes in the oven for a perfectly melty, browned cheese layer on top. You can substitute penne for the ziti. Do not use fat-free mozzarella here.

- 1½ pounds grape tomatoes
- 1 tablespoon extra-virgin olive oil
- Table salt and pepper
- 6 garlic cloves, minced
- 1 teaspoon tomato paste
- ¼ teaspoon red pepper flakes
- 12 ounces (3¾ cups) ziti
- 3 cups water, plus extra as needed
- 1 ounce Parmesan cheese, grated (½ cup)
- ¼ cup chopped fresh basil
- 4 ounces mozzarella cheese, shredded (1 cup)

**1.** Adjust oven rack 6 inches from broiler element and heat broiler. Heat 12-inch cast-iron skillet over medium heat for 5 minutes. Toss tomatoes with oil and 1 teaspoon salt. Add tomatoes to skillet and cook, stirring occasionally, until lightly charred and blistered, about 10 minutes. Stir in garlic, tomato paste, and pepper flakes and cook until fragrant, about 30 seconds. Off heat, coarsely mash tomatoes using potato masher.

**2.** Stir in pasta and water and bring to boil over medium-high heat. Reduce heat to vigorous simmer, cover, and cook, stirring often, until pasta is tender, 15 to 18 minutes.

**3.** Stir in Parmesan and adjust sauce consistency with extra hot water as needed. Stir in basil and season with salt and pepper to taste. Sprinkle with mozzarella. Transfer skillet to oven and broil until cheese is melted and spotty brown, about 5 minutes. Serve.

## Baked Manicotti

**SERVES** 6 to 8

**WHY THIS RECIPE WORKS** Manicotti is composed of a straightforward collection of ingredients (pasta, cheese, and tomato sauce), but it can be surprisingly fussy to prepare. Blanching, shocking, draining, and stuffing slippery pasta requires patience and time. We wanted an easy-to-prepare recipe that produced great-tasting manicotti. Our biggest challenge was filling the slippery manicotti tubes. We solved the problem by discarding the tubes and spreading the filling onto a pliable lasagna noodle, which we then rolled up. No-boil lasagna noodles were ideal for this method. We used part-skim ricotta as the base of our filling; eggs, Parmesan, and mozzarella cheese added richness, flavor, and structure to the ricotta filling. For a quick and bright sauce, we pureed canned diced tomatoes and simmered them with sautéed garlic and red pepper flakes; then we finished the sauce with fresh basil. We prefer Barilla no-boil lasagna noodles for their delicate texture resembling fresh pasta. Note that Pasta Defino and Ronzoni brands contain only 12 no-boil noodles per package; the recipe requires 16 noodles. The manicotti can be prepared through step 5, covered with a sheet of parchment paper, wrapped in aluminum foil, and refrigerated for up to three days or frozen for up to one month. (If frozen, thaw the manicotti in the refrigerator for one to two days.) To bake, remove the parchment, replace the aluminum foil, and increase the baking time to 1 to 1¼ hours.

**TOMATO SAUCE**

- 2 (28-ounce) cans diced tomatoes
- 2 tablespoons extra-virgin olive oil
- 3 garlic cloves, minced
- ½ teaspoon red pepper flakes (optional)
- ½ teaspoon table salt
- 2 tablespoons chopped fresh basil

**CHEESE FILLING AND PASTA**

- 1½ pounds (3 cups) part-skim ricotta cheese
- 4 ounces Parmesan cheese, grated (2 cups), divided
- 8 ounces whole-milk mozzarella cheese, shredded (2 cups)
- 2 large eggs, lightly beaten
- 2 tablespoons chopped fresh parsley
- 2 tablespoons chopped fresh basil
- ¾ teaspoon table salt
- ½ teaspoon pepper
- 16 no-boil lasagna noodles

**1. FOR THE SAUCE:** Adjust oven rack to middle position and heat oven to 375 degrees. Pulse 1 can tomatoes with their juice in food processor until coarsely chopped, 3 to 4 pulses. Transfer to bowl. Repeat with remaining can of tomatoes.

**2.** Heat oil; garlic; and pepper flakes, if using, in large saucepan over medium heat until fragrant but not brown, 1 to 2 minutes. Stir in tomatoes and salt and simmer until slightly thickened, about 15 minutes. Stir in basil; season with salt to taste.

**3. FOR THE CHEESE FILLING AND PASTA:** Combine ricotta, 1 cup Parmesan, mozzarella, eggs, parsley, basil, salt, and pepper in medium bowl; set aside.

**4.** Pour 2 inches boiling water into 13 by 9-inch broiler-safe baking dish. Slip noodles into water, one at a time, and let them soak until pliable, about 5 minutes, separating them with tip of knife to prevent sticking. Remove noodles from water and place in single layer on clean dish towels. Discard water and dry baking dish.

**5.** Spread bottom of baking dish evenly with 1½ cups sauce. Using spoon, spread ¼ cup cheese mixture evenly onto bottom three-quarters of each noodle (with short side facing you), leaving top quarter of noodle exposed. Roll into tube shape and arrange in baking dish, seam side down. Top evenly with remaining sauce, making certain that pasta is completely covered.

**6.** Cover baking dish tightly with aluminum foil and bake until bubbling, about 40 minutes. Remove baking dish from oven and remove foil. Adjust oven rack 6 inches from broiler element and heat broiler. Sprinkle manicotti evenly with remaining 1 cup Parmesan. Broil until cheese is spotty brown, 4 to 6 minutes. Cool for 15 minutes; cut into pieces and serve.

## Hand-Rolled Meat Ravioli

**SERVES** 4 to 6; makes 36 ravioli

**WHY THIS RECIPE WORKS** Handmade ravioli are a treat usually reserved for dinner at a fine Italian restaurant and seldom made at home. But with our supermalleable dough, you don't need a pasta machine or years of pasta-making experience to make tender yet springy ravioli with a delicious meat filling. This dough relies heavily on egg yolks and oil to provide enough fat to limit gluten development so that the dough can be rolled without springing back. The easy-to-make ground pork filling is bound with bread, egg, and Parmesan and infused with the flavors of lemon, fennel, and garlic. If using King Arthur All-Purpose Flour, which is higher in protein, increase the number of egg yolks to seven. To ensure the proper dough texture, it's important to use large eggs and to weigh the flour if possible. The longer the dough rests in step 2, the easier it will be to roll out. When rolling out the dough, don't add too much flour; it can cause excessive snapback. Though a pasta machine is not necessary, you may use one if you like. This recipe produces square ravioli with three cut edges and one folded edge. If using a fluted pasta wheel to cut, you can trim the folded edge so that all sides match. If you don't have a pot that holds 6 quarts or more, cook the ravioli in two batches; toss the first batch with some sauce in a serving bowl, cover it with foil, and keep it warm in a 200-degree oven while the second batch cooks. Serve with your favorite tomato sauce or use our recipe for Quick Tomato Sauce (page 181).

**PASTA DOUGH**

- 2 cups (10 ounces) all-purpose flour, plus extra as needed
- 2 large eggs plus 6 large yolks
- 2 tablespoons extra-virgin olive oil

**FILLING**

- 2 slices hearty white sandwich bread, torn into small pieces
- 1 ounce Parmesan cheese, grated (½ cup), plus extra for serving
- ¼ cup chicken broth
- 1 large egg
- 2 tablespoons minced fresh parsley
- 2 garlic cloves, minced
- 1 teaspoon table salt
- 1 teaspoon ground fennel
- ¾ teaspoon grated lemon zest
- ½ teaspoon pepper
- ½ teaspoon dry mustard
- 1 pound ground pork

**RAVIOLI**

- 1 large egg white, lightly beaten
- Table salt for cooking pasta

**1. FOR THE PASTA DOUGH:** Process all ingredients in food processor until mixture forms cohesive dough that is barely tacky to touch, about 45 seconds. (If any dough sticks to your fingers, add up to ¼ cup extra flour, 1 tablespoon at a time. Process until flour is fully incorporated after each addition, 10 to 15 seconds, before retesting. If dough doesn't become cohesive, add up to 1 tablespoon water, 1 teaspoon at a time, until it just comes together; process 30 seconds longer.)

**2.** Turn out dough onto dry counter and knead until smooth, 1 to 2 minutes. Shape dough into 6-inch-long cylinder. Wrap in plastic wrap and let rest at room temperature for at least 1 hour or up to 4 hours. Wipe processor bowl clean.

**3. FOR THE FILLING:** Process bread, Parmesan, broth, egg, parsley, garlic, salt, fennel, lemon zest, pepper, and mustard in now-empty processor until paste forms, 10 to 15 seconds, scraping down sides of bowl as needed. Add pork and pulse until mixture is well combined, about 5 pulses. Transfer filling to medium bowl, cover with plastic, and refrigerate until needed.

**4. FOR THE RAVIOLI:** Line rimmed baking sheet with parchment paper. Cut dough cylinder crosswise into 6 equal pieces. Working with 1 piece of dough at a time (keep remaining pieces covered), dust both sides with flour, place cut side down on clean counter, and press into 3-inch square. Using heavy rolling pin, roll into 6-inch square.

5. Dust both sides of 1 dough square lightly with flour. Starting at center of square, roll dough away from you in 1 motion. Return rolling pin to center of dough and roll toward you in 1 motion. Repeat rolling steps until dough sticks to counter and measures roughly 12 inches long. Lightly dust both sides of dough with flour and continue to roll out dough until it measures roughly 20 inches long and 6 inches wide, frequently lifting dough to release it from counter. (If dough firmly sticks to counter and wrinkles when rolled out, carefully lift dough and dust counter lightly with flour.) Transfer dough sheet to prepared baking sheet and cover with plastic. Repeat rolling process with remaining 5 dough squares and transfer to prepared sheet (2 dough sheets per layer; place parchment between layers). Keep dough covered with plastic.

6. Line second baking sheet with parchment. Lay 1 dough sheet on clean counter with long side parallel to counter edge (keep others covered). Trim ends of dough with sharp knife so that corners are square and dough is 18 inches long. Brush bottom half of dough with egg white. Starting 1½ inches from left edge of dough and 1 inch from bottom, deposit 1 tablespoon filling. Repeat placing 1-tablespoon mounds of filling, spaced 1½ inches apart, 1 inch from bottom edge of dough. You should be able to fit 6 mounds of filling on 1 dough sheet.

7. Cut dough sheet at center points between mounds of filling, separating it into 6 equal pieces. Working with 1 piece at a time, lift top edge of dough over filling and extend it so that it lines up with bottom edge. Keeping top edge of dough suspended over filling with your thumbs, use your fingers to press dough layers together, working around each mound of filling from back to front, pressing out as much air as possible before sealing completely.

8. Once all edges are sealed, use sharp knife or fluted pastry wheel to cut excess dough from around filling, leaving ¼- to ½-inch border around each mound (it's not necessary to cut folded edge of ravioli, but you may do so, if desired). Transfer ravioli to prepared baking sheet. Refrigerate until ready to cook. Repeat shaping process with remaining dough and remaining filling. (Dough scraps can be frozen and added to soup.)

9. Bring 6 quarts water to boil in large pot. Add ravioli and 1 tablespoon salt. Cook, maintaining gentle boil, until ravioli are just tender, about 13 minutes. (To test, pull 1 ravioli from pot, trim off corner without cutting into filling, and taste. Return ravioli to pot if not yet tender.) Drain well. Using spider skimmer or slotted spoon, transfer ravioli to warmed bowls or plates. Serve immediately, passing extra Parmesan separately. (Freeze uncooked ravioli in single layer on parchment paper–lined rimmed baking sheet. Transfer to zipper-lock bag and freeze for up to 1 month. Cook frozen ravioli with no change to cooking time.)

## PREPARING RAVIOLI PASTA DOUGH AND FILLING

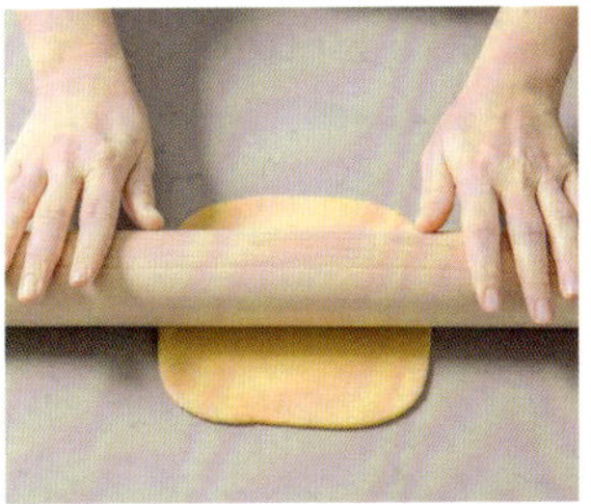

**1.** Cut dough cylinder into 6 equal pieces. Working with 1 piece at a time (keeping remaining pieces covered), dust both sides with flour and roll into 6-inch square.

**2.** Roll from center of dough, dusting with flour if needed, until dough is 6 by 12 inches, lifting frequently to release from counter. Repeat with remaining dough.

**3.** Lay dough sheet on counter, with long side parallel to edge. Trim and brush with egg white. Deposit 6 equally spaced mounds of filling, starting 1½ inches from left edge of dough and placing each mound 1 inch from bottom.

**4.** Cut dough at center points between mounds of filling, separating it into 6 equal pieces. Lift top edge over filling and press to firmly seal in filling, pressing out as much air as possible.

**5.** Once edges are sealed, use knife or fluted pastry wheel to trim excess dough from ravioli.

**6.** Boil, maintaining gentle simmer until ravioli are just tender, about 13 minutes.

## Cheese and Tomato Lasagna

**SERVES 8**

**WHY THIS RECIPE WORKS** While removing both meat and vegetables from lasagna makes it a much simpler affair, it can result in a dish lacking in texture, flavor, and stature. This recipe works by upgrading the basic components—tomato sauce, cheese, and noodles—to star players. Tomato paste, minced anchovies, grated Pecorino Romano, and a dash of sugar boosted the complexity and body of the sauce, while a small can of diced tomatoes added texture to the smoother crushed tomato base. We switched out the usual trio of cheeses for more-flavorful alternatives, replacing ricotta with cottage cheese (mixed into a no-cook sauce with heavy cream, more Pecorino Romano, and seasonings); mozzarella with fontina; and Parmesan with Pecorino Romano. To give the casserole more structure and bite, we used traditional wavy lasagna noodles but treated them like the no-boil variety by briefly soaking them in boiling water. Staggering the noodles in the dish instead of lining them up parallel to one another prevented the casserole from buckling as it baked. Do not substitute no-boil noodles for regular noodles, as they are too thin. For a vegetarian version, omit the anchovies.

**CHEESE SAUCE**

- 4 ounces Pecorino Romano cheese, grated (2 cups)
- 8 ounces (1 cup) cottage cheese
- ½ cup heavy cream
- 2 garlic cloves, minced
- 1 teaspoon cornstarch
- ¼ teaspoon table salt
- ¼ teaspoon pepper

**TOMATO SAUCE**

- ¼ cup extra-virgin olive oil
- 1 onion, chopped fine
- 1½ teaspoons sugar
- ½ teaspoon red pepper flakes
- ½ teaspoon dried oregano
- ½ teaspoon table salt
- 4 garlic cloves, minced
- 8 anchovy fillets, rinsed, patted dry, and minced
- 1 (28-ounce) can crushed tomatoes
- 1 (14.5-ounce) can diced tomatoes, drained
- ¼ cup tomato paste
- 1 ounce Pecorino Romano cheese, grated (½ cup)

**LASAGNA**

- 14 curly-edged lasagna noodles
- 8 ounces fontina cheese, shredded (2 cups)
- ⅛ teaspoon cornstarch
- ¼ cup grated Pecorino Romano cheese
- 3 tablespoons chopped fresh basil

**1. FOR THE CHEESE SAUCE:** Whisk all ingredients in bowl until homogeneous. Set aside.

**2. FOR THE TOMATO SAUCE:** Heat oil in large saucepan over medium heat. Add onion, sugar, pepper flakes, oregano, and salt and cook, stirring frequently, until onions are softened, about 10 minutes. Add garlic and anchovies and cook until fragrant, about 2 minutes. Stir in crushed tomatoes, diced tomatoes, tomato paste, and Pecorino and bring to simmer. Reduce heat to medium-low and simmer until slightly thickened, about 20 minutes.

**3. FOR THE LASAGNA:** While sauce simmers, lay noodles in 13 by 9-inch baking dish and cover with boiling water. Let noodles soak until pliable, about 15 minutes, separating noodles with tip of paring knife to prevent sticking. Place dish in sink, pour off water, and run cold water over noodles. Pat noodles dry with clean dish towel; dry dish. Cut two noodles in half crosswise.

**4.** Adjust oven rack to middle position and heat oven to 375 degrees. Spread 1½ cups tomato sauce in bottom of dish. Lay 3 noodles lengthwise in dish with ends touching 1 short side, leaving space on opposite short side. Lay 1 half noodle crosswise in empty space to create even layer of noodles. Spread half of cheese sauce over noodles, followed by ½ cup fontina. Repeat layering of noodles, alternating which short side gets half noodle (alternating sides will prevent lasagna from buckling). Spread 1½ cups tomato sauce over second layer of noodles, followed by ½ cup fontina. Create third layer using 3½ noodles (reversing arrangement again), remaining cheese sauce, and ½ cup fontina.

**5.** Lay remaining 3½ noodles over cheese sauce. Spread remaining tomato sauce over noodles. Toss remaining ½ cup fontina with cornstarch, then sprinkle over tomato sauce, followed by Pecorino.

**6.** Spray sheet of aluminum foil with vegetable oil spray and cover lasagna. Bake for 35 minutes. Remove lasagna from oven and increase oven temperature to 500 degrees.

**7.** Remove foil from lasagna, return to oven, and continue to bake until top is lightly browned, 10 to 15 minutes longer. Let lasagna cool for 20 minutes. Sprinkle with basil, cut into pieces, and serve.

## Four-Cheese Lasagna

**SERVES 10**

**WHY THIS RECIPE WORKS** Cheese lasagna offers an elegant alternative to meat-laden, red sauce lasagna. Our ideal lasagna was robust with great structure, creamy texture, and maximum flavor. For the best cheese flavor, we settled on a combination of fontina, Parmesan, Gorgonzola, and Gruyère cheeses. We found that making the white sauce (a béchamel) with a high ratio of flour to butter created a binder that kept the lasagna layers together. But the real secret of a great four-cheese lasagna proved to be a fifth cheese: ricotta. It gave the lasagna body without making the dish heavy and starchy. Our final challenge was to keep the baking time short enough to avoid harming this delicate pasta dish. Once the sauce starts bubbling around the edges, uncover the lasagna and turn the oven to broil. If your lasagna pan is not broiler-safe, brown the lasagna at 500 degrees for about 10 minutes. Whole milk is best in the sauce, but skim and low-fat milk also work. We prefer Barilla no-boil lasagna noodles for their delicate texture resembling fresh pasta. Note that Pasta Defino and Ronzoni brands contain only 12 no-boil noodles per package; this recipe requires 15 noodles.

- 6 ounces Gruyère cheese, shredded (about 1½ cups)
- 2 ounces Parmesan cheese, grated (about 1 cup)
- 1½ cups part-skim ricotta cheese
- 1 large egg, lightly beaten
- 2 tablespoons plus 2 teaspoons minced fresh parsley leaves
- ¼ teaspoon ground black pepper
- 3 tablespoons unsalted butter
- 1 medium shallot, minced (about 2 tablespoons)
- 1 medium garlic clove, minced or pressed through a garlic press (about 1 teaspoon)
- ⅓ cup unbleached all-purpose flour
- 2½ cups whole milk
- 1½ cups low-sodium chicken broth
- ½ teaspoon table salt
- 1 bay leaf
- Pinch cayenne pepper
- 15 no-boil lasagna noodles
- 8 ounces fontina cheese, rind removed, shredded (about 2 cups)
- 3 ounces Gorgonzola cheese, crumbled fine (about ¾ cup)

**1.** Place the Gruyère and ½ cup of the Parmesan in a large oven-safe bowl. Combine the ricotta, egg, 2 tablespoons of the parsley, and the black pepper in a medium bowl. Set both bowls aside.

**2.** Melt the butter in a medium saucepan over medium heat; add the shallot and garlic and cook, stirring frequently, until beginning to soften, about 2 minutes. Add the flour and cook, stirring constantly, until thoroughly combined, about 1½ minutes; the mixture should not brown. Gradually whisk in the milk and broth; increase the heat to medium-high and bring to a full boil, whisking frequently. Add the salt, bay leaf, and cayenne; reduce the heat to medium-low and simmer until the sauce thickens and coats the back of a spoon, about 10 minutes, stirring occasionally with a heatproof rubber spatula or wooden spoon and making sure to scrape the bottom and corners of the saucepan.

**3.** Remove the saucepan from the heat and discard the bay leaf. Gradually whisk ¼ cup of the sauce into the ricotta mixture. Pour the remaining sauce over the Gruyère mixture and stir until smooth; set aside.

**4.** Adjust an oven rack to the upper-middle position and heat the oven to 350 degrees. Pour 2 inches boiling water into a 13 by 9-inch broiler-safe baking dish. Slip the noodles into the water, one at a time, and let them soak until pliable, about 5 minutes, separating them with the tip of a knife to prevent sticking. Remove the noodles from the water and place in a single layer on clean kitchen towels. Discard the water, dry the baking dish, and spray lightly with vegetable oil spray.

**5.** Spread the bottom of the baking dish evenly with ½ cup of the sauce. Place 3 noodles in a single layer on top of the sauce. Spread ½ cup of the ricotta mixture evenly over the noodles and sprinkle evenly with ½ cup of the fontina and 3 tablespoons of the Gorgonzola. Drizzle ½ cup of the sauce evenly over the cheese. Repeat the layering of noodles, ricotta, fontina, Gorgonzola, and sauce three more times. Place the final 3 noodles on top and cover completely with the remaining sauce, spreading with a rubber spatula and allowing it to spill over the noodles. Sprinkle evenly with the remaining ½ cup Parmesan.

**6.** Spray a large sheet of foil with vegetable oil spray and cover the lasagna; bake until the edges are just bubbling, 25 to 30 minutes, rotating the pan halfway through the baking time. Remove the foil and turn the oven to broil. Broil until the surface is spotty brown, 3 to 5 minutes. Cool for 15 minutes. Sprinkle with the remaining 2 teaspoons parsley; cut into pieces and serve.

## Spinach Lasagna

**SERVES 8 to 10**

**WHY THIS RECIPE WORKS** Traditional spinach lasagna combines layers of homemade pasta, fresh spinach, béchamel (white sauce), and cheese. For an easier spinach lasagna, we ditched the mozzarella, added cottage cheese, and used no-boil noodles. As for the fresh spinach, the mature curly variety easily stood up to the heat of the oven. Blanching and shocking the spinach allowed it to keep its verdant color and pure flavor. To infuse our luxurious white sauce with flavor, we sautéed a cup of minced shallots and plenty of garlic in butter before whisking in the flour for the roux. Cottage cheese provided pleasing tang and extra creaminess, while nutty fontina replaced bland mozzarella. The real key to our recipe's success was that we parcooked the no-boil noodles by soaking them in boiling water. This cut the baking time down to 20 minutes, which helped the spinach maintain its vibrancy. Italian fontina cheese works best in this dish. If it is not available, substitute whole-milk mozzarella. If your baking dish is not broiler-safe, brown the lasagna at 500 degrees for about 10 minutes.

**SAUCE**

- 1¼ pounds curly-leaf spinach, stemmed
- ½ teaspoon table salt, plus salt for cooking vegetables
- 5 tablespoons unsalted butter
- 6 shallots, minced
- 4 garlic cloves, minced
- ¼ cup all-purpose flour
- 3½ cups whole milk
- 2 bay leaves
- ¾ teaspoon ground nutmeg
- ¼ teaspoon pepper
- 3 ounces Parmesan cheese, grated (1½ cups), divided

**CHEESE FILLING AND PASTA**

- 8 ounces (1 cup) whole-milk cottage cheese
- 1 large egg
- ¼ teaspoon table salt
- 12 no-boil lasagna noodles
- 8 ounces Italian fontina cheese, shredded (2 cups)

**1. FOR THE SAUCE:** Bring 4 quarts water to boil in large pot. Fill large bowl halfway with ice and water. Add spinach and 1 tablespoon salt to boiling water and cook, stirring often, until spinach is just wilted, about 5 seconds. Using slotted spoon, transfer spinach to ice bath and soak until completely cool, about 1 minute; drain spinach and transfer to clean dish towel. Wrap towel tightly around spinach to form ball and wring until dry. Chop spinach and set aside.

**2.** Melt butter in medium saucepan over medium heat. Add shallots and garlic and cook, stirring frequently, until shallots are softened, about 4 minutes. Add flour and cook, stirring constantly, until thoroughly combined, about 1½ minutes; mixture should not brown. Gradually whisk in milk; increase heat to medium-high and bring to boil, whisking often. Stir in bay leaves, nutmeg, pepper, and salt; reduce heat to low; and simmer, whisking occasionally, for 10 minutes. Discard bay leaves, then whisk in ½ cup Parmesan until completely melted. Reserve ½ cup sauce in small bowl; press plastic wrap directly against surface and set aside. Transfer remaining sauce to second bowl and stir in spinach, mixing well to break up any clumps; press plastic directly against surface and set aside.

**3. FOR THE CHEESE FILLING:** Process cottage cheese, egg, and salt in food processor until very smooth, about 30 seconds.

**4. FOR THE PASTA:** Adjust oven rack to middle position and heat oven to 425 degrees. Pour 2 inches boiling water into 13 by 9-inch broiler-safe baking dish. Slip noodles into water, one at a time, and soak until pliable, about 5 minutes, separating noodles with tip of paring knife to prevent sticking. Remove noodles from water and place in single layer on clean dish towels; discard water. Dry and grease dish.

**5.** Spread reserved sauce evenly over bottom of prepared dish. Arrange 3 noodles in single layer on top of sauce. Spread 1 cup spinach mixture evenly over noodles, sprinkle remaining 1 cup Parmesan over spinach mixture, and top cheese with 3 noodles. Spread 1 cup spinach mixture evenly over noodles, sprinkle 1 cup fontina over spinach mixture, and top with 3 noodles. Spread 1 cup spinach mixture evenly over noodles, followed by cheese filling. For final layer, arrange remaining 3 noodles over cheese filling, then cover noodles with remaining spinach mixture. Sprinkle remaining 1 cup fontina over spinach mixture.

**6.** Cover dish tightly with aluminum foil that has been sprayed with vegetable oil spray and bake until edges are just bubbling, about 20 minutes, rotating dish halfway through baking. Remove dish from oven and remove foil. Adjust oven rack 6 inches from broiler element and heat broiler. Broil lasagna until cheese on top becomes spotty brown, 4 to 6 minutes. Let lasagna cool for 15 minutes before serving.

## Vegetable Lasagna

**SERVES** 8 to 10

**WHY THIS RECIPE WORKS** For a complex vegetable lasagna with bold flavor, we started with a summery mix of zucchini, yellow squash, and eggplant. Garlic, spinach, and olives added textural contrast and flavor without much work. We dialed up the typical cheese filling by switching mild-mannered ricotta for tangy cottage cheese mixed with heavy cream for richness and Parmesan and garlic for added flavor. Our creamy, quick no-cook tomato sauce brought enough moisture to our lasagna that we found that we could skip the usual step of soaking the no-boil noodles before assembling the dish. Part-skim mozzarella can also be used in this recipe, but avoid preshredded cheese, as it does not melt well. We prefer kosher salt because it clings best to the eggplant. If using table salt, reduce salt amounts by half. The roasted vegetable filling can be made ahead and stored in the refrigerator for up to one day.

**TOMATO SAUCE**

- 1 (28-ounce) can crushed tomatoes
- ¼ cup minced fresh basil leaves
- 2 tablespoons extra-virgin olive oil
- 2 medium garlic cloves, minced or pressed through a garlic press (about 2 teaspoons)
- 1 teaspoon kosher salt
- ¼ teaspoon red pepper flakes

**CREAM SAUCE**

- 8 ounces whole-milk cottage cheese (about 1 cup)
- 1 cup heavy cream
- 4 ounces Parmesan cheese, grated (about 2 cups)
- 2 medium garlic cloves, minced or pressed through a garlic press (about 2 teaspoons)
- 1 teaspoon cornstarch
- ½ teaspoon kosher salt
- ½ teaspoon ground black pepper

**VEGETABLE FILLING**

- 1½ pounds eggplant, peeled and cut into ½-inch pieces
- Kosher salt and ground black pepper
- 1 pound zucchini, cut into ½-inch pieces

1 pound yellow squash, cut into ½-inch pieces
5 tablespoons plus 1 teaspoon extra-virgin olive oil
4 medium garlic cloves, minced or pressed through a garlic press (about 4 teaspoons)
1 tablespoon minced fresh thyme leaves
12 ounces baby spinach (12 cups)
½ cup pitted kalamata olives, minced
12 ounces whole-milk mozzarella cheese, shredded (about 3 cups)

12 no-boil lasagna noodles
2 tablespoons chopped fresh basil leaves

**1. FOR THE TOMATO SAUCE:** Whisk all the ingredients together in a bowl; set aside.

**2. FOR THE CREAM SAUCE:** Whisk all the ingredients together in a separate bowl; set aside.

**3. FOR THE FILLING:** Adjust an oven rack to the middle position and heat the oven to 375 degrees. Toss the eggplant with 1 teaspoon kosher salt in a large bowl. Line the surface of a large plate with a double layer of coffee filters and lightly spray with vegetable oil spray. Spread the eggplant in an even layer over the coffee filters; wipe out and reserve the bowl. Microwave the eggplant, uncovered, until dry to the touch and slightly shriveled, about 10 minutes, tossing halfway through cooking. Cool slightly. Return the eggplant to the bowl and toss with the zucchini and summer squash.

**4.** Combine 1 tablespoon of the oil, the garlic, and thyme in a small bowl. Heat 2 tablespoons more oil in a 12-inch nonstick skillet over medium-high heat until shimmering. Add half of the eggplant mixture, ¼ teaspoon kosher salt, and ¼ teaspoon pepper and cook, stirring occasionally, until the vegetables are lightly browned, about 7 minutes. Clear the center of the skillet, add half of the garlic mixture, and cook, mashing with a spatula, until fragrant, about 30 seconds. Stir the garlic mixture into the vegetables and transfer to a medium bowl. Repeat with the remaining eggplant mixture, 2 tablespoons more oil, and the remaining garlic mixture; transfer to the bowl.

**5.** Heat the remaining 1 teaspoon oil in the now-empty skillet over medium-high heat until shimmering. Add the spinach and cook, stirring frequently, until wilted, about 3 minutes. Transfer the spinach to a paper towel–lined plate and drain for 2 minutes. Stir into the eggplant mixture.

**6.** Grease a 13 by 9-inch baking dish. Spread 1 cup of the tomato sauce evenly over the bottom of the dish. Arrange 4 noodles on top of the sauce (the noodles will overlap). Spread half of the vegetable mixture over the noodles, followed by half of the olives. Spoon half of the cream sauce over the top and sprinkle with 1 cup of the mozzarella. Repeat the layering with 4 more noodles, 1 cup more tomato sauce, the remaining vegetables, remaining olives, remaining cream sauce and 1 cup more mozzarella. For the final layer, arrange the remaining 4 noodles on top and cover completely with the remaining tomato sauce. Sprinkle with the remaining 1 cup mozzarella.

**7.** Cover the dish tightly with aluminum foil that has been sprayed with vegetable oil spray and bake until the edges are just bubbling, about 35 minutes, rotating the dish halfway through baking. Cool the lasagna for 25 minutes, then sprinkle with the basil and serve.

## Simple Lasagna with Hearty Tomato-Meat Sauce

**SERVES** 6 to 8

**WHY THIS RECIPE WORKS** Traditional meaty lasagna is one of the best comfort foods out there. Unfortunately, this hearty dish takes the better part of a day to make. The noodles must be boiled and the sauce slow-cooked. Then, once the cheese filling is mixed, the ingredients must be carefully layered before the whole thing is baked. We wanted a really good meat lasagna that could be ready in a lot less time. For a meaty tomato sauce, we simmered onion, garlic, and meatloaf mix together for about 15 minutes. Heavy cream created a richer, creamier, more cohesive sauce; we stirred in pureed and diced tomatoes for a luxurious sauce with chunks of tomatoes. Using no-boil lasagna noodles eliminated the tedious process of boiling and draining the pasta. You can substitute equal amounts of 80 percent lean ground beef, ground veal, and ground pork for the meatloaf mix (the total amount of meat should be 1 pound).

**TOMATO-MEAT SAUCE**

1 tablespoon olive oil
1 medium onion, minced
6 medium garlic cloves, minced or pressed through a garlic press (about 2 tablespoons)
1 pound meatloaf mix
½ teaspoon table salt
½ teaspoon ground black pepper
¼ cup heavy cream
1 (28-ounce) can tomato puree
1 (28-ounce) can diced tomatoes, drained

CHEESE FILLING AND PASTA

- 1¾ cups whole-milk or part-skim ricotta cheese
- 2½ ounces Parmesan cheese, grated (about 1¼ cups)
- ½ cup chopped fresh basil leaves
- 1 large egg, lightly beaten
- ½ teaspoon table salt
- ½ teaspoon ground black pepper
- 12 no-boil lasagna noodles
- 1 pound whole-milk mozzarella cheese, shredded (about 4 cups)

**1.** Adjust an oven rack to the middle position and heat the oven to 375 degrees.

**2. FOR THE SAUCE:** Heat the oil in a large Dutch oven over medium heat until shimmering. Add the onion and cook, stirring occasionally, until softened but not browned, about 2 minutes. Add the garlic and cook until fragrant, about 2 minutes. Increase the heat to medium-high and add the meatloaf mix, salt, and pepper; cook, breaking the meat into small pieces with a wooden spoon, until the meat loses its raw color but has not browned, about 4 minutes. Add the cream and simmer, stirring occasionally, until the liquid evaporates and only rendered fat remains, about 4 minutes. Add the tomato puree and diced tomatoes and bring to a simmer; reduce the heat to low and simmer until the flavors have blended, about 3 minutes. Set aside. (The cooled sauce can be refrigerated in an airtight container for up to 2 days; reheat before assembling the lasagna.)

**3. FOR THE CHEESE FILLING:** Combine the ricotta, 1 cup of the Parmesan, the basil, egg, salt, and pepper in a medium bowl; set aside.

**4.** Spread the bottom of a 13 by 9-inch baking dish evenly with ¼ cup of the meat sauce (avoiding large chunks of meat). Place 3 noodles in a single layer on top of the sauce. Spread each noodle evenly with 3 tablespoons of the ricotta mixture and sprinkle the entire layer evenly with 1 cup of the mozzarella cheese. Spread the cheese evenly with 1½ cups of the meat sauce. Repeat the layering of noodles, ricotta, mozzarella, and sauce two more times. Place the remaining 3 noodles on top of the sauce, spread evenly with the remaining sauce, sprinkle with the remaining 1 cup mozzarella, then sprinkle with the remaining ¼ cup Parmesan. Spray a large sheet of foil with vegetable oil spray and cover the lasagna.

**5.** Bake for 15 minutes, then remove the foil. Continue to bake until the cheese is spotty brown and the sauce is bubbling, about 25 minutes longer. Cool the lasagna for 10 minutes; cut into pieces and serve.

## Skillet Lasagna

**SERVES** 4 to 6

**WHY THIS RECIPE WORKS** Lasagna isn't usually a dish you can throw together at the last minute. Even with no-boil noodles, it takes a good amount of time to get the components just right. Our goal was to transform traditional baked lasagna into a stovetop skillet dish without losing any of its flavor or appeal. We built a hearty, flavorful meat sauce with onions, garlic, red pepper flakes, and meatloaf mix (a more flavorful alternative to plain ground beef). Canned diced tomatoes along with tomato sauce provided juicy tomato flavor and a nicely chunky texture. We scattered regular curly-edged lasagna noodles, broken into pieces, over the top of the sauce (smaller pieces are easier to eat). We then diluted the sauce with a little water so that the noodles would cook through. After a 20-minute simmer with the lid on, the pasta was tender, the sauce was properly thickened, and it was time for the cheese. Stirring Parmesan into the dish worked well, but we discovered that the sweet creaminess of ricotta was lost unless we placed it in heaping tablespoonfuls on top of the lasagna. Letting the cheese warm through for several minutes was the final step for this supereasy one-pan dish. Meatloaf mix is a combination of ground beef, pork, and veal, sold prepackaged in many supermarkets. If it's unavailable, use ground beef. A skillet with a tight-fitting lid works best for this recipe. To make this dish a bit richer, sprinkle the lasagna with additional shredded cheese, such as mozzarella or provolone, along with the Parmesan in step 4.

- 1 (28-ounce) can diced tomatoes
- Water
- 1 tablespoon extra-virgin olive oil
- 1 onion, chopped fine
- ½ teaspoon table salt
- 3 garlic cloves, minced
- ⅛ teaspoon red pepper flakes
- 1 pound meatloaf mix
- 10 curly-edged lasagna noodles, broken into 2-inch lengths
- 1 (8-ounce) can tomato sauce
- 1 ounce Parmesan cheese, grated (½ cup), divided, plus extra for serving
- 8 ounces (1 cup) ricotta cheese
- 3 tablespoons chopped fresh basil

1. Pour tomatoes and their juice into 4-cup liquid measuring cup. Add water until mixture measures 4 cups.

2. Heat oil in 12-inch nonstick skillet over medium heat until shimmering. Add onion and salt and cook until onion begins to brown, 6 to 8 minutes. Stir in garlic and pepper flakes and cook until fragrant, about 30 seconds. Add meatloaf mix and cook, breaking apart meat, until no longer pink, about 4 minutes.

3. Scatter noodles over meat but do not stir. Pour diced tomato mixture and tomato sauce over noodles. Cover and bring to simmer. Reduce heat to medium-low and simmer, stirring occasionally, until noodles are tender, about 20 minutes.

4. Remove skillet from heat and stir in all but 2 tablespoons Parmesan. Season with salt and pepper to taste. Dot with heaping tablespoons of ricotta, cover, and let stand off heat for 5 minutes. Sprinkle with basil and remaining 2 tablespoons Parmesan. Serve.

## Turkey Sausage Lasagna

**SERVES** 8 **SEASON 26**

**WHY THIS RECIPE WORKS** This meaty turkey lasagna is destined to become a go-to recipe. We achieved a rich turkey lasagna by using turkey two ways and going big on the cheese. A combination of ground turkey and turkey sausage gave the lasagna lots of savory, herby flavor. And a trio of cheeses—including melty, salty fontina—accounted for the lasagna's creaminess. To give the casserole structure and some bite, we used traditional lasagna noodles but instead of boiling them, we briefly soaked them in boiling water. Using the broiler to brown the lasagna after it baked gave the lasagna a golden-brown topping in just a few minutes. Be sure to use ground turkey, not ground turkey breast (also labeled 99 percent fat-free), in this recipe.

- 1 tablespoon extra-virgin olive oil
- 1 large onion, chopped fine
- 1¼ teaspoons table salt, divided
- 1 pound sweet Italian turkey sausage, casings removed
- 8 ounces ground turkey
- ¾ teaspoon pepper, divided
- 2 tablespoons tomato paste
- 6 garlic cloves, minced
- 2 teaspoon fennel seeds, lightly cracked
- ¼ teaspoon red pepper flakes
- 1 (28-ounce) can crushed tomatoes
- 1 (15-ounce) can tomato sauce
- 1 tablespoon Italian seasoning blend
- 15 curly-edged lasagna noodles
- 1 pound (2 cups) cottage cheese
- 8 ounces block mozzarella cheese, shredded (2 cups), divided
- 4 ounces fontina cheese, shredded (1 cup), divided

1. Heat oil in Dutch oven over medium heat until shimmering. Add onion and 1 teaspoon salt and cook, stirring occasionally, until onion is softened, about 5 minutes. Add turkey sausage, ground turkey, and ½ teaspoon pepper and cook, breaking up meat with wooden spoon, until no longer pink, about 5 minutes.

2. Stir in tomato paste, garlic, fennel seeds, and pepper flakes and cook until fragrant, about 2 minutes. Stir in crushed tomatoes, tomato sauce, and Italian seasoning and bring to simmer. Reduce heat to low, cover, and simmer gently until slightly thickened, about 20 minutes. Season with salt and pepper to taste.

3. While sauce simmers, lay noodles in broiler-safe 13 by 9-inch baking dish and cover with boiling water. Let noodles soak until pliable, about 15 minutes, separating noodles with tip of paring knife occasionally throughout soaking time to prevent sticking. Drain noodles and set aside, patting noodles and now-empty dish dry. Adjust oven rack to middle position and heat oven to 400 degrees.

4. Combine cottage cheese, 1½ cups mozzarella cheese, ½ cup fontina cheese, remaining ¼ teaspoon salt and remaining ¼ teaspoon pepper in bowl; set aside. Combine remaining ½ cup mozzarella cheese and remaining ½ cup fontina cheese in separate bowl; set aside.

5. Spread 1½ cups meat sauce over bottom of now-empty dish. Place 5 noodles side by side over sauce (noodles may overlap slightly), then spread ⅔ cup cottage cheese mixture over top. Repeat layering of meat sauce, noodles, and cottage cheese mixture 2 more times, then top with remaining meat sauce. Sprinkle reserved mozzarella-fontina mixture evenly over top.

6. Spray sheet of aluminum foil with vegetable oil spray and cover lasagna. Bake until sauce is bubbling, about 25 minutes. Remove lasagna from oven and heat broiler element. Discard foil. Broil until cheese is golden, about 3 minutes. Let lasagna cool on wire rack for 15 minutes. Slice and serve.

## Homemade Ricotta Cheese

**MAKES** about 2 pounds (4 cups)

**WHY THIS RECIPE WORKS** Creamy, milky, and luxuriously rich, fresh ricotta bears little-to-no resemblance to the grainy, clumpy cheese sold in supermarkets. The best part of fresh ricotta, however, is how simple it is to make at home. Using fresh homogenized and pasteurized milk yielded the most reliable results because ultrapasteurized or ultra-heat-treated (UHT or long-life) milk wouldn't curdle properly. After lining a colander with butter muslin, we set about curdling a gallon of whole milk, heating it in a Dutch oven with salt. Once the milk reached 185 degrees, we took it off the heat and gently added the curdling agents: lemon juice and distilled white vinegar. Stirring gently and then leaving the mixture alone once the curds appeared allowed the ricotta to fully separate from the whey; adding more vinegar drew out any remaining curds from milky whey, if necessary. To finish, we emptied the pot into the colander to drain and then transferred the ricotta to a bowl to break up the curds and incorporate the whey. For best results, don't stir the milk too hard, and be very gentle with the curds once they form.

- 1/3 cup lemon juice (2 lemons)
- 1/4 cup distilled white vinegar, plus extra as needed
- 1 gallon pasteurized (not ultrapasteurized or UHT) whole milk
- 2 teaspoons table salt

**1.** Line colander with butter muslin or triple layer of cheesecloth and place in sink. Combine lemon juice and vinegar in liquid measuring cup; set aside. Heat milk and salt in Dutch oven over medium-high heat, stirring frequently with rubber spatula to prevent scorching, until milk registers 185 degrees.

**2.** Remove pot from heat and slowly stir in lemon juice mixture until fully incorporated and mixture curdles, about 15 seconds. Let sit undisturbed until mixture fully separates into solid curds and translucent whey, 5 to 10 minutes. If curds do not fully separate and there is still milky whey in pot, stir in extra vinegar, 1 tablespoon at a time, and let sit another 2 to 3 minutes, until curds separate.

**3.** Gently pour mixture into prepared colander. Let sit, undisturbed, until whey has drained from edges of cheese but center is still very moist, about 8 minutes. Working quickly, gently transfer cheese to large bowl, retaining as much whey in center of cheese as possible. Stir well to break up large curds and incorporate whey. Refrigerate ricotta until cold, about 2 hours. Stir cheese before using. (Ricotta can be refrigerated for up to 5 days.)

## Pastitsio

**SERVES 6**

**WHY THIS RECIPE WORKS** Pastitsio is the famous Greek meat and macaroni casserole that features tubular pasta, ground meat, tomato sauce, and a plush blanket of béchamel. We started by treating ground beef with baking soda before cooking, which made it better able to hold on to moisture. Cinnamon, oregano, dried mint, and paprika made the flavor profile distinctly Greek; red wine plus lots of tomato paste added brightness and savoriness. We parcooked ziti (the closest substitute for authentic Greek "number 2" macaroni) in the hot béchamel; doing so hydrated the pasta to ensure that it would be fully cooked after baking, and the pasta's starches helped to thicken the béchamel. Cheese and an egg thickened the rest of the béchamel. Don't use ground beef that's less than 93 percent lean or the dish will be greasy. We like the richness of whole milk for this dish, but you can substitute 2 percent lowfat milk; do not use skim milk. Kasseri is a semifirm sheep's-milk cheese from Greece. If it's unavailable, substitute a mixture of 1½ ounces (¾ cup) grated Pecorino Romano and 3 ounces (¾ cup) shredded provolone, adding ½ cup to the ziti in step 4, ½ cup to the béchamel, and the remaining ½ cup to the top of the béchamel. To accommodate all the components, use a baking dish that is at least 2¼ inches tall.

**MEAT SAUCE**

- 3/4 teaspoon table salt
- 1/4 teaspoon baking soda
- 1 tablespoon plus 1/2 cup water, divided

- 8 ounces 93 percent lean ground beef
- 1 tablespoon vegetable oil
- 1/2 cup finely chopped onion
- 3 garlic cloves, minced
- 1¼ teaspoons ground cinnamon
- 1 teaspoon dried oregano
- 1 teaspoon dried mint
- 1 teaspoon paprika
- 1/8 teaspoon red pepper flakes
- 1/8 teaspoon pepper
- 1/4 cup red wine
- 1/3 cup tomato paste

**BÉCHAMEL AND PASTA**

- 2 tablespoons unsalted butter
- 2 tablespoons all-purpose flour
- 1 garlic clove, minced
- 1/2 teaspoon table salt
- 1/4 teaspoon grated nutmeg
- 1/8 teaspoon pepper
- 4 cups whole milk
- 8 ounces (2½ cups) ziti
- 4 ounces kasseri cheese, shredded (1 cup), divided
- 1 large egg, lightly beaten

**1. FOR THE MEAT SAUCE:** Mix salt, baking soda, and 1 tablespoon water in bowl. Add beef and toss until thoroughly combined. Set aside.

**2.** Heat oil in medium saucepan over medium heat until shimmering. Add onion and cook, stirring frequently, until softened, about 3 minutes. Stir in garlic, cinnamon, oregano, mint, paprika, pepper flakes, and pepper and cook until fragrant, 1 to 2 minutes. Add wine and cook, stirring occasionally, until mixture is thickened, 2 to 3 minutes. Add tomato paste, beef mixture, and remaining ½ cup water and cook, breaking up meat into pieces no larger than ¼ inch with wooden spoon, until beef has just lost its pink color, 3 to 5 minutes. Bring to simmer; cover; reduce heat to low; and simmer for 30 minutes, stirring occasionally. Off heat, season with salt to taste. (Meat sauce can be refrigerated in airtight container for up to 3 days. Heat through before proceeding with step 3.)

**3. FOR THE BÉCHAMEL AND PASTA:** Adjust oven rack to middle position and heat oven to 375 degrees. Spray 8-inch square baking dish with vegetable oil spray and place on rimmed baking sheet. Melt butter in large saucepan over medium heat. Add flour, garlic, salt, nutmeg, and pepper and cook, stirring constantly, until golden and fragrant, about 1 minute. Slowly whisk in milk and bring to boil. Add pasta and return to simmer, stirring frequently to prevent sticking. When mixture reaches simmer, cover and let stand off heat, stirring occasionally, for 15 minutes (pasta will not be fully cooked).

**4.** Using spider skimmer, transfer pasta to prepared dish, leaving excess béchamel in saucepan. Sprinkle ⅓ cup kasseri over pasta and stir to combine. Using spatula, gently press pasta into even layer. Add ⅓ cup kasseri to béchamel and whisk to combine. Whisk egg into béchamel. Spread meat sauce over pasta and, using spatula, spread into even layer. Top with béchamel. Sprinkle remaining kasseri over béchamel. Bake until top of pastitsio is puffed and spotty brown, 40 to 50 minutes. Let cool for 20 minutes. Serve.

## Pasta Frittata with Sausage and Hot Peppers

**SERVES** 6 to 8

**WHY THIS RECIPE WORKS** The classic Neapolitan pasta frittata starts with leftover cooked and sauced pasta and several eggs beaten with salt, pepper, melted lard or butter, and grated Parmigiano-Reggiano cheese. With the right techniques these modest ingredients are transformed into a creamy, golden-brown frittata laced with noodles and small bites of meat or vegetables. Since we rarely find ourselves with leftover pasta, we wanted to find a way to use dried pasta. The solution? Angel hair pasta. We cooked it in the same skillet we used to cook the frittata. By cooking off the water and letting the pasta lightly "fry" after the water evaporated, we were left with a lightly crispy, crunchy crust. We cooked the eggs gently so that the exterior portions didn't overcook and turn rubbery while the interior came up to temperature. We like to serve the frittata warm or at room temperature, with a green salad.

- 8 large eggs
- 1 ounce Parmesan cheese, grated (½ cup)
- 3 tablespoons extra-virgin olive oil
- 3 tablespoons coarsely chopped jarred hot cherry peppers
- 2 tablespoons chopped fresh parsley
- Table salt and pepper
- 8 ounces sweet Italian sausage, casings removed, crumbled
- 2 garlic cloves, sliced thin
- 3 cups water
- 6 ounces angel hair pasta, broken in half
- 3 tablespoons vegetable oil

### MAKING PASTA FRITTATA

**1.** Add water, broken angel hair, and oil to skillet.

**2.** Once pasta is tender, keep cooking until water evaporates and pasta starts sizzling in oil.

**3.** After about 5 minutes, pasta will start to crisp (check progress by lifting up the edge).

**4.** Pour eggs over pasta, then gently pull up top strands to allow eggs to flow into center.

**5.** To brown second side, slide frittata onto plate, invert onto second plate, and return to skillet.

**1.** Whisk eggs, Parmesan, olive oil, cherry peppers, parsley, ½ teaspoon salt, and ½ teaspoon pepper together in large bowl until egg is even yellow color; set aside.

**2.** Cook sausage in 10-inch nonstick skillet over medium heat, breaking up sausage with wooden spoon, until fat renders and sausage is about half cooked, 3 to 5 minutes. Stir in garlic and cook for 30 seconds. Remove skillet from heat. Transfer sausage mixture (some sausage will still be raw) to bowl with egg mixture and wipe out skillet.

3. Bring water, pasta, vegetable oil, and ¾ teaspoon salt to boil in now-empty skillet over high heat, stirring occasionally. Cook, stirring occasionally, until pasta is tender, water has evaporated, and pasta starts to sizzle in oil, 8 to 12 minutes. Reduce heat to medium and continue to cook pasta, swirling pan and scraping under edge of pasta with rubber spatula frequently to prevent sticking (do not stir), until bottom turns golden and starts to crisp, 5 to 7 minutes (lift up edge of pasta to check progress).

4. Using spatula, push some pasta up sides of skillet so entire pan surface is covered with pasta. Pour egg mixture over pasta. Using tongs, lift up loose strands of pasta to allow egg to flow toward pan, being careful not to pull up crispy bottom crust. Cover skillet and continue to cook over medium heat until bottom crust turns golden brown and top of frittata is just set (egg below very top will still be raw), 5 to 8 minutes. Slide frittata onto large plate. Invert frittata onto second large plate and slide it browned side up back into skillet. Tuck edges of frittata into skillet with rubber spatula. Continue to cook second side of frittata until light brown, 2 to 4 minutes longer.

5. Remove skillet from heat and let stand for 5 minutes. Using your hand or pan lid, invert frittata onto cutting board. Cut into wedges and serve.

## Gnocchi alla Romana (Semolina Gnocchi)

**SERVES** 4 to 6

**WHY THIS RECIPE WORKS** Unlike the pillowy dumplings we often associate with gnocchi, Roman-style semolina gnocchi bears a stronger resemblance to polenta. The dough is made from a hearty combination of semolina flour, butter, egg, and cheese. To begin, we whisked flour into hot milk with a touch of woodsy nutmeg. Butter and egg were added to boost the dough's richness. Gruyère added big flavor without watering down the mixture and minced rosemary contributed warm, savory notes. Baking powder promised great lift without compromising the texture. While some traditional recipes stamp out the gnocchi rounds like biscuits, we used a wet measuring cup to portion out the gnocchi onto a tray. Chilling the rounds before baking kept the dumplings from fusing together in the oven. Serve as a side dish or as a light entrée topped with Quick Tomato Sauce (page 181).

- 2½ cups whole milk
- ¾ teaspoon table salt
- Pinch ground nutmeg
- 1 cup (6 ounces) fine semolina flour
- 4 tablespoons unsalted butter
- 1 large egg, lightly beaten
- 1½ ounces Gruyère cheese, shredded (⅓ cup)
- 1 teaspoon minced fresh rosemary
- ½ teaspoon baking powder
- 2 tablespoons grated Parmesan cheese

1. Adjust oven rack to middle position and heat oven to 400 degrees. Heat milk, salt, and nutmeg in medium saucepan over medium-low heat until bubbles form around edges of saucepan. Whisking constantly, slowly add semolina to milk mixture. Reduce heat to low and cook, stirring often with rubber spatula, until mixture forms stiff mass that pulls away from sides when stirring, 3 to 5 minutes. Remove from heat and let cool for 5 minutes.

2. Stir 3 tablespoons butter and egg into semolina mixture until incorporated. (Mixture will appear separated at first but will become smooth and a bit shiny.) Stir in Gruyère, rosemary, and baking powder until incorporated.

3. Fill small bowl with water. Moisten ¼-cup dry measuring cup with water and scoop even portion of semolina mixture. Invert gnocchi onto tray or large plate. Repeat, moistening measuring cup between scoops to prevent sticking. Place tray of gnocchi, uncovered, in refrigerator for 30 minutes. (Gnocchi can be refrigerated, covered, for up to 24 hours.)

4. Rub interior of 8-inch square baking dish with remaining 1 tablespoon butter. Shingle gnocchi in pan, creating 3 rows of 4 gnocchi each. Sprinkle gnocchi with Parmesan. Bake until tops of gnocchi are golden brown, 35 to 40 minutes. Let cool for 15 minutes before serving.

### MAKING SEMOLINA GNOCCHI

1. Slowly whisk semolina into warm milk mixture. Cook over low heat until stiff dough forms. Add butter, egg, cheese, rosemary, and baking powder.

2. Use moistened ¼ cup measure to portion gnocchi, inverting onto tray.

3. Shingle gnocchi in greased 8-inch square dish, then sprinkle with Parmesan and bake.

## Potato Gnocchi with Browned Butter and Sage Sauce

**SERVES 4**

**WHY THIS RECIPE WORKS** Good potato gnocchi are something of a culinary paradox; light, airy pillows created from dense, starchy ingredients. The method is simple: Knead mashed potatoes into a dough with a minimum of flour, shape, and boil for a minute. And yet the potential pitfalls are numerous (lumpy mashed potatoes, too much or too little flour, a heavy hand when kneading, and bland flavor). We wanted a foolproof recipe for impossibly light gnocchi with unmistakable potato flavor. Baking russets (parcooked in the microwave for speed and ease) produced intensely flavored potatoes—an excellent start to our gnocchi base. To avoid lumps, which can cause gnocchi to break apart during cooking, we turned to a ricer for a smooth, supple mash. While many recipes offer a range of flour to use, which ups the chances of overworking the dough (and producing leaden gnocchi), we used an exact amount based on the ratio of potato to flour so that our gnocchi dough was mixed as little as possible. And we found that an egg, while not traditional, tenderized our gnocchi further, delivering delicate pillow-like dumplings. Gnocchi, like many baking recipes, require accurate measurement to achieve the proper texture; it's best to weigh the potatoes and flour. After processing, you may have slightly more than the 3 cups (16 ounces) of potatoes required for this recipe; do not be tempted to use more than 3 cups.

**POTATO GNOCCHI**

- 2 pounds russet potatoes, unpeeled
- 1 large egg, lightly beaten
- ¾ cup plus 1 tablespoon (4 ounces) all-purpose flour
- 1 teaspoon table salt, plus salt for cooking gnocchi

**BROWNED BUTTER AND SAGE SAUCE**

- 4 tablespoons unsalted butter, cut into 4 pieces
- 1 small shallot, minced
- 1 teaspoon minced fresh sage
- 1½ teaspoons lemon juice
- ¼ teaspoon table salt

**1. FOR THE GNOCCHI:** Adjust oven rack to middle position and heat oven to 450 degrees. Poke each potato 8 times with paring knife over entire surface. Place potatoes on plate and microwave until slightly softened at ends, about 10 minutes, flipping potatoes halfway through cooking. Transfer potatoes directly to oven rack and bake until skewer glides easily through flesh and potatoes yield to gentle pressure, 18 to 20 minutes.

**2.** Hold potato with pot holder or dish towel and peel with paring knife. Process potato through ricer or food mill onto rimmed baking sheet. Repeat with remaining potatoes. Gently spread riced potatoes into even layer and let cool for 5 minutes.

**3.** Transfer 3 cups (16 ounces) warm potatoes to large bowl. Using fork, gently stir in egg until just combined. Sprinkle flour and salt over potato mixture. Using fork, gently combine until no pockets of dry flour remain. Press mixture into rough dough, transfer to lightly floured counter and gently knead until smooth but slightly sticky, about 1 minute, lightly dusting counter with flour as needed to prevent sticking.

**4.** Line 2 rimmed baking sheets with parchment paper and dust liberally with flour. Cut dough into 8 pieces. Lightly dust counter with flour. Gently roll 1 piece of dough into ½-inch-thick rope, dusting with flour to prevent sticking. Cut rope into ¾-inch lengths. Hold fork, with tines facing down, in your hand and press side of each piece of dough against ridged surface with your thumb to make indentation in center; roll dough down and off tines to form ridges. Transfer formed gnocchi to prepared sheets and repeat with remaining dough.

**5. FOR THE SAUCE:** Melt butter in 12-inch skillet over medium-high heat, swirling occasionally, until butter is browned and releases nutty aroma, about 1½ minutes. Off heat, add shallot and sage, stirring until shallot is fragrant, about 1 minute. Stir in lemon juice and salt and cover to keep warm.

**6.** Bring 4 quarts water to boil in large pot. Add 1 tablespoon salt. Using parchment paper as sling, add half of gnocchi and cook until firm and just cooked through, about 90 seconds (gnocchi should float to surface after about 1 minute). Remove gnocchi with slotted spoon, transfer to skillet with sauce, and cover to keep warm. Repeat with remaining gnocchi and transfer to skillet. Gently toss gnocchi with sauce to combine; serve.

### MAKING RIDGES ON GNOCCHI

To make ridges on gnocchi, hold fork with tines facing down. Press each dough piece (cut side down) against tines with your thumb to make indentation. Roll dumpling down tines to create ridges on sides.

## Gnocchi à la Parisienne with Arugula, Tomatoes, and Olives

SERVES 4

**WHY THIS RECIPE WORKS** Gnocchi à la Parisienne, the French cousin of Italian potato gnocchi, are made by piping pate a choux (the same dough used to make éclairs and profiteroles) directly into simmering water while cutting off short lengths with a knife, producing tender, ethereal puffs. For the dough,used three large eggs plus equal amounts of water and flour. Two ounces of shredded Gruyère (or Emmentaler) cheese imparted nutty flavor while still keeping the dough light enough to puff. After cooking the lengths of dough, we seared the gnocchi in a hot skillet to brown and puff them to tender, melt-in-your-mouth perfection. To finish, we tossed with sweet tomatoes, briny olives, and peppery arugula dressed with lemon and thyme. You'll need a pastry bag and a ½-inch round tip for this recipe. If these are unavailable, substitute a large zipper-lock bag with one corner snipped off to create a ½-inch opening. For a simpler dish, follow the recipe through step 6 and then toss the sautéed gnocchi with 4 tablespoons of browned butter, 2 teaspoons of minced fresh sage, and a pinch of salt. Or, if you'd prefer, follow the recipe through step 6, plate the sautéed gnocchi on top of a generous layer of Pistou (recipe follows), and serve with extra Parmesan cheese.

- 3 large eggs
- 9 tablespoons unsalted butter, divided
- 1 teaspoon table salt, divided
- ¾ cup (3¾ ounces) all-purpose flour
- 2 ounces Gruyère cheese, shredded (½ cup)
- ⅛ teaspoon pepper
- 20 cherry tomatoes, quartered
- 20 pitted kalamata olives, quartered
- 2 teaspoons minced fresh thyme
- 2 teaspoons lemon juice
- 1½ ounces (1½ cups) baby arugula
- 1 tablespoon minced fresh chives
- Grated Parmesan cheese

**1.** Fit pastry bag with ½-inch round tip. Beat eggs in 2-cup liquid measuring cup.

**2.** Bring ¾ cup water, 4 tablespoons butter, and ¾ teaspoon salt to boil in small saucepan over medium heat, stirring occasionally. As soon as mixture boils, remove saucepan from heat and stir in flour until incorporated. Return saucepan to low heat and cook, stirring constantly, using smearing motion, until mixture looks like shiny, wet sand, about 2 minutes.

**3.** Immediately transfer mixture to food processor. Add Gruyère and pepper and process, with feed tube open, for 10 seconds. With processor running, gradually add eggs in steady stream. When all eggs have been added, scrape down sides of bowl with rubber spatula. Continue to process until smooth, thick, sticky paste forms, about 30 seconds longer.

**4.** Fill prepared pastry bag with warm mixture. Twist top of bag to close and let rest at room temperature for at least 30 minutes or up to 1 hour.

**5.** Lightly grease rimmed baking sheet. Bring 4 quarts water to boil in large Dutch oven. Reduce heat to maintain gentle simmer. Using 1 hand, hold pastry bag at 45-degree angle so tip is about 3 inches away from surface of water and squeeze bag to force dough out of tip. Using paring knife, cut off ¾-inch lengths and let them fall into water. Continue to pipe until 20 to 30 gnocchi are in pot. Simmer until gnocchi float and are slightly firm, about 2 minutes. Using spider skimmer or slotted spoon, transfer gnocchi to prepared sheet. Repeat until all dough is cooked (4 to 6 batches). (If not proceeding immediately, allow gnocchi to cool completely. Transfer to airtight container and refrigerate for up to 3 days. Alternatively, freeze on sheet until solid, then transfer to zipper-lock bag and freeze for up to 2 months; sauté from frozen, adding 1 to 2 minutes to sautéing time.)

**6.** Melt 3 tablespoons butter in 12-inch nonstick skillet over medium heat. Add all gnocchi and shake skillet gently until gnocchi fall into single layer. Cook, tossing every 2 minutes, until gnocchi are golden brown and slightly puffed, about 6 minutes. Return cooked gnocchi to sheet.

**7.** Melt remaining 2 tablespoons butter in now-empty skillet over medium heat. Add tomatoes, olives, thyme, and remaining ¼ teaspoon salt and cook, tossing occasionally, until tomatoes start to soften, about 2 minutes. Add lemon juice and gnocchi to skillet and gently stir until gnocchi are evenly glazed. Off heat, add arugula and stir until it just starts to wilt, about 15 seconds. Top with chives and serve immediately, passing Parmesan separately.

### Pistou

SERVES 4

- 1¼ cups fresh basil leaves
- 1½ ounces Parmesan cheese, grated (¾ cup)
- ½ cup extra-virgin olive oil
- 2 garlic cloves, minced
- 2 anchovy fillets, rinsed, patted dry, and minced
- 1 teaspoon grated lemon zest plus 2 teaspoons juice

Add all ingredients to food processor and process until smooth, about 15 seconds.

## Spinach and Ricotta Gnudi with Tomato-Butter Sauce

SERVES 4

**WHY THIS RECIPE WORKS** Pillowy, verdant gnudi are Italian dumplings created from ricotta and greens, delicately seasoned, and bound with egg and flour and/or bread crumbs. The trick to making them well is water management: Both the cheese and the greens are loaded with moisture, which needs to be removed or the dough will be too difficult to handle or require so much binder that the dumplings will be leaden. We found that "towel-drying" the ricotta sheet drained the cheese in just 10 minutes. A combination of egg whites, flour, and panko bread crumbs bound the mixture into a light, tender

dough. Our sauce was a hybrid of bright tomato sugo and browned butter; we toasted garlic in browning butter and added halved cherry tomatoes, which collapsed, adding their juices to the mix. You can substitute part-skim ricotta for the whole-milk ricotta. You can use either frozen whole-leaf spinach or frozen chopped spinach. Serve with a simple salad.

**GNUDI**

- 12 ounces (1½ cups) whole-milk ricotta cheese
- ½ cup all-purpose flour
- 1 ounce Parmesan cheese, grated (½ cup), plus extra for garnishing
- 1 tablespoon panko bread crumbs
- ¾ teaspoon table salt, plus salt for cooking gnudi
- ½ teaspoon pepper
- ¼ teaspoon grated lemon zest
- 10 ounces frozen whole-leaf spinach, thawed and squeezed dry
- 2 large egg whites, lightly beaten

**SAUCE**

- 4 tablespoons unsalted butter
- 3 garlic cloves, sliced thin
- 12 ounces cherry or grape tomatoes, halved
- 2 teaspoons cider vinegar
- ¼ teaspoon table salt
- ¼ teaspoon pepper
- 2 tablespoons shredded fresh basil

**1. FOR THE GNUDI:** Line rimmed baking sheet with double layer of paper towels. Spread ricotta in even layer over towels; set aside and let sit for 10 minutes. Place flour, Parmesan, panko, salt, pepper, and lemon zest in large bowl and stir to combine. Process spinach in food processor until finely chopped, about 30 seconds, scraping down sides of bowl as needed. Transfer spinach to bowl with flour mixture. Grasp paper towels and fold ricotta in half; peel back towels. Rotate sheet 90 degrees and repeat folding and peeling 2 more times to consolidate ricotta into smaller mass. Using paper towels as sling, transfer ricotta to bowl with spinach mixture. Discard paper towels but do not wash sheet. Add egg whites to bowl and mix gently until well combined.

**2.** Transfer heaping teaspoons of dough to now-empty sheet (you should have 45 to 50 portions). Using your dry hands, gently roll each portion into 1-inch ball.

**3. FOR THE SAUCE:** Melt butter in small saucepan over medium heat. Add garlic and cook, swirling saucepan occasionally, until butter is very foamy and garlic is pale golden brown, 2 to 3 minutes. Off heat, add tomatoes and vinegar; cover and set aside.

**4.** Bring 1 quart water to boil in Dutch oven. Add 1½ teaspoons salt. Using spider skimmer or slotted spoon, transfer all gnudi to water. Return water to gentle simmer. Cook, adjusting heat to maintain gentle simmer, for 5 minutes, starting timer once water has returned to simmer (to confirm doneness, cut 1 dumpling in half; center should be firm).

**5.** While gnudi simmer, add salt and pepper to sauce and cook over medium-high heat, stirring occasionally, until tomatoes are warmed through and slightly softened, about 2 minutes. Divide sauce evenly among 4 bowls. Using spider skimmer or slotted spoon, remove gnudi from pot, drain well, and transfer to bowls with sauce. Garnish with basil and extra Parmesan. Serve immediately.

### MANAGING THE WATER IN GNUDI MAKING

**RICOTTA:** Spread ricotta in even layer over paper towels; set aside for 10 minutes. Grasp paper towels, fold ricotta in half, and peel back towels. Rotate sheet 90 degrees; repeat folding and peeling to turn ricotta into smaller mass.

**SPINACH:** Divide thawed frozen spinach into 3 or 4 portions. Gather 1 portion in your hands and squeeze out as much liquid as possible. Repeat with remaining portions.

## Chilled Soba Noodles with Cucumber, Snow Peas, and Radishes

**SERVES** 4 to 6

**WHY THIS RECIPE WORKS** Soba noodles, made from buckwheat flour or a buckwheat-wheat flour blend, have a chewy texture and nutty flavor and are terrific chilled. After cooking the soba noodles we rinsed them under cold running water to remove excess starch and prevent sticking. We then tossed them with a miso-based dressing, which clung to and flavored the noodles without overpowering their distinct taste. To help keep

the vegetables from collecting at the bottom of the bowl, we cut them into shapes and sizes that would get entwined in the noodles so that they'd incorporate nicely while adding crunch and color. Sprinkling strips of earthy-tasting toasted nori over the top added more texture. Their understated briny taste was the perfect finishing touch to the perfectly cooked noodles; sweet-savory dressing; and cool, crunchy vegetables. Sheets of nori, a dried seaweed that adds a subtle briny umami flavor and crisp texture to this salad, can be found in packets at Asian markets or in the Asian section of the supermarket. Plain pretoasted seaweed snacks can be substituted for the toasted nori, and yellow, red, or brown miso can be substituted for the white miso, if desired. Our favorite soba noodles are Shirakiku Soba Japanese Style Buckwheat Noodles. These chilled noodles pair nicely with salmon, shrimp, tofu, or chicken for lunch or a light dinner.

- 8 ounces dried soba noodles
- 1 (8-inch square) sheet nori (optional)
- 3 tablespoons white miso
- 3 tablespoons mirin
- 2 tablespoons toasted sesame oil
- 1 tablespoon sesame seeds
- 1 teaspoon grated fresh ginger
- ¼–½ teaspoon red pepper flakes
- ⅓ English cucumber, quartered lengthwise, seeded, and sliced thin on bias
- 4 ounces snow peas, strings removed, cut lengthwise into matchsticks
- 4 radishes, trimmed, halved, and sliced into thin half-moons
- 3 scallions, sliced thin on bias

**1.** Bring 4 quarts water to boil in large pot. Stir in noodles and cook according to package directions, stirring occasionally, until noodles are cooked through but still retain some chew. Drain noodles and rinse under cold water until chilled. Drain well and transfer to large bowl.

**2.** Grip nori sheet, if using, with tongs and hold about 2 inches above low flame on gas burner. Toast nori, flipping every 3 to 5 seconds, until nori is aromatic and shrinks slightly, about 20 seconds. If you do not have a gas stove, toast nori on rimmed baking sheet in 275-degree oven until it is aromatic and shrinks slightly, 20 to 25 minutes, flipping nori halfway through toasting. Using scissors, cut nori into four 2-inch strips. Stack strips and cut crosswise into thin strips.

**3.** Combine miso, mirin, oil, 1 tablespoon water, sesame seeds, ginger, and pepper flakes in small bowl and whisk until smooth. Add dressing to noodles and toss to combine. Add cucumber; snow peas; radishes; scallions; and nori, if using, and toss well to evenly distribute. Season with salt to taste, and serve.

## Sesame Noodles with Shredded Chicken

**SERVES** 4 to 6

**WHY THIS RECIPE WORKS** For lunch or dinner on a hot day, cold sesame noodles are unmatched. These toothsome noodles tossed with shreds of tender chicken and fresh sesame sauce are a summertime staple. For this recipe, we set out to avoid sticky noodles, gloppy sauce, and lackluster flavors. We found that rinsing and tossing the noodles (either fresh Chinese noodles or dried spaghetti) with a little sesame oil after cooking prevents a rubbery texture and washes away much of their sticky starch. Boneless, skinless chicken breasts were the obvious choice for easy cooking and shredding, and broiling the meat helped retain the chicken's moisture and flavor. For the sauce, a combination of chunky peanut butter and freshly ground toasted sesame seeds provided nutty, rich flavors. After adding fresh garlic and ginger, as well as soy sauce, rice vinegar, hot sauce, and brown sugar, we achieved the perfect texture by thinning out the sauce with hot water. Although our preference is for fresh Chinese noodles, we found that dried spaghetti works well, too. Because dried pasta swells so much more than fresh pasta during cooking, 12 ounces of dried spaghetti can replace 1 pound of fresh noodles.

- 5 tablespoons soy sauce
- ¼ cup sesame seeds, toasted
- ¼ cup chunky peanut butter
- 2 tablespoons rice vinegar
- 2 tablespoons light brown sugar
- 1 tablespoon minced or grated fresh ginger
- 2 medium garlic cloves, minced or pressed through a garlic press (about 2 teaspoons)
- 1 teaspoon hot sauce
- Hot water
- 1 pound fresh Chinese noodles or 12 ounces dried spaghetti
- 1 tablespoon table salt
- 2 tablespoons toasted sesame oil
- 1½ pounds boneless, skinless chicken breasts, trimmed
- 4 scallions, sliced thin on the bias
- 1 carrot, peeled and shredded

**1.** Process the soy sauce, 3 tablespoons of the sesame seeds, the peanut butter, vinegar, brown sugar, ginger, garlic, and hot sauce together in a blender or food processor until smooth, about 30 seconds. With the machine running, add hot water, 1 tablespoon at a time, until the sauce has the consistency of heavy cream (you should need about 5 tablespoons); set aside.

**2.** Position an oven rack 6 inches from the heating element and heat the broiler.

**3.** Bring 6 quarts water to a boil in a large pot. Add the noodles and salt and cook, stirring often, until tender, about 4 minutes for fresh and 10 minutes for dried. Drain the noodles, rinse them under cold running water until cold, then toss them with the sesame oil.

**4.** Set a wire rack over a foil-lined rimmed baking sheet and lightly coat the rack with vegetable oil spray. Lay the chicken on the rack and broil until lightly browned, 4 to 8 minutes. Flip the chicken over and continue to broil until the thickest part of the breast registers 160 to 165 degrees on an instant-read thermometer, 6 to 8 minutes longer. Transfer the chicken to a carving board and let rest for 5 minutes. Using two forks, shred the chicken into bite-size pieces and set aside.

**5.** Transfer the noodles to a large bowl, add the shredded chicken, sauce, scallions, and carrot and toss to combine. Divide the mixture among individual bowls, sprinkle with the remaining 1 tablespoon sesame seeds, and serve.

## Thai-Style Stir-Fried Noodles with Chicken and Broccolini

SERVES 4

**WHY THIS RECIPE WORKS** Pad see ew is a traditional Thai dish of chewy, lightly charred rice noodles with chicken, crisp broccoli, and moist egg, bound with a sweet and salty soy-based sauce. For our adaptation, we substituted readily available supermarket ingredients for fresh rice noodles, Chinese broccoli, and sweet Thai soy sauce. The flat, generous surface of a 12-inch nonstick skillet worked perfectly for this dish. To achieve the char that characterizes the dish, we eliminated much of the stirring. If you can't find broccolini, you can substitute an equal amount of broccoli, but be sure to trim and peel the stalks before cutting.

**CHILE VINEGAR**

- ⅓ cup white vinegar
- 1 serrano chile, stemmed and sliced into thin rings

**STIR-FRY**

- 2 (6-ounce) boneless, skinless chicken breasts, trimmed and cut against grain into ¼-inch-thick slices
- 1 teaspoon baking soda
- 8 ounces (¼-inch-wide) rice noodles
- ¼ cup vegetable oil
- ¼ cup oyster sauce
- 1 tablespoon plus 2 teaspoons soy sauce
- 2 tablespoons packed dark brown sugar
- 1 tablespoon white vinegar
- 1 teaspoon molasses
- 1 teaspoon fish sauce
- 3 garlic cloves, sliced thin
- 3 large eggs
- 10 ounces broccolini, florets cut into 1-inch pieces, stalks cut on bias into ½-inch pieces (5 cups)

**1. FOR THE CHILE VINEGAR:** Combine vinegar and serrano in bowl. Let stand at room temperature for at least 15 minutes.

**2. FOR THE STIR-FRY:** Combine chicken with 2 tablespoons water and baking soda in bowl. Let sit at room temperature for 15 minutes. Rinse chicken in cold water and drain well.

**3.** Bring 6 cups water to boil. Place noodles in large bowl. Pour boiling water over noodles. Stir, then soak until noodles are almost tender, about 8 minutes, stirring once halfway through soaking. Drain and rinse with cold water. Drain well and toss with 2 teaspoons oil.

**4.** Whisk oyster sauce, soy sauce, sugar, vinegar, molasses, and fish sauce together in bowl.

**5.** Heat 2 teaspoons oil and garlic in 12-inch nonstick skillet over high heat, stirring occasionally, until garlic is deep golden brown, 1 to 2 minutes. Add chicken and 2 tablespoons sauce mixture, toss to coat, and spread chicken into even layer. Cook, without stirring, until chicken begins to brown, 1 to 1½ minutes. Flip chicken and cook, without stirring, until second side begins to brown, 1 to 1½ minutes. Push chicken to 1 side of skillet. Add 2 teaspoons oil to cleared side of skillet. Add eggs to clearing. Using rubber spatula, stir eggs gently and cook until set but still wet. Stir eggs into chicken and continue to cook, breaking up large pieces of egg, until eggs are fully cooked, 30 to 60 seconds. Transfer chicken mixture to bowl.

**6.** Heat 2 teaspoons oil in now-empty skillet until smoking. Add broccolini and 2 tablespoons sauce and toss to coat. Cover skillet and cook for 2 minutes, stirring once halfway through cooking. Remove lid and continue to cook until broccolini is crisp and very brown in spots, 2 to 3 minutes, stirring once halfway through cooking. Transfer broccolini to bowl with chicken mixture.

**7.** Heat 2 teaspoons oil in again-empty skillet until smoking. Add half of noodles and 2 tablespoons sauce and toss to coat. Cook until noodles are starting to brown in spots, about 2 minutes, stirring halfway through cooking. Transfer noodles to bowl with chicken mixture. Repeat with remaining 2 teaspoons oil, noodles, and sauce. When second batch of noodles is cooked, add contents of bowl back to skillet and toss to combine. Cook, without stirring, until everything is warmed through, 1 to 1½ minutes. Transfer to platter and serve immediately, passing chile vinegar separately.

## Japchae (Korean Sweet Potato Starch Noodles with Vegetables and Beef)

SERVES 4

**WHY THIS RECIPE WORKS** Japchae, one of Korea's most popular noodle dishes, is a celebration of colorful vegetables, each of which is cut thin and then lightly sautéed and seasoned separately to preserve its texture and bright color. Briefly blanching and squeezing the spinach and shiitakes before sautéing helped them shed some of their abundant water and collapsed the mushrooms so that they didn't pick up too much oil. Japchae also often includes a bit of beef or pork; thinly slicing, marinating, and sautéing well-marbled boneless short ribs added bites of savory, meaty richness. Dangmyeon, Korea's beloved sweet potato starch noodles, soaked up all the salty-sweet dressing while still retaining their unique springy chew. Korean sweet potato starch noodles are sometimes labeled as japchae noodles or sweet potato starch vermicelli. Do not substitute other noodles or use frozen spinach instead of fresh. Halve lengthwise any scallions wider than ½ inch. To streamline assembly, cut, cover, and refrigerate the vegetables in advance. Serve this dish warm or at room temperature.

- 8 ounces boneless beef short ribs, trimmed
- 2 teaspoons plus ¼ cup soy sauce, divided
- 2 tablespoons plus ¼ teaspoon sugar, divided
- 2¼ teaspoons minced garlic, divided
- 1 teaspoon pepper, divided
- 4¼ teaspoons toasted sesame oil, divided
- 1¾ teaspoons kosher salt, divided
- 1 (10-ounce) bag curly-leaf spinach
- 6 ounces shiitake mushrooms, stemmed and sliced ¼ inch thick
- 8 ounces dangmyeon
- 1¾ teaspoons vegetable oil, divided
- 1 small onion, halved and sliced thin
- 3 scallions, cut into 2-inch pieces
- 2 carrots, peeled and cut into 2- to 2½-inch-long matchsticks (1 cup)
- 1 small red bell pepper, stemmed, seeded, and cut into ⅛-inch-wide strips
- 2 tablespoons sesame seeds, toasted, divided

**1.** Bring 2 quarts water to boil in large pot. Slice beef crosswise ¼ inch thick. Cut slices into ¼-inch-thick strips. Toss beef, 2 teaspoons soy sauce, 2 teaspoons sugar, 2 teaspoons garlic, and ½ teaspoon pepper in bowl until well combined. Add 2 tablespoons soy sauce, 2 teaspoons sugar, 2 teaspoons sesame oil, ½ teaspoon salt, and remaining ½ teaspoon pepper to large bowl.

**2.** Add spinach to boiling water and cook until leaves are just wilted, 5 to 10 seconds. Using spider skimmer or slotted spoon, transfer spinach to colander. Rinse under cold running water until leaves are cool enough to handle, about 30 seconds. Squeeze spinach dry and transfer to cutting board. Return water to boil. Add mushrooms and cook until tender and pliant, about 30 seconds. Using spider skimmer or slotted spoon, transfer mushrooms to colander. Rinse under cold running water until mushrooms are cool, about 1 minute. Squeeze dry and transfer to cutting board.

**3.** Return water to boil. Add dangmyeon and cook, stirring occasionally, until noodles are cooked through but still very chewy, 5 to 8 minutes. Drain noodles in colander and shake to remove excess water. Lift about one-quarter of noodles with tongs and use kitchen shears to cut noodles 8 inches below tongs. Repeat 3 more times with remaining noodles. Transfer noodles to large bowl with soy sauce mixture and toss until noodles are evenly coated. Add spinach to small bowl and use your clean hands to break up into small clumps. Add ¼ teaspoon sesame oil, ¼ teaspoon salt, and remaining ¼ teaspoon garlic and toss with spinach until well combined. Transfer spinach to bowl with noodles.

**4.** Heat ¼ teaspoon vegetable oil, ¼ teaspoon salt, and mushrooms in 10-inch nonstick skillet over medium heat. Cook, stirring frequently, until warmed through but not browned, about 1 minute. Transfer to bowl with noodles. Add onion, scallions, ¼ teaspoon salt, and ½ teaspoon vegetable oil to now-empty skillet and cook, stirring often, until vegetables have lost their raw bite and are crisp but not browned, 3 to 4 minutes. Transfer to bowl with noodles.

**5.** Add carrots, ⅛ teaspoon salt, and ¼ teaspoon vegetable oil to now-empty skillet and cook, stirring constantly, until carrots have lost their raw bite and are crisp but not browned, about 3 minutes. Transfer to bowl with noodles. Add bell pepper, ⅛ teaspoon salt, and ¼ teaspoon vegetable oil to now-empty skillet and cook, stirring constantly, until bell pepper has lost its raw bite and is crisp but not browned, about 1 minute. Transfer to bowl with noodles.

**6.** Increase heat to medium-high and add remaining ½ teaspoon vegetable oil to now-empty skillet. When oil shimmers, add beef and cook, stirring frequently, until cooked through, 3 to 4 minutes. Transfer to bowl with noodles. Let beef rest for 5 minutes. Add 1½ tablespoons sesame seeds, remaining 2 tablespoons soy sauce, remaining 2¼ teaspoons sugar, remaining 2 teaspoons sesame oil, and remaining ¼ teaspoon salt to bowl with noodles. Using your clean hands, toss everything to combine. Mound on serving platter, sprinkle with remaining 1½ teaspoons sesame seeds, and serve.

## Yakisoba (Japanese Stir-Fried Noodles with Beef)

**SERVES** 4 to 6

**WHY THIS RECIPE WORKS** Yakisoba stands out among noodle dishes for its sweet-savory-tangy sauce, tender meat, and hearty vegetables. To start we focused on the beef, coating bite-size strips of flank steak in baking soda and water to tenderize it. Traditionally the dish is seasoned with a Japanese brand of Worcestershire sauce; to mimic it we augmented Worcestershire sauce with ketchup, soy sauce, rice vinegar, and brown sugar. For the vegetable accompaniments to the noodles, sliced shiitakes and carrot cooked in chicken broth were a traditional choice. Sliced napa cabbage and grassy scallions cooked quickly, followed by the beef. A sprinkling of our Sesame-Orange Spice Blend brought the flavors home. If you can find yakisoba noodles, follow the same cooking directions for the lo mein noodles. Garnish the noodles with pickled ginger and our Sesame-Orange Spice Blend, or, if you can find it, commercial shichimi togarashi.

- ⅛ teaspoon baking soda
- 12 ounces flank steak, trimmed, sliced lengthwise into 2- to 2½-inch strips, each strip sliced crosswise ¼ inch thick
- ¼ cup ketchup
- ¼ cup soy sauce
- 2 tablespoons Worcestershire sauce
- 1½ tablespoons packed brown sugar
- 3 garlic cloves, minced
- 3 anchovy fillets, rinsed, patted dry, and minced
- 1 teaspoon rice vinegar
- 1 pound fresh or 8 ounces dried lo mein noodles
- 1 tablespoon vegetable oil
- 6 ounces shiitake mushrooms, stemmed and sliced ¼ inch thick
- 1 carrot, peeled and sliced ⅛ inch thick on bias
- ¾ cup chicken broth
- 6 cups napa cabbage, sliced crosswise into ½-inch strips
- 7 scallions, cut on bias into 1-inch lengths
- Table salt

**1.** Combine 1 tablespoon water and baking soda in medium bowl. Add beef and toss to coat. Let sit at room temperature for 5 minutes.

**2.** Whisk ketchup, soy sauce, Worcestershire, sugar, garlic, anchovies, and vinegar together in second bowl. Stir 2 tablespoons sauce into beef mixture and set aside remaining sauce.

**3.** Bring 4 quarts water to boil in large pot. Add noodles and cook, stirring often, until almost tender (center should still be firm with slightly opaque dot), 3 to 10 minutes (cooking time will vary depending on whether you are using fresh or dry noodles). Drain noodles and rinse under cold running water until water runs clear. Drain well and set aside.

**4.** Heat ½ teaspoon oil in 12-inch nonstick skillet over high heat until just smoking. Add mushrooms and carrot and cook, stirring occasionally, until vegetables are spotty brown, 2 to 3 minutes. Add ¼ cup broth and cook until all liquid has evaporated and vegetables are tender, about 30 seconds. Transfer vegetables to bowl.

**5.** Return skillet to high heat, add ½ teaspoon oil, and heat until just smoking. Add cabbage and scallions and cook, without stirring, for 30 seconds. Cook, stirring occasionally, until cabbage and scallions are spotty brown and crisp-tender, 2 to 3 minutes. Transfer to bowl with mushrooms and carrot.

**6.** Return skillet to high heat, add 1 teaspoon oil, and heat until just smoking. Add half of beef in single layer. Cook, without stirring, for 30 seconds. Continue to cook, stirring occasionally, until beef is spotty brown, 1 to 2 minutes. Transfer to bowl with vegetables. Repeat with remaining beef and remaining 1 teaspoon oil.

**7.** Return skillet to high heat; add reserved sauce, remaining ½ cup broth, and noodles. Cook, scraping up any browned bits, until noodles are warmed through, about 1 minute. Transfer noodles to bowl with vegetables and beef and toss to combine. Season with salt to taste, and serve immediately.

### Sesame-Orange Spice Blend

**MAKES** ¼ cup

In addition to garnishing our stir-fry, this blend makes a great seasoning for eggs, rice, and fish. Store for up to one week.

- ¾ teaspoon grated orange zest
- 2 teaspoons sesame seeds
- 1½ teaspoons paprika
- 1 teaspoon pepper
- ¼ teaspoon garlic powder
- ¼ teaspoon ground ginger
- ⅛ teaspoon cayenne pepper

Place orange zest in small bowl and microwave, stirring every 20 seconds, until zest is dry and no longer clumping together, 1 minute 30 seconds to 2 minutes 30 seconds. Stir in sesame seeds, paprika, pepper, garlic powder, ginger, and cayenne.

## Beef Ho Fun

**SERVES** 4 to 6

**WHY THIS RECIPE WORKS** Beef ho fun is a foundational recipe in Cantonese cooking, but for such a simple dish of noodles, there are a lot of things to get right. We tossed the beef in a cornstarch slurry to keep it velvety and tender when cooked, and we stirred together a simple but balanced sauce of soy sauce, oyster sauce, Shaoxing wine, a bit more cornstarch, and pepper. To keep all the components from sticking together in a gummy mass, we cooked them all separately: first the beef; then the vegetables; and finally the noodles, which we tossed over high heat to achieve the perfect amount of char. This dish is everything you'd want in a stir-fried noodle: savory rice noodles, crunchy veg, and tender wok-fried beef, served up hot and fast. Fresh ho fun noodles (sometimes labeled chow fun) are wide, flat rice noodles; do not substitute other types of fresh or dried noodles. If ho fun noodles are stuck together out of the package, place them on a plate and cover with a wet paper towel. Microwave at 50 percent power 20 seconds at a time until the noodles pull apart.

- 6 ounces flank steak, trimmed
- 1 tablespoon water
- ¼ teaspoon baking soda
- 5 teaspoons soy sauce, divided
- 1 tablespoon oyster sauce, divided
- 1 tablespoon Shaoxing wine, divided
- 1 teaspoon cornstarch
- ¼ teaspoon white pepper
- 2 teaspoons dark soy sauce
- 12 ounces fresh ho fun noodles
- 2 tablespoons vegetable oil, divided
- 6 ounces (3 cups) bean sprouts
- ½ small onion, sliced ¼ inch thick
- 2 garlic cloves, minced
- 1 teaspoon grated fresh ginger
- 3 scallions, green parts only, cut into 1½-inch pieces

**1.** Cut beef with grain into 2½- to 3-inch-wide strips. Transfer to plate and freeze until firm, about 15 minutes. Slice strips crosswise against grain ¼ inch thick. Combine water and baking soda in medium bowl. Add beef and toss to coat; let sit for 5 minutes.

**2.** Whisk 2 teaspoons soy sauce, 1 teaspoon oyster sauce, 1 teaspoon Shaoxing wine, cornstarch, and white pepper together in large bowl. Add beef mixture, toss to coat, and let sit at room temperature for 30 minutes.

**3.** Whisk remaining 1 tablespoon soy sauce, remaining 2 teaspoons oyster sauce, remaining 2 teaspoons Shaoxing wine, and dark soy sauce together in small bowl. Using your fingers, unfurl noodles and transfer to rimmed baking sheet; set sauce and noodles aside.

**4.** Heat empty 14-inch flat-bottomed wok over high heat until just beginning to smoke. Drizzle 1 tablespoon oil around perimeter of wok and heat until just smoking. Add beef mixture and cook, tossing slowly but constantly, until just beginning to brown, about 2 minutes; transfer to clean bowl. Wipe wok clean with damp paper towels.

**5.** Heat now-empty wok over high heat until just beginning to smoke. Drizzle 1½ teaspoons oil around perimeter of wok and heat until just smoking. Add bean sprouts, onion, garlic, and ginger and cook, tossing slowly but constantly, until vegetables begin to soften and lightly char, about 1 minute; transfer to bowl with beef.

**6.** Heat now-empty wok over high heat until just beginning to smoke. Drizzle remaining 1½ teaspoons oil around perimeter of wok and heat until just smoking. Add noodles and cook, tossing gently but constantly, until beginning to char, about 1 minute. Add beef mixture and scallions and toss gently to combine. Drizzle reserved soy sauce mixture around perimeter of hot wok and cook, tossing gently to coat noodles, about 30 seconds. Serve.

## Beijing-Style Meat Sauce and Noodles

**SERVES 6**

**WHY THIS RECIPE WORKS** This easy-to-make and deeply satisfying one-dish meal is based on a popular dish from northern China, zha jiang mian. Our version calls for red miso paste and soy sauce in place of ground bean sauce and a combination of hoisin, molasses, and soy sauce as a substitute for sweet bean sauce. We mixed a baking soda solution into the ground pork to keep it moist and tender. Shiitake mushrooms added even more meaty depth to the dish. We spooned the sauce over chewy lo mein noodles and finished it off with bean sprouts, cucumber matchsticks, and scallion greens for a crisp, fresh contrast. We prefer red miso in this recipe. You can use white miso, but the color will be lighter and the flavor milder. You can substitute 8 ounces of dried linguine for the lo mein noodles, if desired, but be sure to follow the cooking time listed on the package. For a presentation similar to that of zha jiang mian, bring the bowl to the table before tossing the noodles in step 5.

- 8 ounces ground pork
- ⅛ teaspoon baking soda
- 5 tablespoons red miso paste
- 5 tablespoons soy sauce
- 3 tablespoons hoisin sauce
- 1 tablespoon molasses
- 8 scallions, white and light green parts cut into ½-inch pieces, dark green parts sliced thin on bias
- 2 garlic cloves, peeled
- 1 (½-inch) piece ginger, peeled and sliced into ⅛-inch rounds
- 4 ounces shiitake mushrooms, stemmed and sliced ½ inch thick
- 1 tablespoon vegetable oil
- 1 pound fresh lo mein noodles
- ½ English cucumber, unpeeled, cut into 2½-inch-long matchsticks (2 cups)
- 6 ounces (3 cups) bean sprouts

**1.** Toss pork, 2 teaspoons water, and baking soda in bowl until thoroughly combined. Let stand for 5 minutes. Whisk ½ cup water, miso paste, soy sauce, hoisin, and molasses together in second bowl.

**2.** Pulse white and light green scallion parts, garlic, and ginger in food processor until coarsely chopped, 5 to 10 pulses, scraping down sides of bowl as needed. Add mushrooms and pulse until mixture is finely chopped, 5 to 10 pulses.

**3.** Heat oil and pork mixture in large saucepan over medium heat for 1 minute, breaking up meat with wooden spoon. Add mushroom mixture and cook, stirring frequently, until mixture is dry and just begins to stick to saucepan, 5 to 7 minutes. Add miso mixture to saucepan and bring to simmer. Cook, stirring occasionally, until mixture thickens, 8 to 10 minutes. Cover and keep warm while noodles cook.

**4.** Bring 4 quarts water to boil in large pot. Add noodles and cook, stirring often, until almost tender (center should still be firm with slightly opaque dot), 3 to 5 minutes. Drain noodles and transfer to wide, shallow serving bowl.

5. Ladle sauce over center of noodles and sprinkle with cucumber, sprouts, and dark green scallion parts. Toss well and serve.

## Pork Lo Mein

**SERVES 4**

**WHY THIS RECIPE WORKS** We wanted a dish representative of some of the best lo mein: chewy noodles tossed in a salty-sweet sauce and accented with bits of smoky barbecued pork and still-crisp cabbage. First we tackled the pork. We wanted to evoke the flavors of char siu in a stir-fried preparation, since we were already stir-frying the vegetables. Country-style pork ribs won for best cut. Though fatty, these meaty ribs have the same rich flavor of pork shoulder—but don't need to be cooked for hours since they're naturally tender. To avoid an overly greasy dish, we trimmed the fat and cut the meat into thin strips that would allow our flavorful marinade to penetrate effectively. A few drops of liquid smoke mimicked char siu's characteristic smoky flavor. Turning to the noodles, ones labeled "lo mein" at the market won raves. Dried linguine, cooked to al dente, also worked beautifully. For the vegetables, we opted for traditional choices—cabbage, scallions, and shiitake mushrooms—stir-frying them with garlic and fresh ginger. We used our meat marinade as a sauce base, with a little chicken broth and a teaspoon of cornstarch added for body. A cast-iron skillet created the best sear on the pork. If boneless pork ribs are unavailable, substitute 1½ pounds bone-in country-style ribs, followed by the next-best option, pork tenderloin. It is important to cook the noodles at the last minute to avoid clumping.

- 3 tablespoons soy sauce
- 2 tablespoons oyster-flavored sauce
- 2 tablespoons hoisin sauce
- 1 tablespoon toasted sesame oil
- ¼ teaspoon Chinese five-spice powder
- 1 pound boneless country-style pork ribs, trimmed of fat and gristle, sliced crosswise into ⅛-inch pieces
- ¼ teaspoon liquid smoke (optional)
- ½ cup low-sodium chicken broth
- 1 teaspoon cornstarch
- 2 tablespoons plus 1 teaspoon peanut or vegetable oil
- 2 teaspoons minced or grated fresh ginger
- 2 medium garlic cloves, minced or pressed through a garlic press (about 2 teaspoons)
- ¼ cup Chinese rice cooking wine (Shaoxing) or dry sherry
- 8 ounces shiitake mushrooms, stemmed, wiped clean, caps sliced ¼ inch thick
- 2 bunches scallions, whites sliced thin, greens cut into 1-inch pieces
- 1 pound napa cabbage (1 small head), cored and cut into ½-inch strips
- 12 ounces fresh Chinese noodles or 8 ounces dried linguine
- 1 tablespoon Asian chili-garlic sauce

1. Whisk the soy sauce, oyster-flavored sauce, hoisin sauce, sesame oil, and five-spice powder together in a small bowl. Transfer 3 tablespoons of the mixture to a medium bowl and add the pork and liquid smoke (if using). Let marinate for at least 10 minutes or up to 1 hour. Whisk the broth and cornstarch into the remaining soy sauce mixture and set aside. In a small bowl, mix 1 teaspoon of the peanut oil, the ginger, and garlic together and set aside.

2. Heat 2 teaspoons more peanut oil in a 12-inch nonstick or cast-iron skillet over high heat until just smoking. Add half of the pork, break up any clumps, then cook without stirring until the meat is browned at the edges, about 1 minute. Stir the pork and continue to cook until cooked through, about 1 minute longer. Add 2 tablespoons of the wine to the skillet and cook, stirring constantly, until the liquid is reduced and the pork is well coated, 30 to 60 seconds. Transfer the pork to a clean bowl and cover with foil to keep warm. Repeat with 2 teaspoons more peanut oil, the remaining pork, and the remaining 2 tablespoons wine. Wipe out the skillet with a wad of paper towels.

3. Add 1 teaspoon more peanut oil to the skillet and return to high heat until just smoking. Add the mushrooms and cook, stirring occasionally, until light golden brown, 4 to 6 minutes. Add the scallion whites and greens and cook, stirring occasionally, until wilted, 2 to 3 minutes. Transfer the vegetables to the bowl with the pork.

4. Add the remaining 1 teaspoon peanut oil to the skillet and heat over high heat until just smoking. Add the cabbage and cook, stirring occasionally, until spotty brown, 3 to 5 minutes. Clear the center of the skillet, add the ginger mixture, and cook, mashing the mixture into the pan, until fragrant, 15 to 20 seconds. Stir the ginger mixture into the cabbage.

5. Stir in the vegetables and pork with any accumulated juices. Whisk the sauce to recombine, then add to the skillet and cook, tossing constantly, until the sauce is thickened, about 30 seconds.

6. Bring 6 quarts water to a boil in a large pot. Add the noodles and cook, stirring often, until tender, about 4 minutes for fresh and 10 minutes for dried. Drain the noodles and

return them to the pot. Add the cooked stir-fry mixture and the chili-garlic sauce to the noodles and toss to combine. Transfer to a serving platter and serve.

## Dan Dan Mian (Sichuan Noodles with Chili Sauce and Pork)

SERVES 4

**WHY THIS RECIPE WORKS** Sichuan's popular street food consists of chewy noodles bathed in a spicy, fragrant chili sauce and topped with crispy, savory bits of pork and plump lengths of baby bok choy. Gently heating Sichuan chili powder, ground Sichuan peppercorns, and cinnamon in vegetable oil yielded a flavorful chili oil base for the sauce. For ultracrispy pieces of pork, we smeared ground pork into a thin layer across the wok, broke it up into bits, and gave it a hard sear. Stirring in minced garlic and grated ginger, plus a scoop of the Sichuan pickle called ya cai, added unique tang and complexity. Boiling the noodles in the bok choy blanching water was efficient, and thoroughly rinsing the noodles after they were cooked washed away starch that would cause them to stick together. If you can't find Sichuan chili powder, substitute Korean red pepper flakes (gochugaru). Sichuan peppercorns provide a tingly, numbing sensation important to the dish; find them in the spice aisle at Asian markets. We prefer the chewy texture of fresh, eggless Chinese wheat noodles here. If they aren't available, substitute fresh lo mein or ramen noodles or 8 ounces of dried lo mein noodles. Ya cai, Sichuan preserved mustard greens, gives these noodles a savory and pungent boost; you can buy it online or at an Asian market. If ya cai is unavailable, omit it and increase the soy sauce in step 2 to 2 teaspoons. This dish can be served warm or at room temperature.

**SAUCE**

- ¼ cup vegetable oil
- 1 tablespoon Sichuan chili powder
- 2 teaspoons Sichuan peppercorns, ground fine
- ¼ teaspoon ground cinnamon
- 2 tablespoons soy sauce
- 2 teaspoons Chinese black vinegar or balsamic vinegar
- 2 teaspoons sweet wheat paste or hoisin sauce
- 1½ teaspoons Chinese sesame paste or tahini

**NOODLES**

- 8 ounces ground pork
- 2 teaspoons Shaoxing wine or dry sherry
- 1 teaspoon soy sauce
- 2 small heads baby bok choy (3 ounces each)
- 1 tablespoon vegetable oil, divided
- 3 garlic cloves, minced
- 2 teaspoons grated fresh ginger
- 1 pound fresh Chinese wheat noodles
- ⅓ cup ya cai
- 2 scallions, sliced thin on bias

**1. FOR THE SAUCE:** Heat oil, chili powder, peppercorns, and cinnamon in 14-inch wok or 12-inch nonstick skillet over low heat for 10 minutes. Using rubber spatula, transfer oil mixture to bowl (do not wash wok). Whisk soy sauce, vinegar, wheat paste, and sesame paste into oil mixture. Divide evenly among 4 shallow bowls.

**2. FOR THE NOODLES:** Bring 4 quarts water to boil in large pot. While water comes to boil, combine pork, Shaoxing wine, and soy sauce in medium bowl and toss with your hands until well combined. Set aside. Working with 1 head bok choy at a time, trim base (larger leaves will fall off) and halve lengthwise through core. Rinse well.

**3.** Heat 2 teaspoons oil in now-empty wok over medium-high heat until shimmering. Add reserved pork mixture and use rubber spatula to smear into thin layer across surface of wok. Break up meat into ¼-inch chunks with edge of spatula and cook, stirring frequently, until pork is firm and well browned, about 5 minutes. Push pork mixture to far side of wok and add garlic, ginger, and remaining 1 teaspoon oil to cleared space. Cook, stirring constantly, until garlic mixture begins to brown, about 1 minute. Stir to combine pork mixture with garlic mixture. Remove wok from heat.

**4.** Add bok choy to boiling water and cook until leaves are vibrant green and stems are crisp-tender, about 1 minute. Using slotted spoon or spider skimmer, transfer bok choy to plate; set aside. Add noodles to boiling water and cook, stirring often, until almost tender (center should still be firm with slightly opaque dot). Drain noodles. Rinse under hot running water, tossing with tongs, for 1 minute. Drain well.

**5.** Divide noodles evenly among prepared bowls. Return wok with pork to medium heat. Add ya cai and cook, stirring frequently, until warmed through, about 2 minutes. Spoon equal amounts of pork topping over noodles. Divide bok choy evenly among bowls, shaking to remove excess moisture as you portion. Top with scallions and serve, leaving each diner to stir components together before eating.

## Chili Crisp Noodles

**SERVES** 4 to 6 **SEASON 26**

**WHY THIS RECIPE WORKS** This streamlined weeknight recipe was inspired by the Sichuan street food dan dan mian. It features a chili sauce, savory pork, springy noodles, and tender bok choy. We skipped the made-from-scratch chili oil. Instead of cooking the fried pork topping and blanching green vegetables for the topping separately, we cooked the ground pork and bok choy together, creating the noodle topping in one pan. We highly recommend using LAOGANMA Spicy Chili Crisp in the recipe. If using other brands, try to find a neutral one that has onion or garlic for crunch but does not include fermented black beans. We prefer the chewy texture of fresh noodles that are about ⅛ inch thick, but if they are unavailable, substitute 8 ounces of dried Chinese wheat noodles or spaghetti and increase the cooking time to 6 to 10 minutes. A rasp-style grater helps to quickly turn the garlic into a paste. A mortar and pestle is the best tool for grinding a small amount of Sichuan peppercorns. If you only have a spice grinder, grind a larger amount and measure out a heaping ¼ teaspoon for this recipe.

**CHILI CRISP SAUCE AND NOODLES**

- ½ teaspoon Sichuan peppercorns
- ⅓ cup unsweetened natural peanut butter
- ⅓ cup soy sauce
- 3 tablespoons Chinese black vinegar
- ¼ cup chili crisp, plus extra for serving
- 2 tablespoons sugar
- 2 garlic cloves, minced to paste
- 1 teaspoon grated fresh ginger
- 1 pound fresh Chinese wheat noodles

**PORK AND BOK CHOY TOPPING**

- 1 tablespoon vegetable oil
- 8 ounces ground pork
- 1 pound baby bok choy, stalks sliced thin crosswise, greens cut into ¾-inch pieces
- 2 scallions, white and green parts separated and sliced thin
- 2 tablespoons Shaoxing wine
- 2 tablespoons soy sauce
- ½ teaspoon sugar

**1. FOR THE SAUCE AND NOODLES:** Grind Sichuan peppercorns using mortar and pestle until finely ground; transfer to medium bowl. Whisk in peanut butter and soy sauce until fully incorporated, then whisk in vinegar until combined. Add chili crisp, sugar, garlic, and ginger and whisk to combine; set aside. (Sauce should be thick enough to coat a spoon, add 1 to 2 tablespoons water to thin out sauce if needed. Sauce can be refrigerated for up to 1 week.)

**2.** Bring 4 quarts water to boil in large pot. Add noodles; reduce heat to maintain very gentle simmer, and cook, stirring occasionally, until almost tender (center of noodles should be firm with slightly opaque dot), 3 to 5 minutes. Drain noodles in colander then rinse under running water. Drain well. Transfer noodles to bowl with ¾ cup sauce, tossing to coat.

**3. FOR THE TOPPING:** While water comes to boil, heat oil in 12-inch nonstick skillet over medium-high heat until shimmering. Add pork and cook until browned, breaking up meat into small pieces, 5 to 7 minutes. Add bok choy stalks and scallion whites and cook, stirring constantly, for 1 minute.

**4.** Stir in bok choy greens, Shaoxing wine, soy sauce, and sugar, stirring to coat pork and bok choy. Reduce heat to medium and cook until bok choy greens are wilted, about 1 minute. Remove from heat.

**5.** To serve, divide noodles among individual serving bowls. Top with pork mixture then sprinkle with scallion greens. Serve with remaining chili crisp sauce and extra chili crisp, mixing each bowl well before eating.

## Singapore Noodles

**SERVES** 4 to 6

**WHY THIS RECIPE WORKS** This dish is actually native to Hong Kong but it's called Singapore noodles for the rice noodles that are used. Along with the traditional Chinese flavorings of garlic, ginger, and soy sauce, the dish features curry powder, which was brought to Southeast Asia by the British. The spice mixture lends the dish a pervasive aroma and a pleasant chile burn. "Blooming" the spice mix by cooking it in hot oil released lots of complex flavor. This had the added benefit of allowing the spice granules to disperse, eliminating grittiness. A spoonful of sugar dispelled lingering bitter notes. We cut the noodles after soaking to make them less tangle-prone, cut the shrimp into ½-inch pieces that distributed nicely throughout the noodles, and bulked up the protein and vegetables by adding eggs, scallion, and bean sprouts. Look for dried rice vermicelli in the Asian section of the supermarket. A rasp-style grater helps to quickly turn the garlic into a paste.

- 4 tablespoons plus 1 teaspoon vegetable oil
- 2 tablespoons curry powder
- ⅛ teaspoon cayenne pepper (optional)
- 6 ounces rice vermicelli
- 2 tablespoons soy sauce
- 1 teaspoon sugar
- 12 ounces large shrimp (26 to 30 per pound), peeled, deveined (see page 523), tails removed, and cut into ½-inch pieces
- 4 large eggs, lightly beaten
- Table salt
- 1 teaspoon grated fresh ginger
- 3 garlic cloves, minced to paste
- 1 red bell pepper, stemmed, seeded, and cut into 2-inch-long matchsticks
- 2 large shallots, sliced thin
- ⅔ cup chicken broth
- 4 ounces (2 cups) bean sprouts
- 4 scallions, cut into ½-inch pieces
- 2 teaspoons lime juice, plus lime wedges for serving

**1.** Heat 3 tablespoons oil, curry powder, and cayenne (if using) in 12-inch nonstick skillet over medium-low heat, stirring occasionally, until fragrant, about 4 minutes. Remove skillet from heat and set aside.

**2.** Bring 6 cups water to boil. Place noodles in large bowl. Pour boiling water over noodles and stir briefly. Soak noodles until flexible, but not soft, about 2½ minutes, stirring once halfway through. Drain noodles briefly; do not wash bowl. Transfer noodles to cutting board. Using chef's knife, cut pile of noodles roughly into thirds. Return noodles to bowl, add curry mixture, soy sauce, and sugar; using tongs, toss until well combined. Set aside.

**3.** Wipe out skillet with paper towels. Heat 2 teaspoons oil in skillet over medium-high heat until shimmering. Add shrimp in even layer and cook without moving until bottom is browned, about 90 seconds. Stir and continue to cook until just cooked through, about 90 seconds longer. Push shrimp to one side of skillet. Add 1 teaspoon oil to cleared side of skillet. Add eggs to clearing, and sprinkle with ¼ teaspoon salt. Using rubber spatula, stir eggs gently until set but still wet, about 1 minute. Stir eggs into shrimp and continue to cook, breaking up large pieces of egg, until eggs are fully cooked, about 30 seconds longer. Transfer shrimp-egg mixture to second large bowl.

**4.** Lower heat to medium. Heat remaining 1 teaspoon oil in now-empty skillet until shimmering. Add ginger and garlic and cook, stirring constantly, until fragrant, about 15 seconds. Add bell pepper and shallots. Cook, stirring frequently, until vegetables are crisp-tender, about 2 minutes. Transfer to bowl with shrimp.

**5.** Return again-empty skillet to medium-high heat, add chicken broth to skillet, and bring to simmer. Add noodles and cook, stirring frequently, until liquid is absorbed, about 2 minutes. Add noodles to bowl with shrimp and vegetable mixture and toss to combine. Add bean sprouts, scallions, and lime juice, and toss to combine. Transfer to warmed platter and serve immediately, passing lime wedges separately.

## Wor Tip (Pork and Cabbage Dumplings)

**MAKES** 2 dumplings

**WHY THIS RECIPE WORKS** For our version of wor tip, Cantonese potstickers, we wanted a light filling, the right wrapper, and the perfect mix of flavors. In addition to the pork and cabbage, we wanted dumplings spiked with garlic, ginger, and soy sauce. Using ready-made wrappers streamlined the process. To lighten up the filling a bit, we increased the amount of cabbage, after first salting and draining it to get rid of excess moisture, and then added lightly beaten egg whites. A sequence of browning, steaming, then cranking up the heat produced potstickers with a perfect balance of soft and crispy textures. We recommend that you serve the first batch immediately, then cook the second batch.

**SCALLION DIPPING SAUCE**

- ¼ cup soy sauce
- 2 tablespoons rice vinegar
- 2 tablespoons mirin or sweet sherry
- 2 tablespoons water
- 1 teaspoon chili oil (optional)
- ½ teaspoon toasted sesame oil
- 1 scallion, minced

**POTSTICKERS**

- 12 ounces napa cabbage (½ medium head), cored and minced
- ¾ teaspoon table salt
- 12 ounces ground pork
- 4 scallions, minced
- 2 large egg whites, lightly beaten
- 4 teaspoons soy sauce
- 1½ teaspoons minced or grated fresh ginger
- 1 medium garlic clove, minced or pressed through a garlic press (about 1 teaspoon)
- ⅛ teaspoon ground black pepper
- 24 round gyoza wrappers
- 4 teaspoons peanut or vegetable oil

**1. FOR THE SAUCE:** Combine all the ingredients in a small bowl and set aside. (The sauce can be refrigerated in an airtight container for up to 24 hours.)

**2. FOR THE FILLING:** Toss the cabbage and salt together in a colander set over a bowl and let sit until the cabbage begins to wilt, about 20 minutes. Press the cabbage gently with a rubber spatula to squeeze out excess moisture, then transfer to a medium bowl. Stir the pork, scallions, egg whites, soy sauce, ginger, garlic, and pepper into the cabbage until combined. Cover and refrigerate until the mixture is cold, at least 30 minutes or up to 24 hours.

**3.** Working with 4 wrappers at a time (keep the remaining wrappers covered with plastic wrap), follow the photos on page 244 to fill, seal, and shape the dumplings using a generous 1 tablespoon of the chilled filling per dumpling. Transfer the dumplings to a baking sheet. (The filled dumplings can be refrigerated for up to 24 hours in a single layer on a baking sheet wrapped tightly with plastic wrap or frozen for up to 1 month. Once frozen, the dumplings can be transferred to a zipper-lock bag to save space in the freezer; do not thaw before cooking.)

**4.** Brush 2 teaspoons of the peanut oil over the bottom of a 12-inch nonstick skillet and arrange half of the dumplings in the skillet, with a flat side facing down (overlapping just slightly, if necessary). Place the skillet over medium-high heat and cook the dumplings, without moving, until golden brown on the bottom, about 5 minutes.

**5.** Reduce the heat to low, add ½ cup water, and cover immediately. Cook until most of the water is absorbed and the wrappers are slightly translucent, about 10 minutes. Uncover, increase the heat to medium-high, and cook, without stirring, until the dumpling bottoms are well browned and crisp, 3 to 4 minutes. Slide the dumplings from the skillet onto a paper towel–lined plate, browned side down, and let drain briefly.

**6.** Transfer the dumplings to a platter and serve with the sauce. Let the skillet cool until just warm, then wipe out the skillet with a wad of paper towels and repeat with the remaining peanut oil and dumplings.

## Chinese Pork Dumplings

**MAKES** 40 dumplings

---

**WHY THIS RECIPE WORKS** Chinese dumplings are as much fun to make as they are to eat. Our dough has just two ingredients—boiling water and flour—and is easy to roll out and remains moist. For the filling, we started with ground pork, mixing in vegetable oil and sesame oil to mimic the richness of the fatty pork shoulder that is traditionally used. Soy sauce, ginger, Shaoxing wine, hoisin sauce, and white pepper added flavor to the meat, and cabbage and scallions contributed subtle crunch. To shape the dumplings, we developed a simpler two-pleat approach that achieved the appearance and functionality of a traditional multipleat crescent. To ensure even browning, we brushed a cold nonstick skillet with oil and snugly arranged 16 dumplings in it before turning on the heat. For dough that has the right moisture level, we strongly recommend weighing the flour. For an accurate measurement of boiling water, bring a full kettle of water to a boil and then measure out the desired amount. To ensure that the dumplings seal completely, use minimal flour when kneading, rolling, and shaping so that the dough remains slightly tacky. Keep all the dough covered with a damp towel except when rolling and shaping. There is no need to cover the shaped dumplings. A shorter, smaller-diameter rolling pin works well here, but a conventional pin will also work.

**DOUGH**

- 2½ cups (12½ ounces) all-purpose flour
- 1 cup boiling water

**FILLING**

- 5 cups 1-inch napa cabbage pieces
- 1 teaspoon table salt, divided
- 12 ounces ground pork
- 1½ tablespoons soy sauce, plus extra for dipping
- 1½ tablespoons toasted sesame oil
- 1 tablespoon vegetable oil, plus 2 tablespoons for pan-frying (optional)
- 1 tablespoon Shaoxing wine or dry sherry
- 1 tablespoon hoisin sauce
- 1 tablespoon grated fresh ginger
- ¼ teaspoon white pepper
- 4 scallions, chopped fine
- Chinese black vinegar or unseasoned rice vinegar
- Chili oil

**1. FOR THE DOUGH:** Place flour in food processor. With processor running, add boiling water. Continue to process until dough forms ball and clears sides of bowl, 30 to 45 seconds longer. Transfer dough to counter and knead until smooth, 2 to 3 minutes. Wrap dough in plastic wrap and let rest for 30 minutes.

**2. FOR THE FILLING:** While dough rests, scrape any excess dough from now-empty processor bowl and blade. Pulse cabbage in processor until finely chopped, 8 to 10 pulses. Transfer cabbage to medium bowl and stir in ½ teaspoon salt; let sit for 10 minutes. Using your hands, squeeze excess moisture from cabbage. Transfer cabbage to small bowl and set aside.

**3.** Pulse pork, soy sauce, sesame oil, 1 tablespoon vegetable oil, Shaoxing wine, hoisin, ginger, white pepper, and remaining ½ teaspoon salt in now-empty food processor until blended and slightly sticky, about 10 pulses. Scatter cabbage over pork mixture. Add scallions and pulse until vegetables are evenly distributed, about 8 pulses. Transfer pork mixture to small bowl and, using rubber spatula, smooth surface. Cover with plastic and refrigerate.

**4.** Line 2 rimmed baking sheets with parchment paper. Lightly dust with flour and set aside. Unwrap dough and transfer to counter. Roll dough into 12-inch cylinder and cut cylinder into 4 equal pieces. Set 3 pieces aside and cover with plastic. Roll remaining piece into 8-inch cylinder. Cut cylinder in half and cut each half into 5 equal pieces. Place dough pieces on 1 cut side on lightly floured counter and lightly dust with flour. Using palm of your hand, press each dough piece into 2-inch disk. Cover disks with damp towel.

**5.** Roll 1 disk into 3½-inch round (wrappers needn't be perfectly round) and re-cover disk with damp towel. Repeat with remaining disks. (Do not overlap disks.)

6. Using rubber spatula, mark filling with cross to divide into 4 equal portions. Transfer 1 portion to small bowl and refrigerate remaining filling. Working with wrapper at a time (keep remaining wrappers covered), place scant 1 tablespoon filling in center of wrapper. Brush away any flour clinging to surface of wrapper. Lift side of wrapper closest to you and side farthest away and pinch together to form 1½-inch-wide seam in center of dumpling. (When viewed from above, dumpling will have rectangular shape with rounded open ends.) Lift left corner farthest away from you and bring to center of seam. Pinch to seal. Pinch together remaining dough on left side to seal. Repeat pinching on right side. Gently press dumpling into crescent shape and transfer to prepared sheet. Repeat with remaining wrappers and filling in bowl. Repeat dumpling-making process with remaining 3 pieces dough and remaining 3 portions filling.

**7A. TO PAN-FRY:** Brush 12-inch nonstick skillet with 1 tablespoon vegetable oil. Evenly space 16 dumplings, flat sides down, around edge of skillet and place four in center. Cook over medium heat until bottoms begin to turn spotty brown, 3 to 4 minutes. Off heat, carefully add ½ cup water (water will sputter). Return skillet to heat and bring water to boil. Cover and reduce heat to medium-low. Cook for 6 minutes. Uncover, increase heat to medium-high, and cook until water has evaporated and bottoms of dumplings are crispy and browned, 1 to 3 minutes. Transfer dumplings to platter, crispy sides up. (To cook second batch of dumplings, let skillet cool for 10 minutes. Rinse skillet under cool water and wipe dry with paper towels. Repeat cooking process with remaining 1 tablespoon vegetable oil and remaining dumplings.)

**7B. TO BOIL:** Bring 4 quarts water to boil in large Dutch oven over high heat. Add 20 dumplings, a few at a time, stirring gently to prevent them from sticking. Return to simmer, adjusting heat as necessary to maintain simmer. Cook dumplings for 7 minutes. Drain well.

8. Serve dumplings hot, passing vinegar, chili oil, and extra soy sauce separately for dipping.

**TO MAKE AHEAD:** Freeze uncooked dumplings on rimmed baking sheet until solid. Transfer to zipper-lock bag and freeze for up to 1 month. To pan-fry, increase water to ⅔ cup and covered cooking time to 8 minutes. To boil, increase cooking time to 8 minutes.

### ASSEMBLING CHINESE PORK DUMPLINGS

1. Place scant 1 tablespoon filling in center of wrapper.

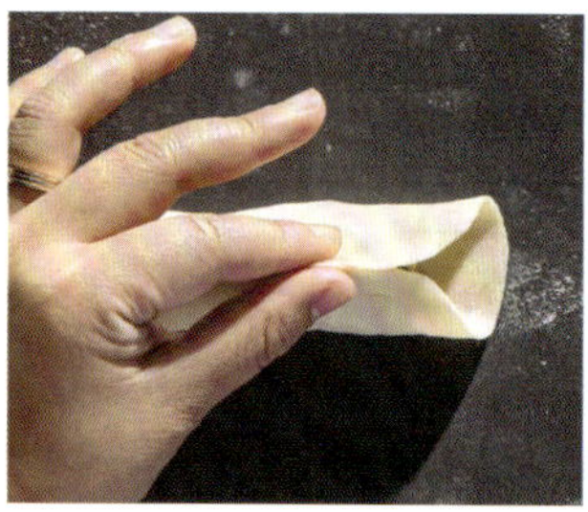

2. Seal top and bottom edges to form 1½-inch-wide seam.

3. Bring far left corner to center of seam and pinch together.

4. Pinch rest of left side to seal. Repeat process on right side.

5. Gently press dumpling into crescent shape.

## Shu Mai (Steamed Chinese Dumplings)

**MAKES** 40 dumplings

**WHY THIS RECIPE WORKS** For moist and tender meat in our Shu Mai recipe, we used our food processor to grind boneless country-style ribs in two batches: one chunky and one fine. Once combined in the filling, the smaller pieces helped hold the larger bits together and added a pleasant textural contrast. A mixture of powdered gelatin and cornstarch to kept our shu mai's filling moist and tender, and we flavored it with cilantro, ginger, and Shaoxing wine. For wrappers, we used square egg roll skins, which we cut into rounds with a biscuit cutter. Finally, we garnished each dumpling's center with finely grated carrot and served our shu mai with a quick dash of chili oil. Do not trim the excess fat from the spareribs, as the fat contributes flavor and moistness. Use any size shrimp except popcorn shrimp; do not halve shrimp smaller than 26 to 30 per pound before processing. The dumplings may be frozen for up to 3 months; cook straight from the freezer for about an extra 5 minutes. Shu mai are traditionally served with a spicy chili oil (page 246), or use store-bought.

- 2 tablespoons soy sauce
- ½ teaspoon unflavored gelatin
- 1 pound boneless country-style pork spareribs, cut into 1-inch pieces, divided
- ½ pound shrimp, peeled, deveined, tails removed, and halved lengthwise (see page 523)
- ¼ cup chopped water chestnuts
- 4 dried shiitake mushroom caps (about ¾ ounce), soaked in hot water for 30 minutes, squeezed dry, and cut into ¼-inch dice
- 2 tablespoons cornstarch
- 2 tablespoons minced fresh cilantro
- 1 tablespoon toasted sesame oil
- 1 tablespoon Shaoxing wine or dry sherry
- 1 tablespoon unseasoned rice vinegar
- 2 teaspoons sugar
- 2 teaspoons grated fresh ginger
- ½ teaspoon table salt
- ½ teaspoon pepper
- 1 (1-pound) package 5½-inch square egg roll wrappers
- ¼ cup finely grated carrot (optional)

**1.** Combine soy sauce and gelatin in small bowl. Set aside to allow gelatin to bloom, about 5 minutes.

**2.** Meanwhile, place half of pork in food processor and pulse until coarsely ground into pieces that are about ⅛ inch, about 10 pulses; transfer to large bowl. Add shrimp and remaining pork to food processor and pulse until coarsely chopped into pieces that are about ¼ inch, about 5 pulses. Transfer to bowl with coarsely ground pork. Stir in soy sauce mixture, water chestnuts, mushrooms, cornstarch, cilantro, oil, Shaoxing wine, vinegar, sugar, ginger, salt, and pepper until well combined.

**3.** Line large baking sheet with parchment paper. Divide egg roll wrappers into 3 stacks (six to seven per stack). Using 3-inch biscuit cutter, cut two 3-inch rounds from each stack of egg roll wrappers (you should have 40 to 42 rounds). Cover rounds with moist paper towels to prevent drying.

**4.** Working with 6 rounds at a time, brush edges of each round lightly with water. Place heaping 1 tablespoon filling in center of each round. Form dumplings by pinching 2 opposing sides of wrapper with your fingers. Rotate dumpling 90 degrees and, again, pinch opposing sides of wrapper with your fingers. Continue to pinch dumpling to form 8 equidistant pinches around circumference. Gather up sides of dumpling and squeeze gently at top to create rounded and open shape with "waist." Gently but firmly pack down filling with back of spoon or butter knife. Transfer to prepared baking sheet, cover with damp dish towel, and repeat with remaining wrappers and filling. Top center of each dumpling with pinch of grated carrot, if using.

**5.** Cut piece of parchment paper slightly smaller than diameter of steamer basket and place in basket. Poke about 20 small holes in parchment to allow steam to pass through and lightly coat with vegetable oil spray. Place batches of dumplings on parchment, making sure they are not touching. Set steamer basket over simmering water and cook, covered, until no longer pink, 8 to 10 minutes. Serve immediately with chili oil.

### FILLING AND FORMING SHU MAI

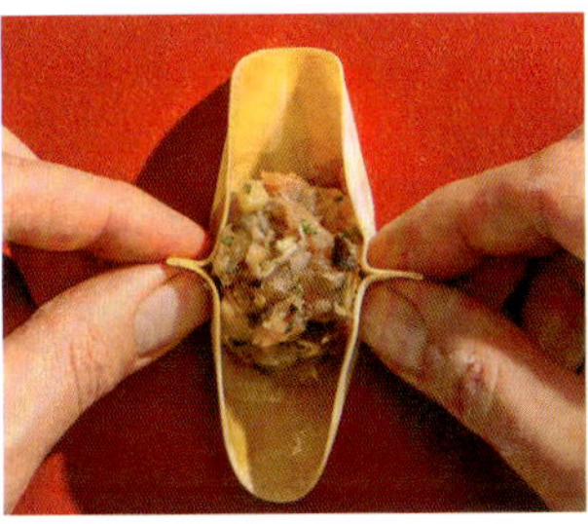

**1.** Place heaping 1 tablespoon filling in center of wrapper. Pinch 2 opposing sides of wrapper with your fingers. Rotate dumpling 90 degrees, and pinch again. Continue to pinch dumpling until you have 8 equidistant pinches around circumference of dumpling.

**2.** Gather up sides of dumpling and squeeze gently at top to create "waist."

**3.** Hold dumpling in your hand and gently but firmly pack filling into dumpling with butter knife.

## Quick Chili Oil

**MAKES ½ CUP**

- 1 tablespoon soy sauce
- 2 teaspoons sugar
- ½ teaspoon table salt
- ½ cup peanut oil
- ¼ cup red pepper flakes
- 2 garlic cloves, peeled

Combine soy sauce, sugar, and salt in small bowl; set aside. Heat oil in small saucepan over medium heat until just shimmering and registers 300 degrees. Remove pan from heat and stir in pepper flakes, garlic, and soy mixture. Let cool to room temperature, stirring occasionally, about 1 hour. Discard garlic before storing.

## Har Gow (Crystal Shrimp Dumplings)

**MAKES** 24 dumplings

**WHY THIS RECIPE WORKS** The meticulously crafted Cantonese crystal shrimp dumplings called har gow are one of the great joys of a dim sum feast. To start, we made a wheat starch and tapioca starch dough in a food processor which produced a translucent wrapper. We added boiling water to the starches and let the starch briefly gelatinize to give the dough structure; we then drizzled in melted lard to make a dough that was easy to flatten into thin rounds and pliable enough to pleat around a filling. Melted lard added richness, along with modest amounts of ginger, garlic, and Shaoxing wine. Minced bamboo shoots or water chestnuts contributed a bit of crunch. Dim sum chefs use the wide side of a cleaver to smear pieces of dough into round wrappers, but we used a tortilla press, which is easier. We developed this recipe with Red Lantern wheat starch and Bob's Red Mill tapioca starch. We strongly recommend weighing the starches. For an accurate measurement of boiling water, bring a kettle of water to a boil and then measure out the desired amount. You can substitute vegetable oil for the lard. Any size shrimp can be used; the larger the shrimp, the more pulses will be required to chop them in step 2. Canned water chestnuts can be substituted for the bamboo shoots. If you don't own a tortilla press, flatten the dough with a 6-inch cake pan or another similar-size clean, flat surface. Serve with DIY Chili Oil (page 247).

**DOUGH**

- 1 cup plus 2 tablespoons (5¼ ounces) wheat starch
- ¼ cup plus 3 tablespoons (1¾ ounces) tapioca starch
- Pinch table salt
- ½ cup plus 1 tablespoon boiling water
- 4 teaspoons lard, melted

**FILLING**

- 6 ounces shrimp, peeled, deveined, and tails removed
- 2 tablespoons finely chopped canned bamboo shoots
- 1 tablespoon lard, melted and cooled
- 1 teaspoon Shaoxing wine
- ½ teaspoon grated fresh ginger
- ½ teaspoon minced garlic
- ¼ teaspoon sugar
- ¼ teaspoon table salt
- ¼ teaspoon white pepper
- ¼ teaspoon soy sauce

**1. FOR THE DOUGH:** Process wheat starch, tapioca starch, and salt in food processor until combined, about 3 seconds. Add boiling water and let rest for 5 seconds. Pulse once. Add melted lard and process until dough forms ball that clears sides of processor bowl, about 1 minute (if dough does not come together, add up to 2 teaspoons hot water, ½ teaspoon at a time, processing for 10 seconds between additions, until dough ball forms). Transfer to lightly greased counter and knead for 1 minute. Dough should be slightly tacky. Shape dough into ball and cover with plastic wrap.

**2. FOR THE FILLING:** In clean, dry workbowl, pulse all filling ingredients until shrimp is finely ground, 10 to 20 pulses. Transfer to bowl; cover; and refrigerate until filling is well chilled, about 20 minutes.

**3.** To shape, divide dough into 4 equal portions. On lightly greased counter, roll 1 portion of dough into 6-inch rope. Divide rope into 6 equal pieces. Cover all pieces with plastic wrap. Use lightly oiled tortilla press to press 1 piece of dough into 3¼-inch round.

**4.** Place dough round on fingers of your nondominant hand. Place heaping ½ tablespoon of filling in center of dough. To create first pleat, use thumb and index finger of your other hand to pinch dough just above pinky and lift pleat toward top of filling.

**5.** Using index finger of hand holding dumpling, push dough toward pinched portion to begin forming second pleat. Use index finger of pleating hand to position second pleat against first pleat. Repeat pleating motion, rotating dough with each pleat, until all of dough is pleated and dumpling has rounded shape.

**6.** Hold dumpling pleated side up, and use your thumb and index finger to press pleats together just above filling to seal dumpling. Gently tear excess dough from dumpling. Place dumpling pleated side up on counter and cover with plastic wrap. Repeat with remaining dough and filling, lightly oiling tortilla press and counter as needed.

**7.** To steam, bring 4 cups water to boil in 14-inch flat-bottomed wok or 12-inch skillet. Meanwhile, lightly grease two 8-inch parchment rounds. Place rounds in two 10-inch bamboo steamer baskets. Arrange dumplings on prepared parchment so that they are not touching; stack baskets and cover. Reduce heat to maintain simmer and set steamer in wok. Steam until har gow wrappers are translucent, about 8 minutes. Off heat, remove steamer from wok and let rest, covered, for 10 minutes. Serve.

## DIY Chili Oil

**MAKES 1¾ CUPS**

Chili oil, neutral oil infused with aromatics and spices and tinted vibrant red by Sichuan chili flakes, features in many traditional Chinese dishes. It also can be used at the table to add color and moderate heat to noodles, soups, or dumplings such as Har Gow. If Sichuan chili flakes are unavailable or you'd prefer a less spicy chili oil, you can substitute gochugaru (Korean chili flakes).

- 1¼ cups vegetable oil
- 1 shallot, sliced into ¼-inch rings
- 1 (2-inch) piece ginger, peeled and sliced into ¼-inch-thick rounds
- 3 garlic cloves, peeled
- 2 bay leaves
- 1 star anise pod
- 1 cinnamon stick
- ½ cup Sichuan chili flakes
- ⅛ teaspoon table salt

**1.** Bring oil, shallot, ginger, garlic, bay leaves, star anise, and cinnamon to simmer in small saucepan over medium heat. Reduce heat to low; tiny bubbles should surround aromatics, but aromatics should not fry. Cook until garlic and shallot are golden brown, taking care to maintain gentle bubbling, 45 minutes to 1 hour.

**2.** Combine Sichuan chili flakes and salt in medium heatproof bowl. Strain oil mixture through fine-mesh strainer over chili flakes (mixture may bubble). Discard solids in strainer. Let chili oil cool completely, about 1½ hours. Once cool, transfer mixture to airtight container. Store in refrigerator for up to 3 months.

### SHAPING HAR GOW

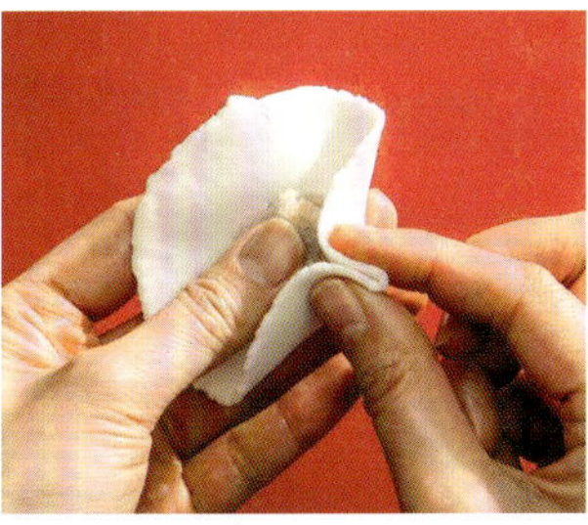

**1.** To create first pleat, use your thumb and index finger to pinch dough.

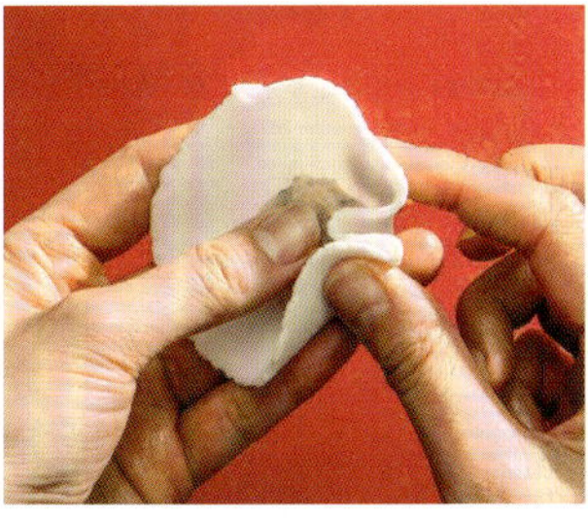

**2.** Use index finger of your other hand to push dough to begin second pleat.

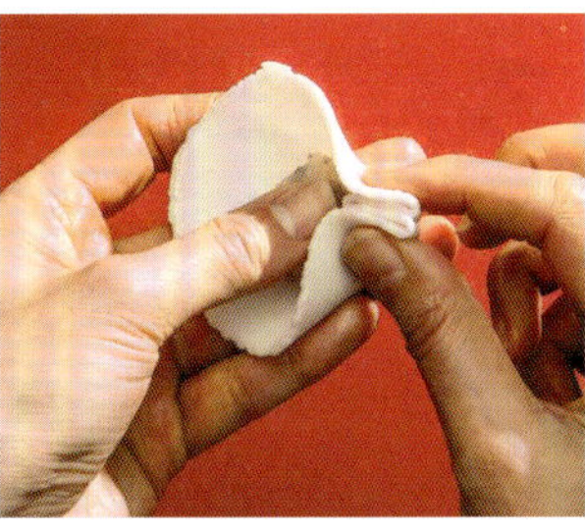

**3.** Position second pleat against first pleat.

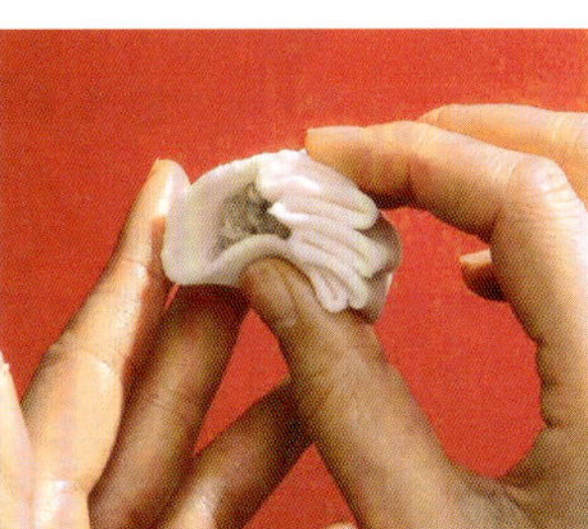

**4.** Repeat, rotating with each pleat, until dumpling has rounded shape. Press pleats above filling to seal.

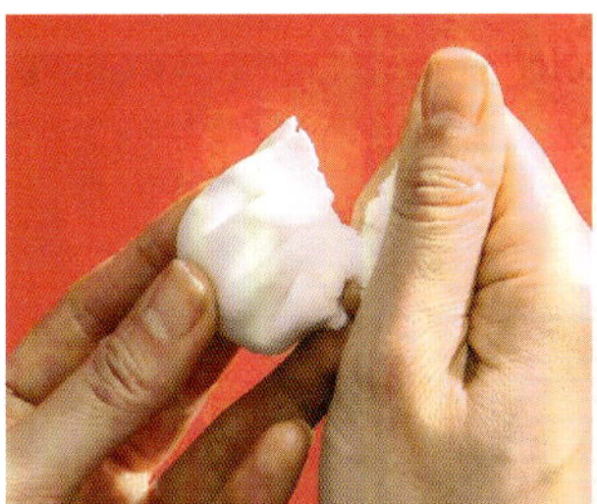

**5.** Gently tear off excess dough.

CHAPTER 6 # Poultry

*Continued on next page*

Photos (left to right): Gongbao Jiding (Sichuan Kung Pao Chicken); Oven-Roasted Chicken Thighs; Murgh Makhani (Indian Butter Chicken); Roast Turkey and Gravy with Herbes de Provence and Lemon; Crispy Pan-Fried Chicken Cutlets; Skillet Turkey Burgers; Chicken Yassa (Senegalese Braised Chicken with Caramelized Onion and Lemon)

CHAPTER 6 **Poultry**

## Perfect Poached Chicken Breasts

**SERVES** 4

**WHY THIS RECIPE WORKS** Poaching can be a perfect way to gently cook delicate chicken breasts, but the standard approach can be fussy and it offers little in the way of flavor. To up the flavor ante, we added salt, soy sauce, garlic, and a bit of sugar to the poaching liquid for rich-tasting chicken. We found that our salty poaching liquid could double as a quick brine, simplifying the recipe and infusing the chicken with flavor. To ensure that the chicken cooked evenly, we used plenty of water and raised the chicken off the bottom of the pot in a steamer basket. Taking the pot off the heat partway through cooking allowed the delicate meat to cook through using residual heat and prevented overcooking. A couple of simple sauces made the perfect accompaniment. To ensure that the chicken cooks through, don't use breasts that weigh more than 8 ounces each. If desired, serve the chicken with our warm tomato vinaigrette or in a salad or sandwich.

- 4 (6- to 8-ounce) boneless, skinless chicken breasts, trimmed
- ½ cup soy sauce
- ¼ cup table salt
- 2 tablespoons sugar
- 6 garlic cloves, smashed and peeled

**1.** Cover chicken breasts with plastic wrap and pound thick ends gently with meat pounder until ¾ inch thick. Whisk 4 quarts water, soy sauce, salt, sugar, and garlic in Dutch oven until salt and sugar are dissolved. Arrange breasts, skinned side up, in steamer basket, making sure not to overlap them. Submerge steamer basket in brine and let sit at room temperature for 30 minutes.

**2.** Heat pot over medium heat, stirring liquid occasionally to even out hot spots, until water registers 175 degrees, 15 to 20 minutes. Turn off heat, cover pot, remove from burner, and let stand until meat registers 160 degrees, 17 to 22 minutes.

**3.** Transfer breasts to cutting board, cover tightly with aluminum foil, and let rest for 5 minutes. Slice each breast on bias into ¼-inch-thick slices, transfer to serving platter or individual plates, and serve.

### Warm Tomato-Ginger Vinaigrette

**MAKES** about 2 cups

Parsley may be substituted for the cilantro.

- ¼ cup extra-virgin olive oil
- 1 shallot, minced
- 1½ teaspoons grated fresh ginger
- ⅛ teaspoon ground cumin
- ⅛ teaspoon ground fennel
- 12 ounces cherry tomatoes, halved
- Table salt and pepper
- 1 tablespoon red wine vinegar
- 1 teaspoon packed light brown sugar
- 2 tablespoons chopped fresh cilantro

Heat 2 tablespoons oil in 10-inch nonstick skillet over medium heat until shimmering. Add shallot, ginger, cumin, and fennel and cook until fragrant, about 15 seconds. Stir in tomatoes and ¼ teaspoon salt and cook, stirring frequently, until tomatoes have softened, 3 to 5 minutes. Off heat, stir in vinegar and sugar and season with salt and pepper to taste; cover to keep warm. Stir in cilantro and remaining 2 tablespoons oil just before serving.

## Sautéed Chicken Cutlets

**SERVES** 4

**WHY THIS RECIPE WORKS** Sautéed chicken cutlets are a breeze to prepare, but they really need a sauce to accompany them. With this in mind, we sought out a sauce that packed big flavor and could be made before the chicken even hit the skillet. Romesco sauce with its bold flavor profile was a great option. We browned the cutlets in a hot oiled pan and, in just under 3 minutes, they were ready to be served with either Romesco or one of our other two simple and quick bold sauces (page 252). The cutlets will be easier to slice in half if you freeze them for about 15 minutes.

- 4 (6- to 8-ounce) boneless, skinless chicken breasts, trimmed, halved horizontally, and pounded ¼ inch thick
- 1 teaspoon kosher salt
- ¼ teaspoon pepper
- 4 teaspoons vegetable oil

Pat cutlets dry with paper towels; sprinkle each side of each cutlet evenly with salt and pepper. Heat 2 teaspoons oil in 12-inch skillet over medium-high heat until just smoking. Place 4 cutlets in skillet and cook, without moving, until browned, about 2 minutes. Flip cutlets and continue to cook until second sides are opaque, about 30 seconds. Transfer to platter and tent with aluminum foil. Repeat with remaining 4 cutlets and remaining 2 teaspoons oil. Serve.

### Romesco Sauce

**MAKES** 1 cup

You will need at least one 12-ounce jar of roasted red peppers for this recipe.

- ½ slice hearty white sandwich bread, cut into ½-inch pieces
- ¼ cup hazelnuts, toasted and skinned
- 2 tablespoons extra-virgin olive oil, divided
- 2 garlic cloves, sliced thin
- 1 cup jarred roasted red peppers, rinsed and patted dry
- 1½ tablespoons sherry vinegar
- 1 teaspoon honey
- ½ teaspoon smoked paprika
- ½ teaspoon table salt
- Pinch cayenne pepper

Heat bread, hazelnuts, and 1 tablespoon oil in 12-inch skillet over medium heat; cook, stirring constantly, until bread and hazelnuts are lightly toasted, 2½ to 3 minutes. Add garlic and cook, stirring constantly, until fragrant, about 30 seconds. Transfer bread mixture to food processor and pulse until coarsely chopped, about 5 pulses. Add red peppers, vinegar, honey, paprika, salt, cayenne, and remaining 1 tablespoon oil to processor. Pulse until finely chopped, 5 to 8 pulses. Transfer to bowl and let stand for at least 10 minutes. (Sauce can be refrigerated in an airtight container for up to 2 days.)

## Quick Sun-Dried Tomato Sauce

**MAKES** 1 cup

For the best taste and texture, make sure to rinse all the dried herbs off the sun-dried tomatoes.

- ½ slice hearty white sandwich bread, cut into ½-inch pieces
- ¼ cup pine nuts
- 2 tablespoons extra-virgin olive oil, divided
- 2 garlic cloves, sliced thin
- 1 small tomato, cored and cut into ½-inch pieces
- ½ cup oil-packed sun-dried tomatoes, rinsed
- 2 tablespoons coarsely chopped fresh basil
- 2 tablespoons balsamic vinegar
- ½ teaspoon table salt

Heat bread, pine nuts, and 1 tablespoon oil in 12-inch skillet over medium heat; cook, stirring constantly, until bread and pine nuts are lightly toasted, 2½ to 3 minutes. Add garlic and cook, stirring constantly, until fragrant, about 30 seconds. Transfer bread mixture to food processor and pulse until coarsely chopped, about 5 pulses. Add tomato, sun-dried tomatoes, basil, vinegar, salt, and remaining 1 tablespoon oil to processor. Pulse until finely chopped, 5 to 8 pulses. Transfer to bowl and let stand for at least 10 minutes. (Sauce can be refrigerated for up to 2 days.)

## Quick Tomatillo Sauce

**MAKES** 1 cup

You will need at least one 15-ounce can of tomatillos for this recipe.

- ½ slice hearty white sandwich bread, cut into ½-inch pieces
- ¼ cup pepitas
- 2 tablespoons extra-virgin olive oil, divided
- 2 garlic cloves, sliced thin
- 1 cup canned tomatillos, rinsed
- 2 tablespoons jarred sliced jalapeños plus 2 teaspoons brine
- 2 tablespoons fresh cilantro leaves
- 1 teaspoon honey
- ½ teaspoon table salt

Heat bread, pepitas, and 1 tablespoon oil in 12-inch skillet over medium heat; cook, stirring constantly, until pepitas and bread are lightly toasted, 2½ to 3 minutes. Add garlic and cook, stirring constantly, until fragrant, about 30 seconds. Transfer bread mixture to food processor and pulse until coarsely chopped, about 5 pulses. Add tomatillos, jalapeños and brine, cilantro, honey, salt, and remaining 1 tablespoon oil to processor. Pulse until finely chopped, 5 to 8 pulses. Transfer to bowl and let stand for at least 10 minutes. (Sauce can be refrigerated in an airtight container for up to 2 days.)

### MAKING CHICKEN CUTLETS

**1.** Remove tenderloin from underside of breast if necessary. Lay chicken smooth side up on cutting board. To make cutlets, place your hand on top of chicken and carefully slice it in half horizontally.

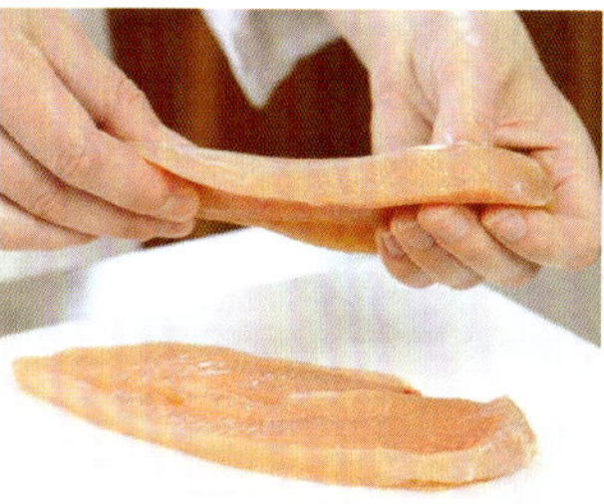

**2.** Separate breast to yield 2 cutlets between ⅜ and ½ inch thick. If necessary, pound to even thickness.

## Sautéed Chicken Cutlets with Mustard-Cider Sauce (Chicken Paillard)

**SERVES** 4

**WHY THIS RECIPE WORKS** Sautéed superthin cutlets are satisfying midweek fare, except when they are tough and dry. We wanted juicy, ultrathin sautéed chicken cutlets, paired with a sauce that complements, rather than overpowers, the meat. For evenly sized cutlets, we took a two-step approach. We halved the chicken breasts horizontally before pounding them to an even thickness under plastic wrap. Halving and pounding the breasts ensured that they cooked at the same rate and turned out moist, tender, and juicy. To further ensure that the cutlets were juicy, we browned them on only one side. And for the sauce, we kept the flavors simple, relying on the sweet, tangy combination of apple cider and cider vinegar complemented with the kick of whole-grain mustard. To make slicing the chicken easier, freeze it for 15 minutes.

**CHICKEN**

- 4 (6- to 8-ounce) boneless, skinless chicken breasts, tenderloins removed and breasts trimmed
- Table salt and ground black pepper
- 2 tablespoons vegetable oil

**MUSTARD-CIDER SAUCE**

- 2 teaspoons vegetable oil
- 1 medium shallot, minced (about 3 tablespoons)
- 1¼ cups apple cider
- 2 tablespoons cider vinegar
- 2 teaspoons whole grain mustard
- 2 teaspoons minced fresh parsley leaves
- 2 tablespoons unsalted butter
- Table salt and ground black pepper

**1. FOR THE CHICKEN:** Adjust an oven rack to the middle position and heat the oven to 200 degrees. Halve the chicken horizontally, then cover the chicken halves with plastic wrap and use a meat pounder to pound the cutlets to an even ¼-inch thickness. Season both sides of each cutlet with salt and pepper. Heat 1 tablespoon of the oil in a 12-inch skillet over medium-high heat until just smoking. Place four cutlets in the skillet and cook without moving them until browned, about 2 minutes. Using a spatula, flip the cutlets and continue to cook until the second sides are opaque, 15 to 20 seconds. Transfer to a large heatproof plate. Add the remaining 1 tablespoon oil to the now-empty skillet and repeat to cook the remaining cutlets. Cover the plate loosely with foil and transfer it to the oven to keep warm while making the sauce.

**2. FOR THE SAUCE:** Off the heat, add the oil and shallot to the hot skillet. Using residual heat, cook, stirring constantly, until softened, about 30 seconds. Set the skillet over medium-high heat and add the cider and vinegar. Bring to a simmer, scraping the pan bottom with a wooden spoon to loosen any browned bits. Simmer until reduced to ½ cup, 6 to 7 minutes. Off the heat, stir in the mustard and parsley; whisk in the butter 1 tablespoon at a time. Season with salt and pepper to taste and serve immediately with the cutlets.

## Crisp Breaded Chicken Cutlets

**SERVES 4**

**WHY THIS RECIPE WORKS** Breaded chicken cutlets, for all their apparent simplicity, can be problematic. Too often, they end up with either an underdone or burnt coating, which falls off the tasteless, rubbery chicken underneath. We wanted chicken cutlets with flavorful meat and a crunchy crust that would adhere nicely to the meat. To ensure even cooking, we flattened the chicken breasts to ½ inch; thin enough to cook evenly, but thick enough to make a hearty, crisp cutlet. To prevent crust separation, we coated the chicken with flour, an egg and oil mixture, and flavorful, fresh bread crumbs. We then let them sit for 5 minutes to help set the crust. For the crispiest coating, we fried the cutlets in batches in vegetable oil. And for a tasty variation, we added Parmesan for a version of the classic Italian dish Chicken Milanese. If you'd rather not prepare fresh bread crumbs, use panko, the extra-crisp Japanese bread crumbs. The chicken is cooked in batches of two because the crust is noticeably more crisp if the pan is not overcrowded. Note that these cutlets are a bit thicker than others in the chapter and should not be halved horizontally.

- 4 (5- to 6-ounce) boneless, skinless chicken breasts, tenderloins removed and breasts trimmed
- Table salt and ground black pepper
- 3 slices high-quality white sandwich bread, torn into quarters
- ¾ cup unbleached all-purpose flour
- 2 large eggs
- 1 tablespoon plus ¾ cup vegetable oil
- Lemon wedges, for serving

**1.** Use a meat pounder to pound the chicken breasts to an even ½-inch thickness. Sprinkle the cutlets with salt and pepper and set aside. Set a large wire rack over a large baking sheet and set aside.

**2.** Adjust an oven rack to the lower-middle position, set a heatproof plate on the rack, and heat the oven to 200 degrees. Process the bread in a food processor until evenly fine-textured, 20 to 30 seconds. Transfer the crumbs to a pie plate or shallow dish. Spread the flour in a second plate. Beat the eggs with 1 tablespoon of the oil in a third plate.

**3.** Working with one cutlet at a time, dredge each cutlet in the flour, shaking off the excess. Using tongs, dip both sides of the cutlets in the egg mixture, allowing the excess to drip off. Dip both sides of the cutlets in the bread crumbs, pressing the crumbs with your fingers to form an even, cohesive coat. Place the breaded cutlets on the wire rack and allow the coating to dry for about 5 minutes.

**4.** Meanwhile, heat 6 tablespoons more oil in a 12-inch nonstick skillet over medium-high heat until shimmering but not smoking, about 2 minutes. Lay 2 cutlets gently in the skillet; cook until deep golden brown and crisp on the first side, gently pressing down on the cutlets with a metal spatula, about 2½ minutes. Using tongs, flip the cutlets, reduce the heat to medium, and continue to cook until the meat feels firm when pressed gently and the second side is deep golden brown and crisp, 2½ to 3 minutes longer. Line the warmed plate with a double layer of paper towels and set the cutlets on top; return the plate to the oven.

**5.** Discard the oil in the skillet and wipe the skillet clean with paper towels. Repeat step 4 using the remaining 6 tablespoons oil and remaining cutlets; serve with lemon wedges.

### Crisp Breaded Chicken Cutlets with Parmesan (Chicken Milanese)

Though Parmesan is classic in this dish, use Pecorino Romano if you prefer a more tangy flavor. Keep a close eye on the cutlets as they brown to make sure the cheese does not burn.

Follow the recipe for Breaded Chicken Cutlets, substituting ¼ cup finely grated Parmesan cheese for an equal amount of bread crumbs.

## Parmesan-Crusted Chicken Cutlets

**SERVES 4**

**WHY THIS RECIPE WORKS** We wanted moist and tender chicken coated with a thin, crispy-yet-chewy, wafer-like sheath of Parmesan cheese. A standard breading in which we merely substituted cheese for the bread crumbs and flour was disappointing; the cheese didn't provide the dry base to which the rest of the coating would stick. So we went back to flour, with a bit of Parmesan for flavor, and we left out the egg yolks to eliminate the eggy taste. For the outermost layer, shredding the cheese on the large holes of a box grater made a sturdier, more even crust, and a little flour added to this cheese helped the coating turn crisp. These cutlets were pale golden rather than deep golden brown, but the nutty, crisp Parmesan crust was everything we hoped it would be. To make slicing the chicken easier, freeze it for 15 minutes. Note that part of the Parmesan is grated on the smallest holes of a box grater (or rasp grater) and the remaining Parmesan is shredded on the largest holes of the box grater. We like the flavor that authentic Parmigiano-Reggiano lends to this recipe. Although the portion size (one cutlet per person) might seem small, these cutlets are rather rich due to the cheese content.

- 2 (7- to 8-ounce) boneless, skinless chicken breasts, tenderloins removed and breasts trimmed (see note)
- Table salt and ground black pepper
- 5 tablespoons unbleached all-purpose flour
- ¼ cup grated Parmesan cheese plus 6 ounces, shredded (about 2 cups; see note)
- 3 large egg whites
- 2 tablespoons minced fresh chives (optional)
- 4 teaspoons olive oil
- Lemon wedges, for serving

**1.** Adjust an oven rack to the middle position and heat the oven to 200 degrees. Halve the chicken horizontally, then cover the chicken halves with plastic wrap and pound the cutlets to an even ¼-inch thickness. Pat the chicken dry with paper towels and season with salt and pepper.

**2.** Whisk ¼ cup of the flour and the ¼ cup grated Parmesan together in a shallow dish. Whisk the egg whites and chives (if using) in a medium bowl until slightly foamy. Combine the 2 cups shredded Parmesan and remaining 1 tablespoon flour in a second shallow dish. Working with 1 chicken cutlet at a time, dredge in the flour mixture, shaking off the excess, then coat with the egg white mixture, allowing the excess to drip off. Finally, coat with the shredded Parmesan mixture, pressing gently so that the cheese adheres. Place the coated cutlets in a single layer on a wire rack set over a rimmed baking sheet.

**3.** Heat 2 teaspoons of the oil in a 12-inch nonstick skillet over medium heat until shimmering. Add 2 of the cutlets and cook until pale golden brown on both sides, 4 to 6 minutes in total. (While the chicken is cooking, use a thin nonstick spatula to gently separate any cheesy edges that have melted together.) Transfer to a clean wire rack set over a rimmed baking sheet and keep warm in the oven. Wipe out the skillet with paper towels. Repeat with the remaining 2 teaspoons oil and chicken. Serve with the lemon wedges.

## Crispy Pan-Fried Chicken Cutlets

**SERVES 4 to 6**

**WHY THIS RECIPE WORKS** Chicken cutlets coated in bread crumbs and pan-fried are quick-cooking and a crowd-pleaser. But the three-step breading process of flour, egg, and crumbs is fussy, so we set out to make a streamlined version. Inspired by Japanese chicken katsu, we ditched the flour step, which made for a more delicate coating. Instead of using homemade bread crumbs, we swapped in Japanese panko bread crumbs that we poured into a zipper-lock bag and crushed with a rolling pin. To avoid any spotty browning or burned bits of panko with our second batch of cutlets, we discarded the cooking oil from the first batch and started over with fresh oil. To punch up the flavor, we made a tonkatsu-style sauce. Be sure to remove any tenderloins from the breasts before halving. The cutlets will be easier to slice in half if you freeze them for about 15 minutes. If you are working with 8-ounce cutlets, the skillet will initially be crowded; the cutlets will shrink slightly as they cook. The first batch of cutlets can be kept warm in a 200-degree oven while the second batch cooks. These cutlets can be sliced into ½-inch-wide strips and served over rice with sauce, in a sandwich, or over a green salad.

- 2 cups panko bread crumbs
- 2 large eggs
- 1 teaspoon table salt
- 4 (6- to 8-ounce) boneless, skinless chicken breasts, trimmed, halved horizontally, and pounded ¼ inch thick
- ½ cup vegetable oil, divided

**1.** Place panko in large zipper-lock bag and finely crush with rolling pin. Transfer crushed panko to shallow dish. Whisk eggs and salt in second shallow dish until well combined.

**2.** Working with 1 cutlet at a time, dredge cutlet in egg mixture, allowing excess egg to drip off, then coat all sides with panko, pressing gently so crumbs adhere. Transfer cutlet to rimmed baking sheet and repeat with remaining cutlets.

**3.** Place wire rack in second rimmed baking sheet. Line rack with layer of paper towels. Heat ¼ cup oil and small pinch of panko in 12-inch skillet over medium-high heat. When panko has turned golden brown, place 4 cutlets in skillet. Cook without moving them until bottoms are crispy and deep golden brown, 2 to 3 minutes. Using tongs, carefully flip cutlets and cook on second side until deep golden brown, 2 to 3 minutes. Transfer cutlets to towel-lined rack and season with salt to taste. Wipe out skillet with paper towels. Repeat with remaining ¼ cup oil and 4 cutlets. Serve immediately.

### Tonkatsu Sauce

**MAKES** ⅓ cup

You can substitute yellow mustard for the Dijon, but do not use a grainy mustard.

- ¼ cup ketchup
- 2 tablespoons Worcestershire sauce
- 2 teaspoons soy sauce
- 1 teaspoon Dijon mustard

Whisk all ingredients together in bowl.

## Best Chicken Parmesan

**SERVES 4**

**WHY THIS RECIPE WORKS** Classic chicken Parmesan should feature juicy chicken cutlets with a crisp pan-fried breaded coating, complemented by creamy mozzarella and a bright, zesty marinara sauce. But more often it ends up dry and overcooked, with a soggy crust and a chewy mass of cheese. To prevent the cutlets from overcooking, we halved them horizontally and pounded them to an even thickness. Then we salted them for 20 minutes to help them hold on to their moisture. To keep the crust crunchy, we replaced more than half of the sogginess-prone bread crumbs with flavorful grated Parmesan cheese. For a cheese topping that didn't turn chewy, we added some creamy fontina to the usual shredded mozzarella and ran it under the broiler for just 2 minutes to melt and brown. Melting the cheese directly on the fried cutlet formed a barrier between the crispy crust and the tomato sauce. Our preferred brand of crushed tomatoes is San Merican. This recipe makes enough sauce to top the cutlets as well as four servings of pasta. Serve with pasta and a simple green salad.

**SAUCE**

- 2 tablespoons extra-virgin olive oil, divided
- 2 garlic cloves, minced
- ¾ teaspoon kosher salt
- ¼ teaspoon dried oregano
- Pinch red pepper flakes
- 1 (28-ounce) can crushed tomatoes
- ¼ teaspoon sugar
- 2 tablespoons coarsely chopped fresh basil

**CHICKEN**

- 2 (6- to 8-ounce) boneless, skinless chicken breasts, trimmed, halved horizontally, and pounded ½ inch thick
- 1 teaspoon kosher salt
- 2 ounces whole-milk mozzarella cheese, shredded (½ cup)
- 2 ounces fontina cheese, shredded (½ cup)
- 1 large egg
- 1 tablespoon all-purpose flour
- 1½ ounces Parmesan cheese, grated (¾ cup)
- ½ cup panko bread crumbs
- ½ teaspoon garlic powder
- ¼ teaspoon dried oregano
- ¼ teaspoon pepper
- ⅓ cup vegetable oil
- ¼ cup torn fresh basil

**1. FOR THE SAUCE:** Heat 1 tablespoon oil in medium saucepan over medium heat until shimmering. Add garlic, salt, oregano, and pepper flakes; cook, stirring occasionally, until fragrant, about 30 seconds. Stir in tomatoes and sugar; increase heat to high and bring to simmer. Reduce heat to medium-low and simmer until thickened, about 20 minutes. Off heat, stir in basil and remaining 1 tablespoon oil; season with salt and pepper to taste. Cover and keep warm.

**2. FOR THE CHICKEN:** Sprinkle each side of each cutlet with ⅛ teaspoon salt and let stand at room temperature for 20 minutes. Combine mozzarella and fontina in bowl; set aside.

**3.** Adjust oven rack 4 inches from broiler element and heat broiler. Whisk egg and flour together in shallow dish or pie plate until smooth. Combine Parmesan, panko, garlic powder, oregano, and pepper in second shallow dish or pie plate. Pat chicken dry with paper towels. Dredge 1 cutlet in egg mixture, allowing excess to drip off. Coat all sides in Parmesan mixture, pressing gently so crumbs adhere. Transfer cutlet to large plate and repeat with remaining cutlets.

**4.** Heat oil in 10-inch nonstick skillet over medium-high heat until shimmering. Carefully place 2 cutlets in skillet and cook without moving them until bottoms are crispy and deep golden brown, 1½ to 2 minutes. Using tongs, carefully flip cutlets and cook on second side until deep golden brown, 1½ to 2 minutes. Transfer cutlets to paper towel–lined plate and repeat with remaining cutlets.

**5.** Place cutlets on rimmed baking sheet and sprinkle cheese mixture evenly over cutlets, covering as much surface area as possible. Broil until cheese is melted and beginning to brown, 2 to 4 minutes. Transfer chicken to serving platter and top each cutlet with 2 tablespoons sauce. Sprinkle with basil and serve immediately, passing remaining sauce separately.

## Lighter Chicken Parmesan

**SERVES** 6

**WHY THIS RECIPE WORKS** Crunchy fried chicken cutlets topped with cheese and tomato sauce, chicken Parmesan isn't exactly a dish for dieters. Not wanting to eliminate it as an option for healthy eating, we looked for a way to get the crispy coating without using all the oil. Baking seemed to be the best alternative to frying. We toasted panko with a little oil for color and to give them "fried" flavor without the fat. Adopting the conventional breading technique of dipping the cutlets in flour, then egg, then bread crumbs, we cut more calories by using only the egg whites. We baked the breasts on a wire rack until they were almost done, then topped them with tomato sauce and shredded low-fat mozzarella to finish. And with 310 calories and 8 grams of fat, they have one-third less calories and two-thirds less fat than traditional versions. To make slicing the chicken easier, freeze it for 15 minutes.

- 1½ cups panko
- 1 tablespoon olive oil
- 1 ounce Parmesan cheese, grated (about ½ cup), plus extra for serving
- ½ cup unbleached all-purpose flour
- 1½ teaspoons garlic powder
- Table salt and ground black pepper
- 3 large egg whites
- 1 tablespoon water
- 3 (7- to 8-ounce) boneless, skinless chicken breasts, tenderloins removed and breasts trimmed (see note)
- 1 recipe Simple Tomato Sauce, warmed (see note)
- 3 ounces low-fat mozzarella cheese, shredded (about ¾ cup)
- 1 tablespoon minced fresh basil leaves

**1.** Adjust an oven rack to the middle position and heat the oven to 475 degrees. Combine the bread crumbs and oil in a 12-inch skillet and toast over medium heat, stirring often, until golden, about 10 minutes. Spread the bread crumbs in a shallow dish and cool slightly; when cool, stir in the Parmesan.

**2.** In a second shallow dish, combine the flour, garlic powder, 1 tablespoon salt, and ½ teaspoon pepper. In a third shallow dish, whisk the egg whites and water together.

**3.** Line a rimmed baking sheet with foil, place a wire rack over the sheet, and spray the rack with vegetable oil spray. Halve the chicken horizontally, then cover the chicken halves with plastic wrap and pound the cutlets to an even ¼-inch thickness. Pat the chicken dry with paper towels, then season with salt and pepper. Lightly dredge the cutlets in the flour, shaking off the excess. Using tongs, dip both sides of the cutlets into the egg whites and allow the excess egg to drip back into the dish. Finally, coat both sides of the chicken with the bread crumbs. Press on the bread crumbs to make sure they adhere. Lay the chicken on the wire rack.

**4.** Spray the tops of the chicken with vegetable oil spray. Bake until the meat is no longer pink in the center and feels firm when pressed with a finger, about 15 minutes.

**5.** Remove the chicken from the oven. Spoon 2 tablespoons of the sauce onto the center of each cutlet and top the sauce with 2 tablespoons of the mozzarella. Return the chicken to the oven and continue to bake until the cheese has melted, about 5 minutes. Sprinkle with the basil and serve, passing the remaining sauce and Parmesan separately.

### Simple Tomato Sauce

**MAKES** about 2 cups

This easy sauce also works well with pasta.

- 1 (28-ounce) can diced tomatoes
- 4 medium garlic cloves, minced or pressed through a garlic press (about 4 teaspoons)
- 1 tablespoon tomato paste
- 1 teaspoon olive oil
- ⅛ teaspoon red pepper flakes
- 1 tablespoon minced fresh basil leaves
- Table salt and ground black pepper

Pulse the tomatoes in a food processor until mostly smooth, about 10 pulses; set aside. Cook the garlic, tomato paste, oil, and red pepper flakes in a medium saucepan over medium heat until the tomato paste begins to brown, about 2 minutes. Stir in the pureed tomatoes and cook until the sauce is thickened and measures 2 cups, about 20 minutes. Off the heat, stir in the basil and season with salt and pepper to taste. Cover and set aside until needed.

## Chicken Schnitzel

**SERVES** 4 to 6

**WHY THIS RECIPE WORKS** Chicken schnitzel is defined by thin, tender, juicy cutlets coated in a fine, wrinkly crust that puffs away from the meat during frying. Halving and pounding chicken breasts ¼ inch thick ensured that they were tender and delicate. Fine store-bought bread crumbs held in place by an egg wash formed a compact crust, and adding oil to the eggs made the coating slightly elastic. A large Dutch oven filled with just 2 cups of oil meant there was plenty of headspace when agitating the pot, so the oil washed over the cutlets without spilling. Bathing the cutlets in oil quickly set the crust so that the breading trapped steam, which then caused the coating to puff away from the meat. We like to serve the schnitzel with our Apple-Fennel Rémoulade (page 267). We used Diamond Crystal Kosher Salt in this recipe; if using Morton Kosher Salt, sprinkle each cutlet with only ½ teaspoon. The oil must wash over the cutlets in waves to achieve

the desired wrinkles and puff, so the ample space provided by a large Dutch oven is necessary; do not attempt to use a smaller pot.

- ½ cup all-purpose flour
- 2 large eggs
- 1 tablespoon vegetable oil
- 2 cups plain dried bread crumbs
- 4 (6- to 8-ounce) boneless, skinless chicken breasts, trimmed
- 2 tablespoons kosher salt
- 1 teaspoon pepper
- 2 cups vegetable oil for frying
- Lemon wedges

**1.** Spread flour in shallow dish. Beat eggs and 1 tablespoon oil in second shallow dish. Place bread crumbs in third shallow dish. Set wire rack in rimmed baking sheet. Line second rimmed baking sheet with double layer of paper towels. Adjust oven rack to middle position and heat oven to 200 degrees.

**2.** Halve chicken breasts horizontally to form 8 cutlets of even thickness. Place 1 cutlet between 2 sheets of plastic wrap and pound to ¼-inch thickness. Repeat with remaining cutlets. Sprinkle each cutlet on both sides with ¾ teaspoon salt and ⅛ teaspoon pepper.

**3.** Working with 1 cutlet at a time, dredge cutlets thoroughly in flour, shaking off excess, then coat with egg mixture, allowing excess to drip back into dish to ensure very thin coating. Coat evenly with bread crumbs, pressing on crumbs to adhere. Place cutlets on prepared wire rack, taking care not to overlap cutlets. Let coating dry for 5 minutes.

**4.** Add 2 cups oil to large Dutch oven and heat over medium-high heat to 350 degrees. Lay 2 or 3 cutlets (depending on size) in oil, without overlapping them, and cook, shaking pot continuously and gently, until cutlets are wrinkled and light golden brown on both sides, 1 to 1½ minutes per side. Transfer cutlets to paper towel–lined sheet, flip to blot excess oil, and transfer sheet to oven to keep warm. Repeat with remaining cutlets. Serve immediately with lemon wedges.

## Apple-Fennel Rémoulade

**SERVES** 6 to 8

Any variety of apple can be used here, but we recommend a crisp-sweet variety such as Fuji, Gala, or Honeycrisp. Our favorite capers are Reese Non Pareil Capers.

- ¼ cup mayonnaise
- 2 tablespoons whole-grain mustard
- 2 tablespoons lemon juice
- 2 tablespoons capers, rinsed, plus 1 tablespoon brine
- 4 celery ribs, sliced thin on bias
- 1 fennel bulb, 1 tablespoon fronds minced, stalks discarded, bulb halved, cored, and sliced thin crosswise
- 1 apple, cored and cut into 2-inch-long matchsticks

Whisk mayonnaise, mustard, lemon juice, and caper brine together in large bowl. Add celery, fennel bulb, apple, and capers and toss to combine. Season with salt and pepper to taste. Top with fennel fronds and serve.

## Nut-Crusted Chicken Breasts with Lemon and Thyme

**SERVES** 4

**WHY THIS RECIPE WORKS** Adding chopped nuts to a coating is a great way to add robust flavor to otherwise lean and mild boneless, skinless chicken breasts. Using a combination of chopped almonds and panko bread crumbs—rather than all nuts—kept the coating light and crunchy, and the bread crumbs helped the coating adhere. Instead of frying the breaded breasts, we found that baking them in the oven was easier, helped the meat stay juicy, and ensured an even golden crust. But it wasn't until we cooked the coating in browned butter prior to breading the chicken that we finally achieved the deep nutty flavor we sought. This recipe is best with almonds but works well with any type of nut. We prefer kosher salt in this recipe. If using table salt, reduce the salt amounts by half.

- 4 (6- to 8-ounce) boneless, skinless chicken breasts, tenderloins removed and breasts trimmed
- Kosher salt
- 1 cup almonds, chopped coarse
- 4 tablespoons (½ stick) unsalted butter
- 1 medium shallot, minced (about 3 tablespoons)
- 1 cup panko bread crumbs
- 2 teaspoons finely grated zest from 1 lemon, zested lemon cut into wedges
- 1 teaspoon minced fresh thyme leaves
- ⅛ teaspoon cayenne pepper
- 1 cup unbleached all-purpose flour
- 3 large eggs
- 2 teaspoons Dijon mustard
- ¼ teaspoon ground black pepper

**1.** Adjust the oven rack to the lower-middle position and heat the oven to 350 degrees. Set a wire rack in a rimmed baking sheet. Pat the chicken dry with paper towels. Using a fork, poke the thickest half of the breasts 5 to 6 times and sprinkle with ½ teaspoon salt. Transfer the breasts to the prepared wire rack and refrigerate, uncovered, while preparing the coating.

**2.** Pulse the almonds in a food processor until they resemble coarse meal, about 20 pulses. Melt the butter in a 12-inch skillet over medium heat, swirling occasionally, until the butter is browned and releases a nutty aroma, 4 to 5 minutes. Add the shallot and ½ teaspoon salt and cook, stirring constantly, until just beginning to brown, about 3 minutes. Reduce the heat to medium-low, add the bread crumbs and ground almonds and cook, stirring often, until golden brown, 10 to 12 minutes. Transfer the panko mixture to a shallow dish or pie plate and stir in the lemon zest, thyme, and cayenne. Place the flour in a second dish. Lightly beat the eggs, mustard, and black pepper together in a third dish.

**3.** Pat the chicken dry with paper towels. Working with one breast at a time, dredge the chicken in the flour, shaking off the excess, then coat with the egg mixture, allowing the excess to drip off. Coat all sides of the breast with the panko mixture, pressing gently so that the crumbs adhere. Return the breaded breasts to the wire rack.

**4.** Bake until the chicken registers 160 degrees on an instant-read thermometer, 20 to 25 minutes. Let the chicken rest for 5 minutes before serving with the lemon wedges.

## Almond-Crusted Chicken Cutlets with Wilted Spinach–Orange Salad

**SERVES 4**

**WHY THIS RECIPE WORKS** When leafy greens are paired with sautéed chicken, a simple salad becomes a satisfying, one-dish meal. We wanted to create an easy recipe for such a dish, and thought incorporating nuts in the coating of the chicken would make for a heartier, more elegant meal. We started by pounding store-bought chicken breasts to the same thickness to ensure that they would cook evenly. Ground almonds paired with panko (Japanese-style bread crumbs) created a rich-tasting crust that was both light and crisp. Much like regular breaded chicken, the breasts had to be pan-fried in a fair amount of oil. Pan-frying can make a mess in a traditional skillet, so we used a nonstick pan. To make a quick salad with bright flavors, we heated orange slices to create a dressing in the skillet, then used the hot dressing to wilt the spinach. Don't process the nuts longer than directed or they will turn pasty and oily.

**CHICKEN**

- 4 (5 to 6-ounce) boneless, skinless chicken breasts, trimmed
  Table salt and ground black pepper
- 1 cup sliced almonds
- ½ cup panko (Japanese-style bread crumbs)
- 2 large eggs
- 1 teaspoon Dijon mustard

- 1¼ teaspoons grated zest from 1 orange
- ¾ cup plus 2 tablespoons vegetable oil

**SALAD**

- 5 ounces baby spinach (about 5 cups)
- 2 medium oranges, peel and pith removed (see page 539), quartered and sliced ¼ inch thick
- 1 small shallot, minced (about 1 tablespoon)

**1. FOR THE CHICKEN:** Adjust an oven rack to the middle position and heat the oven to 200 degrees. Pound each breast between two sheets of plastic wrap to a uniform ½-inch thickness. Pat the chicken dry with paper towels and season with salt and pepper.

**2.** Process the almonds in a food processor to fine crumbs, about 10 seconds (do not over process). Toss the nuts with the panko in a shallow dish. Whisk the eggs, mustard, 1 teaspoon of the orange zest, ½ teaspoon salt, and ¼ teaspoon pepper together in another shallow dish. Working with 1 chicken breast at a time, dip the chicken into the egg mixture, turning to coat well and allowing the excess to drip off, then coat with the nut mixture, pressing gently so that the nuts adhere. Place the breaded chicken in a single layer on a wire rack set over a rimmed baking sheet and let sit for 5 minutes.

**3.** Heat 6 tablespoons of the oil in a 12-inch nonstick skillet over medium heat until shimmering. Add 2 of the chicken breasts and cook until browned on both sides, 4 to 6 minutes total. Drain the chicken briefly on a paper towel–lined plate, then transfer to a clean wire rack set over a rimmed baking sheet and keep warm in the oven. Discard the oil and wipe out the skillet with paper towels. Repeat with 6 tablespoons more oil and the remaining chicken. Discard the oil and wipe out the skillet with paper towels.

**4. FOR THE SALAD:** Place the spinach in a large bowl. Heat 1 tablespoon more oil in the skillet over high heat until just smoking. Add the orange slices and cook until lightly browned around the edges, 1½ to 2 minutes. Remove the pan from the heat and add the remaining 1 tablespoon oil, the shallot, remaining ¼ teaspoon zest, ¼ teaspoon salt, and ⅛ teaspoon pepper and allow residual heat to soften the shallot, about 30 seconds. Pour the warm dressing with the oranges over the spinach and toss gently. Divide the greens among individual plates. Remove the chicken from the oven, set a cutlet over each portion, and serve.

## Pan-Seared Chicken Breasts

**SERVES 4**

**WHY THIS RECIPE WORKS** A boneless, skinless chicken breast inevitably emerges from the pan moist in the middle and dry at the edges, with an exterior that's leathery and tough. We utilized a technique that we'd used successfully with steaks, where we gently parcook the meat in the oven and then sear it on the stovetop. First, we salted the chicken to help it retain more moisture as it cooked. To expedite the process we poked holes in the breasts so the salt could reach the interior of the chicken as it parcooked. We then placed the breasts in a baking dish and covered it tightly with foil. In this enclosed environment, any moisture released by the chicken kept the exterior from drying out without becoming so overly wet that it couldn't brown quickly. To achieve a crisp, even crust, we turned to a Chinese cooking technique called velveting, in which meat is dipped in a mixture of oil and cornstarch to create a thin protective layer. The coating helped the chicken make better contact with the hot skillet, creating a thin, browned, crisp veneer that kept the breast's exterior as moist as the interior. If the breasts include the tenderloin, leave it in place and follow the upper range of time in step 1. Sear chicken immediately after removing it from the oven. Serve with Lemon and Chive Pan Sauce, if desired.

- 4 (6- to 8-ounce) boneless, skinless chicken breasts, trimmed
- 1 teaspoon table salt
- 1 tablespoon vegetable oil
- 2 tablespoons unsalted butter, melted
- 1 tablespoon all-purpose flour
- 1 teaspoon cornstarch
- ½ teaspoon pepper

**1.** Adjust oven rack to lower-middle position and heat oven to 275 degrees. Use fork to poke thickest half of each breast 5 or 6 times, then sprinkle each breast with ¼ teaspoon salt. Place chicken, skin side down, in 13 by 9-inch baking dish and cover tightly with foil. Bake until chicken registers 145 to 150 degrees, 30 to 40 minutes.

**2.** Remove chicken from oven and transfer, skinned side up, to paper towel–lined plate; pat dry. Heat oil in 12-inch skillet over medium-high heat until just smoking. While pan is heating, whisk melted butter, flour, cornstarch, and pepper together in small bowl. Brush tops of chicken with half of butter mixture. Place chicken in skillet, coated side down, and cook until browned, 3 to 4 minutes. While chicken browns, brush second side with remaining butter mixture. Using tongs, flip chicken, reduce heat to medium, and cook until second side is browned and chicken registers 160 to 165 degrees, 3 to 4 minutes. Transfer chicken to platter and let rest while preparing pan sauce. (If not making pan sauce, let chicken rest for 5 minutes before serving.)

### Lemon and Chive Pan Sauce

**MAKES** ¾ cup

- 1 shallot, minced
- 1 teaspoon all-purpose flour
- 1 cup chicken broth
- 1 tablespoon lemon juice
- 1 tablespoon minced fresh chives
- 1 tablespoon unsalted butter, chilled

Add shallot to fond in skillet and cook over medium heat until softened, about 2 minutes. Add flour and cook, stirring constantly, for 30 seconds. Add broth, increase heat to medium-high, and bring to simmer, scraping up any browned bits. Simmer rapidly until reduced to ¾ cup, 3 to 5 minutes. Stir in any accumulated chicken juices, return to simmer, and cook for 30 seconds. Off heat, whisk in lemon juice, chives, and butter; season with salt and pepper to taste.

## Cold-Start Pan-Seared Chicken Breasts with Cherry and Rosemary Pan Sauce

**SERVES 4** SEASON 26

**WHY THIS RECIPE WORKS** With just a few modifications to our tried-and-true "cold-sear" cooking method, we've added boneless, skinless chicken breasts to the list of proteins that cook up beautifully with the technique. Gently flattening the thick part of the breast with a meat pounder encouraged even cooking, while lightly brushing oil on both sides of the breast allowed for even browning without splattering. We put the oiled chicken in an unheated, dry skillet; set it over high heat; and flipped it regularly. Flipping the breasts frequently meant that the meat gently cooked from the outside in: The exterior slowly developed a deep, brown crust while the interior remained juicy. For a ruby pan sauce to dress up our pan-seared chicken breasts, we combined frozen sweet cherries, red wine, and fresh rosemary. For the best results, buy similar-size chicken breasts weighing up to 10 ounces. If using breasts that weigh 10 to 12 ounces, cook only three and increase the cooking time in step 3 to 9 to 12 minutes and slice the chicken for serving. We don't recommend using breasts larger than 12 ounces here as their exteriors will toughen before they cook through. This recipe was developed with Diamond Crystal kosher salt. If using Morton kosher salt, which is denser, use only 1½ teaspoons. A Cabernet Sauvignon or Pinot Noir would work well here.

**CHICKEN**

- 4 boneless, skinless chicken breasts, trimmed
- 2 tablespoons vegetable oil
- 2 teaspoons kosher salt, divided

**CHERRY AND ROSEMARY PAN SAUCE**

- 2 teaspoons extra-virgin olive oil
- 2 tablespoons minced shallot
- ½ teaspoon minced fresh rosemary
- 1 cup dry red wine
- 2 tablespoons balsamic vinegar
- 2 teaspoons sugar
- 5 ounces frozen sweet cherries, thawed and halved (½ cup)
- 2 teaspoons water
- ½ teaspoon cornstarch
- 2 tablespoons unsalted butter, cut into 4 pieces and chilled

**1. FOR THE CHICKEN:** Gently pound thicker end of each breast until ½ inch thick. Pat breasts dry with paper towels. Brush both sides of breasts with oil and evenly sprinkle each breast with ½ teaspoon kosher salt.

**2.** Place breasts, skinned side down, in 12-inch nonstick or carbon-steel skillet, arranging narrow parts of breasts opposite wider parts. Place skillet over high heat and cook for 2 minutes. Flip breasts and cook on second side for 2 minutes (there should be light browning).

**3.** Flip breasts; reduce heat to medium; and continue to cook, flipping breasts every 2 minutes, until exterior is well browned and thickest part of breast registers 155 degrees, 6 to 8 minutes longer. Transfer breasts, skinned side up, to platter; tent with foil; and let rest for at least 10 minutes.

**4. FOR THE PAN SAUCE:** Heat oil in now-empty skillet over medium heat. Add shallot and rosemary and cook, stirring frequently, until shallot is softened and lightly golden, about 2 minutes. Add wine, vinegar, and sugar and bring to simmer, scraping up any browned bits. Cook, stirring frequently, until liquid is reduced by half and shallots are tender, about 5 minutes.

**5.** Stir in cherries and any accumulated chicken juices and cook for 2 minutes. Combine water and cornstarch in small bowl. Add cornstarch mixture to skillet and cook, stirring constantly, until sauce is slightly thickened and glossy, about 1 minute. Off heat, whisk in butter. Season with salt and pepper to taste. Spoon over chicken and serve.

## Skillet Chicken Fajitas

**SERVES 4**

---

**WHY THIS RECIPE WORKS** To create moist and tender chicken fajitas that could be made year-round, we took a fresh look at the key ingredients. For well-charred, juicy chicken we marinated boneless, skinless breasts in a potent mix of smoked paprika, garlic, cumin, cayenne, and sugar before searing them on one side and finishing them gently in a low oven. We revamped the usual mix of bell pepper and onion by charring poblano chiles and thinly sliced onion and then cooking them down with cream and lime. Finally, we finished the dish with moderate amounts of complementary garnishes: pickled radish, queso fresco, and minced cilantro. We like to serve these fajitas with crumbled queso fresco or feta in addition to the other garnishes listed.

**CHICKEN**

- ¼ cup vegetable oil
- 2 tablespoons lime juice
- 4 garlic cloves, peeled and smashed
- 1½ teaspoons smoked paprika
- 1 teaspoon sugar
- 1 teaspoon salt
- ½ teaspoon ground cumin
- ½ teaspoon pepper
- ¼ teaspoon cayenne pepper
- 1½ pounds boneless, skinless chicken breasts, trimmed and pounded to ½-inch thickness

**RAJAS CON CREMA**

- 1 pound (3 to 4) poblano chiles, stemmed, halved, and seeded
- 1 tablespoon vegetable oil
- 1 onion, halved and sliced ¼ inch thick
- 2 garlic cloves, minced
- ¼ teaspoon dried thyme
- ¼ teaspoon dried oregano
- ½ cup heavy cream
- 1 tablespoon lime juice
- ½ teaspoon salt
- ¼ teaspoon pepper

- 8–12 (6-inch) flour tortillas, warmed
- ¼ cup minced fresh cilantro
- Spicy Pickled Radishes
- Lime wedges

**1. FOR THE CHICKEN:** Whisk 3 tablespoons oil, lime juice, garlic, paprika, sugar, salt, cumin, pepper, and cayenne together in bowl. Add chicken and toss to coat. Cover and let stand at room temperature for at least 30 minutes or up to 1 hour.

**2. FOR THE RAJAS CON CREMA:** Meanwhile, adjust oven rack to highest position and heat broiler. Line rimmed baking sheet with aluminum foil, then arrange poblanos skin side up on baking sheet and press to flatten. Broil until skin is charred and puffed, 4 to 10 minutes, rotating baking sheet halfway through cooking. Transfer poblanos to bowl, cover, and let steam for 10 minutes. Rub most of skin from poblanos (leaving a little attached for flavor); slice into ¼-inch-thick strips. Adjust oven racks to middle and lowest positions and heat oven to 200 degrees.

**3.** Heat oil in 12-inch nonstick skillet over high heat until just smoking. Add onion and cook until charred and just softened, about 3 minutes. Add garlic, thyme, and oregano and cook until fragrant, about 15 seconds. Add cream and cook, stirring frequently, until reduced and cream lightly coats onion, 1 to 2 minutes. Add poblano strips, lime juice, salt, and pepper and toss to coat. Transfer vegetables to bowl, cover with foil, and place on middle oven rack. Wipe out skillet with paper towels.

**4.** Remove chicken from marinade and wipe off excess. Heat remaining 1 tablespoon oil in now-empty skillet over high heat until just smoking. Add chicken and cook without moving it until bottom side is well charred, about 4 minutes. Flip chicken; transfer skillet to lower oven rack. Bake until chicken registers 160 degrees, 7 to 10 minutes. Transfer to cutting board and let rest for 5 minutes; do not wash out skillet.

**5.** Slice chicken crosswise into ¼-inch-thick strips. Return chicken strips to skillet and toss to coat with pan juices. To serve, spoon a few pieces of chicken into center of warmed tortilla and top with spoonful of vegetable mixture, cilantro, and pickled radishes. Serve with lime wedges.

### Spicy Pickled Radishes

**MAKES** about 1¾ cups

If you'd like a less spicy version of these pickled radishes, omit the seeds from the jalapeño.

- 10 radishes, trimmed and sliced thin
- ½ cup lime juice (4 limes)
- ½ jalapeño chile, stemmed and sliced thin
- 1 teaspoon sugar
- ¼ teaspoon salt

Combine all ingredients in bowl. Cover and let stand at room temperature for 30 minutes (or refrigerate for up to 24 hours).

## Blackened Chicken

**SERVES** 4

**WHY THIS RECIPE WORKS** Blackening refers to coating proteins in a robust Cajun spice blend and cooking them in a hot skillet until the fat and spices smoke and char to produce a primal savoriness that stops just short of fully burnt. This method, popularized by New Orleans chef Paul Prudhomme and his wife, K. Hinrichs, as a cooking method for fish, is now used to cook all sorts of proteins, from steak to shellfish to the chicken we used in our recipe. Blackening is usually a smoky business, but we controlled the smoke with a few tweaks. Pounding the cutlets very thin helped them cook through quickly, so there was little time for the fat and spices to burn. We arranged the cutlets in the pan to cover as much surface area as possible; this prevented hot spots from forming in the gaps and overheating the chicken's fat and juices. And since butter smokes readily in high-heat applications, we used just 3 tablespoons total—still plenty to produce the rich, deep char we were after. We prefer a 12-inch cast-iron skillet here, but a heavy-bottomed stainless-steel or well-seasoned carbon-steel skillet will also work. Avoid nonstick cookware due to the high cooking temperature. This cooking method will produce a modest amount of smoke, so turn on your exhaust fan or crack open a window prior to cooking. If your chicken breasts weigh more than 8 ounces each, add 15 seconds to the cooking time after the cutlets have been flipped. We developed this recipe using Diamond Crystal kosher salt; if using Morton kosher salt, which is denser, use only 2¼ teaspoons. For a less spicy dish, use only ½ teaspoon of cayenne pepper.

- 1 tablespoon smoked paprika
- 1 tablespoon paprika
- 1 tablespoon kosher salt
- 2 teaspoons garlic powder
- 2 teaspoons onion powder
- 1½ teaspoons pepper
- 1½ teaspoons dried oregano
- 1½ teaspoons dried thyme
- ½–1 teaspoon cayenne pepper
- 4 (6- to 8-ounce) boneless, skinless chicken breasts, trimmed
- 1 teaspoon vegetable oil
- 3 tablespoons unsalted butter, cut into 6 pieces, divided

**1.** Combine smoked paprika, paprika, salt, garlic powder, onion powder, pepper, oregano, thyme, and cayenne in wide, shallow bowl. Set wire rack in rimmed baking sheet. Wad up paper towel and place within reach of stove.

**2.** Working with 1 chicken breast at a time, halve chicken breast crosswise, then cut thicker half in half horizontally, creating 3 cutlets of similar thickness. Place cutlets between sheets of plastic wrap and gently pound to even ⅓-inch thickness.

**3.** Working with 1 cutlet at a time, dredge thoroughly in spice mixture, pressing to adhere, then shake off excess. Place cutlets in single layer on second rimmed baking sheet.

**4.** Heat oil in 12-inch cast-iron skillet over high heat until just smoking. Add 1 tablespoon butter to skillet, then tilt skillet or spread butter with flexible spatula until it coats skillet evenly. Add 6 cutlets to skillet, press on each firmly with spatula, and cook undisturbed for 2 minutes. Using tongs, flip cutlets. Press cutlets against skillet with spatula and cook for 1 minute. Slide skillet off heat (leave burner on) and transfer cutlets to prepared wire rack. Grab paper towel with tongs and wipe out skillet to remove any debris.

**5.** Return skillet to heat. Add remaining 2 tablespoons butter and repeat with remaining cutlets. Let cutlets rest for 3 minutes on rack and serve. (Leftover chicken can be wrapped tightly in plastic wrap and refrigerated for up to 3 days.)

## Chicken Marsala

**SERVES 4**

**WHY THIS RECIPE WORKS** Developed in Italy after a successful 19th-century marketing campaign to promote Marsala wine from Sicily, this combination of chicken and mushrooms in wine sauce has become an Italian restaurant staple. Too often, however, the chicken is dry, the mushrooms flabby, and the sauce nondescript. We wanted a failproof recipe. We browned chicken breasts in a skillet to start and kept them warm while we prepared the mushrooms and sauce. The mushrooms went into the skillet next, but the chicken drippings burned. Our solution was to sauté some pancetta before browning the mushrooms, which rendered additional fat as well as added meaty flavor. We preferred sweet (as opposed to dry) Marsala for its depth of flavor and smooth finish. Some lemon juice tempered the Marsala's sweetness, while a little garlic and tomato paste rounded out the flavors. Finally, we whisked butter into the sauce at the end, for a rich finish and beautiful sheen. Our wine of choice for this dish is Sweet Marsala Fine, an imported wine that gives the sauce body, soft edges, and a smooth finish. To make slicing the chicken easier, freeze it for 15 minutes.

- 2 tablespoons vegetable oil
- 1 cup all-purpose flour
- 4 (5- to 6-ounce) boneless, skinless chicken breasts, tenderloins removed and breasts trimmed
- ½ teaspoon table salt
- ½ teaspoon pepper
- 2½ ounces pancetta (about 3 slices), cut into pieces 1 inch long and ⅛ inch wide
- 8 ounces white mushrooms, trimmed and sliced (about 2 cups)
- 1 garlic clove, minced
- 1 teaspoon tomato paste
- 1½ cups sweet Marsala
- 1½ tablespoons lemon juice
- 4 tablespoons unsalted butter, cut into 4 pieces
- 2 tablespoons minced fresh parsley

**1.** Adjust oven rack to lower-middle position, place large ovensafe dinner plate on oven rack, and heat oven to 200 degrees. Heat oil in 12-inch skillet over medium-high heat until shimmering. Meanwhile, place flour in shallow baking dish or pie plate. Halve chicken horizontally, then cover chicken halves with plastic wrap and pound cutlets to even ¼-inch thickness. Pat chicken breasts dry. Sprinkle both sides of breasts with salt and pepper; working with 1 piece at a time, coat both sides with flour. Place 4 floured cutlets in single layer in skillet and cook until golden brown, about 3 minutes. Using tongs, flip cutlets and cook on second side until golden brown and meat feels firm when pressed with your finger, about 3 minutes longer. Transfer chicken to heated plate and return plate to oven while cooking remaining 4 cutlets.

**2.** Return skillet to low heat and add pancetta; sauté, stirring occasionally and scraping up any browned bits, until pancetta is brown and crisp, about 4 minutes. Using slotted spoon, transfer pancetta to paper towel–lined plate. Add mushrooms and increase heat to medium-high; sauté, stirring occasionally and scraping pan bottom, until liquid released by mushrooms evaporates and mushrooms begin to brown, about 8 minutes. Add garlic, tomato paste, and cooked pancetta; sauté while stirring until tomato paste begins to brown, about 1 minute. Off heat, add Marsala; return pan to high heat and simmer vigorously, scraping up any browned bits, until sauce is slightly syrupy and reduced to about 1¼ cups, about 5 minutes. Off heat, add lemon juice and any accumulated juices from chicken; whisk in butter 1 piece at a time. Season with salt and pepper to taste, and stir in parsley. Pour sauce over chicken and serve immediately.

## Better Chicken Marsala

**SERVES 4 to 6**

**WHY THIS RECIPE WORKS** For this recipe, we decided to create a new approach to making chicken Marsala. First, we cut each chicken breast in half crosswise. Then, we cut the thicker half in half horizontally to make three identically sized pieces that could easily be pounded into cutlets. We salted the cutlets briefly to boost their ability to retain moisture and then dredged them in a light coating of flour, which accelerated browning and helped prevent the meat from overcooking. We seared the cutlets quickly on both sides and set them aside while we made the sauce. Our Marsala sauce used reduced dry Marsala and chicken broth, along with cremini and dried porcini mushrooms for rich flavor and gelatin for a silky texture. Once the Marsala and mushroom sauce was complete, we returned the cutlets to the pan to cook them through and wash any excess starch into the sauce, eliminating gumminess. It is worth spending a little extra for a moderately priced dry Marsala ($10 to $12 per bottle).

- 2¼ cups dry Marsala
- 4 teaspoons unflavored gelatin
- 1 ounce dried porcini mushrooms, rinsed
- 4 (6- to 8-ounce) boneless, skinless chicken breasts, trimmed
- Kosher salt and pepper
- 2 cups chicken broth
- ¾ cup all-purpose flour
- ¼ cup plus 1 teaspoon vegetable oil
- 3 ounces pancetta, cut into ½-inch pieces
- 1 pound cremini mushrooms, trimmed and sliced thin
- 1 shallot, minced
- 1 tablespoon tomato paste
- 1 garlic clove, minced
- 2 teaspoons lemon juice
- 1 teaspoon minced fresh oregano
- 3 tablespoons unsalted butter, cut into 6 pieces
- 2 teaspoons minced fresh parsley

**1.** Bring 2 cups Marsala, gelatin, and porcini mushrooms to boil in medium saucepan over high heat. Reduce heat to medium-high and vigorously simmer until reduced by half, 6 to 8 minutes.

**2.** Meanwhile, cut each chicken breast in half crosswise, then cut thick half in half again horizontally, creating 3 cutlets of about same thickness. Place cutlets between sheets of plastic wrap and pound gently to even ½-inch thickness. Place cutlets in bowl and toss with 2 teaspoons salt and ½ teaspoon pepper. Set aside for 15 minutes.

**3.** Strain Marsala reduction through fine-mesh strainer, pressing on solids to extract as much liquid as possible; discard solids. Return Marsala reduction to saucepan, add broth, and return to boil over high heat. Lower heat to medium-high and simmer until reduced to 1½ cups, 10 to 12 minutes. Set aside.

**4.** Spread flour in shallow dish. Working with 1 cutlet at a time, dredge cutlets in flour, shaking gently to remove excess. Place on wire rack set in rimmed baking sheet. Heat 2 tablespoons oil in 12-inch skillet over medium-high heat until just smoking. Place 6 cutlets in skillet and lower heat to medium. Cook until golden brown on 1 side, 2 to 3 minutes. Flip and cook until golden brown on second side, 2 to 3 minutes. Return cutlets to wire rack. Repeat with 2 tablespoons oil and remaining 6 cutlets.

**5.** Return now-empty skillet to medium-low heat and add pancetta. Cook, stirring occasionally, scraping pan bottom to loosen any browned bits, until pancetta is brown and crisp, about 4 minutes. Add cremini mushrooms and increase heat to medium-high. Cook, stirring occasionally and scraping pan bottom, until liquid released by mushrooms evaporates and mushrooms begin to brown, about 8 minutes. Using slotted spoon, transfer cremini mushrooms and pancetta to bowl. Add remaining 1 teaspoon oil and shallot to pan and cook until softened, about 1 minute. Add tomato paste and garlic and cook until fragrant, about 30 seconds. Add reduced Marsala mixture, remaining ¼ cup Marsala, lemon juice, and oregano and bring to simmer.

**6.** Add cutlets to sauce and simmer for 3 minutes, flipping halfway through simmering. Transfer cutlets to platter. Off heat, whisk in butter. Stir in parsley and cremini mushroom mixture. Season with salt and pepper to taste. Spoon sauce over chicken and serve.

## Chicken Piccata

**SERVES 4**

**WHY THIS RECIPE WORKS** Chicken piccata is one of those appealing Italian recipes that tastes complex but is actually easy to prepare. Our goal was properly cooked chicken with a streamlined sauce that really tasted of lemons and capers. After browning the chicken and sautéing aromatics, we deglazed the pan with chicken broth alone; although wine is sometimes suggested, we found it to be too acidic for this dish. We simmered slices from half a lemon in the broth for a few minutes; this was easier than grating the zest. For maximum lemon flavor in the sauce, we used a full quarter-cup of lemon juice, added when the sauce was nearly done so as not to blunt its impact. Plenty of capers and a bit of parsley finished our ultralemony piccata. To make slicing the chicken easier, freeze it for 15 minutes. If you like, use thinly sliced cutlets available at many supermarkets. These cutlets don't have any tenderloins and can be used as they are.

- 2 large lemons
- 4 boneless, skinless chicken breasts (about 1½ pounds), tenderloins removed and breasts trimmed
- Table salt and ground black pepper
- ½ cup unbleached all-purpose flour
- 4 tablespoons vegetable oil
- 1 small shallot, minced (about 2 tablespoons), or 1 small garlic clove, minced (about 1 teaspoon)
- 1 cup chicken broth
- 2 tablespoons small capers, drained
- 3 tablespoons unsalted butter, softened
- 2 tablespoons minced fresh parsley leaves

**1.** Adjust oven rack to the lower-middle position, set large ovensafe plate on rack, and heat oven to 200 degrees.

**2.** Halve 1 lemon pole to pole. Trim ends from one half and cut it crosswise into slices ⅛ to ¼ inch thick; set aside. Juice remaining half and whole lemon to obtain ¼ cup juice; reserve.

**3.** Halve chicken horizontally, then cover chicken halves with plastic wrap and pound cutlets to even ¼-inch thickness. Sprinkle both sides of cutlets generously with salt and pepper. Place flour in shallow baking dish or pie plate. Working with 1 cutlet at a time, coat with flour and shake to remove excess.

**4.** Heat 2 tablespoons of oil in a heavy-bottomed 12-inch skillet over medium-high heat until shimmering. Lay half of chicken cutlets in skillet. Cook cutlets until lightly browned on first side, 2 to 3 minutes. Flip cutlets and cook until second

side is lightly browned, 2 to 3 minutes longer. Remove pan from heat and transfer cutlets to plate in warm oven. Add remaining 2 tablespoons oil to now-empty skillet and heat until shimmering. Add remaining chicken cutlets and repeat.

**5.** Add shallot or garlic to now-empty skillet and return skillet to medium heat. Sauté until fragrant, about 30 seconds for shallot or 10 seconds for garlic. Add broth and lemon slices, increase heat to high, and scrape pan bottom with wooden spoon or spatula to loosen browned bits. Simmer until liquid reduces to about ⅓ cup, about 4 minutes. Add lemon juice and capers and simmer until sauce reduces again to ⅓ cup, about 1 minute. Remove pan from heat and swirl in butter until it melts and thickens sauce. Stir in parsley and season with salt and pepper to taste. Spoon sauce over chicken and serve immediately.

## Next-Level Chicken Piccata

**SERVES** 4 to 6

**WHY THIS RECIPE WORKS** Chicken piccata needs little introduction—chicken breasts pounded thin, lightly dusted with flour, pan-seared, and bathed in a lemon-butter pan sauce. We wanted an updated recipe for tender chicken and a complex, lemony sauce. First, we used an innovative approach to butchering and cooking chicken cutlets: We cut each chicken breast in half crosswise, and then halved the thicker portion horizontally to make three similar-size pieces that required only minimal pounding to become cutlets. We salted the cutlets briefly to boost their ability to retain moisture and then lightly coated them in flour, which helped with browning. We seared the cutlets quickly and set them aside while making the sauce. We chose to include both lemon juice and lemon slices in the sauce for complexity and textural appeal. We then returned the cutlets to the pan to cook through and to wash any excess starch into the sauce, eliminating a gummy coating. Briny capers and a few tablespoons of butter finished the sauce, while a sprinkling of parsley added freshness.

- 4 (6- to 8-ounce) boneless, skinless chicken breasts, trimmed
- 2 teaspoons kosher salt
- ½ teaspoon pepper
- 2 large lemons
- ¾ cup all-purpose flour
- ¼ cup plus 1 teaspoon vegetable oil, divided
- 1 shallot, minced
- 1 garlic clove, minced
- 1 cup chicken broth
- 3 tablespoons unsalted butter, cut into 6 pieces
- 2 tablespoons capers, drained
- 1 tablespoon minced fresh parsley

**1.** Cut each chicken breast in half crosswise, then cut thick half in half again horizontally, creating 3 cutlets of similar thickness. Place cutlets between sheets of plastic wrap and gently pound to even ½-inch thickness. Place cutlets in bowl and toss with salt and pepper. Set aside for 15 minutes.

**2.** Halve 1 lemon lengthwise. Trim ends from 1 half, halve lengthwise again, then cut crosswise in ¼-inch-thick slices; set aside. Juice remaining half and whole lemon and set aside 3 tablespoons juice.

**3.** Spread flour in shallow dish. Working with 1 cutlet at a time, dredge cutlets in flour, shaking gently to remove excess. Place on wire rack set in rimmed baking sheet. Heat 2 tablespoons oil in 12-inch skillet over medium-high heat until just smoking. Place 6 cutlets in skillet, reduce heat to medium, and cook until golden brown on 1 side, 2 to 3 minutes. Flip and cook until golden brown on second side, 2 to 3 minutes. Return cutlets to wire rack. Repeat with 2 tablespoons oil and remaining 6 cutlets.

**4.** Add remaining 1 teaspoon oil and shallot to skillet and cook until softened, 1 minute. Add garlic and cook until fragrant, 30 seconds. Add broth, reserved lemon juice, and reserved lemon slices and bring to simmer, scraping up any browned bits.

**5.** Add cutlets to sauce and simmer for 4 minutes, flipping halfway through simmering. Transfer cutlets to platter. Sauce should be thickened to consistency of heavy cream; if not, simmer 1 minute longer. Off heat, whisk in butter. Stir in capers and parsley. Season with salt and pepper to taste. Spoon sauce over chicken and serve.

## Quick Chicken Fricassee

**SERVES** 4 to 6

**WHY THIS RECIPE WORKS** In search of a streamlined technique that would give this classic French braise weeknight potential and a brighter sauce, we replaced the bone-in chicken parts with the busy cook's favorite timesaver: boneless, skinless breasts and thighs. Then we found two ways to add richness that we'd lost by omitting the skin and bones: We browned the meat in butter and oil, and we browned the vegetables until they developed fond to serve as the sauce base. Increasing the amount of mushrooms boosted the fricassee's meaty flavor, while finishing the sauce with sour cream added body and tang. Whisking an egg yolk into the sour cream thickened the sauce and made it silky. Two tablespoons of chopped fresh parsley leaves may be substituted for the tarragon in this recipe.

- 2 pounds boneless, skinless chicken breasts and/or thighs, trimmed
- Table salt and ground black pepper
- 1 tablespoon unsalted butter
- 1 tablespoon olive oil
- 1 pound cremini mushrooms, trimmed and sliced ¼ inch thick
- 1 medium onion, chopped fine
- ¼ cup dry white wine
- 1 tablespoon unbleached all-purpose flour
- 1 medium garlic clove, minced or pressed through a garlic press (about 1 teaspoon)
- 1½ cups low-sodium chicken broth
- ⅓ cup sour cream
- 1 large egg yolk
- 2 teaspoons juice from 1 lemon
- 2 teaspoons minced fresh tarragon leaves
- ½ teaspoon freshly grated nutmeg

**1.** Pat the chicken dry with paper towels and season with 1 teaspoon salt and ½ teaspoon pepper. Heat the butter and oil in a 12-inch skillet over medium-high heat until the butter is melted. Place the chicken in a skillet and cook until browned, about 4 minutes. Using tongs, flip the chicken and cook until browned on the second side, about 4 minutes longer. Transfer the chicken to a large plate.

**2.** Add the mushrooms, onion, and wine to the now-empty skillet and cook, stirring occasionally, until the liquid has evaporated and the mushrooms are browned, 8 to 10 minutes. Add the flour and garlic; cook, stirring constantly, for 1 minute. Add the broth and bring the mixture to a boil, scraping up the browned bits from the bottom of the pan. Add the chicken and any accumulated juices to the skillet. Reduce the heat to medium-low, cover, and simmer until the breasts register 160 degrees and the thighs register 175 degrees, 5 to 10 minutes.

**3.** Transfer the chicken to a clean platter and tent loosely with foil. Whisk the sour cream and the egg yolk together in a medium bowl. Whisking constantly, slowly stir ½ cup of the hot sauce from the skillet into the sour cream mixture to temper. Stirring constantly, slowly pour the sour cream mixture into the simmering sauce. Stir in the lemon juice, tarragon and nutmeg; return to a simmer. Season with salt and pepper to taste, pour the sauce over the chicken, and serve.

## Chicken Francese

**SERVES 6**

---

**WHY THIS RECIPE WORKS** Chicken Francese is a timeless Italian American dish of fried chicken cutlets sauced in a lemony beurre blanc. Cutting and pounding each boneless, skinless chicken breast into three ¼-inch cutlets ensured that they cooked through evenly in minutes. For a tender coating for the cutlets, we diluted the eggs with water to prevent their proteins from coagulating tightly and cooking up rubbery. It was important to fry the chicken in enough oil that it crested just above the sides of the cutlets, which prevented the coating from slipping off before it had time to set. We captured complex fruit flavor in the lemony butter sauce by combining juice, zest, and browned lemon slices; the latter also made for a visually striking garnish. Thickening the sauce with flour-dredged cubed butter added lush, silky body. Use a stainless-steel skillet, not cast iron, the seasoning of which can be damaged by the acidic sauce. To ensure that the sauce develops the correct flavor and consistency, transfer the liquid to a heatproof liquid measuring cup once or twice during simmering to monitor the amount.

- 4 (6- to 8-ounce) boneless, skinless chicken breasts, trimmed
- 2 teaspoons table salt
- ½ teaspoon pepper
- 1 large lemon
- 4 tablespoons unsalted butter, divided
- ¾ cup all-purpose flour, divided
- 3 large eggs
- 2 tablespoons water
- ⅓ cup extra-virgin olive oil for frying
- ⅓ cup vegetable oil for frying
- 1 garlic clove, minced
- ⅓ cup dry white wine
- 1½ cups chicken broth
- 2 tablespoons minced fresh parsley

**1.** Adjust oven rack to middle position and heat oven to 200 degrees. Cut each chicken breast in half crosswise, then cut thick half in half again horizontally, creating 3 cutlets of similar thickness. Place cutlets between sheets of plastic wrap and gently pound to even ¼-inch thickness. Place cutlets in bowl and toss with salt and pepper. Set aside for 15 minutes.

**2.** Grate peel from 1 end of lemon to yield 1 teaspoon zest. Cut lemon in half crosswise and juice zested lemon half. Measure out 2 tablespoons juice. Slice remaining (unzested) lemon half into four ¼-inch-thick rounds. Discard end. Cut 3 tablespoons butter into ½-inch cubes and transfer to small bowl. Sprinkle cubes with 1 teaspoon flour and toss until cubes are fully coated and no loose flour remains in bowl; refrigerate until needed.

**3.** Set wire rack in rimmed baking sheet. Spread remaining flour in shallow dish. In medium bowl, whisk eggs with water. Working with 1 cutlet at a time, dredge cutlets in flour, shaking gently to remove excess. Transfer to prepared rack.

**4.** Heat olive oil and vegetable oil in 12-inch skillet over medium-high heat until shimmering. Working with 1 cutlet at a time, coat 4 cutlets with egg mixture and gently place in skillet. Reduce heat to medium and cook until golden brown on 1 side, about 2 minutes. Using tongs, flip and cook until golden brown on second side, about 2 minutes. Arrange cutlets on serving platter and place in oven. Repeat with remaining cutlets in 2 batches.

**5.** Discard oil. Gently wipe out skillet with paper towels. Return skillet to medium heat and add lemon slices and remaining 1 tablespoon butter. Cook, flipping slices occasionally, until lightly browned on both sides, about 3 minutes. Transfer lemon slices to cutting board.

**6.** Add garlic to now-empty skillet and cook, stirring constantly, until fragrant, about 30 seconds. Stir in wine, scraping up any browned bits, and increase heat to medium-high. Bring to rapid simmer and cook until wine is mostly evaporated, 2 to 3 minutes. Stir in broth and continue to simmer, stirring occasionally, until liquid is reduced to ⅔ cup, 6 to 8 minutes longer.

**7.** Reduce heat to low and stir in reserved lemon zest and juice. Whisk in floured butter cubes, a few at a time, until sauce is thickened to consistency of heavy cream, 1½ to 2 minutes. Off heat, stir in parsley. Season with salt and pepper to taste. Cut browned lemon slices in half and scatter over cutlets. Spoon sauce over cutlets and serve.

## Chicken Saltimbocca

**SERVES 4**

---

**WHY THIS RECIPE WORKS** In its classic Italian form, saltimbocca is made with veal, prosciutto, and sage, but chicken is frequently substituted for the veal. The combination of flavors is meant to "jump in the mouth," as the name suggests. Preparing this dish can be complicated, but we wanted to streamline it and ensure that the flavors were well balanced. Flouring only the chicken, rather than the chicken-prosciutto package, avoided gummy spots. The prosciutto is usually secured to the chicken with a toothpick, but we found that searing the prosciutto side of the chicken first worked as well; once browned, the two stuck together just fine. A single sage leaf is the usual garnish, but we wanted more sage flavor, so we sprinkled some minced fresh sage over the floured chicken before adding the prosciutto. With a simple pan sauce of vermouth, lemon juice, butter, and parsley, our chicken saltimbocca was ready to serve and full of flavor. To make slicing the chicken easier, freeze it for 15 minutes. Although whole sage leaves make a beautiful presentation, they are optional and can be left out of step 3. A single fried sage leaf is another pretty but optional garnish. Make sure to buy prosciutto that is thinly sliced, not shaved; also avoid slices that are too thick, as they won't stick to the chicken. The prosciutto slices should be large enough to fully cover one side of each cutlet.

- 4 (5- to 6-ounce) boneless, skinless chicken breasts, tenderloins removed and breasts trimmed
- ½ cup unbleached all-purpose flour
- Ground black pepper
- 1 tablespoon minced fresh sage leaves, plus 8 large leaves (optional; see note)
- 8 thin prosciutto slices (about 3 ounces; see note)
- 4 tablespoons olive oil
- 1¼ cups dry vermouth or white wine
- 2 teaspoons juice from 1 lemon
- 4 tablespoons (½ stick) unsalted butter, cut into 4 pieces and chilled
- 1 tablespoon minced fresh parsley leaves
- Table salt

**1.** Halve the chicken horizontally, then cover the chicken halves with plastic wrap and pound the cutlets to an even ¼-inch thickness.

**2.** Combine the flour and 1 teaspoon pepper in a shallow dish. Pat the chicken dry with paper towels. Dredge the chicken in the flour, shaking off any excess. Lay the cutlets flat and sprinkle evenly with the minced sage. Place 1 prosciutto slice on top of each cutlet, pressing lightly to adhere; set aside.

**3.** Heat 2 tablespoons of the oil in a 12-inch skillet over medium-high heat until shimmering. Add the sage leaves (if using) and cook until the leaves begin to change color and are fragrant, 15 to 20 seconds. Using a slotted spoon, transfer the sage to a paper towel–lined plate and set aside. Add 4 of the cutlets to the pan, prosciutto side down, and cook until lightly browned on one side, about 2 minutes. Flip the chicken over and continue to cook until no longer pink, 30 seconds to 1 minute. Transfer the chicken to a plate and tent loosely with foil. Add the remaining 2 tablespoons oil to the skillet and repeat with the remaining 4 cutlets. Transfer to the plate and tent loosely with foil while making the sauce.

**4.** Pour off the excess fat from the skillet. Stir in the vermouth, scraping up any browned bits, and simmer until reduced to about ⅓ cup, 5 to 7 minutes. Stir in the lemon juice. Turn the heat to low and whisk in the butter, 1 tablespoon at time. Off the heat, stir in the parsley and season with salt and pepper to taste. Spoon the sauce over the chicken, place a sage leaf (if using) on each cutlet, and serve.

## Crispy-Skinned Chicken Breasts with Vinegar-Pepper Pan Sauce

**SERVES 2**

---

**WHY THIS RECIPE WORKS** We set out to develop a foolproof recipe for perfectly cooked chicken with shatteringly crispy, flavorful skin. Boning and pounding the chicken breasts was essential to creating a flat, even surface to maximize the skin's contact with the hot pan. We salted the chicken to both season the meat and dry out the skin; poking holes in the skin and the meat allowed the salt to penetrate deeply. Starting the chicken in a cold pan allowed time for the skin to crisp without overcooking the meat. Weighting the chicken for part of the cooking time with a heavy Dutch oven encouraged even contact with the hot pan for all-over crunchy skin. Finally, we created a vibrant pan sauce to accompany the chicken. This recipe requires refrigerating the salted meat for at least 1 hour before cooking. Two 10- to 12-ounce chicken breasts are ideal, but three smaller ones can fit in the same pan; the skin will be slightly less crispy. To maintain the crispy skin, spoon the sauce around, not over, the breasts when serving.

**CHICKEN**

- 2 (10- to 12-ounce) bone-in split chicken breasts
- 1 teaspoon kosher salt
- ½ teaspoon pepper
- 2 tablespoons vegetable oil

**PAN SAUCE**

- 1 shallot, minced
- 1 teaspoon all-purpose flour
- ½ cup chicken broth
- ¼ cup chopped pickled hot cherry peppers, plus ¼ cup brine
- 1 tablespoon unsalted butter, chilled
- 1 teaspoon minced fresh thyme

**1. FOR THE CHICKEN:** Place 1 chicken breast, skin side down, on cutting board, with ribs facing away from your knife hand. Run tip of knife between breastbone and meat, working from thick end of breast toward thin end. Angling blade slightly and following rib cage, repeat cutting motion several times to remove ribs and breastbone from breast. Find short remnant of wishbone along top edge of breast and run tip of knife along both sides of bone to separate it from meat. Remove tenderloin (reserve for another use) and trim excess fat, taking care not to cut into skin. Repeat with second breast.

**2.** Using tip of paring knife, poke skin on each breast evenly 30 to 40 times. Turn breasts over and poke thickest half of each breast 5 or 6 times. Cover breasts with plastic wrap and pound thick ends gently with meat pounder until ½ inch thick. Evenly sprinkle each breast with ½ teaspoon kosher salt. Place breasts, skin side up, on wire rack set in rimmed baking sheet, cover loosely with plastic, and refrigerate for at least 1 hour or up to 8 hours.

**3.** Pat breasts dry with paper towels and sprinkle each breast with ¼ teaspoon pepper. Pour oil in 12-inch skillet and swirl to coat. Place breasts, skin side down, in oil and place skillet over medium heat. Place heavy skillet or Dutch oven on top of breasts. Cook breasts until skin is beginning to brown and meat is beginning to turn opaque along edges, 7 to 9 minutes.

**4.** Remove weight and continue to cook until skin is well browned and very crispy, 6 to 8 minutes. Flip breasts, reduce heat to medium-low, and cook until second side is lightly browned and meat registers 160 to 165 degrees, 2 to 3 minutes. Transfer breasts to individual plates and let rest while preparing pan sauce.

**5. FOR THE PAN SAUCE:** Pour off all but 2 teaspoons oil from skillet. Return skillet to medium heat and add shallot; cook, stirring occasionally, until shallot is softened, about 2 minutes. Add flour and cook, stirring constantly, for 30 seconds. Increase heat to medium-high; add broth and brine; and bring to simmer, scraping up any browned bits. Simmer until thickened, 2 to 3 minutes. Stir in any accumulated chicken juices; return to simmer and cook for 30 seconds. Remove skillet from heat and whisk in peppers, butter, and thyme; season with salt and pepper to taste. Spoon sauce around breasts and serve.

### BONING A SPLIT CHICKEN BREAST

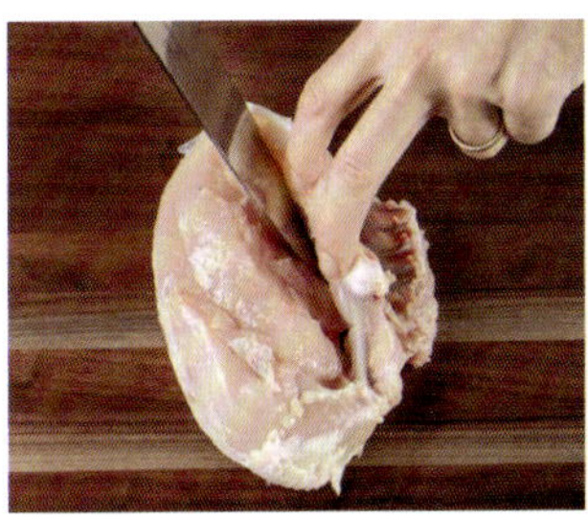

**1.** With chicken breast skin side down, run tip of boning or sharp paring knife between breastbone and meat, working from thick end of breast toward thin end.

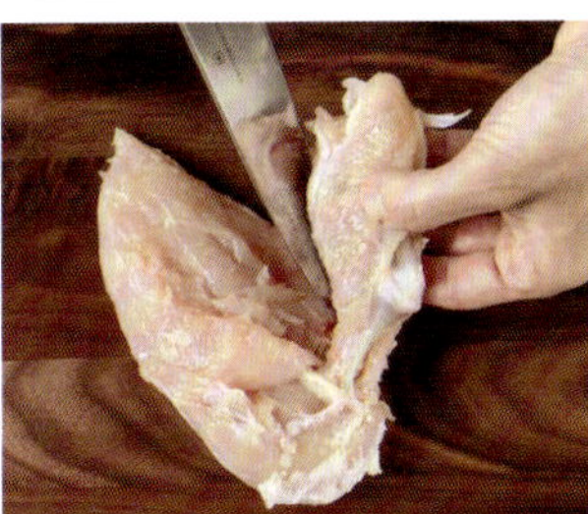

**2.** Angling blade slightly and following rib cage, repeat cutting motion several times to remove ribs and breastbone from breast.

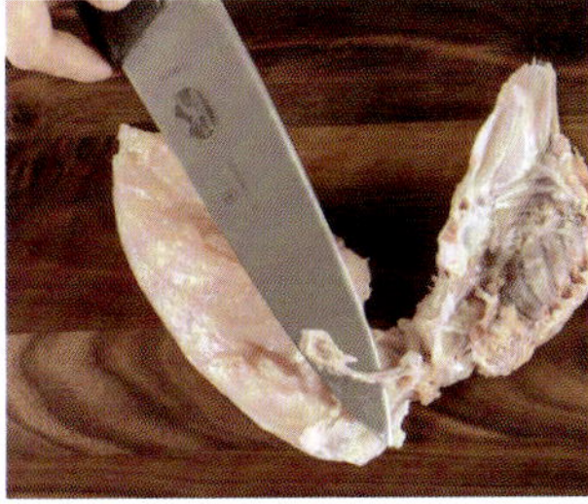

**3.** Find short remnant of wishbone along top edge of breast and run tip of knife along both sides of bone to separate it from meat.

## Pan-Roasted Chicken Breasts with Sage-Vermouth Sauce

**SERVES 4**

**WHY THIS RECIPE WORKS** Cooking bone-in, skin-on chicken breasts can be a challenge. They are difficult to sauté or cook through on the stovetop because of their uneven shape. We wanted to find a method that would produce crisp skin, moist meat, and a quick, flavorful pan sauce. We chose whole breasts, then split them ourselves to control their size. We brined the breasts for maximum moistness and then seared them on the stovetop before letting them cook through in a 450-degree oven. For the pan sauce, we sautéed minced shallot in the same skillet used to cook the chicken, so we could take advantage of the flavorful browned bits left in the pan. We deglazed the pan with chicken broth and vermouth, then added fresh sage for a sauce with deep herbal flavor. Butter whisked into the sauce after it had reduced lent the sauce body and richness—a perfect partner to our moist, juicy chicken. We prefer to split whole chicken breasts ourselves because store-bought split chicken breasts are often sloppily butchered. However, if you prefer to purchase split chicken breasts, try to choose 10- to 12-ounce pieces with skin intact. If split breasts are of different sizes, check the smaller ones a few minutes early to see if they are cooking more quickly, and remove them from the skillet when they are done.

CHICKEN

- ½ cup table salt
- 2 (1½-pound) whole bone-in, skin-on chicken breasts, split in half along breast bone and trimmed of rib sections
- Ground black pepper
- 1 teaspoon vegetable oil

SAGE-VERMOUTH SAUCE

- 1 large shallot, minced (about 4 tablespoons)
- ¾ cup low-sodium chicken broth
- ½ cup dry vermouth
- 4 medium fresh sage leaves, each leaf torn in half
- 3 tablespoons unsalted butter, cut into 3 pieces
- Table salt and ground black pepper

**1. FOR THE CHICKEN:** Dissolve the salt in 2 quarts cold water in a large container; submerge the chicken in the brine, cover, and refrigerate for about 30 minutes. Rinse the chicken well and pat dry with paper towels. Season the chicken with pepper.

**2.** Adjust an oven rack to the lowest position and heat the oven to 450 degrees.

**3.** Heat the oil in a 12-inch ovensafe skillet over medium-high heat until beginning to smoke. Brown the chicken, skin side down, until deep golden, about 5 minutes; turn the chicken and brown until golden on the second side, about 3 minutes longer. Turn the chicken skin side down and place the skillet in the oven. Roast until the thickest part of the breasts registers 160 degrees, 15 to 18 minutes. Transfer the chicken to a platter, and let it rest while making the sauce. (If you're not making the sauce, let the chicken rest for 5 minutes before serving.)

**4. FOR THE SAUCE:** Using a potholder to protect your hands from the hot skillet handle, pour off all but 1 teaspoon of the fat from the skillet; add the shallot, then set the skillet over medium-high heat and cook, stirring frequently, until the shallot is softened, about 1½ minutes. Add the chicken broth, vermouth, and sage; increase the heat to high and simmer rapidly, scraping the skillet bottom with a wooden spoon to loosen the browned bits, until slightly thickened and reduced to about ¾ cup, about 5 minutes. Pour the accumulated chicken juices into the skillet, reduce the heat to medium, and whisk in the butter 1 piece at a time; season with salt and pepper to taste and discard the sage. Spoon the sauce around the chicken breasts and serve immediately.

### TRIMMING SPLIT CHICKEN BREASTS

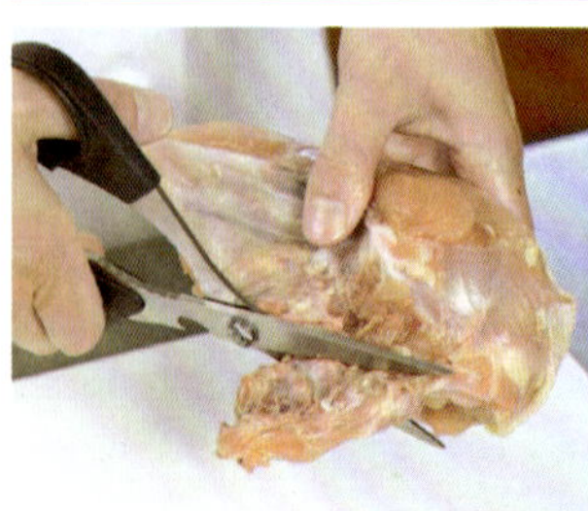

Using kitchen shears, trim off the rib sections from each breast, following the vertical line of fat from the tapered end of the breast up to the socket where the wing was attached.

## Stovetop Roast Chicken with Lemon-Herb Sauce

SERVES 4

**WHY THIS RECIPE WORKS** Roasting chicken in the oven is the usual route to crisp skin and moist meat, but sometimes you want your oven for something else. Cooking chicken pieces in a skillet easily yields a flavorful pan sauce, but the skin on the chicken is often flabby and the meat unevenly cooked. We wanted to combine the best aspects of both roasted and skillet-cooked chicken. We started with four breast halves, two drumsticks, and two thighs. We tested a variety of approaches to achieve moist meat and crisp skin but ran into numerous problems. Steaming the raw chicken in broth and then searing it in a hot pan skin side down crisped the skin but caused it to shrink. To avoid this, we found that searing the chicken first and then steaming was the answer. After steaming, we poured off all the liquid from the pan (reserving it to use for the pan sauce) and returned the chicken to sear again skin side down, which produced deep, russet-hued crisp skin. After removing the finished chicken, we made our pan sauce with shallot, lemon, and herbs. Use a splatter screen when browning the chicken.

CHICKEN

- 3½ pounds bone-in, skin-on chicken pieces (split breasts cut in half, drumsticks, and/or thighs), trimmed
- Table salt and ground black pepper
- 1 tablespoon vegetable oil
- ¾–1¼ cups low-sodium chicken broth

LEMON-HERB SAUCE

- 1 teaspoon vegetable oil
- 1 medium shallot, minced (about 3 tablespoons)
- 1 teaspoon unbleached all-purpose flour
- 1½ tablespoons minced fresh parsley leaves
- 1½ tablespoons minced fresh chives
- 1 tablespoon juice from 1 lemon
- 1 tablespoon unsalted butter, chilled
- Table salt and ground black pepper

**1. FOR THE CHICKEN:** Pat the chicken dry with paper towels and season with salt and pepper. Heat 2 teaspoons of the oil in a 12-inch nonstick skillet over medium-high heat until just smoking. Add the chicken pieces skin side down and cook without moving until golden brown, 5 to 8 minutes.

**2.** Using tongs, flip the chicken pieces skin side up. Reduce the heat to medium-low, add ¾ cup of the broth to the skillet, cover, and cook until the thickest part of the breasts registers 155 degrees and the thickest part of the thighs/drumsticks registers 170 degrees on an instant-read thermometer, 10 to 16 minutes. Transfer the chicken to a plate, skin side up.

**3.** Pour off the liquid from the skillet into a 2-cup measuring cup and reserve. Wipe out the skillet with paper towels. Add the remaining 1 teaspoon oil to the skillet and heat over medium-high heat until shimmering. Return the chicken pieces skin side down and cook undisturbed until the skin is

deep golden brown and crisp, the thickest part of the breasts registers 160 degrees, and the thickest part of the thighs/drumsticks registers 175 degrees, 4 to 7 minutes. Transfer to a serving platter and tent loosely with foil. Using a spoon, skim any fat from the reserved cooking liquid and add enough broth to measure ¾ cup.

**4. FOR THE SAUCE:** Heat the oil in the now-empty skillet over low heat. Add the shallot and cook, stirring frequently, until softened, about 2 minutes. Add the flour and cook, stirring constantly, for 30 seconds. Increase the heat to medium-high, add the reserved cooking liquid, and bring to a simmer, scraping the skillet bottom with a wooden spoon to loosen any browned bits. Simmer rapidly until reduced to ½ cup, 2 to 3 minutes. Stir in any accumulated juices from the resting chicken; return to a simmer and cook for 30 seconds. Off the heat, whisk in the parsley, chives, lemon juice, and butter; season with salt and pepper to taste. Pour the sauce around the chicken and serve immediately.

## Skillet-Roasted Chicken in Lemon Sauce

**SERVES 4**

**WHY THIS RECIPE WORKS** Inspired by Rao's famous roast lemon chicken in New York City, we aspired to re-create this popular dish while making it more accessible to home cooks. We used a mixture of white and dark meat bone-in chicken parts, instead of the small birds Rao's uses, which can be difficult to find. Searing the chicken before transferring it to the oven provided flavorful fond for a pan sauce. Browning the dark meat on both sides ensured that the white and dark meats cooked evenly. To get the right amount of lemony flavor, we introduced zest to the sauce right before the chicken was added. The most successful way to thicken the sauce was with flour, added to the aromatics in the beginning of cooking, which provided a full-bodied gravy. A last-minute sprinkle of oregano, parsley, and more lemon zest finished the dish, adding a fruity brightness that complemented the crisp skin, moist meat, and silky sauce. We serve our version of Rao's chicken with crusty bread, but it can also be served with rice, potatoes, or egg noodles. To ensure crisp skin, dry the chicken well after brining and pour the sauce around, not on, the chicken right before serving.

- ½ cup table salt
- 3 pounds bone-in chicken pieces (2 split breasts cut in half crosswise, 2 drumsticks, and 2 thighs), trimmed
- 1 teaspoon vegetable oil
- 2 tablespoons unsalted butter
- 1 large shallot, minced
- 1 garlic clove, minced
- 4 teaspoons all-purpose flour
- 1 cup chicken broth
- 4 teaspoons grated lemon zest plus ¼ cup juice (2 lemons)
- 1 tablespoon fresh parsley leaves
- 1 teaspoon fresh oregano leaves

**1.** Dissolve salt in 2 quarts cold water in large container. Submerge chicken in brine, cover, and refrigerate for 30 minutes to 1 hour. Remove chicken from brine and pat dry with paper towels.

**2.** Adjust oven rack to lower-middle position and heat oven to 475 degrees. Heat oil in ovensafe 12-inch skillet over medium-high heat until just smoking. Place chicken skin side down in skillet and cook until skin is well browned and crisp, 8 to 10 minutes. Transfer breasts to large plate. Flip thighs and legs and continue to cook until browned on second side, 3 to 5 minutes longer. Transfer thighs and legs to plate with breasts.

**3.** Pour off and discard fat in skillet. Return skillet to medium heat; add butter, shallot, and garlic and cook until fragrant, about 30 seconds. Sprinkle flour evenly over shallot-garlic mixture and cook, stirring constantly, until flour is lightly browned, about 1 minute. Slowly stir in broth and lemon juice, scraping up any browned bits, and bring to simmer. Cook until sauce is slightly reduced and thickened, 2 to 3 minutes. Stir in 1 tablespoon zest and remove skillet from heat. Return chicken, skin side up (skin should be above surface of liquid), and any accumulated juices to skillet and transfer to oven. Cook, uncovered, until breasts register 160 degrees and thighs and legs register 175 degrees, 10 to 12 minutes.

**4.** While chicken cooks, chop parsley, oregano, and remaining 1 teaspoon zest together until finely minced and well combined. Remove skillet from oven and let chicken stand for 5 minutes.

**5.** Transfer chicken to serving platter. Whisk sauce, incorporating any browned bits from sides of pan, until smooth and homogeneous, about 30 seconds. Whisk half of herb-zest mixture into sauce and sprinkle remaining half over chicken. Pour some sauce over chicken. Serve, passing remaining sauce separately.

## Pan-Roasted Chicken Breasts with Potatoes

**SERVES 4**

**WHY THIS RECIPE WORKS** This recipe has all the attributes of a special Sunday dinner when time is not an issue, but our skillet preparation will allow you to put it on your weeknight rotation. To start, we borrowed the restaurant method of browning meat on the stovetop and finishing it in the oven. Meanwhile, we turned to the potatoes. We chose red potatoes because their skins are tender and don't require peeling. This saved some prep time, but we couldn't get them to cook in the same amount of time as the chicken. The microwave turned out to be the solution; while the chicken was browning, we tossed the potatoes with a little olive oil, salt, and pepper and microwaved them for a few minutes to jump-start the cooking process. Placing the potatoes in a single layer in the skillet—the same one in which we'd browned the chicken—helped them cook up creamy and moist inside while their exteriors became crispy and caramelized just when it was time to take the chicken out of the oven. Before serving, we drizzled a mixture of olive oil, lemon juice, garlic, red pepper flakes, and thyme over our chicken and potatoes for an extra hit of moisture and flavor. To complete this recipe in 30 minutes, preheat your oven before assembling the ingredients. If the split breasts are different sizes, check the smaller ones a few minutes early and remove them from the oven if they are done.

- 4 (10 to 12-ounce) bone-in, split chicken breasts
- Table salt and ground black pepper
- 6 tablespoons olive oil
- 1½ pounds red potatoes (4 to 5 medium), cut into 1-inch wedges
- 2 tablespoons juice from 1 lemon
- 1 medium garlic clove, minced or pressed through a garlic press (about 1 teaspoon)
- 1 teaspoon minced fresh thyme leaves
- Pinch red pepper flakes

**1.** Adjust an oven rack to the lowest position and heat the oven to 450 degrees.

**2.** Pat the chicken dry with paper towels and season with salt and pepper. Heat 1 tablespoon of the oil in a 12-inch nonstick skillet over medium-high heat until just smoking. Add the chicken, skin side down, and cook until deep golden, about 5 minutes.

**3.** Meanwhile, toss the potatoes with 1 more tablespoon of the oil, ½ teaspoon salt, and ¼ teaspoon pepper in a microwave-safe bowl. Cover tightly with plastic wrap. Microwave on high power until the potatoes begin to soften, 5 to 10 minutes, shaking the bowl (without removing the plastic) to toss the potatoes halfway through.

**4.** Transfer the chicken, skin side up, to a baking dish and bake until the thickest part of the breasts register 160 degrees, 15 to 20 minutes.

**5.** While the chicken bakes, pour off any fat in the skillet, add 1 tablespoon more oil, and return to medium heat until shimmering. Drain the microwaved potatoes, then add to the skillet and cook, stirring occasionally, until golden brown and tender, about 10 minutes.

**6.** Whisk the remaining 3 tablespoons oil, the lemon juice, garlic, thyme, and red pepper flakes together. Drizzle the oil mixture over the chicken and potatoes before serving.

## Chicken Vesuvio

**SERVES 4 to 6**

**WHY THIS RECIPE WORKS** Chicken Vesuvio is a classic Chicago restaurant dish: crisp-skinned chicken and deeply browned potatoes in a potent garlic and white wine sauce. Line cooks make it one order at a time in a big skillet, which provides plenty of space for browning and for reduction of the sauce, and goes handily from stovetop to oven. To transfer Vesuvio to the home kitchen, we traded the customary skillet for a large, heavy roasting pan, and we swapped the usual half chickens for just thighs. We heated oil in the roasting pan on the stovetop, browned the chicken thighs and halved Yukon Gold potatoes, and added traditional dried herbs and plenty of garlic cloves. We then poured wine into the pan and transferred it to the oven so that the chicken, potatoes, and garlic could finish cooking. After placing the cooked chicken and potatoes on a platter, we returned the pan to the stovetop to further reduce the sauce. Mashing the cooked garlic cloves released polysaccharides, which brought the oil and wine together in a rich emulsion, and fresh minced garlic, tempered with lemon juice, delivered robust flavor. For this recipe you'll need a roasting pan that measures at least 16 by 12 inches. Trim all the skin from the underside of the chicken thighs, but leave the skin on top intact. To ensure that all of the potatoes fit in the pan, halve them crosswise to minimize their surface area. For the most efficient browning, heat the roasting pan over 2 burners. Mixing lemon juice into the garlic in step 1 makes the garlic taste less harsh, but only if the lemon juice is added immediately after the garlic is minced.

8 (5- to 7-ounce) bone-in chicken thighs, trimmed
2½ teaspoons kosher salt, divided
½ teaspoon pepper
2 tablespoons vegetable oil, divided
1½ pounds Yukon Gold potatoes, 2 to 3 inches, halved
14 garlic cloves, peeled (2 whole, 12 halved lengthwise)
1 tablespoon lemon juice
1½ teaspoons dried oregano
½ teaspoon dried thyme
1½ cups dry white wine
2 tablespoons minced fresh parsley, divided

**1.** Adjust oven rack to upper-middle position, and heat oven to 450 degrees. Pat chicken dry with paper towels and season both sides with 1½ teaspoons salt and ½ teaspoon pepper. Toss potatoes with 1 tablespoon oil and remaining 1 teaspoon salt. Mince 2 whole garlic cloves and immediately combine with lemon juice in small bowl and set aside.

**2.** Heat remaining 1 tablespoon oil in large roasting pan over medium-high heat until shimmering. Place chicken skin-side down in single layer in pan and cook without moving until chicken has rendered about 2 tablespoons of fat, 2 to 3 minutes. Place potatoes cut side down in chicken fat, arranging so that cut sides are in complete contact with surface of pan. Sprinkle chicken and potatoes with oregano and thyme. Continue to cook until chicken and potatoes are deeply browned and crisp, 8 to 12 minutes longer, moving chicken and potatoes to ensure even browning and turning pieces over when fully browned. When all pieces have been flipped, tuck halved garlic cloves in between chicken and potatoes. Remove roasting pan from heat and pour wine into pan (do not pour over chicken or potatoes). Transfer to oven. Roast until potatoes are tender when pierced with tip of paring knife and chicken registers 185 to 190 degrees, 15 to 20 minutes.

**3.** Transfer chicken and potatoes to deep platter, browned sides up. Place roasting pan over medium heat (handles will be hot) and stir to incorporate any browned bits. Using slotted spoon, transfer garlic cloves to cutting board. Chop coarse, and then mash to smooth paste with side of knife. Whisk garlic into sauce. Continue to cook until sauce coats back of spoon, 3 to 5 minutes. Remove from heat and whisk in reserved lemon juice mixture and 1 tablespoon parsley. Pour sauce around chicken and potatoes. Sprinkle with remaining 1 tablespoon parsley, and serve.

## Skillet-Roasted Chicken Breasts with Garlicky Green Beans

SERVES 4

**WHY THIS RECIPE WORKS** This recipe is a twofer from one skillet. First, we seasoned bone-in, skin-on chicken breasts under the skin with salt. We placed them skin side down in a cold skillet and then turned on the heat to slowly render and brown the skin without overcooking the delicate flesh just beneath it. Once the skin was well browned, we flipped the breasts and placed them in a 325-degree oven for about 30 minutes to cook through. While the cooked chicken breasts rested, we added sliced garlic, spicy red pepper flakes, and salt to the skillet and cooked them until the chicken juices reduced and the mixture began to sizzle in the chicken fat and release flavor. We then added green beans to the pan along with a little water, covered the pan, and let the green beans cook through. With the skillet uncovered, the savory, chicken-y liquid thickened to coat the beans. A shower of nutty, salty Parmesan shreds enhanced the rich green beans.

4 (10- to 12-ounce) bone-in split chicken breasts, trimmed
2¼ teaspoons kosher salt, divided
Vegetable oil spray
3 garlic cloves, sliced thin
¼ teaspoon red pepper flakes
1¼ pounds green beans, trimmed
⅓ cup water
1½ ounces Parmesan cheese, shredded (½ cup)

**1.** Adjust oven rack to lower-middle position and heat oven to 325 degrees. Working with 1 breast at a time, use your fingers to carefully separate skin from meat. Peel back skin, leaving skin attached at top and bottom of breast and at ribs. Sprinkle 1½ teaspoons salt evenly over chicken (⅜ teaspoon per breast). Lay skin back in place. Using metal skewer or tip of paring knife, poke 6 to 8 holes in fat deposits in skin of each breast. Spray skin with oil spray.

**2.** Place chicken, skin side down, in 12-inch ovensafe skillet and set over medium-high heat. Cook, moving chicken as infrequently as possible, until skin is well browned, 7 to 9 minutes.

**3.** Carefully flip chicken and transfer skillet to oven. Roast until chicken registers 160 degrees, 25 to 30 minutes.

**4.** Transfer chicken to plate; do not discard liquid in skillet. Add garlic, pepper flakes, and remaining ¾ teaspoon salt to skillet and cook over medium-high heat, stirring occasionally and scraping up any browned bits, until moisture has evaporated and mixture begins to sizzle, 2 to 4 minutes. Add green beans and water and bring to simmer. Cover skillet, reduce heat to medium, and cook until green beans are tender, 8 to 10 minutes, stirring halfway through cooking. Uncover and continue to cook, stirring frequently, until sauce begins to coat green beans, 2 to 4 minutes longer. Add any accumulated chicken juices to skillet and toss to combine. Season with salt to taste. Transfer green beans to serving platter and sprinkle with Parmesan. Top with chicken and serve.

### Skillet-Roasted Chicken Breasts with Harissa-Mint Carrots

Substitute 1 thinly sliced shallot for garlic and 2 teaspoons harissa for pepper flakes. Substitute 1½ pounds carrots, peeled and sliced on bias ¼ inch thick, for green beans. Increase salt for vegetables to 1 teaspoon, water to ½ cup, and covered cooking time to 10 to 12 minutes. Add 2 teaspoons lemon juice and 1½ teaspoons chopped fresh mint with accumulated chicken juices. Substitute additional 1½ teaspoons chopped fresh mint for Parmesan.

## Stuffed Chicken Cutlets with Ham and Cheddar

**SERVES 4**

**WHY THIS RECIPE WORKS** Cutlets that are stuffed and breaded are special-occasion food. The filling moistens the chicken from the inside with a creamy, tasty sauce, while the crust makes a crunchy counterpoint. The problem is that these bundles can leak, and getting the right proportion of filling to cutlet can be tricky. We wanted stuffed chicken cutlets with a creamy filling that wouldn't turn runny and flavors that would complement, not overpower, the chicken. And we wanted the crust to be crisp all over and completely seal in the filling so that none leaked out. We pounded the chicken breasts thin so they rolled and cooked evenly. A combination of cream cheese and cheddar mixed with onion, garlic, and fresh thyme gave us a well-flavored filling. Thin-sliced ham added another layer of flavor to our cutlets. Before we breaded the cutlets, we chilled them in the refrigerator to help the filling set and to prevent leaks during cooking. For perfectly cooked stuffed cutlets, we sautéed them just until brown, then moved them into the oven to finish cooking through. To make slicing the chicken easier, freeze it for 15 minutes. To dry fresh bread crumbs, spread them out on a baking sheet and bake in a 200-degree oven, stirring occasionally, for 30 minutes.

**FILLING**

- 1 tablespoon unsalted butter
- 1 small onion, minced
- 1 small garlic clove, minced or pressed through a garlic press (about ½ teaspoon)
- 4 ounces cream cheese, softened
- 1 teaspoon minced fresh thyme leaves
- 2 ounces cheddar cheese, shredded (about ½ cup)
- Table salt and ground black pepper
- 4 slices (about 4 ounces) thin-sliced cooked deli ham

**CHICKEN**

- 4 (5- to 6-ounce) boneless, skinless chicken breasts, tenderloins removed and breasts trimmed
- Table salt and ground black pepper
- ¾ cup unbleached all-purpose flour
- 2 large eggs
- 1 tablespoon plus ¾ cup vegetable oil
- 4 slices high-quality white sandwich bread, pulsed in a food processor to coarse crumbs and dried

**1. FOR THE FILLING:** Melt the butter in a medium skillet over low heat; add the onion and cook, stirring occasionally, until deep golden brown, 15 to 20 minutes. Stir in the garlic and cook until fragrant, about 30 seconds longer; set aside.

**2.** In a medium bowl and using an electric mixer, beat the cream cheese on medium speed until light and fluffy, about 1 minute. Stir in the onion mixture, thyme, and cheddar; season with salt and pepper to taste and set aside.

**3.** Butterfly each chicken breast and pound between two sheets of plastic wrap to a uniform ¼-inch thickness. Pound the outer perimeter to ⅛ inch. Place the chicken cutlets, smooth side down, on a work surface and season with salt and pepper. Spread each cutlet with one-quarter of the cheese mixture, then place 1 slice of ham on top of the cheese, folding the ham as necessary to fit onto the surface of the cutlet. Roll up each cutlet from the tapered end, folding in the edges to form a neat cylinder. Refrigerate until the filling is firm, at least 1 hour.

**4. FOR THE CHICKEN:** Adjust an oven rack to the lower-middle position and heat the oven to 450 degrees. Set a large wire rack over a large baking sheet and set aside. Place the flour in a pie plate or shallow dish. Beat the eggs with 1 tablespoon of the oil in a second plate. Spread the bread crumbs in a third plate. Dredge 1 chicken roll in the flour, shaking off the excess, then coat with the egg mixture, allowing the excess to drip off. Coat all sides of the chicken roll with the bread crumbs, pressing gently so that the crumbs adhere. Place on the wire rack and repeat the flouring and breading with the remaining chicken. Allow the coating to dry for about 5 minutes. Transfer the chicken to a plate. Wipe the wire rack and baking sheet clean and set aside.

**5.** Heat the remaining ¾ cup oil in a 10-inch nonstick skillet over medium-high heat until shimmering, but not smoking. Using tongs, carefully add the chicken, seam side down, to the pan, and cook until medium golden brown, about 2 minutes. Turn each roll and cook until medium golden brown on all sides, 2 to 3 minutes longer. Transfer the chicken rolls, seam side down, to the now-clean wire rack on the baking sheet; bake until deep golden brown and an instant-read thermometer inserted into the center of a roll registers 160 degrees, about 15 minutes. Let stand for 5 minutes before slicing each roll crosswise on the diagonal with a serrated knife into five pieces; arrange on individual dinner plates and serve. (Cutlets can be filled and rolled in advance, wrapped in plastic wrap, then refrigerated for up to 24 hours.)

### BUTTERFLYING CHICKEN BREASTS

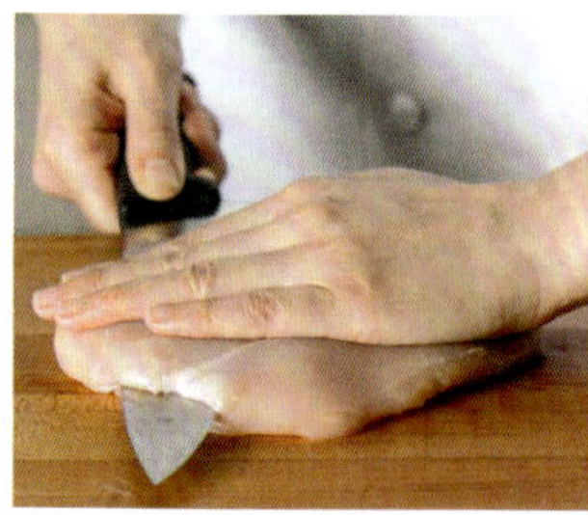

**1.** Starting on the thinnest side, butterfly the breast by slicing it lengthwise almost in half. Open the breast up to create a single flat breast. (To make cutlets, continue to cut through the meat until you have two cutlets.)

**2.** With the breast or cutlet in a zipper-lock bag or between sheets of plastic wrap, pound (starting at the center) to ¼-inch thickness. Pound the outer perimeter to ⅛ inch.

## French-Style Stuffed Chicken Breasts

SERVES 4

**WHY THIS RECIPE WORKS** When it comes to stuffed chicken breasts, the French turn this recipe into a four-star affair that requires some serious labor, and includes skinning and boning a whole chicken, stuffing the breasts with the leg meat, and wrapping them up in the skin. For a simplified approach, that was just as luxurious, we started with boneless, skinless chicken breasts and mimicked a forcemeat stuffing by trimming a bit of meat from each chicken breast; then we and combined the meat with mushrooms, herbs, and leeks. Pureeing the meat trimmings created a cohesive filling that stayed put inside the chicken breasts. After butterflying the chicken breasts, we pounded them and trimmed them into a rectangular shape. This made the stuffing easy to spread on the breasts, which we rolled up and tied with twine. Finally, we browned the chicken in a hot skillet and then added chicken broth and wine to braise the meat in the pan. To make slicing the chicken easier, freeze it for 15 minutes. If your chicken breasts come with the tenderloins attached, pull them off and reserve them to make the puree (along with the breast meat you will trim in step 1). Because the stuffing contains raw chicken, it is important to check its temperature in step 5.

**CHICKEN AND STUFFING**

- 4 (7- to 8-ounce) boneless, skinless chicken breasts, tenderloins removed and breasts trimmed
- 3 tablespoons vegetable oil
- 10 ounces white mushrooms, wiped clean and sliced thin
- 1 small leek, white part only, chopped and rinsed thoroughly (about 1 cup)
- 2 medium garlic cloves, minced or pressed through a garlic press (about 2 teaspoons)
- ½ teaspoon minced fresh thyme leaves
- 1 tablespoon juice from 1 lemon
- ½ cup dry white wine
- 1 tablespoon minced fresh parsley leaves
- Table salt and ground black pepper
- 1 cup low-sodium chicken broth

**SAUCE**

- 1 teaspoon Dijon mustard
- 2 tablespoons unsalted butter
- Table salt and ground black pepper

**1. FOR THE CHICKEN AND STUFFING:** Butterfly the chicken horizontally, stopping ½ inch from the edges so the halves remain attached, then open up each breast, cover with plastic wrap, and pound the cutlets to an even ¼-inch thickness (each cutlet should measure about 8 by 6 inches). Trim about ½ inch from the long sides of the cutlets (1½ to 2 ounces of meat per cutlet, or a total of ½ cup from all 4 cutlets) to form rectangles that measure about 8 by 5 inches. Process all the trimmings in a food processor until smooth, about 20 seconds. Transfer the puree to a medium bowl and set aside. (Do not wash the food processor bowl.)

**2.** Heat 1 tablespoon of the oil in a 12-inch skillet over medium-high heat until shimmering. Add the mushrooms and cook, stirring occasionally, until all the moisture has evaporated and the mushrooms are golden brown, 8 to 11 minutes. Add 1 tablespoon more oil and the leek; continue to cook, stirring frequently, until softened, 2 to 4 minutes. Add the garlic and thyme and cook until fragrant, about 30 seconds. Add 1½ teaspoons of the lemon juice and cook until all the moisture has evaporated, about 30 seconds. Transfer the mixture to the bowl of the food processor. Return the pan to the heat, add the wine, and scrape the pan bottom to loosen any browned bits. Transfer the wine to a small bowl and set aside. Rinse and dry the skillet.

**3.** Pulse the mushroom mixture in the food processor until roughly chopped, about 5 pulses. Transfer the mushroom mixture to the bowl with the pureed chicken. Add 1½ teaspoons of the parsley, ¾ teaspoon salt, and ½ teaspoon pepper. Using a rubber spatula, fold together the stuffing ingredients until well combined (you should have about 1½ cups stuffing).

**4.** Spread one-quarter of the stuffing evenly over each cutlet with a rubber spatula, leaving a ¾-inch border along the short sides of the cutlet and a ¼-inch border along the long sides. Roll each breast up as tightly as possible without squeezing out the filling and place seam side down. Evenly space three pieces of kitchen twine (each about 12 inches long) beneath each breast and tie, trimming any excess.

**5.** Season the chicken with salt and pepper. Heat the remaining 1 tablespoon oil in the skillet over medium-high heat until just smoking. Add the chicken bundles and brown on all four sides, about 2 minutes per side. Add the broth and reserved wine to the pan and bring to a boil. Reduce the heat to low, cover the pan, and cook until the center of the chicken registers 160 degrees, 12 to 18 minutes. Transfer the chicken to a carving board and tent loosely with foil.

**6. FOR THE SAUCE:** While the chicken rests, whisk the mustard into the cooking liquid. Increase the heat to high and simmer, scraping the pan bottom to loosen the browned bits, until dark brown and reduced to ½ cup, 7 to 10 minutes. Off the heat, whisk in the butter and the remaining 1½ teaspoons parsley and 1½ teaspoons lemon juice; season with salt and pepper to taste. Remove the twine and cut each chicken bundle on the bias into six medallions. Spoon the sauce over the chicken and serve.

## Chicken Kyiv

SERVES 4

**WHY THIS RECIPE WORKS** Chicken Kyiv is a recipe that elevates the humdrum boneless, skinless chicken breast to star status. Traditionally, the dish is a crisp fried chicken breast encasing a buttery herb sauce that dramatically oozes out when cut. But it's easy to end up with a greasy, bread crumb–coated chicken breast whose meat is dry and chalky despite the butter filling. We wanted to develop a foolproof recipe that maximized the dish's full potential. We found that butterflying the chicken breasts, then pounding them thin—and even thinner at the

edges—helped create chicken bundles that wouldn't leak the butter filling. Instead of deep-frying the chicken as is traditional, we oven-fried it. Toasting the bread crumbs prior to breading the chicken helped mimic the flavorful, golden brown crust of the original. Traditional recipes stuff the Kyivs with butter spiked with nothing more than parsley and chives, but we found that minced shallots were more flavorful than chives and a small amount of tarragon added a pleasant hint of sweetness. To make slicing the chicken easier, freeze it for 15 minutes.

**HERB BUTTER**

- 8 tablespoons (1 stick) unsalted butter, softened
- 1 tablespoon juice from 1 lemon
- 1 small shallot, minced (about 1 tablespoon)
- 1 tablespoon minced fresh parsley leaves
- ½ teaspoon minced fresh tarragon leaves
- ⅜ teaspoon table salt
- ⅛ teaspoon ground black pepper

**CHICKEN**

- 4 slices high-quality white sandwich bread, torn into quarters
- Table salt and ground black pepper
- 2 tablespoons vegetable oil
- 4 (7- to 8-ounce) boneless, skinless chicken breasts, tenderloins removed and breasts trimmed
- 1 cup unbleached all-purpose flour
- 3 large eggs, beaten
- 1 teaspoon Dijon mustard

**1. FOR THE HERB BUTTER:** Mix the ingredients in a medium bowl with a rubber spatula until thoroughly combined. Form into a 2 by 3-inch rectangle on a sheet of plastic wrap; wrap tightly and refrigerate until firm, about 1 hour.

**2. FOR THE CHICKEN:** Adjust an oven rack to the lower-middle position and heat the oven to 300 degrees. Add half of the bread to a food processor and pulse until the bread is coarsely ground, about 16 pulses. Transfer the crumbs to a large bowl and repeat with the remaining bread. Add ⅛ teaspoon salt and ⅛ teaspoon pepper to the bread crumbs. Add the oil and toss until the crumbs are evenly coated. Spread the crumbs on a rimmed baking sheet and bake until golden brown and dry, about 25 minutes, stirring twice during the baking time. Let cool completely.

**3.** Butterfly each chicken breast and pound between two sheets of plastic wrap to a uniform ¼-inch thickness. Pound the outer perimeter to ⅛ inch. Unwrap the herb butter and cut it into four rectangular pieces. Place a chicken breast, cut side up, on a work surface; season both sides with salt and pepper. Place one piece of butter in the center of the bottom half of the breast. Roll the bottom edge of the chicken over the butter, then fold in the sides and continue rolling to form a neat, tight package, pressing on the seam to seal. Repeat with the remaining butter and chicken. Refrigerate the chicken, uncovered, to allow the edges to seal, about 1 hour.

**4.** Adjust an oven rack to the middle position and heat the oven to 350 degrees. Set a large wire rack over a large baking sheet and set aside. Place the flour, eggs, and bread crumbs in separate pie plates or shallow dishes. Season the flour with ¼ teaspoon salt and ⅛ teaspoon pepper; season the bread crumbs with ½ teaspoon salt and ¼ teaspoon pepper. Add the mustard to the eggs and whisk to combine. Dredge 1 chicken roll in the flour, shaking off the excess, then coat with the egg

### ASSEMBLING CHICKEN KYIV

**1.** Shape the butter mixture into a 2 by 3-inch rectangle on plastic wrap, then wrap tightly and refrigerate until firm, about 1 hour.

**2.** Cut the butter into four rectangular pieces. Place one butter piece near the tapered end of the cutlet.

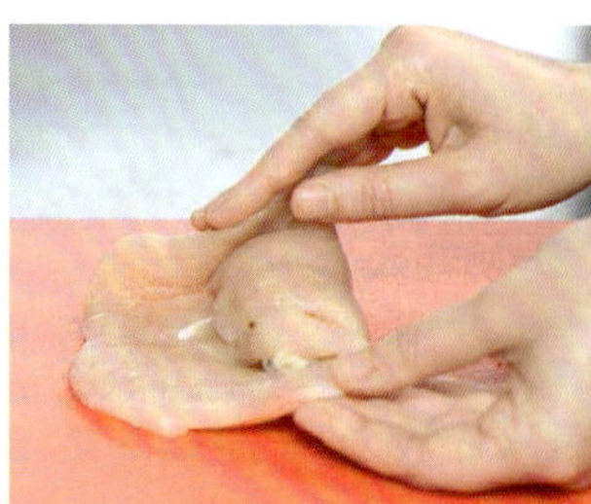

**3.** Roll up the tapered end of the chicken over the butter, then fold in the sides and continue rolling, pressing on the seam to seal. Repeat with the remaining butter pieces and cutlets. The chicken is now ready to be breaded.

mixture, allowing the excess to drip off. Coat all sides of the chicken roll with the bread crumbs, pressing gently so that the crumbs adhere. Place on the wire rack set over a rimmed baking sheet. Repeat the flouring and breading with the remaining chicken rolls.

**5.** Bake until the center of the chicken registers 160 degrees, 40 to 45 minutes. Let rest for 5 minutes on the wire rack before serving. (Unbaked, breaded chicken Kyivs can be wrapped in plastic wrap, refrigerated overnight, and baked the next day or frozen for up to one month. To cook frozen chicken Kyivs, increase the baking time to 50 to 55 minutes; do not thaw the chicken).

## Chicken and Dumplings

**SERVES** 6 to 8

**WHY THIS RECIPE WORKS** Chicken and dumplings is an old-fashioned recipe with a very high comfort food quotient. It is essentially like making a pot pie filling and dumplings that can be steamed on top of it just before serving. But the dumplings are where this recipe tends to go wrong; there is nothing worse than leaden and inedible dumplings or those that just sink into the filling. After much testing we added warm liquid rather than cold to the flour and fat, and our dumplings were great—firm but light and fluffy. The reason? The heat expands and sets the flour so that the dumplings don't absorb liquid in the stew. Don't use low-fat or fat-free milk in this recipe. Be sure to reserve 3 tablespoons of chicken fat for the dumplings in step 1. Start the dumpling dough only when you're ready to top the stew with the dumplings.

**STEW**

- 5 pounds bone-in, skin-on chicken thighs (about 12 thighs)
- Table salt and ground black pepper
- 4 teaspoons vegetable oil
- 4 tablespoons (½ stick) unsalted butter
- 4 carrots, peeled and sliced ¼ inch thick
- 2 celery ribs, sliced ¼ inch thick
- 1 medium onion, minced
- 6 tablespoons unbleached all-purpose flour
- ¼ cup dry sherry
- 4½ cups low-sodium chicken broth
- ¼ cup whole milk
- 1 teaspoon minced fresh thyme leaves
- 2 bay leaves
- 1 cup frozen green peas
- 3 tablespoons minced fresh parsley leaves

**DUMPLINGS**

- 2 cups unbleached all-purpose flour
- 1 tablespoon baking powder
- 1 teaspoon table salt
- 1 cup whole milk
- 3 tablespoons reserved chicken fat

**1. FOR THE STEW:** Pat the chicken dry with paper towels, then season with salt and pepper. Heat 2 teaspoons of the oil in a large Dutch oven over medium-high heat until just smoking. Add half of the chicken and cook until golden on both sides, about 10 minutes. Transfer the chicken to a plate and remove the browned skin. Pour off the chicken fat and reserve. Return the pot to medium-high heat and repeat with the remaining 2 teaspoons oil and the remaining chicken. Pour off and reserve any chicken fat.

**2.** Add the butter to the Dutch oven and melt over medium-high heat. Add the carrots, celery, onion, and ¼ teaspoon salt and cook until softened, about 7 minutes. Stir in the flour. Whisk in the sherry, scraping up any browned bits. Stir in the broth, milk, thyme, and bay leaves. Nestle the chicken, with any accumulated juices, into the pot. Cover and simmer until the chicken is fully cooked and tender, about 1 hour.

**3.** Transfer the chicken to a carving board. Discard the bay leaves. Allow the sauce to settle for a few minutes, then skim the fat from the surface using a wide spoon. Shred the chicken, discarding the bones, then return it to the stew.

**4. FOR THE DUMPLINGS:** Stir the flour, baking powder, and salt together. Microwave the milk and chicken fat in a microwave-safe bowl on high power until just warm (do not overheat), about 1 minute. Stir the warmed milk mixture into the flour mixture with a wooden spoon until incorporated and smooth.

**5.** Return the stew to a simmer, stir in the peas and parsley, and season with salt and pepper to taste. Drop golf ball–sized dumplings over the top of the stew, about ¼ inch apart (you should have about 18 dumplings). Reduce the heat to low, cover, and cook until the dumplings have doubled in size, 15 to 18 minutes. Serve.

## Lighter Chicken and Dumplings

**SERVES** 6

**WHY THIS RECIPE WORKS** Between the very rich chicken stew and the dumplings, this recipe is meant to be ribsticking. We wanted a modern and lighter version with dumplings as airy as drop biscuits in a light broth with concentrated chicken flavor. To start, we poached browned chicken thighs in store-bought broth. To give our broth body, we added chicken wings, since boiling them converts the connective tissue to gelatin and thickens the broth. For light, airy, but sturdy dumplings we made some changes to our drop biscuit recipe: We cut back the buttermilk and eliminated the baking powder (which led to overrising). Adding an egg white kept them from turning mushy. We strongly recommend buttermilk for the dumplings, but you can substitute ½ cup plain yogurt thinned with ¼ cup milk. If you want to include white meat, replace 2 chicken thighs with 2 boneless, skinless chicken breast halves (about 8 ounces each). Brown the chicken breasts along with the thighs and remove them from the stew once they register 160 degrees, 20 to 30 minutes. Do not omit the chicken wings.

STEW

- 2½ pounds bone-in, skin-on chicken thighs, trimmed
- Table salt and ground black pepper
- 2 teaspoons vegetable oil
- 2 small onions, minced
- 2 carrots, peeled and cut into ¾-inch pieces
- 1 celery rib, chopped fine
- ¼ cup dry sherry
- 6 cups low-sodium chicken broth
- 1 teaspoon minced fresh thyme leaves
- 1 pound chicken wings
- ¼ cup chopped fresh parsley leaves

DUMPLINGS

- 2 cups (10 ounces) unbleached all-purpose flour
- 1 teaspoon sugar
- 1 teaspoon table salt
- ½ teaspoon baking soda
- ¾ cup cold buttermilk
- 4 tablespoons (½ stick) unsalted butter, melted and cooled
- 1 large egg white

**1. FOR THE STEW:** Pat the chicken thighs dry with paper towels and season with 1 teaspoon salt and ¼ teaspoon pepper. Heat the oil in a large Dutch oven over medium-high heat until shimmering. Add the chicken thighs, skin side down, and cook until the skin is crisp and well browned, 5 to 7 minutes. Using tongs, turn the chicken pieces and brown the second side, 5 to 7 minutes longer; transfer to a large plate. Discard all but 1 teaspoon fat from the pot.

**2.** Add the onions, carrots, and celery to the pot. Cook, stirring occasionally, until caramelized, 7 to 9 minutes. Stir in the sherry, scraping up any browned bits. Stir in the broth and thyme. Return the chicken thighs, along with any accumulated juices, to the pot and add the chicken wings. Bring to a simmer, cover, and cook until the thigh meat offers no resistance when poked with the tip of a paring knife but still clings to the bones, 45 to 55 minutes.

**3.** Remove the pot from the heat and transfer the chicken to a cutting board. Allow the broth to settle for 5 minutes, then skim the fat from the surface using a wide spoon or ladle. When cool enough to handle, remove and discard the skin from the chicken. Using your fingers or a fork, pull the meat from the chicken thighs (and wings, if desired) and cut into 1-inch pieces. Return the meat to the pot.

**4. FOR THE DUMPLINGS:** Whisk the flour, sugar, salt, and baking soda in a large bowl. Combine the buttermilk and melted butter in a medium bowl, stirring until the butter forms small clumps. Whisk in the egg white. Add the buttermilk mixture to the dry ingredients and stir with a rubber spatula until just incorporated and the batter pulls away from the sides of the bowl.

**5.** Return the stew to a simmer, stir in the parsley, and season with salt and pepper to taste. Using a greased tablespoon measure (or #60 portion scoop), scoop level amounts of batter and drop them into the stew, spacing the dumplings about ¼ inch apart (you should have about 24 dumplings). Wrap the lid of the Dutch oven with a clean dish towel (keeping the towel away from the heat source) and cover the pot. Simmer gently until the dumplings have doubled in size and a toothpick inserted into the center comes out clean, 13 to 16 minutes. Serve immediately. (The stew can be prepared through step 3 up to 2 days in advance; bring the stew back to a simmer before proceeding with the recipe.)

## Skillet Chicken and Rice with Peas and Scallions

SERVES 4

**WHY THIS RECIPE WORKS** There are lots of bad recipes out there for quick chicken and rice. Most contain leftover chicken, instant rice, and canned cream-of-something soup. We aimed to improve this dish and still deliver it quickly. Boneless, skinless chicken breasts are definitely convenient, but we needed to prevent them from drying out. Dredging them in flour not only gave the chicken a nice brown crust but also kept the meat juicy inside. After browning the breasts on one side in a nonstick skillet, we removed them to deal with the rice. We first sautéed minced onion, garlic, and red pepper flakes in butter, then added the rice and stirred to coat the grains. Coating and toasting the rice this way before adding liquid is a technique that imparts deeper flavor and keeps the rice grains distinct and firm. We added a little white wine to the skillet for brightness. We then added chicken broth and returned the chicken to the skillet to cook through. When the chicken was done, we removed it from the skillet and finished cooking the rice. Off the heat, we added the frozen peas.

- 4 (6- to 8-ounce) boneless, skinless chicken breasts, trimmed
- Table salt and ground black pepper
- ½ cup unbleached all-purpose flour
- 2 tablespoons vegetable oil
- 2 tablespoons unsalted butter
- 1 medium onion, minced
- 3 medium garlic cloves, minced or pressed through a garlic press (about 1 tablespoon)
- Pinch red pepper flakes
- 1½ cups long-grain white rice
- ½ cup dry white wine
- 4½ cups low-sodium chicken broth
- 1 cup frozen peas
- 5 scallions, sliced thin
- 2 tablespoons juice from 1 lemon
- Lemon wedges, for serving

**1.** Pat the chicken dry with paper towels and season with salt and pepper. Dredge the chicken in the flour to coat and shake off any excess. Heat the oil in a 12-inch nonstick skillet over medium-high heat just until smoking. Brown the chicken well on one side, about 5 minutes. Transfer the chicken to a plate and set aside.

**2.** Off the heat, add the butter to the skillet, and swirl to melt. Add the onion and ½ teaspoon salt and return to medium-high heat until softened, 2 to 5 minutes. Stir in the garlic and red pepper flakes and cook until fragrant, about 30 seconds. Stir in the rice thoroughly and let toast for about 30 seconds.

**3.** Stir in the wine and let the rice absorb it completely, about 1 minute. Stir in the broth, scraping up any browned bits. Nestle the chicken into the rice, browned side up, and add any accumulated juices. Cover and cook over medium heat until the thickest part of the chicken registers 160 degrees, about 10 minutes.

**4.** Transfer the chicken to a clean plate. Gently brush off and discard any rice clinging to the chicken, then tent the chicken with foil and set aside. Return the skillet of rice to medium-low heat, cover, and continue to cook, stirring occasionally, until the liquid is absorbed and the rice is tender, 8 to 12 minutes longer.

**5.** Off the heat, sprinkle the peas over the rice, cover, and let warm through, about 2 minutes. Add the scallions and lemon juice to the rice. Season with salt and pepper to taste and serve with the chicken and lemon wedges.

## Kare Raisu (Japanese Curry Rice with Chicken)

**SERVES 4** **SEASON 26**

**WHY THIS RECIPE WORKS** Kare raisu, or curry rice, is Japan's go-to comfort food: a bowl filled with fragrant spiced stew (the curry) on one side and a mound of steamed rice on the other. Cooks typically make the curry by adding a commercial curry-roux "brick" to the cooking liquid. But it's easy to make your own curry roux, and the bricks freeze well. In this version, the roux was cooked only until golden brown (not darker, like many commercial versions) to allow the spices to stand out and to maximize the roux's thickening power since browning the fat-flour paste weakens its ability to thicken liquid. Adding sugar and miso rounded out the flavors of the curry roux, and refrigerating it in a loaf pan molded it into a flat "brick" that could easily be halved and used to make two batches of curry rice. To make the stew, we sautéed aromatics and chunks of seasoned boneless, skinless chicken thighs; added chicken broth as well as carrots and potatoes; and simmered until everything was cooked through. The curry-roux brick plus dashes of soy and Worcestershire sauces added during the last few minutes of cooking seasoned and thickened the stew. Fukujinzuke is a traditional mixture of sweet-tart (sometimes vibrantly pink or red) pickled vegetables. Look for it in vacuum-sealed packages in the refrigerated section of your local Japanese or Korean grocery store or make our recipe (page 278).

- 1 pound boneless, skinless chicken thighs, trimmed and cut into 1-inch pieces
- 1¼ teaspoons kosher salt, divided
- 1 tablespoon vegetable oil
- 1 onion, chopped (about 1¼ cups)
- 2½ teaspoons grated fresh ginger
- 1 garlic clove, minced
- 1 pound Yukon Gold potatoes, peeled and cut into ¾-inch pieces
- 2 carrots, peeled and cut into ½-inch pieces (about 1 cup)
- 2⅔ cups chicken broth
- 1 (4-ounce) curry-roux brick
- 2 teaspoons soy sauce
- 1 teaspoon Worcestershire sauce
- 4 cups cooked Japanese short-grain rice
- 1 scallion, sliced thin on bias
- Fukujinzuke (recipe follows) or pickled ginger or lemon wedges

**1.** Toss chicken and 1 teaspoon salt in bowl. Heat oil in medium saucepan over medium heat until shimmering. Add onion and remaining ¼ teaspoon salt and cook, stirring frequently, until onion is browned, about 8 minutes. Add ginger and garlic and cook, stirring constantly, until fragrant, about 30 seconds.

**2.** Add chicken and cook, stirring frequently, until chicken is no longer pink, about 3 minutes. Stir in potatoes and carrots. Add broth and bring to simmer over high heat. Adjust heat to maintain gentle simmer and cook until potatoes are just tender, about 20 minutes.

**3.** Add curry-roux brick, soy sauce, and Worcestershire, and let block dissolve, about 1 minute. Stir gently, scraping curry from bottom of pot, and simmer until liquid thickens, about 3 minutes. Season with salt and pepper to taste.

**4.** Divide rice evenly among 4 shallow bowls, spreading it over half of each bowl. Divide curry evenly among bowls, making sure to ladle curry next to rice. Sprinkle scallion over curry and serve with fukujinzuke, pickled ginger, or lemon wedges.

### Japanese Curry-Roux Bricks

**MAKES** 2 (4-ounce) curry-roux bricks

We prefer commercially ground spices for this recipe because they are very finely ground. If using whole spices, grind each individually until very fine and sift through a fine-mesh strainer before measuring. You can substitute mustard powder for the ground brown mustard. White miso has a sweet flavor and a fine texture we prefer over red miso, which makes a slightly coarse, more robustly savory curry. If using the curry roux immediately in the Kare Raisu, divide the mixture in half at the end of step 2. Use half in the curry rice recipe, transfer the remaining mixture to a loaf pan (the roux will not cover the surface), and proceed with step 3.

- 1½ teaspoons sugar
- 1½ teaspoons ground turmeric
- 1½ teaspoons ground coriander
- 1½ teaspoons ground ginger
- ½ teaspoon ground cardamom
- ½ teaspoon ground cumin
- ½ teaspoon ground cinnamon
- ½ teaspoon ground fennel
- ½ teaspoon ground fenugreek
- ½ teaspoon garlic powder
- ¼ teaspoon ground brown mustard
- ¼ teaspoon pepper
- 8 tablespoons unsalted butter
- ⅔ cup all-purpose flour
- 1 tablespoon white miso

**1.** Stir sugar, turmeric, coriander, ginger, cardamom, cumin, cinnamon, fennel, fenugreek, garlic powder, mustard, and pepper together in bowl.

**2.** Melt butter in 10-inch skillet over low heat. Off heat, sprinkle flour over butter and whisk until smooth. Return skillet to medium heat and cook, whisking very frequently, until flour mixture is pale golden brown, 3 to 4 minutes. Remove from heat and immediately whisk in spices. Add miso and whisk until very well combined (mixture will not be totally smooth).

**3.** Transfer mixture to loaf pan and smooth into even layer. Refrigerate until fully set, about 30 minutes. Run knife around edge of pan to release curry brick. Remove brick and cut into 2 equal pieces. (Bricks can be refrigerated in airtight container for up to 1 week or frozen for up to 3 months.)

### Fukujinzuke (Japanese Pickles for Curry)

**MAKES** 2 cups

The ginger and mushroom are flavoring agents; they are not meant to be eaten. We highly recommend seeking out lotus root, but if it's unavailable, use additional daikon. If daikon is unavailable, another type of radish can be used.

**VEGETABLES**

- ½ cup lotus root, peeled, quartered lengthwise, and sliced ⅛ inch thick (2 ounces)
- 1 cup daikon radish, peeled, quartered lengthwise, and sliced ⅛ inch thick (4½ ounces)
- 1 cup Persian cucumbers, sliced into ⅛-inch rounds (4½ ounces)
- ½ cup Japanese eggplant, peeled, quartered lengthwise, and sliced ⅛ inch thick (1¾ ounces)
- Kosher salt for salting vegetables
- 3 shiso leaves, sliced thin (optional)

**PICKLING LIQUID**

- ⅓ cup unseasoned rice vinegar
- ¼ cup mirin
- ¼ cup water
- ¼ cup sugar
- 3 tablespoons soy sauce
- 1 (2-inch) piece fresh ginger, peeled and quartered
- 1 shiitake mushroom, stemmed
- 1 teaspoon sesame seeds, toasted

**1. FOR THE VEGETABLES:** Bring 2 cups water to boil in small saucepan. Add lotus root and cook until crisp-tender, 2 to 3 minutes. Drain lotus root in fine-mesh strainer and rinse under cold water to cool. Transfer lotus root to medium bowl. Add daikon, cucumbers, and eggplant. Sprinkle 1 tablespoon salt evenly over vegetables and, using your hands, mix and squeeze vegetables until slightly softened, about 45 seconds. Let stand for 20 minutes.

**2.** Transfer vegetables to colander and rinse under cold water to remove salt (rinse out bowl). Squeeze vegetables to remove any excess water and return to bowl. Stir in shiso, if using.

**3. FOR THE PICKLING LIQUID:** Combine vinegar, mirin, water, sugar, soy sauce, ginger, and mushroom in medium saucepan and bring to boil over high heat. Add vegetables and sesame seeds and cook for 30 seconds. In fine-mesh strainer set over bowl, drain vegetables. Return liquid to saucepan and boil until thickened and slightly syrupy, 4 to 5 minutes.

**4.** Transfer vegetables to 2-cup canning jar and cover with pickling liquid. Using chopstick or fork, press on vegetables to make sure they are submerged. Cover and refrigerate overnight or up to 1 week.

### Japanese-Style Steamed Rice

**SERVES** 4

Place 1⅓ cups short-grain rice in fine-mesh strainer and rinse under running water, stirring occasionally, until water runs clear, about 1½ minutes. Drain rice well and transfer to small saucepan. Add 1⅔ cups water. Bring to boil over high heat. Adjust heat to maintain bare simmer. Cover and cook until water is absorbed, about 20 minutes. Remove from heat and let stand, covered, for 10 minutes to finish cooking. Serve.

## Arroz con Pollo (Latin-Style Chicken and Rice)

**SERVES** 4 to 6

**WHY THIS RECIPE WORKS** Arroz con pollo is a popular dish with countless variations throughout Latin America. Many traditional versions require an overnight marinade of the chicken and then a long, slow stewing with rice and vegetables. Could we find a way to achieve similar results in less time? We began by choosing chicken thighs, not only for shopping convenience but also to ensure that all the pieces would cook at the same rate—a problem when using a combination of white and dark meat. We poached the thighs in a broth preseasoned

with a sofrito, a classic Latin American mixture of chopped onions and bell peppers. About half an hour before the chicken finished cooking, we added medium-grain rice (which we preferred over long-grain for its creamy texture). And for maximum flavor, we devised two marinades. Before cooking, we marinated the chicken quickly in garlic, oregano, and distilled white vinegar; after cooking we tossed the cooked chicken with olive oil, vinegar, and cilantro. Some versions of arroz con pollo have a vibrant orange hue that comes from infusing oil with achiote, a tropical seed. Canned tomato sauce gave our dish a similar color and boosted its savory flavor. To use long-grain rice instead of medium-grain, increase the amount of water added in step 2 from ¼ to ¾ cup and add the additional ¼ cup water in step 3 as needed.

- 6 garlic cloves, minced
- 1¾ teaspoons table salt, divided
- 1 tablespoon plus 2 teaspoons distilled white vinegar, divided
- ½ teaspoon dried oregano
- ½ teaspoon pepper
- 4 pounds bone-in chicken thighs, trimmed
- 2 tablespoons extra-virgin olive oil, divided
- 1 onion, chopped fine
- 1 small green bell pepper, stemmed, seeded, and chopped fine
- ¼ teaspoon red pepper flakes
- ¼ cup minced fresh cilantro, divided
- 1¾ cups chicken broth
- 1 (8-ounce) can tomato sauce
- ¼ cup water, plus extra as needed
- 3 cups medium-grain rice
- ½ cup green manzanilla olives, pitted and halved
- 1 tablespoon capers
- ½ cup jarred pimentos, cut into 2 by ¼-inch strips
- Lemon wedges

**1.** Adjust oven rack to middle position and heat oven to 350 degrees. Place garlic and 1 teaspoon salt in large bowl; using rubber spatula, mix to make smooth paste. Add 1 tablespoon vinegar, oregano, and pepper to garlic-salt mixture; stir to combine. Place chicken in bowl with marinade. Coat chicken pieces evenly with marinade; set aside for 15 minutes.

**2.** Heat 1 tablespoon oil in Dutch oven over medium heat until shimmering. Add onion, bell pepper, and pepper flakes; cook, stirring occasionally, until vegetables begin to soften, 4 to 8 minutes. Add 2 tablespoons cilantro; stir to combine. Push vegetables to the sides of pot and increase heat to medium-high. Add chicken to clearing in center of pot, skin side down, in even layer. Cook, without moving chicken, until outer layer of meat becomes opaque, 2 to 4 minutes. (If chicken begins to brown, reduce heat to medium.) Using tongs, flip chicken and cook on second side until opaque, 2 to 4 minutes more. Add broth, tomato sauce, and water; stir to combine. Bring to simmer; cover, reduce heat to medium-low, and simmer for 20 minutes.

**3.** Add rice, olives, capers, and remaining ¾ teaspoon salt; stir well. Bring to simmer, cover, and transfer pot to oven. After 10 minutes, remove pot from oven and stir chicken and rice once from bottom up. Cover and return pot to oven. After another 10 minutes, stir once more, adding another ¼ cup water if rice appears dry and bottom of pot is beginning to burn. Cover and return pot to oven; cook until rice has absorbed all liquid and is tender but still holds its shape and thickest part of thighs registers 175 degrees, about 10 minutes longer.

**4.** Using tongs, remove chicken from pot; replace lid and set pot aside. Remove and discard chicken skin; using 2 spoons, pull meat off bones in large chunks. Using your fingers, remove remaining fat and any dark veins from chicken pieces. Place chicken in large bowl and toss with remaining 1 tablespoon oil, remaining 2 teaspoons vinegar, remaining 2 tablespoons cilantro, and pimentos; season with salt and pepper to taste. Place chicken on top of rice, cover, and let stand until warmed through, about 5 minutes. Serve, passing lemon wedges separately.

## Peruvian Arroz con Pollo

**SERVES** 4 to 6 **SEASON 26**

**WHY THIS RECIPE WORKS** For our version of Peruvian arroz con pollo, the wildly popular dish that's characterized by a substantial amount of cilantro, we started by browning bone-in, skin-on chicken thighs, leaving the fat in the Dutch oven. In the fat, we sizzled an aderezo, the flavorsome base of chopped red onion, garlic, and spices (here, cumin and ají amarillo paste) that is foundational in Peruvian cuisine, before adding dark, malty beer and bright cilantro puree. We cooked the chicken in this deeply flavorful liquid until tender and then used the liquid, augmented by chicken broth, to cook white rice, bell pepper strips, and diced carrots. Before serving, we returned the chicken parts to the pot, along with green peas, to warm through. The dish is served with sarza criolla, a bright onion-lime-cilantro salad that adds punchy acidity to the chicken and rice. Any smooth, malty beer such as Modelo Negra, Newcastle Brown Ale, or Samuel Adams Boston Lager will work here. Ají amarillo paste is available in supermarkets or online. The spice level can vary between brands; taste before using. Thinly sliced onions are key to the sarza criolla; it is best to use a mandoline.

**ARROZ CON POLLO**

- 2 cups (2 ounces) fresh cilantro leaves and stems
- ½ cup water
- 6 (5- to 7-ounce) bone-in chicken thighs, trimmed
- 2¼ teaspoons table salt, divided
- ¾ teaspoon pepper
- 2 tablespoons vegetable oil
- 1 red onion, chopped fine
- 1–2 tablespoons ají amarillo paste
- 1 tablespoon minced garlic
- ½ teaspoon ground cumin
- 1½ cups dark beer
- 2 cups chicken broth, plus extra as needed
- 1½ cups long-grain white rice, rinsed
- 1 red bell pepper, stemmed, seeded, and cut into ½-inch-wide strips
- 2 carrots, peeled and cut into ½-inch pieces (1 cup)
- ½ cup frozen peas

**SARZA CRIOLLA**

- 1 red onion, halved and sliced through root end 1/16 inch thick
- ⅛ teaspoon table salt, plus salt for salting onion
- ¼ cup chopped fresh cilantro
- 2 tablespoons lime juice
- ⅛ teaspoon pepper

**1. FOR THE ARROZ CON POLLO:** Process cilantro and water in blender until cilantro is finely chopped and very loose puree forms, about 1 minute, scraping down sides of blender jar as needed; set aside.

**2.** Pat chicken dry and sprinkle both sides with 1½ teaspoons salt and pepper. Heat oil in large Dutch oven over medium heat until shimmering. Add chicken, skin side down, and cook, without moving, until well browned, 8 to 12 minutes. Using tongs, flip chicken and brown on second side, about 2 minutes. Transfer chicken to large plate.

**3.** Add onion, chile paste, garlic, cumin, and remaining ¾ teaspoon salt to fat left in pot and cook, stirring often, until onion is softened, 5 to 7 minutes. Increase heat to medium-high and add beer, scraping up any browned bits. Cook until mixture is almost dry, 7 to 10 minutes. Stir in cilantro puree and return chicken to pot, skin side up (chicken will be almost entirely above surface of liquid). Adjust heat to maintain simmer, cover, and cook until chicken registers at least 195 degrees, 18 to 20 minutes.

**4.** Using tongs, transfer chicken to clean plate and tent with aluminum foil. Transfer cooking liquid and solids to 4-cup liquid measuring cup (you should have about 1½ cups). Add enough broth to measure 3½ cups. Return broth mixture to pot and stir in rice, bell pepper, and carrots. Bring to boil, adjust heat to simmer, cover, and cook until rice is tender, 20 to 25 minutes.

**5.** Off heat, stir in peas (browning at bottom of rice is OK). Arrange chicken on top of rice and pour any accumulated juices into pot. Cover and let stand until peas and chicken are warmed through, 5 to 10 minutes.

**6. FOR THE SARZA CRIOLLA:** Toss onion and ½ teaspoon table salt in strainer or colander set over bowl. Let stand for 10 minutes. Rinse onion under cold water and pat dry. Combine onion, cilantro, lime juice, pepper, and salt in bowl. (Sarza criolla can be made up to 1 hour ahead.) Serve with chicken and rice.

## Chicken Biryani

**SERVES 4**

**WHY THIS RECIPE WORKS** In biryani, long-grain basmati rice takes center stage, enriched with butter, saffron, and a variety of fresh herbs and pungent spices and layered with pieces of tender chicken and browned onions. For our recipe, we browned bone-in, skin-on chicken thighs; removed the skin; and layered them with basmati rice, caramelized onions, and a blend of spices. To get the most flavor out of the spices, we tied them into cheesecloth and simmered them in the rice cooking water; we then added some of that water to the biryani. For a finishing touch, we added saffron, currants, and plenty of ginger and chiles. This recipe requires a heavy-bottomed 3½- to 4-quart saucepan about 8 inches in diameter. Do not use a large, wide Dutch oven, as it will adversely affect both the layering of the dish and the final cooking times. For more heat, add the jalapeño seeds and ribs when mincing.

**YOGURT SAUCE**

- 1 cup whole-milk or low-fat plain yogurt
- 2 tablespoons minced fresh cilantro
- 2 tablespoons minced fresh mint
- 1 garlic clove, minced

**CHICKEN AND RICE**

- 10 cardamom pods, preferably green, smashed with a chef's knife
- 1 cinnamon stick
- 1 (2-inch) piece fresh ginger, peeled, cut into ½-inch-thick coins, and smashed
- ½ teaspoon cumin seeds
- 3 quarts water
- ¾ teaspoon table salt, divided
- ¼ teaspoon pepper
- 4 (5- to 6-ounce) bone-in chicken thighs, trimmed
- 3 tablespoons unsalted butter
- 2 onions, halved and sliced thin
- 2 jalapeño chiles, stemmed, seeded, and minced
- 4 garlic cloves, minced
- 1¼ cups basmati rice

½ teaspoon saffron threads, lightly crumbled
¼ cup dried currants or raisins
2 tablespoons chopped fresh cilantro
2 tablespoons chopped fresh mint

**1. FOR THE YOGURT SAUCE:** Combine all ingredients in small bowl, season with salt and pepper to taste, and set aside. (Sauce can be refrigerated in airtight container for up to 2 days.)

**2. FOR THE CHICKEN AND RICE:** Wrap cardamom pods, cinnamon stick, ginger, and cumin in small piece of cheesecloth and secure with kitchen twine. In 3½- to 4-quart saucepan, bring spice bundle, water, and 1½ teaspoons salt to boil over medium-high heat. Reduce heat to medium and simmer, partially covered, until spices have infused water, at least 15 minutes (but no longer than 30 minutes).

**3.** Meanwhile, pat chicken thighs dry with paper towels and sprinkle with ¼ teaspoon salt and pepper. Melt butter in 12-inch nonstick skillet over medium-high heat. Add onions and cook, stirring frequently, until soft and dark brown around edges, 10 to 12 minutes. Stir in jalapeños and garlic and cook, stirring frequently, until fragrant, about 2 minutes. Transfer onion mixture to bowl, season with salt to taste, and set aside. Wipe out skillet with wad of paper towels.

**4.** Place chicken, skin side down, in skillet; return skillet to medium-high heat; and cook until well browned on both sides, 8 to 10 minutes, flipping halfway through. Transfer chicken to plate and discard skin. Tent with aluminum foil to keep warm.

**5.** If necessary, return spice-infused water to boil over high heat. Add rice and cook, stirring occasionally, for 5 minutes. Drain rice in fine-mesh strainer, reserving ¾ cup cooking liquid; discard spice bundle. Transfer rice to medium bowl and stir in saffron and currants (rice will turn splotchy yellow).

**6.** Spread half of rice evenly in bottom of saucepan using rubber spatula. Scatter half of onion mixture over rice, then place chicken thighs, skinned side up, on top of onions; add any accumulated juices. Sprinkle evenly with cilantro and mint, scatter remaining onion mixture over herbs, then cover with remaining rice. Pour reserved ¾ cup cooking liquid evenly over rice.

**7.** Cover saucepan and cook over medium-low heat until rice is tender and chicken registers 175 degrees, about 30 minutes (if large amount of steam is escaping from pot, reduce heat to low).

**8.** Run heat-resistant rubber spatula around inside rim of saucepan to loosen any affixed rice. Using large serving spoon, spoon biryani into individual bowls, scooping from bottom of the pot. Serve, passing yogurt sauce separately.

## Skillet Jambalaya

**SERVES** 4 to 6

**WHY THIS RECIPE WORKS** Jambalaya, a hearty mix of chicken, andouille sausage, shrimp, and rice, is typically made in a Dutch oven and can take at least an hour to prepare. We wanted a quicker, easier version without sacrificing any of the complex flavors of this Creole classic. Using bone-in, skin-on chicken thighs rather than the typical whole cut-up chicken saved us time and fuss. To mimic long-simmered flavor, we browned the chicken in the skillet, added the sausage, then cooked the vegetables in some of the rendered fat. We then stirred the rice in to coat it with the fat for deep flavor. For our cooking liquid, we relied on chicken broth and clam juice (to complement the shrimp). To prevent the shrimp from overcooking, we cooked it for only a few minutes and allowed it to finish cooking through off the heat. If you cannot find andouille sausage, either chorizo or linguica can be substituted. For a spicier jambalaya, you can add ¼ teaspoon of cayenne pepper along with the vegetables, and/or serve it with hot sauce.

1½ pounds bone-in chicken thighs, trimmed
¾ teaspoon table salt, divided
⅛ teaspoon pepper
5 teaspoons vegetable oil, divided
8 ounces andouille sausage, halved lengthwise and sliced into ¼-inch pieces
1 onion, chopped
1 red bell pepper, stemmed, seeded, and chopped
5 garlic cloves, minced
1½ cups long-grain white rice
2½ cups chicken broth
1 (14.5-ounce) can diced tomatoes, drained
1 (8-ounce) bottle clam juice
1 pound large shrimp (31 to 40 per pound), peeled and deveined
2 tablespoons chopped fresh parsley

**1.** Pat chicken dry with paper towels, then sprinkle with ¼ teaspoon salt and pepper. Heat 2 teaspoons oil in 12-inch nonstick skillet over medium-high heat until just smoking. Carefully lay chicken thighs in skillet, skin side down, and cook until golden, 4 to 6 minutes. Flip chicken over and continue to cook until second side is golden, about 3 minutes. Remove pan from heat and transfer chicken to plate. Using paper towels, remove and discard browned chicken skin.

**2.** Pour off all but 2 teaspoons fat left in skillet and return to medium-high heat until shimmering. Add andouille and cook until lightly browned, about 3 minutes; transfer sausage to small bowl and set aside.

**3.** Add remaining 1 tablespoon oil to skillet and return to medium heat until shimmering. Add onion, bell pepper, garlic, and remaining ½ teaspoon salt; cook, scraping up any browned bits, until onion is softened, about 5 minutes. Add rice and cook until edges turn translucent, about 3 minutes. Stir in broth, tomatoes, and clam juice; bring to simmer. Gently nestle chicken and any accumulated juices into rice. Cover; reduce heat to low; and cook until chicken is tender and cooked through, 30 to 35 minutes.

**4.** Transfer chicken to plate and cover with aluminum foil to keep warm. Stir shrimp and sausage into rice and continue to cook, covered, over low heat for 2 minutes. Remove skillet from heat and let stand, covered, until shrimp are fully cooked and rice is tender, about 5 minutes. Meanwhile, shred chicken into bite-size pieces. Stir parsley and shredded chicken into rice, season with salt and pepper to taste, and serve.

## Skillet Chicken, Broccoli, and Ziti

**SERVES 4**

**WHY THIS RECIPE WORKS** This classic restaurant dish rarely lives up to its promise. Our challenge would lie in getting the flavors and textures just right: tender chicken, crisp broccoli, and a light, fresh sauce. First we browned pieces of skinless, boneless chicken breasts in the skillet, then we removed the chicken to build our sauce. We started with a base of sautéed onion, garlic, oregano, and red pepper flakes. And to keep all our work limited to the skillet, we cooked the pasta right in the sauce. The broccoli went in next, along with chopped sun-dried tomatoes. We then covered the skillet and simmered everything just until the broccoli turned bright green. At this point, we returned the chicken to the pan to finish cooking. A little heavy cream made the sauce silky without obscuring the flavor of the broccoli and chicken. Grated Asiago cheese enriched the sauce and gave it a pleasantly tangy flavor. And a little lemon juice added a bright note. This recipe also works well with 8 ounces of penne. Parmesan cheese can be substituted for the Asiago.

- 1 pound boneless, skinless chicken breasts, cut into 1-inch pieces
- Table salt and ground black pepper
- 2 tablespoons vegetable or olive oil
- 1 medium onion, minced
- 3 medium garlic cloves, minced or pressed through a garlic press (about 1 tablespoon)
- ¼ teaspoon dried oregano
- ⅛ teaspoon red pepper flakes
- 8 ounces (2½ cups) ziti
- 2¾ cups water
- 1⅔ cups low-sodium chicken broth
- 12 ounces broccoli florets (4 cups)
- ¼ cup oil-packed sun-dried tomatoes, rinsed and chopped coarse
- ½ cup heavy cream
- 1 ounce Asiago cheese, grated (about ½ cup), plus extra for serving
- 1 tablespoon juice from 1 lemon

**1.** Season the chicken with salt and pepper. Heat 1 tablespoon of the oil in a 12-inch nonstick skillet over medium-high heat until just smoking. Add the chicken in a single layer and cook for 1 minute without stirring. Stir the chicken and continue to cook until most, but not all, of the pink color has disappeared and the chicken is lightly browned around the edges, 1 to 2 minutes longer. Transfer the chicken to a clean bowl and set aside.

**2.** Add the remaining 1 tablespoon oil, the onion, and ½ teaspoon salt to the skillet. Return the skillet to medium-high heat and cook, stirring often, until the onion is softened, 2 to 5 minutes. Stir in the garlic, oregano, and red pepper flakes and cook until fragrant, about 30 seconds.

**3.** Add the ziti, 2 cups of the water, and the broth. Bring to a boil over high heat and cook until the liquid is very thick and syrupy and almost completely absorbed, 12 to 15 minutes.

**4.** Add the broccoli, sun-dried tomatoes, and the remaining ¾ cup water. Cover, reduce the heat to medium, and cook until the broccoli turns bright green and is almost tender, 3 to 5 minutes.

**5.** Uncover and return the heat to high. Stir in the cream, Asiago, and reserved chicken with any accumulated juices and continue to simmer, uncovered, until the sauce is thickened and the chicken is cooked and heated through, 1 to 2 minutes. Off the heat, stir in the lemon juice and season with salt and pepper to taste. Serve, passing more grated Asiago at the table, if desired.

## Skillet Chicken Pot Pie with Biscuit Topping

**SERVES 4**

**WHY THIS RECIPE WORKS** Quick versions of chicken pot pie are often plagued by dried-out leftover chicken, bland sauce made with canned soup, and biscuits popped out of a tube. We saw no reason why pot pie couldn't be a whole lot better. We wanted moist chicken, a richly flavored sauce, and a homemade biscuit crust. Instead of the refrigerated biscuit dough used in most recipes, we turned to homemade biscuits, and it was easy enough to put together a simple dough for baking powder biscuits. We just whisked the dry ingredients together and stirred in heavy cream, kneaded the dough briefly, and cut it into rounds (wedges would also work fine). We then popped the biscuits into the oven to bake, while we turned to the filling. Next, we decided to contain all our cooking to a skillet for ease of preparation. We first sautéed skinless, boneless breasts in butter, keeping the heat at medium so the exterior wouldn't toughen. We set the chicken aside after it was browned and started the sauce in the skillet with onion,

celery, thyme, vermouth, and chicken broth—ingredients that contributed lots of flavor. Flour thickened the liquid, and heavy cream gave it richness and a lush texture. Gently simmering the browned chicken in this sauce not only enhanced the flavor of the sauce but also kept the chicken juicy. Using frozen peas and carrots made quick work of the vegetables. All that was left to do was to assemble our pie by placing the hot biscuits over the filling in the skillet. Our flavorful, meaty stew with tender biscuits on top was not only delicious but also fast and easy. If you don't have time to make your own biscuits for the topping, use packaged refrigerated biscuits and bake them according to the package instructions. We prefer the flavor of Immaculate Baking Organic Flaky Biscuits but you can use your favorite brand (you will need anywhere from four to eight biscuits depending on their size). This pot pie can be served in a large pie plate with the biscuits arranged on top, or served directly from the skillet.

**BISCUITS**

- 2 cups (10 ounces) unbleached all-purpose flour, plus extra for the work surface
- 2 teaspoons sugar
- 2 teaspoons baking powder
- ½ teaspoon table salt
- 1½ cups heavy cream

**FILLING**

- 1½ pounds boneless, skinless chicken breasts
- Table salt and ground black pepper
- 4 tablespoons (½ stick) unsalted butter
- 1 medium onion, minced
- 1 celery rib, sliced thin
- ¼ cup unbleached all-purpose flour
- ¼ cup dry vermouth or dry white wine
- 2 cups low-sodium chicken broth
- ½ cup heavy cream
- 1½ teaspoons minced fresh thyme leaves
- 2 cups frozen pea-carrot medley, thawed

1. **FOR THE BISCUITS:** Adjust an oven rack to the upper-middle position and heat the oven to 450 degrees. Line a baking sheet with parchment paper and set aside.

2. Whisk the flour, sugar, baking powder, and salt together in a large bowl. Stir in the cream with a wooden spoon until a dough forms, about 30 seconds. Turn the dough out onto a lightly floured work surface and gather into a ball. Knead the dough briefly until smooth, about 30 seconds.

3. Pat the dough into a ¾-inch-thick circle. Cut the biscuits into rounds using a 2½-inch biscuit cutter or cut into eight wedges using a knife.

4. Place the biscuits on the prepared baking sheet. Bake until golden brown, about 15 minutes. Set aside on a wire rack.

5. **FOR THE FILLING:** While the biscuits bake, pat the chicken dry with paper towels and season with salt and pepper. Melt 2 tablespoons of the butter in a 12-inch skillet over medium heat until the foam subsides. Brown the chicken lightly on both sides, about 5 minutes total. Transfer the chicken to a clean plate.

6. Add the remaining 2 tablespoons butter to the skillet and return to medium heat until melted. Add the onion, celery, and ½ teaspoon salt and cook until the onion is softened, about 5 minutes. Stir in the flour and cook, stirring constantly, until incorporated, about 1 minute.

7. Stir in the vermouth and cook until evaporated, about 30 seconds. Slowly whisk in the broth, cream, and thyme, and bring to a simmer. Nestle the chicken into the sauce, cover, and cook over medium-low heat until the thickest part of the breasts registers 160 degrees, 8 to 10 minutes.

8. Transfer the chicken to a plate. Stir the peas and carrots into the sauce and simmer until heated through, about 2 minutes. When the chicken is cool enough to handle, cut or shred it into bite-size pieces and return it to the skillet. Season the filling with salt and pepper to taste.

9. **FOR SERVING:** Transfer the filling to a large pie plate and arrange the biscuits over the top, or serve directly from the skillet, topping individual portions with the biscuits.

## Cast Iron Chicken Pot Pie

**SERVES** 4 to 6

**WHY THIS RECIPE WORKS** The preparations required for chicken pot pie have largely relegated it to a Sunday treat, but moving this dish to a cast-iron skillet speeds up the process and also improves the results. We started by parbaking the crust separately, which kept it from becoming soggy and ensured that it was done at the same time as the filling. Sautéing the vegetables and aromatics and adding broth created a rich, caramelized base in which we then poached the chicken. Next, we shredded the meat and then stirred it back in with heavy cream, peas, parsley, and dry sherry. We slipped on the parbaked crust and baked the dish for a short time to bring it all together. You can use one of our recipes for single crust pie dough (pages 944–945) or ready-made pie dough in this recipe.

- 1 recipe single-crust pie dough (pages 944 and 945)
- 1 large egg, lightly beaten with 2 tablespoons water
- 4 tablespoons unsalted butter
- 4 carrots, peeled and sliced ¼ inch thick
- 2 celery ribs, cut into ¼-inch pieces
- 1 onion, chopped fine
- ¼ teaspoon table salt
- ¼ teaspoon pepper
- 1 teaspoon minced fresh thyme or ¼ teaspoon dried
- 6 tablespoons all-purpose flour
- 2 cups chicken broth
- 1½ pounds boneless, skinless chicken breasts, trimmed
- ½ cup frozen peas
- ¼ cup heavy cream
- 3 tablespoons minced fresh parsley
- 1 tablespoon dry sherry

**1.** Roll dough between 2 sheets of parchment paper into 11-inch circle. Remove top parchment sheet. Fold in outer ½ inch of dough to make 10-inch circle. Using your fingers, crimp edge of dough to make attractive fluted rim. Using paring knife, cut 4 oval-shaped vents, each about 2 inches long and ½ inch wide, in center of dough. Transfer dough, still on parchment, to baking sheet and refrigerate until firm, about 15 minutes.

**2.** Adjust oven rack to middle position and heat oven to 400 degrees. Brush dough with egg mixture and bake until golden brown, 17 to 20 minutes, rotating sheet halfway through baking. Transfer crust, still on sheet, to wire rack and let cool; do not turn off oven.

**3.** Heat 10-inch cast-iron skillet over medium heat for 3 minutes. Melt butter in skillet. Add carrots, celery, onion, salt, and pepper and cook until softened and lightly browned, 5 to 7 minutes. Stir in thyme and cook until fragrant, about 30 seconds. Stir in flour and cook for 2 minutes. Slowly whisk in broth, scraping up any browned bits and smoothing out any lumps, and bring to simmer.

**4.** Pound thicker ends of chicken breasts as needed to create even thickness. Nestle chicken into skillet. Reduce heat to gentle simmer; cover; and cook until chicken registers 160 degrees and sauce has thickened, 10 to 15 minutes, flipping chicken halfway through.

**5.** Transfer chicken to carving board, let cool slightly, then shred into bite-size pieces using 2 forks. Stir shredded chicken, peas, cream, parsley, and sherry into skillet. Season with salt and pepper to taste.

**6.** Place parbaked pie crust on top of filling; transfer skillet to oven; and bake until crust is deep golden brown and filling is bubbling, about 10 minutes. Let pot pie cool for 10 minutes before serving.

## Chicken Pot Pie with Savory Crumble Topping

SERVES 6

**WHY THIS RECIPE WORKS** We wanted to streamline chicken pot pie and get it on the table in 90 minutes, tops. And, we wanted a completely homemade pie (no prefab crust) full of tender, juicy chicken and bright vegetables. To start, we swapped out a whole chicken for easy-to-poach chicken breasts—and we used the poaching liquid as the base of our sauce. But to boost the sauce's flavor, we turned to a few ingredients rich in glutamates, naturally occurring flavor compounds that accentuate savory qualities. Sautéed mushrooms, soy sauce, and tomato paste did the trick, turning into caramelized fond that gave our sauce deep flavor. Sautéing the vegetables while the chicken rested also boosted the filling's flavor. For the topping, we replaced traditional pastry with a savory crumble topping, enriched with grated cheese and pepper. To increase the crunch factor, we baked the crumble separately from the filling, then scattered it over the pot pie and slid it into the oven to warm through. Minutes later, our homemade pot pie emerged bubbling, fragrant, and topped with a crunchy, flavorful crust. When making the topping, do not substitute milk or half-and-half for the heavy cream.

**CHICKEN AND FILLING**

- 1½ pounds boneless, skinless chicken breasts and/or thighs
- 3 cups low-sodium chicken broth
- 2 tablespoons vegetable oil
- 1 medium onion, minced
- 3 medium carrots, peeled and cut crosswise into ¼-inch-thick slices (about 1 cup)
- 2 small celery ribs, chopped fine
- Table salt and ground black pepper
- 10 ounces cremini mushrooms, stems trimmed, caps wiped clean and sliced thin

- 1 teaspoon soy sauce
- 1 teaspoon tomato paste
- 4 tablespoons (½ stick) unsalted butter
- ½ cup unbleached all-purpose flour
- 1 cup whole milk
- 2 teaspoons juice from 1 lemon
- 3 tablespoons minced fresh parsley leaves
- ¾ cup frozen baby peas

**CRUMBLE TOPPING**

- 2 cups (10 ounces) unbleached all-purpose flour
- 2 teaspoons baking powder
- ¾ teaspoon table salt
- ½ teaspoon ground black pepper
- ⅛ teaspoon cayenne pepper
- 6 tablespoons (¾ stick) unsalted butter, cut into ½-inch cubes and chilled
- 1 ounce Parmesan cheese, finely grated (about ½ cup)
- ¾ cup plus 2 tablespoons heavy cream

**1. FOR THE CHICKEN:** Bring the chicken and broth to a simmer in a covered Dutch oven over medium heat. Cook until the chicken is just done, 8 to 12 minutes. Transfer the cooked chicken to a large bowl. Pour the broth through a fine-mesh strainer into a liquid measuring cup and reserve. Do not wash the Dutch oven. Meanwhile, adjust an oven rack to the upper-middle position and heat the oven to 450 degrees.

**2. FOR THE TOPPING:** Combine the flour, baking powder, salt, black pepper, and cayenne in a large bowl. Sprinkle the butter pieces over the top of the flour. Using your fingers, rub the butter into the flour mixture until it resembles coarse cornmeal. Stir in the Parmesan. Add the cream and stir until just combined. Crumble the mixture into irregularly shaped pieces ranging from ½ to ¾ inch onto a parchment-lined rimmed baking sheet. Bake until fragrant and starting to brown, 10 to 13 minutes. Set aside.

**3. FOR THE FILLING:** Heat 1 tablespoon of the oil in the now-empty Dutch oven over medium heat until shimmering. Add the onion, carrots, celery, ¼ teaspoon salt, and ¼ teaspoon pepper; cover and cook, stirring occasionally, until just tender, 5 to 7 minutes. While the vegetables are cooking, shred the chicken into small bite-size pieces. Transfer the cooked vegetables to the bowl with the chicken; set aside.

**4.** Heat the remaining 1 tablespoon oil in the again-empty Dutch oven over medium heat until shimmering. Add the mushrooms; cover and cook, stirring occasionally, until the mushrooms have released their juices, about 5 minutes. Remove the cover, stir in the soy sauce and tomato paste. Increase the heat to medium-high and cook, stirring frequently, until the liquid has evaporated, the mushrooms are well browned, and a dark fond begins to form on the surface of the pan, about 5 minutes. Transfer the mushrooms to the bowl with the chicken and vegetables. Set aside.

**5.** Heat the butter in the again-empty Dutch oven over medium heat. When the foaming subsides, stir in the flour and cook for 1 minute. Slowly whisk in the reserved chicken broth and the milk. Bring to a simmer, scraping the pan bottom with a wooden spoon to loosen the browned bits, then continue to simmer until the sauce fully thickens, about 1 minute. Season with salt and pepper to taste. Remove from the heat and stir in the lemon juice and 2 tablespoons of the parsley.

**6.** Stir the chicken-vegetable mixture and peas into the sauce. Pour the mixture into a 13 by 9-inch baking dish or casserole dish of similar size. Scatter the crumble topping evenly over the filling. Bake on a rimmed baking sheet until the filling is bubbling and the topping is well browned, 12 to 15 minutes. Sprinkle with the remaining 1 tablespoon parsley and serve.

## Chicken Pot Pie with Spring Vegetables

**SERVES 6**

**WHY THIS RECIPE WORKS** In this inventive pot pie, our trusty Dutch oven proved to be the key to making this recipe easier but also stunning. Boneless, skinless chicken thighs, cut into pieces, were easy to work with and stayed moist through cooking. Leeks, asparagus, peas, and tarragon gave the pot pie fresh spring flavor. As for the crust, we opted to use buttery store-bought puff pastry, weaving it into a simple but stunning lattice. To keep the pastry crispy, we baked it on the overturned Dutch oven lid while the filling simmered in the pot below. Once the filling was cooked, we simply slid the baked crust on top. To thaw frozen puff pastry, let it sit either in the refrigerator for 24 hours or on the counter for 30 minutes to 1 hour. We prefer to place the baked pastry on top of the filling in the pot just before serving for an impressive presentation; however, you can also cut the pastry into wedges and place them over individual portions of the filling.

- 1 (9½ by 9-inch) sheet puff pastry, thawed
- 4 tablespoons unsalted butter
- 1 pound leeks, white and light green parts only, halved lengthwise, cut into ½-inch pieces, and washed thoroughly
- 4 carrots, peeled and cut into ½-inch pieces
- 1 teaspoon table salt
- ½ cup all-purpose flour
- 4 garlic cloves, minced
- 1 teaspoon tomato paste
- 3 cups chicken broth, plus extra as needed
- ¼ cup heavy cream
- 1 teaspoon soy sauce
- 2 bay leaves
- 2 pounds boneless, skinless chicken thighs, trimmed and cut into 1-inch pieces
- 1 large egg, lightly beaten
- 1 pound asparagus, trimmed and cut on bias into 1-inch lengths
- 1 cup frozen peas
- 2 tablespoons chopped fresh tarragon or parsley
- 1 tablespoon grated lemon zest plus 2 teaspoons juice

**1.** Cut sheet of parchment paper to match outline of Dutch oven lid and place on large plate or upturned rimmed baking sheet. Roll puff pastry sheet into 15 by 11-inch rectangle on lightly floured counter. Using pizza cutter or sharp knife, cut pastry widthwise into ten 1½-inch-wide strips.

**2.** Space 5 pastry strips parallel and evenly across parchment circle. Fold back first, third, and fifth strips almost completely. Lay additional pastry strip perpendicular to second and fourth strips, keeping it snug to folded edges of pastry, then unfold strips. Repeat laying remaining 4 pastry strips evenly across parchment circle, alternating between folding back second and fourth strips and first, third, and fifth strips to create lattice pattern. Using pizza cutter, trim edges of pastry following outline of parchment circle. Cover loosely with plastic wrap and refrigerate while preparing filling.

**3.** Adjust oven rack to lower-middle position and heat oven to 400 degrees. Melt butter in Dutch oven over medium heat. Add leeks, carrots, and salt and cook until vegetables are softened, about 5 minutes. Stir in flour, garlic, and tomato paste and cook for 1 minute.

**4.** Slowly stir in broth, scraping up any browned bits and smoothing out any lumps. Stir in cream, soy sauce, and bay leaves. Bring to simmer and cook until mixture is thickened, about 3 minutes. Stir in chicken and return to simmer.

**5.** Off heat, cover pot with inverted lid and carefully place parchment with pastry on lid. Brush pastry with egg and sprinkle with salt. Transfer pot to oven and bake until pastry is puffed and golden brown, 25 to 30 minutes, rotating pot halfway through baking.

### PREPARING A LATTICE TOP

**1.** Space 5 pastry strips parallel and evenly across parchment circle. Fold back first, third, and fifth strips almost completely.

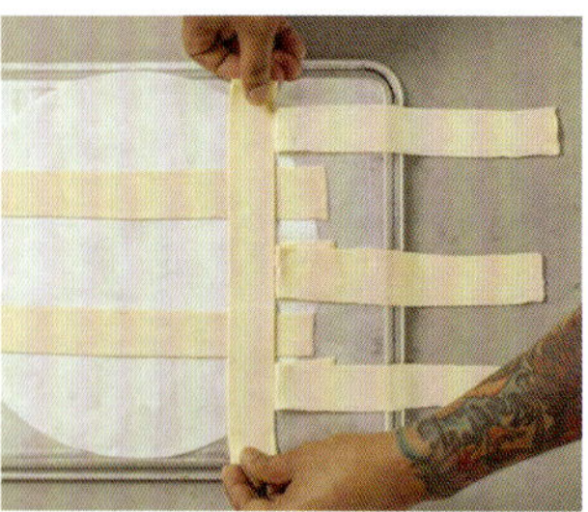

**2.** Lay pastry strip perpendicular to second and fourth strips, keeping it snug to folded edges of pastry, then unfold strips. Fold back second and fourth strips.

**3.** Repeat laying remaining 4 pastry strips evenly across parchment circle, alternating between folding back first, third, and fifth strips and second and fourth strips to create lattice pattern.

**6.** Remove pot from oven. Transfer parchment with pastry to wire rack; discard parchment. Remove lid and discard bay leaves. Stir asparagus into filling and cook over medium heat until crisp-tender, 3 to 5 minutes. Off heat, stir in peas and let sit until heated through, about 5 minutes. Adjust filling consistency with extra hot broth as needed. Stir in tarragon and lemon zest and juice. Season with salt and pepper to taste. Set pastry on top of filling and serve.

## Braised Chicken with Mustard and Herbs

**SERVES** 4 to 6

**WHY THIS RECIPE WORKS** Chicken is great for braising. It's got skin that renders loads of fat and collagen, which adds flavor and lush body to the sauce, and meat that turns tender and gives up savory juices. For well-seasoned, juicy braised chicken pieces, we started by brining them. We then browned the drumsticks, thighs, and larger breast pieces to create a flavorful fond, to which we added aromatics and a bit of flour to emulsify the fat and make the sauce silky. Then we deglazed the pot with water and wine to create a braising liquid. Once we had cooked the chicken (in stages, by cut) we transferred the pot to the oven and let the chicken pieces simmer gently until tender. Chicken breasts are broader at one end than the other, so cut more than halfway up each breast to create two pieces of equal mass. There's no need to take the temperature of the dark meat; it will be properly cooked by the time the white meat reaches its target temperature.

- ½ cup table salt, for brining
- 1½–2 pounds bone-in split chicken breasts, trimmed and each cut crosswise into 2 pieces of equal mass
- 1½–2 pounds chicken leg quarters, separated into drumsticks and thighs, trimmed
- 1 tablespoon vegetable oil
- 1 onion, chopped fine
- 3 garlic cloves, minced
- 1 tablespoon finely chopped fresh thyme
- 1 teaspoon pepper
- 1 tablespoon all-purpose flour
- 1¼ cups water
- ⅓ cup dry white wine
- 3 tablespoons finely chopped fresh parsley
- 1½ tablespoons whole-grain mustard
- 2 teaspoons lemon juice

**1.** Dissolve salt in 2 quarts cold water in large container. Submerge chicken in brine, cover, and refrigerate for 30 minutes to 1 hour. Remove chicken from brine and thoroughly pat dry with paper towels. Set aside tapered breast pieces.

**2.** Adjust oven rack to middle position and heat oven to 300 degrees. Heat oil in Dutch oven over medium-high heat until just smoking. Place all chicken except reserved tapered breast pieces skin side down in pot and cook until skin is well browned, 5 to 8 minutes. (Reduce heat if pot begins to scorch.) Transfer chicken to plate. Pour off all but 2 tablespoons fat from pot, then reduce heat to medium.

**3.** Add onion and cook, stirring occasionally, until softened, 5 to 7 minutes. Stir in garlic, thyme, and pepper and cook until fragrant, about 30 seconds. Stir in flour and cook, stirring constantly, for 1 minute. Stir in water and wine, scraping up any browned bits.

**4.** Place thighs and drumsticks skin side up in pot and bring to simmer over medium heat. Cover and cook for 8 minutes. (Sauce will have consistency of thick gravy but will thin as chicken cooks.) Add broad breast pieces, skin side down, along with any accumulated juices. Cover and cook until broad breast pieces register 105 to 115 degrees, 3 to 5 minutes. Remove pot from heat.

**5.** Using tongs, flip broad breast pieces skin side up. Add tapered breast pieces, skin side up, to pot and cover. Transfer pot to oven and cook until breast pieces register 160 degrees, 15 to 30 minutes.

**6.** Transfer chicken to serving dish. Discard skin from tapered breast pieces (or all skin, if desired). Sauce should thinly coat back of spoon; if necessary, simmer until slightly thickened, 1 to 2 minutes. Stir parsley, mustard, and lemon juice into sauce. Season with salt and pepper to taste. Pour sauce over chicken and serve.

## Chicken Tagine

SERVES 4

---

**WHY THIS RECIPE WORKS** This Moroccan-inspired chicken dish achieves deep flavor in about an hour. We used a mix of skin-on white and dark meat chicken and browned the meat first. After removing the chicken from the pot, we sautéed onion, strips of lemon zest, garlic, and a spice blend in some oil and the browned bits left in the pot; this ensured that no flavor went to waste. A number of spices were necessary to re-create the notes in Moroccan chicken, including paprika, cumin, cayenne, ginger, coriander, and cinnamon; honey filled the bill for the missing sweetness. Greek green olives provided the meatiness and piquant flavor of the traditional Moroccan olives. Chopped cilantro, stirred in right before serving, was the perfect finishing touch to our dish. Bone-in chicken parts can be substituted for the whole chicken. For best results, use four chicken thighs and two chicken breasts, each breast split in half; the dark meat contributes valuable flavor to the broth and should not be omitted. Use a vegetable peeler to remove wide strips of zest from the lemon before juicing it. Make sure to trim any white pith from the zest, as it can impart bitter flavor. If the olives are particularly salty, rinse them first. Serve with Simple Couscous (page 731).

- 1¼ teaspoons paprika
- ½ teaspoon ground cumin
- ½ teaspoon ground ginger
- ¼ teaspoon cayenne pepper
- ¼ teaspoon ground coriander
- ¼ teaspoon ground cinnamon
- 3 (2-inch) strips zest plus 3 tablespoons juice from 1 lemon
- 5 medium garlic cloves, minced or pressed through a garlic press (about 5 teaspoons)
- 1 (3½ to 4-pound) whole chicken, cut into 8 pieces (4 breast pieces, 2 thighs, 2 drumsticks), wings discarded, and trimmed
- Table salt and ground black pepper
- 1 tablespoon olive oil
- 1 large onion, halved and sliced ¼ inch thick
- 1¾ cups low-sodium chicken broth
- 1 tablespoon honey
- 2 medium carrots, peeled and cut crosswise into ½-inch-thick rounds, very large pieces cut into half-moons
- 1 cup cracked green olives, pitted and halved
- 2 tablespoons chopped fresh cilantro leaves

**1.** Combine the paprika, cumin, ginger, cayenne, coriander, and cinnamon in a small bowl and set aside. Mince 1 of the lemon zest strips, combine with 1 teaspoon of the minced garlic, and mince together until reduced to a fine paste; set aside.

**2.** Season both sides of the chicken pieces with salt and pepper. Heat the oil in a Dutch oven over medium-high heat until beginning to smoke. Brown the chicken pieces, skin side down, until deep golden, about 5 minutes; using tongs, flip the chicken pieces and brown on the second side, about 4 minutes longer. Transfer the chicken to a large plate; when cool enough to handle, remove and discard the skin. Pour off and discard all but 1 tablespoon fat from the pot.

**3.** Add the onion and the 2 remaining lemon zest strips to the pot and cook, stirring occasionally, until the onion slices have browned at the edges but still retain their shape, 5 to 7 minutes (add 1 tablespoon water if the pan gets too dark). Add the remaining 4 teaspoons garlic and cook, stirring, until fragrant, about 30 seconds. Add the spices and cook, stirring constantly, until darkened and very fragrant, 45 seconds to 1 minute. Stir in the broth and honey, scraping up the browned bits from the bottom of the pot. Add the thighs and drumsticks, reduce the heat to medium, and simmer for 5 minutes.

**4.** Add the carrots and breast pieces with any accumulated juices to the pot, arranging the breast pieces in a single layer on top of the carrots. Cover, reduce the heat to medium-low, and simmer until the breast pieces register 160 degrees, 10 to 15 minutes.

**5.** Transfer the chicken to a plate and tent with aluminum foil. Add the olives to the pot; increase the heat to medium-high and simmer until the liquid has thickened slightly and the carrots are tender, 4 to 6 minutes. Return the chicken to the pot and stir in the garlic mixture, lemon juice, and cilantro; season with salt and pepper to taste. Serve immediately.

### Chicken Tagine with Chickpeas and Apricots

Follow the recipe for Chicken Tagine, replacing 1 carrot with 1 cup dried apricots, halved, and replacing the olives with one 15-ounce can chickpeas, rinsed.

## Chicken Marbella

**SERVES** 4 to 6

**WHY THIS RECIPE WORKS** More than 25 years ago, this dinner-party mainstay put *The Silver Palate Cookbook* on the map. We wanted to retool the recipe for today's tastes. To save time and boost flavor, we ditched the original marinade and made a paste of the prunes, olives, capers, garlic, and oregano, which we spread on the chicken and caramelized into the sauce. Instead of using whole birds, which require butchering, we chose easy-prep chicken parts. To intensify the dish's meaty flavor and to create complexity, we added anchovies and red pepper flakes and browned the chicken skin in a skillet before baking it through. Any combination of split breasts and leg quarters can be used in this recipe.

**PASTE**

- ⅓ cup pitted green olives, rinsed
- ⅓ cup pitted prunes
- 3 tablespoons extra-virgin olive oil
- 2 tablespoons capers, rinsed
- 4 garlic cloves, peeled
- 3 anchovy fillets, rinsed
- ½ teaspoon dried oregano
- ½ teaspoon pepper
- ¼ teaspoon kosher salt
- Pinch red pepper flakes

**CHICKEN**

- 2½–3 pounds bone-in split chicken breasts and/or leg quarters, trimmed
- Kosher salt and pepper
- 2 teaspoons olive oil
- ¾ cup low-sodium chicken broth
- ⅓ cup white wine
- ⅓ cup pitted green olives, rinsed and halved
- 1 tablespoon capers, rinsed
- 2 bay leaves
- ⅓ cup pitted prunes, chopped coarse
- 1 tablespoon unsalted butter
- 1 teaspoon red wine vinegar
- 2 tablespoons minced fresh parsley

**1. FOR THE PASTE:** Adjust oven rack to middle position and heat oven to 400 degrees. Pulse all ingredients together in food processor until finely chopped, about 10 pulses. Scrape down bowl and continue to process until mostly smooth, 1 to 2 minutes. Transfer to bowl. (Paste can be stored in an airtight container and refrigerated for up to 24 hours.)

**2. FOR THE CHICKEN:** Pat chicken dry with paper towels. Sprinkle chicken pieces with 1½ teaspoons salt and season with pepper.

**3.** Heat oil in 12-inch skillet over medium-high heat until just smoking. Add chicken, skin side down, and cook without moving until well browned, 5 to 8 minutes. Transfer chicken to large plate. Drain off all but 1 teaspoon fat from skillet and return to medium-low heat.

**4.** Add ⅓ cup paste to skillet and cook, stirring constantly, until fragrant and fond forms on bottom of pan, 1 to 2 minutes. Stir in broth, wine, olives, capers, and bay leaves, scraping up any browned bits. Return chicken, skin side up, to pan (skin should be above surface of liquid) and transfer to oven. Cook, uncovered, for 15 minutes.

**5.** Remove skillet from oven and use back of spoon to spread remaining paste over chicken pieces; sprinkle prunes around chicken. Continue to roast until paste begins to brown, breasts register 160 degrees, and leg quarters register 175 degrees, 7 to 12 minutes longer.

**6.** Transfer chicken to serving platter and tent loosely with aluminum foil. Remove bay leaves from sauce and whisk in butter, vinegar, and 1 tablespoon parsley; season with salt and pepper to taste. Pour sauce around chicken, sprinkle with remaining 1 tablespoon parsley, and serve.

## Pollo en Pepitoria (Spanish Braised Chicken with Sherry and Saffron)

**SERVES** 4

**WHY THIS RECIPE WORKS** Nailing the classic Spanish dish called pollo en pepitoria hinges on achieving a balance between the richness and brightness of its creamy, nutty sherry sauce. We began with chicken thighs because their high collagen content breaks down into gelatin the longer they cook, making our slow-braised chicken tender. Onions, softened in rendered fat, created the base into which we added garlic, a bay leaf, and cinnamon. Dry, light-bodied sherries shine in savory applications, so we poured some in along with chicken broth. We also chopped canned peeled tomatoes, adding them for some bright acidity. We braised the chicken in the sauce at a gentle 300 degrees and removed the skin once the thighs were fully cooked. To finish, we poured a portion of the cooking liquid into a blender to create a picada, a flavorful thickener, adding chopped hard-boiled egg yolks, saffron threads, garlic, and almonds. We whirred the mixture into a thick, smooth paste. With a finishing touch of fresh lemon juice for brightness, we thickened the sauce before pouring it over the chicken. Fresh parsley and hard-boiled egg whites made for a classic presentation. Any dry sherry, such as fino or Manzanilla, will work in this dish. Serve with crusty bread.

- 8 (5- to 7-ounce) bone-in chicken thighs, trimmed
- Table salt and pepper
- 1 tablespoon extra-virgin olive oil
- 1 onion, chopped fine
- 3 garlic cloves, minced
- 1 bay leaf
- ¼ teaspoon ground cinnamon
- ⅔ cup dry sherry
- 1 cup chicken broth
- 1 (14.5-ounce) can whole peeled tomatoes, drained and chopped fine
- 2 hard-cooked large eggs, peeled and yolks and whites separated
- ½ cup slivered blanched almonds, toasted
- Pinch saffron threads, crumbled
- 2 tablespoons chopped fresh parsley
- 1½ teaspoons lemon juice

**1.** Adjust oven rack to middle position and heat oven to 300 degrees.

**2.** Pat thighs dry with paper towels and season both sides of each with 1 teaspoon salt and ½ teaspoon pepper. Heat oil in 12-inch skillet over high heat until just smoking. Add thighs and brown on both sides, 10 to 12 minutes. Transfer thighs to large plate and pour off all but 2 teaspoons fat from skillet.

**3.** Return skillet to medium heat, add onion and ¼ teaspoon salt, and cook, stirring frequently, until just softened, about 3 minutes. Add 2 teaspoons garlic, bay leaf, and cinnamon and cook until fragrant, about 1 minute. Add sherry and cook, scraping up any browned bits, until sauce starts to thicken, about 2 minutes. Stir in broth and tomatoes and bring to simmer. Return thighs to skillet, cover, transfer to oven, and cook until chicken registers 195 degrees, 45 to 50 minutes. Transfer thighs to serving platter, remove and discard skin, and cover loosely with aluminum foil to keep warm. While thighs cook, finely chop egg whites.

**4.** Discard bay leaf. Transfer ¾ cup chicken cooking liquid, egg yolks, almonds, saffron, and remaining garlic to blender. Process until smooth, about 2 minutes, scraping down jar as needed. Return almond mixture to skillet. Add 1 tablespoon parsley and lemon juice; bring to simmer over medium heat. Simmer, whisking frequently, until thickened, 3 to 5 minutes. Season with salt and pepper to taste.

**5.** Pour sauce over chicken, sprinkle with remaining 1 tablespoon parsley and egg whites, and serve.

## Mahogany Chicken Thighs

**SERVES** 4 to 6

**WHY THIS RECIPE WORKS** Braising chicken thighs does an excellent job of rendering sneaky pockets of fat and producing luxurious, flavorful meat, but there is one drawback: we miss the crispy skin of roasted chicken. We wanted the best of both worlds. We took a hybrid approach: braise for tenderness, then broil for crispy skin. We oven-braised the thighs in a flavor-infusing combination of soy sauce, sherry, white vinegar, a big piece of smashed ginger, smashed garlic, and sugar and molasses for sweetness (both would also caramelize and boost the mahogany hue). After braising for an hour, the fat was fully rendered, and although the meat was overcooked according to our usual standards, the melted connective tissue had converted to gelatin, which resulted in meat that was supple and juicy. Turning the chicken skin side up halfway through braising allowed the rendered skin to dry before broiling, which helped it crisp a little more. For a simple, streamlined finish, we used a portion of the braising liquid to make a quick sauce (thickened with a little cornstarch for body). For best results, trim all visible fat and skin from the underside of the thighs. Serve with steamed rice and vegetables.

- 1½ cups water
- 1 cup soy sauce
- ¼ cup dry sherry
- 2 tablespoons sugar
- 2 tablespoons molasses
- 1 tablespoon distilled white vinegar
- 8 (5- to 7-ounce) bone-in chicken thighs, trimmed
- 1 (2-inch) piece ginger, peeled, halved, and smashed
- 6 garlic cloves, peeled and smashed
- 1 tablespoon cornstarch

**1.** Adjust oven rack to lower-middle position and heat oven to 300 degrees. Whisk 1 cup water, soy sauce, sherry, sugar, molasses, and vinegar together in ovensafe 12-inch skillet until sugar is dissolved. Arrange chicken, skin side down, in soy mixture and nestle ginger and garlic between pieces of chicken.

**2.** Bring soy mixture to simmer over medium heat and simmer for 5 minutes. Transfer skillet to oven and cook, uncovered, for 30 minutes.

**3.** Flip chicken skin side up and continue to cook, uncovered, until chicken registers 195 degrees, 20 to 30 minutes longer. Transfer chicken to platter, taking care not to tear skin. Pour cooking liquid through fine-mesh strainer into fat separator and let settle for 5 minutes. Heat broiler.

**4.** Whisk cornstarch and remaining ½ cup water together in bowl. Pour 1 cup defatted cooking liquid into now-empty skillet and bring to simmer over medium heat. Whisk cornstarch mixture into cooking liquid and simmer until thickened, about 1 minute. Pour sauce into bowl and set aside for serving.

**5.** Return chicken skin side up to now-empty skillet and broil until well browned, about 4 minutes. Return chicken to platter, and let rest for 5 minutes. Serve, passing reserved sauce separately.

## Braised Chicken Thighs with Fennel, Orange, and Cracked Olives

**SERVES** 4 to 6

**WHY THIS RECIPE WORKS** For this simple chicken braise, we started by searing bone-in, skin-on thighs to crisp the skin. We then transferred the thighs to the oven where they simmered, skin side up, in a flavorful mix of chicken broth, orange juice, fennel, and Pernod until they reached 195 degrees and turned meltingly tender and juicy. To finish the sauce, we reduced the braising liquid to concentrate its flavors before whisking in a cornstarch slurry to thicken it to a luxurious, velvety consistency. Last-minute additions of olives, orange zest, and minced fennel fronds made for a fragrant finish. Serve with potatoes, rice, or buttered noodles.

- 8 (5- to 7-ounce) bone-in chicken thighs, trimmed
- 1¼ teaspoons table salt
- ½ teaspoon pepper
- 1 tablespoon vegetable oil
- 1 small fennel bulb, finely chopped, plus 2 teaspoons fronds, minced
- ¼ teaspoon red pepper flakes
- 1 cup chicken broth
- 1 cup orange juice
- 2 tablespoons Pernod
- 2 teaspoons water
- 1½ teaspoons cornstarch
- 2 tablespoons lemon juice
- ½ teaspoon grated orange zest
- 18 Castelvetrano olives, pitted and cracked

**1.** Adjust oven rack to lower-middle position and heat oven to 325 degrees. Pat chicken dry with paper towels and sprinkle both sides with salt and pepper. Heat oil in 12-inch ovensafe skillet over medium heat until shimmering. Add chicken, skin side down, and cook, without moving it, until well browned, about 8 minutes. Using tongs, flip chicken and brown on second side, about 3 minutes. Transfer chicken to large plate.

**2.** Pour off all but 2 tablespoons fat from skillet. Add chopped fennel and cook, stirring frequently, until lightly browned, about 4 to 5 minutes. Add pepper flakes and cook, stirring constantly, for 1 minute. Add broth, orange juice, and Pernod; bring to simmer, scraping up any browned bits. Return chicken to skillet skin side up (skin will be above surface of liquid). Transfer skillet to oven and bake, uncovered, until chicken registers 195 degrees, 35 to 40 minutes. Whisk water and cornstarch together in small bowl; set aside.

**3.** Using tongs, transfer chicken to serving platter and tent with aluminum foil. Place skillet over high heat. Cook, occasionally scraping side of skillet to incorporate fond, until sauce is thickened and reduced to 1½ cups, 8 to 10 minutes. Adjust heat to medium-low. Whisk cornstarch mixture to recombine and then whisk into sauce and simmer until thickened, about 1 minute. Off heat, whisk in lemon juice, orange zest, and olives. Season with salt and pepper to taste. Pour sauce around chicken, top with fennel fronds, and serve.

### Braised Chicken Thighs with Lemon, Spices, and Torn Basil

**SERVES** 4 to 6

Use a small saucepan or skillet to crush the coriander seeds. Serve with potatoes, rice, or buttered noodles.

- 8 (5- to 7-ounce) bone-in chicken thighs, trimmed
- 1¼ teaspoons table salt
- ½ teaspoon pepper
- 1 tablespoon vegetable oil
- 1 shallot, minced
- 2 garlic cloves, minced
- 1 teaspoon ground cumin
- ½ teaspoon ground coriander
- 1½ cups chicken broth
- ½ teaspoon grated lemon zest plus ½ cup juice (3 lemons)
- 2 teaspoons water
- 1½ teaspoons cornstarch
- 1 teaspoon coriander seeds, lightly crushed
- 2 tablespoons unsalted butter, cut into 2 pieces
- 10 large basil leaves, torn into pieces

**1.** Adjust oven rack to lower-middle position and heat oven to 325 degrees. Pat chicken dry with paper towels and sprinkle both sides with salt and pepper. Heat oil in 12-inch ovensafe skillet over medium heat until shimmering. Add chicken, skin side down, and cook, without moving it, until well browned, about 8 minutes. Using tongs, flip chicken and brown on second side, about 3 minutes. Transfer chicken to large plate.

**2.** Pour off all but 2 tablespoons fat from skillet. Add shallot and garlic and cook, stirring frequently, until garlic is golden brown, about 1½ minutes. Add cumin and ground coriander and cook, stirring constantly, for 1 minute. Add broth and lemon juice; bring to simmer, scraping up any browned bits. Return chicken to skillet skin side up (skin will be above surface of liquid). Transfer skillet to oven and bake, uncovered, until chicken registers 195 degrees, 35 to 40 minutes. Whisk water and cornstarch together in small bowl; set aside.

**3.** Using tongs, transfer chicken to serving platter and tent with aluminum foil. Place skillet over high heat. Stir coriander seeds into liquid and bring to boil. Cook, occasionally scraping side of skillet to incorporate fond, until sauce is thickened and reduced to 1½ cups, 8 to 10 minutes. Adjust heat to medium-low. Whisk cornstarch mixture to recombine and then whisk into sauce and simmer until thickened, about 1 minute. Off heat, whisk in lemon zest and butter. Season with salt and pepper to taste. Pour sauce around chicken, top with basil, and serve.

### Creamy Braised Chicken Thighs with Caraway and Dill

Substitute 2 teaspoons caraway seeds for ground cumin and coriander. Substitute ⅔ cup dry white wine for lemon juice. Omit coriander seeds and butter. Reduce sauce to 1¼ cups, 8 to 10 minutes. Whisk in ⅓ cup crème fraîche over low heat. Substitute 2 teaspoons minced fresh dill for lemon zest and 1 teaspoon minced fresh dill for basil.

## Filipino Chicken Adobo

SERVES 4

**WHY THIS RECIPE WORKS** Adobo is the national dish of the Philippines, and chicken adobo is among the most popular versions. The dish consists of chicken simmered in a mixture of vinegar, soy sauce, garlic, bay leaves, and black pepper. Some versions of chicken adobo include coconut milk; we loved how its richness tempered the bracing acidity of the vinegar and masked the briny soy sauce, bringing the sauce into balance. But the fat from the coconut milk and the chicken skin made the sauce somewhat greasy. To combat this, we borrowed a technique used in French bistros: We placed the meat skin side down in a cold pan and then turned up the heat. As the pan gradually got hotter, the fat under the chicken's skin melted away while the exterior browned. Light coconut milk can be substituted for regular coconut milk. Serve this dish over rice.

- 8 (5- to 7-ounce) bone-in chicken thighs, trimmed
- ⅓ cup soy sauce
- 1 (13.5-ounce) can coconut milk
- ¾ cup cider vinegar
- 8 garlic cloves, peeled
- 4 bay leaves
- 2 teaspoons pepper
- 1 scallion, sliced thin

**1.** Toss chicken with soy sauce in large bowl. Refrigerate for at least 30 minutes or up to 1 hour.

**2.** Remove chicken from soy sauce, allowing excess to drip back into bowl. Transfer chicken, skin side down, to 12-inch nonstick skillet; set aside soy sauce.

**3.** Place skillet over medium-high heat and cook until chicken skin is browned, 7 to 10 minutes. While chicken is browning, whisk coconut milk, vinegar, garlic, bay leaves, and pepper into soy sauce.

**4.** Transfer chicken to plate and discard fat in skillet. Return chicken to skillet skin side down, add coconut milk mixture, and bring to boil. Reduce heat to medium-low and simmer, uncovered, for 20 minutes. Flip chicken skin side up and continue to cook, uncovered, until chicken registers 175 degrees, about 15 minutes. Transfer chicken to platter and tent with aluminum foil.

**5.** Remove bay leaves and skim any fat off surface of sauce. Return skillet to medium-high heat and cook until sauce is thickened, 5 to 7 minutes. Pour sauce over chicken, sprinkle with scallion, and serve.

## Chicken Yassa (Senegalese Braised Chicken with Caramelized Onion and Lemon)

SERVES 4 to 6 SEASON 26

**WHY THIS RECIPE WORKS** Fall-off-the-bone-tender meat smothered in caramelized onions, lemon, mustard, and garlic, chicken yassa is comfort food by way of the Casamance region in Southern Senegal. Briefly marinating chicken thighs in a mixture of lemon juice, mustard, oil, and salt moistened, seasoned, and helped the meat retain moisture during cooking and coated its surface with bright flavor. Braising the chicken in the reserved marinade (along with chicken broth, garlic, and habanero) suffused it with lemony, mustardy tang; we cooked it for the better part of an hour, so it was practically falling off the bone. The sauce was finished with more lemon juice, and it and the chicken were served family-style over a bed of rice along with more lemon wedges for a last-minute burst of flavor. We like the mild-to-moderate heat of half a habanero or serrano. Make it spicier by using a whole chile (poked with a fork) or milder by seeding the chile before use. Braised hibiscus leaves (widely eaten in Senegal) are a traditional accompaniment, but cooked spinach seasoned with lemon juice is a fine alternative.

- ⅓ cup plus 2 tablespoons lemon juice (3 lemons), divided, plus lemon wedges for serving
- 3½ tablespoons vegetable oil, divided
- 2 tablespoons Dijon mustard
- 1½ teaspoons table salt, divided
- 2 pounds bone-in chicken thighs, trimmed
- 2 pounds onions, halved and sliced thin
- 1⅓ cups chicken broth
- 8 garlic cloves, lightly crushed and peeled
- ½–1 habanero chile
- ¼ teaspoon pepper
- 4½ cups cooked long-grain white rice
- 1½ teaspoons minced fresh parsley

**1.** Whisk ⅓ cup lemon juice, 1½ tablespoons oil, mustard, and 1 teaspoon salt together in large bowl. Add chicken and toss to coat. Cover and refrigerate for at least 30 minutes or up to 1 hour.

**2.** Heat remaining 2 tablespoons oil in large Dutch oven over medium heat until shimmering. Using tongs, remove chicken from marinade and drag pieces against rim of bowl to scrape excess marinade back into bowl; do not discard marinade. Transfer chicken to pot, skin side down, and cook until skin is golden brown, 6 to 8 minutes. Flip chicken and brown on second side, 6 to 8 minutes. Transfer chicken to large plate.

**3.** Add onions and remaining ½ teaspoon salt to pot; reduce heat to medium-low; and cook, stirring frequently and scraping browned bits from bottom of pot, until onions are softened and caramelized, 25 to 30 minutes.

**4.** Stir in broth, garlic, habanero, pepper, and reserved marinade and bring to simmer. Return chicken and any accumulated juices to pot. Cover and simmer, stirring occasionally, until sauce has thickened to consistency of heavy cream and chicken is very tender (meat should begin to fall from bone and fork will slip easily in and out of meat), 45 to 55 minutes.

**5.** Spread rice in even layer on large platter. Arrange chicken on top of rice. Stir remaining 2 tablespoons lemon juice into sauce and season with salt and pepper to taste. Spoon sauce and onions over and around chicken and rice. Sprinkle with parsley and serve with lemon wedges.

## Modern Coq au Vin

**SERVES 4**

**WHY THIS RECIPE WORKS** We wanted to return this fancy restaurant classic to its humble roots and create a dish with tender, juicy chicken infused with the flavors of red wine, onions, mushrooms, and bacon. If using a mix of dark and white meat, we found it was essential to start the dark before the white, so that all the meat finished cooking at the same time and nothing was overcooked or undercooked. To thicken the stewing liquid, we sprinkled flour over the sautéed vegetables and whisked in butter toward the end of cooking; the butter also provided a nice richness in the sauce. Chicken broth added a savory note to the sauce and gave it some body; an entire bottle of red wine provided a great base of flavor. A sprinkling of crisp, salty bacon rounded out the acidity of the wine. Use any $10 bottle of fruity, medium-bodied red wine, such as Pinot Noir, Côtes du Rhône, or Zinfandel. The breasts and thighs/drumsticks do not cook at the same rate; if using both, note that the breast pieces are added partway through the cooking time. Serve with egg noodles.

- 5 slices thick-cut bacon, chopped
- Vegetable oil
- 4 pounds bone-in, skin-on chicken pieces (split breasts cut in half, drumsticks, and/or thighs)
- ¾ teaspoon table salt
- ¾ teaspoon pepper
- 2 cups frozen pearl onions
- 10 ounces white mushrooms, trimmed and quartered

- 2 garlic cloves, minced
- 1 tablespoon tomato paste
- 3 tablespoons all-purpose flour
- 1 (750-ml) bottle medium-bodied red wine
- 2½ cups chicken broth
- 1 teaspoon minced fresh thyme or ¼ teaspoon dried
- 2 bay leaves
- 2 tablespoons unsalted butter, cut into 2 pieces, chilled
- 2 tablespoons minced fresh parsley

**1.** Fry bacon in large Dutch oven over medium heat until crisp, 5 to 7 minutes. Transfer bacon to paper towel–lined plate, leaving fat in pot (you should have about 2 tablespoons; if necessary, add vegetable oil to make this amount). Set aside.

**2.** Pat chicken dry with paper towels and sprinkle with salt and pepper. Return pot with bacon fat to medium-high heat until shimmering. Brown half of chicken on both sides, 5 to 8 minutes per side, reducing heat if pan begins to scorch. Transfer chicken to plate, leaving fat in pot. Return pot to medium-high heat and repeat with remaining chicken; transfer chicken to plate.

**3.** Pour off all but 1 tablespoon fat in pot (or add vegetable oil if needed to make this amount). Add onions and mushrooms and cook over medium heat, stirring occasionally, until lightly browned, about 10 minutes. Stir in garlic and tomato paste and cook until fragrant, about 30 seconds. Stir in flour and cook for 1 minute. Stir in wine, broth, thyme, and bay leaves, scraping up any browned bits.

**4.** Nestle chicken, along with any accumulated juices, into pot and bring to simmer. Cover, turn heat to medium-low, and simmer until chicken is tender and thickest part of breasts registers 160 degrees, about 20 minutes, or thickest part of thighs and drumsticks registers 175 degrees, about 1 hour. (If using both types of chicken, simmer thighs and drumsticks for 40 minutes before adding breasts.)

**5.** Transfer chicken to serving dish, tent with aluminum foil, and let rest while finishing sauce. Skim as much fat as possible off surface of sauce and return to simmer until sauce is thickened and measures about 2 cups, about 20 minutes. Off heat, remove bay leaves, whisk in butter, and season with salt and pepper to taste. Pour sauce over chicken, sprinkle with reserved bacon and parsley, and serve.

## Coq au Riesling

**SERVES** 4 to 6

**WHY THIS RECIPE WORKS** For our take on the elegant white wine version of coq au vin, starting with a whole chicken and then breaking it down ourselves was a must, not only to obtain evenly sized parts that would cook at the same rate but also so that we could use the back and wings to enrich the sauce. The fond created from browning the chicken skin was also essential for flavor but required browning the chicken parts in batches. Plus, the skin turned flabby during braising. The solution? Removing the skin from the meat, browning it in one batch, and then discarding it before serving. Adding about three-quarters of a bottle of dry Riesling along with a cup of water produced a sauce that was nuanced and balanced. Finally, we finished the sauce with crème fraîche for just the right silkiness and body. A dry Riesling is the best wine for this recipe, but a Sauvignon Blanc or Chablis will also work. Avoid a heavily oaked wine such as Chardonnay. Serve the stew with egg noodles or mashed potatoes.

- 1 (4- to 5-pound) whole chicken, cut into 8 pieces (4 breast pieces, 2 drumsticks, 2 thighs), wings and back reserved
- Table salt and pepper
- 2 slices bacon, chopped
- 3 shallots, chopped
- 2 carrots, peeled and chopped coarse
- 2 celery ribs, chopped coarse
- 4 garlic cloves, lightly crushed and peeled
- 3 tablespoons all-purpose flour
- 2½ cups dry Riesling
- 1 cup water
- 2 bay leaves
- 6 sprigs fresh parsley, plus 2 teaspoons minced
- 6 sprigs fresh thyme
- 1 pound white mushrooms, trimmed and halved if small or quartered if large
- ¼ cup crème fraîche

**1.** Remove skin from chicken breast pieces, drumsticks, and thighs and set aside. Sprinkle both sides of chicken pieces with 1¼ teaspoons salt and ½ teaspoon pepper; set aside. Cook bacon in large Dutch oven over medium-low heat, stirring occasionally, until beginning to render, 2 to 4 minutes. Add chicken skin, back, and wings to pot; increase heat to medium; and cook, stirring frequently, until bacon is browned, skin is rendered, and chicken back and wings are browned on all sides, 10 to 12 minutes. Remove pot from heat and carefully transfer 2 tablespoons fat to small bowl and set aside.

**2.** Return pot to medium heat. Add shallots, carrots, celery, and garlic and cook, stirring occasionally, until vegetables are softened, 4 to 6 minutes. Add flour and cook, stirring constantly, until no dry flour remains, about 30 seconds. Slowly add wine, scraping up any browned bits. Increase heat to high and simmer until mixture is slightly thickened, about 2 minutes. Stir in water, bay leaves, parsley sprigs, and thyme and bring to simmer. Place chicken pieces in even layer in pot, reduce heat to low, cover, and cook until breasts register 160 degrees and thighs and legs register 175 degrees, 25 to 30 minutes, stirring halfway through cooking. Transfer chicken pieces to plate as they come up to temperature.

**3.** Discard back and wings. Strain cooking liquid through fine-mesh strainer set over large bowl, pressing on solids to extract as much liquid as possible; discard solids. Let cooking liquid settle for 10 minutes. Using wide shallow spoon, skim fat from surface and discard.

**4.** While liquid settles, return pot to medium heat and add reserved fat, mushrooms, and ¼ teaspoon salt; cook, stirring occasionally, until lightly browned, 8 to 10 minutes.

**5.** Return liquid to pot and bring to boil. Simmer briskly, stirring occasionally, until sauce is thickened to consistency of heavy cream, 4 to 6 minutes. Reduce heat to medium-low and stir in crème fraîche and minced parsley. Return chicken to pot along with any accumulated juices, cover, and cook until just heated through, 5 to 8 minutes. Season with salt and pepper to taste, and serve.

## Chicken Provençal

**SERVES** 4

**WHY THIS RECIPE WORKS** Chicken Provençal represents the best of rustic peasant food—bone-in chicken is simmered all day in a tomatoey, garlicky herb broth. We wanted to rejuvenate this dish, and create a chicken dish that was meltingly tender, moist, and flavorful, napped in an aromatic, garlicky tomato sauce that we could mop up with a good loaf of crusty bread. For the best flavor and most tender texture, we used bone-in chicken thighs and browned them in a sheer film of olive oil. Skinless thighs stuck to the pan, and skin-on thighs developed a flabby texture when braised later on. So we settled on a compromise—browning the thighs with the skin on (to develop rich flavor and leave browned bits in the pan), then ditching the skins prior to the braising (to avoid flabby skin). To keep the sauce from becoming greasy, we spooned off the excess fat left behind from browning the chicken, but kept enough to sauté our garlic and onion. Diced tomatoes, white wine, and chicken broth also went into the sauce. We then braised the chicken until it was meltingly tender. As for flavor enhancers, a small amount of niçoise olives added an essential brininess to the dish, and some minced anchovy made the sauce taste richer and fuller. This dish is often served with rice or slices of crusty bread, but soft polenta is also a good accompaniment. Niçoise olives are the preferred olives here; the flavor of kalamatas and other types of brined or oil-cured olives is too potent.

- 8 (5- to 6-ounce) bone-in, skin-on chicken thighs, trimmed
  Table salt
- 1 tablespoon extra-virgin olive oil
- 1 small onion, minced
- 6 medium garlic cloves, minced or pressed through a garlic press (about 2 tablespoons)
- 1 anchovy fillet, minced (about ½ teaspoon)
- ⅛ teaspoon cayenne pepper
- 1 cup dry white wine
- 1 cup low-sodium chicken broth
- 1 (14.5-ounce) can diced tomatoes, drained
- 2½ tablespoons tomato paste
- 1½ tablespoons chopped fresh thyme leaves
- 1 teaspoon chopped fresh oregano leaves
- 1 teaspoon herbes de Provence (optional)
- 1 bay leaf
- 1½ teaspoons grated zest from 1 lemon
- ½ cup pitted niçoise olives
- 1 tablespoon chopped fresh parsley leaves

**1.** Adjust an oven rack to the lower-middle position and heat the oven to 300 degrees. Season both sides of the chicken thighs with salt. Heat 1 teaspoon of the oil in a large Dutch oven over medium-high heat until shimmering. Add 4 chicken thighs, skin side down, and cook, without moving, until the skin is crisp and well browned, about 5 minutes. Flip the chicken pieces and brown on the second side, about 5 minutes longer; transfer to a large plate. Repeat with the remaining 4 chicken thighs, then transfer them to the plate and set aside. Discard all but 1 tablespoon of fat from the pot.

**2.** Add the onion to the pot and cook, stirring occasionally, over medium heat until softened and browned, about 4 minutes. Add the garlic, anchovy, and cayenne; cook, stirring constantly, until fragrant, about 1 minute. Add the wine, scraping up any browned bits. Stir in the chicken broth, tomatoes, tomato paste, thyme, oregano, herbes de Provence (if using), and bay leaf. Remove and discard the skin from the chicken thighs, then submerge the chicken pieces in the liquid and add the accumulated chicken juices to the pot. Increase the heat to high, bring to a simmer, cover, and set the pot in the oven; cook until the chicken offers no resistance when poked with a knife but is still clinging to the bones, about 1¼ hours.

**3.** Using a slotted spoon, transfer the chicken to a serving platter and tent loosely with foil. Discard the bay leaf. Set the pot over high heat, stir in 1 teaspoon of the lemon zest, bring to a boil, and cook, stirring occasionally, until slightly thickened and reduced to 2 cups, about 5 minutes. Stir in the olives and cook until heated through, about 1 minute. Combine the remaining ½ teaspoon zest and the parsley. Spoon the sauce over the chicken, drizzle the chicken with the remaining 2 teaspoons oil, sprinkle with the parsley mixture, and serve.

# Chicken with 40 Cloves of Garlic

**SERVES 4**

---

**WHY THIS RECIPE WORKS** We wanted to revisit this classic French dish so that it would boast well-browned, full-flavored chicken, sweet and nutty garlic, and a savory sauce. Using a cut-up chicken rather than a whole bird ensured that the meat cooked quickly and evenly. We roasted the garlic cloves first to develop their flavor, then added them to the braising liquid. Cooking it all with a pan-roasting/braising technique kept the chicken moist, and finishing the chicken under the broiler made the skin crispy. Shallots and herbs added flavor to the sauce, and several roasted garlic cloves, smashed into a paste, thickened and flavored the sauce. If using a kosher chicken, skip the brining process and begin with step 2. Avoid heads of garlic that have begun to sprout (the green shoots will make the sauce taste bitter). Tie the rosemary and thyme sprigs together with kitchen twine so that they will be easier to retrieve from the pan. Serve the dish with slices of crusty baguette; you can spread them with the roasted garlic cloves.

- ¼ cup table salt for brining
- ¾ teaspoon pepper, divided
- 1 (3½- to 4-pound) whole chicken, cut into 8 pieces (4 breast pieces, 2 drumsticks, 2 thighs)
- 3 garlic heads, outer papery skins removed, cloves separated and unpeeled
- 2 shallots, peeled and quartered
- 1 tablespoon extra-virgin olive oil, divided
- ½ teaspoon table salt
- ¾ cup dry vermouth or dry white wine
- ¾ cup chicken broth
- 2 sprigs fresh thyme
- 1 sprig fresh rosemary
- 1 bay leaf
- 2 tablespoons unsalted butter

**1.** Adjust oven rack to middle position and heat oven to 400 degrees. Dissolve ¼ cup salt in 2 quarts cold water in large container; submerge chicken in brine, cover, and refrigerate for 30 minutes. Remove chicken from brine and pat dry with paper towels. Sprinkle both sides of chicken pieces with ½ teaspoon pepper.

**2.** Meanwhile, combine garlic, shallots, 2 teaspoons oil, salt, and remaining ¼ teaspoon pepper in 9-inch pie plate; cover tightly with aluminum foil and roast until softened and beginning to brown, about 30 minutes, shaking pan once halfway through cooking. Uncover, stir, and continue to roast, uncovered, until browned and fully tender, about 10 minutes longer, stirring once or twice. Remove from oven and increase oven temperature to 450 degrees.

**3.** Heat remaining 1 teaspoon oil in 12-inch ovensafe skillet over medium-high heat until just smoking. Brown chicken, skin side down, until golden, about 5 minutes; flip chicken pieces and brown until golden on second side, about 4 minutes longer. Transfer chicken to large plate and pour off fat from skillet. Off heat, add vermouth, chicken broth, thyme, rosemary, and bay leaf to pan, scraping up any browned bits. Set skillet over medium heat, add garlic mixture, and return chicken, skin side up, to pan, nestling pieces on top of and between garlic cloves. Place skillet in oven and roast until the thickest part of breasts registers 160 degrees; remove skillet from oven.

**4.** Adjust oven rack 6 inches from broiler element and heat broiler. Broil chicken to crisp skin, 3 to 5 minutes. Remove skillet from oven and transfer chicken to serving dish. Transfer 10 to 12 garlic cloves to fine-mesh sieve and reserve. Using slotted spoon, scatter remaining garlic cloves and shallots around chicken; discard herbs. Using rubber spatula, push reserved garlic cloves through sieve and into bowl; discard skins. Add garlic paste to skillet and bring liquid to simmer over medium-high heat, whisking to incorporate garlic. Whisk in butter and season with salt and pepper to taste. Serve chicken, passing sauce separately.

### CUTTING UP A WHOLE CHICKEN

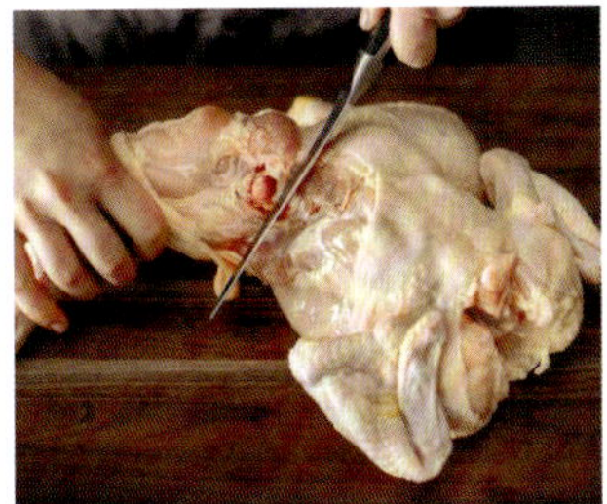

**1.** Using chef's knife, cut off legs, one at a time, by severing joint between leg and body.

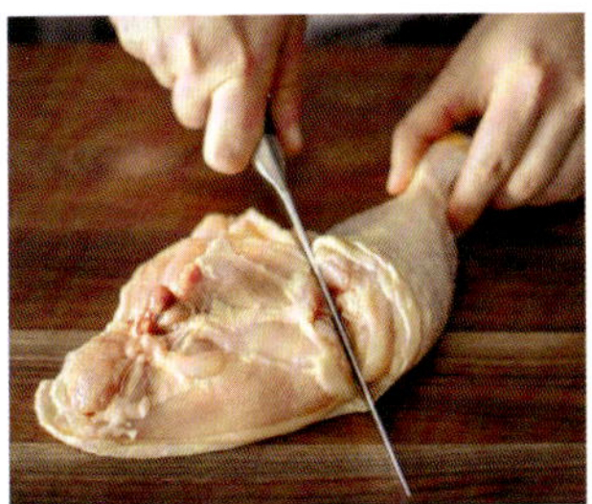

**2.** Cut each leg into 2 pieces—drumstick and thigh—by slicing through joint that connects them (marked by thick white line of fat).

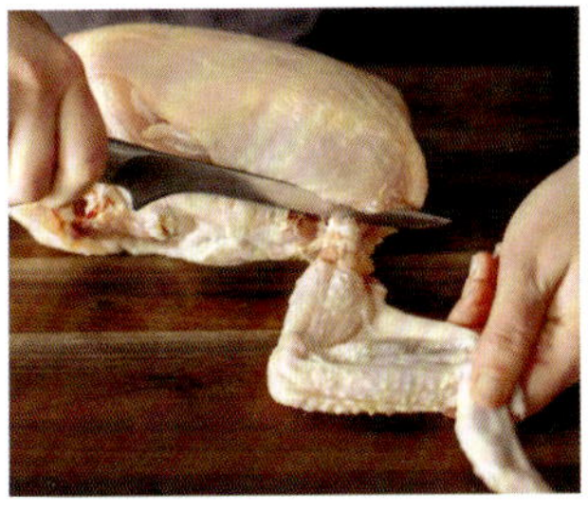

**3.** Flip chicken and remove wings by slicing through each wing joint. Save wings for another purpose.

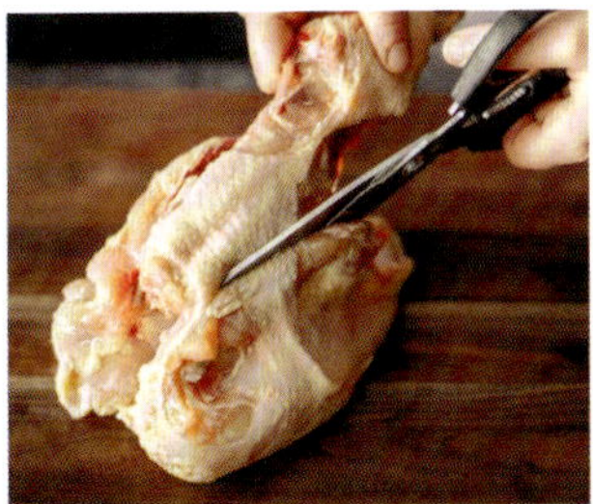

**4.** Turn chicken (now without its legs and wings) on its side and, using scissors, remove back from chicken breast.

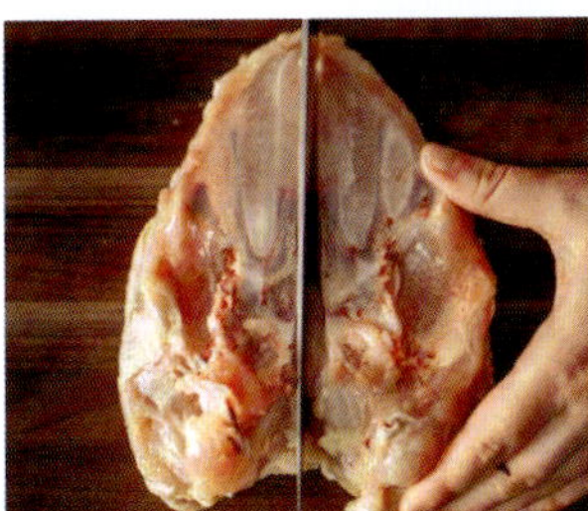

**5.** Flip breast skin side down and, using chef's knife, cut it in half through breast plate (marked by thin white line of cartilage), then cut each piece in half again.

## Poulet au Vinaigre (Chicken with Vinegar)

**SERVES** 4 to 6

**WHY THIS RECIPE WORKS** Our recipe for this classic Lyonnaise dish calls for using just chicken thighs—rather than the usual combination of light and dark meat—to ensure that all the meat cooks at the same rate. We browned the chicken to develop savory flavor and then braised it in a flavorful mix of chicken broth, white wine, and red wine vinegar until it reached 195 degrees, the temperature at which dark meat is silky and succulent because its collagen has turned to supple gelatin. To finish the sauce, we fortified the braising liquid with tomato paste (which we found much less fussy than peeling, seeding, and dicing a fresh tomato) and reduced it to a luxurious, lightly thickened consistency before adding minced fresh tarragon. The sauce is typically finished with heavy cream, but we preferred to whisk in a couple tablespoons of butter instead to help preserve the vibrancy of the sauce. Use an inexpensive dry white wine here.

- 8 (5- to 7-ounce) bone-in chicken thighs, trimmed
- 1¼ teaspoons table salt
- ¾ teaspoon pepper
- 1 tablespoon vegetable oil
- 1 large shallot, minced
- 2 garlic cloves, sliced thin
- 1 cup chicken broth
- 1 cup dry white wine
- ⅓ cup red wine vinegar, plus extra for seasoning
- 1 tablespoon tomato paste
- 2 tablespoons unsalted butter, chilled
- 1 tablespoon minced fresh tarragon

**1.** Adjust oven rack to lower-middle position and heat oven to 325 degrees. Pat chicken dry with paper towels and sprinkle both sides with salt and pepper. Heat oil in 12-inch ovensafe skillet over medium heat until shimmering. Add chicken, skin side down, and cook, without moving it, until well browned, about 8 minutes. Using tongs, flip chicken and brown on second side, about 3 minutes. Transfer chicken to large plate.

**2.** Pour off all but 2 tablespoons fat from skillet. Add shallot and garlic and cook, stirring frequently, until garlic is golden brown, about 1½ minutes. Add broth, wine, and vinegar; bring to simmer, scraping up any browned bits. Return chicken to skillet, skin side up (skin will be above surface of liquid). Transfer skillet to oven and bake, uncovered, until chicken registers 195 degrees, 35 to 40 minutes.

**3.** Using tongs, transfer chicken to clean serving platter and tent with aluminum foil. Place skillet over high heat. Whisk tomato paste into liquid and bring to boil. Cook, occasionally scraping side of skillet to incorporate fond, until sauce is thickened and reduced to 1¼ cups, 5 to 7 minutes. Off heat, whisk in butter and tarragon. Season with salt, pepper, and up to 1 teaspoon extra vinegar (added ¼ teaspoon at a time) to taste. Pour sauce around chicken and serve.

## Chicken Canzanese

**SERVES** 4 to 6

**WHY THIS RECIPE WORKS** Chicken canzanese is a regional Italian braised dish that transforms tough old birds into a moist and tender meal. Today's lean, mass-produced chickens, however, turn dried-out and bland when braised. We wanted old-fashioned results with a modern-day bird: tender, juicy chicken in an intensely flavored, well-developed sauce. To start, we swapped out young, modern chickens for meaty chicken thighs that hold up especially well to braising. Next, we turned to the sauce. We browned diced prosciutto on the stovetop until it rendered enough fat to cook the garlic, which created a rich flavor base. Then we added white wine and chicken broth, and simmered them to concentrate flavors and burn off the raw alcohol flavor. We returned the chicken to the skillet and put it into the oven, uncovered to crisp the skin. To round out the flavors, we added a quick squeeze of lemon juice, a generous pat of butter, and a sprinkling of chopped rosemary. When seasoning the dish at the end, be mindful that the prosciutto adds a fair amount of salt. It is important to use a piece of thickly sliced prosciutto in this recipe; thin strips will become tough and stringy. An equal amount of thickly sliced pancetta or bacon can be used in place of the prosciutto. Serve the chicken with boiled potatoes, noodles, or polenta.

- 1 tablespoon olive oil
- 2 ounces prosciutto (¼ inch thick), cut into ¼-inch cubes (see note)
- 4 medium garlic cloves, sliced thin lengthwise
- 3 pounds bone-in, skin-on chicken thighs (about 8 thighs), trimmed
- Ground black pepper
- 2 teaspoons unbleached all-purpose flour
- 2 cups dry white wine
- 1 cup low-sodium chicken broth
- 4 whole cloves
- 1 (4-inch) sprig fresh rosemary, leaves removed and minced fine (about ½ teaspoon), stem reserved
- 12 whole fresh sage leaves
- 2 bay leaves
- ¼–½ teaspoon red pepper flakes
- 1 tablespoon juice from 1 lemon
- 2 tablespoons unsalted butter
- Table salt

**1.** Adjust an oven rack to the lower-middle position and heat the oven to 325 degrees. Heat 1 teaspoon of the oil in a 12-inch heavy-bottomed ovensafe skillet over medium heat until shimmering. Add the prosciutto and cook, stirring frequently, until just starting to brown, about 3 minutes. Add the garlic slices and cook, stirring frequently, until the garlic is golden brown, about 1½ minutes. Using a slotted spoon, transfer the garlic and prosciutto to a small bowl and set aside. Do not rinse the pan.

**2.** Increase the heat to medium-high; add the remaining 2 teaspoons oil and heat until just smoking. Pat the chicken dry with paper towels and season with black pepper. Add the chicken, skin side down, and cook without moving until well browned, 5 to 8 minutes. Using tongs, turn the chicken and brown on the second side, about 5 minutes longer. Transfer the chicken to a large plate.

**3.** Remove all but 2 tablespoons fat from the pan. Sprinkle the flour over the fat and cook, stirring constantly, for 1 minute. Slowly add the wine and broth; bring to a simmer, scraping the bottom of the pan with a wooden spoon to loosen the browned bits. Cook until the liquid is slightly reduced, 3 minutes. Stir in the cloves, rosemary stem, sage leaves, bay leaves, red pepper flakes, and reserved prosciutto and garlic. Nestle the chicken into the liquid, skin side up (the skin should be above the surface of the liquid), and bake, uncovered, until the meat offers no resistance when poked with a fork but is not falling off the bones, about 1 hour 15 minutes. (Check the chicken after 15 minutes; the broth should be barely bubbling. If bubbling vigorously, reduce the oven temperature to 300 degrees.)

**4.** Using tongs, transfer the chicken to a serving platter and tent with foil. Remove and discard the sage leaves, rosemary stem, cloves, and bay leaves. Place the skillet over high heat and bring the sauce to a boil. Cook until the sauce is reduced to 1¼ cups, 2 to 5 minutes. Off the heat, stir in the minced rosemary, lemon juice, and butter. Season with salt and pepper to taste. Pour the sauce around the chicken and serve.

## Tamales

**MAKES** 18 tamales

**WHY THIS RECIPE WORKS** Tamales take a lot of time to prepare, so they are usually made for holidays and special occasions. We wanted to simplify the process while staying true to the tamales' subtle but hearty flavor and light texture. Although masa dough (made from corn kernels that have been cooked with slaked lime, ground to a flour, and mixed with water) is traditional, it can be difficult to find in some supermarkets. Instead, we turned to widely available masa harina, but when used alone, it was too fine-textured and had bland corn flavor. Grits, on the other hand, had a granular texture similar to traditional tamales and didn't sacrifice any flavor. Frozen corn added more corn flavor and also some texture. For the filling, hearty chicken thighs worked best for the long cooking time. A combination of dried ancho and New Mexican chiles resulted in a sauce with subtle spice and sweetness. We found it easiest to use large corn husks that measure about 8 inches long by 6 inches wide; if the husks are small, you may need to

use two per tamale and shingle them as needed to hold all of the filling. You can substitute butter for the lard if desired, but the tamales will have a distinctive buttery flavor. Be sure to use quick, not instant, grits in this recipe. For an accurate measurement of boiling water, bring a full kettle of water to a boil and then measure out the desired amount.

- 1 cup plus 2 tablespoons quick grits
- 1½ cups boiling water
- 1 cup (4 ounces) plus 2 tablespoons masa harina
- 20 large dried corn husks
- 1½ cups frozen corn, thawed
- 6 tablespoons unsalted butter, cut into ½-inch cubes and softened
- 6 tablespoons lard, softened
- 1 tablespoon sugar
- 2¼ teaspoons baking powder
- ¾ teaspoon table salt
- 1 recipe Red Chile Chicken Filling (recipe follows)

**1.** Place grits in medium bowl; whisk in boiling water; and let stand until water is mostly absorbed, about 10 minutes. Stir in masa harina; cover; and let cool to room temperature, about 20 minutes. Meanwhile, place husks in large bowl; cover with hot water; and let soak until pliable, about 30 minutes.

**2.** Process masa dough, corn, butter, lard, sugar, baking powder, and salt in food processor until mixture is light, sticky, and very smooth, about 1 minute, scraping down sides as necessary. Remove husks from water and pat dry with dish towel.

**3.** Working with 1 husk at a time, lay on counter, cupped side up, with long side facing you and wide end on right side. Spread ¼ cup tamale dough into 4-inch square over bottom right-hand corner, pushing it flush to bottom edge but leaving 1½-inch border at wide edge. Mound scant 2 tablespoons filling in line across center of dough, parallel to bottom edge. Roll husk away from you and over filling, so that dough surrounds filling and forms cylinder. Fold up tapered end, leaving top open, and transfer seam side down to platter.

### ASSEMBLING TAMALES

**1.** Arrange corn husk with long side parallel to counter edge. Spoon scant ¼ cup dough onto center of husk. Spread into 4-inch square, pushing it flush to bottom edge but leaving 1½-inch border at wide end.

**2.** Place scant 2 tablespoons of filling down center of dough. Roll husk away from you so that dough surrounds filling. It is important to roll tamales tightly so that they don't leak while cooking.

**3.** Fold tapered end of tamale up, leaving top open, and transfer to platter, seam side down. Keeping tamales seam side down means that you can skip tedious task of tying each one closed.

**4.** Fit large pot or Dutch oven with steamer basket, removing feet from steamer basket if pot is short. Fill pot with water until it just touches bottom of basket and bring to boil. Gently lay tamales in basket with open ends facing up and seam sides facing down. Cover and steam, checking water level often and adding additional water as needed, until tamales easily come free from husks, about 1 hour. Transfer tamales to large platter. Reheat remaining sauce from filling in covered bowl in microwave, about 30 seconds, and serve with tamales.

## Red Chile Chicken Filling

**MAKES** enough for 18 tamales

- 4 dried ancho chiles, stemmed, seeded, and torn into ½-inch pieces (1 cup)
- 4 dried New Mexican chiles, stemmed, seeded, and torn into ½-inch pieces (1 cup)
- 3 tablespoons vegetable oil
- 1 large onion, chopped
- 6 garlic cloves, minced
- ¾ teaspoon ground cumin
- ¾ teaspoon dried oregano
- 1 teaspoon table salt, divided
- 3 cups chicken broth
- ½ teaspoon pepper
- 1¼ pounds boneless, skinless chicken thighs, trimmed
- 1½ tablespoons cider vinegar
- Sugar

1. Toast anchos and New Mexican chiles in 12-inch skillet over medium heat, stirring frequently, until fragrant, 2 to 6 minutes; transfer to bowl.

2. Heat oil in now-empty skillet over medium heat until shimmering. Add onion and cook until softened, 5 to 7 minutes. Stir in garlic, cumin, oregano, ½ teaspoon salt, and toasted chiles and cook for 30 seconds. Stir in broth and simmer until slightly reduced, about 10 minutes. Transfer mixture to blender and process until smooth, about 20 seconds; return to skillet.

3. Sprinkle chicken with pepper and remaining ½ teaspoon salt, nestle into skillet, and bring to simmer over medium heat. Cover; reduce heat to low; and cook until chicken registers 160 degrees, 20 to 25 minutes.

4. Transfer chicken to carving board and let cool slightly. Using 2 forks, shred chicken into small pieces. Stir vinegar into sauce and season with salt, pepper, and sugar to taste. Toss shredded chicken with 1 cup sauce. Reserve remaining sauce to serve with tamales.

## Tinga de Pollo (Shredded Chicken Tacos)

**SERVES** 6

**WHY THIS RECIPE WORKS** Smoky, earthy tinga de pollo is a traditional taco filling that combines shredded chicken meat with a flavorful tomato-chipotle sauce. At first, we poached chicken breast meat separately from the sauce. We realized, though, that we could achieve a deeper flavor by using boneless thighs and cooking them in the spicy, tomatoey sauce. Fire-roasted tomatoes increased the sauce's smokiness, and a little brown sugar and lime juice and zest further boosted the dish's complexity. Simmering the cooked shredded chicken in the sauce for a full 10 minutes before serving gave the sauce a chance to thicken so it could really cling to the meat, making more cohesive tacos. If you have a little extra time, homemade tortillas will take these tacos to the next level. In addition to the Escabeche and the toppings included here, Mexican crema (or sour cream) and minced onion are also good choices. If you can't find Cotija cheese, substitute feta.

**CHICKEN**

- 2 pounds boneless, skinless chicken thighs, trimmed
- ½ teaspoon table salt
- ½ teaspoon pepper
- 2 tablespoons vegetable oil, divided
- 1 onion, halved and sliced thin
- 3 garlic cloves, minced
- 1 (14.5-ounce) can fire-roasted diced tomatoes
- ½ cup chicken broth
- 2 tablespoons minced canned chipotle chile in adobo sauce plus 2 teaspoons adobo sauce
- 1 teaspoon ground cumin
- ½ teaspoon brown sugar
- ¼ teaspoon cinnamon
- 1 teaspoon grated lime zest plus 2 tablespoons juice

**TACOS**

- 12 (6-inch) corn tortillas, warmed
- 1 avocado, halved, pitted, and cut into ½-inch pieces
- 2 ounces Cotija cheese, crumbled (½ cup)
- 6 scallions, minced
- Fresh cilantro leaves
- Lime wedges

1. **FOR THE CHICKEN:** Pat chicken dry with paper towels and sprinkle with salt and pepper. Heat 1 tablespoon oil in Dutch oven over medium-high heat until shimmering. Add half of chicken and brown on both sides, 3 to 4 minutes per side. Transfer to large plate. Repeat with remaining chicken.

2. Reduce heat to medium, add remaining 1 tablespoon oil to now-empty pot, and heat until shimmering. Add onion and cook, stirring frequently, until browned, about 7 minutes. Add garlic and cook until fragrant, about 1 minute. Add tomatoes and their juice, broth, chipotle and adobo sauce, cumin, sugar, and cinnamon and bring to boil, scraping up any browned bits.

3. Return chicken to pot; reduce heat to medium-low; cover; and simmer until meat registers 195 degrees, about 15 minutes, flipping chicken after 5 minutes. Transfer chicken to cutting board.

4. Transfer cooking liquid to blender and process until smooth, 15 to 30 seconds. Return cooking liquid to pot. When cool enough to handle, use 2 forks to shred chicken into bite-size pieces. Return chicken to pot with cooking liquid. Cook over medium heat, stirring frequently, until sauce is thickened and clings to chicken, about 10 minutes. Stir in lime zest and juice. Season with salt and pepper to taste.

5. **FOR THE TACOS:** Spoon chicken into center of each warm tortilla and serve immediately, passing avocado, Cotija, scallions, cilantro, and lime wedges separately.

### Escabeche (Mexican-Style Pickled Vegetables)

**MAKES** 2 cups

For a less spicy pickle, remove the seeds from the jalapeño.

- ½ teaspoon coriander seeds
- ¼ teaspoon cumin seeds
- 1 cup apple cider vinegar
- ½ cup water
- 1½ teaspoons sugar
- ¼ teaspoon table salt
- 1 red onion, halved and sliced thin
- 2 carrots, peeled and sliced thin
- 1 jalapeño, stemmed and sliced thin into rings

Heat coriander seeds and cumin seeds in medium saucepan over medium heat, stirring frequently, until fragrant, about 2 minutes. Add vinegar, water, sugar, and salt and bring to boil, stirring to dissolve sugar and salt. Remove saucepan from heat and add onion, carrots, and jalapeño, pressing to submerge vegetables. Cover and let cool completely, 30 minutes. (Cooled vegetables can be stored in an airtight container and refrigerated for up to 1 week.)

### Corn Tortillas

**MAKES** twenty-two 5-inch tortillas

Pressing the dough between a zipper-lock bag that has been cut open at the sides prevents it from sticking to the pie plate. Distribute your weight evenly over the dough when pressing. Using a clear pie plate makes it easy to see the tortilla. A tortilla press, of course, can also be used. You can find masa harina in the international aisle or near the flour.

- 2 cups (8 ounces) masa harina
- 2 teaspoons vegetable oil, divided
- ¼ teaspoon table salt
- 1¼ cups warm water, plus extra as needed

**1.** Cut sides of sandwich-size zipper-lock bag but leave bottom seam intact so that bag unfolds completely. Place open bag on counter and line large plate with 2 damp dish towels.

**2.** Mix masa, 1 teaspoon oil, and salt together in medium bowl. Using rubber spatula, stir in warm water to form soft dough. Using your hands, knead dough in bowl, adding extra warm water, 1 tablespoon at a time, until dough is soft and tacky but not sticky (texture is like Play-Doh). Cover dough and set aside for 5 minutes.

**3.** Meanwhile, heat remaining 1 teaspoon oil in 8-inch nonstick skillet over medium-high heat until shimmering. Using paper towel, wipe out skillet, leaving thin film of oil on bottom. Pinch off 1-ounce piece of dough (about 2 tablespoons) and roll into smooth 1¼-inch ball. Cover remaining dough with damp paper towel. Place ball in center of open bag and fold other side of bag over ball. Using clear pie plate, press down on plastic to flatten ball into 5-inch disk, rotating plastic during pressing to ensure even thickness. Working quickly, gently peel plastic away from tortilla.

**4.** Carefully place tortilla in skillet and cook, without moving it, until tortilla moves freely when pan is shaken, about 30 seconds. Flip tortilla and cook until edges curl and bottom surface is spotty brown, about 1 minute. Flip tortilla again and continue to cook until bottom surface is spotty brown and puffs up in center, 30 to 60 seconds. Place toasted tortilla between 2 damp dish towels; repeat shaping and cooking with remaining dough. (Cooled tortillas can be transferred to zipper-lock bag and refrigerated for up to 5 days. Reheat before serving.)

## Chicken Enchiladas with Red Chile Sauce

**SERVES** 4 to 5

**WHY THIS RECIPE WORKS** Chicken enchiladas are a complete meal that offers a rich and complex combination of flavors, textures, and ingredients. The problem with preparing enchiladas at home is that traditional cooking methods require a whole day of preparation. We wanted a recipe for a streamlined version of chicken enchiladas that could be made in 90 minutes from start to finish. To save time preparing the tortillas, we sprayed them with vegetable oil spray and warmed them on a baking sheet in the oven. We created a quick chili sauce with onions, garlic, spices, and tomato sauce, and to further enhance the sauce's flavor, we poached the chicken right in the sauce. This step also made for moist, flavorful meat. And cheddar cheese spiked with canned jalapeños and fresh cilantro made a rich, flavorful filling. Monterey Jack can be used instead of cheddar, or for a mellower flavor and creamier texture, try farmer's cheese. Be sure to cool the chicken before filling the tortillas; otherwise the hot filling will make the enchiladas soggy.

**SAUCE AND FILLING**

- 1½ tablespoons vegetable oil
- 1 medium onion, chopped fine
- 3 medium garlic cloves, minced or pressed through a garlic press (about 1 tablespoon)
- 3 tablespoons chili powder
- 2 teaspoons ground coriander
- 2 teaspoons ground cumin
- 2 teaspoons sugar
- ½ teaspoon table salt
- 12 ounces boneless, skinless chicken thighs (about 4 thighs), trimmed and cut into ¼-inch-wide strips
- 2 (8-ounce) cans tomato sauce
- ¾ cup water
- 8 ounces sharp cheddar cheese, shredded (about 2 cups)
- ½ cup coarsely chopped fresh cilantro leaves
- 1 (4-ounce) can pickled jalapeño chiles, drained and chopped (about ¼ cup)

**TORTILLAS AND TOPPINGS**

- 10 (6-inch) corn tortillas
- Vegetable oil spray
- 3 ounces sharp cheddar cheese, shredded (about ¾ cup)
- ¾ cup sour cream
- 1 medium, ripe avocado, diced medium
- 5 romaine lettuce leaves, shredded
- Lime wedges

**1. FOR THE SAUCE AND FILLING:** Heat the oil in a medium saucepan over medium-high heat until shimmering. Add the onion and cook, stirring occasionally, until softened and beginning to brown, about 5 minutes. Add the garlic, chili powder, coriander, cumin, sugar, and salt and cook, stirring constantly, until fragrant, about 30 seconds. Add the chicken and cook, stirring constantly, until coated with the spices, about 30 seconds. Add the tomato sauce and water, stir to separate the chicken pieces, and bring to a simmer. Reduce the heat to medium-low and simmer, uncovered, stirring occasionally, until the chicken is cooked through and the flavors have melded, about 8 minutes. Pour the mixture through a medium-mesh strainer into a medium bowl, pressing on the chicken and onions to extract as much sauce as possible; set the sauce aside. Transfer the chicken mixture to a large plate; place in the freezer for 10 minutes to cool, then combine with the cheddar, cilantro, and jalapeños in a medium bowl.

**2.** Adjust the oven racks to the upper-middle and lower-middle positions and heat the oven to 300 degrees.

**3. TO ASSEMBLE:** Smear the bottom of a 13 by 9-inch baking dish with ¾ cup of the chili sauce. Place the tortillas in a single layer on two baking sheets. Spray both sides of the tortillas lightly with vegetable oil spray. Bake until the tortillas are soft and pliable, about 4 minutes. Transfer the warm tortillas to a work surface. Increase the oven temperature to 400 degrees. Spread ⅓ cup of the filling down the center of each tortilla. Roll each tortilla tightly by hand and place, seam side down, side by side on the sauce in the baking dish. Pour the remaining chili sauce over the top of the enchiladas. Use the back of a spoon to spread the sauce so it coats the top of each tortilla. Sprinkle the cheese down the center of the enchiladas.

**4.** Cover the baking dish with foil. Bake the enchiladas on the lower-middle rack until heated through and the cheese is melted, 20 to 25 minutes. Uncover and serve immediately, passing the sour cream, avocado, lettuce, and lime wedges separately.

## Enchiladas Verdes

**SERVES 4 to 6**

**WHY THIS RECIPE WORKS** For our version of this classic favorite, we wanted moist, tender chicken and fresh, citrusy flavors wrapped in soft corn tortillas and topped with melted cheese. To infuse the chicken with flavor we poached it in broth enhanced with sautéed onion, garlic, and cumin. The green sauce here is based on tomatillos and poblano chiles, which add more complex herbal notes. To get the characteristic char, we tossed the chiles and fresh tomatillos with a little oil and ran them under the broiler. Pulsed in a food processor and thinned with a bit of the broth left from poaching the chicken, the tomatillos and chiles formed a well-seasoned, chunky sauce. You can substitute 3 (11-ounce) cans tomatillos, drained and rinsed, for the fresh ones in this recipe. Halve large tomatillos (more than 2 inches in diameter) and place them skin side up for broiling in step 2 to ensure even cooking and charring. If you can't find poblanos, substitute four large jalapeño chiles (with seeds and ribs removed). To increase the spiciness of the sauce, reserve some of the chiles' ribs and seeds and add them to the food processor in step 3.

- 4 teaspoons vegetable oil, divided
- 1 onion, chopped
- 3 garlic cloves, minced, divided
- ½ teaspoon ground cumin
- 1½ cups chicken broth
- 1 pound boneless, skinless chicken breasts, trimmed
- 1½ pounds tomatillos (16 to 20 medium), husks and stems removed, rinsed well and dried
- 3 poblano chiles, stemmed, halved, and seeded
- 1–2 teaspoons sugar
- 1 teaspoon table salt
- ½ cup coarsely chopped fresh cilantro
- 8 ounces pepper Jack or Monterey Jack cheese, grated (2 cups), divided
- 12 (6-inch) corn tortillas
- 2 scallions, sliced thin
- Thinly sliced radishes
- Sour cream

**1.** Adjust oven racks to middle and highest positions and heat broiler. Heat 2 teaspoons oil in medium saucepan over medium heat until shimmering; add onion and cook, stirring frequently, until golden, 6 to 8 minutes. Add 2 teaspoons garlic and cumin; cook, stirring frequently, until fragrant, about 30 seconds. Reduce heat to low and stir in broth. Add chicken; cover; and simmer until thickest part of chicken registers 160 degrees, 15 to 20 minutes, flipping chicken halfway through cooking. Transfer chicken to large bowl and place in refrigerator to cool, about 20 minutes. Remove ¼ cup liquid from saucepan and set aside; discard remaining liquid.

**2.** Meanwhile, toss tomatillos and poblanos with remaining 2 teaspoons oil; arrange on rimmed baking sheet lined with aluminum foil, with poblanos skin side up. Broil until vegetables blacken and start to soften, 5 to 10 minutes, rotating pan halfway through cooking. Cool for 10 minutes, then remove skin from poblanos (leave tomatillo skins intact). Transfer tomatillos and chiles to food processor. Reduce oven temperature to 350 degrees. Discard foil from baking sheet and set sheet aside for warming tortillas.

**3.** Add 1 teaspoon sugar, salt, remaining 1 teaspoon garlic, and reserved ¼ cup cooking liquid to food processor; pulse until sauce is somewhat chunky, about 8 pulses. Taste sauce; season with salt and pepper to taste and adjust tartness by stirring in remaining sugar, ½ teaspoon at a time. Set sauce aside (you should have about 3 cups).

**4.** When chicken is cool, pull into shreds using your hands or 2 forks, then chop into bite-size pieces. Combine chicken with cilantro and 1½ cups pepper Jack; season with salt to taste.

**5.** Smear bottom of 13 by 9-inch baking dish with ¾ cup tomatillo sauce. Place tortillas in single layer on two baking sheets. Spray both sides of tortillas lightly with vegetable oil spray. Bake until tortillas are soft and pliable, 2 to 4 minutes. Increase oven temperature to 450 degrees. Place warm tortillas

on counter and spread 1/3 cup filling down center of each tortilla. Roll each tortilla tightly by hand and place in baking dish, seam side down. Pour remaining tomatillo sauce over top of enchiladas. Use back of a spoon to spread sauce so it coats top of each tortilla. Sprinkle with remaining 1/2 cup pepper Jack and cover baking dish with foil.

**6.** Bake enchiladas on middle oven rack until heated through and cheese is melted, 15 to 20 minutes. Uncover, sprinkle with scallions, and serve immediately, passing radishes and sour cream separately.

## Thai Chicken Curry with Potatoes and Peanuts

**SERVES** 4 to 6

**WHY THIS RECIPE WORKS** Warm-spiced, savory-sweet massaman curry is a Thai specialty. We set out to create a streamlined version of the traditional recipe. To make a deeply flavorful curry paste, we broiled chiles, garlic, and shallots per tradition, but we replaced the galangal with readily available ginger and traded out toasted, ground whole spices for preground five-spice powder. Coconut milk and lime juice rounded out the flavor of our curry. We stuck with the traditional potatoes, onion, chicken, and peanuts, simmered in the sauce until they were tender. A final garnish of lime zest and cilantro added a splash of color and brightness. Serve the curry with jasmine rice. The ingredients for the curry paste can be doubled to make extra for future use. Refrigerate the paste for up to one week or freeze it for up to two months.

**CURRY PASTE**

- 6 dried New Mexico chiles
- 4 shallots, unpeeled
- 7 garlic cloves, unpeeled
- 1/2 cup chopped fresh ginger
- 1/4 cup water
- 1 1/2 tablespoons lime juice
- 1 1/2 tablespoons vegetable oil
- 1 tablespoon fish sauce
- 1 teaspoon five-spice powder
- 1/2 teaspoon ground cumin
- 1/2 teaspoon pepper

**CURRY**

- 1 teaspoon vegetable oil
- 1 1/4 cups chicken broth
- 1 (13.5-ounce) can coconut milk
- 1 pound Yukon Gold potatoes, unpeeled, cut into 3/4-inch pieces
- 1 onion, cut into 3/4-inch pieces
- 1/3 cup dry-roasted peanuts
- 3/4 teaspoon table salt
- 1 pound boneless, skinless chicken thighs, trimmed and cut into 1-inch pieces
- 2 teaspoons grated lime zest
- 1/4 cup chopped fresh cilantro

**1. FOR THE CURRY PASTE:** Adjust oven rack to middle position and heat oven to 350 degrees. Line rimmed baking sheet with aluminum foil. Arrange chiles on prepared sheet and toast until puffed and fragrant, 4 to 6 minutes. Transfer chiles to large plate. Heat broiler.

**2.** Place shallots and garlic on now-empty foil-lined sheet and broil until softened and skin is charred, 6 to 9 minutes.

**3.** When cool enough to handle, stem and seed chiles and tear into 1 1/2-inch pieces. Process chiles in blender until finely ground, about 1 minute. Peel shallots and garlic. Add shallots, garlic, ginger, water, lime juice, oil, fish sauce, five-spice powder, cumin, and pepper to blender. Process to smooth paste, scraping down sides of blender jar as needed, 2 to 3 minutes. (You should have 1 cup paste.)

**4. FOR THE CURRY:** Heat oil in large saucepan over medium heat until shimmering. Add curry paste and cook, stirring constantly, until paste begins to brown, 2 1/2 to 3 minutes. Stir in broth, coconut milk, potatoes, onion, peanuts, and salt, scraping up any browned bits. Bring to simmer and cook until potatoes are just tender, 12 to 14 minutes.

**5.** Stir in chicken and continue to simmer until chicken is cooked through, 10 to 12 minutes. Remove pan from heat and stir in lime zest. Serve, passing cilantro separately.

## Thai Green Curry with Chicken, Broccoli, and Mushrooms

**SERVES** 4

**WHY THIS RECIPE WORKS** Like most Thai food, Thai curries embrace a delicate balance of tastes, textures, temperatures, and colors that come together to create a harmonious whole. They usually feature fresh aromatics, which are added in the form of a paste. We wanted to develop a recipe for Thai green curry perfumed with lemongrass, hot chiles, and coconut milk. A food processor made quick work of blending together the curry paste. For the paste, we favored Thai green chiles for heat while shallots, lemongrass, cilantro stems, garlic, ginger, coriander, and cumin rounded out the flavors. And to approximate the flavor of makrut lime leaves( sometimes called the bay leaf of Thai cooking), we added grated lime zest. To make the curry, we skimmed the coconut cream off the coconut milk and cooked it with the curry paste—this added silky body and intense, rich flavor. We paired the green curry with chicken, broccoli, mushrooms, and bell pepper. To make slicing the chicken easier, freeze it for 15 minutes. Serve with rice.

- 2 (14-ounce) cans unsweetened coconut milk, not shaken
- 1 recipe Green Curry Paste (recipe follows) or 2 tablespoons store-bought green curry paste
- 2 tablespoons fish sauce
- 2 tablespoons brown sugar
- 1½ pounds boneless, skinless chicken breasts, trimmed and sliced thin
- Table salt
- 8 ounces broccoli (½ small bunch), florets cut into 1-inch pieces
- 4 ounces white mushrooms, wiped clean and quartered
- 1 red bell pepper, stemmed, seeded, and cut into ¼-inch strips
- 1 Thai chile, stemmed, seeded, and quartered lengthwise (optional)
- ½ cup loosely packed fresh basil leaves
- ½ cup loosely packed fresh mint leaves
- 1 tablespoon juice from 1 lime

**1.** Carefully spoon off about 1 cup of the top layer of cream from one can of the coconut milk. Whisk the coconut cream and curry paste together in a large Dutch oven, bring to a simmer over high heat, and cook until almost all of the liquid evaporates, 5 to 7 minutes. Reduce the heat to medium-high and continue to cook, whisking constantly, until the cream separates into a puddle of colored oil and coconut solids, 3 to 8 minutes. Continue cooking until the curry paste is very aromatic, 1 to 2 minutes.

**2.** Whisk in the remaining coconut milk, the fish sauce, and sugar, bring to a simmer, and cook until the flavors meld and the sauce thickens, about 5 minutes. Season the chicken with salt, stir into the sauce, and cook until evenly coated, about 1 minute. Stir in the broccoli and mushrooms and cook until the vegetables are almost tender, about 5 minutes. Stir in the bell pepper and chile (if using) and cook until the bell pepper is crisp-tender, about 2 minutes. Off the heat, stir in the basil, mint, and lime juice. Serve.

### Green Curry Paste

**MAKES** about ½ cup

We strongly prefer the flavor of Thai chiles here; however, serrano and jalapeño chiles are decent substitutes. For more heat, include the chile seeds and ribs when chopping.

- ⅓ cup water
- 12 fresh green Thai, serrano, or jalapeño chiles, seeds and ribs removed, chiles chopped coarse
- 8 medium garlic cloves, peeled
- 3 medium shallots, peeled and quartered
- 2 stalks lemongrass, bottom 5 inches only, trimmed and sliced thin
- 2 tablespoons grated zest from 2 limes
- 2 tablespoons vegetable oil
- 2 tablespoons minced fresh cilantro stems
- 1 tablespoon minced or grated fresh ginger
- 2 teaspoons ground coriander
- 1 teaspoon ground cumin
- 1 teaspoon table salt

Process all the ingredients in a food processor to a fine paste, about 3 minutes, scraping down the sides of the workbowl as needed.

## Chicken Teriyaki

**SERVES 4**

**WHY THIS RECIPE WORKS** Our version of chicken teriyaki started with bone-in chicken thighs, not because we wanted the bones (we promptly removed them), but because we wanted the skin, which protects the meat from the heat of the skillet and adds succulence and meaty flavor. Cutting the thighs into bite-size pieces not only made them easier to eat with chopsticks but also created plenty of surface area for browning and, eventually, for the glaze. A pretreatment with sake boosted savory flavor. Adding cornstarch to the sake had a triple benefit: It formed an extra layer of protection around the chicken, which left it supple; it provided a surface that "grabbed" the glaze; and some of it sloughed off into the glaze, thickening it a bit more. The glaze used plenty of soy sauce for seasoning, sake for savory depth, sugar for sweetness and luster, and a good amount of fresh ginger for brightness. It's worth deboning the chicken thighs here so that you can retain the skin. Boneless, skin-on thighs are a rare find, but if you do find them, buy 1½ pounds for this recipe; do not use skinless thighs, because they'll be less juicy. Use a Frywall or splatter screen if you have one. Inexpensive sake is fine here; it can often be purchased in small cans. We strain the glaze in step 4 to improve its clarity, but you can skip this process if you prefer. Serve with unseasoned short-grain white rice, peppery greens such as watercress or mizuna, and sliced scallions.

- 1½–2 pounds bone-in chicken thighs
- 3½ tablespoons sake, divided
- 1 tablespoon cornstarch
- 3 tablespoons soy sauce
- 1 tablespoon sugar
- 2 tablespoons grated fresh ginger
- 2 teaspoons vegetable oil

**1.** Place 1 chicken thigh skin side down on cutting board. Using sharp paring knife, trim excess skin and fat, leaving enough skin to cover meat. Cut slit along length of thigh bone to expose bone. Using tip of knife, cut/scrape meat from bone. Slip knife under bone to separate bone from meat. Discard bone and trim any remaining cartilage from thigh. Keeping thigh skin side down, cut into 1½-inch pieces, leaving as much skin attached as possible. Transfer to medium bowl and repeat with remaining thighs. Add 1½ tablespoons sake and cornstarch and stir gently until chicken is evenly coated.

**2.** Combine soy sauce, sugar, and remaining 2 tablespoons sake in small bowl. Microwave until sugar is dissolved, about 30 seconds. Place fine-mesh strainer over bowl containing soy sauce mixture. Add ginger to strainer and press to extract juice. Discard solids, but do not wash strainer.

**3.** Line large plate with paper towels. Heat oil in 12-inch nonstick skillet over medium heat until shimmering. Place chicken skin side down in skillet (skillet may be very full). Increase heat to medium-high; place Frywall or splatter screen, if using, on skillet; and cook, without moving chicken, until all pieces have ¼- to ½-inch perimeter of white, 6 to 8 minutes. Slide skillet off heat and flip chicken. Return skillet to burner and reduce heat to medium. Continue to cook until chicken is just cooked through, 1 to 2 minutes longer.

**4.** Remove skillet from heat. Using slotted spoon, transfer chicken to prepared plate. Pour off fat, scrape any browned bits out of skillet, and wipe skillet clean with paper towels. Return chicken to skillet. Add soy sauce mixture and cook over medium heat, stirring frequently, until chicken is thinly coated and sauce has consistency of maple syrup, 1 to 2 minutes. Using slotted spoon, transfer chicken to serving bowl. Pour glaze in skillet through now-empty strainer set over small serving bowl. Drizzle 2 tablespoons glaze over chicken and serve, passing remaining glaze (there will be only a few tablespoons, but it is potent) separately.

## San Bei Ji (Three-Cup Chicken)

**SERVES 4**

**WHY THIS RECIPE WORKS** Originating in Dadu (modern Beijing), san bei ji, or three-cup chicken, was named for its sparse ingredient list, with a sauce made up of just 1 cup each of soy sauce, sesame oil, and rice wine. Now adopted by Taiwan, it has evolved into a traditional Taiwanese dish of sorts. Its robust, aromatic flavors easily explain its popularity. While traditional recipes involve butchering a whole bird into smaller pieces, we opted for boneless, skinless thighs for easier preparation. The rich flavor of the thighs would stand up to the potent sauce better than that of milder breasts. Marinating the chicken in the sauce helped build deep flavor with minimal effort. We found that scallions, ginger, garlic, and red pepper flakes added even more flavor and complexity to this dish. We prefer the flavor of Thai basil, but Italian sweet basil can be substituted. For a spicier dish, use the larger amount of red pepper flakes. Serve with rice.

- ⅓ cup soy sauce
- ⅓ cup dry sherry
- 1 tablespoon packed brown sugar
- 1½ pounds boneless, skinless chicken thighs, trimmed and cut into 2-inch pieces
- 3 tablespoons vegetable oil
- 1 (2-inch) piece ginger, peeled, halved lengthwise, and sliced into thin half-rounds
- 12 garlic cloves, peeled and halved lengthwise
- ½–¾ teaspoon red pepper flakes
- 6 scallions, white and green parts separated and sliced thin on bias
- 1 tablespoon water
- 1 teaspoon cornstarch
- 1 cup Thai basil leaves, large leaves halved lengthwise
- 1 tablespoon toasted sesame oil

**1.** Whisk soy sauce, sherry, and sugar together in medium bowl. Add chicken and toss to coat; set aside.

**2.** Heat vegetable oil, ginger, garlic, and pepper flakes in 12-inch nonstick skillet over medium-low heat. Cook, stirring frequently, until garlic is golden brown and beginning to soften, 8 to 10 minutes.

**3.** Add chicken and marinade to skillet, increase heat to medium-high, and bring to simmer. Reduce heat to medium-low and simmer, stirring occasionally, for 10 minutes. Stir in scallion whites and continue to cook until chicken registers about 200 degrees, 8 to 10 minutes longer.

**4.** Whisk water and cornstarch together in small bowl, then whisk into sauce; simmer until sauce is slightly thickened, about 1 minute. Remove skillet from heat. Stir in basil, sesame oil, and scallion greens. Transfer to platter and serve.

## Orange-Flavored Chicken

**SERVES 4**

**WHY THIS RECIPE WORKS** Featuring pieces of crispy fried chicken bathed in a citrusy sauce, orange-flavored chicken is one craveable dish. For our version, we wanted substantial, well-seasoned chicken chunks with a crisp, golden brown crust and a sauce that offered a clear hit of fresh orange flavor with balanced sweet, sour, and spicy background notes. We marinated the chicken in a mixture of soy sauce, garlic, ginger, sugar, vinegar, fresh orange juice, and chicken broth, reserving some marinade to become the base for the final sauce. Then, we created a tender/crisp coating by dunking the marinated chicken first in egg white, then cornstarch. The egg white created a thin sheath of protein beneath the cornstarch that kept it dry, helping it to brown more readily than a wet, gluey coating would. A touch of baking soda helped the chicken pieces develop golden color during frying. We prefer the flavor and texture of thigh meat for this recipe, though an equal amount of boneless, skinless chicken breasts can be used. Unless you have a very high spice tolerance, do not eat the whole chiles in the finished dish. Serve with rice.

**MARINADE AND SAUCE**

- ¾ cup low-sodium chicken broth
- ¾ cup juice, 1½ teaspoons grated zest, and 8 strips peel (each about 2 inches long by ½ inch wide) from 2 oranges
- ½ cup packed dark brown sugar
- 6 tablespoons distilled white vinegar
- ¼ cup soy sauce
- 3 medium garlic cloves, minced or pressed through a garlic press (about 1 tablespoon)
- 1 tablespoon minced or grated fresh ginger
- ¼ teaspoon cayenne pepper
- 1½ pounds boneless, skinless chicken thighs, trimmed and cut into 1½-inch pieces
- 2 tablespoons cold water
- 1 tablespoon plus 2 teaspoons cornstarch
- 8 small whole dried red chiles (optional)

**COATING AND FRYING OIL**

- 3 large egg whites
- 1 cup cornstarch
- ½ teaspoon baking soda
- ¼ teaspoon cayenne pepper
- 3 cups peanut or vegetable oil

**1. FOR THE MARINADE AND SAUCE:** Whisk the broth, orange juice, grated zest, sugar, vinegar, soy sauce, garlic, ginger, and cayenne together in a large saucepan until the sugar is fully dissolved. Transfer ¾ cup of the mixture to a medium bowl and add the chicken. Let marinate for at least 10 minutes or up to 1 hour.

**2.** In a small bowl, stir the cold water and cornstarch together. Bring the remaining mixture in the saucepan to a simmer over high heat. Whisk the cornstarch mixture into the sauce, bring to a simmer, and cook, stirring occasionally, until thick and translucent, about 1 minute. Off the heat, stir in the orange peel and chiles (if using) and set aside. (The sauce should measure 1½ cups.)

**3. FOR THE COATING:** Using a fork, lightly beat the egg whites in a shallow dish until frothy. In a second shallow dish, whisk the cornstarch, baking soda, and cayenne together until combined. Drain the chicken and pat dry with paper towels. Place half of the chicken pieces in the egg whites and turn to coat. Transfer the chicken pieces to the cornstarch mixture and coat thoroughly. Place the dredged chicken pieces on a wire rack set over a baking sheet. Repeat with the remaining chicken pieces.

**4. TO FRY THE CHICKEN:** Heat the oil in a Dutch oven over high heat until the oil registers 350 degrees on an instant-read or deep-fry thermometer. Carefully place half of the chicken in the oil and fry until golden brown, about 5 minutes, turning each piece with tongs halfway through. Transfer the chicken pieces to a paper towel–lined plate. Return the oil to 350 degrees and repeat with the remaining chicken.

**5. TO SERVE:** Reheat the sauce over medium heat until simmering, about 2 minutes. Add the chicken and toss gently until evenly coated and heated through. Serve.

## Dry Chili Chicken

**SERVES 4 to 6** **SEASON 26**

**WHY THIS RECIPE WORKS** This magnificent Sichuan dish is a restaurant favorite, and suprisingly easy to execute at home. Dry chili chicken (or Chongqing chicken, named for the Sichuan city) features meaty chunks of chicken thighs that are marinated, battered, and double fried and then stir-fried; what sets this dish apart is that it contains a sea of peppers—a remarkable 3 cups of small, dried Sichuan chiles that are more for decorative effect than for consumption. All the steps are easy here and the ingredients readily available. The batter is a simple mix of cornstarch, flour, baking powder, and water that is refrigerated for 30 minutes to get to the right consistency. Meanwhile, the chicken pieces are marinated in soy sauce and Shaoxing wine and also refrigerated for the same amount of time. When it's time to stir fry, the traditional trio of garlic, scallions, and ginger go first, then the chiles and Sichuan peppercorns, followed by the chicken. The final touch is a spice mix anchored by chili flakes, sugar, and salt that is scattered over the entire dish.

- ⅔ cup cornstarch
- ⅓ cup all-purpose flour
- ½ teaspoon baking powder
- ¾ cup water
- 1½ pounds boneless, skinless chicken thighs, trimmed and cut into 1-inch pieces
- 1 tablespoon soy sauce
- 1 tablespoon Shaoxing wine
- 2 quarts peanut or vegetable oil for frying
- ¼ cup Sichuan chili flakes
- 1½ teaspoons sugar
- ½ teaspoon table salt

- ¼ teaspoon monosodium glutamate (optional)
- 6 garlic cloves, minced
- 4 scallions, sliced thin
- 1 (1-inch) piece ginger, peeled and cut into thin matchsticks (1 tablespoon)
- 4 ounces (3 cups) small dried Sichuan chiles
- 2 tablespoons Sichuan peppercorns
- ½ cup chopped fresh cilantro
- 1 teaspoon sesame seeds, toasted

**1.** Whisk cornstarch, flour, and baking powder together in bowl. Whisk in water until smooth, then refrigerate for 30 minutes. Meanwhile, toss chicken, soy sauce, and Shaoxing wine in second bowl; cover and refrigerate for 30 minutes.

**2.** Set wire rack in rimmed baking sheet. Set second wire rack in second sheet and line with triple layer of paper towels. Add oil to large Dutch oven until it measures about 1½ inches deep and heat over medium-high heat to 400 degrees.

**3.** Whisk batter to recombine. Add chicken and toss to coat. Using hands, remove half of chicken from batter and place in single layer on unlined rack. Let rest for 1 minute to allow excess batter to drip off. Working quickly, use spider skimmer or slotted spoon to lower chicken pieces into hot oil. Using tongs or cooking chopsticks, separate pieces so they fry individually. Fry chicken until light golden brown, about 2 minutes. Adjust burner, if necessary, to maintain oil temperature between 375 and 400 degrees. Using spider skimmer, transfer chicken to towel-lined rack. Return oil to 400 degrees and repeat with remaining chicken; transfer to rack.

**4.** Return oil to 400 degrees over medium-high heat. Working in 2 batches, fry chicken a second time until deep golden brown and crisp, 2 to 4 minutes; return chicken to rack lined with fresh paper towels.

**5.** Whisk chili flakes; sugar; salt; and monosodium glutamate, if using, together in small bowl. Measure out and reserve ¼ cup frying oil; discard remaining oil or save for another use.

**6.** Heat empty 14-inch flat-bottomed wok over medium-high heat until just beginning to smoke. Reduce heat to medium-low, drizzle reserved oil around perimeter of wok and heat until just smoking. Add garlic, scallions, and ginger and cook, tossing constantly, until fragrant, about 2 minutes. Add chiles and peppercorns and cook, tossing constantly, until just toasted, about 1 minute. Add chicken and sprinkle spice mix evenly over top. Cook, tossing constantly, until chicken is well coated, about 1 minute. Off heat, add cilantro and toss gently to incorporate. Sprinkle with sesame seeds and serve.

## Thai-Style Chicken with Basil

**SERVES 4**

**WHY THIS RECIPE WORKS** In Thailand, street vendors have mastered a stir-frying method that uses low flames to produce complex and flavorful dishes such as chicken and basil. Because Thai stir-fries are cooked over a lower temperature, to prevent scorching, we started our aromatics (garlic, chiles, and shallots) in a cold skillet. To ensure moist meat, we added fish sauce to the food processor when we ground the chicken and then rested it in the refrigerator; the fish sauce acted as a brine, seasoning the chicken and sealing in moisture. For our sauce base, we liked oyster sauce brightened with a dash of white vinegar. We spiced up the flavor of the sauce by adding a reserved tablespoon of the raw garlic-chile mixture at the end of cooking. And for intense, bright basil flavor, we cooked a portion of chopped basil with the garlic, chile, and shallot mixture, and stirred in whole basil leaves just before serving. Since tolerance for spiciness can vary, we've kept our recipe relatively mild. For a very mild version, remove the seeds and ribs from the chiles. If fresh Thai chiles are unavailable, substitute two serranos or one medium jalapeño. Serve with rice and vegetables, if desired.

- 2 cups fresh basil leaves, divided
- 6 green or red Thai chiles, stemmed
- 3 garlic cloves, peeled
- 2 tablespoons fish sauce, divided, plus extra for serving
- 1 tablespoon oyster sauce
- 1 tablespoon sugar, plus extra for serving
- 1 teaspoon distilled white vinegar, plus extra for serving
- 1 pound boneless, skinless chicken breasts, trimmed and cut into 2-inch pieces
- 3 shallots, peeled and sliced thin (about ¾ cup)
- 2 tablespoons vegetable oil
- Red pepper flakes

**1.** Pulse 1 cup basil leaves, chiles, and garlic in food processor until chopped fine, 6 to 10 pulses, scraping down sides of bowl once during processing. Transfer 1 tablespoon basil mixture to small bowl, stir in 1 tablespoon fish sauce, oyster sauce, sugar, and vinegar and set aside. Transfer remaining basil mixture to 12-inch heavy-bottomed nonstick skillet.

**2.** Pulse chicken and remaining 1 tablespoon fish sauce in now-empty food processor until meat is chopped into ¼-inch pieces, 6 to 8 pulses. Transfer chicken to medium bowl and refrigerate for 15 minutes.

3. Stir shallots and oil into basil mixture in skillet. Heat mixture over medium-low heat (mixture should start to sizzle after about 1½ minutes; if it doesn't, adjust heat accordingly), stirring constantly, until garlic and shallots are golden brown, 5 to 8 minutes.

4. Add chicken; increase heat to medium; and cook, stirring and breaking up chicken with potato masher or rubber spatula, until only traces of pink remain, 2 to 4 minutes. Add reserved basil–fish sauce mixture and continue to cook, stirring constantly, until chicken is no longer pink, about 1 minute. Stir in remaining 1 cup basil leaves and cook, stirring constantly, until basil is wilted, 30 to 60 seconds. Serve immediately, passing extra fish sauce, sugar, vinegar, and red pepper flakes separately.

## Gōngbǎo Jīdīng (Sichuan Kung Pao Chicken)

**SERVES** 4 to 6

**WHY THIS RECIPE WORKS** Spicy chiles and Sichuan peppercorns team up with lightly sauced chicken and peanuts to make a sensational kung pao chicken. We started our version by toasting peanuts in a skillet to maximize their crunch. Next we toasted crushed Sichuan peppercorns and arbol chiles that we'd halved lengthwise to release their heat. We stirred in plenty of garlic and ginger and then added marinated diced chicken thighs. When it was almost cooked through, we added some celery for crisp freshness and then a concentrated sauce mixture that cooked down to a glaze. Kung pao chicken should be quite spicy. To adjust the heat level, use more or fewer chiles, depending on the size (we used 2-inch-long chiles) and your taste. Have your ingredients prepared and your equipment in place before you begin to cook. Use a spice grinder or mortar and pestle to coarsely grind the Sichuan peppercorns. If Chinese black vinegar is unavailable, substitute sherry vinegar. Serve with white rice and a simple vegetable such as broccoli or bok choy. Do not eat the chiles.

**CHICKEN AND SAUCE**

- 1½ pounds boneless, skinless chicken thighs, trimmed and cut into ½-inch pieces
- ¼ cup soy sauce, divided
- 1 tablespoon cornstarch
- 1 tablespoon Chinese rice wine or dry sherry
- ½ teaspoon white pepper
- 1 tablespoon Chinese black vinegar
- 1 tablespoon packed dark brown sugar
- 2 teaspoons toasted sesame oil

**STIR-FRY**

- 2 tablespoons plus 1 teaspoon vegetable oil, divided
- 3 garlic cloves, minced
- 2 teaspoons grated fresh ginger
- ½ cup dry-roasted peanuts
- 10–15 dried arbol chiles, halved lengthwise and seeded
- 1 teaspoon Sichuan peppercorns, ground coarse
- 2 celery ribs, cut into ½-inch pieces
- 5 scallions, white and light green parts only, cut into ½-inch pieces

1. **FOR THE CHICKEN AND SAUCE:** Combine chicken, 2 tablespoons soy sauce, cornstarch, rice wine, and white pepper in medium bowl and set aside. Stir vinegar, sugar, oil, and remaining 2 tablespoons soy sauce together in small bowl and set aside.

2. **FOR THE STIR-FRY:** Stir 1 tablespoon oil, garlic, and ginger together in second small bowl. Combine peanuts and 1 teaspoon oil in 12-inch nonstick skillet over medium-low heat. Cook, stirring constantly, until peanuts just begin to darken, 3 to 5 minutes. Transfer peanuts to plate and spread into even layer to cool. Return now-empty skillet to medium-low heat. Add remaining 1 tablespoon oil, arbols, and peppercorns and cook, stirring constantly, until arbols begin to darken, 1 to 2 minutes. Add garlic mixture and cook, stirring constantly, until all clumps are broken up and mixture is fragrant, about 30 seconds.

3. Add chicken and spread into even layer. Cover skillet; increase heat to medium-high; and cook, without stirring, for 1 minute. Stir chicken and spread into even layer. Cover and cook, without stirring, for 1 minute. Add celery and cook uncovered, stirring frequently, until chicken is cooked through, 2 to 3 minutes. Add soy sauce mixture and cook, stirring constantly, until sauce is thickened and shiny and coats chicken, 3 to 5 minutes. Stir in scallions and peanuts. Transfer to platter and serve.

## Vietnamese-Style Caramel Chicken with Broccoli

**SERVES** 4 to 6

**WHY THIS RECIPE WORKS** In Vietnamese cooking, caramel sauce has a savory, bittersweet quality that gives a rich, molasses-like hue to meat, fish, and tofu alike. To prep our chicken for this flavorful sauce, we coated boneless, skinless thighs with a mixture of baking soda (to break down the muscle fibers) and water. After making the caramel we transferred it to a skillet and added fish sauce and freshly grated ginger. Simmering the boneless chicken in the sauce produced tender meat fully infused with bold flavor. Once the chicken was cooked, we prepared some steamed broccoli for textural and visual contrast and reduced the caramel, adding some cornstarch to further thicken and finish the sauce. The saltiness of fish sauce can vary by brand; we used Red Boat in this recipe. When taking the temperature of the caramel in step 2, tilt the pan and move the thermometer back and forth to equalize hot and cool spots; also make sure to have hot water at the ready. This dish is intensely seasoned, so serve it with rice.

- 1 tablespoon baking soda
- 2 pounds boneless, skinless chicken thighs, trimmed and halved crosswise
- 7 tablespoons sugar
- ¼ cup fish sauce
- 2 tablespoons grated fresh ginger
- 1 pound broccoli, florets cut into 1-inch pieces, stalks peeled and sliced ¼ inch thick
- 2 teaspoons cornstarch
- ½ teaspoon pepper
- ½ cup chopped fresh cilantro leaves and stems

**1.** Combine baking soda and 1¼ cups cold water in large bowl. Add chicken and toss to coat. Let stand at room temperature for 15 minutes. Rinse chicken in cold water and drain well.

**2.** Meanwhile, combine sugar and 3 tablespoons water in small saucepan. Bring to boil over medium-high heat and cook, without stirring, until mixture begins to turn golden, 4 to 6 minutes. Reduce heat to medium-low and continue to cook, gently swirling saucepan, until sugar turns color of molasses and registers between 390 and 400 degrees, 4 to 6 minutes longer. (Caramel will produce some smoke during last 1 to 2 minutes of cooking.) Immediately remove saucepan from heat and carefully pour in ¾ cup hot water (mixture will bubble and steam vigorously). When bubbling has subsided, return saucepan to medium heat and stir to dissolve caramel.

**3.** Transfer caramel to 12-inch skillet and stir in fish sauce and ginger. Add chicken and bring to simmer over medium-high heat. Reduce heat to medium-low, cover, and simmer until chicken is fork-tender and registers 205 degrees, 30 to 40 minutes, flipping chicken halfway through simmering. Transfer chicken to serving dish and cover to keep warm.

**4.** Bring 1 inch water to boil in Dutch oven. Lower insert or steamer basket with broccoli into pot so it rests above water; cover and simmer until broccoli is just tender, 4½ to 5 minutes. Transfer broccoli to serving dish with chicken.

**5.** While broccoli cooks, bring sauce to boil over medium-high heat and cook until reduced to 1¼ cups, 3 to 5 minutes. Whisk cornstarch and 1 tablespoon water together in small bowl, then whisk into sauce; simmer until slightly thickened, about 1 minute. Stir in pepper. Pour ¼ cup sauce over chicken and broccoli. Sprinkle with cilantro and serve, passing remaining sauce separately.

## Stir-Fried Chicken with Bok Choy and Crispy Noodle Cake

**SERVES 4**

**WHY THIS RECIPE WORKS** Stir-fries are the quintessential weeknight dinner. And while a stir-fry served on top of rice is great, a pan-fried noodle cake—crispy and crunchy on the outside and tender and chewy in the middle—makes an enticing base. For the noodle cake, we had the most success with fresh Chinese egg noodles—they made for a cohesive cake with a crunchy exterior. A nonstick skillet was crucial—it kept the cake from sticking and falling apart and allowed us to use less oil, so the cake wasn't greasy. We found the best way to flip the cake in the skillet was to slide it onto a plate, invert it onto another plate, and then slide it back in the pan to finish cooking. We kept the stir-fry simple; chicken and bok choy are a classic combination. A quick marinade gave our chicken welcome flavor, and a modified version of the Chinese technique called velveting prevented the chicken from drying out over high heat. To make slicing the chicken easier, freeze it for 15 minutes. Fresh Chinese noodles are often kept in the produce section of the grocery store. If you can't find them, substitute an equal amount of fresh spaghetti.

**SAUCE**

- ¼ cup low-sodium chicken broth
- 2 tablespoons soy sauce
- 1 tablespoon dry sherry
- 1 tablespoon oyster-flavored sauce
- 1 teaspoon sugar
- 1 teaspoon cornstarch
- ¼ teaspoon red pepper flakes

**NOODLE CAKE**

- 1 (9-ounce) package fresh Chinese noodles
- 1 teaspoon table salt
- 2 scallions, sliced thin
- ¼ cup peanut or vegetable oil

**CHICKEN AND VEGETABLES**

- 1 pound boneless, skinless chicken breasts, trimmed and sliced thin
- 1 tablespoon soy sauce
- 1 tablespoon dry sherry
- 2 tablespoons toasted sesame oil
- 1 tablespoon cornstarch
- 1 tablespoon unbleached all-purpose flour
- 2 tablespoons plus 2 teaspoons peanut or vegetable oil
- 1 tablespoon minced or grated fresh ginger
- 1 medium garlic clove, minced or pressed through a garlic press (about 1 teaspoon)
- 1 small head bok choy, stalks cut on the bias into ¼-inch pieces and greens cut into ½-inch strips
- 1 small red bell pepper, stemmed, seeded, and cut into ¼-inch strips

**1. FOR THE SAUCE:** Combine all the ingredients in a small bowl and set aside.

**2. FOR THE NOODLE CAKE:** Bring 6 quarts water to a boil in a large pot. Add the noodles and salt and cook, stirring often, until almost tender, 2 to 3 minutes. Drain the noodles, then toss them with the scallions.

**3.** Heat 2 tablespoons of the peanut oil in a 12-inch nonstick skillet over medium heat until shimmering. Spread the noodles evenly across the bottom of the skillet and press with a spatula to flatten into a cake. Cook until crisp and golden brown, 5 to 8 minutes.

**4.** Slide the noodle cake onto a large plate. Add the remaining 2 tablespoons peanut oil to the skillet and swirl to coat. Invert the noodle cake onto a second plate and slide it, browned side up, back into the skillet. Cook until golden brown on the second side, 5 to 8 minutes.

**5.** Slide the noodle cake onto a cutting board and let sit for at least 5 minutes before slicing into wedges and serving. (The noodle cake can be transferred to a wire rack set over a baking sheet and kept warm in a 200-degree oven for up to 20 minutes.) Wipe out the skillet with a wad of paper towels.

**6. FOR THE CHICKEN AND VEGETABLES:** While the noodles boil, toss the chicken with the soy sauce and sherry in a medium bowl and let marinate for at least 10 minutes or up to 1 hour. In a large bowl, whisk the sesame oil, cornstarch, and flour together. In a small bowl, mix 1 teaspoon of the peanut oil, the ginger, and garlic together.

**7.** Stir the marinated chicken into the sesame oil–cornstarch mixture. Heat 2 teaspoons more peanut oil in the skillet over high heat until just smoking. Add half of the chicken, break up any clumps, then cook without stirring until the meat is browned at the edges, about 1 minute. Stir the chicken and continue to cook until cooked through, about 1 minute longer. Transfer the chicken to a clean bowl and cover with foil to keep warm. Repeat with 2 teaspoons more peanut oil and the remaining chicken.

**8.** Add the remaining 1 tablespoon peanut oil to the skillet and return to high heat until just smoking. Add the bok choy stalks and bell pepper and cook until lightly browned, 2 to 3 minutes.

**9.** Clear the center of the skillet, add the ginger mixture, and cook, mashing the mixture into the pan, until fragrant, 15 to 20 seconds. Stir the ginger mixture into the vegetables, then stir in the bok choy greens and cook until beginning to wilt, about 30 seconds.

**10.** Stir in the chicken with any accumulated juices. Whisk the sauce to recombine, then add to the skillet and cook, tossing constantly, until the sauce is thickened, about 30 seconds. Transfer to a serving platter and serve with the noodle cake.

## Tandoori Chicken

**SERVES 4**

**WHY THIS RECIPE WORKS** Traditional tandoors produce moist, smoky meat because the heat allows protein molecules on the meat's surface to contract, trapping moisture. Juices and fat fall on the coals, creating smoky flavor. Trying to mimic the tandoor by cooking chicken in a very hot oven gave us disappointing results. Instead, we baked the chicken in a low-temperature oven until almost done, then quickly broiled it to char the exterior. To get flavor into the meat, we turned to a salt-spice rub made with garam masala, cumin, and chili powder bloomed in oil. We massaged the rub into chicken pieces to lock in juices and infuse flavor. Following a dunk in yogurt flavored with the same spice mix, the chicken was ready for the oven. We prefer this dish with whole-milk yogurt, but low-fat yogurt can be substituted. It is important to remove the chicken from the oven before switching to the broiler setting to allow the heating element to come up to temperature. Serve with Yogurt Sauce (page 280), Onion Relish (page 537), Cilantro-Mint Chutney (page 558), and Simple Rice Pilaf (page 726).

- 2 tablespoons vegetable oil
- 6 medium garlic cloves, minced or pressed through a garlic press (about 2 tablespoons)
- 2 tablespoons minced or grated fresh ginger
- 1 tablespoon garam masala
- 2 teaspoons ground cumin
- 2 teaspoons chili powder
- 1 cup plain whole-milk yogurt
- ¼ cup juice from 2 limes, plus 1 lime, cut into wedges (for serving)
- 2 teaspoons table salt
- 3 pounds bone-in, skin-on chicken pieces (split breasts cut in half, drumsticks, and/or thighs), trimmed and skin removed

**1.** Heat the oil in an 8-inch skillet over medium heat until shimmering. Add the garlic and ginger and cook until fragrant, about 1 minute. Stir in the garam masala, cumin, and chili powder and cook until fragrant, about 30 seconds. Transfer half of the garlic-spice mixture to a medium bowl, stir in the yogurt and 2 tablespoons of the lime juice, and set aside.

**2.** In a large bowl, combine the remaining garlic-spice mixture, remaining 2 tablespoons lime juice, and salt. Using a sharp knife, lightly score the skin side of each piece of chicken, making two or three shallow cuts about 1 inch apart and about ⅛ inch deep. Transfer the chicken to the bowl and gently rub with the salt-spice mixture until evenly coated. Let sit at room temperature for 30 minutes.

**3.** Adjust an oven rack to the upper-middle position (about 6 inches from the heating element) and heat the oven to 325 degrees. Set a wire rack over a foil-lined rimmed baking sheet or broiler pan bottom.

4. Pour the yogurt mixture over the chicken and toss until the chicken is evenly coated with a thick layer. Arrange the chicken pieces, scored side down, on the prepared wire rack. Discard the excess yogurt mixture. Bake the chicken until an instant-read thermometer inserted into the thickest part of the chicken registers 125 degrees for breasts and 130 degrees for legs and thighs, 15 to 25 minutes. (Smaller pieces may cook faster than larger pieces.) Transfer the chicken to a plate.

5. Turn the oven to broil and heat for 10 minutes. Flip the chicken pieces scored side up and broil until lightly charred in spots and the thickest part of the breasts registers 165 degrees and the thickest part of the legs and thighs registers 175 degrees, 8 to 15 minutes.

6. Transfer the chicken to a serving platter, tent loosely with foil, and let rest for 5 minutes. Serve with the lime wedges.

## Chicken Tikka Masala

**SERVES** 4 to 6

**WHY THIS RECIPE WORKS** Chicken tikka masala is arguably the single most popular Indian restaurant dish in the world. Turns out, it's not a traditional Indian dish: It was invented in an Indian restaurant in London. Without historical roots, there is no definitive recipe. We wanted to develop one that would produce moist, tender chunks of chicken in a rich, lightly spiced tomato sauce. To season the chicken, we rubbed it with salt, coriander, cumin, and cayenne. Then we dipped it in yogurt mixed with oil, garlic, and ginger and broiled it. And since large pieces don't dry out as quickly as smaller ones under the broiler, we cooked the chicken breasts whole, cutting them into pieces only after cooking. While the chicken was cooking, we made the sauce using canned crushed tomatoes and cream and added onion, ginger, garlic, chile, and readily available garam masala. This dish is best when prepared with whole-milk yogurt, but low-fat yogurt can be substituted. For more heat, include the chile seeds and ribs when mincing. Serve with rice pilaf.

**CHICKEN**

- 1 teaspoon table salt, divided
- ½ teaspoon ground cumin
- ½ teaspoon ground coriander
- ¼ teaspoon cayenne pepper
- 2 pounds boneless, skinless chicken breasts, trimmed
- 1 cup plain whole-milk yogurt
- 2 tablespoons vegetable oil
- 1 tablespoon minced or grated fresh ginger
- 2 garlic cloves, minced

**SAUCE**

- 3 tablespoons vegetable oil
- 1 onion, chopped fine
- 1 tablespoon garam masala
- 1 tablespoon tomato paste
- 2 garlic cloves, minced
- 2 teaspoons grated fresh ginger
- 1 serrano chile, stemmed, seeded, and minced
- 1 (28-ounce) can crushed tomatoes
- 2 teaspoons sugar
- ½ teaspoon table salt
- ⅔ cup heavy cream
- ¼ cup chopped fresh cilantro

1. **FOR THE CHICKEN:** Combine ½ teaspoon salt, cumin, coriander, and cayenne in small bowl. Pat chicken dry with paper towels and sprinkle with spice mixture, pressing gently so mixture adheres. Place chicken on plate, cover with plastic wrap, and refrigerate for at least 30 minutes or up to 1 hour. In large bowl, whisk yogurt, oil, ginger, and garlic together and set aside.

2. **FOR THE SAUCE:** Heat oil in Dutch oven over medium heat until shimmering. Add onion and cook, stirring frequently, until softened and light golden, 8 to 10 minutes. Stir in garam masala, tomato paste, garlic, ginger, and serrano and cook, stirring frequently, until fragrant, about 3 minutes. Add crushed tomatoes, sugar, and remaining ½ teaspoon salt and bring to a boil. Reduce heat to medium-low, cover, and simmer for 15 minutes, stirring occasionally. Stir in cream and return to simmer. Remove pan from heat and cover to keep warm. (Sauce can be refrigerated in airtight container for up to 4 days and gently reheated before adding hot chicken.)

3. **TO COOK THE CHICKEN:** While sauce simmers, adjust oven rack 6 inches from broiling element and heat broiler. Line rimmed baking sheet or broiler pan with aluminum foil and set wire rack in sheet.

4. Using tongs, dip chicken into yogurt mixture (chicken should be coated with thick layer of yogurt) and arrange on wire rack. Discard excess yogurt mixture. Broil chicken until lightly charred and chicken registers 160 degrees, 10 to 18 minutes, flipping chicken halfway through.

5. Let chicken rest for 5 minutes, then cut into 1-inch chunks and stir into warm sauce (do not simmer chicken in sauce). Stir in cilantro, season with salt to taste, and serve.

## Murgh Makhani (Indian Butter Chicken)

**SERVES** 4 to 6

**WHY THIS RECIPE WORKS** Murgh makhani (butter chicken) should taste rich and creamy but also vibrant and complex, so we started by softening lots of onion, garlic, ginger, and chile in butter followed by aromatic spices such as garam masala, coriander, cumin, and black pepper. Instead of chopped or crushed tomatoes, we opted for a hefty portion of tomato paste and water, which lent the sauce bright acidity, punch, and deep color without making it too liquid-y. A full cup of cream gave the sauce lush, velvety body, and we finished it by whisking in a couple more tablespoons of solid butter for extra richness. To imitate the deep charring produced by a tandoor oven, we broiled chicken thighs coated in yogurt (its milk proteins and lactose brown quickly and deeply) before cutting them into chunks and stirring them into the sauce. Traditionally, butter chicken is mildly spiced. If you prefer a spicier dish, reserve, mince, and add the ribs and seeds from the chile. Serve with Indian-Style Basmati Rice and/or warm naan.

- 4 tablespoons unsalted butter, cut into 4 pieces and chilled, divided
- 1 onion, chopped fine
- 5 garlic cloves, minced
- 4 teaspoons grated fresh ginger
- 1 serrano chile, stemmed, seeded, and minced
- 1 tablespoon garam masala
- 1 teaspoon ground coriander
- ½ teaspoon ground cumin
- ½ teaspoon pepper
- 1½ cups water
- ½ cup tomato paste
- 1 tablespoon sugar
- 2 teaspoons table salt, divided
- 1 cup heavy cream
- 2 pounds boneless, skinless chicken thighs, trimmed
- ½ cup plain Greek yogurt
- 3 tablespoons chopped fresh cilantro, divided

**1.** Melt 2 tablespoons butter in large saucepan over medium heat. Add onion, garlic, ginger, and serrano and cook, stirring frequently, until mixture is softened and onion begins to brown, 8 to 10 minutes. Add garam masala, coriander, cumin, and pepper and cook, stirring frequently, until fragrant, about 3 minutes. Add water and tomato paste and whisk until no lumps of tomato paste remain. Add sugar and 1 teaspoon salt and bring to boil. Off heat, stir in cream. Using immersion blender or blender, process until smooth, 30 to 60 seconds. Return sauce to simmer over medium heat and whisk in remaining 2 tablespoons butter. Remove saucepan from heat and cover to keep warm. (Sauce can be refrigerated for up to 4 days; gently reheat sauce before adding hot chicken.)

**2.** Adjust oven rack 6 inches from broiler element and heat broiler. Combine chicken, yogurt, and remaining 1 teaspoon salt in bowl and toss well to coat. Using tongs, transfer chicken to wire rack set in aluminum foil–lined rimmed baking sheet. Broil until chicken is evenly charred on both sides and registers 175 degrees, 16 to 20 minutes, flipping chicken halfway through broiling.

**3.** Let chicken rest for 5 minutes. While chicken rests, warm sauce over medium-low heat. Cut chicken into ¾-inch chunks and stir into sauce. Stir in 2 tablespoons cilantro and season with salt to taste. Transfer to serving dish, sprinkle with remaining 1 tablespoon cilantro, and serve.

### Indian-Style Basmati Rice

**SERVES** 4 to 6

For basmati rice with a bright yellow color, add ¼ teaspoon of ground turmeric and a pinch of saffron threads with the water in step 3.

- 1½ cups basmati rice
- 3 tablespoons unsalted butter
- 1 teaspoon cumin seeds
- 3 green cardamom pods, lightly crushed
- 3 whole cloves
- 2¼ cups water
- 1 cinnamon stick
- 1 bay leaf
- 1 teaspoon table salt

**1.** Place rice in fine-mesh strainer and rinse under cold running water until water runs clear. Place strainer over bowl and set aside.

**2.** Melt butter in medium saucepan over medium heat. Add cumin, cardamom, and cloves and cook, stirring constantly, until fragrant, about 1 minute. Add rice and cook, stirring constantly, until fragrant, about 1 minute.

**3.** Add water, cinnamon stick, bay leaf, and salt and bring to boil. Reduce heat to low, cover, and simmer until all water is absorbed, about 17 minutes. Let stand, covered, off heat for at least 10 minutes. Discard cardamom, cloves, cinnamon stick, and bay leaf. Fluff rice with fork and serve.

## Indoor Pulled Chicken

**SERVES** 6 to 8

**WHY THIS RECIPE WORKS** Traditional pulled chicken is a true labor of love. We wanted a stovetop version that had the texture and flavor of outdoor slow-smoked pulled chicken but that came together in just a fraction of the time. We started by braising boneless, skinless chicken thighs in a mixture of chicken broth, salt, sugar, molasses, gelatin, and liquid smoke. The liquid smoke simulated the flavor of traditional smoked chicken, while the gelatin and broth mimicked the unctuous texture and intense flavor of whole chicken parts. To mimic the richness of skin-on chicken, we skipped trimming the fat and added the rendered fat back to the finished chicken. Finally, we mixed the shredded meat with a homemade barbecue sauce. Do not trim the fat from the chicken thighs; it contributes to the flavor and texture of the pulled chicken.

If you don't have 3 tablespoons of fat to add back to the pot in step 3, add melted butter to make up the difference. We like mild molasses in this recipe; do not use blackstrap. Serve the pulled chicken on white bread or hamburger buns with pickles and coleslaw.

- 1 cup chicken broth
- 2 tablespoons molasses
- 1 tablespoon sugar
- 1 tablespoon liquid smoke, divided
- 1 teaspoon unflavored gelatin
- 1 teaspoon table salt
- 2 pounds boneless, skinless chicken thighs, halved crosswise
- 1 recipe Sweet and Tangy Barbecue Sauce
- Hot sauce

**1.** Bring broth, molasses, sugar, 2 teaspoons liquid smoke, gelatin, and salt to boil in large Dutch oven over high heat, stirring to dissolve sugar. Add chicken and return to simmer. Reduce heat to medium-low; cover; and cook, stirring occasionally, until chicken is easily shredded with fork, about 25 minutes.

**2.** Transfer chicken to medium bowl and set aside. Strain cooking liquid through fine-mesh strainer set over bowl (do not wash pot). Let liquid settle for 5 minutes; skim fat from surface. Set aside fat and defatted liquid.

**3.** Using tongs, squeeze chicken until shredded into bite-size pieces. Transfer chicken, 1 cup barbecue sauce, ½ cup reserved defatted liquid, 3 tablespoons reserved fat, and remaining 1 teaspoon liquid smoke to now-empty pot. Cook mixture over medium heat, stirring frequently, until liquid has been absorbed and exterior of meat appears dry, about 5 minutes. Season with salt, pepper, and hot sauce to taste. Serve, passing remaining barbecue sauce separately.

### Sweet and Tangy Barbecue Sauce

**MAKES** 2 cups

We like mild molasses in this recipe.

- 1½ cups ketchup
- ¼ cup molasses
- 2 tablespoons Worcestershire sauce
- 1 tablespoon hot sauce
- ½ teaspoon table salt
- ½ teaspoon pepper

Whisk all ingredients together in bowl.

## Sweet and Tangy Oven-Barbecued Chicken

**SERVES** 4

**WHY THIS RECIPE WORKS** What do you do when a craving for this summertime favorite strikes in midwinter? Oven-barbecued chicken is the obvious solution. We started with boneless, skinless chicken breasts; the mild white meat is a perfect backdrop for the sauce. (Skinless breasts also meant that we wouldn't have to deal with the problem of flabby skin.) We lightly seared the chicken breasts in a skillet, then removed them from the pan to make a simple but flavorful barbecue sauce with pantry ingredients like grated onion, ketchup, Worcestershire sauce, mustard, molasses, and maple syrup. When we returned the chicken to the pan, the sauce clung nicely to the meat, thanks to the light searing we had given the chicken. We slid the chicken and sauce, still in the skillet, into the oven to cook through. Finally, for a nicely caramelized coating on the sauce, we finished the chicken under the high heat of the broiler. Real maple syrup is preferable to imitation syrup, and "mild" or "original" molasses is preferable to darker, more bitter types. Use a rasp-style grater or the fine holes of a box grater to grate the onion. Make this recipe only in an in-oven broiler; do not use a drawer-type broiler. Broiling times may differ from one oven to another, so we urge you to check the chicken for doneness after only 3 minutes of broiling. You may also have to lower the oven rack if your broiler runs very hot. It is important to remove the chicken from the oven before switching to the broiler setting to allow the broiler element to come up to temperature.

- 1 cup ketchup
- 3 tablespoons molasses
- 3 tablespoons cider vinegar
- 2 tablespoons finely grated onion
- 2 tablespoons Worcestershire sauce
- 2 tablespoons Dijon mustard
- 2 tablespoons maple syrup
- 1 teaspoon chili powder
- ¼ teaspoon cayenne pepper
- 4 (5- to 6-ounce) boneless, skinless chicken breasts, tenderloins removed and breasts trimmed
- Table salt and ground black pepper
- 1 tablespoon vegetable oil

**1.** Adjust an oven rack to the upper-middle position, about 5 inches from the heating element, and heat the oven to 325 degrees. Whisk the ketchup, molasses, vinegar, onion, Worcestershire sauce, mustard, maple syrup, chili powder, and cayenne together in a small bowl; set aside. Pat the chicken dry with paper towels and season with salt and pepper.

**2.** Heat the oil in a 12-inch ovensafe skillet over high heat until just smoking. Add the chicken, smooth side down, and cook until very light golden, 1 to 2 minutes; using tongs, turn the chicken and cook until very light golden on the second side, 1 to 2 minutes longer. Transfer the chicken to a plate and set aside.

**3.** Discard the fat in the skillet; off the heat, add the sauce mixture and, using a wooden spoon, scrape up the browned bits on the bottom of the skillet. Simmer the sauce over medium heat, stirring frequently with a heatproof spatula, until the sauce is thick and glossy and a spatula leaves a clear trail in the sauce, about 4 minutes. Off the heat, return the chicken to the skillet and turn to coat thickly with the sauce; set the chicken pieces smooth side up and spoon extra sauce over each piece to create a thick coating.

**4.** Place the skillet in the oven and cook until the thickest part of the breasts registers 130 degrees on an instant-read thermometer, 8 to 12 minutes. Remove the skillet from the oven, turn the oven to broil, and heat for 5 minutes. Once the broiler is heated, place the skillet back in the oven and broil the chicken until the thickest part of the breasts registers 160 degrees, 3 to 8 minutes longer. Transfer the chicken to a platter and let rest for 5 minutes. Meanwhile, whisk the sauce in the skillet to recombine and transfer to a small bowl. Serve the chicken, passing the extra sauce separately.

## Spice-Rubbed Picnic Chicken

**SERVES 8**

**WHY THIS RECIPE WORKS** We wanted an easy but delicious recipe for cold barbecued chicken perfect to pack (and eat) for a picnic; chicken with moist, tender meat flavored with robust spicy and slightly sweet barbecue flavors. We first threw out the idea of a sticky sauce, substituting a robust dry rub (brown sugar, chili powder, paprika, and pepper) that reproduced the flavors of a good barbecue sauce. We partly solved the flabby skin problem by diligently trimming the chicken pieces as well as by slitting the skin before cooking. But the skin was still flabby from the moisture contributed by our brine. So we eliminated the brine, added salt to the rub, and applied it the night before. Sure enough, when we oven-roasted the chicken next day, we found the meat well seasoned and very moist. Best of all, the skin was flavorful, delicate, and definitely not flabby. If you plan to serve the chicken later on the same day that you cook it, refrigerate it immediately after it has cooled, then let it come back to room temperature before serving. On the breast pieces, we use toothpicks to secure the skin, which otherwise shrinks considerably in the oven, leaving the meat exposed and prone to drying out. This recipe halves easily.

- 5 pounds bone-in, skin-on chicken parts (split breasts, thighs, drumsticks, or a mix, with breasts cut into 3 pieces or halved if small), trimmed of excess fat and skin
- 3 tablespoons brown sugar
- 2 tablespoons chili powder
- 2 tablespoons sweet paprika
- 2 tablespoons kosher salt
- 2 teaspoons ground black pepper
- ¼–½ teaspoon cayenne pepper

**1.** Use a sharp knife to make two or three short slashes in the skin of each piece of chicken, taking care not to cut into the meat. Combine the sugar, chili powder, paprika, salt, and pepper in a small bowl and mix thoroughly. Coat the chicken pieces with the spices, gently lifting the skin to distribute the spice rub underneath but leaving it attached to the chicken. Transfer the chicken, skin side up, to a wire rack set over a large, rimmed baking sheet, lightly tent it with foil, and refrigerate for at least 6 hours or up to 24 hours.

**2.** If desired, secure the skin of each breast piece with two or three toothpicks placed near the edges of the skin.

**3.** Adjust an oven rack to the middle position and heat the oven to 425 degrees. Roast the chicken until the thickest part of the smallest piece registers 140 degrees on an instant-read thermometer, 15 to 20 minutes. Increase the oven temperature to 500 degrees and continue roasting until the chicken is browned and crisp and the thickest part of the breasts registers 160 degrees, 5 to 8 minutes longer, removing the pieces from the oven and transferring them to a clean wire rack as they finish cooking. Continue to roast the thighs and/or drumsticks, if using, until the thickest part of the meat registers 175 degrees, about 5 minutes longer. Remove from the oven, transfer the chicken to a rack, and cool completely before refrigerating or serving.

## Roasted Bone-In Chicken Breasts

**SERVES 4**

**WHY THIS RECIPE WORKS** People often view the chicken bones and skin as a complication rather than an asset, so we resolved to devise an easy method that would deliver juicy, well-seasoned meat and crispy, brown skin. We ran into some expected problems though: The bone-in chicken breasts roasted at a high temperature achieved a crispy, brown skin, but the resulting meat was dry and bland. Cooking the chicken at a lower temperature kept the meat juicy but left the skin pale and flabby. For the best of both worlds, we adapted a cooking technique that we more commonly use for steaks: reverse searing. We started by applying salt under the skin to season the meat and help it retain moisture. Then we poked small holes in the skin to help drain excess fat. Gently baking the breasts at 325 degrees minimized moisture loss and resulted in even cooking from the breasts' thick ends to their thin ends. It also allowed the surface of the skin to dry out so that a quick sear in a hot skillet was all that was required for a crackly finish. Be sure to remove excess fatty skin from the thick ends of the breasts when trimming. You may serve these chicken breasts on their own or with a sauce like our Jalapeño and Cilantro Sauce.

- 4 (10- to 12-ounce) bone-in chicken breasts, trimmed
- 1½ teaspoons kosher salt
- 1 tablespoon vegetable oil

**1.** Adjust oven rack to lower-middle position and heat oven to 325 degrees. Line rimmed baking sheet with aluminum foil. Working with 1 breast at a time, use your fingers to carefully separate chicken skin from meat. Peel skin back, leaving it attached at top and bottom of breast and at ribs. Sprinkle salt evenly over all chicken, then lay skin back in place. Using metal skewer or tip of paring knife, poke 6 to 8 holes in fat deposits in skin. Arrange breasts skin side up on prepared sheet. Roast until chicken registers 160 degrees, 35 to 45 minutes.

**2.** Heat 12-inch skillet over low heat for 5 minutes. Add oil and swirl to coat surface. Add chicken, skin side down, and increase heat to medium-high. Cook chicken without moving it until skin is well browned and crispy, 3 to 5 minutes. Using tongs, flip chicken and prop against side of skillet so thick side of breast is facing down; continue to cook until browned, 1 to 2 minutes longer. Transfer to platter and let rest for 5 minutes before serving.

### Jalapeño and Cilantro Sauce

**MAKES** 1 cup

For a spicier sauce, reserve and add some of the chile seeds to the blender.

- 1 cup fresh cilantro leaves and stems, trimmed and chopped coarse
- 3 jalapeño chiles, stemmed, seeded, and minced
- ½ cup mayonnaise
- 1 tablespoon lime juice
- 2 garlic cloves, minced
- ½ teaspoon kosher salt
- 2 tablespoons extra-virgin olive oil

Process cilantro, jalapeños, mayonnaise, lime juice, garlic, and salt in blender for 1 minute. Scrape down sides of blender jar and continue to process until smooth, about 1 minute longer. With blender running, slowly add oil until incorporated. Transfer to bowl.

## Oven-Roasted Chicken Thighs

**SERVES 4**

**WHY THIS RECIPE WORKS** More flavorful and less prone to overcooking than lean breasts, chicken thighs are a perfect weeknight dinner. The only problem is that the layer of fat underneath the skin that helps keep them moist during cooking often leads to flabby skin. To combat this, we cooked the thighs, skin side down, on a preheated baking sheet, until the skin was browned and the fat rendered. We then flipped the thighs and put them under the broiler briefly to dry and crisp the skin. The result was chicken thighs with succulent and juicy meat under a sheer layer of crackly crisp, deeply browned skin. For best results, trim all visible fat from the thighs. Use a heavy-duty baking sheet and fully preheat the oven and baking sheet before adding the chicken. Serve with Roasted Garlic Salsa Verde, if desired (page 314).

- 8 (6- to 8-ounce) bone-in chicken thighs, trimmed
- ½ teaspoon table salt
- ½ teaspoon pepper
- Vegetable oil spray

**1.** Adjust oven racks to middle and lowest positions, place rimmed baking sheet on lower rack, and heat oven to 450 degrees.

**2.** Using metal skewer, poke skin side of chicken thighs 10 to 12 times. Sprinkle both sides of thighs with salt and pepper; spray skin lightly with vegetable oil spray. Place thighs skin side down on preheated baking sheet. Return sheet to bottom rack.

**3.** Roast chicken until skin side is beginning to brown and meat registers 160 degrees, 20 to 25 minutes, rotating pan as needed for even browning. Remove chicken from oven and heat broiler.

**4.** While broiler heats, flip chicken skin side up. Broil chicken on middle rack until skin is crisp and well browned and meat registers 175 degrees, about 5 minutes, rotating pan as needed for even browning. Transfer chicken to platter and let rest for 5 minutes. Serve.

## Roasted Garlic Salsa Verde

**MAKES** ½ cup

- 1 garlic head, cloves separated, unpeeled
- 5 tablespoons extra-virgin olive oil, divided
- 2 tablespoons lemon juice
- 1 cup fresh parsley leaves
- 2 anchovy fillets, rinsed and patted dry
- 2 tablespoons capers, rinsed
- ¼ teaspoon table salt
- ¼ teaspoon red pepper flakes

**1.** While oven preheats for Oven-Roasted Chicken Thighs, toss garlic cloves and 1 tablespoon oil in bowl. Cover bowl and microwave until garlic is softened, 2 to 5 minutes, stirring once halfway through. Place garlic in center of 12-inch square of aluminum foil. Cover with second 12-inch square of foil; fold edges together to create packet about 7 inches square. Place packet on middle rack of oven for 10 minutes.

**2.** Remove packet from oven and squeeze garlic cloves out of skins. Process garlic, lemon juice, parsley, anchovies, capers, and salt in food processor until coarsely chopped, about 5 seconds. Add remaining ¼ cup oil and pepper flakes; pulse until combined, scraping bowl as necessary.

## Slow-Roasted Chicken Parts with Shallot-Garlic Pan Sauce

**SERVES** 8

**WHY THIS RECIPE WORKS** Slow roasting keeps chicken nice and juicy, but at a cost: The skin is often a bit flabby, padded with unrendered fat. For ultramoist roast chicken that boasted the shatteringly crisp skin we loved, we bypassed a whole chicken and turned to parts. We seared leg quarters and then split breasts in oil, rendering some of the fat and giving the crisping a head start. We moved the parts to a 250-degree oven, keeping the slower-cooking thighs on the back portion of the wire rack–lined sheet, facing the hotter side of the oven. While the chicken rested, we whisked together a simple pan sauce with butter, shallots, garlic, and coriander, adding a little powdered gelatin and cornstarch to give it the rich body of a jus. Before serving, we gave the skin a final crisping under the broiler. To serve four people, halve the ingredient amounts.

- 5 pounds bone-in chicken pieces (4 split breasts and 4 leg quarters), trimmed
- 2 teaspoons kosher salt
- ½ teaspoon pepper
- ¼ teaspoon vegetable oil
- 1 tablespoon unflavored gelatin
- 2¼ cups chicken broth
- 2 tablespoons water
- 2 teaspoons cornstarch
- 4 tablespoons unsalted butter, cut into 4 pieces
- 4 shallots, sliced thin
- 6 garlic cloves, sliced thin
- 1 teaspoon ground coriander
- 1 tablespoon minced fresh parsley
- 1½ teaspoons lemon juice

**1.** Adjust 1 oven rack to lowest position and second rack 8 inches from broiler element. Heat oven to 250 degrees. Line rimmed baking sheet with aluminum foil and place wire rack on top. Sprinkle chicken pieces with salt and pepper (do not pat chicken dry).

**2.** Heat oil in 12-inch skillet over medium-high heat until shimmering. Place leg quarters skin side down in skillet; cook, turning once, until golden brown on both sides, 5 to 7 minutes total. Transfer to prepared sheet, arranging legs along 1 long side of sheet. Pour off fat from skillet. Place breasts skin side down in skillet; cook, turning once, until golden brown on both sides, 4 to 6 minutes total. Transfer to sheet with legs. Discard fat; do not clean skillet. Place sheet on lower rack, orienting so legs are at back of oven. Roast until breasts register 160 degrees and legs register 175 degrees, 1 hour 25 minutes to 1 hour 45 minutes. Let chicken rest on sheet for 10 minutes.

**3.** While chicken roasts, sprinkle gelatin over broth in bowl and let sit until gelatin softens, about 5 minutes. Whisk water and cornstarch together in small bowl; set aside.

**4.** Melt butter in now-empty skillet over medium-low heat. Add shallots and garlic; cook until golden brown and crisp, 6 to 9 minutes. Stir in coriander and cook for 30 seconds. Stir in gelatin mixture, scraping up any browned bits. Bring to simmer over high heat and cook until reduced to 1½ cups, 5 to 7 minutes. Whisk cornstarch mixture to recombine. Whisk into sauce and simmer until thickened, about 1 minute. Off heat, stir in parsley and lemon juice; season with salt and pepper to taste. Cover to keep warm.

**5.** Heat broiler. Transfer sheet to upper rack and broil chicken until skin is well browned and crisp, 3 to 6 minutes. Serve, passing sauce separately.

## Chicken in Mole-Poblano Sauce

**SERVES** 4 to 6

**WHY THIS RECIPE WORKS** The most famous of Mexico's moles, mole poblano often relies on as many as six types of chiles for its deep richness. We pared our recipe down to two: ancho, for a robust chile base; and chipotle, for smoky, intense chile flavor. Using almond butter instead of ground almonds was a simple shortcut that lent a luxurious, velvety texture to the sauce. Just 1 ounce of chocolate added richness and depth but didn't make the sauce taste chocolaty. We added warmth and a touch of sweetness with cinnamon, cloves, and raisins. Sautéing the chiles, chocolate, and spices along with the onion and garlic deepened the flavor of the final sauce. Simmering the mole for just 10 minutes thickened the sauce to the perfect consistency. Bone-in chicken pieces worked perfectly with our mole, and removing the skin kept it from turning soggy in the sauce. Feel free to substitute ½ teaspoon ground chipotle chile powder or ½ teaspoon minced canned chipotles in adobo sauce for the chipotle chile and add with the cinnamon in step 2. Serve with rice.

- 2 dried ancho chiles, stemmed, seeded, and torn into ½-inch pieces (½ cup)
- ½ dried chipotle chile, stemmed, seeded, and torn into ½-inch pieces (scant tablespoon)
- 3 tablespoons vegetable oil
- 1 onion, chopped fine
- 1 ounce bittersweet, semisweet, or Mexican chocolate, chopped coarse
- ½ teaspoon ground cinnamon
- ⅛ teaspoon ground cloves
- 2 garlic cloves, minced
- 2 cups chicken broth
- 1 (14.5-ounce) can diced tomatoes, drained
- ¼ cup raisins
- ¼ cup almond butter
- 2 tablespoons sesame seeds, plus extra for garnish, toasted
- Sugar
- 3½ pounds bone-in chicken pieces (split breasts, drumsticks, and/or thighs), skin removed, trimmed
- ¼ teaspoon table salt
- ¼ teaspoon pepper

**1.** Toast anchos and chipotle in 12-inch skillet over medium heat, stirring frequently, until fragrant, 2 to 6 minutes; transfer to plate. Add oil and onion to now-empty skillet and cook over medium-high heat until softened, 5 to 7 minutes.

**2.** Stir in chocolate, cinnamon, cloves, and toasted chiles and cook until chocolate is melted and bubbly, about 2 minutes. Stir in garlic and cook until fragrant, about 30 seconds. Stir in broth, tomatoes, raisins, almond butter, and sesame seeds and bring to simmer. Reduce heat to medium and simmer gently, stirring occasionally, until slightly thickened and measures about 3½ cups, about 7 minutes.

**3.** Transfer mixture to blender and process until smooth, about 20 seconds. Season with salt, pepper, and sugar to taste. (Sauce can be refrigerated for up to 3 days; loosen with water as needed before continuing.)

**4.** Adjust oven rack to middle position and heat oven to 400 degrees. Pat chicken dry with paper towels and sprinkle with salt and pepper. Arrange chicken in single layer in shallow baking dish and cover with mole sauce, turning to coat chicken evenly. Bake, uncovered, until breasts register 160 degrees, and thighs or drumsticks register 175 degrees, 35 to 45 minutes.

**5.** Remove chicken from oven, tent with aluminum foil, and let rest for 5 to 10 minutes. Sprinkle with extra sesame seeds and serve.

## Perfect Roast Chicken

**SERVES** 2 to 3

**WHY THIS RECIPE WORKS** Most home-cooked chickens are either grossly overcooked or so underdone that they resemble an avian version of steak tartare. We wanted a method for producing perfectly roasted chicken, where the white meat cooks up juicy and tender, but with a hint of chew, and the dark meat is fully cooked, all the way to the bone. For maximum juiciness and well-seasoned meat, we brined the chicken. And for further flavor and a moisture boost to the delicate breast, we rubbed butter under the skin and over the breast. Trussing and continuous basting both proved unnecessary for this ideal chicken. In fact, basting turned its skin greasy and chewy. We had hoped that the bird wouldn't have to be turned while cooking, but we found it was a must for even cooking. In the end, we found that roasting the bird for 15 minutes on each side and then putting it on its back rendered perfectly cooked white and dark meat as well as golden, crunchy skin. If using a kosher chicken, skip the brining process and begin with step 2. We recommend using a V-rack to roast the chicken. If you don't have a V-rack, set the bird on a regular roasting rack and use balls of aluminum foil to keep the roasting chicken propped up on its side.

- ½ cup table salt
- ½ cup sugar
- 1 (3½- to 4-pound) whole chicken, giblets discarded
- 2 tablespoons unsalted butter, softened
- 1 tablespoon olive oil
- Ground black pepper

**1.** Dissolve the salt and sugar in 2 quarts cold water in a large container. Submerge the chicken in the brine, cover, and refrigerate for 1 hour.

**2.** Adjust an oven rack to the lower-middle position, place a roasting pan on the rack, and heat the oven to 400 degrees. Coat a V-rack with vegetable oil spray and set aside. Remove the chicken from the brine, rinse well, and pat dry with paper towels.

**3.** Use your fingers to gently loosen the center portion of the skin covering each breast; place the butter under the skin, directly on the meat in the center of each breast. Gently press on the skin to distribute the butter over the meat. Tuck the wings behind the back. Rub the skin with the oil, season with pepper, and place the chicken, wing side up, on the prepared V-rack. Place the V-rack in the preheated roasting pan and roast for 15 minutes.

**4.** Remove the roasting pan from the oven and, using two large wads of paper towels, rotate the chicken so that the opposite wing side is facing up. Return the roasting pan to the oven and roast for another 15 minutes.

**5.** Using two large wads of paper towels, rotate the chicken again so that the breast side is facing up and continue to roast until the thickest part of the breasts registers 160 to 165 degrees and the thickest part of the thighs registers 175 degrees on an instant-read thermometer, 20 to 25 minutes longer. Transfer the chicken to a carving board and let rest for 10 minutes. Carve the chicken and serve.

## Weeknight Roast Chicken

**SERVES 4**

**WHY THIS RECIPE WORKS** When done properly, the rich flavor and juicy meat of a roast chicken need little adornment. But the process of preparing and roasting chicken can be surprisingly complicated and time-consuming. We wanted a way to get roast chicken on the table in about an hour without sacrificing flavor. After testing the various components and steps of a typical recipe, we found we could skip trussing and just tie the legs together and tuck the wings underneath. We also discovered that using a preheated skillet and placing the chicken breast side up gave the thighs a jumpstart on cooking. Starting the chicken in a 450-degree oven and then turning the oven off while the chicken finished cooking slowed the evaporation of juices, ensuring moist, tender meat. We prefer to use a 3½- to 4-pound chicken for this recipe; however, this method can be used to cook a larger chicken. If roasting a larger bird, increase the cooking time in step 2 to 35 to 40 minutes. If you choose to serve the chicken with Thyme–Sherry Vinegar Pan Sauce, don't wash the skillet after removing the chicken. Prepare the pan sauce while resting the chicken.

- 1 tablespoon kosher salt
- ½ teaspoon pepper
- 1 (3½- to 4-pound) whole chicken, giblets discarded
- 1 tablespoon extra-virgin olive oil

**1.** Adjust oven rack to middle position, place 12-inch ovensafe skillet on rack, and heat the oven to 450 degrees. Combine salt and pepper in bowl. Pat chicken dry with paper towels and rub entire surface with oil. Sprinkle evenly all over with salt mixture and rub in mixture with your hands to coat evenly. Tie legs together with twine and tuck wingtips behind back.

**2.** Transfer chicken, breast side up, to preheated skillet in oven. Roast chicken until thickest part of breasts registers 120 degrees and the thickest part of thighs registers 135 degrees, 25 to 35 minutes. Turn off oven and leave chicken in oven until breasts register 160 degrees and the thighs register 175 degrees, 25 to 35 minutes.

**3.** Transfer chicken to carving board and let rest, uncovered, for 20 minutes. Carve and serve.

## Thyme–Sherry Vinegar Pan Sauce

**MAKES ¾ cup**

- 1 shallot, minced
- 2 garlic cloves, minced
- 2 teaspoons chopped fresh thyme
- 1 cup chicken broth
- 2 teaspoons Dijon mustard
- 2 tablespoons unsalted butter
- 2 teaspoons sherry vinegar

While chicken rests, remove all but 1 tablespoon fat from now-empty skillet, leaving any browned bits and juices in skillet. Place skillet over medium-high heat; add shallot, garlic, and thyme; and cook until softened, about 2 minutes. Stir in broth and mustard, scraping up any browned bits. Cook until reduced to ¾ cup, about 3 minutes. Off heat, whisk in butter and vinegar. Season with pepper to taste; cover and keep warm.

### CARVING A WHOLE ROAST CHICKEN

**1.** Cut chicken where leg meets breast, then pull leg quarter away. Push up on joint, then carefully cut through it to remove leg quarter.

**2.** Cut through joint that connects drumstick to thigh. Repeat on second side to remove other leg.

**3.** Cut down along 1 side of breastbone, pulling breast meat away from bone.

**4.** Remove wing from breast by cutting through wing joint. Slice breast into attractive slices.

## Crisp Roast Chicken

**SERVES** 2 to 3

**WHY THIS RECIPE WORKS** During roasting, juices and rendered fat can accumulate beneath the chicken skin and turn it wet and flabby. We wanted a juicy roasted chicken with skin that would crackle against your teeth with every bite. We first cut an incision down the chicken's back to allow fat to escape and then loosened the skin from the thighs and breasts, poking holes in the fat deposits to allow multiple channels for excess fat and juices to escape. And we added baking powder to our salt rub, which helped dehydrate the skin and enhanced the effects of next step: overnight air-drying. Finally, we roasted the bird at high heat to speed the browning. To prevent our kitchen from filling with smoke from burning pan drippings, we placed a sheet of foil with holes punched into it under the chicken. Now we had roast chicken with juicy meat and the crispest skin ever. Do not brine the bird; it will prevent the skin from becoming crisp.

- 1 (3½- to 4-pound) whole chicken, giblets discarded
- 1 tablespoon kosher salt or 1½ teaspoons table salt
- 1 teaspoon baking powder
- ½ teaspoon ground black pepper

**1.** Place the chicken, breast side down, on a work surface. Use the tip of a sharp knife to make four 1-inch incisions along the back of the chicken. Using your fingers or the handle of a wooden spoon, separate the skin from the thighs and breast, being careful not to break the skin. Using a metal skewer, poke 15 to 20 holes in the fat deposits on top of the breast halves and thighs. Tuck the wings behind the back.

**2.** Combine the salt, baking powder, and pepper in a small bowl. Pat the chicken dry with paper towels and sprinkle all over with the salt mixture. Rub in the mixture with your hands, coating the entire surface evenly. Set the chicken, breast side up, in a V-rack set on a rimmed baking sheet and refrigerate, uncovered, for at least 12 hours or up to 24 hours.

**3.** Adjust an oven rack to the lowest position and heat the oven to 450 degrees. Using a paring knife, poke 20 holes about 1½ inches apart in a 16 by 12-inch piece of foil. Place the foil loosely in a large roasting pan. Flip the chicken so the breast side faces down, and set the V-rack in the roasting pan on top of the foil. Roast the chicken for 25 minutes.

**4.** Remove the roasting pan from the oven. Using two large wads of paper towels, rotate the chicken breast side up. Continue to roast until the thickest part of the breasts registers 135 degrees on an instant-read thermometer, 15 to 25 minutes.

**5.** Increase the oven temperature to 500 degrees. Continue to roast until the skin is golden brown and crisp and the thickest part of the breasts registers 160 to 165 degrees and the thickest part of the thighs registers 175 degrees, 10 to 20 minutes.

**6.** Transfer the chicken to a carving board and let rest, uncovered, for 20 minutes. Following the photos on page 152, carve the chicken and serve immediately.

## One-Hour Broiled Chicken and Pan Sauce

**SERVES** 4

**WHY THIS RECIPE WORKS** We found that one key to getting a whole chicken on the table efficiently was butterflying it and broiling it. Preheating a skillet first on the stovetop was key to getting the white and dark meat to finish cooking at the same time (it jump-started the cooking of the leg quarters and then sliding that skillet under a cold broiler slowed down the cooking of the breasts). To account for carryover cooking, we pulled the chicken from the oven when the breast meat reached 155 degrees instead of 160 degrees. Finally, the simple addition of garlic and thyme sprigs to the hot pan drippings created a flavorful sauce with almost no effort. If your broiler has multiple settings, choose the highest one. In step 3, if the skin is dark golden brown but the breast has not yet reached 155 degrees, cover the chicken with aluminum foil and continue to broil. To avoid overcooking, monitor the temperature of the chicken in the final 10 minutes. Do not attempt this recipe with a drawer broiler.

- 1 (4-pound) whole chicken, giblets discarded
- 1½ teaspoons vegetable oil
- Kosher salt and pepper
- 4 sprigs fresh thyme
- 1 garlic clove, peeled and crushed
- Lemon wedges

**1.** Adjust oven rack 12 to 13 inches from broiler element (do not preheat broiler). Place chicken breast side down on cutting board. Using kitchen shears, cut through bones on either side of backbone. Trim off any excess fat and skin and discard backbone. Flip chicken over and press on breastbone to flatten. Using tip of paring knife, poke holes through skin over entire surface of chicken, spacing them approximately ¾ inch apart.

**2.** Rub ½ teaspoon oil over skin and sprinkle with 1 teaspoon salt and ½ teaspoon pepper. Flip chicken over, sprinkle bone side with ½ teaspoon salt, and season with pepper. Tie legs together with kitchen twine and tuck wings under breasts.

**3.** Heat remaining 1 teaspoon oil in broiler-safe 12-inch skillet over high heat until just smoking. Place chicken in skillet, skin side up, and transfer to oven, positioning skillet as close to center of oven as handle allows (turn handle so it points toward one of oven's front corners.) Turn on broiler and broil chicken for 25 minutes. Rotate skillet by moving handle to opposite front corner of oven and continue to broil until skin is dark golden brown and thickest part of breast registers 155 degrees, 20 to 30 minutes longer.

**4.** Transfer chicken to carving board and let rest, uncovered, for 15 minutes. While chicken rests, stir thyme sprigs and garlic into juices in pan and let stand for 10 minutes.

**5.** Using spoon, skim fat from surface of pan juices. Carve chicken and transfer any accumulated juices to pan. Strain sauce through fine-mesh strainer and season with salt and pepper to taste. Serve chicken, passing pan sauce and lemon wedges separately.

## Broiled Chicken with Gravy

**SERVES 4**

**WHY THIS RECIPE WORKS** Chicken with gravy is pure comfort food but we wanted to enjoy it on a weeknight, not only on Sundays. First we spatchcocked the chicken (so it would lie flat) and broiled it instead of roasting it. A preheated skillet plays a role here, too, because placing the bird breast side up allows the dark meat to get a head start on the cooking. Because the broiler's heat is more intense than that of the oven, carryover cooking has a bigger impact, so we pulled the chicken from the oven when the breast meat registered 155 degrees instead of 160 degrees. For a gravy that really tasted like the bird, we began by making a full-flavored chicken stock that included the backbone, giblets, and excess skin and fat from the chicken—powerhouses of chicken flavor. Combining the reduced stock with a roux of flour and butter yielded a rich, silky gravy. If your broiler has multiple settings, choose the highest one. The backbone and trimmings provide plenty of flavor for the gravy, but if your chicken comes with the giblets and neck, use them too. Feel free to substitute dry vermouth for the white wine. In step 2, if the skin is dark golden brown but the breast has not yet reached 155 degrees, cover the chicken with foil and continue to broil. Keep a close eye on the temperature of the chicken during the final 10 minutes of cooking, because it can quickly overcook. This recipe won't work with a drawer-style broiler. You will need a 12-inch ovensafe skillet for this recipe.

- 1 (4-pound) whole chicken, giblets and neck reserved
- 1½ teaspoons vegetable oil, divided
- 1½ teaspoons kosher salt, divided
- ½ teaspoon pepper
- 4 cups chicken broth, divided
- ½ onion, chopped fine
- 1 carrot, peeled and chopped fine
- 1 celery rib, chopped fine
- 4 sprigs fresh parsley
- 2 sprigs fresh thyme
- 1 garlic clove, crushed and peeled
- ¼ cup dry white wine
- 2 tablespoons unsalted butter
- 2½ tablespoons all-purpose flour

**1.** Adjust oven rack 12 to 13 inches from broiler element (do not heat broiler). Place chicken breast side down on cutting board. Using kitchen shears, cut through bones on either side of backbone. Cut backbone into 1-inch pieces and reserve. Trim excess fat and skin from chicken and reserve with backbone. Flip chicken and use heel of your hand to press on breastbone to flatten. Using tip of paring knife, poke holes through skin over entire surface of chicken, spacing them approximately ¾ inch apart.

**2.** Rub ½ teaspoon oil over skin and sprinkle with 1 teaspoon salt and pepper. Flip chicken and sprinkle bone side with remaining ½ teaspoon salt. Flip chicken skin side up, tie legs together with kitchen twine, and tuck wings under breasts. Heat remaining 1 teaspoon oil in broiler-safe 12-inch skillet over high heat until just smoking. Place chicken in skillet, skin side up, and transfer to oven, positioning skillet as close to center of oven as handle allows (turn handle so it points toward 1 of oven's front corners). Turn on broiler and broil chicken for 25 minutes. Rotate skillet by moving handle to opposite front corner of oven and continue to broil until skin is dark golden brown and thickest part of breast registers 155 degrees, 20 to 30 minutes longer.

**3.** While chicken broils, bring 1 cup broth and reserved giblets, neck, backbone, and trimmings to simmer in large saucepan over high heat. Cook, adjusting heat to maintain vigorous simmer and stirring occasionally, until all liquid evaporates and trimmings begin to sizzle, about 12 minutes. Continue to cook, stirring frequently, until dark fond forms on bottom of saucepan, 2 to 4 minutes longer. Reduce heat to medium. Add onion, carrot, celery, parsley sprigs, thyme sprigs, and garlic to saucepan and cook, stirring frequently, until onion is translucent, 7 to 8 minutes. Stir in wine and bring to simmer, scraping up any browned bits. Add remaining 3 cups broth and bring to simmer over high heat. Adjust heat to maintain simmer and continue to cook, stirring occasionally, until stock (liquid only) is reduced by half, about 20 minutes longer.

**4.** Strain stock through fine-mesh strainer set over bowl, pressing on solids to extract as much liquid as possible. Melt butter in now-empty saucepan over medium heat. Add flour and cook, stirring constantly, until mixture is deep golden brown, 5 to 8 minutes. Slowly whisk in stock. Increase heat to medium-high and bring to simmer. Simmer until thickened, about 5 minutes.

**5.** Transfer chicken to carving board and let rest, uncovered, for 15 minutes. While chicken rests, transfer fat and drippings in skillet to small bowl and let sit for 5 minutes. Spoon off fat and discard. Whisk drippings into gravy. Season gravy with salt and pepper to taste. Carve chicken and serve, passing gravy separately.

## SPATCHCOCKING A CHICKEN

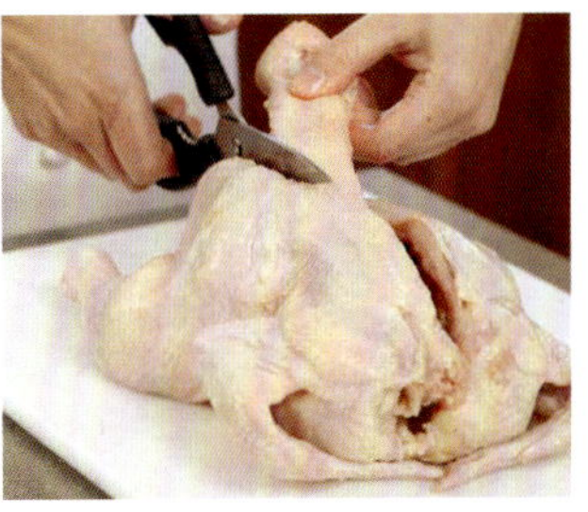

1. Using kitchen shears, cut through bones on either side of backbone and trim any excess fat or skin from chicken, reserving any trimmings.

2. Flip chicken and use heel of your hand to flatten breastbone.

# Classic Roast Lemon Chicken

**SERVES** 3 to 4

**WHY THIS RECIPE WORKS** The idea of a lemon roast chicken and a lemony pan sauce is ultra-appealing, but creating one that is really infused with bright lemon flavor takes a few techniques. The goal? Chicken that's evenly roasted and moist, with crispy skin, lemon flavor that's bright and pure, and no trace of bitterness. We brined the chicken for extra juiciness. Then we filled the chicken cavity with a cut-up lemon and garlic cloves. To further ensure a juicy bird, we found that the roasting technique was key. We started the chicken breast side down in a moderately hot oven, then flipped it breast side up, added some broth to prevent the drippings from burning, and raised the oven temperature for the remainder of the cooking time. Once the chicken was cooked, we cut it into four pieces and broiled the pieces to get an evenly crisped skin. For the truest lemon flavor, we added a squirt of fresh lemon juice to a simple pan sauce of chicken broth, butter, and fresh herbs. If using a kosher chicken, skip the brining process and begin with step 2. Broiling the roasted and quartered chicken skin side up at the end browns the skin while keeping the meat succulent. If you decide to skip the broiling step, go directly from quartering the chicken to finishing the sauce with lemon juice, butter, and herbs.

- ½ cup table salt
- 1 (3½- to 4-pound) whole chicken, giblets discarded
- 2 lemons
- 6 medium garlic cloves, crushed and peeled
- 4 tablespoons (½ stick) unsalted butter, 2 tablespoons melted and 2 tablespoons chilled and cut into 2 pieces
- Ground black pepper
- 1¾ cups low-sodium chicken broth
- 1 tablespoon minced fresh parsley leaves
- 1 teaspoon minced fresh thyme leaves

**1.** Dissolve the salt in 2 quarts cold water in a large container. Submerge the chicken in the brine, cover, and refrigerate for 1 hour. Remove the chicken from the brine, rinse well, and pat dry with paper towels.

**2.** Adjust an oven rack to the lower-middle position; heat the oven to 375 degrees. Spray a V-rack with vegetable oil spray and set in a roasting pan.

**3.** Cut 1 of the lemons lengthwise into quarters. Place the lemon quarters and garlic in the cavity of the chicken. Brush the breast side of the chicken with 1 tablespoon of the melted butter and season generously with pepper. Place the chicken, breast side down, in the V-rack, then brush the back with the remaining 1 tablespoon melted butter and season generously with pepper.

**4.** Roast the chicken for 40 minutes. Remove the roasting pan from the oven; increase the oven temperature to 450 degrees. Using two large wads of paper towels, rotate the chicken breast side up; add 1 cup of the chicken broth to the roasting pan. Return the roasting pan to the oven and continue roasting until the thickest part of the breasts registers 160 degrees and the thickest part of the thighs registers 175 degrees on an instant-read thermometer, 35 to 40 minutes longer. Remove the roasting pan from the oven; tip the V-rack to let the juices from the chicken cavity run into the roasting pan. Transfer the chicken to a carving board and let rest, uncovered, while making the sauce. Remove the V-rack from the roasting pan.

**5.** Adjust the oven rack to the upper-middle position and heat the broiler. Skim the fat from the drippings in the roasting pan, add the remaining ¾ cup chicken broth, and set the roasting pan on a burner over high heat. Simmer the liquid, scraping the pan bottom with a wooden spoon to loosen the browned bits, until reduced to ½ cup, about 4 minutes; set aside off the heat.

**6.** Discard the lemons and garlic from the chicken cavity. Cut the chicken into quarters. Pour the accumulated chicken juices into the roasting pan, then place the chicken quarters, skin side up, into the sauce in the roasting pan; broil the chicken until the skin is crisp and deep golden brown, 3 to 5 minutes. Transfer the chicken to a serving platter.

**7.** Halve the remaining lemon lengthwise; squeeze the juice of one half into the roasting pan; cut the remaining half into four wedges and set aside. Whisk the remaining 2 tablespoons butter into the sauce until combined; stir in the parsley and thyme. Season with salt and pepper to taste. Serve the chicken with the pan sauce and lemon wedges.

# Glazed Roast Chicken

**SERVES** 4 to 6

**WHY THIS RECIPE WORKS** Glazed chicken might sound simple but actually turns up a host of troubles, as the problems inherent in roasting chicken (dry breast meat, flabby skin) are compounded by the glaze (won't stick to the meat, burns in patches, introduces moisture). We started with a large roaster chicken. We separated the skin from the meat and pricked holes in the fat deposits to allow rendered fat to escape, then rubbed it with salt and baking powder—to dehydrate the skin and help it to crisp—and we roasted the chicken straddled on top of a beer can set in a roasting pan. But cutting into the chicken revealed that the breast, now exposed to the high oven heat for the entire cooking time, was dry and tough. To solve these problems, we covered the chicken with a salt mixture and put it uncovered in the refrigerator for 30 to 60 minutes; now the skin came out crisper than before and the breast meat was perfectly cooked. As for the glaze, we thickened it with cornstarch and reduced it to a syrupy consistency, then applied it before the final five minutes of roasting. For best results, use a 16-ounce can of beer. A larger can will work, but avoid using a 12-ounce can, as it will not support the weight of the chicken. Taste your marmalade, and if it is overly sweet, reduce the maple syrup in the glaze by 2 tablespoons. Trappist Seville Orange Marmalade is our preferred brand.

**CHICKEN**

- 1 (6- to 7-pound) whole chicken, giblets discarded
- 2½ teaspoons table salt
- 1 teaspoon baking powder
- 1 teaspoon ground black pepper
- 1 (16-ounce) can beer

**GLAZE**

- 1 tablespoon water
- 1 teaspoon cornstarch
- ½ cup maple syrup
- ½ cup orange marmalade
- ¼ cup cider vinegar
- 2 tablespoons unsalted butter
- 2 tablespoons Dijon mustard
- 1 teaspoon ground black pepper

**1. FOR THE CHICKEN:** Place the chicken, breast side down, on a work surface. Use the tip of a sharp knife to make four 1-inch incisions along the back of the chicken. Using your fingers or the handle of a wooden spoon, separate the skin from the thighs and breast, being careful not to break the skin. Using a metal skewer, poke 15 to 20 holes in the fat deposits on top of the breast halves and thighs. Tuck the wings behind the back.

**2.** Combine the salt, baking powder, and pepper in a small bowl. Pat the chicken dry with paper towels and sprinkle evenly all over with the salt mixture. Rub in the mixture with your hands, coating the entire surface evenly. Set the chicken, breast side up, on a rimmed baking sheet and refrigerate, uncovered, for 30 to 60 minutes. Meanwhile, adjust an oven rack to the lowest position and heat the oven to 325 degrees.

**3.** Open the beer can and pour out (or drink) about half of the liquid. Spray the can lightly with vegetable oil spray and place in the middle of a roasting pan. Slide the chicken over the can so the drumsticks reach down to the bottom of the can, the chicken stands upright, and the breast is perpendicular to the bottom of the pan. Roast until the skin starts to turn golden and the thickest part of the breasts registers 140 degrees on an instant-read thermometer, 75 to 90 minutes. Carefully remove the chicken and pan from the oven and increase the oven temperature to 500 degrees.

**4. FOR THE GLAZE:** While the chicken cooks, stir the water and cornstarch together in a small bowl until no lumps remain; set aside. Bring the remaining glaze ingredients to a simmer in a medium saucepan over medium-high heat. Cook, stirring occasionally, until reduced to ¾ cup, 6 to 8 minutes. Slowly whisk the cornstarch mixture into the glaze. Return to a simmer and cook for 1 minute. Remove the pan from the heat.

**5.** When the oven is heated to 500 degrees, place 1½ cups water in the bottom of the roasting pan and return to the oven. Roast until the entire chicken skin is browned and crisp, the thickest part of the breasts registers 160 degrees, and the thickest part of the thighs registers 175 degrees on an instant-read thermometer, 24 to 30 minutes. Check the chicken halfway through roasting; if the top is becoming too dark, place a 7-inch square piece of foil over the neck and wingtips of the chicken and continue to roast (if the pan begins to smoke and sizzle, add ½ cup water to the roasting pan).

**6.** Brush the chicken with ¼ cup of the glaze and continue to roast until browned and sticky, about 5 minutes. (If the glaze has become stiff, return to low heat to soften.) Carefully remove the chicken from the oven, transfer the chicken, still on the can, to a carving board, and brush with ¼ cup more glaze. Let rest for 20 minutes.

**7.** While the chicken rests, strain the juices from the pan through a fine-mesh strainer into a fat separator; allow the liquid to settle for 5 minutes. Whisk ½ cup juices into the remaining ¼ cup glaze in a saucepan and set over low heat. Using a dish towel, carefully lift the chicken off the can and onto a platter or carving board. Carve the chicken, adding any accumulated juices to the sauce. Serve, passing the sauce separately.

## Peruvian Roast Chicken with Garlic and Lime

**SERVES** 3 to 4

---

**WHY THIS RECIPE WORKS** This robustly flavored roast chicken is inspired by Peruvian pollo a la brasa, which traditionally cooks on a spit in a wood-fired oven. It is seasoned with garlic, spices, lime, chiles, and huacatay, or black mint. We wanted to replicate the chicken using a standard oven. Rubbing a flavorful paste underneath and on top of the skin produced well-seasoned meat and a heady flavor. To this basic paste we added fresh mint (replacing the black mint paste called for in traditional recipes), oregano, pepper, and minced habanero chile for tangy spice, while a little smoked paprika subtly mimicked the smokiness we were missing from the rotisserie. Roasting the chicken vertically allowed it to cook evenly, while using two different oven temperatures helped us achieve both moist meat and well-browned skin. If habanero chiles are unavailable, 1 tablespoon of minced serrano chile can be substituted. Wear gloves when working with hot chiles. This recipe calls for a vertical poultry roaster. If you don't have one, substitute a 12-ounce can of beer. Open the can and pour out (or drink) about half of the beer. Spray the can lightly with vegetable oil spray and proceed with the recipe. Serve with Spicy Mayonnaise and lime wedges.

- ¼ cup fresh mint leaves
- 3 tablespoons extra-virgin olive oil
- 6 garlic cloves, chopped coarse
- 1 tablespoon table salt
- 1 tablespoon pepper
- 1 tablespoon ground cumin
- 1 tablespoon sugar
- 2 teaspoons smoked paprika
- 2 teaspoons dried oregano
- 2 teaspoons finely grated lime zest plus ¼ cup juice (2 limes)
- 1 teaspoon minced habanero chile
- 1 (3½- to 4-pound) whole chicken, giblets discarded
- 1 cup Spicy Mayonnaise

**1.** Process mint, oil, garlic, salt, pepper, cumin, sugar, paprika, oregano, lime zest and juice, and habanero in blender until smooth paste forms, 10 to 20 seconds. Use your fingers to gently loosen skin covering breast and thighs; place half of paste under skin, directly on meat of breast and thighs. Gently press on skin to distribute paste over meat. Spread entire exterior surface of chicken with remaining paste. Tuck wings behind back. Place chicken in 1-gallon zipper-lock bag and refrigerate for at least 6 hours or up to 24 hours.

**2.** Adjust oven rack to lowest position and heat oven to 325 degrees. Place vertical roaster on rimmed baking sheet. Slide chicken onto vertical roaster so drumsticks reach down to bottom of roaster, chicken stands upright, and breast is perpendicular to bottom of pan. Roast chicken until skin just begins to turn golden and thickest part of breast registers 140 degrees, 45 to 55 minutes. Carefully remove chicken and pan from oven and increase oven temperature to 500 degrees.

**3.** Once oven has reached 500 degrees, place 1 cup water in bottom of baking sheet and continue to roast until entire chicken skin is browned and crisp, breast registers 160 degrees, and thighs register 175 degrees, about 20 minutes, rotating pan halfway through roasting. Check chicken halfway through roasting; if top is becoming too dark, place 7-inch square piece of aluminum foil over neck and wingtips of chicken and continue to roast (if pan begins to smoke and sizzle, add additional water to pan).

**4.** Carefully remove chicken from oven and let rest, still on vertical roaster, for 20 minutes. Using 2 large wads of paper towels, carefully lift chicken off vertical roaster and onto carving board. Carve chicken and serve, passing spicy mayonnaise separately.

## Spicy Mayonnaise

**MAKES** 1 cup

If you have concerns about consuming raw eggs, ¼ cup of an egg substitute can be used in place of the egg.

- 1 large egg
- 2 tablespoons water
- 1 tablespoon minced onion
- 1 tablespoon lime juice
- 1 tablespoon minced fresh cilantro
- 1 tablespoon minced jarred jalapeño chiles
- 1 garlic clove, minced
- 1 teaspoon yellow mustard
- ¼ teaspoon table salt
- 1 cup vegetable oil

Process egg, water, onion, lime juice, cilantro, jalapeños, garlic, mustard, and salt in food processor until combined, about 5 seconds. With machine running, slowly drizzle in oil in steady stream until mayonnaise-like consistency is reached, scraping down bowl as needed.

### FLAVORING ROAST CHICKEN

**1.** Use your fingers to gently loosen chicken skin from over thighs and breast and rub half of paste directly over meat.

**2.** Spread remaining paste over skin of entire chicken.

**3.** Place chicken in gallon-size zipper-lock bag; refrigerate for at least 6 or up to 24 hours.

## Roast Chicken with Couscous, Roasted Red Peppers, and Basil

**SERVES 4**

**WHY THIS RECIPE WORKS** For a golden-brown, juicy, and tender roast chicken, we trimmed off excess skin and fat from the cavity and cut small slits in the skin above and below the thigh. Then we brushed the skin with melted butter instead of oil to facilitate browning. Roasting the chicken breast side up in a preheated skillet set in a 400-degree oven helped the legs finish cooking at the same time as the breast. We removed the chicken when the breast registered 150 to 155 degrees and let it rest for 15 minutes so that it could gently rise to the serving temperature of 160 degrees. While the bird rested, we used the umami-rich jus as a base for cooking an ultraflavorful side dish of couscous with roasted red peppers. This recipe was developed with Diamond Crystal Kosher Salt; if using Morton Kosher Salt, which is denser, decrease the amount for the chicken to 1¾ teaspoons and the amount for the couscous to ¼ teaspoon.

- 1 tablespoon kosher salt, divided
- ½ teaspoon pepper
- 1 (4-pound) whole chicken, giblets discarded
- 1 tablespoon unsalted butter, melted
- ½ teaspoon vegetable oil
- 4 garlic cloves, sliced thin
- ¾ cup couscous
- ¾ cup water
- 5 teaspoons red wine vinegar
- ¾ cup jarred roasted red peppers, chopped fine
- 2 tablespoons chopped fresh basil

**1.** Adjust oven rack to middle position and heat oven to 400 degrees. Stir 2½ teaspoons salt and pepper together in small bowl. Place chicken breast side up on cutting board. Using kitchen shears, thoroughly trim excess fat and skin from cavity. Lift 1 drumstick and use paring knife to cut ½-inch slit in skin where drumstick and thigh meet. Turn chicken on side so breast faces edge of counter. Cut ½-inch slit in skin where top of thigh meets breast. Repeat both cuts on opposite side of chicken. Tuck wingtips behind back. Sprinkle about one-third of salt mixture into cavity. Brush top and sides of chicken with melted butter. Sprinkle remaining salt mixture evenly over all sides of chicken.

**2.** Heat oil in 12-inch skillet over medium-high heat until shimmering. Place chicken breast side up in skillet; transfer to oven; and roast until thickest part of breast registers 150 to 155 degrees, 1 hour to 1 hour 10 minutes, rotating skillet halfway through roasting. Transfer chicken to carving board and let rest for 15 minutes (chicken temperature will continue to rise as it rests).

**3.** Meanwhile, pour pan juices into fat separator. Add 2 teaspoons fat to now-empty skillet. Add garlic and cook over medium-low heat, stirring occasionally, until garlic is pale golden brown, about 3 minutes. Add couscous and stir until well combined. Stir in ¼ cup defatted pan juices, water, vinegar, and remaining ½ teaspoon salt and bring to simmer. Spread red peppers in even layer over couscous; turn off heat; cover; and let sit until couscous is just tender and all liquid is absorbed, about 10 minutes.

**4.** Carve chicken and transfer to platter. Fluff couscous, stir in basil, season with salt to taste, and transfer to bowl. Serve chicken with couscous.

## Roast Chicken with Warm Bread Salad

**SERVES 4 to 6**

**WHY THIS RECIPE WORKS** When renowned chef Judy Rogers of Zuni Cafe put her roast chicken with warm bread salad on the menu in the late '80s, it was a real hit. Now, some 30 years later, it still is. We wanted our own take on Zuni Café's roast chicken with bread salad, so we started by butterflying a whole chicken and salting it overnight; this would allow it to cook quickly and evenly and be juicy and well seasoned. Before roasting the chicken, we covered the bottom of a skillet with bread cubes that we had moistened with oil and broth and then draped the chicken on top. The bread cubes toasted and browned beneath the bird while absorbing its juices. To finish, we built a bright vinaigrette that we tossed with peppery arugula and the toasted bread. To ensure the greens didn't wilt, we served the salad alongside the carved chicken. This recipe was developed and tested using Diamond Crystal Kosher Salt. If you have Morton Kosher Salt, which is denser than Diamond Crystal, put only ½ teaspoon of salt onto the cavity. Red wine or white wine vinegar may be substituted for champagne vinegar, if desired. For the bread, we prefer a round rustic loaf with a chewy, open crumb and a sturdy outer crust.

- 1 (4-pound) whole chicken, giblets discarded
- Kosher salt and pepper
- 4 (1-inch-thick) slices country-style bread (8 ounces), bottom crust removed, cut into ¾- to 1-inch pieces (5 cups)
- ¼ cup chicken broth
- 6 tablespoons plus 2 teaspoons extra-virgin olive oil, divided
- 2 tablespoons champagne vinegar
- 1 teaspoon Dijon mustard
- 3 scallions, sliced thin
- 2 tablespoons dried currants
- 5 ounces (5 cups) baby arugula

**1.** Place chicken, breast side down, on cutting board. Using kitchen shears, cut through bones on either side of backbone; discard backbone. Do not trim off any excess fat or skin. Flip chicken over and press on breastbone to flatten.

**2.** Using your fingers, carefully loosen skin covering breast and legs. Rub ½ teaspoon salt under skin of each breast, ½ teaspoon under skin of each leg, and 1 teaspoon salt onto bird's cavity. Tuck wings behind back and turn legs so drumsticks face inward toward breasts. Place chicken on wire rack set in rimmed baking sheet or on large plate and refrigerate, uncovered, for 24 hours.

**3.** Adjust oven rack to middle position and heat oven to 475 degrees. Spray 12-inch skillet with vegetable oil spray. Toss bread with broth and 2 tablespoons oil until pieces are evenly moistened. Arrange bread in skillet in single layer, with majority of crusted pieces near center, crust side up.

**4.** Pat chicken dry with paper towels and place, skin side up, on top of bread. Brush 2 teaspoons oil over chicken skin and sprinkle with ¼ teaspoon salt and ¼ teaspoon pepper. Roast chicken until skin is deep golden brown and thickest part of breast registers 160 degrees and thighs register 175 degrees, 45 to 50 minutes, rotating skillet halfway through roasting.

**5.** While chicken roasts, whisk vinegar, mustard, ¼ teaspoon salt, and ¼ teaspoon pepper together in small bowl. Slowly whisk in remaining ¼ cup oil. Stir in scallions and currants and set aside. Place arugula in large bowl.

**6.** Transfer chicken to carving board and let rest, uncovered, for 15 minutes. Run thin metal spatula under bread to loosen from bottom of skillet. (Bread should be mix of softened, golden-brown, and crunchy pieces.) Carve chicken and whisk any accumulated juices into vinaigrette. Add bread and vinaigrette to arugula and toss to evenly coat. Transfer salad to serving platter and serve with chicken.

## Chicken Under a Brick with Herb-Roasted Potatoes

SERVES 4

**WHY THIS RECIPE WORKS** Cooking a butterflied chicken under a brick in a skillet is a cool culinary trick but not all that practical for home cooks. So we turned to weighting the chicken (which was in a nonstick skillet) by placing a cast-iron skillet with heavy cans on top, which forced all of the skin to make contact with the pan. When pounded to an even thickness, a superflat chicken cooked evenly, and more of the skin made contact with the pan, thus turning crisp. We cooked the chicken, skin side down, underneath the weighted skillet until it had a beautiful color. We then removed the cans and the cast-iron skillet, flipped the chicken, and finished it—still in the skillet—in a 450-degree oven. The hot, dry air of the oven ensured that the skin remained crisp and intact as the meat finished cooking. To include a flavorful side dish of roasted potatoes, we added the potatoes to the pan underneath the browned and seasoned oil–brushed chicken before it went into the oven. While the chicken was resting, the potatoes went back into the oven to finish cooking and take on gorgeous color. Instead of a heavy cast-iron skillet loaded with several cans, you can use a large stockpot partially filled with water to weight the chicken. Note that chickens much larger than 3 pounds will be difficult to fit into a 12-inch skillet.

- 1 (3-pound) whole chicken, giblets discarded
- 1¼ teaspoons table salt, divided
- ¾ teaspoon plus ⅛ teaspoon pepper, divided
- 1 teaspoon plus 2 tablespoons vegetable oil, divided
- 2 tablespoons lemon juice, plus 1 lemon, cut into wedges
- 3 garlic cloves, minced

- 1 tablespoon minced fresh thyme, divided
- ⅛ teaspoon red pepper flakes
- 1½ pounds Red Bliss potatoes (small), scrubbed, dried, and cut into ¾ inch pieces
- 1 tablespoon minced fresh parsley

**1.** Place chicken, breast side down, on cutting board. Using kitchen shears, cut through bones on either side of backbone; discard backbone. Turn chicken breast side up and use palm of your hand to flatten chicken, then pound chicken flat to fairly even thickness. Sprinkle chicken with ½ teaspoon salt and ½ teaspoon pepper.

**2.** Adjust oven rack to lowest position and heat oven to 450 degrees. Heat 1 teaspoon oil in 12-inch ovensafe nonstick skillet over medium-high heat until just smoking. Swirl skillet to coat evenly with oil. Place chicken, skin side down, in pan and reduce heat to medium. Place weighted skillet or pot on chicken and cook, checking every 5 minutes or so, until evenly browned, about 25 minutes. (After 20 minutes, chicken should be fairly crisp and golden; if not, turn heat up to medium-high and continue to cook until well browned.)

**3.** Meanwhile, mix lemon juice, garlic, 1½ teaspoons thyme, pepper flakes, ½ teaspoon salt, ¼ teaspoon pepper, and remaining 2 tablespoons oil in small bowl and set aside.

**4.** Using tongs, carefully transfer chicken, skin side up, to clean plate. Pour off any accumulated fat in pan and add potatoes, sprinkling them with remaining ¼ teaspoon salt, remaining ⅛ teaspoon pepper, and remaining 1½ teaspoons thyme. Place chicken, skin side up, on potatoes and brush skin with reserved thyme–lemon juice mixture.

**5.** Transfer pan to oven and roast until thickest part of breast registers 160 degrees, about 10 minutes longer. Transfer chicken to cutting board and let rest for 10 minutes.

**6.** Return skillet with potatoes to oven and roast until browned and cooked through, about 10 minutes. Using slotted spoon, transfer potatoes to large bowl, leaving fat behind. Toss potatoes with parsley. Cut chicken into pieces. Serve chicken and potatoes immediately with lemon wedges.

## French Chicken in a Pot

**SERVES 4**

**WHY THIS RECIPE WORKS** Poulet en cocotte (chicken in a pot) is a classic French specialty—a whole chicken baked with root vegetables in a covered pot that delivers incredibly tender and juicy meat. One potential problem is too much moisture in the pot, which washes out the flavor; another pitfall is overcooking. We removed the vegetables—the liquid they released made the pot too steamy—and cooked the chicken by itself. We also tightly sealed the pot with foil before adding the lid. To keep the breast meat from drying out and becoming tough, we cooked the chicken very slowly in a low oven. We decided to revisit adding vegetables, and found that a small amount of potently flavored aromatic vegetables could be added if they were lightly browned with the chicken to erase most of their moisture. The cooking times in the recipe are for a 4½- to 5-pound bird. A 3½- to 4½-pound chicken will take about an hour to cook, and a 5- to 6-pound bird will take close to 2 hours. We developed this recipe to work with a 5- to 8-quart Dutch oven with a tight-fitting lid. If using a 5-quart pot, do not cook a chicken larger than 5 pounds. If using a kosher chicken, reduce the amount of table salt to ½ teaspoon. The amount of sauce will vary depending on the size of the chicken; season it with about ¼ teaspoon lemon juice for every ¼ cup. If desired, remove the skin before carving.

- 1 (4½- to 5-pound) whole chicken, giblets discarded, wings tucked under back
- 1 teaspoon table salt
- ¼ teaspoon pepper
- 1 tablespoon extra-virgin olive oil
- 1 small onion, chopped
- 1 small celery rib, chopped
- 6 garlic cloves, peeled and trimmed
- 1 bay leaf
- 1 sprig fresh rosemary (optional)
- ½–1 teaspoon lemon juice

**1.** Adjust oven rack to lowest position and heat oven to 250 degrees. Pat chicken dry with paper towels and sprinkle with salt and pepper.

**2.** Heat oil in large Dutch oven over medium heat until just smoking. Add chicken, breast side down, and scatter onion, celery, garlic cloves, bay leaf, and rosemary (if using) around chicken. Cook until breast is lightly browned, about 5 minutes. Flip chicken breast side up and continue to cook until chicken and vegetables are well browned, 6 to 8 minutes.

**3.** Off heat, place large sheet of aluminum foil over pot and cover tightly with lid. Transfer pot to oven and cook until thickest part of breast registers 160 degrees and thickest part of the thighs registers 175 degrees, 1 hour and 20 minutes to 1 hour and 50 minutes.

**4.** Remove pot from oven. Transfer chicken to carving board, tent with foil, and let rest for 20 minutes. Strain chicken juices from pot into fat separator, pressing on solids to extract liquid; discard solids (you should have about ¾ cup juices). Let liquid settle for 5 minutes, then pour into saucepan and cook over low heat until hot. Carve chicken, adding any accumulated juices to saucepan. Season sauce with lemon juice to taste. Serve chicken, passing sauce separately.

## French-Style Chicken and Stuffing in a Pot

**SERVES 4 to 6**

**WHY THIS RECIPE WORKS** The French classic poule au pot is a rather unique take on stuffed chicken: Instead of being roasted, the stuffed bird is braised with vegetables in a Dutch oven to make a satisfying and hearty one-pot meal. Our first efforts were less than promising. One issue was getting the pork and bread stuffing to cook through before the chicken was overdone; instead of stuffing the bird we patted the stuffing into logs, wrapped them in parchment paper, and nestled them into the pot. We also needed make more room for the chicken and vegetables, so we turned to chicken parts and browned them first to give the broth rich flavor. We layered them on top of the vegetables with broth to cover them so that the breast meat could cook gently above the simmering liquid. A neutral bulk sausage is best here. You'll need a Dutch oven with at least a 7¼-quart capacity. Use red potatoes, measuring 1 to 2 inches in diameter. Serve with crusty bread, cornichons, and Dijon mustard or Herb Sauce.

**SAUSAGE STUFFING**

- 2 slices hearty white sandwich bread, crusts removed, torn into quarters
- 1 large egg
- 1 shallot, minced
- 2 garlic cloves, minced
- 2 tablespoons minced fresh parsley
- 2 tablespoons minced fennel fronds
- 2 teaspoons whole-grain mustard
- 1 teaspoon minced fresh marjoram
- ¼ teaspoon pepper
- 1 pound bulk pork sausage

**CHICKEN**

- 2 celery ribs, halved crosswise
- 8 sprigs plus 1 tablespoon minced fresh parsley
- 6 sprigs fresh marjoram
- 1 bay leaf
- 2 teaspoons vegetable oil
- 2 (12-ounce) bone-in split chicken breasts, trimmed
- 2 (12-ounce) bone-in chicken leg quarters, trimmed
- Table salt and pepper
- 1½ pounds small red potatoes, unpeeled
- 2 carrots, peeled and cut into ½-inch lengths
- 1 fennel bulb, stalks trimmed, bulb quartered
- 8 whole peppercorns
- 2 garlic cloves, peeled
- 3–3½ cups low-sodium chicken broth

**1. FOR THE SAUSAGE STUFFING:** Adjust oven rack to middle position and heat oven to 300 degrees. Pulse bread in food processor until finely ground, 10 to 15 pulses. Add egg, shallot, garlic, parsley, fennel fronds, mustard, marjoram, and pepper to processor and pulse to combine, 6 to 8 pulses, scraping down sides of bowl as needed. Add sausage and pulse to combine, 3 to 5 pulses, scraping down sides of bowl as needed.

**2.** Place 18 by 12-inch piece of parchment paper on counter, with longer edge parallel to edge of counter. Place half of stuffing onto lower third of parchment, shaping it into rough 8 by 2-inch rectangle. Roll up sausage in parchment; gently but firmly twist both ends to compact mixture into 6- to 7-inch-long cylinder, approximately 2 inches in diameter. Repeat with second piece of parchment and remaining stuffing.

**3. FOR THE CHICKEN:** Using kitchen twine, tie together celery, parsley sprigs, marjoram, and bay leaf. Heat oil in large Dutch oven over medium-high heat until just smoking. Pat chicken breasts and leg quarters dry with paper towels, sprinkle with ½ teaspoon salt, and season with pepper. Add chicken, skin side down, and cook without moving it until browned, 4 to 7 minutes. Transfer chicken to large plate. Pour off and discard any fat in pot.

**4.** Remove Dutch oven from heat and carefully arrange celery bundle, potatoes, carrots, and fennel in even layer over bottom of pot. Sprinkle peppercorns, garlic, and ¼ teaspoon salt over vegetables. Add enough broth so that top ½ inch of vegetables is above surface of liquid. Place leg quarters on top of vegetables in center of pot. Place stuffing cylinders on either side of leg quarters. Arrange breasts on top of leg quarters. Place pot over high heat and bring to simmer. Cover, transfer to oven, and cook until breasts register 160 degrees, 60 to 75 minutes.

**5.** Transfer chicken and stuffing cylinders to carving board. Using slotted spoon, transfer vegetables to serving platter, discarding celery bundle. Pour broth through fine-mesh strainer into fat separator; discard solids. Let stand for 5 minutes.

**6.** Unwrap stuffing cylinders and slice into ½-inch-thick disks; transfer slices to platter with vegetables. Remove skin from chicken pieces and discard. Carve breasts from bone and slice into ½-inch-thick pieces. Separate thigh from leg by cutting through joint. Transfer chicken to platter with stuffing and vegetables. Pour ½ cup defatted broth over chicken and stuffing to moisten. Sprinkle with minced parsley. Serve, ladling remaining broth over individual servings.

### Herb Sauce

**MAKES** about ½ cup

- ⅓ cup extra-virgin olive oil
- 6 cornichons, minced
- 2 tablespoons minced fresh parsley
- 1 tablespoon minced fennel fronds
- 2 teaspoons minced shallot
- 2 teaspoons whole-grain mustard
- 1 teaspoon minced fresh marjoram
- ½ teaspoon finely grated lemon zest plus 2 tablespoons juice
- ¼ teaspoon pepper

Whisk all ingredients together in bowl. Let stand for 15 minutes before serving.

## Multicooker Chicken in a Pot with Lemon-Herb Sauce

**SERVES** 4

**WHY THIS RECIPE WORKS** Cooking a whole chicken in a moist, covered environment isn't a new concept. In fact, the classic French method of cooking en cocotte relies on this principle to create unbelievably tender, moist meat and a savory sauce enhanced with the chicken's own concentrated juices. We knew this would be a perfect use for the multicooker, and started with a 4-pound chicken, which fit nicely into the narrow pot. Since we wanted to focus on achieving succulent meat and not on getting crisp skin, we didn't bother with the time-consuming step of browning the chicken; sautéing some onion and garlic in the pot gave the chicken and the jus layers of deep flavor. Both pressure and slow cooking produced a chicken with perfectly cooked light and dark meat. A couple of tablespoons of flour, added at the start, ensured that our jus was transformed into a velvety smooth sauce after cooking. Butter, lemon juice, and fresh herbs gave our sauce a final boost of rich, bright flavor. If using the slow cook function, begin checking the chicken's temperature after 3 hours and continue to monitor until it is done.

- 1 tablespoon vegetable oil
- 1 onion, chopped fine
- 2 tablespoons all-purpose flour
- 3 garlic cloves, minced
- 2 teaspoons minced fresh rosemary
- ½ cup dry white wine
- 1 cup chicken broth
- 1 (4-pound) whole chicken, giblets discarded
- Table salt and pepper
- 2 tablespoons unsalted butter, cut into 2 pieces and chilled
- 2 tablespoons lemon juice
- ¼ cup minced fresh chives, parsley, or tarragon

**1.** Using highest sauté or browning function, heat oil in multicooker until shimmering. Add onion and cook until softened, 3 to 5 minutes. Stir in flour, garlic, and rosemary and cook until fragrant, about 1 minute. Slowly whisk in wine, scraping up any browned bits and smoothing out any lumps, then stir in broth. Season chicken with salt and pepper and place breast side up into multicooker.

**2A. TO PRESSURE COOK:** Lock lid in place and close pressure release valve. Select high pressure cook function and cook for 30 minutes. Turn off multicooker and quick-release pressure. Carefully remove lid, allowing steam to escape away from you.

**2B. TO SLOW COOK:** Lock lid in place and open pressure release valve. Select low slow cook function and cook until breast registers 160 degrees and thighs register 175 degrees, 3 to 4 hours. (If using Instant Pot, select high slow cook function.) Turn off multicooker and carefully remove lid, allowing steam to escape away from you.

**3.** Transfer chicken to carving board, tent with aluminum foil, and let rest for 5 to 10 minutes. Let cooking liquid settle, then skim excess fat from surface using large spoon. Whisk in butter, lemon juice, and chives. Carve chicken, discarding chicken skin, if desired. Serve with sauce.

## Best Roast Chicken with Root Vegetables

**SERVES** 4 to 6

**WHY THIS RECIPE WORKS** Our roast chicken and root vegetables recipe ensures perfect versions of both components by cooking them separately. We brined the chicken to ensure that it stayed juicy and then placed it in a preheated skillet in a hot oven. The dark meat, which needed to be cooked to a higher temperature than the white meat, stayed in contact with the pan, ensuring that it finished cooking at the same time as the more delicate breast meat. We cooked the vegetables below the chicken on a baking sheet until they were tender. Once the chicken was done, we turned the oven up to 500 degrees and finished roasting the vegetables, using the drippings left behind in the skillet to infuse them with flavor. A variety of vegetables works well as long as they are cut to the same size. This recipe requires brining the chicken for 1 hour before cooking. If using a kosher chicken, do not brine in step 1, but season with ½ teaspoon salt in step 3.

- 1 (3½- to 4-pound) whole chicken, giblets discarded
- Table salt and pepper
- ½ cup sugar
- 1½ pounds Yukon Gold potatoes, peeled and cut into 2-inch pieces
- 12 ounces carrots, peeled, halved crosswise, thick ends halved lengthwise
- 12 ounces parsnips, peeled, halved crosswise, thick ends halved lengthwise
- 4 teaspoons extra-virgin olive oil
- ¼ cup water
- 1 teaspoon minced fresh thyme
- 1 tablespoon chopped fresh parsley

**1.** With chicken breast side down, use tip of sharp knife to make four 1-inch incisions along back. Using your fingers, gently loosen skin covering breast and thighs. Use metal skewer to poke 15 to 20 holes in fat deposits on top of breast halves and thighs. Dissolve ½ cup salt and sugar in 2 quarts cold water in large container. Submerge chicken in brine, cover, and refrigerate for 1 hour.

**2.** Adjust oven racks to upper-middle and lower-middle positions and heat oven to 450 degrees. Place 12-inch ovensafe skillet on upper rack and heat for 15 minutes. Spray rimmed baking sheet with vegetable oil spray. Arrange potatoes, carrots, and parsnips with cut surfaces down in single layer on baking sheet and cover sheet tightly with aluminum foil.

**3.** Remove chicken from brine and pat dry with paper towels. Combine 1 tablespoon oil and ½ teaspoon pepper in small bowl. Rub entire surface of chicken with oil-pepper mixture. Tie legs together with twine and tuck wingtips behind back.

**4.** Carefully remove skillet from oven (handle will be hot). Add remaining 1 teaspoon oil to skillet and swirl to coat. Place chicken breast side up in skillet. Return skillet to upper rack and place sheet of vegetables on lower rack. Cook for 30 minutes.

**5.** Remove vegetables from oven, remove foil, and set aside. Rotate skillet and continue to cook chicken until breast registers 160 degrees and thighs register 175 degrees, 15 to 25 minutes longer.

**6.** Transfer chicken to carving board and let rest, uncovered, for 20 minutes. Increase oven temperature to 500 degrees. Add water to skillet. Using whisk, stir until brown bits have dissolved. Strain sauce through fine-mesh strainer into fat separator, pressing on solids to remove any remaining liquid. Let liquid settle for 5 minutes. Pour off liquid from fat separator and reserve. Reserve 3 tablespoons fat, discarding remaining fat.

**7.** Drizzle vegetables with reserved fat. Sprinkle vegetables with thyme, 1 teaspoon salt, and ½ teaspoon pepper and toss to coat. Place sheet on upper rack and roast for 5 minutes. Remove sheet from oven. Using thin, sharp metal spatula, turn vegetables. Continue to roast until browned at edges, 8 to 10 minutes longer.

**8.** Pour reserved liquid over vegetables. Continue to roast until liquid is thick and syrupy and vegetables are tender, 3 to 5 minutes. Toss vegetables to coat, then transfer to serving platter and sprinkle with parsley. Carve chicken and transfer to platter with vegetables. Serve.

## Crisp Roast Butterflied Chicken with Rosemary and Garlic

**SERVES** 4

**WHY THIS RECIPE WORKS** One of the perks of a butterflied chicken is that it takes far less time to cook than a whole bird. Additionally, flattening the chicken encourages crisp skin, since most of the skin is in contact with the hot pan. However, during our testing we found that after initially crisping up, the skin turned soggy as the chicken continued to cook skin side down in its own juices. We set out to produce perfectly cooked chicken with crisp skin that could be on the table in about an

hour. We started by heating a cast-iron skillet in a very hot oven. We then put the chicken into the preheated skillet skin side down and cooked it until the skin was golden brown. Flipping the chicken over for the remainder of the cooking time allowed us to take advantage of the hot, dry air of the oven to ensure that the skin remained crisp and intact. A simple mixture of extra-virgin olive oil, rosemary, and garlic brushed on the chicken during roasting added flavor and crisped the skin further. The chicken may slightly overhang the skillet at first, but once browned it will shrink to fit; do not use a chicken larger than 4 pounds. Serve with lemon wedges.

- 2 tablespoons extra-virgin olive oil, divided
- 1 teaspoon minced fresh rosemary
- 1 garlic clove, minced
- 1 (3½- to 4-pound) whole chicken, giblets discarded
- ½ teaspoon table salt
- ½ teaspoon pepper

**1.** Adjust oven rack to lowest position, place 12-inch cast-iron skillet on rack, and heat oven to 500 degrees. Meanwhile, combine 1 tablespoon oil, rosemary, and garlic in bowl; set aside.

**2.** With chicken breast side down, use kitchen shears to cut through bones on either side of backbone; discard backbone. Flip chicken over, tuck wingtips behind back, and press firmly on breastbone to flatten. Pat chicken dry with paper towels, then rub with remaining 1 tablespoon oil and sprinkle with salt and pepper.

**3.** When oven reaches 500 degrees, place chicken breast side down in hot skillet. Reduce oven temperature to 450 degrees and roast chicken until well browned, about 30 minutes.

**4.** Using pot holders, remove skillet from oven. Being careful of hot skillet handle, gently flip chicken breast side up. Brush chicken with oil mixture, return skillet to oven, and continue to roast chicken until breast registers 160 degrees and thighs register 175 degrees, about 10 minutes. Transfer chicken to carving board, tent with aluminum foil, and let rest for 15 minutes. Carve chicken and serve.

## High-Roast Butterflied Chicken with Potatoes

**SERVES** 2 to 3

**WHY THIS RECIPE WORKS** "High roasting"—cooking a bird at temperatures in excess of 450 degrees—is supposed to produce tastier chicken with crisper skin in record time. But recipes we've tried overcook the bird while producing enough smoke to be mistaken for a five-alarm fire. We wanted to improve upon this method and while we were at it, we wanted roasted potatoes too. We first brined the chicken and then butterflied it, which allowed for even and faster roasting. To add moisture and flavor to the chicken we rubbed flavored herb butter under the skin. We cooked the chicken on top of a broiler pan with a bottom attached. In the bottom of the pan under the chicken, we placed a layer of potatoes. To ensure that the potatoes cooked through, we sliced them very thin. In just one hour we had roast chicken with spectacularly crisp skin and moist meat—and potatoes too. If using a kosher bird, skip the brining process and begin with step 2. Because you'll be cooking the chicken under high heat you must rinse it thoroughly after brining or the sugar remaining on the skin will caramelize and burn. Russet potatoes offer the best flavor, but Yukon Golds retain their shape better after cooking. Either works well in this recipe.

**CHICKEN AND BRINE**

- ½ cup table salt
- ½ cup sugar
- 1 (3½- to 4-pound) whole chicken, giblets discarded
- 1 recipe Mustard-Garlic Butter with Thyme (recipe follows)
- 1 tablespoon olive oil
- Ground black pepper

**POTATOES**

- 2½ pounds russet or Yukon Gold potatoes (4 to 5 medium), peeled and sliced ⅛ to ¼ inch thick
- 1 tablespoon olive oil
- ½ teaspoon table salt
- ⅛ teaspoon ground black pepper

**1. FOR THE CHICKEN AND BRINE:** Dissolve the salt and sugar in 2 quarts cold water in a large container. Submerge the chicken in the brine, cover, and refrigerate for 1 hour.

**2.** Adjust an oven rack to the lower-middle position and heat the oven to 500 degrees. Line a broiler-pan bottom with foil. Remove the chicken from the brine, rinse well, and pat dry with paper towels. Remove the backbone from the chicken, pound the chicken to a fairly even thickness, and tuck the wings behind the back.

**3.** Use your fingers to gently loosen the center portion of skin covering each side of the breast. Place the butter mixture under the skin, directly on the meat in the center of each side. Gently press on the skin to distribute the butter over the meat. Rub the skin with the oil and season with pepper. Place the chicken on the broiler-pan top and push each leg up to rest between the thigh and breast.

**4. FOR THE POTATOES:** Toss the potatoes with the oil, salt, and pepper. Spread the potatoes in an even layer in the prepared broiler-pan bottom. Place the broiler-pan top with the chicken on top.

**5.** Roast the chicken until just beginning to brown, about 20 minutes. Rotate the pan and continue to roast until the skin is crisped and deep brown and the thickest part of the breasts registers 160 to 165 degrees and the thickest part of the thighs registers 175 degrees on an instant-read thermometer, 20 to 25 minutes longer. Transfer the chicken to a carving board and let rest for 10 minutes.

**6.** While the chicken rests, remove the broiler-pan top and, using paper towels, soak up any excess grease from the potatoes. Transfer the potatoes to a serving platter. Carve the chicken, transfer to the platter with the potatoes, and serve.

### Mustard-Garlic Butter with Thyme

**MAKES** about 3 tablespoons

- 2 tablespoons unsalted butter, softened
- 1 tablespoon Dijon mustard
- 1 medium garlic clove, minced or pressed through a garlic press (about 1 teaspoon)
- 1 teaspoon minced fresh thyme leaves
- Pinch ground black pepper

Mash all the ingredients together in a small bowl.

## "Stuffed" Roast Butterflied Chicken

**SERVES** 4 to 6

**WHY THIS RECIPE WORKS** Stuffed roast chicken can be a conundrum—it's either a perfectly cooked bird filled with lukewarm stuffing (risking salmonella) or safe-to-eat stuffing packed in parched poultry. We wanted our stuffed roast chicken to produce both flavorful white and dark chicken meat along with an ample amount of intensely flavored stuffing. And we wanted to solve the problem of cooking the stuffing to a safe temperature without drying out the delicate breast meat of the chicken. We brined the bird to ensure moist meat and while it was brining, we made a savory stuffing. Our most creative solution, however, was to make an aluminum foil bowl, mound the stuffing into it, and place the chicken—after butterflying it—on top. This improvised cooking vessel allowed the stuffing to become moist and flavorful throughout from the chicken juices, while also becoming brown and chewy on the bottom. If using a kosher bird, skip the brining process and begin with step 2. The chicken should extend past the edges of the stuffing bowl so that fat renders into the roasting pan.

- ½ cup table salt
- ½ cup sugar
- 1 (5- to 6-pound) whole chicken, giblets discarded
- 1 tablespoon olive oil
- Ground black pepper
- 1 recipe Mushroom-Leek Bread Stuffing with Herbs

**1.** Dissolve the salt and sugar in 2 quarts cold water in a large container. Submerge the chicken in the brine, cover, and refrigerate for 1½ hours.

**2.** Adjust an oven rack to the lower-middle position and heat the oven to 450 degrees. Remove the chicken from the brine, rinse well, and pat dry with paper towels. Remove the backbone from the chicken, pound the chicken to a fairly even thickness, and tuck the wings behind the back. Rub the skin with the oil and season with pepper.

**3.** To make the foil bowl, place two 12-inch squares of foil on top of each other. Fold the edges to construct an 8 by 6-inch bowl. Coat the inside of the bowl with vegetable oil spray, and place the bowl in a roasting pan. Gently mound and pack the stuffing into the foil bowl and position the chicken over the stuffing. Roast the chicken until just beginning to brown, about 30 minutes. Rotate the pan and continue to roast until the skin is crisped and deep golden brown, the thickest part of the breasts registers 160 degrees, and the thickest part of the thighs registers 175 degrees, 25 to 35 minutes longer. Transfer the chicken to a carving board and let rest for 10 minutes.

**4.** While the chicken rests, transfer the stuffing to a serving bowl and fluff. Cover the stuffing with foil to keep warm. Carve the chicken and serve with the stuffing.

### Mushroom-Leek Bread Stuffing with Herbs

**MAKES** about 6 cups

The dried bread cubes for this stuffing can be stored in an airtight container for up to 1 week.

- 6 slices high-quality white sandwich bread, cut into ¼-inch cubes
- 2 tablespoons unsalted butter
- 1 leek, white and light green parts only, halved lengthwise, sliced ⅛ inch thick, and rinsed thoroughly
- 1 celery rib, chopped fine
- 8 ounces white mushrooms, wiped clean and chopped medium
- ¼ cup minced fresh parsley leaves
- 2 medium garlic cloves, minced or pressed through a garlic press (about 2 teaspoons)
- ½ teaspoon minced fresh sage leaves or ¼ teaspoon dried sage
- ½ teaspoon minced fresh thyme leaves or ¼ teaspoon dried thyme
- ½ cup plus 2 tablespoons low-sodium chicken broth
- 1 large egg
- ½ teaspoon table salt
- ½ teaspoon ground black pepper

**1.** Adjust an oven rack to the middle position and heat the oven to 250 degrees. Spread the bread cubes in a single layer on a rimmed baking sheet. Bake until thoroughly dried but not browned, about 30 minutes, stirring halfway through the baking time.

**2.** Meanwhile, melt the butter in a 12-inch skillet over medium-high heat. Add the leek, celery, and mushrooms and cook, stirring occasionally, until the vegetables begin to brown,

6 to 8 minutes. Stir in the parsley, garlic, sage, and thyme and cook until fragrant, about 30 seconds.

**3.** Whisk the broth, egg, salt, and pepper together in a large bowl. Add the bread cubes and leek-mushroom mixture and toss gently until evenly moistened and combined. Use as directed.

## Roasted Cornish Game Hens

**SERVES 4**

**WHY THIS RECIPE WORKS** Quick-cooking roasted Cornish game hens are an easy, elegant dinner option, but achieving crispy skin and tender meat in the short cooking time can be a challenge. Poking holes in the skin helped the fat to render quickly. To help the skin crisp up and brown, we used a baking powder rub and let the hens air-dry in the refrigerator overnight. To guarantee evenly golden skin, we butterflied the hens and started cooking them skin side down on a preheated baking sheet. Finally, we flipped them over for a final stint under the broiler. To season the meat inside and out, we added a light coating of kosher salt and fragrant spices on the undersides of the birds. This recipe requires refrigerating the salted meat for at least 4 hours or up to 24 hours before cooking (a longer salting time is preferable). If your hens weigh 1½ to 2 pounds, cook three instead of four, and extend the initial cooking time in step 5 to 15 minutes. We prefer Bell and Evans Cornish Game Hens.

- 4 (1¼- to 1½-pound) Cornish game hens, giblets discarded
- Kosher salt and pepper
- ¼ teaspoon vegetable oil
- 1 teaspoon baking powder
- Vegetable oil spray

**1.** Using kitchen shears and working with 1 hen at a time, with hen breast side down, cut through bones on either side of backbone; discard backbone. Lay hens breast side up on counter. Using sharp chef's knife, cut through center of breast to make 2 halves.

**2.** Using your fingers, carefully separate skin from breasts and thighs. Using metal skewer or tip of paring knife, poke 10 to 15 holes in fat deposits on top of breasts and thighs. Tuck wingtips underneath hens. Pat hens dry with paper towels.

**3.** Sprinkle 1 tablespoon salt on underside (bone side) of hens. Combine 1 tablespoon salt and oil in small bowl and stir until salt is evenly coated with oil. Add baking powder and stir until well combined. Turn hens skin side up and rub salt–baking powder mixture evenly over surface. Arrange hens skin side up and in single layer on large platter or plates and refrigerate, uncovered, for at least 4 hours or up to 24 hours.

**4.** Adjust oven racks to upper-middle and lower positions, place rimmed baking sheet on lower rack, and heat oven to 500 degrees.

**5.** Once oven is fully heated, spray skin side of hens with oil spray and season with pepper. Carefully transfer hens, skin side down, to preheated sheet and cook for 10 minutes.

### GETTING CORNISH GAME HENS TO CRISP QUICKLY AND EVENLY

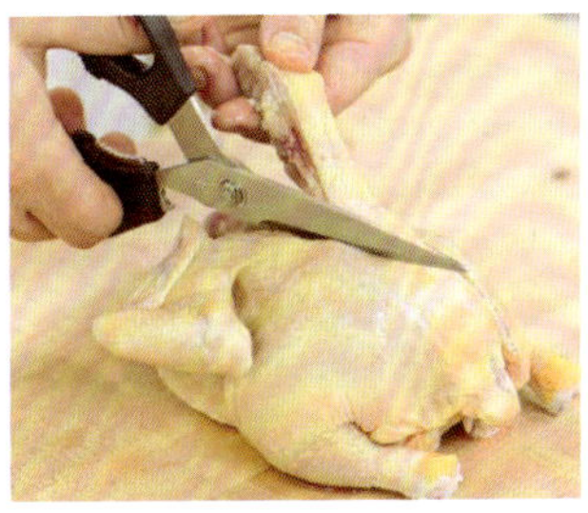

**1.** Cutting out the backbones and flattening the birds promotes uniform browning.

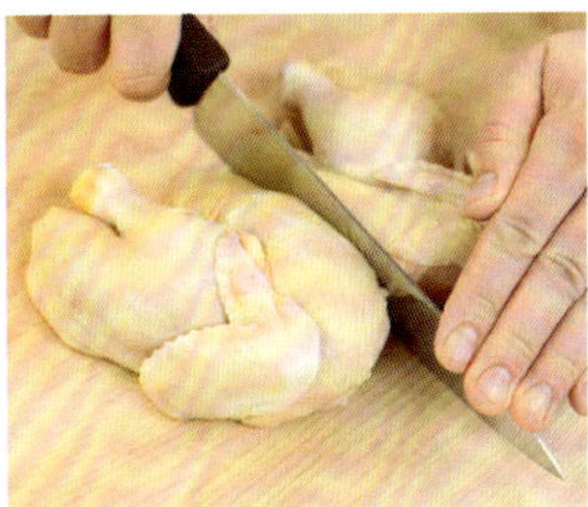

**2.** Halving the flattened hens makes them easier to serve.

**3.** Loosening and poking holes in the skin allows the fat to drain during cooking, aiding crisping. Rubbing the birds with salt and baking powder and then chilling them wicks away moisture.

**6.** Remove hens from oven and heat broiler. Flip hens skin side up. Transfer sheet to upper rack and broil until well browned and breasts register 160 degrees and drumsticks/thighs register 175 degrees, about 5 minutes, rotating sheet as needed to promote even browning. Transfer to platter or individual plates and serve.

## Easier Fried Chicken

**SERVES 4**

**WHY THIS RECIPE WORKS** Crackling-crisp, golden-brown, and juicy—what's not to love about fried chicken? In a word, frying. Heating more than a quart of fat on the stovetop can be daunting for home cooks. We wanted to find a way to prepare fried chicken without having to heat up a pot full of oil. To season the meat and ensure it turned out juicy, we soaked chicken parts in a buttermilk brine. We also incorporated baking powder, an unconventional ingredient in fried chicken, into our dredging mixture. As the chicken fried, the baking powder released carbon dioxide gas, leavening the crust and increasing its surface area, keeping it light and crisp. And while most dredging mixtures contain purely dry ingredients, we added a little buttermilk to our mixture because the small clumps of batter it formed turn ultracrisp once fried. To streamline frying the chicken, we fried the chicken until just lightly browned on both sides in less than half the amount of oil we'd typically use. Then we transferred the chicken to the oven to finish cooking through. Setting the chicken on a rack promoted air circulation all around the meat for an evenly crisp crust. A whole 4-pound chicken, cut into eight pieces, can be used instead of the chicken parts. Skinless chicken pieces are also an acceptable substitute, but the meat will come out slightly drier. A Dutch oven with an 11-inch diameter can be used in place of the straight-sided sauté pan.

- 1¼ cups buttermilk
- Table salt
- Dash of hot sauce
- 3 teaspoons ground black pepper
- 1 teaspoon garlic powder
- 1 teaspoon paprika
- ¼ teaspoon cayenne pepper
- 3½ pounds bone-in, skin-on chicken parts (breasts, thighs, and drumsticks, or a mix, with breasts cut in half), trimmed of excess fat
- 2 cups unbleached all-purpose flour
- 2 teaspoons baking powder
- 1¾ cups vegetable oil

**1.** Whisk 1 cup of the buttermilk, 1 tablespoon salt, the hot sauce, 1 teaspoon of the black pepper, ¼ teaspoon of the garlic powder, ¼ teaspoon of the paprika, and a pinch of cayenne together in a large bowl. Add the chicken pieces and turn to coat. Refrigerate, covered, for at least 1 hour or up to overnight.

**2.** Adjust an oven rack to the middle position and heat the oven to 400 degrees. Whisk the flour, baking powder, 1 teaspoon salt, and the remaining 2 teaspoons black pepper, the remaining ¾ teaspoon garlic powder, the remaining ¾ teaspoon paprika, and the remaining cayenne together in a large bowl. Add the remaining ¼ cup buttermilk to the flour mixture and mix with your fingers until combined and small clumps form. Working with one piece at a time, dredge the chicken pieces in the flour mixture, pressing the mixture onto the pieces to form a thick, even coating. Place the dredged chicken on a large plate, skin side up.

**3.** Heat the oil in an 11-inch straight-sided sauté pan over medium-high heat to 375 degrees, about 5 minutes. Carefully place the chicken pieces in the pan, skin side down, and cook until golden brown, 3 to 5 minutes. Carefully flip the chicken pieces and continue to cook until golden brown on the second side, 2 to 4 minutes longer. Transfer the chicken to a wire rack set over a rimmed baking sheet. Bake the chicken until an instant-read thermometer inserted into the thickest part of the chicken registers 160 degrees for the breasts and 175 for the legs and thighs, 15 to 20 minutes. (Smaller pieces may cook faster than larger pieces. Remove the chicken pieces from the oven as they reach the correct temperature.) Let the chicken rest for 5 minutes before serving.

## Crispy Fried Chicken

**SERVES** 4 to 6

**WHY THIS RECIPE WORKS** Frying chicken at home is a daunting task, with its messy preparation and spattering hot fat. In the end, the chicken often ends up disappointingly greasy, with a peeling crust and dry, tasteless meat. We wanted fried chicken worthy of the mess and splatter: moist, seasoned meat coated with a delicious crispy mahogany crust. We soaked chicken parts in a seasoned buttermilk brine for ultimate flavor and juiciness. Then we air-dried the brined chicken parts to help ensure a crisp skin. Flour made the crispest coating. We found that peanut oil can withstand the demands of frying and had the most neutral flavor of all the oils we tested. Vegetable oil was a close runner-up. As for frying the chicken, we found that a Dutch oven worked best. With its high sides and lid, the Dutch oven minimized splatters and retained heat which helped the chicken cook through. Avoid using kosher chicken in this recipe or it will be too salty. Maintaining an even oil temperature is key. After the chicken is added to the pot, the temperature will drop dramatically, and most of the frying will be done at about 325 degrees. Use an instant-read thermometer with a high upper range; a clip-on candy/deep-fry thermometer is fine, too, though it can be clipped to the pot only for the uncovered portion of frying.

**CHICKEN**

- ½ cup table salt for brining
- ¼ cup sugar for brining
- 2 tablespoons paprika
- 7 cups buttermilk for brining
- 3 garlic heads, cloves separated and smashed
- 3 bay leaves, crumbled
- 4 pounds bone-in chicken pieces (split breasts cut in half, drumsticks, and/or thighs), trimmed
- 3–4 quarts peanut oil or vegetable oil, for frying

COATING

- 4 cups all-purpose flour
- 1 large egg
- 1 teaspoon baking powder
- ½ teaspoon baking soda
- 1 cup buttermilk

**1. FOR THE CHICKEN:** Dissolve salt, sugar, and paprika in buttermilk in large container. Add garlic and bay leaves, submerge chicken in brine, cover, and refrigerate for 2 to 3 hours.

**2.** Remove chicken from brine and place in single layer on wire rack set over rimmed baking sheet. Refrigerate uncovered for 2 hours. (At this point, chicken can be covered with plastic wrap and refrigerated for up to 6 more hours.)

**3.** Adjust oven rack to middle position and heat oven to 200 degrees. In large Dutch oven, heat 2 inches oil over medium-high heat to 375 degrees.

**4. FOR THE COATING:** Place flour in shallow dish. Whisk egg, baking powder, and baking soda together in medium bowl, then whisk in buttermilk (mixture will bubble and foam). Working with 3 chicken pieces at a time, dredge in flour, shaking off excess, then coat with egg mixture, allowing excess to drip off. Finally, coat with flour again, shake off excess, and return to wire rack.

**5.** When oil is hot, add half of chicken pieces to pot, skin side down, cover, and fry until deep golden brown, 7 to 11 minutes, adjusting heat as necessary to maintain oil temperature of about 325 degrees. (After 4 minutes, check chicken pieces for even browning and rearrange if some pieces are browning faster than others.) Turn chicken pieces over and continue to cook until thickest part of breasts registers 160 degrees and thickest part of thighs or drumsticks registers 175 degrees, 6 to 8 minutes. Drain chicken briefly on paper towel–lined plate, then transfer to clean wire rack set in rimmed baking sheet and keep warm in oven.

**6.** Return oil to 375 degrees (if necessary) over medium-high heat and repeat with remaining chicken pieces. Serve.

## Oven-Fried Chicken

SERVES 4

**WHY THIS RECIPE WORKS** Oven-fried chicken never seems to taste as good as the real thing. The coating, often plain bread crumbs or cornflakes, never gets as crunchy or as flavorful as a deep-fried coating does. We wanted a good alternative to regular fried chicken that would have real crunch and good flavor. We soaked bone-in chicken legs and thighs in a buttermilk brine to achieve maximum juiciness. And we removed the skin from the chicken before brining because it didn't render in the oven. A mixture of eggs and mustard helped the crumbs stick to the chicken. Melba toast crumbs made the crispest coating. We baked the chicken on a wire rack set over a baking sheet that we had lined with foil. This method allowed heat to circulate around the chicken during baking, resulting in crisp chicken all over without turning. Avoid using kosher chicken in this recipe or it will be too salty. If you don't want to buy whole chicken legs and cut them into drumsticks and thighs, simply buy four drumsticks and four thighs. To make Melba toast crumbs, place the toasts in a heavy-duty zipper-lock freezer bag, seal, and pound with a meat pounder or other heavy blunt object. Leave some crumbs in the mixture the size of pebbles, but most should resemble coarse sand.

CHICKEN

- ½ cup plus 2 tablespoons table salt
- ¼ cup sugar
- 2 tablespoons paprika
- 3 medium heads garlic, cloves separated
- 3 bay leaves, crumbled
- 7 cups buttermilk
- 4 whole chicken legs, separated into drumsticks and thighs and skin removed

COATING

- ¼ cup vegetable oil
- 1 box (about 5 ounces) plain Melba toast, crushed
- 2 large eggs
- 1 tablespoon Dijon mustard
- 1 teaspoon dried thyme
- ¾ teaspoon table salt
- ½ teaspoon ground black pepper
- ½ teaspoon dried oregano
- ¼ teaspoon garlic powder
- ¼ teaspoon cayenne pepper (optional)

**1. FOR THE CHICKEN:** In a large zipper-lock bag, combine the salt, sugar, paprika, garlic cloves, and bay leaves. With a flat meat pounder, smash the garlic into the salt and spice mixture thoroughly. Pour the mixture into a large container. Add the buttermilk and stir until the salt and sugar are completely dissolved. Submerge the chicken in the brine and refrigerate for 2 to 3 hours. Rinse the chicken well and place on a large wire rack set over a rimmed baking sheet. Refrigerate uncovered for 2 hours. (After 2 hours, the chicken can be covered with plastic wrap and refrigerated up to 6 hours longer.)

**2.** Adjust an oven rack to the upper-middle position and heat the oven to 400 degrees. Line a large, rimmed baking sheet with foil and set a large wire rack over the pan.

**3. FOR THE COATING:** Drizzle the oil over the Melba toast crumbs in a pie plate or shallow dish; toss well to coat. Mix the eggs, mustard, thyme, salt, pepper, oregano, garlic powder, and cayenne (if using) with a fork in a second plate.

**4.** Working with one piece at a time, coat the chicken on both sides with the egg mixture. Set the chicken in the Melba crumbs, sprinkle the crumbs over the chicken, and press to coat. Turn the chicken over and repeat on the other side. Gently shake off the excess and place on the rack. Bake until the chicken is deep nutty brown and the thickest part of a piece registers 175 degrees on an instant-read thermometer, about 40 minutes. Serve.

## Dakgangjeong (Korean Fried Chicken Wings)

**SERVES** 4 to 6

**WHY THIS RECIPE WORKS** A thin, crispy exterior and a spicy-sweet-salty sauce are the hallmarks of dakgangjeong, Korean fried chicken wings. The biggest challenge is preventing the sauce from destroying the crust. We dunked the wings (which offer a high exterior to interior ratio for maximum crunch and also cook quickly) in a loose batter of flour, cornstarch, and water, which clung nicely to the chicken and fried up brown and crispy. To help the coating withstand a wet sauce, we double-fried the wings, which removed more water from the skin, making the coating extra-crispy. Gochujang, Korean chile paste, gave our sauce the proper spicy, fermented notes, while sugar tempered the heat and garlic and ginger provided depth. A rasp-style grater makes quick work of turning the garlic into a paste. If you can't find gochujang, substitute an equal amount of sriracha and add only 2 tablespoons of water to the sauce. For a complete meal, serve these wings with rice and a vegetable.

- 1 tablespoon toasted sesame oil
- 1 teaspoon garlic, minced to paste
- 1 teaspoon grated fresh ginger
- 1¾ cups water, divided
- 3 tablespoons sugar
- 2–3 tablespoons gochujang
- 1 tablespoon soy sauce
- 2 quarts vegetable oil for frying
- 1 cup all-purpose flour
- 3 tablespoons cornstarch
- 3 pounds chicken wings, cut at joints, wingtips discarded

**1.** Combine sesame oil, garlic, and ginger in large bowl and microwave until mixture is bubbly and fragrant but not browned, 40 to 60 seconds. Whisk in ¼ cup water, sugar, gochujang, and soy sauce until smooth and set aside.

**2.** Heat oil in large Dutch oven over medium-high heat to 350 degrees. While oil heats, whisk flour, cornstarch, and remaining 1½ cups water in second large bowl until smooth. Set wire rack in rimmed baking sheet and set aside.

**3.** Place half of wings in batter and stir to coat. Using tongs, remove wings from batter one at a time, allowing any excess batter to drip back into bowl, and add to hot oil. Increase heat to high and cook, stirring occasionally to prevent wings from sticking, until coating is light golden and beginning to crisp, about 7 minutes. (Oil temperature will drop sharply after adding chicken.) Transfer wings to prepared rack. Return oil to 350 degrees and repeat with remaining wings. Reduce heat to medium and let second batch of chicken rest for 5 minutes.

**4.** Return oil to 375 degrees. Carefully return all chicken to oil and cook, stirring occasionally, until exterior is deep golden brown and very crispy, about 7 minutes. Transfer to rack and let stand for 2 minutes. Add chicken to reserved sauce and toss until coated. Return chicken to rack and let stand for 2 minutes to allow surface to set. Transfer to platter and serve.

## Roasted and Glazed Chicken Wings

**SERVES** 4

**WHY THIS RECIPE WORKS** With succulent, savory meat and well-rendered, bronzed skin, the wings are a real treat. To produce an entire trayful of golden-brown, fall-off-the-bone-tender wings, we roasted 4 pounds of flats and drumettes sandwiched between two rimmed baking sheets. The extra weight of the top sheet ensured that both sides of the wings were in close contact with hot metal, helping render the wings' fat and produce evenly browned skin. We also poured off the gelatin-rich juices exuded during roasting (we roasted the wingtips along with the flats and drumettes to produce as many drippings as possible) and then reduced them to a syrupy glaze that we brushed onto the wings after a final skin-browning blast under the broiler. Roasting the wingtips along with the flats and drumettes boosts the flavor and volume of the juices, but if your chicken wings are packaged without wingtips, it's OK to omit them. This recipe was developed with Diamond Crystal kosher salt; if you're using Morton, which is denser, decrease the amount to 2¼ teaspoons. Serve with a green salad and crusty loaf of bread.

- 4 pounds chicken wings, cut at joints, wingtips reserved
- 1 tablespoon vegetable oil
- 1 tablespoon kosher salt
- 1 teaspoon pepper

**1.** Adjust oven racks to lowest and upper-middle positions and heat oven to 400 degrees. Spray rimmed baking sheet with vegetable oil spray and line with parchment paper. Pat chicken dry with paper towels and transfer to large bowl. Add oil, salt, and pepper. Toss well to combine.

**2.** Arrange drumettes along 2 long sides of prepared baking sheet. Place flats rounded side down in center. Tuck wingtips in to fill any gaps on sheet (discard any wingtips that don't fit).

Top chicken with second sheet of parchment, then gently press second rimmed baking sheet on top of parchment to weigh down wings. Roast on lower rack for 45 minutes.

**3.** Remove sheet from oven and heat broiler. Carefully and gently tilt 1 corner of sheet over fat separator or liquid measuring cup and drain off as much liquid as possible; you should have ⅓ to ½ cup. Remove top baking sheet and parchment. Discard wingtips (or save for nibbling). Flip remaining pieces.

**4.** Transfer defatted drippings to small saucepan. Cook over medium heat, swirling saucepan occasionally, until juices are reduced to 2 to 3 tablespoons, 6 to 8 minutes. Cover to keep warm.

**5.** While juices reduce, broil chicken on upper rack until evenly golden brown, 6 to 8 minutes, rotating sheet halfway through broiling. Brush chicken with reduced juices, transfer to platter, and serve.

## Buffalo Wings

**SERVES** 6 to 8

**WHY THIS RECIPE WORKS** Buffalo wings are the ultimate bar snack. Great wings boast juicy meat; a crisp coating; and a spicy, slightly sweet, and vinegary sauce. But dry, flabby wings are often the norm and the sauce can be scorchingly hot. We wanted perfectly cooked wings, coated in a well-seasoned sauce. We coated the wings with cornstarch for a supercrisp exterior and deep-fried the wings for the best texture. Then we deepened the flavor of the traditional hot sauce by adding brown sugar and cider vinegar. For heat, we chose Frank's RedHot Original Sauce, which is traditional, but not very spicy, so we added a little Tabasco for even more kick. Use a Dutch oven that hold 6 quarts or more for this recipe.

**SAUCE**

- 4 tablespoons unsalted butter
- ½ cup Frank's RedHot Original Sauce
- 2 tablespoons Tabasco or other hot sauce, plus more to taste
- 1 tablespoon packed dark brown sugar
- 2 teaspoons cider vinegar

**WINGS**

- 1–2 quarts peanut oil, for frying
- 3 tablespoons cornstarch
- 1 teaspoon table salt
- 1 teaspoon pepper
- 1 teaspoon cayenne pepper
- 3 pounds chicken wings, cut at joints, wingtips discarded

- 2 carrots, peeled and cut into thin sticks
- 4 celery ribs, cut into thin sticks
- Blue cheese dressing

**1. FOR THE SAUCE:** Melt butter in small saucepan over low heat. Whisk in hot sauces, sugar, and vinegar until combined. Remove from heat and set aside.

**2. FOR THE WINGS:** Heat oven to 200 degrees. Line baking sheet with paper towels. In large Dutch oven fitted with clip-on candy thermometer, heat 2½ inches oil over medium-high heat to 360 degrees. While oil heats, combine cornstarch, salt, pepper, and cayenne in a small bowl. Dry chicken with paper towels and place pieces in large bowl. Sprinkle spice mixture over wings and toss with rubber spatula until evenly coated. Fry half of chicken wings until golden and crisp, 10 to 12 minutes. With slotted spoon, transfer fried chicken wings to prepared sheet. Keep first batch of chicken warm in oven while frying remaining wings. (The fried, unsauced wings can be kept warm in the oven for up to 1½ hours. Toss them with the sauce just before serving.)

**3.** Pour sauce mixture into large bowl, add chicken wings, and toss until wings are uniformly coated. Serve immediately with carrot and celery sticks and blue cheese dressing on side.

### CUTTING UP CHICKEN WINGS

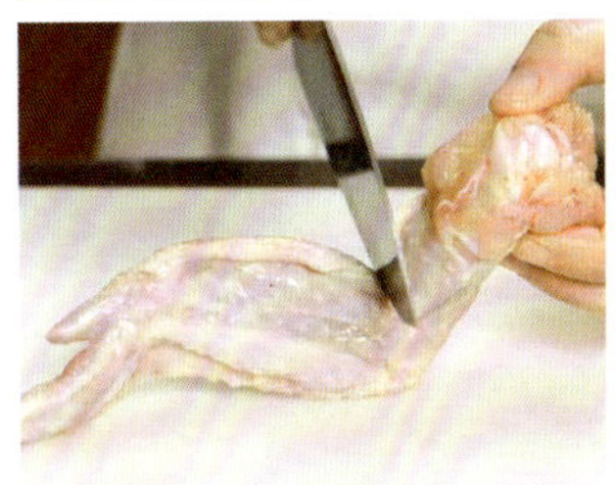

**1.** Cut into skin between larger sections of wing until you hit joint.

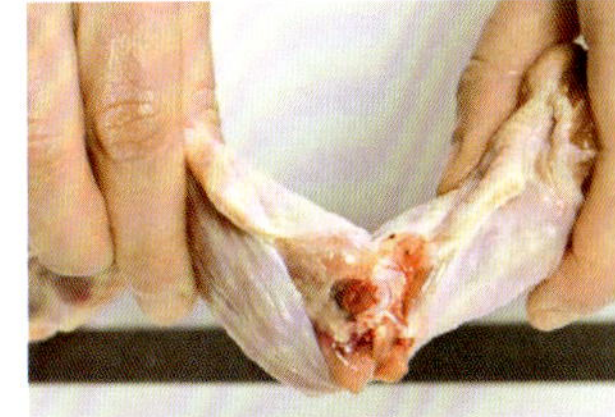

**2.** Bend back 2 sections to pop and break joint.

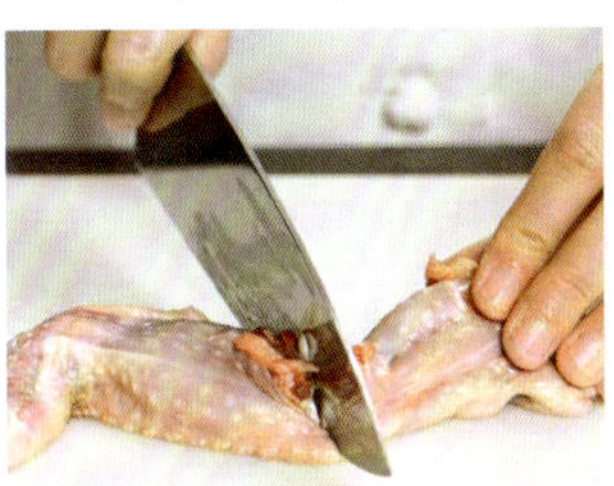

**3.** Cut through skin and flesh to completely separate 2 meaty portions.

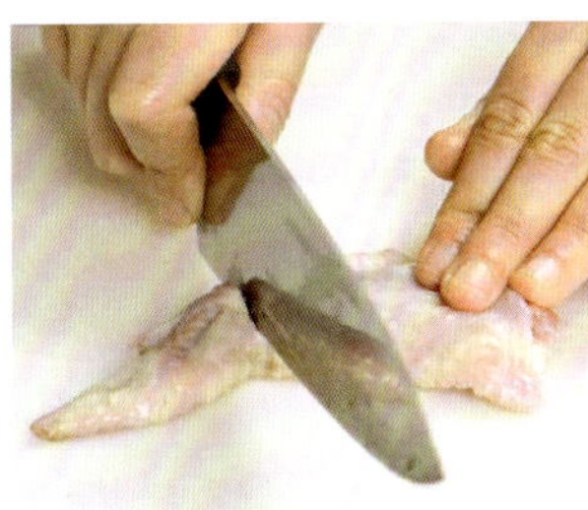

**4.** Hack off wingtip and discard.

# Karaage (Japanese Fried Chicken Thighs)

**SERVES** 4 to 6

**WHY THIS RECIPE WORKS** Juicy, deeply seasoned thigh meat encased in a supercrispy crust makes karaage a fried chicken lover's dream. Our version of this Japanese classic started with boneless, skinless chicken thighs, which eliminated the need to debone the meat at home. Cutting the chicken into narrow strips instead of small chunks created fewer pieces to handle. Briefly marinating the meat in a mixture of soy sauce, sake, ginger, and garlic (seasoned with a little salt and sugar) imbued the chicken with deeply savory, aromatic flavor. Dredging the chicken in cornstarch—instead of traditional potato starch—made for a less sticky coating and shaking off the excess starch and letting the dredged pieces rest while the oil heated gave the starch time to hydrate. Dabbing any dry patches with reserved marinade prevented dustiness. We recommend using a rasp-style grater to grate the ginger. Do not substitute chicken breasts for the thighs; they will dry out during frying. There's no need to take the temperature of the chicken; it will be cooked through by the time it is golden brown and crispy. Leftover frying oil can be cooled, strained, and saved for later use.

- 3 tablespoons soy sauce
- 2 tablespoons sake
- 1 tablespoon grated fresh ginger
- 2 garlic cloves, minced
- ¾ teaspoon sugar
- ⅛ teaspoon table salt
- 1½ pounds boneless, skinless chicken thighs, trimmed and cut crosswise into 1- to 1½-inch-wide strips
- 1¼ cups cornstarch
- 1 quart vegetable oil for frying
- Lemon wedges

**1.** Combine soy sauce, sake, ginger, garlic, sugar, and salt in medium bowl. Add chicken and toss to combine. Let sit at room temperature for 30 minutes. While chicken is marinating, line rimmed baking sheet with parchment paper. Set wire rack in second rimmed baking sheet and line rack with triple layer of paper towels. Place cornstarch in wide bowl.

**2.** Lift chicken from marinade, 1 piece at a time, allowing excess marinade to drip back into bowl but leaving any garlic or ginger bits on chicken. Coat chicken with cornstarch, shake off excess, and place on parchment-lined sheet. Reserve marinade.

**3.** Heat oil in large Dutch oven over medium-high heat to 325 degrees. While oil heats, check chicken pieces for white patches of dry cornstarch. Dip back of spoon in reserved marinade and gently press onto dry spots to lightly moisten.

**4.** Using tongs, add half of chicken, 1 piece at a time, to oil in single layer. Cook, adjusting burner, if necessary, to maintain oil temperature between 300 and 325 degrees, until chicken is golden brown and crispy, 4 to 5 minutes. Using spider skimmer or slotted spoon, transfer chicken to paper towel–lined rack. Return oil to 325 degrees and repeat with remaining chicken. Serve with lemon wedges.

# Sung Choy Bao (Chinese Chicken Lettuce Wraps)

**SERVES** 4 as a main dish or 6 as an appetizer

**WHY THIS RECIPE WORKS** These chicken lettuce wraps, popularized by chain restaurants such as P.F. Chang's, are based on a Cantonese preparation. To ensure flavorful, tender meat, we started with chicken thighs and marinated them in soy sauce and rice wine. To keep the meat from drying out when stir-fried, we coated it in a velvetizing cornstarch slurry, which helped it retain moisture as it cooked. To make it an entrée, serve this dish with rice.

**CHICKEN**

- 1 pound boneless, skinless chicken thighs, trimmed and cut into 1-inch pieces
- 2 teaspoons Chinese rice wine or dry sherry
- 2 teaspoons soy sauce
- 2 teaspoons toasted sesame oil
- 2 teaspoons cornstarch

**SAUCE**

- 3 tablespoons oyster sauce
- 1 tablespoon Chinese rice wine or dry sherry
- 2 teaspoons soy sauce
- 2 teaspoons toasted sesame oil
- ½ teaspoon sugar
- ¼ teaspoon red pepper flakes

**STIR-FRY**

- 2 tablespoons vegetable oil
- 2 celery ribs, cut into ¼-inch pieces
- 6 ounces shiitake mushrooms, stemmed and sliced thin
- ½ cup water chestnuts, cut into ¼-inch pieces
- 2 scallions, white parts minced, green parts sliced thin
- 2 garlic cloves, minced
- 1 head Bibb lettuce (8 ounces), washed and dried, leaves separated and left whole
- Hoisin sauce

**1. FOR THE CHICKEN:** Place chicken pieces on large plate in single layer. Freeze meat until firm and starting to harden around edges, about 20 minutes.

**2.** Whisk rice wine, soy sauce, sesame oil, and cornstarch together in bowl. Pulse half of meat in food processor until coarsely chopped into ¼- to ⅛-inch pieces, about 10 pulses. Transfer meat to bowl with rice wine mixture and repeat with remaining chunks. Toss chicken to coat and refrigerate for 15 minutes.

**3. FOR THE SAUCE:** Whisk all ingredients together in bowl; set aside.

**4. FOR THE STIR-FRY:** Heat 1 tablespoon vegetable oil in 12-inch nonstick skillet over high heat until smoking. Add chicken and cook, stirring constantly, until opaque, 3 to 4 minutes. Transfer to bowl and wipe out skillet.

**5.** Heat remaining 1 tablespoon vegetable oil in now-empty skillet over high heat until smoking. Add celery and mushrooms; cook, stirring constantly, until mushrooms have reduced in size by half and celery is crisp-tender, 3 to 4 minutes. Add water chestnuts, scallion whites, and garlic; cook, stirring constantly, until fragrant, about 1 minute. Whisk sauce to recombine. Return chicken to skillet; add sauce and toss to combine. Spoon into lettuce leaves and sprinkle with scallion greens. Serve, passing hoisin sauce separately.

## Buffalo Chicken Sandwiches

**SERVES 4**

**WHY THIS RECIPE WORKS** This sandwich combines the spicy appeal of buffalo wings with the crunch of classic fried chicken. We used chicken breasts, the leanness of which allows the fiery hot sauce and tangy blue cheese dressing to shine. We dunked the meat in a generously salted egg mixture, not only to help the breading adhere but also to season the meat and keep it juicy. For the breading, we used all-purpose flour for crunch and added some cornstarch for crispness and baking powder for lightness. We mixed a small amount of buttermilk into the seasoned flour to create a shaggy coating that, after a rest in the refrigerator, adhered well to the chicken. This coating fried up into a crunchy crust with lots of surface area for holding the maximum amount of buttery hot sauce, which we cooked down to thicken and intensify it. Freezing the chicken breasts for 15 minutes will make them easier to halve horizontally. Use a Dutch oven that holds 6 quarts or more. If you prefer less spice, reduce or omit the cayenne in the sauce.

**CHICKEN**

- 1 cup all-purpose flour
- ½ cup cornstarch
- 1 teaspoon pepper
- 1 teaspoon cayenne pepper
- 1 teaspoon baking powder
- ¼ cup buttermilk
- 2 large eggs
- 1 teaspoon table salt
- 2 (6- to 8-ounce) boneless, skinless chicken breasts, trimmed, halved horizontally, and pounded ½ inch thick

**BUFFALO SAUCE**

- 1 tablespoon unsalted butter
- ½ teaspoon cayenne pepper
- ½ cup Frank's RedHot Original Cayenne Pepper Sauce
- 2 teaspoons cider vinegar

**BLUE CHEESE SPREAD**

- 2 ounces blue cheese, crumbled (½ cup)
- 2 tablespoons mayonnaise
- 2 tablespoons buttermilk
- 1 teaspoon cider vinegar
- 2 quarts vegetable oil for frying
- 4 hamburger buns, toasted if desired
- 2 cups finely shredded iceberg lettuce

**1. FOR THE CHICKEN:** Set wire rack in rimmed baking sheet. In wide, shallow bowl, whisk together flour, cornstarch, pepper, cayenne, and baking powder. Drizzle buttermilk over flour mixture and mix with your fingers until combined and small clumps form. In medium bowl, whisk together eggs and salt.

**2.** Working with 1 piece at a time, dip chicken in egg mixture and turn to coat. Lift from egg mixture, allowing excess to drip back into bowl. Coat both sides of chicken in flour mixture, pressing to form thick, bumpy coating. Place on prepared rack. Refrigerate, uncovered, for at least 1 hour or up to 8 hours. While chicken rests, make sauce and blue cheese spread.

**3. FOR THE BUFFALO SAUCE:** Melt butter in small saucepan over medium heat. Add cayenne and cook, stirring constantly, until fragrant, about 30 seconds. Add hot sauce (mixture may sputter) and cook, stirring occasionally, until sauce is thickened and spatula drawn across bottom of pan leaves trail that takes longer than 5 seconds to fill in, 4 to 5 minutes. Remove from heat and stir in vinegar.

**4. FOR THE BLUE CHEESE SPREAD:** In small bowl, mash blue cheese with fork until no pieces larger than ¼ inch remain. Add mayonnaise and continue to mash until incorporated. Stir in buttermilk and vinegar until combined. Refrigerate until needed.

**5.** Place second wire rack in second rimmed baking sheet. Heat oil in large Dutch oven over medium-high heat to 425 degrees. Carefully transfer all chicken to oil and fry until chicken registers at least 155 degrees, 2 to 3 minutes. Transfer chicken to prepared rack. Using pastry brush, coat top of chicken with half of buffalo sauce.

**6.** Open buns on cutting board. Transfer 1 chicken piece, sauce side down, to each bun bottom. Brush remaining buffalo sauce over chicken. Top each chicken piece with ½ cup lettuce. Spread each bun top with 2 teaspoons blue cheese spread. Invert bun top onto each sandwich and serve, passing remaining blue cheese spread separately.

## Air-Fryer Spicy Fried Chicken Sandwiches

**SERVES 4**

**WHY THIS RECIPE WORKS** The air fryer gave us a less-greasy route to crunchy, juicy, spicy fried chicken sandwiches that was nearly as convenient as hitting up our favorite lunch spot. For our spicy chicken sandwich to live up to its name, we added heat in three stages. First, we whisked hot sauce into the egg-flour dredging mixture to ensure the heat was directly coating the chicken rather than getting lost in the breading, as it does in many recipes. Combining more hot sauce with mayonnaise for a creamy spread upped the heat level further. An unwritten rule of fried sandwiches states that a pickled element is a must; this was our opportunity to add even more heat with fiery sweet pickled jalapeños in lieu of pickle chips. Shredded lettuce provided a crisp, fresh component that tempered the heat a bit. You can use your air fryer to toast the buns.

- 1 cup panko bread crumbs
- 2 tablespoons extra-virgin olive oil
- 1 large egg
- 3 tablespoons hot sauce, divided
- 1 tablespoon all-purpose flour
- ½ teaspoon garlic powder
- ⅛ teaspoon table salt
- ⅛ teaspoon pepper
- 2 (8-ounce) boneless, skinless chicken breasts, trimmed
- ¼ cup mayonnaise
- 4 hamburger buns, toasted if desired
- 2 cups shredded iceberg lettuce
- ¼ cup jarred sliced jalapeños

**1.** Toss panko with oil in bowl until evenly coated. Microwave, stirring frequently, until light golden brown, 1 to 3 minutes. Transfer to shallow dish and set aside to cool slightly. Whisk egg, 2 tablespoons hot sauce, flour, garlic powder, salt, and pepper together in second shallow dish.

**2.** Pound chicken to uniform thickness as needed. Halve each breast crosswise, pat dry with paper towels, and season with salt and pepper. Working with 1 piece of chicken at a time, dredge in egg mixture, letting excess drip off, then coat with panko mixture, pressing gently to adhere.

**3.** Lightly spray base of air-fryer basket with vegetable oil spray. Arrange chicken pieces in prepared basket, spaced evenly apart. Place basket in air fryer and set temperature to 400 degrees. Cook until chicken is crispy and registers 160 degrees, 12 to 16 minutes, flipping and rotating chicken pieces halfway through cooking.

**4.** Combine mayonnaise and remaining 1 tablespoon hot sauce in small bowl. Spread mayonnaise mixture evenly over bun bottoms, then top with 1 piece chicken, lettuce, jalapeños, and bun tops. Serve.

## Easier Roast Turkey and Gravy

**SERVES 10 to 12**

**WHY THIS RECIPE WORKS** To season the meat and help it retain more juices as it cooked, we loosened the skin of the turkey and applied a mixture of salt and sugar to the flesh. We preheated both a baking stone and roasting pan in the oven before placing the turkey in the pan. The stone absorbed heat and delivered it through the pan to the turkey's legs and thighs, which needed to cook to a higher temperature than the delicate breast meat. The boost of heat provided by the stone also helped the juices brown and reduce into concentrated drippings that could be used in our gravy. After the leg quarters had gotten a jump start on cooking, we reduced the oven temperature from 425 to 325 degrees. Note that this recipe requires salting the bird in the refrigerator for 24 to 48 hours. This recipe was developed and tested using Diamond Crystal Kosher Salt. If you have Morton Kosher Salt, which is denser than Diamond Crystal, reduce the salt in step 1 to 3 tablespoons. Rub 1 tablespoon salt mixture into each breast, 1½ teaspoons into each leg, and remainder into cavity. Do not use table salt here. If you are roasting a kosher or self-basting turkey (such as a frozen Butterball), do not salt it.

- 4 teaspoons sugar
- ¼ cup kosher salt
- 1 (12- to 14-pound) turkey, neck and giblets removed and reserved for gravy
- 2½ tablespoons vegetable oil, divided
- 1 teaspoon baking powder
- 1 small onion, chopped fine
- 1 carrot, peeled and sliced thin
- 5 sprigs fresh parsley
- 2 bay leaves
- 5 tablespoons all-purpose flour
- 3¼ cups water
- ¼ cup dry white wine

**1.** Combine sugar and salt in bowl. With turkey breast side up, use your fingers or handle of wooden spoon to carefully separate skin from thighs and breast. Rub 4 teaspoons salt-sugar mixture under skin of each breast half, 2 teaspoons under skin of each leg, and remaining salt-sugar mixture into cavity. Tie legs together with kitchen twine. Place turkey on rack set in rimmed baking sheet and refrigerate uncovered for 24 to 48 hours.

**2.** At least 30 minutes before roasting turkey, adjust oven rack to lowest position and set pizza stone on oven rack. Place roasting pan on pizza stone and heat oven to 500 degrees. Combine 1½ teaspoons oil and baking powder in small bowl. Pat turkey dry with paper towels. Rub oil mixture evenly over turkey. Cover turkey breast with double layer of aluminum foil.

**3.** Remove roasting pan from oven. Place remaining 2 tablespoons oil in roasting pan. Place turkey into pan breast side up and return pan to oven. Reduce oven temperature to 425 degrees and cook for 45 minutes.

**4.** Remove foil shield, reduce temperature to 325 degrees, and continue to cook until breast registers 160 degrees and thighs register 175 degrees, 1 to 1½ hours longer.

**5.** Using spatula loosen turkey from roasting pan, transfer to carving board, and let rest uncovered for 45 minutes. While turkey rests, use wooden spoon to scrape any browned bits from bottom of roasting pan. Pour mixture through fine-mesh strainer set in bowl. Transfer drippings to fat separator and let rest 10 minutes. Reserve 3 tablespoons fat and defatted liquid (about 1 cup). Discard remaining fat.

**6.** Heat reserved fat in large saucepan over medium-high heat until shimmering. Add reserved neck and giblets and cook until well browned, 10 to 12 minutes. Transfer neck and giblets to large plate. Reduce heat to medium; add onion, carrot, parsley, and bay leaves; and cook, stirring frequently, until vegetables are softened, 5 to 7 minutes. Add flour and cook, stirring constantly, until flour is well coated with fat, about 1 minute. Slowly whisk in reserved defatted liquid and cook until thickened, about 1 minute. Whisk in water and wine, return neck and giblets, and bring to simmer. Simmer for 10 minutes. Season with salt and pepper to taste. Discard neck. Strain mixture through fine-mesh strainer and transfer to serving bowl. Carve turkey and arrange on serving platter. Serve with gravy.

## Classic Roast Turkey

**SERVES** 10 to 12

**WHY THIS RECIPE WORKS** Few of us want to take chances when cooking the holiday bird. We wanted to find a way that guaranteed moist, flavorful meat and bronzed skin—a true holiday table centerpiece. First we brined our turkey, which helped prevent the meat from drying out and also seasoned it right to the bone. After brining, we rinsed the bird of excess salt and let it rest on a wire rack in the refrigerator so that the skin dried out. This step helped ensure the skin would cook up crisp, not flabby. Placing the turkey on a V-rack allowed for air circulation all around so that the bird cooked evenly. And turning the turkey three times also helped to ensure even cooking. Finally, once the turkey was cooked, we waited 30 minutes before carving it. This allowed the juices in the turkey to redistribute so that, once carved, each slice was moist and full of flavor. Resist the temptation to tent the roasted turkey with foil while it rests on the carving board. Covering the bird will make the skin soggy.

- 2 cups table salt
- 1 (12- to 14-pound) turkey; giblets, neck, and tailpiece removed and reserved for gravy
- 2 medium onions, chopped coarse
- 2 medium carrots, chopped coarse
- 2 celery ribs, chopped coarse
- 6 sprigs fresh thyme
- 3 tablespoons unsalted butter, melted
- 1 cup water, plus more as needed
- 1 recipe Giblet Pan Gravy (recipe follows)

**1.** Dissolve the salt in 2 gallons cold water in a large container. Submerge the turkey in the brine, cover, and refrigerate or store in a very cool spot (40 degrees or less) for 4 to 6 hours.

**2.** Set a wire rack over a large rimmed baking sheet. Remove the turkey from the brine and rinse it well. Pat the turkey dry, inside and out, with paper towels. Place the turkey on the prepared baking sheet. Refrigerate, uncovered, for at least 8 hours or overnight.

**3.** Adjust an oven rack to the lowest position and heat the oven to 400 degrees. Line a V-rack with heavy duty foil and poke several holes in the foil. Set the V-rack in a roasting pan and spray the foil with vegetable oil spray.

**4.** Toss half of the onions, carrots, celery, and thyme with 1 tablespoon of the melted butter in a medium bowl and place inside the turkey. Tie the legs together with kitchen twine and tuck the wings under the bird. Scatter the remaining vegetables into the roasting pan.

**5.** Pour 1 cup water over the vegetable mixture. Brush the turkey breast with 1 tablespoon more melted butter, then place the turkey, breast side down, on the V-rack. Brush with the remaining 1 tablespoon melted butter.

**6.** Roast the turkey for 45 minutes. Remove the pan from the oven; baste with juices from the pan. With a dish towel in each hand, turn the turkey leg/thigh side up. If the liquid in the pan has totally evaporated, add another ½ cup water. Return the turkey to the oven and roast for 15 minutes. Remove the turkey from the oven again, baste, and turn the other leg/thigh side up; roast for another 15 minutes. Remove the turkey from the oven for a final time, baste, and turn it breast side up; roast until the thickest part of the breast registers 160 degrees and the thickest part of the thigh registers 175 degrees on an instant-read thermometer, 30 to 45 minutes.

**7.** Remove the turkey from the oven. Gently tip the turkey so that any accumulated juices in the cavity run into the roasting pan. Transfer the turkey to a carving board and let rest, uncovered, for 30 minutes. Carve the turkey and serve with the gravy.

### Giblet Pan Gravy

**MAKES** about 6 cups

Complete step 1 up to a day ahead, if desired. Begin step 3 once the bird has been removed from the oven and is resting on a carving board.

- 1 tablespoon vegetable oil
- Reserved turkey giblets, neck, and tailpiece
- 1 medium onion, chopped
- 4 cups chicken broth
- 2 cups water
- 2 sprigs fresh thyme
- 8 sprigs fresh parsley
- 3 tablespoons unsalted butter
- ¼ cup unbleached all-purpose flour
- 1 cup dry white wine
- Table salt and ground black pepper

**1.** Heat the oil in a large Dutch oven over medium heat until shimmering; add the giblets, neck, and tailpiece, and cook until golden and fragrant, about 5 minutes. Add the onion and continue to cook until softened, 3 to 4 minutes longer. Reduce the heat to low, cover, and cook until the turkey parts and onion release their juices, about 15 minutes. Add the broth, water, and herbs, bring to a boil, and adjust the heat to low. Simmer, uncovered, skimming any impurities that may rise to the surface, until the broth is rich and flavorful, about 30 minutes longer. Strain the broth into a large container and reserve the giblets. When cool enough to handle, chop the giblets. Refrigerate the giblets and broth until ready to use. (The broth can be stored in the refrigerator in an airtight container for up to 1 day.)

**2.** While the turkey is roasting, return the reserved turkey broth to a simmer. Heat the butter in a large saucepan over medium-low heat. Vigorously whisk in the flour (the mixture will froth and then thin out again). Cook slowly, stirring constantly, until nutty brown and fragrant, 10 to 15 minutes. Vigorously whisk all but 1 cup of the hot broth into the flour mixture. Bring to a boil, then continue to simmer, stirring occasionally, until the gravy is lightly thickened and very flavorful, about 30 minutes longer. Set aside until the turkey is done.

**3.** When the turkey has been transferred to a carving board to rest, spoon out and discard as much fat as possible from the roasting pan, leaving the caramelized herbs and vegetables. Place the roasting pan over two burners set on medium-high heat. Return the gravy to a simmer. Add the wine to the roasting pan of caramelized vegetables, scraping up any browned bits with a wooden spoon, and boil until reduced by half, about 5 minutes. Add the remaining 1 cup turkey broth and continue to simmer for 15 minutes; strain the pan juices into the gravy, pressing as much juice as possible out of the vegetables. Stir the reserved giblets into the gravy and return to a boil. Season with salt and pepper to taste and serve.

## Roast Turkey for a Crowd

**SERVES** about 20

**WHY THIS RECIPE WORKS** Unless you have access to multiple ovens, only a very large turkey will do when you've got a crowd coming to dinner. But finding a container large enough to brine a gargantuan bird can be tricky. And turning the bird in the oven, our usual method for evenly cooked meat, can be hot, heavy, and dangerous. We wanted the Norman Rockwell picture of perfection: a crisp, mahogany skin wrapped around tender, moist meat. We chose a Butterball turkey, which has already been brined for juicy flavor (a kosher bird, which has been salted, works well too). A combination of high and low heat resulted in a tender, juicy bird with deeply browned skin. We made the meat and pan drippings more flavorful with the addition of onion, carrot, and celery. A quartered lemon added bright, clean flavor. Serve with Giblet Pan Gravy for a Crowd. Rotating the bird helps produce moist, evenly cooked meat, but you may opt not to rotate it. In that case, do not line the V-rack with foil and roast the bird breast side up for the entire time.

- 3 medium onions, chopped coarse
- 3 medium carrots, chopped coarse
- 3 celery ribs, chopped coarse
- 1 lemon, quartered
- 2 sprigs fresh thyme
- 5 tablespoons unsalted butter, melted
- 1 (18- to 22-pound) frozen Butterball or kosher turkey, fully thawed; giblets, neck, and tailpiece removed and reserved for gravy
- 1 cup water, plus more as needed
- 1 teaspoon table salt
- 1 teaspoon pepper

**1.** Adjust an oven rack to the lowest position. Heat the oven to 425 degrees. Line a large V-rack with heavy-duty foil and poke several holes in the foil. Set the V-rack in a large roasting pan and spray the foil with vegetable oil spray.

**2.** Toss half of the onions, carrots, celery, lemon, and thyme with 1 tablespoon of the melted butter in a medium bowl and place inside the turkey. Tie the legs together with kitchen twine and tuck the wings under the bird. Scatter the remaining vegetables into the roasting pan.

**3.** Pour 1 cup water over the vegetable mixture. Brush the turkey breast with 2 tablespoons more of the melted butter, then sprinkle with half of the salt and half of the pepper. Place the turkey, breast side down, on the V-rack. Brush with the remaining 2 tablespoons melted butter and sprinkle with the remaining salt and pepper.

**4.** Roast the turkey for 1 hour. Remove the pan from the oven; baste with juices from the pan. With a dish towel in each hand, turn the turkey breast side up. If the liquid in the pan has totally evaporated, add another ½ cup water. Lower the oven temperature to 325 degrees. Return the turkey to the oven and continue to roast until the thickest part of the breast registers 160 degrees and the thickest part of the thigh registers 175 degrees on an instant-read thermometer, about 2 hours longer.

5. Remove the turkey from the oven. Gently tip the turkey up so that any accumulated juices in the cavity run into the roasting pan. Transfer the turkey to a carving board. Let rest, uncovered, for 35 to 40 minutes. Carve the turkey and serve with the gravy.

## Giblet Pan Gravy for a Crowd

**MAKES** about 8 cups

Complete step 1 up to a day ahead, if desired. Begin step 3 once the bird has been removed from the oven and is resting on a carving board.

- 1 tablespoon vegetable oil
- Reserved turkey giblets, neck, and tailpiece
- 1 medium onion, unpeeled and chopped
- 6 cups low-sodium chicken broth
- 3 cups water
- 2 sprigs fresh thyme
- 8 sprigs fresh parsley
- 5 tablespoons unsalted butter
- ¼ cup plus 2 tablespoons unbleached all-purpose flour
- 1½ cups dry white wine
- Table salt and pepper

1. Heat the oil in a large Dutch oven over medium heat until shimmering; add the giblets, neck, and tailpiece, and cook until golden and fragrant, about 5 minutes. Add the onion and continue to cook until softened, 3 to 4 minutes longer. Reduce the heat to low, cover, and cook until the turkey parts and onion release their juices, about 15 minutes. Add the broth, water, and herbs, bring to a boil, and adjust the heat to low. Simmer, uncovered, skimming any impurities that may rise to the surface, until the broth is rich and flavorful, about 30 minutes longer. Strain the broth into a large container and reserve the giblets. When cool enough to handle, chop the giblets. Refrigerate the giblets and broth until ready to use. (The broth can be stored in the refrigerator in an airtight container for up to 1 day.)

2. While the turkey is roasting, return the reserved turkey broth to a simmer. Heat the butter in a large saucepan over medium-low heat. Vigorously whisk in the flour (the mixture will froth and then thin out again). Cook slowly, stirring constantly, until nutty brown and fragrant, 10 to 15 minutes. Vigorously whisk all but 2 cups of the hot broth into the flour mixture. Bring to a boil, then continue to simmer, stirring occasionally, until the gravy is lightly thickened and very flavorful, about 35 minutes longer. Set aside until the turkey is done.

3. When the turkey has been transferred to a carving board to rest, spoon out and discard as much fat as possible from the roasting pan, leaving the caramelized herbs and vegetables. Place the roasting pan over two burners set on medium-high heat. Return the gravy to a simmer. Add the wine to the roasting pan of caramelized vegetables, scraping up any browned bits with a wooden spoon, and boil until reduced by half, about 7 minutes. Add the remaining 2 cups turkey broth and continue to simmer for 15 minutes; strain the pan juices into the gravy, pressing as much juice as possible out of the vegetables. Stir the reserved giblets into the gravy and return to a boil. Season with salt and pepper to taste and serve.

## Roast Turkey and Gravy with Herbes de Provence and Lemon

**SERVES** 10 to 12

**WHY THIS RECIPE WORKS** For a roast turkey that combines verdant, savory herb flavor in every bite with an easy, reliable roasting method, we started by making an herb paste that featured delicately floral herbes de Provence and vibrant lemon zest. Adding a generous amount of parsley as well as garlic powder and black pepper gave the paste a complex foundation. Applying the paste in three ways—under the skin with salt and sugar before roasting, over the skin in a basting butter, and stirred into the gravy—ensured that it offered bright, savory flavor in every bite. Applying baking powder to the skin before roasting helped it brown deeply. Roasting the bird in a preheated roasting pan set on a baking stone jump-started the cooking of the legs, while covering the breast with a foil shield for part of the time protected the lean breast meat from overcooking. The baking stone also thoroughly reduced and concentrated the pan drippings, so it didn't take long to make a flavorful gravy. Note that this recipe requires refrigerating the seasoned turkey for at least 24 hours. This recipe was developed using Diamond Crystal Kosher Salt. If you have Morton Kosher Salt, which is denser, reduce the salt in step 2 to 3 tablespoons and rub 1 tablespoon of the herb mixture into each side of the breast, 1½ teaspoons into each leg, and the remainder into the cavity. If using a self-basting turkey (such as a frozen Butterball) or a kosher turkey, omit the salt and sugar; instead, apply 4 teaspoons of the herb paste to each breast side and 2 teaspoons to each leg. When removing the foil in step 5, check the drippings in the roasting pan. If they are very dark or there is no liquid, add ¾ cup of water to the pan. The success of this recipe depends on saturating a baking stone and roasting pan with heat.

HERB PASTE

- ¾ cup chopped fresh parsley
- ¼ cup herbes de Provence
- 2 tablespoons vegetable oil
- 2 teaspoons grated lemon zest
- 2 teaspoons garlic powder
- ½ teaspoon pepper

TURKEY AND GRAVY

- ¼ cup kosher salt
- 4 teaspoons sugar
- 1 (12- to 14-pound) turkey, neck and giblets removed and reserved for gravy
- 2½ tablespoons vegetable oil, divided
- 1 teaspoon baking powder
- 2 tablespoons unsalted butter, melted
- 1 small onion, chopped fine
- 1 carrot, peeled and sliced thin
- 5 tablespoons all-purpose flour
- 3¼ cups water
- ¼ cup dry white wine
- 5 sprigs fresh parsley
- 2 bay leaves

**1. FOR THE HERB PASTE:** Process all ingredients in food processor until finely ground, about 30 seconds, scraping down sides of bowl as necessary.

**2. FOR THE TURKEY AND GRAVY:** Combine ¼ cup herb paste, salt, and sugar in bowl. Place turkey, breast side up, on counter. Using your fingers, carefully loosen skin covering breast and leg quarters. Rub 2 tablespoons herb mixture under skin of each side of breast, 4 teaspoons under skin of each leg, and remaining herb mixture inside cavity. Tuck wings behind back and tie legs together with kitchen twine. Place turkey on wire rack set in rimmed baking sheet and refrigerate, uncovered, for at least 24 hours or up to 2 days.

**3.** At least 30 minutes before roasting turkey, adjust oven rack to lowest position, set baking stone on rack, set roasting pan on baking stone, and heat oven to 500 degrees. Combine 1½ teaspoons oil and baking powder in small bowl. Pat turkey dry with paper towels. Rub oil mixture evenly over turkey. Cover breast with double layer of aluminum foil.

**4.** Remove roasting pan from oven. Drizzle remaining 2 tablespoons oil into roasting pan. Place turkey, breast side up, in pan and return pan to oven. Reduce oven temperature to 425 degrees and roast for 45 minutes. Stir 1 tablespoon herb paste into melted butter.

**5.** Remove turkey from oven. Discard foil and brush herb butter evenly over turkey. Return turkey to oven; reduce oven temperature to 325 degrees; and continue to roast until breast registers 160 degrees and thighs register 175 degrees, 1 to 1½ hours longer.

**6.** Using spatula, loosen turkey from roasting pan; transfer to carving board and let rest, uncovered, for 45 minutes. While turkey rests, using wooden spoon, scrape up any browned bits from bottom of roasting pan. Strain mixture through fine-mesh strainer set over bowl. Transfer drippings to fat separator and let rest for 10 minutes. Reserve defatted liquid (you should have 1 cup; add water if necessary) and 3 tablespoons fat. Discard remaining fat.

**7.** Heat reserved fat in large saucepan over medium-high heat until shimmering. Add neck and giblets and cook until well browned, 10 to 12 minutes. Transfer neck and giblets to large plate. Reduce heat to medium; add onion and carrot; and cook, stirring frequently, until vegetables are softened, 5 to 7 minutes. Add flour and cook, stirring constantly, until flour is well coated with fat, about 1 minute. Slowly whisk in defatted liquid and cook until thickened, about 1 minute.

**8.** Whisk in water, wine, parsley sprigs, and bay leaves. Return neck and giblets to saucepan and bring to simmer. Simmer for 10 minutes. Discard neck. Strain gravy through fine-mesh strainer set over bowl, discarding solids. Stir in remaining herb paste and season with salt and pepper to taste. Transfer to serving bowl. Carve turkey and arrange on serving platter. Serve with gravy.

## Roast Salted Turkey

**SERVES** 10 to 12

**WHY THIS RECIPE WORKS** We wanted an alternative method to brining that would make things more practical for those with limited refrigerator space, so we turned to salting. To make sure the salt penetrated the meat, (and we didn't tear the skin in the process) we found that chopsticks or the handle of a wooden spoon worked to help us gently separate the skin from the meat. To ensure moist breast meat, we chilled the breast by placing a small bag of ice inside the cavity against the breast and setting the turkey, breast side down, on ice. This trick brought down the temperature of the breast, thus allowing it to cook through over a longer period in the oven (more in line with the cooking time of the dark meat) without drying out. This recipe was developed and tested using Diamond Crystal Kosher Salt. If you have Morton's Kosher Salt, which is denser than Diamond Crystal, use only 4½ teaspoons of salt in the cavity, 2¼ teaspoons of salt per each half of the breast, and 1 teaspoon of salt per leg. Table salt is too fine and is not recommended for this recipe. If you are roasting a kosher or self-basting turkey (such as a frozen Butterball), do not salt it. If serving with Giblet Pan Gravy (page 338), note that you can complete step 1 of the gravy recipe up to a day ahead, if desired. Begin step 3 once the bird has been removed from the oven.

- 1 (12- to 14-pound) turkey; giblets, neck, and tailpiece removed and reserved for gravy (see page 338)
- 5 tablespoons kosher salt
- 1 (5-pound) bag ice cubes
- 4 tablespoons (½ stick) unsalted butter, melted
- 3 medium onions, chopped coarse
- 2 medium carrots, chopped coarse
- 2 celery ribs, chopped coarse
- 6 sprigs fresh thyme
- 1 cup water, plus more as needed

**1.** Carefully separate the turkey skin from the meat on the breast, legs, thighs, and back; avoid breaking the skin. Then rub 2 tablespoons of the salt evenly inside the cavity of the turkey, 1 tablespoon more salt under the skin of each breast half, and 1½ teaspoons more salt under the skin of each leg. Wrap the turkey tightly with plastic wrap; refrigerate for 24 to 48 hours.

**2.** Remove the turkey from the refrigerator. Rinse off any excess salt between the meat and skin and in the cavity, then pat dry inside and out with paper towels. Add ice to two 1-gallon zipper-lock bags until each is half full. Place the bags in a large roasting pan and lay the turkey, breast side down, on top of the ice. Add ice to two 1-quart zipper-lock bags until each is one-third full; place one bag of ice in the large cavity of the turkey and the other bag in the neck cavity. (Make sure that the ice touches the breast only, not the thighs or legs; see the photo.) Keep the turkey on ice for 1 hour (the roasting pan should remain on the counter).

**3.** Meanwhile, adjust an oven rack to the lowest position and heat the oven to 425 degrees. Line a large V-rack with heavy-duty foil and poke several holes in the foil. Set the V-rack in a roasting pan and spray the foil with vegetable oil spray.

**4.** Remove the turkey from the ice and pat dry with paper towels (discard the ice). Tuck the tips of the drumsticks into the skin at the tail to secure and tuck the wings under the bird. Brush the turkey breast with 2 tablespoons of the melted butter. Scatter the vegetables and thyme in the roasting pan and pour 1 cup water over the vegetable mixture. Place the turkey, breast side down, on the V-rack. Brush the turkey with the remaining 2 tablespoons melted butter.

### SALTING A TURKEY

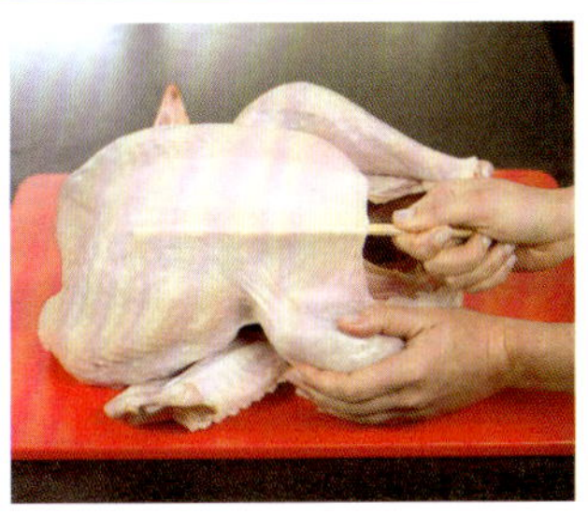

**1.** Use a chopstick or a thin wooden spoon handle to separate the skin from the meat over the breast, legs, thighs, and back. Rub 2 tablespoons kosher salt inside the main cavity.

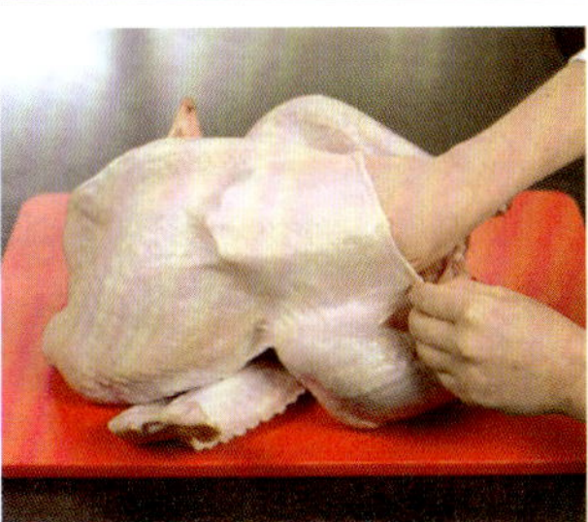

**2.** Lift the skin and apply 1 tablespoon kosher salt over each breast half, placing half of the salt on each end of each breast, then massaging the salt evenly over the meat.

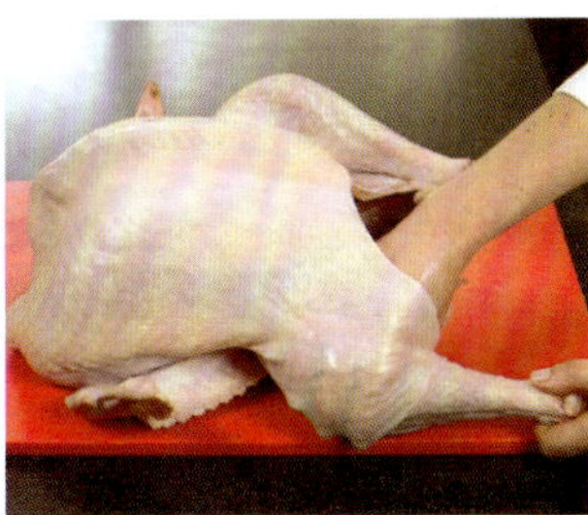

**3.** Apply 1½ teaspoons kosher salt over the top and bottom of each leg.

**5.** Roast the turkey for 45 minutes. Remove the pan from the oven (close the oven door to retain the oven heat) and reduce the oven temperature to 325 degrees. With a dish towel in each hand, rotate the turkey breast side up; continue to roast until the thickest part of the breast registers 160 degrees and the thickest part of the thigh registers 175 degrees on an instant-read thermometer, 1 to 1½ hours longer. Transfer the turkey to a carving board and let rest, uncovered, for 30 minutes. Carve the turkey and serve with the gravy.

## Roasted Brined Turkey

**SERVES** 10 TO 22, depending on turkey size

**WHY THIS RECIPE WORKS** Brining brings out the best in roasted turkey: It helps the bird retain moisture, seasons the meat, and helps the meat withstand hot oven temperatures, making for crisp skin. After brining, we let the turkey dry in the refrigerator for optimal crisping. Brushing the skin with melted butter before placing it breast-side down in a V-rack boosted its browning and added rich, buttery flavor to the finished turkey. To avoid overcooking the breast, we rotated the turkey after 45 minutes to an hour of roasting (depending on its size). We offer two brine formulas: one for a 4- to 6-hour brine and another for a 12- to 14-hour brine. The amount of salt used does not change with turkey size. If you're roasting a kosher or self-basting turkey, do not brine it. If you're roasting a large (18- to 22-pound) bird and are reluctant to rotate it, do not line the V-rack with foil and roast the bird breast-side up for the full time.

Table salt
1 turkey (12–22 pounds gross weight), rinsed thoroughly, giblets and neck reserved for gravy, if making
4 tablespoons unsalted butter, melted

**1.** Dissolve 1 cup salt per gallon cold water for 4- to 6-hour brine or ½ cup salt per gallon cold water for 12- to 14-hour brine in large stockpot or clean bucket. Two gallons of water will be sufficient for most birds; larger birds may require three gallons. Add turkey and refrigerate for predetermined amount of time.

**2.** Set wire rack in large rimmed baking sheet. Remove turkey from brine and pat dry, inside and out, with paper towels. Place turkey on prepared baking sheet. Refrigerate, uncovered, for at least 8 hours or overnight.

**3.** Before removing turkey from refrigerator, adjust oven rack to lowest position; heat oven to 400 degrees for 12- to 18-pound bird or 425 degrees for 18- to 22-pound bird. Line large V-rack with heavy-duty aluminum foil and use paring knife or skewer to poke 20 to 30 holes in foil; set V-rack in large roasting pan. Tuck tips of drumsticks into skin at tail to secure; tuck wing tips behind back. Brush breast with 2 tablespoons butter. Set turkey breast side down on prepared V-rack; brush back with remaining 2 tablespoons butter. Roast 45 minutes for 12- to 18-pound bird or 1 hour for 18- to 22-pound bird.

4. Remove roasting pan with turkey from oven (close oven door to retain oven heat); reduce oven temperature to 325 degrees if roasting 18- to 22-pound bird. Using clean potholders or dish towels, rotate turkey breast side up; continue to roast until thickest part of breast registers 160 degrees and thickest part of thigh registers 175 degrees, 50 to 60 minutes longer for 12- to 15-pound bird, about 1¼ hours for 15- to 18-pound bird, or about 2 hours for 18- to 22-pound bird. Transfer turkey to carving board; let rest for 30 minutes (or up to 40 minutes for 18- to 22-pound bird). Carve and serve.

## Herbed Roast Turkey

**SERVES** 10 to 12

**WHY THIS RECIPE WORKS** Throwing a bunch of herbs into the cavity of a turkey or rubbing the outside of the bird with a savory paste only flirts with great herb flavor—it doesn't infuse that flavor into each and every bite. We wanted an intensely herby turkey, one with a powerful, aromatic flavor that permeated well beyond the meat's surface. First we tried an intense brine, but it made the bird taste more pickled than infused with herbs. Next, we pumped the paste into the bird with a syringe, which created nothing but ugly blobs of overwhelmingly strong, raw-tasting herbs. Then we made a vertical slit in the breast meat and, using a paring knife, created an expansive pocket by sweeping the blade back and forth. This created a void into which we could rub a small amount of herb paste. This along with three other herbal applications—underneath the skin, inside the cavity, and over the skin gave every bite of turkey herb flavor. The herb paste, with small amounts of pungent herbs (sage and rosemary) and greater amounts of softer flavors (thyme and parsley), also included lemon zest, plus olive oil and Dijon mustard for spreadablity. Now we had a moist roast turkey packed with bright herb flavor. If you have the time and the refrigerator space, air-drying produces extremely crisp skin and is worth the effort. Serve with All-Purpose Turkey Gravy.

**TURKEY AND BRINE**

- 2 cups table salt
- 1 (12- to 14-pound) turkey; giblets, neck, and tailpiece removed and discarded

**HERB PASTE**

- 1¼ cups roughly chopped fresh parsley leaves
- 4 teaspoons minced fresh thyme leaves
- 2 teaspoons roughly chopped fresh sage leaves
- 1½ teaspoons minced fresh rosemary leaves
- 1 medium shallot, minced (about 3 tablespoons)
- 2 medium garlic cloves, minced or pressed through a garlic press (about 2 teaspoons)
- ¾ teaspoon grated zest from 1 lemon
- ¾ teaspoon table salt
- 1 teaspoon ground black pepper
- ¼ cup olive oil
- 1 teaspoon Dijon mustard

1. **FOR THE TURKEY AND BRINE:** Dissolve the salt in 2 gallons cold water in a large container. Submerge the turkey in the brine, cover, and refrigerate or store in a very cool spot (40 degrees or less) for 4 to 6 hours.

2. Remove the turkey from the brine and rinse it well. Pat dry inside and out with paper towels. Place the turkey, breast side up, on a wire rack set over a rimmed baking sheet or roasting pan and refrigerate, uncovered, for 30 minutes. (Alternatively, air-dry the turkey.)

3. **FOR THE HERB PASTE:** Pulse the parsley, thyme, sage, rosemary, shallot, garlic, lemon zest, salt, and pepper together in a food processor until a coarse paste is formed, 10 pulses. Add the olive oil and mustard; continue to pulse until the mixture forms a smooth paste, 10 to twelve 2-second pulses; scrape the sides of the processor bowl with a rubber spatula after 5 pulses. Transfer the mixture to a small bowl.

4. **TO PREPARE THE TURKEY:** Adjust an oven rack to the lowest position and heat the oven to 400 degrees. Line a large V-rack with heavy-duty foil and poke several holes in the foil. Set the V-rack in a large roasting pan and spray the foil with vegetable oil spray. Remove the turkey from the refrigerator and wipe away any water collected in the baking sheet; set the turkey, breast side up, on the baking sheet.

5. Use your hands to carefully loosen the skin from the meat of the breast, thighs, and drumsticks. Using your fingers or a spoon, slip 1½ tablespoons of the paste under the breast skin on each side of the turkey. Using your fingers, distribute the paste under the skin over the breast, thigh, and drumstick meat.

6. Using a sharp paring knife, cut a 1½-inch vertical slit into the thickest part of each side of the breast. Starting from the top of the incision, swing the knife tip down to create a 4 to 5-inch pocket within the flesh. Place 1 tablespoon more paste in the pocket of each side of the breast; using your fingers, rub the paste in a thin, even layer.

7. Rub 1 tablespoon more paste inside the turkey cavity. Rotate the turkey breast side down; apply half the remaining herb paste to the turkey skin; flip the turkey breast side up and apply the remaining herb paste to the skin, pressing and patting to make the paste adhere; reapply the herb paste that falls onto the baking sheet. Tuck the tips of the drumsticks into the skin at the tail to secure, and tuck the wings under the bird.

8. **TO ROAST THE TURKEY:** Place the turkey, breast side down, on the V-rack. Roast the turkey for 45 minutes.

9. Remove the pan from the oven (close the oven door to retain the oven heat). With a dish towel in each hand, rotate the turkey breast side up. Continue to roast until the thickest part of the breast registers 160 degrees and the thickest part of the thigh registers 175 degrees on an instant-read thermometer, 50 to 60 minutes longer. Transfer the turkey to a carving board and let rest, uncovered, for 30 minutes. Serve with the gravy.

## All-Purpose Turkey Gravy

**MAKES** about 2 cups

Adding drippings from the roasted turkey will enhance the flavor of the gravy.

- 1 small carrot, peeled and chopped coarse
- 1 small celery rib, chopped coarse
- 1 small onion, chopped coarse
- 3 tablespoons unsalted butter
- ¼ cup unbleached all-purpose flour
- 2 cups low-sodium chicken broth
- 2 cups beef broth
- 1 bay leaf
- 2 sprigs fresh thyme
- 5 whole black peppercorns
- Defatted pan drippings from Herbed Roast Turkey (optional)
- Table salt and ground black pepper

### APPLYING HERB PASTE TO THE TURKEY

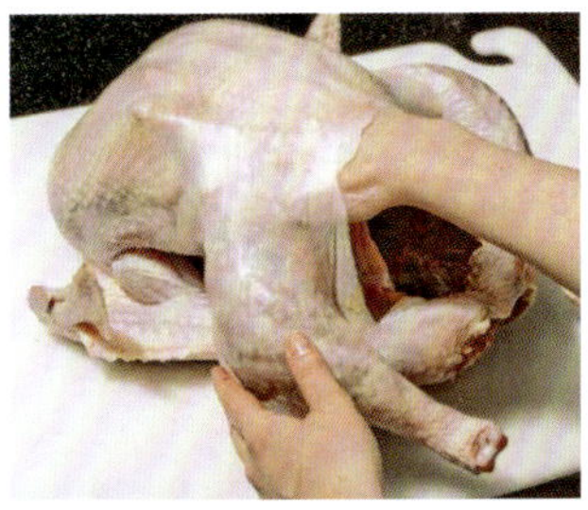

**1.** Carefully separate the skin from the meat on the breast, thigh, and drumstick areas.

**2.** Rub the herb paste under the skin and directly onto the flesh, distributing it evenly.

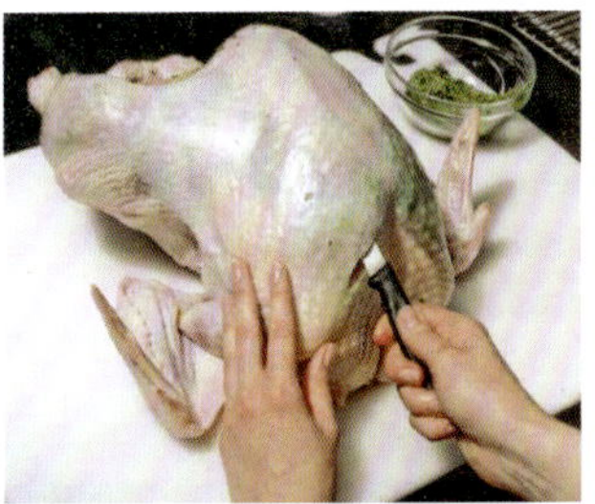

**3.** Make a 1½-inch slit in each breast. Swing a knife tip through the breast to create a large pocket.

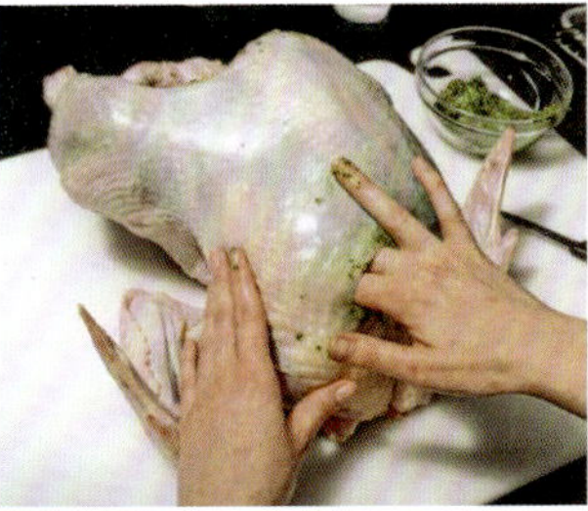

**4.** Place a thin layer of paste inside each pocket.

**5.** Rub the remaining paste inside the turkey cavity and on the skin.

**1.** Pulse the carrot into ¼-inch pieces in a food processor, about 5 pulses. Add the celery and onion and continue to pulse until all of the vegetables are chopped fine, 5 pulses.

**2.** Melt the butter in a large saucepan over medium-high heat. Add the vegetables and cook, stirring often, until softened and well browned, about 7 minutes. Reduce the heat to medium, stir in the flour, and cook, stirring constantly, until well browned, about 5 minutes.

**3.** Gradually whisk in the broths until smooth. Bring to a boil, skimming any foam that rises to the surface. Add the bay leaf, thyme, and peppercorns. Reduce the heat to medium-low and simmer, stirring occasionally, until the gravy is thickened and measures about 3 cups, 20 to 25 minutes. Stir in any juices from the roasted meat (if using) and continue to simmer the gravy as needed to re-thicken.

**4.** Strain the gravy through a fine-mesh strainer into a serving pitcher, pressing on the solids to extract as much liquid as possible; discard the solids. Season the gravy with salt and pepper to taste and cover to keep warm until needed.

## Old-Fashioned Stuffed Turkey

**SERVES** 10 to 12

**WHY THIS RECIPE WORKS** We wanted a turkey with everything: juicy meat, crisply burnished skin, and rich-flavored stuffing that cooked inside the bird. For the crispiest possible skin, we opted for salting over brining. Salting initially draws moisture out of the meat, but after a long rest in the refrigerator, all the moisture gets slowly drawn back in, seasoning the meat and helping it retain moisture. Next we turned to slow roasting and started the bird in a relatively low oven, then cranked the temperature to give it a final blast of skin-crisping heat and to bring the center up to temperature. It worked beautifully, yielding breast meat that was moist and tender. For even crispier skin, we massaged it with a baking powder and salt rub. The baking powder dehydrates the skin and raises its pH, making it more conducive to browning. We also poked holes in the skin to help rendering fat escape. And for extra flavor, we draped the bird with meaty salt pork, which we removed and drained before cranking up the heat so the bird didn't taste too smoky. To make sure the stuffing was cooked through, we started half of it in the bird (in a cheesecloth bag for easy removal) to give it meaty flavor, then combined it with the uncooked batch to finish baking it while the turkey rested. Table salt is not recommended for this recipe because it is too fine. To roast a kosher or self-basting turkey (such as a frozen Butterball), do not salt it in step 1. Look for salt pork that is roughly equal parts fat and lean meat. Serve with Make-Ahead Turkey Gravy (page 344).

**TURKEY**

- 1 (12- to 14-pound) turkey, giblets and neck reserved for gravy, if making
- 3 tablespoons plus 2 teaspoons kosher salt
- 2 teaspoons baking powder
- 12 ounces salt pork, cut into ¼-inch-thick slices and rinsed

STUFFING

- 1½ pounds (about 15 slices) high-quality white sandwich bread, cut into ½-inch cubes (about 12 cups)
- 4 tablespoons (½ stick) unsalted butter, plus extra for the baking dish
- 1 medium onion, minced
- 2 celery ribs, chopped fine
- Kosher salt and ground black pepper
- 2 tablespoons minced fresh thyme leaves
- 1 tablespoon minced fresh marjoram leaves
- 1 tablespoon minced fresh sage leaves
- 1½ cups low-sodium chicken broth
- 1 36-inch square cheesecloth, folded in quarters
- 2 large eggs

**1. FOR THE TURKEY:** Use your fingers or the handle of a wooden spoon to separate the turkey skin from the meat on the breast, legs, thighs, and back; avoid breaking the skin. Rub 1 tablespoon of the salt evenly inside the cavity of the turkey, 1½ teaspoons salt under the skin of each breast half, and 1½ teaspoons salt under the skin of each leg. Wrap the turkey tightly with plastic wrap; refrigerate for 24 to 48 hours.

**2. FOR THE STUFFING:** Adjust an oven rack to the lowest position and heat the oven to 250 degrees. Spread the bread cubes in a single layer on a rimmed baking sheet; bake until the edges have dried but the centers are slightly moist (the cubes should yield to pressure), about 45 minutes, stirring several times during baking. Transfer to a large bowl and increase the oven temperature to 325 degrees. (The bread can be toasted up to 1 day ahead.)

**3.** While the bread dries, heat the butter in a 12-inch skillet over medium-high heat; when the foaming subsides, add the onion, celery, 2 teaspoons salt, and 1 teaspoon pepper; cook, stirring occasionally, until the vegetables begin to soften and brown slightly, 7 to 10 minutes. Stir in the herbs; cook until fragrant, about 1 minute. Add the vegetables to the bowl with the dried bread; add 1 cup of the broth and toss until evenly moistened.

**4. TO ROAST THE TURKEY:** Combine the remaining 2 teaspoons salt and the baking powder in a small bowl. Remove the turkey from the refrigerator and unwrap. Thoroughly dry the turkey inside and out with paper towels. Using a skewer, poke 15 to 20 holes in the fat deposits on top of the breast halves and thighs, 4 to 5 holes in each deposit. Sprinkle the surface of the turkey with the salt–baking powder mixture and rub in the mixture with your hands, coating the skin evenly. Tuck the wings underneath the turkey. Line the turkey cavity with the cheesecloth, pack with 4 to 5 cups stuffing, and tie the ends of the cheesecloth together. Cover the remaining stuffing with plastic wrap and refrigerate. Using kitchen twine, loosely tie the turkey legs together. Place the turkey breast side down in a V-rack set in a roasting pan and drape the salt pork slices over the back.

**5.** Roast the turkey breast side down until the thickest part of the breast registers 130 degrees on an instant-read thermometer, 2 to 2½ hours. Remove the roasting pan from the oven and increase the oven temperature to 450 degrees. Transfer the turkey in the V-rack to a rimmed baking sheet. Remove and discard the salt pork. Using clean potholders or kitchen towels, rotate the turkey breast side up. Cut the twine binding the legs and remove the stuffing bag; empty into the reserved stuffing in the bowl. Pour the drippings from the roasting pan into a fat separator and reserve for gravy.

**6.** Once the oven has come to temperature, return the turkey in the V-rack to the roasting pan and roast until the skin is golden brown and crisp, the thickest part of the breast registers 160 degrees, and the thickest part of the thigh registers 175 degrees, about 45 minutes, rotating the pan halfway through. Transfer the turkey to a carving board and let rest, uncovered, for 30 minutes.

**7.** While the turkey rests, reduce the oven temperature to 400 degrees. Whisk the eggs and remaining ½ cup broth together in a small bowl. Pour the egg mixture over the stuffing and toss to combine, breaking up any large chunks; spread in a buttered 13 by 9-inch baking dish. Bake until the stuffing registers 165 degrees and the top is golden brown, about 15 minutes. Carve the turkey and serve with the stuffing.

## Make-Ahead Turkey Gravy

**MAKES** about 2 quarts

Note that the optional roast turkey drippings may be quite salty—add them carefully to the gravy in step 4 so that the gravy does not become too salty.

- 6 turkey thighs, trimmed, or 9 wings, separated at the joints
- 2 medium carrots, chopped coarse
- 2 medium celery ribs, chopped coarse
- 2 medium onions, chopped coarse
- 1 head garlic, halved
- Vegetable oil spray
- 10 cups low-sodium chicken broth, plus extra as needed
- 2 cups dry white wine
- 12 sprigs fresh thyme
- Unsalted butter, as needed
- 1 cup unbleached all-purpose flour
- Table salt and ground black pepper
- Defatted drippings from Old-Fashioned Stuffed Turkey (page 343) (optional)

**1.** Adjust an oven rack to the middle position and heat the oven to 450 degrees. Toss the thighs, carrots, celery, onions, and garlic together in a roasting pan and spray with vegetable oil spray. Roast, stirring occasionally, until well browned, 1½ to 1¾ hours.

**2.** Transfer the contents of the roasting pan to a large Dutch oven. Add the broth, wine, and thyme and bring to a boil, skimming as needed. Reduce to a gentle simmer and cook until the broth is brown and flavorful and measures about 8 cups when strained, about 1½ hours. Strain the broth through a fine-mesh strainer into a large container, pressing on the solids to extract as much liquid as possible; discard the solids. (The turkey broth can be cooled and refrigerated in an airtight container for up to 2 days or frozen for up to 1 month.)

**3.** Let the strained turkey broth settle (if necessary), then spoon off and reserve ½ cup of the fat that has risen to the top (add butter as needed if short on turkey fat). Heat the fat in a Dutch oven over medium-high heat until bubbling. Whisk in the flour and cook, whisking constantly, until well browned, 3 to 7 minutes.

**4.** Slowly whisk in the turkey broth and bring to a boil. Reduce to a simmer and cook until the gravy is very thick, 10 to 15 minutes. Add the defatted drippings (if using) to taste, then season with salt and pepper to taste and serve. (The gravy can be refrigerated in an airtight container for up to 2 days; reheat gently, adding additional chicken broth as needed to adjust the consistency).

### STUFFING A TURKEY

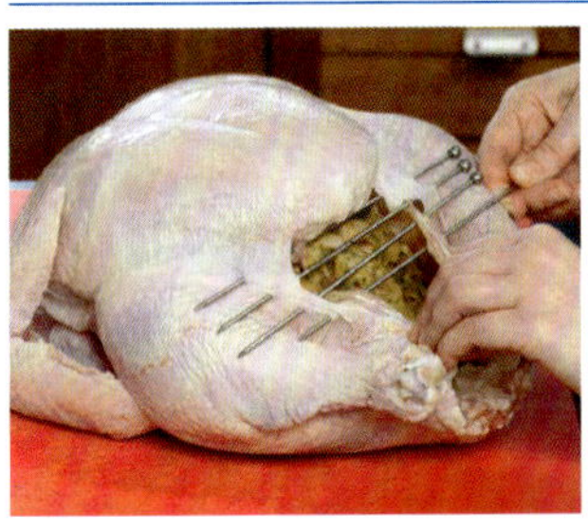

**1.** After placing 4 to 5 cups of the preheated stuffing into the turkey, use metal skewers (or cut bamboo skewers) and thread them through the skin on both sides of the cavity to seal the cavity shut.

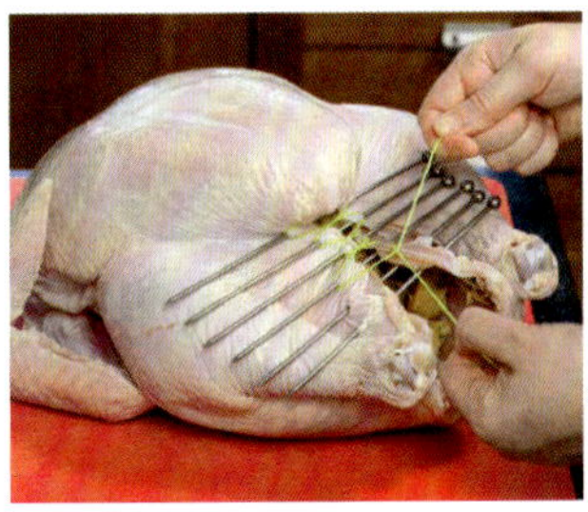

**2.** Center a 2-foot piece of kitchen twine on the top skewer and then cross the twine as you wrap each end of it around and under the skewers. Loosely tie the legs together with another short piece of twine.

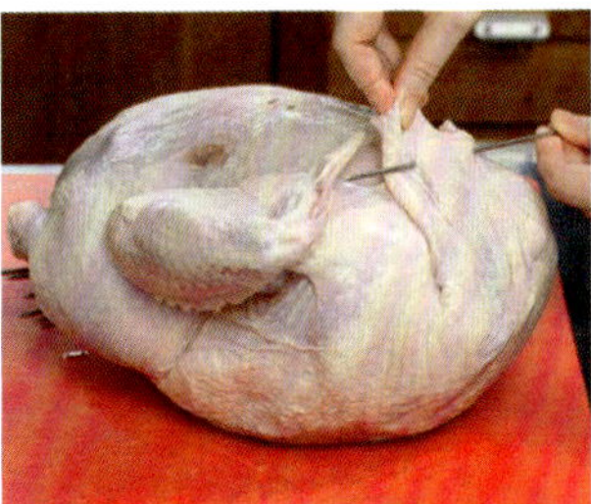

**3.** Flip the turkey over onto its breast. Stuff the neck cavity loosely with approximately 1 cup of stuffing. Pull the skin flap over and use a skewer to pin the flap to the turkey.

## Classic Roast Stuffed Turkey

**SERVES** 10 to 12

**WHY THIS RECIPE WORKS** A stuffed roasted turkey is certainly festive, but more people nowadays roast turkeys unstuffed out of concern for safety. We wanted to find a way to safely and successfully roast a stuffed turkey, so that the breast meat would be succulent and the stuffing fully cooked. This required limiting our turkey to a maximum of 14 pounds, as it is too difficult to safely stuff and roast a larger bird. Often, the breast meat is a bone-dry 180 degrees by the time the stuffing reaches a safe 160 degrees. To solve this, we heated the stuffing in the microwave before placing half of it in the bird to give it a head start on cooking. We baked the remaining stuffing in a casserole dish. We also brined the bird to add flavor and moisture (which did not make the stuffing soggy or overly salty). A 12- to 14-pound turkey will accommodate approximately half of the stuffing. Bake the remainder while the bird rests. If serving with Giblet Pan Gravy (page 338), note that you can complete step 1 up to a day ahead, if desired.

- 2 cups table salt
- 1 (12- to 14-pound) turkey; giblets, neck, and tailpiece removed and reserved for gravy (see page 338)
- 2 medium onions, chopped coarse
- 1 medium carrot, chopped coarse
- 1 celery rib, chopped coarse
- 4 sprigs fresh thyme
- 1 cup water, plus more as needed
- 1 recipe Bread Stuffing with Bacon, Apples, Sage, and Caramelized Onions (page 346)
- 3 tablespoons unsalted butter, plus extra for the casserole dish and foil
- ¼ cup low-sodium chicken broth
- 1 recipe Giblet Pan Gravy (page 338) (optional)

**1.** Dissolve the salt in 2 gallons cold water in a large container. Submerge the turkey in the brine, cover, and refrigerate or store in a very cool spot (40 degrees or less) for 4 to 6 hours.

**2.** Set a wire rack over a large rimmed baking sheet. Remove the turkey from the brine and rinse it well. Pat the turkey dry inside and out with paper towels. Place the turkey on the prepared baking sheet. Refrigerate, uncovered, and air-dry for at least 8 hours or overnight.

**3.** Adjust an oven rack to the lowest position and heat the oven to 400 degrees. Line a V-rack with heavy-duty foil and poke several holes in the foil. Set the V-rack inside a roasting pan and spray the foil with vegetable oil spray. Scatter the onions, carrot, celery, and thyme in the roasting pan. Pour 1 cup water over the vegetable mixture.

**4.** Place half of the stuffing in a buttered medium casserole dish, dot the surface with 1 tablespoon of the butter, cover with foil, and refrigerate until ready to use. Microwave the remaining stuffing on high power, stirring two or three times, until very hot (120 to 130 degrees on an instant-read thermometer), 6 to 8 minutes. Spoon 4 to 5 cups of stuffing into the turkey cavity until very loosely packed. Secure the skin flap over the cavity opening with skewers. Melt the remaining 2 tablespoons butter. Tuck the wings under the bird, brush the turkey breast with half of the melted butter, then turn the turkey breast side down. Fill the neck cavity with the remaining heated stuffing and secure the skin flap over the opening. Place the turkey, breast side down, on the V-rack. Brush with the remaining butter.

**5.** Roast the turkey for 1 hour, then reduce the temperature to 250 degrees and roast for 2 hours longer, adding water if the pan becomes dry. Remove the pan from the oven (close the oven door) and, with a dish towel in each hand, turn the bird breast side up, and baste (the temperature of the thickest part of the breast should be 145 to 150 degrees). Increase the oven temperature to 400 degrees; continue to roast until the thickest part of the breast registers 160 degrees, the thickest part of the thigh registers 175 degrees, and the center of the stuffing registers 165 degrees on an instant-read thermometer, 1 to 1½ hours longer. Remove the turkey from the oven, transfer to a carving board, and let rest for 30 minutes.

**6.** Add the broth to the dish of reserved stuffing, replace the foil, and bake until hot throughout, about 20 minutes. Remove the foil; continue to bake until the stuffing forms a golden brown crust, about 15 minutes longer.

**7.** Carve the turkey and serve with the stuffing and the gravy, if using.

## Bread Stuffing with Bacon, Apples, Sage, and Caramelized Onions

**MAKES** about 12 cups

To dry the bread, spread the cubes out onto 2 large baking sheets and dry in a 300-degree oven for 30 to 60 minutes. Let the bread cool before using in the stuffing.

- 1 pound bacon, cut crosswise into ¼-inch strips
- 6 medium onions, sliced thin (about 7 cups)
- 1 teaspoon table salt
- 2 Granny Smith apples, peeled, cored, and cut into ½-inch cubes (about 2 cups)
- ½ cup fresh parsley leaves, chopped fine
- 3 tablespoons minced fresh sage leaves
- ½ teaspoon ground black pepper
- 3 pounds high-quality white sandwich bread, cut into ¾-inch cubes and dried (about 12 cups)
- 1 cup low-sodium chicken broth
- 3 large eggs, lightly beaten

**1.** Cook the bacon in a large skillet or Dutch oven over medium heat until crisp and browned, about 12 minutes. Remove the bacon from the pan with a slotted spoon and drain on paper towels. Discard all but 3 tablespoons of the rendered bacon fat.

**2.** Increase the heat to medium-high and add the onions and ¼ teaspoon of the salt. Cook the onions until golden in color, making sure to stir occasionally and scrape the sides and bottom of the pan, about 20 minutes. Reduce the heat to medium and continue to cook, stirring more often to prevent burning, until the onions are deep golden brown, another 5 minutes. Add the apples and continue to cook for another 5 minutes. Transfer the contents of the pan to a large bowl.

**3.** Add the parsley, sage, remaining ¾ teaspoon salt, and the pepper to the bowl and mix to combine. Add the bread cubes.

**4.** Whisk the broth and eggs together in a small bowl. Pour the mixture over the bread cubes. Toss gently to evenly distribute the ingredients.

## Stuffed Spatchcocked Turkey

**SERVES** 10 to 12 **SEASON 26**

**WHY THIS RECIPE WORKS** The easiest way to produce perfectly cooked, crisp-skinned turkey and poultry-infused stuffing is to spatchcock the bird and drape it over the stuffing. Spatchcocking, or removing the backbone from the turkey, allowed it to lay flat in the roasting pan so that the rich dark meat and delicate white meat cooked at similar rates (a foil shield prevented the delicate breast meat from overcooking). And because all of the skin was face-up, every inch of it turned brown and crisp in the oven. With the bird arranged on top of the stuffing, its drippings added loads of flavor and moisture to the bread during roasting. We purposely made the stuffing dry, since the bird would exude flavorful juices as it cooked. After transferring the roast turkey to a carving board, we stirred the drippings into the stuffing and baked it briefly to crisp the top. Note that this recipe requires refrigerating the seasoned bird for 24 to 48 hours. Remove any large pockets of fat from the neck cavity. This recipe was developed using Diamond Crystal Kosher Salt. If you have Morton Kosher Salt, which is denser, reduce the salt in step 1 to 3 tablespoons and rub 4 teaspoons of the salt mixture into each side of the breast, 2 teaspoons into each leg, and the remainder onto the cavity. If using a self-basting turkey (such as a frozen Butterball) or a kosher turkey, omit the salt and sugar.

- ¼ cup kosher salt
- 4 teaspoons sugar
- 1 (12- to 14-pound) turkey, neck and giblets removed and reserved for gravy
- 1½ pounds hearty white sandwich bread, cut into ½-inch cubes
- 3 large eggs
- ½ cup water
- 5 tablespoons unsalted butter, divided
- 3 onions, chopped
- 6 celery ribs, chopped fine
- 2 tablespoons minced fresh thyme
- 2 tablespoons minced fresh sage
- 6 garlic cloves, minced
- 1 teaspoon pepper

**1.** Combine salt and sugar in bowl. Place turkey on counter breast side down. Using kitchen shears, cut through bones on either side of backbone, staying as close as possible to backbone. Remove backbone and save for gravy, if making. Flip turkey and press down firmly with heels of your hands to flatten breastbone.

**2.** Using your fingers, carefully loosen skin covering breast and leg quarters. Rub 5 teaspoons salt mixture under skin of each side of breast, 2 teaspoons under skin of each leg, and remaining mixture onto cavity. Tuck wings under turkey and place turkey skin side up on wire rack set in rimmed baking sheet. Refrigerate, uncovered, for at least 24 hours or up to 2 days.

**3.** Adjust oven racks to upper-middle and lower-middle positions and heat oven to 250 degrees. Spread bread cubes in even layer on 2 rimmed baking sheets and bake until mostly dry and very lightly browned, 40 to 50 minutes, stirring halfway through baking. Remove bread from oven and cool on sheets for at least 15 minutes.

**4.** While bread cools, adjust lower oven rack to middle position and increase oven temperature to 425 degrees. Whisk eggs and water in large bowl until combined. When bread is cool, add to egg mixture and toss gently so bread is fully coated but does not break apart; set aside.

**5.** Melt 4 tablespoons butter in 12-inch nonstick skillet over medium heat. Add onions and celery and cook, stirring occasionally, until softened, 8 to 10 minutes. Stir in thyme, sage, garlic, and pepper and cook until fragrant, about 30 seconds. Transfer vegetables to bowl with bread and stir gently to combine (stuffing will seem dry). (Stuffing can be refrigerated for 24 hours.)

**6.** Spray roasting pan with vegetable oil spray. Transfer stuffing to pan and shape into level 9 by 9-inch square. Pat turkey dry with paper towels. Arrange turkey on top of stuffing. Tuck any exposed stuffing under bird, so all of stuffing is covered. Cover breast with double layer of aluminum foil. Roast on middle rack for 45 minutes. Remove turkey from oven and discard foil.

**7.** Reduce oven temperature to 325 degrees. Melt remaining 1 tablespoon butter and brush evenly over turkey. Return turkey to oven and continue to roast until skin is deep golden brown and breast registers 155 degrees and thighs register 175 degrees, 2 to 2½ hours longer.

**8.** Transfer turkey to carving board and let rest, uncovered, for 30 minutes. While turkey rests, stir stuffing well to incorporate drippings and scrape up any browned bits. Redistribute stuffing over bottom of roasting pan in even layer. When turkey has rested for 15 minutes, return stuffing to oven and bake until golden brown, about 15 minutes. Transfer stuffing to serving dish. Carve turkey and arrange on serving platter. Serve turkey with stuffing.

## Crisp-Skin High-Roast Butterflied Turkey with Sausage Dressing

**SERVES** 10 to 12

**WHY THIS RECIPE WORKS** High-roasting (oven-roasting at very high temperatures for the sake of speed and flavor) a turkey presents the home cook with two potential problems: billowing smoke from incinerated pan drippings and torched breast meat. We wanted to find a way to prepare a high-roast turkey with crisp, picture-perfect skin and moist, evenly cooked meat in less than two hours—without setting off the smoke alarm. We butterflied the turkey for crisp skin and evenly cooked meat, and then roasted it on a broiler pan set over the stuffing—which absorbed the drippings. This step helped season the stuffing and kept the kitchen from filling with smoke. To complement our moist, crisp-skinned turkey, we made a cornbread and sausage stuffing that was both rich and easy to prepare. The dressing can be made with cornbread or white bread, but note that they are not used in equal amounts. The turkey is roasted in a broiler pan top, or a sturdy wire rack, set in a 16 by 12-inch disposable aluminum roasting pan. If using a wire rack, choose one about 17 by 11 inches so that it will span the roasting pan and sit above the dressing in the pan.

**TURKEY**

- 1 cup table salt
- 1 cup sugar
- 1 (12- to 14-pound) turkey; giblets, neck, and tailpiece removed and reserved for gravy; turkey butterflied (see page 348) and backbone and rib bones reserved for gravy
- 1 tablespoon unsalted butter, melted

**SAUSAGE DRESSING**

- 12 cups Golden Cornbread (recipe follows) broken into 1-inch pieces (include crumbs), or 18 cups 1-inch challah or Italian bread cubes (from about 1½ loaves)
- 1¾ cups low-sodium chicken broth
- 1 cup half-and-half
- 2 large eggs, beaten lightly
- 12 ounces bulk pork sausage, broken into 1-inch pieces
- 3 medium onions, minced (about 3 cups)
- 3 celery ribs, chopped fine (about 1½ cups)
- 2 tablespoons unsalted butter
- 2 tablespoons minced fresh thyme leaves
- 2 tablespoons minced fresh sage leaves
- 3 medium garlic cloves, minced or pressed through a garlic press (about 1 tablespoon)
- 1½ teaspoons table salt
- 2 teaspoons ground black pepper
- 1 recipe Giblet Pan Gravy (page 338)

**1. TO BRINE THE TURKEY:** Dissolve the salt and sugar in 2 gallons cold water in a large container. Submerge the turkey in the brine and refrigerate or store in a very cool spot (40 degrees or less) for 4 to 6 hours.

**2. TO PREPARE THE DRESSING:** While the turkey brines, adjust the oven racks to the upper-middle and lower-middle positions and heat the oven to 250 degrees. Spread the bread in an even layer on two rimmed baking sheets and dry in the oven for 50 to 60 minutes for cornbread or 40 to 50 minutes for challah or Italian bread.

### PREPARING THE BUTTERFLIED TURKEY

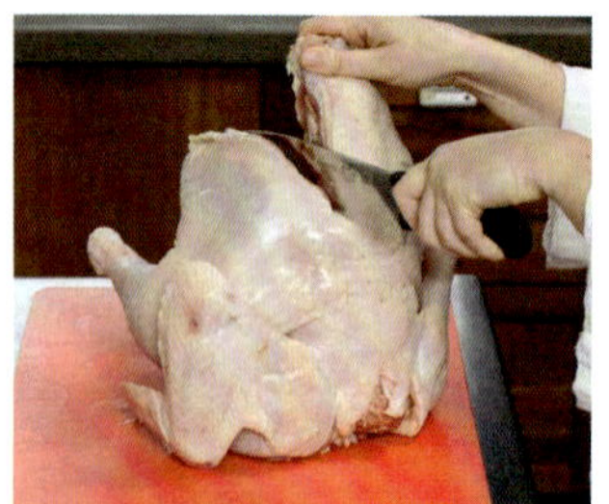

**1.** Holding the turkey upright with the backbone facing front, use a hacking motion to cut through the turkey directly to one side of the backbone with a chef's knife.

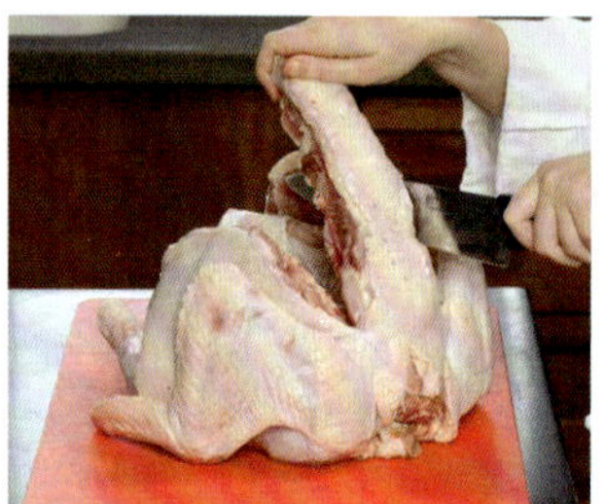

**2.** Holding the backbone with one hand, hack through the turkey directly to the other side of the backbone; the backbone will fall away.

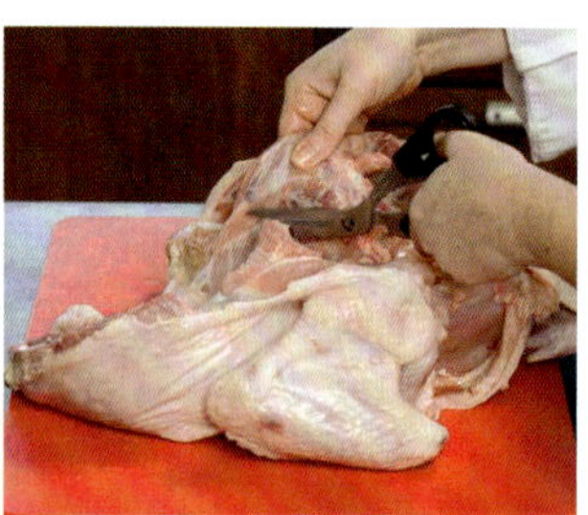

**3.** Using kitchen scissors, cut out the rib plate and remove any small pieces of bone.

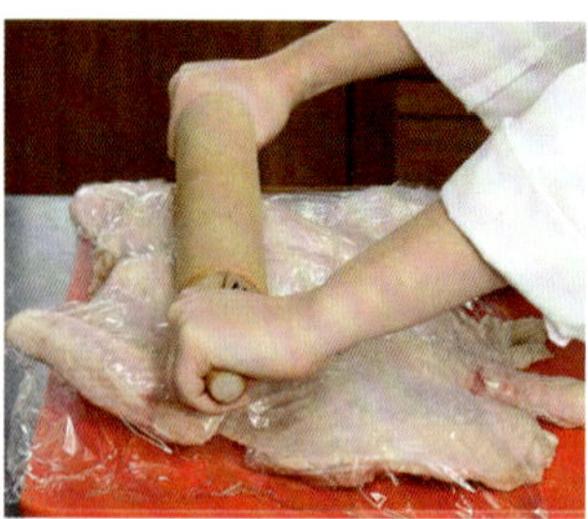

**4.** Place the turkey, breast side up, on a cutting board and cover with plastic wrap. With a large rolling pin, whack the breastbone until it cracks and the turkey flattens.

**5.** After brining and rinsing, place the turkey, breast side up, on a wire rack set over a rimmed baking sheet. Tuck the wings under the turkey. Push the legs up to rest between the thigh and breast. Tie the legs together.

**3.** Place the bread in a large bowl. Whisk the broth, half-and-half, and eggs together in a medium bowl; pour over the bread and toss very gently to coat so that the bread does not break into smaller pieces. Set aside.

**4.** Heat a 12-inch skillet over medium-high heat until hot, about 1½ minutes. Add the sausage and cook, stirring occasionally, until the sausage loses its raw color, 5 to 7 minutes. With a slotted spoon, transfer the sausage to a medium bowl. Add half the onions and celery to the fat in the skillet; sauté, stirring occasionally, over medium-high heat until softened, about 5 minutes. Transfer the onion mixture to the bowl with the sausage. Return the skillet to the heat and add the butter; when melted add the remaining onions and celery and sauté, stirring occasionally, until softened, about 5 minutes. Stir in the thyme, sage, and garlic; cook until fragrant, about 30 seconds; add the salt and pepper. Add this mixture along with the sausage and onion mixture to the bread and stir gently to combine (try not to break the bread into smaller pieces).

**5.** Spray a 16 by 12-inch disposable aluminum roasting pan with vegetable oil spray. Transfer the dressing to the roasting pan and spread in an even layer. Cover the pan with foil and refrigerate while preparing the turkey.

**6. TO PREPARE THE TURKEY FOR ROASTING:** Remove the turkey from the brine and rinse it well. Position the turkey on a broiler pan top or wire rack; thoroughly pat the surface of the turkey dry with paper towels. Place the broiler pan top with the turkey on top of the roasting pan with the dressing; refrigerate, uncovered, for 8 to 24 hours.

**7. TO ROAST THE TURKEY WITH THE DRESSING:** Adjust an oven rack to the lower-middle position and heat the oven to 450 degrees. Remove the broiler pan top with the turkey and remove the foil from the dressing; place the broiler pan top with the turkey on the dressing in the roasting pan. Brush the turkey with the melted butter. Roast the turkey until the turkey skin is crisp and deep brown and the thickest part of the breast registers 160 degrees and the thickest part of the thigh registers 175 degrees, 1 hour 20 minutes to 1 hour 40 minutes, rotating the pan from front to back after 40 minutes.

**8.** Transfer the broiler pan top with the turkey to a carving board, tent loosely with foil, and let rest for 20 minutes. Meanwhile, adjust an oven rack to the upper-middle position, place the roasting pan with the dressing back in the oven, and bake until golden brown, about 10 minutes. Carve the turkey and serve with the dressing and gravy.

## Golden Cornbread

**MAKES** about 16 cups crumbled corn bread

You need about three-quarters of this recipe for the dressing; the rest is for nibbling.

- 4 tablespoons (½ stick) unsalted butter, melted, plus extra for the baking dish
- 4 large eggs
- 1⅓ cups buttermilk
- 1⅓ cups milk
- 2 cups yellow cornmeal
- 2 cups (10 ounces) unbleached all-purpose flour

- 2 tablespoons sugar
- 4 teaspoons baking powder
- 1 teaspoon baking soda
- 1 teaspoon table salt

**1.** Adjust an oven rack to the middle position and heat the oven to 375 degrees. Grease a 13 by 9-inch baking dish with butter.

**2.** Beat the eggs in medium bowl; whisk in the buttermilk and milk.

**3.** Whisk the cornmeal, flour, sugar, baking powder, baking soda, and salt together in a large bowl. Push the dry ingredients up the sides of the bowl to make a well, then pour the egg and milk mixture into the well and stir with a whisk until just combined; stir in the melted butter.

**4.** Pour the batter into the prepared baking dish. Bake until the top is golden brown and the edges have pulled away from the sides of the pan, 30 to 40 minutes.

**5.** Transfer the baking dish to a wire rack and let cool completely before using, about 1 hour.

## Julia Child's Stuffed Turkey, Updated

**SERVES** 10 to 12

**WHY THIS RECIPE WORKS** In her 1989 cookbook, *The Way to Cook*, Julia Child separates a raw turkey into legs and breast to ensure that both white and dark meat are roasted to perfection. Other benefits include a quicker cooking time and a small mound of rich sausage stuffing that tastes as though it has been roasted inside the bird. We loved this idea, but saw a couple opportunities for improvement. In our version, we brined the breast to keep it juicy and flavorful. Jump-starting the cooking of the breast at 425 degrees decreased the overall cooking time, which also helped the meat to retain moisture. To make even more stuffing, we increased the amount of bread, and we swapped the sausage for the brighter flavor of dried cranberries. This recipe calls for a natural, unenhanced turkey and requires brining the turkey breast in the refrigerator for 6 to 12 hours before cooking. If using a self-basting turkey (such as a frozen Butterball) or a kosher turkey, do not brine in step 3 and omit the salt in step 2. Trim any excess fat from the bird before cooking to ensure that the stuffing doesn't become greasy. The bottom of your roasting pan should be 7 to 8 inches from the top of the oven. In this recipe, we leave the stuffing in a warm oven while the turkey rests. Serve with Turkey Gravy for Julia Child's Stuffed Turkey, Updated (page 350).

- 1 (12- to 15-pound) turkey, neck and giblets removed and reserved for gravy
- 1 teaspoon plus 2 tablespoons minced fresh sage
- Table salt and pepper
- Wooden skewers
- 1½ pounds hearty white sandwich bread, cut into ½-inch cubes
- 1 tablespoon vegetable oil
- 3 tablespoons unsalted butter
- 3 onions, chopped fine
- 6 celery ribs, minced
- 1 cup dried cranberries
- 4 large eggs, beaten

**1.** With turkey breast side up, using boning or paring knife, cut through skin around leg quarter where it attaches to breast. Bend leg back to pop leg bone out of socket. Cut through joint to separate leg quarter. Repeat to remove second leg quarter. Working with 1 leg quarter at a time and with skin side down, use tip of knife to cut along sides of thighbone to expose bone, then slide knife under bone to free meat. Cut joint between thigh and leg and remove thighbone. Reserve thighbones for gravy.

**2.** Rub interior of each thigh with ½ teaspoon sage, ½ teaspoon salt, and ¼ teaspoon pepper. Truss each thigh closed using wooden skewers and kitchen twine. Place leg quarters on large plate, cover, and refrigerate for 6 to 12 hours.

**3.** Using kitchen shears, cut through ribs following vertical line of fat where breast meets back from tapered end of breast to wing joint. Using your hands, bend back away from breast to pop shoulder joint out of socket. Cut through joint between bones to separate back from breast. Reserve back for gravy. Trim excess fat from breast. Dissolve ¾ cup salt in 6 quarts cold water in large container. Submerge breast in brine, cover, and refrigerate for 6 to 12 hours.

**4.** Adjust oven racks to upper-middle and lower-middle positions and heat oven to 300 degrees. Spread bread cubes in even layer on 2 rimmed baking sheets and bake until mostly dry and very lightly browned, 25 to 30 minutes, stirring occasionally during baking. Transfer dried bread to large bowl. Increase oven temperature to 425 degrees.

**5.** While bread dries, remove breast from brine and pat dry with paper towels (leave leg quarters in refrigerator). Tuck wings behind back. Brush surface with 2 teaspoons oil. Melt butter in 12-inch nonstick ovensafe skillet over medium heat. Add onions and cook, stirring occasionally, until softened, 10 to 12 minutes. Add celery, remaining 2 tablespoons sage, and 1½ teaspoons pepper; continue to cook until celery is slightly softened, 3 to 5 minutes longer. Transfer vegetables to bowl with bread and wipe out skillet with paper towels. Place turkey breast skin side down in skillet, and roast in oven for 30 minutes.

**6.** While breast roasts, add cranberries and eggs to bread mixture and toss to combine (mixture will be dry). Transfer stuffing to 16 by 13-inch roasting pan and, using rubber spatula, pat stuffing into level 12 by 10-inch rectangle.

**7.** Remove breast from oven, and using 2 wads of paper towels, flip breast and place over two-thirds of stuffing. Arrange leg quarters over remaining stuffing and brush with remaining 1 teaspoon oil. Lightly season breast and leg quarters with salt. Tuck any large sections of exposed stuffing under bird so most of stuffing is covered by turkey. Transfer pan to oven and cook for 30 minutes.

**8.** Reduce oven temperature to 350 degrees. Continue to roast until thickest part of breast registers 160 degrees and thickest part of thigh registers 175 degrees, 40 minutes to

## DECONSTRUCTED TURKEY

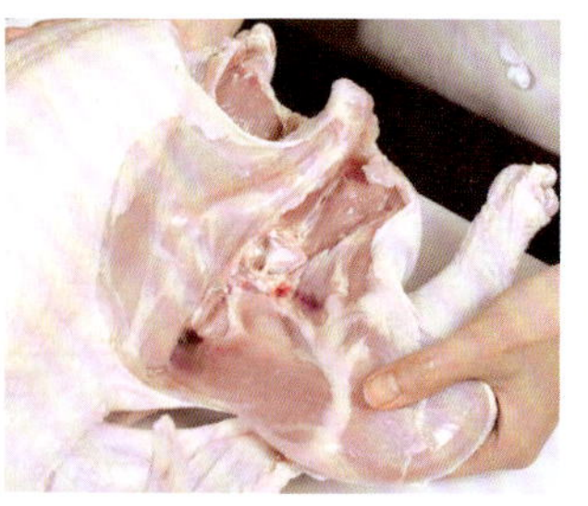

**1.** Using boning or paring knife, cut through skin around leg where it attaches to breast. Bend leg back to pop leg bone out of socket. Cut through joint to separate leg quarter.

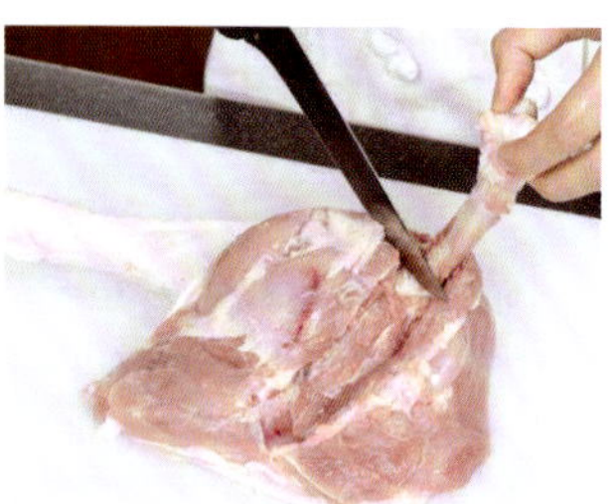

**2.** With tip of knife, cut along sides of thighbone to expose bone, then slide knife under bone to free meat. Without severing skin, cut joint between thigh and leg and remove thighbone.

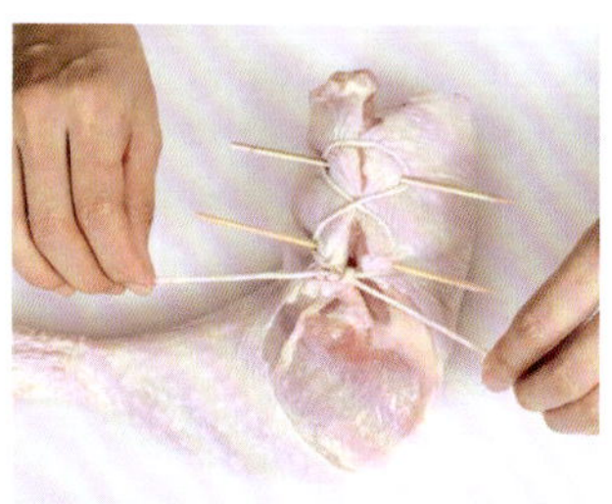

**3.** Rub interior of each thigh with sage, salt, and pepper. Truss thighs closed with wooden skewers and kitchen twine.

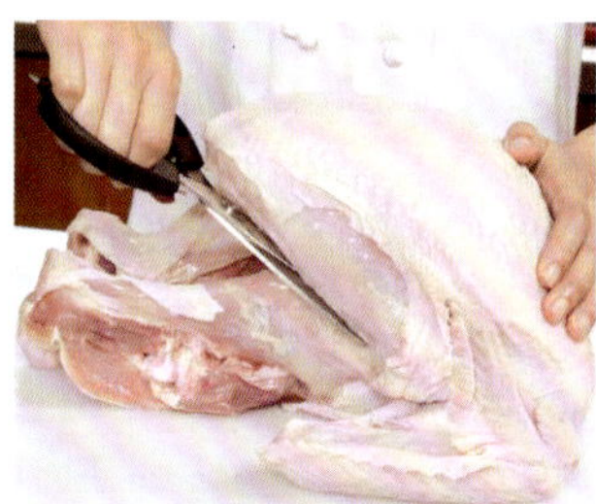

**4.** Using kitchen shears, cut through ribs, following line of fat running from tapered end of breast to wing joint.

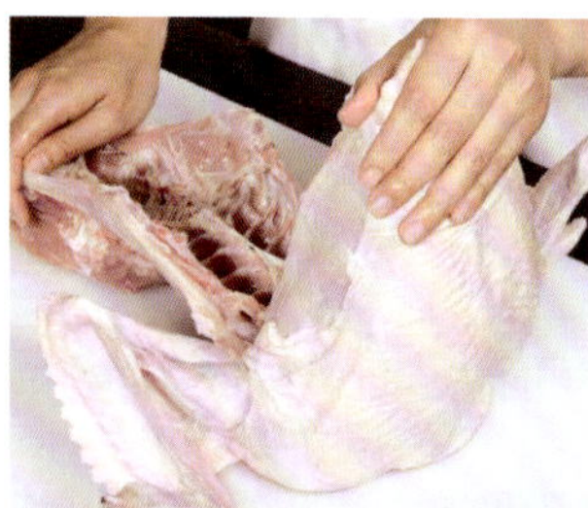

**5.** Using your hands, bend backbone away from breast to pop shoulder joint out of socket.

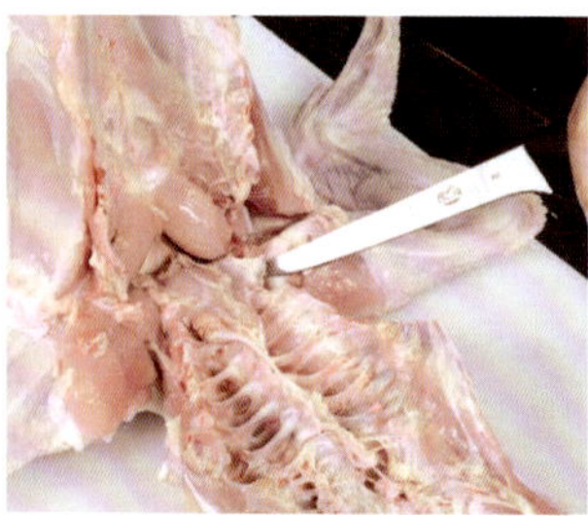

**6.** Cut through shoulder joint to separate back from breast.

1 hour 20 minutes longer. Transfer breast and leg quarters to cutting board and let rest for 30 minutes. While turkey rests, using metal spatula, stir stuffing well, scraping up any browned bits. Redistribute stuffing over bottom of roasting pan, return to oven, and turn off oven.

**9.** Before serving, season stuffing with salt and pepper to taste. Mound stuffing in center of platter. Place breast on top of stuffing with point of breast resting on highest part of mound. Remove skewers and twine from leg quarters and place on each side of breast. Carve and serve.

## Turkey Gravy for Julia Child's Stuffed Turkey, Updated

**MAKES** about 4 cups

If you do not have ¼ cup of reserved turkey fat in step 4, supplement with unsalted butter.

- Reserved turkey giblets, neck, backbone, and thighbones, hacked into 2-inch pieces
- 2 onions, chopped coarse
- 1 carrot, peeled and cut into 1-inch pieces
- 1 celery rib, cut into 1-inch pieces
- 6 garlic cloves, unpeeled
- 1 tablespoon vegetable oil
- 3½ cups chicken broth
- 3 cups water
- 2 cups dry white wine
- 6 sprigs fresh thyme
- ¼ cup all-purpose flour
- Table salt and pepper

**1.** Adjust oven rack to middle position and heat oven to 450 degrees. Place turkey parts, onions, carrot, celery, and garlic in large roasting pan. Drizzle with oil and toss to combine. Roast, stirring occasionally, until well browned, 40 to 50 minutes.

**2.** Remove pan from oven, and place over high heat. Add broth and bring to boil, scraping up any browned bits. Transfer contents of pan to Dutch oven. Add water, wine, and thyme sprigs; bring to boil over high heat. Reduce heat to low and simmer until reduced by half, about 1½ hours.

**3.** Strain contents of pot through fine-mesh strainer set in large bowl. Press solids with back of spatula to extract as much liquid as possible. Discard solids. Transfer liquid to fat separator and let settle, 5 minutes.

**4.** Transfer ¼ cup fat to medium saucepan and heat over medium-high heat until bubbling. Whisk in flour and cook, whisking constantly, until combined and honey-colored, about 2 minutes. Gradually whisk in hot liquid and bring to boil. Reduce heat to medium-low and simmer, stirring occasionally, until thickened, about 5 minutes. Season with salt and pepper to taste. (Gravy can be refrigerated in an airtight container for up to 2 days.)

## Turkey and Gravy for a Crowd

**SERVES** 18 to 20

**WHY THIS RECIPE WORKS** For a low-stress holiday meal to feed a crowd, we cooked turkey parts—leg quarters and bone-in breasts—separately rather than roasting two whole birds. The leg quarters benefited from braising in a flavorful liquid, a step that can be done a few days in advance. We then used the braising liquid as the base for a gravy that could also be made ahead. That left only roasting the breasts (which we salted and refrigerated for 24 hours) and reheating the leg quarters and gravy on Thanksgiving Day. Brushing the skin of the breasts, legs, and thighs with melted butter and heating them in a 500-degree oven ensured that all the parts arrived at the table evenly crisp and bronzed. This recipe requires refrigerating the salted turkey breasts for 24 hours. If using self-basting or kosher turkey breasts, do not salt in step 7, but season with salt in step 8. We used Diamond Crystal Kosher Salt; if you use Morton Kosher Salt, reduce the salt in step 7, rubbing 1 teaspoon onto the side of each breast and ½ teaspoon onto the underside of each breast cavity. Covering the turkey with parchment and then foil will prevent the wine in the braising liquid from "pitting" the foil.

**TURKEY LEGS AND GRAVY**

- 3 onions, chopped
- 4 celery ribs, chopped
- 4 carrots, peeled and chopped
- 10 garlic cloves, crushed and peeled
- 3 tablespoons unsalted butter, melted, plus extra as needed
- 10 sprigs fresh thyme
- 10 sprigs fresh parsley
- 3 bay leaves
- 1 tablespoon black peppercorns
- 4 cups chicken broth
- 1 cup water
- 1 cup dry white wine
- 4 (1½- to 2-pound) turkey leg quarters, trimmed
- 3 tablespoons kosher salt
- ½ teaspoon pepper
- ½ cup all-purpose flour

**TURKEY BREASTS**

- 2 (5- to 6-pound) bone-in turkey breasts, trimmed
- 2 tablespoons plus 2 teaspoons kosher salt, divided
- 7 tablespoons unsalted butter, melted, divided

**1. FOR THE TURKEY LEGS AND GRAVY (UP TO 3 DAYS AHEAD):** Adjust oven rack to lower-middle position and heat oven to 325 degrees. Toss onions, celery, carrots, garlic, melted butter, thyme sprigs, parsley sprigs, bay leaves, and peppercorns together in large roasting pan; spread into even layer. Place pan over medium heat and cook, stirring occasionally, until vegetables are softened and lightly browned and fond forms on bottom of pan, about 15 minutes. Add broth, water, and wine and bring to simmer, scraping up any browned bits. Remove pan from heat.

**2.** Cut leg quarters at joints into thighs and drumsticks, and sprinkle with salt and pepper. Place pieces skin side up in pan (braising liquid should come about three-quarters of way up legs and thighs). Place 12 by 16-inch piece of parchment paper over turkey pieces. Cover pan tightly with aluminum foil. Cook in oven until thighs register 170 degrees, 2½ to 3 hours. Remove pan from oven. Transfer turkey pieces to large, shallow container and let cool completely, about 1 hour. Once cool, cover and refrigerate.

**3.** Using spatula, scrape up any browned bits from bottom and sides of pan. Strain contents of pan through fine-mesh strainer set over large bowl, pressing on solids with spatula to extract as much liquid as possible; discard solids.

**4.** Transfer liquid to fat separator and let settle for 5 minutes. Reserve ½ cup plus 1 tablespoon fat (if there is not enough fat, add extra melted butter to make up difference) and 8 cups liquid; discard remaining liquid.

**5.** Heat reserved fat in large saucepan over medium-high heat. Add flour and cook, stirring constantly, until flour is medium golden brown and fragrant, about 5 minutes. Slowly whisk in reserved liquid and bring to boil. Reduce heat to medium-low and simmer, stirring occasionally, until gravy is thickened and reduced to 6 cups, 15 to 20 minutes. Off heat, season gravy with salt and pepper to taste. Transfer to large container and let cool completely, about 1 hour. (The legs and gravy can be prepared up to 3 days in advance and refrigerated.)

**6. FOR THE TURKEY BREASTS (THE DAY BEFORE):** Place breasts on cutting board skin side down. Using kitchen shears, cut through ribs, following vertical lines of fat where breasts meet backs, from tapered ends of breasts to wing joints. Using your hands, bend backs away from breasts to pop shoulder joints out of sockets. Using paring knife, cut through joints between bones to separate backs from breasts.

**7.** Flip breasts skin side up. Using your fingers, gently loosen skin covering each side of 1 breast. Peel back skin, leaving it attached at top and center. Rub 1 teaspoon salt onto each side of breast, then place skin back over meat. Rub 1 teaspoon salt onto underside of breast cavity. Repeat with second breast. Place breasts on rimmed baking sheet and refrigerate, uncovered, for 24 hours.

**8.** Roast the breasts and reheat the dark meat and gravy (serving day): Adjust oven rack to middle position and heat oven to 325 degrees. Measure out 20-inch piece of foil and roll into loose ball. Unroll foil, place on second rimmed baking sheet, and top with wire rack (crinkled foil will insulate bottom of sheet to keep it from smoking during roasting). Place breasts, skin side up, on prepared wire rack; brush with 4 tablespoons melted butter and sprinkle each whole breast with 1 teaspoon remaining salt. Roast until thickest part of breast registers 130 degrees, about 1½ hours.

**9.** Remove breasts from oven and increase oven temperature to 500 degrees. When oven reaches temperature, return breasts to oven and roast until skin is deeply browned and thickest part of breast registers 160 degrees, 20 to 30 minutes. Transfer to carving board and let rest, uncovered, for 30 minutes. Pour any juices from sheet into bowl and set aside.

**10.** Adjust oven rack to upper-middle position. Place thighs and drumsticks skin side up on now-empty wire rack set in sheet and brush with remaining 3 tablespoons melted butter. Place in oven and reheat until skin is well browned and thighs register 110 degrees, 18 to 22 minutes. Transfer thighs and drumsticks to large platter.

**11.** While thighs reheat, bring gravy to simmer in large saucepan over medium-low heat, whisking occasionally. Add any reserved juices from breasts and season with salt and pepper to taste. Cover and keep warm.

**12.** Carve breasts and transfer to platter with thighs and drumsticks. Serve, passing gravy separately.

## Braised Turkey

**SERVES** 10 to 12

**WHY THIS RECIPE WORKS** Separating turkey into parts and braising it for the holiday meal? It may sound heretical, but this break from tradition has a lot going for it. Roasting a large turkey is always a race to get the denser, fattier thighs and legs to come up to the ideal temperature of around 175 degrees before the leaner, more delicate breast dries out, once its temperature climbs past 160 degrees. So we wondered if there was an easier way to get perfectly cooked turkey on the table without sacrificing flavor. Turkey parts provided a neat solution to the problem by giving both types of meat more even exposure to the heat—and without any cumbersome turning. Better yet, braising the pieces in a flavorful liquid created rich, ready-made gravy and infused the meat with all of its complex flavors. When we tasted this deeply flavored, moist and tender turkey, we found we didn't miss the traditional whole bird at all. Instead of drumsticks and thighs, you may use 2 whole leg quarters, 1½ to 2 pounds each. The recipe will also work with turkey breast alone; in step 1, reduce the amount of salt and sugar to ½ cup each, and the amount of water to 4 quarts. If you are braising kosher or self-basting turkey parts, skip the brining step, and instead season the turkey parts with 1½ teaspoons salt.

**BRAISED TURKEY**

- Table salt and ground black pepper
- 1 cup sugar
- 1 (5- to 7-pound) whole bone-in, skin-on turkey breast, trimmed
- 4 pounds turkey drumsticks and thighs, trimmed
- 3 medium onions, chopped medium
- 3 medium celery ribs, chopped medium
- 2 medium carrots, peeled and chopped medium
- 6 medium garlic cloves, peeled and crushed
- 2 bay leaves
- 6 sprigs fresh thyme
- 6 sprigs fresh parsley
- ½ ounce dried porcini mushrooms, rinsed
- 4 tablespoons (½ stick) unsalted butter, melted
- 4 cups low-sodium chicken broth
- 1 cup dry white wine

**GRAVY**

- 3 tablespoons unbleached all-purpose flour
- Table salt and ground black pepper

**1. FOR THE TURKEY:** Dissolve 1 cup salt and the sugar in 2 gallons cold water in a large container. Submerge the turkey pieces in the brine, cover, and refrigerate for 3 to 6 hours.

**2.** Adjust an oven rack to the lower-middle position and heat the oven to 500 degrees. Remove the turkey from the brine and pat dry with paper towels. Toss the onions, celery, carrots, garlic, bay leaves, thyme, parsley, porcini, and 2 tablespoons of the melted butter in a large roasting pan; arrange in an even layer. Brush the turkey pieces with the remaining 2 tablespoons melted butter and season with pepper. Place the turkey pieces, skin side up, over the vegetables, leaving at least ¼ inch between the pieces. Roast until the skin is lightly browned, about 20 minutes.

**3.** While the turkey is roasting, bring the broth and wine to a simmer in a medium saucepan over medium heat. Cover and keep warm.

**4.** Remove the turkey from the oven and reduce the oven temperature to 325 degrees. Pour the broth mixture around the turkey pieces (it should come about three-quarters of the way up the legs and thighs.) Place a 12 by 16-inch piece of parchment paper over the turkey pieces. Cover the roasting pan tightly with aluminum foil. Return the covered roasting pan to the oven and cook until the breast registers 160 degrees and the thighs register 175 degrees on an instant-read thermometer, 1½ to 2 hours. Transfer the turkey to a carving board, tent loosely with foil, and let rest for 20 minutes.

**5. FOR THE GRAVY:** Strain the vegetables and liquid from the roasting pan through a fine-mesh strainer set in a large bowl. Press the solids with the back of a spatula to extract as much liquid as possible. Discard the vegetables. Transfer the liquid to a fat separator and allow to settle for 5 minutes. Reserve 3 tablespoons fat and measure off 3 cups broth (use any remaining broth for another use.)

**6.** Heat 3 tablespoons reserved turkey fat in a medium saucepan over medium-high heat; add the flour and cook, stirring constantly, until the flour is dark golden brown and fragrant, about 5 minutes. Whisk in 3 cups braising liquid and bring to a boil. Reduce the heat to medium-low and simmer, stirring occasionally, until the gravy is thick and reduced to 2 cups, 15 to 20 minutes. Remove the gravy from the heat and season with salt and pepper to taste.

**7.** Carve the turkey and serve, passing the gravy separately.

## Roast Whole Turkey Breast with Gravy

**SERVES** 6 to 8

**WHY THIS RECIPE WORKS** For an impressive roast turkey breast, we removed (but did not discard) the backbone so the breast lay flat in the oven for even browning and more stability during carving. Salting the breast for 24 hours seasoned it and helped it retain more juices as it cooked. Brushing the skin with melted butter ensured deep browning and great flavor. Roasting the breast in a 12-inch skillet instead of a roasting pan helped contain drippings underneath the bird so they didn't scorch. Starting the breast at 325 degrees helped gently cook the white meat, while finishing it at 500 degrees ensured that it got deeply bronzed. While the turkey cooked, we used the backbone to make a flavorful stock to use as the base for the gravy, which we built directly in the skillet. Note that this recipe requires refrigerating the seasoned breast for 24 hours. This recipe was developed using Diamond Crystal Kosher Salt. If you use Morton Kosher Salt, which is denser, reduce the salt in step 2, rubbing 1 teaspoon of salt into each side of the breast and ½ teaspoon into the cavity. If you're using a self-basting (such as a frozen Butterball) or kosher turkey breast, do not salt in step 2. If your turkey breast comes with the back removed, you can skip making the gravy or substitute 1 pound of chicken wings for the turkey back.

- 1 (5- to 7- pound) bone-in turkey breast
- 4 teaspoons kosher salt, divided
- 2 tablespoons unsalted butter, melted
- 2 teaspoons extra-virgin olive oil, plus extra as needed
- 1 small onion, chopped
- 1 small carrot, chopped
- 1 small celery rib, chopped
- 5 cups water
- 2 sprigs fresh thyme
- 1 bay leaf
- ¼ cup all-purpose flour
- ¼ cup dry white wine

**1.** Place turkey breast on counter skin side down. Using kitchen shears, cut through ribs, following vertical line of fat where breast meets back, from tapered end of breast to wing joint. Using your hands, bend back away from breast to pop shoulder joints out of sockets. Using paring knife, cut through joints between bones to separate back from breast. Reserve back for gravy. Trim excess fat from breast.

**2.** Place turkey breast, skin side up, on counter. Using your fingers, carefully loosen and separate turkey skin from each side of breast. Peel back skin, leaving it attached at top and center of breast. Rub 1 teaspoon salt onto each side of breast, then place skin back over meat. Rub 1 teaspoon salt onto underside of breast cavity. Place turkey on large plate and refrigerate, uncovered, for 24 hours.

**3.** Adjust oven rack to middle position and heat oven to 325 degrees. Pat turkey dry with paper towels. Place turkey, skin side up, in 12-inch ovensafe skillet, arranging so narrow end of breast is not touching skillet. Brush melted butter evenly over turkey and sprinkle with remaining 1 teaspoon salt. Roast until thickest part of breast registers 130 degrees, 1 to 1¼ hours.

**4.** Meanwhile, heat oil in large saucepan over medium-high heat. Add reserved back, skin side down, and cook until well browned, 6 to 8 minutes. Add onion, carrot, and celery and cook, stirring occasionally, until vegetables are softened and lightly browned, about 5 minutes. Add water, thyme sprigs, and bay leaf and bring to boil. Reduce heat to medium-low and simmer for 1 hour. Strain broth through fine-mesh strainer into container. Discard solids; set aside broth (you should have about 4 cups). (Broth can be refrigerated for up to 24 hours.)

**5.** Remove turkey from oven and increase oven temperature to 500 degrees. When oven reaches 500 degrees, return turkey to oven and roast until skin is deeply browned and thickest part of breast registers 160 degrees, 15 to 30 minutes. Using spatula, loosen turkey from skillet; transfer to carving board and let rest, uncovered, for 30 minutes.

### PREPPING THE TURKEY BREAST

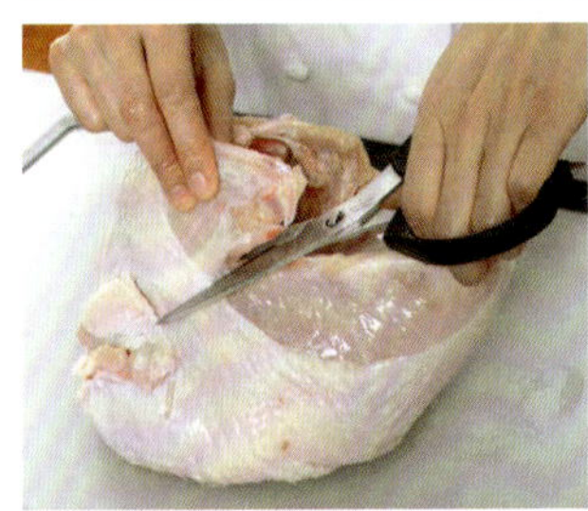

**1.** Cut through ribs following line of fat where breast meets back, from breast's tapered end to wing joint.

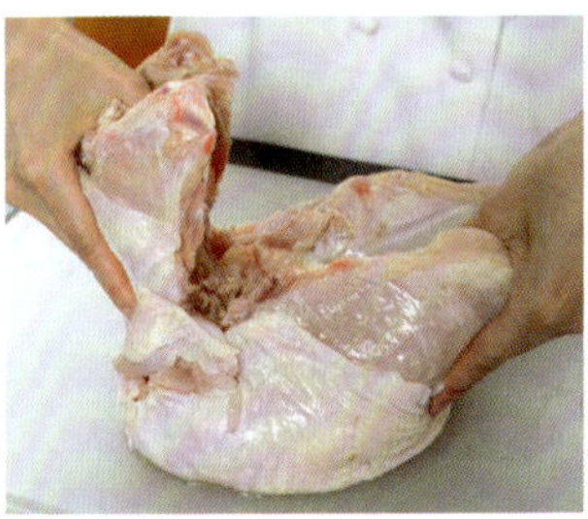

**2.** Bend back away from breast to pop shoulder joints out of sockets. Cut through joints to remove back.

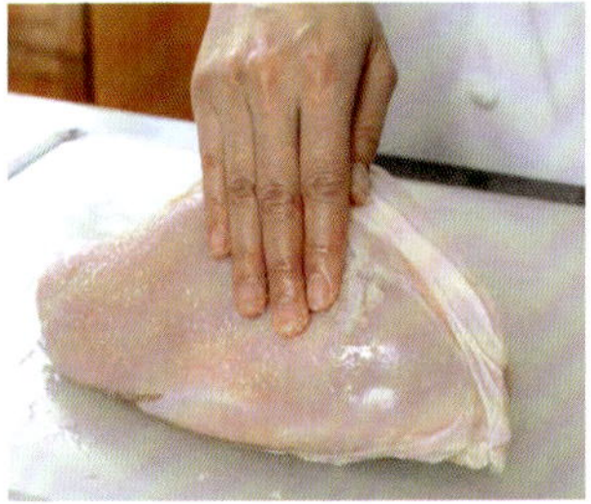

**3.** Without backbone in the way, it's easy to pull back skin so you can evenly season breast meat.

**6.** While turkey rests, pour off fat from skillet. (You should have about ¼ cup; if not, add extra oil as needed to equal ¼ cup.) Return fat to skillet and heat over medium heat until shimmering. Sprinkle flour evenly over fat and cook, whisking constantly, until flour is coated with fat and browned, about 1 minute. Add wine, whisking to scrape up any browned bits, and cook until wine has evaporated, 1 to 2 minutes. Slowly whisk in reserved broth. Increase heat to medium-high and cook, whisking occasionally, until gravy is thickened and reduced to 2 cups, about 20 minutes. Season with salt and pepper to taste. Carve turkey and serve, passing gravy separately.

## Slow-Roasted Turkey with Gravy

**SERVES** 10 to 12

---

**WHY THIS RECIPE WORKS** Roasting a whole turkey is a race to keep the white meat from drying out while the dark meat cooks through. We required moist meat with crisp, crackling skin, accompanied by rich gravy. For a greater challenge, we wanted to do it without salting the turkey or brining it. First, we roasted two nonbrined turkeys, one using our high-heat method and the other at 275 degrees the entire time. The high-heat breast dried out, but the slow-roasted breast cooked through moist, even without a brine. Coordinating the cooking between the breast and legs and thighs, however, was a problem. We discovered that swapping in turkey parts for a whole turkey would help ensure the breast and thighs cooked through at about the same time. We roasted a breast and two leg quarters on a rack over a baking sheet to promote air circulation. The results? Tender, juicy meat. Most recipes achieve crisp skin by starting the bird in a hot oven to brown it, then lowering the heat. But that meant a higher oven temperature, which meant dried-out meat. Instead, we let the turkey cool before popping it back in the oven to crisp the skin. This turned out a perfect turkey surrounded by flawless, crisp skin. Instead of drumsticks and thighs, you can use two whole leg quarters, 1½ to 2 pounds each. The recipe will also work with turkey breast alone; in step 2, reduce the butter to 1½ tablespoons, the salt to 1½ teaspoons, and the pepper to 1 teaspoon. If you are roasting kosher or self-basting turkey parts, season the turkey with only 1½ teaspoons salt.

**TURKEY**

- 3 medium onions, chopped medium
- 3 medium celery ribs, chopped medium
- 2 medium carrots, peeled and chopped medium
- 5 sprigs fresh thyme
- 5 medium garlic cloves, peeled and halved
- 1 cup low-sodium chicken broth
- 1 (5- to 7-pound) whole bone-in, skin-on turkey breast, trimmed
- 4 pounds turkey drumsticks and thighs, trimmed
- 3 tablespoons unsalted butter, melted
- 1 tablespoon table salt
- 2 teaspoons ground black pepper

**GRAVY**

- 2 cups low-sodium chicken broth
- 3 tablespoons unsalted butter
- 3 tablespoons unbleached all-purpose flour
- 2 bay leaves
- Table salt and ground black pepper

**1. FOR THE TURKEY:** Adjust an oven rack to the lower-middle position and heat the oven to 275 degrees. Arrange the onions, celery, carrots, thyme, and garlic in an even layer on a large rimmed baking sheet. Pour the broth into the baking sheet. Place a wire rack on top of the vegetables.

**2.** Pat the turkey pieces dry with paper towels. Brush the turkey pieces on all sides with the melted butter. Sprinkle the salt and pepper evenly over the turkey. Place the breast, skin side down, and the drumsticks and thighs, skin side up, on the rack on the vegetable-filled baking sheet, leaving at least ¼ inch between the pieces.

**3.** Roast the turkey pieces for 1 hour. With a dish towel in each hand, turn the turkey breast skin side up. Continue roasting until the thickest part of the breast registers 160 degrees the thickest part of the thigh registers 175 degrees, 1 to 2 hours longer. Remove the baking sheet from the oven and transfer the rack with the turkey to a second baking sheet. Allow the pieces to rest for at least 30 minutes or up to 1½ hours.

**4. FOR THE GRAVY:** Strain the vegetables and liquid from the baking sheet through a colander set in a large bowl. Press the solids with the back of a spatula to extract as much liquid as possible. Discard the vegetables. Transfer the liquid in the bowl to a 4-cup liquid measuring cup. Add the chicken broth to the measuring cup (you should have about 3 cups liquid).

**5.** In a medium saucepan, heat the butter over medium-high heat; add the flour and cook, stirring constantly, until the flour is dark golden brown and fragrant, about 5 minutes. Whisk in the broth mixture and bay leaves and gradually bring to a boil. Reduce the heat to medium-low and simmer, stirring occasionally, until the gravy is thick and reduced to 2 cups, 15 to 20 minutes. Discard the bay leaves. Remove the gravy from the heat and season with salt and pepper to taste. Keep the gravy warm.

**6. TO SERVE:** Heat the oven to 500 degrees. Place the baking sheet with the turkey in the oven. Roast until the skin is golden brown and crisp, about 15 minutes. Transfer the turkey to a carving board and let rest, uncovered, for 20 minutes. Carve and serve with the gravy.

## Turkey Breast en Cocotte with Pan Gravy

**SERVES** 6 TO 8

---

**WHY THIS RECIPE WORKS** Having successfully developed a recipe for chicken en cocotte, we wondered if we could use this same method (cooking the poultry in a covered pot over low heat for an extended period of time), for cooking a turkey breast. We found that bone-in breasts were more flavorful, and a 6- to 7-pound turkey breast was ideal. Browning the turkey breast was an essential step in developing deep flavor. Adding some aromatics to the pot further rounded out the

flavor. Once the turkey was done, we removed it from the pot and reduced the jus, concentrating flavor and developing a rich fond on the bottom of the pot, which we could use to make a roux as the base of our gravy. We added chicken broth and brought it to a simmer, reducing it to gravy consistency. Try to avoid "hotel-style" turkey breasts which have the wings attached. If this is all you can find, simply remove the wings. Be sure to use a 7- to 8-quart Dutch oven. Turkey breasts larger than 7 pounds will not fit in the pot. Adjust the cooking time for a smaller turkey breast.

- 1 (6- to 7-pound) whole bone-in turkey breast
- Table salt and ground black pepper
- 2 tablespoons olive oil
- 1 medium onion, chopped medium
- 1 medium carrot, chopped medium
- 1 celery rib, chopped medium
- 6 medium garlic cloves, peeled and crushed
- 2 sprigs fresh thyme
- 1 bay leaf
- ¼ cup unbleached all-purpose flour
- 4 cups low-sodium chicken broth

**1.** Adjust an oven rack to the lowest position and heat the oven to 250 degrees. Using kitchen shears or a chef's knife, trim the rib bones and any excess fat on both sides of the breast following the vertical line of fat. Pat the turkey dry with paper towels and season with salt and pepper.

**2.** Heat the oil in a large Dutch oven over medium-high heat until just smoking. Add the turkey, breast side down, and scatter the onion, carrot, celery, garlic, thyme, and bay leaf around the turkey. Cook, turning the breast on its sides and stirring the vegetables as needed, until the turkey and vegetables are well browned, 12 to 16 minutes, reducing the heat if the pot begins to scorch. Turn turkey so breast side is facing up.

**3.** Off the heat, place a large sheet of foil over the pot and press to seal, then cover tightly with the lid. Transfer the pot to the oven and cook until the thickest part of the breast registers 160 degrees on an instant-read thermometer, 1½ to 1¾ hours.

**4.** Remove the pot from the oven. Transfer the turkey to a cutting board, tent loosely with foil, and let rest while making the gravy.

**5.** Place the pot with the juices and vegetables over medium-high heat and simmer until almost all of the liquid has evaporated, 15 to 20 minutes. Stir in the flour and cook, stirring constantly, until browned, 2 to 5 minutes. Slowly whisk in the chicken broth, bring to a simmer, and cook, stirring often, until the gravy is thickened and measures about 2½ cups, 10 to 15 minutes.

**6.** Strain the gravy through a fine-mesh strainer and season with salt and pepper to taste. Carve the turkey and serve, passing the gravy separately.

## Porchetta-Style Turkey Breast

**SERVES** 6 to 8

**WHY THIS RECIPE WORKS** Turkey porchetta, or turchetta, is a turkey breast roast that takes its shape and seasonings from the iconic Italian pork roast called porchetta. Instead of starting with a boneless turkey breast, we deboned a turkey crown roast to keep the skin and meat intact. We tossed the breast halves and tenderloins with an herb-spice paste in a bowl so that, once we wrapped the meat in the skin into a cylinder, the paste was evenly swirled throughout, marbling each slice. Refrigerating the assembled roast for at least 8 hours before cooking allowed the salt in the paste to migrate into the meat, seasoning it and helping it retain its juices during cooking. Starting the roast in a low oven and pulling it out 15 degrees shy of the target temperature meant that carryover cooking could gradually raise its internal temperature to the perfect doneness. We prefer a natural turkey breast here; if you're using a self-basting breast (such as Butterball) or kosher breast, omit the 4 teaspoons of salt in the herb paste. This recipe was developed using Diamond Crystal Kosher Salt; if you're using Morton Kosher Salt, which is denser, use 1 tablespoon in the herb paste and 1½ teaspoons on the exterior of the roast.

- 1 tablespoon fennel seeds
- 2 teaspoons black peppercorns
- ¼ cup fresh rosemary leaves, chopped
- ¼ cup fresh sage leaves, chopped
- ¼ cup fresh thyme leaves
- 6 garlic cloves, chopped
- 2 tablespoons kosher salt, divided
- 3 tablespoons extra-virgin olive oil
- 1 (7- to 8-pound) bone-in turkey breast
- 2 tablespoons unsalted butter, melted

**1.** Grind fennel seeds and peppercorns using spice grinder or mortar and pestle until finely ground. Transfer to food processor and add rosemary, sage, thyme, garlic, and 4 teaspoons salt. Pulse mixture until finely chopped, 15 to 20 pulses, scraping down sides of bowl as needed. Add oil and process until paste forms, 20 to 30 seconds. Cut seven 16-inch lengths and one 30-inch length of kitchen twine and set aside. Measure out 20-inch piece of aluminum foil and crumple into loose ball. Uncrumple foil and place on rimmed baking sheet (crinkled foil will insulate bottom of sheet and minimize smoking during final roasting step). Spray wire rack with vegetable oil spray and place on prepared sheet.

**2.** To remove back, place turkey breast skin side down on cutting board. Using kitchen shears, cut through ribs, following vertical lines of fat where breast meets back, from tapered ends of breast to wing joints. Using your hands, bend back away from breast to pop shoulder joints out of sockets. Using paring knife, cut through joints between bones to separate back from breast.

## ASSEMBLING TURCHETTA

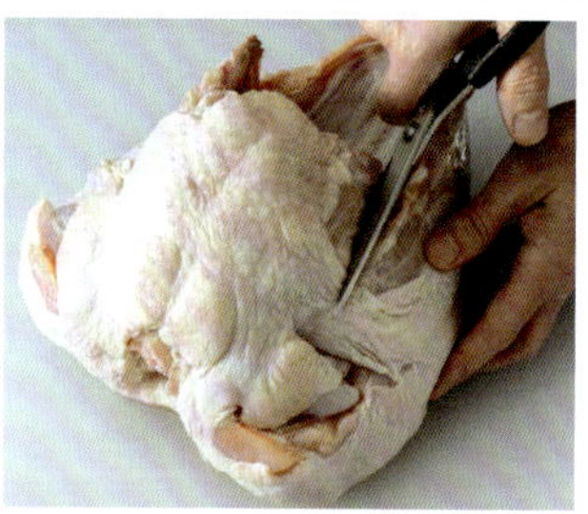

**1.** Using kitchen shears, cut through ribs, following vertical lines of fat where breast meets back, from tapered ends of breast to wing joints.

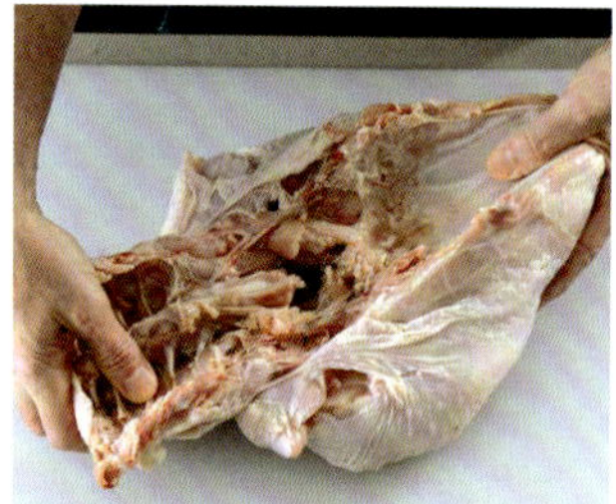

**2.** Using your hands, bend back away from breast to pop shoulder joints out of sockets.

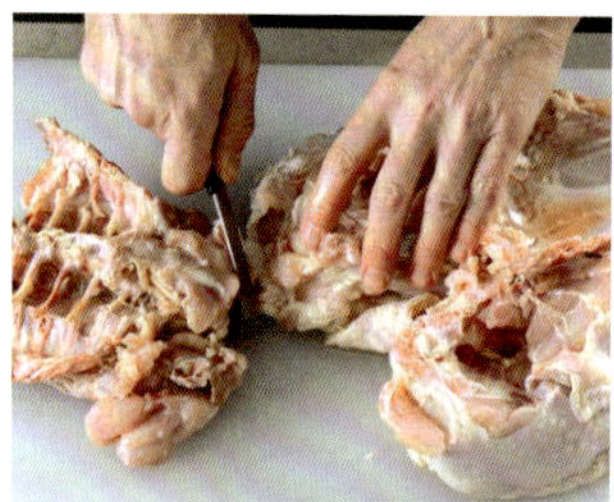

**3.** Using paring knife, cut through joints between bones to separate back from breast.

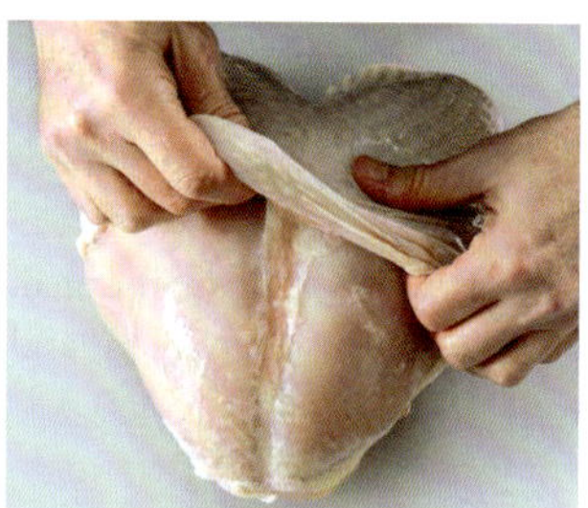

**4.** Starting at tapered side of breast and using your fingers to separate skin from meat, peel skin off breast meat and reserve.

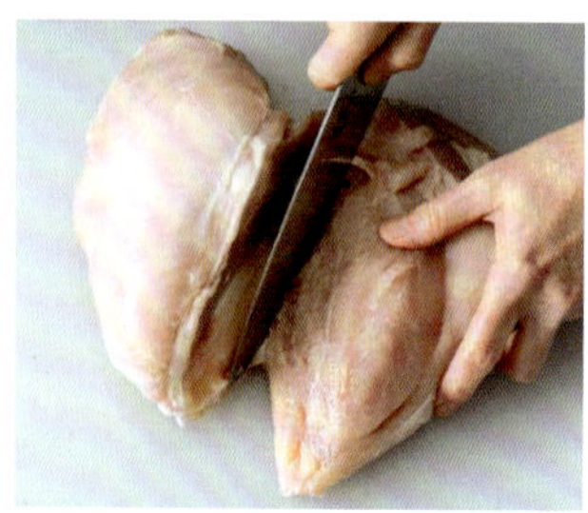

**5.** Using tip of boning knife or chef's knife, cut along rib cage to remove each breast half completely. Peel tenderloins from underside of each breast and use knife to remove exposed part of white tendon from each tenderloin.

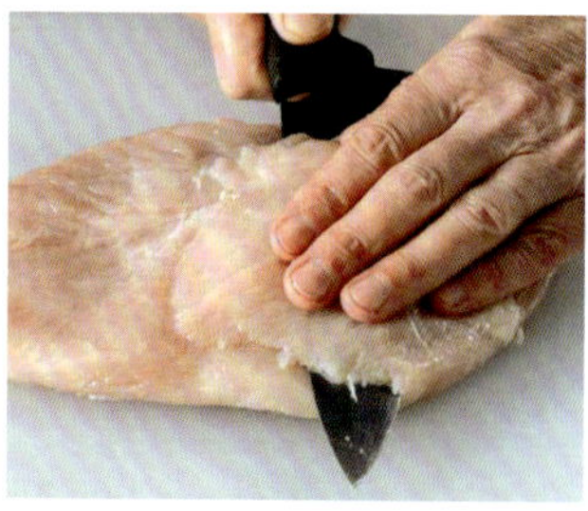

**6.** Holding knife parallel to cutting board, slice into breast starting where breast becomes thicker (about halfway along length). Stop ½ inch from edge of breast and open to create 1 long piece of even thickness. Repeat with remaining breast.

**7.** Massage herb paste into meat. Lay 1 breast half on 1 side of skin with butterflied end closest to you. Lay second breast half next to first with butterflied end farthest away from you. Lay tenderloins between them with thin ends overlapping.

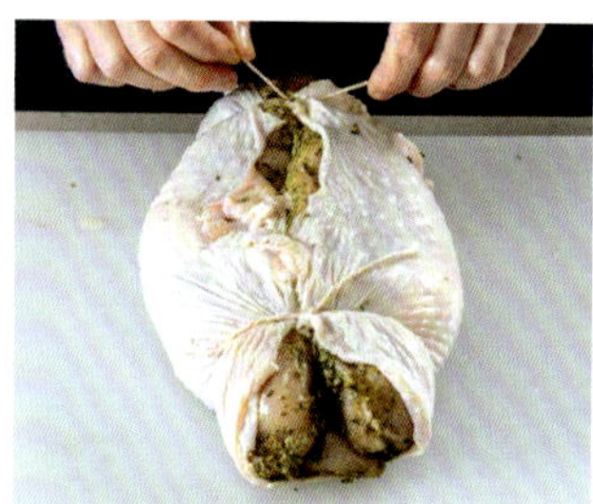

**8.** Fold each side skin up over tenderloins. Slip one 16-inch length of twine under roast 2 inches from 1 end and tie into simple knot; repeat at opposite end.

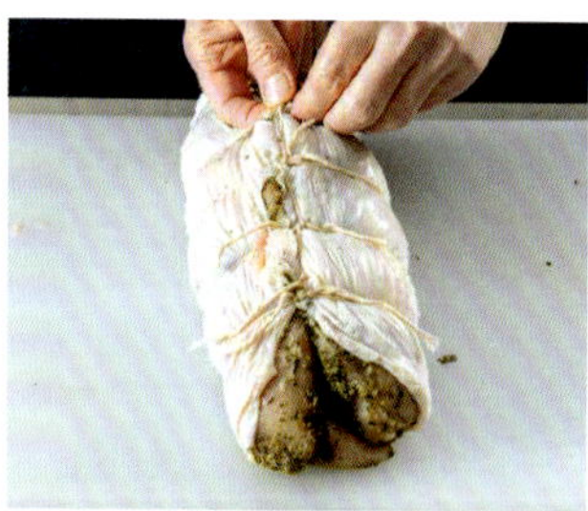

**9.** Tie end of 30-inch length of twine on to loop farthest from you. Working toward you, loop twine over top and around each strand to bottom of roast.

**10.** Flip roast and continue looping to bottom of roast. Flip roast again and tie off where you started. Sprinkle roast with remaining 2 teaspoons salt; place on prepared rack; and refrigerate, uncovered, for at least 8 hours or up to 24 hours.

**3.** Flip breast skin side up. Starting at tapered side of breast and using your fingers to separate skin from meat, peel skin off breast meat and reserve. Using tip of chef's knife or boning knife, cut along rib cage to remove each breast half completely. Reserve bones for making stock, or discard. Peel tenderloins from underside of each breast and use knife to remove exposed part of white tendon from each tenderloin.

**4.** Lay 1 breast half on cutting board, smooth side down and with narrow end pointing toward your knife hand. Holding knife parallel to cutting board, slice into breast starting where breast becomes thicker (about halfway along length). Stop ½ inch from edge of breast and open to create 1 long piece of even thickness. Repeat with remaining breast half. Transfer all meat to large bowl. Add herb paste and massage into meat to coat evenly.

**5.** Pat exterior of skin dry with paper towels and lay flat, exterior side down, on cutting board with long side running parallel to counter. Remove any loose pieces of fat. Lay 1 breast half on 1 side of skin with butterflied end closest to you. Lay second breast half next to first with butterflied end farthest away from you. Spread breast halves slightly apart and lay tenderloins between them with their thin ends overlapping in center.

**6.** Using skin as aid, fold up each breast half over tenderloins so skin meets directly over tenderloins. Slip one 16-inch length of twine under roast about 2 inches from 1 end and tie into simple knot, pinching skin closed as you tighten. Repeat tying at opposite end. Tie remaining five 16-inch lengths of twine evenly between 2 end pieces. Trim excess twine.

**7.** Tie 1 end of 30-inch length of twine onto loop farthest from you. Working toward you, loop twine over top and around each successive strand until you get to bottom of roast. Flip roast and continue looping to bottom of roast. Flip roast again and tie off where you started. Sprinkle roast evenly with remaining 2 teaspoons salt; place on prepared rack; and refrigerate, uncovered, for at least 8 hours or up to 2 days.

**8.** Adjust oven rack to upper-middle position and heat oven to 275 degrees. Brush roast with melted butter. Cook until thickest part of roast registers 125 degrees, 1½ to 1¾ hours. Remove roast from oven and increase oven temperature to 500 degrees. When oven is up to temperature, remove twine from roast; return roast to oven; and cook until skin is browned and roast registers 145 degrees, 15 to 20 minutes.

**9.** Transfer roast to cutting board, tent with foil, and let rest for 30 minutes. Slice ½ inch thick and serve.

## Turkey Thigh Confit with Citrus-Mustard Sauce

**SERVES 6 to 8**

**WHY THIS RECIPE WORKS** This naturally make-ahead confit technique transforms turkey thighs into a silky, dense, and savory revelation. Before refrigeration, confit was used to prolong the shelf life of foods, including duck or goose parts. The poultry was cured in salt and then gently poached in its own fat before being buried beneath the fat and stored in an airtight crock. For silky, supple, evenly seasoned turkey confit, we coated turkey thighs in a flavorful paste and let them cure for at least four days. As the thighs sat, the salt, sugar, and water-soluble compounds in the aromatics gave the turkey a deeply savory flavor. After rinsing away the cure, we oven-poached the thighs in duck fat. The thighs could then be refrigerated for up to six days or immediately browned and served. Start this recipe at least five days or up to 12 days before serving. Be sure to use table salt, not kosher salt, and measure carefully. Make sure that the total weight of the turkey is within 2 ounces of the 4-pound target weight; do not use enhanced or kosher turkey thighs.

- 3 large onions, chopped coarse (4¾ cups)
- 12 sprigs fresh thyme
- 2½ tablespoons table salt for curing
- 1½ tablespoons sugar
- 1½ teaspoons pepper
- 4 pounds bone-in turkey thighs
- 6 cups duck fat, chicken fat, or vegetable oil for confit
- 1 garlic head, halved crosswise
- 2 bay leaves
- ½ cup orange marmalade
- 2 tablespoons whole-grain mustard
- ¾ teaspoon grated lime zest plus 2 tablespoons juice
- ¼ teaspoon table salt
- ⅛ teaspoon cayenne pepper

**1. TO CURE:** Process onions, thyme sprigs, 2½ tablespoons salt, sugar, and pepper in food processor until finely chopped, about 20 seconds, scraping down sides of bowl as needed. Spread one-third of mixture evenly in bottom of 13 by 9-inch baking dish. Arrange turkey thighs, skin side up, in single layer in dish. Spread remaining onion mixture evenly over thighs. Wrap dish tightly with plastic wrap and refrigerate for 4 to 6 days (whatever is most convenient).

**2. TO COOK:** Adjust oven rack to lower-middle position and heat oven to 200 degrees. Remove thighs from onion mixture and rinse well (if you don't have a garbage disposal, do not allow onion pieces to go down drain). Pat thighs dry with paper towels. Heat fat in large Dutch oven over medium heat to 165 degrees. Off heat, add turkey thighs, skin side down and in single layer, making sure thighs are completely submerged. Add garlic and bay leaves. Transfer to oven, uncovered, and cook until metal skewer inserted straight down into thickest part of largest thigh can be easily removed without lifting thigh, 4 to 5 hours. (To ensure that oven temperature remains steady, wait at least 20 minutes before retesting if turkey is not done.) Remove from oven.

**3. TO MAKE AHEAD:** Let turkey cool completely in pot, about 2 hours; cover pot; and refrigerate for up to 6 days.

**4.** Uncover pot. Heat pot over medium-low heat until fat is melted, about 25 minutes. Increase heat to medium, maintaining bare simmer, and continue to cook until thickest part of largest thigh registers 135 to 140 degrees, about 30 minutes longer. (If turkey has been cooked in vegetable oil, heat pot over medium heat, maintaining bare simmer, until thickest part of largest thigh registers 135 to 140 degrees, about 30 minutes.)

**5. TO SERVE:** Adjust oven rack to lower-middle position and heat oven to 500 degrees. While oven heats, crumple 20-inch length of aluminum foil into loose ball. Uncrumple foil, place in rimmed baking sheet, and top with wire rack. Using tongs, gently transfer thighs, skin side up, to prepared wire rack, being careful not to tear delicate skin. Set aside. Strain liquid through fine-mesh strainer into large bowl. Working in batches, pour liquid into fat separator, letting liquid settle for 5 minutes before separating fat from turkey stock. (Alternatively, use bulb baster to extract turkey stock from beneath fat.) Transfer 4 teaspoons turkey stock to small bowl; add marmalade; and microwave until mixture is fluid, about 30 seconds. Stir in mustard, lime zest and juice, salt, and cayenne. Transfer to serving bowl.

**6.** Transfer thighs to oven and roast until well browned, 12 to 15 minutes. Transfer thighs to cutting board, skin side up, and let rest until just cool enough to handle, about 15 minutes.

**7.** Flip 1 thigh skin side down. Using tip of paring knife, cut along sides of thighbone, exposing bone. Carefully remove bone and any stray bits of cartilage. Flip thigh skin side up. Using sharp chef's knife, slice thigh crosswise ¾ inch thick. Transfer to serving platter, skin side up. Repeat with remaining thighs. Serve, passing sauce separately.

### CARVING TURKEY THIGHS

**1.** Place thigh skin side down. Using tip of paring knife, cut along sides of thighbone, exposing bone.

**2.** Carefully remove bone and any stray bits of cartilage. Flip thigh skin side up.

**3.** Using sharp chef's knife, slice thigh crosswise ¾ inch thick.

# Turkey Tetrazzini

**SERVES 8**

**WHY THIS RECIPE WORKS** Overcooking is the inevitable fate of many casseroles, as the contents are usually cooked twice: once on their own and once again when joined with the other casserole ingredients. We wanted a casserole with a silky sauce, a generous portion of turkey meat, and noodles cooked just until done. We found we could cut the second cooking down to just 15 minutes by baking the recipe in a shallow dish that would allow it to heat through quickly. Most recipes for turkey Tetrazzini call for a béchamel sauce, in which milk is added to a roux. In switching to a velouté, which is based on chicken stock rather than milk, we brightened up the texture and the flavor. Still looking for brighter flavor, we spruced things up with a shot of sherry and a little lemon juice and nutmeg. Parmesan cheese provided tang and bite, and a full 2 teaspoons of fresh thyme helped to freshen the overall impression of the dish.

**BREAD CRUMB TOPPING**

- 6 slices high-quality white sandwich bread, torn into quarters
- 4 tablespoons (½ stick) unsalted butter, melted
- Pinch table salt
- ½ ounce Parmesan cheese, grated (about ¼ cup)

**FILLING**

- 8 tablespoons (1 stick) unsalted butter, plus extra for the baking dish
- 8 ounces white mushrooms, wiped cleaned and sliced thin (about 3 cups)
- 2 medium onions, minced
- Table salt and ground black pepper
- 12 ounces spaghetti or other long-strand pasta, strands snapped in half
- 6 tablespoons unbleached all-purpose flour
- 3 cups low-sodium chicken broth
- 1½ ounces Parmesan cheese, grated (about ¾ cup)
- ¼ cup dry sherry
- 1 tablespoon juice from 1 lemon
- 2 teaspoons minced fresh thyme leaves
- ¼ teaspoon grated nutmeg
- 2 cups frozen peas
- 4 cups leftover cooked boneless turkey or chicken meat, cut into ¼-inch pieces

**1. FOR THE TOPPING:** Adjust an oven rack to the middle position and heat the oven to 350 degrees. Pulse the bread in a food processor until coarsely ground, 10 to 15 pulses. Mix the bread crumbs, butter, and salt in a small baking dish; bake until golden brown and crisp, 15 to 20 minutes. Cool to room temperature and mix with the Parmesan in a small bowl. Set aside.

**2. FOR THE FILLING:** Increase the oven temperature to 450 degrees. Melt 2 tablespoons of the butter in a large skillet over medium heat; add the mushrooms and onions and sauté, stirring frequently, until the liquid from the mushrooms evaporates, 12 to 15 minutes. Season with salt and pepper to taste; transfer the vegetables to a medium bowl and set aside. Clean the skillet.

**3.** Meanwhile, bring 4 quarts water to a boil in a large pot. Add 1 tablespoon salt and the pasta and cook until al dente. Reserve ¼ cup cooking water, drain the pasta, and return to the pot with the reserved liquid.

**4.** Melt the remaining 6 tablespoons butter in the clean skillet over medium heat. Whisk in the flour and cook, whisking constantly, until the flour turns golden, 1 to 2 minutes. Whisking constantly, gradually add the chicken broth. Increase the heat to medium-high and simmer until the mixture thickens, 3 to 4 minutes. Off the heat, whisk in the Parmesan, sherry, lemon juice, thyme, nutmeg, and ½ teaspoon salt. Add the sauce, sautéed vegetables, peas, and turkey to the pasta and mix well; season with salt and pepper to taste.

**5.** Turn the mixture into a buttered 13 by 9-inch gratin dish (or other shallow ovensafe baking dish of similar size), sprinkle evenly with the reserved bread crumbs, and bake until the bread crumbs brown and the mixture is bubbly, 13 to 15 minutes. Serve immediately.

## Turkey Meatloaf with Ketchup–Brown Sugar Glaze

**SERVES** 4 to 6

---

**WHY THIS RECIPE WORKS** Store-bought ground turkey is so fine and pasty that it usually produces a dense, mushy meatloaf. So we could not just swap it for beef in our favorite meatloaf recipe. Instead of a panade, we stirred in quick oats, which added a bit of chew and helped open up the texture of the dense turkey. To give the turkey's thin juices fuller body, we added cornstarch, boosted flavor with grated Parmesan cheese and butter, and used egg yolks instead of whole eggs. To avoid overwhelming the mild flavor of the meat with too many add-ins, we stirred in a modest amount of onion, as well as garlic, Worcestershire sauce, thyme, and Dijon mustard. To finish it off, we made a flavor-packed glaze and ensured that it stuck by applying a first coat to the meatloaf and letting it cook until the glaze was tacky. We then added a second coat of glaze, which stuck to this base coat in an even layer. To ensure the loaf cooked evenly, we baked it on an aluminum foil–lined wire rack set in a rimmed baking sheet. Do not use 99 percent lean ground turkey in this recipe. Three tablespoons of rolled oats, chopped fine, can be substituted for the quick oats; do not use steel-cut oats.

**MEATLOAF**

- 3 tablespoons unsalted butter
- Pinch baking soda
- ½ onion, chopped fine
- Table salt and pepper
- 1 garlic clove, minced
- 1 teaspoon minced fresh thyme
- 2 tablespoons Worcestershire sauce
- 3 tablespoons quick oats
- 2 teaspoons cornstarch
- 2 large egg yolks
- 2 tablespoons Dijon mustard
- 2 pounds 85 or 93 percent lean ground turkey
- 1 ounce Parmesan, grated (½ cup)
- ⅓ cup chopped fresh parsley

**GLAZE**

- 1 cup ketchup
- ¼ cup packed brown sugar
- 2½ teaspoons cider vinegar
- ½ teaspoon hot sauce

**1. FOR THE MEATLOAF:** Adjust oven rack to upper-middle position and heat oven to 350 degrees. Line wire rack with aluminum foil and set in rimmed baking sheet. Melt butter in 10-inch skillet over low heat. Stir baking soda into melted butter. Add onion and ¼ teaspoon salt, increase heat to medium, and cook, stirring frequently, until onion is softened and beginning to brown, 3 to 4 minutes. Add garlic and thyme and cook until fragrant, about 1 minute. Stir in Worcestershire and continue to cook until slightly reduced, about 1 minute longer. Transfer onion mixture to large bowl and set aside. Combine oats, cornstarch, ¾ teaspoon salt, and ½ teaspoon pepper in second bowl.

**2. FOR THE GLAZE:** Whisk all ingredients in saucepan until sugar dissolves. Bring mixture to simmer over medium heat and cook until slightly thickened, about 5 minutes; set aside.

**3.** Stir egg yolks and mustard into cooled onion mixture until well combined. Add turkey, Parmesan, parsley, and oat mixture; using your hands, mix until well combined. Transfer turkey mixture to center of prepared rack. Using your wet hands, shape into 9 by 5-inch loaf. Using pastry brush, spread half of glaze evenly over top and sides of meatloaf. Bake meatloaf for 40 minutes.

**4.** Brush remaining glaze onto top and sides of meatloaf and continue to cook until meatloaf registers 160 degrees, 35 to 40 minutes longer. Let meatloaf cool for 20 minutes before slicing and serving.

## Italian-Style Turkey Meatballs

**SERVE** 4 to 6

---

**WHY THIS RECIPE WORKS** Our turkey meatballs rival those made from beef or pork, thanks to a few test kitchen tricks. We started with 85 or 93 percent lean turkey; these fattier options produced moister meatballs. Next, we added an egg and fresh bread crumbs to help bind the meatballs. And a stint in the fridge was key to firming up the gelatin and creating juicy texture. To boost meaty flavor, we added glutamate-rich ingredients such as Parmesan cheese, anchovies, tomato paste, and dried shiitake mushrooms. Braising the meatballs in a quick tomato sauce gave them time to soak up extra flavor. Serve with spaghetti.

1 cup chicken broth
½ ounce dried shiitake mushrooms
2 slices hearty white sandwich bread, torn into 1-inch pieces
1 ounce Parmesan cheese, grated (½ cup), plus extra for serving
1 tablespoon chopped fresh parsley
1½ teaspoons unflavored gelatin
1 teaspoon table salt
½ teaspoon pepper, divided
4 anchovy fillets, rinsed, patted dry, and minced, divided
1½ pounds 85 or 93 percent lean ground turkey
1 large egg, lightly beaten
4 garlic cloves, minced, divided
1 (14.5-ounce) can whole peeled tomatoes
½ teaspoon dried oregano
⅛ teaspoon red pepper flakes
3 tablespoons extra-virgin olive oil
2 tablespoons tomato paste
¼ cup chopped fresh basil
Sugar

**1.** Microwave broth and mushrooms in covered bowl until steaming, about 1 minute. Let sit until softened, about 5 minutes. Drain mushrooms in fine-mesh strainer and reserve liquid.

**2.** Pulse bread in food processor until finely ground, 10 to 15 pulses; transfer bread crumbs to large bowl (do not wash processor bowl). Add Parmesan, parsley, gelatin, salt, and ¼ teaspoon pepper to bowl with bread crumbs and mix until thoroughly combined. Pulse mushrooms and half of anchovies in food processor until chopped fine, 10 to 15 pulses. Add mushroom mixture, turkey, egg, and half of garlic to bowl with bread-crumb mixture and mix with your hands until thoroughly combined. Divide mixture into 16 portions (about ¼ cup each). Using your hands, roll each portion into ball; transfer meatballs to plate and refrigerate for 15 minutes.

**3.** Pulse tomatoes and their juice in food processor to coarse puree, 10 to 15 pulses. Combine oregano, pepper flakes, remaining ¼ teaspoon pepper, remaining anchovies, and remaining garlic in small bowl; set aside.

**4.** Heat oil in 12-inch nonstick skillet over medium-high heat until shimmering. Add meatballs and cook until well browned all over, 5 to 7 minutes. Transfer meatballs to paper towel–lined plate, leaving fat in skillet.

**5.** Add reserved anchovy mixture to skillet and cook, stirring constantly, until fragrant, about 30 seconds. Increase heat to high; stir in tomato paste, reserved mushroom liquid, and pureed tomatoes; and bring to simmer. Return meatballs to skillet, reduce heat to medium-low, cover, and cook until meatballs register 160 degrees, 12 to 15 minutes, turning meatballs once. Transfer meatballs to platter, increase heat to high, and simmer sauce until slightly thickened, 3 to 5 minutes. Stir in basil and season with sugar, salt, and pepper to taste. Pour sauce over meatballs and serve, passing extra Parmesan separately.

## Skillet Turkey Burgers

**SERVES 4**

**WHY THIS RECIPE WORKS** Ground turkey is full of moisture—more so than ground beef—but since you have to cook it to 160 degrees, it's virtually impossible to keep the juices in the meat unless you give it some help. For juicy turkey burgers, we started by adding baking soda and gelatin to help keep the meat moist as it cooked. A few tablespoons of panko bread crumbs broke up the texture to keep the meat from binding together too firmly. Gently tossing the ingredients together and lightly shaping the patties also helped create a texture that was pleasantly coarse, loose, and tender. A bit of melted butter added richness, while soy sauce and Parmesan contributed savoriness. Starting the patties in a cold skillet meant the exteriors could slowly start to brown while the interiors had time to reach the 160-degree serving temperature. Covering the skillet enveloped the burgers in steam so they cooked evenly. When mixing and shaping the patties, do not overwork the meat, or the burgers may become dense. Serve with your favorite burger toppings and Pickled Avocado, if desired.

2 teaspoons vegetable oil
1 teaspoon water
¼ teaspoon baking soda
1 pound 93 percent lean ground turkey
1½ tablespoons soy sauce
1 tablespoon unsalted butter, melted
3 tablespoons panko bread crumbs
3 tablespoons grated Parmesan cheese
½ teaspoon unflavored gelatin
¼ teaspoon pepper
⅛ teaspoon table salt
4 slices American cheese (optional)
4 hamburger buns

**1.** Place oil in 12-inch nonstick skillet and set aside. Combine water and baking soda in small bowl. Place turkey in large bowl. Using your hands, break up meat into rough ½-inch pieces. Drizzle baking soda mixture evenly over turkey, followed by soy sauce and melted butter. Evenly sprinkle panko, Parmesan, gelatin, pepper, and salt over turkey mixture. Using your hands, toss gently to combine.

**2.** Divide meat into 4 lightly packed portions, about 4 ounces each. Gently flatten 1 portion into patty about ½ inch thick and about 4 inches in diameter. Transfer patty directly to prepared skillet and repeat with remaining portions.

**3.** Heat skillet over medium heat. When patties start to sizzle, cover skillet and cook until patties are well browned on bottom, about 2½ minutes (if patties are not browned after 2½ minutes, increase heat). Carefully flip patties, cover, and continue to cook until second side is well browned and burgers register 160 degrees, 2½ to 3 minutes longer. If using cheese, place 1 slice on each burger about 1 minute before burgers finish cooking. Transfer burgers to plate and let rest for 5 minutes, then transfer to buns and serve.

## Pickled Avocado

**SERVES** 4

Use a relatively firm avocado for this recipe.

- ½ cup distilled white vinegar
- ½ cup water
- 1 tablespoon sugar
- 2 teaspoons table salt
- 1 ripe but firm avocado, halved, pitted, and sliced ¼ inch thick

Combine vinegar, water, sugar, and salt in medium bowl and whisk until sugar and salt are dissolved, about 30 seconds. Add avocado (avocado should be submerged) and refrigerate for at least 30 minutes or up to 2 hours. Drain and pat dry before using.

# Turkey Patty Melts

**MAKES** 4 sandwiches

**WHY THIS RECIPE WORKS** Our ground turkey patty melts started with browning a turkey mixture designed to remain juicy and tender even when pressed into very thin patties and seared. We added onions, water, and baking soda to the skillet; covered it; and allowed the water to lift the fond from the pan and steam the juices from the onion. Then, we removed the lid and continued to cook. The baking soda both tenderized the onions and raised the pH in the pan to promote speedy browning. We boosted the sweetness of the onions with brown sugar and added a splash of balsamic vinegar to give them some tang. We built the melts by layering the onions, patties, and pepper Jack between slices of bread and then gently griddled them until the sandwiches were warmed through, the cheese was melty, and the bread was crisply toasted.

- 1 recipe Ground Turkey Mix
- 1 pound onions, halved and sliced thin
- ½ cup water
- 1 tablespoon plus 4 teaspoons unsalted butter, divided
- ½ teaspoon kosher salt
- ¼ teaspoon pepper
- Pinch baking soda
- 2 teaspoons balsamic vinegar
- 1 teaspoon packed brown sugar
- 8 slices hearty sandwich bread
- 2 tablespoons Dijon mustard
- 12 slices pepper Jack cheese (4½ ounces), divided

**1.** Divide ground turkey mix into 4 equal portions. Shape each portion into thin patties that are ¼ inch larger than slices of bread. Place 2 patties in 12-inch nonstick skillet and cook over medium heat until spotty brown on bottom, about 3 minutes. Flip and cook, pressing down on patties frequently, until second side is lightly browned, about 2 minutes. Transfer to plate. Wipe out skillet and add remaining 2 patties. Repeat cooking process and transfer patties to plate, leaving fat in skillet.

**2.** Add onions, water, 1 tablespoon butter, salt, pepper, and baking soda and bring to simmer. Cover and cook for 8 minutes. Uncover and continue to cook, stirring occasionally, until onions are well browned, 7 to 10 minutes. Stir in vinegar and sugar.

**3.** While onions cook, arrange 4 slices of bread on cutting board. Spread 1½ teaspoons mustard on each slice. Top each slice with 1½ slices cheese, breaking up cheese as necessary to keep from hanging over edge. Arrange patties on top of cheese. Divide onions evenly over patties and top with remaining 6 slices cheese and remaining 4 slices bread.

**4.** In clean, dry skillet, melt 1 teaspoon butter over medium-low heat. Add 2 sandwiches and cook until bottoms are well browned, 4 to 5 minutes, moving sandwiches as needed to ensure even browning. Flip, add 1 teaspoon butter to pan, and continue to cook until second side is well browned, 2 to 3 minutes. Remove sandwiches and repeat with remaining 2 teaspoons butter and remaining 2 sandwiches. Serve.

## Ground Turkey Mix

**MAKES** 21 ounces

This mixture can be wrapped tightly in plastic wrap and refrigerated for up to two days or wrapped in foil and frozen for up to 1 month.

- 1 shallot, chopped coarse (⅓ cup)
- ¼ cup panko bread crumbs
- ½ teaspoon kosher salt
- ¼ teaspoon pepper
- 1 pound 93 percent lean ground turkey
- ¼ cup milk
- 2 tablespoons unsalted butter, melted and cooled
- 1 tablespoon Worcestershire sauce

Process shallot, panko, salt, and pepper in food processor, scraping down sides as necessary, until shallot is finely ground, about 20 seconds. Add turkey, milk, melted butter, and Worcestershire and pulse until just combined, 8 to 12 pulses. Transfer to bowl, cover, and refrigerate until ready to use.

*Continued on next page*

Photos (left to right): Grind-Your-Own Sirloin Burger Blend; New York Strip Steaks with Crispy Potatoes and Parsley Sauces; Steak Tacos with Sweet and Spicy Pickled Onions; Plov (Rice Pilaf with Beef and Carrots); Roast Beef Tenderloin with Caramelized Onion and Mushroom Stuffing; Home-Corned Beef with Vegetables; Herb-Crusted Pork Roast

# CHAPTER 7 Meat

## Best Old-Fashioned Burgers

**MAKES** 4 burgers

**WHY THIS RECIPE WORKS** We wanted to create the classic drive-in burger. A thin patty made from freshly ground beef and cooked on a flat griddle, this style of burger is ultracrisp, ultrabrowned, and ultrabeefy. Prepackaged hamburger is ground very fine and packaged tightly, which produced dense and dry patties. For the meat, we settled on short ribs ground up with sirloin steak tips. While beefiness depended on cut, juiciness corresponded to fat. Well-marbled short ribs added the perfect amount of fat to complement the beefy flavor from the sirloin tips. It was easy to grind the meat in the food processor as long as the meat was first chilled until firm but still pliable. To combat a rubbery texture, the meat needed to be loosely packed—not pressed but rather gently shaped into loose patties. Sirloin steak tips are also labeled "flap meat;" flank steak can be used in its place. This recipe yields juicy medium to medium-well burgers. If doubling the recipe, process the meat in three batches in step 2. Because the cooked burgers do not hold well, fry four burgers and serve them immediately before frying more. Or cook them in two pans. Extra patties can be frozen for up to 2 weeks. Stack the patties, separated by parchment paper, and wrap them in three layers of plastic wrap. Thaw burgers in a single layer on a baking sheet at room temperature for 30 minutes before cooking.

- 10 ounces sirloin steak tips, cut into 1-inch chunks
- 6 ounces boneless beef short ribs, cut into 1-inch chunks
- Table salt and ground black pepper
- 1 tablespoon unsalted butter
- 4 soft hamburger buns
- ½ teaspoon vegetable oil
- 4 slices American cheese
- Thinly sliced onion
- 1 recipe Classic Burger Sauce

**1.** Place the beef chunks on a baking sheet in a single layer, leaving ½ inch of space around each chunk. Freeze the meat until very firm and starting to harden around the edges but still pliable, 15 to 25 minutes.

**2.** Place half of the meat in a food processor and pulse until the meat is coarsely ground, 10 to 15 pulses, stopping and redistributing the meat around the bowl as necessary to ensure the beef is evenly ground. Transfer the meat to a baking sheet by overturning the bowl, without touching the meat. Repeat the grinding with the remaining meat. Spread the meat over the sheet and inspect carefully, discarding any long strands of gristle or large chunks of hard meat or fat.

**3.** Gently separate the ground meat into four equal mounds. Without picking the meat up, with your fingers gently shape each mound into a loose patty ½ inch thick and 4 inches in diameter, leaving the edges and surface ragged. Season the top of each patty with salt and pepper. Using a spatula, flip the patties and season the other side. Refrigerate while toasting the buns.

**4.** Melt ½ tablespoon of the butter in a heavy-bottomed 12-inch skillet over medium heat. Add the bun tops, cut side down, and toast until light golden brown, about 2 minutes. Repeat with the remaining ½ tablespoon butter and the bun bottoms. Set the buns aside and wipe out the skillet with paper towels.

**5.** Return the skillet to high heat; add the oil and heat until just smoking. Using a spatula, transfer the burgers to the skillet and cook without moving them for 3 minutes. Using the spatula, flip the burgers over and cook for 1 minute. Top each patty with a slice of the cheese and continue to cook until the cheese is melted, about 1 minute longer.

**6.** Transfer the patties to the bun bottoms and top with the onion. Spread 2 teaspoons of the burger sauce on each bun top. Cover the burgers with the bun tops and serve immediately.

### Classic Burger Sauce

**MAKES** about ¼ cup

- 2 tablespoons mayonnaise
- 1 tablespoon ketchup
- ½ teaspoon sweet pickle relish
- ½ teaspoon sugar
- ½ teaspoon white vinegar
- ¼ teaspoon ground black pepper

Whisk all the ingredients together in a small bowl.

### MAKING LOOSELY PACKED PATTIES

**1.** Chill meat in freezer, separating cubes by at least ½ inch, until firm but still pliable, 15 to 25 minutes. Pulse meat in food processor.

**2.** Spread chopped meat over baking sheet and remove any large chunks or stringy connective tissue. Gently separate meat into 4 piles.

**3.** Without lifting or compressing, gently form meat into thin patties with rough edges and textured surface.

## Smashed Burgers

**SERVES 2**

**WHY THIS RECIPE WORKS** Smashed burgers trade on one simple truth: Crust is king. These burgers share the same thin, verging-on-well-done profile, but their big selling point is an ultrabrown, crispy crust. We used commercial ground beef instead of grinding our own because the former is ground finer and thus exposes more myosin, a sticky meat protein that helps the patties hold together when smashed. Using a small saucepan to press down on the meat ensured that it spread and stuck uniformly to the skillet, resulting in deep browning. Sandwiching an ultramelty slice of American cheese between the two patties helped the cheese melt and seep into the meat. Do not use a stainless-steel or nonstick skillet here. You can use 85 percent lean ground beef, but 90 percent lean will produce a dry burger. Open a window or turn on your exhaust fan before cooking. Be assertive when pressing the patties. To serve four, double the ingredients for the sauce and burgers and use the same amount of oil; once the burgers are cooked, transfer them to a wire rack set in a rimmed baking sheet, adding cheese to the first four burgers, and keep warm in a 200-degree oven.

**SAUCE**

- 2 tablespoons mayonnaise
- 1 tablespoon minced shallot
- 1½ teaspoons finely chopped dill pickles plus ½ teaspoon brine
- 1½ teaspoons ketchup
- ⅛ teaspoon sugar
- ⅛ teaspoon pepper

**BURGERS**

- 2 hamburger buns, toasted if desired
- 8 ounces 80 percent lean ground beef
- ¼ teaspoon vegetable oil
- ¼ teaspoon kosher salt, divided
- 2 slices American cheese (2 ounces)
- Bibb lettuce leaves
- Thinly sliced tomato

1. **FOR THE SAUCE:** Stir all ingredients together in bowl.

2. **FOR THE BURGERS:** Spread 1 tablespoon sauce on cut side of each bun top. Divide beef into 4 equal pieces (2 ounces each); form into loose, rough balls (do not compress). Place oil in 12-inch cast-iron or carbon-steel skillet. Use paper towel to rub oil into bottom of skillet (reserve paper towel). Heat over medium-low heat for 5 minutes. While skillet heats, wrap bottom and sides of small saucepan with large sheet of aluminum foil, anchoring foil on rim, and place large plate next to cooktop.

3. Increase heat to high. When skillet begins to smoke, place 2 balls about 3 inches apart in skillet. Use bottom of prepared saucepan to firmly smash each ball until 4 to 4½ inches in diameter. Place saucepan on plate next to cooktop. Sprinkle patties with ⅛ teaspoon salt and season with pepper. Cook until at least three-quarters of each patty is no longer pink on top, about 2 minutes (patties will stick to skillet). Use thin metal spatula to loosen patties from skillet. Flip patties and cook for 15 seconds. Slide skillet off heat. Transfer 1 burger to each bun bottom and top each with 1 slice American cheese. Gently scrape any browned bits from skillet, use tongs to wipe with reserved paper towel, and return skillet to heat. Repeat with remaining 2 balls and place burgers on top of cheese. Top with lettuce and tomato. Cap with prepared bun tops. Serve immediately.

## Juicy Pub-Style Burgers

**SERVES 4**

**WHY THIS RECIPE WORKS** Few things are as satisfying as a thick, juicy pub-style burger. But by the time the center of these hefty burgers cooks through, there is often an overcooked band of meat. We wanted a patty that was evenly rosy from center to edge. Grinding our own meat in the food processor was a must (freezing the meat until just firm helped the processor chop it cleanly), and we found that sirloin steak tips were ideal. To give the burgers just enough structure, we cut the meat into small ½-inch chunks before grinding and lightly packed the meat into patties. Melted butter improved their flavor and juiciness. Transferring the burgers from the stovetop to the oven to finish cooking eliminated the overcooked gray zone. For extra pub-style appeal, we came up with flavorful topping combinations to finish off our burgers. Sirloin steak tips are also labeled as "flap meat." When stirring the butter and pepper into the ground meat and shaping the patties, take care not to overwork the meat or the burgers will become dense. For the best flavor, season the burgers aggressively just before cooking.

- 2 pounds sirloin steak tips or boneless beef short ribs, trimmed and cut into ½-inch chunks
- 4 tablespoons unsalted butter, melted and cooled slightly
- ½ teaspoon table salt, divided

1½ teaspoons pepper, divided
1 teaspoon vegetable oil
4 large hamburger buns, toasted and buttered
1 recipe Pub-Style Burger Sauce (optional; recipe follows)

1. Place beef chunks on baking sheet in single layer. Freeze meat until very firm and starting to harden around edges but still pliable, 15 to 25 minutes.

2. Place one-quarter of meat in food processor and pulse until finely ground into 1⁄16-inch pieces, about 35 pulses, stopping and redistributing meat around bowl as necessary to ensure beef is evenly ground. Transfer meat to baking sheet by overturning processor bowl and without directly touching meat. Repeat grinding with remaining 3 batches of meat. Spread meat over sheet and inspect carefully, discarding any long strands of gristle or large chunks of hard meat or fat.

3. Adjust oven rack to middle position and heat oven to 300 degrees. Drizzle melted butter over ground meat and add 1 teaspoon pepper. Toss gently with fork to combine. Divide meat into 4 lightly packed balls. Gently flatten into patties ¾ inch thick and about 4½ inches in diameter. (Uncooked patties can be wrapped in plastic wrap and refrigerated for up to 24 hours)

4. Sprinkle 1 side of patties with ¼ teaspoon salt and ¼ teaspoon pepper. Using spatula, flip patties and sprinkle other side with remaining ¼ teaspoon salt and remaining ¼ teaspoon pepper. Heat oil in 12-inch skillet over high heat until just smoking. Using spatula, transfer burgers to skillet and cook without moving for 2 minutes. Using spatula, flip burgers over and cook 2 minutes longer. Transfer patties to rimmed baking sheet and bake until burgers register 120 to 125 degrees (for medium-rare), 3 to 5 minutes.

5. Transfer burgers to plate and let rest for 5 minutes. Transfer to buns, top with Pub-Style Burger Sauce, if using, and serve.

### Pub-Style Burger Sauce

**MAKES** 1 cup, enough to top 4 burgers

¾ cup mayonnaise
2 tablespoons soy sauce
1 tablespoon packed dark brown sugar
1 tablespoon Worcestershire sauce
1 tablespoon minced fresh chives
1 garlic clove, minced
¾ teaspoon pepper

Whisk all ingredients together in bowl.

### Juicy Pub-Style Burgers with Crispy Shallots and Blue Cheese

Heat ½ cup vegetable oil and 3 thinly sliced shallots in a medium saucepan over high heat; cook, stirring frequently, until the shallots are golden, about 8 minutes. Using a slotted spoon, transfer the shallots to a paper towel–lined plate, season with table salt, and let drain until crisp, about 5 minutes. (The cooled shallots can be stored at room temperature in an airtight container for up to 3 days.) Follow the recipe for Juicy Pub-Style Burgers, topping each burger with 1 ounce crumbled blue cheese before transferring to the oven. Top with Pub-Style Burger Sauce and the crispy shallots just before serving.

## Grind-Your-Own Sirloin Burger Blend

**SERVES 4**

**WHY THIS RECIPE WORKS** Although store-bought ground chuck makes a quick and satisfying burger, home-ground meat provides a loose, craggy texture and strong beefy flavor that make for a truly superior burger experience. We started with sirloin steak tips—which have good flavor, contain minimal gristly fat, and are available in small quantities—and turned to our trusty food processor to grind them. Butter gave the meat some much-needed moisture and fat for juicy, tender burgers. Freezing the patties prior to cooking helped them hold together. Sirloin steak tips are often sold as flap meat. When trimming the meat, remove any pieces of fat thicker than ⅛ inch along with any silverskin. After trimming, you should have about 1¾ pounds of meat. To double this recipe, spread beef over two baking sheets in step 1 and pulse in food processor in eight batches.

2 pounds sirloin steak tips, trimmed and cut into ½-inch pieces
4 tablespoons unsalted butter, melted and cooled
½ teaspoon table salt
¼ teaspoon pepper
1 teaspoon vegetable oil, if using skillet
1 (13 by 9-inch) disposable aluminum roasting pan, if using charcoal grill
4 slices cheese (4 ounces) (optional)
4 hamburger buns, toasted if desired

1. **FOR THE BURGER BLEND:** Arrange beef in single layer on rimmed baking sheet and freeze until very firm and starting to harden around edges but still pliable, 35 to 45 minutes.

2. Working in 4 batches, pulse beef in food processor until finely ground into 1⁄16-inch pieces, about 20 pulses, stopping to redistribute meat as needed; return to sheet. Spread ground beef over sheet, discarding any long strands of gristle and large chunks of fat. Drizzle with melted butter and toss gently with fork to combine.

3. Divide beef mixture into 4 lightly packed balls, then gently flatten into ¾-inch-thick patties. Using your fingertips, press center of each patty down until about ½ inch thick, creating slight divot. Cover and refrigerate until ready to cook. (Patties can be wrapped in plastic wrap and refrigerated for up to 24 hours or frozen for up to 2 weeks. To freeze, stack patties, separated by parchment paper, wrap in plastic wrap, and place in zipper-lock freezer bag.)

4A. **FOR A SKILLET:** Adjust oven rack to middle position and heat oven to 300 degrees. Season patties with salt and pepper. (If patties were previously frozen, thaw at room temperature for 30 minutes before seasoning and increase baking time to

6 to 12 minutes.) Heat oil in 12-inch skillet over high heat until just smoking. Using spatula, transfer patties to skillet, divot side up, and cook until well browned on first side, 2 to 4 minutes. Gently flip patties and continue to cook until well browned on second side, 2 to 4 minutes. Transfer patties to rimmed baking sheet, divot side down; top with cheese, if using; and bake until burgers register 120 to 125 degrees (for medium-rare) or 130 to 135 degrees (for medium), 3 to 8 minutes. Transfer burgers to platter and let rest for 5 minutes. Serve burgers on buns.

**4B. FOR A CHARCOAL GRILL:** Freeze patties for 30 minutes. (If patties were previously frozen, thaw at room temperature for 30 minutes.) Using skewer, poke 12 holes in bottom of disposable pan. Open bottom vent completely and place prepared pan in center of grill. Light large chimney starter two-thirds filled with charcoal briquettes (4 quarts). When top coals are partially covered with ash, pour into pan. Set cooking grate in place, cover, and open lid vent completely. Heat grill until hot, about 5 minutes. Clean and oil cooking grate. Season patties with salt and pepper. Using spatula, place patties on grill, divot side up, directly over coals. Cook until well browned on first side and meat easily releases from grill, 4 to 7 minutes. Gently flip patties; top with cheese, if using; and continue to cook until well browned on second side and meat registers 120 to 125 degrees (for medium-rare) or 130 to 135 degrees (for medium), 4 to 7 minutes. Transfer burgers to platter and let rest for 5 minutes. Serve burgers on buns.

**4C. FOR A GAS GRILL:** Freeze patties for 30 minutes. (If patties were previously frozen, thaw at room temperature for 30 minutes.) Turn all burners to high, cover, and heat grill until hot, about 15 minutes. Leave all burners on high. Clean and oil cooking grate. Season patties with salt and pepper. Using spatula, place patties on grill, divot side up, and cook, covered, until well browned on first side and meat easily releases from grill, 4 to 7 minutes. Gently flip patties; top with cheese, if using; and continue to cook until well browned on second side and meat registers 120 to 125 degrees (for medium-rare) or 130 to 135 degrees (for medium), 4 to 7 minutes. Transfer burgers to platter and let rest for 5 minutes. Serve burgers on buns.

## Mushroom-Beef Blended Burgers

**SERVES 4**

**WHY THIS RECIPE WORKS** This blended burger is a great option for those who want to eat less beef but still want the experience of eating a deeply savory, juicy, meaty-textured patty because it replaces a portion of the beef with mushrooms. Our version started with 12 ounces of inexpensive and readily available white mushrooms. We processed them to a paste and microwaved the paste to remove enough excess moisture to allow the burgers to cook up juicy but not wet. We then used a food processor to combine the mushroom paste with 80 percent lean ground beef, which was important to ensure that these burgers tasted meaty. Adding salt to the beef and then mixing it with the mushrooms in a food processor developed a sturdy myosin network that held the patties together. Cooking the patties to 135 to 165 degrees ensured that they had a firm—not floppy—texture. In step 4, if all of the patties do not fit in the skillet, start by cooking three patties until they shrink slightly, about 2 minutes, before adding the remaining patty. Cook these burgers 10 degrees higher than you would an all-beef patty. Serve with your favorite burger toppings.

- 12 ounces white mushrooms, trimmed
- 1 pound 80 percent lean ground beef, broken into rough 1½-inch pieces
- 1¼ teaspoons kosher salt
- ½–2 teaspoons pepper
- 1½ teaspoons vegetable oil
- 4 slices American, Swiss, or cheddar cheese (optional)
- 4 hamburger buns, toasted

**1.** Process mushrooms in food processor until smooth paste forms (paste will resemble thick oatmeal), scraping down sides of bowl as needed, about 1 minute. Transfer to large bowl and cover. (Do not wash out processor bowl.)

**2.** Microwave mushrooms until liquid released begins to boil, about 3 minutes, stirring halfway through microwaving. (Do not walk away during final minute; mushrooms could boil over.) Transfer mushrooms to large fine-mesh strainer set over bowl. Using spatula, press on mushrooms to extract ½ cup liquid (if more than ½ cup is removed, stir extra liquid back into mushrooms). Discard liquid and return mushrooms to bowl. Refrigerate mushrooms until room temperature, about 20 minutes.

### MAKING THE MUSHROOM-BEEF BLEND

**1.** Process raw white mushrooms until they form thick paste resembling cooked oatmeal.

**2.** Microwave mushrooms until their liquid boils, about 3 minutes, then strain off ½ cup of liquid.

**3.** Process mushrooms with ground beef and salt until mixture pulls away from sides of bowl.

**3.** Return mushrooms to processor bowl. Add beef and salt and process until mixture is uniform and begins to pull away from sides of bowl, about 20 seconds. Divide mixture into 4 equal portions and shape into patties that are 4½ inches in diameter. Sprinkle both sides of each patty with pepper. (Patties can be refrigerated overnight or tightly wrapped and frozen for up to 1 month; if frozen, thaw before cooking.)

**4.** Heat oil in 12-inch skillet over medium-high heat until shimmering. Transfer patties to skillet and cook until well browned on both sides and burgers register 120 to 125 degrees (for medium-rare) or 140 to 145 degrees (for medium-well), 6 to 10 minutes. If using cheese, place 1 slice on each burger 1 minute before burgers finish cooking. Transfer burgers to plate and let rest for 5 minutes, then transfer to buns and serve.

## Classic Sloppy Joes

**SERVES 4**

**WHY THIS RECIPE WORKS** This recipe is equally loved by adults and children. Our objective was to develop a recipe with a balanced, less sweet flavor and much less greasy meat. Treating the ground beef with baking soda (so that it retained more moisture when cooked) and then breaking it down to a fine, uniform texture in the skillet delivered a tender and cohesive mixture. Limiting the aromatics to just onion (also treated with baking soda to soften it) made for a beefier-tasting mixture with a rich, luxurious texture. We made ketchup's flavor more complex by adding vinegar, pepper flakes, and sugar and balanced it out with tomato paste, paprika, and Worcestershire. Tossing the beef with baking soda in step 1 helps keep it tender and juicy; adding baking soda to the skillet with the onion in step 2 helps the onion break down. You may substitute 90 percent lean ground beef in this recipe, but the cooked mixture will be a bit less tender. Serve the Sloppy Joes with pickle chips, if desired.

- 2 tablespoons water, divided
- ½ teaspoon plus ⅛ teaspoon baking soda, divided
- 1 pound 85 percent lean ground beef
- ½ teaspoon plus ⅛ teaspoon table salt, divided
- 2 teaspoons vegetable oil
- ½ onion, chopped fine
- 2 garlic cloves, minced
- 2 teaspoons packed brown sugar, plus extra for seasoning
- 2 teaspoons paprika
- ¼ teaspoon red pepper flakes
- ¼ cup tomato paste
- ⅓ cup ketchup
- 1 tablespoon red wine vinegar, plus extra for seasoning
- 1 tablespoon Worcestershire sauce
- ½ teaspoon cornstarch
- 4 hamburger buns

**1.** Combine 1 tablespoon water and ½ teaspoon baking soda in small bowl. In large bowl, toss beef with baking soda mixture and ½ teaspoon salt until thoroughly combined. Set aside.

**2.** Heat oil in 12-inch nonstick skillet over medium heat until shimmering. Add onion and remaining ⅛ teaspoon baking soda and stir to coat. Cook, stirring occasionally, until onion is softened, 3 to 4 minutes. Add garlic and cook, stirring constantly, until fragrant, about 30 seconds. Stir in sugar, paprika, pepper flakes, and remaining ⅛ teaspoon salt and cook, stirring constantly, until paprika is fragrant, about 1 minute. Add tomato paste and cook, stirring constantly, until paste is rust-colored, 3 to 4 minutes.

**3.** Add beef and cook, breaking up meat with wooden spoon, until beef is no longer pink, about 5 minutes. Mash beef with potato masher until fine-textured, about 1 minute. Add ketchup, vinegar, and Worcestershire and stir to combine, scraping up any browned bits.

**4.** Combine cornstarch and remaining 1 tablespoon water in small bowl, then pour cornstarch mixture over beef and stir to incorporate. Cook, stirring constantly, until sauce thickens and coats beef, about 1 minute. Season with salt, extra sugar, and extra vinegar to taste. Spoon beef mixture onto buns and serve.

## Ground Beef Tacos

**SERVES 4**

**WHY THIS RECIPE WORKS** Tacos made from supermarket kits are disappointing substitutes for the real thing. Easy as they may be to prepare, taco fillings made with store-bought spice mixes taste flat and stale, and the shells don't taste much different than the cardboard they're packaged in. We set out to develop a recipe for toasty, not greasy, taco shells filled with a boldly spiced beef mixture and fresh toppings. Home-fried corn tortillas made superior homemade taco shells. For the filling, we seasoned lean ground beef with onions, garlic, and spices (chili powder, cumin, coriander, and oregano). To moisten and further flavor the beef filling, we added chicken broth, brown sugar, and vinegar. Spooned into our fresh, crisp taco shells and topped with tomatoes, lettuce, avocado, Monterey Jack, onion, and cilantro, these tacos have far better flavor than taco-kit versions. Taco toppings are highly individual. We consider the ones listed below essential, but you might also want to consider diced avocado, sour cream, and chopped onion.

**BEEF FILLING**

- 2 teaspoons vegetable oil
- 1 small onion, minced
- 3 medium garlic cloves, minced or pressed through a garlic press (about 1 tablespoon)
- 2 tablespoons chili powder
- 1 teaspoon ground cumin
- 1 teaspoon ground coriander
- ½ teaspoon dried oregano
- ¼ teaspoon cayenne pepper
- Table salt
- 1 pound 90 percent lean ground beef
- ½ cup canned tomato sauce
- ½ cup low-sodium chicken broth
- 2 teaspoons vinegar, preferably cider vinegar
- 1 teaspoon brown sugar
- Ground black pepper

**SHELLS AND TOPPINGS**

- 8 Home-Fried Taco Shells
- Shredded Monterey Jack cheese
- Shredded iceberg lettuce
- Diced tomatoes
- Chopped fresh cilantro leaves

**1. FOR THE FILLING:** Heat the oil in a medium skillet over medium heat until shimmering. Add the onion and cook, stirring occasionally, until softened, about 4 minutes. Add the garlic, spices, and ½ teaspoon salt; cook, stirring constantly, until fragrant, about 30 seconds. Add the ground beef and cook, breaking up the meat with a wooden spoon and scraping the pan bottom to prevent scorching, until the beef is no longer pink, about 5 minutes. Add the tomato sauce, broth, vinegar, and brown sugar; bring to a simmer. Reduce the heat to medium-low and simmer uncovered, stirring frequently and breaking up the meat so that no chunks remain, until the liquid has reduced and thickened (the mixture should not be completely dry), about 10 minutes. Season with salt and pepper to taste.

**2.** Using a wide, shallow spoon, divide the mixture evenly among the taco shells; place two tacos on each plate. Serve immediately, passing the toppings separately.

## Home-Fried Taco Shells

**MAKES** 8 shells

Fry the taco shells before you make the filling, then rewarm them in a 200-degree oven for about 10 minutes before serving.

- ¾ cup corn oil, vegetable oil, or canola oil
- 8 (6-inch) corn tortillas

**1.** Line rimmed baking sheet with double thickness of paper towels and set aside. Heat oil in 8-inch skillet over medium heat to 350 degrees, about 5 minutes (oil should bubble when small piece of tortilla is dropped in; piece should rise to surface in 2 seconds and be light golden brown in about 1 minute).

**2.** Using tongs to hold tortilla, submerge half of tortilla into hot oil and press it down with metal spatula. Fry until just set, about 30 seconds. Flip tortilla and submerge second half. Fry until golden brown, about 1½ minutes. Flip again and fry other side until golden brown, about 30 seconds. Transfer each fried taco shell upside down to prepared baking sheet.

## Tacos Dorados (Crispy Ground Beef Tacos)

**SERVES 4**

**WHY THIS RECIPE WORKS** Frying your own taco shells results in great taste, but the process is messy. Enter tacos dorados, a Mexican preparation in which tortillas are stuffed with a beef filling then folded in half and fried. The tacos are then opened like books and loaded with garnishes. We first tossed ground beef with a bit of baking soda to help it stay juicy before adding it to a savory base of onion, spices, and tomato paste. Next, we stirred in shredded cheddar to make the filling cohesive. To build the tacos, we brushed corn tortillas with oil, warmed them to make them pliable, and stuffed them with the filling. Instead of fussy deep frying, we pan-fried the tacos in two batches until they were crisp and golden. Arrange the tacos so they face the same direction in the skillet to make them easy to fit and flip. To ensure crispy tacos, cook the tortillas until they are deeply browned. To garnish, open each taco like a book and load it with your preferred toppings; close it to eat.

- 1 tablespoon water
- ¼ teaspoon baking soda
- 12 ounces 90 percent lean ground beef
- 7 tablespoons vegetable oil, divided
- 1 onion, chopped fine
- 1½ tablespoons chili powder
- 1½ tablespoons paprika
- 1½ teaspoons ground cumin
- 1½ teaspoons garlic powder
- 1 teaspoon table salt
- 2 tablespoons tomato paste
- 2 ounces cheddar cheese, shredded (½ cup), plus extra for serving
- 12 (6-inch) corn tortillas

- Shredded iceberg lettuce
- Chopped tomato
- Sour cream
- Pickled jalapeño slices
- Hot sauce

**1.** Adjust oven rack to middle position and heat oven to 400 degrees. Combine water and baking soda in large bowl. Add beef and mix until thoroughly combined. Set aside.

**2.** Heat 1 tablespoon oil in 12-inch nonstick skillet over medium heat until shimmering. Add onion and cook, stirring occasionally, until softened, 4 to 6 minutes. Add chili powder, paprika, cumin, garlic powder, and salt and cook, stirring frequently, until fragrant, about 1 minute. Stir in tomato paste and cook until paste is rust-colored, 1 to 2 minutes. Add beef mixture and cook, using wooden spoon to break meat into pieces no larger than ¼ inch, until beef is no longer pink, 5 to 7 minutes. Transfer beef mixture to bowl; stir in cheddar until cheese has melted and mixture is homogeneous. Wipe skillet clean with paper towels.

**3.** Thoroughly brush both sides of tortillas with 2 tablespoons oil. Arrange tortillas, overlapping, on rimmed baking sheet in 2 rows (6 tortillas each). Bake until tortillas are warm and pliable, about 5 minutes. Remove tortillas from oven and reduce oven temperature to 200 degrees.

**4.** Place 2 tablespoons filling on 1 side of 1 tortilla. Fold and press to close tortilla (edges will be open, but tortilla will remain folded). Repeat with remaining tortillas and remaining filling. (Filled tortillas can be wrapped in foil and refrigerated for up to 12 hours.)

**5.** Set wire rack in second rimmed baking sheet and line rack with double layer of paper towels. Heat remaining ¼ cup oil in now-empty skillet over medium-high heat until shimmering. Arrange 6 tacos in skillet with open sides facing away from you. Cook, adjusting heat so oil actively sizzles and bubbles appear around edges of tacos, until tacos are crispy and deeply browned on 1 side, 2 to 3 minutes. Using tongs and thin spatula, carefully flip tacos. Cook until deeply browned on second side, 2 to 3 minutes, adjusting heat as necessary.

**6.** Remove skillet from heat and transfer tacos to prepared wire rack. Blot tops of tacos with double layer of paper towels. Place sheet with fried tacos in oven to keep warm. Return skillet to medium-high heat and cook remaining tacos. Serve tacos immediately, passing extra cheddar, lettuce, tomato, sour cream, jalapeños, and hot sauce separately.

### MAKING THE CRISPIEST TACOS

**1.** Brush corn tortillas with oil; bake until pliable enough to stuff. Stuff warmed tortillas with savory ground beef bound together with melted cheddar cheese.

**2.** Fry tacos in 2 batches until crispy. (Only ¼ cup of oil is needed for 12 tacos.)

## Ground Beef and Cheese Enchiladas

**SERVES** 4 to 6

**WHY THIS RECIPE WORKS** We employed techniques from both Mexican and Tex-Mex cuisines to produce a quicker, but still deeply flavorful, take on this dinnertime staple. This recipe works by elevating a simple Tex-Mex ground beef filling with melted cheese and spices to give it a richness reminiscent of long-braised beef. When crafting the enchilada sauce, we used whole dried chiles for a deeper and more complex flavor than can be achieved when using commercial chili powder. Brushing the tortillas lightly with oil and briefly baking them helped waterproof them so that they didn't get soggy when baked in the enchilada sauce. Fresh cilantro and a spritz of lime brightened the dish and provided balance for the rich, cheesy filling. Do not use ground beef that's fattier than 90 percent lean or the dish will be greasy.

**SAUCE**

- 1½ ounces (3 to 4) dried ancho chiles, stemmed, seeded, and torn into 1-inch pieces
- 2 cups beef broth
- 1 tablespoon minced canned chipotle chile in adobo sauce
- 2 tablespoons vegetable oil
- 2 onions, chopped fine
- 6 garlic cloves, minced
- ¼ cup tomato paste
- 1 teaspoon ground cumin

**ENCHILADAS**

- 3 tablespoons vegetable oil, divided
- 1 pound 90 percent lean ground beef
- 1 teaspoon ground cumin
- 1 teaspoon ground coriander
- ½ teaspoon table salt
- 8 ounces Monterey Jack cheese, shredded (2 cups), divided
- 4 tablespoons minced fresh cilantro, divided
- 12 6-inch corn tortillas
- 2 scallions, sliced thin on bias
- Sour cream
- Lime wedges

**1. FOR THE SAUCE:** Adjust oven rack to middle position and heat oven to 400 degrees. Heat anchos in 12-inch nonstick skillet over medium-high heat, stirring frequently, until fragrant, 2 to 3 minutes. Transfer anchos to bowl, add broth, and microwave, covered, until steaming, about 2 minutes. Let sit until softened, about 5 minutes. Transfer anchos and broth to blender and add chipotle.

**2.** Heat oil in now-empty skillet over medium heat until shimmering. Add onions and cook, stirring occasionally, until translucent, about 5 minutes. Add garlic and cook until fragrant, about 1 minute. Transfer half of onion mixture to large bowl and set aside. Return skillet with remaining onion mixture to medium heat and add tomato paste and cumin. Cook, stirring frequently, until tomato paste starts to darken,

3 to 5 minutes. Transfer onion mixture in skillet to blender with ancho mixture and process until smooth, about 1 minute. Season sauce with salt to taste.

**3. FOR THE ENCHILADAS:** Heat 1 tablespoon oil in now-empty skillet over medium heat until shimmering. Add beef, cumin, coriander, and salt and cook for 2 minutes, breaking meat into ¼-inch pieces with wooden spoon. Add reserved onion mixture (do not wash bowl) and continue to cook until beef is no longer pink, 3 to 4 minutes. Return beef mixture to bowl; add 1½ cups Monterey Jack, 2 tablespoons cilantro, and ¼ cup sauce and stir to combine. Season with salt to taste.

**4.** Spread ½ cup sauce over bottom of 13 by 9-inch baking dish. Brush both sides of tortillas with remaining 2 tablespoons oil. Arrange tortillas, overlapping, on rimmed baking sheet and bake until warm and pliable, about 5 minutes. Spread ¼ cup filling down center of each tortilla. Roll each tortilla tightly around filling and place seam side down in dish, arranging enchiladas in 2 rows across width of dish.

**5.** Spread remaining sauce over top of enchiladas. Sprinkle with remaining ½ cup Monterey Jack. Bake until cheese is lightly browned and sauce is bubbling at edges, about 15 minutes. Let cool for 10 minutes. Sprinkle with scallions and remaining 2 tablespoons cilantro. Serve, passing sour cream and lime wedges separately.

## Cuban-Style Picadillo

SERVES 6

---

**WHY THIS RECIPE WORKS** Traditional recipes for this Cuban dish of spiced ground meat, sweet raisins, and briny olives call for hand-chopping or grinding the beef, but we wanted a quicker version. Store-bought ground beef provided a convenient substitute, and supplementing it with ground pork added a subtle sweetness and complexity. Browning the meat made it tough, so we skipped the extra step and soaked the meat in a mixture of baking soda and water to ensure that it remained tender. Pinching it off into sizable 2-inch chunks before adding it to the pot to simmer also kept it moist. For the spices, we settled on just oregano, cumin, and cinnamon and then bloomed them to heighten their flavor. Beef broth added a savory boost, while drained canned whole tomatoes and white wine provided brightness. We prefer this dish prepared with raisins, but they can be replaced with 2 tablespoons of brown sugar added with the broth in step 2. Picadillo is traditionally served with rice and black beans. It can also be topped with chopped parsley, toasted almonds, and/or chopped hard-cooked egg.

- 1 pound 85 percent lean ground beef
- 1 pound ground pork
- 2 tablespoons water
- ½ teaspoon baking soda
- ¾ teaspoon table salt, divided
- ¼ teaspoon pepper
- 1 green bell pepper, stemmed, seeded, and cut into 2-inch pieces
- 1 onion, halved and cut into 2-inch pieces
- 2 tablespoons vegetable oil
- 1 tablespoon dried oregano
- 1 tablespoon ground cumin
- ½ teaspoon ground cinnamon
- 6 garlic cloves, minced
- 1 (14.5-ounce) can whole tomatoes, drained and chopped coarse
- ¾ cup dry white wine
- ½ cup beef broth
- ½ cup raisins
- 3 bay leaves
- ½ cup pimento-stuffed green olives, chopped coarse
- 2 tablespoons capers, rinsed
- 1 tablespoon red wine vinegar, plus extra for seasoning

**1.** Toss beef and pork with water, baking soda, ½ teaspoon salt, and pepper in bowl until thoroughly combined. Set aside for 20 minutes. Meanwhile, pulse bell pepper and onion in food processor until chopped into ¼-inch pieces, about 12 pulses.

**2.** Heat oil in large Dutch oven over medium-high heat until shimmering. Add chopped vegetables, oregano, cumin, cinnamon, and remaining ¼ teaspoon salt; cook, stirring frequently, until vegetables are softened and beginning to brown, 6 to 8 minutes. Add garlic and cook, stirring constantly, until fragrant, about 30 seconds. Add tomatoes and wine and cook, scraping up any browned bits, until pot is almost dry, 3 to 5 minutes. Stir in broth, raisins, and bay leaves and bring to simmer.

**3.** Reduce heat to medium-low, add meat mixture in 2-inch chunks to pot, and bring to gentle simmer. Cover and cook, stirring occasionally with 2 forks to break meat chunks into ¼- to ½-inch pieces, until meat is cooked through, about 10 minutes.

**4.** Discard bay leaves. Stir in olives and capers. Increase heat to medium-high and cook, stirring occasionally, until sauce is thickened and coats meat, about 5 minutes. Stir in vinegar and season with salt, pepper, and extra vinegar to taste. Serve.

## Pastelón (Puerto Rican Sweet Plantain and Picadillo Casserole)

SERVES 6 to 8

---

**WHY THIS RECIPE WORKS** This Puerto Rican casserole is a savory-sweet mash-up of two island staples—plátanos maduros fritos (fried ripe plantains) and the briny, sofrito-laced filling called picadillo. To ensure evenly thick planks for frying, we cut the peeled fruit in half before slicing it into slabs. For the picadillo, we browned the beef with a healthy dose of sazón (a Puerto Rican seasoning blend) before combining it with the sofrito; tomato sauce; and alcaparrado, a briny blend of olives, capers, and pimentos. Drizzling beaten egg on the first layer of plantains gave the casserole a sturdier structure. We topped the pastelón with a light sprinkling of Monterey Jack. If culantro (also called recao) is unavailable, increase the

cilantro to 1 cup. You can substitute a small green bell pepper for the Cubanelle. Buy the largest plantains you can find; they should be almost completely black and yield to firm pressure. The seasoning mix sazón can be found in the international section of your supermarket; we like versions that include cilantro and achiote for this dish, but any will work. Alcaparrado is a mixture of pitted Manzanilla olives, capers, and pimento strips. If unavailable, substitute pimento-stuffed Manzanilla olives. Serve with rice and beans.

- ¾ cup fresh cilantro leaves and stems
- 1 small Cubanelle pepper, stemmed, seeded, and chopped coarse
- ½ onion, quartered
- ¼ cup fresh culantro, chopped coarse
- 2 tablespoons vegetable oil
- 3 garlic cloves, peeled
- 3–3½ pounds very ripe plantains, peeled, divided
- ¾ cup vegetable oil for frying
- ½ teaspoon plus pinch table salt, divided
- 1 pound 90 percent lean ground beef
- 2½ teaspoons sazón
- 2 teaspoons distilled white vinegar
- 1 (8-ounce) can tomato sauce
- 2 tablespoons pitted alcaparrado
- 2 large eggs
- 4 ounces Monterey Jack cheese, shredded (1 cup)

**1.** Adjust oven rack to middle position and heat oven to 400 degrees. Pulse cilantro, Cubanelle, onion, culantro, 2 tablespoons oil, and garlic in food processor until coarsely chopped, 12 to 14 pulses.

**2.** Line rimmed baking sheet with double layer of paper towels. Halve 1 plantain crosswise; cut each half lengthwise into thirds. Repeat with remaining plantains.

**3.** Heat ¾ cup oil in 12-inch nonstick skillet over medium-high heat until shimmering. Carefully lay one-third of plantain pieces in skillet and fry until deep golden brown on 1 side, 3 to 4 minutes. Using 2 spatulas, flip and fry on second side until deep golden brown, 2 to 3 minutes. Transfer plantains to prepared sheet. Repeat with remaining plantains in 2 batches. Discard excess oil, leaving any browned bits in skillet. Sprinkle ½ teaspoon salt over plantains.

**4.** Add beef to now-empty skillet and cook over medium-high heat, breaking up meat with wooden spoon, until beef is no longer pink and begins to brown. Sprinkle sazón over meat and cook until aromatic, about 1 minute. Drizzle vinegar over meat and stir to combine. Transfer meat to bowl.

**5.** Transfer cilantro mixture to now-empty skillet. Cook over medium-high heat, stirring frequently, until onion softens, 3 to 4 minutes. Add tomato sauce and continue to cook until mixture thickens and fond begins to form on edges and bottom of skillet, 2 to 4 minutes longer. Stir in beef and alcaparrado and continue to cook until sauce is thickened and coats meat, 2 to 3 minutes longer. Off heat, season with salt and pepper to taste.

**6.** Arrange half of plantain pieces in lightly greased 13 by 9-inch baking dish (plantains will not cover bottom of dish completely). Whisk eggs with remaining pinch salt and pour evenly over plantains. Spread beef over plantains. Arrange remaining plantains in single layer over beef. Sprinkle evenly with Monterey Jack. Bake until cheese is melted and beginning to brown, 20 to 25 minutes. Transfer to wire rack; let cool for 5 minutes before serving.

## Keema Aloo (Garam Masala–Spiced Ground Beef with Potatoes)

**SERVES 4 to 6**

**WHY THIS RECIPE WORKS** Keema is a rich and savory spiced ground meat dish that's been a staple of South Asian cuisine for centuries. Whether it's made with ground goat, lamb, beef, or poultry, the meat is broken into small bits and coated with a complexly spiced, velvety sauce. Our version features a garam masala, a warming spice mix, comprising whole cinnamon and black and green cardamom as well as ground coriander, cumin, turmeric, and Kashmiri chile powder. We bloomed the whole spices early to coax out their oil-soluble compounds. Then we carefully browned red onion to deepen its flavor before spiking the mixture with garlic and ginger pastes. Next we added 90 percent lean ground beef, and when it sizzled and browned, we stirred in the ground spices in the masala. As soon as these were fragrant, in went ripe tomatoes, pieces of potato, and whole-milk yogurt. The tomatoes broke down as the keema cooked, and the yogurt added subtle richness. Together they created a clingy sauce that flavored every bite of beef and potato. Have your ingredients in place before you begin to cook. Look for black and green cardamom pods, Kashmiri chile powder, and 4- to 5-inch long green chiles at Indian or Pakistani markets. If you can't find Kashmiri chile powder, toast and grind one large guajillo chile and use 2 teaspoons; if a long green chile is unavailable, substitute a serrano. For a milder keema, omit the fresh chile or use only half of it. A rasp-style grater makes it easy to turn garlic and ginger into pastes. Serve with roti, naan, or basmati rice.

- 2 tablespoons vegetable oil
- 6 black peppercorns
- 4 green cardamom pods
- 2 black cardamom pods
- 1 cinnamon stick
- 1 red onion, halved and sliced thin crosswise
- 1 teaspoon grated garlic
- 1 teaspoon grated fresh ginger
- 1 pound 90 percent lean ground beef
- ¾ teaspoon table salt
- 2 teaspoons ground coriander
- 2 teaspoons Kashmiri chile powder
- ½ teaspoon ground turmeric
- ½ teaspoon ground cumin
- 2 (6-ounce) vine-ripened tomatoes, cored and chopped
- 1 (8-ounce) Yukon Gold potato, peeled and cut into ½-inch pieces
- ¼ cup whole-milk yogurt
- 2 tablespoons water
- 1 long green chile, halved lengthwise (optional)
- ¼ cup chopped fresh cilantro, plus extra for garnish

**1.** Heat oil in medium saucepan over medium heat until shimmering. Add peppercorns, green and black cardamom pods, and cinnamon stick and cook, stirring occasionally, until fragrant, about 30 seconds. Add onion and cook, stirring occasionally, until onion is browned, 7 to 10 minutes.

**2.** Add garlic and ginger and cook, stirring constantly, until fragrant, about 30 seconds. Add beef and salt. Increase heat to medium-high and cook, stirring to break up meat into very small pieces and scraping up any browned bits. Continue to cook, stirring occasionally, until mixture sizzles and bottom of saucepan appears dry, 7 to 12 minutes longer.

**3.** Add coriander, chile powder, turmeric, and cumin and cook, stirring constantly, until spices are well distributed and fragrant, about 1 minute. Add tomatoes; potato; yogurt; water; and chile, if using, and cook, stirring frequently, until tomatoes release their juice and mixture begins to simmer, about 2 minutes. Adjust heat to maintain gentle simmer. Cover and cook, stirring occasionally, until tomatoes have broken down, potatoes are tender, and wooden spoon scraped across bottom of saucepan leaves clear trail, 12 to 18 minutes. Stir in cilantro and season with salt and pepper to taste. If desired, remove cinnamon stick and cardamom pods. Transfer to serving bowl, garnish with extra cilantro, and serve.

## Moussaka

**SERVES 8**

**WHY THIS RECIPE WORKS** This iconic casserole has it all: plush vegetables, spiced meat sauce, and a top coat of satiny béchamel. We microwaved the potatoes to help rid them of their raw edge without rendering them greasy or waterlogged, and they retained enough structural integrity to be shingled in the greased baking dish. We skipped the unnecessary fuss of peeling and salting the eggplant and simply cut it into cubes, which we roasted. The eggplant pieces collapsed without turning mushy or stringy and then fit compactly into the baking dish. To make a rich-tasting meat sauce, we started with 80 percent lean ground beef and cooked off most of the wine and tomato juice; this ensured that the mixture was tight and concentrated. A low ratio of milk to roux, plus egg yolks and plenty of kasseri cheese, made for a custardy béchamel that baked up thick, lush, and beautifully souffléed. Kasseri is a semifirm Greek sheep's-milk cheese. If it's unavailable, substitute 3 ounces (¾ cup) of shredded provolone and 1½ ounces (¾ cup) of grated Pecorino Romano. We like the richness of whole milk for this dish, but you can substitute 2 percent lowfat; do not use skim. Use a mandoline to quickly slice the potatoes, and use a baking dish that is at least 2¼ inches tall.

**VEGETABLES**

- 3½ pounds eggplant, cut into ¾-inch cubes
- ½ cup plus 2 teaspoons plus 3 tablespoons extra-virgin olive oil, divided
- 2 teaspoons table salt, divided
- ¾ teaspoon pepper, divided
- 1½ pounds Yukon Gold potatoes, unpeeled, sliced crosswise ¼ inch thick

**MEAT SAUCE**

- 1 tablespoon extra-virgin olive oil
- 1 onion, chopped fine
- ½ teaspoon table salt
- 4 garlic cloves, minced
- 1 tablespoon tomato paste
- ½ cup dry red wine
- 2 teaspoons paprika
- 2 teaspoons dried oregano
- ½ teaspoon red pepper flakes
- ¼ teaspoon ground cinnamon
- 1 pound 80 percent lean ground beef
- 1 (14.5-ounce) can crushed tomatoes
- 2 teaspoons red wine vinegar

**BÉCHAMEL**

- 6 tablespoons unsalted butter
- ½ cup all-purpose flour
- 2½ cups whole milk
- 4 ounces kasseri cheese, shredded (1 cup)
- ¼ teaspoon table salt
- ⅛ teaspoon ground nutmeg
- 3 large egg yolks, lightly beaten

**1. FOR THE VEGETABLES:** Adjust oven racks to middle and lower-middle positions and heat oven to 450 degrees. Line 2 rimmed baking sheets with aluminum foil and spray with vegetable oil spray. Divide eggplant evenly between prepared sheets. Toss each batch with ¼ cup oil, ½ teaspoon salt, and ¼ teaspoon pepper until evenly coated, and spread eggplant into single layer. Roast until eggplant is softened and lightly browned, about 30 minutes, switching and rotating sheets halfway through roasting. Transfer sheets to wire racks to cool. Reduce oven temperature to 400 degrees.

**2.** While eggplant roasts, grease 13 by 9-inch baking dish with 2 teaspoons oil. In medium bowl, toss potatoes with remaining 3 tablespoons oil, 1 teaspoon salt, and ¼ teaspoon pepper. Cover and microwave until potatoes can be easily pierced with tip of paring knife, 8 to 10 minutes, stirring halfway through microwaving. Transfer potatoes, along with any accumulated liquid, to prepared dish and let rest until cool enough to handle, about 15 minutes. Shingle evenly in dish.

**3. FOR THE MEAT SAUCE:** Heat oil in Dutch oven over medium heat until shimmering. Add onion and salt and cook, stirring occasionally, until just starting to brown, 6 to 8 minutes. Add garlic and stir constantly until fragrant, about 1 minute. Add tomato paste and cook, stirring frequently, until paste darkens, about 2 minutes. Stir in wine, scraping up any browned bits from bottom of pot. Add paprika, oregano, pepper flakes, and cinnamon and cook, stirring frequently, until wine is almost completely evaporated, 2 to 3 minutes. Add beef; increase heat to medium-high; and cook, breaking up meat with wooden spoon, until no pink remains, 4 to 5 minutes. Add tomatoes and cook, stirring occasionally, until liquid has almost completely evaporated and spoon leaves trail when dragged through sauce, 6 to 8 minutes. Stir in vinegar, cover, and remove from heat.

**4. FOR THE BÉCHAMEL:** Melt butter in medium saucepan over medium heat. Whisk in flour and cook until golden, about 1 minute. Slowly whisk in milk and cook, whisking constantly, until mixture is thick, smooth, and comes to boil, about 5 minutes. Off heat, whisk in kasseri, salt, and nutmeg. Cover and let stand for 5 minutes. Whisk in egg yolks and cover to keep warm.

**5.** Cover potatoes with eggplant, lightly pressing into even layer. Spread meat sauce in even layer over eggplant. Top with béchamel. Place dish on rimmed baking sheet and bake on middle rack until top of moussaka is deeply browned in spots and is bubbling at edges, about 30 minutes. Let cool for 30 minutes before serving.

# Mapo Tofu (Sichuan Braised Tofu with Beef)

**SERVES** 4 to 6

**WHY THIS RECIPE WORKS** This braise of custardy tofu cloaked in a garlicky, spicy meat sauce is a signature dish of the Sichuan province. And although the flavors of mapo tofu may be complex, the preparation is fast and easy. We used cubed soft tofu, poached gently in chicken broth to help the cubes stay intact in the braise. For the sauce base, we used plenty of ginger and garlic, along with four Sichuan pantry powerhouses: doubanjiang (broad bean chili paste), fermented black beans, Sichuan chili powder, and Sichuan peppercorns. In place of the chili oil often called for, we used a generous amount of vegetable oil, extra Sichuan chili powder, and toasted sesame oil. Broad bean chili paste (or sauce) is also known as doubanjiang or toban djan; our favorite, Pixian, is available online. Supermarket Lee Kum Kee Chili Bean Sauce is also a good option. If you can't find Sichuan chili powder, an equal amount of gochugaru (Korean red pepper flakes) is a good substitute. In a pinch, use 2½ teaspoons of ancho chile powder and ½ teaspoon of cayenne pepper. If you can't find fermented black beans, you can use an equal amount of fermented black bean paste or sauce or two additional teaspoons of broad bean chili paste. Serve with rice.

- 1 tablespoon Sichuan peppercorns
- 12 scallions
- 28 ounces soft tofu, cut into ½-inch cubes
- 2 cups chicken broth
- 9 garlic cloves, peeled
- 1 (3-inch) piece ginger, peeled and cut into ¼-inch rounds
- ⅓ cup doubanjiang (broad bean chili paste)
- 1 tablespoon fermented black beans
- 6 tablespoons vegetable oil, divided
- 1 tablespoon Sichuan chili powder
- 8 ounces 85 percent lean ground beef
- 2 tablespoons hoisin sauce
- 2 teaspoons toasted sesame oil
- 2 tablespoons water
- 1 tablespoon cornstarch

**1.** Place peppercorns in small bowl and microwave until fragrant, 15 to 30 seconds. Let cool completely. Once cool, grind in spice grinder or mortar and pestle (you should have 1½ teaspoons).

**2.** Using side of chef's knife, lightly crush white parts of scallions, then cut scallions into 1-inch pieces. Place tofu, broth, and scallions in large bowl and microwave, covered, until steaming, 5 to 7 minutes. Let stand while preparing remaining ingredients.

**3.** Process garlic, ginger, chili paste, and black beans in food processor until coarse paste forms, 1 to 2 minutes, scraping down sides of bowl as needed. Add ¼ cup vegetable oil, chili powder, and 1 teaspoon peppercorns and continue to process until smooth paste forms, 1 to 2 minutes longer. Transfer spice paste to bowl.

**4.** Heat 1 tablespoon vegetable oil and beef in large saucepan over medium heat; cook, breaking up meat with wooden spoon, until meat just begins to brown, 5 to 7 minutes. Transfer beef to bowl.

**5.** Add remaining 1 tablespoon vegetable oil and spice paste to now-empty saucepan and cook, stirring frequently, until paste darkens and oil begins to separate from paste, 2 to 3 minutes. Gently pour tofu with broth into saucepan, followed by hoisin, sesame oil, and beef. Cook, stirring gently and frequently, until dish comes to simmer, 2 to 3 minutes. Whisk water and cornstarch together in small bowl. Add cornstarch mixture to saucepan and continue to cook, stirring frequently, until thickened, 2 to 3 minutes longer. Transfer to serving dish, sprinkle with remaining peppercorns, and serve. (Mapo tofu can be stored in an airtight container and refrigerated for up to 24 hours.)

## Shepherd's Pie

**SERVES** 4 to 6

**WHY THIS RECIPE WORKS** Shepherd's pie, a hearty mix of meat, gravy, and mashed potatoes, can take the better part of a day to prepare. And while the dish is indeed satisfying, traditional versions can be very rich. We wanted to scale back its preparation and lighten the dish too. Per other modern recipes, we chose ground beef as our filling over ground lamb. To prevent the beef from turning dry and crumbly, we tossed it with a little baking soda (diluted in water) before browning it. This raised the pH level of the beef, resulting in more tender meat. An onion and mushroom gravy, spiked with Worcestershire sauce, complemented the filling. For the mashed potatoes, we cut way back on the dairy in favor of fresh scallions, which made for a lighter, more flavorful topping that was a good match for the meat filling. This recipe was developed with 93 percent lean ground beef. Using ground beef with a higher percentage of fat will make the dish too greasy.

- 1½ pounds 93 percent lean ground beef
- 2 tablespoons plus 2 teaspoons water, divided
- 1½ teaspoons table salt, divided, plus salt for cooking potatoes
- ½ teaspoon pepper, divided
- ½ teaspoon baking soda
- 2½ pounds russet potatoes, peeled and cut into 1-inch chunks
- 4 tablespoons unsalted butter, melted
- ½ cup milk
- 1 large egg yolk
- 8 scallions, green parts only, sliced thin
- 2 teaspoons vegetable oil
- 1 onion, chopped
- 4 ounces white mushrooms, trimmed and chopped
- 1 tablespoon tomato paste
- 2 garlic cloves, minced
- 2 tablespoons Madeira or ruby port
- 2 tablespoons all-purpose flour
- 1¼ cups beef broth
- 2 teaspoons Worcestershire sauce
- 2 sprigs fresh thyme
- 1 bay leaf
- 2 carrots, peeled and chopped
- 2 teaspoons cornstarch

**1.** Toss beef with 2 tablespoons water, 1 teaspoon salt, ¼ teaspoon pepper, and baking soda in bowl until thoroughly combined. Let sit for 20 minutes.

**2.** Meanwhile, place potatoes in medium saucepan; add water to just cover and 1 tablespoon salt. Bring to boil over high heat. Reduce heat to medium-low and simmer until potatoes are soft and tip of paring knife inserted into potato meets no resistance, 8 to 10 minutes. Drain potatoes and return to saucepan. Return saucepan to low heat and cook, shaking pot occasionally, until any surface moisture on potatoes has evaporated, about 1 minute. Remove pan from heat and mash potatoes well with potato masher. Stir in melted butter. Whisk together milk and egg yolk in small bowl, then stir into potatoes. Stir in scallions and season with salt and pepper to taste. Cover and set aside.

**3.** Heat oil in broiler-safe 10-inch skillet over medium heat until shimmering. Add onion, mushrooms, remaining ½ teaspoon salt, and remaining ¼ teaspoon pepper; cook, stirring occasionally, until vegetables are just starting to soften and dark bits form on bottom of skillet, 4 to 6 minutes. Stir in tomato paste and garlic; cook until bottom of skillet is dark brown, about 2 minutes. Add Madeira and cook, scraping up any browned bits, until evaporated, about 1 minute. Stir in flour and cook for 1 minute. Add broth, Worcestershire, thyme sprigs, bay leaf, and carrots; bring to boil, scraping up any browned bits. Reduce heat to medium-low, add beef in 2-inch pieces to broth, and bring to gentle simmer. Cover and cook until beef is cooked through, 10 to 12 minutes, stirring and breaking up meat chunks with 2 forks halfway through cooking. Stir cornstarch and remaining 2 teaspoons water together in bowl. Stir cornstarch mixture into filling and continue to simmer for 30 seconds. Discard thyme sprigs and bay leaf. Season with salt and pepper to taste.

**4.** Adjust oven rack 5 inches from broiler element and heat broiler. Place mashed potatoes in large zipper-lock bag and snip off 1 corner to create 1-inch opening. Pipe potatoes in even layer over filling, making sure to cover entire surface. Smooth potatoes with back of spoon, then use tines of fork to make ridges over surface. Place skillet on rimmed baking sheet and broil until potatoes are golden brown and crusty and filling is bubbly, 10 to 15 minutes. Let cool for 10 minutes before serving.

## Skillet Tamale Pie

**SERVES 4**

---

**WHY THIS RECIPE WORKS** Tamale pie—lightly seasoned, tomatoey ground beef with cornbread topping—is easy to prepare and makes a satisfying supper. But in many recipes, the filling either tastes bland and one-dimensional or turns heavy. As for the cornbread topping, it's usually from a mix and tastes like it. We wanted a skillet tamale pie with a rich, well-seasoned filling and a cornbread topping with real corn flavor. For the beef, we found 90 percent lean ground sirloin gave us a good balance of richness and flavor. We started by sautéing minced onion and garlic. For seasoning, we used a generous amount of chili powder, which we added to the aromatics in the skillet to "bloom," or intensify, its flavor. The addition of canned black beans made our pie heartier, and canned diced tomatoes contributed additional flavor and texture. Cheddar cheese stirred into the mixture enriched the filling and also helped thicken it, and some minced fresh cilantro contributed a bright, fresh note. And to finish our pie, we skipped the cornbread mix and instead devised an easy homemade version. We spread the cornbread batter over the filling in the skillet, put the skillet in the oven to bake through, and the result was crunchy, corny topping that perfectly complemented the spicy tamale filling. Parsley can be substituted for the cilantro, if desired.

**TAMALE FILLING**

- 2 tablespoons vegetable oil
- 1 medium onion, minced
- 2 tablespoons chili powder
- Table salt
- 2 medium garlic cloves, minced or pressed through a garlic press (about 2 teaspoons)
- 1 pound 90 percent lean ground sirloin
- 1 (15-ounce) can black beans, drained and rinsed
- 1 (14.5-ounce) can diced tomatoes, drained
- 4 ounces cheddar cheese, shredded (about 1 cup)
- 2 tablespoons minced fresh cilantro leaves
- Ground black pepper

**CORNBREAD TOPPING**

- ¾ cup (3¾ ounces) unbleached all-purpose flour
- ¾ cup (3¾ ounces) yellow cornmeal
- 3 tablespoons sugar
- ¾ teaspoon table salt
- ¾ teaspoon baking powder
- ¼ teaspoon baking soda
- ¾ cup buttermilk
- 1 large egg
- 3 tablespoons unsalted butter, melted and cooled

**1.** Adjust an oven rack to the middle position and heat the oven to 450 degrees.

**2. FOR THE TAMALE FILLING:** Heat the oil in a 12-inch ovensafe skillet over medium heat until shimmering. Add the onion, chili powder, and ½ teaspoon salt and cook until the onion is softened, about 5 minutes. Stir in the garlic and cook until fragrant, about 30 seconds.

**3.** Stir in the ground sirloin, beans, and tomatoes and bring to a simmer, breaking up the meat with a wooden spoon, about 5 minutes. Stir the cheddar and cilantro into the filling and season with salt and pepper to taste.

**4. FOR THE CORNBREAD TOPPING:** Whisk the flour, cornmeal, sugar, salt, baking powder, and baking soda together in a large bowl. In a separate bowl, whisk the buttermilk and egg together. Stir the buttermilk mixture into the flour mixture until uniform. Stir in the butter until just combined.

**5.** Dollop the cornbread batter evenly over the filling and spread into an even layer. Bake until the cornbread is cooked through in the center, 10 to 15 minutes. Using potholders (the skillet handle will be hot), remove the skillet from the oven. Serve.

## Glazed All-Beef Meatloaf

**SERVES 6 to 8**

---

**WHY THIS RECIPE WORKS** Every all-beef meatloaf we've tasted has had the same problems—chewy texture and uninteresting flavor, making it more of a hamburger in the shape of a log than bona fide meatloaf. In the past, when we wanted a great meatloaf, we turned to a traditional meatloaf mix consisting of beef, pork, and veal. Could we create an all-beef meatloaf to compete with this classic? Supermarkets offer a wide selection of "ground beef," and after testing them alone and in combination we determined that equal parts of chuck (for moisture) and sirloin (for beefy flavor) were best. Beef has a livery taste that we wanted to subdue, and the usual dairy additions to meatloaf didn't work. Chicken broth, oddly enough, neutralized this off-flavor and provided moisture. For additional moisture and richness, we included mild-tasting Monterey Jack cheese, which also helped bind the mixture. To avoid pockets of oozing hot cheese in the meatloaf, we shredded the cheese and froze it briefly. Crushed saltines, our choice for the starchy filler, provided texture, but we felt our meatloaf needed more "sliceability." Surprisingly, gelatin gave us just the smooth, luxurious texture we sought. We seasoned the mixture with onions, celery, garlic (all sautéed), thyme, paprika, soy sauce, and mustard. A traditional ketchup glaze crowned our flavorful all-beef meatloaf. If you can't find ground chuck and/or sirloin, substitute 85 percent lean ground beef.

MEATLOAF

- 3 ounces Monterey Jack cheese, shredded on small holes of box grater (¾ cup)
- 1 tablespoon unsalted butter
- 1 onion, chopped fine
- 1 celery rib, minced
- 2 teaspoons minced fresh thyme
- 1 teaspoon paprika
- 1 garlic clove, minced
- ¼ cup tomato juice
- ½ cup chicken broth
- 2 large eggs
- ½ teaspoon unflavored gelatin
- ⅔ cup crushed saltines
- 2 tablespoons minced fresh parsley
- 1 tablespoon soy sauce
- 1 teaspoon Dijon mustard
- ¾ teaspoon table salt
- ½ teaspoon pepper
- 1 pound 90 percent lean ground sirloin
- 1 pound 80 percent lean ground chuck

GLAZE

- ½ cup ketchup
- ¼ cup cider vinegar
- 3 tablespoons packed light brown sugar
- 1 teaspoon hot sauce
- ½ teaspoon ground coriander

**1. FOR THE MEATLOAF:** Adjust oven rack to middle position and heat oven to 375 degrees. Spread cheese on plate and place in freezer until ready to use. Set wire rack in rimmed baking sheet. Fold sheet of heavy-duty aluminum foil to form 10 by 6-inch rectangle. Center foil on rack and poke holes in foil with skewer (about half an inch apart). Spray foil with vegetable oil spray.

**2.** Melt butter in 10-inch skillet over medium-high heat; add onion and celery and cook, stirring occasionally, until beginning to brown, 6 to 8 minutes. Add thyme, paprika, and garlic and cook, stirring, until fragrant, about 1 minute. Reduce heat to low and add tomato juice. Cook, stirring to scrape up any browned bits, until thickened, about 1 minute. Transfer mixture to small bowl and set aside to cool.

**3.** Whisk broth and eggs together in large bowl until combined. Sprinkle gelatin over liquid and let stand for 5 minutes. Stir in saltines, parsley, soy sauce, mustard, salt, pepper, and onion mixture. Crumble frozen cheese into coarse powder and sprinkle over mixture. Add sirloin and chuck; mix gently with your hands until thoroughly combined, about 1 minute. Transfer meat to foil rectangle and shape into 10 by 6-inch oval about 2 inches high. Smooth top and edges of meatloaf with moistened spatula. Bake until center of loaf registers 135 to 140 degrees, 55 minutes to 1 hour 5 minutes. Remove meatloaf from oven and heat broiler.

**4. FOR THE GLAZE:** While meatloaf cooks, combine glaze ingredients in small saucepan; bring to simmer over medium heat and cook, stirring, until thick and syrupy, about 5 minutes. Spread half of glaze evenly over cooked meatloaf with rubber spatula; place under broiler and cook until glaze bubbles and begins to brown at edges, about 5 minutes. Remove meatloaf from oven and spread evenly with remaining glaze; place back under broiler and cook until glaze is again bubbling and beginning to brown, about 5 minutes more. Let meatloaf cool for about 20 minutes before slicing.

### MAKING A FREE-FORM LOAF PAN

**1.** Set wire rack in rimmed baking sheet and top with 10 by 6-inch rectangle of aluminum foil.

**2.** Using skewer, poke holes in foil, spacing them about half an inch apart.

## Bacon-Wrapped Meatloaf with Brown Sugar–Ketchup Glaze

SERVES 6 to 8

**WHY THIS RECIPE WORKS** Not all meatloaves resemble Mom's. Some recipes go the canned soup route and, frankly, taste like it. Others become gussied up with ingredients that have no place in this humble family dish—canned pineapple, sun-dried tomatoes, and the like. Our goal was not to develop the ultimate meatloaf but to bring it back to its classic roots—a tender, well-seasoned loaf smothered with tangy sweet glaze. Meatloaf mix—a mixture of ground beef chuck, ground pork, and ground veal—produced the best balance of flavors and textures. A starch turned out to be a necessity for binding the meat and giving it that classic meatloaf texture; cracker crumbs, quick-cooking oatmeal, and fresh bread crumbs all worked well. To prevent the filler from drying out the meatloaf, we added some moisture. After trying a host of options, we determined that whole milk and plain yogurt are equally acceptable. Finally, we realized that the pan in which the meatloaf baked made a big difference. A standard loaf pan traps the fat and stews the meat, and the juice bubbles up and destroys the glaze. Baking the meatloaf free-form in a shallow baking pan gave the loaf a good crust, preserved our sweet-tart glaze, and helped the bacon topping crisp nicely. Lining the baking pan with foil makes for easier cleanup.

**BROWN SUGAR-KETCHUP GLAZE**

- ½ cup ketchup or chili sauce
- ¼ cup brown sugar
- 4 teaspoons cider vinegar or white vinegar

**MEATLOAF**

- 2 teaspoons vegetable oil
- 1 medium onion, chopped
- 2 medium garlic cloves, minced or pressed through a garlic press (about 2 teaspoons)
- 2 large eggs
- ½ cup whole milk or plain yogurt, plus more as needed
- 2 teaspoons Dijon mustard
- 2 teaspoons Worcestershire sauce
- 1 teaspoon table salt
- ½ teaspoon ground black pepper
- ½ teaspoon dried thyme
- ¼ teaspoon hot sauce
- 2 pounds meatloaf mix (50 percent ground chuck, 25 percent ground pork, 25 percent ground veal)
- ⅔ cup crushed saltines (about 16) or quick oatmeal or 1⅓ cups fresh bread crumbs
- ⅓ cup minced fresh parsley leaves
- 6–8 ounces bacon (8 to 12 slices, depending on loaf shape)

**1. FOR THE GLAZE:** Mix all the ingredients together in a small saucepan; set aside.

**2. FOR THE MEATLOAF:** Line a 13 by 9-inch baking pan with foil; set aside. Heat the oven to 350 degrees. Heat the oil in a medium skillet over medium heat until shimmering. Add the onion and garlic; sauté until softened, about 5 minutes. Set aside to cool while preparing the remaining ingredients.

**3.** Mix the eggs with the milk, mustard, Worcestershire sauce, salt, pepper, thyme, and hot sauce. Combine the egg mixture with the meat in a large bowl and add the crackers, parsley, and cooked onion and garlic; mix with a fork until evenly blended and the meat mixture does not stick to the bowl. (If necessary, add more milk, a couple of tablespoons at a time, until the mixture no longer sticks.)

**4.** Turn the meat mixture onto a work surface. With wet hands, pat the mixture into an approximately 9 by 5-inch loaf shape. Place on the prepared baking pan. Brush with half the glaze, then arrange the bacon slices, crosswise, over the loaf, overlapping them slightly and tucking only the bacon tip ends under the loaf.

**5.** Bake the loaf until the bacon is crisp and the center of the loaf registers 160 degrees on an instant-read thermometer, about 1 hour. Cool for at least 20 minutes. Simmer the remaining glaze over medium heat until thickened slightly. Slice the meatloaf and serve with the extra glaze passed separately.

## Classic Stuffed Bell Peppers

**SERVES 4**

**WHY THIS RECIPE WORKS** A vegetable can be more than just a side dish, and stuffed peppers are a perfect case in point. But slimy or too-crunchy peppers and tasteless fillings can ruin the show. We wanted to revamp this dish to be a flavorful option for a weeknight dinner. Cooking the peppers correctly is critical; they need to be sturdy enough to hold the filling but not crunchy and bitter. We found that blanching them before adding the filling gave us peppers that held their shape, had good color, and tasted sweeter. Rice is the classic stuffing for peppers, but alone it didn't have much flavor; a mixture of rice and ground beef did the trick. We cooked the rice in the water we'd used to blanch the peppers and for additional flavor, we included sautéed onion and garlic, tomatoes, cheddar cheese, and ketchup. When shopping for bell peppers to stuff, it's best to choose those with broad bases that will allow the peppers to stand up on their own. It's easier to fill the peppers after they have been placed in the baking dish because the sides of the dish will hold the peppers steady.

- Table salt
- 4 medium red, yellow, or orange bell peppers (about 6 ounces each), ½ inch trimmed off tops, cores and seeds discarded
- ½ cup long-grain white rice
- 1½ tablespoons olive oil
- 1 medium onion, minced
- 12 ounces ground beef, preferably 80 percent lean ground chuck
- 3 medium garlic cloves, minced or pressed through a garlic press (about 1 tablespoon)
- 1 (14.5-ounce) can diced tomatoes, drained, ¼ cup juice reserved
- 5 ounces Monterey Jack cheese, shredded (about 1¼ cups)
- 2 tablespoons chopped fresh parsley leaves
- Ground black pepper
- ¼ cup ketchup

**1.** Bring 4 quarts water to a boil in a large stockpot or Dutch oven over high heat. Add 1 tablespoon salt and the bell peppers. Cook until the peppers just begin to soften, about 3 minutes. Using a slotted spoon, remove the peppers from the pot, drain off the excess water, and place the peppers, cut side up, on paper towels. Return the water to a boil; add the rice and boil until tender, about 13 minutes. Drain the rice and transfer it to a large bowl; set aside.

**2.** Adjust an oven rack to the middle position and heat the oven to 350 degrees.

**3.** Meanwhile, heat the oil in a heavy-bottomed 12-inch skillet over medium-high heat until shimmering. Add the onion and cook, stirring occasionally, until softened and beginning to brown, about 5 minutes. Add the ground beef and cook, breaking the beef into small pieces with a spoon, until no longer pink, about 4 minutes. Stir in the garlic and cook until fragrant, about 30 seconds. Transfer the mixture to the bowl with the rice; stir in the tomatoes, 1 cup of the cheese, the parsley, and salt and pepper to taste.

**4.** Stir together the ketchup and the reserved tomato juice in a small bowl.

**5.** Place the peppers, cut side up, in a 9-inch square baking dish. Using a soup spoon, divide the filling evenly among the peppers. Spoon 2 tablespoons of the ketchup mixture over each filled pepper and sprinkle each with 1 tablespoon of the remaining 1/4 cup cheese. Bake until the cheese is browned and the filling is heated through, 25 to 30 minutes. Serve immediately.

## Cincinnati Chili

**SERVES** 6 to 8

---

**WHY THIS RECIPE WORKS** This Midwestern diner specialty is a unique marriage of American chili and Middle Eastern spices. For an easy weeknight meal, we wanted to pare the list of ingredients down to the essentials without compromising the distinctive character of the dish. The beef in Cincinnati chili isn't sautéed like the beef in other chilis, so there is no way to remove the fat. To avoid greasiness, we blanched ground chuck for half a minute, which got rid of most of the fat but still left plenty of flavor. The spices in this chili vary from recipe to recipe. We settled on chili powder, oregano, cinnamon, and cocoa powder, which we bloomed in hot oil for more depth of flavor. Water and tomato sauce are the traditional base for the sauce; we added chicken broth for balance. Vinegar and brown sugar livened things up. After a long simmer, the chili was ready to be served. We couldn't think of a better way to do it than with a "five-way"—over spaghetti, topped with cheddar cheese, chopped onions, and kidney beans. Use canned tomato sauce for this recipe—do not use jarred spaghetti sauce.

**CHILI**

- 2 teaspoons table salt, plus more to taste
- 1½ pounds 80 percent lean ground chuck
- 2 tablespoons vegetable oil
- 2 medium onions, minced
- 2 medium garlic cloves, minced or pressed through a garlic press (about 2 teaspoons)
- 2 tablespoons chili powder
- 2 teaspoons dried oregano
- 2 teaspoons cocoa powder
- 1½ teaspoons ground cinnamon
- ½ teaspoon cayenne pepper
- ½ teaspoon ground allspice
- ¼ teaspoon ground black pepper
- 2 cups tomato sauce
- 2 cups low-sodium chicken broth
- 2 cups water
- 2 tablespoons cider vinegar
- 2 teaspoons dark brown sugar
- Hot sauce

**ACCOMPANIMENTS**

- 1 pound spaghetti, cooked, drained, and tossed with 2 tablespoons unsalted butter
- 12 ounces sharp cheddar cheese, shredded (about 3 cups)
- 1 (15-ounce) can red kidney beans, drained, rinsed, and warmed
- 1 medium onion, chopped

**1. FOR THE CHILI:** Bring 2 quarts water and 1 teaspoon of the salt to a boil in a large saucepan. Add the ground chuck, stirring vigorously to separate the meat into individual strands. As soon as the foam from the meat rises to the top (this takes about 30 seconds) and before the water returns to a boil, drain the meat into a strainer and set it aside.

**2.** Rinse and dry the empty saucepan. Set the pan over medium heat and add the oil. When the oil is warm, add the onions and cook, stirring frequently, until the onions are soft and browned around the edges, about 8 minutes. Add the garlic and cook until fragrant, about 1 minute. Stir in the chili powder, oregano, cocoa, cinnamon, cayenne, allspice, black pepper, and the remaining 1 teaspoon salt. Cook, stirring constantly, until the spices are fragrant, about 30 seconds. Stir in the tomato sauce, broth, water, vinegar, and sugar, scraping the pan bottom to remove any browned bits.

**3.** Add the blanched ground beef and increase the heat to high. As soon as the liquid boils, reduce the heat to medium-low and simmer, stirring occasionally, until the chili is deep red and has thickened slightly, about 1 hour. Season with salt and hot sauce to taste. (The chili can be refrigerated in an airtight container for up to 3 days. Bring to a simmer over medium-low heat before serving.)

**4. TO SERVE:** Divide the buttered spaghetti among individual bowls. Spoon the chili over the spaghetti and top with the cheese, beans, and onion. Serve immediately.

# Beef Empanadas

**SERVES** 4 to 6

**WHY THIS RECIPE WORKS** In many Latin American countries, crisp pastry pockets stuffed with spiced beef make a savory, light lunch. We wanted an empanada hearty enough for dinner, with a moist, savory filling encased in a tender crust. We initially enhanced ground chuck with a milk-and-bread mixture known as a panade; as the meat and panade cooked, the starches in the bread absorbed moisture from the milk and formed a gel around the protein molecules, which lubricated the meat. But to intensify the meaty flavor, we replaced the milk with chicken broth and then added a hefty dose of aromatics. Inspired by Chilean empanadas de pino, we added hard-cooked eggs, raisins, and green olives. For the crust, we made a few changes to our Foolproof Dough for Double-Crust Pie (page 945), a recipe that combines butter (for flavor) and shortening (for tenderness) with water and vodka for a dough that's both workable and tender. We traded some of the flour for masa harina, the dehydrated cornmeal used to make Mexican tortillas and tamales, which provided nutty richness and rough-hewn texture. The alcohol in the dough is essential to the texture of the crust and imparts no flavor—do not omit it or substitute water. Masa harina can be found in the international aisle of the supermarket with other Latin foods or in the baking aisle with the flour. If you cannot find masa harina, replace it with additional all-purpose flour (for a total of 4 cups).

**FILLING**

- 1 slice high-quality white sandwich bread, torn into quarters
- 2 tablespoons plus ½ cup low-sodium chicken broth
- 1 pound 85 percent lean ground beef
- Table salt and ground black pepper
- 1 tablespoon olive oil
- 2 medium onions, minced
- 4 medium garlic cloves, minced or pressed through a garlic press (about 4 teaspoons)
- 1 teaspoon ground cumin
- ¼ teaspoon cayenne pepper
- ⅛ teaspoon ground cloves
- ½ cup fresh cilantro leaves, chopped coarse
- 2 hard-cooked eggs, chopped coarse (page 147)
- ⅓ cup raisins, chopped coarse
- ¼ cup pitted green olives, chopped coarse
- 4 teaspoons cider vinegar

**DOUGH**

- 3 cups (15 ounces) unbleached all-purpose flour
- 1 cup (5 ounces) masa harina
- 1 tablespoon sugar
- 2 teaspoons table salt
- 12 tablespoons (1½ sticks) unsalted butter, cut into ½-inch pieces and chilled
- ½ cup cold vodka or tequila
- ½ cup cold water
- 5 tablespoons olive oil

## ASSEMBLING EMPANADAS

**1.** Divide the dough in half, then divide each half into six equal pieces.

**2.** Roll each piece of dough into a 6-inch round about ⅛ inch thick.

**3.** Place about ⅓ cup of the filling on each round, then brush the edges with water.

**4.** Fold the dough over the filling, then crimp the edges using a fork to seal.

**1. FOR THE FILLING:** Process the bread and 2 tablespoons of the chicken broth in a food processor until a paste forms, about 5 seconds, scraping down the sides of the bowl as necessary. Add the beef, ¾ teaspoon salt, and ½ teaspoon pepper and pulse until the mixture is well combined, 6 to 8 pulses.

**2.** Heat the oil in a 12-inch nonstick skillet over medium-high heat until shimmering. Add the onions and cook, stirring frequently, until beginning to brown, about 5 minutes. Stir in the garlic, cumin, cayenne, and cloves and cook until fragrant, about 1 minute. Add the beef mixture and cook, breaking the meat into 1-inch pieces with a wooden spoon, until browned, about 7 minutes. Add the remaining ½ cup chicken broth and simmer until the mixture is moist but not wet, 3 to 5 minutes. Transfer the mixture to a bowl and cool for 10 minutes. Stir in the cilantro, eggs, raisins, olives, and vinegar. Season with salt and pepper to taste and refrigerate until cool, about 1 hour.

**3. FOR THE DOUGH:** Pulse 1 cup of the flour, the masa harina, sugar, and salt in a food processor until combined, about 2 pulses. Add the butter and process until the mixture is homogeneous and the dough resembles wet sand, about 10 seconds. Add the remaining 2 cups flour and pulse until the mixture is evenly distributed around the bowl, 4 to 6 quick pulses. Empty the mixture into a medium bowl.

**4.** Sprinkle the vodka and water over the mixture. Using your hands, mix the dough until it forms a tacky mass that sticks together. Divide the dough in half, then divide each half into six equal pieces. Transfer the dough pieces to a plate, cover with plastic wrap, and refrigerate until firm, about 45 minutes.

**5. TO ASSEMBLE:** Adjust the oven racks to the upper-middle and lower-middle positions, place 1 baking sheet on each rack, and heat the oven to 425 degrees. While the baking sheets are preheating, remove the dough from the refrigerator. Roll each dough piece out on a lightly floured work surface into a 6-inch circle about ⅛ inch thick, covering each rolled-out dough round with plastic wrap while rolling out the remaining dough. Place about ⅓ cup of the filling in the center of each dough round. Brush the edges of each round with water and fold the dough over the filling. Trim any ragged edges, then crimp the edges of the empanadas shut using a fork. (Filled empanadas, wrapped tightly in plastic wrap, can be refrigerated for up to 2 days.)

**6.** Drizzle 2 tablespoons of the oil over the surface of each hot baking sheet, then return the sheets to the oven for 2 minutes. Brush the empanadas with the remaining 1 tablespoon oil. Carefully place 6 empanadas on each baking sheet and cook until well browned and crisp, 25 to 30 minutes, switching and rotating the baking sheets halfway through baking. Cool the empanadas on a wire rack for 10 minutes before serving.

## Pan-Seared Steaks

**SERVES 4**

**WHY THIS RECIPE WORKS** We wanted to produce outstanding steaks—indoors—that were every bit as good as those cooked on the grill. We found that heating a heavy-bottomed skillet until very hot is essential for a good sear and, thus, a good crust. Thoroughly drying the steaks is also key—soggy steaks will steam, not sear. For best flavor, we seasoned the steaks with salt and pepper prior to cooking. And we reduced the heat before adding the steaks—the skillet was still hot, but not so hot that it burned the fond, which we used to make a pan sauce. After removing the steaks from the pan, we let them rest for 5 minutes, enough time to prepare a pan sauce. Serve these steaks with either Red Wine Pan Sauce or Shallot Butter Sauce. Prepare all the sauce ingredients before starting the steaks and don't wash the skillet after cooking the steaks; the fat left in the pan will be used for the sauce. Note that the wine reduction used in the red wine sauce should be started before the steaks are cooked.

- 1 tablespoon vegetable oil
- 4 (8-ounce) boneless strip or rib-eye steaks, each 1 to 1¼ inches thick, thoroughly dried with paper towels
- Table salt and ground black pepper

**1.** Heat the oil in a 12-inch skillet over high heat until just smoking. Meanwhile, season both sides of the steaks with salt and pepper.

**2.** Lay the steaks in the pan, leaving ¼ inch of space between them; reduce the heat to medium-high and cook, not moving the steaks until well browned, about 4 minutes. Using tongs, flip the steaks; cook until the center of the steaks registers 115 to 120 degrees (for rare) about 4 minutes, 120 to 125 degrees (for medium-rare), about 5 minutes, or 130 to 135 degrees (for medium), about 6 minutes. Transfer the steaks to a large plate, tent with foil, and let rest for 5 minutes while preparing one of the pan sauces.

### Red Wine Pan Sauce

**MAKES** about ½ cup

Start cooking the steaks when the wine has almost finished reducing. Use a smooth, medium-bodied, fruity wine, such as a Côtes du Rhône.

**WINE REDUCTION**

- 1 cup red wine
- 1 medium shallot, minced (about 3 tablespoons)
- 2 white mushrooms, wiped clean and chopped fine (about 3 tablespoons)
- 1 small carrot, chopped fine (about 2 tablespoons)
- 1 bay leaf
- 3 sprigs fresh parsley

**SAUCE**

- 1 medium shallot, minced (about 3 tablespoons)
- ½ cup low-sodium chicken broth
- ½ cup low-sodium beef broth
- 3 tablespoons cold unsalted butter, cut into 6 pieces
- ½ teaspoon fresh thyme leaves
- Table salt and ground black pepper

**1. FOR THE WINE REDUCTION:** Heat the wine, shallot, mushrooms, carrot, bay leaf, and parsley in a 12-inch skillet over low heat; cook, without simmering (the liquid should be steaming but not bubbling), until the entire mixture reduces to 1 cup, 15 to 20 minutes. Strain through a fine-mesh strainer and return the liquid (about ½ cup) to the clean skillet. Continue to cook over low heat, without simmering, until the liquid is reduced to 2 tablespoons, 15 to 20 minutes. Transfer the reduction to a bowl.

**2. FOR THE SAUCE:** Follow the recipe for Pan-Seared Steaks. After removing the steaks from the skillet, add the shallot and cook over low heat until softened, about 1 minute. Turn the heat to high; add the chicken and beef broths. Bring to a boil, scraping up the browned bits on the pan bottom with a wooden spoon, until the liquid is reduced to 2 tablespoons, about 6 minutes. Turn the heat to medium-low, gently whisk in the reserved wine reduction and any accumulated juices from the plate with the steaks. Whisk in the butter, one piece at a time, until melted and the sauce is thickened and glossy; add the thyme and season with salt and pepper to taste. Spoon the sauce over the steaks and serve immediately.

### Shallot Butter Sauce

**MAKES** about ½ cup

- 2 medium shallots, minced (about ⅓ cup)
- 4 tablespoons (½ stick) cold unsalted butter, cut into 4 pieces
- 1 teaspoon juice from 1 lemon
- 1 teaspoon minced fresh parsley leaves
- Table salt and ground black pepper

Follow the recipe for Pan-Seared Steaks. After removing the steaks from the skillet, add the shallots and cook over low heat until softened, about 1 minute. Turn the heat to medium-low; stir in the butter, scraping up the browned bits on the pan bottom with a wooden spoon. When the butter is just melted, stir in the lemon juice and parsley; season with salt and pepper to taste. Spoon the sauce over the steaks and serve immediately.

## Restaurant-Style Herb Sauce for Pan-Seared Steaks

**SERVES** 4

**WHY THIS RECIPE WORKS** We love the ultrarich flavor and glossy consistency that a classic French demi-glace (a savory, full-bodied reduction traditionally made from veal bones and stock) adds to a sauce, but making it is a time-consuming process usually left to the expertise of professional cooks. We wanted to find a shortcut for making demi-glace at home, so that we could use it as the base of a variety of great sauces for crusty, pan-seared steaks. Chopping up vegetables (to increase their surface area, thus providing more opportunity for flavorful browning) as well as adding mushrooms, tomato paste, and seasonings to red wine and beef broth was a good start, but it wasn't enough. To replicate the meaty flavor and unctuous gelatin given up by roasted bones, we sautéed ground beef with the tomato paste and stirred powdered gelatin into the final reduction. Since the sauce base was easy to freeze and use again, we didn't mind making a batch that would yield enough for two pan sauces. We like this herb sauce with strip or rib-eye steaks, but it will work with any type of pan-seared steak.

- 1 recipe Pan-Seared Steaks
- 1 small shallot, minced (about 1 tablespoon)
- ½ cup white wine
- ¼ cup Sauce Base (½ recipe)
- ¼ teaspoon white wine vinegar
- 1½ teaspoons minced fresh chives
- 1½ teaspoons minced fresh parsley leaves
- 1 teaspoon minced fresh tarragon leaves
- 1 tablespoon unsalted butter
- Table salt and ground black pepper

After transferring the steaks to a plate to rest, return the now-empty skillet to medium-low heat; add the shallot and cook, stirring constantly, until lightly browned, about 2 minutes. Add the wine and bring to a simmer, scraping the bottom of the skillet with a wooden spoon to loosen any browned bits. Add the Sauce Base, vinegar, and any accumulated juices from the steaks; return to a simmer and cook until slightly reduced, about 1 minute. Off the heat, whisk in the chives, parsley, tarragon, and butter; season with salt and pepper to taste. Spoon the sauce over the steaks and serve.

### Sauce Base

**MAKES** ½ cup

The sauce base recipe yields more than called for in the sauce recipes; leftovers can be refrigerated in an airtight container for up to 3 days or frozen for up to 1 month.

- 1 small onion, peeled and cut into rough ½-inch pieces
- 1 small carrot, peeled and cut into rough ½-inch pieces
- 8 ounces cremini mushrooms, trimmed and halved
- 2 medium garlic cloves, peeled
- 1 tablespoon vegetable oil
- 8 ounces 85 percent lean ground beef
- 1 tablespoon tomato paste
- 2 cups dry red wine
- 4 cups beef broth
- 4 sprigs fresh thyme
- 2 bay leaves
- 2 teaspoons whole black peppercorns
- 5 teaspoons unflavored gelatin

**1.** Pulse the onion, carrot, mushrooms, and garlic in a food processor into ⅛-inch pieces, 10 to 12 pulses, scraping down the sides as needed.

**2.** Heat the oil in a Dutch oven over medium-high heat until shimmering; add the beef and tomato paste and cook, stirring frequently, until the beef is well browned, 8 to 10 minutes. Add the vegetable mixture and cook, stirring occasionally, until any exuded moisture has evaporated, about 8 minutes. Add the wine and bring to a simmer, scraping the bottom of the pot with a wooden spoon to loosen any browned bits. Add the broth, thyme, bay leaves, and peppercorns; bring to a boil. Reduce the heat and gently boil, occasionally scraping the bottom and sides of the pot and skimming fat from the surface, until reduced to 2 cups, 20 to 25 minutes.

**3.** Strain the mixture through a fine-mesh strainer set over a small saucepan, pressing on the solids with a rubber spatula to extract as much liquid as possible (you should have about 1 cup stock). Sprinkle the gelatin over the stock and stir to dissolve. Place the saucepan over medium-high heat and bring the stock to a boil. Gently boil, stirring occasionally, until reduced to ½ cup, 5 to 7 minutes. Remove from the heat and cover to keep warm.

## Sous Vide Perfect Seared Steaks

**SERVES 4**

**WHY THIS RECIPE WORKS** Though we often think of the grill when it comes to steaks, sous vide cooking is a game changer. The water bath technique takes all of the risk, guesswork, and stress out of the dinner-preparation equation. With sous vide, steaks are cooked to the same temperature, and thus same doneness (of your choosing), all the way through. This eliminates the gray band of overcooked meat around the exterior of the meat, which often occurs with traditional pan-roasted methods. Once the steaks are taken out of the water bath, all we had to do was give them a quick sear in a screaming-hot pan to create a brown, flavorful crust. Then we created a luscious pan sauce from the drippings left behind in the pan. This recipe was developed for tender steaks such as strip, rib eye, shell sirloin, top sirloin, and tenderloin; avoid tougher cuts such as top round, bottom round, blade, and flank. Serve with Mustard-Fennel Pan Sauce, if desired.

- 2 pounds boneless beef steaks, 1 to 1½ inches thick, trimmed
- Table salt and pepper
- 7 tablespoons vegetable oil

**1.** Using sous vide circulator, bring water to 130 degrees in 7-quart container.

**2.** Season steaks with salt and pepper. Place steaks and ¼ cup oil in 1-gallon zipper-lock freezer bag and toss to coat. Arrange steaks in single layer and seal bag, pressing out as much air as possible. Gently lower bag into prepared water bath until steaks are fully submerged, and then clip top corner of bag to side of water bath container, allowing remaining air bubbles to rise to top of bag. Reopen 1 corner of zipper, release remaining air bubbles, and reseal bag. Cover and cook for at least 1½ hours or up to 3 hours.

**3.** Transfer steaks to paper towel–lined plate and let rest for 5 to 10 minutes. Pat steaks dry with paper towels. Heat remaining 3 tablespoons oil in 12-inch skillet over medium-high heat until just smoking. Sear steaks, about 1 minute per side, until well browned. Transfer to cutting board and slice ½ inch thick. Serve.

### Mustard-Fennel Pan Sauce

**MAKES** about ½ cup

Note that this recipe is meant to be started after you have seared the steaks. Sauvignon Blanc is our preferred white cooking wine.

- Vegetable oil, if needed
- 1 shallot, minced
- ½ teaspoon fennel seeds, cracked
- ½ cup chicken broth
- ¼ cup dry white wine
- 1½ tablespoons Dijon mustard
- 2 tablespoons unsalted butter, cut into 2 pieces and chilled
- 1 teaspoon chopped fresh tarragon
- Table salt and pepper

**1.** Pour off all but 1 tablespoon fat from skillet used to sear steak. (If necessary, add oil to equal 1 tablespoon.) Add shallot and fennel seeds and cook over medium heat until shallot is softened, 1 to 2 minutes. Stir in broth, wine, and mustard, scraping up any browned bits. Bring to simmer and cook until liquid is reduced to ½ cup, about 6 minutes.

**2.** Off heat, whisk in butter, 1 piece at a time, until melted and sauce is thickened and glossy. Whisk in tarragon and any accumulated meat juices and season with salt and pepper to taste. Serve immediately.

## Pan-Seared Strip Steaks

**SERVES 4**

**WHY THIS RECIPE WORKS** Pan-searing strip or rib-eye steaks usually leads to a smoky, grease-splattered kitchen—but it doesn't have to. To devise a fast, mess-free method for achieving deeply seared, rosy meat, we started the steaks in a "cold" (not preheated) nonstick skillet over high heat and flipped them every 2 minutes; that way, the meat's temperature increased gradually, allowing a crust to build up on the outside without overcooking the interior. Because we were cooking in a nonstick skillet, it wasn't necessary to lubricate the skillet with oil; plus, the well-marbled meat exuded enough fat to achieve a good sear, and adding more simply encouraged splatter. We started cooking over high heat to burn off moisture and prevent the steaks from steaming but quickly lowered the heat to medium; at this temperature, the meat kept sizzling, but there was no risk of the fat smoking. Before serving, we sliced the steaks and sprinkled them with coarse sea salt so that every bite was well seasoned. This recipe also works with boneless rib-eye steaks of a similar thickness. If you have time, salt the steaks for at least 45 minutes or up to 24 hours before cooking: Sprinkle each of the steaks with 1 teaspoon of kosher salt, refrigerate them, and pat them dry with paper towels before cooking. Serve with one of the sauces on pages 382–384, if desired.

- 2 (12- to 16-ounce) boneless strip steaks, 1½ inches thick, trimmed
- 1 teaspoon pepper

**1.** Pat steaks dry with paper towels and sprinkle both sides with pepper. Place steaks 1 inch apart in cold nonstick skillet. Place skillet over high heat and cook steaks for 2 minutes. Flip steaks and cook on second side for 2 minutes. (Neither side of steaks will be browned at this point.)

**2.** Flip steaks, reduce heat to medium, and continue to cook, flipping steaks every 2 minutes, until browned and meat registers 120 to 125 degrees (for medium-rare), 4 to 10 minutes longer. (Steaks should be sizzling gently; if not, increase heat slightly. Reduce heat if skillet starts to smoke.)

**3.** Transfer steaks to carving board and let rest for 5 minutes. Slice steaks, season with coarse or flake sea salt to taste, and serve.

## Steak au Poivre with Brandied Cream Sauce

**SERVES 4**

**WHY THIS RECIPE WORKS** Steak au poivre is often nothing more than uninspired skillet steak. We were after the real thing—a perfectly cooked steak with a well-seared crust of pungent, cracked peppercorns and a silky sauce. The trick to successful steak au poivre is coating just one side of the steaks with peppercorns and cooking the steaks on the uncoated side as long as possible to promote browning and prevent scorching of the peppercorns. With the first side browned, we flipped the steaks and cooked them for less time on the peppered side. Pressing the steaks with a cake pan once they were in the hot skillet ensured that the peppercorns stuck. After the steaks were done, we made a simple creamy pan sauce with a mixture of beef broth and chicken broth that we reduced, then flavored with brandy and lemon juice. To save time, crush the peppercorns and trim the steaks while the broth mixture simmers. Many pepper mills do not have a sufficiently coarse setting. In that case, crush peppercorns with the back of a heavy pan. See page 1013 for information on our top-rated pepper mill.

- 4 tablespoons (½ stick) unsalted butter
- 1 medium shallot, minced (about 3 tablespoons)
- 1 cup beef broth
- ¾ cup low-sodium chicken broth
- 4 (8- to 10-ounce) strip steaks, ¾ to 1 inch thick, trimmed
- Table salt
- 4 teaspoons black peppercorns, crushed

- 1 tablespoon vegetable oil
- ¼ cup plus 1 tablespoon brandy
- ¼ cup heavy cream
- 1 teaspoon juice from 1 lemon or 1 teaspoon champagne vinegar

**1.** Melt 1 tablespoon of the butter in a 12-inch skillet over medium heat. Add the shallot and cook, stirring occasionally, until softened, about 2 minutes. Add the beef and chicken broths and bring to a boil over high heat; cook until reduced to ½ cup, about 8 minutes. Transfer the broth mixture to a small bowl; wipe out the skillet with paper towels.

**2.** Meanwhile, pat the steaks dry with paper towels and season with salt. Sprinkle one side of each steak with 1 teaspoon of the crushed peppercorns and press them into the steaks with your fingers to adhere.

**3.** Heat the oil in the skillet over medium-high heat until just smoking. Carefully lay the steaks in the skillet, peppered side up. Press on the steaks with the bottom of a cake pan and cook until well-browned on the first side, 3 to 5 minutes. Flip the steaks over and continue to cook, pressing again with the cake pan, until the center of the steaks registers 115 to 120 degrees (for rare) about 3 minutes, 120 to 125 degrees (for medium-rare about 4 minutes, or 130 to 135 degrees (for medium) about 5 minutes). Transfer the steaks to a plate, tent loosely with foil, and let rest while making the sauce.

**4.** Pour off any fat left in the pan and remove any stray peppercorns. Add the broth mixture, ¼ cup of the brandy, and the cream to the skillet and bring to a boil over high heat, scraping up any browned bits. Simmer until golden brown and thickened, about 5 minutes. Off the heat, whisk in the remaining 3 tablespoons butter, the remaining 1 tablespoon brandy, the lemon juice, and any accumulated meat juices from the plate; season with salt to taste. Spoon the sauce over the steaks and serve immediately.

## Steak Frites

**SERVES 4**

**WHY THIS RECIPE WORKS** Too often, steak frites can miss the mark: The fries are too soggy and the steak just isn't flavorful. To re-create the steak frites of our Parisian dreams, with perfectly cooked steak and fries that were fluffy on the inside and crisp on the outside, we started with high-starch russet potatoes. We found that a double-cooking, blanch-and-fry method yielded the crispiest exterior and fluffiest interior. Cooking small batches of fries and soaking the potatoes in cold water before they were cooked further improved their crispiness, and a "rest" between the first and second frying allowed the fries to develop a thin coating of starch, which made them even crispier. Tossing them with cornstarch made them perfect. We were able to sear four rib-eye steaks at once in a large skillet. Capped with a quick herb butter, the steaks tasted just like the bistro classic. Make sure to dry the potatoes well before tossing them with the cornstarch. For safety, use a Dutch oven with a capacity of at least 7 quarts. A 12-inch skillet is essential for cooking four steaks at once. The ingredients can be halved to serve two—keep the oil amount the same and forgo blanching and frying the potatoes in batches.

Herb Butter

- 4 tablespoons unsalted butter, softened
- ½ shallot, minced
- 1 tablespoon minced fresh parsley
- 1 tablespoon minced fresh chives
- 1 garlic clove, minced
- ¼ teaspoon table salt
- ¼ teaspoon pepper

Potatoes and Steak

- 2½ pounds russet potatoes (about 4 large), scrubbed, sides squared off and cut lengthwise into ¼ by ¼-inch fries
- 2 tablespoons cornstarch
- 3 quarts peanut oil
- 1 tablespoon vegetable oil
- 2 (1-pound) boneless rib-eye steaks, cut in half
- ½ teaspoon table salt
- ½ teaspoon pepper

**1. FOR THE HERB BUTTER:** Combine all ingredients in medium bowl.

**2. FOR THE POTATOES:** Rinse cut potatoes in large bowl under cold running water until water turns clear. Cover with cold water and refrigerate for at least 30 minutes or up to 12 hours.

**3.** Pour off water, spread potatoes onto clean dish towels, and thoroughly dry. Transfer potatoes to large bowl and toss with cornstarch until evenly coated. Transfer potatoes to wire rack set in rimmed baking sheet and let rest until fine white coating forms, about 20 minutes.

**4.** Meanwhile, heat peanut oil over medium heat to 325 degrees in large, heavy-bottomed Dutch oven fitted with a clip-on candy thermometer.

**5.** Add half of potatoes, 1 handful at a time, to hot oil and increase heat to high. Fry, stirring with mesh spider or slotted spoon, until potatoes start to turn from white to blond, 4 to 5 minutes. (Oil temperature will drop about 75 degrees during this frying.) Transfer fries to thick paper bag or paper towels. Return oil to 325 degrees and repeat with remaining potatoes. Reduce heat to medium and let fries cool while cooking steaks, at least 10 minutes. (Fries can be prepared through this step up to 2 hours in advance; shut off the heat under the oil and turn the heat back to medium when you start step 6.)

**6. FOR THE STEAK:** Heat vegetable oil in 12-inch skillet over medium-high heat until just smoking. Meanwhile, sprinkle steaks with salt and pepper. Lay steaks in pan, leaving ¼ inch between them. Cook, without moving steaks, until well browned, about 4 minutes. Flip steaks and continue to cook until meat registers 120 degrees (for rare to medium-rare), 3 to 7 minutes. Transfer steaks to large plate, top with herb butter, and tent with aluminum foil; let rest while finishing fries.

**7.** Increase heat under Dutch oven to high and heat oil to 375 degrees. Add half of fries, 1 handful at a time, and fry until golden brown and puffed, 2 to 3 minutes. Transfer to thick paper bag or paper towels. Return oil to 375 degrees and repeat with remaining fries. Season fries with salt to taste, and serve immediately with steaks.

## New York Strip Steaks with Crispy Potatoes and Parsley Sauce

**SERVES 2**

**WHY THIS RECIPE WORKS** For a steak-and-potatoes recipe that was anything but ordinary, we started with boneless strip steaks and small red potatoes. Cooking everything in a single skillet cut down on cleanup, and the rendered fat from the steak lent the potatoes a rich, meaty flavor. But the potatoes took nearly 40 minutes to cook through on the stovetop—not the simple weeknight meal we had in mind. To speed up the process, we jump-started the potatoes in the microwave, then added them to the skillet for just 10 minutes to develop a crispy, golden-brown crust. A quick parsley sauce seasoned with garlic, vinegar, a dash of red pepper, and a little chopped red onion contributed vibrant flavor to our hearty meal. You will need a 12-inch nonstick skillet for this recipe.

**PARSLEY SAUCE**

- ½ cup fresh parsley leaves
- ¼ cup extra-virgin olive oil
- 2 tablespoons chopped red onion
- 2 tablespoons red wine vinegar
- 1 tablespoon water
- 2 garlic cloves, minced
- ½ teaspoon table salt
- ⅛ teaspoon red pepper flakes

**STEAK AND POTATOES**

- 12 ounces red potatoes, unpeeled, cut into 1-inch wedges
- 3 tablespoons vegetable oil, divided
- ¼ teaspoon table salt
- ⅛ teaspoon pepper
- 2 (8-ounce) boneless strip steaks, ¾ inch thick, trimmed

**1. FOR THE PARSLEY SAUCE:** Process all ingredients in food processor until well combined, about 20 seconds, scraping down sides of bowl as needed. Transfer sauce to bowl and set aside.

**2. FOR THE STEAK AND POTATOES:** Toss potatoes with 1 tablespoon oil, salt, and pepper in bowl. Cover and microwave until potatoes begin to soften, 5 to 7 minutes, stirring potatoes halfway through microwaving. Drain well.

**3.** Meanwhile, pat steaks dry with paper towels and season with salt and pepper. Heat 1 tablespoon oil in 12-inch nonstick skillet over medium-high heat until just smoking. Lay steaks in skillet and cook until well browned on first side, 3 to 5 minutes. Flip steaks, reduce heat to medium, and continue to cook until meat registers 120 to 125 degrees (for medium-rare), 1 to 4 minutes; transfer to plate and tent with aluminum foil.

**4.** Add remaining 1 tablespoon oil to fat left in skillet and heat over medium heat until shimmering. Add drained potatoes and cook until golden brown and tender on all sides, about 10 minutes. Serve steaks with potatoes and sauce.

## Steak Diane

**SERVE 4**

**WHY THIS RECIPE WORKS** For a different spin on pan-seared steaks, we turned to the French classic, steak Diane. But the demanding rich sauce is based on an all-day veal stock reduction—and then the steaks still have to be cooked, and the sauce completed. We aimed to determine the right cut of steak, create a lighter, less labor-intensive sauce, and find a foolproof method for cooking the meat. For a rich sauce base that mimicked the complexity of veal stock in a fraction of the time, we used a combination of sautéed tomato paste, aromatics such as garlic, onion, and carrots, both beef broth and chicken broth, red wine, peppercorns, and herbs. Omitting the traditional cream allowed the sauce to fully develop in intensity, and the inclusion of cognac gave the sauce a slightly sweet, complex flavor. For the meat, we selected strip steaks for great beefy flavor and ease of preparation. To brown the steaks evenly and develop enough fond (the flavorful browned bits that cling to the pan and add rich, meaty flavor), we weighted the steaks with a heavy-bottomed skillet when cooking the second side. If you prefer not to make the sauce base (page 388), mix ½ cup glace de viande with ¾ cup water and ¼ cup red wine and use this mixture in place of the base in step 2. Glace de viande is meat stock, in this case veal stock, that's been reduced to a thick syrup; we recommend Provimi Glace de Veau and CulinArte' Bonewerks Glace de Veau. If you do not wish to flambé, simmer the cognac in step 2 for 10 to 15 seconds for a slightly less sweet flavor profile.

**STEAKS**

- 4 (12-ounce) strip steaks, 1 to 1¼ inches thick, trimmed
- Table salt and ground black pepper
- 2 tablespoons vegetable oil

**SAUCE**

- 1 tablespoon vegetable oil
- 1 small shallot, minced (about 1 tablespoon)
- ¼ cup cognac
- 1 recipe Sauce Base for Steak Diane (page 388)
- 2 teaspoons Dijon mustard
- 2 tablespoons unsalted butter, chilled
- 1 teaspoon Worcestershire sauce
- 2 tablespoons minced fresh chives
- Table salt and ground black pepper

**1. FOR THE STEAKS:** Cover the steaks with plastic wrap and use a meat pounder to pound them to an even ½-inch thickness; season them with salt and pepper. Heat 1 tablespoon of the oil in a 12-inch skillet over medium-high heat until smoking. Place 2 steaks in the skillet and cook until well browned, about 1½ minutes. Flip the steaks and weight with a heavy-bottomed pan; continue to cook until well browned on the second side, about 1½ minutes longer. Transfer the steaks to a plate and tent with foil. Add the remaining 1 tablespoon oil to the skillet and repeat with the remaining 2 steaks; transfer the second batch of steaks to the plate.

**2. FOR THE SAUCE:** Off the heat, add the oil and shallot to the skillet. Using the skillet's residual heat, cook, stirring frequently, until the shallot is slightly softened and browned, about 45 seconds. Add the cognac and let stand until the cognac warms slightly, about 10 seconds, then set the skillet over high heat. Wave a lit match over the skillet until the cognac ignites, shaking the skillet until the flames subside, then simmer the cognac until reduced to about 1 tablespoon, about 10 seconds. Add the sauce base and mustard and simmer until slightly thickened and reduced to 1 cup, 2 to 3 minutes. Whisk in the butter. Off the heat, add the Worcestershire sauce, any accumulated juices from the steaks, and 1 tablespoon of the chives. Season with salt and pepper to taste.

**3.** Serve immediately, spooning 2 tablespoons sauce and sprinkling a portion of the remaining 1 tablespoon chives over each steak, and passing the remaining sauce separately.

### Sauce Base for Steak Diane

**MAKES** 1¼ cups

This sauce base is an excellent facsimile of a demi-glace, a time-consuming classic French sauce base. Ii is critical to use low-sodium chicken and beef broths.

- 2 tablespoons vegetable oil
- 4 teaspoons tomato paste
- 2 small onions, chopped medium
- 1 medium carrot, chopped medium
- 4 medium garlic cloves, peeled
- ¼ cup water
- 4 teaspoons unbleached all-purpose flour
- 1½ cups dry red wine
- 3½ cups low-sodium beef broth
- 1¾ cups low-sodium chicken broth
- 2 teaspoons black peppercorns
- 8 sprigs fresh thyme
- 2 bay leaves

**1.** Heat the oil and tomato paste in a Dutch oven over medium-high heat and cook, stirring constantly, until the paste begins to brown, about 3 minutes. Add the onions, carrot, and garlic and cook, stirring frequently, until the mixture is reddish brown, about 2 minutes. Add 2 tablespoons of the water and continue to cook, stirring constantly, until the mixture is well browned, about 3 minutes, adding the remaining 2 tablespoons water as needed to prevent scorching. Add the flour and cook, stirring constantly, for about 1 minute. Add the wine, scraping up the browned bits on the bottom and sides of the pot; bring to a boil, stirring occasionally (the mixture will thicken slightly). Add the beef and chicken broths, peppercorns, thyme, and bay leaves; bring to a boil and cook, uncovered, occasionally scraping the bottom and sides of the pot with a spatula, until reduced to 2½ cups, 35 to 40 minutes.

**2.** Strain the mixture through a fine-mesh strainer, pressing on the solids to extract as much liquid as possible; you should have about 1¼ cups. (The sauce base can be refrigerated in an airtight container for up to 3 days.)

## Cast Iron Thick-Cut Steaks with Herb Butter

**SERVES** 4

**WHY THIS RECIPE WORKS** We were looking for a way to make a steak with the ultimate crust entirely on the stovetop—so we turned to a cast-iron skillet, since its heat-retention properties are ideal for a perfect sear. We chose the boneless strip steak for its big, beefy flavor. We heated up the skillet in the oven so its surface would be uniformly hot—so hot that it could jump-start the searing process. While it heated we made a compound

butter with shallot, garlic, parsley, and chives—and let the steaks warm to room temperature, which helped them cook more quickly and evenly. Salting the outside of the steaks while they rested pulled moisture from the steaks while also seasoning the meat, helping us get a better sear. After testing flipping techniques and heat levels, we found that flipping the steaks every 2 minutes and lowering the heat from medium-high to medium-low partway through cooking resulted in a perfectly browned, crisp crust and a juicy interior.

- 2 (1-pound) boneless strip steaks, 1½ inches thick, trimmed
- Table salt and pepper
- 4 tablespoons unsalted butter, softened
- 2 tablespoons minced shallot
- 1 tablespoon minced fresh parsley
- 1 tablespoon minced fresh chives
- 1 garlic clove, minced
- 2 tablespoons vegetable oil

**1.** Adjust oven rack to middle position, place 12-inch cast-iron skillet on rack, and heat oven to 500 degrees. Meanwhile, season steaks with salt and let sit at room temperature. Mix butter, shallot, parsley, chives, garlic, ¼ teaspoon pepper, and pinch of salt together in bowl; set aside until needed.

**2.** When oven reaches 500 degrees, pat steaks dry with paper towels and season with pepper. Using potholders, remove skillet from oven and place over medium-high heat; turn off oven. Being careful of hot skillet handle, add oil and heat until just smoking. Cook steaks, without moving, until lightly browned on first side, about 2 minutes. Flip steaks and continue to cook until lightly browned on second side, about 2 minutes.

**3.** Flip steaks, reduce heat to medium-low, and cook, flipping every 2 minutes, until steaks are well browned and meat registers 120 to 125 degrees (for medium-rare), 7 to 9 minutes. Transfer steaks to carving board, dollop 2 tablespoons herb butter on each steak, tent loosely with aluminum foil, and let rest for 5 to 10 minutes. Slice steaks into ½-inch-thick slices and serve.

## Pan-Seared Thick-Cut Strip Steaks

**SERVES 4**

**WHY THIS RECIPE WORKS** A nicely charred thick-cut steak certainly looks appealing. But cutting into the steak to find that the rosy meat is confined to a measly spot in the center—with the rest a thick band of overcooked gray—is a great disappointment. We wanted to find a surefire method for pan-searing thick-cut steaks that could deliver both a flavorful crust and juicy, perfectly pink meat throughout. We found it was essential to sear the steaks quickly to keep the meat directly under the crust from turning gray. But we'd need to take an untraditional approach for these thick-cut steaks and sear them at the end of cooking, rather than at the beginning. We began by moving the steaks straight from the fridge into a 275-degree oven, which not only warmed them to 95 degrees but also dried the meat thoroughly—essential for a well-browned crust. At this temperature, when the steak met the hot skillet, it developed a beautiful brown crust in less than four minutes, while the rest of the meat stayed pink, juicy, and tender. Rib-eye or filet mignon of similar thickness can be substituted for strip steaks. If using filet mignon, buying a 2-pound center-cut tenderloin roast and portioning it into four 8-ounce steaks yourself will produce more consistent results. If using filet mignon, increase the oven time by about 5 minutes. When cooking lean strip steaks (without an external fat cap) or filet mignon, add an extra tablespoon of oil to the pan. Don't wash the skillet before making the pan sauce.

- 2 (1-pound) boneless strip steaks, each 1½ to 1¾ inches thick
- Table salt and ground black pepper
- 1 tablespoon vegetable oil

**1.** Adjust an oven rack to the middle position and heat the oven to 275 degrees. Pat the steaks dry with paper towels. Cut each steak in half vertically to create four 8-ounce steaks. Season the steaks liberally with salt and pepper; using your hands, gently shape into a uniform thickness. Place the steaks on a wire rack set over a rimmed baking sheet; transfer the baking sheet to the oven. Cook until an instant-read thermometer inserted horizontally into the center of the steaks registers 90 to 95 degrees for rare to medium-rare (20 to 25 minutes), or 100 to 105 degrees for medium (25 to 30 minutes).

**2.** Heat the oil in a 12-inch skillet over high heat until smoking. Place the steaks in the skillet and sear until well browned and crusty, 1½ to 2 minutes, lifting once halfway through to redistribute the fat underneath each steak. (Reduce the heat if the fond begins to burn.) Using tongs, turn the steaks and cook until well browned on the second side, 2 to 2½ minutes. Transfer the steaks to a clean rack and reduce the heat under the pan to medium. Use tongs to stand 2 steaks on their sides. Holding the steaks together, return to the skillet and sear on all edges until browned, about 1½ minutes. Repeat with the remaining 2 steaks.

**3.** Return the steaks to the wire rack and let rest, loosely tented with foil, for about 10 minutes. If desired, cook the sauce in the now-empty skillet. Serve immediately.

### Red Wine–Mushroom Pan Sauce

**MAKES** about 1 cup

Prepare all the ingredients for the pan sauce while the steaks are in the oven.

- 1 tablespoon vegetable oil
- 8 ounces white mushrooms, wiped clean and sliced thin (about 3 cups)
- 1 small shallot, minced (about 1 tablespoon)
- 1 cup dry red wine
- ½ cup low-sodium chicken broth
- 1 tablespoon balsamic vinegar
- 1 teaspoon Dijon mustard
- 2 tablespoons cold unsalted butter, cut into 4 pieces
- 1 teaspoon minced fresh thyme leaves
- Table salt and ground black pepper

Follow the recipe for Pan-Seared Thick-Cut Steaks. After removing the steaks from the skillet, pour off the fat from the skillet. Heat the oil over medium-high heat until just smoking. Add the mushrooms and cook, stirring occasionally, until beginning to brown and the liquid has evaporated, about 5 minutes. Add the shallot and cook, stirring frequently, until beginning to soften, about 1 minute. Increase the heat to high; add the red wine and broth, scraping the bottom of the skillet with a wooden spoon to loosen any browned bits. Simmer rapidly until the liquid and mushrooms are reduced to 1 cup, about 6 minutes. Add the vinegar, mustard, and any juices from the resting steaks; cook until thickened, about 1 minute. Off the heat, whisk in the butter and thyme; season with salt and pepper to taste. Spoon the sauce over the steaks and serve immediately.

### SEARING TWO STEAKS AT ONCE

Use tongs to sear the sides of two steaks at the same time.

## Pan-Seared Inexpensive Steaks

**SERVES 4**

**WHY THIS RECIPE WORKS** Buying cheap steak can be a gamble and a lesson in confusion, especially since names differ from region to region. We wanted inexpensive steak with the flavor and texture to rival its pricey counterparts. After we had investigated all the options, we were left with a list of 12 candidates. We cooked them as we would any steak, creating a nice sear on both sides without overcooking or allowing the browned bits in the pan to burn. Tasters judged most to be too tough and/or lacking beefy flavor, while others were livery or gamy. In the end, two cuts earned favored status: boneless shell

sirloin steak (aka top butt) and flap meat steak (aka sirloin tips). To prepare the steak, season with salt and pepper and start and get your skillet very hot. Allow the meat to rest before slicing and do so thinly against the grain on the bias to ensure the tenderest meat. Serve these steaks with Mustard-Cream Pan Sauce; prepare the ingredients before cooking the steaks, and don't wash the skillet after removing them. The fat left in the pan enhances the sauce. To serve two instead of four, use a 10-inch skillet to cook a 1-pound steak and halve the sauce ingredients. Note that these steaks should be cooked to medium-rare or medium for the best texture. The times in the recipe are for 1¼-inch-thick steaks.

- 2 tablespoons vegetable oil
- 2 1-pound whole boneless shell sirloin steaks (top butt) or whole flap meat steaks, each about 1¼ inches thick
- Table salt and ground black pepper

1. Heat the oil in a heavy-bottomed 12-inch skillet over medium-high heat until smoking. Meanwhile, season both sides of the steaks with salt and pepper. Place the steaks in the skillet; cook, without moving the steaks, until well browned, about 2 minutes. Using tongs, flip the steaks; reduce the heat to medium. Cook until well browned on (the second side and the center of the steaks registers 120 to 125 degrees for medium-rare) about 5 minutes or 130 to 135 degrees (for medium) about 6 minutes.
2. Transfer the steaks to a large plate and tent loosely with foil; let rest for about 10 minutes. Meanwhile, prepare the pan sauce, if making.
3. Using a sharp chef's knife or carving knife, slice the steak about ¼ inch thick against the grain on the bias, arrange on a platter or on individual plates, and spoon some sauce (if using) over each steak; serve immediately.

### Mustard-Cream Pan Sauce

**MAKES** about ¾ cup

- 1 medium shallot, minced (about 3 tablespoons)
- 2 tablespoons dry white wine
- ½ cup low-sodium chicken broth
- 6 tablespoons heavy cream
- 3 tablespoons grainy Dijon mustard
- Table salt and ground black pepper

Follow the recipe for Pan-Seared Inexpensive Steaks. After removing the steaks from the skillet, pour off all but 1 tablespoon of the fat. Return the skillet to low heat and add the shallot; cook, stirring frequently, until beginning to brown, 2 to 3 minutes. Add the wine and increase the heat to medium-high; simmer rapidly, scraping up the browned bits on the pan bottom with a wooden spoon. Simmer until the liquid is reduced to a glaze, about 30 seconds; add the broth and simmer until reduced to ¼ cup, about 3 minutes. Add the cream and any meat juices that have accumulated on the plate; cook until heated through, about 1 minute. Stir in the mustard; season with salt and pepper to taste. Spoon over the sliced steak and serve immediately.

## Pan-Seared Filet Mignon

**SERVES** 4

**WHY THIS RECIPE WORKS** Many cooks feel that filet mignon should be reserved for a celebratory restaurant meal. But we knew we could replicate the best restaurant filet at home, with a rich, brown crust and a tender interior, topped with a quick but luscious pan sauce. For a great crust, we patted the steaks dry before searing them in a very hot skillet. Then we transferred the meat to a hot oven to cook through. Finishing the steak in the oven prevented the richly flavored browned bits in the bottom of the pan from burning and allowed us time to start the sauce, which can be made in minutes while the steaks rest. If you are making one of the sauces, don't wash the skillet after removing the steaks and begin the sauce while the steaks are in the oven. To cook six steaks instead of four, use a 12-inch pan and use 6 teaspoons of olive oil.

- 4 (7- to 8-ounce) center-cut filets mignons, 1½ inches thick, trimmed
- 4 teaspoons extra-virgin olive oil
- ½ teaspoon table salt
- ½ teaspoon pepper

1. Adjust oven rack to lower-middle position, place rimmed baking sheet on oven rack, and heat oven to 450 degrees. When oven reaches 450 degrees, heat 12-inch skillet over high heat until just smoking.
2. Meanwhile, pat steaks dry with paper towels; rub each side of steaks with ½ teaspoon oil and sprinkle with salt and pepper. Place steaks in skillet and cook, without moving steaks, until well browned and nice crust has formed, about 3 minutes.

Turn steaks with tongs and cook until well browned and nice crust has formed on second side, about 3 minutes longer. Remove pan from heat and use tongs to transfer steaks to hot baking sheet in oven.

**3.** Roast until center of steaks registers 115 to 120 degrees (for rare) 4 to 5 minutes, 120 to 125 degrees (for medium-rare) 6 to 8 minutes, or 130 to 135 degrees (for medium) 8 to 10 minutes. Transfer steaks to large plate; tent with aluminum foil and let rest for about 10 minutes before serving.

### Madeira Pan Sauce with Mustard and Anchovies

**MAKES** ⅔ cup

If you do not have Madeira on hand, sherry makes a fine substitute. The accumulated pan juices from the steaks in the oven are incorporated into the reduction. If the steaks haven't finished cooking once the sauce has reduced, simply set the sauce aside until the steaks (and accumulated juices) are ready.

- 1 shallot, minced
- 1 cup Madeira
- 2 anchovy fillets, minced to paste
- 1 tablespoon minced fresh parsley
- 1 tablespoon minced fresh thyme
- 1 tablespoon Dijon mustard
- 1 tablespoon lemon juice
- 3 tablespoons unsalted butter, softened

While steaks are in oven, set skillet over medium-low heat; add shallot and cook, stirring constantly, until softened, about 1 minute. Add Madeira, increase heat to high, and scrape up any browned bits. Simmer until liquid is reduced to about ⅓ cup, 6 to 8 minutes. Add accumulated juices from baking sheet and reduce liquid 1 minute longer. Off heat, whisk in anchovies, parsley, thyme, mustard, lemon juice, and butter until butter has melted and sauce is slightly thickened. Season with salt and pepper to taste, spoon sauce over steaks, and serve immediately.

## Pepper-Crusted Filet Mignon

**SERVES** 4

**WHY THIS RECIPE WORKS** Chefs often compensate for the mild flavor of filet mignon by wrapping the delicate meat in bacon or puff pastry, serving it with rich wine sauces or flavored butter, or giving it a crust of cracked black peppercorns. We pursued the peppercorn approach but there were several issues: The peppercorns tend to fall off in the pan, interfere with the meat's browning, and—when used in sufficient quantity to create a real crust—deliver punishing pungency. Our first step was to mellow the peppercorns' heat by gently simmering them in olive oil. We then created a well-browned and attractive pepper crust using a two-step process: First, we rubbed the raw steaks with a paste of the cooked cracked peppercorns, salt, and oil, then we pressed the paste into each steak through a sheet of plastic wrap. We let the steaks sit, covered, for an hour before cooking. The paste added flavor and drew out the meat's beefy flavor. If you prefer a very mild pepper flavor, drain the cooled peppercorns in a fine-mesh strainer in step 1, toss them with 5 tablespoons of fresh oil, add the salt, and proceed. Serve with Port-Cherry Reduction.

- 5 tablespoons black peppercorns, cracked
- 5 tablespoons plus 2 teaspoons olive oil
- 1½ teaspoons table salt
- 4 (7- to 8-ounce) center-cut filets mignons, 1½ to 2 inches thick, each dried thoroughly with paper towels

**1.** Heat the peppercorns and 5 tablespoons of the oil in a small saucepan over low heat until faint bubbles appear. Continue to cook at a bare simmer, swirling the pan occasionally, until the pepper is fragrant, 7 to 10 minutes. Remove from the heat and set aside to cool. When the mixture is at room temperature, add the salt and stir to combine. Rub the steaks with the pepper mixture, thoroughly coating the top and bottom of each steak with the peppercorns. Cover the steaks with plastic wrap and press gently to make sure the peppercorns adhere; let stand at room temperature for 1 hour.

**2.** Meanwhile, adjust an oven rack to the middle position, place a rimmed baking sheet on the oven rack, and heat the oven to 450 degrees. Heat the remaining 2 teaspoons oil in a 12-inch heavy-bottomed skillet over medium-high heat until faint smoke appears. Place the steaks in the skillet and cook, without moving the steaks, until a dark brown crust has formed, 3 to 4 minutes. Using tongs, turn the steaks and cook until well browned on the second side, about 3 minutes. Remove the pan from the heat and transfer the steaks to the hot baking sheet. Roast until the center of the steaks registers 225 to 120 degrees (for rare) 3 to 5 minutes, 120 to 125 degrees (for medium-rare) 5 to 7 minutes, and 130 to 135 degrees (for medium) (7 to 9 minutes. Transfer the steaks to a wire rack and let rest, loosely tented with foil, for about 10 minutes before serving.

### Port-Cherry Reduction

**MAKES** about 1 cup

- 1½ cups port
- ½ cup balsamic vinegar
- ½ cup dried tart cherries
- 1 large shallot, minced (about 4 tablespoons)
- 2 sprigs fresh thyme
- 1 tablespoon unsalted butter
- Table salt

**1.** Combine the port, balsamic vinegar, cherries, shallot, and thyme in a medium saucepan; simmer over medium-low heat until the liquid is reduced to ⅓ cup, about 30 minutes. Set aside, covered.

**2.** While the steaks are resting, reheat the sauce. Off the heat, remove the thyme, then whisk in the butter until melted. Season with salt to taste. Serve, passing the sauce at the table with the steak.

## Pan-Seared Flank Steak with Mustard-Chive Butter

**SERVES** 4 to 6

**WHY THIS RECIPE WORKS** Cooking flank steak indoors often poses challenges—the cut of meat is too long to fit in most skillets, and it's quite thin, so it often overcooks before the exterior is well browned. We wanted a year-round, indoor cooking method that would produce a juicy, well-browned flank steak that was cooked to medium throughout. To start, we cut the flank into four steaks that would fit neatly in the skillet, but we didn't put them there right away. Instead, we sprinkled them with salt for seasoning and sugar for browning and baked them in a very low oven until they reached 120 degrees. Then we seared them in a hot skillet to develop the crust, flipping the steaks three times instead of just once. After enriching the lean steaks with a flavorful compound butter, we sliced them thinly against the grain for maximum tenderness. Open the oven as infrequently as possible in step 1. If the meat is not yet up to temperature, wait at least 5 minutes before taking its temperature again. Slice the steak as thin as possible against the grain.

- 1 (1½- to 1¾-pound) flank steak, trimmed
- 2 teaspoons kosher salt
- 1 teaspoon sugar
- ½ teaspoon pepper
- 3 tablespoons unsalted butter, softened
- 3 tablespoons chopped fresh chives
- 2 teaspoons Dijon mustard
- ½ teaspoon grated lemon zest plus 1 teaspoon juice
- 2 tablespoons vegetable oil

**1.** Adjust oven rack to middle position and heat oven to 225 degrees. Pat steak dry with paper towels. Cut steak in half lengthwise. Cut each piece in half crosswise to create 4 steaks. Combine salt, sugar, and pepper in small bowl. Sprinkle half of salt mixture on 1 side of steaks and press gently to adhere. Flip steaks and repeat with remaining salt mixture. Place steaks on wire rack set in rimmed baking sheet; transfer sheet to oven. Cook until thermometer inserted through side into center of thickest steak registers 120 degrees, 30 to 40 minutes.

**2.** Meanwhile, combine butter, 1 tablespoon chives, mustard, and lemon zest and juice in small bowl.

**3.** Heat oil in 12-inch skillet over medium-high heat until just smoking. Sear steaks, flipping every 1 minute, until brown crust forms on both sides, 4 minutes total. (Do not move steaks between flips.) Return steaks to wire rack and let rest for 10 minutes.

**4.** Transfer steaks to cutting board with grain running from left to right. Spread 1½ teaspoons butter mixture on top of each steak. Slice steak as thin as possible against grain. Transfer sliced steak to warm platter, dot with remaining butter mixture, sprinkle with remaining 2 tablespoons chives, and serve.

## Chicken-Fried Steaks

**SERVES** 6

**WHY THIS RECIPE WORKS** Although this truck-stop favorite often gets a bad rap, chicken-fried steak can be delicious when cooked just right. Poorly prepared versions feature dry, rubbery steaks that snap back with each bite, coated in damp, pale breading and topped with a bland, pasty white sauce. When cooked well, thin cutlets of beef are breaded and fried until a crisp, golden brown and served with a creamy gravy. A thin steak works best here, so we turned to cube steak and pounded the meat evenly. After trying a variety of coatings—Melba toast, corn flakes, panko, and the like—we determined simple was best. We dredged the steaks in heavily seasoned flour, dipped them in a thick buttermilk and egg mixture aerated with baking power and baking soda, and then returned them to the seasoned flour for a second coat. This coating fried up to an impressive dark mahogany color with a resilient texture. For the gravy, we built in flavor by using the fried bits left in the pan after cooking the steaks and by making a roux and adding aromatics. Make sure the initial oil temperature reaches 375 degrees. Use an instant-read thermometer or a clip-on candy/deep-fry thermometer. If your Dutch oven measures 11 inches across, fry the steaks in two batches.

**STEAKS**

- 3 cups unbleached all-purpose flour
- Table salt and ground black pepper
- ⅛ teaspoon cayenne pepper
- 1 large egg
- 1 teaspoon baking powder
- ½ teaspoon baking soda
- 1 cup buttermilk
- 6 (5-ounce) cube steaks, pounded ⅓ inch thick
- 4–5 cups peanut oil

**CREAM GRAVY**

- 1 medium onion, minced
- ⅛ teaspoon dried thyme
- 2 medium garlic cloves, minced or pressed through a garlic press (about 2 teaspoons)
- 3 tablespoons unbleached all-purpose flour
- ½ cup low-sodium chicken broth
- 2 cups whole milk
- ¾ teaspoon table salt
- ¼ teaspoon ground black pepper
- Pinch cayenne pepper

**1. FOR THE STEAKS:** Mix the flour, 5 teaspoons salt, 1 teaspoon black pepper, and the cayenne together in a large shallow dish. In a second large shallow dish, beat the egg, baking powder, and baking soda; stir in the buttermilk.

**2.** Set a wire rack over a large rimmed baking sheet. Pat the steaks dry with paper towels and sprinkle each side with salt and pepper. One at a time, drop the steaks into the flour and shake the dish to coat. Shake excess flour from each steak, then, using tongs, dip each steak into the egg mixture, turning to coat well and allowing the excess to drip off. Coat the steaks with flour again, shake off the excess, and place them on the wire rack.

**3.** Adjust an oven rack to the middle position, set a second wire rack over a second rimmed baking sheet, and place the sheet on the oven rack; heat the oven to 200 degrees. Line a large plate with a double layer of paper towels. Meanwhile, heat 1 inch of oil in a large (11-inch diameter) Dutch oven over medium-high heat to 375 degrees. Place 3 steaks in the oil and fry, turning once, until deep golden brown on each side, about 5 minutes (the oil temperature will drop to around 335 degrees). Transfer the steaks to the paper towel–lined plate to drain, then transfer them to the wire rack in the oven. Bring the oil back to 375 degrees and repeat the cooking and draining process (use fresh paper towels) with the 3 remaining steaks.

**4. FOR THE GRAVY:** Carefully pour the hot oil through a fine-mesh strainer into a clean pot. Return the browned bits from the strainer along with 2 tablespoons of the frying oil to the Dutch oven. Turn the heat to medium, add the onion and thyme, and cook until the onion has softened and is beginning to brown, 4 to 5 minutes. Add the garlic and cook until aromatic, about 30 seconds. Add the flour to the pan and stir until well combined and starting to dissolve, about 1 minute. Whisk in the broth, scraping any browned bits off the bottom of the pan. Whisk in the milk, salt, black pepper, and cayenne; bring to a simmer over medium-high heat. Cook until thickened (the gravy should have a loose consistency—it will thicken as it cools), about 5 minutes.

**5.** Transfer the chicken-fried steaks to individual plates. Spoon a generous amount of gravy over each steak. Serve immediately, passing any remaining gravy separately.

## Beef Satay

**SERVES** 8 to 10

**WHY THIS RECIPE WORKS** Satay is a popular street food throughout Southeast Asia. We wanted tender meat that could easily be pulled apart into small bites right off the skewer, with great flavors such as garlic, chiles, and cilantro. Choosing the right cut of meat proved to be more about texture than flavor: Flank steak was the winner. We used two techniques to slice it, first freezing the meat to firm it up enough to slice cleanly, then cutting the beef across the grain to keep it tender. Since the meat was so thin, cooking it was a breeze. Placing the skewered meat on a wire rack and cooking it 6 inches from the broiler's heating element proved just right. We found our marinade ingredients in the supermarket (sriracha was key) and added generous amounts of cilantro and garlic. Sriracha is available in most supermarkets. Use 6-inch-long skewers for this recipe; you'll need about 24.

- ¼ cup soy sauce
- ¼ cup peanut or vegetable oil
- ¼ cup packed dark brown sugar
- ¼ cup minced fresh cilantro leaves
- 4 scallions, sliced thin

- 2 tablespoons sriracha, or more to taste
- 2 medium garlic cloves, minced or pressed through a garlic press (about 2 teaspoons)
- 1 (1½-pound) flank steak, trimmed, halved lengthwise, frozen for 30 minutes, and sliced across the grain into ¼-inch-thick strips
- 1 recipe Spicy Peanut Dipping Sauce (recipe follows)

**1.** Combine the soy sauce, oil, sugar, cilantro, scallions, sriracha, and garlic in a large bowl. Stir in the beef, cover, and refrigerate for 1 hour.

**2.** Adjust an oven rack 6 inches from the heating element and heat the broiler.

**3.** Weave the meat onto 6-inch bamboo skewers (one piece per skewer). Lay the skewers on a wire rack set over a rimmed baking sheet and cover the skewer ends with foil. Broil the skewers until the meat is browned, 6 to 9 minutes, flipping the skewers over halfway through. Transfer the skewers to a serving platter and serve with the peanut sauce.

### Spicy Peanut Dipping Sauce

**MAKES** about 1½ cups

This sauce can be refrigerated in an airtight container for up to 24 hours; bring to room temperature before serving.

- ½ cup creamy peanut butter
- ¼ cup hot water
- 2 tablespoons juice from 1 lime
- 2 tablespoons sriracha
- 1 tablespoon soy sauce
- 1 tablespoon dark brown sugar
- 1 tablespoon chopped fresh cilantro leaves
- 2 scallions, sliced thin
- 1 medium garlic clove, minced or pressed through a garlic press (about 1 teaspoon)

Whisk the peanut butter and hot water together in a small bowl until smooth. Stir in the remaining ingredients.

## Flank Steak and Arugula Sandwiches with Red Onion

**SERVES 4**

**WHY THIS RECIPE WORKS** Steak sandwiches run the gamut from oversized "bombs" with greasy, gristly meat to precious restaurant concoctions (hold the truffle butter, please) with a price tag to match. We wanted to find a satisfying steak sandwich with some middle ground—easy to eat and gussied up with flavorful, but not costly, ingredients. We started with the choice of steak, and flank steak won out. It's relatively inexpensive, lean, and tender, as long as the meat is cooked correctly. For a flavorful browned crust, we generously seasoned the steak with salt and pepper and then pan-seared it in a very hot skillet on both sides until browned. To keep the steak tender and juicy, we allowed the meat to rest and then sliced it thin across the grain. No soft, squishy bread here; only a crusty baguette or similar artisan-style bread would do. We slathered the bread with mayonnaise doctored with soy sauce, honey, garlic, and ginger. And to finish, thinly sliced onion and arugula scattered on top of the steak provided a little spicy bite. Be sure to let the steak rest for 10 minutes after cooking and slice the steak thin across the grain.

- 1½ pounds flank steak, trimmed of excess fat and patted dry with paper towels
- Table salt and ground black pepper
- 1 tablespoon vegetable oil
- 1 baguette, cut into four 5-inch lengths, each piece split into top and bottom pieces
- 1 recipe Garlic-Soy Mayonnaise (recipe follows)
- ½ small red onion, sliced thin
- 3 ounces arugula, stemmed, washed, and dried (about 3 cups)

**1.** Heat a 12-inch skillet over high heat until very hot, about 4 minutes. While the skillet is heating, season the steak generously with salt and pepper. Add the oil to the pan and swirl to coat the bottom. Lay the steak in the pan and cook without moving it until well browned, about 5 minutes. Using tongs, flip the steak; cook until well browned on the second side, about 5 minutes longer. Transfer the steak to a carving board, tent with foil, and let rest for 10 minutes. Cut the steak into ¼-inch slices on the bias against the grain.

**2.** Spread each baguette piece with 1 tablespoon mayonnaise; portion the steak over the bottom pieces of the bread and sprinkle with salt and pepper to taste. Evenly divide the onion and arugula over the steak; top each with a baguette piece and serve.

### Garlic-Soy Mayonnaise

**MAKES** about ½ cup

Blue Plate is the test kitchen's favorite brand of mayonnaise—read why on page 1051.

- ½ cup mayonnaise
- 1 tablespoon soy sauce
- 1 teaspoon minced or grated fresh ginger
- ½ teaspoon honey
- 1 small garlic clove, minced or pressed through a garlic press (about ½ teaspoon)
- ½ teaspoon toasted sesame oil

Mix all the ingredients together in a small bowl. (The mayonnaise can be covered and refrigerated for up to 1 day.)

## Philly Cheesesteaks

**SERVES 4**

**WHY THIS RECIPE WORKS** Authentic Philly cheesesteak recipes start with a rib eye and require a meat slicer and flat-top griddle to achieve ultrathin slices with crisp edges. To make this sandwich at home, we needed a stand-in for the meat and a way to slice it thin to get it supercrisp, without any fancy equipment. We started by looking for a more economical cut of meat and landed on skirt steak. When partially frozen, skirt steak's thin profile and open-grained texture made for easy slicing, and its flavor was nearest to rib eye. To best approximate the wide griddle typically used in Philadelphia, we cooked the meat in two batches, letting any excess moisture drain off before giving it a final sear. Finally, to bind it all together, we let slices of American cheese melt into the meat; a bit of grated Parmesan boosted the flavor. If skirt steak is unavailable, substitute sirloin steak tips (also called flap meat). Top these sandwiches with chopped pickled hot peppers, sautéed onions or bell peppers, sweet relish, or hot sauce.

- 2 pounds skirt steak, trimmed and sliced with grain into 3-inch-wide strips
- 4 (8-inch) Italian sub rolls, split lengthwise
- 2 tablespoons vegetable oil
- ½ teaspoon table salt
- ⅛ teaspoon pepper
- ¼ cup grated Parmesan cheese
- 8 slices white American cheese (8 ounces)

**1.** Place steak pieces on large plate or baking sheet and freeze until very firm, about 1 hour.

**2.** Meanwhile, adjust oven rack to middle position and heat oven to 400 degrees. Spread split rolls on baking sheet and toast until lightly browned, 5 to 10 minutes.

**3.** Using sharp knife, shave steak pieces as thinly as possible against grain. Mound meat on cutting board and chop coarsely with knife 10 to 20 times.

**4.** Heat 1 tablespoon oil in 12-inch nonstick skillet over high heat until smoking. Add half of meat in even layer and cook without stirring until well browned on 1 side, 4 to 5 minutes. Stir and continue to cook until meat is no longer pink, 1 to 2 minutes. Transfer meat to colander set in large bowl. Wipe out skillet with paper towel. Repeat with remaining 1 tablespoon oil and sliced meat.

**5.** Return now-empty skillet to medium heat. Drain excess moisture from meat. Return meat to skillet (discard any liquid in bowl) and add salt and pepper. Heat, stirring constantly, until meat is warmed through, 1 to 2 minutes. Reduce heat to low, sprinkle with Parmesan, and shingle slices of American cheese over meat. Allow cheeses to melt, about 2 minutes. Using heatproof spatula or wooden spoon, fold melted cheese into meat thoroughly. Divide mixture evenly among toasted rolls. Serve immediately.

## Steak Tacos

**SERVES** 4 to 6

**WHY THIS RECIPE WORKS** Upscale steak tacos usually get their rich, beefy flavor from the grill, but cooking outdoors isn't always possible. We wanted an indoor cooking method that would always yield steak taco meat as tender, juicy, and rich-tasting as the grilled method. We didn't want to use a pricey cut of beef for this recipe, so we explored inexpensive cuts and chose flank steak for its good flavor and ready availability; when sliced against the grain, it can be just as tender as pricier cuts. To add flavor, we poked holes in the meat with a fork and rubbed it with a paste of oil, cilantro, jalapeño, garlic, and scallions; salt helped draw all the flavors into the steak and ensured juiciness. Pan searing, with a sprinkling of sugar to enhance browning, gave us a crust that mimicked the char of the grill. To maximize this effect, we cut the steak into four long pieces, which gave us more sides to brown and turn crispy. For additional flavor, we tossed the cooked steak with some marinade that we had reserved, and garnished the tacos simply with onion, cilantro, and lime wedges. In Mexico, steak tacos are often served with curtido, a relish of pickled vegetables; we devised a quick recipe for pickled onions to accompany our good-as-grilled steak tacos. Our preferred method for warming tortillas is to place each one over the medium flame of a gas burner until slightly charred, about 30 seconds per side (see page 37). We also like toasting them in a dry skillet over medium-high heat until softened and speckled with brown spots, 20 to 30 seconds per side. For a less spicy dish, remove some or all of the ribs and seeds from the jalapeños before chopping them for the marinade. In addition to the toppings suggested below, try serving the tacos with Sweet and Spicy Pickled Onions (recipe follows), thinly sliced radish or cucumber, or salsa.

**MARINADE**

- ½ cup fresh cilantro leaves
- 3 scallions, roughly chopped
- 1 jalapeño chile, stemmed and roughly chopped
- 3 garlic cloves, roughly chopped
- ½ teaspoon ground cumin
- ¼ cup vegetable oil
- 1 tablespoon lime juice

**STEAK**

- 1 (1½- to 1¾-pound) flank steak, trimmed and cut lengthwise (with grain) into 4 equal pieces
- 1 tablespoon kosher salt
- ½ teaspoon sugar
- ½ teaspoon pepper
- 2 tablespoons vegetable oil

**TACOS**

- 12 (6-inch) corn tortillas, warmed
- Fresh cilantro leaves
- Minced white onion
- Lime wedges

**1. FOR THE MARINADE:** Pulse cilantro, scallions, jalapeño, garlic, and cumin in food processor until finely chopped, 10 to 12 pulses, scraping down sides of bowl as necessary. Add oil and process until mixture is smooth and resembles pesto, about 15 seconds, scraping down sides as necessary. Transfer 2 tablespoons herb paste to medium bowl; whisk in lime juice and set aside.

**2. FOR THE STEAK:** Using dinner fork, poke each piece of steak 10 to 12 times on each side. Place in large baking dish; rub all sides of steak pieces evenly with salt and then coat with remaining herb paste. Cover with plastic wrap and refrigerate for at least 30 minutes or up to 1 hour.

**3.** Scrape herb paste off steak and sprinkle all sides of pieces evenly with sugar and pepper. Heat oil in 12-inch nonstick skillet over medium-high heat until just smoking. Place steak in skillet and cook until well browned, about 3 minutes. Flip steak and sear until second side is well browned, 2 to 3 minutes. Using tongs, stand each piece on cut side and cook, turning as necessary, until all cut sides are well browned and steak registers 125 to 130 degrees, 2 to 7 minutes. Transfer steak to cutting board and let rest for 5 minutes.

**4. FOR THE TACOS:** Slice steak against grain ⅛ inch thick. Transfer sliced steak to bowl with herb paste–lime juice mixture and toss to coat. Season with salt to taste. Spoon small amount of sliced steak into center of each warm tortilla and serve immediately, passing toppings separately.

## Sweet and Spicy Pickled Onions

**MAKES** 2 cups

The onions can be refrigerated, tightly covered, for up to one week.

- 1 red onion, halved and sliced thin (about 1½ cups)
- 1 cup red wine vinegar
- ⅓ cup sugar
- 2 jalapeño chiles, stemmed, seeded, and cut into thin rings
- ¼ teaspoon table salt

Place onions in medium heat-resistant bowl. Bring vinegar, sugar, jalapeños, and salt to simmer in small saucepan over medium-high heat, stirring occasionally, until sugar dissolves. Pour vinegar mixture over onions, cover loosely, and let cool to room temperature, about 30 minutes. Once cool, drain and discard the liquid.

## Beef Bulgogi (Korean Marinated Beef)

**SERVES** 4

**WHY THIS RECIPE WORKS** For our bulgogi rib-eye steak offered a nice combination of marbled interior and rich beef flavor. Freezing the meat in pieces firmed it up enough to be shaved superthin and treating the meat with baking soda helped it stay tender. Soy sauce, garlic, sesame oil, pepper, and onion brought savory undertones to the marinade but let the delicate flavor of the beef shine through. We cooked the beef in a moderately hot skillet until it was fully cooked. Ssamjang, a savory and spicy sauce, and daikon pickles offered heat and textural contrast to the sweet beef. To save time, prepare them while the steak is in the freezer. You can substitute 2 cups of bean sprouts and one cucumber, peeled, quartered lengthwise, seeded, and sliced thin on the bias, for the daikon. You can find the Korean fermented bean pastes doenjang and gochujang in Asian markets and online. If you can't find them, you can substitute red or white miso for the doenjang and sriracha for the gochujang. You can eat bulgogi as a plated meal with steamed rice and kimchi or wrap portions of the beef in lettuce leaves with chile sauce and eat them with your hands.

**PICKLES**

- 1 cup rice vinegar
- 2 tablespoons sugar
- 1½ teaspoons table salt
- 1 pound daikon radish, peeled and cut into 1½-inch-long matchsticks

**SSAMJANG**

- 4 scallions, white and light green parts only, minced
- ¼ cup doenjang
- 1 tablespoon gochujang
- 1 tablespoon water
- 2 teaspoons sugar
- 2 teaspoons toasted sesame oil
- 1 garlic clove, minced

**BEEF**

- 1 (1¼-pound) boneless rib-eye steak, cut crosswise into 1½-inch-wide pieces and trimmed
- 1 tablespoon water
- ¼ teaspoon baking soda
- ¼ cup chopped onion
- ¼ cup sugar
- 3 tablespoons soy sauce
- 4 garlic cloves, peeled
- 1 tablespoon toasted sesame oil
- ¼ teaspoon pepper
- 2 teaspoons vegetable oil
- 4 scallions, dark green parts only, cut into 1½-inch pieces

**1. FOR THE PICKLES:** Whisk vinegar, sugar, and salt together in medium bowl. Add daikon and toss to combine. Gently press on daikon to submerge. Cover and refrigerate for at least 30 minutes or up to 24 hours.

**2. FOR THE SSAMJANG:** Combine all ingredients in small bowl. Cover and set aside. (Sauce can be refrigerated for up to 3 days.)

**3. FOR THE BEEF:** Place beef on large plate and freeze until very firm, 35 to 40 minutes. Once firm, stand each piece on 1 cut side on cutting board and, using sharp knife, shave beef against grain as thin as possible. (Slices needn't be perfectly intact.) Combine water and baking soda in medium bowl. Add beef and toss to coat. Let sit at room temperature for 5 minutes.

**4.** Meanwhile, process onion, sugar, soy sauce, garlic, sesame oil, and pepper in food processor until smooth, about 30 seconds, scraping down sides of bowl as needed. Add onion mixture to beef and toss to evenly coat.

**5.** Heat vegetable oil in 12-inch nonstick skillet over medium-high heat until shimmering. Add beef mixture in even layer and cook, without stirring, until browned on 1 side, about 1 minute. Stir and continue to cook until beef is no longer pink, 3 to 4 minutes longer. Add scallion greens and cook, stirring constantly, until fragrant, about 30 seconds. Transfer to platter. Serve with pickles and chile sauce.

## Simple Pot Roast

SERVES 6 to 8

---

**WHY THIS RECIPE WORKS** We wanted a pot roast that was fall-apart tender with a savory sauce—a meal that was worth the wait. We determined that chuck-eye was the best choice for pot roast; its fat and connective tissue broke down and kept the meat moist during the long oven stay. Browning the meat first was important for flavor as well as color. Caramelizing the vegetables added another layer of flavor. For the braising liquid, beef and chicken broths tasted best and we added just enough water for the liquid to come halfway up the sides of the roast. We covered the pot with foil and the lid for a tight seal, so no steam (or flavor) escaped. The secret to tenderness is in the cooking time. Cooking the meat in the oven until it reached 210 degrees, then cooking it for an hour longer rewarded us with flavorful and remarkably tender meat. Most markets sell chuck-eye roast with twine tied around the center; if necessary, do this yourself. Seven-bone and top-blade roasts are also good choices for this recipe. Remember to add only enough water to come halfway up the sides of these thinner roasts, and begin checking for doneness after 2 hours. If using a top-blade roast, tie it before cooking to keep it from falling apart. Mashed or boiled potatoes are nice with pot roast.

- 1 (3½-pound) boneless chuck-eye roast
- Table salt and ground black pepper
- 2 tablespoons vegetable oil
- 1 medium onion, chopped medium
- 1 small carrot, chopped medium
- 1 small celery rib, chopped medium
- 2 medium garlic cloves, minced or pressed through a garlic press (about 2 teaspoons)
- 2 teaspoons sugar
- 1 cup low-sodium chicken broth
- 1 cup beef broth
- 1 sprig fresh thyme
- 1–1½ cups water
- ¼ cup dry red wine

**1.** Adjust an oven rack to middle position and heat oven to 300 degrees. Thoroughly pat roast dry with paper towels; sprinkle generously with salt and pepper.

**2.** Heat oil in large Dutch oven over medium-high heat until shimmering but not smoking. Brown roast thoroughly on all sides, reducing heat if fat begins to smoke, 8 to 10 minutes. Transfer roast to large plate; set aside. Reduce heat to medium; add onion, carrot, and celery to pot and cook, stirring occasionally, until beginning to brown, 6 to 8 minutes. Add garlic and sugar; cook until fragrant, about 30 seconds. Add chicken and beef broths and thyme, scraping bottom of pan with wooden spoon to loosen browned bits. Return roast and any accumulated juices to pot; add enough water to come halfway up sides of roast. Place large piece of foil over pot and cover tightly with lid; bring liquid to simmer over medium heat, then transfer pot to oven. Cook, turning roast every 30 minutes, until fully tender and meat fork or sharp knife easily slips in and out of meat, 3½ to 4 hours.

**3.** Transfer roast to carving board; tent with foil to keep warm. Allow liquid in pot to settle for about 5 minutes, then use wide spoon to skim fat off surface; discard thyme sprig. Boil over high heat until reduced to about 1½ cups, about 8 minutes. Add red wine and reduce again to 1½ cups, about 2 minutes. Season with salt and pepper to taste.

**4.** Using chef's or carving knife, cut meat into ½-inch-thick slices, or pull apart into large pieces; transfer meat to warmed serving platter and pour about ½ cup sauce over meat. Serve, passing remaining sauce separately.

### Simple Pot Roast with Root Vegetables

Add 1½ pounds carrots, sliced ½ inch thick; 1½ pounds small red potatoes, halved if larger than 1½ inches in diameter; and 1 pound parsnips, sliced ½ inch thick, to Dutch oven after cooking beef for about 3 hours, submerging them in liquid. Continue to cook until vegetables are almost tender, 30 minutes to 1 hour longer. Transfer roast to carving board; tent with foil to keep warm. Allow liquid in pot to settle for about 5 minutes, then use wide spoon to skim fat off surface; remove thyme sprig. Add wine and salt and pepper to taste; boil over high heat until vegetables are tender, 5 to 10 minutes. Using slotted spoon, transfer vegetables to warmed serving platter. Using carving knife, cut meat into ½-inch-thick slices or pull apart into large pieces; transfer meat to bowl or platter with vegetables and pour about ½ cup sauce over meat and vegetables. Serve, passing remaining sauce separately.

## Old-Fashioned Pot Roast

SERVES 6 to 8

---

**WHY THIS RECIPE WORKS** This recipe creates a meltingly tender pot roast in a full-bodied gravy. To start, we separated the roast into two pieces, which allowed us to remove the fat in between them. Salting the roast improved its flavor and allowed us to skip browning. Sautéing the onion, celery, carrot, and garlic before we added them to the pot gave them more depth of flavor. We used beef broth as the cooking liquid and boosted the flavor with garlic, tomato paste, red wine, thyme, and bay leaves. Finally, sealing the pot with foil and the lid concentrated the steam for an even simmer and fork-tender meat. The roast can be made up to 2 days ahead: Follow the recipe through step 4, transferring the cooked roasts to a large bowl and straining the liquid as directed in step 5. Transfer the vegetables to the bowl with the roasts, cover with plastic wrap, cut vents in the plastic, and refrigerate overnight or up to 48 hours. One hour before serving, adjust the oven rack to the middle position and heat the oven to 325 degrees. Transfer the cold roasts to a carving board, slice them against the grain into ½-inch-thick slices, place them in a 13 by 9-inch baking dish, cover tightly with foil, and bake until heated through, about 45 minutes. While the roasts heat, puree the sauce and vegetables as directed in step 5. Bring the sauce to a simmer and finish as directed in step 6.

- 1 (3½ to 4-pound) boneless chuck-eye roast, pulled into 2 pieces at the natural seam and fat trimmed
- Table salt and ground black pepper
- 2 tablespoons unsalted butter
- 2 medium onions, halved and sliced thin (about 2 cups)
- 1 large carrot, peeled and chopped medium (about 1 cup)
- 1 celery rib, chopped medium (about ¾ cup)
- 2 medium garlic cloves, minced or pressed through a garlic press (about 2 teaspoons)
- 1 cup beef broth, plus 1 to 2 cups for the sauce
- ½ cup dry red wine, plus ¼ cup for the sauce
- 1 tablespoon tomato paste
- 1 bay leaf
- 1 sprig fresh thyme plus ¼ teaspoon chopped fresh thyme leaves
- 1 tablespoon balsamic vinegar

**1.** Sprinkle the pieces of meat with 1½ teaspoons salt, place on a wire rack set over a rimmed baking sheet and let stand at room temperature for 1 hour.

**2.** Adjust an oven rack to the lower-middle position and heat the oven to 300 degrees. Heat the butter in a heavy-bottomed Dutch oven over medium heat. When the foaming subsides, add the onions and cook, stirring occasionally, until softened and beginning to brown, 8 to 10 minutes. Add the carrot and celery and continue to cook, stirring occasionally, for 5 minutes longer. Add the garlic and cook until fragrant, about 30 seconds. Stir in 1 cup of the broth, ½ cup of the wine, the tomato paste, bay leaf, and thyme sprig; bring to a simmer.

**3.** Season the beef generously with pepper. Using three pieces of kitchen twine, tie each piece of meat into a loaf shape for even cooking.

**4.** Nestle the roasts on top of the vegetables. Place a large piece of foil over the pot and cover tightly with the lid; transfer the pot to the oven. Cook the roasts until fully tender and a sharp knife easily slips in and out of the meat, 3½ to 4 hours, turning the roasts halfway through cooking.

**5.** Transfer the roasts to a carving board and tent loosely with foil. Strain the liquid through a fine-mesh strainer into a 4-cup liquid measuring cup. Discard the thyme sprig and bay leaf. Transfer the vegetables to a blender. Allow the liquid to settle for 5 minutes, then skim any fat off the surface. Add the remaining beef broth as necessary to bring the total amount of liquid to 3 cups. Place the liquid in the blender with the vegetables and blend until smooth, about 2 minutes. Transfer the sauce to a medium saucepan and bring to a simmer over medium heat.

**6.** While the sauce heats, remove the twine from the roasts and slice them against the grain into ½-inch-thick slices. Transfer the meat to a large serving platter. Stir the chopped thyme, remaining ¼ cup wine, and the balsamic vinegar into the sauce and season with salt and pepper to taste. Serve immediately, passing the sauce separately.

### Old-Fashioned Pot Roast with Root Vegetables

Follow the recipe for Old-Fashioned Pot Roast, adding 1 pound carrots, peeled and cut crosswise into 2-inch pieces; 1 pound parsnips, peeled and cut crosswise into 2-inch pieces; and 1½ pounds russet potatoes, peeled, halved lengthwise, and each half quartered, to the pot in step 4 after the roasts have cooked for 3 hours. Once the pot roast and vegetables are fully cooked, transfer any large pieces of carrot, parsnip, and potato to a serving platter using a slotted spoon, cover tightly with foil, and proceed with the recipe as directed.

## Pot Roast with Root Vegetables

**SERVES 6**

**WHY THIS RECIPE WORKS** A good pot roast should be tender. For a supremely tender pot roast with a spoonable sauce, we cooked ours for 3 to 3½ hours, adding root vegetables partway through. A chuck-eye roast is our favorite cut for pot roast; opening it along its natural seam into two lobes and trimming excess fat eliminated greasiness and promised thorough seasoning. A stovetop sear created a caramelized exterior before we moved the roast to the oven where it could braise more evenly. To ensure that the vegetables were perfectly cooked and imbued with beefy flavor, we added them partway through the roast's cooking time. By the time the roast emerged, it was so tender a fork met no resistance. Use a good-quality medium-bodied wine, such as a Côtes du Rhône or a Pinot Noir.

- 1 (3½- to 4-pound) boneless beef chuck-eye roast, pulled into 2 pieces at natural seam, trimmed, and tied at 1-inch intervals
- 1 teaspoon table salt
- ½ teaspoon pepper
- 3 tablespoons vegetable oil, divided
- 1 onion, chopped
- 1 celery rib, chopped
- 4 garlic cloves, minced
- 2 teaspoons sugar
- 1 teaspoon fresh minced thyme or ¼ teaspoon dried
- 1 cup chicken broth
- 1 cup beef broth
- 1 cup water
- 1½ pounds carrots, peeled and cut into 3-inch pieces
- 1½ pounds red potatoes, unpeeled, cut into 1½-inch pieces
- 1½ pounds parsnips, peeled and cut into 3-inch pieces
- ⅓ cup red wine

**1.** Adjust oven rack to lower-middle position and heat oven to 300 degrees. Pat beef dry with paper towels and sprinkle with salt and pepper. Heat 2 tablespoons oil in Dutch oven over medium-high heat until just smoking. Add both beef roasts and brown on all sides, 7 to 10 minutes; transfer to large plate.

**2.** Add remaining 1 tablespoon oil, onion, and celery to now-empty pot and cook over medium heat until vegetables are softened, 5 to 7 minutes. Stir in garlic, sugar, and thyme and cook until fragrant, about 30 seconds. Stir in broths and water, scraping up any browned bits.

**3.** Add browned roasts along with any accumulated juices to pot and bring to simmer. Cover, transfer pot to oven, and cook for 2 hours, flipping roasts halfway through cooking.

4. Remove pot from oven. Nestle carrots into pot around meat and sprinkle potatoes and parsnips over top. Return covered pot to oven and cook until meat and vegetables are very tender, 1 to 1½ hours.

5. Remove pot from oven. Transfer roasts to carving board and tent with foil. Transfer vegetables to large bowl and season with salt and pepper to taste; cover to keep warm.

6. Using large spoon, skim any fat from surface of braising liquid. Stir in wine and simmer until sauce measures 2 cups, about 15 minutes. Season with salt and pepper to taste. Transfer vegetables to serving platter. Remove twine from roasts, slice meat against grain ¼ inch thick, and transfer to serving platter. Spoon half of sauce over meat. Serve, passing remaining sauce separately.

## Beef Braised in Barolo

**SERVES 6**

**WHY THIS RECIPE WORKS** Italian pot roast is comprised of an inexpensive cut of beef braised in wine. We wanted tender meat in a rich, savory sauce that would do justice to the wine. A chuck-eye roast can withstand a long braise, but its line of fat in the middle felt was out of place in this refined dish. Separating one roast into two smaller ones enabled us to discard most of that fat before cooking. We then tied the roasts together and browned them in fat rendered from pancetta. After browning aromatics, we poured a whole bottle of wine into the pot. The Barolo's bold flavor needed tempering, so we added canned diced tomatoes. When the meat was done, we reduced the sauce and strained it. The resulting winey sauce was full-flavored and lustrous. Don't skip tying the roasts—it keeps them intact during the long cooking time. Purchase pancetta that is cut to order, about ¼ inch thick. If pancetta is not available, substitute an equal amount of salt pork (find the meatiest piece possible), cut it into ¼-inch cubes, and boil it in 3 cups of water for about 2 minutes to remove excess salt. After draining, use it as you would pancetta.

- 1 (3½-pound) boneless beef chuck-eye roast
- 1 teaspoon table salt
- ½ teaspoon pepper
- 4 ounces pancetta, cut into ¼-inch cubes
- 2 onions, chopped
- 2 carrots, chopped
- 2 celery ribs, chopped
- 1 tablespoon tomato paste
- 3 garlic cloves, minced
- 1 tablespoon all-purpose flour
- ½ teaspoon sugar
- 1 (750-ml) bottle Barolo wine
- 1 (14.5-ounce) can diced tomatoes, drained
- 1 sprig fresh thyme plus 1 teaspoon minced thyme
- 1 sprig fresh rosemary
- 10 sprigs fresh parsley

1. Adjust oven rack to middle position and heat oven to 300 degrees. Pull roast apart at its major seams (delineated by lines of fat) into 2 halves. Use knife as necessary. With knife, remove large knobs of fat from each piece, leaving thin layer of fat on meat. Tie 3 pieces of kitchen twine around each piece of meat. Thoroughly pat beef dry with paper towels; sprinkle with salt and pepper. Place pancetta in large Dutch oven; cook over medium heat, stirring occasionally, until browned and crisp, about 8 minutes. Using slotted spoon, transfer pancetta to paper towel–lined plate and reserve. Pour off all but 2 tablespoons of fat; set Dutch oven over medium-high heat and heat fat until just smoking. Add beef to pot and cook until well browned on all sides, about 8 minutes total. Transfer beef to large plate; set aside.

2. Reduce heat to medium; add onions, carrots, celery, and tomato paste to pot and cook, stirring occasionally, until vegetables begin to soften and brown, about 6 minutes. Add garlic, flour, sugar, and reserved pancetta; cook, stirring constantly, until combined and fragrant, about 30 seconds. Add wine and tomatoes, scraping up any browned bits; add thyme sprig, rosemary, and parsley. Return roast and any accumulated juice to pot; increase heat to high and bring liquid to boil, then place large sheet of aluminum foil over pot and cover tightly with lid. Set pot in oven and cook, using tongs to turn beef every 45 minutes, until dinner fork easily slips in and out of meat, about 3 hours.

3. Transfer beef to carving board and tent with foil to keep warm. Allow braising liquid to settle for about 5 minutes, then, using wide shallow spoon, skim fat off surface. Add minced thyme, bring liquid to boil over high heat, and cook, whisking vigorously to help vegetables break down, until mixture is thickened and reduced to about 3½ cups, about 18 minutes. Strain liquid through large fine-mesh strainer, pressing on solids with spatula to extract as much liquid as possible; you should have 1½ cups strained sauce (if necessary, return strained sauce to Dutch oven and reduce to 1½ cups). Discard solids in strainer. Season sauce with salt and pepper to taste.

4. Remove kitchen twine from meat and discard. Using chef's knife or carving knife, slice meat against grain ½ inch thick. Divide meat among warmed bowls or plates; pour about ¼ cup sauce over each portion and serve immediately.

## ASSEMBLING BRACIOLE

**1.** Lay 1 steak on cutting board with grain running parallel to counter edge. Slice horizontally to create 2 thin pieces. Repeat with second steak.

**2.** Cover 1 piece with plastic wrap and pound into rough rectangle measuring about ¼ inch thick. Repeat with remaining 3 pieces.

**3.** Cut each piece in half, with grain, to create total of 8 pieces.

**4.** Arrange 4 pieces so grain runs parallel to counter edge. Distribute half of filling over pieces and top with prosciutto slice.

**5.** Keeping filling in place, roll each piece away from you to form tight log.

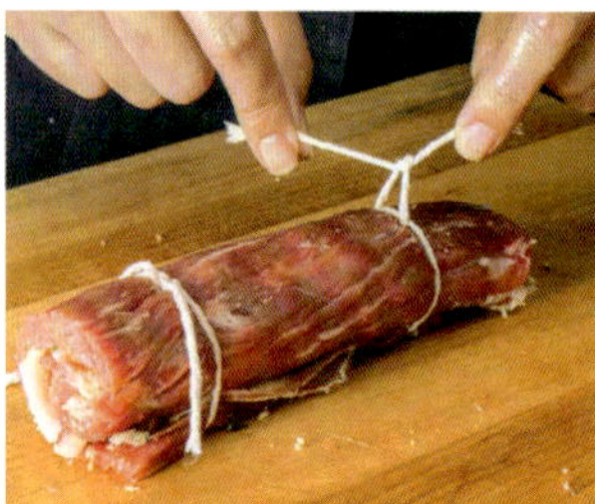

**6.** Tie each roll with 2 pieces kitchen twine to secure. Repeat process with remaining steak pieces, filling, and prosciutto.

# Braciole

**SERVES** 6 to 8

**WHY THIS RECIPE WORKS** For our take on Italian stuffed beef rolls, we chose flank steak rather than top or bottom round (the other common choices) because its loose grain made it easier to pound thin and its higher fat content meant that it emerged from the oven tender and moist. Our filling was on the bold side, including umami-rich ingredients such as prosciutto, anchovies, and fontina, a good melter that also brought much-needed fat to the dish. In addition, a gremolata-inspired mix provided the filling with a jolt of flavor and freshness. Finally, we added beef broth to the tomato sauce to integrate the beef and the sauce into a unified whole. Cut sixteen 10-inch lengths of kitchen twine before starting the recipe. You can substitute sharp provolone for the fontina, if desired. For the most tender braciole, be sure to roll the meat so that the grain runs parallel to the length of the roll. Serve the braciole and sauce together, with pasta or polenta, or separately, as a pasta course with the sauce followed by the meat.

- 7 tablespoons extra-virgin olive oil, divided
- 10 garlic cloves, minced, divided
- 2 teaspoons grated lemon zest
- 3 anchovy fillets, rinsed and minced
- ⅓ cup plus 2 tablespoons chopped fresh basil, divided
- ⅓ cup minced fresh parsley
- ⅓ cup grated Pecorino Romano cheese, plus extra for serving
- ⅓ cup plain dried bread crumbs
- 3 ounces fontina cheese, shredded (¾ cup)
- 1 (2- to 2½-pound) flank steak, trimmed
- 8 thin slices prosciutto (4 ounces)
- 1 teaspoon kosher salt
- ½ teaspoon pepper
- 1 large onion, chopped fine
- ¼ teaspoon red pepper flakes
- ¼ cup tomato paste
- ¾ cup dry red wine
- 1 (28-ounce) can crushed tomatoes
- 2 cups beef broth

**1.** Adjust oven rack to lower-middle position and heat oven to 325 degrees. Stir 3 tablespoons oil, half of garlic, lemon zest, and anchovies together in medium bowl. Add ⅓ cup basil, parsley, Pecorino, and bread crumbs and stir to incorporate. Stir in fontina until evenly distributed and set aside filling.

**2.** Halve steak against grain to create 2 smaller steaks. Lay 1 steak on cutting board with grain running parallel to counter edge. Holding blade of chef's knife parallel to counter, halve steak horizontally to create 2 thin pieces. Repeat with remaining steak. Cover 1 piece with plastic wrap and, using meat pounder, flatten into rough rectangle measuring no more than ¼ inch thick. Repeat pounding with remaining 3 pieces. Cut each piece in half, with grain, to create total of 8 pieces.

**3.** Lay 4 pieces on cutting board with grain running parallel to counter edge (if 1 side is shorter than the other, place shorter side closer to you). Distribute half of filling evenly over pieces.

Top filling on each piece with 1 slice of prosciutto, folding to fit, and press firmly. Keeping filling in place, roll each piece away from you to form tight log. Tie each roll with 2 pieces kitchen twine to secure. Repeat process with remaining steak pieces, filling, and prosciutto. Sprinkle rolls on both sides with salt and pepper.

**4.** Heat remaining ¼ cup oil in large Dutch oven over medium-high heat until shimmering. Brown rolls on 2 sides, 8 to 10 minutes. Transfer rolls to plate. Add onion to pot and cook, stirring occasionally, until softened and browned, 5 to 7 minutes. Stir in pepper flakes and remaining garlic; cook until fragrant, 30 seconds. Stir in tomato paste and cook until slightly darkened, 3 to 4 minutes. Add wine and cook, scraping up any browned bits. Stir in tomatoes and broth. Return rolls to pot; bring to simmer. Cover and transfer to oven. Braise until meat is fork-tender, 2½ to 3 hours, using tongs to flip rolls halfway through braising.

**5.** Transfer braciole to serving dish and discard twine. Stir remaining 2 tablespoons basil into tomato sauce and season with salt and pepper to taste. Pour sauce over braciole and serve, passing extra Pecorino separately.

## Pressure-Cooker Pot Roast

**SERVES 6 TO 8**

**WHY THIS RECIPE WORKS** Pressure-cooker pot roast recipes can produce fatty meat and bland, watery gravy. In order to put the pressure cooker to work for us, we made a few key adjustments. First we split the roast into two smaller pieces to speed cooking and allow for better trimming of fat. We decreased the liquid in the pot to account for very little evaporation and we also overcooked the vegetables and pureed them into the gravy for better flavor and consistency. Finally, we added some baking soda to encourage the Maillard reaction in the pressurized pot. If using an electric pressure cooker, turn off the cooker immediately after the pressurized cooking time and let the pressure release naturally for 10 minutes; do not let the cooker switch to the warm setting. To adjust for differences among pressure cookers, cook the roasts for the recommended time, check for doneness, and, if needed, repressurize and cook up to 10 minutes longer. A half teaspoon of red wine vinegar can be substituted for the wine.

- 1 (3½- to 4-pound) boneless beef chuck-eye roast, pulled into 2 pieces at natural seam and trimmed of large pieces of fat
- Kosher salt and pepper
- 4 tablespoons unsalted butter, cut into 4 pieces
- 1 onion, sliced thick
- 1 celery rib, sliced thick
- 1 carrot, peeled and sliced thick
- ¼ teaspoon baking soda
- 1 cup beef broth
- 2 teaspoons soy sauce
- 2 bay leaves
- 1 tablespoon red wine
- 1 sprig fresh thyme

**1.** Using 3 pieces of kitchen twine per roast, tie each roast crosswise at equal intervals into loaf shape. Season roasts with salt and pepper and set aside.

**2.** Melt 2 tablespoons butter in pressure cooker over medium heat; refrigerate remaining 2 tablespoons butter. Add onion, celery, carrot, and baking soda to pot and cook until onion breaks down and liquid turns golden brown, about 5 minutes. Stir in broth, soy sauce, and bay leaves, scraping up any browned bits. Nestle roasts side by side on top of vegetables in cooker.

**3.** Lock lid in place and bring pot to high pressure over high heat, 3 to 8 minutes. As soon as indicator signals that pot has reached high pressure, reduce heat to medium-low and cook for 55 minutes, adjusting heat as needed to maintain high pressure.

**4.** Remove pot from heat and let pressure release naturally for 10 minutes. Quick-release any remaining pressure, then remove lid, allowing steam to escape away from you. Transfer roasts to carving board, tent with aluminum foil, and let rest for 20 minutes.

**5.** Meanwhile, strain liquid through fine-mesh strainer into fat separator; discard bay leaves. Transfer vegetables in strainer to blender. Let liquid settle for 5 minutes, then pour defatted liquid into blender with vegetables. Blend until smooth, about 1 minute. Transfer sauce to medium saucepan. Add wine, thyme sprig, and 2 tablespoons chilled butter and bring to boil over high heat. Cook until sauce is thickened and measures 2 cups, 5 to 8 minutes.

**6.** Remove twine from roasts and slice against grain into ½-inch-thick slices. Transfer meat to serving platter and season with salt to taste. Remove thyme sprig from sauce and season sauce with salt and pepper to taste. Spoon half of sauce over meat. Serve, passing remaining sauce separately.

## Easy Beef Tenderloin with Harissa Spice Rub and Cilantro-Mint Relish

**SERVES 8** **SEASON 26**

**WHY THIS RECIPE WORKS** This impressive beef tenderloin is simply rubbed with spices and then roasted in a low oven to a perfect medium-rare. The spices not only add flavor but also give the tenderloin a beautiful, deep red crust, so there is no need to sear the roast. Rubbing a little honey over the tenderloin helps the spices stick nicely and adds a welcome counterpoint to the savory spices. A final burst of broiler heat at the end of cooking helps toast the spice crust before serving. Look for a fatter, shorter roast over a longer, skinnier one. If your roast is particularly narrow, begin checking for doneness at least 30 minutes early in step 2. If you're buying an untrimmed tenderloin to trim yourself, be sure it weighs 6 to 7 pounds. You may need to tuck the tapered end of the roast underneath by 3 to 5 inches to create a more even shape before tying. Serve with Cilantro-Mint Relish (recipe follows).

- 1 (4- to 5-pound) trimmed beef tenderloin roast, tied at 1-inch intervals
- 1 tablespoon kosher salt
- Vegetable oil spray
- 2 tablespoons paprika
- 1 tablespoon ground coriander
- 1 tablespoon ground dried Aleppo pepper
- 1 teaspoon ground cumin
- 1 teaspoon garlic powder
- ¾ teaspoon caraway seeds
- 3 tablespoons honey, warmed

**1.** Pat roast dry with paper towels, then rub with salt. Wrap roast with plastic wrap and refrigerate for at least 6 hours or up to 24 hours.

**2.** Adjust oven rack to middle position and heat oven to 250 degrees. Spray wire rack with oil spray and set inside aluminum foil–lined rimmed baking sheet. Combine paprika, coriander, Aleppo pepper, cumin, garlic powder, and caraway seeds in small bowl. Unwrap roast, pat dry with paper towels, and set on prepared rack. Brush top and sides of roast with honey, then sprinkle evenly with spice mixture, pressing gently to adhere. Spray roast lightly with oil spray. Roast until meat registers 115 degrees (for medium-rare) or 125 degrees (for medium), 1½ to 2 hours.

**3.** Remove roast from oven and heat broiler. Broil roast until spice crust has toasted slightly and meat registers 120 to 125 degrees (for medium-rare) or 130 to 135 degrees (for medium), 5 to 10 minutes. Transfer roast to carving board and let rest for 20 minutes before slicing and serving.

### Cilantro-Mint Relish

**MAKES** 1¼ cups

Mincing the garlic to a paste mellows out its sharp bite.

- 1 cup chopped fresh cilantro
- ½ cup chopped fresh mint
- 4 scallions, sliced thin
- ½ cup extra-virgin olive oil
- 3 garlic cloves, minced to a paste
- 2 tablespoons lemon juice
- ¼ teaspoon table salt

Combine all ingredients in serving bowl and set aside until ready to serve. (Sauce can be refrigerated for up to 24 hours; bring to room temperature before serving.)

## Roast Beef Tenderloin

**SERVES** 4 to 6

**WHY THIS RECIPE WORKS** There's nothing like the buttery texture of a roasted beef tenderloin. Ideally, it has rosy meat all the way through and a deep brown crust. We wanted a technique that produced perfectly cooked and deeply flavored meat. We opted for a center-cut piece; it's already trimmed and lacks the narrow "tail" of the whole cut. We first tried searing the meat in the oven, but it never browned evenly. Stovetop browning was better for producing a crust, but the roast still came out of the oven with a gray band. The trick was to reverse the process, first roasting the meat in the oven, then searing it. Lowering the oven temperature eliminated the ring of overcooked meat. To add flavor to this mild cut of beef, simply salting it before roasting worked wonders; rubbing the roast with softened butter added richness. A flavored butter served alongside was the final touch. With its uniformly rosy meat, deep brown crust, and beefy flavor, this tenderloin was worthy of its price tag. Ask your butcher to prepare a trimmed, center-cut Châteaubriand from the whole tenderloin, as this cut is not usually available without special ordering. If you are cooking for a crowd, this recipe can be doubled to make two roasts. Sear the roasts one after the other, wiping out the pan and adding new oil after searing the first roast. Both pieces of meat can be roasted on the same rack.

- 1 (2-pound) beef tenderloin center-cut Châteaubriand, trimmed
- 1 teaspoon table salt
- 1 teaspoon coarsely ground black pepper
- 2 tablespoons unsalted butter, softened
- 1 tablespoon vegetable oil
- 1 recipe flavored butter (recipes follow)

**1.** Using 12-inch lengths of kitchen twine, tie the roast crosswise at 1½-inch intervals. Sprinkle the roast evenly with the salt, cover loosely with plastic wrap, and let stand at room temperature for 1 hour. Meanwhile, adjust an oven rack to the middle position and heat the oven to 300 degrees.

**2.** Pat the roast dry with paper towels. Sprinkle the roast evenly with the pepper and spread the butter evenly over the surface. Transfer the roast to a wire rack set over a rimmed baking sheet. Roast until the center of the roast registers 125 degrees on an instant-read thermometer for medium-rare (40 to 55 minutes), or 135 degrees for medium (55 to 70 minutes), flipping the roast halfway through cooking.

**3.** Heat the oil in a 12-inch heavy-bottomed skillet over medium-high heat until just smoking. Place the roast in the skillet and sear until well browned on four sides, 1 to 2 minutes per side (a total of 4 to 8 minutes). Transfer the roast to a carving board and spread 2 tablespoons of the flavored butter evenly over the top of the roast; let rest for 15 minutes. Remove the twine and cut the meat crosswise into ½-inch-thick slices. Serve, passing the remaining flavored butter separately.

### Shallot and Parsley Butter

**MAKES** about ½ cup

- 4 tablespoons (½ stick) unsalted butter, softened
- 1 small shallot, minced (about 1 tablespoon)
- 1 medium garlic clove, minced or pressed through a garlic press (about 1 teaspoon)
- 1 tablespoon finely chopped fresh parsley leaves
- ¼ teaspoon table salt
- ¼ teaspoon ground black pepper

Combine all the ingredients in a medium bowl.

### Chipotle and Garlic Butter with Lime and Cilantro

**MAKES** about ½ cup

- 5 tablespoons unsalted butter, softened
- 1 medium chipotle chile in adobo sauce, seeded and minced, with 1 teaspoon adobo sauce
- 1 medium garlic clove, minced or pressed through a garlic press (about 1 teaspoon)
- 1 teaspoon honey
- 1 teaspoon grated zest from 1 lime
- 1 tablespoon minced fresh cilantro leaves
- ½ teaspoon table salt

Combine all the ingredients in a medium bowl.

## Horseradish-Crusted Beef Tenderloin

**SERVES** 6

**WHY THIS RECIPE WORKS** A crisp horseradish crust contrasts nicely with the mild flavor of beef tenderloin. We wanted the bracing flavor of horseradish with a crisp, golden crust that would add textural contrast to rosy, medium-rare meat—and we wanted it to stick. We chose to use a center-cut roast, also called a Châteaubriand, because its uniform shape cooks evenly. After lightly flouring the meat and applying a thin wash of egg white, we rolled the roast in crushed potato chips and panko bread crumbs mixed with horseradish, mayonnaise, shallot, garlic, and herbs. Potato chips may seem unusual, but they kept their crunch and contributed lots of flavor, particularly when we made our own by frying shredded potato in oil. To make the crust adhere to the meat after being sliced, we replaced the egg white with gelatin. Because both meat and gelatin are made up of linear proteins that form tight bonds with each other, the gelatin mixture bound the bread crumbs firmly to the meat, yet yielded slightly as we cut it. And to prevent the crust from turning soggy from meat juices, we seared the meat in a hot skillet and let it rest so that its juices could drain off before applying the paste and the crumbs. Then we coated only the top and sides of the tenderloin, leaving an "opening" on the bottom for meat juices to escape as it roasted. If using table salt, reduce the amount in step 1 to 1½ teaspoons. Add the gelatin to the horseradish paste at the last moment or the mixture will become unspreadable. If desired, serve the roast with Horseradish Cream Sauce (page 413; you will need 2 jars of prepared horseradish for both the roast and sauce). If you choose to salt the tenderloin in advance, remove it from the refrigerator 1 hour before cooking. To make this recipe 1 day in advance, prepare it through step 3, but in step 2 do not toss the bread crumbs with the other ingredients until you are ready to sear the meat.

- 1 (2-pound) beef tenderloin center-cut Châteaubriand, trimmed of fat and silver skin
- Kosher salt
- 3 tablespoons panko (Japanese-style bread crumbs)
- 1 cup plus 2 teaspoons vegetable oil
- 1¼ teaspoons ground black pepper
- 1 small shallot, minced (about 1 tablespoon)
- 2 medium garlic cloves, minced or pressed through a garlic press (about 2 teaspoons)
- ¼ cup well-drained prepared horseradish
- 2 tablespoons minced fresh parsley leaves
- ½ teaspoon minced fresh thyme leaves
- 1 small russet potato (about 6 ounces), peeled and grated on the large holes of a box grater
- 1½ teaspoons mayonnaise
- 1½ teaspoons Dijon mustard
- ½ teaspoon powdered gelatin

**1.** Sprinkle the roast with 1 tablespoon salt, cover with plastic wrap, and let stand at room temperature for 1 hour or refrigerate for up to 24 hours. Adjust an oven rack to the middle position and heat the oven to 400 degrees.

**2.** Toss the bread crumbs with 2 teaspoons of the oil, ¼ teaspoon salt, and ¼ teaspoon of the pepper in a 10-inch nonstick skillet. Cook over medium heat, stirring frequently, until deep golden brown, 3 to 5 minutes. Transfer to a rimmed baking sheet and cool to room temperature (wipe out the skillet). Once cool, toss the bread crumbs with the shallot, garlic, 2 tablespoons of the horseradish, the parsley, and thyme.

**3.** Rinse the grated potato under cold water, then squeeze dry in a dish towel. Transfer the potatoes and remaining 1 cup oil to the skillet. Cook over high heat, stirring frequently, until the potatoes are golden brown and crisp, 6 to 8 minutes. Using a slotted spoon, transfer the potatoes to a paper towel–lined plate and season lightly with salt; let cool for 5 minutes. Reserve 1 tablespoon oil from the skillet and discard the remainder. Once the potatoes are cool, transfer to a quart-size zipper-lock bag and crush until coarsely ground. Transfer the potatoes to the baking sheet with the bread-crumb mixture and toss to combine.

**4.** Pat the exterior of the tenderloin dry with paper towels and sprinkle evenly with the remaining 1 teaspoon pepper. Heat the reserved 1 tablespoon oil in a 12-inch nonstick skillet over medium-high heat until just smoking. Sear the tenderloin until well browned on all sides, 5 to 7 minutes. Transfer to a wire rack set over a rimmed baking sheet and let rest for 10 minutes.

**5.** Combine the remaining 2 tablespoons horseradish, mayonnaise, and mustard in a small bowl. Just before coating the tenderloin, add the gelatin and stir to combine. Spread the horseradish paste on the top and sides of the meat, leaving the bottom and ends bare. Roll the coated sides of the tenderloin in the bread-crumb mixture, pressing gently so the crumbs adhere in an even layer that just covers the horseradish paste; pat off any excess.

**6.** Return the tenderloin to the wire rack. Roast until an instant-read thermometer inserted into the center of the roast registers 120 to 125 degrees for medium-rare, 25 to 30 minutes.

**7.** Transfer the roast to a carving board and let rest for 20 minutes. Carefully cut the meat crosswise into ½-inch-thick slices and serve.

## Roast Beef Tenderloin with Caramelized Onion and Mushroom Stuffing

**SERVES** 4 to 6

**WHY THIS RECIPE WORKS** Add a rich stuffing to beef tenderloin and you've got the ultimate main course—at least in theory. We found three problems with stuffed tenderloin. The tenderloin's thin, tapered shape made for uneven cooking; in the time it took to develop a nice crust, the meat overcooked; and "deluxe" fillings such as lobster and chanterelles were so chunky they fell out of the meat when sliced. We had determined for our Roast Beef Tenderloin recipe (page 402) that a center-cut tenderloin cooks more evenly than a whole one, and its cylindrical shape had an added advantage here as it made the roast easier to stuff. But making a slit in the roast didn't give us much room for stuffing; double-butterflying the meat, to open it up like a book, gave us more space. After we stuffed, rolled, and tied it, we rubbed the roast with salt, pepper, and olive oil, which added flavor and helped develop a good crust when we seared the meat. We could fit just a cupful of stuffing in the meat, so we knew the flavors had to be intense. We finally decided on woodsy cremini mushrooms and caramelized onions, seasoned with Madeira and garlic; this combination made a savory-sweet jam-like filling that spread easily on the meat and held together well. Baby spinach added color and freshness. This roast was juicy and flavorful, and the filling was the ultimate touch of luxury. The roast can be stuffed, rolled, and tied a day ahead, but don't season the exterior until you are ready to cook it. This recipe can be doubled to make two roasts. Sear the roasts one after the other, cleaning the pan and adding new oil after searing the first roast. Both pieces of meat can be roasted on the same rack.

**STUFFING**

- 8 ounces cremini mushrooms, cleaned, stems trimmed, and broken into rough pieces
- 1½ teaspoons unsalted butter
- 1½ teaspoons olive oil
- 1 medium onion, halved and sliced ¼ inch thick
- ¼ teaspoon table salt
- ⅛ teaspoon ground black pepper
- 1 medium garlic clove, minced or pressed through a garlic press (about 1 teaspoon)
- ½ cup Madeira or sweet Marsala wine

**BEEF ROAST**

- 1 (2- to 3-pound) beef tenderloin center-cut Châteaubriand, trimmed and butterflied
- Table salt and ground black pepper
- ½ cup lightly packed baby spinach
- 3 tablespoons olive oil

**HERB BUTTER**

- 4 tablespoons (½ stick) unsalted butter, softened
- 1 tablespoon chopped fresh parsley leaves
- ¾ teaspoon chopped fresh thyme leaves
- 1 medium garlic clove, minced or pressed through a garlic press (about 1 teaspoon)
- 1 tablespoon whole grain mustard
- ⅛ teaspoon table salt
- ⅛ teaspoon ground black pepper

**1. FOR THE STUFFING:** Pulse the mushrooms in a food processor until coarsely chopped, about 6 pulses. Heat the butter and oil in a 12-inch nonstick skillet over medium-high heat. Add the onion, salt, and pepper; cook, stirring occasionally, until the onion begins to soften, about 5 minutes. Add the mushrooms and cook, stirring occasionally, until all the moisture has evaporated, 5 to 7 minutes. Reduce the heat to medium and continue to cook, stirring frequently, until the vegetables are deeply browned and sticky, about 10 minutes. Stir in the garlic and cook until fragrant, about 30 seconds. Slowly stir in the Madeira and cook, scraping the bottom of the skillet to loosen any browned bits, until the liquid has evaporated, 2 to 3 minutes. Transfer the onion-mushroom mixture to a plate and cool to room temperature.

**2. FOR THE ROAST:** Pat the tenderloin dry and season the cut side of the tenderloin liberally with salt and pepper. Spread the cooled stuffing mixture over the interior of the beef, leaving a ½-inch border on all sides; press the spinach leaves on top of the stuffing. Roll the roast lengthwise, making it as compact as possible without squeezing out any filling. Evenly space eight pieces of kitchen twine (each about 14 inches) beneath the roast. Tie each strand tightly around the roast, starting with the ends.

**3.** In a small bowl, stir together 1 tablespoon of the olive oil, 1½ teaspoons salt, and 1½ teaspoons pepper. Rub the roast with the oil mixture and let stand at room temperature for 1 hour.

**4.** Adjust an oven rack to the middle position and heat the oven to 450 degrees. Heat the remaining 2 tablespoons olive oil in a 12-inch skillet over medium-high heat until smoking.

Add the beef to the pan and cook until well browned on all sides, 8 to 10 minutes total. Transfer the beef to a wire rack set over a rimmed baking sheet and place in the oven. Roast until the thickest part of the roast registers 120 degrees on an instant-read thermometer for rare (16 to 18 minutes), or 125 degrees for medium-rare (20 to 22 minutes).

**5. FOR THE BUTTER:** While the meat roasts, combine all the ingredients in a small bowl. Transfer the tenderloin to a carving board; spread half of the butter evenly over the top of the roast. Loosely tent the roast with foil; let rest for 15 minutes. Cut the roast between the pieces of twine into thick slices. Remove the twine and serve, passing the remaining butter separately.

### STUFFING AND TYING A TENDERLOIN

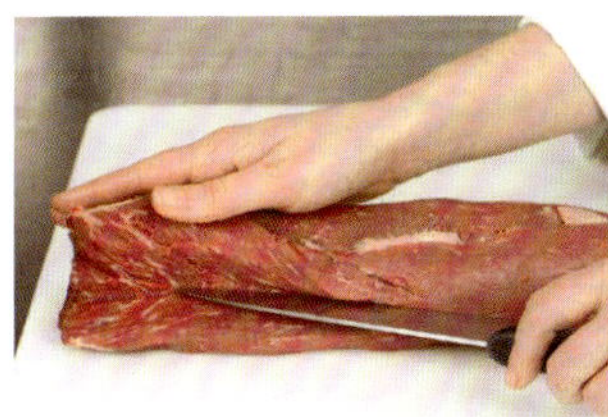

**1.** Insert a chef's knife about 1 inch from the bottom of the roast and cut horizontally, stopping just before the edge. Open the meat like a book.

**2.** Make another cut diagonally into the thicker portion of the roast. Open up this flap, smoothing out the butterflied rectangle of meat.

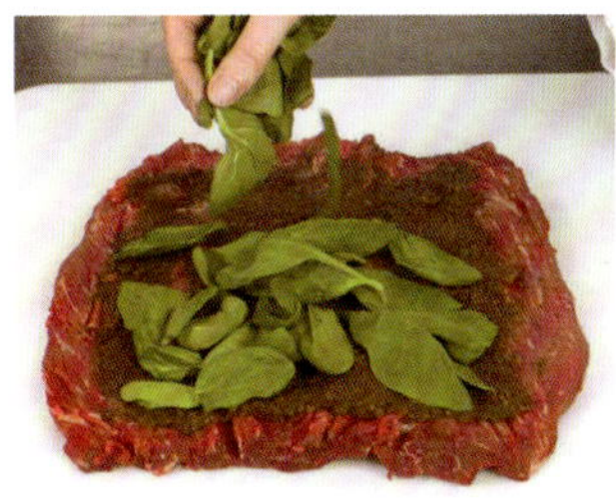

**3.** Spread the filling evenly over the entire surface, leaving a ½-inch border on all sides. Press the spinach leaves evenly on top of the filling.

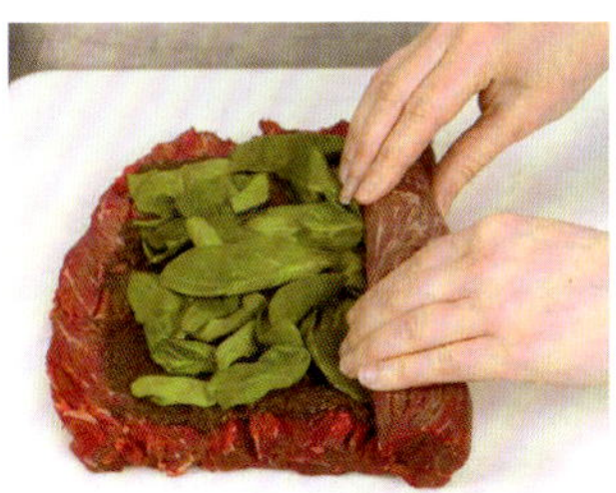

**4.** Using both hands, gently but firmly roll up the stuffed tenderloin, making it as compact as possible without squeezing out the filling.

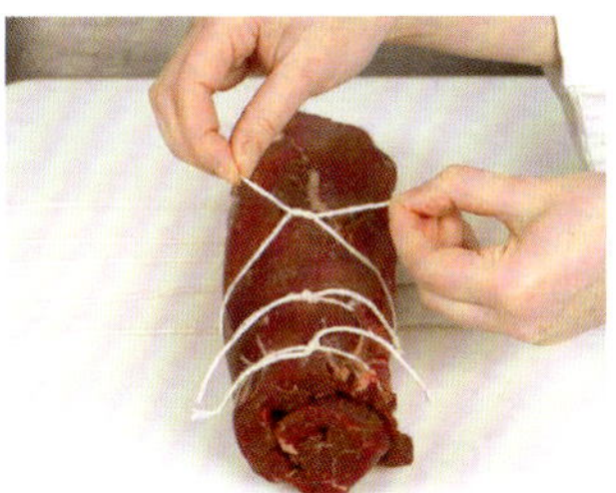

**5.** Evenly space eight pieces of kitchen twine (each about 14 inches) beneath the roast. Tie each strand tightly around the roast, starting with the ends.

## Beef Tenderloin with Smoky Potatoes and Persillade Relish

**SERVES** 6 to 8

**WHY THIS RECIPE WORKS** For special occasions, few cuts top a beef tenderloin. This elegant roast cooks quickly and serves a crowd, and its rich, buttery slices are fork-tender. We found that a hot oven delivered rich, roasted flavor and perfectly rosy meat. Tying the roast helped to ensure even cooking. To accompany the roast, small whole red potatoes were a perfect pairing. To punch up the flavor, we tossed the potatoes with smoked paprika, which added a pleasant smokiness to complement our meat, along with garlic and scallions for a flavorful backbone. To add a sauce too, we made a simple yet bold persillade relish, which featured parsley, capers, and cornichons. We prefer to use extra-small red potatoes measuring less than 1 inch in diameter. Larger potatoes can be used, but it may be necessary to return the potatoes to the oven to finish cooking, while the roast is resting in step 5. Center-cut beef tenderloin roasts are sometimes sold as Châteaubriand.

**BEEF AND POTATOES**

- 1 (3-pound) center-cut beef tenderloin roast, trimmed
- 3¼ teaspoons kosher salt, divided
- 1¼ teaspoons pepper, divided
- 1 teaspoon baking soda
- 3 tablespoons extra-virgin olive oil, divided
- 3 pounds extra-small red potatoes, unpeeled
- 5 scallions, minced
- 4 garlic cloves, minced
- 1 tablespoon smoked paprika
- ½ cup water

**PERSILLADE RELISH**

- ¾ cup minced fresh parsley
- ½ cup extra-virgin olive oil
- 6 tablespoons minced cornichons plus 1 teaspoon brine
- ¼ cup capers, rinsed and chopped coarse
- 3 garlic cloves, minced
- 1 scallion, minced
- 1 teaspoon sugar
- ¼ teaspoon table salt
- ¼ teaspoon pepper

**1. FOR THE BEEF AND POTATOES:** Pat roast dry with paper towels. Combine 2¼ teaspoons salt, 1 teaspoon pepper, and baking soda in small bowl. Rub salt mixture evenly over roast and let stand for 1 hour. After 1 hour, tie roast with kitchen twine at 1½ inch intervals. Adjust oven rack to middle position and heat oven to 425 degrees.

**2.** Heat 2 tablespoons oil in 16 by 12-inch roasting pan over medium-high heat (over 2 burners, if possible) until shimmering. Add potatoes, scallions, garlic, paprika, remaining 1 teaspoon salt, and remaining ¼ teaspoon pepper and cook until scallions are softened, about 1 minute. Off heat, stir in water, scraping up any browned bits. Transfer roasting pan to oven and roast potatoes for 15 minutes.

3. Brush remaining 1 tablespoon oil over surface of roast. Remove roasting pan from oven, stir potato mixture, and lay beef on top. Reduce oven temperature to 300 degrees. Return pan to oven and roast until beef registers 120 to 125 degrees (for medium-rare), 45 to 55 minutes, rotating roasting pan halfway through cooking.

4. **FOR THE PERSILLADE RELISH:** While beef roasts, combine all ingredients in bowl.

5. Remove pan from oven. Transfer roast to carving board, tent with aluminum foil, and let rest for 15 minutes. Cover potatoes left in pan with foil to keep warm. Remove twine from roast, slice ½ inch thick, and serve with potatoes and persillade relish.

## Pepper-Crusted Beef Tenderloin Roast

**SERVES** 10 to 12

**WHY THIS RECIPE WORKS** For a tender, rosy roast with a spicy, yet not harsh-tasting, peppercorn crust that didn't fall off, we relied on a few tricks. Rubbing the raw tenderloin with an abrasive mixture of kosher salt, sugar, and baking soda transformed its surface into a magnet for the pepper crust. To tame the heat of the pepper crust, we simmered cracked peppercorns in oil, then strained them from the oil. To replace some of the subtle flavors we had simmered away, we added some orange zest and nutmeg. With the crust in place, we gently roasted the tenderloin in the oven until it was perfectly rosy, then served it with a tangy, fruity sauce to complement the rich beef. Not all pepper mills produce a coarse enough grind for this recipe. Coarsely cracked peppercorns are each about the size of a halved whole one.

- 4½ teaspoons kosher salt
- 1½ teaspoons sugar
- ¼ teaspoon baking soda
- 9 tablespoons olive oil
- ½ cup coarsely cracked black peppercorns
- 1 tablespoon finely grated orange zest
- ½ teaspoon ground nutmeg
- 1 (6-pound) whole beef tenderloin, trimmed

1. Adjust oven rack to middle position and heat oven to 300 degrees. Combine salt, sugar, and baking soda in bowl; set aside. Heat 6 tablespoons oil and peppercorns in small saucepan over low heat until faint bubbles appear. Continue to cook at bare simmer, swirling pan occasionally, until pepper is fragrant, 7 to 10 minutes. Using fine-mesh strainer, drain cooking oil from peppercorns. Discard cooking oil and mix peppercorns with remaining 3 tablespoons oil, orange zest, and nutmeg.

2. Set tenderloin on sheet of plastic wrap. Sprinkle salt mixture evenly over surface of tenderloin and rub into tenderloin until surface is tacky. Tuck tail end of tenderloin under about 6 inches to create more even shape. Rub top and side of tenderloin with peppercorn mixture, pressing to make sure peppercorns adhere. Spray three 12-inch lengths kitchen twine with vegetable oil spray; tie head of tenderloin to maintain even shape, spacing twine at 2-inch intervals.

3. Transfer prepared tenderloin to wire rack set in rimmed baking sheet, keeping tail end tucked under. Roast until thickest part of meat registers about 120 degrees for rare and about 125 degrees for medium-rare (thinner parts of tenderloin will be slightly more done), 60 to 70 minutes. Transfer to carving board and let rest for 30 minutes.

4. Remove twine and slice meat into ½-inch-thick slices. Serve.

### Red Wine–Orange Sauce

**MAKES** 1 cup

- 2 tablespoons unsalted butter, plus 4 tablespoons cut into 4 pieces and chilled
- 2 shallots, minced
- 1 tablespoon tomato paste
- 2 teaspoons sugar
- 3 garlic cloves, minced
- 2 cups beef broth
- 1 cup red wine
- ¼ cup orange juice
- 2 tablespoons balsamic vinegar
- 1 tablespoon Worcestershire sauce
- 1 sprig fresh thyme
- Table salt and pepper

1. Melt 2 tablespoons butter in medium saucepan over medium-high heat. Add shallots, tomato paste, and sugar; cook, stirring frequently, until deep brown, about 5 minutes. Add garlic and cook until fragrant, about 1 minute. Add broth, wine, orange juice, vinegar, Worcestershire, and thyme sprig, scraping up any browned bits. Bring to simmer and cook until reduced to 1 cup, 35 to 40 minutes.

2. Strain sauce through fine-mesh strainer and return to saucepan. Return saucepan to medium heat and whisk in remaining 4 tablespoons butter, 1 piece at a time. Season with salt and pepper to taste.

## Beef Wellington

**SERVES** 8 to 10

**WHY THIS RECIPE WORKS** We developed a failproof process that produces a stunningly beautiful—and delicious—beef Wellington wrapped in buttery pastry and cooked to rosy perfection every time. We first salted beef tenderloin overnight and then slathered it with Dijon mustard before wrapping it in prosciutto spread with a savory mixture of mushrooms, shallots, and garlic known as duxelles. We traded the traditional puff pastry for sturdier, easier-to-work-with pâte brisée, which produces a firm yet flaky and tender crust that slices neatly. Finally, we tackled the biggest challenge of all: producing both a perfectly baked crust and uniformly medium-rare beef. To accomplish this, we roasted the Wellington in a 450-degree oven and removed it when the beef registered a mere 85 degrees. Carryover cooking did the rest of the work, gradually raising the meat's temperature to 130 degrees. A dollop of creamy sauce gives this dish an elegant finish. We recommend using a probe thermometer for this recipe. Center-cut beef tenderloin roasts are sometimes sold as Châteaubriand. Request a Châteaubriand from the thicker end of the tenderloin; some butchers refer to this as the "cannon cut." Dry sherry can be substituted for the Madeira. Use packaged prosciutto rather than freshly sliced deli prosciutto, as the slices will be easier to handle. Although the timing for many of the components is flexible, we recommend making the Wellington over a three-day period: Prepare the components on the first day, assemble it on the second day (remember to reserve your leftover egg wash so that you can give the pastry a final coat before roasting it), and bake and serve it on the third day. Serve with Creamy Green Peppercorn Sauce (recipe follows).

**BEEF**

- 1 center-cut beef tenderloin roast, 3 pounds trimmed weight, 12 to 13 inches long and 4 to 4½ inches in diameter
- 1 tablespoon kosher salt
- 1 tablespoon Dijon mustard
- 1 teaspoon pepper

**PASTRY**

- 3¼ cups (17¾ ounces) bread flour
- 22 tablespoons (2¾ sticks) unsalted butter, cut into ½-inch cubes and chilled
- 1 teaspoon table salt
- ½ cup plus 1 tablespoon ice water

**DUXELLES**

- 8 shallots, chopped
- 4 garlic cloves, peeled
- 2 pounds cremini mushrooms, trimmed and quartered, divided
- 8 tablespoons unsalted butter
- ¼ teaspoon pepper
- ⅛ teaspoon table salt
- 1 tablespoon Madeira
- 2 teaspoons minced fresh thyme

**ASSEMBLY**

- 12 slices prosciutto
- 1 large egg plus 1 large yolk

### Day One: Prep Components

**1. FOR THE BEEF:** Sprinkle all sides of beef evenly with salt. Wrap in plastic wrap and refrigerate for at least 12 hours or up to 3 days.

**2. FOR THE PASTRY:** Using stand mixer fitted with paddle, mix flour, butter, and salt on medium-low speed until mixture is crumbly and pieces of butter are no larger than peas, 4 to 5 minutes. With mixer running, add ice water in steady stream. Increase speed to medium and continue to mix until smooth dough comes together around paddle, 1 to 3 minutes longer. Transfer dough to lightly floured counter. Remove one-quarter (about 8 ounces) of dough and shape into 6-inch square. Shape remaining dough into 6-inch square. Wrap both pieces in plastic and refrigerate for at least 8 hours or up to 2 days.

**3. FOR THE DUXELLES:** Process shallots and garlic in food processor until very finely chopped, about 30 seconds, scraping down sides of bowl as needed. Transfer to small bowl. Pulse half of mushrooms until mushrooms resemble couscous, about 10 pulses, scraping down sides of bowl halfway through processing (do not overprocess). Transfer to large bowl and repeat with remaining mushrooms.

**4.** Melt butter in 12-inch nonstick skillet over medium-low heat. Add shallot mixture and cook, stirring frequently, until softened, 3 to 5 minutes. Stir in mushrooms, pepper, and salt and cook, stirring occasionally, until liquid given off by mushrooms has evaporated and mushrooms begin to sizzle, about 45 minutes. Add Madeira to mushroom mixture and cook, stirring constantly, until evaporated, about 2 minutes. Off heat, stir in thyme. (If making duxelles ahead, let cool completely and refrigerate in airtight container for up to 3 days.)

### Day Two: Assemble

**5. TO ASSEMBLE:** Overlap 2 or 3 pieces of plastic on counter to form 30-inch square (it's OK if up to 2 inches of plastic hangs off edge of counter). Shingle prosciutto in center of plastic in 2 rows of 6 slices, slightly overlapping to form 14 by 15-inch rectangle, with shorter side parallel to edge of counter. Transfer duxelles to prosciutto and use offset spatula to spread in even layer, leaving 1-inch border of prosciutto on all sides (if duxelles is cold, microwave for 1 minute to soften before spreading).

**6.** Unwrap beef and pat dry with paper towels. Brush all sides of beef with mustard and sprinkle with pepper. Arrange roast parallel to edge of counter, about one-third of way up duxelles. Using both hands, lift bottom edge of plastic to begin wrapping roast. Continue to roll roast, leaving plastic behind, until roast is completely wrapped in prosciutto. Tuck overhanging slices of prosciutto over each end of roast.

**7.** Tightly roll roast in plastic and twist plastic tightly at each end to seal. Continue to twist ends of plastic and roll roast on counter until formed into snug cylinder. Refrigerate for at least 30 minutes or up to 2 days before cooking.

**8.** Line 2 rimmed baking sheets with parchment paper. Roll out larger piece of dough on generously floured counter into

18 by 16-inch rectangle. Drape dough over rolling pin, transfer to prepared sheet, and refrigerate for 15 minutes. Roll smaller piece of dough into 16 by 7-inch rectangle. Transfer to second prepared sheet and refrigerate.

**9.** Whisk together egg and yolk. Lay large pastry sheet directly on counter with long side parallel to edge of counter. Brush entire surface with egg wash; set aside remaining egg wash. Unwrap beef and place on pastry, arranging it parallel to edge of counter and 2 inches from pastry edge closest to you. Wrap edge of pastry closest to you over beef. Holding edge in place, slowly roll roast away from you, keeping pastry snug to meat, until roast is covered.

**10.** Allow pastry to overlap by 1 inch and trim away excess. Roll roast so seam is on top. Gently press and pinch overlapping dough to seal. Roll roast so seam is on bottom.

**11.** To seal ends of roast, tuck sides of pastry tightly against meat as though you are wrapping a present, then fold top of pastry down, pressing snugly.

**12.** Using rolling pin, roll excess dough at end of roast against counter to make it thinner and longer. Trim rolled end to 2-inch length and tuck under roast. Repeat process on other end of roast. Transfer roast seam side down to lightly greased rimmed baking sheet and refrigerate for at least 15 minutes or up to overnight (if refrigerating longer than 1 hour, wrap in plastic).

**13.** Transfer smaller rectangle of dough, still on parchment, to counter, with short side parallel to edge of counter. Using ruler and sharp knife or pizza cutter, cut dough lengthwise into ¼-inch-wide strips.

**14.** Brush top, sides, and ends of roast with some of reserved egg wash; set aside remaining egg wash. Lay strips of dough diagonally across top of roast, leaving ¼ to ½ inch between strips. Gently press strips to adhere to roast and trim excess at each end to ¼ inch. Using bench scraper, tuck ends of strips under roast. Refrigerate roast for at least 10 minutes. (Roast can be loosely covered with plastic and refrigerated for up to 24 hours.)

## Day Three: Bake and Serve

**15.** Adjust oven rack to lower-middle position and heat oven to 450 degrees. Brush roast thoroughly with reserved egg wash. Place thermometer probe, if using, through 1 end of roast so tip of probe is positioned at center of roast. Roast until beef registers 85 degrees and crust is well browned and crisp, 40 to 45 minutes. Transfer sheet to wire rack, leaving probe in place to monitor temperature. Let rest, uncovered, until internal temperature reaches 130 degrees, 40 to 45 minutes.

**16. TO SERVE:** Slide large metal spatula under roast to loosen from sheet. Use both hands to transfer roast to carving board. Using serrated knife, cut roast into 1-inch-thick slices (to keep pastry intact, score through decorative strips before cutting each slice) and serve.

## Creamy Green Peppercorn Sauce

**SERVES** 8 to 10

The sauce can be made as the roast is resting; alternatively, prepare it up to three days ahead and warm it right before serving.

- 2 tablespoons unsalted butter
- ¼ cup jarred green peppercorns
- 2 tablespoons minced shallot
- 1 tablespoon all-purpose flour
- 1½ cups beef broth
- ¼ cup brandy
- 2 tablespoons soy sauce
- 1 cup heavy cream

**1.** Melt butter in medium saucepan over medium-low heat. Add peppercorns and shallot and cook, stirring frequently, until shallot is softened, 3 to 5 minutes. Add flour and cook, stirring constantly, for 2 minutes. Increase heat to medium and whisk in broth, brandy, and soy sauce. Bring to boil. Cook, whisking occasionally, until mixture is reduced to 1½ cups, 12 to 15 minutes.

**2.** Add cream and cook, whisking occasionally, until reduced to 2 cups, about 10 minutes. Season with salt and pepper to taste.

### ASSEMBLING BEEF WELLINGTON

**1.** Lay large pastry sheet directly on counter and brush entire surface of pastry with egg wash.

**2.** Unwrap beef and place on pastry. Holding edge in place, slowly roll roast keeping pastry snug to meat.

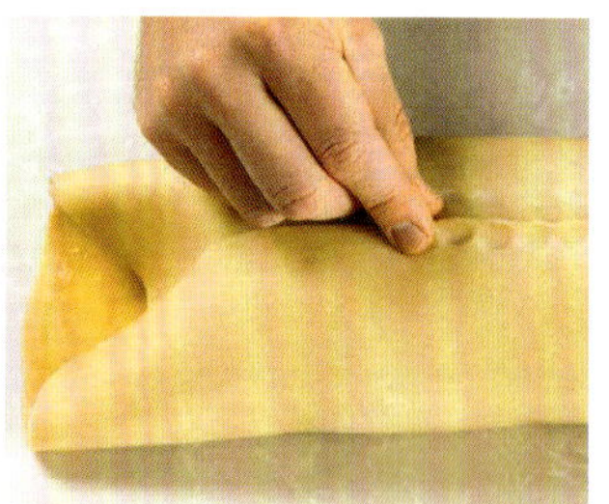

**3.** With seam on top, gently pinch dough to seal; roll seam to bottom. Tuck sides to seal ends. Brush with egg wash.

**4.** Lay thin strips of dough diagonally across top of roast, leaving space between strips. Press strips to adhere.

## Beef en Cocotte with Mushroom Sauce

**SERVES** 6 to 8

**WHY THIS RECIPE WORKS** We push the limits of what you might think can come out of one Dutch oven with this impressive ultra-beefy roast and earthy mushroom sauce. En cocotte simply means cooking in a covered pot. We browned the roast in a Dutch oven, removed it, and then started the savory sauce in the drippings using both cremini and porcini mushrooms. Once all the ingredients were incorporated, we returned the roast to the pot, sealed it, covered it, and let everything cook in the oven until the meat was medium-rare. Trim the beef well to keep the sauce from turning greasy.

- 1 (3- to 4-pound) top sirloin beef roast, trimmed and tied once around middle
- 3 tablespoons vegetable oil, divided
- 5 ounces cremini mushrooms, trimmed, wiped clean, and sliced ¼ inch thick
- 1 onion, minced
- 3 garlic cloves, peeled and crushed
- ½ ounce dried porcini mushrooms, rehydrated, liquid strained and reserved, and mushrooms minced
- 2 sprigs fresh tarragon
- 1 tablespoon tomato paste
- ¼ cup dry white wine
- 2 tablespoons cognac
- 1½ cups chicken broth
- 1 tablespoon unsalted butter

**1.** Adjust oven rack to lowest position and heat oven to 250 degrees. Pat roast dry with paper towels and season with salt and pepper. Heat 2 tablespoons oil in Dutch oven over medium-high heat until just smoking. Add roast and brown well on all sides, 7 to 10 minutes; transfer to plate.

**2.** Add remaining 1 tablespoon oil to now-empty pot and heat over medium heat until shimmering. Add cremini mushrooms, onion, garlic, porcini mushrooms, and tarragon, cover, and cook until mushrooms are softened and wet, about 5 minutes. Remove lid and continue to cook, stirring often, until mushrooms are dry and well-browned, 10 to 12 minutes.

**3.** Stir in tomato paste and cook until lightly browned, about 30 seconds. Stir in reserved porcini soaking liquid, wine, and cognac, scraping up any browned bits, and cook until almost completely evaporated, about 5 minutes.

**4.** Off heat, return roast and any accumulated juices to pot. Place large sheet of aluminum foil over pot and press to seal, then cover tightly with lid. Transfer pot to oven and cook until beef registers 120 to 125 degrees (for medium-rare), 45 to 75 minutes.

**5.** Remove pot from oven. Transfer roast to carving board, tent with foil, and let rest for 20 minutes. Stir broth into vegetables and simmer over medium-high heat until slightly thickened, about 2 minutes. Off heat, remove tarragon, whisk in butter, season with salt and pepper to taste, and cover to keep warm. Remove twine from roast. Slice meat against grain ¼ inch thick. Spoon sauce over meat and serve.

## Fennel-Coriander Top Sirloin Roast

**SERVES** 8 to 10

**WHY THIS RECIPE WORKS** Top sirloin offers great beefy flavor and decent tenderness, but this cheap cut has its challenges. We began by splitting the roast into two smaller roasts, salting them, and air-drying them in the refrigerator. This seasoned the meat, maximized its juiciness, and dried the surfaces for optimal browning. After 24 hours, we kick-started the browning by searing all sides of the roasts in a skillet. Tying the roasts with kitchen twine turned them into two uniform cylinders. We created a richly seasoned paste to further boost browning. We processed garlic, fennel, olive oil, and anchovy fillets, then added coriander, paprika, and oregano for extra flavor. After applying the paste, we roasted the meat in a 225-degree oven for 2 hours. To give it an attractive browned crust, we ramped up the temperature to 500 degrees, and returned the roasts for a final crisping. This recipe requires refrigerating the salted meat for at least 24 hours. The roast, also called a top sirloin roast, top butt roast, center-cut roast, spoon roast, shell roast, or shell sirloin roast, should not be confused with a whole top sirloin butt roast or top loin roast. Do not omit the anchovies; they provide great depth of flavor with no overt fishiness. Monitoring the roast with a meat-probe thermometer is best. If you use an instant-read thermometer, open the oven door as little as possible and remove the roast from the oven to take its temperature.

- 1 (5- to 6-pound) boneless top sirloin center-cut roast, trimmed
- 2 tablespoons kosher salt
- 4 teaspoons plus ¼ cup extra-virgin olive oil, divided
- 4 garlic cloves, minced
- 6 anchovy fillets, rinsed and patted dry
- 2 teaspoons ground fennel
- 2 teaspoons ground coriander
- 2 teaspoons paprika
- 1 teaspoon dried oregano
- 1 teaspoon pepper

**1.** Cut roast lengthwise along grain into 2 equal pieces. Rub 1 tablespoon kosher salt over each piece. Transfer to large plate and refrigerate, uncovered, for at least 24 hours or up to 4 days.

**2.** Adjust oven rack to middle position and heat oven to 225 degrees. Heat 2 teaspoons oil in 12-inch skillet over high heat until just smoking. Brown 1 roast on all sides, 6 to 8 minutes. Return browned roast to plate. Repeat with 2 teaspoons oil and remaining roast. Let cool for 10 minutes.

**3.** While roasts cool, process garlic, anchovies, fennel, coriander, paprika, oregano, and remaining ¼ cup oil in food processor until smooth paste forms, about 30 seconds, scraping down sides of bowl as needed. Add pepper and pulse to combine, 2 or 3 pulses.

**4.** Using 5 pieces of kitchen twine per roast, tie each roast crosswise at equal intervals into loaf shape. Transfer roasts to wire rack set in rimmed baking sheet and rub roasts evenly with paste.

**5.** Roast until meat registers 125 degrees (for medium-rare) or 130 degrees (for medium), 2 to 2¼ hours. Remove roasts from oven, leaving on wire rack, and tent with aluminum foil; let rest for at least 30 minutes or up to 40 minutes.

**6.** Heat oven to 500 degrees. Remove foil from roasts and cut and discard twine. Return roasts to oven and cook until exteriors of roasts are well browned, 6 to 8 minutes.

**7.** Transfer roasts to carving board. Slice meat ¼ inch thick. Season with coarse sea salt to taste, and serve.

## Beef Top Loin Roast with Potatoes

**SERVES** 8 to 10

**WHY THIS RECIPE WORKS** To create a tender, juicy roast and beefy-tasting potatoes worthy of being a holiday centerpiece, we started with a top loin roast and trimmed the ribbons of fat that run along its sides. Browning the trimmings along with the roast yielded loads of rendered fat (and flavorful fond), which we then used to brown the potatoes. From there, we covered the potatoes with aluminum foil, which allowed us to roast the beef on top of them. While the roast rested, we flipped the potatoes; added broth that we fortified with the seared beef scraps, herbs, seasonings, and gelatin for unctuous body; and braised them in a 500-degree oven. Finally, we strained and defatted the remaining broth to serve as a jus alongside the meat and potatoes. Top loin roast is also known as strip roast. Use potatoes that are about 1½ inches in diameter and at least 4 inches long. The browned surfaces of the potatoes are very delicate; take care when flipping the potatoes in step 7. To make flipping easier, flip two potatoes and remove them from the pan to create space before flipping the rest.

- 1 (5- to 6-pound) boneless top loin roast
- 2 tablespoons plus 2 teaspoons kosher salt, divided
- 2 teaspoons pepper, divided
- 5 pounds Yukon Gold potatoes, peeled
- ¼ cup vegetable oil
- 5 cups beef broth
- 6 sprigs fresh thyme
- 2 small sprigs fresh rosemary
- 2 tablespoons unflavored gelatin
- 4 garlic cloves, lightly crushed and peeled

**1.** Pat roast dry with paper towels. Place roast fat cap side down and trim off strip of meat that is loosely attached to thicker side of roast. Rotate roast 180 degrees and trim off strip of meat and fat from narrow side of roast. (After trimming, roast should be rectangular with roughly even thickness.) Cut trimmings into 1-inch pieces. Transfer trimmings to small bowl, wrap tightly in plastic wrap, and refrigerate.

**2.** Using sharp knife, cut slits ½ inch apart and ¼ inch deep in crosshatch pattern in fat cap of roast. Sprinkle all sides of roast evenly with 2 tablespoons salt and 1 teaspoon pepper. Wrap in plastic and refrigerate for 6 to 24 hours.

**3.** Adjust oven rack to lowest position and heat oven to 300 degrees. Trim and discard ¼ inch from end of each potato. Cut each potato in half crosswise. Toss potatoes with remaining 2 teaspoons salt and remaining 1 teaspoon pepper and set aside.

**4.** Place oil in large roasting pan. Place roast, fat cap side down, in center of pan and scatter trimmings around roast. Cook over medium heat, stirring trimmings frequently but not moving roast, until fat cap is well browned, 8 to 12 minutes. Flip roast and continue to cook, stirring trimmings frequently, until bottom of roast is lightly browned and trimmings are rendered and crisp, 6 to 10 minutes. Remove pan from heat and transfer roast to plate. Using slotted spoon, transfer trimmings to medium saucepan, leaving fat in pan.

**5.** Arrange potatoes in single layer, broad side down, in pan. Return pan to medium heat and cook, without moving potatoes, until well browned around edges, 15 to 20 minutes. (Do not flip potatoes.) Off heat, lay 22 by 18-inch sheet of aluminum foil over potatoes. Using oven mitts, crimp edges of foil to rim of pan. With paring knife, poke 5 holes in center of foil. Lay roast, fat side up, in center of foil. Transfer pan to oven and cook until meat registers 115 degrees, 1 to 1¼ hours.

**6.** While roast cooks, add broth, thyme sprigs, rosemary sprigs, gelatin, and garlic to saucepan with trimmings. Bring to boil over medium-high heat. Reduce heat and simmer for 15 minutes. Strain mixture through fine-mesh strainer into 4-cup liquid measuring cup, pressing on solids to extract as much liquid as possible; discard solids. (You should have 4 cups liquid; if necessary, add water to equal 4 cups.)

**7.** When meat registers 115 degrees, remove pan from oven and increase oven temperature to 500 degrees. Transfer roast to carving board. Remove foil and use to tent roast. Using offset spatula, carefully flip potatoes. Pour strained liquid around potatoes and return pan (handles will be hot) to oven (it's OK if oven has not yet reached 500 degrees). Cook until liquid is reduced by half, 20 to 30 minutes.

**8.** Carefully transfer potatoes to serving platter. Pour liquid into fat separator and let settle for 5 minutes. Slice roast and transfer to platter with potatoes. Transfer defatted juices to small bowl. Serve, passing juices separately.

## Classic Prime Rib

**SERVES** 6 to 8

**WHY THIS RECIPE WORKS** Most of us cook prime rib only once a year, if that, and don't want to risk experimenting with the cooking method—especially when the results are no better than mediocre. We thought that a special-occasion roast deserved better and wanted to find the best way to get the juicy, tender, rosy meat that prime rib should have. The principal question for roasting prime rib was oven temperature, and our research turned up a wide range of recommendations. Most delivered meat that was well-done on the outside but increasingly rare toward the center—not too bad, but not exactly great. Surprisingly, the roast we cooked at a temperature of only 250 degrees was rosy from the center all the way out. Additionally, it retained more juice than a roast cooked at a higher temperature, and the internal temperature rose less during resting, so we had more control over the final degree of doneness. Searing before roasting gave us a crusty brown exterior. For seasoning, prime rib needs nothing more than salt and pepper. Now that we'd found a dependable cooking method, we could serve this once-a-year roast with confidence. With two pieces of kitchen twine running parallel to the bone, tie the roast at both ends to prevent the outer layer of meat from pulling away from the rib-eye muscle and overcooking.

- 1 (7-pound; 3-rib) standing rib roast, trimmed and tied
- Table salt and ground black pepper

**1.** Pat the roast dry with paper towels and season with salt and pepper. Cover the roast loosely with plastic wrap and let sit at room temperature for 1 to 2 hours.

**2.** Adjust an oven rack to the lowest position and heat the oven to 250 degrees. Heat a large roasting pan over two burners set at medium-high heat until hot, about 4 minutes. Place the roast in the hot pan and cook on all sides until nicely browned and about ½ cup fat has rendered, 6 to 8 minutes.

**3.** Remove the roast from the pan. Set a wire rack in the pan, then set the roast on the rack.

**4.** Place the roast in the oven and roast until the meat registers 125 degrees on an instant-read thermometer for rare, 130 degrees for medium-rare, and 140 degrees for medium, 3 to 3½ hours. Remove the roast from the oven and tent with foil. Let stand for 20 to 30 minutes to allow the juices to redistribute evenly throughout the roast.

**5.** Remove the twine and set the roast on a carving board, with the rib bones at a 90-degree angle to the board. Carve and serve immediately.

## Best Prime Rib

**SERVES** 6 to 8

**WHY THIS RECIPE WORKS** The perfect prime rib should have a deep-colored, substantial crust encasing a tender, juicy rosy-pink center. To achieve superior results, we cut slits in the layer of fat to help it render efficiently, then salted the roast overnight. The long salting time enhanced the beefy flavor while dissolving some of the proteins, yielding a buttery-tender roast. To further enhance tenderness, we cooked the roast at a very low temperature, which allowed the meat's enzymes to act as natural tenderizers, breaking down its tough connective tissue. A brief stint under the broiler before serving ensured a crisp, flavorful crust. Look for a roast with an untrimmed fat cap (ideally ½ inch thick). We prefer the flavor and texture of Prime beef, but Choice grade will work as well. Monitoring the roast with a meat-probe thermometer is best. If you use an instant-read thermometer, open the oven door as little as possible and remove the roast from the oven while taking its temperature. If the roast has not reached the correct temperature in the time range specified in step 3, heat the oven to 200 degrees, wait for 5 minutes, then shut it off, and continue to cook the roast until it reaches the desired temperature.

- 1 (7-pound) first-cut beef standing rib roast (3 bones), meat removed from bones, bones reserved
- 2 tablespoons kosher salt
- 2 teaspoons vegetable oil
- 1 teaspoon pepper

**1.** Using sharp knife, cut through roast's fat cap in 1-inch crosshatch pattern, being careful not to cut into meat. Rub salt over entire roast and into slits. Place meat back on bones (to save space in refrigerator), transfer to large plate, and refrigerate, uncovered, for at least 24 hours or up to 4 days.

### PREPARING BEST PRIME RIB

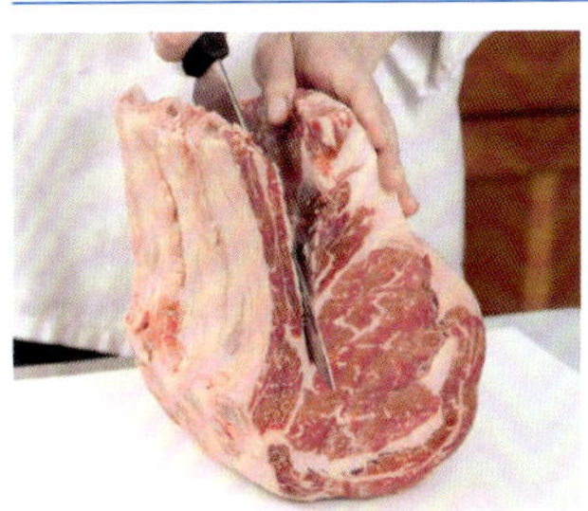

**1.** Remove ribs to make it easier to sear prime rib in skillet. Run sharp knife down length of bones, following contours as closely as possible to remove ribs.

**2.** Score fat cap in 1-inch crosshatch pattern to allow salt to contact meat directly and to improve fat rendering and crisping.

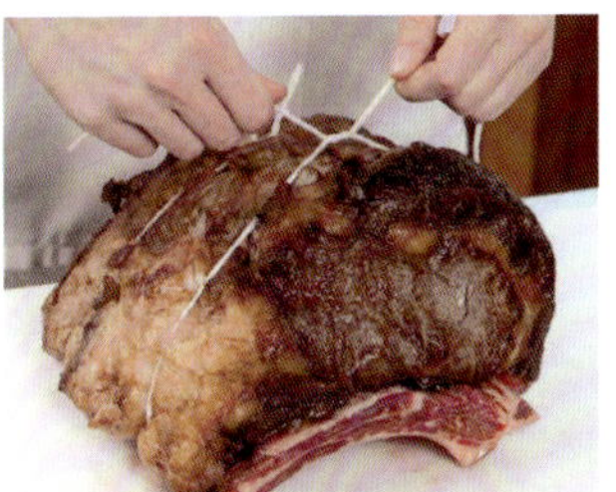

**3.** After searing meat, place meat back on ribs so bones fit where they were cut and let cool for 10 minutes; tie meat to bones with 2 lengths of kitchen twine between ribs. Bones provide insulation to meat so it cooks evenly.

2. Adjust oven rack to middle position and heat oven to 200 degrees. Set wire rack in rimmed baking sheet. Heat oil in 12-inch skillet over high heat until just smoking. Sear sides and top of roast (reserving bones) until browned, 6 to 8 minutes total (do not sear side where roast was cut from bones). Place meat back on ribs so bones fit where they were cut and let cool for 10 minutes; tie meat to bones with 2 lengths of kitchen twine between ribs. Transfer roast, fat side up, to prepared wire rack and sprinkle with pepper. Roast until meat registers 110 degrees, 3 to 4 hours.

3. Turn off oven; leave roast in oven, opening door as little as possible, until meat registers 120 degrees for rare or 125 degrees for medium-rare, 30 minutes to 1¼ hours longer.

4. Remove roast from oven (leave roast on baking sheet), tent with aluminum foil, and let rest for at least 30 minutes or up to 1¼ hours.

5. Adjust oven rack to about 8 inches from broiler element and heat broiler. Remove foil from roast, form into 3-inch ball, and place under ribs to elevate fat cap. Broil until top of roast is well browned and crisp, 2 to 8 minutes.

6. Transfer roast to carving board; cut twine and remove ribs from roast. Slice meat ¾ inch thick. Season with salt to taste, and serve.

## Sous Vide Prime Rib

**SERVES** 6 to 8

**WHY THIS RECIPE WORKS** In the land of celebratory roasts, quality prime rib stands as king. But cooking this cut of beef properly is a challenge. Luckily, sous vide allows you to cook it well. We started by removing the ribs to expose all sides of the roast before salting it and letting it sit overnight. The salt slowly moved toward the center of the meat, enhancing the beefy flavor while dissolving some of the proteins. Presearing the roast built flavor before it went into its low-temperature bath. After 16 to 24 hours at 133°F, the roast's connective tissue had broken down, producing a buttery texture. A flash under the broiler crisped up the fat cap to create a nice crust. To gild the lily, we also whipped up a quick herby persillade (a French sauce that, in its simplest form, is just parsley and garlic). Our version is a bright, zesty accompaniment to the rich, crusty roast. Look for a roast with an untrimmed fat cap ideally ½ inch thick. We prefer the flavor and texture of prime-grade prime rib, but a choice-grade roast will work. Serve with Mint Persillade. Note that this recipe requires salting and refrigerating the roast at least 24 hours before cooking.

- 1 7-pound first-cut beef standing rib roast (3 bones)
- Kosher salt and pepper
- 1 tablespoon vegetable oil

1. To remove bones from roast, use sharp knife and run it down length of bones, following contours as closely as possible; set bones aside. Cut slits in surface layer of fat on roast, spaced 1 inch apart, in crosshatch pattern, being careful to cut down to, but not into, meat. Rub 2 tablespoons salt over entire roast and into slits. Place meat back on bones (to save space in refrigerator), transfer to plate, and refrigerate, uncovered, at least 24 hours or up to 96 hours.

2. Using sous vide circulator, bring water to 133°F/56°C in 12-quart container.

3. Separate meat and bones; set aside bones. Heat oil in 12-inch skillet over medium-high heat until just smoking. Sear sides and top of roast until browned, 6 to 8 minutes (do not sear side where roast was cut from bone). Place meat back on ribs so bones fit where they were cut, and let cool for 10 minutes. Tie meat to bones between ribs with 2 lengths of kitchen twine.

4. Season roast with pepper and place in 2-gallon zipper-lock freezer bag. Seal bag, pressing out as much air as possible. Gently lower bag into prepared water bath until roast is fully submerged, and then clip top corner of bag to side of water bath container, allowing remaining air bubbles to rise to top of bag. Reopen 1 corner of zipper, release remaining air bubbles, and reseal bag. Cover and cook for at least 16 hours or up to 24 hours.

5. Adjust oven rack to middle position and heat broiler. Set wire rack in aluminum foil–lined rimmed baking sheet and spray with vegetable spray. Transfer roast, fat side up, to prepared rack and let rest for 10 to 15 minutes. Pat roast dry with paper towels. Broil until surface of roast is browned and crisp, 4 to 8 minutes.

6. Transfer roast to carving board and discard ribs. Slice meat into ¾-inch-thick slices. Serve.

### Mint Persillade

**SERVES** 4 (makes about 1 cup)

You can substitute 1½ teaspoons of anchovy paste for the fillets, if desired.

- 1 cup fresh mint leaves
- 1 cup fresh parsley leaves
- 3 garlic cloves, peeled
- 3 anchovy fillets, rinsed and patted dry

1 teaspoon grated lemon zest plus 1 tablespoon juice
½ teaspoon table salt
⅛ teaspoon pepper
⅓ cup extra-virgin olive oil

Pulse mint, parsley, garlic, anchovies, lemon zest, salt, and pepper in food processor until finely chopped, 15 to 20 pulses. Add lemon juice and pulse briefly to combine. Transfer mixture to medium bowl and slowly whisk in oil until fully incorporated.

## Slow-Roasted Beef

**SERVES** 6 to 8

**WHY THIS RECIPE WORKS** Roasting inexpensive beef usually yields tough meat. We wanted to take an inexpensive cut and turn it into a tender, rosy roast worthy of Sunday dinner. Our favorite cut, the eye round, has good flavor and tenderness and a uniform shape that guarantees even cooking. Next, we chose between the two classic methods for roasting meat: high and fast or low and slow. Low temperature was the way to go. Keeping the meat's internal temperature below 122 degrees as long as possible allowed the meat's enzymes to act as natural tenderizers. Since most ovens don't heat below 200 degrees, we needed to devise a special method to lengthen this tenderizing period. We roasted the meat at 225 degrees (after searing it) and shut off the oven when the roast reached 115 degrees. The meat stayed below 122 degrees an extra 30 minutes. We found that salting the meat a full 24 hours before roasting made it even more tender and seasoned throughout. This recipe requires salting the roast for 18 to 24 hours before cooking. We don't recommend cooking this roast past medium. Open the oven door as little as possible and remove the roast from the oven while taking its temperature. If the roast has not reached the desired temperature in the time specified in step 3, heat the oven to 225 degrees for 5 minutes, shut it off, and continue to cook the roast to the desired temperature. For a smaller (2½- to 3½-pound) roast, reduce the amount of pepper to 1½ teaspoons. For a 4½- to 6-pound roast, cut in half crosswise before cooking to create two smaller roasts. Slice the roast as thin as possible and serve with Horseradish Cream Sauce (recipe follows), if desired.

1 (3½- to 4½-pound) boneless eye-round roast, trimmed
4 teaspoons kosher salt
1 tablespoon plus 2 teaspoons vegetable oil, divided
2 teaspoons pepper

**1.** Sprinkle all sides of roast evenly with salt. Wrap with plastic wrap and refrigerate for 18 to 24 hours.

**2.** Adjust oven rack to middle position and heat oven to 225 degrees. Pat roast dry with paper towels; rub with 2 teaspoons oil and sprinkle all sides evenly with pepper. Heat remaining 1 tablespoon oil in 12-inch skillet over medium-high heat until just smoking. Sear roast until browned on all sides, 3 to 4 minutes per side. Transfer roast to wire rack set in rimmed baking sheet. Roast until center of roast registers 115 degrees (for medium-rare), 1¼ to 1¾ hours, or 125 degrees (for medium), 1¾ to 2¼ hours.

**3.** Turn off oven; leave roast in oven, without opening door, until center of roast registers 130 degrees (for medium-rare) or 140 degrees (for medium), 30 to 50 minutes longer. Transfer roast to carving board and let rest for 15 minutes. Slice meat crosswise as thin as possible and serve with sauce, if using.

### Horseradish Cream Sauce

**MAKES** 1 cup

½ cup heavy cream, chilled
½ cup prepared horseradish
1 teaspoon table salt
⅛ teaspoon pepper

Whisk cream in medium bowl until thickened but not yet holding soft peaks, 1 to 2 minutes. Gently fold in horseradish, salt, and pepper. Transfer to serving bowl and refrigerate for at least 30 minutes or up to 1 hour before serving.

## Sous Vide Rosemary–Mustard Seed Crusted Roast Beef

**SERVES** 10 to 12

**WHY THIS RECIPE WORKS** When it comes to holiday beef roasts, chuck isn't really known for being the go-to for medium-rare resplendence. But that's a shame since chuck is among the most flavorful cuts of beef available—and the cheapest per pound, to boot. This cut has plenty of fat and connective tissue, making it tough and chewy when it's cooked to medium-rare in a conventional oven. With most traditional methods of cooking, you have two options: low and slow until it's tender, or braised and broken down. Neither method gives you pink, tender, juicy meat. But with sous vide we can have it all: A fork-tender, juicy, medium-rare chuck roast. Circulating the roast at a low temperature for 24 hours allows enough time to break down intramuscular collagen, tenderizing the meat while preserving a rosy, medium-rare interior from edge to edge. We were inspired to pair this roast with an herb, mustard seed, and peppercorn crust, making it easily customizable and ready to serve with all sorts of sauces. Serve with Yogurt-Herb Sauce (recipe follows), if desired.

1 (5-pound) boneless beef chuck-eye roast, pulled into 2 pieces at natural seam and trimmed of large pieces of fat
4 teaspoons kosher salt
2 tablespoons vegetable oil
1¼ teaspoons pepper
1 egg white
¼ cup mustard seeds
3 tablespoons peppercorns
⅓ cup finely chopped fresh rosemary
2 tablespoons flake sea salt

**1.** Sprinkle beef with kosher salt. Arrange pieces side by side along natural seam, and then tie together at 1-inch intervals with kitchen twine to create 1 evenly shaped roast. Wrap roast in plastic wrap, transfer to large plate, and refrigerate for at least 24 hours or up to 96 hours.

**2.** Using sous vide circulator, heat water to 133 degrees in 12-quart container.

**3.** Heat oil in 12-inch skillet over medium-high heat until just smoking. Brown roast on all sides, 6 to 8 minutes. Season roast with pepper and place into 2-gallon zipper-lock freezer bag. Seal bag, pressing out as much air as possible. Gently lower bag into prepared water bath until roast is fully submerged, and then clip top corner of bag to side of water bath container, allowing remaining air bubbles to rise to top of bag. Reopen 1 corner of zipper, release remaining air bubbles, and reseal bag. Cover and cook for at least 18 hours or up to 24 hours.

**4.** Adjust oven rack to middle position and heat oven to 475 degrees. Set wire rack in aluminum foil–lined rimmed baking sheet and spray with vegetable spray. Transfer roast to prepared rack and let rest for 10 to 15 minutes. Pat roast dry with paper towels.

**5.** Whisk egg white in bowl until frothy, about 30 seconds. Grind mustard seeds and peppercorns in spice grinder under coarsely ground. Transfer to shallow dish and stir in rosemary and flake sea salt. Brush roast on all sides with egg white, then coat with mustard seed mixture, pressing to adhere. Return roast to prepared rack and roast until surface is evenly browned and fragrant, 15 to 20 minutes, rotating sheet halfway through roasting.

**6.** Transfer roast to carving board and slice into ½-inch-thick slices, removing pieces of twine as you slice, and serve.

## Yogurt-Herb Sauce

**MAKES** about 2 cups

Do not substitute low-fat or nonfat yogurt here.

- 2 cups plain whole-milk yogurt
- ¼ cup finely chopped fresh parsley
- ¼ cup finely chopped fresh chives
- 2 teaspoons grated lemon zest plus ¼ cup juice
- 2 garlic cloves, minced

Whisk all ingredients together in bowl and season with salt and pepper to taste. Cover and refrigerate for at least 30 minutes to allow flavors to meld. (Sauce can be refrigerated for up to 4 days.)

## Simple Pot-au-Feu

**SERVES** 6 to 8

**WHY THIS RECIPE WORKS** Pot-au-feu is a French boiled dinner of meltingly tender beef in a flavorful broth with an array of perfectly cooked vegetables. We developed a pot-au-feu brimming with tradition but suited to today's modern kitchen. Boneless chuck roast won out for its relative tenderness and big meaty flavor. Marrow bones gave the broth a buttery, beefy quality. We transferred the pot to the oven to cook low and slow and, in the meantime, stirred together a sauce of traditional pot-au-feu accompaniments. The zesty combination of parsley, Dijon, chives, white wine vinegar, minced cornichons, and pepper was deepened with the addition of the beefy marrow extracted from the bones after cooking. Marrow bones (also called soup bones) can be found in the freezer section or the meat counter at most supermarkets. Use small red potatoes measuring 1 to 2 inches in diameter.

**MEAT**

- 1 (3½- to 4-pound) boneless beef chuck-eye roast, pulled into two pieces at natural seam and trimmed
- 1 tablespoon kosher salt
- 1½ pounds marrow bones
- 1 onion, quartered
- 1 celery rib, sliced thin
- 3 bay leaves
- 1 teaspoon black peppercorns

**PARSLEY SAUCE**

- ⅔ cup minced fresh parsley
- ¼ cup Dijon mustard
- ¼ cup minced fresh chives
- 3 tablespoons white wine vinegar
- 10 cornichons, minced
- 1½ teaspoons pepper

**VEGETABLES**

- 1 pound small red potatoes, unpeeled, halved
- 6 carrots, peeled and halved crosswise, thick halves quartered lengthwise, thin halves halved lengthwise
- 1 pound asparagus, trimmed

**1. FOR THE MEAT:** Adjust oven rack to lower-middle position and heat oven to 300 degrees. Sprinkle beef with salt. Using 3 pieces of kitchen twine per piece, tie each into loaf shape for even cooking. Place beef, bones, onion, celery, bay leaves, and peppercorns in Dutch oven. Add 4 cups cold water (water should come halfway up roasts). Bring to simmer over high heat. Partially cover pot and transfer to oven. Cook until beef is fully tender and sharp knife easily slips in and out of meat (meat will not be shreddable), 3¼ to 3¾ hours, flipping beef over halfway through cooking.

**2. FOR THE PARSLEY SAUCE:** While beef cooks, combine all ingredients in bowl. Cover and set aside.

**3.** Remove pot from oven and turn off oven. Transfer beef to large platter, cover tightly with aluminum foil, and return to oven to keep warm. Transfer bones to cutting board and use end of spoon to extract marrow. Mince marrow into paste and add 2 tablespoons to parsley sauce (reserve any remaining marrow for other applications). Using ladle or large spoon, skim fat from surface of broth and discard fat. Strain broth through fine-mesh strainer into large liquid measuring cup; add water to make 6 cups. Return broth to pot. (Meat can be returned to broth, cooled, and refrigerated for up to 2 days. Skim fat from cold broth, then gently reheat and proceed with recipe.)

**4. FOR THE VEGETABLES:** Add potatoes to broth and bring to simmer over high heat. Reduce heat to medium and simmer for 6 minutes. Add carrots and cook for 10 minutes. Add asparagus and continue to cook until all vegetables are tender, 3 to 5 minutes.

**5.** Using slotted spoon, transfer vegetables to large bowl. Toss with 3 tablespoons parsley sauce and season with salt and pepper to taste. Season broth with salt to taste.

**6.** Transfer beef to cutting board, remove twine, and slice against grain ½ inch thick. Arrange servings of beef and vegetables in large, shallow bowls. Dollop beef with parsley sauce, drizzle with ⅓ cup broth, and sprinkle with flake sea salt. Serve, passing remaining parsley sauce and flake sea salt separately.

### PULLING APART A ROAST

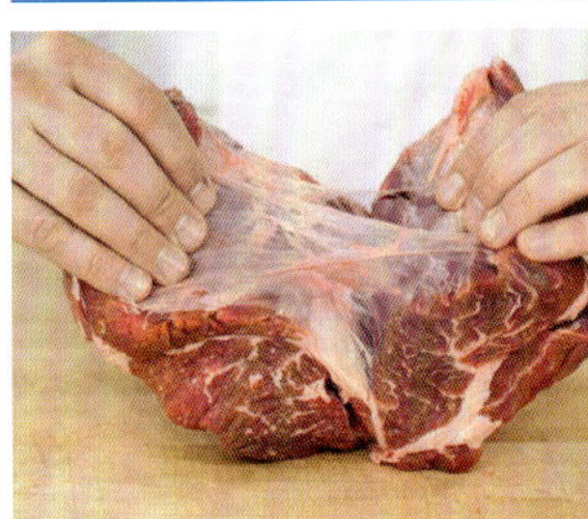

Pull roast apart at seam to make 2 smaller roasts and trim any large knobs of fat.

## New England–Style Home-Corned Beef and Cabbage

**SERVES 8**

**WHY THIS RECIPE WORKS** Corned beef and cabbage is a hearty winter favorite, but too many recipes result in overly salty beef and washed-out, mushy vegetables. To control the salt level in our beef, we eschewed commercially corned beef and set out to cure our own with an easy dry rub. We cooked our corned beef in the oven so it would benefit from the oven's slow, steady, and gentle heat. Cooking the vegetables separately in the meat's broth (while the meat rested) allowed the vegetables to be enriched by the meat's juices, but still retain their own flavor. Leave a bit of fat attached to the brisket for better texture and flavor. A similar size point-cut brisket can be used in this recipe. The meat is cooked fully when it is tender, the muscle fibers have loosened visibly, and a skewer slides in with minimal resistance. Serve this dish with horseradish, either plain or mixed with whipped cream or sour cream, or with grainy mustard.

**CORNED BEEF**

- ½ cup kosher salt
- 1 tablespoon cracked black peppercorns
- 1 tablespoon dried thyme
- 2¼ teaspoons ground allspice
- 1½ teaspoons paprika
- 2 bay leaves, crumbled
- 1 (4- to 5-pound) beef brisket, flat cut, trimmed

**VEGETABLES**

- 1½ pounds carrots, peeled and halved crosswise, thick end halved lengthwise
- 1½ pounds small red potatoes
- 1 small rutabaga (1 pound), peeled and halved crosswise; each half cut into 6 chunks
- 1 small head green cabbage (2 pounds), uncored, cut into 8 wedges

**1. FOR THE CORNED BEEF:** Combine salt, peppercorns, thyme, allspice, paprika, and bay leaves in bowl.

**2.** Using metal skewer, poke about 30 holes on each side of brisket. Rub each side evenly with salt mixture. Place brisket in 2-gallon zipper-lock bag, forcing out as much air as possible. Place in 13 by 9-inch baking dish, cover with second, similar-size pan, and weight with 2 bricks or heavy cans of similar weight. Refrigerate for 5 to 7 days, turning once a day.

**3.** Rinse brisket and pat it dry. Place brisket in Dutch oven and cover brisket with water by 1 inch. Bring to boil over high heat, skimming any scum that rises to surface. Reduce heat to medium-low, cover, and simmer until skewer inserted in thickest part of brisket slides in and out with ease, 2 to 3 hours.

**4.** Adjust oven rack to middle position and heat oven to 200 degrees. Transfer meat to large platter, ladle 1 cup cooking liquid over meat, cover with aluminum foil, and place in oven to keep warm.

**5. FOR THE VEGETABLES:** Add carrots, potatoes, and rutabaga to Dutch oven and bring to a boil over high heat. Reduce heat to medium-low, cover, and simmer until vegetables begin to soften, about 7 minutes.

**6.** Add cabbage, increase heat to high and return to boil. Reduce heat to medium-low, cover, and simmer until all vegetables are tender, 13 to 18 minutes.

**7.** Meanwhile, remove meat from oven, transfer to carving board, and slice against grain into ¼-inch slices. Return meat to platter. Transfer vegetables to meat platter, moisten with additional broth, and serve.

## Home-Corned Beef with Vegetables

**SERVES** 8 to 10

**WHY THIS RECIPE WORKS** Making corned beef at home is actually quite simple. And though the process takes several days, it's almost entirely hands-off. We chose to go with a wet cure, which was considerably faster and easier than dry-curing. We soaked a flat-cut brisket for six days in a brine made with table and pink curing salts, which improved both the flavor and color of the meat. To break down the brisket's abundant collagen, we simmered the meat gently in a low oven. We added the classic carrots, potatoes, and cabbage to the pot while the meat rested so that they simmered in the seasoned cooking liquid. To add some last-minute depth, we added more garlic and curing spices and steeped them in the cooking liquid before serving. Pink curing salt #1, which can be purchased online or in stores specializing in meat curing, is a mixture of table salt and nitrites; it is also called Prague Powder #1, Insta Cure #1, or DQ Curing Salt #1. In addition to the pink salt, we use table salt here. If using Diamond Crystal kosher salt, increase the salt to 1½ cups; if using Morton kosher salt, increase to 1⅛ cups. This recipe requires six days to corn the beef, and you will need cheesecloth. Look for a uniformly thick brisket to ensure that the beef cures evenly. The brisket will look gray after curing but will turn pink once cooked.

**CORNED BEEF**

- 1 (4½- to 5-pound) beef brisket, flat cut
- ¾ cup table salt
- ½ cup packed brown sugar
- 2 teaspoons pink curing salt #1
- 6 garlic cloves, peeled
- 6 bay leaves
- 5 allspice berries
- 2 tablespoons peppercorns
- 1 tablespoon coriander seeds

**VEGETABLES**

- 6 carrots, peeled, halved crosswise, thick ends halved lengthwise
- 1½ pounds small red potatoes, unpeeled
- 1 head green cabbage (2 pounds), uncored, cut into 8 wedges

**1. FOR THE CORNED BEEF:** Trim fat on surface of brisket to ⅛ inch. Dissolve salt, sugar, and curing salt in 4 quarts water in large container. Add brisket, 3 garlic cloves, 4 bay leaves, allspice berries, 1 tablespoon peppercorns, and coriander seeds to brine. Weigh brisket down with plate, cover, and refrigerate for 6 days.

**2.** Adjust oven rack to middle position and heat oven to 275 degrees. Remove brisket from brine, rinse, and pat dry with paper towels. Cut 8-inch square triple thickness of cheesecloth. Place remaining 3 garlic cloves, remaining 2 bay leaves, and remaining 1 tablespoon peppercorns in center of cheesecloth and tie into bundle with kitchen twine. Place brisket, spice bundle, and 2 quarts water in Dutch oven. (Brisket may not lie flat but will shrink slightly as it cooks.)

**3.** Bring to simmer over high heat, cover, and transfer to oven. Cook until fork inserted into thickest part of brisket slides in and out with ease, 2½ to 3 hours.

**4.** Remove pot from oven and turn off oven. Transfer brisket to large ovensafe platter, ladle 1 cup of cooking liquid over meat, cover, and return to oven to keep warm.

**5. FOR THE VEGETABLES:** Add carrots and potatoes to pot and bring to simmer over high heat. Reduce heat to medium-low, cover, and simmer until vegetables begin to soften, 7 to 10 minutes.

**6.** Add cabbage to pot, increase heat to high, and return to simmer. Reduce heat to low, cover, and simmer until all vegetables are tender, 12 to 15 minutes.

**7.** While vegetables cook, transfer beef to carving board and slice ¼ inch thick against grain. Return beef to platter. Using slotted spoon, transfer vegetables to platter with beef. Moisten with additional broth and serve.

## Onion-Braised Beef Brisket

**SERVES** 6

**WHY THIS RECIPE WORKS** Brisket is naturally flavorful, but because it is so lean, it requires long, slow braising to become tender. The fat in a brisket is all on the surface; there's no marbling to keep the interior moist. Could the answer lie in adding moisture after the long braise? We left the meat in the sauce after cooking it and there was a noticeable difference. Taking this discovery further, we refrigerated the cooked meat and sauce overnight. The meat reabsorbed some of the liquid, becoming moister and easier to carve without shredding. The sauce had improved as well. All we had to do was reheat the sliced meat in the defatted sauce, and this hearty dish was ready. This recipe requires advance preparation. The brisket must stand overnight in the braising liquid that later becomes the sauce. Defatting the sauce is essential. If the fat has congealed into a layer on top of the sauce, it can be easily removed while cold. If fragments of solid fat are dispersed throughout the sauce, the sauce should be skimmed of fat after reheating. If you prefer a spicy sauce, increase the cayenne to ¼ teaspoon. You will need 18-inch-wide heavy-duty foil for this recipe. If you own an electric knife, it will make easy work of slicing the cold brisket. If you would like to make and serve the brisket on the same day, after removing the brisket from the oven in step 4, reseal the foil and let the brisket stand at room temperature for an hour. Then transfer the brisket to a carving board and continue with the recipe to strain, defat, and reheat the sauce and slice the meat; because the brisket will still be hot, there will be no need to put it back into the oven once the reheated sauce is poured over it.

- 1 (4- to 5-pound) beef brisket, preferably flat cut
- 1¼ teaspoons table salt, divided
- 1 teaspoon pepper
- 1 teaspoon vegetable oil, plus extra as needed
- 3 large onions (about 2½ pounds), halved and sliced ½ inch thick

- 1 tablespoon packed brown sugar
- 3 garlic cloves, minced
- 1 tablespoon tomato paste
- 1 tablespoon paprika
- ⅛ teaspoon cayenne pepper
- 2 tablespoons all-purpose flour
- 1 cup chicken broth
- 1 cup dry red wine
- 3 bay leaves
- 3 sprigs fresh thyme
- 2 teaspoons cider vinegar

**1.** Adjust oven rack to lower-middle position and heat oven to 300 degrees. Line 13 by 9-inch baking dish with two 24-inch-long sheets of 18-inch-wide heavy-duty aluminum foil, positioning sheets perpendicular to each other and allowing excess foil to extend beyond edges of pan. Pat brisket dry with paper towels. Place brisket, fat side up, on cutting board; using dinner fork, poke holes in meat through fat layer about 1 inch apart. Sprinkle both sides of brisket with 1 teaspoon salt and pepper.

**2.** Heat oil in 12-inch skillet over medium-high heat until just smoking. Place brisket, fat side up, in skillet (brisket may climb up sides of skillet); weight brisket with heavy Dutch oven or cast-iron skillet and cook until well browned, about 7 minutes. Remove Dutch oven; using tongs, flip brisket and cook on second side without weight until well browned, about 7 minutes longer. Transfer brisket to platter.

**3.** Pour off all but 1 tablespoon fat from pan (or, if brisket is lean, add enough oil to fat in skillet to equal 1 tablespoon); stir in onions, sugar, and remaining ¼ teaspoon salt and cook over medium-high heat, stirring occasionally, until onions are softened and golden, 10 to 12 minutes. Add garlic and cook, stirring frequently, until fragrant, about 1 minute; add tomato paste and cook, stirring to combine, until paste darkens, about 2 minutes. Add paprika and cayenne and cook, stirring constantly, until fragrant, about 1 minute. Sprinkle flour over onions and cook, stirring constantly, until well combined, about 2 minutes. Add broth, wine, bay leaves, and thyme, stirring to scrape up any browned bits; bring to simmer and simmer for about 5 minutes to fully thicken.

**4.** Pour sauce and onions into foil-lined baking dish. Nestle brisket, fat side up, in sauce and onions. Fold foil extensions over and seal (do not tightly crimp foil because it must later be opened to test for doneness). Place in oven and cook until fork can be inserted into and removed from center of brisket with no resistance, 3½ to 4 hours (when testing for doneness, open foil with caution as contents will be steaming). Carefully open foil and let brisket cool at room temperature for 20 to 30 minutes.

**5.** Transfer brisket to large bowl; set mesh strainer over bowl and strain sauce over brisket. Discard bay leaves and thyme and transfer onions to small bowl. Cover both bowls with plastic wrap, cut vents in plastic with paring knife, and refrigerate overnight.

**6.** About 45 minutes before serving, adjust oven rack to lower-middle position and heat oven to 350 degrees. While oven heats, transfer cold brisket to carving board. Scrape off and discard any congealed fat from sauce, then transfer sauce to medium saucepan and heat over medium heat until warm, skimming any fat on surface with wide shallow spoon (you should have about 2 cups of sauce without onions; if necessary, simmer sauce over medium-high heat until reduced to 2 cups). While sauce heats, use electric knife, chef's knife, or carving knife to slice brisket against grain ¼ inch thick, trimming and discarding any excess fat, if desired; place slices in 13 by 9-inch baking dish. Stir reserved onions and vinegar into warmed sauce and season with salt and pepper to taste. Pour sauce over brisket slices, cover baking dish with foil, and bake until heated through, 25 to 30 minutes. Serve immediately.

## Braised Brisket with Pomegranate, Cumin, and Cilantro

**SERVES** 6 to 8

**WHY THIS RECIPE WORKS** Braising brisket breaks down what can be a tough cut into something satisfyingly tender. For a foolproof modern take, we spared no detail to create the ultimate brisket dish. For braised brisket that would be both tender and moist, we started by salting the meat (halved lengthwise for quicker cooking and easier slicing and poked all over to allow the salt to penetrate) and letting it sit for at least 16 hours, which helped it retain moisture as it cooked; the salt also seasoned it. From there, we brought the meat to 180 degrees—the sweet spot for the collagen breakdown that turns the meat tender—relatively quickly in a 325-degree oven and then lowered the temperature to 250 degrees so that the brisket finished cooking gently and retained as much moisture as possible. We reduced the braising liquid in the pan to achieve rich flavor and enhanced its body with flour and gelatin for a velvety consistency. This recipe requires salting the brisket for at least 16 hours; if you have time, you can salt it for up to 48 hours. We recommend using a remote probe thermometer to monitor the temperature of the brisket. Serve with boiled or mashed potatoes or buttered noodles.

1 (4- to 5-pound) beef brisket, flat cut, fat trimmed to ¼ inch
Kosher salt and pepper
2 tablespoons vegetable oil
2 large onions, chopped
¼ teaspoon baking soda
6 garlic cloves, minced
4 anchovy fillets, rinsed, patted dry, and minced to paste
1 tablespoon tomato paste
1 tablespoon ground cumin
1½ teaspoons ground cardamom
⅛ teaspoon cayenne pepper
¼ cup all-purpose flour
2 cups pomegranate juice
1½ cups chicken broth
3 bay leaves
2 tablespoons unflavored gelatin
1 cup pomegranate seeds
3 tablespoons chopped fresh cilantro

**1.** Place brisket, fat side down, on cutting board and cut in half lengthwise with grain. Using paring knife or metal skewer, poke each roast 20 times, pushing all the way through roast. Flip roasts and repeat on second side.

**2.** Sprinkle each roast evenly on all sides with 2½ teaspoons salt (5 teaspoons salt total). Wrap each roast in plastic wrap and refrigerate for at least 16 hours or up to 48 hours.

**3.** Adjust oven rack to middle position and heat oven to 325 degrees. Heat oil in large roasting pan over medium heat until shimmering. Add onions and baking soda and cook, stirring frequently, until onions have started to soften and break down, 4 to 5 minutes. Add garlic and cook until fragrant, about 30 seconds. Stir in anchovies, tomato paste, cumin, cardamom, cayenne, and ½ teaspoon pepper. Add flour and cook, stirring constantly, until onions are evenly coated and flour begins to stick to pan, about 2 minutes. Stir in pomegranate juice, broth, and bay leaves, scraping up any browned bits. Stir in gelatin. Increase heat to medium-high and bring to boil.

**4.** Unwrap roasts and place in pan. Cover pan tightly with aluminum foil, transfer to oven, and cook until meat registers 180 to 185 degrees at center, about 1½ hours. Reduce oven temperature to 250 degrees and continue to cook until fork slips easily in and out of meat, 2 to 2½ hours longer. Transfer roasts to baking sheet and wrap sheet tightly in foil.

**5.** Strain braising liquid through fine-mesh strainer set over large bowl, pressing on solids to extract as much liquid as possible; discard solids. Let liquid settle for 10 minutes. Using wide, shallow spoon, skim fat from surface and discard. Wipe roasting pan clean with paper towels and return defatted liquid to pan.

**6.** Increase oven temperature to 400 degrees. Return pan to oven and cook, stirring occasionally, until liquid is reduced by about one-third, 30 to 40 minutes. Remove pan from oven and use wooden spoon to draw liquid up sides of pan and scrape browned bits around edges of pan into liquid.

**7.** Transfer roasts to carving board and slice against grain ¼ inch thick; transfer to wide serving platter. Season sauce with salt and pepper to taste and pour over brisket. Tent platter with foil and let stand for 5 to 10 minutes to warm brisket through. Sprinkle with pomegranate seeds and cilantro and serve.

**TO MAKE AHEAD:** Follow recipe through step 6 and let sauce and brisket cool completely. Cover and refrigerate sauce and roasts separately for up to 2 days. To serve, slice each roast against grain ¼ inch thick and transfer to 13 by 9-inch baking dish. Heat sauce in small saucepan over medium heat until just simmering. Pour sauce over brisket, cover dish with aluminum foil, and cook in 325-degree oven until meat is heated through, about 20 minutes.

## Ropa Vieja (Cuban Braised and Shredded Beef)

**SERVES** 6 to 8

**WHY THIS RECIPE WORKS** Tender yet hearty strands of beef napped in a bright and deeply savory sauce define ropa vieja. For braised and shredded beef dishes, we usually turn to chuck roast and short ribs, but this Cuban specialty calls for thicker, more fibrous shreds, so we used brisket. Slicing the beef into strips made for faster cooking and easy shredding, and a quick sear before braising gave the meat some ultrasavory browning. The accompanying vegetables would get overly soft if braised, so we cooked them ahead of time, browning sliced onions and red bell peppers then using their fond (as well as the beef's) to build the sauce. A fragrant combination of minced anchovies, minced garlic, ground cumin, and dried oregano created the meaty, aromatic base to which we added dry white wine for brightness. After letting the mixture reduce, we added chicken broth, tomato sauce, and bay leaves. We cooked the brisket in this seasoned sauce for 2 hours and it emerged juicy and richly flavored. Green olives are a traditional finishing touch, so we chopped and added them to the sauce while the beef cooled, stirring them in with the cooked onions and peppers. A splash of white wine vinegar made the flavors in our perfectly chewy Cuban beef pop. Look for a brisket that is 1½ to 2½ inches thick. Serve with steamed white rice and beans. Another good accompaniment is Plátanos Maduros (Fried Sweet Plantains) (page 693).

1 (2-pound) beef brisket, fat trimmed to ¼ inch
Table salt and pepper
5 tablespoons vegetable oil
2 onions, halved and sliced thin
2 red bell peppers, stemmed, seeded, and sliced into ¼-inch-wide strips
2 anchovy fillets, rinsed, patted dry, and minced
4 garlic cloves, minced
2 teaspoons ground cumin
1½ teaspoons dried oregano
½ cup dry white wine
2 cups chicken broth
1 (8-ounce) can tomato sauce
2 bay leaves
¾ cup pitted green olives, chopped coarse
¾ teaspoon white wine vinegar, plus extra for seasoning

**1.** Adjust oven rack to middle position and heat oven to 300 degrees. Cut brisket against grain into 2-inch-wide strips. Cut any strips longer than 5 inches in half crosswise. Season beef on all sides with salt and pepper. Heat 4 tablespoons oil in Dutch oven over medium-high heat until just smoking. Brown beef on all sides, 7 to 10 minutes; transfer to large plate and set aside. Add onions and bell peppers and cook until softened and pan bottom develops fond, 10 to 15 minutes. Transfer vegetables to bowl and set aside. Add remaining 1 tablespoon oil to now-empty pot, then add anchovies, garlic, cumin, and oregano and cook until fragrant, about 30 seconds. Stir in wine, scraping up any browned bits, and cook until mostly evaporated, about 1 minute. Stir in broth, tomato sauce, and bay leaves. Return beef and any accumulated juices to pot and bring to simmer over high heat. Transfer to oven and cook, covered, until beef is just tender, 2 to 2¼ hours, flipping beef halfway through cooking.

**2.** Transfer beef to cutting board; when cool enough to handle, shred into ¼-inch-thick pieces. Meanwhile, add olives and reserved vegetables to pot and bring to boil over medium-high heat; simmer until thickened and measures 4 cups, 5 to 7 minutes. Stir in beef. Add vinegar. Season with salt, pepper, and extra vinegar to taste; serve.

## Cuban Shredded Beef

**SERVES** 4 to 6

**WHY THIS RECIPE WORKS** Vaca frita is a Cuban classic that features beef (usually flank steak) that's been boiled, shredded, and fried so that the exterior develops a deep crust; a bit of lime juice and garlic contribute bright, tart, and robust flavors. For our recipe, we were after meat with some textural contrast—we wanted a good exterior crust, plus a moister, more tender interior. We started with a collagen-rich chuck-eye roast and cut it into 1½-inch cubes to reduce the cooking time. Gently simmering it helped keep it moist. Pounding the meat flat was much more efficient than shredding it by hand. To reinforce the beefy flavor, we fried it, along with some thin-sliced onion, in its own fat before finishing everything with a mixture of garlic, cumin, oil, and citrus juices (lime as well as orange, to mellow the lime's acidity but maintain brightness). Use a well-marbled chuck-eye roast in this recipe. When trimming the beef, don't remove all visible fat—some of it will be used in lieu of oil later in the recipe. If you don't have enough reserved fat in step 3, use vegetable oil. This dish pairs well with rice and beans, or it can be used as a filling for tacos, empanadas, or sandwiches.

- 2 pounds boneless beef chuck-eye roast, pulled apart at seams, trimmed, and cut into 1½-inch cubes
- Kosher salt and pepper
- 3 garlic cloves, minced
- 1 teaspoon vegetable oil
- ¼ teaspoon ground cumin
- 2 tablespoons orange juice
- 1½ teaspoons grated lime zest plus 1 tablespoon juice

- 1 onion, halved and sliced thin
- 2 tablespoons dry sherry
- Lime wedges

**1.** Bring beef, 2 cups water, and 1¼ teaspoons salt to boil in 12-inch nonstick skillet over medium-high heat. Reduce heat to low, cover, and simmer gently until beef is very tender, about 1 hour 45 minutes. (Check beef every 30 minutes, adding water so that bottom third of beef is submerged.) While beef simmers, combine garlic, oil, and cumin in bowl. Combine orange juice and lime zest and juice in second bowl.

**2.** Remove lid from skillet, increase heat to medium, and simmer until water evaporates and beef starts to sizzle, 3 to 8 minutes. Using slotted spoon, transfer beef to rimmed baking sheet. Pour off and reserve fat from skillet. Rinse skillet clean and dry with paper towels. Place sheet of aluminum foil over beef and, using meat pounder or heavy sauté pan, pound to flatten beef into ⅛-inch-thick pieces, discarding any large pieces of fat or connective tissue. (Some of beef should separate into shreds. Larger pieces that do not separate can be torn in half.)

**3.** Heat 1½ teaspoons reserved fat in now-empty skillet over high heat. When fat begins to sizzle, add onion and ¼ teaspoon salt. Cook, stirring occasionally, until onion is golden brown and charred in spots, 5 to 8 minutes. Add sherry and ¼ cup water and cook until liquid is absorbed, about 2 minutes. Transfer onion to bowl. Return skillet to high heat, add 1½ teaspoons reserved fat, and heat until it begins to sizzle. Add beef and cook, stirring frequently, until dark golden brown and crusty, 2 to 4 minutes.

**4.** Reduce heat to low and push beef to sides of skillet. Add garlic mixture to center and cook, stirring frequently, until fragrant and golden brown, about 30 seconds. Remove pan from heat, add orange juice mixture and onion, and toss to combine. Season with pepper to taste. Serve immediately with lime wedges.

## Braised Beef Short Ribs

**SERVES 6**

**WHY THIS RECIPE WORKS** Short ribs have great flavor and luscious texture, but their excess fat can be a problem. Most recipes call for resting the ribs in the braising liquid overnight, so that the fat solidifies into an easy-to-remove layer. However, the meat and sauce can come out greasy. We wanted a grease-free sauce and fork-tender meat. We used boneless short ribs, which rendered significantly less fat. To replace the body that the bones' connective tissue adds we sprinkled a bit of gelatin into the sauce. To ramp up the richness of the sauce, we reduced wine with browned aromatics before using the liquid to cook the meat. We needed another cup of liquid to keep the meat half-submerged so we used beef broth. As for the excess fat, the level was low enough that we could strain and defat the liquid in a fat separator. Reducing the liquid concentrated the flavors and made for a rich, luxurious sauce. Make sure that the ribs are at least 4 inches long and 1 inch thick. If boneless ribs are unavailable, substitute 7 pounds of bone-in beef short ribs at least 4 inches long with 1 inch of meat above the bone and bone them yourself.

- 3½ pounds boneless beef short ribs, trimmed
- 2 teaspoons kosher salt
- 1 teaspoon pepper
- 2 tablespoons vegetable oil
- 2 large onions, sliced thin (about 4 cups)
- 1 tablespoon tomato paste
- 6 garlic cloves, peeled
- 2 cups red wine, such as Cabernet Sauvignon or Côtes du Rhône
- 1 cup beef broth
- 4 carrots, peeled and cut crosswise into 2-inch pieces
- 4 sprigs fresh thyme
- 1 bay leaf
- ¼ cup cold water
- ½ teaspoon unflavored gelatin

**1.** Adjust oven rack to lower-middle position and heat oven to 300 degrees. Pat beef dry with paper towels and sprinkle with salt and pepper. Heat 1 tablespoon oil in large Dutch oven over medium-high heat until just smoking. Add half of beef and cook, without stirring, until well browned, 4 to 6 minutes. Turn beef and continue to cook on second side until well browned, 4 to 6 minutes longer, reducing heat if fat begins to smoke. Transfer beef to medium bowl. Repeat with remaining 1 tablespoon oil and remaining meat.

**2.** Reduce heat to medium; add onions; and cook, stirring occasionally, until softened and beginning to brown, 12 to 15 minutes. (If onions begin to darken too quickly, add 1 to 2 tablespoons water to pan.) Add tomato paste and cook, stirring constantly, until it browns on sides and bottom of pan, about 2 minutes. Add garlic and cook until fragrant, about 30 seconds. Increase heat to medium-high, add wine, and simmer, scraping up any browned bits, until reduced by half, 8 to 10 minutes. Add broth, carrots, thyme sprigs, and bay leaf. Add beef and any accumulated juices to pot; cover and bring to simmer. Transfer pot to oven and cook, using tongs to turn meat twice during cooking, until fork slips easily in and out of meat, 2 to 2½ hours.

**3.** Place water in small bowl and sprinkle gelatin on top; let stand for at least 5 minutes. Using tongs, transfer meat and carrots to serving platter and tent with aluminum foil. Strain cooking liquid through fine-mesh strainer into fat separator or bowl, pressing on solids to extract as much liquid as possible; discard solids. Allow liquid to settle for about 5 minutes and strain off fat. Return cooking liquid to Dutch oven and cook over medium heat until reduced to 1 cup, 5 to 10 minutes. Remove from heat and stir in gelatin mixture; season with salt and pepper to taste. Pour sauce over meat and carrots and serve.

### BONING SHORT RIBS

**1.** With chef's knife as close as possible to bone, carefully remove meat.

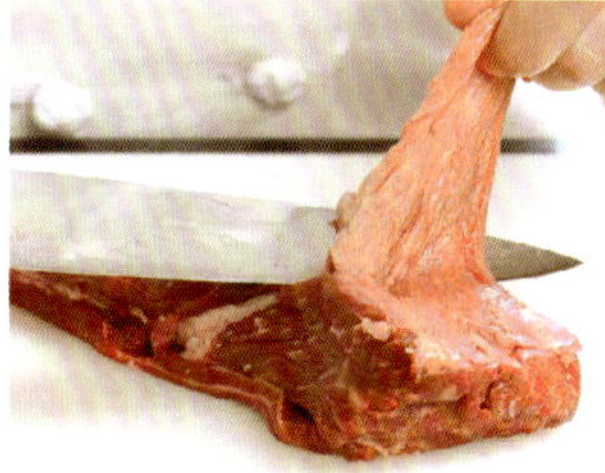

**2.** Trim excess hard fat and silverskin from both sides of meat.

## Glazed Boneless Beef Short Ribs

**SERVES 6 to 8** **SEASON 26**

**WHY THIS RECIPE WORKS** To turn boneless beef short ribs into a company-worthy entrée, we started by braising the rich, beefy meat in advance. In addition to red wine and beef broth, we incorporated umami-rich miso and soy sauce into the braising liquid. Once cooked, the meat was refrigerated in its braising liquid overnight. After the meat was removed and the fat skimmed off, the braising liquid was reduced to concentrate its flavor. Adding molasses and balsamic vinegar created a sweet-tart glaze to lacquer the ribs. For even cooking, buy ribs that are at least 4 inches long and 1 inch thick. Do not substitute bone-in short ribs. This recipe requires refrigerating the braised ribs overnight. Use a Dutch oven that holds 6 quarts or more. This recipe was developed using Diamond Crystal Kosher Salt. If you have Morton Kosher Salt, which is denser, reduce the salt to 1 tablespoon. Use a medium- to full-bodied dry red wine such as Pinot Noir or Cabernet Sauvignon. Serve with mashed potatoes or polenta and a green vegetable or Apple–Celery Root Salad (recipe follows).

- 4 pounds boneless beef short ribs, trimmed
- 4 teaspoons kosher salt
- 2 teaspoons pepper
- 2 cups beef broth
- 2 cups dry red wine
- 3 tablespoons packed brown sugar
- 2 tablespoons white miso
- 2 tablespoons soy sauce
- 1 large onion, halved and sliced thin
- 2 carrots, peeled and sliced ¼ inch thick
- 6 sprigs fresh thyme
- ⅓ cup balsamic vinegar
- 3 tablespoons molasses
- 2½ teaspoons cornstarch
- 2 teaspoons water
- 1½ teaspoons hot sauce
- 2 tablespoons minced fresh parsley or chives

**1.** Adjust oven rack to middle position and heat oven to 275 degrees. Pat beef dry with paper towels and sprinkle with salt and pepper.

**2.** Whisk broth, wine, sugar, miso, and soy sauce together in Dutch oven. Add onion, carrots, and thyme. Nestle short ribs into pot so that they are nearly submerged. Bring to simmer over high heat, cover, and transfer to oven. Cook until fork can be easily slipped in and out of ribs, 2¼ to 2¾ hours, using tongs to turn meat halfway through cooking. Cool ribs completely in braising liquid and refrigerate overnight or up to 3 days.

**3.** Remove solidified fat from top of braising liquid and discard. Transfer ribs to large plate and refrigerate until ready to use. Strain braising liquid through fine-mesh strainer set over large bowl, pressing on solids to extract as much liquid as possible. Discard solids.

**4.** Transfer 3 cups braising liquid to medium saucepan (discard remaining liquid) and bring to simmer over medium-high heat. Cook, stirring occasionally, until reduced to 1 cup, 20 to 25 minutes. Off heat, stir in vinegar and molasses.

**5.** Combine cornstarch and water in bowl. Stir cornstarch mixture into glaze and bring to simmer over medium heat. Cook until slightly thickened, about 2 minutes. Stir in hot sauce and set aside to cool slightly.

**6.** While glaze cools, adjust oven rack to middle position and heat oven to 450 degrees. Line rimmed baking sheet with parchment paper. Transfer beef to cutting board and use paring knife to trim any large pieces of fat from surface of ribs. Blot ribs dry with paper towels and evenly space on prepared sheet. Brush all surfaces of each rib with glaze.

**7.** Transfer sheet to oven and cook until beef registers 140 degrees, 20 to 25 minutes. Every 5 minutes, brush all sides of ribs with glaze and turn ribs so different side is touching pan. Apply 1 more coat of glaze to top of each rib and sprinkle with parsley. Serve, passing remaining glaze separately.

### Apple–Celery Root Salad

This creamy, crunchy, fragrant salad comes together in 15 minutes. Slicing the celery root thin and cutting the apple into matchsticks made the pieces easy to spear with a fork. Spiking the mayonnaise with cider vinegar, whole-grain mustard, and capers produced a rich, yet bright and tangy slaw.

- ¼ cup cider vinegar
- ¼ cup mayonnaise
- 1 tablespoon whole-grain mustard
- 2 Granny Smith apples, cored and cut into 2-inch-long matchsticks
- 1 small celery root, peeled and cut into 2-inch-long matchsticks
- 2 ounces (2 cups) baby arugula, roughly chopped
- 2 tablespoons capers, chopped

Whisk vinegar, mayonnaise, and mustard together in large bowl. Add apples, celery root, arugula, and capers and toss to combine. Season with salt and pepper to taste. Serve.

## Slow-Cooker Beer-Braised Short Ribs

**SERVES** 4 to 6

**WHY THIS RECIPE WORKS** Beef short ribs, which contain lots of fat and connective tissue, are ideal for the slow cooker. This recipe produces meaty ribs in a rich, oniony sauce. Browning the ribs gave us a good start; next we browned lots of onions. We chose beer as the braising liquid, and dark beer worked best. Since flavors tend to become muted after hours in a slow cooker, we intensified the taste and color of the sauce with tomato paste and soy sauce. Our dish lacked balance but we found our solution in an unusual source: prunes. They melted into the sauce and were unidentifiable, but their sweetness balanced the other flavors nicely. Livened up with Dijon mustard and fresh thyme, these slow-cooker short ribs had rich, complex flavor. The only way to remove fat from the braising liquid is to prepare this recipe a day or two before you want to serve it. Luckily, the short ribs actually taste better if cooked in advance and then reheated in the defatted braising liquid.

- 5 pounds English-style beef short ribs (6 to 8 ribs), trimmed of excess fat
- Table salt and ground black pepper
- 2 tablespoons vegetable oil
- 2 tablespoons unsalted butter
- 3 pounds yellow onions (about 6 medium), halved and sliced thin
- 2 tablespoons tomato paste
- 2 (12-ounce) bottles dark beer
- 12 pitted prunes
- 2 tablespoons soy sauce
- 2 tablespoons Minute tapioca
- 2 bay leaves
- 2 teaspoons minced fresh thyme leaves
- 3 tablespoons Dijon mustard
- 2 tablespoons minced fresh parsley leaves

**1.** Season the ribs with salt and pepper. Heat the oil in a 12-inch skillet over medium-high heat until just smoking. Add half of the ribs, meaty side down, and cook until well browned, about 5 minutes. Turn each rib on one side and cook until well browned, about 1 minute. Repeat with the remaining sides. Transfer the ribs to a slow-cooker insert, arranging them meaty side down. Repeat with the remaining ribs.

**2.** Pour off all but 1 teaspoon fat from the skillet. Add the butter and reduce the heat to medium. When the butter has melted, add the onions and cook, stirring occasionally, until well browned, 25 to 30 minutes. Stir in the tomato paste and cook, coating the onions with the tomato paste, until the paste begins to brown, about 5 minutes. Stir in the beer, bring to a simmer, and cook, scraping the browned bits from the pan bottom with a wooden spoon, until the foaming subsides, about 5 minutes. Remove the skillet from the heat and stir in the prunes, soy sauce, tapioca, bay leaves, and 1 teaspoon of the thyme. Transfer to the slow-cooker insert.

**3.** Set the slow cooker on low, cover, and cook until the ribs are fork-tender, 10 to 11 hours. (Alternatively, cook on high for 4 to 5 hours.) Transfer the ribs to a baking dish and strain the liquid through a fine-mesh strainer into a bowl. Cover and refrigerate for at least 8 hours or up to 2 days.

**4.** When ready to serve, use a spoon to skim off the hardened fat from the liquid. Place the short ribs, meaty side down, and the liquid in a Dutch oven and reheat over medium heat until warmed through, about 20 minutes. Transfer the ribs to a serving platter. Whisk the mustard and remaining 1 teaspoon thyme into the sauce and season with salt and pepper to taste. Pour 1 cup of the sauce over the ribs. Sprinkle with the parsley and serve, passing the remaining sauce separately.

## Pub-Style Steak and Ale Pie

SERVES 6

**WHY THIS RECIPE WORKS** Savory steak pie is a classic British comfort food, but making it is a multistep procedure. Our streamlined version has all the flavor and texture of the original dish, with less work. We skipped browning the meat and

browned the mushrooms and onion instead, building a flavorful fond. Adding flour early and limiting the amount of beef broth meant that the gravy formed as the meat cooked. To intensify the flavor, we added bacon, garlic, and thyme. We substituted beer for some of the broth and boosted browning with baking soda. Our sturdy dough included an egg for structure, which together with sour cream also contributed fat. The dough could be placed over the filling while hot and still bake up flaky. Do not substitute bone-in short ribs. Instead, use a 4-pound chuck-eye roast, well trimmed of fat. Use a good-quality beef broth for this recipe. If you don't have a deep-dish pie plate, use an 8 by 8-inch baking dish and roll the pie dough into a 10-inch square. We prefer pale and brown ales for this recipe.

**FILLING**

- 3 tablespoons water
- ½ teaspoon baking soda
- 3 pounds boneless beef short ribs, trimmed and cut into ¾-inch chunks
- ½ teaspoon table salt
- ½ teaspoon pepper
- 2 slices bacon, chopped
- 1 pound cremini mushrooms, trimmed and halved if medium or quartered if large
- 1½ cups beef broth, divided
- 1 large onion, chopped
- 1 garlic clove, minced
- ½ teaspoon dried thyme
- ¼ cup all-purpose flour
- ¾ cup beer

**CRUST**

- 1 large egg, lightly beaten, divided
- ¼ cup sour cream, chilled
- 1¼ cups (6¼ ounces) all-purpose flour
- ½ teaspoon table salt
- 6 tablespoons unsalted butter, cut into ½-inch pieces and chilled

**1. FOR THE FILLING:** Combine water and baking soda in large bowl. Add beef, salt, and pepper and toss to combine. Adjust oven rack to lower-middle position and heat oven to 350 degrees.

**2.** Cook bacon in large Dutch oven over high heat, stirring occasionally, until partially rendered but not browned, about 3 minutes. Add mushrooms and ¼ cup broth and stir to coat. Cover and cook, stirring occasionally, until mushrooms are reduced to about half their original volume, about 5 minutes. Add onion, garlic, and thyme and cook, uncovered, stirring occasionally, until onion is softened and fond begins to form on bottom of pot, 3 to 5 minutes. Sprinkle flour over mushroom mixture and stir until all flour is moistened. Cook, stirring occasionally, until fond is deep brown, 2 to 4 minutes. Stir in beer and remaining 1¼ cups broth, scraping up any browned bits. Stir in beef and bring to simmer, pressing as much beef as possible below surface of liquid. Cover pot tightly with aluminum foil, then lid; transfer to oven. Cook for 1 hour.

**3.** Remove lid and discard foil. Stir filling, cover, return to oven, and continue to cook until beef is tender and liquid is thick enough to coat beef, 15 to 30 minutes longer. Transfer filling to deep-dish pie plate. (Once cool, filling can be covered with plastic wrap and refrigerated for up to 2 days.) Increase oven temperature to 400 degrees.

**4. FOR THE CRUST:** While filling is cooking, measure out 2 tablespoons beaten egg and set aside. Whisk remaining egg and sour cream together in bowl. Process flour and salt in food processor until combined, about 3 seconds. Add butter and pulse until only pea-size pieces remain, about 10 pulses. Add half of sour cream mixture and pulse until combined, about 5 pulses. Add remaining sour cream mixture and pulse until dough begins to form, about 10 pulses. Transfer mixture to lightly floured counter and knead briefly until dough comes together. Form into 4-inch disk, wrap in plastic, and refrigerate for at least 1 hour or up to 2 days.

**5.** Roll dough into 11-inch round on lightly floured counter. Using knife or 1-inch round biscuit cutter, cut round from center of dough. Drape dough over filling (it's OK if filling is hot). Trim overhang to ½ inch beyond lip of plate. Tuck overhang under itself; folded edge should be flush with edge of plate. Crimp dough evenly around edge of plate using your fingers or press with tines of fork to seal. Brush crust with reserved egg. Place pie on rimmed baking sheet. Bake until filling is bubbling and crust is deep golden brown and crisp, 25 to 30 minutes. (If filling has been refrigerated, increase baking time by 15 minutes and cover with foil for last 15 minutes to prevent overbrowning.) Let cool for 10 minutes before serving.

## Carne Deshebrada (Shredded Beef Tacos)

**SERVES** 6 to 8

**WHY THIS RECIPE WORKS** The Mexican taco filling called carne deshebrada (shredded meat) is made by braising a large cut of beef until ultratender then shredding the meat and tossing it with a red or green sauce. Our version has a robust rojo (red) sauce. Traditionally, the beef is cooked in water, which is then discarded. We put the braising liquid to use in the sauce which added flavor and streamlined the recipe. We swapped in beer and cider vinegar and swapped the roast for short ribs. Propping the cubes of meat on slices of onion allowed them to brown in ambient heat. Tomato paste lent savory depth, and ancho chiles a spicy kick. Cumin, cinnamon, and cloves provided earthy backbone. For a bright topping, we made a curtido, a pickled slaw from El Salvador. Queso fresco added a salty, creamy finish. Use a full-bodied lager or ale such as Dos Equis or Sierra Nevada. If you can't find queso fresco, substitute feta. To warm tortillas, place them on a plate, cover with a damp dish towel, and microwave for 60 to 90 seconds.

**BEEF**

- 1½ cups beer
- ½ cup cider vinegar
- 2 ounces (4 to 6) dried ancho chiles, stemmed, seeded, and torn into 1-inch pieces
- 2 tablespoons tomato paste
- 6 garlic cloves, lightly crushed and peeled
- 3 bay leaves
- 2 teaspoons ground cumin
- 2 teaspoons dried oregano
- Table salt and pepper
- ½ teaspoon ground cloves
- ½ teaspoon ground cinnamon
- 1 large onion, sliced into ½-inch-thick rounds
- 3 pounds boneless beef short ribs, trimmed and cut into 2-inch cubes

**CABBAGE-CARROT SLAW**

- 1 cup cider vinegar
- ½ cup water
- 1 tablespoon sugar
- 1½ teaspoons table salt
- ½ head green cabbage, cored and sliced thin (6 cups)
- 1 onion, sliced thin
- 1 large carrot, peeled and shredded
- 1 jalapeño chile, stemmed, seeded, and minced
- 1 teaspoon dried oregano
- 1 cup chopped fresh cilantro

- 18 (6-inch) corn tortillas, warmed
- 4 ounces queso fresco, crumbled (1 cup)
- Lime wedges

**1. FOR THE BEEF:** Adjust oven rack to lower-middle position and heat oven to 325 degrees. Combine beer, vinegar, anchos, tomato paste, garlic, bay leaves, cumin, oregano, 2 teaspoons salt, ½ teaspoon pepper, cloves, and cinnamon in Dutch oven. Arrange onion rounds in single layer on bottom of pot. Place beef on top of onion rounds in single layer. Cover and cook until meat is well browned and tender, 2½ to 3 hours.

**2. FOR THE CABBAGE-CARROT SLAW:** While beef cooks, whisk vinegar, water, sugar, and salt in large bowl until sugar is dissolved. Add cabbage, onion, carrot, jalapeño, and oregano and toss to combine. Cover and refrigerate for at least 1 hour or up to 24 hours. Drain slaw and stir in cilantro right before serving.

**3.** Using slotted spoon, transfer beef to large bowl, cover loosely with aluminum foil, and set aside. Strain liquid through fine-mesh strainer into 2-cup liquid measuring cup (do not wash pot). Discard onion rounds and bay leaves. Transfer remaining solids to blender. Let strained liquid settle for 5 minutes, then skim any fat off surface. Add water as needed to equal 1 cup. Pour liquid in blender with reserved solids and blend until smooth, about 2 minutes. Transfer sauce to now-empty pot.

**4.** Using two forks, shred beef into bite-size pieces. Bring sauce to simmer over medium heat. Add shredded beef and stir to coat. Season with salt to taste. (Beef can be refrigerated for up to 2 days; gently reheat before serving.)

**5.** Spoon small amount of beef into each warm tortilla and serve, passing slaw, queso fresco, and lime wedges separately.

## Hóng Shāo Niú Ròu (Chinese Braised Beef)

**SERVES 6**

**WHY THIS RECIPE WORKS** Chinese braised beef (also called red-cooked beef) is a slow-braised dish in which a thick, ultra-flavorful sauce envelops tender pieces of beef. We wanted our version to maintain the deeply complex flavors of the original. We used readily available boneless beef short ribs in place of the traditional shank of beef. To streamline the classic cooking method, we skipped blanching the meat, and we moved the pot from the stovetop to the even heat of the oven. A pair of thickeners—gelatin and cornstarch—added body to the sauce. Five-spice powder provided characteristic flavor without the need for whole spices, and hoisin sauce and molasses contributed an underlying sweetness that completed the dish. With its generous amount of soy sauce, this dish is meant to taste salty, which is why we like to serve it with white rice. A simple steamed vegetable like bok choy or broccoli completes the meal. Boneless beef short ribs require little trimming, but you can also use a 4-pound chuck roast. Trim the roast of large pieces of fat and sinew, cut it across the grain into 1-inch-thick slabs, and cut the slabs into 4 by 2-inch pieces.

- 1½ tablespoons unflavored gelatin
- 2½ cups plus 1 tablespoon water
- ½ cup dry sherry
- ⅓ cup soy sauce
- 2 tablespoons hoisin sauce
- 2 tablespoons molasses
- 3 scallions, white and green parts separated, green parts sliced thin on bias
- 1 (2-inch) piece ginger, peeled, halved lengthwise, and crushed
- 4 garlic cloves, peeled and smashed
- 1½ teaspoons five-spice powder
- 1 teaspoon red pepper flakes
- 3 pounds boneless beef short ribs, trimmed and cut into 4-inch lengths
- 1 teaspoon cornstarch

**1.** Sprinkle gelatin over 2½ cups water in Dutch oven and let sit until gelatin softens, about 5 minutes. Adjust oven rack to middle position and heat oven to 300 degrees.

**2.** Heat softened gelatin over medium-high heat, stirring occasionally, until melted, 2 to 3 minutes. Stir in sherry, soy sauce, hoisin, molasses, scallion whites, ginger, garlic, five-spice powder, and pepper flakes. Stir in beef and bring to simmer. Remove pot from heat. Cover tightly with sheet of heavy-duty aluminum foil, then lid. Transfer to oven and cook until beef is tender, 2 to 2½ hours, stirring halfway through cooking.

**3.** Using slotted spoon, transfer beef to cutting board. Strain sauce through fine-mesh strainer into fat separator. Wipe out pot with paper towels. Let liquid settle for 5 minutes, then return defatted liquid to now-empty pot. Cook liquid over medium-high heat, stirring occasionally, until thickened and reduced to 1 cup, 20 to 25 minutes.

**4.** While sauce reduces, using 2 forks, break beef into 1½-inch pieces. Whisk cornstarch and remaining 1 tablespoon water together in small bowl.

**5.** Reduce heat to medium-low, whisk cornstarch mixture into reduced sauce, and cook until sauce is slightly thickened, about 1 minute. Return beef to sauce and stir to coat. Cover and cook, stirring occasionally, until beef is heated through, about 5 minutes. Sprinkle scallion greens over top. Serve.

## Panang Beef Curry

**SERVES 6**

**WHY THIS RECIPE WORKS** Panang curry is a sweeter, more unctuous derivative of red curry. Our panang curry is rich and flavorful but quicker to make than traditional versions. We doctored jarred red curry paste with the distinct flavors of makrut lime leaves, fish sauce, sugar, a Thai chile, and peanuts. We cooked thin-sliced boneless beef short ribs separately in plain water until tender. This ensured that the beef's flavor didn't overpower the other flavors in the dish. Once the beef was cooked (which can be done in advance), we added it to the coconut milk–based sauce and simmered it briefly. Red curry pastes vary in spiciness, so start by adding 2 tablespoons and then taste the sauce and add up to 2 tablespoons more. Makrut lime leaves are well worth seeking out. If you can't find them, substitute three 3-inch strips each of lemon zest and lime zest, adding them to the sauce with the beef in step 2 (remove the zest strips before serving). Do not substitute light coconut milk. Serve this rich dish with rice and vegetables.

- 2 pounds boneless beef short ribs, trimmed
- 2 tablespoons vegetable oil
- 2–4 tablespoons Thai red curry paste
- 1 (14-ounce) can unsweetened coconut milk
- 4 teaspoons fish sauce
- 2 teaspoons sugar
- 1 Thai red chile, halved lengthwise (optional)
- 6 makrut lime leaves, middle vein removed, sliced thin
- ⅓ cup unsalted dry-roasted peanuts, chopped fine

**1.** Cut each rib crosswise with grain into 3 equal pieces. Slice each piece against grain ¼ inch thick. Place beef in large saucepan and add water to cover. Bring to boil over high heat. Cover, reduce heat to low, and cook until beef is fork-tender, 1 to 1¼ hours. Using slotted spoon, transfer beef to bowl; discard water. (Beef can refrigerated for up to 24 hours; when ready to use, add it to curry as directed in step 2.)

**2.** Heat oil in 12-inch nonstick skillet over medium heat until shimmering. Add 2 tablespoons curry paste and cook, stirring frequently, until paste is fragrant and darkens in color to brick red, 5 to 8 minutes. Add coconut milk, fish sauce, sugar, and chile, if using; stir to combine and dissolve sugar. Taste sauce and add up to 2 tablespoons more curry paste to achieve desired spiciness. Add beef, stir to coat with sauce, and bring to simmer.

**3.** Rapidly simmer, stirring occasionally, until sauce is thickened and reduced by half and coats beef, 12 to 15 minutes. (Sauce should be quite thick, and streaks of oil will appear. Sauce will continue to thicken as it cools.) Add makrut lime leaves and simmer until fragrant, 1 to 2 minutes. Transfer to serving platter, sprinkle with peanuts, and serve.

## Plov (Rice Pilaf with Beef and Carrots)

SERVES 4

**WHY THIS RECIPE WORKS** Plov is a revered beef-and-carrot rice dish from Uzbekistan. The challenge is to get the meat to reach perfect tenderness at the same time that the rice finishes cooking. We removed the beef from the pan when it was tender and added it back when the rice was nearly done. A tight seal on the saucepan ensured that the flavorful cooking liquid was retained and absorbed into the rice. A grated carrot plus carrot chunks provided sweet, earthy flavor. Traditional dried barberries supplied bracing pops of acidity. We simmered a head of garlic with the meat; diners can mix cloves into their pilaf. Grate the largest carrot on the large holes of a box grater. You can substitute 1¼ pounds of blade steak, about 1 inch thick, for the boneless short ribs; halve the steak along the central line of connective tissue, and then remove the tissue. Don't substitute bone-in short ribs. If barberries are unavailable, combine 2 tablespoons of dried currants and 1 tablespoon of lemon juice in a small bowl. Microwave, covered, until very steamy, about 1 minute. Add the currants (and any residual lemon juice) to the plov as directed.

- 5 carrots, peeled
- 1 pound boneless beef short ribs, trimmed
- 1½ teaspoons table salt, divided
- 1 tablespoon vegetable oil
- 2 onions, quartered through root end and sliced ¼ inch thick
- 2 tablespoons dried barberries, divided
- 3 garlic cloves, minced, plus 1 head garlic, outer papery skin removed and top ½ inch cut off
- 1 tablespoon ground cumin
- 2 teaspoons ground coriander
- ½ teaspoon pepper
- 1¾ cups water
- 1 cup basmati rice, rinsed and drained
- 2 scallions, sliced thin

**1.** Adjust oven rack to middle position and heat oven to 350 degrees. Grate largest carrot. Cut remaining 4 carrots into 2 by ½-inch pieces. Pat beef dry with paper towels and sprinkle all over with ½ teaspoon salt. Heat oil in large ovensafe saucepan over medium-high heat until shimmering. Add beef and cook until well browned on all sides, 10 to 12 minutes. Using tongs, transfer beef to bowl.

**2.** Add onions and remaining 1 teaspoon salt to saucepan. Cover and cook, stirring occasionally and scraping up any browned bits, until onions are soft, about 5 minutes. Add grated carrot, 1 tablespoon barberries, minced garlic, cumin, coriander, and pepper and cook, stirring constantly, until garlic and spices are fragrant, 1 to 2 minutes. Spread mixture into even layer. Return beef to saucepan, nestling it into vegetables. Add water and any accumulated beef juices. Place garlic head in center of saucepan. Increase heat to high and bring mixture to vigorous simmer. Remove saucepan from heat; place large sheet of aluminum foil over saucepan, crimp tightly to seal, and cover tightly with lid. Transfer saucepan to oven and cook until meat is fork-tender, 1¼ to 1½ hours.

**3.** Transfer beef and garlic head to cutting board. Stir rice and remaining carrots into cooking liquid (saucepan handle will be hot). Bring to simmer over medium heat. Adjust heat to maintain simmer; replace foil, cover, and cook until liquid level has dropped below rice and rice is half cooked, about 10 minutes. While rice cooks, cut beef into ½-inch cubes. Gently fold beef into rice mixture, making sure to incorporate rice on bottom of saucepan. Replace foil, cover, and continue to cook until rice is tender and moisture is fully absorbed, 10 to 15 minutes longer. (Check rice every 5 minutes by sliding butter knife to bottom of center of saucepan and gently pushing rice aside; if bottom appears to be drying out, reduce heat slightly.)

**4.** Pile pilaf on platter. Sprinkle with scallions and remaining 1 tablespoon barberries. Garnish with garlic head and serve.

## Skillet Beef Stroganoff

**SERVES 4**

**WHY THIS RECIPE WORKS** Originally, beef stroganoff was quite elegant and was even made with filet mignon. Our goal was twofold: find a less expensive option for the beef to turn it into a within-reach weeknight supper, and refine the too-rich, often gloppy sauce. We started with the beef: Sirloin tips became tender and held their shape well, after we pounded the meat before cutting it into strips. We first seared the meat, then sautéed mushrooms and onion in the same pan. To finish cooking the beef, we built a braising liquid of both chicken and beef broth and a little flour to thicken the sauce. We didn't want to over season the dish but found that some brandy was essential. We then returned the meat to the sauce to cook through. To avoid cooking the noodles separately, we added them directly to the braising liquid. When the noodles were tender and the beef was cooked through, we added sour cream and lemon juice, off the heat so that they wouldn't curdle. To prepare the beef, pound it with a meat pounder to an even ½-inch thickness. Slice the meat, with the grain, into 2-inch strips, then slice each piece against the grain into ½-inch strips. Brandy can ignite if added to a hot, empty skillet. Be sure to add the brandy to the skillet after stirring in the broth.

- 1½ pounds sirloin tips, pounded and cut into ½-inch strips
- Table salt and ground black pepper
- 4 tablespoons vegetable oil
- 10 ounces white mushrooms, wiped clean and sliced thin
- 1 medium onion, minced
- 2 tablespoons unbleached all-purpose flour
- 1½ cups low-sodium chicken broth
- 1½ cups beef broth
- ⅓ cup brandy
- 6 ounces wide egg noodles (4 cups)
- ⅔ cup sour cream
- 2 teaspoons juice from 1 lemon

**1.** Pat the beef dry with paper towels and season with salt and pepper. Heat 1 tablespoon of the oil in a 12-inch skillet over medium-high heat until just smoking. Cook half of the beef until well browned, 3 to 4 minutes per side. Transfer to a medium bowl and repeat with 1 tablespoon more oil and the remaining beef.

**2.** Heat the remaining 2 tablespoons oil in the now-empty skillet until shimmering. Cook the mushrooms, onion, and ½ teaspoon salt until the liquid from the mushrooms has evaporated, about 8 minutes. (If the pan becomes too brown, pour the accumulated beef juices into the skillet.) Stir in the flour and cook for 30 seconds. Gradually stir in the broths, then the brandy, and return the beef and accumulated juices to the skillet. Bring to a simmer, cover, and cook over low heat until the beef is tender, 30 to 35 minutes.

**3.** Stir the noodles into the beef mixture, cover, and cook, stirring occasionally, until the noodles are tender, 10 to 12 minutes. Off the heat, stir in the sour cream and lemon juice. Season with salt and pepper to taste and serve.

## Steak Tips with Mushroom-Onion Gravy

**SERVES 4 to 6**

**WHY THIS RECIPE WORKS** This classic supper promises juicy beef and hearty flavors but often delivers overcooked meat in a generic brown sauce or a greasy, gloppy gravy. To rescue the dish, we started with tender sirloin steak tips. To build flavor without adding any fat, we marinated the tips in a mixture of sugar for sweetness and soy sauce for saltiness. Browning the beef in a skillet leaves behind plenty of flavorful browned bits with which we built a rich gravy. Cremini mushrooms can be used in place of the white mushrooms. This dish can be served over rice or mashed potatoes, or with egg noodles. Steak tips, also known as flap meat, are sold as whole steak, cubes, and strips. To ensure evenly sized chunks, we prefer to purchase whole steak tips and cut them ourselves.

- 1 tablespoon soy sauce
- 1 teaspoon sugar
- 1½ pounds sirloin steak tips, trimmed and cut into 1½-inch chunks
- 1¾ cups beef broth, divided
- ¼ ounce dried porcini mushrooms, rinsed
- ½ teaspoon pepper
- 2 tablespoons vegetable oil, divided
- 1 pound white mushrooms, trimmed and sliced ¼ inch thick
- ½ teaspoon table salt, divided
- 1 large onion, halved and sliced thin
- 4 teaspoons all-purpose flour
- 1 garlic clove, minced
- ½ teaspoon minced fresh thyme
- 1 tablespoon chopped fresh parsley

**1.** Combine soy sauce and sugar in medium bowl. Add beef, toss well, and marinate for at least 30 minutes or up to 1 hour, tossing once more.

**2.** Meanwhile, microwave ¼ cup broth and porcini mushrooms in covered bowl until steaming, about 1 minute. Let sit until softened, about 5 minutes. Drain porcini mushrooms in fine-mesh strainer lined with coffee filter, reserve liquid, and mince porcini mushrooms. Set aside porcini mushrooms and liquid.

**3.** Pat beef dry with paper towels and sprinkle with pepper. Heat 1 tablespoon oil in 12-inch skillet over medium-high heat until just smoking. Add beef and cook until well browned on all sides, 6 to 8 minutes. Transfer to large plate and set aside.

**4.** Add remaining 1 tablespoon oil to now-empty skillet and heat over medium-high heat. Add white mushrooms, minced porcini mushrooms, and ¼ teaspoon salt; cook, stirring frequently, until all liquid has evaporated and mushrooms start to brown, 7 to 9 minutes, scraping up any browned bits. Add onion and remaining ¼ teaspoon salt; cook, stirring frequently, until onion begins to brown and dark bits form on pan bottom, 6 to 8 minutes longer. Add flour, garlic, and thyme; cook, stirring constantly, until vegetables are coated with flour mixture, about 1 minute. Stir in porcini soaking liquid and remaining 1½ cups broth, scraping up any browned bits, and bring to boil.

5. Nestle beef into mushroom-onion mixture and add any accumulated juices to skillet. Reduce heat to medium-low and simmer until beef registers 130 to 135 degrees (for medium), 3 to 5 minutes, turning beef several times. Season with salt and pepper to taste, sprinkle with parsley, and serve.

## Bò Lúc Lắc (Shaking Beef)

**SERVES 4**

**WHY THIS RECIPE WORKS** Bò lúc lắc (shaking beef) is a Vietnamese cross between a beef stir-fry and a watercress salad. We used sirloin steak tips (aka flap meat) for their beefy flavor and pleasant chewy texture. We first marinated the meat in a mixture of soy sauce, fish sauce, and molasses and then reserved the marinade to make the glaze. We coated the meat with oil (to prevent splattering) and then cooked it in two batches to give it ample room in the skillet. True to the dish's name, we shook and stirred the beef to develop good browning and to deglaze the skillet, which prevented the fond from burning. After setting aside the meat, we lightly softened a red onion in butter, added the reserved marinade (along with garlic, water, and cornstarch) to the skillet, and cooked it down to a glossy consistency. We coated the meat with the sauce and then placed it atop the watercress, which we had lightly dressed with a mixture of lime juice and pepper. We used more of the lime juice mixture as a dipping sauce for the meat. Sirloin steak tips are often sold as flap meat. They can be packaged as whole steaks, cubes, or strips. We prefer to buy whole steaks so we can cut our own steak tips. Maggi Seasoning can be used in place of the soy sauce, if desired. Serve with Cơm Đỏ (recipe follows) or steamed white rice.

- 4 teaspoons fish sauce
- 4 teaspoons soy sauce
- 2 teaspoons molasses
- 1 pound sirloin steak tips, trimmed and cut into ¾-inch cubes
- 4 ounces (4 cups) watercress, torn into bite-size pieces
- ¼ cup lime juice (2 limes)
- 1 teaspoon pepper
- ¼ cup water
- 2 garlic cloves, minced
- ¾ teaspoon cornstarch
- 4 teaspoons vegetable oil, divided
- 1 tablespoon unsalted butter
- 1 small red onion, sliced thin

1. Whisk fish sauce, soy sauce, and molasses together in medium bowl. Add beef and toss to coat. Let sit at room temperature for 15 minutes. Spread watercress in shallow serving bowl. Combine lime juice and pepper in small bowl and set aside.

2. Using tongs, transfer beef to second medium bowl, letting as much marinade as possible drain back into first bowl. Add water, garlic, and cornstarch to marinade in first bowl and whisk to combine; set aside. Add 2 teaspoons oil to beef and toss to coat.

3. Heat 1 teaspoon oil in 12-inch nonstick skillet over medium-high heat until just smoking. Using tongs, wipe skillet clean with paper towels. Add half of beef to skillet, leaving space between pieces. Cook, swirling skillet gently and occasionally to capture any fond that collects on bottom of skillet, until beef is browned on first side, 3 to 4 minutes. Continue to cook, stirring and shaking skillet frequently, until beef is coated and browned and center is just pink (to check for doneness, remove larger piece and cut in half), 2 to 4 minutes longer. Transfer beef to clean bowl. Wipe skillet clean with wet paper towels and repeat with remaining 1 teaspoon oil and remaining beef.

4. Melt butter in now-empty skillet over medium heat. Add onion and cook, stirring occasionally, until just beginning to soften, about 1 minute. Add reserved marinade and bring to boil. Cook, stirring occasionally, until thickened and glossy, about 2 minutes. Add beef and any accumulated juices and toss to coat. Scatter beef mixture and sauce over watercress. Drizzle 2 teaspoons lime juice mixture over salad. Divide remaining lime juice mixture among small bowls for dipping and serve with salad.

### Cơm Đỏ (Vietnamese Red Rice)

**SERVES 4 to 6**

Red rice is an ultrasavory Vietnamese dish normally made by stir-frying precooked rice, but we made ours from scratch in one pot, using tomato paste and soy sauce for umami and butter for richness. We based this recipe on a version made by Vietnamese cooking authority Andrea Nguyen. If jasmine rice is unavailable, substitute another long-grain white rice. Maggi Seasoning can be used in place of the soy sauce.

- 1½ cups jasmine rice
- 2 tablespoons unsalted butter
- 4 garlic cloves, minced
- 3 tablespoons tomato paste
- 1¾ cups water
- 2 teaspoons soy sauce
- ½ teaspoon table salt

**1.** Place rice in fine-mesh strainer and rinse under cold running water until water runs clear. Drain well. Melt butter in medium saucepan over medium-high heat. Add rice and cook, stirring constantly, until grains become chalky and opaque, 1 to 3 minutes. Add garlic and cook, stirring constantly, until fragrant, about 30 seconds. Add tomato paste and cook, stirring constantly, until tomato paste is evenly distributed, about 1 minute.

**2.** Add water, soy sauce, and salt and bring to boil. Cover, reduce heat to low, and cook until liquid is absorbed and rice is tender, about 20 minutes. Let stand off heat, covered, for 10 minutes. Fluff rice with fork and stir to combine. Serve.

## Stir-Fried Cumin Beef

**SERVES 4**

**WHY THIS RECIPE WORKS** With roots in Hunan cuisine, cumin beef typically features tender pieces of meat stir-fried with onions and/or peppers and aromatics, glossed in a soy sauce–based glaze, seasoned with spices, and finished with cilantro. We first briefly treated slices of beefy flank steak with baking soda, which raised the meat's pH so that it stayed moist and tender during cooking. We stir-fried the meat in two batches until its juices reduced to a sticky fond that coated each slice. Quickly stir-frying sliced onion allowed it to soften but retain a hint of its raw bite and crunch. Grinding cumin seeds and Sichuan peppercorns released aromatic compounds that gave the dish plenty of fragrance, while Sichuan chili powder added moderate heat. We developed this recipe for a 14-inch wok, but a 12-inch nonstick or carbon-steel skillet can be used instead. You can substitute 1 tablespoon of ground cumin for the cumin seeds. If you can't find Sichuan chili powder, Korean red pepper flakes (gochugaru) are a good substitute. Another alternative is 1¾ teaspoons of ancho chile powder plus ¼ teaspoon of cayenne pepper. There is no substitute for Sichuan peppercorns. We like this stir-fry with steamed white rice and stir-fried baby bok choy.

- 1 tablespoon water
- ¼ teaspoon baking soda
- 1 pound flank steak, trimmed, cut with grain into 2- to 2½-inch-wide strips, each strip sliced against grain ¼ inch thick
- 4 garlic cloves, minced
- 1 tablespoon grated fresh ginger
- 1 tablespoon cumin seeds, ground
- 2 teaspoons Sichuan chili powder
- 1¼ teaspoons Sichuan peppercorns, ground
- ½ teaspoon table salt, divided
- 1 tablespoon Shaoxing wine or dry sherry
- 1 tablespoon soy sauce
- 2 teaspoons molasses
- ½ teaspoon cornstarch
- ¼ cup vegetable oil, divided
- ½ small onion, sliced thin
- 2 tablespoons coarsely chopped fresh cilantro

**1.** Combine water and baking soda in medium bowl. Add beef and toss to coat. Let sit at room temperature for 5 minutes.

**2.** While beef rests, combine garlic and ginger in small bowl. Combine cumin, chili powder, peppercorns, and ¼ teaspoon salt in second small bowl. Add Shaoxing wine, soy sauce, molasses, cornstarch, and remaining ¼ teaspoon salt to beef mixture. Toss until well combined.

**3.** Heat 1 tablespoon oil in wok over medium-high heat until just smoking. Add half of beef mixture and increase heat to high. Using tongs, toss beef slowly but constantly until exuded juices have evaporated and meat begins to sizzle, 2 to 6 minutes. Transfer to clean bowl. Repeat with 1 tablespoon oil and remaining beef mixture.

**4.** Heat remaining 2 tablespoons oil in now-empty wok over medium heat until shimmering. Add garlic mixture (oil will splatter) and cook, stirring constantly, until fragrant, 15 to 30 seconds. Add onion and cook, tossing slowly but constantly with tongs, until onion begins to soften, 1 to 2 minutes. Return beef to wok and toss to combine. Sprinkle cumin mixture over beef and toss until onion takes on pale orange color. Transfer to serving platter, sprinkle with cilantro, and serve immediately.

## Stir-Fried Beef and Gai Lan

**SERVES 4**

**WHY THIS RECIPE WORKS** Our take on this ever-evolving Chinese American standard features gai lan (Chinese broccoli) and filet mignon. The luxe cut is ideal for the quick, high-heat cooking of stir-frying; is readily available in small portions; and needs only a brief chill in the freezer to firm up for easy slicing. While the meat chilled, we sliced the gai lan stalks thin on the bias and cut the tender leaves into wide ribbons; together, the sweeter-tasting stalks and earthier, pleasantly bitter-tasting blue-green leaves created complexly layered flavor. To avoid sodden leaves, we stir-fried the leaves first, transferred them to a serving dish, and then stir-fried the heartier stalks and the meat with the sauce. Once the sauce thickened, we arranged the beef mixture over the leaves, ensuring that each bite was perfectly sauced. We developed this recipe for a 14-inch wok, but a 12-inch carbon-steel or cast-iron skillet can be used. If gai lan is unavailable, you can use broccolini, substituting the florets for the gai lan leaves. Do not use standard broccoli. This recipe was developed with Lee Kum Kee oyster sauce. Serve with white rice.

- 1 (8-ounce) center-cut filet mignon, trimmed
- 1 pound gai lan, stalks trimmed
- 5 teaspoons Shaoxing wine or dry sherry, divided
- 1 tablespoon soy sauce, divided
- 2 teaspoons cornstarch, divided
- ¾ cup chicken broth, divided
- 2 tablespoons oyster sauce
- 1½ teaspoons toasted sesame oil, divided
- 2 tablespoons vegetable oil, divided
- 1½ teaspoons grated fresh ginger
- ¾ teaspoon minced garlic, divided

**1.** Cut beef into 4 equal wedges. Transfer to plate and freeze until very firm, 20 to 25 minutes. While beef freezes, prepare gai lan. Remove leaves, small stems, and florets from stalks; slice leaves crosswise into 1½-inch strips (any florets and stems can go into pile with leaves); and cut stalks on bias into ½-inch-thick pieces. Set aside. When beef is firm, stand 1 piece on its side and slice against grain ¼ inch thick. Repeat with remaining pieces. Transfer to bowl. Add 1 teaspoon Shaoxing wine, 1 teaspoon soy sauce, and 1 teaspoon cornstarch and toss until beef is evenly coated. Set aside.

**2.** In second bowl, whisk together ½ cup broth, oyster sauce, ½ teaspoon sesame oil, remaining 4 teaspoons Shaoxing wine, remaining 2 teaspoons soy sauce, and remaining 1 teaspoon cornstarch; set aside. In third bowl, combine 4 teaspoons vegetable oil, ginger, and ¼ teaspoon garlic.

**3.** Heat 1 teaspoon vegetable oil in wok over high heat until just smoking. Add stalks and cook, stirring slowly but constantly, until spotty brown and crisp-tender, 3 to 4 minutes. Transfer to bowl.

**4.** Add remaining 1 teaspoon sesame oil, remaining 1 teaspoon vegetable oil, and remaining ½ teaspoon garlic to wok and cook, stirring constantly, until garlic is fragrant, about 15 seconds. Add leaves and cook, stirring frequently, until vibrant green, about 1 minute. Add remaining ¼ cup broth and cook, stirring constantly, until broth evaporates, 2 to 3 minutes. Spread evenly on serving dish.

**5.** Add ginger-garlic mixture to wok and cook, stirring constantly, until fragrant, about 30 seconds. Add beef and cook, stirring slowly but constantly, until no longer pink, about 2 minutes. Return stalks to wok and add oyster sauce mixture. Cook, stirring constantly, until sauce thickens, 30 to 60 seconds. Place mixture on top of leaves. Serve.

### PREPPING GAI LAN

**1.** Remove leaves, small stems, and florets from stalks.

**2.** Slice leaves crosswise into 1½-inch strips.

**3.** Slice stalks on bias into ½-inch-thick pieces.

## Stir-Fried Beef and Broccoli with Oyster Sauce

**SERVES 4**

**WHY THIS RECIPE WORKS** For our beef and broccoli recipe, we wanted to make sure that our beef was tender and our sauce deeply flavored and silky. For the meat, we found that flank steak offered the biggest beefy taste and slicing it thin made it tender. We cooked the beef in two batches over high heat to make sure that it browned and didn't steam. Then we cooked the broccoli until crisp-tender using a combination of methods—sautéing and steaming—and added some red bell pepper for sweetness and color. For the sauce, we made a simple mixture of oyster-flavored sauce, chicken broth, dry sherry, sugar, and sesame oil, which we lightly thickened with cornstarch so that it clung beautifully to the beef and vegetables. Now we had it: Every component of the dish—the beef, the broccoli, and the sauce—was distinct and cooked to the best of its ability. To make slicing the flank steak easier, freeze it for 15 minutes. Serve with rice.

**SAUCE**

- 5 tablespoons oyster-flavored sauce
- 2 tablespoons low-sodium chicken broth
- 1 tablespoon dry sherry
- 1 tablespoon light brown sugar
- 1 teaspoon toasted sesame oil
- 1 teaspoon cornstarch

**BEEF AND BROCCOLI**

- 1 (1-pound) flank steak, trimmed and cut into 2-inch-wide strips with the grain, then sliced across the grain into ⅛-inch-thick slices
- 3 tablespoons soy sauce
- 3 tablespoons peanut or vegetable oil
- 6 medium garlic cloves, minced or pressed through a garlic press (about 2 tablespoons)
- 1 tablespoon minced or grated fresh ginger
- 1¼ pounds broccoli, florets cut into 1-inch pieces, stems trimmed and sliced thin
- ⅓ cup water
- 1 small red bell pepper, stemmed, seeded, and cut into ½-inch pieces
- 3 scallions, sliced ½ inch thick on the bias

**1. FOR THE SAUCE:** Combine all the ingredients in a small bowl and set aside.

**2. FOR THE BEEF AND BROCCOLI:** Toss the beef with the soy sauce in a medium bowl and let marinate for at least 10 minutes or up to 1 hour. In a small bowl, mix 1 teaspoon of the peanut oil, the garlic, and ginger together.

**3.** Heat 2 teaspoons more peanut oil in a 12-inch nonstick skillet over high heat until just smoking. Add half of the beef, break up any clumps, then cook without stirring until the meat is browned at the edges, about 1 minute. Stir the beef and continue to cook until cooked through, about 1 minute longer. Transfer the beef to a clean bowl and cover with foil to keep warm. Repeat with 2 teaspoons more peanut oil and the remaining beef.

**4.** Add 1 tablespoon more peanut oil to the skillet and return to high heat until just smoking. Add the broccoli and cook for 30 seconds. Add the water, cover the pan, and lower the heat to medium. Cook the broccoli until crisp-tender, about 2 minutes. Transfer the broccoli to a paper towel–lined plate.

**5.** Add the remaining 1 teaspoon peanut oil to the skillet and return to high heat until just smoking. Add the bell pepper and cook, stirring frequently, until spotty brown, about 1½ minutes. Clear the center of the skillet, add the garlic mixture, and cook, mashing the mixture into the pan, until fragrant, 15 to 20 seconds. Stir the garlic mixture into the bell pepper.

**6.** Stir in the broccoli and beef with any accumulated juices. Whisk the sauce to recombine, then add to the skillet and cook, tossing constantly, until the sauce is thickened, about 30 seconds. Transfer to a serving platter, sprinkle with the scallions, and serve.

## Beef Stir-Fry with Bell Peppers and Black Pepper Sauce

**SERVES 4**

**WHY THIS RECIPE WORKS** We discovered that in order to produce a stir-fry with velvety, tender beef, we needed to choose the right cut of meat and treat it correctly. Flank steak, cut across the grain into bite-size pieces, delivered great beef flavor and a moderate chew. Then, our combination of meat tenderizing techniques—soaking the meat briefly in a mild baking soda solution and adding some cornstarch to the marinade before flash-searing the steak in a very hot pan—finished the job of delivering a supertender beef stir-fry. Prepare the vegetables and aromatics while the beef is marinating. Serve with rice.

- 1 tablespoon plus ¼ cup water
- ¼ teaspoon baking soda
- 1 pound flank steak, trimmed, cut into 2- to 2½-inch strips with grain, each strip cut crosswise against grain into ¼-inch-thick slices
- 3 tablespoons soy sauce
- 3 tablespoons dry sherry or Chinese rice wine
- 3 teaspoons cornstarch
- 2½ teaspoons packed light brown sugar
- 1 tablespoon oyster sauce
- 2 teaspoons rice vinegar
- 1½ teaspoons toasted sesame oil
- 2 teaspoons coarsely ground pepper
- 3 tablespoons plus 1 teaspoon vegetable oil
- 1 red bell pepper, stemmed, seeded, and cut into ¼-inch-wide strips
- 1 green bell pepper, stemmed, seeded, and cut into ¼-inch-wide strips
- 6 scallions, white parts sliced thin on bias, green parts cut into 2-inch pieces
- 3 garlic cloves, minced
- 1 tablespoon grated fresh ginger

**1.** Combine 1 tablespoon water and baking soda in medium bowl. Add beef and toss to coat. Let sit at room temperature for 5 minutes.

**2.** Whisk 1 tablespoon soy sauce, 1 tablespoon sherry, 1½ teaspoons cornstarch, and ½ teaspoon sugar together in small bowl. Add soy sauce mixture to beef, stir to coat, and let sit at room temperature for 15 to 30 minutes.

**3.** Whisk remaining ¼ cup water, remaining 2 tablespoons soy sauce, remaining 2 tablespoons sherry, remaining 1½ teaspoons cornstarch, remaining 2 teaspoons sugar, oyster sauce, vinegar, sesame oil, and pepper together in second bowl.

**4.** Heat 2 teaspoons vegetable oil in 12-inch nonstick skillet over high heat until just smoking. Add half of beef in single layer. Cook without stirring for 1 minute. Continue to cook, stirring occasionally, until spotty brown on both sides, about 1 minute longer. Transfer to bowl. Repeat with 2 teaspoons vegetable oil and remaining beef.

**5.** Return skillet to high heat, add 2 teaspoons vegetable oil, and heat until just beginning to smoke. Add bell peppers and scallion greens and cook, stirring occasionally, until vegetables are spotty brown and crisp-tender, about 4 minutes. Transfer vegetables to bowl with beef.

**6.** Return now-empty skillet to medium-high heat and add remaining 4 teaspoons vegetable oil, scallion whites, garlic, and ginger. Cook, stirring frequently, until lightly browned, about 2 minutes. Return beef and vegetables to skillet and stir to combine.

**7.** Whisk sauce to recombine. Add to skillet and cook, stirring constantly, until sauce has thickened, about 30 seconds. Serve immediately.

## Jamaican Pepper Steak

**SERVES 4**

**WHY THIS RECIPE WORKS** Pepper steak is a clear snapshot of Jamaican Chinese cooking: The beef-and–bell pepper stir-fry is lavished with heady seasonings and brown gravy. We briefly soaked the meat in a baking soda solution to raise its pH, which helped it hold on to moisture during cooking. Adding a little cornstarch to the soy sauce marinade sheathed the meat in a thin, protective coating, loosely mimicking Chinese velveting. To cook everything to its ideal doneness, we stir-fried in batches: first the steak, then the peppers, the scallions, and finally the aromatics. The beef browned, the vegetables charred lightly but retained their crisp bite, and the aromatics toasted just enough to turn fragrant. Deglazing the steak fond with a splash of rum released those savory bits for the sauce. Marinating the meat in dark soy sauce and stirring oyster and Worcestershire sauces into the beef broth captured savory

depth and color. We coarsely ground allspice berries so the small bits weren't jarring to bite into. Prepare the vegetables and aromatics while the beef rests. Dark soy sauce is thicker and a bit sweeter than the all-purpose kind; shop for it online or at an Asian market. You can substitute a habanero chile for the Scotch bonnet. We prefer coarsely ground allspice berries (use a spice grinder or mortar and pestle), but ½ teaspoon ground allspice can be used. Serve over rice or rice and peas.

- 1 (1¼-pound) boneless strip steak, trimmed
- 1 tablespoon water
- ¼ teaspoon baking soda
- 4 teaspoons cornstarch, divided
- 1 tablespoon dark soy sauce
- 1 teaspoon pepper, divided
- ½ teaspoon table salt
- 2 cups beef broth
- 2 tablespoons Worcestershire sauce
- 2 tablespoons oyster sauce
- 1 teaspoon packed brown sugar
- ½ teaspoon garlic powder
- ½ teaspoon onion powder
- 2 tablespoons plus 2 teaspoons vegetable oil, divided
- 2 tablespoons dark rum or brandy
- ½ large red bell pepper, cut into ¼-inch-wide strips
- ½ large yellow bell pepper, cut into ¼-inch-wide strips
- ½ large green bell pepper, cut into ¼-inch-wide strips
- 3 scallions, cut into 2-inch pieces
- 5 garlic cloves, sliced
- 1 teaspoon whole allspice berries, coarsely ground
- ½ teaspoon grated fresh ginger
- ½ teaspoon minced fresh thyme
- ½ teaspoon minced Scotch bonnet chile

**1.** Slice beef crosswise ¼ inch thick. Cut slices into ¼-inch-thick strips. Combine water and baking soda in medium bowl. Add beef and toss to coat. Let sit at room temperature for 5 minutes.

**2.** Add 1 teaspoon cornstarch, soy sauce, ½ teaspoon pepper, and salt to beef and toss until well combined. Refrigerate for at least 1 hour or up to 2 hours.

**3.** Whisk beef broth, Worcestershire, oyster sauce, sugar, garlic powder, onion powder, remaining 1 tablespoon cornstarch, and remaining ½ teaspoon pepper in bowl.

**4.** Heat 2 teaspoons oil in 12-inch nonstick or carbon-steel skillet over medium-high heat until just smoking. Add half of beef in single layer. Cook without stirring for 1 minute. Continue to cook, stirring occasionally, until spotty brown on both sides, about 1 minute longer. Transfer to clean bowl. Repeat with 2 teaspoons oil and remaining beef. Remove now-empty skillet from heat. Add rum and, using spatula, scrape any browned bits from skillet. Transfer any remaining liquid and browned bits to bowl with beef.

**5.** Return skillet to medium-high heat, add 2 teaspoons oil, and heat until just smoking. Add bell peppers and cook, stirring occasionally, until peppers are spotty brown but still crisp, 2 to 3 minutes. Transfer peppers to bowl with beef.

**6.** Return skillet to medium-high heat, add remaining 2 teaspoons oil, and heat until just smoking. Add scallions and cook, stirring occasionally, until spotty brown, 1 to 2 minutes. Add garlic, allspice, ginger, thyme, and Scotch bonnet. Cook, stirring frequently, until garlic is lightly browned and fragrant, about 1 minute. Transfer scallion mixture to bowl with beef and peppers.

**7.** Whisk beef broth mixture to recombine. Add mixture to skillet; reduce heat to medium; and cook, stirring occasionally, until thickened (spatula will start to leave trail that quickly fills in), 4 to 6 minutes. Stir in beef and vegetables and cook until heated through, about 1 minute. Season with salt and pepper to taste. Serve.

## Teriyaki Stir-Fried Beef with Green Beans and Shiitakes

SERVES 4

**WHY THIS RECIPE WORKS** With beef and vegetable stir-fries, it's easy to overcook the beef and overreduce the sauce, resulting in chewy, gray beef smothered in a gloppy sauce. We wanted browned, tender beef and crisp-tender vegetables coated in a deep-flavored, silky sauce. We chose flank steak for the best texture and flavor. We sliced the steak thin and then marinated it in soy sauce and sugar before cooking it over high heat to achieve a good sear. We cooked the vegetables in batches for the best texture. For this stir-fry, we paired the beef with green beans, shiitakes, and a teriyaki sauce, along with garlic and ginger. We lightly thickened the sauce with just 1 teaspoon of cornstarch so that it clung to the beef and vegetables but was not overly thick. To make slicing the flank steak easier, freeze it for 15 minutes. Serve with rice.

SAUCE

- ½ cup low-sodium chicken broth
- 2 tablespoons soy sauce
- 2 tablespoons sugar
- 1 tablespoon mirin or sweet sherry
- 1 teaspoon cornstarch
- ¼ teaspoon red pepper flakes

BEEF AND VEGETABLES

- 12 ounces flank steak, trimmed and cut into 2-inch-wide strips with the grain, then sliced across the grain into ⅛-inch-thick slices
- 2 tablespoons soy sauce
- 1 teaspoon sugar
- 2 tablespoons peanut or vegetable oil
- 1 tablespoon minced or grated fresh ginger
- 3 medium garlic cloves, minced or pressed through a garlic press (about 1 tablespoon)
- 8 ounces shiitake mushrooms, stemmed, wiped clean, caps cut into 1-inch pieces
- 12 ounces green beans, ends trimmed, cut into 2-inch lengths
- ¼ cup water
- 3 scallions, quartered lengthwise and cut into 1½-inch pieces

**1. FOR THE SAUCE:** Combine all the ingredients in a small bowl and set aside.

**2. FOR THE BEEF AND VEGETABLES:** Toss the beef with the soy sauce and sugar in a medium bowl and let marinate for at least 10 minutes or up to 1 hour. In a small bowl, mix 1 teaspoon of the oil, the ginger, and garlic together.

**3.** Heat 2 teaspoons more oil in a 12-inch nonstick skillet over high heat until just smoking. Add the beef, break up any clumps, then cook without stirring until the meat is browned at the edges, about 1 minute. Stir the beef and continue to cook until cooked through, about 1 minute longer. Transfer the beef to a clean bowl and cover with foil to keep warm.

**4.** Add the remaining 1 tablespoon oil to the skillet and return to high heat until just smoking. Add the mushrooms and cook until beginning to brown, about 2 minutes. Add the green beans and cook, stirring frequently, until spotty brown, 3 to 4 minutes. Add the water, cover the pan, and lower the heat to medium. Cook the green beans until crisp-tender, about 2 minutes.

**5.** Clear the center of the skillet, add the ginger mixture, and cook, mashing the mixture into the pan, until fragrant, 15 to 20 seconds. Stir the ginger mixture into the vegetables.

**6.** Stir in the beef with any accumulated juices. Whisk the sauce to recombine, then add to the skillet and cook, tossing constantly, until the sauce is thickened, about 30 seconds. Stir in the scallions. Transfer to a serving platter and serve.

## Stir-Fried Thai-Style Beef with Chiles and Shallots

SERVES 4

**WHY THIS RECIPE WORKS** We wanted to create a sophisticated Thai-style stir-fried beef recipe built around the traditional Thai flavors—spicy, sweet, sour, and salty—using readily available ingredients and requiring minimal cooking time. A cheap and readily available cut—blade steak—won our taste test for its tenderness and very beefy flavor. We added the beef to our stir-fry marinade made with fish sauce for its briny flavor, white pepper for its spicy flavor, citrusy coriander, and light brown sugar for both sweetness and help in developing caramelization. The beef needed to marinate for only 10 minutes to develop full flavor. To add some wanted heat, we used both a jalapeño and Asian chili-garlic paste. More fish sauce, brown sugar, rice vinegar, fresh mint and cilantro, a few crunchy peanuts, and a bright squirt of lime juice finished the dish. To make slicing the blade steaks easier, freeze them for 15 minutes. If you cannot find blade steak, use flank steak; because flank steak requires less trimming, you will need only about 1¾ pounds. To cut a flank steak into the proper size slices for stir-frying, first cut the steak with the grain into 2-inch strips, then cut the strips against the grain into ⅛-inch-thick slices. Serve with rice.

SAUCE

- 2 tablespoons fish sauce
- 2 tablespoons rice vinegar
- 2 tablespoons water
- 1 tablespoon light brown sugar
- 1 tablespoon Asian chili-garlic paste

BEEF AND VEGETABLES

- 2 pounds blade steaks, halved lengthwise, trimmed, and sliced into ⅛-inch-thick slices
- 1 tablespoon fish sauce
- 1 teaspoon light brown sugar

¾ teaspoon ground coriander
⅛ teaspoon ground white pepper
3 tablespoons peanut or vegetable oil
3 medium garlic cloves, minced or pressed through a garlic press (about 1 tablespoon)
3 serrano or jalapeño chiles, halved, seeds and ribs removed, chiles sliced thin
3 medium shallots, ends trimmed, peeled, quartered lengthwise, and layers separated
½ cup fresh mint leaves, large leaves torn into bite-size pieces
½ cup fresh cilantro leaves
⅓ cup unsalted roasted peanuts, chopped coarse
Lime wedges, for serving

1. **FOR THE SAUCE:** Combine all the ingredients in a small bowl and set aside.

2. **FOR THE BEEF AND VEGETABLES:** Toss the beef with the fish sauce, sugar, coriander, and white pepper in a medium bowl and let marinate for at least 10 minutes or up to 1 hour. In a small bowl, mix 1 teaspoon of the oil and the garlic together.

3. Heat 2 teaspoons more oil in a 12-inch nonstick skillet over high heat until just smoking. Add one-third of the beef, break up any clumps, then cook without stirring until the meat is browned at the edges, about 1 minute. Stir the beef and continue to cook until cooked through, about 1 minute longer. Transfer the beef to a clean bowl and cover with foil to keep warm. Repeat with 4 teaspoons more oil and the remaining beef in two batches.

4. Add the remaining 2 teaspoons oil to the skillet and return to medium heat until shimmering. Add the chiles and shallots and cook until beginning to soften, 3 to 4 minutes. Clear the center of the skillet, add the garlic mixture, and cook, mashing the mixture into the pan, until fragrant, 15 to 20 seconds. Stir the garlic mixture into the shallots and chiles.

5. Stir in the beef with any accumulated juices. Whisk the sauce to recombine, then add to the skillet and cook, tossing constantly, until the sauce is thickened, about 30 seconds. Stir in the half of the mint and half of the cilantro. Transfer to a serving platter, sprinkle with the remaining mint, remaining cilantro, and peanuts, and serve with the lime wedges.

## Crispy Orange Beef

**SERVES 4**

**WHY THIS RECIPE WORKS** The crunchy batter coating of crispy orange beef seems impossible to achieve without a deep fryer. To make this recipe on the stovetop without diminishing its big flavor and shatteringly crisp crust, we started with the beef. Tender flap meat cut into matchsticks maximized the surface area for extra crunch in each bite. Tossing the beef in soy sauce and cornstarch created a clingy, delicate coating, and 45 minutes in the freezer dried the prepped beef's surface to boost crisping. We needed only 3 cups of oil to fry the beef to a beautiful golden brown, and thanks to the dry cornstarch coating, very little oil was absorbed, so the beef never turned greasy. For a sauce to complement the crispy beef, we recreated the bitter, citrusy tang of traditional dried tangerine peels by using the juice and peels of two oranges. We whisked the fresh juice with soy sauce, molasses, dry sherry, rice vinegar, and sesame oil for a complex, complementary sauce and then, for some bite and heat, browned the peels with jalapeños in a skillet. Garlic, ginger, and red pepper flakes reinforced the spicy bite before the soy sauce mixture was added to the pan. We cooked the mixture until it thickened slightly, and then tossed in our beef along with sliced scallions for a finishing touch of brightness. We prefer to buy flap meat and cut our own steak tips. Use a vegetable peeler on the oranges and make sure that your strips contain some pith. Do not use low-sodium soy sauce. Serve this dish with rice.

1½ pounds beef flap meat, trimmed
3 tablespoons soy sauce
6 tablespoons cornstarch
10 (3-inch) strips orange peel, sliced thin lengthwise (¼ cup), plus ¼ cup juice (2 oranges)
3 tablespoons molasses
2 tablespoons dry sherry
1 tablespoon rice vinegar
1½ teaspoons toasted sesame oil
3 cups vegetable oil
1 jalapeño chile, stemmed, seeded, and sliced thin lengthwise
3 garlic cloves, minced
2 tablespoons grated fresh ginger
½ teaspoon red pepper flakes
2 scallions, sliced thin on bias

1. Cut beef with grain into 2½- to 3-inch-wide lengths. Slice each piece against grain into ½-inch-thick slices. Cut each slice lengthwise into ½-inch-wide strips. Toss beef with 1 tablespoon soy sauce in bowl. Add cornstarch and toss until evenly coated. Spread beef in single layer on wire rack set in rimmed baking sheet. Transfer sheet to freezer until meat is very firm but not completely frozen, about 45 minutes.

2. Whisk remaining 2 tablespoons soy sauce, orange juice, molasses, sherry, vinegar, and sesame oil together in bowl.

3. Line second rimmed baking sheet with triple layer of paper towels. Heat vegetable oil in large Dutch oven over medium heat until oil registers 375 degrees. Carefully add one-third of beef and fry, stirring occasionally to keep beef from sticking together, until golden brown, about 1½ minutes. Using spider, transfer beef to paper towel–lined sheet. Return oil to 375 degrees and repeat twice more with remaining beef. After frying, reserve 2 tablespoons frying oil.

4. Heat reserved oil in 12-inch skillet over medium-high heat until shimmering. Add orange peel and jalapeño and cook, stirring occasionally, until about half of orange peel is golden brown, 1½ to 2 minutes. Add garlic, ginger, and pepper flakes; cook, stirring frequently, until garlic is beginning to brown, about 45 seconds. Add soy sauce mixture and cook, scraping up any browned bits, until slightly thickened, about 45 seconds. Add beef and scallions and toss. Transfer to platter and serve immediately.

## Braised Oxtails with White Beans, Tomatoes, and Aleppo Pepper

**SERVES** 6 to 8

**WHY THIS RECIPE WORKS** Succulent, beefy oxtails star in our spin on the Turkish dish etli kuru fasulye (which means "white beans with meat"). In our version, navy beans offer a creamy counterpoint to hearty oxtails. We started by roasting the oxtails in the oven, rather than browning them in a Dutch oven; this way we rendered and discarded another half-cup of fat. We then transferred the oxtails to a bowl and deglazed the roasting pan with chicken broth to create a flavorful liquid for braising. We added a trio of eastern Mediterranean elements to give the braising liquid its character: sweet whole tomatoes, warm and earthy Aleppo pepper, and pungent oregano. After braising, we removed another half-cup of fat from the cooking liquid. We added canned navy beans, sherry vinegar, and fresh oregano to create a hearty sauce in which we reheated the oxtails. Try to buy oxtails that are approximately 2 inches thick and 2 to 4 inches in diameter. Oxtails can often be found in the freezer section of the grocery store; if using frozen oxtails, be sure to thaw them completely before using. If you can't find Aleppo pepper, you can substitute 1½ teaspoons paprika and 1½ teaspoons finely chopped red pepper flakes.

- 4 pounds oxtails, trimmed
- Table salt and pepper
- 4 cups chicken broth
- 2 tablespoons extra-virgin olive oil
- 1 onion, chopped fine
- 1 carrot, peeled and chopped fine
- 6 garlic cloves, minced
- 2 tablespoons tomato paste
- 2 tablespoons ground dried Aleppo pepper
- 1 tablespoon minced fresh oregano, divided
- 1 (28-ounce) can whole peeled tomatoes
- 1 (15-ounce) can navy beans, rinsed
- 1 tablespoon sherry vinegar

**1.** Adjust oven rack to lower-middle position and heat oven to 450 degrees. Pat oxtails dry with paper towels and season with salt and pepper. Arrange oxtails cut side down in single layer in large roasting pan and roast until meat begins to brown, about 45 minutes.

**2.** Discard any accumulated fat and juices in pan and continue to roast until meat is well browned, 15 to 20 minutes. Transfer oxtails to bowl and tent loosely with aluminum foil; set aside. Stir chicken broth into pan, scraping up any browned bits; set aside.

**3.** Reduce oven temperature to 300 degrees. Heat oil in Dutch oven over medium heat until shimmering. Add onion and carrot and cook until softened, about 5 minutes. Stir in garlic, tomato paste, Aleppo pepper, and 1 teaspoon oregano and cook until fragrant, about 30 seconds.

**4.** Stir in broth mixture from roasting pan and tomatoes and their juice and bring to simmer. Nestle oxtails into pot and bring to simmer. Cover, transfer pot to oven, and cook until oxtails are tender and fork slips easily in and out of meat, about 3 hours.

**5.** Transfer oxtails to bowl and tent loosely with aluminum foil. Strain braising liquid through fine-mesh strainer into fat separator; return solids to now-empty pot. Let braising liquid settle for 5 minutes, then pour defatted liquid into pot with solids.

**6.** Stir in beans, vinegar, and remaining 2 teaspoons oregano. Return oxtails and any accumulated juices to pot, bring to gentle simmer over medium heat, and cook until oxtails and beans are heated through, about 5 minutes. Season with salt and pepper to taste. Transfer oxtails to serving platter and spoon 1 cup sauce over top. Serve, passing remaining sauce separately.

## Osso Buco

**SERVES** 6

**WHY THIS RECIPE WORKS** Osso buco, veal shanks braised in a rich sauce until tender, is incredibly rich and hearty. We felt that this time-honored recipe shouldn't be altered much, but we hoped to identify the keys to flavor so that we could perfect it. To serve one shank per person, we searched for medium-size shanks, and we tied them around the equator to keep the meat attached to the bone for an attractive presentation. Most recipes suggest flouring the veal before browning it, but we got better flavor when we simply seared the meat, liberally seasoned with just salt and pepper. Browning in two batches enabled us to deglaze the pan twice, thus enriching the sauce. Celery, onion, and carrots formed the basis of the sauce; for the liquid we used a combination of chicken broth and white wine, along with canned tomatoes. The traditional garnish of gremolata—minced garlic, lemon, and parsley—required no changes; we stirred half into the sauce and sprinkled the rest over individual servings for a fresh burst of citrus flavor. To keep the meat attached to the bone during the long simmering process, tie a piece of kitchen twine around the thickest portion of each shank before it is browned. Just before serving, taste the liquid and, if it seems too thin, simmer it on the stovetop as you remove the strings from the osso buco and arrange them in individual bowls. Serve with rice or polenta.

OSSO BUCO

- ¼ cup vegetable oil, divided
- 6 (8- to 10-ounce) veal shanks, 1½ inches thick, patted dry with paper towels and tied with kitchen twine at 1½-inch intervals
- ¾ teaspoon table salt, divided
- ⅜ teaspoon pepper, divided
- 2½ cups dry white wine, divided
- 2 onions, cut into ½-inch pieces
- 2 carrots, cut into ½-inch pieces
- 2 celery ribs, cut into ½-inch pieces
- 6 garlic cloves, minced
- 2 cups chicken broth
- 2 small bay leaves
- 1 (14.5-ounce) can diced tomatoes, drained

GREMOLATA

- ¼ cup minced fresh parsley
- 3 garlic cloves, minced
- 2 teaspoons grated lemon zest

**1. FOR THE OSSO BUCO:** Adjust oven rack to lower-middle position and heat oven to 325 degrees. Heat 1 tablespoon oil in large Dutch oven over medium-high heat until shimmering. Meanwhile, sprinkle both sides of shanks with ½ teaspoon salt and ½ teaspoon pepper. Place 3 shanks in pan and cook until golden brown on one side, about 5 minutes. Using tongs, flip shanks and cook until golden brown on second side, about 5 minutes longer. Transfer shanks to bowl and set aside. Off heat, add ½ cup wine to Dutch oven, scraping up any browned bits. Pour liquid into bowl with browned shanks. Return pot to medium-high heat, add 1 tablespoon oil, and heat until shimmering. Brown remaining shanks, about 5 minutes for each side. Transfer shanks to bowl. Off heat, add 1 cup wine to pot, scraping up any browned bits. Pour liquid into bowl with shanks.

**2.** Set pot over medium heat. Add remaining 2 tablespoons oil and heat until shimmering. Add onions, carrots, celery, remaining ¼ teaspoon salt, and remaining ⅛ teaspoon pepper and cook, stirring occasionally, until soft and lightly browned, about 9 minutes. Stir in garlic and cook until fragrant, about 30 seconds. Increase heat to high and stir in broth, remaining 1 cup wine, and bay leaves. Add tomatoes; return veal shanks to pot along with any accumulated juices (liquid should just cover shanks). Bring liquid to simmer. Cover pot and transfer pot to oven. Cook shanks until meat is easily pierced with fork but not falling off bone, about 2 hours. (At this point osso buco can be refrigerated for up to 2 days. Bring to simmer over medium-low heat.)

**3.** For the gremolata: Combine parsley, garlic, and lemon zest in small bowl. Stir half of gremolata into pot, reserving rest for garnish. Season with salt and pepper to taste. Let osso buco stand, uncovered, for 5 minutes.

**4.** Using tongs, remove shanks from pot, cut off and discard twine, and place 1 veal shank in each of 6 bowls. Ladle some of braising liquid over each shank and sprinkle each serving with remaining gremolata. Serve immediately.

## Sautéed Pork Cutlets with Mustard-Cider Sauce

SERVES 4

**WHY THIS RECIPE WORKS** Lean pork cutlets are flavorless without proper browning, but by the time the cutlets take on any color, they're dry and lacking any tenderness. We wanted tender, browned cutlets with meaty flavor and a rich pan sauce. Instead of cutlets, we opted for a meatier-tasting cut: boneless country-style spare ribs. These ribs combine a large portion of the flavorful shoulder meat with minimal connective tissue. Even better, because the ribs are sold portioned into small pieces, they require little work to fashion into cutlets. To guard against dry meat, we brined our cutlets to help them retain moisture. To trigger faster browning, we added sugar to the brine. And for a darker crust, we cooked the cutlets in olive oil and butter. The sugars and milk proteins in the butter promoted browning and boosted flavor. We prefer natural to enhanced pork (pork that has been injected with a salt solution to increase moistness and flavor). If the pork is enhanced, do not brine. Look for ribs that are 3 to 5 inches long. Cut ribs over 5 inches in half crosswise before slicing them lengthwise to make pounding more manageable.

- Table salt and ground black pepper
- 1½ teaspoons sugar
- 1½ pounds boneless country-style pork spareribs, trimmed
- 1½ tablespoons unsalted butter, cut into 6 equal pieces
- 1 small shallot, minced (about 1 tablespoon)
- 1 teaspoon unbleached all-purpose flour
- 1 teaspoon dry mustard
- ½ cup low-sodium beef or chicken broth
- ¼ cup apple cider
- ½ teaspoon minced fresh sage
- 1 tablespoon olive oil
- 2 teaspoons whole-grain mustard

**1.** Dissolve 1 tablespoon salt and the sugar in 2 cups water in a medium bowl. Cut each pork rib lengthwise into 2 or 3 cutlets about ⅜ inch wide. Gently pound the cutlets to ¼-inch thickness between two layers of plastic wrap. Submerge the cutlets in the brine, cover with plastic wrap, and refrigerate for 30 minutes. (Do not overbrine.)

**2.** Meanwhile, melt 2 pieces of the butter in a small saucepan over medium heat. Add the shallot and cook until softened, about 1½ minutes. Stir in the flour and dry mustard and cook for 30 seconds. Gradually whisk in the broth, smoothing out any lumps. Stir in the cider and sage, bring to a boil, then reduce to a gentle simmer and cook for 5 minutes. Remove the pan from the heat, cover, and set aside.

**3.** Adjust an oven rack to the middle position and heat the oven to 200 degrees. Remove the cutlets from the brine, dry thoroughly with paper towels, and season with pepper. Heat the oil in a 12-inch skillet over medium-high heat until just smoking. Add 1 piece more butter, let it melt, then quickly lay half of the cutlets in the skillet. Cook until browned on the first side, 1 to 2 minutes.

**4.** Using tongs, flip the cutlets and continue to cook until browned on the second side, 1 to 2 minutes. Transfer the cutlets to a large plate and keep warm in the oven. Repeat with the remaining cutlets and 1 piece more butter.

**5.** Return the empty skillet to medium heat, add the reserved broth mixture, and bring to a simmer. Cook, scraping up the browned bits, until the sauce is slightly thickened and has reduced to about ½ cup, about 2 minutes. Stir in any accumulated pork juices and simmer for 30 seconds longer.

**6.** Off the heat, whisk in the whole-grain mustard and remaining 2 pieces butter. Season the sauce with salt and pepper to taste, spoon it over the cutlets, and serve immediately.

#### CUTTING COUNTRY-STYLE RIBS INTO CUTLETS

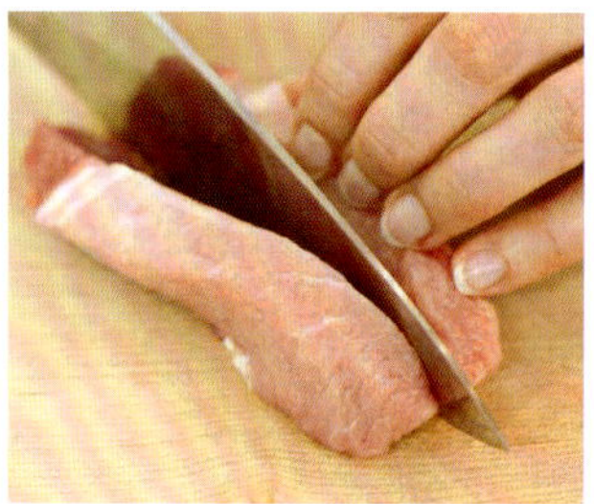

**1.** Slice each rib lengthwise to create 2 or 3 cutlets, each about ⅜ inch wide.

**2.** Lay each piece between 2 sheets of plastic wrap and pound until roughly ¼ inch thick.

## Pork Schnitzel (Breaded Pork Cutlets)

**SERVES 4**

**WHY THIS RECIPE WORKS** Classic Wiener schnitzel features veal cutlets but many recipes substitute pork. We wanted tender cutlets with the crisp, wrinkled coating that is schnitzel's signature. We chose to use pork tenderloin. We cut the tenderloin crosswise on an angle into four pieces, which we then pounded thin. To get the characteristic puffiness and crisp "rumpled" appearance of good schnitzel we made extra-dry bread crumbs and also whisked a little vegetable oil into the egg to help separate the coating from the meat. We cooked the cutlets in a Dutch oven in an inch of oil, shaking the pot to get some of the oil over the top of the meat. The extra heat quickly solidified the egg in the coating, so that the steam from the meat couldn't escape and puffed the coating instead. To make cutlets, cut the tenderloin in half on a 20-degree angle, then cut each piece in half again at the same angle. Cut the tapered tail pieces slightly thicker than the middle ones. Using 2 cups of oil for cooking is necessary to get the desired wrinkled texture on the finished cutlets. It is essential to use a Dutch oven with a large surface area. Although spaetzle is the traditional side dish, boiled potatoes or egg noodles are also good.

- 7 slices high-quality white sandwich bread, crusts removed, cut into ¾-inch cubes (about 4 cups)
- ½ cup unbleached all-purpose flour
- 2 large eggs
- 2 cups plus 1 tablespoon vegetable oil
- 1 (1¼-pound) pork tenderloin, trimmed of fat and silver skin and tenderloin cut on an angle into 4 equal pieces
- Table salt and ground black pepper

**GARNISHES**

- 1 lemon, cut into wedges
- 2 tablespoons chopped fresh parsley leaves
- 2 tablespoons capers, rinsed
- 1 large hard-cooked egg (page 5), yolk and white separated and passed separately through a fine-mesh strainer (optional)

**1.** Place the bread cubes on a large microwave-safe plate. Microwave on high power for 4 minutes, stirring well halfway through the cooking time. Microwave on medium power until the bread is dry and a few pieces start to lightly brown, 3 to 5 minutes longer, stirring every minute. Process the dry bread in a food processor to very fine crumbs, about 45 seconds. Transfer the bread crumbs to a shallow dish (you should have about 1¼ cups crumbs). Spread the flour in a second shallow dish. Beat the eggs with 1 tablespoon of the oil in a third shallow dish.

**2.** Place the pork, with one cut side down, between two sheets of plastic wrap and pound to an even thickness of between ⅛ and ¼ inch. Season the cutlets with salt and pepper. Working with one cutlet at a time, dredge the cutlets thoroughly in flour, shaking off the excess, then coat with the egg, allowing the excess to drip back into the dish to ensure a very thin coating, and coat evenly with the bread crumbs, pressing on the crumbs to adhere. Place the breaded cutlets in a single layer on a wire rack set over a baking sheet; let the coating dry for 5 minutes.

**3.** Heat the remaining 2 cups oil in a large Dutch oven over medium-high heat until it registers 375 degrees on an instant-read thermometer. Lay two cutlets, without overlapping, in the pan and cook, shaking the pan continuously and gently, until wrinkled and light golden brown on both sides, 1 to 2 minutes per side. Transfer the cutlets to a paper towel–lined plate and flip the cutlets several times to blot the excess oil. Repeat with the remaining cutlets. Serve immediately with the garnishes.

## Crispy Pan-Fried Pork Chops

**SERVES 4**

**WHY THIS RECIPE WORKS** A breaded coating can be just the thing to give lean, bland pork chops a flavor boost. Using boneless chops was fast and easy. Dipping the chops in cornstarch helped to create an ultracrisp sheath. Buttermilk brought a lighter texture and tang to the breading, and garlic and mustard perked up the breading's flavor. Crushed cornflakes added a craggy texture to the pork chops. To ensure that

the breading adhered, we gave the meat a short rest and we lightly scored the chops before adding them to the pan. We prefer natural to enhanced pork (pork that has been injected with a salt solution to increase moistness and flavor) for this recipe. Don't let the cooked chops drain for longer than 30 seconds, or the heat will steam the crust and make it soggy. You can substitute ¾ cup store-bought cornflake crumbs for the whole cornflakes. If using crumbs, omit the processing step and mix the crumbs with the cornstarch, salt, and pepper.

- ⅔ cup cornstarch
- 1 cup buttermilk
- 2 tablespoons Dijon mustard
- 1 garlic clove, minced (about 1 teaspoon)
- 3 cups cornflakes
- Table salt and ground black pepper
- 8 (3- to 4-ounce) boneless pork chops, ½ to ¾ inch thick, trimmed
- ⅔ cup vegetable oil
- Lemon wedges, for serving

**1.** Place ⅓ cup of cornstarch in shallow dish or pie plate. In second shallow dish, whisk buttermilk, mustard, and garlic until combined. Process cornflakes, ½ teaspoon salt, ½ teaspoon pepper, and remaining ⅓ cup cornstarch in food processor until cornflakes are finely ground, about 10 seconds. Transfer cornflake mixture to third shallow dish.

### HELPING THE COATING STICK

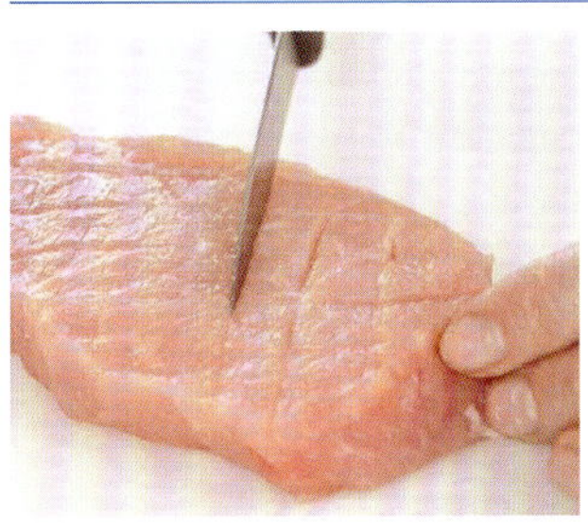

Making shallow slits on both sides of chops, spaced ½ inch apart, in a crosshatch pattern releases juices and sticky meat proteins that dampen the cornstarch, helping the cornflake coating adhere.

**2.** Adjust oven rack to middle position and heat oven to 200 degrees. With sharp knife, cut 1/16-inch-deep slits on both sides of chops, spaced ½ inch apart, in crosshatch pattern. Season chops with salt and pepper. Dredge 1 chop in cornstarch; shake off excess. Using tongs, coat with buttermilk mixture; let excess drip off. Coat with cornflake mixture; gently pat off excess. Transfer coated chop to wire rack set in rimmed baking sheet and repeat with remaining 7 chops. Let coated chops stand for 10 minutes.

**3.** Heat ⅓ cup of oil in 12-inch nonstick skillet over medium-high heat until shimmering. Place 4 chops in skillet and cook until golden brown and crisp, 2 to 5 minutes. Carefully flip chops and continue to cook until second side is golden brown, crispy, and chops register 145 degrees on instant-read thermometer, 2 to 5 minutes longer. Transfer chops to paper towel–lined plate and let drain for 30 seconds on each side. Transfer to clean wire rack set in rimmed baking sheet, then transfer to oven to keep warm. Discard oil in skillet and wipe clean with paper towels. Repeat process with remaining ⅓ cup oil and 4 pork chops. Serve with lemon wedges.

## Pan-Seared Thick-Cut Boneless Pork Chops

**SERVES 4**

**WHY THIS RECIPE WORKS** Searing pork chops in a screaming-hot pan is an obvious way to brown them deeply. What we discovered is that it's also the trick to keeping this lean cut juicy. Superthick pork chops can be hard to find, so we cut them ourselves from a boneless center-cut pork loin roast. To maximize the crust, we avoided brining or salting and patted the chops dry with paper towels so that the exteriors were as dry as possible before the chops went into the pan. We also used a cast-iron skillet, preheated in a 500-degree oven, and a generous 2 tablespoons of oil to maximize heat transfer to the chops' exteriors. Finally, to keep the interiors juicy, we flipped the chops every 2 minutes and removed them from the pan once they hit 125 degrees, relying on carryover cooking to bring them to the serving temperature of 140 degrees. Our easy no-cook sauces add richness to the lean chops, and a little bit goes a long way. Look for a pork loin that is 7 to 8 inches long and 3 to 3½ inches in diameter. We strongly prefer using natural pork here. Using pork that is enhanced (injected with a salt solution) will inhibit browning. This recipe works best in a cast-iron skillet, but a 12-inch stainless-steel skillet will work. Serve the chops with Roasted Red Pepper–Vinegar Sauce (recipe follows), if desired.

- 1 (2½- to 3-pound) boneless center-cut pork loin roast, trimmed
- ½ teaspoon kosher salt
- ½ teaspoon pepper
- 2 tablespoons vegetable oil

1. Adjust oven rack to middle position, place 12-inch cast-iron skillet on rack, and heat oven to 500 degrees. Meanwhile, cut roast crosswise into 4 chops of equal thickness.

2. When oven reaches 500 degrees, pat chops dry with paper towels and sprinkle with salt and pepper. Using pot holders, remove skillet from oven and place over high heat. Being careful of hot skillet handle, add oil and heat until just smoking. Add chops and cook, without moving them, until lightly browned on first side, about 2 minutes. Flip chops and cook until lightly browned on second side, about 2 minutes.

3. Flip chops and continue to cook, flipping every 2 minutes and adjusting heat as necessary if chops brown too quickly or slowly, until exteriors are well browned and meat registers 125 to 130 degrees, 10 to 12 minutes longer. Transfer chops to platter, tent with aluminum foil, and let rest for 15 minutes (temperature will climb to 140 degrees). Serve.

### Roasted Red Pepper–Vinegar Sauce

**MAKES** 1 cup

Red wine vinegar or sherry vinegar can be substituted for the white wine vinegar, if desired.

- ¾ cup jarred roasted red peppers, rinsed and patted dry
- 2 jarred hot cherry peppers, stems removed
- 2 garlic cloves, peeled
- 2 teaspoons dried rosemary, lightly crushed
- 2 anchovy fillets, rinsed and patted dry
- ½ teaspoon table salt
- ⅛ teaspoon pepper
- ¼ cup water
- 2 tablespoons white wine vinegar
- ⅓ cup extra-virgin olive oil
- 2 tablespoons minced fresh parsley

Pulse red peppers, cherry peppers, garlic, rosemary, anchovies, salt, and pepper in food processor until finely chopped, 15 to 20 pulses. Add water and vinegar and pulse briefly to combine. Transfer mixture to medium bowl and slowly whisk in oil until fully incorporated. Stir in parsley.

## Sous Vide Boneless Thick-Cut Pork Chops

**SERVES** 4

**WHY THIS RECIPE WORKS** Sous vide pork chops are guaranteed to be uniformly juicy and tender. The temperature-controlled water bath gradually raises the meat to its 140-degree target, maximizing collagen breakdown and minimizing moisture loss for consistently perfect results with practically zero hands-on work. We sealed thick chops in a zipper-lock freezer bag and submerged them in 140-degree water; the meat was cooked through by the 2-hour mark (although it could sit for up to an hour longer with no ill effect). Thoroughly drying the surface of the cooked chops and briefly searing them produced a flavorful brown crust. For a company-worthy dish, we served them with a stir-together roasted red pepper–almond relish. Buy chops of similar thickness so that they cook at the same rate. If desired, you can sous vide the chops ahead of time; chill them in an ice bath after step 2, and then refrigerate them in their zipper-lock bag for up to three days. To reheat, return the sealed bag to a water bath set to 140°F/60°C for 30 minutes, and then proceed with step 3.

- 4 boneless center-cut pork chops, about 1½ inches thick, trimmed
- 1 teaspoon table salt
- ½ teaspoon pepper
- 6 tablespoons vegetable oil, divided
- 1 recipe Red Pepper and Almond Relish (recipe follows)

1. Using sous vide circulator, bring water to 140°F/60°C in 7-quart container.

2. Sprinkle chops on both sides with salt and pepper. Arrange chops in single layer in 1-gallon zipper-lock freezer bag. Add ¼ cup oil and seal bag, pressing out as much air as possible. Gently lower bag into prepared water bath until chops are fully submerged, and then clip top corner of bag to side of water bath container, allowing remaining air bubbles to rise to top of bag. Reopen 1 corner of zipper, release remaining air bubbles, and reseal bag. Cover and cook for at least 2 hours or up to 3 hours.

3. Transfer chops to paper towel–lined plate and let rest for 5 to 10 minutes. Pat chops dry with paper towels. Heat 1 tablespoon oil in 10-inch skillet over medium-high heat until just smoking. Place 2 chops in skillet and cook until well browned on first side, 1 to 2 minutes, lifting halfway through cooking to redistribute fat underneath each chop. Flip chops and continue to cook until well browned on second side, 1 to 2 minutes longer. Transfer chops to plate and tent with aluminum foil. Repeat with remaining 1 tablespoon oil and remaining chops. Serve, passing relish separately.

### Red Pepper and Almond Relish

**MAKES** ¾ cup

We like Dunbars Sweet Roasted Peppers.

- ½ cup finely chopped jarred roasted red peppers
- ¼ cup slivered almonds, toasted and chopped coarse
- 2 tablespoons extra-virgin olive oil
- 2 tablespoons minced fresh parsley
- 1 tablespoon white wine vinegar
- 1 teaspoon minced fresh oregano
- ¼ teaspoon table salt

Combine all ingredients in bowl.

## Pan-Seared Thick-Cut Pork Chops

SERVES 4

**WHY THIS RECIPE WORKS** Pan-seared thick-cut pork chops should boast a juicy interior and crisp, browned exterior. We wanted a simple skillet-roasting recipe that would give us juicy meat and a well-formed crust every time. Instead of brining our chops, we salted the meat and let it rest for almost an hour. This drew out additional moisture to produce juicy, well-seasoned meat. Slow-roasting the chops in the oven broke down connective tissue and tenderized the meat. This step also dried the exterior of the chops, creating a thin outer layer that, when seared, caramelized and turned into the crisp crust that we were after. For a completely browned crust, we seared the sides of the chops as well, using tongs to hold them up on their edges. While the cooked chops rested, we created a simple rich wine and garlic sauce using the browned bits left behind in the pan. We prefer natural to enhanced pork (pork that has been injected with a salt solution to increase moistness and flavor) for this recipe. If using enhanced pork, skip the salting in step 1. To make Garlic and Thyme Sauce (recipe follows), have all the ingredients ready to go and don't wash the skillet after browning the chops. Use the fat left behind from the chops, when you set them aside to rest.

- 4 (12-ounce) bone-in rib loin pork chops, about 1½ inches thick, trimmed of excess fat
- Table salt and ground black pepper
- 1-2 tablespoons vegetable oil

**1.** Adjust an oven rack to the middle position and heat the oven to 275 degrees. Pat the chops dry with paper towels. Use a sharp knife to cut two slits, about 2 inches apart, through the outer layer of fat and silver skin of each chop (do not cut into the meat of the chops). Sprinkle each chop with ½ teaspoon salt. Place the chops on a wire rack set over a rimmed baking sheet and let stand at room temperature for 45 minutes.

**2.** Season the chops with pepper; transfer the baking sheet to the5 to the skillet, and sear the sides (do not sear the bone side) until browned and the center of the chops registers 140 to 145 degrees on an instant-read thermometer, about 1½ minutes. Repeat with the remaining 2 chops. Transfer the chops to a platter, cover loosely with foil, and let rest until the internal temperature reaches 150 degrees, about 5 minutes, or while preparing the pan sauce.

### Garlic and Thyme Sauce

MAKES about ½ cup

- 1 large shallot, minced (about 4 tablespoons)
- 2 medium garlic cloves, minced or pressed through a garlic press (about 2 teaspoons)
- ¾ cup low-sodium chicken broth
- ½ cup dry white wine
- 1 teaspoon minced fresh thyme leaves
- ¼ teaspoon white wine vinegar
- 3 tablespoons unsalted butter, chilled and cut into 3 pieces
- Table salt and ground black pepper

Follow the recipe for Pan-Seared Thick-Cut Pork Chops. Pour off all but 1 teaspoon oil from the pan used to cook the chops and return the pan to medium heat. Add the shallot and garlic and cook, stirring constantly, until softened, about 1 minute. Add the broth and wine, scraping up any browned bits. Bring to a simmer and cook until the sauce measures ½ cup, 6 to 7 minutes. Off heat, stir in thyme and vinegar; whisk in butter, 1 tablespoon at a time. Season with salt and pepper to taste, and serve with the pork chops.

## Pan-Seared Thick-Cut, Bone-In Pork Chops

SERVES 4

**WHY THIS RECIPE WORKS** With a cold pan and the right cut, you can achieve deeply browned, juicy bone-in pork chops in minutes. This cold-sear method is especially beneficial for leaner cuts that are prone to drying out. We settled on 1½-inch-thick bone-in rib chops, which were thick enough to build up a browned exterior before cooking through; the bone also insulates the meat so it stays juicy. Placing the chops in a cold nonstick skillet over high heat and flipping them every 2 minutes allowed the meat to heat up slowly and build a crust. If you have time, salt the chops for at least 1 hour before cooking: Sprinkle each chop with 1½ teaspoons of Diamond Crystal Kosher Salt (if using Morton, which is denser, use only 1⅛ teaspoons), refrigerate them, and pat them dry with paper towels before cooking. If the pork is enhanced (injected with a salt solution), do not salt the chops ahead. Make sure to include the bones when serving; they're great for nibbling. The chops can be served plain or with a sauce (recipe follows).

- 2 (14- to 16-ounce) bone-in pork rib chops, 1½ inches thick, trimmed
- ½ teaspoon pepper

**1.** Pat chôps dry with paper towels and sprinkle both sides with pepper. Place chops 1 inch apart in cold 12-inch nonstick or carbon-steel skillet, arranging so narrow part of 1 chop is opposite wider part of second. Place skillet over high heat and cook chops for 2 minutes. Flip chops and cook on second side for 2 minutes. (Neither side of chops will be browned at this point.)

**2.** Flip chops; reduce heat to medium; and continue to cook, flipping chops every 2 minutes, until exterior is well browned and meat registers 140 degrees, 10 to 15 minutes longer. (Chops should be sizzling; if not, increase heat slightly. Reduce heat if skillet starts to smoke.)

**3.** Transfer chops to carving board and let rest for 5 minutes. Carve meat from bone and slice ½ inch thick. (When carved, meat at tapered end near bone may retain slightly pink hue despite being cooked.) Season meat with coarse or flake sea salt to taste. Serve with bones.

### Maple Agrodolce

**MAKES** ⅓ cup

- ¼ cup balsamic vinegar
- 2 tablespoons maple syrup
- 2 tablespoons minced shallot
- 2 tablespoons chopped golden raisins
- Pinch red pepper flakes
- Pinch table salt

Bring all ingredients to boil in small saucepan over medium heat. Reduce heat to low and simmer until reduced and slightly thickened, 8 to 10 minutes (sauce will continue to thicken as it cools). Cover to keep warm until ready to serve.

## Cider-Glazed Pork Chops

**SERVES** 4

**WHY THIS RECIPE WORKS** Thin boneless pork chops cook fast and are a bargain compared to other meats. But they are prone to overcooking. We wanted to combine the convenience and speed of thin boneless pork chops with the flavor and juicy interior of their thicker, bone-in counterparts. Before searing the chops, it's important to cut through the fat and silver skin, which creates a bowing effect as it contracts. We found the chops needed a quick sear, for a nicely browned side. A sweet and sticky glaze went into the pan to finish cooking the chops. Not only did the glaze give the chops rich flavor, but it also perfectly coated the juicy, tender chops. We prefer natural to enhanced pork (pork that has been injected with a salt solution to increase moistness and flavor) for this recipe, though either will work here. If your chops are on the thinner side, check their internal temperature after the initial sear. If they are already at the 140-degree mark, remove them from the skillet and allow them to rest, covered loosely with foil, for 5 minutes, then add the accumulated juices and glaze ingredients to the skillet and proceed with step 4. If your chops are a little thicker than we specify, you may need to increase the simmering time in step 3.

**GLAZE**

- ½ cup distilled white vinegar or cider vinegar
- ⅓ cup (2⅓ ounces) light brown sugar
- ⅓ cup apple cider or apple juice
- 2 tablespoons Dijon mustard
- 1 tablespoon soy sauce
- Pinch cayenne pepper

**PORK CHOPS**

- 4 (5- to 7-ounce) boneless center-cut or loin pork chops, ½ to ¾ inch thick, trimmed of excess fat
- Table salt and ground black pepper
- 1 tablespoon vegetable oil

**1. FOR THE GLAZE:** Combine the glaze ingredients in a medium bowl and set aside.

**2. FOR THE PORK CHOPS:** Use a sharp knife to cut two slits, about 2 inches apart, through the outer layer of fat and silver skin of each chop (do not cut into the meat of the chops). Pat the chops dry with paper towels and season with salt and pepper. Heat the oil in a 12-inch skillet over medium-high heat until smoking. Add the chops to the skillet and cook until well browned, 4 to 6 minutes. Flip the chops and cook 1 minute longer; transfer the chops to a platter and pour off any oil in the skillet. (Check the internal temperature of the thinner chops.)

**3.** Return the chops to the skillet, browned side up, and add the glaze mixture; cook over medium heat until the center of the chops registers 140 to 145 degrees on an instant-read thermometer, 5 to 8 minutes. Remove the skillet from the heat; transfer the chops to a clean platter, cover loosely with foil, and let rest until the center of the chops registers 150 degrees on an instant-read thermometer, about 5 minutes.

**4.** Stir any accumulated meat juices from the plate into the glaze in the skillet and simmer, whisking constantly, until the glaze has thickened, 2 to 6 minutes. Return the chops to the skillet and turn to coat both sides with the glaze. Transfer the chops back to the plate, browned side up, spread the remaining glaze over the top, and serve.

**HOW TO PREVENT CURLED PORK CHOPS**

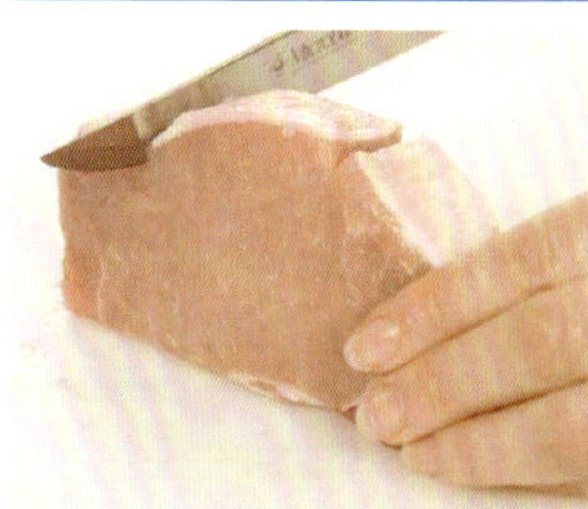

Whether your pork chops are boneless or bone-in, you can use the same technique to prevent them from buckling in a hot pan or oven. Simply cut two slits, about 2 inches apart, through one side of each chop.

## Mustardy Apple Butter–Glazed Pork Chops

**SERVES** 4

**WHY THIS RECIPE WORKS** Low-fuss boneless pork chops make for a great weeknight dinner, but gussying them up with a flavorful glaze can be a challenge. By the time a glazed chop reaches your plate, its coating has often ended up everywhere but on the meat. For a stay-put solution, we started by stirring together apple butter and Dijon mustard—thick and intensely flavored ingredients that wouldn't run off the chops when heated. Next, we adjusted the balance of flavors with maple syrup, soy sauce, and cider vinegar. We applied a thin coating of the glaze to the pork chops and slow-roasted them in a low oven. The low, ambient heat of slow roasting cooked the pork more gently than pan searing would, helping the chops retain their juices rather than exude too much liquid and dilute the glaze. After the first coat of glaze fused to the chops, we applied a second coating to the tacky, grippy surface and broiled the chops until the glaze was bubbly and started to char. If your broiler has multiple temperature settings, use the highest. We like the consistency that Musselman's Apple Butter gives the glaze; if you're using another brand, you may need to thin the glaze with up to 1 tablespoon of water.

- 3 tablespoons apple butter
- 2 tablespoons maple syrup
- 1 tablespoon Dijon mustard
- 1 teaspoon soy sauce
- ½ teaspoon cider vinegar
- 1 teaspoon kosher salt
- 4 (6- to 8-ounce) boneless pork chops, ¾ to 1 inch thick, trimmed
- 2 teaspoons minced fresh parsley

**1.** Adjust oven rack to middle position and heat oven to 275 degrees. Line rimmed baking sheet with aluminum foil and set wire rack in sheet. Spray rack with vegetable oil spray. Stir apple butter, maple syrup, mustard, soy sauce, and vinegar together in small bowl.

**2.** Sprinkle salt evenly over both sides of chops. Place chops on prepared wire rack and brush 1 teaspoon glaze on top and sides of each chop. Roast until meat registers 135 to 137 degrees, 40 to 45 minutes.

**3.** Remove sheet from oven and heat broiler. Brush 1 tablespoon glaze on top and sides of each chop. Return sheet to oven and broil until glaze is bubbly and slightly charred in spots, 3 to 6 minutes. Let rest for 5 minutes. Sprinkle with parsley and serve.

## Deviled Pork Chops

SERVES 4

WHY THIS RECIPE WORKS Most recipes call for pan-searing or broiling pork chops, but those techniques often yield dried-out meat, so we wanted to slow-roast them in a low oven, which wouldn't require fussy flipping and would allow them to cook evenly and retain as much moisture as possible—a must for lean cuts to taste juicy. To punch up their mild flavor, we "deviled" them by painting the tops and sides of the chops with a bold, balanced, complex-tasting paste of spicy, sharp Dijon mustard mixed with dry mustard (for an extra jolt of heat), minced garlic, and cayenne and black peppers. A bit of brown sugar and salt balanced the paste's heat and acidity. For textural contrast and visual appeal, we coated the tops of the chops with crispy panko bread crumbs, which we toasted in butter to render them deep golden brown and make them water-resistant so that they didn't absorb too much moisture from the mustard coating and turn soggy. For the best results, be sure to buy chops of similar size. This recipe was developed using natural pork; if using enhanced pork (injected with a salt solution), do not add salt to the mustard paste in step 2. Serve the pork chops with mashed potatoes, rice, or buttered egg noodles.

- 2 tablespoons unsalted butter
- ½ cup panko bread crumbs
- Kosher salt and pepper
- ¼ cup Dijon mustard
- 2 teaspoons packed brown sugar
- 1½ teaspoons dry mustard
- ½ teaspoon garlic, minced to paste
- ¼ teaspoon cayenne pepper
- 4 (6- to 8-ounce) boneless pork chops, ¾ to 1 inch thick

**1.** Adjust oven rack to middle position and heat oven to 275 degrees.

**2.** Melt butter in 10-inch skillet over medium heat. Add panko and cook, stirring frequently, until golden brown, 3 to 5 minutes. Transfer to bowl and sprinkle with ⅛ teaspoon salt. Stir Dijon, sugar, dry mustard, garlic, cayenne, 1 teaspoon salt, and 1 teaspoon pepper in second bowl until smooth.

**3.** Set wire rack in rimmed baking sheet and spray with vegetable oil spray. Pat chops dry with paper towels. Transfer chops to prepared wire rack, spacing them 1 inch apart. Brush 1 tablespoon mustard mixture over top and sides of each chop (leave bottoms uncoated). Spoon 2 tablespoons toasted panko evenly over top of each chop and press lightly to adhere.

**4.** Roast until meat registers 140 degrees, 40 to 50 minutes. Remove from oven and let rest on rack for 10 minutes before serving.

## Crunchy Baked Pork Chops

**SERVES 4**

**WHY THIS RECIPE WORKS** When done right, baked, breaded pork chops are juicy, tender chops covered with a well-seasoned, crunchy crust. We were on a mission to perfect these chops and avoid a soggy, flavorless crust, flabby meat, and a coating that just won't stay on. We used center-cut boneless loin chops—which are easy to find and affordable—and brined them so the meat would stay moist and juicy. For the coating, only fresh bread crumbs would do; we toasted them first for crispness, then doctored them with garlic, shallots, Parmesan cheese, and fresh herbs for flavor. To form a strong adhering agent for the crumbs, we made a quick batterlike mixture by whisking flour and mustard into egg whites; whole eggs were a no-go because their higher amount of fat made for a soft, puffy layer under the bread crumbs. Baking the breaded chops on a wire rack set over a baking sheet allowed air to circulate completely around the chops, keeping the bottom crumbs crisp. Out of the oven, these chops were tender and moist, with a crisp coating that stayed put. We prefer natural to enhanced pork (pork that has been injected with a salt solution to increase moistness and flavor) for this recipe. If using enhanced pork, skip the brining in step 1. The breaded chops can be frozen for up to 1 week. They don't need to be thawed before baking; simply increase the cooking time in step 5 to 35 to 40 minutes.

- Table salt
- 4 (6- to 8-ounce) boneless center-cut or loin pork chops, ¾ to 1 inch thick, trimmed of excess fat
- 4 slices high-quality white sandwich bread, torn into 1-inch pieces
- 2 tablespoons vegetable oil
- 1 small shallot, minced (about 1 tablespoon)
- 3 medium garlic cloves, minced or pressed through a garlic press (about 1 tablespoon)
- Ground black pepper
- 2 tablespoons grated Parmesan cheese
- 2 tablespoons minced fresh parsley leaves
- ½ teaspoon minced fresh thyme leaves
- ¼ cup plus 6 tablespoons unbleached all-purpose flour
- 3 large egg whites
- 3 tablespoons Dijon mustard
- Lemon wedges, for serving

**1.** Adjust an oven rack to the middle position and heat the oven to 350 degrees. Dissolve ¼ cup salt in 4 cups cold water in a medium bowl or gallon-sized zipper-lock bag. Submerge the chops in the brine, cover the container with plastic wrap or seal the bag, and refrigerate for 30 minutes. Remove the chops from the brine, rinse, and pat dry with paper towels.

**2.** Meanwhile, pulse the bread in a food processor to coarse crumbs, about 8 pulses (you should have about 3½ cups crumbs). Transfer the crumbs to a rimmed baking sheet, add the oil, shallot, garlic, ¼ teaspoon salt, and ¼ teaspoon pepper, and toss until the crumbs are evenly coated with the oil. Bake until golden brown and dry, about 15 minutes, stirring twice during the baking time. (Do not turn off the oven.) Cool to room temperature. Toss the crumbs with the Parmesan, parsley, and thyme. (The bread-crumb mixture can be stored in an airtight container for up to 3 days.)

**3.** Place ¼ cup of the flour in a pie plate. In a second pie plate, whisk the egg whites and mustard together; add the remaining 6 tablespoons flour and whisk until almost smooth, with pea-sized lumps remaining.

**4.** Increase the oven temperature to 425 degrees. Spray a wire rack with vegetable oil spray and place over a rimmed baking sheet. Season the chops with pepper. Dredge 1 pork chop in the flour; shake off the excess. Using tongs, coat with the egg mixture; let the excess drip off. Coat all sides of the chop with the bread-crumb mixture, pressing gently so that a thick layer of crumbs adheres to the chop. Transfer the breaded chop to the wire rack. Repeat with the remaining 3 chops.

**5.** Bake until the center of the chops registers 140 to 145 degrees on an instant-read thermometer, about 20 minutes. Let rest on the rack for 5 minutes; serve with the lemon wedges.

## Tonkatsu (Japanese Fried Pork Chops)

**SERVES 4** **SEASON 26**

**WHY THIS RECIPE WORKS** Our crisp, juicy, well-browned pork tonkatsu starts with ¾-inch-thick boneless chops with a thin fat cap. We cut slits in the fat to prevent the chops from buckling and then sprinkled them with salt. We revamped the bound breading process so that a triple dip—first in flour, then in egg, and finally in panko—coated the chops with the least possible mess and fuss. We found that shallow-frying the chops in a cast-iron skillet produced the best results with the least amount of oil, and a unique setup for resting the chops helped keep them crispy from edge to edge. The cooking time is dependent on the thickness of the pork chops. Do not substitute chops of another thickness. If you can, purchase chops with a ¼-inch-thick fat cap. If your pork chops do not have a fat cap, skip step 3. Panko may be sold in boxes or bags, some of which have windows showing the size and shape of the crumbs; for the crispest texture, look for crumbs that are large and flaked rather than small and pebbly. If you don't have a cast-iron skillet, use stainless steel and increase the oil to 1 cup. If desired, serve the tonkatsu with our DIY Bull-Dog Sauce (recipe follows) and/or lemon, soy sauce, and wasabi.

- 2 cups finely shredded green cabbage
- ¼ cup all-purpose flour
- 2 large eggs
- 2½ cups panko bread crumbs
- 4 (6-ounce) boneless pork chops, ¾ inch thick
- 1 teaspoon kosher salt
- ¾ cup vegetable oil for frying
- 4 cups cooked Japanese short-grain rice
- Lemon wedges
- Soy sauce
- Prepared wasabi or Japanese mustard

1. Place cabbage in salad spinner basket. Add single layer of ice cubes to salad spinner bowl. Set basket on ice and add cold water to cover cabbage. Let sit until cabbage is cold and crisp, 10 minutes. Drain and spin until very dry. Cover and refrigerate until ready to use. (Cabbage can be prepared up to 3 hours in advance.)

2. Place flour in medium bowl. Beat eggs in second medium bowl until no streaks remain. Spread panko in even layer over 1 half of 13 by 9-inch baking dish. Set wire rack in rimmed baking sheet. Invert loaf pan onto center of rack.

3. Place pork chops on cutting board. Working with 1 chop at a time, and starting at 1 end of chop, insert paring knife at 45-degree angle through fat cap to create ¼-inch slit, pushing knife through until you reach cutting board (do not cut from edge to edge). Repeat around perimeter of fat cap, spacing slits ¾ inch apart.

4. Sprinkle chops all over with salt. Dredge chops thoroughly in flour, shaking off excess and returning to cutting board. Use your hand to dip 1 chop in egg and allow excess to drip back into bowl to ensure very thin coating. Place chop on top of panko and, using your other hand, cover pork with crumbs, pressing firmly so crumbs stick to all sides. Return to cutting board. Repeat with remaining chops, tilting dish to rearrange panko on 1 side before coating.

5. Heat oil in 12-inch cast-iron skillet over medium heat to 340 degrees (to take temperature, tilt skillet slightly so oil collects on 1 side). Place chops in skillet and cook, using tongs to lift 1 edge of each chop occasionally to allow steam to escape, until deep golden brown on both sides, about 4 minutes per side. Transfer chops to prepared rack, leaning them against loaf pan. Let rest for 5 minutes.

6. Divide cabbage evenly among 4 serving plates and portion rice into 4 bowls. Slice chops crosswise ½ inch thick and transfer to plates. Serve with lemon wedges, soy sauce, and wasabi.

### DIY Bull-Dog Sauce

**MAKES** ⅔ cup

Bull-Dog Sauce is a sweet and tangy bottled Japanese condiment that's commonly drizzled over tonkatsu or chicken katsu. We use a combination of Worcestershire sauce, ketchup, and molasses to mimic the product's acidity, sweetness, and body. Garlic powder adds a touch of savoriness while cinnamon, pepper, and cloves add dimension. Do not use blackstrap molasses here, as it is too bitter.

- ⅓ cup Worcestershire sauce
- ⅓ cup ketchup
- ¼ cup molasses
- 1 teaspoon garlic powder
- ¼ teaspoon kosher salt
- ¼ teaspoon ground cinnamon
- ¼ teaspoon pepper
- Pinch ground cloves

Whisk all ingredients in small saucepan until no lumps remain. Bring to simmer over medium-high heat. Reduce heat to maintain gentle simmer and cook until slightly thickened, about 5 minutes. Let cool completely before using. (Sauce can be refrigerated for up to 1 month.)

## Zha Paigu (Taiwanese Fried Pork Chops)

**SERVES 4**

**WHY THIS RECIPE WORKS** Taiwan's zha paigu, or fried pork chops, are juicy, fragrant with five-spice powder, and unsurpassed in their crispiness. We started with bone-in rib chops. Pounding the chops ¼ inch thick ensured that they cooked quickly. We soaked the chops in a superflavorful marinade then dipped them in beaten egg before dredging them in coarse sweet potato starch to create a shattery crust. Sweet potato starch develops an exceptionally crispy crust, especially after the chops are double-fried. If rib chops are unavailable, blade chops may be used. The bones of the chops are great for nibbling, which is why we include them for serving. Coarse (or "thick") sweet potato starch gives the chops their distinct crunch. You can substitute coarse tapioca starch. We developed this recipe with michiu, Taiwanese rice wine; if it's unavailable, clear rice wine and sake make good substitutes. Fry the chops in a 14-inch wok or a Dutch oven that holds 6 quarts or more. To make paigu fan, serve the chops with white rice; a stir-fried vegetable; a pickled vegetable, such as mustard greens; and Lu Dan (recipe follows).

- 1 tablespoon soy sauce
- 1 tablespoon michiu
- 2 garlic cloves, minced to paste
- 1½ teaspoons sugar
- 1½ teaspoons water
- ¾ teaspoon five-spice powder
- ½ teaspoon table salt
- ¼ teaspoon white pepper
- 2 (8- to 10-ounce) bone-in pork rib chops, ¾ to 1 inch thick
- 2 large eggs
- 1 cup coarse sweet potato starch
- 3 cups vegetable oil for frying

**1.** Whisk soy sauce, michiu, garlic, sugar, water, five-spice powder, salt, and white pepper together in large bowl.

**2.** Place 1 chop on cutting board; cover with sheet of plastic wrap; and pound to ¼-inch thickness, being careful to avoid bone. Repeat with remaining chop. Add chops to bowl with marinade and toss to evenly coat. Cover and refrigerate for 1 hour or up to 4 hours.

**3.** Beat eggs in shallow dish. Spread sweet potato starch in second shallow dish. Working with 1 chop at a time, remove from marinade (do not pat dry) and dip into egg, turning to coat well and allowing excess egg to drip back into dish. Coat evenly on all sides with sweet potato starch, pressing on chop to adhere. Transfer chops to rimmed baking sheet.

**4.** Set wire rack in second rimmed baking sheet. Add oil to wok or large Dutch oven and heat over medium-high heat to 350 degrees. Place 1 chop in oil and cook until just starting to brown on both sides, 1 minute per side. Transfer chop to prepared rack. Return oil to 350 degrees and repeat with remaining chop.

**5.** Heat oil to 375 degrees. Return 1 chop to oil and cook until golden brown on both sides, about 1 minute per side. Transfer chop to rack. Return oil to 375 degrees and repeat with remaining chop. Let chops rest for 5 minutes. Carve meat from bone and slice ½ inch thick. Serve meat with bones.

### Lu Dan (Braised Eggs)

**SERVES 4 to 6**

Taiwanese braised eggs ("lu" means "braised," and "dan" means "egg") are eggs cooked or marinated in a soy sauce broth. They are eaten as an appetizer or as a side dish alongside proteins such as zha paigu. If you don't have a steamer basket, use a spoon or tongs to gently place the eggs in the water. It does not matter if the eggs are above the water or partially submerged. You can use this method for fewer eggs without altering the timing. You can also double this recipe as long as you use a pot and steamer basket large enough to hold the eggs in a single layer. We developed this recipe with michiu, Taiwanese rice wine; if it's unavailable, clear rice wine and sake make good substitutes. The soy marinade can be reused to marinate up to three batches of eggs; it can be refrigerated for up to one week or frozen for up to one month.

- 4–6 large eggs
- ¾ cup soy sauce
- 1 tablespoon michiu
- 1 tablespoon sugar
- 1½ teaspoons five-spice powder

**1.** Bring 1 inch water to rolling boil in medium saucepan over high heat. Place eggs in steamer basket. Transfer basket to saucepan. Cover, reduce heat to medium (small wisps of steam should escape from beneath lid), and cook until eggs reach desired doneness (6½ minutes for soft-cooked eggs or 13 minutes for hard-cooked eggs).

**2.** When eggs are almost finished cooking, fill large bowl halfway with ice and water. Using tongs or spoon, transfer eggs to ice bath. Discard water in saucepan. Let eggs sit for 15 minutes, then peel eggs. Discard ice bath and wipe out bowl.

**3.** Meanwhile, combine 2 cups water, soy sauce, michiu, sugar, and five-spice in now-empty saucepan and bring to boil over high heat. Reduce heat to low and simmer for 10 minutes. Remove saucepan from heat and add eggs. Let eggs sit in marinade until cool enough to handle, about 30 minutes.

**4.** Carefully add eggs and soy sauce mixture to large zipper-lock bag and place bag in now-empty bowl. Press out as much air as possible from bag so eggs are fully submerged in liquid, then seal bag. Refrigerate for at least 4 hours or up to 12 hours (the longer the eggs marinate, the more seasoned they will be). Remove eggs from marinade and serve.

## Skillet-Barbecued Pork Chops

**SERVES 4**

**WHY THIS RECIPE WORKS** One of our favorite summer flavors is that of charred, salty-sweet grilled pork chops coated with spicy barbecue sauce. But because winter sometimes seems endless, we wanted to come up with an indoor method for replicating the tangy, sweet burnished crust and juicy meat of grilled chops. Brining the chops first ensured that our meat would be juicy and well seasoned. Instead of searing the chops in a blazing hot skillet and then turning the heat down, we coated the chops with a dry spice rub—the rub charred rather than the pork chops and gave the meat the flavor and appearance of real barbecue. To prevent the rub from blackening, we cooked the chops over medium heat and used a nonstick skillet. Homemade barbecue sauce provided a tangy flavor that contrasted nicely with the tender meat, and some reserved spice rub gave the sauce a spicy kick. A touch of liquid smoke gave our barbecue sauce more grill flavor. Finally, we brushed our chops with a small amount of sauce for a second sear so the sauce would caramelize and intensify in flavor—just as it would on the grill. We prefer natural to enhanced pork (pork that has been injected with a salt solution to increase moistness and flavor) for this recipe. If using enhanced pork, skip the brining in step 1 and add ½ teaspoon salt to the spice rub. Grate the onion on the large holes of a box grater. In step 5, check your chops after 3 minutes. If you don't hear a definite sizzle and the chops have not started to brown on the underside, increase the heat to medium-high and continue cooking as directed (follow the indicated temperatures for the remainder of the recipe).

**PORK CHOPS**

- ½ cup table salt
- 4 (8- to 10-ounce) bone-in rib loin pork chops, ¾ to 1 inch thick, trimmed of excess fat
- 4 teaspoons vegetable oil

**SPICE RUB**

- 1 tablespoon paprika
- 1 tablespoon brown sugar
- 2 teaspoons ground coriander
- 1 teaspoon ground cumin
- 1 teaspoon ground black pepper

**SAUCE**

- ½ cup ketchup
- 3 tablespoons light or mild molasses
- 2 tablespoons grated onion
- 2 tablespoons Worcestershire sauce
- 2 tablespoons Dijon mustard
- 1 tablespoon cider vinegar
- 1 tablespoon brown sugar
- 1 teaspoon liquid smoke

1. **FOR THE PORK CHOPS:** Dissolve the salt in 2 quarts cold water in a large bowl or container. Submerge the chops in the brine, cover with plastic wrap, and refrigerate for 30 minutes.

2. **FOR THE SPICE RUB:** Combine the rub ingredients in a small bowl. Measure 2 teaspoons of the mixture into a medium bowl and set aside for the sauce. Transfer the remaining spice rub to a large plate.

3. **FOR THE SAUCE:** Whisk the sauce ingredients in the bowl with the reserved spice mixture until thoroughly combined; set aside.

4. Remove the chops from the brine, rinse, and pat dry with paper towels. Use a sharp knife to cut two slits, about 2 inches apart, through the outer layer of fat and silver skin of each chop (do not cut into the meat of the chops). Coat both sides of the chops with the spice rub, pressing gently so the rub adheres. Shake off the excess rub.

5. Heat 1 tablespoon of the oil in a 12-inch nonstick skillet over medium heat until just smoking. Place the chops in the skillet in a pinwheel pattern, with the ribs pointing toward the center, and cook until browned and charred in spots, 5 to 8 minutes. Flip the chops and continue to cook until the second side is browned and the center of the chops registers 130 degrees on an instant-read thermometer, 4 to 8 minutes. Remove the skillet from the heat and transfer the chops to a plate. Lightly brush the top of each chop with 2 teaspoons of the sauce.

6. Wipe out the pan with paper towels and return to medium heat. Add the remaining 1 teaspoon oil and heat until just smoking. Add the chops to the pan, sauce side down, and cook without moving them until the sauce has caramelized and charred in spots, about 1 minute. While cooking, lightly brush the top of each chop with 2 more teaspoons sauce. Flip the chops and cook until the second side is charred and caramelized and the center of the chops registers 140 to 145 degrees on an instant-read thermometer, 1 to 2 minutes.

7. Transfer the chops back to the plate, cover loosely with foil, and let rest until the center of the chops registers 150 degrees on an instant-read thermometer, about 5 minutes.

8. Meanwhile, add the remaining sauce to the pan and cook over medium heat, scraping up any browned bits, until thickened and it measures ⅔ cup, about 3 minutes. Brush each chop with 1 tablespoon of the sauce and serve, passing the remaining sauce separately.

## Red Wine–Braised Pork Chops

**SERVES 4**

**WHY THIS RECIPE WORKS** Braising promises flavorful, tender pork chops and a rich, glossy sauce. To get juicy meat and a silky sauce, we first had to pick the right chop. For moist, tender chops, we began with blade chops, which have a larger amount of fat and connective tissue. We brined our chops to ensure seasoning and juiciness then trimmed them of excess fat and connective tissue to prevent buckling when cooking. We used the trimmings to generate fond, which is crucial to building a flavorful braising liquid. The fond was so impressive that we found we did not need to sear the chops themselves. Deglazing the pot with red wine, ruby port, and red wine vinegar added acidity, sweetness, and complexity. The trimmings also provided a nest for the chops, so that they rested above the liquid where they cooked more gently. Blade chops may be a little harder to find in the store, but they are worth seeking out. Look for chops with a small eye and a large amount of marbling, as these are the best suited to braising. The pork scraps can be removed when straining the sauce in step 4 and served alongside the chops. (They taste great.)

- Table salt and pepper
- 4 (10- to 12-ounce) bone-in pork blade chops, 1 inch thick
- 2 teaspoons vegetable oil
- 2 onions, halved and sliced thin
- 5 sprigs fresh thyme plus ¼ teaspoon minced
- 2 garlic cloves, peeled
- 2 bay leaves
- 1 (½-inch) piece ginger, peeled and crushed
- ⅛ teaspoon ground allspice
- ½ cup red wine
- ¼ cup ruby port
- 2 tablespoons plus ½ teaspoon red wine vinegar
- 1 cup low-sodium chicken broth
- 2 tablespoons unsalted butter
- 1 tablespoon minced fresh parsley

**1.** Dissolve 3 tablespoons salt in 1½ quarts cold water in large container. Submerge chops in brine, cover, and refrigerate for 30 minutes or up to 1 hour.

**2.** Adjust oven rack to lower-middle position and heat oven to 275 degrees. Remove chops from brine and pat dry with paper towels. Trim off meat cap and any fat and cartilage opposite rib bones. Cut trimmings into 1-inch pieces. Heat oil in Dutch oven over medium-high heat until shimmering. Add trimmings and brown on all sides, 6 to 9 minutes.

**3.** Reduce heat to medium and add onions, thyme sprigs, garlic, bay leaves, ginger, and allspice. Cook, stirring occasionally, until onions are golden brown, 5 to 10 minutes. Stir in wine, port, and 2 tablespoons vinegar and cook until reduced to thin syrup, 5 to 7 minutes. Add chicken broth, spread onions and pork scraps into even layer, and bring to simmer. Arrange pork chops on top of pork scraps and onions.

**4.** Cover, transfer to oven, and cook until meat is tender, 1¼ to 1½ hours. Remove from oven and let chops rest in pot, covered, for 30 minutes. Transfer chops to serving platter and tent with aluminum foil. Strain braising liquid through fine-mesh strainer; discard solids. Transfer braising liquid to fat separator and let stand for 5 minutes.

**5.** Wipe out now-empty pot with wad of paper towels. Return defatted braising liquid to pot and cook over medium-high heat until reduced to 1 cup, 3 to 7 minutes. Off heat, whisk in butter, minced thyme, and remaining ½ teaspoon vinegar. Season with salt and pepper to taste. Pour sauce over chops, sprinkle with parsley, and serve.

## Smothered Pork Chops

SERVES 4

---

**WHY THIS RECIPE WORKS** Tender, flavorful chops stand up very well to rich, hearty gravy. We wanted a foolproof recipe for juicy chops smothered in rich gravy with a satiny, thick texture. For a nice balance with the gravy and to allow for the best absorption of the gravy's flavors, we used thin, not thick, rib chops. Browning them well left meaty browned bits in the pan, essential for making a flavorful gravy. To build further flavor, we made a nut-brown, bacony roux. Thinly sliced yellow onions contributed a significant amount of moisture to the gravy. Garlic, thyme, and bay leaves rounded out the flavorful gravy. For the tenderest chops, we combined the sauce and browned chops in the pan and braised them for half an hour. Not only did the lengthy braise result in moist, tender chops, it also allowed the gravy to thicken and its flavors to meld, so the chops had a rich, velvety coating when served. We prefer natural to enhanced pork (pork that has been injected with a salt solution to increase moistness and flavor) for this recipe, though either will work here. Serve smothered chops with egg noodles or mashed potatoes to soak up the rich gravy.

- 3 ounces bacon (about 3 slices), cut into ¼-inch pieces
- 2 tablespoons unbleached all-purpose flour
- 1¾ cups low-sodium chicken broth
- 2 tablespoons vegetable oil, plus more as needed
- 4 (7-ounce) bone-in rib loin pork chops, ½ to ¾ inch thick, trimmed of excess fat
- Ground black pepper
- 2 medium yellow onions, halved and sliced thin (about 3½ cups)
- Table salt
- 2 tablespoons water
- 2 medium garlic cloves, minced or pressed through a garlic press (about 2 teaspoons)
- 1 teaspoon minced fresh thyme leaves
- 2 bay leaves
- 1 tablespoon minced fresh parsley leaves

**1.** Fry the bacon in small saucepan over medium heat, stirring occasionally, until crispy, 8 to 10 minutes. Using slotted spoon, transfer bacon to paper towel–lined plate, leaving fat in saucepan (you should have 2 tablespoons bacon fat; if not, add oil to make this amount). Whisk in flour and cook over medium-low heat until golden, about 5 minutes. Whisk in broth and bring to boil, stirring occasionally, over medium-high heat; cover and set aside off heat.

**2.** Heat 1 tablespoon of oil in 12-inch skillet over high heat until smoking. Pat chops dry with paper towels. Use sharp knife to cut two slits, about 2 inches apart, through outer layer of fat and silver skin of each chop (do not cut into meat of chops). Sprinkle each chop with ½ teaspoon pepper. Brown chops in single layer until browned on first side, about 3 minutes. Flip chops and cook until second side is browned, about 3 minutes longer. Transfer chops to plate and set aside.

**3.** Add remaining 1 tablespoon oil to skillet and return to medium heat until shimmering. Add onions, ¼ teaspoon salt, and water, scraping up any browned bits, and cook until lightly browned, about 5 minutes. Stir in garlic and thyme and cook until fragrant, about 30 seconds longer. Return chops to skillet and cover with onions. Add reserved sauce, bay leaves, and any accumulated meat juices from plate to skillet. Cover and simmer over low heat until chops are tender and paring knife inserted into chops meets little resistance, about 30 minutes.

**4.** Transfer chops to platter and cover loosely with foil. Simmer sauce over medium-high heat, stirring frequently, until thickened, about 5 minutes. Discard bay leaves, stir in parsley, and season with salt and pepper to taste. Cover chops with sauce, sprinkle with reserved bacon, and serve.

## French-Style Pork Chops with Apples and Calvados

SERVES 4

---

**WHY THIS RECIPE WORKS** For pork chops with big apple flavor, we took cues from the French. While our salted pork chops rested in the refrigerator, we created a base by frying up bacon, adding shallots and nutmeg to bloom and cook in the rendered fat. After adding a hit of Calvados, the woodsy apple brandy, we carefully ignited the sauce to eliminate the alcohol's bite. We repeated this step, flambéing a total of ½ cup of Calvados, and then rounded out the sauce's herbal, fruity

flavors with apple cider, chicken broth, thyme, butter, and chopped apples. Once the sauce reduced and the apples softened, we turned to the chops. After browning the chops, we then browned the apple rings. We arranged the chops atop the rings, elevating the meat to finish cooking in the oven. We added minced thyme and cider vinegar to the sauce to reinforce its apple flavor. We prefer natural pork, but if the pork is enhanced (injected with a salt solution), decrease the salt in step 1 to ½ teaspoon per chop. To ensure that they fit in the skillet, choose apples that are approximately 3 inches in diameter. Applejack or regular brandy can be used in place of the Calvados. Before flambéing, be sure to roll up long shirtsleeves, tie back long hair, and turn off the exhaust fan and any lit burners. Use a long match or wooden skewer to flambé the Calvados. The amount of vinegar to add in step 4 will vary depending on the sweetness of your cider.

- 4 (12- to 14-ounce) bone-in pork rib chops, 1 inch thick, trimmed
- Kosher salt and pepper
- 4 Gala or Golden Delicious apples, peeled and cored
- 2 slices bacon, cut into ½-inch pieces
- 3 shallots, sliced
- Pinch ground nutmeg
- ½ cup Calvados
- 1¾ cups apple cider
- 1¼ cups chicken broth
- 4 sprigs fresh thyme, plus ¼ teaspoon minced
- 2 tablespoons unsalted butter
- 2 teaspoons vegetable oil
- ½–1 teaspoon apple cider vinegar

**1.** Evenly sprinkle each chop with ¾ teaspoon salt. Place chops on large plate, cover loosely with plastic wrap, and refrigerate for 1 hour.

**2.** While chops rest, cut 2 apples into ½-inch pieces. Cook bacon in medium saucepan over medium heat until crisp, 5 to 7 minutes. Add shallots, nutmeg, and ¼ teaspoon salt; cook, stirring frequently, until shallots are softened and beginning to brown, 3 to 4 minutes. Off heat, add ¼ cup Calvados and let warm through, about 5 seconds. Wave lit match over pan until Calvados ignites, then shake pan gently to distribute flames. When flames subside, 30 to 60 seconds, cover pan to ensure flame is extinguished, 15 seconds. Add remaining ¼ cup Calvados and repeat flambéing (flames will subside after 1½ to 2 minutes). (If you have trouble igniting second addition, return pan to medium heat, bring to bare simmer, and remove from heat and try again.) Once flames have extinguished, increase heat to medium-high; add cider, 1 cup broth, thyme sprigs, butter, and chopped apples; and bring to rapid simmer. Cook, stirring occasionally, until apples are very tender and mixture has reduced to 2⅓ cups, 25 to 35 minutes. Cover and set aside.

**3.** Adjust oven rack to middle position and heat oven to 300 degrees. Slice remaining 2 apples into ½-inch-thick rings. Pat chops dry with paper towels and evenly sprinkle each chop with pepper. Heat oil in 12-inch skillet over medium heat until just beginning to smoke. Increase heat to high and brown chops on both sides, 6 to 8 minutes total. Transfer chops to large plate and reduce heat to medium. Add apple rings and cook until lightly browned, 1 to 2 minutes. Add remaining ¼ cup broth and cook, scraping up any browned bits with rubber spatula, until liquid has evaporated, about 30 seconds. Remove pan from heat, flip apple rings, and place chops on top of apple rings. Place skillet in oven and cook until chops register 135 to 140 degrees, 11 to 15 minutes.

**4.** Transfer chops and apple rings to serving platter, tent loosely with aluminum foil, and let rest for 10 minutes. While chops rest, strain apple-brandy mixture through fine-mesh strainer set in large bowl, pressing on solids with ladle or rubber spatula to extract liquid; discard solids. (Make sure to use rubber spatula to scrape any apple solids on bottom of strainer into sauce.) Stir in minced thyme and season sauce with vinegar, salt, and pepper to taste. Transfer sauce to serving bowl. Serve chops and apple rings, passing sauce separately.

## Pork Chops with Vinegar and Sweet Peppers

**SERVES 4**

**WHY THIS RECIPE WORKS** This Italian American dish was devised when pork chops had plenty of fat to keep them juicy; the leaner pork we have today tends to dry out and ruin the dish. But the thought of succulent pork with a tangy vinegar and pepper sauce spurred us to search for a way to make this dish taste the way it should. Bone-in rib chops of medium thickness had the best flavor, and the bone helped keep the meat juicy. Brining the chops in a solution of salt and sugar added moisture and flavor, and the sugar enhanced browning. We discovered that browning the chops, removing them from the pan to build the sauce, then finishing everything together in the oven worked best to get the flavors of the sauce into the meat. Jarred vinegar peppers are traditional but we made our own. We prefer natural to enhanced pork (pork that has been injected with a salt solution to increase moistness and flavor) for this recipe, though enhanced pork can be used. If using enhanced pork, skip the brining in step 1. To keep the chops from overcooking and becoming tough, remove them from the oven when they are just shy of fully cooked; as they sit in the hot skillet, they will continue to cook with residual heat.

- 1 cup sugar
- Table salt and ground black pepper
- 4 (8- to 10-ounce) bone-in rib loin pork chops, ¾ to 1 inch thick, trimmed of excess fat (see note)
- 2 tablespoons olive oil
- 1 large onion, chopped fine (about 1¼ cups)
- 1 large red bell pepper, stemmed, seeded, and cut into ¼-inch-wide strips (about 1½ cups)
- 1 large yellow bell pepper, stemmed, seeded, and cut into ¼-inch-wide strips (about 1½ cups)
- 2 anchovy fillets, minced (about 2 teaspoons)
- 1 sprig fresh rosemary, about 5 inches long
- 2 medium garlic cloves (about 2 teaspoons)
- ¾ cup water
- ½ cup white wine vinegar, plus optional 2 tablespoons to finish sauce
- 2 tablespoons cold unsalted butter
- 2 tablespoons chopped fresh parsley leaves

**1.** Dissolve sugar and ½ cup table salt in 2 quarts water in large container; add pork chops and refrigerate 30 minutes. Remove chops from brine; thoroughly pat dry with paper towels. Using a sharp knife, cut two slits, about 2 inches apart, through outer layer of fat and silver skin of each chop (do not cut into meat of chops). Season chops with ¾ teaspoon pepper and set aside.

**2.** Adjust oven rack to middle position; heat oven to 400 degrees. Heat oil in heavy-bottomed ovensafe 12-inch nonreactive skillet over medium-high heat until oil begins to smoke; swirl skillet to coat with oil. Place chops in skillet; cook until well browned, 3 to 4 minutes, using spoon or spatula to press down on center of chops to aid in browning. Using tongs, flip chops and brown lightly on second side, about 1 minute. Transfer chops to large plate; set aside.

**3.** Set skillet over medium-high heat. Add onion and cook, stirring occasionally, until just beginning to soften, about 2 minutes. Add peppers, anchovies, and rosemary; cook, stirring frequently, until peppers just begin to soften, about 4 minutes. Add garlic; cook, stirring constantly, until fragrant, about 30 seconds. Add water and ½ cup of vinegar and bring to a boil, scraping up browned bits with wooden spoon. Reduce heat to medium; simmer until liquid is reduced to about ⅓ cup, 6 to 8 minutes. Off heat, discard rosemary.

**4.** Return pork chops, browner side up, to skillet; nestle chops in peppers, but do not cover them. Add any accumulated juices to skillet; set skillet in oven and cook until center of chops registers 140 to 145 degrees, 8 to 12 minutes (begin checking temperature after 6 minutes). Using potholders, carefully remove skillet from oven (handle will be very hot) and cover skillet with lid or foil; let stand until center of chops registers 150 degrees, 5 to 7 minutes. Transfer chops to platter or individual plates. Swirl butter into sauce and peppers in skillet; taste and stir in remaining 2 tablespoons vinegar (if using) and parsley. Season with salt and pepper to taste, then pour or spoon sauce and peppers over chops. Serve immediately.

## Oven-Roasted Pork Chops

**SERVES 4**

**WHY THIS RECIPE WORKS** Roasting thick-cut chops in a blazing hot oven (their thickness prevents them from drying out) cuts down on cooking time and frees up the stovetop so you can make an easy pan sauce at the same time. We chose extra-thick rib loin pork chops and flavored them with a brown sugar and salt brine. We found that our thick chops couldn't go straight into the oven—they had to be cooked in three stages. First, we seared them in a hot pan to give them a nicely browned crust, then we transferred them to a preheated pan in the oven to cook most of the way through, and finally we moved them to a platter and covered them with foil to gently come up to serving temperature (while the meat stayed moist and tender). This last step also gave us time to make a speedy lemon-caper sauce right in the pan using the fond (browned bits) left behind from searing the chops. We prefer natural to enhanced pork (pork that has been injected with a salt solution to increase moistness and flavor) for this recipe. If using enhanced pork, skip the brining in step 1. To serve the pork chops with the Lemon-Caper Sauce (recipe follows), have all the sauce ingredients ready to go and don't wash the skillet after browning the chops; begin the sauce, using the fat left behind from browning the chops, after the pork chops come out of the oven and are resting.

- ¾ cup (5¼ ounces) dark brown sugar
- ¼ cup table salt
- 10 medium garlic cloves, crushed
- 4 bay leaves, crumbled
- 8 whole cloves
- 3 tablespoons whole black peppercorns, crushed
- 4 (12-ounce) bone-in rib loin pork chops, about 1½ inches thick, trimmed of excess fat
- 2 tablespoons vegetable oil

**1.** Dissolve sugar and salt in 6 cups cold water in large bowl or container. Add garlic, bay leaves, cloves, and peppercorns. Submerge chops in brine, cover with plastic wrap, and refrigerate for 1 hour. Remove chops from brine, rinse, and pat dry with paper towels. Use sharp knife to cut two slits, about 2 inches apart, through outer layer of fat and silver skin of each chop (do not cut into meat of chops).

**2.** Adjust oven rack to lower-middle position, place rimmed baking sheet on rack, and heat oven to 450 degrees. When oven reaches 450 degrees, heat oil in 12-inch skillet over high heat until shimmering. Place chops in skillet and cook until well browned, about 2 minutes. Flip chops and continue to cook until second side is well browned, about 2 minutes longer.

**3.** Transfer chops to baking sheet in oven. Roast until center of chops registers 140 to 145 degrees on instant-read thermometer, about 15 minutes, turning chops over once halfway through cooking time. Transfer chops to platter, cover loosely with foil, and let rest until internal temperature registers 150 degrees on instant-read thermometer, 5 to 10 minutes or while preparing pan sauce.

### Lemon-Caper Sauce

**MAKES** about ½ cup

- 1 medium shallot, minced (about 3 tablespoons)
- 1 cup low-sodium chicken broth
- ¼ cup juice from 2 lemons
- 2 tablespoons capers, drained
- 3 tablespoons unsalted butter, softened

Follow recipe for Oven-Roasted Pork Chops. After removing chops from pan, add shallot and cook over medium heat until softened, about 30 seconds. Increase heat to high and stir in broth, scraping up any browned bits. Add lemon juice and capers, bring to simmer, and cook until sauce measures ⅓ cup, 3 to 4 minutes. Off heat, whisk in butter; serve with pork chops.

## Stuffed Pork Chops

**SERVES** 4

**WHY THIS RECIPE WORKS** Thick-cut pork chops make the perfect home for a simple stuffing. We wanted the stuffing to be especially flavorful and rich to offset the mildness of the pork, and we wanted the chops to be moist and juicy. Our stuffing was easy enough to make—we used a simple combination of aromatic vegetables, herbs, and fresh bread. But the stuffing was so loose, it crumbled and spilled out over the plate when the chops were served. Clearly, we needed a binder. Instead of eggs, we chose cream, which added richness and enough moisture to bring the stuffing together. Because the stuffing didn't contain eggs, the chops could be cooked to a lower (and more palatable) internal temperature, making for tender and juicy meat. After brining the chops and creating a small "pocket" to hold the stuffing, we started them in a skillet to develop a nice brown crust but finished cooking them through on a baking sheet in a hot oven. Flavorful gravy (sans big roast) is ideal for draping over the stuffed chops. Thoroughly browning both the aromatic vegetables and the flour added significant flavor, as did the inclusion of two kinds of broth: beef and chicken. We prefer natural to enhanced pork (pork that has been injected with a salt solution to increase moistness and flavor) for this recipe, though either will work here. Serve these pork chops with Quick All-Purpose Gravy (recipe follows). The gravy is best made before you start the chops and reheated as needed.

**PORK CHOPS**

- 4 (12-ounce) bone-in rib loin pork chops, about 1½ inches thick, trimmed of excess fat
- ¾ cup packed light brown sugar
- ¼ cup table salt
- Ground black pepper
- 1 tablespoon vegetable oil

**STUFFING**

- 3 tablespoons unsalted butter
- 1 small onion, minced
- 1 celery rib, chopped fine
- ½ teaspoon table salt
- 1 tablespoon minced fresh parsley leaves
- 2 medium garlic cloves, minced or pressed through a garlic press (about 2 teaspoons)
- 2 teaspoons minced fresh thyme leaves
- 2 slices high-quality white sandwich bread, cut into ¼-inch cubes (about 2 cups)
- 2 tablespoons heavy cream
- Ground black pepper

**1. FOR THE PORK CHOPS:** Cut a small pocket through the side of each chop. Dissolve the sugar and salt in 6 cups cold water in a large bowl or container. Submerge the chops in the brine, cover with plastic wrap, and refrigerate for 1 hour.

**2. FOR THE STUFFING:** Melt the butter in a 12-inch skillet over medium heat. Add the onion, celery, and salt and cook until the vegetables are softened, 6 to 8 minutes. Add the parsley,

### STUFFING PORK CHOPS

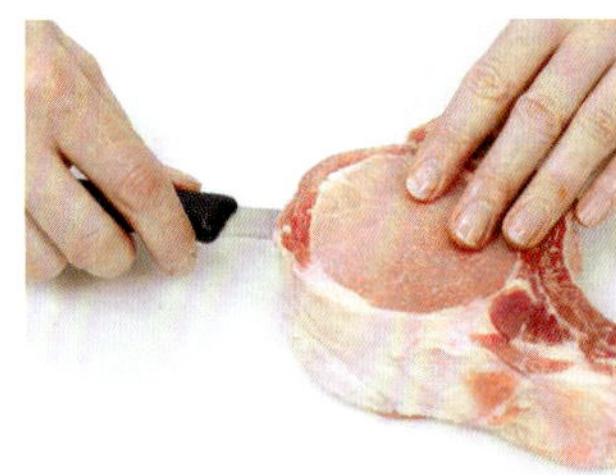

**1.** Using paring knife, trim away excess fat and connective tissue around edge of meat. With knife positioned as shown, insert blade through center of side of chop until tip touches bone.

**2.** Swing tip of blade through middle of chop to create pocket (opening should be about 1 inch wide).

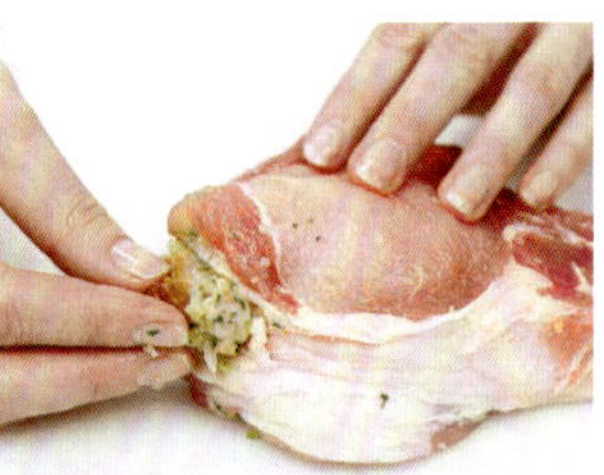

**3.** With your fingers, gently press stuffing mixture into pocket, without enlarging opening.

garlic, and thyme and cook until fragrant, about 30 seconds. Transfer to a medium bowl and toss with the bread cubes, cream, and ⅛ teaspoon pepper. Mix, lightly pressing the mixture against the sides of the bowl, until it comes together.

**3.** Adjust an oven rack to the lower-middle position, place a rimmed baking sheet on the rack, and heat the oven to 450 degrees. Remove the chops from the brine, rinse, and pat dry with paper towels. Place one-quarter of the stuffing (about ⅓ cup) in the pocket of each pork chop. Season the chops with pepper.

**4.** Heat the oil in a 12-inch skillet over high heat until shimmering. Place the chops in the skillet and cook until well browned, about 3 minutes. Flip the chops and cook until the second side is well browned, about 2 minutes longer.

**5.** Transfer the chops to the baking sheet in the oven. Roast until the center of the chops registers 140 degrees on an instant-read thermometer, about 15 minutes, turning the chops over halfway through the cooking time. Transfer the chops to a plate, cover loosely with foil, and let rest for 5 to 10 minutes. Serve.

## Quick All-Purpose Gravy

**MAKES** 2 cups

This gravy can be served with almost any type of meat and with mashed potatoes as well. The recipe can be doubled. If doubling it, use a Dutch oven so that the vegetables brown properly and increase the cooking times by roughly half. The finished gravy can be frozen. To thaw it, place the gravy and 1 tablespoon of water in a saucepan over low heat and slowly bring it to a simmer. It may appear broken or curdled as it thaws, but a vigorous whisking will recombine it.

- 3 tablespoons unsalted butter
- 1 onion, minced
- 1 small carrot, peeled and chopped fine
- 1 celery rib, chopped fine
- ¼ cup unbleached all-purpose flour
- 2 cups low-sodium chicken broth
- 2 cups beef broth
- 1 bay leaf
- ¼ teaspoon dried thyme
- 5 whole black peppercorns
- Table salt and ground black pepper

**1.** Melt the butter in a large saucepan over medium-high heat. Add the onion, carrot, and celery and cook, stirring frequently, until softened, about 7 minutes. Reduce the heat to medium, add the flour, and cook, stirring constantly, until thoroughly browned, about 5 minutes. Gradually whisk in the broths and bring to a boil, skimming off any foam that forms on the surface. Add the bay leaf, thyme, and peppercorns and simmer, stirring occasionally, until thickened and reduced to 3 cups, 20 to 25 minutes.

**2.** Strain the gravy through a fine-mesh strainer into a clean saucepan, pressing on the solids to extract as much liquid as possible; discard the solids. Season with salt and pepper to taste and serve with the pork chops.

# Thick-Cut Pork Tenderloin Medallions

**SERVES** 4 to 6

**WHY THIS RECIPE WORKS** When cooked properly, pork tenderloin has a tenderness rivaling that of beef tenderloin; unfortunately it also has ultra-mild flavor. Long marinades and hybrid searing and roasting techniques help remedy the flavor deficiency, but they take the home cook a long way from the realm of the no-fuss meal. We wanted a recipe for a fast weeknight dinner that still offered maximum flavor. We needed to deal with the tenderloin's oblong, tapered shape as well as the fact that the tenderloins (which are usually sold in a pair in a vacuum pack) were almost guaranteed to be substantially different in weight and length. The solution was to cut them into 1½-inch-thick medallions (the end pieces were scored, creating a small flap of meat that folded underneath the larger half to yield the right-sized medallion). To preserve their tidy cylindrical shape, we developed two approaches: tying the medallions or wrapping blanched bacon around them, fastened with toothpicks. We found we could create a beautiful sear on all sides of these neat packages in the time it took to reach an internal temperature of 140 to 145 degrees, and the searing process had the extra benefit of producing enough fond (flavorful browned bits) to create a few easy, flavorful pan sauces. We prefer natural to enhanced pork (pork that has been injected with a salt solution to increase moistness and flavor), though both will work in this recipe. Begin checking the doneness of smaller medallions 1 or 2 minutes early; they may need to be taken out of the pan a little sooner. Be sure not to rinse out the skillet if serving with a pan sauce (recipe follows).

- 2 (1- to 1¼-pound) pork tenderloins, trimmed, cut crosswise into 1½-inch pieces, and tied; thinner end pieces removed and tied together
- Table salt and ground black pepper
- 2 tablespoons vegetable oil

**1.** Pat pork medallions dry and season with salt and pepper.

**2.** Heat oil in 12-inch skillet over medium-high heat until shimmering. Add pork and cook, without moving pieces, until well browned, 3 to 5 minutes. Turn pork and brown on second side, 3 to 5 minutes more. Reduce heat to medium. Using tongs, stand each piece on its side and cook, turning pieces as necessary, until sides are well browned and internal temperature registers 140 to 145 degrees on instant-read thermometer, 8 to 12 minutes. Transfer pork to platter, tent loosely with foil, and let rest until temperature registers 150 degrees on instant-read thermometer, while making pan sauce. Serve with sauce.

## Apple Cider Sauce

**MAKES** about 1¼ cups

Complete step 1 of this recipe either before or during the cooking of the pork, then finish the sauce while the pork rests.

- 1½ cups apple cider
- 1 cup chicken broth
- 2 teaspoons cider vinegar

1 cinnamon stick
4 tablespoons (½ stick) unsalted butter, cut into 4 pieces
2 large shallots, minced (about ½ cup)
1 tart apple, such as Granny Smith, peeled, cored, and diced small
¼ cup Calvados or apple-flavored brandy
1 teaspoon minced fresh thyme leaves
Table salt and ground black pepper

**1.** Combine cider, broth, vinegar, and cinnamon stick in medium saucepan; simmer over medium-high heat until liquid is reduced to 1 cup, 10 to 12 minutes. Remove cinnamon stick and discard. Set sauce aside until pork is cooked.

**2.** Pour off any fat from skillet in which pork was cooked. Add 1 tablespoon of butter and heat over medium heat until melted. Add shallots and apple and cook, stirring occasionally, until softened and beginning to brown, 1 to 2 minutes. Remove skillet from heat and add Calvados. Return skillet to heat and cook for about 1 minute, scraping bottom of skillet with wooden spoon to loosen any browned bits. Add reduced cider mixture, any juices from resting meat, and thyme; increase heat to medium-high and simmer until thickened and reduced to 1¼ cups, 3 to 4 minutes. Off heat, whisk in remaining 3 tablespoons butter and season with salt and pepper to taste. Pour sauce over pork and serve immediately.

## Perfect Pan-Seared Pork Tenderloin Steaks

**SERVES 4**

**WHY THIS RECIPE WORKS** Techniques using high heat typically overcook lean pork tenderloin. We wanted a way to guarantee juicy, fork-tender meat. We began by lightly pounding the pork to create two flat sides that would be easy to sear. Halving the tenderloins crosswise created moderately sized steaks that were easy to maneuver. We raised the pork off the hot baking sheet to help it cook evenly. Slowly cooking the pork in a low oven ensured that the meat was moist and tender. After searing the pork and letting it rest, we sliced into pork tenderloin perfection: juicy, tender, and evenly rosy meat with a mahogany crust. Choose tenderloins that are equal in size to ensure that the pork cooks at the same rate. We prefer natural pork in this recipe. If using enhanced pork (injected with a salt solution), reduce the salt in step 2 to ¼ teaspoon per steak. Open the oven as infrequently as possible in step 2. If the meat is not yet up to temperature, wait at least 5 minutes before taking its temperature again. Serve the pork with Scallion-Ginger Relish (recipe follows), if desired.

2 (1-pound) pork tenderloins, trimmed
Kosher salt and pepper
2 tablespoons vegetable oil

**1.** Adjust oven rack to middle position and heat oven to 275 degrees. Set wire rack in rimmed baking sheet and lightly spray rack with vegetable oil spray.

### TYING THICK MEDALLIONS

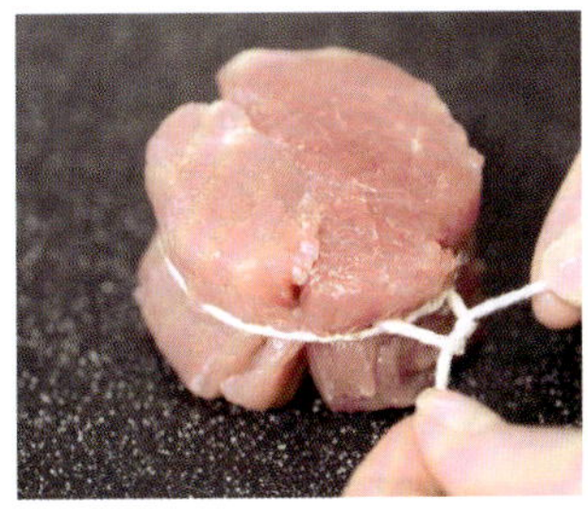

Thick medallions allow for more browning, but they can flop over in the pan. To prevent this, tie each piece with kitchen twine.

### TURNING THE TAILPIECE INTO A MEDALLION

**1.** Score the tenderloin's tapered tail end.

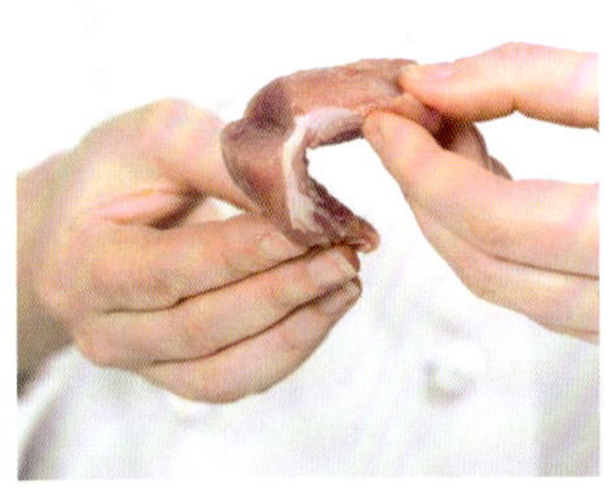

**2.** Fold in half at the incision.

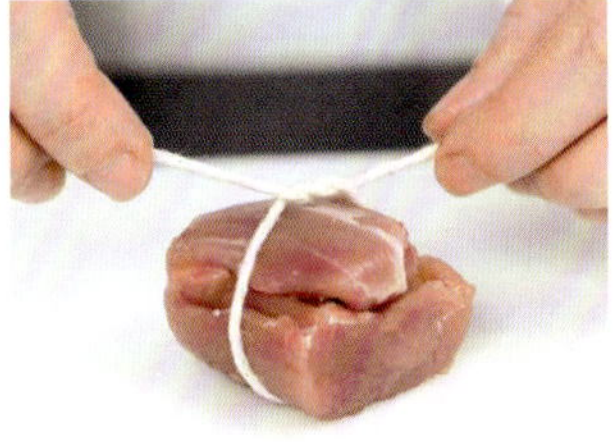

**3.** Tie the medallion with kitchen twine, making sure the outer surfaces are flat.

**2.** Pound each tenderloin to 1-inch thickness. Halve each tenderloin crosswise. Sprinkle each steak with ½ teaspoon salt and ⅛ teaspoon pepper. Place steaks on prepared wire rack and cook until meat registers between 137 and 140 degrees, 25 to 35 minutes.

**3.** Move steaks to 1 side of rack. Line cleared side with double layer of paper towels. Transfer steaks to paper towels, cover with another double layer of paper towels, and let stand for 10 minutes.

**4.** Pat steaks until surfaces are very dry. Heat oil in 12-inch skillet over medium-high heat until just smoking. Increase heat to high, place steaks in skillet, and sear until well browned on both sides, 1 to 2 minutes per side. Transfer to carving board and let stand for 5 minutes. Slice steaks against grain ¾ inch thick and transfer to serving platter. Season with salt to taste, and serve.

## Scallion-Ginger Relish

**MAKES** about ⅔ cup

We like the complexity of white pepper in this recipe.

- 6 scallions, white and green parts separated and sliced thin
- 2 teaspoons grated fresh ginger
- ½ teaspoon ground white pepper
- ½ teaspoon grated lime zest plus 2 teaspoons juice
- ¼ cup vegetable oil
- 2 teaspoons soy sauce

Combine scallion whites, ginger, white pepper, and lime zest in heatproof bowl. Heat oil in small saucepan over medium heat until shimmering. Pour oil over scallion mixture. (Mixture will bubble.) Stir until well combined. Let cool completely, about 15 minutes. Stir in scallion greens, lime juice, and soy sauce. Let mixture sit for 15 minutes to allow flavors to meld.

# Pan-Seared Oven-Roasted Pork Tenderloin

**SERVES** 4

**WHY THIS RECIPE WORKS** Pork tenderloins are so lean, they tend to overcook, and there's also less flavor. We wanted a preparation for whole pork tenderloins that would deliver a flavor boost to this quick-cooking roast. Searing the meat in a skillet, then transferring the pork to the oven to finish cooking, produced a flavorful crust and well-cooked meat. The browned crust added some flavor, but we wanted more. A dry rub of just salt and pepper, left on for half an hour before searing, provided enough seasoning and further encouraged a browned crust; a pan sauce made with the browned bits left from sautéing added additional flavor. These pork tenderloins were delicious and were also on the dinner table in about half an hour. We prefer natural to enhanced pork (pork that has been injected with a salt solution to increase moisture and flavor) for this recipe. Enhanced pork can be used, but the meat won't brown as well. Because two are cooked at once, tenderloins larger than 1 pound apiece will not fit comfortably in a 12-inch skillet. If time permits, season the tenderloins up to 30 minutes before cooking; the seasonings will better penetrate the meat. The recipe will work in a nonstick or a traditional skillet. A pan sauce can be made while the tenderloins are in the oven (recipe follows); make sure to prepare all of the sauce ingredients before cooking the pork.

- 2 (12- to 16-ounce) pork tenderloins, trimmed of fat and silver skin
- 1¼ teaspoons table salt
- ¾ teaspoon ground black pepper
- 2 teaspoons vegetable oil
- 1 recipe pan sauce (optional; recipes follow)

**1.** Adjust an oven rack to middle position and heat oven to 400 degrees. Sprinkle tenderloins evenly with salt and pepper; rub seasoning into meat. Heat oil in 12-inch skillet over medium-high heat until smoking. Place both tenderloins in skillet; cook until well browned, about 3 minutes. Using tongs, rotate tenderloins quarter-turn; cook until well browned, 45 to 60 seconds. Repeat until all sides are browned, about 1 minute longer. Transfer tenderloins to rimmed baking sheet and place in oven (reserve skillet if making pan sauce); roast until internal temperature registers 140 to 145 degrees on instant-read thermometer, 10 to 16 minutes. (Begin pan sauce, if making, while meat roasts.)

**2.** Transfer tenderloins to carving board and tent loosely with foil (continue with pan sauce, if making); let rest until internal temperature registers 150 degrees, 8 to 10 minutes. Cut tenderloins crosswise into ½-inch-thick slices, arrange on platter or individual plates, and spoon sauce (if using) over; serve immediately.

## Dried Cherry–Port Sauce with Onions and Marmalade

**MAKES** about ½ cup

The flavors in this sauce are especially suited to the winter holiday season.

- 1 teaspoon vegetable oil
- 1 large onion, halved and sliced ½ inch thick (about 1½ cups)
- ¾ cup port
- ¾ cup dried cherries
- 2 tablespoons orange marmalade
- 3 tablespoons unsalted butter, cut into 3 pieces
- Table salt and ground black pepper

**1.** Immediately after placing pork in oven, add oil to still-hot skillet, swirl to coat, and set skillet over medium-high heat; add onion and cook, stirring frequently, until softened and browned around edges, 5 to 7 minutes. (If drippings are browning too quickly, add 2 tablespoons water and scrape up browned bits with wooden spoon.) Set skillet aside off heat.

**2.** While the pork is resting, set the skillet over medium-high heat and add the port and cherries; simmer, scraping up the browned bits with a wooden spoon, until the mixture is slightly thickened, 4 to 6 minutes. Add any accumulated pork juices and continue to simmer until thickened and reduced to about ⅓ cup, 2 to 4 minutes longer. Off the heat, whisk in the orange marmalade and butter, one piece at a time. Season with salt and pepper to taste.

## Maple-Glazed Pork Tenderloin

**SERVES 6**

**WHY THIS RECIPE WORKS** On its own, pork tenderloin can lack flavor. We thought a thick, sweet glaze would be just the solution. To give the glaze something to hold on to, we rolled the tenderloins in a mixture of cornstarch and sugar before searing them. When we'd built a good crust in the skillet, we painted on some glaze and transferred the pork to the oven. When the meat was nearly done, we put on more glaze, and added yet another coat when it was done. Finally, after the tenderloins rested, we glazed them one last time. We prefer natural to enhanced pork (pork that has been injected with a salt solution to increase moistness) for this recipe. If your tenderloins are smaller than 1¼ pounds, reduce the cooking time in step 3 (and use an instant-read thermometer for best results). If the tenderloins don't fit in the skillet initially, let their ends curve toward each other; the meat will shrink as it cooks. Make sure to cook the tenderloins until they turn deep golden brown in step 2 or they will appear pale after glazing. Be sure to pat off the cornstarch mixture thoroughly in step 1, as any excess will leave gummy spots on the tenderloins.

- ¾ cup maple syrup, preferably grade B
- ¼ cup light or mild molasses
- 2 tablespoons bourbon or brandy
- ⅛ teaspoon ground cinnamon
- Pinch ground cloves
- Pinch cayenne pepper
- ¼ cup cornstarch
- 2 tablespoons sugar
- 1 tablespoon table salt
- 2 teaspoons ground black pepper
- 2 (1¼- to 1½-pound) pork tenderloins, trimmed of fat and silver skin
- 2 tablespoons vegetable oil
- 1 tablespoon whole grain mustard

**1.** Adjust oven rack to middle position and heat oven to 375 degrees. Stir ½ cup of maple syrup, molasses, bourbon, cinnamon, cloves, and cayenne together in 2-cup liquid measure; set aside. Whisk cornstarch, sugar, salt, and black pepper in small bowl until combined. Transfer cornstarch mixture to rimmed baking sheet. Pat tenderloins dry with paper towels, then roll them in cornstarch mixture until evenly coated on all sides. Thoroughly pat off excess cornstarch mixture.

**2.** Heat oil in 12-inch heavy-bottomed nonstick skillet over medium-high heat until just beginning to smoke. Reduce heat to medium and place both tenderloins in skillet, leaving at least 1 inch between them. Cook until well browned on all sides, 8 to 12 minutes. Transfer tenderloins to wire rack set over rimmed baking sheet.

**3.** Pour off fat from skillet and return to medium heat. Add syrup mixture to skillet, scraping up browned bits with wooden spoon, and cook until reduced to ½ cup, about 2 minutes. Transfer 2 tablespoons of glaze to small bowl and set aside. Using remaining glaze, brush each tenderloin with approximately 1 tablespoon glaze. Roast pork until thickest part of tenderloins registers 130 degrees on instant-read thermometer, 12 to 20 minutes. Brush each tenderloin with another tablespoon of glaze and continue to roast until thickest part of tenderloins registers 140 degrees, 2 to 4 minutes longer. Remove tenderloins from oven and brush each with remaining glaze; let rest, uncovered, until temperature reaches 150 degrees, about 10 minutes.

**4.** While tenderloins rest, stir remaining ¼ cup maple syrup and mustard into reserved 2 tablespoons glaze. Brush each tenderloin with 1 tablespoon mustard glaze. Transfer meat to carving board and slice into ¼-inch-thick pieces. Serve, passing extra mustard glaze at table.

## Broiled Pork Tenderloin

**SERVES 4 to 6**

**WHY THIS RECIPE WORKS** An easy way to prepare pork tenderloin is to simply put it under the broiler. The intense heat of the broiler promises to deeply brown the exterior and cook the roast through in one fell swoop. But the problem is that no two broilers behave exactly the same way. We needed to figure out a way to minimize the differences so that every oven would produce the same richly browned, juicy pork tenderloins. To ensure that the tip of the tenderloin cooked at the same rate as the middle, we folded the thinner tail end underneath and tied the meat at 2-inch intervals to give it a rounded shape that would cook evenly. The best browning came from cooking the roasts in a disposable roasting pan, which effectively reflected the heat of the broiler. A baking soda rub further enhanced browning. To correct for differences in broilers, we preheated the oven to 325 degrees, then turned on the broiler at the same time that we put the pork in the oven. We pulled the roasts from the oven when they reached a lower-than-normal internal temperature to account for the increased carryover cooking from the broiler's intense heat. We prefer natural pork, but enhanced pork (injected with a salt solution) can be used. If you're using enhanced pork, reduce the amount of salt in step 2 to 1½ teaspoons. A 13 by 9-inch aluminum roasting pan that is at least 3 inches deep is critical to the success of this recipe. We do not recommend broiling the pork in a pan that is a different size or material. This lean cut can be served by itself, but it's best accompanied by a richly flavored sauce (recipes follow). We developed this recipe with an in-oven broiler; do not attempt this with a drawer broiler (one that is below the oven compartment).

- 2 (1-pound) pork tenderloins, trimmed
- 2 teaspoons kosher salt
- 1¼ teaspoons vegetable oil
- ½ teaspoon pepper
- ¼ teaspoon baking soda
- 1 (13 by 9-inch) disposable aluminum roasting pan

**1.** Adjust oven rack 4 to 5 inches from broiler element and heat oven to 325 degrees. Fold thin tip of each tenderloin under about 2 inches to create uniformly shaped roast. Tie tenderloins crosswise with kitchen twine at 2-inch intervals, making sure folded tip is secured underneath. Trim any excess twine close to meat to prevent it from scorching under broiler.

**2.** Mix salt, oil, and pepper in small bowl until salt is evenly coated with oil. Add baking soda and stir until well combined. Rub salt mixture evenly over pork. Place tenderloins in disposable pan, evenly spaced between sides of pan and each other.

**3.** Turn oven to broil. Broil tenderloins for 5 minutes. Flip tenderloins and continue to broil until golden brown and meat registers 125 to 130 degrees, 8 to 14 minutes. Remove disposable pan from oven, tent loosely with aluminum foil, and let rest for 10 minutes. Remove twine, slice tenderloins into ½-inch-thick slices, and serve.

### Mustard–Crème Fraîche Sauce

**MAKES** about 1 cup

- ½ cup crème fraîche
- 3 tablespoons Dijon mustard
- 3 tablespoons chopped fresh parsley
- Table salt and pepper

Whisk crème fraîche, mustard, and parsley together in bowl. Season with salt and pepper to taste.

### Sun-Dried Tomato and Basil Salsa

**MAKES** about 1 cup

- ¼ cup oil-packed sun-dried tomatoes, rinsed and chopped fine
- ¼ cup chopped fresh basil
- ¼ cup chopped fresh parsley
- ¼ cup extra-virgin olive oil
- 2 tablespoons balsamic vinegar
- 1 small shallot, minced
- Table salt and pepper

Combine all ingredients in bowl and season with salt and pepper to taste.

## Stir-Fried Pork, Eggplant, and Onion with Garlic and Black Pepper

**SERVES** 4

**WHY THIS RECIPE WORKS** This take on a classic Thai pork and vegetable stir-fry has tender, flavorful pork and perfectly cooked vegetables. We chose pork tenderloin because it is so tender. Marinating improved the pork's flavor, and cooking quickly over high heat ensured browning. We batch-cooked the vegetables and added aromatics at the end so they would develop their flavors but not burn. For the sauce, we used chicken broth as the backbone and added lime juice to brighten the flavors. Cornstarch created a thickened sauce that lightly cloaked the pork and vegetables. To make slicing the pork easier, freeze it for 15 minutes. Serve with rice.

**SAUCE**

- 2½ tablespoons soy sauce
- 2½ tablespoons fish sauce
- 2½ tablespoons light brown sugar
- 2 tablespoons chicken broth
- 2 teaspoons juice from 1 lime
- 1 teaspoon cornstarch

**PORK AND VEGETABLES**

- 1 (12-ounce) pork tenderloin, trimmed of fat and silver skin and cut into ¼-inch strips
- 1 teaspoon soy sauce
- 1 teaspoon fish sauce
- 3 tablespoons peanut or vegetable oil
- 12 medium garlic cloves, minced or pressed through a garlic press (about ¼ cup)
- 2 teaspoons ground black pepper
- 1 medium eggplant (1 pound), cut into ¾-inch cubes
- 1 large onion, halved and cut into ¼-inch wedges
- ½ cup chopped fresh cilantro leaves

**1. FOR THE SAUCE:** Combine all ingredients in small bowl and set aside.

**2. FOR THE PORK AND VEGETABLES:** Toss pork with soy sauce and fish sauce in medium bowl and let marinate for at least 10 minutes or up to 1 hour. In small bowl, mix 2 teaspoons of oil, garlic, and pepper together.

**3.** Heat 2 teaspoons more oil in 12-inch nonstick skillet over high heat until just smoking. Add pork, break up any clumps, then cook without stirring until the meat is browned at the edges, about 1 minute. Stir pork and continue to cook until cooked through, about 1 minute longer. Transfer pork to clean bowl and cover with foil to keep warm.

**4.** Add 1 tablespoon more oil to skillet and return to high heat until just smoking. Add eggplant and cook, stirring frequently, until browned and no longer spongy, about 5 minutes. Transfer eggplant to bowl with pork. Add remaining 2 teaspoons peanut oil to skillet and return to high heat until just smoking. Add onion and cook until beginning to brown and soften, about 2 minutes.

**5.** Clear center of skillet, add garlic mixture, and cook, mashing mixture into pan, until fragrant, 15 to 20 seconds. Stir garlic mixture into onion.

**6.** Stir in eggplant and pork with any accumulated juices. Whisk sauce to recombine, then add to skillet and cook, tossing constantly, until sauce is thickened, about 30 seconds. Transfer to serving platter, sprinkle with cilantro, and serve.

## Sichuan Stir-Fried Pork in Garlic Sauce

**SERVES** 4 to 6

**WHY THIS RECIPE WORKS** To re-create the succulent pork found in the best Chinese stir-fries (usually achieved by low-temperature deep frying), we soaked the pork in a baking soda solution, which tenderized and moisturized the meat, and then coated it in a velvetizing cornstarch slurry, which helped it retain moisture as it cooked. And the secret to our sauce's silken texture and rich flavor? Ketchup and fish sauce, both high in flavor-enhancing glutamates. If Chinese black vinegar is unavailable, substitute 2 teaspoons balsamic vinegar and 2 teaspoons rice vinegar. If Asian broad-bean chili paste is unavailable, substitute 2 teaspoons chili-garlic paste or sriracha. Serve with rice.

**SAUCE**

- ½ cup low-sodium chicken broth
- 2 tablespoons sugar
- 2 tablespoons soy sauce
- 4 teaspoons Chinese black vinegar
- 1 tablespoon toasted sesame oil
- 1 tablespoon Chinese rice wine or dry sherry
- 2 teaspoons ketchup
- 2 teaspoons fish sauce
- 2 teaspoons cornstarch

**PORK**

- 12 ounces boneless country-style pork ribs, trimmed
- 1 teaspoon baking soda
- 2 teaspoons Chinese rice wine or dry sherry
- 2 teaspoons cornstarch

**STIR-FRY**

- 2 scallions, white parts minced, green parts sliced thin
- 4 garlic cloves, minced
- 2 tablespoons Asian broad-bean chili paste
- ¼ cup vegetable oil
- 6 ounces shiitake mushrooms, stemmed and sliced thin
- 2 celery ribs, cut on bias into ¼-inch slices

**1. FOR THE SAUCE:** Whisk all ingredients together in bowl; set aside.

**2. FOR THE PORK:** Cut pork into 2-inch lengths, then cut each length into ¼-inch matchsticks. Combine pork with ½ cup cold water and baking soda in bowl. Let sit at room temperature for 15 minutes.

**3.** Rinse pork in cold water. Drain well and pat dry with paper towels. Whisk rice wine and cornstarch together in bowl. Add pork and toss to coat.

**4. FOR THE STIR-FRY:** Combine scallion whites, garlic, and chili paste in bowl.

**5.** Heat 1 tablespoon vegetable oil in 12-inch nonstick skillet over high heat until just smoking. Add mushrooms and cook, stirring frequently, until tender, 2 to 4 minutes. Add celery and continue to cook until celery is crisp-tender, 2 to 4 minutes. Transfer vegetables to separate bowl.

**6.** Add remaining 3 tablespoons vegetable oil to now-empty skillet and place over medium-low heat. Add scallion-garlic mixture and cook, stirring frequently, until fragrant, about 30 seconds. Transfer 1 tablespoon scallion-garlic oil to small bowl and set aside. Add pork to skillet and cook, stirring frequently, until no longer pink, 3 to 5 minutes. Whisk sauce mixture to recombine and add to skillet. Increase heat to high and cook, stirring constantly, until sauce is thickened and pork is cooked through, 1 to 2 minutes. Return vegetables to skillet and toss to combine. Transfer to serving platter, sprinkle with scallion greens and reserved scallion-garlic oil, and serve.

## Khua Kling (Southern Thai Pork Stir-Fry)

**SERVES** 6 to 8

**WHY THIS RECIPE WORKS** Khua kling, a dry-fried minced pork curry, is one of the spiciest dishes of southern Thailand. Dried and fresh chiles bring plenty of heat. We stir-fried a fresh and complex curry paste to soften its raw edge, then added ground pork, sugar and fish sauce, and black pepper. Toss the fiery khua kling with steamed jasmine rice and alternate bites of the mixture with chilled cucumber slices. You'll need an immersion blender (or mortar and pestle) for this recipe. We developed this recipe for a 14-inch wok, but a 12-inch nonstick or carbon-steel skillet can be used. Lemongrass, galangal, kapi (Thai shrimp paste), and lime leaves can be found at a well-stocked supermarket or Asian market; they freeze well. You can substitute 1½ teaspoons of dried turmeric for fresh. Prepare the other curry paste ingredients while the arbols hydrate. To avoid inhaling spicy fumes while stir-frying, use an exhaust fan or open a window. This dish is meant to be intensely spicy and should be eaten with rice in a ratio of 1 part pork to 2 parts rice. The sliced chiles enable diners to customize the spice level, but they can be omitted. To make a half batch of khua kling, make a full recipe of curry paste and freeze half of it; cut all the other ingredients in half.

CURRY PASTE

- 10 dried arbol chiles, stemmed, halved lengthwise, and seeds removed
- 2 large shallots, chopped coarse
- 2 lemongrass stalks, trimmed to bottom 6 inches, halved lengthwise, and sliced thin
- 4 garlic cloves, chopped coarse
- 1 (2-inch) piece fresh galangal, chopped coarse
- 1 (2-inch) piece fresh turmeric, chopped coarse
- 4 Thai red chiles, stemmed and chopped coarse
- 4 makrut lime leaves, middle vein removed and sliced thin crosswise
- 2 teaspoons kapi
- ¾ teaspoon table salt

PORK

- 1 tablespoon vegetable oil
- 1 pound ground pork, broken into 1-inch chunks
- 2 teaspoons fish sauce
- 2 teaspoons brown sugar
- 1 teaspoon pepper
- 4 Thai red chiles, stemmed and sliced ¼ inch thick on bias (optional)
- 3 makrut lime leaves, middle vein removed and sliced thin crosswise

Steamed jasmine rice

- 1 English cucumber, peeled if desired, sliced into ¼-inch rounds, and chilled

**1. FOR THE CURRY PASTE:** Place arbols in small bowl and cover with 1 cup boiling water. Let sit for 20 minutes. Drain, reserving liquid. Combine arbols, shallots, lemongrass, garlic, galangal, turmeric, Thai chiles, lime leaves, kapi, and salt in 2-cup liquid measure. Use immersion blender in mashing, up-and-down motion, to blend to coarse paste, about 2 minutes, stirring and scraping down sides halfway through blending. (Paste can be refrigerated for 4 days or frozen for up to 4 months.)

**2. FOR THE PORK:** Heat oil in wok over medium heat until shimmering. Add curry paste and cook, stirring constantly with wok spatula or wooden spoon, until paste just begins to stick, about 2 minutes. Add pork and mash and chop until meat and paste are mostly combined. Increase heat to medium-high and continue to cook, stirring and chopping constantly, until pork breaks into small pieces and is mostly cooked but some pink bits remain, about 3 minutes (if mixture starts to stick, deglaze with reserved arbol liquid, using 1 tablespoon at a time).

**3.** Add fish sauce, sugar, and pepper and cook, stirring constantly, until pork is fully cooked and no moisture remains. Off heat, stir in sliced chiles, if using, and lime leaves. Transfer to serving bowl. Serve with rice and cucumber slices.

## Mu Shu Pork

SERVES 4

---

**WHY THIS RECIPE WORKS** Mu shu pork's thin, stretchy pancakes are the hallmark of the Chinese classic, so we started there. Stirring boiling water into flour kept the dough from turning sticky and made it easy to roll. After resting the dough, we rolled it into a log and cut it into 12 pieces, pressing them into rounds and brushing one side of 6 disks with sesame oil. After placing the unoiled disks on top of the oiled ones, we rolled the doubled-up disks to a 7-inch diameter and cooked each in a warm skillet. These browned, puffed pancakes were easily peeled into two thinner pancakes. We loaded up the filling with flavor-builders, first microwaving dried shiitakes in water for an earthy component. We saved the shiitakes' soaking liquid to boost our sauce. To season the sliced pork tenderloin, we tossed it in a blend of soy sauce, dry sherry, sugar, fresh ginger, and white pepper. Next, we scrambled eggs, browned sliced scallion whites, and cooked the pork—1 to 2 minutes a side—then finished up the vegetables. Simply heating the shiitakes and bamboo shoots sufficed before adding in sliced green cabbage and scallion greens, cooking them in the mushroom liquid mixture. A smear of hoisin sauce on the pancakes tied the flavors together. We strongly recommend weighing the flour for the pancakes.

PANCAKES

- 1½ cups (7½ ounces) all-purpose flour
- ¾ cup boiling water
- 2 teaspoons toasted sesame oil
- ½ teaspoon vegetable oil

STIR-FRY

- 1 ounce dried shiitake mushrooms, rinsed
- ¼ cup soy sauce
- 2 tablespoons dry sherry
- 1 teaspoon sugar
- 1 teaspoon grated fresh ginger
- ¼ teaspoon white pepper
- 1 (12-ounce) pork tenderloin, trimmed, halved horizontally, and sliced thin against grain
- 2 teaspoons cornstarch
- 2 tablespoons plus 2 teaspoons vegetable oil
- 2 large eggs, beaten
- 6 scallions, white and green parts separated and sliced thin on bias
- 1 (8-ounce) can bamboo shoots, rinsed and sliced into matchsticks
- 3 cups thinly sliced green cabbage
- ¼ cup hoisin sauce

**1. FOR THE PANCAKES:** Using wooden spoon, mix flour and boiling water in bowl to form rough dough. When cool, transfer dough to lightly floured surface and knead until it forms ball that is tacky but no longer sticky, about 4 minutes (dough will not be perfectly smooth). Cover loosely with plastic wrap and let rest for 30 minutes.

**2.** Roll dough into 12-inch-long log on lightly floured surface and cut into 12 equal pieces. Turn each piece cut side up and pat into rough 3-inch disk. Brush 1 side of 6 disks with sesame oil; top each oiled side with unoiled disk and press lightly to form 6 pairs. Roll disks into 7-inch rounds, lightly flouring work surface as needed.

**3.** Heat vegetable oil in 12-inch nonstick skillet over medium heat until shimmering. Using paper towels, carefully wipe out oil. Place pancake in skillet and cook without moving it until air pockets begin to form between layers and underside is dry, 40 to 60 seconds. Flip pancake and cook until few light brown spots appear on second side, 40 to 60 seconds. Transfer to plate and, when cool enough to handle, peel apart into 2 pancakes. Stack pancakes moist side up and cover loosely with plastic. Repeat with remaining pancakes. Cover pancakes tightly and keep warm. Wipe out skillet with paper towel. (Pancakes can be wrapped tightly in plastic wrap, then aluminum foil, and refrigerated for up to 3 days or frozen for up to 2 months. Thaw wrapped pancakes at room temperature. Unwrap and place on plate. Invert second plate over pancakes and microwave until warm and soft, 60 to 90 seconds.)

**4. FOR THE STIR-FRY:** Microwave 1 cup water and mushrooms in covered bowl until steaming, about 1 minute. Let sit until softened, about 5 minutes. Drain mushrooms through fine-mesh strainer and reserve ⅓ cup liquid. Discard mushroom stems and slice caps thin.

**5.** Combine 2 tablespoons soy sauce, 1 tablespoon sherry, sugar, ginger, and pepper in large bowl. Add pork and toss to combine. Whisk together reserved mushroom liquid, remaining 2 tablespoons soy sauce, remaining 1 tablespoon sherry, and cornstarch; set aside.

**6.** Heat 2 teaspoons oil in now-empty skillet over medium-high heat until shimmering. Add eggs and scramble quickly until set but not dry, about 15 seconds. Transfer to bowl and break eggs into ¼- to ½-inch pieces with fork. Return now-empty skillet to medium-high heat and heat 1 tablespoon oil until shimmering. Add scallion whites and cook, stirring frequently, until well browned, 1 to 1½ minutes. Add pork mixture. Spread into even layer and cook without moving it until well browned on 1 side, 1 to 2 minutes. Stir and continue to cook, stirring frequently, until all pork is opaque, 1 to 2 minutes longer. Transfer to bowl with eggs.

**7.** Return now-empty skillet to medium-high heat and heat remaining 1 tablespoon oil until shimmering. Whisk mushroom liquid mixture to recombine. Add mushrooms and bamboo shoots to skillet and cook, stirring frequently, until heated through, about 1 minute. Add cabbage, all but 2 tablespoons scallion greens, and mushroom liquid mixture and cook, stirring constantly, until liquid has evaporated and cabbage is wilted but retains some crunch, 2 to 3 minutes. Add pork and eggs and stir to combine. Transfer to platter and top with remaining scallion greens.

**8.** Spread about ½ teaspoon hoisin in center of each warm pancake. Spoon stir-fry over hoisin and serve.

### MAKING TWO PANCAKES AT A TIME

**1.** Brush 6 disks with sesame oil. Top with unoiled disks. Press pairs together, then roll into thin rounds.

**2.** Heat each round until air pockets form between layers and underside is dry. Flip and cook second side.

**3.** When pancakes are cool enough to handle, peel apart into 2 pieces.

## Thai Pork Lettuce Wraps

**SERVES 6**

**WHY THIS RECIPE WORKS** Larb, a classic Thai salad, is made with finely chopped meat and nutty rice powder tossed with fresh herbs and a light dressing. The dish embodies the cuisine's signature balance of sweet, sour, hot, and salty flavors. Many recipes we found called for ground pork, but inconsistent results with supermarket ground pork inspired us to grind our own, using pork tenderloin and a food processor. To impart flavor and moisture to this lean cut, we marinated the meat in fish sauce. Toasted rice powder, which adds a nutty flavor and texture to the pork, can be found in Asian markets, but we found that it was just as easy to make our own by toasting rice until golden brown and grinding it in a mini food processor or with a mortar and pestle. As for the aromatic components, we found that the pungency of sliced shallots and the bright flavor of chopped mint and cilantro yielded a very flavorful salad. For serving, the pork is spooned into lettuce leaves and wrapped. We preferred the crisp spine, tender leaf, and mild taste of Bibb lettuce. We prefer natural pork in this recipe. If using enhanced pork (pork that has been injected with a salt solution to increase moistness and flavor), skip the marinating in step 1 and reduce the amount of fish sauce to 2 tablespoons, adding it all in step 4.

- 1 (1-pound) pork tenderloin, trimmed of silver skin and fat, cut into 1-inch chunks, and frozen for 20 minutes
- 2½ tablespoons fish sauce
- 1 tablespoon white rice
- ¼ cup low-sodium chicken broth
- 3 medium shallots, peeled and sliced into thin rings (about ½ cup)
- 3 tablespoons roughly chopped fresh mint leaves
- 3 tablespoons roughly chopped fresh cilantro leaves
- 3 tablespoons juice from 2 limes
- 2 teaspoons sugar
- ¼ teaspoon red pepper flakes
- 1 head Bibb lettuce, washed and dried, leaves separated and left whole

**1.** Pulse half of the pork in a food processor until coarsely chopped, about 6 pulses. Transfer the ground pork to a medium bowl and repeat with the remaining chunks. Stir 1 tablespoon of the fish sauce into the ground pork, cover, refrigerate, and let marinate for 15 minutes.

**2.** Toast the rice in a small skillet over medium-high heat, stirring constantly, until deep golden brown, about 5 minutes. Transfer to a small bowl and cool for 5 minutes. Grind the rice with a spice grinder, mini food processor, or mortar and pestle until it resembles fine meal, 10 to 30 seconds (you should have about 1 tablespoon rice powder).

**3.** Bring the broth to a simmer in a 12-inch nonstick skillet over medium-high heat. Add the pork and cook, stirring frequently, until about half of the pork is no longer pink, about 2 minutes. Sprinkle 1 teaspoon of the rice powder over the pork and continue to cook, stirring constantly, until the remaining pork is no longer pink, 1 to 1½ minutes longer. Transfer the pork to a large bowl and cool for 10 minutes.

**4.** Add the remaining 1½ tablespoons fish sauce, remaining 2 teaspoons rice powder, the shallots, mint, cilantro, lime juice, sugar, and red pepper flakes to the pork and toss to combine. Serve with the lettuce leaves, spooning the meat into the leaves at the table.

## Maple-Glazed Pork Roast

**SERVES** 4 to 6

**WHY THIS RECIPE WORKS** Maple-glazed pork roast often falls short of its savory-sweet promise. Many roasts turn out dry, but the glazes often present even bigger problems. Most are too thin to coat the pork properly, some are too sweet, and few have a pronounced maple flavor. We wanted a glistening roast, which, when sliced, would combine the juices from tender, well-seasoned pork with a rich maple glaze to create complex flavor in every bite. For this dish we chose a blade-end loin roast, which has a deposit of fat that helps keep the meat moist. We tied it at intervals to make a neat bundle. Searing the roast first on the stovetop was a must for a flavorful exterior. We then removed the pork so that we could use the browned bits in the skillet to build the glaze. Maple syrup, with complementary spices and cayenne pepper for heat, made a thick, clingy glaze. Instead of brushing the glaze onto the pork, however, we decided to keep things simple and returned the pork to the skillet, rolled it in the glaze to coat it, and put the whole thing into the oven. The smaller area of the skillet kept the glaze from spreading out and burning, and the glaze reduced nicely while the roast cooked. Rolling the roast in the glaze periodically ensured even coverage and resulted in a tender, juicy roast. We prefer natural to enhanced pork (pork that has been injected with a salt solution to increase moisture and flavor) for this recipe. We prefer a nonstick ovensafe skillet because it is much easier to clean than a traditional one. Whichever you use, remember that the handle will be blistering hot when you take it out of the oven, so be sure to use a potholder or oven mitt. Note that you should not trim the pork of its thin layer of fat. This dish is unapologetically sweet, so we recommend side dishes that take well to the sweetness. Garlicky sautéed greens, braised cabbage, and soft polenta are good choices.

- ⅓ cup maple syrup, preferably grade B
- ⅛ teaspoon ground cinnamon
- Pinch ground cloves
- Pinch cayenne pepper
- 1 (2½-pound) boneless blade-end pork loin roast, tied at 1½-inch intervals
- ¾ teaspoon table salt
- ½ teaspoon ground black pepper
- 2 teaspoons vegetable oil

**1.** Adjust an oven rack to the middle position and heat the oven to 325 degrees. Stir the maple syrup, cinnamon, cloves, and cayenne together in a measuring cup or small bowl and set aside. Pat the roast dry with paper towels, then sprinkle evenly with the salt and pepper.

**2.** Heat the oil in a heavy-bottomed ovensafe 10-inch nonstick skillet over medium-high heat until just beginning to smoke, about 3 minutes. Place the roast, fat side down, in the skillet and cook until well browned, about 3 minutes. Using tongs, rotate the roast a quarter-turn and cook until well browned, about 2½ minutes; repeat until the roast is well browned on all sides. Transfer the roast to a large plate. Reduce the heat to medium and pour off the fat from the skillet; add the maple syrup mixture and cook until fragrant, about 30 seconds (the syrup will bubble immediately). Turn off the heat and return the roast to the skillet; using tongs, roll the roast to coat with the glaze on all sides.

**3.** Place the skillet in the oven and roast until the center of the pork registers 140 to 145 degrees on an instant-read thermometer, 35 to 45 minutes, using tongs to roll and spin the roast to coat with the glaze twice during the roasting time. Transfer the roast to a carving board; set the skillet aside to cool slightly to thicken the glaze, about 5 minutes. Pour the glaze over the roast and let rest for 15 minutes longer (the center of the loin should register 150 degrees on an instant-read thermometer). Remove the twine, cut the meat into ¼-inch slices, and serve immediately.

## Herb-Crusted Pork Roast

**SERVES** 6

**WHY THIS RECIPE WORKS** A fresh herb crust is a classic way to enliven a boneless pork roast and infuse the meat with bold herb presence in every bite. To add flavor from the inside out, we started by cutting a deep, wide pocket in the roast and filling it with a paste packed full of fresh herbs, garlic, and nutty Parmesan. We also scored the fat cap on top of the roast before searing it briefly in a very hot skillet. The seared, crosshatched layer provided the perfect canvas for our bread-crumb and herb-paste crust. It gave the paste something to grip and helped unify the crust and meat. After applying the crust to our seared roast, we transferred the whole dish to a relatively low oven, which allowed the roast to cook evenly and the crust to get beautifully crisp and golden brown. Center-cut pork loin roast is also called center-cut roast. Look for a roast with a thin fat cap (about ¼ inch thick) and don't trim this thin layer of fat. We strongly prefer natural pork in this recipe. If the pork is enhanced (injected with a salt solution to increase moisture and flavor), do not brine, and season the exterior of the roast with 1¼ teaspoons salt.

- 1 (2½- to 3-pound) boneless center-cut pork loin roast
- ½ cup table salt, for brining
- ¼ cup sugar, for brining
- 1 slice hearty white sandwich bread, torn into quarters
- 1 ounce Parmesan or Pecorino Romano cheese, grated (½ cup), divided
- 1 shallot, minced
- ¼ cup plus 2 teaspoons extra-virgin olive oil, divided
- ¼ teaspoon table salt, divided
- ¾ teaspoon pepper, divided
- ⅓ cup fresh parsley or basil leaves
- 2 tablespoons finely chopped fresh thyme
- 1 teaspoon finely chopped fresh rosemary or ½ teaspoon dried
- 1 garlic clove, minced

**1.** Using sharp knife, cut slits ¼ inch apart in crosshatch pattern in fat cap of roast, being careful not to cut into meat. Create pocket in roast by inserting knife ½ inch from end of roast and cutting along side of pork, stopping ½ inch short of other end. Pull open roast and use gentle strokes to cut deeper pocket.

**2.** Dissolve ½ cup salt and sugar in 2 quarts water in large container; submerge roast, cover, and refrigerate for 1 hour. Remove from brine and pat dry with paper towels.

**3.** Adjust oven rack to lower-middle position and heat oven to 325 degrees. Set wire rack in rimmed baking sheet lined with aluminum foil. Pulse bread in food processor until coarsely ground, about 16 pulses (you should have 1 cup crumbs). Transfer crumbs to bowl and add 2 tablespoons Parmesan, shallot, 1 tablespoon oil, ⅛ teaspoon salt, and ⅛ teaspoon pepper. Using fork, toss mixture until crumbs are evenly coated with oil.

**4.** Pulse parsley, thyme, rosemary, garlic, remaining 6 tablespoons Parmesan, 3 tablespoons oil, remaining ⅛ teaspoon salt, and ⅛ teaspoon pepper in now-empty processor until smooth, about 12 pulses. Transfer herb paste to bowl.

**5.** Spread ¼ cup herb paste inside roast and tie roast at 1½-inch intervals with kitchen twine. Season roast with remaining ½ teaspoon pepper.

**6.** Heat remaining 2 teaspoons oil in 12-inch skillet over medium-high heat until just smoking. Brown roast well on all sides, about 10 minutes. Transfer roast, fat side up, to prepared sheet.

**7.** Remove twine from roast. Spread remaining herb paste over roast and top with bread-crumb mixture. Transfer sheet with roast to oven and cook until pork registers 140 degrees, 50 minutes to 1¼ hours. Remove roast from oven and let rest on sheet for 20 minutes. Transfer roast to carving board, taking care not to squeeze juices out of pocket in roast. Slice roast into ½-inch-thick slices. Serve.

### STUFFING A PORK LOIN ROAST

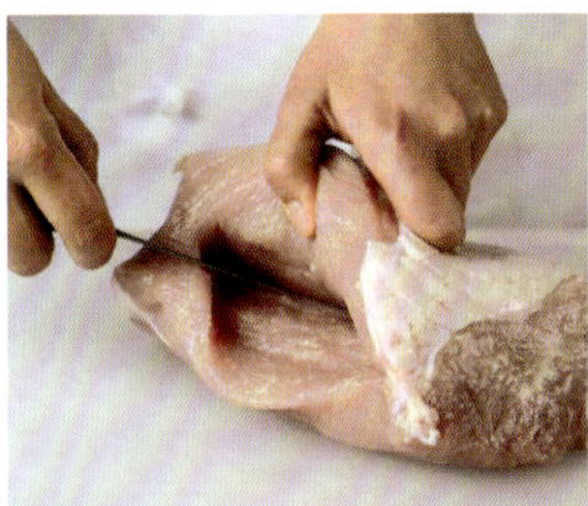

**1.** Starting ½ inch from end of roast, cut along side of pork, stopping ½ inch short of other end. Pull open roast and use gentle strokes to cut deeper pocket.

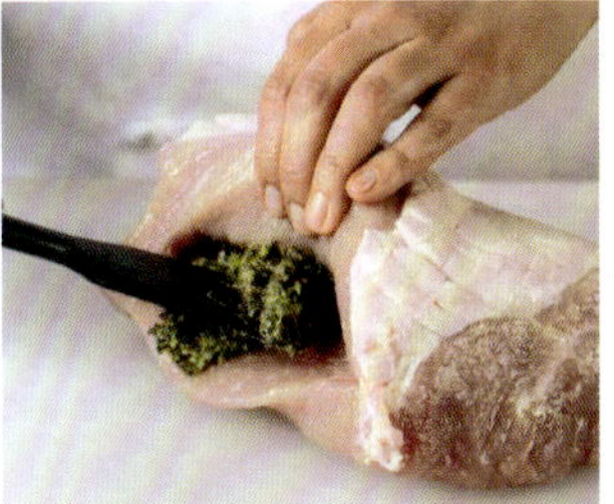

**2.** To stuff roast, spread ¼ cup herb paste evenly into pocket, using spatula and your fingers to make sure paste reaches corners of pocket.

**3.** Fold roast over to original shape and tie it at 1½-inch intervals along its length with kitchen twine.

## Garlic-Studded Roast Pork Loin

**SERVES** 4 to 6

**WHY THIS RECIPE WORKS** Although it has a little more fat than pork tenderloin, a center loin pork roast is still quite lean and requires special handling to roast without drying out. We sought the best way to roast this cut so that the juices would remain inside the meat. It turned out that a two-step roasting process was the key to juicy pork loin. After poking slivers of garlic into the meat and rubbing the surface with a mixture of thyme, cloves, salt, and pepper for extra flavor, we refrigerated the roast overnight. The next day we cranked up the oven and added the pork directly from the fridge. After we rested the roast, we returned it to the oven, this time at a lower temperature, to finish cooking. The texture of the meat was remarkably tender, and it had lost very little juice. When the meat went back into the oven, the center cooked through but the outside didn't overcook. A mustard-shallot sauce provides additional moisture and flavor. We prefer natural to enhanced pork (pork that has been injected with a salt solution to increase moisture and flavor) for this recipe.

- 2 teaspoons dried thyme
- 2 teaspoons table salt
- 1 teaspoon ground black pepper
- ¼ teaspoon ground cloves or allspice
- 2 large garlic cloves, peeled and cut into slivers
- 1 (2¼-pound) boneless center loin pork roast, fat trimmed to about ⅛ inch thick and roast tied at 1½-inch intervals
- 1 recipe Mustard-Shallot Sauce with Thyme (optional; recipe follows)

**1.** Mix together thyme, salt, pepper, and cloves. Coat garlic slivers in spice mixture. Poke slits in roast with point of paring knife; insert garlic slivers. Rub remaining spice mixture onto meat. Tie roast with kitchen twine into tight cylinder. Wrap roast in plastic wrap and refrigerate for at least 2 hours or up to 24 hours.

**2.** Adjust oven rack to middle position and heat oven to 475 degrees. Take meat directly from refrigerator, remove plastic wrap, and place it on wire rack set in shallow roasting pan. Roast for exactly 30 minutes.

**3.** Remove meat from oven; immediately reduce oven temperature to 325 degrees. Insert instant-read thermometer at one end of roast, going into thickest part at center (temperature will range from 80 to 110 degrees); let roast rest at room temperature, uncovered, for exactly 30 minutes. (At this point roast's internal temperature will range from 115 to 140 degrees.) After this 30-minute rest, remove thermometer, return meat to oven, and roast until thickest part of roast reaches internal temperature of 140 to 145 degrees, 15 to 30 minutes longer, depending on roast's internal temperature at end of resting period. Since roast may cook unevenly, take temperature readings from couple of locations, each time plunging thermometer into center of meat and waiting 15 seconds.

**4.** Let roast stand at room temperature, uncovered, for 15 to 20 minutes to finish cooking. (The temperature should register 150 degrees.) Remove twine, slice meat thin, and serve with sauce (if using).

### Mustard-Shallot Sauce with Thyme

**MAKES** about 1 cup

Start making the sauce as soon as the roast comes out of the oven for the second time. Use a grainy, or country-style, mustard in this recipe. For extra body and richness, swirl another tablespoon or two of softened butter into the finished sauce.

- 2 tablespoons unsalted butter
- 4 medium shallots, minced (about ¾ cup)
- ¾ cup dry white wine or dry vermouth
- 1 cup low-sodium chicken broth
- ¾ teaspoon minced fresh thyme leaves or ¼ teaspoon dried thyme, crumbled
- ¼ cup whole grain mustard

Melt butter in medium skillet over medium-high heat. Add shallots and sauté until softened, 3 to 4 minutes. Add wine and boil until nearly evaporated, 8 to 10 minutes. Add broth and thyme; boil until reduced by one third, about 5 minutes. Remove pan from heat and stir in mustard. Serve immediately.

## French-Style Pot-Roasted Pork Loin

**SERVES** 4 to 6

**WHY THIS RECIPE WORKS** Enchaud périgourdin is a fancy name for a simple French dish: slow-cooked pork loin. Cooked in the oven in a covered casserole dish, the roast turns incredibly moist and flavorful, with a rich jus. To improve the flavor and texture of a lean center-cut loin, we lowered the oven temperature and removed the roast from the oven when it was medium-rare. Searing just three sides of the roast prevented the bottom of it from overcooking. Butterflying the pork allowed us to salt a maximum amount of surface area. Butter added richness while gelatin lent body to the sauce. We strongly prefer the flavor of natural pork in this recipe, but enhanced pork (injected with a salt solution) can be used. If using enhanced pork, reduce the salt to 2 teaspoons (1 teaspoon per side) in step 2. The pork can be prepared through step 2, wrapped in plastic wrap, and refrigerated for up to 2 days.

- 2 tablespoons unsalted butter, cut into 2 pieces
- 6 medium garlic cloves, sliced thin
- 1 (2½-pound) boneless center-cut pork loin roast, trimmed
- Kosher salt and ground black pepper
- 1 teaspoon sugar
- 2 teaspoons herbes de Provence
- 2 tablespoons vegetable oil
- 1 Granny Smith apple, peeled, cored, and cut into ¼-inch pieces
- 1 medium onion, chopped fine
- ⅓ cup dry white wine
- 2 sprigs fresh thyme
- 1 bay leaf
- 1 tablespoon unflavored gelatin
- ¼–¾ cup low-sodium chicken broth
- 1 tablespoon chopped fresh parsley

**1.** Adjust oven rack to lower-middle position and heat oven to 225 degrees. Melt 1 tablespoon butter in 8-inch skillet over medium-low heat. Add half of garlic and cook, stirring frequently, until golden, 5 to 7 minutes. Transfer mixture to bowl and refrigerate.

**2.** Position roast fat side up. Insert knife one-third of way up from bottom of roast along 1 long side and cut horizontally, stopping ½ inch before edge. Open up flap. Keeping knife parallel to cutting board, cut through thicker portion of roast about ½ inch from bottom of roast, keeping knife level with first cut and stopping about ½ inch before edge. Open up this flap. If uneven, cover with plastic wrap and use meat pounder to even out. Sprinkle 1 tablespoon salt over both sides of loin (½ tablespoon per side) and rub into pork until slightly tacky. Sprinkle sugar over inside of loin, then spread with cooled toasted garlic mixture. Starting from short side, fold roast back together like business letter (keeping fat on outside) and tie with twine at 1-inch intervals. Sprinkle tied roast evenly with herbes de Provence and season with pepper.

**3.** Heat 1 tablespoon oil in Dutch oven over medium heat until just smoking. Add roast, fat side down, and brown on fat side and sides (do not brown bottom of roast), 5 to 8 minutes. Transfer to large plate. Add remaining 1 tablespoon oil, apple, and onion; cook, stirring frequently, until onion is softened and browned, 5 to 7 minutes. Stir in remaining sliced garlic and cook until fragrant, about 30 seconds. Stir in wine, thyme, and bay leaf, and cook for 30 seconds. Return roast, fat side up, to pot; place large sheet of aluminum foil over pot and cover tightly with lid. Transfer pot to oven and cook until pork registers 140 degrees, 50 to 90 minutes (short, thick roasts will take longer than long, thin ones).

**4.** Transfer roast to carving board, tent loosely with foil, and let rest for 20 minutes. While pork rests, sprinkle gelatin over ¼ cup chicken broth and let sit until gelatin softens, about 5 minutes. Remove and discard thyme sprigs and bay leaf from jus. Pour jus into 2-cup measuring cup and, if necessary, add chicken broth to measure 1¼ cups. Return jus to pot and bring to simmer over medium heat. Whisk softened gelatin mixture, remaining 1 tablespoon butter, and parsley into jus and season with salt and pepper to taste; remove from heat and cover to keep warm. Slice pork into ½-inch-thick slices, adding any accumulated juices to sauce. Serve pork, passing sauce separately.

### DOUBLE-BUTTERFLYING A ROAST

**1.** Holding a chef's knife parallel to the cutting board, insert the knife one-third of the way up from the bottom of the roast and cut horizontally, stopping ½ inch before the edge. Open up the flap.

**2.** Make another horizontal cut into the thicker portion of the roast. Open up this flap, smoothing out the butterflied rectangle of meat.

## Spice-Rubbed Pork Roast en Cocotte with Caramelized Onions

**SERVES** 4 to 6

**WHY THIS RECIPE WORKS** Roasting pork en cocotte combines the best of both braising and roasting. We prefer a boneless cut, which fits more easily into the pot. A blade-end loin is a good choice for its flavor and juiciness; a shorter, wider piece is ideal. We tied the meat, for easier browning and more even cooking. To add flavor to the pork, we used a spice rub that combined coriander, paprika, cumin, and anise, a pinch of cayenne for heat, and a touch of brown sugar for sweetness. Caramelized sliced onions provided a sweet contrast to the potent spice rub. Browning the meat on the stovetop, covering the pot, and cooking it slowly in a low oven produced just what we wanted—an incredibly juicy, tender roast. This recipe works best prepared with a pork roast that is about 7 to 8 inches long and 4 to 5 inches wide. We found that leaving a ¼-inch-thick layer of fat on top of the roast is ideal; if your roast has a thicker fat cap, trim it back to about a ¼-inch thickness. To prevent the spices from burning when browning the pork in step 2, be sure to use medium heat.

- 1 (2½- to 3-pound) boneless pork loin roast, trimmed and tied at 1½-inch intervals
- 5 teaspoons ground coriander
- 2 teaspoons paprika
- 1 teaspoon table salt
- 1 teaspoon packed brown sugar
- ¾ teaspoon ground anise seeds
- ¾ teaspoon ground cumin
- Pinch cayenne pepper
- 3 tablespoons vegetable oil, divided
- 2 onions halved and sliced thin
- 3 garlic cloves, minced
- 1 tablespoon unsalted butter

1. Adjust oven rack to lowest position and heat oven to 250 degrees. Pat pork dry with paper towels. Toss coriander, paprika, salt, sugar, anise, cumin, and cayenne together in small bowl, then rub mixture evenly over pork.

2. Heat 2 tablespoons oil in large Dutch oven over medium heat until just smoking. Lightly brown pork on all sides, 5 to 7 minutes, reducing heat if pot begins to scorch or spices begin to burn. Transfer pork to large plate.

3. Add remaining 1 tablespoon oil to pot and heat over medium heat until shimmering. Add onions; cover; and cook until softened and wet, about 5 minutes. Remove lid and continue to brown onions, stirring often, until dry and well browned, 10 to 12 minutes. Stir in garlic and cook until fragrant, about 30 seconds.

4. Off heat, nestle pork, along with any accumulated juices, into pot. Place large sheet of aluminum foil over pot and press to seal, then cover tightly with lid. Transfer pot to oven and cook until very center of roast registers 140 to 145 degrees, 35 to 55 minutes.

5. Remove pot from oven. Transfer pork to cutting board; tent with foil; and let rest until center of roast registers 150 degrees, about 20 minutes. Stir butter into onions, season with salt and pepper to taste, and cover to keep warm.

6. Remove twine, slice pork thin, and transfer to serving platter. Spoon onions over pork and serve.

## Milk-Braised Pork Loin

**SERVES** 4 to 6

**WHY THIS RECIPE WORKS** Braising pork in milk is an Italian technique that produces moist pork paired with a rich, savory sauce. To maximize the pork loin roast's seasoning and moisture, we brined it in salt and sugar for 90 minutes. To load the sauce with porky flavor, we rendered salt pork before introducing the roast to the pot. We browned the roast, removed it, and then built the sauce. Adding baking soda to the pot deepened the sauce's color and enriched its savory flavors. Once the sauce had thickened, we added the roast back to the pot and transferred it to a 275-degree oven. Adding white wine brightened the sauce, and we finished it with mustard for heat and parsley for freshness. The milk will bubble up when added to the pot. If necessary, remove the pot from the heat and stir to break up the foam before returning it to the heat. We prefer natural pork, but if your pork is enhanced (injected with a salt solution), do not brine. Instead, skip to step 2.

- Table salt and pepper
- ¼ cup sugar
- 1 (2- to 2½-pound) boneless pork loin roast, trimmed
- 2 ounces salt pork, chopped coarse
- 3 cups whole milk
- 5 garlic cloves, peeled
- 1 teaspoon minced fresh sage
- ¼ teaspoon baking soda
- ½ cup dry white wine
- 3 tablespoons chopped fresh parsley
- 1 teaspoon Dijon mustard

1. Dissolve ¼ cup salt and sugar in 2 quarts cold water in large container. Submerge roast in brine, cover, and refrigerate for at least 1½ hours or up to 2 hours. Remove roast from brine and pat dry with paper towels.

2. Adjust oven rack to middle position and heat oven to 275 degrees. Bring salt pork and ½ cup water to simmer in Dutch oven over medium heat. Simmer until water evaporates and salt pork begins to sizzle, 5 to 6 minutes. Continue to cook, stirring frequently, until salt pork is lightly browned and fat has rendered, 2 to 3 minutes. Using slotted spoon, discard salt pork, leaving fat in pot.

3. Increase heat to medium-high, add roast to pot, and brown on all sides, 8 to 10 minutes. Transfer roast to large plate. Add milk, garlic, sage, and baking soda to pot and bring to simmer, scraping up any browned bits. Cook, stirring frequently, until milk is lightly browned and has consistency of heavy cream, 14 to 16 minutes. Reduce heat to medium-low and continue to cook, stirring and scraping bottom of pot constantly, until milk thickens to consistency of thin batter, 1 to 3 minutes longer. Remove pot from heat.

4. Return roast to pot, cover, and transfer to oven. Cook until meat registers 140 degrees, 40 to 50 minutes, flipping roast once halfway through cooking. Transfer roast to carving board, tent with aluminum foil, and let rest for 20 to 25 minutes.

5. Once roast has rested, pour any accumulated juices into pot. Add wine and return sauce to simmer over medium-high heat, whisking vigorously to smooth out sauce. Simmer until sauce has consistency of thin gravy, 2 to 3 minutes. Off heat, stir in 2 tablespoons parsley and mustard and season with salt and pepper to taste. Slice roast into ¼-inch-thick slices. Transfer slices to serving platter. Spoon sauce over slices, sprinkle with remaining 1 tablespoon parsley, and serve.

## Slow-Cooker Pork Loin with Cranberries and Orange

**SERVES** 6

**WHY THIS RECIPE WORKS** Cooking a lean roast like a pork loin in a slow cooker is tricky because it can quickly turn overcooked and dry. The key to this recipe was to monitor the temperature of the roast after a few hours and take it out of the slow cooker as soon as it reached 145 degrees. Whether you're cooking a pork loin in the oven or the slow cooker, pairing the lean meat with a sauce gives it a lot more appeal. We paired our loin with both dried cranberries and whole canned cranberries. Cinnamon, orange juice, and orange zest livened up our easy-to-make sauce, which goes directly into the slow cooker. After cooking the loin, we reduced the braising liquid until it became a sweet sauce that paired perfectly with our juicy pork loin. When choosing a pork loin, we prefer the blade-end—be sure to choose a fatter, shorter loin over a longer, skinnier one. Use a vegetable peeler to remove wide strips of zest from the orange. Make sure to trim any white pith from the zest, as it can impart a bitter flavor.

- 1 (4½- to 5-pound) boneless pork loin roast, trimmed and tied at 1-inch intervals
- Table salt and ground black pepper
- 1 tablespoon vegetable oil
- 1 (14-ounce) can whole berry cranberry sauce
- ½ cup dried cranberries
- ½ cup juice and 3 (3-inch-long) strips zest from 1 orange
- ⅛ teaspoon ground cinnamon

**1.** Dry the pork with paper towels and season with salt and pepper. Heat the oil in a 12-inch skillet over medium-high heat until just smoking. Brown the pork well on all sides, 7 to 10 minutes.

**2.** Stir the cranberry sauce, cranberries, orange juice, orange zest, and cinnamon into the slow cooker. Nestle the browned pork into the slow cooker. Cover and cook until the pork is tender and registers 140 to 145 degrees on an instant-read thermometer, about 4 hours on low.

**3.** Transfer the pork to a cutting board, tent loosely with aluminum foil, and let rest for 10 minutes. Let the braising liquid settle for 5 minutes, then remove the fat from the surface using a large spoon. Discard the orange zest. Transfer the braising liquid to a saucepan and simmer until reduced to 2 cups, about 12 minutes. Season with salt and pepper to taste.

**4.** Remove the twine from the pork, slice into ½-inch-thick slices, and arrange on a serving platter. Spoon 1 cup sauce over the meat and serve with the remaining sauce.

## Arista (Tuscan-Style Roast Pork with Garlic and Rosemary)

**SERVES** 4 to 6

**WHY THIS RECIPE WORKS** The Tuscan roast pork dish known as arista promises to turn lean, mild pork loin into a juicy roast flavored with plenty of garlic and rosemary and featuring a deeply browned crust. To boost both flavor and juiciness, we salted the meat for 1 hour before cooking, using a double-butterfly technique to expose plenty of surface area and then salting both sides and rolling it back up. This technique also allowed maximum distribution of the garlic and rosemary. Briefly simmering the herb-garlic mixture before spreading it over the pork tempered any raw flavors, and using plenty of oil and a nonstick skillet kept the garlic from browning. To enhance the overall porky flavor, we processed pancetta with the garlic and rosemary (plus red pepper flakes and lemon zest) to make a paste. Using a low oven ensured that the meat was evenly cooked. And instead of roasting, browning, and then resting the roast under foil, we let it rest after it came out of the oven and then browned it and served it immediately; this approach helped keep the crust crisp. For a finishing touch, we made a bright, rich sauce by combining the reserved oil with lemon juice that we quickly caramelized. We strongly prefer natural pork in this recipe, but if enhanced pork is used, reduce the salt to 2 teaspoons (1 teaspoon per side) in step 3. After applying the seasonings, the pork needs to rest, refrigerated, for 1 hour before cooking.

- 1 lemon
- ⅓ cup extra-virgin olive oil
- 8 garlic cloves, minced
- ¼ teaspoon red pepper flakes
- 1 tablespoon chopped fresh rosemary
- 2 ounces pancetta, cut into ½-inch pieces
- 1 (2½-pound) center-cut boneless pork loin roast, trimmed
- Kosher salt

**1.** Finely grate 1 teaspoon zest from lemon. Cut lemon in half and reserve. Combine lemon zest, oil, garlic, and pepper flakes in 10-inch nonstick skillet. Cook over medium-low heat, stirring frequently, until garlic is sizzling, about 3 minutes. Add rosemary and cook, about 30 seconds. Strain mixture through fine-mesh strainer set over bowl, pushing on garlic-rosemary mixture to extract oil. Set oil aside and let garlic-rosemary mixture cool. Using paper towels, wipe out skillet.

**2.** Process pancetta in food processor until smooth paste forms, 20 to 30 seconds, scraping down sides of bowl as needed. Add garlic-rosemary mixture and continue to process until mixture is homogeneous, 20 to 30 seconds longer, scraping down sides of bowl as needed.

**3.** Position roast fat side up. Insert knife one-third of way up from bottom of roast along 1 long side and cut horizontally, stopping ½ inch before edge. Open up flap. Keeping knife parallel to cutting board, cut through thicker portion of roast about ½ inch from bottom of roast, keeping knife level with first cut and stopping about ½ inch before edge. Open up this flap. If uneven, cover with plastic wrap and use meat pounder to even out. Sprinkle 1 tablespoon salt over both sides of roast (½ tablespoon per side) and rub into meat to adhere. Spread inside of roast evenly with pancetta-garlic paste, leaving about ¼-inch border on all sides. Starting from short side, roll roast (keeping fat on outside) and tie with twine at 1-inch intervals. Set wire rack in rimmed baking sheet and spray with vegetable oil spray. Set roast fat side up on prepared rack and refrigerate for 1 hour.

**4.** Adjust oven rack to middle position and heat oven to 275 degrees. Transfer roast to oven and cook until meat registers 135 degrees, 1½ to 2 hours. Remove roast from oven, tent with aluminum foil, and let rest for 20 minutes.

**5.** Heat 1 teaspoon reserved oil in now-empty skillet over high heat until just smoking. Add reserved lemon halves, cut side down, and cook until softened and cut surfaces are browned, 3 to 4 minutes. Transfer lemon halves to small plate.

**6.** Pat roast dry with paper towels. Heat 2 tablespoons reserved oil in now-empty skillet over high heat until just smoking. Brown roast on fat side and sides (do not brown bottom of roast), 4 to 6 minutes. Transfer roast to carving board and remove twine.

**7.** Once lemon halves are cool enough to handle, squeeze into fine-mesh strainer set over bowl. Press on solids to extract all pulp; discard solids. Whisk 2 tablespoons strained lemon juice into bowl with remaining reserved oil. Slice roast into ¼-inch-thick slices and serve, passing vinaigrette separately.

## Porchetta

**SERVES** 8 to 10

**WHY THIS RECIPE WORKS** To make porchetta, we opted for pork butt since it offered the right balance of meat and fatty richness. We cut slits in the meat, coated it with salt and an intensely flavored paste, and let it sit overnight in the refrigerator. For quicker cooking, we cut and tied the roast into two pieces. We used a two-stage cooking method: First, we covered the pan with foil, which trapped steam to cook the meat evenly and keep it moist. We then uncovered the pan and returned it to a hot oven to brown and crisp the baking soda–pasted outer "skin" of the roasts. Pork butt roast is often labeled Boston butt in the supermarket. Look for a roast with a substantial fat cap. If fennel seeds are unavailable, substitute ¼ cup of ground fennel. The porchetta needs to be refrigerated for 6 to 24 hours once it is rubbed with the paste; it is best when it sits for a full 24 hours.

- 3 tablespoons fennel seeds
- ½ cup fresh rosemary leaves (2 bunches)
- ¼ cup fresh thyme leaves (2 bunches)
- 12 garlic cloves, peeled
- 2 tablespoons plus 1 teaspoon kosher salt, divided
- 4 teaspoons pepper, divided
- ½ cup extra-virgin olive oil
- 1 (5- to 6-pound) boneless pork butt roast, trimmed
- ¼ teaspoon baking soda

**1.** Grind fennel seeds in spice grinder or mortar and pestle until finely ground. Transfer ground fennel to food processor and add rosemary, thyme, garlic, 2 teaspoons salt, and 1 tablespoon pepper. Pulse mixture until finely chopped, 10 to 15 pulses. Add oil and process until smooth paste forms, 20 to 30 seconds.

**2.** Using sharp knife, cut through roast's fat cap in 1-inch crosshatch pattern, being careful not to cut into meat. Cut roast in half with grain into 2 equal pieces.

**3.** Turn each roast on its side so fat cap is facing away from you, bottom of roast is facing toward you, and newly cut side is facing up. Starting 1 inch from short end of each roast, use boning or paring knife to make slit that starts 1 inch from top of roast and ends 1 inch from bottom, pushing knife completely through roast. Repeat making slits, spaced 1 to 1½ inches apart, along length of each roast, stopping 1 inch from opposite end (you should have 6 to 8 slits, depending on size of roast).

**4.** Turn each roast so fat cap is facing down. Rub sides and bottom of each roast with 2 teaspoons salt, taking care to work salt into slits from both sides. Rub herb paste onto sides and bottom of each roast, taking care to work paste into slits from both sides. Flip each roast so that fat cap is facing up. Using 3 pieces of kitchen twine per roast, tie each roast into compact cylinder.

**5.** Combine remaining 1 tablespoon salt, remaining 1 teaspoon pepper, and baking soda in small bowl. Rub fat cap of each roast with salt–baking soda mixture, taking care to work mixture into crosshatches. Transfer roasts to wire rack set in rimmed baking sheet and refrigerate, uncovered, for at least 6 hours or up to 24 hours.

**6.** Adjust oven rack to middle position and heat oven to 325 degrees. Transfer roasts, fat side up, to large roasting pan, leaving at least 2 inches between roasts. Cover tightly with aluminum foil. Cook until pork registers 180 degrees, 2 to 2½ hours.

**7.** Remove pan from oven and increase oven temperature to 500 degrees. Carefully remove and discard foil and transfer roasts to large plate. Discard liquid in pan. Line pan with foil. Remove twine from roasts; return roasts to pan, directly on foil; and return pan to oven. Cook until exteriors of roasts are well browned and interiors register 190 degrees, 20 to 30 minutes.

**8.** Transfer roasts to carving board and let rest for 20 minutes. Slice roasts ½ inch thick, transfer to serving platter, and serve.

## Slow-Roasted Bone-In Pork Rib Roast

**SERVES** 6 to 8

**WHY THIS RECIPE WORKS** Some butchers call a center-cut pork rib roast the "pork equivalent of prime rib." Treated right, it can be truly impressive: moist, tender, and full of rich, meaty taste. To start, we pretreated the pork with a salt–brown sugar rub. The salt seasoned the meat and drew moisture into the flesh, helping to keep it juicy. The brown sugar contributed deep molasses notes and a gorgeous mahogany color, which allowed us to skip searing. We removed the bones from the meat so we could season it from all sides, then tied it back onto the bones to roast. The bones helped keep the roast moist. And free of bones, the roast was easier to carve. Scoring crosshatch marks into the fat helped it melt and baste the meat during roasting. Cooking the roast in a gentle oven ensured that the pork was evenly cooked. We crisped up the fat by blasting it under the broiler. To finish, a classic fruit and herb sauce balanced the meaty roast. This recipe requires refrigerating the salted meat for at least 6 hours before cooking. For easier carving, ask the butcher to remove the chine bone. Monitoring the roast with an oven probe thermometer is best. If you use an instant-read thermometer, open the oven door as infrequently as possible and remove the roast from the oven while taking its temperature. The sauce may be prepared in advance or while the roast rests in step 3.

- 1 (4- to 5-pound) center-cut bone-in pork rib roast, chine bone removed
- 2 tablespoons packed dark brown sugar
- 1 tablespoon kosher salt
- 1½ teaspoons pepper
- 1 recipe Port Wine–Cherry Sauce (recipe follows)

**1.** Using sharp knife, remove roast from bones, running knife down length of bones and following contours as closely as possible. Reserve bones. Combine sugar and salt in small bowl. Pat roast dry with paper towels. If necessary, trim thick spots of fat cap to about ¼-inch thickness. Using sharp knife, cut through fat cap in 1-inch crosshatch pattern, being careful not to cut into meat. Rub roast evenly with sugar mixture. Wrap roast and ribs in plastic wrap and refrigerate for at least 6 hours or up to 24 hours.

**2.** Adjust oven rack to lower-middle position and heat oven to 250 degrees. Sprinkle roast evenly with pepper. Place roast back on ribs so bones fit where they were cut; tie roast to bones with lengths of kitchen twine between ribs. Transfer roast, fat side up, to wire rack set in rimmed baking sheet. Roast until meat registers 145 degrees, 3 to 4 hours.

**3.** Remove roast from oven (leave roast on sheet), tent with aluminum foil, and let rest for 30 minutes.

**4.** Adjust oven rack 8 inches from broiler element and heat broiler. Return roast to oven and broil until top of roast is well browned and crispy, 2 to 6 minutes.

**5.** Transfer roast to carving board; cut twine and remove meat from ribs. Slice meat ¾ inch thick and serve, passing sauce separately.

### Port Wine–Cherry Sauce

**MAKES** 1¾ cups

- 2 cups tawny port
- 1 cup dried cherries
- ½ cup balsamic vinegar
- 4 sprigs fresh thyme, plus 2 teaspoons minced
- 2 shallots, minced
- ¼ cup heavy cream
- 16 tablespoons unsalted butter, cut into ½-inch pieces and chilled
- 1 teaspoon table salt
- ½ teaspoon pepper

**1.** Combine port and cherries in bowl and microwave until steaming, 1 to 2 minutes. Cover and let stand until plump, about 10 minutes. Strain port through fine-mesh strainer into medium saucepan, reserving cherries.

**2.** Add vinegar, thyme sprigs, and shallots to port and bring to boil over high heat. Reduce heat to medium-high and reduce mixture until it measures ¾ cup, 14 to 16 minutes. Add cream and reduce again to ¾ cup, about 5 minutes. Discard thyme sprigs. Off heat, whisk in butter, few pieces at a time, until fully incorporated. Stir in cherries, minced thyme, salt, and pepper. Cover pan and hold, off heat, until serving. Alternatively, let sauce cool completely and refrigerate for up to 2 days. Reheat in small saucepan over medium-low heat, stirring frequently, until warm.

## Slow-Roasted Pork Shoulder with Peach Sauce

**SERVES** 8 to 12

**WHY THIS RECIPE WORKS** Although most modern pork is leaner than it used to be, this is not true of every cut. We wanted to celebrate the glories of rich old-fashioned pork with the shoulder roast (also called Boston butt or pork butt). This tough cut is loaded with intramuscular fat that builds flavor and bastes the meat during roasting; outside, its thick fat cap renders to a bronze, bacon-like crust. Plus, at around $2 per pound, the shoulder offers value. First, we salted the meat overnight—a technique we frequently use with large, tough roasts for improved texture and flavor. This helped, but to improve the roast's flavor even more, we turned to an idea taken from Chinese barbecued pork, where the meat is rubbed with a salt and sugar rub (we preferred brown sugar over white for its subtle molasses flavor and hints of caramel). As we hoped, the sugar caramelized and helped crisp the fat cap, giving it a bronze hue. An accompanying sauce made from peaches, white wine, sugar, vinegar, fresh thyme, mustard, and the drippings delivered on all fronts. We prefer natural pork to enhanced pork (pork that has been injected with a salt solution to increase moistness and flavor), though both will work in this recipe. Add more water to the roasting pan as necessary during the last hours of cooking to prevent the fond from burning.

PORK ROAST

1 (6- to 8-pound) bone-in pork butt
⅓ cup kosher salt
⅓ cup packed light brown sugar
Ground black pepper

PEACH SAUCE

10 ounces frozen peaches, cut into 1-inch chunks (about 2 cups) or 2 fresh peaches cut into ½-inch wedges
2 cups dry white wine
½ cup granulated sugar
¼ cup plus 1 tablespoon unseasoned rice vinegar
2 sprigs fresh thyme
1 tablespoon whole-grain mustard

**1. FOR THE ROAST:** Using a sharp knife, cut slits 1 inch apart in the fat cap of the roast in a crosshatch pattern, being careful not to cut into the meat. Combine the salt and brown sugar in a medium bowl. Rub the salt mixture over the entire pork shoulder and into the slits. Wrap the roast tightly in a double layer of plastic wrap, place on a rimmed baking sheet, and refrigerate for at least 12 hours or up to 24 hours.

**2.** Adjust an oven rack to the lowest position and heat the oven to 325 degrees. Unwrap the roast and brush off any excess salt mixture from the surface. Season the roast with pepper. Transfer the roast to a V-rack coated with vegetable oil spray set in a large roasting pan. Add 1 quart water to the roasting pan.

**3.** Cook the roast, basting twice during cooking, until the meat is extremely tender and an instant-read thermometer inserted into the roast near, but not touching, the bone registers 190 degrees, 5 to 6 hours. Transfer the roast to a carving board and let rest, loosely tented with foil, for 1 hour. Transfer the liquid in the roasting pan to a fat separator and let stand for 5 minutes. Pour off ¼ cup jus and reserve, then discard any remaining jus and fat.

**4. FOR THE SAUCE:** Bring the peaches, wine, granulated sugar, ¼ cup of the vinegar, the reserved defatted jus, and the thyme to a simmer in a small saucepan; cook, stirring occasionally, until reduced to 2 cups, about 30 minutes. Stir in the remaining 1 tablespoon vinegar and the mustard. Remove the thyme sprigs, cover the pan, and keep warm.

**5.** Using a sharp paring knife, cut around the inverted T-shaped bone, until it can be pulled free from the roast (use a clean dish towel to grasp the bone). Using a serrated knife, slice the roast. Serve, passing the sauce separately.

## Indoor Pulled Pork with Sweet and Tangy Barbecue Sauce

SERVES 6 to 8

**WHY THIS RECIPE WORKS** "Indoor barbecue" is usually code for "braised in a Dutch oven with bottled barbecue sauce," which results in mushy meat and candy-sweet sauce. We wanted tender, shreddable meat with deep smoke flavor, plus a dark, richly seasoned crust, often referred to as bark. With barbecue a good amount of fat is necessary for moisture and flavor, so we chose to use boneless pork butt because of its high level of marbling. To mimic the moist heat of a covered grill, we came up with a dual cooking method, covering the pork for part of the oven time to speed up cooking and keep it moist and uncovering it for the remainder of the time to help the meat develop a crust. To achieve smoky flavor, we turned to liquid smoke, adding it to the brine. For even more smokiness, we employed a dry rub and a wet rub, which we fortified with smoky flavorings. Lastly, we developed a classic sweet and tangy sauce to serve alongside the pork, which we flavored with some of the pork's defatted cooking liquid. Sweet paprika may be substituted for smoked paprika. Covering the pork with parchment and then foil prevents the acidic mustard from eating holes in the foil. Serve the pork on hamburger rolls with pickle chips and thinly sliced onion. In place of Sweet and Tangy Barbecue Sauce or the variations that follow, you can use 2 cups of your favorite barbecue sauce thinned with ½ cup of the defatted pork cooking liquid in step 5. The shredded and sauced pork can be cooled, tightly covered, and refrigerated for up to 2 days. Reheat it gently before serving.

PORK

1 cup table salt for brining
½ cup sugar for brining
3 tablespoons plus 2 teaspoons liquid smoke, divided
1 (5-pound) boneless pork butt roast, cut in half horizontally
¼ cup yellow mustard
2 tablespoons pepper
2 tablespoons smoked paprika
2 tablespoons sugar
2 teaspoons table salt
1 teaspoon cayenne pepper

SWEET AND TANGY BARBECUE SAUCE

1½ cups ketchup
¼ cup light or mild molasses
2 tablespoons Worcestershire sauce
1 tablespoon hot sauce
½ teaspoon table salt
½ teaspoon pepper

**1. FOR THE PORK:** Dissolve 1 cup salt, ½ cup sugar, and 3 tablespoons liquid smoke in 1 gallon cold water in large container. Submerge pork in brine, cover with plastic wrap, and refrigerate for 2 hours.

**2.** While pork brines, combine mustard and remaining 2 teaspoons liquid smoke in small bowl; set aside. Combine pepper, paprika, sugar, salt, and cayenne in second small bowl; set aside. Adjust oven rack to lower-middle position and heat oven to 325 degrees.

**3.** Remove pork from brine and dry thoroughly with paper towels. Rub mustard mixture over entire surface of each piece of pork. Sprinkle entire surface of each piece with spice mixture. Place pork on wire rack set in aluminum foil–lined rimmed baking sheet. Place piece of parchment paper over pork, then cover with sheet of foil, sealing edges to prevent moisture from escaping. Roast pork for 3 hours.

4. Remove pork from oven; discard foil and parchment. Carefully pour off liquid in bottom of baking sheet into fat separator and reserve for sauce. Return pork to oven and cook, uncovered, until well browned, tender, and center of roast registers 200 degrees, about 1½ hours. Transfer pork to serving dish, tent with foil, and let rest for 20 minutes.

5. **FOR THE SAUCE:** While pork rests, pour ½ cup defatted cooking liquid from fat separator into medium bowl; whisk in sauce ingredients.

6. Using 2 forks, shred pork into bite-size pieces. Toss with 1 cup sauce and season with salt and pepper to taste. Serve, passing remaining sauce separately.

### Lexington Vinegar Barbecue Sauce

**MAKES** about 2½ cups

- 1 cup cider vinegar
- ½ cup ketchup
- ½ cup water
- 1 tablespoon sugar
- ¾ teaspoon table salt
- ¾ teaspoon red pepper flakes
- ½ teaspoon ground black pepper

Combine all the ingredients in a medium bowl with ½ cup of the defatted cooking liquid in step 5 and whisk to combine.

#### CUTTING A PORK BUTT IN HALF

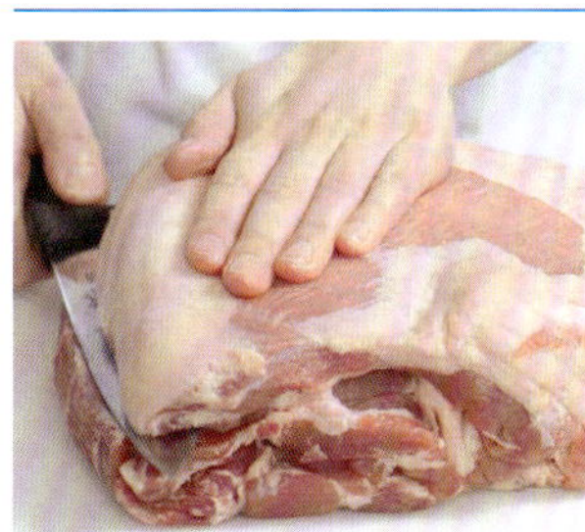

To increase surface area, hold knife parallel to cutting board; press your hand flat against top of pork while cutting horizontally.

### South Carolina Mustard Barbecue Sauce

**MAKES** about 2½ cups

- 1 cup yellow mustard
- ½ cup white vinegar
- ¼ cup packed light brown sugar
- ¼ cup Worcestershire sauce
- 2 tablespoons hot sauce
- 1 teaspoon table salt
- 1 teaspoon ground black pepper

Combine all the ingredients in a medium bowl with ½ cup of the defatted cooking liquid in step 5 and whisk to combine.

## Spicy Mexican Shredded Pork Tostadas

**SERVES** 4 to 6

**WHY THIS RECIPE WORKS** True Mexican shredded pork, or tinga, features fall-apart-tender meat bathed in a savory, complex sauce. We set out to perfect its characteristic crisp texture and smoky tomato flavor. We trimmed and cubed a pork butt (chosen for its good marbling), then simmered the pieces in water that we flavored with garlic, thyme, and onion. Once the pork was tender, we drained the meat (reserving some of the cooking liquid for the sauce) and returned it to the pot to shred. We then sautéed the meat along with the requisite additions of chopped onion and oregano. Minutes later, the pork had crackling edges crisp enough to survive simmering in tomato sauce. For our version, we diluted canned tomato sauce with the reserved flavorful cooking liquid from the pork and added bay leaves. For tinga's all-important smokiness, we turned to ground chipotle powder. The trimmed pork should weigh about 1½ pounds. The shredded pork is traditionally served on tostadas (crisp fried corn tortillas), but you can also use the meat in tacos or burritos or simply served over rice. Make sure to buy tortillas made only with corn, lime, and salt—preservatives will compromise quality. We prefer the complex flavor of chipotle powder, but two minced canned chipotle chiles can be used in its place. The pork can be prepared through step 1 and refrigerated in an airtight container for up to 2 days. The tostadas can be made up to a day in advance and stored in an airtight container.

**SHREDDED PORK**

- 2 pounds boneless pork butt roast, trimmed of excess fat and cut into 1-inch pieces
- 2 medium onions, 1 quartered and 1 chopped fine
- 5 medium garlic cloves, 3 peeled and smashed and 2 minced or pressed through a garlic press (about 2 teaspoons)
- 4 sprigs fresh thyme
- Table salt
- 2 tablespoons olive oil
- ½ teaspoon dried oregano
- 1 (14.5-ounce) can tomato sauce
- 1 tablespoon ground chipotle powder
- 2 bay leaves

**TOSTADAS**

- ¾ cup vegetable oil
- 12 (6-inch) corn tortillas
- Table salt

**GARNISHES**

- Queso fresco or feta cheese
- Fresh cilantro leaves
- Sour cream
- Diced avocado
- Lime wedges

**1. FOR THE SHREDDED PORK:** Bring the pork, quartered onion, smashed garlic cloves, thyme, 1 teaspoon salt, and 6 cups water to a simmer in a large saucepan over medium-high heat, skimming off any foam that rises to the surface. Reduce the heat to medium-low, partially cover, and cook until the pork is tender, 1¼ to 1½ hours. Drain the pork, reserving 1 cup cooking liquid. Discard the onion, garlic, and thyme. Return the pork to the saucepan and, using a potato masher, mash until shredded into rough ½-inch pieces; set aside.

**2.** Heat the olive oil in a 12-inch nonstick skillet over medium-high heat until shimmering. Add the shredded pork, chopped onion, and oregano; cook, stirring often, until the pork is well browned and crisp, 7 to 10 minutes. Add the minced garlic and cook until fragrant, about 30 seconds.

**3.** Stir in the tomato sauce, chipotle powder, reserved pork cooking liquid, and bay leaves; simmer until almost all the liquid has evaporated, 5 to 7 minutes. Remove and discard the bay leaves and season with salt to taste.

**4. TO FRY THE TOSTADAS:** Heat the vegetable oil in an 8-inch heavy-bottomed skillet over medium heat to 350 degrees. Using a fork, poke the center of each tortilla three or four times (to prevent puffing and allow for even cooking). Fry one at a time, holding a metal potato masher in the upright position on top of the tortilla to keep it submerged, until crisp and lightly browned, 45 to 60 seconds (no flipping is necessary). Drain on a paper towel–lined plate and season with salt to taste. Repeat with the remaining tortillas.

**5. TO SERVE:** Spoon a small amount of shredded pork onto the center of each tostada and serve, passing the garnishes separately.

## Carnitas (Mexican Pulled Pork)

**SERVES 6**

**WHY THIS RECIPE WORKS** Spanish for "little meats," carnitas offer fall-apart-tender hunks of pork with lightly crispy, caramelized exteriors. The chunks of meat are often deep-fried in lard or oil. We wanted tender chunks of lightly crisped, caramelized pork—without the need for deep frying. Our initial recipe for carnitas started by simmering the meat (we found boneless pork butt had the best flavor) in a seasoned broth in the oven and then sautéing it in some of the rendered fat. The flavor was OK, but too much of the pork flavor was lost when we discarded the cooking liquid. So we reduced the liquid to a thick, syrupy glaze that was perfect for coating the meat. Broiled on a rack set over a baking sheet, the glazed meat developed a wonderfully rich flavor, and the rack allowed the excess fat to drip off. We emulated the flavor of the Mexican sour oranges used in traditional carnitas with a mixture of fresh lime and orange juices. Bay leaves and oregano provided aromatic notes, and cumin brought a complementary earthiness. We like serving carnitas spooned into tacos, but you can also use it as a filling for tamales, enchiladas, and burritos.

- 1 (3½- to 4-pound) boneless pork butt roast, fat cap trimmed to ⅛ inch thick, cut into 2-inch chunks
- 1 small onion, halved
- 2 bay leaves
- 1 teaspoon dried oregano
- 1 teaspoon ground cumin
- 1 teaspoon table salt
- ½ teaspoon pepper
- 2 cups water
- 2 tablespoons lime juice
- 1 orange, halved

- 18 (6-inch) corn tortillas, warmed
- Lime wedges
- Minced white or red onion
- Fresh cilantro leaves
- Thinly sliced radishes
- Sour cream

**1.** Adjust oven rack to lower-middle position and heat oven to 300 degrees. Combine pork, onion, bay leaves, oregano, cumin, salt, pepper, water, and lime juice in large Dutch oven (liquid should just barely cover meat). Juice orange into medium bowl and remove any seeds (you should have about ⅓ cup juice). Add juice and spent orange halves to pot. Bring mixture to simmer over medium-high heat, stirring occasionally. Cover pot and transfer it to oven; cook until meat is soft and falls apart when prodded with fork, about 2 hours, flipping pieces of meat once during cooking.

**2.** Remove pot from oven and turn oven to broil. Using slotted spoon, transfer pork to bowl; remove orange halves, onion, and bay leaves from cooking liquid and discard (do not skim fat from liquid). Place pot over high heat (use caution, as handles will be very hot) and simmer liquid, stirring frequently, until thick and syrupy (heat-resistant spatula should leave wide trail when dragged through glaze), 8 to 12 minutes. You should have about 1 cup reduced liquid.

**3.** Using 2 forks, pull each piece of pork in half. Fold in reduced liquid; season with salt and pepper to taste. Spread pork in even layer on wire rack set in rimmed baking sheet or on broiler pan (meat should cover almost entire surface of rack or broiler pan). Place baking sheet on lower-middle oven rack and broil until top of meat is well browned (but not charred) and edges are slightly crisp, 5 to 8 minutes. Using wide metal spatula, flip pieces of meat and continue to broil until top is well browned and edges are slightly crisp, 5 to 8 minutes longer. Serve immediately with warm tortillas and garnishes.

## Carne Adovada (Braised New Mexico–Style Pork in Red Chile Sauce)

**SERVES 6**

**WHY THIS RECIPE WORKS** To make carne adovada, a classic, ultrasimple New Mexican pork braise in a brick-red sauce of chiles, aromatics, and vinegar, we started by cutting boneless pork shoulder into large chunks and salting them (so that they would be well seasoned and retain moisture during cooking). We started with a generous 4 ounces of dried red New Mexican chiles, which are fruity and relatively mild. But rather than toast them, we simply steeped them in water to preserve their bright flavor. When they were pliable, we blended them with aromatics and spices, as well as honey, white vinegar, and just enough of the chile soaking liquid to form a thick paste; when the paste was smooth, we added the remaining water to form a puree, making sure to leave in small bits of chile skin that contributed rustic texture and vibrant flavor. We tossed the pork with the puree in a Dutch oven, then braised it in a low oven until the meat was very tender. A squeeze of lime added brightness and acidity. Pork butt roast is often labeled Boston butt. If you can't find New Mexican chiles, substitute dried California chiles. Dried chiles should be pliable and smell slightly fruity. Kitchen shears can be used to cut them. If you can't find Mexican oregano, substitute Mediterranean oregano. Serve with rice and beans, crispy potatoes, or flour tortillas with shredded lettuce and chopped tomato. Alternatively, shred the pork as a filling for tacos and burritos.

- 1 (3½- to 4-pound) boneless pork butt roast, trimmed and cut into 1½-inch pieces
- 4 teaspoons kosher salt, divided
- 4 ounces dried New Mexican chiles, wiped clean, stemmed, seeded, and torn into 1-inch pieces
- 2 tablespoons honey
- 2 tablespoons distilled white vinegar
- 5 garlic cloves, peeled
- 2 teaspoons dried Mexican oregano
- 2 teaspoons ground cumin
- ½ teaspoon cayenne pepper
- ⅛ teaspoon ground cloves
- Lime wedges

**1.** Toss pork and 1 tablespoon salt together in bowl; refrigerate for 1 hour.

**2.** Bring 4 cups water to boil. Place chile pieces in medium bowl. Pour boiling water over chiles, making sure they are completely submerged, and let stand until chiles are softened, 30 minutes. Adjust oven rack to lower-middle position and heat oven to 325 degrees.

**3.** Drain chiles and reserve 2 cups of soaking liquid (discard remaining soaking liquid). Process chiles, honey, vinegar, garlic, oregano, cumin, cayenne, cloves, and remaining 1 teaspoon salt in blender until chiles are finely ground and thick paste forms, about 30 seconds. With blender running, add 1 cup soaking liquid and blend until puree is smooth, 1½ to

2 minutes, adding up to additional ¼ cup liquid to maintain vortex. Add remaining soaking liquid and continue to blend sauce at high speed, 1 minute longer.

**4.** Add pork and chile sauce to Dutch oven, stirring to make sure pork is evenly coated. Bring to boil over high heat. Cover pot, transfer to oven, and cook until pork is tender and fork inserted into pork meets little to no resistance, 2 to 2½ hours.

**5.** Using wooden spoon, scrape any browned bits from sides of pot and stir until pork and sauce are recombined, and sauce is smooth and homogeneous. Let stand, uncovered, for 10 minutes. Season with salt to taste. Serve, passing lime wedges separately.

## Goan Pork Vindaloo

**SERVES 8**

**WHY THIS RECIPE WORKS** Disregard vindaloo's reputation for extreme heat. The word "vindaloo" has evolved to indicate a searingly hot curry because of its adoption into British cuisine, but the original Goan vindaloo is a brightly flavored but relatively mild and more nuanced pork braise that's aromatic with spices. It's made with dried Kashmiri chiles and spices such as cinnamon, cloves, and cardamom. Vindaloo should have a pronounced vinegary tang, but we found that adding the vinegar at the beginning made the meat chalky. We withheld it until halfway through cooking so that we could use less but still enjoy the characteristic acidity. Moving the cooking from the stovetop to the oven made this dish hands-off and foolproof. Kashmiri chile powder should have a brilliant red hue, a fruity flavor, and a slightly tannic edge, but very little heat. Pork butt roast is often labeled Boston butt. Cider vinegar can be used in place of the coconut vinegar. Traditional Goan vindaloo is not very spicy, but if you prefer more heat, add up to ½ teaspoon of cayenne pepper. Serve with white rice, naan, or Goan pao.

- ¾ cup water
- 1 (2-inch) piece ginger, peeled and sliced crosswise ⅛ inch thick
- 6 garlic cloves
- 3 tablespoons Kashmiri chile powder
- 1 tablespoon paprika
- 1 tablespoon ground cumin
- 2 teaspoons table salt
- 1 teaspoon pepper
- ¼–½ teaspoon cayenne pepper (optional)
- ½ teaspoon ground cinnamon
- ½ teaspoon ground cardamom
- ¼ teaspoon ground cloves
- ¼ teaspoon ground nutmeg
- 1 (3- to 3½-pound) boneless pork butt roast, trimmed and cut into 1-inch pieces
- 1 tablespoon vegetable oil
- 1 large onion, chopped fine
- ⅓ cup coconut vinegar

**1.** Adjust oven rack to middle position and heat oven to 325 degrees. Process water; ginger; garlic; chile powder; paprika; cumin; salt; pepper; cayenne, if using; cinnamon; cardamom; cloves; and nutmeg in blender on low speed until rough paste forms, about 1 minute. Scrape down sides and blend on high speed until paste is smooth, about 1 minute. Place pork in large bowl. Add spice paste and mix thoroughly.

**2.** Heat oil in Dutch oven over medium heat until shimmering. Add onion and cook, stirring frequently, until soft and golden, 7 to 9 minutes. Add pork mixture and stir to combine. Spread mixture into even layer. Continue to cook until mixture begins to bubble, about 2 minutes longer. Cover pot, transfer to oven, and cook for 40 minutes. Stir in vinegar. Cover, return pot to oven, and cook for 20 minutes. Uncover and cook until fork inserted into pork meets little or no resistance, 20 to 30 minutes longer. Let stand, uncovered, for 10 minutes. Stir and serve. (Pork can be cooked up to 3 days in advance.)

## Chinese Barbecued Pork

SERVES 6

**WHY THIS RECIPE WORKS** For Chinese barbecued pork that could be made in the oven, we started by slicing a boneless pork butt into strips. Our marinade of soy sauce, sherry, hoisin, five-spice powder, sesame oil, ginger, and garlic introduced the dish's signature flavors. For optimal browning and intense flavor, we first cooked the meat, covered, at a low temperature to render fat and then cranked up the heat to develop a burnished crust. The classic lacquered appearance was achieved by applying a ketchup-honey glaze right before broiling, which gave our pork its traditional red color. To facilitate cleanup, spray the rack and pan with vegetable oil spray. The pork will release liquid and fat during the cooking process, so be careful when removing the pan from the oven. If you don't have a wire rack that fits in a rimmed baking sheet, substitute a broiler pan, although the meat may not darken as much. Pay close attention to the meat when broiling—you are looking for it to darken and caramelize, not blacken. Do not use a drawer broiler; the heat source will be too close to the meat. Instead, increase the oven temperature in step 5 to 500 degrees and cook for 8 to 12 minutes before glazing and 6 to 8 minutes once the glaze has been applied; flip meat and repeat on second side. This recipe can be made with boneless country-style ribs, but the meat will be slightly drier and less flavorful. To use ribs, reduce the uncovered cooking time in step 4 to 20 minutes and increase the broiling and glazing times in step 5 by 2 to 3 minutes per side.

- 4 pounds boneless pork butt (Boston butt), cut into 8 strips and excess fat removed
- ½ cup sugar
- ½ cup soy sauce
- 6 tablespoons hoisin sauce
- ¼ cup dry sherry
- ¼ teaspoon ground white pepper
- 1 teaspoon Chinese five-spice powder
- 1 tablespoon toasted sesame oil
- 2 tablespoons grated fresh ginger (from 4- to 6-inch piece)
- 2 medium cloves garlic, minced or pressed through a garlic press (about 2 teaspoons)
- ¼ cup ketchup
- ⅓ cup honey

**1.** Using fork, prick pork 10 to 12 times on each side. Place pork in large plastic zipper-lock bag. Combine sugar, soy, hoisin, sherry, pepper, five-spice powder, sesame oil, ginger, and garlic in medium bowl. Measure out ½ cup marinade and set aside. Pour remaining marinade into bag with pork. Press out as much air as possible; seal bag. Refrigerate for at least 30 minutes or up to 4 hours.

**2.** While meat marinates, combine ketchup and honey with reserved marinade in small saucepan. Cook glaze over medium heat until syrupy and reduced to 1 cup, 4 to 6 minutes.

**3.** Adjust oven rack to middle position and heat oven to 300 degrees. Line rimmed baking sheet with aluminum foil and set wire rack on sheet.

**4.** Remove pork from marinade, letting any excess drip off, and place on wire rack. Pour ¼ cup water into bottom of pan. Cover pan with heavy-duty aluminum foil, crimping edges tightly to seal. Cook pork for 20 minutes. Remove foil and continue to cook until edges of pork begin to brown, 40 to 45 minutes.

**5.** Turn on broiler. Broil pork until evenly caramelized, 7 to 9 minutes. Remove pan from oven and brush pork with half of glaze; broil until deep mahogany color, 3 to 5 minutes. Using tongs, flip meat and broil until other side caramelizes, 7 to 9 minutes. Brush meat with remaining glaze and continue to broil until second side is deep mahogany, 3 to 5 minutes. Cool for at least 10 minutes, then cut into thin strips and serve.

## Chinese-Style Barbecued Spareribs

**SERVES** 6 to 8 as an appetizer or 4 to 6 as a main dish

**WHY THIS RECIPE WORKS** Chinese barbecued spareribs are usually marinated for several hours and then slow-roasted and basted repeatedly to build up a thick crust. For a faster version, we instead braised the ribs, which we cut into individual pieces to speed up cooking and create more surface area. We also made a highly seasoned liquid, which helped the flavor penetrate the meat. Then we strained, defatted, and reduced the braising liquid to make a full-bodied glaze in which we tossed the ribs before roasting them. It's not necessary to remove the membrane on the bone side of the ribs. These ribs are chewier than American-style ribs; if you prefer them more tender, cook them for an additional 15 minutes in step 1. Adding water to the baking sheet during roasting helps prevent smoking. Serve the ribs alone or with vegetables and rice. You can serve the first batch immediately or tent them with foil to keep them warm.

- 1 (6-inch) piece fresh ginger, peeled and sliced thin
- 8 garlic cloves, peeled
- 1 cup honey
- ¾ cup hoisin sauce
- ¾ cup soy sauce
- ½ cup Shaoxing wine or dry sherry
- 2 teaspoons five-spice powder
- 1 teaspoon red food coloring (optional)
- 1 teaspoon white pepper
- 2 (2½- to 3-pound) racks St. Louis–style spareribs, cut into individual ribs
- 2 tablespoons toasted sesame oil

**1.** Pulse ginger and garlic in food processor until finely chopped, 10 to 12 pulses, scraping down sides of bowl as needed. Transfer ginger-garlic mixture to Dutch oven. Add honey; hoisin; soy sauce; ½ cup water; Shaoxing wine; five-spice powder; food coloring, if using; and white pepper and whisk until combined. Add ribs and stir to coat (ribs will not be fully submerged). Bring to simmer over high heat, then reduce heat to low, cover, and cook for 1¼ hours, stirring occasionally.

**2.** Adjust oven rack to middle position and heat oven to 425 degrees. Using tongs, transfer ribs to large bowl. Strain braising liquid through fine-mesh strainer set over large container, pressing on solids to extract as much liquid as possible; discard solids. Let cooking liquid settle for 10 minutes. Using wide, shallow spoon, skim fat from surface and discard.

**3.** Return braising liquid to pot and add sesame oil. Bring to boil over high heat and cook until syrupy and reduced to 2½ cups, 16 to 20 minutes.

**4.** Set wire rack in aluminum foil–lined rimmed baking sheet and pour ½ cup water into sheet. Transfer half of ribs to pot with braising liquid and toss to coat. Arrange ribs, bone sides up, on prepared rack, letting excess glaze drip off. Roast until edges of ribs start to caramelize, 5 to 7 minutes. Flip ribs and continue to roast until second side starts to caramelize, 5 to 7 minutes longer. Transfer ribs to serving platter; repeat process with remaining ribs. Serve.

## Oven-Barbecued Spareribs

**SERVES** 4

**WHY THIS RECIPE WORKS** To make this recipe, you will need a baking stone. It's fine if the ribs overlap slightly on the wire rack. Removing the surface fat keeps the ribs from being too greasy and removing the membrane from the ribs allows the smoke to penetrate both sides of the racks and also makes the ribs easier to eat. Note that the ribs must be coated with the rub and refrigerated at least 8 hours or up to 24 hours ahead of cooking. Be careful when opening the crimped foil to add the juice, as hot steam and smoke will billow out. Serve ribs with Quick Barbecue Sauce (recipe follows), if desired.

- 6 tablespoons yellow mustard
- 2 tablespoons ketchup
- 3 garlic cloves, minced
- 3 tablespoons packed brown sugar
- 1½ tablespoons kosher salt
- 1 tablespoon sweet paprika
- 1 tablespoon chili powder
- 2 teaspoons pepper
- ½ teaspoon cayenne pepper
- 2 (2½- to 3-pound) racks St. Louis–style spareribs, trimmed, membrane removed, and each rack cut in half
- ¼ cup finely ground Lapsang Souchong tea leaves (from about 10 tea bags, or ½ cup loose tea leaves ground to a powder in a spice grinder)
- ½ cup apple juice

**1.** Combine mustard, ketchup, and garlic in bowl; combine sugar, salt, paprika, chili powder, pepper, and cayenne in separate bowl. Spread mustard mixture in thin, even layer over both sides of ribs; coat both sides with spice mixture, then wrap ribs in plastic and refrigerate for 8 to 24 hours.

**2.** Transfer ribs from refrigerator to freezer for 45 minutes. Adjust oven racks to lowest and upper-middle positions (at least 5 inches below broiler). Place baking stone on lower rack; heat oven to 500 degrees. Sprinkle ground tea evenly over bottom of rimmed baking sheet; set wire rack in baking sheet. Place ribs meat side up on rack and cover with heavy-duty aluminum foil, crimping edges tightly to seal. Place baking sheet on stone and roast ribs for 30 minutes, then reduce oven temperature to 250 degrees, leaving oven door open for 1 minute to cool. While oven is open, carefully open 1 corner of foil and pour apple juice into bottom of baking sheet; reseal foil. Continue to roast until meat is very tender and begins to pull away from bones, about 1½ hours. (Begin to check ribs after 1 hour; leave loosely covered with foil for remaining cooking time.)

**3.** Remove foil and carefully flip racks bone side up; place baking sheet on upper-middle rack. Turn on broiler; cook ribs until well browned and crispy in spots, 5 to 10 minutes. Flip ribs meat side up and cook until second side is well browned and crispy, 5 to 7 minutes more. Cool for at least 10 minutes before cutting into individual ribs. Serve with Quick Barbecue Sauce, if desired.

## Quick Barbecue Sauce

**MAKES** about 1½ cups

Classic barbecue sauce must simmer for a long time for the whole tomatoes in it to break down. However, we found that starting with ketchup can shorten the process.

- 1 medium onion, peeled and quartered
- ¼ cup water
- 1 cup ketchup
- 5 tablespoons molasses
- 2 tablespoons cider vinegar
- 2 tablespoons Worcestershire sauce
- 2 tablespoons Dijon mustard
- 1½ teaspoons liquid smoke (optional)
- 1 teaspoon hot sauce
- ¼ teaspoon pepper
- 2 tablespoons vegetable oil
- 1 garlic clove, minced
- 1 teaspoon chili powder
- ¼ teaspoon cayenne pepper

**1.** Process onion and water in a food processor until pureed and mixture resembles slush, about 30 seconds. Strain mixture through fine mesh strainer into liquid measuring cup, pressing on solids with rubber spatula to obtain ½ cup juice. Discard solids.

**2.** Whisk onion juice, ketchup, molasses, vinegar, Worcestershire sauce, mustard, liquid smoke (if using), hot sauce, and pepper together in medium bowl.

**3.** Heat oil in large saucepan over medium heat until shimmering but not smoking. Add garlic, chili powder, and cayenne and cook until fragrant, about 30 seconds. Whisk in ketchup mixture and bring to a boil; reduce heat to medium-low and simmer gently, uncovered, until flavors meld and sauce is thickened, about 25 minutes. Cool sauce to room temperature before using. (Sauce can be refrigerated for up to 1 week.)

# Fried Brown Rice with Pork and Shrimp

**SERVES** 6

**WHY THIS RECIPE WORKS** Using brown rice offers several advantages. Because of its bran, brown rice holds up well if cooked aggressively in boiling water. To balance its nuttier flavor, we used plenty of ginger, garlic, and soy sauce. To turn our fried brown rice into a main course, we cut boneless country-style pork ribs across the grain into bite-size slices and tossed them in hoisin sauce, honey, and five-spice powder. We chopped scallions and shrimp, beat some eggs, grated some ginger, and minced some garlic, then stir-fried these components in batches. This yielded perfectly cooked ingredients ready to stir together with the fried brown rice. Boiling the rice gives it the proper texture for this dish. Do not use a rice cooker. The most efficient way to make this dish is to start the rice boiling and then to assemble the remaining ingredients while the rice cooks. The stir-fry portion of this recipe moves quickly, so make sure to have all your ingredients in place before starting. This recipe works best in a nonstick skillet with a slick surface. If your skillet is a bit worn, add an additional teaspoon of oil with the eggs in step 3. Serve with a simple steamed vegetable like broccoli, bok choy, or snow peas, if desired.

- 2 cups short grain brown rice
- Table salt
- 10 ounces boneless country-style pork ribs, trimmed
- 1 tablespoon hoisin sauce
- 2 teaspoons honey
- ⅛ teaspoon five-spice powder
- Small pinch cayenne pepper
- 4 teaspoons vegetable oil
- 8 ounces large shrimp (26 to 30 per pound), peeled, deveined (see page 613), tails removed, and cut into ½-inch pieces
- 3 large eggs, lightly beaten
- 1 tablespoon toasted sesame oil
- 6 scallions, whites and greens separated, sliced thin on bias
- 1½ teaspoons garlic, minced
- 1½ teaspoons grated fresh ginger
- 2 tablespoons soy sauce
- 1 cup frozen peas

**1.** Bring 3 quarts water to boil in large pot. Add rice and 2 teaspoons salt. Cook, stirring occasionally, until rice is tender, about 35 minutes. Drain well, and return to pot. Cover and set aside.

**2.** While rice cooks, cut pork into 1-inch pieces, and cut each piece into ¼-inch slices against grain. Combine pork with hoisin, honey, five-spice, cayenne, and ½ teaspoon salt, and toss to coat. Set aside.

**3.** Heat 1 teaspoon vegetable oil in 12-inch nonstick skillet over medium-high heat until shimmering. Add shrimp in even layer and cook without moving them until bottoms are browned, about 90 seconds. Stir and continue to cook until just cooked through, about 90 seconds longer. Push shrimp to 1 side of skillet. Add 1 teaspoon vegetable oil to cleared side of skillet.

Add eggs to clearing and sprinkle with ¼ teaspoon salt. Using rubber spatula, stir eggs gently until set but still wet, about 30 seconds. Stir eggs into shrimp and continue to cook, breaking up large pieces of egg, until eggs are fully cooked, about 30 seconds longer. Transfer shrimp-egg mixture to clean bowl.

**4.** Heat remaining 2 teaspoons vegetable oil in now-empty skillet over medium-high heat until shimmering. Add pork in even layer. Cook without moving until pork is well browned on underside, 2 to 3 minutes. Flip pork and cook without moving until pork is cooked through and caramelized on second side, 2 to 3 minutes. Transfer to bowl with shrimp-egg mixture.

**5.** Heat sesame oil in now-empty skillet over medium-high heat until shimmering. Add scallion whites and cook, stirring frequently, until well-browned, about 1 minute. Add ginger and garlic and cook, stirring frequently, until fragrant and beginning to brown, 30 to 60 seconds. Add soy sauce and half of rice and stir until all ingredients are fully incorporated, making sure to break up clumps of ginger and garlic. Reduce heat to medium-low and add remaining rice, pork, shrimp, eggs, and peas. Stir until all ingredients are evenly incorporated and heated through, 2 to 4 minutes. Remove from heat and stir in scallion greens. Transfer to heated platter and serve.

## Crispy Slow-Roasted Pork Belly

**SERVES** 8 to 10

**WHY THIS RECIPE WORKS** Pork belly is a boneless cut featuring alternating layers of flavorful, well-marbled meat and buttery fat which, when properly cooked, turn sumptuous, with crisp skin. To tackle this special cut, we started by scoring the skin and rubbing the meat with salt and brown sugar. We then air-dried the belly overnight to dehydrate the skin. Roasting the pork belly low and slow further dried the skin and broke down the tough collagen. We finished by frying the belly skin side down, which caused it to dramatically puff up and crisp. A bracing mustard sauce balanced the richness of the pork belly. This recipe requires refrigerating the seasoned pork belly for at least 12 hours or up to 24 hours before cooking (a longer time is preferable). Be sure to ask for a flat, rectangular center-cut section of skin-on pork belly that's 1½ inches thick with roughly equal amounts of meat and fat. Serve with white rice and steamed greens or boiled potatoes and salad.

**PORK**

- 1 (3-pound) skin-on center-cut fresh pork belly, about 1½ inches thick
- 2½ tablespoons kosher salt
- 2 tablespoons packed dark brown sugar
- Vegetable oil

**MUSTARD SAUCE**

- ⅔ cup Dijon mustard
- ⅓ cup cider vinegar
- ¼ cup packed dark brown sugar
- 1 tablespoon hot sauce
- 1 teaspoon Worcestershire sauce

**1. FOR THE PORK:** Using sharp chef's knife, slice pork belly lengthwise into 3 strips about 2 inches wide, then cut slits, spaced 1 inch apart in crosshatch pattern, in surface fat layer, being careful not to cut into meat. Combine 2 tablespoons salt and sugar in bowl. Rub salt mixture into bottom and sides of pork belly (do not rub into skin). Season skin of each strip evenly with ½ teaspoon salt. Place pork belly, skin side up, in 13 by 9-inch baking dish and refrigerate, uncovered, for at least 12 hours or up to 24 hours.

**2.** Adjust oven rack to middle position and heat oven to 250 degrees. Set wire rack in rimmed baking sheet and spray with vegetable oil spray. Transfer pork belly, skin side up, to

### COOKING PORK BELLY

**1.** Cutting pork belly into 3 strips provides more surface area for seasoning. Smaller pieces of meat and skin also cook more quickly and evenly.

**2.** Seasoning meat with salt and brown sugar adds flavor, encourages browning, and helps it retain moisture. Sprinkling salt on skin (scored for deeper penetration) helps it dehydrate.

**3.** Letting seasoned meat sit overnight in refrigerator gives rub time to penetrate. It also dries out surface of skin so that it can crisp.

**4.** Slow roasting browns meat and further dehydrates skin while converting rigid collagen in both to gelatin. Gelatin keeps meat moist and helps skin puff when crisped.

**5.** Frying just skin portion of pork belly (start it in cold oil so that all skin heats at same pace) forces its remaining water to evaporate, leaving it puffed up and ultracrisp.

wire rack and roast until pork registers 195 degrees and paring knife inserted in pork meets little resistance, 3 to 3½ hours, rotating sheet halfway through roasting.

**3. FOR THE MUSTARD SAUCE:** Whisk all ingredients together in bowl; set aside.

**4.** Transfer pork belly, skin side up, to large plate. (Pork belly can be held at room temperature for up to 1 hour.) Pour fat from sheet into 1-cup liquid measuring cup. Add vegetable oil as needed to equal 1 cup and transfer to 12-inch skillet. Arrange pork belly, skin side down, in skillet (strips can be sliced in half crosswise if skillet won't fit strips whole) and place over medium heat until bubbles form around pork belly. Continue to fry, tilting skillet occasionally to even out hot spots, until skin puffs, crisps, and turns golden, 6 to 10 minutes. Transfer pork belly, skin side up, to carving board and let rest for 5 minutes. Flip pork belly skin side down and slice ½ inch thick (being sure to slice through original score marks). Reinvert slices and serve with sauce.

## Gua Bao (Taiwanese Steamed Buns with Braised Pork Belly)

**SERVES** 6 to 8 **SEASON 26**

**WHY THIS RECIPE WORKS** Gua bao is a popular street food in Taiwan that's become even more common in the United States. We made our bao with a combination of yeast, baking powder, and vegetable shortening to give the buns superior tenderness and loft. All-purpose flour, milk, and modest amounts of sugar and salt delivered a tender bun with a well-balanced flavor that paired well with a savory filling. For our Americanized filling, we braised pork belly with deeply savory ingredients such as soy sauce and hoisin sauce. Fresh ginger, garlic, and dried chiles provided aromatic complexity and depth. Texturally contrasting garnishes such as daikon, scallions, and cilantro offered crispness, crunch, and freshness. Like most braises, the pork belly freezes beautifully, so it can be made well in advance of serving. Similarly, the bao, once fully cooled, can be frozen and easily reheated (from frozen) in a steamer in just 7 to 8 minutes. The sauces, seasoned vegetables, and fresh garnishes can be prepped hours in advance, and when paired with quickly reheated buns and fillings, yield a make-ahead star. This recipe requires a bamboo steamer basket; a steamer insert can be used, but the buns will need to be steamed in several batches. Be sure to ask for a flat, rectangular section of skin-on pork belly with roughly equal amounts of meat and fat. We prefer to use a chopstick for shaping and moving the buns, which relaxes the dough so the buns maintain their shape when steamed, but you can also use a bamboo skewer. We strongly recommend that you measure the flour for the bao by weight. An equal amount of lard or vegetable oil can be substituted for the shortening, though the buns will not be as tender and fluffy if made with vegetable oil. Two percent low-fat milk can be used instead of whole milk. We recommend making the pork belly and garnishes before preparing the buns.

**BRAISED PORK BELLY**

- 1 (2-pound) skin-on center-cut fresh pork belly, about 1½ inches thick
- 1 tablespoon vegetable oil
- 3 cups water
- ¼ cup Shaoxing wine or dry sherry
- 3 tablespoons hoisin sauce
- 3 tablespoons soy sauce
- 3 tablespoons oyster sauce
- 3 tablespoons packed brown sugar
- 3 whole dried arbol chiles
- 3 garlic cloves, smashed and peeled
- 2 star anise pods
- 1 (1-inch) piece ginger, peeled and cut into thirds

**SEASONED DAIKON**

- 8 ounces daikon radish, peeled, halved lengthwise, and sliced crosswise ⅛ inch thick
- 1 tablespoon sugar
- ½ teaspoon table salt

**HOISIN-SOY SAUCE**

- ¼ cup hoisin sauce
- 1 tablespoon soy sauce

**BAO**

- 2½ cups (12½ ounces) all-purpose flour
- 1 tablespoon sugar
- 1¾ teaspoons instant or rapid-rise yeast
- 1 teaspoon baking powder
- ½ teaspoon table salt
- 1 cup warm whole milk (100 degrees)
- 2 tablespoons vegetable shortening
- ¼ teaspoon plus 2 tablespoons vegetable oil, divided
- 1¼ cups fresh cilantro leaves and stems, trimmed
- 3 scallions, halved lengthwise and cut into 2-inch pieces
- ⅓ cup dry-roasted peanuts, chopped
- 2 Thai chiles, stemmed, seeded, and minced (optional)

**1. FOR THE PORK BELLY:** Using sharp chef's knife, slice pork into ¾-inch-wide strips. Cut strips crosswise to make 16 evenly sized pieces (2 to 2½ inches long). Heat oil in Dutch oven over medium-high heat until shimmering. Add pork in single layer (if needed, wait for some pieces to render fat and shrink before adding remainder) and cook until golden brown, 15 to 20 minutes, flipping pieces halfway through cooking.

**2.** Meanwhile, combine water, Shaoxing wine, hoisin, soy sauce, oyster sauce, and sugar in bowl.

**3.** Add water mixture, arbols, garlic, star anise, and ginger to pot with pork. Bring to boil over high heat, then adjust heat to maintain vigorous simmer. Cover and cook, stirring occasionally and adjusting heat as necessary to maintain vigorous simmer, until pork is tender and fork inserted into meat meets little resistance, about 1 hour.

**4.** Off heat, use slotted spoon to transfer pork to bowl. Pour liquid into fat separator and let settle for 5 minutes; discard solids. Return defatted liquid to pot and cook over medium heat until reduced to 1 cup, about 15 minutes. Stir in pork, cover, and keep warm until ready to serve. (Braised pork belly can be refrigerated for up to 2 days. To reheat, cook over low heat in covered Dutch oven until warmed through.)

**5. FOR THE SEASONED DAIKON:** Toss daikon, sugar, and salt together in bowl. Cover and refrigerate until ready to use. (Daikon can be refrigerated for up to 24 hours.)

**6. FOR THE HOISIN-SOY SAUCE:** Combine hoisin and soy sauces in small bowl.

**7. FOR THE BAO:** Using stand mixer fitted with dough hook, mix flour, sugar, yeast, baking powder, and salt on low speed until combined, about 30 seconds. Add milk and shortening and continue to mix until no dry flour remains and dough has formed ball around hook, about 2 minutes longer. Increase speed to medium-low and knead until dough is smooth and pulls away from sides of bowl, 5 minutes.

**8.** Transfer dough to counter and knead briefly to form smooth ball. Grease medium bowl with ¼ teaspoon oil. Place dough in bowl and roll in oil to coat. Arrange dough in bowl seam side down and cover. Let rise until doubled in volume, about 1 hour.

**9.** While dough rises, cut sixteen 4-inch squares of parchment paper. Divide squares evenly between 2 rimmed baking sheets (8 squares per sheet). Place remaining 2 tablespoons oil in small bowl.

**10.** Transfer dough to counter. Press dough gently but firmly to expel all air. Knead briefly to form smooth ball. Using bench scraper or chef's knife, cut dough in half. Return half of dough to bowl and cover.

**11.** Roll remaining dough into 8-inch log. Cut log into 8 equal portions (about 1⅓ ounces each) and cover. Using your fingertips, pat 1 portion to ¼-inch-thick disk (keep remaining portions covered). Fold edges toward center and pinch to form ball. Turn ball pinched side down and round to form smooth sphere. Cover and repeat with remaining 7 portions.

**12.** Roll 1 dough ball into 6-inch oval. Transfer to small cutting board or plate and brush lightly with oil. Lightly brush chopstick with oil and lay it horizontally across center of oval. Fold oval in half over chopstick to form bun. Using chopstick, lift dough

## SHAPING THE BUNS

**1.** Cut, then pat into disks.

**2.** Pinch to form ball.

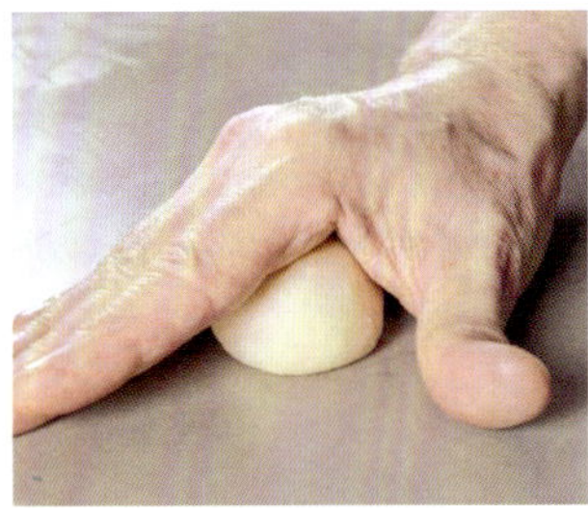

**3.** Round into smooth sphere.

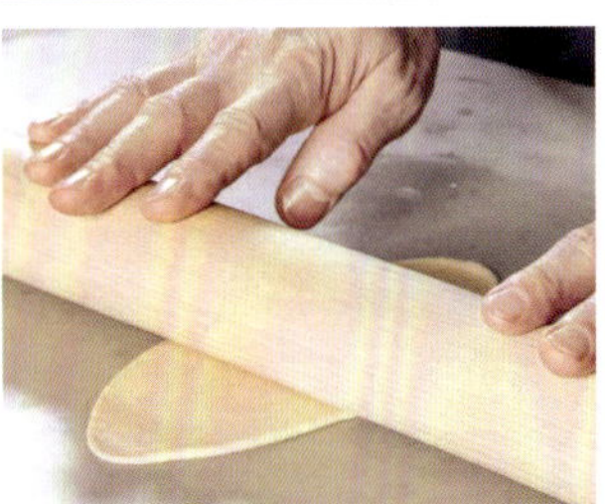

**4.** Roll into oval.

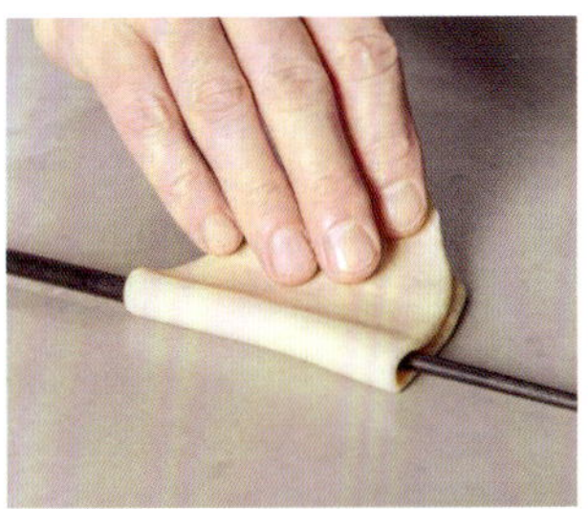

**5.** Fold over chopstick.

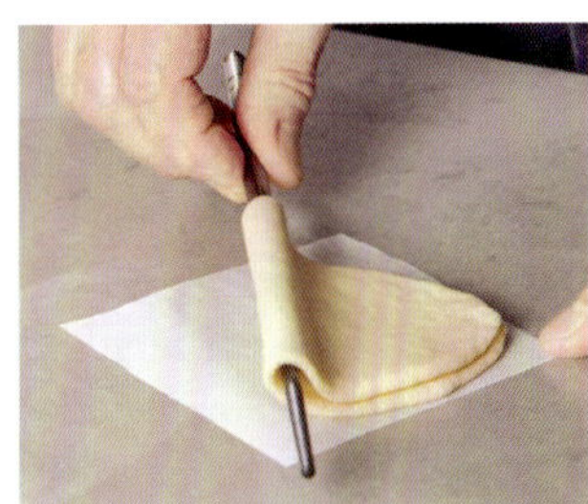

**6.** Transfer to parchment.

(it should drape evenly over both sides) and transfer to parchment square. Gently pull out chopstick, leaving bun folded. Repeat with remaining dough balls. Cover buns and let rise until slightly puffy, about 30 minutes. Repeat steps 11 and 12 with remaining dough, placing buns on second prepared sheet.

**13.** Meanwhile, bring 4 cups water to boil in 14-inch flat-bottomed wok or 12-inch skillet. Arrange first batch of buns, on parchment squares, in two 10-inch bamboo steamer baskets (4 buns per basket). Stack baskets and cover. Reduce heat to maintain simmer and set steamer in wok. Steam buns for 10 minutes (do not uncover, as buns might collapse; small wisps of steam should escape from beneath lid during cooking). Off heat, remove steamer from wok and let rest, covered, for 5 minutes. Transfer buns, still on parchment, to wire rack. Steam remaining buns.

**14.** To serve, place slice of pork inside bun. Garnish with seasoned daikon; hoisin-soy sauce; cilantro; scallions; peanuts; and Thai chiles, if using. Serve immediately.

**STORAGE AND REHEATING:** Bao can be kept covered at room temperature for up to 3 hours or refrigerated for up to 3 days. To serve, resteam (on parchment squares) for 2 to 3 minutes. Alternatively, bao can be frozen for up to 1 month. Arrange cooled bao (on parchment squares) in zipper-lock bag. To serve, steam from frozen (on parchment squares) until warmed through, 7 to 8 minutes.

## Simplified Cassoulet with Pork and Kielbasa

SERVES 8

**WHY THIS RECIPE WORKS** Comforting and delectable as it is, cassoulet takes patience to prepare. The recipe requires careful shopping for ingredients, and it can take three days to make. We wanted to see if there was a way to streamline the preparation of this dish without compromising its essential character. Instead of duck confit, we brined chicken thighs and cooked them in bacon fat to simulate the smoky flavor and moist texture of the confit. With our mock confit in place, we decided on flavorful, fatty blade-end pork roast for stewing, dried beans instead of canned (canned beans fell apart during cooking), and smoky kielbasa for the sausage (the classically correct French sausage wasn't readily available). We cooked the beans with onion and garlic to season them, then added crisp bacon to infuse them with a salty smokiness. Slowly simmering the dish on the stove, with a quick finish to brown the croutons, gave us a quicker and easier cassoulet. This dish can be made without brining the chicken, but we recommend that you do so. To ensure the most time-efficient preparation of the cassoulet, while the chicken is brining and the beans are simmering, prepare the remaining ingredients. Look for dried flageolet beans in specialty food stores. You can substitute a boneless Boston butt for the boneless blade-end pork loin roast. Additional salt is not necessary because the brined chicken adds a good deal of it, but if you skip the brining step, add salt to taste before serving.

**CHICKEN**

- 1 cup sugar
- ½ cup table salt
- 10 (5- to 6-ounce) bone-in, skin-on chicken thighs, trimmed and skin removed

**BEANS**

- 1 pound dried flageolet or great Northern beans, picked over and rinsed
- 1 medium onion, peeled, plus 1 small onion, minced
- 1 medium head garlic, outer papery skin removed and top ½ inch sliced off, plus 2 medium garlic cloves, minced or pressed through a garlic press (about 2 teaspoons)
- 1 teaspoon table salt
- Ground black pepper
- 6 ounces (about 6 slices) bacon, cut into ¼-inch pieces
- 1 (1-pound) boneless blade-end pork loin roast, trimmed and cut into 1-inch pieces
- 1 (14.5-ounce) can diced tomatoes, drained
- 1 tablespoon tomato paste
- 1 large sprig fresh thyme
- 1 bay leaf
- ¼ teaspoon ground cloves
- 3½ cups low-sodium chicken broth
- 1½ cups dry white wine
- ½ pound kielbasa, halved lengthwise and cut into ¼-inch slices

**CROUTONS**

- 6 slices high-quality white sandwich bread, cut into ½-inch cubes
- 3 tablespoons unsalted butter, melted

**1. FOR THE CHICKEN:** Dissolve the sugar and salt in 1 quart cold water in a gallon-size zipper-lock bag. Add the chicken, pressing out as much air as possible, seal the bag, and refrigerate for 1 hour. Remove the chicken from the brine, rinse, and pat dry with paper towels. Refrigerate until ready to use.

**2. FOR THE BEANS:** Bring the beans, the peeled onion, head of garlic, salt, ¼ teaspoon pepper, and 8 cups water to a boil in a large Dutch oven over high heat. Cover, reduce the heat to medium-low, and simmer until the beans are almost tender, 1¼ to 1½ hours. Drain the beans; discard the onion and garlic.

**3.** While the beans are cooking, fry the bacon in a large Dutch oven over medium heat until just beginning to crisp and most of the fat has rendered, 5 to 6 minutes. Using a slotted spoon, add half of the bacon to the pot with the beans; transfer the remaining bacon to a paper towel–lined plate and set aside. Increase the heat to medium-high and add half of the chicken, skinned side down; cook until lightly browned, 4 to 5 minutes. Flip the chicken thighs and cook until lightly browned on the second side, 3 to 4 minutes longer. Transfer the chicken to a large plate; repeat with the remaining thighs and set aside. Pour off all but 2 tablespoons fat from the pot. Return the pot to medium heat; add the pork pieces and cook, stirring occasionally, until lightly browned, about 5 minutes. Add the minced onion and cook, stirring occasionally, until softened, 3 to 4 minutes. Add the minced garlic, tomatoes, tomato paste, thyme, bay leaf, cloves, and pepper to taste and cook until fragrant, about 1 minute. Stir in the chicken broth and wine, scraping up any browned bits. Submerge the chicken in the pot, adding any accumulated juices, increase the heat to high, and bring to a boil. Reduce the heat to low, cover, and simmer for 40 minutes. Uncover and continue to simmer until the chicken and pork are fully tender, 20 to 30 minutes more.

**4. FOR THE CROUTONS:** While the chicken is simmering, adjust an oven rack to the lower-middle position and heat the oven to 400 degrees. Toss the bread cubes with the melted butter and spread out over a rimmed baking sheet. Bake until light golden brown and crisp, 8 to 12 minutes. Cool to room temperature; set aside (do not turn off the oven).

**5.** Gently stir the kielbasa, drained beans, and reserved bacon into the pot with the chicken and pork; remove and discard the thyme and bay leaf and season with pepper to taste. Sprinkle the croutons evenly over the surface and bake, uncovered, until the croutons are deep golden brown, about 15 minutes. Let stand for 10 minutes; serve.

## Italian Sausage with Grapes and Balsamic Vinegar

**SERVES** 4 to 6

**WHY THIS RECIPE WORKS** Italian sausage with grapes is a great example of the affinity that pork and fruit flavors have for one another. We wanted to pay homage to this simple Italian dish and highlight the attributes that make it so appealing. We used a combination of sautéing and steaming to produce sausages that were nicely browned but moist and juicy. Building the sauce in the same skillet, we cooked down seedless red grapes and thinly sliced onion until caramelized to create a sweet but complex sauce. White wine, in addition to balsamic vinegar, gave the dish acidity and complemented the grapes. Oregano and pepper contributed earthiness and a touch of spice, while a finish of fresh mint added brightness. Serve this dish with crusty bread and salad or over polenta for a heartier meal.

- 1 tablespoon vegetable oil
- 1½ pounds sweet Italian sausage
- 1 pound red seedless grapes, halved lengthwise (3 cups)
- 1 onion, halved and sliced thin (1½ cups)
- ¼ cup water
- ⅛ teaspoon table salt
- ¼ teaspoon pepper
- ¼ cup dry white wine
- 1 tablespoon chopped fresh oregano
- 2 teaspoons balsamic vinegar
- 2 tablespoons chopped fresh mint

**1.** Heat oil in 12-inch skillet over medium heat until shimmering. Arrange sausage links in pan and cook, turning once, until browned on both sides, about 5 minutes. Tilt skillet and carefully remove excess fat with paper towel. Distribute grapes and onion over and around sausages. Add water and immediately cover. Cook, turning sausages once, until they register between 160 and 165 degrees and onions and grapes have softened, about 10 minutes.

**2.** Transfer sausages to paper towel–lined plate and tent with aluminum foil. Return skillet to medium-high heat and stir salt and pepper into grape-onion mixture. Spread grape-onion mixture in even layer in skillet and cook without stirring until browned, 3 to 5 minutes. Continue to cook, stirring frequently, until mixture is well browned and grapes are soft but still retain their shape, 3 to 5 minutes longer. Reduce heat to medium, stir in wine and oregano, and cook, scraping up any browned bits, until wine is reduced by half, 30 to 60 seconds. Remove pan from heat and stir in vinegar.

**3.** Arrange sausages on serving platter and spoon grape-onion mixture over top. Sprinkle with mint and serve.

## Bangers with Onion Gravy

**SERVES 4 TO 6** SEASON 26

**WHY THIS RECIPE WORKS** Great bangers and mash with onion gravy, the iconic British pub staple, revolves around plump, well-browned links napped with an ultrasavory sauce. Searing the sausages ensured that the links developed attractive, flavorful browning; steaming cooked them through gently so that they were plump and juicy. Adding the onions (thin-sliced so that they softened quickly) to the pan to steam with the sausages jump-started their cooking. Continuing to sauté them after the sausage came out further softened them and caramelized their sugars; doing so also developed a deep, flavor-packed fond on the bottom of the skillet. Deglazing the pan with a highly seasoned beef broth captured the fond, and simmering the onions in the broth tenderized them more and concentrated the flavor of the gravy. A cornstarch slurry and butter, whisked in just before serving, gave the gravy the requisite viscosity, shine, and richness. If Cumberland sausage is unavailable, you can substitute bratwurst or any mildly spiced

fresh pork sausage. Marmite, a British yeast extract, is sold at most grocery stores. For the best-tasting gravy, cook the onions until a dark fond forms in the skillet. Serve the sausages and gravy with our Fastest, Easiest Mashed Potatoes (page 705).

- 1 tablespoon vegetable oil
- 1½ pounds Cumberland sausage (6 links)
- 2 onions, halved and sliced thin (3 cups)
- ½ cup plus 1 tablespoon water, divided
- 2½ cups beef broth
- 1 tablespoon Marmite
- 1 teaspoon dry mustard
- 1 teaspoon minced fresh thyme
- ½ teaspoon minced fresh rosemary
- 1¼ teaspoons sugar
- ½ teaspoon pepper
- ¼ teaspoon table salt
- 1 tablespoon cornstarch
- 2 tablespoons unsalted butter, cut into 2 pieces
- 1 teaspoon red wine vinegar
- 1 tablespoon minced fresh parsley

**1.** Heat oil in 12-inch skillet over medium heat until shimmering. Arrange sausages in pan and cook, turning once, until browned on 2 sides, about 5 minutes. Move sausages to 1 side of skillet. Add onions, evenly distributing around bottom of pan, and nestle sausages on top. Add ½ cup water and immediately cover. Cook, turning sausages once until they register between 160 and 165 degrees and onions have softened, about 10 minutes.

**2.** While sausages cook, whisk broth, Marmite, mustard, thyme, and rosemary in 4-cup liquid measuring cup until Marmite dissolves.

**3.** Transfer sausages to plate and tent with aluminum foil. Make sure onions are spread evenly; cook without stirring until beginning to brown, about 5 minutes (if onions have not browned, increase heat to medium-high). Continue to cook, stirring occasionally, until onions are tender and well browned, and dark fond forms on bottom of skillet, 3 to 5 minutes longer. Stir in sugar, pepper, and salt and cook for 1 minute.

**4.** Add broth mixture, increase heat to medium-high, and bring to boil. Cook, scraping up any browned bits from bottom and sides of skillet and stirring back into sauce, until sauce is slightly reduced, about 5 minutes. Combine cornstarch and remaining 1 tablespoon water in small bowl. Whisk cornstarch mixture into sauce and cook until sauce is glossy and has consistency of heavy cream, about 2 minutes.

**5.** Off heat, whisk in butter, 1 piece at a time. Stir in vinegar and season with salt and pepper to taste. Sprinkle with parsley and serve.

## Chorizo and Potato Tacos

**SERVES 4**

**WHY THIS RECIPE WORKS** Juicy, seasoned Mexican chorizo is the key to this classic taco, but it isn't available in some supermarkets, so we devised a quick method for making our own. We started by toasting ancho chili powder, paprika, and spices in oil to intensify their flavors, and then we mixed the spiced oil into preground pork along with some cider vinegar. We cooked the mixture in a skillet and added parboiled diced potatoes to absorb the flavorful juices as they finished cooking. Mashing some of the potatoes and mixing them into the filling made it more cohesive and easier to eat. A creamy, cooling puree of tomatillos, avocado, cilantro, and jalapeños complemented the richness and spiciness of the filling. If you can purchase a good quality Mexican-style chorizo, skip step 2 and cook the chorizo as directed in step 3. The raw onions complement the soft, rich taco filling, so we do not recommend omitting them.

**FILLING**

- 1 pound Yukon Gold potatoes, peeled and cut into ½-inch chunks
- Table salt and pepper
- 1 tablespoon ancho chili powder
- 1 tablespoon paprika
- 1½ teaspoons ground coriander
- 1½ teaspoon dried oregano
- ¼ teaspoon ground cinnamon
- Pinch cayenne pepper
- Pinch ground allspice
- 3 tablespoons vegetable oil
- 3 tablespoons apple cider vinegar
- 1½ teaspoons sugar
- 1 garlic clove, minced
- ½ pound ground pork

**SAUCE**

- 8 ounces tomatillos, husks and stems removed, rinsed well and dried, and cut into 1-inch pieces
- 1 avocado, halved, pitted, and cut into 1-inch pieces
- 1-2 jalapeño chile(s), stemmed, seeded, and chopped

¼ cup chopped fresh cilantro leaves and stems
1 tablespoon lime juice
1 garlic clove, minced
¾ teaspoon table salt

TACOS
12 (6-inch) corn tortillas, warmed
Finely chopped white onion
Fresh cilantro leaves
Lime wedges

1. **FOR THE FILLING:** Bring 4 cups water to boil in 12-inch nonstick skillet over high heat. Add potatoes and 1 teaspoon salt. Reduce heat to medium, cover, and cook until just tender, 3 to 5 minutes. Drain and set aside. Wipe out skillet.

2. Combine chili powder, paprika, coriander, oregano, cinnamon, cayenne, allspice, ¾ teaspoon salt, ½ teaspoon pepper, and oil in now-empty skillet. Cook over medium heat, stirring constantly, until mixture is bubbling and fragrant. Remove from heat and carefully stir in vinegar, sugar, and garlic (mixture will sputter). Let stand until steam subsides and skillet cools slightly, about 5 minutes. Add pork to skillet. Mash and mix with rubber spatula until spice mixture is evenly incorporated.

3. Return skillet to medium-high heat and cook pork mixture over medium-high heat, mashing and stirring until pork has broken into fine crumbles and juices are bubbling over entire surface of skillet, about 3 minutes.

4. Stir in potatoes, cover, and reduce heat to low. Cook until potatoes are fully softened and have soaked up most of the pork juices, 6 to 8 minutes, stirring halfway through cooking time. Remove skillet from heat and, using spatula, mash approximately one-eighth of potatoes. Stir mashed potatoes into mixture until lightly coated with juices. Cover and keep warm.

5. **FOR THE SAUCE:** Process all ingredients in food processor until smooth, about 1 minute, scraping down sides of bowl as needed. Transfer to serving bowl.

6. **FOR THE TACOS:** Spoon filling into center of each warm tortilla and serve with sauce, onion, cilantro, and lime wedges.

## Chiles en Nogada

SERVES 6 to 8 **SEASON 26**

**WHY THIS RECIPE WORKS** Chiles en nogada, widely considered to be Mexico's national dish, features picadillo-stuffed poblanos napped in creamy walnut sauce and bejeweled with pomegranate seeds. It's a patriotic feast prepared every September for the country's Independence Day festivities. We broiled the chiles until their skins blistered and then peeled them, slit them lengthwise, and hollowed them out for stuffing. The extravagant picadillo contains three distinct components: a tomato-based salsa, minced pork and/or beef, and seasonal fresh fruit and nuts. Broiling the salsa vegetables on the same baking sheet used to cook the chiles and then buzzing them in a blender until smooth with herbs, warm spices, and a little chipotle in adobo for smokiness was efficient. Stirring the fruit and nuts into the cooked meat—rather than simmering them along with it—ensured that their flavors melded while allowing the items to retain juiciness, chew, and crunch. The nogada came together quickly in the blender: Equal parts walnuts and Mexican crema made for a creamy base; chèvre added richness and complexity; and honey, dry sherry, and nutmeg provided subtle sweetness. Use poblanos that measure about 6 inches in length. For efficiency, broil the picadillo vegetables while the poblanos cool. When preparing the poblanos in step 2, it's helpful to have a bowl of water nearby for cleaning your hands and tools. Crème fraîche can be substituted for Mexican crema; if necessary, adjust its consistency with water to make it thick but pourable. The picadillo can be refrigerated for up to two days; microwave it until warm to the touch before stuffing the chiles. Serve this dish at room temperature.

CHILES
8 large poblano chiles (5 to 6 ounces each)

PICADILLO
2 plum tomatoes (4 ounces each)
8 ounces tomatillos, husks and stems removed, rinsed well and dried
½ large white onion, peeled and quartered through root end
1 jalapeño chile, stemmed
3 garlic cloves, unpeeled
2 teaspoons minced canned chipotle chile in adobo sauce
2 teaspoons chopped fresh oregano
1¾ teaspoons table salt, divided
1 teaspoon ground cinnamon
¼ teaspoon ground cloves
¼ teaspoon ground cumin
1 tablespoon lard or vegetable oil
1 pound ground pork
¼ cup dry sherry
1 Bosc pear, peeled, halved, cored, and cut into ¼-inch pieces (1 cup)
1 peach, peeled, halved, pitted, and cut into ¼-inch pieces (½ cup)
⅓ cup raisins
⅓ cup pitted green olives, sliced thin
⅓ cup pine nuts, toasted
¼ cup fresh parsley leaves plus ¼ cup chopped, divided
½ teaspoon grated lemon zest plus 2 tablespoons juice

NOGADA
1½ cups Mexican crema
1½ cups walnuts
2 ounces goat cheese
¼ cup water
1 tablespoon honey
1 teaspoon dry sherry
¼ teaspoon ground nutmeg
¼ teaspoon table salt
1 cup pomegranate seeds

**1. FOR THE CHILES:** Adjust oven rack 6 inches from broiler element and heat broiler. Line rimmed baking sheet with aluminum foil and spray with vegetable oil spray. Evenly space poblanos on prepared sheet and broil until skins just begin to blister on first side, 4 to 6 minutes. Flip poblanos and continue to broil until skins are just beginning to blister on second side, 3 to 5 minutes longer. Transfer poblanos to second rimmed baking sheet and let stand until cool enough to handle, about 10 minutes (do not wash foiled-lined sheet).

**2.** Using your fingers and paring knife, carefully peel poblanos and discard skins. Working with 1 poblano at a time, leaving stem intact and starting just beneath stem, cut slit lengthwise down 1 side of chile, stopping ½ inch before end. Using kitchen shears, cut away interior seed bulb and discard, then use spoon to scoop out any remaining seeds. Return cleaned poblanos to baking sheet.

**3. FOR THE PICADILLO:** While poblanos are cooling, place tomatoes, tomatillos, onion, jalapeño, and garlic on now-empty foil-lined sheet. Broil, turning every 4 minutes, until vegetables are lightly charred, 12 to 14 minutes. Let vegetables cool on sheet for 10 minutes.

**4.** Peel garlic, trim root end from onion, and remove seeds from jalapeño. Add garlic, onion, and jalapeño to blender along with tomatoes, tomatillos, chipotle, oregano, 1¼ teaspoons salt, cinnamon, cloves, and cumin, and process until smooth, 1 to 2 minutes.

**5.** Heat lard in 12-inch skillet over medium-high heat until shimmering. Add pork and remaining ½ teaspoon salt and, using heat-resistant spatula, mash to even layer that covers bottom of skillet. Cook pork without moving until lightly browned around edges, about 2 minutes. Continue to cook, stirring constantly and breaking up meat into ¼-inch pieces with side of spatula, until meat is almost cooked through but still slightly pink, about 2 minutes longer. Carefully add sherry and cook until reduced by half, 30 seconds. Add tomato mixture and bring to simmer. (Rinse out blender jar.) Adjust heat to maintain gentle simmer and cook, stirring occasionally, until sauce has thickened and spatula leaves trail that does not fill in when dragged through sauce, 10 to 12 minutes.

**6.** Stir in pear, peach, raisins, olives, pine nuts, chopped parsley, lemon zest, and juice. Remove skillet from heat and let stand until mixture has cooled and fruit has softened, about 10 minutes (picadillo should be moist, without large pools of liquid remaining). Season with salt to taste.

**7. FOR THE NOGADA:** Add all ingredients to blender and process until smooth, about 2 minutes, scraping down sides of blender jar as needed.

**8.** Using spoon, carefully fill each poblano with about ¾ cup of picadillo, gently pressing filling into cavity so poblano is full but not bursting. Place filled poblanos on platter or individual plates. Spoon about ½ cup sauce over each poblano to cover entirely. Sprinkle with parsley leaves and pomegranate seeds. Serve.

## Shīzi Tóu (Lion's Head Meatballs)

**SERVES** 4 to 6

**WHY THIS RECIPE WORKS** Shīzi tóu, giant lion's head meatballs, are tender-yet-springy pork meatballs from eastern China. For a streamlined approach, we started with commercial ground pork and treated the meat with a baking soda solution before cooking, which helped it retain juices over the relatively long cooking time. We lightly seasoned the meat for a well-rounded savory flavor that still tasted distinctly porky. Beating the pork mixture in a stand mixer caused its sticky proteins to link up into a strong network that trapped fat and moisture, resulting in a texture that was resilient and unctuous. Braising the meatballs in the oven broke down the pork's collagen so that the meatballs were tender. Adding the cabbage for the last 30 minutes of cooking allowed it to soften and absorb the flavor of the broth without turning mushy. Soaking rice vermicelli in just-boiled water softened but did not overcook them. Fully cooked ground pork may retain a slightly pink hue. Don't be concerned if the meatballs crack while cooking.

- ¾ teaspoon baking soda
- ½ teaspoon table salt
- 2 pounds ground pork
- 1 large egg, lightly beaten
- 2 scallions, white parts minced, green parts sliced thin
- 2 tablespoons soy sauce
- 2 tablespoons Shaoxing wine
- 4 teaspoons sugar
- 2 teaspoons grated fresh ginger
- ½ teaspoon white pepper
- 4 cups chicken broth
- 1 small head napa cabbage (1½ pounds), quartered lengthwise, cored, and cut crosswise into 2-inch pieces
- 4 ounces rice vermicelli

**1.** Adjust oven rack to lower-middle position and heat oven to 325 degrees. Whisk baking soda, salt, and 2 tablespoons water together in bowl of stand mixer. Add pork to baking soda mixture and toss to combine. Add egg, scallion whites, soy sauce, Shaoxing wine, sugar, ginger, and white pepper. Fit stand mixer with paddle and beat on medium speed until mixture is well combined and has stiffened and started to pull away from sides of bowl and pork has slightly lightened in color, 45 to 60 seconds. Using your wet hands, form about ½ cup (4½ ounces) pork mixture into 3-inch round meatball; repeat with remaining mixture to form 8 meatballs.

**2.** Bring broth to boil in large Dutch oven over high heat. Off heat, carefully arrange meatballs in pot (seven around perimeter and one in center; meatballs will not be totally submerged). Cover pot, transfer to oven, and cook for 1 hour.

**3.** Transfer meatballs to large plate. Add cabbage to pot in even layer and arrange meatballs over cabbage, paler side up. Cover, return pot to oven, and continue to cook until meatballs are lightly browned and cabbage is softened, about 30 minutes longer.

**4.** While meatballs and cabbage cook, bring 4 quarts water to boil in large pot. Off heat, add vermicelli and let sit, stirring occasionally, until vermicelli is fully tender, 10 to 15 minutes. Drain, rinse with cold water, drain again, and distribute evenly among 4 to 6 large soup bowls.

**5.** Ladle meatballs, cabbage, and broth into bowls of noodles. Sprinkle with scallion greens and serve.

## Quick Taiwanese Pork Rice

SERVES 4 SEASON 26

WHY THIS RECIPE WORKS Our simplified Taiwanese lu rou fan, or pork rice, uses ground pork instead of pork belly to create a rich, savory meat sauce in just 30 minutes instead of the usual two hours. We simmered ground pork with several flavor-packed ingredients, including dried shiitake mushrooms and the liquid they were rehydrated in, fried shallots, two types of soy sauce, and five-spice powder, all of which gave the meat a deep, complex flavor in a short amount of time. Dark soy sauce lent the pork sauce a sweet roastiness and a dark color. If you can't find Shaoxing wine, you can use dry sherry. Serve with steamed rice and top with soft-cooked eggs, steamed vegetables, fried shallots, and scallions, if desired.

- 2 cups hot water
- ¼ ounce dried shiitake mushrooms, rinsed
- 2 tablespoons vegetable oil, divided
- 2 garlic cloves, minced
- ½ teaspoon grated fresh ginger
- 1 pound ground pork
- Pinch table salt
- 2 tablespoons Shaoxing wine
- 2 cups chicken broth
- 1 tablespoon soy sauce
- 1 tablespoon dark soy sauce
- 1 tablespoon packed brown sugar
- ¼ teaspoon five-spice powder
- ½ cup fried shallots
- 4 cups cooked white rice

Soft-cooked eggs
Steamed vegetables
Fried shallots
Thinly sliced scallions

**1.** Combine hot water and mushrooms in bowl. Let sit until mushrooms are tender, about 15 minutes. Drain mushrooms, reserving liquid, and discard mushroom stems. Finely chop mushrooms.

**2.** Heat 1 tablespoon oil in 12-inch nonstick skillet over medium-high heat until shimmering. Add mushrooms, reduce heat to medium, and cook until golden brown, 1 to 2 minutes, stirring constantly. Add garlic and ginger and cook until fragrant, about 1 minute, stirring constantly. Add remaining 1 tablespoon oil, pork, and salt to skillet and cook over medium-high heat until browned, breaking up meat into small pieces, 5 to 7 minutes.

**3.** Add Shaoxing wine, scraping up any browned bits, then stir in broth, soy sauce, dark soy sauce, sugar, five-spice powder, and ¼ cup reserved mushroom soaking liquid. Bring to boil and add fried shallots. Cover skillet, reduce heat to medium, and simmer vigorously, until broth is mostly absorbed and pork is tender, about 20 minutes. (If sauce reduces too quickly, add more water, 1 tablespoon at a time.)

**4.** Serve pork sauce with steamed rice and desired toppings.

## Roast Fresh Ham

SERVES 8 to 10

WHY THIS RECIPE WORKS Some people think there's no such thing as "fresh" ham. There is—and we wanted to find the best way to cook it for a roasted ham that boasted rich, moist meat and crackling crisp skin. Fresh hams are large, so they're usually cut in half and sold as either the sirloin or the shank end; we chose the latter for its ease of carving. But even cut into these smaller roasts, fresh ham needs a long time in the oven, so the danger is drying out the meat. To prevent this, we brined the ham overnight. A garlic and herb rub added further flavor. We positioned the ham wide cut side down on a rack in a roasting pan; the rack allowed the heat to circulate all around the ham for more even cooking. A brief roasting at a high temperature followed by longer cooking at a lower temperature produced crunchy skin and succulent meat. The crowning touch was a sweet glaze, which we brushed on while the meat roasted. Fresh ham comes from the pig's hind leg. Because a whole leg is quite large, it is usually cut into two sections. The sirloin, or butt, end is harder to carve than our favorite, the shank end. If you don't have room in your refrigerator, brine the ham in an insulated cooler or a small plastic garbage can; add five or six freezer packs to the brine to keep it well cooled.

**ROAST**

1 (6- to 8-pound) bone-in fresh half ham with skin, preferably shank end, rinsed

**BRINE**

3 cups packed brown sugar
2 cups table salt
2 heads garlic, cloves separated, lightly crushed and peeled
10 bay leaves
½ cup black peppercorns, crushed

**GARLIC AND HERB RUB**

1 cup fresh sage leaves
½ cup parsley leaves
¼ cup extra-virgin olive oil
8 garlic cloves, peeled
½ tablespoon pepper
1½ teaspoons table salt

**GLAZE**

1 recipe glaze (recipes follow)

**1. FOR THE ROAST:** Using sharp knife, cut through roast's skin and fat cap in 1-inch crosshatch pattern, being careful not to cut into meat.

**2. FOR THE BRINE:** In large container, dissolve sugar and 2 cups salt in 2 gallons cold water. Add garlic, bay leaves, and crushed peppercorns. Submerge ham in brine and refrigerate for 8 to 24 hours.

**3.** Set large disposable aluminum roasting pan on rimmed baking sheet for extra support; set wire rack in roasting pan. Remove ham from brine; rinse under cold water and dry thoroughly with paper towels. Place ham, wide cut side down, on rack. (If using sirloin end, place ham skin side up.) Let ham stand uncovered at room temperature for 1 hour.

**4. FOR THE RUB:** Meanwhile, adjust oven rack to lowest position and heat oven to 500 degrees. Process sage, parsley, oil, garlic, pepper, and salt in food processor until mixture forms smooth paste, about 30 seconds. Rub all sides of ham with paste.

**5.** Roast ham at 500 degrees for 20 minutes. Reduce oven temperature to 350 degrees and continue to roast, brushing ham with glaze every 45 minutes, until center of ham registers 145 to 150 degrees, about 2½ hours longer. Remove from oven; tent ham with aluminum foil; and let stand until center of ham registers 155 to 160 degrees, 30 to 40 minutes. Carve and serve.

## Coca-Cola Glaze with Lime and Jalapeño

**MAKES** 1⅓ cups

1 cup Coca-Cola
¼ cup lime juice (2 limes)
2 cups packed brown sugar
2 jalapeño chiles, cut crosswise into ¼-inch-thick slices

Bring Coca-Cola, lime juice, sugar, and jalapeños to boil in small nonreactive saucepan over high heat; reduce heat to medium-low and simmer until syrupy and reduced to about 1⅓ cups, 5 to 7 minutes. (Glaze will thicken as it cools between bastings; cook over medium heat for about 1 minute, stirring once or twice, before using.)

## Glazed Spiral-Sliced Ham

**SERVES** 12 to 14

**WHY THIS RECIPE WORKS** We revisited the way to cook a cured ham to get moist meat accompanied by a glaze that didn't overwhelm it. We have found that bone-in hams, labeled "with natural juices," have the best flavor, and spiral-sliced ones make carving a cinch. We knew that the longer the ham spent in the oven, the greater the chances of dried-out meat, so we focused on reducing the cooking time. First we soaked the ham in hot water so that it wouldn't be ice-cold when it went into the oven; this step saved a full hour. Roasting the ham in an oven bag further reduced the cooking time, and the bag had the added advantage of holding in moisture. We made a fruit-based glaze with just a touch of sweetness to complement the ham. You can bypass the 90-minute soaking time, but the heating time will increase to 18 to 20 minutes per pound for a cold ham. If there is a tear or hole in the ham's inner covering, wrap the ham in several layers of plastic wrap before soaking it in hot water. Instead of using the plastic oven bag, the ham may be placed cut side down in the roasting pan and covered tightly with foil, but you will need to add 3 to 4 minutes per pound to the heating time. If using an oven bag, be sure to cut slits in the bag so it does not burst.

1 (7- to 10-pound) spiral-sliced bone-in half ham
1 large plastic oven bag
1 recipe glaze (recipes follow)

**1.** Leaving the ham's inner plastic or foil covering intact, place the ham in a large container and cover with hot tap water; set aside for 45 minutes. Drain and cover again with hot tap water; set aside for another 45 minutes.

**2.** Adjust an oven rack to the lowest position and heat the oven to 250 degrees. Unwrap the ham; remove and discard the plastic disk covering the bone. Place the ham in the oven bag. Gather the top of the bag tightly so the bag fits snugly around the ham, tie the bag, and trim the excess plastic. Set the ham, cut side down, in a large roasting pan and cut four slits in the top of the bag with a paring knife.

**3.** Bake the ham until the center registers 100 degrees on an instant-read thermometer, 1 to 1½ hours (about 10 minutes per pound).

**4.** Remove the ham from the oven and increase the oven temperature to 350 degrees. Cut open the oven bag and roll back the sides to expose the ham. Brush the ham with

one-third of the glaze and return to the oven until the glaze becomes sticky, about 10 minutes (if the glaze is too thick to brush, return it to the heat to loosen).

**5.** Remove the ham from the oven, transfer it to a carving board, and brush the entire ham with another third of the glaze. Let the ham rest, loosely tented with foil, for 15 minutes. While the ham rests, heat the remaining third of the glaze with 4 to 6 tablespoons of the ham juices until it forms a thick but fluid sauce. Carve and serve the ham, passing the sauce at the table.

### Maple-Orange Glaze

**MAKES** 1 cup

- ¾ cup maple syrup
- ½ cup orange marmalade
- 2 tablespoons unsalted butter
- 1 tablespoon Dijon mustard
- 1 teaspoon ground black pepper
- ¼ teaspoon ground cinnamon

Combine all the ingredients in a small saucepan. Cook over medium heat, stirring occasionally, until the mixture is thick, syrupy, and reduced to 1 cup, 5 to 10 minutes; set aside.

## Spiral-Sliced Ham with Cider-Vinegar Caramel

**SERVES** 12 to 14

**WHY THIS RECIPE WORKS** Many recipes for spiral ham produce meat that's parched and leathery on the exterior with a glaze that flavors only the outermost edge. Our ham is moist and juicy—and every bite benefits from the flavors of the glaze. For moist meat throughout, we placed our ham in an oven bag, which traps juices and creates a moist environment that cooks it in less time than the dry air of the oven would, and reheated it in a 250-degree oven. We then brushed it with a sweet-tart caramel glaze. Since the sugar in the mixture was already caramelized, the glaze needed only a few minutes in a hot oven to acquire a deep mahogany sheen. Finally, we thinned some of the remaining caramel with ham juices to create a sauce to accompany to the smoky, salty ham. We recommend a shank-end ham because the bone configuration makes it easier to carve; look for a half ham with a tapered, pointed end. We developed this recipe using Turkey Size Reynolds Kitchens Oven Bags.

- 1 (7- to 10-pound) spiral-sliced, bone-in half ham, preferably shank end
- 1 large oven bag
- 1¼ cups sugar
- ½ cup water
- 3 tablespoons light corn syrup
- 1¼ cups cider vinegar
- ½ teaspoon pepper
- ¼ teaspoon five-spice powder

**1.** Adjust oven rack to lower-middle position and heat oven to 250 degrees. Line rimmed baking sheet with aluminum foil and set wire rack in sheet. Unwrap ham and, if necessary, discard plastic disk covering bone. Place ham cut side down in oven bag. Insert temperature probe (if using) through top of ham into center. Tie bag shut and place ham cut side down on prepared wire rack. Bake until center registers 110 degrees, 3½ to 4½ hours.

**2.** Bring sugar, water, and corn syrup to boil in large heavy-bottomed saucepan over medium-high heat. Cook, without stirring, until mixture is straw-colored, 6 to 8 minutes. While sugar mixture cooks, microwave vinegar in bowl until steaming, about 90 seconds; set aside. Once sugar mixture is straw-colored, reduce heat to low and continue to cook, swirling saucepan occasionally, until mixture is dark amber–colored and just smoking and registers 360 to 370 degrees, 2 to 5 minutes longer. Off heat, add warm vinegar a little at a time, whisking after each addition (some caramel may harden but will melt as sauce continues to cook). When bubbling subsides, add pepper and five-spice powder. Cook over medium-high heat, stirring occasionally, until reduced to 1⅓ cups, 5 to 7 minutes.

**3.** Remove sheet from oven and increase oven temperature to 450 degrees. Once oven reaches temperature, remove ham from bag and transfer to carving board. Reserve ¼ cup juices from bag; discard bag and remaining juices. Remove wire rack, leaving foil in place, and return ham to sheet, cut side down. Brush ham evenly with ⅓ cup caramel. Transfer sheet to oven and cook until glaze is bubbling and starting to brown in places, 5 to 7 minutes. Add reserved juices to remaining 1 cup caramel and whisk to combine.

**4.** Slice ham and serve, passing caramel sauce separately.

## Kimchi Bokkeumbap (Kimchi Fried Rice)

**SERVES** 4 to 6

**WHY THIS RECIPE WORKS** Iconic, quick-cooking Korean comfort food, kimchi bokkeumbap is typically made with leftover cooked short-grain rice and well-fermented kimchi, but from there the seasonings and additions vary widely from cook to cook. We started by stir-frying some aromatics (chopped onion and sliced scallions) with chopped ham—a popular addition that we liked for its smoky flavor and pleasantly springy texture. Then we added lots of chopped cabbage kimchi along with some of its savory, punchy juice and a little water and seasoned it with soy sauce, toasted sesame oil, and gochujang to add savoriness, rich nuttiness, and a little more heat. We simmered the cabbage leaves so that they softened a bit; stirred in the rice and cooked the mixture until the liquid had been absorbed; and topped the rice with small strips of gim, sesame seeds, and scallion greens. This recipe works best with day-old rice; alternatively, cook your rice 2 hours ahead, spread it on a rimmed baking sheet, and let it cool completely before chilling it for 30 minutes. Plain pretoasted seaweed snacks can be substituted for the gim (seaweed paper); omit the toasting in step 1. You'll need at least a 16-ounce jar of kimchi; if it doesn't yield ¼ cup of juice, make up the difference with water. If using soft, well-aged kimchi, omit the water and reduce the cooking time at the end of step 2 to 2 minutes. We developed this recipe with a 12-inch nonstick skillet, but a well-seasoned carbon-steel skillet or 14-inch flat-bottomed wok can be used instead. If desired, top each portion of rice with a fried egg.

- 1 (8-inch square) sheet gim
- 2 tablespoons vegetable oil, divided
- 2 (¼-inch-thick) slices deli ham, cut into ¼-inch pieces (about 4 ounces)
- 1 large onion, chopped
- 6 scallions, white and green parts separated and sliced thin on bias
- 1¼ cups cabbage kimchi, drained with ¼ cup juice reserved, cut into ¼-inch strips
- ¼ cup water
- 4 teaspoons soy sauce
- 4 teaspoons gochujang
- ½ teaspoon pepper
- 3 cups cooked short-grain white rice
- 4 teaspoons toasted sesame oil
- 1 tablespoon sesame seeds, toasted

**1.** Grip gim with tongs and hold 2 inches above low flame on gas burner. Toast gim, turning every 3 to 5 seconds, until gim is aromatic and shrinks slightly, about 20 seconds. (If you do not have a gas stove, toast gim on rimmed baking sheet in 275-degree oven until gim is aromatic and shrinks slightly, 20 to 25 minutes, flipping gim halfway through toasting.) Using kitchen shears, cut gim into four 2-inch-wide strips. Stack strips and cut crosswise into thin strips.

**2.** Heat 1 tablespoon vegetable oil in 12-inch nonstick skillet over medium-high heat until shimmering. Add ham, onion, and scallion whites and cook, stirring frequently, until onion is softened and ham is beginning to brown at edges, 6 to 8 minutes. Stir in kimchi and reserved juice, water, soy sauce, gochujang, and pepper. Cook, stirring occasionally, until kimchi turns soft and translucent, 4 to 6 minutes.

**3.** Add rice; reduce heat to medium-low; and cook, stirring and folding constantly until mixture is evenly coated, about 3 minutes. Stir in sesame oil and remaining 1 tablespoon vegetable oil. Increase heat to medium-high and cook, stirring occasionally, until mixture begins to stick to skillet, about 4 minutes. Transfer to serving bowl. Sprinkle with sesame seeds, scallion greens, and gim and serve.

## Cuban-Style Black Beans and Rice

**SERVES** 6 to 8

**WHY THIS RECIPE WORKS** Beans and rice is a familiar combination the world over, but Cuban black beans and rice is unique in that the rice is cooked in the inky concentrated liquid left over from cooking the beans, which renders the grains just as flavorful. We expanded on this method, simmering a portion of the sofrito (the trio of garlic, bell pepper, and onion) with our beans to infuse them with flavor and then using the liquid to cook our rice and beans. Lightly browning the remaining sofrito vegetables and spices with rendered salt pork added complex, meaty flavor, and finishing the dish in the oven eliminated the crusty bottom that can form when the dish is cooked on the stove. It is important to use lean—not fatty—salt pork. If you can't find it, substitute six slices of bacon. If using bacon, decrease the cooking time in step 4 to 8 minutes. You will need a Dutch oven with a tight-fitting lid for this recipe. For a vegetarian version of this recipe, use water instead of chicken broth, omit the salt pork, add 1 tablespoon tomato paste with the vegetables in step 4, and increase the amount of salt in step 5 to 1½ teaspoons.

- 1½ tablespoons table salt for soaking beans
- 1 cup dried black beans, picked over and rinsed
- 2 cups chicken broth
- 2 large green bell peppers, stemmed, seeded, and halved, divided
- 1 large onion, halved crosswise, root end left intact, divided
- 1 garlic head (5 cloves minced, remaining head halved crosswise with skin left intact)
- 2 bay leaves
- 1½ teaspoons table salt, divided
- 1½ cups long-grain white rice
- 2 tablespoons extra-virgin olive oil, divided
- 6 ounces lean salt pork, cut into ¼-inch pieces
- 4 teaspoons ground cumin
- 1 tablespoon minced fresh oregano
- 2 tablespoons red wine vinegar
- 2 scallions, sliced thin
- Lime wedges

**1.** Dissolve 1½ tablespoons salt in 2 quarts cold water in large bowl or container. Add beans and soak at room temperature for at least 8 hours or up to 24 hours. Drain and rinse well.

**2.** In Dutch oven, stir together drained beans, broth, 2 cups water, 1 bell pepper half, 1 onion half (with root end), halved garlic head, bay leaves, and 1 teaspoon salt. Bring to simmer over medium-high heat, cover, and reduce heat to low. Cook until beans are just soft, 30 to 35 minutes. Using tongs, discard pepper, onion, garlic, and bay leaves. Drain beans in colander set over large bowl, reserving 2½ cups bean cooking liquid. (If you don't have enough bean cooking liquid, add water to equal 2½ cups.) Do not wash Dutch oven.

**3.** Adjust oven rack to middle position and heat oven to 350 degrees. Place rice in large fine-mesh strainer and rinse under cold running water until water runs clear, about 1½ minutes. Shake strainer vigorously to remove all excess water; set rice aside. Cut remaining peppers and onion into 2-inch pieces and process in food processor until broken into rough ¼-inch pieces, about 8 pulses, scraping down bowl as necessary; set vegetables aside.

**4.** In now-empty Dutch oven, heat 1 tablespoon oil and salt pork over medium-low heat and cook, stirring frequently, until lightly browned and rendered, 15 to 20 minutes. Add remaining 1 tablespoon oil, chopped bell peppers and onion, cumin, and oregano. Increase heat to medium and continue to cook, stirring frequently, until vegetables are softened and beginning to brown, 10 to 15 minutes longer. Add minced garlic and cook, stirring constantly, until fragrant, about 1 minute. Add rice and stir to coat, about 30 seconds.

**5.** Stir in beans, reserved bean cooking liquid, vinegar, and remaining ½ teaspoon salt. Increase heat to medium-high and bring to simmer. Cover and transfer to oven. Cook until liquid is absorbed and rice is tender, about 30 minutes. Fluff with fork and let rest, uncovered, for 5 minutes. Serve, passing scallions and lime wedges separately.

## Red Beans and Rice

**SERVES** 6 to 8

**WHY THIS RECIPE WORKS** To replicate the traditional New Orleans red beans and rice recipe using ingredients easily found in supermarkets, we made some simple substitutions: small red beans for Camellia-brand dried red beans and bacon for the tasso. Fine-tuning the proportions of sautéed green peppers, onions, and celery gave the recipe balance, and the right ratio of chicken broth to water added complexity to the dish. If you are pressed for time you can "quick-brine" your beans. In step 1, combine the salt, water, and beans in a large Dutch oven and bring to a boil over high heat. Remove the pot from the heat, cover, and let stand 1 hour. Drain and rinse the beans and proceed with the recipe. If you can't find andouille sausage, substitute kielbasa. If you want to use tasso, omit the bacon and paprika in step 2 and cook 4 ounces finely chopped tasso in 2 teaspoons vegetable oil until lightly browned, 4 to 6 minutes, then proceed. It is important to maintain a vigorous simmer in step 2. The beans can be cooled, covered tightly, and refrigerated for up to 2 days. To reheat, add enough water to the beans to thin them slightly.

- Table salt and pepper
- 1 pound (about 2 cups) dried small red beans, picked over and rinsed
- 4 slices bacon, chopped fine
- 1 onion, chopped fine
- 1 small green bell pepper, stemmed, seeded and chopped fine
- 1 celery rib, chopped fine
- 3 garlic cloves, minced
- 1 teaspoon minced fresh thyme
- 1 teaspoon sweet paprika
- 2 bay leaves
- ¼ teaspoon cayenne pepper
- 3 cups chicken broth
- 6 cups water
- 8 ounces andouille sausage, halved lengthwise and cut into ¼-inch slices
- 5 cups cooked white rice
- 1 teaspoon red wine vinegar, plus extra for seasoning
- 3 scallions, sliced thin
- Hot sauce (optional)

**1.** Dissolve 3 tablespoons salt in 4 quarts cold water in large container. Add beans and soak at room temperature at least 8 hours or up to 24 hours. Drain and rinse well.

**2.** Heat bacon in Dutch oven over medium heat, stirring occasionally, until browned and almost fully rendered, 5 to 8 minutes. Add onion, bell pepper, and celery; cook, stirring frequently, until vegetables are softened, 6 to 7 minutes. Stir in garlic, thyme, paprika, bay leaves, cayenne pepper, and ¼ teaspoon black pepper; cook until fragrant, about 30 seconds. Stir in beans, broth, and water, and bring to boil over high heat. Reduce heat and vigorously simmer, stirring occasionally, until beans are just soft and liquid begins to thicken, 45 to 60 minutes.

**3.** Stir in sausage and 1 teaspoon vinegar and cook until liquid is thick and beans are fully tender and creamy, about 30 minutes. Season with salt, pepper, and additional vinegar to taste. Serve over rice, sprinkling with scallions and passing hot sauce separately, if using.

## Paniscia (Red Wine Risotto with Beans)

**SERVES** 6 to 8

**WHY THIS RECIPE WORKS** This deeply flavored, hearty winter specialty from northern Italy is essentially a merger of two dishes: risotto—flavored with red wine and cured meats—and a minestrone-like soup. Typically, paniscia is made by first preparing the soup and then slowly incorporating it into the rice in several additions as the risotto cooks. To simplify its preparation, we departed from the established risotto method by adding nearly all of the liquid at the outset and covering the pot to cook the rice. This had the benefit of more evenly distributing the heat, so every grain of rice became tender with just the occasional stir, and the dish was now a one-pot affair to boot. We used mild Italian-style salami in place of the traditional salam d'la duja (which can be hard to source in the United States), sautéing it with the Arborio rice before adding red wine and broth. Near the end of cooking, we added chopped cabbage and creamy canned pinto beans. We finished the dish with butter for even more richness and red wine vinegar to brighten the meaty flavors. We prefer to use a smaller, individually packaged, dry Italian-style salami such as Genoa or soppressata, but unsliced deli salami can be used.

- 2 tablespoons extra-virgin olive oil
- 2 ounces pancetta, chopped fine
- 1 onion, chopped fine
- 1 carrot, chopped fine
- 1 celery rib, chopped fine
- ½ teaspoon table salt
- ¼ teaspoon pepper
- 6 garlic cloves, minced
- 1½ cups Arborio rice
- 6 ounces salami, cut into ¼-inch dice
- 2 tablespoons tomato paste
- 1 cup dry red wine
- 4 cups chicken broth
- 1 small head green cabbage, halved, cored, and cut into ½-inch pieces (4 cups)
- 1 (15-ounce) can pinto beans, rinsed
- 1 cup hot water, plus extra as needed
- 1 ounce Parmesan cheese, grated (½ cup), plus extra for serving
- 2 tablespoons unsalted butter
- 2 teaspoons red wine vinegar
- 2 tablespoons chopped fresh parsley

**1.** Heat oil in Dutch oven over medium heat until shimmering. Add pancetta and cook, stirring occasionally, until beginning to brown, 3 to 5 minutes. Add onion, carrot, celery, salt, and pepper and cook, stirring occasionally, until vegetables are softened, 5 to 7 minutes. Add garlic and cook until fragrant, 30 seconds. Add rice and salami and cook, stirring frequently, until rice grains are translucent around edges, about 3 minutes.

**2.** Stir in tomato paste and cook until fragrant, about 1 minute. Add wine and cook, stirring constantly, until fully absorbed, 2 to 3 minutes. Stir in broth; reduce heat to medium-low; cover; and simmer for 10 minutes, stirring halfway through simmering.

**3.** Stir in cabbage and continue to cook, covered, until almost all liquid has been absorbed and rice is just al dente, 6 to 9 minutes longer.

**4.** Add beans and hot water and stir gently and constantly until risotto is creamy, about 3 minutes. Remove from heat, cover, and let stand for 5 minutes. Stir in Parmesan and butter. If desired, add up to 1 cup extra hot water to create fluid, pourable consistency. Stir in vinegar and season with salt and pepper to taste. Sprinkle with parsley and serve immediately, passing extra Parmesan separately.

## Tartiflette (French Potato and Cheese Gratin)

**SERVES** 4

**WHY THIS RECIPE WORKS** Hailing from the Haute-Savoie region of the French Alps, tartiflette is a luscious potato gratin with smoked bacon and nutty Reblochon cheese. For the potatoes, we used half-moon slices of Yukon Golds since they maintained their shape well and cooked evenly. We left their skins on and steamed them to maximize their earthy taste. Chopped thick-cut bacon delivered the requisite meaty smokiness, and a modest amount of cream contributed silkiness. Reblochon isn't available in the United States due to restrictions on raw-milk cheeses, so we evoked its flavor with a ripe, semisoft cow's-milk cheese such as Camembert or Taleggio. Other alternatives include Pont l'Évêque, Delice du Jura, and Vacherin Mont d'Or or domestic cheeses such as Jasper Hill's Harbison and Winnimere. If your cheese is very runny, chill it before cutting it and hold the pieces in the freezer until you're ready to use them. A 2-quart baking dish of any dimensions can be used in place of the 8-inch square baking dish. Serve the tartiflette with bread and a crisp green salad.

8 ounces ripe Camembert or Taleggio cheese, rind left on
1¾ pounds Yukon Gold potatoes, unpeeled, halved lengthwise and sliced into ¼-inch half-moons
6 slices thick-cut bacon, cut into ½-inch pieces
1 large onion, chopped fine
1¼ teaspoons table salt, divided
2½ teaspoons minced fresh thyme
2 garlic cloves, minced
½ cup dry white wine
½ cup heavy cream
¼ teaspoon pepper
Crème fraîche (optional)

**1.** Adjust oven rack to middle position and heat oven to 400 degrees. Line large plate with paper towels. Grease 8-inch square baking dish. Cut Camembert in half horizontally to create 2 pieces of equal thickness. Cut each half into ¾-inch pieces.

**2.** Place steamer basket in large saucepan. Add water to barely reach bottom of steamer and bring to boil over high heat. Add potatoes, cover, and reduce heat to medium (small wisps of steam should escape from beneath lid). Cook until potatoes are just cooked through and tip of paring knife inserted into potatoes meets little resistance, 15 to 17 minutes. Leaving potatoes in steamer, remove steamer from saucepan; set aside and let cool slightly, at least 10 minutes.

**3.** While potatoes cool, cook bacon in 12-inch skillet over medium heat, stirring occasionally, until browned and chewy-crisp, 4 to 6 minutes. Using slotted spoon, transfer bacon to prepared plate; pour off all but 2 tablespoons bacon fat. Add onion and ½ teaspoon salt to fat left in skillet and cook over medium heat, stirring occasionally, until onion is softened and beginning to brown, about 7 minutes. Add thyme and garlic and continue to cook, stirring occasionally, until fragrant, about 2 minutes longer. Add wine and cook until reduced by half, about 2 minutes. Off heat, stir in cream, pepper, and remaining ¾ teaspoon salt.

**4.** Add potatoes to skillet and stir gently to coat with onion mixture. Transfer half of potato mixture to prepared dish and spread into even layer. Top evenly with half of bacon. Add remaining potatoes and top evenly with remaining bacon. Arrange Camembert, rind side up, in even layer on top. Bake until bubbling and lightly browned, about 20 minutes. Let cool for 10 minutes before serving. Top each serving with spoonful of crème fraîche, if using.

## Roast Rack of Lamb with Roasted Red Pepper Relish

**SERVES** 4 to 6

**WHY THIS RECIPE WORKS** When you really think about it, roasting a rack of lamb is a simple process, but there's a fine line between a showstopper and a dried-out disappointment. For a rack that would make us proud at our next fête, the seasoning needed to be spot-on, the meat had to be juicy, and we'd need a bold relish to serve alongside it. Starting with the lamb, carving a shallow cross-hatch into the fat cap and rubbing the racks' surfaces with a blend of kosher salt and ground cumin ensured that our lamb would be loaded with flavor. We heated the oven to 250 degrees and arranged the lamb on a wire rack–lined baking sheet. In just over an hour, our racks emerged at a rosy medium-rare with big flavor to boot. While the racks roasted in the oven, we whipped up a relish to dress up the lamb, combining chopped roasted red pepper, minced parsley, olive oil, fresh lemon juice, and minced garlic. This simple sauce steeped while the lamb cooked. Because meat always tastes best with a bit of char, we browned the racks in a skillet before slicing and serving. We prefer the milder taste and bigger size of domestic lamb, but you may substitute imported lamb from New Zealand or Australia. Since imported racks are generally smaller, in step 1 season each rack with ½ teaspoon of salt and reduce the cooking time to 50 to 70 minutes. A rasp-style grater makes quick work of turning the garlic into a paste.

**LAMB**

2 racks of lamb (1¾ to 2 pounds each), fat trimmed to ⅛ to ¼ inch, rib bones frenched
Kosher salt and pepper
1 teaspoon ground cumin
1 teaspoon vegetable oil

**RELISH**

½ cup jarred roasted red peppers, rinsed, patted dry, and chopped fine
½ cup minced fresh parsley
¼ cup extra-virgin olive oil
¼ teaspoon lemon juice
⅛ teaspoon garlic, minced to paste
Kosher salt and pepper

1. **FOR THE LAMB:** Adjust oven rack to middle position and heat oven to 250 degrees. Using sharp knife, cut slits in surface layer of fat, spaced ½-inch apart, in crosshatch pattern, being careful to cut down to, but not into, meat. Combine 2 tablespoons salt and cumin in bowl. Rub ¾ teaspoon salt mixture over entire surface of each rack and into slits. Reserve remaining salt mixture for serving. Place racks, bone-side down, on wire rack set in rimmed baking sheet. Roast until meat registers 125 degrees for medium-rare or 130 degrees for medium, 1 hour 5 minutes to 1 hour 25 minutes.

2. **FOR THE RELISH:** While lamb roasts, combine red peppers, parsley, olive oil, lemon juice, and garlic in bowl. Season with salt and pepper to taste. Let stand at room temperature at least 1 hour before serving.

3. Heat vegetable oil in 12-inch skillet over high heat until just smoking. Place one rack, bone-side up, in skillet and cook until well-browned, 1 to 2 minutes. Transfer to carving board. Pour off all but 1 teaspoon fat from skillet and repeat with second rack. Tent racks loosely with aluminum foil and let rest for 20 minutes. Cut between ribs to separate chops and sprinkle cut side of chops with ½ teaspoon salt mixture. Serve, passing relish and remaining salt mixture separately.

### Roast Rack of Lamb with Sweet Mint-Almond Relish

Substitute ground anise for cumin in salt mixture. Omit red pepper relish. While lamb roasts, combine ½ cup minced fresh mint; ¼ cup sliced almonds, toasted and chopped fine; ¼ cup extra-virgin olive oil; 2 tablespoons red currant jelly; 4 teaspoons red wine vinegar; and 2 teaspoons Dijon mustard in bowl. Season with salt and pepper to taste. Let stand at room temperature for at least 1 hour before serving with lamb.

## Roast Butterflied Leg of Lamb with Coriander, Cumin, and Mustard Seeds

**SERVES** 8 to 10

**WHY THIS RECIPE WORKS** Roast leg of lamb is both delicious and daunting. The usual bone-in or boned, rolled, and tied leg options cook unevenly and are tricky to carve. Choosing a butterflied leg of lamb did away with these problems; we simply pounded it to an even thickness and salted it for an hour to encourage juicy, evenly cooked meat. We first roasted it gently in the oven until it was just medium-rare; we then passed it under the broiler to give it a crisp crust. A standard spice rub scorched under the broiler, so we opted for a spice-infused oil, which seasoned the lamb during cooking and then became a quick sauce for serving. We prefer the subtler flavor and larger size of lamb labeled "domestic" or "American" for this recipe. The amount of salt (2 tablespoons) in step 1 is for a 6-pound leg. If using a larger leg (7 to 8 pounds), add an additional teaspoon of salt for every pound.

**LAMB**

- 1 (6- to 8-pound) butterflied leg of lamb
- 2 tablespoons kosher salt
- ⅓ cup vegetable oil
- 3 shallots, sliced thin
- 4 garlic cloves, peeled and smashed
- 1 (1-inch) piece ginger, sliced into ½-inch-thick rounds and smashed
- 1 tablespoon coriander seeds
- 1 tablespoon cumin seeds
- 1 tablespoon mustard seeds
- 3 bay leaves
- 2 (2-inch) strips lemon zest

**SAUCE**

- ⅓ cup chopped fresh mint
- ⅓ cup chopped fresh cilantro
- 1 shallot, minced
- 2 tablespoons lemon juice

1. **FOR THE LAMB:** Place lamb on cutting board with fat cap facing down. Using sharp knife, trim any pockets of fat and connective tissue from underside of lamb. Flip lamb over, trim fat cap so it's between ⅛ and ¼ inch thick, and pound roast to even 1-inch thickness. Cut slits, spaced ½ inch apart, in fat cap in crosshatch pattern, being careful to cut down to but not into meat. Rub salt over entire roast and into slits. Let stand, uncovered, at room temperature for 1 hour.

2. Meanwhile, adjust oven racks 4 to 5 inches from broiler element and to lower-middle position and heat oven to 250 degrees. Stir together oil, shallots, garlic, ginger, coriander seeds, cumin seeds, mustard seeds, bay leaves, and lemon zest on rimmed baking sheet and bake on lower rack until spices are softened and fragrant and shallots and garlic turn golden, about 1 hour. Remove sheet from oven and discard bay leaves.

**3.** Thoroughly pat lamb dry with paper towels and transfer, fat side up, to sheet (directly on top of spices). Roast on lower rack until lamb registers 120 degrees, 30 to 40 minutes. Remove sheet from oven and heat broiler. Broil lamb on upper rack until surface is well browned and charred in spots and lamb registers 125 degrees, 3 to 8 minutes for medium-rare.

**4.** Remove sheet from oven and, using 2 pairs of tongs, transfer lamb to carving board (some spices will cling to bottom of roast); tent with aluminum foil and let rest for 20 minutes.

**5. FOR THE SAUCE:** Meanwhile, carefully pour pan juices through fine-mesh strainer into medium bowl, pressing on solids to extract as much liquid as possible; discard solids. Stir in mint, cilantro, shallot, and lemon juice. Add any accumulated lamb juices to sauce and season with salt and pepper to taste.

**6.** With long side facing you, slice lamb with grain into 3 equal pieces. Turn each piece and slice across grain into ¼-inch-thick slices. Serve with sauce. (Briefly warm sauce in microwave if it has cooled and thickened.)

## Roast Boneless Leg of Lamb with Garlic, Herb, and Bread Crumb Crust

**SERVES** 6 to 8

**WHY THIS RECIPE WORKS** A boneless leg of lamb is an easy shortcut to a great roast dinner—as long as you treat it correctly. We started by pounding it to an even thickness. Next we introduced extra flavor and textural interest to the roast. First, we made a potent herb and garlic paste. We spread a portion of the paste over the lamb before rolling up and tying the roast so it would infuse the lamb with flavor from the inside out. The rest of the herb paste was combined with fresh bread crumbs and Parmesan. A quick sear on the stovetop jump-started the cooking process and ensured our lamb would have a golden-brown crust. After searing, we moved the roast to a 375-degree oven, which was perfect for cooking the meat to a juicy, tender medium-rare. Partway through cooking, we took the roast out of the oven, removed the twine, brushed the meat with zingy Dijon mustard, and applied the bread crumb mixture. This ensured that the crust wouldn't peel off with the twine but also gave the tied lamb enough roasting time to hold its shape when we removed the twine, resulting in perfect slices with a crunchy, savory crust. We prefer the sirloin end rather than the shank end for this recipe, though either will work well. We prefer the subtler flavor and larger size of lamb labeled "domestic" or "American," but you may substitute lamb imported from New Zealand or Australia. Leg of lamb is often sold in elastic netting that must be removed.

- 1 slice hearty white sandwich bread
- ¼ cup extra-virgin olive oil, divided
- ¼ cup finely chopped fresh parsley
- 3 tablespoons finely chopped fresh rosemary
- 2 tablespoons finely chopped fresh thyme
- 3 garlic cloves, peeled
- 1 ounce Parmesan cheese, grated (½ cup)
- 1 (3½- to 4-pound) boneless half leg of lamb, trimmed and pounded to ¾-inch thickness
- 1 tablespoon kosher salt, divided
- 1 teaspoon pepper, divided
- 1 tablespoon Dijon mustard

**1.** Adjust oven rack to lower-middle position and heat oven to 375 degrees. Pulse bread in food processor until coarsely ground, about 10 pulses (you should have about 1 cup crumbs). Transfer to bowl and set aside. Process 1 teaspoon oil, parsley, rosemary, thyme, and garlic in now-empty processor until minced, scraping down sides of bowl as needed, about 1 minute. Transfer 1½ tablespoons herb mixture to bowl and reserve. Scrape remaining mixture into bowl of bread crumbs; stir in Parmesan and 1 tablespoon oil and set aside.

**2.** Lay roast on cutting board with rough interior side (which was against bone) facing up, rub with 2 teaspoons oil, and sprinkle with 1½ teaspoons salt and ½ teaspoon pepper. Spread reserved herb mixture evenly over lamb, leaving 1-inch border around edge. Roll roast and tie with kitchen twine at 1½-inch intervals. Sprinkle roast with remaining 1½ teaspoons salt and remaining ½ teaspoon pepper, then rub with 1 tablespoon oil.

**3.** Set wire rack in rimmed baking sheet. Heat remaining 1 tablespoon oil in 12-inch skillet over medium-high heat until just smoking. Brown roast well on all sides, about 10 minutes. Transfer to prepared rack and roast until lamb registers 105 to 110 degrees, 30 to 35 minutes. Transfer roast to carving board; remove twine. Brush roast exterior with mustard, then carefully press bread crumb mixture onto top and sides of roast with your hands, pressing firmly to form solid, even coating that adheres to roast. Return coated roast to prepared rack; roast until lamb registers 125 degrees (for medium-rare), 10 to 15 minutes longer. Transfer roast to carving board and let rest for 20 minutes. Slice roast into ½-inch-thick slices. Serve.

## Braised Lamb Shanks with Red Wine and Herbes de Provence

**SERVES** 6

**WHY THIS RECIPE WORKS** Braising lamb shanks turns this richly flavored but tough cut of meat meltingly tender. However, the high fat content of lamb all too often leads to a greasy sauce. We avoided this pitfall by trimming the shanks well and then browning them before adding liquid (a complex and savory mix of broth and wine) to get a head start on rendering their fat. We also defatted the braising liquid after the shanks were cooked to significantly cut down on the greasiness. We used more liquid than is called for in many braises to guarantee that plenty of flavorful cooking liquid remains in the pot even after about an hour of uncovered cooking. Côtes du Rhône works particularly well here. If you can't locate herbes de Provence, substitute a mixture of 1 teaspoon each of dried thyme, rosemary, and marjoram. If you're using smaller shanks than the ones called for in this recipe, reduce the braising time.

6 (12- to 16-ounce) lamb shanks, trimmed
1 teaspoon plus pinch table salt, divided
2 tablespoons vegetable oil, divided
3 carrots, peeled and cut into 2-inch pieces
2 onions, sliced thick
2 celery ribs, cut into 2-inch pieces
2 tablespoons tomato paste
4 garlic cloves, minced
2 tablespoons herbes de Provence
2 cups dry red wine
3 cups chicken broth
Ground black pepper

**1.** Adjust oven rack to middle position and heat oven to 350 degrees. Pat lamb shanks dry with paper towels and sprinkle with 1 teaspoon salt. Heat 1 tablespoon oil in Dutch oven over medium-high heat until just smoking. Brown 3 shanks on all sides, 7 to 10 minutes. Transfer shanks to large plate and repeat with remaining 1 tablespoon oil and remaining 3 shanks.

**2.** Pour off all but 2 tablespoons fat from pot. Add carrots, onions, celery, tomato paste, garlic, herbes de Provence, and remaining pinch salt and cook until vegetables just begin to soften, 3 to 4 minutes. Stir in wine, then broth, scraping up any browned bits; bring to simmer. Nestle shanks, along with any accumulated juices, into pot.

**3.** Return to simmer and cover; transfer pot to oven. Cook for 1½ hours. Uncover and continue to cook until tops of shanks are browned, about 30 minutes. Flip shanks and continue to cook until remaining sides are browned and fork slips easily in and out of shanks, 15 to 30 minutes longer.

**4.** Remove pot from oven and let rest for 15 minutes. Using tongs, transfer shanks and vegetables to large plate and tent with aluminum foil. Skim fat from braising liquid and season liquid with salt and pepper to taste. Return shanks to braising liquid to warm through before serving.

## Lamb Barbacoa

**SERVES 8**

**WHY THIS RECIPE WORKS** Barbacoa is a pit-cooking method traditional to Mexico that produces tender bites of meat and consomé de barbacoa that's flavored by the meat drippings. Our barbacoa begins by coating 1½-inch-thick slabs of lamb or beef in a marinade made by pureeing guajillo chiles with garlic, spices, salt, and vinegar. To mimic a traditional barbacoa setup, we placed the ingredients for consomé de barbacoa in a Dutch oven along with a small ramekin. We placed the meat on a plate on top of the ramekin. After bringing the broth to a simmer on the stove, we covered the pot tightly and placed it in a 325-degree oven, where the meat cooked gently until its collagen broke down and its drippings imbued the broth, beans, and potatoes with a rich savory flavor. We chopped the meat, moistened it with some of the broth, and seasoned it. Then, we served it with corn tortillas; an ancho chile–tomatillo salsa; and lime, cilantro, onion, and radish. Barbacoa is traditionally steamed underground in a pit or in a specially constructed pot. For our barbacoa setup, you'll need a 6-quart or larger round Dutch oven with a tight-fitting lid, a 1½- to 2-inch-tall ramekin, and an 8- to 9-inch-wide heatproof plate. If you prefer a mild salsa, omit the arbol chiles; for a spicier salsa, use two arbols. Because tomatillos can vary in acidity, we adjust the salsa's seasoning with sugar and vinegar. We developed our recipe using lamb, but you can substitute an equivalent weight of boneless beef chuck-eye roast (or boneless leg of goat).

**LAMB AND CONSOMÉ DE BARBACOA**

6 dried guajillo chiles, stemmed, seeded, and torn into ½-inch pieces (¾ cup)
1 (2½- to 3-pound) boneless leg of lamb, fat cap trimmed to ⅛ to ¼ inch
6 garlic cloves, peeled, divided
5 teaspoons kosher salt, divided
2½ teaspoons dried Mexican oregano
2 teaspoons cider vinegar
½ teaspoon pepper
2 whole cloves
¼ teaspoon ground cumin
1 (15-ounce) can chickpeas, undrained
8 ounces red potatoes, unpeeled, cut into ½-inch pieces
½ small white onion, halved through root end
2 carrots, peeled and halved crosswise
2 bay leaves

**SPICY TOMATILLO SALSA**

2 dried ancho chiles, stemmed, seeded, and torn into ½-inch pieces (½ cup)
6 ounces tomatillos, husks and stems removed, rinsed well and dried
1 small plum tomato
¼ small white onion, quartered through root end
2 garlic cloves, unpeeled
1-2 dried arbol chiles, stemmed (optional)
1¼ teaspoons kosher salt
½-1 teaspoon cider vinegar (optional)
Pinch to ½ teaspoon sugar (optional)

24 (6-inch) corn tortillas, warmed
Finely chopped white onion
Thinly sliced radishes
Fresh cilantro leaves
Lime wedges

**1. FOR THE LAMB AND CONSOMÉ DE BARBACOA:** Adjust oven rack to lower-middle position and heat oven to 325 degrees. Toast guajillos in 10-inch cast-iron skillet over medium-high heat, stirring frequently, until fragrant, 2 to 6 minutes. Transfer to bowl (reserve skillet). Add 2 cups hot water to guajillos, making sure they're completely submerged, and let stand until softened, about 20 minutes.

**2.** Meanwhile, place lamb on cutting board with fat cap facing down. Using sharp knife, trim any pockets of fat and connective tissue from underside of lamb. If lamb is thicker than 1½ inches, cover with plastic wrap and pound until it is no more than 1½ inches thick (thickness does not need to be uniform; some areas may be thinner). Cut lamb crosswise into 3 pieces. Add lamb to large bowl.

**3.** Drain guajillos and reserve ⅔ cup soaking liquid (discard remaining liquid). Process guajillos, reserved liquid, 4 garlic cloves, 1½ tablespoons salt, oregano, vinegar, pepper, cloves, and cumin in blender until smooth, about 3 minutes. Pour chile sauce over lamb and, using tongs, toss until lamb is well coated. Rinse out blender.

**4.** Place 1½- to 2-inch-tall ramekin right side up in center of Dutch oven. Avoiding ramekin, add 3 cups water, chickpeas and their liquid, potatoes, onion, carrots, bay leaves, remaining 2 garlic cloves, and remaining ½ teaspoon salt. Place 8- to 9-inch-wide plate on top of ramekin.

**5.** Arrange lamb on plate, placing 2 pieces side by side with third piece on top. Scrape any excess marinade from bowl onto top of meat. Bring to simmer over high heat. Cover tightly with lid and transfer to oven. Cook until paring knife inserted into lamb slides in and out with little resistance, about 3 hours. Let meat rest, covered, for 30 minutes.

**6. FOR THE SPICY TOMATILLO SALSA:** While lamb cooks, toast anchos in now-empty skillet over medium-high heat, stirring frequently, until fragrant, 2 to 6 minutes. Transfer to bowl (reserve skillet). Add 2 cups hot water to anchos, making sure they're completely submerged, and let stand until softened, about 20 minutes.

**7.** Place tomatillos, tomato, onion, and garlic in skillet and cook over medium-low heat, turning ingredients occasionally. Cook garlic until skins are lightly charred and interior is soft, about 5 minutes. Cook onion until 2 cut sides are lightly charred and onion has softened slightly, 12 to 15 minutes. Cook tomatillos and tomato until exteriors are spotty brown and flesh is soft, 20 to 25 minutes.

**8.** Peel garlic and trim root end from onion. Add garlic and onion to clean blender along with tomatillos; tomato; arbol chiles, if using; and salt. Drain anchos and reserve ⅔ cup soaking liquid (discard remaining liquid). Add anchos and reserved liquid to blender and process until smooth, 1 to 2 minutes. Transfer to serving bowl and let sit at room temperature so flavors meld, about 30 minutes. Season with salt; vinegar; and sugar, if using, to taste.

**9.** Transfer lamb to cutting board. Pour accumulated lamb juices from plate into Dutch oven. Remove ramekin and discard onion, carrots, and bay leaves. Bring consomé to simmer over medium heat. Slice lamb crosswise ½ inch thick. Transfer lamb to bowl and add ½ cup consomé. Using tongs, toss meat, breaking it up into bite-size pieces. Season consomé and lamb with salt to taste. Transfer lamb to serving platter. Ladle consomé into individual serving bowls. Serve, passing salsa, warm tortillas, onion, radishes, cilantro, and lime wedges separately.

## Indian Curry

**SERVES** 4 to 6

---

**WHY THIS RECIPE WORKS** For a deeply flavored curry, we found that allowing the spices to cook completely provided the intense flavor we were after. We used a combination of whole spices—cinnamon sticks, cloves, green cardamom pods, black peppercorns, and a bay leaf—and toasted them in oil before adding aromatics, jalapeño, and ground spices. Instead of browning the lamb, we stirred it into the pot along with crushed tomatoes and cooked the mixture until the liquid evaporated and the oil separated. This is a classic Indian technique that allows the spices to further develop their flavors in the oil, flavors which are then cooked into the meat. We added water and simmered the mixture until the meat was tender, at which point we stirred in the spinach and channa dal (yellow split peas) and cooked the dish until all the ingredients were melded and tender. If desired, 1½ pounds boneless, skinless chicken thighs, trimmed and cut into ¾-inch chunks, can be substituted for the lamb. For more heat, add the jalapeño seeds and ribs when mincing. For a creamier curry, choose yogurt over the crushed tomatoes. Serve with Yogurt Sauce (page 550), Onion Relish (page 557), Cilantro-Mint Chutney (page 558), and Simple Rice Pilaf (page 726).

SPICE BLEND

- 1½ cinnamon sticks
- 4 whole cloves
- 4 green cardamom pods
- 8 whole black peppercorns
- 1 bay leaf

CURRY

- ¼ cup vegetable oil
- 1 medium onion, halved and sliced thin
- 5 medium garlic cloves, minced or pressed through a garlic press (about 5 teaspoons)
- 1 tablespoon minced or grated fresh ginger
- 1 jalapeño chile, stemmed and halved lengthwise, seeds and ribs removed
- 2 teaspoons ground cumin
- 2 teaspoons ground coriander
- 1 teaspoon ground turmeric
- Table salt
- 1½ pounds boneless leg of lamb, trimmed and cut into ¾-inch cubes
- ⅔ cup crushed tomatoes or ½ cup plain low-fat yogurt
- 2 cups water
- 1½ pounds spinach, stemmed, washed, and chopped coarse (optional)
- ½ cup channa dal (yellow split peas)
- ¼ cup chopped fresh cilantro leaves

**1. FOR THE SPICE BLEND:** Combine all the ingredients in a small bowl and set aside.

**2. FOR THE CURRY:** Heat the oil in a Dutch oven over medium heat until shimmering. Add the spice blend and cook, stirring frequently, until the cinnamon stick unfurls and the cloves pop, about 5 seconds. Add the onion and cook, stirring occasionally, until softened, 5 to 7 minutes. Stir in the garlic, ginger, jalapeño, cumin, coriander, turmeric, and ½ teaspoon salt and cook until fragrant, about 30 seconds.

**3.** Stir in the lamb and the tomatoes. Bring to a simmer and cook, stirring frequently, until the liquid evaporates and the oil separates and turns orange, 5 to 7 minutes. Continue to cook until the spices are sizzling, about 30 seconds longer.

**4.** Stir in the water and bring to a simmer over medium heat. Reduce the heat to medium-low, cover, and cook until the lamb is almost tender, about 40 minutes.

**5.** Stir in the spinach (if using) and channa dal and cook until the channa dal are tender, about 15 minutes. Season with salt to taste, stir in the cilantro, and serve.

## Kousa Mihshi (Lebanese Stuffed Squash)

**SERVES** 4 to 6

**WHY THIS RECIPE WORKS** Kousa mihshi, which translates as "stuffed squash" in Arabic, consists of hollowed-out zucchini stuffed with a mixture of spiced ground lamb and rice called hashweh. The squash is slowly braised in cinnamon-accented tomato sauce until the meat is succulent, the rice tender, and the zucchini is yielding but not mushy. Soaking the rice for 10 minutes before combining it with the lamb ensured that the grains cooked evenly and thoroughly. Browning the stuffing and breaking it up with the back of a spatula created small, distinct pieces that packed lightly into the squash cavities. To give the sauce a meaty underpinning, we sautéed the aromatics in the fatty juices we drained from the lamb. For this recipe, you'll need an apple corer that removes only the core but does not create wedges; the small end of a melon baller or a long handled bar spoon is also helpful. We like ground lamb here, but you can substitute 90 percent lean ground beef, if preferred. Select zucchini that are similarly sized to ensure even cooking; and to make them easier to core, choose the straightest ones you can find. Use fresh, in-season tomatoes for the best flavor.

HASHWEH

- ½ cup long-grain white rice
- 8 ounces ground lamb
- 2 tablespoons extra-virgin olive oil, divided
- 1 teaspoon table salt
- ½ teaspoon pepper
- ¼ teaspoon ground cinnamon

**SAUCE**

- 2 tablespoons extra-virgin olive oil
- ½ teaspoon pepper
- ¼ teaspoon ground cinnamon
- 1 small onion, chopped coarse
- 2 garlic cloves, minced
- 2 pounds tomatoes, cored and chopped coarse
- 2 tablespoons tomato paste
- 2 teaspoons cider vinegar
- 1 teaspoon table salt

**ZUCCHINI**

- 6 zucchini (6 to 7 inches long and at least 1½ inches wide)
- 2 tablespoons extra-virgin olive oil
- ¼ cup fresh parsley leaves
- 2 cups plain whole-milk yogurt

**1. FOR THE HASHWEH:** Place rice in fine-mesh strainer and rinse under cold running water until water runs clear. Place rice in bowl and cover with 2 cups hot water; let stand for 10 minutes. Drain rice in now-empty strainer and return to bowl (do not wash strainer). Add lamb, 1 tablespoon oil, salt, pepper, and cinnamon and mix until rice is well dispersed. Heat remaining 1 tablespoon oil in 12-inch nonstick skillet over medium-high heat until shimmering. Add lamb mixture to skillet (do not wash bowl) and, using heat-resistant spatula, mash to thin layer. Cook, stirring constantly and breaking up meat with side of spatula, until meat is almost cooked through but still slightly pink, 3 to 4 minutes. Transfer mixture to now-empty strainer set over bowl. Return juices and fat to skillet. Transfer lamb mixture to now-empty bowl and, using fork, break up mixture until meat is reduced to pieces no larger than ¼ inch.

**2. FOR THE SAUCE:** Add oil to juices and fat in skillet and heat over medium-low heat until sizzling. Stir in pepper and cinnamon and cook until just fragrant, about 30 seconds. Add onion and garlic and cook, stirring occasionally, until very soft and light golden, 7 to 9 minutes.

**3.** Transfer onion mixture to food processor. Add tomatoes, tomato paste, vinegar, and salt to processor and process until smooth, 1½ to 2 minutes. Transfer tomato mixture to now-empty skillet. Bring to boil over medium-high heat. Reduce heat to simmer and cook, uncovered and stirring occasionally, until sauce is thickened and heat-resistant spatula dragged across bottom of skillet leaves trail, 25 to 30 minutes. While sauce cooks, prepare zucchini.

**4. FOR THE ZUCCHINI:** Remove stem end of 1 zucchini and discard. Holding zucchini with 1 hand, insert apple corer into stemmed end and press and turn until cutting end of corer is about ½ inch from bottom of zucchini (or as far as corer will go), being careful not to damage walls of zucchini. (If stemmed end is too narrow to accommodate corer without damaging walls, remove additional inch of stemmed end.) Remove corer. Using melon baller or long-handled bar spoon, scoop out any remaining core in pieces until farthest part of hollow is ½ inch from bottom of zucchini. Repeat with remaining zucchini. Rinse hollows and drain zucchini on dish towel.

**5.** Hold 1 zucchini stemmed side up on counter. Using your hand or small spoon, drop small portions of stuffing into hollow, tapping bottom of zucchini on counter to settle stuffing, until it is ½ inch from top of zucchini. Do not compact stuffing. Repeat with remaining zucchini and stuffing.

**6.** Remove sauce from heat. Gently arrange stuffed zucchini in single layer in skillet. Return skillet to medium-high heat and bring to boil. Adjust heat to maintain low simmer, cover, and cook for 20 minutes (small wisps of steam should escape from beneath skillet lid, but sauce should not boil). Turn zucchini over gently. Cover and continue to simmer until rice and meat are fully cooked and zucchini are tender but not mushy, 20 to 25 minutes longer. Drizzle zucchini and sauce with oil; sprinkle with parsley; and serve, passing yogurt separately.

## CORING ZUCCHINI

**1.** Core zucchini with apple corer, pressing apple corer into squash as far down as it will go.

**2.** Scoop out more pieces of core using melon baller or long-handled bar spoon until hollow is ½ inch from bottom.

**3.** Rinse cavity to remove seeds and debris clinging to walls. Let zucchini drain on dish towel.

**CHAPTER 8** 
# Seafood

Photos (from left to right): Poached Salmon with Herb and Caper Vinaigrette; Nasi Goreng; Oven-Steamed Mussels; Crispy Salmon Cakes with Smoked Salmon, Capers, and Dill for Two; Fisherman's Pie; New England Lobster Roll; Shrimp Tempura

## Pan-Seared Brined Salmon

**SERVES 4**

**WHY THIS RECIPE WORKS** Harnessing the intense heat of a skillet, you can produce a golden-brown, ultracrisp crust on salmon fillets while keeping their interiors moist. We first brined the fish to season it and to keep it moist. Instead of adding the fish to an already-hot skillet, we placed it in a cold, dry nonstick skillet skin side down and then turned on the heat. The skin protected the fish from drying out while cooking and later was easy to peel off, if desired. Also, because the skin released fat into the pan as it cooked, no extra oil was needed to sear the second side of the fish. To ensure even cooking, buy a whole center-cut fillet and cut it into four pieces. Using skin-on salmon is important here, as we rely on the fat underneath the skin as the cooking medium (as opposed to adding extra oil). It is important to keep the skin on during cooking; once the salmon is cooked, the skin will be easy to remove. If using wild salmon, cook until it registers 120 degrees. Serve with Mango-Mint Salsa if desired.

- ¼ cup table salt for brining
- 1 (1½- to 2-pound) skin-on salmon fillet, sliced crosswise into 4 equal pieces
- ½ teaspoon table salt, divided
- ½ teaspoon pepper, divided
- Lemon wedges

**1.** Dissolve ¼ cup salt in 2 quarts cold water in large container. Submerge salmon in brine and let sit at room temperature for 15 minutes. Remove salmon from brine and pat dry with paper towels.

**2.** Sprinkle bottom of 12-inch nonstick skillet evenly with ¼ teaspoon salt and ¼ teaspoon pepper. Place fillets, skin side down, in skillet and sprinkle tops of fillets with remaining ¼ teaspoon salt and remaining ¼ teaspoon pepper. Heat skillet over medium-high heat and cook fillets without moving them until fat begins to render, skin begins to brown, and bottom ¼ inch of fillets turns opaque, 6 to 8 minutes.

**3.** Using tongs and thin spatula, flip fillets and continue to cook without moving them until fillets register 125 degrees (for medium-rare), 6 to 8 minutes longer. Transfer fillets skin side down to serving platter and let rest for 5 minutes before serving with lemon wedges.

### Mango-Mint Salsa

**MAKES** 1 cup

Adjust the salsa's heat level by reserving and adding the jalapeño seeds, if desired.

- 1 mango, peeled, pitted, and cut into ¼-inch pieces
- 1 shallot, minced
- 3 tablespoons lime juice (2 limes)
- 2 tablespoons chopped fresh mint
- 1 jalapeño chile, stemmed, seeded, and minced
- 1 tablespoon extra-virgin olive oil
- 1 garlic clove, minced
- ½ teaspoon table salt

Combine all ingredients in bowl.

## Saumon aux Lentilles (Pan-Seared Salmon with Braised Lentilles du Puy)

**SERVES 4**

**WHY THIS RECIPE WORKS** For our version of the classic French pairing of salmon and lentils, we started by building a flavorful base for the lentils, gently cooking onion, carrots, and celery in olive oil until soft. Fruity tomato paste and plenty of garlic added even more depth before the lentils and water went in. When the lentils were fully softened and most of the moisture in the pot had either evaporated or been absorbed, we set them aside to focus on the salmon, which we'd briefly brined in a saltwater solution to season the fish and to ensure that it retained plenty of moisture as it cooked. We employed our tried-and-true method of placing the salmon skin side down in a cold nonstick skillet that had been strewn with salt and pepper. As the pan heated up, the salmon released some of the fat just beneath the skin, crisping it, and enabling us to cook the fish without any additional fat. A bit of mustard and sherry vinegar stirred into the lentils brightened their flavor, making them an ideal pairing for the rich fish, and a final addition of extra-virgin olive oil added grassy top notes. To ensure uniform cooking, buy a 1½-pound center-cut salmon fillet and cut it into four pieces. Using skin-on salmon is important here, as we rely on the fat underneath the skin as the cooking medium. If using wild salmon, cook until it registers 120 degrees. Small, olive-green lentilles du Puy are worth seeking out for their meaty texture, but if you can't find them, substitute another small green lentil. Do not use red or brown lentils.

**LENTILS**

- 2 tablespoons extra-virgin olive oil, divided
- 1 large onion, chopped fine
- 1 celery rib, chopped fine
- 1 carrot, peeled and chopped fine
- ¾ teaspoon table salt
- 1 tablespoon minced garlic
- 1 tablespoon tomato paste
- ½ teaspoon dried thyme
- ½ teaspoon pepper
- 2½ cups water
- 1 cup dried lentilles du Puy (French green lentils), picked over and rinsed
- 1 tablespoon sherry vinegar, plus extra for seasoning
- 2 teaspoons Dijon mustard

**SALMON**

- ¼ cup table salt for brining
- 1 (1½- to 2-pound) skin-on salmon fillet, sliced crosswise into 4 equal pieces
- ¾ teaspoon table salt, divided
- ¾ teaspoon pepper, divided

**1. FOR THE LENTILS:** Heat 1 tablespoon oil in medium saucepan over medium heat until shimmering. Add onion, celery, carrot, and salt and stir to coat vegetables. Cover and cook, stirring occasionally, until vegetables are softened but not browned, 8 to 10 minutes. Add garlic, tomato paste, thyme, and pepper and cook, stirring constantly, until fragrant, about 2 minutes. Stir in water and lentils. Increase heat and bring to boil. Adjust heat to simmer. Cover and cook, stirring occasionally, until lentils are tender but not mushy and have consistency of thick risotto, 40 to 50 minutes. Remove from heat and keep covered.

**2. FOR THE SALMON:** While lentils are cooking, dissolve ¼ cup salt in 1 quart water in narrow container. Submerge salmon in brine and let stand for 15 minutes. Remove salmon from brine and pat dry with paper towels. Allow to stand while lentils finish cooking.

**3.** Sprinkle bottom of 12-inch nonstick skillet evenly with ½ teaspoon salt and ½ teaspoon pepper. Place fillets, skin side down, in skillet and sprinkle tops of fillets with remaining ¼ teaspoon salt and remaining ¼ teaspoon pepper. Heat skillet over medium-high heat and cook fillets, without moving them, until fat begins to render, skin begins to brown, and bottom ¼ inch of fillets turns opaque, 6 to 8 minutes.

**4.** Using tongs and thin spatula, flip fillets and continue to cook without moving them until fillets register 125 degrees (for medium-rare), 5 to 8 minutes longer. Transfer fillets, skin side up, to clean plate.

**5.** Warm lentils briefly if necessary. Stir in vinegar, mustard, and remaining 1 tablespoon oil. Season with salt, pepper, and vinegar to taste. Divide lentils among wide, shallow serving bowls. Arrange salmon skin side up on lentils and serve.

## Pan-Seared Salmon Steaks

**SERVES** 4

**WHY THIS RECIPE WORKS** In this recipe, we prepared salmon steaks in a way that encouraged a well-browned, crisp crust; promoted even cooking; and delivered a beautiful presentation. Deboning and then tying each steak into a round produced a structurally sound parcel that cooked evenly and resulted in two large surfaces on which to develop a well-browned crust. A light coating of cornstarch enhanced the crispness of the crust. Serve the salmon steaks with lemon wedges or top them with Tarragon Chimichurri if desired.

- Table salt and pepper
- 4 (8- to 10-ounce) salmon steaks, ¾ to 1 inch thick
- ¼ cup cornstarch
- 2 tablespoons vegetable oil
- Lemon wedges

**1.** Dissolve ¼ cup salt in 2 quarts cold water in large container. Submerge salmon in brine and let stand at room temperature for 15 minutes. Remove salmon from brine and pat dry with paper towels.

**2.** Place 1 salmon steak on counter with belly flaps facing you. Locate white line at top of salmon steak. Using paring knife, cut along 1 side of white line, around spine, then along membrane inside belly flap. Repeat process on other side of white line.

**3.** Using kitchen shears, cut out spine and membrane; discard. Run your fingers along each steak where spinal structure was removed and locate any pin bones; remove pin bones using tweezers. Remove 1½ inches of skin from 1 flap of steak. Tuck skinned portion into center of steak. Wrap other flap around steak and tie with kitchen twine. Repeat with remaining steaks.

**4.** Lightly season both sides of salmon with salt and pepper. Spread cornstarch in even layer on large plate. Lightly press both sides of salmon into cornstarch. Using pastry brush, remove excess cornstarch.

**5.** Heat oil in 12-inch nonstick skillet over medium-high heat until shimmering. Place salmon in skillet and cook until first side is browned, about 3 minutes. Flip salmon and cook until second side is browned, 3 minutes. Continue to cook, flipping salmon every 2 minutes, until it register 125 degrees (for medium-rare), 2 to 6 minutes longer. Transfer salmon to serving platter, discard twine, and serve with lemon wedges.

### Tarragon Chimichurri

**MAKES** about 1 cup

Carapelli Original Extra Virgin Olive Oil is our favorite supermarket brand.

- ½ cup minced fresh parsley
- ¼ cup extra-virgin olive oil
- 2 tablespoons minced fresh tarragon
- 2 tablespoons white wine vinegar
- 2 garlic cloves, minced
- ¼ teaspoon red pepper flakes
- Table salt and pepper

Combine all ingredients in bowl and season with salt and pepper to taste.

## Glazed Salmon

**SERVES 4**

**WHY THIS RECIPE WORKS** The traditional method for glazed salmon calls for broiling, but reaching into a broiling-hot oven every minute to baste the fish is a hassle and, even worse, the fillets often burn if your timing isn't spot-on. We wanted a foolproof method for glazed salmon that was succulent and pink throughout while keeping the slightly crusty, flavorful browned exterior typically achieved with broiling. First we found that reducing the temperature and gently baking the fish, instead of broiling, cooked the salmon perfectly. To rapidly caramelize the exterior of the fillets before they had a chance to toughen, we sprinkled the fillets with sugar and quickly pan-seared each side before transferring them to the oven. To make sure the glaze stayed put, we rubbed the fish with a mixture of cornstarch, brown sugar, and salt before searing. To ensure uniform pieces of fish that cook at the same rate, buy a whole center-cut fillet and cut it into 4 pieces. Prepare the glaze before you cook the salmon. You will need a 12-inch ovensafe nonstick skillet for this recipe. If your nonstick skillet isn't ovensafe, sear the salmon as directed in step 2, then transfer it to a rimmed baking sheet, glaze it, and bake as directed in step 3. If using wild salmon cook until it registers 120 degrees.

- 1 teaspoon light brown sugar
- ½ teaspoon kosher salt
- ¼ teaspoon cornstarch
- 1 (1½- to 2-pound) skin-on salmon fillet, sliced crosswise into 4 equal pieces
- 1 teaspoon vegetable oil
- 1 recipe glaze (recipes follow)

**1.** Adjust oven rack to middle position and heat oven to 300 degrees. Combine brown sugar, salt, and cornstarch in small bowl. Pat fillets dry with paper towels and season with pepper. Sprinkle brown sugar mixture evenly over flesh side of salmon, rubbing to distribute.

**2.** Heat oil in 12-inch ovensafe nonstick skillet over medium-high heat until just smoking. Place salmon, flesh side down, in skillet and cook until well browned, about 1 minute. Using tongs and thin spatula, carefully flip salmon and cook on skin side for 1 minute.

**3.** Remove skillet from heat and spoon glaze evenly over salmon fillets. Transfer skillet to oven and cook until fillets register 125 degrees (for medium-rare), 7 to 10 minutes. Transfer fillets to platter or individual plates and serve.

### Soy-Mustard Glaze

**MAKES ½ cup**

Mirin, a sweet Japanese rice wine, can be found in Asian markets and the international section of most supermarkets.

- 3 tablespoons light brown sugar
- 2 tablespoons soy sauce
- 2 tablespoons mirin
- 1 tablespoon sherry vinegar
- 1 tablespoon whole-grain mustard
- 1 tablespoon water
- 1 teaspoon cornstarch
- ⅛ teaspoon red pepper flakes

Whisk all ingredients together in small saucepan. Bring to boil over medium-high heat; simmer until thickened, about 1 minute. Remove from heat and cover to keep warm.

## Double-Glazed Salmon with Lemon and Thyme

**SERVES 4** **SEASON 26**

**WHY THIS RECIPE WORKS** For a quick, high-impact salmon entrée, we started by brining center-cut fillets in a salt and sugar solution and making a full-flavored, glossy glaze. We built that glaze on lemon juice, adding complexity to its flavor with fresh thyme sprigs and seasoning it with soy sauce. Rather than relying on lots of sugar to thicken the glaze, we stirred in a little cornstarch. We applied the glaze to fillets that we had seared on the stovetop until they were well browned and then let the fish finish cooking gently in the oven. We finished our fillets by painting on another coating of the clingy, lemony glaze just before serving. To ensure uniform cooking, buy a 1½- to 2-pound center-cut salmon fillet and cut it into four pieces. If your salmon is less than 1 inch thick at its thickest point, check for doneness after 10 minutes of roasting in step 3. If using wild salmon cook until it registers 120 degrees.

- ¼ cup table salt for brining
- ¼ cup sugar for brining
- 4 (6- to 8-ounce) skin-on salmon fillets
- ¼ cup lemon juice (2 lemons)
- 3 tablespoons water
- 2 tablespoons sugar
- 4 teaspoons soy sauce
- 1½ teaspoons cornstarch
- 6 sprigs fresh thyme
- ½ teaspoon vegetable oil
- 1 tablespoon minced fresh parsley or chives

1. Adjust oven rack to middle position and heat oven to 300 degrees. Dissolve salt and ¼ cup sugar in 2 quarts cold water in large container. Submerge salmon fillets in brine and let stand at room temperature for 15 minutes. Remove salmon from brine and pat dry with paper towels.

2. Meanwhile, combine lemon juice, water, sugar, soy sauce, and cornstarch in small saucepan and stir until no lumps remain. Add thyme sprigs and bring to simmer over medium-high heat, stirring frequently. Continue to cook, stirring frequently, until thickened, about 1 minute longer. Remove from heat and let thyme sprigs steep for 5 minutes. Discard thyme sprigs and transfer 2 tablespoons glaze to small bowl.

3. Heat oil in 12-inch ovensafe nonstick skillet over medium-high heat until just smoking. Place fillets, flesh side down, in skillet and cook until flesh side is well browned, 2 to 3 minutes. Flip fillets and reduce heat to low. Brush tops of fillets with reserved 2 tablespoons glaze. Transfer skillet to oven and cook until fillets register 125 degrees (for medium-rare), 10 to 15 minutes. Wash and dry brush.

4. Brush remaining glaze on top and sides of each fillet and sprinkle with parsley. Transfer to platter or individual plates and serve.

## Sesame-Crusted Salmon with Lemon and Ginger

SERVES 4

**WHY THIS RECIPE WORKS** The combination of fish and sesame shows up in cuisines from Asia to California to the Middle East. The simplest approach is to coat fillets with the seeds and then pan-sear the fish. But the duo of salmon and sesame often suffers from a common problem: Both salmon and sesame have a monotonous richness, so finishing a whole serving is a chore. We wanted a lively dish in which the salmon and sesame would be offset with bolder, brighter flavors. Brining the fish for just 15 minutes took care of any dryness. We dunked the seeds in the fish brine, which woke up the nutty flavor by infusing each with salt. Toasting the seeds gave them nice crunch. For extra sesame flavor, we "thickened" tahini with some lemon juice and used the thick paste to adhere the seeds. We also added scallion whites, lemon zest, fresh ginger, and a dash of cayenne for more layers of flavor. For even cooking, purchase fillets that are about the same size and shape. If any of your fillets have a thin belly flap, fold it over to create a more even thickness. If using wild salmon cook until it registers 120 degrees.

Table salt
¾ cup sesame seeds
4 (6- to 8-ounce) skinless salmon fillets
2 scallions, white parts minced, green parts sliced thin
1 tablespoon grated lemon zest plus 2 teaspoons juice
4 teaspoons tahini
2 teaspoons grated fresh ginger
⅛ teaspoon cayenne pepper
1 teaspoon vegetable oil

1. Adjust oven rack to middle position and heat oven to 325 degrees. Dissolve 5 tablespoons salt in 2 quarts water. Transfer 1 cup brine to bowl, stir in sesame seeds, and let stand at room temperature for 5 minutes. Submerge fillets in remaining brine and let stand at room temperature for 15 minutes.

2. Drain seeds and place in 12-inch nonstick skillet. Cook seeds over medium heat, stirring constantly, until golden brown, 2 to 4 minutes. Transfer seeds to pie plate and wipe out skillet with paper towels. Remove fillets from brine and pat dry.

3. Place scallion whites and lemon zest on cutting board and chop until whites and zest are finely minced and well combined. Transfer scallion-zest mixture to bowl and stir in lemon juice, tahini, ginger, cayenne, and ⅛ teaspoon salt.

4. Evenly distribute half of paste over bottoms (skinned sides) of fillets. Press coated sides of fillets in seeds and transfer, seed side down, to plate. Evenly distribute remaining paste over tops of fillets and coat with remaining seeds.

5. Heat oil in now-empty skillet over medium heat until shimmering. Place fillets in skillet, skinned side up, and reduce heat to medium-low. Cook until seeds begin to brown, 1 to 2 minutes. Remove skillet from heat and, using 2 spatulas, carefully flip fillets over. Transfer skillet to oven. Bake until fillets register 125 degrees (for medium-rare), 10 to 15 minutes. Transfer to serving platter and let rest for 5 minutes. Sprinkle with scallion greens and serve.

## Miso-Marinated Salmon

SERVES 4

**WHY THIS RECIPE WORKS** Miso-marinated salmon promises firm, flavorful fish with a savory-sweet, lacquer-like exterior, but it takes three days to prepare. We wanted to make a dish that pulled back on the traditional approach (and shortened the process) but still achieved the depth of flavor that this dish is known for. And instead of a dense interior, we wanted fish that was silky and moist, contrasting with the texture of the

crust. By reducing the marinating to between 6 and 24 hours, we found a window that allowed us to achieve such a goal. A marinade composed of miso, sugar, mirin, and sake allowed for flavor penetration, moisture retention, and better browning by firming up the fish's surface. Broiling the fish at a distance from the heating element allowed the fish to caramelize and cook to tender at the same time. Note that the fish needs to marinate for at least 6 or up to 24 hours before cooking. Use center-cut salmon fillets of similar thickness. Yellow, red, or brown miso paste can be used instead of white. If using wild salmon cook until it registers 120 degrees.

- ½ cup white miso paste
- ¼ cup sugar
- 3 tablespoons sake
- 3 tablespoons mirin
- 4 (6- to 8-ounce) skin-on salmon fillets
- Lemon wedges

**1.** Whisk miso, sugar, sake, and mirin in medium bowl until sugar and miso are dissolved (mixture will be thick). Dip each fillet into miso mixture to evenly coat all flesh sides. Place fish skin side down in baking dish and pour any remaining miso mixture over fillets. Cover with plastic wrap and refrigerate for at least 6 hours or up to 24 hours.

**2.** Adjust oven rack 8 inches from broiler element and heat broiler. Place wire rack in rimmed baking sheet and cover with aluminum foil. Using your fingers, scrape miso mixture from fillets (do not rinse) and place fish skin side down on foil, leaving 1 inch between fillets.

**3.** Broil salmon until deeply browned and centers of fillets are still translucent when checked with tip of paring knife and register 125 degrees (for medium-rare), 8 to 12 minutes, rotating sheet halfway through cooking and shielding edges of fillets with foil if necessary. Transfer to platter and serve with lemon wedges.

## Tandoori Salmon

**SERVES 4** **SEASON 26**

**WHY THIS RECIPE WORKS** To produce the traditional flavor and look of tandoori cooking for salmon, we first built a fragrant marinade around garam masala. Using garam masala, a spice blend, streamlined creating a complex earthy flavor profile for our salmon. We used a baking soda brine to keep the salmon moist during cooking and the high heat of the broiler to achieve the characteristic char of a superhot tandoor oven. Instead of using red dye for the distinctive ruby hue like many restaurants do, we used a spicy, smoky spice paste that included two crimson ingredients: Kashmiri chile powder and beet juice. Brushing the salmon with some lemon juice preserved the color during cooking, even after the baking soda brine. If you can't find kasoori methi (dried fenugreek leaves), omit it.

- 2 tablespoons baking soda for brining
- 4 (6- to 8-ounce) skin-on salmon fillets, 1 to 1½ inches thick
- 2 teaspoons garam masala
- 1 small red beet, trimmed and peeled
- 1½ tablespoons plus ¼ cup lemon juice (2 lemons)
- 1 tablespoon vegetable oil
- 2 garlic cloves, minced
- 2 teaspoons grated fresh ginger
- 2 teaspoons Kashmiri chile powder
- 1 teaspoon kasoori methi, crushed
- 1 teaspoon table salt
- ¼ teaspoon ground cardamom

**1.** Dissolve baking soda in 1 quart water in large bowl. Submerge salmon in brine and let stand at room temperature for 15 minutes.

**2.** Meanwhile, toast garam masala in dry 8-inch skillet over medium heat until fragrant, about 1 minute. Transfer to medium bowl. Place fine-mesh strainer over second bowl. Using rasp-style grater, grate beet over strainer set in bowl to yield about 3 tablespoons grated beet. Press on grated beet in strainer to extract about 2 tablespoons juice. (Discard solids and any extra juice.) Add beet juice, 1½ tablespoons lemon juice, oil, garlic, ginger, chile powder, kasoori methi, salt, and cardamom to bowl with garam masala, stirring to combine. Set aside.

**3.** Adjust oven rack 8 inches from broiler element and heat broiler. Remove salmon from brine, rinse fillets well under cold water, then pat dry with paper towels. Space salmon fillets evenly over aluminum foil–lined rimmed baking sheet, then brush salmon all over with remaining ¼ cup lemon juice (let excess lemon juice drip off onto sheet). Without patting salmon dry, coat top and sides of fillets with spice mixture. (Use all of spice mixture.)

**4.** Transfer sheet to oven and broil until center of salmon is still translucent when checked with tip of paring knife and registers 125 degrees (for medium- rare), 8 to 10 minutes, rotating sheet halfway through broiling. Serve.

## Broiled Salmon with Mustard and Crisp Dilled Crust

**SERVES** 8 to 10

**WHY THIS RECIPE WORKS** We wanted to pull off a crowd-pleasing side of salmon that was moist and firm, with a golden crumb crust that contrasted with the flavorful fish. Most of the time, we achieve a crisp crust on salmon through pan-searing in a skillet on the stovetop. With a crumb crust, it made sense to use the broiler. A plain bread crumb topping seemed bland, but when we toasted the crumbs and mixed in crushed potato chips and chopped dill, the result was a crisp and flavorful coating. To get the crumb mixture to adhere to the fish, we relied on a thin layer of mustard. But the crust burned by the time the fish was cooked through. We switched gears and broiled the fish almost unadorned until it was nearly done, then spread on the mustard and crumbs for a second run under the broiler. To get the fish onto a platter in one piece, we lined a baking sheet with heavy-duty foil, creating a sling with which we could move the fish. If you prefer to cook a smaller 2-pound fillet, ask to have it cut from the thick center of the fillet, not the thin tail end, and begin checking doneness a minute earlier.

- 3 slices high-quality white sandwich bread, torn into quarters
- 4 ounces plain high-quality potato chips, crushed into rough ⅛-inch pieces (about 1 cup)
- 6 tablespoons chopped fresh dill
- 1 whole side salmon fillet, about 3½ pounds, white belly fat trimmed
- 1 teaspoon olive oil
- Table salt and ground black pepper
- 3 tablespoons Dijon mustard

**1.** Adjust one oven rack to the top position (about 3 inches from the heat source) and the second rack to the upper-middle position; heat the oven to 400 degrees.

**2.** Pulse the bread in a food processor to fairly even ¼-inch pieces about the size of Grape-Nuts cereal (you should have about 1 cup), about 10 pulses. Spread the crumbs evenly on a rimmed baking sheet; toast on the lower oven rack, shaking the pan once or twice, until golden brown and crisp, 4 to 5 minutes. Toss the bread crumbs, crushed potato chips, and dill together in a small bowl; set aside.

**3.** Change the oven setting to broil. Cut a piece of heavy-duty foil 6 inches longer than the fillet. Fold the foil lengthwise in thirds and place lengthwise on a rimmed baking sheet; position the salmon lengthwise on the foil, allowing the excess foil to overhang the baking sheet. Rub the fillet evenly with the oil; sprinkle with salt and pepper. Broil the salmon on the upper rack until the surface is spotty brown and the outer ½ inch of the thick end is opaque when gently flaked with a paring knife, 9 to 11 minutes. Remove the baking sheet from the oven, spread the fish evenly with the mustard, and press the bread-crumb mixture onto the fish. Return the baking sheet to the lower oven rack and continue broiling until the crust is deep golden brown, about 1 minute longer.

**4.** Grasping the ends of the foil sling, lift the salmon, sling and all, onto a platter. Slide an offset spatula under the thick end. Grasp the foil, press the spatula against the foil, and slide it under the fish down to the thin end, loosening the entire side of fish. Grasp the foil again, hold the spatula perpendicular to the fish to stabilize it, and pull the foil out from under the fish. Wipe the platter clean with a damp paper towel. Serve the salmon immediately.

## Oven-Roasted Salmon

**SERVES** 4

**WHY THIS RECIPE WORKS** Roasting a salmon fillet can create a brown exterior, but often at the risk of a dry, overcooked interior. The best roasted salmon should have moist, flavorful flesh inside, with a contrasting crisp texture on the outside. To ensure that the salmon fillets would cook evenly, we cut a whole center-cut fillet into four pieces. We roasted the fish at a low temperature and achieved the buttery flesh we were after, but no browning—and the fillets were a little mushy from the rendered fat. Taking the opposite approach, we put the fish on a preheated baking sheet and started the oven at a high temperature to firm up and brown the exterior. This gave us a crust, but we still needed to get rid of the fat; cutting slits in the skin released the fat rendered by the high heat. Lowering the temperature as soon as we put the fish in the oven enabled it to cook through gradually after the initial blast of heat, so it didn't dry out. Now we had the contrast between moist interior and crisp brown exterior that we wanted. To ensure uniform pieces of fish that cook at the same rate, buy a whole center-cut fillet and cut it into four pieces. If your knife is not sharp enough to easily cut through the skin, try a serrated knife. It is important to keep the skin on during cooking; remove it afterward if you choose not to serve it. If using wild salmon cook until it registers 120 degrees.

- 1 (1¾- to 2-pound) skin-on salmon fillet, about 1½ inches at the thickest part
- 2 teaspoons olive oil
- Table salt and ground black pepper
- 1 recipe relish (recipes follow)

**1.** Adjust an oven rack to the lowest position, place a rimmed baking sheet on the rack, and heat the oven to 500 degrees. Remove any whitish fat from the belly of the fillet and cut it into four equal pieces. Make four or five shallow slashes about an inch apart along the skin side of each piece, being careful not to cut into the flesh.

**2.** Pat the salmon dry with paper towels. Rub the fillets evenly with the oil and season liberally with salt and pepper. Reduce the oven temperature to 275 degrees and remove the baking sheet. Carefully place the salmon, skin-side down, on the baking sheet. Roast until fillets registers 125 degrees (for medium-rare), 9 to 13 minutes. Transfer the fillets to individual plates or a platter. Top with relish and serve.

## Tangerine and Ginger Relish

**MAKES** about 1¼ cups

- 4 tangerines, rind and pith removed and segments cut into ½-inch pieces (about 1 cup)
- 1 scallion, sliced thin (about ¼ cup)
- 1½ teaspoons minced or grated fresh ginger
- 2 teaspoons juice from 1 lemon
- 2 teaspoons extra-virgin olive oil
- Table salt and ground black pepper

**1.** Place the tangerines in a fine-mesh strainer set over a medium bowl and drain for 15 minutes.

**2.** Pour off all but 1 tablespoon tangerine juice from the bowl; whisk in the scallion, ginger, lemon juice, and oil. Stir in the tangerines and season with salt and pepper to taste.

### REMOVING PIN BONES FROM SALMON

Drape whole fillet over inverted mixing bowl to help any pin bones protrude. Working from head end to tail end, locate pin bones by running fingers along length of fillet. Use pliers or tweezers to grasp bone and pull slowly but firmly at slight angle.

## Roasted Whole Side of Salmon

**SERVES** 8 to 10

**WHY THIS RECIPE WORKS** A whole roasted salmon fillet is ideal for entertaining. To start, we salted the fillet for an hour, which helped the flesh retain moisture and protein. An aluminum foil sling ensured easy transfer to a serving platter. We set the salmon on a wire rack set in a rimmed baking sheet to encourage air circulation. Brushing the surface with honey encouraged browning. We preheated the oven to 250 degrees, then broiled the fillet until it just began to brown. Last, we again turned the oven heat to 250 degrees to allow the fillet to gently cook through. A squeeze of fresh lemon juice was all it took to temper the richness of the salmon, but a vibrant, no-cook pesto offers dress-up potential. This recipe requires salting the fish for at least 1 hour. Look for a fillet that is uniformly thick from end to end. The surface will continue to brown after the oven temperature is reduced in step 4; if the surface starts to darken too much before the fillet's center registers 125 degrees, shield the dark portion with foil. If using wild salmon cook until it registers 120 degrees. Serve as is or with Arugula and Almond Pesto (recipe follows).

- 1 (4-pound) skin-on side of salmon, pin bones removed and belly fat trimmed
- 1 tablespoon kosher salt
- 2 tablespoons honey
- Lemon wedges

**1.** Sprinkle flesh side of salmon evenly with salt and refrigerate, uncovered, for at least 1 hour or up to 4 hours.

**2.** Adjust oven rack 7 inches from broiler element and heat oven to 250 degrees. Line rimmed baking sheet with aluminum foil and place wire rack in sheet. Fold 18 by 12-inch piece of foil lengthwise to create 18 by 6-inch sling. Place sling on wire rack and spray with vegetable oil spray.

**3.** Heat broiler. Pat salmon dry with paper towels and place, skin side down, on foil sling. Brush salmon evenly with honey and broil until surface is lightly but evenly browned, 8 to 12 minutes, rotating sheet halfway through broiling.

**4.** Return oven temperature to 250 degrees and continue to cook until center registers 125 degrees (for medium-rare), 10 to 15 minutes longer, rotating sheet halfway through cooking. Using foil sling, transfer salmon to serving platter, then carefully remove foil. If using wild salmon cook until it registers 120 degrees. Serve with lemon wedges.

## Arugula and Almond Pesto

**MAKES** 1½ cups

For a spicier pesto, reserve, mince, and add the ribs and seeds from the chile. The pesto can be refrigerated for up to 24 hours. If refrigerated, let the pesto sit at room temperature for 30 minutes before serving.

- ¼ cup almonds, lightly toasted
- 4 garlic cloves, peeled
- 4 anchovy fillets, rinsed and patted dry
- 1 serrano chile, stemmed, seeded, and halved lengthwise
- 6 ounces (6 cups) arugula
- ¼ cup lemon juice (2 lemons)
- ¼ cup extra-virgin olive oil
- 1½ teaspoons kosher salt

Process almonds, garlic, anchovies, and serrano in food processor until finely chopped, about 15 seconds, scraping down sides of bowl as needed. Add arugula, lemon juice, oil, and salt and process until smooth, about 30 seconds.

## Herb-Crusted Salmon

**SERVES** 4

**WHY THIS RECIPE WORKS** To make the best herb-crusted salmon, we first brined the salmon to keep it moist. For the herb, we thought the sweet, woodsy notes of tarragon paired well with salmon. To protect its delicate flavor in the oven, we mixed the herb with mustard and mayonnaise, layered it on the fish, then sprinkled on bread crumbs, which we'd seasoned with thyme. Toasting the bread crumbs in butter gave them some color and flavor. Beaten egg helped them adhere, and a low oven kept the crust from scorching while the salmon cooked. For the fillets to cook at the same rate, they must be the same size and shape. To ensure uniformity, we prefer to purchase a 1½- to 2-pound center-cut salmon fillet and cut it into four pieces. Dill or basil can be substituted for the tarragon. If using wild salmon cook until it registers 120 degrees.

Table salt and pepper
4 (6- to 8-ounce) skin-on salmon fillets
2 tablespoons unsalted butter
½ cup panko bread crumbs
2 tablespoons beaten egg
2 teaspoons minced fresh thyme
¼ cup chopped fresh tarragon
1 tablespoon whole-grain mustard
1½ teaspoons mayonnaise
Lemon wedges

**1.** Adjust oven rack to middle position and heat oven to 325 degrees. Dissolve 5 tablespoons salt in 2 quarts water in large container. Submerge salmon in brine and let stand at room temperature for 15 minutes. Remove salmon from brine, pat dry, and set aside.

**2.** Meanwhile, melt butter in 10-inch skillet over medium heat. Add panko and ⅛ teaspoon salt and season with pepper; cook, stirring frequently, until panko is golden brown, 4 to 5 minutes. Transfer to bowl and let cool completely. Stir in egg and thyme until thoroughly combined. Stir tarragon, mustard, and mayonnaise together in second bowl.

**3.** Set wire rack in rimmed baking sheet. Place 12 by 8-inch piece of aluminum foil on wire rack and lightly coat with vegetable oil spray. Evenly space fillets, skin side down, on foil. Using spoon, spread tarragon mixture evenly over top of each fillet. Sprinkle panko mixture evenly over top of each fillet, pressing with your fingers to adhere. Bake until fillets center register 125 degrees (for medium-rare), 18 to 25 minutes. Transfer salmon to serving platter and let rest for 5 minutes before serving with lemon wedges.

## Brown Rice Bowls with Vegetables and Salmon

**SERVES 4**

**WHY THIS RECIPE WORKS** Rice and grain bowls are healthy and delicious and offer an array of options for packing proteins and vegetables into a one-bowl meal. For this brown rice bowl, the chewy, nutty brown rice that forms the base was supereasy to make: We just poured it into plenty of boiling salted water and cooked it like pasta. While the rice cooked, we started roasting carrots and shiitakes in a hot oven and prepared pickled cucumbers to add crisp brightness to our bowl. When the vegetables were half-roasted, we added four small salmon fillets, brushed with hoisin sauce to boost their flavor and color. We mixed a portion of the pickling liquid with scallion-ginger oil and more hoisin to make a potent dressing. We stirred some into the drained rice to ensure that every bite was flavorful. If your knife is too dull to cut through the salmon skin, try a serrated knife. It is important to keep the skin on during cooking; once the salmon is cooked, the skin will be easy to remove. Toast the sesame seeds in a dry skillet over medium heat until fragrant (about 1 minute), and then remove the skillet from the heat so the seeds won't scorch. If using wild salmon cook until it registers 120 degrees.

¼ cup vegetable oil, divided
3 scallions, white and green parts separated and sliced thin on bias
2 teaspoons grated fresh ginger, divided
⅓ cup distilled white vinegar
1 tablespoon sugar
1¾ teaspoons table salt, divided, plus salt for cooking rice
1 English cucumber, quartered lengthwise, seeded, and sliced on bias ¼ inch thick
1¾ cups short-grain brown rice
1 pound carrots, peeled and sliced on bias ½ inch thick
1 pound shiitake mushrooms, stemmed, caps larger than 2 inches halved
1 (1-pound) skin-on salmon fillet, 1½ inches thick, sliced crosswise into 4 equal pieces
4 teaspoons hoisin sauce, divided
1 tablespoon sesame seeds, toasted
Sriracha (optional)

**1.** Adjust oven rack to lowest position and heat oven to 500 degrees. Heat 2 tablespoons oil in large saucepan over medium heat until shimmering. Add scallion whites and 1½ teaspoons ginger and cook, stirring constantly, until fragrant, about 30 seconds. Transfer scallion mixture to small bowl.

**2.** Bring 6 cups water to boil in now-empty saucepan. While water is coming to boil, whisk vinegar, sugar, ¾ teaspoon salt, and remaining ½ teaspoon ginger in medium bowl until sugar is dissolved. Add cucumber and stir until coated. Set aside, stirring occasionally.

**3.** Add rice and 1 teaspoon salt to boiling water. Reduce heat and simmer until rice is tender, about 30 minutes. Drain rice well and return it to saucepan. Cover and set aside.

**4.** While rice is cooking, toss carrots with 1 tablespoon oil and ½ teaspoon salt. Spread in even layer on half of rimmed baking sheet. Toss mushrooms with 2 tablespoons water, remaining 1 tablespoon oil, and remaining ½ teaspoon salt and spread in even layer on other half of sheet. Roast until vegetables are just beginning to soften and brown, about 10 minutes.

**5.** While vegetables are cooking, make 2 shallow slashes about 1 inch apart along skin side of each piece of salmon, being careful not to cut into flesh. Brush flesh side of each piece with ½ teaspoon hoisin.

**6.** Reduce oven temperature to 275 degrees and remove baking sheet. Push vegetables to either side to clear space in middle of sheet. Carefully place salmon, skin side down, in clearing. Return sheet to oven and roast until vegetables are tender and browned and fillets register 125 degrees (for medium-rare), 10 to 12 minutes.

**7.** Measure out ¼ cup cucumber liquid and add to scallion mixture. Whisk in remaining 2 teaspoons hoisin. Stir 2 tablespoons dressing into rice.

**8.** Spoon rice into 4 wide bowls. Place 1 piece of salmon on top of rice. Arrange carrots, mushrooms, and cucumbers in piles that cover rice. Drizzle salmon and vegetables with remaining dressing. Sprinkle with sesame seeds and scallion greens. Serve, passing sriracha separately, if using.

## Fresh Salmon Burgers with Sriracha Mayonnaise

**SERVES 4** **SEASON 26**

**WHY THIS RECIPE WORKS** The fat in salmon is very delicate and prone to liquefying when the fish is mechanically ground, so most salmon burger recipes call for mincing the salmon for burgers by hand. Instead, we cut our salmon into ¾-inch chunks and par-froze it before chopping it in the food processor. This brief chill fortified the fat against the heated friction of the processor. Sprinkling salt over the salmon before grinding drew a sticky protein called myosin out of the cut surfaces of the salmon, making our patties more cohesive. Starting the burgers in a cold skillet brought the temperature of the fish up more slowly, so our burgers retained their moisture. We halted the cooking when the burgers reached 110 degrees; carryover cooking during a 5-minute rest brought them to an ideal 125 degrees (for wild salmon, stop cooking at 105 degrees and let rest until they reach 120). If buying a skin-on salmon fillet, purchase 1⅓ pounds fish to yield 1¼ pounds after skinning. If using wild salmon, grease the skillet with 2 teaspoons of vegetable oil before adding the burgers. If you prefer a spicier mayonnaise, use the full 2 tablespoons of sriracha.

- 1 (1¼-pound) skinless salmon fillet, cut into ¾-inch pieces
- 3 tablespoons panko bread crumbs
- 2 tablespoons minced fresh parsley
- 2 tablespoons plus ¼ cup mayonnaise, divided
- 1 tablespoon lemon juice
- 1 tablespoon minced shallot
- 1 teaspoon Dijon mustard
- ¼ teaspoon pepper
- 1–2 tablespoons sriracha
- ¾ teaspoon table salt
- 4 hamburger buns, toasted
- Bibb lettuce leaves

**1.** Spread salmon pieces on parchment-lined rimmed baking sheet and freeze until very firm and starting to harden around edges but still pliable, 20 to 25 minutes. Combine panko, parsley, 2 tablespoons mayonnaise, lemon juice, shallot, mustard, and pepper in medium bowl. Mix remaining ¼ cup mayonnaise with sriracha in small bowl and set aside. Line plate with paper towel.

**2.** Transfer salmon to food processor and sprinkle with salt (reserve parchment). Pulse until coarsely chopped into ¼-inch pieces, 13 to 18 pulses. Transfer to bowl with panko mixture. Mix vigorously until uniformly combined. Smooth salmon into even layer and use edge of spatula to divide into 4 equal portions. Transfer portions to reserved parchment.

**3.** Shape each portion into patty about 3½ inches in diameter and transfer to unheated 12-inch nonstick skillet. Heat skillet over medium-high heat and cook patties, without moving, until undersides are well browned and bottom ⅓ inch turns opaque, 5 to 6 minutes. Carefully flip patties and continue to cook until second side is well browned and burgers register 110 degrees at center, 4 to 5 minutes longer. Transfer to prepared plate and let rest for 5 minutes.

**4.** Spread bun bottoms with sriracha mayonnaise. Top with lettuce, burgers, and bun tops and serve.

## Easy Salmon Cakes

**SERVES 4**

**WHY THIS RECIPE WORKS** Salmon cakes can be mushy and overly fishy, with gluey binders and heavy-handed seasoning. Our goal was a quick and simple recipe for salmon cakes that really tasted like salmon, with a delicate texture. To simplify preparation, we broke out our food processor. Pulsing small pieces of raw salmon (cooked salmon turned fishy) allowed for more even chopping and resulted in discrete pieces of fish. We also found a way to ditch the egg and flour steps of the breading process. Instead, we coated the salmon cakes with panko, which we had also used as a binder. If buying a skin-on salmon fillet, purchase 1⅓ pounds fish to yield 1¼ pounds after skinning. When processing the salmon, it is OK to have some pieces that are larger than ¼ inch. It is important to avoid overprocessing the fish. Serve the salmon cakes with lemon wedges and/or Sweet and Tangy Tartar Sauce (page 519).

- 3 tablespoons plus ¾ cup panko bread crumbs
- 2 tablespoons minced fresh parsley
- 2 tablespoons mayonnaise
- 4 teaspoons lemon juice
- 1 scallion, sliced thin
- 1 small shallot, minced
- 1 teaspoon Dijon mustard
- ¾ teaspoon table salt
- ¼ teaspoon pepper
- Pinch cayenne pepper
- 1 (1¼-pound) skinless salmon fillet, cut into 1-inch pieces
- ½ cup vegetable oil

**1.** Combine 3 tablespoons panko, parsley, mayonnaise, lemon juice, scallion, shallot, mustard, salt, pepper, and cayenne in bowl. Working in 3 batches, pulse salmon in food processor until coarsely chopped into ¼-inch pieces, about 2 pulses, transferring each batch to bowl with panko mixture. Gently mix until uniformly combined.

**2.** Place remaining ¾ cup panko in shallow dish. Using ⅓-cup measure, scoop level amount of salmon mixture and transfer to baking sheet; repeat to make 8 cakes. Carefully coat each cake with bread crumbs, gently patting into disk measuring 2¾ inches in diameter and 1 inch high. Return coated cakes to baking sheet.

**3.** Heat oil in 12-inch skillet over medium-high heat until shimmering. Place salmon cakes in skillet and cook without moving until bottoms are golden brown, about 2 minutes. Carefully flip cakes and cook until second side is golden brown, 2 to 3 minutes. Transfer cakes to paper towel–lined plate to drain for 1 minute. Serve.

## Crispy Salmon Cakes with Smoked Salmon, Capers, and Dill for Two

**SERVES 2**

**WHY THIS RECIPE WORKS** We wanted to give classic salmon cakes a new spin by creating an appealing, crispy coating. In addition, we used fresh salmon plus just a small amount of chopped smoked salmon which amped up the flavor. To keep this flavor center stage, we selected just a few choice ingredients and used a minimal amount of binder—mayonnaise and bread crumbs. To chop the salmon, we quickly pulsed 1-inch pieces in the food processor. This gave us both larger chunks for a substantial texture and smaller pieces that helped the cakes hold together. Coating the cakes in ultracrisp panko bread crumbs ensured a good crust. Dijon mustard, shallot, lemon juice, and dill boosted the flavor of the cakes, and a quick tartar sauce completed our dish. Be sure to use raw salmon here; do not substitute cooked salmon. Do not overprocess the salmon in step 2 or the cakes will have a pasty texture. If you purchase skin-on fillets, you can easily remove the skin yourself.

**TARTAR SAUCE**

- ⅓ cup mayonnaise
- 1 tablespoon sweet pickle relish
- 1½ teaspoons capers, rinsed and minced
- 1 teaspoon white wine vinegar
- ¼ teaspoon Worcestershire sauce

**SALMON CAKES**

- 1 (8-ounce) skinless salmon fillet, cut into 1-inch pieces
- 2 tablespoons plus ½ cup panko bread crumbs, divided
- 2 ounces smoked salmon, finely chopped
- 1 tablespoon chopped fresh dill
- 1 tablespoon mayonnaise
- 1 small shallot, minced
- 2 teaspoons lemon juice
- 1½ teaspoons capers, rinsed and minced
- ½ teaspoon Dijon mustard
- ¼ teaspoon pepper
- ⅛ teaspoon table salt
- Pinch cayenne pepper
- ⅓ cup vegetable oil

**1. FOR THE TARTAR SAUCE:** Whisk all ingredients together in bowl and season with salt and pepper to taste; set aside.

**2. FOR THE SALMON CAKES:** Pulse salmon in food processor until there is an even mix of finely minced and coarsely chopped pieces of salmon, about 2 pulses, scraping down sides of bowl as needed.

**3.** Combine 2 tablespoons panko, smoked salmon, dill, mayonnaise, shallot, lemon juice, capers, mustard, pepper, salt, and cayenne in bowl. Gently fold in processed salmon until just combined.

**4.** Spread remaining ½ cup panko in shallow dish. Scrape salmon mixture onto small baking sheet. Divide mixture into 4 equal portions and gently flatten each portion into 1-inch-thick patty. Carefully coat each cake with panko, then return to sheet.

**5.** Line large plate with triple layer of paper towels. Heat oil in 10-inch skillet over medium-high heat until shimmering. Gently place salmon cakes in skillet and cook, without moving, until golden brown and crisp on both sides, 2 to 3 minutes per side. Drain cakes briefly on paper towel–lined plate. Serve with Sweet and Tangy Tartar Sauce (page 519).

### SKINNING A SALMON FILLET

Insert blade of sharp knife just above skin about 1 inch from end of fillet. Cut through nearest end, away from yourself, keeping blade just above skin. Rotate fish and grab loose skin. Run knife between flesh and skin until skin is completely removed.

## Poached Salmon with Herb and Caper Vinaigrette

**SERVES 4**

**WHY THIS RECIPE WORKS** For a supple poached salmon with a delicately flavored poaching liquid, we started with a classic court-bouillon made by boiling water, wine, herbs, vegetables, and aromatics. Discarding all those vegetables seemed wasteful so we used less liquid and cut back on the vegetables and aromatics; shallots, a few herbs, and wine were all we needed. The salmon that wasn't submerged needed to be steamed to cook through, but the low cooking temperature required to poach the salmon evenly didn't create enough steam. Increasing the ratio of wine to water lowered the liquid's boiling point, producing more vapor. Meanwhile, the bottom of the fillets overcooked due to direct contact with the pan. Resting the fillets on top of lemon slices provided insulation. For a finishing touch, we reduced the liquid and added olive oil to create an easy sauce. To ensure uniform pieces of fish that cook at the same rate, buy a whole center-cut fillet and cut it into four pieces. If a skinless whole fillet is unavailable, remove the skin yourself or follow the recipe as directed with a skin-on fillet, adding 3 to 4 minutes to the cooking time in step 2. If using wild salmon, cook until it registers 120 degrees.

- 2 lemons
- 1 large shallot, minced (about ¼ cup), divided
- 2 tablespoons minced fresh parsley, stems reserved
- 2 tablespoons minced fresh tarragon, stems reserved
- ½ cup dry white wine
- ½ cup water
- 1 (1¾- to 2-pound) skinless salmon fillet, about 1½ inches at the thickest part
- 2 tablespoons capers, rinsed and chopped coarse
- 2 tablespoons extra-virgin olive oil
- 1 tablespoon honey

**1.** Cut top and bottom off 1 lemon; cut lemon into eight to ten ¼-inch-thick slices. Cut remaining lemon into 8 wedges and set aside. Arrange lemon slices in single layer across bottom of 12-inch skillet. Scatter 2 tablespoons of shallot and herb stems evenly over lemon slices. Add wine and water.

**2.** Use sharp knife to trim any whitish fat from belly of fillet and cut it into 4 equal pieces. Place salmon fillets in skillet, skinned side down, on top of lemon slices. Set pan over high heat and bring liquid to simmer. Reduce heat to low, cover, and cook fillets register 125 degrees (for medium-rare), 11 to 16 minutes. Remove pan from heat and, using spatula, carefully transfer salmon and lemon slices to paper towel–lined plate. Tent with foil.

**3.** Return pan to high heat and simmer cooking liquid until slightly thickened and reduced to 2 tablespoons, 4 to 5 minutes. Meanwhile, combine remaining shallot, minced herbs, capers, olive oil, and honey in medium bowl. Strain reduced cooking liquid through fine-mesh strainer into bowl with herb-caper mixture, pressing on solids to extract as much liquid as possible. Whisk to combine and season with salt and pepper to taste.

**4.** Season salmon lightly with salt and pepper. Using spatula, carefully lift and tilt salmon fillets to remove lemon slices. Place salmon on serving platter or individual plates and spoon vinaigrette over top. Serve, with reserved lemon wedges.

## Pesce all'Acqua Pazza (Southern Italian-Style Poached Fish)

**SERVES 4**

**WHY THIS RECIPE WORKS** Pesca all'acqua pazza, or "fish in crazy water," refers to the centuries-old southern Italian tradition of cooking the day's catch in seawater. Following the lead of modern Italian cooks, we spiked our water-based broth with white wine for brightness and acidity and halved cherry tomatoes for sweetness and pops of color. For the fish, we chose skin-on haddock fillets, which held up nicely during simmering and (due to the abundant collagen in the skin) suffused the broth with rich flavor and body. To ensure perfectly cooked fillets, we poached them over low heat until they were nearly done and then slid the pan off the burner to finish the cooking at a gentler pace. After just a few minutes, the haddock absorbed the heady flavor of the broth and the broth was enriched by the fish. You may substitute skin-on fillets of other firm, white-fleshed species such as sea bass, branzino, and red snapper. Serve with crusty bread.

- 1½ pounds skin-on haddock fillets, ¾ to 1 inch thick
- 1 teaspoon kosher salt, divided
- 2 tablespoons extra-virgin olive oil
- 3 garlic cloves, sliced thin
- ¼ teaspoon crushed red pepper flakes
- 1 small onion, chopped fine
- 1 bay leaf
- 8 ounces cherry or grape tomatoes, halved
- 1¼ cups water
- ¼ cup dry white wine
- 12 parsley stems, plus 3 tablespoons chopped fresh parsley leaves

**1.** Season fish fillets all over with ½ teaspoon salt and pepper to taste and set aside.

**2.** Heat oil, garlic, and red pepper flakes in 12-inch skillet over medium heat, stirring constantly, until garlic begins to sizzle gently, 1½ to 2 minutes. Add onion, bay leaf, and remaining ½ teaspoon salt and cook, stirring constantly, until onion just starts to soften, 2 to 3 minutes. Add tomatoes and cook, stirring constantly, until they begin to soften, 2 to 3 minutes. Stir in water, wine, parsley stems and half of chopped parsley and bring to boil. Nestle fillets skin side down in liquid, moving aside solids as much as possible (it's fine if fillets fold over slightly at ends; liquid will not quite cover fillets). Spoon some liquid and solids over fillets. Adjust heat to low, cover, and simmer gently until fillets register 110 at thickest point, 4 to 7 minutes. Remove skillet from heat and let stand, covered, until fish is opaque and just cooked through (fish should register at least 135 degrees), 3 to 7 minutes.

3. Divide fish among 4 shallow soup plates. Remove bay leaf and parsley stems from skillet; stir in remaining parsley. Season broth with salt and pepper to taste. Spoon a portion of broth and solids over each serving of fish and serve immediately.

## Poached Fish Fillets with Sherry-Tomato Vinaigrette

SERVES 4

**WHY THIS RECIPE WORKS** Restaurant-style poached fish requires a potful of pricey olive oil and promises supermoist, delicately cooked fish. Using a small skillet and flipping the fish halfway through cooking allowed us to cut back to ¾ cup of oil, which we employed to crisp flavorful garnishes and finally blended into a vinaigrette. Fillets of meaty white fish like cod, halibut, sea bass, or snapper work best in this recipe. Just make sure the fillets are at least 1 inch thick. A neutral oil such as canola can be substituted for the olive oil. The onion half in step 3 is used to displace the oil; a 4-ounce porcelain ramekin may be used instead. Serve with couscous or steamed white rice.

**FISH**

- 4 (6-ounce) skinless white fish fillets, 1 inch thick
- Kosher salt
- 4 ounces frozen artichoke hearts, thawed, patted dry, and sliced in half lengthwise
- 1 tablespoon cornstarch
- ¾ cup olive oil
- 3 garlic cloves, minced
- ½ onion, peeled

**VINAIGRETTE**

- 4 ounces cherry tomatoes
- ½ small shallot, peeled
- 4 teaspoons sherry vinegar
- Kosher salt and pepper
- 2 ounces cherry tomatoes, cut into ⅛-inch-thick rounds
- 1 tablespoon minced fresh parsley

1. **FOR THE FISH:** Adjust oven racks to middle and lower-middle positions and heat oven to 250 degrees. Pat fish dry with paper towels and season each fillet with ¼ teaspoon salt. Let sit at room temperature for 20 minutes.

2. Meanwhile, toss artichokes with cornstarch in bowl to coat. Heat ½ cup oil in 10-inch nonstick ovensafe skillet over medium heat until shimmering. Shake excess cornstarch from artichokes and add to skillet; cook, stirring occasionally, until crisp and golden, 2 to 4 minutes. Add garlic and continue to cook until garlic is golden, 30 to 60 seconds. Strain oil through fine-mesh strainer into bowl. Transfer artichokes and garlic to ovensafe paper towel–lined plate and season with salt. Do not wash strainer.

3. Return strained oil to skillet and add remaining ¼ cup oil. Place onion half in center of pan. Let oil cool until it registers about 180 degrees, 5 to 8 minutes. Arrange fish fillets, skinned side up, around onion (oil should come roughly halfway up fillets). Spoon a little oil over each fillet, cover skillet, transfer to middle oven rack, and cook for 15 minutes.

4. Remove skillet from oven (skillet handle will be hot). Using 2 spatulas, carefully flip fillets. Cover skillet, return to middle rack, and place plate with artichokes and garlic on lower-middle rack. Continue to cook until fish registers 135 degrees, 9 to 14 minutes longer. Gently transfer fish to serving platter, reserving ½ cup oil, and tent fish loosely with aluminum foil. Turn off oven, leaving plate of artichokes in oven.

5. **FOR THE VINAIGRETTE:** Process cherry tomatoes, shallot, vinegar, ¾ teaspoon salt, and ½ teaspoon pepper with reserved ½ cup fish cooking oil in blender until smooth, 1 to 2 minutes. Add any accumulated fish juices from platter, season with salt to taste, and blend for 10 seconds. Strain sauce through fine-mesh strainer; discard solids.

6. To serve, pour vinaigrette around fish. Garnish each fillet with warmed crisped artichokes and garlic, tomato rounds, and parsley. Serve immediately.

## Butter-Basted Fish Fillets with Garlic and Thyme

SERVES 2

**WHY THIS RECIPE WORKS** Butter basting, a technique that involves spooning sizzling butter over food as it cooks, is great for mild, flaky fish such as cod, haddock, or snapper. The butter helps cook the top of the fillet as the skillet heats the bottom, allowing you to flip the fish only once during cooking—before the flesh becomes too fragile—so it stays intact. The nutty, aromatic butter, which we enhanced with thyme sprigs and crushed garlic cloves, bathed the fish in savory flavor. We alternated basting with direct-heat cooking on the burner, taking the temperature of the fish so we knew exactly when the fillets were done. You can substitute red snapper or haddock for the cod. The "skinned" side of a skinless fillet can be identified by its streaky, slightly darker appearance.

- 2 (6-ounce) skinless cod fillets, about 1 inch thick
- ½ teaspoon kosher salt
- ⅛ teaspoon pepper
- 1 tablespoon vegetable oil
- 3 tablespoons unsalted butter, cut into ½-inch cubes
- 2 garlic cloves, crushed and peeled
- 4 sprigs fresh thyme
- Lemon wedges

**1.** Pat all sides of fillets dry with paper towels. Sprinkle on all sides with salt and pepper. Heat oil in 12-inch nonstick or carbon-steel skillet over medium-high heat until just smoking. Reduce heat to medium and place fillets skinned side down in skillet. Gently press on each fillet with spatula for 5 seconds to ensure good contact with skillet. Cook fillets, without moving them, until underside is light golden brown, 4 to 5 minutes.

**2.** Using 2 spatulas, gently flip fillets. Cook for 1 minute. Scatter butter around fillets. When butter is melted, tilt skillet slightly toward you so butter pools at front of skillet. Using large spoon, scoop up melted butter and pour over fillets repeatedly for 15 seconds. Place skillet flat on burner and continue to cook 30 seconds longer. Tilt skillet and baste for 15 seconds. Place skillet flat on burner and take temperature of thickest part of each fillet. Continue to alternate basting and cooking until fillets register 130 degrees. Add garlic and thyme sprigs to skillet at 12 o'clock position (butter will spatter). When spattering has subsided, continue basting and cooking until fillets register 135 degrees at thickest point. (Total cooking time will range from 8 to 10 minutes.)

**3.** Transfer fillets to individual plates. Discard garlic. Top each fillet with thyme sprigs, pour butter over fillets, and serve with lemon wedges.

## Fish Meunière with Browned Butter and Lemon

**SERVES 4**

**WHY THIS RECIPE WORKS** The best fish meunière consists of perfectly cooked fillets that are delicately crisp and golden brown, moist and flavorful on the inside, napped in a buttery yet light sauce. Whole Dover sole is the traditional choice, but it's not widely available so sole or flounder fillets make good stand-ins. To prevent overcooking, the fillets needed to be no less than ⅜ inch thick and they must be patted dry before being seasoned and dredged in flour. Using a nonstick skillet for pan-frying meant there was less chance for the fillets to fall apart; lubricating the pan with oil and butter added extra insurance. Removing the pan from the heat just before the fish was cooked kept the fish moist since it continued to cook off the heat. Browning the butter in a traditional skillet made it easier to monitor the browning. Try to purchase fillets that are of similar size, and avoid those that weigh less than 5 ounces as they cook too quickly. When placing the fillets in the skillet, place them skinned side up so that the opposite side, which had bones, will brown first. You will need both a 12-inch nonstick skillet and a 10-inch traditional skillet for this recipe.

**FISH**

- ½ cup unbleached all-purpose flour
- 4 (5- to 6-ounce) sole or flounder fillets, ⅜ inch thick
- Table salt and ground black pepper
- 2 tablespoons vegetable oil
- 2 tablespoons unsalted butter, cut into 2 pieces

**BROWNED BUTTER**

- 4 tablespoons (½ stick) unsalted butter, cut into 4 pieces
- 1 tablespoon chopped fresh parsley leaves
- 1½ tablespoons juice from 1 lemon
- Table salt
- Lemon wedges, for serving

**1. FOR THE FISH:** Adjust an oven rack to the lower-middle position, set four heatproof dinner plates on the rack, and heat the oven to 200 degrees. Place the flour in a large baking dish. Pat the fillets dry with paper towels and season with salt and pepper; let stand until the fillets are glistening with moisture, about 5 minutes. Coat both sides of the fillets with flour, shake off the excess, and place in a single layer on a rimmed baking sheet.

**2.** Heat 1 tablespoon of the oil in a 12-inch nonstick skillet over high heat until shimmering; add 1 tablespoon of the butter and swirl to coat the pan bottom. Carefully place 2 fillets, skinned side up, in the skillet. Immediately reduce the heat to medium-high and cook, without moving the fish, until the edges of the fillets are opaque and the bottoms are golden brown, about 3 minutes. Using two spatulas, gently flip the fillets and cook on the second side until the thickest part of the fillet easily separates into flakes when a toothpick is inserted, about 2 minutes longer. Transfer the fillets to two of the heated dinner plates, keeping them boned side up, and return the plates to the oven. Wipe out the skillet and repeat with the remaining 1 tablespoon oil, remaining 1 tablespoon butter, and the remaining fish fillets.

**3. FOR THE BROWNED BUTTER:** Melt the butter in a 10-inch traditional skillet over medium-high heat. Continue to cook, swirling the pan constantly, until the butter is golden brown and has a nutty aroma, 1 to 1½ minutes; remove the skillet from the heat. Remove the plates from the oven and sprinkle the fillets with the parsley. Add the lemon juice to the browned butter and season with salt to taste. Spoon the sauce over the fish and serve immediately, garnished with the lemon wedges.

## Skillet-Roasted Fish Fillets

**SERVES 4**

**WHY THIS RECIPE WORKS** Pan-roasted fish seems like a simple dish, but in reality it is usually only well executed by practiced chefs. At home, the dish often results in dry, overbaked fillets. We set out to develop a foolproof recipe for producing succulent, well-browned fillets. From an initial round of testing, we knew we needed thick fillets; skinnier pieces end up overcooked by the time they achieved a serious sear. We then turned to a common restaurant method to cook the fish: Sear the fillet in a hot pan, flip, then transfer it to a hot oven to finish cooking. The technique was sound, but to brown the fish quickly before the hot pan had a chance to dry out the fish's exterior we turned to a sprinkling of sugar. The idea is that sugar commingles with exuded juices from the fish, accelerating browning and giving the fish a rich color and deep flavor that's anything but sweet. We dusted a few fillets with a touch of granulated sugar and placed them in a hot skillet. A well-browned crust formed almost immediately, leaving no time for the interior to dry out. And after a short stay in the oven to finish cooking through, the fish emerged well-browned, tender and moist, and best of all, not one taster detected any out-of-place sweetness. Thick white fish fillets with a meaty texture, like halibut, cod, sea bass, or red snapper, work best in this recipe. Because most fish fillets differ in thickness, some pieces may finish cooking before others—be sure to immediately remove any fillet that reaches 135 degrees. You will need an ovensafe nonstick skillet for this recipe. If you can't find skinless fillets, see page 505 for information on skinning fillets. Serve with lemon wedges.

- 4 (6 to 8-ounce) skinless white fish fillets, 1 to 1½ inches thick
- Table salt and ground black pepper
- ½ teaspoon sugar
- 1 tablespoon vegetable oil
- Lemon wedges

Adjust an oven rack to the middle position and heat the oven to 425 degrees. Dry the fish thoroughly with paper towels and season with salt and pepper. Sprinkle ⅛ teaspoon sugar evenly over one side of each fillet. Heat the oil in a 12-inch ovensafe nonstick skillet over high heat until smoking. Place the fillets in the skillet, sugared side down, and press down lightly to ensure even contact with the pan. Cook until browned, 1 to 1½ minutes. Using two spatulas, flip the fillets and transfer the skillet to the oven. Roast until fillets register 135 degrees, 7 to 10 minutes. Immediately transfer the fish to individual plates and serve with lemon wedges or a fresh relish.

## Moroccan Fish Tagine

SERVES 4

**WHY THIS RECIPE WORKS** With its vibrant colors, punchy flavors, and straightforward technique, a tagine is just the thing to perk up mild white fish. For a bright, flavorful fish tagine, we started by salting chunks of cod to season the flesh and help it retain moisture. We coated the fish in chermoula, a flavorful herb-spice paste of cilantro, garlic, cumin, paprika, cayenne, lemon juice, and olive oil, just before cooking to season its exterior. Softening bell pepper, onion, and carrot before adding the tomatoes and fish ensured that the vegetables would be soft and tender by the time the fish was cooked through. Preserved lemon and olives added acidity, complexity, and salty punch to the broth. To produce moist, flaky cod, we turned off the heat once the broth was bubbling at the bottom of the pot and allowed the fish to cook in the residual heat. You can substitute red snapper or haddock for the cod as long as the fillets are 1 to 1½ inches thick. Picholine or Cerignola olives work well in this recipe. Serve this dish with flatbread, couscous, or rice.

- 1½ pounds skinless cod fillets (1 to 1½ inches thick), cut into 1½- to 2-inch pieces
- ¾ teaspoon table salt, divided
- ½ cup fresh cilantro leaves, plus ¼ cup chopped
- 4 garlic cloves, peeled
- 1¼ teaspoons ground cumin
- 1¼ teaspoons paprika
- ¼ teaspoon cayenne pepper
- 1½ tablespoons lemon juice
- 6 tablespoons extra-virgin olive oil, divided
- 1 onion, halved and sliced through root end ¼ inch thick
- 1 green bell pepper, stemmed, seeded, and cut into ¼-inch strips
- 1 carrot, peeled and sliced on bias ¼ inch thick
- 1 (14.5-ounce) can diced tomatoes
- ⅓ cup pitted green olives, quartered lengthwise
- 2 tablespoons finely chopped preserved lemon

**1.** Place cod in bowl and toss with ½ teaspoon salt. Set aside.

**2.** Pulse cilantro leaves, garlic, cumin, paprika, and cayenne in food processor until cilantro and garlic are finely chopped, about 12 pulses. Add lemon juice and pulse briefly to combine. Transfer mixture to small bowl and stir in 2 tablespoons oil. Set aside.

**3.** Heat remaining ¼ cup oil in large Dutch oven over medium heat until shimmering. Add onion, bell pepper, carrot, and remaining ¼ teaspoon salt and cook, stirring frequently, until softened, 5 to 7 minutes. Stir in tomatoes and their juice, olives, and preserved lemon. Spread mixture in even layer on bottom of pot.

**4.** Toss cod with cilantro mixture until evenly coated, then arrange cod over vegetables in single layer. Cover and cook until cod starts to turn opaque and juices released from cod are simmering vigorously, 3 to 5 minutes. Remove pot from heat and let stand, covered, until cod registers 135 degrees, 3 to 5 minutes. Sprinkle with chopped cilantro and serve.

## Oven-Steamed Fish with Scallions and Ginger

**SERVES 4**

**WHY THIS RECIPE WORKS** Classic Chinese and French cuisines both use techniques for steaming fish that ensure moist, flavorful results. We borrowed from each approach to come up with an entirely new method that produces fish fillets infused with the flavors of soy sauce, garlic, and ginger. We spread scallions and ginger over the bottom of a baking pan to infuse the fish with flavor as it steamed. We poured in a mixture of soy sauce, rice wine, sesame oil, sugar, salt, and white pepper; covered the pan; and placed it in a hot oven. After just 12 minutes the fish was perfectly cooked. To coat the fish in a fragrant sauce, we strained the aromatic liquid left behind in the pan and poured it over the fish. Following the Chinese tradition, to finish we sautéed thin matchsticks of ginger in oil and then poured the mixture over the fish. A smattering of cilantro sprigs over the top provided a final, elegant touch. Haddock, red snapper, halibut, and sea bass will also work in this recipe as long as the fillets are about 1 inch thick. If one end of the fillet is thinner, fold it under when placing it in the pan. This recipe works best in a metal baking pan; if using a glass baking dish, add 5 minutes to the cooking time. To ensure that the fish doesn't overcook, remove it from the oven when it registers between 125 and 130 degrees; it will continue to cook as it is plated. Serve with steamed rice and vegetables.

- 8 scallions, trimmed, divided
- 1 (3-inch) piece ginger, peeled, divided
- 3 garlic cloves, sliced thin
- 4 (6-ounce) skinless cod fillets, about 1 inch thick
- 3 tablespoons soy sauce
- 2 tablespoons rice wine or dry sherry
- 1½ teaspoons toasted sesame oil
- 1½ teaspoons sugar
- ¼ teaspoon table salt
- ¼ teaspoon white pepper
- 2 tablespoons vegetable oil
- ⅓ cup cilantro leaves and thin stems

**1.** Adjust oven rack to middle position and heat oven to 450 degrees. Chop 6 scallions coarse and spread evenly in 13 by 9-inch baking pan. Slice remaining scallions thin on bias, and set aside. Chop 2 inches of ginger coarse and spread in baking pan with scallions. Slice remaining 1 inch of ginger into thin matchsticks and reserve. Sprinkle garlic over scallions and ginger.

**2.** Fold 18 by 12-inch piece of aluminum foil lengthwise to create 18 by 6-inch sling and spray lightly with vegetable oil spray. Place in pan lengthwise, allowing excess to hang over each end. Arrange fish on sling. If fillets vary in thickness, place thinner fillets in middle and thicker fillets at ends.

**3.** Whisk soy sauce, rice wine, sesame oil, sugar, salt, and white pepper in small bowl until combined. Pour around fish. Cover pan tightly with aluminum foil. Bake until fish registers 135 degrees, 12 to 14 minutes.

**4.** Grasping sling at each end, carefully transfer sling and fish to deep platter. Place spatula at 1 end of fillet to hold in place, and carefully slide foil out from under fish. Pour cooking liquid into fine-mesh strainer set over bowl and press on solids to extract liquid. Discard solids. Pour cooking liquid over fish. Sprinkle remaining scallions over fish. Heat vegetable oil in skillet over high heat until just smoking. Remove from heat and add remaining ginger (ginger will sizzle). Stir until ginger is beginning to brown and crisp. Drizzle oil and ginger over fish. Top with cilantro and serve.

## Cod Baked in Foil with Leeks and Carrots

**SERVES 4**

**WHY THIS RECIPE WORKS** Cooking mild fish like cod en papillote—in a tightly sealed, artfully folded parchment package so it can steam in its own juices—is an easy, mess-free way to enhance its delicate flavor. If you throw in vegetables, it should add up to a light but satisfying meal. However, without the right blend of flavorings, the fish can taste lean and bland, and not all vegetables pair well with cod. We found that foil was easier to work with than parchment. Placing the packets on the oven's lower-middle rack concentrated the exuded liquid and deepened the flavor. Leeks, carrots, fennel, and zucchini all worked well as the vegetable component and complemented the mild fish. Haddock, red snapper, halibut, and sea bass also work well in this recipe and those that follow as long as the fillets are 1 to 1¼ inches thick. The packets may be assembled several hours ahead of time and refrigerated until ready to cook. If the packets have been refrigerated for more than 30 minutes, increase the cooking time by 2 minutes. Open each packet promptly after baking to prevent overcooking. Zest the lemon before cutting it into wedges.

- 4 tablespoons unsalted butter, softened
- 1¼ teaspoons finely grated zest from 1 lemon, divided; lemon cut into wedges
- 2 medium garlic cloves, minced (about 2 teaspoons), divided
- 1 teaspoon minced fresh thyme leaves
- Table salt and pepper
- 2 tablespoons minced fresh parsley leaves
- 2 medium carrots, peeled and cut into matchsticks (about 1½ cups)
- 2 medium leeks, white and light green parts halved lengthwise, washed, and cut into matchsticks (about 2 cups)
- 4 tablespoons vermouth or dry white wine
- 4 skinless cod fillets, 1 to 1¼ inches thick (about 6 ounces each)

**1.** Combine butter, ¼ teaspoon zest, 1 teaspoon garlic, thyme, ¼ teaspoon salt, and ⅛ teaspoon pepper in small bowl. Combine parsley, remaining 1 teaspoon zest, and remaining 1 teaspoon garlic in another small bowl; set aside. Place carrots and leeks in medium bowl, season with salt and pepper, and toss together.

**2.** Adjust oven rack to lower-middle position and heat oven to 450 degrees. Cut eight 12-inch sheets of foil; arrange four flat on counter. Divide carrot and leek mixture among foil sheets, mounding in center of each. Pour 1 tablespoon vermouth over each mound of vegetables. Pat fish dry with paper towels; season with salt and pepper and place one fillet on top of each vegetable mound. Spread one-quarter of butter mixture on top of each fillet. Place second square of foil on top of fish; crimp edges together in ½-inch fold, then fold over three more times to create a packet about 7 inches square. Place packets on rimmed baking sheet (overlapping slightly if necessary).

**3.** Bake packets for 15 minutes. Carefully open foil, allowing steam to escape away from you. Using thin metal spatula, gently slide fish and vegetables onto plate with any accumulated juices; sprinkle with parsley mixture. Serve immediately, passing lemon wedges separately.

## Pan-Roasted Halibut Steaks

**SERVES** 4 to 6

**WHY THIS RECIPE WORKS** Chefs often choose to braise halibut instead of pan-roasting or sautéing because this moist-heat cooking technique keeps the fish from drying out. The problem is that braising doesn't allow for browning. We didn't want to make any compromises on either texture or flavor, so we set out to develop a technique for pan-roasting halibut that would produce perfectly cooked, moist, and tender fish. Halibut is most frequently sold as steaks, but there is quite a bit of range in size; to ensure that they cooked at the same rate, we chose steaks that were as close in size to each other as possible. We knew we could get a crust on the fish by pan-searing or oven-roasting, but neither technique proved satisfactory. A combination of the two—browning on the stovetop and roasting in the oven—worked best. To be sure the steaks wouldn't overcook, we seared them on one side in a piping-hot skillet and turned them over before placing them in the oven to finish cooking through. When they were done, the steaks were browned but still moist inside. To complement the lean fish, we paired the halibut with a rich flavored butter. If you plan to serve the fish with Chipotle-Garlic Butter with Lime and Cilantro (recipe follows), prepare it before cooking the fish. Even well-dried fish can cause the hot oil in the pan to splatter. You can minimize splattering by laying the halibut steaks in the pan gently and putting the edge closest to you in the pan first so that the far edge falls away from you.

- 2 tablespoons olive oil
- 2 (full) halibut steaks, about 1¼ inches thick and 10 to 12 inches long (about 2½ pounds total), gently rinsed, dried well with paper towels, and trimmed of cartilage at both ends
- ¾ teaspoon table salt
- ¾ teaspoon pepper
- 1 recipe Chipotle-Garlic Butter with Lime and Cilantro

**1.** Adjust oven rack to middle position and heat oven to 425 degrees. When oven reaches 425 degrees, heat oil in 12-inch ovensafe skillet over high heat until oil just begins to smoke.

**2.** Meanwhile, sprinkle both sides of halibut steaks with salt and pepper. Reduce heat to medium-high and swirl oil in pan to distribute; carefully lay steaks in pan and sear, without moving them, until spotty brown, about 4 minutes. (If steaks are thinner than 1¼ inches, check browning at 3½ minutes; thicker steaks of 1½ inches may require extra time, so check at 4½ minutes.) Off heat, flip steaks over in pan using 2 thin-bladed metal spatulas.

### TRIMMING AND SERVING FULL HALIBUT STEAKS

**1.** Cut off cartilage at each end of steaks to ensure they will fit neatly in pan and prevent small bones located there from winding up on your plate.

**2.** Remove skin from cooked steaks and separate quadrants of meat from bone by slipping knife gently between them.

**3.** Transfer skillet to oven and roast until centers are just steaks register 130 degrees, about 9 minutes (thicker steaks may take up to 10 minutes). Remove skillet from oven. Remove skin from cooked steaks and separate each quadrant of meat from bones by slipping spatula or knife gently between them. Transfer fish to warm platter and serve with chipotle-garlic butter.

### Chipotle-Garlic Butter with Lime and Cilantro

**MAKES** ¼ cup

- 4 tablespoons unsalted butter, softened
- 1 medium chipotle chile in adobo sauce, seeded and minced, plus 1 teaspoon adobo sauce
- 2 teaspoons minced fresh cilantro
- 1 garlic clove, minced
- 1 teaspoon honey
- 1 teaspoon grated lime zest
- ½ teaspoon table salt

Beat butter with fork until light and fluffy. Stir in chipotle and adobo sauce, cilantro, garlic, honey, lime zest, and salt until thoroughly combined. Dollop a portion of butter over each piece of hot cooked fish and allow butter to melt. Serve immediately.

## Braised Halibut with Leeks and Mustard

**SERVES** 4

**WHY THIS RECIPE WORKS** Braising is a technique usually reserved for tough cuts of meat, but the gentle, moist-heat cooking method also works wonders on fish. Halibut's dense flesh made it an easy fillet to manipulate and its clean, sweet flavor paired well with a simple wine sauce. We began by gently cooking just one side of the fillets in butter in a skillet, then removing the fish to establish the braising liquid. We cooked sliced leeks in Dijon and their exuded moisture added to the thin sauce. Once the leeks had softened, we added some dry white wine, brought it to a simmer, and placed the halibut atop the vegetables with the uncooked side facing down. This arrangement allowed the parcooked side to steam while the rest of the fillet cooked through to perfection. To finish the sauce, we transferred the cooked fish and vegetables to a serving platter and let the wine sauce reduce, adding lemon juice for a burst of bright acidity. We prefer to prepare this recipe with halibut, but a similar firm-fleshed white fish such as striped bass or sea bass that is between ¾ and 1 inch thick can be substituted. To ensure that your fish cooks evenly, purchase fillets that are similarly shaped and uniformly thick.

- 4 (6- to 8-ounce) skinless halibut fillets, ¾ to 1 inch thick
- Table salt and pepper
- 6 tablespoons unsalted butter
- 1 pound leeks, white and light green parts only, halved lengthwise, sliced thin, and washed thoroughly
- 1 teaspoon Dijon mustard
- ¾ cup dry white wine
- 1 teaspoon lemon juice, plus lemon wedges for serving
- 1 tablespoon minced fresh parsley

**1.** Sprinkle fish with ½ teaspoon salt. Melt butter in 12-inch skillet over low heat. Place fish in skillet, skinned side up, increase heat to medium, and cook, shaking pan occasionally, until butter begins to brown (fish should not brown), 3 to 4 minutes. Using spatula, carefully transfer fish to large plate, raw side down.

**2.** Add leeks, mustard, and ½ teaspoon salt to skillet and cook, stirring frequently, until leeks begin to soften, 2 to 4 minutes. Add wine and bring to gentle simmer. Place fish, raw side down, on top of leeks. Cover skillet and cook, adjusting heat to maintain gentle simmer, until fish registers 130 degrees, 10 to 14 minutes. Remove skillet from heat and, using 2 spatulas, transfer fish and leeks to serving platter or individual plates. Tent loosely with aluminum foil.

**3.** Return skillet to high heat and simmer briskly until sauce is thickened, 2 to 3 minutes. Remove pan from heat, stir in lemon juice, and season with salt and pepper to taste. Spoon sauce over fish and sprinkle with parsley. Serve immediately with lemon wedges.

## Halibut à la Nage with Parsnips and Tarragon

**SERVES** 4

**WHY THIS RECIPE WORKS** Our easy, elegant poached halibut is inspired by the classic French preparation called à la nage, in which fish is delicately cooked and served in a well-seasoned, lightly acidulated broth. For a nontraditional Western European riff, we made a broth infused with parsnip, Parmesan, lemon, vanilla, and tarragon. Gently poaching the fish until it reached 110 degrees, then letting it sit, covered, off the heat, ensured that it came up to temperature (135 degrees) gradually and didn't overshoot the mark. Garnishing the plated fish and broth with a rich, verdant herb oil and additional fresh herbs added pops of flavor and color. For the most vibrant sauce, tightly pack the parsley in the measuring cup. Process the oil in a blender; an immersion blender will not process the herbs finely enough and will produce a paler colored oil. You can substitute other flaky white fish such as cod, haddock, pollock, or hake for the halibut; choose uniformly thick fillets to ensure even cooking.

**TARRAGON OIL**

- Kosher salt for blanching herbs
- ⅓ cup fresh parsley leaves
- 1 tablespoon fresh tarragon leaves
- ⅓ cup vegetable oil

**FISH**

- 4 (5- to 6-ounce) skinless halibut fillets, ¾ to 1 inch thick
- 2 teaspoons kosher salt, divided
- 2 cups water

- 6 ounces parsnips, peeled and sliced thin
- 1 shallot, sliced thin
- 1 piece Parmesan cheese rind, about 2½ inches by 1 inch
- 2 (3-inch) strips lemon zest plus 2 teaspoons lemon juice, plus extra juice for seasoning
- ½ teaspoon black peppercorns
- ¼ teaspoon vanilla extract
- 3 sprigs fresh tarragon, plus extra for garnish
- 1 tablespoon whole-grain mustard

**1. FOR THE TARRAGON OIL:** Bring 6 cups water and 2 teaspoons salt to boil in large saucepan. Add parsley and cook until leaves are tender but still bright green, about 30 seconds. Stir in tarragon, then drain herbs in fine-mesh strainer. Run under cold water until herbs are cool, about 10 seconds. Squeeze dry and transfer to blender. (Reserve strainer.) Add oil and process until herbs are finely ground and oil is bright green, about 2 minutes. (Oil can be refrigerated for up to 24 hours.)

**2. FOR THE FISH:** Sprinkle halibut all over with 1 teaspoon salt and set aside. Add water, parsnips, shallot, cheese rind, lemon zest, 2 teaspoons lemon juice, peppercorns, vanilla, and remaining 1 teaspoon salt to 12-inch skillet and bring to boil over high heat. Adjust heat to maintain gentle simmer, cover, and cook for 25 minutes.

**3.** Return liquid to boil over medium-high heat. Nestle halibut skinned side down in liquid, moving aside solids as much as possible (liquid will not quite cover fillets). Add tarragon and spoon some liquid over halibut. Reduce heat to low; cover and simmer gently until fish registers 110 degrees at thickest point, 4 to 7 minutes. Let stand off heat, covered, until fish is opaque when checked with the tip of a pairing knife and registers 130 degrees, 3 to 7 minutes.

**4.** Divide halibut among 4 shallow bowls. Season broth with salt and lemon juice to taste. Strain broth into 4-cup liquid measuring cup (you should have about 1⅔ cups broth) and discard solids. Divide broth evenly among bowls. Garnish with tarragon leaves. Top each piece halibut with ¾ teaspoon mustard. At table, drizzle about 1 tablespoon tarragon oil into each bowl. Serve immediately.

## Braised Monkfish with Saffron and Cured Olives

**SERVES** 4 to 6

**WHY THIS RECIPE WORKS** A North African specialty, a tagine is both the name for the traditional conical clay cooking vessel and the stew that is cooked inside it. We found, however, that we could get similar results when using a Dutch oven with a heavy lid. We set out to create a Moroccan-style fish tagine with the signature sweet and sour flavors of the region. Meaty monkfish fillets were our go-to choice, as their firm texture helped them keep their shape while simmering. For sweetness, we turned to orange zest, onion, carrots, and tomato paste, which, along with fragrant paprika, cumin, dried mint, and saffron, built the base for the tagine's broth. Deglazing

the sautéed aromatics with clam juice brought in a salty, briny element and created a rich braising broth. Monkfish fillets are surrounded by a thin membrane that needs to be removed before cooking; to do it yourself see page 514.

- 3 (2-inch) strips orange zest, divided
- 5 garlic cloves, minced, divided
- 2 tablespoons extra-virgin olive oil
- 1 large onion, halved and sliced ¼ inch thick
- 3 carrots, peeled, halved lengthwise, and sliced ¼ inch thick
- ¼ teaspoon table salt
- 1 tablespoon tomato paste
- 1¼ teaspoons paprika
- 1 teaspoon ground cumin
- ½ teaspoon dried mint
- ¼ teaspoon saffron threads, crumbled
- 1 (8-ounce) bottle clam juice
- 1½ pounds skinless monkfish fillets, 1 to 1½ inches thick, trimmed and cut into 3-inch pieces
- ¼ cup pitted oil-cured black olives, quartered
- 2 tablespoons minced fresh mint
- 1 teaspoon sherry vinegar

**1.** Mince 1 strip orange zest and combine with 1 teaspoon garlic in bowl; set aside.

**2.** Heat oil in Dutch oven over medium heat until shimmering. Add onion, carrots, salt, and remaining 2 strips orange zest and cook until vegetables are softened and lightly browned, 10 to 12 minutes. Stir in remaining garlic, tomato paste, paprika, cumin, dried mint, and saffron and cook until fragrant, about 30 seconds. Stir in clam juice, scraping up any browned bits.

**3.** Pat monkfish dry with paper towels and season with salt and pepper. Nestle monkfish into pot, spoon some cooking liquid over top, and bring to simmer. Reduce heat to medium-low, cover, and simmer gently until monkfish is opaque when checked with tip of paring knife in center and registers 140 degrees, 8 to 12 minutes.

**4.** Discard orange zest. Gently stir in olives, fresh mint, vinegar, and garlic–orange zest mixture. Season with salt and pepper to taste. Serve

### REMOVING THE MONKFISH MEMBRANE

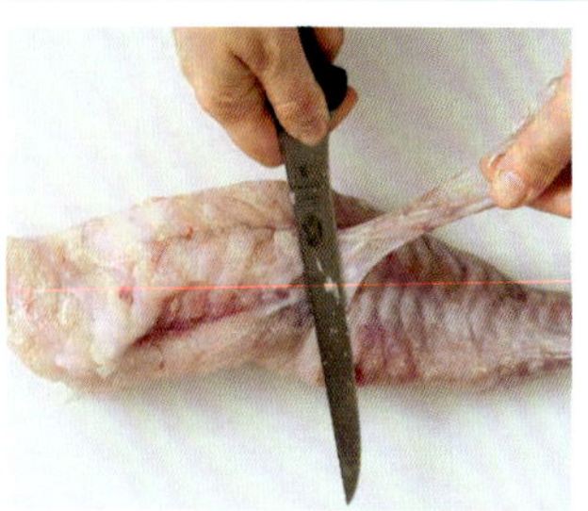

Slip boning knife underneath membrane, then angle knife slightly upward and use back-and-forth motion to cut it away from fish.

## Pan-Seared Halibut with Wilted Bitter Salad

**SERVES 4** **SEASON 26**

**WHY THIS RECIPE WORKS** This recipe is inspired by a memorable meal eaten at a restaurant in Paris. It is light but flavorful, a little cheffy but easy to pull off at home. It pairs meaty fish and caramelized fennel with a bitter salad of radicchio, Belgian endive, and arugula. After cooking the fish and fennel and topping them with the greens, we spooned a bright pan sauce over it all, wilting some of the salad and countering some of its bitterness. Building the pan sauce around the fennel in the skillet imbued the fennel wedges with a lemony punch. You can substitute cod for the halibut in this recipe; cod tends to be more delicate, so take care when flipping and transferring to serving plates. Trim the base of the fennel very lightly, and do not remove the core so that the wedges remain intact.

- 4 (6- to 8-ounce) skinless halibut fillets, 1 inch thick
- ½ teaspoon table salt
- ¼ teaspoon pepper
- 7 tablespoons extra-virgin olive oil, divided, plus extra for drizzling
- 1 small fennel bulb, base lightly trimmed, ¼ cup fronds reserved and torn, stalks discarded, bulb halved and sliced into ½-inch thick wedges
- 1 large shallot, minced
- 3 garlic cloves, minced
- ¾ cup dry white wine
- ⅔ cup plus 1½ teaspoons lemon juice (4 lemons)
- 3 tablespoons water
- 2 tablespoons Dijon mustard
- 1 small head radicchio (6 ounces), torn into bite-size pieces
- 1 head Belgian endive (4 ounces), leaves separated and halved crosswise
- 2 ounces (2 cups) baby arugula
- ½ teaspoon flake sea salt

**1.** Pat halibut dry with paper towels and sprinkle with table salt and pepper. Heat 3 tablespoons oil in 12-inch nonstick skillet over medium-high heat until just smoking. Add halibut and cook until browned on both sides, fish flakes apart when gently prodded with paring knife, and registers 130 degrees, 8 to 10 minutes, flipping halfway through.

**2.** Divide halibut among 4 individual serving plates; set aside. Heat 2 tablespoons oil in now-empty skillet over medium heat until shimmering. Add fennel wedges and cook until golden, about 10 minutes, flipping once halfway through.

**3.** Stir shallot and garlic into skillet with fennel and cook until softened and fragrant, about 2 minutes. Stir in wine, ⅔ cup lemon juice, and water and bring to simmer. Cook over medium heat until slightly reduced, about 2 minutes. Stir in mustard until well combined, then remove from heat. Season with table salt and pepper to taste.

**4.** Toss radicchio, endive, arugula, remaining 2 tablespoons oil, and remaining 1½ teaspoons lemon juice together in bowl. Divide fennel wedges evenly among reserved serving plates, then top fish in plate with radicchio mixture, creating mound on top of each fish fillet. Spoon sauce directly from skillet over top of each mound of greens, sprinkle with fennel fronds and sea salt, and drizzle with extra oil. Serve immediately.

## Pan-Roasted Cod with Green Olive, Almond, and Orange Relish

**SERVES 4**

**WHY THIS RECIPE WORKS** We set out to develop a recipe for producing moist pan-roasted fish fillets with a bright-meets-briny Greek relish. We chose thick fillets of semifirm cod; thinner fish overcooked by the time they achieved a serious sear. We then turned to a common restaurant method to cook the fish: We seared the fillets in a hot pan, flipped them, and then transferred the pan to the oven to finish cooking. Sprinkling the fillets with sugar accelerated browning on the stovetop, shortening the cooking time and thus ensuring that the fish didn't dry out. After a short stay in the oven, the fish emerged browned, tender, and moist. Any firm-fleshed white fish like halibut, haddock, red snapper, or sea bass will work well in this recipe as long the fillets are 1 to ½ inches thick.

**RELISH**

- ½ cup pitted brine-cured green olives, chopped coarse
- ½ cup toasted slivered almonds
- 1 small garlic clove, minced
- 1 teaspoon grated zest plus ¼ cup juice from 1 large orange
- ¼ cup extra-virgin olive oil
- ¼ cup minced fresh mint
- 2 teaspoons white wine vinegar
- Cayenne pepper

COD

- 4 (4- to 6-ounce) skinless cod fillets, 1 to 1½ inches thick
- ½ teaspoon sugar
- 1 tablespoon extra-virgin olive oil

**1. FOR THE RELISH:** Adjust oven rack to middle position and heat oven to 425 degrees. Pulse olives, nuts, garlic, and orange zest in food processor until finely chopped, 10 to 12 pulses. Transfer to bowl and stir in orange juice, oil, mint, and vinegar. Season with salt and cayenne to taste. Set aside.

**2. FOR THE COD:** Pat cod dry with paper towels, season with salt and pepper, and sprinkle sugar evenly on 1 side of each fillet.

**3.** Heat oil in 12-inch ovensafe skillet over medium-high heat until just smoking. Place cod sugared side down in skillet and press lightly to ensure even contact with skillet. Cook until browned on first side, about 2 minutes. Gently flip cod using 2 spatulas, transfer skillet to oven, and roast until fillets register 135 degrees, 7 to 10 minutes. Serve with relish.

## Red Snapper Ceviche with Radishes and Orange

**SERVES** 4 to 6 as a main dish or 6 to 8 as an appetizer

**WHY THIS RECIPE WORKS** Ceviche, the Latin American dish in which pieces of raw fish are "cooked" in an acidic marinade until the flesh firms and turns opaque, is a great summertime go-to dinner because it's easy and quick, it doesn't require turning on the stove or oven or firing up the grill, and it's the only dish that truly allows the fresh, clean, delicate flavor of seafood to shine. To create a flavorful yet balanced "cooking" liquid for our fish ceviche, we made what's known as a leche de tigre by blending lime juice, ají amarillo chile paste, garlic, extra-virgin olive oil, and a small amount of fish. Once strained, the mixture became an intensely flavorful and silky-textured emulsion. We then soaked thinly sliced and briefly salted fish (red snapper, sea bass, halibut, and grouper were all good options) in the leche for 30 to 40 minutes until the fish was just opaque and slightly firm. To complete the dish, we added sweet oranges, peppery radishes, and chopped cilantro. We served the ceviche with corn nuts and popcorn, which provided a customizable salty crunch. It is imperative to use the freshest fish possible in this recipe. Do not use frozen fish. Sea bass, halibut, or grouper can be substituted for the snapper, if desired. Ají amarillo chile paste can be found in the Latin section of grocery stores; if you can't find it, you can substitute 1 stemmed and seeded habanero chile.

- 1 pound skinless red snapper fillets, ½ inch thick
- Kosher salt
- ¾ cup lime juice (6 limes)
- 3 tablespoons extra-virgin olive oil, divided
- 1 tablespoon ají amarillo chile paste
- 2 garlic cloves, peeled
- 3 oranges
- 8 ounces radishes, trimmed, halved, and sliced thin
- ¼ cup coarsely chopped fresh cilantro
- 1 cup corn nuts
- 1 cup lightly salted popcorn

**1.** Using sharp knife, cut fish lengthwise into ½-inch-wide strips. Slice each strip crosswise ⅛ inch thick. Set aside ⅓ cup (2½ ounces) fish pieces. Toss remaining fish with 1 teaspoon salt and refrigerate for at least 10 minutes or up to 30 minutes.

**2.** Meanwhile, process reserved fish pieces, 2½ teaspoons salt, lime juice, 2 tablespoons oil, chile paste, and garlic in blender until smooth, 30 to 60 seconds. Strain mixture through fine-mesh strainer set over large bowl, pressing on solids to extract as much liquid as possible. Discard solids. (Sauce can be refrigerated for up to 24 hours. It will separate slightly; whisk to recombine before proceeding with recipe.)

**3.** Cut away peel and pith from oranges. Holding fruit over bowl, use paring knife to slice between membranes to release segments. Cut orange segments into ¼-inch pieces. Add oranges, salted fish, and radishes to bowl with sauce and toss to combine. Refrigerate for 30 to 40 minutes (for more-opaque fish, refrigerate for 45 minutes to 1 hour).

**4.** Add cilantro to ceviche and toss to combine. Portion ceviche into individual bowls and drizzle with remaining 1 tablespoon oil. Serve, passing corn nuts and popcorn separately.

## Baked Sole Fillets with Herbs and Bread Crumbs

**SERVES** 6

**WHY THIS RECIPE WORKS** For a fuss-free sole preparation that was suitable for a weeknight yet elegant enough for company, we rolled fillets into compact bundles. To ramp up the fillets' mild flavor, we brushed them with Dijon mustard; seasoned them with salt, pepper, fresh herbs, and lemon zest; and drizzled them with melted butter and garlic. Then we rolled them up, drizzled them with more butter, and baked them. For texture, we added a mixture of herbs, butter, and panko to the sole at two intervals. We removed the foil before the fish was done cooking, basted the fillets with pan juices, topped them with most of the bread crumb mixture, and then returned them to the oven uncovered. Just before serving, we sprinkled the remaining crumbs over the fillets. Try to purchase fillets of similar size. If using smaller fillets (about 3 ounces each), serve 2 fillets per person and reduce the baking time in step 3 to 20 minutes. Do not use frozen fish in this recipe. Fresh basil or dill can be used in place of the tarragon.

- 3 tablespoons minced fresh parsley leaves
- 3 tablespoons minced fresh chives
- 1 tablespoon minced fresh tarragon leaves
- 1 teaspoon grated zest from 1 lemon
- 5 tablespoons unsalted butter, cut into 5 pieces
- 2 medium garlic cloves, minced or pressed through a garlic press (about 2 teaspoons)
- 6 (6-ounce) boneless, skinless sole or flounder fillets
- Table salt and ground black pepper
- 1 tablespoon Dijon mustard
- ⅔ cup panko bread crumbs
- Lemon wedges, for serving

**1.** Adjust an oven rack to the middle position and heat the oven to 325 degrees. Combine the parsley, chives, and tarragon in a small bowl. Reserve 1 tablespoon herb mixture; stir the lemon zest into the remaining herb mixture.

**2.** Heat 4 tablespoons of the butter in an 8-inch skillet over medium heat until just melted. Add half of the garlic and cook, stirring frequently, until fragrant, 1 to 2 minutes. Remove from the heat and set aside.

**3.** Pat the fillets dry with paper towels and season both sides with salt and pepper. Arrange the fillets, skinned side up, with the tail end pointing away from you. Spread ½ teaspoon mustard on each fillet, sprinkle each evenly with about 1 tablespoon of the herb–lemon zest mixture, and drizzle each with about 1½ teaspoons of the garlic butter. Tightly roll the fillets from the thick end to form cylinders. Set the fillets, seam side down, in a 13 by 9-inch baking dish. Drizzle the remaining garlic butter over the fillets, cover the baking dish with aluminum foil, and bake for 25 minutes. Wipe out the skillet but do not wash.

**4.** While the fillets are baking, melt the remaining 1 tablespoon butter in the now-empty skillet over medium heat. Add the panko and cook, stirring frequently, until the crumbs are deep golden brown, 5 to 8 minutes. Reduce the heat to low, add the remaining garlic, and cook, stirring constantly, until the garlic is fragrant and evenly distributed in the crumbs, about 1 minute. Transfer to a small bowl, stir in ¼ teaspoon salt, and season with pepper to taste. Let cool, then stir in the reserved 1 tablespoon herb mixture.

**5.** After the fillets have baked for 25 minutes, remove the baking dish from oven. Baste the fillets with melted garlic butter from the baking dish, sprinkle with all but 3 tablespoons of the bread crumbs, and continue to bake, uncovered, fillets register 135 degrees, 6 to 10 minutes longer. Using a thin metal spatula, transfer the fillets to plates, sprinkle with the remaining bread crumbs, and serve with the lemon wedges.

## Pan-Seared Swordfish Steaks

**SERVES 4**

---

**WHY THIS RECIPE WORKS** Swordfish, unlike silky salmon or flaky halibut, offers a unique dense meatiness, making it an appealing option even for a staunch carnivore. But it isn't that easy to turn out swordfish steaks with a gorgeous brown crust and a tender yet firm interior. Like meats, fish contain enzymes called cathepsins. In the right circumstances, such as slow cooking, the cathepsins will break down the proteins that give swordfish its sturdy texture, rendering the dense steaks mushy. We learned that the key to perfectly cooked swordfish steaks was to cook them quickly in a skillet over high heat, flipping them frequently so that they cooked from both the bottom up and the top down. To keep each bite juicy, we removed the steaks from the heat when they reached 130 degrees and let carryover cooking bring them up to the desired temperature of 140 degrees. For the best results, purchase swordfish steaks that are ¾ to 1 inch thick. Look for four steaks that weigh 7 to 9 ounces each or two steaks that weigh about 1 pound each. If you purchase the latter, cut them in half to create four steaks. We've found that skin-on swordfish often buckles in the hot skillet. Ask your fishmonger to remove the skin or trim it yourself with a thin, sharp knife. These steaks are great with just a squeeze of lemon or dressed up with a savory relish.

- 2 teaspoons vegetable oil
- 2 pounds skinless swordfish steaks, ¾ to 1 inch thick
- 1½ teaspoons kosher salt
- Lemon wedges

**1.** Heat oil in 12-inch nonstick skillet over medium-high heat until shimmering. While oil heats, pat steaks dry with paper towels and sprinkle on both sides with salt.

**2.** Place steaks in skillet and cook, flipping every 2 minutes, until golden brown and centers register 130 degrees, 7 to 11 minutes. Transfer to serving platter or individual plates and let rest for 10 minutes. Serve with lemon wedges.

### Caper-Currant Relish

**MAKES ½ cup**

In classic Italian agrodolce style, we balanced sweet currants, salty capers, fresh parsley, and savory garlic in this relish that's perfect for delicately flavored fish and poultry. Golden raisins can be substituted for the currants.

- 3 tablespoons finely chopped fresh parsley
- 3 tablespoons extra-virgin olive oil
- 2 tablespoons capers, rinsed and chopped fine
- 2 tablespoons currants, chopped fine
- 1 garlic clove, minced
- 1 teaspoon grated lemon zest plus 2 tablespoons juice

Combine all ingredients in bowl. Let sit at room temperature for at least 20 minutes before serving.

## Sautéed Tilapia with Chive-Lemon Miso Butter

**SERVES 4**

**WHY THIS RECIPE WORKS** Most tilapia is responsibly raised and features moist, firm flesh with a clean, mild taste. We quickly cooked our tilapia in a nonstick skillet over high heat to maximize flavorful browning without overcooking and drying out the fillets. We found that this fish is firm and resilient enough to cook over aggressive heat without falling apart. Dividing each fillet into a thick and a thin portion and sautéing them separately allowed for more precise cooking and even browning. The fish was top-notch with just a squeeze of lemon but we finished it with a chive-lemon miso butter, which added flavor and richness to this lean fish. We also developed an olive oil–based Cilantro Chimichurri that features fresh cilantro and parsley. You can use fresh or frozen tilapia in this recipe (if frozen, thaw before cooking). There is no need to take the temperature of the thin halves of the fillets; they will be cooked through by the time they are golden brown. We like the delicate flavor of white miso in this recipe, but red miso can be substituted.

**FISH**

- 4 (5- to 6-ounce) skinless tilapia fillets
- 1 teaspoon kosher salt
- 2 tablespoons vegetable oil

**CHIVE-LEMON MISO BUTTER**

- 2 tablespoons white miso
- 1 teaspoon grated lemon zest plus 2 teaspoons juice
- ⅛ teaspoon pepper
- 4 tablespoons unsalted butter, softened
- 2 tablespoons minced fresh chives

1. **FOR THE FISH:** Place tilapia on cutting board and sprinkle both sides with salt. Let sit at room temperature for 15 minutes.

2. **FOR THE CHIVE-LEMON MISO BUTTER:** While tilapia rests, combine miso, lemon zest and juice, and pepper in small bowl. Add butter and stir until fully incorporated. Stir in chives and set aside.

3. Pat tilapia dry with paper towels. Using seam that runs down middle of fillet as guide, cut each fillet in half lengthwise to create 1 thick half and 1 thin half.

4. Heat oil in 12-inch nonstick skillet over high heat until just smoking. Add thick halves of fillets to skillet. Cook, tilting and gently shaking skillet occasionally to distribute oil, until undersides are golden brown, 2 to 3 minutes. Using thin spatula, flip fillets. Cook until second sides are golden brown and tilapia registers 130 to 135 degrees, 2 to 3 minutes. Transfer tilapia to serving platter. Dot tilapia with two-thirds of miso butter.

5. Return skillet to high heat. When oil is just smoking, add thin halves of fillets and cook until undersides are golden brown, about 1 minute. Flip and cook until second sides are golden brown, about 1 minute. Transfer to serving platter. Top thin halves with remaining miso butter and serve.

### Cilantro Chimichurri

**SERVES 4**

Soaking the dried oregano in hot water and vinegar helps soften it and release its flavor. Top the tilapia with ¼ cup of chimichurri before serving, passing the rest separately.

- 2 tablespoons hot water
- 2 tablespoons red wine vinegar
- 1 teaspoon dried oregano
- ½ cup minced fresh parsley
- ¼ cup minced fresh cilantro
- 3 garlic cloves, minced
- 1 teaspoon kosher salt
- ¼ teaspoon red pepper flakes
- ¼ cup extra-virgin olive oil

Combine hot water, vinegar, and oregano in medium bowl; let stand for 5 minutes. Add parsley, cilantro, garlic, salt, and pepper flakes and stir to combine. Whisk in oil until incorporated.

## Pan-Seared Sesame-Crusted Tuna Steaks

**SERVES 4**

**WHY THIS RECIPE WORKS** Moist and rare in the middle with a seared crust, pan-seared tuna is a popular entrée in restaurants. Starting with high-quality tuna—sushi grade if possible—is paramount; we prefer the flavor of yellowfin. A thickness of at least an inch is necessary for the center of the tuna to be rare while the exterior browns. Before searing the tuna in a nonstick skillet, we rubbed the steaks with oil, then coated them with sesame seeds; the oil helped the seeds stick to the fish. The sesame seeds browned in the skillet and formed a beautiful, nutty-tasting crust. We learned that tuna, like beef, will continue to cook from residual heat when removed from the stove, so when the interior of the tuna was near the desired degree of doneness (about 110 degrees), we transferred it to a platter. If you plan to serve the fish with Ginger-Soy Sauce with Scallions (recipe follows), prepare it before cooking the fish. Most members of the test kitchen staff prefer their tuna steaks rare to medium-rare; the cooking times given in this recipe are for tuna steaks cooked to these two degrees of doneness. For tuna steaks cooked medium, observe the timing for medium-rare, then tent the steaks loosely with foil for 5 minutes before slicing. If you prefer tuna steaks cooked so rare that they are still cold in the center, try to purchase steaks that are 1½ inches thick and cook them according to the timing in step 2 for rare steaks. Bear in mind, though, that the cooking times given are estimates; check for doneness by nicking the fish with a paring knife. To cook only two steaks, use half as many sesame seeds, reduce the amount of oil to 2 teaspoons both on the fish and in the pan, use a 10-inch nonstick skillet, and follow the same cooking times.

- ¾ cup sesame seeds
- 4 (8-ounce) tuna steaks, preferably yellowfin, about 1 inch thick
- 2 tablespoons vegetable oil
- Table salt and ground black pepper
- 1 recipe Ginger-Soy Sauce with Scallions (recipe follows)

**1.** Spread the sesame seeds in a shallow baking dish or pie plate. Pat the tuna steaks dry with a paper towel; use 1 tablespoon of the oil to rub both sides of the steaks, then sprinkle them with salt and pepper. Press both sides of each steak in the sesame seeds to coat.

**2.** Heat the remaining 1 tablespoon oil in a 12-inch nonstick skillet over high heat until just beginning to smoke and swirl to coat the pan. Add the tuna steaks and cook 30 seconds without moving the steaks. Reduce the heat to medium-high and continue to cook until the seeds are golden brown, about 1½ minutes. Using tongs, flip the tuna steaks carefully and cook, without moving them, until golden brown on the second side and the centers register 110 degree (for rare), about 1½ minutes, or 120 degrees for medium-rare (about 3 minutes). Serve with Ginger-Soy Sauce with Scallions.

### Ginger-Soy Sauce with Scallions

**MAKES** about 1 cup

If available, serve pickled ginger and wasabi, passed separately, with the tuna and this sauce.

- ¼ cup soy sauce
- ¼ cup rice vinegar
- ¼ cup water
- 1 medium scallion, sliced thin
- 2½ teaspoons sugar
- 2 teaspoons minced or grated fresh ginger
- 1½ teaspoons toasted sesame oil
- ½ teaspoon red pepper flakes

Combine all the ingredients in a small bowl, stirring to dissolve the sugar.

## Crunchy Oven-Fried Fish

**SERVES 4**

**WHY THIS RECIPE WORKS** The golden brown coating and moist, flaky flesh of batter-fried fish come at a price: the oil. Cooks have turned to the oven to avoid the bother of deep-fat frying, but oven-frying often falls short with soggy coating and overcooked fish. We used thick fillets so that the fish and coating would finish cooking at the same time. Flaky cod and haddock provided the best contrast to the crunchy exterior we envisioned. A conventional bound breading—flour, egg, and fresh bread crumbs—wasn't as crisp as we wanted, so we toasted the bread crumbs with a little butter. (Precooking the crumbs also ensured we wouldn't have to overcook the fish to get really crunchy crumbs.) Placing the coated fish on a wire rack while baking allowed air to circulate all around the fish, crisping all sides. We boosted flavor in two ways, adding shallots and parsley to the breading and horseradish, cayenne, and paprika to the egg wash. To prevent overcooking, buy fish fillets that are at least 1 inch thick. The bread crumbs can be made up to 3 days in advance and stored at room temperature in a tightly sealed container (allow to cool fully before storing). Serve with Sweet and Tangy Tartar Sauce.

- 4 slices high-quality white sandwich bread, torn into quarters
- 2 tablespoons unsalted butter, melted
- Table salt and ground black pepper
- 2 tablespoons minced fresh parsley leaves
- 1 small shallot, minced (about 1 tablespoon)
- ¼ cup plus 5 tablespoons unbleached all-purpose flour
- 2 large eggs
- 3 tablespoons mayonnaise
- 2 teaspoons prepared horseradish (optional)
- ½ teaspoon paprika
- ¼ teaspoon cayenne pepper (optional)
- 1¼ pounds cod, haddock, or other thick whitefish fillets (1 to 1½ inches thick), cut into 4 pieces
- Lemon wedges, for serving

**1.** Adjust an oven rack to the middle position and heat the oven to 350 degrees. Pulse the bread, butter, ¼ teaspoon salt, and ¼ teaspoon black pepper in a food processor until the bread is coarsely ground, about 8 pulses. Transfer to a rimmed baking sheet and bake until deep golden brown and dry, about 15 minutes, stirring twice during the baking time. Cool the crumbs to room temperature, about 10 minutes. Transfer the crumbs to a pie plate and toss with the parsley and shallot. Increase the oven temperature to 425 degrees.

**2.** Place ¼ cup of the flour in a second pie plate. In a third pie plate, whisk together the eggs, mayonnaise, horseradish (if using), paprika, cayenne (if using), and ¼ teaspoon black pepper until combined; whisk in the remaining 5 tablespoons flour until smooth.

**3.** Spray a wire rack with vegetable oil spray and place over a rimmed baking sheet. Dry the fish thoroughly with paper towels and season with salt and black pepper. Dredge 1 fillet in the flour; shake off the excess. Using tongs, coat the fillet with the egg mixture. Coat all sides of the fillet with the bread-crumb mixture, pressing gently so that a thick layer of crumbs adheres to the fish. Transfer the breaded fish to the wire rack. Repeat with the remaining 3 fillets.

**4.** Bake until fillets register 135 degrees, 18 to 25 minutes. Using a thin spatula, transfer the fillets to individual plates and serve immediately with the lemon wedges.

## Sweet and Tangy Tartar Sauce

**MAKES** about 1 cup

This sauce can be refrigerated, tightly covered, for up to 1 week.

- ¾ cup mayonnaise
- 2 tablespoons drained capers, minced
- 2 tablespoons sweet pickle relish
- 1 small shallot, minced (about 1 tablespoon)
- 1½ teaspoons distilled white vinegar
- ½ teaspoon Worcestershire sauce
- ½ teaspoon ground black pepper

Mix all the ingredients together in a small bowl. Cover the bowl with plastic wrap and let sit until the flavors meld, about 15 minutes. Stir again before serving.

### PREVENTING STICKING

Spear each piece of battered fish with a fork, let the excess batter drip off, and then drag the fish along the oil's surface before releasing it. This gives the batter a chance to set up and harden so that it won't adhere to other pieces it touches in the oil.

## Crispy Fish Sandwiches

**SERVES** 4

**WHY THIS RECIPE WORKS** In New England, a fish sandwich is a coastal favorite that's all about the succulent fish and its shatteringly crispy coating. For our version, we started by coating the fish in a batter of beer, flour, cornstarch, and baking powder. The proteins in the flour helped the batter fuse to the fish and brown deeply, the cornstarch helped it crisp up nicely, and the baking powder and the beer contributed airiness. Frying the battered fillets in 375-degree peanut oil crisped and browned the batter while steaming the fish to perfection; briefly dragging each fillet along the surface of the oil at the start of frying prevented sticking. Cod or halibut can be substituted for the haddock; you can substitute plain seltzer for the beer. Do not use a dark beer in this recipe. Use a Dutch oven that holds 6 quarts or more here. Slather bun bottoms with Sweet and Tangy Tartar Sauce.

- ½ cup all-purpose flour
- ½ cup cornstarch
- ½ teaspoon table salt
- ½ teaspoon baking powder
- ¾ cup beer
- 2 quarts peanut or vegetable oil for frying
- 4 (4- to 6-ounce) skinless haddock fillets, 1 inch thick
- 4 brioche buns, toasted
- 4 leaves Bibb lettuce
- Lemon wedges

**1.** Whisk flour, cornstarch, salt, and baking powder together in large bowl. Whisk in beer until smooth. Cover and refrigerate for 20 minutes.

**2.** Set wire rack in rimmed baking sheet. Add oil to large Dutch oven until it measures about 1½ inches deep and heat over medium-high heat to 375 degrees. Pat haddock dry with paper towels and transfer to batter, tossing gently to coat. Using fork, remove haddock from batter, 1 piece at a time, allowing excess batter to drip back into bowl; add to hot oil, briefly dragging haddock along surface of oil to set batter before gently dropping into oil. Adjust burner, if necessary, to maintain oil temperature between 350 and 375 degrees.

**3.** Cook, stirring gently to prevent pieces from sticking together, until deep golden brown and crispy, about 4 minutes per side. Using spider skimmer or slotted spoon, transfer haddock to prepared rack. Divide tartar sauce evenly among bun bottoms, followed by haddock and lettuce. Cover with bun tops. Serve with lemon wedges.

## Fried Whole Branzino with Cheesy Grits

**SERVES** 2 to 4

**WHY THIS RECIPE WORKS** Upgrade your fried fish game with whole branzino and cheesy grits. This sophisticated but homey recipe is a real standout. It was created by Antoinette Johnson, the winner of the first season of *America's Test*

*Kitchen: The Next Generation*. Here we used branzino, a mild white fish that is a great candidate for deep frying whole. Grits, made from dried corn, are mild on their own so to bump up their flavor, we added sharp cheddar and Parmesan along with both garlic and onion powders. We prefer sharp white cheddar, but other types of cheddar can be used. To speed preparation, ask your fishmonger to prepare the fish. Serve with Texas Pete's Hot Sauce.

**BRANZINO**

- 2 teaspoons kosher salt
- 2 teaspoons garlic powder
- 1 teaspoon black pepper
- ½ teaspoon paprika
- 1 cup all-purpose flour
- 2 (1 to 1½—pound each) whole branzino, about 15 inches long, scaled, gutted, gills removed, fins snipped off with scissors
- 2 tablespoons yellow mustard
- 1 quart vegetable oil, for frying

**CHEESY GRITS**

- 2 cups water
- 2 cups heavy cream
- ½ teaspoon kosher salt
- 1 cup quick-cooking grits
- 4 ounces sharp white cheddar cheese, shredded (1 cup)
- 1 ounce Parmesan cheese, grated (½ cup)
- 4 tablespoons unsalted butter, cut into 4 pieces
- 1 teaspoon garlic powder
- 1 teaspoon onion powder
- ¼ teaspoon pepper

Hot Sauce
Lemon wedges

**1. FOR THE BRANZINO:** Adjust oven rack to middle position and heat oven to 200 degrees. Combine salt, garlic powder, pepper, and paprika in small bowl. Place flour in shallow dish, add 2 teaspoons salt-spice mixture, and whisk to combine. Rinse each branzino under cold running water and pat dry inside and out with paper towels. Using sharp knife, cut each fish in half crosswise. Using sharp knife, make three ½-inch deep slashes about 1 inch apart along skin sides of each fish. Sprinkle remaining salt-spice mixture evenly over both the exterior and interior cavity of each piece. Brush both sides of each piece evenly with ½ tablespoon mustard. Working with one piece at a time, coat both sides lightly with flour mixture, shaking off excess, and place on wire rack set in rimmed baking sheet.

**2.** Set wire rack in second rimmed baking sheet. Heat oil in Dutch oven over medium-high heat until it registers 350 degrees. Using tongs and working with 1 piece at a time, add fish to oil holding for 5 to 10 seconds below surface of oil to set coating before gently dropping into oil. Repeat with second piece of fish. Adjust burner, if necessary, to maintain oil temperature between 350 and 375 degrees. Fry branzino until golden brown, crisp, and registers 140 degrees, 3 to 5 minutes per side. Using 2 spatulas, carefully remove each piece from oil and place on prepared rack. Season with salt. Transfer fish to oven, return oil to 350 degrees, and repeat with remaining fish.

**3. FOR THE GRITS:** Bring water, cream and salt to boil in large saucepan over high heat. Whisk in grits. Cover, reduce heat to low, and cook whisking occasionally, until grits are tender and have consistency of thick pancake batter, 5 to 7 minutes. Off heat, add cheddar, Parmesan, butter, garlic powder, onion powder, and pepper and stir until cheddar and butter have melted. Season with salt to taste. (Adjust consistency with 1 to 2 tablespoons water as needed).

**4.** Divide grits evenly among individual plates, spreading into even layer. Place fish on top of grits. Serve passing hot sauce and lemon wedges separately.

## Fish and Chips

**SERVES 4**

**WHY THIS RECIPE WORKS** Making fish and chips at home can be a hassle. By the time the fries finish frying, the fish is cold. We wanted to serve both at their prime. Our first challenge was to create a batter that protected the fish as it cooked and also provided a crisp contrast. For this, we discovered that a wet batter was best. We liked beer—the traditional choice—as the liquid component. For a crisp coating we used a 3:1 ratio of flour to cornstarch, along with a teaspoon of baking powder. A final layer of flour on top of the battered fish prevented the coating from puffing away from the fish as it cooked. To deliver both hot fish and fries, we cooked them alternately. First, we precooked the fries in the microwave, which lessened the cooking time and also removed excess moisture that could diminish crisping. After giving the fries their first fry, we battered and fried the fish while the potatoes were draining. Then, as the fish drained, we gave the fries a final fry. Use a Dutch oven with at least a 7-quart capacity. Serve with traditional malt vinegar or with Sweet and Tangy Tartar Sauce (page 519).

- 3 pounds russet potatoes (about 4 large potatoes), peeled, ends and sides squared off, and cut lengthwise into ½-inch by ½-inch fries
- 3 quarts plus ¼ cup peanut oil or canola oil, divided, for frying
- 1½ cups all-purpose flour
- ½ cup cornstarch
- 2 teaspoons table salt
- ½ teaspoon cayenne pepper
- ½ teaspoon paprika
- ⅛ teaspoon pepper
- 1 teaspoon baking powder
- 1½ pounds cod, hake, or haddock, cut into eight 3-ounce pieces about 1 inch thick
- 1½ cups cold beer, divided

**1.** Place cut fries in large microwave-safe bowl, toss with ¼ cup oil, and cover with plastic wrap. Microwave on high power until potatoes are partially translucent and pliable but still offer some resistance when pierced with tip of paring knife, 6 to 8 minutes, tossing them with rubber spatula

halfway through cooking time. Carefully pull back plastic wrap from side farthest from you and drain potatoes into large mesh strainer set over sink. Rinse well under cold running water. Spread potatoes on few clean dish towels and pat dry. Let rest until fries have reached room temperature, at least 10 minutes or up to 1 hour.

**2.** While fries cool, whisk flour, cornstarch, salt, cayenne, paprika, and pepper in large bowl; transfer ¾ cup of mixture to rimmed baking sheet. Add baking powder to bowl and whisk to combine.

**3.** In large Dutch oven heat 2 quarts oil over medium heat to 350 degrees. Add fries to hot oil and increase heat to high. Fry, stirring with a mesh spider or slotted metal spoon, until potatoes turn light golden and just begin to brown at corners, 6 to 8 minutes. Transfer fries to thick paper bag or paper towels to drain.

**4.** Reduce heat to medium-high, add remaining 1 quart oil, and heat oil to 375 degrees. Meanwhile, thoroughly dry fish with paper towels and dredge each piece in flour mixture on sheet; transfer pieces to wire rack, shaking off any excess flour. Add 1¼ cups beer to flour mixture in bowl and stir until mixture is just combined (batter will be lumpy). Add remaining ¼ cup beer as needed, 1 tablespoon at a time, whisking after each addition, until batter falls from whisk in thin, steady stream and leaves faint trail across surface of batter. Using tongs, dip 1 piece fish in batter and let excess run off, shaking gently. Place battered fish back on sheet with flour mixture and turn to coat both sides. Repeat with remaining fish, keeping pieces in single layer on sheet.

**5.** When oil reaches 375 degrees, increase heat to high and add battered fish to oil with tongs, gently shaking off any excess flour. Fry, stirring occasionally, until golden brown, 7 to 8 minutes. Transfer fish to thick paper bag or paper towels to drain. Allow oil to return to 375 degrees.

**6.** Add all of fries back to oil and fry until golden brown and crisp, 3 to 5 minutes. Transfer to fresh paper bag or paper towels to drain. Season fries with salt to taste and serve immediately with fish.

## Pan-Seared Scallops

SERVES 4

**WHY THIS RECIPES WORKS** For restaurant-style pan-seared scallops with golden-brown crusts and tender interiors, we needed to compensate for the weaker heating power of home stovetops. We started with a nonstick skillet so that the browned bits would form a crust on the fish instead of sticking to the skillet. But it wasn't until we tried a common restaurant technique—butter basting—that our scallops really improved. We seared the scallops in oil on one side and added butter to the skillet after flipping them. We then spooned the foaming butter over the scallops. Waiting to add the butter ensured that it had just enough time to work its browning magic, but not enough time to burn. We strongly recommend purchasing "dry" scallops, which don't contain chemical additives and taste better than "wet" scallops. Dry scallops will look ivory or pinkish; wet scallops are bright white. If you can find only wet scallops, soak them in a solution of 1 quart cold water, ¼ cup lemon juice, and 2 tablespoons table salt for 30 minutes before proceeding with step 1, and season the scallops with pepper only in step 2. Prepare the sauce (if serving) while the scallops dry (between steps 1 and 2) and keep it warm while cooking them.

- 1½ pounds large sea scallops, tendons removed
- ½ teaspoon table salt
- ¼ teaspoon pepper
- 2 tablespoons vegetable oil, divided
- 2 tablespoons unsalted butter, cut into 2 pieces, divided
- Lemon wedges or Lemon Browned Butter Sauce (recipe follows)

**1.** Place scallops on rimmed baking sheet lined with clean dish towel. Place second clean dish towel on top of scallops and press gently on towel to blot liquid. Let scallops sit at room temperature for 10 minutes while towels absorb moisture.

**2.** Remove second towel and sprinkle scallops on both sides with salt and pepper. Heat 1 tablespoon oil in 12-inch nonstick skillet over high heat until just smoking. Add half of scallops in single layer, flat side down, and cook, without moving, until well browned, 1½ to 2 minutes.

**3.** Add 1 tablespoon butter to skillet. Using tongs, flip scallops and continue to cook, using large spoon to baste scallops with melted butter, tilting skillet so butter runs to one side, until sides of scallops are firm and centers are opaque, 30 to

### PREPPING SCALLOPS

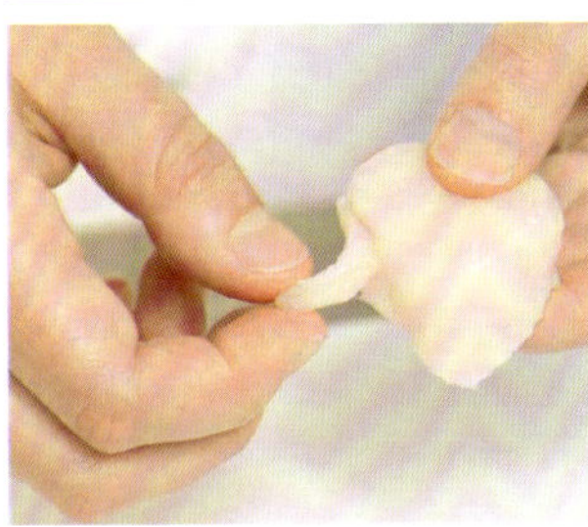

Using your fingers, peel away small, rough-textured, crescent-shaped muscle attached to side of scallop before cooking.

90 seconds longer (remove smaller scallops from the pan as they finish cooking).

**4.** Transfer scallops to large plate and tent with aluminum foil. Wipe out skillet with paper towels and repeat with remaining 1 tablespoon oil, remaining scallops, and remaining 1 tablespoon butter. Serve immediately with lemon wedges or sauce.

### Lemon Browned Butter Sauce

**MAKES** ¼ cup

- 4 tablespoons unsalted butter, cut into 4 pieces
- 1 small shallot, minced
- 1 tablespoon minced fresh parsley
- ½ teaspoon minced fresh thyme
- 2 teaspoons lemon juice

Heat butter in small heavy-bottomed saucepan over medium heat and cook, swirling pan constantly, until butter turns dark golden brown and has a nutty aroma, 4 to 5 minutes. Add shallot and cook until fragrant, about 30 seconds. Remove pan from heat and stir in parsley, thyme, and lemon juice. Season with salt and pepper to taste. Cover to keep warm.

## Pan-Seared Scallops with Wilted Spinach, Watercress, and Orange Salad

**SERVES** 4

**WHY THIS RECIPE WORKS** Attempts to make perfectly seared, caramelized sea scallops usually result in overcooking these tender mollusks, rendering them rubbery and tough. We wanted a nutty, rich-colored crust encasing an interior of creamy, perfectly cooked scallop meat. And for a complete meal, we incorporated our scallops into a main course salad that was both elegant and satisfying. To get scallops with a crusty exterior, using the unprocessed variety is a must. We found it was essential to dry the scallops thoroughly before adding them to the pan, to further guard against the scallops steaming rather than searing. Equally important is to avoid crowding the pan. We cooked the scallops in batches, browning each batch on just one side, then returned them all to the skillet at once to cook through on the other side, so that each salad would have hot scallops. For the salad, we liked baby spinach and watercress for easy prep and tender greens. A bright dressing with sherry vinegar and fresh orange complemented the rich scallops. For a finishing touch, toasted sliced almonds lent our salad nutty flavor and welcome crunch. Sea scallops can vary dramatically in size from 1 to 1½ ounces each. A dinner portion, therefore, can range from four to six scallops per person. To ensure that the scallops cook at the same rate, be sure to buy scallops of similar size. Be sure to peel away the small muscle from the side of each scallop before cooking.

**SALAD**

- 5 ounces baby spinach (about 5 cups)
- 4 ounces watercress or arugula (about 4 cups)
- ¾ cup sliced almonds, toasted

**SCALLOPS**

- 1½ pounds large sea scallops (16 to 24 scallops), tendons removed (see page 521)
- Table salt and ground black pepper
- ¼ cup vegetable oil

**DRESSING**

- 3 tablespoons extra-virgin olive oil
- ½ medium red onion, sliced thin
- 1 teaspoon minced fresh thyme leaves
- 2 large oranges, peel and pith removed (see page 539), quartered and sliced ¼ inch thick
- 2 tablespoons sherry vinegar

**1. FOR THE SALAD:** Toss the spinach, watercress, and almonds together in a large bowl; set aside.

**2. FOR THE SCALLOPS:** Place the scallops on a dish towel–lined plate or baking sheet and season with salt and pepper. Lay a single layer of paper towels over the scallops; set aside.

**3.** Add 2 tablespoons of the vegetable oil to a 12-inch skillet and heat over high heat until just smoking. Meanwhile, press the paper towel flush to the scallops to dry. Add half of the scallops to the skillet, dry side facing down, and cook until evenly golden, 1 to 2 minutes. Using tongs, transfer the scallops, browned side facing up, to a large plate; set aside. Wipe out the skillet using a wad of paper towels. Repeat with the remaining 2 tablespoons oil and the remaining scallops. Once the first side is golden, turn the heat to medium, turn the scallops over with tongs, and return the first batch of scallops to the pan, golden side facing up. Cook until the sides on all the scallops have firmed up and all but the middle third of each scallop is opaque, 30 to 60 seconds longer. Transfer all the scallops to a clean, large plate; set aside.

**4. FOR THE DRESSING:** Wipe the skillet clean with a wad of paper towels. Add the olive oil, onion, thyme, and ½ teaspoon salt to the skillet and return to medium-high heat; cook until the onion is slightly softened, about 1 minute. Add the oranges and vinegar to the pan and swirl to incorporate. Remove from the heat.

**5. TO FINISH THE SALAD:** Pour the warm dressing over the salad mixture and toss gently to wilt. Divide the spinach salad among four plates and arrange the scallops on top. Serve immediately.

## Pan-Seared Shrimp

**SERVES 4**

**WHY THIS RECIPE WORKS** A good recipe for pan-seared shrimp is hard to find. Of the handful of recipes we uncovered, the majority resulted in shrimp that were either dry and flavorless or pale, tough, and gummy. We wanted shrimp that were well caramelized but still moist, briny, and tender. We peeled the shrimp first and tried using a brine to add moisture, but found that it inhibited browning. Instead, we seasoned the shrimp with salt, pepper, and sugar, which brought out their natural sweetness and aided in browning. We cooked the shrimp in batches in a large, piping-hot skillet and then paired them with a thick, glaze-like sauce with assertive ingredients and plenty of acidity as a foil for the shrimp's richness. This recipe can also be prepared with large shrimp (31 to 40 per pound); the cooking time will be slightly shorter. Either a nonstick or a traditional skillet will work for this recipe, but a nonstick simplifies cleanup.

- 2 tablespoons vegetable oil
- 1½ pounds extra-large shrimp (21 to 25 per pound), peeled and deveined (see below)
- ¼ teaspoon table salt
- ¼ teaspoon ground black pepper
- ⅛ teaspoon sugar

Heat 1 tablespoon of the oil in a 12-inch skillet over high heat until smoking. Meanwhile, toss the shrimp, salt, pepper, and sugar in a medium bowl. Add half of the shrimp to the pan in a single layer and cook until spotty brown and the edges turn pink, about 1 minute. Remove the pan from the heat. Using tongs, flip each shrimp and let stand until all but the very center is opaque, about 30 seconds. Transfer the shrimp to a large plate. Repeat with the remaining 1 tablespoon oil and the remaining shrimp. After the second batch has stood off the heat, return the first batch to the skillet and toss to combine. Cover the skillet and let stand until the shrimp are cooked through, 1 to 2 minutes. Serve immediately.

### DEVEINING SHRIMP

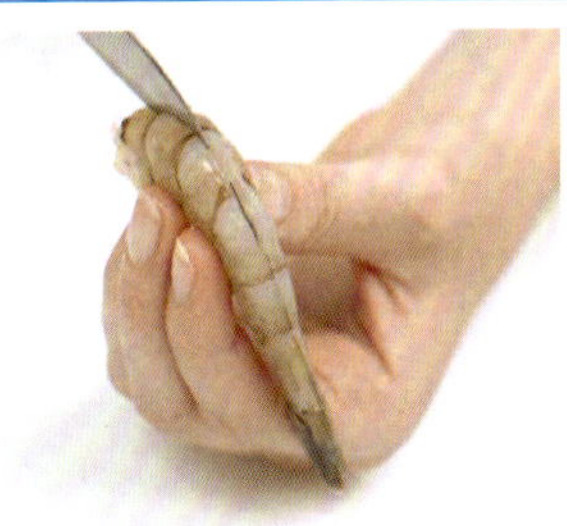

**1.** After removing the shell, use a paring knife to make a shallow cut along the back of the shrimp so that the vein is exposed.

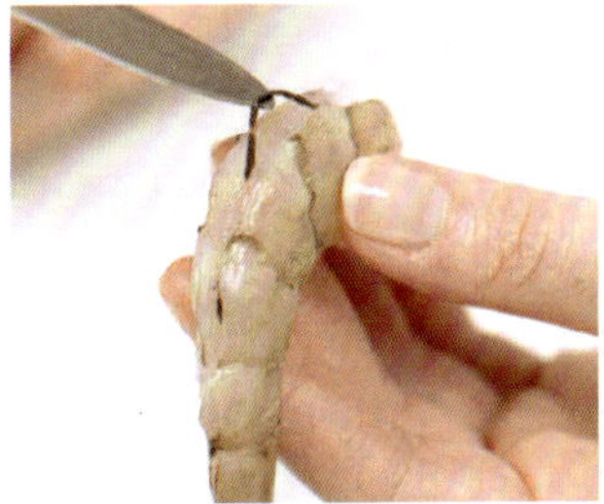

**2.** Use the tip of the knife to lift the vein out of the shrimp. Discard the vein by wiping the blade against a paper towel.

### Pan-Seared Shrimp with Garlic-Lemon Butter

Beat 3 tablespoons softened unsalted butter with a fork in a small bowl until light and fluffy. Stir in 1 medium garlic clove, minced or pressed through a garlic press, 1 tablespoon juice from 1 lemon, 2 tablespoons chopped fresh parsley leaves, and ⅛ teaspoon salt until combined. Follow the recipe for Pan-Seared Shrimp, adding the flavored butter when returning the first batch of shrimp to the skillet. Serve with lemon wedges, if desired.

## Pan-Seared Shrimp with Peanuts, Black Pepper, and Lime

**SERVES 4**

**WHY THIS RECIPE WORKS** Shrimp cook quickly so it's difficult to brown them before they become dry and rubbery. That's why we start them in a cold skillet and sprinkle them with sugar. Salting them helped them to retain their moisture. We arranged the shrimp in a single layer, making even contact with the pan. They heated up gradually, so they didn't buckle and thus browned uniformly; slower searing also ensured that they didn't overcook. Once the shrimp were spotty brown and pink at the edges, we removed them from the heat, letting residual heat gently finish cooking them. A flavorful spice mixture came together in the same pan. We prefer untreated shrimp; if yours are treated with additives such as sodium tripolyphosphate, skip salting in step 1. You can substitute jumbo shrimp (16 to 20 per pound) for the extra-large shrimp; simply increase the cooking time by 1 to 2 minutes. To use the plain seared shrimp in rice bowls or salads, skip steps 2 and 4.

- 1½ pounds extra-large shrimp (21 to 25 per pound), peeled, deveined, and tails removed (see left)
- 1 teaspoon kosher salt, divided
- 2 teaspoons coriander seeds
- 1 teaspoon black peppercorns
- 1 teaspoon paprika
- 1 garlic clove, minced
- 1⅛ teaspoons sugar, divided
- ⅛ teaspoon red pepper flakes
- 4 teaspoons vegetable oil, divided
- ½ cup fresh cilantro leaves and tender stems, chopped
- 1 tablespoon lime juice, plus lime wedges for serving
- 3 tablespoons dry-roasted peanuts, chopped coarse

**1.** Toss shrimp and ½ teaspoon salt together in bowl; set aside for 15 to 30 minutes.

**2.** Meanwhile, grind coriander seeds and peppercorns using spice grinder or mortar and pestle until coarsely ground. Transfer to small bowl. Add paprika, garlic, 1 teaspoon sugar, pepper flakes, and remaining ½ teaspoon salt and stir until combined.

**3.** Pat shrimp dry with paper towels. Add 1 tablespoon oil and remaining ⅛ teaspoon sugar to bowl with shrimp and toss to coat. Add shrimp to cold 12-inch nonstick or well-seasoned carbon-steel skillet in single layer and cook over high heat until undersides of shrimp are spotty brown and edges turn pink, 3 to 4 minutes. Remove skillet from heat. Working quickly, use tongs to flip each shrimp; let stand until second side is opaque, about 2 minutes. Transfer shrimp to platter.

**4.** Add remaining 1 teaspoon oil to now-empty skillet. Add spice mixture and cook over medium heat until fragrant, about 30 seconds. Off heat, return shrimp to skillet. Add cilantro and lime juice and toss to combine. Transfer to platter; sprinkle with peanuts; and serve, passing lime wedges separately.

## Garlicky Shrimp with Bread Crumbs

**SERVES 4**

**WHY THIS RECIPE WORKS** A casserole of shrimp in a sherry-garlic sauce topped with bread crumbs certainly has its appeal, but the ones we tried produced rubbery shrimp and gluey toppings. We wanted tender, moist shrimp infused with garlic and blanketed with crisp, buttery bread crumbs. Most recipes call for cooking the shrimp twice, first poaching them on the stovetop and then baking them in the casserole dish. No wonder they're usually overdone. Our experiments with skipping the poaching weren't very successful—the shrimp were just plain bland—so we abandoned the oven altogether and decided to make the entire dish in a skillet on top of the stove. After searing the shrimp on one side, sprinkled with a pinch of sugar to promote browning, we removed them to build the sauce. For the sauce, we started with garlic. Sherry alone tasted too boozy, so we cut it with clam juice, which underscored the briny flavor of the shrimp. A pinch of flour and some butter thickened the sauce, and lemon juice brightened everything up. A chewy supermarket baguette made the perfect buttery bread crumbs; sprinkled on at the last minute, they were sturdy enough to stay crisp on the saucy shrimp. Vermouth can be substituted for the sherry; if using, increase the amount to ½ cup and reduce the amount of clam juice to ½ cup. Serve the shrimp with rice and either broccoli or asparagus.

- 1 (3-inch) piece baguette, cut into small pieces
- 5 tablespoons unsalted butter, cut into 5 pieces
- 1 small shallot, minced (about 1 tablespoon)
- Table salt and ground black pepper
- 2 tablespoons minced fresh parsley leaves
- 2 pounds extra-large shrimp (21 to 25 per pound), peeled and deveined (see page 523)
- ¼ teaspoon sugar
- 4 teaspoons vegetable oil
- 4 medium garlic cloves, minced or pressed through a garlic press (about 4 teaspoons)
- ⅛ teaspoon red pepper flakes
- 2 teaspoons unbleached all-purpose flour
- ⅔ cup bottled clam juice
- ⅓ cup dry sherry
- 2 teaspoons juice from 1 lemon, plus lemon wedges for serving

**1.** Pulse the bread in a food processor until coarsely ground, about 8 pulses; you should have about 1 cup crumbs. Melt 1 tablespoon of the butter in a 12-inch nonstick skillet over medium heat. Add the crumbs, shallot, ⅛ teaspoon salt, and ⅛ teaspoon pepper. Cook, stirring occasionally, until the bread crumbs are golden brown, 7 to 10 minutes. Stir in 1 tablespoon of the parsley and transfer to a plate to cool. Wipe out the skillet with paper towels.

**2.** Pat the shrimp dry with paper towels and toss with the sugar, ¼ teaspoon salt, and ¼ teaspoon pepper in a bowl. Return the skillet to high heat, add 2 teaspoons of the oil, and heat until shimmering. Add half of the shrimp in a single layer and cook until spotty brown and the edges turn pink, about 3 minutes (do not flip the shrimp). Remove the pan from heat and transfer the shrimp to a large plate. Wipe out the skillet with paper towels. Repeat with the remaining 2 teaspoons oil and remaining shrimp; transfer the shrimp to the plate.

**3.** Return the skillet to medium heat and add 1 tablespoon more butter. When melted, add the garlic and red pepper flakes; cook, stirring frequently, until the garlic just begins to color, about 1 minute. Add the flour and cook, stirring frequently, for 1 minute. Increase the heat to medium-high and slowly whisk in the clam juice and sherry. Bring to a simmer and cook until the mixture reduces to ¾ cup, 3 to 4 minutes. Whisk in the remaining 3 tablespoons butter, 1 tablespoon at a time. Stir in the lemon juice and remaining 1 tablespoon parsley.

**4.** Reduce the heat to medium-low, return the shrimp to the pan, and toss to combine. Cook, covered, until the shrimp are pink and cooked through, 2 to 3 minutes. Uncover and sprinkle with the toasted bread crumbs. Serve with the lemon wedges.

## Garlicky Roasted Shrimp with Parsley and Anise

**SERVES 4 to 6**

**WHY THIS RECIPE WORKS** The flavor of shrimp concentrates through roasting, but it's worth it only if the flesh stays moist and tender. First we chose jumbo-size shrimp, which were the least likely to dry out and overcook. Butterflying the shrimp increased their surface area, giving us more room to add flavor. After brining the shrimp briefly to help them hold on to more moisture, we tossed them in a potent mixture of aromatic spices, garlic, herbs, butter, and oil. Then we roasted them under the broiler to get lots of color as quickly as possible, elevating them on a wire rack so they'd brown all over. To further protect them as they cooked and to produce a more

deeply roasted flavor, we left their shells on; the sugar- and protein-rich shells browned quickly in the heat of the oven and transferred flavor to the shrimp itself. Don't be tempted to use smaller shrimp with this cooking technique; they will be overseasoned and prone to overcook.

- ¼ cup table salt for brining
- 2 pounds shell-on jumbo shrimp (16 to 20 per pound)
- 4 tablespoons unsalted butter, melted
- ¼ cup vegetable oil
- 6 garlic cloves, minced
- 1 teaspoon anise seeds
- ½ teaspoon red pepper flakes
- ¼ teaspoon pepper
- 2 tablespoons minced fresh parsley
- Lemon wedges

**1.** Dissolve salt in 1 quart cold water in large container. Using kitchen shears or sharp paring knife, cut through shell of shrimp and devein but do not remove shell. Using paring knife, continue to cut shrimp ½ inch deep, taking care not to cut in half completely. Submerge shrimp in brine, cover, and refrigerate for 15 minutes.

**2.** Adjust oven rack 4 inches from broiler element and heat broiler. Combine melted butter, oil, garlic, anise seeds, pepper flakes, and pepper in large bowl. Remove shrimp from brine and pat dry with paper towels. Add shrimp and parsley to butter mixture; toss well, making sure butter mixture gets into interior of shrimp. Arrange shrimp in single layer on wire rack set in rimmed baking sheet.

**3.** Broil shrimp until opaque and shells are beginning to brown, 2 to 4 minutes, rotating sheet halfway through broiling. Flip shrimp and continue to broil until second side is opaque and shells are beginning to brown, 2 to 4 minutes longer, rotating sheet halfway through broiling. Transfer shrimp to serving platter and serve immediately, passing lemon wedges separately.

## Garlicky Broiled Shrimp

**SERVES** 4 as a Main Course or 6 as an Appetizer

**WHY THIS RECIPE WORKS** Broiling is a hands-off way to get succulent, spotty-brown shrimp in minutes. We started by briefly salting the shrimp so that they retained moisture as they cooked under high heat. A coating of butter and honey added richness, boosted browning, and underscored the shrimp's sweetness. We arranged the shrimp in a single layer on a wire rack set in a rimmed baking sheet to allow for airflow, which promoted even cooking. The biggest key to achieving snappy, lightly charred shrimp through broiling was determining how close the sheet should be to the broiler element. The sweet spot turned out to be 4 inches from the broiler, which ensured that the shrimp had enough distance to cook evenly and brown quickly without needing to be turned. We prefer untreated shrimp; if yours are treated with salt or additives such as sodium tripolyphosphate, skip the salting in step 1. This recipe was developed with Diamond Crystal kosher salt. If you're using Morton, which is denser, use a little less than ½ teaspoon. A rasp-style grater makes quick work of turning the garlic into a paste. For a simpler flavor profile suitable for serving with cocktail sauce or adding to salad or pasta, omit the garlic and red pepper flakes.

- 1½ pounds extra-large shrimp (21 to 25 per pound), peeled and deveined, tails left on (see page 523)
- ½ teaspoon kosher salt
- 4 tablespoons unsalted butter
- 1 tablespoon honey
- 6 garlic cloves, minced to paste
- ½–¾ teaspoon red pepper flakes
- Lemon wedges

**1.** Toss shrimp and salt together in bowl; set aside and let sit for 15 to 30 minutes.

**2.** Combine butter and honey in small bowl. Cover and microwave until butter is melted, 30 to 60 seconds. Add garlic and pepper flakes and stir to combine. Let cool slightly, about 5 minutes. While mixture cools, adjust oven rack 4 inches from broiler element and heat broiler. Line rimmed baking sheet with aluminum foil and set wire rack in sheet.

**3.** Spread out shrimp on large plate or cutting board and pat dry with paper towels. Return to bowl and pour butter mixture over shrimp. Toss until shrimp are thoroughly and evenly coated, including where they are split from deveining (it's OK if butter starts to solidify). Arrange shrimp in single layer on prepared rack.

**4.** Broil until shrimp are opaque throughout and beginning to lightly char in spots, 3 to 5 minutes. Transfer shrimp to serving platter and serve, passing lemon wedges separately.

### Smoky, Spiced Broiled Shrimp

Omit garlic and pepper flakes. Stir 1½ teaspoons smoked paprika, 1 teaspoon ground cumin, and 1 teaspoon ground coriander into warm honey-butter mixture before cooling. Sprinkle cooked shrimp with 2 tablespoons chopped fresh cilantro.

## Crispy Salt and Pepper Shrimp

**SERVES** 4 to 6

**WHY THIS RECIPE WORKS** In this traditional Chinese dish, shell-on shrimp are seasoned and flash-fried until the meat is plump and the shells are as deliciously crispy as fried chicken skin. To keep our deep-fried salt and pepper shrimp shells crisp and crunchy, we employed several tricks. First, we chose shrimp that were not overly large, which ensured that the shells were thinner relative to those on more jumbo specimens. Next, we coated them in a layer of cornstarch to dry out their shells, which helped make them brittle upon frying. Then we cooked them in small batches in very hot oil, which drove off any remaining water in the shells. To season the shrimp and keep them moist, we tossed them with salt and rice wine and let them sit briefly before dredging and frying. For an extra jolt of spiciness, we also fried a couple of sliced jalapeños. To give the dish depth, we added black peppercorns, Sichuan peppercorns, cayenne, and sugar to the coating and fried more of the same with ginger and garlic. Finally, we tossed the shrimp in the aromatic paste to unify the dish. In this recipe the shrimp are meant to be eaten shell and all. To ensure that the shells fry up crisp, avoid using shrimp that are overly large or jumbo. We prefer 31- to 40-count shrimp, but 26- to 30-count may be substituted. Serve with steamed rice.

- 1½ pounds shell-on shrimp (31 to 40 per pound)
- 2 tablespoons Shaoxing wine or dry sherry
- 1½ teaspoons kosher salt, divided
- 2½ teaspoons black peppercorns
- 2 teaspoons Sichuan peppercorns
- 2 teaspoons sugar
- ¼ teaspoon cayenne pepper
- 1 quart vegetable oil, for frying
- 5 tablespoons cornstarch, divided
- 2 jalapeño chiles, stemmed, seeded, and sliced into ⅛-inch-thick rings
- 3 garlic cloves, minced
- 1 tablespoon grated fresh ginger
- 2 scallions, sliced thin on bias
- ¼ head iceberg lettuce, shredded (1½ cups)

**1.** Adjust oven rack to upper-middle position and heat oven to 225 degrees. Toss shrimp, Shaoxing wine, and 1 teaspoon salt together in large bowl and set aside for 10 to 15 minutes.

**2.** Grind black peppercorns and Sichuan peppercorns in spice grinder or mortar and pestle until coarsely ground. Transfer peppercorns to small bowl and stir in sugar and cayenne.

**3.** Heat oil in large Dutch oven over medium heat until oil registers 385 degrees. While oil is heating, drain shrimp and pat dry with paper towels. Transfer shrimp to bowl, add 3 tablespoons cornstarch and 1 tablespoon peppercorn mixture, and toss until well combined.

**4.** Carefully add one-third of shrimp to oil and fry, stirring occasionally to keep shrimp from sticking together, until light brown, 2 to 3 minutes. Using wire skimmer or slotted spoon, transfer shrimp to paper towel–lined plate. Once paper towels absorb any excess oil, transfer shrimp to wire rack set in rimmed baking sheet and place in oven. Return oil to 385 degrees and repeat in 2 more batches, tossing each batch thoroughly with coating mixture before frying.

**5.** Toss jalapeño rings and remaining 2 tablespoons cornstarch in medium bowl. Shaking off excess cornstarch, carefully add jalapeño rings to oil and fry until crispy, 1 to 2 minutes. Using wire skimmer or slotted spoon, transfer jalapeño rings to paper towel–lined plate. After frying, reserve 2 tablespoons frying oil.

**6.** Heat reserved oil in 12-inch skillet over medium-high heat until shimmering. Add garlic, ginger, and remaining peppercorn mixture and cook, stirring occasionally, until mixture is fragrant and just beginning to brown, about 45 seconds. Add shrimp, scallions, and remaining ½ teaspoon salt and toss to coat. Line platter with lettuce. Transfer shrimp to platter, sprinkle with jalapeño rings, and serve immediately.

## Kung Pao Shrimp

**SERVES** 4

**WHY THIS RECIPE WORKS** Kung pao is meant to have a fiery personality. We wanted our version of this classic Sichuan stir-fry to boast large, tender shrimp; crunchy peanuts; and an assertive, well-balanced sauce. For tender, flavorful shrimp, we stir-fried marinated extra-large shrimp for just a few seconds, then added small whole red chiles and whole unsalted roasted peanuts. For vegetables, we kept things simple and added just one diced red bell pepper (we found other vegetables to be superfluous) and the usual aromatics, garlic and ginger. We made a potently flavored, syrupy sauce using a mixture of chicken broth, rice vinegar, toasted sesame oil, oyster-flavored sauce, hoisin sauce, and cornstarch. Stirring in sliced scallions just before serving put on the final touch. Roasted unsalted cashews can be substituted for the peanuts. Unless you have a high tolerance for spicy food, do not eat the whole chiles in the finished dish. Serve with steamed rice.

SAUCE

- ¾ cup chicken broth
- 1 tablespoon oyster-flavored sauce
- 1 tablespoon hoisin sauce
- 2 teaspoons rice vinegar
- 2 teaspoons toasted sesame oil
- 1½ teaspoons cornstarch

SHRIMP AND VEGETABLES

- 1 pound extra-large shrimp (21 to 25 per pound), peeled and deveined (see page 523)
- 1 tablespoon Chinese rice cooking wine (Shaoxing) or dry sherry
- 2 teaspoons soy sauce
- 2 tablespoons plus 1 teaspoon peanut or vegetable oil
- 3 garlic cloves, minced (about 1 tablespoon)
- 2 teaspoons minced or grated fresh ginger
- ½ cup unsalted roasted peanuts
- 6 small whole dried red chiles
- 1 red bell pepper, stemmed, seeded, and cut into ½-inch pieces
- 3 scallions, sliced thin

**1. FOR THE SAUCE:** Combine all the ingredients in a small bowl and set aside.

**2. FOR THE SHRIMP AND VEGETABLES:** Toss the shrimp with the rice cooking wine and soy sauce in a medium bowl and let marinate for at least 10 minutes or up to 1 hour. In a small bowl, mix 1 teaspoon of the peanut oil, the garlic, and ginger together.

**3.** Heat 1 tablespoon more peanut oil in a 12-inch nonstick skillet over high heat until just smoking. Add the shrimp and cook until barely opaque, 30 to 40 seconds, stirring halfway through. Add the peanuts and chiles and continue to cook until the shrimp are bright pink and the peanuts have darkened slightly, 30 to 40 seconds longer. Transfer the shrimp, peanuts, and chiles to a clean bowl and cover with foil to keep warm.

**4.** Add the remaining 1 tablespoon peanut oil to the skillet and return to high heat until just smoking. Add the bell pepper and cook, stirring frequently, until spotty brown, about 1½ minutes. Clear the center of the skillet, add the garlic mixture, and cook, mashing the mixture into the pan, until fragrant, 15 to 20 seconds. Stir the garlic mixture into the bell pepper.

**5.** Stir in the peanuts, chiles, and shrimp with any accumulated juices. Whisk the sauce to recombine, then add to the skillet and cook, tossing constantly, until the sauce is thickened, about 30 seconds. Stir in the scallions, transfer to a serving platter, and serve.

## Shrimp Tempura

SERVES 4

**WHY THIS RECIPE WORKS** Creating shrimp tempura that is so light and crisp that it barely seems fried hinges almost entirely on the batter. We used the largest shrimp available, since it's easy to overcook small shrimp. Cooking the tempura in 400-degree oil helped limit grease absorption. To prevent the batter from clumping on the shrimp, we made two cuts in the flesh. For the batter, we replaced a bit of the flour with cornstarch to improve the structure and lightness. For a supertender coating, we used seltzer and vodka. Do not omit the vodka; it is critical for a crisp coating. For safety, use a Dutch oven with a capacity of at least 7 quarts. Begin mixing the batter when the oil reaches 385 degrees (the final temperature should reach 400 degrees). It is important to maintain a high oil temperature throughout cooking. If you are unable to find colossal shrimp, jumbo (16 to 20 per pound) or extra-large (21 to 25 per pound) may be substituted. Fry smaller shrimp in three batches, reducing the cooking time to 1½ to 2 minutes per batch.

- 3 quarts peanut or vegetable oil
- 1½ pounds colossal shrimp (8 to 12 per pound), peeled and deveined, tails left on (see page 523)
- 1½ cups (7½ ounces) all-purpose flour
- ½ cup (2 ounces) cornstarch
- 1 cup vodka
- 1 large egg
- 1 cup seltzer water
- 1 recipe Scallion Dipping Sauce

**1.** Adjust oven rack to upper-middle position and heat oven to 200 degrees. In large Dutch oven, heat oil over high heat to 385 degrees, 18 to 22 minutes.

**2.** While oil heats, make 2 shallow cuts about ¼ inch deep and 1 inch apart on underside of each shrimp. Whisk flour and cornstarch together in large bowl. Whisk vodka and egg together in second large bowl, then whisk in seltzer water.

**3.** When oil reaches 385 degrees, whisk vodka mixture into bowl with flour mixture until just combined (it is OK if small lumps remain). Submerge half of shrimp in batter. Using tongs, remove shrimp from batter one at a time, allowing excess batter to drip off, and carefully place in oil (temperature should now be at 400 degrees). Fry, stirring with chopstick or wooden skewer to prevent sticking, until light brown, 2 to 3 minutes. Using slotted spoon, transfer shrimp to paper towel–lined plate and season with kosher salt. Once paper towels absorb excess oil, transfer shrimp to wire rack set over rimmed baking sheet and place in oven to keep warm.

**4.** Return oil to 400 degrees, about 4 minutes, then repeat with remaining shrimp. Serve with dipping sauce.

### Scallion Dipping Sauce

MAKES ¾ cup

- ¼ cup soy sauce
- 2 tablespoons rice vinegar
- 2 tablespoons mirin or sweet sherry
- 2 tablespoons water
- 1 teaspoon chili oil (optional)
- ½ teaspoon toasted sesame oil
- 1 scallion, minced

Combine all ingredients in small bowl and set aside. (Sauce can be refrigerated in airtight container for up to 24 hours.)

## Stir-Fried Shrimp with Snow Peas and Red Bell Pepper in Hot and Sour Sauce

SERVES 4

**WHY THIS RECIPE WORKS** Stir-fries are typically cooked over high heat to sear the food and develop flavor. This works well with chicken, beef, and pork, but delicate shrimp can turn to rubber very quickly. We wanted a stir-fry with plump, juicy, well-seasoned shrimp in a balanced, flavorful sauce. We wondered if browning was really necessary. Abandoning the high-heat method, we turned down the burner to medium-low and gently parcooked a batch of shrimp, removed them from the skillet, then turned up the heat to sear the vegetables, sauté the aromatics, and finish cooking the shrimp with the sauce. This worked beautifully. Reversing the approach—cooking the veggies followed by the aromatics over high heat, then turning the heat down before adding the shrimp—made the process more efficient. We reduced our sweet and spicy sauce so that it tightly adhered to the shellfish. Serve with white rice.

- 1 pound extra-large shrimp (21 to 25 per pound), peeled, deveined, and tails removed (see page 523)
- 3 tablespoons vegetable oil, divided
- 1 tablespoon grated fresh ginger
- 2 garlic cloves (1 minced, 1 sliced thin)
- ½ teaspoon table salt
- 3 tablespoons sugar
- 3 tablespoons white vinegar
- 1 tablespoon chili-garlic sauce
- 1 tablespoon Shaoxing wine or dry sherry
- 1 tablespoon ketchup
- 2 teaspoons toasted sesame oil
- 2 teaspoons cornstarch
- 1 teaspoon soy sauce
- 1 large shallot, sliced thin (about ⅓ cup)
- 8 ounces snow peas or sugar snap peas, strings removed
- 1 red bell pepper, stemmed, seeded, and cut into ¾-inch dice

**1.** Combine shrimp with 1 tablespoon vegetable oil, ginger, minced garlic, and salt in medium bowl. Let shrimp marinate at room temperature for 30 minutes.

**2.** Meanwhile, whisk sugar, vinegar, chili-garlic sauce, Shaoxing wine, ketchup, sesame oil, cornstarch, and soy sauce in small bowl. Combine sliced garlic with shallot in second small bowl.

**3.** Heat 1 tablespoon vegetable oil in 14-inch flat-bottomed wok or 12-inch nonstick skillet over high heat until just smoking. Add snow peas and bell pepper and cook, tossing slowly but constantly, until vegetables begin to brown, 1½ to 2 minutes. Transfer vegetables to medium bowl.

**4.** Add remaining 1 tablespoon vegetable oil to now-empty skillet and heat until just smoking. Add garlic-shallot mixture and cook, stirring frequently, until just beginning to brown, about 30 seconds. Reduce heat to medium-low; add shrimp; and cook, stirring frequently, until shrimp are light pink on both sides, 1 to 1½ minutes. Whisk soy sauce mixture to recombine and add to skillet; return to high heat and cook, stirring constantly, until sauce is thickened and shrimp are cooked through, 1 to 2 minutes. Return vegetables to skillet, toss to combine, and serve.

## Spanish-Style Garlic Shrimp

SERVES 6

**WHY THIS RECIPE WORKS** Sizzling gambas al ajillo is a tempting tapas dish. We re-created it to serve at home, so we could savor juicy shrimp in spicy, garlic-infused oil. The shrimp in the Spanish original are completely submerged in oil and cooked slowly. We didn't want to use that much oil, so we added just enough to a skillet to come halfway up the sides of the shrimp. We cooked them over very low heat and turned them halfway through; these shrimp cooked as evenly as if completely covered with oil. We built heady garlic flavor in three ways: We added minced garlic to a marinade, we browned smashed cloves in the shrimp's cooking oil, and we cooked slices of garlic along with the shrimp. We included bay leaf and red chile, and added sherry vinegar and parsley, all of which brightened the richness of the oil. Serve the shrimp with crusty bread for dipping in the flavorful oil. This dish can be served directly from the skillet or, for a sizzling effect, transferred to an 8-inch cast-iron skillet that's been heated for 2 minutes over medium-high heat. We prefer the slightly sweet flavor of dried chiles in this recipe, but ¼ teaspoon sweet paprika can be substituted. If sherry vinegar is unavailable, use 2 teaspoons dry sherry and 1 teaspoon white vinegar.

- 14 medium garlic cloves, peeled
- 1 pound large shrimp (31 to 40 per pound), peeled, deveined and tails removed (see page 523)
- 8 tablespoons olive oil
- ½ teaspoon table salt
- 1 bay leaf
- 1 (2-inch) piece mild dried chile, such as New Mexico, roughly broken, seeds included
- 1½ teaspoons sherry vinegar
- 1 tablespoon minced fresh parsley leaves

**1.** Mince 2 of the garlic cloves with a chef's knife or garlic press. Toss the minced garlic with the shrimp, 2 tablespoons of the olive oil, and salt in a medium bowl. Let the shrimp marinate at room temperature for 30 minutes.

**2.** Meanwhile, using the flat side of a chef's knife, smash 4 more garlic cloves. Heat the smashed garlic with the remaining 6 tablespoons olive oil in a 12-inch skillet over medium-low heat, stirring occasionally, until the garlic is light golden brown, 4 to 7 minutes. Remove the pan from the heat and allow the oil to cool to room temperature. Using a slotted spoon, remove the smashed garlic from the skillet and discard.

**3.** Slice the remaining 8 garlic cloves thin. Return the skillet to low heat and add the sliced garlic, bay leaf, and chile. Cook, stirring occasionally, until the garlic is tender but not browned, 4 to 7 minutes. (If the garlic has not begun to sizzle after

3 minutes, increase the heat to medium-low.) Increase the heat to medium-low and add the shrimp with the marinade to the pan in a single layer. Cook the shrimp, undisturbed, until the oil starts to gently bubble, about 2 minutes. Using tongs, flip the shrimp and continue to cook until almost cooked through, about 2 minutes longer. Increase the heat to high and add the sherry vinegar and parsley. Cook, stirring constantly, until the shrimp are cooked through and the oil is bubbling vigorously, 15 to 20 seconds. Serve immediately, discarding the bay leaf.

## Greek-Style Shrimp with Tomatoes and Feta

**SERVES** 4 to 6

**WHY THIS RECIPE WORKS** The unlikely combination of seafood and cheese marry well in Greece's shrimp saganaki. Sweet, briny shrimp are covered with a garlic-and-herb- accented tomato sauce and topped with creamy, salty feta cheese. We set out to develop a foolproof version of this dish—one that is perfectly cooked and captures the bold and exuberant essence of Greek cuisine. We started with the tomato sauce. Canned diced tomatoes along with sautéed onion and garlic provided our base. Dry white wine added acidity. Ouzo, the slightly sweet anise-flavored Greek liqueur, added welcome complexity when simmered in the sauce. Since this should be a quick and easy dish, we cooked the shrimp right in the sauce, which infused them with bright flavor. And for even more flavor, we marinated the shrimp with olive oil, ouzo, garlic, and lemon zest first. This recipe works equally well with either jumbo shrimp (16 to 20 per pound) or extra-large shrimp (21 to 25 per pound); the cooking times in step 3 will vary slightly. Serve with crusty bread for soaking up the sauce.

- 1½ pounds shrimp, peeled and deveined, tails left on, if desired (see page 523)
- ¼ cup extra-virgin olive oil, divided
- 3 tablespoons ouzo, divided
- 5 garlic cloves, minced, divided
- 1 teaspoon grated lemon zest
- ½ teaspoon table salt, divided
- ⅛ teaspoon pepper
- 1 small onion, chopped
- ½ red bell pepper, chopped
- ½ green bell pepper, chopped
- ½ teaspoon red pepper flakes
- 1 (28-ounce) can diced tomatoes, drained with ⅓ cup juice reserved
- ¼ cup dry white wine
- 2 tablespoons coarsely chopped fresh parsley
- 6 ounces feta cheese, preferably sheep's and/or goat's milk, crumbled (about 1½ cups)
- 2 tablespoons chopped fresh dill

**1.** Toss shrimp, 1 tablespoon oil, 1 tablespoon ouzo, 1 teaspoon garlic, lemon zest, ¼ teaspoon salt, and pepper in small bowl until well combined. Set aside while preparing sauce.

**2.** Heat 2 tablespoons oil in 12-inch skillet over medium heat until shimmering. Add onion, red and green bell peppers, and remaining ¼ teaspoon salt and stir to combine. Cover skillet and cook, stirring occasionally, until vegetables release their moisture, 3 to 5 minutes. Uncover and continue to cook, stirring occasionally, until moisture cooks off and vegetables have softened, about 5 minutes longer. Add pepper flakes and remaining garlic and cook until fragrant, about 1 minute. Add tomatoes and reserved juice, wine, and remaining 2 tablespoons ouzo; increase heat to medium-high and bring to simmer. Reduce heat to medium and simmer, stirring occasionally, until flavors have melded and sauce is slightly thickened (sauce should not be completely dry), 5 to 8 minutes. Stir in parsley and season with salt and pepper to taste.

**3.** Reduce heat to medium-low and add shrimp along with any accumulated liquid to pan; stir to coat and distribute evenly. Cover and cook, stirring occasionally, until shrimp are opaque throughout, 6 to 9 minutes for extra-large shrimp or 7 to 11 minutes for jumbo shrimp, adjusting heat as needed to maintain bare simmer. Remove pan from heat and sprinkle evenly with feta. Drizzle remaining 1 tablespoon oil evenly over top and sprinkle with dill. Serve immediately.

## Tacos Gobernador

**SERVES** 4 **SEASON 26**

**WHY THIS RECIPE WORKS** Tacos gobernador are shrimp and vegetable tacos from Mexico's Baja region that are toasted briefly in a skillet. We sautéed the shrimp first to help us control its doneness, as well as to drain its excess moisture from the filling to avoid sogging out the tacos. Creating a layer of cheese atop the tortilla ensured that it had maximum contact with the pan's heat and melted readily. Fresh cilantro, crema, a spritz of lime, and a few dashes of hot sauce added welcome freshness and zing. For a spicier dish, leave the seeds and ribs in the serrano. If desired, small (6-inch) flour tortillas can be

substituted for the corn tortillas. Oaxaca is a mild, semisoft Mexican cheese; if it's unavailable, queso asadero or Monterey Jack can be substituted.

- 3 tablespoons unsalted butter, divided
- 1 pound medium shrimp (41 to 50 per pound), peeled, deveined, and tails removed, chopped (see page 523)
- 1 large poblano chile, stemmed, seeded, and cut into 2-inch-long matchsticks
- 1 onion, halved and sliced thin
- 1 serrano chile, stemmed, seeded, and minced
- 2 garlic cloves, minced
- 1 teaspoon dried Mexican oregano
- ½ teaspoon ground coriander
- ½ teaspoon ground cumin
- ½ teaspoon table salt
- 2 plum tomatoes, cored and chopped fine
- ⅓ cup chopped fresh cilantro, plus extra for serving
- 8 (6-inch) corn tortillas
- 2 tablespoons vegetable oil
- 8 ounces Oaxaca cheese, shredded (2 cups)
- Lime wedges
- Mexican crema or sour cream
- Hot sauce

**1.** Adjust oven rack to middle position and heat oven to 200 degrees. Set wire rack in rimmed baking sheet and place in oven. Place colander inside medium bowl; set aside.

**2.** Melt 1 tablespoon butter in 12-inch nonstick skillet over medium heat. Add shrimp and cook, stirring frequently, until just opaque, about 2 minutes. Transfer shrimp to prepared colander to drain.

**3.** Return skillet to heat and melt remaining 2 tablespoons butter. Add poblano, onion, and serrano and cook, stirring frequently, until onion is softened and starting to brown, 6 to 8 minutes. Stir in garlic, oregano, coriander, cumin, and salt and cook for 1 minute. Add tomatoes and cook until vegetable mixture is dry, 4 to 5 minutes. Off heat, stir in cilantro.

**4.** Discard any shrimp juices that have collected in bowl. Transfer shrimp and vegetable mixture to now-empty bowl and stir to combine. Season with salt to taste. Wipe out skillet.

**5.** Stack tortillas, wrap in damp dish towel, and place on plate; microwave until warm and pliable, about 30 seconds. Place 1 tortilla on cutting board (keep others covered) and brush top lightly with oil. Flip tortilla over, then sprinkle evenly with ¼ cup cheese. Spread ¼ cup shrimp mixture over half of tortilla, leaving ⅛-inch border at edge. Fold and press to close tortilla. Repeat with remaining tortillas, oil, and filling.

**6.** Arrange 4 tacos in now-empty skillet with open sides facing toward center of pan. Place skillet over medium-high heat and cook until cheese has melted and tacos are spotty golden brown on 1 side, 2 to 3 minutes. Using tongs and thin spatula, carefully flip tacos. Cook until spotty golden brown on second side, 2 to 3 minutes, adjusting heat as necessary.

**7.** Remove skillet from heat and transfer tacos to prepared sheet in oven to keep warm. Arrange remaining 4 tacos in skillet, return pan to medium-high heat, and cook remaining tacos. Serve tacos immediately, passing lime wedges, crema, hot sauce, and cilantro separately. Open tacos to add garnishes.

## Simple Shrimp Scampi

**SERVES** 4 to 6

**WHY THIS RECIPE WORKS** Shrimp scampi can run the gamut from boiled shrimp and tomato sauce on a bed of pasta to rubbery shrimp overloaded in butter or olive oil. We wanted moist shrimp in a light garlic and lemon sauce. A quick sauté in batches was all the shrimp needed to cook fully without becoming rubbery; we then set them aside to build the sauce. We cooked minced garlic briefly in butter, so as not to scorch it, then added lemon juice and vermouth for depth of flavor; the liquids also protected the garlic from burning. Additional butter thickened the sauce, and parsley and cayenne provided the finishing touches to this flavorful Italian favorite. Serve the scampi over long pasta such as linguine or spaghetti or with chewy bread to soak up the extra juices.

- 2 tablespoons olive oil
- 2 pounds extra-large shrimp (21 to 25 per pound), peeled and deveined (see page 523)
- 3 tablespoons unsalted butter
- 4 medium garlic cloves, minced or pressed through a garlic press (about 4 teaspoons)
- 2 tablespoons juice from 1 lemon
- 1 tablespoon dry vermouth
- 2 tablespoons minced fresh parsley leaves
- Pinch cayenne pepper
- Table salt and ground black pepper

**1.** Heat 1 tablespoon of the oil in a 12-inch skillet over high heat until shimmering. Add 1 pound of the shrimp and cook, stirring occasionally, until just opaque, about 1 minute; transfer to a medium bowl. Return the pan to high heat and repeat with the remaining 1 tablespoon oil and remaining 1 pound shrimp.

**2.** Return the skillet to medium-low heat; melt 1 tablespoon of the butter. Add the garlic and cook, stirring constantly, until fragrant, about 30 seconds. Off the heat, add the lemon juice and vermouth. Whisk in the remaining 2 tablespoons butter; add the parsley and cayenne, and season with salt and black pepper to taste. Return the shrimp and any accumulated juices to the skillet. Toss to combine; serve immediately.

## Shrimp Scampi

**SERVES** 4

**WHY THIS RECIPE WORKS** Our ultimate shrimp scampi recipe uses a few test kitchen tricks to ensure flavorful and well-cooked shrimp, as well as a creamy, robust sauce to pair them with. First, we brined the shrimp in salt and sugar to season them and to keep them moist and juicy. Because sautéing can lead to uneven cooking, we instead gently poached the shrimp in wine. To get more shrimp flavor into the sauce, we used the shells as the base of a stock and added wine and thyme. The key was to let it simmer for only 5 minutes. For potent but clean garlic flavor, we used a generous amount of sliced, rather than minced, garlic. A teaspoon of cornstarch at the end of cooking kept the sauce emulsified and silky. Extra-large shrimp (21 to 25 per pound) can be substituted for jumbo shrimp. If you use them, reduce the cooking time in step 3 by 1 to 2 minutes. We prefer untreated shrimp, but if your shrimp are treated with sodium or preservatives like sodium tripolyphosphate, skip the brining in step 1 and add ¼ teaspoon of salt to the sauce in step 4. Serve with crusty bread.

- 3 tablespoons table salt for brining
- 2 tablespoons sugar for brining
- 1½ pounds jumbo shrimp (16 to 20 per pound), peeled, deveined, and tails removed, shells reserved (see page 523)
- 2 tablespoons extra-virgin olive oil, divided
- 1 cup dry white wine
- 4 sprigs fresh thyme
- 3 tablespoons lemon juice, plus lemon wedges for serving
- 1 teaspoon cornstarch
- 8 garlic cloves, sliced thin
- ½ teaspoon red pepper flakes
- ¼ teaspoon pepper
- 4 tablespoons unsalted butter, cut into ½-inch pieces
- 1 tablespoon chopped fresh parsley

**1.** Dissolve salt and sugar in 1 quart cold water in large container. Submerge shrimp in brine, cover, and refrigerate for 15 minutes. Remove shrimp from brine and pat dry with paper towels.

**2.** Heat 1 tablespoon oil in 12-inch skillet over high heat until shimmering. Add shrimp shells and cook, stirring frequently, until they begin to turn spotty brown and skillet starts to brown, 2 to 4 minutes. Remove skillet from heat and carefully add wine and thyme sprigs. When bubbling subsides, return skillet to medium heat and simmer gently, stirring occasionally, for 5 minutes. Strain mixture through colander set over large bowl. Discard shells and reserve liquid (you should have about ⅔ cup). Wipe out skillet with paper towels.

**3.** Combine lemon juice and cornstarch in small bowl. Heat remaining 1 tablespoon oil, garlic, pepper flakes, and pepper in now-empty skillet over medium-low heat, stirring occasionally, until garlic is fragrant and just beginning to brown at edges, 3 to 5 minutes. Add reserved wine mixture, increase heat to high, and bring to simmer. Reduce heat to medium, add shrimp, cover, and cook, stirring occasionally, until shrimp are just opaque, 5 to 7 minutes. Remove skillet from heat and, using slotted spoon, transfer shrimp to bowl.

**4.** Return skillet to medium heat, add lemon juice–cornstarch mixture, and cook until slightly thickened, about 1 minute. Remove from heat and whisk in butter and parsley until combined. Return shrimp and any accumulated juices to skillet and toss to combine. Serve, passing lemon wedges separately.

## Shrimp Risotto

**SERVES** 4 to 6

**WHY THIS RECIPE WORKS** For a simplified shrimp risotto, we started by making a quick stock: We seared the shrimp shells to extract their flavorful compounds, added water and seasonings, and simmered it all for just 5 minutes. Next we sautéed onion and fennel and then added the rice to the pot, followed by white wine and almost all the stock. We simmered the risotto covered to help it cook evenly and stirred it only occasionally. Adding the chopped, salted shrimp off the heat ensured that they would cook through very gently and retain their delicate texture. Final additions of butter, lemon, chives, and Parmesan contributed complexity while keeping things light. Accompanied by a salad, this risotto makes a great dinner, but it can also be served in eight smaller portions as a first course.

- 1 pound extra-large shrimp (21 to 25 per pound), peeled, deveined, and tails removed, shells reserved (see page 523)
- 1¾ teaspoons table salt, divided
- 1 tablespoon vegetable oil
- 7 cups water
- 15 black peppercorns
- 2 bay leaves
- 4 tablespoons unsalted butter, divided
- 1 onion, chopped fine
- 1 fennel bulb, stalks discarded, bulb halved, cored, and chopped fine
- ⅛ teaspoon baking soda
- 2 garlic cloves, minced
- 1½ cups Arborio rice
- ¾ cup dry white wine
- 1 ounce Parmesan cheese, grated (½ cup), plus extra for serving
- ¼ cup minced fresh chives
- ½ teaspoon grated lemon zest plus 1 tablespoon juice, plus lemon wedges for serving

1. Cut each shrimp crosswise into thirds. Toss with ½ teaspoon salt and set aside. Heat oil in Dutch oven over high heat until shimmering. Add reserved shrimp shells and cook, stirring frequently, until shells begin to turn spotty brown, 2 to 4 minutes. Add water, peppercorns, bay leaves, and 1 teaspoon salt and bring to boil. Reduce heat to low and simmer for 5 minutes. Strain stock through fine-mesh strainer set over large bowl, pressing on solids with rubber spatula to extract as much liquid as possible; discard solids.

2. Melt 2 tablespoons butter in now-empty pot over medium heat. Add onion, fennel, baking soda, and remaining ¼ teaspoon salt. Cook, stirring frequently, until vegetables are softened but not browned, 8 to 10 minutes (volume will be dramatically reduced and onion will have mostly disintegrated). Add garlic and stir until fragrant, about 30 seconds. Add rice and cook, stirring frequently, until grains are translucent around edges, about 3 minutes.

3. Add wine and cook, stirring constantly, until fully absorbed, 2 to 3 minutes. Stir 4 cups stock into rice mixture; reduce heat to medium-low, cover, and simmer until almost all liquid has been absorbed and rice is just al dente, 16 to 18 minutes, stirring twice during simmering.

4. Add ¾ cup stock to risotto and stir gently and constantly until risotto becomes creamy, about 3 minutes. Stir in Parmesan and shrimp. Cover pot and let stand off heat for 5 minutes.

5. Gently stir chives, lemon zest and juice, and remaining 2 tablespoons butter into risotto. Season with salt and pepper to taste. If desired, stir in additional stock to loosen texture of risotto. Serve, passing lemon wedges and extra Parmesan separately.

## Pad Thai

**SERVES 4**

**WHY THIS RECIPE WORKS** We hoped to develop a pad thai with clean, fresh, not-too-sweet flavors; perfectly cooked noodles; and plenty of plump, juicy shrimp with tender bits of scrambled egg. Soaking the rice sticks in boiling water for 10 minutes before stir-frying made for tender but not sticky noodles. We created the salty, sweet, sour, and spicy flavor profile of pad thai by combining fish sauce, sugar, ground chiles, and vinegar. For the fresh, bright, fruity taste that is essential to the dish, we used tamarind paste, which we soaked in hot water and passed through a fine-mesh strainer to make a smooth puree. Tossed with fresh and dried shrimp and eggs, and garnished with scallions, peanuts, and cilantro, this dish was a delicious rendition of the Thai classic. Although this pad thai cooks very quickly, the ingredient list is long, and everything must be prepared and within easy reach at the stovetop when you begin cooking. For maximum efficiency, use the time during which the tamarind and noodles soak to prepare the other ingredients. If tamarind paste is unavailable, substitute ⅓ cup lime juice and ⅓ cup water and use light brown sugar instead of granulated sugar.

**SAUCE**

- ¾ cup boiling water
- 2 tablespoons tamarind paste
- 3 tablespoons fish sauce
- 3 tablespoons sugar
- 2 tablespoons peanut or vegetable oil
- 1 tablespoon rice vinegar
- ¾ teaspoon cayenne pepper

**NOODLES, SHRIMP, AND GARNISH**

- 8 ounces dried rice stick noodles, ⅛ to ¼ inch wide
- 2 tablespoons peanut or vegetable oil
- 12 ounces medium shrimp (41 to 50 per pound), peeled and deveined (see page 523)
- Table salt
- 1 medium shallot, minced (about 2 tablespoons)
- 3 garlic cloves, minced or pressed through a garlic press (about 1 tablespoon)
- 2 large eggs, lightly beaten
- 2 tablespoons chopped Thai salted preserved radish (optional)
- 1 tablespoon dried shrimp, chopped fine (optional)
- 3 cups bean sprouts
- ½ cup unsalted roasted peanuts, chopped coarse
- 5 scallions, green parts only, sliced thin on the bias
- ¼ cup loosely packed fresh cilantro leaves (optional)
- Lime wedges, for serving

1. **FOR THE SAUCE:** Combine the water and tamarind paste in a small bowl and let sit until the tamarind is softened and mushy, 10 to 30 minutes. Mash the tamarind to break it up, then push it through a fine-mesh strainer into a medium bowl to remove the seeds and fibers and extract as much pulp as possible. Stir in the remaining sauce ingredients and set aside.

2. **FOR THE NOODLES, SHRIMP, AND GARNISH:** Bring 4 quarts water to a boil in a large pot. Remove the boiling water from the heat, add the rice noodles, and let sit, stirring occasionally, until almost tender, about 10 minutes. Drain the noodles and set aside.

**3.** Heat 1 tablespoon of the oil in a 12-inch nonstick skillet over high heat until just smoking. Add the shrimp, sprinkle with 1/8 teaspoon salt, and cook without stirring until bright pink, about 1 minute. Stir the shrimp and continue to cook until cooked through, 15 to 30 seconds longer. Transfer the shrimp to a clean bowl and cover with foil to keep warm.

**4.** Add the remaining 1 tablespoon oil to the skillet and return to medium heat until shimmering. Add the shallot and garlic and cook, stirring constantly, until light golden brown, about 1½ minutes. Stir in the eggs and cook, stirring constantly, until scrambled and barely moist, about 20 seconds.

**5.** Add the noodles and the salted radish and dried shrimp (if using) to the eggs and toss to combine. Add the sauce, increase the heat to high, and cook, tossing constantly, until the noodles are evenly coated, about 1 minute.

**6.** Add the cooked shrimp, bean sprouts, ¼ cup of the peanuts, and all but ¼ cup of the scallions and continue to cook, tossing constantly, until the noodles are tender, about 2½ minutes. (If not yet tender add 2 tablespoons water to the skillet and continue to cook until tender.) Transfer the noodles to a serving platter, sprinkle with the remaining ¼ cup peanuts, remaining ¼ cup scallions, and cilantro (if using) and serve with the lime wedges.

## Shrimp Pad Thai

**SERVES 4**

**WHY THIS RECIPE WORKS** Thai cuisine is known for its symphony of salty, sweet, and sour flavors, and this hugely popular street food is no different. In our version, we achieved those flavors with a careful balance of fish sauce, sugar, and tamarind juice concentrate. Lime juice squeezed over the finished dish, along with a quick-to-make chile vinegar, added even more tangy kick. Soaking rice noodles in boiling water, versus cooking them in the hot water, prevented the delicate strands from getting too soft. Shrimp and egg bulked up the dish while bean sprouts, scallion greens, and peanuts added crunch. Finally, we pickled regular red radishes in a nod to the traditional addition of preserved daikon, and we created our own faux dried shrimp by microwaving and then frying small pieces of fresh shrimp. Since pad thai cooks very quickly, prepare everything before you begin to cook. If you cannot find tamarind juice concentrate, substitute 1½ tablespoons lime juice and 1½ tablespoons water and omit the lime wedges.

**CHILE VINEGAR**

- ⅓ cup distilled white vinegar
- 1 serrano chile, stemmed and sliced into thin rings

**STIR-FRY**

- ½ teaspoon table salt for pickling
- ¼ teaspoon sugar for pickling
- 2 radishes, trimmed and cut into 1½-inch by ¼-inch matchsticks
- 8 ounces (¼-inch-wide) rice noodles
- 3 tablespoons plus 2 teaspoons vegetable oil, divided
- ¼ cup fish sauce
- 3 tablespoons tamarind juice concentrate
- 3 tablespoons plus ⅛ teaspoon sugar, divided
- 1 pound large shrimp (26 to 30 per pound), peeled and deveined (see page 523)
- ⅛ teaspoon table salt
- 4 scallions, white and light green parts minced, dark green parts cut into 1-inch lengths
- 1 garlic clove, minced
- 4 large eggs, beaten
- 4 ounces (2 cups) bean sprouts
- ¼ cup roasted unsalted peanuts, chopped coarse
- Lime wedges

**1. FOR THE CHILE VINEGAR:** Combine vinegar and chile in bowl and let stand at room temperature for at least 15 minutes.

**2. FOR THE STIR-FRY:** Combine ¼ cup water, ½ teaspoon salt, and ¼ teaspoon sugar in small bowl. Microwave until steaming, about 30 seconds. Add radishes and let stand for 15 minutes. Drain and pat dry with paper towels.

**3.** Bring 6 cups water to boil. Place noodles in large bowl. Pour boiling water over noodles. Stir, then let soak until noodles are almost tender, about 8 minutes, stirring once halfway through soaking. Drain noodles and rinse with cold water. Drain noodles well, then toss with 2 teaspoons oil.

**4.** Combine fish sauce, tamarind concentrate, and 3 tablespoons sugar in bowl and whisk until sugar is dissolved. Set sauce aside.

**5.** Remove tails from 4 shrimp. Cut shrimp in half lengthwise, then cut each half into ½-inch pieces. Toss shrimp pieces with salt and remaining ⅛ teaspoon sugar. Arrange pieces in single layer on large plate and microwave at 50 percent power until shrimp are dried and have reduced in size by half, 4 to 5 minutes. (Check halfway through microwaving and separate any pieces that may have stuck together.)

**6.** Heat 2 teaspoons oil in 12-inch nonstick skillet over medium heat until shimmering. Add dried shrimp and cook, stirring frequently, until golden brown and crispy, 3 to 5 minutes. Transfer to large bowl.

**7.** Heat 1 teaspoon oil in now-empty skillet over medium heat until shimmering. Add minced scallions and garlic and cook, stirring constantly, until garlic is golden brown, about 1 minute. Transfer to bowl with dried shrimp.

**8.** Heat 2 teaspoons oil in now-empty skillet over high heat until just smoking. Add remaining whole shrimp and spread into even layer. Cook, without stirring, until shrimp turn opaque and brown around edges, 2 to 3 minutes, flipping halfway through cooking. Push shrimp to sides of skillet. Add 2 teaspoons oil to center, then add eggs to center. Using rubber spatula, stir eggs gently and cook until set but still wet. Stir eggs into shrimp and continue to cook, breaking up large pieces of egg, until eggs are fully cooked, 30 to 60 seconds longer. Transfer shrimp-egg mixture to bowl with scallion-garlic mixture and dried shrimp.

**9.** Heat remaining 2 teaspoons oil in now-empty skillet over high heat until just smoking. Add noodles and sauce and toss with tongs to coat. Cook, stirring and tossing often, until noodles are tender and have absorbed sauce, 2 to 4 minutes. Transfer noodles to bowl with shrimp mixture. Add 2 teaspoons chile vinegar, drained radishes, scallion greens, and bean sprouts and toss to combine.

**10.** Transfer to platter and sprinkle with peanuts. Serve immediately, passing lime wedges and remaining chile vinegar separately.

## Nasi Goreng (Indonesian-Style Fried Rice)

**SERVES** 4 to 6

**WHY THIS RECIPE WORKS** For a different take on Indonesian-style nasi goreng, a classic Southeast Asian fried rice dish, we tweaked the cooking process so that we could avoid cooking the rice the day before or waiting until we had leftover rice on hand. To mimic the firmness of leftover rice, we rinsed the raw grains and sautéed them in some oil. We then cooked the rice in less water and let it cool in the refrigerator. All our Indonesian-style fried rice needed was the traditional garnishes: frizzled shallots; cucumbers; tomatoes; and an egg, which we turned into an omelet, cut into strips, and rolled up for an attractive presentation. If Thai chiles are unavailable, substitute two serranos or two medium jalapeños. Reduce the spiciness of this dish by removing the ribs and seeds from the chiles. This dish progresses very quickly at step 4; it's imperative that your ingredients are in place by then and ready to go. If desired, serve the rice with sliced cucumbers and tomato wedges.

- 5 green or red Thai chiles, stemmed
- 7 large shallots, peeled
- 4 large garlic cloves, peeled
- 2 tablespoons dark brown sugar
- 2 tablespoons light or mild molasses
- 2 tablespoons soy sauce
- 2 tablespoons fish sauce
- Table salt
- 4 large eggs
- ½ cup vegetable oil
- 1 recipe Faux Leftover Rice
- 12 ounces extra-large shrimp (21 to 25 per pound), peeled, deveined (see page 523), tails removed, and cut crosswise into thirds
- 4 large scallions, sliced thin
- 2 limes, cut into wedges

**1.** Pulse the chiles, 4 of the shallots, and the garlic in a food processor until a coarse paste is formed, about 15 pulses, scraping down the sides of the bowl as necessary. Transfer the mixture to a small bowl and set aside. In a second small bowl, stir together the brown sugar, molasses, soy sauce, fish sauce, and 1¼ teaspoons salt. Whisk the eggs and ¼ teaspoon salt together in a medium bowl.

**2.** Thinly slice the remaining 3 shallots and place in a 12-inch nonstick skillet with the oil. Cook over medium heat, stirring constantly, until the shallots are golden and crisp, 6 to 10 minutes. Using a slotted spoon, transfer the shallots to a paper towel–lined plate and season with salt to taste. Pour off the oil and reserve. Wipe out the skillet with paper towels.

**3.** Heat 1 teaspoon of the reserved oil in the now-empty skillet over medium heat until shimmering. Add half of the eggs to the skillet, gently tilting the pan to evenly coat the bottom. Cover and cook until the bottom of the omelet is spotty golden brown and the top is just set, about 1½ minutes. Slide the omelet onto a cutting board and gently roll up into a tight log. Using a sharp knife, cut the log crosswise into 1-inch segments (leaving the segments rolled). Repeat with 1 teaspoon more reserved oil and the remaining egg.

**4.** Remove the rice from the refrigerator and break up any large clumps with your fingers. Heat 3 tablespoons more reserved oil in the now-empty skillet over medium heat until just shimmering. Add the chile mixture and cook until the mixture turns golden, 3 to 5 minutes. Add the shrimp, increase the heat to medium-high, and cook, stirring constantly, until the exterior of the shrimp is just opaque, about 2 minutes. Push the shrimp to the sides of the skillet to clear the center; stir the molasses mixture to recombine and pour into the center of the skillet. When the molasses mixture bubbles, add the rice and cook, stirring and folding constantly, until the shrimp is cooked, the rice is heated through, and the mixture is evenly coated, about 3 minutes. Stir in the scallions, remove from the heat, and transfer to a serving platter. Garnish with the egg segments, fried shallots, and lime wedges; serve immediately.

### Faux Leftover Rice

**MAKES** 6 cups

To rinse the rice, place it in a fine-mesh strainer and rinse under cool water until the water runs clear.

- 2 tablespoons vegetable oil
- 2 cups jasmine or long-grain white rice, rinsed
- 2⅔ cups water

Heat the oil in a large saucepan over medium heat until shimmering. Add the rice and stir to coat the grains with oil, about 30 seconds. Add the water, increase the heat to high, and bring to a boil. Reduce the heat to low, cover, and simmer until all the liquid is absorbed, about 18 minutes. Off the heat, remove the lid and place a clean dish towel, folded in half, over the saucepan; replace the lid. Let stand until the rice is just tender, about 8 minutes. Spread the cooked rice onto a rimmed baking sheet, set on a wire rack, and cool for 10 minutes. Transfer to the refrigerator and chill for 20 minutes.

## Fried Rice with Shrimp, Pork, and Shiitakes

**SERVES** 4 to 6

**WHY THIS RECIPE WORKS** Fried rice is the perfect solution for leftover rice. We wanted fried rice with firm, separate grains, and we wanted to distinguish the dish's many different flavors in every bite. For fried rice that is light and flavorful rather than sodden and greasy, we found it essential to start with cold, dry rice (like leftover rice). We added a small amount of soy sauce in conjunction with complex oyster-flavored sauce to yield well-seasoned but not soggy rice. Cooking the vegetables and shrimp separately ensured that everything was cooked to perfection—no rubbery shrimp or mushy peas. And frying the rice in just a couple tablespoons of oil kept it from being greasy. Lastly, we finished the dish with tender vegetables including bean sprouts and a sprinkling of scallions. See the Faux Leftover Rice recipe (left) for any easy way to make cool rice for this recipe,

- ½ ounce (5 to 6 medium) dried shiitake mushrooms
- ¼ cup oyster-flavored sauce
- 1 tablespoon soy sauce
- 3 tablespoons plus 1½ teaspoons peanut or vegetable oil
- 2 large eggs, lightly beaten
- 8 ounces small shrimp (51 to 60 per pound), peeled and deveined (see page 523)
- 1 cup frozen peas, thawed
- 8 ounces sliced smoked ham, cut into ½-inch pieces
- 2 medium garlic cloves, minced or pressed through a garlic press (about 2 teaspoons)
- 5 cups cold cooked white rice, large clumps broken up with fingers
- 1 cup bean sprouts
- 5 scallions, sliced thin

**1.** Cover the dried shiitakes with 1 cup hot tap water in a small microwave-safe bowl. Cover the bowl with plastic wrap and microwave on high power for 30 seconds. Let sit until the mushrooms soften, about 5 minutes. Lift the mushrooms from the liquid with a fork. Trim the stems, slice into ¼-inch strips, and set aside.

**2.** Combine the oyster-flavored sauce and soy sauce in a small bowl and set aside.

**3.** Heat 1½ teaspoons of the oil in a 12-inch nonstick skillet over medium heat until shimmering. Add the eggs and cook, without stirring, until they just begin to set, about 20 seconds. Scramble and break into small pieces with a wooden spoon and continue to cook, stirring constantly, until the eggs are cooked through but not browned, about 1 minute longer. Transfer the eggs to a small bowl and set aside.

**4.** Add 1½ teaspoons more oil to the skillet and heat over medium heat until shimmering. Add the shrimp and cook, stirring constantly, until opaque and just cooked through, about 30 seconds. Transfer the shrimp to the bowl with the eggs and set aside.

**5.** Add the remaining 2½ tablespoons oil to the skillet and heat over medium heat until shimmering. Add the mushrooms, peas, and ham and cook, stirring constantly, for 1 minute. Stir in the garlic and cook until fragrant, about 30 seconds. Add the rice and oyster-flavored sauce mixture and cook, stirring constantly and breaking up any rice clumps, until the mixture is heated through, about 3 minutes. Stir in the eggs, shrimp, bean sprouts, and scallions and cook until heated through, about 1 minute. Serve.

## Bánh Xèo (Sizzling Vietnamese Crepes)

**SERVES** 4

**WHY THIS RECIPE WORKS** Vietnamese bánh xèo are crispy rice flour and coconut milk crepes studded with pork and shrimp that are cut into pieces, tucked inside lettuce leaves with fresh Thai basil and cilantro, and then dipped in a bold and zesty nước chấm sauce. It's a spectacular jumble of flavors, colors, textures, fragrances and temperatures. Although they are made like French crepes, this dish is one of a kind and so incredibly good we think everyone should know how to make it. Our crepe batter contains hot water, white rice flour, cornstarch, turmeric, and coconut milk. Using hot water helped minimize the gritty texture that rice flour can have, and cornstarch absorbed extra moisture so that the crepe could crisp properly. To preserve the texture of the first few crepes while making the last one, we held them on a rack in a 275-degree oven. Stir the coconut milk thoroughly to combine before measuring. Although we prefer the flavor of regular coconut milk, light coconut milk can be substituted. Use plain white rice flour (ground from long-or medium-grain rice), not glutinous rice flour (ground from glutinous, aka "sweet" rice) for this recipe. If you can't find Thai basil leaves, substitute regular basil. Serve with Do Chua (Daikon-Carrot Pickle), if desired.

NƯỚC CHẤM

- 3 tablespoons sugar, divided
- 1 small Thai chile, stemmed and minced
- 1 garlic clove, minced
- ⅔ cup hot water
- 5 tablespoons fish sauce
- ¼ cup lime juice (2 limes)

CREPES

- 1 head Boston lettuce (8 ounces), leaves separated and left whole
- 1 cup fresh Thai basil leaves
- 1 cup fresh cilantro leaves and thin stems
- 1 cup hot water (120 to 130 degrees)
- ½ cup (3 ounces) white rice flour
- 3 tablespoons cornstarch
- ½ teaspoon ground turmeric
- ½ teaspoon table salt, divided
- 3 tablespoons vegetable oil, divided
- 4 ounces boneless country-style pork ribs, trimmed and cut into 2-inch-long matchsticks
- 1 small red onion, halved and sliced thin
- 6 ounces medium-large shrimp (31 to 40 per pound), peeled, deveined, halved lengthwise, and halved crosswise
- ⅓ cup canned coconut milk
- 6 ounces (3 cups) bean sprouts, divided

**1. FOR THE NƯỚC CHẤM:** Using mortar and pestle (or using flat side of chef's knife on cutting board), mash 1 tablespoon sugar, Thai chile, and garlic to fine paste. Transfer to medium bowl and add hot water and remaining 2 tablespoons sugar. Stir until sugar is dissolved. Stir in fish sauce and lime juice. Divide sauce among 4 individual small serving bowls.

**2. FOR THE CREPES:** Adjust oven rack to middle position and heat oven to 275 degrees. Set wire rack in rimmed baking sheet, spray rack with vegetable oil spray, and set aside. Arrange lettuce, basil, and cilantro on serving platter. Whisk hot water, rice flour, cornstarch, turmeric, and ¼ teaspoon salt in bowl until smooth.

**3.** Heat 1 teaspoon oil in 12-inch nonstick skillet over medium-high heat until shimmering. Add pork and onion and cook, stirring occasionally, until pork is no longer pink and onion is softened, 5 to 7 minutes. Add shrimp and remaining ¼ teaspoon salt and continue to cook, stirring occasionally, until shrimp just begin to turn pink, about 2 minutes longer. Transfer mixture to second bowl. Wipe skillet clean with paper towels. Add coconut milk and 2 teaspoons oil to crepe batter and stir to combine.

**4.** Heat 2 teaspoons oil in now-empty skillet over medium-high heat until just smoking. Add one-third of pork mixture and heat through until sizzling, about 30 seconds. Spread pork mixture over half of skillet. Pour ½ cup batter evenly over entire skillet. (Batter poured over filling will drain to skillet surface. If needed, tilt skillet gently to fill gaps.) Spread 1 cup bean sprouts over filling. Cook until crepe loosens completely from bottom of skillet with gentle shake, 4 to 5 minutes. Reduce heat to medium-low and continue to cook, shaking skillet occasionally, until edges of crepe are lacy and crisp and underside is golden brown, 2 to 4 minutes longer.

**5.** Gently fold unfilled side of crepe over sprouts. Slide crepe onto prepared wire rack and transfer to oven to keep warm. Repeat 2 more times with remaining oil, pork mixture, batter, and bean sprouts. When final crepe is cooked, use 2 spatulas to transfer all 3 crepes to cutting board and cut each crosswise into 1¼-inch-wide strips.

**6. TO SERVE:** Place crepes and greens in center of table, and give each diner 1 bowl of sauce. To eat, wrap individual strip of crepe and several leaves of basil and cilantro in lettuce leaf and dip into sauce.

## Do Chua (Daikon-Carrot Pickle)

SERVES 6

Do chua is a Vietnamese quick pickled carrot and daikon condiment that is served as an accompaniment to bánh xèo crepes, summer rolls, or bún cha. To crisp the shredded carrots and daikon, we let them sit with a small amount of salt and sugar and then rinsed and drained them. Then we added them to a tangy-sweet mixture of white vinegar, salt, and sugar. This pickle is quite pungent. Cover it tightly before storing it in the refrigerator. The aroma will dissipate soon after the pickle is uncovered.

- 12 ounces daikon radish, peeled and shredded (about 3 cups)
- 3 carrots, peeled and shredded (about 2 cups)
- 1 teaspoon plus ⅓ cup sugar, divided
- 1¼ teaspoons table salt, divided
- ¾ cup distilled white vinegar
- ½ cup water

**1.** Combine daikon, carrots, 1 teaspoon sugar, and ½ teaspoon salt in large bowl and let sit until vegetables are partially wilted and reduced in volume by half, about 30 minutes. Meanwhile, in second bowl, whisk vinegar, water, remaining ⅓ cup sugar, and remaining ¾ teaspoon salt until sugar and salt are dissolved.

**2.** Transfer daikon mixture to colander and drain, pressing on solids to remove excess moisture. Add daikon mixture to vinegar mixture and toss to combine. Let sit for 30 minutes at room temperature, then serve. (Pickle can be refrigerated for up to 1 week.)

### MAKING BÁNH XÈO

**1.** After stir-frying the pork, onion, and shrimp, make each crepe. Heat oiled skillet over medium-high heat and spread one-third of pork mixture over half of skillet.

**2.** Pour ½ cup batter evenly over entire skillet. Spread 1 cup bean sprouts over filling.

**3.** Cook until crepe loosens from skillet bottom with gentle shake, 4 to 5 minutes.

**4.** Reduce heat to medium-low; cook until underside is brown and edges are lacy and crisp, 2 to 4 minutes. Gently fold unfilled crepe in half. Cook until crepe loosens completely from bottom of skillet. Transfer to oven to keep warm; repeat 2 more times.

## Best Crab Cakes

**SERVES 4**

**WHY THIS RECIPE WORKS** We wanted to come up with a recipe for crab cakes that were chock-full of sweet, plump meat delicately seasoned and seamlessly held together with a binder that didn't mask the seafood flavor. And we didn't want shopping to be an issue—we wanted our crab cakes to work with either fresh crabmeat or the pasteurized variety found at the supermarket. To highlight and enhance the crabmeat's sweetness, we bound our cakes with a delicate shrimp mousse. Classic components like Old Bay seasoning and lemon juice bolstered the crab's flavor, and panko bread crumbs helped ensure a crisp crust. Either fresh or pasteurized crabmeat can be used in this recipe. With packaged crab, if the meat smells clean and fresh when you first open the package, skip steps 1 and 4 and simply blot away any excess liquid. Serve the crab cakes with lemon wedges.

- 1 pound lump crabmeat, picked over for shells
- 1 cup milk
- 1½ cups panko bread crumbs, divided
- ¾ teaspoon table salt, divided
- 2 celery ribs, chopped
- ½ cup chopped onion
- 1 garlic clove, peeled and smashed
- 1 tablespoon unsalted butter
- ⅛ teaspoon pepper
- 4 ounces shrimp, peeled, deveined, and tails removed (see page 523)
- ¼ cup heavy cream
- 2 teaspoons Dijon mustard
- 1 teaspoon lemon juice
- ½ teaspoon hot sauce
- ½ teaspoon Old Bay seasoning
- ¼ cup vegetable oil

**1.** Place crabmeat and milk in bowl, making sure crab is totally submerged. Cover and refrigerate for 20 minutes.

**2.** Meanwhile, place ¾ cup panko in small zipper-lock bag and finely crush with rolling pin. Transfer crushed panko to 10-inch nonstick skillet and add remaining ¾ cup panko. Toast over medium-high heat, stirring constantly, until golden brown, about 5 minutes. Transfer panko to shallow dish and stir in ¼ teaspoon salt and pepper to taste. Wipe out skillet.

**3.** Pulse celery, onion, and garlic in food processor until finely chopped, 5 to 8 pulses, scraping down bowl as needed. Transfer vegetables to large bowl. Rinse processor bowl and blade. Melt butter in now-empty skillet over medium heat. Add chopped vegetables, pepper, and remaining ½ teaspoon salt; cook, stirring frequently, until vegetables are softened and all moisture has evaporated, 4 to 6 minutes. Return vegetables to large bowl and let cool to room temperature. Rinse out pan and wipe clean.

**4.** Drain crabmeat in fine-mesh strainer, pressing firmly to remove milk but being careful not to break up lumps of crabmeat.

**5.** Pulse shrimp in now-empty food processor until finely ground, 12 to 15 pulses, scraping down bowl as needed. Add cream and pulse to combine, 2 to 4 pulses, scraping down bowl as needed. Transfer shrimp puree to bowl with cooled vegetables. Add mustard, lemon juice, hot sauce, and Old Bay; stir until well combined. Add crabmeat and fold gently with rubber spatula, being careful not to overmix, and break up lumps of crabmeat. Divide mixture into 8 balls and firmly press into ½-inch-thick patties. Place cakes in rimmed baking sheet lined with parchment paper, cover tightly with plastic wrap, and refrigerate for 30 minutes.

**6.** Coat each cake with panko, firmly pressing to adhere crumbs to exterior. Heat 1 tablespoon oil in now-empty skillet over medium heat until shimmering. Place 4 cakes in skillet and cook without moving them until golden brown, 3 to 4 minutes. Using 2 spatulas, carefully flip cakes. Add 1 tablespoon oil, reduce heat to medium-low, and continue to cook until second side is golden brown, 4 to 6 minutes. Transfer cakes to platter. Wipe out skillet and repeat with remaining 4 cakes and remaining 2 tablespoons oil. Serve immediately.

## Maryland Crab Cakes—Pan-Fried Crab Cakes with Old Bay Seasoning

**SERVES 4**

**WHY THIS RECIPE WORKS** Making crab cakes at home is the only way to avoid the pricey crab-flecked dough balls that pass for crab cakes in many restaurants. We wanted traditional Maryland-style crab cakes with a crisp brown exterior and well-seasoned filling that tasted of sweet crab, not filler. Fresh crabmeat provided superior taste and texture, and jumbo lump crabmeat was worth the high price tag. After experimenting with different binders, we settled on fine dry bread crumbs; their flavor is mild, they held the cakes together well, and they mixed easily with the crab. We used just a few tablespoons of crumbs so that the crab's flavor and texture would shine. An egg and some mayonnaise bound the cakes together. Old Bay is the traditional seasoning for crab; some herbs and white pepper were the only additions we found necessary. Carefully folding the ingredients together rather than stirring them kept the texture chunky, and a short chill in the refrigerator ensured that the cakes wouldn't fall apart. Pan-frying in vegetable oil gave our crab cakes the crisp exterior we wanted. The amount of bread crumbs you add will depend on the crabmeat's juiciness. Start with the smallest amount, adjust the seasonings, then add the egg. If the cakes won't bind at this point, add more bread crumbs, 1 tablespoon at a time. If you can't find fresh jumbo lump crabmeat, pasteurized crabmeat, though not as good, is a decent substitute. At all costs, avoid the canned crabmeat sold near canned tuna. Either a nonstick or a traditional skillet will work for this recipe, but a nonstick simplifies cleanup.

- 1 pound fresh jumbo lump crabmeat, carefully picked over to remove cartilage and shell fragments
- 4 scallions, green parts only, minced (about ½ cup)
- 1 tablespoon chopped fresh herb, such as cilantro, dill, basil, or parsley
- 1½ teaspoons Old Bay seasoning
- 2-4 tablespoons plain dry bread crumbs
- ¼ cup mayonnaise
- Table salt and ground white pepper
- 1 large egg
- ¼ cup unbleached all-purpose flour
- ¼ cup vegetable oil
- Sweet and Tangy Tartar Sauce (page 519), Creamy Chipotle Chile Sauce, or lemon wedges

**1.** Gently mix the crabmeat, scallions, herb, Old Bay, 2 tablespoons of the bread crumbs, and the mayonnaise in a medium bowl, being careful not to break up the lumps of crab. Season with salt and white pepper to taste. Carefully fold in the egg with a rubber spatula until the mixture just clings together. Add more bread crumbs if necessary.

**2.** Divide the crab mixture into four portions and shape each into a fat, round cake, about 3 inches across and 1½ inches high. Arrange the cakes on a baking sheet lined with waxed or parchment paper; cover with plastic wrap and chill for at least 30 minutes. (The crab cakes can be refrigerated for up to 24 hours.)

**3.** Place the flour in a pie plate. Lightly dredge the crab cakes in the flour. Heat the oil in a large skillet over medium-high heat until hot but not smoking. Gently place the chilled crab cakes in the skillet; pan-fry until the outsides are crisp and browned, 4 to 5 minutes per side. Serve immediately with Creamy Chipotle-Chile Sauce, Sweet and Tangy Tartar Sauce (page 519), or a classic Cocktail Sauce (page 23).

## Creamy Chipotle-Chile Sauce

**MAKES** about ½ cup

The addition of sour cream makes this sauce richer than traditional tartar sauce. The chipotles add smoky and spicy flavors.

- ¼ cup mayonnaise
- ¼ cup sour cream
- 2 teaspoons canned minced chipotle chiles in adobo sauce
- 1 small garlic clove, minced or pressed through a garlic press (about ½ teaspoon)
- 2 teaspoons minced fresh cilantro leaves
- 1 teaspoon juice from 1 lime

Mix all of the ingredients in a small bowl. Cover and refrigerate until the flavors blend, about 30 minutes. (The sauce can be refrigerated for up to 2 days.)

### SEGMENTING ORANGES

**1.** Start by slicing a ½-inch piece from the top and bottom of the orange. With the fruit resting flat against a work surface, use a very sharp paring knife to slice off the rind, including the white pith.

**2.** Slip the knife blade between a membrane and one section of the fruit and slice to the center. Turn the blade so that it is facing out and slide the blade from the center out along the membrane to completely free the section.

## Crab Towers with Avocado and Gazpacho Salsas

**SERVES** 6

**WHY THIS RECIPE WORKS** Sometimes a dish served in a restaurant is so delicious and impressive-looking that we just have to try to make it ourselves. A crab salad molded into towers, from the Mayflower Park Hotel in Seattle, is one such dish, but a hotel restaurant can easily handle the recipe's 35 ingredients. Was there a way to re-create the flavors and presentation at home, with fewer ingredients and a lot less effort? By breaking down the recipe for this appetizer into its components—crab salad, avocado–hearts of palm salsa, and gazpacho salsa—we were able to address each one separately. For the crab salad, we used lump crabmeat mixed with a little mayonnaise and champagne vinaigrette. We eliminated the hearts of palm from the salsa; the avocado alone worked quite well. For the gazpacho salsa, we used only one kind of bell pepper rather than two and omitted the diced lime and orange segments that were in the original recipe; we also cut back on the seasonings, limiting ourselves to sherry vinegar and olive oil. To assemble the dish the restaurant uses timbale rings, but we found our workaday biscuit cutter did the job just fine. You can prepare the crabmeat salad and gazpacho salsa several hours ahead of serving, but the avocado salsa should be prepared just before assembly.

**CRABMEAT SALAD**

- 3 tablespoons extra-virgin olive oil
- 1 tablespoon champagne vinegar
- 1 teaspoon minced or grated lemon zest
- ½ teaspoon Dijon mustard
- ½ teaspoon table salt
- ⅛ teaspoon ground black pepper
- 2 tablespoons mayonnaise
- 12 ounces lump or backfin Atlantic blue crabmeat, carefully picked over to remove cartilage and shell fragments

**GAZPACHO SALSA**

- 1 small yellow bell pepper, cored, seeded, and cut into ⅛-inch pieces (about ½ cup)
- ½ small cucumber, peeled if desired, seeded, and cut into ⅛-inch pieces (about ½ cup)
- 1 medium plum tomato, cored, seeded, and cut into ⅛-inch pieces (about ½ cup)
- 1 small celery rib, cut into ⅛-inch pieces (about ½ cup)
- ½ small red onion, minced (about ¼ cup)
- ½ small jalapeño chile, stemmed, seeded, and minced
- 1 tablespoon minced fresh cilantro leaves
- 2 tablespoons extra-virgin olive oil
- 1 tablespoon sherry vinegar
- ¾ teaspoon table salt
- ¼ teaspoon ground black pepper

**AVOCADO SALSA**

- 3 ripe avocados, pitted, peed, and cut into ¼-inch dice
- 2 tablespoons juice from 1 lime
- ¼ teaspoon ground coriander
- ½ teaspoon table salt
- ⅛ teaspoon ground black pepper

**GARNISH**

- 1 cup frisée
- 2 oranges, peeled using a paring knife and segmented (optional)

**1. FOR THE CRABMEAT SALAD:** Whisk the olive oil, champagne vinegar, lemon zest, mustard, salt, and pepper together in a small bowl. Measure 3 tablespoons of the vinaigrette into a medium bowl and mix with the mayonnaise. Add the crabmeat to the mayonnaise mixture and toss to coat. Cover with plastic wrap and refrigerate until needed. Set the remaining vinaigrette aside.

**2. FOR THE GAZPACHO SALSA:** Toss the bell pepper, cucumber, tomato, celery, red onion, jalapeño, cilantro, olive oil, sherry vinegar, salt, and pepper in a medium bowl and set aside.

**3. FOR THE AVOCADO SALSA:** Toss the avocados, lime juice, coriander, salt, and pepper in a medium bowl and set aside.

**4. TO ASSEMBLE:** Place a 3-inch-wide round biscuit cutter in the center of an individual plate. Press ⅓ cup of the Avocado Salsa into the bottom of the cutter using the back of a soup spoon. Lift the cutter off the plate slightly to reveal some but not all of the avocado. Holding the cutter aloft, press ⅓ cup of the Crabmeat Salad evenly into the cutter on top of the avocado. Lift the cutter further to reveal some but not all of the crab salad. Holding the cutter aloft, use a soup spoon to press ⅓ cup of the Gazpacho Salsa evenly into the cutter on top of the crab. Gently lift the cutter up and away from the plate to reveal the crab tower. Repeat the procedure five more times with the remaining ingredients.

**5.** Dress the frisée with the remaining champagne vinaigrette. Place a few sprigs of the dressed frisée on top of each crab tower and arrange the orange segments (if using) around the towers. Serve immediately.

### ASSEMBLING CRAB TOWERS

**1.** Place the biscuit cutter in the center of the plate and, using the back of a soup spoon, press ⅓ cup of the Avocado Salsa evenly into the cutter. Lift the cutter off the plate slightly to reveal some but not all of the avocado.

**2.** Holding the cutter aloft, press ⅓ cup of the Crabmeat Salad evenly into the cutter, on top of the avocado. Lift the cutter farther off the plate and press ⅓ cup of the Gazpacho Salsa evenly into the cutter, on top of the crab.

**3.** Gently lift the cutter up and away from the plate to reveal the crab tower. Repeat with the remaining salsas and crabmeat salad.

## New England Lobster Roll

SERVES 6

**WHY THIS RECIPE WORKS** We wanted to bring home a true New England–style lobster roll, complete with tender meat coated in a light dressing and tucked into a buttery toasted bun, but first we had to deal with the lobster. To make things easier, we sedated the lobster by placing it in the freezer for 30 minutes. Boiling was the easiest way to cook it, and removing it from the water when the tail registered 175 degrees ensured it was perfectly tender. For the lobster roll, we adhered mostly to tradition, tossing our lobster with just a bit of mayonnaise and adding a hint of crunch with lettuce leaves and a small amount of minced celery. Onion and shallot were overpowering, but minced chives offered bright herb flavor. Lemon juice and a pinch of cayenne provided a nice counterpoint to the rich lobster and mayo. This recipe is best when made with lobster you've cooked yourself. Use a very small pinch of cayenne pepper, as it should not make the dressing spicy. We prefer New England–style top-loading hot dog buns, as they provide maximum surface on the sides for toasting. If using other buns, butter, salt, and toast the interior of each bun instead of the exterior.

- 2 tablespoons mayonnaise
- 2 tablespoons minced celery
- 1½ teaspoons lemon juice
- 1 teaspoon minced fresh chives
- Table salt
- Pinch cayenne pepper
- 1 pound lobster meat, tail meat cut into ½-inch pieces and claw meat cut into 1-inch pieces
- 2 tablespoons unsalted butter, softened
- 6 New England–style hot dog buns
- 6 leaves Boston lettuce

**1.** Whisk mayonnaise, celery, lemon juice, chives, ⅛ teaspoon salt, and cayenne together in large bowl. Add lobster and toss gently to combine.

**2.** Place 12-inch nonstick skillet over low heat. Butter both sides of hot dog buns and sprinkle lightly with salt. Place buns in skillet, with 1 buttered side down; increase heat to medium-low; and cook until crisp and brown, 2 to 3 minutes. Flip and cook second side until crisp and brown, 2 to 3 minutes longer. Transfer buns to large platter. Line each bun with lettuce leaf. Spoon lobster salad into buns and serve immediately.

### Boiled Lobster

SERVES 4; yields 1 pound meat

To cook four lobsters at once, you will need a pot with a capacity of at least 3 gallons. If your pot is smaller, boil the lobsters in batches. Start timing the lobsters from the moment they go into the pot.

- 4 (1¼-pound) live lobsters
- ⅓ cup table salt

**1.** Place lobsters in large bowl and freeze for 30 minutes. Meanwhile, bring 2 gallons water to boil in large pot over high heat.

**2.** Add lobsters and salt to pot, arranging with tongs so that all lobsters are submerged. Cover pot, leaving lid slightly ajar, and adjust heat to maintain gentle boil. Cook for 12 minutes, until thickest part of tail registers 175 degrees (insert thermometer into underside of tail to take temperature). If temperature registers lower than 175 degrees, return lobster to pot for 2 minutes longer, until tail registers 175 degrees, using tongs to transfer lobster in and out of pot.

**3.** Serve immediately or transfer lobsters to rimmed baking sheet and set aside until cool enough to remove meat, about 10 minutes. (Lobster meat can be refrigerated in airtight container for up to 24 hours.)

## Flambéed Pan-Roasted Lobster

**SERVES 2**

**WHY THIS RECIPE WORKS** Boiling and steaming are the usual ways of preparing lobster, and they're just fine. But we wanted an alternative cooking method that would be even tastier, and we didn't want to spend a whole lot more time in the kitchen. Our solution was a restaurant dish adapted for home cooking. The New England restaurant chef Jasper White created a pan-roasted lobster dish that we took as our starting point. We quartered the lobsters and tossed them into a very hot skillet—shells down, so the meat wouldn't overcook—to pan-roast. The heat roasted the shells and permeated the lobster meat with intense flavor. To cook the exposed meat, we put the skillet under the broiler, returning it to the stovetop when the meat was cooked through. Then we flambéed the lobster with bourbon (carefully, of course!). A quick pan sauce, made in the skillet after we removed the lobsters, was the final touch; we used shallots, white wine, herbs, and, for unusual and intense flavor, the lobster tomalley. This way of cooking lobsters is a little more trouble than dunking them in a pot of boiling water, but we think the results are well worth it. If you want to prepare more than two lobsters, we suggest that you engage some help monitoring and juggle two very hot pans. Before flambéing, make sure to roll up long shirtsleeves, tie back long hair, turn off the exhaust fan (so it cannot pull up the flames), and turn off any lit burners. You will need a large ovensafe skillet, oven mitts, a pair of tongs, and long fireplace or grill matches.

- 2 (1½- to 2-pound) live lobsters
- 2 tablespoons peanut or canola oil
- ¼ cup bourbon or cognac
- 6 tablespoons (¾ stick) unsalted butter, cut into 6 pieces
- 2 medium shallots, minced (about 6 tablespoons)
- 3 tablespoons dry white wine
- 1 teaspoon minced fresh tarragon leaves
- 1 tablespoon minced fresh chives
- Table salt and ground black pepper
- Lemon wedges, for serving (optional)

### REMOVING LOBSTER MEAT FROM THE SHELL

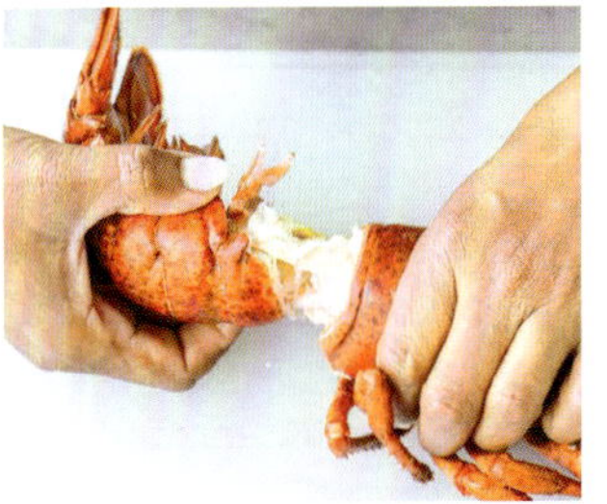

**1.** Once cooked lobster is cool enough to handle, set it on cutting board. Grasp tail with your hand and grab body with your other hand and twist to separate.

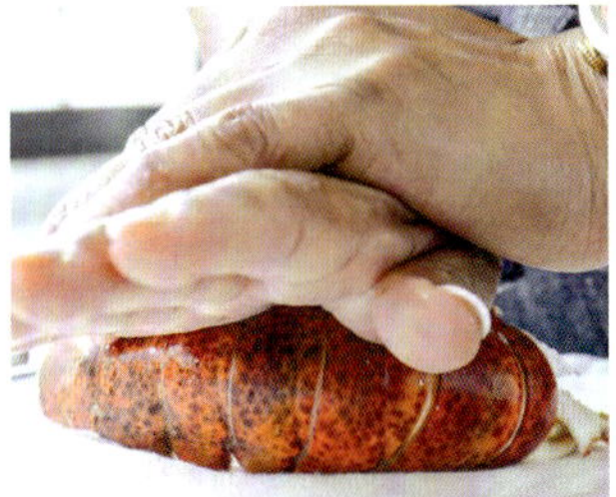

**2.** Lay tail on its side on counter and use both hands to press down on tail until shell cracks.

**3.** Hold tail, flippers facing you and shell facing down. Pull back on sides to crack open shell and remove meat. Rinse meat under water to remove green tomalley if you wish; pat meat dry with paper-towels and remove dark vein.

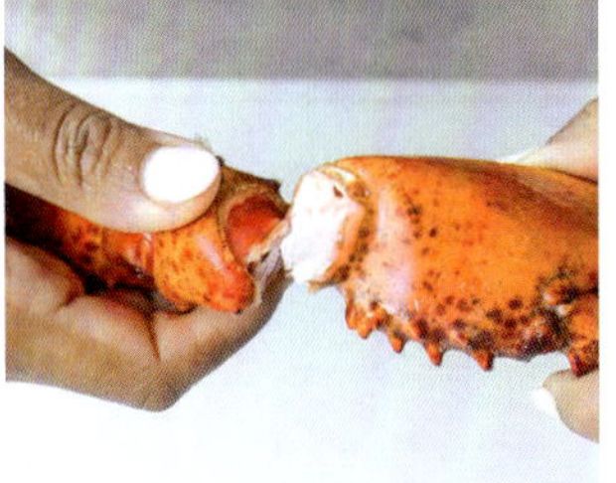

**4.** Twist "arms" to remove both claws and attached "knuckles." Twist knuckle to remove from claw. Break knuckles at joint using back of chef's knife or lobster-cracking tool. Use handle of teaspoon to push out meat.

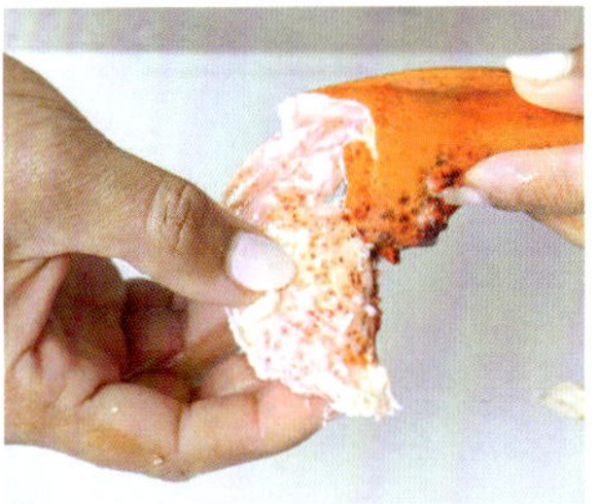

**5.** Wiggle hinged portion of each claw to separate. If meat is stuck inside small part, remove it with skewer. Break open claws, cracking 1 side and then flipping them to crack other side, and remove meat.

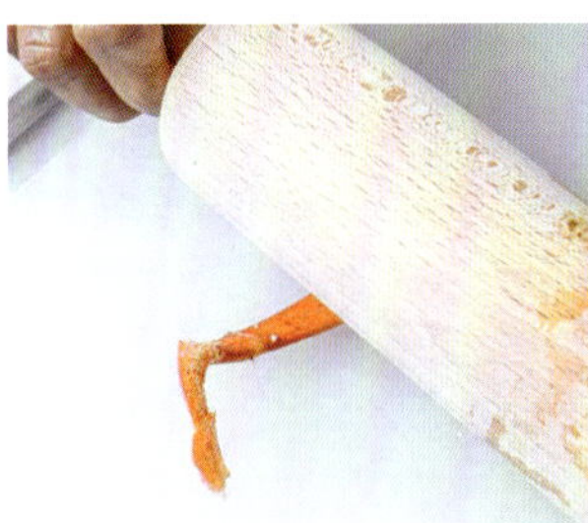

**6.** Twist legs to remove them. Lay legs flat on counter. Using rolling pin, start from claw end and roll toward open end, pushing out meat. Stop rolling before reaching end of leg; otherwise, leg can crack and release pieces of shell.

**1.** Use a large heavy-duty chef's knife to quarter the lobsters. (Don't be put off if the lobsters continue to twitch a little after quartering; it's a reflexive movement.)

**2.** Adjust an oven rack so it is 6 inches from the broiler element and heat the broiler. Heat the peanut oil in a large ovensafe skillet over high heat until smoking. Add the lobster pieces, shell-side down, in a single layer and cook, without disturbing, until the shells are bright red and lightly browned, 2 to 3 minutes. Transfer the skillet to the broiler and cook until the tail meat is just opaque, about 2 minutes.

**3.** Carefully remove the pan from the oven and return it to the stovetop. Off the heat, pour the bourbon over the lobsters. Wait for 10 seconds, then light a long match and wave it over the skillet until the bourbon ignites. Return the pan to medium-high heat and shake it until the flames subside. Transfer the lobster pieces to a warmed serving bowl and tent with foil to keep warm.

**4.** Using tongs, remove any congealed albumin (white substance) from the skillet and add 2 tablespoons of the butter and the shallots. Cook, stirring constantly, until the shallots are softened and lightly browned, 1 to 2 minutes. Add the tomalley (if using) and white wine and stir until completely combined. Remove the skillet from the heat and add the tarragon and chives. Stirring constantly, add the remaining 4 tablespoons butter, 1 piece at a time, until fully emulsified. Season with salt and pepper to taste. Pour the sauce over the lobster pieces. Serve immediately, accompanied by the lemon wedges, if desired.

### PREPARING LOBSTER FOR PAN-ROASTING

**1.** Freeze the lobster for 5 to 10 minutes to sedate it. Plunge a chef's knife into the body at the point where the shell forms a "T" to kill the lobster. Move the blade straight down through the head.

**2.** Turn the lobster around and, while holding the upper body with one hand, cut through the body toward the tail.

**3.** Remove and discard the stomach and intestinal tract. Reserve the green tomalley for the sauce, if desired.

**4.** Cut the tail from the body.

**5.** Twist off the claws from the body. Remove the rubber bands from the claws. (Don't be put off if the lobster continues to twitch a little; it's a reflexive movement.)

## Oven-Steamed Mussels

**SERVES 4**

**WHY THIS RECIPE WORKS** Mussels come in a range of sizes, making it a challenge to cook them evenly. This method guarantees that the mussels cook through at the same rate, even if they are different sizes. First, we moved them from the stovetop to the oven, where the even heat ensured that they cooked through more gently, and we traded the Dutch oven for a large roasting pan so they weren't crowded. Covering the pan with aluminum foil trapped the moisture so the mussels didn't dry out. For a flavorful cooking liquid, we reduced white wine to concentrate its flavor and added thyme, garlic, and red pepper flakes for aromatic complexity. To avoid dirtying another pan, we simply cooked the aromatics and wine on the stovetop in the roasting pan before tossing in our mussels and transferring the pan to the oven. A few pats of butter, stirred in at the end, gave the sauce richness and body. Occasionally, mussels will have a harmless fibrous piece (known as the beard) protruding from between the shells. To remove it, trap the beard between the side of a paring knife and your thumb and pull. The flat surface of the knife gives you leverage to remove the beard. Unopened cooked mussels just need more cooking time. To open them, microwave briefly for 30 seconds or so. Serve mussels with crusty bread to sop up the flavorful broth.

- 1 tablespoon extra-virgin olive oil
- 3 garlic cloves, minced
- Pinch red pepper flakes
- 1 cup dry white wine
- 3 sprigs fresh thyme
- 2 bay leaves
- 4 pounds mussels, scrubbed and debearded
- ¼ teaspoon table salt
- 2 tablespoons unsalted butter, cut into 4 pieces
- 2 tablespoons minced fresh parsley

1. Adjust oven rack to lowest position and heat oven to 500 degrees. Heat oil, garlic, and pepper flakes in large roasting pan over medium heat; cook, stirring constantly, until fragrant, about 30 seconds. Add wine, thyme sprigs, and bay leaves and bring to boil. Cook until wine is slightly reduced, about 1 minute. Add mussels and salt. Cover pan tightly with aluminum foil and transfer to oven. Cook until most mussels have opened (a few may remain closed), 15 to 18 minutes.

2. Remove pan from oven. Push mussels to sides of pan. Add butter to center and whisk until melted. Discard thyme sprigs and bay leaves, sprinkle parsley over mussels, and toss to combine. Serve immediately.

### DEBEARDING MUSSELS

If your mussel has a beard (a harmless fibrous piece protruding from between the shells), hold it and use back of paring knife to remove it with a stern yank.

## Paella

**SERVES 6**

**WHY THIS RECIPE WORKS** We wanted a recipe for a streamlined version of this Spanish classic that still stayed true to the dish's heritage. We started by substituting a Dutch oven for a single-purpose paella pan. Next we pared down our ingredients, dismissing lobster, diced pork, fish, rabbit, and snails. We were left with chorizo, chicken, shrimp, and mussels. We then simplified our sofrito—in this Spanish version, a combination of onions, garlic, and tomatoes—by mincing a can of drained diced tomatoes rather than seeding and grating a fresh tomato. For the rice, we found that we preferred short-grain varieties. Valencia was our favorite, with Italian Arborio a close second. Sautéing the rice in the same pot used to brown the meat and make the sofrito boosted its flavor. For the cooking liquid and seasonings, we chose chicken broth, white wine, saffron, and a bay leaf. Once the rice had absorbed almost all the liquid, we added the mussels, shrimp, and peas to the mix. The result? A colorful, streamlined, yet flavorful rendition of the Spanish classic. Use a Dutch oven that is 11 to 12 inches in diameter with at least a 6-quart capacity. Dry-cured Spanish chorizo is the sausage of choice for paella, but fresh chorizo or linguica is an acceptable substitute. Socarrat, a layer of crusty browned rice that forms on the bottom of the pan, is a traditional part of paella. In our version, socarrat does not develop because most of the cooking is done in the oven. We have provided instructions to develop socarrat in step 5; if you prefer, skip this step and go directly from step 4 to step 6.

- 1 pound extra-large shrimp (21 to 25 per pound), peeled and deveined (page 523)
- 2 tablespoons extra-virgin olive oil, divided, plus extra as needed
- 8 garlic cloves, minced, divided
- 1 teaspoon table salt, divided
- ½ teaspoon pepper, divided
- 1 pound boneless, skinless chicken thighs, trimmed and halved crosswise
- 1 red bell pepper, stemmed, seeded, and cut into ½-inch-wide strips
- 8 ounces Spanish chorizo, sliced ½ inch thick on bias
- 1 onion, chopped fine
- 1 (14.5-ounce) can diced tomatoes, drained, minced, and drained again
- 2 cups Valencia or Arborio rice
- 3 cups chicken broth
- ⅓ cup dry white wine
- ½ teaspoon saffron threads, crumbled
- 1 bay leaf
- 1 dozen mussels, scrubbed and debearded
- ½ cup frozen peas, thawed
- 2 tablespoons chopped fresh parsley
- Lemon wedges

1. Adjust oven rack to lower-middle position and heat oven to 350 degrees. Toss shrimp, 1 tablespoon oil, 1 teaspoon garlic, ¼ teaspoon salt, and ¼ teaspoon pepper in medium bowl; cover with plastic wrap and refrigerate until needed. Season chicken thighs with ¼ teaspoon salt and remaining ¼ teaspoon pepper; set aside.

2. Heat 2 teaspoons oil in large Dutch oven over medium-high heat until shimmering but not smoking. Add pepper strips and cook, stirring occasionally, until skin begins to blister and turn spotty black, 3 to 4 minutes. Transfer pepper to small plate and set aside.

**3.** Add remaining 1 teaspoon oil to now-empty Dutch oven; heat oil until shimmering but not smoking. Add chicken pieces in single layer; cook, without moving pieces, until browned, about 3 minutes. Turn pieces and brown on second side, about 3 minutes longer; transfer chicken to medium bowl. Reduce heat to medium and add chorizo to pot; cook, stirring frequently, until deeply browned and fat begins to render, 4 to 5 minutes. Transfer chorizo to bowl with chicken and set aside.

**4.** Add enough oil to fat in Dutch oven to equal 2 tablespoons; heat over medium heat until shimmering but not smoking. Add onion and cook, stirring frequently, until softened, about 3 minutes; stir in remaining garlic and cook until fragrant, about 1 minute. Stir in tomatoes; cook until mixture begins to darken and thicken slightly, about 3 minutes. Stir in rice and cook until grains are well coated with tomato mixture, 1 to 2 minutes. Stir in chicken broth, wine, saffron, bay leaf, and remaining ½ teaspoon salt. Return chicken and chorizo to pot, increase heat to medium-high, and bring to boil, uncovered, stirring occasionally. Cover pot and transfer it to oven; cook until rice absorbs almost all of liquid, about 15 minutes. Remove pot from oven (close oven door to retain heat). Uncover pot; scatter shrimp over rice, insert mussels, hinged side down, into rice (so they stand upright), arrange bell pepper strips, and scatter peas over top. Cover and return to oven; cook until shrimp are opaque and mussels have opened, 10 to 12 minutes.

**5. OPTIONAL:** If socarrat is desired, set Dutch oven, uncovered, over medium-high heat for about 5 minutes, rotating pot 180 degrees after about 2 minutes for even browning.

**6.** Let paella stand, covered, for about 5 minutes. Discard any mussels that have not opened and bay leaf, if it can be easily removed. Sprinkle with parsley and serve, passing lemon wedges separately.

## Indoor Clambake

**SERVES** 4 to 6

**WHY THIS RECIPE WORKS** A clambake is perhaps the ultimate seafood meal: clams, mussels, and lobster, nestled with sausage, corn, and potatoes, all steamed together with hot stones in a sand pit by the sea. A genuine clambake is an all-day affair and, of course, requires a beach. But we wanted to re-create the great flavors of the clambake indoors, so we could enjoy this flavorful feast anywhere, without hours of preparation. A large stockpot was our cooking vessel of choice. Many recipes suggest cooking the ingredients separately before adding them to the pot, but we found that with careful layering, we could cook everything in the same pot and have it all finish at the same time. And we didn't need to add water, because the shellfish released enough liquid to steam everything else. Sliced sausage went into the pot first (we liked kielbasa), so that it could sear before the steam was generated. Clams and mussels were next, wrapped in cheesecloth for easy removal. Then in went the potatoes, which would take the longest to cook; they were best placed near the heat source, and we cut them into 1-inch pieces to cook more quickly. Corn, with the husks left on to protect it from seafood flavors and lobster foam, was next, followed by the lobsters. It took less than half an hour for everything to cook—and we had all the elements of a clambake (minus the sand and surf) without having spent all day preparing them. Choose a large, narrow stockpot in which you can easily layer the ingredients. The recipe can be cut in half and layered in an 8-quart Dutch oven, but it should cook for the same amount of time. We prefer small littlenecks for this recipe. If your market carries larger clams, use 4 pounds. Mussels sometimes contain a small weedy beard between their shells. To remove it easily, trap the beard between the side of a small paring knife and your thumb and pull to remove it. The flat surface of the knife gives you some leverage to remove the beard.

- 2 pounds small littleneck or cherrystone clams, scrubbed
- 2 pounds mussels, scrubbed and debearded (see page 543)
- 1 pound kielbasa, sliced into ⅓-inch-thick rounds
- 1 pound small new or red potatoes, scrubbed and cut into 1-inch pieces
- 6 medium ears corn, silk and all but last layer of husk removed
- 2 (1½-pound) live lobsters
- 8 tablespoons salted butter, melted

**1.** Place clams and mussels on large piece of cheesecloth and tie ends together to secure; set aside. In heavy-bottomed 12-quart stockpot, layer sliced kielbasa, sack of clams and mussels, potatoes, corn, and lobsters on top of one another. Cover with lid and place over high heat. Cook until potatoes are tender (paring knife can be slipped into and out of center of potato with little resistance), and lobsters are bright red, 17 to 20 minutes.

**2.** Remove pot from heat and remove lid (watch out for scalding steam). Remove lobsters and set aside until cool enough to handle. Remove corn from pot and peel off husks; arrange ears on large platter. Using slotted spoon, remove potatoes and arrange them on platter with corn. Transfer clams and mussels to large bowl and cut open cheesecloth with scissors. Using slotted spoon, remove kielbasa from pot and arrange it on platter with potatoes and corn. Pour remaining steaming liquid in pot over clams and mussels. Twist and remove lobster tails, claws, and legs (if desired). Arrange lobster parts on platter. Serve immediately with melted butter and napkins.

## Fisherman's Pie

**SERVES** 4 to 6

**WHY THIS RECIPE WORKS** We hewed close to tradition when selecting the seafood for our Fisherman's Pie, landing on a trio that offered a variety of flavors and textures: flaky, white-fleshed cod; delicate cold-smoked salmon; and snappy jumbo shrimp. A roux-thickened mixture of heavy cream, clam juice, and white wine produced a light, elegant sauce. We kept the flavorings simple, using just leek, thyme, and parsley so as not to overwhelm the delicate fish. Gently simmering the seafood in the sauce on the stovetop before topping it with fluffy mashed potatoes ensured that the seafood would be perfectly cooked. We use an 8-inch square broiler-safe baking dish for this recipe, but any broiler-safe dish that holds 2 quarts will work here. At the end of step 3, the base for the pie should look quite thick; it will loosen to the perfect consistency as the seafood cooks. We prefer cold-smoked salmon here because it's less likely to overcook, but you can substitute hot-smoked salmon if you prefer it. Making a pattern on the topping not only looks attractive but also provides textural contrast when the pie is broiled.

**TOPPING**

- 2 pounds russet potatoes, peeled and cut into 1-inch chunks
- Table salt for cooking potatoes
- 3 tablespoons unsalted butter, cut into 3 pieces
- ⅓ cup heavy cream
- 1 large egg yolk

**FILLING**

- 12 ounces jumbo shrimp (16 to 20 per pound), peeled, deveined, tails removed, and cut in half crosswise
- ¾ teaspoon table salt, divided
- ⅛ teaspoon baking soda
- 4 tablespoons unsalted butter, divided
- 1 leek, white and light-green parts only, halved lengthwise, sliced thin, and washed thoroughly
- 1 teaspoon minced fresh thyme
- ⅓ cup dry white wine or dry vermouth
- 3 tablespoons all-purpose flour
- 2 (8-ounce) bottles clam juice
- ⅔ cup heavy cream
- ¼ teaspoon pepper
- 1 pound skinless cod fillets, cut into 1-inch chunks
- 4 ounces cold-smoked salmon, cut into ½-inch pieces
- ¼ cup minced fresh parsley

**1. FOR THE TOPPING:** Place potatoes in large saucepan and add water to just cover. Add 1 tablespoon salt and bring to boil over high heat. Reduce heat to maintain simmer and cook until tip of paring knife inserted into potato meets no resistance, 8 to 10 minutes. Drain potatoes and return to saucepan over low heat. Cook, shaking saucepan occasionally, until any surface moisture on potatoes has evaporated, about 1 minute. Off heat, mash potatoes well. Stir in butter until melted. Whisk cream and egg yolk together in bowl; stir into potatoes. Season with salt and pepper to taste. Cover to keep warm and set aside.

**2. FOR THE FILLING:** Set 8-inch square broiler-safe baking dish on rimmed baking sheet. Sprinkle shrimp with ¼ teaspoon salt and baking soda in bowl and toss to combine. Refrigerate until needed.

**3.** Melt 3 tablespoons butter in medium saucepan over medium-low heat. Add leek and thyme and cook, stirring occasionally, until leek is softened, 6 to 7 minutes. Add wine and cook, stirring occasionally, until wine has evaporated, about 5 minutes. Add flour and cook, stirring constantly, for 1 minute. Add clam juice and stir until mixture is smooth. Stir in cream, pepper, and remaining ½ teaspoon salt. Increase heat to medium-high and bring to simmer. Lower heat to maintain simmer and cook, stirring frequently, until mixture resembles thick chowder, 10 to 13 minutes.

**4.** Stir cod, salmon, and shrimp into sauce and return to simmer. Cover and cook, stirring every 2 minutes and adjusting heat if needed to maintain simmer, until shrimp are opaque and just cooked through, 4 to 6 minutes. Off heat, stir in parsley. Transfer filling to prepared dish.

**5.** Adjust oven rack 8 inches from broiler element and heat broiler. Spoon topping over filling, starting at edges and working toward center. Smooth with rubber spatula, making sure to seal around edges of dish so no seafood or sauce is exposed. Using back of spoon or tines of fork, make pattern on topping. Melt remaining 1 tablespoon butter and drizzle over topping. Broil pie, still on sheet, until topping is golden brown and crusty and filling is bubbly, 6 to 7 minutes (watch closely). Let cool for 10 minutes before serving.

### CLEANING LEEKS

Cut root end of leeks and upper portion of dark green leaves. Cut in half horizontally and then cut crosswise into pieces. Rinse in a bowl of water and drain or place in a colander or salad spinner and rinse thoroughly.

CHAPTER 9 # Vegetarian Mains

Photos (from left to right): Grown-Up Grilled Cheese Sandwiches with Cheddar and Shallot; Chana Masala; Vegan Pinto Bean-Beet Burgers; Tomato and Mozzarella Tart; Palak Dal; Mushroom and Leek Galette with Gorgonzola; Red Lentil Kibbeh

## Best Vegetarian Chili

**SERVES** 6 to 8

**WHY THIS RECIPE WORKS** Vegetarian chilis can be little more than a mishmash of beans and vegetables. To create a robust, complex-flavored chili—not just a bean and vegetable stew—we found vegetarian replacements for the different ways in which meat adds depth and savory flavor to chili. Walnuts, soy sauce, dried shiitake mushrooms, and tomatoes added hearty savoriness. Bulgur filled out the chili, giving it a substantial texture. The added oil and nuts lent a richness to the chili, for full, lingering flavor. We prefer to use whole dried chiles, but the chili can be prepared with jarred chili powder. If using chili powder, grind the shiitakes and oregano and add them to the pot with ¼ cup of chili powder in step 4. Pinto, black, red kidney, small red, cannellini, or navy beans can be used in this recipe, either a single variety or a combination of beans. For a spicier chili use both jalapeños. Serve with diced avocado, chopped red onion, lime wedges, sour cream, and shredded Monterey Jack or cheddar cheese.

- 1¼ teaspoons table salt, plus salt for soaking beans
- 1 pound (2½ cups) dried beans, rinsed and picked over
- 2 dried ancho chiles
- 2 dried New Mexico chiles
- ½ ounce dried shiitake mushrooms, chopped coarse
- 4 teaspoons dried oregano
- ½ cup walnuts, toasted
- 1 (28-ounce) can diced tomatoes, drained with juice reserved
- 3 tablespoons tomato paste
- 1–2 jalapeño chiles, stemmed and chopped coarse
- 6 garlic cloves, minced
- 3 tablespoons soy sauce
- ¼ cup vegetable oil
- 2 pounds onions, chopped fine
- 1 tablespoon ground cumin
- ⅔ cup medium-grain bulgur
- ¼ cup chopped fresh cilantro

**1.** Bring 4 quarts water, 3 tablespoons salt, and beans to boil in Dutch oven over high heat. Remove pot from heat, cover, and let stand for 1 hour. Drain beans and rinse well.

**2.** Adjust oven rack to middle position and heat oven to 300 degrees. Arrange ancho and New Mexico chiles on rimmed baking sheet and toast until fragrant and puffed, about 8 minutes. Transfer to plate and let cool, about 5 minutes. Stem and seed toasted chiles. Working in batches, grind toasted chiles, shiitakes, and oregano in spice grinder or with mortar and pestle until finely ground.

**3.** Process walnuts in food processor until finely ground, about 30 seconds. Transfer to bowl. Process drained tomatoes, tomato paste, jalapeño(s), garlic, and soy sauce in food processor until tomatoes are finely chopped, about 45 seconds, scraping down bowl as needed.

**4.** Heat oil in Dutch oven over medium-high heat until shimmering. Add onions and salt; cook, stirring occasionally until onions begin to brown, 8 to 10 minutes. Lower heat to medium, add ground chile mixture and cumin, and cook, stirring constantly, until fragrant, about 1 minute. Add rinsed beans and 7 cups water and bring to boil. Cover pot, transfer to oven, and cook for 45 minutes.

**5.** Remove pot from oven. Stir in bulgur, ground walnuts, tomato mixture, and reserved tomato juice. Return to oven and cook until beans are fully tender, about 2 hours.

**6.** Remove pot from oven, stir chili well, and let stand, uncovered, for 20 minutes. Stir in cilantro and serve. (Chili can be made up to 3 days in advance.)

## Mushroom Bourguignon

**SERVES** 6 to 8

**WHY THIS RECIPE WORKS** Mushrooms are inherently savory; have the ability to build fond; and offer a balance of tenderness and resilience that allows them to turn supple when simmered without losing structural integrity. For all those reasons, they're great for featuring in a luxurious, wintery braise such as bourguignon. We started with chunks of meaty, satisfying portobellos, while dried porcini offered a heavy-hitting boost of umami. We added plenty of savory supports such as miso, tomato paste, and soy sauce and classic aromatics and herbs such as carrot, shallot, garlic, and thyme. For body and gloss, we made a modified roux with olive oil and flour. Use a good-quality light- to medium-body red wine, such as a Pinot Noir or Grenache. You can substitute dried shiitake mushrooms for the porcini and yellow or red miso for white. Leave the mushroom gills intact; they enhance the stew's color and flavor. Serve the bourguignon over polenta, noodles, or mashed potatoes.

- 4¾ cups water, divided
- ¼ cup extra-virgin olive oil, divided
- 2½ pounds portobello mushroom caps, cut into 1-inch pieces
- ½ teaspoon table salt
- ¼ teaspoon pepper
- 2 carrots, peeled and sliced ¼ inch thick
- 1 large shallot, chopped
- 4 garlic cloves, smashed and peeled
- 3 tablespoons all-purpose flour
- 1 cup plus 2 tablespoons dry red wine, divided
- 2 tablespoons white miso
- 2 tablespoons soy sauce
- 1 tablespoon tomato paste
- 6 sprigs fresh thyme
- 2 bay leaves
- 1 ounce dried porcini mushrooms, rinsed
- 1 cup frozen pearl onions, thawed
- ¼ cup minced fresh parsley

**1.** Bring ¼ cup water and 2 tablespoons oil to simmer in Dutch oven over medium-high heat. Add portobello mushrooms, salt, and pepper. Cover and cook, stirring occasionally, until mushrooms have released their moisture, about 10 minutes.

2. Uncover and continue to cook, stirring occasionally, until pot is dry and dark fond forms, 10 to 12 minutes longer. Transfer mushrooms to bowl. Add carrots, shallot, and remaining 2 tablespoons oil to pot and cook, stirring frequently, until vegetables start to brown, 3 to 4 minutes. Add garlic and cook for 1 minute. Stir in flour and cook for 30 seconds. Whisk in 1 cup wine.

3. Add miso, soy sauce, tomato paste, and remaining 4½ cups water and whisk to combine. Add thyme sprigs, bay leaves, and porcini mushrooms and bring to boil over high heat. Reduce heat to maintain vigorous simmer and cook, stirring occasionally and scraping bottom of pot to loosen any browned bits, until sauce is reduced and has consistency of heavy cream, about 25 minutes.

4. Strain sauce through fine-mesh strainer set over large bowl, pressing on solids to extract as much liquid as possible; discard solids. You should have 2 cups sauce. (If you have more, return sauce to pot and continue to cook over medium heat until reduced. If you have less, add enough water to yield 2 cups.) Return sauce to pot. Stir in onions, portobello mushrooms, and remaining 2 tablespoons wine. Cover and cook over low heat, stirring occasionally, until onions are tender, about 20 minutes. Stir in parsley. Season with salt and pepper to taste, and serve.

## Chana Masala

**SERVES** 4 to 6

**WHY THIS RECIPE WORKS** Chana masala is arguably one of North India's most popular vegetarian dishes, and it can be quick and easy to prepare. We started by using the food processor to grind the aromatic paste that formed the base of our dish. We opted for canned chickpeas because their flavor and texture were nearly indistinguishable from those of chickpeas that were cooked from dried, and we didn't drain them because the canning liquid added body and savory depth to the dish. The canned chickpeas still retained a bit of snap, so we simmered them in the sauce until they turned soft. Adding stronger foundational spices such as cumin, turmeric, and fennel seeds at the beginning of cooking ensured that they permeated the dish, and reserving the sweet, delicate garam masala until near the end preserved its aroma. A generous garnish of chopped onion, sliced chile, and cilantro added so much vibrancy, texture, and freshness that you'd never guess that most of the ingredients in the recipe were from the pantry. Because the sodium contents of canned chickpeas and tomatoes vary, we include only a small amount of salt in this recipe; season with additional salt at the end of cooking if needed. If you prefer a spicier dish, leave the seeds in the serrano chiles. If you can't find Kashmiri chile powder, substitute 1 teaspoon paprika. This dish is often paired with bhature, deep-fried breads that puff up as they cook; alternatively, serve it with rice or naan.

- 1 small red onion, quartered, divided
- 10 sprigs fresh cilantro, stems and leaves separated
- 1 (1½-inch) piece ginger, peeled and chopped coarse
- 2 garlic cloves, chopped coarse
- 2 serrano chiles, stemmed, halved, seeded, and sliced thin crosswise, divided
- 3 tablespoons vegetable oil
- 1 (14.5-ounce) can whole peeled tomatoes
- 1 teaspoon Kashmiri chile powder
- 1 teaspoon ground cumin
- ½ teaspoon ground turmeric
- ½ teaspoon fennel seeds
- 2 (15-ounce) cans chickpeas, undrained
- 1½ teaspoons garam masala
- ½ teaspoon table salt
- Lime wedges

1. Chop three quarters of onion coarse; reserve remaining quarter for garnish. Cut cilantro stems into 1-inch lengths. Process chopped onion, cilantro stems, ginger, garlic, and half of serranos in food processor until finely chopped, scraping down sides of bowl as necessary, about 20 seconds. Combine onion mixture and oil in large saucepan. Cook over medium-high heat, stirring frequently, until onion is fully softened and beginning to stick to saucepan, 5 to 7 minutes.

2. While onion mixture cooks, process tomatoes and their juice in now-empty food processor until smooth, about 30 seconds. Add chile powder, cumin, turmeric, and fennel seeds to onion mixture and cook, stirring constantly, until fragrant, about 1 minute. Stir in chickpeas and their liquid and processed tomatoes and bring to boil. Adjust heat to maintain simmer, then cover and simmer for 15 minutes. While mixture cooks, chop reserved onion quarter fine.

3. Stir garam masala and salt into chickpea mixture and continue to cook, uncovered and stirring occasionally, until chickpeas are softened and sauce is thickened, 8 to 12 minutes longer. Season with salt to taste. Transfer to wide, shallow serving bowl. Sprinkle with chopped onion, remaining serranos, and cilantro leaves and serve, passing lime wedges separately.

## Espinacas con Garbanzos (Andalusian Spinach and Chickpeas)

**SERVES** 4

**WHY THIS RECIPE WORKS** Espinacas con garbanzos is a hyper-regional dish—native to Seville with strong Moorish influence—that's substantive and full of flavor. Briefly simmering canned chickpeas in a combination of chicken broth and chickpea canning liquid tenderized them and infused them with savory flavor. A picada (a paste of garlic and bread cooked in plenty of olive oil) thickened and seasoned the sauce. Smoked paprika and Moorish spices such as cumin, cinnamon, and saffron imbued the picada with heady aromas, and tomatoes and vinegar boosted its tang. Thawed frozen chopped spinach was perfect here; already fine and tender, it dispersed beautifully throughout the dish. You can substitute water or chicken broth for the vegetable broth. If using chickpeas that you've cooked from dried, use 3⅓ cups of cooked chickpeas and ⅔ cup of the cooking liquid. Use a fruity, spicy, high-quality olive oil here. Red wine vinegar can be substituted for the sherry vinegar.

- 1 loaf crusty bread, divided
- 2 (15-ounce) cans chickpeas (1 can drained, 1 can undrained)
- 1½ cups vegetable broth
- 6 tablespoons extra-virgin olive oil, divided
- 6 garlic cloves, minced
- 1 tablespoon smoked paprika
- 1 teaspoon ground cumin
- ¼ teaspoon table salt
- ⅛ teaspoon ground cinnamon
- ⅛ teaspoon cayenne pepper
- 1 small pinch saffron
- 2 small plum tomatoes, halved lengthwise, flesh shredded on large holes of box grater and skins discarded
- 4 teaspoons sherry vinegar, plus extra for seasoning
- 10 ounces frozen chopped spinach, thawed and squeezed dry

**1.** Cut 1½-ounce piece from loaf of bread (thickness will vary depending on size of loaf) and tear into 1-inch pieces. Process in food processor until finely ground (you should have ¾ cup crumbs). Combine chickpeas and broth in large saucepan and bring to boil over high heat. Adjust heat to maintain simmer and cook until level of liquid is just below top layer of chickpeas, about 10 minutes.

**2.** While chickpeas cook, heat ¼ cup oil in 10-inch nonstick or carbon-steel skillet over medium heat until just shimmering. Add bread crumbs and cook, stirring frequently, until deep golden brown, 3 to 4 minutes. Add garlic, paprika, cumin, salt, cinnamon, cayenne, and saffron and cook until fragrant, 30 seconds. Stir in tomatoes and vinegar; remove from heat.

**3.** Stir bread mixture and spinach into chickpeas. Continue to simmer, stirring occasionally, until mixture is thick and stew-like, 5 to 10 minutes longer. Off heat, stir in remaining 2 tablespoons oil. Cover and let stand for 5 minutes. Season with salt and extra vinegar to taste. Transfer to serving bowl and serve with remaining bread.

## Mujaddara (Rice and Lentils with Crispy Onions)

**SERVES** 4 to 6

**WHY THIS RECIPE WORKS** Mujaddara is a hearty, warm-spiced rice and lentil pilaf from the Middle East that contains large brown or green lentils and crispy fried onion strings. We wanted a version of this dish in which all of the elements were cooked perfectly. We found that precooking the lentils and soaking the rice in hot water before combining them ensured that both components cooked evenly. For the crispiest possible onions, we removed some moisture by salting and microwaving them before frying. This allowed us to pare down the fussy process of batch-frying in several cups of oil to a single batch. And using some of the oil from the onions to dress our pilaf gave it ultrasavory depth. Large green or brown lentils will work interchangeably in this recipe; do not substitute smaller French lentils. When preparing the Crispy Onions, be sure to reserve 3 tablespoons of the onion cooking oil for cooking the rice and lentils.

**YOGURT SAUCE**

- 1 cup plain whole-milk yogurt
- 2 tablespoons lemon juice
- ½ teaspoon minced garlic
- ½ teaspoon table salt

**RICE AND LENTILS**

- 8½ ounces (1¼ cups) green or brown lentils, picked over and rinsed
- 1 teaspoon table salt, plus salt for cooking lentils
- 1¼ cups basmati rice
- 1 recipe Crispy Onions, plus 3 tablespoons reserved oil (recipe follows)
- 3 garlic cloves, minced
- 1 teaspoon ground coriander
- 1 teaspoon ground cumin

- ½ teaspoon ground cinnamon
- ½ teaspoon ground allspice
- ¼ teaspoon pepper
- ⅛ teaspoon cayenne pepper
- 1 teaspoon sugar
- 3 tablespoons minced fresh cilantro

1. **FOR THE YOGURT SAUCE:** Whisk all ingredients together in bowl. Refrigerate while preparing rice and lentils.

2. **FOR THE RICE AND LENTILS:** Bring lentils, 4 cups water, and 1 teaspoon salt to boil in medium saucepan over high heat. Reduce heat to low and cook until lentils are tender, 15 to 17 minutes. Drain and set aside. While lentils cook, place rice in medium bowl and cover by 2 inches with hot tap water; let stand for 15 minutes.

3. Using your hands, gently swish rice grains to release excess starch. Carefully pour off water, leaving rice in bowl. Add cold tap water to rice and pour off water. Repeat adding and pouring off cold tap water 4 or 5 times, until water runs almost clear. Drain rice in fine-mesh strainer.

4. Heat reserved onion oil, garlic, coriander, cumin, cinnamon, allspice, pepper, and cayenne in Dutch oven over medium heat until fragrant, about 2 minutes. Add rice and cook, stirring occasionally, until edges of rice begin to turn translucent, about 3 minutes. Add 2¼ cups water, sugar, and salt and bring to boil. Stir in lentils, reduce heat to low, cover, and cook until all liquid is absorbed, about 12 minutes.

5. Off heat, remove lid, fold clean dish towel in half, and place over pot; replace lid. Let stand for 10 minutes. Fluff rice and lentils with fork and stir in cilantro and half of crispy onions. Transfer to serving platter, top with remaining crispy onions, and serve, passing yogurt sauce separately.

## Crispy Onions

**MAKES** 1½ cups

It is crucial to thoroughly dry the microwaved onions after rinsing. The best way to accomplish this is to use a salad spinner. Reserve 3 tablespoons of oil when draining the onions to use in Mujaddara. Remaining oil may be stored in an airtight container and refrigerated for up to 4 weeks.

- 2 pounds onions, halved and sliced crosswise into ¼-inch-thick pieces
- 2 teaspoons table salt, for salting onions
- 1½ cups vegetable oil

1. Toss onions and salt together in large bowl. Microwave for 5 minutes. Rinse thoroughly, transfer to paper towel–lined baking sheet, and dry well.

2. Heat onions and oil in Dutch oven over high heat, stirring frequently, until onions are golden brown, 25 to 30 minutes. Drain onions in colander set in large bowl. Transfer onions to paper towel–lined baking sheet to drain. Serve.

# Palak Dal (Spinach Dal with Cumin and Mustard Seeds)

**SERVES** 4 to 6

**WHY THIS RECIPE WORKS** Dal is an Indian staple that is quick, nourishing, and—most important—incredibly flavorful. Quick-cooking red lentils are the centerpiece of our spinach dal. Once they had softened, a vigorous whisk transformed them into a porridge-like stew without requiring us to break out a blender or food processor. Seasoning the lentils with a tadka (whole spices sizzled in ghee with aromatics) right before serving gave the dish loads of complexity and an enticing aroma. For less heat, remove the ribs and seeds of the serrano. Fresh curry leaves add a wonderful aroma to this dal, but if they're unavailable, you can omit them. Monitor the spices and aromatics during frying to prevent scorching. Serve with naan and basmati or another long-grain white rice.

- 4½ cups water
- 1½ cups (10½ ounces) dried red lentils, picked over and rinsed
- 1 tablespoon grated fresh ginger
- ¾ teaspoon ground turmeric
- 6 ounces (6 cups) baby spinach
- 1½ teaspoons table salt
- 3 tablespoons ghee
- 1½ teaspoons brown or yellow mustard seeds
- 1½ teaspoons cumin seeds
- 1 large onion, chopped
- 15 curry leaves, roughly torn (optional)
- 6 garlic cloves, sliced
- 4 whole dried arbol chiles
- 1 serrano chile, halved lengthwise
- 1½ teaspoons lemon juice, plus extra for seasoning
- ⅓ cup chopped fresh cilantro

1. Bring 4½ cups water, lentils, ginger, and turmeric to boil in large saucepan over medium-high heat. Reduce heat to maintain vigorous simmer. Cook, uncovered, stirring occasionally, until lentils are soft and starting to break down, 18 to 20 minutes.

2. Whisk lentils vigorously until coarsely pureed, about 30 seconds. Continue to cook until lentils have consistency of loose polenta or oatmeal, up to 5 minutes longer. Stir in spinach and salt and continue to cook until spinach is fully wilted, 30 to 60 seconds longer. Cover and set aside off heat.

3. Melt ghee in 10-inch skillet over medium-high heat. Add mustard seeds and cumin seeds and cook, stirring constantly, until seeds sizzle and pop, about 30 seconds. Add onion and cook, stirring frequently, until onion is just starting to brown, about 5 minutes. Add curry leaves, if using; garlic; arbols; and serrano and cook, stirring frequently, until onion and garlic are golden brown, 3 to 4 minutes.

4. Add lemon juice to lentils and stir to incorporate. (Dal should have consistency of loose polenta. If too thick, loosen with hot water, adding 1 tablespoon at a time.) Season with salt and extra lemon juice to taste. Transfer dal to serving bowl and spoon onion mixture on top. Sprinkle with cilantro and serve.

## Red Lentil Kibbeh

**SERVES** 4 to 6

**WHY THIS RECIPE WORKS** Kibbeh is a popular Middle Eastern dish made from bulgur, onions, spices, and, typically, ground meat. During Lent, however, this meal is often prepared with lentils. We wanted to develop this flavor-packed mixture into something that could be served either on its own with Bibb lettuce and yogurt or as a showstopping addition to a larger spread. We chose red lentils for their vibrant hue and enhanced both their color and flavor with two red pastes: Tomato paste brought sweetness and an umami quality, and harissa, a smoky, spicy chile paste, added complexity. We gave the bulgur a head start before adding the quick-cooking lentils to the same saucepan. Fresh lemon juice and parsley balanced the deep flavors. This kibbeh would go great on a meze platter alongside baba ghanoush, hummus, nuts, pickled radishes, and/or pita. You can use our homemade harissa or store-bought; note that spiciness can vary greatly by brand. If your harissa is spicy, omit the cayenne.

- 3 tablespoons extra-virgin olive oil, divided
- 1 onion, chopped fine
- 1 red bell pepper, stemmed, seeded, and chopped fine
- 1 teaspoon table salt
- 2 tablespoons harissa
- 2 tablespoons tomato paste
- ½ teaspoon cayenne pepper (optional)
- 1 cup medium-grind bulgur
- 4 cups water
- ¾ cup dried red lentils, picked over and rinsed
- ½ cup chopped fresh parsley
- 2 tablespoons lemon juice
- 1 head Bibb lettuce (8 ounces), leaves separated
- ½ cup plain yogurt
- Lemon wedges

**1.** Heat 1 tablespoon oil in large saucepan over medium heat until shimmering. Add onion, bell pepper, and salt and cook until softened, about 5 minutes. Stir in harissa; tomato paste; and cayenne, if using, and cook, stirring frequently, until fragrant, about 1 minute.

**2.** Stir in bulgur and water and bring to simmer. Reduce heat to low; cover; and simmer gently until bulgur is barely tender, about 8 minutes. Stir in lentils; cover; and continue to cook, stirring occasionally, until lentils and bulgur are tender, 8 to 10 minutes.

**3.** Off heat, lay clean dish towel underneath lid and let mixture sit for 10 minutes. Stir in 1 tablespoon oil, parsley, and lemon juice and stir vigorously until mixture is cohesive. Season with salt and pepper to taste. Transfer to platter and drizzle with remaining 1 tablespoon oil. Spoon kibbeh into lettuce leaves and drizzle with yogurt. Serve with lemon wedges.

### Harissa

**MAKES** ½ cup

This spicy, aromatic chile paste is used both as an ingredient and as a condiment throughout North Africa; use it to enliven vegetables, eggs, lamb, soups, and more. If you can't find Aleppo pepper, substitute ¾ teaspoon of paprika and ¾ teaspoon of finely chopped red pepper flakes.

- 6 tablespoons extra-virgin olive oil
- 6 garlic cloves, minced
- 2 tablespoons paprika
- 1 tablespoon ground coriander
- 1 tablespoon ground dried Aleppo pepper
- 1 teaspoon ground cumin
- ¾ teaspoon caraway seeds
- ½ teaspoon table salt

Combine all ingredients in bowl and microwave until bubbling and very fragrant, about 1 minute, stirring halfway through microwaving; let cool completely. (Harissa can be refrigerated for up to 4 days.)

## Vospov Kofte (Red Lentil Kofte)

**SERVES** 4 to 6

**WHY THIS RECIPE WORKS** Vospov (red lentil) kofte is the vegetarian analog to chi kofte, the canonical Armenian dish of minced raw beef or lamb that's bound with bulgur, seasoned with tomato paste and spices, formed into logs or balls, served with a mixture of chopped herbs, and eaten inside a shroud of pita or lavash. The meatless version is popular during Lent (as well as on many other occasions during the year when Armenians avoid meat) and is typically served at room temperature with herbs and bread. We opted for a 3:1:1 ratio of water to lentils to bulgur, which yielded a mixture that was tender, moist but not pasty, and easy to shape. A combination of olive oil and butter enriched the mixture and added complexity and depth, especially since the butter developed nutty flavor as it thoroughly softened the onions and bloomed the spices. For the herb component, we mixed a modest amount of chopped parsley into the kofte and then turned much more of it into a vibrant chopped herb salad along with mint, scallions, Aleppo pepper, sumac, lemon juice, and olive oil. Fine-grind bulgur (labeled "#1") is ideal here but can be hard to find; if you can't find it, process ¾ cup plus 2 tablespoons of any size bulgur in a blender until at least half is finely ground, about 2 minutes. If sumac is unavailable, increase the lemon juice to 1 tablespoon and the salt to ½ teaspoon in the salad. We like the gentle heat and raisiny sweetness of Aleppo pepper, but if it's unavailable, substitute ¾ teaspoon paprika and ¼ teaspoon cayenne pepper in the kofte and ⅜ teaspoon paprika and ⅛ teaspoon cayenne pepper in the salad. Serve the kofte on their own or with pita or lavash.

KOFTE

- 3 cups water
- 1 cup dried red lentils, picked over and rinsed
- ¼ cup extra-virgin olive oil
- 1¼ teaspoons table salt, divided
- 1 cup fine-grind bulgur
- 4 tablespoons unsalted butter
- 1 onion, chopped fine
- 1 teaspoon ground dried Aleppo pepper
- 1 teaspoon ground cumin
- ¼ teaspoon pepper
- ¼ teaspoon ground allspice
- 2 tablespoons chopped fresh parsley

SALAD

- ¾ cup chopped fresh parsley
- 4 scallions, sliced thin
- ¼ cup chopped fresh mint
- 1 tablespoon extra-virgin olive oil
- 2 teaspoons lemon juice
- 1 teaspoon ground sumac
- ½ teaspoon ground dried Aleppo pepper
- ¼ teaspoon table salt

**1. FOR THE KOFTE:** Bring water, lentils, oil, and 1 teaspoon salt to boil in large saucepan over high heat. Adjust heat to maintain gentle simmer. Cover and cook, stirring occasionally, until lentils are fully broken down, 20 to 25 minutes. Place bulgur in large bowl.

**2.** Pour lentil mixture over bulgur, stir until uniform, and set aside. Wipe out saucepan with paper towel. Melt butter in now-empty saucepan over medium-high heat. Add onion, Aleppo pepper, cumin, pepper, allspice, and remaining ¼ teaspoon salt. Cook, stirring frequently, until onion is softened and just beginning to brown, 8 to 10 minutes. Add parsley and onion mixture to lentil mixture and stir until uniform. Let cool completely, 30 to 45 minutes. Refrigerate until stiffened enough to mold, about 30 minutes.

**3.** Using ¼-cup dry measuring cup sprayed with vegetable oil spray, divide mixture into 16 portions (respray cup if mixture starts to stick). Using your slightly moistened hands, press and roll each portion into 3-inch log. Arrange around perimeter of platter.

**4. FOR THE SALAD:** Toss all ingredients together in bowl.

**5.** Top kofte with salad; serve at room temperature.

## Falafel

**MAKES** 24 falafel

**WHY THIS RECIPES WORKS** The best falafel are moist, tender, packed with vibrant fresh herbs and aromatics, and sturdy enough to form and fry. We started by soaking dried chickpeas overnight to soften them slightly and then ground them into coarse bits along with onion, herbs, garlic, and spices. Though many recipes call for mixing starch (flour, cornstarch, or chickpea flour) into the dough, we found success using a technique associated with Asian bread baking called tang-zhong, a cooked flour paste. This paste added moisture without making the batter too fragile to form and fry. Adding a bit of baking powder to the dough helped to lighten the fritters as they fried. Frying the fritters at 325 degrees allowed the moist interiors to fully cook through just as the exteriors turned brown and crisp. This recipe requires that the chick-peas be soaked for at least 8 hours. Use a Dutch oven that holds 6 quarts or more. An equal amount of chickpea flour can be substituted for the all-purpose flour; if using, increase the amount of water to ½ cup in step 4. Do not substitute canned beans or quick-soaked chickpeas. They will make stodgy falafel. Serve the falafel with the tahini sauce as an appetizer or in pita bread with lettuce, chopped tomatoes, chopped cucumbers, fresh cilantro, and pickled turnips. Serve the first batch of falafel immediately or hold them in a 200-degree oven while the second batch cooks.

FALAFEL

- 8 ounces dried chickpeas, picked over and rinsed
- ¾ cup fresh cilantro leaves and stems
- ¾ cup fresh parsley leaves
- ½ onion, chopped fine (½ cup)
- 2 garlic cloves, minced
- 1½ teaspoons ground coriander
- 1 teaspoon ground cumin
- 1 teaspoon table salt
- ¼ teaspoon cayenne pepper
- ¼ cup all-purpose flour
- 2 teaspoons baking powder
- 2 quarts vegetable oil for frying

TAHINI SAUCE

- ⅓ cup tahini
- ⅓ cup plain Greek yogurt
- ¼ cup lemon juice (2 lemons)
- ¼ cup water

**1. FOR THE FALAFEL:** Place chickpeas in large container and cover with 2 to 3 inches of cold water. Let soak at room temperature for at least 8 hours or up to 24 hours. Drain well.

**2. FOR THE TAHINI SAUCE:** Whisk tahini, yogurt, and lemon juice in medium bowl until smooth. Whisk in water to thin sauce as desired. Season with salt to taste; set aside. (Sauce can be refrigerated for up to 4 days. Let come to room temperature and stir to combine before serving.)

**3.** Process cilantro, parsley, onion, garlic, coriander, cumin, salt, and cayenne in food processor for 5 seconds. Scrape down sides of bowl. Continue to process until mixture resembles pesto, about 5 seconds longer. Add chickpeas and pulse 6 times. Scrape down sides of bowl. Continue to pulse until chickpeas are coarsely chopped and resemble sesame seeds, about 6 pulses more. Transfer mixture to large bowl and set aside.

**4.** Whisk flour and ⅓ cup water in bowl until no lumps remain. Microwave, whisking every 10 seconds, until mixture thickens to stiff, smooth, pudding-like consistency that forms mound when dropped from end of whisk into bowl, 40 to 80 seconds. Stir baking powder into flour paste.

**5.** Add flour paste to ground chickpea mixture and, using rubber spatula, mix until fully incorporated. Divide mixture into 24 pieces and gently roll into golf ball–size spheres, transferring spheres to parchment paper–lined rimmed baking sheet once they are formed. (Formed falafel can be refrigerated for up to 2 hours.)

**6.** Heat oil in large Dutch oven over medium-high heat to 325 degrees. Add half of falafel and fry, stirring occasionally, until deep brown, about 5 minutes. Adjust burner, if necessary, to maintain oil temperature of 325 degrees. Using slotted spoon or wire skimmer, transfer to paper towel–lined baking sheet. Return oil to 325 degrees and repeat with remaining falafel. Serve immediately with tahini sauce.

## Vegetable Bibimbap with Nurungji

**SERVES 6**

**WHY THIS RECIPE WORKS** Bibimbap, an iconic Korean dish with many regional variations, features rice mixed with various toppings. In dolsot bibimbap, the combination of the hot stone bowl called a dolsot and a splash of fragrant sesame oil causes the rice to develop a delicious, crunchy crust called nurungji wherever it touches the dolsot. We wanted to create a bibimbap recipe that could be made without a dolsot but still result in plenty of nurungji. We also wanted to cut down on the sautéing and knife work. First we substituted one cast-iron Dutch oven for a set of stone bowls. To shorten the prep time and simplify the knife work, we made three sautéed vegetable toppings instead of the usual six or more. We also turned the pickles, sauce, and vegetables into make-ahead options. We skipped the traditional step of rinsing the rice before steaming it to save time. A quickly pickled mixture of bean sprouts and cucumbers added crisp brightness. For a quick dinner, prepare the pickles, chile sauce, and vegetables a day ahead (warm the vegetables to room temperature in the microwave before adding them to the rice). You can also substitute store-bought kimchi for the pickles to save time. For a family-style bibimbap experience, bring the pot to the table before stirring the vegetables into the rice in step 9.

**PICKLES**

- 1 cup cider vinegar
- 2 tablespoons sugar
- 1½ teaspoons table salt
- 1 cucumber, peeled, quartered lengthwise, seeded, and sliced thin on bias
- 4 ounces (2 cups) bean sprouts

**CHILE SAUCE**

- ¼ cup gochujang
- 3 tablespoons water
- 2 tablespoons toasted sesame oil
- 1 teaspoon sugar

**RICE**

- 2½ cups short-grain white rice
- 2½ cups water
- ¾ teaspoon table salt

**VEGETABLES**

- ½ cup water
- 3 scallions, minced
- 3 tablespoons soy sauce
- 3 garlic cloves, minced
- 1 tablespoon sugar
- 1 tablespoon vegetable oil, divided
- 3 carrots, peeled and shredded (2 cups)
- 8 ounces shiitake mushrooms, stemmed, caps sliced thin
- 1 (10-ounce) bag curly-leaf spinach, stemmed and chopped coarse

BIBIMBAP

- 2 tablespoons plus 2 teaspoons vegetable oil, divided
- 1 tablespoon toasted sesame oil
- 4 large eggs

1. **FOR THE PICKLES:** Whisk vinegar, sugar, and salt together in medium bowl. Add cucumber and bean sprouts and toss to combine. Gently press on vegetables to submerge. Cover and refrigerate for at least 30 minutes or up to 24 hours.

2. **FOR THE CHILE SAUCE:** Whisk all ingredients together in small bowl. Cover and set aside.

3. **FOR THE RICE:** Bring rice, water, and salt to boil in medium saucepan over high heat. Cover, reduce heat to low, and cook for 7 minutes. Remove rice from heat and let sit, covered, until tender, about 15 minutes.

4. **FOR THE VEGETABLES:** While rice cooks, stir together water, scallions, soy sauce, garlic, and sugar. Heat 1 teaspoon oil in Dutch oven over high heat until shimmering. Add carrots and stir until coated. Add ⅓ cup scallion mixture and cook, stirring frequently, until carrots are slightly softened and moisture has evaporated, 1 to 2 minutes. Using slotted spoon, transfer carrots to small bowl.

5. Heat 1 teaspoon oil in now-empty pot until shimmering. Add mushrooms and stir until coated with oil. Add ⅓ cup scallion mixture and cook, stirring frequently, until mushrooms are tender and moisture has evaporated, 3 to 4 minutes. Using slotted spoon, transfer mushrooms to second small bowl.

6. Heat remaining 1 teaspoon oil in now-empty pot until shimmering. Add spinach and remaining ⅓ cup scallion mixture and stir to coat spinach. Cook, stirring frequently, until spinach is completely wilted but still bright green, 1 to 2 minutes. Using slotted spoon, transfer spinach to third small bowl. Discard any remaining liquid and wipe out pot with paper towel.

7. **FOR THE BIBIMBAP:** Heat 2 tablespoons vegetable oil and sesame oil in now-empty pot over high heat until shimmering. Carefully add cooked rice and gently press into even layer. Cook, without stirring, until rice begins to form crust on bottom of pot, about 2 minutes. Using slotted spoon, transfer carrots, spinach, and mushrooms to pot and arrange in piles that cover surface of rice. Reduce heat to low.

8. While crust forms, heat remaining 2 teaspoons vegetable oil in 10-inch nonstick skillet over low heat for 5 minutes. Crack eggs into small bowl. Pour eggs into skillet; cover and cook (about 2 minutes for runny yolks, 2½ minutes for soft but set yolks, and 3 minutes for firmly set yolks). Slide eggs onto vegetables in pot.

9. Drizzle 2 tablespoons chile sauce over eggs. Without disturbing crust, use wooden spoon to stir rice, vegetables, and eggs until combined. Just before serving, scrape large pieces of crust from bottom of pot and stir into rice. Serve in individual bowls, passing pickles and extra chile sauce separately.

## Paella de Verduras (Cauliflower and Bean Paella)

SERVES 4

**WHY THIS RECIPE WORKS** Rather than using vegetables merely as a flavoring agent, paella de verduras—a common, versatile approach to the beloved rice dish that's prepared throughout Spain—places them front and center. This hearty version features green and butter beans plus chunky cauliflower florets. In lieu of the flavorful fond that lends a meaty backbone to protein-based paellas, we retooled a Spanish sofrito to make a complex and supersavory flavor base: We browned the bell pepper instead of sautéing it, swapped in umami-rich tomato paste for the fresh tomatoes, loaded up on garlic, and omitted the sweet-tasting onion. Mixing in smoked paprika, saffron, and dry sherry added brightness and depth. Letting the paella rest for a few minutes before serving it helped the socarrat firm up enough to release easily from the pan. If neither Calasparra nor bomba rice is available, use Arborio rice. You can use chicken broth instead of vegetable broth. It's worth seeking out butter beans for their large size; do not substitute small white beans. We've included instructions for creating a socarrat—a chewy, well-browned bottom layer of rice—but it's optional.

- 3 tablespoons extra-virgin olive oil, divided
- 8 ounces cauliflower, cut into 2- to 2½-inch florets
- ¾ teaspoon table salt, divided
- 6 ounces green beans, trimmed and cut into 2- to 2½-inch pieces
- 1 red bell pepper, stemmed, seeded, and chopped fine
- 1 tablespoon tomato paste
- 3 garlic cloves, minced
- 1 teaspoon smoked paprika
- ¼ teaspoon saffron
- ¼ cup dry sherry
- 1 cup Calasparra or bomba rice
- 1 (15-ounce) can butter beans, rinsed
- 3½ cups vegetable broth
- Lemon wedges (optional)

1. Heat 1½ tablespoons oil in 12-inch skillet over medium heat until shimmering. Add cauliflower and ¼ teaspoon salt and cook, stirring frequently, until cauliflower is spotty brown, 3 to 5 minutes. Add green beans and ¼ teaspoon salt. Continue to cook, stirring frequently, until beans are dark green, 2 to 4 minutes. Transfer vegetables to bowl.

2. Heat remaining 1½ tablespoons oil in now-empty skillet over medium heat until shimmering. Add bell pepper and remaining ¼ teaspoon salt and cook, stirring occasionally, until pepper starts to brown, 7 to 10 minutes. Add tomato paste and cook, stirring constantly, until pepper pieces are coated in tomato paste, about 1 minute. Add garlic, smoked paprika, and saffron and cook, stirring constantly until fragrant, about 30 seconds. Stir in sherry and cook, stirring frequently, until excess moisture has evaporated and pepper mixture forms large clumps, 1 to 2 minutes.

**3.** Add rice and stir until very well combined. Off heat, smooth into even layer. Scatter butter beans evenly over rice. Scatter cauliflower and green beans evenly over butter beans. Gently pour broth all over, making sure rice is fully submerged (it's okay if parts of vegetables aren't submerged).

**4.** Bring to boil over high heat. Adjust heat to maintain gentle simmer and cook until broth is just below top of rice, 12 to 17 minutes. Cover and cook until rice is cooked through, about 5 minutes. Uncover and cook until rice pops and sizzles and all excess moisture has evaporated (to test, use butter knife to gently push aside some rice and vegetables), 3 to 7 minutes. (If socarrat is desired, continue to cook, rotating skillet one-quarter turn every 20 seconds, until rice at bottom of skillet is well browned and slightly crusty, 2 to 5 minutes.) Let rest off heat for 5 minutes. Serve, passing lemon wedges, if using.

## Saag Paneer (Indian-Style Spinach with Fresh Cheese)

**SERVES** 4 to 6

**WHY THIS RECIPE WORKS** Saag paneer, soft cubes of creamy cheese in a spicy pureed spinach sauce, is a popular Indian dish. Even if you've never made cheese at home, our method for making paneer is very simple, and the flavor payoff is well worth the effort. We started our paneer by heating a combination of whole milk and buttermilk, squeezing the curds of moisture, and then weighing the cheese down until it was firm enough to slice. We simply wilted the spinach in the microwave. Mustard greens gave our sauce additional complexity. Canned diced tomatoes brightened the dish, and buttery cashews gave our dish a subtle nutty richness. To ensure that the cheese is firm, wring it tightly in step 2 and be sure to use two plates that nestle together snugly. Use commercially produced cultured buttermilk in this recipe. We found that some locally produced buttermilks didn't sufficiently coagulate the milk. Serve with basmati rice and/or naan.

### MAKING PANEER

**1.** Bring milk to boil, curdle it with buttermilk, and let rest for 1 minute off heat. Pour curdled milk through cheesecloth-lined colander; let drain. Twist cheesecloth to squeeze out liquid.

**2.** Press cheese between plates topped with Dutch oven; let drain until firm. Slice into ½-inch pieces.

**CHEESE**

- 3 quarts whole milk
- 3 cups buttermilk
- 1 tablespoon table salt

**SPINACH SAUCE**

- 1 (10-ounce) bag curly-leaf spinach, rinsed
- 12 ounces mustard greens, stemmed and rinsed
- 3 tablespoons unsalted butter
- 1 teaspoon cumin seeds
- 1 teaspoon ground coriander
- 1 teaspoon paprika
- ½ teaspoon ground cardamom
- ¼ teaspoon ground cinnamon
- 1 onion, chopped fine
- ¾ teaspoon table salt
- 3 garlic cloves, minced
- 1 tablespoon grated fresh ginger
- 1 jalapeño chile, stemmed, seeded, and minced
- 1 (14.5-ounce) can diced tomatoes, drained and chopped coarse
- ½ cup roasted cashews, chopped coarse, divided
- 1 cup water
- 1 cup buttermilk
- 3 tablespoons chopped fresh cilantro

**1. FOR THE CHEESE:** Line colander with triple layer of cheesecloth and set in sink. Bring milk to boil in Dutch oven over medium-high heat. Whisk in buttermilk and salt, turn off heat, and let stand for 1 minute. Pour milk mixture through cheesecloth and let curds drain for 15 minutes.

**2.** Pull edges of cheesecloth together to form pouch. Twist edges of cheesecloth together, firmly squeezing out as much liquid as possible from cheese curds. Place taut, twisted cheese pouch between 2 large plates and weigh down top plate with heavy Dutch oven. Set aside at room temperature until cheese is firm and set, at least 45 minutes. Remove cheesecloth and cut cheese into ½-inch pieces. (Left uncut, cheese can be wrapped in plastic wrap and refrigerated for up to 3 days.)

**3. FOR THE SPINACH SAUCE:** Place spinach in large bowl, cover, and microwave until wilted, about 3 minutes. When cool enough to handle, chop enough spinach to measure ⅓ cup and set aside. Transfer remaining spinach to blender and wipe out bowl. Place mustard greens in now-empty bowl, cover, and microwave until wilted, about 4 minutes. When cool enough to handle, chop enough mustard greens to measure ⅓ cup and transfer to bowl with chopped spinach. Transfer remaining mustard greens to blender.

**4.** Meanwhile, melt butter in 12-inch skillet over medium-high heat. Add cumin seeds, coriander, paprika, cardamom, and cinnamon and cook until fragrant, about 30 seconds. Add onion and salt; cook, stirring frequently, until softened, about 3 minutes. Add garlic, ginger, and jalapeño; cook, stirring frequently, until lightly browned and just beginning to stick to pan, 2 to 3 minutes. Stir in tomatoes and cook mixture until pan is dry and tomatoes are beginning to brown, 3 to 4 minutes. Remove skillet from heat.

**5.** Transfer half of onion mixture to blender with greens. Add ¼ cup cashews and water; process until smooth, about 1 minute. Return puree to skillet.

**6.** Return skillet to medium-high heat, stir in chopped greens and buttermilk, and bring to simmer. Reduce heat to low; cover; and cook until flavors have blended, 5 minutes. Season with salt and pepper to taste. Gently fold in cheese cubes and cook until just heated through, 1 to 2 minutes. Transfer to serving dish, sprinkle with cilantro and remaining ¼ cup cashews, and serve.

## Indian-Style Curry with Potatoes, Cauliflower, Peas, and Chickpeas

**SERVES** 4 to 6

**WHY THIS RECIPE WORKS** We wanted a vegetable curry we could make on a weeknight in less than an hour—without sacrificing flavor. Although we were initially reluctant to use store-bought curry powder, we found that toasting the curry powder in a skillet turned it into a flavor powerhouse. Further experimentation proved that adding a few pinches of garam masala added even more flavor. To build the rest of our flavor base we started with a generous amount of sautéed onion, vegetable oil, garlic, ginger, fresh chile, and tomato paste for sweetness. When we chose our vegetables (chickpeas and potatoes for heartiness and cauliflower and peas for texture and color), we found that sautéing the spices and main ingredients together enhanced and melded the flavors. Finally, we rounded out our sauce with a combination of water, pureed canned tomatoes, and a splash of heavy cream or coconut milk. This curry is moderately spicy when made with one chile. For more heat, include the chile seeds and ribs when mincing. Serve with Yogurt-Herb Sauce (page 414) and Simple Rice Pilaf (page 726).

- 2 tablespoons sweet or mild curry powder
- 1½ teaspoons garam masala
- 4 tablespoons vegetable oil
- 3 medium garlic cloves, minced or pressed through a garlic press (about 1 tablespoon)
- 1 tablespoon minced or grated fresh ginger
- 1 serrano chile, seeds and ribs removed, chile minced
- 1 tablespoon tomato paste
- 1 (14.5-ounce) can diced tomatoes
- 2 medium onions, minced (about 2 cups)
- 12 ounces red potatoes (about 2 medium), scrubbed and cut into ½-inch pieces
- 1¼ pounds cauliflower (½ medium head), trimmed, cored, and cut into 1-inch florets
- 1¼ cups water
- 1 (15-ounce) can chickpeas, drained and rinsed
- Table salt
- 1½ cups frozen peas
- ¼ cup heavy cream or coconut milk

**CONDIMENTS**

- Onion Relish
- Cilantro-Mint Chutney (page 558) or mango chutney

**1.** Toast the curry powder and garam masala in a small skillet over medium-high heat, stirring constantly, until the spices darken slightly and become fragrant, about 1 minute. Transfer the spices to a small bowl and set aside. In a separate small bowl, stir 1 tablespoon of the oil, the garlic, ginger, serrano, and tomato paste together. Pulse the tomatoes with their juice in a food processor until coarsely chopped, 3 to 4 pulses.

**2.** Heat the remaining 3 tablespoons oil in a large Dutch oven over medium-high heat until shimmering. Add the onions and potatoes and cook, stirring occasionally, until the onions are caramelized and the potatoes are golden brown around the edges, about 10 minutes. (Reduce the heat to medium if the onions darken too quickly.)

**3.** Reduce the heat to medium. Clear the center of the pot, add the garlic mixture, and cook, mashing the mixture into the pan, until fragrant, 15 to 20 seconds. Stir the garlic mixture into the vegetables. Add the toasted spices and cook, stirring constantly, for 1 minute longer. Add the cauliflower and cook, stirring constantly, until the spices coat the florets, about 2 minutes longer.

**4.** Add the tomatoes, water, chickpeas, and 1 teaspoon salt, scraping up any browned bits. Bring to a boil over medium-high heat. Cover, reduce the heat to medium, and cook, stirring occasionally, until the vegetables are tender, 10 to 15 minutes. Stir in the peas and cream and continue to cook until heated through, about 2 minutes longer. Season with salt to taste and serve, passing the condiments separately.

### Onion Relish

**MAKES** about 1 cup

If using a regular yellow onion, increase the sugar to 1 teaspoon. This relish can be refrigerated in an airtight container for up to 24 hours.

- 1 medium Vidalia onion, minced (about 1 cup)
- 1 tablespoon juice from 1 lime
- ½ teaspoon sweet paprika
- ½ teaspoon sugar
- ⅛ teaspoon table salt
- Pinch cayenne pepper

Combine all the ingredients in a small bowl.

### Cilantro-Mint Chutney

**MAKES** about 1 cup

This chutney can be refrigerated in an airtight container for up to 24 hours.

- 2 cups packed fresh cilantro leaves
- 1 cup packed fresh mint leaves
- ⅓ cup plain yogurt
- ¼ cup minced onion
- 1 tablespoon juice from 1 lime
- 1½ teaspoons sugar
- ½ teaspoon ground cumin
- ¼ teaspoon table salt

Process all the ingredients together in a food processor until smooth, about 20 seconds, scraping down the sides of the workbowl as needed.

## Stir-Fried Portobellos with Ginger-Oyster Sauce

**SERVES** 3 to 4

**WHY THIS RECIPE WORKS** For a satisfying vegetable stir-fry, we chose meaty portobello mushrooms as the main vegetable. After removing the gills (to keep the mushrooms from tasting leathery and raw), we cut the mushrooms into substantial 2-inch wedges. We cooked the mushrooms over medium-high heat until browned and tender, then added a mixture of broth, soy sauce, and sugar and reduced it to a glaze for an intense flavor boost. For this stir-fry, we bulked up the amount of vegetables in our traditional stir-fries, mixing carrots, snow peas, and napa cabbage. Finally, the sauce—a mixture of broth, oyster sauce, soy sauce, cornstarch, and sesame oil—and a heavy dose of ginger tied the dish together, and nobody missed the meat. Serve with white rice.

**GLAZE**

- ¼ cup vegetable broth
- 2 tablespoons soy sauce
- 2 tablespoons sugar

**SAUCE**

- 1 cup vegetable broth
- 3 tablespoons vegetarian oyster sauce
- 1 tablespoon soy sauce
- 1 tablespoon cornstarch
- 2 teaspoons toasted sesame oil

**VEGETABLES**

- ¼ cup peanut or vegetable oil, divided
- 4 teaspoons minced or grated fresh ginger
- 2 garlic cloves, minced
- 6–8 portobello mushrooms (each 4 to 6 inches), stemmed, gills removed, and cut into 2-inch wedges
- 4 carrots, peeled and sliced ¼ inch thick on bias
- ½ cup vegetable broth
- 3 ounces snow peas, strings removed
- 1 pound napa cabbage (1 small head), cored and cut into ¾-inch strips
- 1 tablespoon sesame seeds, toasted (optional)

**1. FOR THE GLAZE:** Combine broth, soy sauce, and sugar in small bowl and set aside.

**2. FOR THE SAUCE:** Combine all ingredients in small bowl and set aside.

**3. FOR THE VEGETABLES:** In small bowl, mix 1 teaspoon oil, ginger, and garlic together; set aside.

**4.** Heat 3 tablespoons oil in 12-inch nonstick skillet over medium-high heat until shimmering. Add mushrooms and cook without stirring until browned on 1 side, 2 to 3 minutes. Using tongs, flip mushrooms, reduce heat to medium, and cook until second sides are browned and mushrooms are tender, about 5 minutes. Increase heat to medium-high, add glaze, and cook, stirring frequently, until glaze is thick and mushrooms are coated, 1 to 2 minutes. Transfer mushrooms to plate. Rinse skillet clean and wipe dry with paper towels.

**5.** Add 1 teaspoon oil to skillet and return to high heat until just smoking. Add carrots and cook, stirring frequently, until beginning to brown, 1 to 2 minutes. Add broth, cover, and lower heat to medium. Cook carrots until just tender, 2 to 3 minutes. Uncover and cook until liquid evaporates, about 30 seconds. Transfer carrots to plate with mushrooms.

**6.** Add remaining 1 teaspoon oil to skillet and return to high heat until just smoking. Add snow peas and cook until spotty brown, about 2 minutes. Add cabbage and cook, stirring frequently, until wilted, about 2 minutes.

**7.** Clear center of skillet, add ginger mixture, and cook, mashing mixture into pan, until fragrant, 15 to 20 seconds. Stir ginger mixture into vegetables.

**8.** Stir in mushrooms and carrots. Whisk sauce to recombine, then add to skillet and cook, tossing constantly, until sauce is thickened, 2 to 3 minutes. Transfer to serving platter; sprinkle with sesame seeds, if using; and serve.

## Stir-Fried Tofu, Snow Peas, and Red Onion with Hot and Sour Sauce

**SERVES** 4

**WHY THIS RECIPE WORKS** We aimed to create a tofu and vegetable stir-fry recipe that harmonized their flavors and textures with a complementary sauces. To enhance the mild-flavored tofu, we selected an assertive hot and sour sauce which also paired well with the snow peas and bright red onion. As with most of our stir-fries, we marinated the tofu, in a combination of soy sauce and dry sherry to add flavor. After cooking the tofu and removing it from the pan, we stir-fried the vegetables in batches, quickly cooked the garlic and ginger, and returned the tofu to the pan along with the sauce. This final mixture needed less than a minute over medium heat to finish. Make sure to buy firm or extra-firm tofu; silken or soft tofu will crumble if stir-fried. To promote caramelization on the exterior of the tofu, turn the cubes as little as possible so that they have time to brown on several sides. For more heat, include the jalapeño seeds and ribs when mincing. Serve with rice.

**SAUCE**

- 3 tablespoons cider vinegar
- 1 tablespoon low-sodium chicken broth
- 1 tablespoon soy sauce
- 2 teaspoons sugar

**TOFU AND VEGETABLES**

- 1 (14-ounce) block firm or extra-firm tofu, drained and cut into 1-inch cubes
- 1 tablespoon soy sauce
- 1 tablespoon dry sherry
- 2 tablespoons plus 1 teaspoon peanut or vegetable oil
- 1 tablespoon minced or grated fresh ginger
- 3 garlic cloves, minced or pressed through a garlic press (about 1 tablespoon)
- 2 scallions, white parts only, minced
- 1 jalapeño chile, seeds and ribs removed, chile minced
- 1 medium red onion, halved and sliced thin
- 1 pound snow peas, tips and strings removed
- 2 tablespoons water

**1. FOR THE SAUCE:** Combine all the ingredients in a small bowl and set aside.

**2. FOR THE TOFU AND VEGETABLES:** Toss the tofu with the soy sauce and sherry in a medium bowl and let marinate for at least 10 minutes or up to 1 hour. In a small bowl, mix 1 teaspoon of the oil, the ginger, garlic, scallions, and jalapeño together.

**3.** Heat 1 tablespoon more oil in a 12-inch nonstick skillet over high heat until just smoking. Add the tofu and cook until golden brown on several sides, 2 to 3 minutes, turning as needed. Transfer the tofu to a clean bowl and cover with foil to keep warm.

**4.** Add the remaining 1 tablespoon oil to the skillet and return to high heat until just smoking. Add the onion and cook, stirring frequently, until beginning to brown, about 2 minutes. Add the snow peas and cook until spotty brown, about 2 minutes. Add the water, cover the pan, and lower the heat to medium. Cook the snow peas until crisp-tender, about 1 minute.

**5.** Clear the center of the skillet, add the ginger mixture, and cook, mashing the mixture into the pan, until fragrant, 15 to 20 seconds. Stir the ginger mixture into the vegetables.

**6.** Stir in the tofu. Whisk the sauce to recombine, then add to the skillet and cook, tossing constantly, until the sauce is thickened, about 30 seconds. Transfer to a serving platter and serve.

## Cheese Soufflé

**SERVES** 4 to 6

**WHY THIS RECIPE WORKS** Making a truly great cheese soufflé is like finding the Holy Grail for most cooks—unattainable. But this classic French dish doesn't have to be relegated to the realm of professional chefs. We wanted a cheese soufflé with bold cheese flavor, good stature, and a light but not-too-airy texture—all without the fussiness of most recipes. To bump up the cheese flavor without weighing down the soufflé, we added lightweight-but-flavorful Parmesan cheese to the traditional Gruyère. Reducing the amount of butter and flour also amplified the cheese flavor. Filling the soufflé dish to an inch below the rim allowed ample room for the soufflé to rise high. To get the texture just right while keeping the preparation simple, we beat egg whites to stiff peaks, and then—rather than carefully folding them into the cheese sauce—added the sauce right to the stand mixer, and beat everything until uniform. When the center reached 170 degrees, our soufflé had a perfect luscious creamy center and lightly bronzed edges. Comté, sharp cheddar, or Gouda cheese can be substituted for the Gruyère. To prevent the soufflé from overflowing the soufflé dish, leave at least 1 inch of space between the top of the batter and the rim of the dish; any excess batter should be discarded. The most foolproof way to test for doneness is with an instant-read thermometer. To judge doneness without an instant-read thermometer, use two large spoons to pry open the soufflé so that you can peer inside it; the center should appear thick and creamy but not soupy. Serve this soufflé with a green salad for a light dinner.

- 1 ounce Parmesan cheese, grated (½ cup)
- ¼ cup (1¼ ounces) all-purpose flour
- ¼ teaspoon paprika
- ¼ teaspoon table salt
- ⅛ teaspoon cayenne pepper
- ⅛ teaspoon white pepper
- Pinch ground nutmeg
- 4 tablespoons unsalted butter
- 1⅓ cups whole milk
- 6 ounces Gruyère cheese, shredded (1½ cups)
- 6 large eggs, separated
- 2 teaspoons minced fresh parsley
- ¼ teaspoon cream of tartar

**1.** Adjust oven rack to middle position and heat oven to 350 degrees. Spray 8-inch round (2-quart) soufflé dish with vegetable oil spray, then sprinkle with 2 tablespoons Parmesan.

**2.** Combine flour, paprika, salt, cayenne, white pepper, and nutmeg in bowl. Melt butter in small saucepan over medium heat. Stir in flour mixture and cook for 1 minute. Slowly whisk in milk and bring to simmer. Cook, whisking constantly, until mixture is thickened and smooth, about 1 minute. Remove pan from heat and whisk in Gruyère and 5 tablespoons Parmesan until melted and smooth. Let cool for 10 minutes, then whisk in egg yolks and 1½ teaspoons parsley.

**3.** Using stand mixer fitted with whisk, whip egg whites and cream of tartar on medium-low speed until foamy, about 1 minute. Increase speed to medium-high and whip until stiff peaks form, 3 to 4 minutes. Add cheese mixture and continue to whip until fully combined, about 15 seconds.

**4.** Pour mixture into prepared dish and sprinkle with remaining 1 tablespoon Parmesan. Bake until risen above rim, top is deep golden brown, and interior registers 170 degrees, 30 to 35 minutes. Sprinkle with remaining ½ teaspoon parsley and serve immediately.

## Make-Ahead Cheese Soufflés

**SERVES 6**

**WHY THIS RECIPE WORKS** Wouldn't it be nice to produce a batch of rich, cheesy soufflés without having to arrange your schedule around them? With this recipe, it's easily achieved. We began with a standard béchamel sauce and then added plenty of nutty Comté, which we supplemented with Parmesan to add extra-cheesy oomph without a lot of moisture that might otherwise cause the soufflé to collapse. After folding in egg whites that had been whipped to stiff peaks, we portioned the mixture into individual ramekins, which we baked in a water bath until the structure was softly set. The water bath ensured that the soufflés cooked evenly from edge to edge instead of becoming dry and stiff on the sides. When they were cool, we removed them from their ramekins and refrigerated them on a baking sheet. Just before serving, we transferred the baking sheet to a hot oven, where the soufflés became puffy and crisp. You'll need six 4-ounce ramekins for this recipe. Sharp cheddar, Gruyère, or gouda can be substituted for the Comté. The cooled soufflés can be frozen for up to two weeks before the second bake; thaw them at room temperature before baking. Serve the soufflés with Pickled Mustard Seeds and lightly dressed salad greens, if desired.

- 2 tablespoons unsalted butter
- 3 tablespoons all-purpose flour
- ¼ teaspoon table salt
- Pinch ground nutmeg
- 1 cup milk, divided
- 3 ounces Comté cheese, shredded (¾ cup)
- 1 ounce Parmesan cheese, grated (½ cup)
- 3 large eggs, separated
- 2 teaspoons minced fresh parsley
- ¼ teaspoon cream of tartar

**1.** Adjust oven rack to middle position and heat oven to 350 degrees. Generously spray six 4-ounce ramekins with vegetable oil spray. Bring kettle of water to boil.

**2.** Melt butter in medium saucepan over medium heat. Stir in flour, salt, and nutmeg and cook for 1 minute. Add ½ cup milk and whisk until smooth. Whisk in remaining ½ cup milk and cook, whisking constantly, until mixture is thickened and bubbling, about 2 minutes. Off heat, whisk in Comté and Parmesan until melted and smooth (mixture will be thick). Transfer to large bowl and whisk in egg yolks and parsley.

**3.** Using stand mixer fitted with whisk attachment, whip egg whites and cream of tartar on medium-low speed until foamy, about 1 minute. Increase speed to medium-high and whip until stiff peaks form, about 2 minutes. Gently whisk one-third of whites into cheese mixture. Using rubber spatula, gently fold in remaining whites.

**4.** Distribute mixture evenly among prepared ramekins and smooth tops. Transfer ramekins to 13 by 9-inch baking pan and add boiling water until it comes halfway up sides of ramekins. Bake until soufflés are puffed and register 170 to 175 degrees, 14 to 17 minutes. Using tongs, transfer ramekins to wire rack and let cool completely, 30 to 40 minutes (soufflés will shrink). While soufflés cool, line rimmed baking sheet with parchment paper and grease parchment lightly.

**5.** Invert 1 ramekin onto your hand and shake sharply until soufflé releases. Reinvert soufflé onto prepared sheet. Repeat with remaining soufflés. Cover tightly with plastic wrap and refrigerate for at least 1 hour or up to 3 days.

**6.** Adjust oven rack to middle position and heat oven to 400 degrees. Bake soufflés until puffed and deeply browned, 15 to 18 minutes. While soufflés bake, set out 6 plates. Using thin spatula, transfer 1 soufflé to each plate. Serve immediately.

### Pickled Mustard Seeds

**MAKES** ½ cup

With their piquant flavor and caviar-like pop, these seeds make a perfect accompaniment to our Make-Ahead Cheese Soufflés. They are also a great addition to sandwiches, cheese or charcuterie boards, or even a vinaigrette. You can substitute cider vinegar for the white wine vinegar, if desired.

- ½ cup white wine vinegar
- ½ cup water
- ⅓ cup yellow mustard seeds
- 2 tablespoons maple syrup
- ½ teaspoon table salt

**1.** Whisk all ingredients together in small saucepan and bring to boil over medium-high heat. Lower heat to maintain simmer and cook, stirring frequently, until mustard seeds are swollen and softened and mixture is nearly dry, about 40 minutes (if mixture starts to dry out before mustard seeds have softened, add extra water, 1 tablespoon at a time).

**2.** Transfer to container and let cool completely. Cover and refrigerate for up to 1 month. Let come to room temperature before serving.

## White Bean and Mushroom Gratin

**SERVES** 4 to 6

**WHY THIS RECIPE WORKS** Our complexly flavored gratin features creamy white beans, meaty cremini mushrooms, tender carrots, and a crisp layer of bread. The gravy's flavor is created from the fond left by sautéing mushrooms and aromatics and deglazing with nutty dry sherry. Flour and the starchy canned bean liquid thickened the gravy. We baked the gratin in a low oven after topping it with seasoned bread cubes. As it baked, the lower portion of the bread merged with the gratin, creating a lovely soft texture, while the upper portion dried out. Then, using the broiler, we toasted the bread until it was golden brown. We prefer a round rustic loaf (also known as a boule) with a chewy, open crumb and a sturdy crust for this recipe. Cannellini or navy beans can be used in place of great Northern beans, if desired.

- ½ cup extra-virgin olive oil, divided
- 10 ounces cremini mushrooms, trimmed and sliced ½ inch thick
- ¾ teaspoon table salt
- ½ teaspoon pepper, divided
- 4–5 slices country-style bread, cut into ½-inch cubes (5 cups)
- ¼ cup minced fresh parsley, divided
- 1 cup water
- 1 tablespoon all-purpose flour
- 1 small onion, chopped fine
- 5 garlic cloves, minced
- 1 tablespoon tomato paste
- 1½ teaspoons minced fresh thyme
- ⅓ cup dry sherry
- 2 (15-ounce) cans great Northern beans, undrained
- 3 carrots, peeled, halved lengthwise, and cut into ¾-inch pieces

**1.** Adjust oven rack to middle position and heat oven to 300 degrees. Heat 1/4 cup oil in 12-inch ovensafe skillet over medium-high heat until shimmering. Add mushrooms, salt, and 1/4 teaspoon pepper and cook, stirring occasionally, until mushrooms are well browned, 8 to 12 minutes.

**2.** While mushrooms cook, toss bread, 3 tablespoons parsley, remaining 1/4 cup oil, and remaining 1/4 teaspoon pepper together in bowl. Set aside. Stir water and flour in second bowl until no lumps of flour remain. Set aside.

**3.** Reduce heat to medium, add onion to skillet, and continue to cook, stirring frequently, until onion is translucent, 4 to 6 minutes. Reduce heat to medium-low; add garlic, tomato paste, and thyme; and cook, stirring constantly, until bottom of skillet is dark brown, 2 to 3 minutes. Add sherry and cook, scraping up any browned bits.

**4.** Add beans and their liquid, carrots, and flour mixture. Bring to boil over high heat. Off heat, arrange bread mixture over surface in even layer. Transfer skillet to oven and bake for 40 minutes. (Liquid should have consistency of thin gravy.)

**5.** Leave skillet in oven and turn on broiler. Broil until crumbs are golden brown, 4 to 7 minutes. Remove gratin from oven and let stand for 20 minutes. Sprinkle with remaining 1 tablespoon parsley; serve.

## Rajas Poblanas con Crema (Charred Poblano Strips with Cream)

**SERVES** 4

**WHY THIS RECIPE WORKS** To make rajas poblanas con crema, a Mexican favorite that features tender strips of roasted chiles and sliced onion cooked with crema, we broiled poblanos until they were completely charred and then wrapped them in foil to steam. This imbued the chiles with smoky flavor and made them easy to peel. White onion gently cooked in butter added sweetness, and garlic contributed savoriness. Mexican crema makes the dish creamy, lightly salty, and tangy and balances the mild heat of the poblanos. Broilers vary, so watch the chiles carefully. Mexican crema can be found in the dairy section of many grocery stores. If you cannot find crema, substitute heavy cream. Rajas con crema is a versatile dish that can be enjoyed alongside grilled meat or fish, rice, or beans or as a filling for tacos or quesadillas.

- 1 pound (3 to 4) poblano chiles, stemmed, halved, and seeded
- 2 tablespoons unsalted butter
- ½ white onion, sliced through root end ¼ inch thick
- 2 garlic cloves, minced
- ½ teaspoon table salt
- ¼ teaspoon pepper
- ¾ cup Mexican crema

**1.** Line rimmed baking sheet with aluminum foil. Arrange poblanos skin side up on prepared sheet and press to flatten. Adjust oven rack 3 to 4 inches from broiler element and heat broiler. Broil until skin is puffed and most of surface is well charred, 5 to 10 minutes, rotating sheet halfway through broiling.

**2.** Using tongs, pile poblanos in center of foil. Gather foil over poblanos and crimp to form pouch. Let steam for 10 minutes. Open foil packet carefully and spread out poblanos. When cool enough to handle, peel poblanos (it's OK if some bits of skin remain intact) and discard skins. Slice lengthwise into ½-inch-thick strips. (Rajas can be refrigerated for up to 3 days.)

**3.** Melt butter in 12-inch nonstick skillet over medium heat. Add onion and cook, stirring occasionally, until onion has softened and edges are just starting to brown, 6 to 8 minutes. Add garlic and cook until fragrant, about 30 seconds. Add rajas, salt, and pepper and cook until warmed through, about 1 minute. Add crema and cook, stirring gently but frequently, until crema has thickened and clings to vegetables, 2 to 3 minutes. Serve immediately.

## Roasted Poblano and Black Bean Enchiladas

**SERVES** 4 to 6

**WHY THIS RECIPE WORKS** For great vegetarian enchiladas, we wanted a bright sauce featuring sweet-tart tomatillos. We rounded out the sauce with onion, garlic, cilantro, lime juice, and a splash of cream for richness. For the filling, we started with spicy, fruity, roasted poblano chiles. We smashed canned black beans to create a quick "refried" bean base and stirred in a little of the tomatillo sauce, Monterey Jack cheese, and some heady seasonings. When choosing tomatillos, look for pale-green orbs with firm flesh that fills and splits open the fruit's outer papery husk, which must be removed before cooking. Serve with sour cream, diced avocado, sliced radishes, shredded romaine lettuce, and lime wedges.

- 1 pound tomatillos, husks and stems removed, rinsed well, dried, and halved
- 4 poblano chiles, halved, stemmed, and seeded
- 1 teaspoon plus ¼ cup vegetable oil, divided
- 2 onions, chopped fine, divided
- 1 cup fresh cilantro leaves, divided
- ⅓ cup vegetable broth
- ¼ cup heavy cream
- 4 garlic cloves, minced, divided
- 1 tablespoon lime juice
- 1¼ teaspoons table salt, divided

- 1 teaspoon sugar
- 1 teaspoon chili powder
- ½ teaspoon ground coriander
- ½ teaspoon ground cumin
- 1 (15-ounce) can black beans, rinsed, half of beans mashed smooth
- 8 ounces Monterey Jack cheese, shredded (2 cups), divided
- 12 (6-inch) corn tortillas

**1.** Adjust oven rack 6 inches from broiler element and heat broiler. Line rimmed baking sheet with aluminum foil. Toss tomatillos and poblanos with 1 teaspoon oil. Arrange tomatillos cut side down and poblanos skin side up on prepared sheet. Broil until vegetables are blackened and beginning to soften, 5 to 10 minutes. Let vegetables cool slightly. Remove skins and seeds from poblanos (leave tomatillo skins intact), then chop into ½-inch pieces.

**2.** Process broiled tomatillos, 1 cup onion, ½ cup cilantro, broth, cream, 1 tablespoon oil, half of garlic, lime juice, 1 teaspoon salt, and sugar in food processor until sauce is smooth, about 2 minutes. Season with salt and pepper to taste.

**3.** Heat 1 tablespoon oil in 12-inch skillet over medium heat until shimmering. Add remaining onion and remaining ¼ teaspoon salt and cook until softened, 5 to 7 minutes. Stir in chili powder, coriander, cumin, and remaining garlic and cook until fragrant, about 30 seconds. Stir in mashed and whole beans and chopped poblanos and cook until warmed through, about 2 minutes. Transfer mixture to large bowl and let cool slightly. Stir in 1 cup Monterey Jack, ½ cup tomatillo sauce, and remaining ½ cup cilantro. Season with salt and pepper to taste.

**4.** Adjust oven rack to middle position and heat oven to 400 degrees. Spread ½ cup tomatillo sauce over bottom of 13 by 9-inch baking dish. Brush both sides of tortillas with remaining 2 tablespoons oil. Arrange tortillas, overlapping, on rimmed baking sheet in 2 rows (6 tortillas each). Bake until tortillas are warm and pliable, about 5 minutes.

5. Working with 1 warm tortilla at a time, spread ¼ cup bean-cheese filling across center of tortilla. Roll tortilla tightly around filling and place seam side down in baking dish; arrange enchiladas in 2 rows across width of dish.

6. Pour remaining sauce over top to cover completely and sprinkle remaining 1 cup cheese down center of enchiladas. Cover dish tightly with greased aluminum foil. Bake until enchiladas are heated through and cheese is melted, about 25 minutes. Let cool for 5 minutes before serving.

## Eggplant Parmesan

**SERVES** 6 to 8

**WHY THIS RECIPE WORKS** Frying the eggplant for eggplant Parm is not only time-consuming but can also make the dish heavy and dull. In hopes of eliminating the grease as well as some prep time, we cooked the eggplant in the oven and looked for other ways to freshen up this Italian classic. We salted and drained the eggplant slices to improve their texture. A traditional bound breading worked best for giving the eggplant a crisp coating. Baking the eggplant on preheated and oiled baking sheets resulted in crisp, golden-brown slices. While the eggplant was in the oven, we made a quick tomato sauce using canned diced tomatoes. We layered the sauce, eggplant, and mozzarella in a baking dish and left the top layer of eggplant mostly unsauced, so that it would crisp up in the oven. Use kosher salt when salting the eggplant. The coarse grains don't dissolve as readily as the fine grains of regular table salt, so any excess can be easily wiped away. It's necessary to divide the eggplant into two batches when tossing it with the salt. To be time-efficient, use the 30 to 45 minutes during which the salted eggplant sits to prepare the breading.

**EGGPLANT**

- 2 pounds globe eggplant (2 medium eggplants), cut crosswise into ¼-inch-thick rounds
- 1 tablespoon kosher salt, for salting eggplant
- 8 slices high-quality white sandwich bread, torn into quarters
- 2 ounces Parmesan cheese, grated (1 cup)
- 1½ teaspoons pepper, divided
- ¼ teaspoon table salt
- 1 cup unbleached all-purpose flour
- 4 large eggs
- 6 tablespoons vegetable oil

**TOMATO SAUCE**

- 3 (14.5-ounce) cans diced tomatoes, divided
- 2 tablespoons extra-virgin olive oil
- 4 garlic cloves, minced
- ¼ teaspoon red pepper flakes
- ½ cup coarsely chopped fresh basil leaves
- 8 ounces whole-milk or part-skim mozzarella cheese, shredded (2 cups)
- 1 ounce Parmesan cheese, grated (½ cup)
- 10 fresh basil leaves, torn, for garnish

1. **FOR THE EGGPLANT:** Toss half of eggplant slices and 1½ teaspoons kosher salt in a large bowl until combined; transfer salted eggplant to large colander set over bowl. Repeat with remaining eggplant and kosher salt, placing second batch on top of first. Let stand until eggplant releases about 2 tablespoons liquid, 30 to 45 minutes. Spread eggplant slices on triple thickness of paper towels; cover with another triple thickness of paper towels. Press firmly on each slice to remove as much liquid as possible, then wipe off excess salt.

2. While eggplant is draining, adjust oven racks to upper-middle and lower-middle positions, place rimmed baking sheet on each rack, and heat oven to 425 degrees. Process bread in food processor to fine, even crumbs, about 20 to 30 seconds. Transfer crumbs to shallow dish and stir in Parmesan, ½ teaspoon pepper, and salt; set aside. Wipe out workbowl (do not wash) and set aside.

3. Combine flour and remaining 1 teaspoon pepper in large zipper-lock bag; shake to combine. Beat eggs in second shallow dish. Place 8 to 10 eggplant slices in bag with flour; seal bag and shake to coat slices. Remove slices, shaking off excess flour, dip into eggs, let excess egg run off, then coat evenly with bread-crumb mixture; set breaded slices on wire rack set over baking sheet. Repeat with remaining eggplant.

4. Remove preheated baking sheets from oven; add 3 tablespoons vegetable oil to each sheet, tilting to coat evenly with oil. Place half of breaded eggplant slices on each sheet in single layer; bake until eggplant is well browned and crisp, about 30 minutes, switching and rotating baking sheets after 10 minutes, and flipping eggplant slices with wide spatula after 20 minutes. Do not turn off oven.

**5. FOR THE TOMATO SAUCE:** While eggplant bakes, process 2 cans diced tomatoes in food processor until almost smooth, about 5 seconds. Heat olive oil, garlic, and red pepper flakes in large heavy-bottomed saucepan over medium-high heat, stirring occasionally, until fragrant and garlic is light golden, about 3 minutes; stir in processed tomatoes and remaining can of diced tomatoes. Bring sauce to boil, then reduce heat to medium-low and simmer, stirring occasionally, until slightly thickened and reduced, about 15 minutes (you should have about 4 cups). Stir in basil and season with table salt and pepper to taste.

**6. TO ASSEMBLE:** Spread 1 cup of tomato sauce in bottom of 13 by 9-inch baking dish. Layer in half eggplant slices, overlapping slices to fit; distribute 1 cup more sauce over eggplant; sprinkle with half of mozzarella. Layer in remaining eggplant and dot with 1 cup more sauce, leaving majority of eggplant exposed so it will remain crisp; sprinkle with Parmesan and remaining mozzarella. Bake until bubbling and cheese is browned, 13 to 15 minutes. Let cool for 10 minutes, scatter basil over top, and serve, passing remaining tomato sauce separately.

## Eggplant Involtini

SERVES 4 to 6

**WHY THIS RECIPE WORKS** Making eggplant involtini ("little bundles" in Italian) can be a labor-intensive and messy affair, but one bite of the resulting dish—charmingly tidy involtini with homemade tomato sauce and a pleasantly cheesy filling—and you'll know why it's still made by home cooks. We wanted to streamline the process and create a version of involtini that would emphasize the eggplant. First up for fixing: the eggplant. Generally this recipe calls for frying, but in order to fry eggplant, you must first get rid of the excess water or the eggplant will turn mushy and oily. Salting can fix this problem, but it's time-consuming. Instead, we opted for a lighter and more hands-off option: baking. We brushed the planks with oil, seasoned them, and then baked them for 30 minutes. They emerged light brown and tender, with a compact texture that was neither mushy nor sodden. To lighten up the filling, we decreased the amount of ricotta and replaced it with more flavorful Pecorino Romano. To ensure that our filling stayed creamy and didn't toughen up, we added bread crumbs to the mix. After making a bare-bones tomato sauce, we added the eggplant rolls directly to the sauce. Select shorter, wider eggplants for this recipe. Part-skim ricotta may be used, but do not use fat-free ricotta. Serve the eggplant with crusty bread and a salad.

- 2 large eggplants (1½ pounds each), peeled
- 6 tablespoons vegetable oil, divided
- 2 teaspoons kosher salt, divided
- ½ teaspoon pepper, divided
- 2 garlic cloves, minced
- ¼ teaspoon dried oregano
- Pinch red pepper flakes
- 1 (28-ounce) can whole peeled tomatoes, drained with juice reserved, chopped coarse

- 1 slice hearty white sandwich bread, torn into 1-inch pieces
- 8 ounces (1 cup) whole-milk ricotta cheese
- 1½ ounces grated Pecorino Romano (¾ cup), divided
- ¼ cup plus 1 tablespoon chopped fresh basil, divided
- 1 tablespoon lemon juice

**1.** Slice each eggplant lengthwise into ½-inch-thick planks (you should have 12 planks). Trim rounded surface from each end piece so it lies flat.

**2.** Adjust 1 oven rack to lower-middle position and second rack 8 inches from broiler element. Heat oven to 375 degrees. Line 2 rimmed baking sheets with parchment paper and spray generously with vegetable oil spray. Arrange eggplant slices in single layer on prepared sheets. Brush 1 side of eggplant slices with 2½ tablespoons oil and sprinkle with ½ teaspoon salt and ¼ teaspoon pepper. Flip eggplant slices and brush with 2½ tablespoons oil and sprinkle with ½ teaspoon salt and remaining ¼ teaspoon pepper. Bake until tender and lightly browned, 30 to 35 minutes, switching and rotating sheets halfway through baking. Let cool for 5 minutes. Using thin spatula, flip each slice over. Heat broiler.

**3.** While eggplant cooks, heat remaining 1 tablespoon oil in 12-inch broiler-safe skillet over medium-low heat until just shimmering. Add garlic, oregano, pepper flakes, and ½ teaspoon salt and cook, stirring occasionally, until fragrant, about 30 seconds. Stir in tomatoes and their juice. Increase heat to high and bring to simmer. Reduce heat to medium-low and simmer until thickened, about 15 minutes. Cover and set aside.

**4.** Pulse bread in food processor until finely ground, 10 to 15 pulses. Combine bread crumbs, ricotta, ½ cup Pecorino, ¼ cup basil, lemon juice, and remaining ½ teaspoon salt in medium bowl.

**5.** With widest short sides of eggplant slices facing you, evenly distribute ricotta mixture on bottom third of each slice. Gently roll up each eggplant slice and place seam side down in tomato sauce.

**6.** Bring sauce to simmer over medium heat. Simmer for 5 minutes. Transfer skillet to oven and broil until eggplant is well browned and cheese is heated through, 5 to 10 minutes. Sprinkle with remaining ¼ cup Pecorino and let stand for 5 minutes. Sprinkle with remaining 1 tablespoon basil and serve.

## Silky Roasted Eggplant with Tomato and Feta

**SERVES** 4 to 6 **SEASON 26**

**WHY THIS RECIPE WORKS** This riff on shrimp saganaki—a Greek dish of shrimp stewed in a tomato sauce infused with red pepper flakes and oregano and dotted with chunks of sheep's milk feta—swaps the seafood for vegetarian-friendly eggplant, a substantial vegetable that gives this dish the feeling of a hearty main course. Roasting the eggplant slices allowed us to skip the salting and draining step because their excess moisture evaporated in the oven. Baking the browned slices in tomato sauce made them melt-in-your-mouth tender. Slicing the eggplant at an angle cut across their fibers so that there were no stringy bits. You can prep and cook the eggplant and the tomato sauce up to 3 days ahead. We developed this recipe with Diamond Crystal kosher salt. If using Morton Kosher salt, which is denser, use only 1½ teaspoons in step 1. Before flambéing, make sure to roll up long shirt sleeves, tie back long hair, turn off the exhaust fan (otherwise the fan may pull the flames up). and turn off any lit burners (this is critical if you have a gas stove). If flambéing, do not use a nonstick skillet; the heat produced by flambéing (igniting) the contents of the skillet can damage nonstick coatings.

- ½ cup extra-virgin olive oil, divided
- 2½ pounds eggplant, peeled and sliced ½-inch-thick on bias
- 2 teaspoons kosher salt
- ¾ teaspoon pepper
- 1 onion, chopped fine
- 1 tablespoon tomato paste
- 2 garlic cloves, minced
- 1 teaspoon dried oregano
- ½ teaspoon red pepper flakes
- ½ cup dry white wine
- 1 (28-ounce) can crushed tomatoes
- ½ teaspoon sugar
- 8 ounces feta cheese, crumbled (2 cups)
- 2 tablespoons ouzo, grappa, brandy, or vodka (optional)
- Crusty bread

**1.** Adjust oven rack to upper-middle and lower-middle positions. Heat oven to 450 degrees. Drizzle 2 tablespoons oil over 2 rimmed baking sheets (1 tablespoon per sheet), then use pastry brush to evenly coat sheets. Arrange eggplant slices in even layer over sheets, then brush eggplant evenly with ¼ cup oil. Sprinkle eggplant with salt and pepper.

**2.** Bake until slices are golden brown on bottom and tender throughout, about 30 minutes, switching and rotating sheets halfway through baking. Remove sheets from oven and reduce oven temperature to 375 degrees. Let eggplant cool for 5 minutes. Using thin metal spatula, flip each slice and let cool completely on sheets.

**3.** While eggplant cooks, heat remaining2 tablespoons oil in 12-inch skillet over medium heat until shimmering. Add onion and cook until softened and beginning to caramelize at edges, 16 to 18 minutes, stirring occasionally. Stir in tomato paste, garlic, oregano, and pepper flakes and cook, stirring occasionally, until fragrant, about 2 minutes. Stir in wine, scraping up any browned bits, and cook until mostly evaporated, about 1 minute. Stir in tomatoes and sugar, increase heat to high, and bring to simmer. Reduce heat to medium-low and simmer until slightly thickened, about 5 minutes. Remove from heat and season with salt and pepper to taste. Set aside about two-thirds of sauce and spread remaining sauce in even layer in skillet.

**4.** Arrange one-third of cooled eggplant slices in skillet in single layer, spooning some sauce in skillet over eggplant and spreading to cover. Use remaining eggplant slices and reserved sauce, repeat layering 2 more times to make 3 layers. Sprinkle feta evenly over top layer.

**5.** Transfer skillet to upper rack in oven and bake until sauce is bubbling in center, feta is well browned on top, and tomato sauce is caramelizing at edges of skillet, 35 to 40 minutes. Being careful of hot skillet handle, transfer skillet to wire rack and, if using, drizzle ouzo over top. Wave lit match over skillet until ouzo ignites. When flames subside (15 to 30 seconds), serve immediately with crusty bread. (If omitting ouzo, skip flambéing.)

## Alu Parathas (Punjabi Potato-Stuffed Griddle Breads)

**MAKES** 8 parathas

**WHY THIS RECIPE WORKS** These potato-stuffed flatbreads hail from Punjab and are a staple across the northern part of the Indian subcontinent and in big cities such as Mumbai and Delhi. Alu parathas are made by wrapping circles of dough around a boldly spiced potato stuffing, rolling the stuffed balls into slim disks, and browning the disks (brushed with ghee) until crisp brown patches develop. The steamy, pliable breads are typically enjoyed as the center of a meal, and frankly, there is no more satisfying breakfast, lunch, or dinner than a stack of piping hot alu parathas. We started by making a compact, flavorful potato stuffing of mashed russets, aromatics, and a bold mix of spices and seeds: amchoor, cumin, kalonji, and ajwain (all of which can be found in a South Asian market or online). Next, we mixed a quick dough in the food processor, letting it rest for 30 minutes to allow the gluten to relax. After stuffing the potato balls into rounds of dough, we rolled the packages thin and griddled them in a cast-iron skillet. These Punjabi flatbreads are typically enjoyed with spicy-sweet mango pickle, cooling raita, or a tomato-onion salad. If you cannot fined

ajwain, it's OK to leave it out. You can substitute ¼ teaspoon of cayenne pepper for the Thai chile in the stuffing. We strongly recommend weighing the flour for this recipe. Serve the parathas as an entrée with raita, prepared mango pickle, or Tamatya-Kandyachi Koshimbir (page 567).

**POTATO STUFFING**

- 1 pound russet potatoes, peeled and cut into 1-inch pieces
- 2 tablespoons minced fresh cilantro
- 1 tablespoon grated fresh ginger
- 1½ teaspoons amchoor
- 1 teaspoon ground cumin
- ¾ teaspoon table salt
- 1 Thai chile, stemmed and minced
- ¼ teaspoon kalonji
- ¼ teaspoon ajwain

**DOUGH**

- 1⅔ cups (8⅓ ounces) all-purpose flour
- ½ teaspoon table salt
- ½ teaspoon sugar
- 2 tablespoons vegetable oil
- ½ cup plus 1 tablespoon cold water
- ¼ cup ghee, melted

**1. FOR THE POTATO STUFFING:** Place potatoes in large saucepan, add cold water to cover by 1 inch, and bring to boil over high heat. Reduce heat to maintain simmer and cook until potatoes are very tender, about 16 minutes. Drain well and process through ricer or mash with potato masher until completely smooth. Set aside and let partially cool, about 20 minutes.

**2.** Stir cilantro, ginger, amchoor, cumin, salt, Thai chile, kalonji, and ajwain into potatoes. Season with salt to taste. Cover and set aside. (Potato stuffing can be refrigerated for up to 24 hours; let come to room temperature before using.)

**3. FOR THE DOUGH:** Pulse flour, salt, and sugar in food processor until combined, about 5 pulses. Add oil and pulse until incorporated, about 5 pulses. With processor running, slowly add cold water and process until dough is combined and no dry flour remains, about 30 seconds. Transfer dough to clean counter and knead by hand to form smooth, round ball, about 30 seconds; transfer to bowl, cover with plastic wrap, and let rest for 30 minutes.

**4.** Divide potato stuffing into 8 equal portions and roll into balls (they will be about 1½ inches wide); cover with plastic. Divide dough into 8 equal pieces, about 1¾ ounces each, and cover loosely with plastic. Working with 1 piece of dough at a time, form dough pieces into smooth, taut balls. (To round, set piece of dough on unfloured counter. Loosely cup your hand around dough and, without applying pressure to dough, move your hand in small circular motions. Tackiness of dough against counter and circular motion should work dough into smooth ball.) Let dough balls rest, covered, for 15 minutes. While dough balls rest, line rimmed baking sheet with parchment paper.

**5.** Roll 1 dough ball into 4-inch disk on lightly floured counter. Place 1 stuffing ball in center of dough disk. Gather edges of dough around stuffing to enclose completely; pinch to seal. Place seam side down on lightly floured counter, gently flatten, and lightly and gently roll to even ⅛-inch-thick round (about 8 inches wide). Transfer to prepared sheet and cover loosely with plastic. Repeat with remaining dough balls, stacking parathas between layers of parchment.

**6.** Heat 10-inch cast-iron skillet over medium heat for 5 minutes, then reduce heat to low. Brush any remaining flour from both sides of 1 paratha, then gently place in hot skillet, being careful not to stretch paratha. Cook until large bubbles begin to form on surface, underside of paratha is light blond, and

### FILLING ALU PARATHAS

**1.** Place stuffing in center of dough.

**2.** Pinch edges tightly to seal. Turn ball seam side down.

**3.** To prevent edges from tearing, press gently as you roll. Roll stuffed dough to ⅛-inch-thick 8-inch round.

paratha moves freely in skillet, 30 to 60 seconds. (Paratha may puff.) Using metal spatula, flip paratha; brush with ghee. Cook until underside is spotty brown and moves freely in skillet, 20 to 60 seconds, pressing any puffed edges firmly onto skillet with spatula to ensure even contact.

**7.** Flip paratha back onto first side. Repeat brushing with ghee, pressing, cooking, and flipping once more until paratha is even more spotty brown on both sides and no longer looks raw, about 30 seconds per side. Transfer cooked paratha to second rimmed baking sheet, let cool slightly, then cover loosely with dish towel.

**8.** Repeat with remaining parathas, wiping out skillet with paper towels between each paratha and briefly removing skillet from heat if it begins to smoke or if paratha browns too quickly. Serve hot. (Parathas can be stacked between layers of parchment paper, placed in zipper-lock bag, and refrigerated for up to 2 days; to refresh, heat 10-inch cast-iron skillet over medium heat for 5 minutes, then reduce heat to low. Cook paratha until warmed through, flipping 3 times, 10 to 15 seconds per side.)

### Tamatya-Kandyachi Koshimbir (Tomato-Onion Salad)

**SERVES** 4

If you are not fond of raw onion, substitute 1/4 cup of crushed peanuts.

- 4 large, firm tomatoes, cored and cut into ¼-inch dice
- ½ teaspoon table salt
- 1 Thai green chile, sliced
- Pinch sugar
- 1 large onion, chopped fine
- ¼ teaspoon ground cumin
- 2 tablespoons grated fresh coconut (optional)
- 2 tablespoons finely chopped fresh cilantro (optional)

Stir tomatoes, salt, Thai chile, and sugar together in bowl. Let sit for 5 minutes to allow flavors to meld. Stir in onion and cumin. Serve, garnishing with coconut and cilantro, if using.

## Spanakopita (Greek Spinach and Feta Pie)

**SERVES** 6 to 8

**WHY THIS RECIPE WORKS** The roots of spinach pie run deep in Greek culture. For our version, we wanted a casserole-style pie with a perfect balance of zesty spinach filling and shatteringly crisp phyllo crust—and we didn't want it to take all day. Using store-bought phyllo dough was an easy time-saver. Among the various spinach options, tasters favored the bold flavor of fresh curly-leaf spinach that had been microwaved, chopped, and squeezed of moisture. Crumbling the feta into fine pieces ensured a salty tang in every bite, while Greek yogurt buffered its assertiveness. We found that Pecorino Romano (a good stand-in for the traditional Greek hard sheep's milk cheese) added complexity to the filling and, when sprinkled between the sheets of phyllo, helped the flaky layers hold together. Using a baking sheet rather than a baking dish allowed excess moisture to easily evaporate, ensuring a crisp crust. It is important to rinse the feta; this step removes some of its salty brine. Full-fat sour cream can be substituted for whole-milk Greek yogurt. Phyllo is also available in 14 by 18-inch sheets; if using, cut them in half to make 14 by 9-inch sheets. Don't thaw the phyllo in the microwave; let it sit in the refrigerator overnight or on the countertop for 4 to 5 hours. The filling can be made up to 24 hours in advance and refrigerated. The assembled, unbaked spanakopita can be frozen on a baking sheet, wrapped well in plastic wrap, or cut in half crosswise and frozen in smaller sections on a plate. To bake, unwrap and increase the baking time by 5 to 10 minutes.

**FILLING**

- 1¼ pounds curly-leaf spinach, stemmed
- ¼ cup water
- 12 ounces feta cheese, rinsed, patted dry, and crumbled into fine pieces (about 3 cups)
- ¾ cup whole-milk Greek yogurt
- 4 scallions, sliced thin
- 2 large eggs, beaten
- ¼ cup minced fresh mint leaves
- 2 tablespoons minced fresh dill leaves
- 3 medium garlic cloves, minced (about 1 tablespoon)
- 1 teaspoon grated zest plus 1 tablespoon juice from 1 lemon
- 1 teaspoon ground nutmeg
- ½ teaspoon ground black pepper
- ¼ teaspoon table salt
- ⅛ teaspoon cayenne pepper

**PHYLLO LAYERS**

- 7 tablespoons unsalted butter, melted
- 8 ounces (14 by 9-inch) phyllo, thawed
- 1½ ounces Pecorino Romano cheese, grated (¾ cup)
- 2 teaspoons sesame seeds (optional)

**1. FOR THE FILLING:** Place spinach and water in large bowl and cover with large dinner plate. Microwave until spinach is wilted and decreased in volume by half, about 5 minutes. Using pot holders, remove bowl from microwave and keep covered for 1 minute. Carefully remove plate and transfer spinach to colander. Using back of rubber spatula, gently press spinach against colander to release excess liquid. Transfer spinach to cutting board and chop coarse. Transfer the spinach to clean dish towel and squeeze to remove excess water. Place drained spinach in large bowl. Add remaining filling ingredients and mix until thoroughly combined.

**2. FOR THE PHYLLO LAYERS:** Adjust oven rack to lower-middle position and heat oven to 425 degrees. Line rimmed baking sheet with parchment paper. Using pastry brush, lightly brush a 14 by 9-inch rectangle in center of parchment with melted butter to cover area same size as phyllo. Lay 1 phyllo sheet on buttered parchment and brush thoroughly with melted butter. Repeat with 9 more phyllo sheets, brushing each with butter (you should have a total of 10 layers of phyllo).

**3.** Spread spinach mixture evenly over phyllo, leaving ¼-inch border on all sides. Cover spinach with 6 more phyllo sheets, brushing each with butter and sprinkling each with about 2 tablespoons Pecorino cheese. Lay 2 more phyllo sheets on top, brushing each with butter (do not sprinkle these layers with Pecorino).

**4.** Working from center outward, use palms of your hands to compress layers and press out any air pockets. Using sharp knife, score spanakopita through top 3 layers of phyllo into 24 equal pieces. Sprinkle with sesame seeds, if using. Bake until phyllo is golden and crisp, 20 to 25 minutes. Let cool on baking sheet for 10 minutes or up to 2 hours. Slide spanakopita, still on parchment, onto cutting board. Cut into squares and serve.

## Tomato and Mozzarella Tart

**SERVES** 4 to 6

**WHY THIS RECIPE WORKS** Falling somewhere in between pizza and quiche, tomato and mozzarella tart shares the flavors of both but features unique problems. For starters, some sort of pastry crust is required. Second, the moisture in the tomatoes almost guarantees a soggy crust. Third, despite their good looks, tomato tarts often fall short on flavor. We wanted a solid bottom crust and great vine-ripened flavor. Frozen puff pastry was the solution to an easy crust, and prebaking it was a start to solving the problem of sogginess. Sealing the puff pastry shell with an egg wash helped but tomato juice still found its way into the crust. To extract more moisture from the tomatoes before baking, we sliced and salted them, then pressed them lightly between paper towels. But even with a layer of grated mozzarella cheese between tomatoes and crust, the tart shell still came out a bit soggy. Our breakthrough came when we added a layer of grated nutty Parmesan cheese, which sealed the crust fully and repelled moisture. To keep the frozen dough from cracking, it's best to let it thaw slowly in the refrigerator overnight. For the best flavor, use authentic Parmesan cheese and very ripe, flavorful tomatoes. Fresh mozzarella will make the crust soggy, so be sure to use low-moisture, shrink-wrapped mozzarella.

- 1 (9 by 9½-inch) sheet frozen puff pastry, thawed
- 1 large egg, lightly beaten
- 1 ounce Parmesan cheese, grated (½ cup)
- 8 ounces plum tomatoes, cored and sliced ¼ inch thick
- ½ teaspoon table salt
- 4 ounces whole-milk mozzarella cheese, shredded (1 cup)
- 2 tablespoons extra-virgin olive oil
- 1 garlic clove, minced
- 2 tablespoons minced fresh basil

**1.** Adjust oven rack to lowest position and heat oven to 425 degrees. Line large baking sheet with parchment paper. Lay pastry in center of prepared baking sheet. Brush pastry with beaten egg. To form rimmed crust, fold long edges of pastry over by ½ inch, then brush with egg. Fold short edges of pastry over by ½ inch and brush with egg. Use paring knife to cut through folded edges and corner of pastry. Sprinkle Parmesan evenly over crust bottom. Poke dough uniformly with fork. Bake until golden brown and crisp, 15 to 20 minutes. Transfer to wire rack to cool.

**2.** Meanwhile, spread tomatoes over several layers of paper towels. Sprinkle with salt and let drain for 30 minutes.

**PREPARING TOMATO TART PASTRY SHELL**

**1.** Fold short edges of pastry over by ½ inch and brush with egg. Then fold long edges of pastry over by ½ inch, making sure to keep edges flush and square. Brush with egg.

**2.** Using paring knife, cut through folded edges and corners of tart shell. Sprinkle bottom of tart with Parmesan, poke dough repeatedly with fork, and bake.

3. Sprinkle mozzarella evenly over crust bottom. Press excess moisture from tomatoes, using additional paper towels. Shingle tomatoes evenly over mozzarella. Whisk olive oil and garlic together and drizzle over tomatoes. Bake until shell is deep golden, 10 to 15 minutes.

4. Let cool on wire rack for 5 minutes, then sprinkle with basil. Slide tart onto cutting board, slice into pieces, and serve.

## Upside-Down Tomato Tart

**SERVES** 4 to 6

**WHY THIS RECIPE WORKS** A traditional tarte Tatin is prepared with apples, but here we use the formula for tomatoes. The savory-sweet fruit pairs beautifully with buttery pastry and a tangy-sweet sherry vinegar syrup in lieu of caramel. To ensure a crisp—not soggy—crust, we removed the jelly and seeds from plum tomatoes and then roasted them in the syrup for a full hour, which evaporated any excess moisture, concentrated their fruity taste, gave their edges some browning, and enhanced their meaty texture. We topped the roasted tomatoes with puff pastry, a convenient alternative to pie or biscuit dough that needed only to be thawed, rolled, and cut before it was ready to go in the oven. After about 30 minutes of baking, the pastry was puffed, crisp, and golden brown. If you don't have sherry vinegar, cider vinegar is the next best thing. For the proper moisture balance in the tomatoes, use your fingers or a teaspoon to remove as much of the gel and seeds as you can. To thaw frozen puff pastry, let it sit either in the refrigerator for 24 hours or on the counter for 30 minutes to 1 hour. Dimensions of puff pastry sheets vary by brand; if your pastry will accommodate a 10-inch circle, skip the rolling in step 2. This tart is at its best within a couple of hours of baking. Cut the tart into four wedges and serve with salad as a main course or cut it into six wedges and serve as an appetizer.

- ⅓ cup sherry vinegar
- 2½ tablespoons sugar
- ¾ teaspoon table salt, divided
- ½ teaspoon pepper, divided
- 1 medium shallot, chopped fine
- 1 tablespoon unsalted butter
- 2½ teaspoons minced fresh thyme, divided
- 2 pounds plum tomatoes (about 10), cored, halved lengthwise, seeds and gel removed
- 1 sheet puff pastry, thawed but still cool

1. Adjust oven rack to middle position and heat oven to 400 degrees. Bring vinegar, sugar, ½ teaspoon salt, and ¼ teaspoon pepper to simmer in 10-inch ovensafe skillet over medium-high heat, swirling skillet to dissolve sugar. Simmer vigorously, swirling skillet occasionally, until consistency resembles that of maple syrup, about 2 minutes. Add shallot, butter, and 2 teaspoons thyme and whisk until butter is fully incorporated, about 1 minute. Off heat, add tomatoes and toss to coat lightly with syrup. Arrange tomatoes cut sides up in as close to single layer as possible (some overlap is OK; tomatoes will shrink as they cook) and sprinkle with remaining ¼ teaspoon salt and remaining ¼ teaspoon pepper. Transfer to oven and cook until liquid has evaporated and tomatoes are very lightly browned around edges and softened but not fully collapsed, about 1 hour. While tomatoes are cooking, prepare pastry.

2. On lightly floured counter, roll pastry to 10-inch square. Using plate, bowl, or pot lid as template, cut out 10-inch round. Discard trim. Transfer round to large plate and refrigerate until needed. Remove skillet from oven, and place pastry over tomatoes. Bake until pastry is puffed, crisp, and deep golden brown, about 30 minutes, rotating skillet halfway through baking.

3. Let tart cool for 8 minutes. Run paring knife around edge of crust to loosen and invert plate over skillet. Using pot holders, swiftly and carefully invert tart onto plate (if tomatoes or shallots shift or stick to skillet, arrange with spoon). Let cool for 10 minutes and sprinkle with remaining ½ teaspoon thyme. Serve warm or at room temperature.

## Mushroom and Leek Galette with Gorgonzola

**SERVES** 6

**WHY THIS RECIPE WORKS** Most vegetable tarts rely on the same pastry dough used for fruit tarts. But vegetable tarts are more prone to leaking liquid into the crust or falling apart when the tart is sliced. We needed a crust that was extra-sturdy and boasted a complex flavor of its own. To increase the flavor of the crust and keep it tender, we swapped out part of the white flour for nutty whole wheat, and we used butter rather than shortening. To punch up its flaky texture and introduce more structure, we gave the crust a series of folds to create numerous interlocking layers. For a filling that was both flavorful and cohesive, we paired mushrooms and leeks with rich, potent binders like Gorgonzola cheese and crème fraîche. Cutting a few small holes in the dough prevents it from lifting off the pan as it bakes. A pizza stone helps to crisp the crust but is not essential. An overturned baking sheet can be used in place of the pizza stone.

**DOUGH**

- 1¼ cups (6¼ ounces) all-purpose flour
- ½ cup (2¾ ounces) whole-wheat flour
- 1 tablespoon sugar
- ¾ teaspoon table salt
- 10 tablespoons unsalted butter, cut into ½-inch pieces and chilled
- 7 tablespoons ice water
- 1 teaspoon distilled white vinegar

**FILLING**

- 1¼ pounds shiitake mushrooms, stemmed and sliced thin
- 5 teaspoons olive oil, divided
- 1 pound leeks, white and light green parts only, sliced ½ inch thick and washed thoroughly (3 cups)
- 1 teaspoon minced fresh thyme
- 2 tablespoons crème fraîche
- 1 tablespoon Dijon mustard

- 3 ounces Gorgonzola cheese, crumbled (¾ cup)
- 1 large egg, lightly beaten
- Kosher salt
- 2 tablespoons minced fresh parsley

**1. FOR THE DOUGH:** Pulse all-purpose flour, whole-wheat flour, sugar, and salt in food processor until combined, 2 to 3 pulses. Add butter and pulse until it forms pea-size pieces, about 10 pulses. Transfer mixture to medium bowl.

**2.** Sprinkle water and vinegar over mixture. With rubber spatula, use folding motion to mix until loose, shaggy mass forms with some dry flour remaining (do not overwork). Transfer mixture to center of large sheet of plastic wrap, press gently into rough 4-inch square, and wrap tightly. Refrigerate for at least 45 minutes.

**3.** Transfer dough to lightly floured counter. Roll into 11 by 8-inch rectangle with short side of rectangle parallel to edge of counter. Using bench scraper, bring bottom third of dough up, then fold upper third over it, folding like business letter into 8 by 4-inch rectangle. Turn dough 90 degrees counterclockwise. Roll out dough again into 11 by 8-inch rectangle and fold into thirds again. Turn dough 90 degrees counterclockwise and repeat rolling and folding into thirds. After last fold, fold dough in half to create 4-inch square. Press top of dough gently to seal. Wrap in plastic and refrigerate for at least 45 minutes or up to 2 days.

**4. FOR THE FILLING:** Microwave mushrooms in covered bowl until just tender, 3 to 5 minutes. Transfer to colander to drain; return to bowl. Meanwhile, heat 1 tablespoon oil in 12-inch skillet over medium heat until shimmering. Add leeks and thyme, cover, and cook, stirring occasionally, until leeks are tender and beginning to brown, 5 to 7 minutes. Transfer to bowl with mushrooms. Stir in crème fraîche and mustard. Season with salt and pepper to taste. Set aside.

**5.** Adjust oven rack to lower-middle position, place pizza stone on rack, and heat oven to 400 degrees. Line rimmed baking sheet with parchment paper. Remove dough from refrigerator and let stand at room temperature for 15 to 20 minutes. Roll out on generously floured counter (use up to ¼ cup flour) to 14-inch circle about ⅛ inch thick. (Trim edges as needed to form rough circle.) Transfer dough to prepared baking sheet. With tip of paring knife, cut five ¼-inch circles in dough (one at center and four evenly spaced halfway from center to edge of dough). Brush top of dough with 1 teaspoon oil.

**6.** Spread half of filling evenly over dough, leaving 2-inch border around edge. Sprinkle with half of Gorgonzola, cover with remaining filling, and top with remaining Gorgonzola. Drizzle remaining 1 teaspoon oil over filling. Gently grasp 1 edge of dough and fold up outer 2 inches over filling. Repeat around circumference of tart, overlapping dough every 2 to 3 inches; gently pinch pleated dough to secure but do not press dough into filling. Brush dough with egg and sprinkle evenly with kosher salt.

**7.** Lower oven temperature to 375 degrees. Bake until crust is deep golden brown and filling is beginning to brown, 35 to 45 minutes. Let tart cool on baking sheet on wire rack for 10 minutes. Using offset or wide metal spatula, loosen tart from parchment and carefully slide tart off parchment onto cutting board. Sprinkle with parsley, cut into wedges, and serve.

### PLEATING A FREE-FORM TART

Gently grasp 1 edge of dough and make 2-inch-wide fold over filling. Lift and fold another segment of dough over first fold to form pleat. Repeat every 2 to 3 inches.

## Tourte aux Pommes de Terre (French Potato Pie)

**SERVES** 6 to 8

**WHY THIS RECIPE WORKS** Myriad versions of this decadent and delicious potato and cream pie recipe—known as tourte aux pommes de terre or pâté aux pommes de terre—exist throughout central France. Though many are made using puff pastry, we opted for somewhat less common pâte brisée (aka pie dough) for its crisp, sturdy texture. While many traditional recipes call for adding the cream through a vent hole in the top crust, we found it more practical to parboil the potatoes in water, drain them, and return them to the pot to simmer for a

few minutes with the cream. This eliminated the guesswork of determining exactly how much cream the potato slices could absorb without the pie ending up runny or loose. To ensure that the cream fully coated the potatoes, we added a pinch of baking soda to the cooking water to help break down the potatoes' exteriors and release starch that would thicken the cream. We strongly recommend measuring the flour for the pie crust by weight. The potatoes can be sliced on a mandoline. Serve as a main course with a salad or in small slices as a side dish.

**CRUST**

- 20 tablespoons (2½ sticks) unsalted butter, chilled, divided
- 2½ cups (12½ ounces) all-purpose flour, divided
- 1 teaspoon table salt
- ½ cup ice water, divided

**FILLING**

- 1 onion, halved and sliced thin
- 1½ teaspoons table salt
- 2 pounds Yukon Gold potatoes, peeled and sliced crosswise ⅛ inch thick
- ½ teaspoon baking soda
- 1¼ cups heavy cream
- 3 garlic cloves, minced
- ½ teaspoon pepper
- ¼ teaspoon ground nutmeg
- 2 tablespoons minced fresh parsley
- 1 egg, lightly beaten

**1. FOR THE CRUST:** Shred 4 tablespoons butter on large holes of box grater and place in freezer. Cut remaining 16 tablespoons butter into ½-inch cubes.

**2.** Pulse 1½ cups flour and salt in food processor until combined, 2 pulses. Add cubed butter and process until homogeneous paste forms, 40 to 50 seconds. Using your hands, carefully break paste into 2-inch chunks and redistribute evenly around processor blade. Add remaining 1 cup flour and pulse until mixture is broken into pieces no larger than 1 inch (most pieces will be much smaller), 4 to 5 pulses. Transfer mixture to medium bowl. Add shredded butter and toss until butter pieces are separated and coated with flour.

**3.** Sprinkle ¼ cup ice water over mixture. Toss with rubber spatula until mixture is evenly moistened. Sprinkle remaining ¼ cup ice water over mixture and toss to combine. Press dough with spatula until dough sticks together. Use spatula to divide dough into 2 portions. Transfer each portion to sheet of plastic wrap. Working with 1 portion at a time, draw edges of plastic over dough and press firmly on sides and top to form compact, fissure-free mass; wrap in plastic and form into 5-inch disk. Refrigerate dough for at least 2 hours or up to 2 days. Let chilled dough sit on counter until softened slightly, about 10 minutes, before rolling. (Wrapped dough can be frozen for up to 1 month. If frozen, let dough thaw completely on counter before rolling.)

**4. FOR THE FILLING:** One hour before baking pie, make filling. Toss onion and salt in bowl and set aside. Bring 4 quarts water to boil in Dutch oven over high heat. Add potatoes and baking soda. Return to boil and cook for 1 minute. Drain potatoes. Return potatoes to pot; add cream, garlic, pepper, nutmeg, and onion and any accumulated liquid; and bring to simmer over high heat. Adjust heat to maintain simmer and cook, stirring gently and frequently (it's OK if some slices break), until cream thickens and begins to coat potatoes, about 5 minutes. Let cool off heat for at least 30 minutes or up to 2 hours.

**5.** Roll 1 disk of dough into 12-inch round on well-floured counter. Loosely roll dough around rolling pin and gently unroll onto 9-inch pie plate, letting excess dough hang over edge. Ease dough into plate by gently lifting edge of dough with your hand while pressing into plate bottom with your other hand. Refrigerate until dough is firm, about 30 minutes. Roll second disk of dough into 12-inch round on well-floured counter, then transfer to parchment paper–lined baking sheet; refrigerate for 30 minutes. Adjust oven rack to lower-middle position and heat oven to 450 degrees.

**6.** Stir parsley into potato mixture, transfer mixture to dough-lined pie plate, and spread into even layer (it's OK if potato mixture is still slightly warm). Using paring knife or round cutter, cut ½-inch hole in center of second dough round. Loosely roll dough round around rolling pin and gently unroll it over filling, aligning hole with center of pie and leaving at least ½-inch overhang all around. Fold dough under itself so edge of fold is flush with outer rim of pie plate. Flute edges using your thumb and forefinger or press with tines of fork to seal. Place pie on parchment-lined rimmed baking sheet and brush with egg. Bake until top is light golden brown, 18 to 20 minutes.

**7.** Reduce oven temperature to 325 degrees and continue to bake until crust is deep golden brown and potatoes at vent hole are tender when pricked with paring knife, 30 to 40 minutes longer. If pie begins to get too brown before potatoes are softened, cover loosely with aluminum foil. Let pie cool on wire rack for at least 30 minutes. Serve warm or at room temperature.

## Summer Vegetable Gratin

**SERVES** 6 to 8

**WHY THIS RECIPE WORKS** Layering summer's best vegetables into a gratin can lead to a memorable side dish—or a soggy mess. Juicy vegetables like zucchini and tomatoes can exude a torrent of liquid that washes away flavors. We wanted a simple, Provençal-style vegetable gratin, where a golden brown, cheesy topping provides a rich contrast to the fresh, bright flavor of the vegetables. The typical combination of tomatoes, zucchini, and yellow summer squash won out. To eliminate excess moisture, we baked the casserole uncovered. Salting both seasoned and dried out the zucchini and summer squash, but proved insufficient to deal with all the tomato juice. The watery jelly and seeds from the tomatoes were crucial for full tomato flavor, so we moved the tomatoes to the top layer, to roast and caramelize. The roasting added flavor as did garlic-thyme oil. We also added a layer of caramelized onions between the zucchini-squash and tomato layers. The success of this recipe depends on good-quality produce. Buy zucchini and summer squash of roughly the same diameter. If desired, you can also use just one or the other. A similarly sized oven-safe gratin dish can be substituted for the 13 by 9-inch baking dish. Serve the gratin alongside grilled fish or meat, accompanied by bread to soak up any flavorful juices.

- 6 tablespoons extra-virgin olive oil
- 1 pound zucchini, ends trimmed and cut crosswise into ¼-inch-thick slices
- 1 pound yellow summer squash, ends trimmed and cut crosswise into ¼-inch-thick slices
- 2 teaspoons table salt
- 1½ pounds ripe tomatoes (3 to 4 large), cut into ¼-inch-thick slices
- 2 medium onions, halved pole to pole and sliced thin (about 3 cups)
- ¾ teaspoon ground black pepper
- 2 medium garlic cloves, minced or pressed through a garlic press (about 2 teaspoons)
- 1 tablespoon minced fresh thyme leaves
- 1 slice high-quality white sandwich bread, torn into quarters
- 2 ounces grated Parmesan cheese (about 1 cup)
- 2 medium shallots, minced (about 6 tablespoons)
- ¼ cup chopped fresh basil leaves

**1.** Adjust an oven rack to the upper-middle position and heat the oven to 400 degrees. Brush a 13 by 9-inch baking dish with 1 tablespoon of the oil; set aside.

**2.** Toss the zucchini and summer squash slices with 1 teaspoon of the salt in a large bowl; transfer to a colander set over a bowl. Let stand until the zucchini and squash release at least 3 tablespoons of liquid, about 45 minutes. Arrange the slices on a triple layer of paper towels; cover with another triple layer of paper towels. Firmly press each slice to remove as much liquid as possible.

**3.** Place the tomato slices in a single layer on a double layer of paper towels and sprinkle evenly with ½ teaspoon more salt; let stand for 30 minutes. Place a second double layer of paper towels on top of the tomatoes and press firmly to dry the tomatoes.

**4.** Meanwhile, heat 1 tablespoon more oil in a 12-inch nonstick skillet over medium heat until shimmering. Add the onions, the remaining ½ teaspoon salt, and ¼ teaspoon of the pepper; cook, stirring occasionally, until the onions are softened and dark golden brown, 20 to 25 minutes. Set the onions aside.

**5.** Combine the garlic, 3 tablespoons more oil, the remaining ½ teaspoon pepper, and the thyme in a small bowl. In a large bowl, toss the zucchini and summer squash in half of the oil mixture, then arrange in the greased baking dish. Arrange the caramelized onions in an even layer over the squash. Slightly overlap the tomato slices in a single layer on top of the onions. Spoon the remaining garlic-oil mixture evenly over the tomatoes. Bake until the vegetables are tender and the tomatoes are starting to brown on the edges, 40 to 45 minutes.

**6.** Meanwhile, process the bread in a food processor until finely ground, about 10 seconds. (You should have about 1 cup crumbs.) Combine the bread crumbs, remaining 1 tablespoon oil, the Parmesan, and shallots in a medium bowl. Remove the baking dish from the oven and increase the heat to 450 degrees. Sprinkle the bread crumb mixture evenly on top of the tomatoes. Bake the gratin until bubbling and the cheese is lightly browned, 5 to 10 minutes. Sprinkle with the basil and cool for 10 minutes before serving.

## Walkaway Ratatouille

**SERVES** 6 to 8

**WHY THIS RECIPE WORKS** Classic ratatouille recipes call for cutting vegetables into small pieces, labor- and time-intensive pretreatments like salting and/or pressing the vegetables to remove excess moisture, and cooking them in batches on the stovetop. Our secret to great yet easy ratatouille? Overcook some of the vegetables, barely cook the others—and let the oven do the work. Our streamlined recipe starts by sautéing onions and aromatics and then adding chunks of eggplant and tomatoes before moving the pot to the oven, where the dry, ambient heat thoroughly evaporated moisture, concentrated flavors, and caramelized some of the veggies. After 45 minutes, the tomatoes and eggplant became meltingly soft and could be mashed into a thick, silky sauce. Zucchini and bell peppers went into the pot last so that they retained some texture. Finishing the dish with fresh herbs, a splash of sherry vinegar, and a drizzle of extra-virgin olive oil tied everything together. This dish is best prepared using ripe, in-season tomatoes. If good tomatoes are not available, substitute 1 (28-ounce) can of whole peeled tomatoes that have been drained, rinsed, and chopped coarse. Ratatouille can be served as an accompaniment to meat or fish. It can also be served on its own with crusty bread, topped with an egg, or over pasta or rice. This dish can be served warm, at room temperature, or chilled.

- ⅓ cup extra-virgin olive oil, plus extra for serving
- 2 large onions, cut into 1-inch pieces
- 8 large garlic cloves, peeled and smashed
- Table salt and pepper
- 1½ teaspoons herbes de Provence
- ¼ teaspoon red pepper flakes
- 1 bay leaf
- 1½ pounds eggplant, peeled and cut into 1-inch pieces
- 2 pounds plum tomatoes, peeled and chopped coarse
- 2 small zucchini, halved lengthwise and cut into 1-inch pieces
- 1 red bell pepper, stemmed, seeded, and cut into 1-inch pieces
- 1 yellow bell pepper, stemmed, seeded, and cut into 1-inch pieces
- 2 tablespoons chopped fresh basil
- 1 tablespoon minced fresh parsley
- 1 tablespoon sherry vinegar

**1.** Adjust oven rack to middle position and heat oven to 400 degrees. Heat oil in Dutch oven over medium-high heat until shimmering. Add onions, garlic, 1 teaspoon salt, and ¼ teaspoon pepper and cook, stirring occasionally, until onions are starting to soften and have become translucent, about 10 minutes. Add herbes de Provence, pepper flakes, and bay leaf and cook, stirring frequently, for 1 minute. Stir in eggplant and tomatoes. Sprinkle with ½ teaspoon salt and ¼ teaspoon pepper and stir to combine. Transfer pot to oven and cook, uncovered, until vegetables are very tender and spotty brown, 40 to 45 minutes.

**2.** Remove pot from oven and, using potato masher or heavy wooden spoon, smash and stir eggplant mixture until broken down into sauce-like consistency. Stir in zucchini, bell peppers, ¼ teaspoon salt, and ¼ teaspoon pepper and return to oven. Cook, uncovered, until zucchini and peppers are just tender, 20 to 25 minutes.

**3.** Remove pot from oven, cover, and let stand until zucchini is translucent and easily pierced with tip of paring knife, 10 to 15 minutes. Using wooden spoon, scrape any browned bits from sides of pot and stir back into ratatouille. Stir in 1 tablespoon basil, parsley, and vinegar. Season with salt and pepper to taste. Transfer to large platter, drizzle with 1 tablespoon oil, sprinkle with remaining 1 tablespoon basil, and serve.

## Classic Grilled Cheese Sandwiches

**SERVES 2**

**WHY THIS RECIPE WORKS** The perfect grilled cheese consists of evenly melted cheese between crisp bread, but most don't turn out that way. We set out to find the keys to the ideal sandwich. We found that grating the cheese on a box grater enabled us to get an even layer of cheese onto the bread. Butter melted in the pan sometimes burned and didn't always coat the bread evenly, so we opted to butter the bread rather than the pan. And to coat the bread evenly and prevent it from tearing, we melted the butter first. Finally, we learned that the secret of a crisp exterior is low heat; the longer it takes for the bread to become golden, the crispier the bread will become—these are grilled cheese sandwiches worth the wait. The traditional grilled cheese sandwich usually uses a mild cheddar cheese, but our technique for this sandwich works with most any cheese. Grilled cheese sandwiches are best served hot out of the pan, though in a pinch they can be held, unsliced, for up to 20 minutes in a warm oven. If you want to make more than two sandwiches at once, get two skillets going or use an electric griddle set at medium-low (about 250 degrees), grilling 10 minutes per side. The possible variations on the basic grilled cheese sandwich are endless, but the extras are best sandwiched between the cheese. Try a few very thin slices of baked ham, prosciutto, turkey breast, or ripe, in-season tomato. Condiments such as Dijon mustard, pickle relish, or chutney can be spread on the bread instead of sandwiched in the cheese.

- 3 ounces cheese (preferably mild cheddar) or a combination of cheeses, shredded on the large holes of a box grater (about ¾ cup)
- 4 slices high-quality white sandwich bread
- 2 tablespoons unsalted butter, melted

**1.** Heat a heavy 12-inch skillet over low to medium-low heat. Meanwhile, sprinkle the cheese evenly over two bread slices. Top each with a remaining bread slice, pressing down gently to set.

**2.** Brush the sandwich tops completely with half of the melted butter; place each sandwich, buttered side down, in the skillet. Brush the remaining side of each sandwich completely with the remaining butter. Cook until crisp and deep golden brown, 5 to 10 minutes per side, flipping the sandwiches back to the first side to reheat and crisp, about 15 seconds. Serve immediately.

## Grown-Up Grilled Cheese Sandwiches with Cheddar and Shallots

**SERVES** 4

**WHY THIS RECIPE WORKS** Melty American cheese on fluffy white bread is a childhood classic, but we wanted a grilled cheese for adults that offered more robust flavor. Aged cheddar gave us the complexity we were after, but it made for a greasy sandwich with a grainy filling. Adding a splash of wine and some Brie helped the aged cheddar melt evenly without separating or becoming greasy. Using a food processor to combine the ingredients ensured our cheese-and-wine mixture was easy to spread. A little bit of shallot ramped up the flavor without detracting from the cheese, and a smear of mustard butter livened up the bread. For the best flavor, look for a cheddar aged for about one year (avoid cheddar aged for longer; it won't melt well in this recipe). To quickly bring the cheese to room temperature, microwave the pieces until warm, about 30 seconds. The first two sandwiches can be held in a 200-degree oven on a wire rack set in a baking sheet while the second batch cooks.

- 7 ounces aged cheddar cheese, cut into 24 equal pieces, room temperature
- 2 ounces Brie cheese, rind removed
- 2 tablespoons dry white wine or dry vermouth
- 4 teaspoons minced shallot
- 3 tablespoons unsalted butter, softened
- 1 teaspoon Dijon mustard
- 8 slices hearty white sandwich bread

**1.** Process cheddar, Brie, and wine in food processor until smooth paste is formed, 20 to 30 seconds. Add shallot and pulse to combine, 3 to 5 pulses. Combine butter and mustard in small bowl.

**2.** Working on parchment paper–lined counter, divide mustard butter evenly among slices of bread. Spread butter evenly over surface of bread. Flip 4 slices of bread over and spread cheese mixture evenly over slices. Top with remaining 4 slices of bread, buttered sides up.

**3.** Preheat 12-inch nonstick skillet over medium heat for 2 minutes. (Droplets of water should just sizzle when flicked onto pan.) Place 2 sandwiches in skillet, reduce heat to medium-low, and cook until both sides are crisp and golden brown, 6 to 9 minutes per side, moving sandwiches to ensure even browning. Remove sandwiches from skillet and let stand for 2 minutes before serving. Repeat with remaining 2 sandwiches.

### Grown-Up Grilled Cheese Sandwiches with Gruyère and Chives

Substitute Gruyère cheese for cheddar, chives for shallot, and rye sandwich bread for white sandwich bread.

## Quesadillas

**MAKES** 2 folded 8-inch quesadillas

**WHY THIS RECIPE WORKS** A traditional quesadilla is meant to be a quick snack, not an overstuffed tortilla with complicated fillings. We wanted a simple toasted tortilla, crisp and hot, filled with just the right amount of cheese. We kept the tortillas crisp by lightly toasting them in a dry skillet. We then filled them with cheese and pickled jalapeños, lightly coated the tortillas with oil, and returned them to the skillet until they were well browned and the cheese was fully melted. Not yet satisfied that our recipe was speedy enough, we made the process even more convenient by switching to 8-inch tortillas and folding them in half around the filling. This allowed us to cook two at one time in the same skillet, and the fold also kept our generous cheese filling from oozing out. Cooling the quesadillas before cutting and serving them is important; straight from the skillet, the melted cheese will ooze out. Finished quesadillas can be held on a baking sheet in a 200-degree oven for up to 20 minutes.

- 2 (8-inch) flour tortillas
- 2 ounces Monterey Jack or cheddar cheese, shredded (½ cup)
- 1 tablespoon minced pickled jalapeños (optional)
- Vegetable oil for brushing tortillas
- Kosher salt

**1.** Heat 10-inch nonstick skillet over medium heat until hot, about 2 minutes. Place 1 tortilla in skillet and toast until soft and puffed slightly at the edges, about 2 minutes. Flip tortilla and toast until puffed and slightly browned, 1 to 2 minutes longer. Transfer tortilla to cutting board. Repeat to toast second tortilla while assembling first quesadilla. Sprinkle ¼ cup cheese and half of jalapeños, if using, over half of tortilla, leaving ½-inch border around edge. Fold tortilla in half and press to flatten. Brush top generously with oil, sprinkle lightly with kosher salt, and set aside. Repeat to form second quesadilla.

**2.** Place both quesadillas in skillet, oiled sides down; cook over medium heat until crisp and well browned, 1 to 2 minutes. Brush tops with oil and sprinkle lightly with kosher salt. Flip quesadillas and cook until second sides are crisp, 1 to 2 minutes. Transfer quesadillas to cutting board; let cool for 3 minutes, halve each quesadilla, and serve.

### Corn and Black Bean Quesadillas with Pepper Jack Cheese

Heat 10-inch nonstick skillet over medium-high heat until hot, about 2 minutes. Add ⅓ cup thawed frozen corn kernels and cook, stirring occasionally, until kernels begin to brown and pop, 3 to 5 minutes; transfer corn to medium bowl. Heat 2 teaspoons vegetable oil in now-empty skillet over medium heat until shimmering; add ⅓ cup minced red onion and cook, stirring occasionally, until softened, about 3 minutes. Add 1 teaspoon minced garlic and ½ teaspoon chili powder and cook until fragrant, about 1 minute; stir in ⅓ cup drained canned black beans and cook until heated through, about 1 minute. Return corn to skillet and toss to combine; gently press mixture with spatula to lightly crush black beans. Transfer mixture to now-empty bowl, stir in 2 teaspoons lime juice, and season to taste with salt. Wipe out skillet with paper towels and return pan to medium heat until hot, about 2 minutes. After toasting tortillas as directed, assemble first quesadilla by sprinkling ⅓ cup cheese, half the corn and bean mixture, and half of jalapeños, if using, over half of tortilla, leaving ½-inch border around edge. Fold tortilla in half and press to flatten. Brush surface generously with oil, sprinkle lightly with salt, and set aside. Repeat to form second quesadilla. Place both quesadillas in skillet, oiled sides down, and cook as directed.

## Pupusas

**MAKES** 8 pupusas

**WHY THIS RECIPE WORKS** These savory stuffed corn cakes have a long history in Honduras and El Salvador, where they're made by stuffing cheese, beans, braised meat, or a combination thereof into a ball of corn flour dough called masa. For smooth, well-hydrated dough that was easy to work with and didn't dry out when cooked, we hydrated the masa harina with boiling water which allowed the starches in the flour to absorb it quickly and completely. We pressed the stuffed pupusas into 4-inch disks between sheets of plastic to create a uniform thickness; this size also allowed us to cook four pupusas at once in a 12-inch skillet. The crunch and acidic brightness of curtido and salsa perfectly complemented the tender, savory patties. For an accurate measurement of boiling water, bring a full kettle of water to a boil and then measure out the desired amount. Properly hydrated masa dough should be tacky, requiring damp hands to keep it from sticking to your palms. An occasional leak while frying the pupusas is to be expected, and the browned cheese is delicious. Feta cheese can be substituted for the cotija; if you can find quesillo, use 10 ounces in place of the cotija and Monterey Jack.

- 2 cups (8 ounces) masa harina
- ½ teaspoon table salt
- 2 cups boiling water, plus warm tap water as needed
- 2 teaspoons vegetable oil, divided
- 2 ounces cotija cheese, cut into 2 pieces
- 8 ounces Monterey Jack cheese, cut into 8 pieces
- 1 recipe Quick Salsa (page 576)
- 1 recipe Curtido (page 576)

1. Using marker, draw 4-inch circle in center of 1 side of 1-quart or 1-gallon zipper-lock bag. Cut open seams along both sides of bag, but leave bottom seam intact so bag opens completely.

### SHAPING PUPUSAS

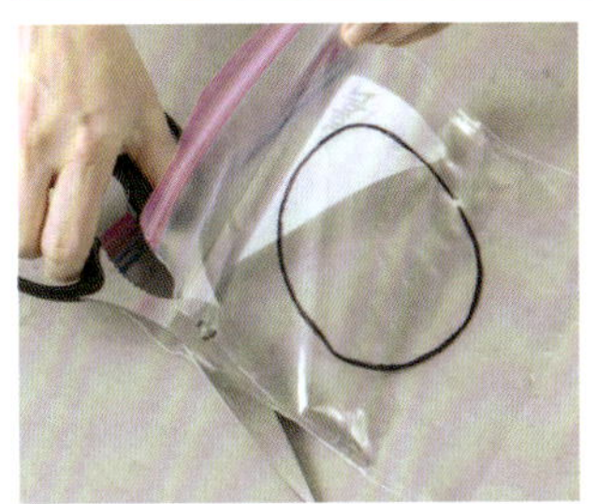

**1.** Using marker, draw 4-inch circle in center of 1 side of 1-quart or 1-gallon zipper-lock bag. Cut open seams along both sides of bag, but leave bottom seam intact so bag opens completely.

**2.** Place open cut bag marked side down on counter. Place dough ball in center of circle. Fold other side of bag over ball. Using glass pie plate, gently press dough to 4-inch diameter.

**3.** Turn out disk into your palm and place cheese ball in center. Bring sides of dough up around filling; pinch to seal. Remoisten your hands and roll ball, smoothing any cracks with your damp fingertip.

**4.** Return ball to zipper-lock bag and use pie plate to slowly press to 4-inch diameter. Pinch closed any small cracks that form at edges. Repeat steps 2 through 4 with remaining dough and filling.

**2.** Mix masa harina and salt together in medium bowl. Add boiling water and 1 teaspoon oil and mix with rubber spatula until soft dough forms. Cover dough and let rest for 20 minutes.

**3.** While dough rests, line rimmed baking sheet with parchment paper. Process cotija in food processor until cotija is finely chopped and resembles wet sand, about 20 seconds. Add Monterey Jack and process until mixture resembles wet oatmeal, about 30 seconds (it will not form cohesive mass). Remove processor blade. Form cheese mixture into 8 balls, weighing about 1¼ ounces each, and place balls on 1 half of prepared sheet.

**4.** Knead dough in bowl for 15 to 20 seconds. Test dough's hydration by flattening golf ball–size piece. If cracks larger than ¼ inch form around edges, add warm tap water, 2 teaspoons at a time, until dough is soft and slightly tacky. Transfer dough to counter, shape into large ball, and divide into 8 equal pieces. Using your damp hands, roll 1 dough piece into ball and place on empty half of prepared sheet. Cover with damp dish towel. Repeat with remaining dough pieces.

**5.** Place open cut bag marked side down on counter. Place 1 dough ball in center of circle. Fold other side of bag over ball. Using glass pie plate or 8-inch square baking dish, gently press dough to 4-inch diameter, using circle drawn on bag as guide. Turn out disk into your palm and place 1 cheese ball in center. Bring sides of dough up around filling and pinch top to seal. Remoisten your hands and roll ball until smooth, smoothing any cracks with your damp fingertip. Return ball to bag and slowly press to 4-inch diameter. Pinch closed any small cracks that form at edges. Return pupusa to sheet and cover with damp dish towel. Repeat with remaining dough and filling.

**6.** Heat remaining 1 teaspoon oil in 12-inch nonstick skillet over medium-high heat until shimmering. Wipe skillet clean with paper towels. Carefully lay 4 pupusas in skillet and cook until spotty brown on both sides, 2 to 4 minutes per side. Transfer to platter and repeat with remaining 4 pupusas. Serve warm with salsa and curtido.

### Quick Salsa

**SERVES 4**

For a spicier salsa, add the jalapeño seeds as desired.

- ¼ small red onion
- 2 tablespoons minced fresh cilantro
- ½ small jalapeño chile, seeded and minced
- 1 (14.5-ounce) can diced tomatoes, drained
- 2 teaspoons lime juice, plus extra for seasoning
- 1 small garlic clove, minced
- ¼ teaspoon table salt
- Pinch pepper

Pulse onion, cilantro, and jalapeño in food processor until finely chopped, 5 pulses, scraping down sides of bowl as needed. Add tomatoes, lime juice, garlic, salt, and pepper and process until smooth, 20 to 30 seconds. Season with salt and extra lime juice to taste.

### Curtido

**SERVES 4**

For a spicier slaw, add the jalapeño seeds as desired.

- 1 cup cider vinegar
- ½ cup water
- 1 tablespoon sugar
- 1½ teaspoons table salt
- ½ head green cabbage, cored and sliced thin (6 cups)
- 1 onion, sliced thin
- 1 large carrot, peeled and shredded
- 1 jalapeño chile, stemmed, seeded, and minced
- 1 teaspoon dried oregano
- 1 cup chopped fresh cilantro

Whisk vinegar, water, sugar, and salt in large bowl until sugar is dissolved. Add cabbage, onion, carrot, jalapeño, and oregano and toss to combine. Cover and refrigerate for at least 1 hour or up to 24 hours. Toss slaw, then drain. Return slaw to bowl and stir in cilantro.

## Vegan Baja-Style Cauliflower Tacos

**SERVES 4 to 6**

---

**WHY THIS RECIPE WORKS** Battered cauliflower bites, drizzled with a cool and creamy sauce, can serve as an incredible vegan stand-in for the fried fish traditionally served in Baja-style tacos. We wanted to avoid the mess of deep frying, so we cut the cauliflower into large florets and roasted it. To boost the cauliflower's flavor, we first dunked the pieces in canned coconut milk seasoned with garlic and spices and then rolled them in a mixture of panko bread crumbs and shredded coconut. Not only did this add richness and tropical flavor, but it also mimicked the crisp exterior texture of batter-fried fish. A bed of crunchy slaw with juicy mango and spicy jalapeño provided the perfect balance of sweetness and heat. By using equal parts vegan mayonnaise and dairy-free sour cream, plus cilantro, we were able to whip up a vegan crema to top it all off. Just add cerveza and sunshine. For a spicier slaw, mince and add the jalapeño ribs and seeds. Serve with lime wedges.

- 3 cups (7½ ounces) coleslaw mix
- ½ mango, peeled and cut into ¼-inch pieces (¾ cup)
- 1 tablespoon chopped fresh cilantro
- 2 tablespoons lime juice
- 1 tablespoon minced jalapeño chile
- 1¼ teaspoons table salt, divided
- 1 cup unsweetened shredded coconut
- 1 cup panko bread crumbs
- 1 cup canned coconut milk
- 1 teaspoon garlic powder
- 1 teaspoon ground cumin
- ¼ teaspoon cayenne
- ½ head cauliflower (1 pound), trimmed and cut into 1-inch pieces
- 8–12 (6-inch) corn tortillas, warmed
- 1 recipe Vegan Cilantro Sauce

1. Adjust oven rack to middle position and heat oven to 450 degrees. Combine coleslaw mix, mango, cilantro, lime juice, jalapeño, and ¼ teaspoon salt in bowl; cover and refrigerate.

2. Spray rimmed baking sheet with vegetable oil spray. Combine coconut and panko in shallow dish. Whisk coconut milk, garlic powder, cumin, cayenne, and remaining 1 teaspoon salt together in bowl. Add cauliflower to coconut milk mixture; toss to coat well. Working with 1 piece cauliflower at a time, remove from coconut milk, letting excess drip back into bowl, then coat well with coconut-panko mixture, pressing gently to adhere; transfer to prepared sheet.

3. Bake until cauliflower is tender, golden, and crisp, 20 to 25 minutes, flipping cauliflower and rotating sheet halfway through baking.

4. Divide slaw evenly among warm tortillas and top with cauliflower. Drizzle with cilantro sauce and serve.

## Vegan Cilantro Sauce

**MAKES** about ¾ cup

We prefer the flavor and texture of Tofutti Better Than Sour Cream. Other dairy-free sour creams will add their distinctive flavor, and you may need to adjust the consistency with water. Our favorite vegan mayonnaise brands are Hellman's Plant Based Mayo Spread and Dressing and Follow Your Heart Original Vegenaise

- ¼ cup vegan mayonnaise
- ¼ cup dairy-free sour cream
- 3 tablespoons water
- 3 tablespoons minced fresh cilantro
- ¼ teaspoon table salt

Whisk all ingredients together in bowl.

# Ultimate Veggie Burgers

**MAKES** 12 patties

**WHY THIS RECIPE WORKS** For veggie burgers with complex, savory flavor and a satisfyingly robust texture good enough to be worth the effort, we used a combination of quick-cooking, meaty lentils and bulgur as the base. As a bonus, these burgers can be made ahead and frozen for a quick weeknight meal. An earthy mix of lentils, bulgur, and panko paired with aromatic onions, celery, leek, and garlic gave these burgers a deeply flavorful base. Cremini mushrooms lent meaty flavor, and a surprising addition of ground cashews amplified the meatiness even more. Pulsing everything in the food processor made for a cohesive and even-textured mix, and mayonnaise provided necessary fat to bind our burgers. After forming the mixture into patties, we seared them in a skillet to develop a crunchy, browned exterior. Do not confuse bulgur for cracked wheat, which has a much longer cooking time and will not work in this recipe.

- ¾ cup brown lentils, picked over and rinsed
- 1 teaspoon table salt, plus salt for cooking lentils and bulgur
- ¾ cup medium-grind bulgur, rinsed
- ¼ cup vegetable oil, divided, plus extra as needed
- 2 onions, chopped fine
- 1 celery rib, chopped fine
- 1 small leek, white and light green parts only, halved lengthwise, chopped fine, and washed thoroughly
- 2 garlic cloves, minced
- 1 pound cremini or white mushrooms, trimmed and sliced ¼ inch thick
- 1 cup raw cashews
- ⅓ cup mayonnaise
- 2 cups panko bread crumbs
- 4–12 hamburger buns, toasted if desired

1. Bring 3 cups water, lentils, and 1 teaspoon salt to boil in medium saucepan over high heat. Reduce heat to medium-low and simmer gently, stirring occasionally, until lentils are just beginning to fall apart, about 25 minutes. Drain lentils, spread out over paper towel–lined rimmed baking sheet, and pat dry; let cool to room temperature.

### RINSING GRAINS

We recommend rinsing and draining grains before cooking to remove excess surface starch. Place grain (or rice) in fine-mesh strainer and rinse under cool water until water runs clear, occasionally stirring lightly with your hand. Let drain briefly.

**2.** Bring 2 cups water and ½ teaspoon salt to boil in small saucepan. Off heat, stir in bulgur, cover, and let sit until tender, 15 to 20 minutes. Drain bulgur, pressing with rubber spatula to remove excess moisture, and transfer to large bowl; let cool slightly.

**3.** Heat 1 tablespoon oil in 12-inch nonstick skillet over medium-high heat until shimmering. Add onions, celery, leek, and garlic and cook, stirring occasionally, until vegetables begin to brown, about 10 minutes. Spread vegetable mixture onto second rimmed baking sheet.

**4.** Heat 1 tablespoon oil in now-empty skillet over high heat until shimmering. Add mushrooms and cook, stirring occasionally, until golden brown, about 12 minutes; add to baking sheet with other vegetables and let cool to room temperature, about 20 minutes.

**5.** Pulse cashews in food processor until finely chopped, about 15 pulses. Stir cashews into bulgur, then stir in cooled lentils, vegetable-mushroom mixture, and mayonnaise. Working in 2 batches, pulse mixture in now-empty food processor until coarsely chopped, 15 to 20 pulses (mixture should be cohesive but roughly textured); transfer to clean bowl.

**6.** Stir in panko and salt. Divide mixture into 12 equal portions (about ½ cup each), then tightly pack each portion into ½-inch-thick patty. (Patties can be refrigerated for up to 3 days or frozen for up to 1 month.) To freeze, transfer patties to 2 parchment paper–lined rimmed baking sheets and freeze until firm, about 1 hour. Stack patties, separated by parchment paper; wrap in plastic.

**7. TO COOK BURGERS:** Heat remaining 2 tablespoons oil in 12-inch nonstick skillet over medium-high heat until shimmering. Place 4 patties in skillet and cook until well browned on first side, about 4 minutes. Using 2 spatulas, gently flip patties and continue to cook until well browned on second side, about 4 minutes, adding extra oil as needed if skillet looks dry. Transfer burgers to platter, wipe skillet clean with paper towels, and repeat with extra oil and remaining patties as desired. (If patties were previously frozen, transfer to wire rack set in rimmed baking sheet and bake in 350-degree oven until heated through, about 10 minutes.) Serve burgers on buns.

## Black Bean Burgers

**SERVES 6**

**WHY THIS RECIPE WORKS** As with many meatless patties, black bean burgers often get their structure from fillers that rob them of any trace of black bean flavor. We wanted that key ingredient to shine in our burgers. For convenient and reliable beans, we turned to canned, rinsing and drying them completely to eliminate cohesion-compromising moisture. Eggs and flour served as our binding agents, and adding minced scallions, cilantro, and garlic contributed some personality. We stirred in a couple of spices with major impact—cumin and coriander—plus a hit of hot sauce for zip. In keeping with our Latin American flavor profile, we turned to the bright corn flavor of tortilla chips to build up our burger mix. After blitzing crushed chips in the food processor, we added in the beans and pulsed them into coarsely chopped pieces. We combined the beans with the flour-egg binder and refrigerated the mixture, allowing the starches to absorb some of the eggs' moisture. After an hour, we formed patties and cooked the burgers in an oiled skillet. After a quick browning on each side, these burgers were ready to serve with all of our favorite fixings. When forming the patties it is important to pack them firmly together. Serve the burgers with your favorite toppings or with Chipotle Mayonnaise (recipe follows).

- 2 (15-ounce) cans black beans, rinsed
- 2 large eggs
- 2 tablespoons all-purpose flour
- 4 scallions, minced (¼ cup)
- 3 tablespoons minced fresh cilantro
- 2 garlic cloves, minced
- 1 teaspoon ground cumin
- ½ teaspoon ground coriander
- ¼ teaspoon table salt
- ¼ teaspoon pepper
- 1 teaspoon hot sauce (optional)
- 1 ounce tortilla chips, crushed coarse (½ cup)
- 8 teaspoons vegetable oil, divided
- 6 burger buns

**1.** Line rimmed baking sheet with triple layer of paper towels and spread black beans over towels. Let stand for 15 minutes.

**2.** Whisk eggs and flour in large bowl until uniform paste forms. Stir in scallions; cilantro; garlic; cumin; coriander; salt; pepper; and hot sauce, if using, until well combined.

**3.** Process tortilla chips in food processor until finely ground, about 30 seconds. Add black beans and pulse until beans are roughly broken down, about 5 pulses. Transfer black bean mixture to bowl with egg mixture and mix until well combined. Cover and refrigerate for at least 1 hour or up to 24 hours.

**4.** Divide bean mixture into 6 equal portions. Firmly pack each portion into tight ball, then flatten to 3½-inch patty. (Patties can be wrapped individually in plastic wrap, placed in a zipper-lock bag, and frozen for up to 2 weeks. Thaw patties before cooking.)

**5.** Heat 2 teaspoons oil in 10-inch nonstick skillet over medium heat until shimmering. Carefully lay 3 patties in skillet and cook until bottoms are well-browned and crisp, about 5 minutes. Flip patties, add 2 teaspoons oil, and cook second sides until well-browned and crisp, 3 to 5 minutes. Transfer patties to buns and repeat with remaining 3 patties and 4 teaspoons oil. Serve.

### Chipotle Mayonnaise

**MAKES** about ⅓ cup

- 3 tablespoons mayonnaise
- 3 tablespoons sour cream
- 2 teaspoons minced canned chipotle chile in adobo sauce
- 1 garlic clove, minced
- ⅛ teaspoon table salt

Combine all ingredients. Cover and refrigerate for at least 1 hour.

## Vegan Pinto Bean–Beet Burgers

**SERVES** 8

**WHY THIS RECIPE WORKS** Vegan burgers are often bean-based; starchy, protein-packed beans taste great, hold together well, and are satisfying. For a twist on the typical bean burger, we combined pinto beans with vibrant shredded beets, and we packed in a generous amount of basil. The result was a substantial fresh-tasting burger with some sweetness from the beets and the bright aroma of basil. We added bulgur for heft and ground nuts for meaty richness while garlic and mustard deepened the savory flavors. To bind the burgers, we turned to a surprising ingredient: carrot baby food. The carrot added tackiness, and its subtle sweetness heightened that of the beets; plus, it was already conveniently pureed. Panko bread crumbs further bound the mixture and helped the patties sear up with a crisp crust. When shopping, don't confuse bulgur with cracked wheat, which has a much longer cooking time and will not work in this recipe. Use a coarse grater or the shredding disk of a food processor to shred the beets.

- Table salt and pepper
- ⅔ cup medium-grind bulgur, rinsed
- 1 large beet (9 ounces), peeled and shredded
- ¾ cup walnuts
- ½ cup fresh basil leaves
- 2 garlic cloves, minced
- 1 (15-ounce) can pinto beans, rinsed
- 1 (4-ounce) jar carrot baby food
- 1 tablespoon whole-grain mustard
- 1½ cups panko bread crumbs
- 6 tablespoons vegetable oil, plus extra as needed
- 8 burger buns

**1.** Bring 1½ cups water and ½ teaspoon salt to boil in small saucepan. Off heat, stir in bulgur, cover, and let stand until tender, 15 to 20 minutes. Drain bulgur, spread onto rimmed baking sheet, and let cool slightly.

**2.** Meanwhile, pulse beet, walnuts, basil, and garlic in food processor until finely chopped, about 12 pulses, scraping down sides of bowl as needed. Add beans, carrot baby food, 2 tablespoons water, mustard, 1½ teaspoons salt, and ½ teaspoon pepper and pulse until well combined, about 8 pulses. Transfer mixture to large bowl and stir in panko and cooled bulgur.

**3.** Adjust oven rack to middle position and heat oven to 200 degrees. Divide mixture into 8 equal portions and pack into 3½-inch-wide patties.

**4.** Heat 3 tablespoons oil in 12-inch nonstick skillet over medium-high heat until shimmering. Gently lay 4 patties in skillet and cook until crisp and well browned on first side, about 4 minutes. Gently flip patties and cook until crisp and well browned on second side, about 4 minutes, adding extra oil if skillet looks dry.

**5.** Transfer burgers to wire rack set in rimmed baking sheet and place in oven to keep warm. Wipe out skillet with paper towels and repeat with remaining 3 tablespoons oil and remaining patties. Transfer to buns and serve.

### Vegan Pub-Style Burger Sauce

**MAKES** 1 cup

- ¾ cup vegan mayonnaise
- 2 tablespoons soy sauce
- 1 tablespoon packed dark brown sugar
- 1 tablespoon vegan Worcestershire sauce
- 1 tablespoon minced fresh chives
- 1 garlic clove, minced
- ¾ teaspoon ground black pepper

Whisk all ingredients together in bowl. (Sauce can be refrigerated for up to 4 days.)

# CHAPTER 10 Grilling

*Continued on next page*

Photos (left to right): Grilled Flank Steak; Grilled Lemon Chicken with Rosemary; Grilled Rack of Lamb; Grilled Pork Tenderloin with Grilled Pineapple–Red Onion Salsan; Barbecued Pulled Pork; Grilled Well-Done Hamburgers; Mexican-Style Grilled Corn

# CHAPTER 10 Grilling

## Grilled Hamburgers

SERVES 4

**WHY THIS RECIPE WORKS** We wanted a grilled burger with a flavorful, deeply caramelized reddish brown crust with an even surface capable of holding as many condiments as we could pile on. Ground chuck gave us the most robustly flavored burgers when pitted head to head against burgers made from other cuts of ground beef. We selected meat with a ratio of 20 percent fat to 80 percent lean; more fat than that, and the burgers were too greasy. Burgers made with less fat lacked in juiciness and moisture. We formed the meat into 6-ounce patties that were fairly thick, with a depression in the middle. Rounds of testing taught us that indenting the center of each burger ensured that the patties would come off the grill with an even thickness instead of puffed up like a tennis ball. Cooking the burgers over the fire for just a few minutes kept them tender, and lightly oiling the cooking grate prevented them from sticking. Weighing the meat on a kitchen scale is the most accurate way to portion it. If you don't own a scale, do your best to divide the meat evenly into quarters. Eighty percent lean ground chuck is our favorite for flavor, but 85 percent lean works too.

- 1½ pounds 80 percent lean ground chuck
- 1 teaspoon table salt
- ½ teaspoon pepper
- 4 hamburger rolls, toasted

**1.** Using hands, gently break up meat, season with salt and pepper, and toss lightly to incorporate. Divide meat into 4 portions and lightly toss 1 portion from hand to hand to form ball, then lightly flatten ball with fingertips into ¾-inch-thick patty. Press center of patty down with fingertips until it is about ½ inch thick, creating slight depression. Repeat with remaining portions.

**2A. FOR A CHARCOAL GRILL:** Open bottom vent completely. Light large chimney starter filled with charcoal briquettes (6 quarts). When top coals are partially covered with ash, pour evenly over grill. Set cooking grate in place, cover, and open lid vent completely. Heat grill until hot, about 5 minutes.

**2B. FOR A GAS GRILL:** Turn all burners to high, cover, and heat grill until hot, about 15 minutes.

**3.** Clean and oil cooking grate. Place burgers on grill and cook, without pressing on them, until well browned on first side, 2 to 3 minutes. Flip burgers and continue to grill until meat registers 115 to 120 (for rare) 2 to 3 minutes, 120 to 125 (for medium-rare) 2½ to 3½ minutes, or 130 to 135 (for medium), 3 to 4 minutes.

**4.** Transfer burgers to serving platter, tent loosely with aluminum foil, and let rest for 5 to 10 minutes before serving on buns.

### Grilled Cheeseburgers

Since the cheese is evenly distributed in these burgers, just a little goes a long way.

Mix ¾ cup shredded cheddar, Swiss, or Monterey Jack cheese or ¾ cup crumbled blue cheese into meat with salt and pepper.

## Tender, Juicy Grilled Burgers

SERVES 4

**WHY THIS RECIPE WORKS** For us, the ideal burger has an ultra-craggy charred crust; a rich, beefy taste; and an interior so juicy and tender that it practically falls apart at the slightest pressure—a particularly difficult achievement when grilling. While the typical burger may have a nicely browned crust, it's also heavy and dense, with a pebbly texture that comes from using preground beef. We knew we wanted to grind our own meat to make the ultimate burger. First we trimmed gristle and excess fat from the meat, cut it into ½-inch pieces, froze it for about 30 minutes to firm it up so that the blades cut it cleanly, and finally processed it in a food processor in small batches to ensure an even, precise grind. We chose to use beefy steak tips since they are decently tender, require virtually no trimming, and are relatively inexpensive. Adding a bit of butter to the food processor when grinding added richness but not buttery flavor. To form the burgers so that they wouldn't fall apart on the grate but at the same time achieve that essential open texture, we froze them briefly before putting them on the grill. By the time they'd thawed at their centers, they had developed enough crust to ensure that they held together. A few minutes over a hot grill was all our burgers needed to achieve a perfect medium-rare. This recipe requires freezing the meat twice, for a total of 65 to 80 minutes, before grilling. Take care not to overwork the meat or the burgers will become dense. Sirloin steak tips are also sold as flap meat. Serve the burgers with your favorite toppings or our creamy Grilled Scallion Topping.

- 1½ pounds sirloin steak tips, trimmed and cut into ½-inch chunks
- 4 tablespoons unsalted butter, cut into ¼-inch pieces
- 1 teaspoon kosher salt, divided
- 1¼ teaspoons pepper, divided
- 1 (13 by 9-inch) disposable aluminum pan (if using charcoal)
- 4 hamburger buns

**1.** Place beef chunks and butter on large plate in single layer. Freeze until meat is very firm and starting to harden around edges but still pliable, about 35 minutes.

**2.** Place one-quarter of meat and one-quarter of butter cubes in food processor and pulse until finely ground into pieces size of rice grains (about $1/_{32}$ inch), 15 to 20 pulses, stopping and redistributing meat around bowl as necessary to ensure beef is evenly ground. Transfer meat to baking sheet. Repeat grinding with remaining 3 batches of meat and butter. Spread mixture over sheet and inspect carefully, discarding any long strands of gristle or large chunks of hard meat, fat, or butter.

**3.** Sprinkle 1 teaspoon pepper and ¾ teaspoon salt over meat and toss gently with fork to combine. Divide meat into 4 balls. Toss each between your hands until uniformly but lightly packed. Gently flatten into patties ¾ inch thick and about 4½ inches in diameter. Using your thumb, make 1-inch-wide by ¼-inch-deep depression in center of each patty. Transfer patties to platter and freeze for 30 to 45 minutes.

**4A. FOR A CHARCOAL GRILL:** Using skewer, poke 12 holes in bottom of disposable pan. Open bottom vent completely and place disposable pan in center of grill. Light large chimney starter two-thirds filled with charcoal briquettes (4 quarts). When top coals are partially covered with ash, pour into disposable pan. Set cooking grate in place, cover, and open lid vent completely. Heat grill until hot, about 5 minutes.

**4B. FOR A GAS GRILL:** Turn all burners to high; cover; and heat grill until hot, about 15 minutes. Leave all burners on high.

**5.** Clean and oil cooking grate. Sprinkle 1 side of patties with ⅛ teaspoon salt and ⅛ teaspoon pepper. Using spatula, flip patties and sprinkle other side with remaining ⅛ teaspoon salt and remaining ⅛ teaspoon pepper. Grill patties (directly over coals if using charcoal), without moving them, until browned and meat easily releases from grate, 4 to 7 minutes. Flip burgers and continue to grill until browned on second side and meat registers 120 to 125 degrees (for medium-rare), or 130 to 135 degrees (for medium), 4 to 7 minutes longer.

**6.** Transfer burgers to plate and let rest for 5 minutes. While burgers rest, lightly toast buns on grill, 1 to 2 minutes. Transfer burgers to buns and serve.

## Grilled Scallion Topping

**MAKES** ½ cup

- 2 tablespoons sour cream
- 2 tablespoons mayonnaise
- 2 tablespoons buttermilk
- 1 tablespoon cider vinegar
- 1 tablespoon minced fresh chives
- 2 teaspoons Dijon mustard
- ¼ teaspoon sugar
- ½ teaspoon table salt
- ⅛ teaspoon pepper
- 20 scallions
- 2 tablespoons vegetable oil

**1.** Combine sour cream, mayonnaise, buttermilk, vinegar, chives, mustard, sugar, salt, and pepper in medium bowl. Set aside.

**2.** Toss scallions with oil in large bowl. Grill scallions over hot fire until lightly charred and softened, 2 to 4 minutes per side. Return to bowl and let cool for 5 minutes. Slice scallions thin, then transfer to bowl with reserved sour cream mixture. Toss to combine and season with salt and pepper to taste.

## Grilled Well-Done Hamburgers

**SERVES 4**

**WHY THIS RECIPE WORKS** We know that many backyard cooks grill their burgers to medium-well and beyond, but we aren't willing to accept the usual outcome of tough, desiccated hockey pucks with no beefy flavor. We wanted to work with supermarket ground beef to produce a tender and moist-as-can-be burger, with perfect grill marks and all, even when well-done. Taste tests proved that well-done burgers made with 80 percent lean chuck were noticeably moister than burgers made from leaner beef, but they still weren't juicy enough. Because we couldn't force the meat to retain moisture, we opted to pack the patties with a panade, a paste made from bread and milk that's often used to keep meat loaf and meatballs moist. To punch up the flavor, we also added minced garlic and tangy steak sauce. To keep our burgers from puffing up the way most burgers do, we made use of a previous test kitchen discovery: If you make a slight depression in the center of the patty, it will puff slightly as it cooks and level out to form a flat top. For cheeseburgers, follow the optional instructions.

- 1 slice hearty white sandwich bread, crust removed, bread cut into ¼-inch pieces
- 2 tablespoons whole milk
- 2 teaspoons steak sauce
- 1 garlic clove, minced
- ¾ teaspoon table salt
- ¾ teaspoon pepper
- 1½ pounds 80 percent lean ground chuck
- 6 ounces sliced cheese (optional)
- 4 hamburger buns, toasted

**1.** Mash bread and milk in large bowl with fork until homogeneous. Stir in steak sauce, garlic, salt, and pepper. Using hands, gently break up meat over bread mixture and toss lightly to distribute. Divide meat into 4 portions and lightly toss 1 portion from hand to hand to form ball, then lightly flatten ball with fingertips into ¾-inch-thick patty. Press center of patty down with fingertips until it is about ½ inch thick, creating slight depression. Repeat with remaining portions.

**2A. FOR A CHARCOAL GRILL:** Open bottom vent completely. Light large chimney starter filled with charcoal briquettes (6 quarts). When top coals are partially covered with ash, pour evenly over grill. Set cooking grate in place, cover, and open lid vent completely. Heat grill until hot, about 5 minutes.

**2B. FOR A GAS GRILL:** Turn all burners to high, cover, and heat grill until hot, about 15 minutes.

**3.** Clean and oil cooking grate. Place burgers on grill (on hot side if using charcoal) and cook, without pressing on them, until well browned on first side, 2 to 4 minutes. Flip burgers and cook until meat registers 140 to 145 degrees (for medium-well done) 3 to 4 minutes or 150 to 155 degrees (for well done), 4 to 5 minutes, adding cheese, if using, about 2 minutes before reaching desired doneness and covering grill to melt cheese.

**4.** Transfer burgers to serving platter, tent loosely with aluminum foil, and let rest for 5 to 10 minutes before serving on buns.

### Well-Done Bacon Cheeseburgers

Most bacon burgers simply top the burgers with bacon. We also add bacon fat to the ground beef, which adds juiciness and unmistakable bacon flavor throughout the burger.

Cook 8 slices bacon in skillet over medium heat until crisp, 7 to 9 minutes. Transfer bacon to paper towel–lined plate and set aside. Reserve 2 tablespoons fat and refrigerate until just warm. Follow recipe for Grilled Well-Done Hamburgers, including optional cheese and adding reserved bacon fat to beef mixture. Top each burger with 2 slices bacon before serving.

## Grilled Flank Steak

**SERVES** 4 to 6 **SEASON 26**

**WHY THIS RECIPE WORKS** Flank steak, a relatively thin cut, tends to cook through well before its abundant surface area has a chance to brown. So we applied a modified sugar steak approach not only to season the meat but also to encourage faster, deeper browning on the grill. After dividing the steak into quadrants to allow the tapered portions to be pulled off the grill sooner and to shorten the steak's muscle fibers and thus minimize its tendency to shrink and buckle during cooking, we rubbed it with a 1:1 ratio of sugar and kosher salt twice before cooking, which encouraged rich Maillard browning and caramelization. Flipping it every 2 minutes during cooking further minimized any buckling; prevented either side from developing a band of gray, overcooked meat just below the surface; and developed some attractive grill marks. We cooked the meat until it registered to 130 to 135 degrees (for medium) because collagen-rich cuts such as flank are more tender when cooked to medium versus medium-rare. We let it rest uncovered on a wire rack set to avoid steaming the crust and finished it with butter seasoned with a Montreal-inspired blend of spices to add bold flavor. This recipe was developed using Diamond Crystal kosher salt. If you have Morton kosher salt, which is denser, use 2 teaspoons of salt and sprinkle 1¾ teaspoons of salt mixture per side of the steaks in step 1. Serve with Montreal Steak Butter and flake salt, if desired.

- 1 (1½- to 1¾-pound) flank steak, trimmed
- 2½ teaspoons kosher salt
- 2½ teaspoons sugar
- 1 teaspoon pepper

**1.** Pat steak dry with paper towels. Cut steak in half lengthwise. Cut each piece in half crosswise to create 4 steaks. Place steaks in 13 by 9-inch baking dish. Combine salt and sugar in small bowl. Sprinkle 2 teaspoons salt mixture on 1 side of steaks and press gently to adhere. Flip steaks and repeat with another 2 teaspoons salt mixture. Cover and let sit at room temperature for 1 hour.

**2A. FOR A CHARCOAL GRILL:** Open bottom vent completely. Light large chimney starter mounded with charcoal briquettes (7 quarts). When top coals are partially covered with ash, pour evenly over grill. Set cooking grate in place, cover, and open lid vent completely. Heat grill until hot, about 5 minutes.

**2B. FOR A GAS GRILL:** Turn all burners to high; cover; and heat grill until hot, about 15 minutes.

**3.** Clean and oil cooking grate. Sprinkle both sides of steaks with pepper and remaining 1 teaspoon salt mixture. (Steaks will be moist; do not pat dry.)

**4.** Set wire rack in rimmed baking sheet. Arrange steaks on grill and cook (covered if using gas), flipping steaks every 2 minutes and moving steaks as needed for even cooking, until meat registers 125 to 130 degrees, 6 to 12 minutes. (Start checking temperature of thinner pieces after 6 minutes.) Transfer steaks to prepared rack and let rest for 10 minutes.

**5.** Transfer steaks to cutting board and, using sharp knife, slice steak as thin as possible on bias against grain. Transfer to platter and serve.

### Montreal Steak Butter

**MAKES** ½ cup

You can substitute 1½ teaspoons of dried dill for the fresh.

- 6 tablespoons unsalted butter, softened
- 1 tablespoon minced fresh dill
- ½ teaspoon paprika
- ½ teaspoon pepper
- ½ teaspoon kosher salt
- ½ teaspoon garlic powder
- ¼ teaspoon onion powder
- ¼ teaspoon ground coriander
- ¼ teaspoon red pepper flakes

Combine all ingredients in bowl.

## Grilled Marinated Flank Steak

**SERVES** 4 to 6

**WHY THIS RECIPE WORKS** An acidic marinade—such as one made with vinegar—can ruin the texture of flank steak, making the exterior mushy and gray. We wanted an aromatic, acid-free marinade that would boost flavor without overtenderizing the meat. We knew oil would be a key ingredient because fat carries flavor so well—the challenge was to infuse garlic, shallots, and rosemary into the oil and then into the steak. To do so, we first minced the aromatics and combined them with the oil in a blender to create a marinade paste. To grill our steak to perfection, we used a two-level fire (which lets you move the thin part of the steak to the cooler side of the grill once it is done), cooked the steak only to medium-rare to keep it from getting tough. Other thin steaks with a loose grain, such as skirt steak or steak tips, can be substituted for the flank steak.

- 1 (2- to 2½-pound) flank steak, trimmed
- 1 teaspoon table salt
- 1 recipe wet paste marinade
- ½ teaspoon pepper

**1.** Pat steak dry with paper towels and place in large baking dish. Using dinner fork, prick steak about 20 times on each side. Rub both sides of steak evenly with salt, then with paste. Cover with plastic wrap and refrigerate for at least 1 hour or up to 24 hours.

**2A. FOR A CHARCOAL GRILL:** Open bottom vent completely. Light large chimney starter filled with charcoal briquettes (6 quarts). When top coals are partially covered with ash, pour two-thirds of coals over half of grill, then pour remaining coals over other half. Set cooking grate in place, cover, and open lid vent completely. Heat grill until hot, about 5 minutes.

**2B. FOR A GAS GRILL:** Turn all burners to high; cover; and heat grill until hot, about 15 minutes.

**3.** Clean and oil cooking grate. Using paper towels, wipe paste off steak and sprinkle with pepper. Place steak on grill (hotter side if using charcoal) and cook (covered if using gas) until well browned on first side, 4 to 6 minutes. Flip steak and cook (covered if using gas) until meat registers 120 to 125 degrees (for medium-rare) or 130 to 135 degrees (for medium), 3 to 6 minutes. If exterior of meat is browned but steak is not yet cooked through, move to cooler side of grill (if using charcoal) or turn down burners (if using gas) and continue to cook to desired doneness.

**4.** Transfer steak to carving board, tent with aluminum foil, and let rest for 10 minutes. Slice steak against grain on bias ¼ inch thick and serve.

### Garlic-Shallot-Rosemary Wet Paste Marinade

**MAKES** ⅔ cup

- 6 tablespoons extra-virgin olive oil
- 1 shallot, minced
- 6 garlic cloves, minced
- 2 tablespoons minced fresh rosemary

Process all ingredients in blender until smooth, about 30 seconds, scraping down bowl as needed.

## Grilled Stuffed Flank Steak

**SERVES** 4 to 6

**WHY THIS RECIPE WORKS** Stuffed steak originated with Italian American cooking as a way to transform an inexpensive steak into something special. But when we tried a few of the premade stuffed "pinwheels," the cheese oozed out all over the grill, and the stuffing fell out in clumps. Thanks to its uniform shape and good beefy taste, flank steak was clearly the best bet when tackling this recipe. To guarantee the filling stayed in place, we butterflied and pounded the steak, so we were starting with the flattest and widest surface possible. As for the filling, the classic combo of prosciutto and provolone won raves for its salty savor and the way the dry cheese melted inside the pinwheel yet turned crisp where exposed to the grill. To prevent the meat from shrinking, and squeezing the centers of the pinwheels, we rolled up the flank steak, tied it with twine, and skewered it at 1-inch intervals before slicing and grilling. The twine kept the steak from unraveling, while the skewers prevented the meat from shrinking. Look for a flank steak measuring approximately 8 by 6 inches, with the grain running the long way. Depending on the steak's size, you may have more or less than 8 slices of meat at the end of step 2. You will need both wooden skewers and kitchen twine for this recipe.

- 2 tablespoons olive oil
- 2 tablespoons minced fresh parsley
- 1 small shallot, minced
- 2 garlic cloves, minced
- 1 teaspoon minced fresh sage
- 1 (2- to 2½-pound) flank steak, trimmed
- 4 ounces thinly sliced prosciutto
- 4 ounces thinly sliced provolone cheese
- Table salt and pepper

**1.** Combine oil, parsley, shallot, garlic, and sage in bowl.

**2.** Soak 8 to 12 wooden skewers in warm water to cover (you will need 1 skewer per inch of rolled steak length) for 30 minutes. Drain, dry, and set aside.

**3.** Lay steak on cutting board with grain running parallel to counter edge. Cut horizontally through meat, leaving ½-inch "hinge" along top edge. Open up steak and pound flat into rough rectangle, trimming any ragged edges. Rub herb mixture evenly over opened side of steak. Lay prosciutto evenly over steak, leaving 2-inch border along top edge. Cover prosciutto with even layer of cheese, leaving 2-inch border along top edge. Starting from short edge, roll beef into tight log and place on cutting board seam side down.

**4.** Starting ½ inch from end of rolled steak, evenly space eight to twelve 14-inch pieces of kitchen twine at 1-inch intervals underneath steak. Tie middle piece first, then, working from outer pieces toward center, tightly tie roll and turn tied steak 90 degrees so seam is facing you.

**5.** Skewer beef directly through outer flap of steak near seam through each piece of twine, allowing skewers to extend ½ inch on other side. Using chef's knife, slice roll between each piece of twine into 1-inch-thick pinwheels. Season pinwheels with salt and pepper.

**6A. FOR A CHARCOAL GRILL:** Open bottom vent completely. Light large chimney starter three-quarters filled with charcoal briquettes (4½ quarts). When top coals are partially covered with ash, pour evenly over half of grill. Set cooking grate in place, cover, and open lid vent completely. Heat grill until hot, about 5 minutes.

**6B. FOR A GAS GRILL:** Turn all burners to high, cover, and heat grill until hot, about 15 minutes.

**7.** Clean and oil cooking grate. Place pinwheels on grill (hot side if using charcoal) and cook (covered if using gas) until well browned on both sides, 6 to 12 minutes, flipping halfway through cooking. Move pinwheels to cool side of grill (if using charcoal) or turn all burners to medium (if using gas). Cover and cook until meat registers 120 to 125 degrees (for medium-rare) or 130 to 135 degrees (for medium), 1 to 5 minutes.

**8.** Transfer pinwheels to serving platter, tent loosely with aluminum foil, and let rest for 5 to 10 minutes. Remove and discard skewers and twine and serve.

### HOW TO BUTTERFLY AND STUFF FLANK STEAK

**1.** Lay the flank steak on the edge of a cutting board. Slice the steak horizontally, making sure to leave a ½-inch "hinge" along the top edge.

**2.** Open up the steak, cover with plastic wrap, and pound it to a 12 by 8-inch rectangle of even thickness.

**3.** Leaving the steak in place with the grain running perpendicular to the edge of the cutting board, rub the steak evenly with the herb mixture, and layer it with the prosciutto and cheese, leaving a 2-inch border along the top edge.

**4.** Roll the steak away from you into a tight log, then tie it at even 1-inch intervals. Skewer the meat directly through each string, making sure to insert the skewer through the seam in the roll to prevent the beef from unraveling during cooking.

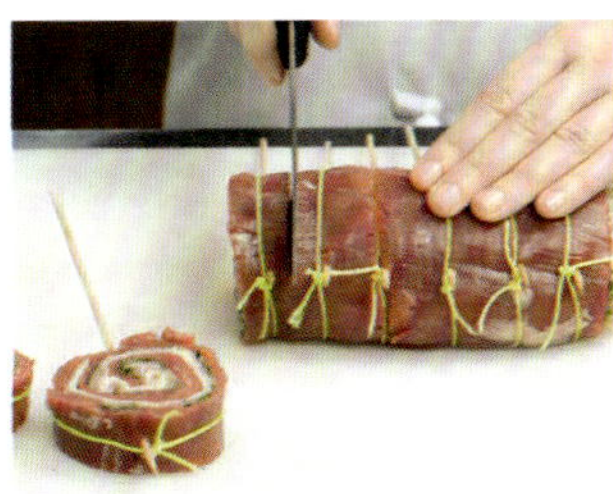

**5.** Slice the beef into 1-inch-thick pinwheels. Each spiral should be held together with a skewer and a piece of twine.

## Steak Fajitas

**SERVES 8**

**WHY THIS RECIPE WORKS** Recipes for fajitas are fairly straightforward: Grill the meat and vegetables and serve them in a warm tortilla. But many versions are either lackluster or ruined by unnecessary complexity. We want fajitas that boasted flawless, flavorful meat with a rosy interior and browned crust. We learned that flank steak is plenty tender without a marinade if sliced thin against the grain after being cooked. But we did want to add flavor. A squeeze of lime juice and a generous dose of salt and pepper just before grilling added all the extra flavor we wanted. The tried-and-true way of cooking flank steak—over high heat for a short period of time—required no changes. Served in tortillas with freshly made guacamole, these fajitas delivered. The ingredients go on the grill in order as the fire dies down: steak over a medium-hot fire, vegetables over a medium fire, and tortillas around the edge of a medium to low fire just to warm them. When you head outside to grill, bring a clean dish towel in which to wrap the tortillas and keep them warm. Chunky Guacamole (page 2) and fresh salsa make good accompaniments.

- 1 (2- to 2½-pound) flank steak, trimmed
- ¼ cup lime juice
- Table salt and pepper
- 1 large red onion, peeled and cut into ½-inch-thick rounds (do not separate rings)
- 2 large bell peppers, quartered, stemmed, and seeded
- 8–12 (6-inch) flour tortillas

**1A. FOR A CHARCOAL GRILL:** Open bottom vent completely. Light large chimney starter mounded with charcoal briquettes (7 quarts). When top coals are partially covered with ash, pour evenly over half of grill. Set cooking grate in place, cover, and open lid vent completely. Heat grill until hot, about 5 minutes.

**1B. FOR A GAS GRILL:** Turn all burners to high, cover, and heat grill until hot, about 15 minutes.

**2.** Clean and oil cooking grate. Pat steak dry with paper towels and sprinkle with lime juice, salt, and pepper. Place steak on grill (hot side if using charcoal) and cook (covered if using gas) until well browned on first side, 4 to 7 minutes. Flip steak and continue to cook until meat registers 120 to 125 degrees (for medium-rare) or 130 to 135 degrees (for medium), 3 to 8 minutes. Transfer steak to cutting board, tent loosely with aluminum foil, and let rest for 10 minutes.

**3.** While steak rests, place onion rounds and peppers (skin side down) on hot side of grill (if using charcoal) or turn all burners to medium (if using gas). Cook until tender and charred on both sides, 8 to 12 minutes, flipping every 3 minutes. Transfer onions and peppers to carving board with beef.

**4.** Place tortillas in single layer on hot side of grill (if using charcoal) or turn all burners to low (if using gas). Cook until warm and lightly browned, about 20 seconds per side (do not grill too long or tortillas will become brittle). As tortillas are done, wrap in clean dish towel or large sheet of foil.

**5.** Separate onions into rings and slice peppers into ¼-inch strips. Slice steak, against grain, ¼-inch-thick. Transfer beef and vegetables to serving platter and serve with warmed tortillas.

## Tacos al Carbón (Grilled Steak Tacos)

**SERVES** 4 to 6

**WHY THIS RECIPE WORKS** Grilled steak tacos, feature meat seasoned with a marinade or spices, cooked over a live fire, tucked into soft corn tortillas, and topped with garnishes like charred scallions and lime juice. We chose inexpensive and widely available flank steak for these tacos. Instead of a marinade, we opted for a spice paste made with chipotle chiles in adobo sauce for spicy, smoky, and savory notes. Cumin, oil, and a little salt turned the minced chipotles into a paste. Grilled directly over the coals (a gas grill works, too), the thickest part of the steak registered 120 to 125 degrees (for medium-rare), about 10 minutes. The chipotle paste was a keeper, but the thinner areas of the steak were overdone. What's more, it was unevenly browned and didn't have much grill flavor. So next time around we divided the steak into thirds lengthwise. This separated the thinner portions from the thicker ones so we could grill each to the proper doneness. The mediocre browning was because the steak's fibers contracted during the first few minutes of cooking. Frequent flipping helped the top and bottom shrink at about the same rate so the steaks stayed flat and browned evenly. As for the deficit of grill flavor, if we wanted deep grill flavor, we needed drippings. Next time around, we trimmed less fat. Problem solved. Inspired by the charred scallions that often adorn tacos al carbón, we whipped up a grilled scallion salsa. For the sake of efficiency, we grilled the vegetables alongside the steak, and they picked up some flavor from the meat vapors. Finally, we blistered the corn tortillas on the hot side of the grill until they developed a toasty, popcorn-like aroma and then wrapped them tightly in foil so they would stay warm and soft. This steak's grill flavor is created when some of the fat and juices land on the fire and create small, controlled flare-ups, so choose a steak that has some fat deposits. For a spicier scallion salsa, add the reserved jalapeño seeds in step 5. Sour cream can be substituted for the crema, if desired.

- 3 tablespoons extra-virgin olive oil, divided
- 2 teaspoons minced canned chipotle chile in adobo sauce, plus 1 teaspoon adobo sauce, divided
- 2 teaspoons kosher salt, divided
- ¾ teaspoon ground cumin
- 1 (1½- to 1¾-pound) flank steak
- 2 jalapeño chiles
- 20 scallions
- 12 (6-inch) corn tortillas
- 1½ tablespoons lime juice, plus more to taste, plus lime wedges for serving
- Fresh cilantro
- Mexican crema

**1.** Combine 1 tablespoon oil, chipotles, 1½ teaspoons salt, and cumin in bowl. Trim fat deposits on steak to ⅛-inch thickness. Cut steak lengthwise (with grain) into three 2- to 3-inch-wide strips. Rub chipotle mixture into all surfaces of steak and transfer to rimmed baking sheet.

**2A. FOR A CHARCOAL GRILL:** Open bottom vent completely. Light large chimney starter mounded with charcoal briquettes (7 quarts). When top coals are partially covered with ash, pour evenly over half of grill. Set cooking grate in place, cover, and open lid vent completely. Heat grill until hot, about 5 minutes.

**2B. FOR A GAS GRILL:** Turn all burners to high, cover, and heat grill until hot, about 15 minutes. Turn off 1 burner (if using grill with more than 2 burners, turn off burner farthest from primary burner) and leave other burner(s) on high.

**3.** Clean and oil cooking grate. Arrange steak and jalapeños on hotter side of grill. (If using gas, cover grill.) Cook steak, flipping every 2 minutes, until meat is well browned and registers 120 to 125 degrees (for medium-rare), 7 to 12 minutes. Cook jalapeños until skins are blistered and charred in spots, 7 to 10 minutes. Transfer steak to clean cutting board and tent with aluminum foil. Transfer jalapeños to medium bowl and cover tightly with plastic wrap.

**4.** Grill scallions on hotter side of grill until greens are well charred on 1 side, 1 to 2 minutes. Flip scallions, arranging so that greens are on cooler side while white and pale green parts are on hotter side. Continue to cook until whites are well charred, 1 to 2 minutes. Transfer to bowl with jalapeños and cover tightly with plastic wrap. Arrange half of tortillas over hotter side of grill and cook until lightly charred, about 45 to 60 seconds per side. Tightly wrap warmed tortillas in foil. Repeat with remaining tortillas.

**5.** Without peeling, stem and seed jalapeños and reserve seeds. Chop jalapeños fine, chop scallions coarse, and transfer to bowl. Stir in remaining 2 tablespoons oil, lime juice, remaining adobo sauce, and remaining ½ teaspoon salt. Season with lime juice, salt, and jalapeño seeds to taste. Slice steak thin across grain and transfer to serving platter. Serve, passing scallion salsa, tortillas, lime wedges, cilantro, and sour cream separately.

## Negimaki (Japanese Grilled Steak and Scallion Rolls)

**SERVES** 8 to 10 as an appetizer or 4 to 6 as a main dish

**WHY THIS RECIPE WORKS** Negimaki pairs the flavor of grilled beef, grassy scallions, and a salty-sweet teriyaki glaze with an elegant bite-size presentation, making a summer dish that can be served as an appetizer or entrée. For our version, we opted for flank steak (briefly frozen first to firm it up for easy slicing), which was affordable, flavorful, and mostly uniform. We pounded the pieces until they were thin and arranged the slices in an overlapping pattern to form rectangular meat "wrappers." Then we laid 4 scallion halves on each wrapper in alternating directions so that the green and white portions were evenly distributed, tightly rolled the meat around the scallions, and pinned the roll shut with toothpicks. To char the meat quickly, we grilled the rolls over a hot fire, turning them so all sides browned evenly, and glazed the meat partway through cooking with a salty-sweet teriyaki-like reduction of sake, mirin, soy sauce, and sugar. The meat slices were too thin to probe for doneness, so instead we took the temperature of the scallion core; when it registered between 150 and 155 degrees, the meat was fully cooked. Finally, we sliced the rolls, drizzled them with extra glaze, and sprinkled them with toasted sesame seeds. Look for a flank steak that is as rectangular as possible as this will yield the most uniform slices. Depending on how you slice the steak you may end up with extra slices; you can grill these alongside the rolls or make several smaller rolls. Serve either as an appetizer or as an entrée with steamed white rice and a vegetable.

- 1 (2-pound) flank steak, trimmed
- ⅓ cup soy sauce
- 3 tablespoons sugar
- 2 tablespoons mirin
- 2 tablespoons sake
- 16 scallions, trimmed and halved crosswise
- 1 tablespoon sesame seeds, toasted

**1.** Place flank steak on large plate and freeze until firm, about 30 minutes.

**2.** Bring soy sauce, sugar, mirin, and sake to simmer in small saucepan over high heat, stirring to dissolve sugar. Reduce heat to medium and cook until slightly syrupy and reduced to ½ cup, 3 to 5 minutes. Divide evenly between two bowls and let cool. Cover one bowl with plastic wrap and set aside for serving.

**3.** Place flank steak on cutting board. Starting at thinner end, slice steak ⅜ inch thick, against grain, on bias until width of steak is about 7 inches across (usually 2 to 3 slices). Cut steak in half lengthwise. Continue to slice each half, against grain, on bias. You should end up with at least 24 slices. Pound each slice into 3⁄16-inch thickness between two sheets of plastic wrap.

**4.** Arrange 3 slices on cutting board, overlapping slices by ¼ inch and alternating tapered ends as needed, to form rough rectangle that measures 4 to 6 inches wide and at least 4 inches long. Place 4 scallion halves along edge of rectangle nearest to edge of work surface, with white tips slightly overhanging edges on either side. Starting from bottom edge and rolling away from you, roll into tight log. Insert three equally spaced toothpicks into end flaps and through center of roll. Transfer to platter and repeat with remaining steak and scallions. (Rolls can be assembled, wrapped tightly in plastic wrap, and refrigerated for up to 24 hours.)

**5A. FOR A CHARCOAL GRILL:** Open bottom vent completely. Light large chimney starter three-quarters filled with charcoal briquettes (5 quarts). When top coals are partially covered with ash, pour evenly over half of grill. Set cooking grate in place, cover, and open lid vent completely. Heat grill until hot, about 5 minutes.

**5B. FOR A GAS GRILL:** Turn all burners to high, cover, and heat grill until hot, about 15 minutes.

**6.** Clean and oil cooking grate. Place rolls over hot part of grill and cook until first side is beginning to char, 4 to 6 minutes. Flip rolls, brush cooked sides with glaze, and continue to cook until second side is beginning to char, 4 to 6 minutes. Cook remaining two sides, glazing after each turn, until all 4 sides of rolls are evenly charred and thermometer inserted from end of roll into scallions at core registers 150 to 155 degrees, 16 to 24 minutes total. Transfer rolls to cutting board, tent loosely with foil, and let rest for 5 minutes. Discard remaining glaze.

**7.** Remove toothpicks from rolls and cut rolls crosswise into 1-inch pieces. Arrange rolls cut-side down on clean platter, drizzle with 2 tablespoons reserved glaze, sprinkle with sesame seeds, and serve, passing remaining reserved glaze separately.

## WRAPPING AND ROLLING NEGIMAKI

**1.** Slice chilled steak against grain on bias into 24 pieces.

**2.** Pound slices to 3⁄16-inch thickness.

**3.** Arrange slices like jigsaw puzzle, overlapping them by ¼ inch to form rough 4- to 6-inch by 4-inch rectangle.

**4.** Lay scallion halves head to toe over beef, letting white tips overhang edge.

**5.** Roll steak away from you into tight log and fasten with three toothpicks.

## Thai Grilled-Beef Salad

SERVES 4 to 6

**WHY THIS RECIPE WORKS** This traditional grilled Thai salad features slices of charred steak tossed with shallots, mint, and cilantro in a bright dressing. We chose flank steak for its marbling and moderate price. Grilling the steak over a modified two-level fire and flipping it just when moisture beaded on the surface yielded perfectly charred, juicy meat. Adding a fresh Thai chile, toasted cayenne, and paprika gave the dressing a fruity, fiery heat. Toasted rice powder is a traditional Thai tableside condiment that gives the dressing fuller body and a subtle crunch; we made our own by toasting rice in a skillet on the stovetop and then grinding it in a food processor, spice grinder, or even with a mortar and pestle. If fresh Thai chiles are unavailable, substitute ½ serrano chile. Don't skip the toasted rice; it's integral to the texture and flavor of the dish. Any variety of white rice can be used. Toasted rice powder (kao kua) can also be found in many Asian markets; substitute 1 tablespoon rice powder for the white rice. Serve with rice if desired.

- 1 teaspoon paprika
- 1 teaspoon cayenne pepper
- 1 tablespoon white rice
- 3 tablespoons lime juice (2 limes)
- 2 tablespoons fish sauce
- 2 tablespoons water
- ½ teaspoon sugar
- 1 (1½-pound) flank steak, trimmed
- Table salt and coarsely ground white pepper
- 1 seedless English cucumber, sliced ¼ inch thick on bias
- 4 shallots, sliced thin
- 1½ cups fresh mint leaves, torn
- 1½ cups fresh cilantro leaves
- 1 Thai chile, stemmed, seeded, and sliced thin into rounds

**1.** Heat paprika and cayenne in 8-inch skillet over medium heat; cook, shaking pan, until fragrant, about 1 minute. Transfer to small bowl. Return skillet to medium-high heat, add rice and toast, stirring constantly, until deep golden brown, about 5 minutes. Transfer to small bowl and let cool 5 minutes. Grind rice with spice grinder, mini food processor, or mortar and pestle until it resembles fine meal, 10 to 30 seconds (you should have about 1 tablespoon rice powder).

**2.** Whisk lime juice, fish sauce, water, sugar, and ¼ teaspoon toasted paprika mixture in large bowl and set aside.

**3A. FOR A CHARCOAL GRILL:** Open bottom vent completely. Light large chimney starter filled with charcoal briquettes (6 quarts). When top coals are partially covered with ash, pour in even layer over half of grill. Set cooking grate in place, cover, and open lid vent completely. Heat grill until hot, about 5 minutes.

**3B. FOR A GAS GRILL:** Turn all burners to high, cover, and heat grill until hot, about 15 minutes. Leave primary burner on high and turn off other burner(s).

**4.** Clean and oil grate. Season steak with salt and pepper. Place steak on grate over hot part of grill and cook until beginning to char and beads of moisture appear on outer edges of meat, 5 to 6 minutes. Flip steak, continue to cook on second side until meat registers 120 to 125 degrees (for medium-rare), about 5 minutes longer. Transfer to carving board, tent loosely with aluminum foil, and rest for 10 minutes (or allow to cool to room temperature, about 1 hour).

**5.** Line large platter with cucumber slices. Slice meat, against grain, on bias, into ¼-inch-thick slices. Transfer sliced steak to bowl with fish sauce mixture, add shallots, mint, cilantro, chile, and half of rice powder, and toss to combine. Arrange steak over cucumber-lined platter. Serve, passing remaining rice powder and toasted paprika mixture separately.

## Grilled Sirloin Steak Tips

SERVES 4 to 6

**WHY THIS RECIPE WORKS** Steak tips have long been the darling of all-you-can-eat restaurant chains where quantity takes precedence over quality. We wanted to improve this classic bar food and instill it with deep flavor and a tender texture. To stay true to the inexpensive nature of this dish, we set our sights on finding the best affordable (read: cheap) cut of meat that would stay tender and moist during a brief stint on the grill. The best cut, we found, is what butchers call flap meat. To tenderize and flavor the meat, we used a soy sauce–based marinade and let the meat marinate for at least an hour—just the right amount of time to allow the thicker parts of the meat to become tender while preventing the thinner sections from becoming too salty. Grilling the tips over a two-level fire, which has hotter and cooler areas, helps to cook this often unevenly shaped cut evenly. We let the meat rest for five minutes after grilling to ensure juicy meat, then sliced it thin so the meat would be tender and flavorful. Lime, orange, or lemon wedges provided a bright acidic counterpoint to the steak tips. Sirloin steak tips are sometimes labeled "flap meat."Serve with orange wedges.

- 1 recipe Garlic and Herb Marinade
- 2 pounds sirloin steak tips, trimmed
- orange wedges

**1.** Combine marinade and beef in 1-gallon zipper-lock bag and toss to coat; press out as much air as possible and seal bag. Refrigerate for 1 hour, flipping bag halfway through marinating.

**2A. FOR A CHARCOAL GRILL:** Open bottom vent completely. Light large chimney starter filled with charcoal briquettes (6 quarts). When top coals are partially covered with ash, pour two-thirds evenly over grill, then pour remaining coals over half of grill. Set cooking grate in place, cover, and open lid vent completely. Heat grill until hot, about 5 minutes.

**2B. FOR A GAS GRILL:** Turn all burners to high, cover, and heat grill until hot, about 15 minutes.

**3.** Clean and oil cooking grate. Remove beef from bag and pat dry with paper towels. Place steak tips on grill (on hotter side if using charcoal) and cook (covered if using gas) until well browned on first side, about 4 minutes. Flip steak tips and continue to cook (covered if using gas) until meat registers 120 to 125 degrees (for medium-rare) or 130 to 135 degrees (for medium), 6 to 10 minutes longer. If exterior of meat is browned but steak is not yet cooked through, move to cooler side of grill (if using charcoal) or turn down burners to medium (if using gas) and continue to cook to desired doneness.

**4.** Transfer steak tips to carving board, tent loosely with aluminum foil, and let rest for 5 to 10 minutes. Slice steak tips very thin on bias and serve with lime, orange, or lemon wedges.

### Garlic and Herb Marinade

- ⅓ cup soy sauce
- ⅓ cup olive oil
- 3 cloves garlic, minced
- 1 tablespoon minced fresh rosemary
- 1 tablespoon minced fresh thyme leaves
- 1 tablespoon dark brown sugar
- 1 tablespoon tomato paste
- 1 teaspoon ground black pepper

Combine all ingredients in bowl, stirring until sugar is dissolved.

## Grilled Strip or Rib-Eye Steaks

SERVES 6

**WHY THIS RECIPE WORKS** Grilled steaks have many tempting qualities—rich, beefy flavor; a thick, caramelized crust; and almost zero prep. But the rendered fat can cause flare-ups, leaving pricey cuts of meat charred and tasting like the inside of a smokestack. We wanted a surefire technique for grilling premium steaks so that they would turn out juicy and tender every time. To get a good crust, a very hot fire was essential. But cooking these thick steaks over consistently high heat led to burned steaks and the dreaded flare-ups from fat dripping down onto the charcoal. The solution was to cook the steaks over a two-level fire, searing them first over high heat and then moving them to the cooler part of the grill to cook through. For strip and rib-eye steaks, lightly oiling the cooking grate was enough to keep them from sticking; we rubbed the lean filets mignons with olive oil to encourage browning. Otherwise, we didn't fuss with our steaks before cooking them—a little salt and pepper was sufficient. To add some richness to our steaks, we topped them with a compound butter before serving. Try to buy steaks of even thickness so they cook at the same rate.

- 4 (12- to 16-ounce) strip or rib-eye steaks, with or without bone, 1¼ to 1½ inches thick, trimmed
- 1 teaspoon table salt
- ½ teaspoon pepper

**1A. FOR A CHARCOAL GRILL:** Open bottom vent completely. Light large chimney starter filled with charcoal briquettes (6 quarts). When top coals are partially covered with ash, pour two-thirds of coals over half of grill, then pour remaining coals over other half. Set cooking grate in place, cover, and open lid vent completely. Heat grill until hot, about 5 minutes.

**1B. FOR A GAS GRILL:** Turn all burners to high; cover; and heat grill until hot, about 15 minutes. Leave 1 burner on high and turn other burner(s) to medium.

**2.** Clean and oil cooking grate. Pat steaks dry with paper towels and sprinkle with salt and pepper. Place steaks on grill (hotter side if using charcoal) and cook, uncovered, until well browned on both sides, 4 to 6 minutes, flipping steaks halfway through cooking. Move steaks to cooler side of grill (if using charcoal) or turn all burners to medium (if using gas) and continue to cook until meat registers 115 to 120 degrees (for rare) or 120 to 125 degrees (for medium-rare) 5 to 8 minutes longer.

**3.** Transfer steaks to serving platter, tent with aluminum foil, and let rest for 10 minutes before serving.

### Classic Steak Sauce

Raisins may seem unusual, but they add depth and sweetness.

- ⅓ cup raisins
- ½ cup boiling water
- ¼ cup ketchup
- 3 tablespoons Worcestershire sauce
- 2 tablespoons Dijon mustard
- 2 tablespoons white vinegar

Combine raisins and boiling water in bowl and let sit, covered, until raisins are plump, about 5 minutes. Puree raisin mixture, ketchup, Worcestershire, mustard, and vinegar in blender until smooth. Season with salt and pepper. (Sauce can be refrigerated in airtight container for 1 week.

## Ultimate Charcoal-Grilled Steaks

**SERVES** 4

**WHY THIS RECIPE WORKS** For a thick steak that delivered a perfectly browned crust, even doneness, and only a minimal gray band—plus, great charred flavor from the grill—we ditched the actual grill in favor of a superhot charcoal chimney. After trimming the steaks' fat caps in order to eliminate flare-ups, we scored the steaks for better browning. We salted the steaks to ensure seasoning throughout and then baked them slowly in a low oven to cook them evenly and dehydrate their surfaces. Skewering them ahead of time made for easy handling and setup. Moving to the grill, we blasted the steaks over the chimney for about 60 seconds per side, and kept the seasoning simple with just a bit of black pepper to finish. Rib-eye steaks of a similar thickness can be substituted for strip steaks, although they may produce more flare-ups. You will need a charcoal chimney starter with a 7½-inch diameter and four 12-inch metal skewers for this recipe. If your chimney starter has a smaller diameter, skewer each steak individually and cook in four batches. It is important to remove the fat caps on the steaks to limit flare-ups during grilling.

- 2 (1-pound) boneless strip steaks, 1¾ inches thick, fat caps removed
- Kosher salt and pepper

**1.** Adjust oven rack to middle position and heat oven to 200 degrees. Cut each steak in half crosswise to create four 8-ounce steaks. Cut 1⁄16-inch-deep slits on both sides of steaks, spaced ¼ inch apart, in crosshatch pattern. Sprinkle both sides of each steak with ½ teaspoon salt (2 teaspoons total). Lay steak halves with tapered ends flat on counter and pass two 12-inch metal skewers, spaced 1½ inches apart, horizontally through steaks, making sure to keep ¼-inch space between steak halves. Repeat skewering with remaining steak halves.

**2.** Place skewered steaks on wire rack set in rimmed baking sheet, transfer to oven, and cook until centers of steaks register 120 degrees, flipping steaks over halfway through cooking and removing them as they come to temperature, 1½ hours to 1 hour 50 minutes. Tent skewered steaks (still on rack) with aluminum foil.

**3.** Light large chimney starter filled halfway with charcoal briquettes (3 quarts). When top coals are completely covered in ash, uncover steaks (reserving foil) and pat dry with paper towels. Using tongs, place 1 set of steaks directly over chimney so skewers rest on rim of chimney (meat will be suspended over coals). Cook until both sides are well browned and charred, about 1 minute per side. Using tongs, return first set of steaks to wire rack in sheet, season with pepper, and tent with reserved foil. Repeat with second set of skewered steaks. Remove skewers from steaks and serve.

## Grilled Steak with New Mexican Chile Rub

**SERVES** 6 to 8

**WHY THIS RECIPE WORKS** In this recipe, we used a two-stage rub to make the most of a comparatively inexpensive steak, the shell sirloin. We started with a savory rub of salt, onion powder, garlic powder, fish sauce, and tomato paste. This umami-rich rub made the steaks more savory and enhanced juiciness. For the second stage, we made our own coarsely ground rub based on toasted whole spices and dried chiles. By grinding our own spices, instead of using store-bought ground spices, we created a rub with much deeper flavor. Shell sirloin steak is also known as top butt, butt steak, top sirloin butt, top sirloin steak, and center-cut roast. Spraying the rubbed steaks with oil helps the spices bloom, preventing a raw flavor.

**STEAK**

- 2 teaspoons tomato paste
- 2 teaspoons fish sauce
- 1½ teaspoons kosher salt
- ½ teaspoon onion powder
- ½ teaspoon garlic powder
- 2 (1½- to 1¾-pound) boneless shell sirloin steaks, 1 to 1¼ inches thick

**SPICE RUB**

- 2 dried New Mexican chiles, stemmed, seeded, and flesh torn into ½-inch pieces
- 4 teaspoons cumin seeds
- 4 teaspoons coriander seeds
- ½ teaspoon red pepper flakes
- ½ teaspoon black peppercorns
- 1 tablespoon sugar
- 1 tablespoon paprika
- ¼ teaspoon ground cloves
- Vegetable oil spray

**1. FOR THE STEAK:** Combine tomato paste, fish sauce, salt, onion powder, and garlic powder in bowl. Pat steaks dry with paper towels. With sharp knife, cut 1/16-inch-deep slits on both sides of steaks, spaced ½ inch apart, in crosshatch pattern. Rub salt mixture evenly on both sides of steaks. Place steaks on wire rack set in rimmed baking sheet; let stand at room temperature for at least 1 hour. After 30 minutes, prepare grill.

**2. FOR THE SPICE RUB:** Toast chiles, cumin, coriander, pepper flakes, and peppercorns in 10-inch skillet over medium-low heat, stirring frequently, until just beginning to smoke, 3 to 4 minutes. Transfer to plate to cool, about 5 minutes. Grind spices in spice grinder or in mortar with pestle until coarsely ground. Transfer spices to bowl and stir in sugar, paprika, and cloves.

**3A. FOR A CHARCOAL GRILL:** Open bottom vent completely. Light large chimney starter mounded with charcoal briquettes (7 quarts). When top coals are partially covered with ash, pour two-thirds evenly over grill, then pour remaining coals over half of grill. Set cooking grate in place, cover, and open lid vent completely. Heat grill until hot, about 5 minutes.

**3B. FOR A GAS GRILL:** Turn all burners to high, cover, and heat grill until hot, about 15 minutes. Leave primary burner on high and turn other burner(s) to medium.

**4.** Clean and oil cooking grate. Sprinkle half of spice rub evenly over 1 side of steaks and press to adhere until spice rub is fully moistened. Lightly spray rubbed side of steak with vegetable oil spray, about 3 seconds. Flip steaks and repeat process of sprinkling with spice rub and coating with vegetable oil spray on second side.

**5.** Place steaks over hotter part of grill and cook until browned and charred on both sides and center registers 120 to 125 degrees (for medium-rare), 130 to 135 degrees (for medium) 3 to 4 minutes per side. If steaks have not reached desired temperature, move to cooler side of grill and continue to cook. Transfer steaks to clean wire rack set in rimmed baking sheet, tent loosely with aluminum foil, and let rest for 10 minutes. Slice meat thin against grain and serve.

## Grilled Argentine Steaks with Chimichurri

**SERVES** 6 to 8

**WHY THIS RECIPE WORKS** In Argentina, large 2-pound steaks are grilled low and slow over hardwood logs, which imbues them with a smokiness that is subtle and complex. With the piquant parsley, garlic, and olive oil sauce known as chimichurri served alongside, it's a world favorite. For our choice of steak, we selected well-marbled New York strip steak for its big beefy flavor and meaty chew. To mimic a wood fire, we added unsoaked wood chunks to the perimeter of our grill fire. Setting the lid down on the grill for the first few minutes of cooking helped to quickly trap smoke flavor. To get a deep brown char on the meat without overcooking it, we used two strategies. First, we rubbed the meat with a mixture of salt and cornstarch. Salt seasons the meat and draws out moisture, as does cornstarch. A trip to the freezer robbed them of their moisture. The par-frozen steaks browned within moments of hitting the grill and they could stand about five more minutes of fire, adding up to more char and more flavor. A less expensive strip steak alternative is a boneless shell sirloin steak (or top sirloin steak).

**SAUCE**

- ¼ cup hot water
- 2 teaspoons dried oregano
- 1 teaspoon table salt
- 1⅓ cups fresh parsley leaves
- ⅔ cup fresh cilantro leaves
- 6 garlic cloves, minced
- ½ teaspoon red pepper flakes
- ¼ cup red wine vinegar
- ½ cup extra-virgin olive oil

**STEAKS**

- 1 tablespoon cornstarch
- table salt and pepper
- 4 (1-pound) boneless strip steaks, 1½ inches thick, trimmed
- 4 (2-inch) wood chunks
- 1 (9-inch) disposable aluminum pie plate (if using gas)

**1. FOR THE SAUCE:** Combine water, oregano, and salt in small bowl and let sit until oregano is softened, about 15 minutes. Pulse parsley, cilantro, garlic, and pepper flakes in food processor until coarsely chopped, about 10 pulses. Add water mixture and vinegar and pulse to combine. Transfer mixture to bowl and slowly whisk in oil until emulsified. Cover with plastic wrap and let sit at room temperature for 1 hour.

**2. FOR THE STEAKS:** Combine cornstarch and 1½ teaspoon salt in bowl. Pat steaks dry with paper towels and place on wire rack set in rimmed baking sheet. Rub entire surface of steaks with cornstarch mixture and place steaks, uncovered, in freezer until very firm, about 30 minutes.

**3A. FOR A CHARCOAL GRILL:** Open bottom vent halfway. Light large chimney starter filled with charcoal briquettes (6 quarts). When top coals are partially covered with ash, pour evenly over grill. Place wood chunks around perimeter of coals. Set cooking grate in place, cover, and open lid vent halfway. Heat grill until hot and wood chips are smoking, about 5 minutes.

**3B. FOR A GAS GRILL:** Using metal skewer, poke holes in bottom of disposable pie plate. Place wood chunks in pie plate and set on cooking grate. Turn all burners to high, cover, and heat grill until hot, about 15 minutes. Leave all burners on high.

**4.** Clean and oil cooking grate. Season steaks with pepper. Place steaks on grill (alongside pie plate if using gas), cover, and cook until beginning to brown on both sides, 4 to 6 minutes, flipping halfway through cooking.

**5.** Flip steaks again and cook, uncovered, until well browned on first side, 2 to 4 minutes. Flip steaks once more and continue to cook until meat registers 115 to 120 degrees (for rare) or 120 to 125 degrees (for medium-rare), 2 to 6 minutes longer.

**6.** Transfer steaks to carving board, tent loosely with aluminum foil, and let rest for 10 minutes. Cut each steak crosswise into ¼-inch-thick slices. Transfer to serving platter and serve, passing sauce separately.

# Carne Asada (Mexican-Style Grilled Steak)

**SERVES** 4 to 6

**WHY THIS RECIPE WORKS** Created around 1940 at the Tampico Club in Mexico City, carne asada is typically served with a bevy of sides. We wanted to stick close to the original. A juicy, thin, well-charred steak was a must. We decided to use skirt steak, since it stayed tender when grilled to medium (the ideal doneness for both adequate charring and tender beef). A rub made with salt and cumin not only added flavor, but the salt dried out the steaks' exteriors to promote browning. For our grill setup, we used a disposable aluminum roasting pan with the bottom removed to corral the coals and ensure high heat for fast browning and char. Two pounds of sirloin steak tips, also sold as flap meat, may be substituted for the skirt steak. Serve with Red Chile Salsa, Simple Refried Beans, and Folded Enchiladas (recipes follow), if desired.

- 2 teaspoons kosher salt
- ¾ teaspoon ground cumin
- 1 (2-pound) skirt steak, trimmed, pounded ¼ inch thick, and cut with grain into 4 equal steaks
- 1 (13 by 9-inch) disposable aluminum roasting pan (if using charcoal)
- 1 garlic clove, peeled and smashed
- Lime wedges

**1.** Combine salt and cumin in small bowl. Sprinkle salt mixture evenly over both sides of steaks. Transfer steaks to wire rack set in rimmed baking sheet and refrigerate, uncovered, for at least 45 minutes or up to 24 hours. Meanwhile, if using charcoal, use kitchen shears to remove bottom of disposable pan and discard, reserving pan collar.

**2A. FOR A CHARCOAL GRILL:** Open bottom vent completely. Light large chimney starter filled with charcoal briquettes (6 quarts). When top coals are partially covered with ash, place disposable pan collar in center of grill over bottom vent and pour coals into even layer in collar. Set cooking grate in place, cover, and open lid vent completely. Heat grill until hot, about 5 minutes.

**2B. FOR A GAS GRILL:** Turn all burners to high; cover; and heat grill until hot, about 15 minutes. Leave all burners on high.

**3.** Clean and oil cooking grate. Place steaks on grill (if using charcoal, arrange steaks over coals in collar) and cook, uncovered, until well browned on first side, 2 to 4 minutes. Flip steaks and continue to cook until well browned on second side and meat registers 130 degrees, 2 to 4 minutes longer. Transfer steaks to cutting board, tent with aluminum foil, and let rest for 5 minutes.

**4.** Rub garlic thoroughly over 1 side of steaks. Slice steaks against grain ¼ inch thick and serve with lime wedges.

## Simple Refried Beans

**MAKES** 1½ cups

Using the canning liquid from the beans helps develop a creamy texture.

- 2 slices bacon
- 1 small onion, chopped fine
- 2 garlic cloves, minced
- 1 (15-ounce) can pinto beans
- ¼ cup water

Cook bacon in 10-inch nonstick skillet over medium-low heat until fat is rendered and bacon crisps, 7 to 10 minutes, flipping bacon halfway through. Remove bacon and reserve for another use. Increase heat to medium, add onion to fat in skillet, and cook until lightly browned, 5 to 7 minutes. Add garlic and cook until fragrant, about 30 seconds. Add beans and their canning liquid and water and bring to simmer. Cook, mashing beans with potato masher, until mixture is mostly smooth, 5 to 7 minutes. Season with kosher salt to taste, and serve.

## Red Chile Salsa

**MAKES** 2 cups

Guajillo chiles are tangy with just a bit of heat. Serve the salsa alongside the steak as a dipping sauce.

- 1¼ ounces dried guajillo chiles, wiped clean
- 1 (14.5-ounce) can fire-roasted diced tomatoes
- ¾ cup water
- ¾ teaspoon table salt
- 1 garlic clove, peeled and smashed
- ½ teaspoon distilled white vinegar
- ¼ teaspoon dried oregano
- ⅛ teaspoon pepper
- Pinch ground cloves
- Pinch ground cumin

Toast guajillos in 10-inch nonstick skillet over medium-high heat until softened and fragrant, 1 to 2 minutes per side. Transfer to large plate and, when cool enough to handle, remove stems and seeds. Place guajillos in blender and process until finely ground, 60 to 90 seconds, scraping down sides of blender jar as needed. Add tomatoes and their juice, water, salt, garlic, vinegar, oregano, pepper, cloves, and cumin to blender and process until very smooth, 60 to 90 seconds, scraping down sides of blender jar as needed. (Salsa can be stored in refrigerator in airtight container for up to 5 days or frozen for up to 1 month.)

### Folded Enchiladas

**SERVES** 4 to 6

Feta cheese can be substituted for the queso fresco. Guajillo chiles are tangy, with just a bit of heat.

- ⅔ ounce dried guajillo chiles, wiped clean
- 1 (8-ounce) can tomato sauce
- 1 cup chicken broth
- 1 tablespoon vegetable oil
- 1 garlic clove, peeled and smashed
- 1 teaspoon distilled white vinegar
- ¼ teaspoon ground cumin
- 12 (6-inch) soft corn tortillas
- Vegetable oil spray
- 1 small onion, chopped fine
- 2 ounces queso fresco, crumbled (½ cup)

**1.** Toast guajillos in 10-inch nonstick skillet over medium-high heat until softened and fragrant, 1 to 2 minutes per side. Transfer to large plate and, when cool enough to handle, remove stems and seeds. Place guajillos in blender and process until finely ground, 60 to 90 seconds, scraping down sides of blender jar as needed. Add tomato sauce, broth, oil, garlic, vinegar, and cumin to blender and process until very smooth, 60 to 90 seconds, scraping down sides of blender jar as needed. Season with salt to taste.

**2.** Place 1 cup enchilada sauce in large bowl. Spray both sides of tortillas with oil spray and stack on plate. Microwave, covered, until softened and warm, 60 to 90 seconds. Working with 1 tortilla at a time, dip into sauce in bowl to coat both sides, fold in quarters, and place in 8-inch square baking dish (enchiladas will overlap slightly in dish).

**3.** When ready to serve, pour remaining sauce evenly over enchiladas. Microwave enchiladas until hot throughout, 3 to 5 minutes. Sprinkle evenly with onion and queso fresco. Serve.

## Grilled Mojo-Marinated Skirt Steak

**SERVES** 4 to 6

**WHY THIS RECIPE WORKS** If you're not grilling skirt steak, you should be: It's a great cut for marinating, it cooks in minutes, and it's beefy, tender, and juicy. We chose the outside skirt steak, which is 3 to 4 inches wide, and avoided the wider, far less tender inside skirt steak. To make the most of this steak's ample surface area, we submerged it in a citrusy, garlicky Cuban-style mojo marinade. Adding soy sauce, though untraditional, helped season the meat and added even more savory flavor. We also added baking soda to the oil we rubbed onto the steak, which created even more browning during cooking. We reused the marinade as a bright serving sauce. Skirt steak is most tender when cooked to medium (130 to 135 degrees).

- 6 garlic cloves, minced
- 2 tablespoons soy sauce
- 1 teaspoon grated lime zest plus ¼ cup juice (2 limes), divided
- 1 teaspoon ground cumin
- 1 teaspoon dried oregano
- Table salt
- ½ teaspoon grated orange zest plus ½ cup juice
- ¼ teaspoon red pepper flakes
- 2 pounds skirt steak, trimmed and cut with grain into 6- to 8-inch-long steaks
- 2 tablespoons extra-virgin olive oil, divided
- 1 teaspoon baking soda

**1.** Combine garlic, soy sauce, 2 tablespoons lime juice, cumin, oregano, ¾ teaspoon salt, orange juice, and pepper flakes in 13 by 9-inch baking dish. Place steaks in dish. Flip steaks to coat both sides with marinade. Cover and refrigerate for 1 hour, flipping steaks halfway through refrigerating.

**2.** Remove steaks from marinade and transfer marinade to small saucepan. Pat steaks dry with paper towels. Combine 1 tablespoon oil and baking soda in small bowl. Rub oil mixture evenly onto both sides of each steak.

**3.** Bring marinade to boil over high heat and boil for 30 seconds. Transfer to bowl and stir in lime zest, orange zest, remaining 2 tablespoons lime juice, and remaining 1 tablespoon oil. Set aside sauce.

**4A. FOR A CHARCOAL GRILL:** About 25 minutes before grilling, open bottom vent completely. Light large chimney starter filled with charcoal briquettes (6 quarts). When top coals are partially covered with ash, pour evenly over half of grill. Set cooking grate in place, cover, and open lid vent completely. Heat grill until hot, about 5 minutes.

**4B. FOR A GAS GRILL:** Turn all burners to high, cover, and heat grill until hot, about 15 minutes. Turn off 1 burner (if using grill with more than 2 burners, turn off burner farthest from primary burner) and leave other burner(s) on high.

**5.** Clean and oil cooking grate. Cook steaks on hotter side of grill until well browned and meat registers 130 to 135 degrees (for medium), 2 to 4 minutes per side. (Move steaks to cooler side of grill before taking temperature to prevent them from overcooking.) Transfer steaks to cutting board, tent with aluminum foil, and let rest for 10 minutes. Cut steaks on bias against grain into ½-inch-thick slices. Arrange slices on serving platter, drizzle with 2 tablespoons sauce, and serve, passing extra sauce separately.

## Grill-Roasted Beef Short Ribs

**SERVES** 4 to 6

**WHY THIS RECIPE WORKS** Beef short ribs can require a lot of time and tending on the grill. We began our testing by coating our ribs with a simple spice rub. We jump-started the cooking process by giving the ribs a pit stop in the oven. In a foil-covered baking dish, the fat was rendered from the ribs, and the tough, chewy collagen began to transform into moisture-retaining gelatin. Then we headed out to the grill to complete the cooking while lacquering on our Mustard Glaze. Make sure to choose ribs that are 4 to 6 inches in length and have at least 1 inch of meat on top of the bone.

**SPICE RUB**

- 2 tablespoons kosher salt
- 1 tablespoon packed brown sugar
- 2 teaspoons pepper
- 2 teaspoons ground cumin
- 2 teaspoons garlic powder
- 1¼ teaspoons paprika
- ¾ teaspoon ground fennel
- ⅛ teaspoon cayenne pepper

**SHORT RIBS**

- 5 pounds bone-in English-style beef short ribs, trimmed
- 2 tablespoons red wine vinegar
- 1 recipe Mustard Glaze (recipe follows)

**1. FOR THE SPICE RUB:** Combine all ingredients in bowl. Measure out 1 teaspoon rub and set aside for glaze.

**2. FOR THE SHORT RIBS:** Adjust oven rack to middle position and heat oven to 300 degrees. Sprinkle ribs with spice rub, pressing into all sides of ribs. Arrange ribs, bone side down, in 13 by 9-inch baking dish, placing thicker ribs around perimeter of baking dish and thinner ribs in center. Sprinkle vinegar evenly over ribs. Cover baking dish tightly with aluminum foil. Bake until thickest ribs register 165 to 170 degrees, 1½ to 2 hours.

**3A. FOR A CHARCOAL GRILL:** Open bottom vent halfway. Arrange 2 quarts unlit charcoal into steeply banked pile against 1 side of grill. Light large chimney starter half filled with charcoal (3 quarts). When top coals are partially covered with ash, pour on top of unlit charcoal to cover one-third of grill with coals steeply banked against side of grill. Set cooking grate in place, cover, and open lid vent halfway. Heat grill until hot, about 5 minutes.

**3B. FOR A GAS GRILL:** Turn all burners to high, cover, and heat grill until hot, about 15 minutes. Leave primary burner on medium and turn off other burner(s). Adjust primary burner as needed to maintain grill temperature of 275 to 300 degrees.

**4.** Clean and oil cooking grate. Place short ribs, bone side down, on cooler side of grill about 2 inches from flames. Brush with ¼ cup glaze. Cover and cook until ribs register 195 degrees, 1¾ to 2¼ hours, rotating and brushing ribs with ¼ cup glaze every 30 minutes. Transfer ribs to large platter, tent loosely with foil, and let rest for 5 to 10 minutes before serving.

### Mustard Glaze

**MAKES** about 1 cup

- ½ cup Dijon mustard
- ½ cup red wine vinegar
- ¼ cup packed brown sugar
- 1 teaspoon reserved spice rub
- ⅛ teaspoon cayenne pepper

Whisk all ingredients together in bowl.

## Grilled Boneless Beef Short Ribs

**SERVES** 4 to 6

**WHY THIS RECIPE WORKS** The best steaks for searing over hot coals are those that have enough fat and beefy flavor to support the smoky, charred aromas that the meat acquires during grilling. Enter boneless beef short ribs: With their rich marbling and intense, beefy flavor, they can rival a rib eye on the grill—at about half the cost. Instead of flavoring just the surface of the ribs with a marinade, we salted them for an hour to ensure that they were seasoned throughout. We grilled the ribs over high heat, intentionally allowing the drippings to flare up, to impart that charred, savory grill flavor to the meat. Frequent flipping cooked the meat evenly and gently. Finally, we sliced the ribs against the grain so that they were as tender as possible. This recipe was developed using Diamond Crystal kosher salt. If you're using Morton kosher salt, which is denser, use only 1¾ teaspoons of salt. We like these ribs cooked to 130 to 135 degrees (medium). If you prefer them medium-rare, remove the ribs from the grill when they register 125 degrees. Serve with lemon wedges and flake sea salt or with Preserved Lemon-Almond Sauce.

- 2 pounds boneless beef short ribs, trimmed
- 2½ teaspoons kosher salt
- 1 teaspoon pepper

**1.** Cut ribs into 3- to 4-inch lengths. Sprinkle all sides with salt and pepper. Let sit at room temperature for 1 hour.

**2A. FOR A CHARCOAL GRILL:** Open bottom vent completely. Light large chimney starter mounded with charcoal briquettes (7 quarts). When top coals are partially covered with ash, pour evenly over half of grill. Set cooking grate in place, cover, and open lid vent completely. Heat grill until hot, about 5 minutes.

**2B. FOR A GAS GRILL:** Turn all burners to high; cover; and heat grill until hot, about 15 minutes. Turn off 1 burner (if using grill with more than 2 burners, turn off burner farthest from primary burner) and leave other burner(s) on high.

**3.** Clean and oil cooking grate. Arrange ribs on hotter side of grill. Cook (covered if using gas), flipping ribs every minute, until meat is well browned on all sides and registers about 130 degrees at thickest part, 8 to 14 minutes. (Ribs will be very pale after first flip but will continue to brown as they cook. This cut can quickly overcook; start checking temperature of smaller ribs after 8 minutes.)

**4.** Transfer ribs to cutting board, tent with aluminum foil, and let rest for 10 minutes. Slice ribs as thin as possible against grain. (Grain runs diagonally, so as long as you slice lengthwise, you will be cutting against grain.) Serve.

### Preserved Lemon–Almond Sauce

**MAKES** 1 cup

Sliced almonds provide a delicate crunch; do not substitute slivered or whole almonds.

5 tablespoons extra-virgin olive oil, divided
¼ cup sliced almonds, chopped
½ cup minced fresh parsley
2 tablespoons finely chopped preserved lemon plus 2 tablespoons brine
2 tablespoons lemon juice
¼ teaspoon sugar

Combine 1 tablespoon oil and almonds in 8-inch skillet; toast over medium-high heat, stirring constantly, until almonds are golden brown, 1 to 2 minutes. Immediately transfer to bowl. Stir in parsley, preserved lemon and brine, lemon juice, sugar, and remaining ¼ cup oil. Let sit for 15 minutes. Stir well before using. (Sauce can be refrigerated in airtight container for up to 24 hours. Let sit at room temperature for 15 minutes before serving.)

## Inexpensive Grill-Roasted Beef with Garlic and Rosemary

**SERVES** 6 to 8

**WHY THIS RECIPE WORKS** Grilling an uneven piece of meat can result in a fibrous, chewy, and woefully dry roast. We wanted to turn an inexpensive cut of meat into a juicy, evenly cooked roast with a substantial garlic-rosemary crust. After extensively testing five "cheap" roast beef options and subjecting each to a 24-hour salt rub, we settled on top sirloin, a beefy, relatively tender cut from the back half of the cow. To grill our roast, we set up a fire in which the coals cover one-third of the grill. In effect, this created hot zones for searing and cooler zones for gentler, indirect cooking. To prevent the meat from cooking too quickly, we placed the roast inside a disposable aluminum pan on the cooler side of the grill after searing it. Poking a few escape channels in the bottom of the aluminum allowed any liquid to drain away, preserving the meat's sear. We also found that cutting the roast into thin slices made the meat taste even more tender. A pair of kitchen shears works well for punching the holes in the aluminum pan. We prefer a top sirloin roast, but you can substitute a top round or bottom round roast. Start this recipe the day before you plan to grill so the salt rub has time to flavor and tenderize the meat.

6 garlic cloves, minced
2 tablespoons minced fresh rosemary
4 teaspoons kosher salt
1 tablespoon pepper
1 (3- to 4-pound) top sirloin roast
1 (13 by 9-inch) disposable aluminum roasting pan

**1.** Combine garlic, rosemary, salt, and pepper in bowl. Sprinkle all sides of roast evenly with garlic mixture, wrap tightly in plastic wrap, and refrigerate for 18 to 24 hours.

**2A. FOR A CHARCOAL GRILL:** Open bottom vent halfway. Light large chimney starter half filled with charcoal briquettes (3 quarts). When top coals are partially covered with ash, pour evenly over one-third of grill. Set cooking grate in place, cover, and open lid vent halfway. Heat grill until hot, about 5 minutes.

**2B. FOR A GAS GRILL:** Turn all burners to high, cover, and heat grill until hot, about 15 minutes.

**3.** Clean and oil cooking grate. Place roast on grill (hotter side if using charcoal) and cook (covered if using gas) until well browned on all sides, 10 to 12 minutes, turning as needed. (If flare-ups occur, move roast to cooler side of grill until flames die down.)

**4.** Meanwhile, punch fifteen ¼-inch holes in center of disposable pan in area roughly same size as roast. Once browned, place beef in pan over holes and set pan over cooler side of grill (if using charcoal) or turn primary burner to medium and other burner(s) off (if using gas). (Adjust burners as needed to maintain grill temperature of 250 to 300 degrees.) Cover and cook until meat registers 120 to 125 degrees (for medium-rare) or 130 to 135 degrees (for medium), 40 minutes to 1 hour, rotating pan halfway through cooking.

**5.** Transfer roast to wire rack set in rimmed baking sheet, tent loosely with aluminum foil, and let rest for 20 minutes. Transfer roast to carving board, slice thin against grain, and serve.

### GRILLING TOP SIRLOIN ROAST

**1.** Place roast over hot part of grill and cook until well browned on all sides, about 10 minutes.

**2.** Punch fifteen ¼-inch holes in center of 13 by 9-inch disposable aluminum roasting pan in area roughly same size as roast. Place browned beef in pan.

**3.** Set pan over cool side of grill and cover. After about 20 minutes, rotate pan 180 degrees and continue roasting until center of roast registers 120 to 125 degrees (for medium-rare) or 130 to 135 degrees (for medium), 20 to 40 minutes more.

**4.** Transfer meat to wire rack set in rimmed baking sheet. Tent loosely with aluminum foil and let rest for 20 minutes.

## Grill-Roasted Beef Tenderloin

**SERVES** 4 to 6

**WHY THIS RECIPE WORKS** Grilling is a great way to add flavor that enhances but doesn't overwhelm beef tenderloin's delicate beefiness. Producing deep browning was the first step toward delivering flavor. To do this without overcooking the tenderloin's interior, we rubbed the exterior of the roast with baking soda. This raised the meat's pH, which sped up browning by allowing the Maillard reaction to occur more quickly. "Grilled" flavor also depends on drippings from the food, which hit the coals (charcoal) or heat diffusers (gas), transform into new compounds, vaporize, and then waft up and stick to the meat. Because lean tenderloin produces very little in the way of drippings, we looked to an outside source: bacon. Threading three strips onto a metal skewer and placing the skewer directly over the heat source while the tenderloin cooked, low and slow away from direct heat, allowed the bacon to slowly render and produce the "grilled" flavor the tenderloin needed. Center-cut beef tenderloin roasts are sometimes sold as Châteaubriand. You will need one metal skewer for this recipe. The bacon will render slowly during cooking, creating a steady stream of smoke that flavors the beef. Serve the roast as is or with Chermoula Sauce (recipe follows).

- 2¼ teaspoons kosher salt
- 1 teaspoon pepper
- 2 teaspoons vegetable oil
- 1 teaspoon baking soda
- 1 (3-pound) center-cut beef tenderloin roast, trimmed and tied at 1½-inch intervals
- 3 slices bacon

**1.** Combine salt, pepper, oil, and baking soda in small bowl. Rub mixture evenly over roast and let stand while preparing grill.

**2.** Stack bacon slices. Keeping slices stacked, thread metal skewer through bacon 6 or 7 times to create accordion shape. Push stack together to compact into about 2-inch length.

**3A. FOR A CHARCOAL GRILL:** Open bottom vent halfway. Light large chimney starter two-thirds filled with charcoal briquettes (4 quarts). When top coals are partially covered with ash, pour evenly over half of grill. Set cooking grate in place, cover, and open lid vent halfway. Heat grill until hot, about 5 minutes.

**3B. FOR A GAS GRILL:** Turn all burners to high; cover; and heat grill until hot, about 15 minutes. Turn primary burner to medium and turn off other burner(s). (Adjust primary burner as necessary to maintain grill temperature of 300 degrees.)

**4.** Clean and oil cooking grate. Place roast on hotter side of grill and cook until lightly browned on all sides, about 12 minutes. Slide roast to cooler side of grill, arranging so roast is about 7 inches from heat source. Place skewered bacon on hotter side of grill. (For charcoal, place near center of grill, above edge of coals. For gas, place above heat diffuser of primary burner. Bacon should be 4 to 6 inches from roast and drippings should fall on coals or heat diffuser and produce steady stream of smoke and minimal flare-ups. If flare-ups are large or frequent, slide bacon skewer 1 inch toward roast.)

**5.** Cover and cook until beef registers 120 to 125 degrees (for medium-rare), 50 minutes to 1¼ hours. Transfer roast to carving board, tent with aluminum foil, and let rest for 20 minutes. Discard twine and slice roast ½ inch thick. Serve.

### Chermoula Sauce

**MAKES** 1 cup

To keep the sauce from becoming bitter, whisk in the olive oil by hand.

- ¾ cup fresh cilantro leaves
- 4 garlic cloves, minced
- 1 teaspoon ground cumin
- 1 teaspoon paprika
- ¼ teaspoon cayenne pepper
- ¼ teaspoon table salt
- 3 tablespoons lemon juice
- ½ cup extra-virgin olive oil

Pulse cilantro, garlic, cumin, paprika, cayenne, and salt in food processor until coarsely chopped, about 10 pulses. Add lemon juice and pulse briefly to combine. Transfer mixture to medium bowl and slowly whisk in oil until incorporated and mixture is emulsified. Cover with plastic wrap and let stand at room temperature for at least 1 hour. (Sauce can be refrigerated in airtight container for up to 2 days; bring to room temperature and rewhisk before serving.)

## Grill-Roasted Beef Tenderloin for a Crowd

**SERVES** 10 to 12

**WHY THIS RECIPE WORKS** Grilled tenderloin should be an even, rosy pink throughout; have a browned, crusty exterior; and boast a well-seasoned flavor. We found beef at wholesale clubs to be more wallet-friendly. Though these tenderloins needed some home butchering, they were well worth the modest time and effort it took to trim them. Flavor-enhancement came next through salting the meat. Tucking the narrow tip end of the tenderloin under and tying gave the tenderloin a more consistent thickness to cook through more evenly. Direct fire was too hot for the roast to endure throughout the cooking stages, so after a brief sear, we moved it to grill-roast via indirect heat. We removed it from the grill while still rare, and let the meat rest before slicing. Beef tenderloins from wholesale clubs require a good amount of trimming before cooking. At the grocery store, however, the butcher might trim it for you. Once trimmed, and with the butt tenderloin still attached (the butt tenderloin is the lobe attached to the large end of the roast), the roast should weigh 4½ to 5 pounds. If you purchase an already-trimmed tenderloin without the butt attached, begin checking for doneness about 5 minutes early. When using a charcoal grill, we prefer wood chunks to wood chips whenever possible; substitute 2 medium wood chunks, soaked in water for 1 hour, for the wood chip packet (if using). Serve with Salsa Verde, if desired.

- 1 (6-pound) beef tenderloin, trimmed of fat and silver skin, tail end tucked and tied with kitchen twine at 2-inch intervals
- 1½ tablespoons kosher salt
- 2 cups wood chips, soaked in water for 15 minutes and drained (optional)
- 2 tablespoons olive oil
- 1 tablespoon pepper

**1.** Pat tenderloin dry with paper towels and rub with salt. Cover loosely with plastic wrap and let sit at room temperature for 1 hour.

**2.** Using large piece of heavy-duty aluminum foil, wrap soaked wood chips, if using, in foil packet and cut several vent holes in top.

**3A. FOR A CHARCOAL GRILL:** Open bottom vent halfway. Light large chimney starter filled with charcoal briquettes (6 quarts). When top coals are partially covered with ash, pour evenly over half of grill. Place wood chip packet, if using, on coals. Set cooking grate in place, cover, and open lid vent halfway. Heat grill until hot and wood chips are smoking, about 5 minutes.

**3B. FOR A GAS GRILL:** Place wood chip packet, if using, opposite primary burner. Turn all burners to high, cover, and heat grill until hot and wood chips are smoking, about 15 minutes.

**4.** Clean and oil cooking grate. Rub tenderloin with oil and season with pepper. Place roast on hot side of grill if using charcoal or opposite primary burner if using gas and cook (covered if using gas) until well browned on all sides, 8 to 10 minutes, turning as needed.

**5.** For gas grill, leave primary burner on, turning off other burner(s). (Adjust primary burner as needed during cooking to maintain grill temperature around 350 degrees.) Move roast to cool side of grill, cover (position lid vent over meat if using charcoal), and cook until meat registers 115 to 120 degrees (for rare) or 120 to 125 degrees (for medium-rare), 15 to 30 minutes.

**6.** Transfer roast to carving board, tent loosely with foil, and let rest for 10 to 15 minutes. Remove twine, cut into ½-inch-thick slices, and serve.

### Salsa Verde

**MAKES** 1½ cups

Salsa verde is excellent with grilled or roasted meats, fish, or poultry; poached fish; boiled or steamed potatoes; or sliced tomatoes. It is also good on sandwiches.

- 2–3 slices hearty white sandwich bread, lightly toasted and cut into ½-inch pieces (about 1½ cups)
- 1 cup extra-virgin olive oil
- ¼ cup lemon juice (2 lemons)
- 4 cups parsley leaves
- ¼ cup capers, rinsed
- 4 anchovy fillets, rinsed
- 1 garlic clove, minced
- ¼ teaspoon table salt

Process bread, oil, and lemon juice in food processor until smooth, about 10 seconds. Add parsley, capers, anchovies, garlic, and salt and pulse until finely chopped (mixture should not be smooth), about 5 pulses. Transfer to serving bowl. (Salsa verde can be stored in an airtight container and refrigerated for up to 2 days.)

## Grill-Smoked Herb-Rubbed Flat-Iron Steaks

**SERVES** 4 to 6

**WHY THIS RECIPE WORKS** Smoking steaks can lend them complexity, but treating them like larger, collagen-rich barbecue cuts like brisket can overwhelm the meat's delicate flavor with too much smoke. We found that the key was using a small amount of wood chips and cooking the steaks quickly over direct heat so that they were just kissed with smoke. To make sure we had a consistent amount of smoke, we weighed the wood chips for more control over the smoke quantity. We salted the steaks for an hour before cooking and coated them with an herb-spice rub. We also grilled lemons to serve with the steaks for a hit of brightness. This recipe requires rubbing the steaks with salt and letting them sit at room temperature for 1 hour before cooking. You can substitute blade steaks for the flat-iron steaks, if desired. We like hickory chips in this recipe, but other kinds of wood chips will work. Gas grills are not as efficient at smoking meat as charcoal grills, so we recommend using 1½ cups of wood chips if using a gas grill.

- 2 teaspoons dried thyme
- 1 teaspoon dried rosemary
- ¾ teaspoon fennel seeds
- ½ teaspoon black peppercorns
- ¼ teaspoon red pepper flakes
- 4 (6- to 8-ounce) flat-iron steaks, ¾ to 1 inch thick, trimmed
- 1 tablespoon kosher salt
- 1–1½ cups (2½–3¾ ounces) wood chips
- Vegetable oil spray
- 2 lemons, quartered lengthwise

**1.** Grind thyme, rosemary, fennel seeds, peppercorns, and pepper flakes in spice grinder or with mortar and pestle until coarsely ground. Transfer to small bowl. Pat steaks dry with paper towels. Rub steaks evenly on both sides with salt and place on wire rack set in rimmed baking sheet. Let stand at room temperature for 1 hour. (After 30 minutes, prepare grill.)

**2.** Using large piece of heavy-duty aluminum foil, wrap wood chips (1 cup if using charcoal; 1½ cups if using gas) in 8 by 4½-inch foil packet. (Make sure chips do not poke holes in sides or bottom of packet.) Cut 2 evenly spaced 2-inch slits in top of packet.

**3A. FOR A CHARCOAL GRILL:** Open bottom vent completely. Light large chimney starter filled with charcoal briquettes (6 quarts). When top coals are partially covered with ash, pour evenly over half of grill. Place wood chip packet on coals. Set cooking grate in place, cover, and open lid vent completely. Heat grill until hot and wood chips are smoking, about 5 minutes.

**3B. FOR A GAS GRILL:** Remove cooking grate and place wood chip packet directly on primary burner. Set grate in place, turn all burners to high, cover, and heat grill until hot and wood chips are smoking, about 15 minutes. Leave primary burner on high and turn other burner(s) to medium.

**4.** Clean and oil cooking grate. Sprinkle half of herb rub evenly over 1 side of steaks and press to adhere. Lightly spray herb-rubbed side of steaks with oil spray, about 3 seconds. Flip steaks and repeat process of sprinkling and pressing steaks with remaining herb rub and coating with oil spray on second side.

**5.** Place lemons and steaks on hotter side of grill, cover (position lid vent over steaks if using charcoal), and cook until lemons and steaks are well browned on both sides and meat registers 130 to 135 degrees (for medium), 4 to 6 minutes per side. (If steaks are fully charred before reaching desired temperature, move to cooler side of grill, cover, and continue to cook.) Transfer lemons and steaks to clean wire rack set in rimmed baking sheet, tent with foil, and let rest for 10 minutes. Slice steaks thin against grain and serve, passing lemons separately.

## Barbecued Whole Beef Brisket with Spicy Chili Rub

**SERVES** 18 to 24

**WHY THIS RECIPE WORKS** Brisket starts out as a very tough cut of meat. It's also big, sometimes weighing upward of 13 pounds, which is why most butchers separate it into two cuts: the "point" and the "flat." Slow cooking for as many as six to 12 hours at a low temperature tends to be the norm for cooking brisket, but we wanted to jump-start the cooking on the grill. First, we cooked the meat for two hours to let in those smoky flavors; barbecuing the brisket fat side up allowed the fat to melt slowly over the meat. Then we moved it to the oven to cook for a few more hours unattended. For flavor, we turned to a dry rub. Our grill-to-oven approach gave us fork-tender meat with real barbecue flavor in about half the time it would take to cook the meat entirely on the grill. Cooking a whole brisket, which weighs about 10 pounds, may seem like overkill. However, the process is easy, and the leftovers keep well in the refrigerator for up to 4 days. (Leave leftover brisket unsliced, and reheat the foil-wrapped meat in a 300-degree oven until warm.) If you don't want a big piece of meat or if your grill has fewer than 400 square inches of cooking space, see the variation for Barbecued Half Beef Brisket (recipe follows). No matter what size piece you cook, it's a good idea to save the juices the meat gives off while in the oven to enrich the barbecue sauce. If you'd like to use wood chunks instead of wood chips when using a charcoal grill, substitute 2 medium wood chunks, soaked in water for 1 hour, for the wood chip packet. You can either use store-bought barbecue sauce or Quick Barbecue Sauce (page 472) in this recipe. If you cannot abide spicy food, reduce or eliminate cayenne.

- ¼ cup paprika
- 2 tablespoons chili powder
- 2 tablespoons ground cumin
- 2 tablespoons table salt
- 2 tablespoons dark brown sugar
- 1 tablespoon granulated sugar
- 1 tablespoon ground oregano
- 1 tablespoon ground black pepper
- 1 tablespoon ground white pepper
- 2 teaspoons cayenne pepper
- 1 (9- to 11-pound) whole beef brisket, fat trimmed to ¼ inch
- 2 cups wood chips
- 3 cups barbecue sauce, warmed

**1.** Combine paprika, chili powder, cumin, salt, brown sugar, granulated sugar, oregano, black pepper, white pepper, and cayenne in bowl. (Rub can be stored in airtight container at room temperature for up to 1 month.) Rub brisket thoroughly with spice mixture. Wrap brisket in plastic wrap and refrigerate for at least 2 hours, or up to 2 days.

**2.** Just before grilling, soak wood chips in water for 15 minutes, then drain. Using large piece of heavy-duty aluminum foil, wrap soaked chips in foil packet and cut several vent holes in top.

**3A. FOR A CHARCOAL GRILL:** Open bottom vent halfway. Light large chimney starter half filled with charcoal briquettes (3 quarts). When top coals are partially covered with ash, pour into steeply banked pile against side of grill. Place wood chip packet on coals. Set cooking grate in place, cover, and open lid vent halfway. Heat grill until hot and wood chips are smoking, about 5 minutes.

**3B. FOR A GAS GRILL:** Remove cooking grate and place wood chip packet directly on primary burner. Set grate in place, turn all burners to high, cover, and heat grill until hot and wood chips are smoking, about 15 minutes. Turn primary burner to medium and turn off other burner(s). (Adjust primary burner as needed to maintain grill temperature around 275 degrees.)

**4.** Clean and oil cooking grate. Place brisket, fat side up, on cooler side of grill. Cover (position lid vent over meat if using charcoal) and cook for 2 hours without removing lid.

**5.** During final 20 minutes of grilling time, adjust oven rack to middle position and heat oven to 300 degrees. Assemble 4 by 3-foot rectangle of heavy-duty aluminum foil by piecing two, 4-foot-long pieces of foil together and folding over edges two or three times to seal.

**6.** Remove brisket from grill, place lengthwise in center of foil, then fold and crimp edges of foil together to completely seal brisket. Place brisket on rimmed baking sheet and cook in oven until meat is fork-tender, 3 to 3½ hours.

**7.** Remove brisket from oven, loosen foil at one end to release steam, and let rest for 30 minutes. Unwrap brisket and transfer to carving board, pouring any meat juices into fat separator. Separate meat into two sections and slice each thinly on bias against grain. Stir 1 cup of defatted juices into barbecue sauce, and serve with brisket.

### Barbecued Half Beef Brisket with Spicy Chili Rub

This smaller brisket will serve 8 to 10 people. Either a point cut or a flat cut brisket will work well here.

Substitute 4½- to 5½-pound brisket (either point cut or flat cut) for whole brisket and rub with only half of spice rub. Reduce cooking time on grill to 1½ hours and cooking time in oven to 2 hours. Reserve ½ cup of meat juices and reduce barbecue sauce to 1½ cups.

## Texas-Style Barbecued Beef Ribs

**SERVES 4**

**WHY THIS RECIPE WORKS** In Texas, good beef ribs are all about intense meat flavor—not just smoke and spice. Can a backyard cook replicate this Lone Star classic? We first debated whether to trim the fatty membrane along the back side of the ribs. It turns out that the juiciest meat with the most flavor was accomplished by leaving the membrane in place. To turn our grill into a backyard smoker, we made a slow, even fire with a single pile of coals on one side of the grill and kept the temperature in the range of 250 to 300 degrees. About an hour and a half of slow cooking was enough to render some of the fat and make the ribs juicy and slightly toothy. We prepared a Texas-style barbecue sauce to pair with the ribs. Worcestershire added depth while tomato juice provided tangy flavor and helped thin the sauce out. Beef ribs are sold in slabs with up to seven bones, but slabs with three to four bones are easier to manage on the grill. If you cannot find ribs with a substantial amount of meat on the bones, don't bother making this recipe. One medium wood chunk, soaked in water for one hour, can be substituted for the wood chips on a charcoal grill.

**TEXAS BARBECUE SAUCE**

- 2 tablespoons unsalted butter
- ½ small onion, chopped fine
- 2 garlic cloves, minced
- 1½ teaspoons chili powder
- 1½ teaspoons pepper
- ½ teaspoon dry mustard
- 2 cups tomato juice
- 6 tablespoons distilled white vinegar
- 2 tablespoons Worcestershire sauce
- 2 tablespoons packed brown sugar
- 2 tablespoons molasses
- Table salt

**RIBS**

- 3 tablespoons packed brown sugar
- 4 teaspoons chili powder
- 1 tablespoon table salt
- 2 teaspoons pepper
- ½ teaspoon cayenne pepper
- 3–4 beef rib slabs (3 to 4 ribs per slab, about 5 pounds total), trimmed
- 1 cup wood chips, soaked in water for 15 minutes and drained

**1. FOR THE SAUCE:** Melt butter in medium saucepan over medium heat. Add onion and cook until softened, about 5 minutes. Stir in garlic, chili powder, pepper, and dry mustard and cook until fragrant, about 30 seconds. Stir in tomato juice, vinegar, Worcestershire, sugar, and molasses and simmer until sauce is reduced to 2 cups, about 20 minutes. Season with salt to taste. (Sauce can be refrigerated in airtight container for up to 1 week.)

**2. FOR THE RIBS:** Combine sugar, chili powder, salt, pepper, and cayenne in bowl. Pat ribs dry with paper towels and rub them evenly with spice mixture. Cover ribs with plastic wrap and let sit at room temperature for 1 hour.

**3.** Adjust oven rack to middle position and heat oven to 300 degrees. Set wire rack set in rimmed baking sheet and add just enough water to cover pan bottom. Arrange ribs on rack and cover tightly with aluminum foil. Bake until fat has rendered and meat begins to pull away from bones, about 2 hours. Using large piece of heavy-duty foil, wrap soaked chips in foil packet and cut several vent holes in top.

**4A. FOR A CHARCOAL GRILL:** Open bottom vent halfway. Light large chimney starter filled with charcoal briquettes (6 quarts). When top coals are partially covered with ash, pour into steeply banked pile against 1 side of grill. Place wood chip packet on coals. Set cooking grate in place, cover, and open lid vent halfway. Heat grill until hot and wood chips are smoking, about 5 minutes.

**4B. FOR A GAS GRILL:** Place wood chip packet directly on primary burner. Turn all burners to high, cover, and heat grill until hot and wood chips are smoking, about 15 minutes. Leave primary burner on high and turn other burner(s) off. (Adjust primary burner as needed to maintain grill temperature between 250 and 300 degrees.)

**5.** Clean and oil cooking grate. Place ribs meat side down on cool side of grill; ribs may overlap slightly. Cover (positioning lid vent over meat if using charcoal) and cook until ribs are lightly charred and smoky, about 1½ hours, flipping and rotating racks halfway through grilling. Transfer to cutting board, tent with foil, and let rest for 10 minutes. Serve with barbecue sauce.

## Grilled Beef Kebabs with Lemon and Rosemary Marinade

**SERVES 4 to 6**

**WHY THIS RECIPE WORKS** Kebabs take a bit of technique to live up to the expectation of chunks of beef with a caramelized char on the outside and a juicy interior, all thoroughly seasoned by a marinade and paired with tender-firm vegetables. For the meat, we chose well-marbled steak tips for their beefy flavor and tender texture. For the marinade, we included salt for moisture, oil for flavor, and sugar for browning. For even more depth, we used tomato paste, a host of seasonings and herbs, and beef broth. For the vegetables, we settled on peppers, onions, and zucchini. Grilling the beef kebabs and vegetables on separate skewers and building a fire with hotter and cooler areas allowed us to cook both the vegetables and the meat perfectly. If you can't find sirloin steak tips, sometimes labeled "flap meat," substitute 2½ pounds of blade steak; if you use blade steak, cut each steak in half to remove the gristle. You will need four 12-inch metal skewers for this recipe. If you have long, thin pieces of meat, roll or fold them into approximate 2-inch cubes before skewering.

**MARINADE**

- 1 onion, chopped
- ⅓ cup beef broth
- ⅓ cup vegetable oil
- 3 tablespoons tomato paste
- 6 garlic cloves, chopped
- 2 tablespoons chopped fresh rosemary
- 2 teaspoons grated lemon zest
- 2 teaspoons table salt
- 1½ teaspoons sugar
- ¾ teaspoon pepper

**BEEF AND VEGETABLES**

- 2 pounds sirloin steak tips, trimmed and cut into 2-inch chunks
- 1 large zucchini or summer squash, halved lengthwise and sliced 1 inch thick
- 1 large red or green bell pepper, stemmed, seeded, and cut into 1½-inch pieces
- 1 large red or sweet onion, halved lengthwise, each half cut into 4 wedges and each wedge cut crosswise into thirds

**1. FOR THE MARINADE:** Process all ingredients in blender until smooth, about 45 seconds. Transfer ¾ cup marinade to large bowl and set aside.

**2. FOR THE BEEF AND VEGETABLES:** Place remaining marinade and beef in 1-gallon zipper-lock bag and toss to coat; press out as much air as possible and seal bag. Refrigerate for at least 1 to 2 hours, flipping bag every 30 minutes.

**3.** Add zucchini, bell pepper, and onion to bowl with reserved marinade and toss to coat. Cover and let sit at room temperature for at least 30 minutes.

**4.** Remove beef from bag and pat dry with paper towels. Thread beef tightly onto two 12-inch metal skewers. Alternating pattern of zucchini, bell pepper, and onion, thread vegetables onto two 12-inch metal skewers.

**5A. FOR A CHARCOAL GRILL:** Open bottom vent completely. Light large chimney starter mounded with charcoal briquettes (7 quarts). When top coals are partially covered with ash, pour evenly over center of grill, leaving 2-inch gap between grill wall and charcoal. Set cooking grate in place, cover, and open lid vent completely. Heat grill until hot, about 5 minutes.

**5B. FOR A GAS GRILL:** Turn all burners to high, cover, and heat grill until hot, about 15 minutes. Leave primary burner on high and turn other burner(s) to medium-low.

**6.** Clean and oil cooking grate. Place beef skewers on grill (directly over coals if using charcoal or over hotter side of grill if using gas). Place vegetable skewers on grill (near edge of coals but still over coals if using charcoal or over cooler side of grill if using gas). Cook (covered if using gas), turning skewers every 3 to 4 minutes, until beef is well browned and registers 120 to 125 degrees (for medium-rare) or 130 to 135 degrees (for medium), 12 to 16 minutes. Transfer beef skewers to platter and tent loosely with aluminum foil. Continue to cook vegetable skewers until tender and lightly charred, about 5 minutes; serve with beef skewers.

## Grilled Beef Satay

**SERVES 6**

**WHY THIS RECIPE WORKS** For our version of this popular street food, we started by slicing beefy-flavored flank steak thin across the grain and threading it onto skewers. To add flavor, we used a basting sauce consisting of coconut milk, fish sauce, aromatics, and warm spices rather than the overtenderizing marinade used in many recipes. And to ensure that the quick-cooking beef achieved a burnished exterior, we corralled the coals in an aluminum pan in the center of the grill to bring them closer to the meat. You will need ten to twelve 12-inch metal skewers for this recipe. Bamboo skewers soaked in water for 30 minutes can be substituted for metal skewers. The aluminum pan used for charcoal grilling should be at least 2¾ inches deep; you will not need the pan for a gas grill. Kitchen shears work well for punching the holes in the pan. Unless you have a very high-powered gas grill, these skewers will not be as well seared as they would be with charcoal. Serve with Peanut Sauce and rice.

BASTING SAUCE

- ¾ cup regular or light coconut milk
- 3 tablespoons packed dark brown sugar
- 3 tablespoons fish sauce
- 2 tablespoons vegetable oil
- 3 shallots, minced
- 2 lemon grass stalks, trimmed to bottom 6 inches and minced
- 2 tablespoons grated fresh ginger
- 1½ teaspoons ground coriander
- ¾ teaspoon red pepper flakes
- ½ teaspoon ground cumin
- ½ teaspoon table salt

BEEF

- 2 tablespoons vegetable oil
- 2 tablespoons packed dark brown sugar
- 1 tablespoon fish sauce
- 1 (1½- to 1¾-pound) flank steak, halved lengthwise and sliced on slight angle against grain into ¼-inch-thick slices
- Disposable aluminum deep roasting pan (if using charcoal)

**1. FOR THE BASTING SAUCE:** Whisk all ingredients together in bowl. Reserve one-third of sauce in separate bowl.

**2. FOR THE BEEF:** Whisk oil, sugar, and fish sauce together in medium bowl. Toss beef with marinade and let stand at room temperature for 30 minutes. Weave beef onto 12-inch metal skewers, 2 to 4 pieces per skewer, leaving 1½ inches at top and bottom of skewer exposed. You should have 10 to 12 skewers.

**3A. FOR A CHARCOAL GRILL:** Punch twelve ½-inch holes in bottom of disposable roasting pan. Open bottom vent completely and place roasting pan in center of grill. Light large chimney starter mounded with charcoal briquettes (7 quarts). When top coals are partially covered with ash, pour into roasting pan. Set cooking grate over coals with grates parallel to long side of roasting pan, cover, and open lid vent completely. Heat grill until hot, about 5 minutes.

**3B. FOR A GAS GRILL:** Turn all burners to high, cover, and heat grill until hot, about 15 minutes. Leave all burners on high.

**4.** Clean and oil cooking grate. Place beef skewers on grill (directly over coals if using charcoal) perpendicular to grate. Brush meat with reserved one-third of basting sauce and cook (covered if using gas) until browned, about 3 minutes. Flip skewers, brush with half of remaining basting sauce, and cook until browned on second side, about 3 minutes. Brush meat with remaining basting sauce and cook 1 minute longer. Transfer to large platter and serve with Peanut Sauce.

### Peanut Sauce

**MAKES** about 1½ cups

- 1 tablespoon vegetable oil
- 1 tablespoon Thai red curry paste
- 1 tablespoon packed dark brown sugar
- 2 garlic cloves, minced
- 1 cup regular or light coconut milk
- ⅓ cup chunky peanut butter
- ¼ cup dry-roasted unsalted peanuts, chopped
- 1 tablespoon lime juice
- 1 tablespoon fish sauce
- 1 teaspoon soy sauce

Heat oil in small saucepan over medium heat until shimmering. Add curry paste, sugar, and garlic; cook, stirring constantly, until fragrant, about 1 minute. Add coconut milk and bring to simmer. Whisk in peanut butter until smooth. Remove from heat and stir in peanuts, lime juice, fish sauce, and soy sauce. Cool to room temperature.

## Easy Grilled Boneless Pork Chops

**SERVES** 4 to 6

**WHY THIS RECIPE WORKS** Pork chops are a prime candidate for the grill, which can imbue the lean chops with smoky, savory flavor, but too often, the results are disappointing. To produce juicy, well-charred boneless pork chops on the grill, we used a two-pronged approach. We brined the chops to improve their ability to hold on to juices during cooking, provide seasoning throughout, and increase their tenderness. To ensure that we'd get a substantial browned crust before the interior overcooked, we looked to a unique coating of anchovy paste and honey. The anchovies' amino acids couple with the fructose from honey to rapidly begin the flavorful Maillard browning reaction. If your pork is enhanced, do not brine it in step 1. Very finely mashed anchovy fillets (rinsed and dried before mashing) can be used instead of anchovy paste. Serve with Onion, Olive, and Caper Relish (page 604) if desired.

- 6 (6- to 8-ounce) boneless pork chops, ¾ to 1 inch thick
- 3 tablespoons table salt for brining
- 1 tablespoon vegetable oil
- 1½ teaspoons honey
- 1 teaspoon anchovy paste
- ½ teaspoon pepper
- 1 recipe Onion, Olive, and Caper Relish (optional) (page 604)

**1.** Cut 2 slits about 1 inch apart through outer layer of fat and connective tissue on each chop to prevent buckling. Dissolve salt in 1½ quarts cold water in large container. Submerge chops in brine and let stand at room temperature for 30 minutes.

**2.** Whisk together oil, honey, anchovy paste, and pepper to form smooth paste. Remove pork from brine and pat dry with paper towels. Using spoon, spread half of oil mixture evenly over 1 side of each chop (about ¼ teaspoon per side).

**3A. FOR A CHARCOAL GRILL:** Open bottom vent completely. Light chimney starter filled with charcoal briquettes (6 quarts). When top coals are partially covered with ash, pour evenly over half of grill. Set cooking grate in place, cover, and open lid vent completely. Heat grill until hot, about 5 minutes.

**3B. FOR A GAS GRILL:** Turn all burners to high; cover; and heat grill until hot, about 15 minutes. Leave primary burner on high and turn off other burner(s).

**4.** Clean and oil cooking grate. Place chops, oiled side down, over hotter part of grill and cook, uncovered, until well browned on first side, 4 to 6 minutes. While chops are grilling, spread remaining oil mixture evenly over second side of chops. Flip chops and continue to cook until chops register 140 to 145 degrees, 4 to 6 minutes longer (if chops are well browned but register less than 140 degrees, move to cooler part of grill to finish cooking). Transfer chops to plate and let rest for 5 minutes. Serve with relish, if using.

### Onion, Olive, and Caper Relish

**MAKES** 2 cups

- ¼ cup extra-virgin olive oil, divided
- 2 onions, cut into ¼-inch pieces
- 6 garlic cloves, sliced thin
- ½ cup pitted kalamata olives, chopped coarse
- ¼ cup capers, rinsed
- 3 tablespoons balsamic vinegar
- 2 tablespoons minced fresh parsley
- 1 teaspoon minced fresh marjoram
- 1 teaspoon sugar
- ½ teaspoon anchovy paste
- ½ teaspoon pepper
- ¼ teaspoon table salt

Heat 2 tablespoons oil in 10-inch nonstick skillet over medium heat until shimmering. Add onions and cook until softened, about 5 minutes. Stir in garlic and cook until fragrant, about 30 seconds. Transfer onion mixture to medium bowl; stir in remaining 2 tablespoons oil, olives, capers, vinegar, parsley, marjoram, sugar, anchovy paste, pepper, and salt. Serve warm or at room temperature.

## Grilled Pork Chops

**SERVES** 4

**WHY THIS RECIPE WORKS** Too many grilled pork chops are burnt on the outside and raw on the inside. And even if they are cooked evenly, they can still be tough and bland. We wanted great-looking and great-tasting chops with a perfectly grilled, crisp crust and juicy, flavorful meat. What's more, we wanted our chops plump and meaty, not thin and tough. We started with the right chops—tender and flavorful bone-in rib loin or center-cut loin chops worked best—and brined them to pump up their flavor and lock in moisture. To brown the pork chops, only a really hot fire would do. So we grilled the chops over a two-level fire, with one side of the grill intensely hot to sear the chops, and the other only moderately hot to allow the chops to cook through without burning the exterior. So they wouldn't overcook, we pulled the chops from the grill when they were just underdone, and let the chops rest until the temperature rose to serving temperature and the juices were redistributed in the meat. A spice rub, made with potent spices and applied before grilling, added big flavor and gave our chops a nice crust. Rib loin chops are our top choice for their big flavor and juiciness. If the pork is enhanced, do not brine and add 2 teaspoons salt along with spice rub or pepper.

- 3 tablespoons table salt
- 3 tablespoons sugar
- 4 (12-ounce) bone-in pork rib or center-cut chops, 1½ inches thick, trimmed
- 1 recipe Basic Spice Rub for Pork Chops (recipe follows) or 2 teaspoons pepper

**1.** Dissolve salt and sugar in 1½ quarts cold water in large container. Submerge chops in brine, cover, and refrigerate for 30 minutes to 1 hour. Remove chops from brine and pat dry with paper towels. Rub chops with spice rub.

**2A. FOR A CHARCOAL GRILL:** Open bottom vent completely. Light large chimney starter filled with charcoal briquettes (6 quarts). When top coals are partially covered with ash, pour two-thirds evenly over grill, then pour remaining coals over half of grill. Set cooking grate in place, cover, and open lid vent completely. Heat grill until hot, about 5 minutes.

**2B. FOR A GAS GRILL:** Turn all burners to high, cover, and heat grill until hot, about 15 minutes. Leave primary burner on high and turn off other burner(s).

**3.** Clean and oil cooking grate. Place chops on hotter side of grill and cook (covered if using gas) until browned on both sides, 4 to 8 minutes. Move chops to cool side of grill, cover, and continue to cook, turning once, until meat registers 140 to 145 degrees, 7 to 9 minutes longer. Transfer chops to serving platter, tent loosely with aluminum foil, and let rest for 5 to 10 minutes. Serve.

### Basic Spice Rub for Pork Chops

**MAKES** ¼ cup

- 1 tablespoon ground cumin
- 1 tablespoon chili powder
- 1 tablespoon curry powder
- 2 teaspoons packed brown sugar
- 1 teaspoon pepper

Combine all ingredients in bowl.

## Grill-Smoked Pork Chops

**SERVES 4**

**WHY THIS RECIPE WORKS** Getting good smoke flavor and a charred crust is an elusive grilling goal. Smokiness generally requires a lengthy exposure to a slow fire, while a charred crust requires a blast of high heat to quickly sear the exterior of the meat before the interior turns dry. We wanted chops that had it all: charred crust, ultra-moist meat, and true smoke flavor. We decided to employ a technique we had used in previous pork chop recipes: reversing the cooking by starting low and finishing with a quick sear. To reap the benefits of both high and low heat on a charcoal grill, we used a double-banked fire (made by placing a disposable aluminum pan between two mounds of coals) and started our chops under cover on the cooler center of the grill, allowing the smoke to do its job for about 25 minutes. We then applied a few coats of sauce and finished by searing them, uncovered, over hot coals. As for arranging the chops on the grill, we found it best to rest each chop on its bone instead of laying it flat. To keep them from toppling over, we speared the chops together with skewers, making sure to leave a good inch between each one to allow smoke to circulate, then stood them upright in the center of the grill with bone, not meat, touching the grill. This allowed us to keep the chops over the fire for a full 30 minutes, after which we removed the skewers, applied the glaze, and finished the chops over hot coals for that crusty char. Buy chops of the same thickness so they will cook uniformly. Use the large holes on a box grater to grate the onion for the sauce. Two medium wood chunks, soaked in water for 1 hour, can be substituted for the wood chip packet on a charcoal grill. You will need two 10-inch metal skewers for this recipe.

**SAUCE**

- ½ cup ketchup
- ¼ cup molasses
- 2 tablespoons grated onion
- 2 tablespoons Worcestershire sauce
- 2 tablespoons Dijon mustard
- 2 tablespoons cider vinegar
- 1 tablespoon packed light brown sugar

**CHOPS**

- 2 cups wood chips, soaked in water for 15 minutes and drained
- 4 (12-ounce) bone-in pork rib chops, 1½ inches thick, trimmed
- 2 teaspoons table salt
- 2 teaspoons pepper
- 1 (13 by 9-inch) disposable aluminum roasting pan (if using charcoal)

**1. FOR THE SAUCE:** Bring all ingredients to simmer in small saucepan over medium heat and cook, stirring occasionally, until reduced to about 1 cup, 5 to 7 minutes. Transfer ½ cup sauce to small bowl and set aside remaining sauce for serving.

**2. FOR THE CHOPS:** Using large piece of heavy-duty aluminum foil, wrap soaked chips in foil packet and cut several vent holes in top. Pat pork chops dry with paper towels. Use sharp knife to cut 2 slits about 1 inch apart through outer layer of fat and connective tissue. Season each chop with ½ teaspoon salt and ½ teaspoon pepper. Place chops side by side, facing in same direction, on cutting board with curved rib bone facing down. Pass 2 skewers through loin muscle of each chop, close to bone, about 1 inch from each end, then pull apart to create 1-inch space between each.

**3A. FOR A CHARCOAL GRILL:** Open bottom vent halfway and place roasting pan in center of grill. Light large chimney starter filled with charcoal briquettes (6 quarts). When top coals are partially covered with ash, pour into 2 even piles on either side of roasting pan. Place wood chip packet on 1 pile of coals. Set cooking grate in place, cover, and open lid vent halfway. Heat grill until hot and wood chips are smoking, about 5 minutes.

**3B. FOR A GAS GRILL:** Place wood chip packet over primary burner. Turn all burners to high, cover, and heat grill until hot and wood chips are smoking, about 15 minutes. Turn all burners to medium-high. (Adjust burners as needed during cooking to maintain grill temperature between 300 and 325 degrees.)

**4.** Clean and oil cooking grate. Place skewered chops bone side down on grill (over pan if using charcoal). Cover and cook until meat registers 120 degrees, 28 to 32 minutes.

**5.** Remove skewers from chops, tip chops onto flat side and brush surface of each with 1 tablespoon sauce. Transfer chops, sauce side down, to hotter parts of grill (if using charcoal) or turn all burners to high (if using gas) and cook until browned on first side, 2 to 6 minutes. Brush top of each chop with 1 tablespoon sauce, flip, and continue to cook until browned on second side and meat registers 140 to 145 degrees, 2 to 6 minutes longer.

**6.** Transfer chops to serving platter, tent loosely with aluminum foil, and let rest for 5 to 10 minutes. Serve, passing reserved sauce separately.

### SKEWERING PORK CHOPS FOR THE GRILL

**1.** Pass two skewers through the loin muscle of each chop to provide stability when standing on the grill.

**2.** Stand the skewered chops, bone side down, on the cooking grate in the center of the grill so smoke can reach all sides.

## Garlic-Lime Grilled Pork Tenderloin Steaks

**SERVES** 4 to 6

**WHY THIS RECIPE WORKS** Although pork tenderloin medallions make for a nice presentation and offer lots of surface area to crisp and brown on the grill, they are inherently fussy. We wanted to take the spirit of the medallion approach but find a shape and a technique that, while it reliably delivered a flavorful, nicely browned crust, still kept this lean cut tender. We started by cutting two tenderloin roasts in half and pounding them to an even thickness to make pork tenderloin "steaks." A two-level grill fire, with both hotter and cooler areas, allowed us to sear the steaks on the hotter side and then let them gently finish cooking on the cooler side. We added both bold seasoning and richness through a marinade. Plenty of salt ensured thorough seasoning and tender meat. Oil, lime juice and zest, garlic, fish sauce (which provided a savory boost without tasting fishy), and honey (the sugars in which would encourage browning) rounded out the marinade. A bit of reserved marinade, whisked with some mayo for body and cilantro for freshness, completed our tenderloin steaks. Since marinating is a key step in this recipe, we don't recommend using enhanced pork (injected with a salt solution).

- 2 (1-pound) pork tenderloins, trimmed
- 1 tablespoon grated lime zest plus ¼ cup juice (2 limes)
- 4 garlic cloves, minced
- 4 teaspoons honey
- 2 teaspoons fish sauce
- ¾ teaspoon table salt
- ½ teaspoon pepper
- ½ cup vegetable oil
- 4 teaspoons mayonnaise
- 1 tablespoon chopped fresh cilantro

**1.** Slice each tenderloin in half crosswise to create 4 steaks total. Pound each half to ¾-inch thickness. Using sharp knife, cut ⅛-inch-deep slits spaced ½ inch apart in crosshatch pattern on both sides of steaks.

**2.** Whisk lime zest and juice, garlic, honey, fish sauce, salt, and pepper together in large bowl. Whisking constantly, slowly drizzle oil into lime mixture until smooth and slightly thickened. Transfer ½ cup lime mixture to small bowl and whisk in mayonnaise; set aside sauce. Add steaks to bowl with remaining marinade and toss thoroughly to coat; transfer steaks and marinade to large zipper-lock bag, press out as much air as possible, and seal bag. Let steaks sit at room temperature for 45 minutes.

**3A. FOR A CHARCOAL GRILL:** Open bottom vent completely. Light large chimney starter filled with charcoal briquettes (6 quarts). When top coals are partially covered with ash, pour evenly over half of grill. Set cooking grate in place, cover, and open lid vent completely. Heat grill until hot, about 5 minutes.

**3B. FOR A GAS GRILL:** Turn all burners to high; cover; and heat grill until hot, about 15 minutes. Leave primary burner on high and turn off other burner(s).

**4.** Clean and oil cooking grate. Remove steaks from marinade (do not pat dry) and place over hotter part of grill. Cook, uncovered, until well browned on first side, 3 to 4 minutes. Flip steaks and cook until well browned on second side, 3 to 4 minutes. Transfer steaks to cooler part of grill, with wider end of each steak facing hotter part of grill. Cover and cook until meat registers 140 to 145 degrees, 3 to 8 minutes longer (remove steaks as they come to temperature). Transfer steaks to cutting board and let rest for 5 minutes.

**5.** While steaks rest, microwave reserved sauce until warm, 15 to 30 seconds; stir in cilantro. Slice steaks against grain ½ inch thick. Drizzle with half of sauce; sprinkle with flake sea salt, if desired; and serve, passing remaining sauce separately.

## Grilled Glazed Pork Tenderloin Roast

**SERVES** 6

**WHY THIS RECIPE WORKS** Too often, delicate pork tenderloin turns out disappointing: The lean meat dries out easily, and it is plagued by uneven cooking because of its tapered shape. To make the pork cook more evenly and to create a more presentation-worthy roast, we tied two tenderloins together. Scraping the insides of the tenderloins with a fork created a sticky protein network that helped the tenderloins bind together. To ensure that our pork retained maximum juiciness, we brined the meat and cooked it mostly over indirect heat. Since brining is a key step in having the two tenderloins stick together, we don't recommend using enhanced pork (injected with a salt solution) in this recipe.

- 2 (1-pound) pork tenderloins, trimmed
- Table salt and pepper
- Vegetable oil
- 1 recipe Miso Glaze

**1.** Lay tenderloins on cutting board, flat side (side opposite where silverskin was) up. Holding thick end of 1 tenderloin with paper towels and using dinner fork, scrape flat side lengthwise from end to end 5 times, until surface is completely covered with shallow grooves. Repeat with second tenderloin. Dissolve 3 tablespoons salt in 1½ quarts cold water in large container. Submerge tenderloins in brine and let stand at room temperature for 1 hour.

**2.** Remove tenderloins from brine and pat completely dry with paper towels. Lay 1 tenderloin, scraped side up, on cutting board and lay second tenderloin, scraped side down, on top so that thick end of 1 tenderloin matches up with thin end of other. Spray five 14-inch lengths of kitchen twine thoroughly with vegetable oil spray; evenly space twine underneath tenderloins and tie. Brush roast with vegetable oil and season with pepper. Transfer ⅓ cup glaze to bowl for grilling; reserve remaining glaze for serving.

**3A. FOR A CHARCOAL GRILL:** Open bottom vent completely. Light large chimney starter filled with charcoal briquettes (6 quarts). When top coals are partially covered with ash, pour

into steeply banked pile against side of grill. Set cooking grate in place, cover, and open lid vent completely. Heat grill until hot, about 5 minutes.

**3B. FOR A GAS GRILL:** Turn all burners to high, cover, and heat grill until hot, about 15 minutes. Leave primary burner on high and turn off other burner(s).

**4.** Clean and oil cooking grate. Place roast on cooler side of grill, cover, and cook until meat registers 115 degrees, 22 to 28 minutes, flipping and rotating halfway through cooking.

**5.** Slide roast to hotter side of grill and cook until lightly browned on all sides, 4 to 6 minutes. Brush top of roast with about 1 tablespoon glaze and grill, glaze side down, until glaze begins to char, 2 to 3 minutes; repeat glazing and grilling with remaining 3 sides of roast, until meat registers 135 to 140 degrees.

**6.** Transfer roast to carving board, tent loosely with aluminum foil, and let rest for 10 minutes. Carefully remove twine and slice roast into ½-inch-thick slices. Serve with remaining glaze.

## Miso Glaze

**MAKES** about ¾ cup

- 3 tablespoons sake
- 3 tablespoons mirin
- ⅓ cup white miso paste
- ¼ cup sugar
- 2 teaspoons Dijon mustard
- 1 teaspoon rice vinegar
- ¼ teaspoon grated fresh ginger
- ¼ teaspoon toasted sesame oil

Bring sake and mirin to boil in small saucepan over medium heat. Whisk in miso and sugar until smooth, about 30 seconds. Remove pan from heat and continue to whisk until sugar is dissolved, about 1 minute. Whisk in mustard, vinegar, ginger, and sesame oil until smooth.

## Grilled Pork Tenderloin with Grilled Pineapple–Red Onion Salsa

**SERVES** 4 to 6

**WHY THIS RECIPE WORKS** To produce pork tenderloin with a rich crust and a tender, juicy interior, we used a half-grill fire and seared the roast on the hotter side of the grill. This allowed the exterior to develop flavorful browning before the interior was cooked through. Then we moved the meat to the cooler side of the grill to finish cooking gently. Seasoning the meat with a mixture of salt, cumin, and chipotle chile powder added smoky, savory flavor, and a touch of sugar encouraged browning. To add bright flavor and make the most of the fire, we grilled pineapple and red onion and, while the cooked pork rested, combined them with cilantro, a serrano chile, lime juice, and a bit of reserved spice mixture to make a quick salsa. We prefer unenhanced pork in this recipe, but enhanced pork (injected with a salt solution) can be used.

**PORK**

- 1½ teaspoons kosher salt
- 1½ teaspoons sugar
- ½ teaspoon ground cumin
- ½ teaspoon chipotle chile powder
- 2 (12- to 16-ounce) pork tenderloins, trimmed

**SALSA**

- ½ pineapple, peeled, cored, and cut lengthwise into 6 wedges
- 1 red onion, cut into 8 wedges through root end
- 4 teaspoons extra-virgin olive oil, divided
- ½ cup minced fresh cilantro
- 1 serrano chile, stemmed, seeded, and minced
- 2 tablespoons lime juice, plus extra for seasoning

**1. FOR THE PORK:** Combine salt, sugar, cumin, and chile powder in small bowl. Reserve ½ teaspoon spice mixture. Rub remaining spice mixture evenly over surface of both tenderloins. Transfer to large plate or rimmed baking sheet and refrigerate while preparing grill.

**2A. FOR A CHARCOAL GRILL:** Open bottom vent completely. Light large chimney starter filled with charcoal briquettes (6 quarts). When top coals are partially covered with ash, pour evenly over half of grill. Set cooking grate in place, cover, and open lid vent completely. Heat grill until hot, about 5 minutes.

**2B. FOR A GAS GRILL:** Turn all burners to high; cover; and heat grill until hot, about 15 minutes. Leave primary burner on high and turn off other burner(s).

**3.** Clean and oil cooking grate. Place tenderloins on hotter side of grill. Cover and cook, turning tenderloins every 2 minutes, until well browned on all sides, about 8 minutes.

**4. FOR THE SALSA:** Brush pineapple and onion with 1 teaspoon oil. Move tenderloins to cooler side of grill (6 to 8 inches from heat source) and place pineapple and onion on hotter side of grill. Cover and cook until pineapple and onion are charred on both sides and softened, 8 to 10 minutes, and until pork registers 135 to 140 degrees, 12 to 17 minutes, turning tenderloins every 5 minutes. As pineapple and onion and tenderloins reach desired level of doneness, transfer pineapple and onion to plate and transfer tenderloins to carving board. Tent tenderloins with aluminum foil and let rest for 10 minutes.

**5.** While tenderloins rest, chop pineapple coarse. Pulse pineapple, onion, cilantro, serrano, lime juice, reserved spice mixture, and remaining 1 tablespoon oil in food processor until mixture is roughly chopped, 4 to 6 pulses. Transfer to bowl and season with salt and extra lime juice to taste.

**6.** Slice tenderloins crosswise ½ inch thick. Serve with salsa.

## Grilled Stuffed Pork Tenderloin

**SERVES** 6 to 8

**WHY THIS RECIPE WORKS** Pork tenderloin is quick cooking, extremely tender, and has a uniform shape that allows for even cooking. But this cut is also mild and lean, making it prone to drying out. Stuffing this roast solves these problems by adding flavor and moisture. For more surface area for the filling, we pounded, filled, then rolled the tenderloins. And for our filling, we pulsed bold ingredients in a food processor for an intense paste that didn't leak. When it came time to fire up the grill, we found that a two-level fire, with the coals spread over half the grill, allowed the pork to cook evenly without drying out. A brown sugar rub on the exterior of each tenderloin boosted browning significantly. We prefer natural to enhanced pork (pork that has been injected with a salt solution to increase moistness and flavor) for this recipe.

- 4 teaspoons packed dark brown sugar
- Table salt and pepper
- 2 (1¼- to 1½-pound) pork tenderloins, trimmed
- 1 recipe Olive and Sun-Dried Tomato Stuffing
- 1 cup baby spinach
- 2 tablespoons olive oil

**1.** Combine sugar, 1 teaspoon salt, and 1 teaspoon pepper in bowl. Cut each tenderloin in half horizontally, stopping ½ inch from edge so halves remain attached. Open up tenderloins, cover with plastic wrap, and pound to ¼-inch thickness. Trim any ragged edges to create rough rectangle about 10 inches by 6 inches. Season interior of pork with salt and pepper.

**2.** With long side of pork facing you, spread half of stuffing mixture over bottom half of pork followed by ½ cup of spinach. Roll away from you into tight cylinder, taking care not to squeeze stuffing out ends. Position tenderloin seam side down, evenly space 5 pieces kitchen twine underneath, and tie. Repeat with remaining tenderloin, stuffing, and spinach.

**3A. FOR A CHARCOAL GRILL:** Open bottom vent completely. Light large chimney starter filled with charcoal briquettes (6 quarts). When top coals are partially covered with ash, pour evenly over half of grill. Set cooking grate in place, cover, and open lid vent completely. Heat grill until hot, about 5 minutes.

**3B. FOR A GAS GRILL:** Turn all burners to high, cover, and heat grill until hot, about 15 minutes. Leave primary burner on high and turn off other burner(s). (Adjust primary burner as needed during cooking to maintain grill temperature between 325 and 350 degrees.)

**4.** Clean and oil cooking grate. Coat pork with oil, then rub entire surface with brown sugar mixture. Place pork on cool side of grill, cover, and cook until meat registers 135 to 140 degrees, 25 to 30 minutes, rotating pork halfway through cooking.

**5.** Transfer pork to carving board, tent loosely with aluminum foil, and let rest for 20 minutes. Remove twine, slice pork into ½-inch-thick slices, and serve.

### Olive and Sun-Dried Tomato Stuffing

**MAKES** about 1 cup

- ½ cup pitted kalamata olives
- ½ cup oil-packed sun-dried tomatoes, rinsed and chopped coarse
- 4 anchovy fillets, rinsed
- 2 garlic cloves, minced
- 1 teaspoon minced fresh thyme
- 1 teaspoon grated lemon zest
- Table salt and pepper

Pulse all ingredients except salt and pepper in food processor until coarsely chopped, 5 to 10 pulses; season with salt and pepper to taste.

## Grilled Pork Loin with Apple-Cranberry Filling

**SERVES** 6

**WHY THIS RECIPE WORKS** Center-cut pork loin is an especially lean cut, making it difficult to cook without drying out. We wanted to cook our pork loin on the grill but keep it moist using an approach other than traditional brines or sauces. We decided to use a moist, well-seasoned stuffing. We bought a short and wide roast, more square than cylindrical. This shape required only a few straight, short cuts to open to a long, flat sheet that was easy to fill and roll up. The best stuffing required both a deep flavor to counter the pork's rather bland taste and a texture thick enough to stay put. Poaching apples and cranberries in a blend of apple cider, apple cider vinegar, and spices developed a filling with the consistency we wanted. And we had ample poaching liquid left, which could be reduced to a glaze. We had already decided not to give the loin a preliminary sear, which can create a tough exterior, but found we missed the brown color that searing produces. Rolling the loin in our glaze gave it a beautifully burnished finish. This recipe is best prepared with a loin that is 7 to 8 inches long and 4 to 5 inches wide and not enhanced (injected with a salt solution). To make cutting the pork easier, freeze it for 30 minutes. If mustard seeds are unavailable, stir an equal amount of whole grain mustard into the filling after the apples have been processed. If you'd like to use wood chunks instead of wood chips when using a charcoal grill, substitute 2 medium wood chunks, soaked in water for 1 hour, for the wood chip packet.

**FILLING**

- 1½ cups (4 ounces) dried apples
- 1 cup apple cider
- ¾ cup packed light brown sugar
- ½ cup cider vinegar
- ½ cup dried cranberries
- 1 large shallot, halved lengthwise and sliced thin crosswise
- 1 tablespoon grated fresh ginger
- 1 tablespoon yellow mustard seeds
- ½ teaspoon ground allspice
- ⅛–¼ teaspoon cayenne pepper

**PORK**

- 1 (2½-pound) boneless center-cut pork loin roast, trimmed
- Table salt and pepper
- 2 cups wood chips, soaked in water for 15 minutes and drained

1. **FOR THE FILLING:** Bring all ingredients to simmer in medium saucepan over medium-high heat. Cover, reduce heat to low, and cook until apples are very soft, about 20 minutes. Pour mixture through fine-mesh strainer set over bowl, pressing with back of spoon to extract as much liquid as possible. Return liquid to saucepan and simmer over medium-high heat until reduced to ⅓ cup, about 5 minutes; reserve for glazing. Pulse apple mixture in food processor until coarsely chopped, about 15 pulses. Transfer filling to bowl and refrigerate until needed.

2. **FOR THE PORK:** Position roast fat side up. Insert knife ½ inch from bottom of roast and cut horizontally, stopping ½ inch before edge. Open up this flap. Cut through thicker half of roast about ½ inch from bottom, stopping about ½ inch before edge. Open up this flap. Repeat until pork is even ½-inch thickness throughout. If uneven, cover with plastic wrap and use meat pounder to even out. Season interior with salt and pepper and spread filling in even layer, leaving ½-inch border. Roll tightly and tie with kitchen twine at 1-inch intervals. Season with salt and pepper. (Pork loin can be stuffed and tied and wrapped tightly in plastic wrap for up to 1 day ahead; do not season until ready to grill.)

3. Using large piece of heavy-duty aluminum foil, wrap soaked chips in foil packet and cut several vent holes in top.

4A. **FOR A CHARCOAL GRILL:** Open bottom vent halfway. Light large chimney starter three-quarters filled with charcoal briquettes (4½ quarts). When top coals are partially covered with ash, pour evenly over half of grill. Place wood chip packet on coals. Set cooking grate in place, cover, and open lid vent halfway. Heat grill until hot and wood chips are smoking, about 5 minutes.

4B. **FOR A GAS GRILL:** Place wood chip packet over primary burner. Turn all burners to high, cover, and heat grill until hot and wood chips are smoking, about 15 minutes. Leave primary burner on medium-high and turn off other burner(s). (Adjust primary burner as needed to maintain grill temperature of 300 to 325 degrees.)

5. Clean and oil cooking grate. Place pork, fat side up, on cooler side of grill, cover (position lid vent over roast if using charcoal), and cook until meat registers 130 to 135 degrees, 55 minutes to 1 hour 10 minutes, flipping halfway through cooking.

6. Brush roast evenly with reserved glaze. (Reheat glaze, if necessary, to make it spreadable.) Continue to cook until glaze is glossy and meat registers 135 to 140 degrees, 5 to 10 minutes longer. Transfer to carving board, tent loosely with foil, and let rest for 15 minutes. Remove twine, cut roast into ½-inch-thick slices, and serve.

## STUFFING A PORK LOIN

**1.** Position the roast fat side up. Insert a knife ½ inch from the bottom of the roast and cut horizontally, stopping ½ inch before the edge. Open up this flap.

**2.** Cut through the thicker half of the roast about ½ inch from the bottom, stopping about ½ inch before the edge. Open up this flap.

**3.** Repeat until the pork loin is an even ½-inch thickness throughout. If uneven, cover with plastic wrap and use a meat pounder to even out.

**4.** With the long side of the meat facing you, season the meat and spread the filling, leaving a ½-inch border on all sides.

**5.** Starting from the short side, roll the pork loin tightly, then tie the roast with kitchen twine at 1-inch intervals.

## Grill-Roasted Pork Loin

**SERVES** 4 to 6

**WHY THIS RECIPE WORKS** When we're looking to dress up an outdoor dinner—and offer guests more than burgers or grilled chicken—we like to serve a juicy, crisp-crusted pork loin. But because the roasts available at the supermarket nowadays are so lean, this cut can dry out considerably when grilled. We planned to produce a succulent roast with a deep brown crust and aromatic, smoke-flavored meat. First, we chose the best cut. Our top choice—the blade-end roast—was moist and flavorful and was the hands-down winner over center-cut, sirloin, and tenderloin roasts. Brining ensured that our finished roast met with rave reviews from testers and stayed juicy and moist. We used a two-step grilling process, searing the roast directly over hot coals for a nice crust and finishing it over indirect heat, so as not to overcook it. The final step was removing the roast from the grill when the internal temperature was just shy of done, then allowing it to rest until the temperature rose and the meat was juicy and tender. If the pork is enhanced (injected with a salt solution), do not brine, and add 1 tablespoon salt to the pepper or spice rub. Two medium wood chunks, soaked in water for 1 hour, can be substituted for the wood chip packet on a charcoal grill.

- ¼ cup table salt
- 1 (2½- to 3-pound) boneless blade-end pork loin roast, trimmed and tied with kitchen twine at 1½-inch intervals
- 2 tablespoons olive oil
- 1 tablespoon pepper or 1 recipe spice rub (recipes follow)
- 2 cups wood chips, soaked in water for 15 minutes and drained

**1.** Dissolve salt in 2 quarts cold water in large container. Submerge pork loin in brine, cover, and refrigerate for 1 to 1½ hours. Remove pork from brine and pat dry with paper towels. Rub pork loin with oil and coat with pepper. Let sit at room temperature for 1 hour.

**2.** Using large piece of heavy-duty aluminum foil, wrap soaked chips in foil packet and cut several vent holes in top.

**3A. FOR A CHARCOAL GRILL:** Open bottom vent halfway. Light large chimney starter three-quarters filled with charcoal briquettes (4½ quarts). When top coals are partially covered with ash, pour evenly over half of grill. Place wood chip packet on coals. Set cooking grate in place, cover, and open lid vent halfway. Heat grill until hot and wood chips are smoking, about 5 minutes.

**3B. FOR A GAS GRILL:** Place wood chip packet directly on primary burner. Turn all burners to high, cover, and heat grill until hot and wood chips are smoking, about 15 minutes. Leave primary burner on high and turn off other burner(s). (Adjust primary burner as needed during cooking to maintain grill temperature between 300 and 325 degrees.)

**4.** Clean and oil cooking grate. Place pork loin on hot side of grill, fat side up, and cook (covered if using gas) until well browned on all sides, 10 to 12 minutes, turning as needed. Move to cool side of grill, positioning roast parallel with and as close as possible to heat. Cover (position lid vent over roast if using charcoal) and cook for 20 minutes.

**5.** Rotate roast 180 degrees, cover, and continue to cook until meat registers 135 to 140 degrees, 10 to 30 minutes longer, depending on thickness of roast.

**6.** Transfer roast to carving board, tent loosely with aluminum foil, and let rest for 15 minutes. Remove twine, cut roast into ½-inch-thick slices, and serve.

## Smoked Pork Loin with Dried Fruit Chutney

**SERVE** 6

**WHY THIS RECIPE WORKS** For a company-worthy pork roast, look to a pork loin. Choosing a blade-end roast meant more fat and thus more flavor. An overnight rub of salt and brown sugar seasoned the roast, kept it juicy, and delivered a nicely caramelized exterior. Low-and-slow indirect cooking was key for an evenly cooked, tender roast, so we poured lit coals over a layer of unlit coals to create a fire that wouldn't require refueling. Two cups of wood chips (in a single packet) provided just enough smoke to enhance the roast's meaty flavor. A dried fruit chutney was the perfect complement to the smoky meat. A blade roast is our preferred cut, but a center-cut boneless loin roast can be used. If the pork is enhanced (injected with a salt solution) skip step 1, but season with sugar-salt mixture in step 4. Any variety of wood chip except mesquite will work; we prefer hickory. If you'd like to use wood chunks instead of wood chips when using a charcoal grill, substitute two medium wood chunk(s), soaked in water for 1 hour, for the wood chip packet. To maintain a constant charcoal grill temperature, do not remove the lid unless necessary.

**PORK**

- ½ cup packed light brown sugar
- ¼ cup kosher salt
- 1 (3½- to 4-pound) blade-end boneless pork loin roast, trimmed
- 2 cups wood chips
- 1 (13 by 9-inch) disposable aluminum roasting pan (if using charcoal) or 1 (9-inch) disposable aluminum pie plate (if using gas)

**CHUTNEY**

- ¾ cup dry white wine
- ½ cup dried apricots, diced
- ½ cup dried cherries
- ¼ cup white wine vinegar
- 3 tablespoons water
- 3 tablespoons packed light brown sugar
- 1 shallot, minced
- 2 tablespoons grated fresh ginger
- 1 tablespoon unsalted butter
- 1 tablespoon Dijon mustard
- 1½ teaspoons dry mustard

**1. FOR THE PORK:** Combine sugar and salt in small bowl. Tie roast with twine at 1-inch intervals. Rub sugar-salt mixture over entire surface of roast, making sure roast is evenly coated. Wrap roast tightly in plastic wrap, set in rimmed baking sheet, and refrigerate for at least 6 hours or up to 24 hours.

**2.** Just before grilling, soak wood chips in water for 15 minutes, then drain. Using large piece of heavy-duty aluminum foil, wrap soaked chips in 8 by 4½-inch foil packet. (Make sure chips do not poke holes in sides or bottom of packet.) Cut 2 evenly spaced 2-inch slits in top of packet.

**3A. FOR A CHARCOAL GRILL:** Open bottom vent halfway. Arrange 25 unlit charcoal briquettes over half of grill and place disposable pan filled with 3 cups water on other side of grill. Light large chimney starter two-thirds filled with charcoal briquettes (4 quarts). When top coals are partially covered with ash, pour evenly over unlit briquettes. Place wood chip packet on coals. Set cooking grate in place, cover, and open lid vent halfway. Heat grill until hot and wood chips are smoking, about 5 minutes. (Adjust top and bottom vents as needed to maintain grill temperature of 300 degrees.)

**3B. FOR A GAS GRILL:** Remove cooking grate and place wood chip packet directly on primary burner. Place disposable pie plate filled with 1 inch water directly on other burner(s). Set grate in place; turn all burners to high; cover; and heat grill until hot and wood chips are smoking, about 15 minutes. Turn primary burner to medium and turn off other burner(s). (Adjust primary burner as needed to maintain grill temperature of 300 degrees.)

**4.** Clean and oil cooking grate. Unwrap roast and pat dry with paper towels. Place roast on grill (cooler side if using charcoal), directly over water pan. Cover (position lid vent over roast if using charcoal) and cook until meat registers 135 to 140 degrees, 1½ to 2 hours, rotating roast 180 degrees after 45 minutes.

**5. FOR THE CHUTNEY:** Combine wine, apricots, cherries, vinegar, water, sugar, shallot, and ginger in medium saucepan. Bring to simmer over medium heat. Cover and cook until fruit is softened, 10 minutes. Remove lid and reduce heat to medium-low. Add butter, Dijon, and dry mustard and continue to cook until slightly thickened, 4 to 6 minutes. Remove from heat and season with salt to taste. Transfer to bowl and let stand at room temperature.

**6.** Transfer roast to carving board, tent with foil, and let rest for 30 minutes. Remove and discard twine. Slice ¼ inch thick and serve, passing chutney separately.

## Grill-Roasted Bone-In Pork Roast

**SERVES** 6 to 8

**WHY THIS RECIPE WORKS** Grilling a bulky cut of meat like a pork roast may sound difficult, but we found that a tender, quick-cooking center-cut rib roast and a simple salt rub were all that we needed for a juicy grilled roast with a thick mahogany crust. Scoring the fat on the roast helped the rendered drippings baste the meat during grill-roasting. We grilled the roast over indirect heat (on the cooler side of the grill) so it could cook through slowly. For the perfect counterpoint to the roast's richness, we whipped up a fresh orange salsa with fresh herbs, jalapeño, and a warm touch of cumin. If you buy a blade-end roast (sometimes called a "rib-end roast"), tie it into a uniform shape with kitchen twine at 1-inch intervals; this step is unnecessary with a center-cut roast. For easier carving, ask the butcher to remove the tip of the chine bone and to cut the remainder of the chine bone between each rib. If you'd like to use wood chunks instead of wood chips when using a charcoal grill, substitute one medium wood chunk, soaked in water for 1 hour, for the wood chip packet.

- 1 (4- to 5-pound) bone-in center-cut pork rib or blade-end roast, tip of chine bone removed, fat trimmed to ¼-inch thickness
- 4 teaspoons kosher salt
- 1 cup wood chips
- 1½ teaspoons pepper
- 1 recipe Orange Salsa with Cuban Flavors (optional) (page 612)

**1.** Pat roast dry with paper towels. Using sharp knife, cut slits in surface fat layer, spaced 1 inch apart, in crosshatch pattern, being careful not to cut into meat. Sprinkle roast with salt. Wrap with plastic wrap and refrigerate for at least 6 hours or up to 24 hours.

**2.** Just before grilling, soak wood chips in water for 15 minutes, then drain. Using large piece of heavy-duty aluminum foil, wrap soaked chips in 8 by 4½-inch foil packet. (Make sure chips do not poke holes in sides or bottom of packet.) Cut 2 evenly spaced 2-inch slits in top of packet.

**3A. FOR A CHARCOAL GRILL:** Open bottom vent halfway. Light large chimney starter filled with charcoal briquettes (6 quarts). When top coals are partially covered with ash, pour into steeply banked pile against side of grill. Place wood chip packet on coals. Set cooking grate in place, cover, and open lid vent halfway. Heat grill until hot and wood chips are smoking, about 5 minutes.

**3B. FOR A GAS GRILL:** Place wood chip packet over primary burner. Turn all burners to high; cover; and heat grill until hot and wood chips are smoking, about 15 minutes. Turn primary burner to medium-high and turn off other burner(s). (Adjust primary burner as needed during cooking to maintain grill temperature around 325 degrees.)

**4.** Clean and oil cooking grate. Unwrap roast and season with pepper. Place roast on grate with meat near, but not over, coals and flames and bones facing away from coals and flames. Cover (position lid vent over meat if using charcoal) and cook until meat registers 135 to 140 degrees, 1¼ to 1½ hours.

**5.** Transfer roast to carving board, tent with foil, and let rest for 30 minutes. Carve into thick slices by cutting between ribs. Serve, passing salsa, if using, separately.

### Orange Salsa with Cuban Flavors

**MAKES** about 2½ cups

To make this salsa spicier, add the reserved chile seeds.

- ½ teaspoon grated orange zest plus 5 oranges peeled and segmented; each segment quartered crosswise
- ½ cup minced red onion
- 1 jalapeño chile, stemmed, seeds reserved, and minced
- 2 tablespoons lime juice
- 2 tablespoons minced fresh parsley
- 1 tablespoon extra-virgin olive oil
- 2 teaspoons packed brown sugar
- 1½ teaspoons distilled white vinegar
- 1½ teaspoons minced fresh oregano
- 1 garlic clove, minced
- ½ teaspoon ground cumin
- ½ teaspoon table salt
- ½ teaspoon pepper

Combine all ingredients in medium bowl.

## Grilled Pork Kebabs with Hoisin Glaze

**SERVES** 4

**WHY THIS RECIPE WORKS** To bring out the best in mild pork tenderloins, we cut the meat into chunks and let them soak in salt. This simple mixture changed the structure of the raw meat's exterior proteins so that it wouldn't lose moisture on the grill. For a flavorful, sticky glaze that clung to the pork (and not to the grill), we combined five-spice powder, garlic powder, cornstarch, and hoisin sauce. Applying the glaze twice meant the pork developed great char from the sweet hoisin sauce during grilling and still had a thick, tasty coating when the kebabs were served. You will need four 12-inch metal skewers for this recipe. We prefer natural pork, but if your pork is enhanced (injected with a salt solution), do not salt it in step 1.

- 2 (12-ounce) pork tenderloins, trimmed and cut into 1-inch chunks
- 1 teaspoon kosher salt
- 1½ teaspoons five-spice powder
- ¾ teaspoon garlic powder
- ½ teaspoon cornstarch
- 4½ tablespoons hoisin sauce
- Vegetable oil spray
- 2 scallions, thinly sliced

**1.** Toss pork and salt together in large bowl and let sit for 20 minutes. Meanwhile, whisk five-spice powder, garlic powder, and cornstarch together in bowl. Add hoisin to five-spice mixture and stir to combine. Set aside 1½ tablespoons hoisin mixture.

**2.** Add remaining hoisin mixture to pork and toss to coat. Thread pork onto four 12-inch metal skewers, leaving ¼ inch between pieces. Spray both sides of meat generously with oil spray.

**3A. FOR A CHARCOAL GRILL:** Open bottom vent completely. Light large chimney starter filled with charcoal briquettes (6 quarts). When top coals are partially covered with ash, pour evenly over half of grill. Set cooking grate in place, cover, and open lid vent completely. Heat grill until hot, about 5 minutes.

**3B. FOR A GAS GRILL:** Turn all burners to high, cover, and heat grill until hot, about 15 minutes. Leave primary burner on high and turn off other burner(s).

**4.** Clean and oil cooking grate. Place skewers on hotter side of grill and grill until well charred, 3 to 4 minutes. Flip skewers, brush with reserved hoisin mixture, and continue to grill until second side is well charred and meat registers 140 degrees, 3 to 4 minutes longer. Transfer to serving platter, tent loosely with aluminum foil, and let rest for 5 minutes. Sprinkle with scallions and serve.

## Pinchos Morunos (Spanish Grilled Pork Kebabs)

**SERVES 4**

**WHY THIS RECIPE WORKS** Pinchos morunos are Spanish pork kebabs that are heavily seasoned with a bright, heady spice paste (lemon, garlic, smoked paprika, cumin, and coriander are common components); skewered; charred over hot coals; and served as part of a tapas spread. For our version, we used country-style ribs for their convenience and their ability to remain juicy and tender when grilled. To increase the meat's juiciness, we brined the pork for 30 minutes before cutting it into cubes and coating it with a robust spice paste. And because country-style ribs contain a mix of lighter loin meat and darker shoulder meat, we were careful to place the light meat and dark meat on separate skewers so that we could cook each to its ideal temperature. You will need four or five 12-inch metal skewers for this recipe. Look for country-style ribs with an even distribution of light and dark meat. We prefer natural pork, but if your pork is enhanced (injected with a salt solution), do not brine it in step 1.

- 3 tablespoons table salt for brining
- 2 pounds boneless country-style pork ribs, trimmed
- ¼ cup vegetable oil
- 2 tablespoons lemon juice, plus lemon wedges for serving
- 6 garlic cloves, minced
- 1 tablespoon grated fresh ginger
- 2 teaspoons minced fresh oregano, divided
- 2 teaspoons smoked paprika
- 1 teaspoon ground coriander
- 1 teaspoon table salt
- ½ teaspoon ground cumin
- ½ teaspoon pepper
- ¼ teaspoon cayenne pepper

**1.** Dissolve 3 tablespoons salt in 1½ quarts cold water in large container. Submerge ribs in brine and let stand at room temperature for 30 minutes. Meanwhile, whisk oil, lemon juice, garlic, ginger, 1 teaspoon oregano, paprika, coriander, salt, cumin, pepper, and cayenne in small bowl until combined.

**2.** Remove pork from brine and pat dry with paper towels. Cut ribs into 1-inch chunks; place dark meat and light meat in separate bowls. Divide spice paste proportionately between bowls and toss to coat. Thread light and dark meat onto separate skewers (do not crowd pieces). Place dark meat kebabs on left side of rimmed baking sheet and light meat kebabs on right side.

**3A. FOR A CHARCOAL GRILL:** Open bottom vent completely. Light large chimney starter filled with charcoal briquettes (6 quarts). When top coals are partially covered with ash, pour evenly over half of grill. Set cooking grate in place, cover, and open lid vent completely. Heat grill until hot, about 5 minutes.

**3B. FOR A GAS GRILL:** Turn all burners to high; cover; and heat grill until hot, about 15 minutes. Leave primary burner on high and turn off other burner(s).

**4.** Clean and oil cooking grate. Place dark meat on hotter side of grill and cook for 6 minutes. Flip dark meat and add light meat to hotter side of grill. Cook for 4 minutes, then flip all kebabs. Continue to cook, flipping kebabs every 4 minutes, until dark meat is well charred and registers 155 degrees and light meat is lightly charred and registers 140 degrees, 4 to 8 minutes longer. Transfer to serving platter, tent with aluminum foil, and let rest for 5 minutes. Remove pork from skewers; toss to combine; sprinkle with remaining 1 teaspoon oregano; and serve, passing lemon wedges separately.

## Tacos al Pastor (Spicy Pork Tacos)

**SERVES 6 to 8**

**WHY THIS RECIPE WORKS** In Mexico, superthin slices of pork butt and pork fat are marinated in chiles and tomato, roasted on a spit, and shaved, hot and crispy, into a corn tortilla. To mimic this popular filling, we started by braising ½-inch-thick slabs of pork butt in a mix of guajillo chiles, tomatoes, and spices until tender, before basting them with sauce on the grill until crisped and charred. Chopped into bite-size strips and topped with grilled pineapple, our tacos al pastor lives up to the original. Boneless pork butt is often labeled Boston butt in the supermarket. If you can't find guajillo chiles, New Mexican chiles may be substituted, although the dish may be spicier. To warm tortillas, place them on a plate, cover with a damp dish towel, and microwave for 60 to 90 seconds. Keep tortillas covered and serve immediately.

- 10 large dried guajillo chiles, wiped clean
- 1½ cups water
- 1¼ pounds plum tomatoes, cored and quartered
- 8 garlic cloves, peeled
- 4 bay leaves
- Table salt and pepper
- ¾ teaspoon sugar
- ½ teaspoon ground cumin
- ⅛ teaspoon ground cloves
- 1 (3-pound) boneless pork butt roast
- 1 lime, cut into 8 wedges
- ½ pineapple, peeled, cored, and cut into ½-inch-thick rings
- Vegetable oil
- 18 (6-inch) corn tortillas, warmed
- 1 small onion, chopped fine
- ½ cup coarsely chopped fresh cilantro

**1.** Toast guajillos in large Dutch oven over medium-high heat until softened and fragrant, 2 to 4 minutes. Transfer to large plate and, when cool enough to handle, remove stems.

**2.** Return toasted guajillos to now-empty Dutch oven, add water, tomatoes, garlic, bay leaves, 2 teaspoons salt, ½ teaspoon pepper, sugar, cumin, and cloves, and bring to simmer over medium-high heat. Cover, reduce heat, and simmer, stirring occasionally, until guajillos are softened and tomatoes mash easily, about 20 minutes.

3. While sauce simmers, trim excess fat from exterior of pork, leaving ¼-inch-thick fat cap. Slice pork against grain into ½-inch-thick slabs.

4. Transfer guajillo-tomato mixture to blender and process until smooth, about 1 minute. Strain puree through fine-mesh strainer, pressing on solids to extract as much liquid as possible. Return puree to pot, submerge pork slices in liquid, and bring to simmer over medium heat. Partially cover, reduce heat, and simmer gently until pork is tender but still holds together, 1½ to 1¾ hours, flipping and rearranging pork halfway through cooking. (Pork can be left in sauce, cooled to room temperature, and refrigerated for up to 2 days.)

5. Transfer pork to large plate, season both sides with salt, and cover tightly with aluminum foil. Whisk sauce to combine. Transfer ½ cup sauce to bowl for grilling; pour off all but ½ cup remaining sauce from pot and reserve for another use. Squeeze 2 lime wedges into sauce in pot and add spent wedges; season with salt to taste.

**6A. FOR A CHARCOAL GRILL:** Open bottom vent halfway. Light large chimney starter filled with charcoal briquettes (6 quarts). When top coals are partially covered with ash, pour evenly over grill. Set cooking grate in place, cover, and open lid vent halfway. Heat grill until hot, about 5 minutes.

**6B. FOR A GAS GRILL:** Turn all burners to high, cover, and heat grill until hot, about 15 minutes. Turn all burners to medium.

7. Clean and oil cooking grate. Brush 1 side of pork with ¼ cup reserved sauce. Place pork on 1 side of grill, sauce side down, and cook until well browned and crisp, 5 to 7 minutes. Brush pork with remaining ¼ cup reserved sauce, flip, and continue to cook until second side is well browned and crisp, 5 to 7 minutes longer. Transfer to carving board. Meanwhile, brush both sides of pineapple rings with vegetable oil and season with salt to taste. Place on other half of grill and cook until pineapple is softened and caramelized, 10 to 14 minutes; transfer pineapple to carving board.

8. Coarsely chop grilled pineapple and transfer to serving bowl. Using tongs or carving fork to steady hot pork, slice each piece crosswise into ⅛-inch pieces. Bring remaining ½ cup sauce in pot to simmer, add sliced pork, remove pot from heat, and toss to coat pork well. Season with salt to taste.

9. Spoon small amount of pork into each warm tortilla and serve, passing chopped pineapple, remaining 6 lime wedges, onion, and cilantro separately.

## Sous Vide Cochinita Pibil

**SERVES** 8 to 10

**WHY THIS RECIPE WORKS** Cochinita pibil is the pride of the Yucatán—a dish of smoky, slow-roasted pork marinated in a special blend including cinnamon, allspice, and annatto seeds. Cochinita means "baby pig," and the real-deal recipes use a whole suckling pig wrapped in banana leaves and then buried in a pib, a pit with a fire at the bottom. We used Boston butt and employed a two-stage cooking process to make things convenient and a lot juicier. Pregrilling the meat added great flavor, while low and slow cooking in a water bath produced succulent meat. Pork butt roast is often labeled Boston butt in the supermarket. We prefer the flavor of canela cinnamon and Mexican oregano here, but conventional varieties will work. Serve with white rice or in warmed corn tortillas with any combination of the following: spicy salsa, pickled red onions, thinly sliced radishes, thinly sliced scallions, crumbled queso fresco or cotija cheese, and lime wedges.

- 25 garlic cloves, unpeeled
- 2 tablespoons vegetable oil
- ¼ cup annatto seeds
- 1 tablespoon peppercorns
- 1 (4-inch) stick canela cinnamon
- 1 tablespoon allspice berries
- 2 tablespoons Mexican oregano
- ¼ cup orange juice
- ¼ cup cider vinegar
- Table salt and pepper
- 1 teaspoon liquid smoke
- 1 4-pound boneless pork butt roast, trimmed and halved
- 1 onion, sliced into ¾-inch-thick rounds
- 8 ounces banana leaf, cut into long strips and bruised
- 8 bay leaves

1. Cook garlic in 12-inch skillet over high heat, shaking occasionally, until blackened on most sides, 8 to 10 minutes. Transfer garlic to bowl, let cool slightly, then peel away skins; wipe skillet clean with paper towels.

2. Heat oil in now-empty skillet over medium heat until shimmering. Add annatto seeds, peppercorns, cinnamon stick, allspice berries, and oregano, cover, and cook, shaking skillet frequently, for 30 seconds. Transfer spice mixture to blender along with garlic, orange juice, vinegar, 1 tablespoon salt, and liquid smoke. Process until smooth paste forms, about 3 minutes, scraping down sides of blender jar as needed. Transfer ¼ cup spice paste to large bowl, add pork, and toss to coat; reserve remaining spice paste. (Pork can be rapidly chilled in ice bath and then refrigerated in zipper-lock bag after step 2

for up to 3 days. To reheat, return sealed bag to water bath set to 155 degrees for 30 to 45 minutes and then proceed with step 3.

**3A. FOR A CHARCOAL GRILL:** Open bottom vent completely. Light large chimney starter filled with charcoal briquettes (6 quarts). When top coals are partially covered with ash, pour evenly over half of grill. Set cooking grate in place, cover, and open lid vent completely. Heat grill until hot, about 5 minutes.

**3B. FOR A GAS GRILL:** Turn all burners to high, cover, and heat grill until hot, about 15 minutes. Leave all burners on high.

**4.** Clean and oil cooking grate. Place pork and onions on grill over flames and cook until well charred on first side, 3 to 4 minutes. Flip pork and onions and continue to cook until well charred on second side, 2 to 3 minutes. Return pork to now-empty bowl. Continue to cook onions, flipping as needed, until softened, about 4 minutes; transfer to small bowl.

**5.** Meanwhile, using sous vide circulator, bring water to 155 degrees in 12-quart container.

**6.** Add onions to blender with reserved spice paste and process until smooth, 1 to 2 minutes. Divide pork, spice paste, banana leaves, and bay leaves between two 1-gallon zipper-lock bags and toss to coat. Seal bags, pressing out as much air as possible. Gently lower bags into prepared water bath until pork is fully submerged, and then clip top corner of bags to side of water bath container, allowing remaining air bubbles to rise to top of bag. Reopen 1 corner of zipper, release remaining air bubbles, and reseal bag. Cover and cook for at least 22 hours or up to 26 hours.

**7.** Transfer pork to cutting board, let cool slightly, and then chop into rough ½-inch pieces. Strain cooking liquid through fine-mesh strainer set over large bowl; discard solids. Add pork to cooking liquid and toss to combine. Season with salt and pepper to taste and serve.

## Barbecued Pulled Pork

**SERVES 8**

**WHY THIS RECIPE WORKS** Pulled pork is classic summertime party food: slow-cooked pork roast, shredded and seasoned, served on the most basic of hamburger buns (or sliced white bread), with just enough of your favorite barbecue sauce, a couple of dill pickle chips, and a topping of coleslaw. However, many barbecue procedures demand the regular attention of the cook for eight hours or more. We wanted to find a way to make moist, fork-tender pulled pork without the marathon cooking time and constant attention to the grill. After testing shoulder roasts (also called Boston butt), fresh ham, and picnic roasts, we determined that the shoulder roast, which has the most fat, retained the most moisture and flavor during a long, slow cook. We massaged a spicy chili rub into the meat, then wrapped the roast in plastic wrap and refrigerated it for at least three hours to "marinate." The roast is first cooked on the grill to absorb smoky flavor (from wood chips—no smoker required), then finished in the oven. Finally, we let the pork rest in a paper bag so the meat would steam and any remaining collagen would break down, allowing the flavorful juices to be reabsorbed. We also developed a sauce recipe. Pulled pork can be made with a fresh ham or picnic roast, although our preference is for Boston butt. If using a fresh ham or picnic roast, remove the skin by cutting through it with the tip of a chef's knife; slide the blade just under the skin and work around to loosen it while pulling it off with your other hand. Four medium wood chunks, soaked in water for 1 hour, can be substituted for the wood chip packets on a charcoal grill. Serve on plain white bread or warmed rolls with dill pickle chips and coleslaw.

- 1 (6- to 8-pound) bone-in Boston butt roast
- ¾ cup Dry Rub for Barbecue (recipe follows)
- 4 cups wood chips, soaked in water for 15 minutes and drained
- 1 (13 by 9-inch) disposable aluminum roasting pan
- 2 cups barbecue sauce (recipe follows)

**1.** Pat pork dry with paper towels, then massage dry rub into meat. Wrap meat in plastic wrap and refrigerate for at least 3 hours or up to 3 days.

**2.** At least 1 hour prior to cooking, remove roast from refrigerator, unwrap, and let sit at room temperature. Using 2 large pieces of heavy-duty aluminum foil, wrap soaked chips in 2 foil packets and cut several vent holes in tops.

**3A. FOR A CHARCOAL GRILL:** Open bottom vent halfway. Light large chimney starter three-quarters filled with charcoal briquettes (4½ quarts). When top coals are partially covered with ash, pour evenly over half of grill. Place wood chip packets on coals. Set cooking grate in place, cover, and open lid vent halfway. Heat grill until hot and wood chips are smoking, about 5 minutes.

**3B. FOR A GAS GRILL:** Place wood chip packets directly on primary burner. Turn all burners to high, cover, and heat grill until hot and wood chips are smoking, about 15 minutes. Turn primary burner to medium-high and turn off other burner(s). (Adjust primary burner as needed to maintain grill temperature around 325 degrees.)

**4.** Set roast in disposable pan, place on cool side of grill, and cook for 3 hours. During final 20 minutes of cooking, adjust oven rack to lower-middle position and heat oven to 325 degrees.

**5.** Wrap disposable pan with heavy-duty foil and cook in oven until meat is fork-tender, about 2 hours.

**6.** Carefully slide foil-wrapped pan with roast into brown paper bag. Crimp end shut and let rest for 1 hour.

**7.** Transfer roast to carving board and unwrap. Separate roast into muscle sections, removing fat, if desired, and tearing meat into shreds with your fingers. Place shredded meat in large bowl and toss with 1 cup barbecue sauce. Serve, passing remaining sauce separately.

### Dry Rub for Barbecue

**MAKES** about 1 cup

You can adjust the proportions of spices in this all-purpose rub or add or subtract a spice, as you wish.

- ¼ cup paprika
- 2 tablespoons chili powder
- 2 tablespoons ground cumin
- 2 tablespoons packed dark brown sugar
- 2 tablespoons table salt
- 1 tablespoon dried oregano
- 1 tablespoon granulated sugar
- 1 tablespoon black pepper
- 1 tablespoon white pepper
- 1–2 teaspoons cayenne pepper

Combine all ingredients in small bowl.

### Eastern North Carolina Barbecue Sauce

**MAKES** about 2 cups

This sauce can be refrigerated in an airtight container for up to 4 days.

- 1 cup distilled white vinegar
- 1 cup cider vinegar
- 1 tablespoon sugar
- 1 tablespoon red pepper flakes
- 1 tablespoon hot sauce
- Table salt and pepper

Mix all ingredients except salt and pepper together in bowl and season with salt and pepper to taste.

## Smoky Pulled Pork on a Gas Grill

**SERVES** 8 to 10

**WHY THIS RECIPE WORKS** Pulled pork is traditionally best made on a charcoal grill. But the reality is that most home cooks rely on a gas grill. And simply using a charcoal recipe on a gas grill is a total failure in this case. That's because it is so difficult to imbue pulled pork with rich, smoky flavor when cooking on a gas grill. We cut our pork butt into three pieces to increase the surface area that the smoke could cling to. After salting the pork overnight, we took it directly from the fridge to the grill: The meat's cool temperature allowed more smoke to condense onto its surface. Instead of inundating the meat with smoke at the beginning, we got the most out of the wood chips by soaking half of them in water to delay when they began to smoke. Finally, we stirred together a bright and spicy vinegar sauce that highlighted the pungent smoke flavors of our pulled pork. Pork butt is ideal because it's collagen-rich and has the right amount of intramuscular fat. Pork butt roast is often labeled Boston butt in the supermarket. We developed this recipe with hickory chips, though other varieties of hardwood can be used. (We do not recommend mesquite chips.) Before beginning, check your propane tank to make sure that you have at least a half-tank of fuel. If you happen to run out of fuel, you can move the pork to a preheated 300-degree oven to finish cooking. Serve the pulled pork on white bread or hamburger buns with pickles and coleslaw.

**PORK**

- 5 teaspoons kosher salt
- 2½ teaspoons pepper
- 2 teaspoons paprika
- 2 teaspoons packed light brown sugar
- 1 (5-pound) boneless pork butt roast, trimmed
- 4 cups wood chips
- 2 (9-inch) disposable aluminum pie plates
- 1 (13 by 9-inch) disposable aluminum roasting pan

**VINEGAR SAUCE**

- 2 cups cider vinegar
- 2 tablespoons ketchup
- 2 teaspoons packed light brown sugar
- 1 teaspoon red pepper flakes
- 1 teaspoon kosher salt

**1. FOR THE PORK:** Combine salt, pepper, paprika, and sugar in small bowl. Cut pork against grain into 3 equal slabs. Rub salt mixture into pork, making sure meat is evenly coated. Wrap pork tightly in plastic wrap and refrigerate for at least 6 hours or up to 24 hours.

**2.** Just before grilling, soak 2 cups wood chips in water for 15 minutes, then drain. Using large piece of heavy-duty aluminum foil, wrap soaked chips in 8 by 4½-inch foil packet. (Make sure chips do not poke holes in sides or bottom of packet.) Repeat with remaining 2 cups unsoaked chips. Cut 2 evenly spaced 2-inch slits in top of each packet.

**3.** Remove cooking grate and place wood chip packets directly on primary burner. Place disposable pie plates, each filled with 3 cups water, directly on other burner(s). Set grate in place, turn all burners to high, cover, and heat grill until hot and wood chips are smoking, about 15 minutes. Turn primary burner to medium and turn off other burner(s). (Adjust primary burner as needed to maintain grill temperature of 300 degrees.)

**4.** Clean and oil cooking grate. Place pork on cooler side of grill, directly over water pans; cover and smoke for 1½ hours.

**5.** Transfer pork to disposable pan. Place pork in pan on cooler side of grill and continue to cook until meat registers 200 degrees, 2½ to 3 hours.

**6.** Transfer pork to carving board and let rest for 20 minutes. Pour juices from disposable pan into fat separator and let sit for 5 minutes.

**7. FOR THE VINEGAR SAUCE:** While pork rests, whisk all ingredients together in bowl. Using 2 forks, shred pork into bite-size pieces. Stir ⅓ cup defatted juices and ½ cup sauce into pork. Serve, passing remaining sauce separately.

## Rosticciana (Tuscan Grilled Pork Ribs)

**SERVES** 4 to 6

**WHY THIS RECIPE WORKS** Tuscan grilled pork spareribs are unlike any ribs we've had: They are seasoned simply with salt, pepper, and a hint of garlic or rosemary to allow the natural flavors of the ribs to shine. For our version, we started with two racks of St. Louis–style spareribs and cut ribs into two-rib

sections, creating more surface area for browning; and salting them prior to grilling ensured that they would be juicy and well seasoned. We grilled the ribs over a medium-hot fire to avoid drying them out. Drizzling the pork with a simple vinaigrette balanced its richness. When portioning the meat into two-rib sections, start at the thicker end of the rack. If you are left with a three-rib piece at the tapered end, grill it as such. Take the temperature of the meat between the bones. Since these ribs cook quickly, we like to use the still-hot fire to grill a vegetable. Radicchio's bitterness and crunch made it a perfect partner for the rich meat.

**RIBS**

- 2 (2½- to 3-pound) racks St. Louis–style spareribs, trimmed, membrane removed, and each rack cut into 2-rib sections
- 2 teaspoons kosher salt
- 1 tablespoon vegetable oil
- 1 teaspoon pepper

**VINAIGRETTE**

- ¼ cup extra-virgin olive oil
- 2 garlic cloves, minced
- 1 teaspoon finely chopped fresh rosemary
- 2 tablespoons lemon juice

**1. FOR THE RIBS:** Pat ribs dry with paper towels. Rub evenly on both sides with salt and place on wire rack set in rimmed baking sheet. Let sit at room temperature for 1 hour. Brush meat side of ribs with oil and sprinkle with pepper.

**2. FOR THE VINAIGRETTE:** Combine oil, garlic, and rosemary in small bowl and microwave until fragrant and just starting to bubble, about 30 seconds. Stir in lemon juice and set aside.

**3A. FOR A CHARCOAL GRILL:** Open bottom vent completely. Light large chimney starter filled with charcoal briquettes (6 quarts). When top coals are partially covered with ash, pour evenly over grill. Set cooking grate in place, cover, and open lid vent completely. Heat grill until hot, about 5 minutes.

**3B. FOR A GAS GRILL:** Turn all burners to high; cover; and heat grill until hot, about 15 minutes. Turn all burners to medium-high.

**4.** Clean and oil cooking grate. Place ribs meat side down on grill. Cover and cook until meat side begins to develop spotty browning and light but defined grill marks, 4 to 6 minutes. Flip ribs and cook, covered, until second side is lightly browned, 4 to 6 minutes, moving ribs as needed to ensure even browning. Flip again and cook, covered, until meat side is deeply browned with slight charring and thick ends of ribs register 175 to 185 degrees, 4 to 6 minutes.

**5.** Transfer ribs to cutting board and let rest for 10 minutes. Cut ribs between bones and serve, passing vinaigrette separately.

## Grilled Radicchio

**SERVES 4**

Turning the wedges during cooking ensures that all sides, including the rounded one, spend time facing the fire.

- 3 heads radicchio (10 ounces each), quartered
- ¼ cup extra-virgin olive oil
- 1 teaspoon table salt
- ½ teaspoon pepper
- Balsamic vinegar

**1.** Place radicchio on rimmed baking sheet, brush with oil, and sprinkle with salt and pepper.

**2.** Grill radicchio over medium-hot fire (covered if using gas), turning every 1½ minutes, until edges are browned and wilted but centers are still slightly firm, about 5 minutes. Transfer radicchio to serving dish, drizzle with vinegar, and serve.

### CUTTING RIBS TWO BY TWO

Starting at thicker end of rack, portion meat into 2-rib sections. If left with 3-rib piece at tapered end of rack, it can be grilled as such.

## Sweet and Tangy Grilled Country-Style Pork Ribs

**SERVES 4 to 6**

**WHY THIS RECIPE WORKS** Since country-style ribs feature a combination of light, lean loin meat and richly flavored, fattier shoulder, the trick is figuring out how to grill them to cook the white and dark meat perfectly. We applied a salty dry rub to boost the ribs' seasoning and help them stay moist, particularly the faster-drying light meat. Starting the ribs over high heat and then finishing on the cooler side of the grill ensured good browning and an evenly cooked interior. While the ribs

were on the cooler side of the grill, we basted them with a sweet and tangy sauce that included ketchup, molasses, Worcestershire sauce, cider vinegar, and Dijon mustard. Trim the pork carefully to reduce flare-ups during grilling. Note that the spice-rubbed ribs must be refrigerated for at least 1 hour or up to 24 hours before grilling.

**PORK**

- 4 teaspoons packed brown sugar
- 1 tablespoon kosher salt
- 1 tablespoon chili powder
- ⅛ teaspoon cayenne pepper
- 4 pounds bone-in country-style pork ribs, trimmed

**SAUCE**

- 1 cup ketchup
- 5 tablespoons molasses
- 3 tablespoons cider vinegar
- 2 tablespoons Worcestershire sauce
- 2 tablespoons Dijon mustard
- ¼ teaspoon pepper
- 2 tablespoons vegetable oil
- ⅓ cup grated onion
- 1 garlic clove, minced
- 1 teaspoon chili powder
- ¼ teaspoon cayenne pepper

**1. FOR THE PORK:** Combine sugar, salt, chili powder and cayenne in bowl. Rub mixture all over ribs. Wrap tightly in plastic wrap and refrigerate for at least 1 hour or up to 24 hours.

**2. FOR THE SAUCE:** Whisk ketchup, molasses, vinegar, Worcestershire, mustard, and pepper together in bowl. Heat oil in medium saucepan over medium heat until shimmering. Add onion and garlic; cook until onion is softened, 2 to 4 minutes. Add chili powder and cayenne and cook until fragrant, about 30 seconds. Whisk in ketchup mixture and bring to boil. Reduce heat to medium-low and simmer gently for 5 minutes. Set aside ½ cup of sauce for basting pork and reserve remaining sauce for serving. (Sauce can be refrigerated in an airtight container for up to 1 week.)

**3A. FOR A CHARCOAL GRILL:** Open bottom vent halfway. Light large chimney starter filled with charcoal briquettes (6 quarts). When top coals are partially covered with ash, pour evenly over half of grill. Set cooking grate in place, cover, and open lid vent halfway. Heat grill until hot, about 5 minutes.

**3B. FOR A GAS GRILL:** Turn all burners to high, cover and heat grill until hot, about 15 minutes. Leave primary burner on high and turn other burner(s) off to maintain grill temperature around 350 degrees.

**4.** Clean and oil cooking grate. Place ribs over hotter part of grill and cook until well browned on both sides, 4 to 7 minutes. Move ribs to cooler part of grill and brush top sides with ¼ cup sauce. Cover and cook 6 minutes. Flip ribs and brush with remaining ¼ cup sauce. Cover and continue to cook until pork registers 150 degrees, 5 to 10 minutes longer. Transfer ribs to serving platter, tent loosely with aluminum foil and let rest for 10 minutes. Serve, passing sauce separately.

## Kansas City Sticky Ribs

**SERVES** 4 to 6

**WHY THIS RECIPE WORKS** Kansas City ribs, slow-smoked pork ribs, are slathered in an irresistible thick, sweet, and sticky sauce; but these ribs can take all day to prepare. We knew we could come up with a faster method for Kansas City ribs—one that would produce the same fall-off-the-bone tender, smoky meat of the long-cooked original recipe. We learned that spareribs, which are well marbled with fat, produce moist, tender ribs, but some racks are so big they barely fit on the grill. We turned to a more manageable cut, "St. Louis" ribs, which is a narrower, rectangular rack that offers all the taste of whole spareribs without any of the trouble. A spice rub added flavor and encouraged a savory crust on the meat. We barbecued the ribs, covered with foil, over indirect heat for 4 hours—the foil traps some of the steam over the meat, so that it cooks up tender. Using wood chips on the grill imparted great smoky flavor to the meat. For sticky, saucy ribs, we brushed the ribs all over with barbecue sauce and finished them in the gentle heat of the oven until tender. We like St. Louis–style racks, but if you can't find them, baby back ribs will work fine; reduce the oven time in step 6 to 1 to 2 hours. If you'd like to use wood chunks instead of wood chips when using a charcoal grill, substitute two medium wood chunks, soaked in water for 1 hour, for the wood chip packet.

**RIBS**

- 3 tablespoons paprika
- 2 tablespoons packed brown sugar
- 1 tablespoon table salt
- 1 tablespoon pepper
- ¼ teaspoon cayenne pepper
- 2 (2½- to 3-pound) full racks pork spareribs, trimmed of any large pieces of fat and membrane removed
- 2 cups wood chips

**SAUCE**

- 1 tablespoon vegetable oil plus more for cooking grate
- 1 onion, chopped fine
- Pinch table salt
- 4 cups chicken broth
- 1 cup root beer
- 1 cup cider vinegar
- 1 cup dark corn syrup
- ½ cup light or mild molasses
- ½ cup tomato paste
- ½ cup ketchup
- 2 tablespoons brown mustard
- 1 tablespoon hot sauce
- ½ teaspoon garlic powder
- ¼ teaspoon liquid smoke

**1. FOR THE RIBS:** Combine paprika, sugar, salt, black pepper, and cayenne in bowl. Pat ribs dry with paper towels and rub evenly with spice mixture. Wrap ribs in plastic wrap and let sit at room temperature for at least 1 hour, or refrigerate for up to 24 hours. (If refrigerated, let sit at room temperature for 1 hour before grilling.) Just before grilling, soak wood chips in water for 15 minutes, then drain. Using large piece of heavy-duty aluminum foil, wrap soaked chips in 8 by 4½-inch foil packet. (Make sure chips do not poke holes in sides or bottom of packet.) Cut 2 evenly spaced 2-inch slits in top of packet.

**2. FOR THE SAUCE:** Meanwhile, heat oil in large saucepan over medium heat until shimmering. Add onion and salt and cook until softened, 5 to 7 minutes. Whisk in broth, root beer, vinegar, corn syrup, molasses, tomato paste, ketchup, mustard, hot sauce, and garlic powder. Bring sauce to simmer and cook, stirring occasionally, until reduced to 4 cups, about 1 hour. Stir in liquid smoke. Let cool to room temperature and season with salt and pepper to taste. Measure out 1 cup barbecue sauce for cooking; set aside remaining sauce for serving. (Sauce can be refrigerated in an airtight container for up to 4 days.)

**3A. FOR A CHARCOAL GRILL:** Open bottom grill vent halfway. Light large chimney starter three-quarters filled with charcoal briquettes (4½ quarts). When top coals are partially covered with ash, pour into steeply banked pile against side of grill. Place wood chip packet on coals. Set cooking grate in place, cover, and open lid vent halfway. Heat grill until hot and wood chips are smoking, about 5 minutes.

**3B. FOR A GAS GRILL:** Remove cooking grate and place wood chip packet directly on primary burner. Set grate in place; turn all burners to high; cover; and heat grill until hot and wood chips are smoking, about 15 minutes. Turn primary burner to medium-high and turn off other burner(s). (Adjust primary burner as needed to maintain grill temperature of 325 degrees.)

**4.** Clean and oil cooking grate. Place ribs, meat side down, on cooler side of grill; ribs may overlap slightly. Place sheet of foil on top of ribs. Cover (position lid vent over meat if using charcoal) and cook until ribs are deep red and smoky, about 2 hours, flipping and rotating racks halfway through. During final 20 minutes of grilling, adjust oven rack to middle position and heat oven to 250 degrees.

**5.** Remove ribs from grill, brush evenly with 1 cup sauce reserved for cooking, and wrap tightly with foil. Lay foil-wrapped ribs on rimmed baking sheet and continue to cook in oven until tender and fork inserted into ribs meets no resistance, 1½ to 2½ hours.

**6.** Remove ribs from oven and let rest, still wrapped, for 30 minutes. Unwrap ribs and brush them thickly with 1 cup sauce set aside for serving. Slice ribs between bones and serve with remaining sauce.

### REMOVING THE MEMBRANE FOR KANSAS CITY RIBS

Before cooking, loosen papery membrane with tip of paring knife and, with aid of paper towel, pull it off slowly, all in 1 piece.

## Memphis-Style Barbecued Spareribs

**SERVES** 4 to 6

**WHY THIS RECIPE WORKS** Memphis pit masters pride themselves on their all-day barbecued pork ribs with a dark, bark-like crust and distinctive chew. Up for a challenge, we decided to come up with our own version, but one that wouldn't involve tending a grill all day. After failing to grill the ribs in a reasonable amount of time (less than 7 hours), we opted for a grill-to-oven approach. We started first with the grill. For a fire that would maintain the key amount of indirect heat (roughly 250 to 275 degrees), we turned to a half-grill fire where the hot coals are arranged over half the grill. In addition, we stowed a pan of water underneath the cooking grate on the cooler side of the grill, where it would absorb heat and work to keep the temperature stable, as well as help keep the meat moister. Then we transferred the ribs to a wire rack set over a rimmed baking sheet and cooked them in a moderate oven until tender and thick-crusted. We even mimicked our grill setup by pouring 1½ cups water into the rimmed baking sheet. In all, we'd shaved more than three hours off of our shortest recipe. In the charcoal version, the wood chips are sprinkled over coals. Don't remove the membrane that runs along the bone side of the ribs; it prevents some of the fat from rendering out and is authentic to this style of ribs.

- 1 recipe Spice Rub
- 2 (2½- to 3-pound) racks St. Louis–style spareribs, trimmed
- ½ cup apple juice
- 3 tablespoons cider vinegar
- 1 (13 by 9-inch) disposable aluminum roasting pan (if using charcoal) or 2 (9-inch) disposable aluminum pie plates (if using gas)
- ¾ cup wood chips, soaked in water for 15 minutes and drained

**1.** Rub 2 tablespoons spice rub on each side of each rack of ribs. Let ribs sit at room temperature while preparing grill.

**2.** Combine apple juice and vinegar in small bowl and set aside.

**3A. FOR A CHARCOAL GRILL:** Open bottom vent halfway and evenly space 15 unlit charcoal briquettes on 1 side of grill. Place disposable pan filled with 2 cups water on other side of grill. Light large chimney starter one-third filled with charcoal briquettes (2 quarts). When top coals are partially covered with ash, pour evenly over unlit coals. Sprinkle soaked wood chips over lit coals. Set cooking grate in place, cover, and open lid vent halfway. Heat grill until hot and wood chips are smoking, about 5 minutes.

**3B. FOR A GAS GRILL:** Place soaked wood chips in pie plate with ¼ cup water and set over primary burner. Place second pie plate filled with 2 cups water on other burner(s). Turn all burners to high; cover; and heat grill until hot and wood chips are smoking, about 15 minutes. Turn primary burner to medium-high and turn off other burner(s). (Adjust primary burner as needed to maintain grill temperature between 250 to 275 degrees.)

**4.** Clean and oil cooking grate. Place ribs meat side down on cooler side of grill over water-filled pan. Cover (position lid vent over meat if using charcoal) and cook until ribs are deep red and smoky, about 1½ hours, brushing with apple juice mixture and flipping and rotating racks halfway through cooking. About 20 minutes before removing ribs from grill, adjust oven rack to lower-middle position and heat oven to 300 degrees.

**5.** Set wire rack in rimmed baking sheet and transfer ribs to rack. Brush top of each rack with 2 tablespoons apple juice mixture. Pour 1½ cups water into bottom of sheet; roast for 1 hour. Brush ribs with remaining apple juice mixture and continue to cook until meat is tender and registers 195 degrees, 1 to 2 hours. Transfer ribs to cutting board and let rest for 15 minutes. Slice ribs between bones and serve.

## Spice Rub

**MAKES ½ cup**

For less spiciness, reduce the amount of cayenne to ½ teaspoon.

- 2 tablespoons paprika
- 2 tablespoons packed light brown sugar
- 1 tablespoon table salt
- 2 teaspoons chili powder
- 1½ teaspoons pepper
- 1½ teaspoons garlic powder
- 1½ teaspoons onion powder
- 1½ teaspoons cayenne pepper
- ½ teaspoon dried thyme

Combine all ingredients in bowl.

## Barbecued Baby Back Ribs

**SERVES 4**

**WHY THIS RECIPE WORKS** Dry, flavorless ribs are a true culinary disaster. We wanted ribs that were juicy, tender, and fully seasoned, with an intense smokiness, ribs that would be well worth the time, money, and effort. Meaty ribs—racks as close to 2 pounds as possible—provided substantial, satisfying portions. For ribs that were so good and moist they didn't even need barbecue sauce, they needed to be brined first—we used a salt, sugar, and water solution—then rubbed with a spice mix before barbecuing. Chili powder, cayenne pepper, cumin, and dark brown sugar formed a nice, crisp crust on the ribs and provided the best balance of sweet and spicy. For even more flavor, we placed wood chips or chunks on top of the coals before barbecuing and used the "low and slow" cooking method: Barbecue the ribs for a few hours on the cool side of the grill, then add fresh briquettes to the coals and continue to cook for another hour or two. For a more potent spice flavor, coat the ribs with the spice rub as directed and refrigerate them overnight, wrapped tightly in plastic wrap, If you'd like to use wood chunks rather than wood chips when using a charcoal grill, substitute 2 medium wood chunks, soaked in water for 1 hour, for the wood chip packet.

- Table salt and pepper
- ½ cup granulated sugar
- 2 (2-pound) racks baby back or loin back ribs, trimmed, membrane removed
- 1 tablespoon plus ½ teaspoon paprika
- 1¾ teaspoons ground cumin
- 1½ teaspoons chili powder
- 1½ teaspoons packed dark brown sugar
- 1 teaspoon white pepper
- ¾ teaspoon dried oregano
- ½ teaspoon cayenne pepper
- 2 cups wood chips, soaked in water for 15 minutes and drained

**1.** Dissolve ½ cup salt and granulated sugar in 4 quarts cold water in a large bowl or container. Submerge ribs in brine, cover, and refrigerate for 1 hour. Remove ribs from brine and pat dry with paper towels.

**2.** Combine paprika, cumin, chili powder, brown sugar, white pepper, ¾ teaspoon salt, ¾ teaspoon pepper, oregano, and cayenne in a small bowl. Rub each rack with 1 tablespoon of spice rub and refrigerate for 30 minutes. Using large piece of heavy-duty aluminum foil, wrap soaked chips in foil packet and cut several vent holes in top.

**3A. FOR A CHARCOAL GRILL:** Open bottom vent halfway. Light large chimney starter three-quarters filled with charcoal briquettes (4½ quarts). When top coals are partially covered with ash, pour evenly over half of grill. Place wood chip packet on coals. Set cooking grate in place, cover, and open lid vent halfway. Heat grill until hot, about 5 minutes.

**3B. FOR A GAS GRILL:** Place wood chip packet over primary burner. Turn all burners to high, cover, and heat grill until hot and wood chips are smoking, about 15 minutes. Leave primary burner on high and turn off other burner(s).

**4.** Clean and oil cooking grate. Place ribs on cooler side of grill and cook for 2 hours, covered, until grill temperature drops to about 250 degrees, flipping, switching, and rotating ribs every 30 minutes so that rack that was nearest fire is on outside. Add 10 fresh briquettes to pile of coals (if using charcoal). Cover and continue to cook (grill temperature should register 275 to 300 degrees on grill thermometer), flipping, switching, and rotating ribs every 30 minutes, until meat easily pulls away from bone, 1½ to 2 hours longer. Transfer ribs to cutting board, cut between bones to separate ribs, and serve.

## Grilled Glazed Baby Back Ribs

**SERVES** 4 to 6

---

**WHY THIS RECIPE WORKS** Instead of spending hours tending a grill for flavorful, tender ribs, we started ours on the stovetop, then moved them outside. Boiling is an established rib-cooking shortcut, but we found this led to unevenly cooked ribs, so we turned down the heat and simmered them; the gentler heat kept the thinner ends from overcooking and becoming dry. Salting the water prevented them from losing too much of their pork flavor to the cooking liquid. Once they reached 195 degrees, we removed our ribs from the pot, applied a flavorful glaze, and tossed them on the grill for tender-chewy ribs that were ready in a fraction of the time. Use 1 cup of your favorite glaze or barbecue sauce.

- 2 tablespoons table salt
- 2 (2-pound) racks baby back or loin back ribs, trimmed, membrane removed, and each rack cut in half
- 1 recipe glaze

**1.** Dissolve salt in 2½ quarts water in Dutch oven; place ribs in pot so they are fully submerged. Bring to simmer over high heat. Reduce heat to low, cover, and cook at bare simmer until thickest part of ribs registers 195 degrees, 15 to 25 minutes. While ribs are simmering, set up grill. (If ribs come to temperature before grill is ready, leave in pot, covered, until ready to use.)

**2A. FOR A CHARCOAL GRILL:** Open bottom vent halfway. Light large chimney starter filled with charcoal briquettes (6 quarts). When top coals are partially covered with ash, pour evenly over grill. Set cooking grate in place, cover, and open lid vent halfway. Heat grill until hot, about 5 minutes.

**2B. FOR A GAS GRILL:** Turn all burners to high, cover, and heat grill until hot, about 15 minutes. Turn all burners to medium-high.

**3.** Clean and oil cooking grate. Remove ribs from pot and pat dry with paper towels. Brush both sides of ribs with ⅓ cup glaze. Grill ribs, uncovered, flipping and rotating as needed, until glaze is caramelized and charred in spots, 15 to 20 minutes, brushing with another ⅓ cup glaze halfway through cooking. Transfer ribs to cutting board, brush both sides with remaining glaze, tent loosely with aluminum foil, and let rest for 10 minutes. Cut ribs between bones to separate, and serve.

### Lime Glaze

**MAKES** about 1 cup

- ⅔ cup lime juice (6 limes)
- ⅓ cup ketchup
- ¼ cup packed brown sugar
- 1 teaspoon table salt

Whisk all ingredients together in bowl.

## Bún Chả

**SERVES** 4 to 6

---

**WHY THIS RECIPE WORKS** Vietnamese *bún chả* features grilled pork patties, crisp vegetables, springy noodles, and a vibrant sauce. We started by boiling dried rice vermicelli, after which we rinsed the noodles well and spread them on a platter to dry. Then we mixed up the bold and zesty sauce known as *nước chấm* from lime juice, sugar, and fish sauce. To ensure that every drop of the sauce was flavored with garlic and chile, we used a portion of the sugar to help grind the pungent ingredients into a fine paste. Mixing baking soda into ground pork helped the meat retain moisture and brown during the brief grilling time. We also seasoned the pork with shallot, fish sauce, sugar, and pepper. Briefly dunking the grilled patties in the sauce further flavored them, and their meaty char flavors infused the sauce. Look for dried rice vermicelli in the Asian section of your supermarket. We prefer the more delicate springiness of vermicelli made from 100 percent rice flour. For a less spicy sauce, use only half the Thai chile. For the cilantro, use the leaves and the thin, delicate stems, not the thicker ones close to the root. To serve, place platters of noodles, salad, sauce, and pork patties on the table and allow diners to combine components to their taste.

NOODLES AND SALAD

- 8 ounces rice vermicelli
- 1 head Boston lettuce (8 ounces), torn into bite-size pieces
- 1 English cucumber, peeled, quartered lengthwise, seeded, and sliced thin on bias
- 1 cup fresh cilantro leaves and stems
- 1 cup fresh mint leaves, torn if large

SAUCE

- 1 small Thai chile, stemmed and minced
- 3 tablespoons sugar, divided
- 1 garlic clove, minced
- ⅔ cup hot water
- 5 tablespoons fish sauce
- ¼ cup lime juice (2 limes)

PORK PATTIES

- 1 large shallot, minced
- 1 tablespoon fish sauce
- 1½ teaspoons sugar
- ½ teaspoon baking soda
- ½ teaspoon pepper
- 1 pound ground pork

**1. FOR THE NOODLES AND SALAD:** Bring 4 quarts water to boil in large pot. Stir in noodles and cook until tender but not mushy, 4 to 12 minutes. Drain noodles and rinse under cold running water until cool. Drain noodles very well, spread on large plate, and let stand at room temperature to dry. Arrange lettuce, cucumber, cilantro, and mint separately on large platter and refrigerate until needed.

**2. FOR THE SAUCE:** Using mortar and pestle (or on cutting board using flat side of chef's knife), mash Thai chile, 1 tablespoon sugar, and garlic to fine paste. Transfer to medium bowl and add hot water and remaining 2 tablespoons sugar. Stir until sugar is dissolved. Stir in fish sauce and lime juice. Set aside.

**3. FOR THE PORK PATTIES:** Combine shallot, fish sauce, sugar, baking soda, and pepper in medium bowl. Add pork and mix until well combined. Shape pork mixture into 12 patties, each about 2½ inches wide and ½ inch thick.

**4A. FOR A CHARCOAL GRILL:** Open bottom vent completely. Light large chimney starter filled with charcoal briquettes (6 quarts). When top coals are partially covered with ash, pour over half of grill. Set cooking grate in place, cover, and open lid vent completely. Heat grill until hot, about 5 minutes.

**4B. FOR A GAS GRILL:** Turn all burners to high; cover; and heat grill until hot, about 15 minutes. Leave all burners on high.

**5.** Clean and oil cooking grate. Cook patties (directly over coals if using charcoal; covered if using gas) until well charred, 3 to 4 minutes per side. Transfer grilled patties to bowl with sauce and toss gently to coat. Let stand for 5 minutes.

**6.** Transfer patties to serving plate, reserving sauce. Serve noodles, salad, sauce, and pork patties separately.

# Grilled Lamb Kebabs

SERVES 6

**WHY THIS RECIPE WORKS** Kebabs, for all their popularity and convenience, can be hard to cook right, leaving you with vegetables and meat that are either burnt or raw and falling off the skewer. We decided to revisit the kebab. So we grabbed some metal skewers and headed to the grill in search of perfectly cooked lamb and crisp, slightly charred vegetables. To avoid the raw lamb and burnt vegetables, we cut the meat (boneless leg of lamb, trimmed of fat and silverskin) into 1-inch cubes and narrowed the vegetable field. Onions and peppers were the vegetable combination most preferred by tasters; they aren't incredibly watery like tomatoes, which were out from the beginning, and they cooked at the same rate as the meat. Marinating the meat for 2 hours added extra flavor. You can use red, yellow, orange, or green bell peppers in this recipe. You will need four 12-inch metal skewers for this recipe. If you have long, thin pieces of meat, roll or fold them into approximate 1-inch cubes before skewering.

- 1 recipe Rosemary-Mint Marinade
- 1 (2¼-pound) shank end boneless leg of lamb, trimmed and cut into 1-inch chunks
- 1 large bell pepper, stemmed, seeded, and cut into 1-inch pieces
- 1 large red or sweet onion, peeled, halved lengthwise, each half cut into 4 wedges and each wedge cut crosswise into thirds
- Lemon or lime wedges (optional)

**1.** Place marinade and lamb in 1-gallon zipper-lock bag and toss to coat; press out as much air as possible and seal bag. Refrigerate for at least 2 hours or up to 24 hours, flipping bag every hour.

**2.** Remove lamb from bag and pat dry with paper towels. Starting and ending with meat, thread 4 pieces of meat, 3 pieces of onion (three 3-layer stacks), and 6 pieces of pepper in mixed order on four 12-inch metal skewers.

**3A. FOR A CHARCOAL GRILL:** Open bottom vent completely. Light large chimney starter mounded with charcoal briquettes (7 quarts). When top coals are partially covered with ash, pour evenly over grill. Set cooking grate in place, cover, and open lid vent completely. Heat grill until hot, about 5 minutes.

**3B. FOR A GAS GRILL:** Turn all burners to high, cover, and heat grill until hot, about 15 minutes.

**4.** Clean and oil cooking grate. Place skewers on grill and cook (covered if using gas), turning skewers every 3 to 4 minutes, until well browned and lamb registers 120 to 125 degrees (for medium-rare) or 130 to 135 degrees (for medium), 7 to 12 minutes.

**5.** Transfer skewers to serving platter, tent loosely with aluminum foil, and let rest for 5 to 10 minutes before serving with lemon wedges, if using.

## Rosemary-Mint Marinade

- 10 fresh mint leaves
- 1½ teaspoons chopped fresh rosemary
- 2 tablespoons lemon juice
- ½ tablespoon grated lemon zest
- 3 cloves garlic, peeled
- ½ cup olive oil
- 1 teaspoon table salt
- ⅛ teaspoon pepper

Process all ingredients in food processor until smooth, about 1 minute.

# Grilled Lamb Kofte

**SERVES** 4 to 6

**WHY THIS RECIPE WORKS** In the Middle East, kebabs called kofte feature ground meat, not chunks, mixed with lots of spices and fresh herbs. For ours, we started with preground lamb for convenience. Kneading the meat ensured the kofte had a sausage-like spring. To help keep the meat firm, we added a small amount of gelatin and then refrigerated it. Ground pine nuts gave the kofte a noticeably richer flavor and added moisture for a perfect texture. Hot smoked paprika, cumin, and cloves contributed warm spice notes, while parsley and mint offered bright, grassy flavors. Adding a little tahini to the tangy garlic and yogurt serving sauce gave it more complexity. You will need 8 (12-inch) metal skewers for this recipe. Serve with Rice Pilaf (page 726) or make sandwiches with warm pita bread, sliced red onion, and chopped fresh mint.

**YOGURT-GARLIC SAUCE**

- 1 cup plain whole-milk yogurt
- 2 tablespoons lemon juice
- 2 tablespoons tahini
- 1 garlic clove, minced
- ½ teaspoon table salt

**KOFTE**

- ½ cup pine nuts
- 4 garlic cloves, peeled
- 1½ teaspoons hot smoked paprika
- 1 teaspoon table salt
- 1 teaspoon ground cumin
- ½ teaspoon pepper
- ¼ teaspoon ground coriander
- ¼ teaspoon ground cloves
- ⅛ teaspoon ground nutmeg
- ⅛ teaspoon ground cinnamon
- 1½ pounds ground lamb
- ½ cup grated onion, drained
- ⅓ cup minced fresh parsley
- ⅓ cup minced fresh mint
- 1½ teaspoons unflavored gelatin
- 1 large disposable aluminum roasting pan (if using charcoal)

**1. FOR THE YOGURT-GARLIC SAUCE:** Whisk all ingredients together in bowl. Set aside.

**2. FOR THE KOFTE:** Process pine nuts, garlic, paprika, salt, cumin, pepper, coriander, cloves, nutmeg, and cinnamon in food processor until coarse paste forms, 30 to 45 seconds. Transfer mixture to large bowl. Add lamb, onion, parsley, mint, and gelatin; knead with your hands until thoroughly combined and mixture feels slightly sticky, about 2 minutes. Divide mixture into 8 equal portions. Shape each portion into 5-inch-long cylinder about 1 inch in diameter. Using 8 (12-inch) metal skewers, thread 1 cylinder onto each skewer, pressing gently to adhere. Transfer skewers to lightly greased baking sheet, cover with plastic wrap, and refrigerate for at least 1 hour or up to 24 hours.

**3A. FOR A CHARCOAL GRILL:** Using skewer, poke 12 holes in bottom of disposable pan. Open bottom vent completely and place pan in center of grill. Light large chimney starter filled two-thirds with charcoal briquettes (4 quarts). When top coals are partially covered with ash, pour into pan. Set cooking grate in place, cover, and open lid vent completely. Heat grill until hot, about 5 minutes.

**3B. FOR A GAS GRILL:** Turn all burners to high; cover; and heat grill until hot, about 15 minutes. Leave all burners on high.

**4.** Clean and oil cooking grate. Place skewers on grill (directly over coals if using charcoal) at 45-degree angle to grate. Cook (covered if using gas) until browned and meat easily releases from grill, 4 to 7 minutes. Flip skewers and continue to cook until browned on second side and meat registers 160 degrees, about 6 minutes longer. Transfer skewers to platter and serve, passing yogurt-garlic sauce separately.

## Grilled Beef Kofte

Substitute 80 percent lean ground beef for lamb. Increase garlic to 5 cloves, paprika to 2 teaspoons, and cumin to 2 teaspoons.

## Grilled Arayes (Grilled Lamb-Stuffed Pita with Yogurt Sauce)

**SERVES** 4 to 6

**WHY THIS RECIPE WORKS** Inspired by Middle Eastern arayes, these lamb sandwiches are seasoned with warm spices and herbs, pressed between pita, and grilled. To help balance the richness of the sandwiches, we served them with a bright and cooling yogurt-tahini sauce. To determine which side of the pita is thicker, look closely at the pattern of browning across its surface; the less-fragile side is usually covered with char marks in a dotted-line pattern.

**SAUCE**

- 1 cup plain Greek yogurt
- ½ cup minced fresh mint
- 2 tablespoons lemon juice
- 2 tablespoons tahini
- 2 tablespoons extra-virgin olive oil
- ½ teaspoon table salt

**SANDWICHES**

- 1 onion, cut into 1-inch pieces
- 1 cup fresh cilantro leaves
- ¼ cup extra-virgin olive oil
- 1 tablespoon grated lemon zest plus 3 tablespoons juice
- 1 tablespoon ground coriander
- 1 tablespoon ground cumin
- 1 tablespoon paprika
- 2 teaspoons table salt
- 1½ teaspoons pepper
- ½ teaspoon cayenne pepper
- ¼ teaspoon ground cinnamon
- 2 pounds ground lamb
- 4 (8-inch) pita breads

**1. FOR THE SAUCE:** Whisk all ingredients together in bowl. Set aside.

**2. FOR THE SANDWICHES:** Pulse onion and cilantro in food processor until finely chopped, 10 to 12 pulses, scraping down sides of bowl as needed. Transfer mixture to large bowl. Stir in oil, lemon zest and juice, coriander, cumin, paprika, salt, pepper, cayenne, and cinnamon. Add lamb and knead gently with your hands until thoroughly combined.

**3.** Using kitchen shears, cut around perimeter of each pita and separate into 2 halves. Place 4 thicker halves on counter with interiors facing up. Divide lamb mixture into 4 equal portions and place 1 portion in center of each pita half. Using spatula, gently spread lamb mixture into even layer, leaving ½-inch border around edge. Top each with thinner pita half. Press each sandwich firmly until lamb mixture spreads to ¼ inch from edge of pita. Transfer assembled sandwiches to large plate, cover with plastic wrap, and set aside. (Sandwiches may be held for up to 1 hour before grilling.)

**4A. FOR A CHARCOAL GRILL:** Open bottom vent completely. Light large chimney starter two-thirds filled with charcoal briquettes (4 quarts). When top coals are partially covered with ash, spread coals in single layer over bottom of grill. Set cooking grate in place, cover, and open lid vent completely. Heat grill until hot, about 5 minutes.

**4B. FOR A GAS GRILL:** Turn all burners to high; cover; and heat grill until hot, about 15 minutes. Turn all burners to medium-high.

**5.** Clean and oil cooking grate. Place sandwiches on grill; cover; and cook until bottoms are evenly browned and edges are starting to crisp, 7 to 10 minutes, moving sandwiches as needed to ensure even cooking. Flip sandwiches; cover grill; and continue to cook until second sides are evenly browned and edges are crisp, 7 to 10 minutes longer. Transfer sandwiches to cutting board and cut each in half crosswise. Transfer sandwiches to platter and serve, passing sauce separately.

## Grilled Rack of Lamb

**SERVES** 4 to 6

**WHY THIS RECIPE WORKS** With its juicy, pink meat, rich crust, and classic stand-up-straight presentation, rack of lamb is a bona fide showstopper—and it has the price tag to prove it. But grill this piece of meat improperly and you've made a very costly mistake. That's why we wanted to come up with a foolproof technique for grilling rack of lamb—one that would deliver a great crust and flavorful, tender meat, every time. Our first challenge was choosing just the right cut. While the racks from butcher shops and high-end specialty stores cost more than those from the supermarket, they come already trimmed. And once we trimmed all the excess fat from our supermarket samples, we found this meat wasn't actually much cheaper. However, even the trimmed lamb needed additional butchering, both to remove the "cap" of fat that creates meat-scorching flare-ups and to trim away any excess meat and fat. (For perfect grilling results, we needed fairly lean racks of uniform thickness.) To cook the lamb evenly as well as to effectively render its fat, we placed a disposable aluminum pan in the middle of the grill and heaped a small pile of coals on either side of the pan. Placing the lamb in the middle of the grill, over the pan, ensured the pan would catch the rendering fat, preventing flare-ups. A wet rub (garlic, rosemary, thyme, and olive oil) was the best way to flavor the meat—marinades turned the lamb mushy and dry rubs simply didn't work with our grilling method. For a rich crust that wasn't charred, we applied the wet rub during the last few minutes of grilling, keeping the surface crisp. We prefer the milder taste and bigger size of domestic lamb, but you may substitute lamb from New Zealand or Australia. Since imported racks are generally smaller, follow the shorter cooking times given in the recipe. While most lamb is sold frenched (meaning part of each rib bone is exposed), chances are there will still be some extra fat between the bones. Remove the majority of this fat, leaving an inch at the top of the small eye of meat. Also, make sure that the chine bone (along the bottom of the rack) has been removed to ensure that it will be easy to cut between the ribs after cooking. Ask the butcher to do it; it's very hard to cut off at home.

- 1 (13 by 9-inch) disposable aluminum pan (if using charcoal)
- 4 teaspoons olive oil
- 4 teaspoons chopped fresh rosemary
- 2 teaspoons chopped fresh thyme
- 2 garlic cloves, minced
- 2 (1½- to 1¾-pound) racks of lamb (8 ribs each), frenched and trimmed
- Table salt and pepper

**1A. FOR A CHARCOAL GRILL:** Open bottom vent completely and place pan in center of grill. Light large chimney starter filled with charcoal briquettes (6 quarts). When top coals are partially covered with ash, pour into two even piles on either side of pan. Set cooking grate in place, cover, and open lid vent completely. Heat grill until hot, about 5 minutes.

**1B. FOR A GAS GRILL:** Turn all burners to high, cover, and heat grill until hot, about 15 minutes. Leave primary burner on high, turning off other burners.

**2.** Combine 1 tablespoon oil, rosemary, thyme, and garlic in bowl. Pat lamb dry with paper towels, rub with remaining teaspoon oil, and season with salt and pepper. Place racks bone side up on cooler part of grill with meaty side of racks very close to, but not quite over, hot coals or lit burner. Cover and cook until meat is lightly browned, faint grill marks appear, and fat has begun to render, 8 to 10 minutes.

**3.** Flip racks over, bone side down, and move to hotter parts of grill. Cook until well browned, 3 to 4 minutes. Brush racks with herb mixture. Flip racks bone side up and continue to cook until well browned, 3 to 4 minutes longer. Stand racks up and lean them against each other; continue to cook (over hotter side of grill if using charcoal) until bottom is well browned and meat registers 120 to 125 degrees (for medium-rare) or 130 to 135 degrees (for medium), 3 to 8 minutes longer.

**4.** Transfer lamb to carving board, tent loosely with aluminum foil, and let rest for 15 minutes. Cut between ribs to separate chops and serve.

### TRIMMING FAT FROM RACK OF LAMB

Use a boning or paring knife to cut away any thick portions of fat until a thin layer remains.

## Grilled Boneless, Skinless Chicken Breasts

**SERVES 4**

**WHY THIS RECIPE WORKS** Boneless, skinless chicken breasts are a tremendously practical cut for grilling. They cook quickly and evenly and don't tend to cause flare-ups; plus, their neutral flavor goes well with anything—bold sauces, sandwiches, salads, taco fixings, you name it. That said, lean chicken breasts can easily dry out if you're not careful. We perfected the method to ensure juicy, savory, and well-browned meat. We started by pounding the breasts to a ½-inch thickness so that they cooked through evenly. Soaking the chicken for 30 minutes in a potent saltwater solution seasoned it and added moisture that helped keep it juicy during cooking; we spiked the solution with umami-rich fish sauce to add savory depth and honey to encourage browning. Coating the chicken in a little oil before grilling kept it from sticking to the grate, and cooking it over a hot fire ensured that it browned deeply. Serve this chicken with Red Pepper–Almond Sauce (page 626), pair it with a vegetable, use it in sandwiches or tacos, or slice it and add it to a salad. This recipe can be easily doubled. Red Boat makes one of our favorite fish sauces.

- 4 (6- to 8-ounce) boneless, skinless chicken breasts, trimmed
- ⅓ cup water
- 3 tablespoons fish sauce
- 2 tablespoons honey
- 1 teaspoon table salt
- ⅛ teaspoon pepper
- 1 tablespoon vegetable oil

**1.** Cover chicken breasts with plastic wrap and pound gently with meat pounder until ½ inch thick. Whisk water, fish sauce, honey, salt, and pepper together in bowl. Transfer mixture to 1-gallon zipper-lock bag. Add chicken, press out air, seal bag, and turn bag so contents are evenly distributed. Refrigerate for 30 minutes.

**2A. FOR A CHARCOAL GRILL:** Open bottom vent completely. Light large chimney starter filled with charcoal briquettes (6 quarts). When top coals are partially covered with ash, pour evenly over grill. Set cooking grate in place, cover, and open lid vent completely. Heat grill until hot, about 5 minutes.

**2B. FOR A GAS GRILL:** Turn all burners to high; cover; and heat grill until hot, about 15 minutes. Leave all burners on high.

**3.** Remove chicken from brine, letting excess drip off (do not pat dry), then toss with oil in second bowl until evenly coated.

**4.** Clean and oil cooking grate. Place chicken, skinned side down, on grill and cook (covered if using gas) until chicken develops dark grill marks, 3 to 5 minutes. Gently release chicken from cooking grate; flip; and continue to cook until chicken registers 160 degrees, 3 to 5 minutes longer. Transfer chicken to cutting board and tent with aluminum foil. Let rest for 5 minutes before serving.

### Red Pepper–Almond Sauce

SERVES 4

We like the complexity that toasted sesame oil gives to this sauce, but extra-virgin olive oil can be substituted.

- 5 teaspoons sherry vinegar
- 1 garlic clove, minced
- ¾ teaspoon table salt
- 2 red bell peppers, stemmed, seeded, and quartered
- 1 tablespoon vegetable oil
- ¼ cup whole almonds, toasted
- 2 teaspoons toasted sesame oil
- ½ teaspoon smoked paprika
- Pinch cayenne pepper

**1.** Combine vinegar, garlic, and salt in small bowl and set aside.

**2.** Toss bell peppers with vegetable oil in bowl until evenly coated. Grill bell peppers, skin side down, over hot fire (covered if using gas) until most of surface is well charred, 5 to 7 minutes. Flip and cook until lightly charred on second side, about 2 minutes. Transfer bell peppers to bowl and cover tightly with aluminum foil.

**3.** Pulse almonds in food processor until finely chopped, 10 to 12 pulses. Add sesame oil, paprika, cayenne, vinegar mixture, and bell peppers (do not remove skins) and process until smooth, about 45 seconds, scraping down sides of bowl as needed. Loosen with water as needed and season with salt to taste.

## Grilled Glazed Boneless, Skinless Chicken Breasts

SERVES 4

**WHY THIS RECIPE WORKS** Grilled glazed boneless chicken breasts are a quick and easy summer dinner, but too often the glaze burns or the chicken overcooks. To produce perfectly cooked chicken, we briefly brined the meat to keep it moist during cooking and used a two-level grill fire to prevent the glaze from singeing. Lightly coating the chicken with milk powder hastened browning during the quick cooking time. We developed a sweet-savory glaze that complemented but didn't overpower the chicken. A small amount of corn syrup provided a mild sweetness and just enough viscosity to help the glaze cling to the meat.

- ¼ cup table salt
- ¼ cup sugar
- 4 (6- to 8-ounce) boneless, skinless chicken breasts, trimmed
- 2 teaspoons nonfat dry milk powder
- ¼ teaspoon pepper
- Vegetable oil spray
- 1 recipe Spicy Hoisin Glaze

**1.** Dissolve salt and sugar in 1½ quarts cold water. Submerge chicken in brine, cover, and refrigerate for at least 30 minutes or up to 1 hour. Remove chicken from brine and pat dry with paper towels. Combine milk powder and pepper in bowl.

**2A. FOR A CHARCOAL GRILL:** Open bottom vent completely. Light large chimney starter mounded with charcoal briquettes (7 quarts). When top coals are partially covered with ash, pour two-thirds evenly over half of grill, then pour remaining coals over other half of grill. Set cooking grate in place, cover, and open lid vent completely. Heat grill until hot, about 5 minutes.

**2B. FOR A GAS GRILL:** Turn all burners to high, cover, and heat grill until hot, about 15 minutes. Leave primary burner on high and turn other burner(s) to medium-high.

**3.** Clean and oil cooking grate. Sprinkle half of milk powder mixture over 1 side of chicken. Lightly spray coated side of chicken with oil spray until milk powder is moistened. Flip chicken and sprinkle remaining milk powder mixture over second side. Lightly spray with oil spray.

**4.** Place chicken, skinned side down, on hotter side of grill and cook until browned on first side, 2 to 2½ minutes. Flip chicken, brush with 2 tablespoons glaze, and cook until browned on second side, 2 to 2½ minutes. Flip chicken, move to cooler side of grill, brush with 2 tablespoons glaze, and cook for 2 minutes. Repeat flipping and brushing 2 more times, cooking for 2 minutes on each side. Flip chicken, brush with remaining glaze, and cook until chicken registers 160 degrees, 1 to 3 minutes. Transfer chicken to plate and let rest for 5 minutes before serving.

### Spicy Hoisin Glaze

MAKES about ⅔ cup

For a spicier glaze, use the larger amount of sriracha.

- 2 tablespoons rice vinegar
- 1 teaspoon cornstarch
- ⅓ cup hoisin sauce
- 2 tablespoons light corn syrup
- 1–2 tablespoons sriracha sauce
- 1 teaspoon grated fresh ginger
- ¼ teaspoon five-spice powder

Whisk vinegar and cornstarch together in small saucepan until cornstarch has dissolved. Whisk in hoisin, corn syrup, sriracha, ginger, and five-spice powder. Bring mixture to boil over high heat. Cook, stirring constantly, until thickened, about 1 minute. Transfer glaze to bowl.

## Grilled Glazed Bone-In Chicken Breasts

**SERVES 4**

**WHY THIS RECIPE WORKS** We wanted glazed chicken breasts with tender meat and crisp, lacquered skin. Brining the bone-in chicken breasts before grilling helped ensure juicy, well-seasoned meat. For the glaze, we balanced sweet molasses and chipotle chiles. To keep the glaze from burning on the grill, we first seared the breasts over high heat and then moved them to the cool side of the grill, where we brushed them with the glaze in the last few minutes. For extra flavor, we reserved half of the glaze for serving. If using kosher chicken, do not brine in step 1, and season with salt as well as pepper. Remember to reserve half of the glaze for serving.

- ½ cup table salt for brining
- 4 (10- to 12-ounce) bone-in split chicken breasts, trimmed
- ½ teaspoon pepper
- 1 recipe Orange-Chipotle Glaze

**1.** Dissolve salt in 2 quarts cold water in large container. Submerge chicken breasts in brine, cover, and refrigerate for 30 minutes to 1 hour. Remove chicken from brine and pat dry with paper towels. Sprinkle chicken with pepper.

**2A. FOR A CHARCOAL GRILL:** Open bottom vent completely. Light large chimney starter filled with charcoal briquettes (6 quarts). When top coals are partially covered with ash, pour evenly over half of grill. Set cooking grate in place, cover, and open lid vent completely. Heat grill until hot, about 5 minutes.

**2B. FOR A GAS GRILL:** Turn all burners to high; cover; and heat grill until hot, about 15 minutes. Leave primary burner on high and turn off other burner(s). (Adjust primary burner as needed during cooking to maintain grill temperature of 350 degrees.)

**3.** Clean and oil cooking grate. Place chicken on hotter side of grill, skin side up, and cook (covered if using gas) until lightly browned on both sides, 6 to 8 minutes, flipping halfway through cooking. Move chicken, skin side down, to cooler side of grill, with thicker end of breasts facing coals and flames. Cover and continue to cook until chicken registers 150 degrees, 15 to 20 minutes longer.

**4.** Brush bone side of chicken generously with half of glaze; move to hotter side of grill; and cook until browned, 5 to 10 minutes. Brush skin side of chicken with remaining glaze; flip chicken; and continue to cook until chicken registers 160 degrees, 2 to 3 minutes longer.

**5.** Transfer chicken to serving platter, tent with aluminum foil, and let rest for 5 to 10 minutes before serving, passing reserved glaze separately.

### Orange-Chipotle Glaze

**MAKES** ¾ cup

For a spicier glaze, use the greater amount of chipotle chiles.

- 1 teaspoon grated orange zest plus ⅔ cup juice (2 oranges)
- 1–2 tablespoons minced canned chipotle chile in adobo sauce
- 1 small shallot, minced
- 2 teaspoons minced fresh thyme
- 1 tablespoon molasses
- ¾ teaspoon cornstarch

Combine orange zest and juice, chipotle, shallot, and thyme in small saucepan. Whisk in molasses and cornstarch, bring to simmer, and cook over medium heat until thickened, about 5 minutes. Season with salt to taste. Reserve half of glaze for serving and use remaining glaze to brush on chicken.

## Thai-Style Grilled Chicken with Spicy Sweet-and-Sour Dipping Sauce

**SERVES 4**

**WHY THIS RECIPE WORKS** We wanted to develop a recipe for Thai-style grilled chicken to offer a delicious alternative to typical American-style barbecue fare. After testing numerous rub combinations, we liked cilantro, black pepper, lime juice, garlic, coriander, and ginger. We took some of the rub and placed it in a thick layer under the skin as well as on top of it. For perfectly cooked chicken, we made a modified two-level fire, first browning the chicken directly over the coals and then moving it to the cool side of the grill to finish cooking. The true flavors of this dish come through in the sauce, a classic combination of sweet and spicy. For even cooking, the chicken breasts should be of comparable size. Some of the rub is inevitably lost to the grill, but the chicken will still be flavorful.

**CHICKEN AND BRINE**

- ½ cup sugar
- ½ cup table salt
- 4 (12-ounce) bone-in split chicken breasts, trimmed

DIPPING SAUCE

- ⅓ cup sugar
- ¼ cup distilled white vinegar
- ¼ cup lime juice (2 limes)
- 2 tablespoons fish sauce
- 3 small garlic cloves, minced
- 1 teaspoon red pepper flakes

RUB

- ⅔ cup chopped fresh cilantro
- 12 garlic cloves, minced
- ¼ cup lime juice (2 limes)
- 2 tablespoons grated fresh ginger
- 2 tablespoons pepper
- 2 tablespoons ground coriander
- 2 tablespoons vegetable oil

- 1 disposable aluminum roasting pan (if using charcoal)

**1. FOR THE CHICKEN AND BRINE:** Dissolve sugar and salt in 2 quarts cold water in large container. Submerge chicken in brine, cover, and refrigerate for at least 30 minutes or up to 1 hour. Remove chicken from brine and pat dry with paper towels.

**2. FOR THE DIPPING SAUCE:** Whisk all ingredients together in bowl until sugar dissolves. Let stand for 1 hour at room temperature to allow flavors to meld.

**3. FOR THE RUB:** Combine all ingredients in small bowl; work mixture with your fingers to thoroughly combine. Slide your fingers between chicken skin and meat to loosen skin, taking care not to detach skin. Rub about 2 tablespoons rub under skin of each breast. Thoroughly rub even layer of rub onto all exterior surfaces, including bottom and sides. Place chicken in bowl, cover with plastic wrap, and refrigerate while preparing grill.

**4A. FOR A CHARCOAL GRILL:** Open bottom vent completely. Light large chimney starter filled with charcoal briquettes (6 quarts). When top coals are partially covered with ash, pour evenly over half of grill. Set cooking grate in place, cover, and open lid vent completely. Heat grill until hot, about 5 minutes.

**4B. FOR A GAS GRILL:** Turn all burners to high, cover, and heat grill until hot, about 15 minutes. Leave primary burner on high and turn other burner(s) to low.

**5.** Clean and oil cooking grate. Place chicken, skin side down, on hotter side of grill; cook until browned, about 3 minutes (1 to 2 minutes longer for gas grill). Using tongs, flip chicken and cook until browned on second side, about 3 minutes longer. Move chicken, skin side up, to cooler side of grill and cover with disposable pan (or close lid if using gas grill). Continue to cook until thickest part of breast (not touching bone) registers 160 degrees, 10 to 15 minutes longer. Transfer chicken to platter; let rest for 10 minutes. Serve, passing dipping sauce separately.

## Grilled Stuffed Chicken Breasts with Prosciutto and Fontina

SERVES 4

**WHY THIS RECIPE WORKS** Chicken cordon bleu solves the problem of dry, mild-flavored chicken breasts with a flavorful stuffing of sharp, nutty melted cheese and salty sliced ham. We wanted to bring this concept to the grill, but leaky cheese can cause flare-ups as it drips from the chicken and into the coals. We wanted great grilled chicken breasts with a flavorful stuffing that stayed put. For the stuffing, we settled on more flavorful prosciutto and fontina cheese rather than the usual deli ham and Swiss cheese. And we chose bone-in, skin-on breasts since the skin acts as a natural protector of the meat. We butterflied the breasts—cutting them horizontally nearly halfway through so the meat opened like a book. We placed prosciutto-wrapped fontina inside, folded over the breast to enclose it and tied each breast up with kitchen twine. Encasing the fontina in prosciutto, rather than layering it on top, prevented the cheese from leaking. We also chose to add a simple compound butter enlivened by shallots and tarragon for additional moisture and flavor. Cooking the stuffed breasts over a modified two-level fire (in which all the coals are banked on one side of the grill) allowed us to first sear the breasts over the hot coals for color and flavor, then finish cooking them over more moderate indirect heat. If using kosher chicken, do not brine in step 1. You can serve the chicken on the bone, but we prefer to carve it off and slice it before serving.

- 4 (10- to 12-ounce) bone-in split chicken breasts, trimmed
  Table salt and pepper
- 4 tablespoons unsalted butter, softened
- 1 shallot, minced
- 4 teaspoons chopped fresh tarragon
- 2 ounces fontina cheese, rind removed, cut into four 3 by ½-inch sticks
- 4 thin slices prosciutto

**1.** Using sharp knife and starting on thick side of breast closest to breastbone, cut horizontal pocket in each breast, stopping ½ inch from edge so halves remain attached. Dissolve ¼ cup salt in 2 quarts cold water in large container. Submerge chicken breasts in brine, cover, and refrigerate for 30 minutes to 1 hour. Remove chicken from brine and pat dry with paper towels. Season chicken with pepper.

**2A. FOR A CHARCOAL GRILL:** Open bottom vent completely. Light large chimney starter filled with charcoal briquettes (6 quarts). When top coals are partially covered with ash, pour evenly over half of grill. Set cooking grate in place, cover, and open lid vent completely. Heat grill until hot, about 5 minutes.

**2B. FOR A GAS GRILL:** Turn all burners to high, cover, and heat grill until hot, about 15 minutes. Leave primary burner on high and turn off other burner(s). (Adjust primary burner as needed during cooking to maintain grill temperature around 350 degrees.)

**3.** Meanwhile, combine butter, shallot, and tarragon in bowl. Roll each piece of fontina in 1 slice prosciutto. Spread equal amount of butter mixture inside each breast. Place 1 prosciutto-wrapped piece of fontina inside each breast and fold breast over to enclose. Evenly space 3 pieces kitchen twine (each about 12 inches long) beneath each breast and tie, trimming any excess.

**4.** Clean and oil cooking grate. Place chicken on hot side of grill, skin side down. Cook (covered if using gas) until well browned on first side, 4 to 6 minutes. Flip chicken and cook until second side is just opaque, about 2 minutes. Move chicken to cool side of grill, skin side up with thicker side of breasts facing coals and flames. Cover and continue to cook until chicken registers 160 degrees, 25 to 35 minutes longer.

**5.** Transfer chicken to carving board, tent loosely with aluminum foil, and let rest for 5 to 10 minutes. Remove twine, cut meat from bone, slice ½ inch thick, and serve.

### ASSEMBLING STUFFED CHICKEN BREASTS FOR GRILLING

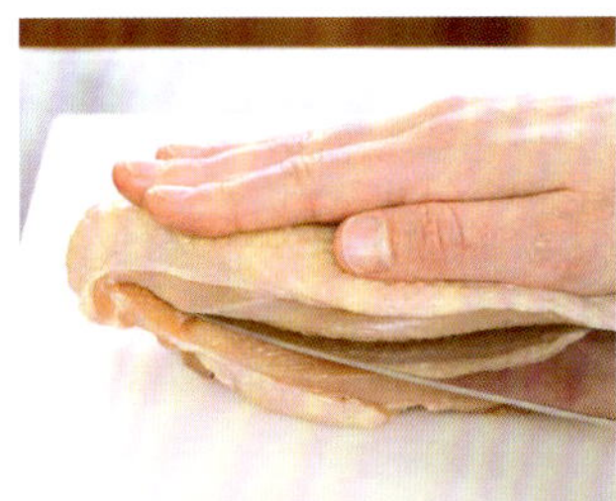

**1.** Starting on the thick side closest to the breastbone, cut a horizontal pocket in each breast, stopping ½ inch from the edge.

**2.** Spread an equal portion of compound butter inside each breast.

**3.** Place one prosciutto-wrapped piece of cheese inside each breast and fold the breast over to enclose.

**4.** Tie each breast with three 12-inch pieces of kitchen twine at even intervals.

## Grilled Chicken Fajitas

**SERVES** 4 to 6

**WHY THIS RECIPE WORKS** Some chicken fajitas need to be slathered with guacamole, sour cream, and salsa to compensate for the bland flavor of the main ingredients. We wanted the chicken and vegetables to be flavorful enough to make condiments unnecessary. To boost the flavor of the chicken, we used a marinade of lime juice and oil. We added jalapeño and cilantro for some bright spice and herbal flavor, and a surprising addition—Worcestershire sauce—lent a subtle but complex savory note. We marinated the chicken only briefly, so the acid wouldn't turn the delicate chicken to mush. Bell peppers and onions are the customary vegetables, and we found that their sweet-bitter flavors contrasted well with the chicken. To prepare the vegetables for grilling, we quartered the peppers, so they'd lie flat on the grill, and cut the onion into thick rounds that would hold together during cooking. A two-level fire enabled us to grill the chicken and vegetables at the same time, the latter on the cooler part so they wouldn't burn. We saved some of the marinade to toss with everything at the end for a bright flavor burst; nestled in a warm tortilla, the smoky vegetables and well-seasoned chicken were so good on their own that we forgot all about toppings. You can use red, yellow, orange, or green bell peppers in this recipe. The chicken tenderloins can be reserved for another use or marinated and grilled along with the breasts. When you head outside to grill, bring a clean dish towel in which to wrap the tortillas and keep them warm. The chicken and vegetables have enough flavor on their own, but accompaniments (guacamole, salsa, sour cream, shredded cheddar or Monterey Jack cheese, and lime wedges) can be offered at the table.

- 6 tablespoons vegetable oil
- ⅓ cup lime juice (3 limes)
- 1 jalapeño chile, stemmed, seeded, and minced
- 1½ tablespoons minced fresh cilantro
- 3 garlic cloves, minced
- 1 tablespoon Worcestershire sauce
- 1½ teaspoons packed brown sugar
- Table salt and pepper
- 1½ pounds boneless, skinless chicken breasts, tenderloins removed, trimmed, pounded to ½-inch thickness
- 1 large red onion, peeled and cut into ½-inch-thick rounds (do not separate rings)
- 2 large bell peppers, quartered, stemmed, and seeded
- 8–12 (6-inch) flour tortillas

**1.** Whisk ¼ cup oil, lime juice, jalapeño, cilantro, garlic, Worcestershire, sugar, 1 teaspoon salt, and ¾ teaspoon pepper together in bowl. Reserve ¼ cup marinade and set aside. Add 1 teaspoon salt to remaining marinade. Place marinade and chicken in 1-gallon zipper-lock bag and toss to coat; press out as much air as possible and seal bag. Refrigerate for at least 15 minutes, flipping bag halfway through marinating. Brush both sides of onion rounds and peppers with remaining 2 tablespoons oil and season with salt and pepper to taste.

**2A. FOR A CHARCOAL GRILL:** Open bottom vent completely. Light large chimney starter filled with charcoal briquettes (6 quarts). When top coals are partially covered with ash, pour coals over two-thirds of grill, leaving remaining one-third empty. Set cooking grate in place, cover, and open lid vent completely. Heat grill until hot, about 5 minutes.

**2B. FOR A GAS GRILL:** Turn all burners to high, cover, and heat grill until hot, about 15 minutes. Leave primary burner on high and turn other burner(s) to medium.

**3.** Clean and oil cooking grate. Remove chicken from bag, allowing excess marinade to drip off. Place chicken on hotter side of grill, smooth side down. Cook (covered if using gas) until well browned on first side, 4 to 6 minutes. Flip and continue to cook until chicken registers 160 degrees, 4 to 6 minutes longer. Transfer chicken to cutting board, tent loosely with aluminum foil, and let rest for 5 to 10 minutes.

**4.** While chicken cooks, place onion rounds and peppers (skin side down) on cooler side of grill and cook until tender and charred on both sides, 8 to 12 minutes, flipping every 3 minutes. Transfer onions and peppers to cutting board with chicken.

**5.** Working in 2 or 3 batches, place tortillas in single layer on cooler side of grill. Cook until warm and lightly browned, about 20 seconds per side (do not grill too long or tortillas will become brittle). As tortillas are done, wrap in dish towel or large sheet of foil.

**6.** Separate onions into rings and place in medium bowl. Slice peppers into ¼-inch-thick strips and place in bowl with onions. Add 2 tablespoons reserved marinade and toss to combine. Slice each breast on bias into ¼-inch-thick slices, place in second bowl, and toss with remaining 2 tablespoons reserved marinade.

**7.** Transfer chicken and vegetables to serving platter and serve with warmed tortillas.

## Best Grilled Chicken Thighs

**SERVES** 4 to 6

**WHY THIS RECIPE WORKS** We wanted a recipe that would produce juicy, flavorful grilled chicken thighs that had well-rendered, crispy skin—minus the all-too-frequent inferno. Cooking the chicken over indirect heat for a relatively long time (about 40 minutes), until it registered between 185 to 190 degrees, allowed collagen in the meat to break down into gelatin, which lubricated the meat so that it tasted moist and silky. We also grilled the thighs skin side down for all but the last few minutes of cooking, which thoroughly rendered the fat under the surface of the skin and allowed the collagen in the skin to break down, both of which led to thin, crispy, well-browned skin. For extra flavor, we coated the chicken with a bold paste, spreading two-thirds of the paste on the flesh side of each thigh. We then rubbed the remaining third of the paste over the skin, which seasoned and flavored it without adding moisture that inhibited crisping.

- 8 (5- to 7-ounce) bone-in chicken thighs, trimmed
- ½ teaspoon kosher salt
- 1 recipe Mustard-Tarragon Paste

**1.** Place chicken, skin side up, on large plate. Sprinkle skin side with salt and spread evenly with one-third of spice paste. Flip chicken and spread remaining two-thirds of paste evenly over flesh side. Refrigerate while preparing grill. (Chicken can be wrapped in plastic wrap and refrigerated for up to 2 hours.)

**2A. FOR A CHARCOAL GRILL:** Open bottom vent halfway. Light large chimney starter mounded with charcoal briquettes (7 quarts). When top coals are partially covered with ash, pour evenly over half of grill. Set cooking grate in place, cover, and open lid vent halfway. Heat grill until hot, about 5 minutes.

**2B. FOR A GAS GRILL:** Turn all burners to high; cover; and heat grill until hot, about 15 minutes. Leave primary burner on high and turn off other burner(s). (Adjust primary burner [or, if using 3-burner grill, primary burner and second burner] as needed to maintain grill temperature of 350 degrees.)

**3.** Clean and oil cooking grate. Place chicken, skin side down, on cooler side of grill. Cover and cook for 20 minutes. Rearrange chicken, keeping skin side down, so that pieces that were positioned closest to edge of grill are now closer to heat source and vice versa. Cover and continue to cook until chicken registers 185 to 190 degrees, 15 to 20 minutes longer.

**4.** Move all chicken, skin side down, to hotter side of grill and cook until skin is lightly charred, about 5 minutes. Flip chicken and cook until flesh side is lightly browned, 1 to 2 minutes. Transfer to platter, tent with aluminum foil, and let rest for 10 minutes. Serve.

### Mustard-Tarragon Paste

**MAKES** ⅓ cup

Rosemary or thyme can be substituted for the tarragon, if desired. When using this paste, we like to serve the chicken with lemon wedges.

- 3 tablespoons Dijon mustard
- 5 garlic cloves, minced
- 1 tablespoon grated lemon zest
- 2 teaspoons minced fresh tarragon
- 1½ teaspoons kosher salt
- 1 teaspoon water
- ½ teaspoon pepper

Combine all ingredients in bowl.

## Grilled Chicken Satay

**SERVES** 4 to 6

**WHY THIS RECIPE WORKS** This Malaysian-style chicken satay features pieces of chicken coated in a deeply fragrant paste, skewered, and charred on the grill. Cutting the chicken thighs into strips and stretching them between two skewers created more surface area for the paste to coat and for charring. An aromatic paste of lemongrass, ginger, galangal, garlic, shallots, and spices developed savory character when charred. We used a portion of the paste as the base for a dipping sauce. You will need eight 12-inch metal skewers for this recipe. If galangal is unavailable, increase the ginger to one 1½-inch piece. The aromatic paste can also be prepared using a mortar and pestle. Lime juice can be substituted for the tamarind paste.

**AROMATIC PASTE**

- 2 lemongrass stalks, trimmed to bottom 6 inches
- 3 shallots, chopped (⅔ cup)
- 3 tablespoons water
- 1 tablespoon vegetable oil
- 1 tablespoon packed brown sugar
- 3 garlic cloves, chopped
- 1 (1-inch) piece galangal, peeled and minced
- 1 (1-inch) piece ginger, peeled and sliced into ⅛-inch-thick coins
- 2 teaspoons table salt
- 1 teaspoon ground turmeric
- ½–¾ teaspoon red pepper flakes
- ½ teaspoon ground coriander
- ½ teaspoon ground cumin

**PEANUT SAUCE**

- ⅓ cup dry-roasted peanuts
- 2 tablespoons vegetable oil
- ¾ cup water, plus extra as needed
- 1 tablespoon tamarind paste
- 1 tablespoon packed brown sugar

**CHICKEN**

- 2 pounds boneless, skinless chicken thighs, trimmed and cut crosswise into 1- to 1½-inch-wide strips
- 2 tablespoons vegetable oil

**1. FOR THE AROMATIC PASTE:** Halve lemongrass lengthwise and, using meat pounder, lightly crush on cutting board to soften. Mince lemongrass and transfer to food processor. Add shallots, water, oil, sugar, garlic, galangal, ginger, salt, turmeric, and pepper flakes and process until uniform paste forms, about 2 minutes, scraping down sides of bowl as necessary. Measure out ⅓ cup paste and set aside. Transfer remaining paste to bowl and stir in coriander and cumin. Cover bowl and microwave paste for 1½ minutes, stirring halfway through microwaving. Transfer bowl to refrigerator and let paste cool while preparing sauce.

**2. FOR THE PEANUT SAUCE:** Place peanuts in now-empty processor and process until coarsely ground, about 15 seconds. Heat oil and reserved ⅓ cup paste in medium saucepan over medium-low heat until fond begins to form on bottom of saucepan and paste starts to darken, about 5 minutes. Stir in water, tamarind, sugar, and ground peanuts and bring to boil, scraping up any browned bits. Reduce heat to maintain gentle simmer and cook, stirring occasionally, until sauce is reduced to about 1 cup, 8 to 10 minutes. Season with salt to taste, cover, and set aside.

**3. FOR THE CHICKEN:** Add chicken to cooled paste and toss to combine. Thread chicken onto 4 sets of two 12-inch metal skewers. (Hold 2 skewers 1 inch apart and thread chicken onto both skewers at once so strips of chicken are perpendicular to skewers.) Do not crowd skewers; each set of skewers should hold 6 to 8 pieces of chicken. Transfer kebabs to large plate and refrigerate while preparing grill. (Kebabs can be refrigerated for up to 4 hours.)

**4A. FOR A CHARCOAL GRILL:** Open bottom vent completely. Light large chimney starter mounded with charcoal briquettes (7 quarts). When top coals are partially covered with ash, pour evenly over grill. Set cooking grate in place, cover, and open lid vent completely. Heat grill until hot, about 5 minutes.

**4B. FOR A GAS GRILL:** Turn all burners to high; cover; and heat grill until hot, about 15 minutes. Turn all burners to medium.

**5.** Clean and oil cooking grate. Brush both sides of kebabs with oil. Place kebabs on grill and cook (covered if using gas) until browned and char marks appear on first side, about 5 minutes. Using large metal spatula, gently release chicken from grill; flip; and continue to cook until chicken registers 175 to 180 degrees, 3 to 5 minutes longer. Transfer to large platter. Gently reheat peanut sauce, thinning with extra water, 1 tablespoon at a time, to desired consistency. Serve chicken, passing peanut sauce separately.

## Grilled Spice-Rubbed Chicken Drumsticks

**SERVES 6**

**WHY THIS RECIPE WORKS** Chicken drumsticks are usually neglected unless they are eaten as part of a whole bird. But their built-in handles and conveniently small size make them tailor-made for a cookout. With the right treatment, economical chicken drumsticks can be a delicious choice for the grill. We started by soaking them in a saltwater brine to season them and help them retain their juices during cooking, then coated our drumsticks with a flavorful rub (after deciding that a glaze would make them too messy to eat out of hand). We cooked them to between 185 and 190 degrees over indirect heat, to ensure this collagen-rich cut turned tender. We finished by cooking the drumsticks briefly over the coals to capture some char and crispiness. Before applying the spice rub, smooth the skin over the drumsticks so it is covering as much surface area as possible.

- ½ cup table salt
- 5 pounds chicken drumsticks
- 1 recipe Barbecue Spice Rub (recipe follows)

**1.** Dissolve salt in 2 quarts cold water in large container. Submerge drumsticks in brine, cover, and refrigerate for 30 minutes to 1 hour.

**2.** Place spice rub on plate. Remove drumsticks from brine and pat dry with paper towels. Holding 1 drumstick by bone end, press lightly into rub on all sides. Pat gently to remove excess rub. Repeat with remaining drumsticks.

**3A. FOR A CHARCOAL GRILL:** Open bottom vent halfway. Light large chimney starter filled with charcoal briquettes (6 quarts). When top coals are partially covered with ash, pour evenly over half of grill. Set cooking grate in place, cover, and open lid vent halfway. Heat grill until hot, about 5 minutes.

**3B. FOR A GAS GRILL:** Turn all burners to high, cover, and heat grill until hot, about 15 minutes. Leave primary burner on high and turn off other burner(s). (Adjust primary burner [or, if using three-burner grill, primary burner and second burner] as needed to maintain grill temperature between 325 and 350 degrees.)

**4.** Clean and oil cooking grate. Place drumsticks, skin side down, on cooler side of grill. Cover and cook for 25 minutes. Rearrange pieces so that drumsticks that were closest to edge are now closer to heat source and vice versa. Cover and cook until drumsticks register 185 to 190 degrees, 20 to 30 minutes.

**5.** Move all drumsticks to hotter side of grill and cook, turning occasionally, until skin is nicely charred, about 5 minutes. Transfer to platter, tent with aluminum foil, and let rest for 10 minutes. Serve.

### Barbecue Spice Rub

**MAKES** about ⅓ cup

You can substitute granulated garlic for the garlic powder.

- 3 tablespoons packed brown sugar
- 1 tablespoon paprika
- 1 tablespoon chili powder
- 2 teaspoons garlic powder
- ¾ teaspoon table salt
- ¾ teaspoon pepper
- ¼ teaspoon cayenne pepper

Combine all ingredients in small bowl.

## Grilled Chicken with Adobo and Sazón

**SERVES** 4 to 6

**WHY THIS RECIPE WORKS** This intensely flavored chicken gets its punch from two dried seasonings from the Puerto Rican pantry: adobo, a blend made from granulated garlic, salt, pepper, and oregano; and sazón, a mixture that includes all the ingredients of adobo as well as achiote, dried onion, cumin, and more herbs. We crafted a homemade adobo but used a commercial sazón. Breaking down a chicken gave us proportionately sized legs and breasts, which cooked more evenly, and the grilled backbone to enjoy. After tossing the chicken in oil and vinegar, we rubbed the seasoning over and under the skin as well as into pockets slashed into the legs. Applied after grilling, a punchy marinade added another layer of bright flavor. Look for sazón with culantro and achiote (also called annatto) at the supermarket, and avoid sazón without salt. You can substitute garlic powder for the granulated garlic. Breaking down a whole chicken lets you enjoy the delicacy that is the grilled backbone, but the recipe works fine with 4 to 4½ pounds of bone-in leg quarters and split breasts.

**ADOBO AND SAZÓN**

- 4 teaspoons granulated garlic
- 2½ teaspoons commercial sazón
- 1 teaspoon table salt
- ½ teaspoon pepper
- ¼ teaspoon dried oregano

**CHICKEN**

- 1 (4- to 4½-pound) whole chicken, giblets discarded
- 5 tablespoons distilled white vinegar, divided
- 5 tablespoons extra-virgin olive oil, divided
- 6 garlic cloves, minced
- ½ teaspoon table salt
- 1 (13 by 9-inch) disposable aluminum roasting pan
- ¼ cup chopped fresh cilantro
- ½ teaspoon pepper

**1. FOR THE ADOBO AND SAZÓN:** Combine all ingredients in bowl.

**2. FOR THE CHICKEN:** Place chicken breast side down on cutting board. Using kitchen shears, cut through bones on either side of backbone. Reserve backbone. Using chef's knife, cut through breastbone to split chicken in half.

**3.** Working with 1 half of chicken, slice through skin connecting leg quarter to breast, cutting close to leg quarter to ensure skin completely covers breast and rib meat. Leave split breast whole and tuck wing behind back. Flip leg quarter and remove and discard any rib bone connected to thigh bone. Repeat with second half of chicken.

**4.** Place 1 leg quarter skin side up on cutting board. Using sharp knife, make 3 slashes: 1 across thigh, 1 across joint, and 1 across drumstick (each slash should reach bone). Flip leg quarter and make 1 more diagonal slash across back of drumstick. Repeat with second leg quarter.

**5.** Toss chicken (including backbone) with 1 tablespoon vinegar and 1 tablespoon oil in large bowl, using your hands to loosen skin from meat. Sprinkle adobo-sazón mixture over chicken pieces. Toss with your hands, rubbing mixture all over chicken, into slashes, and under skin. Cover and refrigerate chicken for at least 3 hours or up to 24 hours.

**6A. FOR A CHARCOAL GRILL:** Open bottom vent completely. Light large chimney starter filled with charcoal briquettes (6 quarts). When top coals are partially covered with ash, pour evenly over half of grill. Set cooking grate in place, cover, and open lid vent completely. Heat grill until hot, about 5 minutes.

**6B. FOR A GAS GRILL:** Turn all burners to high; cover; and heat grill until hot, about 15 minutes. Turn primary burner to medium and turn other burner(s) to low. (Adjust primary burner as needed to maintain grill temperature between 400 and 425 degrees.)

**7.** While grill heats, place garlic on cutting board and sprinkle with salt. Mash to paste with side of knife. Transfer garlic paste to disposable pan. Add cilantro, pepper, remaining ¼ cup vinegar, and remaining ¼ cup oil and mix to form paste.

**8.** Clean and oil cooking grate. Place chicken (including backbone) on cooler side of grill, skin side up. Cover and cook until underside of chicken is lightly browned, 15 to 20 minutes. Flip chicken; cover; and continue to cook on cooler side of grill until thickest part of breast registers 150 degrees, 15 to 20 minutes longer. While chicken cooks, place disposable pan with paste on hotter side of grill and heat until liquid begins to simmer and garlic begins to cook, 2 to 3 minutes. Remove disposable pan from grill.

**9.** Transfer chicken to hotter side of grill, skin side down, and cook (covered if using gas) until skin is well browned, 2 to 3 minutes. As chicken browns, place disposable pan on cooler side of grill.

**10.** Flip chicken and cook until breasts register 155 degrees and leg quarters register 175 degrees, about 2 to 3 minutes. As chicken reaches temperature, transfer to disposable pan. Once all chicken is in disposable pan, cover with aluminum foil and slide to hotter side of grill. Cook until marinade is sizzling, 3 to 4 minutes. Let stand off heat for 10 minutes.

**11.** Cut each breast in half crosswise through bone. Cut leg quarters through joint to separate thigh and drumstick. Place chicken, including backbone, on serving platter. Pour marinade from disposable pan into serving bowl. Serve, passing marinade separately.

## Peri Peri Grilled Chicken

**SERVES** 6 to 8

**WHY THIS RECIPE WORKS** To make this bold African chicken dish, we started with a spice paste. We blended garlic, shallot, bay leaves, lemon zest and juice, and pepper. Five-spice powder and tomato paste brought complexity and richness. Fruity-tasting arbol chiles, along with some cayenne pepper, replaced peri peri peppers, which aren't widely available in the States. We tossed chicken pieces in the mixture along with chopped peanuts and let it sit overnight. We set up the grill with a cooler side and a hotter side. After rendering and charring the skin on the hotter side of the grill, we finished cooking the chicken on the cooler side. This recipe requires refrigerating the spice paste–coated chicken for at least 6 hours or up to 24 hours prior to cooking. When browning the chicken over the hotter side of the grill, move it away from the direct heat if any flare-ups occur. Serve with white rice.

- 4–10 arbol chiles, stemmed
- 3 tablespoons extra-virgin olive oil
- 2 tablespoons salt
- 8 garlic cloves, peeled
- 2 tablespoons tomato paste
- 1 shallot, chopped
- 1 tablespoon sugar
- 1 tablespoon paprika
- 1 tablespoon five-spice powder
- 2 teaspoons grated lemon zest plus ¼ cup juice (2 lemons)
- 1 teaspoon pepper
- ½ teaspoon cayenne pepper
- 3 bay leaves, crushed
- 6 pounds bone-in chicken pieces (breasts, thighs, and/or drumsticks), trimmed
- ½ cup dry-roasted peanuts, chopped fine
- 1 (13 by 9-inch) disposable aluminum pan (if using charcoal) or 2 (9-inch) disposable aluminum pie plates (if using gas)
- Lemon wedges

**1.** Process 4 arbols, oil, salt, garlic, tomato paste, shallot, sugar, paprika, five-spice powder, lemon zest and juice, pepper, cayenne, and bay leaves in blender until smooth, 10 to 20 seconds. Taste paste and add up to 6 additional arbols, depending on desired level of heat (spice paste should be slightly hotter than desired heat level of cooked chicken), and process until smooth. Using metal skewer, poke skin side of each chicken piece 8 to 10 times. Place chicken pieces, peanuts, and spice paste in large bowl or container and toss until chicken is evenly coated. Cover and refrigerate for at least 6 hours or up to 24 hours.

**2A. FOR A CHARCOAL GRILL:** Open bottom vent halfway and place disposable pan filled with 3 cups water on 1 side of grill. Light large chimney starter filled with charcoal briquettes (6 quarts). When top coals are partially covered with ash, pour evenly over other half of grill (opposite disposable pan). Set cooking grate in place, cover, and open lid vent halfway. Heat grill until hot, about 5 minutes.

**2B. FOR A GAS GRILL:** Place 2 disposable pie plates, each filled with 1½ cups water, directly on 1 burner of gas grill (opposite primary burner). Turn all burners to high, cover, and heat grill until hot, about 15 minutes. Turn primary burner to medium-high and turn off other burner(s). (Adjust primary burner as needed to maintain grill temperature between 325 and 350 degrees.)

**3.** Clean and oil cooking grate. Place chicken, skin side down, on hotter side of grill and cook until browned and blistered in spots, 2 to 5 minutes. Flip chicken and cook until second side is browned, 4 to 6 minutes. Move chicken to cooler side of grill and arrange, skin side up, with legs and thighs closest to fire and breasts farthest away. Cover (positioning lid vent over chicken if using charcoal) and cook until breasts register 160 degrees and legs and thighs register 175 degrees, 50 to 60 minutes.

**4.** Transfer chicken to serving platter, tent with aluminum foil, and let rest for 10 minutes before serving, passing lemon wedges separately.

## Jerk Chicken

**SERVES 4**

**WHY THIS RECIPE WORKS** We were able to achieve the characteristic spicy-sweet-fresh-smoky balance of jerk chicken with the right combination of spices and herbs. Keeping the marinade paste-like and cooking the meat first over indirect heat prevented the jerk flavors from dripping or peeling off during grilling. Enhancing our hickory chip packet with a few spice-cabinet ingredients allowed our jerk chicken recipe to mimic the unique smoke of traditional pimento wood. For a milder dish, use one seeded chile. If you prefer your food very hot, use up to all three chiles, including their seeds and ribs. Scotch bonnet chiles can be used in place of the habaneros, if desired. Wear gloves when working with the chiles.

**JERK MARINADE**

- 1½ tablespoons whole coriander seeds
- 1 tablespoon whole allspice berries
- 1 tablespoon whole peppercorns
- 1-3 habanero chiles, stemmed, quartered, and seeds and ribs reserved, if using
- 8 scallions, chopped
- 6 garlic cloves, peeled
- 3 tablespoons vegetable oil
- 2 tablespoons soy sauce
- 2 tablespoons finely grated lime zest (3 limes), plus lime wedges for serving
- 2 tablespoons yellow mustard
- 1 tablespoon dried thyme
- 1 tablespoon ground ginger
- 1 tablespoon packed brown sugar
- 2¼ teaspoons table salt
- 2 teaspoons dried basil
- ½ teaspoon dried rosemary
- ½ teaspoon ground nutmeg

**CHICKEN**

- 3 pounds bone-in chicken pieces (split breasts cut in half, drumsticks, and/or thighs)
- 2 tablespoons whole allspice berries
- 2 tablespoons dried thyme
- 2 tablespoons dried rosemary
- 2 tablespoons water
- 1 cup wood chips, soaked in water for 15 minutes and drained

**1. FOR THE JERK MARINADE:** Grind coriander seeds, allspice berries, and peppercorns in spice grinder or mortar and pestle until coarsely ground. Transfer spices to blender jar. Add habanero(s), scallions, garlic, oil, soy sauce, lime zest, mustard, thyme, ginger, sugar, salt, basil, rosemary, and nutmeg and process until smooth paste forms, 1 to 3 minutes, scraping down sides as necessary. Transfer marinade to gallon-size zipper-lock bag.

**2. FOR THE CHICKEN:** Place chicken pieces in bag with marinade and toss to coat; press out as much air as possible and seal bag. Let stand at room temperature for 30 minutes while preparing grill, flipping bag after 15 minutes. (Marinated chicken can be refrigerated for up to 24 hours.)

**3.** Combine allspice berries, thyme, rosemary, and water in bowl and set aside to moisten for 15 minutes. Using large piece of heavy-duty aluminum foil, wrap soaked chips and moistened allspice mixture in foil packet and cut several vent holes in top.

**4A. FOR A CHARCOAL GRILL:** Open bottom vent halfway. Arrange 1 quart unlit charcoal briquettes in single layer over half of grill. Light large chimney starter one-third filled with charcoal briquettes (2 quarts). When top coals are partially covered with ash, pour evenly over unlit briquettes, keeping coals arranged over half of grill. Place wood chip packet on coals. Set cooking grate in place, cover, and open lid vent halfway. Heat grill until hot and wood chips are smoking, about 5 minutes.

**4B. FOR A GAS GRILL:** Place wood chip packet over primary burner. Turn all burners to high, cover, and heat grill until hot and wood chips begin to smoke, 15 to 25 minutes. Turn primary burner to medium and turn off other burner(s).

**5.** Clean and oil cooking grate. Place chicken, with marinade clinging and skin side up, as far away from fire as possible, with thighs closest to fire and breasts farthest away. Cover (positioning lid vent over chicken if using charcoal) and cook for 30 minutes.

**6.** Move chicken, skin side down, to hotter side of grill; cook until browned and skin renders, 3 to 6 minutes. Using tongs, flip chicken pieces and cook until browned on second side and breasts register 160 degrees and thighs/drumsticks register 175 degrees, 5 to 12 minutes longer.

**7.** Transfer chicken to serving platter, tent loosely with foil, and let rest for 5 to 10 minutes. Serve warm or at room temperature with lime wedges.

## Smoked Chicken

**SERVES** 6 to 8

**WHY THIS RECIPE WORKS** We wanted perfectly cooked meat with a pervasive smoky flavor and crisp skin. A salt and sugar brine guaranteed moist, well-seasoned meat. Chicken parts were easier than whole chickens; the breasts could cook evenly on the coolest part of the grill and more of the bird was exposed to the smoke and heat, adding flavor and rendering more fat from the skin. To keep the skin moist, we brushed it with oil and added a pan of water to the grill. Two wood chip packets produced the ideal amount of smoke. If using kosher chicken, do not brine in step 1. Two medium wood chunks, soaked in water for 1 hour, can be substituted for the wood chip packet on a charcoal grill.

- 1 cup table salt
- 1 cup sugar
- 6 pounds bone-in chicken parts (breasts, thighs, and/or drumsticks), trimmed
- 3 tablespoons vegetable oil
- Pepper
- 3 cups wood chips, 1½ cups soaked in water for 15 minutes and drained, plus 1½ cups unsoaked
- 1 (16 by 12-inch) disposable aluminum roasting pan (if using charcoal) or 1 disposable aluminum pie plate (if using gas)

**1.** Dissolve salt and sugar in 4 quarts cold water in large container. Submerge chicken pieces in brine, cover, and refrigerate for 30 minutes to 1 hour. Remove chicken from brine and pat dry with paper towels. Brush chicken evenly with oil and season with pepper.

**2.** Using large piece of heavy-duty aluminum foil, wrap soaked chips in foil packet and cut several vent holes in top. Repeat with another sheet of foil and unsoaked wood chips.

**3A. FOR A CHARCOAL GRILL:** Open bottom vent halfway. Arrange 2 quarts unlit charcoal banked against 1 side of grill and disposable pan filled with 2 cups water on empty side of grill. Light large chimney starter half filled with charcoal briquettes (3 quarts). When top coals are partially covered with ash, pour on top of unlit charcoal, to cover one-third of grill with coals steeply banked against side of grill. Place wood chip packets on top of coals. Set cooking grate in place, cover, and open lid vent halfway. Heat grill until hot and wood chips begin to smoke, about 5 minutes.

**3B. FOR A GAS GRILL:** Place wood chip packets directly on primary burner. Place disposable pie plate filled with 2 cups water on other burner(s). Turn all burners to high, cover, and heat grill until hot and wood chips begin to smoke, about 15 minutes. Turn primary burner to medium-high and turn off other burner(s). (Adjust primary burner as needed to maintain grill temperature around 325 degrees.)

**4.** Clean and oil cooking grate. Place chicken on cool side of grill, skin side up, as far away from heat as possible with thighs closest to heat and breasts farthest away. Cover (positioning lid vents over chicken if using charcoal) and cook until breasts register 160 degrees and thighs/drumsticks register 175 degrees, 1¼ to 1½ hours.

**5.** Transfer chicken to serving platter, tent loosely with foil, and let rest for 5 to 10 minutes before serving.

## Sweet and Tangy Barbecued Chicken

**SERVES** 6 to 8

**WHY THIS RECIPE WORKS** To produce juicy, evenly cooked chicken parts on the grill, indirect cooking is key, as it provides a hotter side for briefly searing the parts and a cooler side for them to cook through gently. We lined up the fattier leg quarters closer to the coals and the leaner white meat farther from the heat, as well as adding a water pan underneath the cooler side, to help the dark and white pieces cook slowly and evenly. Applying a simple spice rub deeply seasoned the meat, and the salt in it helped retain moisture, while brushing on a homemade sauce in stages allowed it to cling nicely to the skin and also develop layers of tangy-sweet flavor. When browning the chicken over the hotter side of the grill, move it away from any flare-ups. Try to select similar-size chicken parts for even cooking.

**CHICKEN**

- 2 tablespoons packed dark brown sugar
- 4½ teaspoons kosher salt
- 1½ teaspoons onion powder
- 1½ teaspoons garlic powder
- 1½ teaspoons paprika
- ¼ teaspoon cayenne pepper
- 6 pounds bone-in chicken pieces (split breasts and/or leg quarters), trimmed

SAUCE

- 1 cup ketchup
- 5 tablespoons molasses
- 3 tablespoons cider vinegar
- 2 tablespoons Worcestershire sauce
- 2 tablespoons Dijon mustard
- ¼ teaspoon pepper
- 2 tablespoons vegetable oil
- ⅓ cup grated onion
- 1 garlic clove, minced
- 1 teaspoon chili powder
- ¼ teaspoon cayenne pepper

- 1 large disposable aluminum roasting pan (if using charcoal) or 2 disposable aluminum pie plates (if using gas)

**1. FOR THE CHICKEN:** Combine sugar, salt, onion powder, garlic powder, paprika, and cayenne in bowl. Arrange chicken on rimmed baking sheet and sprinkle both sides evenly with spice rub. Cover with plastic wrap and refrigerate for at least 6 hours or up to 24 hours.

**2. FOR THE SAUCE:** Whisk ketchup, molasses, vinegar, Worcestershire, mustard, and pepper together in bowl. Heat oil in medium saucepan over medium heat until shimmering. Add onion and garlic; cook until onion is softened, 2 to 4 minutes. Add chili powder and cayenne and cook until fragrant, about 30 seconds. Whisk in ketchup mixture and bring to boil. Reduce heat to medium-low and simmer gently for 5 minutes. Set aside ⅔ cup sauce to baste chicken and reserve remaining sauce for serving. (Sauce can be refrigerated for up to 1 week.)

**3A. FOR A CHARCOAL GRILL:** Open bottom vent halfway and place disposable pan filled with 3 cups water on 1 side of grill. Light large chimney starter filled with charcoal briquettes (6 quarts). When top coals are partially covered with ash, pour evenly over other half of grill (opposite disposable pan). Set cooking grate in place, cover, and open lid vent halfway. Heat grill until hot, about 5 minutes.

**3B. FOR A GAS GRILL:** Place 2 disposable pie plates, each filled with 1½ cups water, directly on 1 burner of gas grill (opposite primary burner). Turn all burners to high, cover, and heat grill until hot, about 15 minutes. Turn primary burner to medium-high and turn off other burner(s). (Adjust primary burner as needed to maintain grill temperature of 325 to 350 degrees.)

**4.** Clean and oil cooking grate. Place chicken, skin side down, over hotter part of grill and cook until browned and blistered in spots, 2 to 5 minutes. Flip chicken and cook until second side is browned, 4 to 6 minutes. Move chicken to cooler side of grill and brush both sides of chicken with ⅓ cup sauce. Arrange chicken, skin side up, with leg quarters closest to fire and breasts farthest away. Cover (positioning lid vent over chicken if using charcoal) and cook for 25 minutes.

**5.** Brush both sides of chicken with remaining ⅓ cup sauce and continue to cook, covered, until breasts register 160 degrees and leg quarters register 175 degrees, 25 to 35 minutes longer.

**6.** Transfer chicken to serving platter, tent loosely with aluminum foil, and let rest for 10 minutes. Serve, passing reserved sauce separately.

## Barbecued Pulled Chicken

**SERVES** 6 to 8

**WHY THIS RECIPE WORKS** This recipe takes pulled chicken seriously—using tender, smoky meat pulled off the bone in moist, soft shreds and tossed with a tangy, sweet sauce. We chose whole chicken legs for great flavor, low cost, and resistance to overcooking. The legs cooked gently over indirect heat, absorbing plenty of smoke flavor along the way. Chicken leg quarters consist of drumsticks attached to thighs; often also attached are backbone sections that must be trimmed away. If you'd like to use wood chunks instead of wood chips when using a charcoal grill, substitute two medium wood chunks, soaked in water for 1 hour, for the wood chip packet. Serve on hamburger rolls or sandwich bread, with pickles and coleslaw.

CHICKEN

- 2 cups wood chips, soaked in water for 15 minutes and drained
- 1 (16 by 12-inch) disposable aluminum roasting pan (if using charcoal)
- 1 tablespoon vegetable oil
- 8 (14-ounce) chicken leg quarters, trimmed
- 2 teaspoons table salt
- 1 teaspoon pepper

SAUCE

- 1 large onion, quartered
- ¼ cup water
- 1½ cups ketchup
- 1½ cups apple cider
- ¼ cup molasses
- ¼ cup apple cider vinegar, divided
- 3 tablespoons Worcestershire sauce
- 3 tablespoons Dijon mustard
- ½ teaspoon pepper
- 1 tablespoon vegetable oil
- 1½ tablespoons chili powder
- 2 garlic cloves, minced
- ½ teaspoon cayenne pepper
- Hot sauce

**1.** For the chicken: Using large piece of heavy-duty aluminum foil, wrap soaked chips in 8 by 4½-inch foil packet. (Make sure chips do not poke holes in sides or bottom of packet.) Cut 2 evenly spaced 2-inch slits in top of packet.

**2A. FOR A CHARCOAL GRILL:** Open bottom vent halfway and place disposable pan in center of grill. Light large chimney starter three-quarters filled with charcoal briquettes (4½ quarts). When top coals are partially covered with ash, pour into 2 even piles on either side of pan. Place wood chip packet on 1 pile of coals. Set cooking grate in place, cover, and open lid vent halfway. Heat grill until hot and wood chips are smoking, about 5 minutes.

**2B. FOR A GAS GRILL:** Place wood chip packet directly on primary burner. Turn all burners to high; cover; and heat grill until hot and wood chips are smoking, about 15 minutes. Turn all burners to medium. (Adjust burners as needed during cooking to maintain grill temperature between 250 and 300 degrees.)

**3.** Clean and oil cooking grate. Pat chicken dry with paper towels and sprinkle with salt and pepper. Place chicken in single layer on center of grill (over roasting pan if using charcoal), skin side up, or evenly over grill (if using gas). Cover (position lid vent over meat if using charcoal) and cook until chicken registers 185 degrees, 1 to 1½ hours, rotating chicken pieces halfway through cooking. Transfer chicken to carving board, tent with foil, and let rest until cool enough to handle.

**4. FOR THE SAUCE:** Meanwhile, process onion and water in food processor until mixture resembles slush, about 30 seconds. Pass through fine-mesh strainer into liquid measuring cup, pressing on solids with rubber spatula (you should have ¾ cup strained onion juice). Discard solids in strainer.

**5.** Whisk onion juice, ketchup, cider, molasses, 3 tablespoons vinegar, Worcestershire, mustard, and pepper together in bowl. Heat oil in large saucepan over medium heat until shimmering. Stir in chili powder, garlic, and cayenne and cook until fragrant, about 30 seconds. Stir in ketchup mixture, bring to simmer, and cook over medium-low heat until slightly thickened, about 15 minutes (you should have about 4 cups of sauce). Transfer 2 cups sauce to serving bowl; leave remaining sauce in saucepan.

**6. TO SERVE:** Remove and discard skin from chicken legs. Using your fingers, pull meat off bones, separating larger pieces (which should fall off bones easily) from smaller, drier pieces into 2 equal piles.

**7.** Pulse smaller chicken pieces in food processor until just coarsely chopped, 3 to 4 pulses, stirring chicken with rubber spatula after each pulse. Add chopped chicken to sauce in saucepan. Using your fingers or 2 forks, pull larger chicken pieces into long shreds and add to saucepan. Stir in remaining 1 tablespoon vinegar, cover, and heat chicken over medium-low heat, stirring occasionally, until heated through, about 10 minutes. Add hot sauce to taste, and serve, passing remaining sauce separately.

### Barbecued Pulled Chicken for a Crowd

**SERVES** 10 to 12

This technique works best on a charcoal grill. If your gas grill can accommodate more than 8 legs, follow the master recipe, adding as many legs as will fit in a single layer.

Increase amount of charcoal briquettes to 6 quarts. Use 12 chicken legs and slot them into V-shaped roasting rack set on top of cooking grate over disposable aluminum pan. Increase cooking time in step 3 to 1½ to 1¾ hours. In step 5, remove only 1 cup of sauce from saucepan. In step 7, pulse chicken in food processor in 2 batches.

## Charcoal-Grilled Barbecued Chicken Kebabs

**SERVES** 6

**WHY THIS RECIPE WORKS** In theory, barbecued chicken kebabs sound pretty great: char-streaked chunks of juicy meat lacquered with sweet and tangy barbecue sauce. But without an insulating layer of skin, even the fattiest thigh meat can dry out and toughen when exposed to the blazing heat of the grill—and forget about ultralean skinless breast meat. Our goal was simple: juicy, tender chicken with plenty of sticky-sweet, smoke-tinged flavor. Brining is one common way to safeguard against dry meat, but in this case the brine made the meat so slick that the barbecue sauce refused to stick. A salt rub worked much better; the rub crisped up on the chicken's exterior as it cooked, forming a craggy surface that the sauce could really cling to. For incredible depth of flavor as well as juicy meat, we turned to an unusual technique: grinding bacon to a paste and applying it to the salted meat. Combined with both sweet and smoked paprika and a little sugar, our bacony rub created chicken that was juicy, tender, and full-flavored, with a smoky depth that complemented the barbecue sauce. We prefer flavorful thigh meat for these kebabs, but you can use white meat. Whichever you choose, don't mix white and dark meat on the same skewer, since they cook at different rates. If you have thin pieces of chicken, cut them larger than 1 inch and roll or fold them into approximately 1-inch cubes. Use the large holes on a box grater to grate the onion.

**SAUCE**

- ½ cup ketchup
- ¼ cup light or mild molasses
- 2 tablespoons grated onion
- 2 tablespoons Worcestershire sauce
- 2 tablespoons Dijon mustard
- 2 tablespoons cider vinegar
- 1 tablespoon packed light brown sugar

KEBABS

- 2 pounds boneless, skinless chicken thighs or breasts, trimmed and cut into 1-inch cubes
- 2 teaspoons kosher salt
- 2 tablespoons sweet paprika
- 4 teaspoons sugar
- 2 teaspoons smoked paprika
- 2 slices bacon, cut into ½-inch pieces
- 4 12-inch metal skewers

**1. FOR THE SAUCE:** Bring all ingredients to simmer in small saucepan over medium heat; cook, stirring occasionally, until sauce reaches ketchup-like consistency and is reduced to about 1 cup, 5 to 7 minutes. Transfer ½ cup sauce to small bowl and set aside remaining sauce to serve with cooked chicken.

**2. FOR THE KEBABS:** Toss chicken and salt in large bowl; cover with plastic wrap and refrigerate for at least 30 minutes and up to 1 hour.

**3.** Open bottom vent completely. Light large chimney starter three-quarters filled with charcoal (4½ quarts). When top coals are partially covered with ash, pour evenly over half of grill. Set cooking grate in place, cover, and open lid vent completely. Heat grill until hot, about 5 minutes.

**4.** While grill heats, pat chicken dry with paper towels. Combine sweet paprika, sugar, and smoked paprika in small bowl. Process bacon in food processor until smooth paste forms, 30 to 45 seconds, scraping down bowl twice during processing. Add bacon paste and spice mixture to chicken; mix with hands or rubber spatula until ingredients are thoroughly blended and chicken is completely coated. Thread meat onto skewers, rolling or folding meat as necessary to maintain 1-inch cubes.

**5.** Clean and oil cooking grate. Place kebabs over coals and cook, turning one-quarter turn every 2 to 2½ minutes until well browned and slightly charred, 8 minutes for breasts or 10 minutes for thighs. (If flare-ups occur, slide kebabs to cool side of grill until fire dies down.) Brush top surface of kebabs with ¼ cup sauce; flip and cook until sauce is brown in spots, about 1 minute. Brush second side with remaining ¼ cup sauce; flip and continue to cook until brown in spots and breasts register 160 degrees or thighs register 175 degrees, about 1 minute. Remove kebabs from grill and let rest for 5 minutes. Serve, passing reserved barbecue sauce separately.

## Grilled Chicken Souvlaki

SERVES 4

**WHY THIS RECIPE WORKS** In Greece, souvlaki is usually made with pork, but at Greek restaurants here in the United States, boneless, skinless chicken breast is common. The chunks of white meat are marinated in a tangy mixture of lemon juice, olive oil, oregano, parsley, and garlic before being skewered and grilled until charred. The chicken is often placed on a lightly grilled pita, slathered with a yogurt-based tzatziki sauce, wrapped, and eaten out of hand. Instead of a long marinating time, which made the meat mushy and didn't add

much flavor, we brined the chicken for a mere 30 minutes, then tossed it with olive oil, lemon juice, dried oregano, parsley, black pepper, and honey. The honey added complexity and encouraged browning. We also reserved a bit of the mixture to season the meat after cooking. We found that the meat on the outside of the skewers cooked faster than the chunks in the middle, so we made "shields" by threading bell peppers and onions onto the ends of the skewers. They steamed and softened while the chicken cooked. This tzatziki is fairly mild; if you like a more assertive flavor, double the garlic. A rasp-style grater makes quick work of turning the garlic into a paste. You will need four 12-inch metal skewers.

TZATZIKI SAUCE

- 1 tablespoon lemon juice
- 1 small garlic clove, minced to paste
- ¾ cup plain Greek yogurt
- ½ cucumber, peeled, halved lengthwise, seeded, and diced fine (½ cup)
- 3 tablespoons minced fresh mint
- 1 tablespoon minced fresh parsley
- ⅜ teaspoon table salt

CHICKEN

- Table salt and pepper
- 1½ pounds boneless, skinless chicken breasts, trimmed and cut into 1-inch pieces
- ⅓ cup extra-virgin olive oil
- 2 tablespoons minced fresh parsley
- 1 teaspoon finely grated lemon zest plus ¼ cup juice (2 lemons)
- 1 teaspoon honey
- 1 teaspoon dried oregano
- 1 green bell pepper, quartered, stemmed, and seeded, each quarter cut into 4 chunks
- 1 small red onion, ends trimmed, peeled, and halved lengthwise, each half cut into 4 chunks
- 4 (8-inch) pitas

**1. FOR THE TZATZIKI SAUCE:** Whisk lemon juice and garlic together in small bowl. Let stand for 10 minutes. Stir in yogurt, cucumber, mint, parsley, and salt. Cover and set aside.

**2. FOR THE CHICKEN:** Dissolve 2 tablespoons salt in 1 quart cold water. Submerge chicken in brine, cover, and refrigerate for 30 minutes. While chicken is brining, combine oil, parsley, lemon zest and juice, honey, oregano, and ½ teaspoon pepper in medium bowl. Transfer ¼ cup oil mixture to large bowl and set aside to toss with cooked chicken.

**3.** Remove chicken from brine and pat dry with paper towels. Toss chicken with remaining oil mixture. Thread 4 pieces of bell pepper, concave side up, onto one 12-inch metal skewer. Thread one-quarter of chicken onto skewer. Thread 2 chunks of onion onto skewer, and place skewer on plate. Repeat skewering remaining chicken and vegetables on 3 more skewers. Lightly moisten 2 pita breads with water. Sandwich 2 unmoistened pita breads between moistened pita breads and wrap stack tightly in lightly greased heavy-duty aluminum foil.

**4A. FOR A CHARCOAL GRILL:** Open bottom vent completely. Light large chimney starter mounded with charcoal briquettes (7 quarts). When top coals are partially covered with ash, pour evenly over half of grill. Set cooking grate in place, cover, and open lid vent completely. Heat grill until hot, about 5 minutes.

**4B. FOR A GAS GRILL:** Turn all burners to high, cover, and heat grill until hot, about 15 minutes. Leave primary burner on high and turn off other burner(s).

**5.** Clean and oil cooking grate. Place skewers on hotter side of grill and cook, turning occasionally, until chicken and vegetables are well browned on all sides and chicken registers 160 degrees, 15 to 20 minutes. Using fork, push chicken and vegetables off skewers into bowl of reserved oil mixture. Stir gently, breaking up onion chunks; cover with foil and let sit for 5 minutes.

**6.** Meanwhile, place packet of pitas on cooler side of grill. Flip occasionally to heat, about 5 minutes.

**7.** Lay each warm pita on 12-inch square of foil. Spread each pita with 2 tablespoons tzatziki. Place one-quarter of chicken and vegetables in middle of each pita. Roll into cylindrical shape and serve.

## Grilled Lemon Chicken with Rosemary

**SERVES 4**

**WHY THIS RECIPE WORKS** Grilling a whole chicken can be a recipe for disaster thanks to flare-ups caused by the fatty skin. To solve the problem we removed the skin before grilling. Then we butterflied the chicken it so it was an even thickness, and brined it for juicy meat. For flavor that penetrated all the way to the bone, we cut deep channels in the meat and rubbed it with lemon and herb seasoning. Basting the chicken with a flavorful butter sauce and tenting it with aluminum foil partway through cooking kept the surface moist and tender as it cooked. We quickly charred lemon wedges to squeeze over each portion before serving. For a better grip when removing the chicken skin, use a paper towel.

- 1 (3½- to 4-pound) whole chicken, giblets discarded
- ¾ cup sugar
- Table salt and pepper
- 2 lemons
- 1 tablespoon vegetable oil
- 2 teaspoons minced fresh rosemary
- 1½ teaspoons Dijon mustard
- 2 tablespoons unsalted butter

**1.** With chicken breast side down, using kitchen shears, cut through bones on either side of backbone; discard backbone. Flip chicken over and press on breastbone to flatten. Using fingers and shears, peel skin off chicken, leaving skin on wings.

**2.** Tuck wings behind back. Turn legs so drumsticks face inward toward breasts. Using chef's knife, cut ½-inch-deep slits, spaced ½ inch apart, in breasts and legs. Insert skewer through thigh of 1 leg, into bottom of breast, and through thigh of second leg. Insert second skewer, about 1 inch lower, through thigh and drumstick of 1 leg and then through thigh and drumstick of second leg.

**3.** Dissolve sugar and ¾ cup salt in 3 quarts cold water in large, wide container. Submerge chicken in brine, cover, and refrigerate for at least 30 minutes or up to 1 hour.

**4.** Zest lemons (you should have 2 tablespoons grated zest). Juice 1 lemon (you should have 3 tablespoons juice) and quarter remaining lemon lengthwise. Combine zest, oil, 1½ teaspoons rosemary, 1 teaspoon mustard, and ½ teaspoon pepper in small bowl; set aside. Heat butter, remaining ½ teaspoon rosemary, remaining ½ teaspoon mustard, and ½ teaspoon pepper in small saucepan over low heat, stirring occasionally, until butter is melted and ingredients are combined. Remove pan from heat and stir in lemon juice; leave mixture in saucepan.

**5.** Remove chicken from brine and pat dry with paper towels. With chicken skinned side down, rub ½ teaspoon zest mixture over surface of legs. Flip chicken over and rub remaining zest mixture evenly over entire surface, making sure to work mixture into slits.

**6A. FOR A CHARCOAL GRILL:** Open bottom vent completely. Light large chimney starter mounded with charcoal briquettes (7 quarts). When top coals are partially covered with ash, pour evenly over half of grill. Set cooking grate in place, cover, and open lid vent completely. Heat grill until hot, about 5 minutes.

**6B. FOR A GAS GRILL:** Turn all burners to high, cover, and heat grill until hot, about 15 minutes. Leave primary burner on high and turn off other burner(s).

**7.** Clean and oil cooking grate. Place chicken, skinned side down, and lemon quarters over hotter side of grill. Cover and cook until chicken and lemon quarters are well browned, 8 to 10 minutes. Transfer lemon quarters to bowl and set aside. Flip chicken over and brush with one-third of butter mixture (place saucepan over cooler side of grill if mixture has solidified). Cover chicken loosely with aluminum foil. Continue to cook, covered, until chicken is well browned on second side, 8 to 10 minutes.

**8.** Remove foil and slide chicken to cooler side of grill. Brush with half of remaining butter mixture, and re-cover with foil. Continue to cook, covered, until breasts register 160 degrees and thighs/drumsticks register 175 degrees, 8 to 10 minutes longer.

**9.** Transfer chicken to carving board, brush with remaining butter mixture, tent loosely with foil, and let rest for 5 to 10 minutes. Carve into pieces and serve with reserved lemon quarters.

**PREPPING A WHOLE CHICKEN FOR THE GRILL**

For even, fast cooking, we remove the backbone, then flip the chicken and crack and flatten the breastbone. We peel off the skin, leaving it on the wings, and deeply slash the meat. Skewers inserted through the thighs and legs provide stability.

## Grill-Roasted Whole Chicken

**SERVES 4**

**WHY THIS RECIPE WORKS** Our ideal grill-roasted chicken has succulent, subtly smoky meat encased in a well-rendered and deeply golden skin. But cooking a whole chicken that hasn't been flattened by spatchcocking over direct heat can be disastrous: Thanks to the bird's bulbous shape, its exterior can easily dry out before the interior cooks through. Our solution was a two-zone fire with heat sources on either side of the grill and a cooler zone down the middle and cooking the chicken breast side up over indirect heat until it hit 130 degrees. Then we finished cooking it directly over the fire, flipping it breast side down so that both sides saw direct heat. We found we needed just ¼ to ½ cup of wood chips to generate the understated flavor we wanted. We also made sure to use dry wood chips; they ignite quickly while the bird is still relatively cold and best able to absorb smoke flavor. We developed this recipe on a three-burner gas grill. If using a two-burner grill, use one side—the side with the wood chips—as the primary burner and the other as the secondary burner. Adjust the primary burner to maintain a grill temperature of 375 to 400 degrees. Place the chicken 6 inches from the primary burner and rotate it after 25 minutes of cooking in step 4 so that it cooks evenly.

- 1 tablespoon kosher salt
- ½ teaspoon pepper
- 1 (3½- to 4½-pound) whole chicken, giblets discarded
- 1 tablespoon vegetable oil
- ¼–½ cup wood chips

**1.** Combine salt and pepper in bowl. Pat chicken dry with paper towels. Rub entire surface with oil. Sprinkle evenly all over with salt mixture and rub in mixture with your hands to coat evenly. Tie legs together with twine and tuck wing tips behind back.

**2.** Using large piece of heavy-duty aluminum foil, wrap chips (½ cup if using gas; ¼ cup if using charcoal) in 8 by 4½-inch foil packet. (Make sure chips do not poke holes in sides or bottom of packet.) Cut 2 evenly spaced 2-inch slits in top of packet.

**3A. FOR A CHARCOAL GRILL:** Open bottom vent halfway. Light large chimney starter mounded with charcoal briquettes (7 quarts). When top coals are partially covered with ash, pour into 2 even banked piles on either side of grill. Place wood chip packet on 1 pile of coals. Set cooking grate in place, cover, and open lid vent halfway. Heat grill until hot and wood chips are smoking, about 5 minutes. (Temperature of grill will start around 400 degrees and will fall to about 350 degrees by end of cooking.)

**3B. FOR A GAS GRILL:** Place wood chip packet directly on primary burner. Turn all burners to high, cover, and heat grill until hot and wood chips are smoking, about 15 minutes. Turn primary burners (2 outside burners) to medium-high and turn off center (secondary) burner. (Adjust primary burners as needed to maintain grill temperature between 400 and 425 degrees.)

**4.** Clean and oil cooking grate. Place chicken, breast side up with cavity facing toward you, in center of grill, making sure bird is centered between heat sources on either side. Cover (placing vent over chicken on charcoal grill) and cook until breast registers 130 degrees, about 45 to 55 minutes.

**5.** Using long grill tongs, reach into cavity and carefully lift chicken by breast. Holding chicken over bowl or container, tilt toward you to allow fat and juices to drain from cavity. Transfer chicken, breast side up, to hotter side of grill (without wood chip packet) and cook, covered, until back is deep golden brown, about 5 minutes. Using tongs, flip chicken breast side down; cover and continue to cook over hotter side of grill until breast is deep golden brown, about 5 minutes longer. Using tongs, flip chicken breast side up, return to center of grill; take internal temperature of breast. If breast registers 155 degrees, transfer chicken to carving board. If breast registers less than 155 degrees, cover and continue to cook in center of grill, checking temperature every 2 minutes until it registers 155 degrees, 2 to 10 minutes longer. Let chicken rest, uncovered, for 20 minutes. Carve chicken and serve.

## Pollo a la Brasa (Peruvian Grill-Roasted Chicken)

**SERVES 4**

**WHY THIS RECIPE WORKS** In Peru, poultry masters make the wildly popular chickens known as pollo a la brasa by grill-roasting chickens on rotisseries to produce meat that's encased in tawny, paper-thin skin and dripping with juices. Our version calls for marinating the bird for 24 hours in a beer-based marinade. We used a half-empty beer can to prop the chicken up vertically and then set it in the center of a kettle grill outfitted with a split fire. As it cooked, we rotated the chicken a quarter turn every 15 minutes; about five turns produced remarkably succulent, smoky meat Our gas grill instructions are for a three-burner grill. If using a two-burner grill, turn both burners to high and place the wood chips on the primary burner while the grill heats. When the grill is hot, turn the primary burner to medium and turn the secondary burner off; stand the chicken on the cooler side of the grill, about 4 inches from the primary burner, and proceed with the recipe, adjusting the primary burner as needed to maintain 350 to 375 degrees. Inexpensive beer is fine; avoid those with strong hoppy or bitter flavors. Do not use a 16-ounce can; its height will make the chicken less stable. If you'd like to use wood chunks instead of wood chips when using a charcoal grill, substitute one medium wood chunk the wood chip packet. Serve with Peruvian Green Chile Sauce or Yellow Sauce (page 642).

- 1 (12-ounce) can beer, divided
- 2 tablespoons finely grated garlic
- 2 tablespoons lime juice
- 2 tablespoons soy sauce
- 2 teaspoons table salt
- 2 teaspoons yellow mustard
- 1 teaspoon pepper
- 1 teaspoon dried thyme
- 1 teaspoon ground cumin
- 1 (4- to 4½-pound) whole chicken, giblets discarded
- 1 cup wood chips
- 1 (13 by 9-inch) disposable aluminum roasting pan

**1.** Whisk ½ cup beer, garlic, lime juice, soy sauce, salt, mustard, pepper, thyme, and cumin together in liquid measuring cup. Refrigerate remaining beer, still in can, until ready to grill. Using your fingers or handle of wooden spoon, gently loosen skin covering chicken breast and leg quarters. Using paring knife, poke 10 to 15 holes in fat deposits on skin of back. Tuck wingtips underneath chicken.

**2.** Place chicken in bowl with cavity end facing up. Slowly pour marinade between skin and meat and rub marinade inside cavity, outside skin, and under skin to distribute. Cover and refrigerate for 24 hours, turning chicken halfway through marinating.

**3.** Using large piece of heavy-duty aluminum foil, wrap wood chips in 8 by 4½-inch foil packet. (Make sure chips do not poke holes in packet.) Cut 2 evenly spaced 2-inch slits in top of packet.

**4.** Place beer can in large, shallow bowl. Spray can all over with vegetable oil spray. Slide chicken over can so drumsticks reach down to bottom of can and chicken stands upright; set aside at room temperature while preparing grill.

**5A. FOR A CHARCOAL GRILL:** Open bottom vent completely and place disposable pan in center of grill. Light large chimney starter two-thirds filled with charcoal briquettes (4 quarts). When top coals are partially covered with ash, pour into 2 even piles on either side of disposable pan. Place wood chip packet on 1 pile of coals. Set cooking grate in place, cover, and open lid vent completely. Heat grill until hot and wood chips are smoking, about 5 minutes.

**5B. FOR A GAS GRILL:** Remove cooking grate and place wood chip packet directly on one of outside burners. Set grate in place; turn all burners to high; cover; and heat grill until hot and wood chips are smoking, about 15 minutes. Turn 2 outside burners to medium and turn off center burner. (Adjust outside burners as needed to maintain grill temperature between 350 and 375 degrees.)

**6.** Clean and oil cooking grate. Transfer chicken with can to center of cooking grate with wings facing piles of coals (or outer burners on gas grill) at 3 and 9 o'clock (ends of drumsticks should rest on grate to help steady bird). Cover grill (with top vent open for charcoal grill) and cook for 15 minutes. Using tongs and wad of paper towels, rotate chicken 90 degrees so wings are at 6 and 12 o'clock. Continue cooking and turning chicken at 15-minute intervals until thickest part of thigh registers 170 to 175 degrees, 1 hour to 1¼ hours longer.

**7.** With large wad of paper towels in each hand, transfer chicken and can to clean bowl, keeping can upright; let rest for 15 minutes (do not discard paper towels). Using wads of paper towels, carefully lift chicken off can and onto cutting board. Discard can. Carve chicken, transfer to platter, and serve.

## Ají Verde (Peruvian Green Chile Sauce)

**MAKES** ¾ cup

Zippy ají sauces are mandatory with pollo a la brasa, and they're not just for the chicken: Peruvians also pour them all over the salad and fries that Usually share the plate. Huacatay is a Peruvian herb sometimes called black mint. You can find it jarred in supermarkets or online. If it's unavailable, increase the cilantro to 5 tablespoons.

- ½ cup mayonnaise
- 1 jalapeño chile, stemmed, seeded, and chopped coarse
- 3 tablespoons minced fresh cilantro
- 2 tablespoons grated cotija cheese
- 2 tablespoons lime juice
- 1 tablespoon jarred huacatay paste
- 1 garlic clove, minced

Combine all ingredients in blender and process until smooth, about 1 minute. (Sauce can be refrigerated for up to 1 week.)

## Ají Amarillo (Peruvian Yellow Chile Sauce)

**MAKES** ⅔ cup

Ají amarillo paste, made from yellow Peruvian chiles, is available in supermarkets or online. If huacatay paste is unavailable, it can be omitted.

- ½ cup mayonnaise
- 2 tablespoons ají amarillo paste
- 1 tablespoon lime juice
- 1 garlic clove, minced
- 1 teaspoon jarred huacatay paste

Combine all ingredients in blender and process until smooth, about 1 minute. (Sauce can be refrigerated for up to 1 week.)

# Grill-Roasted Beer Can Chicken

**SERVES** 4

**WHY THIS RECIPE WORKS** We found that beer can chicken is the real deal—why? The beer in the open can simmers and turns to steam as the chicken roasts, which makes the meat remarkably juicy and rich-textured, similar to braised chicken. As an added bonus, the dry heat of the grill crisps the skin and renders the fat away. To perfect the technique, we added a few hardwood chunks or chips to the fire for smoky flavor. The best grilling setup (for a charcoal grill) proved to be banking the lit coals on either side of the grill and propping the chicken up on an open can of beer on the grill in the center, using the bird's drumsticks to form a tripod. For the gas grill, a medium fire did the trick. Finally, we found we didn't have to spend money on an expensive beer—the beer flavor wasn't really detectable in the chicken, so a cheap brew worked just fine (so does lemonade, which proved an acceptable substitute for the beer). Two medium wood chunks, soaked in water for 1 hour, can be substituted for the wood chip packet on a charcoal grill. If you prefer, use lemonade instead of beer; fill an empty 12-ounce soda or beer can with 10 ounces (1¼ cups) of lemonade and proceed as directed.

- 1 (12-ounce) can beer
- 2 bay leaves
- 1 (3½- to 4-pound) whole chicken
- 3 tablespoons Spice Rub (recipe follows)
- 2 cups wood chips, soaked in water for 15 minutes and drained
- 1 (13 by 9-inch) disposable aluminum roasting pan (if using charcoal)

**1.** Open beer can and pour out (or drink) about ¼ cup. With church key can opener, punch 2 more large holes in the top of can (for total of 3 holes). Crumble bay leaves into beer.

**2.** Pat chicken dry with paper towels. Rub chicken evenly, inside and out, with spice rub, lifting up skin over breast and rubbing spice rub directly onto meat. Using skewer, poke skin all over. Slide chicken over beer can so that drumsticks reach down to bottom of can and chicken stands upright; set aside at room temperature.

**3.** Using large piece of heavy-duty aluminum foil, wrap soaked chips in foil packet and cut several vent holes in top.

**4A. FOR A CHARCOAL GRILL:** Open bottom vent halfway and place roasting pan in center of grill. Light large chimney starter two-thirds filled with charcoal briquettes (4 quarts). When top coals are partially covered with ash, pour into 2 even piles on either side of roasting pan. Place wood chip packet on 1 pile of coals. Set cooking grate in place, cover, and open lid vent halfway. Heat grill until hot and wood chips are smoking, about 5 minutes.

**4B. FOR A GAS GRILL:** Place wood chip packet directly on primary burner. Turn all burners to high, cover, and heat grill until hot and wood chips are smoking, about 15 minutes. Turn all burners to medium. (Adjust burners as needed to maintain grill temperature around 325 degrees.)

**5.** Clean and oil cooking grate. Place chicken (with can) in center of grill (over roasting pan if using charcoal), using drumsticks to help steady bird. Cover (position lid vent over chicken if using charcoal) and cook until breast registers 160 degrees and thighs register 175 degrees, 1 to 1½ hours.

**6.** Using large wad of paper towels, carefully transfer chicken (with can) to tray, making sure to keep can upright. Tent loosely with foil and let rest for 15 minutes. Carefully lift chicken off can and onto carving board. Discard remaining beer and can. Carve chicken and serve.

## Spice Rub

**MAKES** 1 cup

Store leftover spice rub in an airtight container for up to 3 months.

- ½ cup paprika
- 2 tablespoons kosher salt
- 2 tablespoons garlic powder
- 1 tablespoon dried thyme

2 teaspoons ground celery seeds
2 teaspoons pepper
2 teaspoons cayenne pepper

Combine all ingredients in bowl.

## Italian-Style Grilled Chicken

SERVES 4

**WHY THIS RECIPE WORKS** Many cuisines have developed methods to overcome the problems of chicken cooked over a fire; the Italian way is to cook the chicken under bricks. This was one method we had to try. One attempt to grill a butterflied chicken the Italian way was enough to let us know that we needed more than just bricks to make this recipe work. We thought of brining to keep the meat moist, but it produced burnt chicken when the liquid dripped into the fire. An alternative way to retain moisture in meat is salting; we rubbed the flesh under the skin with salt, mixed with garlic, red pepper flakes, and herbs for Italian flavor. With a modified two-level fire in the grill, we cooked the chicken under preheated bricks on the cooler side, skin side down, to firm up the flesh and release fat and liquid where the fire wouldn't cause flare-ups. We flipped the chicken and finished cooking it on the hot side; another flip and a few minutes without the bricks crisped up the skin. The combination of flipping and moving the chicken from the cool side to the hot side guaranteed even cooking, and the salting had kept the meat juicy. With a finishing embellishment of a quick vinaigrette, we had perfectly cooked chicken with zesty Italian flavor, and not a burnt piece in sight. Use an oven mitt or dish towel to safely grip and maneuver the hot bricks. You will need two standard-size bricks for this recipe. Placing the bricks on the chicken while it cooks ensures that the skin will be evenly browned and well rendered. A cast-iron skillet or other heavy pan can be used in place of the bricks.

⅓ cup extra-virgin olive oil
8 garlic cloves, minced
1 teaspoon grated lemon zest plus 2 tablespoons juice
Pinch red pepper flakes
4 teaspoons minced fresh thyme
1 tablespoon minced fresh rosemary
1 (3½- to 4-pound) whole chicken
Table salt and pepper

**1.** Heat oil, garlic, lemon zest, and pepper flakes in small saucepan over medium-low heat until sizzling, about 3 minutes. Stir in 1 tablespoon thyme and 2 teaspoons rosemary and continue to cook for 30 seconds longer. Strain mixture through fine-mesh strainer set over small bowl, pushing on solids to extract oil. Transfer solids to bowl and cool; set oil and solids aside.

**2. TO BUTTERFLY CHICKEN:** Use kitchen shears to cut along both sides of backbone to remove it. Flatten breastbone and tuck wings behind back. Use hands or handle of wooden spoon to loosen skin over breast and thighs and remove any excess fat.

**3.** Combine 1½ teaspoons salt and 1 teaspoon pepper in bowl. Mix 2 teaspoons salt mixture with cooled garlic solids. Spread salt-garlic mixture evenly under skin over chicken breast and thighs. Sprinkle remaining ½ teaspoon salt mixture on exposed meat of bone side. Place chicken skin side up on wire rack set in rimmed baking sheet and refrigerate for 1 to 2 hours.

**4A. FOR A CHARCOAL GRILL:** Open bottom vent halfway. Light large chimney starter three-quarters filled with charcoal briquettes (4½ quarts). When top coals are partially covered with ash, pour evenly over half of grill. Set cooking grate in place, wrap 2 bricks tightly in aluminum foil, and place on cooking grate. Cover and open lid vent halfway. Heat grill until hot, about 5 minutes.

**4B. FOR A GAS GRILL:** Wrap 2 bricks tightly in aluminum foil and place on cooking grate. Turn all burners to high, cover, and heat grill until hot, about 15 minutes. Leave primary burner on high and turn off other burner(s). (Adjust primary burner as needed during cooking to maintain grill temperature around 350 degrees.)

**5.** Clean and oil cooking grate. Place chicken on cooler side of grill, skin side down, with legs facing coals and flames. Place hot bricks lengthwise over each breast half, cover, and cook until skin is lightly browned and faint grill marks appear, 22 to 25 minutes. Remove bricks from chicken. Using tongs, grip legs and flip chicken (chicken should release freely from grill; use thin metal spatula to loosen if stuck), then transfer to hot side of grill, skin side up. Place bricks over breast, cover, and cook until chicken is well browned, 12 to 15 minutes.

**6.** Remove bricks, flip chicken skin side down, and continue to cook until skin is well browned and breast registers 160 degrees and thighs register 175 degrees, 5 to 10 minutes longer. Transfer chicken to carving board, tent loosely with foil, and let rest for 15 minutes.

**7.** Whisk lemon juice, remaining 1 teaspoon thyme, and remaining 1 teaspoon rosemary into reserved oil and season with salt and pepper to taste. Carve chicken and serve, passing sauce separately.

## Grill-Roasted Cornish Game Hens

SERVES 4

**WHY THIS RECIPE WORKS** Grilled Cornish game hens provide an attractive, elegant alternative to grilled chicken. By butterflying the birds we kept all of the skin on one side, which meant it crisped more quickly when placed facing the coals. Butterflying also produced a uniformly thick bird, which promoted even cooking. We needed to secure the legs to the body to keep the skin from tearing, so we developed a special skewering procedure that stabilized the legs, made it easier to fit the birds on the cooking grate, and created a restaurant-worthy presentation. A seven-ingredient rub gave the hens a sweet and savory complexity and helped crisp the skin even further, giving it a rich mahogany hue. A quick glaze provided the crowning touch. To add smoke flavor to the hens, use the optional wood chips; however, when using a charcoal grill, we prefer wood chunks to wood chips; substitute 4 medium wood chunks, soaked in water for 1 hour, for the wood chip packets. You will need four 8- to 10-inch flat metal skewers for this recipe.

- ½ cup table salt
- 4 (1¼- to 1½-pound) whole Cornish game hens
- 2 tablespoons packed brown sugar
- 1 tablespoon paprika
- 2 teaspoons garlic powder
- 2 teaspoons chili powder
- 1 teaspoon ground black pepper
- 1 teaspoon ground coriander
- ⅛ teaspoon cayenne pepper
- 4 cups wood chips, soaked in water for 15 minutes and drained (optional)
- 1 (16 by 12-inch) disposable aluminum roasting pan
- 1 recipe glaze (recipes follow)

**1. TO BUTTERFLY GAME HENS:** Use kitchen shears to cut along both sides of backbone to remove it. With skin side down, make ¼-inch cut into bone separating breast halves. Lightly press on ribs to flatten hen. Fold wing tips behind bird to secure them.

**2.** Dissolve salt in 4 quarts cold water in large container. Submerge hens in brine, cover, and refrigerate for 30 minutes to 1 hour.

**3.** Combine sugar, paprika, garlic powder, chili powder, pepper, coriander, and cayenne in bowl. Remove hens from brine and pat dry with paper towels.

**4. TO SKEWER HENS:** Insert flat metal skewer ½ inch from end of drumstick through skin and meat and out other side. Turn leg so that end of drumstick faces wing, then insert tip of skewer into meaty section of thigh under bone. Press skewer all the way through breast and second thigh. Fold end of drumstick toward wing and insert skewer ½ inch from end. Press skewer so that blunt end rests against bird and stretch skin tight over legs, thighs, and breast halves. Rub hens evenly with spice mixture and refrigerate while preparing grill.

**5.** Using 2 large pieces of heavy-duty aluminum foil, wrap soaked chips, if using, in 2 foil packets and cut several vent holes in tops.

**6A. FOR A CHARCOAL GRILL:** Open bottom vent completely and place roasting pan in center of grill. Light large chimney starter filled with charcoal briquettes (6 quarts). When top coals are partially covered with ash, pour into 2 even piles on either side of roasting pan. Place 1 wood chip packet, if using, on each pile of coals. Set cooking grate in place, cover, and open lid vent completely. Heat grill until hot and wood chips are smoking, about 5 minutes.

**6B. FOR A GAS GRILL:** Place wood chip packets, if using, directly on primary burner. Turn all burners to high, cover, and heat grill until hot and wood chips are smoking, about 15 minutes. Turn all burners to medium. (Adjust burners as needed during cooking to maintain grill temperature around 325 degrees.)

**7.** Clean and oil cooking grate. Place hens in center of grill (over roasting pan if using charcoal), skin side down. Cover (position lid vent over birds if using charcoal) and cook until thighs register 160 degrees, 20 to 30 minutes.

**8.** Using tongs, move the birds to the hot sides of the grill (if using charcoal; 2 hens per side), keeping them skin side down, or turn all burners to high (if using gas). Cover and continue to cook until browned, about 5 minutes. Brush the birds with half of glaze, flip, and cook for 2 minutes. Brush remaining glaze over hens, flip, and continue to cook until breasts register 160 degrees and thighs register 175 degrees, 1 to 3 minutes longer.

**9.** Transfer hens to carving board, tent loosely with foil, and let rest for 5 to 10 minutes. Cut hens in half through the breastbone and serve.

## Barbecue Glaze

**MAKES** about ½ cup

- ½ cup ketchup
- 2 tablespoons brown sugar
- 1 tablespoon soy sauce
- 1 tablespoon distilled white vinegar
- 1 tablespoon yellow mustard
- 1 garlic clove, minced

Combine all ingredients in small saucepan, bring to simmer, and cook, stirring occasionally, until thickened, about 5 minutes.

### SKEWERING GAME HENS

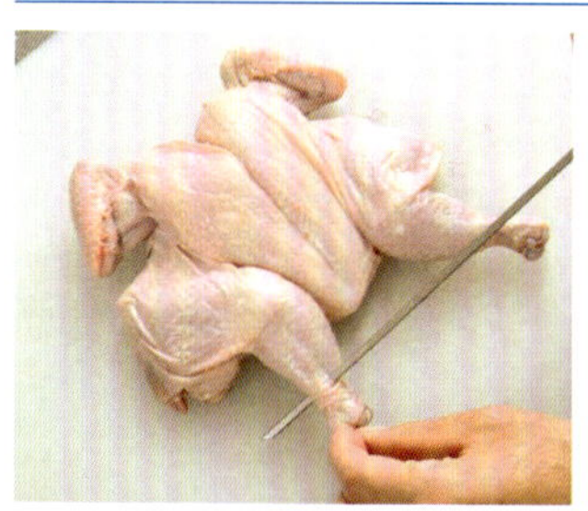

**1.** Insert a flat metal skewer ½ inch from the end of a drumstick through the skin and meat and out the other side.

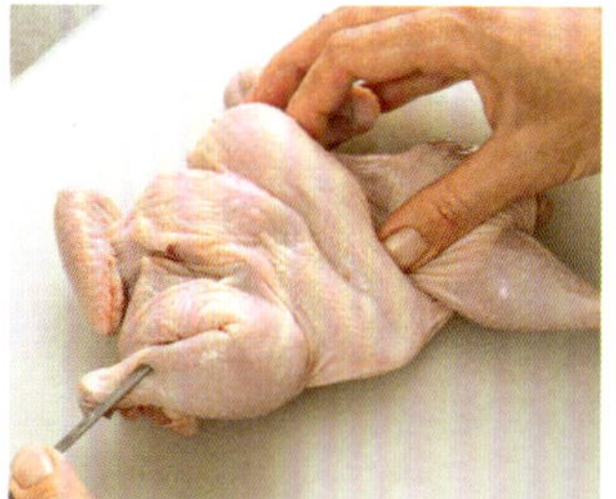

**2.** Turn the leg so that the end of the drumstick faces the wing, then insert the tip of the skewer into the meaty section of the thigh under the bone.

**3.** Press the skewer all the way through the breast and second thigh. Fold the end of the drumstick toward the wing and insert the skewer ½ inch from the end. Press the skewer so that the blunt end rests against the bird and stretch the skin tight.

# Gai Yang (Thai Grilled Cornish Game Hens with Chili Dipping Sauce)

**SERVES 4**

**WHY THIS RECIPE WORKS** For our take on gai yang, Thai grilled chicken, we started with Cornish hens, which are similar in size to the hens traditionally used by street vendors in Thailand. Butterflying and flattening the hens helped them cook more quickly and evenly on the grill. We created a marinade consisting of cilantro leaves and stems (a substitute for the traditional cilantro root), lots of garlic, white pepper, ground coriander, brown sugar, and fish sauce; thanks to its pesto-like consistency, it clung to the hens instead of sliding off. We set up a half-grill fire and started cooking the hens skin side up over the cooler side of the grill so the fatty skin had time to slowly render while the meat cooked; then we finished them over the hotter side to crisp the skin. We whipped up a version of the traditional sweet-tangy-spicy dipping sauce. Plenty of minced garlic and Thai chiles balanced the sauce with savory, fruity heat. The hens need to marinate for at least 6 hours before cooking (a longer marinating time is preferable). If your hens weigh 1½ to 2 pounds, grill three hens instead of four and extend the initial cooking time in step 6 by 5 minutes. If you can't find Thai chiles, substitute Fresno or red jalapeño chiles. Serve with steamed white rice.

**HENS**

- 4 Cornish game hens (1¼ to 1½ pounds each), giblets discarded
- 1 cup fresh cilantro leaves and stems, chopped coarse
- 12 garlic cloves, peeled
- ¼ cup packed light brown sugar
- 2 teaspoons ground white pepper
- 2 teaspoons ground coriander
- 2 teaspoons table salt
- ¼ cup fish sauce

**DIPPING SAUCE**

- ½ cup distilled white vinegar
- ½ cup granulated sugar
- 1 tablespoon minced Thai chiles
- 3 garlic cloves, minced
- ¼ teaspoon table salt

**1. FOR THE HENS:** Working with 1 hen at a time, place hen breast side down on cutting board and use kitchen shears to cut through bones on either side of backbone; discard backbone. Flip hen and press on breastbone to flatten. Trim off any excess fat and skin.

**2.** Pulse cilantro leaves and stems, garlic, sugar, pepper, coriander, and salt in food processor until finely chopped, 10 to 15 pulses; transfer to small bowl. Add fish sauce and stir until marinade has consistency of loose paste.

**3.** Rub hens all over with marinade. Transfer hens and any excess marinade to large zipper-lock bag and refrigerate for at least 6 hours or up to 24 hours, turning bag halfway through marinating.

**4. FOR THE DIPPING SAUCE:** Bring vinegar to boil in small saucepan. Add sugar and stir to dissolve. Reduce heat to medium-low and simmer until vinegar mixture is slightly thickened, 5 minutes. Remove from heat and let vinegar mixture cool to room temperature. Add chiles, garlic, and salt and stir until combined. Transfer sauce to airtight container and refrigerate until ready to use. (Sauce can be refrigerated for up to 2 weeks. Bring to room temperature before serving.)

**5A. FOR A CHARCOAL GRILL:** Open bottom vent completely. Light large chimney starter filled with charcoal briquettes (6 quarts). When top coals are partially covered with ash, pour evenly over half of grill. Set cooking grate in place, cover, and open lid vent completely. Heat grill until hot, about 5 minutes.

**5B. FOR A GAS GRILL:** Turn all burners to high, cover, and heat grill until hot, about 15 minutes. Leave primary burner and secondary burner (next to primary burner) on high and turn off other burner(s). Adjust secondary burner as needed to maintain grill temperature between 400 and 450 degrees.

**6.** Clean and oil cooking grate. Remove hens from bag, leaving any marinade that sticks to hens in place. Tuck wingtips behind backs and turn legs so drumsticks face inward toward breasts. Place hens, skin side up, on cooler side of grill (if using charcoal, arrange hens so that legs and thighs are facing coals). Cover and cook until skin has browned and breasts register 145 to 150 degrees, 30 to 35 minutes, rotating hens halfway through cooking.

**7.** Using tongs, carefully flip hens and place skin side down on hotter side of grill. Cover and cook until skin is crisp, deeply browned, and charred in spots and breasts register 160 degrees, 3 to 5 minutes, being careful to avoid burning.

**8.** Transfer hens, skin side up, to cutting board, tent with aluminum foil, and let rest for 10 minutes. Carve each hen in half or into 4 pieces and serve, passing dipping sauce separately.

## Juicy Grilled Turkey Burgers

**SERVES** 6

**WHY THIS RECIPE WORKS** To create juicy, well-textured turkey burgers, we ditched store-bought ground turkey in favor of home-ground turkey thighs, which boast more fat and flavor. To ensure that our turkey burger recipe delivered maximum juiciness, we incorporated a paste with a portion of the ground turkey, gelatin, soy sauce, and baking soda, which trapped juice within the burgers. Finally, we added coarsely chopped raw white mushrooms to keep the meat from binding together too firmly. If you are able to purchase boneless, skinless turkey thighs, substitute 1½ pounds for the bone-in thigh. To ensure the best texture, don't let the burgers stand for more than an hour before cooking. Serve the burgers with Malt Vinegar–Molasses Burger Sauce.

- 1 (2-pound) bone-in turkey thigh, skinned, boned, trimmed, and cut into ½-inch pieces
- 1 tablespoon unflavored gelatin
- 3 tablespoons low-sodium chicken broth
- 6 ounces white mushrooms, trimmed
- 1 tablespoon soy sauce
- Pinch baking soda
- 2 tablespoons vegetable oil, plus extra for brushing
- Kosher salt and pepper
- 6 large hamburger buns

**1.** Place turkey pieces on large plate in single layer. Freeze meat until very firm and hardened around edges, 35 to 45 minutes. Meanwhile, sprinkle gelatin over chicken broth in small bowl and let sit until gelatin softens, about 5 minutes. Pulse mushrooms in food processor until coarsely chopped, about 7 pulses, stopping and redistributing mushrooms around bowl as needed to ensure even grinding. Set mushrooms aside; do not wash food processor.

**2.** Pulse one-third of turkey in food processor until coarsely chopped into ⅛-inch pieces, 18 to 22 pulses, stopping and redistributing turkey around bowl as needed to ensure even grinding. Transfer meat to large bowl and repeat two more times with remaining turkey.

**3.** Return ½ cup (about 3 ounces) ground turkey to bowl of food processor along with softened gelatin, soy sauce, and baking soda. Process until smooth, about 2 minutes, scraping down bowl as needed. With processor running, slowly drizzle in oil, about 10 seconds; leave paste in food processor. Return mushrooms to food processor with paste and pulse to combine, 3 to 5 pulses, stopping and redistributing mixture as needed to ensure even mixing. Transfer mushroom mixture to bowl with ground turkey and use hands to evenly combine.

**4.** With lightly greased hands, divide meat mixture into 6 balls. Flatten into ¾-inch-thick patties about 4 inches in diameter; press shallow indentation into center of each burger to ensure even cooking. (Shaped patties can be frozen for up to 1 month. Frozen patties can be cooked straight from freezer.)

**5A. FOR A CHARCOAL GRILL:** Open bottom vent completely. Light large chimney starter filled with charcoal briquettes (6 quarts). When top coals are partially covered with ash, pour evenly over half of grill. Set cooking grate in place, cover, and open lid vent completely. Heat grill until hot, about 5 minutes.

**5B. FOR A GAS GRILL:** Turn all burners to high, cover, and heat grill until hot, about 15 minutes. Leave primary burner on high and turn off other burner(s).

**6.** Clean and oil cooking grate. Brush 1 side of patties with oil and season with salt and pepper. Using spatula, flip patties, brush with oil, and season second side. Place burgers over hot part of grill and cook until burgers are well browned on both sides and register 160 degrees, 4 to 7 minutes per side. (If cooking frozen burgers: After burgers are browned on both sides, transfer to cool side of grill, cover, and continue to cook until burgers register 160 degrees.)

**7.** Transfer burgers to plate and let rest for 5 minutes. While burgers rest, grill buns over hot side of grill. Transfer burgers to buns, add desired toppings, and serve.

### Malt Vinegar–Molasses Burger Sauce

**MAKES** about 1 cup

- ¾ cup mayonnaise
- 4 teaspoons malt vinegar
- ½ teaspoon molasses
- ¼ teaspoon Worcestershire sauce
- ¼ teaspoon table salt
- ¼ teaspoon pepper

Whisk all ingredients together in bowl.

## Simple Grill-Roasted Turkey

**SERVES** 10 to 12

**WHY THIS RECIPE WORKS** Besides freeing up your oven for other dishes, roasting your turkey out on the grill also means that you don't have to constantly monitor the bird to ensure a perfectly juicy, tender turkey. To make grilling turkey failproof, we divided our coals into two piles on either side of the grill so that the turkey thighs would receive the highest heat. A combination of lit coals and unlit briquettes yielded a longer-burning fire, making replenishing coals unnecessary. The addition of a pan of water stabilized the temperature inside the grill for even cooking, and a quick salt rub before grilling yielded seasoned meat and crispy skin. Table salt is not recommended for this recipe because it is too fine. If using a kosher or self-basting turkey (such as a frozen Butterball), do not salt it in step 1. Check the wings halfway through roasting; if they are getting too dark, fold a 12 by 8-inch piece of foil in half lengthwise and then again crosswise and slide the foil between the wing and the cooking grate to shield the wings from the flame. As an accompaniment, try our Gravy for Simple Grill-Roasted Turkey or Cranberry Chutney with Apples and Crystallized Ginger (recipes follow).

- 1 (12- to 14-pound) turkey, neck and giblets removed and reserved for gravy
- ¼ cup plus 1 teaspoon kosher salt, divided
- 1 teaspoon pepper
- 1 teaspoon baking powder
- 1 tablespoon vegetable oil
- Large disposable aluminum roasting pan (if using charcoal) or 2 disposable aluminum pie plates (if using gas)

**1.** Place turkey breast side down on work surface. Make two 2-inch incisions below each thigh and breast along back of turkey (4 incisions total). Using your fingers or handle of wooden spoon, carefully separate skin from thighs and breast. Rub 4 teaspoons salt evenly inside cavity of turkey, 1 tablespoon salt under skin of each side of breast, and 1 teaspoon salt under skin of each leg.

**2.** Combine pepper, baking powder, and remaining 1 teaspoon salt in bowl. Pat turkey dry with paper towels and sprinkle surface with pepper mixture; rub in with your hands to coat evenly. Wrap turkey tightly with plastic wrap; refrigerate for at least 24 hours or up to 2 days.

**3.** Discard plastic. Tuck wings underneath turkey. Using your hands, rub oil evenly over entire surface of turkey.

**4A. FOR A CHARCOAL GRILL:** Open bottom vent halfway and place disposable pan filled with 3 cups water in center of grill. Arrange 1½ quarts unlit charcoal briquettes on either side of pan in even layer. Light large chimney starter two-thirds filled with charcoal briquettes (4 quarts). When top coals are partially covered with ash, pour 2 quarts of lit coals on top of each pile of unlit coals. Set cooking grate in place, cover, and open lid vent halfway. Heat grill until hot, about 5 minutes.

**4B. FOR A GAS GRILL:** Place 2 disposable pie plates with 2 cups water in each directly on 1 burner over which turkey will be cooked. Turn all burners to high; cover; and heat grill until hot, about 15 minutes. Turn primary burner (burner opposite pie plates) to medium and turn other burner(s) off. Adjust primary burner as needed to maintain grill temperature of 325 degrees.

**5.** Clean and oil cooking grate. Place turkey, breast side up, in center of charcoal grill or on cooler side of gas grill, making sure bird is over disposable pans and not over flame. Cover (placing vents over turkey on charcoal grill) and cook until breast registers 160 degrees and thighs/drumsticks register 175 degrees, 2½ to 3 hours, rotating turkey after 1¼ hours if using gas grill.

**6.** Transfer turkey to carving board and let rest, uncovered, for 45 minutes. Carve turkey and serve.

## Gravy for Simple Grill-Roasted Turkey

**MAKES** 6 cups

- 1 tablespoon vegetable oil
- Reserved turkey neck, cut into 1-inch pieces, and giblets
- 1 pound onions, chopped coarse, divided
- 4 cups chicken broth
- 4 cups beef broth
- 2 small carrots, peeled and chopped coarse
- 2 small celery ribs, chopped coarse
- 6 tablespoons unsalted butter
- ½ cup all-purpose flour
- 2 bay leaves
- ½ teaspoon dried thyme
- 10 whole black peppercorns

**1.** Heat oil in Dutch oven over medium-high heat until shimmering. Add turkey neck and giblets; cook, stirring occasionally, until browned, about 5 minutes. Add half of onions and cook, stirring occasionally, until softened, about 3 minutes. Reduce heat to low; cover and cook, stirring occasionally, until turkey parts and onions release their juices, about 20 minutes.

**2.** Add chicken broth and beef broth; increase heat to high and bring to boil. Reduce heat to low and simmer, uncovered, skimming any scum that rises to surface, until broth is rich and flavorful, about 30 minutes. Strain broth into large bowl (you should have about 8 cups), reserving giblets, if desired; discard neck. Reserve broth. When cool enough to handle, remove gristle from giblets, if using; dice; and set aside. (Broth can be refrigerated in airtight container for up to 2 days.)

**3.** Pulse carrots in food processor until broken into rough ¼-inch pieces, about 5 pulses. Add celery and remaining onions; pulse until all vegetables are broken into ⅛-inch pieces, about 5 pulses.

**4.** Melt butter in now-empty Dutch oven over medium-high heat. Add vegetables and cook, stirring frequently, until softened and well browned, about 10 minutes. Reduce heat to medium; stir in flour and cook, stirring constantly, until thoroughly browned and fragrant, 5 to 7 minutes. Whisking constantly, gradually add reserved broth; bring to boil, skimming off any foam that forms on surface. Reduce heat to medium-low and add bay leaves, thyme, and peppercorns; simmer, stirring occasionally, until thickened and reduced to 6 cups, 30 to 35 minutes.

**5.** Strain gravy through fine-mesh strainer into clean saucepan, pressing on solids to extract as much liquid as possible; discard solids. Stir in diced giblets, if using. Season with salt and pepper to taste.

### Cranberry Chutney with Apples and Crystallized Ginger

**MAKES** about 3 cups

If using frozen cranberries, thaw them before cooking.

- 1 teaspoon vegetable oil
- 1 shallot, minced
- 2 teaspoons finely grated fresh ginger
- ½ teaspoon table salt
- ⅔ cup water
- ¼ cup cider vinegar
- 1 cup packed brown sugar
- 12 ounces (3 cups) fresh or frozen cranberries
- 2 Granny Smith apples, peeled, cored, and cut into ¼-inch pieces
- ⅓ cup minced crystallized ginger

**1.** Heat oil in medium saucepan over medium heat until shimmering. Add shallot, fresh ginger, and salt; cook, stirring occasionally, until shallot has softened, 1 to 2 minutes.

**2.** Add water, vinegar, and sugar. Increase heat to high and bring to simmer, stirring to dissolve sugar. Add 1½ cups cranberries and apples; return to simmer. Reduce heat to medium-low and simmer, stirring occasionally, until cranberries have almost completely broken down and mixture has thickened, about 15 minutes.

**3.** Add remaining 1½ cups cranberries and crystallized ginger; continue to simmer, stirring occasionally, until cranberries just begin to burst, 5 to 7 minutes. Transfer to serving bowl and cool for at least 1 hour before serving. (Sauce can be refrigerated in airtight container for up to 3 days.)

## Grill-Roasted Turkey

**SERVES** 10 to 12

**WHY THIS RECIPE WORKS** Grill-roasting a turkey can be hard to manage. Cooking times can vary depending on the weather, and it's much easier to burn the bird's skin on a grill. There also remain the usual problems inherent to roasting a turkey: dry, overcooked breast meat and undercooked thighs. But grill-roasting can produce the best-tasting, best-looking turkey ever, with crispy skin and moist meat wonderfully perfumed with smoke. We wanted to take the guesswork out of preparing the holiday bird on the grill. Because the skin on larger birds will burn before the meat is done, we chose a small turkey (less than 14 pounds). We ditched stuffing the turkey or trussing it—both can lead to burnt skin and undercooked meat. To season the meat and help prevent it from drying out on the grill, we brined the turkey. To protect the skin and promote slow cooking, we placed the turkey on the opposite side of the glowing coals or lit gas burner. Using a V-rack also helped, as it improved air circulation. And we turned the turkey three times instead of twice; this way, all four sides received equal exposure to the hot side of the grill for evenly bronzed skin. If using a self-basting turkey or kosher turkey, do not brine in step 1, and season with salt after brushing with melted butter in step 2. When using a charcoal grill, we prefer wood chunks to wood chips whenever possible; substitute 6 medium wood chunks, soaked in water for 1 hour, for the wood chip packets. The total cooking time is 2 to 2½ hours, depending on the size of the bird, the ambient conditions (the bird will require more time on a cool, windy day), and the intensity of the fire.

- 1 cup table salt
- 1 (12- to 14-pound) turkey, trimmed, neck, giblets, and tailpiece removed, and wings tucked behind back
- 2 tablespoons unsalted butter, melted
- 6 cups wood chips, soaked in water for 15 minutes and drained

**1.** Dissolve salt in 2 gallons cold water in large container. Submerge turkey in brine, cover, and refrigerate or store in very cool spot (40 degrees or less) for 6 to 12 hours.

**2.** Lightly spray V-rack with vegetable oil spray. Remove turkey from brine and pat dry, inside and out, with paper towels. Brush both sides of turkey with melted butter and place breast side down in prepared V-rack.

**3.** Using 3 large pieces of heavy-duty aluminum foil, wrap soaked chips in 3 foil packets and cut several vent holes in top.

**4A. FOR A CHARCOAL GRILL:** Open bottom vent halfway. Light large chimney mounded with charcoal briquettes (7 quarts). When top coals are partially covered with ash, pour into steeply banked pile against side of grill. Place 1 wood chip packet on pile of coals. Set cooking grate in place, cover, and open lid vent halfway. Heat grill until hot and wood chips are smoking, about 5 minutes.

**4B. FOR A GAS GRILL:** Place 1 wood chip packet directly on primary burner. Turn all burners to high, cover, and heat grill until hot and wood chips are smoking, about 15 minutes. Turn primary burner to medium-high and turn off other burner(s). (Adjust primary burner as needed during cooking to maintain grill temperature around 325 degrees.)

**5.** Clean and oil cooking grate. Place V-rack with turkey on cool side of grill with leg and wing facing coal, cover (position lid vent over turkey if using charcoal), and cook for 1 hour.

**6.** Using potholders, transfer V-rack with turkey to rimmed baking sheet or roasting pan. If using charcoal, remove cooking grate and add 12 new briquettes and second wood chip packet to pile of coals; set cooking grate in place. If using gas, place remaining wood chip packets directly on primary burner. With wad of paper towels in each hand, flip turkey breast side up in rack and return V-rack with turkey to cool side of grill, with other leg and wing facing heat. Cover (position lid vent over turkey if using charcoal) and cook for 45 minutes.

**7.** Using potholders, carefully rotate V-rack with turkey (breast remains up) 180 degrees. Cover and continue to cook until breast registers 160 degrees and thighs register 175 degrees, 15 to 45 minutes longer. Transfer turkey to carving board, tent loosely with foil, and let rest for 20 to 30 minutes. Carve and serve.

## Grill-Roasted Boneless Turkey Breast

**SERVES** 6 to 8

**WHY THIS RECIPE WORKS** Grill-roasting a turkey breast makes a nice change from the same old oven-roasted holiday bird. The problem is that unlike fatty pork butt or brisket, which turns moist and tender after a stint on the grill, ultra-lean turkey breast easily dries out. Plus its irregular shape can lead to uneven cooking. We wanted to develop a recipe that would deliver a grill-roasted breast with all the richness and juiciness we associate with the thighs and legs, along with crisp, well-rendered skin, and meat that was moist all the way through. We began by salting our turkey breast. When meat is salted, its juices are initially drawn out of the flesh and beads of liquid pool on its surface. Eventually, the salty liquid slowly migrates back into the meat, keeping it moist as it cooks. We grill-roasted the turkey breast over a modified two-level fire, starting the meat over the cool side of the grill and later moving it to the hot side to finish cooking. Although most of the meat turned out moist and flavorful, there were still desiccated spots on the tapered ends of the breast and in places where the skin didn't completely cover the meat. Inspired by a restaurant technique, we reshaped our turkey breast like a roulade so that it would cook through evenly. We prefer either a natural (unbrined) or kosher turkey breast for this recipe. Using a kosher turkey breast (rubbed with salt and rinsed during processing) or self-basting turkey breast (injected with salt and water) eliminates the need for salting in step 2. If the breast has a pop-up timer, remove it before cooking. When using a charcoal grill, we prefer wood chunks to wood chips whenever possible; substitute 1 small wood chunk, soaked in water for 1 hour, for the wood chip packet.

- ½ cup wood chips, soaked in water for 15 minutes and drained (optional)
- 1 (5- to 7-pound) whole bone-in turkey breast, trimmed
- 2 teaspoons table salt
- 1 teaspoon vegetable oil
- Pepper

**1.** Using large piece of heavy-duty aluminum foil, wrap soaked chips, if using, in foil packet and cut several vent holes in top.

**2.** Remove skin from breast meat and then cut along rib cage to remove breast halves (discard bones or save for stock). Pat turkey breast halves dry with paper towels and season with salt. Stack breast halves on top of one another with cut sides facing, and alternating thick and tapered ends. Stretch skin over exposed meat and tuck in ends. Tie kitchen twine lengthwise around roast. Then tie 5 to 7 pieces of twine at 1-inch intervals crosswise along roast. Transfer roast to wire rack set in rimmed baking sheet and refrigerate for 1 hour.

**3A. FOR A CHARCOAL GRILL:** Open bottom vent halfway. Light large chimney starter filled with charcoal briquettes (6 quarts). When top coals are partially covered with ash, pour evenly over half of grill. Place wood chip packet, if using, on coals. Set cooking grate in place, cover, and open lid vent halfway. Heat grill until hot and wood chips are smoking, about 5 minutes.

**3B. FOR A GAS GRILL:** Place wood chip packet, if using, directly on primary burner. Turn all burners to high, cover, and heat grill until hot and wood chips are smoking, about 15 minutes. Turn all burners to medium-low. (Adjust burner(s) as needed during cooking to maintain grill temperature around 300 degrees.)

**4.** Clean and oil cooking grate. Rub surface of roast with oil and season with pepper. Place roast on grill (cool side if using charcoal). Cover (position lid vents over meat if using charcoal) and cook until roast registers 150 degrees, 40 minutes to 1 hour, turning 180 degrees halfway through cooking.

**5.** Slide roast to hot side of grill (if using charcoal) or turn all burners to medium-high (if using gas). Cook until roast is browned and skin is crisp on all sides, 8 to 10 minutes, rotating every 2 minutes.

**6.** Transfer roast to carving board, tent loosely with foil, and let rest for 15 minutes. Cut into ½-inch-thick slices, removing twine as you cut. Serve.

### TURNING A BONE-IN TURKEY BREAST INTO A BONELESS TURKEY ROAST

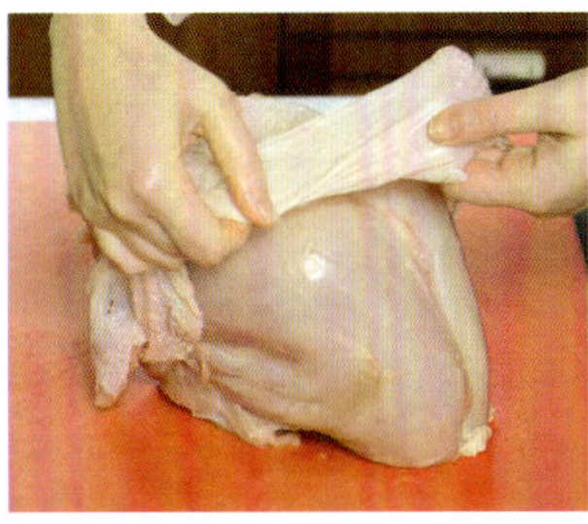

**1.** Starting at one side of the breast and using your fingers to separate the skin from the meat, peel the skin off the breast meat and reserve.

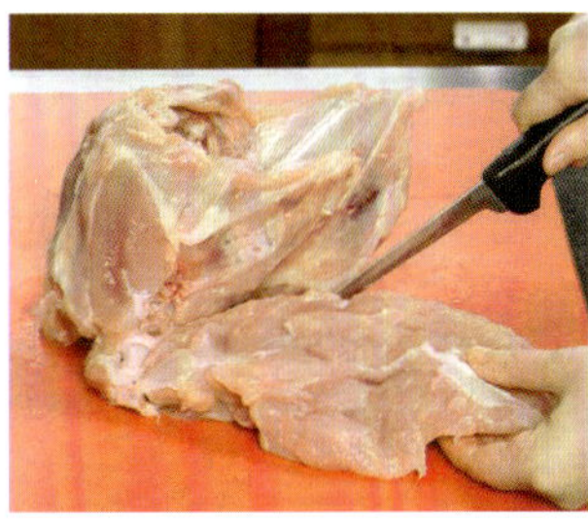

**2.** Using the tip of a knife, cut along the rib cage to remove each breast half completely.

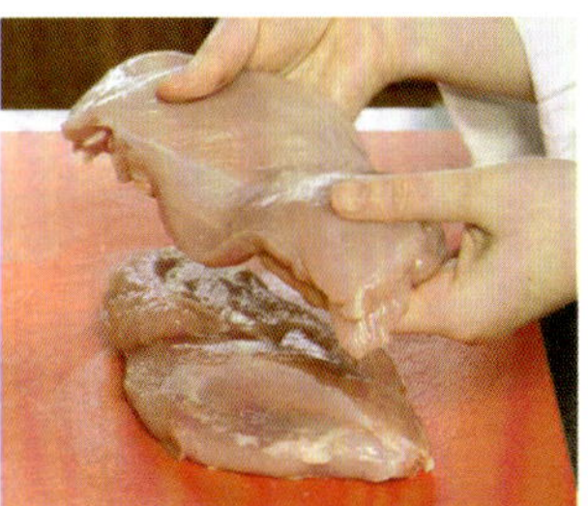

**3.** Arrange one breast, cut side up; top with the second breast, cut side down, the thick end over the tapered end. Drape the skin over the breasts and tuck the ends under.

**4.** Tie a 3-foot piece of kitchen twine lengthwise around the roast. Then, tie five to seven pieces of twine at 1-inch intervals crosswise along the roast, starting at its center, then at either end, and then filling in the rest.

## Grilled Salmon Fillets

**SERVES 4**

**WHY THIS RECIPE WORKS** Cooking delicate salmon can be tricky. Even using a nonstick skillet, it's still easy to break the occasional fillet. Introduce that same fillet to a grill, and you've got a real challenge. We wanted grilled salmon with a tender interior and crisp skin, and with each fillet perfectly intact. We chose thicker salmon fillets, which could stand the heat of the grill for a little while longer before the first turn. To prevent the fish from sticking, we dried the fish's exterior by wrapping it in dish towels and "seasoned" our cooking grate by brushing it over and over with multiple layers of oil until it developed a dark, shiny coating. After laying the fillets on the grate, we easily flipped each fillet without even the tiniest bit of sticking. This recipe can be used with any thick, firm-fleshed white fish, including red snapper, grouper, halibut, and sea bass (cook white fish to 140 degrees, up to 2 minutes longer per side). If you are using skinless fillets, treat the skinned side of each as if it were the skin side. If desired, serve with Almond Vinaigrette.

- 1 (1½- to 2-pound) skin-on salmon fillet, 1½ inches thick
- Vegetable oil
- Table salt and pepper
- Lemon wedges

**1.** Use sharp knife to remove any whitish fat from belly of salmon and cut fillet into 4 equal pieces. Place fillets skin side up on large plate lined with clean dish towel. Place second clean dish towel on top of fillets and press down to blot liquid. Refrigerate fish, wrapped in towels, while preparing grill, at least 20 minutes.

**2A. FOR A CHARCOAL GRILL:** Open bottom vent completely. Light large chimney starter two-thirds filled with charcoal briquettes (4 quarts). When top coals are partially covered with ash, pour evenly over half of grill. Set cooking grate in place, cover, and open lid vent completely. Heat grill until hot, about 5 minutes.

**2B. FOR A GAS GRILL:** Turn all burners to high, cover, and heat grill until hot, about 15 minutes.

**3.** Clean cooking grate, then repeatedly brush grate with well-oiled paper towels until grate is black and glossy, 5 to 10 times. Lightly brush both sides of fish with oil and season with salt and pepper. Place fish skin side down on hot side of grill (if using charcoal) or turn all burners to medium (if using gas) with fillets diagonal to grate. Cover and cook until skin is well browned and crisp, 3 to 5 minutes. (Try lifting fish gently with spatula after 3 minutes; if it doesn't cleanly lift off grill, continue to cook, checking at 30-second intervals, until it releases.)

**4.** Flip fish and continue to cook, covered, until center is still translucent when checked with tip of paring knife and registers 125 degrees (for medium-rare) and is still translucent when cut into with paring knife, 2 to 6 minutes longer. Serve immediately with lemon wedges.

### Almond Vinaigrette

**MAKES** about ½ cup

- ⅓ cup whole almonds, toasted
- 1 small shallot, minced
- 4 teaspoons white wine vinegar
- 2 teaspoons honey
- 1 teaspoon Dijon mustard
- ⅓ cup extra-virgin olive oil
- 1 tablespoon cold water
- 1 tablespoon chopped fresh tarragon
- Table salt and pepper

Place almonds in zipper-lock bag and, using rolling pin or bottom of skillet, pound until pieces no larger than ⅛ inch remain. Combine pounded almonds, shallot, vinegar, honey, and mustard in medium bowl. Whisking constantly, slowly drizzle in oil until smooth emulsion forms. Add water and tarragon and whisk to combine, then season with salt and pepper to taste. Whisk to recombine before serving.

## Sweet and Saucy Grilled Salmon with Lime-Jalapeño Glaze

**SERVES 4**

**WHY THIS RECIPE WORKS** A burnt, stuck-to-the-grill crust and flavorless interior are too often the reality of glazed salmon. But truly great glazed salmon right off the grill is a thing of beauty—the sweet glaze not only forms a glossy, deeply caramelized crust, but it also permeates the flesh. This was the salmon that we wanted to re-create—sweet, crisp, moist, and flavorful. Our recipe coup came early on in development—we realized that the best way to prevent the glazed salmon from sticking to the cooking grate was by not letting it touch the grate at all. We grilled the salmon fillets in individual aluminum trays set over the grill. We simply folded heavy-duty foil into 7 by 5-inch trays. This way, the fish still picked up great smoky flavor, but didn't stick to the cooking grate. Jelly was the best base ingredient for a sweet and sticky glaze. For the deepest flavor, we brushed some glaze over the fish toward the end of grilling, so it caramelized, and spooned the remaining glaze, enriched with butter, over the fish just before serving. Be sure to spray the foil trays with vegetable oil spray. You can also use Reynolds Wrap nonstick aluminum foil and skip the vegetable oil spray.

- ½ cup jalapeño jelly
- ½ cup packed fresh cilantro leaves and stems
- 1 teaspoon grated fresh lime zest and
- 2 tablespoons fresh lime juice
- 2 scallions, chopped coarse
- 2 garlic cloves, minced
- 2 tablespoons unsalted butter
- 4 (6- to 8-ounce) skinless salmon fillets, about 1¼ inches thick
- Table salt and pepper

**1.** Process jelly, cilantro, lime zest, lime juice, scallions, and garlic in food processor or blender to a smooth glaze. Transfer glaze to small saucepan and cook over medium heat until just bubbling, 2 to 3 minutes. Measure out and reserve ¼ cup glaze. Stir butter into remaining glaze.

**2.** Cut 4 rectangles of heavy-duty foil and crimp edges to make four 7 by 5-inch trays. Coat trays with vegetable oil spray. Season fillets with salt and pepper, and brush each thoroughly, on both sides, with 1 tablespoon of the reserved ¼ cup glaze. Place fillets, skinned side up, on trays.

**3A. FOR A CHARCOAL GRILL:** Open bottom grill vents completely. Light large chimney starter filled with charcoal briquettes (100 briquettes; 6 quarts). When coals are hot, pour evenly over grill. Set cooking grate in place, cover, and heat grill until hot, about 5 minutes.

**3B. FOR A GAS GRILL:** Turn all burners to high, cover, and heat grill until hot, about 15 minutes. (Adjust the burners as needed to maintain a hot fire.)

**4.** Clean and oil cooking grate. Place trays on grill. Cook (covered if using gas) until glaze forms a golden-brown crust, 6 to 8 minutes. Flip fillets, keeping them in trays, and spoon half of buttered glaze over salmon. Continue to cook until fish is opaque and flakes apart when gently prodded with paring knife, about 2 to 4 minutes longer.

**5.** Transfer trays to wire rack, tent loosely with foil, and let rest for 5 minutes. Transfer salmon to platter, spoon remaining buttered glaze over the top, and serve.

### MAKING FOIL TRAYS

Cut four rectangles of heavy-duty aluminum foil, then crimp the edges of each piece to make a 7 by 5-inch tray.

## Barbecued Salmon

**SERVES** 4 to 6

**WHY THIS RECIPE WORKS** Store-bought smoked salmon is inconsistent in quality and also incredibly expensive. We wanted to create our own easy recipe for this dish and make moist (but not too moist), nicely crusted salmon with a hint of smoked flavor—in just two hours. Instead of the traditional cold-smoking technique, which keeps the salmon moist but lacks flavor, we developed a "hot-smoked" method, and kept the salmon moist by brining. We achieved full smoked salmon flavor on the grill using a whole side of salmon. To get a firm but not overly dry texture, complemented by a strong hit of smoke and wood, we slow-cooked the salmon with wood chips or chunks for more than an hour over a modified two-level fire, but kept the fish on the cooler part of the grill the whole time. Using two spatulas to transfer the cooked fish from the grill prevented it from falling apart, and cutting through the pink flesh, not the skin, to divide individual portions kept the meat intact while leaving the skin behind. The cooking grate must be hot and thoroughly clean before you place the salmon on it; otherwise the fish might stick. Use foil or the back of a large rimmed baking sheet to get the fish onto the grill. If you'd like to use wood chunks instead of wood chips when using a charcoal grill, substitute 2 medium wood chunks, soaked in water for 1 hour, for the wood chip packet.

- 1 cup sugar
- ½ cup table salt
- 1 (2½-pound) skin-on salmon fillet
- 2 cups wood chips, soaked in water for 15 minutes and drained
- 2 tablespoons vegetable oil
- 1½ teaspoons sweet paprika
- 1 teaspoon ground white pepper

**1.** Dissolve sugar and salt in 7 cups cold water in gallon-size zipper-lock bag. Add salmon, seal bag, and refrigerate for 3 hours. Remove salmon from brine, pat dry with paper towels, and rub thoroughly with oil. Lay salmon skin side down on 30-inch sheet of heavy-duty aluminum foil and season top and sides with paprika and pepper.

**2A. FOR A CHARCOAL GRILL:** Open bottom grill vent halfway. Light large chimney starter half filled with charcoal briquettes (3 quarts). When top coals are partially covered with ash, pour evenly over half of grill. Place wood chip packet on coals. Set cooking grate in place, cover, and open lid vent completely halfway. Heat grill until hot and wood chips are smoking, about 5 minutes.

**2B. FOR A GAS GRILL:** Remove cooking grate and place wood chip packet directly on primary burner. Set cooking grate in place, turn all burners to high, cover, and heat grill until hot and wood chips are smoking, about 15 minutes. Leave primary burner on medium and turn off other burner(s). (Adjust primary burner as needed to maintain grill temperature around 275 degrees.)

**3.** Clean cooking grate, then repeatedly brush grate with well-oiled paper towels until black and glossy, 5 to 10 times. Gently slide salmon off foil onto cooler side of grill, skin-side down and perpendicular to grill grate. Cover (position lid vent over meat if using charcoal) and cook until heavily flavored with smoke, about 1½ hours.

**4.** Using two spatulas, gently remove salmon from grill. Serve hot or at room temperature.

## Grill-Smoked Salmon

**SERVES 6**

**WHY THIS RECIPE WORKS** We wanted to capture the intense, smoky flavor of hot-smoked fish and the firm but silky texture of the cold-smoked type, but we also wanted to skip specialized equipment and make this dish less of a project. We quick-cured the fish with a mixture of salt and sugar to draw moisture from the flesh, and we seasoned it inside and out. Cooking it over a gentle fire with ample smoke produced salmon that was sweet, smoky, and tender. Cutting a large fillet into individual portions created more surface area for smoke exposure. Plus, the smaller pieces of salmon were far easier to remove from the grill intact. Use center-cut salmon fillets of similar thickness so that they cook at the same rate. The best way to ensure uniformity is to buy a 2½- to 3-pound whole center-cut fillet and cut it into six pieces. If you'd like to use wood chunks instead of wood chips when using a charcoal grill, substitute two medium wood chunks, soaked in water for 1 hour, for the wood chip packet. Avoid mesquite wood chunks for this recipe. Serve with lemon wedges.

- 2 tablespoons sugar
- 1 tablespoon kosher salt
- 6 (6- to 8-ounce) center-cut skin-on salmon fillets
- 2 cups wood chips, half of chips soaked in water for 15 minutes and drained

**1.** Combine sugar and salt in bowl. Set wire rack in rimmed baking sheet, set salmon on rack, and sprinkle flesh side evenly with sugar mixture. Refrigerate, uncovered, for 1 hour. With paper towels, brush any excess salt and sugar from salmon and blot dry. Return fish on wire rack to refrigerator, uncovered, while preparing grill.

**2.** Combine soaked and unsoaked chips. Using large piece of heavy-duty aluminum foil, wrap chips in 8 by 4½-inch foil packet. (Make sure chips do not poke holes in sides or bottom of packet.) Cut 2 evenly spaced 2-inch slits in top of packet.

**3A. FOR A CHARCOAL GRILL:** Open bottom vent halfway. Light large chimney starter one-third filled with charcoal briquettes (2 quarts). When top coals are partially covered with ash, pour into steeply banked pile against side of grill. Place wood chip packet on top of coals. Set cooking grate in place, cover, and open lid vent halfway. Heat grill until hot and wood chips are smoking, about 5 minutes.

**3B. FOR A GAS GRILL:** Place wood chip packet directly on primary burner. Turn primary burner to high (leave other burners off); cover; and heat grill until hot and wood chips are smoking, about 15 minutes. Turn primary burner to medium. (Adjust primary burner as needed to maintain grill temperature between 275 to 300 degrees.)

**4.** Clean and oil cooking grate. Fold piece of heavy-duty foil into 18 by 6-inch rectangle. Place foil rectangle over cooler side of grill and place salmon pieces on foil, spaced at least ½ inch apart. Cover grill (positioning lid vent over fish if using charcoal) and cook until center of thickest part of fillet is still translucent when checked with tip of paring knife and registers 125 degrees (for medium-rare), 30 to 40 minutes. Transfer to platter and serve, or let cool to room temperature.

### "Smoked Salmon Platter" Sauce

**MAKES 1½ cups**

This sauce incorporates the three garnishes that are commonly served on a smoked salmon platter—hard-cooked egg, capers, and dill.

- 1 large egg yolk, plus 1 large hard-cooked egg, chopped fine
- 2 teaspoons Dijon mustard
- 2 teaspoons sherry vinegar
- ½ cup vegetable oil
- 2 tablespoons capers, rinsed, plus 1 teaspoon caper brine
- 2 tablespoons minced shallot
- 2 tablespoons minced fresh dill

Whisk egg yolk, mustard, and vinegar together in medium bowl. Whisking constantly, slowly drizzle in oil until emulsified, about 1 minute. Gently fold in capers and brine, hard-cooked egg, shallot, and dill.

## Grilled Tuna Steaks with Vinaigrette

**SERVES 6**

**WHY THIS RECIPE WORKS** Most grilled tuna steaks are either rare in the center with no char or have a great sear enveloping a dry, mealy interior. We wanted a thick layer of hot, grilled tuna with an intense smoky char wrapped around a cool, delicately flavored, tender, and moist center. We began by selecting tuna steaks that were thick enough to stay on the grill long enough to achieve a decent crust without overcooking. Our initial test of cooking methods proved that using direct heat with a hot fire and getting the tuna on and off the grill as quickly as possible worked well. For the charred flavor we were after, we turned to an ingredient that can enhance browning—oil. Oil helped to distribute heat evenly over the surface of the fish, including those areas not actually touching the cooking grate, and it added a little fat to the lean tuna, which kept the exterior from getting too dry and stringy. But oil alone didn't infuse our fish with grill flavor. We discovered that to moisten the tuna's flesh, the oil needed to penetrate the meat's tiny muscle fibers. Instead, we turned to a vinaigrette. The dressing (and its oil) clung to the fish, moistening its

exterior and solving the problem of dry flesh. To improve browning we added honey to our vinaigrette. The sugars caramelized quickly on the grill, helping deliver a perfectly browned crust on our tuna steaks. We prefer our tuna served rare or medium-rare. If you like your fish cooked medium, observe the timing for medium-rare, then tent the steaks loosely with aluminum foil for 5 minutes before serving.

- 3 tablespoons plus 1 teaspoon red wine vinegar
- 2 tablespoons chopped fresh thyme or rosemary
- 2 tablespoons Dijon mustard
- 2 teaspoons honey
- Table salt and pepper
- ¾ cup olive oil
- 6 (8-ounce) tuna steaks, 1 inch thick

**1A. FOR A CHARCOAL GRILL:** Open bottom vent completely. Light large chimney starter filled with charcoal briquettes (6 quarts). When top coals are partially covered with ash, pour evenly over half of grill. Set cooking grate in place, cover, and open lid vent completely. Heat grill until hot, about 5 minutes.

**1B. FOR A GAS GRILL:** Turn all burners to high, cover, and heat grill until hot, about 15 minutes. (Adjust burners as needed to maintain hot fire.)

**2.** Clean cooking grate, then repeatedly brush grate with well-oiled paper towels until grate is black and glossy, 5 to 10 times.

**3.** Meanwhile, whisk vinegar, thyme, mustard, honey, ½ teaspoon salt, and pinch pepper together in large bowl. Whisking constantly, slowly drizzle oil into vinegar mixture until lightly thickened and emulsified. Measure out ¾ cup vinaigrette and set aside for cooking fish. Reserve remaining vinaigrette for serving.

**4.** Pat fish dry with paper towels. Generously brush both sides of fish with vinaigrette and season with salt and pepper. Place fish on grill (hot side if using charcoal) and cook (covered if using gas) until grill marks form and bottom surface is opaque, 1 to 3 minutes.

**5.** Flip fish and cook until opaque at perimeter and translucent red at center when checked with tip of paring knife and registers 110 degrees (rare), about 1½ minutes, or until opaque at perimeter and reddish pink at center when checked with tip of paring knife and registers 125 degrees (medium-rare), about 3 minutes. Serve, passing reserved vinaigrette.

## Grilled Blackened Red Snapper

**SERVES 4**

**WHY THIS RECIPE WORKS** Blackened fish is usually prepared in a cast-iron skillet, but it can lead to one smoky kitchen. So we turned to the grill. Unfortunately, this move created a host of other problems, including fish stuck to the grate, the outside of the fish being way overdone by the time the flesh had cooked through, and the skin-on fillets curling midway through cooking. We were done with the smoke—and were ready for our fillets to have a dark brown, crusty, sweet-smoky, toasted spice exterior, providing a rich contrast to the moist, mild-flavored fish inside. The curling problem was easy to fix. We simply needed to score the skin. To prevent sticking, we made sure the grill was hot when we put the fish on and oiled the grate multiple times to ensure a clean surface. Finally, to give the fish its flavorful "blackened but not burned" coating, we bloomed our spice mixture in melted butter, allowed it to cool, and then applied the coating to the fish. Once on the grill, the spice crust acquired the proper depth and richness while the fish cooked through. Striped bass, halibut, or grouper can be substituted for the snapper; if the fillets are thicker or thinner, they will have slightly different cooking times. Serve with lemon wedges or Rémoulade (page 654).

- 2 tablespoons paprika
- 2 teaspoons onion powder
- 2 teaspoons garlic powder
- ¾ teaspoon ground coriander
- ¾ teaspoon table salt
- ¼ teaspoon cayenne pepper
- ¼ teaspoon black pepper
- ¼ teaspoon white pepper
- 3 tablespoons unsalted butter
- 4 (6- to 8-ounce) skin-on red snapper fillets, ¾ inch thick

**1.** Combine paprika, onion powder, garlic powder, coriander, salt, cayenne, black pepper, and white pepper in bowl. Melt butter in 10-inch skillet over medium heat. Stir in spice mixture and cook, stirring frequently, until fragrant and spices turn dark rust color, 2 to 3 minutes. Transfer mixture to pie plate and let cool to room temperature. Use a fork to break up any large clumps.

**2A. FOR A CHARCOAL GRILL:** Open bottom vent completely. Light large chimney starter two-thirds filled with charcoal briquettes (4 quarts). When top coals are partially covered with ash, pour evenly over half of grill. Set cooking grate in place, cover, and open lid vent completely. Heat grill until hot, about 5 minutes.

**2B. FOR A GAS GRILL:** Turn all burners to high, cover, and heat grill until hot, about 15 minutes.

**3.** Clean cooking grate, then repeatedly brush grate with well-oiled paper towels until black and glossy, 5 to 10 times.

**4.** Meanwhile, pat fillets dry with paper towels. Using sharp knife, make shallow diagonal slashes every inch along skin side of fish, being careful not to cut into flesh. Place fillets skin side up on large plate. Using your fingers, rub spice mixture in thin, even layer on top and sides of fish. Flip fillets over and repeat on other side (you should use all of spice mixture).

**5.** Place fish skin side down on grill (hot side if using charcoal) with fillets diagonal to grate. Cook until skin is very dark brown and crisp, 3 to 5 minutes. Carefully flip fish and continue to cook until dark brown and beginning to flake and center is opaque but still moist, about 5 minutes longer. Serve.

### Rémoulade

**MAKES** about ½ cup

The rémoulade can be refrigerated in an airtight container for up to 3 days.

- ½ cup mayonnaise
- 1½ teaspoons sweet pickle relish
- 1 teaspoon hot sauce
- 1 teaspoon lemon juice
- 1 teaspoon minced fresh parsley
- ½ teaspoon capers, rinsed
- ½ teaspoon Dijon mustard
- 1 small garlic clove, minced
- Table salt and pepper

Pulse all ingredients in food processor until well combined but not smooth, about 10 pulses. Season with salt and pepper to taste. Transfer to serving bowl.

## Grilled Whole Trout with Marjoram and Lemon

**SERVES** 4

**WHY THIS RECIPE WORKS** This recipe teaches that whole fish should not be feared, and grill-roasting trout is an immaculate example why. The grill infuses the trout with complementary smoky flavor, and the intense heat crisps the skin beautifully. The dish is simple, because whole trout are almost always sold cleaned, scaled, and gutted. And one fish serves one person for nice portioning. We brush mayonnaise and honey, neither of which you can taste, over the fish to brown it quickly. Fresh marjoram and lemon zest go inside. A concentrated fire, with an aluminum pan to corral the coals and focus their heat, cooks the trout in a flash. To take the temperature, insert the thermometer into the fillets through the opening by the gills. We prefer marjoram in this recipe, but thyme or oregano can be substituted. Do not flip the fish over in one motion. Instead, use two thin metal spatulas to gently lift the fish from the grate and then slide it from the spatula back onto the grate. The heads can be removed before serving, if desired.

- 2 teaspoons minced fresh marjoram
- 2 teaspoons kosher salt
- 1 teaspoon grated lemon zest, plus lemon wedges for serving
- ½ teaspoon pepper
- 4 (10- to 12-ounce) whole trout, gutted, fins snipped off with scissors
- 2 tablespoons mayonnaise
- ½ teaspoon honey
- 1 (13 by 9-inch) disposable aluminum pan (if using charcoal)

**1.** Place marjoram, lemon zest, and salt on cutting board and chop until finely minced and well combined. Rinse each fish under cold running water and pat dry with paper towels inside and out. Open up each fish and sprinkle marjoram mixture evenly over flesh of fish. Sprinkle each fish with pepper. Close up fish and let stand for 10 minutes. Stir mayonnaise and honey together. Brush mayonnaise mixture evenly over entire exterior of each fish.

**2A. FOR A CHARCOAL GRILL:** Using kitchen shears, poke twelve ½-inch holes in bottom of disposable pan. Open bottom vent completely and place disposable pan in center of grill. Light large chimney starter two-thirds filled with charcoal briquettes (4 quarts). When top coals are partially covered with ash, pour into even layer in disposable pan. Set cooking grate over coals with bars parallel to long side of disposable pan, cover, and open lid vent completely. Heat grill until hot, about 5 minutes.

**2B. FOR A GAS GRILL:** Turn all burners to high; cover; and heat grill until hot, about 15 minutes. Leave all burners on high.

#### FLIPPING WHOLE FISH ON THE GRILL

**1.** Slide spatula scant 1 inch under backbone edge and lift edge up.

**2.** Slide second spatula under, then remove first spatula, allowing fish to ease onto second spatula.

**3.** Place first spatula on top of fish, in same direction as second spatula; flip fish so it rests on second spatula, then ease fish onto grill.

**3.** Clean and oil cooking grate. Grill fish (directly over coals if using charcoal and with lid closed if using gas) until skin is browned and beginning to blister, 2 to 4 minutes. Using thin metal spatula, lift bottom of thick backbone edge of fish from cooking grate just enough to slide second thin metal spatula under fish. Remove first spatula, then use it to support raw side of fish as you use second spatula to flip fish over. Grill until second side is browned, beginning to blister, and thickest part of fish registers 130 to 135 degrees, 2 to 4 minutes. Transfer fish to platter and let rest for 5 minutes. Serve with lemon wedges.

## Grilled Fish Tacos

SERVES 6

WHY THIS RECIPE WORKS For a fish taco with fresh, bold flavors, we fired up the grill. For simplicity, we opted for skinless fillets instead of the traditional whole butterflied fish. Meaty swordfish held up on the grill better than flaky options like hake and cod. A thick paste featuring ancho and chipotle chile powders, oregano, and just a touch of citrus juice developed deep, flavorful charring on the grill without promoting sticking. Refreshing grilled pineapple salsa, avocado, and crunchy iceberg lettuce completed our tacos with flavor and texture contrasts. Mahi-mahi, tuna, and halibut fillets are all suitable substitutes for the swordfish; to ensure the best results, buy 1-inch-thick fillets and cut them in a similar fashion to the swordfish.

- 3 tablespoons vegetable oil
- 1 tablespoon ancho chile powder
- 2 teaspoons chipotle chile powder
- 1 teaspoon dried oregano
- 1 teaspoon ground coriander
- 2 garlic cloves, minced
- 1 teaspoon table salt
- 2 tablespoons tomato paste
- ½ cup orange juice
- 6 tablespoons lime juice (3 limes)
- 2 pounds skinless swordfish steaks, 1 inch thick, cut lengthwise into 1-inch-wide strips
- 1 pineapple, peeled, quartered lengthwise, cored, and each quarter halved lengthwise
- 1 jalapeño chile
- 18 (6-inch) corn tortillas
- 1 red bell pepper, stemmed, seeded, and cut into ¼-inch pieces
- 2 tablespoons minced fresh cilantro, plus extra for serving
- ½ head iceberg lettuce (4½ ounces), cored and sliced thin
- 1 avocado, halved, pitted, and sliced thin
- Lime wedges

**1.** Heat 2 tablespoons oil, ancho chile powder, and chipotle chile powder in 8-inch skillet over medium heat, stirring constantly, until fragrant and some bubbles form, 2 to 3 minutes. Add oregano, coriander, garlic, and salt and continue to cook until fragrant, about 30 seconds longer. Add tomato paste and, using spatula, mash tomato paste with spice mixture until combined, about 20 seconds. Stir in orange juice and 2 tablespoons lime juice. Cook, stirring constantly, until thoroughly mixed and reduced slightly, about 2 minutes. Transfer chile mixture to large bowl and cool for 15 minutes.

**2.** Add swordfish to bowl with chile mixture, and stir gently with rubber spatula to coat fish. Cover and refrigerate for at least 30 minutes or up to 2 hours.

**3A. FOR A CHARCOAL GRILL:** Open bottom vent completely. Light large chimney starter mounded with charcoal briquettes (7 quarts). When top coals are partially covered with ash, pour evenly over grill. Set cooking grate in place, cover, and open lid vent completely. Heat grill until hot, about 5 minutes.

**3B. FOR A GAS GRILL:** Turn all burners to high; cover; and heat grill until hot, about 15 minutes. Turn all burners to medium-high.

**4.** Clean cooking grate, then repeatedly brush grate with well-oiled paper towels until grate is black and glossy, 5 to 10 times. Brush both sides of pineapple with remaining 1 tablespoon oil. Place fish on half of grill. Place pineapple and jalapeño on other half. Cover and cook until fish, pineapple, and jalapeño have begun to brown, 3 to 5 minutes. Using thin spatula, flip fish, pineapple, and jalapeño. Cover and continue to cook until second sides of pineapple and jalapeño are browned and swordfish registers 130 degrees, 3 to 5 minutes. Transfer fish to large platter, flake into pieces, and tent with aluminum foil. Transfer pineapple and jalapeño to cutting board.

**5.** Clean cooking grate. Place half of tortillas on grill. Grill until softened and speckled with brown spots, 30 to 45 seconds per side. Wrap tortillas in dish towel or foil to keep warm until ready to use. Repeat with remaining tortillas.

**6.** When cool enough to handle, finely chop pineapple and jalapeño. Transfer to medium bowl and stir in bell pepper, cilantro, and remaining ¼ cup lime juice. Season with salt to taste. Top tortillas with flaked fish, pineapple salsa, lettuce, and avocado. Serve with lime wedges and extra cilantro.

## Grilled Scallops

SERVES 4

**WHY THIS RECIPE WORKS** Scallops are tricky to cook on the grill as they are usually overcooked by the time they develop a good sear, not to mention their tendency to stick to the grill. For great grilled scallops, we needed the hottest fire possible. The solution for a charcoal grill was a disposable aluminum pan—it corralled the coals in the center of the grill for a super-hot fire that gave us scallops with impressive char and juicy centers. Drying the scallops before cooking helped ensure browning, and threading them onto two side-by-side skewers made them easy to flip. To combat sticking, we lightly coated the scallops in a mixture of flour, cornstarch, oil, and sugar. We recommend buying "dry" scallops, which don't have additives and taste better than "wet." You will need eight to twelve 12-inch metal skewers. Serve with lemon wedges or Chile-Lime Vinaigrette (recipe follows).

- 1½ pounds large sea scallops, tendons removed
- 8–12 12-inch metal skewers
- 1 (13 by 9-inch) disposable aluminum roasting pan (if using charcoal)
- 2 tablespoons vegetable oil, plus extra for cooking grate
- 1 tablespoon all-purpose flour
- 1 teaspoon cornstarch
- 1 teaspoon sugar
- 1 teaspoon kosher salt
- ¼ teaspoon pepper
- Lemon wedges

**1.** Place scallops on rimmed baking sheet lined with clean dish towel. Place second clean dish towel on top of scallops and press gently on towel to blot liquid. Let scallops sit at room temperature, covered with towel, for 10 minutes. Thread 4 to 6 scallops, 1 flat side down, onto 1 skewer and then place second skewer through scallops parallel to and about ¼ inch from first. Return skewered scallops to towel- lined baking sheet; refrigerate, covered with second towel, while preparing grill.

**2A. FOR A CHARCOAL GRILL:** Open bottom vent completely. Light large chimney starter mounded with charcoal briquettes (7 quarts). Meanwhile, poke twelve ½-inch holes in bottom of disposable pan and place in center of grill. When top coals are partially covered with ash, empty coals into pan. Set cooking grate in place, cover, and open lid vent completely. Heat grill until hot, about 5 minutes.

**2B. FOR A GAS GRILL:** Turn all burners to high; cover; and heat grill until hot, about 15 minutes.

**3.** While grill heats, whisk oil, flour, cornstarch, and sugar together in small bowl. Remove towels from scallops. Brush both sides of skewered scallops with oil mixture and sprinkle with salt and pepper.

**4.** Clean cooking grate, then repeatedly brush grate with well-oiled paper towels until grate is black and glossy, 5 to 10 times.

**5.** Place skewered scallops directly on grill (directly over coals if using charcoal). Cook (covered if using gas) without moving scallops until lightly browned, 2½ to 4 minutes. Carefully flip skewers and continue to cook until second side of scallops is browned, sides are firm, and centers are opaque, 2 to 4 minutes longer. Serve immediately.

### Chile-Lime Vinaigrette

MAKES 1 cup

- 1 teaspoon grated lime zest plus 3 tablespoons juice (2 limes)
- 2 tablespoons honey
- 1 tablespoon sriracha
- 2 teaspoons fish sauce
- ½ cup vegetable oil

Whisk lime zest and juice, honey, sriracha, and fish sauce in medium bowl until combined. Whisking constantly, slowly drizzle in oil until emulsified.

## Grilled Scallops with Fennel and Orange Salad for Two

SERVES 2

**WHY THIS RECIPE WORKS** Grilled scallops need little embellishment—their sweet, briny richness becomes even more intense on a hot grill, and their exterior develops a flavorful, nicely charred crust. With just oil, salt, and pepper plus a sprinkling of ground pink peppercorns for color and fruity flavor, our scallops were ready for the grill. To turn our tender scallops into a satisfying supper, we created a simple salad of grilled fennel, orange pieces, and chopped mint to go with them. You will need four 12-inch metal skewers for this recipe. We recommend buying "dry" scallops, which don't have chemical additives and taste better than "wet." Dry scallops will look ivory or pinkish; wet scallops are bright white.

- 1 orange
- 1 fennel bulb, stalks discarded, bulb halved, cored, and sliced thin
- 1 tablespoon chopped fresh mint
- 2 tablespoons extra-virgin olive oil
- Table salt and pepper
- 8 large sea scallops, tendons removed
- 2 teaspoons pink peppercorns, crushed

**1.** Cut away peel and pith from orange. Quarter orange, then slice crosswise into ¼-inch-thick pieces. Toss orange, fennel, basil, and 1 tablespoon oil in bowl and season with salt and pepper to taste; set aside for serving.

**2.** Pat scallops dry with paper towels and thread onto doubled 12-inch metal skewers, 4 scallops per doubled skewer. Brush scallops with remaining 1 tablespoon oil and season with peppercorns, salt, and pepper.

**3A. FOR A CHARCOAL GRILL:** Open bottom vent completely. Light large chimney starter mounded with charcoal briquettes (7 quarts). When top coals are partially covered with ash, pour evenly over grill. Set cooking grate in place, cover, and open lid vent completely. Heat grill until hot, about 5 minutes.

**3B. FOR A GAS GRILL:** Turn all burners to high, cover, and heat grill until hot, about 15 minutes.

**4.** Clean cooking grate, then repeatedly brush grate with well-oiled paper towels until grate is black and glossy, 5 to 10 times. Place scallop skewers on grill and cook (covered if using gas), turning as needed, until lightly charred and centers of scallops are opaque, about 6 minutes. Serve with salad.

## Grilled Bacon-Wrapped Scallops

**SERVES 4**

**WHY THIS RECIPE WORKS** Smoky, salty bacon beautifully accents sweet, succulent scallops, and we thought taking it to the grill would make a great thing even better. We set out to make this classic appetizer into a grilled entrée. We knew we needed to parcook the bacon to prevent the grease from dripping into the fire and incinerating our scallops. Microwaving proved a perfect solution: We layered strips of bacon between paper towels (to absorb grease) and weighed them down with a second plate to prevent curling. We wrapped each strip of bacon around two scallops for an ideal scallop to bacon ratio. Tossing the scallops in melted butter added richness, and pressing the scallops firmly together on the skewers prevented them from spinning when flipped. A two-level fire cooked both scallops and bacon to perfection. A spritz of grilled lemon juice and a sprinkling of chopped chives gave the dish a bright finish. Use ordinary bacon, as thick-cut bacon will take too long to crisp on the grill. When wrapping the scallops, the bacon slice should fit around both scallops, overlapping just enough to be skewered through both ends. We recommend buying "dry" scallops, which don't have chemical additives and taste better than "wet." Dry scallops will look ivory or pinkish; wet scallops are bright white. This recipe was developed with large sea scallops (sold 10 to 20 per pound).

- 12 slices bacon
- 24 large sea scallops, tendons removed
- 3 tablespoons unsalted butter, melted
- ½ teaspoon table salt
- ⅛ teaspoon pepper
- 2 lemons, halved
- ¼ cup chopped fresh chives

**1.** Place 4 layers paper towels on large plate and arrange 6 slices bacon over towels in single layer. Top with 4 more paper towels and remaining 6 slices bacon. Cover with 2 layers of paper towels; place second large plate on top and press gently to flatten. Microwave until fat begins to render but bacon is still pliable, about 4 minutes. Toss scallops, butter, salt, and pepper together in bowl until scallops are thoroughly coated with butter.

**2.** Press 2 scallops together, side to side, and wrap with 1 slice bacon, trimming excess as necessary. Thread onto skewer through bacon. Repeat with remaining scallops and bacon, threading 3 bundles onto each of 4 skewers.

**3A. FOR A CHARCOAL GRILL:** Open bottom vent completely. Light large chimney starter filled with charcoal briquettes (6 quarts). When top coals are partially covered with ash, pour two-thirds evenly over half of grill, then pour remaining coals over other half of grill. Set cooking grate in place, cover, and open lid vent completely. Heat grill until hot, about 5 minutes.

**3B. FOR A GAS GRILL:** Turn all burners to high, cover, and heat grill until hot, about 15 minutes. Leave primary burner on high and turn other burner(s) to medium.

**4.** Clean and oil cooking grate. Place skewers, bacon side down, and lemon halves, cut side down, on cooler side of grill. Cook (covered, if using gas) until bacon is crispy on first side, about 4 minutes. Flip skewers onto other bacon side and cook until crispy, about 4 minutes longer. Flip skewers scallop side down and move to hot side of grill. Grill until sides of scallops are firm and centers are opaque, about 4 minutes on 1 side only. Transfer skewers to platter, squeeze lemon over, and sprinkle with chives. Serve.

## Grilled Shrimp Skewers

**SERVES 4**

**WHY THIS RECIPE WORKS** Really great grilled shrimp—tender, moist, and flavorful—are hard to come by. Usually, they're overcooked and rubbery, giving the jaws a workout, thanks to their quick cooking time and the high temperature of the grill. Grilling shrimp in their shells can guarantee juiciness, but the seasoning tends to be lost when the shells are pulled off. We wanted tender, juicy, boldly seasoned grilled shrimp, with the flavor in the shrimp and not on our fingers. Our decision to go with peeled shrimp for this recipe meant we had to revisit how we traditionally grilled shrimp. First we eliminated brining, which created waterlogged shrimp and hindered caramelization. Then we set the shrimp over a screaming-hot fire. This worked well with jumbo shrimp, but smaller shrimp overcooked before charring. With jumbo shrimp costing as much as $25 per pound, we decided against them. They did give us an idea, though. For our next step, we created faux jumbo shrimp by cramming a skewer with several extra-large shrimp pressed tightly together. Our final revision was to take the shrimp off the fire before they were completely cooked (but after they had picked up attractive grill marks). We finished cooking them in a heated sauce waiting on the cool side of the grill; this final simmer gave them tons of flavor. Prepare the sauce ingredients while the grill is heating. To fit all the shrimp on the cooking grate at once, you will need three 14-inch metal skewers. Serve with grilled bread.

- 1½ pounds extra-large shrimp (21 to 25 per pound), peeled and deveined (see page 523)
- 2–3 tablespoons olive oil
- Table salt and pepper
- ¼ teaspoon sugar
- 1 recipe sauce (recipe follows)
- Lemon wedges

**1.** Pat shrimp dry with paper towels. Thread the shrimp onto 3 skewers, alternating direction of heads and tails. Brush both sides of shrimp with oil and season with salt and pepper. Sprinkle 1 side of each skewer evenly with sugar.

**2A. FOR A CHARCOAL GRILL:** Open bottom vent completely. Light large chimney starter filled with charcoal briquettes (6 quarts). When top coals are partially covered with ash, pour evenly over half of grill. Set cooking grate in place, cover, and open lid vent completely. Heat grill until hot, about 5 minutes.

**2B. FOR A GAS GRILL:** Turn all burners to high, cover, and heat grill until hot, about 15 minutes. Leave primary burner on high and turn other burner(s) to medium-low.

**3.** Clean cooking grate, then repeatedly brush grate with well-oiled paper towels until grate is black and glossy, 5 to 10 times. Place disposable pan with sauce ingredients on hot side of grill and cook, stirring occasionally, until hot, 1 to 3 minutes. Move pan to cool side of grill.

**4.** Place shrimp skewers sugared side down on hot side of grill and use tongs to push shrimp together on skewers if they have separated. Cook shrimp until lightly charred, 4 to 5 minutes. Using tongs, flip and continue to cook until second side is pink and slightly translucent, 1 to 2 minutes longer.

**5.** Using potholder, carefully lift each skewer from grill and use tongs to slide shrimp off skewers into pan with sauce. Toss shrimp and sauce to combine. Place pan on hot side of grill and cook, stirring, until shrimp are opaque throughout, about 30 seconds. Remove from the grill, add remaining sauce ingredients, and toss to combine. Transfer to serving platter and serve with lemon wedges.

### ARRANGING SHRIMP ON A SKEWER

Pass the skewer through the center of each shrimp. As you add shrimp to the skewer, alternate the directions of the heads and tails for a compact arrangement of shrimp. The shrimp should fit snugly against one another.

### Chermoula Sauce for Shrimp Skewers

- 1 small red bell pepper, stemmed, seeded, and diced very small (about ½ cup)
- 4 tablespoons extra-virgin olive oil
- ½ small red onion, minced (about ⅓ cup)
- 1 teaspoon paprika
- ½ teaspoon ground cumin
- ¼ teaspoon cayenne pepper
- 3 cloves garlic, minced
- ⅛ teaspoon table salt
- Disposable 10-inch aluminum pie plate
- ⅓ cup minced fresh cilantro leaves
- 2 tablespoons fresh lemon juice from 1 lemon

Combine bell pepper, oil, onion, paprika, cumin, cayenne, garlic, and salt in pan. Cook over hot side of grill, stirring occasionally, until vegetables soften, about 5 minutes (2 or 3 minutes longer if using gas grill); transfer to cooler side of grill and proceed to grill shrimp, adding cilantro and lemon juice just before serving.

## Grilled Shrimp and Vegetable Kebabs

**SERVES** 4 to 6

**WHY THIS RECIPE WORKS** Combined shrimp and vegetable kebabs are notoriously difficult to cook because the shrimp inevitably overcooks in the time it takes most vegetables to pass from raw to their crisp-tender ideal. As a result, you end up with either overcooked shrimp or undercooked vegetables. This recipe works by pairing slower cooking jumbo shrimp with soft, quick-cooking vegetables. We nestled mushrooms into the curve of the shrimp on the skewer to better insulate the shrimp and extend their cooking time, and we cut the vegetables to mimic the profile of the shrimp, so the entire skewer made contact with the grill, promoting even cooking. Finally, we precooked some vegetables in the microwave before skewering them to give them a head start. Simply seasoning with oil and pepper allowed the kebabs to char beautifully on the grill, and dressing them with a fresh lemon-herb vinaigrette while still hot from the fire finished the dish in style. Small mushrooms about 1¼ to 1½ inches in diameter work best here. If using larger mushrooms, halve them before microwaving. You will need eight 12-inch metal skewers for this recipe.

**SHRIMP**

- 2 tablespoons table salt for brining
- 2 tablespoons sugar for brining
- 1½ pounds jumbo shrimp (16 to 20 per pound), peeled and deveined

- 3 large red or yellow bell peppers, stemmed, seeded, and cut into ¾-inch-wide by 3-inch-long strips
- ¼ teaspoon plus ⅛ teaspoon table salt, divided
- 24 cremini mushrooms, trimmed
- 12 scallions, cut into 3-inch lengths
- 2 tablespoons vegetable oil
- ¼ teaspoon pepper

VINAIGRETTE

- ¼ cup lemon juice (2 lemons)
- ¼ cup extra-virgin olive oil
- 2 teaspoons minced fresh thyme
- 1 garlic clove, minced
- ½ teaspoon table salt
- ¼ teaspoon Dijon mustard
- ⅛ teaspoon pepper

**1. FOR THE SHRIMP:** Dissolve 2 tablespoons salt and sugar in 1 quart cold water in large container. Submerge shrimp in brine, cover, and refrigerate for 15 minutes. Remove shrimp from brine and pat dry with paper towels.

**2.** Line large microwave-safe plate with double layer of paper towels. Spread half of bell peppers skin side down in even layer on plate and sprinkle with ⅛ teaspoon salt. Microwave for 2 minutes. Transfer peppers, still on towels, to cutting board and let cool. Repeat with fresh paper towels and remaining bell peppers and ⅛ teaspoon salt.

**3.** Line second plate with double layer of paper towels. Spread mushrooms in even layer and sprinkle with remaining ⅛ teaspoon salt. Microwave for 3 minutes. Transfer mushrooms, still on towels, to cutting board and let cool.

**4.** Lay one shrimp on cutting board and run 12-inch metal skewer through center. Thread mushroom onto skewer through sides of cap, pushing so it nestles tightly into curve of shrimp. Follow mushroom with 2 pieces scallion and 2 pieces bell pepper, skewering so vegetables and shrimp form even layer. Repeat shrimp and vegetable sequence two more times. When skewer is full, gently press ingredients so they fit snugly together in center of each skewer. Skewer remaining shrimp and vegetables on 7 more skewers for total of 8 kebabs. Brush each side of kebabs with vegetable oil and sprinkle with pepper.

**5A. FOR A CHARCOAL GRILL:** Open bottom vent completely. Light large chimney starter mounded with charcoal briquettes (7 quarts). When top coals are partially covered with ash, pour evenly over grill. Set cooking grate in place, cover, and open lid vent completely. Heat grill until hot, about 5 minutes.

**5B. FOR A GAS GRILL:** Turn all burners to high; cover; and heat grill until hot, about 15 minutes. Leave all burners on high.

**6.** For the vinaigrette: While grill heats, whisk all ingredients together in bowl.

**7.** Clean and oil cooking grate. Place kebabs on grill and grill (covered if using gas) until charred, about 2½ minutes. Flip skewers and grill until second side is charred and shrimp are cooked through, 2 to 3 minutes, moving skewers as needed to ensure even cooking. Transfer skewers to serving platter. Rewhisk vinaigrette and drizzle over kebabs. Serve.

## Grilled Swordfish Skewers with Tomato-Scallion Caponata

**SERVES** 4 to 6

**WHY THIS RECIPE WORKS** Swordfish is a favorite fish to grill along the Mediterranean and beyond. It has a robust taste all its own and needs costarring ingredients with just as much oomph. For our skewers, we paired swordfish with a Sicilian-inspired grilled caponata. As a base for the caponata, we grilled cherry tomatoes, lemons, and scallions alongside the swordfish and added an aromatic blend of warm spices for a potent sauce to complement the fish. Once grilled, the lemon transformed from tart and acidic to sweet. Rubbing the swordfish with a bit of ground coriander added complexity and provided flavor that popped with the tomato, scallions, and a final sprinkling of fresh basil. If swordfish isn't available, you can substitute halibut. You will need six 12-inch metal skewers for this recipe.

- 1½ pounds skinless swordfish steaks, 1¼ to 1½ inches thick, cut into 1¼-inch pieces
- 5 teaspoons ground coriander
- Table salt and pepper
- 12 ounces cherry tomatoes
- 1 small eggplant (12 ounces), cut crosswise on bias into ½-inch-thick ovals
- 6 scallions, trimmed
- ¼ cup extra-virgin olive oil
- 1 tablespoon grated lemon zest, plus 2 lemons, halved
- 1½ tablespoons honey
- 2 garlic cloves, minced
- 1 teaspoon ground cumin
- ¼ teaspoon ground cinnamon
- ⅛ teaspoon ground nutmeg
- ¼ cup pitted kalamata olives, chopped
- 2 tablespoons minced fresh basil

1. Pat swordfish dry with paper towels, rub with 1 tablespoon coriander, and season with salt and pepper. Thread fish onto three 12-inch metal skewers. Thread tomatoes onto three 12-inch metal skewers. Brush swordfish, tomatoes, eggplant, and scallions with 2 tablespoons oil.

2A. **FOR A CHARCOAL GRILL:** Open bottom vent completely. Light large chimney starter filled with charcoal briquettes (6 quarts). When top coals are partially covered with ash, pour evenly over grill. Set cooking grate in place, cover, and open lid vent completely. Heat grill until hot, about 5 minutes.

2B. **FOR A GAS GRILL:** Turn all burners to high, cover, and heat grill until hot, about 15 minutes. Leave all burners on high.

3. Clean cooking grate, then repeatedly brush grate with well-oiled paper towels until black and glossy, 5 to 10 times. Place swordfish, tomatoes, eggplant, scallions, and lemon halves on grill. Cook (covered if using gas), turning as needed, until swordfish flakes apart when gently prodded with paring knife and registers 130 degrees and tomatoes, eggplant, scallions, and lemon halves are softened and lightly charred, 5 to 15 minutes. Transfer items to serving platter as they finish grilling and tent loosely with aluminum foil. Let swordfish rest while finishing caponata.

4. Whisk remaining 2 teaspoons coriander, remaining 2 tablespoons oil, lemon zest, honey, garlic, cumin, ¾ teaspoon salt, ¼ teaspoon pepper, cinnamon, and nutmeg together in large bowl. Microwave, stirring occasionally, until fragrant, about 1 minute. Once lemons are cool enough to handle, squeeze into fine-mesh strainer set over bowl with oil-honey mixture, extracting as much juice as possible; whisk to combine. Stir in olives.

5. Using tongs, slide tomatoes off skewers onto cutting board. Coarsely chop tomatoes, eggplant, and scallions, transfer to bowl with dressing, and toss gently to combine. Season with salt and pepper to taste. Remove swordfish from skewers, sprinkle with basil, and serve with caponata.

## Grilled Southern Shrimp Burgers

**MAKES** 4 burgers

**WHY THIS RECIPE WORKS** Shrimp burgers are a long-standing specialty in coastal towns in South Carolina and Georgia. We set out to develop a recipe for our ideal shrimp burger that would hold up on the grill and packed with flavors. After early testing we decided we needed a combination of textures—finely chopped shrimp to help bind the burgers, as well as some larger, bite-size chunks. Pulsing the shrimp in the food processor easily produced an inconsistent texture. As for a binder, we wanted as little as possible. Most recipes use some combination of mayonnaise, egg, and bread crumbs. The mayonnaise was adding much-needed fat and moisture (shrimp have little fat of their own), but we found we could eliminate the egg and decrease the bread crumbs. Since packing the patties makes them rubbery, we handled them as little as possible, instead allowing them to firm up in the refrigerator. Be sure to use raw, not cooked, shrimp here. Dry the shrimp thoroughly before processing, or the burgers will be mushy. Handle the burgers gently when shaping and grilling or they will be dense and may break apart during cooking. Serve with Chipotle Chili Mayonnaise if desired. If using shrimp with sodium added as a preservative, omit the salt in the recipe.

- 1 slice hearty white sandwich bread, torn into large pieces
- 1½ pounds extra-large shrimp (21 to 25 per pound), peeled, deveined (see page 523), and patted dry
- ¼ cup mayonnaise
- 2 scallions, minced
- 2 tablespoons minced fresh parsley
- 2 teaspoons grated fresh lemon zest
- Pinch cayenne pepper
- ¼ teaspoon table salt
- ⅛ teaspoon pepper

1. Pulse bread in food processor to fine crumbs, 10 to 15 pulses; transfer to bowl. Pulse shrimp in now-empty food processor until some pieces are finely minced and others are coarsely chopped, about 7 pulses. Transfer shrimp to large bowl.

2. Combine mayonnaise, scallions, parsley, lemon zest, cayenne, salt, and pepper in large bowl until uniform, then gently fold into processed shrimp until just combined. Sprinkle bread crumbs over mixture and gently fold until thoroughly incorporated.

3. Divide shrimp mixture into 4 equal portions and shape each into 1-inch-thick patty. Cover and refrigerate patties for at least 30 minutes or up to 3 hours.

4A. **FOR A CHARCOAL GRILL:** Open bottom grill vents completely. Light large chimney starter three-quarters full with charcoal briquettes (75 briquettes; 4½ quarts). When coals are hot, pour evenly over grill. Set cooking grate in place, cover, and heat grill until hot, about 5 minutes.

4B. **FOR A GAS GRILL:** Turn all burners to high, cover, and heat grill until hot, about 15 minutes. Turn all burners to medium-high. (Adjust burners as needed to maintain medium-hot fire.)

5. Clean and oil cooking grate. Lightly brush tops of burgers with oil, lay them on grill, oiled side down, and lightly brush other side with oil. Cook burgers, without pressing on them, until lightly browned and register 140 to 145 degrees, 10 to 14 minutes, flipping halfway through. Transfer burgers to platter, tent loosely with foil, and let rest for 5 minutes before serving.

### Chipotle Chile Mayonnaise

- ½ cup mayonnaise
- ½ cup sour cream
- 4 teaspoons minced chipotle chile in adobo sauce
- 1 tablespoon minced fresh cilantro
- 2 teaspoons lime juice
- 1 garlic clove, minced
- ½ teaspoon salt

Whisk all ingredients together in bowl. Cover and refrigerate until flavors meld, about 30 minutes. (Mayonnaise can be refrigerated in an airtight container for up to 4 days.)

## Paella on the Grill

SERVES 8

**WHY THIS RECIPE WORKS** Grilling paella lends the dish subtle smoke flavor and a particularly rich crust and makes it a great dish for summer entertaining. In place of a traditional paella pan, we cooked ours in a large, sturdy roasting pan that maximized the amount of socarrat, the prized caramelized rice crust that forms on the bottom of the pan. Building a large fire and fueling it with fresh coals (which ignited during cooking) ensured that the heat output would last throughout cooking. To ensure that the various components finished cooking at the same time, we staggered the addition of the proteins. This recipe was developed with a light-colored 16 by 13.5-inch triply roasting pan; however, it can be made in any heavy roasting pan that measures at least 14 by 11 inches. If your roasting pan is dark in color, the cooking times will be on the lower end of the ranges given. The recipe can also be made in a 15- to 17-inch paella pan. If littlenecks are unavailable, use 1½ pounds shrimp in step 1 and season them with ½ teaspoon salt.

- 1½ pounds boneless, skinless chicken thighs, trimmed and halved crosswise
- 1¾ teaspoons table salt, divided
- 1 teaspoon pepper
- 12 ounces jumbo shrimp (16 to 20 per pound), peeled and deveined
- 6 tablespoons extra-virgin olive oil, divided
- 6 garlic cloves, minced, divided
- 1¾ teaspoons smoked hot paprika, divided
- 3 tablespoons tomato paste
- 4 cups chicken broth
- ⅔ cup dry sherry
- 1 (8-ounce) bottle clam juice
- Pinch saffron threads (optional)
- 1 onion, chopped fine
- ½ cup roasted red peppers, chopped fine
- 3 cups Arborio rice
- 1 pound littleneck clams, scrubbed
- 1 pound Spanish-style chorizo, cut into ½-inch pieces
- 1 cup frozen peas, thawed
- Lemon wedges

**1.** Place chicken on large plate and sprinkle both sides with 1 teaspoon salt and pepper. Toss shrimp with 1 tablespoon oil, ½ teaspoon garlic, ¼ teaspoon paprika, and ¼ teaspoon salt in bowl until evenly coated. Set aside.

**2.** Heat 1 tablespoon oil in medium saucepan over medium heat until shimmering. Add remaining garlic and cook, stirring constantly, until garlic sticks to bottom of saucepan and begins to brown, about 1 minute. Add tomato paste and remaining 1½ teaspoons paprika and continue to cook, stirring constantly, until dark brown bits form on bottom of saucepan, about 1 minute. Add broth; sherry; clam juice; and saffron, if using. Increase heat to high and bring to boil. Remove pan from heat and set aside.

**3A. FOR A CHARCOAL GRILL:** Open bottom vent completely. Light large chimney starter mounded with charcoal briquettes (7 quarts). When top coals are partially covered with ash, pour evenly over grill. Using tongs, arrange 20 unlit briquettes evenly over coals. Set cooking grate in place, cover, and open lid vent completely. Heat grill until hot, about 5 minutes.

**3B. FOR A GAS GRILL:** Turn all burners to high; cover; and heat grill until hot, about 15 minutes. Leave all burners on high.

**4.** Clean and oil cooking grate. Place chicken on grill and cook until both sides are lightly browned, 5 to 7 minutes total. Return chicken to plate. Clean cooking grate.

**5.** Place roasting pan on grill (turning burners to medium-high if using gas) and add remaining ¼ cup oil. When oil begins to shimmer, add onion, red peppers, and remaining ½ teaspoon salt. Cook, stirring frequently, until onion begins to brown, 4 to 7 minutes. Add rice (turning burners to medium if using gas) and stir until grains are well coated with oil.

**6.** Arrange chicken around perimeter of pan. Pour broth mixture and any accumulated juices from chicken over rice. Smooth rice into even layer, making sure nothing sticks to sides of pan and no rice rests atop chicken. When liquid reaches gentle simmer, place shrimp in center of pan in single layer. Arrange clams in center of pan, evenly distributing with shrimp and pushing hinge sides of clams into rice slightly so they stand up. Distribute chorizo evenly over surface of rice. Cook, moving and rotating pan to maintain gentle simmer across entire surface of pan, until rice is almost cooked through, 12 to 18 minutes. (If using gas, heat can also be adjusted to maintain simmer.)

**7.** Sprinkle peas evenly over paella; cover grill; and cook until liquid is fully absorbed and rice on bottom of pan sizzles, 5 to 8 minutes. Continue to cook, uncovered, checking frequently, until uniform golden-brown crust forms on bottom of pan, 8 to 15 minutes longer. (Rotate and slide pan around grill as necessary to ensure even crust formation.) Remove from grill, cover with foil, and let stand for 10 minutes. Serve with lemon wedges.

## New England Clambake

**SERVES** 4 **SEASON 26**

**WHY THIS RECIPE WORKS** Clambakes are a rite of summer all along the East Coast. Shellfish and vegetables are layered with seaweed and piled on top of white-hot rocks in a wide sandpit. The food then steams beneath a wet tarp until it's done. The biggest challenge in moving this operation to the grill was that our grill was only big enough to handle half the ingredients at a time. Since charcoal dies down as it burns, we had to decide which items would need the hotter temperature of the first round of grilling but could also sit the longest before serving. We chose to lead off with the corn, sausage, and potatoes and follow with the lobsters and clams. We also gave the potatoes a jump-start in the microwave and skewered them to make them more manageable. This grilled clambake captured all the smoky flavor of the traditional version—with no shovel required. Look for potatoes that are 1 to 2 inches in diameter; if your potatoes are larger, quarter them and increase the microwaving time as needed in step 2. Because the skewers go into the microwave, use wooden, not metal, skewers.

- ½ cup table salt, for brining
- 4 ears corn, husks and silk removed
- ½ teaspoon plus ⅛ teaspoon pepper, divided
- 1 pound small red potatoes, unpeeled, halved
- 2 (12-inch) wooden skewers
- 4 tablespoons unsalted butter, melted, divided, plus extra for serving
- ¾ teaspoon table salt, divided
- 2 (1¼- to 1½-pound) live lobsters
- 1 pound kielbasa
- 2 pounds littleneck clams, scrubbed
- Lemon wedges

**1.** Dissolve ½ cup salt in 4 quarts cold water in large pot. Add corn and soak for at least 30 minutes or up to 8 hours. Before grilling, remove corn from water, pat dry with paper towels, and sprinkle with ¼ teaspoon pepper.

**2.** Skewer potatoes, then lay them in single layer on large plate. Brush with 1 tablespoon melted butter and sprinkle with ¼ teaspoon salt and ⅛ teaspoon pepper. Microwave until potatoes begin to soften, about 6 minutes, flipping them halfway through microwaving. Brush with 1 tablespoon melted butter.

**3.** Split lobsters in half lengthwise, removing internal organs. Using back of chef's knife, whack 1 side of each claw to crack shell. Brush tail meat with 1 tablespoon melted butter, and sprinkle with remaining ½ teaspoon salt and remaining ¼ teaspoon pepper.

**4A. FOR A CHARCOAL GRILL:** Open bottom vent completely. Light large chimney starter filled with charcoal briquettes (6 quarts). When top coals are partially covered with ash, pour evenly over grill. Set cooking grate in place, cover, and open lid vent completely. Heat grill until hot, about 5 minutes.

**4B. FOR A GAS GRILL:** Turn all burners to high, cover, and heat grill until hot, about 15 minutes. Adjust burners as needed to maintain grill temperature at 325 degrees.

**5.** Clean and oil cooking grate. Place kielbasa, corn, and skewered potatoes on grill. Cook until kielbasa is seared and hot throughout, corn is lightly charred, and potatoes are brown and tender, 10 to 16 minutes, turning as needed. Transfer vegetables and sausage as they finish cooking to serving platter, and tent with aluminum foil.

**6.** Lay lobsters, flesh side down, and clams on grill. Cook until clams have opened and lobsters are cooked through, 8 to 14 minutes, flipping lobsters and brushing lobster tail meat with remaining 1 tablespoon butter halfway through grilling. As lobsters and clams finish cooking, transfer them to serving platter with vegetables and sausage, preserving any juices that have accumulated inside their shells.

**7.** Slice kielbasa into 1-inch pieces and remove skewers from potatoes. Serve with lemon wedges and extra melted butter. Use lobster picks to reach meat inside claws and knuckles.

## Grilled Cauliflower

**SERVES** 4 to 6

**WHY THIS RECIPE WORKS** Char, caramelization, and smoke bring new dimension to cauliflower. To make grilled cauliflower with a tender interior and a nicely browned exterior, we first microwaved it until it was cooked through and then briefly grilled it to pick up color and flavor. To ensure that the cauliflower held up on the grill and to provide sufficient surface area for browning, we cut the head into large wedges. Dunking the cauliflower in a salt and sugar solution before microwaving seasoned it, even in the nooks and crannies. Look for cauliflower with densely packed florets that feels heavy for its size. Using tongs or a thin metal spatula to gently flip the wedges helps keep them intact. This dish stands well on its own, but to dress it up, serve it sprinkled with 1 tablespoon of Pistachio Dukkah; Almond, Raisin, and Caper Relish; or Za'atar.

- 1 head cauliflower (2 pounds)
- ¼ cup table salt
- 2 tablespoons sugar
- 2 tablespoons extra-virgin olive oil
- 1 tablespoon minced fresh chives
- Lemon wedges

**1.** Trim outer leaves of cauliflower and cut stem flush with bottom. Cut head through core into 6 equal wedges so that core and florets remain intact.

**2.** Whisk 2 cups water, salt, and sugar in medium bowl until salt and sugar dissolve. Holding wedges by core, gently dunk in salt-sugar mixture until evenly moistened (do not dry—residual water will help cauliflower steam). Transfer wedges, rounded side down, to large plate and cover with inverted large bowl. Microwave until cauliflower is translucent and tender and paring knife inserted in thickest stem of florets (not into core) meets no resistance, 14 to 16 minutes.

**3.** Carefully (bowl and cauliflower will be very hot) transfer cauliflower to paper towel–lined plate and pat dry. (Microwaved cauliflower can be held at room temperature for up to 2 hours.)

**4.** Brush cut sides of wedges with 1 tablespoon oil. Place cauliflower, cut side down, on grill over medium-high heat and cook, covered, until well browned with spots of charring, 3 to 4 minutes. Using tongs or thin metal spatula, flip cauliflower and cook second cut side until well browned with spots of charring, 3 to 4 minutes. Flip again so cauliflower is sitting on rounded edge and cook until browned, 1 to 2 minutes.

**5.** Transfer cauliflower to large platter. Drizzle with remaining 1 tablespoon oil, sprinkle with chives, and serve with lemon wedges.

### Pistachio Dukkah

**MAKES** about ⅓ cup

This Egyptian spice blend can be sprinkled on a plate of extra-virgin olive oil and served as a dip for bread or sprinkled over soups, grain dishes, or bean salads as a garnish. If you do not own a spice grinder, you can process the spices in a mini food processor.

- 1½ tablespoons sesame seeds, toasted
- 1½ teaspoons coriander seeds, toasted
- ¾ teaspoon cumin seeds, toasted
- ½ teaspoon fennel seeds, toasted
- 2 tablespoons shelled pistachios, toasted and chopped fine
- ½ teaspoon table salt
- ½ teaspoon pepper

Process sesame seeds in spice grinder or mortar and pestle until coarsely ground; transfer to bowl. Process coriander seeds, cumin seeds, and fennel seeds in now-empty grinder until finely ground. Transfer to bowl with sesame seeds. Stir pistachios, salt, and pepper into sesame mixture until combined. (Dukkah can be refrigerated in an airtight container for up to 1 month.)

### Almond, Raisin, and Caper Relish

**MAKES** about ½ cup

Champagne vinegar can be used in place of white wine vinegar and regular raisins in place of golden raisins, if desired.

- 2 tablespoons golden raisins
- 2 tablespoons hot water
- 1 teaspoon white wine vinegar
- ¼ cup almonds, toasted and chopped fine
- 1 tablespoon capers, rinsed, drained, and chopped fine
- 1 teaspoon minced fresh parsley
- Pinch red pepper flakes
- 3–4 tablespoons extra-virgin olive oil
- Table salt and pepper

Combine raisins and hot water in small bowl and let stand for 5 minutes. Drain raisins and chop fine. Toss raisins and vinegar in bowl, then stir in almonds, capers, parsley, and pepper flakes. Stir in 3 tablespoons oil; mixture should be well moistened. If still dry, add remaining 1 tablespoon oil. Season with salt and pepper to taste.

### Za'atar

**MAKES** about ⅓ cup

Try sprinkling some of this Middle Eastern spice mix over olive oil as a dip for bread. You can also use it in grain dishes or as a flavorful topping for hummus or other dips.

- 2 tablespoons dried thyme
- 1 tablespoon dried oregano
- 1½ tablespoons sumac
- 1 tablespoon sesame seeds, toasted
- ¼ teaspoon table salt

Process thyme and oregano in spice grinder or mortar and pestle until finely ground and powdery. Transfer to bowl and stir in sumac, sesame seeds, and salt. (Za'atar can be stored at room temperature in airtight container for up to 1 year.)

## Grilled Corn with Flavored Butter

**SERVES** 4 to 6

**WHY THIS RECIPE WORKS** Grilled corn is a go-to summer treat, but we wanted a way to spice it up—literally. To incorporate flavorful herbs and spices into the corn, we found that a two-step approach worked best. First, we brushed the ears with vegetable oil and seared them over a hot grill fire. When the corn had a nice char, we moved the ears to a disposable pan on the grill and added a dollop of butter seasoned with herbs and other aromatic ingredients. The butter infused every kernel with extra flavor, and the disposable pan made the process simple and prevented butter-induced flare-ups on the grill. Use a disposable aluminum roasting pan that is at least 2¾ inches deep.

- 1 recipe Basil and Lemon Butter
- 1 (13 by 9-inch) disposable aluminum roasting pan
- 8 ears corn, husks and silk removed
- 2 tablespoons vegetable oil

**1.** Place flavored butter in disposable pan. Brush corn evenly with oil and sprinkle with salt and pepper.

**2.** Grill corn over hot fire, turning occasionally, until lightly charred on all sides, 5 to 9 minutes. Transfer corn to pan and cover tightly with aluminum foil.

**3.** Place pan on grill and cook, shaking pan frequently, until butter is sizzling, about 3 minutes. Remove pan from grill and carefully remove foil, allowing steam to escape away from you. Serve corn, spooning any butter in pan over individual ears.

### Basil and Lemon Butter

Serve with lemon wedges, if desired.

- 6 tablespoons unsalted butter, softened
- 2 tablespoons chopped fresh basil
- 1 tablespoon minced fresh parsley
- 1 teaspoon grated lemon zest
- ½ teaspoon table salt
- ¼ teaspoon pepper

Combine all ingredients in small bowl.

## Mexican-Style Grilled Corn

**SERVES** 6

**WHY THIS RECIPE WORKS** In Mexico, street vendors add kick to grilled corn by slathering it with a creamy, spicy sauce. The corn takes on a sweet, charred flavor, which is heightened by the lime juice and chili powder in the cheesy sauce. We wanted to develop our own rendition of this street fare. We ditched the husks, coated the ears with oil to prevent sticking, and grilled them directly on the grate. Over a single-level fire, the corn emerged nicely smoky but insufficiently charred, so we pushed all the coals to one side to create a modified two-level fire, allowing the ears to cook closer to the coals. The traditional base for the sauce is crema, a thick, soured Mexican cream but we used a combination of mayonnaise and sour cream. Most recipes call for queso fresco or cotija, but if these aren't available, Pecorino Romano is a good substitute. We included the usual seasonings of cilantro, lime juice, garlic, and chili powder. To provide more depth, we added chili powder to the oil used for coating the corn; once heated on the grill, the chili powder bloomed with a full flavor that penetrated the corn kernels. If you can find queso fresco or cotija, use either in place of the Pecorino Romano. If you prefer the corn spicy, add the optional cayenne pepper.

- 1½ ounces Pecorino Romano cheese, grated (¾ cup)
- ¼ cup mayonnaise
- 3 tablespoons sour cream
- 3 tablespoons minced fresh cilantro
- 4 teaspoons lime juice
- 1 garlic clove, minced
- ¾ teaspoon chili powder
- ¼ teaspoon pepper
- ¼ teaspoon cayenne pepper (optional)
- 4 teaspoons vegetable oil
- ¼ teaspoon table salt
- 6 ears corn, husks and silk removed

**1A. FOR A CHARCOAL GRILL:** Open bottom vent completely. Light large chimney starter filled with charcoal briquettes (6 quarts). When top coals are partially covered with ash, pour evenly over half of grill. Set cooking grate in place, cover, and open lid vent completely. Heat grill until hot, about 5 minutes.

**1B. FOR A GAS GRILL:** Turn all burners to high, cover, and heat grill until hot, about 15 minutes.

**2.** Meanwhile, combine Pecorino, mayonnaise, sour cream, cilantro, lime juice, garlic, ¼ teaspoon chili powder, pepper, and cayenne, if using, in large bowl and set aside. In second large bowl, combine oil, salt, and remaining ½ teaspoon chili powder. Add corn to oil mixture and toss to coat evenly.

**3.** Clean and oil cooking grate. Place corn on grill (hot side if using charcoal) and cook (covered if using gas) until lightly charred on all sides, 7 to 12 minutes, turning as needed. Place corn in bowl with cheese mixture, toss to coat evenly, and serve.

## Grilled Baba Ghanoush

**MAKES** 2 cups

**WHY THIS RECIPE WORKS** Baba ghanoush showcases eggplant's full potential. We were after a dip that was full of smoky eggplant flavor and brightened with garlic and lemon juice. And one certain way to produce this creation was to start off by grilling our eggplant. For the best flavor, it's imperative to start out with firm, shiny, and unblemished eggplants. We grilled the eggplants directly over a hot fire until they were wrinkled and soft. To avoid a watery texture and any bitterness, we drained the pulp of excess fluid, but didn't bother spending time deseeding the eggplants. We processed the pulp with a modest amount of garlic, tahini paste, and lemon juice for the creaminess and bright flavor that baba ghanoush is known for. When buying eggplants, select those with shiny, taut, and unbruised skins and an even shape (eggplants with a bulbous shape won't cook evenly). Grill until the eggplant walls have collapsed and the insides feel sloshy when pressed with tongs. We prefer to serve baba ghanoush only lightly chilled; if cold, let it stand at room temperature for about 20 minutes before serving. Baba ghanoush does not keep well, so plan to make it the day you want to serve it. Serve with pita bread, black olives, tomato wedges, or cucumber slices.

2 pounds eggplant, pricked all over with fork
2 tablespoons tahini
1 tablespoon lemon juice
1 tablespoon extra-virgin olive oil, plus extra for serving
1 small garlic clove, minced
¼ teaspoon table salt
¼ teaspoon pepper
2 teaspoons chopped fresh parsley

**1A. FOR A CHARCOAL GRILL:** Open bottom vent completely. Light large chimney starter filled with charcoal briquettes (6 quarts). When top coals are partially covered with ash, pour evenly over grill. Set cooking grate in place, cover, and open lid vent completely. Heat grill until hot, about 5 minutes.

**1B. FOR A GAS GRILL:** Turn all burners to high; cover; and heat grill until hot, about 15 minutes. Turn all burners to medium. (Adjust burners as needed to maintain grill temperature of 350 degrees.)

**2.** Clean and oil cooking grate. Set eggplants on cooking grate and cook until skins darken and wrinkle on all sides and eggplants are uniformly soft when pressed with tongs, about 25 minutes, turning every 5 minutes and reversing direction of eggplants on grill with each turn. Transfer eggplants to rimmed baking sheet and let cool for 5 minutes.

**3.** Set small colander over bowl. Trim top and bottom off each eggplant. Slit eggplants lengthwise and use spoon to scoop hot pulp from skins; place pulp in colander (you should have about 2 cups packed pulp); discard skins. Let pulp drain for 3 minutes.

**4.** Transfer pulp to food processor. Add tahini, lemon juice, oil, garlic, salt, and pepper. Pulse until mixture has coarse, choppy texture, about 8 pulses. Season with salt and pepper to taste. Transfer to serving bowl, cover with plastic wrap flush with surface of dip, and refrigerate for 45 minutes to 1 hour. Make trough in center of dip using large spoon and spoon olive oil into it. Sprinkle with parsley and serve.

## Grilled Potatoes with Garlic and Rosemary

**SERVES 4**

**WHY THIS RECIPE WORKS** We wanted to put a new spin on grilled potatoes by adding rosemary and garlic for a more savory side. To avoid burnt, bitter garlic and charred rosemary, we learned that we needed to introduce the potatoes to a garlic-oil mixture not once, but three times. First we pierced the potatoes, skewered them, brushed on a garlic-rosemary oil, and precooked them in the microwave. We brushed them again with the infused oil before grilling. After grilling, we tossed the potatoes with the oil yet again for serious flavor without any bitterness. This recipe allows you to grill an entrée while the hot coals burn down in step 4. Once that item is done, start grilling the potatoes. This recipe works best with small potatoes that are about 1½ inches in diameter. If using medium potatoes, 2 to 3 inches in diameter, cut them into quarters. If the potatoes are larger than 3 inches in diameter, cut each potato into eighths. Since the potatoes are first cooked in the microwave, use wooden skewers.

¼ cup extra-virgin olive oil
9 garlic cloves, minced
1 teaspoon chopped fresh rosemary
1 teaspoon table salt, divided
2 pounds small red potatoes, unpeeled, halved and skewered
½ teaspoon pepper
2 tablespoons chopped fresh chives

**1.** Heat oil, garlic, rosemary, and ½ teaspoon salt in small skillet over medium heat until sizzling, about 3 minutes. Reduce heat to medium-low and continue to cook until garlic is light blond, about 3 minutes. Pour mixture through fine-mesh strainer into small bowl; press on solids. Measure 1 tablespoon of solids and 1 tablespoon of oil into large bowl and set aside. Discard remaining solids but reserve remaining oil.

**2.** Place skewered potatoes in single layer on large plate and poke each potato several times with skewer. Brush with 1 tablespoon of strained oil and sprinkle with ¼ teaspoon salt. Microwave until potatoes offer slight resistance when pierced with paring knife, about 8 minutes, turning halfway through microwaving. Transfer potatoes to baking sheet coated with 1 tablespoon strained oil. Brush with remaining 1 tablespoon strained oil and sprinkle with remaining ¼ teaspoon salt and pepper.

**3A. FOR A CHARCOAL GRILL:** Open bottom vent completely. Light large chimney starter filled with charcoal briquettes (6 quarts). When top coals are partially covered with ash, pour two-thirds evenly over grill, then pour remaining coals over half of grill. Set cooking grate in place, cover, and open lid vent completely. Heat grill until hot, about 5 minutes.

**3B. FOR A GAS GRILL:** Turn all burners to high; cover; and heat grill until hot, about 15 minutes. Turn all burners down to medium-high.

**4.** Clean and oil cooking grate. Place potatoes on grill (hotter side if using charcoal) and cook (covered if using gas) until grill marks appear, 3 to 5 minutes, flipping halfway through cooking. Move potatoes to cooler side of grill (if using charcoal) or turn all burners to medium-low (if using gas). Cover and continue to cook until paring knife slips in and out of potatoes easily, 5 to 8 minutes longer.

**5.** Remove potatoes from skewers and transfer to bowl with reserved garlic-oil mixture. Add chives, season with salt and pepper to taste, and toss until thoroughly coated. Serve.

## Grilled Tomatoes

**MAKES** about 2 cups

**WHY THIS RECIPE WORKS** Grilling enhances tomatoes with smoky char while preserving their summery taste. But you can't simply throw them on the fire or you'll end up with a mushy mess. We started by cutting tomatoes in half so both the interiors and exteriors could pick up flavorful charring before the interiors got too soft. To ensure that the tomatoes held their shape, we cut them through their equators. We used tomatoes that were ripe but firm, since softer tomatoes were more likely to fall apart during grilling. Salting the tomatoes allowed some of their juice to be drawn out so that they'd be less wet on the grill for better browning. Grilling the tomatoes cut sides down first allowed them to caramelize before we flipped them; the cradle-like skins helped to hold the tomatoes together as they continued to soften. For the best results, use in-season, round tomatoes that are ripe yet a bit firm so that they will hold their shape on the grill. Plum tomatoes can be used, but they will be drier in texture. If using plum tomatoes, halve them lengthwise. Supermarket vine-ripened tomatoes will work but won't be as flavorful. To serve the tomatoes as a simple side dish, top them with the reserved juice, 2 tablespoons of torn fresh basil leaves, 1 tablespoon of extra-virgin olive oil, and flake sea salt to taste. This recipe can easily be doubled.

- 2 pounds ripe tomatoes, cored and halved along equator
- 1 tablespoon extra-virgin olive oil
- ½ teaspoon table salt
- ¼ teaspoon pepper

**1.** Toss tomatoes with oil, salt, and pepper in large bowl. Let stand for at least 15 minutes or up to 1 hour.

**2A. FOR A CHARCOAL GRILL:** Open bottom vent completely. Light large chimney starter filled with charcoal briquettes (6 quarts). When top coals are partially covered with ash, pour evenly over grill. Set cooking grate in place, cover, and open lid vent completely. Heat grill until hot, about 5 minutes.

**2B. FOR A GAS GRILL:** Turn all burners to high, cover, and heat grill until hot, about 15 minutes. Leave all burners on high.

**3.** Clean and oil cooking grate. Place tomatoes, cut sides down, on grill (reserve any juice left behind in bowl) and cook (covered if using gas) until tomatoes are charred and beginning to soften, 4 to 6 minutes.

**4.** Using tongs or thin metal spatula, carefully flip tomatoes and continue to cook (covered if using gas) until skin sides are charred and juice bubbles, 4 to 6 minutes longer. Transfer tomatoes to large plate. (Tomatoes can be refrigerated for up to 2 days.)

## Mechouia (Tunisian-Style Grilled Vegetables)

**SERVES** 4 to 6

**WHY THIS RECIPE WORKS** Grilling brings out the best in summer vegetables, calling forth their sweetness and adding an accent of smoke. We took inspiration from the robustly flavored Tunisian dish called mechouia. We opted to use bell peppers, eggplant, zucchini, and plum tomatoes. To avoid a waterlogged salad, we halved the zucchini and eggplant and cut deep crosshatch marks in their flesh to allow them to release their moisture. We also halved the tomatoes and opened the peppers into long planks so they would cook evenly all the way through. We sprinkled the vegetables with salt and oil flavored with traditional tabil seasonings. The spices bloomed on the grill and became full-flavored and aromatic. More tabil, plus lemon zest and a trio of fresh herbs, brought a tangy, lively taste to our finishing vinaigrette. Serve as a side dish to grilled meats and fish; with grilled pita as a salad course; or with hard-cooked eggs, olives, and premium canned tuna as a light lunch. Equal amounts of ground coriander and cumin can be substituted for the whole spices.

**VINAIGRETTE**

- 2 teaspoons coriander seeds
- 1½ teaspoons caraway seeds
- 1 teaspoon cumin seeds
- 5 tablespoons olive oil
- ½ teaspoon sweet paprika
- ⅛ teaspoon cayenne pepper
- 3 garlic cloves, minced
- ¼ cup chopped fresh parsley
- ¼ cup chopped fresh cilantro
- 2 tablespoons chopped fresh mint
- 1 teaspoon grated lemon zest plus 2 tablespoons juice
- Table salt

**VEGETABLES**

- 2 bell peppers (1 red and 1 green)
- 1 small eggplant, halved lengthwise
- 1 zucchini (8 to 10 ounces), halved lengthwise
- 4 plum tomatoes, cored and halved lengthwise
- Table salt and pepper
- 2 medium shallots, unpeeled

**1. FOR THE VINAIGRETTE:** Grind coriander seeds, caraway seeds, and cumin seeds in spice grinder until finely ground. Whisk ground spices, oil, paprika, and cayenne together in bowl. Reserve 3 tablespoons oil mixture. Heat remaining oil mixture and garlic in small skillet over low heat, stirring occasionally, until fragrant and small bubbles appear, 8 to 10 minutes. Transfer to large bowl and let cool, about 10 minutes. Whisk parsley, cilantro, mint, and lemon zest and juice into oil mixture; season with salt to taste.

**2. FOR THE VEGETABLES:** Slice ¼ inch off tops and bottoms of bell peppers and remove cores. Make slit down 1 side of each bell pepper and then press flat into 1 long strip, removing ribs and remaining seeds with knife as needed. Using sharp knife, cut slits in flesh of eggplant and zucchini, spaced ½ inch apart, in crosshatch pattern, being careful to cut into but not through skin. Brush cut sides of bell peppers, eggplant, zucchini, and tomatoes with reserved oil mixture and season with salt to taste.

**3.** Grill vegetables, starting with cut sides down, over medium-hot fire, until tender and well browned and skins of bell peppers, eggplant, tomatoes, and shallots are charred, 8 to 16 minutes, turning and moving vegetables as necessary. Transfer vegetables to baking sheet as they are done. Place bell peppers in bowl, cover with plastic wrap, and let steam to loosen skins.

**4.** When cool enough to handle, peel bell peppers, eggplant, tomatoes, and shallots. Chop all vegetables into ½-inch pieces and transfer to bowl with vinaigrette; toss to coat. Season with salt and pepper to taste, and serve warm or at room temperature.

## Grilled Vegetable Platter

**SERVES** 4 to 6

---

**WHY THIS RECIPE WORKS** A bounteous assortment of grilled vegetables served with a citrus-kissed vinaigrette makes for a casual and fabulously charry spread. The vegetables are even better at room temperature than they are hot, so you can easily make this ahead, if you like. It makes an excellent starter to keep everybody happy at the outdoor table while you continue to grill up more goodies, or you can easily customize the platter with add-ons to make this the centerpiece of your meal. The burrata is a great start; its creamy insides will mingle with the vegetables on guests' plates. Also consider additions such as crusty bread slices toasted on the grill, marinated olives, marinated white beans, high-quality tuna packed in oil, and/or grilled lemon halves to squeeze over whatever you please. If burrata is unavailable, sliced fresh mozzarella makes a suitable substitute.

**LEMON-BASIL VINAIGRETTE**

- 2 tablespoons lemon juice
- 4 teaspoons Dijon mustard
- 2 garlic cloves, minced
- ½ teaspoon table salt
- ¼ teaspoon pepper
- 6 tablespoons extra-virgin olive oil
- ¼ cup chopped fresh basil, plus basil leaves for garnish

**GRILLED VEGETABLE PLATTER**

- 2 red bell peppers
- 1 red onion, cut into ½-inch-thick rounds
- 4 plum tomatoes, cored and halved lengthwise
- 2 zucchini, ends trimmed, sliced lengthwise into ¾-inch-thick planks
- 1 eggplant, ends trimmed, cut crosswise into ½-inch-thick rounds
- 3 tablespoons extra-virgin olive oil
- ½ teaspoon table salt
- ½ teaspoon pepper
- 8 ounces burrata cheese, room temperature

**1. FOR THE LEMON-BASIL VINAIGRETTE:** Whisk lemon juice, mustard, garlic, salt, and pepper together in bowl. Whisking constantly, slowly drizzle in oil. Stir in basil and season with salt and pepper to taste. (Vinaigrette can be refrigerated in an airtight container for up to 2 days. Bring to room temperature and whisk to recombine before serving.)

**2. FOR THE GRILLED VEGETABLE PLATTER:** Slice ¼ inch off tops and bottoms of bell peppers and remove cores. Make slit down 1 side of each bell pepper, then press flat into 1 long strip, removing ribs and remaining seeds with knife as needed. Cut strips in half crosswise (you should have 4 bell pepper pieces).

**3.** Push toothpick horizontally through each onion round to keep rings intact while grilling. Brush onion, bell peppers, tomatoes, and zucchini all over with oil, then brush eggplant with remaining oil (it will absorb more oil than other vegetables). Sprinkle vegetables with salt and pepper.

**4A.** For a charcoal grill: Open bottom vent completely. Light large chimney starter filled with charcoal briquettes (6 quarts). When top coals are partially covered with ash, pour evenly over grill. Set cooking grate in place, cover, and open lid vent completely. Heat grill until hot, about 5 minutes.

**4B. FOR A GAS GRILL:** Turn all burners to high; cover; and heat grill until hot, about 15 minutes. Turn all burners to medium-high.

**5.** Clean and oil cooking grate. Grill vegetables until skins of bell peppers and tomatoes are well browned and onions, eggplant, and zucchini are tender, 10 to 16 minutes, flipping and moving vegetables as necessary to ensure even cooking and transferring vegetables to baking sheet as they finish cooking. Place bell peppers in bowl, cover with plastic wrap, and let steam to loosen skins, about 5 minutes.

**6.** Remove toothpicks from onion and separate rings. When cool enough to handle, peel bell peppers, discarding skins; slice into 1-inch-thick strips. Arrange vegetables and burrata attractively on serving platter with lemon-basil vinaigrette. Garnish platter with basil leaves. Serve warm or at room temperature.

## Grilled Halloumi Wraps

**SERVES 4**

**WHY THIS RECIPE WORKS** Firm and easy to brown, halloumi cheese is a natural on the grill. To offset the cheese's salty richness, we combined it with bright, crisp, sumac-spiked onion; smoky grilled bell pepper; and peppery arugula. While the cheese and peppers cooked, we steamed some moistened pitas in a foil packet on the cooler side of the grill so that they would be soft and flexible enough to wrap. For a yogurt spread that was garlicky without being harsh, we combined the garlic with some lemon juice to deactivate its alliinase before combining it with the yogurt. The saltiness of halloumi varies; for the best results, select a product that has less than 260 milligrams of sodium per serving. Because the cooking time is so brief, using a charcoal grill is impractical here; if you don't have a gas grill, cook the halloumi and bell pepper in a grill pan on the stovetop over medium-high heat, and wrap the moistened pitas in paper towels and warm them in the microwave.

- 1 red onion, halved and sliced thin
- 3 tablespoons red wine vinegar
- 1 tablespoon ground sumac
- ¾ teaspoon table salt, divided
- 2 tablespoons lemon juice
- 1 garlic clove
- ½ cup plain Greek yogurt
- 1 large red bell pepper
- 4 (8-inch) pitas, divided
- 12 ounces halloumi cheese, sliced crosswise ½ inch thick
- 1 tablespoon extra-virgin olive oil
- ¼ teaspoon red pepper flakes
- 2 ounces (2 cups) arugula

**1.** Combine onion, vinegar, sumac, and ¼ teaspoon salt in medium bowl. Stir until well combined; set aside. Place lemon juice in small bowl. Mince or grate garlic and add to juice. Add ¼ teaspoon salt and whisk to combine. Whisk in yogurt until smooth.

**2.** Slice ½ inch from top and bottom of bell pepper. Gently remove stem from top. Twist and pull out core, using knife to loosen at edges if necessary. Cut slit down 1 side of bell pepper. Turn bell pepper skin side down and gently press so it opens to create long strip. Slide knife along insides to remove remaining ribs and seeds.

**3.** Lightly moisten 2 pitas with water. Sandwich remaining pitas between moistened pitas and wrap tightly in lightly greased heavy-duty aluminum foil.

**4.** Turn all burners on gas grill to high; cover; and heat grill until hot, about 15 minutes. Leave primary burner on high and turn off other burner(s). Clean and oil cooking grate. Arrange halloumi slices and bell pepper pieces, skin side up, on hotter side of grill. Cook, covered, until undersides of cheese and bell pepper are lightly browned, 3 to 5 minutes. Using tongs, flip cheese and bell pepper and continue to cook until second side of cheese and bell pepper are lightly browned, 3 to 5 minutes longer.

**5.** Meanwhile, place packet of pitas on cooler side of grill. Flip occasionally to heat, about 5 minutes. Transfer cheese and bell pepper to cutting board. Cut bell pepper into ½-inch pieces and transfer to second small bowl. Add oil, pepper flakes, and remaining ¼ teaspoon salt and toss to combine.

**6.** Lay each warm pita on 12-inch square of foil or parchment paper. Spread each pita with one-quarter of yogurt mixture. Place one-quarter of cheese in middle of each pita. Top with pepper, onion, and arugula. Drizzle with any remaining onion liquid. Roll pita into cylinder. Wrap in foil, cut in half, and serve.

## Grilled Fresh Corn Cornbread with Charred Jalapeños and Cheddar

**SERVES 6 to 8** SEASON 26

**WHY THIS RECIPE WORKS** Fire does amazing things for corn, taking it from mild and sweet to earthy and nutty. Toasting cornmeal as well as grilling whole ears of corn makes this skillet bread hearty enough to take on the bold flavors of charred jalapeños and sharp cheddar. The batter is easy to mix outdoors, and the finished bread comes out lofty and golden, with a delectably crisp bottom and a cheese-laced top. Cut into hearty wedges, it's the perfect side for ribs, chili, or really anything off the grill. Don't use stone-ground cornmeal. You will need a 10-inch cast-iron skillet.

- 4 jalapeño chiles
- 2 ears corn, husks and silk removed
- 2¼ cups (11¼ ounces) cornmeal
- 1 tablespoon sugar
- 1 teaspoon baking powder
- 1 teaspoon baking soda
- ¾ teaspoon table salt
- 1½ cups sour cream

½ cup whole milk
¼ cup vegetable oil
5 tablespoons unsalted butter, melted, divided
2 large eggs
8 ounces sharp cheddar cheese, shredded (2 cups), divided

**1A. FOR A CHARCOAL GRILL:** Open bottom vent completely. Light large chimney starter mounded with charcoal briquettes (7 quarts). When top coals are partially covered with ash, pour into steeply banked pile against 1 side of grill. Set cooking grate in place, cover, and open lid vent completely. Heat grill until hot, about 5 minutes.

**1B. FOR A GAS GRILL:** Turn all burners to high; cover; and heat grill until hot, about 15 minutes. Leave primary burner on high and turn off other burner(s). (Adjust primary burner as needed to maintain grill temperature between 400 and 450 degrees; if using 3-burner grill, adjust primary burner and second burner.)

**2.** Clean and oil cooking grate. Grill jalapeños and corn on hotter side of grill (covered if using gas), turning as needed, until jalapeños are blistered and charred in spots, 7 to 10 minutes, and corn is charred on all sides, 10 to 12 minutes. Transfer jalapeños to cutting board and let cool slightly; stem, seed, and chop fine. Transfer corn to cutting board and let cool slightly; cut kernels from corn. (You should have about 1½ cups.)

**3.** Place 10-inch cast-iron skillet on hotter side of grill. Add cornmeal and toast, stirring frequently, until fragrant, about 5 minutes. Transfer cornmeal to large bowl. Whisk sugar, baking powder, baking soda, and salt into cornmeal. Whisk in sour cream, milk, oil, ¼ cup melted butter, and eggs until combined. Stir in jalapeños, corn, and 1½ cups cheddar.

**4.** Brush skillet with remaining 1 tablespoon melted butter. Quickly scrape batter into skillet and smooth top. Sprinkle remaining ½ cup cheddar on top of batter. Place skillet on cooler side of grill and bake, covered, until top is golden brown and toothpick inserted into center comes out clean, 20 to 35 minutes, rotating skillet halfway through baking. Transfer skillet to wire rack and let cornbread cool for 30 minutes. Slice into wedges and serve.

## Grilled Tomato and Cheese Pizza

**MAKES** four 9-inch pizzas, serving 4 to 6

**WHY THIS RECIPE WORKS** Most homemade versions of this restaurant classic disappoint with charred crusts and sauce and cheese that drip onto the coals. We set out to find the secret to great grilled pizza at home. Regular pizza dough stuck to the cooking grate and burned easily. We found that the dough has to be both thinner and sturdier to work on the grill. We used high-protein bread flour to strengthen the dough, and adding water made it easier to stretch. The crust also needed more flavor to stand up to the heat of the fire, so we added extra salt, a little whole-wheat flour, and some olive oil. The oil in the dough also kept the crust from sticking to the cooking grate. Salted chopped tomatoes rather than sauce and a mixture of soft fontina (which has more flavor than mozzarella) and nutty Parmesan made a flavorful but light topping that didn't weigh down the crust or make it soggy. Spicy garlic oil and a scattering of fresh basil added complexity without heaviness. Full of flavor and with a cracker-crisp crust, these grilled pizzas are as good as any we've had in a restaurant. The pizzas cook very quickly on the grill, so before you begin, be sure to have all the equipment and ingredients you need at hand. Equipment includes a pizza peel (or baking sheet), a pair of tongs, a paring knife, a large cutting board, and a pastry brush. Ingredients includes all the toppings and a small bowl of flour for dusting. The pizzas are best served hot off the grill but can be kept warm for 20 to 30 minutes on a wire rack in a 200-degree oven.

**DOUGH**

1 cup water, room temperature
2 tablespoons olive oil
2 cups (11 ounces) bread flour
1 tablespoon whole-wheat flour (optional)
2 teaspoons sugar
1¼ teaspoons table salt
1 teaspoon instant or rapid-rise yeast

**TOPPING**

1½ pounds plum tomatoes, cored, seeded, and cut into ½-inch pieces
¾ teaspoon table salt
6 ounces fontina cheese, shredded (1½ cups)
1½ ounces Parmesan cheese, grated fine (¾ cup)
1 recipe Spicy Garlic Oil (recipe follows)
½ cup chopped fresh basil
Kosher salt

**1. FOR THE DOUGH:** Combine water and 2 tablespoons oil in liquid measuring cup. Pulse 1¾ cup bread flour, whole wheat flour, if using, sugar, salt, and yeast in food processor (fitted with dough blade if possible) until combined, about 5 pulses. With food processor running, slowly add water mixture; process until dough forms ball, about 1½ minutes. (If after

1½ minutes dough is sticky and clings to blade, add remaining ¼ cup flour 1 tablespoon at a time.) Transfer dough to large, lightly greased bowl; cover tightly with plastic wrap and let rise at room temperature until doubled in size, 1½ to 2 hours.

**2.** Gently press down on center of dough to deflate. Transfer dough to clean counter and divide into 4 equal pieces. With cupped palms, form each piece into smooth, tight ball. Set dough balls on well-floured counter. Press dough rounds by hand to flatten; cover loosely with plastic and let rest for 15 minutes.

**3. FOR THE TOPPING:** Meanwhile, toss tomatoes and salt in bowl; transfer to colander and drain for 30 minutes (wipe out and reserve bowl). Shake colander to drain off excess liquid; transfer tomatoes to now-empty bowl and set aside. Combine fontina and Parmesan in second bowl and set aside.

**4.** Gently stretch 1 dough round (keep other rounds covered) into disk about ½ inch thick and 5 to 6 inches in diameter. Roll disk out to ⅛-inch thickness, 9 to 10 inches in diameter, on well-floured sheet of parchment paper, dusting with additional flour as needed to prevent sticking. (If dough shrinks when rolled out, cover with plastic and let rest until relaxed, 10 to 15 minutes.) Dust surface of rolled dough with flour and set aside. Repeat with remaining dough rounds, stacking sheets of rolled dough on top of each other (with parchment in between) and covering stack with plastic; set aside until grill is ready.

**5A. FOR A CHARCOAL GRILL:** Open bottom vent completely. Light large chimney starter filled with charcoal briquettes (6 quarts). When top coals are partially covered with ash, pour evenly over three-quarters of grill. Set cooking grate in place, cover, and open lid vent completely. Heat grill until hot, about 5 minutes.

**5B. FOR A GAS GRILL:** Turn all burners to high, cover, and heat grill until hot, about 15 minutes. Leave primary burner on high and turn off other burner(s).

**6.** Clean and oil cooking grate. Lightly flour pizza peel or baking sheet; invert 1 dough round onto peel, gently stretching it as needed to retain its shape (do not stretch dough too thin; thin spots will burn quickly). Peel off and discard parchment; carefully slide round onto hotter side of grill. Immediately repeat with another dough round. Cook (covered if using gas) until tops are covered with bubbles (pierce larger bubbles with paring knife) and bottoms are grill-marked and charred in spots, 1 to 4 minutes; while rounds cook, check undersides and slide to cooler area of grill if browning too quickly. Transfer crusts to cutting board, browned sides up. Repeat with 2 remaining dough rounds.

**7.** Brush 2 crusts generously with garlic oil; top each evenly with one-quarter of cheese mixture and one-quarter of tomatoes. Return pizzas to hotter side of grill and cover grill with lid; cook until bottoms are well browned and cheese is melted, 2 to 6 minutes, checking bottoms frequently to prevent burning. Transfer pizzas to cutting board; repeat with remaining 2 crusts. Sprinkle pizzas with basil and season with salt to taste; cut into wedges and serve.

### Spicy Garlic Oil

**MAKES** enough for 4 pizzas

- ⅓ cup extra-virgin olive oil
- 4 medium garlic cloves, minced or pressed through a garlic press (about 4 teaspoons)
- ½–¾ teaspoon red pepper flakes

Cook all the ingredients in a small saucepan over medium heat, stirring occasionally, until the garlic begins to sizzle, 2 to 3 minutes. Transfer to a small bowl.

## Ultimate Grilled Pizza

**SERVES** 4 to 6

**WHY THIS RECIPE WORKS** We let the food processor do the work making the dough for our grilled pizza, before letting it proof for at least 24 hours in the refrigerator to develop complex flavor. To ensure that the dough cooked up thin, we used a tiny amount of yeast to reduce air bubbles and a relatively high percentage of water that made a relatively slack dough that easily stretched. Stretching the dough on a generously oiled baking sheet prevented it from sticking to our hands and the grill and also helped the exterior fry and crisp. To ensure that the toppings cooked quickly on a grill, we preheated the sauce and used a combination of fast-melting fresh mozzarella and finely grated Parmesan; we also sprinkled the Parmesan evenly over the dough to create a flavorful barrier against moisture before dolloping (rather than slathering on) the sauce and scattering chunks of cheese, all of which helped maintain the dough's crisp texture. To prevent a hotspot at the center that would burn the crust, we placed the coals only around the perimeter of the grill rather than in an even layer. The dough must sit for at least 24 hours before shaping. We prefer the high protein content of King Arthur bread flour for this recipe, though other bread flours are acceptable. For best results, weigh your ingredients. It's important to use ice water in the dough to prevent it from overheating in the food processor. Grilled pizza cooks quickly, so it's critical to have all of your ingredients and tools ready ahead of time. We recommend pargrilling, topping, and grilling in quick succession and serving the pizzas one at a time, rather than all at once.

**DOUGH**

- 3 cups (16½ ounces) King Arthur bread flour
- 1 tablespoon sugar
- ¼ teaspoon instant or rapid-rise yeast
- 1¼ cups plus 2 tablespoons ice water (11 ounces)
- Vegetable oil
- 1½ teaspoons table salt

**SAUCE**

- 1 (14-ounce) can whole peeled plum tomatoes, drained, juice reserved
- 2 tablespoons extra-virgin olive oil
- 2 teaspoons minced fresh oregano
- ¼ teaspoon red pepper flakes
- Table salt
- Sugar

**PIZZA**

- Extra-virgin olive oil
- 3 ounces Parmesan cheese, grated (1½ cups)
- 8 ounces fresh whole-milk mozzarella cheese, torn into grape-size pieces (about 2 cups)
- 3 tablespoons shredded fresh basil
- Coarse sea salt

**1. FOR THE DOUGH:** Process flour, sugar, and yeast in food processor until combined, about 2 seconds. With processor running, slowly add ice water; process until dough is just combined and no dry flour remains, about 10 seconds. Let dough stand for 10 minutes.

**2.** Add 1 tablespoon oil and salt to dough and process until dough forms satiny, sticky ball that clears sides of bowl, 30 to 60 seconds. Transfer dough to lightly oiled counter and knead until smooth, about 1 minute. Divide dough into 3 equal pieces (about 9⅓ ounces each). Shape each piece into tight ball and transfer to well-oiled baking sheet (alternatively, place dough balls in individual well-oiled bowls). Cover tightly with plastic wrap (taking care not to compress dough) and refrigerate for at least 24 hours or up to 3 days.

**3. FOR THE SAUCE:** Pulse tomatoes in food processor until finely chopped, 12 to 15 pulses. Transfer to medium bowl and stir in oil, oregano, pepper flakes, reserved juice, ½ teaspoon salt, and ½ teaspoon sugar. Season with additional salt and sugar to taste, cover, and refrigerate until ready to use.

**4.** One hour before cooking pizza, remove tray of dough from refrigerator and let stand at room temperature.

**5A. FOR A CHARCOAL GRILL:** Open bottom vent halfway. Light large chimney starter three-quarters filled with charcoal briquettes (4½ quarts). When top coals are partially covered with ash, pour into ring around perimeter of grill, leaving 8-inch clearing in center. Set cooking grate in place, cover, and open lid vent halfway. Heat grill until hot, about 5 minutes.

**5B. FOR A GAS GRILL:** Turn all burners to high, cover, and heat grill until hot, about 15 minutes. Leave all burners on high.

**6.** While grill is heating, place sauce in small saucepan and bring to simmer over medium heat. Cover and keep warm.

**7. FOR THE PIZZA:** Clean and oil cooking grate. Pour ¼ cup oil onto center of rimmed baking sheet. Transfer 1 dough round to sheet and coat both sides of dough with oil. Using your fingertips and palms, gently press and stretch dough toward edges of sheet to form rough 16 by 12-inch oval of even thickness. Using both of your hands, lift dough and carefully transfer to grill. (When transferring dough from sheet to grill, it will droop slightly to form half-moon or snowshoe shape.) Cook (over clearing if using charcoal and covered if using gas) until grill marks form, 2 to 3 minutes. Using tongs and spatula, carefully peel dough from grill grates, then rotate dough 90 degrees and continue to cook (covered if using gas) until second set of grill marks appears, 2 to 3 minutes longer. Flip dough and cook (covered if using gas) until second side of dough is lightly charred in spots, 2 to 3 minutes. Using tongs or pizza peel, transfer crust to cutting board, inverting so side that was grilled first is facing down. Repeat with remaining 2 dough rounds, adding 1 tablespoon oil to baking sheet for each round and keeping grill cover closed when not in use to retain heat.

**8.** Drizzle top of 1 crust with 1 tablespoon oil. Sprinkle one-third of Parmesan evenly over surface. Arrange one-third of mozzarella pieces, evenly spaced, on surface of pizza. Dollop one-third of sauce in evenly spaced 1-tablespoon mounds over surface of pizza. Using pizza peel or overturned rimmed baking sheet, transfer pizza to grill, cover, and cook until bottom is well browned and mozzarella is melted, 3 to 5 minutes, checking bottom and turning frequently to prevent burning. Transfer pizza to cutting board; repeat with remaining 2 crusts. Sprinkle pizzas with basil, drizzle lightly with oil, and season with salt to taste. Cut into wedges and serve.

### DON'T SKIMP ON THE OIL

Stretching the dough in a generous amount of olive oil not only prevents it from sticking to your hands and to the cooking grate but also crisps the exterior without rendering it greasy.

CHAPTER 11 # Sides

Photos (left to right): Braised Collard Greens; Perfect Roasted Root Vegetables; Beer-Battered Onion Rings with Jalapeño Dipping Sauce; Simplified Potato Galette; Broiled Smashed Zucchini with Herbed Sour Cream; Pan-Roasted Asparagus; Suan La Bai Cai (Sour and Hot Napa Cabbage)

# Carciofi alla Giudia (Roman Jewish Fried Artichokes)

**SERVES 4**

**WHY THIS RECIPE WORKS** To make the fried artichokes that Roman Jews have prepared for centuries during the thistle's spring harvest, cooks trim the thistles to expose their tender, inner leaves, and then they deep-fry the artichokes a few at a time—twice. The first round softens up the vegetable's dense heart, and the second makes the petals unfurl and crisp. After plucking off the tough outer bracts, we made four angled cuts with a sharp knife to remove the top half of the remaining leaves. Halving the artichoke exposed its hairy choke, which we scooped out with a spoon after the first fry, when it had softened considerably. Using very fresh, tightly closed blossoms minimized the amount of leaves lost during prep. Double frying delivered a stunning range of textures: The first fry, done low and slow, rendered the dense heart soft and creamy. The second, a 1-minute flash in hot oil, browned and crisped up the leaves. The leaves also unfurled so that the finished product resembled a copper-dipped chrysanthemum. Straining the used oil meant that it could be reused more than half a dozen times. Look for artichokes that are uniformly green, have tightly closed leaves, feel heavy for their size, and squeak a little when squeezed—all indications of freshness; avoid any that are browning and dried out. Don't worry when the artichokes discolor as you prep them; any oxidation won't be visible after frying. If your large saucepan holds less than 4 quarts, use a large Dutch oven and add 2 cups more canola oil so that the artichokes are completely covered.

- 4 artichokes (10 to 12 ounces each)
- 6 cups canola oil for frying
- 2 cups extra-virgin olive oil for frying
- Lemon wedges

**1.** Working with 1 artichoke at a time, snap off tough outer leaves until you reach tender inner leaves (they'll be pale yellow at their base). Trim stem to 1½-inch length. Peel stem and base with paring or bird's beak knife to remove dark-green layer. Starting halfway up leaves, use chef's knife to make 45-degree angled cut toward top of artichoke to remove tips of leaves. Repeat same cut 3 more times, rotating artichoke quarter turn before each cut.

**2.** Set wire rack in rimmed baking sheet and line with double layer of paper towels. Heat canola oil and olive oil in large saucepan over medium-high heat to 275 degrees. Cut each artichoke in half through stem.

**3.** Using spider skimmer or slotted spoon, carefully add artichokes to oil. Cook until paring knife slipped into thickest part of base meets little resistance and leaves are medium brown, 10 to 12 minutes. Using spider skimmer or slotted spoon, transfer artichokes to prepared rack cut side down to drain. Remove saucepan from heat. Let artichokes cool for 15 minutes. (Artichoke halves can be wrapped well and refrigerated for up to 24 hours.)

**4.** Using spoon, scoop out choke from center of each artichoke half, being careful not to dislodge leaves attached to base. Replace paper towels with double layer of fresh paper towels. Heat oil over high heat to 350 degrees.

**5.** Place 2 artichoke halves cut side down in oil and, using spider skimmer or slotted spoon, lightly press on artichokes to submerge. Cook until outer leaves are dark brown, 45 to 60 seconds. Transfer to prepared rack cut side down to drain. Return oil to 350 degrees and repeat with remaining artichoke halves in 3 batches. Sprinkle artichokes on both sides with flake sea salt to taste. Serve, passing lemon wedges separately.

## PREPPING ARTICHOKES FOR FRYING

**1.** Snap off outer leaves.

**2.** Trim and peel stem.

**3.** Cut top at 45-degree angle.

**4.** Rotate quarter turn; repeat 3 times.

**5.** Halve lengthwise through stem.

## Broiled Asparagus

SERVES 6

**WHY THIS RECIPE WORKS** Broiling can intensify the flavor of asparagus, turning it sweet and nutty. But getting the asparagus to cook through evenly can be tricky. We wanted a foolproof broiling method for turning out browned, tender spears every time. To start, we found that with thicker asparagus, the exterior began to char before the interior of the spears became fully tender. When we used thinner spears, however, the interior was tender by the time the exterior was browned. Keeping the spears about four inches away from the broiling element allowed them to caramelize properly without charring. To encourage browning, we tossed the asparagus with olive oil before broiling. Shaking the pan with the asparagus as it cooked ensured that the spears cooked evenly. The intense dry heat of the broiler concentrated the flavor of the asparagus, and the exterior caramelization made the spears especially sweet. Broilers vary significantly in intensity, thus the wide range of cooking times in this recipe. Choose asparagus no thicker than ½ inch near the base for this recipe.

- 2 pounds thin asparagus (about 2 bunches), tough ends trimmed
- 1 tablespoon olive oil
- Table salt and ground black pepper

Adjust an oven rack to the highest position (about 4 inches from the heating element) and heat the broiler. Toss the asparagus with the oil and salt and pepper to taste, then lay the spears in a single layer on a rimmed baking sheet. Broil, shaking the pan halfway through cooking to turn the spears, until the asparagus is tender and lightly browned, 6 to 10 minutes. Serve hot or warm.

## Pan-Roasted Asparagus

SERVES 3 to 4

**WHY THIS RECIPE WORKS** Our simple stovetop method for pan-roasted asparagus delivers crisp, nicely browned spears. We quickly learned to choose thick spears because thinner spears overcooked too quickly. Taking a cue from restaurant chefs who blanch asparagus first, we developed a method to lightly steam and then brown the asparagus in the same skillet. For both flavor and browning, we used olive oil and butter. Positioning half the spears in one direction and the other half in the opposite direction ensured a better fit in the pan. Browning just one side of the asparagus provided a contrast in texture and guaranteed that the asparagus were firm and tender, never limp. This recipe works best with asparagus that is at least ½ inch thick near the base. If using thinner spears, reduce the covered cooking time to 3 minutes and the uncovered cooking time to 5 minutes. Do not use pencil-thin asparagus; it cannot withstand the heat and overcooks too easily.

- 1 tablespoon olive oil
- 1 tablespoon unsalted butter
- 2 pounds thick asparagus (2 bunches), tough ends trimmed
- ½ lemon (optional)

**1.** Heat oil and butter in 12-inch skillet over medium-high heat. When butter has melted, add half of asparagus to skillet with tips pointed in 1 direction; add remaining asparagus with tips pointed in opposite direction. Using tongs, distribute spears in even layer (spears will not quite fit into single layer); cover and cook until asparagus is bright green and still crisp, about 5 minutes.

**2.** Uncover and increase heat to high; season asparagus with salt and pepper to taste. Cook until spears are tender and well browned along 1 side, 5 to 7 minutes, using tongs to occasionally move spears from center of pan to edge of pan to ensure all are browned. Transfer asparagus to dish, adjust seasonings with salt and pepper, and squeeze lemon half, if using, over spears. Serve.

### Pan-Roasted Asparagus with Toasted Garlic and Parmesan

Before cooking asparagus, cook 2 tablespoons extra-virgin olive oil and 3 thinly sliced garlic cloves in 12-inch skillet over medium heat, stirring occasionally, until garlic is crisp and golden, about 5 minutes. Using slotted spoon, transfer garlic to paper towel–lined plate. Add butter to oil left in skillet and cook asparagus as directed. Sprinkle asparagus with toasted garlic and 2 tablespoons grated Parmesan cheese before serving.

## Stir-Fried Asparagus with Shiitake Mushrooms

SERVES 4

**WHY THIS RECIPE WORKS** To achieve stir-fried asparagus with a flavorful browned exterior and a crisp-tender texture, we had to start with a hot pan and only stir the asparagus occasionally. This allowed the vegetables to char and caramelize. To ensure that the asparagus cooked evenly, we diluted the sauce with water. This diluted sauce created a small amount of steam, cooking the spears through, before evaporating and leaving behind a flavorful glaze. To allow it to brown, stir the asparagus only occasionally. Look for spears that are no thicker than ½ inch.

- 2 tablespoons water
- 1 tablespoon soy sauce
- 1 tablespoon dry sherry
- 2 teaspoons packed brown sugar
- 2 teaspoons grated fresh ginger
- 1 teaspoon toasted sesame oil
- 1 tablespoon vegetable oil
- 1 pound asparagus, tough ends trimmed and cut on bias into 2-inch lengths
- 4 ounces shiitake mushrooms, stemmed and sliced thin
- 2 scallions, green parts only, sliced thin on bias

1. Combine water, soy sauce, sherry, sugar, ginger, and sesame oil in bowl.

2. Heat vegetable oil in 12-inch nonstick skillet over high heat until smoking. Add asparagus and mushrooms and cook, stirring occasionally, until asparagus is spotty brown, 3 to 4 minutes. Add soy sauce mixture and cook, stirring once or twice, until pan is almost dry and asparagus is crisp-tender, 1 to 2 minutes. Transfer to serving platter, sprinkle with scallion greens, and serve.

## Buttery Spring Vegetables

**SERVES 6**

---

**WHY THIS RECIPE WORKS** Crisp-tender spring vegetables coated in a rich yet light butter sauce sounds ideal, but many of these recipes wind up dull, waterlogged, and ultimately lacking in buttery flavor. We wanted spring vegetables that retained their vibrant colors and crisp textures and a butter sauce that would cling to the vegetables, not the platter. To prevent our medley of vegetables from becoming soggy, we cooked them in a steamer basket, staggering their additions so that each ended up perfectly crisp-tender. Spreading the vegetables on a platter immediately after cooking allowed excess heat to dissipate, so the vegetables didn't overcook while we made the sauce. Instead of plain melted butter, which had a tendency to slip off the vegetables, we made a version of the creamy, tangy French butter sauce beurre blanc by emulsifying chilled butter into a mixture of sautéed shallot, vinegar, salt, and sugar. To ensure that the turnips are tender, peel them thoroughly to remove not only the tough outer skin but also the fibrous layer of flesh just beneath. This recipe works best with thick asparagus spears that are between ½ and ¾ inch in diameter.

- 1 pound turnips, peeled and cut into ½-inch by ½-inch by 2-inch batons
- 1 pound asparagus, trimmed and cut on bias into 2-inch lengths
- 8 ounces sugar snap peas, strings removed, trimmed
- 4 large radishes, halved and sliced thin
- 1 tablespoon minced shallot
- 1½ teaspoons white wine vinegar
- ¾ teaspoon table salt
- ¼ teaspoon sugar
- 6 tablespoons unsalted butter, cut into 6 pieces and chilled
- 1 tablespoon minced fresh chives

1. Bring 1 cup water to boil in large saucepan over high heat. Place steamer basket over boiling water. Add turnips and asparagus to basket, cover saucepan, and reduce heat to medium. Cook until vegetables are slightly softened, about 2 minutes. Add snap peas, cover, and cook until snap peas are crisp-tender, about 2 minutes. Add radishes, cover, and cook for 1 minute. Lift basket out of saucepan and transfer vegetables to platter. Spread into even layer to allow steam to dissipate. Discard all but 3 tablespoons liquid from saucepan.

2. Return saucepan to medium heat. Add shallot, vinegar, salt, and sugar and cook until mixture is reduced to 1½ tablespoons (it will barely cover bottom of saucepan), about 2 minutes. Reduce heat to low. Add butter, 1 piece at a time, whisking vigorously after each addition, until butter is incorporated and sauce has consistency of heavy cream, 4 to 5 minutes. Remove saucepan from heat. Add vegetables and stir to coat. Dry platter and return vegetables to platter. Sprinkle with chives and serve.

## Beets with Lemon and Almonds

**SERVES 4 to 6**

---

**WHY THIS RECIPE WORKS** This streamlined recipe for beets maximizes their sweet, earthy flavor. To achieve our goal, we braised the halved beets on the stovetop in minimal water, reduced the residual cooking liquid, and added light brown sugar and vinegar. This flavor-packed glaze was just thick enough to coat the wedges of peeled beets. For flavor and texture contrast, we added toasted nuts (or pepitas), fresh herbs, and aromatic citrus zest just before serving. To ensure even cooking, we recommend using beets that are of similar size—roughly 2 to 3 inches in diameter. The beets can be served warm or at room temperature. If serving at room temperature, wait until right before serving to sprinkle on the almonds and herbs.

- 1½ pounds beets, trimmed and halved horizontally
- 1¼ cups water
- ¾ teaspoon table salt, divided
- 3 tablespoons distilled white vinegar
- 1 tablespoon packed light brown sugar
- 1 shallot, sliced thin
- 1 teaspoon grated lemon zest
- ¼ teaspoon pepper
- ½ cup whole almonds, toasted and chopped
- 2 tablespoons chopped fresh mint
- 1 teaspoon chopped fresh thyme

1. Place beets, cut side down, in single layer in 11-inch straight-sided sauté pan or Dutch oven. Add water and ¼ teaspoon salt; bring to simmer over high heat. Reduce heat to low; cover; and simmer until beets are tender and tip of paring knife inserted into beets meets no resistance, 45 to 50 minutes.

2. Transfer beets to cutting board. Increase heat to medium-high and reduce cooking liquid, stirring occasionally, until pan is almost dry, 5 to 6 minutes. Add vinegar and sugar, return to boil, and cook, stirring constantly with heat-resistant spatula, until spatula leaves wide trail when dragged through glaze, 1 to 2 minutes. Remove pan from heat.

3. When beets are cool enough to handle, rub off skins with paper towel or clean dish towel and cut into ½-inch wedges. Add beets, shallot, lemon zest, pepper, and remaining ½ teaspoon salt to glaze and toss to coat. Transfer beets to serving dish; sprinkle with almonds, mint, and thyme; and serve.

## Roasted Broccoli

**SERVES 4**

**WHY THIS RECIPE WORKS** Roasting can concentrate flavor to turn dull vegetables into something great, but roasting broccoli usually makes for spotty browning and charred, bitter florets. We figured out how to roast broccoli so that it turned out perfectly browned and deeply flavorful every time. To ensure that the broccoli would brown evenly, we cut the crown into uniform wedges that lay flat on the baking sheet, increasing contact with the pan. To promote even cooking of the stem, we sliced away the exterior and cut the stalk into rectangular pieces slightly smaller than the more delicate wedges. Preheating the baking sheet helped the broccoli cook faster, crisping but not charring the florets, while a very hot oven delivered the best browning. Sprinkling a little sugar over the broccoli along with the salt and pepper helped it brown even more deeply. We finally had roasted broccoli with crispy-tipped florets and sweet, browned stems. It is important to trim away the outer peel from the broccoli stalks; otherwise, they will turn tough when cooked.

- 1¾ pounds broccoli (1 large bunch)
- 3 tablespoons extra-virgin olive oil
- ½ teaspoon table salt
- ½ teaspoon sugar
- Lemon wedges

**1.** Adjust oven rack to lowest position, place rimmed baking sheet on rack, and heat oven to 500 degrees. Cut broccoli at juncture of florets and stems; remove outer peel from stalk. Cut stalk into 2- to 3-inch lengths and each length into ½-inch-thick pieces. Cut crowns into 4 wedges (if 3 to 4 inches in diameter) or 6 wedges (if 4 to 5 inches in diameter). Place broccoli in large bowl; drizzle with oil and toss well until evenly coated. Sprinkle with salt and sugar and season with pepper to taste; toss to combine.

**2.** Carefully remove baking sheet from oven. Working quickly, transfer broccoli to baking sheet and spread into even layer, placing flat sides down. Return baking sheet to oven and roast until stalks are well browned and tender and florets are lightly browned, 9 to 11 minutes. Transfer to dish and serve with lemon wedges.

## Skillet-Roasted Broccoli

**SERVES 4**

**WHY THIS RECIPE WORKS** Deeply browned broccoli has a nutty flavor and a hint of crisp texture. To make it quickly on the stovetop, we cut broccoli crowns into wedges to expose more surface area for browning, arranged the pieces in oiled skillet so that the flat sides sat flush with the pan's surface, and sprinkled on some water to help the broccoli steam and cook through as it browned. Pressing on the broccoli with the back of a spatula ensured maximum contact with the pan. When the water evaporated, the oil filled any gaps between the broccoli and the skillet for optimal heat transfer and browning. We found that sauces and vinaigrettes sogged out the beautifully crisped tops of the florets, so we whipped up a dry topping to accompany the broccoli for a bit of variety and textural interest. Make the topping recipe before cooking the broccoli, if desired.

- 1 recipe topping (optional) (recipe follows)
- 1¼ pounds broccoli crowns
- 5 tablespoons vegetable oil
- ¾ teaspoon kosher salt
- 2 tablespoons water

**1.** Sprinkle one-third of topping, if using, onto platter. Cut broccoli crowns into 4 wedges if 3 to 4 inches in diameter or 6 wedges if 4 to 5 inches in diameter.

**2.** Add oil to 12-inch nonstick or carbon-steel skillet and tilt skillet until oil covers surface. Add broccoli, cut side down (pieces will fit snugly; if a few pieces don't fit in bottom layer, place on top). Sprinkle evenly with salt and drizzle with water. Cover and cook over high heat, without moving broccoli, until broccoli is bright green, about 4 minutes.

**3.** Uncover and press gently on broccoli with back of spatula. Cover and cook until undersides of broccoli are deeply browned and stems are crisp-tender, 4 to 6 minutes. Off heat, uncover and turn broccoli so second cut side is touching skillet. Move any pieces that were on top so they are flush with skillet surface. Continue to cook, uncovered, pressing gently on broccoli with back of spatula, until second cut side is deeply browned, 3 to 5 minutes longer. Transfer to platter; sprinkle with remaining topping, if using; and serve.

### Smoky Sunflower Seed Topping

**MAKES** about 3 tablespoons

Nutritional yeast is a nonleavening form of yeast with a nutty flavor; look for it in natural foods stores.

- 2 tablespoons raw sunflower seeds, toasted
- 1 tablespoon nutritional yeast
- ½ teaspoon grated lemon zest
- ¼ teaspoon smoked paprika
- ¼ teaspoon kosher salt

Using spice grinder or mortar and pestle, grind all ingredients to coarse powder.

## Roasted Brussels Sprouts

**SERVES** 6 to 8

**WHY THIS RECIPE WORKS** Roasting is a simple and quick way to produce brussels sprouts that are well caramelized on the outside and tender on the inside. To ensure that we achieved this balance, we started out roasting the "tiny cabbages" covered with a little bit of water. This created a steamy environment which cooked the vegetables through. We then removed the foil and allowed the exteriors to dry out and caramelize. If you are buying loose brussels sprouts, select those that are about 1½ inches long. Quarter brussels sprouts longer than 2½ inches; don't cut sprouts shorter than 1 inch.

- 2¼ pounds brussels sprouts, trimmed and halved
- 3 tablespoons extra-virgin olive oil
- 1 tablespoon water
- ¾ teaspoon table salt
- ¼ teaspoon pepper

**1.** Adjust oven rack to upper-middle position and heat oven to 500 degrees. Toss all ingredients in large bowl until sprouts are coated. Transfer sprouts to rimmed baking sheet and arrange cut sides down.

**2.** Cover baking sheet tightly with aluminum foil and roast for 10 minutes. Remove foil and continue to cook until brussels sprouts are well browned and tender, 10 to 12 minutes longer. Transfer to serving platter, season with salt and pepper to taste, and serve.

## Skillet-Roasted Brussels Sprouts with Lemon and Pecorino Romano

**SERVES** 4

**WHY THIS RECIPE WORKS** We wanted a foolproof stovetop recipe that would produce Brussels sprouts that were deeply browned on the cut sides, while still bright green on the uncut sides and crisp-tender within. After several unsuccessful attempts in a hot skillet, we tried starting the sprouts in a cold skillet, adding plenty of oil, and cooking them covered. This gently heated the sprouts and created a steamy environment that cooked them through without adding any extra moisture. We then removed the lid and continued to cook the sprouts cut sides down so they had time to develop a substantial, caramelized crust. Look for Brussels sprouts that are similar in size, with small, tight heads that are no more than 1½ inches in diameter, as they're likely to be sweeter and more tender than larger sprouts. Parmesan cheese can be substituted for the Pecorino, if desired.

- 1 pound small (1 to 1½ inches in diameter) Brussels sprouts, trimmed and halved
- 5 tablespoons extra-virgin olive oil
- 1 tablespoon lemon juice
- Table salt and pepper
- ¼ cup shredded Pecorino Romano cheese

**1.** Arrange Brussels sprouts in single layer, cut sides down, in 12-inch nonstick skillet. Drizzle oil evenly over sprouts. Cover skillet, place over medium-high heat, and cook until sprouts are bright green and cut sides have started to brown, about 5 minutes.

**2.** Uncover and continue to cook until cut sides of sprouts are deeply and evenly browned and paring knife slides in with little to no resistance, 2 to 3 minutes longer, adjusting heat and moving sprouts as necessary to prevent them from overbrowning. While sprouts cook, combine lemon juice and 1/4 teaspoon salt in small bowl.

**3.** Off heat, add lemon juice mixture to skillet and stir to evenly coat sprouts. Season with salt and pepper to taste. Transfer sprouts to large plate, sprinkle with Pecorino, and serve.

### Skillet-Roasted Brussels Sprouts with Maple Syrup and Smoked Almonds

Omit pepper. Substitute 1 tablespoon maple syrup and 1 tablespoon sherry vinegar for lemon juice and 1/4 cup smoked almonds, chopped fine, for Pecorino.

### Skillet-Roasted Brussels Sprouts with Chile, Peanuts, and Mint

Substitute 1 Fresno chile, stemmed, seeded, and minced; 2 teaspoons lime juice; and 1 teaspoon fish sauce for lemon juice. Omit pepper. Substitute 2 tablespoons finely chopped dry-roasted peanuts and 2 tablespoons chopped fresh mint for Pecorino.

## Roasted Carrots

**SERVES** 4 to 6

**WHY THIS RECIPE WORKS** Roasted carrots should have a pleasingly al dente chew and earthy, sweet flavor. Roasting draws out their natural sugars and intensifies their flavor, but too often carrots shrivel up and turn jerky-like under the high heat of the oven. To compensate for the oven's arid heat, we tried adding liquid to the roasting pan. While our carrots turned out moist, they weren't browned and lacked the intense roasted flavor we wanted. Our science editor then explained that no additional moisture was necessary. While a carrot's hard, woody structure doesn't suggest it, the average carrot is actually 87.5 percent water by weight. For our next test we tossed the carrots with melted butter, spread them onto a

baking sheet, and covered the sheet tightly with foil. We roasted the carrots, covered, just until softened; we then removed the foil and continued to roast them to draw out their moisture and brown them. The result? Rich-tasting, tender carrots with a nutty flavor. Best of all, the technique worked just as well when we paired the carrots with other roasted root vegetables such as parsnips, fennel, and shallots. Most bagged carrots come in a variety of sizes and must be cut lengthwise for evenly cooked results. After halving the carrots crosswise, leave small (less than ½ inch in diameter) pieces whole; halve medium pieces (½- to 1-inch diameter) and quarter large pieces (over 1 inch).

- 1½ pounds carrots, peeled, halved crosswise, and cut lengthwise if necessary
- 2 tablespoons unsalted butter, melted
- ½ teaspoon table salt
- ¼ teaspoon pepper

**1.** Adjust oven rack to middle position and heat oven to 425 degrees. Line rimmed baking sheet with parchment paper or aluminum foil. Toss all ingredients in large bowl until carrots are coated. Transfer carrots to prepared baking sheet and spread in single layer.

**2.** Cover baking sheet tightly with foil and roast for 15 minutes. Remove foil and continue to roast carrots, stirring twice, until well browned and tender, 30 to 35 minutes. Transfer to serving platter, season with salt and pepper to taste, and serve.

## Glazed Carrots

**SERVES** 4

**WHY THIS RECIPE WORKS** Glazing is probably the most popular way to prepare carrots, but they often turn out saccharine, with a limp and soggy fibrous texture. We wanted fully tender, well-seasoned carrots with a glossy and clingy—yet modest—glaze. Peeling regular bagged carrots and cutting them on the bias yielded uniform ovals that cooked evenly. We cooked and glazed the carrots in one single operation, starting by cooking the sliced carrots in a covered skillet with chicken broth, salt, and sugar. After the carrots were almost tender, we removed the lid and reduced the liquid. Adding a little butter and a bit more sugar resulted in a pale amber glaze with light caramel flavor. Fresh lemon juice gave the dish sparkle, and a pinch of pepper provided depth.

- 1 pound carrots (about 6 medium), peeled and sliced ¼ inch thick on the bias
- ½ cup low-sodium chicken broth
- 3 tablespoons sugar
- ½ teaspoon table salt
- 1 tablespoon unsalted butter, cut into 4 pieces
- 2 teaspoons juice from 1 lemon
- Ground black pepper

**1.** Bring the carrots, broth, 1 tablespoon of the sugar, and the salt to a boil in a 12-inch nonstick skillet, covered, over medium-high heat. Reduce the heat to medium and simmer, stirring occasionally, until the carrots are almost tender when poked with the tip of a paring knife, about 5 minutes. Uncover, increase the heat to high, and simmer rapidly, stirring occasionally, until the liquid is reduced to about 2 tablespoons, 1 to 2 minutes.

**2.** Add the remaining 2 tablespoons sugar and the butter to the skillet. Toss the carrots to coat and cook, stirring frequently, until the carrots are completely tender and the glaze is light gold, about 3 minutes. Off the heat, add the lemon juice and toss to coat. Transfer the carrots to a dish, scraping the glaze from the pan into the dish. Season with pepper to taste and serve.

## Slow-Cooked Whole Carrots

**SERVES** 4 to 6

**WHY THIS RECIPE WORKS** We wanted a technique for cooking whole carrots that would yield a sweet and meltingly tender vegetable without the carrots becoming mushy. Cooking the tapered vegetable evenly from end to end was a challenge, so we looked to techniques that promised carrots with concentrated flavor and uniformly dense texture. Gently "steeping" the carrots in warm water, butter, and salt before cooking them firmed up the vegetable's cell walls so that they could be cooked for a long time without falling apart. We also took a tip from restaurant cooking and topped the carrots with a cartouche (a circle of parchment that sits directly on the food) during cooking to regulate the reduction of moisture. An easy relish finished the dish on a high note. Use carrots that measure ¾ to 1¼ inches across at the thickest end. The carrots can be served plain, but we recommend topping them with Pine Nut Relish (recipe follows).

- 3 cups water
- 1 tablespoon unsalted butter
- ½ teaspoon table salt
- 12 carrots (1½ to 1¾ pounds), peeled

**1.** Fold 12-inch square of parchment paper into quarters to create 6-inch square. Fold bottom right corner of square to top left corner to create triangle. Fold triangle again, right side over left, to create narrow triangle. Cut off ¼ inch of tip of triangle to create small hole. Cut base of triangle straight across where it measures 5 inches from hole. Open paper round.

**2.** Bring water, butter, and salt to simmer in 12-inch skillet over high heat. Remove pan from heat, add carrots in single layer, and place parchment round on top of carrots. Cover skillet and let stand for 20 minutes.

**3.** Remove lid from skillet, leaving parchment round in place, and bring to simmer over high heat. Reduce heat to medium-low and simmer until almost all water has evaporated and carrots are very tender, about 45 minutes.

**4.** Discard parchment round, increase heat to medium-high, and continue to cook carrots, shaking pan frequently, until they are lightly glazed and no water remains in skillet, 2 to 4 minutes longer. Transfer carrots to platter and serve.

### Pine Nut Relish

**MAKES** about ¾ cup

Pine nuts burn easily, so be sure to shake the pan frequently while toasting them.

- ⅓ cup pine nuts, toasted
- 1 shallot, minced
- 1 tablespoon sherry vinegar
- 1 tablespoon minced fresh parsley
- 1 teaspoon honey
- ½ teaspoon minced fresh rosemary
- ¼ teaspoon smoked paprika
- ¼ teaspoon table salt
- Pinch cayenne pepper

Combine all ingredients in bowl.

## Modern Cauliflower Gratin

**SERVES** 8 to 10

**WHY THIS RECIPE WORKS** For a fresh spin on cauliflower gratin, we relied on cauliflower's ability to become an ultracreamy puree and used it as the base for the sauce. We removed the cores and stems from two heads of cauliflower, steamed them until soft, and then blended them to make the sauce. We cut each head into slabs for a more compact casserole and even cooking. For an efficient cooking setup, we placed the cauliflower cores and stems in water in the bottom of a Dutch oven and set a steamer basket filled with the florets on top. Butter and Parmesan gave the sauce a rich flavor and texture without making it too heavy. A crisp topping of Parmesan and panko gave the gratin savory crunch. This recipe can be halved to serve four to six; cook the cauliflower in a large saucepan and bake the gratin in an 8-inch square baking dish.

- 2 heads cauliflower (2 pounds each)
- 3 cups water, plus extra as needed
- 8 tablespoons unsalted butter, divided
- ½ cup panko bread crumbs
- 2 ounces Parmesan cheese, grated (1 cup), divided
- 2 teaspoons table salt
- ½ teaspoon pepper
- ½ teaspoon dry mustard
- ⅛ teaspoon ground nutmeg
- Pinch cayenne pepper
- 1 teaspoon cornstarch dissolved in 1 teaspoon water
- 1 tablespoon minced fresh chives

**1.** Adjust oven rack to middle position and heat oven to 400 degrees.

**2.** Pull off outer leaves of 1 head of cauliflower and trim stem. Using paring knife, cut around core to remove; halve core lengthwise and slice thin crosswise. Slice head into ½-inch-thick slabs. Cut stems from slabs to create florets that are about 1½ inches tall; slice stems thin and reserve along with sliced core. Transfer florets to bowl, including any small pieces that may have been created during trimming, and set aside. Repeat with remaining head of cauliflower. (After trimming you should have about 3 cups of sliced stems and cores and 12 cups of florets.)

**3.** Combine sliced stems and cores, 2 cups florets, and 6 tablespoons butter in Dutch oven and bring to boil over high heat. Place remaining florets in steamer basket (do not rinse bowl). Once mixture is boiling, place steamer basket in pot, cover, and reduce heat to medium. Steam florets in basket until translucent and stem ends can be easily pierced with paring knife, 10 to 12 minutes. Remove steamer basket and drain florets. Re-cover pot; reduce heat to low; and continue to cook stem mixture until very soft, about 10 minutes longer. Transfer drained florets to now-empty bowl.

**4.** While cauliflower is cooking, melt remaining 2 tablespoons butter in 10-inch skillet over medium heat. Add panko and cook, stirring frequently, until golden brown, 3 to 5 minutes. Transfer to bowl and let cool. Once cool, add ½ cup Parmesan and toss to combine.

**5.** Transfer stem mixture and cooking liquid to blender and add salt, pepper, mustard, nutmeg, cayenne, and remaining ½ cup Parmesan. Process until smooth and velvety, about 1 minute (puree should be pourable; adjust consistency with additional water as needed). With blender running, add cornstarch slurry. Season with salt and pepper to taste. Pour puree over cauliflower florets and toss gently to evenly coat. Transfer mixture to 13 by 9-inch baking dish (it will be quite loose) and smooth top with spatula.

**6.** Scatter bread crumb mixture evenly over top. Transfer dish to oven and bake until sauce bubbles around edges, 13 to 15 minutes. Let stand for 20 to 25 minutes. Sprinkle with chives and serve.

## Braised Collard Greens

**SERVES** 4 to 6

**WHY THIS RECIPE WORKS** Tender, silky, and flavorful collard greens, a Southern favorite, require a long cook time with traditional flavor enhancers to create savory, smoky flavor and tenderness. Starting with ham hocks allowed us to create the richly flavorful broth known as pot liquor or pot likker. Boiling the hocks for 45 minutes, or until the water turned slightly opaque, ensured that the pork's fat and gelatin had diffused into the water, imparting its rich, smoky flavor and body. Cooking the collards for an extended period of time over high heat made them silky, tender, and richly flavorful, consistent with tradition. Select collards that are vibrant green; avoid those that are wilted or yellow. If you can't find two 12-ounce ham hocks, it's fine to buy one larger and one smaller as long as they total about 24 ounces. Use a Dutch oven with a capacity of at least 7¼ quarts. We like to serve these collards with hot sauce, as well as cornbread for dunking or crumbling into the pot liquor.

- 1 tablespoon vegetable oil
- 5 garlic cloves, smashed and peeled
- 12 cups water, divided
- 2 (12-ounce) smoked ham hocks, rinsed
- 2 pounds collard greens
- 2 cups chicken broth
- ¼ teaspoon pepper
- Pinch cayenne pepper

**1.** Heat oil in large Dutch oven over medium heat until shimmering. Add garlic and cook, stirring occasionally, until fragrant, about 1 minute.

**2.** Add 8 cups water and ham hocks. Increase heat to high, cover, and bring to boil. Continue to boil, covered, until water has turned slightly opaque and is reduced by about half, about 45 minutes. While ham hocks cook, prepare collards.

**3.** Using sharp knife, remove stem and central vein from each leaf. Stack 4 or 5 leaves, roll lengthwise, and slice roll crosswise to create ½-inch ribbons. Repeat with remaining collards. Transfer ribbons to large bowl and cover with cool water. Swish with your hand to dislodge grit. Repeat with fresh water, as needed, until grit no longer appears in bottom of bowl. Remove collards from water and set aside.

**4.** Add collards, remaining 4 cups water, broth, pepper, and cayenne to pot (it will be full) and cover. Cook until collards wilt, 4 to 5 minutes. Stir well. Cover and continue to boil, turning ham hocks and stirring halfway through cooking, until collards are very tender, about 1½ hours. (If liquid is more than 2 inches deep at this point, continue to cook, uncovered, until liquid has reduced to about 1 inch, about 30 minutes longer. If liquid is less than 1 inch deep, add enough water to measure 1 inch.)

**5.** Transfer hocks to cutting board and let cool for 10 minutes. Remove meat from bones. Chop meat and stir into collards; discard skin and bones. Season collards with salt to taste, and serve.

## Boiled Corn

**MAKES** 6 to 8 ears

**WHY THIS RECIPE WORKS** You might think you don't need a recipe for boiled corn, but it's easy to overcook. For perfectly crisp, juicy corn, we figured out that the ideal doneness range for it is 150 to 170 degrees—when the starches have gelatinized but a minimum amount of the pectin has dissolved. Consistently cooking the corn to that temperature was easy using a sous vide method: Bring water to a boil, drop in the corn, and shut off the heat. The temperature of the water decreased quickly so the corn didn't overcook, while the temperature of the corn increased to the ideal zone. This recipe's success depends on using the proper ratio of hot water to corn. Use a Dutch oven with a capacity of at least 7 quarts and bring the water to a rolling boil. Eight ears of corn can be prepared using this recipe, but let the corn sit for at least 15 minutes before serving. Serve with Chile-Lime salt, if desired.

- 6 ears corn, husks and silk removed
- Unsalted butter, softened

**1.** Bring 4 quarts water to boil in large Dutch oven. Turn off heat, add corn to water, cover, and let stand for at least 10 minutes or up to 30 minutes.

**2.** Transfer corn to large platter and serve immediately, passing butter, salt, and pepper.

### Chili-Lime Salt

**MAKES** 3 tablespoons

This spice blend can be refrigerated for up to one week.

- 2 tablespoons kosher salt
- 4 teaspoons chili powder
- ¾ teaspoon grated lime zest

Combine salt, chili powder, and lime zest in small bowl.

## Corn Risotto

**SERVES** 6 to 8

**WHY THIS RECIPE WORKS** To make risotto that features truly vibrant corn flavor, we started by blending 3 cups of fresh corn kernels with a little water and the pulpy "milk" we scraped from the cobs to yield a supersweet, bright-tasting puree that infused the rice with corn flavor. Adding the puree near the end of cooking preserved its freshness. The puree also contributed extra liquid as well as naturally occurring cornstarch: The liquid loosened up the risotto to an appropriately fluid consistency, and the cornstarch gelled and acted like a sauce, making the dish especially creamy. Instead of adding the traditional white wine, which overwhelmed the corn's flavor, we stirred in crème fraîche; it added a touch of acidity, and its flavor and richness underscored the risotto's luxurious profile. Serve this risotto as an accompaniment to seared scallops or shrimp or grilled meat. If crème fraîche is unavailable, you can substitute sour cream. A large ear of corn should yield 1 cup of kernels, but if the ears you find are smaller, buy at least six.

- 4–6 ears corn, kernels cut from cobs (4 cups), divided, cobs reserved
- 5½ cups hot water, divided
- 2 tablespoons unsalted butter
- 1 shallot, minced
- 2 teaspoons table salt
- 1 garlic clove, minced
- ½ teaspoon pepper
- 1½ cups arborio rice
- 3 sprigs fresh thyme
- 1 ounce Parmesan cheese, grated (½ cup)
- ¼ cup crème fraîche
- 2 tablespoons chopped fresh chives
- ½ teaspoon lemon juice

**1.** Stand 1 reserved corn cob on end on cutting board and firmly scrape downward with back of butter knife to remove any pulp remaining on cob. Repeat with remaining reserved cobs. Transfer pulp to blender. Add 3 cups corn kernels.

**2.** Process corn and pulp on low speed until thick puree forms, about 30 seconds. With blender running, add ½ cup hot water. Increase speed to high and continue to process until smooth, about 3 minutes longer. Pour puree into fine-mesh strainer set over large liquid measuring cup or bowl. Using back of ladle or rubber spatula, push puree through strainer, extracting as much liquid as possible (you should have about 2 cups corn liquid). Discard solids.

**3.** Melt butter in large Dutch oven over medium heat. Add shallot, salt, garlic, and pepper and cook, stirring frequently, until softened but not browned, about 1 minute. Add rice and thyme sprigs and cook, stirring frequently, until grains are translucent around edges, 2 to 3 minutes.

**4.** Stir in 4½ cups hot water. Reduce heat to medium-low, cover, and simmer until liquid is slightly thickened and rice is just al dente, 16 to 19 minutes, stirring twice during cooking.

**5.** Add corn liquid and continue to cook, stirring gently and constantly, until risotto is creamy and thickened but not sticky, about 3 minutes longer (risotto will continue to thicken as it sits). Stir in Parmesan and remaining 1 cup corn kernels. Cover pot and let stand off heat for 5 minutes. Stir in crème fraîche, chives, and lemon juice. Discard thyme sprigs and season with salt and pepper to taste. Adjust consistency with remaining ½ cup hot water as needed. Serve immediately.

## Corn Fritters

**MAKES** 12 fritters

**WHY THIS RECIPE WORKS** Less is more when making good corn fritters full of fresh corn flavor. These fritters are light, with crispy exteriors and pillow-soft centers. We minimized the number of fillers we added. We processed some of the kernels to act as a thickener rather than bulk up the batter with more flour or cornmeal. This step also let the fresh corn flavor shine through. Browning the corn puree in a skillet drove off excess moisture and deepened the flavor even more. Adding cayenne, nutty Parmesan cheese, and oniony chives balanced the natural sweetness of the corn, and a touch of cornstarch helped crisp the exterior and provide a textural contrast with the creamy interior. Serve these fritters as a side dish with steaks, chops, or poultry or as an appetizer with a dollop of sour cream or with Maple-Chipotle Mayonnaise or Red Pepper Mayonnaise.

- 4 ears corn, kernels cut from cobs (3 cups), divided
- 1 teaspoon plus ½ cup vegetable oil, divided
- ⅛ teaspoon plus ¼ teaspoon table salt, divided
- ¼ cup all-purpose flour
- ¼ cup finely minced chives, divided
- 2 tablespoons grated Parmesan cheese
- 1 tablespoon cornstarch

- 1/8 teaspoon pepper
- Pinch cayenne pepper
- 1 large egg, lightly beaten

**1.** Process 1½ cups corn kernels in food processor to uniformly coarse puree, 15 to 20 seconds, scraping down bowl halfway through processing. Set aside.

**2.** Heat 1 teaspoon oil in 12-inch nonstick skillet over medium-high heat until shimmering. Add remaining 1½ cups corn kernels and 1/8 teaspoon salt, and cook, stirring frequently, until light golden, 3 to 4 minutes. Transfer to medium bowl.

**3.** Return skillet to medium heat, add corn puree, and cook, stirring frequently with heatproof spatula, until puree is consistency of thick oatmeal (puree clings to spatula rather than dripping off), about 5 minutes. Transfer puree to bowl with kernels and stir to combine. Rinse skillet and dry with paper towels.

**4.** Stir flour, 3 tablespoons chives, Parmesan, cornstarch, pepper, cayenne, and remaining ¼ teaspoon salt into corn mixture until well combined. Gently stir in egg until incorporated.

**5.** Line rimmed baking sheet with paper towels. Heat remaining ½ cup oil in now-empty skillet over medium heat until shimmering. Drop six 2-tablespoon portions batter into skillet. Press with spatula to flatten into 2½- to 3-inch disks. Fry until deep golden brown on both sides, 2 to 3 minutes per side. Transfer fritters to prepared sheet. Repeat with remaining batter.

**6.** Transfer fritters to large plate or platter, sprinkle with remaining 1 tablespoon chives, and serve immediately.

### Maple-Chipotle Mayonnaise

**MAKES** ⅔ cup

For the fullest maple flavor, use maple syrup labeled "Grade A Dark Amber."

- ½ cup mayonnaise
- 1 tablespoon maple syrup
- 1 tablespoon minced canned chipotle chile in adobo sauce
- ½ teaspoon Dijon mustard

Combine all ingredients in small bowl.

### Red Pepper Mayonnaise

**MAKES** 1¼ cups

Letting the minced garlic sit in the lemon juice mellows its flavor.

- 1½ teaspoons lemon juice
- 1 clove garlic, minced
- ¾ cup jarred roasted red peppers, rinsed and patted dry
- ½ cup mayonnaise
- 2 teaspoons tomato paste

Combine lemon juice and garlic in small bowl and let stand for 15 minutes. Process red peppers, mayonnaise, tomato paste, and lemon juice mixture in food processor until smooth, about 15 seconds, scraping down sides of bowl as needed. Season with salt to taste. Refrigerate until thickened, about 2 hours.

## Southern Corn Fritters

**MAKES** twelve 2-inch fritters

**WHY THIS RECIPE WORKS** Good corn fritters should be light—creamy in the middle and crisp on the outside. This is rarely the case, however; most corn fritters have little corn flavor and cook up dense and greasy. We wanted to make perfect corn fritters—light, crisp, and packed with fresh corn flavor. We found that combining whole corn kernels and grated kernels worked best for visual appeal, textural contrast, and fullest corn flavor. Running the back of a knife over the cobs from which the corn had been grated helped us extract the flavorful pulp. Equal amounts of flour and cornmeal bound the mixture together without making the fritters heavy and kept the corn flavor strong. A bit of heavy cream added welcome richness. For pan-frying the cakes, vegetable oil was the cooking medium of choice for its high smoke point and neutral flavor, which didn't overpower the corn. Keeping the oil hot helped the fritters brown quickly. Serve these fritters with hot sauce, salsa, or even maple syrup.

- 4 ears corn, husks and silk removed
- 1 large egg, lightly beaten
- 3 tablespoons unbleached all-purpose flour
- 3 tablespoons cornmeal
- 2 tablespoons heavy cream
- 1 small shallot, minced (about 1 tablespoon)
- ½ teaspoon table salt
- Pinch cayenne pepper
- ¼ cup vegetable oil, plus more as needed

**1.** Stand the corn upright inside a large bowl and, using a paring knife, carefully cut the kernels from 2 ears of the corn; you should have about 1 cup. Transfer the kernels to a medium bowl. Use the back of a butter knife to scrape off any pulp remaining on the cobs and transfer it to the bowl. Grate the kernels from the remaining 2 ears of corn on the large holes of a box grater, then firmly scrape off any pulp remaining on the cobs with the back of a butter knife; you should have a generous cup of kernels and pulp. Transfer the grated kernels and pulp to the bowl with the cut kernels.

**2.** Mix the egg, flour, cornmeal, cream, shallot, salt, and cayenne into the corn mixture to form a thick batter.

**3.** Heat the oil in a 12-inch skillet over medium-high heat until almost smoking, about 2 minutes. Drop heaping tablespoons of batter into the oil (half the batter, or six fritters, should fit into the pan at once). Fry until golden brown, about 1 minute. Using a thin metal spatula, turn the fritters and fry until the second side is golden brown, about 1 minute longer. Transfer the fritters to a paper towel–lined plate. Repeat with the remaining batter, adding more oil to the skillet if necessary. Serve.

## Braised Eggplant with Paprika, Coriander, and Yogurt

**SERVES** 4 to 6

**WHY THIS RECIPE WORKS** Braised eggplant develops a meltingly tender, creamy texture, yet the pieces remain meaty and intact. Eggplant is easy to prep and mild in flavor, with extremely porous flesh that soaks up seasonings. We cut the eggplant into slim wedges, making sure that each piece had some skin attached to it, which gave it structural integrity even after the flesh became tender. We braised the eggplant in a single batch in a skillet. As the eggplant cooked, its uniquely air-filled flesh collapsed and became denser and firmer. We cooked the eggplant until it softened and the savory braising liquid—made with tomato paste, garlic, and a mix of warm spices—reduced to a thick sauce. We served our eggplant and sauce with a drizzle of cool yogurt and a refreshing sprinkle of cilantro. Large globe and Italian eggplants disintegrate when braised, so do not substitute a single 1- to 1¼-pound eggplant here. You can substitute 1 to 1¼ pounds of long, slim Chinese or Japanese eggplants if they are available; cut them as directed.

- 2 (8- to 10-ounce) globe or Italian eggplants
- 3 tablespoons vegetable oil
- 2 garlic cloves, minced
- 1 tablespoon tomato paste
- 2 teaspoons paprika
- 1 teaspoon table salt
- 1 teaspoon ground coriander
- ½ teaspoon sugar
- ½ teaspoon ground cumin
- ½ teaspoon ground cinnamon
- ½ teaspoon ground nutmeg
- ½ teaspoon ground ginger
- 2¾ cups water
- ⅓ cup plain whole-milk yogurt
- 2 tablespoons minced fresh cilantro

**1.** Trim ½ inch from top and bottom of 1 eggplant. Halve eggplant crosswise. Cut each half lengthwise into 2 pieces. Cut each piece into ¾-inch-thick wedges. Repeat with remaining eggplant.

**2.** Heat oil in 12-inch nonstick skillet over medium heat until shimmering. Add garlic and cook, stirring constantly, until fragrant, about 30 seconds. Add tomato paste, paprika, salt, coriander, sugar, cumin, cinnamon, nutmeg, and ginger and cook, stirring constantly, until mixture starts to darken, 1 to 2 minutes. Spread eggplant evenly in skillet (pieces will not form single layer). Pour water over eggplant. Increase heat to high and bring to boil. Reduce heat to maintain gentle boil. Cover and cook until eggplant is soft and has decreased in volume enough to form single layer on bottom of skillet, about 15 minutes, gently shaking skillet to settle eggplant halfway through cooking (some pieces will remain opaque).

**3.** Uncover and continue to cook, swirling skillet occasionally, until liquid is thickened and reduced to just a few tablespoons, 12 to 14 minutes longer. Off heat, season with salt and pepper to taste. Transfer to platter, drizzle with yogurt, sprinkle with cilantro, and serve.

## Roasted Fennel

**SERVES** 4 to 6

**WHY THIS RECIPE WORKS** Roasting coaxes out fennel's hidden flavors, turning it nutty and savory-sweet and making it the perfect accompaniment to any dish. We began by cutting the bulbs into wedges, which provided good surface area for browning and kept the layers intact. Covering the pieces with foil for most of the cooking time allowed them to steam and turn creamy; we then removed the foil for the last 10 minutes so that they caramelized. Look for fennel bulbs that measure 3½ to 4 inches in diameter and weigh around 1 pound with the stalks (12 to 14 ounces without); trim the bases very lightly so that the bulbs remain intact.

- 2 fennel bulbs, bases lightly trimmed, 2 tablespoons fronds chopped coarse, stalks discarded
- 2 tablespoons water
- 1 teaspoon kosher salt
- 3 tablespoons vegetable oil
- ¼ teaspoon pepper
- 1 recipe topping (optional) (recipe follows)

**1.** Adjust oven rack to lower-middle position and heat oven to 450 degrees. Spray rimmed baking sheet with vegetable oil spray.

**2.** Cut each fennel bulb lengthwise through core into 8 wedges (do not remove core). Whisk water and salt in large bowl until salt is dissolved. Add fennel wedges to bowl and toss gently to coat. Drizzle with oil, sprinkle with pepper, and toss gently to coat. Arrange fennel wedges cut side down along 2 longer sides of prepared sheet. Drizzle any water in bowl evenly over fennel wedges. Cover sheet tightly with aluminum foil and roast for 20 minutes.

**3.** Remove foil from sheet and continue to roast until side of fennel touching sheet is browned, 5 to 8 minutes longer, rotating sheet halfway through roasting. Flip each fennel wedge to second cut side. Continue to roast until second side is browned, 3 to 5 minutes longer. Transfer to plate; sprinkle with topping, if using, and fennel fronds; and serve.

### Orange-Honey Dressing

**MAKES** ¼ cup

Vinegar boosts the acidity in this dressing.

- 1 tablespoon extra-virgin olive oil
- 2 teaspoons honey
- 1½ teaspoons white wine vinegar
- ⅛ teaspoon grated orange zest plus 1 tablespoon juice
- Pinch kosher salt

Whisk all ingredients together in bowl

## Blanched Green Beans

**SERVES** 4

**WHY THIS RECIPE WORKS** Most vegetable side dishes require last-minute preparation, but green beans are an ideal side dish that can be prepared largely beforehand without sacrificing texture or flavor. We wanted a foolproof way of cooking beans ahead of time and then simply reheating and seasoning them just before serving. The easiest way to do this was to blanch the beans in salted water, shock them in ice water to stop the cooking process, and then towel-dry and refrigerate them until needed—a process that could be completed up to three days before serving. To serve, we reheated the beans in a skillet with a little water and flavored them with a butter sauce. The small amount of water came to a boil quickly and evaporated almost completely, helping to heat the beans in just a minute or two for a quick and flavorful side dish. Blanched and cooled beans can be refrigerated in a zipper-lock bag for up to 3 days.

- 1 teaspoon table salt
- 1 pound green beans, trimmed

Bring 2½ quarts water to a boil in a large saucepan over high heat; add the salt and green beans, return to a boil, and cook until the beans are bright green and crisp-tender, 3 to 4 minutes. Drain the beans and transfer them immediately to a large bowl filled with ice water. When the beans have cooled to room temperature, drain again and dry thoroughly with paper towels. Set aside (or refrigerate) until needed.

## Green Beans Amandine

**SERVE** 8

**WHY THIS RECIPE WORKS** A simple dish of green beans tossed with toasted almonds and a light lemon-butter sauce, green beans amandine, is refined yet not intimidating. Unfortunately, recipes too often yield limp beans swimming in pools of overly acidic sauce, with soft, pale almonds thrown on as an afterthought. We wanted to revive this side dish with tender green beans, crisp almonds, and a balanced sauce. For maximum flavor, we toasted the almonds then added some butter to the skillet and allowed it to brown for further nuttiness. Adding some lemon juice off the heat brightened our sauce considerably. After steaming the green beans in a little water in a covered skillet until they were crisp-tender, we tossed them with our sauce for a simple, flavorful take on this classic side. Use a light-colored traditional skillet instead of a darker nonstick skillet for this recipe to easily monitor the butter's browning.

- ⅓ cup sliced almonds
- 3 tablespoons unsalted butter, cut into pieces
- 2 teaspoons juice from 1 lemon
- 2 pounds green beans, trimmed
- Table salt

**1.** Toast the almonds in a large skillet over medium-low heat, stirring often, until just golden, about 6 minutes. Add the butter and cook, stirring constantly, until the butter is golden brown and has a nutty aroma, about 3 minutes. Transfer the almond mixture to a bowl and stir in the lemon juice.

**2.** Add the beans, ½ cup water, and ½ teaspoon salt to the now-empty skillet. Cover and cook over medium-low heat, stirring occasionally, until the beans are nearly tender, 8 to 10 minutes. Remove the lid and cook over medium-high heat until the liquid evaporates, 3 to 5 minutes. Off the heat, add the reserved almond mixture to the skillet and toss to combine. Season with salt to taste, and serve.

## Skillet-Charred Green Beans with Crispy Bread Crumb Topping

**SERVES** 4

**WHY THIS RECIPE WORKS** Sichuan cooks have a method for preparing green beans called dry frying, which is a two-step process where the beans are deep-fried, and then stir-fried with aromatics and maybe a little ground pork. We love this dish and wanted to re-create what we love about it—deeply browned, blistered green beans with a satisfying chew and concentrated flavor—without the deep frying. The secret, we learned, to truly charred beans was to steam the beans first (which we did in the microwave to keep things easy and avoid having to wash out the skillet before cooking them, as steaming them leaves a residue in the pan). Then we charred them in a skillet with just a couple tablespoons of hot oil. We didn't stir the beans for the first few minutes so that they developed deep color and flavor on one side; then we tossed them in the

pan so that they blistered all over. Once they were charred, we seasoned them with a crispy bread crumb topping, which offered great contrast to their tender chew. Microwave thinner, more tender beans for 6 to 8 minutes and thicker, tougher beans for 10 to 12 minutes. To make the beans without a microwave, bring 1/4 cup of water to a boil in a skillet over high heat. Add the beans, cover, and cook for 5 minutes. Transfer the beans to a paper towel–lined plate to drain and wash the skillet before proceeding with the recipe.

- 2 tablespoons panko bread crumbs
- 3 tablespoons vegetable oil, divided
- 3/4 teaspoon kosher salt
- 1/4 teaspoon pepper
- 1/4 teaspoon red pepper flakes
- 1 pound green beans, trimmed

**1.** Process panko in spice grinder or mortar and pestle until uniformly ground to medium-fine consistency that resembles couscous. Transfer panko to 12-inch skillet, add 1 tablespoon oil, and stir to combine. Cook over medium-low heat, stirring frequently, until light golden brown, 5 to 7 minutes. Remove skillet from heat; add salt, pepper, and pepper flakes; and stir to combine. Transfer panko mixture to bowl and set aside. Wash out skillet thoroughly and dry with paper towels.

**2.** Rinse green beans but do not dry. Place in medium bowl, cover, and microwave until tender, 6 to 12 minutes, stirring every 3 minutes. Using tongs, transfer green beans to paper towel–lined plate and let drain.

**3.** Heat remaining 2 tablespoons oil in now-empty skillet over high heat until just smoking. Add green beans in single layer. Cook, without stirring, until green beans begin to blister and char, 4 to 5 minutes. Toss green beans and continue to cook, stirring occasionally, until green beans are softened and charred, 4 to 5 minutes longer. Using tongs, transfer green beans to serving bowl, leaving any excess oil in skillet. Sprinkle with panko mixture and toss to coat. Serve.

## Roasted Green Beans

**SERVES 4**

**WHY THIS RECIPE WORKS** Mature supermarket green beans are often tough and dull, needing special treatment to become tender and flavorful. Braising works, but the stovetop can get awfully crowded as dinnertime approaches. Roasting is a great option for many vegetables, and we wanted to find out if this technique could help transform older green beans, giving them a flavor comparable to sweet, fresh-picked beans. A remarkably simple test produced outstanding results: Beans roasted in a 450-degree oven with only oil, salt, and pepper transformed aged specimens into deeply caramelized, full-flavored beans. Just 20 minutes of roasting reversed the aging process (converting starch back to sugar) and encouraged flavorful browning. Just 1 tablespoon of oil was enough to lend flavor and moisture without making the beans greasy. Lining the pan with foil prevented scorching and made for easy cleanup.

- 1 pound green beans, trimmed
- 1 tablespoon olive oil
- Table salt and ground black pepper

**1.** Adjust an oven rack to the middle position and heat the oven to 450 degrees. Line a large rimmed baking sheet with foil; spread the beans on the baking sheet. Drizzle with the oil; using your hands, toss to coat evenly. Sprinkle with 1/2 teaspoon salt, toss to coat, and distribute in an even layer. Roast for 10 minutes.

**2.** Remove the baking sheet from the oven. Using tongs, redistribute the beans. Continue roasting until the beans are dark golden brown in spots and have started to shrivel, 10 to 12 minutes longer. Season with salt and pepper to taste and serve.

### Roasted Green Beans with Red Onion and Walnuts

Combine 1 tablespoon balsamic vinegar, 1 teaspoon honey, 1 teaspoon minced fresh thyme leaves, and 2 thin-sliced garlic cloves in bowl; set aside. Follow recipe for Roasted Green Beans through step 1, roasting 1/2 red onion, cut into 1/2-inch-thick wedges, along with beans. Remove baking sheet from oven. Using tongs, coat beans and onion evenly with vinegar-honey mixture; redistribute in even layer. Continue roasting until onion and beans are dark golden brown in spots and beans have started to shrivel, 10 to 12 minutes longer. Adjust seasoning with salt and pepper and toss well to combine. Transfer to serving dish, sprinkle with 1/3 cup toasted and chopped walnuts. Serve.

## Classic Green Bean Casserole

**SERVES 8 to 10**

**WHY THIS RECIPE WORKS** We wanted to upgrade green bean casserole to give it fresh, homemade flavor. A preliminary blanching and shocking prepared the beans to finish cooking perfectly in the casserole, enabling them to keep a consistent texture and retain their beautiful green color. For our sauce, we made a mushroom variation of the classic French velouté sauce (where broth is thickened with a roux and finished with heavy cream). Our biggest challenge was the onion topping. Ultimately we found that the canned onions couldn't be entirely replaced without sacrificing the level of convenience we thought this dish needed, but we jazzed them up with freshly made buttered bread crumbs. All the components of this dish can be cooked ahead of time.

**TOPPING**

- 4 slices high-quality white sandwich bread, torn into quarters
- 2 tablespoons unsalted butter, softened
- ¼ teaspoon table salt
- ⅛ teaspoon ground black pepper
- 3 cups canned fried onions (about 6 ounces)

**BEANS**

- Table salt
- 2 pounds green beans, ends trimmed, cut on the diagonal into 2-inch pieces
- ½ ounce dried porcini mushrooms
- 6 tablespoons (¾ stick) unsalted butter
- 1 medium onion, minced
- 3 medium garlic cloves, minced or pressed through a garlic press (about 1 tablespoon)
- 12 ounces white button mushrooms, wiped clean and sliced ¼ inch thick
- 12 ounces cremini mushrooms, wiped clean and sliced ¼ inch thick
- 2 tablespoons minced fresh thyme leaves
- ¼ teaspoon ground black pepper
- 2 tablespoons unbleached all-purpose flour
- 1 cup low-sodium chicken broth
- 2 cups heavy cream

**1. FOR THE TOPPING:** Pulse the bread, butter, salt, and pepper in a food processor until the mixture resembles coarse crumbs, 10 to 15 pulses. Transfer to a large bowl and toss with the onions; set aside.

**2. FOR THE BEANS:** Heat the oven to 375 degrees. Bring 4 quarts water to a boil in a large pot. Add 2 tablespoons salt and the beans. Cook until bright green and slightly crunchy, 4 to 5 minutes. Drain the beans and plunge immediately into a large bowl filled with ice water to stop cooking. Spread the beans out onto a paper towel–lined baking sheet to drain.

**3.** Meanwhile, cover the dried porcini with ½ cup hot tap water in a small microwave-safe bowl; cover with plastic wrap, cut several steam vents with a paring knife, and microwave on high power for 30 seconds. Let stand until the mushrooms soften, about 5 minutes. Lift the mushrooms from the liquid with a fork and mince using a chef's knife (you should have about 2 tablespoons). Pour the liquid through a paper towel–lined sieve and reserve.

**4.** Melt the butter in a large nonstick skillet over medium-high heat. Add the onion, garlic, button mushrooms, and cremini mushrooms and cook until the mushrooms release their moisture, about 2 minutes. Add the porcini mushrooms along with their strained soaking liquid, the thyme, 1 teaspoon salt, and the pepper and cook until all the mushrooms are tender and the liquid has reduced to 2 tablespoons, about 5 minutes. Add the flour and cook for 1 minute. Stir in the chicken broth and reduce the heat to medium. Stir in the cream and simmer gently until the sauce has the consistency of dense soup, about 15 minutes.

**5.** Arrange the beans in a 3-quart gratin dish. Pour the mushroom mixture over the beans and mix to coat the beans evenly. Sprinkle with the bread-crumb mixture and bake until the top is golden brown and the sauce is bubbling around the edges, about 15 minutes. Serve immediately.

## Quick Green Bean "Casserole"

**SERVES 8**

**WHY THIS RECIPE WORKS** We love traditional green bean casserole, but we wanted one with tender beans in a tasty sauce worthy of a holiday spread and yet speedy enough for a last-minute supper. First, we built a sauce in a skillet with onion, garlic, chicken broth, cream, and a little flour; then we added the beans along with thyme and bay leaves, covered them, and allowed them to steam until the beans were almost done. We then stirred in meaty browned cremini mushrooms and thickened the sauce by uncovering the skillet during the final phase of cooking. And instead of canned fried onions, we sprinkled crunchy fried sliced shallots over our easy, tasty skillet casserole.

- 3 large shallots, sliced thin (about 1 cup)
- Table salt and ground black pepper
- 3 tablespoons unbleached all-purpose flour
- 5 tablespoons vegetable oil
- 10 ounces cremini mushrooms, wiped clean and sliced ¼ inch thick
- 2 tablespoons unsalted butter
- 1 medium onion, minced
- 2 medium garlic cloves, minced or pressed through a garlic press (about 2 teaspoons)
- 1½ pounds green beans, trimmed
- 3 sprigs fresh thyme
- 2 bay leaves
- ¾ cup heavy cream
- ¾ cup low-sodium chicken broth

**1.** Toss shallots with ¼ teaspoon salt, ⅛ teaspoon pepper, and 2 tablespoons flour in bowl. Heat 3 tablespoons of oil in 12-inch nonstick skillet over medium-high heat until smoking; add shallots and cook, stirring frequently, until golden and crisp, about 5 minutes. Transfer shallots with oil to baking sheet lined with paper towels.

**2.** Wipe out skillet and return to medium-high heat. Add remaining 2 tablespoons oil, mushrooms, and ¼ teaspoon salt; cook, stirring occasionally, until mushrooms are well browned, about 8 minutes. Transfer to plate and set aside.

**3.** Wipe out skillet. Heat butter in skillet over medium heat; when foaming subsides, add onion, and cook, stirring occasionally, until edges begin to brown, about 2 minutes. Stir in garlic and remaining 1 tablespoon flour; toss in green beans, thyme, and bay leaves. Add cream and chicken broth, increase heat to medium-high, cover, and cook until beans are partly tender but still crisp at center, about 4 minutes. Add mushrooms and continue to cook, uncovered, until green beans are tender and sauce has thickened slightly, about 4 minutes. Off heat, discard bay leaves and thyme; adjust seasonings with salt and pepper. Transfer to serving dish, sprinkle with shallots, and serve.

## Ultimate Green Bean Casserole

**SERVES** 10 to 12

**WHY THIS RECIPE WORKS** This beloved green bean casserole gets high marks for its from-scratch creamy mushroom sauce infused with garlic, freshly made buttery bread crumbs topping the fried onions, and the fact that it serves a crowd and many components can be made ahead. This recipe can be halved and baked in a 2-quart (or 8-inch square) baking dish. If making a half batch, reduce the cooking time of the sauce in step 3 to about 6 minutes (until the sauce measures about 1¾ cups) and the baking time in step 4 to 10 minutes.

**TOPPING**

- 4 slices hearty white sandwich bread, torn into quarters
- 2 tablespoons unsalted butter, softened
- ¼ teaspoon table salt
- ⅛ teaspoon pepper
- 1 (6-ounce) can fried onions (3 cups)

**GREEN BEANS AND SAUCE**

- 2 pounds green beans, trimmed and halved crosswise
- ¾ teaspoon table salt, plus salt for cooking green beans
- 3 tablespoons unsalted butter
- 1 pound white mushrooms, trimmed and broken into ½-inch pieces
- 3 garlic cloves, minced
- ⅛ teaspoon pepper
- 3 tablespoons all-purpose flour
- 1½ cups chicken broth
- 1½ cups heavy cream

**1. FOR THE TOPPING:** Pulse bread, butter, salt, and pepper in food processor until mixture resembles coarse crumbs, about 10 pulses. Transfer to large bowl and toss with onions; set aside. (The topping can be refrigerated in an airtight container for up to 2 days; combine with the onions just before baking.)

**2.** For the green beans and sauce: Adjust oven rack to middle position and heat oven to 425 degrees. Line baking sheet with paper towels. Fill large bowl halfway with ice and water. Bring 4 quarts water to boil in Dutch oven. Add green beans and 2 tablespoons salt and cook until bright green and crisp-tender, about 6 minutes. Drain green beans and transfer to ice bath to cool. Drain again, then spread green beans on prepared sheet and let dry.

**3.** Melt butter in now-empty pot over medium-high heat. Add mushrooms, garlic, pepper, and salt and cook until mushrooms release their moisture and liquid evaporates, about 6 minutes. Add flour and cook for 1 minute, stirring constantly. Stir in broth and bring to simmer, stirring constantly. Add cream, reduce heat to medium, and simmer until sauce is thickened and reduced to 3½ cups, about 12 minutes. Season with salt and pepper to taste.

**4.** Add green beans to sauce and stir until evenly coated. Spread in even layer in 3-quart (or 13 by 9-inch) baking dish. Sprinkle with topping and bake until topping is golden brown and sauce is bubbling around edges, about 15 minutes. Serve immediately. (After green beans and cooled sauce are transferred to baking dish, wrap dish tightly in plastic wrap and refrigerate for up to 24 hours. To serve, remove plastic and bake casserole in 425-degree oven for 10 minutes, then sprinkle with topping and bake as directed.)

## Quick-Cooked Tough Greens

**SERVES** 4

**WHY THIS RECIPE WORKS** Unlike tender greens, tougher greens such as kale, mustard, turnip, and collard greens don't have enough moisture to be wilted in a hot pan; they'll simply scorch before they wilt. Their flavor is much more assertive, even peppery in some cases, and can be overwhelming. We wanted a technique for cooking Southern-style greens that would mellow their assertive bite and render them tender—while still retaining just the right amount of chew. Because they are relatively dry, these greens required the addition of some liquid as they cooked. Steaming the greens produced a texture tasters liked, but it didn't help tame their bitter flavor. Shallow blanching removed enough bitterness to make these assertive greens palatable, but didn't rob them of their character. After blanching the greens, we drained and then briefly cooked them with a little garlic and red pepper flakes for a spicy kick. To prevent them from becoming too dry, we added a little chicken broth to the pan for moistness and extra flavor. Shallow-blanched greens should be shocked in cold water to stop the cooking process, drained, and then braised.

- Table salt
- 2 pounds assertive greens, such as kale, collards, or mustard, stemmed, washed in several changes of cold water, and chopped coarse
- 3 tablespoons extra-virgin olive oil
- 3 medium garlic cloves, sliced thin crosswise (about 3 teaspoons)
- Red pepper flakes
- ⅓–½ cup low-sodium chicken broth
- Lemon wedges, for serving

**1.** Bring 2 quarts water to a boil in a large pot. Add 1½ teaspoons salt and the greens and stir until wilted, 1 to 2 minutes. Cover and cook until the greens are just tender, about 7 minutes. Drain the greens and pour them into a large bowl filled with ice water. Working with a handful of greens at a time, thoroughly squeeze them dry. (Shocked and drained greens can be held for up to an hour before being braised.)

**2.** Heat the oil, garlic, and ¼ teaspoon red pepper flakes in a large skillet over medium heat until the garlic starts to sizzle, about 1 minute. Add the greens and toss to coat with the oil. Add ⅓ cup of the broth, cover, and cook over medium-high heat, adding more broth if necessary, until the greens are tender and juicy and most of the broth has been absorbed, about 5 minutes. Season with salt and additional red pepper flakes to taste. Serve with the lemon wedges.

## Braised Greens with Bacon and Onion

**SERVES 4**

**WHY THIS RECIPE WORKS** This one-pot approach to turning meaty greens like kale and collards tender works perfectly and doesn't require hours of braising or leaving the greens awash in liquid. And these greens are also deeply flavored with smoky bacon and red onion. To start, we cooked the pieces of bacon until crispy, removing them to add later. The onion went into the skillet next and once it was softened we added garlic and pepper flakes. At this point we added half the greens and cooked them until they were beginning to wilt before adding the rest of the greens, along with broth and water. We covered the pot to let them cook through; when the greens had the tender-firm texture we wanted, we removed the lid to cook off the liquid. The result: a winter greens recipe that highlights the greens' cabbage-like flavor and firm texture. Cider vinegar added brightness to our greens and the crispy bacon added big flavor and texture. For the best results, be sure the greens are fully cooked and tender in step 1 before moving on to step 2.

- 6 slices bacon, cut into ¼-inch pieces
- 1 red onion, halved and cut into ¼-inch slices
- 5 garlic cloves, minced
- ⅛ teaspoon red pepper flakes
- 2 pounds kale or collard greens, stemmed and leaves chopped into 3-inch pieces
- 1 cup chicken broth
- 1 cup water
- ¼ teaspoon table salt
- 1 tablespoon extra-virgin olive oil
- 3–4 teaspoons cider vinegar

**1.** Cook bacon in Dutch oven over medium heat until crisp, 5 to 7 minutes. Transfer bacon to paper towel–lined plate and pour off all but 2 tablespoons fat. Add onion and cook, stirring frequently, until softened and beginning to brown, 4 to 5 minutes. Add garlic and pepper flakes and cook until garlic is fragrant, about 1 minute. Add half of greens and stir until beginning to wilt, about 1 minute. Add remaining greens, broth, water, and salt. Quickly cover pot and reduce heat to medium-low. Cook, stirring occasionally, until greens are tender, 25 to 35 minutes for kale or 35 to 45 minutes for collards.

**2.** Remove lid and increase heat to medium-high. Cook, stirring occasionally, until most of liquid has evaporated (bottom of pot will be almost dry and greens will begin to sizzle), 8 to 12 minutes. Off heat, stir in oil, vinegar, and reserved bacon. Season with salt, pepper, and vinegar to taste, and serve.

## Sautéed Mushrooms with Red Wine and Rosemary

**SERVES 4**

**WHY THIS RECIPE WORKS** These deeply flavored mushrooms are a game changer—they make a fantastic side dish or a topping for steak, polenta, or crostini. And it is a counterintuitive trick—starting by adding water, not oil—that makes all the difference. Usually, sautéing mushrooms means piling them in a skillet slicked with oil and waiting patiently for them to release their moisture, which then must evaporate before the mushrooms can brown. We accelerated this process by adding a little water to the pan to steam the mushrooms, which allowed them to release their moisture more quickly. The added benefit of steaming them was that the collapsed mushrooms didn't absorb much oil; in fact, ½ teaspoon of oil was enough to prevent sticking and encourage browning. And because we used so little fat to sauté the mushrooms, we were able to sauce them with a butter-based reduction without making them overly rich. Adding broth to the sauce and simmering the mixture ensured that the butter emulsified, creating a flavorful glaze that clung to the mushrooms. Use one variety of mushroom or a combination. Stem and halve portobello mushrooms and cut each half crosswise into ½-inch pieces. Trim white or cremini mushrooms; quarter them if large or medium or halve them if small. Tear trimmed oyster

mushrooms into 1- to 1½-inch pieces. Stem shiitake mushrooms; quarter large caps and halve small caps. Cut trimmed maitake (hen-of-the-woods) mushrooms into 1- to 1½-inch pieces. You can substitute vegetable broth for the chicken broth, if desired.

- 1¼ pounds mushrooms
- ¼ cup water
- ½ teaspoon vegetable oil
- 1 tablespoon unsalted butter
- 1 shallot, minced
- 1 teaspoon finely chopped fresh rosemary
- ¼ teaspoon table salt
- ¼ teaspoon pepper
- ¼ cup red wine
- 1 tablespoon cider vinegar
- ½ cup chicken broth

**1.** Cook mushrooms and water in 12-inch nonstick skillet over high heat, stirring occasionally, until skillet is almost dry and mushrooms begin to sizzle, 4 to 8 minutes. Reduce heat to medium-high. Add oil and toss until mushrooms are evenly coated. Continue to cook, stirring occasionally, until mushrooms are well browned, 4 to 8 minutes longer. Reduce heat to medium.

**2.** Push mushrooms to sides of skillet. Add butter to center. When butter has melted, add shallot, rosemary, salt, and pepper to center and cook, stirring constantly, until aromatic, about 30 seconds. Add wine and vinegar and stir mixture into mushrooms. Cook, stirring occasionally, until liquid has evaporated, 2 to 3 minutes. Add broth and cook, stirring occasionally, until glaze is reduced by half, about 3 minutes. Season with salt and pepper to taste, and serve.

## Roasted Mushrooms with Parmesan and Pine Nuts

**SERVES** 4

**WHY THIS RECIPE WORKS** Serving up a side of juicy, full-flavored roasted mushrooms started with an unusual step: brining. Soaking earthy cremini and meaty, smoky shiitakes in salty water for 10 minutes allowed the mushrooms' water-resistant proteins to break down, inviting in moisture and perfect seasoning. In order to cook the mushrooms evenly, we spread them on a baking sheet, drizzled them with olive oil, and roasted them; the mushrooms emerged deeply browned but supremely juicy. As a final flourish before serving, we glossed them with butter and a touch of lemon juice and added Parmesan, pine nuts, and parsley to round out the side's hearty, herbal notes. Quarter large (more than 2 inches) cremini mushrooms, halve medium (1 to 2 inches) ones, and leave small (less than 1 inch) ones whole.

- Table salt and pepper
- 1½ pounds cremini mushrooms, trimmed and left whole if small, halved if medium, or quartered if large
- 1 pound shiitake mushrooms, stemmed, caps larger than 3 inches halved
- 2 tablespoons extra-virgin olive oil
- 2 tablespoons unsalted butter, melted
- 1 teaspoon lemon juice
- 1 ounce Parmesan cheese, grated (½ cup)
- 2 tablespoons pine nuts, toasted
- 2 tablespoons chopped fresh parsley

**1.** Adjust oven rack to lowest position and heat oven to 450 degrees. Dissolve 5 teaspoons salt in 2 quarts room-temperature water in large container. Add cremini mushrooms and shiitake mushrooms to brine, cover with plate or bowl to submerge, and let stand for 10 minutes.

**2.** Drain mushrooms in colander and pat dry with paper towels. Spread mushrooms evenly on rimmed baking sheet, drizzle with oil, and toss to coat. Roast until liquid from mushrooms has completely evaporated, 35 to 45 minutes.

**3.** Remove sheet from oven (be careful of escaping steam when opening oven) and, using thin metal spatula, carefully stir mushrooms. Return to oven and continue to roast until mushrooms are deeply browned, 5 to 10 minutes longer.

**4.** Combine melted butter and lemon juice in large bowl. Add mushrooms and toss to coat. Add Parmesan, pine nuts, and parsley and toss. Season with salt and pepper to taste; serve immediately.

## Mushroom Risotto

**SERVES** 4 to 6

**WHY THIS RECIPE WORKS** Earthy mushrooms nestled in a creamy risotto make for a decidedly luxurious dish. But we wanted to reproduce it with supermarket mushrooms, not expensive foraged ones. The key was to turn to aromatic dried porcini, which pack quite a flavor punch, but also add fresh cremini for their substantive texture. We added extra wine to our basic risotto so that its acidity would balance the richness of the mushrooms, and used a decidedly un-Italian ingredient, soy sauce, to intensify the earthiness of the mushrooms and round out the flavors.

- 2 bay leaves
- 6 sprigs fresh thyme
- 4 sprigs fresh parsley, plus 2 tablespoons minced parsley leaves
- 3½ cups low-sodium chicken broth
- 3½ cups water
- 1 ounce dried porcini mushrooms, rinsed in a mesh strainer under running water
- 2 teaspoons soy sauce
- 6 tablespoons (¾ stick) unsalted butter
- 1¼ pounds cremini mushrooms, wiped clean and cut into quarters if small or sixths if medium or large
- 2 medium onions, minced (about 2 cups)
- Table salt
- 3 medium garlic cloves, minced or pressed through a garlic press (about 1 tablespoon)
- 2⅛ cups Arborio rice
- 1 cup dry white wine or dry vermouth
- 2 ounces Parmesan cheese, grated fine (about 1 cup)
- Ground black pepper

**1.** Tie the bay leaves, thyme sprigs, and parsley sprigs together with kitchen twine. Bring the bundled herbs, chicken broth, water, porcini mushrooms, and soy sauce to a boil in a medium saucepan over medium-high heat; reduce the heat to medium-low and simmer until the dried mushrooms are softened and fully hydrated, about 15 minutes. Remove and discard the herb bundle and strain the broth through a fine-mesh strainer set over a medium bowl (you should have about 6½ cups strained liquid); return the liquid to the saucepan and keep warm over low heat. Finely mince the porcini and set aside.

**2.** Adjust an oven rack to the middle position and heat the oven to 200 degrees. Heat 2 tablespoons of the butter in a 12-inch nonstick skillet over medium-high heat. Add the cremini mushrooms, 1 cup of the onions, and ½ teaspoon salt; cook, stirring occasionally, until the moisture released by the mushrooms evaporates and the mushrooms are well browned, about 7 minutes. Stir in the garlic until fragrant, about 1 minute, then transfer the mushroom mixture to an ovensafe bowl and keep warm in the oven. Off the heat, add ¼ cup water to the now-empty skillet and scrape with a wooden spoon to loosen any browned bits on the pan bottom; pour the liquid from the skillet into the saucepan with the broth.

**3.** Melt 3 tablespoons more butter in a large saucepan over medium heat. Add the remaining 1 cup onions and ¼ teaspoon salt; cook, stirring occasionally, until the onions are softened and translucent, about 9 minutes. Add the rice and cook, stirring frequently, until the edges of the grains are transparent, about 4 minutes. Add the wine and cook, stirring frequently, until the rice absorbs the wine. Add the minced porcini and 3½ cups of the broth and cook, stirring every 2 to 3 minutes, until the liquid is absorbed, 9 to 11 minutes. Stir in ½ cup more broth every 2 to 3 minutes until the rice is cooked through but the grains are still somewhat firm at the center, 10 to 12 minutes (the rice may not require all of the broth). Stir in the remaining 1 tablespoon butter, then stir in the mushroom mixture (and any accumulated juice), cheese, and reserved chopped parsley. Season with salt and pepper to taste; serve immediately in warmed bowls.

## Suan La Bai Cai (Sour and Hot Napa Cabbage)

**SERVES** 4 to 6 **SEASON 26**

**WHY THIS RECIPE WORKS** Suan la bai cai, the napa cabbage stir-fry prepared in the sour-hot style (suan means sour; "la," spicy) that is iconic in Sichuan and northern Chinese cuisines, is fast to make, economical, and glossed with an aromatic, vinegary, gently spicy, savory-sweet sauce. Separating the stiff white ribs from the more tender greens and staggering their additions to the wok ensured that both components cooked as quickly and evenly as possible—critical factors that prevented the cabbage from shedding too much of its abundant water and diluting the sauce. Slicing the cabbage ribs on a sharp bias exposed their capillary structure, allowing them to soak up the sauce. Malty black vinegar, combined with soy and oyster sauces, sugar, dried chiles, and plenty of aromatics (garlic, ginger, scallions) added up to an umami-packed, acid-forward sauce with undercurrents of heat and sweetness. We developed this recipe in a 14-inch wok, but you can use a 12-inch nonstick or carbon-steel skillet instead. If using a skillet, use tongs to toss the cabbage greens and increase their cooking time by 1 minute. Sichuan Facing Heaven chiles are traditional, but you can use any small, dried hot chile such as arbol. For a spicier dish, use the larger amount of chiles. Serve with rice.

- 1 head napa cabbage (2 pounds)
- 2 tablespoons soy sauce
- 2 tablespoons Zhenjiang (also called Chinkiang) black vinegar
- 1 tablespoon oyster sauce
- 1 tablespoon cornstarch
- 2½ teaspoons sugar
- 2 tablespoons peanut or vegetable oil
- 3–5 small dried chiles, stemmed, halved, and seeded
- 1 scallion, white and green parts separated and sliced thin
- 1 tablespoon grated fresh ginger
- 1 tablespoon minced garlic

**1.** Discard any outer leaves from cabbage that are bruised or torn. Peel away enough leaves to yield 1½ pounds (16 to 20 leaves). Reserve smaller leaves near core for other use. Stack three similar-size leaves and, using sharp knife, remove white portion from center. Keeping pieces stacked, cut cabbage whites crosswise at 45-degree angle into 1-inch-thick slices and place in medium bowl. Cut cabbage greens into 2-inch pieces and place in second medium bowl. Repeat with remaining leaves.

**2.** Whisk soy sauce, vinegar, oyster sauce, cornstarch, and sugar together in small bowl.

**3.** Heat oil in wok over medium heat until just smoking. Add chiles and cook, stirring constantly with wok spatula or wooden spoon, until they begin to brown, about 30 seconds. Add scallion whites, ginger, and garlic, and cook, stirring constantly, until fragrant, about 1 minute.

**4.** Increase heat to high and add sliced cabbage whites. Cook, stirring constantly, until cabbage begins to turn translucent at edges, about 2 minutes. Add chopped cabbage greens, and cook, stirring constantly, until greens begin to collapse and wilt, about 1½ minutes longer.

**5.** Whisk soy sauce mixture to recombine and pour over cabbage. Cook, stirring constantly, until cabbage is evenly coated and sauce has thickened, about 30 seconds. Immediately transfer cabbage to large serving bowl. Garnish with scallion greens and serve.

## Roasted Okra

**SERVES 4**

**WHY THIS RECIPE WORKS** Roasted okra is a revelation: the pods emerge from the oven brown and delicately crispy at the edges, with a nutty-sweet, green bean–esque flavor. First we arranged split pods cut sides down on a rimmed baking sheet and covered them with foil so that the thicker parts could steam and turn tender before the thin tips scorched. Finally, we uncovered the okra to allow their cut sides, which rested flush against the baking sheet, to brown and crisp lightly. Don't use frozen okra in this recipe. For even cooking and browning, select okra pods that have approximately the same diameter. If you use a dark baking sheet, the browning time after removing the foil will be on the shorter end of the range. If desired, squeeze lemon or lime juice onto the roasted okra and/or sprinkle it with your favorite spice blend.

- 1 pound fresh okra, caps trimmed and halved lengthwise
- 2 teaspoons vegetable oil
- ½ teaspoon table salt

**1.** Adjust oven rack to middle position and heat oven to 425 degrees.

**2.** Toss okra with oil and salt in bowl until well combined. Arrange okra, cut sides down, in single layer on rimmed baking sheet. Cover tightly with aluminum foil and roast until okra is bright green, 12 to 15 minutes (cut sides of a few pieces may be beginning to brown). Remove foil and roast until cut sides are well browned, 7 to 12 minutes.

**3.** Let okra rest on sheet for 5 minutes. Serve.

## Beer-Battered Onion Rings with Jalapeño Dipping Sauce

**SERVES 6**

**WHY THIS RECIPE WORKS** For crisp, flavorful onion rings we started by adding a bit of flavor to the onions themselves by coating them lightly with a mixture of confectioners' sugar, salt, and onion powder. For the batter, we used a combination of all-purpose flour, which clings and browns nicely, and cornstarch, which crisps beautifully. Cold beer provided plenty of bubbles to lighten the batter, and a hefty dose of baking powder boosted those bubbles even more. Cutting the onions to a ½-inch thickness and cooking them briefly in 375-degree oil ensured that the inner onion softened perfectly as the batter crisped, producing onion rings that were easy to bite through without experiencing the dreaded "onion escape." These rings were great on their own, but a cool, creamy, jalapeño-spiked sauce made a complementary accompaniment. Use a Dutch oven that holds 6 quarts or more. We like large yellow onions here, about 1 pound each, but sweet onions such as Vidalia or Walla Walla can be used. If using sweet onions, which are smaller and flatter, do not trim the ends (trimming will reduce the yield too much), and increase the salt to 2 teaspoons. We like an inexpensive lager for this recipe, but nonalcoholic beer works well too.

**SAUCE**

- ½ cup mayonnaise
- 3 tablespoons ketchup
- 2 tablespoons minced jarred jalapeño chiles, plus 1 tablespoon brine
- ½ teaspoon granulated sugar
- ¼ teaspoon cayenne pepper

**ONION RINGS**

- 2 quarts vegetable oil for frying
- 2 teaspoons plus 3 tablespoons cornstarch, divided
- 1 tablespoon confectioners' sugar
- 1½ teaspoons table salt
- 1 teaspoon onion powder
- 2 large yellow onions, peeled
- 2 cups (10 ounces) all-purpose flour
- 2 teaspoons baking powder
- 2 cups cold beer

**1. FOR THE SAUCE:** Whisk all ingredients in bowl until combined. Refrigerate until needed.

**2. FOR THE ONION RINGS:** Heat oil in large Dutch oven over medium-high heat to 380 degrees. While oil heats, combine 2 teaspoons cornstarch, sugar, salt, and onion powder in small bowl.

**3.** Adjust oven rack to middle position and heat oven to 200 degrees. Set wire rack in rimmed baking sheet and line with triple layer of paper towels. With sharp knife, remove ½-inch slice from each end of 1 onion and save for other use. Cut onion crosswise into ½-inch-thick rounds. Repeat with remaining onion. Separate onion rounds into rings, saving 3 innermost layers of each round for other use. Transfer rings to bowl. Sprinkle with 1 tablespoon confectioners' sugar mixture and toss to coat.

**4.** Whisk flour, baking powder, remaining 3 tablespoons cornstarch, and remaining 1½ tablespoons sugar mixture in medium bowl to combine. Whisk in beer until almost smooth (small lumps are OK). Add one-quarter of rings to batter and stir to coat. Using your fingers or tongs, transfer rings to oil one at a time until surface of oil is covered. Fry rings, turning occasionally and adjusting heat to keep oil temperature between 360 and 375, until deep golden brown and crisp, about 4 minutes. Transfer rings to prepared rack and place in oven. Return oil to 380 degrees and repeat with remaining onion rings and batter. Serve with sauce.

## Oven-Fried Onion Rings

**SERVES** 4 to 6

**WHY THIS RECIPE WORKS** Fried onion rings are the perfect accompaniment to burgers, barbecue, and other casual fare. We wanted an oven method that produced tender, sweet onions with a supercrunchy coating. We made a batter with buttermilk, egg, and flour, but when we put the baking sheet in the oven the batter slid right off the onions. Coating the onion rings with flour first gave the batter something to cling to. But we wanted even more crunch. For an extra layer of coating, we turned to crushed saltines and crushed potato chips. We preheated the oil in the baking sheet before adding the coated onions so they'd start crisping right away. The result: crispy, crunchy oven-fried onion rings with deep-fried flavor. Slice the onions into ½-inch-thick rounds, separate the rings, and discard any rings smaller than 2 inches in diameter.

- ½ cup unbleached all-purpose flour
- 1 large egg, at room temperature
- ½ cup buttermilk, at room temperature
- ½ teaspoon table salt
- ¼ teaspoon ground black pepper
- ¼ teaspoon cayenne pepper
- 30 saltine crackers
- 4 cups kettle-cooked potato chips
- 2 large yellow onions, cut into 24 large rings
- 6 tablespoons vegetable oil

**1.** Adjust the oven racks to the lower-middle and upper-middle positions and heat the oven to 450 degrees. Place ¼ cup of the flour in a shallow baking dish. Beat the egg and buttermilk in a medium bowl. Whisk the remaining ¼ cup flour, the salt, black pepper, and cayenne into the buttermilk mixture. Pulse the saltines and chips together in a food processor until finely ground; place in a separate shallow baking dish.

**2.** Working one at a time, dredge each onion ring in the flour, shaking off the excess. Dip in the buttermilk mixture, allowing the excess to drip back into the bowl, then drop into the crumb coating, turning the ring over to coat evenly. Transfer to a large plate. (At this point, the onion rings can be refrigerated for up to 1 hour. Let them sit at room temperature for 30 minutes before baking.)

**3.** Pour 3 tablespoons of the oil onto each of two rimmed baking sheets. Place in the oven and heat until just smoking, about 8 minutes. Carefully tilt the heated sheets to coat evenly with the oil, then arrange the onion rings on the sheets. Bake, flipping the onion rings over and switching and rotating the baking sheets halfway through baking, until golden brown on both sides, about 15 minutes. Briefly drain the onion rings on paper towels. Serve immediately.

## Plátanos Maduros (Fried Sweet Plantains)

**SERVES** 6 to 8

**WHY THIS RECIPE WORKS** In Cuban restaurants, rich, meaty dishes are often accompanied by plátanos maduros, or fried sweet plantains. This savory-sweet side features thick, soft slices of very ripe plantains that are fried in oil to create a caramel-like browned crust encasing a soft, sweet interior; a sprinkling of salt balances the sweetness. We deep-fried our plantains and stirred the slices occasionally so that they would brown evenly. Make sure to use plantains that are very ripe and black.

- 3 cups vegetable oil for frying
- 5 very ripe black plantains (8½ ounces each), peeled and sliced on bias into ½-inch pieces

Heat oil in medium saucepan over medium-high heat until it registers 350 degrees. Carefully add one-third of plantains and cook until dark brown on both sides, 3 to 5 minutes, stirring occasionally. Using wire skimmer or slotted spoon, transfer plantains to wire rack set in rimmed baking sheet. (Do not place plantains on paper towel or they will stick.) Season with kosher salt to taste. Repeat with remaining plantains in 2 more batches. Serve immediately.

## Classic French Fries

**SERVES 4**

**WHY THIS RECIPE WORKS** Efforts to re-create restaurant-style fries at home have always disappointed, with fries that were greasy, droopy, or burnt on the outside and raw on the inside. We wanted to find a method for the home cook that would rival those cooked by professionals—crunchy fries with deep potato flavor. We chose russet potatoes for their dense texture and hearty flavor. Because these are starchy potatoes, it was important to rinse the starch off the surface after cutting the potatoes into fries. For evenly cooked fries, we first refrigerated the cut potatoes in a bowl of ice water for at least 30 minutes and then took a double-fry approach. During the first fry, because the potatoes are nearly frozen, the potatoes can cook long and slow, which ensures a soft, rich-tasting interior. A quick second fry at a higher temperature crisped and colored the exterior. A little strained bacon grease, added to the oil, gave our fries a touch of meaty flavor just like those found in our favorite restaurant fries. We prefer to peel the potatoes. Leaving the skin on keeps the potato from forming those little airy blisters that we like. Once the potatoes are peeled and cut, plan on at least an hour before the fries are ready to eat.

- 2½ pounds russet potatoes (about 4 large), peeled and cut into ¼-inch by ¼-inch lengths
- 2 quarts peanut oil
- ¼ cup bacon fat, strained (optional)
- Table salt and ground black pepper

**1.** Place the cut potatoes in a large bowl, cover with at least 1 inch of water, then cover with ice cubes. Refrigerate for at least 30 minutes or up to 3 days.

**2.** In a large Dutch oven fitted with a clip-on candy thermometer, heat the oil over medium-low heat to 325 degrees. (The oil will bubble up when you add the potatoes, so be sure you have at least 3 inches of room at the top of the pot.) Add the bacon grease (if using).

**3.** Pour off the ice and water, quickly wrap the potatoes in a clean dish towel, and thoroughly pat them dry. Increase the heat to medium-high and add the potatoes, one handful at a time, to the hot oil. Fry, stirring with a spider skimmer or large-holed slotted spoon, until the potatoes are limp and soft and have turned from white to gold, about 10 minutes. (The oil temperature will drop 50 to 60 degrees during this frying.) Use the skimmer or slotted spoon to transfer the fries to a triple thickness of paper towels to drain; let rest for at least 10 minutes. (The fries can stand at room temperature for up to 2 hours.)

**4.** When ready to serve the fries, reheat the oil to 350 degrees. Using the paper towels as a funnel, pour the potatoes into the hot oil. Discard the paper towels and line a wire rack with another triple thickness of paper towels. Fry the potatoes, stirring fairly constantly, until medium brown and puffed, about 1 minute. Transfer to the paper towel–lined rack to drain. Season with salt and pepper to taste. Serve immediately.

## Easier French Fries

**SERVES 4**

**WHY THIS RECIPE WORKS** We challenged ourselves to devise a streamlined recipe for crisp, golden fries without the usual work. We began with an unorthodox procedure of starting the cut potatoes in a few cups of cold oil. To our surprise, the fries were pretty good, if a little dry. When we swapped russets, which are fairly dry, for Yukon Golds, which have more water and less starch, the fries came out creamy and smooth inside and crisp outside. Leaving the fries undisturbed for 15 minutes, then stirring them, kept them from sticking or breaking apart. Thinner batons were also less likely to stick. These fries have all the qualities of classic french fries, without all the bother. Use a Dutch oven that holds 6 quarts or more. For those who like it, flavoring the oil with bacon fat gives the fries a mild meaty flavor. This recipe will not work with sweet potatoes or russets.

- 2½ pounds Yukon Gold potatoes, unpeeled, sides squared off, cut lengthwise into ¼-inch by ¼-inch batons
- 6 cups peanut or vegetable oil for frying
- ¼ cup bacon fat, strained (optional)

**1.** Combine potatoes; oil; and bacon fat, if using, in large Dutch oven. Cook over high heat until oil has reached rolling boil, about 5 minutes. Continue to cook, without stirring, until potatoes are pale golden and exteriors are beginning to crisp, about 15 minutes.

### CUTTING POTATOES FOR FRENCH FRIES

**1.** Square off potato by cutting ¼-inch-thick slice from each of its 4 long sides.

**2.** Cut potato lengthwise into ¼-inch-thick planks.

**3.** Stack 3 or 4 planks and cut into ¼-inch-thick batons. Repeat with remaining planks.

2. Using tongs, stir potatoes, gently scraping up any that stick, and continue to cook, stirring occasionally, until golden and crisp, 5 to 10 minutes longer. Using spider skimmer or slotted spoon, transfer fries to thick paper bag or paper towels. Season with salt to taste; serve immediately.

## Steak Fries

**SERVES 4**

**WHY THIS RECIPE WORKS** Getting steak fries crisp on the outside and tender inside can be tricky—soggy steak fries are too often the norm. We found that the dense starchiness of russet potatoes makes them the best variety for frying. We got the proper ratio of crisp exterior to tender interior when we cut them into ¾-inch wedges. As for the frying oil, peanut oil was our top choice. Chilling the potatoes in cold water before frying proved to be essential as they then cooked more slowly and evenly, without burning. Even after chilling, though, our fries were overcooked when we simply fried them in oil. A two-step process worked wonders. After chilling and drying the potatoes, we par-fried them at a lower temperature to cook the interiors without browning them. Following a brief rest, we fried them again at a higher temperature to brown and crisp the exteriors. Neither greasy nor soggy, these fries boasted great flavor and crunch. The potatoes must be soaked in cold water, fried once, cooled, and then fried a second time—so start this recipe at least one hour before dinner.

- 2½ pounds russet potatoes (about 4 large), scrubbed and cut lengthwise into ¾-inch-thick wedges (about 12 wedges per potato)
- 2 quarts peanut oil
- Table salt and ground black pepper

1. Place the cut potatoes in a large bowl, cover with cold water by at least 1 inch, and then cover with ice cubes. Refrigerate for at least 30 minutes or up to 3 days.

2. In a large Dutch oven fitted with a clip-on candy thermometer, heat the oil over medium-low heat to 325 degrees. (The oil will bubble up when you add the potatoes, so be sure you have at least 3 inches of room at the top of the pot.)

3. Pour off the ice and water, quickly wrap the potatoes in a clean dish towel, and thoroughly pat them dry. Increase the heat to medium-high and add the potatoes, one handful at a time, to the hot oil. Fry, stirring with a spider skimmer or large-holed slotted spoon, until the potatoes are limp and soft and have turned from white to gold, about 10 minutes. (The oil temperature will drop 50 to 60 degrees during this frying.) Use the skimmer or slotted spoon to transfer the fries to a triple thickness of paper towels to drain; let rest for at least 10 minutes. (The fries can stand at room temperature for up to 2 hours.)

4. When ready to serve the fries, reheat the oil to 350 degrees. Using the paper towels as a funnel, pour the potatoes into the hot oil. Discard the paper towels and line a wire rack with another triple thickness of paper towels. Fry the potatoes, stirring fairly constantly, until medium brown and puffed, 8 to 10 minutes. Transfer to the paper towel–lined rack to drain. Season with salt and pepper to taste. Serve immediately.

## Thick-Cut Oven Fries

**SERVES 4**

**WHY THIS RECIPE WORKS** Most people's alternative to deep-fried fries is oven fries, which are usually less fussy to make and often less greasy. We wanted the flavor and crispiness of deep-fried fries with no more work than roasting potatoes. Since oven fries don't heat fast enough for air pockets to form, we instead coated the potatoes in a cornstarch slurry that crisped up like a deep-fried fry would. We arranged the coated planks on a rimmed baking sheet that we coated with both vegetable oil spray and vegetable oil; the former contains a surfactant called lecithin, which prevented the oil from pooling and, in turn, prevented the potatoes from sticking. Covering the baking sheet with foil to start ensured that the potatoes were fully tender by the time they browned to perfection. Choose potatoes that are 4 to 6 inches in length to ensure well-proportioned fries. Trimming thin slices from the ends of the potatoes in step 2 ensures that each fry has two flat surfaces for even browning. You will need a heavy-duty rimmed baking sheet for this recipe. After removing the foil from the baking sheet in step 5, monitor the color of the potatoes carefully to prevent scorching.

- 3 tablespoons vegetable oil
- 2 pounds Yukon Gold potatoes, unpeeled
- 3 tablespoons cornstarch
- Table salt

1. Adjust oven rack to lowest position and heat oven to 425 degrees. Generously spray rimmed baking sheet with vegetable oil spray. Pour oil into prepared sheet and tilt sheet until surface is evenly coated with oil.

2. Halve potatoes lengthwise and turn halves cut sides down on cutting board. Trim thin slice from both long sides of each potato half; discard trimmings. Slice potatoes lengthwise into ⅓- to ½-inch-thick planks.

3. Combine ¾ cup water and cornstarch in large bowl, making sure no lumps of cornstarch remain on bottom of bowl. Microwave, stirring every 20 seconds, until mixture begins to thicken, 1 to 3 minutes. Remove from microwave and continue to stir until mixture thickens to pudding-like consistency. (If necessary, add up to 2 tablespoons water to achieve correct consistency.)

4. Transfer potatoes to bowl with cornstarch mixture and toss until each plank is evenly coated. Arrange planks on prepared sheet, leaving small gaps between planks. (Some cornstarch mixture will remain in bowl.) Cover sheet tightly with lightly greased aluminum foil and bake for 12 minutes.

5. Remove foil from sheet and bake until bottom of each fry is golden brown, 10 to 18 minutes. Remove sheet from oven and, using thin metal spatula, carefully flip each fry. Return sheet to oven and continue to bake until second sides are golden brown, 10 to 18 minutes longer. Sprinkle fries with ½ teaspoon salt. Using spatula, carefully toss fries to distribute salt. Transfer fries to paper towel–lined plate and season with salt to taste. Serve.

## Thick-Cut Sweet Potato Fries

**SERVES** 4 to 6

**WHY THIS RECIPE WORKS** For thick-cut sweet potato fries with crispy exteriors and creamy interiors, we took a cue from commercial frozen fries and dunked the potato wedges in a slurry of water and cornstarch. Blanching the potatoes with salt and baking soda before dipping them in the slurry helped the coating stick to the potatoes, giving the fries a super-crunchy crust that stayed crispy. To keep the fries from sticking to the pan, we used a nonstick skillet, which had the added benefit of allowing us to use less oil. Use a Dutch oven that holds 6 quarts or more. If your sweet potatoes are shorter than 4 inches in length, do not cut the wedges crosswise. Leftover frying oil may be saved for further use; strain the cooled oil into an airtight container and store it in a cool, dark place for up to one month or in the freezer for up to two months. Serve with Spicy Fry Sauce, if desired.

- ½ cup cornstarch
- Kosher salt, for cooking potatoes
- 1 teaspoon baking soda
- 3 pounds sweet potatoes, peeled and cut into ¾-inch-thick wedges, wedges cut in half crosswise
- 3 cups peanut or vegetable oil for frying

1. Adjust oven rack to middle position and heat oven to 200 degrees. Set wire rack in rimmed baking sheet. Whisk cornstarch and ½ cup cold water together in large bowl.

2. Bring 2 quarts water, ¼ cup salt, and baking soda to boil in Dutch oven. Add potatoes and return to boil. Reduce heat to simmer and cook until exteriors turn slightly mushy (centers will remain firm), 3 to 5 minutes. Whisk cornstarch slurry to recombine. Using spider skimmer or slotted spoon, transfer potatoes to bowl with slurry.

3. Using rubber spatula, fold potatoes with slurry until slurry turns light orange, thickens to paste, and clings to potatoes.

4. Heat oil in 12-inch nonstick skillet over high heat to 325 degrees. Using tongs, carefully add one-third of potatoes to oil, making sure that potatoes aren't touching one another. Fry until crispy and lightly browned, 7 to 10 minutes, using tongs to flip potatoes halfway through frying (adjust heat as necessary to maintain oil temperature between 280 and 300 degrees). Using spider skimmer or slotted spoon, transfer fries to prepared wire rack (fries that stick together can be separated with tongs or forks). Season with salt to taste and transfer to oven to keep warm. Return oil to 325 degrees and repeat with remaining potatoes in 2 batches. Serve immediately.

### Spicy Fry Sauce

**MAKES** ½ cup

For a less spicy version, use only 2 teaspoons of chili-garlic sauce. The sauce can be stored in an airtight container and refrigerated for up to 4 days.

- 6 tablespoons mayonnaise
- 1 tablespoon chili-garlic sauce
- 2 teaspoons distilled white vinegar

Whisk all ingredients together in small bowl.

## Air Fryer Parmesan, Rosemary, and Black Pepper French Fries

**SERVES** 2 to 4

**WHY THIS RECIPE WORKS** To give air-fryer French fries a delectable Parmesan-rosemary coating, we cooked some of the cheese onto the fries, creating an adhesive, crispy crust, and then tossed the rest of the cheese with the cooked fries to contribute a blast of pure Parmesan flavor undulled by heat. Adding the rosemary both during and after cooking also best highlighted the herb's aroma. To gild the lily, we added a background of black pepper and sprinkled a third handful of cheese onto the finished fry pile; the fries' heat melted the cheese into a lacy coating. Frequently tossing the fries while they cooked ensured the most even cooking and the best browning. We found tossing the fries in a bowl, rather than in the air-fryer basket, yielded the best results and the fewest broken fries. Do not clean out the tossing bowl while you are cooking; the residual oil helps the crisping process.

1½ pounds russet potatoes, unpeeled
2 tablespoons vegetable oil, divided
1½ ounces Parmesan cheese, grated (¾ cup), divided
4 teaspoons minced fresh rosemary, divided
¼ teaspoon table salt
¼ teaspoon pepper

1. Cut potatoes lengthwise into ½-inch-thick planks. Stack 3 or 4 planks and cut into ½-inch-thick sticks; repeat with remaining planks.

2. Submerge potatoes in large bowl of water and rinse to remove excess starch. Drain potatoes and repeat process as needed until water remains clear. Cover potatoes with hot tap water and let sit for 10 minutes. Drain potatoes, transfer to paper towel–lined rimmed baking sheet, and thoroughly pat dry.

3. Toss potatoes with 1 tablespoon oil in clean, dry bowl, then transfer to air-fryer basket. Place basket in air fryer, set temperature to 350 degrees, and cook for 8 minutes. Transfer potatoes to now-empty bowl and toss gently to redistribute. Return potatoes to air fryer and cook until softened and potatoes have turned from white to blond (potatoes may be spotty brown at tips), 5 to 10 minutes.

4. Transfer potatoes to now-empty bowl and toss with ¼ cup Parmesan, 1 tablespoon rosemary, remaining 1 tablespoon oil, salt, and pepper. Return potatoes to air fryer, increase temperature to 400 degrees, and cook until golden brown and crispy, 15 to 20 minutes, tossing gently in bowl to redistribute every 5 minutes.

5. Transfer fries to bowl and toss with ¼ cup Parmesan and remaining 1 teaspoon rosemary. Season with salt and pepper to taste. Transfer to larger plate and sprinkle with remaining ¼ cup Parmesan. Serve immediately.

## Crispy Potato Latkes

**SERVES** 4 to 6

**WHY THIS RECIPE WORKS** We wanted latkes that were light, not greasy, with buttery soft interiors and crisp outer crusts. We started with high-starch russet potatoes, shredded them, mixed them with some grated onion, and then wrung out the mixture in a dish towel to rid it of excess moisture, which would prevent the latkes from crisping. To ensure that the latkes' centers were cooked before their crusts were too dark, we parcooked the potato-onion mixture in the microwave. We prefer shredding the potatoes on the large holes of a box grater, but you can also use the large shredding disk of a food processor; cut the potatoes into 2-inch lengths first so you are left with short shreds. Serve with applesauce, sour cream, or gravlax.

2 pounds russet potatoes, unpeeled, shredded
½ cup grated onion
1 teaspoon table salt
2 large eggs, lightly beaten
2 teaspoons minced fresh parsley
¼ teaspoon pepper
Vegetable oil

1. Adjust oven rack to middle position, place rimmed baking sheet on rack, and heat oven to 200 degrees. Toss potatoes, onion, and salt in bowl. Place half of potato mixture in center of clean dish towel. Gather ends together and twist tightly to drain as much liquid as possible, reserving liquid in liquid measuring cup. Transfer drained potato mixture to second bowl and repeat process with remaining potato mixture. Set potato liquid aside and let stand so starch settles to bottom, at least 5 minutes.

2. Cover potato mixture and microwave until just warmed through but not hot, 1 to 2 minutes, stirring mixture with fork every 30 seconds. Spread potato mixture evenly over second rimmed baking sheet and let cool for 10 minutes. Don't wash out bowl.

3. Pour off water from reserved potato liquid, leaving potato starch in measuring cup. Add eggs and stir until smooth. Return cooled potato mixture to bowl. Add parsley, pepper, and potato starch mixture and toss until evenly combined.

4. Set wire rack in clean rimmed baking sheet and line with triple layer of paper towels. Heat ¼-inch depth of oil in 12-inch skillet over medium-high heat until shimmering but not smoking (350 degrees). Place ¼-cup mound of potato mixture in oil and press with nonstick spatula into ⅓-inch-thick disk. Repeat until 5 latkes are in pan. Cook, adjusting heat so fat bubbles around latke edges, until golden brown on bottom, about 3 minutes. Turn and continue cooking until golden brown on second side, about 3 minutes longer. Drain on paper towels and transfer to baking sheet in oven. Repeat with remaining potato mixture, adding oil to maintain ¼-inch depth and returning oil to 350 degrees between batches. Season with salt and pepper to taste; serve immediately. (Cooled latkes can be covered loosely with plastic wrap and held at room temperature for up to 4 hours. To freeze, transfer to zipper-lock bag, and freeze for up to 1 month. Reheat in 375-degree oven 3 minutes per side for room-temperature latkes and 6 minutes per side for frozen latkes.)

## Potato Roesti

SERVES 4

**WHY THIS RECIPE WORKS** Achieving a crisp crust and creamy, not gummy, interior is easier said than done in this simple Swiss potato cake. Producing a golden-brown crust for our roesti recipe wasn't much of a problem, but the inside always came out gluey and half-cooked So we eliminated moisture by wringing the raw grated potatoes in a towel rather than patting them with a paper towel. Our final breakthrough came when we tried removing excess starch with a rinse in cold water before squeezing, but then added back just enough starch to hold the cake together by tossing the rinsed, squeezed-dry grated potato with a teaspoon of cornstarch. It is best to shred the potatoes using a food processor to get long shreds. It is imperative to squeeze the potatoes as dry as possible. A well-seasoned cast-iron skillet can be used in place of the nonstick skillet.

- 1½ pounds Yukon Gold potatoes, peeled and shredded
- 1 teaspoon cornstarch
- ½ teaspoon table salt
- Pepper
- 4 tablespoons unsalted butter

1. Place potatoes in large bowl and fill with cold water. Using your hands, swirl to remove excess starch, then drain.
2. Wipe bowl dry. Place half of potatoes in center of dish towel. Gather ends together and twist as tightly as possible to expel maximum moisture. Transfer potatoes to bowl and repeat process with remaining potatoes.
3. Sprinkle cornstarch, salt, and pepper to taste over potatoes. Using hands or fork, toss ingredients together until well blended.
4. Melt 2 tablespoons butter in 10-inch nonstick skillet over medium heat. Add potato mixture and spread into even layer. Cover and cook for 6 minutes. Remove cover and, using spatula, gently press potatoes down to form round cake. Cook, occasionally pressing on potatoes to shape into uniform round cake, until bottom is deep golden brown, 4 to 6 minutes longer.
5. Shake skillet to loosen roesti and slide onto large plate. Add remaining 2 tablespoons butter to skillet and swirl to coat pan. Invert roesti onto second plate and slide it, browned side up, back into skillet. Cook, occasionally pressing down on cake, until bottom is well browned, 7 to 9 minutes. Remove pan from heat and allow cake to cool in pan for 5 minutes. Transfer roesti to cutting board, cut into 4 pieces, and serve immediately.

### Family-Size Potato Roesti

SERVES 6

Increase amount of potatoes to 2½ pounds. Squeeze potatoes in 3 batches and increase salt to ¾ teaspoon and cornstarch to 1½ teaspoons. Cook roesti in 12-inch nonstick skillet, adding additional 1½ teaspoons butter per side (5 tablespoons total). Increase uncovered cooking time in step 4 to 8 to 10 minutes and cooking time in step 5 to 8 to 10 minutes.

## Patatas Panaderas (Spanish Potatoes with Olive Oil and Wine)

SERVES 6

**WHY THIS RECIPE WORKS** Patatas panaderas, a simple yet luxurious dish of thinly sliced potatoes accented with onions and garlic and baked in white wine and plenty of olive oil, is little known outside of Spain, but it deserves a place among the iconic potato dishes of Europe. For our version, we started by peeling and slicing a pile of Yukon Gold potatoes—their moderately waxy, buttery flesh makes them the closest thing we have to the yellow Monalisa and Álava varieties most commonly used in Spain. We covered the potatoes tightly with aluminum foil before sliding them into the oven to help them soften while remaining tender and moist. We also withheld the wine for the first 40 minutes of cooking to prevent its acid from interfering with the softening of the potatoes. Loosening the foil for the last 20 minutes of cooking allowed any excess moisture to evaporate while keeping the potatoes moist, blond, and tender throughout. For the best results, be sure to use a fresh, high-quality extra-virgin olive oil here. Our favorite supermarket product is Carapelli Original Extra Virgin Olive Oil. We developed this recipe using Diamond Crystal kosher salt; if using Morton kosher salt, decrease the amount to 2⅝ teaspoons. To make peeling and slicing easier, choose larger potatoes. These potatoes make an excellent accompaniment to roasted fish or pork.

- 2½ pounds Yukon Gold potatoes, peeled and sliced crosswise ¼ inch thick
- ⅓ cup extra-virgin olive oil
- 3½ teaspoons kosher salt
- ¼ teaspoon pepper
- 1 onion, halved and sliced thin
- 2 garlic cloves, minced
- ½ cup dry white wine

1. Adjust oven rack to middle position and heat oven to 400 degrees. Stir potatoes and oil in large bowl until potatoes are evenly coated. Stir in salt and pepper until well distributed. Stir in onion and garlic. Transfer potato mixture to 13 by 9-inch baking dish and spread into even layer. Cover tightly with aluminum foil and bake until potatoes can be easily pierced with tip of paring knife, about 40 minutes. Reduce oven temperature to 350 degrees.
2. Carefully remove foil and set aside. Pour wine evenly over potatoes. Lightly place reserved foil on top of dish, leaving sides open so moisture can escape, and return dish to oven. Bake until wine has evaporated or been absorbed (there will still be some oil bubbling around edges of dish), about 20 minutes. Carefully remove foil. Let cool for 10 minutes and serve.

## Patatas Bravas

**SERVES** 4 to 6

**WHY THIS RECIPE WORKS** The best versions of patatas bravas showcase crispy, well-browned potatoes served with a smoky, spicy tomato-based sauce. To create an ultracrispy crust without the need for double frying, we first parboiled russet potatoes with baking soda. We also tossed the parcooked potatoes with kosher salt, which roughs up the surfaces of the potatoes, creating nooks and crannies through which steam can escape. As the steam escaped, the nooks and crannies trapped oil, making an even more substantial crust. For our sauce, tomato paste, cayenne, smoked sweet paprika, garlic, and water made a smooth, smoky, and spicy mixture, which we finished with sherry vinegar for tang. While this dish is traditionally served as part of a tapas spread, it can also be served as a side dish with grilled or roasted meat. Bittersweet or smoked hot paprika can be used in place of sweet, but sure be sure to taste the sauce before deciding how much cayenne to add, if any. A rasp-style grater makes quick work of turning the garlic into a paste.

**SAUCE**

- 1 tablespoon vegetable oil
- 2 teaspoons garlic, minced to paste
- 1 teaspoon smoked sweet paprika
- ½ teaspoon kosher salt
- ½–¾ teaspoon cayenne pepper
- ¼ cup tomato paste
- ½ cup water
- 2 teaspoons sherry vinegar
- ¼ cup mayonnaise

**POTATOES**

- 2¼ pounds russet potatoes, peeled and cut into 1-inch pieces
- ½ teaspoon baking soda
- Kosher salt
- 3 cups vegetable oil

**1. FOR THE SAUCE:** Heat oil in small saucepan over medium-low heat until shimmering. Add garlic, paprika, salt, and cayenne and cook until fragrant, about 30 seconds. Add tomato paste and cook for 30 seconds. Whisk in water and bring to boil over high heat. Reduce heat to medium-low and simmer until slightly thickened, 4 to 5 minutes. Transfer sauce to bowl, stir in vinegar, and let cool completely. Once cool, whisk in mayonnaise. (Sauce can be refrigerated for up to 24 hours. Bring to room temperature before serving.)

**2. FOR THE POTATOES:** Bring 8 cups water to boil in large saucepan over high heat. Add potatoes and baking soda. Return to boil and cook for 1 minute. Drain potatoes.

**3.** Return potatoes to saucepan and place over low heat. Cook, shaking saucepan occasionally, until any surface moisture has evaporated, 30 seconds to 1 minute. Remove from heat. Add 1½ teaspoons salt and stir with rubber spatula until potatoes are coated with thick, starchy paste, about 30 seconds. Transfer potatoes to rimmed baking sheet in single layer to cool. (Potatoes can stand at room temperature for up to 2 hours.)

**4.** Heat oil in large Dutch oven over high heat to 375 degrees. Add all potatoes (they should just be submerged in oil) and cook, stirring occasionally with wire skimmer or slotted spoon, until deep golden brown and crispy, 20 to 25 minutes.

**5.** Transfer potatoes to paper towel–lined wire rack set in rimmed baking sheet. Season with salt to taste. Spoon ½ cup sauce onto bottom of large platter or 1½ tablespoons sauce onto individual plates. Arrange potatoes over sauce and serve immediately, passing remaining sauce separately.

## Simplified Potato Galette

**SERVES** 6 to 8

**WHY THIS RECIPE WORKS** Pommes Anna, the classic French potato cake (or galette) in which thinly sliced potatoes are tossed with butter, tightly shingled in a skillet, and cooked slowly on the stovetop, delivers showstopping results, but it requires so much labor that we don't make it very often. We wanted a potato galette with a crisp, deeply bronzed crust encasing a creamy center that tasted of earthy potatoes and sweet butter—and we wanted one we could make on a weeknight. We started by neatly arranging just the first layer of potatoes in the skillet and then casually packed the rest of the potatoes into the pan; once the galette was inverted onto the plate, only the tidy layer was visible. For a galette that held together but wasn't gluey, we rinsed the potatoes to rid them of excess starch, and we incorporated a little cornstarch for just the right amount of adhesion. And in lieu of tamping down on the galette during cooking as is traditional, we simply filled a cake pan with pie weights and set it on the galette for a portion of the baking time. For the potato cake to hold together, it is important to slice the potatoes no more than ⅛ inch thick and dry them thoroughly before assembling the cake. Use a mandoline slicer or the slicing attachment of a food processor to slice the potatoes uniformly thin. You will need a 10-inch ovensafe nonstick skillet for this recipe.

- 2½ pounds Yukon Gold potatoes, unpeeled, sliced ⅛ inch thick
- 5 tablespoons unsalted butter, melted, divided
- 1 tablespoon cornstarch
- 1½ teaspoons chopped fresh rosemary leaves (optional)
- 1 teaspoon table salt
- ½ teaspoon pepper

**1.** Adjust oven rack to lowest position and heat oven to 450 degrees. Place potatoes in large bowl and fill with cold water. Using your hands, swirl to remove excess starch, drain, then spread potatoes onto dish towels and dry thoroughly.

**2.** Whisk 4 tablespoons melted butter; cornstarch; rosemary, if using; salt; and pepper together in large bowl. Add dried potatoes and toss to thoroughly coat. Place remaining 1 tablespoon butter in 10-inch ovensafe nonstick skillet and swirl to coat. Place 1 potato slice in center of skillet, then overlap slices in circle around center slice, followed by outer circle of overlapping slices. Gently place remaining sliced potatoes on top of first layer, arranging so they form even thickness.

**3.** Place skillet over medium-high heat and cook until sizzling and potatoes around edge of skillet start to turn translucent, about 5 minutes. Spray 12-inch square of aluminum foil with vegetable oil spray. Place foil, sprayed side down, on top of potatoes. Place 9-inch cake pan on top of foil and fill with 2 cups pie weights. Firmly press down on cake pan to compress potatoes. Transfer skillet to oven and bake for 20 minutes.

### INVERTING A GALETTE

**1.** Using spatula, loosen galette and slide it out of skillet onto large plate.

**2.** Gently place cutting board over galette. (Do not use an overly heavy board, which may crush the cake.)

**3.** Flip plate over so board is on bottom. Remove plate; galette is now ready to be sliced and served.

**4.** Remove cake pan and foil from skillet. Continue to bake until potatoes are tender when paring knife is inserted in center, 20 to 25 minutes. Return skillet to stovetop and cook over medium heat, gently shaking pan, until galette releases from sides of pan, 2 to 3 minutes.

**5.** Invert galette onto cutting board. Using serrated knife, gently cut into wedges and serve immediately.

## Pommes Anna

**SERVES** 6 to 8

**WHY THIS RECIPE WORKS** Traditional pommes Anna is a crisp, deep brown potato cake with a glassine crust and soft creamy layers within. It's rarely made at home or seen on restaurant menus these days because it takes a long time to prepare and it is hard to remove cleanly from the pan. A nonstick ovenproof skillet ensured easy release every time. Most recipes for pommes Anna call for clarified butter, but we decided to cut down on time and waste (a good portion of the butter is lost with clarifying) and instead tossed the sliced potatoes with melted butter. To accelerate cooking, we arranged the potatoes in elegant, layered circles in the skillet as it was heating on the stovetop; when we were done layering the slices, we pressed the potatoes with the bottom of a cake pan to compact them into a cohesive cake. To unmold, we simply inverted the potato cake onto a baking sheet and then slid it onto a serving dish. Use a food processor fitted with a fine slicing disk or a mandoline to slice the potatoes, but do not slice them until you are ready to start assembling. Start timing when you begin arranging the potatoes in the skillet; they need 30 minutes on the stovetop to brown properly.

- 3 pounds russet or Yukon Gold potatoes (about 6 medium), peeled and sliced ⅛ inch thick (see note)
- 5 tablespoons unsalted butter, melted
- ¼ cup vegetable oil or peanut oil
- Table salt and ground black pepper

**1.** Adjust an oven rack to the lower-middle position and heat the oven to 450 degrees. Toss the potatoes with the butter to coat.

**2.** Heat the oil in an ovensafe 10-inch nonstick skillet over medium-low heat. Begin timing, and arrange the potato slices in the skillet, using the most attractive slices to form the bottom layer, by placing one slice in the center of the skillet and overlapping more slices in a circle around the center slice; form another circle of overlapping slices to cover the pan bottom. Season with ¼ teaspoon salt and pepper to taste. Arrange the second layer of potatoes, working in the opposite direction of the first layer; season with ¼ teaspoon salt and pepper to taste. Repeat, layering the potatoes in opposite directions and seasoning with ¼ teaspoon salt and pepper to taste, until no slices remain (broken or uneven slices can be pieced together to form a single slice; potatoes will mound in the center of the skillet). Continue to cook until 30 minutes elapse from when you began arranging the potatoes in the skillet.

3. Using the bottom of a 9-inch cake pan, press on the potatoes firmly to compact. Cover the skillet and place in the oven; bake until the potatoes begin to soften, about 15 minutes. Uncover and continue to bake until the potatoes are tender when pierced with the tip of a paring knife and the edge of the potatoes near the skillet is browned, about 10 minutes longer. Meanwhile, line a rimless baking sheet or an inverted rimmed baking sheet with foil and spray lightly with vegetable oil spray. Carefully drain off the excess fat from the potatoes by pressing the bottom of the cake pan against the potatoes while tilting the skillet. (Be sure to use heavy potholders.)

4. Set the baking sheet, foil side down, on top of the skillet. Using potholders, hold the baking sheet in place with one hand and carefully invert the skillet and baking sheet together. Lift the skillet off the potatoes; slide the potatoes from the baking sheet onto a platter. Cut into wedges and serve immediately.

## Potatoes Lyonnaise

SERVES 4

WHY THIS RECIPE WORKS Originally conceived as a way to use up leftover boiled potatoes, potatoes Lyonnaise came to represent the best of classic French bistro cuisine: buttery, browned potato slices with strands of sweet, caramelized onion and fresh parsley. We wanted a return to the original, elegant version but one that didn't require leftover potatoes to make. First, we had to choose the right potato. Yukon Golds beat out high-starch russets and low-starch Red Bliss. We precooked the potatoes in the microwave so that, once added to the skillet, they would cook through in the time they took to brown. While the potatoes were in the microwave, we cooked the onions just long enough to release moisture and cook in their own juices. To finish, we united the onions and potatoes in a brief sauté for the perfect melding of flavors. Toss the potatoes halfway through the microwave session to prevent uneven cooking. If using a lightweight skillet, you will need to stir the potatoes more frequently to prevent burning.

- 3 tablespoons unsalted butter
- 1 large onion, halved pole to pole and sliced ¼ inch thick (about 3 cups)
- ½ teaspoon table salt
- 2 tablespoons water
- 1½ pounds Yukon Gold potatoes (about 3 medium), peeled and sliced crosswise into ¼-inch rounds
- ¼ teaspoon ground black pepper
- 1 tablespoon minced fresh parsley leaves

1. Melt 1 tablespoon of the butter in a 12-inch heavy nonstick skillet over medium-high heat. Add the onion and ¼ teaspoon of the salt and stir to coat; cook, stirring occasionally, until the onion begins to soften, about 3 minutes. Reduce the heat to medium and cook, covered, stirring occasionally, until the onion is light brown and soft, about 12 minutes longer, deglazing with the water when the pan gets dry, about halfway through the cooking time. Transfer to a bowl and cover. Do not wash the skillet.

2. While the onion cooks, microwave 1 tablespoon more butter on high power in a large microwave-safe bowl until melted, about 15 seconds. Add the potatoes to the bowl and toss to coat with the melted butter. Microwave on high power until the potatoes just start to turn tender, about 6 minutes, tossing halfway through the cooking time. Toss the potatoes again and set aside.

3. Melt the remaining 1 tablespoon butter in the now-empty skillet over medium-high heat. Add the potatoes and shake the skillet to distribute evenly. Cook, without stirring, until browned on the bottom, about 3 minutes. Using a spatula, stir the potatoes carefully and continue to cook, stirring every 2 to 3 minutes, until the potatoes are well browned and tender when pierced with the tip of a paring knife, 8 to 10 minutes more. Season with the remaining salt and the pepper.

4. Add the onion back to the skillet and stir to combine. Cook until the onion is heated through and the flavors have melded, 1 to 2 minutes. Transfer to a large plate, sprinkle with the parsley, and serve.

## Best Baked Potatoes

SERVES 4

WHY THIS RECIPE WORKS For baked potatoes with an evenly fluffy interior, their center should reach an ideal doneness temperature of 205 degrees. Baking them in a hot (450-degree) oven prevented a leathery "pellicle" or film from forming underneath the peel. To season the potato skin, we coated the potatoes in salty water before baking them. We also achieved a crisp skin by painting the potatoes with vegetable oil once they were cooked through and then baking the potatoes for an additional 10 minutes. Open up the potatoes immediately after removing them from the oven in step 3 so that steam can escape. Top them as desired; try our Herbed Goat Cheese Topping (page 702).

- Table salt for salting potatoes
- 4 (7- to 9-ounce) russet potatoes, unpeeled, each lightly pricked with fork in 6 places
- 1 tablespoon vegetable oil

1. Adjust oven rack to middle position and heat oven to 450 degrees. Dissolve 2 tablespoons salt in ½ cup water in large bowl. Place potatoes in bowl and toss so exteriors of potatoes are evenly moistened. Transfer potatoes to wire rack set in rimmed baking sheet and bake until center of largest potato registers 205 degrees, 45 minutes to 1 hour.

2. Remove potatoes from oven and brush tops and sides with oil. Return potatoes to oven and continue to bake for 10 minutes.

3. Remove potatoes from oven and, using paring knife, make 2 slits, forming X, in each potato. Using clean dish towel, hold ends and squeeze slightly to push flesh up and out. Season with salt and pepper to taste. Serve immediately.

### Herbed Goat Cheese Topping

**MAKES** ¾ cup

Our favorite goat cheese is Laura Chenel's Original Fresh Goat Cheese Log.

- 4 ounces goat cheese, softened
- 2 tablespoons extra-virgin olive oil
- 2 tablespoons minced fresh parsley
- 1 tablespoon minced shallot
- ½ teaspoon grated lemon zest

Mash goat cheese with fork. Stir in oil, parsley, shallot, and lemon zest. Season with salt and pepper to taste.

## Salt-Baked Potatoes with Roasted Garlic and Rosemary Butter

**SERVES** 4

**WHY THIS RECIPE WORKS** Sometimes baked potatoes could use a flavor boost. And instead of light and fluffy, they are often dense and crumbly. Salt-baking potatoes promises to remedy these problems. We tried burying potatoes under a mound of salt, cooking them on a bed of salt, covering them with foil, and making a salt crust on the potatoes with an egg wash. The bed of salt was best. Moisture that escaped during baking was absorbed by the salt and reabsorbed by the potatoes, making their skins tender and their flesh light. Uncovering the potatoes toward the end of cooking ensured dry, crisp skin. A 13 by 9-inch baking dish provided plenty of space, and 2½ cups of salt allowed us to thoroughly cover the bottom of it. A little rosemary and garlic added good flavor. Kosher salt or table salt can be used in this recipe. The salt may be sifted through a strainer to remove any solid bits and reused for this recipe. These potatoes can be prepared without the roasted garlic butter and topped with your favorite potato toppings such as sour cream, chives, crumbled bacon, or shredded cheese.

- 2½ cups plus ⅛ teaspoon table salt
- 4 medium russet potatoes (about 8 ounces each), well scrubbed and dried
- 2 sprigs fresh rosemary plus ¼ teaspoon minced leaves
- 1 whole garlic head, outer papery skin removed and top quarter of head cut off and discarded
- 4 teaspoons olive oil
- 4 tablespoons (½ stick) unsalted butter, softened

**1.** Adjust an oven rack to the middle position and heat the oven to 450 degrees. Spread the salt into an even layer in a 13 by 9-inch baking dish. Gently nestle the potatoes in the salt, broad side down, leaving space between each potato. Add the rosemary sprigs and the garlic, cut side up, to the baking dish. Cover the baking dish with aluminum foil and crimp the edges to tightly seal. Bake for 1 hour and 15 minutes; remove the pan from the oven. Increase the oven temperature to 500 degrees.

**2.** Carefully remove the foil. Remove the garlic head from the baking dish and set aside to cool. Brush the exposed portion of each potato with 1 teaspoon oil. Return the uncovered baking dish to the oven and continue to bake until the potatoes are tender and the skins are glossy, 15 to 20 minutes.

**3.** Meanwhile, once the garlic is cool enough to handle, squeeze the root end until the cloves slip out of their skins. Using a fork, mash the garlic, butter, minced rosemary, and remaining ⅛ teaspoon salt to a smooth paste. Remove any clumped salt from the potatoes (holding the potatoes with a kitchen mitt if necessary), split lengthwise, top with a portion of the butter and serve immediately.

## Twice-Baked Potatoes

**SERVES** 6 to 8

**WHY THIS RECIPE WORKS** Twice-baked potatoes are often plagued by chewy skins and pasty, bland fillings. We wanted to perfect the process and have twice-baked potatoes with slightly crisp, chewy skins and a rich, creamy filling. We found that we could prevent the hollowed-out shells from turning soggy by keeping them in the oven while making the filling. And for the filling we found it best to combine the potato with tangy dairy ingredients—sour cream and buttermilk were ideal—a small amount of butter, and sharp cheddar cheese for its bold flavor. For a perfect finish, we placed the filled potatoes under the broiler, where they turned brown and crisp. Most potatoes have two relatively flat, blunt sides and two curved sides. Halve the baked potatoes lengthwise so the blunt sides are down once the shells are stuffed, making the potatoes much more stable in the pan during final baking. Feel free to substitute other types of cheese, such as Gruyère, fontina, or feta, for the cheddar. Yukon Gold potatoes can be substituted for the russets.

- 4 medium russet potatoes (about 8 ounces each), scrubbed, dried, and rubbed lightly with vegetable oil
- 4 ounces sharp cheddar cheese, shredded (about 1 cup)
- ½ cup sour cream
- ½ cup buttermilk
- 2 tablespoons unsalted butter, softened
- 3 scallions, sliced thin
- ½ teaspoon table salt
- Ground black pepper

**1.** Adjust an oven rack to the upper-middle position and heat the oven to 400 degrees. Bake the potatoes on a foil-lined baking sheet until the skin is crisp and deep brown and a skewer easily pierces the flesh, about 1 hour. Transfer the potatoes to a wire rack and cool slightly, about 10 minutes. (Leave the oven on.)

**2.** Using an oven mitt or folded dish towel to handle the hot potatoes, cut each potato in half so that the long, blunt sides rest on the work surface. Using a small spoon, scoop the flesh from each half into a medium bowl, leaving a ⅛ to ¼-inch thickness of the flesh in each shell. Arrange the shells on the foil-lined baking sheet and return to the oven until dry and slightly crisp, about 10 minutes. Meanwhile, mash the potato flesh with a fork until smooth. Stir in the remaining ingredients, including pepper to taste, until well combined.

**3.** Remove the shells from the oven and increase the oven setting to broil. Holding the shells steady on the pan with an oven mitt or towel-protected hand, spoon the mixture into the crisped shells, mounding it slightly at the center, and return the potatoes to the oven. Broil until spotty brown and crisp on top, 10 to 15 minutes. Cool for 10 minutes and serve warm.

## Smashed Potatoes

**SERVES** 4

**WHY THIS RECIPE WORKS** Bold flavors and a rustic, chunky texture make smashed potatoes a satisfying side dish. But good smashed potatoes are hard to find. We were after a good contrast of textures, with the rich, creamy puree of mashed potatoes accented by chunks of potato and skins. Testing revealed that low-starch, high-moisture red potatoes were the best choice for this dish. Their compact structure held up well under pressure, maintaining its integrity. The thin skins were pleasantly tender and paired nicely with the chunky potatoes. Cooked whole in salted water, the potatoes became lightly seasoned while also retaining their naturally creamy texture, as the skins protected the potato flesh from the water. For the best chunky texture, we smashed the potatoes with a rubber spatula or the back of a wooden spoon. Cream cheese and butter lent tang and body to the dish, and stirring in a little of the potato cooking water added moisture to give it a creamy consistency. Seasoned with salt, freshly ground black pepper, and chopped chives, these potatoes are a quick, no-fuss side dish. Try to get potatoes of equal size; if that's not possible, test the larger potatoes for doneness (use a paring knife). If only large potatoes are available, increase the cooking time by about 10 minutes.

- 2 pounds red potatoes (about 12 small), scrubbed
- Table salt
- 1 bay leaf
- 4 tablespoons (½ stick) unsalted butter, melted
- 4 ounces cream cheese, at room temperature
- 3 tablespoons minced fresh chives (optional)
- Ground black pepper

**1.** Place the potatoes in a large saucepan and add cold water to cover by 1 inch; add 1 teaspoon salt and the bay leaf. Bring to a boil over high heat, then reduce the heat to medium-low and simmer gently until a paring knife can be inserted into the potatoes with no resistance, 35 to 45 minutes. Reserve ½ cup of the cooking water, then drain the potatoes. Return the potatoes to the pot, discard the bay leaf, and allow the potatoes to stand in the pot, uncovered, until the surfaces are dry, about 5 minutes.

**2.** While the potatoes dry, whisk the melted butter and softened cream cheese in a medium bowl until smooth and fully incorporated. Add ¼ cup of the reserved cooking water, the chives (if using), ½ teaspoon pepper, and ½ teaspoon salt. Using a rubber spatula or the back of a wooden spoon, smash the potatoes just enough to break the skins. Fold in the butter–cream cheese mixture until most of the liquid has been absorbed and chunks of potatoes remain. Add more cooking water as needed, 1 tablespoon at a time, until the potatoes are slightly looser than desired (the potatoes will thicken slightly with standing). Season with salt and pepper to taste and serve.

## Crispy Smashed Potatoes

**SERVES** 4 to 6

**WHY THIS RECIPE WORKS** Crispy smashed potatoes deliver the best of both worlds: mashed potato creaminess and the crackling-crisp crust of roasted potatoes. Typically, skin-on spuds are parcooked in water. Once squashed, the potatoes are oiled and either pan-fried on the stovetop or roasted in the oven to render the roughened edges browned and crispy and the interior flesh creamy. But we found that parcooking the potatoes in water diluted their flavor. To fix the flavor problem and streamline cooking, we turned to one pan—a baking sheet. Its roomy surface allowed us to prepare all the potatoes at once rather than in batches. We spread them out on the sheet, added a little water, covered the pan, and baked them until tender. To smash all the potatoes at once, we used a second sheet, which we pressed firmly on top of the pan of parcooked potatoes. To crisp the potatoes we simply coated the baking sheet and drizzled the broken spuds with olive oil. This recipe is designed to work with potatoes that are 1½ to 2 inches in diameter; don't use potatoes that are over 2 inches. Remove the potatoes from the baking sheet as soon as they are done browning—they will toughen if left on the sheet for too long. A potato masher can also be used to "smash" the potatoes.

- 2 pounds small red potatoes, unpeeled
- 6 tablespoons extra-virgin olive oil, divided
- 1 teaspoon chopped fresh thyme

**1.** Adjust oven racks to top and lowest positions and heat oven to 500 degrees. Spread potatoes on rimmed baking sheet, pour ¾ cup water into baking sheet, and wrap tightly with aluminum foil. Cook on bottom rack until skewer or paring knife slips in and out of potatoes easily, 25 to 30 minutes (poke skewer through foil to test). Remove foil and let cool for 10 minutes. If any water remains on pan, blot dry with paper towel.

**2.** Drizzle 3 tablespoons oil over potatoes and roll to coat. Space potatoes evenly on sheet. Place second baking sheet on top; press down uniformly on sheet until potatoes are roughly ⅓ to ½ inch thick. Sprinkle with thyme and season with salt and pepper to taste; drizzle evenly with remaining 3 tablespoons oil. Roast potatoes on top rack for 15 minutes. Transfer potatoes to bottom rack and continue to roast until well browned, 20 to 30 minutes. Serve immediately.

#### MAKING SMASHED POTATOES

After rolling cooled, oven-steamed potatoes in olive oil, space them evenly on baking sheet and place second baking sheet on top; press down uniformly on baking sheet until potatoes are roughly ⅓ to ½ inch thick.

## Classic Mashed Potatoes

**SERVES** 4

**WHY THIS RECIPE WORKS** Many people would never consider consulting a recipe when making mashed potatoes, instead adding chunks of butter and spurts of cream until their conscience tells them to stop. Little wonder then that mashed potatoes made this way are consistently mediocre. We wanted mashed potatoes that were perfectly smooth and creamy, with great potato flavor and plenty of buttery richness every time. We began by selecting russet potatoes for their high starch content. Through trial and error, we learned to boil them whole and unpeeled—this method yielded mashed potatoes that were rich, earthy, and sweet. We used a food mill or ricer for the smoothest texture imaginable, but a potato masher can be used if you prefer your potatoes a little chunky. For smooth, velvety potatoes, we added melted butter first and then half-and-half. Melting, rather than merely softening, the butter enabled it to coat the starch molecules quickly and easily, so the potatoes turned out creamy and light. Russet potatoes make fluffier mashed potatoes, but Yukon Golds have an appealing buttery flavor and can be used. This recipe yields smooth mashed potatoes. If you don't mind lumps, use a potato masher.

- 2 pounds russet potatoes (about 4 medium), scrubbed
- 8 tablespoons (1 stick) unsalted butter, melted
- 1 cup half-and-half, warmed
- 1½ teaspoons table salt
- Ground black pepper

**1.** Place the potatoes in a large saucepan and add cold water to cover by 1 inch. Bring to a boil over high heat, reduce the heat to medium-low, and simmer until the potatoes are just tender when pricked with a fork, 20 to 30 minutes. Drain the potatoes.

**2.** Set a ricer or food mill over the now-empty saucepan. Using a potholder (to hold the potatoes) and a paring knife, peel the skins from the potatoes. Working in batches, cut the peeled potatoes into large chunks and press or mill into the saucepan.

**3.** Stir in the butter until incorporated. Gently whisk in the half-and-half, and season with the salt and pepper to taste. Serve.

## Make-Ahead Mashed Potatoes

**SERVES** 8 to 10

**WHY THIS RECIPE WORKS** Mashed potatoes are a must-have at a holiday dinner, but as a side dish they need to be quick and easy enough to leave plenty of time for preparing the main event. We wanted a recipe for mashed potatoes that we could make in advance (up to two days ahead of time)—but one that also yielded fluffy and flavorful potatoes. For light and smooth potatoes, we used high-starch russets; gave them a head start in the microwave; and finished them in the oven, where the dry heat cooked off their excess moisture. We then beat the potatoes in a stand mixer to remove every lump before stirring in a generous amount of heavy cream and butter. To serve, all we needed to do was pull the potatoes from the fridge and zap them in the microwave. We prefer to buy loose potatoes rather than bagged potatoes, as their quality is far superior. Be sure to bake the potatoes until they are completely tender; err on the side of overbaking rather than underbaking. The texture of the mash will be quite loose after you introduce the remaining ½ cup of cream in step 5; the potatoes will thicken once refrigerated and reheated. This recipe can be easily halved to serve four to six, but the mixing times in step 4 may be slightly shorter.

- 5 pounds russet potatoes, unpeeled
- 3 cups heavy cream, hot, divided
- 8 tablespoons unsalted butter, melted
- 2 teaspoons table salt

**1.** Adjust oven rack to middle position and heat oven to 450 degrees.

**2.** Pierce skins of potatoes all over with fork. Microwave for 16 minutes, turning over potatoes halfway through microwaving. Transfer potatoes directly to oven rack and bake, flipping halfway through baking, until paring knife slides easily in and out of potatoes, about 30 minutes (do not underbake).

3. Remove potatoes from oven and cut each potato in half lengthwise. Using oven mitt or folded dish towel to hold hot potatoes, scoop out all flesh from each potato half into medium bowl. Using fork, potato masher, or rubber spatula, mash flesh into small pieces.

4. Transfer half of potatoes to bowl of stand mixer fitted with paddle. Beat on high speed until smooth, about 30 seconds. Gradually add remaining potatoes and continue beating, scraping down bowl as needed, until completely smooth and no lumps remain, 1 to 2 minutes.

5. Remove bowl from mixer. Using rubber spatula, gently fold in 2 cups cream until combined, followed by melted butter and salt. Gently fold in ½ cup cream until combined, then gently fold in remaining ½ cup cream (potatoes will be quite loose).

6. Transfer mashed potatoes to large bowl and cover bowl tightly with plastic wrap. Refrigerate for up to 2 days.

7. When ready to serve, evenly poke small holes in plastic with tip of knife and microwave until potatoes are hot, about 14 minutes, stirring halfway through microwaving. Season with salt and pepper to taste, and serve.

## Fastest, Easiest Mashed Potatoes

SERVES 4 SEASON 26

WHY THIS RECIPE WORKS You can make great mashed potatoes efficiently and any way you like—smooth or chunky, fluffy or creamy, earthy or buttery—as long as you start with properly cooked spuds. It's crucial to avoid overcooking, which results in too much free starch that gelatinizes and renders the mash gluey. To avoid overcooking and also make the cooking go as quickly as possible, we started by slicing the potatoes thin to ensure that they'd cook through more quickly and evenly. We also packed them tightly into a moderately sized pot, which reduced the amount of water needed to cover them and thus the time it took for the water to come to a boil. Yukon Gold potatoes will deliver buttery flavor and color; for earthier flavor, use russets. For a smooth mash, use a ricer or food mill; for a chunkier texture, use a potato masher. For lean mashed potatoes, use milk; for a richer result, use half-and-half.

- 2 pounds Yukon Gold or russet potatoes, peeled and sliced ¼ inch thick
- 8–10 tablespoons half-and-half or milk, divided
- 4 tablespoons unsalted butter, cut into ¼-inch slices
- 1 teaspoon table salt

1. Bring 1 quart water to boil in medium saucepan over high heat. Add potatoes, making sure they are fully submerged in water. (If not, add just enough water to cover). Return water to boil, then adjust heat to maintain very gentle simmer. Cover and cook until paring knife meets no resistance when slipped into center of potatoes, about 12 minutes.

2. Drain potatoes and return to saucepan. Use potato masher, ricer, or food mill to process potatoes to desired consistency. Stir in ½ cup half-and-half, butter, and salt until combined. If desired, adjust consistency with remaining half-and-half as desired. Season with salt and pepper to taste, and serve.

## Garlic and Olive Oil Mashed Potatoes

SERVE 6

WHY THIS RECIPE WORKS The Mediterranean approach of flavoring mashed potatoes with olive oil and garlic is an appealing one, but it's not as simple as replacing the dairy with oil: Olive oil can turn the texture pasty and garlic can be harsh and overpowering. We wanted to translate these bold flavors into a light and creamy mashed potato side dish that would partner well with simple grilled meats or fish. We chose to use russets in this dish for their light, fluffy texture. We first simmered the potatoes and then put the drained, peeled, still-hot potatoes through a ricer or food mill for a smooth texture. We created a mild flavor base by slowly cooking minced garlic in oil, then heightened the garlic flavor a bit by adding just a little garlic, mashed to a paste. Fruity extra-virgin olive oil and a splash of fresh lemon juice brightened the final dish.

- 2 pounds russet potatoes (about 4 medium), scrubbed
- 5 medium garlic cloves, minced or pressed through a garlic press (about 5 teaspoons)
- 2⅛ teaspoons table salt
- ½ cup plus 2 tablespoons extra-virgin olive oil
- ½ teaspoon ground black pepper
- 2 teaspoons juice from 1 lemon

1. Place the potatoes in a large saucepan and add cold water to cover by 1 inch. Bring to a boil over high heat; reduce the heat to medium-low and cook at a bare simmer until just tender (the potatoes will offer very little resistance when poked with a paring knife), 40 to 45 minutes.

2. Meanwhile, place 1 teaspoon of the garlic on a cutting board and sprinkle with ⅛ teaspoon of the salt. Using the flat side of a chef's knife, drag the garlic and salt back and forth across the cutting board in small circular motions until the garlic is ground into a smooth paste. Transfer to a medium bowl and set aside.

3. Place the remaining 4 teaspoons garlic in a small saucepan with ¼ cup of the oil and cook over low heat, stirring constantly, until the garlic begins to sizzle and is soft, fragrant, and golden, about 5 minutes. Transfer the oil and garlic to the bowl with the raw garlic paste.

4. Drain the cooked potatoes; set a ricer or food mill over the now-empty saucepan. Using a potholder (to hold the potatoes) and a paring knife, peel the skins from the potatoes. Working in batches, cut the peeled potatoes into large chunks and press or mill into the saucepan.

5. Add the remaining 2 teaspoons salt, the pepper, lemon juice, and remaining 6 tablespoons oil to the bowl with the cooked garlic and oil and whisk to combine. Fold the mixture into the potatoes and serve.

## Mashed Potatoes with Blue Cheese and Port-Caramelized Onions

**SERVES 4**

**WHY THIS RECIPE WORKS** When it comes to mashed potatoes, most cooks worry so much about getting the texture right that they forget about the flavor. Butter and half-and-half make for mashed potatoes that are rich tasting but not terribly exciting. Our goal was to jazz up the flavor of our classic mashed potatoes. Slowly cooking thinly sliced onions brought out their sweetness, which was further complemented by a reduced port glaze. The onions' sweetness paired well with the tanginess of blue cheese, which we stirred in just before serving. The port adds a sweet depth to the onions that perfectly complements the blue cheese.

**ONIONS**

- 1½ teaspoons unsalted butter
- 1½ teaspoons vegetable oil
- ½ teaspoon light brown sugar
- ¼ teaspoon table salt
- 1 pound onions, halved and sliced ¼ inch thick
- 1 cup ruby port

**POTATOES**

- ¾ cup half-and-half
- 1 teaspoon chopped fresh thyme
- 2 pounds russet potatoes
- 6 tablespoons unsalted butter, melted
- 1¼ teaspoons table salt
- ½ teaspoon pepper
- 4 ounces blue cheese, crumbled (1 cup)

1. **FOR THE ONIONS:** Heat butter and oil in 8-inch nonstick skillet over high heat until butter melts, then stir in sugar and salt. Add onions, stir to coat, and cook, stirring occasionally, until onions begin to soften and release some moisture, about 5 minutes. Reduce heat to medium and cook, stirring frequently, until onions are deeply browned and sticky, about 35 minutes longer (if onions are sizzling or scorching, reduce heat; if onions are not browning after 15 minutes, increase heat). Stir in port and continue to cook until port reduces to glaze, 4 to 6 minutes.

2. **FOR THE POTATOES:** While onions are cooking, bring half-and-half and thyme to boil in small saucepan; cover to keep warm.

3. Place potatoes in large saucepan and cover with 1 inch cold water. Bring to boil over high heat, reduce heat to medium-low, and simmer until potatoes are just tender (paring knife can be slipped in and out of potatoes with very little resistance), 20 to 30 minutes. Drain.

4. Set ricer or food mill over now-empty saucepan. Using potholder (to hold potatoes) and paring knife, peel skins from potatoes. Working in batches, cut peeled potatoes into large chunks and press or mill into saucepan.

5. Stir in butter until just incorporated. Add salt and pepper, then gently stir in half-and-half and blue cheese until just combined. Serve immediately topped with onions.

## Creamy Mashed Potatoes

**SERVES** 8 to 10

**WHY THIS RECIPE WORKS** Sometimes we want a luxurious mash, one that is silky smooth and loaded with cream and butter. But there's a fine line between creamy and gluey. We wanted lush, creamy mashed potatoes, with so much richness and flavor they could stand on their own—no gravy necessary. For a creamier, substantial mash, we found that Yukon Golds were perfect—creamier than russets but not as heavy as red potatoes. Slicing the peeled potatoes into rounds and then rinsing away the surface starch before boiling helped intensify their creamy texture without making them gluey. Setting the boiled and drained potatoes in their pot over a low flame helped further evaporate any excess moisture. Using 1½ sticks of butter and 1½ cups of heavy cream gives these potatoes luxurious flavor and richness without making the mash too thin. We found that melting the butter and warming the cream before adding them to the potatoes ensured that the finished dish arrived at the table piping hot. This recipe can be cut in half, if desired.

- 4 pounds Yukon Gold potatoes (about 8 medium), scrubbed, peeled, and sliced ¾ inch thick
- 1½ cups heavy cream
- 12 tablespoons (1½ sticks) unsalted butter, cut into 6 pieces
- 2 teaspoons table salt

**1.** Place the potatoes in a colander and rinse under cool running water, tossing with your hands, for 30 seconds. Transfer the potatoes to a large Dutch oven, add cold water to cover by 1 inch, and bring to a boil over high heat. Reduce the heat to medium and boil until the potatoes are tender, 20 to 25 minutes.

**2.** Meanwhile, heat the heavy cream and butter in a small saucepan over medium heat until the butter is melted, about 5 minutes. Set aside and keep warm.

**3.** Drain the potatoes and return to the Dutch oven. Stir over low heat until the potatoes are thoroughly dried, 1 to 2 minutes. Set a ricer or food mill over a large bowl and press or mill the potatoes into the bowl. Gently fold in the warm cream mixture and salt with a rubber spatula until the cream is absorbed and the potatoes are thick and creamy. Serve.

## Fluffy Mashed Potatoes

SERVES 4

WHY THIS RECIPE WORKS Cooking potatoes in their skins as opposed to cooking and then peeling them preserves their earthy flavor and keeps the starch granules from absorbing too much water, which prevents gluey mashed potatoes. To give peeled potatoes the same protection, the secret was to steam rather than boil them, which exposed the potato pieces to less water, reducing the chance of the granules swelling to the point of bursting. Because potatoes cooked using this method are so full of rich potato flavor, we were able to use less butter and substitute whole milk for cream. This recipe works best with either a metal colander that sits easily in a Dutch oven or a large pasta pot with a steamer insert. To prevent excess evaporation, it is important for the lid to fit snugly over the colander or steamer. For the lightest, fluffiest texture, use a ricer. A food mill is the next best alternative. Russets will also work in this recipe, but avoid red potatoes.

- 2 pounds Yukon Gold potatoes (about 4 medium), peeled, cut into 1-inch chunks, rinsed well, and drained
- 4 tablespoons (½ stick) unsalted butter, melted
- Table salt
- ⅔ cup whole milk, warmed
- Ground black pepper

**1.** Place a metal colander or steamer insert in a large pot or Dutch oven. Add enough water to barely reach the bottom of the colander. Bring the water to a boil over high heat. Add the potatoes, cover, and reduce the heat to medium-high. Cook the potatoes for 10 minutes. Transfer the colander to the sink and rinse the potatoes under cold water until no longer hot, 1 to 2 minutes. Return the colander and potatoes to the pot, cover, and continue to cook until the potatoes are soft and the tip of a paring knife inserted into the potatoes meets no resistance, 10 to 15 minutes longer. Drain the potatoes.

**2.** Set a ricer or food mill over the now-empty pot. Working in batches, transfer the potatoes to the hopper and process or mill, removing any potatoes stuck to the bottom. Using a rubber spatula, stir in the butter and ½ teaspoon salt until incorporated. Stir in the milk until incorporated. Season with salt and pepper to taste and serve.

## Buttermilk Mashed Potatoes

SERVES 4

WHY THIS RECIPE WORKS Merely replacing butter and cream with buttermilk to create tangy, creamy buttermilk mashed potatoes doesn't work—the finished potatoes are curdled, crumbly, chalky, and dry. We wanted easy mashed potatoes with buttermilk's trademark distinctive tang, but we didn't want to sacrifice texture or richness. We started by restoring just enough butter to save our mashed potatoes from this fate. We then tackled the curdling problem. Buttermilk curdles at 160 degrees, a temperature reached almost instantly when the cold liquid hits steaming-hot potatoes. By adding the butter, melted, to room-temperature buttermilk, we coated the proteins in the buttermilk and protected them from the heat shock that causes curdling. We also simplified the recipe by choosing peeled and cut Yukon Gold potatoes rather than using unpeeled russets (which we have used in other mashed potato recipes). Because Yukon Golds have less starch and are less absorbent than russets, they didn't become soggy and thinned out when simmered without their jackets. To achieve the proper texture, it is important to cook the potatoes thoroughly; they are done if they break apart when a knife is inserted and gently wiggled. Buttermilk substitutes such as clabbered milk do not produce sufficiently tangy potatoes.

- 2 pounds Yukon Gold potatoes (about 4 medium), peeled and cut into 1-inch chunks
- Table salt
- 6 tablespoons (¾ stick) unsalted butter, melted and cooled
- ⅔ cup buttermilk, room temperature
- Ground black pepper

**1.** Place the potatoes in a large saucepan and add cold water to cover by 1 inch; add 1 tablespoon salt. Bring to a boil over high heat, then reduce the heat to medium and simmer until the potatoes break apart very easily when a paring knife is inserted, about 18 minutes. Drain the potatoes briefly, then immediately return them to the saucepan set on the still-hot (but off) burner.

**2.** Using a potato masher, mash the potatoes until a few small lumps remain. Gently mix the melted butter and buttermilk in a small bowl until combined. Add the buttermilk mixture to the potatoes; using a rubber spatula, fold gently until just incorporated. Season with salt and pepper to taste and serve.

## Aligot (French Mashed Potatoes with Garlic and Cheese)

**SERVES 6**

**WHY THIS RECIPE WORKS** Aligot is French cookery's intensely rich, cheesy take on mashed potatoes. These potatoes get their elastic, satiny texture through prolonged, vigorous stirring—which can easily go awry. We wanted to re-create these potatoes with the same signature stretch as the French original. We boiled the potatoes (Yukon Golds), then used a food processor to "mash" them. Traditional aligot uses butter and crème fraîche to add flavor and creaminess and loosen the texture before mixing in the cheese. But crème fraîche isn't always easy to find, so we substituted whole milk, which provided depth without going overboard. For the cheese, a combination of mild mozzarella and nutty Gruyère proved just right. As for the stirring, we needed to monitor the consistency closely: too much stirring and the aligot turned rubbery, too little and the cheese didn't marry with the potatoes for that essential elasticity. White cheddar can be substituted for the Gruyère. For richer, stretchier aligot, double the mozzarella.

- 2 pounds Yukon Gold potatoes, peeled, cut into ½-inch-thick slices, rinsed well, and drained
- 1½ teaspoons table salt, plus salt for cooking potatoes
- 6 tablespoons unsalted butter
- 2 garlic cloves, minced
- 1–1½ cups whole milk
- 4 ounces mozzarella cheese, shredded (1 cup)
- 4 ounces Gruyère cheese, shredded (1 cup)

**1.** Place potatoes and 1 tablespoon salt in large saucepan; add water to cover by 1 inch. Partially cover saucepan with lid and bring to boil over high heat. Reduce heat to medium-low and simmer until potatoes are tender and just break apart when poked with fork, 12 to 17 minutes. Drain potatoes and dry saucepan.

**2.** Add potatoes, butter, garlic, and salt to food processor. Pulse until butter is melted and incorporated, about 10 pulses. Add 1 cup milk and continue to process until potatoes are smooth and creamy, about 20 seconds, scraping down sides of bowl halfway through.

**3.** Return potato mixture to saucepan and set over medium heat. Stir in mozzarella and Gruyère 1 cup at a time, until incorporated. Continue to cook potatoes, stirring vigorously, until cheese is fully melted and mixture is smooth and elastic, 3 to 5 minutes. If mixture is difficult to stir and seems thick, stir in 2 tablespoons milk at a time (up to ½ cup) until potatoes are loose and creamy. Season with salt and pepper to taste. Serve immediately.

## Duchess Potato Casserole

**SERVES 8 to 10**

**WHY THIS RECIPE WORKS** Pommes duchesse is a classic French preparation of piped mounds of egg-enriched mashed potatoes. They can be made in advance, they look festive, and they taste great with a variety of entrées; however, they are rather fussy to prepare, require a pastry bag and cool rapidly. To simplify things, we skipped the piping and baked the mashed potatoes in a larger casserole-style dish, which kept them hotter longer. We enhanced mashed Yukon Golds with butter, egg yolks, half-and-half, and nutmeg, being sure to add the butter first to coat the potatoes' starch granules and protect them from being overworked and turning gluey. For an attractive finish and crust, we coated the top with a mixture of butter and egg white and scored the surface. Freshly ground nutmeg contributes heady flavor, so be sure to use it sparingly.

- 3½ pounds Yukon Gold potatoes, peeled and sliced ½ inch thick
- ⅔ cup half-and-half
- 1 large egg, separated, plus 2 large yolks
- Table salt and pepper
- Pinch nutmeg
- 10 tablespoons unsalted butter, melted

**1.** Adjust oven rack to middle position and heat oven to 450 degrees. Grease 13 by 9-inch baking dish. Place potatoes in large saucepan and add cold water to cover by 1 inch. Bring to simmer over medium-high heat. Adjust heat to maintain gentle simmer and cook until paring knife can be slipped into and out of centers of potatoes with no resistance, 18 to 22 minutes. Drain potatoes.

**2.** While potatoes cook, combine half-and-half, 3 egg yolks, 1¾ teaspoons salt, ½ teaspoon pepper, and nutmeg in bowl. Set aside.

**3.** Place now-empty saucepan over low heat; set ricer or food mill over saucepan. Working in batches, transfer potatoes to hopper and process. Using rubber spatula, stir in 8 tablespoons melted butter until incorporated. Stir in reserved half-and-half mixture until combined. Transfer potatoes to prepared dish and smooth into even layer. (The casserole can be wrapped in plastic wrap and refrigerated for up to 24 hours. To serve, top and score casserole as directed in step 4 and bake in 375-degree oven for 45 to 50 minutes.)

4. Combine egg white, remaining 2 tablespoons melted butter, and pinch salt in bowl and beat with fork until combined. Pour egg white mixture over potatoes, tilting dish so mixture evenly covers surface. Using flat side of paring knife, make series of ½-inch-deep, ¼-inch-wide parallel grooves across surface of casserole. Make second series of parallel grooves across surface, at angle to first series, to create crosshatch pattern. Bake casserole until golden brown, 25 to 30 minutes, rotating dish halfway through baking. Let cool for 20 minutes. Serve.

## Potato Casserole with Bacon and Caramelized Onion

**SERVES** 6 to 8

**WHY THIS RECIPE WORKS** This casserole of potatoes and onions is traditionally baked beneath a roast, which allows the casserole to be seasoned by the savory fat and juices of the roast. To get the same luxurious results without the roast, we started by rendering a small amount of bacon, which lent the dish a meaty flavor with a hint of smokiness. We then browned the onions in the rendered bacon fat, which gave the dish remarkable complexity. Do not rinse or soak the potatoes, as this will wash away their starch, which is essential to the dish. A mandoline makes slicing the potatoes much easier. Let the casserole stand for 20 minutes before serving.

- 3 slices thick-cut bacon, cut into ½-inch pieces
- 1 large onion, halved and sliced thin
- 1¼ teaspoons table salt
- 2 teaspoons chopped fresh thyme
- ½ teaspoon pepper
- 1¼ cups low-sodium chicken broth
- 1¼ cups beef broth
- 3 pounds Yukon Gold potatoes, peeled
- 2 tablespoons unsalted butter, cut into 4 pieces

1. Adjust oven rack to lower-middle position and heat oven to 425 degrees. Grease 13 by 9-inch baking dish.

2. Cook bacon in medium saucepan over medium-low heat until crisp, 10 to 13 minutes. Using slotted spoon, transfer bacon to paper towel–lined plate. Remove and discard all but 1 tablespoon fat from pot. Return pot to medium heat and add onion and ¼ teaspoon salt; cook, stirring frequently, until onion is soft and golden brown, about 25 minutes, adjusting heat and adding water 1 tablespoon at a time if onion or bottom of pot becomes too dark. Transfer onion to large bowl; add bacon, thyme, remaining 1 teaspoon salt, and pepper. Add broths to now-empty saucepan and bring to simmer over medium-high heat, scraping bottom of pan to loosen any browned bits.

3. Slice potatoes ⅛ inch thick. Transfer to bowl with onion mixture and toss to combine. Transfer to prepared baking dish. Firmly press down on mixture to compress into even layer. Carefully pour hot broth over top of potatoes. Dot surface evenly with butter.

4. Bake, uncovered, until potatoes are tender and golden brown on edges and most of liquid has been absorbed, 45 to 55 minutes. Transfer to wire rack and let stand for 20 minutes to fully absorb broth before cutting and serving.

## Mashed Potatoes and Root Vegetables

**SERVES** 4

**WHY THIS RECIPE WORKS** Root vegetables such as carrots, parsnips, turnips, and celery root can add an earthy, intriguing flavor to mashed potatoes, but because root vegetables and potatoes have different starch levels and water content, treating them the same way creates a bad mash. We wanted a potato and root vegetable mash with a creamy consistency and a balanced flavor that highlights the natural earthiness of these humble root cellar favorites. We found that a 1:3 ratio of root vegetables to potatoes provided an optimal consistency, although the root vegetable flavor was barely recognizable. Caramelizing the root vegetables first in a little butter helped bring out their natural earthy sweetness; this step also boosted the flavor of the overall dish. To use just one pot, we first sautéed the root vegetables in butter until caramelized and then added the potatoes with a little chicken broth. This gave us great flavor, but the mash had a gluey texture. The answer was to remove the starch from the potatoes by rinsing the peeled, sliced potatoes in several changes of water ahead of time. Russet potatoes will yield a slightly fluffier, less creamy mash, but they can be used in place of the Yukon Gold potatoes if desired. Rinsing the potatoes in several changes of water reduces the amount of starch and prevents the mashed potatoes from becoming gluey. It is important to cut the potatoes and root vegetables into even-sized pieces so that they cook at the same rate. This recipe can be doubled and cooked in a large Dutch oven. If doubling, increase the cooking time in step 2 to 40 minutes.

4 tablespoons (½ stick) unsalted butter
8 ounces carrots, parsnips, turnips, or celery root, peeled; carrots or parsnips cut into ¼-inch-thick half-moons; turnips or celery root cut into ½-inch dice (about 1½ cups)
1½ pounds Yukon Gold potatoes (about 3 medium), peeled, quartered lengthwise, and cut crosswise into ¼-inch-thick slices; rinsed well in 3 to 4 changes of cold water and drained well
⅓ cup low-sodium chicken broth
Table salt
¾ cup half-and-half, warmed
3 tablespoons minced fresh chives
Ground black pepper

**1.** Melt the butter in a large saucepan over medium heat. Add the root vegetables and cook, stirring occasionally, until the butter is browned and the vegetables are dark brown and caramelized, 10 to 12 minutes. (If after 4 minutes the vegetables have not started to brown, increase the heat to medium-high.)

**2.** Add the potatoes, broth, and ¾ teaspoon salt and stir to combine. Cook, covered, over low heat (the broth should simmer gently; do not boil), stirring occasionally, until the potatoes fall apart easily when poked with a fork and all the liquid has been absorbed, 25 to 30 minutes. (If the liquid does not simmer gently after a few minutes, increase the heat to medium-low.) Remove the pan from the heat; remove the lid and allow the steam to escape for 2 minutes.

**3.** Gently mash the potatoes and root vegetables in the saucepan with a potato masher (do not mash vigorously). Gently fold in the half-and-half and chives. Season with salt and pepper to taste and serve.

## Perfect Roasted Root Vegetables

**SERVES 6**

**WHY THIS RECIPE WORKS** Roasted root vegetables develop complex flavors with just a quick toss in oil, salt, and pepper and a stint in a hot oven—until you try to roast different vegetables at the same time. We wanted a medley of vegetables that would cook through evenly. The trick was to carefully prep each vegetable according to how long it took to cook through. With each vegetable cut into the right size and shape, we could roast them together in one batch for uniformly tender results. To speed up the roasting, we briefly microwaved the vegetables and then placed them on a preheated baking sheet to jump-start the browning. Use turnips that are roughly 2 to 3 inches in diameter. Sprinkling the roasted vegetables with chopped herbs, makes these roasted vegetables extra special.

1 celery root (14 ounces), peeled
4 carrots, peeled and cut into 2½-inch lengths, halved or quartered lengthwise if necessary to create pieces ½ to 1 inch in diameter
12 ounces parsnips, peeled and sliced on bias 1 inch thick
5 ounces small shallots, peeled
1 teaspoon kosher salt
12 ounces turnips, peeled, halved horizontally, and each half quartered
3 tablespoons vegetable oil
2 tablespoons chopped fresh parsley, tarragon, or chives

**1.** Adjust oven rack to middle position, place rimmed baking sheet on rack, and heat oven to 425 degrees. Cut celery root into ¾-inch-thick rounds. Cut each round into ¾-inch-thick planks about 2½ inches in length.

**2.** Place celery root, carrots, parsnips, and shallots in large bowl, sprinkle with salt and season with pepper to taste, and toss to combine. Cover bowl and microwave until small pieces of carrot are just pliable enough to bend, 8 to 10 minutes, stirring once halfway through microwaving. Drain vegetables well. Return vegetables to bowl, add turnips and oil, and toss to coat.

**3.** Working quickly, remove baking sheet from oven and carefully transfer vegetables to baking sheet; spread into even layer. Roast for 25 minutes.

**4.** Using thin metal spatula, stir vegetables and spread into even layer. Rotate pan and continue to roast until vegetables are golden brown and celery root is tender when pierced with tip of paring knife, 15 to 25 minutes longer. Transfer to platter, sprinkle with parsley, and serve.

## Root Vegetable Gratin

**SERVES 6 to 8**

**WHY THIS RECIPE WORKS** For a lighter alternative to classic potato gratin, we supplemented the starchy potatoes with more flavorful root vegetables. To keep the potatoes from breaking down before the celery root and rutabaga slices were finished, we added dry white wine to the creamy cooking liquid. Incorporating flour into the liquid bound the layers of sliced vegetables. Dijon mustard offered a spicy, savory boost. A sprinkling of bold aromatics—chopped onion, fresh thyme, minced garlic, and black pepper—between the alternating layers infused the gratin with hearty flavors. Pressing the layers down after adding the liquid compacted the gratin, ensuring that the slices clung together nicely. A sprinkling of panko bread crumbs, Parmesan, and melted butter added with 15 minutes left in the oven created a golden crust. Uniformly thin slices are necessary for a cohesive gratin. We recommend a mandoline for quick and even slicing, but a sharp chef's knife will also work. Because the vegetables in the gratin are tightly packed into the casserole dish, it will still be plenty hot after a 25-minute rest.

1 tablespoon plus 1½ cups water
1½ teaspoons Dijon mustard
2 teaspoons all-purpose flour
Table salt and pepper
⅔ cup dry white wine
½ cup heavy cream

½ onion, chopped fine
1¼ teaspoons minced fresh thyme
1 garlic clove, minced
2 pounds large Yukon Gold potatoes, peeled and sliced lengthwise ⅛ inch thick
1 large celery root (1 pound), peeled, quartered, and sliced ⅛ inch thick
1 pound rutabaga, peeled, quartered, and sliced ⅛ inch thick
¾ cup panko bread crumbs
1½ ounces Parmesan cheese, grated (¾ cup)
4 tablespoons unsalted butter, melted and cooled

**1.** Adjust oven rack to middle position and heat oven to 375 degrees. Grease 13 by 9-inch baking dish. Whisk 1 tablespoon water, mustard, flour, and 1½ teaspoons salt in medium bowl until smooth. Add wine, cream, and remaining 1½ cups water; whisk to combine. Combine onion, thyme, garlic, and ¼ teaspoon pepper in second bowl.

**2.** Arrange half of potatoes in even layer in prepared dish. Sprinkle half of onion mixture evenly over potatoes. Arrange celery root and rutabaga slices in even layer over onions. Sprinkle remaining onion mixture over celery root and rutabaga. Layer remaining potatoes over onions. Slowly pour water mixture over vegetables. Using rubber spatula, gently press down on vegetables to create even, compact layer. Cover tightly with aluminum foil and bake for 50 minutes. Remove foil and continue to bake until knife inserted into center of gratin meets no resistance, 20 to 25 minutes longer.

**3.** While gratin bakes, combine panko, Parmesan, and butter in bowl and season with salt and pepper to taste. Remove gratin from oven and sprinkle evenly with panko mixture. Continue to bake until panko is golden brown, 15 to 20 minutes longer. Remove gratin from oven and let stand for 25 minutes. Serve.

## Duck Fat–Roasted Potatoes

**SERVES 6**

**WHY THIS RECIPE WORKS** For the ultimate side of roasted potatoes, we needed spuds that could take on meaty duck fat flavor and a crisp crust before drying out. Briefly boiling peeled, cut Yukon Golds in a solution of water, salt, and baking soda broke down the potatoes' pectin, causing them to release a wet starch that rapidly browns. After draining, we returned the pot to the stove to evaporate any moisture and then, off heat, stirred in enough duck fat to give the potatoes some distinct flavor. Stirring the potatoes released a thick paste that ensured a crunchy shell and roasting the pieces on a preheated baking sheet kick-started the crisping. To infuse the potatoes with richness and herbal flavors, we stirred in a mixture of rosemary and more duck fat toward the end of cooking. Duck fat is available in the meat department in many supermarkets. Alternatively, substitute chicken fat, lard, or a mixture of 3 tablespoons of bacon fat and 3 tablespoons of extra-virgin olive oil.

3½ pounds Yukon Gold potatoes, peeled and cut into 1½-inch pieces
Kosher salt and pepper
½ teaspoon baking soda
6 tablespoons duck fat
1 tablespoon chopped fresh rosemary

**1.** Adjust oven rack to top position, place rimmed baking sheet on rack, and heat oven to 475 degrees.

**2.** Bring 10 cups water to boil in Dutch oven over high heat. Add potatoes, ⅓ cup salt, and baking soda. Return to boil and cook for 1 minute. Drain potatoes. Return potatoes to pot and place over low heat. Cook, shaking pot occasionally, until surface moisture has evaporated, about 2 minutes. Remove from heat. Add 5 tablespoons fat and 1 teaspoon salt; mix with rubber spatula until potatoes are coated with thick paste, about 30 seconds.

**3.** Remove sheet from oven, transfer potatoes to sheet, and spread into even layer. Roast for 15 minutes.

**4.** Remove sheet from oven. Using thin, sharp, metal spatula, turn potatoes. Roast until golden brown, 12 to 15 minutes. While potatoes roast, combine rosemary and remaining 1 tablespoon fat in bowl.

**5.** Remove sheet from oven. Spoon rosemary-fat mixture over potatoes and turn again. Continue to roast until potatoes are well browned and rosemary is fragrant, 3 to 5 minutes. Season with salt and pepper to taste. Serve immediately.

## Crispy Roasted Potatoes

**SERVES 4 to 6**

**WHY THIS RECIPE WORKS** The aroma of roasting potatoes draws everyone into the kitchen come meal time. Too often, though, the potatoes turn out brown and leathery with a mealy interior, or soft with no crisp crust at all. We wanted oven-roasted potatoes that had a crisp crust with a silky interior. We tested using different potatoes and found that we liked Yukon

Golds best. When we switched from cubing the potatoes to slicing them thick, we created more surface area for crisping but enough heft for a creamy interior. We boiled the potatoes very briefly before roasting to prevent them from breaking up on the baking sheet, and we tossed the precooked potatoes with some olive oil to rough up the exteriors and increase crispiness. Note that the potatoes should be just undercooked when removed from the boiling water—this helps ensure that they will roast up crispy.

- 2½ pounds Yukon Gold potatoes (about 5 medium), rinsed and cut into ½-inch-thick slices
- Table salt
- 5 tablespoons olive oil
- Ground black pepper

**1.** Adjust an oven rack to the lowest position, place a rimmed baking sheet on the rack, and heat the oven to 450 degrees. Place the potatoes and 1 tablespoon salt in a Dutch oven; add cold water to cover by 1 inch. Bring to a boil over high heat; reduce the heat and simmer gently until the exterior of a potato has softened, but the center offers resistance when pierced with a paring knife, about 5 minutes. Drain the potatoes well, and transfer to a large bowl. Drizzle with 2 tablespoons of the oil and sprinkle with ½ teaspoon salt; using a rubber spatula, toss to combine. Drizzle with 2 tablespoons more oil and ½ teaspoon more salt; continue to toss until the exteriors of the potato slices are coated with a starchy paste.

**2.** Working quickly, remove the baking sheet from the oven and drizzle the remaining 1 tablespoon oil over the surface. Carefully transfer the potatoes to the baking sheet and spread them into an even layer (skin side up for the end pieces). Bake until the bottoms of the potatoes are golden brown and crisp, 15 to 25 minutes, rotating the baking sheet after 10 minutes.

**3.** Remove the baking sheet from the oven and, using a metal spatula and tongs, loosen the potatoes from the pan and carefully flip each slice. Continue to roast until the second side is golden and crisp, 10 to 20 minutes longer, rotating the pan as needed to ensure the potatoes brown evenly. Season with salt and pepper to taste and serve.

## Roasted Fingerling Potatoes with Mixed Herbs

SERVES 4

**WHY THIS RECIPE WORKS** Roasting is a great way to enhance the nutty flavor of fingerling potatoes, and their diminutive shape means they can be cooked whole. The only problem is, they can vary widely in shape (from crescent-like to knobby) and length (from 1 inch to nearly 5 inches). Our challenge would be to get a typical bag of assorted sizes to cook at the same rate. We first tried tossing the potatoes with oil and salt and roasting them in a very hot oven, but at such high heat, the exteriors were drying out before the larger potatoes had a chance to cook through. Instead we moved the fingerlings to a 13 by 9-inch baking pan, where they fit snugly in a single layer. To solve the textural problems, we covered the pan with foil to trap steam: Since the potatoes were crowded together, they would be bathed in moist air from their neighbors, helping them cook evenly without turning leathery. After 15 minutes, the tip of a knife easily pierced the largest potato, so we removed the foil to let the skins take on some color. To dress up these perfectly roasted fingerlings, we coated them with herbs minced with salt so that they would stick to their skins. Fingerlings vary in size; to ensure that they are all cooked through, check the doneness of the largest potato. If using a glass or ceramic baking dish, increase the baking time in step 1 by 5 minutes. This recipe can be doubled; use two 13 by 9-inch baking pans on the same oven rack.

- 2 pounds fingerling potatoes, scrubbed, unpeeled
- 3 tablespoons vegetable oil
- 2 teaspoons chopped fresh thyme
- 2 teaspoons chopped fresh sage
- ½ teaspoon table salt

**1.** Adjust oven rack to middle position and heat oven to 450 degrees. In 13 by 9-inch baking pan, toss potatoes with oil until evenly coated. Arrange potatoes in even layer. Cover pan tightly with aluminum foil. Transfer to oven and cook for 15 minutes.

**2.** Carefully remove foil (steam will escape). Shake pan and continue to roast until potatoes are spotty brown and tender, and largest potato can be pierced easily with tip of paring knife, about 20 minutes, shaking pan halfway through cooking. While potatoes roast, chop thyme, sage, and salt together until finely minced and well combined. Transfer potatoes to bowl, along with oil, and toss with topping until evenly coated. Transfer potatoes and topping to platter. Let cool for 5 minutes and serve.

## Skillet-Roasted Potatoes

**SERVES** 3 to 4

**WHY THIS RECIPE WORKS** Skillet-roasted potatoes often cook up unevenly, with a mixture of scorched and pallid potatoes. We wanted to be able to make truly outstanding skillet-roasted potatoes, as good as oven-roasted—extra-crisp on the outside and moist and creamy on the inside, evenly browned, and never greasy. This would be the recipe we'd turn to when we craved roasted potatoes but there was no room in the oven for the conventional kind. The solution turned out to be choosing the right potato and cutting it uniformly. Red Bliss potatoes, cut in half if small or quartered if medium, offered a great crust and a moist interior, thanks to their high moisture content. We rinsed the cut potatoes to remove surface starch, which otherwise caused the potatoes to stick to the pan and inhibited browning. Olive oil added flavor and richness to the dish. The winning cooking technique was to first brown the potatoes over high heat, then cover and finish cooking over low heat. This allowed the insides to cook through while the outsides stayed crisp. Small and medium potatoes can be used in this recipe, but they must be cut differently. Small potatoes (1½ to 2 inches in diameter) should be cut in half and medium potatoes (2 to 3 inches in diameter) should be cut into quarters to create ¾- to 1-inch chunks. Large potatoes should not be used because the cut pieces will be uneven and won't cook at the same rate. For even cooking and proper browning, the potatoes must be cooked in a single layer and should not be crowded in the pan.

- 1½ pounds small or medium red potatoes (about 9 small or 4 to 5 medium), scrubbed, halved if small, quartered if medium
- 2 tablespoons olive oil
- ¾ teaspoon table salt
- ¾ teaspoon ground black pepper

**1.** Rinse the potatoes in cold water and drain well; spread on a clean dish towel and thoroughly pat dry.

**2.** Heat the oil in a 12-inch skillet over medium-high heat until shimmering. Add the potatoes, cut side down, in a single layer. Cook, without stirring, until the potatoes are golden brown (the oil should sizzle but not smoke), 5 to 7 minutes. Using tongs, turn the potatoes skin side down if halved or second cut side down if quartered. Cook, without stirring, until the potatoes are deep golden brown, 5 to 6 minutes longer. Stir the potatoes, then redistribute in a single layer. Reduce the heat to medium-low, cover, and cook until the potatoes are tender (a paring knife can be inserted into the potatoes with no resistance), 6 to 9 minutes.

**3.** When the potatoes are tender, sprinkle with the salt and pepper and toss gently to combine; serve.

## Braised Red Potatoes with Lemon and Chives

**SERVES** 4 to 6

**WHY THIS RECIPE WORKS** What if you could get red potatoes with the creamy interiors created by steaming and the crispy browned exteriors produced by roasting—without doing either? That's the result promised by recipes for braised red potatoes, but they rarely deliver. To make good on the promise, we combined halved small red potatoes, butter, and salted water (plus thyme for flavoring) in a 12-inch skillet and simmered the spuds until their interiors were perfectly creamy and the water was fully evaporated. Then we let the potatoes continue to cook in the now-dry skillet until their cut sides browned in the butter, developing the rich flavor and crisp edges of roasted potatoes. These crispy, creamy potatoes were so good they needed only a minimum of seasoning: We simply tossed them with some minced garlic (softened in the simmering water along with the potatoes), lemon juice, chives, and pepper. Use small red potatoes measuring about 1½ inches in diameter for this recipe.

- 1½ pounds small red potatoes, unpeeled, halved
- 2 cups water
- 3 tablespoons unsalted butter
- 3 garlic cloves, peeled
- 3 sprigs fresh thyme
- ¾ teaspoon table salt
- 1 teaspoon lemon juice
- ¼ teaspoon pepper
- 2 tablespoons minced fresh chives

**1.** Arrange potatoes in single layer, cut side down, in 12-inch nonstick skillet. Add water, butter, garlic, thyme, and salt and bring to simmer over medium-high heat. Reduce heat to medium, cover, and simmer until potatoes are just tender, about 15 minutes.

**2.** Remove lid and use slotted spoon to transfer garlic to cutting board; discard thyme. Increase heat to medium-high and vigorously simmer, swirling pan occasionally, until water evaporates and butter starts to sizzle, 15 to 20 minutes. When cool enough to handle, mince garlic to paste. Transfer paste to bowl and stir in lemon juice and pepper.

**3.** Continue to cook potatoes, swirling pan frequently, until butter browns and cut sides of potatoes turn spotty brown, 4 to 6 minutes longer. Off heat, add garlic mixture and chives and toss to thoroughly coat. Serve immediately.

## Boiled Potatoes with Black Olive Tapenade

**SERVES** 4 to 6

**WHY THIS RECIPE WORKS** Tapenade is a bold spread that shines as a topping for bruschetta or tossed with pasta or potatoes. A paste of processed pine nuts created a buttery base to keep the tapenade spreadable. Using brine-cured kalamata olives and salt-cured black olives created a perfect balance of tang. Anchovies bumped up the spread's subtle meatiness and some Dijon mustard and garlic contributed a sharp kick. Once the tapenade was at the ready, we boiled halved red potatoes until just tender. Once drained, we folded in a mixture of tapenade, lemon juice, and cooking water. Use potatoes measuring about 1½ inches in diameter for this recipe.

- 2 pounds small red potatoes, unpeeled, halved
- 1 tablespoon table salt
- ⅓ cup Black Olive Tapenade
- 1 tablespoon lemon juice
- 1 tablespoon chopped fresh parsley
- Extra-virgin olive oil

**1.** Bring 6 cups water, potatoes, and salt to boil in large saucepan over medium-high heat. Reduce heat to medium-low and simmer until potatoes are just tender when pierced with knife, 10 to 15 minutes.

**2.** Reserve ¼ cup cooking water. Drain potatoes and return them to pan. Combine tapenade, lemon juice, and 2 tablespoons cooking water in bowl. Add tapenade mixture to potatoes and fold gently to incorporate. Add remaining 2 tablespoons cooking water as needed to adjust consistency. Transfer potatoes to serving bowl, sprinkle with parsley, drizzle with oil, and serve.

### Black Olive Tapenade

**MAKES** about 1½ cups

The tapenade must be refrigerated for at least 18 hours before using. Use untoasted pine nuts in this recipe so that they provide creaminess but little flavor of their own. We prefer the rich flavor of kalamata olives, but any high-quality brine-cured black olive, such as niçoise, Sicilian, or Greek, can be substituted. Do not substitute brine-cured olives for the salt-cured olives. Serve extra tapenade as a spread with sliced crusty bread or as a dip with raw vegetables.

- ⅓ cup pine nuts
- 1½ cups pitted kalamata olives
- ½ cup pitted salt-cured black olives
- 3 tablespoons capers, rinsed
- 2 anchovy fillets, rinsed and patted dry
- 2 teaspoons Dijon mustard
- ½ garlic clove, minced
- ¼ cup extra-virgin olive oil

**1.** In food processor fitted with metal blade, process pine nuts until reduced to paste that clings to walls and avoids blade, about 20 seconds. Scrape down bowl to redistribute paste and process until paste again clings to walls and avoids blade, about 5 seconds. Repeat scraping and processing once more (pine nuts should form mostly smooth, tahini-like paste).

**2.** Scrape down bowl to redistribute paste and add olives capers, anchovies, mustard, and garlic. Pulse until finely chopped, about 15 pulses, scraping down bowl halfway through pulsing. Transfer mixture to medium bowl and stir in oil until well combined.

**3.** Transfer to container, cover, and refrigerate for at least 18 hours or up to 2 weeks. Bring to room temperature and stir thoroughly before serving.

## Scalloped Potatoes

**SERVES** 8 to 10

**WHY THIS RECIPE WORKS** Thinly sliced potatoes layered with cream and baked until they are bubbling and browned are a classic accompaniment to baked ham or roast beef. But scalloped potatoes can occupy the oven for over two hours and still produce unevenly cooked potatoes in a heavy, curdled sauce. We wanted to minimize the cooking time while turning out layers of thinly sliced, tender potatoes, a creamy sauce, and a nicely browned, cheesy crust. We tried using flour to thicken the sauce, but this produced a thick, pasty sauce. Instead we relied on heavy cream lightened with whole milk. To cut the cooking time, we simmered the potatoes briefly in the cream in a covered pot, before transferring the mixture to a baking dish and finishing the potatoes in the oven. We found russet potatoes had the best texture and flavor, and we sliced them thin so they formed neat layers. For the fastest and most consistent results, slice the potatoes in a food processor or on a mandoline or V-slicer.

- 2 tablespoons unsalted butter
- 1 small onion, minced
- 2 medium garlic cloves, minced or pressed through a garlic press (about 2 teaspoons)
- 4 pounds russet potatoes (about 8 medium), peeled and cut into ⅛-inch-thick slices
- 3 cups heavy cream
- 1 cup whole milk
- 4 sprigs fresh thyme
- 2 bay leaves
- 2 teaspoons table salt
- ½ teaspoon ground black pepper
- 4 ounces cheddar cheese, shredded (about 1 cup)

**1.** Adjust an oven rack to the middle position and heat the oven to 350 degrees. Melt the butter in a large Dutch oven over medium-high heat. Add the onion and cook until softened and lightly browned, 5 to 7 minutes. Add the garlic and cook until fragrant, about 30 seconds. Add the potatoes, cream, milk, thyme, bay leaves, salt, and pepper, and bring to a simmer. Cover, adjusting the heat as necessary to maintain a light simmer, and cook until the potatoes are almost tender (a paring knife can be slipped into and out of the center of a potato slice with some resistance), about 15 minutes.

**2.** Remove and discard the thyme sprigs and bay leaves. Transfer the potato mixture to a 3-quart gratin dish and sprinkle with the cheese. Bake until the cream has thickened and is bubbling around the sides, and the top is golden brown, about 20 minutes. Cool for 5 minutes before serving.

## Crunchy Kettle Potato Chips

SERVES 6

**WHY THIS RECIPE WORKS** To produce deeply crunchy kettle-style chips, we started by cutting russet potatoes into substantial 1/16-inch-thick slices. Leaving the potatoes unpeeled saved prep time and gave them rustic appeal. Frying them in moderately hot oil ensured that they cooked up crunchy—not hard or delicate. Initially heating the oil to a relatively hot 375 degrees quickly dried out the potatoes' exterior starches so they were less sticky; stirring them frequently also prevented them from fusing together. For our toppings, we ground the spice mixtures to a fine powder and tossed them with the chips while hot to ensure that the spices stuck. We strongly recommend using a mandoline to slice the potatoes. A heavy 7-quart Dutch oven safely accommodates the full batch of chips and helps the oil retain heat; do not use a smaller, lighter pot.

- 2 quarts vegetable oil, for frying
- 1 pound russet potatoes, unpeeled
- ½ teaspoon table salt or 1 recipe topping (recipes follow)

**1.** Set wire rack in rimmed baking sheet and line with double layer of paper towels. Heat oil in large Dutch oven over medium heat to 375 degrees. While oil heats, slice potatoes crosswise 1/16 inch (1½ millimeters) thick. Carefully add all potatoes to oil, 1 small handful at a time, separating slices as much as possible (oil will bubble vigorously). Cook, stirring constantly with wooden spoon, until bubbling has calmed (it will not completely stop) and slices begin to stiffen, 2 to 4 minutes.

**2.** Continue to cook, stirring frequently, until shape of chips is set and slices are rigid at edges (chips will make rustling sound when stirred), about 5 minutes longer, adjusting heat as needed to maintain oil temperature between 240 and 250 degrees.

**3.** Continue to cook, stirring and flipping potatoes frequently with spider skimmer or slotted spoon, until all bubbling ceases and chips are crisp and lightly browned, 6 to 8 minutes longer, adjusting heat as needed during final minutes of cooking to maintain oil temperature between 280 and 300 degrees. Using spider skimmer or slotted spoon, transfer chips to prepared rack. Sprinkle with salt or, if using topping, let chips cool for 30 seconds, then transfer chips to large bowl with topping and toss until evenly coated. Serve. (Chips can be stored in zipper-lock bag at room temperature for up to 5 days.)

### Buttermilk and Chive Topping

Look for buttermilk powder in the baking aisle of your supermarket.

- 4 teaspoons buttermilk powder
- 1 teaspoon garlic powder
- ½ teaspoon onion powder
- ½ teaspoon table salt
- ¼ teaspoon pepper
- 1 teaspoon dried chives

Grind buttermilk powder, garlic powder, onion powder, salt, and pepper in spice grinder to fine powder. Add chives and pulse until finely chopped, about 3 pulses.

### Salt and Vinegar Topping

Look for vinegar powder online.

- 1 tablespoon vinegar powder
- ½ teaspoon table salt

Grind vinegar powder and salt in spice grinder to fine powder.

### Smoky Barbecue Topping

- 1 tablespoon smoked paprika
- 2 teaspoons sugar
- 1 teaspoon garlic powder
- ½ teaspoon onion powder
- ½ teaspoon table salt
- Pinch cayenne pepper

Grind all ingredients in spice grinder to fine powder.

## Mashed Sweet Potatoes

SERVES 4

**WHY THIS RECIPE WORKS** Mashed sweet potatoes often turn out overly thick and gluey or, at the other extreme, sloppy and loose. We wanted a recipe that would push sweet potatoes' deep, earthy sweetness to the fore and that would produce a silky puree with enough body to hold its shape on a fork. We braised the sweet potatoes in a mixture of butter and heavy cream to impart a smooth richness. Adding a little salt brought out the sweet potatoes' delicate flavor, and just a teaspoon of sugar bolstered their sweetness. Once the potatoes were tender, we mashed them in the saucepan with a potato masher.

We skipped the typical pumpkin pie seasoning and instead let the simple sweet potato flavor shine through. Cutting the sweet potatoes into slices of even thickness is important so that they cook at the same rate. The potatoes are best served immediately, but they can be covered tightly with plastic wrap and kept warm for 30 minutes. This recipe can be doubled and prepared in a Dutch oven; the cooking time will need to be doubled as well.

- 4 tablespoons (½ stick) unsalted butter, cut into 4 pieces
- 2 tablespoons heavy cream
- 1 teaspoon sugar
- ½ teaspoon table salt
- 2 pounds sweet potatoes (2 to 3 medium), peeled, quartered lengthwise, and cut crosswise into ¼-inch-thick slices
- Ground black pepper

**1.** Melt the butter in a large saucepan over low heat. Stir in the cream, sugar, and salt; add the sweet potatoes and cook, covered, stirring occasionally, until the potatoes fall apart when poked with a fork, 35 to 45 minutes.

**2.** Off the heat, mash the sweet potatoes in the saucepan with a potato masher or transfer the mixture to a food mill and process into a warmed serving bowl. Season with pepper to taste and serve.

## Candied Sweet Potato Casserole

**SERVES** 10 to 12

**WHY THIS RECIPE WORKS** Kids love this sweet, sticky dish, served so often at Thanksgiving, but adults long for a side dish with a more restrained sweetness. We set out to develop a sweet potato casserole with a bit of a savory accent to please everyone. For the best texture and flavor, we steamed the sweet potatoes on the stovetop with a little water, butter, and brown sugar. We kept the other flavorings simple—just salt and pepper. In the topping, we used whole pecans instead of chopped; this gave the casserole a better texture and appearance. And a little cayenne and cumin lent a hit of spice to the topping that offset the sweetness of the potato. For a more intense molasses flavor, use dark brown sugar in place of light brown sugar.

**SWEET POTATOES**

- 8 tablespoons (1 stick) unsalted butter, cut into 1-inch chunks
- 5 pounds sweet potatoes (about 8 medium), peeled and cut into 1-inch cubes
- 1 cup (7 ounces) packed light brown sugar
- ½ cup water
- 1½ teaspoons table salt
- ½ teaspoon ground black pepper

**PECAN TOPPING**

- 2 cups pecan halves
- ½ cup packed (3½ ounces) light brown sugar
- 1 egg white, lightly beaten
- ⅛ teaspoon table salt
- Pinch cayenne pepper
- Pinch ground cumin

**1. FOR THE SWEET POTATOES:** Melt the butter in a large Dutch oven over medium-high heat. Add the sweet potatoes, brown sugar, water, salt, and black pepper; bring to a simmer. Reduce the heat to medium-low, cover, and cook, stirring often, until the sweet potatoes are tender (a paring knife can be slipped into and out of the center of the potatoes with very little resistance), 45 to 60 minutes.

**2.** When the sweet potatoes are tender, remove the lid and bring the sauce to a rapid simmer over medium-high heat. Continue to simmer until the sauce has reduced to a glaze, 7 to 10 minutes.

**3. FOR THE TOPPING:** Meanwhile, mix all the ingredients for the topping together in a medium bowl; set aside.

**4.** Adjust an oven rack to the middle position and heat the oven to 450 degrees. Pour the potato mixture into a 13 by 9-inch baking dish (or a shallow casserole dish of similar size). Spread the topping over the potatoes. Bake until the pecans are toasted and crisp, 10 to 15 minutes. Serve immediately.

## Roasted Radishes with Yogurt-Tahini Sauce

**SERVES** 4 to 6

**WHY THIS RECIPE WORKS** Radishes hold up well to high-heat roasting, yielding a tender but meaty interior. Roasting also mellows ther spiciness, concentrating their natural sugars for nutty sweetness. To facilitate browning and complement the nuttiness of the radishes, we tossed them in a mixture of melted butter and white miso and then roasted them on the bottom rack of the oven. The butter produced superior browning on the cut side while the miso added a pleasing savory quality. To make the most of our radishes, we used the mild, peppery green tops in a simple salad, pairing them with a tangy yogurt-tahini sauce and a sprinkling of pistachios and sesame seeds for crunch. If you can't find radishes with their greens, substitute baby arugula or watercress.

- ½ cup plain whole-milk yogurt
- 2 tablespoons tahini
- 1 teaspoon grated lemon zest plus 4 teaspoons juice, divided
- 1 garlic clove, minced
- ¾ teaspoon plus ⅛ teaspoon table salt, divided
- ¼ teaspoon pepper, divided
- 2 tablespoons chopped toasted pistachios or almonds
- 1½ teaspoons sesame seeds, toasted
- ⅛ teaspoon ground cumin
- 3 tablespoons unsalted butter, melted
- 5½ teaspoons white miso, divided
- 1½ teaspoons honey, divided
- 2 pounds radishes with their greens, radishes trimmed and halved lengthwise, 8 cups greens reserved
- 1 teaspoon extra-virgin olive oil

1. Adjust oven rack to lowest position and heat oven to 500 degrees. Whisk yogurt, tahini, lemon zest and 1 tablespoon juice, garlic, ¼ teaspoon salt, and ⅛ teaspoon pepper together in bowl; set aside for serving. Combine pistachios, sesame seeds, cumin, and ⅛ teaspoon salt in small bowl; set aside for serving.

2. Line rimmed baking sheet with aluminum foil. Whisk melted butter, 5 teaspoons miso, 1 teaspoon honey, and ¼ teaspoon salt in large bowl until smooth. Add radishes and toss to coat. Arrange radishes cut side down on prepared sheet and roast until tender and well browned on cut side, 10 to 15 minutes.

3. Whisk oil, remaining 1 teaspoon lemon juice, remaining ¼ teaspoon salt, remaining ⅛ teaspoon pepper, remaining ½ teaspoon miso, and remaining ½ teaspoon honey in clean large bowl until smooth. Add radish greens and toss to coat. Season with salt and pepper to taste.

4. To serve, spread portions of yogurt-tahini sauce over bottom of individual serving plates. Top with roasted radishes and radish greens, then sprinkle with pistachio mixture.

## Sautéed Garlic-Lemon Spinach

SERVES 4

WHY THIS RECIPE WORKS Overcooked spinach, bitter burnt garlic, and pallid lemon flavor are all too often the hallmarks of this simple side dish. Instead, we sought tender sautéed spinach, seasoned with a perfect balance of garlic and lemon. We preferred the hearty flavor and texture of curly-leaf spinach in this classic dish. We cooked the spinach in extra-virgin olive oil with slivered garlic (lightly browned in the pan before the spinach was added), which gave the spinach a sweet nuttiness. Once the spinach was cooked, we used tongs to squeeze the spinach in a colander over the sink to get rid of all the excess moisture. As for seasoning, a squeeze of lemon juice and some grated lemon zest, as well as a pinch of red pepper flakes gave the spinach some gentle heat. And finally, a drizzle of extra-virgin olive oil boosted the fruitiness of the dish. The amount of spinach may seem excessive, but the spinach wilts considerably with cooking. We like to use a salad spinner to wash and dry the spinach.

- 2 tablespoons extra-virgin olive oil, plus 1 teaspoon for drizzling
- 4 medium garlic cloves, sliced thin crosswise (about 4 teaspoons)
- 3 (10-ounce) bags curly-leaf spinach, stems removed, leaves washed and dried
- Table salt
- Pinch red pepper flakes
- ½ teaspoon grated zest plus 2 teaspoons juice from 1 lemon

1. Heat 2 tablespoons of the oil and the garlic in a large Dutch oven over medium-high heat until shimmering; cook until the garlic is light golden brown, shaking the pan back and forth when the garlic begins to sizzle, about 3 minutes. Add the spinach by the handful, using tongs to stir and coat the spinach with the oil.

2. Once all the spinach is added, sprinkle ¼ teaspoon salt, the red pepper flakes, and lemon zest over the top and continue stirring with the tongs until the spinach is uniformly wilted and glossy, about 2 minutes. Using the tongs, transfer the spinach to a colander set in a sink and gently squeeze the spinach with the tongs to release the excess liquid. Return the spinach to the Dutch oven; sprinkle with the lemon juice and stir to coat. Drizzle with the remaining 1 teaspoon olive oil and season with salt to taste. Serve.

## Sautéed Baby Spinach with Almonds and Golden Raisins

SERVES 4

WHY THIS RECIPE WORKS Baby spinach is convenient—no stems to remove or grit to rinse out—but cooking often turns this tender green into a watery, mushy mess. We were determined to find a method for cooking baby spinach that would give us a worthwhile side dish. Wilting, blanching, and steaming proved to be unsuccessful in removing excess water from baby spinach, but parcooking the spinach in the microwave with a little water added to the bowl worked great. After three minutes, the spinach had softened and shrunk to half its size, thanks to the release of a great deal of liquid. But there was still more water to remove. We found that pressing the spinach against the colander before roughly chopping it on a cutting board and then pressing it again removed any remaining excess liquid. The spinach was now tender, sweet, and ready to be combined with complementary ingredients. Pairing almonds and raisins introduced bold flavors and textures that enlivened this quick-cooking green. If you don't have a microwave-safe bowl large enough to accommodate the entire amount of spinach, cook it in a smaller bowl in two batches. Reduce the amount of water to 2 tablespoons per batch and cook each batch for about 1½ minutes.

- 3 (6-ounce) bags baby spinach (about 18 cups)
- ¼ cup water
- 2 tablespoons extra-virgin olive oil, plus 2 teaspoons for drizzling
- ½ cup golden raisins
- 4 medium garlic cloves, sliced thin crosswise (about 4 teaspoons)
- ¼ teaspoon red pepper flakes
- Table salt
- 2 teaspoons sherry vinegar
- ⅓ cup slivered almonds, toasted

**1.** Place the spinach and water in a large microwave-safe bowl. Cover the bowl with a large microwave-safe dinner plate (the plate should completely cover the bowl and not rest on the spinach). Microwave on high power until the spinach is wilted and decreased in volume by half, 3 to 4 minutes. Using potholders, remove the bowl from the microwave and keep covered for 1 minute. Carefully remove the plate and transfer the spinach to a colander set in the sink. Using the back of a rubber spatula, gently press the spinach against the colander to release excess liquid. Transfer the spinach to a cutting board and roughly chop. Return to the colander and press a second time.

**2.** Heat 2 tablespoons of the oil, the raisins, garlic, and red pepper flakes in a 10-inch skillet over medium-high heat. Cook, stirring constantly, until the garlic is light golden brown and beginning to sizzle, 3 to 6 minutes. Add the spinach to the skillet, using tongs to stir and coat with the oil. Sprinkle with ¼ teaspoon salt and continue stirring with the tongs until the spinach is uniformly wilted and glossy, about 2 minutes. Sprinkle with the vinegar and almonds; stir to combine. Drizzle with the remaining 2 teaspoons oil and season with salt to taste. Serve.

## Roasted Butternut Squash with Browned Butter and Hazelnuts

**SERVES** 4 to 6

**WHY THIS RECIPE WORKS** Taking a cue from famed chef Yotam Ottolenghi, we sought to create a savory recipe for roasted butternut squash that was simple yet presentation-worthy. We chose to peel the squash thoroughly to remove not only the tough outer skin but also the rugged fibrous layer of white flesh just beneath, ensuring supremely tender squash. To encourage the squash slices to caramelize, we used a hot 425-degree oven, placed the squash on the lowest oven rack, and increased the baking time to evaporate the water. We also swapped in melted butter for olive oil to promote the flavorful Maillard reaction. Finally, we selected a topping that added crunch, creaminess, brightness, and visual appeal. For plain roasted squash, omit the topping. This dish can be served warm or at room temperature. For the best texture, it's important to remove the fibrous flesh just below the squash's skin.

**SQUASH**

- 1 large (2½- to 3-pound) butternut squash
- 3 tablespoons unsalted butter, melted
- ½ teaspoon table salt
- ½ teaspoon pepper

**TOPPING**

- 3 tablespoons unsalted butter, cut into 3 pieces
- ⅓ cup hazelnuts, toasted, skinned, and chopped coarse
- 1 tablespoon water
- 1 tablespoon lemon juice
- Pinch table salt
- 1 tablespoon minced fresh chives

**1. FOR THE SQUASH:** Adjust oven rack to lowest position and heat oven to 425 degrees. Using sharp vegetable peeler or chef's knife, remove skin and fibrous threads from squash just below skin (peel until squash is completely orange with no white flesh remaining, roughly ⅛ inch deep). Halve squash lengthwise and scrape out seeds. Place squash, cut side down, on cutting board and slice crosswise ½ inch thick.

**2.** Toss squash with melted butter, salt, and pepper until evenly coated. Arrange squash on rimmed baking sheet in single layer. Roast squash until side touching sheet toward back of oven is well browned, 25 to 30 minutes. Rotate sheet and continue to bake until side touching sheet toward back of oven is well browned, 6 to 10 minutes. Remove squash from oven and use metal spatula to flip each piece. Continue to roast until squash is very tender and side touching sheet is browned, 10 to 15 minutes longer.

**3. FOR THE TOPPING:** While squash roasts, melt butter with hazelnuts in 8-inch skillet over medium-low heat. Cook, stirring frequently, until butter and hazelnuts are brown and fragrant, about 2 minutes. Immediately remove skillet from heat and stir in water (butter will foam and sizzle). Let cool for 1 minute; stir in lemon juice and salt.

**4.** Transfer squash to large serving platter. Spoon butter mixture evenly over squash. Sprinkle with chives and serve.

## Butternut Squash Risotto

**SERVES** 4 to 6

**WHY THIS RECIPE WORKS** Butternut squash and risotto should make a perfect culinary couple, but too often the squash and rice never become properly intertwined. The squash is reduced to overly sweet orange blobs or the whole dish becomes a gluey squash paste. We wanted to create a creamy, orange-tinged rice fully infused with deep squash flavor. We started with our basic risotto recipe, then addressed the squash. We decided to brown the diced squash in a skillet and set it aside while we sautéed the aromatics and toasted the rice. We added only half of the squash with the first addition of liquid. This squash broke down somewhat during cooking and infused the rice with its flavor; the remaining squash, added when the rice was finished, retained its shape and texture. Chicken broth cut with water was the basis of the liquid in which we simmered the squash seeds and fibers to intensify the squash flavor without adding more squash. We found that a 2-pound squash often yields more than the 3½ cups in step 1; this can be added to the skillet along with the squash scrapings in step 2.

- 2 tablespoons olive oil
- 1 medium butternut squash (about 2 pounds), peeled, seeded (reserve fibers and seeds), and cut into ½-inch cubes (about 3½ cups; see note)
- ¾ teaspoon table salt
- ¾ teaspoon ground black pepper
- 4 cups low-sodium chicken broth
- 1 cup water
- 4 tablespoons (½ stick) unsalted butter
- 2 small onions, minced (about 1½ cups)
- 2 medium garlic cloves, minced or pressed through a garlic press (about 2 teaspoons)
- 2 cups Arborio rice
- 1½ cups dry white wine
- 1½ ounces Parmesan cheese, grated fine (about ¾ cup)
- 2 tablespoons minced fresh sage leaves
- ¼ teaspoon grated nutmeg

**1.** Heat the oil in a 12-inch nonstick skillet over medium-high heat until shimmering but not smoking. Add the squash in an even layer and cook without stirring until golden brown, 4 to 5 minutes; stir in ¼ teaspoon of the salt and ¼ teaspoon of the pepper. Continue to cook, stirring occasionally, until the squash is tender and browned, about 5 minutes longer. Transfer the squash to a bowl and set aside.

**2.** Return the skillet to medium heat; add the reserved squash fibers and seeds and any leftover diced squash. Cook, stirring frequently to break up the fibers, until lightly browned, about 4 minutes. Transfer to a large saucepan and add the chicken broth and water; cover the saucepan and bring the mixture to a simmer over high heat, then reduce the heat to medium-low to maintain a bare simmer.

**3.** Melt 3 tablespoons of the butter in the now-empty skillet over medium heat; add the onions, garlic, remaining ½ teaspoon salt, and remaining ½ teaspoon pepper. Cook, stirring occasionally, until the onions are softened, 4 to 5 minutes. Add the rice to the skillet and cook, stirring frequently, until the grains are translucent around the edges, about 3 minutes. (To prevent the rice from spilling out of the pan, stir inward, from the edges of the pan toward the center, not in a circular motion.) Add the wine and cook, stirring frequently, until the liquid is fully absorbed, 4 to 5 minutes. Meanwhile, strain the hot broth through a fine-mesh strainer into a medium bowl, pressing on the solids to extract as much liquid as possible. Return the strained broth to the saucepan and discard the solids in the strainer; cover the saucepan and set over low heat to keep the broth hot.

**4.** When the wine is fully absorbed, add 3 cups of the hot broth and half of the reserved squash to the rice. Simmer, stirring every 3 to 4 minutes, until the liquid is absorbed and the bottom of the pan is almost dry, about 12 minutes.

**5.** Stir in ½ cup more of the hot broth and cook, stirring constantly, until absorbed, about 3 minutes; repeat with additional broth until the rice is cooked through but the grains are still somewhat firm at the center. Off the heat, stir in the remaining 1 tablespoon butter, the Parmesan, sage, and nutmeg; gently fold in the remaining cooked squash. If desired, add up to ¼ cup more broth to loosen the texture of the risotto. Serve immediately in warmed bowls.

## Quick Roasted Acorn Squash with Brown Sugar

**SERVES 4**

**WHY THIS RECIPE WORKS** Cooked properly, acorn squash develops a sweet, almost nutty flavor and moist, smooth flesh. But after what seems like eons in the oven, acorn squash often lands on the table with little flavor and a stringy texture. We wanted better slow-roasted acorn squash in a fraction of the time. To our astonishment, microwaving was the ideal cooking method. Microwaved on high power for 20 minutes, the squash was perfectly cooked. It was best to halve and seed the squash before cooking. Filling in the only remaining gap, equal portions of butter and dark brown sugar gave the squash ample, but not excessive, sweetness. And for a smooth, cohesive filling mixture, combining the butter and sugar with a pinch of salt and briefly broiling the final product eliminated the nagging sticky glaze problem. Finishing the squash under the broiler also gave it a welcome roasted texture and great caramelized flavor. Squash smaller than 1½ pounds will likely cook a little faster than the recipe indicates, so begin checking for doneness a few minutes early. Likewise, larger squash will take slightly longer to cook. However, keep in mind that the cooking time is largely dependent on the microwave. If microwaving the squash in Pyrex, the manufacturer recommends adding water to the dish (or bowl) prior to cooking. To avoid a steam burn when uncovering the cooked squash, peel back the plastic wrap very carefully, starting from the side that is farthest away from you.

- 2 acorn squash (about 1½ pounds each), halved pole to pole and seeded
- Table salt
- 3 tablespoons unsalted butter
- 3 tablespoons dark brown sugar

**1.** Sprinkle the squash halves with salt and place the halves, cut side down, in a 13 by 9-inch microwave-safe baking dish or arrange the halves in a large (4-quart) microwave-safe bowl so that the cut sides face out. (If using Pyrex, add ¼ cup water to the dish or bowl.) Cover tightly with plastic wrap, using multiple sheets, if necessary; with a paring knife, poke four steam vents in the wrap. Microwave on high power until the squash is very tender and offers no resistance when pierced with a paring knife, 15 to 25 minutes. Using potholders, remove the baking dish or bowl from the microwave and set on a clean, dry surface (avoid damp or cold surfaces).

**2.** While the squash is cooking, adjust an oven rack to the highest position (about 6 inches from the broiler element) and heat the broiler. Melt the butter, brown sugar, and ⅛ teaspoon salt in a small saucepan over low heat, whisking occasionally, until combined.

**3.** When the squash is cooked, carefully pull back the plastic wrap from the side farthest from you. Using tongs, transfer the cooked squash halves, cut side up, to a rimmed baking sheet. Spoon a portion of the butter-sugar mixture onto each squash half. Broil until brown and caramelized, 5 to 8 minutes, rotating the baking sheet halfway through the cooking time and removing the squash halves as they are done. Serve immediately.

## Best Summer Tomato Gratin

**SERVES** 6 to 8

**WHY THIS RECIPE WORKS** A summer tomato gratin should burst with bright tomato flavor and contrasting firm texture from the bread, but most recipes lead to mushy results. Starting our gratin on the stovetop drove off some moisture that would otherwise have sogged out the bread, and shortened the overall cooking time. Toasting large cubes of crusty artisan-style baguette ensured that the bread didn't get too soggy once combined with the tomatoes. After toasting the bread, we added garlic and then coarsely chopped tomatoes, a small amount of sugar, and salt and pepper. Just before moving the skillet to the oven, we folded in most of the toasted bread and scattered the remainder over the top along with some Parmesan. Use the ripest in-season tomatoes you can find. Do not use plum tomatoes, which contain less juice than regular round tomatoes and will result in a dry gratin. Serve the gratin hot, warm, or at room temperature.

- 6 tablespoons extra-virgin olive oil, divided
- 6 ounces crusty baguette, cut into ¾-inch cubes (4 cups)
- 3 garlic cloves, sliced thin
- 3 pounds tomatoes, cored and cut into ¾-inch pieces
- 2 teaspoons sugar
- 1 teaspoon table salt
- 1 teaspoon pepper
- 1½ ounces Parmesan cheese, grated (¾ cup)
- 2 tablespoons chopped fresh basil

**1.** Adjust oven rack to middle position and heat oven to 350 degrees. Heat ¼ cup oil in 12-inch ovensafe skillet over medium-low heat until shimmering. Add bread and stir to coat. Cook, stirring constantly, until bread is browned and toasted, about 5 minutes. Transfer bread to bowl.

**2.** Return now-empty skillet to low heat and add remaining 2 tablespoons oil and garlic. Cook, stirring constantly, until garlic is golden at edges, 30 to 60 seconds. Add tomatoes, sugar, salt, and pepper and stir to combine. Increase heat to medium-high and cook, stirring occasionally, until tomatoes have started to break down and have released enough juice to be mostly submerged, 8 to 10 minutes.

**3.** Remove skillet from heat and gently stir in 3 cups bread until completely moistened and evenly distributed. Using spatula, press down on bread until completely submerged. Arrange remaining 1 cup bread evenly over surface, pressing to partially submerge. Sprinkle evenly with Parmesan.

**4.** Bake until top of gratin is deeply browned, tomatoes are bubbling, and juice has reduced, 40 to 45 minutes; after 30 minutes, run spatula around edge of skillet to loosen crust and release any juice underneath. (Gratin will appear loose and jiggle around outer edges but will thicken as it cools.)

**5.** Remove skillet from oven and let sit for 15 minutes. Sprinkle gratin with basil and serve.

## Briam

**SERVES** 8

**WHY THIS RECIPE WORKS** Here's the magic of Greek briam: A rainbow of summer produce—tomatoes, zucchini, bell peppers, onions, and potatoes—enters the oven simply sliced, seasoned, and bathed in garlic-infused olive oil and emerges as a meltingly soft and velvety mélange in which each vegetable is an amplified version of itself. We sliced our vegetables ¼ inch thick and strategically layered them in a 13 by 9-inch baking dish, with the potatoes serving as a sturdy base and the tomatoes an attractive, browned top. Loosely covering the dish with aluminum foil for the first 30 minutes of cooking allowed just the right amount of moisture to evaporate, hyperconcentrating the vegetables' flavor. We then removed the foil to encourage browning. Use small or medium zucchini, which contain more flesh and fewer seeds, for this recipe. We prefer local seasonal tomatoes here, but supermarket tomatoes will work; plum tomatoes are too dry for this dish. High-quality olive oil is vital. Some oil will pool in the bottom of the baking dish; spoon it over the portioned briam or sop it up with bread. Briam is usually served with crusty bread and feta cheese, but it can also be served over pasta or rice or alongside meat or fish. Serve this dish warm, at room temperature, or chilled.

- 1 pound Yukon Gold potatoes, peeled and sliced crosswise ¼ inch thick
- ⅔ cup extra-virgin olive oil, divided
- 6 garlic cloves (3 minced, 3 sliced thin)
- 1¼ teaspoons table salt, divided
- 1 onion, halved and sliced through root end ¼ inch thick, divided
- 1 teaspoon pepper, divided
- 1 teaspoon dried oregano, divided
- 1 green bell pepper, stemmed, seeded, and cut into 2-inch-long matchsticks
- 12 ounces zucchini (2 small), sliced crosswise ¼ inch thick
- 1½ pounds tomatoes (3 large), cored and sliced ¼ inch thick
- ¼ cup chopped fresh parsley

**1.** Adjust oven rack to middle position and heat oven to 400 degrees. Place potatoes, ⅓ cup oil, minced garlic, and ½ teaspoon salt in 13 by 9-inch baking dish and toss to combine thoroughly. Spread into even layer. Scatter half of onion slices over potatoes. Sprinkle with ½ teaspoon pepper and ½ teaspoon oregano.

**2.** Scatter bell pepper over surface, followed by remaining onion, sliced garlic, ¼ teaspoon salt, ¼ teaspoon pepper, and remaining ½ teaspoon oregano. Arrange zucchini in single layer. Top with tomato slices, overlapping pieces slightly so they cover entire surface (it should be snug). Pour remaining ⅓ cup oil evenly over tomatoes and sprinkle with remaining ½ teaspoon salt and remaining ¼ teaspoon pepper.

**3.** Cover dish loosely with aluminum foil, leaving sides open so moisture can escape. Bake for 30 minutes. Remove foil and bake until potatoes can be easily pierced with tip of paring knife and tomatoes have collapsed slightly and started to brown at edges, 40 to 50 minutes. Let cool for at least 20 minutes. Sprinkle parsley over top and serve.

## Simple Sautéed Swiss Chard

**SERVES** 4

**WHY THIS RECIPE WORKS** Swiss chard, like spinach, is delicate and has an earthy flavor that mellows once cooked. A thick stalk runs through the center of each leaf, however, and can make cooking the greens a challenge. We set out to find a simple method for preparing Swiss chard—one that would yield tender, evenly cooked greens (both stalks and leaves) with deep flavor. After testing blanching, steaming, microwaving, and wilting, the simplest, most straightforward method of cooking proved to be wilting our greens on the stovetop. First, however, we separated the leaves from the stalks and tossed the stalks, wet from washing, into the pan first. We added garlic for flavor, then added the leaves, covered the pan, and cooked, stirring occasionally, until the greens were wilted by the steam created by their own liquid. We then found that we got even better results when combining this technique with sautéing. To do this, we heated oil in the pan, then proceeded as before, adding the stalks before the leaves. Once the leaves wilted, we removed the lid, seasoned with salt and pepper, and sautéed the greens over high heat until all the liquid evaporated. A thick stalk runs through each Swiss chard leaf, so the leaf must be cut away from it.

- 3 tablespoons extra-virgin olive oil
- 2 pounds Swiss chard, stemmed, washed in several changes of cold water, stalks chopped medium and leaves chopped coarse
- 2 medium garlic cloves, minced or pressed through a garlic press (about 2 teaspoons)
- Table salt and ground black pepper
- Lemon wedges, for serving

**1.** Heat the oil in a large Dutch oven over medium heat until shimmering. Add the chard stalks and cook, stirring occasionally, until just tender, about 5 minutes. Add the garlic and cook until fragrant, about 30 seconds. Add the chard leaves, cover, increase the heat to medium-high, and cook, stirring occasionally, until the greens completely wilt, 2 to 3 minutes.

**2.** Uncover and season with salt and pepper to taste. Cook over high heat until the liquid evaporates, about 2 minutes. Serve with the lemon wedges.

## Swiss Chard and Kale Gratin

**SERVES** 8 to 10

**WHY THIS RECIPE WORKS** For a rich gratin with a crisp, flavorful bread crumb topping, we started with a mixture of kale and Swiss chard. Sturdy kale kept the gratin fluffy and tall; Swiss chard collapsed when cooked, but its tender stems added bulk. Steaming the greens in a Dutch oven cooked them quickly and eliminated the need for multiple batches. To keep the gratin from being liquid-y or making the crumb topping soggy, we kept the amount of cream to 1 cup, just enough to give the dish a silky richness. For a craggy and flavorful topping, we used rustic bread, pulsed to a coarse texture in a food processor, along with Parmesan and garlic. Do not use rainbow chard for this recipe; it will have a muddy- brown color when cooked. The greens should not be completely dry after pressing in step 4.

- 2 pounds Swiss chard
- 1 pound curly kale, stemmed and cut into 1-inch-wide strips
- 2 garlic cloves, peeled
- 4 ounces rustic white bread, cut into ¾-inch cubes (3 cups)
- 5 tablespoons extra-virgin olive oil, divided
- 2 ounces Parmesan cheese, grated (1 cup)
- ¾ teaspoon table salt, divided
- ½ teaspoon pepper, divided
- 1 onion, chopped coarse
- 1½ teaspoons minced fresh thyme
- 1 cup heavy cream
- ⅛ teaspoon ground nutmeg

**1.** Adjust oven rack to upper-middle position and heat oven to 375 degrees. Stem chard, then cut stems into 2-inch lengths and set aside. Slice leaves into 1-inch-wide strips. Bring 2 cups water to boil in Dutch oven over high heat. Add kale, cover, and reduce heat to medium-high. Cook until kale is wilted, about 5 minutes, stirring halfway through cooking. Add chard leaves, cover, and continue to cook until chard is wilted, about 4 minutes longer, stirring halfway through cooking. Transfer to colander set in sink and let drain. (Do not wash pot.)

**2.** Pulse garlic in food processor until coarsely chopped, 5 to 7 pulses. Add bread and 3 tablespoons oil and pulse until largest crumbs are smaller than ¼ inch (most will be much smaller), 8 to 10 pulses. Add Parmesan, ¼ teaspoon salt, and ¼ teaspoon pepper and pulse to combine. Transfer to bowl.

**3.** Add onion and chard stems to now-empty processor and process until finely chopped, scraping down sides of bowl as needed, 20 to 30 seconds. Transfer to now-empty pot. Add thyme, remaining 2 tablespoons oil, remaining ½ teaspoon salt, and remaining ¼ teaspoon pepper. Cook over medium-high heat, stirring occasionally, until moisture has evaporated and mixture is just beginning to brown, 8 to 10 minutes.

**4.** Using spatula, press gently on greens in colander to remove excess moisture. Transfer greens to pot with onion mixture. Add cream and nutmeg and stir to combine. Transfer mixture to 13 by 9-inch baking dish. Sprinkle breadcrumb mixture evenly over surface. Bake until topping is golden brown and filling bubbles around edges, 20 to 25 minutes. Let cool for 10 minutes before serving.

## Fried Yuca

**SERVES** 4 to 6 as a side dish

**WHY THIS RECIPE WORKS** Yuca, also known as manioc or cassava, is the starchy root of a woody shrub native to South America. When boiled and then fried, it has a satisfying interior and a crisp exterior. Its delicate, potato-like flavor needs little more than salt to enhance it, though it is also delicious paired with Cuban mojo sauce. Yuca's tough skin must be removed before cooking, a job that calls for a sharp knife, not a vegetable peeler. We also removed the woody core to ensure that the fried yuca would be tender throughout. Frying at a relatively high heat helped create wedges that were crisp on the outside, not greasy. Serve plain or with Cuban mojo sauce.

- 2 pounds yuca roots
- 1 teaspoon table salt
- 2 quarts vegetable oil

**1.** Bring 3 quarts water to boil in Dutch oven over medium heat. While water is coming to boil, use sharp knife to remove 1 to 2 inches of woody stem from yuca. Cut remaining yuca crosswise into 3-inch lengths. Place pieces cut side down and use knife to remove skin in sections, cutting away any flesh that isn't pure white. Halve yuca pieces lengthwise. Pop out any woody core with spoon. Place each piece cut side down and cut lengthwise into ¾-inch-thick wedges.

**2.** Add yuca and salt to boiling water and cook, adjusting heat to maintain vigorous simmer, until yuca is tender and mostly translucent, 20 to 25 minutes. While yuca is cooking, place wire cooling rack in rimmed baking sheet. Drain yuca well in colander. Spread on wire rack. (Boiled yuca can be cooled on rack, wrapped in plastic wrap, and refrigerated for up to 24 hours before frying.) Rinse Dutch oven and dry very well.

### PREPPING YUCA

**1.** Use sharp knife to remove 1 to 2 inches of woody stem. Cut remaining yuca crosswise into 3-inch lengths.

**2.** Place yuca pieces cut side down and use knife to remove skin in sections, cutting away any flesh that isn't pure white.

**3.** Halve yuca pieces lengthwise. Pop out any woody core with spoon. Place each piece cut side down and cut lengthwise into ¾ -inch-thick wedges.

**3.** Heat oil in Dutch oven over medium-high heat to 350 degrees. Pat yuca wedges dry, then add to oil and cook, stirring occasionally, until evenly golden brown, 6 to 8 minutes. While yuca is cooking, remove wire rack and line baking sheet with paper towels. Transfer yuca to paper towel–lined baking sheet. Season with salt to taste, and serve.

## Broiled Smashed Zucchini with Herbed Sour Cream

**SERVES** 4 **SEASON 26**

**WHY THIS RECIPE WORKS** Give zucchini a good whack—then slide it under the broiler. Not only will you create a range of textures but you'll also unlock a surprising variety of flavors. For a side dish that showcases the full spectrum of zucchini, we used a meat pounder to smash the squash and then break it into a couple of large pieces. After seasoning the craggy pieces with salt, lemon juice, and extra-virgin olive oil, we broiled them until they were charred in spots and then let them cool before cutting them into chunks. We served them atop a schmear of creamy dressing garnished with crunchy nuts, pepper, fresh herbs, and a drizzle of extra-virgin olive oil. The zucchini do not need to be the same size, though for this recipe, we prefer ones that are 7 to 12 ounces each.

- 2 pounds zucchini
- 2 tablespoons extra-virgin olive oil, plus extra for drizzling
- ¼ teaspoon grated lemon zest plus 4 teaspoons juice
- 2¼ teaspoons kosher salt, divided
- ½ cup sour cream
- 2 teaspoons water
- 1 tablespoon minced fresh chives
- 1 tablespoon minced fresh dill, plus extra for serving
- ¼ cup pine nuts, toasted and chopped
- Coarsely ground pepper

**1.** Adjust oven rack 5 inches from broiler element and heat broiler. Using meat pounder or rolling pin, firmly but gently smash zucchini until flattened and cracked lengthwise. Trim and discard ends. Break each zucchini into 2 to 4 large pieces. Transfer zucchini pieces to large bowl, including any smaller pieces that have been created during smashing and breaking. Add oil and lemon juice and toss until zucchini is evenly coated.

**2.** Arrange zucchini, skin side down, on aluminum foil–lined rimmed baking sheet. Sprinkle with 2 teaspoons salt, making sure to season thicker pieces more heavily than thiner pieces. Broil until zucchini are lightly charred in spots, 9 to 12 minutes, rotating pan halfway through broiling. Let cool until zucchini are warm to touch, 15 to 20 minutes.

**3.** Meanwhile, stir sour cream, water, chives, 1 tablespoon dill, lemon zest, and remaining ¼ teaspoon salt together in small bowl. Let sit at room temperature so flavors meld, about 10 minutes. Spread sour cream mixture on serving platter. Cut zucchini into bite-size pieces. Arrange zucchini on top of sour cream mixture. Sprinkle with pine nuts, pepper, and additional dill. Drizzle with oil and serve.

## Succotash with Butter Beans, Corn, and Red Pepper

**SERVES** 4 to 6

**WHY THIS RECIPE WORKS** The secret to our fresh, light succotash comes in a can. For the beans, we used canned butter beans instead of limas, as they were superquick and had a creamy consistency and pleasant mild flavor. Some of the canning liquid from the beans created a "sauce" that bound the succotash's ingredients together, creating a dish with a cohesive texture. For the corn, crisp kernels fresh from the cob were the only option for this dish. Do not use frozen or canned corn in this dish.

- 1 (15-ounce) can butter beans, 2 tablespoons liquid reserved, rinsed
- 2 teaspoons lemon juice
- 3 tablespoons unsalted butter
- 1 small onion, chopped fine
- ½ red bell pepper, cut into ¼-inch pieces
- Table salt and pepper
- 2 garlic cloves, minced
- Pinch cayenne pepper
- 4 ears corn, kernels cut from cobs (3 cups)
- 2 tablespoons minced fresh parsley

**1.** Stir reserved bean liquid and lemon juice together in small bowl; set aside. Melt butter in 12-inch nonstick skillet over medium-high heat. Add onion, bell pepper, and ½ teaspoon salt and cook, stirring frequently, until softened and beginning to brown, 4 to 5 minutes. Add garlic and cayenne and cook until fragrant, about 30 seconds.

**2.** Reduce heat to medium and add corn and beans. Cook, stirring occasionally, until corn and beans have cooked through, about 4 minutes. Add bean liquid mixture and cook, stirring constantly, for 1 minute. Remove skillet from heat, stir in parsley, and season with salt and pepper to taste. Serve.

## New England Baked Beans

**SERVES** 4 to 6

**WHY THIS RECIPE WORKS** For a pot of classic New England baked beans, we made a few tweaks while keeping the traditional flavor. Brining the beans overnight jump-started hydration and softened their skins, so they cooked in the oven with few blowouts. Uncovering the pot for the last hour of cooking ensured that the liquid reduced sufficiently to coat the beans in a rich, molasses-based sauce, while salt pork added meatiness. You'll get fewer blowouts if you soak the beans overnight, but you can quick-salt-soak your beans. In step 1, combine the salt, water, and beans in a large Dutch oven and bring them to a boil over high heat. Remove the pot from the heat, cover it, and let it stand for 1 hour. Drain and rinse the beans and proceed with the recipe.

- 1½ tablespoons table salt for brining
- 1 pound (2½ cups) dried navy beans, picked over and rinsed
- 6 ounces salt pork, rinsed and cut into 3 pieces
- 1 onion, halved
- ½ cup molasses
- 2 tablespoons packed dark brown sugar
- 1 tablespoon soy sauce
- 2 teaspoons dry mustard
- ½ teaspoon pepper
- ¼ teaspoon table salt
- 1 bay leaf

**1.** Dissolve 1½ tablespoons salt in 2 quarts cold water in large container. Add beans and let soak at room temperature for at least 8 hours or up to 24 hours. Drain and rinse well.

**2.** Adjust oven rack to lower-middle position and heat oven to 300 degrees. Combine beans, salt pork, onion, molasses, sugar, soy sauce, mustard, pepper, salt, bay leaf, and 4 cups water in large Dutch oven. (Liquid should cover beans by about ½ inch. Add more water if necessary.) Bring to boil over high heat. Cover pot, transfer to oven, and cook until beans are softened and bean skins curl up and split when you blow on them, about 2 hours. (After 1 hour, stir beans and check amount of liquid. Liquid should just cover beans. Add water if necessary.)

**3.** Remove lid and continue to cook until beans are fully tender, browned, and slightly crusty on top, about 1 hour longer. (Liquid will reduce slightly below top layer of beans.)

**4.** Remove pot from oven, cover, and let stand for 5 minutes. Using wooden spoon or rubber spatula, scrape any browned bits from sides of pot and stir into beans. Discard onion and bay leaf. (Salt pork can be eaten, if desired.) Let beans stand, uncovered, until liquid has thickened slightly and clings to beans, 10 to 15 minutes, stirring once halfway through. Season with salt and pepper to taste, and serve. (Cooled beans can be stored in an airtight container and refrigerated for up to 4 days.)

## Boston Baked Beans

**SERVES** 4 to 6

**WHY THIS RECIPE WORKS** Boston baked beans are both sweet and savory, and made with the simplest ingredients. Unfortunately, recipes with lengthy lists of untraditional ingredients and mushy beans abound. We wanted tender beans in a thick, smoky, slightly sweet sauce. For depth of flavor, we started by browning a combination of salt pork and bacon in a Dutch oven. Small white beans were preferred for their creamy texture and ability to remain intact during the long simmer. Molasses provided sweetness, while brown mustard and cider vinegar added welcome spice and tanginess.

- 4 ounces salt pork, trimmed of rind and cut into ½-inch cubes
- 2 ounces (about 2 slices) bacon, cut into ¼-inch pieces
- 1 medium onion, minced
- 9 cups water
- 1 pound (2 cups) dried small white beans, rinsed and picked over
- ½ cup plus 1 tablespoon mild molasses
- 1½ tablespoons prepared brown mustard, such as Gulden's
- Table salt
- 1 teaspoon cider vinegar
- Ground black pepper

**1.** Adjust an oven rack to the lower-middle position and heat the oven to 300 degrees. Place the salt pork and bacon in a large Dutch oven; cook over medium heat, stirring occasionally, until lightly browned and most of the fat is rendered, about 7 minutes. Add the onion and continue to cook, stirring occasionally, until the onion is softened, 5 to 7 minutes. Add the water, beans, ½ cup of the molasses, the mustard, and 1¼ teaspoons salt; increase the heat to medium-high and bring to a boil. Cover the pot and place in the oven.

**2.** Bake until the beans are tender, about 4 hours, stirring once after 2 hours. Remove the lid and continue to bake until the liquid has thickened to a syrupy consistency, 1 to 1½ hours longer. Remove the beans from the oven; stir in the remaining 1 tablespoon molasses, the vinegar, and salt and pepper to taste. Serve. (Cooled beans can be refrigerated in an airtight container for up to 4 days.)

## Drunken Beans

**SERVES** 6 as a main dish

**WHY THIS RECIPE WORKS** To give our drunken beans a rich, complex flavor without imparting booziness or bitterness, we turned to a mixture of beer and tequila. Canned beans were out of the question because this recipe required a full-flavored bean cooking liquid that only dried beans could impart. To preserve the bacon's flavor, we removed it from the pot after crisping it (to use as a garnish). Sautéing onion, garlic, and poblano chiles in the bacon fat created a flavorful base. Off heat, we poured in the tequila and let it evaporate, cooking off some of the alcohol and leaving behind its smoky sweetness. To ensure that our beans remained intact, we brined them overnight. Cilantro leaves are a classic garnish for drunken beans, but the stems also have an aromatic quality, so we tied the stems into a bundle and added them to the pot. We cooked the beans gently in the oven, and held back the acidic beer and tomatoes until the beans were tender. A vigorous simmer to finish caused the beans to release starches that gave the cooking liquid body. You'll get fewer blowouts if you soak the beans overnight, but if you are pressed for time, you can quick-brine your beans: In step 1, combine the salt, water, and beans in a large Dutch oven and bring to a boil over high heat. Remove the pot from the heat, cover, and let stand for 1 hour. Drain and rinse the beans and proceed with the recipe. Serve with rice.

- Table salt
- 1 pound (2½ cups) dried pinto beans, picked over and rinsed
- 30 sprigs fresh cilantro (1 bunch)

- 4 slices bacon, cut into ¼-inch pieces
- 1 onion, chopped fine
- 2 poblano chiles, stemmed, seeded, and chopped fine
- 3 garlic cloves, minced
- ½ cup tequila
- 2 bay leaves
- 1 cup Mexican lager
- ¼ cup tomato paste
- 2 limes, quartered
- 2 ounces cotija cheese, crumbled (½ cup)

**1.** Dissolve 3 tablespoons salt in 4 quarts cold water in large bowl or container. Add beans and soak at room temperature for at least 8 hours or up to 24 hours. Drain and rinse well.

**2.** Adjust oven rack to lower-middle position and heat oven to 275 degrees. Pick leaves from 20 cilantro sprigs (reserve stems), mince, and refrigerate until needed. Using kitchen twine, tie remaining 10 cilantro sprigs and reserved stems into bundle.

**3.** Cook bacon in Dutch oven over medium heat, stirring occasionally, until crisp, 5 to 8 minutes. Using slotted spoon, transfer bacon to paper towel–lined bowl and set aside. Add onion, poblanos, and garlic to fat in pot and cook, stirring frequently, until vegetables are softened, 6 to 7 minutes. Remove from heat. Add tequila and cook until evaporated, 3 to 4 minutes. Return to heat. Increase heat to high; stir in 3½ cups water, bay leaves, 1 teaspoon salt, beans, and cilantro bundle; and bring to boil. Cover, transfer to oven, and cook until beans are just soft, 45 to 60 minutes.

**4.** Remove pot from oven. Discard bay leaves and cilantro bundle. Stir in beer and tomato paste and bring to simmer over medium-low heat. Simmer vigorously, stirring frequently, until liquid is thick and beans are fully tender, about 30 minutes. Season with salt to taste. Serve, passing minced cilantro, lime wedges, cotija, and reserved bacon separately. (Cooled beans can be refrigerated in an airtight container for up to 2 days. Before reheating, thin beans slightly with water.)

## Fava Beans with Artichokes, Asparagus, and Peas

**SERVES 6**

**WHY THIS RECIPE WORKS** This vibrant Italian braise highlights the best of spring produce. Since fresh fava beans are traditional, we started there, but it was clear that they needed tenderizing due to their tough fibrous skins. The solution was to blanch the beans in a baking soda solution. However, the baking soda solution had one drawback: The high pH of the water caused the favas to slowly turn purple during cooking—and they continued to change color after draining. We found that the most effective way to counteract this was to simply rinse them thoroughly after cooking. With our skin-on favas perfected, we turned to the remaining vegetables. Sweet peas, savory baby artichokes, and grassy asparagus added layers of springtime flavor. A speedy stovetop braise was the ideal method for cooking each vegetable perfectly; we added the artichokes first to allow them time to cook almost all the way through before adding the more delicate asparagus and peas, and finally the favas to warm through. This recipe works best with fresh, in-season vegetables; however, if you can't find fresh fava beans and peas, you can substitute 1 cup of frozen, thawed fava beans and 1¼ cups of frozen peas; add the peas to the skillet with the beans in step 4.

- 2 teaspoons grated lemon zest, plus 1 lemon
- 4 baby artichokes (3 ounces each)
- 1 teaspoon baking soda
- 1 pound fava beans, shelled (1 cup)
- 1 tablespoon extra-virgin olive oil, plus extra for serving
- 1 leek, white and light green parts only, halved lengthwise, sliced thin, and washed thoroughly
- Table salt and pepper
- 3 garlic cloves, minced
- 1 cup chicken or vegetable broth
- 1 pound asparagus, trimmed and cut on bias into 2-inch lengths
- 1 pound fresh peas, shelled (1¼ cups)
- 2 tablespoons shredded fresh basil
- 1 tablespoon chopped fresh mint

**1.** Cut lemon in half, squeeze halves into container filled with 2 quarts water, then add spent halves. Working with 1 artichoke at a time, trim stem to about ¾ inch and cut off top quarter of artichoke. Break off bottom 3 or 4 rows of tough outer leaves by pulling them downward. Using paring knife, trim outer layer of stem and base, removing any dark green parts. Cut artichoke into quarters and submerge in lemon water.

**2.** Bring 2 cups water and baking soda to boil in small saucepan. Add beans and cook until edges begin to darken, 1 to 2 minutes. Drain and rinse well with cold water.

**3.** Heat oil in 12-inch skillet over medium heat until shimmering. Add leek, 1 tablespoon water, and 1 teaspoon salt and cook until softened, about 3 minutes. Stir in garlic and cook until fragrant, about 30 seconds.

**4.** Remove artichokes from lemon water, shaking off excess water, and add to skillet. Stir in broth and bring to simmer. Reduce heat to medium-low, cover, and cook until artichokes are almost tender, 6 to 8 minutes. Stir in asparagus and peas, cover, and cook until crisp-tender, 5 to 7 minutes. Stir in beans and cook until heated through and artichokes are fully tender, about 2 minutes. Off heat, stir in basil, mint, and lemon zest. Season with salt and pepper to taste and drizzle with extra oil. Serve immediately.

## Simple Rice Pilaf

**SERVES 4**

**WHY THIS RECIPE WORKS** To make rice pilaf, rice is toasted or browned in fat to build flavor before being cooked through in liquid. Traditional recipes insist that for a truly great pilaf you must soak or at least repeatedly rinse the rice before cooking. We wondered if there was more to making perfect rice pilaf as there seemed to be many variables: the kind of rice to use, the ratio of rice to cooking water, and whether or not to soak the rice before cooking. Testing revealed that using basmati rice was preferable, as was using a lower amount of water than is traditional for cooking rice. Rinsing the rice was key for tender grains. We also sautéed the rice in plenty of butter before adding the water. After the rice was cooked, we covered it with a dish towel and a lid and let it steam off the heat. If you like, olive oil can be substituted for the butter depending on what you are serving with the pilaf. For evenly cooked rice, use a wide-bottomed saucepan with a tight-fitting lid.

- 1½ cups basmati or long-grain rice
- 2½ cups water
- 1½ teaspoons table salt
- Pinch ground black pepper
- 3 tablespoons unsalted butter
- 1 small onion, minced (about ½ cup)

**1.** Place the rice in a medium bowl and add enough water to cover by 2 inches; using your hands, gently swish the grains to release the excess starch. Carefully pour off the water, leaving the rice in the bowl. Repeat four to five times, until the water runs almost clear. Using a colander or fine-mesh strainer, drain the rice; place the colander over a bowl and set aside.

**2.** Bring the water to a boil, covered, in a small saucepan over medium-high heat. Add the salt and pepper; cover to keep hot. Meanwhile, melt the butter in a large saucepan over medium heat; add the onion and cook until softened but not browned, about 4 minutes. Stir in the rice until coated with the butter; cook until the edges of the rice grains begin to turn translucent, about 3 minutes. Stir the hot seasoned water into the rice; return to a boil, then reduce the heat to low, cover, and simmer until all the liquid is absorbed, 16 to 18 minutes. Off the heat, remove the lid and place a clean dish towel folded in half over the saucepan; replace the lid. Let stand for 10 minutes; fluff the rice with a fork and serve.

## Wild Rice Pilaf with Pecans and Dried Cranberries

**SERVES 6 to 8**

**WHY THIS RECIPE WORKS** Sometimes wild rice turns out undercooked and difficult to chew, other times the rice is overcooked and gluey. Through trial and error, we learned to simmer the rice slowly in plenty of liquid, making sure to stop the cooking process at just the right moment by checking it for doneness every couple of minutes past the 35-minute mark. For a simmering liquid, we used chicken broth—its mild yet rich profile tempered the rice's muddy flavor to a pleasant earthiness and affirmed its subdued nuttiness. To further tame the strong flavor of the wild rice, we added some white rice to the mixture, then added onions, carrots, dried cranberries, and toasted pecans for a winning pilaf. Wild rice quickly goes from tough to pasty, so begin testing the rice at the 35-minute mark and drain the rice as soon as it is tender.

- 1¾ cups low-sodium chicken broth
- 2½ cups water
- 2 bay leaves
- 8 sprigs fresh thyme, divided into 2 bundles, each tied together with kitchen twine
- 1 cup wild rice, rinsed well in a strainer
- 1½ cups long-grain white rice
- 3 tablespoons unsalted butter
- 1 medium onion, minced
- 2 carrots, peeled and chopped fine
- Table salt
- ¾ cup sweetened or unsweetened dried cranberries
- ¾ cup pecans, toasted and chopped coarse
- 1½ tablespoons minced fresh parsley leaves
- Ground black pepper

**1.** Bring the chicken broth, ¼ cup of the water, the bay leaves, and 1 bundle of the thyme to a boil in a medium saucepan over medium-high heat. Add the wild rice, cover, and reduce the heat to low; simmer until the rice is plump and tender and has absorbed most of the liquid, 35 to 45 minutes. Drain the rice in a fine-mesh strainer. Return the rice to the saucepan; cover to keep warm and set aside.

**2.** While the wild rice is cooking, place the white rice in a medium bowl and add water to cover by 2 inches; gently swish the grains to release excess starch. Carefully pour off the water, leaving the rice in the bowl. Repeat four to five times, until the water runs almost clear. Drain the rice in a fine-mesh strainer.

**3.** Melt the butter in a medium saucepan over medium-high heat. Add the onion, carrots, and 1 teaspoon salt; cook, stirring frequently, until softened but not browned, about 4 minutes. Stir in the rinsed white rice until coated with the butter; cook, stirring frequently, until the grains begin to turn translucent, about 3 minutes. Meanwhile, bring the remaining 2¼ cups water to a boil in a small saucepan or a microwave. Add the boiling water and the second thyme bundle to the white rice; return to a boil, then reduce the heat to low, sprinkle the cranberries evenly over the rice, and cover. Simmer until all of the liquid is absorbed, 16 to 18 minutes. Off the heat, fluff the rice with a fork and discard the bay leaves and thyme bundles.

**4.** Combine the wild rice, white rice mixture, pecans, and parsley in a large bowl; toss with a rubber spatula until the ingredients are evenly mixed. Season with salt and pepper to taste and serve.

## Rice and Pasta Pilaf

**SERVES** 4 to 6

**WHY THIS RECIPE WORKS** Typically, rice pilaf combines rice with pieces of vermicelli that have been toasted in butter to add richness and a nutty flavor. To produce rice that was as tender and fluffy as the pasta, we needed both elements to cook at the same rate. Jump-starting the rice by soaking it in hot water for a mere 10 minutes softened its outer coating and let it absorb water quickly. Once the pasta and rice were cooked perfectly, we let the pilaf stand for 10 minutes with a towel under the lid to absorb steam. A handful of fresh parsley lent brightness to the finished pilaf. Use long, straight vermicelli or vermicelli nests.

- 1½ cups basmati or other long-grain white rice
- 3 tablespoons unsalted butter
- 2 ounces vermicelli, broken into 1-inch pieces
- 1 onion, grated
- 1 garlic clove, minced
- 2½ cups chicken broth
- 1¼ teaspoons table salt
- 3 tablespoons minced fresh parsley

**1.** Place rice in medium bowl and cover with hot tap water by 2 inches; let stand for 15 minutes.

**2.** Using your hands, gently swish grains to release excess starch. Carefully pour off water, leaving rice in bowl. Add cold tap water to rice and pour off water. Repeat adding and pouring off cold water 4 to 5 times, until water runs almost clear. Drain rice in fine-mesh strainer.

**3.** Melt butter in saucepan over medium heat. Add pasta and cook, stirring occasionally, until browned, about 3 minutes. Add onion and garlic and cook, stirring occasionally, until onion is softened but not browned, about 4 minutes. Add rice and cook, stirring occasionally, until edges of rice begin to turn translucent, about 3 minutes. Add broth and salt and bring to boil. Reduce heat to low, cover, and cook until all liquid is absorbed, about 10 minutes. Off heat, remove lid, fold clean dish towel in half, and place over pan; replace lid. Let stand for 10 minutes. Fluff rice with fork, stir in parsley, and serve.

## Chelow ba Tahdig (Persian-Style Rice with Golden Crust)

**SERVES** 6

**WHY THIS RECIPE WORKS** This classic Iranian dish takes rice to a whole new level, marrying light and fluffy steamed rice (chelow) with a golden-brown, crispy crust known as tahdig. Rinsing the rice and then soaking it for 15 minutes in hot salted water produced fluffy grains. Parboiling the rice and then steaming it created the best texture for the rice and the crunchy crust. Combining a portion of the rice with yogurt, oil, and saffron water created a nicely browned, flavorful crust, while chunks of butter added before steaming enriched the steamed rice portion, and more saffron water added bright yellow color to some of the rice. Plain Greek yogurt will also work here. For the best results, use a Dutch oven with a bottom diameter between 8½ and 10 inches. If you own a nonstick pot, this is a good place to use it. Skip oiling the pot in step 3 and omit 1 tablespoon of oil in step 4. It is important not to overcook the rice during the parboiling step, as it will continue to cook during steaming. Begin checking the rice at the lower end of the given time range. Do not skip placing the pot on a damp towel in step 7—doing so will help free the crust from the pot. Serve with stews or grilled meats.

- ¼ teaspoon saffron threads, crumbled
- 2 cups basmati rice
- Table salt for soaking and cooking rice
- 5 tablespoons vegetable oil, divided
- ¼ cup plain yogurt
- 2 tablespoons unsalted butter, cut into 8 cubes

**1.** Stir saffron threads in ⅓ cup water. Place rice in large fine-mesh strainer and rinse under cold running water until water runs clear. Place rice and 1 tablespoon salt in medium bowl and cover with 4 cups hot tap water. Stir gently to dissolve salt; let stand for 15 minutes. Drain rice in fine-mesh strainer.

**2.** Bring 8 cups water to boil in large Dutch oven over high heat. Add rice and 2 tablespoons salt. Boil briskly until rice is mostly tender with slight bite in center and grains are floating toward top of pot, 3 to 5 minutes.

**3.** Drain rice in fine-mesh strainer and rinse with cold water to stop cooking, about 30 seconds. Rinse and dry pot well to remove any residual starch. Brush bottom and 1 inch up sides of pot with 1 tablespoon oil.

4. Combine yogurt, 1 tablespoon saffron water, 2 cups parcooked rice, and remaining ¼ cup oil in medium bowl. Stir until rice is evenly coated. Spread yogurt-rice mixture evenly over bottom of prepared pot, packing it down well.

5. Mound remaining rice in center of pot on top of yogurt-rice base (it should look like cone or small hill). Poke 8 equally spaced holes through rice mound but not into yogurt-rice base. Place 1 butter cube in each hole. Drizzle remaining saffron water over rice mound.

6. Wrap pot lid with clean dish towel and cover pot tightly, making sure towel is secure on top of lid and away from heat. Cook over medium-high heat until rice on bottom is crackling and steam is coming from sides of pot, 8 to 10 minutes, rotating pot halfway through for even cooking.

7. Reduce heat to medium-low and continue to cook until rice is tender and fluffy, 30 to 35 minutes longer. Remove covered pot from heat and place on damp dish towel set in rimmed baking sheet; let stand for 5 minutes.

8. Gently fluff rice and spoon onto serving platter. Using thin metal spatula, loosen edges of crust from pot, then break crust into large pieces. Transfer pieces to serving platter, arranging evenly around rice. Serve.

## Mexican Rice

**SERVES** 6 to 8

**WHY THIS RECIPE WORKS** Rice cooked the Mexican way is a flavorful pilaf-style dish. For our version, we wanted tender rice infused with well-balanced, fresh flavor. Texture proved to be the backbone of this dish. To keep the rice grains distinct, we found it important to rinse the rice of excess starch before cooking it. And sautéing the rice in vegetable oil before adding the cooking liquid produced superior grains. The best texture for the rice was achieved by properly balancing the grain-to-liquid ratio. We found that equal portions of chicken broth and fresh tomatoes were ideal for a flavorful liquid base, To further guarantee the right flavor, color, and texture, we added a little tomato paste and stirred the rice midway through cooking to reincorporate the tomato mixture. The garlic and jalapeños, meanwhile, fared best sautéed and then combined with a raw puree of tomato and onion. More than a garnish, fresh cilantro, minced jalapeño, and squirt of fresh lime juice complemented the richer tones of the cooked tomatoes, garlic, and onions. It is important to use an ovensafe pot about 12 inches in diameter so that the rice cooks evenly and in the time indicated. The pot's depth is less important than its diameter; note that you will need a pot with a tight-fitting, ovensafe lid. Vegetable broth can be substituted for the chicken broth.

- 2 medium ripe tomatoes (about 12 ounces), cored and quartered
- 1 medium onion, preferably white, peeled and quartered
- 3 medium jalapeño chiles
- 2 cups long-grain white rice
- ⅓ cup vegetable oil
- 4 medium garlic cloves, minced or pressed through a garlic press (about 4 teaspoons)
- 2 cups low-sodium chicken broth
- 1 tablespoon tomato paste
- 1½ teaspoons table salt
- ½ cup minced fresh cilantro leaves
- Lime wedges, for serving

1. Adjust an oven rack to the middle position and heat the oven to 350 degrees. Process the tomatoes and onion in a food processor until smooth and thoroughly pureed, about 15 seconds, scraping down the bowl if necessary. Transfer the mixture to a liquid measuring cup; you should have 2 cups (if necessary, spoon off the excess so that the volume equals 2 cups). Remove the ribs and seeds from 2 of the jalapeños and discard; mince the flesh and set aside. Mince the remaining jalapeño, including the ribs and seeds; set aside.

2. Place the rice in a large fine-mesh strainer and rinse under cold running water until the water runs clear, about 1½ minutes. Shake the rice vigorously in the strainer to remove all excess water.

3. Heat the oil in a heavy-bottomed straight-sided 12-inch ovenproof sauté pan or Dutch oven with a tight-fitting lid over medium-high heat for 1 to 2 minutes. Drop 3 or 4 grains of rice into the oil; if the grains sizzle, the oil is ready. Add the rice and fry, stirring frequently, until the rice is light golden and translucent, 6 to 8 minutes. Reduce the heat to medium, add the garlic and seeded minced jalapeños, and cook, stirring constantly, until fragrant, about 1½ minutes. Stir in the pureed tomato mixture, chicken broth, tomato paste, and salt. Increase the heat to medium-high and bring to a boil. Cover the pan and transfer to the oven. Bake until the liquid is absorbed and the rice is tender, 30 to 35 minutes, stirring well after 15 minutes.

4. Stir in the cilantro and reserved minced jalapeño with seeds to taste. Serve immediately, passing the lime wedges separately.

## Almost Hands-Free Risotto with Parmesan and Herbs

SERVES 6

**WHY THIS RECIPE WORKS** Classic risotto can demand half an hour of stovetop tedium for the best creamy results. Our goal was 5 minutes of stirring, tops. First, we chose to cook our risotto in a Dutch oven not a saucepan; its thick, heavy bottom, deep sides, and tight-fitting lid are made to trap and distribute heat evenly. We added most of the broth after the risotto absorbed the wine and simmered it, with only a few stirs during the process. And to make sure the bottom of our risotto didn't cook more quickly than the top, we stirred the pot for just a few minutes and turned off the heat. The rice turned perfectly al dente from the heat retained in the pot, giving us a foolproof risotto recipe. This more hands-off method does require precise timing, so we strongly recommend using a timer. The consistency of risotto is largely a matter of personal taste; if you prefer a brothy risotto, add extra broth in step 4. This makes a great side dish for braised meats.

- 5 cups chicken broth
- 1½ cups water
- 4 tablespoons unsalted butter, divided
- 1 large onion, chopped fine
- ¾ teaspoon table salt
- 1 garlic clove, minced
- 2 cups arborio rice
- 1 cup dry white wine
- 2 ounces Parmesan cheese, grated (1 cup)
- 2 tablespoons minced fresh parsley
- 2 tablespoons minced fresh chives
- 1 teaspoon lemon juice

**1.** Bring broth and water to boil in large saucepan over high heat. Reduce heat to medium-low to maintain gentle simmer.

**2.** Melt 2 tablespoons butter in Dutch oven over medium heat. Add onion and salt and cook, stirring frequently, until onion is softened but not browned, 5 to 7 minutes. Add garlic and stir until fragrant, about 30 seconds. Add rice and cook, stirring frequently, until grains are translucent around edges, about 3 minutes.

**3.** Add wine and cook, stirring constantly, until fully absorbed, 2 to 3 minutes. Stir 5 cups hot broth mixture into rice; reduce heat to medium-low; cover; and simmer until almost all liquid has been absorbed and rice is just al dente, 16 to 19 minutes, stirring twice during cooking.

**4.** Add ¾ cup broth mixture and stir gently and constantly until risotto becomes creamy, about 3 minutes. Stir in Parmesan. Remove pot from heat, cover, and let stand for 5 minutes. Stir in parsley, chives, lemon juice, and remaining 2 tablespoons butter. Season with salt and pepper to taste. If desired, add up to ½ cup remaining broth mixture to loosen texture of risotto. Serve immediately.

## Parmesan Farrotto

SERVES 6

**WHY THIS RECIPE WORKS** Italian farrotto is a risotto-style dish made with farro in place of rice. Although the method is similar, farro's more robust, nutty flavor gives the dish new dimension. But because much of farro's starch is trapped inside the outer bran, achieving a creamy, velvety consistency can be a challenge. We found that cracking about half the farro in a blender was the key to freeing enough starch from the grains to create a creamy, risotto-like consistency. Adding most of the liquid up front and cooking the farrotto in a lidded Dutch oven helped the grains cook evenly and meant we didn't have to stir constantly—just twice before stirring in the flavorings. We prefer the flavor and texture of whole farro. Do not use quick-cooking or pearled farro. The consistency of farrotto is a matter of personal taste; if you prefer a looser texture, add more of the hot broth mixture in step 6.

- 1½ cups whole farro
- 3 cups chicken broth
- 3 cups water
- 4 tablespoons unsalted butter, divided
- ½ onion, chopped fine
- 1 garlic clove, minced
- 2 teaspoons minced fresh thyme
- 1 teaspoon table salt
- ¾ teaspoon pepper
- 2 ounces Parmesan cheese, grated (1 cup)
- 2 tablespoons minced fresh parsley
- 2 teaspoons lemon juice

**1.** Pulse farro in blender until about half of grains are broken into smaller pieces, about 6 pulses.

**2.** Bring broth and water to boil in large saucepan over high heat. Reduce heat to medium-low to maintain gentle simmer.

**3.** Melt 2 tablespoons butter in large Dutch oven over medium-low heat. Add onion and cook, stirring frequently, until softened, 3 to 4 minutes. Add garlic and stir until fragrant, about 30 seconds. Add farro and cook, stirring frequently, until grains are lightly toasted, about 3 minutes.

**4.** Stir 5 cups hot broth mixture into farro mixture; reduce heat to low; cover; and cook until almost all liquid has been absorbed and farro is just al dente, about 25 minutes, stirring twice during cooking.

**5.** Add thyme, salt, and pepper and continue to cook, stirring constantly, until farro becomes creamy, about 5 minutes.

**6.** Off heat, stir in Parmesan, parsley, lemon juice, and remaining 2 tablespoons butter. Season with salt and pepper to taste. Adjust consistency with remaining hot broth mixture as needed. Serve immediately.

## Quinoa Pilaf with Herbs and Lemon

SERVES 4 to 6

**WHY THIS RECIPE WORKS** Most recipes for quinoa pilaf turn out woefully overcooked because they call for nearly twice as much liquid as they should. We cut the water back to ensure tender grains with a satisfying bite, and gave it a stir partway through cooking to ensure the grains cooked evenly. We let the quinoa rest for several minutes before fluffing to help further improve the texture. We also pre-toasted the quinoa in a dry skillet before simmering to develop its natural nutty flavor, and finished our pilaf with a judicious amount of boldly flavored ingredients. If you buy unwashed quinoa, rinse the grains in a fine-mesh strainer, drain them, and then spread them on a rimmed baking sheet lined with a clean dish towel and let them dry for 15 minutes before proceeding with the recipe. Any soft herbs, such as cilantro, parsley, chives, mint, and tarragon, can be used.

- 1½ cups prewashed quinoa
- 2 tablespoons unsalted butter, cut into 2 pieces
- 1 small onion, chopped fine
- ¾ teaspoon table salt
- 1¾ cups water
- 3 tablespoons chopped fresh herbs
- 1 tablespoon lemon juice

**1.** Toast quinoa in medium saucepan over medium-high heat, stirring frequently, until quinoa is very fragrant and makes continuous popping sound, 5 to 7 minutes. Transfer quinoa to bowl and set aside.

**2.** Return now-empty pan to medium-low heat and melt butter. Add onion and salt; cook, stirring frequently, until onion is softened and light golden, 5 to 7 minutes.

**3.** Increase heat to medium-high, stir in water and quinoa, and bring to simmer. Cover, reduce heat to low, and simmer until grains are just tender and liquid is absorbed, 18 to 20 minutes, stirring once halfway through cooking. Remove pan from heat and let sit, covered, for 10 minutes. Fluff quinoa with fork, stir in herbs and lemon juice, and serve.

### Quinoa Pilaf with Chipotle, Queso Fresco, and Peanuts

Add 1 teaspoon chipotle chile powder and ¼ teaspoon ground cumin with onion and salt. Substitute ½ cup crumbled queso fresco; ½ cup roasted unsalted peanuts, chopped coarse; and 2 thinly sliced scallions for herbs. Substitute 4 teaspoons lime juice for lemon juice.

## Basic Polenta

SERVES 4 to 6

**WHY THIS RECIPE WORKS** A creamy mound of hot polenta can be a comforting dish, especially when served with a stew or saucy braise. Composed of little more than cornmeal and water, it should be easy to prepare. But often it's lumpy or gummy, and getting it right requires constant stirring. We wanted the smooth, creamy texture and great corn flavor of real polenta, but without the hassle. It turned out that the type of cornmeal made a difference in the end result, and we found that a medium-grind meal worked best. The traditional method of making polenta requires half an hour or more of constant stirring after the cornmeal is added to boiling salted water. The way to avoid this continuous attention was very low heat. We added the cornmeal (very gradually, so it wouldn't seize up) to barely simmering water with the flame set as low as possible. With the cover on the pot to keep in moisture, the cornmeal had time to release its starches gradually and develop flavor, and we needed to stir it only every five minutes or so. Our polenta was smooth and creamy with lots of corn flavor, and we were able to serve it in half an hour without standing at the stove the whole time. You will need a heavy-bottomed saucepan for this recipe. Use this polenta as the base for any stew or braise, especially Osso Buco (page 434), or serve with a chunk of Gorgonzola cheese. Cooked leafy greens also make an excellent topping for soft polenta.

- 6 cups water
- Table salt
- 1½ cups medium-grind cornmeal, preferably stone-ground
- 3 tablespoons unsalted butter, cut into large chunks
- Ground black pepper

**1.** Bring the water to a rolling boil in a 4-quart heavy-bottomed saucepan over medium-high heat. Reduce the heat to the lowest possible setting, add 1½ teaspoons salt, and pour the cornmeal into the water in a very slow stream from a measuring cup, all the while whisking in a circular motion to prevent lumps.

**2.** Cover and cook, vigorously stirring the polenta with a wooden spoon for about 10 seconds once every 5 minutes and making sure to scrape clean the bottom and corners of the pot, until the polenta has lost its raw cornmeal taste and becomes soft and smooth, about 30 minutes. Stir in the butter, season with salt and pepper to taste, and serve immediately.

## Creamy Parmesan Polenta

SERVES 6 to 8

**WHY THIS RECIPE WORKS** If you don't stir polenta almost constantly, it forms intractable lumps. We wanted creamy, smooth polenta with rich corn flavor, but we wanted to find a way around the fussy process. The prospect of stirring continuously for an hour made our arms ache, so we set out to find a way to give the water a head start on penetrating the cornmeal (we prefer the soft texture and nutty flavor of degerminated cornmeal in polenta). Our research led us to consider the similarities between cooking dried beans and dried corn. With beans, water has to penetrate the hard outer skin to gelatinize the starch within. In a corn kernel, the water has to penetrate the endosperm. To soften bean skins and speed up cooking, baking soda is sometimes added to the cooking liquid. Sure enough, a pinch was all it took to cut the cooking time in

half without affecting the texture or flavor. Baking soda also helped the granules break down and release their starch in a uniform way, so we could virtually eliminate the stirring if we covered the pot and adjusted the heat to low. Parmesan cheese and butter stirred in at the last minute finishes our polenta, which is satisfying and rich. Coarse-ground degerminated cornmeal such as yellow grits (with grains the size of couscous) works best in this recipe. Avoid instant and quick-cooking products, as well as whole grain, stone-ground, and regular cornmeal. Do not omit the baking soda—it reduces the cooking time and makes for a creamier polenta. The polenta should do little more than release wisps of steam. If it bubbles or sputters even slightly after the first 10 minutes, the heat is too high and you may need a flame tamer. A flame tamer can be purchased at most kitchen supply stores, or there are ways you can improvise your own. For a main course, serve the polenta with a wedge of rich cheese, meat sauce, or cooked leafy greens. Served plain, the polenta makes a great accompaniment to stews and braises.

- 7½ cups water
- 1½ teaspoons table salt
- Pinch baking soda
- 1½ cups coarse-ground cornmeal
- 4 ounces Parmesan cheese, grated (about 2 cups), plus extra for serving
- 2 tablespoons unsalted butter
- Ground black pepper

**1.** Bring the water to a boil in a heavy-bottomed 4-quart saucepan over medium-high heat. Stir in the salt and baking soda. Slowly pour the cornmeal into the water in a steady stream, while stirring back and forth with a wooden spoon or rubber spatula. Bring the mixture to a boil, stirring constantly, about 1 minute. Reduce the heat to the lowest possible setting and cover.

**2.** After 5 minutes, whisk the polenta to smooth out any lumps that may have formed, about 15 seconds. (Make sure to scrape the sides and bottom of the pan.) Cover and continue to cook, without stirring, until the grains of polenta are tender but slightly al dente, about 25 minutes longer. (The polenta should be loose and barely hold its shape; it will continue to thicken as it cools.)

**3.** Remove from the heat, stir in the Parmesan and butter, and season with pepper to taste. Let stand, covered, for 5 minutes. Serve, passing extra Parmesan separately.

## Simple Couscous

**SERVES** 4 to 6

**WHY THIS RECIPE WORKS** Although couscous traditionally serves as a sauce absorber under North African–style stews and braises, it can work equally well as a lighter, quicker alternative to everyday side dishes like rice pilaf. We wanted to develop a classic version as convenient as the box kind but much fresher tasting, as well as a variation with a few flavorful add-ins. The box instructions—measure and boil water, stir in couscous, cover and let stand off heat for five minutes—gave us bland, clumpy grains. Toasting the couscous grains in butter deepened their flavor and helped them cook up fluffy and separate. And to bump up the flavor even further, we replaced half of the water with chicken broth.

- 2 tablespoons unsalted butter
- 2 cups couscous
- 1 cup water
- 1 cup low-sodium chicken broth
- 1 teaspoon table salt
- Ground black pepper

Melt the butter in a medium saucepan over medium-high heat. Add the couscous and cook, stirring frequently, until the grains are just beginning to brown, about 5 minutes. Add the water, broth, and salt and stir briefly to combine. Cover and remove the pan from the heat. Let stand until the grains are tender, about 7 minutes. Uncover and fluff the grains with a fork. Season with pepper to taste and serve.

### Couscous with Shallots, Garlic, and Almonds

Follow the recipe for Simple Couscous, increasing the butter to 3 tablespoons. Once the foaming subsides, add 3 thinly sliced shallots and cook, stirring frequently, until softened and lightly browned, about 5 minutes. Add 1 minced garlic clove and cook until fragrant, about 30 seconds. Continue with recipe, stirring ¾ cup toasted sliced almonds, ¾ cup minced fresh parsley, and ½ teaspoon grated zest and 2 teaspoons juice from 1 lemon into the couscous before serving.

## Simple Pearl Couscous

**MAKES** about 4 cups

**WHY THIS RECIPE WORKS** Pearl couscous is nuttier than its North African cousin, thanks to the practice of drying the pasta-like pearls over a flame. To prepare pearl couscous, we toasted the spheres in oil to accentuate their earthy, nutty flavor. We then added water, brought it to a boil, and cooked the couscous covered and at a simmer, allowing it to slowly and evenly absorb the liquid. To turn the couscous into a salad, we spread the spheres on a baking sheet to cool (and to prevent it from cooking further in its own steam). Meanwhile, we quickly pickled shallots, dissolving sugar in red wine vinegar over medium-high heat before removing the pan from heat and stirring in the shallots. We dressed the couscous in a bold vinaigrette, whisking together olive oil, lemon juice, Dijon, and red pepper flakes. Once the couscous was coated in the vinaigrette, we finished off the salad with mint, peas, toasted pistachios, and feta. Warm couscous can be tossed with butter or extra-virgin olive oil and salt and pepper for a simple side dish. If you're using it in a salad, transfer the couscous to a rimmed baking sheet and let it cool completely, about 15 minutes.

- 2 cups pearl couscous
- 1 tablespoon extra-virgin olive oil
- 2½ cups water
- ½ teaspoon table salt

Heat couscous and oil in medium saucepan over medium heat, stirring frequently, until about half of grains are golden brown, 5 to 6 minutes. Carefully add water and salt; stir briefly to combine. Increase heat to high and bring to boil. Reduce heat to medium-low, cover, and simmer, stirring occasionally, until water is absorbed, 9 to 12 minutes. Remove saucepan from heat and let stand, covered, for 3 minutes. Serve.

### Pearl Couscous with Lemon, Mint, Peas, Feta, and Pickled Shallots

**SERVES** 6

For efficiency, let the shallots pickle while you prepare the remaining ingredients.

- ⅓ cup red wine vinegar
- 2 tablespoons sugar
- Table salt and pepper
- 2 shallots, sliced thin
- 3 tablespoons extra-virgin olive oil
- 3 tablespoons lemon juice
- 1 teaspoon Dijon mustard
- ⅛ teaspoon red pepper flakes
- 1 recipe Simple Pearl Couscous, cooled
- 4 ounces (4 cups) baby arugula, roughly chopped
- 1 cup fresh mint leaves, torn
- ½ cup frozen peas, thawed
- ½ cup shelled pistachios, toasted and chopped
- 3 ounces feta cheese, crumbled (¾ cup)

**1.** Bring vinegar, sugar, and pinch salt to simmer in small saucepan over medium-high heat, stirring occasionally, until sugar dissolves. Remove pan from heat, add shallots, and stir to combine. Cover and let cool completely, about 30 minutes. Drain and discard liquid.

**2.** Whisk oil, lemon juice, mustard, pepper flakes, and ⅛ teaspoon salt together in large bowl. Add cooled couscous, arugula, mint, peas, 6 tablespoons pistachios, ½ cup feta, and shallots and toss to combine. Season with salt and pepper to taste and transfer to serving bowl. Let stand for 5 minutes. Sprinkle with remaining ¼ cup feta and remaining 2 tablespoons pistachios and serve.

## Rustic Bread Stuffing with Cranberries and Walnuts

**SERVES** 6 to 8

**WHY THIS RECIPE WORKS** A lighter, more loosely textured stuffing is a welcome addition to the various hefty, moist side dishes that dominate the holiday meal. With this recipe, we steered away from the usual custardy stuffing by eliminating the eggs and cutting back on the broth. We swapped the usual cubes of toasted white sandwich bread for torn chunks of baguette, which retained some crispness and chew through cooking. In homage to traditional stuffing flavors, we stirred in sautéed onions, celery, dried cranberries, and sage. Baguettes from the bakery section of the supermarket, which have a slightly soft crust, work well in this recipe. The weight should be listed on the wrapper.

- 3 tablespoons unsalted butter, divided
- 2 baguettes (10 ounces each), bottom crust and ends trimmed and discarded
- 3 tablespoons extra-virgin olive oil
- 2 cups chicken broth
- 3 celery ribs, cut into ½-inch pieces
- 1 teaspoon table salt
- ¼ teaspoon pepper
- 2 large onions, cut into ½-inch pieces
- ½ cup dried cranberries
- 3 tablespoons chopped fresh sage
- 3 tablespoons chopped fresh parsley
- ¼ cup walnuts, toasted and chopped coarse

**1.** Adjust oven rack to upper-middle position and heat oven to 450 degrees. Grease 13 by 9-inch baking dish with 1 tablespoon butter and set aside. Tear baguettes into bite-size pieces (you should have about 12 cups) and spread into even layer on rimmed baking sheet. Drizzle with oil and toss with spatula until oil is well distributed. Toast in oven for 5 minutes. Stir bread, then continue to toast until edges are lightly browned and crisped, about 5 minutes longer. Transfer sheet to wire rack. Drizzle broth over bread and stir to combine.

**2.** Melt remaining 2 tablespoons butter in 10-inch skillet over medium heat. Add celery, salt, and pepper. Cook, stirring frequently, until celery begins to soften, 3 to 5 minutes. Add onions and cook until vegetables are soft but not browned, about 8 minutes. Add cranberries and sage and cook until fragrant, about 1 minute.

**3.** Add vegetable mixture to bread and toss with spatula until well combined. Transfer stuffing mixture to prepared dish and spread into even layer. Bake for 20 minutes. Stir with spatula, turning crisp edges into middle, and spread into even layer. Continue to bake until top is crisp and brown, about 10 minutes longer. Stir in parsley, sprinkle with walnuts, and serve. (To make the stuffing ahead, wrap it with plastic wrap immediately after transferring it to the baking dish, and refrigerate for up to 24 hours. Add 5 minutes to the baking time.)

## Baked Bread Stuffing with Sausage, Dried Cherries, and Pecans

**SERVES** 10 to 12

**WHY THIS RECIPE WORKS** Stuffing baked in a dish definitely has appeal—you can make as much as you want and you don't have to time its doneness to coincide with the doneness of the meat—but it lacks the rich flavor from the bird's juices. As the base for our stuffing we chose ordinary sandwich bread, which we "staled" in a low oven; this would allow it to soak up plenty of liquid. To infuse the stuffing with meaty turkey flavor, we browned turkey wings on the stovetop, then we used the same pan to sauté the aromatics. When we placed the stuffing in a baking dish, we arranged the seared wings on top—as they cooked, their rendered fat infused the stuffing with rich flavor. Covering the baking dish with foil prevented the top of the stuffing from drying out, while placing a baking sheet underneath the dish protected the bottom layer from the oven's heat. Two pounds of chicken wings can be substituted for the turkey wings. If using chicken wings, separate them into 2 sections (it's not necessary to separate the tips) and poke each segment 4 to 5 times. Also, increase the amount of broth to 3 cups, reduce the amount of butter to 2 tablespoons, and cook the stuffing for only 60 minutes (the wings should register over 175 degrees at the end of cooking). Use the meat from the cooked wings to make salad or soup.

- 2 pounds hearty white sandwich bread, cut into ½-inch cubes (16 cups)
- 3 pounds turkey wings, divided at joints
- 2 teaspoons vegetable oil
- 1 pound bulk pork sausage
- 4 tablespoons (½ stick) unsalted butter
- 1 large onion, chopped fine
- 3 medium celery ribs, minced
- Table salt
- 2 tablespoons minced fresh thyme
- 2 tablespoons minced fresh sage
- 1 teaspoon ground black pepper
- 2½ cups low-sodium chicken broth
- 3 large eggs
- 1 cup dried cherries
- 1 cup pecan halves, toasted and chopped fine

**1.** Adjust the oven racks to the upper-middle and lower-middle positions and heat the oven to 250 degrees. Spread the bread cubes in an even layer on 2 rimmed baking sheets. Bake until the edges have dried but the centers are slightly moist (the cubes should yield to pressure), 45 to 60 minutes, stirring several times during baking. Transfer the dried bread to a large bowl and increase the oven temperature to 375 degrees. (Bread can be stored in an airtight container for up to 1 day ahead.)

**2.** While the bread dries, use a paring knife to poke 10 to 15 holes in each wing segment. Heat the oil in a 12-inch skillet over medium-high heat until shimmering. Add the wings in a single layer and cook until golden brown on both sides, 8 to 12 minutes. Transfer the wings to a separate bowl and set aside.

**3.** Return the now-empty skillet to medium-high heat, add the sausage, and cook, breaking it up into ½-inch pieces with a wooden spoon, until browned, 5 to 7 minutes. Remove the sausage with a slotted spoon and transfer to a paper towel–lined plate.

**4.** Melt the butter in the fat left in the skillet over medium heat. Add the onion, celery, and ½ teaspoon salt and cook, stirring occasionally, until the vegetables are softened, 7 to 9 minutes. Stir in the thyme, sage, and pepper and cook until fragrant, about 30 seconds. Stir in 1 cup of the broth, scraping up any browned bits, and bring to a simmer. Add the vegetable mixture to the bowl with the dried bread and toss to combine.

**5.** Grease a 13 by 9-inch baking dish. Whisk the eggs, remaining 1½ cups broth, 1½ teaspoons salt, and any accumulated juices from the wings together in a bowl. Add the egg mixture, cherries, pecans, and sausage to the bread mixture and toss to combine; transfer to the prepared baking dish. Arrange the wings on top of the stuffing, cover tightly with aluminum foil, and place the baking dish on a rimmed baking sheet.

**6.** Bake on the lower rack until the wings register 175 degrees, 60 to 75 minutes. (The stuffing can be held at room temperature for up to 4 hours. To finish, remove the wings from the stuffing and re-cover the stuffing tightly with foil. Heat on a rimmed baking sheet in a 375-degree oven until hot, 20 to 25 minutes. Remove the foil, fluff with a fork, and serve immediately.)

**7.** Remove the foil and transfer the wings to a dinner plate to reserve for another use. Gently fluff the stuffing with a fork. Let rest for 5 minutes before serving.

## Simple Applesauce

**MAKES** about 3½ cups

**WHY THIS RECIPE WORKS** Applesauce should taste like apples, but all too often the tart, sweet, and fruity nuances of fresh apple flavor are overpowered by sweeteners and spices, and the sauce ends up tasting like bad pie filling. The texture, too, can vary from dry and chunky to loose and thin. We wanted a smooth, thick sauce that showcased fresh apple flavor without too much sweetness or spice—the perfect partner to pork chops or as a snack. The first step was to find the right variety of apple. We began by gathering 18 varieties and making each into applesauce. We found that Jonagold, Jonathan, Pink Lady, and Macoun varieties all produce a sauce with a pleasing balance of tart and sweet. We tried blending varieties in combination with each other, but concluded that single-variety sauces had more character. Cooking the apples with their skins on saved us the step of peeling and enhanced the flavor of the sauce. Processing the cooked apples through a food mill, not a food processor or blender, removed the skins and produced a sauce with the silky-smooth, thick texture we were after. Adding a little water, sugar, and a pinch of salt—and no spices—resulted in a perfectly sweetened sauce that tasted first and foremost of apples. If you do not own a food mill or prefer applesauce with a coarse texture, peel the apples before coring and cutting them and, after cooking, mash them against the side of the pot with a wooden spoon or against the bottom of the pot with a potato masher. Applesauce made with out-of-season apples may be somewhat drier than sauce made with peak-season apples, so it's likely that in step 2 of the recipe you will need to add more water to adjust the texture. If you double the recipe, the apples will need 10 to 15 minutes of extra cooking time.

- 4 pounds apples (about 10 medium), preferably Jonagold, Pink Lady, Jonathan, or Macoun, unpeeled, cored, and cut into rough 1½-inch pieces
- 1 cup water, plus more as needed
- ¼ cup sugar, plus more to taste
- Pinch table salt

**1.** Toss the apples, water, sugar, and salt in a large Dutch oven. Cover the pot and cook the apples over medium-high heat until they begin to break down, 15 to 20 minutes, checking and stirring occasionally with a wooden spoon to break up any large chunks.

**2.** Process the cooked apples through a food mill fitted with the medium disk. Season with extra sugar to taste or add water to adjust the consistency as desired. Serve hot, warm, at room temperature, or chilled.

## Classic Cranberry Sauce

**MAKES** 2¼ cups

**WHY THIS RECIPE WORKS** The best cranberry sauce has a clean, pure cranberry flavor, with enough sweetness to temper the assertively tart fruit but not so much that the sauce is cloying or candylike. The texture should be that of a soft gel, neither too liquid-y nor too stiff, cushioning some softened but still intact berries. For the most part, it turned out that simpler was better. We used white table sugar, which, unlike brown sugar, honey, or syrup, balanced the tartness of the cranberries without adding a flavor profile of its own. Simpler was also better when it came to liquid: water proved the best choice. We also discovered that adding just a pinch of salt brought out an unexpected sweetness in the berries, heightening the flavor of the sauce overall. If you've got frozen cranberries, do not defrost them before use; just pick through them and add about 2 minutes to the simmering time.

- 1 cup (7 ounces) sugar
- ¾ cup water
- ¼ teaspoon table salt
- 1 (12-ounce) bag cranberries, picked through

Bring the sugar, water, and salt to a boil in a medium saucepan over high heat, stirring occasionally to dissolve the sugar. Stir in the cranberries; return to a boil. Reduce the heat to medium; simmer until saucy and slightly thickened, and about two-thirds of the berries have popped open, about 5 minutes. Transfer to a medium bowl, cool to room temperature, and serve. (The cranberry sauce can be covered and refrigerated for up to 7 days; let stand at room temperature for 30 minutes before serving.)

## Bread-and-Butter Pickles

**MAKES** four 1-pint jars

**WHY THIS RECIPE WORKS** We wanted a bread-and-butter pickle with a crisp texture and a balance of sweet and sour. Most recipes combine cucumbers and onions in a spiced, syrupy brine; we cut back on the sugar and added red bell pepper. Cucumbers can lose their crunch when processed in a boiling-water bath; combining several crisping techniques gave us the best results. We tossed our sliced vegetables in salt to draw out excess water. Then we added a small amount of Ball Pickle Crisp to each jar, which helps keep the natural pectin from breaking down. Next, we employed low-temperature pasteurization, which involved maintaining our pickles in a hot-water bath at a temperature of 180 to 185 degrees Fahrenheit for 30 minutes—in this temperature range microorganisms are destroyed and pectin remains largely intact.

- 2 pounds pickling cucumbers, ends trimmed, sliced ¼ inch thick
- 1 onion, quartered and sliced thin
- 1 red bell pepper, stemmed, seeded, and cut into 1½-inch matchsticks
- 2 tablespoons canning and pickling salt
- 3 cups apple cider vinegar
- 2 cups sugar
- 1 cup water
- 1 tablespoon yellow mustard seeds
- ¾ teaspoon ground turmeric
- ½ teaspoon celery seeds
- ¼ teaspoon ground cloves
- ½ teaspoon Ball Pickle Crisp

**1.** Toss cucumbers, onion, and bell pepper with salt in large bowl and refrigerate for 3 hours. Drain vegetables in colander (do not rinse), then pat dry with paper towels.

**2.** Meanwhile, set canning rack in large pot, place four 1-pint jars in rack, and add water to cover by 1 inch. Bring to simmer over medium-high heat, then turn off heat and cover to keep hot.

**3.** Bring vinegar, sugar, water, mustard seeds, turmeric, celery seeds, and cloves to boil in large saucepan over medium-high heat; cover and remove from heat.

**4.** Place dish towel flat on counter. Using jar lifter, remove jars from pot, draining water back into pot. Place jars upside down on towel and let dry for 1 minute. Add ⅛ teaspoon Pickle Crisp to each hot jar, then pack tightly with vegetables.

**5.** Return brine to brief boil. Using funnel and ladle, pour hot brine over cucumbers to cover, distributing spices evenly and leaving ½ inch headspace. Slide wooden skewer along inside of jar, pressing slightly on vegetables to remove air bubbles, and add extra brine as needed.

**6A. FOR SHORT-TERM STORAGE:** Let jars cool to room temperature, cover with lids, and refrigerate for 1 day before serving. (Pickles can be refrigerated for up to 3 months; flavor will continue to mature over time.)

**6B. FOR LONG-TERM STORAGE:** While jars are warm, wipe rims clean, add lids, and screw on rings until fingertip-tight; do not overtighten. Before processing jars, heat water in canning pot to temperature between 120 and 140 degrees. Lower jars into water, bring water to 180 to 185 degrees, then cook for 30 minutes, adjusting heat as needed to maintain water between 180 and 185 degrees. Remove jars from pot and let cool for 24 hours. Remove rings, check seal, and clean rims. (Sealed jars can be stored for up to 1 year.)

### MAKING BREAD-AND-BUTTER PICKLES

**1.** We add ⅛ teaspoon of Ball Pickle Crisp to each jar before adding cucumbers and brine to help pickles retain their crispness. Pickle Crisp is simply a form of calcium chloride, which helps keep natural pectin in the cucumbers from softening.

**2.** It is key to have brine hot when pouring it over pickles. Be sure to distribute spices evenly among jars and leave ½ inch of headspace.

**3.** To remove any air bubbles trapped between layers of cucumbers, slide a wooden skewer along inside of jar and press it gently against vegetables. Once air bubbles have been dispersed, add extra brine as needed until headspace measures ½ inch.

**4.** Using low-temperature pasteurization processing means jars of pickles need to cook in 180- to 185-degree water. If water climbs above 185, pickles will turn mushy. If water falls below 180 degrees, harmful bacteria could grow inside jars.

CHAPTER 12 # Bread and Pizza

Photos (left to right): Challah; Popovers; Croissants; Pizza Bianca with Tomatoes and Mozzarella; Southern-Style Cornbread; Deli Rye Bread; Cinnamon Swirl Bread

## Easiest-Ever Biscuits

**MAKES** 10 biscuits

**WHY THIS RECIPE WORKS** A fresh, warm biscuit instantly doubles the coziness quotient of practically anything you serve it with: chicken stew, vegetable soup, fried eggs, just to name a few. We wanted to combine the ease of cream biscuits (which eliminate the step of cutting cold fat into dry ingredients) with the ease of drop biscuits (which skip the rolling and cutting) to create the easiest biscuits ever. But the most obvious solution—increasing the amount of cream in a cream biscuit recipe until the dough had a droppable consistency—produced biscuits that spread too much and were greasy. Instead of increasing the amount of cream, we found a way to increase its fluidity: We heated it to between 95 and 100 degrees, which melted the solid particles of butterfat dispersed throughout. This made a dough that was moister and scoopable but that rose up instead of spreading out in the oven, producing biscuits that were appropriately rich and tender but not greasy. These biscuits come together very quickly, so in the interest of efficiency, start heating your oven before gathering your ingredients. We like these biscuits brushed with a bit of melted butter, but you can skip that step if you're serving the biscuits with a rich accompaniment such as sausage gravy. Biscuits can be stored in a zipper-lock bag at room temperature for up to 24 hours; reheat in 300-degree oven for 10 minutes.

- 3 cups (15 ounces) all-purpose flour
- 4 teaspoons sugar
- 1 tablespoon baking powder
- ¼ teaspoon baking soda
- 1¼ teaspoons table salt
- 2 cups heavy cream
- 2 tablespoons unsalted butter, melted (optional)

**1.** Adjust oven rack to upper-middle position and heat oven to 450 degrees. Line rimmed baking sheet with parchment paper. In medium bowl, whisk together flour, sugar, baking powder, baking soda, and salt. Microwave cream until just warmed to body temperature (95 to 100 degrees), 60 to 90 seconds, stirring halfway through microwaving. Stir cream into flour mixture until soft, uniform dough forms.

**2.** Spray ⅓-cup dry measuring cup with vegetable oil spray. Drop level scoops of batter 2 inches apart on prepared sheet (biscuits should measure about 2½ inches wide and 1¼ inches tall). Respray measuring cup after every 3 or 4 scoops. If portions are misshapen, use your fingertips to gently reshape dough into level cylinders. Bake until tops are light golden brown, 10 to 12 minutes, rotating sheet halfway through baking. Brush hot biscuits with melted butter, if using. Serve warm.

## Best Drop Biscuits

**MAKES** 12 biscuits

**WHY THIS RECIPE WORKS** Oftentimes the simplest biscuits are lacking in flavor, not to mention lean and dry or gummy. Drop biscuits should, by nature, be simple to make and tender. While oil-based biscuits were easy to work with, they lacked flavor, so butter was a must. Buttermilk further enhanced the flavor while also allowing us to replace some of the baking powder (too much can cause bitterness) with baking soda (buttermilk provides the acid that soda needs to react). These biscuits had a rich, buttery tang and were crisper on the exterior and fluffier on the interior. Once the ingredients had been identified, we were left with only one problem. Properly combining the butter and buttermilk required that both ingredients be at just the right temperature; if they weren't, the melted butter clumped in the buttermilk. But when we had trouble avoiding this, we made a batch with lumpy buttermilk anyway. The result was a surprisingly better biscuit, slightly higher and with better texture. The water in the lumps of butter (butter is 20 percent water) had turned to steam in the oven, helping create additional height. A ¼-cup (#16) portion scoop can be used to portion the batter. Biscuits can be stored in a zipper-lock bag at room temperature for up to 24 hours; reheat in a 300-degree oven for 10 minutes.

- 2 cups (10 ounces) unbleached all-purpose flour
- 2 teaspoons baking powder
- 1 teaspoon sugar
- ¾ teaspoon table salt
- ½ teaspoon baking soda
- 1 cup buttermilk, chilled
- 8 tablespoons (1 stick) unsalted butter, melted and cooled slightly, plus 2 tablespoons melted butter for brushing the biscuits

**1.** Adjust an oven rack to the middle position and heat the oven to 475 degrees. Line a large rimmed baking sheet with parchment paper. Whisk the flour, baking powder, sugar, salt, and baking soda together in a large bowl. Combine the buttermilk and 8 tablespoons of the melted butter in a medium bowl, stirring until the butter forms small clumps.

**2.** Add the buttermilk mixture to the dry ingredients and stir with a rubber spatula until just incorporated and the batter pulls away from the sides of the bowl. Using a greased ¼-cup measuring cup, scoop a level amount of batter and drop onto the prepared baking sheet. Repeat with the remaining batter, spacing the biscuits about 1½ inches apart. Bake until the tops are golden brown and crisp, 12 to 14 minutes.

**3.** Brush the biscuit tops with the remaining 2 tablespoons melted butter. Transfer to a wire rack and cool for 5 minutes before serving.

## Cream Biscuits

**MAKES** 8 biscuits

**WHY THIS RECIPE WORKS** With a high rise, light texture, and rich flavor, fresh-from-the-oven biscuits tend to disappear quicker than cookies. We wanted to make great biscuits that eliminated the strenuous step of cutting butter into flour or the messy move of rolling out dough time and again to get every last piece into a round. We started with a basic combination of heavy cream, flour, baking powder, and salt. Instead of cutting butter into flour, we included a generous amount of heavy cream in our biscuits, which gave them a lighter and more tender texture. Kneading for just 30 seconds was enough to get our dough smooth and uniform. And we used an extra bit of cream to soak up all the last bits of flour in the bowl. To enhance the light flavor of our biscuits, we added a small amount of sugar. Although it is easy enough to pat out this dough and cut it into rounds with a biscuit cutter, we devised a strategy of simply pressing the dough into an 8-inch cake pan, turning out the dough, and then slicing it into wedges. Bake the biscuits immediately after cutting them; letting them stand for any length of time can decrease the leavening power and thereby prevent the biscuits from rising properly in the oven.

- 2 cups (10 ounces) all-purpose flour
- 2 teaspoons sugar
- 2 teaspoons baking powder
- ½ teaspoon table salt
- 1½ cups heavy cream, divided

**1.** Adjust oven rack to upper-middle position and heat oven to 425 degrees. Line large rimmed baking sheet with parchment paper. Whisk flour, sugar, baking powder, and salt together in medium bowl.

**2.** Add 1¼ cups cream to flour mixture and stir with wooden spoon until dough forms, about 30 seconds. Transfer dough to lightly floured work surface, leaving all dry, floury bits behind in the bowl. Add remaining ¼ cup cream, 1 tablespoon at a time, to bowl, mixing with wooden spoon after each addition, until all loose flour is just moistened; add these moistened bits to dough. Knead dough briefly just until smooth, about 30 seconds.

**3.** Pat dough into ¾-inch-thick circle or press it into 8-inch cake pan and turn it out onto lightly floured surface. Cut biscuits into rounds using 2½-inch biscuit cutter or into 8 wedges using knife. Place rounds or wedges on prepared sheet and bake until golden brown, about 15 minutes. Serve immediately.

## Ultimate Flaky Buttermilk Biscuits

**MAKES** 9 biscuits

**WHY THIS RECIPE WORKS** For the ultimate flaky biscuits with innumerable, ethereally thin layers, we grated the butter so that it would be evenly distributed in the flour mixture, which we learned was key for ideal flakiness. Freezing the butter prior to grating ensured that it stayed in individual pieces throughout the mixing and shaping process. Using a higher-protein all-purpose flour (such as King Arthur) provided the right amount of structure for flakiness (rather than fluffiness, which you'd get with a lower-protein flour) without toughness, while buttermilk gave the biscuits tang, and sugar lent complexity. To produce the maximum number of layers, we rolled out and folded the dough like a letter five times. Cutting the biscuits into squares was easy and avoided any wasted scraps (or tough rerolls). And finally, we learned that letting the dough rest for 30 minutes and trimming away the edges ensured that the biscuits rose up tall in the oven. We prefer King Arthur all-purpose flour for this recipe, but other brands will work. Use sticks of butter. In hot or humid environments, chill the flour mixture, grater, and work bowls before use. The dough will start out very crumbly and dry in pockets but will be smooth by the end of the folding process; do not be tempted to add extra buttermilk. Flour the counter and the top of the dough as needed to prevent sticking, but be careful not to incorporate large pockets of flour into the dough when folding.

- 3 cups (15 ounces) King Arthur all-purpose flour
- 2 tablespoons sugar
- 4 teaspoons baking powder
- ½ teaspoon baking soda
- 1½ teaspoons table salt
- 16 tablespoons (2 sticks) unsalted butter, frozen for 30 minutes, divided
- 1¼ cups buttermilk, chilled

**1.** Line rimmed baking sheet with parchment paper and set aside. Whisk flour, sugar, baking powder, baking soda, and salt together in large bowl. Coat sticks of butter in flour mixture, then grate 7 tablespoons from each stick on large holes of box grater directly into flour mixture. Toss gently to combine. Set aside remaining 2 tablespoons butter.

**2.** Add buttermilk to flour mixture and fold with spatula until just combined (dough will look dry). Transfer dough to liberally floured counter. Dust surface of dough with flour; using your floured hands, press dough into rough 7-inch square.

**3.** Roll dough into 12 by 9-inch rectangle with short side parallel to edge of counter. Starting at bottom of dough, fold into thirds like business letter, using bench scraper or metal spatula to release dough from counter. Press top of dough firmly to seal folds. Turn dough 90 degrees clockwise. Repeat rolling into 12 by 9-inch rectangle, folding into thirds, and turning clockwise 4 more times, for total of 5 sets of folds. After last set of folds, roll dough into 8½-inch square about 1 inch thick. Transfer dough to prepared sheet, cover with plastic wrap, and refrigerate for 30 minutes. Adjust oven rack to upper-middle position and heat oven to 400 degrees.

**4.** Transfer dough to lightly floured cutting board. Using sharp, floured chef's knife, trim ¼ inch of dough from each side of square and discard. Cut remaining dough into 9 squares, flouring knife after each cut. Arrange biscuits at least 1 inch apart on sheet. Melt reserved butter; brush tops of biscuits with melted butter.

**5.** Bake until tops are golden brown, 22 to 25 minutes, rotating sheet halfway through baking. Transfer biscuits to wire rack and let cool for 15 minutes before serving.

## Popovers

**MAKES** 6 popovers

**WHY THIS RECIPE WORKS** The ideal popover is crisp and well browned on the outside and hollow on the inside, with inner walls that are lush and custardy. Bread flour gave our batter extra gluten-forming proteins so that it was stretchy enough to accommodate the expanding steam within the popover. Though many recipes call for preheating the popover pan to jump-start the "pop," we found it equally effective to warm the batter instead by adding heated milk. Lightly greasing the cold cups of the popover pan allowed the batter to "climb" the sides of the cups for bases that were full and round instead of shrunken. This batter comes together quickly, so start heating your oven before gathering your ingredients and equipment. Our recipe works best in a 6-cup popover pan, but you can substitute a 12-cup muffin tin, distributing the batter evenly among the 12 cups; start checking these smaller popovers after 25 minutes. Whole or skim milk can be used in place of the low-fat milk. We strongly recommend weighing the flour for this recipe. Do not open the oven during the first 30 minutes of baking; if possible, use the oven window and light to monitor the popovers. Popovers can be stored in a zipper-lock bag at room temperature for up to 2 days; reheat directly on middle rack of 300-degree oven for 5 minutes

- 1¼ cups (6¾ ounces) bread flour
- ¾ teaspoon table salt
- 1½ cups 2 percent low-fat milk, heated to 110 to 120 degrees
- 3 large eggs
- Salted butter

**1.** Adjust oven rack to middle position and heat oven to 400 degrees. Lightly spray cups of popover pan with vegetable oil spray. Using paper towel, wipe out cups, leaving thin film of oil on bottom and sides.

**2.** Whisk together flour and salt in 8-cup liquid measuring cup or medium bowl. Add milk and eggs and whisk until mostly smooth (some small lumps are OK). Distribute batter evenly among prepared cups in popover pan. Bake until popovers are lofty and deep golden brown all over, 40 to 45 minutes. Serve hot, passing butter separately..

## Pão de Queijo (Brazilian Cheese Bread)

**MAKES** 8 rolls

**WHY THIS RECIPE WORKS** Pão de queijo are traditional Brazilian rolls made using a classic French pate a choux dough. Comprised of butter, water, flour, and eggs, choux pastry relies on steam rather than chemical leavening agents to create rise; this type of dough is used for items both sweet (éclairs, profiteroles) and savory (Parisian gnocchi, gougères). But in developing our own recipe for this bread, many of the recipes we tried baked up with a too-gooey interior. So we played with the hydration level until we nailed our favorite version. At 91 percent hydration (most recipes have hydration levels well over 100 percent, which makes them more of a batter than a dough), our rolls baked up crackly on the outsides, bready just under the crusts, and gooey at the very centers. As an added bonus, these little rolls are gluten-free.

- 3 cups tapioca starch
- 2¼ teaspoons kosher salt, divided
- ¼ teaspoon baking powder
- ⅔ cup plus 2 tablespoons whole milk
- ½ cup vegetable oil
- 1½ tablespoons unsalted butter
- 3 large eggs, divided
- 3½ ounces Parmesan cheese, finely grated (1¾ cups)
- 3½ ounces Pecorino Romano, finely grated (1¾ cups)
- 1 teaspoon water

**1.** Using stand mixer fitted with paddle, mix tapioca starch, 2 teaspoons salt, and baking powder on low speed until combined, about 30 seconds.

**2.** Combine milk, oil, and butter in medium saucepan and bring to boil over high heat. With mixer running on low speed, working quickly, pour milk mixture over tapioca mixture and continue to mix on low speed until all ingredients are incorporated, about 3 minutes longer.

**3.** Add 2 eggs and mix on low speed until dough comes together, turns shiny and sticky, and clings to sides of bowl, about 8 minutes, scraping down paddle and bowl halfway through mixing.

**4.** Add Parmesan and Pecorino and mix on low speed until cheeses are incorporated, 30 to 60 seconds. Mix with rubber spatula to ensure mixture is fully incorporated. Remove

bowl from stand mixer and press plastic wrap directly onto surface of dough. Refrigerate for at least 2 hours or overnight.

**5.** Adjust oven rack to middle position and heat oven to 450 degrees. Stack 2 baking sheets and line top sheet with parchment paper. Divide dough into 8 balls (about 3½ ounces each). To form rolls, lightly dampen your hands with water and roll balls between your palms until smooth. Evenly space rolls on prepared sheet.

**6.** Whisk remaining egg, water, and remaining ¼ teaspoon salt together in small bowl. Brush egg mixture over tops of rolls. Place rolls in oven and immediately reduce oven temperature to 375 degrees. Bake for 20 minutes. Rotate sheet and continue to bake until rolls are deep golden brown and outer crusts are dry and crunchy, about 20 minutes longer. Transfer rolls to serving platter and let cool for 5 minutes. Serve.

## Quick Cheese Bread

**MAKES** one 8-inch loaf

**WHY THIS RECIPE WORKS** Run-of-the-mill cheese bread is both dry and greasy, with almost no cheese flavor. We wanted to create a rich loaf topped with a bold crust. We started with all-purpose flour and added whole milk and sour cream for a creamy flavor and moist texture. Just a few tablespoons of butter added enough richness without greasiness, and using less fat made the texture heartier. A single egg gave rise and structure without an overly eggy flavor. As for cheese, small chunks of Asiago or cheddar mixed into the dough offered rich, cheesy pockets throughout the bread; a moderate amount added plenty of flavor without weighing it down. For added cheesy flavor and a crisp crust, we coated the pan and sprinkled the top of the loaf with shredded Parmesan. If using Asiago, choose a mild supermarket cheese that yields to pressure when pressed. Aged Asiago that is as firm as Parmesan is too sharp and piquant for this bread. If, when testing the bread for doneness, the toothpick comes out with what looks like uncooked batter clinging to it, try again in a different, but still central, spot; if the toothpick hits a pocket of cheese, it may give a false indication.

- 3 ounces Parmesan cheese, shredded on the large holes of a box grater (about 1 cup)
- 3 cups (15 ounces) unbleached all-purpose flour
- 1 tablespoon baking powder
- 1 teaspoon table salt
- ¼ teaspoon cayenne pepper
- ⅛ teaspoon ground black pepper
- 4 ounces extra-sharp cheddar cheese, cut into ½-inch cubes, or mild Asiago, crumbled into ¼- to ½-inch pieces (about 1 cup)
- 1¼ cups whole milk
- 3 tablespoons unsalted butter, melted
- 1 large egg, lightly beaten
- ¾ cup sour cream

**1.** Adjust an oven rack to the middle position and heat the oven to 350 degrees. Spray an 8½ by 4½-inch loaf pan with vegetable oil spray; sprinkle ½ cup of the Parmesan evenly over the bottom of the pan.

**2.** Whisk the flour, baking powder, salt, cayenne, and black pepper together in a large bowl. Using a rubber spatula, mix in the cheddar, breaking up clumps. Whisk the milk, melted butter, egg, and sour cream together in a medium bowl. Using a rubber spatula, gently fold the wet ingredients into the dry ingredients until just combined (the batter will be heavy and thick); do not overmix. Scrape the batter into the prepared loaf pan; smooth the surface with a rubber spatula. Sprinkle the remaining ½ cup Parmesan evenly over the surface.

**3.** Bake until deep golden brown and a toothpick inserted in the center comes out clean, 45 to 50 minutes. Cool on a wire rack for 5 minutes; invert the loaf onto the wire rack, then turn right side up and continue to cool until warm, about 45 minutes. Cut into slices and serve.

### Quick Cheese Bread with Bacon, Onion, and Gruyère

Cook 5 ounces (about 5 slices) bacon, cut into ½-inch pieces, in a 10-inch nonstick skillet over medium heat, stirring occasionally, until crispy, about 8 minutes. Using a slotted spoon, transfer the bacon to a paper towel–lined plate and pour off all but 3 tablespoons fat from the skillet. Add ½ cup minced onion to the skillet and cook, stirring frequently, until softened, about 3 minutes; set the skillet with the onion aside. Follow the recipe for Quick Cheese Bread, substituting Gruyère for the cheddar, adding the bacon and onion to the flour mixture with the cheese, and omitting the butter.

## Classic American Garlic Bread

**SERVES** 6 to 8

**WHY THIS RECIPE WORKS** Garlic bread is a classic accompaniment to spaghetti and meatballs, baked ziti, and countless other Italian favorites. It seems so simple, yet it often goes so wrong. We wanted to banish greasy, bland, and bitter-tasting garlic bread forever in favor of crisp toasted bread imbued with sweet, nutty garlic flavor. Starting with the bread, we chose a substantial loaf of football-shaped Italian bread, the best quality we could find, to give us generous slices. We cut it in half horizontally, so that the surfaces would crisp up in the oven. We tamed the garlic's harshness by toasting whole cloves, which turned them rich and mellow. We cut out the step of melting butter and simply spread it, after softening and mixing in the garlic, on the bread—not too much, so the bread wouldn't be greasy or soggy. The addition of grated Parmesan cheese was nearly undetectable, but it added a deep and complex flavor. We found that leaving the bread unwrapped on a baking sheet gave us the crisp crust we wanted, and the oven's heat further mellowed the garlic. Plan to pull the garlic bread from the oven when you are ready to serve the other dishes—it is best served piping hot.

- 9–10 medium garlic cloves, unpeeled
- 6 tablespoons (¾ stick) unsalted butter, softened
- 2 tablespoons grated Parmesan cheese
- ½ teaspoon table salt
- 1 (1-pound) loaf high-quality Italian bread (preferably football-shaped), halved horizontally
- Ground black pepper

**1.** Adjust an oven rack to the middle position and heat the oven to 500 degrees. Meanwhile, toast the garlic cloves in a small skillet over medium heat, shaking the pan occasionally, until fragrant and the color of the cloves deepens slightly, about 8 minutes. When cool enough to handle, peel and mince the cloves (you should have about 3 tablespoons). Using a dinner fork, mash the garlic, butter, cheese, and salt in a small bowl until thoroughly combined.

**2.** Spread the cut sides of the loaf evenly with the butter mixture; season with pepper to taste. Transfer the loaf halves, buttered side up, onto a rimmed baking sheet; bake, reversing the position of the baking sheet in the oven from front to back halfway through the baking time, until the surface of the bread is golden brown and toasted, 5 to 10 minutes. Cut each half into 2-inch slices; serve immediately.

## Really Good Garlic Bread

**SERVES** 8

**WHY THIS RECIPE WORKS** There are many ways to achieve really good, really garlicky bread that your company will clamor for, and this recipe delivers just that. The keys are to use two types of garlic: garlic powder and fresh garlic and to create a garlicky butter mixture that can be slathered on the cut sides of the bread. First, we briefly microwaved fresh garlic in butter and combined it with garlic powder, which provided sweet, roasty notes; some solid butter; and just a bit of cayenne and salt to make a smooth paste with just the right balance of full, complex garlic flavor. We then baked the garlic bread halves between two baking sheets to create a griddle-like setup that crisped and browned the crust while keeping the interior soft and chewy. A 12 by 5-inch loaf of Italian bread from the bakery section of the supermarket, which has a soft, thin crust and fine crumb, works best in this recipe. We do not recommend using a rustic or crusty artisan-style loaf. A rasp-style grater makes quick work of turning the garlic into a paste. If you bake the bread on a dark baking sheet, start checking for doneness 4 minutes after flipping the bread in step 3.

- 1 teaspoon garlic powder
- 1 teaspoon water
- 8 tablespoons unsalted butter
- ½ teaspoon table salt
- ⅛ teaspoon cayenne pepper
- 4–5 garlic cloves, minced to paste (1 tablespoon)
- 1 (1-pound) loaf soft Italian bread, halved horizontally

**1.** Adjust oven rack to lower-middle position and heat oven 450 degrees. Combine garlic powder and water in medium bowl. Add 4 tablespoons butter, salt, and cayenne to bowl; set aside.

**2.** Place remaining 4 tablespoons butter in small bowl and microwave, covered, until melted, about 30 seconds. Stir in garlic and continue to microwave, covered, until mixture is bubbling around edges, about 1 minute, stirring halfway through. Transfer garlic-butter mixture to bowl with garlic powder mixture and whisk together until it forms homogeneous loose paste. (If mixture melts, set aside until it solidifies before using.)

**3.** Spread cut sides of loaf evenly with butter mixture. Transfer bread, cut side up, to baking sheet. Bake until butter has melted into surface of bread and bread is hot, 3 to 4 minutes. Remove baking sheet from oven. Flip bread, cut side down, place second rimmed baking sheet on top and gently press. Return bread to oven, with second baking sheet on top of bread, and continue to bake until cut side of bread is golden brown and crisp, 5 to 10 minutes longer, rotating sheet halfway through baking. Transfer bread to cutting board. Using serrated knife, cut each half into 8 slices and serve immediately.

## Cheesy Garlic Bread

**SERVES** 6 to 8

**WHY THIS RECIPE WORKS** Garlic bread is a balancing act between the butter, garlic, and bread. Add cheese to the mix and things get complicated. We wanted cheese-topped garlic bread that was crisp on the outside but chewy within, buttery all the way through, and with no bitter garlic aftertaste. Supermarket baguettes already have a chewy interior and crisp crust, so we started there. Grating the garlic cloves made for a smoother butter, and to tone down the garlic's harshness we sautéed it in butter with a little water (to prevent burning). We mixed the garlic into more softened butter, spread it on our split baguette, and wrapped the bread in foil. Baking it this way "steamed" the bread and infused it with garlic-butter flavor. To crisp the crust, we took the bread out of the foil and baked it a little longer. The final adornment was the cheese; rather than shredding several different kinds ourselves, we took a shortcut and used a prepackaged mixture of shredded Italian cheeses. The last step was to run it under the broiler, which gave us both melted cheese and an extra-crisp crust. The serrated edges on a bread knife can pull off the cheesy crust. To prevent this, place the finished garlic bread cheese side down on a cutting board. Slicing through the crust first (rather than the cheese) will keep the cheese in place.

- 5 medium garlic cloves, peeled and grated
- 8 tablespoons (1 stick) unsalted butter, softened
- ½ teaspoon water
- ¼ teaspoon table salt
- ¼ teaspoon ground black pepper
- 1 (18- to 20-inch) baguette, sliced in half horizontally
- 1½ cups shredded Italian cheese blend (see note)

**1.** Adjust an oven rack to the lower-middle position and heat the oven to 400 degrees. Cook the garlic, 1 tablespoon of the butter, and the water in a small nonstick skillet over low heat, stirring occasionally, until straw-colored, 7 to 10 minutes.

**2.** Mix the hot garlic, remaining 7 tablespoons butter, the salt, and pepper in a bowl and spread on the cut sides of the bread. Sandwich the bread back together and wrap the loaf in foil. Place on a baking sheet and bake for 15 minutes.

**3.** Carefully unwrap the bread and place the halves, buttered sides up, on a baking sheet. Bake until just beginning to color, about 10 minutes. Remove from the oven and set the oven to broil.

**4.** Sprinkle the bread with the cheese. Broil until the cheese has melted and the bread is crisp, 1 to 2 minutes. Transfer the bread to a cutting board with the cheese side facing down. Cut into pieces and serve.

## Classic Irish Soda Bread

**MAKES** 1 loaf

**WHY THIS RECIPE WORKS** Traditional Irish soda bread has a tender, dense crumb, and a rough-textured, thick crust—a classic accompaniment to a pub-style lunch or dinner. We wanted to try our hand at making a traditional version. A loaf made with all-purpose flour produced a doughy, heavy bread with an overly thick crust. To soften the crumb, we added some cake flour. A version made with all cake flour, however, was heavy and compact. A ratio of 3 parts all-purpose flour to 1 part cake flour proved best. But this bread was tough and lacking in flavor. Traditionally, very small amounts of butter and sugar are sometimes added, so we felt justified in using

a minuscule amount of each. The sugar added flavor without making the bread sweet, and the butter softened the dough without making it overly rich. If you do not have a cast-iron skillet, the bread can be baked on a baking sheet, although the crust won't be quite as crunchy. This bread is best eaten on the day it is baked but it can be covered with plastic wrap and stored at room temperature for up to 2 days.

- 3 cups (15 ounces) unbleached all-purpose flour
- 1 cup (4 ounces) cake flour
- 2 tablespoons sugar
- 1½ teaspoons baking soda
- 1½ teaspoons cream of tartar
- 1½ teaspoons table salt
- 2 tablespoons unsalted butter, softened, plus 1 tablespoon melted butter for brushing the loaf (optional)
- 1¾ cups buttermilk

**1.** Adjust an oven rack to the middle position and heat the oven to 400 degrees. Whisk the flours, sugar, baking soda, cream of tartar, and salt together in a large bowl. Add the softened butter and rub it into the flour using your fingers until it is completely incorporated. Make a well in the center of the flour mixture and add 1½ cups of the buttermilk. Work the buttermilk into the flour mixture using a fork until the dough comes together in large clumps and there is no dry flour in the bottom of the bowl, adding up to ¼ cup more buttermilk, 1 tablespoon at a time, until all the loose flour is just moistened. Turn the dough onto a lightly floured work surface and pat together to form a 6-inch round. The dough will be scrappy and uneven.

**2.** Place the dough in a 12-inch cast-iron skillet. Score a deep cross, about 5 inches long and ¾ inch deep, on the top of the loaf and place in the oven. Bake until nicely browned and a knife inserted in the center of the loaf comes out clean, 40 to 45 minutes. Remove from the oven and brush with the melted butter (if using). Cool for at least 30 minutes before slicing.

## Irish Brown Soda Bread

**MAKES** one 8-inch loaf

**WHY THIS RECIPE WORKS** Robust, moist, and permeated with wheaty sweetness, Irish brown soda bread combines a high proportion of whole-wheat flour with extra wheat germ and bran to produce a rustic loaf with nutty flavor and an appropriately coarse crumb. We balanced the strong wheat flavor with white flour and a touch of sugar. The addition of baking powder guaranteed a nicely risen loaf, while baking soda lent the characteristic mineral-y tang that it gives to soda breads. Acidic buttermilk also contributed welcome flavor. To produce a loaf with pleasing stature, we baked the soft dough in a cake pan. Our favorite whole-wheat flour is King Arthur Premium. To ensure the best flavor, use fresh whole-wheat flour. Wheat bran can be found at natural foods stores or in the baking aisle of your supermarket. This bread is best eaten on the day it is made, but it can be wrapped in plastic wrap and stored at room temperature for up to 3 days or frozen for up to 2 weeks.

- 2 cups (11 ounces) whole-wheat flour
- 1 cup (5 ounces) all-purpose flour
- 1 cup wheat bran
- ¼ cup wheat germ
- 2 teaspoons sugar
- 1½ teaspoons baking powder
- 1½ teaspoons baking soda
- 1 teaspoon table salt
- 2 cups buttermilk

**1.** Adjust oven rack to middle position and heat oven to 375 degrees. Lightly grease 8-inch round cake pan. Whisk whole-wheat flour, all-purpose flour, wheat bran, wheat germ, sugar, baking powder, baking soda, and salt together in medium bowl.

**2.** Add buttermilk and stir with rubber spatula until all flour is moistened and dough forms soft, ragged mass. Transfer dough to counter and gently shape into 6-inch round (surface will be craggy). Using serrated knife, cut ½-inch-deep cross about 5 inches long on top of loaf. Transfer to prepared pan. Bake until loaf is lightly browned and center registers 185 degrees, 40 to 45 minutes, rotating pan halfway through baking.

**3.** Invert loaf onto wire rack. Reinvert loaf and let cool for at least 1 hour. Slice and serve.

## Boston Brown Bread

**MAKES** 2 small loaves; serves 6 to 8

**WHY THIS RECIPE WORKS** When the colonists started making this unyeasted, one-bowl bread in the 18th century, the cooking happened open hearth. To make it less tricky they turned to making it in lidded tin pudding molds in a kettle of simmering water over an open fire, giving the loaves a distinctive shape and a smooth, crustless exterior—and a moist whole-grain crumb. To get the right balance of flavor in our brown bread, we combined whole-wheat flour, rye flour, and finely ground cornmeal in equal amounts. Molasses, the traditional sweetener, added the right hint of bitterness. Baking soda and baking powder reacted with the acid in the batter to lighten the bread, and melted butter added richness. We steamed the batter on the stovetop in two 28-ounce tomato cans. Use cans that are labeled "BPA-free." We prefer Quaker white cornmeal in this recipe, though other types will work; do not use coarse grits. Any style of molasses will work except for blackstrap. This recipe requires a 10-quart or larger stockpot that is at least 7 inches deep. Brown bread is traditionally served with baked beans but is also good toasted and buttered.

- ¾ cup (4⅛ ounces) rye flour
- ¾ cup (4⅛ ounces) whole-wheat flour
- ¾ cup (3¾ ounces) fine white cornmeal
- 1¾ teaspoons baking soda
- ½ teaspoon baking powder
- 1 teaspoon table salt
- 1⅔ cups buttermilk
- ½ cup molasses
- 3 tablespoons butter, melted and cooled slightly
- ¾ cup raisins

**1.** Bring 3 quarts water to simmer in large stockpot over high heat. Fold two 16 by 12-inch pieces of aluminum foil in half to yield two rectangles that measure 8 by 12 inches. Spray 4-inch circle in center of each rectangle with vegetable oil spray. Spray insides of two clean 28-ounce cans with vegetable oil spray.

**2.** Whisk rye flour, whole-wheat flour, cornmeal, baking soda, baking powder, and salt together in large bowl. Whisk buttermilk, molasses, and melted butter together in second bowl. Stir raisins into buttermilk mixture. Add buttermilk mixture to flour mixture and stir until combined and no dry flour remains. Divide batter evenly between cans. Wrap tops of cans tightly with prepared foil, positioning sprayed side of foil over can openings.

**3.** Place cans in stockpot (water should come about halfway up sides of cans). Cover pot and cook, maintaining gentle simmer, until skewer inserted in center of loaves comes out clean, about 2 hours. Check pot occasionally and add hot water as needed to maintain water level.

**4.** Using jar lifter, carefully transfer cans to wire rack set in rimmed baking sheet and let cool for 20 minutes. Slide loaves from cans onto rack and let cool completely, about 1 hour. Slice and serve.

## All-Purpose Cornbread

**MAKES** one 8-inch square

**WHY THIS RECIPE WORKS** For this cornbread, we wanted a version that was a combination of the Northern (sweet and cakey) and Southern (savory and light) versions. We found that the secret to cornbread with real corn flavor was simple: Use corn, not just cornmeal. While fresh corn was best, we wanted to be able to make this cornbread year round. Frozen kernels were nearly as good as fresh; pureeing the kernels in a food processor made them easy to use while minimizing chewy kernels. Buttermilk provided a tangy flavor, while light brown sugar enhanced the flavor of the corn. When corn is in season, fresh cooked kernels can be substituted for the frozen corn. This recipe was developed with Quaker yellow cornmeal; a stone-ground whole-grain cornmeal will work but will yield a drier cornbread. We prefer using a Pyrex glass baking dish because it yields a nice golden brown crust, but a metal baking dish (nonstick or traditional) will also work. Cornbread can be wrapped in plastic wrap and stored at room temperature for up to 2 days; to reheat, wrap in aluminum foil and place in 350-degree oven for 10 to 15 minutes.

- 1½ cups (7½ ounces) unbleached all-purpose flour
- 1 cup (about 5 ounces) yellow cornmeal
- 2 teaspoons baking powder
- ¾ teaspoon table salt
- ¼ teaspoon baking soda
- 1 cup buttermilk
- ¾ cup frozen corn kernels, thawed
- ¼ cup packed (1¾ ounces) light brown sugar
- 2 large eggs
- 8 tablespoons (1 stick) unsalted butter, melted and cooled slightly

**1.** Adjust an oven rack to the middle position and heat the oven to 400 degrees. Spray an 8-inch square baking dish with vegetable oil spray. Whisk the flour, cornmeal, baking powder, salt, and baking soda together in a medium bowl until combined; set aside.

**2.** Process the buttermilk, thawed corn kernels, and brown sugar in a food processor or blender until combined, about 5 seconds. Add the eggs and process until well combined (corn lumps will remain), about 5 seconds longer.

**3.** Using a rubber spatula, make a well in the center of the dry ingredients; pour the wet ingredients into the well. Begin folding the dry ingredients into the wet ingredients, giving the mixture only a few turns to barely combine; add the melted butter and continue folding until the dry ingredients are just moistened. Pour the batter into the prepared baking dish; smooth the surface with a rubber spatula. Bake until deep golden brown and a toothpick inserted in the center comes out clean, 25 to 35 minutes. Cool on a wire rack for 10 minutes; invert the cornbread onto the wire rack, then turn right side up and continue to cool until warm, about 10 minutes longer. Cut into pieces and serve

## Southern-Style Cornbread

**MAKES** one 8-inch loaf

**WHY THIS RECIPE WORKS** Classic Southern cornbread is made in a ripping-hot skillet greased with bacon fat, which causes it to develop a thin, crispy crust as the bread bakes. Traditionally, Southern-style cornbread is made from white cornmeal and has only trace amounts of sugar and flour. We wanted to perfect the proportions of ingredients and come up with our own crusty, savory Southern-style cornbread. Departing from tradition, we chose yellow cornmeal over white—cornbreads made with yellow cornmeal consistently had a more potent corn flavor than those made with white cornmeal. We used a rustic method to incorporate the cornmeal, combining part of the cornmeal with boiling water to create a cornmeal "mush." Cornbread that started with some mush had the most corn flavor, and a fine, moist crumb. We then stirred the buttermilk and egg into the mush before adding the remaining cornmeal and other dry ingredients. As for sugar, a small amount enhanced the natural sweetness of the corn. Finally, we poured the batter into a hot, greased cast-iron skillet to bake until crusty and fragrant. Cornmeal mush of just the right texture is essential to this bread. Make sure that the water is at a rapid boil when it is added to the cornmeal. And for an accurate measurement of boiling water, bring a kettle of water to a boil, then measure out the desired amount. Though we prefer to make cornbread in a preheated cast-iron skillet, a 9-inch round cake pan or 9-inch square baking pan, greased lightly with butter and not preheated, will also produce acceptable results if you double the recipe and bake the bread for 25 minutes. Cornbread can be wrapped in plastic wrap and stored at room temperature for up to 2 days; to reheat, wrap in aluminum foil and place in 350-degree oven for 10 to 15 minutes.

- 4 teaspoons bacon drippings or vegetable oil
- 1 cup (5 ounces) yellow cornmeal, preferably stone-ground, divided
- 2 teaspoons sugar
- 1 teaspoon baking powder
- ½ teaspoon table salt
- ¼ teaspoon baking soda
- ⅓ cup boiling water
- ¾ cup buttermilk
- 1 large egg, lightly beaten

**1.** Adjust oven rack to lower-middle position and heat oven to 450 degrees. Add bacon drippings to 8-inch cast-iron skillet and place skillet in heating oven. Whisk ⅔ cup cornmeal, sugar, baking powder, salt, and baking soda together in small bowl; set aside.

**2.** Place remaining ⅓ cup cornmeal in medium bowl, add boiling water, and stir to make stiff mush. Whisk in buttermilk gradually, breaking up lumps until smooth, then whisk in egg.

**3.** When oven is preheated and skillet is very hot, add dry ingredients to cornmeal mush and stir until just moistened. Carefully remove skillet from oven (skillet handle will be hot). Pour hot bacon fat from pan into batter and stir to incorporate, then quickly pour batter into heated skillet. Bake until golden brown, about 20 minutes. Invert cornbread onto wire rack and let cool for 5 minutes; serve.

## Fresh Corn Cornbread

**SERVES** 6 to 8

**WHY THIS RECIPE WORKS** For cornbread packed with fresh, concentrated corn flavor, we pureed fresh corn kernels and cooked them down into a "corn butter" that we incorporated into the batter. Buttermilk added tang, while egg yolks and a little bit of extra butter ensured that the bread would be moist. We prefer to use a well-seasoned cast-iron skillet in this recipe, but an ovensafe 10-inch skillet can be used in its place. Alternatively, in step 4 you can add 1 tablespoon of butter to a 9-inch cake pan and place it in the oven until the butter melts, about 3 minutes.

- 1⅓ cups (6⅔ ounces) stone-ground cornmeal
- 1 cup (5 ounces) all-purpose flour
- 2 tablespoons sugar
- 1½ teaspoons baking powder
- ¼ teaspoon baking soda
- 1¼ teaspoons table salt
- 3 ears corn, kernels cut from cobs (2¼ cups)
- 6 tablespoons unsalted butter, cut into 6 pieces
- 1 cup buttermilk
- 2 large eggs plus 1 large yolk

**1.** Adjust oven rack to middle position and heat oven to 400 degrees. Whisk cornmeal, flour, sugar, baking powder, baking soda, and salt together in large bowl.

**2.** Process corn kernels in blender until very smooth, about 2 minutes. Transfer puree to medium saucepan (you should have about 1½ cups). Cook puree over medium heat, stirring constantly, until very thick and deep yellow and it measures ¾ cup, 5 to 8 minutes.

**3.** Remove pan from heat. Add 5 tablespoons butter and whisk until melted and incorporated. Add buttermilk and whisk until incorporated. Add eggs and yolk and whisk until incorporated. Transfer corn mixture to bowl with cornmeal mixture and, using rubber spatula, fold together until just combined.

**4.** Melt remaining 1 tablespoon butter in 10-inch cast-iron skillet over medium heat. Scrape batter into skillet and spread into even layer. Bake until top is golden brown and toothpick inserted in center comes out clean, 23 to 28 minutes. Let cool on wire rack for 5 minutes. Remove cornbread from skillet and let cool for 20 minutes before cutting into wedges and serving.

## Banana Muffins with Coconut and Macadamia

**MAKES** 12 muffins

**WHY THIS RECIPE WORKS** With plenty of mashed bananas in the batter, these muffins pack potent fruit flavor. To prevent the extra liquid and mass from weighing down the crumb and making our muffins dense and gummy, we used bread flour instead of all-purpose flour; its higher protein content not only makes it more absorbent and better able to accommodate the moisture but also provides extra strength, so our muffins have a uniformly light crumb. Adding extra baking powder ensured that each muffin's volume was maximized. Baking the muffins at a higher-than-normal temperature caused the outer edges to set before the middle, resulting in dramatic peaks. Macadamia nuts added subtle crunch and richness, and coconut underscored the tropical theme. Use bananas that are very heavily speckled or even black; less-ripe bananas will produce dry muffins with less flavor. You should have 1¾ to 2 cups of mashed bananas. You can substitute thawed frozen bananas; be sure to add any juice that is released as the bananas thaw.

- ⅓ cup macadamia nuts, toasted and chopped fine
- ⅓ cup (⅔ ounce) sweetened flaked coconut, toasted
- 1⅔ cups (9⅛ ounces) bread flour
- 1 tablespoon baking powder
- ½ teaspoon baking soda
- ½ teaspoon table salt
- 4-5 very ripe large bananas, peeled and mashed (2 cups)
- ½ cup (3½ ounces) plus 1 tablespoon sugar, divided
- 2 large eggs
- ⅓ cup vegetable oil
- 2 teaspoons vanilla extract

**1.** Adjust oven rack to middle position and heat oven to 425 degrees. Grease 12-cup muffin tin. Combine macadamia nuts and coconut in small bowl. Whisk flour, baking powder, baking soda, and salt together in medium bowl.

**2.** Whisk bananas, ½ cup sugar, eggs, oil, and vanilla in large bowl until fully combined. Add flour mixture and whisk until fully combined. Set aside 2 tablespoons macadamia nut mixture for topping. Fold remaining macadamia nut mixture into batter. Using portion scoop or large spoon, divide batter evenly among prepared muffin cups (about ½ cup batter per cup; cups will be very full). Sprinkle with remaining 1 tablespoon sugar and reserved macadamia nut mixture.

**3.** Bake until tops are light golden brown and toothpick inserted in center comes out clean, 14 to 18 minutes. Let muffins cool in muffin tin on wire rack for 10 minutes. Remove muffins from muffin tin and let cool for at least 5 minutes. Serve warm or at room temperature.

## Best Blueberry Muffins

**MAKES** 12 muffins

**WHY THIS RECIPE WORKS** These muffins have an intense blueberry flavor that will shine through whether you use freshly picked wild berries or supermarket berries. To intensify the blueberry in our muffins, we tried combining blueberry jam with supermarket blueberries, but the jam made them too sweet. To solve this, we made our own low-sugar berry jam by simmering fresh blueberries with a bit of sugar. Adding our cooled jam to the batter along with uncooked berries gave us the best of both worlds: intense blueberry flavor and the liquid burst that only fresh berries could provide. We found that the quick-bread method—whisking together eggs and sugar before adding milk and melted butter, and then gently folding in the dry ingredients—produced a hearty, substantial crumb that could support a generous amount of fruit. An equal amount of butter and oil gave our muffins just the right combination of buttery flavor and moist, tender texture. For added richness, we swapped the whole milk for buttermilk. Finally, a sprinkling of lemon-scented sugar provided a pleasant crunch. For finely grated lemon zest, use a rasp-style grater.

**LEMON-SUGAR TOPPING**

- ⅓ cup (2⅓ ounces) sugar
- 1½ teaspoons finely grated lemon zest

**MUFFINS**

- 10 ounces (2 cups) blueberries, divided
- 1 teaspoon plus 1⅛ cups (8 ounces) sugar, divided
- 2½ cups (12½ ounces) all-purpose flour
- 2½ teaspoons baking powder
- 1 teaspoon table salt
- 2 large eggs
- 4 tablespoons unsalted butter, melted and cooled slightly
- 4 tablespoons vegetable oil
- 1 cup buttermilk
- 1½ teaspoons vanilla extract

**1. FOR THE TOPPING:** Stir sugar and lemon zest in small bowl until combined and set aside.

**2. FOR THE MUFFINS:** Adjust oven rack to upper-middle position and heat oven to 425 degrees. Spray 12-cup muffin tin with vegetable oil spray. Bring 1 cup blueberries and 1 teaspoon sugar to simmer in small saucepan over medium heat. Cook, mashing berries with spoon several times and stirring frequently, until berries have broken down and mixture is thickened and reduced to ¼ cup, about 6 minutes. Transfer to small bowl and let cool to room temperature, 10 to 15 minutes.

**3.** Whisk flour, baking powder, and salt together in large bowl. Whisk remaining 1⅛ cups sugar and eggs in medium bowl until thick and homogeneous, about 45 seconds. Slowly whisk in melted butter and oil until combined. Whisk in buttermilk and vanilla until combined. Using rubber spatula, fold egg mixture and remaining 1 cup blueberries into flour mixture until just moistened. (Batter will be very lumpy with few spots of dry flour; do not overmix.)

**4.** Using ⅓-cup measure or an ice cream scoop, divide batter equally among prepared muffin cups (batter should completely fill cups and mound slightly). Spoon 1 teaspoon of cooked berry mixture into center of each mound of batter. Using chopstick or skewer, gently swirl berry filling into batter using figure-eight motion. Sprinkle lemon sugar evenly over muffins.

**5.** Bake until muffin tops are golden and just firm, 17 to 19 minutes, rotating muffin tin halfway through baking. Let muffins cool in muffin tin on wire rack for 5 minutes. Remove muffins from muffin tin and let cool for 5 minutes before serving.

## From-the-Freezer Blueberry-Cinnamon Muffins

**MAKES** 12 muffins

**WHY THIS RECIPE WORKS** Freezing a batch of muffin batter and baking off individual portions sounds great, but the extreme cold temperatures and freeze-thaw cycle negatively impact a batter's leavening, browning, and moisture. But this batter is designed to be baked from frozen and supports a range of mix-ins—from fresh or frozen berries. To maximize the rise, we loaded up on leavening agents—baking powder did most of the leavening, and baking soda further aerated the batter and encouraged flavorful browning. We leaned on oil (a pure fat) instead of butter and included a generous dose of sugar to boost moisture. Partially freezing the portions in the tin set their shape enough for them to be transferred and stored in a zipper-lock bag. Baking the frozen muffins in the tin at a moderate 350 degrees for the better part of 40 minutes allowed the batter to rise and bake evenly from edge to center. We sprinkled coarse-grained turbinado sugar on the portioned batter before freezing because it wouldn't dissolve or melt when frozen or baked the way granulated sugar would, so the muffins' crust baked up with a sweet, sparkly crunch. This recipe requires paper or foil muffin-tin liners. You can replace the buttermilk with ½ cup of plain Greek yogurt (any fat level) mixed with 1 cup of water, measuring out 1¼ cups of the mixture. Do not use buttermilk powder or a mixture of milk and lemon juice. A toaster oven works well for baking the muffins if you're using a 6-cup muffin tin; they will cook a bit faster, so begin checking for doneness 5 minutes earlier than the lower end of the time range.

- 2 large eggs
- ½ cup vegetable oil
- 1¼ cups buttermilk
- 1 cup (7 ounces) granulated sugar
- 2 teaspoons grated lemon zest, divided
- 2½ cups (12½ ounces) all-purpose flour
- 1 tablespoon baking powder
- ½ teaspoon ground cinnamon
- ½ teaspoon baking soda
- ½ teaspoon table salt
- 1½ cups (7½ ounces) fresh or frozen blueberries
- 2 tablespoons turbinado sugar

**1.** Line 12-cup muffin tin with paper or foil liners.

**2.** Whisk eggs and oil in large bowl until thoroughly combined. Add buttermilk, granulated sugar, and 1 teaspoon lemon zest and whisk to combine. Whisk flour, baking powder, cinnamon, baking soda, and salt together in medium bowl. Gently whisk one-third of flour mixture into egg mixture until no lumps remain. Whisk in half of remaining flour mixture until smooth. Using rubber spatula, gently fold in remaining flour mixture until few streaks of flour remain. Stir in blueberries until evenly distributed and no dry streaks of flour remain.

**3.** Using portion scoop or large spoon, divide batter evenly among prepared muffin cups (about ⅓ cup batter per liner). In small bowl, stir turbinado sugar and remaining 1 teaspoon zest together. Evenly sprinkle sugar-zest mixture over batter.

**4.** Cover tin and transfer to freezer and freeze batter until solid, at least 3 hours. Transfer frozen batter portions (in liners) to zipper-lock bag and freeze for up to 2 months. (If liners freeze to tin, place muffin tin in rimmed baking sheet filled with ⅛ inch warm water for 1 minute. Twist and lift to release, then transfer to bag for freezing.)

**5. TO BAKE:** Adjust oven rack to middle position and heat oven to 350 degrees. Arrange desired number of (frozen) batter portions in muffin tin and bake until muffins have risen and are lightly browned and toothpick inserted into center comes out clean, 33 to 36 minutes. Let muffins cool in muffin tin on wire rack for 5 minutes. Remove muffins from muffin tin and let cool for 5 minutes before serving.

## Better Bran Muffins

**MAKES** 12 muffins

**WHY THIS RECIPE WORKS** There is no reason that eating a bran muffin should feel like a punishment for trying to eat healthfully. We wanted to create bran muffins that were tender and packed with earthy bran flavor. Back-of-the-cereal-box recipes advise soaking the twigs in milk to soften but this also soaks up all the moisture leaving the muffins dense and dry. Instead, we stirred together the wet ingredients first and then added the cereal; grinding half of the twigs in the food processor and leaving the rest whole gave us the rustic texture we wanted, and the cereal softened in just a few minutes. Whole-milk yogurt added needed moisture to the batter. Molasses and brown sugar reinforced the earthy bran flavor. To improve the texture, we swapped baking soda for baking powder and used one egg plus a yolk—two eggs made the muffins too springy. To ensure that they would soften fully, we plumped the raisins in water in the microwave. The test kitchen prefers Kellogg's All-Bran Original cereal in this recipe. Dried cranberries or dried cherries may be substituted for the raisins. Low-fat or nonfat yogurt can be substituted for whole-milk yogurt, though the muffins will be slightly less flavorful.

- 1 cup raisins
- 1 teaspoon water
- 2¼ cups (5 ounces) All-Bran Original cereal
- 1¼ cups (6¼ ounces) unbleached all-purpose flour
- ½ cup (2½ ounces) whole-wheat flour
- 2 teaspoons baking soda
- ½ teaspoon table salt
- 1 large whole egg plus 1 large egg yolk
- ⅔ cup packed (4⅔ ounces) light brown sugar
- 3 tablespoons mild or light molasses
- 1 teaspoon vanilla extract
- 6 tablespoons (¾ stick) unsalted butter, melted and cooled
- 1¾ cups plain whole-milk yogurt

**1.** Adjust an oven rack to the middle position and heat the oven to 400 degrees. Spray a standard-size muffin pan with vegetable oil spray. Combine the raisins and water in a small microwave-safe bowl, cover with plastic wrap, cut several steam vents in the plastic with a paring knife, and microwave on high power for 30 seconds. Let stand, covered, until the raisins are softened and plump, about 5 minutes. Transfer the raisins to a paper towel–lined plate to cool.

**2.** Process half of the bran cereal in a food processor until finely ground, about 1 minute. Whisk the flours, baking soda, and salt in a large bowl to combine; set aside. Whisk the egg and egg yolk together in a medium bowl until well combined and light-colored, about 20 seconds. Add the sugar, molasses, and vanilla; whisk until the mixture is thick, about 30 seconds. Add the melted butter and whisk to combine; add the yogurt and whisk to combine. Stir in the processed cereal and unprocessed cereal; let the mixture sit until the cereal is evenly moistened (there will still be some small lumps), about 5 minutes.

**3.** Add the wet ingredients to the dry ingredients and gently mix with a rubber spatula until the batter is combined and evenly moistened. Do not overmix. Gently fold the raisins into the batter. Using a ⅓-cup measure or an ice cream scoop, divide the batter evenly among the prepared muffin cups, dropping the batter to form mounds. Do not level or flatten the surfaces of the mounds.

**4.** Bake until the muffins are dark golden and a toothpick inserted into the center of a muffin comes out with a few crumbs attached, 16 to 20 minutes, rotating the pan halfway through the baking time. Cool the muffins in the pan for 5 minutes, then transfer to a wire rack and cool for 10 minutes before serving.

## Corn Muffins

**MAKES** 12 muffins

**WHY THIS RECIPE WORKS** A corn muffin shouldn't be as sweet and fluffy as a cupcake, nor dense and "corny" like corn bread. It should taste like corn and be moist with a tender crumb and a crunchy top. Our mission was to come up with a recipe for these seemingly simple muffins that struck just the right balance in both texture and flavor. The cornmeal itself proved to be an important factor, and degerminated meal just didn't have enough corn flavor. A fine-ground, whole-grain meal provided better flavor and texture. To avoid dry muffins, we experimented with ways to add moisture; butter, sour cream, and milk provided the moisture, fat (for richness), and acidity (for its tenderizing effect) that we wanted. We mixed the ingredients with the quick-bread method; not only was it the easier way to go, but it also resulted in less airy, cakey muffins. We got our crunchy top from a 400-degree oven. We'd resolved all of our issues with corn muffins; these were subtly sweet, rich but not dense. Whole-grain cornmeal has a fuller flavor than regular cornmeal milled from degerminated corn. To determine what kind of cornmeal a package contains, look closely at the label.

- 2 cups (10 ounces) unbleached all-purpose flour
- 1 cup (5 ounces) fine-ground, whole-grain yellow cornmeal
- 1½ teaspoons baking powder
- 1 teaspoon baking soda
- ½ teaspoon table salt
- 2 large eggs
- ¾ cup (5¼ ounces) sugar
- 8 tablespoons (1 stick) unsalted butter, melted
- ¾ cup sour cream
- ½ cup milk

**1.** Adjust an oven rack to the middle position and heat the oven to 400 degrees. Spray a standard-size muffin pan with vegetable oil spray.

**2.** Whisk the flour, cornmeal, baking powder, baking soda, and salt together in a medium bowl; set aside. Whisk the eggs in a second medium bowl. Add the sugar to the eggs; whisk vigorously until thick and homogeneous, about 30 seconds; add the melted butter in three additions, whisking to combine after each addition. Add half of the sour cream and half of the milk and whisk to combine; whisk in the remaining sour cream and milk until combined. Add the wet ingredients to the dry ingredients; mix gently with a rubber spatula until the batter is just combined and evenly moistened. Do not overmix. Using a ⅓-cup measure or ice cream scoop, divide the batter evenly among the prepared muffin cups, dropping the batter to form mounds. Do not level or flatten the surface of the mounds.

**3.** Bake until the muffins are light golden brown and a skewer inserted into the center of the muffins comes out clean, about 18 minutes, rotating the pan halfway through the baking time. Cool the muffins in the pan for 5 minutes, then transfer to a wire rack and cool for 10 minutes before serving.

### Corn and Apricot Muffins with Orange Essence

**MAKES** 12 muffins

**1.** In a food processor, process ⅔ cup granulated sugar and 1½ teaspoons grated orange zest until pale orange, about 10 seconds. Transfer to a small bowl and set aside.

**2.** In a food processor, pulse 1½ cups (10 ounces) dried apricots for 10 pulses, until chopped fine. Transfer to a medium microwave-safe bowl; add ⅔ cup orange juice to the apricots, cover the bowl tightly with plastic wrap, and microwave on high power until simmering, about 1 minute. Let the apricots stand, covered, until softened and plump, about 5 minutes. Strain the apricots and discard the juice.

**3.** Follow the recipe for Corn Muffins, substituting ¼ cup packed dark brown sugar for an equal amount of the granulated sugar and stirring ½ teaspoon grated orange zest and the strained apricots into the wet ingredients before adding them to the dry ingredients. Before baking, sprinkle a portion of the orange sugar over each mound of batter. Cool the muffins in the pan for 5 minutes, then gently lift them out using the tip of a paring knife. Cool on a wire rack for 10 minutes before serving.

## Savory Corn Muffins

**MAKES** 12 muffins

**WHY THIS RECIPE WORKS** For a corn muffin with great cornmeal flavor and proper muffin structure, we used a ratio of 2 parts cornmeal to 1 part flour for the former's big flavor and the latter's gluten-forming power. Cutting back on sugar promised a perfectly savory muffin, but we needed to keep a few tablespoons of the sweet stuff in order to boost the batter's moisture retention. To make up for the moisture that extra sugar normally provides, we used a mix of milk, butter, and sour cream for the right amount of water and fat. We incorporated extra liquid into the batter by precooking a portion of the cornmeal with additional milk to make a polenta-like porridge. With this technique, we were able to add nearly double the liquid in the batter, promising a supermoist crumb while still allowing the batter to rise into a pretty dome. Don't use coarse-ground or white cornmeal.

- 2 cups (10 ounces) cornmeal, divided
- 1 cup (5 ounces) all-purpose flour
- 1½ teaspoons baking powder
- 1 teaspoon baking soda
- 1¼ teaspoons table salt
- 1¼ cups whole milk
- 1 cup sour cream
- 8 tablespoons unsalted butter, melted and cooled slightly
- 3 tablespoons sugar
- 2 large eggs, beaten

**1.** Adjust oven rack to upper-middle position and heat oven to 425 degrees. Spray 12-cup muffin tin with vegetable oil spray. Whisk 1½ cups cornmeal, flour, baking powder, baking soda, and salt together in medium bowl.

**2.** Combine milk and remaining ½ cup cornmeal in large bowl. Microwave milk-cornmeal mixture for 1½ minutes. Whisk thoroughly and continue to microwave, whisking every 30 seconds, until thickened to batter-like consistency (whisk will leave channel in bottom of bowl that slowly fills in), 1 to 3 minutes longer. Whisk in sour cream, melted butter, and sugar until combined. Whisk in eggs until combined. Fold in flour mixture until thoroughly combined. Using portion scoop or large spoon, divide batter evenly among prepared muffin cups (about ½ cup batter per cup; batter will mound slightly above rim).

**3.** Bake until tops are golden brown and toothpick inserted in center comes out clean, 13 to 17 minutes, rotating muffin tin halfway through baking. Let muffins cool in muffin tin on wire rack for 5 minutes. Remove muffins from muffin tin and let cool for 5 minutes before serving.

## Cranberry-Pecan Muffins

**MAKES** 12 muffins

**WHY THIS RECIPE WORKS** Cranberry-nut muffins can make a quick and hearty breakfast, but all too often they are dense and leaden, with an overwhelming sour berry flavor and soggy nuts distributed haphazardly throughout. We wanted a moist, substantial muffin accented—but not overtaken—by tart cranberries and toasted, crunchy nuts. Hand mixing the batter was quick and gave our muffins enough structure to accommodate the fruit and nuts. Grinding some of the nuts and using them in place of some of the flour added complexity and nutty flavor throughout. Chopping the berries and tossing them with a little sugar toned down their tartness. Finally, adding a streusel topping added back the crunch lost from grinding up the nuts. If fresh cranberries aren't available, substitute frozen cranberries. Before using, place the cranberries in a microwave-safe bowl and microwave on high power until the cranberries are partially thawed, 30 to 45 seconds. Do not overthaw the cranberries.

**STREUSEL TOPPING**

- 3 tablespoons unbleached all-purpose flour
- 1 tablespoon packed light brown sugar
- 1 tablespoon plus 1 teaspoon granulated sugar
- Table salt
- 2 tablespoons unsalted butter, cut into ½-inch pieces, softened
- ½ cup pecan halves

**MUFFINS**

- 1⅓ cups (6⅔ ounces) unbleached all-purpose flour
- 1½ teaspoons baking powder
- 1 teaspoon table salt
- 1¼ cups pecan halves, toasted and cooled
- 1 cup plus 1 tablespoon (7½ ounces) granulated sugar
- 2 large eggs
- 6 tablespoons (¾ stick) unsalted butter, melted and cooled
- ½ cup whole milk
- 2 cups fresh cranberries
- 1 tablespoon confectioners' sugar

1. Adjust an oven rack to the upper-middle position and heat the oven to 425 degrees. Spray a 12-cup muffin tin with vegetable oil spray.

2. **FOR THE STREUSEL:** Pulse the flour, brown sugar, granulated sugar, a pinch of salt, and the butter in a food processor until the mixture resembles coarse sand, 4 to 5 pulses. Add the pecans and pulse until the pecans are chopped coarse, about 4 pulses. Transfer to a small bowl; set aside.

3. **FOR THE MUFFINS:** Whisk the flour, baking powder, and ¾ teaspoon of the salt together in a bowl; set aside.

4. Process the toasted pecans and granulated sugar until the mixture resembles coarse sand, 10 to 15 seconds. Transfer to a large bowl and whisk in the eggs, butter, and milk until combined. Whisk the flour mixture into the egg mixture until just moistened and no streaks of flour remain. Set the batter aside for 30 minutes to thicken.

5. Pulse the cranberries, remaining ¼ teaspoon salt, and confectioners' sugar in the food processor until very coarsely chopped, 4 to 5 pulses. Using a rubber spatula, fold the cranberries into the batter. Using an ice cream scoop or large spoon, divide the batter equally among the prepared muffin cups (the batter should completely fill the cups and mound slightly). Evenly sprinkle the streusel topping over the muffins, gently pressing into the batter to adhere. Bake until the muffin tops are golden and just firm, 17 to 18 minutes, rotating the muffin tin halfway through baking. Cool the muffins in the muffin tin on a wire rack for 10 minutes. Remove the muffins from the tin and cool for 10 minutes before serving.

## Oatmeal Muffins

**MAKES** 12 muffins

**WHY THIS RECIPE WORKS** For an oatmeal muffin that is packed with oats but also has a fine, tender texture, we processed old-fashioned rolled oats into a flour in the food processor. To boost oat flavor, we first toasted the oats in a couple of tablespoons of butter and eliminated extraneous spices from the batter. To ensure a lump-free batter, we used a whisk to fold the wet and dry ingredients together and allowed the batter to sit and hydrate for 20 minutes before baking. Finally, we made an apple crisp–inspired topping of crunchy oats, nuts, and brown sugar. Do not use quick or instant oats in this recipe. Walnuts can be substituted for the pecans. The easiest way to grease and flour the muffin tin is with a baking spray with flour.

**TOPPING**

- ½ cup (1½ ounces) old-fashioned rolled oats
- ⅓ cup (1⅔ ounces) all-purpose flour
- ⅓ cup pecans, chopped fine
- ⅓ cup packed (2⅓ ounces) light brown sugar
- 1¼ teaspoons ground cinnamon
- ⅛ teaspoon table salt
- 4 tablespoons unsalted butter, melted

**MUFFINS**

- 2 tablespoons unsalted butter, plus 6 tablespoons melted
- 2 cups (6 ounces) old-fashioned rolled oats
- 1¾ cups (8¾ ounces) all-purpose flour
- 1½ teaspoons table salt
- ¾ teaspoon baking powder
- ¼ teaspoon baking soda
- 1⅓ cups packed (9⅓ ounces) light brown sugar
- 1¾ cups milk
- 2 large eggs, beaten

1. **FOR THE TOPPING:** Combine oats, flour, pecans, sugar, cinnamon, and salt in medium bowl. Drizzle melted butter over mixture and stir to thoroughly combine; set aside.

2. **FOR THE MUFFINS:** Grease and flour 12-cup muffin tin. Melt 2 tablespoons butter in 10-inch skillet over medium heat. Add oats and cook, stirring frequently, until oats turn golden brown and smell of cooking popcorn, 6 to 8 minutes. Transfer oats to food processor and process into fine meal, about 30 seconds. Add flour, salt, baking powder, and baking soda to oats and pulse until combined, about 3 pulses.

3. Stir 6 tablespoons melted butter and sugar together in large bowl until smooth. Add milk and eggs and whisk until smooth. Using whisk, gently fold half of oat mixture into wet ingredients, tapping whisk against side of bowl to release clumps. Add remaining oat mixture and continue to fold with whisk until no streaks of flour remain. Set aside batter for 20 minutes to thicken. Meanwhile, adjust oven rack to middle position and heat oven to 375 degrees.

4. Using ice cream scoop or large spoon, divide batter equally among prepared muffin cups (about ½ cup batter per cup; cups will be filled to rim). Evenly sprinkle topping over muffins (about 2 tablespoons per muffin). Bake until toothpick inserted in center comes out clean, 18 to 25 minutes, rotating muffin tin halfway through baking.

5. Let muffins cool in muffin tin on wire rack for 10 minutes. Remove muffins from muffin tin and serve or let cool completely before serving.

## Best Banana Bread

**MAKES** one 9-inch loaf

**WHY THIS RECIPE WORKS** Overripe bananas are a good excuse to make banana bread, but the loaf can be dry, heavy, and bland. We wanted a banana bread with deep banana flavor, plenty of moisture, and a nice, light texture. Very ripe, darkly speckled bananas contributed moisture as well as flavor to this bread (they're sweeter, too); unripe ones did not work. Pureeing the bananas kept the bread from rising well, so instead we mashed them thoroughly by hand. For additional moisture we included yogurt, which contributed a nice tang without masking the flavor of the bananas. The quick-bread method of mixing—melting the butter and folding the wet ingredients into the dry ones—produced a golden brown loaf and delicate texture; when we tried creaming the butter and sugar first, the bread came out more like butter cake and wasn't as golden brown. However, we found it was important not to overmix the batter; overly vigorous stirring developed excess gluten that turned the loaf tough and dense. For the best flavor, use bananas that are very ripe.

- 2 cups (10 ounces) unbleached all-purpose flour
- ¾ cup (5¼ ounces) sugar
- ¾ teaspoon baking soda
- ½ teaspoon table salt
- 3 very ripe bananas, mashed well (about 1½ cups)
- ¼ cup plain yogurt
- 2 large eggs, lightly beaten
- 6 tablespoons (¾ stick) unsalted butter, melted and cooled
- 1 teaspoon vanilla extract
- 1¼ cup walnuts, toasted and chopped coarse

**1.** Adjust an oven rack to the lower-middle position and heat the oven to 350 degrees. Grease and flour a 9 by 5-inch loaf pan; set aside.

**2.** Whisk the flour, sugar, baking soda, and salt together in a large bowl; set aside.

**3.** Mix the mashed bananas, yogurt, eggs, butter, and vanilla together with a wooden spoon in a medium bowl. Lightly fold the banana mixture into the dry ingredients with a rubber spatula until just combined and the batter looks thick and chunky. Fold in the walnuts. Scrape the batter into the prepared loaf pan and smooth the surface with a rubber spatula.

**4.** Bake until the loaf is golden brown and a toothpick inserted in the center comes out clean, about 55 minutes. Cool in the pan for 5 minutes, then transfer to a wire rack. Serve warm or at room temperature.

## Ultimate Banana Bread

**MAKES** one 9-inch loaf

**WHY THIS RECIPE WORKS** Recipes for ultimate banana bread abound, but they to use too many bananas for flavor, leading to a soggy, unappealing texture. We also used a generous amount of bananas, but to rid them of excess moisture we microwaved them then drained the now-pulpy fruit and mixed it into the batter. We reduced the flavorful liquid and added it to the batter which infused the bread with ripe, intense banana flavor. We also added toasted walnuts to the batter; their crunch provided a pleasing contrast to the moist crumb. To add a little embellishment to the crust, we sliced a banana and shingled it on top of the batter. A final sprinkle of sugar helped the banana slices caramelize and gave the loaf an enticingly crisp, crunchy top. Be sure to use very ripe, heavily speckled (or even black) bananas in this recipe. This recipe can be made using five thawed frozen bananas; since they release a lot of liquid naturally, they can bypass the microwaving in step 2 and go directly into the fine-mesh strainer. Do not use a thawed frozen banana in step 4; it will be too soft to slice. Instead, simply sprinkle the top of the loaf with sugar. The test kitchen's preferred loaf pan measures 8½ by 4½ inches; if you use a 9 by 5-inch loaf pan, start checking for doneness 5 minutes earlier than advised in the recipe. This loaf is best eaten the day it is made, but it can be cooled completely and stored, covered tightly with plastic wrap, for up to three days.

- 1¾ cups (8¾ ounces) all-purpose flour
- 1 teaspoon baking soda
- ½ teaspoon table salt
- 6 large very ripe bananas (about 2¼ pounds), peeled, divided
- 8 tablespoons unsalted butter, melted and cooled slightly
- 2 large eggs
- ¾ cup packed (5¼ ounces) light brown sugar
- 1 teaspoon vanilla extract
- ½ cup walnuts, toasted and chopped coarse (optional)
- 2 teaspoons granulated sugar

**1.** Adjust oven rack to middle position and heat oven to 350 degrees. Spray 8½ by 4½-inch loaf pan with vegetable oil spray. Whisk flour, baking soda, and salt together in large bowl.

**2.** Place 5 bananas in a microwave-safe bowl; cover with plastic wrap and cut several steam vents in plastic with paring knife. Microwave on high power until bananas are soft and have released their liquid, about 5 minutes. Transfer bananas to fine-mesh strainer placed over medium bowl and allow to drain, stirring occasionally, for 15 minutes (you should have ½ to ¾ cup liquid).

**3.** Transfer liquid to medium saucepan and cook over medium-high heat until reduced to ¼ cup, about 5 minutes. Return drained bananas to bowl. Stir reduced liquid into bananas and mash them with potato masher until fairly smooth. Whisk in melted butter, eggs, brown sugar, and vanilla.

**4.** Pour banana mixture into flour mixture and stir until just combined with some streaks of flour remaining. Gently fold in walnuts, if using. Scrape batter into prepared pan. Slice remaining 1 banana diagonally into ¼-inch-thick slices. Shingle banana slices on top of either side of loaf, leaving 1½-inch-wide space down center to ensure even rise. Sprinkle granulated sugar evenly over loaf.

**5.** Bake until toothpick inserted in center of loaf comes out clean, 55 minutes to 1¼ hours. Let cool in pan on wire rack for 15 minutes, then remove from pan and continue to cool on wire rack. Serve warm or at room temperature.

## Pumpkin Bread

**MAKES** 2 loaves

**WHY THIS RECIPE WORKS** Although most recipes for pumpkin bread are pleasantly sweet and spicy, they're nothing to write home about. For a bread with rich pumpkin flavor and enough spices to enhance rather than overwhelm the flavor of our pumpkin, we used a few strategies. To rid canned pumpkin puree of its raw flavor and bring out its richness, we cooked it on top of the stove just until it began to caramelize. To replace some of the lost moisture from cooking the puree and offset some of the sweetness, we added softened cream cheese to the mix. A modest hand with spices and a sweet streusel sprinkled over the top of the loaf gave us perfect pumpkin bread. The test kitchen's preferred loaf pan measures 8½ by 4½ inches; if using a 9 by 5-inch loaf pan, start checking for doneness 5 minutes early.

**TOPPING**

- 5 tablespoons packed (2¼ ounces) light brown sugar
- 1 tablespoon all-purpose flour
- 1 tablespoon unsalted butter, softened
- 1 teaspoon ground cinnamon
- ⅛ teaspoon table salt

**BREAD**

- 2 cups (10 ounces) all-purpose flour
- 1½ teaspoons baking powder
- ½ teaspoon baking soda
- 1 (15-ounce) can unsweetened pumpkin puree
- 1 teaspoon table salt
- 1½ teaspoons ground cinnamon
- ¼ teaspoon ground nutmeg
- ⅛ teaspoon ground cloves
- 1 cup (7 ounces) granulated sugar
- 1 cup packed (7 ounces) light brown sugar
- ½ cup vegetable oil
- 4 ounces cream cheese, cut into 12 pieces
- 4 large eggs
- ¼ cup buttermilk
- 1 cup walnuts, toasted and chopped fine

**1. FOR THE TOPPING:** Using your fingers, mix all ingredients together in bowl until well combined and topping resembles wet sand; set aside.

**2. FOR THE BREAD:** Adjust oven rack to middle position and heat oven to 350 degrees. Grease two 8½ by 4½-inch loaf pans. Whisk flour, baking powder, and baking soda together in bowl.

**3.** Combine pumpkin puree, salt, cinnamon, nutmeg, and cloves in large saucepan over medium heat. Cook mixture, stirring constantly, until reduced to 1½ cups, 6 to 8 minutes. Remove pot from heat; stir in granulated sugar, brown sugar, oil, and cream cheese until combined. Let mixture stand for 5 minutes. Whisk until no visible pieces of cream cheese remain and mixture is homogeneous.

**4.** Whisk together eggs and buttermilk. Add egg mixture to pumpkin mixture and whisk to combine. Fold flour mixture into pumpkin mixture until combined (some small lumps of flour are OK). Fold walnuts into batter. Scrape batter into prepared pans. Sprinkle topping evenly over top of each loaf. Bake until skewer inserted in center of loaf comes out clean, 45 to 50 minutes. Let loaves cool in pans on wire rack for 20 minutes. Remove loaves from pans and let cool for at least 1½ hours. Serve warm or at room temperature.

## Zucchini Bread

**MAKES** 1 loaf

**WHY THIS RECIPE WORKS** In the 1960s and '70s, recipes for zucchini bread popped up everywhere. With bits of green vegetable speckling the crumb, the bread was touted as a healthier option for a sweet treat. But zucchini can also be a liability, as too much leads to a soggy loaf. That's why, in spite of the oft-stated goal of using up surplus squash, most recipes top out at a mere 10 to 12 ounces. And despite being associated with healthy foods, the recipes tend to call for copious amounts of oil that turn the loaf greasy and overly rich. We found that coarsely grated, thoroughly squeezed squash produced a crumb that was supermoist but not gummy. This had the added benefit of removing some of the key compounds in zucchini—called Amadori compounds—which are responsible for zucchini's vegetal flavor, giving our loaf a sweet, mildly earthy (but not vegetal) flavor. For deeper flavor, we switched from granulated sugar to molasses-y brown sugar, increased the cinnamon to 1 tablespoon, and added nutmeg and vanilla. Swapping some of the all-purpose flour for whole-wheat gave the loaf even better structure and ensured that it wasn't soggy. Use the large holes of a box grater to shred the zucchini. The test kitchen's preferred loaf pan measures 8½ by 4½ inches; if you use a 9 by 5-inch loaf pan, start checking for doneness 5 minutes early.

- 1½ pounds zucchini, shredded
- 1¼ cups (8¾ ounces) packed brown sugar
- ¼ cup vegetable oil
- 2 large eggs
- 1 teaspoon vanilla extract
- 1½ cups (7½ ounces) all-purpose flour
- ½ cup (2¾ ounces) whole-wheat flour
- 1 tablespoon ground cinnamon
- 1½ teaspoons table salt
- 1 teaspoon baking powder
- 1 teaspoon baking soda
- ½ teaspoon ground nutmeg
- ¾ cup walnuts, toasted and chopped (optional)
- 1 tablespoon granulated sugar

1. Adjust oven rack to middle position and heat oven to 325 degrees. Grease 8½ by 4½-inch loaf pan.

2. Place zucchini in center of clean dish towel. Gather ends together and twist tightly to drain as much liquid as possible, discarding liquid (you should have ½ to ⅔ cup liquid). Whisk brown sugar, oil, eggs, and vanilla together in medium bowl. Fold in zucchini.

3. Whisk all-purpose flour, whole-wheat flour, cinnamon, salt, baking powder, baking soda, and nutmeg together in large bowl. Fold in zucchini mixture until just incorporated. Fold in walnuts, if using. Pour batter into prepared pan and sprinkle with granulated sugar.

4. Bake until top bounces back when gently pressed and toothpick inserted in center comes out with a few moist crumbs attached, 65 to 75 minutes. Let bread cool in pan on wire rack for 30 minutes. Remove bread from pan and cool completely on wire rack. Serve.

## Cream Scones

**MAKES** 8 scones

**WHY THIS RECIPE WORKS** Cream scones are delicate and light, much like a biscuit. We set out to perfect a technique for making these tea-time (or breakfast) favorites. Experimentation with different kinds of flour revealed that all-purpose was the best choice for these scones, and even better, for maximum tenderness, was a lower-protein brand of flour. Butter was important for flavor, but only a modest amount or the scones would practically melt in the oven. Cream won out for the liquid; it made our scones rich and kept them tender. We increased the amount of sugar from that used in traditional recipes, but only slightly to keep them from being too sweet. The discovery that the food processor did a great job of cutting the butter into the flour was a boon, making it even easier to make these treats.

Use a low-protein all-purpose flour, such as Gold Medal or Pillsbury. The easiest and most reliable approach to mixing the butter into the dry ingredients is to use a food processor fitted with the metal blade. If you want a light glaze on the scones, brush the tops with 1 tablespoon heavy cream and then sprinkle them with 1 tablespoon sugar just before you put them in the oven. Resist the urge to eat the scones hot out of the oven. Letting them cool for at least 10 minutes firms them up and improves their texture.

- 2 cups (10 ounces) unbleached all-purpose flour
- 3 tablespoons sugar
- 1 tablespoon baking powder
- ½ teaspoon table salt
- 5 tablespoons unsalted butter, chilled and cut into ¼-inch cubes
- ½ cup currants
- 1 cup heavy cream

1. Adjust an oven rack to the middle position and heat the oven to 425 degrees.

2. Place the flour, sugar, baking powder, and salt in a food processor and pulse to combine, about 6 pulses.

3. Scatter the butter evenly over the top and continue to pulse until the mixture resembles coarse cornmeal with a few slightly larger butter lumps, about 12 more pulses. Transfer the mixture to a large bowl and stir in the currants. Stir in the heavy cream with a rubber spatula until a dough begins to form, about 30 seconds.

4. Transfer the dough and any dry, floury bits to a work surface and knead the dough by hand just until it comes together into a rough, slightly sticky ball, 5 to 10 seconds. Cut the dough into eight wedges. Place the wedges on an ungreased baking sheet. (The baking sheet can be covered in plastic wrap and refrigerated for up to 2 hours.)

5. Bake until the scone tops are light brown, 12 to 15 minutes. Cool on a wire rack for at least 10 minutes. Serve warm or at room temperature.

## Blueberry Scones

**MAKES** 8 scones

**WHY THIS RECIPE WORKS** Berry scones can be a treat—moist, sweet berries throughout a tender, light biscuit—but more often the berries weigh down the scone and impart little flavor. We wanted a rich, flaky scone studded with sweet, juicy blueberries. Starting with traditional scone recipes, we increased the amounts of sugar and butter to add sweetness and richness. A combination of sour cream and milk lent both richness and tang. But now our scones were heavier than we wanted. We found two ways to lighten them. First, we borrowed a technique from puff pastry, where the dough is turned, rolled, and folded multiple times to create layers that are forced apart by steam when baked, and added a few quick folds to our scone dough. Then, to ensure that the butter would stay as cold and solid while baking, we froze the butter and grated it into the dry ingredients; this made for lighter, flakier scones.

The solution for incorporating the blueberries without mashing them or destroying the pockets of butter was pressing the berries into the dough, rolling the dough into a log, then pressing the log into a rectangle and cutting the scones. It is important to work the dough as little as possible—work quickly and knead and fold the dough only the number of times called for. The butter should be frozen solid before grating. If your kitchen is hot and humid, chill the flour mixture and bowls before use. The recipe calls for two whole sticks of butter, but only 10 tablespoons are actually used (see step 1). If fresh berries are unavailable, an equal amount of frozen berries, unthawed, can be substituted. An equal amount of raspberries, blackberries, or strawberries can also be used in place of the blueberries. Cut larger berries into ¼- to ½-inch pieces.

- 16 tablespoons (2 sticks) unsalted butter, frozen whole
- 1½ cups (about 7½ ounces) fresh blueberries, picked over
- ½ cup whole milk
- ½ cup sour cream
- 2 cups (10 ounces) unbleached all-purpose flour, plus extra for the work surface
- ½ cup (3½ ounces) sugar, plus 1 tablespoon for sprinkling
- 2 teaspoons baking powder
- ½ teaspoon table salt
- ¼ teaspoon baking soda
- 1 teaspoon grated zest from 1 lemon

**1.** Adjust an oven rack to the middle position and heat the oven to 425 degrees. Score and remove half of the wrapper from each stick of frozen butter. Grate the unwrapped ends on the large holes of a box grater (you should grate a total of 8 tablespoons). Place the grated butter in the freezer until needed. Melt 2 tablespoons of the remaining ungrated butter and set aside. Save the remaining 6 tablespoons butter for another use. Place the blueberries in the freezer until needed.

**2.** Whisk the milk and sour cream together in a medium bowl; refrigerate until needed. Whisk the flour, ½ cup of the sugar, the baking powder, salt, baking soda, and lemon zest together in a medium bowl. Add the frozen butter to the flour mixture and toss with your fingers until the butter is thoroughly coated.

**3.** Add the milk mixture to the flour mixture; fold with a rubber spatula until just combined. Using the spatula, transfer the dough to a liberally floured work surface. Dust the surface of the dough with flour; with floured hands, knead the dough six to eight times, until it just holds together in a ragged ball, adding flour as needed to prevent sticking.

**4.** Roll the dough into an approximate 12-inch square. Fold the dough into thirds like a business letter, using a bench scraper or metal spatula to release the dough if it sticks to the work surface. Lift the short ends of the dough and fold into thirds again to form an approximate 4-inch square. Transfer the dough to a plate lightly dusted with flour and chill in the freezer for 5 minutes.

**5.** Transfer the dough to a floured work surface and roll into an approximate 12-inch square again. Sprinkle the blueberries evenly over the surface of the dough, then press down so they are slightly embedded in the dough. Using a bench scraper or a thin metal spatula, loosen the dough from the work surface. Roll the dough, pressing to form a tight log. Lay the log seam side down and press it into a 12 by 4-inch rectangle. Using a sharp, floured knife, cut the rectangle crosswise into four equal rectangles. Cut each rectangle diagonally to form two triangles and transfer to a parchment-lined baking sheet.

**6.** Brush the tops of the scones with the melted butter and sprinkle with the remaining 1 tablespoon sugar. Bake until the tops and bottoms are golden brown, 18 to 25 minutes. Transfer to a wire rack and cool for 10 minutes before serving.

## Oatmeal Scones

**MAKES** 8 scones

**WHY THIS RECIPE WORKS** The oatmeal scones served in a typical coffeehouse are so dry and leaden that they seem like a ploy to get people to buy more coffee to wash them down. We wanted rich toasted oat flavor in a tender, flaky, not-too-sweet scone. Whole rolled oats and quick oats performed better than instant and steel-cut oats. Toasting the oats brought out their nutty flavor. We used a minimal amount of sugar and baking powder, but plenty of cold butter. A mixture of milk and heavy cream added richness without making the scones too heavy. Cutting the cold butter into the flour, instead of using melted butter, resulted in a lighter texture; we were careful not to overmix the dough, which toughened the scones. A very hot oven made the scones rise spectacularly and also gave them a craggy appearance; the high heat meant less time in the oven and therefore less time to dry out. You can substitute half-and-half for the milk-cream combination.

- 1½ cups (4½ ounces) old-fashioned oats or quick oats
- ¼ cup whole milk
- ¼ cup heavy cream
- 1 large egg
- 1½ cups (7½ ounces) unbleached all-purpose flour
- ⅓ cup (2⅓ ounces) sugar, plus 1 tablespoon for sprinkling
- 2 teaspoons baking powder
- ½ teaspoon table salt
- 10 tablespoons (1¼ sticks) unsalted butter, chilled and cut into ½-inch cubes

**1.** Adjust an oven rack to the middle position and heat the oven to 375 degrees. Spread the oats evenly on a rimmed baking sheet and toast in the oven until fragrant and lightly browned, 7 to 9 minutes; cool the oats on the baking sheet on a wire rack. Increase the oven temperature to 450 degrees. Line a second baking sheet with parchment paper. When the oats are cooled, measure out 2 tablespoons (for dusting the work surface and the dough) and set aside.

**2.** Whisk the milk, cream, and egg together in a large measuring cup; remove 1 tablespoon of the mixture and reserve for glazing.

**3.** Pulse the flour, ⅓ cup of the sugar, the baking powder, and salt in a food processor until combined, about 4 pulses. Scatter the cold butter evenly over the dry ingredients and pulse until the mixture resembles coarse cornmeal, about 12 pulses. Transfer the mixture to a medium bowl and stir in the cooled oats. Using a rubber spatula, fold in the liquid ingredients until large clumps form. Mix the dough by hand in the bowl until the dough forms a cohesive mass.

**4.** Dust a work surface with half of the reserved oats, turn the dough out onto the work surface, and dust the top with the remaining oats. Gently pat into a 7-inch circle about 1 inch thick. Using a bench scraper or chef's knife, cut the dough into eight wedges and set on the prepared baking sheet, spacing the scones about 2 inches apart. Brush the surfaces with the reserved egg mixture and sprinkle with the remaining 1 tablespoon sugar. Bake until golden brown, 12 to 14 minutes; cool the scones on the baking sheet on a wire rack for 5 minutes, then transfer the scones to the rack and cool to room temperature, about 30 minutes. Serve.

### Glazed Maple-Pecan Oatmeal Scones

Follow the recipe for Oatmeal Scones, toasting ½ cup chopped pecans with the oats, whisking ¼ cup maple syrup into the milk mixture, and omitting the sugar. When the scones are cooled, whisk 3 tablespoons maple syrup and ½ cup confectioners' sugar together in a small bowl until combined; drizzle the glaze over the scones.

## British-Style Currant Scones

**MAKES** 12 scones

**WHY THIS RECIPE WORKS** Compared to American scones, British scones are lighter, fluffier, and less sweet; perfect for serving with butter and jam. Rather than leaving pieces of cold butter in the dry ingredients as we would with American scones, we thoroughly worked in softened butter until it was fully integrated. This protected some of the flour granules from moisture, which in turn limited gluten development and kept the crumb tender and cakey. For a higher rise, we added more than the usual amount of leavening and started the scones in a 500-degree oven to boost their lift before turning the temperature down. We brushed some reserved milk and egg on top for enhanced browning, and added currants for tiny bursts of fruit flavor throughout. We prefer whole milk in this recipe, but low-fat milk can be used. The dough will be quite soft and wet; dust your work surface and your hands liberally with flour. For a tall, even rise, use a sharp-edged biscuit cutter and push straight down; do not twist the cutter. Serve these scones with jam as well as salted butter or clotted cream. Scones are best eaten the day they are made.

- 3 cups (15 ounces) all-purpose flour
- ⅓ cup (2⅓ ounces) sugar
- 2 tablespoons baking powder
- ½ teaspoon table salt
- 8 tablespoons unsalted butter, cut into ½-inch pieces and softened
- ¾ cup dried currants
- 1 cup whole milk
- 2 large eggs

**1.** Adjust oven rack to upper-middle position and heat oven to 500 degrees. Line rimmed baking sheet with parchment paper. Pulse flour, sugar, baking powder, and salt in food processor until combined, about 5 pulses. Add butter and pulse until fully incorporated and mixture looks like very fine crumbs with no visible butter, about 20 pulses. Transfer mixture to large bowl and stir in currants.

**2.** Whisk milk and eggs together in second bowl. Set aside 2 tablespoons milk mixture. Add remaining milk mixture to flour mixture and, using rubber spatula, fold together until almost no dry bits of flour remain.

**3.** Transfer dough to well-floured counter and gather into ball. With your floured hands, knead until surface is smooth and free of cracks, 25 to 30 times. Press gently to form disk. Using floured rolling pin, roll disk into 9-inch round, about 1 inch thick. Using floured 2½-inch round cutter, stamp out 8 rounds, recoating cutter with flour if it begins to stick. Arrange scones on prepared sheet. Gather dough scraps, form into ball, and knead gently until surface is smooth. Roll dough to 1-inch thickness and stamp out 4 rounds. Discard remaining dough.

**4.** Brush tops of scones with reserved milk mixture. Reduce oven temperature to 425 degrees and bake scones until risen and golden brown, 10 to 12 minutes, rotating sheet halfway through baking. Transfer scones to wire rack and let cool for at least 10 minutes. Serve scones warm or at room temperature.

## Quick Cinnamon Buns with Buttermilk Icing

**MAKES** 8 buns

**WHY THIS RECIPE WORKS** A tender, fluffy bun with a sweet filling and glaze is a brunch treat no one will turn down. Most recipes, though, require yeast, which makes them time-consuming. Eliminating the yeast would reduce the prep time substantially, so we started with the assumption that our leavener would be baking powder. A cream biscuit recipe, which could be mixed all in one bowl, was our starting point; buttermilk rather than cream (plus baking soda to balance the acidity of the buttermilk) made the interior of the buns light and airy. Melted butter restored some of the richness we lost by eliminating the cream. A brief kneading ensured that the rolls would rise. We patted out the dough rather than rolling it out and covered it with the filling of brown and granulated sugars, cinnamon, cloves, and salt, with melted butter to help the mixture adhere. We rolled up the dough, cut the buns, and put them in a nonstick cake pan to bake. A glaze was the crowning glory. These cinnamon buns were on the table in less than a quarter of the time it would have taken for yeast buns—and they were just as tasty. Melted butter is used in both the filling and the dough and to grease the pan; melt the total amount (8 tablespoons) at once and measure it out as you need it. The buns are best eaten warm, but they will hold for up to 2 hours.

1 tablespoon unsalted butter, melted, for the pan

**CINNAMON-SUGAR FILLING**

¾ cup packed (5¼ ounces) dark brown sugar
¼ cup (1¾ ounces) granulated sugar
2 teaspoons ground cinnamon
⅛ teaspoon ground cloves
⅛ teaspoon table salt
1 tablespoon unsalted butter, melted

**BISCUIT DOUGH**

2½ cups (12½ ounces) unbleached all-purpose flour, plus extra for the work surface
2 tablespoons granulated sugar
1¼ teaspoons baking powder
½ teaspoon baking soda
½ teaspoon table salt
1¼ cups buttermilk
6 tablespoons (¾ stick) unsalted butter, melted

**ICING**

2 tablespoons cream cheese, softened
2 tablespoons buttermilk
1 cup (4 ounces) confectioners' sugar

1. Adjust an oven rack to the upper-middle position and heat the oven to 425 degrees. Pour 1 tablespoon of the melted butter into a 9-inch nonstick cake pan; brush to coat the pan. Spray a wire rack with vegetable oil spray and set aside.

2. **FOR THE CINNAMON-SUGAR FILLING:** Combine the sugars, spices, and salt in a small bowl. Add the melted butter and stir with a fork or your fingers until the mixture resembles wet sand; set the filling mixture aside.

3. **FOR THE BISCUIT DOUGH:** Whisk the flour, sugar, baking powder, baking soda, and salt together in a large bowl. Whisk the buttermilk and 2 tablespoons of the melted butter together in a measuring cup or small bowl. Add the liquid to the dry ingredients and stir with a wooden spoon until the liquid is absorbed (the dough will look very shaggy), about 30 seconds. Transfer the dough to a lightly floured work surface and knead until just smooth and no longer shaggy.

4. Pat the dough with your hands into a 12 by 9-inch rectangle. Brush the dough with 2 tablespoons more melted butter. Sprinkle evenly with the filling, leaving a ½-inch border of plain dough around the edges. Press the filling firmly into the dough. Using a bench scraper or metal spatula, loosen the dough from the work surface. Starting at a long side, roll the dough, pressing lightly, to form a tight log. Pinch the seam to seal. Roll the log seam side down and cut it evenly into eight pieces. With your hand, slightly flatten each piece of dough to seal the open edges and keep the filling in place. Place one roll in the center of the prepared pan, then place the remaining seven rolls around the perimeter of the pan. Brush with the remaining 2 tablespoons melted butter.

5. Bake until the edges are golden brown, 23 to 25 minutes. Use an offset metal spatula to loosen the buns from the pan. Wearing an oven mitt, place a large plate over the pan and invert the buns onto a plate. Place the greased wire rack over the plate and invert the buns onto the rack. Cool for 5 minutes.

6. **FOR THE ICING:** While the buns are cooling, line a rimmed baking sheet with parchment paper; set the rack with the buns over the baking sheet. Whisk the cream cheese and buttermilk together in a large nonreactive bowl until thick and smooth (the mixture will look like cottage cheese at first). Sift the confectioners' sugar over the mixture; whisk until a smooth glaze forms, about 30 seconds. Spoon the glaze evenly over the buns and serve.

## Blueberry Boy Bait

**SERVES** 12

**WHY THIS RECIPE WORKS** This coffee cake, a moist cake with blueberries and a light streusel topping, is so called because the girl who created it for the Pillsbury Grand National Baking Contest said that teenage boys found it irresistible. We tracked down a version of the contest-winning recipe and decided to see if we could improve it. The original recipe called for shortening and granulated sugar. We swapped butter for the shortening and brown sugar for some of the granulated sugar. Both exchanges resulted in richer, deeper flavor in the cake. We doubled the amount of blueberries; half went into the cake batter and the other half on top. An extra egg in the cake batter firmed up the structure so that the extra fruit wouldn't make the cake mushy. The topping couldn't be simpler: in addition to the blueberries, just sugar and cinnamon instead of a streusel, which baked into a light, crisp, sweet coating. If using frozen blueberries, do not let them thaw, as they will turn the batter a blue-green color.

**CAKE**

- 2 cups (10 ounces) plus 1 teaspoon unbleached all-purpose flour
- 1 tablespoon baking powder
- 1 teaspoon table salt
- 16 tablespoons (2 sticks) unsalted butter, softened
- ¾ cup packed (5¼ ounces) light brown sugar
- ½ cup (3½ ounces) granulated sugar
- 3 large eggs
- 1 cup whole milk
- ½ cup blueberries, fresh or frozen

**TOPPING**

- ½ cup blueberries, fresh or frozen
- ¼ cup (1¾ ounces) granulated sugar
- ½ teaspoon ground cinnamon

**1. FOR THE CAKE:** Adjust an oven rack to the middle position and heat the oven to 350 degrees. Grease and flour a 13 by 9-inch baking pan.

**2.** Whisk 2 cups of the flour, the baking powder, and salt together in a medium bowl. With an electric mixer, beat the butter and sugars on medium-high speed until fluffy, about 2 minutes. Add the eggs, one at a time, beating until just incorporated. Reduce the speed to medium and beat in one-third of the flour mixture until incorporated; beat in ½ cup of the milk. Beat in half of the remaining flour mixture, then the remaining ½ cup milk, and finally the remaining flour mixture. Toss the blueberries in a small bowl with the remaining 1 teaspoon flour. Using a rubber spatula, gently fold in the blueberries. Spread the batter into the prepared pan.

**3. FOR THE TOPPING:** Scatter the blueberries over the top of the batter. Stir the sugar and cinnamon together in a small bowl and sprinkle over the batter. Bake until a toothpick inserted in the center of the cake comes out clean, 45 to 50 minutes. Cool in the pan for 20 minutes, then turn out and place on a serving platter (topping side up). Serve warm or at room temperature. The cake can be stored in an airtight container at room temperature for up to 3 days.

## New York–Style Crumb Cake

**SERVES 8 to 10**

**WHY THIS RECIPE WORKS** The original crumb cake was brought to New York by German immigrants; sadly, the bakery-fresh versions have all but disappeared, and most people know only the commercially baked (and preservative-laden) type. We wanted a recipe closer to the original version. The essence of this cake is the balance between the tender, buttery cake and the thick, lightly spiced crumb topping. Starting with our favorite yellow cake recipe, we realized we needed to reduce the amount of butter or the richness would be overwhelming. We compensated for the resulting dryness by substituting buttermilk for milk, which also helped make the cake sturdy enough to support the crumbs. We wanted our crumb topping to be soft and cookie-like, not a crunchy streusel, so we mixed granulated and brown sugars and melted the butter for a dough-like consistency, flavoring the mixture only with cinnamon. If you can't find buttermilk, you can use an equal amount of plain low-fat yogurt, but do not substitute powdered buttermilk because it will make a sunken cake. When topping the cake, take care to not push the crumbs into the batter. This recipe can be easily doubled and baked in a 13 by 9-inch baking dish; increase the baking time to about 45 minutes.

**CRUMB TOPPING**

- ⅓ cup (2⅓ ounces) granulated sugar
- ⅓ cup packed (2⅓ ounces) dark brown sugar
- ¾ teaspoon ground cinnamon
- ⅛ teaspoon table salt
- 8 tablespoons (1 stick) unsalted butter, melted and still warm
- 1¾ cups (7 ounces) cake flour

**CAKE**

- 1¼ cups (5 ounces) cake flour
- ½ cup (3½ ounces) granulated sugar
- ¼ teaspoon baking soda
- ¼ teaspoon table salt
- 6 tablespoons (¾ stick) unsalted butter, cut into 6 pieces, softened but still cool
- 1 large whole egg plus 1 large egg yolk
- ⅓ cup buttermilk
- 1 teaspoon vanilla extract
- Confectioners' sugar, for dusting

**1. FOR THE CRUMB TOPPING:** Whisk the sugars, cinnamon, salt, and butter together in a medium bowl to combine. Add the flour and stir with a rubber spatula or wooden spoon until the mixture resembles a thick, cohesive dough; set aside to cool to room temperature, 10 to 15 minutes.

**2. FOR THE CAKE:** Adjust an oven rack to the upper-middle position and heat the oven to 325 degrees. Cut a 16-inch length of parchment paper or aluminum foil and fold lengthwise to a 7-inch width. Spray an 8-inch square baking dish with vegetable oil spray and fit the parchment into the dish, pushing it into the corners and up the sides; allow the excess to overhang the edges of the dish.

**3.** In the bowl of a stand mixer fitted with the paddle attachment, mix the flour, sugar, baking soda, and salt on low speed to combine. With the mixer running at low speed, add the butter one piece at a time; continue beating until the mixture resembles moist crumbs, with no visible butter chunks remaining, 1 to 2 minutes. Add the egg, egg yolk, buttermilk, and vanilla; beat on medium-high speed until light and fluffy, about 1 minute, scraping once if necessary.

4. Transfer the batter to the prepared baking pan; using a rubber spatula, spread the batter into an even layer. Break apart the crumb topping into large pea-size pieces, rolling them between your thumb and forefinger to form crumbs, and spread in an even layer over the batter, beginning with the edges and then working toward the center. Bake until the crumbs are golden and a wooden skewer inserted into the center of the cake comes out clean, 35 to 40 minutes. Cool on a wire rack for at least 30 minutes. Remove the cake from the pan by lifting the parchment overhang. Dust with confectioners' sugar before serving.

## Coffee Cake with Pecan-Cinnamon Streusel

**SERVES** 8 to 10

**WHY THIS RECIPE WORKS** We wanted to streamline the process for this breakfast treat and still produce a soft, tender crumb crowned with a crunchy, nutty streusel. We decided to use a food processor to mix both the cake and the topping. To make sure our cake was tender despite the aggressive action of the food processor's blades, we opted to use the reverse-creaming method (combining butter and flour before adding the wet ingredients). This mixing method coated the flour's proteins with fat and prevented them from linking up and forming gluten when water was added to the batter. Building a thick batter kept it from rising over and covering the streusel at the edges of the pan. And adding just a teaspoon of water to the streusel ingredients while pulsing them helped the mixture adhere to the cake. Finally, baking the cake in a springform pan instead of the typical round cake pan allowed for fuss-free unmolding that kept the streusel intact. Each bite of this coffee cake offered an appealing combination of crunchy cinnamon-pecan streusel and rich, tender cake. And, as an added bonus, it could be made quickly and using a single kitchen appliance. For the best results, we recommend weighing the flour in this recipe. Do not insert a skewer into this cake to test for doneness until the center appears firm when the pan is shaken. If you do, the weight of the streusel may squeeze out air and the cake may sink. The cake can be wrapped in plastic wrap and stored at room temperature for up to 24 hours.

**STREUSEL**

- 1 cup pecans, toasted
- ⅓ cup packed (2⅓ ounces) brown sugar
- ½ cup (2½ ounces) all-purpose flour
- ¾ teaspoon ground cinnamon
- ¼ teaspoon table salt
- 4 tablespoons unsalted butter, melted and cooled
- 1 teaspoon water

**CAKE**

- 1⅔ cups (8⅓ ounces) all-purpose flour
- 1 cup (7 ounces) sugar
- 1 teaspoon ground cinnamon

- 1 teaspoon baking powder
- ½ teaspoon baking soda
- ¾ teaspoon table salt
- 7 tablespoons unsalted butter, cut into 7 pieces and softened
- ¾ cup milk
- 1 large egg plus 1 large yolk
- 1 teaspoon vanilla extract

1. Adjust oven rack to lower-middle position and heat oven to 350 degrees. Grease and flour 9-inch springform pan and place on rimmed baking sheet.

2. **FOR THE STREUSEL:** Process pecans and sugar in food processor until finely ground, about 10 seconds. Add flour, cinnamon, and salt and pulse to combine, about 5 (1-second) pulses. Add melted butter and water and pulse until butter is fully incorporated and mixture begins to form clumps, 8 to 10 (1-second) pulses. Transfer streusel to bowl and set aside.

3. **FOR THE CAKE:** In now-empty processor, process flour, sugar, cinnamon, baking powder, baking soda, and salt until combined, about 10 seconds. Add butter and pulse until very small but visible pieces of butter remain, 5 to 8 (5-second) pulses. Add milk, egg and yolk, and vanilla; pulse until dry ingredients are moistened, 4 to 5 (1-second) pulses. Scrape down sides of bowl. Pulse until mixture is well combined, 4 to 5 (1-second) pulses (some small pieces of butter will remain). Transfer batter to prepared pan and smooth top with rubber spatula.

4. Starting at edges of pan, sprinkle streusel in even layer over batter. Bake cake on sheet until center is firm and skewer inserted into center of cake comes out clean, 45 to 55 minutes. Transfer pan to wire rack and let cake cool in pan for 15 minutes. Remove side of pan and let cake cool completely, about 2 hours. Using offset spatula, transfer cake to serving platter. Using serrated knife, cut cake into wedges and serve.

## Sour Cream Coffee Cake with Brown Sugar–Pecan Streusel

**SERVES** 12 to 16

**WHY THIS RECIPE WORKS** Sour cream coffee cakes should be buttery and rich. But some recipes yield a heavy cake that borders on greasy. We wanted a pleasantly rich cake with lots of streusel. All-purpose flour gave us a better texture than the cake flour specified in many recipes. For richness, we used plenty of butter, sour cream, and eggs; the eggs also contributed a tight crumb. Baking powder and baking soda were necessary to make this hefty batter rise. Rather than creaming the butter and sugar, which made the cake too light and airy, we cut softened butter and some of the sour cream into the dry ingredients, then added the eggs and the rest of the sour cream. In addition to the streusel in the middle of the cake, we wanted more on top, so we started with a mixture of brown and granulated sugars and added a big hit of cinnamon and some flour (to keep the streusel from congealing). We then divided the mixture—some for the interior streusel layers, which we sweetened further with more brown sugar, and the rest for the topping. To the latter, we added pecans and butter; the nuts toasted as the cake baked, so we didn't have to toast them first. With two layers of streusel in our moist, rich cake and another layer on top with toasty, crunchy nuts, this was a coffee cake worth getting up for. A 10-inch tube pan is best for this recipe. The cake can be wrapped in foil and stored at room temperature for up to 5 days.

**STREUSEL**

- ¾ cup (3¾ ounces) unbleached all-purpose flour
- ¾ cup (5¼ ounces) granulated sugar
- ½ cup packed (3½ ounces) dark brown sugar
- 2 tablespoons ground cinnamon
- 1 cup pecans, chopped
- 2 tablespoons unsalted butter, chilled and cut into 2 pieces

**CAKE**

- 12 tablespoons (1½ sticks) unsalted butter, softened but still cool, cut into ½-inch cubes, plus 2 tablespoons softened butter, for greasing the pan
- 4 large eggs
- 1½ cups sour cream
- 1 tablespoon vanilla extract
- 2¼ cups (11½ ounces) unbleached all-purpose flour
- 1¼ cups (8¾ ounces) granulated sugar
- 1 tablespoon baking powder
- ¾ teaspoon baking soda
- ¾ teaspoon table salt

**1. FOR THE STREUSEL:** In a food processor, process the flour, granulated sugar, ¼ cup of the brown sugar, and the cinnamon until combined, about 15 seconds. Transfer 1¼ cups of the flour-sugar mixture to a small bowl; stir in the remaining ¼ cup brown sugar and set aside to use for the streusel filling. Add the pecans and butter to the flour-sugar mixture in the food processor; pulse until the nuts and butter resemble small pebbly pieces, about 10 pulses; set aside.

**2. FOR THE CAKE:** Adjust an oven rack to the lowest position and heat the oven to 350 degrees. Grease a 10-cup tube pan with 2 tablespoons of the softened butter. Whisk the eggs, 1 cup of the sour cream, and the vanilla together in a medium bowl until combined.

**3.** Mix the flour, granulated sugar, baking powder, baking soda, and salt in the bowl of a stand mixer on low speed until combined, about 30 seconds. Add the remaining 12 tablespoons butter and remaining ½ cup sour cream; mix on low speed until the dry ingredients are moistened and the mixture resembles wet sand, with a few large butter pieces remaining, about 1½ minutes. Increase the speed to medium and beat until the batter comes together, about 10 seconds, scraping down the sides of the bowl with a rubber spatula as necessary. Lower the speed to medium-low and gradually add the egg mixture in three additions, beating for 20 seconds after each addition and scraping down the sides of the bowl as necessary. Increase the speed to medium-high and beat until the batter is light and fluffy, about 1 minute.

**4.** Using a rubber spatula, spread 2 cups of the batter in the bottom of the prepared pan, smoothing the surface. Sprinkle evenly with ¾ cup of the streusel filling without butter or nuts. Repeat with 2 cups more batter and the remaining ¾ cup streusel filling without butter or nuts. Spread the remaining batter over, then sprinkle with the streusel topping with butter and nuts.

**5.** Bake until the cake feels firm to the touch and a long toothpick or skewer inserted into the center comes out clean (bits of sugar from the streusel may cling to the tester), 50 to 60 minutes. Cool the cake in the pan on a wire rack for 30 minutes. Invert the cake onto a rimmed baking sheet (the cake will be streusel side down); remove the tube pan, place a wire rack on top of the cake, and reinvert the cake streusel side up. Cool to room temperature, about 2 hours. Cut into wedges and serve.

## Cream Cheese Coffee Cake

**SERVES** 12 to 16

**WHY THIS RECIPE WORKS** This brunch staple is fraught with pitfalls, from dry, bland cake to lackluster fillings that sink to the bottom. For the filling, we settled on a base mixture of softened cream cheese and sugar and then added lemon juice to cut the richness and a hint of vanilla extract for depth. Incorporating a small amount of the cake batter into the cheese ensured our filling wasn't grainy. The filling not only stayed creamy, but it fused to the cake during baking; this eliminated any gaps and guaranteed perfect swirls of filling. Sliced almonds, sugar, and lemon zest formed a glistening, crackly crust on top of our rich, moist cake.

**LEMON SUGAR–ALMOND TOPPING**

- ¼ cup (1¾ ounces) sugar
- 1½ teaspoons finely grated zest from 1 lemon
- ½ cup sliced almonds

**CAKE**

- 2¼ cups (11¼ ounces) unbleached all-purpose flour
- 1⅛ teaspoons baking powder
- 1⅛ teaspoons baking soda
- 1 teaspoon table salt
- 10 tablespoons (1¼ sticks) unsalted butter, softened but still cool
- 1 cup (7 ounces) plus 7 tablespoons sugar
- 1 tablespoon finely grated zest plus 4 teaspoons juice from 1 to 2 lemons
- 4 large eggs
- 5 teaspoons vanilla extract
- 1¼ cups sour cream
- 8 ounces cream cheese, softened

**1. FOR THE TOPPING:** Adjust an oven rack to the middle position and heat the oven to 350 degrees. Stir together the sugar and lemon zest in a small bowl until combined and the sugar is moistened. Stir in the almonds; set aside.

**2. FOR THE CAKE:** Spray a 10-inch tube pan with vegetable oil spray. Whisk the flour, baking powder, baking soda, and salt together in a medium bowl; set aside. In a stand mixer fitted with the paddle attachment, beat the butter, 1 cup plus 2 tablespoons of the sugar, and the lemon zest at medium speed until light and fluffy, about 3 minutes, scraping down the sides and bottom of the bowl with a rubber spatula. Add the eggs one at a time, beating well after each addition, about 20 seconds, and scraping down the beater and sides of the bowl as necessary. Add 4 teaspoons of the vanilla and mix to combine. Reduce the speed to low and add one-third of the flour mixture, followed by half of the sour cream, mixing until incorporated after each addition, 5 to 10 seconds. Repeat, using half of the remaining flour mixture and all of the remaining sour cream. Scrape the bowl and add the remaining flour mixture; mix at low speed until the batter is thoroughly combined, about 10 seconds. Remove the bowl from the mixer and fold the batter once or twice with a rubber spatula to incorporate any remaining flour.

**3.** Reserve 1¼ cups of the batter and set aside. Spoon the remaining batter into the prepared pan and smooth the top. Return the now-empty bowl to the mixer and beat the cream cheese, remaining 5 tablespoons sugar, lemon juice, and remaining 1 teaspoon vanilla on medium speed until smooth and slightly lightened, about 1 minute. Add ¼ cup of the reserved batter and mix until incorporated. Spoon the cheese filling mixture evenly over the batter, keeping the filling about 1 inch from the edges of the pan; smooth the top. Spread the remaining 1 cup reserved batter over the filling and smooth the top. With a butter knife or offset spatula, gently swirl the filling into the batter using a figure-eight motion, being careful not to drag the filling to the bottom or edges of the pan. Firmly tap the pan on the counter two or three times to dislodge any bubbles. Sprinkle the lemon sugar–almond topping evenly over the batter and gently press into the batter to adhere.

**4.** Bake until the top is golden and just firm and a long skewer inserted into the cake comes out clean (a skewer will be wet if inserted into the cheese filling), 45 to 50 minutes. Remove the pan from the oven and firmly tap on the counter two or three times (the top of the cake may sink slightly). Cool the cake in the pan on a wire rack for 1 hour. Gently invert the cake onto a rimmed baking sheet (the cake will be topping side down); remove the tube pan, place a wire rack on top of the cake, and invert the cake sugar side up. Cool to room temperature, about 1½ hours, before serving.

## Make-Way-Ahead Dinner Rolls

**MAKES** 16 rolls **SEASON 26**

**WHY THIS RECIPE WORKS** With this brown-and-serve recipe, you'll never be more than 15 minutes away from the comforts of fluffy homemade bread. Ours are an improvement over traditional recipes because we included a cooked flour paste commonly called by its Chinese name (though it originated in Japan), tangzhong, which added extra moisture to the dough, ensuring moist and light rolls. Because the rolls were very delicate when parbaked, we cooled them and then froze them still on their baking sheet. Once firm, they went into a zipper-lock bag to be frozen for up to six weeks. To serve, simply place the desired number of frozen rolls on a baking sheet and bake them in a very hot oven (or a toaster oven); the insides of the rolls thawed and softened while the outsides became beautifully browned. We strongly recommend weighing the flour for this recipe. If you prefer, portion the dough by weight in step 5 (1¾ ounces per roll). Do not handle the rolls until they're fully frozen. To prevent the rolls from touching as they expand in the oven, use a baking sheet that is at least 18 by 13 inches. This recipe can be easily doubled, but you'll need enough freezer space for two baking sheets.

**FLOUR PASTE**

- ½ cup water
- 3 tablespoons bread flour

**DOUGH**

- ¾ cup milk, chilled
- 2⅔ cups (14⅔ ounces) bread flour
- 1 large egg
- 2 teaspoons instant or rapid-rise yeast
- 2 tablespoons sugar
- 1¼ teaspoons table salt
- 2 tablespoons unsalted butter, softened
- Vegetable oil spray

**1. FOR THE FLOUR PASTE:** Whisk water and flour in small bowl until no lumps remain. Microwave, whisking every 20 seconds, until mixture thickens to stiff, pasty consistency, 40 to 80 seconds.

**2. FOR THE DOUGH:** In bowl of stand mixer, whisk flour paste and milk until smooth. Add flour, egg, and yeast. Fit mixer with dough hook and mix on low speed until all flour is moistened, 1 to 2 minutes. Let stand for 15 minutes.

**3.** Add sugar and salt and mix on medium-low speed for 5 minutes. With mixer running, add butter, 1 tablespoon at a time. Continue to mix on medium-low speed until dough is smooth and elastic, about 5 minutes longer.

**4.** Transfer dough to lightly floured counter. Knead briefly to form ball and transfer, seam side down, to lightly greased bowl; coat surface of dough lightly with oil spray and cover. Let rise until doubled in volume, about 1 hour.

**5.** Line rimmed baking sheet with parchment paper. Press dough to expel air, then transfer dough to counter. Pat into 8-inch square of even thickness. Using bench scraper or chef's knife, cut dough into 16 equal pieces (4 rows by 4 rows). Working with 1 piece of dough at a time, form dough into smooth, taut balls. (To round, set piece of dough on unfloured counter. Loosely cup your lightly floured hand around dough and, without applying pressure to dough, move your hand in small circular motions. Tackiness of dough against counter and circular motion should work dough into smooth ball.) Arrange dough balls seam side down on prepared sheet, placing 5 balls down each long side and 6 down center. Cover and let rise until almost doubled in size, 45 minutes to 1 hour.

**6.** When rolls are almost doubled in size, adjust oven rack to middle position and heat oven to 300 degrees. Bake until rolls are risen and register 170 to 175 degrees, 14 to 16 minutes (rolls will have little to no color). Transfer sheet to wire rack and let cool completely, 30 to 45 minutes (rolls will wrinkle slightly). Transfer sheet to freezer and freeze rolls until solid, 30 minutes to 1 hour. Transfer rolls to zipper-lock bag and freeze for up to 6 weeks.

**7. TO SERVE:** Adjust oven rack to middle position and heat oven to 425 degrees. Arrange desired number of frozen rolls on parchment-lined baking sheet and bake until deep golden brown, 8 to 10 minutes. Transfer rolls to wire rack and let cool for at least 5 minutes before serving.

## Fluffy Dinner Rolls

**MAKES** 12 rolls

**WHY THIS RECIPE WORKS** Moist, fluffy American dinner rolls are great when fresh but lose those qualities as they sit. We took a classic dinner roll recipe and applied a Japanese bread-making method called tangzhong, which adds extra moisture to the dough in the form of a flour paste. The added liquid extends the rolls' shelf life so they maintain their fluffy texture for more than a day. To support the weight of the extra moisture, we built a strong gluten structure by changing the mixing method—adding a resting period and withholding the butter until the gluten was established. Flattening each portion of dough and rolling it up in a spiral organized the gluten strands into coiled layers, which baked up into feathery sheets. We strongly recommend weighing the flour for the dough. The slight tackiness of the dough aids in flattening and stretching it in step 5, so do not dust your counter with flour. Rolls can be wrapped in a double layer of plastic wrap and stored at room temperature for 1 day. To reheat, wrap in aluminum foil and heat in a 350-degree oven for 15 minutes.

**FLOUR PASTE**

- ½ cup water
- 3 tablespoons bread flour

**DOUGH**

- ½ cup cold milk
- 1 large egg
- 2 cups (11 ounces) bread flour
- 1½ teaspoons instant or rapid-rise yeast
- 2 tablespoons sugar
- 1 teaspoon table salt
- 4 tablespoons unsalted butter, softened, plus ½ tablespoon, melted

**1. FOR THE FLOUR PASTE:** Whisk water and flour in small bowl until no lumps remain. Microwave, whisking every 20 seconds, until mixture thickens to stiff, smooth, pudding-like consistency that forms mound when dropped from end of whisk into bowl, 40 to 80 seconds.

**2. FOR THE DOUGH:** In bowl of stand mixer, whisk flour paste and milk together until smooth. Add egg and whisk until incorporated. Add flour and yeast. Fit stand mixer with dough hook and mix on low speed until all flour is moistened, 1 to 2 minutes. Let stand for 15 minutes.

**3.** Add sugar and salt and mix on medium-low speed for 5 minutes. With mixer running, add softened butter, 1 tablespoon at a time. Continue to mix on medium-low speed 5 minutes longer, scraping down dough hook and sides of bowl occasionally (dough will stick to bottom of bowl).

**4.** Transfer dough to very lightly floured counter. Knead briefly to form ball and transfer, seam side down, to lightly greased bowl; lightly coat surface of dough with vegetable oil spray and cover with plastic wrap. Let rise until doubled in volume, about 1 hour.

5. Grease 9-inch round cake pan and set aside. Transfer dough to counter. Press dough gently but firmly to expel all air. Pat and stretch dough to form 8 by 9-inch rectangle with short side facing you. Cut dough lengthwise into 4 equal strips and cut each strip crosswise into 3 equal pieces. Working with 1 piece at a time, stretch and press dough gently to form 8 by 2-inch strip. Starting on short side, roll dough to form snug cylinder and arrange shaped rolls seam side down in prepared pan, placing 10 rolls around edge of pan, pointing inward, and remaining 2 rolls in center. Cover with plastic and let rise until doubled, 45 minutes to 1 hour.

6. When rolls are nearly doubled, adjust oven rack to lowest position and heat oven to 375 degrees. Bake rolls until deep golden brown, 25 to 30 minutes. Let rolls cool in pan on wire rack for 3 minutes; invert rolls onto rack, then reinvert. Brush tops and sides of rolls with melted butter. Let rolls cool for at least 20 minutes before serving.

## Rustic Dinner Rolls

**MAKES** 16 rolls

**WHY THIS RECIPE WORKS** We wanted to create a reliable recipe for rustic dinner rolls with a crisp crust and chewy crumb. Using bread flour produced a dense, bland crumb beneath a leathery crust. The flavor improved when we replaced a few tablespoons of bread flour with whole-wheat flour, which contributed earthiness, while honey added sweetness. A little extra yeast improved the crumb slightly, but making the dough wetter was the fix. Lots of water in the dough created more steam bubbles during baking, which produced an airier crumb. Giving the dough a couple of turns also encouraged the yeast to produce more carbon dioxide, creating more bubbles and a lighter crumb. Our two-step baking process mimicked a steam-injected oven: First, we misted the rolls with water before baking them for a crispier crust. We then partially baked them in a cake pan to help set their shape. Halfway through baking, we removed the cake pan from the oven, lowered the temperature, pulled the rolls apart, and returned them to the oven for uniformly golden rolls with the crust and crumb we were looking for. Because this dough is sticky, keep your hands well floured when handling it. Use a spray bottle to mist the rolls with water. The rolls can be stored at room temperature in a zipper-lock bag for up to 2 days; to recrisp, place in a 450-degree oven for 6 to 8 minutes. To freeze, wrap rolls in foil and place in a large zipper-lock bag. Rolls can be frozen for several months; thaw at room temperature and recrisp using the instructions above.

- 1½ cups plus 1 tablespoon water, at room temperature
- 2 teaspoons honey
- 1½ teaspoons instant or rapid-rise yeast
- 3 cups plus 1 tablespoon (16½ ounces) bread flour, plus extra for the dough and work surface
- 3 tablespoons whole-wheat flour
- 1½ teaspoons table salt

1. Whisk the water, honey, and yeast in the bowl of a stand mixer until well combined, making sure no honey sticks to the bottom of the bowl. Add the flours and mix on low speed with the dough hook until a cohesive dough is formed, about 3 minutes. Cover the bowl with plastic wrap and let sit at room temperature for 30 minutes.

2. Remove the plastic wrap and sprinkle the salt evenly over the dough. Knead on low speed for 5 minutes. (If the dough creeps up on the attachment, stop the mixer and scrape it down.) Increase the speed to medium and continue to knead until the dough is smooth and slightly tacky, about 1 minute. If the dough is very sticky, add 1 to 2 tablespoons flour and continue mixing for 1 minute. Lightly oil a medium bowl; transfer the dough to the bowl and cover with plastic wrap. Let the dough rise in a warm, draft-free place until doubled in size, about 1 hour.

3. Fold the dough over itself; rotate the bowl a quarter turn and fold again. Rotate the bowl again and fold once more. Cover with plastic wrap and let rise for 30 minutes. Repeat the folding, replace the plastic wrap, and let the dough rise until doubled in size, about 30 minutes. Spray two 9-inch round cake pans with vegetable oil spray and set aside.

4. Transfer the dough to a floured work surface and sprinkle the top with more flour. Using a bench scraper, cut the dough in half and gently stretch each half into a 16-inch log. Divide each log into quarters, then each quarter into two pieces (you should have 16 pieces total), and dust the top of each piece with more flour. With floured hands, gently pick up each piece and roll it in your palms to coat with flour, shaking off the excess, and place in the prepared cake pan. Arrange eight dough pieces in each cake pan, placing one piece in the middle and the others around it, with the long side of each piece running from the center of the pan to the edge and making sure the cut side faces up. Loosely cover the cake pans with plastic wrap and let the rolls rise until doubled in size, about 30 minutes (the dough is ready when it springs back slowly when pressed lightly with a knuckle). Thirty minutes before baking, adjust an oven rack to the middle position and heat the oven to 500 degrees.

**5.** Remove the plastic wrap from the cake pans, spray the rolls lightly with water, and place in the oven. Bake until the tops of the rolls are brown, 10 minutes, then remove them from the oven. Reduce the oven temperature to 400 degrees; using kitchen towels or oven mitts, invert the rolls from both cake pans onto a rimmed baking sheet. When the rolls are cool enough to handle, turn them right side up, pull apart, and space evenly on the baking sheet. Continue to bake until the rolls develop a deep golden brown crust and sound hollow when tapped on the bottom, 10 to 15 minutes, rotating the baking sheet halfway through baking. Transfer the rolls to a wire rack and cool to room temperature, about 1 hour.

## Oatmeal Dinner Rolls

**MAKES** 12 rolls

**WHY THIS RECIPE WORKS** For dinner rolls that boast nutty whole-grain flavor and are also fluffy and moist, we started by soaking old-fashioned rolled oats in hot water. During a short rest the oats absorbed most of the water, effectively locking it away. We stirred in whole-wheat flour to boost the nutty flavor profile, white bread flour for structure, and molasses for its complexity and sweetness. And we added even more water, making a dough with a high proportion of water to flour that could be rolled into balls without sticking to our hands because the oats' starch matrix held on to the extra moisture. Nestling the dough balls close together ensured that they supported each other in upward rather than outward expansion. Along with the transformation of water to steam during the bake, this yielded dinner rolls that contained the best of both worlds: light, soft, plush texture along with whole-grain complexity of flavor. The added liquid also extended the rolls' shelf life, so they could be enjoyed for a few days before going stale, or even frozen for later use. For an accurate measurement of boiling water, bring a kettle of water to a boil and then measure out the desired amount. We strongly recommend measuring the flour by weight. Avoid blackstrap molasses here, as it's too bitter. If you prefer, you can portion the rolls by weight in step 2 (2¼ ounces of dough per roll). To make 24 rolls, double this recipe and bake the rolls in two 9-inch round cake pans. Rolls can be wrapped in a double layer of plastic wrap and stored at room temperature for 1 day. To freeze, wrap rolls in aluminum foil and freeze for up to 1 month; reheat thawed rolls in a 350-degree oven for 8 minutes.

- ¾ cup (2¼ ounces) old-fashioned rolled oats, plus 4 teaspoons for sprinkling
- ⅔ cup boiling water, plus ½ cup cold water
- 2 tablespoons unsalted butter, cut into 4 pieces
- 1½ cups (8¼ ounces) bread flour
- ¾ cup (4⅛ ounces) whole-wheat flour
- ¼ cup molasses
- 1½ teaspoons instant or rapid-rise yeast
- 1 teaspoon table salt
- 1 large egg, beaten with 1 teaspoon water and pinch table salt

**1.** Stir ¾ cup oats, boiling water, and butter together in bowl of stand mixer and let sit until butter is melted and most of water has been absorbed, about 10 minutes. Add bread flour, whole-wheat flour, cold water, molasses, yeast, and salt. Fit mixer with dough hook and mix on low speed until flour is moistened, about 1 minute (dough may look dry). Increase speed to medium-low and mix until dough clears sides of bowl (it will still stick to bottom), about 8 minutes, scraping down dough hook halfway through mixing (dough will be sticky). Transfer dough to counter, shape into ball, and transfer to lightly greased bowl. Cover with plastic wrap and let rise until doubled in volume, 1 to 1¼ hours.

**2.** Grease 9-inch round cake pan and set aside. Transfer dough to lightly floured counter, reserving plastic. Pat dough gently into 8-inch square of even thickness. Using bench scraper or chef's knife, cut dough into 12 pieces (3 rows by 4 rows). Working with 1 piece of dough at a time, form dough pieces into smooth, taut balls. (To round, set piece of dough on unfloured counter. Loosely cup your lightly floured hand around dough and, without applying pressure to dough, move your hand in small circular motions. Tackiness of dough against counter and circular motion should work dough into smooth ball.) Arrange seam side down in prepared pan, placing 9 dough balls around edge of pan and remaining 3 dough balls in center. Cover with reserved plastic and let rise until rolls are doubled in size and no gaps are visible between them, 45 minutes to 1 hour.

**3.** When rolls are nearly doubled in size, adjust oven rack to lower-middle position and heat oven to 375 degrees. Brush rolls with egg wash and sprinkle with remaining 4 teaspoons oats. Bake until rolls are deep brown and register at least 195 degrees at center, 25 to 30 minutes. Let rolls cool in pan on wire rack for 3 minutes; invert rolls onto rack, then reinvert. Let rolls cool for at least 20 minutes before serving.

## Potato Burger Buns

**MAKES** 9 rolls

**WHY THIS RECIPE WORKS** Although mashed potatoes are hefty, when used in these buns they are the secret to a light, tender, moist texture. That's because the starches in potatoes dilute the gluten-forming proteins in flour, which weakens the structural network of the dough and makes it softer, moister, and more tender. For the lightest potato rolls, we combined ½ pound of mashed russet potatoes with high-protein bread flour. This created a potato roll dough with a stable structure, producing rolls that were not only perfectly risen but also light and airy. Don't salt the cooking water for the potatoes. A pound of russet potatoes should yield just over 1 very firmly packed cup (½ pound) of mash. To ensure the optimum rise, your dough should be warm; if your potatoes or potato water are too hot to touch, let cool before proceeding with the recipe. This dough looks very dry when mixing begins but will soften as mixing progresses. If you prefer, you may portion the rolls by weight in step 5 (2.75 ounces of dough per roll).

- 1 pound russet potatoes, peeled and cut into 1-inch pieces
- 2 tablespoons unsalted butter, cut into 4 pieces
- 2¼ cups (12⅓ ounces) bread flour
- 1 tablespoon sugar
- 2 teaspoons instant or rapid-rise yeast
- 1 teaspoon table salt
- 2 large eggs, 1 lightly beaten with 1 teaspoon water and pinch table salt
- 1 tablespoon sesame seeds (optional)

**1.** Place potatoes in medium saucepan and add water to just cover. Bring to boil over high heat; reduce heat to medium-low and simmer until potatoes are cooked through, 8 to 10 minutes.

**2.** Transfer 5 tablespoons cooking water to bowl to cool; drain potatoes. Return potatoes to saucepan and place over low heat. Cook, shaking pot occasionally, until any surface moisture has evaporated, about 1 minute. Remove from heat. Process potatoes through ricer or food mill or mash well with potato masher. Measure 1 very firmly packed cup potatoes and transfer to bowl. Reserve any remaining potatoes for another use. Stir in butter until melted.

**3.** Combine flour, sugar, yeast, and salt in bowl of stand mixer. Add warm potato mixture to flour mixture and mix with hands until combined (some large lumps are OK). Add 1 egg and reserved potato water; mix with dough hook on low speed until dough is soft and slightly sticky, 8 to 10 minutes.

**4.** Shape dough into ball and place in lightly greased container. Cover tightly with plastic wrap and allow to rise at room temperature until almost doubled in volume, 30 to 40 minutes.

**5.** Turn out dough onto counter, dusting with flour only if dough is too sticky to handle comfortably. Pat gently into 8-inch square of even thickness. Using bench scraper or chef's knife, cut dough into 9 pieces (3 rows by 3 rows). Separate pieces and cover loosely with plastic.

**6.** Working with 1 piece of dough at a time and keeping remaining pieces covered, form dough pieces into smooth, taut rounds. (To round, set piece of dough on unfloured work surface. Loosely cup hand around dough and, without applying pressure to dough, move hand in small circular motions. Tackiness of dough against work surface and circular motion should work dough into smooth, even ball, but if dough sticks to hands, lightly dust fingers with flour.) Cover rounds with plastic and allow to rest for 15 minutes.

**7.** Line 2 rimmed baking sheets with parchment paper. On lightly floured surface, firmly press each dough round into 3½-inch disk of even thickness, expelling large pockets of air. Arrange on prepared baking sheets. Cover loosely with plastic and let rise at room temperature until almost doubled in size, 30 to 40 minutes. While rolls rise, adjust oven racks to middle and upper-middle positions and heat oven to 425 degrees.

**8.** Brush rolls gently with egg wash and sprinkle with sesame seeds, if using. Bake rolls until deep golden brown, 15 to 18 minutes, rotating and switching baking sheets halfway through baking. Transfer baking sheets to wire racks and let cool for 5 minutes. Transfer rolls from baking sheets to wire racks. Serve warm or at room temperature.

### Potato Dinner Rolls

**MAKES** 12 rolls

Line rimmed baking sheet with parchment paper. In step 5, divide dough square into 12 pieces (3 rows by 4 rows). Shape pieces into smooth, taut rounds as directed in step 6. Transfer rounds to prepared baking sheet and let rise at room temperature until almost doubled in size, 30 to 40 minutes. Bake on upper-middle rack until rolls are deep golden brown, 12 to 14 minutes, rotating baking sheet halfway through baking.

## Almost No-Knead Bread

**MAKES** 1 large round loaf

**WHY THIS RECIPE WORKS** This revolutionary bread recipe simplifies the process, with only 15 seconds of kneading time, all while keeping maximum flavor. To produce a loaf with a consistent shape, we strengthened the dough by lowering the hydration in addition to the quick kneading time. To give the bread more flavor than the standard no-knead recipe, we added acidic tang with vinegar, and a shot of yeasty flavor with mild-flavored lager. When we started the baking process in a covered pot, the lid trapped released steam, creating a springy loaf. By finishing the baking with the loaf uncovered, we created a beautifully browned crust. This bread is best eaten the day it is baked, but it can be wrapped in aluminum foil and stored for up to 2 days.

- 3 cups (15 ounces) all-purpose flour
- 1½ teaspoons table salt
- ¼ teaspoon instant or rapid-rise yeast
- ¾ cup plus 2 tablespoons water, room temperature
- 6 tablespoons mild-flavored lager
- 1 tablespoon distilled white vinegar
- Vegetable oil spray

**1.** Whisk flour, salt, and yeast together in large bowl. Add water, lager, and vinegar. Using rubber spatula, fold mixture, scraping up dry flour from bottom of bowl, until shaggy ball forms. Cover bowl with plastic wrap and let dough sit at room temperature for at least 8 hours or up to 18 hours.

**2.** Lay 18 by 12-inch sheet of parchment paper on counter and coat lightly with vegetable oil spray. Transfer dough to lightly floured counter and knead by hand to form smooth, round ball, 10 to 15 times. Shape dough into ball by pulling edges into middle. Transfer dough, seam side down, to center of parchment and spray surface of dough with oil spray. Pick up dough by lifting parchment overhang and lower into heavy-bottomed Dutch oven (let any excess parchment hang over pot edge). Cover loosely with plastic and let rise at room temperature until dough has doubled in size and does not readily spring back when poked with finger, about 2 hours.

**3.** Adjust oven rack to middle position. Remove plastic from pot. Lightly flour top of dough and, using razor blade or sharp knife, make one 6-inch-long, ½-inch-deep slit along top of dough. Cover pot and place in oven. Heat oven to 425 degrees. Bake bread for 30 minutes.

**4.** Remove lid and continue to bake until loaf is deep brown and registers 210 degrees, 20 to 30 minutes. Carefully remove bread from pot; transfer to wire rack and let cool completely, about 2 hours.

### MAKING ALMOST NO-KNEAD BREAD

**1.** Mix dough by stirring wet ingredients into dry ingredients with rubber spatula, then leave dough to rest for 8 to 18 hours.

**2.** Turn dough out onto lightly floured surface and knead 10 to 15 times. After kneading dough, shape into ball by pulling edges into middle.

**3.** Transfer loaf, seam side down, to large sheet of greased parchment and, using paper, transfer to Dutch oven. Cover loosely with plastic and let rise until doubled in size, 1½ to 2 hours.

**4.** Sprinkle dough with flour and cut ½-inch-deep X into loaf. Cover pot, place in oven, and turn oven to 425 degrees. Bake for 30 minutes, then remove lid and bake until loaf registers 205 to 210 degrees.

## Almost No-Knead Sourdough Bread

**MAKES 1 LARGE ROUND LOAF**

**WHY THIS RECIPE WORKS** Making one's own sourdough culture (starter) is a commitment, but it's rewarding. For a simple sourdough starter, we began by mixing all-purpose flour with whole-wheat flour, which provided extra nutrition for the developing bacteria and yeasts. We then added enough water to form a wet dough and let it sit at room temperature. After 3 days or so, when it started to show signs of life in the form of gas bubbles and a pungent aroma, we began a routine of daily feedings, mixing some of the culture with fresh flour and water. After 10 to 14 days, it smelled pleasantly yeasty and doubled in volume 8 to 12 hours after refreshing, a sign that it was mature enough to use. For a simple recipe in which to use the culture, we developed a sourdough version of our Almost No-Knead Bread, which rises overnight and is baked in a Dutch oven. To maintain the culture between uses, refresh the food supply once a week by letting the culture sit for 5 hours at room temperature after feeding it and then moving it to the refrigerator. We prefer King Arthur all-purpose flour here; if you can't find it, you can substitute bread flour. For the best results, weigh your ingredients. The dough can rise at room temperature in step 3 (instead of in the oven), but it will take 3 to 4 hours. Do not wait until the oven has preheated in step 4 to start timing 30 minutes or the bread will burn.

- 3⅔ cups (18⅓ ounces) King Arthur all-purpose flour
- 1¾ teaspoons table salt
- 1½ cups plus 4 teaspoons (12⅔ ounces) water, room temperature
- ⅓ cup (3 ounces) mature sourdough starter

**1.** Whisk flour and salt together in medium bowl. Whisk room-temperature water and starter in large bowl until smooth. Add flour mixture to water mixture and stir using wooden spoon, scraping up dry flour from bottom of bowl, until dough comes together, and then knead by hand in bowl until shaggy ball forms and no dry flour remains. Cover bowl with plastic wrap and let sit at room temperature for at least 12 hours or up to 18 hours.

2. Lay 12 by 12-inch sheet of parchment paper on counter and spray generously with vegetable oil spray. Transfer dough to lightly floured counter and knead 10 to 15 times. Shape dough into ball by pulling edges into middle. Transfer dough, seam side down, to center of parchment. Pick up dough by lifting parchment edges and lower into heavy-bottomed Dutch oven. Cover with plastic wrap.

3. Adjust oven rack to middle position and place loaf pan or cake pan in bottom of oven. Place Dutch oven on middle rack and pour 3 cups of boiling water into pan below. Close oven door and let dough rise until doubled in size and does not readily spring back when poked with your floured finger, 2 to 3 hours.

4. Remove Dutch oven and water pan from oven; discard plastic from Dutch oven. Lightly flour top of dough and, using razor blade or sharp knife, make one 7-inch-long, ½-inch-deep slit along top of dough. Cover pot and place on middle rack in oven. Heat oven to 425 degrees. Bake bread for 30 minutes (starting timing as soon as you turn on oven).

5. Remove lid and continue to bake until bread is deep brown and registers 210 degrees, 20 to 30 minutes longer. Carefully remove bread from pot; transfer to wire rack and let cool completely before serving.

## Sourdough Starter

**MAKES** About 2 cups

It's okay to occasionally miss a daily feeding in step 2, but don't let it go for more than 48 hours. For the best results, weigh your ingredients and use organic flour and bottled or filtered water to create the starter. Once the starter is mature, all-purpose flour should be used to maintain it. Placing the starter in a glass bowl will allow for easier observation of activity beneath the surface. Discarding some starter before each feeding gets rid of waste and keeps the amount of starter manageable.

- 4½ cups (24¾ ounces) whole-wheat flour
- 5 cups (25 ounces) all-purpose flour, plus extra for maintaining starter
- Water, room temperature

1. Combine whole-wheat flour and all-purpose flour in large container. Using wooden spoon, mix 1 cup (5 ounces) flour mixture and ⅔ cup (5⅓ ounces) room-temperature water in glass bowl until no dry flour remains (reserve remaining flour mixture). Cover with plastic wrap and let sit at room temperature until bubbly and fragrant, 48 to 72 hours.

2. **FEED STARTER:** Measure out ¼ cup (2 ounces) starter and transfer to clean bowl or jar; discard remaining starter. Stir ½ cup (2½ ounces) flour mixture and ¼ cup (2 ounces) water into starter until no dry flour remains. Cover with plastic wrap and let sit at room temperature for 24 hours.

3. Repeat step 2 every 24 hours until starter is pleasantly aromatic and doubles in size 8 to 12 hours after being refreshed, about 10 to 14 days. At this point starter is mature and ready to be baked with, or it can be moved to storage. (If baking, use starter once it has doubled in size during 8- to 12-hour window. Use starter within 1 hour after it starts to deflate once reaching its peak.)

4A. **TO STORE AND MAINTAIN MATURE STARTER:** Measure out ¼ cup (2 ounces) starter and transfer to clean bowl; discard remaining starter. Stir ½ cup (2½ ounces) all-purpose flour and ¼ cup (2 ounces) room-temperature water into starter until no dry flour remains. Transfer to clean container that can be loosely covered (plastic container or mason jar with its lid inverted) and let sit at room temperature for 5 hours. Cover and transfer to refrigerator. If not baking regularly, repeat process weekly.

4B. **TO PREPARE FOR BAKING:** Eighteen to 24 hours before baking, measure out ½ cup (4 ounces) starter and transfer to clean bowl; discard remaining starter. Stir 1 cup (5 ounces) all-purpose flour and ½ cup (4 ounces) room-temperature water into starter until no dry flour remains. Cover and let sit at room temperature for 5 hours. Measure out amount of starter called for in bread recipe and transfer to second bowl. Cover and transfer to refrigerator for at least 12 hours or up to 18 hours. Remaining starter should be refrigerated and maintained as directed.

## Rustic Country Bread

**MAKES** 1 large round loaf

**WHY THIS RECIPE WORKS** The secret to a crusty, rough-textured country loaf with big-league chew and a great crust is a very wet dough. And authentic rustic country bread should be made with little more than flour, water, yeast, and salt. We decided to focus our tests around using a sponge starter—a mixture of flour, water, and yeast, left to ferment and then combined with additional flour, water, and other ingredients. A sponge starter gave our bread a complex flavor that yeast alone could not provide. We soon learned that bread with a high water content produces a chewier texture. So we ended up working with a wet dough, to which we could add more flour if necessary. This wet dough was tricky to work with but resulted in a bread with a texture that was appealingly rough, chewy, and substantial. For a finishing touch, we added both whole-wheat and rye flours to the ingredients, which enhanced the bread's flavor and texture. To ensure doneness, make sure the bread's internal temperature registers 210 degrees and the crust is very dark brown, almost black. Bread can be wrapped in a double layer of plastic wrap and stored at room temperature for up to 3 days. To freeze, wrap with an additional layer of aluminum foil, and freeze for up to 1 month. To recrisp, place the unwrapped, thawed bread in a 450-degree oven for 10 minutes.

**SPONGE**

- 1 cup water, at room temperature
- ½ teaspoon instant or rapid-rise yeast
- 1 cup (5½ ounces) bread flour
- 1 cup (5½ ounces) whole-wheat flour

**DOUGH**

- 3–3½ cups (16½ to 19¼ ounces) bread flour, plus extra for the dough and work surface
- ½ cup (2¾ ounces) rye flour
- 1⅓ cups water, at room temperature
- 2 tablespoons honey
- 2 teaspoons table salt

**1. FOR THE SPONGE:** Combine the water and yeast in a medium bowl and stir until the yeast is dissolved. Add the flours and stir with a rubber spatula to create a stiff, wet dough. Cover the bowl with plastic wrap and let sit at room temperature for at least 5 hours or up to 24 hours. (The sponge can be refrigerated for up to 24 hours; return to room temperature before continuing with the recipe.)

**2. FOR THE DOUGH:** Using a rubber spatula, combine 3 cups of the bread flour, the rye flour, water, honey, and sponge in the bowl of a stand mixer. Knead the dough on low speed with the dough hook until smooth, about 15 minutes, adding the salt during the final 3 minutes. If more flour is needed, add the remaining ½ cup bread flour, 1 tablespoon at a time, until the dough clears the sides of the bowl but sticks to the bottom. Lightly oil a large bowl; transfer the dough to the bowl and cover with plastic wrap. Let the dough rise until tripled in size, about 2 hours.

**3.** Transfer the dough to a lightly floured work surface. Flour the top of the dough. With floured hands, shape the dough into a round by pulling the edges into the middle and gathering it loosely together. Transfer the dough, seam side down, to an inverted baking sheet lined with parchment paper. Cover with plastic wrap and let rise until almost doubled in size, about 45 minutes. (The dough should barely spring back when poked with a knuckle.)

**4.** Meanwhile, adjust an oven rack to the lower-middle position, place a baking stone on the rack, and heat the oven to 450 degrees at least 30 minutes before baking.

**5.** Use a razor blade or sharp knife to cut three slashes on the top of the dough. With scissors, trim the excess parchment around the dough. Lightly spray the dough with water.

**6.** Carefully slide the parchment with the dough onto the baking stone using a jerking motion. Bake until the crust is very dark brown and the center registers 210 degrees on an instant-read thermometer, 35 to 40 minutes, rotating the bread halfway through baking. Turn the oven off, open the oven door, and let the bread remain in the oven 10 minutes longer. Remove from the oven, transfer to a wire rack, and cool to room temperature, about 2 hours.

## Pane Francese

**MAKES** 2 loaves

**WHY THIS RECIPE WORKS** The Italian cousin to the baguette, pane francese is a long loaf with a moist and open crumb. It has a crisp yet forgiving exterior, and it's slightly fatter in shape than a baguette. A sponge gave the loaf structure, depth of favor, and a hint of tang. After preparing this mixture (made with water, yeast, and 20 percent of the bread's total weight of flour), we let it sit on the counter for 6 to 24 hours. During this period the yeast consumed sugars in the flour. Extending the overall fermentation time for the dough provides great flavor. A repeated series of gentle folds helped develop the gluten structure even further and also incorporated air for an open crumb. We proofed the loaf on a couche—a heavy linen cloth—to help the wet dough keep its shape. We slash the top of rustic loaves like pane francese with a lame, a curved-blade tool that gives our scores a dramatic crispy raised edge. Finally, we preheated pans filled with lava rocks and added water to them to create a steamy oven, which encouraged a crisp crust. Lava rocks are available at many hardware stores for use in gas grills.

**SPONGE**

- ⅔ cup (3⅔ ounces) bread flour
- ½ cup (4 ounces) water, room temperature
- ⅛ teaspoon instant or rapid-rise yeast

**DOUGH**

- 2⅔–3 cups (14⅔ to 6½ ounces) bread flour
- 1½ teaspoons instant or rapid-rise yeast
- 1¼ cups (10 ounces) water, room temperature
- 1 tablespoon extra-virgin olive oil
- 2¼ teaspoons table salt

**1. FOR THE SPONGE:** Stir all ingredients in 4-cup liquid measuring cup with wooden spoon until well combined. Cover tightly with plastic wrap and let sit at room temperature until sponge has risen and begins to collapse, about 6 hours (sponge can sit at room temperature for up to 24 hours).

**2. FOR THE DOUGH:** Whisk 2⅔ cups flour and yeast together in bowl of stand mixer. Stir water into sponge with wooden spoon until well combined. Using dough hook on low speed, slowly add sponge mixture to flour mixture and mix until cohesive dough starts to form and no dry flour remains, about 2 minutes, scraping down bowl as needed. Cover bowl tightly with plastic and let dough rest for 20 minutes.

**3.** Add oil and salt to dough and knead on medium-low speed until dough is smooth and elastic and clears sides of bowl, about 10 minutes. If more flour is needed, add remaining ⅓ cup flour, 1 tablespoon at a time, until dough clears sides of bowl but sticks to bottom. Transfer dough to lightly greased large bowl or container, cover tightly with plastic, and let rise for 30 minutes.

**4.** Using greased bowl scraper (or your fingertips), fold dough over itself by gently lifting and folding edge of dough toward middle. Turn bowl 45 degrees and fold dough again; repeat turning bowl and folding dough 6 more times (total of 8 folds). Cover tightly with plastic and let rise for 30 minutes. Repeat folding, then cover bowl tightly with plastic and let dough rise until nearly doubled in size, 1 to 1½ hours.

**5.** Mist underside of couche with water, drape over inverted rimmed baking sheet, and dust evenly with flour. Transfer dough to lightly floured counter. Using lightly floured hands press and stretch dough into 12 by 6-inch rectangle, deflating any gas pockets larger than 1 inch, and divide in half crosswise. Cover loosely with greased plastic.

**6.** Gently press and stretch 1 piece of dough (keep remaining piece covered) into 7-inch square. Fold top corners of dough diagonally into center of square and press gently to seal. Stretch and fold upper third of dough toward center and press seam gently to seal.

**7.** Stretch and fold dough in half toward you to form rough loaf with tapered ends and pinch seam closed. Roll loaf seam side down. Starting at center of loaf and working toward ends, gently and evenly roll and stretch dough until it measures 15 inches long by 2½ inches wide. Moving your hands in opposite directions, use back and forth motion to roll ends of loaf under your palms to form sharp points.

**8.** Gently slide your hands underneath each end of loaf and transfer seam side up to prepared couche. On either side of loaf, pinch couche into pleat, then cover loosely with large plastic garbage bag. Repeat steps 6 through 7 with remaining piece of dough and place on opposite side of 1 pleat. Fold edges of couche over loaves to cover completely, then carefully place sheet inside garbage bag. Tie, or fold under, open end of bag to fully enclose. Let rise until loaves increase in size by about half and dough springs back minimally when poked gently with your knuckle, 30 minutes to 1 hour (remove loaf from bag to test).

**9.** One hour before baking, adjust oven racks to lower-middle and lowest positions. Place baking stone on upper rack, place 2 disposable aluminum pie plates filled with 1 quart lava rocks each on lower rack, and heat oven to 450 degrees. Line pizza peel with 16 by 12-inch piece of parchment paper, with long edge perpendicular to handle. Bring 1 cup water to boil.

**10.** Remove sheet with loaves from bag. Unfold couche, pulling from ends to remove pleats. Dust top of loaves with flour. (If any seams have reopened, pinch closed before dusting with flour.) Gently pushing with side of flipping board, roll 1 loaf over, away from other loaf, so it is seam side down. Using your hand, hold long edge of flipping board between loaf and couche at 45-degree angle, then lift couche with your other hand and flip loaf seam side up onto board. Invert loaf seam side down onto prepared pizza peel, about 2 inches from long edge of parchment, then use flipping board to straighten loaf and reshape as needed. Repeat with second loaf, leaving at least 3 inches between loaves.

**11.** Carefully pour ½ cup boiling water into 1 disposable pie plate of preheated rocks and close oven door for 1 minute to create steam. Meanwhile, holding lame concave side up at 30-degree angle to loaf, make one ½-inch deep slash with swift, fluid motion lengthwise along top of loaf, starting and stopping about ½ inch from ends. Repeat with second loaf.

**12.** Working quickly, slide parchment with loaves onto baking stone and pour remaining ½ cup boiling water into second disposable pie plate of preheated rocks. Bake until crust is golden brown and loaves register 205 to 210 degrees, 20 to 25 minutes, rotating loaves halfway through baking. Transfer loaves to wire rack, discard parchment, and let cool completely, about 3 hours, before serving.

## SHAPING CLASSIC ITALIAN BREAD

**1.** Gently press and stretch dough into 7-inch square. Fold top corners of dough diagonally into center of square; press gently to seal.

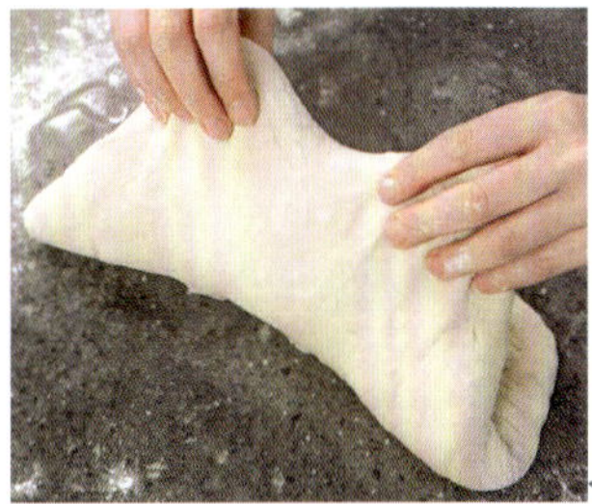

**2.** Stretch and fold upper third of dough toward center; press seam gently to seal.

**3.** Stretch and fold dough in half toward you to form rough loaf with tapered ends. Pinch seam closed, then roll loaf seam side down.

**4.** Roll and stretch loaf until it measures 15 inches long by 2½ inches wide. Moving your hands in opposite directions, use back and forth motion to roll ends of loaf under your palms to form sharp points.

## Ciabatta

**MAKES** 2 loaves

**WHY THIS RECIPE WORKS** This Italian loaf boasts a crisp, flavorful crust and a chewy, open crumb. For a ciabatta recipe with airy texture and perfect lift, we chose all-purpose flour. A sponge fermented for 12 hours gave the bread its tangy flavor. A combination of kneading and turning lent the dough just the right amount of gluten for the medium-size bubbles that are the hallmark of this bread. The bread can be wrapped in a double layer of plastic wrap and stored at room temperature for up to 3 days; wrapped with an additional layer of aluminum foil, it can be frozen for 1 month. To serve, place the unwrapped, thawed bread in a 450-degree oven for 6 to 8 minutes.

**SPONGE**

- 1 cup (5 ounces) unbleached all-purpose flour
- ⅛ teaspoon instant or rapid-rise yeast
- ½ cup water, at room temperature

**DOUGH**

- 2 cups (10 ounces) unbleached all-purpose flour, plus extra for the dough and work surface
- 1½ teaspoons table salt
- ½ teaspoon instant or rapid-rise yeast
- ¾ cup water, at room temperature
- ¼ cup milk, at room temperature

**1. FOR THE SPONGE:** Combine the flour, yeast, and water in a medium bowl and stir with a wooden spoon until a uniform mass forms, about 1 minute. Cover the bowl tightly with plastic wrap and let stand at room temperature (about 70 degrees) for at least 8 hours or up to 24 hours.

**2. FOR THE DOUGH:** Place the sponge and dough ingredients in the bowl of a stand mixer fitted with the paddle attachment. Mix on low speed until roughly combined and a shaggy dough forms, about 1 minute; scrape down the sides of the bowl as necessary. Increase the speed to medium-low and continue mixing until the dough becomes a uniform mass that collects on the paddle and pulls away from the sides of the bowl, 4 to 6 minutes. Change to the dough hook and knead the bread on medium speed until smooth and shiny (the dough will be very sticky), about 10 minutes. (If the dough creeps up on the attachment, stop the mixer and scrape it down.) Transfer the dough to a large bowl and cover tightly with plastic wrap. Let the dough rise at room temperature until doubled in size, about 1 hour. (The dough should barely spring back when poked with a knuckle.)

**3.** Spray a rubber spatula or bowl scraper with vegetable oil spray; fold the partially risen dough over itself by gently lifting and folding the edge of the dough toward the middle. Turn the bowl 90 degrees; fold again. Turn the bowl and fold the dough six more times (for a total of eight turns). Cover with plastic wrap and let rise for 30 minutes. Repeat folding, replace the plastic wrap, and let rise until doubled in size, about 30 minutes longer. Meanwhile, adjust an oven rack to the lower-middle position, place a baking stone on the rack, and heat the oven to 450 degrees at least 30 minutes before baking.

**4.** Cut two 12 by 6-inch pieces of parchment paper and liberally dust with flour. Transfer the dough to a floured work surface, being careful not to deflate it completely. Liberally flour the top of the dough and divide it in half with a bench scraper. Turn one piece of dough cut side up and dust with flour. With well-floured hands, press the dough into a rough 12 by 6-inch shape. Fold the shorter sides of the dough toward the center, overlapping them like a business letter to form a 7 by 4-inch loaf. Repeat with the second dough piece. Gently transfer each loaf, seam side down, to the parchment sheets, dust with flour, and cover with plastic wrap. Let the loaves sit at room temperature for 30 minutes (the surface of the loaves will develop small bubbles).

**5.** Slide the parchment with the loaves onto an inverted rimmed baking sheet or pizza peel. Using floured fingertips, evenly poke the entire surface of each loaf to form a 10 by 6-inch rectangle; spray the loaves lightly with water. Carefully slide the parchment with the loaves onto the baking stone

### MAKING CIABATTA

**1.** Using greased spatula or bowl scraper, fold dough over itself by gently lifting and folding edge of dough toward middle. Turn bowl 45 degrees and fold dough again; repeat 6 more times (total of 8 folds).

**2.** After rising, divide dough in half on well-floured counter. Press and stretch each half into a 12 by 6-inch rectangle, being careful not to deflate dough completely.

**3.** Fold top and bottom thirds of dough over middle to form 7 by 4-inch loaf. Pinch seams closed. Transfer loaf seam side down to prepared parchment; cover with greased plastic. Repeat with remaining dough.

**4.** Transfer parchment with loaves to pizza peel. Using your floured fingertips, evenly poke entire surface of each loaf to form 10 by 6-inch rectangle.

using a jerking motion. Bake, spraying the loaves with water twice more during the first 5 minutes of baking time, until the crust is a deep golden brown and the center of the loaves registers 210 degrees, 22 to 27 minutes. Transfer to a wire rack, discard the parchment, and cool the loaves to room temperature, about 1 hour, before slicing and serving.

## Authentic Baguettes at Home

**MAKES** four 15-inch-long baguettes

**WHY THIS RECIPE WORKS** A great baguette is hard to come by, at least outside of France. The ideal: a moist, wheaty interior punctuated with irregular holes and a deeply browned crust so crisp it shatters into millions of tiny shards. For the ideal structure and open crumb, we opted for a hybrid mixing approach: We mixed the dough in a stand mixer, then folded the dough several times during the initial proofing. As for fermentation, the best flavor was a slow rise in the fridge. At least 24 hours, or up to 72, produced the most flavorful loaves. As a bonus, this dough could be portioned out to make baguettes as desired within that window. Some sifted wheat flour provided extra depth of flavor without any bitterness. The key to shaping was a three-stage process, starting with pressing the dough into a square and then rolling it like a log. Leaving the ends of the loaves unsealed until the very end allowed air bubbles to escape. For slashes with the right wide almond shape, we found that we needed to keep the blade at a shallow angle while making the cuts. Using a lame, which has a slightly curved blade, made this job easy and also created a ridge, or "ear" along the edge of the slash that baked up deliciously crisp. For a shatteringly crisp crust, we covered the bread with a disposable pan while it baked to allow it to begin cooking in its own steam, which promoted good color and flavor as well as crispiness. We recommend using a couche, lame, flipping board, and diastatic malt powder for this recipe (see page 772). You will also need a baking stone and a baking peel (see pages 1021–1022 for our recommended brands). If you can't find King Arthur all-purpose flour, substitute bread flour, not another all-purpose flour. For the best results, weigh your ingredients. This recipe makes enough dough for four loaves, which can be baked anytime during the 24- to 72-hour window after placing the dough in the fridge.

- ¼ cup (1⅓ ounces) whole-wheat flour
- 3 cups (15 ounces) King Arthur all-purpose flour
- 1 teaspoon instant or rapid-rise yeast
- 1 teaspoon diastatic malt powder (optional)
- 1½ teaspoons table salt
- 1½ cups (12 ounces) water
- 2 (16 by 12-inch) disposable aluminum roasting pans

**1.** Sift whole-wheat flour through fine-mesh strainer into bowl of stand mixer; discard bran remaining in strainer. Add all-purpose flour; yeast; malt, if using; and salt to mixer bowl. Fit stand mixer with dough hook, add water, and knead on low speed until cohesive dough forms and no dry flour remains, 5 to 7 minutes. Transfer dough to lightly oiled large bowl, cover with plastic wrap, and let rest at room temperature for 30 minutes.

**2.** Holding edge of dough with your fingertips, fold dough over itself by gently lifting and folding edge of dough toward center. Turn bowl 45 degrees; fold again. Turn bowl and fold dough 6 more times (total of 8 folds). Cover with plastic and let rise for 30 minutes. Repeat folding and rising every 30 minutes, 3 more times. After fourth set of folds, cover bowl tightly with plastic and refrigerate for at least 24 hours or up to 72 hours.

**3.** Transfer dough to lightly floured counter, pat into 8-inch square (do not deflate), and divide in half. Return 1 piece of dough to container, wrap tightly with plastic, and refrigerate (dough can be shaped and baked anytime within 72-hour window). Divide remaining dough in half crosswise, transfer to lightly floured rimmed baking sheet, and cover loosely with plastic. Let rest for 45 minutes.

**4.** On lightly floured counter, roll each piece into loose 3- to 4-inch-long cylinder; return to floured baking sheet and cover with plastic. Let rest at room temperature for 30 minutes.

**5.** Lightly mist underside of couche with water, drape over inverted baking sheet and dust with flour. Gently press 1 piece of dough into 6 by 4-inch rectangle on lightly floured counter, with long edge facing you. Fold upper quarter of dough toward center and press gently to seal. Rotate dough 180 degrees and repeat folding step to form 8 by 2-inch rectangle.

**6.** Fold dough in half toward you, using thumb of your other hand to create crease along center of dough, sealing with heel of your hand as you work your way along the loaf. Without pressing down on loaf, use heel of your hand to reinforce seal (do not seal ends of loaf).

**7.** Cup your hand over center of dough and roll dough back and forth gently to tighten (it should form dog-bone shape).

**8.** Starting at center of dough and working toward ends, gently and evenly roll and stretch dough until it measures 15 inches long by 1¼ inches wide. Moving your hands in opposite directions, use back and forth motion to roll ends of loaf under your palms to form sharp points.

**9.** Transfer dough to floured couche, seam side up. Gather edges of couche into 2 pleats on either side of loaf, then cover loosely with large plastic garbage bag.

**10.** Repeat steps 4 through 9 with second piece of dough and place on opposite side of pleat. Fold edges of couche over loaves to cover completely, then carefully place sheet inside bag, and tie or fold under to enclose.

**11.** Let stand until loaves have nearly doubled in size and dough springs back minimally when poked gently with your fingertip, 45 to 60 minutes. While bread rises, adjust oven rack to middle position, place baking stone on rack, and heat oven to 500 degrees.

**12.** Line pizza peel with 16 by 12-inch piece parchment paper with long edge perpendicular to handle. Unfold couche, pulling from ends to remove pleats. Gently pushing with side of flipping board, roll 1 loaf over, away from other loaf, so it is seam side down. Using your hand, hold long edge of flipping board between loaf and couche at 45-degree angle, then lift couche with your other hand and flip loaf seam side up onto board.

**13.** Invert loaf onto parchment-lined peel, seam side down, about 2 inches from long edge of parchment, then use flipping board to straighten loaf. Repeat with remaining loaf, leaving at least 3 inches between loaves.

**14.** Holding lame concave side up at 30-degree angle to loaf, make series of three 4-inch-long, ½-inch-deep slashes along length of loaf, using swift, fluid motion, overlapping each slash slightly. Repeat with second loaf.

**15.** Transfer loaves, on parchment, to baking stone, cover with stacked inverted disposable pans, and bake for 5 minutes. Carefully remove pans and bake until loaves are evenly browned, 12 to 15 minutes longer, rotating parchment halfway through baking. Transfer to cooling rack and let cool for at least 20 minutes before serving. Consume within 3 to 4 hours.

## SHAPING AND BAKING BAGUETTES

**1.** On lightly floured counter, roll each piece of refrigerated and rested dough into loose 3- to 4-inch-long cylinder. Move dough to floured baking sheet and cover with plastic. Let rest at room temperature for 30 minutes.

**2.** Gently press 1 piece of dough into 6 by 4-inch rectangle with long edge facing you. Fold upper quarter of dough toward center and press gently to seal. Rotate dough 180 degrees and repeat folding step to form 8 by 2-inch rectangle.

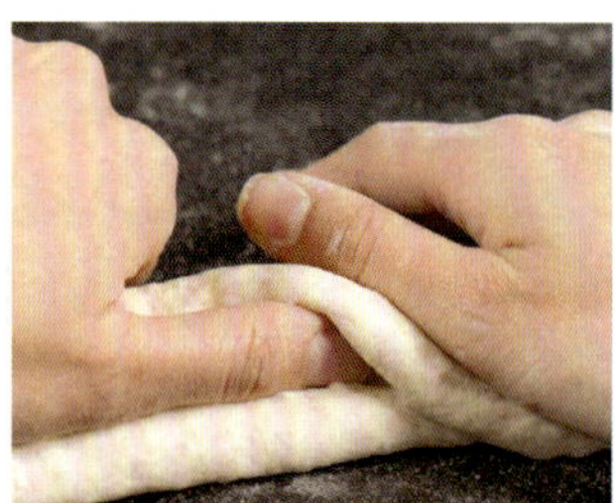

**3.** Fold dough in half toward you, using thumb of your other hand to create crease along center of dough, sealing with heel of your hand as you work your way along the loaf. Do not seal ends of loaf.

**4.** Cup your hand over center of dough and roll dough back and forth gently to form dog-bone shape. Working toward ends, gently roll and stretch dough until it measures 15 inches long by 1¼ inches wide.

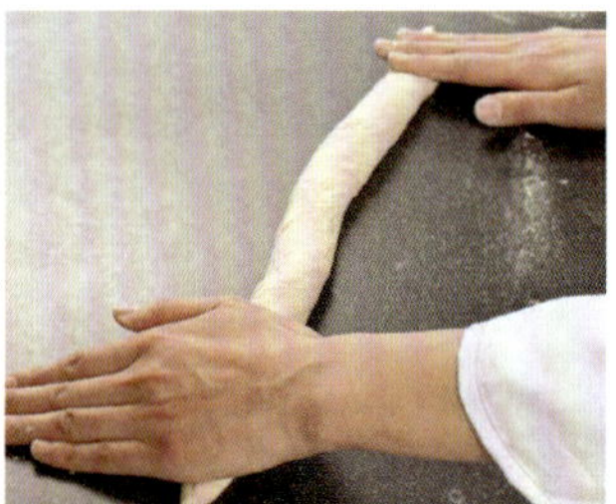

**5.** Moving your hands in opposite directions, use back and forth motion to roll ends of loaf under your palms to form sharp points.

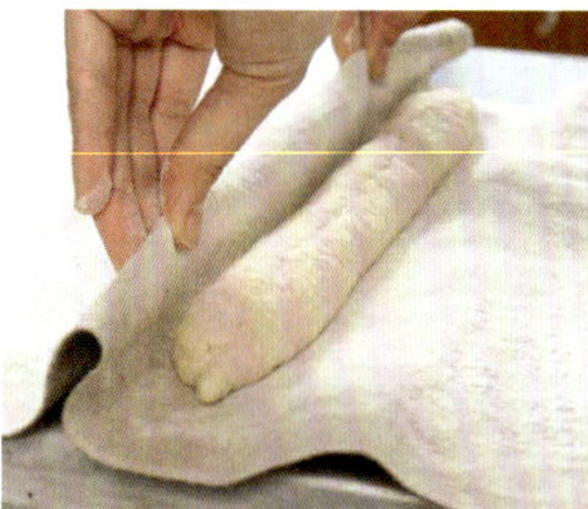

**6.** Transfer dough to floured couche, seam side up. On either side of loaf, pinch edges of couche into pleat. Cover loosely with large plastic garbage bag.

**7.** Place second loaf on opposite side of pleat. Fold edges of couche over loaves to cover, then carefully place sheet inside bag, and tie or fold under to enclose. Let rise for 45 to 60 minutes. While bread rises, preheat baking stone.

**8.** Unfold couche. For each loaf, use flipping board to roll loaf over so it is seam side down. Hold long edge of flipping board between loaf and couche at 45-degree angle. Lift couche and flip loaf seam side up onto board. Invert loaf onto parchment-lined peel.

**9.** Holding lame concave side up at 30-degree angle to loaf, make series of three 4-inch-long, ½-inch-deep slashes along length of each loaf, using swift, fluid motion, overlapping each slash slightly.

**10.** Transfer loaves, on parchment, to baking stone, cover with stacked inverted disposable pans, and bake for 5 minutes. Carefully remove pans and bake until loaves are evenly browned, 12 to 15 minutes longer, rotating parchment halfway through baking.

# Fougasse

**SERVES** 8 (Makes 2 loaves)

**WHY THIS RECIPE WORKS** If ever there was a bread made for crust lovers, it has to be fougasse. First created in Provence, this loaf is related by name and pedigree to Italian focaccia. But unlike its Italian cousin, fougasse gets an elegant twist: After being stretched and flattened, the dough is given a series of cuts, usually in fanciful geometric patterns, to create multiple openings in the finished flatbread and give it a leaf shape. As pretty as the sculpted breads are, the openings are not just for aesthetics: They dramatically increase the crust-to-crumb ratio so that nearly every bite includes an equal share of crisp crust and tender, airy interior. The cuts also help the bread bake very quickly. Most bakeries don't make a separate dough for fougasse. Instead, they simply repurpose extra dough from some other product, such as baguettes. We decided to follow suit and used our bakery-style French baguette recipe as a starting point, eliminating the diastatic malt powder, and then changing up the shaping. To make shaping the fougasse easy, we rolled it out with a rolling pin so that the dough was level, transferred it to parchment, and cut into it with a pizza cutter, which proved the perfect-size implement. The fougasse looked flawless, but the substantial crust was too hard and tough. We tried adding olive oil to the dough, as we'd seen in some recipes, to soften it, but this eliminated any crispness. Brushing the dough with oil before it went into the oven worked much better, producing a delicate, almost fried crunch and even browning that complemented a rosemary and sea salt topping. You'll need to plan ahead: The dough needs to rise in the refrigerator for at least 16 hours. If you can't find King Arthur all-purpose flour, you can substitute bread flour, not another all-purpose flour. The fougasses are best eaten within 4 hours of baking. If you don't have a baking stone, bake the bread on an overturned and preheated rimmed baking sheet set on the lowest oven rack.

- ¼ cup (1⅓ ounces) whole-wheat flour
- 3 cups (15 ounces) King Arthur all-purpose flour
- 1½ teaspoons table salt
- 1 teaspoon instant or rapid-rise yeast
- 1½ cups water, room temperature
- Cornmeal or semolina flour
- ¼ cup extra-virgin olive oil, divided
- 1 tablespoon chopped fresh rosemary, divided
- 2 teaspoons coarse sea salt, divided

**1.** Sift whole-wheat flour through fine-mesh strainer into bowl of stand mixer; discard bran remaining in strainer. Add all-purpose flour, salt, and yeast to mixer bowl. Using dough hook on low speed, slowly add water to flour mixture and mix until cohesive dough starts to form and no dry flour remains, 5 to 7 minutes, scraping down bowl as needed. Transfer dough to lightly oiled large bowl or container, cover tightly with plastic wrap, and let rise for 30 minutes.

**2.** Holding edge of dough with your fingertips, fold dough over itself by gently lifting and folding edge of dough toward center. Turn bowl 45 degrees and fold dough again; repeat turning bowl and folding dough 6 more times (total of 8 folds). Cover tightly with plastic and let rise for 30 minutes. Repeat folding and rising every 30 minutes, 3 more times. After fourth set of folds, cover bowl tightly with plastic and refrigerate for at least 16 hours or up to 2 days.

**3.** Transfer dough to lightly floured counter, stretch gently into 8-inch round (do not deflate), and divide in half. Working with 1 piece of dough at a time, gently stretch and fold over 3 sides of dough to create rough triangle with 5-inch sides.

## SHAPING FOUGASSE

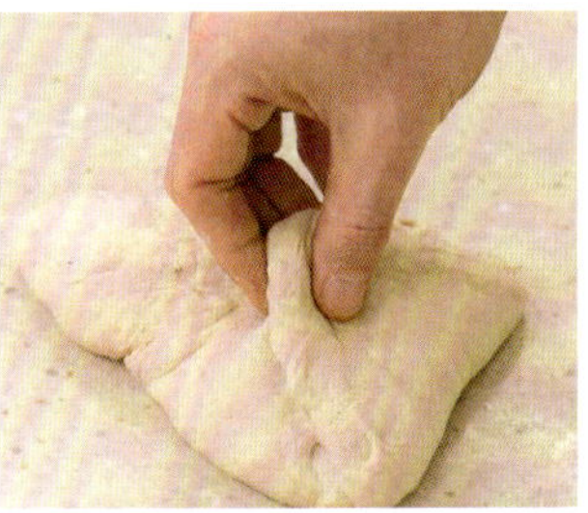

**1.** Working with one 8-inch round of dough at a time, stretch and fold over 3 sides of dough to create triangle with 5-inch sides. Transfer to baking sheet, cover with plastic, and let rest 30 minutes to 1 hour.

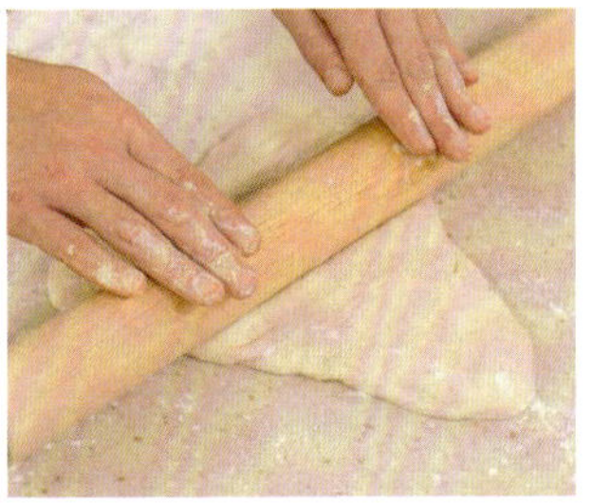

**2.** Transfer 1 piece of dough to floured counter and roll into triangular shape with 8-inch base and 10-inch sides, about ½ inch thick. Transfer to parchment-lined baking sheet dusted with cornmeal.

**3.** Using pizza cutter, make 6-inch-long cut down center of triangle, through dough to sheet, leaving about 1½ inches at either end.

**4.** Make three 2- to 3-inch diagonal cuts through dough on each side of center cut, leaving 1-inch border on each side to create leaf-vein pattern.

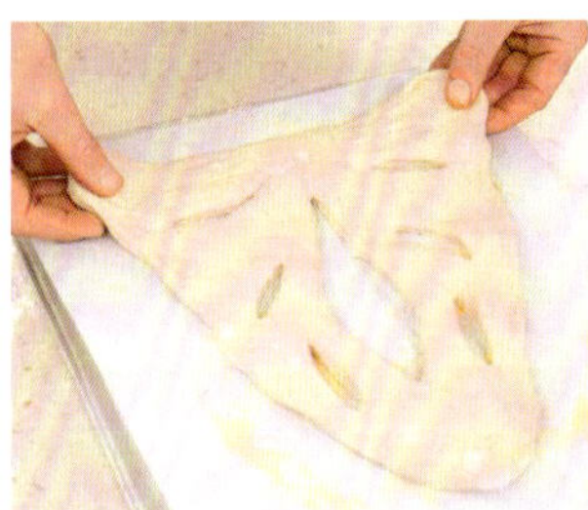

**5.** Gently stretch dough toward sides of sheet to widen cuts and emphasize leaf shape; overall leaf should measure about 10 by 12 inches. Let rise 30 to 45 minutes.

Transfer triangles seam side down to lightly floured rimmed baking sheet, cover loosely with lightly oiled plastic, and let rest until no longer cool to the touch, 30 minutes to 1 hour.

**4.** Place baking stone on lower-middle rack of oven and heat oven to 450 degrees. Line 2 overturned rimmed baking sheets with parchment paper, and dust liberally with cornmeal. Transfer 1 piece of dough to lightly floured counter and gently roll into triangular shape with 8-inch base and 10-inch sides, about ½ inch thick. Transfer dough to prepared sheet, with base facing short side of sheet.

**5.** Using pizza cutter, make 6-inch-long cut down center of triangle, through dough to sheet, leaving about 1½ inches at either end. Make three 2- to 3-inch diagonal cuts through dough on eqch side of center cut, leaving 1-inch border on each end of cuts, to create leaf-vein pattern (cuts shoul not connect to one another or to edges of dough).

**6.** Gently stretch dough toward sides of sheet to widen cuts and emphasize leaf shape; overall size of loaf should measure about 10 by 12 inches. Cover loosely with lightly oiled plastic and let rise until nearly doubled in size, 30 to 45 minutes. Twenty minutes after shaping first loaf, repeat rolling, cutting, and shaping with second piece of dough. (Staggering shaping of leaves will allow them to be baked in succession.)

**7.** Brush top and sides of first loaf with 2 tablespoons oil. Sprinkle loaf evenly with 1½ teaspoons rosemary and 1 teaspoon coarse salt. Slide parchment with loaf onto baking stone and bake until golden brown, 18 to 22 minutes, rotating loaf halfway through baking. Transfer load to wire rack, discard parchment, and let cool for 20 minutes. Repeat topping and baking with second loaf. Serve warm or at room temperature.

### Fougasse with Bacon and Gruyère

Cook 4 slices thick-cut bacon, cut into ½-inch pieces, in 10-inch nonstick skillet over medium heat, stirring occasionally, until crispy, 6 to 8 minutes. Using slotted spoon, transfer bacon to paper towel–lined plate. Omit rosemary and sea salt. Add bacon to mixer bowl with flour in step 1. Sprinkle each loaf with ½ cup shredded Gruyère cheese before baking.

### Olive Fougasse

Add 1 cup coarsely chopped pitted kalamata olives to mixer bowl with flour in step 1.

## Rosemary Focaccia

**MAKES** two 9-inch round loaves

**WHY THIS RECIPE WORKS** Most focaccia in the States is heavy, thick, and strewn with pizza-like toppings. We wanted a lighter loaf, airy on the inside and topped with just a smattering of herbs. To start, we focused on flavor. To get the benefits of a long fermentation with minimal effort, many bakers use a "pre-ferment" (also known as a "sponge" or "starter" or, in Italian, "biga"): a mixture of flour, water, and yeast that rests before being incorporated into the dough. We followed suit, but the interiors of the loaves weren't as tender and airy as we wanted. We wondered if our stand mixer was developing too much gluten (the network of proteins that give bread its structure). We tried a more gentle approach, where a high hydration level (the weight of the water in relation to the weight of the flour) and a long autolyse (the dough resting process) take advantage of the enzymes naturally present in the wheat to produce the same effect as kneading. Our loaves were now light and airy, but squat. To improve the structure, we turned the dough at regular intervals while it proofed. To hasten gluten development and shorten our proofing time, we held back the salt when mixing our dough, adding it later. For a crisp crust, we oiled the baking pans and added coarse salt for flavor and crunchy texture. If you don't have a baking stone, bake the bread on an overturned, preheated rimmed baking sheet set on the upper-middle oven rack.

**BIGA**

- ½ cup (2½ ounces) all-purpose flour
- ⅓ cup (2⅔ ounces) warm water (100–110 degrees)
- ¼ teaspoon instant or rapid-rise yeast

**DOUGH**

- 2½ cups (12½ ounces) all-purpose flour
- 1¼ cups (10 ounces) warm water (100–110 degrees)
- 1 teaspoon instant or rapid-rise yeast
- 1 tablespoon kosher salt, divided
- ¼ cup extra-virgin olive oil
- 2 tablespoons chopped fresh rosemary

**1. FOR THE BIGA:** Combine flour, water, and yeast in large bowl and stir with wooden spoon until uniform mass forms and no dry flour remains, about 1 minute. Cover bowl tightly with plastic wrap and let stand at room temperature (about 70 degrees) at least 8 hours or up to 24 hours. Use immediately or store in refrigerator for up to 3 days (allow to stand at room temperature for 30 minutes before proceeding with recipe).

**2. FOR THE DOUGH:** Stir flour, water, and yeast into biga with wooden spoon until uniform mass forms and no dry flour remains, about 1 minute. Cover with plastic wrap and let rise at room temperature for 15 minutes.

**3.** Sprinkle 2 teaspoons salt over dough; stir into dough until thoroughly incorporated, about 1 minute. Cover with plastic wrap and let rise at room temperature for 30 minutes. Spray rubber spatula or bowl scraper with vegetable oil spray; fold partially risen dough over itself by gently lifting and folding the edge of the dough toward the middle. Turn bowl 90 degrees; fold again. Turn bowl and fold dough 6 more times (total of 8 turns). Cover with plastic wrap and let rise for 30 minutes. Repeat folding, turning, and rising 2 more times, for a total of three 30-minute rises. Meanwhile, adjust oven rack to upper-middle position, place baking stone on the rack, and heat oven to 500 degrees, at least 30 minutes before baking.

**4.** Gently transfer dough to lightly floured work surface. Lightly dust top of dough with flour and divide it in half. Shape each piece of dough into 5-inch round by gently tucking under edges. Coat two 9-inch round cake pans with 2 tablespoons olive oil each. Sprinkle each pan with ½ teaspoon kosher salt. Place round of dough in 1 pan, top side down; slide dough around pan to coat bottom and sides, then flip dough over. Repeat with second piece of dough and second pan. Cover pans with plastic wrap and let rest for 5 minutes.

**5.** Using your fingertips, press dough out toward edges of pan, taking care not to tear it. (If dough resists stretching, let it relax for 5 to 10 minutes before trying to stretch it again.) Using dinner fork, poke entire surface of dough 25 to 30 times, popping any large bubbles. Sprinkle rosemary evenly over top of dough. Let dough rest in pan until slightly bubbly, 5 to 10 minutes.

**6.** Place pans on baking stone and lower oven temperature to 450 degrees. Bake until tops are golden brown, 25 to 28 minutes, switching placement of pans halfway through baking time. Transfer pans to wire rack and let cool for 5 minutes. Remove loaves from pans and place on wire rack. Brush tops with any oil remaining in pans. Let cool for 30 minutes before serving. Focaccia can be wrapped in a double layer of plastic wrap and stored room temperature or frozen for up to 2 months.

## Piadine (Italian Flatbreads)

**MAKES** 4 flatbreads

**WHY THIS RECIPE WORKS** Meet piadine: the rustic, tender-chewy rounds from Emilia-Romagna, tailor-made for filling with cured meat, cheese, and/or vegetables, that are made without yeast, lengthy rising times, or even your oven. For chewy-tender piadine with an open crumb, we added baking powder to the dough, as well as ample amounts of fat and water that diluted the gluten strands, keeping the dough soft and pliable without making it too rich. Rolling the dough into 9-inch rounds made for substantial breads that fit perfectly in a cast-iron pan, which we preheated thoroughly so that they would brown quickly without drying out. If you'd prefer to use lard (which is traditional) rather than vegetable oil, increase the amount to ¼ cup to account for its lower density. Do not substitute butter or olive oil; their flavors are obtrusive here. A nonstick skillet can be used in place of cast iron; increase the heat to medium-high and preheat the empty skillet with ½ teaspoon of oil until shimmering; wipe out the oil before proceeding with the recipe.

- 2 cups (10 ounces) all-purpose flour
- ¾ teaspoon baking powder
- ½ teaspoon table salt
- 3 tablespoons vegetable oil
- ¾ cup water

**1.** Process flour, baking powder, and salt in food processor until combined, about 5 seconds. Add oil and process until no visible bits of fat remain, about 10 seconds. With processor running, slowly add water; process until most of dough forms soft, slightly tacky ball that clears sides of workbowl, 30 to 60 seconds (there may be small bits of loose dough).

**2.** Transfer dough to counter and gently knead until smooth, about 15 seconds. Divide dough into 4 equal pieces and shape each into ball. Working with 1 dough ball at a time, place ball seam side down on clean counter and, using your cupped hand, drag in small circles until ball is taut and smooth. Cover dough balls loosely with plastic wrap. Let rest for 30 minutes.

**3.** Pat 1 dough ball into 5-inch disk on lightly floured counter (keep remaining dough balls covered). Roll disk into 9-inch round, flouring counter as needed to prevent sticking. Repeat with remaining dough balls.

**4.** Heat 12-inch cast-iron skillet over medium heat until drop of water dripped onto surface sizzles immediately, about 3 minutes. Prick 1 dough round all over with fork, then carefully place in skillet. Cook until underside is spotty brown, 1 to 2 minutes, using fork to pop any large bubbles that form. Flip round and cook until second side is spotty brown, 1 to 2 minutes (flatbread should still be pliable). Transfer piadina to plate, gently fold in half, and cover with clean dish towel to keep warm. Repeat with remaining dough rounds, stacking piadine and re-covering with towel as they finish. Serve warm. Piadine can be stored in zipper-lock bag for 2 days; reheat in cast-iron skillet over medium-high heat for 20 to 30 seconds per side, until warmed through.

## Homemade Naan

**MAKES** 4 pieces

**WHY THIS RECIPE WORKS** We wanted a light and tender naan that could be made at home without a tandoor. We started with a moist dough with a fair amount of fat, which created a soft bread that was pleasantly chewy, but the real secret was the cooking method. While we thought a grill or preheated pizza stone would be the best cooking method, we discovered that they cooked the bread unevenly. A much better option was a covered skillet. The skillet delivered heat to the bottom and the top of the bread, producing naan that were nicely charred but still moist. This recipe works best with a high-protein all-purpose flour such as King Arthur brand. Do not use non-fat yogurt in this recipe. A 12-inch nonstick skillet may be used in place of the cast-iron skillet. For efficiency, stretch the next ball of dough while each naan is cooking.

- ½ cup ice water
- ⅓ cup plain whole-milk yogurt
- 3 tablespoons plus 1 teaspoon vegetable oil, divided
- 1 large egg yolk
- 2 cups (10 ounces) all-purpose flour
- 1¼ teaspoons sugar
- ½ teaspoon instant or rapid-rise yeast
- 1¼ teaspoons table salt
- 1½ tablespoons unsalted butter, melted

**1.** In measuring cup or small bowl, combine water, yogurt, 3 tablespoons oil, and egg yolk. Process flour, sugar, and yeast in food processor until combined, about 2 seconds. With processor running, slowly add water mixture; process until dough is just combined and no dry flour remains, about 10 seconds. Let dough stand for 10 minutes.

**2.** Add salt to dough and process until dough forms satiny, sticky ball that clears sides of workbowl, 30 to 60 seconds. Transfer dough to lightly floured work surface and knead until smooth, about 1 minute. Shape dough into tight ball and place in large, lightly oiled bowl. Cover tightly with plastic wrap and refrigerate for 16 to 24 hours.

**3.** Adjust oven rack to middle position and heat oven to 200 degrees. Place heatproof plate on rack. Transfer dough to lightly floured work surface and divide into 4 equal pieces. Shape each piece into smooth, tight ball. Place dough balls on lightly oiled baking sheet, at least 2 inches apart; cover loosely with plastic coated with vegetable oil spray. Let stand for 15 to 20 minutes.

**4.** Transfer 1 ball to lightly floured work surface and sprinkle with flour. Using your hands and rolling pin, press and roll piece of dough into 9-inch round of even thickness, sprinkling dough and work surface with flour as needed to prevent sticking. Using fork, poke entire surface of round 20 to 25 times. Heat remaining 1 teaspoon oil in 12-inch cast-iron skillet over medium heat until shimmering. Wipe oil out of skillet completely with paper towels. Mist top of dough lightly with water. Place dough in pan, moistened side down; mist top surface of dough with water; and cover. Cook until bottom is browned in spots across surface, 2 to 4 minutes. Flip naan, cover, and continue to cook on second side until lightly browned, 2 to 3 minutes. (If naan puffs up, gently poke with fork to deflate.) Flip naan, brush top with about 1 teaspoon melted butter, transfer to plate in oven, and cover plate tightly with aluminum foil. Repeat rolling and cooking remaining 3 dough balls. Once last naan is baked, serve immediately.

## Pita Bread

**MAKES** eight 7-inch pita breads

**WHY THIS RECIPE WORKS** The tender chew and complex flavor of fresh-baked pitas are revelatory. Our recipe creates tender, chewy pitas with perfect pockets, every time. We started with high-protein bread flour, which encouraged pocket formation and increased the pita's chew. A high hydration level and a generous amount of oil helped keep the pita tender, and honey added a touch of sweetness. After quickly making the dough in the stand mixer, we shaped it into balls and let them proof overnight in the refrigerator to develop complex flavor. We then rolled the dough balls into thin, even disks before baking them on a hot baking stone placed on the lowest oven rack, which ensured that they would puff up quickly and fully. We prefer King Arthur bread flour for this recipe for its high protein content. If using another bread flour, reduce the amount of water in the dough by 2 tablespoons (1 ounce). If you don't have a baking stone, bake the pitas on an overturned and preheated rimmed baking sheet.

- 2⅔ cups (14⅔ ounces) bread flour
- 2¼ teaspoons instant or rapid-rise yeast
- 1⅓ cups (10½ ounces) ice water
- ¼ cup extra-virgin olive oil
- 4 teaspoons honey
- 1¼ teaspoons table salt
- Vegetable oil spray

**1.** Whisk flour and yeast together in bowl of stand mixer. Add ice water, oil, and honey on top of flour mixture. Fit stand mixer with dough hook and mix on low speed until all flour is moistened, 1 to 2 minutes. Let dough sit for 10 minutes.

**2.** Add salt to dough and mix on medium speed until dough forms satiny, sticky ball that clears sides of bowl, 6 to 8 minutes. Transfer dough to lightly oiled counter and knead until smooth, about 1 minute. Divide dough into 8 equal pieces (about 3⅜ ounces each). Shape dough pieces into tight, smooth balls and transfer, seam side down, to rimmed baking sheet coated with oil spray. Spray tops of balls lightly with oil spray, then cover tightly with plastic wrap and refrigerate for at least 16 hours or up to 24 hours.

**3.** One hour before baking pitas, adjust oven rack to lowest position, set baking stone on rack, and heat oven to 425 degrees.

**4.** Remove dough from refrigerator. Coat 1 dough ball generously on both sides with flour and place on well-floured counter, seam side down. Use heel of your hand to press dough ball into 5-inch circle. Using rolling pin, gently roll into 7-inch circle, adding flour as necessary to prevent sticking. Roll slowly and gently to prevent any creasing. Repeat with second dough ball. Brush both sides of each dough round with pastry brush to remove any excess flour. Transfer dough rounds to unfloured peel, making sure side that was facing up when you began rolling is faceup again.

**5.** Slide both dough rounds carefully onto stone and bake until evenly inflated and lightly browned on undersides, 1 to 3 minutes. Using peel, slide pitas off stone and, using your hands or spatula, gently invert. (If pitas do not puff after 3 minutes, flip immediately to prevent overcooking.) Return pitas to stone and bake until lightly browned in center of second side, 1 minute. Transfer pitas to wire rack to cool, covering loosely with clean dish towel. Repeat shaping and baking with remaining 6 pitas in 3 batches. Let pitas cool for 10 minutes before serving. (Pitas are best eaten within 24 hours of baking; to reheat wrap pitas in aluminum foil and place in a cold oven; set the temperature to 300 degrees and bake for 15 to 20 minutes.)

## Za'atar Finger Bread

**SERVES** 6 to 8

**WHY THIS RECIPE WORKS** Inspired by mana'eesh, a round Arabic flatbread almost completely covered with a thick coating of zesty, herbal za'atar, we set out to develop a recipe for a finger-licking-good snack bread to eat alone or to dip in a yogurt sauce. To showcase the za'atar, we started by kneading together a simple dough; stretching it across a baking sheet; and slathering it with the oil-moistened za'atar. The top was a delight, but the bottom of the bread paled in comparison—it was blond and limp. Coating the pan with a generous amount of olive oil essentially fried the bottom of the flatbread as it baked, and shifting the oven rack to the lower-middle position created a crisp, golden base. We prefer to use our homemade Za'atar (page 663) but you can use store-bought, though different za'atar blends include varying salt amounts. Use your preferred coarse sea salt in this recipe. Plan ahead; you will need to refrigerate the dough for at least 24 hours or up to 3 days before baking.

- 3½ cups (19¼ ounces) bread flour
- 2½ teaspoons instant or rapid-rise yeast
- 2½ teaspoons sugar
- 1⅓ cups ice water
- ½ cup plus 2 tablespoons extra-virgin olive oil, divided
- 2 teaspoons table salt
- ⅓ cup za'atar
- Coarse sea salt

**1.** Pulse flour, yeast, and sugar in food processor until combined, about 5 pulses. With processor running, slowly add ice water and process until dough is just combined and no dry flour remains, about 10 seconds. Let dough rest for 10 minutes.

**2.** Add 2 tablespoons oil and salt to dough and process until dough forms satiny, sticky ball that clears sides of bowl, 30 to 60 seconds. Transfer dough to lightly floured counter and knead by hand to form smooth, round ball, about 30 seconds. Place seam side down in lightly greased large bowl or container, cover tightly with plastic wrap, and refrigerate for at least 24 hours. (Dough can be refrigerated for or up to 3 days before baking.)

**3.** Remove dough from refrigerator and let sit at room temperature for 1 hour. Coat rimmed baking sheet with 2 tablespoons oil. Gently press down on dough to deflate any large gas pockets. Transfer dough to prepared sheet and, using your fingertips, press out to uniform thickness, taking care not to tear dough. (Dough may not fit snugly into corners.) Cover loosely with greased plastic and let dough rest for 1 hour.

**4.** Adjust oven rack to lower-middle position and heat oven to 375 degrees. Using your fingertips, gently press dough into corners of sheet and dimple entire surface. Combine remaining 6 tablespoons oil and za'atar in bowl. Using back of spoon, spread oil mixture in even layer over entire surface of dough to edge. Bake until bottom crust is evenly browned and edges are crisp, 20 to 25 minutes, rotating sheet halfway through baking. Let bread cool in sheet for 10 minutes, then transfer to cutting board with metal spatula. Sprinkle with coarse salt to taste, tear into large pieces, and serve warm.

## Easy Sandwich Bread

**MAKES** 1 loaf

**WHY THIS RECIPE WORKS** A freshly baked loaf of bread is one of life's great pleasures. But most people don't have 4 hours to devote to mixing dough, waiting for it to rise, kneading, shaping, and baking. Could we find a quicker way? We started with basic batter bread, which relies on a high hydration level and a single rise, but falls short on flavor. Adding melted butter was a good start toward a tastier loaf, and substituting some whole-wheat flour provided nutty depth. Swapping the rest of the all-purpose flour for bread flour lent better structure. We also traded 1 tablespoon of honey for sugar, which contributed complexity and encouraged browning. Two 20-minute proofs were enough for flavor development. Adding salt only after the initial rise allowed the bread to rise high. An egg wash before baking and a brush of melted butter provided a shiny, tender crust. The test kitchen's preferred loaf pan measures 8½ by 4½ inches; if using a 9 by 5-inch pan, check for doneness 5 minutes early. To prevent the loaf from deflating as it rises, do not let the batter come in contact with the plastic wrap.

- 2 cups (11 ounces) bread flour
- 6 tablespoons (2 ounces) whole-wheat flour
- 2¼ teaspoons instant or rapid-rise yeast
- 1¼ cups plus 2 tablespoons warm water (120 degrees), divided
- 3 tablespoons unsalted butter, melted, divided
- 1 tablespoon honey
- ¾ teaspoon table salt
- 1 large egg, lightly beaten with 1 teaspoon water and pinch table salt

**1.** In bowl of stand mixer, whisk bread flour, whole-wheat flour, and yeast together. Add 1¼ cups warm water, 2 tablespoons melted butter, and honey. Fit stand mixer with paddle and mix on low speed for 1 minute. Increase speed to medium and mix for 2 minutes. Scrape down bowl and paddle with greased rubber spatula. Continue to mix 2 minutes longer. Remove bowl and paddle from mixer. Scrape down bowl and paddle, leaving paddle in batter. Cover with plastic wrap and let batter rise in warm place until doubled in size, about 20 minutes.

**2.** Adjust oven rack to lower-middle position and heat oven to 375 degrees. Spray 8½ by 4½-inch loaf pan with vegetable oil spray. Dissolve salt in remaining 2 tablespoons warm water. When batter has doubled, attach bowl and paddle to mixer. Add salt-water mixture and mix on low speed until water is mostly incorporated, about 40 seconds. Increase speed to medium and mix until thoroughly combined, about 1 minute, scraping down paddle if necessary. Transfer batter to prepared pan and smooth surface with greased rubber spatula. Cover and leave in warm place until batter reaches ½ inch below edge of pan, 15 to 20 minutes. Uncover and let rise until center of batter is level with edge of pan, 5 to 10 minutes longer.

**3.** Gently brush top of risen loaf with egg mixture. Bake until deep golden brown and loaf registers 208 to 210 degrees, 40 to 45 minutes. Using clean dish towels, carefully invert bread onto wire rack. Reinvert loaf and brush top and sides with remaining 1 tablespoon melted butter. Let cool completely before slicing. (This bread is best eaten the day it is made; but it can be wrapped in plastic wrap and stored for up to 2 days at room temperature or frozen for up to 1 month.)

## Whole-Wheat Sandwich Bread

**MAKES** two 8-inch loaves

**WHY THIS RECIPE WORKS** Most whole-wheat bread recipes turn out either squat bricks or white bread in disguise. We wanted a nutty, light-textured sandwich loaf. We started with a good white-flour recipe and worked our way backward to "unrefine" it. We made a series of white bread loaves, replacing different amounts of all-purpose flour with whole-wheat to find the highest percentage of whole-wheat flour we could use before the texture suffered, landing on 60 percent. We also substituted bread flour for the all-purpose flour. Next, we soaked the flour overnight in milk, with some wheat germ for added flavor. This softened the grain's fiber, kept the dough moist, and coaxed out some sweetness. Finally, we turned to a sponge, a mixture of flour, water, and yeast left to sit overnight to develop a full range of flavor. Adding honey lent complexity and swapping out some of the butter for vegetable oil cut the richness. If you don't have a baking stone, bake the bread on an overturned and preheated rimmed baking sheet set on the lowest oven rack.

**SPONGE**

- 2 cups (11 ounces) bread flour
- 1 cup water, heated to 110 degrees
- ½ teaspoon instant or rapid-rise yeast

**SOAKER**

- 3 cups (16½ ounces) whole-wheat flour
- ½ cup wheat germ
- 2 cups whole milk

**DOUGH**

- 6 tablespoons unsalted butter, softened
- ¼ cup honey
- 2 tablespoons instant or rapid-rise yeast
- 2 tablespoons vegetable oil
- 4 teaspoons table salt

**1. FOR THE SPONGE:** Combine the flour, water, and yeast in a large bowl and stir with a wooden spoon until a uniform mass forms and no dry flour remains, about 1 minute. Cover the bowl tightly with plastic wrap and let sit at room temperature for at least 8 hours or up to 24 hours.

**2. FOR THE SOAKER:** Combine the flour, wheat germ, and milk in a separate large bowl and stir with a wooden spoon until a shaggy mass forms, about 1 minute. Transfer the dough to a lightly floured work surface and knead by hand until smooth, 2 to 3 minutes. Return the soaker to the bowl, cover tightly with plastic wrap, and refrigerate for at least 8 hours or up to 24 hours.

**3. FOR THE DOUGH:** Tear the soaker apart into 1-inch pieces and place in the bowl of a stand mixer fitted with the dough hook. Add the sponge, butter, honey, yeast, oil, and salt and mix on low speed until a cohesive mass starts to form, about 2 minutes. Increase the speed to medium and knead until the dough is smooth and elastic, 8 to 10 minutes. Transfer the dough to a lightly floured work surface and knead by hand to form a smooth, round ball, about 1 minute. Place the dough in a large, lightly greased bowl. Cover tightly with plastic wrap and let rise at room temperature for 45 minutes.

**4.** Gently press down on the center of the dough to deflate. Spray a rubber spatula or bowl scraper with vegetable oil spray; fold the partially risen dough over itself by gently lifting and folding the edge of the dough toward the middle. Turn the bowl 90 degrees; fold again. Turn the bowl and fold the dough 6 more times (for a total of 8 folds). Cover tightly with plastic wrap and allow to rise at room temperature until doubled in size, about 45 minutes.

**5.** Grease two 8½ by 4½-inch loaf pans. Transfer the dough to a well-floured work surface and divide in half. Press 1 piece of the dough into a 17 by 8-inch rectangle, with the short side facing you. Roll the dough toward you into a firm cylinder, keeping the roll taut by tucking it under itself as you go. Turn the loaf seam side up and pinch it closed. Place the loaf seam side down in a prepared pan, pressing gently into the corners. Repeat with the second piece of dough. Cover the loaves loosely with greased plastic wrap and let rise at room temperature until nearly doubled in size, 1 to 1½ hours (the top of the loaves should rise about 1 inch over the lip of the pan).

**6.** Thirty minutes before baking, adjust the oven racks to the middle and lowest positions, place a baking stone on the middle rack, place an empty loaf pan or other heatproof pan on the bottom rack, and heat the oven to 400 degrees. Bring 2 cups water to boil on the stovetop.

**7.** Using a sharp serrated knife or a single-edge razor blade, make one ¼-inch-deep slash lengthwise down the center of each loaf. Working quickly, pour the boiling water into the empty loaf pan in the oven and set the loaves on the baking stone. Reduce the oven temperature to 350 degrees. Bake until the crust is dark brown and the loaves register 200 degrees on an instant-read thermometer, 40 to 50 minutes, rotating the loaves front to back and side to side halfway through baking. Transfer the pans to a wire rack and let cool for 5 minutes. Remove the loaves from the pans, return to the rack, and let cool to room temperature, about 2 hours, before slicing and serving. Bread can be wrapped in a double layer of plastic wrap and stored at room temperature for up to 3 days; wrapped with an additional layer of aluminum foil, the bread can be frozen for up to 1 month.

### FOLDING AND FORMING WHOLE-WHEAT SANDWICH BREAD

**1.** Deflate the center of the dough, then fold it in on itself. Turn the bowl 90 degrees; fold again. Repeat for a total of 8 folds. Let rise for 45 minutes.

**2.** Halve the dough and pat each portion into an 8 by 17-inch rectangle, with the short side facing you.

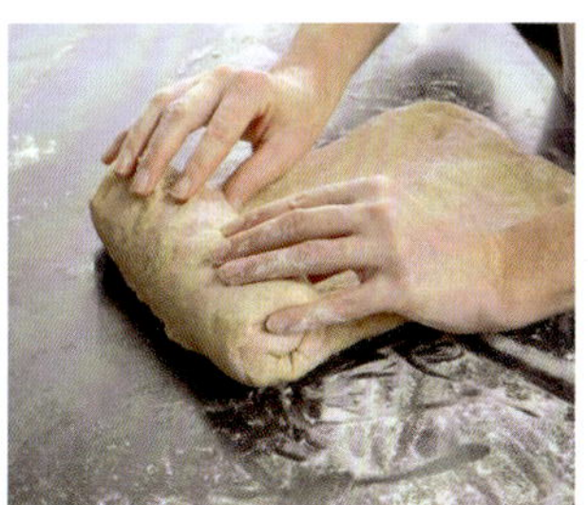

**3.** Roll each sheet toward you into a tight cylinder. Keep the roll taut by tucking it under itself as you go. Pinch the seams to seal.

**4.** Place each loaf seam side down in the prepared loaf pans. Let the dough rise until almost doubled in size, 60 to 90 minutes.

**5.** Using a knife, make a shallow slash down the center of each loaf to stop the bread from tearing when it rises. Bake for 40 to 50 minutes.

## Multigrain Bread

**MAKES** two 8-inch loaves

**WHY THIS RECIPE WORKS** Most multigrain breads are either dense and heavy or have so little grain that they are not much different from white bread. We wanted a multigrain bread with great flavor and balanced texture. Our first challenge was to develop more gluten in the dough. Because the protein content of any flour is an indicator of how much gluten it will produce, we thought first to switch out all-purpose flour for bread flour, but this move only made the bread chewier. The solution was twofold: long kneading preceded by an autolyse, a resting period just after the initial mixing of water and flour that gives flour time to hydrate. The result was a loaf that baked up light yet chewy, without being tough. To incorporate grains into the bread, we turned to packaged seven-grain hot cereal. To soften the grains, we made a thick porridge with the cereal before adding it to the dough. A final step of rolling the shaped loaves in oats yielded a finished, professional look. Don't confuse seven-grain hot cereal mix with boxed, cold breakfast cereals. Our favorite brands of seven-grain mix are Bob's Red Mill and Arrowhead Mills. For an accurate measurement of boiling water, bring a kettle of water to a boil, then measure out the desired amount. See page 1020 for information on our top-rated loaf pan.

- 1¼ cups (6¼ ounces) seven-grain hot cereal mix
- 2½ cups boiling water
- 3 cups (15 ounces) unbleached all-purpose flour, plus extra for the dough and work surface
- 1½ cups (8¼ ounces) whole-wheat flour
- ¼ cup honey
- 4 tablespoons (½ stick) unsalted butter, melted and cooled slightly
- 1 envelope (2¼ teaspoons) instant or rapid-rise yeast
- 1 tablespoon table salt
- ¾ cup unsalted pumpkin seeds or sunflower seeds
- ½ cup old-fashioned rolled oats or quick oats

**1.** Place the cereal mix in the bowl of a stand mixer and pour the boiling water over it; let stand, stirring occasionally, until the mixture cools to 100 degrees and resembles thick porridge, about 1 hour. Whisk the flours together in a medium bowl.

**2.** Once the grain mixture has cooled, add the honey, melted butter, and yeast and stir to combine. Attach the bowl to a stand mixer fitted with the dough hook. With the mixer running on low speed, add the flours, ½ cup at a time, and knead until the dough forms a ball, 1½ to 2 minutes; cover the bowl with plastic wrap and let the dough rest for 20 minutes. Add the salt and knead on medium-low speed until the dough clears the sides of the bowl, 3 to 4 minutes (if it does not clear the sides, add 2 to 3 tablespoons additional all-purpose flour and continue mixing); continue to knead the dough for 5 more minutes. Add the seeds and knead for another 15 seconds. Transfer the dough to a floured work surface and knead by hand until the seeds are dispersed evenly and the dough forms a smooth, taut ball. Place the dough in a greased container with a 4-quart capacity; cover with plastic wrap and allow to rise until doubled in size, 45 to 60 minutes.

**3.** Adjust an oven rack to the middle position and heat the oven to 375 degrees. Spray two 9 by 5-inch loaf pans with vegetable oil spray. Transfer the dough to a lightly floured work surface and pat into a 12 by 9-inch rectangle; cut the dough in half crosswise with a knife or bench scraper. With a short side facing you, starting at the farthest end, roll one dough piece into a log, keeping the roll taut by tucking it under itself as you go. Seal the loaf by pinching the seam together gently with your thumb and forefinger; repeat with the remaining dough. Spray the loaves lightly with water or vegetable oil spray. Roll each dough log in oats to coat evenly and place, seam side down, in the greased loaf pans, pressing gently into the corners; cover lightly with plastic wrap and let rise until almost doubled in size, 30 to 40 minutes. (The dough should barely spring back when poked with a knuckle.) Bake until the center of the loaves registers 200 degrees on an instant-read thermometer, 35 to 40 minutes. Remove the loaves from the pans and cool on a wire rack before slicing, about 3 hours.

## Deli Rye Bread

**MAKES** 1 loaf

**WHY THIS RECIPE WORKS** To pack more rye flour into our Deli Rye Bread without making it dry or crumbly, we add more water than most recipes call for. Adding a small amount of vegetable oil also helps keep the crumb tender. To provide adequate structure without weighing down the loaf, we use King Arthur all-purpose flour rather than lower-protein all-purpose flour or higher-protein bread flour. For a hint of sweetness and complexity, we add a small amount of molasses. Finally, for a glossy finish and a tender crust, we brush the loaf with a cooked cornstarch wash. We prefer King Arthur all-purpose flour for this recipe; if you have trouble finding it at your supermarket, you can use any brand of bread flour instead. Any grade of rye flour will work in this recipe, but for the best flavor and texture we recommend using medium or dark rye flour. Do not use blackstrap molasses here; its flavor is too intense.

- 2½ cups (12½ ounces) King Arthur all-purpose flour
- 1½ cups (8¼ ounces) rye flour
- 1 tablespoon caraway seeds
- 2½ teaspoons instant or rapid-rise yeast
- 1⅔ cups (13⅓ ounces) plus ½ cup (4 ounces) water, room temperature, divided
- 1 tablespoon vegetable oil
- 2 teaspoons molasses
- 1½ teaspoons table salt
- 4 teaspoons cornstarch

**1.** Whisk all-purpose flour, rye flour, caraway seeds, and yeast together in bowl of stand mixer. Whisk 1⅔ cups water, oil, and molasses in 4-cup liquid measuring cup until molasses has dissolved.

**2.** Fit stand mixer with dough hook; add water mixture to flour mixture and knead on low speed until cohesive dough starts to form and no dry flour remains, about 2 minutes, scraping down bowl as needed. Cover bowl tightly with plastic wrap and let dough rest for 20 minutes.

**3.** Add salt to dough and knead on medium-low speed until dough is smooth and elastic and clears sides of bowl, about 5 minutes.

**4.** Transfer dough to lightly floured counter and knead by hand to form smooth, round ball, about 30 seconds. Place dough seam side down in lightly oiled large bowl, cover tightly with plastic, and let rise until doubled in size, 1½ to 2 hours.

**5.** Transfer dough to lightly floured counter and gently press into 8-inch disk, then fold edges toward middle to form round. Cover loosely with plastic and let rest for 15 minutes.

### SHAPING A LOAF OF DELI RYE

**1.** With short end facing edge of counter, fold top left and right edges of dough diagonally into center and press to seal.

**2.** Fold point of dough toward center and press to seal. Rotate 180 degrees and repeat folding and sealing.

**3.** Fold dough in half toward you to form 8 by 4-inch crescent shape. Using heel of your hand, press seam closed.

**4.** Roll loaf seam side down. Tuck ends under loaf to form rounded torpedo shape.

**6.** Adjust oven racks to middle and lowest positions, place baking stone on upper rack, and heat oven to 450 degrees. Line overturned rimmed baking sheet with parchment paper and dust lightly with rye flour. Gently press and stretch dough into 12 by 9-inch oval, with short end of oval facing edge of counter. Fold top left and right edges of dough diagonally into center of oval and press gently to seal. Fold point of dough into center of oval and press seam gently to seal. Rotate dough 180 degrees and repeat folding and sealing top half of dough.

**7.** Fold dough in half toward you to form rough 8 by 4-inch crescent-shaped loaf. Using heel of your hand, press seam closed against counter. Roll loaf seam side down. Tuck ends under loaf to form rounded torpedo shape. Gently slide your hands underneath loaf and transfer, seam side down, to prepared sheet.

**8.** Spray sheet of plastic with vegetable oil spray and cover loaf loosely. Let loaf rise until increased in size by about half and dough springs back minimally when poked gently with your knuckle, 45 minutes to 1¼ hours.

**9.** Place empty loaf pan on bottom oven rack. Using sharp paring knife or single-edge razor blade, make six to eight 4-inch-long, ½-inch-deep slashes with swift, fluid motion across width of loaf, spacing slashes about 1 inch apart. Pour 2 cups boiling water into empty loaf pan in oven.

**10.** Slide parchment and loaf from sheet onto baking stone. Bake until deep golden brown and loaf registers 205 to 210 degrees, 25 to 30 minutes, rotating loaf halfway through baking. Transfer loaf to wire rack.

**11.** Whisk cornstarch and remaining ½ cup water in bowl until cornstarch has dissolved. Microwave, whisking frequently, until mixture is thickened, 1 to 2 minutes.

**12.** Brush top and sides of loaf with 3 tablespoons cornstarch mixture (you will have extra cornstarch mixture). Let cool completely, about 3 hours, before slicing and serving. (Bread can be wrapped in a double layer of plastic wrap and stored at room temperature for up to 3 days; wrapped with an additional layer of aluminum foil, it can be frozen for up to 1 month.)

## Cinnamon Swirl Bread

**MAKES** 2 loaves

**WHY THIS RECIPE WORKS** This American classic frequently disappoints due to either precious little cinnamon flavor or, just as bad, a gloppy, oozing filling reminiscent of sticky buns. The bread itself is often an afterthought of pedestrian white bread, or else it's a cakey, dense affair. We swapped in an airy, cottony Japanese white bread called shokupan and created a filling with a balanced mixture of cinnamon, confectioners' sugar, and vanilla. To ensure that our filling stayed put and could be tasted with every bite, we traded the traditional swirl shape for a simple yet elegant Russian braid. To achieve the proper dough consistency, make sure to weigh your ingredients. The dough will appear very wet and sticky until the final few minutes of kneading; do not be tempted to add supplemental flour.

**DOUGH**

- 8 tablespoons unsalted butter
- 3¾ cups (20⅔ ounces) bread flour
- ¾ cup (2¾ ounces) nonfat dry milk powder
- ⅓ cup (2⅓ ounces) granulated sugar
- 1 tablespoon instant or rapid-rise yeast
- 1½ cups (12 ounces) water, heated to 110 degrees
- 1 large egg, lightly beaten
- 1½ teaspoons table salt
- 1½ cups (7½ ounces) golden raisins

**FILLING**

- 1 cup (4 ounces) confectioners' sugar
- 3 tablespoons ground cinnamon
- 1 teaspoon vanilla extract
- ½ teaspoon table salt
- 1 large egg, lightly beaten with pinch table salt

**1. FOR THE DOUGH:** Cut butter into 32 pieces and toss with 1 tablespoon flour; set aside to soften while mixing dough. Whisk remaining flour, milk powder, sugar, and yeast together in bowl of stand mixer fitted with dough hook. Add water and egg and mix on medium-low speed until cohesive mass forms, about 2 minutes, scraping down bowl as needed. Cover mixing bowl with plastic wrap and let stand for 20 minutes.

**2.** Adjust oven rack to middle position and place loaf or cake pan on bottom of oven. Grease large bowl. Remove plastic from mixer bowl, add salt, and mix on medium-low speed until dough is smooth and elastic and clears sides of bowl, 7 to 15 minutes. With mixer running, add butter a few pieces at a time, and continue to knead until butter is fully incorporated and dough is smooth and elastic and clears sides of bowl, 3 to 5 minutes longer. Add raisins and mix until incorporated, 30 to 60 seconds. Transfer dough to prepared bowl and, using bowl scraper or rubber spatula, fold dough over itself by gently lifting and folding edge of dough toward middle. Turn bowl 90 degrees; fold again. Turn bowl and fold dough 6 more times (total of 8 folds). Cover tightly with plastic and transfer to middle rack of oven. Pour 3 cups boiling water into loaf pan in oven, close oven door, and allow dough to rise for 45 minutes.

**3.** Remove bowl from oven and gently press down on center of dough to deflate. Repeat folding (making total of 8 folds), re-cover, and return to oven until doubled in volume, about 45 minutes.

**4. FOR THE FILLING:** Whisk all ingredients together in bowl until well combined; set aside.

**5.** Grease two 8½ by 4½-inch loaf pans. Transfer dough to lightly floured counter and divide into 2 pieces. Working with 1 piece of dough, pat into rough 6 by 11-inch rectangle. With short side facing you, fold long sides in like a business letter to form 3 by 11-inch rectangle. Roll dough away from you into ball. Dust ball with flour and flatten with rolling pin into 7 by 18-inch rectangle with even ¼-inch thickness. Using spray bottle, spray dough lightly with water. Sprinkle half of filling mixture evenly over dough, leaving ¼-inch border on sides and ¾-inch border on top and bottom; spray filling lightly with water. (Filling should be speckled with water over entire surface.) With short side facing you, roll dough away from you into firm cylinder. Turn loaf seam side up and pinch closed; pinch ends closed. Dust loaf lightly on all sides with flour and let rest for 10 minutes. Repeat with second ball of dough and remaining filling.

**6.** Working with 1 loaf at a time, use bench scraper to cut loaf in half lengthwise; turn halves so cut sides are facing up. Gently stretch each half into 14-inch length. Line up pieces of dough and pinch 2 ends of strips together. Take piece on left and lay over piece on right. Repeat, keeping cut side up, until pieces of dough are tightly twisted. Pinch ends together. Transfer loaf, cut side up, to prepared loaf pan; push any exposed raisins into seams of braid. Repeat with second loaf. Cover loaves loosely with plastic, return to oven, and allow to rise for 45 minutes. Remove loaves and water pan from oven; heat oven to 350 degrees. Allow loaves to rise at room temperature until almost doubled in size, about 45 minutes (tops of loaves should rise about 1 inch over lip of pans).

**7.** Brush loaves with egg mixture. Bake until crust is well browned, about 25 minutes. Reduce oven temperature to 325 degrees, tent loaves with aluminum foil, and continue to bake until internal temperature registers 200 degrees, 15 to 25 minutes longer.

**8.** Transfer pans to wire rack and let cool for 5 minutes. Remove loaves from pans, return to rack, and cool to room temperature before slicing, about 2 hours.

### WEAVING CINNAMON SWIRL BREAD, RUSSIAN-STYLE

**1.** Using bench scraper or sharp chef's knife, cut filled dough in half lengthwise. Turn halves so cut sides are facing up.

**2.** With cut sides up, stretch each half into 14-inch length.

**3.** Pinch 2 ends of strips together. To braid, take left strip of dough and lay it over right strip of dough. Repeat braiding, keeping cut sides face up, until pieces are tightly twisted. Pinch ends together.

## No-Knead Brioche

**MAKES** 2 loaves

**WHY THIS RECIPE WORKS** The average brioche recipe is 50 percent butter, and the high fat content can make the brioche incredibly tender—or it can cause the dough to separate into a greasy mess. We made brioche not only a simple process but a failproof one by eliminating the hassle of adding softened butter to the dough little by little. Instead, we melted the butter and added it directly to the eggs. Then we dispensed with the stand mixer and opted for an equally effective no-knead approach that lets time do most of the work: An overnight rest in the fridge developed both structure and flavor. We used two simple loaf pans and then, to build structure and ensure a fine, even crumb, we shaped the dough into four balls before placing two in each pan. The dough can also be divided to make brioche buns or traditionally shaped loaves using fluted brioche molds. High-protein King Arthur Bread Flour works best with this recipe, though other bread flours will suffice. If you don't have a baking stone, bake the bread on a preheated rimmed baking sheet.

- 3¼ cups (17¾ ounces) bread flour
- 2¼ teaspoons instant or rapid-rise yeast
- 1½ teaspoons salt
- 7 large eggs (1 lightly beaten with pinch salt)
- ½ cup water, room temperature
- ⅓ cup (2⅓ ounces) sugar
- 16 tablespoons unsalted butter, melted and cooled slightly

**1.** Whisk flour, yeast, and salt together in large bowl. Whisk 6 eggs, water, and sugar together in medium bowl until sugar has dissolved. Whisk in melted butter until smooth. Add egg mixture to flour mixture and stir with wooden spoon until uniform mass forms and no dry flour remains, about 1 minute. Cover bowl with plastic wrap and let stand for 10 minutes.

**2.** Holding edge of dough with your fingertips, fold dough over itself by gently lifting and folding edge of dough toward middle. Turn bowl 45 degrees; fold again. Turn bowl and fold dough 6 more times (total of 8 folds). Cover with plastic and let rise for 30 minutes. Repeat folding and rising every 30 minutes, 3 more times. After fourth set of folds, cover bowl tightly with plastic and refrigerate for at least 16 hours or up to 48 hours.

**3.** Transfer dough to well-floured counter and divide into 4 pieces. Working with 1 piece of dough at a time, pat dough into 4-inch disk. Working around circumference of dough, fold edges of dough toward center until ball forms. Flip dough over and, without applying pressure, move your hands in small circular motions to form dough into smooth, taut round. (If dough sticks to your hands, lightly dust top of dough with flour.) Repeat with remaining dough. Cover dough rounds loosely with plastic and let rest for 5 minutes.

**4.** Grease two 8½ by 4½-inch loaf pans. After 5 minutes, flip each dough ball so seam side is facing up, pat into 4-inch disk, and repeat rounding step. Place 2 rounds, seam side down, side by side into prepared pans and press gently into corners. Cover loaves loosely with plastic and let rise at room temperature until almost doubled in size (dough should rise to about ½ inch below top edge of pan), 1½ to 2 hours. Thirty minutes before baking, adjust oven rack to middle position, place baking stone on rack, and heat oven to 350 degrees.

**5.** Remove plastic and brush loaves gently with remaining 1 egg beaten with salt. Set loaf pans on stone and bake until golden brown and internal temperature registers 190 degrees, 35 to 45 minutes, rotating pans halfway through baking. Transfer pans to wire rack and let cool for 5 minutes. Remove loaves from pans, return to wire rack, and let cool completely before slicing and serving, about 2 hours.

## Challah

**MAKES** 1 loaf

**WHY THIS RECIPE WORKS** To make challah dough that was moist but malleable, we combined a short rest during kneading with a long fermentation; this built a sturdy but stretchy gluten network that made the dough easy to handle. We also employed a Japanese dough-mixing technique called tangzhong, incorporating a cooked flour-water paste that bound up water in the dough so that it was moist but not sticky. Ample amounts of oil and eggs made the baked bread plush. Pointing the four dough strands in different directions, rather than lining them up parallel to one another, made them easier to keep track of during braiding. Brushing an egg wash—lightly salted to make the eggs more fluid—over the braided dough encouraged rich browning as the loaf baked. We strongly recommend weighing the flour for this recipe. This dough will be firmer and drier than most bread doughs, which makes it easy to braid. Some friction is necessary for rolling and braiding the ropes, so resist the urge to dust your counter with flour. If your counter is too narrow to stretch the ropes, slightly bend the pieces at the 12 o'clock and 6 o'clock positions. Bake this loaf on two nested baking sheets to keep the bottom of the loaf from getting too dark.

## BRAIDING CHALLAH

**1.** After arranging ropes in cross shape following recipe, lift rope at 12 o'clock, bring over center, and place in 5 o'clock position.

**2.** Lift rope at 6 o'clock, bring over center, and place in 12 o'clock position.

**3.** Lift rope at 9 o'clock, bring over center, and place in 4 o'clock position.

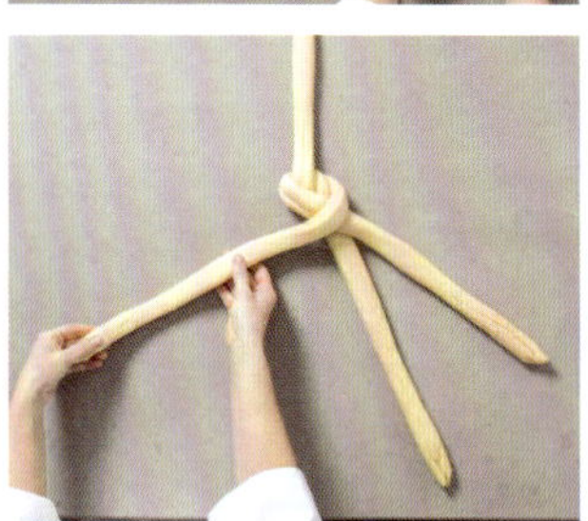

**4.** Lift rope at 3 o'clock and, working toward yourself, bring over braid and place in 8 o'clock position.

**5.** Adjust ropes so they are at 12, 3, 6, and 9 o'clock positions. Repeat steps 1 through 5.

**6.** Continue braiding, working toward yourself, until you can no longer braid. Loaf will naturally list to 1 side. Pinch ends of ropes together. Tuck both ends under braid.

**FLOUR PASTE**

- ½ cup water
- 3 tablespoons bread flour

**DOUGH**

- 1 large egg plus 2 large yolks
- ¼ cup water
- 2 tablespoons vegetable oil
- 2¾ cups (15⅛ ounces) bread flour
- 1¼ teaspoons instant or rapid-rise yeast
- ¼ cup (1¾ ounces) sugar
- 1 teaspoon table salt
- Vegetable oil spray

**EGG WASH**

- 1 large egg
- Pinch table salt
- 1 tablespoon sesame seeds or poppy seeds (optional)

**1. FOR THE FLOUR PASTE:** Whisk water and flour in small bowl until no lumps remain. Microwave, whisking every 20 seconds, until mixture thickens to stiff, smooth, pudding-like consistency that forms mound when dropped from end of whisk into bowl, 40 to 80 seconds.

**2. FOR THE DOUGH:** In bowl of stand mixer, whisk flour paste, egg and yolks, water, and oil until well combined. Add flour and yeast. Fit mixer with dough hook and mix on low speed until all flour is moistened, 3 to 4 minutes. Let stand for 20 minutes.

**3.** Add sugar and salt and mix on medium speed for 9 minutes (dough will be quite firm and dry). Transfer dough to counter and lightly spray now-empty mixer bowl with oil spray. Knead dough briefly to form ball and return it to prepared bowl. Lightly spray dough with oil spray and cover bowl with plastic wrap. Let dough rise until about doubled in volume, about 1½ hours.

**4.** Line rimmed baking sheet with parchment paper and nest in second rimmed baking sheet. Transfer dough to counter and press into 8-inch square, expelling as much air as possible. Cut dough in half lengthwise to form 2 rectangles. Cut each rectangle in half lengthwise to form 4 equal strips of dough. Roll 1 strip of dough into 16-inch rope. Continue rolling, tapering ends, until rope is 18 inches long. Repeat with remaining dough strips. Arrange ropes in plus-sign shape, with 4 ends overlapping in center by ½ inch. Firmly press center of cross into counter to seal ropes to each other and to counter.

**5.** Lift rope at 12 o'clock, bring over center, and place in 5 o'clock position. Lift rope at 6 o'clock, bring over center, and place in 12 o'clock position.

**6.** Lift rope at 9 o'clock, bring over center, and place in 4 o'clock position. Lift rope at 3 o'clock and, working toward yourself, bring over braid and place in 8 o'clock position. Adjust ropes so they are at 12, 3, 6, and 9 o'clock positions.

**7.** Repeat steps 5 and 6, working toward yourself, until you can no longer braid. Loaf will naturally list to 1 side.

**8.** Pinch ends of ropes together and tuck both ends under braid. Carefully transfer braid to prepared sheets. Cover loosely with plastic and let rise until dough does not spring back fully when gently pressed with your knuckle, about 3 hours.

**9. FOR THE EGG WASH:** Thirty minutes before baking, adjust oven rack to middle position and heat oven to 350 degrees. Whisk together egg and salt. Brush loaf with egg wash and sprinkle with sesame seeds, if using. Bake until loaf is deep golden brown and registers at least 195 degrees, 35 to 40 minutes. Let cool on sheets for 20 minutes. Transfer loaf to wire rack and let cool completely before slicing, about 2 hours.

## Stollen

**MAKES** 2 loaves

**WHY THIS RECIPE WORKS** Stollen is a rich, sweet yeasted bread served at Christmas throughout Germany and Austria. It features dried and candied fruit as well as nuts and spirits. We enriched the dough with milk, brandy, egg, and butter, melting the butter before stirring it in to produce the short crumb we wanted. We do not recommend mixing this dough by hand. If the dough becomes too soft to work with at any point, refrigerate it until it's firm enough to handle easily.

**FILLING**

1 tube (7 ounces) almond paste, cut into 4 pieces
1 tablespoon unsalted butter, softened
1 tablespoon water
Pinch nutmeg

**DOUGH**

1 cup raisins
½ cup (4 ounces) brandy
½ cup chopped candied lemon peel
½ cup chopped candied orange peel
½ cup slivered almonds, toasted
3½ cups (17½ ounces) all-purpose flour
4 teaspoons instant or rapid-rise yeast
1¼ teaspoons table salt
1 cup (8 ounces) whole milk, room temperature
10 tablespoons unsalted butter, melted, divided
½ cup (3½ ounces) granulated sugar
1 large egg, room temperature
1 teaspoon vanilla extract
Confectioners' sugar

**1. FOR THE FILLING:** Using stand mixer fitted with paddle, beat almond paste, butter, water, and nutmeg on medium speed until smooth, about 1 minute. Transfer to bowl, cover, and refrigerate until ready to use.

**2. FOR THE DOUGH:** Microwave raisins and brandy in covered bowl until steaming, about 1 minute. Let sit until raisins have softened, about 15 minutes. Drain raisins and reserve brandy. Combine raisins, candied lemon peel, candied orange peel, and almonds in bowl.

**3.** Whisk flour, yeast, and salt together in clean, dry mixer bowl. Whisk milk, 8 tablespoons melted butter, granulated sugar, egg, vanilla, and reserved brandy in 4-cup liquid measuring cup until sugar has dissolved. Using paddle on low speed, slowly add milk mixture to flour mixture and mix until cohesive dough starts to form and no dry flour remains, about 2 minutes, scraping down bowl as needed. Slowly add fruit mixture and mix until incorporated, about 30 seconds. Transfer dough to lightly greased large bowl or container, cover tightly with plastic wrap, and refrigerate for at least 12 hours or up to 24 hours.

**4.** Stack 2 rimmed baking sheets, line with aluminum foil, and spray with vegetable oil spray. Transfer filling to well-floured counter, divide in half, and press each half into 7 by 2-inch rectangle; set aside.

**5.** Transfer dough to well-floured counter, divide in half, and cover loosely with greased plastic. Using your well-floured hands, press 1 piece of dough into 10 by 8-inch rectangle (keep remaining piece covered), with short side parallel to counter edge. Place 1 piece of filling across top edge of dough, leaving 2-inch border at top. Fold dough away from you over filling until folded edge is snug against filling and dough extends 2 inches beyond top edge.

**6.** Fold top 2 inches of dough back toward center of loaf. Pinch side seams together to seal. Repeat with remaining dough and filling. Transfer loaves to prepared sheet, spaced about 4 inches apart. Cover loosely with greased plastic and let rest for 30 minutes.

### SHAPING STOLLEN

**1.** Working with 1 piece of dough at a time, press into 10 by 8-inch rectangle, with short side parallel to counter edge.

**2.** Place 1 piece of filling across top edge of dough, leaving 2-inch border at top. Fold dough away from you over filling until folded edge is snug against filling and dough extends 2 inches beyond top edge.

**3.** Fold top 2 inches of dough back toward center of loaf. Pinch side seams together to seal.

**7.** Adjust oven rack to middle position and heat oven to 350 degrees. Bake until golden brown and loaves register 190 to 195 degrees, 40 to 45 minutes, rotating sheet halfway through baking. Brush loaves with remaining 2 tablespoons melted butter and dust liberally with confectioners' sugar. Transfer to wire rack and let cool completely, about 3 hours. Dust with additional confectioners' sugar before serving. (Stollen can be wrapped in plastic wrap and stored at room temperature for up to 1 month.)

## Breton Kouign Amann

**SERVES** 8 to 10

**WHY THIS RECIPE WORKS** A little bit croissant and a little bit sticky bun, Brittany's traditional kouign amann is easier and quicker to make than either one. A lean yeasted dough made with all-purpose flour provided strength and workability. Embedding the sugar (and a little extra salt) into the butter block by paddling the ingredients together in a stand mixer limited contact between the sugar and dough, thus preventing the sugar from drawing moisture out of the dough and making it unworkably sticky; it also limited abrasion during rolling, which would otherwise tear the dough. It helped to enclose and shape the butter mixture in a parchment paper "envelope." The parchment kept the mixture contained which helped shaping and made it easy to roll during lamination. Kouign amman is best eaten on the day it is made; leftovers can be wrapped in plastic wrap and stored at room temperature for up to 3 days. Warm gently in the oven before serving.

- 2¼ cups (11¼ ounces) all-purpose flour
- 1¼ teaspoons table salt, divided
- ½ teaspoon instant or rapid-rise yeast
- 1 cup water, room temperature
- 16 tablespoons salted butter, softened
- ¾ cup (5¼ ounces) plus 1 tablespoon sugar, divided
- 1 tablespoon milk

**1.** Using rubber spatula, stir together flour, ¾ teaspoon salt, and yeast in bowl of stand mixer. Add water and mix until most flour is moistened. Attach dough hook and knead on low speed until cohesive dough forms, about 1 minute. Increase speed to medium-low and knead until dough is smooth and elastic, about 5 minutes. Shape dough into ball (scrape out mixer bowl but do not wash). Flatten into rough 5-inch square and transfer to lightly greased plate. Cover dough and refrigerate for at least 1 hour or up to 24 hours. While dough rests, make butter packet.

**2.** Fold 18-inch length of parchment in half to create rectangle. Fold over 3 open sides of rectangle to form 6 by 9-inch rectangle with enclosed sides. Crease folds firmly. Open parchment packet and set aside. Combine butter, ¾ cup sugar, and remaining ½ teaspoon salt in now-empty mixer bowl. Using paddle, mix on low speed until thoroughly combined, about 1 minute. Transfer butter mixture to prepared parchment rectangle, fold parchment over mixture, and press to ½-inch thickness. Refold parchment at creases to enclose mixture. Turn packet over so flaps are underneath and roll gently until butter mixture fills packet, taking care to achieve even thickness. Refrigerate for at least 45 minutes or up to 24 hours.

**3.** Transfer butter block to counter. Transfer dough to freezer and freeze for 10 minutes. Meanwhile, adjust oven rack to middle position and heat oven to 375 degrees. Lightly grease 9-inch round cake pan and line with 12-inch parchment square, pleating parchment so it lines bottom and sides of pan.

**4.** Transfer dough to well-floured counter and roll into 18 by 6½-inch rectangle with short side parallel to counter edge. Unwrap butter block and place in center of dough. Fold upper and lower sections of dough over butter so they meet in center

### MAKING THE BUTTER BLOCK FOR KOUIGN AMANN

**1.** Fold 18-inch length of parchment in half to create rectangle.

**2.** Fold over 3 open sides of rectangle to form 6 by 9-inch rectangle with enclosed sides. Crease folds firmly.

**3.** Open parchment packet and place butter mixture in center.

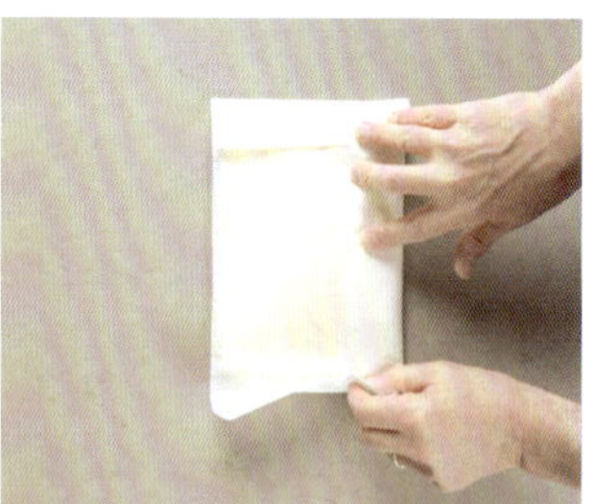

**4.** Fold parchment over mixture and press to ½-inch thickness. Refold parchment at creases to enclose mixture.

**5.** Turn packet over so flaps are underneath and roll until butter fills packet, taking care to achieve even thickness.

## LAMINATING AND SHAPING KOUIGN AMANN

**1.** Transfer dough to well-floured counter and roll into 18 by 6½-inch rectangle with short side parallel to counter edge. Unwrap butter block and place in center of dough.

**2.** Fold upper and lower sections of dough over butter so they meet in center (it's OK to gently stretch dough). Press center seam and side seams closed.

**3.** Place rolling pin at top edge of dough and press gently to make slight depression across top. Lift pin, move it 1 inch closer to you, and press again. Continue pressing and lifting to bottom edge.

**4.** Turn rolling pin 90 degrees and make similar depressions across width of dough.

**5.** Roll dough out lengthwise into 21 by 7-inch rectangle. Pop any bubbles that form and dust off any flour clinging to surface of dough using dry pastry brush.

**6.** Starting at bottom of dough, fold into thirds like business letter to form 7-inch square. Turn square 90 degrees. Roll out lengthwise into 21 by 7-inch rectangle, popping any bubbles that form.

**7.** Using dry pastry brush, dust off any flour clinging to surface of dough. Fold dough into thirds.

**8.** Roll dough into 11-inch square.

**9.** Fold each corner to center, overlapping slightly, and press to adhere.

**10.** Push right and left corners toward center, and then push top and bottom corners toward center to form rough, crumpled round.

**11.** Press top to compress. Flip dough so smoother side is facing up, then tuck edges under to form round. Flatten gently with your hands, then roll dough into 9½-inch round. Transfer to prepared pan.

**12.** Using sharp paring knife, score top of pastry in diamond pattern.

(it's OK to gently stretch dough). Press center seam and side seams closed. Dust counter with more flour if necessary. Place rolling pin at top edge of dough and press gently to make slight depression across top. Lift pin, move it 1 inch closer to you, and press again. Continue pressing and lifting to bottom edge. Turn rolling pin 90 degrees and make similar depressions across width of dough. Roll dough out lengthwise into 21 by 7-inch rectangle (it's OK if it becomes slightly wider). Pop any bubbles that form. Using dry pastry brush, dust off any flour clinging to surface of dough. Starting at bottom of dough, fold into thirds like business letter to form 7-inch square. Turn square 90 degrees. Dust counter with more flour if necessary. Roll out lengthwise into 21 by 7-inch rectangle, and pop any bubbles. Using dry pastry brush, dust off any flour clinging to surface of dough, and fold into thirds.

**5.** Dust counter with more flour if necessary. Roll dough into 11-inch square. Fold each corner to center, overlapping slightly, and press to adhere. Push right and left corners toward center, and then push top and bottom corners toward center to form rough, crumpled round. Press top to compress. Flip dough so smoother side is facing up, then tuck edges under to form round. Flatten gently with your hands, then roll dough into 9½-inch round. Transfer to prepared pan (it's OK if dough is slightly sticky), squishing edges to fit.

**6.** Brush top with milk. Using sharp paring knife, score top of pastry in diamond pattern. Sprinkle evenly with remaining 1 tablespoon sugar. Using paring knife, pierce dough all the way down to pan surface in 4 places to create air vents. Bake until pastry is deeply browned and crisp, 50 minutes to 1 hour. Let cool in pan on wire rack for 10 minutes. Invert, remove parchment, and reinvert. Let cool for at least 30 minutes before serving.

## Croissants

**MAKES** 22 croissants

**WHY THIS RECIPE WORKS** We wanted to create an approachable croissant recipe for home bakers that would deliver rich, buttery flavor. The layered structure that characterizes croissants is formed through a process called lamination. First, a basic dough of flour, water, yeast, sugar, salt, and a small amount of butter is made. Then a larger amount of butter is formed into a block and encased in the relatively lean dough. This dough and butter package is rolled out and folded multiple times (each is called a "turn") to form paper-thin layers of dough separated by even thinner layers of butter. Once baked, it's these layers that make croissants so flaky and decadent. To start, we found that more turns didn't necessarily produce more layers; we stopped at three turns, as any more produced a bready texture. As for the butter, we found that great croissants demanded higher-fat European-style butter. And one essential tip we discovered during recipe development was to give the dough a quick freeze to firm it to the consistency of the butter, thus ensuring perfectly distinct layers. These croissants take at least 10 hours to make from start to finish, but the process can be spread over 2 days. European-style cultured butters have a higher butterfat content, which makes it easier to fold them into the dough (we like Plugrá). Any brand of all-purpose flour will produce acceptable croissants, but we recommend using King Arthur All-Purpose Flour, which has a slightly higher protein content. Do not attempt to make these croissants in a room that is warmer than 80 degrees. If at any time during rolling the dough retracts, dust it lightly with flour, fold it loosely, cover it, and return it to the freezer to rest for 10 to 15 minutes. This recipe makes 22 croissants, but only 12 are baked. Shaped croissants can be evenly spaced 1 inch apart on a parchment-lined baking sheet, wrapped with plastic wrap, and frozen until solid, about 2 hours. (Once frozen, transfer the croissants from the baking sheet to a zipper-lock bag; croissants can be frozen for up to 2 months. Bake frozen croissants as directed in step 8, increasing the rising time by 1 to 2 hours.)

- 24 tablespoons European-style unsalted butter, very cold, plus 3 tablespoons unsalted butter at room temperature
- 1¾ cups whole milk
- 4 teaspoons instant or rapid-rise yeast
- 4¼ cups (21¼ ounces) unbleached all-purpose flour
- ¼ cup (1¾ ounces) sugar
- Table salt
- 1 large egg
- 1 teaspoon cold water

**1.** Melt 3 tablespoons of the butter in a medium saucepan over low heat. Remove from the heat and immediately stir in the milk (the temperature should be lower than 90 degrees). Whisk in yeast; transfer the milk mixture to the bowl of a stand mixer. Add the flour, sugar, and 2 teaspoons salt. Using the mixer's dough hook, knead on low speed until a cohesive dough forms, 2 to 3 minutes. Increase the speed to medium-low and knead for 1 minute. Remove the bowl from the mixer, remove the dough hook, and cover the bowl with plastic wrap. Let the dough rest at room temperature for 30 minutes.

**2.** Transfer the dough to a parchment paper–lined baking sheet and shape into a 10 by 7-inch rectangle about 1 inch thick. Wrap tightly with plastic and refrigerate for 2 hours.

**3.** To make the butter block: While the dough chills, fold a 24-inch length of parchment in half to create a 12-inch rectangle. Fold over 3 open sides of the rectangle to form an 8-inch square with enclosed sides. Crease the folds firmly. Place the cold butter directly on the work surface and beat with a rolling pin for about 60 seconds until the butter is just pliable, but not warm, folding the butter in on itself using a bench scraper. Beat into a rough 6-inch square. Unfold the parchment envelope. Using the bench scraper, transfer the butter to the center of the parchment square, re-folding at the creases to enclose. Turn the packet over so that the flaps are underneath and gently roll the butter packet until the butter fills the parchment square, taking care to achieve an even thickness. Refrigerate for at least 45 minutes.

**4. TO LAMINATE THE DOUGH:** Transfer the dough to the freezer. After 30 minutes, transfer the dough to a lightly floured work surface and roll into a 17 by 8-inch rectangle with the long side of the rectangle parallel to the edge of the work surface. Unwrap the butter and place it in the center of the dough so that the butter and dough are flush at the top and bottom. Fold 2 sides of the dough over the butter square so they meet in the center. Press the seam together. With the rolling pin, press firmly on each open end of the packet. Roll out the dough, perpendicular to the edge of the work surface, until it is 24 inches long and 8 inches wide. Bring the bottom third of the dough up, then fold the upper third over it, folding like a business letter into an 8-inch square. Turn the dough 90 degrees counterclockwise. Roll out the dough again, perpendicular to the edge of the work surface, into a 24 by 8-inch rectangle and fold into thirds. Place the dough on the baking sheet, wrap tightly with plastic wrap, and return to the freezer for 30 minutes.

**5.** Transfer the dough to a lightly floured work surface so that the top flap of the dough is facing right. Roll once more, perpendicular to the edge of the work surface, into a 24 by 8-inch rectangle and fold into thirds. Place the dough on the baking sheet, wrap tightly with plastic wrap, and refrigerate for 2 hours.

**6.** Transfer the dough to the freezer. After 30 minutes, transfer to a lightly floured work surface and roll into an 18 by 16-inch rectangle with the long side of the rectangle parallel to the edge of the work surface. Fold the upper half of the dough over the lower half. Using a ruler, mark the dough at 3-inch intervals along the bottom edge with a bench scraper (you should have 5 marks). Move the ruler to the top of the dough, measure in 1½ inches from the left, then use this mark to measure out 3-inch intervals (you should have 6 marks). Starting at the lower left corner, use a pizza wheel or knife to cut the dough into triangles from mark to mark. You will have 12 single triangles and 5 double triangles; discard any scraps. Unfold the double triangles and cut into 10 single triangles (making 22 equal-size triangles in total). If the dough begins to soften, return to the freezer for 10 minutes.

**7.** To shape the croissants: Position 1 triangle on the work surface. (Keep the remaining triangles covered with plastic while shaping.) Cut a ½-inch slit in the center of the short end of the triangle. Grasp the triangle by 2 corners on either side of the slit and stretch gently, then grasp the bottom point and stretch. Fold both sides of the slit down. Positioning your palms on the folds, roll partway toward the point. Gently stretch the point again; continue to roll, tucking the point underneath. Curve the ends gently toward one another to create a crescent shape. Repeat with the remaining triangles.

**8.** Place 12 croissants on 2 parchment-lined baking sheets, leaving at least 2½ inches between the croissants, 6 croissants per sheet. Lightly wrap the baking sheets with plastic, leaving room for the croissants to expand. Let stand at room temperature until nearly doubled in size, 2½ to 3 hours. (Shaped croissants can be refrigerated on trays for up to 18 hours. Remove from the refrigerator to rise and add at least 30 minutes to the rising time.)

## MAKING THE BUTTER BLOCK FOR CROISSANTS

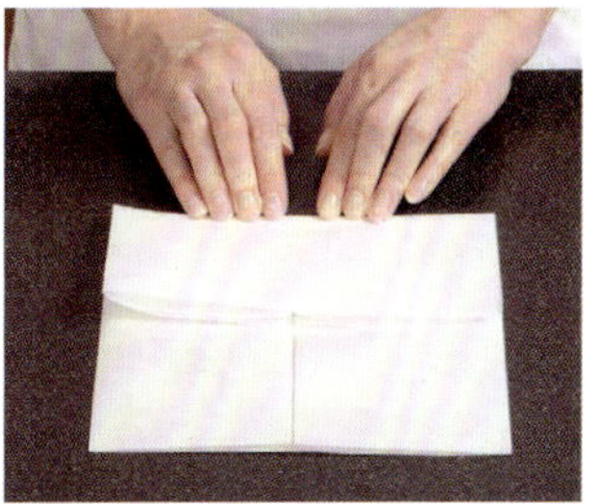

**1.** Fold a 24-inch length of parchment in half to create a 12-inch rectangle. Fold over 3 open sides of the rectangle to form an 8-inch enclosed square. Crease the folds firmly.

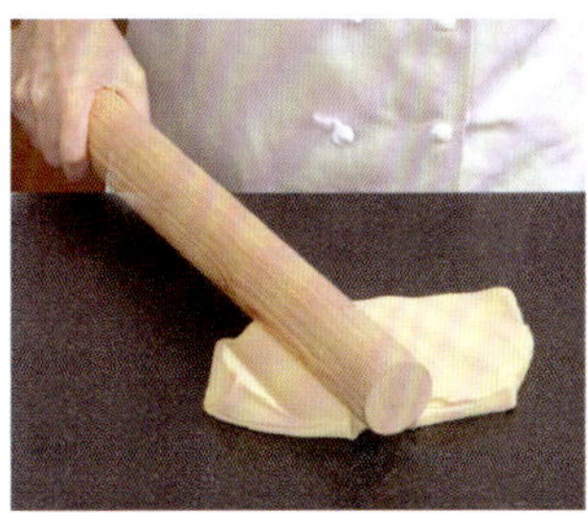

**2.** Using a rolling pin, beat the butter until it is just pliable, then fold the butter in on itself using a bench scraper. Beat the butter into a rough 6-inch square.

**3.** Unfold the envelope and, using a bench scraper, transfer the butter to the parchment, re-folding at the creases to enclose. Turn the packet over; gently roll the butter to fill the parchment square, taking care to achieve an even thickness.

## LAMINATING THE CROISSANT DOUGH

**1.** Roll the dough into a 17 by 8-inch rectangle. Unwrap the butter and place in the center of the dough so that the edges of the butter and dough are flush at the top and bottom. Fold two sides of the dough over the butter so they meet in the center of the butter square.

**2.** Using your fingertips, press the seam together. Using a rolling pin, press firmly on each open end of the packet. Roll the dough out lengthwise until it is 24 inches long and 8 inches wide.

**3.** Starting at the bottom of the dough, fold it into thirds. Turn the dough 90 degrees; roll and fold again. Place it on a baking sheet, wrap with plastic wrap, and return to the freezer for 30 minutes. Roll and fold into thirds one more time.

## SHAPING THE CROISSANTS

**1.** Transfer the dough from the freezer to a lightly floured work surface and roll it into an 18 by 12-inch rectangle. (If it begins to retract, fold it into thirds, wrap it, and return it to the freezer for 10 to 15 minutes.) Fold the upper half of the dough over the lower half.

**2.** Using a ruler, mark the dough at 3-inch intervals along the bottom edge. Move the ruler to the top of the dough, measure in 1½ inches from the left, then use this mark to measure out 3-inch intervals.

**3.** Using a sharp pizza wheel or knife, cut the dough into triangles from mark to mark; discard any scraps.

**4.** You should have 12 single triangles and 5 double triangles. Unfold the double triangles and cut in half to form 10 single triangles (making 22 triangles in all).

**5.** Cut a ½-inch slit in the center of the short end of a triangle. If the dough begins to soften, return it to the freezer for 10 minutes.

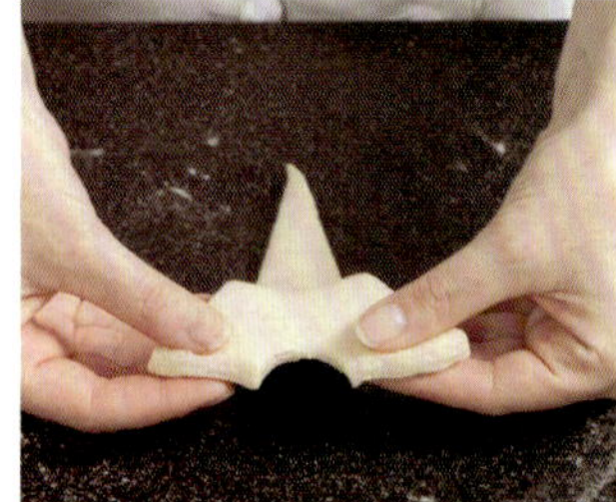

**6.** Grasp the triangle by the 2 corners on either side of the slit and stretch gently, then grasp the point and stretch.

**7.** Place the triangle on the work surface so the point is facing toward you. Fold both sides of the slit down.

**8.** Positioning your palms on the folds, roll partway toward the point.

**9.** Gently grasp the point with one hand and stretch again. Resume rolling, tucking the point underneath.

**10.** Curve the ends gently toward one another to form a crescent shape. Repeat with the remaining triangles.

**9.** After the croissants have been rising for 2 hours, adjust the oven racks to the upper-middle and lower-middle positions and heat the oven to 425 degrees. In a small bowl, whisk together the egg, water, and a pinch of salt. Brush the croissants with the egg wash using a pastry brush. Place the croissants in the oven and reduce the temperature to 400 degrees. Bake for 12 minutes then switch and rotate the baking sheets. Continue to bake until deep golden brown, 8 to 12 minutes longer. Transfer the croissants to a wire rack and allow to cool until just warm, about 15 minutes. Serve warm or at room temperature.

# Kanelbullar (Swedish Cinnamon Buns)

**MAKES** 12 buns

**WHY THIS RECIPE WORKS** The Swedish cinnamon buns known as kanelbullar are soft and fluffy, with lightly crisp swirled edges, and are filled with buttery cinnamon sugar and suffused with cardamom. They're a favorite feature of fika, the daily social ritual of sharing coffee and a snack with friends or colleagues. For our version of this iconic sweet, we started by incorporating a tangzhong (a cooked paste of flour and milk) into the dough. The paste helped lock in moisture so our high-hydration dough was workable and not too sticky. The water in the dough converted to steam during baking, which made the buns fluffy and light. Refrigerating the dough allowed the flour to fully absorb moisture and the butter to firm up, making the dough easier to handle, and preshaping it in a baking pan made it easier to roll out later. Starting with a long strip of dough was important when shaping each bun. Instead of stretching, we cut each strip almost in half and then opened it up to a 2-foot length. Shaping the buns loosely gave them the space to expand during baking without becoming misshapen. We strongly recommend using a scale to measure the flour. It's well worth seeking out cardamom seeds at a South Asian market or online. Alternatively, crack open whole green cardamom pods and remove the seeds yourself. Coarsely grind the seeds using a spice grinder or mortar and pestle. Swedish pearl sugar is available online; you can substitute turbinado sugar (sometimes sold as Sugar in the Raw) if you prefer, though it may soften on the buns during storage.

**FLOUR PASTE**

- ¾ cup milk
- ¼ cup (1⅓ ounces) bread flour

**DOUGH**

- ½ cup milk, chilled
- 2 cups (11 ounces) bread flour
- 1 tablespoon instant or rapid-rise yeast
- ¼ cup (1¾ ounces) granulated sugar
- 1 teaspoon table salt
- 6 tablespoons unsalted butter, cut into 6 pieces and softened
- 2 teaspoons cardamom seeds, ground coarse

**FILLING**

- ¾ cup (5¼ ounces) granulated sugar
- 6 tablespoons unsalted butter, softened
- 2 tablespoons ground cinnamon
- 1 tablespoon bread flour
- ¼ teaspoon table salt
- 1 large egg beaten with 1 tablespoon water and pinch table salt
- ¼ cup Swedish pearl sugar

**1. FOR THE FLOUR PASTE:** Whisk milk and flour in small bowl until no lumps remain. Microwave, whisking every 20 seconds, until mixture has thick, stiff consistency, 1 to 2 minutes.

**2. FOR THE DOUGH:** In bowl of stand mixer, whisk flour paste and milk until smooth. Add flour and yeast. Fit mixer with dough hook and mix on low speed until all flour is moistened, 1 to 2 minutes (dough will look quite dry). Let stand for 15 minutes. Add sugar and salt and mix on medium-low speed for 5 minutes. Stop mixer and add butter and cardamom. Continue to mix on medium-low speed 5 minutes longer, scraping down dough hook and sides of bowl halfway through mixing (dough may stick to bottom of bowl but should clear sides).

**3.** Lightly grease 13 by 9-inch baking pan. Transfer dough to prepared pan (scrape bowl but do not wash). Flip dough, then press and stretch dough until it reaches edges of pan. Cover with plastic wrap and refrigerate for 1 hour. While dough chills, make filling.

**4. FOR THE FILLING:** Add all ingredients to now-empty mixer bowl. Fit mixer with paddle and mix on low speed until fully combined, about 1 minute.

**5.** Line 18 by 13-inch rimmed baking sheet with parchment paper. Transfer dough to well-floured counter. Roll dough into 18 by 10-inch rectangle, with shorter side parallel to edge of counter. Using offset spatula, spread filling over lower two-thirds of rectangle, going all the way to edges (if filling is too stiff to spread, transfer to smaller bowl and microwave for 5 to 10 seconds). Fold upper third of dough over middle third. Fold lower third over middle third to create 10 by 6-inch rectangle. Roll into 12-inch square.

**6.** Cut dough into twelve 1-inch strips. Cut each strip in half lengthwise, leaving it attached at very top (each strip will look like a pair of legs). Extend 1 strip to 24-inch length, but do not stretch. Starting at 1 end, wrap strip around tips of your first 3 fingers, loosely coiling strands side by side along length of your fingers. Continue to wrap loosely until you have just 4 to 6 inches left. Use your thumb to pin dough to side of bundle closest to you, then loop remaining strip over bundle. Transfer to prepared sheet, tucking end of strip under bun. Repeat with remaining strips. Cover sheet with plastic or damp dish towel. Let sit until slightly puffed, about 1 hour.

**7.** About 15 minutes before baking, adjust oven rack to middle position and heat oven to 425 degrees. Brush buns with egg mixture (you won't need all of it) and sprinkle 1 teaspoon pearl sugar on top of each bun. Bake until buns are golden brown and register at least 200 degrees, 13 to 17 minutes, rotating sheet halfway through baking. Transfer buns, still on sheet, to wire rack and let sit for 5 minutes. Use spatula to transfer buns to wire rack (some filling may leak out and form crisp frill around bun). Let cool for at least 10 minutes before serving. (Buns can be cooled completely and stored in a zipper-lock bag at room temperature for up to 2 days or frozen for up to 2 weeks.)

### SHAPING KANELBULLAR

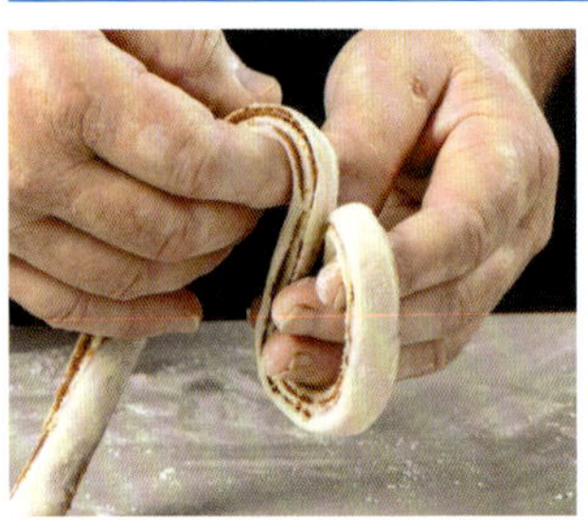

**1.** Starting at 1 end, wrap strip around tips of your first 3 fingers, coiling strands side by side along length of your fingers.

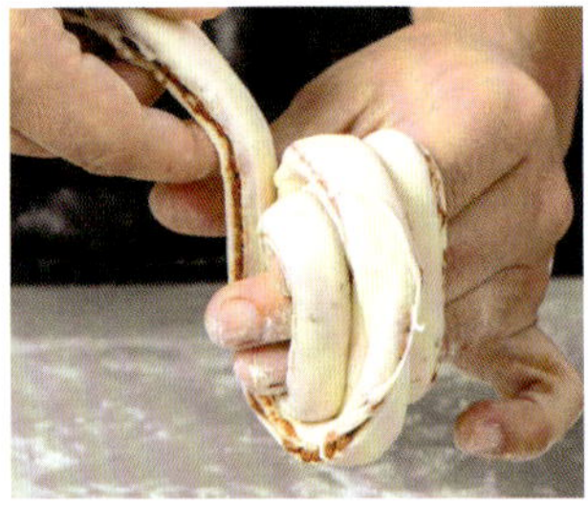

**2.** Continue to wrap loosely until you have just 4 to 6 inches left.

**3.** Use your thumb to pin dough to side of bundle closest to you.

**4.** Loop remaining strip over bundle and tuck into underside of bun.

## Ultimate Sticky Buns

**MAKES** 12 buns

**WHY THIS RECIPE WORKS** We wanted a sticky bun that fulfilled its promise of being both soft and sticky. To make a soft, tender, and moist sticky bun, we added a cooked flour-and-water paste (called a tangzhong) to the dough. The paste traps water, so the dough isn't sticky or difficult to work with, and the increased hydration converts to steam during baking, which makes the buns fluffy. The added water also keeps the crumb moist and tender. To ensure that the soft bread wouldn't collapse under the weight of the topping, we strengthened the crumb by adding a resting period and withholding the sugar and salt until the gluten was firmly established. Dark corn syrup plus water was the key to a gooey, sticky topping that was substantial enough to sit atop the buns without sinking in. These buns take about 4 hours to make from start to finish. We strongly recommend that you measure the flour for the dough by weight. The slight tackiness of the dough aids in flattening and stretching it in step 6, so resist the urge to use a lot of dusting flour. Rolling the dough cylinder tightly in step 7 will result in misshapen rolls; keep the cylinder a bit slack. Bake these buns in a metal, not glass or ceramic, baking pan. We like dark corn syrup and pecans here, but light corn syrup may be used, and the nuts may be omitted, if desired.

**FLOUR PASTE**

- ⅔ cup water
- ¼ cup (1⅓ ounces) bread flour

**DOUGH**

- ⅔ cup milk
- 1 large egg plus 1 large yolk
- 2¾ cups (15⅛ ounces) bread flour
- 2 teaspoons instant or rapid-rise yeast
- 3 tablespoons granulated sugar
- 1½ teaspoons table salt
- 6 tablespoons unsalted butter, softened

**TOPPING**

- 6 tablespoons unsalted butter, melted
- ½ cup packed (3½ ounces) dark brown sugar
- ¼ cup (1¾ ounces) granulated sugar
- ¼ cup dark corn syrup
- ¼ teaspoon table salt
- 2 tablespoons water
- 1 cup pecans, toasted and chopped (optional)

**FILLING**

- ¾ cup packed (5¼ ounces) dark brown sugar
- 1 teaspoon ground cinnamon

**1. FOR THE FLOUR PASTE:** Whisk water and flour in small bowl until no lumps remain. Microwave, whisking every 25 seconds, until mixture thickens to stiff, smooth, pudding-like consistency that forms mound when dropped from end of whisk into bowl, 50 to 75 seconds.

**2. FOR THE DOUGH:** In bowl of stand mixer, whisk flour paste and milk until smooth. Add egg and yolk and whisk until incorporated. Add flour and yeast. Fit stand mixer with dough hook and mix on low speed until all flour is moistened, 1 to 2 minutes. Let stand for 15 minutes. Add sugar and salt and mix on medium-low speed for 5 minutes. Stop mixer and add butter. Continue to mix on medium-low speed for 5 minutes longer, scraping down dough hook and sides of bowl halfway through (dough will stick to bottom of bowl).

**3.** Transfer dough to lightly floured counter. Knead briefly to form ball and transfer seam side down to lightly greased bowl; lightly coat surface of dough with vegetable oil spray and cover bowl with plastic wrap. Let dough rise until just doubled in volume, 40 minutes to 1 hour.

**4. FOR THE TOPPING:** While dough rises, grease 13 by 9-inch metal baking pan. Whisk melted butter, brown sugar, granulated sugar, corn syrup, and salt in medium bowl until smooth. Add water and whisk until incorporated. Pour mixture into prepared pan and tilt pan to cover bottom. Sprinkle evenly with pecans, if using.

**5. FOR THE FILLING:** Stir sugar and cinnamon in small bowl until thoroughly combined; set aside.

**6.** Turn out dough onto lightly floured counter. Press dough gently but firmly to expel air. Working from center toward edge, pat and stretch dough to form 18 by 15-inch rectangle with long edge nearest you. Sprinkle filling over dough, leaving 1-inch border along top edge; smooth filling into even layer with your hand, then gently press mixture into dough to adhere.

**7.** Beginning with long edge nearest you, roll dough into cylinder, taking care not to roll too tightly. Pinch seam to seal and roll cylinder seam side down. Mark gently with knife to create 12 equal portions. To slice, hold strand of dental floss taut and slide underneath cylinder, stopping at first mark. Cross ends of floss over each other and pull. Slice cylinder into 12 portions and transfer, cut sides down, to prepared baking pan. Cover tightly with plastic wrap and let rise until buns are puffy and touching one another, 40 minutes to 1 hour. (Buns may be refrigerated immediately after shaping for up to 14 hours. To bake, remove baking pan from refrigerator and let sit until buns are puffy and touching one another, 1 to 1½ hours.) Meanwhile, adjust oven racks to lowest and lower-middle positions. Place rimmed baking sheet on lower rack to catch any drips and heat oven to 375 degrees.

**8.** Bake buns on upper rack until golden brown, about 20 minutes. Tent with aluminum foil and bake until center of dough registers at least 200 degrees, 10 to 15 minutes longer. Let buns cool in pan on wire rack for 5 minutes. Place rimmed baking sheet over buns and carefully invert. Using spoon, scoop any glaze from baking pan onto buns. Let cool for at least 10 minutes longer before serving.

## Sticky Buns with Pecans

**MAKES** 12 buns

**WHY THIS RECIPE WORKS** Sticky buns are often too sweet and much too big. We wanted a bun that was neither dense nor bready, but tender and feathery with a gooey glaze and a flavor that was buttery and not too sweet. To keep the glaze from hardening into a taffy-like shell, we included cream, which kept the glaze supple. The yeast dough for these buns should be rich, so we added buttermilk, which gave the buns a complex flavor and a little acidity that balanced the sweetness. After the first rise, we spread the filling over the dough, rolled it, cut the individual buns, and laid them in the pan with caramel to rise once more before being baked. Setting the pan on a baking stone in the oven ensured that the bottoms of the buns (which would end up on top) baked completely. To preserve the crispness of the toasted pecans, we topped the rolls with them before serving. This recipe has four components: the dough that is shaped into buns, the filling that creates the swirl in the shaped buns, the caramel glaze that bakes in the bottom of the baking dish along with the buns, and the pecan topping.

**DOUGH**

- 3 large eggs, at room temperature
- ¾ cup buttermilk, at room temperature
- ¼ cup (1¾ ounces) granulated sugar
- 1¼ teaspoons table salt
- 2¼ teaspoons (1 envelope) instant or rapid-rise yeast
- 4¼ cups (21¼ ounces) unbleached all-purpose flour, plus extra for the work surface
- 6 tablespoons (¾ stick) unsalted butter, melted and still warm

**CARAMEL GLAZE**

- ¾ cup packed (5¼ ounces) light brown sugar
- 6 tablespoons (¾ stick) unsalted butter
- 3 tablespoons light or dark corn syrup
- 2 tablespoons heavy cream
- Pinch table salt

**CINNAMON-SUGAR FILLING**

- ¾ cup packed (5¼ ounces) light brown sugar
- 2 teaspoons ground cinnamon
- ¼ teaspoon ground cloves
- Pinch table salt
- 1 tablespoon unsalted butter, melted

**PECAN TOPPING**

- ¼ cup packed (1¾ ounces) light brown sugar
- 3 tablespoons light or dark corn syrup
- 3 tablespoons unsalted butter
- Pinch table salt
- ¾ cup (3 ounces) pecans, toasted in a small, dry skillet over medium heat until fragrant and browned, about 5 minutes, then cooled and chopped coarse
- 1 teaspoon vanilla extract

**1. FOR THE DOUGH:** In the bowl of a stand mixer, whisk the eggs to combine; add the buttermilk and whisk to combine. Whisk in the granulated sugar, salt, and yeast. Add about 2 cups of the flour and the butter; stir with a wooden spoon or rubber spatula until evenly moistened and combined. Add all but about ¼ cup of the remaining flour and knead with the dough hook at low speed for 5 minutes. Check the consistency of the dough (it should feel soft and moist but should not be wet and sticky; add more flour, if necessary); knead at low speed 5 minutes longer (the dough should clear the sides of the bowl but stick to the bottom). Turn the dough out onto a lightly floured work surface; knead by hand for about 1 minute to ensure that the dough is uniform (the dough should not stick to the work surface during hand kneading; if it does, knead in additional flour 1 tablespoon at a time).

**2.** Lightly spray a large bowl or plastic container with vegetable oil spray. Transfer the dough to the bowl, spray the dough lightly with vegetable oil spray, then cover the bowl tightly with plastic wrap and set in a warm, draft-free spot until doubled in volume, 2 to 2½ hours.

**3. FOR THE CARAMEL GLAZE:** Meanwhile, combine all the glaze ingredients in a small saucepan; cook over medium heat, whisking occasionally, until the butter is melted and the mixture is thoroughly combined. Pour the mixture into a nonstick metal 13 by 9-inch baking dish; using a rubber spatula, spread the mixture to cover the surface of the baking dish; set the baking dish aside.

**4. FOR THE FILLING:** Combine the brown sugar, cinnamon, cloves, and salt in a small bowl and mix until thoroughly combined, using your fingers to break up any sugar lumps; set aside.

**5. TO ASSEMBLE AND BAKE THE BUNS:** Turn the dough out onto a lightly floured work surface. Gently shape the dough into a rough rectangle with a long side nearest you. Lightly flour the dough and roll to a 16 by 12-inch rectangle. Brush the dough with the melted butter, leaving a ½-inch border along the top edge; brush the sides of the baking dish with the butter remaining on the brush. Sprinkle the filling mixture over the dough, leaving a ¾-inch border along the top edge; smooth the filling in an even layer with your hand, then gently press the mixture into the dough to adhere. Beginning with the long edge nearest you, roll the dough into a taut cylinder. Firmly pinch the seam to seal and roll the cylinder seam side down. Very gently stretch to form a cylinder of even diameter and 18-inch length; push the ends in to create an even thickness. Using a serrated knife and gentle sawing motion, slice the cylinder in half, then slice each half in half again to create evenly sized quarters. Slice each quarter evenly into thirds, yielding 12 buns (the end pieces may be slightly smaller).

**6.** Arrange the buns cut side down in the prepared baking dish; cover tightly with plastic wrap and set in a warm, draft-free spot until puffy and pressed against one another, about 1½ hours. Meanwhile, adjust an oven rack to the lowest position, place a baking stone on the rack, and heat the oven to 350 degrees.

**7.** Place the baking pan on the baking stone; bake until golden brown and the center of the dough registers 180 degrees on an instant-read thermometer, 25 to 30 minutes. Cool on a wire rack for 10 minutes; invert onto a rimmed baking sheet, large rectangular platter, or cutting board. With a rubber spatula, scrape any glaze remaining in the baking pan onto the buns; cool while making the pecan topping.

**8. FOR THE PECAN TOPPING:** Combine the brown sugar, corn syrup, butter, and salt in a small saucepan and bring to a simmer over medium heat, whisking occasionally to thoroughly combine. Off the heat, stir in the pecans and vanilla until the pecans are evenly coated. Using a soup spoon, spoon a heaping tablespoon of nuts and topping over the center of each sticky bun. Continue to cool until the sticky buns are warm, 15 to 20 minutes. Pull apart or use a serrated knife to cut apart the sticky buns; serve. (Buns can be wrapped in foil or plastic wrap and refrigerated for up to 3 days; warm through in the oven before serving.)

## Yeasted Doughnuts

**MAKES** 12 doughnuts

**WHY THIS RECIPE WORKS** Our yeasted doughnuts are moist but light with a tender chew and restrained sweetness, thanks to a careful balance of fat, sugar, and moisture in the dough. We chilled the dough overnight—a step called cold fermentation—so that it was faster to make the doughnuts in the morning. The dough also developed more complex flavor and was easier to handle when cold. Shutting the cut doughnuts in the oven with a loaf pan of boiling water—a makeshift baker's proof box—encouraged them to rise quickly; we then briefly fried them on both sides in moderately hot oil until they turned golden brown. We dipped them in a thin, fluid confectioners' sugar–based glaze, which set into a sheer, matte shell. You'll need two large baking sheets and two wire racks for this recipe. You'll also need 3-inch and 1-inch round cutters. For the best results, weigh the flour for the doughnuts and the confectioners' sugar for the glaze. Heating the oil slowly will make it easier to control the temperature when frying. Use a Dutch oven that holds 6 quarts or more. You can omit the glaze and frost the doughnuts with our Chocolate Frosting or Raspberry Frosting (recipes follow).

**DOUGHNUTS**

- 4½ cups (22½ ounces) all-purpose flour
- ½ cup (3½ ounces) granulated sugar
- 1 teaspoon instant or rapid-rise yeast
- 1½ cups milk
- 1 large egg
- 1½ teaspoons table salt
- 8 tablespoons unsalted butter, cut into ½-inch pieces and softened
- 2 quarts vegetable oil for frying

**GLAZE**

- 3¼ cups (13 ounces) confectioners' sugar
- ½ cup hot water
- Pinch table salt

**1. FOR THE DOUGHNUTS:** Stir flour, sugar, and yeast together in bowl of stand mixer. Add milk and egg and mix with rubber spatula until all ingredients are moistened. Fit stand mixer with dough hook and mix on medium-low speed until cohesive mass forms, about 2 minutes, scraping down bowl if necessary. Cover bowl with plastic wrap and let stand for 20 minutes.

**2.** Add salt and mix on medium-low speed until dough is smooth and elastic and clears sides of bowl, 5 to 7 minutes. With mixer running, add butter, a few pieces at a time, and continue to mix until butter is fully incorporated and dough is smooth and elastic and clears sides of bowl, 7 to 13 minutes longer, scraping down bowl halfway through mixing. Transfer dough to lightly greased large bowl, flip dough, and form into ball. Cover bowl with plastic. Let sit at room temperature for 1 hour. Transfer to refrigerator and chill overnight (or up to 48 hours).

**3.** Adjust oven racks to lowest and middle positions. Place loaf pan on lower rack. Line rimmed baking sheet with parchment paper and grease parchment. Transfer dough to lightly floured counter. Press into 8-inch square of even thickness, expelling as much air as possible. Roll dough into 10 by 13-inch rectangle, about ½ inch thick. Using 3-inch round cutter dipped in flour, cut 12 rounds. Using 1-inch cutter dipped in flour, cut hole out of center of each round. Transfer doughnuts and holes to prepared sheet. (If desired, use 1-inch cutter to cut small rounds from remaining dough. Transfer to sheet with doughnuts.) Bring kettle or small saucepan of water to boil.

**4.** Pour 1 cup boiling water into loaf pan. Place sheet on upper rack, uncovered. Close oven and allow doughnuts to rise until dough increases in height by 50 percent and springs back very slowly when pressed with your knuckle, 45 minutes to 1 hour.

**5. FOR THE GLAZE:** Whisk sugar, water, and salt in medium bowl until smooth.

**6.** About 20 minutes before end of rising time, add oil to large Dutch oven until it measures about 1½ inches deep and heat over medium-low heat to 360 degrees. Set wire rack in second rimmed baking sheet and line with triple layer of paper towels. Using both your hands, gently place 4 risen doughnuts in oil. Cook until golden brown on undersides, 1 to 1½ minutes, adjusting burner as necessary to maintain oil temperature between 350 and 365 degrees. Using spider skimmer, flip

## MAKING YEASTED DOUGHNUTS

**1.** Roll dough into 10 by 13-inch, ½-inch-thick rectangle. Cut 12 rounds and holes using 3- and 1-inch cutters.

**2.** Let rise until dough slowly springs back when pressed.

**3.** Fry in 360-degree oil until golden brown; flip and repeat.

**4.** Dip in glaze and let stand on wire rack until dry.

doughnuts and cook until second sides are browned, 1 to 1½ minutes. Transfer doughnuts to prepared rack. Return oil to 360 degrees and repeat with remaining doughnuts. For doughnut holes, transfer all to oil and stir gently and constantly until golden brown, about 2 minutes. Transfer to prepared rack to cool. Let doughnuts sit until cool enough to handle, at least 5 minutes.

**7.** Set clean wire rack in now-empty sheet. Working with 1 doughnut at a time, dip both sides of doughnut in glaze, allowing excess to drip back into bowl. Place on unlined rack. Repeat with doughnut holes. Let doughnuts and holes stand until glaze has become slightly matte and dry to touch, 15 to 30 minutes, before serving.

## Chocolate Frosting

**MAKES** 1½ cups

If the frosting stiffens before you use it, microwave it at 50 percent power, stirring every 30 seconds, until it is smooth and fluid. This frosting can be made up to 48 hours in advance. To frost the doughnuts, dip the top half of one cooled doughnut at a time into the frosting until it is evenly coated, allowing the excess to drip back into the bowl. Invert the doughnut and place it on a wire rack. Let the doughnuts stand until the frosting is dry to the touch, 15 to 30 minutes, before serving.

- 4 ounces bittersweet chocolate, chopped fine
- ½ cup water
- 2 cups (8 ounces) confectioners' sugar
- 2 tablespoons unsweetened cocoa powder
- Pinch table salt

Microwave chocolate and water in medium bowl at 50 percent power until chocolate is melted, about 30 seconds. Whisk in sugar, cocoa, and salt until smooth and fluid. Let cool slightly before using.

## Raspberry Frosting

**MAKES** 1 cup

If the frosting stiffens before you use it, add hot water, 1 teaspoon at a time, until the frosting is thick but fluid.

- 8 ounces (1⅔ cups) frozen raspberries, thawed
- 2 cups (8 ounces) confectioners' sugar
- Pinch table salt

Process raspberries in blender until smooth. Strain puree through fine-mesh strainer into bowl or measuring cup. Measure out 6 tablespoons puree for frosting (reserve remaining puree for another use). In medium bowl, whisk sugar, salt, and puree until smooth.

# New York Bagels

**MAKES** 8 bagels

**WHY THIS RECIPE WORKS** Our bagels are as good as those found in the best New York bagel bakeries. They're chewy yet tender, with a fine crumb, and they have a crisp, glossy, evenly browned exterior and a complex, slightly malty flavor. For the right chew, we used high-protein bread flour, supplemented with vital wheat gluten, and a minimum amount of water. To further increase the chew, we incorporate a number of gluten-strengthening rolling and shaping techniques. And to ensure even, rapid browning, we added baking soda to the boiling water. To create a crisp crust, we baked the bagels on a rack set in a rimmed baking sheet; boiling water poured onto the pan created steam. We prefer King Arthur bread flour for this recipe. Vital wheat gluten and malt syrup are available in many supermarkets and online. If you cannot find malt syrup, substitute 4 teaspoons of molasses.

- 1 cup plus 2 tablespoons ice water (9 ounces)
- 2 tablespoons malt syrup
- 2⅔ cups (14⅔ ounces) bread flour
- 4 teaspoons vital wheat gluten
- 2 teaspoons instant or rapid-rise yeast
- 2 teaspoons table salt
- ¼ cup (1¼ ounces) cornmeal
- ¼ cup (1¾ ounces) sugar
- 1 tablespoon baking soda

**1.** Stir ice water and malt syrup in 2-cup liquid measuring cup until malt syrup has fully dissolved. Process flour, wheat gluten, and yeast in food processor until combined, about 2 seconds. With processor running, slowly add ice water mixture; process until dough is just combined and no dry flour remains, about 20 seconds. Let dough stand for 10 minutes.

**2.** Add salt to dough and process, stopping processor and redistributing dough as needed, until dough forms shaggy mass that clears sides of workbowl (dough may not form one single mass),

45 to 90 seconds. Transfer dough to unfloured counter and knead until smooth, about 1 minute. Divide dough into 8 equal pieces (3½ ounces each) and cover loosely with plastic wrap.

**3.** Working with 1 piece of dough at a time and keeping remaining pieces covered, form dough pieces into smooth, taut rounds. (To round, set piece of dough on unfloured counter. Loosely cup your hand around dough and, without applying pressure to dough, move your hand in small circular motions. Tackiness of dough against counter and circular motion should work dough into smooth, even ball, but if dough sticks to your hands, lightly dust your fingers with flour.) Let dough balls rest on counter, covered, for 15 minutes.

**4.** Sprinkle rimmed baking sheet with cornmeal. Working with 1 dough ball at a time and keeping remaining pieces covered, coat dough balls lightly with flour and then, using your hands and rolling pin, pat and roll dough balls into 5-inch rounds. Starting with edge of dough farthest from you, roll into tight cylinder. Starting at center of cylinder and working toward ends, gently and evenly roll and stretch dough into 8- to 9-inch-long rope. Do not taper ends. Rolling ends of dough under your hands in opposite directions, twist rope to form tight spiral. Without unrolling spiral, wrap rope around your fingers, overlapping ends of dough by about 2 inches under your palm, to create ring shape. Pinch ends of dough gently together. With overlap under your palm, press and roll seam using circular motion on counter to fully seal. Transfer rings to prepared sheet and cover loosely with plastic, leaving at least 1 inch between bagels. Let bagels stand at room temperature for 1 hour. Cover sheet tightly with plastic and refrigerate for at least 16 hours or up to 24 hours.

**5.** One hour before baking, adjust oven rack to upper-middle position, place baking stone on rack, and heat oven to 450 degrees.

**6.** Bring 4 quarts water, sugar, and baking soda to boil in large Dutch oven. Set wire rack in rimmed baking sheet and spray rack with vegetable oil spray.

**7.** Transfer 4 bagels to boiling water and cook for 20 seconds. Using wire skimmer or slotted spoon, flip bagels over and cook 20 seconds longer. Using wire skimmer or slotted spoon, transfer bagels to prepared wire rack, with cornmeal side facing down. Repeat with remaining 4 bagels.

**8.** Place sheet with bagels on preheated baking stone and pour ½ cup boiling water into bottom of sheet. Bake until tops of bagels are beginning to brown, 10 to 12 minutes. Using metal spatula, flip bagels and continue to bake until golden brown, 10 to 12 minutes longer. Remove sheet from oven and let bagels cool on wire rack for at least 15 minutes. Serve warm or at room temperature. Bagels are best eaten within a day of baking; to freeze, transfer cooled bagels to heavy-duty zipper-lock bags. Bagels can be frozen for up to 1 month.

### SHAPING BAGELS LIKE A PRO

**1.** Pat and roll dough ball (lightly coated with flour) with rolling pin into 5-inch round. Roll into tight cylinder, starting with far side of dough.

**2.** Roll and stretch dough into 8- to 9-inch-long rope, starting at center of cylinder (don't taper ends). Twist rope to form tight spiral by rolling ends of dough under hands in opposite directions.

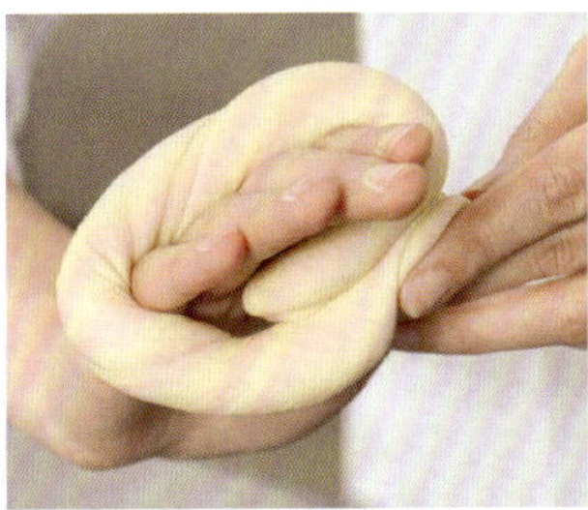

**3.** Wrap rope around your fingers, overlapping ends by 2 inches, to create ring. Pinch ends together. Press and roll seam (positioned under your palm) using circular motion on counter to fully seal.

### Bagel Toppings

Place ½ cup poppy seeds, sesame seeds, caraway seeds, dehydrated onion flakes, dehydrated garlic flakes, or coarse/pretzel salt in small bowl. Press tops of just-boiled bagels (side without cornmeal) gently into topping and return to wire rack, topping side up.

## Laugenbrezeln (German Lye Pretzels)

**MAKES** 6 pretzels

**WHY THIS RECIPE WORKS** Making pretzels the way German bakers do combines science and arts and crafts with a frisson of (manageable) risk. We shaped the pretzels in stages, giving the dough short rests to keep the gluten relaxed so that our pretzels would remain large and elegant instead of small and chunky. A quick dip in either a room-temperature lye solution or a simmering baking soda solution accelerated the Maillard reaction, breaking up proteins on the surface of the pretzel so that they interacted more readily with sugars for quick and deep browning during the brief, hot bake. Dipping pretzels in a lye solution before baking gives them their characteristic flavor and texture, but lye is caustic and can be dangerous if used incorrectly. (See page 798) (Lye-dipped pretzels are perfectly safe to eat after baking; the heat of the oven neutralizes the alkali.) Alternatively, use the baking soda dip. Food-safe lye and pretzel salt are available at specialty baking shops and online. Kosher salt can be substituted for the pretzel salt, but it will melt more easily. We strongly recommend measuring the flour by weight. Eat the pretzels plain or like the Germans do: sliced horizontally and spread with butter.

## WORKING WITH LYE SAFELY

Dipping the dough in a lye solution gives traditional German pretzels their characteristic salinity, chew, and smooth mahogany exterior; but the strong alkali (sodium hydroxide) is corrosive and can burn your skin, so it must be handled with caution. (Don't worry about eating it: Baking neutralizes lye and makes it perfectly safe to consume.) Follow this guide to make your experience safe and comfortable.

### LYE-DIPPING STATION SETUP

Work in a well-ventilated room, on a stable and roomy counter near an empty sink, if possible. Do not use lye around small children or pets.

### KEY SUPPLIES

- Food-grade lye (also known as sodium hydroxide), available at baking shops or online
- Long sleeves with long rubber gloves (such as for dish washing; before wearing, blow up each glove like a balloon to ensure that there are no holes)
- Eyeglasses or safety goggles
- Digital scale that measures in grams
- Rags in case of spills or drips
- Counter protection (plastic wrap or large plastic bag)

### METHOD

**1.** Cover counter with plastic wrap or large plastic bag. Put on rubber gloves, making sure no skin on your arms is showing. Put on eyeglasses or safety goggles.

**2.** Measure out exactly 40 grams of lye crystals into small bowl on scale. Set aside small bowl with lye crystals. Cover container of lye crystals and store in safe location per package instructions.

**3.** Place large bowl on scale. Add 1,000 grams cold water to large bowl. Add reserved 40 grams lye crystals to water and whisk gently to dissolve. Order of operations is important: Always add lye to water instead of adding water to lye. (Lye solution in bowl will heat up slightly and will give off some vapors, which are barely noticeable, but it's not advisable to put your face directly over solution.) Rinse whisk well with cool water. Remove scale.

**4.** Set wire rack in rimmed baking sheet and place to right of lye solution. Unwrap sheet of chilled pretzels, place to left of lye solution, and proceed with recipe. (Clear counter while pretzels bake.)

### CLEANUP

**1.** Still wearing gloves and eyewear, transfer bowl of lye solution to sink.

**2.** Run cold water into bowl in gentle stream to dilute solution. Pour solution down drain. Flush drain and rinse bowl and sink thoroughly with plenty of cold water.

**3.** Rinse rimmed baking sheets and wire rack with plenty of cold water. Dispose of plastic wrap or plastic bag on counter. Rinse gloves before removing. Once gloves are off, remove eyewear.

### IF YOUR SKIN TOUCHES LYE

Avoid touching anything but the pretzels while working with the lye solution. Before touching something else, rinse your gloved hands with cool water and dry them with rags.

**If you get lye solution on your skin:** Rinse your skin immediately with cool running water for 15 minutes.

**If you touch lye crystals:** Brush them off with a dry cloth, and then rinse your skin with cool running water for 10 minutes.

2⅓ cups (12¾ ounces) bread flour
1 teaspoon table salt
1 teaspoon instant or rapid-rise yeast
1 cup room temperature water
2 tablespoons unsalted butter, softened
40 grams lye crystals or ½ cup baking soda
Pretzel salt

**1.** Combine flour, table salt, and yeast in bowl of stand mixer and stir to combine. Add water and butter. Fit mixer with dough hook and mix on low speed until all flour is moistened, about 1 minute. Increase speed to medium-low and continue to mix until dough is smooth and elastic, about 6 minutes longer, scraping down bowl and dough hook halfway through mixing. Shape dough into ball and transfer to lightly greased bowl. Cover and let rise until almost doubled in size, about 1 hour.

**2.** Divide dough into 6 equal portions. Working with 1 piece of dough at a time, form into smooth balls. Cover with damp dish towel and let rest for 10 minutes. While dough rests, line rimmed baking sheet with parchment paper.

**3.** Place 1 dough ball seam side up on unfloured counter and flatten with your hand, pressing out as much air as possible. Using rolling pin, roll out dough to expel remaining air. Stretch and pat dough into roughly 8 by 4-inch rectangle with short side parallel to edge of counter. Starting at short side farthest away from you, roll dough into tight cylinder. Pinch seam to seal. Roll cylinder into 9-inch rope and place under damp dish towel. Repeat with remaining dough balls.

**4.** Working from center outward, roll first 9-inch rope into 28-inch rope, expelling any lingering air pockets as you go. Shape rope into inverted U with ends facing toward you. Cross rope ends once, and then again. Lift ends and attach them to other side of inverted U at about 10 o'clock and 2 o'clock. Press ends firmly into body of pretzel. Transfer to prepared sheet. Repeat with remaining 9-inch ropes. If pretzels have contracted, stretch each gently and return to sheet. Let sit for 10 minutes, uncovered. Cover with plastic wrap and refrigerate for at least 2 hours or up to 24 hours.

**5.** Adjust oven rack to middle position and heat oven to 475 degrees. Line second rimmed baking sheet with silicone baking mat or parchment. If using parchment, spray very generously with vegetable oil spray.

**6A. FOR THE LYE DIP:** Set up station as directed in "Working with Lye Safely." Grasp 1 pretzel with your gloved hands, pinching where ends meet body of pretzel, and transfer gently, presentation side down, to prepared lye bath. Let pretzel soak for 15 seconds, pressing occasionally to submerge. Using your gloved hands, grasp pretzel gently where ends meet body of pretzel and transfer, presentation side up, to prepared wire rack. Repeat with remaining pretzels. With your gloved hands, transfer pretzels to silicone-lined sheet.

**6B. FOR THE BAKING SODA DIP:** Set wire rack in third rimmed baking sheet. Dissolve baking soda in 8 cups water in Dutch oven and bring to boil over medium-high heat. Reduce heat to simmer. Grasp 1 pretzel with your hands, pinching where ends meet body of pretzel, and transfer gently, presentation side down, to simmering water. Cook for 30 seconds, pressing occasionally with slotted spatula to submerge. Carefully flip pretzel with spatula, then lift with spatula and transfer to prepared wire rack. Repeat with remaining pretzels. Transfer pretzels to silicone-lined sheet.

**7.** Sprinkle pretzels evenly with pretzel salt. Bake until deeply browned, about 12 minutes. Transfer to second wire rack and let cool for at least 5 minutes before serving.

### DOING THE TWIST

**1.** After making inverted U with dough rope, cross rope ends once, and then again.

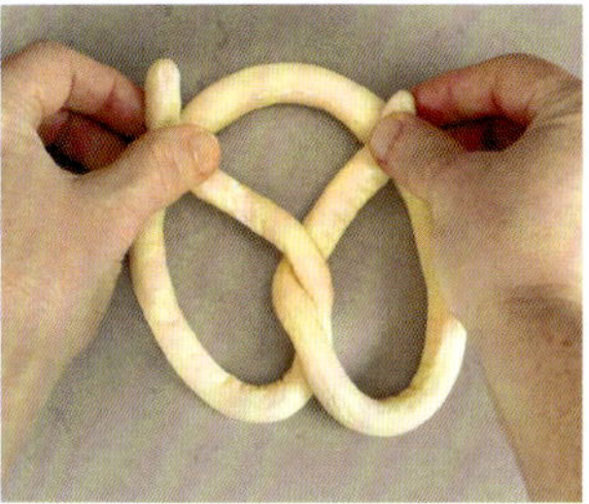

**2.** Lift ends and attach them to curve of inverted U at about 10 o'clock and 2 o'clock. Press ends firmly into body of pretzel.

## One-Hour Pizza

**MAKES** two 11½-inch pizzas

**WHY THIS RECIPE WORKS** We were determined to make a really good pizza from scratch in just one hour. Doing so required a handful of tricks to get a crust that was crisp, tender, and light without prolonged proofing. First, we used a high percentage of yeast and warm water in the dough to make sure it proofed in 30 minutes. We also found that a combination of semolina and all-purpose flours worked best, providing crispness, stretch, and enough structure. Finally, we rolled the dough between sheets of oiled parchment paper immediately after mixing so that the air bubbles that developed during proofing wouldn't be knocked out by shaping. We made our quick no-cook pizza sauce in the food processor. We sprinkled grated Parmesan on the sauce, then creamy shredded mozzarella. In just a few minutes the crust browned to perfection, while the cheese melted and turned bubbly. For the best results, weigh your ingredients. We like the depth anchovies add to the sauce, but you can omit them, if desired. For the mild lager, we recommend Budweiser or Stella Artois. Extra sauce can be refrigerated for up to a week or frozen for up to a month. Some baking stones can crack under the intense heat of the broiler. Our recommended stone from Pizzacraft won't, but if you're using another stone, check the manufacturer's website. If you don't have a pizza peel, use an overturned rimmed baking sheet instead.

**DOUGH**

- 1⅓ cups (7⅓ ounces) bread flour
- ½ cup (3 ounces) semolina flour
- 2 teaspoons instant or rapid-rise yeast
- 2 teaspoons sugar
- ½ cup plus 2 tablespoons (5 ounces) warm water (115 degrees)
- ¼ cup (2 ounces) mild lager
- 2 teaspoons distilled white vinegar
- 1½ teaspoons extra-virgin olive oil
- 1 teaspoon table salt
- Vegetable oil spray
- All-purpose flour

**SAUCE**

- 1 (28-ounce) can whole peeled tomatoes, drained
- 1 tablespoon extra-virgin olive oil
- 3 anchovy fillets, rinsed and patted dry (optional)
- 1 teaspoon table salt
- 1 teaspoon dried oregano
- ½ teaspoon sugar
- ¼ teaspoon pepper
- ⅛ teaspoon red pepper flakes

**PIZZA**

- 1 ounce Parmesan cheese, grated fine (½ cup)
- 6 ounces whole-milk mozzarella, shredded (1½ cups)

**1. FOR THE DOUGH:** Adjust oven rack 4 to 5 inches from broiler element, set pizza stone on rack, and heat oven to 500 degrees.

**2.** While oven heats, process bread flour, semolina flour, yeast, and sugar in food processor until combined, about 2 seconds. With processor running, slowly pour warm water, lager, vinegar, and oil through feed tube; process until dough is just combined and no dry flour remains, about 10 seconds. Let dough stand for 10 minutes.

**3.** Add salt to dough and process until dough forms satiny, sticky ball that clears sides of workbowl, 30 to 60 seconds. Transfer dough to lightly floured counter and gently knead until smooth, about 15 seconds. Divide dough into 2 equal pieces and shape each into smooth ball.

**4.** Spray 11-inch circle in center of large sheet of parchment paper with oil spray. Place 1 ball of dough in center of parchment. Spray top of dough with oil spray. Using rolling pin, roll dough into 10-inch circle. Cover with second sheet of parchment. Using rolling pin and your hands, continue to roll and press dough into 11½-inch circle. Set aside and repeat rolling with second ball of dough. Let dough stand at room temperature until slightly puffy, 30 minutes.

**5. FOR THE SAUCE:** Process all ingredients in food processor until smooth, about 30 seconds. Transfer to medium bowl.

**6. FOR THE PIZZA:** When dough has rested for 20 minutes, heat broiler for 10 minutes. Remove top piece of parchment from 1 disk of dough and dust top of dough lightly with all-purpose flour. Using your hands or pastry brush, spread flour evenly over dough, brushing off any excess. Liberally dust pizza peel with all-purpose flour. Flip dough onto peel, parchment side up. Carefully remove parchment and discard.

**7.** Using back of spoon or ladle, spread ½ cup sauce in thin layer over surface of dough, leaving ¾-inch border around edge. Sprinkle ¼ cup Parmesan evenly over sauce, followed by ¾ cup mozzarella. Slide pizza carefully onto stone and return oven to 500 degrees. Bake until crust is well browned and cheese is bubbly and beginning to brown, 8 to 12 minutes, rotating pizza halfway through baking.

**8.** Transfer pizza to wire rack and let cool for 5 minutes before slicing and serving. Repeat steps 6 and 7 to top and bake second pizza.

## Thin-Crust Pizza

**SERVES** 4 to 6

**WHY THIS RECIPE WORKS** With home ovens that reach only 500 degrees and dough that springs back when stretched, it's a challenge to produce parlor-quality pies at home. This recipe changes that. Kneading our thin-crust pizza dough's ingredients in the food processor was quicker and just as efficient as using a stand mixer. To keep our Thin-Crust Pizza recipe from puffing as it cooked and to infuse it with flavor, we let it proof in the refrigerator for at least 24 hours and up to three days. Finally, placing our pizza stone as close to the upper heating element as possible crisped our thin-crust pizza and browned it. If you don't own a baking stone, bake the pizzas on a rimless or overturned baking sheet that has been preheated just like the pizza stone. If you don't own a pizza peel, stretch the dough on a large sheet of lightly floured parchment paper, transfer to a rimless or overturned baking sheet, and slide the pizza with the parchment onto the hot pizza stone. You can shape the second dough round while the first pizza bakes, but don't add the toppings until just before baking. Semolina flour is ideal for dusting the peel; use it in place of bread flour if you have it. Extra sauce can be refrigerated for up to one week or frozen for up to one month.

**DOUGH**

- 3 cups (16½ ounces) bread flour
- 2 teaspoons sugar
- ½ teaspoon instant or rapid-rise yeast
- 1⅓ cups ice water
- 1 tablespoon vegetable oil
- 1½ teaspoons table salt

**SAUCE**

- 1 (28-ounce) can whole tomatoes, drained
- 1 tablespoon extra-virgin olive oil
- 2 garlic cloves, minced
- 1 teaspoon red wine vinegar
- 1 teaspoon table salt
- 1 teaspoon dried oregano
- ¼ teaspoon pepper

- 1 ounce Parmesan cheese, grated fine (½ cup), divided
- 8 ounces whole-milk mozzarella, shredded (2 cups), divided

**1. FOR THE DOUGH:** Pulse flour, sugar, and yeast in food processor (fitted with dough blade, if possible) until combined, about 5 pulses. With food processor running, slowly add water; process until dough is just combined and no dry flour remains, about 10 seconds. Let dough sit for 10 minutes.

**2.** Add oil and salt to dough and process until dough forms satiny, sticky ball that clears sides of bowl, 30 to 60 seconds. Transfer dough to lightly oiled work surface and knead briefly by hand until smooth, about 1 minute. Shape dough into tight ball and place in large, lightly oiled bowl; cover bowl tightly with plastic wrap and refrigerate for at least 24 hours or up to 3 days.

**3. FOR THE SAUCE:** Process all ingredients in clean bowl of food processor until smooth, about 30 seconds. Transfer to bowl and refrigerate until ready to use.

**4.** One hour before baking, adjust oven rack to upper-middle position (rack should be 4 to 5 inches from broiler), set baking stone on rack, and heat oven to 500 degrees. Transfer dough to clean work surface and divide in half. With your cupped palms, form each half into smooth, tight ball. Place balls of dough on lightly greased baking sheet, spacing them at least 3 inches apart; cover loosely with greased plastic wrap and let sit for 1 hour.

**5.** Coat 1 ball of dough generously with flour and place on well-floured work surface (keep other ball covered). Use your fingertips to gently flatten dough into 8-inch disk, leaving 1 inch of outer edge slightly thicker than center. Using your hands, gently stretch disk into 12-inch round, working along edges and giving disk quarter turns. Transfer dough to well-floured pizza peel and stretch into 13-inch round. Using back of spoon or ladle, spread ½ cup tomato sauce in thin layer over surface of dough, leaving ¼-inch border around edge. Sprinkle ¼ cup Parmesan evenly over the sauce, followed by 1 cup of mozzarella. Slide pizza carefully onto baking stone and bake until crust is well browned and cheese is bubbly and beginning to brown, 10 to 12 minutes, rotating pizza halfway through baking. Transfer pizza to a wire rack and let cool for 5 minutes before slicing and serving. Repeat step 5 to shape, top, and bake second pizza.

## Thin-Crust Whole-Wheat Pizza with Garlic Oil, Three Cheeses, and Basil

**MAKES** two 13-inch pizzas

**WHY THIS RECIPE WORKS** For a whole-wheat pizza that was crisp and chewy and offered a good, but not overwhelming, wheat flavor, we used a combination of 60 percent whole-wheat flour and 40 percent bread flour. To ensure that this higher-than-normal ratio of whole-wheat to bread flour still produced a great crust, we increased the hydration, which resulted in better gluten development and chew. To compensate for the added moisture, we employed the broiler to speed the baking process and guarantee a crisp crust and a tender interior. We recommend King Arthur brand bread flour for this recipe. Some baking stones, especially thinner ones, can crack under the intense heat of the broiler. Our recommended stone, by Pizzacraft, is fine if you're using this technique. If you use another stone, you might want to check the manufacturer's website for guidance.

**DOUGH**

- 1½ cups (8¼ ounces) whole-wheat flour
- 1 cup (5½ ounces) bread flour
- 2 teaspoons honey
- ¾ teaspoon instant or rapid-rise yeast
- 1¼ cups ice water
- 2 tablespoons extra-virgin olive oil
- 1¾ teaspoons table salt

**GARLIC OIL**

- ¼ cup extra-virgin olive oil
- 2 garlic cloves, minced
- 2 anchovy fillets, rinsed, patted dry, and minced (optional)
- ½ teaspoon pepper
- ½ teaspoon dried oregano
- ⅛ teaspoon red pepper flakes
- ⅛ teaspoon table salt

- 1 cup fresh basil leaves
- 1 ounce Pecorino Romano cheese, grated (½ cup)
- 8 ounces whole-milk mozzarella cheese, shredded (2 cups)
- 6 ounces (¾ cup) whole-milk ricotta cheese

**1. FOR THE DOUGH:** Process whole-wheat flour, bread flour, honey, and yeast in food processor until combined, about 2 seconds. With processor running, add water and process until dough is just combined and no dry flour remains, about 10 seconds. Let dough stand for 10 minutes.

**2.** Add oil and salt to dough and process until it forms satiny, sticky ball that clears sides of workbowl, 45 to 60 seconds. Remove from bowl and knead on oiled countertop until smooth, about 1 minute. Shape dough into tight ball and place in large, lightly oiled bowl. Cover tightly with plastic wrap and refrigerate for at least 18 hours or up to 2 days.

**3. FOR THE GARLIC OIL:** Heat oil in 8-inch skillet over medium-low heat until shimmering. Add garlic; anchovies, if using; pepper; oregano; pepper flakes; and salt. Cook, stirring constantly, until fragrant, about 30 seconds. Transfer to bowl and let cool completely before using.

**4.** One hour before baking pizza, adjust oven rack 4½ inches from broiler element, set pizza stone on rack, and heat oven to 500 degrees. Divide dough in half. Shape each half into smooth, tight ball. Place balls on lightly oiled baking sheet, spacing them at least 3 inches apart. Cover loosely with plastic coated with vegetable oil spray; let stand for 1 hour.

**5.** Heat broiler for 10 minutes. Meanwhile, coat 1 ball of dough generously with flour and place on well-floured countertop. Using your fingertips, gently flatten into 8-inch disk, leaving 1 inch of outer edge slightly thicker than center. Lift edge of dough and, using back of your hands and knuckles, gently stretch disk into 12-inch round, working along edges and giving disk quarter turns as you stretch. Transfer dough to well-floured peel and stretch into 13-inch round. Using back of spoon, spread half of garlic oil over surface of dough, leaving ¼-inch border. Layer ½ cup basil leaves over pizza. Sprinkle with ¼ cup Pecorino, followed by 1 cup mozzarella. Slide pizza carefully onto stone and return oven to 500 degrees. Bake until crust is well browned and cheese is bubbly and partially browned, 8 to 10 minutes, rotating pizza halfway through baking. Remove pizza and place on wire rack. Dollop half of ricotta over surface of pizza. Let pizza rest for 5 minutes, slice, and serve.

**6.** Heat broiler for 10 minutes. Repeat process of stretching, topping, and baking with remaining dough and toppings, returning oven to 500 degrees when pizza is placed on stone.

## Pizza al Taglio with Arugula and Fresh Mozzarella

**SERVES** 4 to 6

**WHY THIS RECIPE WORKS** Tender and airy yet substantial, this Roman pie is often topped like an open-faced sandwich. Roman pizzerias display it behind glass cases, where it is sold by the length and cut with scissors ("al taglio" means "by the cut"). Because the dough is so wet, we folded it by hand to develop gluten. We placed the dough in a baking pan to proof overnight in the refrigerator for 16 to 24 hours to develop flavor and allow the dough to relax for easy stretching. We then coated the top of the dough with olive oil, turned it out onto a baking sheet and stretched it to the edges of the sheet; we allowed it to proof for an hour. You'll get the crispest texture by using high-protein King Arthur bread flour, but other bread flours will also work. For the best results, weigh your flour and water. Anchovies give the sauce depth, so don't omit them.

**DOUGH**

- 2⅔ cups (14⅔ ounces) bread flour
- 1 teaspoon instant or rapid-rise yeast
- 1½ cups (12 ounces) water, room temperature
- 2 tablespoons extra-virgin olive oil
- 1¼ teaspoons table salt
- Vegetable oil spray

**SAUCE**

- 1 (14.5-ounce) can whole peeled tomatoes, drained
- 1 tablespoon extra-virgin olive oil
- 2 anchovy fillets, rinsed
- 1 teaspoon dried oregano
- ½ teaspoon table salt
- ¼ teaspoon red pepper flakes

**TOPPING**

- ¼ cup extra-virgin olive oil, divided
- 4 ounces (4 cups) baby arugula
- 8 ounces fresh mozzarella cheese, torn into bite-size pieces (about 2 cups)
- 1½ ounces Parmesan cheese, shredded (½ cup)

**1. FOR THE DOUGH:** Whisk flour and yeast together in medium bowl. Add room-temperature water and oil and stir with wooden spoon until shaggy mass forms and no dry flour remains. Cover bowl with plastic wrap and let sit for 10 minutes. Sprinkle salt over dough and mix until fully incorporated. Cover bowl with plastic and let dough rest for 20 minutes.

**2.** Using your wet hands, fold dough over itself by gently lifting and folding edge of dough toward middle. Turn bowl 90 degrees; fold again. Turn bowl and fold dough 4 more times (total of 6 turns). Cover bowl with plastic and let dough rest for 20 minutes. Repeat folding technique, turning bowl each time, until dough tightens slightly, 3 to 6 turns total. Cover bowl with plastic and let dough rest for 10 minutes.

**3.** Spray bottom of 13 by 9-inch baking pan liberally with oil spray. Transfer dough to prepared pan and spray top of dough lightly with oil spray. Gently press dough into 10 by 7-inch oval of even thickness. Cover pan tightly with plastic and refrigerate for at least 16 hours or up to 24 hours.

**FOLDING DOUGH**

**1.** To fold dough in on itself, grasp section of dough with your wet fingertips and gently lift.

**2.** Place edge down in middle of dough. Rotate bowl 90 degrees and repeat for total of 6 turns.

**4. FOR THE SAUCE:** While dough rests, process all ingredients in blender until smooth, 20 to 30 seconds. Transfer sauce to bowl, cover, and refrigerate until needed. (Sauce can be refrigerated for up to 2 days.)

**5. FOR THE TOPPING:** Brush top of dough with 2 tablespoons oil. Spray rimmed baking sheet (including rim) with oil spray. Invert prepared sheet on top of pan and flip, allowing dough to fall onto sheet (you may need to lift pan and nudge dough at 1 end to release). Using your fingertips, gently dimple dough into even thickness and stretch toward edges of sheet to form 15 by 11-inch oval. Spray top of dough lightly with oil spray, cover loosely with plastic, and let rest until slightly puffy, 1 to 1¼ hours.

**6.** Thirty minutes before baking, adjust oven rack to lowest position and heat oven to 450 degrees. Just before baking, use your fingertips to gently dimple dough into even thickness, pressing into corners of sheet. Using back of spoon or ladle, spread ½ cup sauce in even layer over surface of dough. (Leftover sauce can be frozen in an airtight container for up to 2 months.)

**7.** Drizzle 1 tablespoon oil over top of sauce and use back of spoon to spread evenly over surface. Transfer sheet to oven and bake until bottom of crust is evenly browned and top is lightly browned in spots, 20 to 25 minutes, rotating sheet halfway through baking. Transfer sheet to wire rack and let cool for 5 minutes. Run knife around rim of sheet to loosen pizza. Transfer pizza to cutting board and cut into 8 rectangles. Toss arugula with remaining 1 tablespoon oil in bowl. Top pizza with arugula, followed by mozzarella and Parmesan, and serve.

## Pissaladière (Provençal Pizza)

**MAKES** 2 tarts, serving 6

**WHY THIS RECIPE WORKS** Pissaladière is the classic olive, anchovy, and onion tart from Provence. We made the dough in a food processor and kneaded it as little as possible to create a pizza-like dough with a cracker-like exterior and a chewy crumb, a dough that could stand up to the heavy toppings. Using a combination of high and low heat to cook the onions—starting the onions on high to release their juices and soften them, then turning the heat to medium-low to caramelize them—gave us perfectly browned and caramelized, but not burnt, onions. Adding a bit of water before spreading them on the crust kept them from clumping. If desired, you can slow down the dough's rising time by letting it rise in the refrigerator for 8 to 16 hours in step 1; let the refrigerated dough soften at room temperature for 30 minutes before using. The caramelized onions can be made a day ahead and refrigerated.

**DOUGH**

- 2 cups (11 ounces) bread flour, plus extra for dusting the work surface
- 1 teaspoon instant or rapid-rise yeast
- 1 teaspoon table salt
- 1 tablespoon olive oil, plus extra for brushing the dough and greasing hands
- 1 cup warm water (110 degrees)

**CARAMELIZED ONIONS**

- 2 tablespoons olive oil
- 2 pounds onions (about 4 medium), halved and sliced ¼ inch thick
- 1 teaspoon brown sugar
- ½ teaspoon table salt
- 1 tablespoon water

- Olive oil
- ½ teaspoon ground black pepper
- ½ cup niçoise olives, pitted and chopped coarse
- 8 anchovy fillets, rinsed, patted dry, and chopped coarse (about 2 tablespoons), plus 12 fillets, rinsed and patted dry for garnish (optional)
- 2 teaspoons minced fresh thyme leaves
- 1 teaspoon fennel seeds (optional)
- 1 tablespoon minced fresh parsley leaves (optional)

**1. FOR THE DOUGH:** Pulse the flour, yeast, and salt in a food processor (fitted with a dough blade, if possible) until combined, about 5 pulses. With the machine running, slowly add the oil, then the water, through the feed tube; continue to process until the dough forms a ball, about 15 seconds. Turn the dough out onto a lightly floured work surface and form it into a smooth, round ball. Place the dough in a large lightly oiled bowl and cover tightly with greased plastic wrap. Let rise in a warm place until doubled in volume, 1 to 1½ hours.

**2. FOR THE CARAMELIZED ONIONS:** While the dough is rising, heat the oil in a 12-inch nonstick skillet over medium-low heat until shimmering. Stir in the onions, sugar, and salt. Cover and cook, stirring occasionally, until the onions are softened and have released their juice, about 10 minutes. Remove the lid, increase the heat to medium-high, and continue to cook, stirring often, until the onions are deeply browned, 10 to

15 minutes. Off the heat, stir in the water, then transfer the onions to a bowl and set aside. Adjust the oven rack to the lowest position, set a baking stone on the rack, and heat the oven to 500 degrees. (Let the baking stone heat for at least 30 minutes but no longer than 1 hour.)

**3.** To shape, top, and bake the dough: Turn the dough out onto a lightly floured work surface, divide it into two equal pieces, and cover with greased plastic wrap. Working with one piece at a time (keep the other piece covered), form each piece into a rough ball by gently pulling the edges of the dough together and pinching to seal. With floured hands, turn the dough ball seam side down. Cupping the dough with both hands, gently push the dough in a circular motion to form a taut ball. Repeat with the second piece. Brush each piece lightly with oil, cover with plastic wrap, and let rest for 10 minutes. Meanwhile, cut two 20-inch lengths of parchment paper and set aside.

**4.** Coat your fingers and palms generously with oil. Working with one piece of dough at a time, hold the dough up and gently stretch it to a 12-inch length. Place the dough on the parchment sheet and gently dimple the surface of the dough with your fingertips. Using your oiled palms, push and flatten the dough into a 14 by 8-inch oval. Brush the dough with oil and sprinkle with ¼ teaspoon of the pepper. Leaving a ½-inch border around the edge, sprinkle ¼ cup of the olives, 1 tablespoon of the chopped anchovies, and 1 teaspoon of the thyme evenly over the dough, then evenly scatter with half of the onions. Arrange 6 whole anchovy fillets (if using) on the tart and sprinkle with ½ teaspoon of the fennel seeds (if using). Slip the parchment with the tart onto a pizza peel (or inverted baking sheet), then slide it onto the hot baking stone. Bake until deep golden brown, 13 to 15 minutes. While the first tart bakes, shape and top the second tart.

**5.** Remove the first tart from the oven with a peel (or pull the parchment onto a baking sheet). Transfer the tart to a cutting board and slide the parchment out from under the tart; cool for 5 minutes. While the first tart cools, bake the second tart. Sprinkle with the parsley (if using) and cut each tart into 8 pieces before serving.

## Lahmajun (Armenian Flatbread)

**SERVES 4 to 6**

**WHY THIS RECIPE WORKS** Thin and crispy lahmajun are meat-and-vegetable-topped flatbreads that are eaten whole, cut or folded in half, or wrapped around a salad to make a sandwich. This dough starts with a higher-protein all-purpose flour to create an ample amount of gluten for both crispness and tenderness. Using very little yeast and letting the dough ferment slowly in the refrigerator allowed the gluten to relax so the dough could be stretched thin. A mixture of spices and biber salçası (Turkish red pepper paste) added earthy warmth, sweetness, and heat to the savory lamb topping. We heated a baking stone at 500 degrees for an hour to ensure that there was intense heat both underneath the flatbreads and reflecting onto them from above, guaranteeing crispness and browning in the few minutes it took the flatbreads to bake. If you don't have a baking peel, use an overturned rimmed baking sheet to slide the lahmajun onto the baking stone. If you don't have a baking stone, use a preheated rimless or overturned baking sheet (the breads will be less crisp). We prefer King Arthur All-Purpose Flour for these flatbreads We strongly recommend weighing the flour and the water. Jarred biber salçası can be found in Middle Eastern grocery stores or online. Be sure to use the mild variety; if it's unavailable, increase the tomato paste in the topping to 2 tablespoons and increase the paprika to 4 teaspoons. Eighty-five percent lean ground beef can be substituted for the lamb, if desired. Fold the outer thirds of the lahmajun over the filling, one side at a time. Turn the rolled lahmajun seam side down and cut in half crosswise. Serve with lemon wedges or Cucumber-Tomato Salad.

**DOUGH**

- 3¼ cups (16¼ ounces) King Arthur All-Purpose Flour
- ⅛ teaspoon instant or rapid-rise yeast
- 1¼ cups (10 ounces) ice water
- 1 tablespoon vegetable oil
- 1½ teaspoons table salt
- Vegetable oil spray

**TOPPING**

- 1 red bell pepper, stemmed, seeded, and cut into 1-inch pieces
- ¼ small onion
- ¼ cup fresh parsley leaves and tender stems
- 2 tablespoons mild biber salçası
- 1 tablespoon tomato paste
- 1 garlic clove, peeled
- 1 teaspoon ground allspice
- 1 teaspoon paprika
- ½ teaspoon ground cumin
- ½ teaspoon table salt
- ⅛ teaspoon pepper
- ⅛ teaspoon cayenne pepper
- 6 ounces ground lamb, broken into small pieces
- Lemon wedges

**1. FOR THE DOUGH:** Process flour and yeast in food processor until combined, about 2 seconds. With processor running, slowly add ice water; process until dough is just combined and no dry flour remains, about 10 seconds. Let dough rest for 10 minutes.

**2.** Add oil and salt and process until dough forms shaggy ball, 30 to 60 seconds. Transfer dough to lightly oiled counter and knead until uniform, about 1 minute (texture will remain slightly rough). Divide dough into 4 equal pieces, about 6⅔ ounces each. Shape dough pieces into tight balls and transfer, seam side down, to rimmed baking sheet coated with oil spray. Spray tops of balls lightly with oil spray. Cover tightly with plastic wrap and refrigerate for at least 16 hours or up to 2 days.

**3. FOR THE TOPPING:** In now-empty processor, process bell pepper, onion, parsley, biber salçası, tomato paste, garlic, allspice, paprika, cumin, salt, pepper, and cayenne until smooth, scraping down sides of bowl as needed, about 15 seconds. Add lamb and pulse to combine, 8 to 10 pulses. Transfer to container, cover, and refrigerate until needed. (Topping can be refrigerated for up to 24 hours).

**4.** One hour before baking lahmajun, remove dough from refrigerator and let stand at room temperature until slightly puffy and no longer cool to touch. Meanwhile, adjust oven rack to upper-middle position (rack should be 4 to 5 inches from broiler element), set baking stone on rack, and heat oven to 500 degrees.

**5.** Place 1 dough ball on unfloured counter and dust top lightly with flour. Using heel of your hand, press dough ball into 5-inch disk. Using rolling pin, gently roll into 12-inch round of even thickness. (Use tackiness of dough on counter to aid with rolling; if dough becomes misshapen, periodically peel round from counter, reposition, and continue to roll.) Dust top of round lightly but evenly with flour and, starting at 1 edge, peel dough off counter and flip, floured side down, onto floured baking peel (dough will spring back to about 11 inches in diameter). Place one-quarter of topping (about ½ cup) in center of dough. Cover dough with 12 by 12-inch sheet of plastic and, using your fingertips and knuckles, gently spread filling evenly across dough, leaving ⅛-inch border. Starting at 1 edge, peel away plastic, leaving topping in place (reserve plastic for topping remaining lahmajun).

**6.** Carefully slide lahmajun onto stone and bake until bottom crust is browned, edges are lightly browned, and topping is steaming, 4 to 6 minutes. While lahmajun bakes, begin rolling next dough ball.

**7.** Transfer baked lahmajun to wire rack. Repeat rolling, topping, and baking remaining 3 dough balls.

**8.** Serve with lemon wedges or Cucumber-Tomato Salad.

## Cucumber-Tomato Salad

**SERVES** 4 to 6

Use the ripest in-season tomatoes you can find. This salad is best eaten within 1 hour of being dressed. Be sure to drain excess liquid before placing the salad on the lahmajun.

- 1 English cucumber, quartered lengthwise and cut into ¼-inch pieces
- 2 tomatoes, cored and cut into ¼-inch pieces
- ¾ teaspoon table salt
- ½ cup pitted green olives, chopped coarse
- ¼ cup fresh mint leaves, shredded
- 2 tablespoons extra-virgin olive oil
- 2 tablespoons lemon juice
- ½ teaspoon pepper

Toss cucumber, tomatoes, and salt together in colander set over bowl. Let drain for 15 minutes, then discard liquid. Transfer cucumber-tomato mixture to medium bowl. Add olives, mint, oil, lemon juice, and pepper and toss to combine.

## Deep-Dish Pizza

**SERVES** 4

**WHY THIS RECIPE WORKS** Unlike its thin-crust cousin, deep-dish pizza has a soft, chewy, thick crust and can stand up to substantial toppings. We wanted to try our hand at making this restaurant-style pizza at home. We focused on the dough since these pizzas are 75 percent crust. The secret to a perfect crust came from an unlikely source: a potato which contributed moisture as well as extra richness and sweetness to the dough. We baked the crust untopped for a few minutes so it would start to rise and not be weighed down by the toppings at first. Prepare the topping while the dough is rising so the two will be ready at the same time. If you don't have a pizza stone, use an overturned or heavy rimless baking sheet. If you don't have a 14-inch deep-dish pizza pan, use two 10-inch cake pans. Grease them with 2 tablespoons oil each; divide the pizza dough in half and pat each half into a 9-inch round. Use shrink-wrapped supermarket cheese rather than fresh mozzarella.

**DOUGH**

- 1 medium russet potato (about 9 ounces), peeled and quartered
- 3¼–3½ cups (16¼ to 17½ ounces) unbleached all-purpose flour
- 1¾ teaspoons table salt
- 1½ teaspoons instant or rapid-rise yeast
- 6 tablespoons olive oil, plus extra for oiling the bowl
- 1 cup warm water (110 degrees)

**TOPPING**

- 1½ pounds plum tomatoes (5 to 6 medium), cored, seeded, and cut into 1-inch pieces
- 2 medium garlic cloves, minced or pressed through a garlic press (about 2 teaspoons)
- Table salt and ground black pepper
- 6 ounces whole-milk mozzarella cheese, shredded (about 1½ cups; see note)
- 1¼ ounces Parmesan cheese, grated (about ⅔ cup)
- 3 tablespoons shredded fresh basil leaves

**1. FOR THE DOUGH:** Bring 4 cups water and the potato to a boil in a small saucepan over medium-high heat; cook until tender, 10 to 15 minutes. Drain and cool until the potato can be handled; press the potato through the fine disk of a potato ricer or grate it on the large holes of a box grater. Measure 1⅓ cups lightly packed potato; discard the remaining potato.

**2.** Process 3¼ cups of the flour, the potato, salt and yeast in a food processor (fitted with the dough blade, if possible) until combined, about 5 seconds. With the motor running, pour 2 tablespoons of the oil and then the water through the feed tube and process until the dough comes together in a ball, about 30 seconds. If after 30 seconds the dough is sticky and clings to the blade, add the remaining ¼ cup flour 1 tablespoon at a time. Lightly coat a medium bowl with oil. Transfer the dough to the bowl; cover tightly with plastic wrap and set in a warm spot until doubled in volume, 1½ to 2 hours.

**3. FOR THE TOPPING:** Meanwhile, mix the tomatoes and garlic together in a medium bowl; season with salt and pepper to taste and set aside.

**4.** Oil the bottom of a 14-inch deep-dish pizza pan with the remaining 4 tablespoons olive oil. Remove the dough from the oven and gently punch it down; turn the dough onto a clean, dry work surface and pat it into a 12-inch round. Transfer the round to the oiled pan, cover with plastic wrap, and let rest until the dough no longer resists shaping, about 10 minutes.

**5.** Adjust the oven racks to the lowest and top positions, set a pizza stone on the lower rack, and heat the oven to 500 degrees. Uncover the dough and pull it into the edges and up the sides of the pan to form a 1-inch-high lip. Cover with plastic wrap; let rise in a warm, draft-free spot until doubled in size, about 30 minutes. Uncover the dough and prick it generously with a fork. Reduce the oven temperature to 425 degrees, place the pan with the pizza on the hot pizza stone, and bake until dry and lightly browned, about 15 minutes. Add the tomato mixture, followed by the mozzarella, then the Parmesan. Bake the pizza on the stone or baking sheet until the cheese melts, 10 to 15 minutes (5 to 10 minutes for 10-inch pizzas). Move the pizza to the top rack and bake until the cheese is spotty golden brown, about 5 minutes longer. Cool for 5 minutes, then, holding the pizza pan at an angle with a potholder, use a wide spatula to slide the pizza from the pan to a cutting board, cut into wedges, and serve.

## Chicago-Style Deep-Dish Pizza

**MAKES** two 9-inch pizzas

**WHY THIS RECIPE WORKS** Recipes for Chicago-style deep-dish pizzas—the kind with crusts like buttery pastries you can only get in Chicago pizzerias—are staunchly protected by the people who make them. We would have to invent our own recipe for the best deep-dish pizza Chicago has to offer: one that boasts a thick, crisp crust with an airy, flaky interior, and a rich taste that can hold its own under any kind of topping. The recipes we came across in our research sounded a lot like classic pizza dough, with cornmeal added for crunch and butter for tenderness and flavor. These crusts weren't bad, but they weren't as flaky as a Chicago-made crust. To increase the flakiness factor, we turned to laminating. This baking term refers to the layering of butter and dough to create ultraflaky pastries through a sequence of rolling and folding. A combination of adding melted butter to the dough and spreading the rolled out dough with softened butter before folding it did the trick. For the toppings we followed Chicago tradition: We covered the dough with freshly shredded mozzarella and then topped the cheese with a thick, quick-to-make tomato sauce. You will need a stand mixer with a dough hook for this recipe. Place a damp dish towel under the mixer and watch it at all times during kneading to prevent it from wobbling off the counter. Avoid using preshredded cheese here.

**DOUGH**

- 3¼ cups (16¼ ounces) unbleached all-purpose flour
- ½ cup (2¾ ounces) yellow cornmeal
- 2¼ teaspoons (about 1 envelope) instant or rapid-rise yeast
- 2 teaspoons sugar
- 1½ teaspoons table salt
- 1¼ cups water, room temperature
- 3 tablespoons unsalted butter, melted, plus 4 tablespoons, softened
- 1 teaspoon plus 4 tablespoons olive oil

**SAUCE**

- 2 tablespoons unsalted butter
- ¼ cup grated onion
- ¼ teaspoon dried oregano
- Table salt and ground black pepper
- 2 medium garlic cloves, minced or pressed through a garlic press (about 2 teaspoons)
- 1 (28-ounce) can crushed tomatoes
- ¼ teaspoon sugar
- 2 tablespoons chopped fresh basil
- 1 tablespoon extra-virgin olive oil

**TOPPINGS**

- 1 pound mozzarella, shredded (about 4 cups; see note)
- ¼ cup grated Parmesan cheese

**1. FOR THE DOUGH:** Mix the flour, cornmeal, yeast, sugar, and salt in the bowl of a stand mixer fitted with the dough hook on low speed until incorporated, about 1 minute. Add the water and melted butter and mix on low speed until fully combined, 1 to 2 minutes, scraping the sides and bottom of the bowl as needed. Increase the speed to medium and knead until the dough is glossy and smooth and pulls away from sides of the bowl, 4 to 5 minutes. (The dough will only pull away from the sides while the mixer is on. When the mixer is off, the dough will fall back to the sides.)

**2.** Using your fingers, coat a large bowl with 1 teaspoon of the olive oil, rubbing excess oil from your fingers onto the blade of a rubber spatula. Using the oiled spatula, transfer the dough to the oiled bowl, turning once to oil the top. Cover the bowl tightly with plastic wrap. Let the dough rise at room temperature until nearly doubled in volume, 45 to 60 minutes.

**3. FOR THE SAUCE:** While the dough rises, heat the butter in a medium saucepan over medium heat until melted. Add the onion, oregano, and ½ teaspoon salt and cook, stirring occasionally, until the liquid has evaporated and the onion is golden brown, about 5 minutes. Add the garlic and cook until fragrant, about 30 seconds. Stir in the tomatoes and sugar, increase the heat to high, and bring to a simmer. Lower the heat to medium-low and simmer until the sauce has reduced to 2½ cups, 25 to 30 minutes. Off the heat, stir in the basil and oil, then season with salt and pepper to taste.

**4. TO LAMINATE THE DOUGH:** Adjust an oven rack to the lowest position and heat the oven to 425 degrees. Using a rubber spatula, turn the dough out onto a dry work surface and roll into a 15 by 12-inch rectangle. Use an offset spatula to spread the softened butter over the surface of the dough, leaving a ½-inch border along the edges. Starting at the short end, roll the dough into a tight cylinder. With the seam side down, flatten the cylinder into an 18 by 4-inch rectangle. Cut the rectangle in half crosswise. Working with one half, fold the dough into thirds like a business letter, then pinch the seams together to form a ball. Repeat with the remaining half of the dough. Return the dough balls to the oiled bowl, cover tightly with plastic wrap, and let rise in the refrigerator until nearly doubled in volume, 40 to 50 minutes.

**5.** Coat two 9-inch round cake pans with 2 tablespoons olive oil each. Transfer one dough ball to a dry work surface and roll out into a 13-inch disk about ¼ inch thick. Transfer the dough round to a cake pan by rolling the dough loosely around the rolling pin, then unrolling the dough into the pan. Lightly press the dough into the pan, working it into the corners and 1 inch up the sides. If the dough resists stretching, let it relax for 5 minutes before trying again. Repeat with the remaining dough ball.

**6.** For each pizza, sprinkle 2 cups of the mozzarella evenly over the surface of the dough. Spread 1¼ cups of the tomato sauce over the cheese and sprinkle 2 tablespoons of the Parmesan over the sauce for each pizza. Bake until the crust is golden brown, 20 to 30 minutes. Remove the pizza from the oven and let rest for 10 minutes before slicing and serving.

### MAKING CHICAGO-STYLE DEEP-DISH PIZZA CRUST

**1.** After rolling out the dough into a 15 by 12-inch rectangle, spread the softened butter over the dough, leaving a ½-inch border along the edges.

**2.** Roll the dough into a tight cylinder, starting at the short end closest to you.

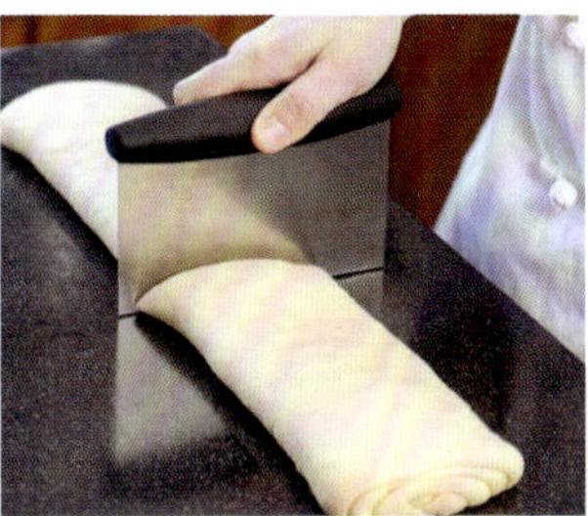

**3.** Flatten the dough cylinder into an 18 by 4-inch rectangle, then halve the cylinder crosswise.

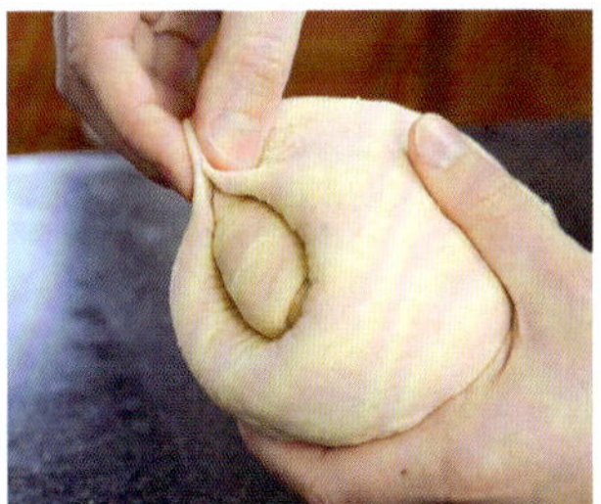

**4.** Fold each dough half into thirds to form a ball, pinch the seams shut, and let the dough balls rise in the refrigerator for 40 to 50 minutes.

**5.** After rolling each ball of dough into a 13-inch disk about ¼ inch thick, transfer the dough disks to the oiled pans and lightly press the dough into the pans, working it into the corners and up the sides.

## Thick-Crust Sicilian-Style Pizza

**SERVES** 6 to 8

**WHY THIS RECIPE WORKS** Unlike the thin pies you can get at any pizza parlor in town, Sicilian-style pizza boasts a thick crust with a tight, even crumb and a delicately crisp underside. To replicate that crust, we created a dough with all-purpose and semolina flours, the latter contributing the distinct yellow color and cake-like crumb. Letting the dough proof for 24 hours under plastic wrap in the refrigerator helped create flavor: The cold kept carbon dioxide from forming bubbles while the extended fermentation period allowed an array of flavor compounds to form. To ensure bubbles didn't form during the second proof, we rolled the dough out with a rolling pin, moved it onto a rimmed baking sheet, and covered it with plastic wrap and a second baking sheet. Before baking, we topped the compressed dough with a boldly seasoned, slow-cooked homemade tomato sauce and a blend of gooey mozzarella and salty, sharp Parmesan. This recipe requires refrigerating the dough for at least 24 hours before shaping it. King Arthur all-purpose flour and Bob's Red Mill semolina flour work best in this recipe. It is important to use ice water in the dough to prevent overheating during mixing. Anchovies give the sauce depth without a discernible fishy taste; if you decide not to use them, add an additional ¼ teaspoon of salt.

**DOUGH**

- 2¼ cups (11¼ ounces) all-purpose flour
- 2 cups (12 ounces) semolina flour
- 1 teaspoon sugar
- 1 teaspoon instant or rapid-rise yeast
- 1⅔ cups (13⅓ ounces) ice water
- 3 tablespoons extra-virgin olive oil
- 2¼ teaspoons table salt

**SAUCE**

- 1 (28-ounce) can whole peeled tomatoes, drained
- 2 teaspoons sugar
- ¼ teaspoon table salt
- ¼ cup extra-virgin olive oil
- 3 garlic cloves, minced
- 1 tablespoon tomato paste
- 3 anchovy fillets, rinsed, patted dry, and minced
- 1 teaspoon dried oregano
- ¼ teaspoon red pepper flakes

**PIZZA**

- ¼ cup extra-virgin olive oil
- 2 ounces Parmesan cheese, grated (1 cup)
- 12 ounces whole-milk mozzarella, shredded (3 cups)

**1. FOR THE DOUGH:** Using stand mixer fitted with dough hook, mix all-purpose flour, semolina flour, sugar, and yeast on low speed until combined, about 10 seconds. With machine running, slowly add water and oil until dough forms and no dry flour remains, 1 to 2 minutes. Cover with plastic wrap and let dough stand for 10 minutes.

**2.** Add salt to dough and mix on medium speed until dough forms satiny, sticky ball that clears sides of bowl, 6 to 8 minutes. Remove dough from bowl and knead briefly on lightly floured counter until smooth, about 1 minute. Shape dough into tight ball and place in large, lightly oiled bowl. Cover tightly with plastic wrap and refrigerate for at least 24 hours or up to 2 days.

**3. FOR THE SAUCE:** Process tomatoes, sugar, and salt in food processor until smooth, about 30 seconds. Heat oil and garlic in medium saucepan over medium-low heat, stirring occasionally, until garlic is fragrant and just beginning to brown, about 2 minutes. Add tomato paste, anchovies, oregano, and pepper flakes and cook until fragrant, about 30 seconds. Add tomato mixture and cook, stirring occasionally, until sauce measures 2 cups, 25 to 30 minutes. Transfer to bowl, let cool, and refrigerate until needed.

**4. FOR THE PIZZA:** One hour before baking pizza, place baking stone on upper-middle rack and heat oven to 500 degrees. Spray rimmed baking sheet (including rim) with vegetable oil spray, then coat bottom of a second baking sheet with oil. Remove dough from refrigerator and transfer to lightly floured counter. Lightly flour top of dough and gently press into 12 by 9-inch rectangle. Using rolling pin, roll dough into 18 by 13-inch rectangle. Transfer dough to prepared baking sheet, fitting dough into corners. Spray top of dough with oil spray and lay sheet of plastic wrap over dough. Place second baking sheet on dough and let stand for 1 hour.

**5.** Remove top baking sheet and plastic wrap. Gently stretch and lift dough to fill pan. Using back of spoon or ladle, spread sauce in even layer over surface of dough, leaving ½-inch border. Sprinkle Parmesan evenly over entire surface of dough to edges followed by mozzarella.

**6.** Place pizza on stone; reduce oven temperature to 450 degrees and bake until bottom crust is evenly browned and cheese is bubbly and browned, 20 to 25 minutes, rotating pizza halfway through baking. Remove pan from oven and let cool on wire rack for 5 minutes. Run knife around rim of pan to loosen pizza. Transfer pizza to cutting board, cut into squares, and serve.

## Cast-Iron Pan Pizza

**SERVES 4**

**WHY THIS RECIPE WORKS** This pizza recipe is dead simple: no rolling, stretching, or baking stone required. The crumb is thick, plush, and encased in a golden, crispy crust. We started with an easy stir-together dough of bread flour, salt, yeast, and warm water. Instead of kneading the dough, we let it rest overnight in the refrigerator. During this rest, the dough's gluten strengthened enough for the crust to support the toppings but still have a tender crumb. Baking the pie in a generously oiled cast-iron skillet "fried" the outside of the crust. We also moved the skillet to the stove for the last few minutes of cooking to crisp up the underside of the crust. For the crispy cheese edge known as frico, we pressed shredded Monterey Jack cheese around the edge of the dough and up the sides of the skillet. For the sauce, we crushed canned whole tomatoes by hand and then pureed them in the food processor with classic seasonings—no cooking required. We strongly recommend measuring the flour by weight. Use a block cheese, not fresh mozzarella, for this recipe. Avoid preshredded cheese; it contains added starch, which gives the melted cheese a drier, chewier texture.

**DOUGH**

- 2 cups (11 ounces) bread flour
- 1 teaspoon table salt
- 1 teaspoon instant or rapid-rise yeast
- 1 cup (8 ounces) warm water (105 to 110 degrees)
- Vegetable oil spray

**SAUCE**

- 1 (14.5-ounce) can whole peeled tomatoes
- 1 teaspoon extra-virgin olive oil
- 1 garlic clove, minced
- ¼ teaspoon sugar
- ¼ teaspoon table salt
- ¼ teaspoon dried oregano
- Pinch red pepper flakes

**PIZZA**

- 3 tablespoons extra-virgin olive oil
- 4 ounces Monterey Jack cheese, shredded (1 cup)
- 7 ounces whole-milk mozzarella cheese, shredded (1¾ cups)

**1. FOR THE DOUGH:** Using wooden spoon or spatula, stir flour, salt, and yeast together in bowl. Add warm water and mix until most of flour is moistened. Using your hands, knead dough in bowl until dough forms sticky ball, about 1 minute. Spray 9-inch pie plate or cake pan with oil spray. Transfer dough to prepared plate and press into 7- to 8-inch disk. Spray top of dough with oil spray. Cover tightly with plastic wrap and refrigerate for 12 to 24 hours.

**2. FOR THE SAUCE:** Place tomatoes in fine-mesh strainer and crush with your hands. Drain well, then transfer to food processor. Add oil, garlic, sugar, salt, oregano, and pepper flakes and process until smooth, about 30 seconds. (Sauce can be refrigerated in an airtight container for up to 3 days.)

**3. FOR THE PIZZA:** Two hours before baking, remove dough from refrigerator and let sit at room temperature for 30 minutes.

**4.** Coat bottom of 12-inch cast-iron skillet with oil. Transfer dough to prepared skillet and use your fingertips to flatten dough until it is ⅛ inch from edge of skillet. Cover tightly with plastic and let rest until slightly puffy, about 1½ hours.

**5.** Thirty minutes before baking, adjust oven rack to lowest position and heat oven to 400 degrees. Spread ½ cup sauce evenly over top of dough, leaving ½-inch border (save remaining sauce for another use). Sprinkle Monterey Jack evenly over border. Press Monterey Jack into side of skillet, forming ½- to ¾-inch-tall wall. (Not all cheese will stick to side of skillet.) Evenly sprinkle mozzarella over sauce. Bake until cheese at edge of skillet is well browned, 25 to 30 minutes.

**6.** Transfer skillet to stovetop and let sit until sizzling stops, about 3 minutes. Run butter knife around rim of skillet to loosen pizza. Using thin metal spatula, gently lift edge of pizza and peek at underside to assess browning. Cook pizza over medium heat until bottom crust is well browned, 2 to 5 minutes (skillet handle will be hot). Using 2 spatulas, transfer pizza to wire rack and let cool for 10 minutes. Slice and serve.

## Pepperoni Pan Pizza

**MAKES** two 9-inch pizzas

**WHY THIS RECIPE WORKS** Great pan pizza—named for the pan in which the dough rises and is cooked—has an irresistible crust that's crisp on the bottom and soft and chewy in the middle. A generous amount of oil poured into the pan creates the crisp bottom; getting the soft interior is harder to figure out. We found the secret in a novel ingredient: skim milk. Milk is often used in tender yeast breads, and when we tried it in our pan pizza dough, we got a tender crust with just the right chew. Whole milk worked fine as well, but dough made with skim milk rose better and baked up especially soft and light. Rising the dough in a warmed oven sped up the process to just 30 minutes. We were determined to top our pizza with the quintessential pepperoni, but when just plopped on the pizza and baked, the pepperoni floated in pools of orange grease. The solution was to use the microwave to render the excess fat before baking. Topped with chewy, spicy pepperoni, mozzarella, and a quick, fresh tomato sauce (and ready in just 90 minutes), this pizza beat delivery hands down.

**DOUGH**

- ½ cup olive oil
- ¾ cup skim milk plus 2 additional tablespoons, warmed to 110 degrees
- 2 teaspoons sugar
- 2⅓ cups (11⅝ ounces) unbleached all-purpose flour, plus extra for the work surface
- 1 envelope instant yeast
- ½ teaspoon table salt

**QUICK TOMATO SAUCE FOR PIZZA**

- 1 (14.5-ounce) can crushed tomatoes
- 1 tablespoon olive oil
- 1 garlic clove, minced

**TOPPING**

- 1 (3.5-ounce) package sliced pepperoni
- 1½ cups Quick Tomato Sauce for Pizza
- 12 ounces shredded part-skim mozzarella cheese (about 3 cups)

**1. TO MAKE THE DOUGH:** Adjust an oven rack to the lowest position and heat the oven to 200 degrees. When the oven reaches 200 degrees, turn it off. Lightly coat a large bowl with vegetable oil spray. Coat each of two 9-inch cake pans with 3 tablespoons of the oil.

**2.** Mix the milk, sugar, and remaining 2 tablespoons oil in a measuring cup. Mix the flour, yeast, and salt in a stand mixer fitted with the dough hook. Turn the machine to low and slowly add the milk mixture. After the dough comes together, increase the speed to medium-low and mix until the dough is shiny and smooth, about 5 minutes. Turn the dough onto a lightly floured work surface, gently shape into a ball, and place in the greased bowl. Cover with plastic wrap and place in the warm oven until doubled in size, about 30 minutes.

**3. TO MAKE THE SAUCE:** Process tomatoes in food processor until smooth, about 5 pulses. Heat oil and garlic in medium saucepan over medium heat until garlic is fragrant, about 30 seconds. Stir in tomatoes; bring to simmer and cook, uncovered, until sauce thickens, about 15 minutes. Season with salt and pepper to taste.

**4. TO SHAPE AND TOP THE DOUGH:** Transfer the dough to a lightly floured work surface, divide it in half, and lightly roll each half into a ball. Working with 1 dough ball at a time, roll and shape the dough into a 9½-inch round and press into the oiled pans. Cover with plastic wrap and set in a warm spot (not in the oven) until puffy and slightly risen, about 20 minutes. Meanwhile, heat the oven to 400 degrees.

**5.** While the dough rises, put half of the pepperoni in a single layer on a microwave-safe plate lined with 2 paper towels. Cover with 2 more paper towels and microwave on high for 30 seconds. Discard the towels and set the pepperoni aside; repeat with new paper towels and the remaining pepperoni.

**6.** Remove the plastic wrap from the dough. Ladle ¾ cup of the sauce on each round, leaving a ½-inch border around the edges. Sprinkle each with 1½ cups of the cheese and top with the pepperoni. Bake until the cheese is melted and the pepperoni is browning around the edges, about 20 minutes. Remove from the oven; let the pizzas rest in the pans for 1 minute. Using a spatula, transfer the pizzas to a cutting board and cut each into 8 wedges. Serve.

## Pizza Bianca

**SERVES** 6 to 8

**WHY THIS RECIPE WORKS** This Roman pizza has a crust like no other we've ever tasted: crisp but extraordinarily chewy. It's so good on its own that it is usually topped with just olive oil, rosemary, and kosher salt. But the challenge of devising a pizza bianca recipe for the home cook was to figure out how to handle the super-hydrated dough. Forming the dough required both a 20-minute resting time and 10 minutes of machine kneading at high speed. Rather than rolling it, we pressed the dough onto a baking sheet and placed the sheet on top of a preheated pizza stone on the middle rack of a 450-degree oven. Place a towel or shelf liner under the mixer while kneading as it has a tendency to wobble on the counter. If using a sheet pan smaller than 18 by 13 inches, baking times will be longer as the pizza with be thicker. If you don't have a pizza stone, bake the pizza on a rimless or overturned baking sheet that has been preheated just like the pizza stone.

- 3 cups (15 ounces) unbleached all-purpose flour
- 1⅔ cups water, at room temperature
- 1¼ teaspoons table salt
- 1½ teaspoons instant or rapid-rise yeast
- 1¼ teaspoons sugar
- 5 tablespoons extra-virgin olive oil
- 1 teaspoon kosher salt
- 2 tablespoons whole fresh rosemary leaves

**1.** Mix the flour, water, and table salt in the bowl of a stand mixer fitted with the dough hook on low speed until no areas of dry flour remain, 3 to 4 minutes, occasionally scraping down the sides of the bowl. Turn off the mixer and let the dough rest for 20 minutes.

**2.** Sprinkle the yeast and sugar over the dough. Knead on low speed until fully combined, 1 to 2 minutes, occasionally scraping down the sides of the bowl. Increase the mixer speed to high and knead until the dough is glossy and smooth and pulls away from the sides of the bowl, 6 to 10 minutes. (The dough will pull away from the sides only while the mixer is on. When the mixer is off, the dough will fall back to the sides.)

**3.** Using your fingers, coat a large bowl with 1 tablespoon of the oil, rubbing the excess oil from your fingers onto the blade of a rubber spatula. Using the oiled spatula, transfer the dough to the bowl and pour 1 tablespoon more oil over the top. Flip the dough over once so that it is well coated with the oil; cover tightly with plastic wrap. Once the dough has been placed in the oiled bowl, it can be refrigerated for up to 24 hours. Bring the dough to room temperature, 2 to 2½ hours, before proceeding with step 4 of the recipe. Let the dough rise at room temperature until nearly tripled in volume and large bubbles have formed, 2 to 2½ hours.

**4.** One hour before baking the pizza, adjust an oven rack to the middle position, place a pizza stone on the rack, and heat the oven to 450 degrees.

**5.** Coat a rimmed baking sheet with 2 tablespoons more oil. Using a rubber spatula, turn the dough out onto the baking sheet along with any oil in the bowl. Using your fingertips, press the dough out toward the edges of the baking sheet, taking care not to tear it. (The dough will not fit snugly into corners. If the dough resists stretching, let it relax for 5 to 10 minutes before trying to stretch it again.) Let the dough rest until slightly bubbly, 5 to 10 minutes. Using a dinner fork, poke the surface of the dough 30 to 40 times and sprinkle with the kosher salt.

**6.** Bake until golden brown, 20 to 30 minutes, sprinkling the rosemary over the top and rotating the baking sheet halfway through baking. Using a metal spatula, transfer the pizza to a cutting board. Brush the dough lightly with the remaining 1 tablespoon oil. Slice and serve immediately.

### Pizza Bianca with Tomatoes and Mozzarella

Place 28-ounce can of crushed tomatoes in fine-mesh strainer set over medium bowl. Let sit 30 minutes, stirring 3 times to allow juices to drain. Combine ¾ cup tomato solids, 1 tablespoon extra-virgin olive oil, and ⅛ teaspoon table salt. (Save remaining solids and juice for another use.) Follow recipe for Pizza Bianca, omitting kosher salt and rosemary. In step 6, bake pizza until spotty brown, 15 to 17 minutes. Remove pizza from oven, spread tomato mixture evenly over surface, and sprinkle with 6 ounces (1½ cups) shredded mozzarella (do not brush pizza with oil). Return pizza to oven and continue to bake until cheese begins to brown in spots, 5 to 10 minutes longer.

## The Best Gluten-Free Pizza

**MAKES** two 12-inch pizzas

**WHY THIS RECIPE WORKS** Gluten-free pizza crusts are almost always a disappointment. Our starting point to fix this issue and make a great gluten-free crust was to use our own all-purpose gluten-free flour blend, one that mimicked many of the properties of wheat flour. To strengthen the structure of a dough lacking gluten we added psyllium husk. You can substitute 16 ounces (2⅔ cups plus ¼ cup) King Arthur Gluten-Free Multi-Purpose Flour or 16 ounces (2⅔ cup plus ½ cup) Bob's Red Mill GF All-Purpose Baking Flour for the America's Test Kitchen All-Purpose Gluten-Free Flour Blend. (Note that pizza crust made with King Arthur will be slightly denser and not as chewy, while pizza crust made with Bob's Red Mill will be thicker, more airy and will have a distinct bean flavor.).

**CRUST**

- 16 ounces (3⅓ cups plus ¼ cup) The America's Test Kitchen All-Purpose Gluten-Free Flour Blend
- 2½ ounces (½ cup plus 1 tablespoon) almond flour
- 1½ tablespoons powdered psyllium husk
- 2½ teaspoons baking powder
- 2 teaspoons table salt
- 1 teaspoon instant or rapid-rise yeast
- 2½ cups warm water (100 degrees)
- ¼ cup vegetable oil
- Vegetable oil spray

**SAUCE**

- 1 (28-ounce) can whole peeled tomatoes, drained
- 1 tablespoon extra-virgin olive oil
- 1 teaspoon red wine vinegar
- 1 garlic clove, minced
- 1 teaspoon dried oregano
- ½ teaspoon table salt
- ¼ teaspoon pepper

- 1 ounce Parmesan cheese, grated fine (½ cup)
- 8 ounces whole-milk mozzarella cheese, shredded (2 cups)

**1. FOR THE CRUST:** Using stand mixer fitted with paddle, mix flour blend, almond flour, psyllium, baking powder, salt, and yeast on low speed until combined. Slowly add warm water and oil in steady stream until incorporated. Increase speed to medium and beat until dough is sticky and uniform, about 6 minutes. (Dough will resemble thick batter.)

**2.** Remove bowl from mixer, cover with plastic wrap, and let stand until inside of dough is bubbly (use spoon to peer inside dough), about 1½ hours. (Dough will puff slightly but will not rise.)

**3.** Adjust oven racks to middle and lower positions. Line 2 rimmed baking sheets with parchment paper and spray liberally with oil spray. Transfer half of dough to center of 1 prepared sheet. Using oil-sprayed rubber spatula, spread dough into 8-inch circle. Spray top of dough with oil spray, cover with large sheet of plastic, and, using your hands, press out dough to 11½-inch round, about ¼ inch thick, leaving outer ¼ inch slightly thicker than center; discard plastic. Repeat with remaining dough and second prepared sheet.

**4.** Place prepared sheets in oven and heat oven to 325 degrees. Bake dough until firm to touch, golden brown on underside, and just beginning to brown on top, 45 to 50 minutes, switching and rotating sheets halfway through baking. Transfer crusts to wire rack and let cool. (Parbaked and cooled crusts can be held at room temperature for up to 4 hours. To freeze, wrap crusts in plastic wrap and aluminum foil and freeze for up to two weeks; do not thaw before topping and baking.)

**5.** For the Sauce: Process all ingredients in food processor until smooth, about 30 seconds. Transfer to bowl and refrigerate until ready to use.

**6.** One hour before baking pizza, adjust oven rack to upper-middle position, set baking stone on rack, and heat oven to 500 degrees.

**7.** Transfer 1 parbaked crust to pizza peel. Using back of spoon or ladle, spread ½ cup tomato sauce in thin layer over surface of crust, leaving ¼-inch border around edge. Sprinkle ¼ cup Parmesan evenly over sauce, followed by 1 cup mozzarella. Carefully slide crust onto stone and bake until crust is well browned and cheese is bubbly and beginning to brown, 10 to 12 minutes. Transfer pizza to wire rack and let cool for 5 minutes before slicing and serving. Repeat with second crust, ½ cup tomato sauce (you will have extra sauce), remaining ¼ cup Parmesan, and remaining 1 cup mozzarella.

### The America's Test Kitchen All-Purpose Gluten-Free Flour Blend

**MAKES** 42 ounces (about 9⅓ cups)

Be sure to use potato starch, not potato flour, with this recipe. Tapioca starch is also sold as tapioca flour; they are interchangeable. We strongly recommend that you use Bob's Red Mill white and brown rice flours. We also recommend that you weigh your ingredients; if you measure by volume, spoon each ingredient into the measuring cup and scrape off the excess.

- 24 ounces (4½ cups plus ⅓ cup) white rice flour
- 7½ ounces (1⅔ cups) brown rice flour
- 7 ounces (1⅓ cups) potato starch
- 3 ounces (¾ cup) tapioca starch
- ¾ ounce (¼ cup) nonfat dry milk powder

Whisk all ingredients in large bowl until well combined. Transfer to airtight container and refrigerate for up to 3 months.

CHAPTER 13 

# Cookies and Bars

Photos (left to right): Baci di Dama; Chocolate Crinkle Cookies; Ultranutty Pecan Bars; Perfect Chocolate Chip Cookies; Best Lemon Bars; Peanut Butter Sandwich Cookies; Profiteroles

## Perfect Chocolate Chip Cookies

**MAKES** 16 large cookies

**WHY THIS RECIPE WORKS** Since Nestlé first began printing the recipe for Toll House cookies on chocolate chip bags in 1939, generations of bakers have packed them into lunches and taken them to potlucks. But we wondered if this was really the best that a chocolate chip cookie could be. We wanted a moist and chewy cookie with crisp edges and deep notes of toffee and butterscotch to balance its sweetness. Melting the butter before combining it with the other ingredients gave us the chewy texture we wanted, and browning a portion of it added nutty flavor. Upping the brown sugar enhanced chewiness, while a combination of one whole egg and one egg yolk gave us supremely moist cookies. For crisp edges and deep toffee flavor, we allowed the sugar to dissolve and rest in the melted butter. Avoid using a nonstick skillet to brown the butter as its color makes it difficult to gauge when the butter is browned.

- 1¾ cups (8¾ ounces) all-purpose flour
- ½ teaspoon baking soda
- 14 tablespoons unsalted butter, divided
- ¾ cup packed (5¼ ounces) dark brown sugar
- ½ cup (3½ ounces) granulated sugar
- 1 teaspoon table salt
- 2 teaspoons vanilla extract
- 1 large egg plus 1 large yolk
- 1¼ cups (7½ ounces) semisweet chocolate chips or chunks
- ¾ cup chopped pecans or walnuts, toasted (optional)

**1.** Adjust oven rack to middle position and heat oven to 375 degrees. Line 2 rimmed baking sheets with parchment paper. Whisk flour and baking soda together in medium bowl; set aside.

**2.** Melt 10 tablespoons butter in 10-inch skillet over medium-high heat, about 2 minutes. Continue cooking, stirring and scraping constantly with rubber spatula until milk solids are dark golden brown and butter has nutty aroma, 1 to 3 minutes. Immediately transfer browned butter to large heatproof bowl. Add remaining 4 tablespoons butter and stir until completely melted.

**3.** Add brown sugar, granulated sugar, salt, and vanilla to melted butter; whisk until fully incorporated. Add whole egg and egg yolk; whisk until mixture is smooth and no sugar lumps remain, about 30 seconds. Let mixture stand for 3 minutes, then whisk for 30 seconds. Repeat process of resting and whisking 2 more times until mixture is thick, smooth, and shiny. Using rubber spatula, stir in flour mixture until just combined, about 1 minute. Stir in chocolate chips and nuts, if using, giving dough final stir to ensure that no flour pockets remain.

**4.** Divide dough into 16 equal pieces, about 3 tablespoons each. Using your hands, roll dough into balls and space about 2 inches apart on prepared sheets.

**5.** Bake cookies, 1 sheet at a time, until golden brown and still puffy and edges have begun to set but centers are still soft, 10 to 14 minutes, rotating sheet halfway through baking. Transfer sheet to wire rack; let cool completely before serving.

## Crispy Chocolate Chip Cookies

**MAKES** 48 cookies

**WHY THIS RECIPE WORKS** Too often, thin and crispy chocolate chip cookies are brittle and crumbly or tough and lacking flavor. We wanted cookies that were thin and packed a big crunch without shattering into a million pieces when eaten. And they had to have the flavors of deeply caramelized sugar and rich butter. To achieve notable butterscotch flavor and sufficient crunch, we turned to a combination of light brown sugar and white sugar. To ensure thin cookies, we used melted butter and milk to create a batter that would spread (not rise) in the oven, resulting in cookies with the perfect thin crispiness. A bit of baking soda and corn syrup promoted maximum browning and caramelization, and vanilla and salt gave our cookies the best flavor. The dough, en masse or shaped into balls and wrapped well, can be refrigerated for up to two days or frozen for up to one month; bring it to room temperature before baking.

- 1½ cups (7½ ounces) all-purpose flour
- ¾ teaspoon baking soda
- ¼ teaspoon table salt
- 8 tablespoons unsalted butter, melted and cooled
- ½ cup (3½ ounces) granulated sugar
- ⅓ cup packed (2⅓ ounces) light brown sugar
- 2 tablespoons light corn syrup
- 1 large egg yolk
- 2 tablespoons milk
- 1 tablespoon vanilla extract
- ¾ cup (4½ ounces) semisweet chocolate chips

**1.** Adjust oven rack to middle position and heat oven to 375 degrees. Line 2 rimmed baking sheets with parchment paper. Whisk flour, baking soda, and salt together in medium bowl; set aside.

**2.** In stand mixer fitted with paddle, beat melted butter, granulated sugar, brown sugar, and corn syrup at low speed until thoroughly blended, about 1 minute. Add egg yolk, milk, and vanilla; mix until fully incorporated and smooth, about 1 minute, scraping down bowl and beater as needed. With mixer still running on low, slowly add dry ingredients and mix until just combined. Do not overbeat. Add chocolate chips and mix until evenly distributed throughout batter, about 5 seconds.

**3.** Divide dough into 48 equal pieces, about 1 tablespoon each. Using your hands, roll dough into balls and space about 2 inches apart on prepared sheets. Bake, 1 sheet at a time, until cookies are deep golden brown and flat, about 12 minutes, rotating sheet halfway through baking.

**4.** Let cookies cool on sheets for 3 minutes, then transfer to wire rack and let cool completely before serving.

spatula. Add the dry ingredients and mix on low speed until combined, about 30 seconds. Mix in the chocolate chips until just incorporated.

**4.** Divide the dough into 18 portions, each about ¼ cup, and roll them between your hands into balls. Holding one dough ball with your fingers, pull the dough apart into two equal halves. Rotate the halves 90 degrees and, with the jagged surfaces facing up, join the halves together at their base, again forming a single ball, being careful not to smooth the dough's uneven surface. Place the cookies on the prepared baking sheets, spacing them about 2½ inches apart.

**5.** Bake until the cookies are light golden brown and the edges start to harden but the centers are still soft and puffy, 15 to 18 minutes, switching and rotating the baking sheets halfway through the baking time. Cool the cookies on the baking sheets.

## Thick and Chewy Chocolate Chip Cookies

**MAKES** about 18 large cookies

**WHY THIS RECIPE WORKS** Chocolate chip cookies sold in gourmet shops and cafés always seem to come jumbo-sized. These cookies are incredibly appealing and satisfying; one key element in achieving this cookie was melting the butter, which created a chewy texture. But to keep the cookie from becoming tough, we had to add a little extra fat, the form of an egg yolk; the added fat acts a tenderizer and prevents the cookies from hardening after several hours. Finally, we formed the dough into balls, then pulled each ball into two pieces and rejoined them with the uneven surface facing up; now our cookies had the rustic, craggy appearance we wanted.

- 2 cups plus 2 tablespoons (about 10⅔ ounces) unbleached all-purpose flour
- ½ teaspoon baking soda
- ½ teaspoon table salt
- 12 tablespoons (1½ sticks) unsalted butter, melted and cooled
- 1 cup packed (7 ounces) light or dark brown sugar
- ½ cup (3½ ounces) granulated sugar
- 1 large whole egg
- 1 large egg yolk
- 2 teaspoons vanilla extract
- 1½ cups (9 ounces) semisweet chocolate chips

**1.** Adjust the oven racks to the upper-middle and lower-middle positions and heat the oven to 325 degrees. Line 2 large baking sheets with parchment paper.

**2.** Whisk the flour, baking soda, and salt together in a medium bowl; set aside.

**3.** In a stand mixer fitted with the paddle attachment, beat the butter and sugars at medium speed until smooth, about 1 minute. Add the whole egg, egg yolk, and vanilla and beat on medium-low speed until fully incorporated, about 30 seconds, scraping down the bowl and beater as needed with a rubber spatula. Add the dry ingredients and mix on low speed until combined, about 30 seconds. Mix in the chocolate chips until just incorporated.

## Gluten-Free Chocolate Chip Cookies

**MAKES** about 24 cookies

**WHY THIS RECIPE WORKS** Most gluten-free chocolate chip cookies turn out crumbly, gritty, and greasy. Using the test kitchen's gluten-free flour blend, we set out to create a great gluten-free cookie. Cutting back on butter helped to minimize greasiness. Melting the butter, rather than creaming (as called for in traditional recipes), gave the cookies a chewier texture. Some xanthan gum helped give the cookies structure. To alleviate grittiness, we added more liquid in the form of milk and let the batter rest for 30 minutes so that the starches had time to hydrate and soften. Upping the ratio of brown sugar to granulated sugar made our cookies crispy on the edges and chewy in the center, and also gave the cookies more complex, toffee-like flavor. Not all brands of chocolate chips are processed in a gluten-free facility, so read labels carefully. We recommend you weigh the ingredients for this recipe, rather than rely on cup measurements. You can substitute 8 ounces (¾ cup plus ⅔ cup) King Arthur Gluten-Free Multi-Purpose Flour or 8 ounces (1½ cups plus 2 tablespoons) Bob's Red Mill GF All-Purpose Baking Flour for the ATK blend. Note that cookies made with King Arthur will spread more and be more delicate, while cookies made with Bob's Red Mill will spread more and have a distinct bean flavor.

- 8 ounces (1¾ cups) America's Test Kitchen All-Purpose Gluten-Free Flour Blend (page 811)
- 1 teaspoon baking soda
- ¾ teaspoon xanthan gum
- ½ teaspoon table salt
- 8 tablespoons unsalted butter, melted
- 5¼ ounces (¾ cup packed) light brown sugar
- 2⅓ ounces (⅓ cup) granulated sugar
- 1 large egg
- 2 tablespoons milk
- 1 tablespoon vanilla extract
- 7½ ounces (1¼ cups) semisweet chocolate chips

**1.** Whisk flour blend, baking soda, xanthan gum, and salt together in medium bowl; set aside. Whisk melted butter, brown sugar, and granulated sugar together in large bowl until well combined and smooth. Whisk in egg, milk, and vanilla and continue to whisk until smooth. Stir in flour mixture with rubber spatula and mix until soft, homogeneous dough forms. Fold in chocolate chips. Cover bowl with plastic wrap and let dough rest for 30 minutes. (Dough will be sticky and soft.)

**2.** Adjust oven rack to middle position and heat oven to 350 degrees. Line 2 baking sheets with parchment paper. Using 2 soupspoons and working with about 1½ tablespoons of dough at a time, portion dough and space 2 inches apart on prepared sheets. Bake cookies, 1 sheet at a time, until golden brown and edges have begun to set but centers are still soft, 11 to 13 minutes, rotating sheet halfway through baking.

**3.** Let cookies cool on sheet for 5 minutes, then transfer to wire rack. Serve warm or at room temperature. (Cookies are best eaten on day they are baked, but they can be cooled and placed immediately in airtight container and stored at room temperature for up to 1 day.)

## Chocolate Chip Cookie Ice Cream Sandwiches

**MAKES** 12 sandwiches

**WHY THIS RECIPE WORKS** The stars of this updated nostalgic treat are the thin, rich chocolate chip cookies whose texture and pliability make them the perfect partner for the ice cream. Since a moister cookie was key, so we replaced the white sugar in our chocolate chip cookie recipe with dark brown sugar, since the molasses it contains is a source of both water and simple sugars which attract water. This dough was encouragingly moist, and the frozen cookies noticeably more tender, though still harder than we wanted. Next we added various amounts of water along with the egg and vanilla. Ultimately, we settled on 2 tablespoons of water, which, when combined with a good 8 hours in the freezer, made for cookies that were sturdy enough to sandwich the ice cream, but tender enough to bite through with just a hint of snap. Using mini chips added delicately crunchy bursts of chocolate. These sandwiches should be made at least 8 hours before serving. If you have it, a #16 scoop works well for portioning the ice cream.

- 10 tablespoons unsalted butter
- ¾ cup (5¼ ounces) dark brown sugar
- ¾ teaspoon table salt
- 1 cup plus 2 tablespoons (5⅔ ounces) all-purpose flour
- ¼ teaspoon baking soda
- 1 large egg
- 2 tablespoons water
- 2 teaspoons vanilla extract
- ½ cup (3 ounces) mini semisweet chocolate chips, plus 1 cup for optional garnish
- 3 pints ice cream

**1.** Adjust oven rack to middle position and heat oven to 325 degrees. Melt butter in 10-inch skillet over medium-high heat, about 2 minutes. Continue cooking, stirring and scraping constantly with rubber spatula until milk solids are dark golden brown and butter has nutty aroma, 1 to 3 minutes. Immediately transfer to large heatproof bowl. Whisk in sugar and salt until fully incorporated and let mixture cool for 10 minutes. Meanwhile, line 2 rimmed baking sheets with parchment paper. Stir flour and baking soda together in bowl; set aside.

**2.** Add egg, water, and vanilla to browned butter mixture and whisk until smooth, about 30 seconds. Using rubber spatula, stir in flour mixture until combined. Stir in ½ cup chocolate chips. (Dough will be very soft.)

**3.** Using 1-tablespoon measure or #60 scoop, space 12 mounds of dough evenly on each prepared sheet. Bake, 1 sheet at a time, until cookies are puffed and golden brown, 9 to 12 minutes, rotating sheet halfway through baking. Let cookies cool on sheet for 5 minutes, then transfer to wire rack and let cool completely. Place 1 sheet, without discarding parchment, in freezer.

**4.** Place 4 cookies upside down on work surface. Quickly deposit 2-inch-tall and 2-inch-wide scoop of ice cream onto center of each cookie. Place 1 cookie from rack, right side up, on top of each scoop. Gently press and twist each sandwich between your hands until ice cream spreads to edges (this doesn't have to be perfect; ice cream can be neatened after chilling). Transfer sandwiches to sheet in freezer. Repeat with remaining cookies and ice cream. Place 1 cup chocolate chips, if using, in shallow bowl or pie plate.

**5.** Remove first 4 sandwiches from freezer. Hold 1 sandwich at a time over bowl of chips and gently press chips into sides with your other hand, neatening ice cream if needed. Return garnished sandwiches to freezer, and repeat with remaining 8 sandwiches in 2 batches. Freeze sandwiches for at least 8 hours before serving. (For longer storage, wrap each sandwich tightly with plastic wrap. Transfer wrapped sandwiches to zipper-lock bag and freeze for up to 2 months.

## Classic Chewy Oatmeal Cookies

**MAKES** 20 cookies

**WHY THIS RECIPE WORKS** Many oatmeal cookies are dry, cakey, and overly spiced. To make ours dense and chewy, we combined unsaturated fat (vegetable oil) and saturated fat (butter) in a ratio of nearly 3 to 1, and we decreased the proportion of flour. Adding an extra egg yolk boosted moistness and richness, while a touch more salt than most recipes call for tempered the sweetness and complemented the oaty flavor. Most recipes call for using a stand mixer, but we found this counterproductive to our goal of chewy, dense cookies because the mixer beats air into the dough. Instead we made our dough by hand. Browning the butter delivered more complexity, and blooming a small amount of cinnamon in the butter rounded out its flavor. Regular old-fashioned rolled oats worked best in this recipe. Do not use extra-thick rolled oats.

- 1 cup (5 ounces) all-purpose flour
- ¾ teaspoon table salt
- ½ teaspoon baking soda
- 4 tablespoons unsalted butter
- ¼ teaspoon ground cinnamon
- ¾ cup packed (5¼ ounces) dark brown sugar
- ½ cup (3½ ounces) granulated sugar
- ½ cup vegetable oil
- 1 large egg plus 1 large yolk
- 1 teaspoon vanilla extract
- 3 cups (9 ounces) old-fashioned rolled oats
- ½ cup raisins (optional)

**1.** Adjust oven rack to middle position and heat oven to 375 degrees. Line 2 rimmed baking sheets with parchment paper. Whisk flour, salt, and baking soda together in medium bowl; set aside.

**2.** Melt butter in 8-inch skillet over medium-high heat, swirling pan occasionally, until foaming subsides. Continue to cook, stirring and scraping bottom of pan with heatproof spatula, until milk solids are dark golden brown and butter has nutty aroma, 1 to 2 minutes. Immediately transfer browned butter to large heatproof bowl, scraping skillet with spatula. Stir in cinnamon.

**3.** Add brown sugar, granulated sugar, and oil to bowl with butter and whisk until combined. Add egg and yolk and vanilla and whisk until mixture is smooth. Using wooden spoon, stir in flour mixture until fully combined, about 1 minute. Add oats and raisins, if using, and stir until evenly distributed (mixture will be stiff).

**4.** Divide dough into 20 portions, each about 3 tablespoons (or use #24 cookie scoop). Arrange dough balls 2 inches apart on prepared sheets, 10 dough balls per sheet. Using your damp hand, press each ball into 2½-inch disk.

**5.** Bake, 1 sheet at a time, until cookie edges are set and lightly browned and centers are still soft but not wet, 8 to 10 minutes, rotating sheet halfway through baking. Let cookies cool on sheet on wire rack for 5 minutes; using wide metal spatula, transfer cookies to wire rack and let cool completely.

## Big and Chewy Oatmeal-Raisin Cookies

**MAKES** 18 large cookies

**WHY THIS RECIPE WORKS** Big, moist, and craggy, oatmeal raisin cookies are so good and so comforting, but also so hard to get just right. Too often, they have textural issues and other times the flavor is off, with cookies that lack any sign of oatiness. For an oversize, chewy cookie with buttery oat flavor, we discovered three key changes that made a significant difference. First, we substituted baking powder for baking soda, which gave the dough more lift and made the cookies less dense and a bit chewier. Second, we eliminated the cinnamon recommended in lots of recipes; by taking away the cinnamon, we revealed more oat flavor. We wanted some spice, however, and chose nutmeg, which has a cleaner, subtler flavor that we like with oats. Finally, we increased the sugar in our cookies, and this made a huge difference in terms of texture and moistness. If you prefer a less sweet cookie, you can reduce the granulated sugar to ¾ cup, but you will lose some crispness. Do not overbake these cookies. The edges should be brown, but the rest of the cookie should be very light in color.

- 1½ cups (7½ ounces) all-purpose flour
- ½ teaspoon table salt
- ½ teaspoon baking powder
- ¼ teaspoon freshly grated nutmeg
- 16 tablespoons unsalted butter, softened
- 1 cup packed (7 ounces) light brown sugar
- 1 cup (7 ounces) granulated sugar
- 2 eggs
- 3 cups (9 ounces) old-fashioned rolled oats
- 1½ cups (7½ ounces) raisins (optional)

**1.** Adjust oven racks to upper-middle and lower-middle positions and heat oven to 350 degrees. Line 2 large baking sheets with parchment paper. Whisk flour, salt, baking powder, and nutmeg together in medium bowl; set aside.

**2.** Using stand mixer fitted with paddle, beat butter, brown sugar, and granulated sugar at medium speed until light and fluffy, about 2 minutes. Add eggs, one at a time, and mix until combined, about 30 seconds.

**3.** Decrease speed to low and slowly add dry ingredients until combined, about 30 seconds. Mix in oats and raisins, if using, until just incorporated.

**4.** Divide dough into 18 equal pieces, generous 2 tablespoons each. Using your hands, roll them into balls and space about 2 inches apart on prepared sheets.

**5.** Bake until cookies turn golden brown around edges, 22 to 25 minutes, switching and rotating sheets halfway through baking. Let cookies cool on sheets for 2 minutes, then transfer to wire rack and let cool completely before serving.

### Big and Chewy Oatmeal-Date Cookies

Substitute 1½ cups chopped dates for raisins.

## Chocolate-Chunk Oatmeal Cookies with Pecans and Dried Cherries

**MAKES** about 16 large cookies

**WHY THIS RECIPE WORKS** Oatmeal cookies can be great vehicles for additional flavors, but it's easy to get carried away and overload the dough with a crazy jumble of ingredients resulting in a poorly textured cookie monster. Our ultimate oatmeal cookie would have just the right amount of added ingredients and an ideal texture—crisp around the edges and chewy in the middle. We wanted to add four flavor components—sweet, tangy, nutty, and chocolaty—to the underlying oat flavor. Bittersweet chocolate, dried sour cherries (or cranberries), and toasted pecans gave the right balance of flavors. We also analyzed the cookie dough ingredients and discovered that cookies made with brown sugar were moister and chewier than cookies made with granulated sugar. A combination of baking powder and baking soda (we doubled the usual amount) produced cookies that were light and crisp on the outside, but chewy, dense, and soft in the center. Finally, we focused on appearance to decide when to remove the cookies from the oven—they should be set but still look wet between the fissures; if they look matte rather than shiny, they've been overbaked. We like these cookies made with pecans and dried sour cherries, but walnuts or skinned hazelnuts can be substituted for the pecans, and dried cranberries for the cherries. Quick oats used in place of the old-fashioned oats will yield a cookie with slightly less chewiness. These cookies keep for 4 to 5 days stored in an airtight container or zipper-lock bag, but they will lose their crisp exterior and become uniformly chewy after a day or so. To recrisp the cookies, place them on a baking sheet and in a 425-degree oven for 4 to 5 minutes. Make sure to let the cookies cool on the baking sheet for a few minutes before removing them, and eat them while they're warm.

- 1¼ cups (6¼ ounces) unbleached all-purpose flour
- ¾ teaspoon baking powder
- ½ teaspoon baking soda
- ½ teaspoon table salt
- 1¼ cups (3¾ ounces) old-fashioned oats
- 1 cup (4 ounces) pecans, toasted and chopped
- 1 cup dried sour cherries, chopped coarse
- 4 ounces bittersweet chocolate, chopped into chunks about the size of chocolate chips (about ¾ cup)
- 12 tablespoons (1½ sticks) unsalted butter, softened
- 1½ cups packed (10½ ounces) brown sugar, preferably dark
- 1 large egg
- 1 teaspoon vanilla extract

**1.** Adjust the oven racks to the upper-middle and lower-middle positions and heat the oven to 350 degrees. Line 2 large baking sheets with parchment paper.

**2.** Whisk the flour, baking powder, baking soda, and salt together in a medium bowl. In a second medium bowl, stir together the oats, pecans, cherries, and chocolate.

**3.** In a stand mixer fitted with the paddle attachment, beat the butter and sugar at medium speed until no sugar lumps remain, about 1 minute, scraping down the bowl and beater as needed with a rubber spatula. Add the egg and vanilla and beat on medium-low until fully incorporated, about 30 seconds, scraping down the bowl and beater as needed. Decrease the speed to low, add the flour mixture, and mix until just combined, about 30 seconds. With the mixer still running on low, gradually add the oat-nut mixture; mix until just incorporated. Give the dough a final stir to ensure that no flour pockets remain and the ingredients are evenly distributed.

**4.** Divide the dough into 16 portions, each about ¼ cup, and roll them between your hands into balls; stagger eight balls on each prepared baking sheet, spacing them about 2½ inches apart. Using your fingertips, gently press each dough ball to a 1-inch thickness. Bake the cookies for 20 to 22 minutes, switching and rotating the baking sheets halfway through the baking time, until the cookies are medium brown and the edges have begun to set but the centers are still soft (the cookies will seem underdone and will appear raw, wet, and shiny in the cracks).

**5.** Cool the cookies on the baking sheets for 5 minutes; using a wide metal spatula, transfer the cookies to a wire rack and cool to room temperature.

## Thin and Crispy Oatmeal Cookies

**MAKES** about 24 cookies

**WHY THIS RECIPE WORKS** Thin and crispy oatmeal cookies really let the flavor of the oats take center stage. But the usual ingredients that give thick, chewy oatmeal cookies great texture—generous amounts of sugar and butter, a high ratio of oats to flour, raisins, and nuts—won't all fit in a thin, crispy cookie. We wanted to adjust the ingredients to create a crispy, delicate cookie in which the simple flavor of buttery oats really stands out. Given this cookie's simplicity, creating a rich butter flavor was critical, so we kept almost the same amount of butter as in our standard big, chewy oatmeal cookie, but we scaled back the amount of sugar. During baking, large carbon dioxide bubbles created by the baking soda and baking powder caused the cookies to puff up, collapse, and spread out, producing the thin, flat cookies. Baking the cookies until they were fully set and evenly browned from center to edge made them crisp throughout but not tough. Place them on the baking sheet in three rows, with three cookies in the outer rows and two cookies in the center row. We developed this recipe using Quaker Old Fashioned Oats. Other brands of old-fashioned oats can be substituted, but may cause the cookies to spread more. Do not use instant or quick oats.

- 1 cup (5 ounces) unbleached all-purpose flour
- ¾ teaspoon baking powder
- ½ teaspoon baking soda
- ½ teaspoon table salt
- 14 tablespoons (1¾ sticks) unsalted butter, softened but still cool

- 1 cup (7 ounces) granulated sugar
- ¼ cup packed (1¾ ounces) light brown sugar
- 1 large egg
- 1 teaspoon vanilla extract
- 2½ cups (7½ ounces) old-fashioned oats

**1.** Adjust an oven rack to the middle position and heat the oven to 350 degrees. Line 3 large baking sheets with parchment paper. Whisk the flour, baking powder, baking soda, and salt in a medium bowl; set aside.

**2.** In a stand mixer fitted with the paddle attachment, beat the butter and sugars at medium-low speed until just combined, about 20 seconds. Increase the speed to medium and continue to beat until light and fluffy, about 1 minute longer, scraping down the bowl and beater as needed with a rubber spatula. Add the egg and vanilla and beat on medium-low until fully incorporated, about 30 seconds, scraping down the bowl and beater as needed. Decrease the speed to low, add the flour mixture, and mix until just incorporated and smooth, about 10 seconds. With the mixer still running on low, gradually add the oats and mix until well incorporated, about 20 seconds. Give the dough a final stir to ensure that no flour pockets remain and the ingredients are evenly distributed.

**3.** Divide the dough into 24 portions, each about 2 tablespoons, and roll them between your hands into balls. Place the cookies on the prepared baking sheets, spacing them about 2½ inches apart, eight dough balls per sheet. Using your fingertips, gently press each dough ball to a ¾-inch thickness.

**4.** Bake one sheet at a time until the cookies are deep golden brown, the edges are crisp, and the centers yield to slight pressure when pressed, 13 to 16 minutes, rotating the sheet halfway through the baking time. Cool the cookies completely on the sheet.

## Chewy Sugar Cookies

**MAKES** about 24 cookies

**WHY THIS RECIPE WORKS** Traditional recipes for sugar cookies require incredible attention to detail. The butter must be at precisely the right temperature and it must be creamed to the proper degree of airiness. Slight variations in measures can result in cookies that spread or cookies that become brittle and hard upon cooling. We didn't want a cookie that depended on such a finicky process, we wanted an approachable recipe for great sugar cookies that anyone could make anytime. We melted the butter so our sugar cookie dough could easily be mixed together with a spoon—no more fussy creaming. Replacing a portion of the melted butter with vegetable oil ensured a chewy cookie without affecting flavor. And incorporating cream cheese into the cookie dough kept our cookies tender, while its tang made for a rich, not-too-sweet cookie. The final dough will be slightly softer than most cookie doughs. For best results, handle the dough as briefly and gently as possible when shaping the cookies. Overworking the dough will result in flatter cookies.

- 2¼ cups (11¼ ounces) unbleached all-purpose flour
- 1 teaspoon baking powder
- ½ teaspoon baking soda
- ½ teaspoon table salt
- 1½ cups (10½ ounces) sugar, plus ⅓ cup for rolling
- 2 ounces cream cheese, cut into 8 pieces
- 6 tablespoons (¾ stick) unsalted butter, melted and still warm
- ⅓ cup vegetable oil
- 1 large egg
- 1 tablespoon whole milk
- 2 teaspoons vanilla extract

**1.** Adjust an oven rack to the middle position and heat the oven to 350 degrees. Line 2 large rimmed baking sheets with parchment paper. Whisk the flour, baking powder, baking soda, and salt together in a medium bowl. Set aside.

**2.** Place 1½ cups of the sugar and the cream cheese in a large bowl. Place the remaining ⅓ cup sugar in a shallow baking dish or pie plate and set aside. Pour the warm butter over the sugar and cream cheese and whisk to combine (some small lumps of cream cheese will remain but will smooth out later). Whisk in the oil until incorporated. Add the egg, milk, and vanilla; continue to whisk until smooth. Add the flour mixture and mix with a rubber spatula until a soft homogeneous dough forms.

**3.** Divide the dough into 24 equal pieces, about 2 tablespoons each. Using your hands, roll each piece of dough into a ball. Working in batches, roll the balls in sugar to coat and set on the prepared baking sheet, 12 dough balls per sheet. Using the bottom of a drinking glass, flatten the dough balls until 2 inches in diameter. Sprinkle the tops of the cookies evenly with the remaining sugar, using 2 teaspoons for each sheet. (Discard the remaining sugar.)

**4.** Bake the cookies, one sheet at a time, until the edges are set and beginning to brown, 11 to 13 minutes, rotating the sheet after 7 minutes. Cool the cookies on the baking sheet for 5 minutes; using a wide metal spatula, transfer the cookies to a wire rack and cool to room temperature.

## Brown Sugar Cookies

**MAKES** 24 cookies

**WHY THIS RECIPE WORKS** We wanted to turn up the volume on the sugar cookie by switching out the granulated sugar in favor of brown sugar. We were after an oversized cookie, with a crackling crisp exterior and a chewy interior, one that would scream "brown sugar." We wanted butter for optimal flavor, but the traditional creaming method gave us a cakey texture. Cutting the butter into the flour produced crumbly cookies. What worked was first melting the butter. We then tweaked the amount of eggs, dark brown sugar, flour, and leavener to give us a good cookie, but we wanted even more brown sugar flavor. We made progress by rolling the dough balls in a combination of brown and granulated sugar and adding a healthy amount of vanilla and table salt. But our biggest success came from an unlikely refinement. Browning the melted butter added a complex nuttiness that made a substantial difference. Avoid using a nonstick skillet to brown the butter; the color of the nonstick coating makes it difficult to gauge when the butter is sufficiently browned. It's hard to judge the cookies' doneness by color. Instead, gently press halfway between the edge and center of the cookie. When it's done, it will form an indentation with slight resistance.

- 14 tablespoons unsalted butter, divided
- 1¾ cups packed (12¼ ounces) dark brown sugar, plus ¼ cup for rolling
- ¼ cup granulated sugar
- 2 cups plus 2 tablespoons (10⅔ ounces) all-purpose flour
- ½ teaspoon baking soda
- ¼ teaspoon baking powder
- ½ teaspoon table salt
- 1 large whole egg plus 1 large egg yolk
- 1 tablespoon vanilla extract

**1.** Melt 10 tablespoons butter in 10-inch skillet over medium-high heat, about 2 minutes. Continue cooking, stirring and scraping constantly with rubber spatula until milk solids are dark golden brown and butter has nutty aroma, 1 to 3 minutes. Immediately transfer to large heatproof bowl. Stir remaining 4 tablespoons butter into hot butter to melt; set aside for 15 minutes.

**2.** Meanwhile, adjust oven rack to middle position and heat oven to 350 degrees. Line 2 large baking sheets with parchment paper. In shallow dish, mix ¼ cup brown sugar and granulated sugar, rubbing mixture between your fingers until well combined; set aside. Whisk flour, baking soda, and baking powder together in medium bowl; set aside.

**3.** Add remaining 1¾ cups brown sugar and salt to bowl with cooled butter; mix until no sugar lumps remain, about 30 seconds. Scrape down bowl with rubber spatula; add egg, egg yolk, and vanilla and mix until fully incorporated, about 30 seconds. Scrape down the bowl. Add flour mixture and mix until just combined, about 1 minute. Give dough final stir to ensure that no flour pockets remain and ingredients are evenly distributed.

**4.** Divide dough into 24 equal pieces, about 2 tablespoons each. Using your hands, roll them into balls. Working in batches, drop 12 dough balls into baking dish with sugar mixture and toss to coat. Space dough balls about 2 inches apart on prepared sheet; repeat with second batch of 12.

**5.** Bake 1 sheet at a time until cookies are browned and still puffy and edges have begun to set but centers are still soft (cookies will look raw between cracks and seem underdone), 12 to 14 minutes, rotating sheet halfway through baking. Do not overbake.

**6.** Let cookies cool on sheet for 5 minutes, then transfer to wire rack and let cool completely before serving.

## Easy Holiday Sugar Cookies

**MAKES** 40 cookies

**WHY THIS RECIPE WORKS** For holiday cookies with a crisp and sturdy texture, we made superfine sugar by grinding granulated sugar briefly in the food processor, and we added small amounts of baking powder and baking soda to the dough. We skipped creaming softened butter and sugar in favor of whizzing cold butter with sugar in the food processor, which let the dough come together in just minutes. In step 3, use a rolling pin and a combination of rolling and pushing or a smearing motion to form the soft dough into an oval. A rimless cookie sheet helps achieve evenly baked cookies; if you do not have one, use an overturned rimmed baking sheet. If desired, stir 1 or 2 drops of food coloring into the icing. For a pourable icing, whisk in milk, 1 teaspoon at a time, until the desired consistency is reached. You can also decorate the shapes with sanding sugar or sprinkles before baking.

**COOKIES**

- 1 large egg
- 1 teaspoon vanilla extract
- ¾ teaspoon table salt
- ¼ teaspoon almond extract
- 2½ cups (12½ ounces) all-purpose flour
- ¼ teaspoon baking powder
- ¼ teaspoon baking soda
- 1 cup (7 ounces) granulated sugar
- 16 tablespoons unsalted butter, cut into ½-inch pieces and chilled

**ROYAL ICING**

- 2⅔ cups (10⅔ ounces) confectioners' sugar
- 2 large egg whites
- ½ teaspoon vanilla extract
- ⅛ teaspoon table salt

**1. FOR THE COOKIES:** Whisk egg, vanilla, salt, and almond extract together in small bowl. Whisk flour, baking powder, and baking soda together in second bowl.

**2.** Process sugar in food processor until finely ground, about 30 seconds. Add butter and process until uniform mass forms and no large pieces of butter are visible, about 30 seconds,

scraping down sides of bowl as needed. Add egg mixture and process until smooth and paste-like, about 10 seconds. Add flour mixture and process until no dry flour remains but mixture remains crumbly, about 30 seconds, scraping down sides of bowl as needed.

**3.** Turn out dough onto counter and knead gently by hand until smooth, about 10 seconds. Divide dough in half. Place 1 piece of dough in center of large sheet of parchment paper and press into 9 by 7-inch oval. Place second large sheet of parchment over dough and roll dough into 14 by 10-inch oval of even ⅛-inch thickness. Transfer dough with parchment to rimmed baking sheet. Repeat pressing and rolling with second piece of dough, then stack on top of first piece on sheet. Refrigerate until dough is firm, at least 1½ hours (or freeze for 30 minutes). (Rolled dough can be wrapped in plastic wrap and refrigerated for up to 5 days.)

**4.** Adjust oven rack to lower-middle position and heat oven to 300 degrees. Line rimless baking sheet with parchment. Working with 1 piece of rolled dough, gently peel off top layer of parchment. Replace parchment, loosely covering dough. (Peeling off parchment and returning it will make cutting and removing cookies easier.) Turn over dough and parchment and gently peel off and discard second piece of parchment. Using cookie cutter, cut dough into shapes. Transfer shapes to prepared sheet, spacing them about ½ inch apart. Bake until cookies are lightly and evenly browned around edges, 14 to 17 minutes, rotating sheet halfway through baking. Let cookies cool on sheet for 5 minutes, then transfer to wire rack and let cool completely. Repeat cutting and baking with remaining dough. (Dough scraps can be patted together, rerolled, and chilled once before cutting and baking.)

**5. FOR THE ROYAL ICING:** Using stand mixer fitted with whisk attachment, whip all ingredients on medium-low speed until combined, about 1 minute. Increase speed to medium-high and whip until glossy, soft peaks form, 3 to 4 minutes, scraping down bowl as needed.

**6.** Spread icing onto cooled cookies. Let icing dry completely, about 1½ hours, before serving.

## Spritz Cookies

**MAKES** about 72 small cookies

**WHY THIS RECIPE WORKS** Spritz cookies, those golden-swirled holiday cookies, often end up bland and tasteless. We set out to make them light, crisp, buttery treats. Creaming the butter and sugar produced a dough light enough to easily press or pipe the cookies. As for shaping, either a cookie press or a pastry bag can be used. If using a pastry bag, use a star tip to create the various shapes. For stars, a ½ to ⅝-inch tip (measure the diameter of the tip at the smallest point) works best, but for rosettes and S shapes, use a ⅜-inch tip. Stars should be about 1 inch in diameter. To create rosettes, pipe the dough while moving the bag in a circular motion, ending at the center of the rosette; rosettes should be about 1¼ inches in diameter. To create S shapes, pipe the dough into compact S's; they should be about 2 inches long and 1 inch wide. If you make an error while piping, scraped the dough off the baking sheet and re-pipe it.. Unbaked dough can be refrigerated in an airtight container for up to 4 days; to use, let it stand at room temperature until softened, about 45 minutes. Baked cookies will keep for more than a week if stored in an airtight container or zipper-lock bag.

- 1 large egg yolk
- 1 tablespoon heavy cream
- 1 teaspoon vanilla extract
- 16 tablespoons (2 sticks) unsalted butter, softened but still cool
- ⅔ cup (4⅔ ounces) granulated sugar
- ¼ teaspoon table salt
- 2 cups (10 ounces) unbleached all-purpose flour

**1.** Adjust an oven rack to the middle position and heat the oven to 375 degrees. Line 2 large baking sheets with parchment paper. Whisk the egg yolk, cream, and vanilla in a small bowl until combined; set aside.

**2.** In a stand mixer fitted with the paddle attachment, beat the butter, sugar, and salt at medium-high speed until light and fluffy, about 3 minutes, scraping down the bowl and beater as needed with a rubber spatula. With the mixer running at medium speed, add the yolk-cream mixture and beat until incorporated, about 30 seconds. With the mixer running at low speed, gradually beat in the flour until combined, scraping down the bowl and beater as needed. Give the dough a final stir to ensure that no flour pockets remain.

**3.** If using a cookie press to form the cookies, follow the manufacturer's instructions to fill the press. If using a pastry bag, fit it with a star tip and fill the bag with half of the dough. Press or pipe cookies onto the prepared baking sheet, spacing them about 1½ inches apart, refilling the cookie press or pastry bag as needed. Bake one sheet at a time, until the cookies are light golden brown, 10 to 12 minutes, rotating the baking sheet halfway through the baking time. Cool the cookies on the baking sheet for 10 to 15 minutes; using a metal spatula, transfer them to a wire rack and cool to room temperature.

## Snickerdoodles

**MAKES** 24 COOKIES

**WHY THIS RECIPE WORKS** With their crinkly tops and liberal dusting of cinnamon sugar, snickerdoodles are a New England favorite. Cream of tartar is essential to these cookies, as it provided their subtle tang, and, when combined with baking soda, it created a short-lived leavening effect that caused the cookies to rise and fall quickly while baking, leaving them with a distinctive crinkly appearance. We found that using equal amounts of shortening and butter gave us nicely shaped cookies that were chewy and buttery. Rolling the balls of dough in cinnamon sugar imparted a spicy sweet crunch. We baked the cookies one sheet at a time and pulled them from the oven just as they were beginning to brown but were still soft and puffy in the middle. They continued to cook as they cooled on the baking sheet and were perfectly done and chewy once cooled. Cream of tartar is essential to the flavor of these cookies, and it works in combination with the baking soda to give the cookies lift; do not substitute baking powder.

- 2½ cups (12½ ounces) all-purpose flour
- 2 teaspoons cream of tartar
- 1 teaspoon baking soda
- ½ teaspoon table salt
- 8 tablespoons unsalted butter, softened
- 8 tablespoons vegetable shortening
- 1½ cups (10½ ounces) sugar, plus ¼ cup for rolling
- 2 large eggs
- 1 tablespoon ground cinnamon

**1.** Adjust oven rack to middle position and heat oven to 375 degrees. Line 3 baking sheets with parchment paper. Whisk flour, cream of tartar, baking soda, and salt together in bowl.

**2.** Using stand mixer fitted with paddle, beat butter, shortening, and 1½ cups sugar together on medium speed until light and fluffy, about 3 minutes. Beat in eggs, one at a time, until incorporated, about 30 seconds, scraping down bowl as needed.

**3.** Reduce speed to low and slowly add flour mixture until combined, about 30 seconds. Give dough final stir by hand to ensure no flour pockets remain.

**4.** Combine remaining ¼ cup sugar and cinnamon in shallow dish. Working with 2 tablespoons dough at a time, roll into balls, then roll in sugar to coat; measure and space 2 inches apart on prepared baking sheets. (Dough balls can be frozen for up to 1 month; bake frozen cookies in 300-degree oven for 18 to 20 minutes.)

**5.** Bake cookies, 1 sheet at a time, with 8 cookies per sheet, until edges are just set and beginning to brown but centers are still soft, puffy, and cracked (cookies will look raw between cracks and seem underdone), 8 to 12 minutes, rotating sheet halfway through baking. Let cookies cool on sheet for 10 minutes, then transfer to wire rack and let cool completely before serving.

## Molasses Spice Cookies

**MAKES** 22 cookies

**WHY THIS RECIPE WORKS** We wanted to create the ultimate molasses spice cookie—soft, chewy, and gently spiced with deep, dark molasses flavor. We also wanted it to have the traditional cracks and crinkles so characteristic of these charming cookies. Using just the right amount of molasses and brown sugar and flavoring the cookies with a combination of vanilla, ginger, cinnamon, cloves, black pepper, and allspice gave these spiced cookies the warm tingle that we were after. We pulled the cookies from the oven when they still looked a bit underdone; residual heat finished the baking and kept the cookies chewy. Light or mild molasses give the cookies a milder flavor; for a stronger flavor, use dark molasses. Either way, measure molasses in a liquid measure. If you find that the dough sticks to your palms as you shape the balls, moisten your hands occasionally in a bowl filled with cold tap water and shake off the excess. Bake the cookies one sheet at a time; if baked two sheets at a time, the cookies started on the bottom rack won't develop attractive crackly tops.

- ⅓ cup (2⅓ ounces) granulated sugar, plus ½ cup for rolling
- 2¼ cups (11¼ ounces) all-purpose flour
- 1 teaspoon baking soda
- 1½ teaspoons ground cinnamon
- 1½ teaspoons ground ginger
- ½ teaspoon ground cloves
- ¼ teaspoon ground allspice
- ¼ teaspoon pepper
- ¼ teaspoon table salt
- 12 tablespoons unsalted butter, softened
- ⅓ cup packed (2⅓ ounces) dark brown sugar
- 1 large egg yolk
- 1 teaspoon vanilla extract
- ½ cup light or dark molasses

**1.** Adjust oven rack to middle position and heat oven to 375 degrees. Line 2 large baking sheets with parchment paper. Place ½ cup granulated sugar in shallow dish; set aside.

**2.** Whisk flour, baking soda, cinnamon, ginger, cloves, allspice, pepper, and salt together in medium bowl; set aside.

**3.** Using stand mixer fitted with paddle, beat butter, brown sugar, and remaining ⅓ cup granulated sugar on medium-high speed until light and fluffy, about 3 minutes. Decrease speed to medium-low and add egg yolk and vanilla; increase speed to medium and beat until incorporated, about 20 seconds. Decrease speed to medium-low and add molasses; beat until fully incorporated, about 20 seconds, scraping down bowl once with rubber spatula. Decrease speed to low and add flour mixture; beat until just incorporated, about 30 seconds, scraping down bowl once. Give dough final stir to ensure that no flour pockets remain. (Dough will be soft.)

**4.** Divide dough into 22 equal pieces, about 1 tablespoon each. Using your hands, roll them into balls. Working in batches of five, drop dough balls into baking dish with sugar and roll to coat. Space dough balls about 2 inches apart on prepared sheets.

**5.** Bake cookies, 1 sheet at a time, until cookies are browned, still puffy, and edges have begun to set but centers are still soft (cookies will look raw between cracks and seem underdone), about 11 minutes, rotating sheet halfway through baking. Do not overbake.

**6.** Let cookies cool on sheets for 5 minutes, then transfer cookies to wire rack and let cool completely before serving.

### Molasses Spice Cookies with Dark Rum Glaze

If the glaze is too thick to drizzle, whisk in up to an additional ½ tablespoon rum. Whisk 1 cup (4 ounces) confectioners' sugar and 2½ tablespoons dark rum together in medium bowl until smooth. Drizzle or spread glaze using back of spoon on cooled cookies. Allow glazed cookies to dry for at least 15 minutes.

## Speculoos (Belgian Spice Cookies)

**MAKES** 32 cookies

**WHY THIS RECIPE WORKS** Speculoos boast warm spice notes, nuanced caramel flavor, and a crisp texture. The widely available packaged version of these Belgian treats, Biscoff cookies, gained a huge following when Delta Airlines started giving them away during flights. We aimed to create a homemade version that mimicked their caramel taste but improved the spice flavor. To achieve the appropriate texture, we rolled the dough thin so it would bake up dry and crisp, used only enough sugar to lightly sweeten the dough since sugar is hygroscopic and makes cookies moist, and added baking powder along with the usual baking soda to produce an open, airy crumb. For a subtle caramel taste, we chose turbinado sugar rather than molasses-based brown sugar or traditional Belgian brown sugar. To nail the spice flavor, we used a large amount of cinnamon along with small amounts of cardamom and cloves for complexity. For the proper flavor, we strongly recommend using turbinado sugar (commonly sold as Sugar in the Raw). If you can't find it, use ¾ cup plus 2 tablespoons (6 ounces) of packed light brown sugar and skip the sugar grinding in step 2. In step 3, use a rolling pin and a combination of rolling and a smearing motion to form the rectangle. If the dough spreads beyond the rectangle, trim it and use the scraps to fill in the corners; then, replace the parchment and continue to roll.

- 1½ cups (7½ ounces) all-purpose flour
- 5 teaspoons ground cinnamon
- 1 teaspoon ground cardamom
- ¼ teaspoon ground cloves
- ¼ teaspoon baking soda
- ¼ teaspoon baking powder
- ¼ teaspoon table salt
- ¾ cup (6 ounces) turbinado sugar

- 8 tablespoons unsalted butter, cut into ½-inch pieces and chilled
- 1 large egg

**1.** Whisk flour, cinnamon, cardamom, cloves, baking soda, baking powder, and salt together in bowl. Using pencil and ruler, draw 12 by 10-inch rectangle in center of each of 2 large sheets of parchment paper, crisscrossing lines at corners. (Use crisscrosses to help line up top and bottom sheets as dough is rolled.)

**2.** Process sugar in food processor for 30 seconds (some grains will be smaller than granulated sugar; others will be larger). Add butter and process until uniform mass forms and no large pieces of butter are visible, about 30 seconds, scraping down sides of bowl as needed. Add egg and process until smooth and paste-like, about 10 seconds, scraping down sides of bowl as needed. Add flour mixture and process until no dry flour remains but mixture remains crumbly, about 30 seconds, scraping down sides of bowl as needed.

**3.** Transfer dough to bowl and knead gently with spatula until uniform and smooth, about 10 seconds. Place 1 piece of parchment on counter with pencil side facing down (you should be able to see rectangle through paper). Place dough in center of marked rectangle and press into 9 by 6-inch rectangle. Place second sheet of parchment over dough, with pencil side facing up, so dough is in center of marked rectangle. Using pencil marks as guide, use rolling pin and bench scraper to shape dough into 12 by 10-inch rectangle of even ⅜-inch thickness. Transfer dough with parchment to rimmed baking sheet. Refrigerate until dough is firm, at least 1½ hours (or freeze for 30 minutes). (Rolled dough can be wrapped in plastic wrap and refrigerated for up to 5 days.)

**4.** Adjust oven racks to upper-middle and lower-middle positions and heat oven to 300 degrees. Line 2 rimless baking sheets with parchment. Transfer chilled dough to counter. Gently peel off top layer of parchment from dough. Using fluted pastry wheel (or sharp knife or pizza cutter) and ruler, trim off rounded edges of dough that extend over marked edges of

12 by 10-inch rectangle. Cut dough lengthwise into 8 equal strips about 1¼ inches wide. Cut each strip crosswise into equal pieces about 3 inches long. Transfer cookies to prepared sheets, spacing them at least ½ inch apart. Bake until cookies are lightly and evenly browned, 30 to 32 minutes, switching and rotating sheets halfway through baking. Let cookies cool completely on sheets before serving. (Cookies can be stored at room temperature for up to 3 weeks.)

## Gingersnaps

**MAKES** 80 1½-inch cookies

**WHY THIS RECIPE WORKS** We wanted to put the "snap" back in gingersnap cookies. This meant creating a cookie that not only breaks cleanly in half and crunches satisfyingly with every bite but also has an assertive ginger flavor and heat. The key to texture was reducing the moisture in the final baked cookie. We achieved this by reducing the amount of sugar (which holds on to moisture), increasing the baking soda (which created cracks in the dough where more moisture could escape), and lowering the oven temperature (which increased the baking time). For flavor we doubled the normal amount of dried ginger but also added fresh ginger, black pepper, and cayenne to ensure our cookie had real "snap." For the best results, use fresh spices. For efficiency, form the second batch of cookies while the first batch bakes. The 2 teaspoons of baking soda are essential to getting the right texture.

- 2½ cups (12½ ounces) all-purpose flour
- 2 teaspoons baking soda
- ½ teaspoon table salt
- 12 tablespoons unsalted butter
- 2 tablespoons ground ginger
- 1 teaspoon ground cinnamon
- ¼ teaspoon ground cloves
- ¼ teaspoon pepper
- Pinch cayenne pepper
- 1¼ cups packed (8¾ ounces) dark brown sugar
- ¼ cup molasses
- 2 tablespoons finely grated fresh ginger
- 1 large egg plus 1 large yolk
- ½ cup (3½ ounces) granulated sugar

**1.** Whisk flour, baking soda, and salt together in bowl. Heat butter in 10-inch skillet over medium heat until melted. Lower heat to medium-low and continue to cook, swirling pan frequently, until foaming subsides and butter is just beginning to brown, 2 to 4 minutes. Transfer butter to large bowl and whisk in ground ginger, cinnamon, cloves, pepper, and cayenne. Let cool slightly, about 2 minutes. Add brown sugar, molasses, and fresh ginger to butter mixture and whisk to combine. Add egg and yolk and whisk to combine. Add flour mixture and stir until just combined. Cover dough tightly with plastic wrap and refrigerate until firm, about 1 hour.

**2.** Adjust oven racks to upper-middle and lower-middle positions and heat oven to 300 degrees. Line 2 baking sheets with parchment paper. Place granulated sugar in shallow dish. Divide dough into heaping teaspoon portions; roll dough into 1-inch balls. Working in batches of 10, roll balls in sugar to coat. Evenly space dough balls on prepared baking sheets, 20 dough balls per sheet.

**3.** Place 1 sheet on upper rack and bake for 15 minutes. Transfer partially baked top sheet to lower rack, rotating 180 degrees, and place second sheet of dough balls on upper rack. Continue to bake until cookies on lower tray just begin to darken around edges, 10 to 12 minutes longer. Remove lower sheet of cookies and transfer upper sheet to lower rack, rotating 180 degrees, and continue to bake until cookies begin to darken around edges, 15 to 17 minutes longer. Slide baked cookies, still on parchment, to wire rack and let cool completely before serving. Let baking sheets cool slightly and line with parchment again. Repeat step 2 with remaining dough balls. (Cooled cookies can be stored at room temperature for up to 2 weeks.)

**TO MAKE AHEAD:** Dough can be refrigerated for up to 2 days or frozen for up to 1 month. Let frozen dough thaw overnight in refrigerator before proceeding with recipe. Let dough stand at room temperature for 30 minutes before shaping.

## Chocolate Cookies

**MAKES** about 16 cookies

**WHY THIS RECIPE WORKS** We set out to make an exceptionally rich chocolate cookie that we could sink our teeth into—without having it fall apart. Our first batch, with modest amounts of cocoa powder and melted chocolate, baked up too cakey and tender—just what we didn't want. The chocolate was the culprit; its fat was softening the dough. Cutting out the chocolate made the cookies less cakey and tender, and more like cookies. To restore chocolate flavor without adding too much fat, we increased the cocoa powder and reduced the flour. Using an egg white rather than a whole egg gave us the structure we wanted, and adding dark corn syrup gave the cookies a nice chewiness and lent a hint of caramel flavor. For more richness, we folded in chopped bittersweet chocolate; the chunks stayed intact and added intense chocolate flavor. A dip in granulated sugar before baking gave the cookies a sweet crunch and an attractive crackled appearance. We recommend using one of the test kitchen's favorite baking chocolates, Ghirardelli 60% Cacao Bittersweet Chocolate or Callebaut Intense Dark Chocolate, but any high-quality dark, bittersweet, or semisweet chocolate will work.

- ⅓ cup (2⅓ ounces) granulated sugar, plus ½ cup for coating
- 1½ cups (7½ ounces) unbleached all-purpose flour
- ¾ cup Dutch-processed cocoa powder
- ½ teaspoon baking soda
- ¼ teaspoon plus ⅛ teaspoon table salt
- ½ cup dark corn syrup
- 1 large egg white
- 1 teaspoon vanilla extract

- 12 tablespoons (1½ sticks) unsalted butter, softened
- ⅓ cup packed (2⅓ ounces) dark brown sugar
- 4 ounces bittersweet chocolate, chopped into ½-inch pieces

**1.** Adjust the oven racks to the upper-middle and lower-middle positions and heat the oven to 375 degrees. Line 2 large baking sheets with parchment paper. Place ½ cup of the granulated sugar in a shallow baking dish or pie plate. Whisk the flour, cocoa powder, baking soda, and salt together in a medium bowl. Whisk the corn syrup, egg white, and vanilla together in a small bowl.

**2.** In a stand mixer fitted with the paddle attachment, beat the butter, brown sugar, and remaining ⅓ cup granulated sugar at medium-high speed until light and fluffy, about 2 minutes. Decrease the speed to medium-low, add the corn syrup mixture, and beat until fully incorporated, about 20 seconds, scraping down the bowl and beater as needed with a rubber spatula. Decrease the speed to low, add the flour mixture and chopped chocolate, and mix until just incorporated, about 30 seconds, scraping down the bowl and beater as needed. Give the dough a final stir to ensure that no pockets of flour remain. Chill the dough for 30 minutes to firm slightly (do not chill longer than 30 minutes).

**3.** Divide the dough into 16 equal portions, each a generous 2 tablespoons, and roll them between your hands into balls about 1½ inches in diameter. Working in batches, drop eight dough balls into the baking dish with the sugar and toss to coat. Place the dough balls on the prepared baking sheet, spacing them about 2 inches apart; repeat with the second batch of eight. Bake, switching and rotating the sheets halfway through the baking time, until the cookies are puffed and cracked and the edges have begun to set but the centers are still soft (the cookies will look raw between the cracks and seem underdone), 10 to 11 minutes. Do not overbake.

**4.** Cool the cookies on the baking sheets for 5 minutes; using a wide metal spatula, transfer the cookies to a wire rack and cool to room temperature.

## Thick and Chewy Double-Chocolate Cookies

**MAKES** about 42 cookies

**WHY THIS RECIPE WORKS** Our goal in creating a traditional double-chocolate cookie recipe seemed more like a fantasy: The first bite of the cookie would reveal a center of hot fudge sauce, the texture would call to mind chocolate bread pudding, and the overall flavor would be of deep and complex chocolate. In the end, the fulfillment of our fantasy relied on very basic ingredients: chocolate, sugar, eggs, butter, flour, baking powder, and salt. We used a modified creaming method with minimal beating to produce moist cookies that weren't cakey, and we let the batter rest for a half-hour to develop a certain fudginess. Ingredient proportions were all-important—for moist, rich cookies, we used more chocolate than flour. The more highly processed semisweet chocolate tasted smoother and richer than unsweetened, and Dutch-processed cocoa and instant coffee further enriched the chocolate flavor. Resist the urge to bake the cookies longer than indicated; they will firm up as they cool.

- 2 cups (10 ounces) unbleached all-purpose flour
- ½ cup Dutch-processed cocoa powder
- 2 teaspoons baking powder
- ½ teaspoon table salt
- 16 ounces semisweet chocolate, chopped
- 4 large eggs
- 2 teaspoons vanilla extract
- 2 teaspoons instant coffee or espresso powder
- 10 tablespoons (1¼ sticks) unsalted butter, softened
- 1½ cups packed (10½ ounces) light brown sugar
- ½ cup (3½ ounces) granulated sugar

**1.** Whisk the flour, cocoa powder, baking powder, and salt together in a medium bowl; set aside.

**2.** Melt the chocolate in a medium heatproof bowl set over a saucepan of barely simmering water, stirring occasionally, until smooth; set aside to cool slightly. Whisk the eggs and vanilla together in a medium bowl, sprinkle the coffee powder over the top to dissolve, and set aside.

**3.** In a stand mixer fitted with the paddle attachment, beat the butter and sugars at medium speed until combined, about 45 seconds; the mixture will look granular. Decrease the speed to low, gradually add the egg mixture, and mix until incorporated, about 45 seconds. Add the melted chocolate in a steady stream and mix until combined, about 40 seconds, scraping down the bowl and beater as needed with a rubber spatula. With the mixer still running on low, add the dry ingredients and mix until just combined. Do not over beat. Cover the bowl of dough with plastic wrap and let stand at room temperature until the consistency is scoopable and fudge-like, about 30 minutes.

**4.** Meanwhile, adjust the oven racks to the upper-middle and lower-middle positions and heat the oven to 350 degrees. Line 2 baking sheets with parchment paper. Divide the dough into 42 equal portions, each about 2 tablespoons, and roll them between your hands into balls about 1¾ inches in diameter. Set the dough balls on the prepared baking sheets, spacing them about 1½ inches apart.

**5.** Bake two sheets at a time, switching and rotating the baking sheets halfway through the baking time, until the edges have just begun to set but the centers are still very soft, about 10 minutes. Cool the cookies on the baking sheets for 10 minutes; using a wide metal spatula, transfer the cookies to a wire rack and cool to room temperature.

## Chocolate Crinkle Cookies

**MAKES** 22 cookies

**WHY THIS RECIPE WORKS** When done well, chocolate crinkle cookies are eye-catching, with an irresistible deep chocolaty richness and a crackling top. But too often, these cookies turn out tooth-achingly sweet, with just a couple of gaping cracks instead of a crackly surface. For the best chocolate flavor, we used a combination of unsweetened chocolate and cocoa powder, which got an additional flavor boost from espresso powder. Using brown sugar instead of granulated lent a more complex, tempered sweetness with a bitter molasses edge that complemented the chocolate. A combination of baking powder and baking soda gave us cookies with the right amount of lift and spread and contributed to a crackly surface. But the real key was rolling the cookies in granulated sugar before the traditional powdered sugar. It not only helped produce the perfect crackly exterior by creating a "shell" that broke into numerous fine fissures as the cookie rose and spread, but it also helped the powdered sugar coating stay in place for chocolate crinkle cookies that lived up to their name. Both natural and Dutch-processed cocoa will work in this recipe.

- 1 cup (5 ounces) all-purpose flour
- ½ cup (1½ ounces) unsweetened cocoa powder
- 1 teaspoon baking powder
- ¼ teaspoon baking soda
- ½ teaspoon table salt
- 1½ cups packed (10½ ounces) brown sugar
- 3 large eggs
- 4 teaspoons instant espresso powder (optional)
- 1 teaspoon vanilla extract
- 4 ounces unsweetened chocolate, chopped
- 4 tablespoons unsalted butter
- ½ cup (3½ ounces) granulated sugar
- ½ cup (2 ounces) confectioners' sugar

**1.** Adjust oven rack to middle position and heat oven to 325 degrees. Line 2 baking sheets with parchment paper. Whisk flour, cocoa, baking powder, baking soda, and salt together in medium bowl; set aside.

**2.** Whisk brown sugar; eggs; espresso powder, if using; and vanilla together in large bowl. Microwave chocolate and butter in bowl at 50 percent power, stirring occasionally, until melted, 2 to 3 minutes.

**3.** Whisk chocolate mixture into egg mixture until combined. Fold in flour mixture until no dry streaks remain. Let dough sit at room temperature for 10 minutes.

**4.** Place granulated sugar and confectioners' sugar in 2 separate shallow dishes. Divide dough into equal pieces, about 2 tablespoons each. Using your hands, roll into balls (or use #30 scoop). Drop balls of dough into granulated sugar and roll to coat. Transfer balls to confectioners' sugar and roll to coat. Evenly space dough balls on prepared sheets, 11 dough balls per sheet.

**5.** Bake cookies, 1 sheet at a time, until cookies are puffed and cracked and edges have begun to set but centers are still soft (cookies will look raw between cracks and will seem underdone), about 12 minutes, rotating sheet halfway through baking. Let cool completely on baking sheet before serving.

## Peanut Butter Cookies

**MAKES** about 36 cookies

**WHY THIS RECIPE WORKS** Recipes for peanut butter cookies tend to fall into one of two categories: sweet and chewy with a mild peanut flavor, and sandy and crumbly with a strong peanut flavor. What we wanted, of course, was the best of both worlds—that is, cookies that were crisp on the edges and chewy in the center, with lots of peanut flavor. Granulated sugar was necessary for crisp edges and chewy centers, while dark brown sugar enriched the peanut flavor. As for flour, too little resulted in an oily cookie, whereas too much made for dry cookies. Baking soda contributed to browning and amplified the peanut flavor and baking powder provided lift, making both leaveners necessary. Extra-crunchy peanut butter also helped the cookie rise and achieve a crisper edge and a softer center. But the best way to get the true peanut flavor we sought was to use peanuts and salt. Adding some roasted, salted peanuts, ground in a food processor, and then adding still more salt (directly to the batter as well in the form of salted rather than unsalted butter) produced a strong roasted nut flavor without sacrificing anything in terms of texture. If using unsalted butter, increase the salt to 1 teaspoon.

- 2½ cups (12½ ounces) unbleached all-purpose flour
- ½ teaspoon baking soda
- ½ teaspoon baking powder
- ½ teaspoon table salt
- 16 tablespoons (2 sticks) salted butter, softened
- 1 cup packed (7 ounces) dark brown sugar
- 1 cup (7 ounces) granulated sugar
- 1 cup extra-crunchy peanut butter, at room temperature
- 2 large eggs
- 2 teaspoons vanilla extract
- 1 cup (5 ounces) roasted salted peanuts, ground in a food processor to resemble bread crumbs, about 14 pulses

**1.** Adjust the oven racks to the upper-middle and lower-middle positions and heat oven to 350 degrees. Line 2 large baking sheets with parchment paper.

2. Whisk the flour, baking soda, baking powder, and salt together in a medium bowl; set aside.

3. In a stand mixer fitted with the paddle attachment, beat the butter and sugars at medium speed until light and fluffy, about 2 minutes, scraping down the bowl and beater as needed with a rubber spatula. Add the peanut butter and mix until fully incorporated, about 30 seconds; add the eggs, one at a time, and the vanilla and mix until combined, about 30 seconds. Decrease the speed to low and add the dry ingredients; mix until combined, about 30 seconds. Mix in the ground peanuts until just incorporated.

4. Divide the dough into 36 portions, each a generous 2 tablespoons, and roll them between your hands into balls about 2 inches in diameter. Place the dough balls on the prepared baking sheets, spacing them about 2½ inches apart. Press each dough ball twice, at perpendicular angles, with a dinner fork dipped in cold water to make a crisscross design.

5. Bake, switching and rotating the sheets halfway through the baking time, until the cookies are puffy and slightly brown around the edges but not on top, 10 to 12 minutes; the cookies will not look fully baked. Cool the cookies on the baking sheets for 5 minutes; using a wide metal spatula, transfer the cookies to a wire rack and cool to room temperature.

## Chewy Peanut Butter Cookies

**MAKES** 24 cookies

**WHY THIS RECIPE WORKS** Commonplace ingredients and a quick mixing method make these peanut butter cookies convenient; the chewy texture and robust peanut flavor make them irresistible. We wanted peanutty peanut butter cookies with crisp edges and moist, chewy centers, but because peanut butter has a fair amount of starch, more peanut butter in the dough resulted in drier, more stunted cookies. So in pursuit of more chew, we examined the fat ratios. In the past, we've found that a ratio of about 30 percent saturated fat to 70 percent unsaturated fat yielded the chewiest cookies, so we've used a combination of butter (mostly saturated) and vegetable oil (mostly unsaturated). In this recipe, peanut butter, which is mostly unsaturated, replaced the oil, and melting the butter meant that there was no mixer required. Dark brown sugar deepened the color of the dough, and honey aided in browning as the cookies baked. A half-cup of finely chopped dry-roasted peanuts provided another layer of nutty flavor and a bit of crunch. To ensure that the cookies have the proper texture, use a traditional creamy peanut butter in this recipe. We developed this recipe with Skippy Creamy Peanut Butter. You can substitute light brown sugar for dark, but your cookies will be lighter in color.

- 1½ cups (7½ ounces) all-purpose flour
- 1 teaspoon baking soda
- ½ teaspoon table salt
- 1½ cups packed (10½ ounces) dark brown sugar
- 1 cup (9 ounces) creamy peanut butter
- 2 large eggs

- 4 tablespoons unsalted butter, melted and cooled
- 2 tablespoons honey
- 1 teaspoon vanilla extract
- ½ cup dry-roasted peanuts, chopped fine

1. Adjust oven rack to middle position and heat oven to 350 degrees. Line two 18 by 13-inch rimmed baking sheets with parchment paper. Whisk flour, baking soda, and salt together in medium bowl.

2. In large bowl, whisk sugar, peanut butter, eggs, melted butter, honey, and vanilla until smooth. Add flour mixture and stir with rubber spatula until soft, homogeneous dough forms. Stir in peanuts until evenly distributed.

3. Working with 2 tablespoons dough at a time (or using #30 portion scoop), roll dough into balls and evenly space on prepared sheets (12 dough balls per sheet). Using your fingers, gently flatten dough balls until 2 inches in diameter.

4. Bake cookies, 1 sheet at a time, until edges are just set and just beginning to brown, 10 to 12 minutes, rotating sheet after 6 minutes. Let cookies cool on sheet for 5 minutes. Using wide metal spatula, transfer cookies to wire rack and let cool completely before serving.

## Peanut Butter Sandwich Cookies

**MAKES** 24 cookies

**WHY THIS RECIPE WORKS** If you love peanut butter cookies, then these cookies with a rich peanut butter filling in the middle will be your new favorite. For the filling, creamy peanut butter, unsalted butter, and a full cup of confectioners' sugar made the perfect rich but cohesive filling, one that stayed in place between two crisp cookies; we balanced the sweetness of the filling with a relatively low-sugar cookie component. Extra liquid and extra baking soda gave our cookies the thin, flat dimensions and sturdy crunch that are vital to a sandwich cookie. Do not use unsalted peanut butter for this recipe.

**COOKIES**

- 1¼ cups (6¼ ounces) raw peanuts, toasted and cooled
- ¾ cup (3¾ ounces) all-purpose flour
- 1 teaspoon baking soda
- ½ teaspoon table salt
- 3 tablespoons unsalted butter, melted
- ½ cup creamy peanut butter
- ½ cup (3½ ounces) granulated sugar
- ½ cup packed (3½ ounces) light brown sugar
- 3 tablespoons whole milk
- 1 large egg

**FILLING**

- ¾ cup creamy peanut butter
- 3 tablespoons unsalted butter
- 1 cup (4 ounces) confectioners' sugar

**1. FOR THE COOKIES:** Adjust oven racks to upper-middle and lower-middle positions and heat oven to 350 degrees. Line 2 baking sheets with parchment paper. Pulse peanuts in food processor until finely chopped, about 8 pulses. Whisk flour, baking soda, and salt together in bowl. Whisk melted butter, peanut butter, granulated sugar, brown sugar, milk, and egg together in second bowl. Stir flour mixture into peanut butter mixture with rubber spatula until combined. Stir in peanuts until evenly distributed.

**2.** Using #60 scoop or tablespoon measure, place 12 mounds, evenly spaced, on each prepared baking sheet. Using damp hand, flatten mounds until 2 inches in diameter.

**3.** Bake until deep golden brown and firm to touch, 15 to 18 minutes, switching and rotating baking sheets halfway through baking. Let cookies cool on baking sheets for 5 minutes. Transfer cookies to wire rack and let cool completely, about 30 minutes. Repeat portioning and baking remaining dough.

**4. FOR THE FILLING:** Microwave peanut butter and butter together until butter is melted and warm, about 40 seconds. Using rubber spatula, stir in confectioners' sugar until combined.

**5. TO ASSEMBLE:** Place 24 cookies upside down on counter. Place 1 level tablespoon (or #60 scoop) warm filling in center of each cookie. Place second cookie on top of filling, right side up, pressing gently until filling spreads to edges. Allow filling to set for 1 hour before serving. Assembled cookies can be stored at room temperature for up to 3 days.

## Florentine Lace Cookies

**MAKES** 24 cookies

**WHY THIS RECIPE WORKS** Wafer-thin Florentines have a reputation for being fussy, but they don't have to be. The key was to grind the almonds and decrease the flour to allow the cookies to spread more. To simplify making the caramel-like base of the dough, we removed the pan from the heat when the sugar mixture thickened and began to brown. A flourish of faux-tempered chocolate completed the professional pastry shop effect. Do not be concerned if some butter separates from the dough while you're portioning the cookies. When melting the chocolate, pause the microwave and stir the chocolate often to ensure that it doesn't get much warmer than body temperature.

- 2 cups slivered almonds
- ¾ cup heavy cream
- 4 tablespoons unsalted butter, cut into 4 pieces
- ½ cup (3½ ounces) sugar
- ¼ cup orange marmalade
- 3 tablespoons all-purpose flour
- 1 teaspoon vanilla extract
- ¼ teaspoon grated orange zest
- ¼ teaspoon table salt
- 4 ounces bittersweet chocolate, chopped fine

**1.** Adjust oven racks to upper-middle and lower-middle positions and heat oven to 350 degrees. Line 2 baking sheets with parchment paper. Process almonds in food processor until they resemble coarse sand, about 30 seconds.

**2.** Bring cream, butter, and sugar to boil in medium saucepan over medium-high heat. Cook, stirring frequently, until mixture begins to thicken, 5 to 6 minutes. Continue to cook, stirring constantly, until mixture begins to brown at edges and is thick enough to leave trail that doesn't immediately fill in when spatula is scraped along pan bottom, 1 to 2 minutes longer (it's OK if some darker speckles appear in mixture). Remove pan from heat and stir in almonds, marmalade, flour, vanilla, orange zest, and salt until combined.

**3.** Drop 6 level tablespoons dough at least 3½ inches apart on prepared sheets. When cool enough to handle, use damp fingers to press each portion into 2½-inch circle.

**4.** Bake until deep brown from edge to edge, 15 to 17 minutes, switching and rotating sheets halfway through baking. Transfer cookies, still on parchment, to wire racks and let cool. Let baking sheets cool for 10 minutes, line with fresh parchment, and repeat portioning and baking with remaining dough.

**5.** Microwave 3 ounces chocolate in bowl at 50 percent power, stirring frequently, until about two-thirds melted, 1 to 2 minutes. Remove bowl from microwave, add remaining 1 ounce chocolate, and stir until melted, returning to microwave for no more than 5 seconds at a time to complete melting if necessary. Transfer chocolate to small zipper-lock bag and snip off corner, making hole no larger than 1/16 inch.

**6.** Transfer cooled cookies directly to wire racks. Pipe zigzag of chocolate over each cookie, distributing chocolate evenly among all cookies. Refrigerate until chocolate is set, about 30 minutes, before serving. (Cookies can be stored at cool room temperature for up to 4 days.)

## Best Shortbread

**MAKES** 16 wedges

**WHY THIS RECIPE WORKS** We wanted well-made, superlative shortbread with a tawny brown crumb and pure, buttery richness. In initial tests we found that reverse creaming—mixing the flour and sugar before adding the butter, creating less aeration—yielded the most reliable results. To smooth out the granular texture, we swapped the white sugar for confectioners' sugar. Still, our shortbread was unpleasantly tough; the problems were gluten and moisture. To curb gluten development, we replaced some of our flour with powdered old-fashioned oats and a modest amount of cornstarch. As for the moisture problem, we cooked the dough briefly, then shut off the heat and let it sit in the still-warm oven. Use the collar of a springform pan to form the shortbread into an even round. Mold the shortbread with the collar in the closed position, then open the collar, but leave it in place. This allows the shortbread to expand slightly but keeps it from spreading too far. Wrapped well and stored at room temperature, the shortbread will keep for up to 7 days.

- ½ cup (1½ ounces) old-fashioned oats
- 1½ cups (7½ ounces) unbleached all-purpose flour
- ¼ cup cornstarch
- ⅔ cup (2⅔ ounces) confectioners' sugar
- ½ teaspoon table salt
- 14 tablespoons (1¾ sticks) unsalted butter, chilled, cut into ⅛-inch-thick slices

**1.** Adjust an oven rack to the middle position and heat the oven to 450 degrees. Pulse the oats in a spice grinder or blender until reduced to a fine powder, about ten 5-second pulses (you should have ¼ to ⅓ cup oat flour). In a stand mixer fitted with the paddle attachment, mix the oat flour, all-purpose flour, cornstarch, sugar, and salt on low speed until combined, about 5 seconds. Add the butter to the dry ingredients and continue to mix on low speed until the dough just forms and pulls away from the sides of the bowl, 5 to 10 minutes.

**2.** Place a 9- or 9½-inch springform pan on a parchment-lined rimmed baking sheet (do not use the springform pan bottom). Press the dough into the collar in an even ½-inch-thick layer, smoothing the top of the dough with the back of a spoon. Place a 2-inch biscuit cutter in the center of the dough and cut out the center. Place the extracted round alongside the springform collar on the baking sheet and replace the cutter in the center of the dough. Open the springform collar, but leave it in place.

**3.** Bake the shortbread for 5 minutes, then reduce the oven temperature to 250 degrees. Continue to bake until the edges turn pale golden, 10 to 15 minutes longer. Remove the baking sheet from the oven; turn off the oven. Remove the springform pan collar; use a chef's knife to score the surface of the shortbread into 16 even wedges, cutting halfway through the shortbread. Using a wooden skewer, poke 8 to 10 holes in each wedge. Return the shortbread to the oven and prop the door open with the handle of a wooden spoon, leaving a 1-inch gap at the top. Allow the shortbread to dry in the turned-off oven until pale golden in the center (the shortbread should be firm but giving to the touch), about 1 hour.

**4.** Transfer the baking sheet to a wire rack; cool the shortbread to room temperature, at least 2 hours. Cut the shortbread at the scored marks to separate and serve.

### FORMING AND BAKING THE SHORTBREAD

**1.** Cut a hole in the center of the dough with a 2-inch biscuit cutter and remove the round of dough—place it on the baking sheet next to the collar; replace the cutter in the hole.

**2.** Open the collar, but leave it in place. Bake 5 minutes at 450 degrees, then 10 to 15 minutes at 250 degrees.

**3.** Score the partially baked shortbread into wedges, then poke 8 to 10 holes in each wedge.

**4.** Return the shortbread to the turned-off oven to dry; prop the door open with a wooden spoon or stick.

## Sablés (French Butter Cookies)

**MAKES** about 40 cookies

**WHY THIS RECIPE WORKS** During the holidays, these French butter cookies offer sophistication and style. That is, if you can capture their elusive sandy texture (sablé is French for sandy), which separates them from sturdy American butter cookies. To create the hallmark sandy texture of sablés—light, with an inviting granular quality similar to shortbread—we would have to do some detective work. We started with a basic recipe using the typical method of creaming butter and sugar, then adding egg and flour. We found that we needed to decrease the liquid in the dough so there would be less moisture to dissolve the sugar particles. Cutting back on butter helped, as did the inclusion of a hard-cooked egg yolk. Adding the mashed yolk during creaming eliminated moisture and perfected the texture of the cookies. Brushing the cookies with a beaten egg white and sprinkling them with coarse sugar before baking added a delicate crunch and an attractive sparkle. Turbinado sugar is commonly sold as Sugar in the Raw. Demerara sugar, sanding sugar, or another coarse sugar can be substituted. Make sure that the cookie dough is well chilled and firm so that it can be uniformly sliced. After the dough has been wrapped in parchment, it can be double-wrapped in plastic wrap and frozen for up to 2 weeks.

- 1 large egg
- 10 tablespoons (1¼ sticks) unsalted butter, softened
- ⅓ cup plus 1 tablespoon (2¾ ounces) granulated sugar
- ¼ teaspoon table salt
- 1 teaspoon vanilla extract
- 1½ cups (7½ ounces) unbleached all-purpose flour
- 1 large egg white, lightly beaten with 1 teaspoon water
- 4 teaspoons turbinado sugar

**1.** Place the egg in a small saucepan, cover with water by 1 inch, and bring to a boil over high heat. Remove the pan from the heat, cover, and let sit for 10 minutes. Meanwhile, fill a small bowl with ice water. Using a slotted spoon, transfer the egg to the ice water and let stand for 5 minutes. Crack the egg and peel the shell. Separate the yolk from the white; discard the white. Press the yolk through a fine-mesh strainer into a small bowl.

**2.** In a stand mixer fitted with the paddle attachment, beat the butter, granulated sugar, salt, and cooked egg yolk on medium speed until light and fluffy, about 4 minutes, scraping down the bowl and beater as needed with a rubber spatula. Decrease the speed to low, add the vanilla, and mix until incorporated. Stop the mixer; add the flour and mix on low speed until just combined, about 30 seconds. Using a rubber spatula, press the dough into a cohesive mass.

**3.** Divide the dough in half; roll each piece into a log about 6 inches long and 1¾ inches in diameter. Wrap each log in a 12-inch square of parchment paper and twist the ends to seal and firmly compact the dough into a tight cylinder. Chill until firm, about 1 hour.

**4.** Adjust the oven racks to the upper-middle and lower-middle positions and heat the oven to 350 degrees. Line 2 large baking sheets with parchment paper. Using a chef's knife, slice the dough into ¼-inch-thick rounds, rotating the dough so that it won't become misshapen from the weight of the knife. Place the cookies 1 inch apart on the baking sheets. Using a pastry brush, gently brush the cookies with the egg white mixture and sprinkle evenly with the turbinado sugar.

**5.** Bake until the centers of the cookies are pale golden brown with edges slightly darker than the centers, about 15 minutes, switching and rotating the baking sheets halfway through the baking time. Cool the cookies on the baking sheets for 5 minutes; using a thin metal spatula, transfer the cookies to a wire rack and cool to room temperature. (The cookies can be stored between sheets of parchment paper in an airtight container for up to 1 week.)

### Chocolate Sablés

Follow the recipe for Sablés, reducing the flour to 1⅓ cups (6⅔ ounces) and adding ¼ cup Dutch-processed cocoa powder with the flour in step 2.

### Black and White Spiral Cookies

**MAKES** about 80 cookies

Follow the recipes for Sablés and Chocolate Sablés through step 2. Following the "Forming Spiral Cookies" photos, form the dough into spiral logs. Proceed with the Sablés recipe from step 4, slicing the logs into ¼-inch-thick rounds, omitting the egg white mixture and turbinado sugar in both recipes, and baking as directed.

### Chocolate Sandwich Cookies

**MAKES** about 40 cookies

Follow the recipe for Sablés through step 3. In step 4, slice one dough log into ⅛-inch-thick rounds, omitting the egg white mixture and turbinado sugar. Bake the cookies as directed in step 5, reducing the baking time to 10 to 13 minutes. Repeat with the second dough log. When all the cookies are completely cool, melt 3½ ounces dark or milk chocolate and cool slightly. Spread the melted chocolate on the bottom of one cookie. Place a second cookie on top, slightly off-center, so some chocolate shows. Repeat with the remaining melted chocolate and cookies.

### Vanilla Pretzel Cookies

**MAKES** about 40 cookies

Follow the recipe for Sablés through step 3, increasing the vanilla extract to 1 tablespoon and reducing the chilling time to 30 minutes (the dough will not be fully hardened). Slice the dough into ¼-inch-thick rounds and roll into balls. Roll each ball into a 6-inch rope, tapering the ends. Following the "Forming Pretzel Cookies" photos on page 831, form the ropes into pretzel shapes. Proceed with the recipe, brushing with the egg white mixture, sprinkling with the turbinado sugar, and baking as directed.

### FORMING SPIRAL COOKIES

**1.** Halve each batch of dough. Roll out each portion on parchment paper into an 8 by 6-inch rectangle, ¼ inch thick. Briefly chill the dough until firm enough to handle.

**2.** Using a bench scraper, place one plain cookie dough rectangle on top of one chocolate dough rectangle. Repeat to make two double rectangles.

**3.** Roll out each double rectangle on parchment into a 9 by 6-inch rectangle (if too firm, let rest until malleable). Then, starting at the long end, roll each into a tight log.

**4.** Twist the ends of the parchment to seal. Chill the logs for 1 hour. Slice the logs into ¼-inch-thick rounds.

### FORMING PRETZEL COOKIES

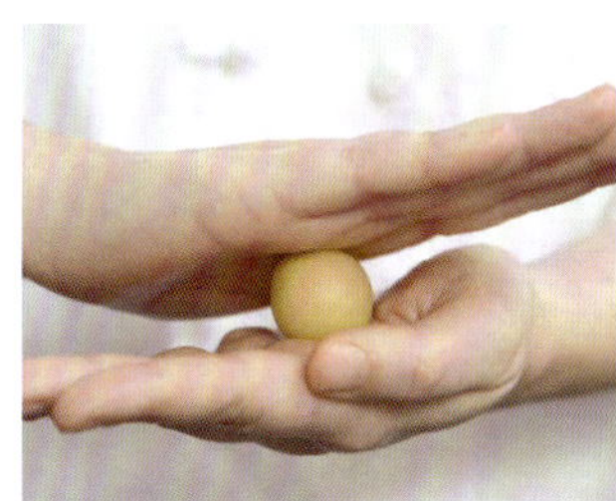

**1.** Slice slightly chilled dough into ¼-inch-thick rounds and roll into balls.

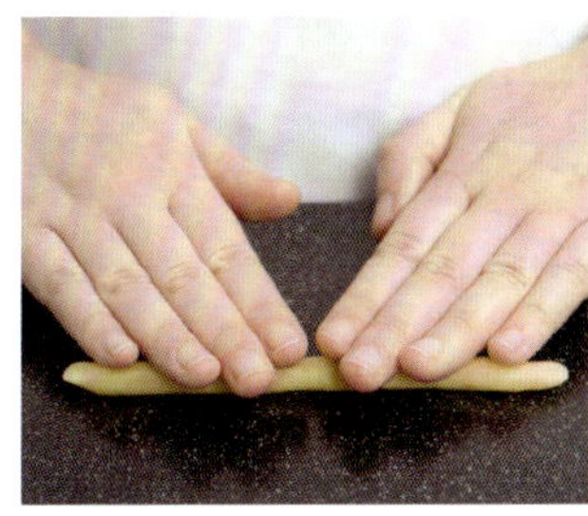

**2.** Roll each ball into a 6-inch rope, tapering the ends.

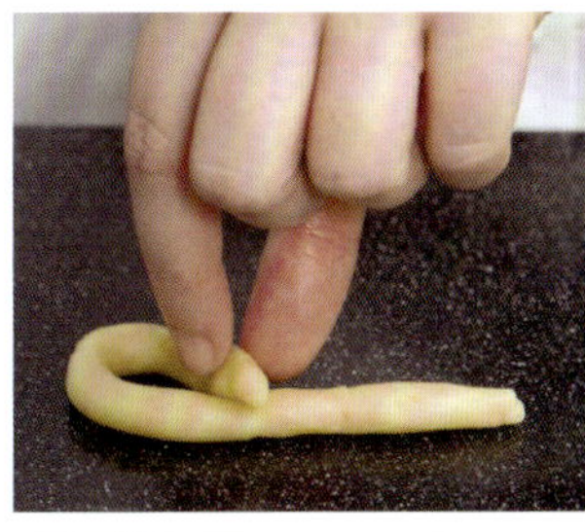

**3.** Pick up one end of the rope and cross it over to form half of a pretzel shape.

**4.** Bring the second end over to complete the pretzel shape.

## Holiday Rolled Cookies

**MAKES** about 38 cookies

**WHY THIS RECIPE WORKS** Baking holiday cookies should be a fun endeavor but so often it's an exercise in frustration. The dough clings to the rolling pin, it rips and tears as it is rolled out, and the tactic of moving the dough in and out of the fridge to make it easier to work with turns a simple one-hour process into a half-day project. We wanted a simple recipe that would yield a forgiving, workable dough, producing cookies that would be sturdy enough to decorate yet tender enough to be worth eating. Our first realization was that we had to use enough butter to stay true to the nature of a butter cookie but not so much that the dough became greasy. All-purpose flour had enough gluten to provide structure, while superfine sugar provided a fine, even crumb and a compact, crisp cookie. Cream cheese—a surprise ingredient—gave the cookies flavor and richness without altering their texture. If you cannot find superfine sugar, process granulated sugar in a food processor for 30 seconds. If desired, the cookies can be finished with sprinkles or other decorations immediately after glazing (see page 832).

**BUTTER COOKIE DOUGH**

- 2½ cups (12½ ounces) unbleached all-purpose flour
- ¾ cup (5⅔ ounces) superfine sugar
- ¼ teaspoon table salt
- 16 tablespoons (2 sticks) unsalted butter, cut into 16 pieces, softened
- 2 tablespoons cream cheese, at room temperature
- 2 teaspoons vanilla extract

**GLAZE**

- 1 tablespoon cream cheese, at room temperature
- 3 tablespoons milk
- 1½ cups (6 ounces) confectioners' sugar

**1. FOR THE COOKIES:** In a stand mixer fitted with the paddle attachment, mix the flour, sugar, and salt at low speed until combined, about 5 seconds. With the mixer running on low, add the butter 1 piece at a time; continue to mix until the mixture looks crumbly and slightly wet, 1 to 2 minutes longer. Beat in the cream cheese and vanilla until the dough just begins to form large clumps, about 30 seconds.

**2.** Knead the dough by hand in the bowl, about two to three turns, until it forms a large, cohesive mass. Transfer the dough to a clean work surface and divide it into two even pieces. Press each piece into a 4-inch disk, wrap the disks in plastic wrap, and refrigerate until the dough is firm but malleable, about 30 minutes. (The disks can be refrigerated for up to 3 days or frozen for up to 2 weeks; defrost in the refrigerator before using.)

**3.** Adjust an oven rack to the middle position and heat the oven to 375 degrees. Working with one piece of dough at a time, roll out the dough to an even ⅛-inch thickness between 2 large sheets of parchment paper; slide the rolled dough, still on the parchment, onto a baking sheet and refrigerate until firm, about 10 minutes.

**4.** Line 2 large baking sheets with parchment paper. Working with 1 sheet of dough at a time, cut into desired shapes using cookie cutters and place the cookies on the prepared sheet, spacing them about 1½ inches apart. Bake 1 sheet at a time, until the cookies are light golden brown, about 10 minutes, rotating the sheet halfway through the baking time. (The dough scraps can be patted together, chilled, and rerolled once.) Cool the cookies on the baking sheet for 3 minutes; using a wide metal spatula, transfer the cookies to a wire rack and cool to room temperature.

**5. FOR THE GLAZE:** Whisk the cream cheese and 2 tablespoons of the milk together in a medium bowl until combined and no lumps remain. Add the confectioners' sugar and whisk until smooth, adding the remaining 1 tablespoon milk as needed until the glaze is thin enough to spread easily. Using the back of a spoon, drizzle or spread a scant teaspoon of the glaze onto each cooled cookie. Allow the glazed cookies to dry for at least 30 minutes.

### DECORATING HOLIDAY COOKIES

**1.** For a smooth, evenly glazed cookie, spoon a little glaze on the center of the cookie, then spread it out in an even layer using the back of a spoon.

**2.** After glazing the cookies, sprinkle with crushed candy canes, colored sugar, or chopped nuts.

**3.** To add detail to a cut-out cookie, make a piping bag by spooning some glaze into a zipper-lock bag, pushing the glaze to a bottom corner, and snipping off the corner of the bag with scissors.

**4.** After you've piped outlines onto a cookie, go back and fill in with colored glazes.

**5.** Use the zipper-lock bag to pipe small dots on the cookie, then top with shiny bead-like decorations. When set, the glaze will hold the beads in place.

## Almond Biscotti

**MAKES** 30 cookies

**WHY THIS RECIPE WORKS** We wanted biscotti that were hard and crunchy, but not hard to eat, and bold in flavor. To keep the crumb crisp, we used just a small amount of butter (4 tablespoons), and to keep the biscotti from being too hard, we ground some of the nuts to a fine meal, which helped minimize gluten development in the crumb. To ensure bold flavor in a biscuit that gets baked twice, we increased the quantity of almond extract. The almonds will continue to toast while the biscotti bake, so toast the nuts only until they are just fragrant.

- 1¼ cups whole almonds, lightly toasted
- 1¾ cups (8¾ ounces) all-purpose flour
- 2 teaspoons baking powder
- ¼ teaspoon table salt
- 2 large eggs, plus 1 large white beaten with pinch table salt
- 1 cup (7 ounces) sugar
- 4 tablespoons unsalted butter, melted and cooled
- 1½ teaspoons almond extract
- ½ teaspoon vanilla extract
- Vegetable oil spray

1. Adjust oven rack to middle position and heat oven to 325 degrees. Using ruler and pencil, draw two 8 by 3-inch rectangles, spaced 4 inches apart, on piece of parchment paper. Grease baking sheet and place parchment on it, marked side down.

2. Pulse 1 cup almonds in food processor until coarsely chopped, 8 to 10 pulses; transfer to bowl and set aside. Process remaining ¼ cup almonds in food processor until finely ground, about 45 seconds. Add flour, baking powder, and salt; process to combine, about 15 seconds. Transfer flour mixture to second bowl. Process 2 eggs in now-empty food processor until lightened in color and almost doubled in volume, about 3 minutes. With processor running, slowly add sugar until thoroughly combined, about 15 seconds. Add melted butter, almond extract, and vanilla and process until combined, about 10 seconds. Transfer egg mixture to medium bowl. Sprinkle half of flour mixture over egg mixture and, using spatula, gently fold until just combined. Add remaining flour mixture and chopped almonds and gently fold until just combined.

3. Divide batter in half. Using floured hands, form each half into 8 by 3-inch rectangle, using lines on parchment as guide. Spray each loaf lightly with oil spray. Using rubber spatula lightly coated with oil spray, smooth tops and sides of rectangles. Gently brush tops of loaves with egg white wash. Bake until loaves are golden and just beginning to crack on top, 25 to 30 minutes, rotating pan halfway through baking.

4. Let loaves cool on baking sheet for 30 minutes. Transfer loaves to cutting board. Using serrated knife, slice each loaf on slight bias into ½-inch-thick slices. Lay slices, cut side down, about ¼ inch apart on wire rack set in rimmed baking sheet. Bake until crisp and golden brown on both sides, about 35 minutes, flipping slices halfway through baking. Let cool completely before serving. Biscotti can be stored in airtight container for up to 1 month.

## Pistachio-Spice Biscotti

**MAKES** 30 cookies

**WHY THIS RECIPE WORKS** We wanted biscotti that were hard and crunchy, but not hard to eat, and bold in flavor. To keep the crumb hard, we used just a small amount of butter (4 tablespoons); to keep it from being too hard, we ground some of the nuts to a fine meal, which helped minimize gluten development in the crumb. To ensure bold flavor in a biscuit that gets baked twice, we increased the quantities of aromatic ingredients. The pistachios will continue to toast while the biscotti bake, so toast the nuts only until they are just fragrant.

- 1¼ cups (5½ ounces) shelled pistachios, lightly toasted, divided
- 1¾ cups (8¾ ounces) all-purpose flour
- 2 teaspoons baking powder
- 1 teaspoon ground cardamom
- ½ teaspoon ground cloves
- ½ teaspoon pepper
- ¼ teaspoon cinnamon
- ¼ teaspoon ground ginger
- ¼ teaspoon table salt
- 2 large eggs, plus 1 large white beaten with pinch table salt
- 1 cup (7 ounces) sugar
- 4 tablespoons unsalted butter, melted and cooled
- 1 teaspoon water
- 1 teaspoon vanilla extract
- Vegetable oil spray

1. Adjust oven rack to middle position and heat oven to 325 degrees. Using ruler and permanent marker, draw two 8 by 3-inch rectangles, spaced 4 inches apart, on piece of parchment paper. Grease rimmed baking sheet and place parchment on it ink side down.

2. Pulse 1 cup pistachios in food processor until coarsely chopped, 8 to 10 pulses; transfer to bowl and set aside. Process remaining ¼ cup pistachios in processor until finely ground, about 45 seconds. Add flour, baking powder, cardamom, cloves, pepper, cinnamon, ginger, and salt; process to combine, about 15 seconds. Transfer flour mixture to bowl. Process 2 eggs in now-empty processor until lightened in color and almost doubled in volume, about 3 minutes. With processor running, slowly add sugar until thoroughly combined, about 15 seconds. Add melted butter, water, and vanilla; process until combined, about 10 seconds. Transfer egg mixture to medium bowl. Sprinkle half of flour mixture over egg mixture and, using spatula, gently fold until just combined. Add remaining flour mixture and chopped pistachios and gently fold until just combined.

3. Divide batter in half. Using your floured hands, form each half into 8 by 3-inch rectangle, using lines on parchment as guide. Spray each loaf lightly with oil spray. Using rubber spatula lightly coated with oil spray, smooth tops and sides of rectangles. Gently brush tops of loaves with egg white wash. Bake until loaves are golden and just beginning to crack on top, 25 to 30 minutes, rotating sheet halfway through baking.

**4.** Let loaves cool on baking sheet for 30 minutes. Transfer loaves to cutting board. Using serrated knife, slice each loaf on slight bias ½ inch thick. Lay slices, cut side down, about ¼ inch apart on wire rack set in second rimmed baking sheet. Bake until crisp and golden brown on both sides, about 35 minutes, flipping slices halfway through baking. Let cool completely before serving. (Biscotti can be stored in airtight container for up to 1 month.)

## Madeleines

**MAKES** 24 cookies

**WHY THIS RECIPE WORKS** Some know the madeleine as a symbol of involuntary memory, laid out by French writer Marcel Proust in *Swann's Way*, the first volume of his famous novel, *In Search of Lost Time*. The light, airy treats are unlike any other cookie; they're sponge cakes in cookie form, with a beautiful ridged exterior formed by the shell-shaped tins in which they are baked. But despite their appeal, madeleines aren't easy to find. Fortunately, this French treat is easy to prepare, so we felt confident that making them in our American kitchen would be a simple task. For madeleines with a light, tight crumb, we used downy-soft cake flour rather than all-purpose flour, which made our madeleines too tough. To cool the baked madeleines without ruining their ridged exteriors, we let them sit in the greased molds for 10 minutes after baking to set their exteriors before transferring them to a wire rack. This way, the rack didn't imprint lines on our cookies as they cooled. This recipe calls for a 12-cookie madeleine mold; even if you have two molds, be sure to bake them one at a time.

- 1 cup (4 ounces) cake flour
- ¼ teaspoon table salt
- 2 large eggs plus 1 large yolk
- ½ cup (3½ ounces) sugar
- 1 tablespoon vanilla extract
- 10 tablespoons unsalted butter, melted and cooled

**1.** Adjust oven rack to middle position and heat oven to 375 degrees. Grease 12-cookie madeleine mold. Whisk flour and salt together in small bowl.

**2.** Using stand mixer fitted with paddle, beat eggs and yolk on medium-high speed until frothy, 3 to 5 minutes. Add sugar and vanilla and beat until very thick, 3 to 5 minutes. Using rubber spatula, gently fold in flour mixture, followed by melted butter.

**3.** Spoon half of batter into prepared mold, filling mold to rim. Bake until madeleines are golden and spring back when pressed lightly, about 10 minutes, rotating mold halfway through baking.

**4.** Let cookies cool in mold for 10 minutes. Remove madeleines from mold and transfer to wire rack. Repeat with remaining batter. Let madeleines cool completely before serving.

## Raspberry Diagonals

**MAKES** 32 cookies

**WHY THIS RECIPE WORKS** Our jam diagonals are a slightly more sophisticated form of thumbprint cookies, but they're even easier and quicker to make. We started by mixing together a simple shortbread dough, but instead of portioning, rolling, and filling individual cookies, we formed four long logs, made a channel down the center of each, and filled the channels with jam. A little lemon juice added to the jam prevented it from drying out during baking and kept the flavor tangy, making it a great match for the buttery cookie. A quick postbake drizzle with a simple icing made these cookies fancy enough to grace a holiday cookie platter, and their nearly one-week shelf life means they can be baked well in advance—a boon for the busy holiday baker. It's best to measure the flour and sugar by weight. You can swap an overturned rimmed baking sheet for a rimless baking sheet and a small spoon for a pastry bag.

- 16 tablespoons unsalted butter, softened
- ½ cup (3½ ounces) granulated sugar
- 2 teaspoons vanilla extract
- ½ teaspoon table salt
- 2½ cups (12½ ounces) all-purpose flour
- ¾ cup seedless raspberry jam
- 1 teaspoon lemon juice
- ¾ cup (3 ounces) confectioners' sugar
- 1 tablespoon hot water

**1.** Adjust oven rack to middle position and heat oven to 350 degrees. Line rimless baking sheet with parchment paper.

**2.** Using stand mixer fitted with paddle, beat butter, sugar, vanilla, and salt on medium-high speed until light and fluffy, 3 to 5 minutes. Stop mixer. Add flour and mix on low speed until mixture comes together in crumbly dough, about 2 minutes, scraping down bowl halfway through mixing. Transfer to work surface and knead gently until dough forms smooth ball.

**3.** Divide dough into 4 equal pieces. Gently roll and pinch each piece into 14-inch log (if dough cracks, pinch it back together). Arrange logs lengthwise on prepared sheet. Press your index finger along length of 1 log to create trough that is ¾ inch wide and ¼ inch to ⅓ inch deep, using fingers of your other hand to mold sides. Repeat with remaining logs.

**4.** Whisk jam and lemon juice in bowl until smooth. Transfer mixture to piping bag fitted with ¼-inch round tip and pipe evenly among troughs. Bake until logs are lightly browned and firm to touch, about 30 minutes, rotating sheet halfway through baking. Cool on sheet until just warm to touch.

**5.** Gently slide logs into center of sheet until touching. Whisk confectioners' sugar and water in small bowl until smooth. (If mixture is too thick to drizzle, whisk in more water, ½ teaspoon at a time.) Using spoon, drizzle icing over cookies. Let sit until icing is set, 25 to 30 minutes.

**6.** Run thin spatula under 1 log to release from parchment. Carefully transfer log to cutting board. Using sharp chef's knife at 45-degree angle, trim ½ inch from each end of log and discard trim. Slice remaining length on diagonal into 8 pieces. Repeat with remaining logs. Serve. (Store cookies at room temperature for up to 6 days.)

### Apricot-Cardamom Diagonals

Substitute ½ teaspoon ground cardamom for vanilla and apricot preserves for raspberry jam.

### Blackberry-Cinnamon Diagonals

Substitute ½ teaspoon ground cinnamon for vanilla and seedless blackberry jam for raspberry jam.

## Ma'amoul

**MAKES** 30 cookies **SEASON 26**

**WHY THIS RECIPE WORKS** Ma'amoul are cookies served for Easter, Purim, and Eid al-Fitr in Levantine countries. To make them, a buttery semolina dough is scented with rose and orange blossom waters and mahlab (the ground cherry kernels used widely in Middle Eastern baking) and stuffed with a spiced date or nut filling. To give the dough some structure, we augmented the semolina flour with all-purpose flour. For the filling, we whizzed Medjool dates in the food processor along with butter, honey, mahlab, cinnamon, and anise. In a break from tradition, we also incorporated chopped pistachios for an additional layer of flavor and texture. To shape the cookies, we rolled portions of dough into disks, wrapped them around balls of filling, and pressed them into a qalab—a mold that imprints a fanciful design on the dough. This recipe requires resting the dough for 4 hours. Mahlab (or mahleb), ground cherry seed kernels, can be found at Middle Eastern grocery stores or online. If it's unavailable, omit it or substitute an additional ¼ teaspoon of cinnamon in both the filling and the dough. If you don't have a qalab (ma'amoul mold), a bowl with about ⅛-cup capacity lined with plastic wrap can be used to shape the cookies. Store ma'amoul for up to two weeks at room temperature or freeze them for up to one month.

**DOUGH**

- 2 cups plus 3 tablespoons (12½ ounces) semolina flour
- 6 tablespoons (1¾ ounces) all-purpose flour
- ¼ teaspoon ground mahlab
- 12 tablespoons unsalted butter, cut into ½-inch pieces and softened
- ⅓ cup honey
- 3 tablespoons orange blossom water
- 3 tablespoons rose water
- 3 tablespoons whole milk
- ¼ teaspoon table salt
- ½ teaspoon instant or rapid-rise yeast

**FILLING**

- ¾ cup raw shelled pistachios
- ½ teaspoon ground anise seeds
- ½ teaspoon ground cinnamon
- ¼ teaspoon ground mahlab

- ¼ teaspoon table salt
- 7 ounces pitted Medjool dates (9 to 10 dates)
- 3 tablespoons unsalted butter, softened
- 1 tablespoon honey
- Confectioners' sugar for dusting

**1. FOR THE DOUGH:** Whisk semolina, all-purpose flour, and mahlab together in large bowl. Add butter, honey, orange blossom water, and rose water. Using your hands, gently fold semolina mixture over wet ingredients until rough dough forms. Continue folding dough over itself into center while turning bowl, rubbing butter into semolina mixture until cohesive dough forms. (Do not knead dough; it should feel like wet sand.) Cover bowl tightly and let dough stand at room temperature for 4 hours.

**2. FOR THE FILLING:** Pulse pistachios, anise, cinnamon, mahlab, and salt in food processor until pistachios are chopped into rough ¼-inch pieces, 5 to 7 pulses. Add dates, butter, and honey and process until mixture is smooth paste and pistachio pieces are ⅛ to 1⁄16 inch, about 20 seconds. Transfer to bowl, cover, and refrigerate until ready to use.

**3.** Microwave milk and salt for dough in bowl until just warm (about 110 degrees), 30 to 45 seconds. Sprinkle yeast over warm milk and stir to combine. Add milk mixture to dough and mix with hands until combined, about 30 seconds. Transfer dough to counter (don't wash bowl) and knead until smooth, about 2 minutes. Return dough to bowl, cover tightly, and let stand at room temperature for 30 minutes.

**4.** While dough rests, line 2 rimmed baking sheets with parchment paper. Divide filling into 30 equal portions, weighing about ½ ounce each, and roll into balls. Place balls on 1 half of 1 prepared sheet. Cover with damp dish towel.

**5.** Divide dough into 2 equal portions (dough will be slightly tacky, soft, and somewhat elastic). Roll each piece into 15-inch log and cut into 15 equal pieces. Roll each portion into ball and place on sheet with filling. Cover with damp dish towel.

**6.** Adjust oven rack to middle position and heat oven to 350 degrees. Place 1 dough ball in palm of your hand and gently press into 3-inch round of even thickness. Place 1 filling ball in center of dough. Bring sides of dough up around filling and pinch top to seal. Roll ball until smooth, place on second prepared baking sheet, and cover with damp dish towel. Repeat with remaining dough and filling.

**7.** Place 1 filled ball in ma'amoul mold and gently press until cookie fills crevices and top is flat. Turn mold over and tap edge on edge of counter so cookie releases onto palm of hand. (If cookie sticks, line mold with plastic wrap.) Return cookie, pattern side up, to baking sheet. Repeat, placing 15 cookies, evenly spaced, on each sheet.

**8.** Bake cookies, 1 sheet at a time, until bottoms are light golden, 15 to 20 minutes, rotating sheet halfway through baking. Transfer baking sheet to wire rack and let cool on sheet for 20 minutes. Dust liberally with confectioners' sugar before serving.

## Macarons with Raspberry Buttercream

**MAKES** 30 cookies **SEASON 26**

**WHY THIS RECIPE WORKS** Few confections have captured the world's attention quite like Parisian macarons. For our version, we started by sifting finely ground almond flour together with confectioners' sugar to eliminate lumps. Next we prepared a sturdy Italian meringue. Then we piped it into rounds and let the shells rest for 20 minutes. While the shells sat, a skin formed that prohibited steam from escaping during baking. Since even the slightest puff of air trapped under the parchment can impact the even rise of the cookie, we stuck the parchment to the sheet with vegetable oil spray. A kitchen scale that weighs in grams is essential for this recipe; you'll also need a large piping bag and ½-inch round tip. Be sure to use finely ground almond flour; Blue Diamond or Bob's Red Mill products work well. Do not use liquid food coloring as it will add too much water to the batter. Use 3 drops of gel for pastel shells and 7 drops for a more vibrant color. The finished cookies need to chill for at least 24 hours before serving.

**MACARON SHELLS**

- 150 grams blanched, finely ground almond flour
- 150 grams confectioners' sugar
- ⅛ teaspoon table salt
- 113 grams egg whites (measure from lightly beaten whites of 4 large eggs), divided
- ⅛ teaspoon cream of tartar
- 150 grams granulated sugar
- 60 grams water
- 3–7 drops gel food coloring

**RASPBERRY BUTTERCREAM**

- 10 tablespoons unsalted butter, softened
- 1¼ cups (5 ounces) confectioners' sugar
- Pinch table salt
- 1 tablespoon heavy cream
- ½ teaspoon vanilla extract
- ⅓ cup freeze-dried raspberries

**1. FOR THE MACARON SHELLS:** Using pencil and 1½-inch round biscuit cutter as guide, trace thirty 1½-inch circles on each of 2 pieces of parchment (5 evenly spaced rows of 6 circles on each piece of parchment). Spray 2 baking sheets with vegetable oil spray. Place templates pencil side down on sheets and smooth to adhere. Sift flour, confectioners' sugar, and salt through fine-mesh strainer into large bowl and set aside.

**2.** Measure 75 grams of egg whites into bowl of stand mixer fitted with whisk attachment (reserve remaining whites). Add cream of tartar. Start mixer on medium-high speed and whip until soft peaks form, 2 to 3 minutes. Turn mixer to lowest speed and let run while you make sugar syrup.

**3.** Using heatproof spatula, gently stir sugar and water together in small saucepan. Cook over medium-high heat, without stirring, until sugar dissolves. Continue to cook, checking temperature frequently, until sugar syrup reaches 245 degrees, 4 to 5 minutes.

**4.** When syrup reaches 245 degrees, quickly remove pan from heat; adjust mixer speed to medium; and carefully pour syrup into whites in thin, steady stream (avoid hitting whisk; aim for side of bowl just above whites). Add food coloring; increase speed to medium-high; and continue to whip until meringue is just shy of stiff peaks (very tip of peak should bend to 2 or 3 o'clock), 3 to 5 minutes.

**5.** Transfer meringue and reserved 38 grams egg whites to almond flour mixture. Using large rubber spatula, stir to incorporate. Turning bowl, stir and smear batter against sides of bowl, scraping sides and bottom frequently until batter loosens and flows from spatula in slow, wide stream for 8 to 10 seconds and reincorporates into batter within about 30 seconds. (To test consistency, place spoonful of batter on prepared sheet and let sit for 1 minute. If batter spreads into flat, smooth-topped disk, continue with recipe; if it remains domed, continue stirring, taking care not to overmix, and retest.)

**6.** Transfer batter to pastry bag fitted with ½-inch round tip. Hold bag perpendicular to sheet and about ½ inch above sheet. Using template as guide, pipe batter into 1½-inch-wide disks, keeping bag still as batter flows from tip. To finish each disk, use quick flick of your wrist to cut off batter stream. Rap sheets firmly on counter 6 times to release air bubbles. Let rest until shells form skin that can be touched gently with your finger without marring surface, about 20 minutes. While shells dry, adjust oven rack to lower-middle position and heat oven to 325 degrees.

**7.** Bake 1 sheet of shells for 13 minutes. To test for doneness, place your finger gently on top of 1 shell and move it side to side; if center feels loose and jiggly, continue to bake, checking every minute, until firm. Transfer sheet to wire rack and bake remaining shells. Let shells cool completely on sheets. While shells cool, make filling.

**8. FOR THE RASPBERRY BUTTERCREAM:** Using stand mixer fitted with paddle attachment, beat butter at medium-high speed until smooth, about 20 seconds. Add sugar and salt; beat at medium-low speed until most of sugar is moistened, about 45 seconds. Scrape down sides of bowl and beat at medium speed until mixture is fully combined, about 15 seconds; scrape down bowl. Add heavy cream and vanilla and beat at medium

speed until incorporated, about 10 seconds. Increase speed to medium-high and beat until light and fluffy, about 4 minutes, scraping down bowl once or twice during mixing.

**9.** Meanwhile, grind raspberries in spice grinder until reduced to fine powder. Sift powder through fine-mesh strainer set over small bowl. Add 1 tablespoon powder to buttercream and beat on medium speed until fully incorporated, about 30 seconds. Add more raspberry powder to taste, as desired. Transfer to pastry bag fitted with ½-inch round or star tip. (Buttercream can be refrigerated for up to 2 days; let stand at room temperature for 30 minutes before using.)

**10. TO ASSEMBLE:** Gently peel shells from parchment. (If shells don't release cleanly, place sheets in freezer for 10 minutes.) Holding 1 upturned shell in your hand, pipe about 2 teaspoons filling on top, leaving ⅛-inch border. Place second shell on top of filling, pressing gently until filling spreads to edges. Repeat with remaining shells and filling. Arrange cookies on clean parchment-lined sheet and wrap well. Refrigerate for at least 24 hours or up to 1 week or freeze for up to 2 months. Bring to room temperature before serving.

## Baci di Dama (Italian Hazelnut Cookies)

**MAKES** 32 sandwich cookies

**WHY THIS RECIPE WORKS** These tiny Italian hazelnut chocolate sandwich cookies are typically made from a very rich, fragile dough that easily softens and crumbles when you roll it. Reducing the amount of butter and nuts in the dough made it firmer but still plenty rich and tender. We left bits of skin on the nuts to help firm up the dough and add complex flavor and attractive color. Instead of scooping and weighing dozens of individual pieces of dough, we found that it was much faster and easier to press the dough into a parchment paper–lined square baking pan, briefly freeze it to firm it up, and cut a "portion grid" into the resulting dough block. Toast the hazelnuts on a rimmed baking sheet in a 325-degree oven until fragrant, 13 to 15 minutes, shaking the sheet halfway through toasting. To skin them, gather the warm hazelnuts in a dish towel and rub to remove some of the skins. A square-cornered metal baking pan works best for shaping the dough. We prefer Ghirardelli 60% Cacao Bittersweet Chocolate Premium Baking Bar here. To assemble, gently press the second cookie on top to spread the filling just to the edges.

- ¾ cup hazelnuts, toasted and partially skinned
- ⅔ cup (3⅓ ounces) all-purpose flour
- ⅓ cup (2⅓ ounces) sugar
- ⅛ teaspoon table salt
- 6 tablespoons unsalted butter, cut into ½-inch pieces and chilled
- 2 ounces bittersweet chocolate, chopped

**1.** Adjust oven rack to middle position and heat oven to 325 degrees. Line 2 rimmed baking sheets with parchment paper. Line bottom of 8-inch square baking pan with parchment. Process hazelnuts, flour, sugar, and salt in food processor until hazelnuts are very finely ground, 20 to 25 seconds. Add butter and pulse until dough just comes together, 20 to 25 pulses.

**2.** Transfer dough to counter, knead briefly to form smooth ball, place in prepared pan, and press into even layer that covers bottom of pan. Freeze for 10 minutes. Run knife or bench scraper between dough and edge of pan to loosen. Turn out dough onto counter and discard parchment. Cut dough into 64 squares (8 rows by 8 rows). Roll dough squares into balls and evenly space 32 dough balls on each prepared sheet. Bake, 1 sheet at a time, until cookies look dry and are fragrant (cookies will settle but not spread), about 20 minutes, rotating sheet halfway through baking. Transfer sheet to wire rack and let cookies cool completely.

**3.** Microwave chocolate in small bowl at 50 percent power, stirring every 20 seconds, until melted, 1 to 2 minutes. Let chocolate cool at room temperature until it is slightly thickened and registers 80 degrees, about 10 minutes. Invert half of cookies on each sheet. Using ¼-teaspoon measure, spoon chocolate onto flat surfaces of all inverted cookies. Top with remaining cookies, pressing lightly to adhere. Let chocolate set for at least 15 minutes before serving. (Cookies can be stored in airtight container at room temperature for up to 10 days.)

## Alfajores de Maicena (Buttery Cornstarch Cookies Filled with Dulce de Leche)

**MAKES** 24 cookies

**WHY THIS RECIPE WORKS** Beloved across Latin America, alfajores de maicena are buttery sandwich cookies that are often filled with the region's caramelized milk jam, dulce de leche. We used slightly more cornstarch than flour by volume in our dough for cookies with enough structure to hold together when filled. Plenty of butter contributed tenderness and rich flavor. We opted for yolks instead of whole eggs, since the proteins in the whites would bind the dough and make the cookies less delicate. For the filling, we took a common shortcut and used Nestlé La Lechera Dulce de Leche, doctoring it with a little vanilla and salt. It's essential to buy this brand of canned dulce de leche, or the filling won't have the right consistency. You can also make your own filling by following the multicooker instructions in our recipe for Dulce de Leche (recipe follows). The brandy complements the flavors of the vanilla and lemon zest, but you can omit it, if preferred. Alfajores are fragile, so we've designed this recipe to make a few extra cookies in case some break. Refrigerate any leftover dulce de leche in an airtight container for up to one month.

**FILLING**

- 2 (13.4-ounce) cans Nestlé La Lechera Dulce de Leche
- 1 teaspoon vanilla extract
- ¼ teaspoon table salt

**COOKIES**

- 1½ cups (6 ounces) cornstarch
- 1⅓ cups (6⅔ ounces) all-purpose flour
- 1 teaspoon baking powder
- ¼ teaspoon table salt
- 16 tablespoons unsalted butter, softened
- ½ cup (3½ ounces) sugar
- 3 large egg yolks
- 1 tablespoon brandy (optional)
- 1 teaspoon grated lemon zest
- 1 teaspoon vanilla extract
- 1 cup (3 ounces) unsweetened shredded coconut

**1. FOR THE FILLING:** Transfer dulce de leche to medium bowl. Stir in vanilla and salt until thoroughly incorporated. Cover and refrigerate until mixture is completely chilled, at least 2 hours.

**2. FOR THE COOKIES:** While filling chills, whisk cornstarch, flour, baking powder, and salt together in medium bowl. Using stand mixer fitted with paddle, beat butter and sugar on medium-high speed until pale and fluffy, 2 to 3 minutes. Add egg yolks; brandy, if using; lemon zest; and vanilla and beat until combined. Add cornstarch mixture; reduce speed to low; and mix until dough is smooth, scraping down bowl as needed.

**3.** Divide dough in half. Place 1 piece of dough in center of large sheet of parchment paper and press with your hand to ½-inch thickness. Place second large sheet of parchment over dough and roll dough to ¼-inch thickness. Using your flat hand on parchment, smooth out wrinkles on both sides. Transfer dough with parchment to rimmed baking sheet. Repeat pressing, rolling, and smoothing second piece of dough, then stack on top of first piece on sheet. Freeze until dough is firm, about 30 minutes.

**4.** Adjust oven racks to upper-middle and lower-middle positions and heat oven to 350 degrees. Transfer 1 piece of dough to counter. Peel off top layer of parchment and replace loosely. Flip dough and parchment. Peel away second piece of parchment and place on rimmed baking sheet. Using 2-inch round cutter, cut dough into rounds. Transfer rounds to prepared sheet, spaced about ½ inch apart. Repeat with remaining dough and second rimmed baking sheet. Reroll, chill, and cut scraps until you have 26 rounds on each sheet.

**5.** Bake until tops are set but still pale and bottoms are light golden, 10 to 12 minutes, switching and rotating sheets halfway through baking. Let cookies cool on sheets for 5 minutes, then carefully transfer to wire rack and let cool completely.

**6.** To assemble, place half of cookies upside down on counter. Place about 2 teaspoons filling on each upside-down cookie. Hold 1 topped cookie on fingers of 1 hand. Place second, untopped cookie on top of filling, right side up, and press gently with fingers of your other hand until filling spreads to edges. Repeat with remaining cookies.

**7.** Place coconut in small bowl. Working with 1 cookie at a time, roll sides of cookies in coconut, pressing gently to help coconut adhere to exposed filling. Serve immediately or refrigerate in airtight container for up to 5 days. Allow refrigerated cookies to sit out at room temperature for 10 minutes before serving.

## Dulce de Leche

**MAKES** 3⅓ cups

This recipe can be made in the oven or in an electric pressure cooker to produce slightly different consistencies. Dulce de leche cooked in the oven will be thick but pourable when warm—perfect for drizzling over pancakes, waffles, or ice cream or as a milky sweetener for coffee. Made in a multicooker, it will be thick enough to fill cookies (such as alfajores) or cakes or to spread on toast; note that you'll need a rack that fits inside your multicooker model.

- 2 (14-ounce) cans sweetened condensed milk
- 1 teaspoon vanilla extract
- ¼ teaspoon table salt

**1A. FOR THE OVEN:** Adjust oven rack to middle position and heat oven to 350 degrees. Pour condensed milk into 13 by 9-inch baking pan. Cover pan tightly with aluminum foil. Pour 1 inch boiling water into large roasting pan and carefully set baking pan inside (water should come about halfway up sides of baking pan). Bake, topping up roasting pan with boiling water every 45 minutes, until condensed milk is brown and has jiggly, flan-like consistency, 2¼ to 2½ hours.

**1B. FOR THE MULTICOOKER:** Set rack into 6- or 8-quart multicooker and add 8 cups water. If using a 6-quart multicooker use only 6 cups water (or bowl will float). Pour condensed milk into 8-inch-diameter stainless-steel bowl. Cover tightly with foil; set on rack. Lock lid into place and close pressure-release valve. Select high pressure-cook function and cook for 1 hour. Turn off multicooker and quick-release pressure. Carefully remove lid, allowing steam to escape away from you.

**2.** Carefully transfer cooked condensed milk (it will look broken and grainy) to fine-mesh strainer set over bowl. Stir and press solids with back of small ladle or spoon. Stir in vanilla and salt. Transfer to airtight container. (Dulce de leche can be refrigerated for up to 2 weeks.)

## Crescent-Shaped Rugelach with Raisin-Walnut Filling

**MAKES** 32 cookies

**WHY THIS RECIPE WORKS** Part cookie, part pastry, rugelach are a traditional Jewish party snack. Their tight curls can contain a variety of bounteous sweet fillings, from nuts and jam to dried fruit and even chocolate. The dough is made with tangy cream cheese and bakes up tender and flaky; however, many rugelach doughs are sticky and hard to work with, so solving this problem was our first order of business. We started by adding more flour to the dough than traditional recipes call for, which helped make it more workable. A couple tablespoons of sour cream in addition to the cream cheese gave the cookies more tang and tenderized them further. For the filling, we settled on a generous combination of apricot preserves, raisins, and walnuts. To abate leaking, we finely chopped the nuts; smaller pieces were less likely to tear the dough. We also processed the preserves in a food processor to eliminate any large chunks.

**DOUGH**

- 2¼ cups (11¼ ounces) all-purpose flour
- 1½ tablespoons sugar
- ¼ teaspoon table salt
- 16 tablespoons unsalted butter, chilled and cut into ¼-inch pieces
- 8 ounces cream cheese, chilled and cut into ½-inch chunks
- 2 tablespoons sour cream

**FRUIT FILLING**

- 1 cup (7 ounces) sugar
- 1 tablespoon ground cinnamon
- ⅔ cup apricot preserves, processed briefly in food processor until smooth
- 1 cup raisins, preferably golden
- 2 cups walnuts, chopped fine

**GLAZE**

- 2 large egg yolks
- 2 tablespoons milk

**1. FOR THE DOUGH:** Pulse flour, sugar, and salt in food processor until combined, about 3 pulses. Add butter, cream cheese, and sour cream; pulse until dough comes together in small, uneven pebbles the size of cottage cheese curds, about 16 pulses. Transfer dough to counter, press into 9 by 6-inch log, and divide log into 4 equal pieces. Form each piece into 4½ by ¾-inch disk. Place each disk between 2 sheets plastic wrap and roll into 8½-inch circle. Stack dough circles, between pieces of parchment paper, on plate; freeze for 30 minutes.

**2. FOR THE FRUIT FILLING:** Meanwhile, combine sugar and cinnamon in small bowl; set aside. Line 2 rimmed baking sheets with parchment. Working with 1 dough circle at a time, remove dough from freezer and spread with 2½ tablespoons preserves. Sprinkle 2 tablespoons cinnamon sugar, ¼ cup raisins, and ½ cup walnuts over preserves and pat down gently with your fingers. Cut circle into 8 wedges. Roll each wedge into crescent shape; space crescents 2 inches apart on prepared sheets. Repeat with remaining dough rounds. Freeze crescents on sheets for 15 minutes. (To make ahead, cover baking sheet loosely with plastic and freeze crescents until firm, about 1¼ hours. Once frozen, transfer crescents to airtight container or zipper-lock bag and freeze for up to 6 weeks. To bake frozen rugelach, place on parchment-lined baking sheets and glaze and bake immediately, increasing baking time by 6 to 7 minutes.)

**3. FOR THE GLAZE:** Adjust oven racks to upper-middle and lower-middle positions and heat oven to 375 degrees. Whisk egg yolks and milk in bowl. Brush crescents with glaze. Bake until rugelach are pale golden and slightly puffy, 21 to 23 minutes, switching and rotating sheets halfway through baking. Sprinkle each cookie with scant teaspoon cinnamon sugar. Transfer rugelach to wire rack with metal spatula and let cool completely before serving. (Rugelach can be stored at room temperature for up to 4 days.)

## Pecan or Walnut Crescent Cookies

**MAKES** about 48 small cookies

**WHY THIS RECIPE WORKS** When nut crescent cookies are well made, they can be delicious: buttery, nutty, slightly crisp, slightly crumbly, with a melt-in-your mouth quality. Too often, however, they turn out bland and dry. We wanted to develop a recipe that would put them back in their proper place. The ratio of 1 cup butter to 2 cups flour in almost all of the recipes we looked at is what worked for us. We tried three kinds of sugar in the batter: granulated, confectioners', and superfine. The last resulted in just what we wanted: cookies that melted in our mouths. If you cannot find superfine sugar, you can obtain a close approximation by processing regular granulated sugar in a food processor for about 30 seconds.

- 2 cups (8 ounces) whole pecans or walnuts, chopped fine
- 2 cups (10 ounces) unbleached all-purpose flour
- ½ teaspoon table salt
- 16 tablespoons (2 sticks) unsalted butter, softened
- ⅓ cup (2½ ounces) superfine sugar
- 1½ teaspoons vanilla extract
- 1½ cups (6 ounces) confectioners' sugar

**1.** Adjust the oven racks to the upper-middle and lower-middle positions and heat the oven to 325 degrees. Line 2 large baking sheets with parchment paper.

**2.** Whisk 1 cup of the chopped nuts, the flour, and salt together in a medium bowl; set aside. Process the remaining 1 cup chopped nuts in a food processor until they are the texture of coarse cornmeal, 10 to 15 seconds (do not over process). Stir the nuts into the flour mixture and set aside.

**3.** In a stand mixer fitted with the paddle attachment, beat the butter and superfine sugar at medium-low speed until light and fluffy, about 2 minutes; add the vanilla, scraping down the bowl and beater with a rubber spatula. Add the flour mixture and beat on low speed until the dough just begins to come together but still looks scrappy, about 15 seconds. Scrape down the bowl and beater again with a rubber spatula; continue beating at low speed until the dough is cohesive, 6 to 9 seconds longer. Do not over beat.

**4.** Divide the dough into 48 portions, each about 1 tablespoon, and roll them between your hands into 1¼-inch balls. Roll each ball between your palms into a rope that measures 3 inches long. Place the ropes on the prepared baking sheets and turn up the ends to form a crescent shape. Bake until the tops are pale golden and the bottoms are just beginning to brown, 17 to 19 minutes, switching and rotating the baking sheets halfway through the baking time.

**5.** Cool the cookies on the baking sheets for 2 minutes; using a wide metal spatula, transfer the cookies to a wire rack and cool to room temperature, about 30 minutes. Place the confectioners' sugar in a shallow baking dish or pie plate. Working with three or four cookies at a time, roll the cookies in the sugar to coat them thoroughly; gently shake off the excess. (The cookies can be stored in an airtight container for up to 5 days.) Before serving, roll the cookies in the confectioners' sugar again and tap off the excess.

### Almond or Hazelnut Crescent Cookies

Almonds can be used raw for cookies that are light in both color and flavor or toasted to enhance the almond flavor and darken the crescents. Follow the recipe for Pecan or Walnut Crescent Cookies, substituting 1¾ cups (7¾ ounces) whole blanched almonds (toasted, if desired) or 2 cups (8 ounces) toasted, skinned hazelnuts for the pecans or walnuts. If using almonds, add ½ teaspoon almond extract along with the vanilla extract.

## Triple-Coconut Macaroons

**MAKES** about 48 cookies

**WHY THIS RECIPE WORKS** We set out to create a great coconut macaroon, with a pleasing texture and real, honest coconut flavor. We knew that the choice of coconut and other flavorings would make a big difference in both taste and texture. After rounds of testing, we determined that unsweetened shredded coconut resulted in a less sticky, more appealing texture. But sweetened shredded coconut packed more flavor than the unsweetened coconut, so we decided to use both. To add one more layer of coconut flavor, we tried cream of coconut and hit the jackpot. As for the structure of our cookie, a few egg whites and some corn syrup ensured that the macaroons held together well and were moist and chewy. If you are unable to find unsweetened, dessicated coconut, use all sweetened flaked or shredded coconut, but reduce the amount of cream of coconut to ½ cup, omit the corn syrup, and toss 2 tablespoons cake flour with the coconut before adding the liquid ingredients.

- 1 cup cream of coconut
- 2 tablespoons light corn syrup
- 4 large egg whites
- 2 teaspoons vanilla extract
- ½ teaspoon table salt
- 3 cups unsweetened, shredded, desiccated (dried) coconut
- 3 cups sweetened flaked or shredded coconut

**1.** Adjust the oven racks to the upper-middle and lower-middle positions and heat the oven to 375 degrees. Line 2 baking sheets with parchment paper and lightly spray the parchment with vegetable oil spray.

**2.** Whisk the cream of coconut, corn syrup, egg whites, vanilla, and salt together in a small bowl; set aside. Combine the unsweetened and sweetened coconuts in a large bowl; toss together, breaking up clumps with your fingertips. Pour the liquid ingredients over the coconut and mix with a rubber spatula until evenly moistened. Chill for 15 minutes.

**3.** Drop heaping tablespoons of batter onto the prepared baking sheets, spacing them about 1 inch apart. Using moistened fingertips, form the cookies into loose haystacks. Bake until light golden brown, about 15 minutes, switching and rotating the sheets halfway through the baking time.

**4.** Cool the cookies on the baking sheets until slightly set, about 2 minutes; using a wide metal spatula, transfer the cookies to a wire rack and cool to room temperature.

### Chocolate-Dipped Triple-Coconut Macaroons

Using the two-stage melting process for the chocolate helps ensure that it will be at the proper consistency for dipping the cookies. To melt the 8 ounces of chocolate in a microwave, heat it at 50 percent power for 2 minutes; stir the chocolate and continue heating until melted, stirring once every additional minute. Follow the recipe for Triple-Coconut Macaroons. Cool the baked macaroons to room temperature; line two large baking sheets with parchment paper. Chop 10 ounces semisweet chocolate; melt 8 ounces of the chocolate in a small heatproof bowl set over a saucepan of barely simmering water, stirring occasionally, until smooth. Off the heat, stir in the remaining 2 ounces of chocolate until smooth. Holding a macaroon by its pointed top, dip the bottom ½ inch up the sides in the chocolate, scrape off the excess, and place the macaroon on the prepared baking sheet. Repeat with the remaining macaroons. Refrigerate until the chocolate sets, about 15 minutes.

## Classic Meringue Cookies

**MAKES** about 48 small cookies

**WHY THIS RECIPE WORKS** A classic meringue cookie may have only two ingredients—egg whites and sugar—but it requires precise timing. A great meringue cookie should emerge from the oven glossy with a shatteringly crisp texture that dissolves instantly in your mouth. We chose a basic French meringue over a fussier Italian meringue. The French version, in which egg whites are whipped with sugar, is the simpler of the two. The key to glossy, evenly textured meringue was adding the sugar when the whites have been whipped enough to gain some volume, but still have enough free water left in them for the sugar to dissolve completely. It was also important to form the cookies in a uniform shape, so we piped them from either a pastry bag or a zipper-lock bag with a corner cut off. Meringues may be soft after being removed from the oven but will stiffen as they cool. To minimize stickiness on humid or rainy days, allow the meringues to cool in a turned-off oven for an additional hour (for a total of 2 hours) without opening the door, then transfer them immediately to airtight containers and seal. Cooled cookies can be kept in an airtight container for up to 2 weeks.

- ¾ cup (5¼ ounces) sugar
- 2 teaspoons cornstarch
- 4 large egg whites
- ¾ teaspoon vanilla extract
- ⅛ teaspoon table salt

**1.** Adjust the oven racks to the upper-middle and lower-middle positions and heat the oven to 225 degrees. Line 2 large baking sheets with parchment paper. Combine the sugar and cornstarch in a small bowl.

**2.** In a stand mixer fitted with the whisk attachment, beat the egg whites, vanilla, and salt together at high speed until very soft peaks start to form (the peaks should slowly lose their shape when the whip is removed), 30 to 45 seconds. Decrease the speed to medium and slowly add the sugar mixture in a steady stream down the side of the mixer bowl (the process should take about 30 seconds). Stop the mixer and scrape down the sides and bottom of the bowl with a rubber spatula. Increase the speed to high and beat until glossy and stiff peaks have formed, 30 to 45 seconds.

**3.** Working quickly, place the meringue in a pastry bag fitted with a ½-inch plain tip or a large zipper-lock bag with ½ inch of the corner cut off. Pipe meringues into 1¼-inch-wide mounds about 1 inch high on the baking sheets, six rows of four meringues on each sheet. Bake for 1 hour, switching and rotating the baking sheets halfway through the baking time. Turn off the oven and allow the meringues to cool in the oven for at least 1 hour. Remove the meringues from the oven and let cool to room temperature before serving, about 10 minutes.

## Meringue Christmas Trees

**MAKES** about 50 cookies

**WHY THIS RECIPE WORKS** This standout holiday cookie pairs crisp, sweet meringue with milk chocolate kisses and colorful, festive decorations for a showstopping treat. We whipped egg whites to stiff peaks and then incorporated green food coloring before piping the glossy mixture onto baking sheets. To trim the tree with colorful "lights" and "ornaments," we chose multicolor nonpareils and yellow sugar stars. To finish, we cut a small hole in the bottom of each tree and snugly affixed a Hershey's Kiss to serve as the tree trunk. You'll need a 12-ounce bag of Hershey's Kisses for this recipe (you'll have a few left over).

- ¾ cup (5¼ ounces) granulated sugar
- 2 teaspoons cornstarch
- 4 large egg whites
- ¾ teaspoon vanilla extract
- 8–10 drops green food coloring
- ⅛ teaspoon table salt
- Sugar stars
- Multicolored nonpareils
- 62 Hershey's Kisses, unwrapped
- Confectioners' sugar

**1.** Adjust oven racks to upper-middle and lower-middle positions and heat oven to 225 degrees. Line 2 baking sheets with parchment paper. Combine granulated sugar and cornstarch in small bowl. Using stand mixer fitted with whisk attachment, whip egg whites, vanilla, food coloring, and salt on medium-low speed until foamy, about 1 minute. Increase speed to medium-high and whip whites to soft, billowy mounds, about 1 minute. Gradually add sugar mixture and whip until glossy, stiff peaks form, 2 to 3 minutes.

**2.** Working quickly, fill pastry bag fitted with ¼- to ⅝-inch star tip with meringue. Pipe 1-inch-wide stars, spaced 1 inch apart, on prepared sheets. Top each star with another smaller star; then pipe even smaller star on top (trees should be 1½ inches tall). Place sugar star on top of each tree and sprinkle nonpareils around sides.

**3.** Bake meringues for 1 hour, switching and rotating sheets halfway through baking. Turn off oven and let meringues cool in oven for at least 1 hour. Transfer sheets to wire rack and let meringues cool completely.

**4.** Microwave 12 candies at 50 percent power until melted, 1 to 2 minutes. Using paring knife, gently cut small hole in bottom of each tree. Press tips of remaining candies into melted chocolate and then snugly into each hole. Dust trees with confectioners' sugar before serving.

## Profiteroles

**SERVES** 6 to 8 (Makes 24 puffs)

**WHY THIS RECIPE WORKS** Profiteroles are among the world's great desserts: crisp, tender, airy pastry encasing cold, creamy ice cream, drizzled all over with a luxurious chocolate sauce. We used both water and milk in the dough so that they crisped up well and colored nicely. For lighter, puffier puffs, we incorporated the eggs all at once using the high speed of a food processor to mix plenty of air into the dough. An initial blast of heat from a hot oven jump-started browning; we then lowered the heat to let the interiors finish cooking. We slit the puffs immediately after removing them from the oven to release the steam trapped inside and then returned them to the turned-off, propped-open oven to dry out in the gentle residual heat. Prescooping the ice cream makes serving quick and neat.

**CREAM PUFFS**

- 2 large eggs plus 1 large white
- 5 tablespoons unsalted butter, cut into 10 pieces
- 6 tablespoons water
- 2 tablespoons whole milk
- 1½ teaspoons sugar
- ¼ teaspoon table salt
- ½ cup (2½ ounces) all-purpose flour, sifted

**CHOCOLATE SAUCE**

- ¾ cup heavy cream
- 3 tablespoons light corn syrup
- 3 tablespoons unsalted butter, cut into 3 pieces
- Pinch table salt
- 6 ounces bittersweet chocolate, chopped fine
- 1 quart vanilla or coffee ice cream

**1. FOR THE CREAM PUFFS:** Adjust oven rack to middle position and heat oven to 425 degrees. Spray rimmed baking sheet with vegetable oil spray and line with parchment paper; set aside. Beat eggs and white in measuring cup. (You should have about ½ cup; discard excess.)

**2.** Bring butter, water, milk, sugar, and salt to boil in small saucepan over medium heat. When mixture reaches full boil (butter should be fully melted), immediately remove saucepan from heat and stir in flour with heat-resistant spatula until combined and mixture clears sides of pan. Return saucepan to low heat and cook, stirring constantly, using smearing motion, for 3 minutes, until mixture is slightly shiny with wet-sand appearance and tiny beads of fat appear on bottom of saucepan (temperature should register 175 to 180 degrees on instant-read thermometer).

**3.** Immediately transfer mixture to food processor and process with feed tube open for 10 seconds to cool slightly. With machine running, gradually add eggs in steady stream. When all eggs have been added, scrape down sides of bowl, then process for 30 seconds until smooth, sticky paste forms. (If not using immediately, transfer paste to bowl, press sheet of plastic wrap sprayed with oil spray directly on surface, and store at room temperature for up to 2 hours.)

**4A. TO PORTION USING PASTRY BAG:** Fold down top 3 or 4 inches of 14- or 16-inch pastry bag fitted with ½-inch plain tip to form a cuff. Hold bag open with one hand in cuff and fill bag with paste. Unfold cuff, lay bag on work surface, and, using hands or bench scraper, push paste into lower portion of pastry bag. Twist top of bag and pipe paste into 1½-inch mounds on prepared baking sheet, spacing them 1 to 1¼ inches apart (you should be able to fit all 24 mounds on baking sheet).

**4B. TO PORTION USING SPOONS:** Scoop 1 level tablespoon of dough. Using second small spoon, scrape dough onto prepared sheet into 1½-inch mound. Repeat, spacing mounds 1 to 1¼ inches apart (you should be able to fit all 24 mounds on baking sheet).

**5.** Use back of teaspoon dipped in bowl of cold water to smooth shape and surface of piped mounds. Bake for 15 minutes (do not open oven door), then reduce oven temperature to 375 degrees and continue to bake until puffs are golden brown and fairly firm (puffs should not be soft and squishy), 8 to 10 minutes longer. Remove baking sheet from oven. With paring knife, cut ¾-inch slit into side of each puff to release steam; return puffs to oven, turn off oven, and prop oven door open with handle of wooden spoon. Dry puffs in turned-off oven until centers are just moist (not wet) and puffs are crisp, about 45 minutes. Transfer puffs to wire rack to cool. (Cooled puffs can be stored in airtight container at room temperature for up to 24 hours or frozen in zipper-lock bag for up to 1 month. Before serving, crisp room temperature puffs in 300-degree oven for 5 to 8 minutes, or 8 to 10 minutes for frozen puffs.

**6. FOR THE CHOCOLATE SAUCE:** Bring cream, corn syrup, butter, and salt to boil in small saucepan over medium-high heat. Off heat, add chocolate while gently swirling saucepan. Cover pan and let stand until chocolate is melted, about 5 minutes. Uncover and whisk gently until combined. (Sauce can be cooled to room temperature, placed in airtight container, and refrigerated for up to 3 weeks. To reheat, transfer sauce to heatproof bowl set over saucepan of simmering water. Alternatively, microwave at 50 percent power, stirring once or twice, for 1 to 3 minutes.)

**7. TO ASSEMBLE:** Line baking sheet with parchment paper; freeze until cold, about 20 minutes. Using 2-inch ice cream scoop (about same diameter as puffs), scoop ice cream onto cold sheet and freeze until firm, then cover with plastic wrap; keep frozen until ready to serve. (Ice cream can be scooped and frozen for up to 1 week.)

**8.** When ready to serve, use paring knife to split open puffs about ⅜ inch from bottom; set 3 or 4 bottoms on each dessert plate. Place scoop of ice cream on each bottom and gently press tops into ice cream. Pour sauce over profiteroles and serve immediately.

### PREPARING PROFITEROLES

**1A. TO PIPE PUFFS:** Twist top of pastry bag and pipe paste into 1½-inch mounds on prepared baking sheet.

**1B. TO SPOON PUFFS:** Scoop 1 level tablespoon of dough and, using second spoon, scrape dough onto sheet into 1½-inch mounds.

**2.** Use back of teaspoon dipped in water to smooth pastry mounds.

**3.** Immediately after baking, cut slit into side of each puff to release steam. Return puffs to turned-off oven to dry.

## Choux au Craquelin

**MAKES 24 CHOUX**

**WHY THIS RECIPE WORKS** For our choux au craquelin recipe—airy, crispy shells encasing smooth, lush pastry cream—we began by making our pastry cream, which we reinforced with a little extra flour so that it could be lightened with whipped cream later on. While it chilled and set, we mixed the craquelin dough—a combination of flour, butter, and sugar—and rolled it into a thin sheet from which we cut 24 disks before freezing the dough. Before sliding the piped mounds of batter into the oven, we topped them with slim disks of the craquelin dough, which transformed into crackly shells as the puffs baked. Slitting the baked puffs released steam before we returned them to the oven (now turned off) for 45 minutes to ensure crispness. You'll need a 2-inch round cutter, a pastry bag, and two pastry tips—one with a ¼-inch round opening and one with a ½-inch round opening—for this recipe. If desired, this recipe can be made over two days: Make the pastry cream and craquelin on day 1 and the puffs on day 2. We prefer whole milk in the pastry cream, but you can use low-fat milk; do not use skim milk. Use a mixer to whip the cream if you prefer.

**PASTRY CREAM**

- 2½ cups whole milk, divided
- ⅔ cup (3⅓ ounces) all-purpose flour
- ½ cup (3½ ounces) granulated sugar
- ¼ teaspoon table salt
- 6 large egg yolks
- 4 tablespoons unsalted butter, cut into 4 pieces and chilled
- 1 tablespoon vanilla extract

**CRAQUELIN**

- 6 tablespoons unsalted butter, softened
- ½ cup packed (3½ ounces) light brown sugar
- ¾ cup (3¾ ounces) all-purpose flour
- Pinch table salt

CHOUX

- 2 large eggs plus 1 large white
- 6 tablespoons water
- 5 tablespoons unsalted butter, cut into ½-inch pieces
- 2 tablespoons milk
- 1½ teaspoons granulated sugar
- ¼ teaspoon table salt
- ½ cup (2½ ounces) all-purpose flour
- 1 cup heavy cream

1. **FOR THE PASTRY CREAM:** Heat 2 cups milk in medium saucepan over medium heat until just simmering. Meanwhile, whisk flour, sugar, and salt in medium bowl until combined. Add egg yolks and remaining ½ cup milk to flour mixture and whisk until smooth. Remove saucepan from heat and, whisking constantly, slowly add ½ cup milk to yolk mixture to temper. Whisking constantly, add tempered yolk mixture to milk in saucepan.

2. Return saucepan to medium heat and cook, whisking constantly, until mixture thickens slightly, about 1 minute. Reduce heat to medium-low and continue to simmer, whisking constantly, for 8 minutes longer. Increase heat to medium and cook, whisking vigorously, until very thick (mixture dripped from whisk should mound on surface), 1 to 2 minutes. Off heat, whisk in butter and vanilla until butter is melted and incorporated. Transfer to wide bowl. Press lightly greased parchment paper directly on surface and refrigerate until set, at least 2 hours or up to 24 hours.

3. **FOR THE CRAQUELIN:** Mix butter and sugar in medium bowl until combined. Mix in flour and salt. Transfer mixture to large sheet of parchment and press into 6-inch square. Cover with second piece of parchment and roll dough into 13 by 9-inch rectangle (it's fine to trim and patch dough to achieve correct dimensions). Remove top piece of parchment and use 2-inch round cutter to cut 24 circles. Leaving circles and trim in place, replace top parchment and transfer to rimless baking sheet. Freeze until firm, at least 30 minutes or up to 2 days.

4. **FOR THE CHOUX:** Adjust oven rack to middle position and heat oven to 400 degrees. Spray rimmed baking sheet with vegetable oil spray and dust lightly and evenly with flour, discarding any excess. Using 2-inch round cutter, mark 24 circles on sheet. Fit pastry bag with ½-inch round tip. Beat eggs and white together in 2-cup liquid measuring cup.

5. Bring water, butter, milk, sugar, and salt to boil in small saucepan over medium heat, stirring occasionally. Off heat, stir in flour until incorporated. Return saucepan to low heat and cook, stirring constantly and using smearing motion, until mixture looks like shiny, wet sand, about 3 minutes (mixture should register between 175 and 180 degrees).

6. Immediately transfer hot mixture to food processor and process for 10 seconds to cool slightly. With processor running, add beaten eggs in steady stream and process until incorporated, about 30 seconds. Scrape down sides of bowl and continue to process until smooth, thick, sticky paste forms, about 30 seconds longer.

7. Fill pastry bag with warm mixture and pipe into 1½-inch-wide mounds on prepared sheet, using circles as guide. Using small, thin spatula, transfer 1 frozen craquelin disk to top of each mound. Bake for 15 minutes; then, without opening oven door, reduce oven temperature to 350 degrees and continue to bake until golden brown and firm, 7 to 10 minutes longer.

8. Remove sheet from oven and cut ¾-inch slit into side of each pastry with paring knife to release steam. Return pastries to oven, turn off oven, and prop open oven door with handle of wooden spoon. Let pastries dry until center is mostly dry and surface is crisp, about 45 minutes. Transfer pastries to wire rack and let cool completely.

9. Fit pastry bag with ¼-inch round tip. In large bowl, whisk cream to stiff peaks. Gently whisk pastry cream until smooth. Fold pastry cream into whipped cream until combined. Transfer one-third of mixture to pastry bag. To fill choux buns, insert pastry tip ¾ inch into opening and squeeze gently until cream just starts to appear around opening, about 2 tablespoons cream per bun. Refill bag as needed. Serve. (Choux are best eaten up to 2 hours after filling. Leftovers can be refrigerated for up to 3 days but will soften over time.)

## Classic Brownies

**MAKES** 24 brownies

---

**WHY THIS RECIPE WORKS** Chewy and chocolaty, brownies should be a simple and utterly satisfying affair. But too often, brownies are heavy, dense, and remarkably low on chocolate flavor. First, for a texture and delicate chew, we swapped all-purpose flour for cake flour. Getting the number of eggs just right prevented our brownies from being cakey or dry. As for chocolatiness, plenty of unsweetened chocolate provided maximum chocolate flavor. Finally, for nut-lovers, we toasted pecans and topped the brownies with them just before baking. To melt the chocolate using a microwave, heat it with the butter at 50 percent power for 2 minutes; stir the chocolate and continue heating until melted, stirring once every additional minute.

- 1¼ cups (5 ounces) cake flour
- ¾ teaspoon baking powder
- ½ teaspoon table salt
- 6 ounces unsweetened chocolate, chopped fine
- 12 tablespoons (1½ sticks) unsalted butter, cut into 6 pieces
- 2¼ cups (15¾ ounces) sugar
- 4 large eggs
- 1 tablespoon vanilla extract
- 1 cup (4 ounces) pecans or walnuts, toasted and coarsely chopped (optional)

1. Adjust an oven rack to the middle position and heat the oven to 325 degrees. Line a 13 by 9-inch baking pan with 2 pieces of foil perpendicular to each other with extra foil hanging over edges; spray with vegetable oil spray.

2. Whisk the flour, baking powder, and salt in a medium bowl until combined; set aside.

3. Melt the chocolate and butter in a medium heatproof bowl set over a saucepan of barely simmering water, stirring occasionally, until smooth. Off the heat, gradually whisk in the sugar. Add the eggs, one at a time, whisking after each addition, until thoroughly combined. Whisk in the vanilla. Add the flour mixture in three additions, folding with a rubber spatula until the batter is completely smooth and homogeneous.

4. Transfer the batter to the prepared pan; using a spatula, spread the batter into the corners of the pan and smooth the surface. Sprinkle the toasted nuts (if using) evenly over the batter. Bake until a toothpick or wooden skewer inserted into the center of the brownies comes out with a few moist crumbs attached, 30 to 35 minutes. Cool on a wire rack to room temperature, about 2 hours; loosen the edges with a paring knife and lift the brownies from the pan using the foil sling. Cut the brownies into 2-inch squares and serve. (The brownies can be stored in an airtight container at room temperature for up to 3 days.)

## Chewy, Fudgy Triple-Chocolate Brownies

**MAKES** 64 small brownies

**WHY THIS RECIPE WORKS** Classic Brownies boast a balance of cakey and chewy. We wanted a brownie that was distinctly chewy and fudgy—a moist, dark brownie with a firm, smooth texture. To develop a rich, deep chocolate flavor, we ultimately found it necessary to use three types of chocolate: Unsweetened chocolate, semisweet chocolate, and cocoa powder. We focused on flour, butter, and eggs to arrive at the chewy texture we wanted. Too little flour and the batter was goopy; too much made the brownies dry and muted the flavor. We melted the butter instead of creaming softened butter with the sugar and eggs; the melted butter produced a more dense and fudgy texture. To melt the chocolates in a microwave, heat them with the butter at 50 percent power for 2 minutes; stir the chocolate and continue heating until melted, stirring once every additional minute. Either Dutch-processed or natural cocoa powder works well in this recipe. These brownies are very rich, so we prefer to cut them into very small squares for serving.

- 5 ounces semisweet or bittersweet chocolate, chopped
- 2 ounces unsweetened chocolate, chopped
- 8 tablespoons (1 stick) unsalted butter, cut into quarters
- 3 tablespoons cocoa powder
- 3 large eggs
- 1¼ cups (8¾ ounces) sugar
- 2 teaspoons vanilla extract
- ½ teaspoon table salt
- 1 cup (5 ounces) unbleached all-purpose flour

1. Adjust an oven rack to the lower-middle position and heat the oven to 350 degrees. Line an 8-inch square baking pan with 2 pieces of foil perpendicular to each other and extra foil hanging over edges; spray with vegetable oil spray.

2. Melt the chocolates and butter in a medium heatproof bowl set over a saucepan of barely simmering water, stirring occasionally, until smooth. Whisk in the cocoa powder until smooth. Set aside to cool slightly.

3. Whisk the eggs, sugar, vanilla, and salt together in a medium bowl until combined, about 15 seconds. Whisk the warm chocolate mixture into the egg mixture. Using a wooden spoon, stir in the flour until just combined. Transfer the batter to the prepared pan; using a spatula, spread the batter into the corners and smooth the surface. Bake until slightly puffed and a toothpick or wooden skewer inserted into the center of the brownies comes out with a few moist crumbs attached, 35 to 40 minutes. Cool the brownies on a wire rack to room temperature, about 2 hours; loosen the edges with a paring knife and lift the brownies from the pan using the foil sling. Cut the brownies into 1-inch squares and serve. (Do not cut the brownies until ready to serve; the brownies can be wrapped in plastic wrap and refrigerated for up to 5 days.)

### MAKING A FOIL SLING

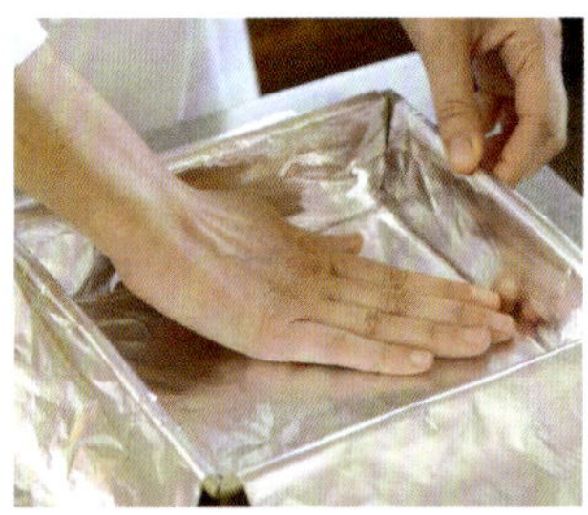

**1.** Place two sheets of aluminum foil perpendicular to each other in the baking pan, with the extra foil hanging over the edges of the pan. Push the foil into the corners and up the sides of the pan, smoothing out any wrinkles in the foil.

**2.** After the bars or brownies have baked and cooled, use the foil sling to lift and transfer them to a cutting board before cutting into squares.

## Chewy Brownies

**MAKES** 24 brownies

**WHY THIS RECIPE WORKS** Our goal was clear: a homemade brownie with chewiness to rival the boxed-mix standard—but flush with a rich, deep chocolate flavor. To get the right chewiness, we tested and tested until we finally homed in on the ratio of butter and oil that produced the chewiest brownie. To combat greasiness, we replaced some of the oil with egg yolks, whose emulsifiers prevented fat from separating and leaking out during baking. To ramp up the chocolate flavor, we replaced some of the butter with unsweetened chocolate. Espresso powder improved the chocolate taste as well. And finally, folding in bittersweet chocolate chunks just before baking gave our chewy, fudgy brownies pockets of melted chocolate. For an accurate measurement of boiling water, bring a full kettle of water to a boil, then measure out the desired amount. If your baking dish is glass, let the brownies cool for 10 minutes, then remove them promptly from the pan (otherwise, the superior heat retention of glass can lead to overbaking). While any high-quality chocolate can be used, our preferred brand of bittersweet chocolate is Ghirardelli 60% Cacao Bittersweet Chocolate Premium Baking Bar. Our preferred brand of unsweetened chocolate is Baker's.

- ⅓ cup (1 ounce) Dutch-processed cocoa powder
- 1½ teaspoons instant espresso powder (optional)
- ½ cup plus 2 tablespoons boiling water
- 2 ounces unsweetened chocolate, chopped fine
- ½ cup plus 2 tablespoons vegetable oil
- 4 tablespoons unsalted butter, melted
- 2 large eggs plus 2 large yolks
- 2 teaspoons vanilla extract
- 2½ cups (17½ ounces) sugar
- 1¾ cups (8¾ ounces) all-purpose flour
- ¾ teaspoon table salt
- 6 ounces bittersweet chocolate, cut into ½-inch pieces

**1.** Adjust oven rack to lowest position and heat oven to 350 degrees. Make foil sling for 13 by 9-inch baking pan by folding 2 long sheets of aluminum foil; first sheet should be 13 inches wide and second sheet should be 9 inches wide. Lay sheets of foil in pan perpendicular to each other, with extra foil hanging over edges of pan. Push foil into corners and up sides of pan, smoothing foil flush to pan. Lightly spray foil with vegetable oil spray.

**2.** Whisk cocoa; espresso powder, if using; and boiling water in large bowl until smooth. Add unsweetened chocolate and whisk until chocolate is melted. Whisk in oil and melted butter. (Mixture may look curdled.) Add eggs and yolks and vanilla and continue to whisk until smooth and homogeneous. Whisk in sugar until fully incorporated. Add flour and salt and mix with rubber spatula until combined. Fold in bittersweet chocolate pieces.

**3.** Scrape batter into prepared pan and bake until toothpick inserted halfway between edge and center comes out with few moist crumbs attached, 30 to 35 minutes. Transfer pan to wire rack and let cool for 1½ hours.

**4.** Loosen edges with paring knife. Using foil overhang, lift brownies out of pan. Return brownies to wire rack and let cool completely. Cut into 2-inch squares and serve. (Brownies can be stored in airtight container at room temperature for up to 4 days.)

## Ultimate Turtle Brownies

**MAKES** 25 brownies

**WHY THIS RECIPE WORKS** Dark chocolate brownies, rich caramel, and crunchy pecans—this irresistible combination featured in turtle brownies is hard to beat. So our first step to make brownies reminiscent of the classic turtle candy started with a basic recipe: Whole eggs, a modest amount of flour, and baking powder gave us brownies with a structure that was partway between cakey and chewy—perfect for supporting a blanket of caramel. A combination of bittersweet and unsweetened chocolate struck just the right balance. Garnishing each brownie with a pecan half made them look like turtles, but they didn't taste like turtles until we stirred chopped pecans into the brownie batter as well. Caramel made with cream, butter, and sugar was pleasantly chewy and gooey, and a little corn syrup prevented it from crystallizing. Swirling some caramel into the batter and pouring more over the top ensured plenty of rich, gooey caramel in every bite. If the caramel is too cool to be fluid, reheat it in the microwave. Be sure to use a metal baking pan and not a glass baking dish in this recipe.

**CARAMEL**

- 6 tablespoons heavy cream
- ¼ teaspoon table salt
- ¼ cup water
- 2 tablespoons light corn syrup
- 1¼ cups (8¾ ounces) sugar
- 2 tablespoons unsalted butter
- 1 teaspoon vanilla extract

**BROWNIES**

- 8 tablespoons unsalted butter, cut into 8 pieces
- 4 ounces bittersweet chocolate, chopped
- 2 ounces unsweetened chocolate, chopped
- ¾ cup (3¾ ounces) all-purpose flour
- ½ teaspoon baking powder
- 2 large eggs, room temperature
- 1 cup (7 ounces) sugar
- 2 teaspoons vanilla extract
- ¼ teaspoon table salt
- ⅔ cup chopped pecans, plus 25 toasted pecan halves, divided
- ⅓ cup (2 ounces) semisweet chocolate chips (optional)

**1. FOR THE CARAMEL:** Combine cream and salt in small bowl; stir well to dissolve salt. Combine water and corn syrup in medium saucepan; pour sugar into center of saucepan, taking care not to let sugar granules touch sides of saucepan. Gently stir with spatula to moisten sugar thoroughly. Cover and bring to boil over medium-high heat and cook, covered and without stirring, until sugar is completely dissolved and liquid is clear, 3 to 5 minutes. Uncover and continue to cook, without stirring, until bubbles show faint golden color, 3 to 5 minutes longer. Reduce heat to medium-low and continue to cook, swirling saucepan occasionally, until caramel is light amber and registers about 360 degrees, 1 to 3 minutes longer. Off heat, carefully add cream mixture to center of saucepan; stir (mixture will bubble and steam vigorously) until cream is fully incorporated and bubbling subsides. Stir in butter and vanilla until combined. Transfer caramel to liquid measuring cup or bowl; set aside.

**2. FOR THE BROWNIES:** Adjust oven rack to lower-middle position and heat oven to 325 degrees. Make foil sling for 9-inch square baking pan by folding 2 long sheets of aluminum foil so each is 9 inches wide. Lay sheets of foil in pan perpendicular to each other, with extra foil hanging over edges of pan. Push foil into corners and up sides of pan, smoothing foil flush to pan. Grease foil.

**3.** Microwave butter, bittersweet chocolate, and unsweetened chocolate in bowl at 50 percent power, stirring occasionally, until melted and smooth, 2 to 4 minutes; set aside and let cool slightly. Meanwhile, whisk flour and baking powder together in second bowl; set aside. Whisk eggs in large bowl to combine; add sugar, vanilla, and salt and whisk until incorporated. Add cooled chocolate mixture to egg mixture and whisk until combined. Using rubber spatula, stir in flour mixture until almost combined. Stir in chopped pecans and chocolate chips, if using, until incorporated and no flour streaks remain.

**4.** Spread half of brownie batter in even layer in prepared pan. Using greased ¼-cup dry measuring cup, drizzle ¼ cup caramel over batter. Using spoon, dollop remaining batter in large mounds over caramel layer and spread into even layer. Drizzle another ¼ cup caramel over top. Using butter knife, swirl brownie batter through caramel. Bake until toothpick inserted in center comes out with few moist crumbs attached, 35 to 40 minutes, rotating pan halfway through baking. Let brownies cool completely in pan on wire rack, about 1½ hours.

**5.** Heat remaining caramel (you should have about ¾ cup) in microwave until warm and pourable but still thick (do not boil), 45 to 60 seconds, stirring once or twice; pour caramel over brownies. Spread caramel to cover surface. Refrigerate brownies, uncovered, for 2 hours.

**6.** Using foil overhang, lift brownies out of pan, loosening sides with paring knife if needed, and transfer to cutting board. Using chef's knife, cut brownies into 25 pieces. Press pecan half onto surface of each brownie. Serve chilled or at room temperature. (Brownies can be refrigerated for up to 3 days.)

## Cream Cheese Brownies

**MAKES** sixteen 2-inch brownies

**WHY THIS RECIPE WORKS** Decadent cream cheese brownies are hard to get just right: They are plagued by chalky cream cheese, dry brownie, and uneven distribution of each element. To fix these issues, we started with a cakey brownie, which would absorb some of the moisture from the cream cheese. Unsweetened chocolate gave us the most intense chocolate flavor, and a bit of extra sugar eliminated bitter notes. For the cream cheese swirl, we mixed in some sour cream for tang and richness. Dolloping the cream cheese into the brownie batter made for unevenly dispersed swirls; we fixed this by layering some brownie batter, then the cream cheese, then more brownie batter on top and giving the whole construction a few quick swirls with a knife. To accurately test the doneness of the brownies, be sure to stick the toothpick into the brownie portion, not the cream cheese. Leftover brownies should be stored in the refrigerator. Let leftovers stand at room temperature for 1 hour before serving.

**CREAM CHEESE FILLING**

- 4 ounces cream cheese, cut into 8 pieces
- ½ cup sour cream
- 2 tablespoons sugar
- 1 tablespoon all-purpose flour

**BROWNIE BATTER**

- ⅔ cup (3⅓ ounces) all-purpose flour
- ½ teaspoon baking powder
- ½ teaspoon table salt
- 4 ounces unsweetened chocolate, chopped fine
- 8 tablespoons unsalted butter
- 1¼ cups (8¾ ounces) sugar
- 2 large eggs
- 1 teaspoon vanilla extract

**1. FOR THE CREAM CHEESE FILLING:** Microwave cream cheese until soft, 20 to 30 seconds. Add sour cream, sugar, and flour and whisk to combine. Set aside.

**2.** Adjust oven rack to middle position and heat oven to 325 degrees. Make foil sling for 8-inch square baking pan by folding 2 long sheets of aluminum foil so each is 8 inches wide. Lay sheets of foil in pan perpendicular to each other, with extra foil hanging over edges of pan. Push foil into corners and up sides of pan, smoothing foil flush to pan. Grease foil.

**3. FOR THE BROWNIE BATTER:** Whisk flour, baking powder, and salt together in bowl and set aside. Microwave chocolate and butter in bowl at 50 percent power, stirring occasionally, until melted, 1 to 2 minutes.

**4.** Whisk sugar, eggs, and vanilla together in medium bowl. Add melted chocolate mixture (do not clean bowl) and whisk until incorporated. Add flour mixture and fold to combine.

**5.** Transfer ½ cup batter to bowl used to melt chocolate. Spread remaining batter in prepared pan. Spread cream cheese filling evenly over batter.

**6.** Microwave bowl of reserved batter until warm and pourable, 10 to 20 seconds. Using spoon, dollop softened batter over cream cheese filling, 6 to 8 dollops. Using knife, swirl batter through cream cheese filling, making marbled pattern, 10 to 12 strokes, leaving ½-inch border around edges.

**7.** Bake until toothpick inserted in center comes out with a few moist crumbs attached, 35 to 40 minutes, rotating pan halfway through baking. Let cool in pan on wire rack for 1 hour.

**8.** Using foil overhang, lift brownies out of pan. Return brownies to wire rack and let cool completely, about 1 hour. Cut into 2-inch squares and serve.

## Fudgy Low-Fat Brownies

**MAKES** 16 brownies

**WHY THIS RECIPE WORKS** We have tried many recipes for "healthy" brownies, but it usually takes just one bite to regret the effort. We wanted a moist, fudgy, chocolaty brownie that had a lower fat and calorie count than a traditional brownie, which can weigh in at over 200 calories and 12 grams of fat. We started our tests with "alternative" ingredients, such as prune puree, applesauce, and yogurt, but they resulted in everything from oddly flavored brownies to flavorless hockey pucks. We had more success replacing some of the butter with low-fat sour cream, which yielded moist, fudgy brownies. A blend of cocoa powder and bittersweet chocolate (which has less fat per ounce than unsweetened chocolate) added deep chocolate flavor. And to boost both the brownies' chocolate flavor and moisture without adding any fat, we used a shot of chocolate syrup. Our brownies were now rich and decadent, but with half the calories (just 110 per serving) and less than half the fat (only 4.5 grams) of traditional brownies. For a fudgy consistency, don't overbake the brownies; as soon as a toothpick inserted into the center comes out with moist crumbs attached, the brownies are done. If the toothpick emerges with no crumbs, the brownies will be cakey. To melt the chocolate in a microwave, heat it with the butter at 50 percent power for 2 minutes; stir and continue heating until melted, stirring once every additional minute.

- ¾ cup (3¾ ounces) unbleached all-purpose flour
- ⅓ cup Dutch-processed cocoa powder
- ½ teaspoon baking powder
- ¼ teaspoon table salt
- 2 ounces bittersweet chocolate, chopped
- 2 tablespoons unsalted butter
- 1 cup (7 ounces) sugar
- 2 tablespoons low-fat sour cream
- 1 tablespoon chocolate syrup
- 2 teaspoons vanilla extract
- 1 large whole egg
- 1 large egg white

**1.** Adjust an oven rack to the middle position and heat the oven to 350 degrees. Line an 8-inch square baking pan with 2 pieces of foil perpendicular to each other and extra foil hanging over edges; spray with vegetable oil spray.

**2.** Whisk the flour, cocoa powder, baking powder, and salt together in a medium bowl. Melt the chocolate and butter in a large heatproof bowl set over a saucepan of barely simmering water, stirring occasionally, until smooth. Set aside to cool slightly, 2 to 3 minutes. Whisk in the sugar, sour cream, chocolate syrup, vanilla, whole egg, and egg white. Using a rubber spatula, fold the dry ingredients into the chocolate mixture until combined.

**3.** Transfer the batter to the prepared pan; using a spatula, spread the batter into the corners and smooth the surface. Bake until slightly puffed and a toothpick or wooden skewer inserted into the center of the brownies comes out with a few moist crumbs attached, 20 to 25 minutes. Cool the brownies on a wire rack to room temperature, about 1 hour. Loosen the edges with a paring knife and lift the brownies from the pan using the foil sling. Cut the brownies into 2-inch squares and serve. (Do not cut the brownies until ready to serve; the brownies can be wrapped in plastic wrap and refrigerated for up to 3 days.)

## Blondies

**MAKES** 36 bars

**WHY THIS RECIPE WORKS** Blondies are first cousins to both brownies and chocolate chip cookies. Although blondies are baked in a pan like brownies, the flavorings are similar to those in chocolate chip cookies. They're sometimes laced with nuts and chocolate chips or butterscotch chips. But even with these extras, blondies can be pretty bland, floury, and dry. We set out to fix the blondie so it would be chewy but not dense, sweet but not cloying, and loaded with nuts and chocolate. We found that the key to chewy blondies was using melted, not creamed, butter because the creaming process incorporated too much air into the batter. Light brown sugar lent the right amount of molasses flavor. And combined with vanilla

extract and salt, the light brown sugar developed a rich butterscotch flavor. To add both texture and flavor, we included chocolate chips and pecans. We also tried butterscotch chips, but we found that they did little for this recipe. On a whim, we included white chocolate chips with the semisweet chips, and we were surprised that they produced the best blondie yet. If you have trouble finding white chocolate chips, chop a bar of white chocolate into small chunks.

- 1½ cups (7½ ounces) unbleached all-purpose flour
- 1 teaspoon baking powder
- ½ teaspoon table salt
- 1½ cups packed (10½ ounces) light brown sugar
- 12 tablespoons (1½ sticks) unsalted butter, melted and cooled
- 2 large eggs
- 1½ teaspoons vanilla extract
- 1 cup (4 ounces) pecans, toasted and chopped coarse
- ½ cup (3 ounces) semisweet chocolate chips
- ½ cup (3 ounces) white chocolate chips

**1.** Adjust an oven rack to the middle position and heat the oven to 350 degrees. Line a 13 by 9-inch baking pan with 2 pieces of foil (see the photos on page 845) and spray with vegetable oil spray.

**2.** Whisk the flour, baking powder, and salt together in a medium bowl; set aside.

**3.** Whisk the brown sugar and melted butter together in a medium bowl until combined. Add the eggs and vanilla and mix well. Using a rubber spatula, fold the dry ingredients into the egg mixture until just combined. Do not overmix. Fold in the nuts and semisweet and white chocolate chips and turn the batter into the prepared pan, smoothing the top with a rubber spatula.

**4.** Bake until the top is shiny and cracked and feels firm to the touch, 22 to 25 minutes. Transfer the pan to a wire rack and cool completely. Loosen the edges with a paring knife and lift the bars from the pan using the foil sling. Cut into 2 by 1½-inch bars.

### Congo Bars

If you have trouble locating unsweetened shredded coconut, try a natural foods store or an Asian market. Keep a close eye on the coconut when toasting, as it can burn quickly. Toast 1½ cups unsweetened shredded coconut on a rimmed baking sheet on the middle oven rack at 350 degrees, stirring two to three times, until light golden, 4 to 5 minutes. Transfer to a small bowl to cool. Follow the recipe for Blondies, adding the toasted coconut with the chocolate chips and nuts in step 3.

## Browned Butter Blondies

**MAKES** 24 blondies

**WHY THIS RECIPE WORKS** For a blondie that's chewy but not too sweet, we found that you can't simply swap in a cookie dough or brownie batter. Using melted rather than creamed butter made for a blondie that was dense and chewy instead of cakey. To boost the blondie's flavor with nutty complexity, we browned the butter first. Brown sugar was a must for its underlying caramel notes, and its moistness contributed to a chewy texture. To tone down the sweetness, we replaced a portion of the sugar with corn syrup. A full 2 tablespoons of vanilla brought more complexity to the bars, and a generous amount of salt in the batter and sprinkled on top brought all the flavors into focus. Chopped pecans and milk chocolate chips complemented the butterscotch flavor without overwhelming it. We developed this recipe using a metal baking pan; using a glass baking dish may cause the blondies to overbake. Toast the pecans on a rimmed baking sheet in a 350-degree oven until fragrant, 8 to 12 minutes, stirring them halfway through.

- 2¼ cups (11¼ ounces) all-purpose flour
- 1¼ teaspoons table salt
- ½ teaspoon baking powder
- 12 tablespoons unsalted butter
- 1¾ cups packed (12¼ ounces) light brown sugar
- 3 large eggs
- ½ cup corn syrup
- 2 tablespoons vanilla extract
- 1 cup pecans, toasted and chopped coarse
- ½ cup (3 ounces) milk chocolate chips
- ¼–½ teaspoon flake sea salt, crumbled (optional)

**1.** Adjust oven rack to middle position and heat oven to 350 degrees. Make foil sling for 13 by 9-inch baking pan by folding 2 long sheets of aluminum foil; first sheet should be 13 inches wide and second sheet should be 9 inches wide. Lay sheets of foil in pan perpendicular to each other, with extra foil hanging over edges of pan. Push foil into corners and up sides of pan, smoothing foil flush to pan. Lightly spray foil with vegetable oil spray.

**2.** Whisk flour, table salt, and baking powder together in medium bowl.

**3.** Heat butter in 10-inch skillet over medium-high heat until melted, about 2 minutes. Continue cooking, stirring and scraping constantly with rubber spatula until milk solids are dark golden brown and butter has nutty aroma, 1 to 3 minutes. Immediately transfer to large heatproof bowl.

**4.** Add sugar to hot butter and whisk until combined. Add eggs, corn syrup, and vanilla and whisk until smooth. Using rubber spatula, stir in flour mixture until fully incorporated. Stir in pecans and chocolate chips. Transfer batter to prepared pan; using spatula, spread batter into corners of pan and smooth surface. Sprinkle with sea salt, if using. Bake until top is deep golden brown and springs backs when lightly pressed, 35 to 40 minutes, rotating pan halfway through baking (blondies will firm as they cool).

**5.** Let blondies cool completely in pan on wire rack, about 2 hours. Using foil overhang, lift blondies out of pan and transfer to cutting board. Remove foil. Cut into 24 bars and serve. (Blondies can be wrapped tightly in plastic wrap and stored at room temperature for up to 5 days.)

## Millionaire's Shortbread

**MAKES** 40 cookies

**WHY THIS RECIPE WORKS** Millionaire's shortbread has a lot going for it: a crunchy shortbread base topped with a chewy, caramel-like layer, all covered in shiny, snappy chocolate. We started by making a quick pat-in-the-pan shortbread with melted butter. Sweetened condensed milk was important to the creaminess of the middle layer, but we needed to add a little heavy cream to keep it from separating. Gently heating the chocolate in the microwave and stirring in grated chocolate created a firm top layer, which made a suitably elegant finish for this refined cookie. For the caramel filling, monitor the temperature with an instant-read thermometer. We prefer Ghirardelli 60% Cacao Bittersweet Chocolate Premium Baking Bar for this recipe. When grating the chocolate use the small holes of a box grater. Stir often while melting the chocolate and don't overheat it.

**CRUST**

- 2½ cups (12½ ounces) all-purpose flour
- ½ cup (3½ ounces) granulated sugar
- ¾ teaspoon table salt
- 16 tablespoons unsalted butter, melted

**FILLING**

- 1 (14-ounce) can sweetened condensed milk
- 1 cup packed (7 ounces) brown sugar
- ½ cup heavy cream
- ½ cup corn syrup
- 8 tablespoons unsalted butter
- ½ teaspoon table salt

**CHOCOLATE**

- 8 ounces bittersweet chocolate (6 ounces chopped fine, 2 ounces grated)

**1. FOR THE CRUST:** Adjust oven rack to lower-middle position and heat oven to 350 degrees. Make foil sling for 13 by 9-inch baking pan by folding 2 long sheets of aluminum foil; first sheet should be 13 inches wide and second sheet should be 9 inches wide. Lay sheets of foil in pan perpendicular to each other, with extra foil hanging over edges of pan. Push foil into corners and up sides of pan, smoothing foil flush to pan. Combine flour, sugar, and salt in medium bowl. Add melted butter and stir with rubber spatula until flour is evenly moistened. Crumble dough evenly over bottom of prepared pan. Using your fingertips and palm of your hand, press and smooth dough into even thickness. Using fork, pierce dough at 1-inch intervals. Bake until light golden brown and firm to touch, 25 to 30 minutes. Transfer pan to wire rack. Using sturdy metal spatula, press on entire surface of warm crust to compress (this will make finished bars easier to cut). Let crust cool until it is just warm, at least 20 minutes.

**2. FOR THE FILLING:** Stir all ingredients together in large, heavy-bottomed saucepan. Cook over medium heat, stirring frequently, until mixture registers between 236 and 239 degrees (temperature will fluctuate), 16 to 20 minutes. Pour over crust and spread to even thickness (mixture will be very hot). Let cool completely, about 1½ hours.

**3. FOR THE CHOCOLATE:** Microwave chopped chocolate in bowl at 50 percent power, stirring every 15 seconds, until melted but not much warmer than body temperature (check by holding in palm of your hand), 1 to 2 minutes. Add grated chocolate and stir until smooth, returning to microwave for no more than 5 seconds at a time to finish melting if necessary. Spread chocolate evenly over surface of filling. Refrigerate shortbread until chocolate is just set, about 10 minutes.

**4.** Using foil overhang, lift shortbread out of pan and transfer to cutting board; discard foil. Using serrated knife and gentle sawing motion, cut shortbread in half crosswise to create two 9 by 6½-inch rectangles. Cut each rectangle in half to make four 9 by 3½-inch strips. Cut each strip crosswise into 10 equal pieces and serve. (Shortbread can be stored at room temperature, between layers of parchment, for up to 1 week.)

## Raspberry Squares

**MAKES** 25 squares

**WHY THIS RECIPE WORKS** Raspberry squares are one of the best, and easiest, bar cookies to prepare, especially since the filling is ready-made (a jar of raspberry preserves). But sometimes the proportions are uneven, leaving you feeling parched from too much sandy crust, or puckered up from an overload of tart filling. We were after a buttery, tender, golden brown crust and crumb topping with just the right amount of sweet and tart raspberry preserves in the middle. For the tender, almost (but not quite) sandy crumb, we had to get the right combination of ingredients, especially the butter and sugar. Too much butter made the raspberry squares greasy, but too little left them on the dry side. We found that equal amounts of white and light brown sugar made for a deeper flavor than white alone; oats and nuts made a subtle contribution to flavor while also adding some textural interest. For a golden brown bottom crust, we prebaked it before layering it with raspberry preserves and sprinkling on the top crust, which was a small amount of the reserved bottom crust mixture. For a nice presentation, trim 1/4 inch off the outer rim of the uncut baked block. The outside edges of all cut squares will then be neat.

- 1½ cups (7½ ounces) all-purpose flour
- 1¼ cups (3¾ ounces) quick oats
- ½ cup pecans or almonds, chopped fine
- ⅓ cup (2⅓ ounces) granulated sugar
- ⅓ cup packed (2⅓ ounces) light brown sugar
- ¼ teaspoon baking soda
- ¼ teaspoon table salt
- 12 tablespoons unsalted butter, cut into 12 pieces and softened
- 1 cup raspberry preserves

**1.** Adjust oven rack to lower-middle position and heat oven to 350 degrees. Make foil sling for 9-inch square baking pan by folding 2 long sheets of aluminum foil so each is 9 inches wide. Lay sheets of foil in pan perpendicular to each other, with extra foil hanging over edges of pan. Push foil into corners and up sides of pan, smoothing foil flush to pan. Spray with vegetable oil spray.

**2.** Whisk flour, oats, pecans, granulated sugar, brown sugar, baking soda, and salt together in large bowl. Using stand mixer fitted with paddle, beat flour mixture and butter at low speed until well blended and mixture resembles wet sand, about 2 minutes.

**3.** Transfer two-thirds of mixture to prepared pan. Press crumbs evenly and firmly into bottom of pan. Bake until just starting to brown, about 20 minutes. Using rubber spatula, spread preserves evenly over hot crust; sprinkle remaining flour mixture evenly over preserves. Bake until bubbling around edges and top is golden brown, about 30 minutes, rotating pan halfway through baking. Let cool completely in pan on wire rack. Using foil overhang, lift bars out of pan and transfer to cutting board. Cut bars into 25 squares and serve.

## Best Lemon Bars

**MAKES** 12 bars

**WHY THIS RECIPE WORKS** For the lemoniest lemon bars with a sweet-tart flavor, a silky-smooth filling, and a crisp, well-browned crust, we started at the bottom. Our pat-in-the-pan crust is made with melted—not cold—butter and can therefore be stirred together instead of requiring a food processor. For a truly crisp texture, we used granulated sugar instead of the usual confectioners' sugar and baked the crust until it was dark golden brown to ensure that it retained its crispness even after we topped it with the lemon filling. We cooked our lemon filling on the stove to shorten the oven time and keep it from curdling or browning at the edges when it baked. A combination of lemon juice and lemon zest provided complex flavor and aroma, and a unique ingredient—cream of tartar (tartaric acid)—gave the bars a bold sharpness and bright, lingering finish. Do not substitute bottled lemon juice for fresh here.

**CRUST**

- 1 cup (5 ounces) all-purpose flour
- ¼ cup (1¾ ounces) granulated sugar
- ½ teaspoon table salt
- 8 tablespoons unsalted butter, melted

**FILLING**

- 1 cup (7 ounces) granulated sugar
- 2 tablespoons all-purpose flour
- 2 teaspoons cream of tartar
- ¼ teaspoon table salt
- 3 large eggs plus 3 large yolks
- 2 teaspoons grated lemon zest plus ⅔ cup juice (4 lemons)
- 4 tablespoons unsalted butter, cut into 8 pieces

Confectioners' sugar (optional)

**1. FOR THE CRUST:** Adjust oven rack to middle position and heat oven to 350 degrees. Make foil sling for 8-inch square baking pan by folding 2 long sheets of aluminum foil so each is 8 inches wide. Lay sheets of foil in pan perpendicular to each other, with extra foil hanging over edges of pan. Push foil into corners and up sides of pan, smoothing foil flush to pan.

**2.** Whisk flour, sugar, and salt together in bowl. Add melted butter and stir until combined. Transfer mixture to prepared pan and press into even layer over entire bottom of pan (do not wash bowl). Bake crust until dark golden brown, 19 to 24 minutes, rotating pan halfway through baking.

**3. FOR THE FILLING:** While crust bakes, whisk sugar, flour, cream of tartar, and salt together in now-empty bowl. Whisk in eggs and yolks until no streaks of egg remain. Whisk in lemon zest and juice. Transfer mixture to saucepan and cook over medium-low heat, stirring constantly, until mixture thickens and registers 160 degrees, 5 to 8 minutes. Off heat, stir in butter. Strain filling through fine-mesh strainer set over bowl.

4. Pour filling over hot crust and tilt pan to spread evenly. Bake until filling is set and barely jiggles when pan is shaken, 8 to 12 minutes. (Filling around perimeter of pan may be slightly raised.) Let bars cool completely in pan about 1½ hours. Using foil overhang, lift bars out of pan and transfer to cutting board. Cut into bars, wiping knife clean between cuts as necessary. Before serving, dust bars with confectioners' sugar, if using.

## Key Lime Bars

**MAKES** 16 bars

**WHY THIS RECIPE WORKS** Key lime pie is a luscious dessert, but it's not very portable. Thus, we decided to create a key lime bar, a cookie that balanced tart and creamy flavors as well as soft and crispy textures. To support our handheld bars, we needed a thick, sturdy crust. We found the traditional graham cracker flavor too assertive in such a crust and preferred the more neutral flavor of animal crackers. The filling also had to be firmer. By adding cream cheese and an egg yolk to sweetened condensed milk and lime juice and zest, we created a firm, rich filling that didn't fall apart when the bars were picked up. Two issues remained: Were key limes key? Did we need a topping? While we preferred key lime juice, regular lime juice was judged acceptable. For a topping, the favorite was an optional toasted-coconut topping. If you cannot find fresh key limes, use regular (Persian) limes. Do not use bottled lime juice. Grate the zest from the limes before juicing them, avoiding the bitter white pith that lies just beneath the outer skin. The optional coconut garnish adds textural interest and tames the lime flavor for those who find it too intense. The recipe can be doubled and baked in a 13 by 9-inch baking pan; you will need a double layer of extra-wide foil for the pan (each sheet about 20 inches in length) and to increase the baking times by a minute or two.

**CRUST**

- 5 ounces animal crackers
- 3 tablespoons brown sugar
- Pinch table salt
- 4 tablespoons (½ stick) unsalted butter, melted and cooled slightly

**FILLING**

- 2 ounces cream cheese, at room temperature
- 1 tablespoon grated zest from 1 lime
- Pinch table salt
- 1 (14-ounce) can sweetened condensed milk
- 1 large egg yolk
- ½ cup juice from about 20 key limes or from about 3 Persian limes

**GARNISH (OPTIONAL)**

- ¾ cup sweetened shredded coconut, toasted until golden and crisp

1. Adjust an oven rack to the middle position and heat the oven to 325 degrees. Line an 8-inch square baking pan with 2 pieces of foil perpendicular to each other and extra foil hanging over edges; spray with vegetable oil spray.

2. **FOR THE CRUST:** Pulse the animal crackers in a food processor until broken down, about 10 pulses; process the crumbs until evenly fine, about 10 seconds (you should have about 1¼ cups crumbs). Add the brown sugar and salt; process to combine, 10 to 12 pulses (if large sugar lumps remain, break them apart with your fingers). Drizzle the butter over the crumbs and pulse until the crumbs are evenly moistened with the butter, about 10 pulses. Press the crumbs evenly and firmly into the bottom of the prepared pan. Bake until deep golden brown, 18 to 20 minutes. Cool on a wire rack while making the filling. Do not turn off the oven.

3. **FOR THE FILLING:** While the crust cools, in a medium bowl, stir the cream cheese, zest, and salt with a rubber spatula until softened, creamy, and thoroughly combined. Add the sweetened condensed milk and whisk vigorously until incorporated and no lumps of cream cheese remain; whisk in the egg yolk. Add the lime juice and whisk gently until incorporated (the mixture will thicken slightly).

4. Pour the filling into the crust; spread to the corners and smooth the surface with a rubber spatula. Bake until set and the edges begin to pull away slightly from the sides, 15 to 20 minutes. Cool on a wire rack to room temperature, 1 to 1½ hours. Cover with foil and refrigerate until thoroughly chilled, at least 2 hours.

5. Loosen the edges with a paring knife and lift the bars from the baking pan using the foil sling; cut the bars into 16 squares. Sprinkle with the toasted coconut (if using) and serve. (Leftovers can be refrigerated for up to 2 days; the crust will soften slightly. Let the bars stand at room temperature for about 15 minutes before serving.)

## Ultranutty Pecan Bars

**MAKES** 24 bars

**WHY THIS RECIPE WORKS** Pecan bars usually are more about the custardy filling than the pecans but we wanted a bar cookie that emphasized the star ingredient. We increased the amount of pecans to a full pound and tossed them in a thick mixture of brown sugar, corn syrup, and melted butter for a filling that spread itself evenly in the heat of the oven. Using so many nuts gave these pecan bars a variety of textures; some parts were chewy and some crunchy—a quality we enjoyed. Instead of making a crust using cold butter in a food processor, we found that melted butter helped form an easy press-in crust—no parbaking needed. It is important to use pecan halves, not pieces. The edges of the bars will be slightly firmer than the center. If desired, trim ¼ inch from the edges before cutting into bars. Toast the pecans on a rimmed baking sheet in a 350-degree oven until fragrant, 8 to 12 minutes, shaking the sheet halfway through.

CRUST

- 1¾ cups (8¾ ounces) all-purpose flour
- 6 tablespoons (2⅔ ounces) granulated sugar
- ½ teaspoon table salt
- 8 tablespoons unsalted butter, melted

TOPPING

- ¾ cup packed (5¼ ounces) light brown sugar
- ½ cup light corn syrup
- 7 tablespoons unsalted butter, melted and hot
- 1 teaspoon vanilla extract
- ½ teaspoon table salt
- 4 cups (1 pound) pecan halves, toasted
- ½ teaspoon flake sea salt (optional)

**1. FOR THE CRUST:** Adjust oven rack to lowest position and heat oven to 350 degrees. Make foil sling for 13 by 9-inch baking pan by folding 2 long sheets of aluminum foil; first sheet should be 13 inches wide and second sheet should be 9 inches wide. Lay sheets of foil in pan perpendicular to each other, with extra foil hanging over edges of pan. Push foil into corners and up sides of pan, smoothing foil flush to pan. Lightly spray foil with vegetable oil spray.

**2.** Whisk flour, sugar, and salt together in medium bowl. Add melted butter and stir with wooden spoon until dough begins to form. Using your hands, continue to combine until no dry flour remains and small portion of dough holds together when squeezed in palm of your hand. Evenly scatter tablespoon-size pieces of dough over surface of pan. Using your fingertips and palm of your hand, press and smooth dough into even thickness in bottom of pan.

**3. FOR THE TOPPING:** Whisk sugar, corn syrup, melted butter, vanilla, and salt in medium bowl until smooth (mixture will look separated at first), 20 seconds. Fold pecans into sugar mixture until nuts are evenly coated.

**4.** Pour topping over crust. Using spatula, spread topping over crust, pushing to edges and into corners (there will be bare patches). Bake until topping is evenly distributed and rapidly bubbling across entire surface, 23 to 25 minutes.

**5.** Transfer pan to wire rack and lightly sprinkle with flake sea salt, if using. Let bars cool completely in pan, about 1½ hours. Using foil overhang, lift bars out of pan and transfer to cutting board. Cut into 24 bars and serve. (Bars can be stored at room temperature for up to 5 days.)

### TOASTING NUTS

Spread nuts in single layer on rimmed baking sheet and toast in 350-degree oven until fragrant and slightly darkened, 8 to 12 minutes, shaking sheet halfway through baking.

## Baklava

MAKES 32 TO 40 PIECES

**WHY THIS RECIPE WORKS** Baklava is rich with butter, sugar, and nuts, but it can be too soggy and too sweet. We wanted our baklava to be crisp, flaky, and buttery, light yet decadent, filled with fragrant nuts and spices, and sweetened just assertively enough. To achieve this goal, we sprinkled store-bought phyllo dough with three separate layers of nuts (a combination of almonds and walnuts) flavored with cinnamon and cloves and clarified butter for even browning. Fully cutting the baklava rather than just scoring it before baking helped it to absorb the sugar syrup. A low oven and slow baking time proved best. Finally, allowing the baklava to stand overnight before serving improved both its flavor and texture. A straight-sided traditional (not nonstick) metal baking pan works best for making baklava; the straight sides ensure that the pieces will have nicely shaped edges, and the surface of a traditional pan will not be marred by the knife during cutting, as would a nonstick surface. If you don't have this type of pan, a glass baking dish will work. Make sure that the phyllo is fully thawed before use; leave it in the refrigerator overnight or on the countertop for four to five hours. When assembling, use the nicest, most intact phyllo sheets for the bottom and top layers; use sheets with tears or ones that are smaller than the size of the pan in the middle layers, where their imperfections will go unnoticed.

SUGAR SYRUP

- 1¼ cups granulated sugar
- ¾ cup water
- ⅓ cup honey
- 1 tablespoon lemon juice from 1 lemon, plus 3 strips zest, removed in large strips with vegetable peeler
- 1 cinnamon stick
- 5 whole cloves
- ⅛ teaspoon table salt

NUT FILLING

- 8 ounces blanched slivered almonds
- 4 ounces walnuts
- 1¼ teaspoons ground cinnamon
- ¼ teaspoon ground cloves
- 2 tablespoons granulated sugar
- ⅛ teaspoon table salt

PASTRY AND BUTTER

- 24 tablespoons (3 sticks) unsalted butter, cut into 1-inch pieces
- 1 pound frozen phyllo, thawed

**1. FOR THE SUGAR SYRUP:** Combine syrup ingredients in small saucepan and bring to full boil over medium-high heat, stirring occasionally to ensure that sugar dissolves. Transfer to 2-cup liquid measuring cup and set aside to cool while making and baking baklava; when syrup is cool, discard spices and lemon zest. (Cooled syrup can be refrigerated in airtight container for up to 4 days.)

**2. FOR THE NUT FILLING:** Pulse almonds in food processor until very finely chopped, about twenty 1-second pulses; transfer to medium bowl. Pulse walnuts in food processor until very finely chopped, about fifteen 1-second pulses; transfer to bowl with almonds and toss to combine. Measure out 1 tablespoon nuts and set aside for garnish. Add cinnamon, cloves, sugar, and salt; toss well to combine.

**3. TO ASSEMBLE AND BAKE:** Melt butter in small saucepan over medium-low heat. Remove pan from heat and let stand for 10 minutes. Using spoon, carefully skim off foam from surface. Spoon butterfat into bowl, leaving water and milk solids in saucepan and tipping saucepan gently and only when it becomes necessary. Brush 13 by 9-inch traditional (not non-stick) baking pan with some of melted butter. Adjust oven rack to lower-middle position and heat oven to 300 degrees. Unwrap and unfold phyllo on large cutting board; carefully smooth with hands to flatten. Using baking pan as guide, cut sheets crosswise with chef's knife, yielding two roughly evenly sized stacks of phyllo (one may be narrower than other). Cover with plastic wrap, then damp dish towel to prevent drying.

**4.** Place one phyllo sheet (from wider stack) in bottom of baking pan and brush until completely coated with butter. Repeat with 7 more phyllo sheets (from wider stack), brushing each with butter.

**5.** Evenly distribute about 1 cup nuts over phyllo. Cover nuts with phyllo sheet (from narrower stack) and dab with butter (phyllo will slip if butter is brushed on). Repeat with 5 more phyllo sheets (from narrower stack), staggering sheets slightly if necessary to cover nuts, and brushing each with butter. Repeat layering with additional 1 cup nuts, 6 sheets phyllo, and remaining 1 cup nuts. Finish with 8 to 10 sheets phyllo (from wider stack), using nicest and most intact sheets for uppermost layers and brushing each except final sheet with butter. Use palms of hands to compress layers, working from center outward to press out any air pockets. Spoon 4 tablespoons butter on top layer and brush to cover all surfaces. Use bread knife or other serrated knife with pointed tip in gentle sawing motion to cut baklava into diamonds, rotating pan as necessary to complete cuts. (Cut on bias into eighths on both diagonals.)

**6.** Bake until golden and crisped, about 1½ hours, rotating baking pan halfway through baking. Immediately after removing baklava from oven, pour cooled syrup over cut lines until about 2 tablespoons remain (syrup will sizzle when it hits hot pan); drizzle remaining syrup over surface. Garnish center of each piece with pinch of reserved ground nuts. Cool to room temperature on wire rack, about 3 hours, then cover with foil and let stand at least 8 hours before serving. (Once cooled, baklava can be served, but flavor and texture improve if left to stand at least 8 hours. Baklava can be wrapped tightly in foil and kept at room temperature for up to 10 days.)

## Chocolate Truffles

MAKES 64 truffles

**WHY THIS RECIPE WORKS** The problem with many homemade truffles is that they have a dry, grainy texture. There are three keys to creating creamy, silky-smooth truffles. First, start with melted chocolate. Melting the chocolate before adding the cream allowed us to stir—rather than whisk—the two together, reducing the incorporation of air that can cause grittiness. Second, add corn syrup and butter. Corn syrup smoothed over the gritty texture of the sugar, and butter introduced silkiness. Finally, cooling down the ganache gradually before chilling prevented the formation of grainy crystals. In step 5, running your knife under hot water and wiping it dry makes cutting the chocolate easier. We recommend using Callebaut Intense Dark L-60-40NV or Ghirardelli 60% Cacao Bittersweet Chocolate Baking Bar. If giving the truffles as a gift, set them in 1½-inch candy cup liners in a gift box and keep them chilled.

GANACHE

- 2 cups (12 ounces) bittersweet chocolate, roughly chopped
- ½ cup heavy cream
- 2 tablespoons light corn syrup
- ½ teaspoon vanilla extract
- Pinch table salt
- 1½ tablespoons unsalted butter, cut into 8 pieces and softened

COATING

- 1 cup (3 ounces) Dutch-processed cocoa
- ¼ cup (1 ounce) confectioners' sugar

**1. FOR THE GANACHE:** Lightly coat 8-inch baking dish with vegetable oil spray. Make parchment sling by folding 2 long sheets of parchment so that they are as wide as baking pan. Lay sheets of parchment in pan perpendicular to each other, with extra hanging over edges of pan. Push parchment into corners and up sides of pan, smoothing flush to pan.

**2.** Microwave chocolate in medium bowl at 50 percent power, stirring occasionally, until mostly melted and a few small chocolate pieces remain, 2 to 3 minutes; set aside. Microwave cream in measuring cup until warm to touch, about 30 seconds. Stir corn syrup, vanilla, and salt into cream and pour mixture over chocolate. Cover bowl with plastic wrap, set aside for 3 minutes, and then stir with wooden spoon to combine. Stir in butter, one piece at a time, until fully incorporated.

**3.** Using rubber spatula, transfer ganache to prepared pan and set aside at room temperature for 2 hours. Cover pan and transfer to refrigerator; chill for at least 2 hours. (Ganache can be stored, refrigerated, for up to 2 days.)

**4. FOR THE COATING:** Sift cocoa and sugar through fine-mesh strainer into large bowl. Sift again into large cake pan and set aside.

**5.** Gripping overhanging parchment, lift ganache from pan. Cut ganache into sixty-four 1-inch squares (8 rows by 8 rows). (If ganache cracks during slicing, let sit at room temperature for 5 to 10 minutes and then proceed.) Dust hands lightly with cocoa mixture to prevent ganache from sticking and roll each square into ball. Transfer balls to cake pan with cocoa mixture and roll to evenly coat. Lightly shake truffles in hand over pan to remove excess coating. Transfer coated truffles to airtight container and repeat until all ganache squares are rolled and coated. Cover container and refrigerate for at least 2 hours or up to 1 week. Let truffles sit at room temperature for 5 to 10 minutes before serving.

## Chocolate-Toffee Bark

**MAKES** about 1½ pounds

**WHY THIS RECIPE WORKS** We found three keys to ensure toffee-making triumph. First, we were careful not to get any sugar on the sides of the pan, which can result in undissolved sugar crystals and gritty toffee. Second, we took care not to agitate the pan while the sugar dissolved, which can also cause crystals to form. Third, because the toffee will turn from lightly browned to burnt quickly, we reduced the heat as soon as we saw a faint golden color start to develop. Once the toffee hits 350 degrees, we added the nuts, poured it into a pan lined with greased foil, and smoothed the surface with a spatula. With the toffee set, we just needed to coat both sides with melted chocolate. You will need a thermometer that registers high temperatures for this recipe.

- 8 tablespoons unsalted butter
- ½ cup water
- 1 cup (7 ounces) sugar
- 3 tablespoons corn syrup
- ¼ teaspoon table salt
- 1½ cups pecans or walnuts, toasted and chopped, divided
- 8 ounces semisweet chocolate, chopped fine, divided

**1.** Make foil sling for 13 by 9-inch baking pan by folding 2 long sheets of aluminum foil; first sheet should be 13 inches wide and second sheet should be 9 inches wide. Lay sheets of foil in pan perpendicular to each other, with extra foil hanging over edges of pan. Push foil into corners and up sides of pan, smoothing foil flush to pan. Spray foil lightly with vegetable oil spray.

**2.** Heat butter and water in medium saucepan over medium-high heat until butter is melted. Add sugar, corn syrup, and salt to saucepan. Bring mixture to boil and cook, without stirring, until sugar is completely dissolved and syrup is faint golden color, about 10 to 14 minutes.

**3.** Reduce heat to medium-low and continue to cook, gently swirling saucepan, until toffee is amber-colored and registers 350 to 360 degrees, 2 to 4 minutes longer. Off heat, stir in ½ cup pecans until incorporated and thoroughly coated.

**4.** Pour toffee into prepared pan and smooth into even layer with spatula. Cool to room temperature, about 30 min.

**5.** Microwave 3 ounces chocolate in bowl at 50 percent power, stirring frequently, until about two-thirds melted, 1 to 2 minutes. Remove bowl from microwave, add 1 ounce chocolate, and stir until melted, returning to microwave for no more than 5 seconds at a time to complete melting, if necessary. Pour chocolate over hardened toffee and smooth with spatula, making sure to cover toffee layer evenly and completely. Sprinkle with ½ cup pecans and press lightly to adhere. Refrigerate, uncovered, until chocolate has hardened, about 15 minutes.

**6.** Line rimmed baking sheet with parchment paper. Using foil sling, invert toffee onto prepared sheet. Discard foil.

**7.** Microwave 3 ounces chocolate in bowl at 50 percent power, stirring frequently, until about two-thirds melted, 1 to 2 minutes. Remove bowl from microwave, add remaining 1 ounce chocolate, and stir until melted, returning to microwave for no more than 5 seconds at a time to complete melting, if necessary. Pour chocolate over hardened toffee and smooth with spatula, making sure to cover toffee layer evenly and completely. Sprinkle with remaining ½ cup pecans and press lightly to adhere. Refrigerate, uncovered, until chocolate has hardened, about 15 minutes.

**8.** Break bark into rough squares and serve. (Bark can be stored at room temperature for up to 2 weeks.)

# CHAPTER 14 Cakes and More

Photos (left to right): Pear-Walnut Upside-Down Cake; Lemon Posset; Chocolate-Raspberry Torte; Ice Cream Cake; Sous Vide Crème Brûlée; Dark Chocolate Cupcakes; Raspberry Sorbet

## Olive Oil Cake

**SERVES** 8 to 10

**WHY THIS RECIPE WORKS** Our popular olive oil cake has a light yet plush crumb, with a subtle but noticeable olive oil flavor. Whipping the sugar with whole eggs, rather than just the whites, produced a fine texture that was airy but sturdy enough to support the olive oil–rich batter. To emphasize the defining flavor, we opted for a good-quality extra-virgin olive oil and accentuated its fruitiness with a tiny bit of lemon zest. Sugar created a crackly topping that added a touch of sweetness and sophistication. For the best flavor, use fresh high-quality extra-virgin olive oil. If your springform pan is prone to leaking, place a rimmed baking sheet on the oven floor to catch any drips.

- 1¾ cups (8¾ ounces) all-purpose flour
- 1 teaspoon baking powder
- ¾ teaspoon table salt
- 3 large eggs
- 1¼ cups (8¾ ounces) plus 2 tablespoons sugar, divided
- ¼ teaspoon grated lemon zest
- ¾ cup extra-virgin olive oil
- ¾ cup milk

**1.** Adjust oven rack to middle position and heat oven to 350 degrees. Grease 9-inch springform pan. Whisk flour, baking powder, and salt together in bowl.

**2.** Using stand mixer fitted with whisk attachment, whip eggs on medium speed until foamy, about 1 minute. Add 1¼ cups sugar and lemon zest; increase speed to high; and whip until mixture is fluffy and pale yellow, about 3 minutes. Reduce speed to medium and, with mixer running, slowly pour in oil. Mix until oil is fully incorporated, about 1 minute. Add half of flour mixture and mix on low speed until incorporated, about 1 minute, scraping down bowl as needed. Add milk and mix until combined, about 30 seconds. Add remaining flour mixture and mix until just incorporated, about 1 minute, scraping down bowl as needed.

**3.** Transfer batter to prepared pan; sprinkle remaining 2 tablespoons sugar over entire surface. Bake until cake is deep golden brown and toothpick inserted in center comes out with few crumbs attached, 40 to 45 minutes. Transfer pan to wire rack and let cool for 15 minutes. Remove side of pan and let cake cool completely, about 1½ hours. Cut into wedges and serve. (Leftover cake can be wrapped in plastic wrap and stored at room temperature for up to 3 days.)

## Chocolate Olive Oil Cake

**SERVES** 8 to 10

**WHY THIS RECIPE WORKS** Our Olive Oil cake is a reader favorite, and many have requested that we create a chocolate version. Doing so required several changes to the original recipe, but the new version turned out to be even easier than the original since it's mixed by hand rather than in a stand mixer. A combination of unsweetened cocoa powder and melted bittersweet chocolate provided deep, rich flavor. By replacing some of the flour with cocoa powder, we reduced the overall gluten content, making the cake soft and tender. We wiped any excess grease from the sides of the pan to ensure that the batter could climb as the cake baked, and we omitted a single egg white to make the batter just viscous enough to hold the cake's crackly sugar crust in place. We strongly recommend measuring your ingredients by weight. If your cocoa is lumpy, sift it before using. You can use any fresh, mild olive oil and milk of any fat level or even nondairy milk. If your springform pan is prone to leaking, place a rimmed baking sheet on the lowest rack to catch any drips. A plastic disposable knife works well for loosening the edge of the cake without damaging your pan. Serve this cake on its own or dressed up with berries and whipped cream, crème fraîche, or ice cream.

- ½ cup extra-virgin olive oil
- 3 ounces bittersweet chocolate, chopped
- ¾ cup (3¾ ounces) all-purpose flour
- ¼ cup (¾ ounce) Dutch-processed cocoa powder
- ¾ teaspoon baking powder
- ¼ teaspoon baking soda
- ½ teaspoon table salt
- 1 cup (7 ounces) sugar plus 2 tablespoons, divided
- 2 large eggs plus 1 large yolk
- ½ cup milk

**1.** Adjust oven rack to middle position and heat oven to 350 degrees. Lightly spray bottom and sides of 9-inch springform pan with vegetable oil spray. Using paper towel, wipe sides of pan, leaving only thin film of oil. Combine olive oil and chocolate in bowl and microwave until chocolate is melted, about 1 minute. Stir until combined. Whisk flour, cocoa, baking powder, baking soda, and salt together in medium bowl.

**2.** Whisk 1 cup sugar, eggs, and yolk in large bowl until combined. Whisk in olive oil mixture until fully incorporated. Whisk in milk until incorporated. Whisk in flour mixture until smooth. Transfer batter to prepared pan; sprinkle remaining 2 tablespoons sugar over surface. Secure pan clip with your hand to prevent pan from opening and rap pan gently on counter to dislodge surface air bubbles. Bake until skewer inserted diagonally into crack and aimed toward center of cake comes out with few crumbs attached, 30 to 35 minutes.

**3.** Transfer pan to wire rack and let cake cool completely, about 2 hours. Run knife around edge of cake to loosen. Remove side of pan. Cut cake into wedges and serve. (Leftover cake can be wrapped and stored at room temperature for up to 3 days.)

## Cider-Glazed Apple Bundt Cake

**SERVES** 12 to 16

**WHY THIS RECIPE WORKS** We were able to pack the equivalent of 4½ pounds of fruit into our apple cake and its glaze with the help of a Bundt pan. This specialty pan is a practical vessel for baking moist cakes: The central hole allows heat to reach the center of the batter, which would remain dense and underbaked by the time the exterior was cooked through if baked in a conventional round cake pan. An apple cider reduction bolstered the apple flavor of our cake without making the crumb dense or soggy. Mixing the reduced apple cider into the batter, brushing it onto the cake, and using it to flavor the icing drizzled on top provided layers of pervasive apple flavor. Being selective with our spices—opting for just cinnamon and allspice—and using a light hand allowed the true apple flavor to shine. For the sake of efficiency, we recommend that you begin boiling the cider before assembling the rest of the ingredients. Reducing the cider to exactly 1 cup is important to the success of this recipe. If you accidentally overreduce the cider, make up the difference with water. Spray the pan well in step 1 to prevent sticking. If you don't have nonstick baking spray with flour, mix 1 tablespoon melted butter and 1 tablespoon flour into a paste and brush inside the pan. We like the tartness of Granny Smith apples in this recipe, but any variety of apple will work. You may shred the apples with the large shredding disk of a food processor or with the large holes of a box grater.

- 4 cups apple cider
- 3¾ cups (18¾ ounces) all-purpose flour
- 1½ teaspoons table salt
- 1½ teaspoons baking powder
- ½ teaspoon baking soda
- ¾ teaspoon ground cinnamon
- ¼ teaspoon ground allspice
- ¾ cup (3 ounces) confectioners' sugar
- 16 tablespoons unsalted butter, melted
- 1½ cups packed (10½ ounces) dark brown sugar
- 3 large eggs
- 2 teaspoons vanilla extract
- 1½ pounds Granny Smith apples, peeled, cored, and shredded (3 cups)

**1.** Boil cider in 12-inch skillet over high heat until reduced to 1 cup, 20 to 25 minutes. While cider is reducing, adjust oven rack to middle position and heat oven to 350 degrees. Heavily spray 12-cup nonstick Bundt pan with baking spray with flour. Whisk flour, salt, baking powder, baking soda, cinnamon, and allspice in large bowl until combined. Place confectioners' sugar in small bowl.

**2.** Add 2 tablespoons reduced cider to confectioners' sugar and whisk to form smooth icing. Cover icing with plastic wrap and set aside. Pour ½ cup reduced cider into second large bowl. Set remaining 6 tablespoons reduced cider aside to brush over baked cake.

**3.** Add melted butter, brown sugar, eggs, and vanilla to ½ cup cider reduction and whisk until smooth. Pour cider mixture over flour mixture and stir with rubber spatula until almost fully combined (some streaks of flour will remain). Stir in apples and any accumulated juices until evenly distributed. Transfer mixture to prepared Bundt pan and smooth top. Bake until skewer inserted in center of cake comes out clean, 55 minutes to 1 hour 5 minutes.

**4.** Transfer pan to wire rack set in rimmed baking sheet. Brush exposed surface of cake lightly with 1 tablespoon reserved cider reduction. Let cake cool for 10 minutes. Invert cake onto wire rack. Brush top and sides with remaining 5 tablespoons reserved cider reduction. Let cake for cool 20 minutes. Stir icing to loosen and drizzle over cake. Let cake cool completely, at least 2 hours, before serving. (Leftover cake can be wrapped loosely and stored at room temperature for up to 3 days.)

## Marbled Blueberry Bundt Cake

**SERVES** 12

**WHY THIS RECIPE WORKS** Switching from flavor-packed wild Maine blueberries to oversized, bland cultivated blueberries wreaks havoc in a cake. The berries refuse to stay suspended in the batter and burst into bland, soggy pockets in the heat of the oven. We solved these problems by pureeing the fruit, seasoning it with sugar and lemon, and bumping up its natural pectin content with low-sugar pectin for a thickened, fresh-tasting filling that could be marbled throughout the cake. Spray the pan well in step 1 to prevent sticking. If you don't have nonstick baking spray with flour, mix 1 tablespoon melted butter and 1 tablespoon flour into a paste and brush inside the pan. For fruit pectin we recommend Sure-Jell for Less or No Sugar Needed Recipes. Ball Fruit Pectin will not work. If using frozen berries, thaw them before blending in step 3. This cake can be served plain or with Cinnamon Whipped Cream (recipe follows).

**CAKE**

- 3 cups (15 ounces) all-purpose flour
- 1½ teaspoons baking powder
- ¾ teaspoon baking soda
- 1 teaspoon table salt
- ½ teaspoon ground cinnamon
- ¾ cup buttermilk
- 2 teaspoons grated lemon zest, plus 3 tablespoons juice
- 2 teaspoons vanilla extract
- 3 large eggs, plus 1 large yolk, room temperature
- 18 tablespoons (2¼ sticks) unsalted butter, softened
- 2 cups (14 ounces) sugar

**FILLING**

- ¾ cup (5¼ ounces) sugar
- 3 tablespoons low- or no-sugar-needed fruit pectin
- Pinch table salt
- 10 ounces (2 cups) fresh or thawed frozen blueberries
- 1 teaspoon grated lemon zest, plus 1 tablespoon juice

**1. FOR THE CAKE:** Adjust oven rack to lower-middle position and heat oven to 325 degrees. Heavily spray 12-cup nonstick Bundt pan with baking spray with flour. Whisk flour, baking powder, baking soda, salt, and cinnamon together in large bowl. Whisk buttermilk, lemon zest and juice, and vanilla together in medium bowl. Gently whisk eggs and yolk to combine in third bowl.

**2.** Using stand mixer fitted with paddle, beat butter and sugar on medium-high speed until pale and fluffy, about 3 minutes, scraping down bowl as needed. Reduce speed to medium and beat in half of eggs until incorporated, about 15 seconds. Repeat with remaining eggs, scraping down bowl after incorporating. Reduce speed to low and add one-third of flour mixture, followed by half of buttermilk mixture, mixing until just incorporated after each addition, about 5 seconds. Repeat using half of remaining flour mixture and all of remaining buttermilk mixture. Scrape down bowl, add remaining flour mixture, and mix at medium-low speed until batter is thoroughly combined, about 15 seconds. Remove bowl from mixer and fold batter once or twice with rubber spatula to incorporate any remaining flour. Cover bowl with plastic wrap and set aside while preparing filling (batter will inflate a bit).

**3. FOR THE FILLING:** Whisk sugar, pectin, and salt together in small saucepan. Process blueberries in blender until mostly smooth, about 1 minute. Transfer ¼ cup puree and lemon zest to saucepan with sugar mixture and stir to thoroughly combine. Heat sugar-blueberry mixture over medium heat until just simmering, about 3 minutes, stirring frequently to dissolve sugar and pectin. Transfer mixture to medium bowl and let cool for 5 minutes. Add remaining puree and lemon juice to cooled mixture and whisk to combine. Let sit until slightly set, about 8 minutes.

**4.** Spoon half of batter into prepared pan and smooth top. Using back of spoon, create ½-inch-deep channel in center of batter. Spoon half of filling into channel. Using butter knife or small offset spatula, thoroughly swirl filling into batter (there should be no large pockets of filling remaining). Repeat swirling step with remaining batter and filling.

**5.** Bake until top is golden brown and skewer inserted in center comes out with no crumbs attached, 1 hour to 1 hour 10 minutes. Let cake cool in pan on wire rack for 10 minutes, then invert cake directly onto wire rack. Let cake cool completely, at least 3 hours, before serving.

### Cinnamon Whipped Cream

**MAKES** 2 cups

For the best texture, whip the cream until soft peaks just form. Do not overwhip.

- 1 cup heavy cream
- 2 tablespoons confectioners' sugar
- ¼ teaspoon ground cinnamon
- Pinch table salt

Using stand mixer fitted with whisk attachment, whip all ingredients on medium-low speed until foamy, about 1 minute. Increase speed to high and whip until soft peaks form, 1 to 3 minutes.

## Chocolate Sour Cream Bundt Cake

**SERVES** 12

**WHY THIS RECIPE WORKS** A Bundt cake is the pinnacle of cake-baking simplicity. With its decorative shape, this cake doesn't require frosting or fussy finishing techniques. We wanted a cake that delivered pure chocolate ecstasy with the first bite—a chocolate Bundt cake with a fine crumb, moist texture, and rich chocolate flavor. We intensified the chocolate flavor by using both bittersweet chocolate and natural cocoa and dissolving them in boiling water, which "bloomed" their flavor. We used sour cream and brown sugar instead of white to add moisture and flavor. Finally, we further enhanced flavor with a little espresso powder and a generous amount of vanilla extract, both of which complemented the floral nuances of the chocolate. We prefer natural cocoa here because Dutch-processed cocoa will result in a compromised rise. For an accurate measurement of boiling water, bring a kettle of water to a boil, then measure out the desired amount. The cake can be served with just a dusting of confectioners' sugar but is easily made more impressive with lightly sweetened whipped cream and raspberries.

- 12 tablespoons (1½ sticks) unsalted butter, softened, plus 1 tablespoon, melted, for the pan
- ¾ cup natural cocoa powder, plus 1 tablespoon for the pan
- 6 ounces bittersweet chocolate, chopped coarse
- 1 teaspoon instant espresso powder (optional)
- ¾ cup boiling water
- 1 cup sour cream, at room temperature
- 1¾ cups (8¾ ounces) unbleached all-purpose flour
- 1 teaspoon table salt
- 1 teaspoon baking soda
- 2 cups packed (14 ounces) light brown sugar
- 1 tablespoon vanilla extract
- 5 large eggs, at room temperature
- Confectioners' sugar, for dusting

**1.** Stir together the 1 tablespoon melted butter and 1 tablespoon of the cocoa in a small bowl until a paste forms. Using a pastry brush, coat all the interior surfaces of a standard 12-cup Bundt pan. (If the mixture becomes too thick to brush on, microwave it for 10 to 20 seconds, or until warm and softened.) Adjust an oven rack to the lower-middle position and heat the oven to 350 degrees.

**2.** Combine the remaining ¾ cup cocoa, the chocolate, and espresso powder (if using) in a medium heatproof bowl. Pour the boiling water over and whisk until smooth. Cool to room temperature; then whisk in the sour cream. Whisk the flour, salt, and baking soda in a second bowl to combine.

**3.** In a stand mixer fitted with the paddle attachment, beat the remaining 12 tablespoons butter, the brown sugar, and vanilla on medium-high speed until pale and fluffy, about 3 minutes. Reduce the speed to medium and add the eggs one at a time, mixing for about 30 seconds after each addition and scraping down the bowl with a rubber spatula after the first two additions. Reduce to medium-low speed (the batter may appear separated); add about one-third of the flour mixture and half of the chocolate mixture and mix until just incorporated, about 20 seconds. Scrape the bowl and repeat using half of the remaining flour mixture and all of the remaining chocolate mixture; add the remaining flour mixture and beat until just incorporated, about 10 seconds. Scrape the bowl and mix on medium-low speed until the batter is thoroughly combined, about 30 seconds.

**4.** Transfer the batter to the prepared pan, smoothing the top with a rubber spatula. Lightly tap the pan against the countertop two or three times to settle the batter. Bake until a toothpick inserted into the center comes out with a few crumbs attached, 45 to 50 minutes, rotating the pan halfway through the baking time. Cool the cake in the pan on a wire rack for 10 minutes, then invert the cake directly onto the wire rack; cool to room temperature, about 2 hours. Dust with confectioners' sugar, transfer to a serving platter, cut into slices, and serve.

## Lemon Bundt Cake

**SERVES 12**

**WHY THIS RECIPE WORKS** Lemons are tart, brash, and aromatic. Why, then, is it so hard to capture their assertive flavor in a straightforward Bundt cake? The flavor of lemon juice is drastically muted when exposed to the heat of an oven, and its acidity can wreak havoc on the delicate nature of baked goods. We wanted to develop a Bundt cake with potent lemon flavor without ruining its texture. We developed a battery of tests challenging classic lemon Bundt cake ingredient proportions, finally deciding to increase the butter and to replace the milk with buttermilk. We also found that creaming was necessary to achieve a light and even crumb. But we still needed to maximize the lemon flavor; we couldn't get the flavor we needed from lemon juice alone without using so much that the cake fell apart when sliced. We turned to zest and found that three lemons' worth gave the cake a perfumed lemon flavor, though we needed to give the zest a brief soak in lemon juice to eliminate its fibrous texture. The final challenge was the glaze, and a simple mixture of lemon juice, buttermilk, and confectioners' sugar made the grade.

**CAKE**

- 18 tablespoons (2¼ sticks) unsalted butter, at room temperature, plus 1 tablespoon, melted, for the pan
- 3 cups (15 ounces) unbleached all-purpose flour, plus 1 tablespoon for the pan
- 3 tablespoons grated zest plus 3 tablespoons juice from 3 lemons
- 1 teaspoon baking powder
- ½ teaspoon baking soda
- 1 teaspoon table salt
- ¾ cup buttermilk
- 1 teaspoon vanilla extract
- 3 large eggs plus 1 large egg yolk, at room temperature
- 2 cups (14 ounces) granulated sugar

**GLAZE**

- 2 cups (8 ounces) confectioners' sugar
- 2–3 tablespoons juice from 1 lemon
- 1 tablespoon buttermilk

**1. FOR THE CAKE:** Adjust an oven rack to the lower-middle position and heat the oven to 350 degrees. Stir together the 1 tablespoon melted butter and 1 tablespoon of the flour in a small bowl until a paste forms. Using a pastry brush, coat all the interior surfaces of a standard 12-cup Bundt pan. (If the mixture becomes too thick to brush on, microwave it for 10 to 20 seconds, or until warm and softened.) Mince the lemon zest to a fine paste (you should have about 2 tablespoons). Combine the zest and lemon juice in a small bowl; set aside to soften, 10 to 15 minutes.

**2.** Whisk the remaining 3 cups flour, the baking powder, baking soda, and salt in a large bowl. Combine the lemon juice mixture, buttermilk, and vanilla in a medium bowl. In a small bowl, gently whisk the whole eggs and yolk to combine. In a stand mixer fitted with the paddle attachment, beat the remaining 18 tablespoons butter and the granulated sugar at medium-high speed until pale and fluffy, about 3 minutes. Reduce to medium speed and add half of the eggs, mixing until incorporated, about 15 seconds; scrape down the bowl with a rubber spatula. Repeat with the remaining eggs; scrape down the bowl again. Reduce to low speed; add about one-third of the flour mixture, followed by half of the buttermilk mixture, mixing until just incorporated after each addition (about 5 seconds). Repeat using half of the remaining flour mixture and all of the remaining buttermilk mixture. Scrape down the bowl and add the remaining flour mixture; mix at medium-low speed until the batter is thoroughly combined, about 15 seconds. Transfer the batter to the prepared pan, smoothing the top with a rubber spatula. Lightly tap the pan against the countertop two or three times to settle the batter.

**3.** Bake until the top is golden brown and a toothpick inserted into the center comes out with no crumbs attached, 45 to 50 minutes, rotating the pan halfway through the baking time.

**4. FOR THE GLAZE:** While the cake is baking, whisk the confectioners' sugar, 2 tablespoons of the lemon juice, and the buttermilk until smooth, adding more lemon juice gradually as needed until the glaze is thick but still pourable. Cool the cake in the pan on a wire rack set over a baking sheet for 10 minutes, then invert the cake directly onto the rack. Pour half of the glaze over the warm cake and cool for 1 hour; pour the remaining glaze evenly over the top of the cake and continue to cool to room temperature, at least 2 hours. Cut into slices and serve. (This cake has a light, fluffy texture when eaten the day it is baked, but if well wrapped and held at room temperature overnight its texture becomes more dense—like that of pound cake—the following day.)

## Lemon Pound Cake

**MAKES** one 8-inch loaf

**WHY THIS RECIPE WORKS** Pound cakes often turn out spongy, rubbery, heavy, and dry—and lemon pound cakes often lack true lemon flavor. We wanted to produce a superior pound cake (fine-crumbed, rich, moist, and buttery) while making the process as simple and foolproof as possible. After less-than-successful results with a stand mixer and a hand mixer, we turned to the food processor to mix our cake. It ensured a

perfect emulsification of the eggs, sugar, and melted butter (we found that a blender worked, too). Cake flour produced a tender crumb, but our cake was still a bit heavy. We fixed matters with the addition of baking powder, which increased lift and produced a consistent, fine crumb. Finally, in addition to mixing lemon zest into the cake batter, we glazed the finished cake with lemon sugar syrup—but first we poked holes all over the cake to ensure that the tangy, sweet glaze infused the cake with a blast of bright lemon flavor. You can use a blender instead of a food processor to mix the batter. To add the butter, remove the center cap of the lid so it can be drizzled into the whirling blender with minimal splattering. This batter looks almost like a thick pancake batter and is very fluid.

**CAKE**

- 1½ cups (6 ounces) cake flour
- 1 teaspoon baking powder
- ½ teaspoon table salt
- 16 tablespoons unsalted butter, melted
- 1¼ cups (8¾ ounces) sugar
- 2 tablespoons grated lemon zest plus 2 teaspoons juice
- 4 large eggs, room temperature
- 1½ teaspoons vanilla extract

**GLAZE**

- ½ cup (3½ ounces) sugar
- ¼ cup lemon juice (2 lemons)

**1. FOR THE CAKE:** Adjust oven rack to middle position and heat oven to 350 degrees. Grease and flour 8½ by 4½-inch loaf pan. In medium bowl, whisk together flour, baking powder, and salt; set aside.

**2.** In food processor, pulse sugar and lemon zest until combined, about 5 pulses. Add lemon juice, eggs, and vanilla; process until combined, about 5 seconds. Whisk melted butter thoroughly to reincorporate any separated milk solids. With machine running, add melted butter through feed tube in steady stream (this should take about 20 seconds). Transfer mixture to large bowl. Sift flour mixture over egg mixture in 3 additions, whisking gently after each addition until just combined.

**3.** Pour batter into prepared pan and bake for 15 minutes. Reduce oven temperature to 325 degrees and continue to bake until deep golden brown and toothpick inserted in center comes out clean, about 35 minutes, rotating pan halfway through baking. Let cool in pan for 10 minutes, then turn onto wire rack. Poke top and sides of cake throughout with toothpick. Let cake cool completely, at least 1 hour. (Cooled cake can be wrapped tightly in plastic wrap and stored at room temperature for up to 5 days.)

**4. FOR THE GLAZE:** While cake is cooling, bring sugar and lemon juice to boil in small saucepan, stirring occasionally to dissolve sugar. Reduce heat to low and simmer until thickened slightly, about 2 minutes. Brush top and sides of cake with glaze and let cool to room temperature before serving.

## Applesauce Snack Cake

**SERVES 9**

**WHY THIS RECIPE WORKS** Applesauce cakes run the gamut from dense, chunky fruitcakes to gummy "health" cakes without much flavor. We wanted a moist and tender cake that actually tasted like its namesake. It was easy to achieve the looser, more casual crumb that is best suited to a rustic snack cake. Since this texture is similar to that of quick breads and muffins, we used the same technique, i.e., mixing the wet ingredients separately and then gently adding the dry ingredients by hand. For a boost in apple flavor without adding more moisture, plumping dried apples in cider while reducing it to a syrup was the secret and did not make the cake chunky. With such great apple flavor, we rejected the idea of topping the cake with a sweet glaze or rich frosting. But we found we liked the modicum of textural contrast provided by a simple sprinkling of spiced granulated sugar. This recipe can be easily doubled and baked in a 13 by 9-inch baking dish. If doubling the recipe, give the cider and dried apple mixture about 20 minutes to reduce, and bake the cake for about 45 minutes. The cake is very moist, so it is best to err on the side of overdone when testing its doneness. The test kitchen prefers the rich flavor of cider, but apple juice can be substituted.

- 1 cup apple cider
- ¾ cup (2 ounces) dried apples, cut into ½-inch pieces
- 1½ cups (7½ ounces) unbleached all-purpose flour
- 1 teaspoon baking soda
- ⅔ cup (4⅔ ounces) sugar
- ½ teaspoon ground cinnamon
- ¼ teaspoon ground nutmeg
- ⅛ teaspoon ground cloves
- 1 cup unsweetened applesauce, at room temperature
- 1 large egg, at room temperature, lightly beaten
- ½ teaspoon table salt
- 8 tablespoons (1 stick) unsalted butter, melted and cooled slightly
- 1 teaspoon vanilla extract

**1.** Adjust an oven rack to the middle position and heat the oven to 325 degrees. Cut a 16-inch length of parchment paper or foil and fold lengthwise to a 7-inch width. Grease an 8-inch square baking dish and fit the parchment into the dish, pushing it into the corners and up the sides; allow the excess to overhang the edges of the dish.

**2.** Bring the cider and dried apples to a simmer in a small saucepan over medium heat; cook until the liquid evaporates and the mixture appears dry, about 15 minutes. Cool to room temperature.

**3.** Whisk the flour and baking soda in a medium bowl to combine; set aside. In a second medium bowl, whisk the sugar, cinnamon, nutmeg, and cloves together. Measure 2 tablespoons of the sugar-spice mixture into a small bowl and set aside for the topping.

**4.** In a food processor, process the cooled dried-apple mixture and applesauce until smooth, 20 to 30 seconds, scraping down the sides of the bowl as needed; set aside. Whisk the egg and salt in a large bowl to combine. Add the sugar-spice mixture and whisk continuously until well combined and light colored, about 20 seconds. Add the butter in three additions, whisking after each addition. Add the applesauce mixture and vanilla and whisk to combine. Add the flour mixture to the wet ingredients; using a rubber spatula, fold gently until just combined and evenly moistened.

**5.** Transfer the batter to the prepared pan, smoothing the top with a rubber spatula. Lightly tap the pan against the countertop two or three times to settle the batter. Sprinkle the reserved 2 tablespoons sugar-spice mixture evenly over the batter. Bake until a toothpick inserted into the center comes out clean, 35 to 40 minutes, rotating the pan halfway through the baking time. Cool the cake to room temperature in the pan on a wire rack, about 2 hours. Remove the cake from the pan by lifting the parchment overhang and transfer to a cutting board. Cut the cake into squares and serve.

## Oatmeal Cake with Broiled Icing

**SERVES 9**

**WHY THIS RECIPE WORKS** For this snack cake recipe, we were after a moist, classic oatmeal snack cake with buttery undertones topped by a broiled icing with chewy coconut, crunchy nuts, and a butterscotch-like flavor. To solve the problem of denseness we replaced some of the brown sugar with granulated sugar—less moist than brown sugar, granulated sugar lightened the cake's texture. We also reduced the proportion of flour to oats, using the minimum amount of flour needed to keep the cake from collapsing. We still had to tackle the gumminess, however, which was created partly by soaking the oats in water; the hydrated oats were a sticky mess when we stirred them into the batter. But simply folding in dried oats didn't work; they never fully hydrated during baking, and tasted raw and chewy in the finished cake. The answer proved to be soaking the oats in room-temperature rather than boiling water, minimizing the amount of released starch. Quick-cooking oats worked best. Cutting back on the sugar in

the icing brought the sweetness in line, using melted butter (rather than creaming the butter into the sugar) simplified the recipe, and adding a splash of milk made the icing more pliable. Do not use old-fashioned or instant oats for this recipe. Be sure to use a metal baking dish; glass pans are not recommended when broiling. If you have a drawer-style broiler (underneath the oven), position the rack as far as possible from the broiler element and monitor the icing carefully as it cooks in step 5. A vertical sawing motion with a serrated knife works best for cutting through the crunchy icing and tender crumb.

**CAKE**

- 1 cup (3 ounces) quick-cooking oats
- ¾ cup water, at room temperature
- ¾ cup (3¾ ounces) unbleached all-purpose flour
- ½ teaspoon baking soda
- ½ teaspoon baking powder
- ½ teaspoon table salt
- ¼ teaspoon ground cinnamon
- ⅛ teaspoon ground nutmeg
- 4 tablespoons (½ stick) unsalted butter, softened
- ½ cup (3½ ounces) granulated sugar
- ½ cup packed (3½ ounces) light brown sugar
- 1 large egg, at room temperature
- ½ teaspoon vanilla extract

**BROILED ICING**

- ¼ cup packed (1¾ ounces) light brown sugar
- 3 tablespoons unsalted butter, melted and cooled
- 3 tablespoons milk
- ¾ cup sweetened shredded coconut
- ½ cup (2½ ounces) pecans, chopped

**1. FOR THE CAKE:** Adjust an oven rack to the middle position and heat the oven to 350 degrees. Cut two 16-inch lengths of aluminum foil and fold both lengthwise to 5-inch widths. Grease an 8-inch square metal baking dish. Fit the foil pieces into the baking dish, one overlapping the other, pushing them into the corners and up the sides of the pan; allow the excess to overhang the pan edges. Spray the foil lightly with vegetable oil spray.

**2.** Combine the oats and water in a medium bowl and let sit until the water is absorbed, about 5 minutes. In a second medium bowl, whisk the flour, baking soda, baking powder, salt, cinnamon, and nutmeg together.

**3.** In the bowl of a stand mixer fitted with the paddle attachment, beat the butter and sugars on medium speed until combined and the mixture has the consistency of damp sand, 2 to 4 minutes, scraping down the bowl with a rubber spatula halfway through mixing. Add the egg and vanilla; beat until combined, about 30 seconds. Add the flour mixture in two additions and mix until just incorporated, about 30 seconds. Add the soaked oats and mix until combined, about 15 seconds.

**4.** Give the batter a final stir with a rubber spatula to make sure it is thoroughly combined. Transfer the batter to the prepared pan and lightly tap it against the countertop two or three times to settle the batter; smooth the surface with the spatula. Bake the cake until a toothpick inserted into the center comes out with a few crumbs attached, 30 to 35 minutes, rotating the pan halfway through the baking time. Cool the cake slightly in the pan, at least 10 minutes.

**5. FOR THE BROILED ICING:** While the cake cools, adjust an oven rack about 9 inches from the broiler element and heat the broiler. In a medium bowl, whisk the brown sugar, melted butter, and milk together; stir in the coconut and pecans. Spread the mixture evenly over the warm cake. Broil until the topping is bubbling and golden, 3 to 5 minutes.

**6.** Cool the cake in the pan for 1 hour. To remove the cake from the pan, pick up the overhanging edges of the foil and transfer the cake to a platter. Gently push the side of the cake with a knife and remove the foil, one piece at a time. Cut the cake into squares and serve.

## Pear-Walnut Upside-Down Cake

**SERVES** 8 to 10

**WHY THIS RECIPE WORKS** Pears have a subtle floral flavor and graceful shape, but their popularity in desserts has always been a distant second to apples. We wanted to create an elegant cake that really showcased the pears. We settled on Bosc pears, which have dense flesh and hold their shape after baking; cutting the pears into wedges allowed them to be baked raw. For the cake, we opted for a walnut-based version, which was light but sturdy, earthy-tasting, and not too sweet. Lining the cake pan with parchment and removing the cake from the pan after 15 minutes allowed the top to set while preventing the bottom from steaming and turning soggy. We strongly recommend baking this cake in a light-colored cake pan with sides that are at least 2 inches tall. If using a dark-colored pan, start checking for doneness at 1 hour, and note that the cake may dome in the center and the topping may become too sticky. Serve with crème fraîche or lightly sweetened whipped cream.

TOPPING

- 4 tablespoons unsalted butter, melted
- ½ cup packed (3½ ounces) dark brown sugar
- 2 teaspoons cornstarch
- ⅛ teaspoon table salt
- 3 ripe but firm Bosc pears (8 ounces each)

CAKE

- 1 cup walnuts, toasted
- ½ cup (2½ ounces) all-purpose flour
- ½ teaspoon table salt
- ¼ teaspoon baking powder
- ⅛ teaspoon baking soda
- 3 large eggs
- 1 cup (7 ounces) granulated sugar
- 4 tablespoons unsalted butter, melted
- ¼ cup vegetable oil

1. **FOR THE TOPPING:** Adjust oven rack to middle position and heat oven to 300 degrees. Grease 9-inch round cake pan and line bottom with parchment paper. Pour melted butter over bottom of pan and swirl to evenly coat. Combine sugar, cornstarch, and salt in bowl and sprinkle over butter.

2. Peel, halve, and core pears. Set aside 1 pear half and reserve for other use. Cut remaining 5 pear halves into 4 wedges each. Arrange pears in circular pattern around cake pan with tapered ends pointing inward. Arrange 2 smallest pear wedges in center.

3. **FOR THE CAKE:** Pulse walnuts, flour, salt, baking powder, and baking soda in food processor until walnuts are finely ground, 8 to 10 pulses. Transfer walnut mixture to bowl.

4. Process eggs and sugar in now-empty processor until very pale yellow, about 2 minutes. With processor running, add melted butter and oil in steady stream until incorporated. Add walnut mixture and pulse to combine, 4 or 5 pulses. Pour batter evenly over pears (some pear may show through; cake will bake up over fruit).

5. Bake until center of cake is set and bounces back when gently pressed and toothpick inserted in center comes out clean, 1 hour 10 minutes to 1¼ hours, rotating pan after 40 minutes. Let cake cool in pan on wire rack for 15 minutes. Carefully run paring knife or offset spatula around sides of pan. Invert cake onto wire rack set in rimmed baking sheet; discard parchment. Let cake cool completely, about 2 hours. Transfer to serving platter, cut into wedges, and serve.

### UNMOLDING AN UPSIDE-DOWN CAKE

Lining pan with parchment paper ensures that fruit releases cleanly. Let cake rest in pan for just 15 minutes before turning it out onto wire rack.

## Apple Upside-Down Cake

SERVES 8

**WHY THIS RECIPE WORKS** Ever since pineapple came to town, apple upside-down cake has been a bit player and we wanted to change that. This meant creating a rich, buttery cake topped with tightly packed, burnished, sweet apples. Most apples turned mushy and watery and were simply too sweet, but crisp, tart Granny Smiths made the cut. Following the lead of recipes found in our research, we shingled the apples in the pan and poured the cake batter over the top. But once baked and inverted, our apple layer was shrunken and dry. The solution turned out to be increasing the number of apples, for a hefty layer of fruit. This effort yielded better results, but we still found that the apples were overcooked. So we precooked half the apples by sautéing them on the stovetop, then we cut the remainder thin, so they baked through evenly. For the butter cake, we tested milk, buttermilk, yogurt, and sour cream. Sour cream won hands down—its subtle tang balanced the sweetness of the cake and complemented the caramelized apples. And another addition—cornmeal—gave the cake a hint of earthy flavor and a pleasantly coarse texture. We like the slight coarseness that cornmeal adds to the cake, but it's fine to omit it. Golden Delicious apples can be substituted for the Granny Smiths. You will need a 9-inch nonstick cake pan with sides that are at least 2 inches high; anything shallower and the cake will overflow. Alternatively, a 10-inch ovensafe stainless-steel skillet (don't use cast iron) can be used to both cook the apples and bake the cake, with the following modifications: Cook the apples in the skillet and set them aside while mixing the batter (it's OK if the skillet is still warm when the batter is added) and increase the baking time by 7 to 9 minutes. If you don't have either a 2-inch-high cake pan or an ovensafe skillet, use an 8-inch square pan.

TOPPING

- 4 tablespoons (½ stick) unsalted butter, cut into 4 pieces, plus extra for the pan
- 4 Granny Smith apples (about 2 pounds), peeled and cored
- ⅔ cup packed (4⅔ ounces) light brown sugar
- 2 teaspoons juice from 1 lemon

CAKE

- 1 cup (5 ounces) unbleached all-purpose flour
- 1 tablespoon cornmeal (optional)
- 1 teaspoon baking powder
- ½ teaspoon table salt
- ¾ cup (5¼ ounces) granulated sugar
- ¼ cup packed (1¾ ounces) light brown sugar
- 2 large eggs, at room temperature
- 6 tablespoons (¾ stick) unsalted butter, melted and cooled slightly
- ½ cup sour cream
- 1 teaspoon vanilla extract

**1. FOR THE TOPPING:** Butter the bottom and sides of a nonstick 9-inch-wide by 2-inch-high round cake pan; set aside. Adjust an oven rack to the lowest position and heat the oven to 350 degrees.

**2.** Halve the apples from pole to pole. Cut 2 apples into ¼-inch-thick slices; set aside. Cut the remaining 2 apples into ½-inch-thick slices. Melt the butter in a 12-inch skillet over medium-high heat. Add the ½-inch-thick apple slices and cook, stirring two or three times, until the apples begin to caramelize, 4 to 6 minutes. (Do not fully cook the apples.) Add the ¼-inch-thick apple slices, brown sugar, and lemon juice; continue cooking, stirring constantly, until the sugar dissolves and the apples are coated, about 1 minute longer. Transfer the apple mixture to the prepared pan and lightly press into an even layer. Set aside while preparing the cake.

**3. FOR THE CAKE:** Whisk the flour, cornmeal (if using), baking powder, and salt together in a medium bowl; set aside. Whisk the sugars and eggs together in a large bowl until thick and homogeneous, about 45 seconds. Slowly whisk in the butter until combined. Add the sour cream and vanilla; whisk until combined. Add the flour mixture and whisk until just combined. Pour the batter into the pan and spread evenly over the fruit. Lightly tap the pan against the countertop two or three times to settle the batter. Bake until the cake is golden brown and a toothpick inserted into the center comes out clean, 35 to 40 minutes, rotating the pan halfway through the baking time.

**4.** Cool the pan on a wire rack for 20 minutes. Run a small knife around the sides of the cake to loosen. Place a wire rack over the cake pan. Holding the rack tightly, invert the cake pan and wire rack together; lift off the cake pan. Place the wire rack over a baking sheet or large plate to catch any drips. If any fruit sticks to the pan bottom, remove and position it on top of the cake. Cool the cake for 20 minutes (or longer to cool it completely), then transfer it to a serving platter, cut into pieces, and serve.

## Rhubarb Upside-Down Cake

**SERVES 8**

**WHY THIS RECIPE WORKS** This recipe combines the best attributes of two of our favorite rhubarb cakes: a Scandinavian butter cake perfumed with cardamom and lemon and dotted with almonds and crimson-green rhubarb, and a humble upside-down cake. An almond streusel reminiscent of the sugary almond topping of the former provided a substantial, crunchy foundation, and lemon and cardamom in the batter delivered warm, floral notes to highlight the tart, vegetal rhubarb. Enriching the cake with butter, eggs, and sour cream yielded a rich, tender texture with enough structure to support the generous rhubarb topping. Making this cake in an upside-down style encouraged the rhubarb to break down and achieve a sweet, compote-like consistency. You can substitute thawed, drained frozen rhubarb for the fresh. Serve the cake with unsweetened whipped cream, if desired. Red currant jelly is worth seeking out; strawberry and raspberry jam won't produce the same effect.

**STREUSEL**

- ½ cup (2½ ounces) all-purpose flour
- ½ cup sliced almonds
- ¼ cup (1¾ ounces) sugar
- 4 tablespoons unsalted butter, melted
- ¼ teaspoon table salt

**RHUBARB**

- ¾ cup (5¼ ounces) sugar
- 1½ teaspoons cornstarch
- 1 teaspoon grated lemon zest
- 1 pound rhubarb, trimmed and cut into ½-inch pieces
- 2 tablespoons unsalted butter, melted

**CAKE**

- 1 cup (5 ounces) all-purpose flour
- 1½ teaspoons ground cardamom
- 1 teaspoon baking powder
- ½ teaspoon table salt
- 1 cup (7 ounces) sugar
- 2 large eggs
- 6 tablespoons unsalted butter, melted and cooled
- ½ cup sour cream
- 1 teaspoon grated lemon zest plus 1 tablespoon juice
- 1 teaspoon vanilla extract
- 2 tablespoons red currant jelly

**1.** Adjust oven rack to lower-middle position and heat oven to 350 degrees. Grease 8-inch square baking pan, line bottom with parchment paper, and grease parchment.

**2. FOR THE STREUSEL:** Stir all ingredients in medium bowl until well combined. Set aside.

**3. FOR THE RHUBARB:** Whisk sugar, cornstarch, and lemon zest together in large bowl. Add rhubarb and stir well to coat. Drizzle with melted butter and stir to incorporate. Transfer rhubarb mixture to prepared pan and press rhubarb pieces into bottom of pan, making sure there are no large gaps (pieces may not fit in single layer).

**4. FOR THE CAKE:** Whisk flour, cardamom, baking powder, and salt together in medium bowl; set aside. Whisk sugar and eggs in large bowl until thick and homogeneous, about 45 seconds. Whisk in melted butter until combined. Add sour cream, lemon zest and juice, and vanilla; whisk until combined. Add flour mixture and whisk until just combined. Pour batter into pan and spread evenly over rhubarb mixture. Break up streusel with your hands and sprinkle in even layer over batter. Bake until cake is golden brown and toothpick inserted in center comes out clean, 45 to 50 minutes.

**5.** Transfer pan to wire rack and let cool for 20 minutes. Run knife around edges of pan to loosen cake, then invert onto serving platter. Let cool for about 10 minutes. Microwave jelly in small bowl until fluid, about 20 seconds. Using pastry brush, gently dab jelly over rhubarb topping. Serve warm or at room temperature.

## French Apple Cake

**SERVES** 8 to 10

**WHY THIS RECIPE WORKS** For our own version of this classic French dessert, we wanted the best of both worlds: a dessert with a custardy, apple-rich base beneath a light, cakey topping. To ensure that the apple slices softened fully, we microwaved them briefly to break down the enzyme responsible for firming up pectin. And to create two differently textured layers from one batter, we divided the batter and added egg yolks to one part to make the custardy base and added flour to the rest to form the cake layer above it. The microwaved apples should be pliable but not completely soft when cooked. To test for doneness, take one apple slice and try to bend it. If it snaps in half, it's too firm; microwave it for an additional 30 seconds and test again. If Calvados is unavailable, 1 tablespoon of apple brandy or white rum can be substituted.

- 1½ pounds Granny Smith apples, peeled, cored, cut into 8 wedges, and sliced ⅛ inch thick crosswise
- 1 tablespoon Calvados
- 1 teaspoon lemon juice
- 1 cup (5 ounces) plus 2 tablespoons all-purpose flour, divided
- 1 cup (7 ounces) plus 1 tablespoon granulated sugar, divided
- 2 teaspoons baking powder
- ½ teaspoon table salt
- 1 large egg plus 2 large yolks
- 1 cup vegetable oil
- 1 cup whole milk
- 1 teaspoon vanilla extract
- Confectioners' sugar

**1.** Adjust oven rack to lower-middle position and heat oven to 325 degrees. Spray 9-inch springform pan with vegetable oil spray. Place prepared pan on rimmed baking sheet lined with aluminum foil. Place apple slices in microwave-safe pie plate; cover; and microwave until apples are pliable and slightly translucent, about 3 minutes. Toss apple slices with Calvados and lemon juice and let cool for 15 minutes.

**2.** Whisk 1 cup flour, 1 cup granulated sugar, baking powder, and salt together in bowl. Whisk egg, oil, milk, and vanilla in second bowl until smooth. Add dry ingredients to wet ingredients and whisk until just combined. Transfer 1 cup batter to separate bowl and set aside.

**3.** Add egg yolks to remaining batter and whisk to combine. Using spatula, gently fold in cooled apples. Transfer batter to prepared pan; using offset spatula, spread batter evenly to pan edges, gently pressing on apples to create even, compact layer, and smooth surface.

**4.** Whisk remaining 2 tablespoons flour into reserved batter. Pour over batter in pan, spread batter evenly to pan edges, and smooth surface. Sprinkle remaining 1 tablespoon granulated sugar evenly over cake. Bake until center of cake is set, toothpick inserted in center comes out clean, and top is golden brown, about 1¼ hours. Let cake cool in pan on wire rack for 5 minutes. Run thin knife around edge of pan to loosen cake, then let cool completely, 2 to 3 hours. Remove sides of pan and slide thin metal spatula between cake bottom and pan bottom to loosen, then slide cake onto platter. Dust cake lightly with confectioners' sugar before serving.

## Summer Peach Cake

**SERVES** 8

**WHY THIS RECIPE WORKS** Marrying cake with fresh summer peaches, this dessert is a bakery favorite, yet most versions are plagued by soggy cake and barely noticeable peach flavor. We wanted a buttery cake that was moist and not at all soggy, with a golden-brown exterior and plenty of peach flavor. Roasting chunks of peaches tossed in sugar and a little lemon juice helped concentrate their flavor and expel excess moisture before we combined them with our cake batter. However, during roasting, the peach chunks became swathed in a flavorful but unpleasantly gooey film. Coating our roasted peaches in panko bread crumbs before combining them with the batter ensured the film was absorbed by the crumbs, which then dissolved into the cake during baking. To amplify the peach flavor, we tossed the fruit with peach schnapps before roasting, and a little almond extract added to the batter lent a subtle complementary note. Fanning peach slices (macerated with a little more of the schnapps) over the top, sprinkled with almond extract–flavored sugar for a light glaze, ensured our cake looked as good as it tasted. To crush the panko bread crumbs, place them in a zipper-lock bag and smash them with a rolling pin. Orange liqueur can be substituted for the peach schnapps. If using peak-of-season, farm-fresh peaches, omit the peach schnapps.

- 2½ pounds peaches, halved, pitted, and cut into ½-inch wedges
- 5 tablespoons peach schnapps
- 4 teaspoons juice from 1 lemon
- 6 tablespoons plus ⅓ cup (5 ounces) granulated sugar
- 1 cup (5 ounces) unbleached all-purpose flour
- 1¼ teaspoons baking powder
- ¾ teaspoon table salt
- ½ cup packed (3½ ounces) light brown sugar
- 2 large eggs, at room temperature
- 8 tablespoons (1 stick) unsalted butter, melted and cooled
- ¼ cup sour cream
- 1½ teaspoons vanilla extract
- ¼ teaspoon plus ⅛ teaspoon almond extract
- ⅓ cup panko bread crumbs, crushed fine

**1.** Adjust an oven rack to the middle position and heat the oven to 425 degrees. Line a rimmed baking sheet with aluminum foil and spray with vegetable oil spray. Grease and flour a 9-inch springform pan. Gently toss 24 peach wedges with 2 tablespoons of the schnapps, 2 teaspoons of the lemon juice, and 1 tablespoon of the granulated sugar in a bowl; set aside.

**2.** Cut the remaining peach wedges crosswise into 3 chunks. In a large bowl, gently toss the chunks with the remaining 3 tablespoons schnapps, remaining 2 teaspoons lemon juice, and 2 tablespoons more granulated sugar. Spread the peach chunks in a single layer on the prepared baking sheet and bake until the exuded juices begin to thicken and caramelize at the edges of the pan, 20 to 25 minutes. Transfer the pan to a wire rack and let the peaches cool to room temperature, about 30 minutes. Reduce the oven temperature to 350 degrees.

**3.** Whisk the flour, baking powder, and salt together in a bowl. Whisk ⅓ cup more granulated sugar, the brown sugar, and eggs together in a bowl until thick and thoroughly combined, about 45 seconds. Slowly whisk in the butter until combined. Add the sour cream, vanilla, and ¼ teaspoon of the almond extract; whisk until combined. Add the flour mixture and whisk until just combined.

**4.** Pour half of the batter into the prepared pan. Using an offset spatula, spread the batter evenly to the pan edges and smooth the top. Sprinkle the crushed panko evenly over the cooled peach chunks and toss gently to coat. Arrange the peach chunks on the batter in the pan in an even layer, gently pressing the peaches into the batter. Gently spread the remaining batter over the peach chunks and smooth the top. Arrange the reserved peach wedges, slightly overlapped, in a ring over the surface of the batter, placing the smaller wedges in the center. Stir the remaining 3 tablespoons granulated sugar and the remaining ⅛ teaspoon almond extract together in a small bowl until the sugar is moistened. Sprinkle the sugar mixture evenly over the top of the cake.

**5.** Bake until the center of the cake is set and a toothpick inserted in the center comes out clean, 50 to 60 minutes. Transfer the pan to a wire rack and let cool for 5 minutes. Run a thin knife between the cake and the sides of the pan; remove the sides of the pan. Let the cake cool completely, 2 to 3 hours, before serving.

## Simple Carrot Cake with Cream Cheese Frosting

**SERVES** 15 to 18

**WHY THIS RECIPE WORKS** Once considered a healthier dessert option, carrot cake was heralded for its use of vegetable oil in place of butter and carrots as a natural sweetener. Sure, the carrots add some sweetness, but they also add a lot of moisture, which is why carrot cake is invariably soggy. And oil? It makes this cake dense and, well, oily. We wanted a moist, rich cake with a tight and tender crumb and balanced spice. For lift, we liked a combination of baking soda and baking powder. Some carrot cakes use a heavy hand with the spices and taste too much like spice cake. We took a conservative approach and used modest amounts of cinnamon, nutmeg, and cloves. After trying varying amounts of grated carrots, we settled on 3 cups for a pleasantly moist texture. One and one-half cups of vegetable oil gave us a rich, but not greasy, cake. Cream cheese frosting is the perfect partner to carrot cake—we enriched our version with sour cream for extra tang and vanilla for depth of flavor. You can serve the cake right out of the pan, in which case you'll only need 3 cups of frosting for the top of the cake.

- 2½ cups (12½ ounces) unbleached all-purpose flour
- 1¼ teaspoons ground cinnamon
- 1¼ teaspoons baking powder
- 1 teaspoon baking soda
- ½ teaspoon table salt
- ½ teaspoon ground nutmeg
- ⅛ teaspoon ground cloves
- 4 large eggs, at room temperature
- 1½ cups (10½ ounces) granulated sugar
- ½ cup packed (3½ ounces) light brown sugar
- 1½ cups vegetable oil
- 1 pound carrots (about 6 medium), peeled and grated (about 3 cups)
- 4 cups Cream Cheese Frosting

**1.** Adjust an oven rack to the middle position and heat the oven to 350 degrees. Grease a 13 by 9-inch baking pan, then line the bottom with parchment paper. Whisk the flour, cinnamon, baking powder, baking soda, salt, nutmeg, and cloves together in a medium bowl.

**2.** In a large bowl, whisk the eggs and sugars together until the sugars are mostly dissolved and the mixture is frothy. Continue to whisk, while slowly drizzling in the oil, until thoroughly combined and emulsified. Whisk in the flour mixture until just incorporated. Stir in the carrots.

**3.** Give the batter a final stir with a rubber spatula to make sure it is thoroughly combined. Scrape the batter into the prepared pan, smooth the top, and lightly tap the pan against the countertop two or three times to settle the batter. Bake the cake until a toothpick inserted in the center comes out with a few moist crumbs attached, 35 to 40 minutes, rotating the pan halfway through the baking time.

**4.** Cool the cake completely in the pan, set on a wire rack, about 2 hours. Run a small knife around the edge of the cake and flip the cake out onto a wire rack. Peel off the parchment paper, then flip the cake right side up onto a serving platter. Spread the frosting evenly over the top and sides of the cake and serve.

### Cream Cheese Frosting

**MAKE** about 4 cups

If the frosting becomes too soft to work with, let it chill in the refrigerator until firm.

- 2 (8-ounce) packages cream cheese, softened
- 10 tablespoons (1¼ sticks) unsalted butter, cut into chunks and softened
- 2 tablespoons sour cream
- 1½ teaspoons vanilla extract
- ¼ teaspoon table salt
- 2 cups (8 ounces) confectioners' sugar

**1.** Beat the cream cheese, butter, sour cream, vanilla, and salt together in a large bowl with an electric mixer on medium-high speed until smooth, 2 to 4 minutes.

**2.** Reduce the mixer speed to medium-low, slowly add the confectioners' sugar, and beat until smooth, 4 to 6 minutes. Increase the mixer speed to medium-high and beat until the frosting is light and fluffy, 4 to 6 minutes.

## Classic Gingerbread Cake

**SERVES** 8

**WHY THIS RECIPE WORKS** Most recipes for gingerbread suffer from a dense, sunken center, and flavors range from barely gingery to over-the-top spicy. Our ideal gingerbread should be moist through and through and utterly simple. Focusing on flavor first, we bumped up the ginger with both a hefty dose of ground ginger and grated fresh ginger. Cinnamon and freshly ground pepper produced a complex, lingering heat. Dark stout, gently heated to minimize its booziness, had a bittersweet flavor that brought out the caramel undertones of the molasses. Finally, swapping out the butter for vegetable oil and replacing some of the brown sugar with granulated let the spice flavors come through. To prevent a sunken center, we looked at our leaveners first. Baking powder isn't as effective at leavening if too many other acidic ingredients are present in the batter. Incorporating the baking soda with the wet ingredients instead of the other dry ones helped to neutralize those acidic ingredients before they got incorporated into the batter and allowed the baking powder to do a better job. While stirring is typically the enemy of tenderness since it develops the flour's gluten, our batter was so loose that vigorous stirring actually gave our gingerbread the structure necessary to further ensure the center didn't collapse. With that, we had a flawless cake with plenty of spice and warmth. This cake packs potent yet well-balanced spice. If you prefer less spice, you can decrease the amount of ground ginger to 1 tablespoon. Avoid opening the oven door until the minimum baking time has elapsed. Serve the gingerbread plain or with lightly sweetened whipped cream.

- ¾ cup stout, such as Guinness
- ½ teaspoon baking soda
- ⅔ cup molasses
- ¾ cup (5¼ ounces) packed light brown sugar
- ¼ cup (1¾ ounces) granulated sugar
- 1½ cups (7½ ounces) unbleached all-purpose flour
- 2 tablespoons ground ginger
- ½ teaspoon baking powder
- ½ teaspoon table salt
- ¼ teaspoon ground cinnamon
- ¼ teaspoon ground black pepper
- 2 large eggs, at room temperature
- ⅓ cup vegetable oil
- 1 tablespoon grated fresh ginger

**1.** Adjust an oven rack to the middle position and heat the oven to 350 degrees. Grease an 8-inch square baking pan, line with parchment paper, grease the parchment, and flour the pan.

**2.** Bring the stout to a boil in a medium saucepan over medium heat, stirring occasionally. Remove from the heat and stir in the baking soda (the mixture will foam vigorously). When the foaming subsides, stir in the molasses, brown sugar, and granulated sugar until dissolved; set aside. Whisk the flour, ground ginger, baking powder, salt, cinnamon, and pepper together in a large bowl.

**3.** Transfer the stout mixture to a second large bowl. Whisk in the eggs, oil, and grated ginger until combined. Whisk the wet mixture into the flour mixture in thirds, stirring vigorously until completely smooth after each addition.

**4.** Scrape the batter into the prepared pan, smooth the top with a rubber spatula, and gently tap the pan on the counter to release any air bubbles. Bake until the top of the cake is just firm to the touch and a toothpick inserted into the center comes out clean, 35 to 45 minutes. Let the cake cool in the pan on a wire rack, about 1½ hours, before serving.

## Spice Cake

**SERVES** 15 to 18

**WHY THIS RECIPE WORKS** The problem with spice cakes? Spice. Some variations suffer from spice overload, which makes them gritty and dusty. Others are so lacking in spice flavor that it seems as if a cinnamon stick has only been waved in their general direction. We wanted an old-fashioned, moist, and substantial spice cake with spices that were warm and bold without being overpowering. We needed a less-than-tender cake, one with a substantial and open crumb that could stand up to the spices. We found that all-purpose flour, rather than cake flour, added volume and heft. Butter and eggs contributed richness. We bloomed the spices in butter, a process that intensified their aromas and gave the cake a heightened spice impact throughout. We used the classic mixture of cinnamon, cloves, cardamom, allspice, and nutmeg, but found that a tablespoon of grated fresh ginger and a couple of tablespoons of molasses gave the cake an extra zing. And reserving a little of the spice mixture to add to the cream cheese frosting united the frosting and the cake. You can serve the cake right out of the pan, in which case you'll only need 3 cups of frosting for the top of the cake.

- 1 tablespoon ground cinnamon
- ¾ teaspoon ground cardamom
- ½ teaspoon ground allspice
- ½ teaspoon ground cloves
- ¼ teaspoon ground nutmeg
- 16 tablespoons (2 sticks) unsalted butter, cut into 16 pieces and softened
- 2¼ cups (11¼ ounces) all-purpose flour
- ½ teaspoon baking powder
- ½ teaspoon baking soda
- ½ teaspoon table salt
- 2 large whole eggs plus 3 large egg yolks, at room temperature
- 1 teaspoon vanilla extract
- 1¾ cups (12¼ ounces) sugar
- 2 tablespoons light or mild molasses
- 1 tablespoon minced or grated fresh ginger
- 1 cup buttermilk, room temperature
- 4 cups Cream Cheese Frosting (page 869)

**1.** Adjust an oven rack to the middle position and heat the oven to 350 degrees. Grease a 13 by 9-inch baking pan, then line the bottom with parchment paper.

**2.** Combine the cinnamon, cardamom, allspice, cloves, and nutmeg in a small bowl; reserve ½ teaspoon of the spice mixture for the frosting. Melt 4 tablespoons of the butter in a small skillet over medium heat and continue to cook, swirling the pan constantly, until the butter is light brown, 3 to 6 minutes. Stir in the spice mixture and cook until fragrant, about 15 seconds. Set the mixture aside to cool slightly.

**3.** In a medium bowl, whisk the flour, baking powder, baking soda, and salt together. In a small bowl, whisk the whole eggs, egg yolks, and vanilla together.

**4.** In a stand mixer fitted with the paddle attachment, beat the remaining 12 tablespoons butter, the sugar, and molasses on medium-high speed until light and fluffy, 3 to 6 minutes; scrape down the bowl with a rubber spatula. Beat in the ginger, cooled butter-spice mixture, and half of the egg mixture until combined, about 30 seconds. Beat in the remaining egg mixture until combined, about 30 seconds, and scrape down the bowl again.

**5.** Reduce the mixer speed to low and beat in one-third of the flour mixture, followed by half of the buttermilk. Repeat with half of the remaining flour mixture and the remaining buttermilk. Beat in the remaining flour mixture until just combined; scrape down the bowl.

**6.** Give the batter a final stir with a rubber spatula to make sure it is thoroughly combined. Scrape the batter into the prepared pan, smooth the top, and lightly tap the pan against the countertop two or three times to settle the batter. Bake the cake until a toothpick inserted in the center comes out with a few moist crumbs attached, 30 to 35 minutes, rotating the pan halfway through the baking time.

**7.** Cool the cake completely in the pan, set on a wire rack, about 2 hours. Run a small knife around the edge of the cake and flip the cake out onto a wire rack. Peel off the parchment paper, then flip the cake right side up onto a serving platter. Stir the reserved spice mixture into the frosting, spread the frosting evenly over the top and sides of the cake, and serve.

## Best Almond Cake

**SERVES** 8 to 10

**WHY THIS RECIPE WORKS** Simple, rich almond cake makes a sophisticated dessert, but traditional European versions can be heavy and dense. For a slightly cakier version with plenty of nutty flavor, we swapped out traditional almond paste for toasted, blanched sliced almonds and added a bit of almond extract for extra depth. Lemon zest in the batter provided citrusy brightness. For a lighter crumb, we increased the flour slightly and added baking powder. Making the batter in a food processor broke down some of the protein structure in the eggs, ensuring that the cake had a level, not domed, top. We swapped some butter for oil and lowered the oven temperature to produce an evenly baked, moist cake. For a finishing touch, we topped the cake with sliced almonds and lemon-infused sugar. If you can't find blanched sliced almonds, grind slivered almonds for the batter and use unblanched sliced almonds for the topping. Serve plain or with Orange Crème Fraîche (recipe follows).

- 1½ cups (5¼ ounces) plus ⅓ cup blanched sliced almonds, toasted, divided
- ¾ cup (3¾ ounces) all-purpose flour
- ¾ teaspoon table salt
- ¼ teaspoon baking powder
- ⅛ teaspoon baking soda
- 4 large eggs
- 1¼ cups (8¾ ounces) plus 2 tablespoons sugar, divided

- 1 tablespoon plus ½ teaspoon grated lemon zest (2 lemons), divided
- ¾ teaspoon almond extract
- 5 tablespoons unsalted butter, melted
- ⅓ cup vegetable oil

**1.** Adjust oven rack to middle position and heat oven to 300 degrees. Grease 9-inch round cake pan and line with parchment paper. Pulse 1½ cups almonds, flour, salt, baking powder, and baking soda in food processor until almonds are finely ground, 5 to 10 pulses. Transfer almond mixture to bowl.

**2.** Process eggs, 1¼ cups sugar, 1 tablespoon lemon zest, and almond extract in now-empty processor until very pale yellow, about 2 minutes. With processor running, add melted butter and oil in steady stream, until incorporated. Add almond mixture and pulse to combine, 4 or 5 pulses. Transfer batter to prepared pan.

**3.** Using your fingers, combine remaining 2 tablespoons sugar and remaining ½ teaspoon lemon zest in small bowl until fragrant, 5 to 10 seconds. Sprinkle top of cake evenly with remaining ⅓ cup almonds followed by sugar-zest mixture.

**4.** Bake until center of cake is set and bounces back when gently pressed and toothpick inserted in center comes out clean, 55 minutes to 1 hour 5 minutes, rotating pan after 40 minutes. Let cake cool in pan on wire rack for 15 minutes. Run paring knife around sides of pan. Invert cake onto greased wire rack, discard parchment, and reinvert cake onto second wire rack. Let cake cool completely, about 2 hours. Cut into wedges and serve. (Leftover cake can be wrapped tightly in plastic wrap and stored at room temperature for up to 3 days.)

## Orange Crème Fraîche

**MAKES** 2 cups

- 2 oranges
- 1 cup crème fraîche
- 2 tablespoons sugar
- ⅛ teaspoon salt

Grate 1 teaspoon zest from 1 orange. Cut away peel and pith from oranges. Slice between membranes to release segments and cut segments into ¼-inch pieces. Combine orange pieces and zest, crème fraîche, sugar, and salt in bowl and mix well. Refrigerate for 1 hour.

## Financiers (Almond–Browned Butter Cakes)

**MAKES** 24 cakes

**WHY THIS RECIPE WORKS** It is said that financiers were created in the late 19th century by a pâtissier whose shop was located near the Paris stock exchange as treats for bankers to enjoy on the go. Making these elegant little cakes requires only six ingredients and they bake in less than 15 minutes. For financiers with complex almond flavor and contrasting textures, we started by spraying a mini-muffin tin with baking spray with flour. The flour in the spray helped the sides of the cakes rise along with the center, preventing doming. We then stirred together almond flour, sugar, all-purpose flour, and egg whites. We opted for granulated sugar, which doesn't totally dissolve in the egg whites, to ensure a pleasantly coarse texture. Once these ingredients were whisked together, it was just a matter of stirring in nutty browned butter and baking the cakes. These two-bite treats were easy to customize so we created a variety of add-ins including fresh fruit, dark chocolate chunks, and nuts. You'll need a 24-cup mini-muffin tin for this recipe. Because egg whites can vary in size, measuring the whites by weight or volume is essential. Baking spray with flour ensures that the cakes bake up with appropriately flat tops; we don't recommend substituting vegetable oil spray in this recipe.

- 5 tablespoons unsalted butter
- ¾ cup (3 ounces) finely ground almond flour
- ½ cup plus 1 tablespoon (4 ounces) sugar
- 2 tablespoons all-purpose flour
- ⅛ teaspoon table salt
- ⅓ cup (3 ounces) egg whites (3 to 4 large eggs)

**1.** Adjust oven rack to middle position and heat oven to 375 degrees. Generously spray 24-cup mini-muffin tin with baking spray with flour. Melt butter in 10-inch skillet over medium-high heat. Cook, stirring and scraping skillet constantly with rubber spatula, until milk solids are dark golden brown and butter has nutty aroma, 1 to 3 minutes. Immediately transfer butter to heatproof bowl.

**2.** Whisk almond flour, sugar, all-purpose flour, and salt together in second bowl. Add egg whites. Using rubber spatula, stir until combined, mashing any lumps against side of bowl until mixture is smooth. Stir in butter until incorporated. Distribute batter evenly among prepared muffin cups (cups will be about half full).

**3.** Bake until edges are well browned and tops are golden, about 14 minutes, rotating muffin tin halfway through baking. Remove tin from oven and immediately invert wire rack on top of tin. Invert rack and tin; carefully remove tin. Turn cakes right side up and let cool for at least 20 minutes before serving. (To enjoy the crisp edges of the cakes, the cakes are best eaten on the day they are baked; leftovers can be stored in an airtight container at room temperature for up to 3 days.)

### Fresh Fruit Financiers

Place 1 small raspberry on its side on top of each cake (do not press into batter). Or pit 1 small firm plum, peach, apricot, or nectarine and cut into 6 wedges. Slice each wedge crosswise ¼ inch thick. Shingle 2 slices on top of each cake (do not press into batter) before baking.

### Chocolate Chunk Financiers

Place one ½-inch dark chocolate chunk on top of each cake (do not press into batter) before baking.

### Nut Financiers

Sprinkle lightly toasted sliced almonds on top of batter. Or substitute ¾ cup (3 ounces) shelled untoasted pistachios, hazelnuts, pecans, or whole unblanched almonds for almond flour. Process nuts and all-purpose flour in food processor until finely ground, about 1 minute, scraping down sides of bowl twice during processing.

## Pouding Chômeur (Maple Syrup Cake)

**SERVES** 6 to 8

**WHY THIS RECIPE WORKS** This Quebecois dessert was born during the cold winters of the Great Depression, when it transformed a few humble ingredients—stale bread, milk, and brown sugar—into a sweet, comforting treat. As the economy improved, the frugal recipe evolved into something quite decadent, as the sugar was traded for maple syrup, the milk for cream, and a coarse-crumbed egg-and-butter-rich cake batter took the place of the bread. To make it, we whisked together the batter, spread it into a baking dish, and then poured the maple syrup–heavy cream mixture on top; the two layers mingled and then inverted during baking, so the cake became lusciously gooey, floating atop a bubbling pool of maple cream sauce. To ensure that the cake and sauce stayed mostly separate, we added more flour to provide structure and more butter to "waterproof" the batter. Making the cake in the top half of a 375-degree oven made sure that the top of the cake caramelized thanks to the reflected heat. The cake is best served hot; for this reason, we prefer using a glass baking dish, which retains heat well, but a metal baking pan will also work. The color of syrup labeled Grade A Dark Amber will contrast best against the yellow cake. Serve with a dollop of crème fraîche or a scoop of vanilla or coffee ice cream.

- 1 cup maple syrup, preferably dark amber
- 1 cup heavy cream
- 1 teaspoon table salt, divided
- 1¼ cups (6¼ ounces) all-purpose flour
- 3 tablespoons sugar

- 1½ teaspoons baking powder
- ⅔ cup milk
- 2 large eggs
- ½ teaspoon vanilla extract
- 6 tablespoons unsalted butter, melted

**1.** Adjust oven rack 6 inches from top of oven and heat oven to 375 degrees. Heat maple syrup, cream, and ½ teaspoon salt in medium saucepan over medium heat until simmering, about 5 minutes. Off heat, whisk to combine, then transfer to heatproof 2-cup liquid measuring cup.

**2.** Whisk flour, sugar, baking powder, and remaining ½ teaspoon salt together in large bowl. Whisk milk, eggs, and vanilla in second bowl until combined. Whisk milk mixture into flour mixture until combined. Add melted butter and whisk until smooth. Transfer batter to 8-inch square baking dish set in rimmed baking sheet and spread into even layer with spatula. Pour syrup mixture slowly down corner of baking dish so it flows gently over top of cake batter.

**3.** Bake until deep golden brown and toothpick inserted in center of cake layer comes out clean, 30 to 35 minutes. Let cool on wire rack for 10 minutes. Use serving spoon to scoop onto plates, inverting each spoonful so sauce is on top. Serve.

## Gâteau Breton with Apricot Filling

**SERVES** 8

**WHY THIS RECIPE WORKS** The rich, dense texture of gâteau Breton lies somewhere between shortbread and pound cake. To avoid introducing too much air into the batter of our French butter cake, which would lead to a fluffy, airy texture, we creamed the butter and sugar for only 3 minutes before adding the egg yolks and flour. Briefly freezing a layer of the batter in the cake pan helped us spread a bright homemade apricot filling onto the batter. The pan then went back into the freezer to firm so that the top layer of batter could also easily be added. All that was left to do was pretty up the cake with an egg wash and diamond-patterned design. We strongly prefer the flavor of California apricots in the filling. Mediterranean (or Turkish) apricots can be used, but increase the amount of lemon juice to 2 tablespoons. This cake is traditionally served plain with coffee or tea but can be dressed up with fresh berries, if desired.

**FILLING**

- ⅔ cup water
- ½ cup dried California apricots, chopped
- ⅓ cup (2⅓ ounces) sugar
- 1 tablespoon lemon juice

**CAKE**

- 16 tablespoons (2 sticks) unsalted butter, softened
- ¾ cup plus 2 tablespoons (6⅛ ounces) sugar
- 6 large egg yolks (1 lightly beaten with 1 teaspoon water)
- 2 tablespoons dark rum
- 1 teaspoon vanilla extract
- 2 cups (10 ounces) all-purpose flour
- ½ teaspoon table salt

**1. FOR THE FILLING:** Process water and apricots in blender until uniformly pureed, about 2 minutes. Transfer puree to 10-inch nonstick skillet and stir in sugar. Set skillet over medium heat and cook, stirring frequently, until puree has darkened slightly and rubber spatula leaves distinct trail when dragged across bottom of pan, 10 to 12 minutes. Transfer filling to bowl and stir in lemon juice. Refrigerate filling until cool to touch, about 15 minutes.

**2. FOR THE CAKE:** Adjust oven rack to lower-middle position and heat oven to 350 degrees. Grease 9-inch round cake pan.

**3.** Using stand mixer fitted with paddle, beat butter on medium-high speed until smooth and lightened in color, 1 to 2 minutes. Add sugar and continue to beat until pale and fluffy, about 3 minutes longer. Add 5 egg yolks, one at a time, and beat until combined. Scrape down bowl, add rum and vanilla, and mix until incorporated, about 1 minute. Reduce speed to low, add flour and salt, and mix until flour is just incorporated, about 30 seconds. Give batter final stir by hand.

**4.** Spoon half of batter into bottom of prepared pan. Using small offset spatula, spread batter into even layer. Freeze for 10 minutes.

**5.** Spread ½ cup filling in even layer over chilled batter, leaving ¾-inch border around edge (reserve remaining filling for another use). Freeze for 10 minutes.

**6.** Gently spread remaining batter over filling. Using offset spatula, carefully smooth top of batter. Brush with egg yolk wash. Using tines of fork, make light scores in surface of cake, spaced about 1½ inches apart, in diamond pattern, being careful not to score all the way to sides of pan. Bake until top is golden brown and edges of cake start to pull away from sides of pan, 45 to 50 minutes. Let cake cool in pan on wire rack for 30 minutes. Run paring knife between cake and sides of pan, remove cake from pan, and let cool completely on rack, about 1 hour. Cut into wedges and serve.

## Carrot Layer Cake

**SERVES** 10 to 12

**WHY THIS RECIPE WORKS** We wanted to reengineer the humble carrot cake as a four-tier, nut-crusted confection that could claim its place among the most glamorous desserts. To start, we found that baking this cake in a half sheet pan meant that it baked and cooled in far less time than a conventional layer cake, and—cut into quarters—it produced four thin, level layers that did not require splitting or trimming. Extra baking soda raised the pH of the batter, ensuring that the coarsely shredded carrots softened during the shortened baking time. Shred the carrots on the large holes of a box grater or in a food processor fitted with the shredding disk. Do not substitute liquid buttermilk for the buttermilk powder. To ensure the proper spreading consistency for the frosting, use cold cream cheese. If your baked cake is of an uneven thickness, adjust the orientation of the layers as they are stacked to produce a level cake. Assembling this cake on a cardboard cake round trimmed to about an 8 by 6-inch rectangle makes it easy to press the pecans onto the sides of the frosted cake.

**CAKE**

- 1¾ cups (8¾ ounces) all-purpose flour
- 2 teaspoons baking powder
- 1 teaspoon baking soda
- 1½ teaspoons ground cinnamon
- ¾ teaspoon ground nutmeg
- ½ teaspoon table salt
- ¼ teaspoon ground cloves
- 1¼ cups packed (8¾ ounces) light brown sugar
- ¾ cup vegetable oil
- 3 large eggs
- 1 teaspoon vanilla extract
- 2⅔ cups shredded carrots (4 carrots)
- ⅔ cup dried currants

**FROSTING**

- 3 cups (12 ounces) confectioners' sugar
- 16 tablespoons unsalted butter, softened
- ⅓ cup buttermilk powder
- 2 teaspoons vanilla extract
- ¼ teaspoon table salt
- 12 ounces cream cheese, chilled and cut into 12 equal pieces
- 2 cups (8 ounces) pecans, toasted and chopped coarse

**1. FOR THE CAKE:** Adjust oven rack to middle position and heat oven to 350 degrees. Grease 18 by 13-inch rimmed baking sheet, line with parchment paper, and grease parchment. Whisk flour, baking powder, baking soda, cinnamon, nutmeg, salt, and cloves together in large bowl.

**2.** Whisk sugar, oil, eggs, and vanilla in second bowl until mixture is smooth. Stir in carrots and currants. Add flour mixture and fold with rubber spatula until mixture is just combined.

**3.** Transfer batter to prepared sheet and smooth surface with offset spatula. Bake until center of cake is firm to touch, 15 to 18 minutes. Let cool in pan on wire rack for 5 minutes. Invert cake onto wire rack (do not remove parchment), then reinvert onto second wire rack. Let cake cool completely, about 30 minutes.

**4. FOR THE FROSTING:** Using stand mixer fitted with paddle, beat sugar, butter, buttermilk powder, vanilla, and salt on low speed until smooth, about 2 minutes, scraping down bowl as needed. Increase speed to medium-low; add cream cheese, 1 piece at a time; and mix until smooth, about 2 minutes.

**5.** Transfer cooled cake to cutting board, parchment side down. Using sharp chef's knife, cut cake and parchment in half crosswise, then lengthwise into 4 even quarters.

**6.** Place 8 by 6-inch cardboard rectangle on cake platter. Place 1 cake layer, parchment side up, on cardboard and carefully remove parchment. Using offset spatula, spread ⅔ cup frosting evenly over top, right to edge of cake. Repeat with 2 more layers of cake, pressing lightly to adhere and frosting each layer with ⅔ cup frosting. Top with last cake layer and spread 1 cup frosting evenly over top. Spread remaining frosting evenly over sides of cake. (It's fine if some crumbs show through frosting on sides, but if you go back to smooth top of cake, be sure that spatula is free of crumbs.)

**7.** Hold cake with your hand and gently press chopped pecans onto sides with your other hand. Chill for at least 1 hour before serving. (Frosted cake can be refrigerated for up to 24 hours before serving.)

## Coconut Layer Cake

**SERVES** 10 to 12

**WHY THIS RECIPE WORKS** Our coconut cake is perfumed inside and out with the cool, subtle essence of coconut. Its layers of snowy white cake are moist and tender, with a delicate, yielding crumb, and the icing is a silky, gently sweetened coat covered with a deep drift of downy coconut. For this type of cake, we found a traditional butter cake to be best. To infuse the cake with maximum coconut flavor, we relied on coconut extract and cream of coconut in the cake and the buttercream icing. We coated the cake with a generous amount of toasted shredded coconut for textural interest and a final dose of flavor. Be sure to use cream of coconut (such as Coco López), and not coconut milk here. One 15-ounce can of cream of coconut is enough for both the cake and the frosting.

**CAKE**

- 1 large egg plus 5 large whites
- ¾ cup cream of coconut
- ¼ cup water
- 1 teaspoon coconut extract
- 1 teaspoon vanilla extract
- 2¼ cups (9 ounces) cake flour
- 1 cup (7 ounces) granulated sugar
- 1 tablespoon baking powder
- ¾ teaspoon table salt
- 12 tablespoons unsalted butter, cut into 12 pieces and softened
- 2 cups (6 ounces) sweetened shredded coconut

**FROSTING**

- 4 large egg whites
- 1 cup (7 ounces) granulated sugar
- Pinch table salt
- 1 pound (4 sticks) unsalted butter, each stick cut into 6 pieces and softened
- ¼ cup cream of coconut
- 1 teaspoon coconut extract
- 1 teaspoon vanilla extract

**1. FOR THE CAKE:** Adjust oven rack to lower-middle position and heat oven to 325 degrees. Grease two 9-inch round cake pans, line with parchment paper, grease parchment, and flour pans. Whisk egg and whites together in 4-cup liquid measuring cup. Whisk in cream of coconut, water, coconut extract, and vanilla.

**2.** Using stand mixer fitted with paddle, mix flour, sugar, baking powder, and salt on low speed until combined. Add butter, 1 piece at a time, until only pea-size pieces remain, about 1 minute. Add half of egg mixture, increase speed to medium-high, and beat until light and fluffy, about 1 minute. Reduce speed to medium-low, add remaining egg mixture, and beat until incorporated, about 30 seconds. Give batter final stir by hand.

**3.** Divide batter evenly between prepared pans and smooth tops with rubber spatula. Gently tap pans on counter to settle batter. Bake until toothpick inserted in center comes out clean, about 30 minutes, switching and rotating pans halfway through baking.

**4.** Let cakes cool in pans on wire rack for 10 minutes. Remove cakes from pans, discarding parchment, and let cool completely on rack, about 2 hours. (Cake layers can be wrapped tightly in plastic wrap and stored at room temperature for up to 24 hours. To freeze, wrap layers in plastic wrap and aluminum foil for up to 1 month; defrost cakes at room temperature.) Meanwhile spread shredded coconut on rimmed baking sheet and toast in oven until shreds are mix of golden brown and white, 15 to 20 minutes, stirring 2 or 3 times; let cool.

**5. FOR THE FROSTING:** Combine egg whites, sugar, and salt in bowl of stand mixer and set over medium saucepan filled with 1 inch barely simmering water, making sure that water does not touch bottom of bowl. Cook, whisking constantly, until mixture is opaque and registers 120 degrees, about 2 minutes.

**6.** Remove bowl from heat and transfer to stand mixer fitted with whisk attachment. Whip egg white mixture on high speed until glossy, sticky, and barely warm (80 degrees), about 7 minutes. Reduce speed to medium-high and whip in butter, 1 piece at a time, followed by cream of coconut, coconut extract, and vanilla, scraping down bowl as needed. Continue to whip until combined, about 1 minute.

**7.** Using long serrated knife, cut 1 horizontal line around sides of each layer; then, following scored lines, cut each layer into 2 even layers.

**8.** Line edges of cake platter with 4 strips of parchment to keep platter clean. Place 1 cake layer on platter. Spread ¾ cup frosting evenly over top, right to edge of cake. Repeat with 2 more cake layers, pressing lightly to adhere and spreading ¾ cup frosting evenly over each layer. Top with remaining cake layer and spread remaining frosting evenly over top and sides of cake. Sprinkle top of cake evenly with toasted coconut, then gently press remaining toasted coconut onto sides. Carefully remove parchment strips before serving. (Frosted cake can be refrigerated for up to 24 hours. Bring to room temperature before serving.)

## Gingerbread Layer Cake

**SERVES** 12 to 16

**WHY THIS RECIPE WORKS** We wanted the dark, moist crumb and spicy bite of gingerbread in a tender, sophisticated layer cake. For fiery flavor, we added 2 tablespoons each of ground ginger and freshly grated ginger, and we enhanced that heat with both white pepper and cayenne pepper. Molasses and coffee contributed moisture, rich color, and pleasantly bitter notes that worked well with the spices and sweetness. Cocoa powder, an unexpected ingredient in gingerbread, added depth to the color and the flavor and, as it is mostly gluten-free starch and fat, it increased the cake's tenderness. To avoid the challenge of slicing thicker layers in half horizontally, we baked four thin layers in two batches. Finally, a silky, fluffy, and not-too-sweet ermine frosting, made by beating softened butter into a cooked gel made with milk, sugar, and starch, showed off the spicy, tender cake to its best advantage. Transferring the milk mixture to a wide bowl will ensure that it cools within 2 hours. A rasp-style grater makes quick work of grating the ginger. Use a 2-cup liquid measuring cup to portion the cake batter. Baking four thin cake layers two at a time eliminates the need to halve thicker layers. Do not use blackstrap molasses here, as it is too bitter.

**FROSTING**

- 1½ cups (10½ ounces) sugar
- ¼ cup (1¼ ounces) all-purpose flour
- 3 tablespoons cornstarch
- ½ teaspoon table salt
- 1½ cups milk
- 24 tablespoons (3 sticks) unsalted butter, softened
- 2 teaspoons vanilla extract

**CAKE**

- 1¾ cups (8¾ ounces) all-purpose flour
- ¼ cup (¾ ounce) unsweetened cocoa powder
- 2 tablespoons ground ginger
- 1½ teaspoons baking powder
- 1 teaspoon ground cinnamon
- ¾ teaspoon table salt
- ½ teaspoon ground white pepper
- ⅛ teaspoon cayenne pepper
- 1 cup brewed coffee
- ¾ cup molasses
- ½ teaspoon baking soda
- 1½ cups (10½ ounces) sugar
- ¾ cup vegetable oil
- 3 large eggs, beaten
- 2 tablespoons finely grated fresh ginger
- ¼ cup chopped crystallized ginger (optional)

**1. FOR THE FROSTING:** Whisk sugar, flour, cornstarch, and salt together in medium saucepan. Slowly whisk in milk until smooth. Cook over medium heat, whisking constantly and scraping corners of saucepan, until mixture is boiling and is very thick, 5 to 7 minutes. Transfer milk mixture to wide bowl and let cool completely, about 2 hours.

**2. FOR THE CAKE:** Adjust oven rack to middle position and heat oven to 350 degrees. Grease and flour two 8-inch round cake pans and line pans with parchment paper. Whisk flour, cocoa, ground ginger, baking powder, cinnamon, salt, white pepper, and cayenne together in large bowl. Whisk coffee, molasses, and baking soda in second large bowl until combined. Add sugar, oil, eggs, and fresh ginger to coffee mixture and whisk until smooth.

**3.** Whisk coffee mixture into flour mixture until smooth. Pour 1⅓ cups batter into each prepared pan. Bake until toothpick inserted in center of cake comes out clean, 12 to 14 minutes. Let cakes cool in pans on wire rack for 10 minutes. Invert cakes onto wire rack and peel off parchment; reinvert cakes. Wipe pans clean with paper towels. Grease and flour pans and line with fresh parchment. Repeat baking and cooling process with remaining batter.

**4.** Using stand mixer fitted with paddle, beat butter on medium-high speed until light and fluffy, about 5 minutes. Add cooled milk mixture and vanilla; mix on medium speed until combined, scraping down bowl if necessary. Increase speed to medium-high and beat until frosting is light and fluffy, 3 to 5 minutes.

**5.** Place 1 cake layer on platter or cardboard round. Using offset spatula, spread ¾ cup frosting evenly over top, right to edge of cake. Repeat stacking and frosting with 2 more cake layers and 1½ cups frosting. Place final cake layer on top and spread remaining frosting evenly over top and sides of cake. Garnish top of cake with crystallized ginger, if using. Refrigerate cake until frosting is set, about 30 minutes. (Cake can be refrigerated, covered, for up to 2 days. Let cake come to room temperature before serving.)

## Easy Caramel Cake

**SERVES 8**

---

**WHY THIS RECIPE WORKS** A Southern favorite, caramel cake boasts a rich toffee-flavored caramel frosting spread over yellow cake layers. But the best part—the caramel frosting that develops a thin, crystalline crust on its exterior while remaining silky-smooth closer to the cake—is notoriously troublesome to make. We wanted an easier, even foolproof, caramel icing that would stay creamy long enough to frost a two-layer cake. First, we needed a cake sturdy enough to support the thick frosting. Using the reverse creaming method—beating the butter into the dry ingredients—and switching from cake flour to all-purpose flour gave us a tender, fine-crumbed cake with enough structure. For a truly easy frosting, we simmered brown sugar and butter before adding cream, and rather than use a candy thermometer we relied on simple visual cues to know when to add the cream and when to remove the mixture from the heat. To ensure that the frosting wouldn't stiffen before we frosted the cake, we beat in a little softened butter. The fat from the butter kept the frosting soft and spreadable for a few precious extra minutes. After about 30 minutes, it transformed into the classic coating of frosting that we were after. In step 5, the cooled frosting stays soft and spreadable longer than with other recipes, but it will harden over time. If the frosting does begin to stiffen, you can microwave it for about 10 seconds (or until it returns to a spreadable consistency).

**CAKE**

- ½ cup buttermilk, at room temperature
- 4 large eggs, at room temperature
- 2 teaspoons vanilla extract
- 2¼ cups (11¼ ounces) unbleached all-purpose flour
- 1½ cups (10⅕ ounces) granulated sugar
- 1½ teaspoons baking powder
- ½ teaspoon baking soda
- ¾ teaspoon table salt
- 16 tablespoons (2 sticks) unsalted butter, cut into 16 pieces and softened

**FROSTING**

- 12 tablespoons (1½ sticks) unsalted butter, cut into 12 pieces and softened
- 2 cups packed (14 ounces) dark brown sugar
- ½ teaspoon table salt
- ½ cup heavy cream
- 1 teaspoon vanilla extract
- 2½ cups (10 ounces) confectioners' sugar, sifted

**1. FOR THE CAKE:** Adjust an oven rack to the middle position and heat the oven to 350 degrees. Grease and flour two 9-inch cake pans, then line the bottoms with parchment paper. Whisk the buttermilk, eggs, and vanilla in a large measuring cup. With an electric mixer on low speed, mix the flour, granulated sugar, baking powder, baking soda, and salt until combined. Beat in the butter, 1 piece at a time, until only pea-size pieces remain. Pour in half of the buttermilk mixture and beat over medium-high speed until light and fluffy, about 1 minute. Slowly add the remaining buttermilk mixture to the bowl and beat until incorporated, about 15 seconds.

**2.** Scrape equal amounts of the batter into the prepared pans and bake until golden and a toothpick inserted in the center comes out clean, 20 to 25 minutes. Cool the cakes in the pans for 10 minutes, then turn out onto wire racks. Cool completely, at least 1 hour.

**3. FOR THE FROSTING:** Heat 8 tablespoons of the butter, the brown sugar, and salt in a large saucepan over medium heat until small bubbles appear around the perimeter of the pan, 4 to 8 minutes. Whisk in the cream and cook until the ring of bubbles reappears, about 1 minute. Off the heat, whisk in the vanilla.

**4.** Transfer the hot frosting mixture to a bowl and, with the electric mixer on low speed, gradually mix in the confectioners' sugar until incorporated. Increase the speed to medium and beat until the frosting is pale brown and just warm, about 5 minutes. Add the remaining butter, 1 piece at a time, and beat until light and fluffy, about 2 minutes.

**5.** Line the edges of a cake platter with strips of parchment paper to keep the platter clean. Place 1 cake round on a serving platter. Spread ¾ cup of the frosting over the cake, then top with the second cake round. Spread the remaining frosting evenly over the top and sides of the cake. Serve.

## Old-Fashioned Chocolate Layer Cake

**SERVES** 10 to 12

**WHY THIS RECIPE WORKS** Over the years, chocolate cakes have become denser and intensely rich. We wanted an old-style, mile-high chocolate layer cake with a tender, airy, open crumb and a soft, billowy frosting. The mixing method was the key to getting the right texture. After trying a variety of techniques, we turned to ribboning, which involves whipping eggs with sugar until they double in volume, then adding the butter, dry ingredients, and milk. The egg foam aerated the cake, giving it both structure and tenderness. To achieve a moist cake with rich chocolate flavor, we looked to historical sources, which suggested using buttermilk and making a "pudding" with a mixture of chocolate, water, and sugar. For the frosting, we wanted the intense chocolate flavor of a ganache (a mixture of chocolate and cream) and the volume of a meringue or buttercream. Reversing the conventional ganache method, we poured cold (rather than heated) cream into warm (rather than room-temperature) chocolate, waited for it to cool to room temperature, then whipped until fluffy. For a smooth, spreadable frosting use chopped semisweet chocolate; do not use chocolate chips which will not melt as readily. For best results, make the frosting when the cakes are cooled, and use the frosting as soon as it is ready.

**CAKE**

- 1¾ cups (8¾ ounces) unbleached all-purpose flour, plus extra for the pans
- 4 ounces unsweetened chocolate, chopped coarse
- ¼ cup Dutch-processed cocoa powder
- ½ cup hot water
- 1¾ cups (12¼ ounces) sugar
- 1½ teaspoons baking soda
- 1 teaspoon table salt
- 1 cup buttermilk
- 2 teaspoons vanilla extract
- 4 large whole eggs plus 2 large egg yolks, at room temperature
- 12 tablespoons (1½ sticks) unsalted butter, very soft

**FROSTING**

- 1 pound semisweet chocolate, chopped fine
- 8 tablespoons (1 stick) unsalted butter
- ⅓ cup (2⅓ ounces) sugar
- 2 tablespoons corn syrup
- 2 teaspoons vanilla extract
- ¼ teaspoon table salt
- 1¼ cups heavy cream, chilled

**1. FOR THE CAKE:** Adjust an oven rack to the middle position and heat the oven to 350 degrees. Grease and flour two 9-inch-wide by 2-inch-high round cake pans and line with parchment paper. Combine the chocolate, cocoa powder, and hot water in a medium heatproof bowl set over a saucepan filled with 1 inch of barely simmering water, stirring occasionally until smooth. Add ½ cup of the sugar to the chocolate mixture and stir until thick and glossy, 1 to 2 minutes. Remove the bowl from the heat and set aside to cool.

**2.** Whisk the flour, baking soda, and salt in a medium bowl. Combine the buttermilk and vanilla in a small bowl. In the bowl of a stand mixer fitted with the whisk attachment, whisk the whole eggs and egg yolks on medium-low speed until combined, about 10 seconds. Add the remaining 1¼ cups sugar, increase the speed to high, and whisk until fluffy and lightened in color, 2 to 3 minutes. Replace the whisk with the paddle attachment. Add the cooled chocolate mixture to the egg-sugar mixture and mix on medium speed until thoroughly incorporated, 30 to 45 seconds, pausing to scrape down the sides of the bowl with a rubber spatula as needed. Add the softened butter 1 tablespoon at a time, mixing for about 10 seconds after each addition. Add about one-third of the flour mixture followed by half of the buttermilk mixture, mixing until incorporated after each addition (about 15 seconds). Repeat, using half of the remaining flour mixture and all of the remaining buttermilk mixture (the batter may appear separated). Scrape down the sides of the bowl and add the remaining flour mixture; mix at medium-low speed until the batter is thoroughly combined, about 15 seconds. Remove the bowl from the mixer and fold the batter once or twice with a rubber spatula to incorporate any remaining flour. Divide the batter evenly between the prepared pans, smoothing the tops with a rubber spatula. Lightly tap the pans against the countertop two or three times to settle the batter.

**3.** Bake the cakes until a toothpick inserted into the center comes out with a few crumbs attached, 25 to 30 minutes, rotating the pans halfway through the baking time. Cool the cakes in the pans on a wire rack for 15 minutes. Run a small knife around the edge of the cakes, then flip them out onto a wire rack. Peel off the parchment paper, flip the cakes right side up, and cool completely before frosting, about 2 hours.

**4.** For the frosting: Melt the chocolate in a heatproof bowl set over a saucepan containing 1 inch of barely simmering water, stirring occasionally until smooth. Remove from the heat and set aside. Meanwhile, heat the butter in a small saucepan over medium-low heat until melted. Increase the heat to medium; add the sugar, corn syrup, vanilla, and salt and stir with a heatproof spatula until the sugar is dissolved, 4 to 5 minutes. Add the melted chocolate, butter mixture, and cream to the clean bowl of a stand mixer and stir to thoroughly combine.

**5.** Place the mixer bowl over an ice bath and stir the mixture constantly with a rubber spatula until the frosting is thick and just beginning to harden against the sides of the bowl, 1 to 2 minutes (the frosting should be at 70 degrees). Place the bowl on a stand mixer fitted with the paddle attachment and beat on medium-high speed until the frosting is light and fluffy, 1 to 2 minutes. Stir with a rubber spatula until completely smooth.

**6.** Line the edges of a cake platter with strips of parchment to keep the platter clean while you assemble the cake. Place one cake layer on the platter. Spread 1½ cups of the frosting evenly across the top of the cake with a spatula. Place the second cake layer on top, then spread the remaining frosting evenly over the top and sides of the cake. Remove the parchment strips from the platter before serving.

## Chocolate-Caramel Layer Cake

**SERVES 12**

**WHY THIS RECIPE WORKS** Many chocolate-caramel cakes barely contain enough caramel flavor to merit the name. To ensure a hit of caramel flavor in each and every bite, we sandwiched three layers of thick but spreadable caramel filling between layers of deep, dark, moist chocolate cake. We started with a simple chocolate cake recipe and added a little extra water and swapped melted butter for more neutral-tasting vegetable oil. For a not-too-sweet caramel that was spreadable but thick enough to stand out between the layers, we cooked it until it turned dark (but not burnt) and added extra butter to ensure that it set up at room temperature without any unpleasant oozing. For the frosting, we used a food processor: We combined softened butter, confectioners' sugar, cocoa powder, corn syrup (for a guaranteed smooth texture), vanilla, and melted bittersweet chocolate. For a dramatic layered look, we split our two cake rounds in half, creating four layers, and sandwiched our lush caramel filling between each before spreading the thick chocolate frosting over the sides and top of the cake. Baking spray with flour can be used to grease and flour the pans. Both natural and Dutch-processed cocoa will work in this recipe. We like Hershey's Natural Unsweetened Cocoa; our favorite Dutch-processed cocoa is Droste Cacao. When taking the temperature of the caramel in steps 3 and 4, remove the pot from heat and tilt the pan to one side. Use your thermometer to stir the caramel back and forth to equalize hot and cool spots to make sure you are getting an accurate reading.

**CAKE**

- 1½ cups (7½ ounces) all-purpose flour
- ¾ cup (2¼ ounces) unsweetened cocoa powder
- 1½ cups (10½ ounces) granulated sugar
- 1¼ teaspoons baking soda
- ¾ teaspoon baking powder
- ¾ teaspoon salt
- ¾ cup buttermilk
- ½ cup water
- ¼ cup vegetable oil
- 2 large eggs
- 1 teaspoon vanilla extract

**CARAMEL FILLING**

- 1¼ cups (8¾ ounces) granulated sugar
- ¼ cup light corn syrup
- ¼ cup water
- 1 cup heavy cream
- 8 tablespoons unsalted butter, cut into 8 pieces
- 1 teaspoon vanilla extract
- ¾ teaspoon salt

**FROSTING**

- 16 tablespoons unsalted butter, softened
- ¾ cup (3 ounces) confectioners' sugar
- ½ cup (1½ ounces) unsweetened cocoa powder
- Pinch salt
- ½ cup light corn syrup
- ¾ teaspoon vanilla extract
- 6 ounces bittersweet chocolate, melted and cooled

¼–½ teaspoon coarse sea salt (optional)

**1. FOR THE CAKE:** Adjust oven rack to middle position and heat oven to 325 degrees. Grease two 9-inch round cake pans, line with parchment paper, grease parchment, and flour pans. Sift flour and cocoa into large bowl. Whisk in sugar, baking soda, baking powder, and salt. Whisk buttermilk, water, oil, eggs, and vanilla together in second bowl. Whisk buttermilk mixture into flour mixture until smooth batter forms. Divide batter evenly between prepared pans and smooth tops with rubber spatula.

2. Bake until toothpick inserted in center comes out clean, 22 to 28 minutes, rotating and switching pans halfway through baking. Let cakes cool in pans on wire rack for 15 minutes. Remove cakes from pans, discard parchment, and let cool completely on rack, at least 2 hours.

3. **FOR THE CARAMEL FILLING:** Lightly grease 8-inch square baking pan. Combine sugar, corn syrup, and water in medium saucepan. Bring to boil over medium-high heat and cook, without stirring, until mixture is amber colored, 8 to 10 minutes. Reduce heat to low and continue to cook, swirling saucepan occasionally, until dark amber, 2 to 5 minutes longer. (Caramel will register between 375 and 380 degrees.)

4. Off heat, carefully stir in cream, butter, vanilla, and salt (mixture will bubble and steam). Return saucepan to medium heat and cook, stirring frequently, until smooth and caramel reaches 240 to 245 degrees, 3 to 5 minutes. Carefully transfer caramel to prepared pan and let cool until just warm to touch (100 to 105 degrees), 20 to 30 minutes.

5. **FOR THE FROSTING:** Process butter, sugar, cocoa, and salt in food processor until smooth, about 30 seconds, scraping down sides of bowl as needed. Add corn syrup and vanilla and process until just combined, 5 to 10 seconds. Scrape down sides of bowl, then add chocolate and pulse until smooth and creamy, 10 to 15 seconds. (Frosting can be made 3 hours in advance. For longer storage, cover and refrigerate frosting. Let stand at room temperature for 1 hour before using.)

6. Using long serrated knife, score 1 horizontal line around sides of each cake layer; then, following scored lines, cut each layer into 2 even layers.

7. Using rubber spatula or large spoon, transfer ⅓ of caramel to center of 1 cake layer and use small offset spatula to spread over surface, leaving ½-inch border around edge. Repeat with remaining caramel and 2 of remaining cake layers. (Three of your cake layers should be topped with caramel.)

8. Line edges of cake platter with 4 strips of parchment to keep platter clean. Place 1 caramel-covered cake layer on platter. Top with second caramel-covered layer. Repeat with third caramel-covered layer and top with final layer. Spread frosting evenly over sides and top of cake. Carefully remove parchment strips. Let cake stand for at least 1 hour. (The cake can be made up to 2 days ahead and refrigerated. Let stand at room temperature for at least 5 hours before serving.),Sprinkle with coarse sea salt, if using. Cut and serve.

## German Chocolate Cake with Coconut-Pecan Filling

**SERVES** 12 to 16

**WHY THIS RECIPE WORKS** This cake has made it into the dessert hall of fame, but a closer look reveals shortcomings: faint chocolate flavor, microsuede-like texture, and a complicated mixing process. We wanted a streamlined German chocolate cake recipe that would be less sweet and more chocolaty than the original. After testing, we discovered that the texture of the cake actually improved when we used whole eggs instead of laboriously separating the eggs, beating the whites, and folding them into the batter. We enhanced the chocolate flavor with a combination of cocoa powder and high-quality semisweet or bittersweet chocolate. Finally, we adjusted the level and proportions of the sugar (both brown and white) and butter in the cake and filling, and toasted the pecans, for a German chocolate cake that was easier to make and had better texture and flavor than the original. When you assemble the cake, the filling should be cool or cold. To be time-efficient, first make the filling, then use the refrigeration time to prepare, bake, and cool the cakes. For an accurate measurement of boiling water, bring a kettle of water to a boil, then measure out the desired amount.

**FILLING**

- 4 large egg yolks, at room temperature
- 1 (12-ounce) can evaporated milk
- 1 cup (7 ounces) granulated sugar
- ¼ cup packed (1¾ ounces) light brown sugar
- 6 tablespoons (¾ stick) unsalted butter, cut into 6 pieces
- ⅛ teaspoon table salt
- 2 teaspoons vanilla extract
- 2⅓ cups sweetened shredded coconut
- 1½ cups (6 ounces) finely chopped pecans, toasted

**CAKE**

- 4 ounces semisweet or bittersweet chocolate, chopped fine
- ¼ cup Dutch-processed cocoa powder
- ½ cup boiling water
- 2 cups (10 ounces) unbleached all-purpose flour, plus extra for the pans
- ¾ teaspoon baking soda
- 12 tablespoons (1½ sticks) unsalted butter, softened
- 1 cup (7 ounces) granulated sugar
- ⅔ cup packed (4⅔ ounces) light brown sugar
- ¾ teaspoon table salt
- 4 large whole eggs, at room temperature
- 1 teaspoon vanilla extract
- ¾ cup sour cream, at room temperature

1. **FOR THE FILLING:** Whisk the egg yolks in a medium saucepan; gradually whisk in the evaporated milk. Add the sugars, butter, and salt and cook over medium-high heat, whisking constantly, until the mixture is boiling, frothy, and slightly thickened, about 6 minutes. Transfer the mixture to a bowl, whisk in the vanilla, then stir in the coconut. Cool until just warm, cover with plastic wrap, and refrigerate until cool or cold, at least 2 hours or up to 3 days. (The pecans are stirred in just before cake assembly.)

2. **FOR THE CAKE:** Adjust an oven rack to the lower-middle position; heat the oven to 350 degrees. Combine the chocolate and cocoa in a small bowl; pour the boiling water over and let stand to melt the chocolate, about 2 minutes. Whisk until smooth; set aside until cooled to room temperature.

3. Meanwhile, grease and flour two 9-inch-wide by 2-inch-high round cake pans and line with parchment paper. Sift the flour and baking soda into a medium bowl or onto a sheet of parchment or waxed paper.

4. In a stand mixer fitted with the paddle attachment, beat the butter, sugars, and salt at medium-low speed until the sugar is moistened, about 30 seconds. Increase the speed to medium-high and beat until the mixture is light and fluffy, about 4 minutes, scraping down the bowl with a spatula halfway through. With the mixer running at medium speed, add the eggs one at a time, beating well after each addition and scraping down the bowl halfway through. Beat in the vanilla; increase the speed to medium-high and beat until light and fluffy, about 45 seconds. With the mixer running at low speed, add the chocolate mixture, then increase the speed to medium and beat until combined, about 30 seconds, scraping down the bowl once (the batter may appear curdled). Add about one-third of the flour mixture, followed by half of the sour cream, mixing until just incorporated after each addition (about 5 seconds). Repeat using half of the remaining flour mixture and all of the remaining sour cream. Scrape down the bowl and add the remaining flour mixture; mix at medium-low speed until the batter is thoroughly combined, about 15 seconds. Divide the batter evenly between the prepared cake pans, smoothing the tops with a rubber spatula. Lightly tap the pans against the countertop two or three times to settle the batter.

5. Bake the cakes until a toothpick inserted into the centers comes out clean, about 30 minutes, rotating the pans halfway through the baking time. Cool the cakes in the pans on a wire rack for 10 minutes. Run a small knife around the edges of the cakes, then flip them out onto a wire rack. Peel off the parchment, flip the cakes right side up, and cool completely before frosting, about 2 hours.

6. **TO ASSEMBLE:** Stir the toasted pecans into the chilled filling. Line the edges of a cake platter with strips of parchment paper to keep the platter clean while you assemble the cake. Use a serrated knife to cut each cake horizontally into two even layers. Place one bottom layer on the platter. Spread about 1 cup of the filling evenly across the top of the cake with a spatula. Carefully place the upper cake layer on top of the filling; repeat using the remaining filling and cake layers. Remove the parchment strips before serving.

## Strawberry Cream Cake

**SERVES** 8 to 10

**WHY THIS RECIPE WORKS** What could possibly ruin the heavenly trio of cake, cream, and ripe strawberries? How about soggy cake, bland berries, and squishy cream? We wanted a sturdy cake, a firm filling, and strawberry flavor fit for a starring role. To start, we had to solve three crucial problems. First, we realized that tender butter cakes couldn't support a substantial strawberry filling, so we developed a chiffon-style cake that combined the rich flavor of a butter cake with the light-yet-sturdy texture of a sponge cake. Second, we made a flavorful berry "mash" with half of the berries and then reduced the macerated juice in a saucepan (with a little kirsch) to help concentrate and round out the flavor. We sliced the rest of the berries and placed them around the edges of the cake for visual appeal. Another problem arose when the cake was sliced: The filling squirted out and the layers fell apart. To correct the problem, we reduced the number of layers from four to three and fortified the whipped-cream filling with cream cheese. This filling stayed put and didn't mar the glorious layers of this spectacular summertime cake. You will need a cake pan with straight sides that are at least 2 inches high.

**CAKE**

- 1¼ cups (5 ounces) cake flour, plus extra for the pan
- 1½ teaspoons baking powder
- ¼ teaspoon table salt
- 1 cup (7 ounces) sugar
- 5 large eggs (2 whole and 3 separated), at room temperature
- 6 tablespoons (¾ stick) unsalted butter, melted and cooled slightly
- 2 tablespoons water
- 2 teaspoons vanilla extract

**STRAWBERRY FILLING**

- 2 pounds fresh strawberries (medium or large, about 2 quarts), washed, dried, and stemmed
- 4–6 tablespoons sugar
- 2 tablespoons kirsch
- Pinch table salt

**WHIPPED CREAM**

- 8 ounces cream cheese, at room temperature
- ½ cup (3½ ounces) sugar
- 1 teaspoon vanilla extract
- ⅛ teaspoon table salt
- 2 cups heavy cream

1. **FOR THE CAKE:** Adjust an oven rack to the lower-middle position and heat the oven to 325 degrees. Grease and flour a 9-inch-wide by 2-inch-high round cake pan or 9-inch springform pan and line it with parchment paper. Whisk the flour, baking powder, salt, and all but 3 tablespoons of the sugar in a mixing bowl. Whisk in 2 whole eggs and 3 yolks (reserving the whites), the butter, water, and vanilla; whisk until smooth.

**2.** In the clean bowl of a stand mixer fitted with the whisk attachment, beat the remaining 3 egg whites at medium-low speed until frothy, 1 to 2 minutes. With the machine running, gradually add the remaining 3 tablespoons sugar, increase the speed to medium-high, and beat until soft peaks form, 60 to 90 seconds. Stir one-third of the whites into the batter to lighten; add the remaining whites and gently fold into the batter until no white streaks remain. Transfer the batter to the prepared pan, smoothing the top with a rubber spatula. Lightly tap the pan against the countertop two or three times to settle the batter. Bake until a toothpick inserted into the center comes out clean, 30 to 40 minutes, rotating the pan halfway through the baking time. Cool the cake in the pan on a wire rack for 10 minutes, then invert onto the wire rack and peel off the parchment. Invert the cake again and cool completely on the rack, about 2 hours.

**3. FOR THE STRAWBERRY FILLING:** Halve 24 of the best-looking berries and reserve. Quarter the remaining berries; toss with 4 to 6 tablespoons sugar (depending on the sweetness of the berries) in a medium bowl and let sit for 1 hour, stirring occasionally. Strain the juices from the berries and reserve (you should have about ½ cup). In a food processor, give the macerated berries 5 pulses (you should have about 1½ cups). In a small saucepan over medium-high heat, simmer the reserved juices and the kirsch until syrupy and reduced to about 3 tablespoons, 3 to 5 minutes. Pour the reduced syrup over the processed, macerated berries, add the salt, and toss to combine. Set aside until the cake has cooled.

**4. FOR THE WHIPPED CREAM:** When the cake has cooled, place the cream cheese, sugar, vanilla, and salt in the clean bowl of a stand mixer fitted with the whisk attachment. Whisk at medium-high speed until light and fluffy, 1 to 2 minutes, scraping down the bowl with a rubber spatula as needed. Reduce the speed to low and add the heavy cream in a slow, steady stream; when almost fully combined, increase the speed to medium-high and beat until the mixture holds stiff peaks, 2 to 2½ minutes more, scraping down the bowl as needed (you should have about 4½ cups).

**5. TO ASSEMBLE THE CAKE:** Line the edges of a cake platter with strips of parchment paper to keep the platter clean. Use a serrated knife to cut the cake horizontally into three even layers. Place the bottom layer on the platter and arrange a ring of 20 strawberry halves, cut sides down and stem ends facing out, around the perimeter of the cake layer. Pour one-half of the pureed berry mixture (about ¾ cup) in the center, then spread to cover any exposed cake. Gently spread about one-third of the whipped cream (about 1½ cups) over the berry layer, leaving a ½-inch border from the edge. Place the middle cake layer on top and press down gently (the whipped cream layer should become flush with the cake edge). Repeat with 20 additional strawberry halves, the remaining berry mixture, and half of the remaining whipped cream; gently press the last cake layer on top. Spread the remaining whipped cream over the top; decorate with the remaining cut strawberries. Remove the parchment strips from the platter and serve.

### BUILDING A STRAWBERRY CREAM CAKE

**1.** With a serrated knife, use a sawing motion to cut the cake into three layers, rotating the cake as you go. Place sliced berries evenly around the edges (they will be visible once the layers are assembled).

**2.** Cover the center of the cake completely with half of the pureed strawberries.

**3.** Spread one-third of the whipped cream over the berries, leaving a ½-inch border. Repeat the layering.

**4.** Press the last layer into place, spread with the remaining cream, and decorate with the remaining berries.

## Lemon Layer Cake

**SERVES** 10 to 12

**WHY THIS RECIPE WORKS** Most versions of lemon layer cake are poorly executed concoctions of heavy cake stacked with filling and frosting that taste more like butter than lemon. We wanted an old-fashioned cake in which tangy, creamy lemon filling divides layers of tender, delicate cake draped in sweet frosting—an ideal contrast of sweet and tart. Most layer cakes are substantial butter cakes, but we suspected that the light, fresh flavor of lemon would be better served by something more ethereal. After trying a sponge cake and a classic yellow cake, we found that a white butter cake was the perfect compromise: a cake nicely flavored by butter yet still light with a fine crumb and tender texture. Instead of the usual lemon-scented buttercream, we preferred the brightness of lemon curd. And the same was true for our frosting: We chose an old-fashioned seven-minute icing, cutting back on the sugar and adding a squeeze of lemon juice. After some trial and error, we learned that if we heated the mixture to at least 160 degrees and then transferred it to the stand mixer for whipping (rather than holding a hand mixer for seven minutes), the end result was just as billowy and shiny as the old-fashioned version. You will need a cake pan with straight sides that are at least 2 inches high. For neater slices, dip a knife into hot water before cutting the cake.

**LEMON CURD FILLING**

- 1 cup juice from about 6 lemons
- 1 teaspoon powdered gelatin
- 1½ cups (10½ ounces) sugar
- ⅛ teaspoon table salt
- 4 large whole eggs plus 6 large egg yolks (reserve the egg whites for the cake)
- 8 tablespoons (1 stick) unsalted butter, cut into ½-inch cubes and frozen

**CAKE**

- 2¼ cups (9 ounces) cake flour, plus extra for the pans
- 1 cup whole milk, at room temperature
- 6 large egg whites, at room temperature
- 2 teaspoons vanilla extract
- 1¾ cups (12¼ ounces) sugar
- 4 teaspoons baking powder
- 1 teaspoon table salt
- 12 tablespoons (1½ sticks) unsalted butter, cut into 12 pieces, softened but still cool

**FLUFFY WHITE ICING**

- 1 cup (7 ounces) sugar
- 2 large egg whites, at room temperature
- ¼ cup water
- 1 tablespoon juice from 1 lemon
- 1 tablespoon corn syrup

**1. FOR THE FILLING:** Measure 1 tablespoon of the lemon juice into a small bowl; sprinkle the gelatin over the top. Heat the remaining lemon juice, the sugar, and salt in a medium saucepan over medium-high heat, stirring occasionally, until the sugar dissolves and the mixture is hot but not boiling. Whisk the eggs and yolks in a large bowl. Whisking constantly, slowly pour the hot lemon-sugar mixture into the eggs, then return the mixture to the saucepan. Cook over medium-low heat, stirring constantly with a heatproof spatula, until the mixture registers 170 degrees on an instant-read thermometer and is thick enough to leave a trail when the spatula is scraped along the pan bottom, 4 to 6 minutes. Immediately remove the pan from the heat and stir in the gelatin mixture until dissolved. Stir in the frozen butter until incorporated. Pour the filling through a fine-mesh strainer into a bowl (you should have 3 cups). Lay a sheet of plastic wrap directly on the surface and refrigerate until firm enough to spread, at least 4 hours.

**2. FOR THE CAKE:** Adjust an oven rack to the middle position and heat the oven to 350 degrees. Grease and flour two 9-inch-wide by 2-inch-high round cake pans and line with parchment paper. In a 2-cup liquid measure or medium bowl, whisk together the milk, egg whites, and vanilla.

**3.** In a stand mixer fitted with the paddle attachment, mix the flour, sugar, baking powder, and salt at low speed until combined, about 30 seconds. With the mixer running at low speed, add the butter one piece at a time; continue beating until the mixture resembles moist crumbs with no visible butter chunks. Add all but ½ cup of the milk mixture to the crumbs and beat at medium speed until the mixture is pale and fluffy, about 1½ minutes. With the mixer running at low speed, add the remaining ½ cup milk mixture; increase the speed to medium and beat for 30 seconds more. Stop the mixer and scrape the sides of the bowl. Return the mixer to medium speed and beat for 20 seconds longer. Divide the batter evenly between the pans, smoothing the tops with a rubber spatula. Lightly tap the pan against the countertop two or three times to settle the batter.

**4.** Bake until a toothpick inserted in the center of the cakes comes out clean, 23 to 25 minutes, rotating the pans halfway through the baking time. Cool the cakes in the pans on a wire rack for 10 minutes. Run a small knife around the edges of the cakes, then flip them out onto a wire rack. Peel off the parchment paper, flip the cakes right side up, and cool completely before frosting, about 2 hours.

**5. TO ASSEMBLE:** Line the edges of a cake platter with strips of parchment paper to keep the platter clean while you assemble the cake. Use a serrated knife to cut each cake horizontally into two even layers. Place the bottom layer of one cake on the platter. Using a spatula, spread 1 cup of the lemon filling evenly on the cake, leaving a ½-inch border around the edge. Carefully place the upper cake layer on top of the filling. Spread 1 cup of the filling on top; repeat using the remaining filling and cake layers. Smooth out any filling that has leaked from the sides of the cake; cover with plastic wrap and refrigerate while making the icing.

**6. FOR THE ICING:** Combine all the ingredients in the bowl of a stand mixer or a large heatproof bowl and set over a medium saucepan filled with 1 inch of barely simmering water (do not let the bowl touch the water). Cook, stirring constantly, until the mixture registers 160 degrees on an instant-read thermometer, 5 to 10 minutes. Remove the bowl from the heat and transfer the mixture to a stand mixer fitted with the whisk attachment. Beat on medium speed until soft peaks form, about 5 minutes. Increase the speed to medium-high and continue to beat until the mixture has cooled to room temperature and stiff peaks form, 5 minutes longer. Using a spatula, spread the frosting evenly over the top and sides of the cake. Remove the parchment strips from the platter and serve.

## Classic Yellow Layer Cake with Vanilla Buttercream

**SERVES** 8 to 10

**WHY THIS RECIPE WORKS** Traditional yellow layer cake should melt in the mouth and taste of butter and eggs. But many recipes we tried came out crumbly, sugary, and hard. We wanted a yellow cake that was tender and buttery and could stand up to a slathering of frosting, if desired. Most versions of yellow layer cake rely on the classic 1–2–3–4 formula (1 cup butter, 2 cups sugar, 3 cups flour, and four eggs—plus milk, baking powder, vanilla, and salt) and follow the classic way of mixing together the ingredients—creaming the butter and sugar, adding the eggs one at a time, and finally adding the milk and dry ingredients alternately. This worked OK, but we wanted something easier. The two-stage method fit the bill. In this technique, the dry ingredients are combined and then two-thirds of the milk and eggs are added and beaten until thick and fluffy. Then in the second stage, the rest of the milk and eggs are poured in and the batter is beaten again. This technique is simpler and quicker, and produced a tender cake. Now we had a tender cake but the flavor needed improvement. Increasing the proportions of butter, eggs, and sugar turned out a fine-grained, soft, and meltingly rich cake. As for the frosting, we chose a traditional vanilla buttercream. Rich with egg yolks, butter, sugar, and corn syrup for sheen, this supple frosting is the perfect complement to our cake. Cake flour gives this buttery yellow cake its tender crumb; do not substitute all-purpose flour. For a decorative finish, press toasted sliced almonds on the sides of the cake.

**CAKE**

- 1¾ cups (7 ounces) cake flour, plus extra for the pans
- ½ cup whole milk, at room temperature
- 4 large eggs, at room temperature
- 2 teaspoons vanilla extract
- 1½ cups (10½ ounces) sugar
- 2 teaspoons baking powder
- ¾ teaspoon table salt
- 16 tablespoons (2 sticks) unsalted butter, cut into 16 pieces and softened

**VANILLA BUTTERCREAM**

- 6 large egg yolks, at room temperature
- ¾ cup (5¼ ounces) sugar
- ½ cup light corn syrup
- 2½ teaspoons vanilla extract
- ¼ teaspoon table salt
- 4 sticks unsalted butter, cut into chunks and softened

**1. FOR THE CAKE:** Adjust an oven rack to the middle position and heat the oven to 350 degrees. Grease and flour two 8- or 9-inch round cake pans, then line the bottoms with parchment paper. Whisk the milk, eggs, and vanilla together in a small bowl.

**2.** In a stand mixer fitted with the paddle attachment, whisk the flour, sugar, baking powder, and salt together on low speed until combined, about 30 seconds. Increase the speed to medium-low and beat the butter into the flour mixture, one piece at a time, about 30 seconds. Continue to beat the mixture until it resembles moist crumbs, about 1 minute.

**3.** Beat in all but ½ cup of the milk mixture, then increase the mixer speed to medium and beat the batter until smooth, light, and fluffy, about 1 minute. Reduce the mixer speed to low and slowly beat in the remaining ½ cup milk mixture until the batter looks slightly curdled, about 15 seconds.

**4.** Give the batter a final stir with a rubber spatula to make sure it is thoroughly combined. Scrape the batter into the prepared pans and smooth the tops with a rubber spatula. Lightly tap the pans against the countertop two or three times to settle the batter. Bake the cakes until a toothpick inserted in the center comes out with a few crumbs attached, 20 to 25 minutes, rotating the pans halfway through the baking time.

**5.** Cool the cakes in the pans for 10 minutes. Run a small knife around the edge of the cakes, then flip them out onto a wire rack. Peel off the parchment paper, flip the cakes right side up, and cool completely before frosting, about 2 hours.

**6. FOR THE BUTTERCREAM:** Whip the egg yolks in a large bowl with an electric mixer on medium speed until slightly thickened and pale yellow, 4 to 6 minutes.

**7.** Meanwhile, bring the sugar and corn syrup to a boil in a small saucepan over medium heat, stirring occasionally to dissolve the sugar, about 3 minutes.

**8.** Without letting the hot sugar mixture cool off, turn the mixer to low and slowly pour the warm sugar syrup into the whipped egg yolks without hitting the side of the bowl or the beaters. Increase the mixer speed to medium-high and whip the mixture until it is light and fluffy and the bowl is no longer warm, 5 to 10 minutes.

**9.** Reduce the mixer speed to medium-low and add the vanilla and salt. Gradually add the butter, one piece at a time, until completely incorporated, about 2 minutes. Increase the mixer speed to medium-high and whip the buttercream until smooth and silky, about 2 minutes. (If the mixture looks curdled, wrap a hot wet towel around the bowl and continue to whip until smooth, 1 to 2 minutes.)

**10.** Line the edges of a cake platter with strips of parchment to keep the platter clean while you assemble the cake. Place one cake layer on the platter. Spread 1½ cups of the frosting evenly across the top of the cake with a spatula. Place the second cake layer on top, then spread the remaining frosting evenly over the top and sides of the cake. Remove the parchment strips from the platter before serving.

## Fluffy Yellow Layer Cake

**SERVES** 10 to 12

**WHY THIS RECIPE WORKS** Most fluffy layer cakes made entirely from natural ingredients are either unpleasantly dense or too fragile to support layers of frosting. We wanted a frosted yellow layer cake with an ethereal texture and the great flavor of real butter and eggs. Chiffon cakes are especially weightless, springy, and moist. But unlike butter cakes, they are too light to stand up to serious frosting. We decided to blend the two types of cake. We adapted a chiffon technique (using a large quantity of whipped egg whites to get a high volume and light texture) to combine the ingredients from our butter cake recipe. This worked beautifully, creating a light, porous cake that was hefty enough to hold the frosting's weight. But the cake lacked moistness and some tenderness. A combination of fats (butter plus vegetable oil), kept the butter flavor intact while improving the moistness of the cake. For extra tenderness, we increased the sugar and substituted buttermilk for milk. The buttermilk allowed us to replace some of the baking powder with a little baking soda to ensure an even rise. A fluffy chocolate frosting is the perfect partner to this cake. A hefty amount of cocoa powder combined with melted chocolate gave the frosting a deep chocolate flavor. A combination of confectioners' sugar and corn syrup made it smooth and glossy. To keep the frosting from separating and turning greasy, we moved it out of the stand mixer and into the food processor. The faster machine minimized any risk of over beating, as it blended the ingredients quickly. Bring all the ingredients to room temperature before beginning. For the frosting, cool the chocolate to between 85 and 100 degrees before adding it to the butter mixture.

**CAKE**

- 2½ cups (10 ounces) cake flour, plus extra for the pans
- 1¾ cups (12¼ ounces) granulated sugar
- 1¼ teaspoons baking powder
- ¼ teaspoon baking soda
- ¾ teaspoon table salt
- 1 cup buttermilk, at room temperature
- 10 tablespoons (1¼ sticks) unsalted butter, melted and cooled slightly
- 3 tablespoons vegetable oil
- 2 teaspoons vanilla extract
- 6 large egg yolks plus 3 large egg whites, at room temperature

**FROSTING**

- 20 tablespoons (2½ sticks) unsalted butter, softened
- 1 cup (4 ounces) confectioners' sugar
- ¾ cup Dutch-processed cocoa powder
- Pinch table salt
- ¾ cup light corn syrup
- 1 teaspoon vanilla extract
- 8 ounces milk chocolate, melted and cooled slightly

**1. FOR THE CAKE:** Adjust an oven rack to the middle position and heat the oven to 350 degrees. Grease and flour two 9-inch-wide by 2-inch-high round cake pans and line with parchment paper. Whisk the flour, 1½ cups of the granulated sugar, the baking powder, baking soda, and salt together in a large bowl. In a 4-cup liquid measuring cup or medium bowl, whisk together the buttermilk, melted butter, oil, vanilla, and egg yolks.

**2.** In a stand mixer fitted with the whisk attachment, beat the egg whites at medium-high speed until foamy, about 30 seconds. With the machine running, gradually add the remaining ¼ cup granulated sugar; continue to beat until stiff peaks just form, 30 to 60 seconds (the whites should hold a peak but the mixture should appear moist). Transfer to a bowl and set aside.

**3.** Add the flour mixture to the now-empty mixing bowl. With the mixer still fitted with the whisk attachment, and running at low speed, gradually pour in the butter mixture and mix until almost incorporated (a few streaks of dry flour will remain), about 15 seconds. Stop the mixer and scrape the whisk and the sides of the bowl. Return the mixer to medium-low speed and beat until smooth and fully incorporated, 10 to 15 seconds.

**4.** Using a rubber spatula, stir one-third of the whites into the batter to lighten, then add the remaining whites and gently fold into the batter until no white streaks remain. Divide the batter evenly between the prepared pans, smoothing the tops with a rubber spatula. Lightly tap the pans against the countertop two or three times to settle the batter.

**5.** Bake until the cake layers begin to pull away from the sides of the pans and a toothpick inserted into the centers comes out clean, 20 to 22 minutes, rotating the pans halfway through the baking time. Cool the cakes in the pans on a wire rack for 10 minutes. Run a small knife around the edge of the cakes, then flip them out onto a wire rack. Peel off the parchment paper, flip the cakes right side up, and cool completely before frosting, about 2 hours. (The frosting can be made up to 3 hours ahead. For longer storage, refrigerate the frosting, covered, and let it stand at room temperature for 1 hour before using.)

**6. FOR THE FROSTING:** In a food processor, process the butter, confectioners' sugar, cocoa, and salt until smooth, about 30 seconds, scraping down the sides of the bowl as needed. Add the corn syrup and vanilla and process until just combined, 5 to 10 seconds. Scrape down the sides of the bowl, then add the chocolate and process until smooth and creamy, 10 to 15 seconds. The frosting can be used immediately or held.

**7.** Line the edges of a cake platter with strips of parchment to keep the platter clean while you assemble the cake. Place one cake layer on the platter. Spread 1½ cups of the frosting evenly across the top of the cake with a spatula. Place the second cake layer on top, then spread the remaining frosting evenly over the top and sides of the cake. Remove the parchment strips from the platter before serving.

### FROSTING A LAYER CAKE

**1.** Dollop a portion of frosting in the center of the cake and spread into an even layer right to the edge.

**2.** Lay the second layer on top. Brush away any large crumbs, dollop more frosting in the center, and spread slightly over the edge.

**3.** Gather a few tablespoons of frosting onto the top of the spatula, then gently smear it onto the side of the cake. Repeat to frost the sides completely.

**4.** For smooth sides, gently run the edge of the spatula around the cake. Or, to create billows in the frosting, press the back of a soupspoon into the frosting, then twirl the spoon as you lift it away.

## Wicked Good Boston Cream Pie

**SERVES 8 TO 10**

**WHY THIS RECIPE WORKS** This triple-component dessert deserved a revival—if only we could make the filling foolproof and keep the glaze from cracking off. A hot-milk sponge cake made a good base because it didn't require any finicky folding or separating of eggs. Baking the batter in two pans eliminated the need to slice a single cake horizontally before adding the filling. We used butter to firm up our pastry cream, and added corn syrup to heavy cream and melted chocolate to make a smooth glaze that clung to the top of our Boston Cream Pie and dripped artistically down its sides. Chill the assembled cake for at least 3 hours to make it easy to cut and serve.

**PASTRY CREAM**

- 2 cups half-and-half
- 6 large egg yolks
- ½ cup (3½ ounces) sugar
- Pinch table salt
- ¼ cup all-purpose flour
- 4 tablespoons cold unsalted butter, cut into four pieces
- 1½ teaspoons vanilla extract

**CAKE**

- 1½ cups (7½ ounces) all-purpose flour
- 1½ teaspoons baking powder
- ¾ teaspoon table salt
- ¾ cup whole milk
- 6 tablespoons unsalted butter
- 1½ teaspoons vanilla extract
- 3 large eggs
- 1½ cups (10½ ounces) sugar

**GLAZE**

- ½ cup heavy cream
- 2 tablespoons light corn syrup
- 4 ounces bittersweet chocolate, chopped fine

**1. FOR THE PASTRY CREAM:** Heat half-and-half in medium saucepan over medium heat until just simmering. Meanwhile, whisk yolks, sugar, and salt in medium bowl until smooth. Add flour to yolk mixture and whisk until incorporated. Remove half-and-half from heat and, whisking constantly, slowly add ½ cup to yolk mixture to temper. Whisking constantly, return tempered yolk mixture to half-and-half in saucepan.

**2.** Return saucepan to medium heat and cook, whisking constantly, until mixture thickens slightly, about 1 minute. Reduce heat to medium-low and continue to simmer, whisking constantly, 8 minutes.

**3.** Increase heat to medium and cook, whisking vigorously, until bubbles burst on surface, 1 to 2 minutes. Remove saucepan from heat; whisk in butter and vanilla until butter is melted and incorporated. Strain pastry cream through fine-mesh strainer set over medium bowl. Press lightly greased parchment paper directly on surface and refrigerate until set, at least 2 hours and up to 24 hours.

**4. FOR THE CAKE:** Adjust oven rack to middle position and heat oven to 325 degrees. Lightly grease two 9-inch round cake pans with vegetable oil spray and line with parchment. Whisk flour, baking powder, and salt together in medium bowl. Heat milk and butter in small saucepan over low heat until butter is melted. Remove from heat, add vanilla, and cover to keep warm.

**5.** In stand mixer fitted with whisk attachment, whip eggs and sugar at high speed until light and airy, about 5 minutes. Remove mixer bowl from stand. Add hot milk mixture and whisk by hand until incorporated. Add dry ingredients and whisk until incorporated.

**6.** Working quickly, divide batter evenly between prepared pans. Bake until tops are light brown and toothpick inserted in center of cakes comes out clean, 20 to 22 minutes.

**7.** Transfer cakes to wire rack and cool completely in pan, about 2 hours. Run small plastic knife around edge of pans, then invert cakes onto wire rack. Carefully remove parchment, then reinvert cakes.

**8. TO ASSEMBLE:** Place one cake round on large plate. Whisk pastry cream briefly, then spoon onto center of cake. Using offset spatula, spread evenly to cake edge. Place second layer on pastry cream, bottom side up, making sure layers line up properly. Press lightly on top of cake to level. Refrigerate cake while preparing glaze.

**9. FOR THE GLAZE:** Bring cream and corn syrup to simmer in small saucepan over medium heat. Remove from heat and add chocolate. Whisk gently until smooth, 30 seconds. Let stand, whisking occasionally, until thickened slightly, about 5 minutes.

**10.** Pour glaze onto center of cake. Use offset spatula to spread glaze to edge of cake, letting excess drip decoratively down sides. Chill finished cake for 3 hours before slicing. (Cake may be made up to 24 hours before serving.)

### LINING CAKE PANS

**1.** Trace the outline of the bottom of the pan onto a sheet of parchment paper. Cut out the outline, cutting on the inside of the line so that the round fits snugly inside the pan.

**2.** Fit the trimmed piece of parchment into the pan.

## Classic White Layer Cake with Butter Frosting and Raspberry-Almond Filling

**SERVES** 10 to 12

**WHY THIS RECIPE WORKS** White layer cakes have been the classic birthday cake for more than 100 years. Unfortunately, the white cakes that we have baked over the years always fell short of our high expectations. They came out a little dry and chewy and riddled with tunnels and small holes. Every traditional recipe for white cake calls for stiffly beaten egg whites folded into the batter at the end. We suspected that it was the beaten egg whites that were forming the large air pockets and those unsightly holes. The solution was to mix the egg whites with the milk before beating them into the flour-and-butter mixture. To make this cake birthday-special, we iced it with an easy butter frosting and added a layer of raspberry jam and chopped toasted almonds. There will be enough frosting left to pipe a border around the base and top of the cake; to decorate the cake more elaborately, you should make 1½ times the frosting recipe. If desired, finish the sides of the cake with 1 cup of sliced almonds.

**CAKE**

- 2¼ cups (9 ounces) cake flour, plus extra for the pans
- 1 cup whole milk, at room temperature
- 6 large egg whites, at room temperature
- 1 teaspoon vanilla extract
- 1 teaspoon almond extract
- 1¾ cups (12¼ ounces) granulated sugar
- 4 teaspoons baking powder
- 1 teaspoon table salt
- 12 tablespoons (1½ sticks) unsalted butter, cut into 12 pieces and softened

**FROSTING AND FILLING**

- 16 tablespoons (2 sticks) unsalted butter, softened
- 4 cups (1 pound) confectioners' sugar
- 1 tablespoon vanilla extract
- 1 tablespoon milk
- Pinch table salt
- ½ cup (2¼ ounces) blanched slivered almonds, toasted and chopped coarse
- ⅓ cup seedless raspberry jam

**1. FOR THE CAKE:** Adjust an oven rack to the middle position and heat the oven to 350 degrees. Grease and flour two 8- or 9-inch round cake pans, then line the bottoms with parchment paper. Whisk the milk, egg whites, and both extracts together in a small bowl.

**2.** In a stand mixer fitted with the paddle attachment, mix the flour, sugar, baking powder, and salt together on low speed until combined, about 30 seconds. Increase the speed to medium-low and beat the butter into the flour mixture, one piece at a time, about 30 seconds. Continue to beat the mixture until it resembles moist crumbs, about 1 minute.

**3.** Beat in all but ½ cup of the milk mixture, then increase the mixer speed to medium and beat until smooth, light, and fluffy, about 1 minute. Reduce the mixer speed to low and slowly beat in the remaining ½ cup milk mixture until the batter looks slightly curdled, about 15 seconds.

**4.** Give the batter a final stir with a rubber spatula to make sure it is thoroughly combined. Scrape the batter into the prepared pans, smooth the tops, and lightly tap the pans against the countertop two or three times to settle the batter. Bake the cakes until a toothpick inserted in the center comes out with a few crumbs attached, 20 to 25 minutes, rotating the pans halfway through the baking time.

**5.** Cool the cakes in the pans for 10 minutes. Run a small knife around the edge of the cakes, then flip them out onto a wire rack. Peel off the parchment paper, flip the cakes right side up, and cool completely before frosting, about 2 hours.

**6. FOR THE FROSTING AND FILLING:** In the bowl of a stand mixer fitted with the paddle attachment, beat the butter, confectioners' sugar, vanilla, milk, and salt on low speed until the sugar is moistened, about 30 seconds. Increase the speed to medium-high; beat, stopping twice to scrape down the bowl, until creamy and fluffy, about 1½ minutes.

**7.** Line the edges of a cake platter with strips of parchment to keep the platter clean while you assemble the cake. Place one cake layer on the platter. Combine ½ cup of the frosting with the almonds in a small bowl. Spread the almond frosting over the first layer. Carefully spread the jam on top, then cover with the second cake layer. Spread the remaining frosting evenly over the top and sides of the cake. Remove the parchment strips from the platter before serving.

## Rainbow Cake

**SERVES** 20 to 24

**WHY THIS RECIPE WORKS** If it's possible that just looking at a cake can make you happy, this is the cake to do it. The array of vibrant colors will liven up the mood at any celebration and is sure to appeal to guests of all ages. We started with our classic white layer cake recipe as the base. It's rich and tender and, most importantly for a cake of this stature, has the structure to stand tall in six layers; plus, it was the obvious choice for easy dyeing. We separated the batter into six portions and stirred in food dye right before baking. Baking our colorful layers in multiple batches ensured they were evenly cooked. To finish, we gave the cake a demure coat of vanilla frosting, leaving the cake's colorful layers to be dramatically revealed after it was cut. We had the best luck using Betty Crocker Food Gel Colors. The amount of food dye required and the resulting color will differ from brand to brand. We strongly recommend using food gel coloring over liquid food dye for best results. Be sure to let the cake pans cool completely before repeating with more batter. To make 10 cups of frosting, prepare the 5-cup recipe for Vanilla Frosting (page 888) twice. (Do not try doubling the recipe; it won't fit in the mixer.) You may have leftover frosting after decorating.

- 2 cups whole milk, room temperature, divided
- 12 large egg whites, room temperature, divided
- 2 teaspoons vanilla extract, divided
- 4½ cups (18 ounces) cake flour, divided
- 3½ cups (24½ ounces) sugar, divided
- 2 tablespoons plus 2 teaspoon baking powder, divided
- 2 teaspoons table salt, divided
- 24 tablespoons (3 sticks) unsalted butter, cut into 24 pieces and softened, divided
- Gel food dye (red, orange, yellow, green, blue, and purple)
- 10 cups Vanilla Frosting (page 888)

**1.** Adjust oven racks to upper-middle and lower-middle positions and heat oven to 350 degrees. Grease three 9-inch round cake pans, line with parchment paper, grease parchment, and flour pans.

**2.** Whisk 1 cup milk, 6 egg whites, and 1 teaspoon vanilla together in 2-cup liquid measuring cup. Using stand mixer fitted with paddle, mix 2¼ cups (9 ounces) flour, 1¾ cups (12¼ ounces) sugar, 4 teaspoons baking powder, and 1 teaspoon salt on low speed until combined. Add 12 tablespoons butter, 1 piece at a time, and mix until only pea-size pieces remain, about 1 minute. Add half of milk mixture, increase speed to medium-high, and beat until light and fluffy, about 1 minute. Reduce speed to medium-low, add remaining milk mixture, and beat until incorporated, about 30 seconds (batter may look slightly curdled). Give batter final stir by hand.

**3.** Divide batter evenly among three bowls. Add ½ teaspoon red gel food dye to one bowl, ¼ teaspoon yellow to second bowl, and ¼ teaspoon orange to third bowl. Stir each to combine. Transfer each colored batter to separate prepared pans. Smooth tops with rubber spatula and gently tap pans on counter to release air bubbles. Place 2 pans on upper rack and one pan on lower rack. Bake until toothpick inserted in center comes out clean, 18 to 22 minutes, switching and rotating pans halfway through baking. Let cakes cool in pans on wire rack for 10 minutes. Remove cakes from pans, discarding parchment, and let cool completely on rack, about 2 hours.

**4.** Repeat steps 1 through 3 with remaining ingredients, using ½ teaspoon blue, ½ teaspoon green, and ½ teaspoon purple gel food dye in each bowl of batter. (Cakes can be stored at room temperature for up to 24 hours or frozen for up to 1 month; defrost cakes at room temperature.)

**5.** Line edges of cake platter with 4 strips of parchment to keep platter clean and place small dab of frosting in center of platter to anchor cake. Place purple cake layer on platter. Spread ¾ cup frosting evenly over top, right to edge of cake. Top with blue cake layer, pressing lightly to adhere, and repeat process with green, yellow, orange, and red layers, pressing lightly to adhere and spreading ¾ cup frosting evenly over each layer. Place ¾ cup frosting in center of top of cake and spread to outer edges, letting any excess hang over edges; smooth top. Spread half of remaining frosting along sides of cake with short side-by-side strokes until entire side is covered with thin coat of frosting. Refrigerate cake until frosting is set, about 15 minutes.

**6.** Spread remaining frosting evenly over top and sides of cake. Carefully remove parchment strips before serving.

### Vanilla Frosting

**MAKES** 5 cups, enough for two-layer cake

For colored frosting, stir in drops of food coloring at the end, but be sure to use a light hand—a little goes a long way.

- 1 pound (4 sticks) unsalted butter, each stick cut into quarters and softened
- ¼ cup heavy cream
- 1 tablespoon vanilla extract
- ¼ teaspoon table salt
- 4 cups (16 ounces) confectioners' sugar

**1.** Using stand mixer fitted with paddle, beat butter, cream, vanilla, and salt on medium-high speed until smooth, about 1 minute. Reduce speed to medium-low, slowly add sugar, and beat until incorporated and smooth, about 4 minutes.

**2.** Increase speed to medium-high and beat until frosting is light and fluffy, about 5 minutes. (Frosting can be refrigerated for up to 3 days; let soften at room temperature, about 2 hours, then rewhip on medium speed until smooth, 2 to 5 minutes.)

## Yellow Sheet Cake with Chocolate Frosting

**SERVES** 12 to 15

**WHY THIS RECIPE WORKS** Yellow sheet cake is a darling of American desserts: It's classic, universally liked, and just right for serving by the square. For a tender cake with a fine, plush texture, we started by using bleached cake flour. Its altered starch is more absorbent than the starch in unbleached flour, so it can accommodate more liquid, sugar, and fat (we use butter for flavor and vegetable oil for moistness) without collapsing under the extra weight. We combined the ingredients using the two-stage reverse-creaming method: The first stage combines everything into a homogeneous mixture and incorporates air, and the high-speed second stage divides that air into progressively smaller bubbles, producing a cake with a fine, uniform crumb. We decided to crown our cake with a rich chocolate frosting. Use a metal baking pan for this recipe; a glass dish will cause the edges of the cake to overbake as it cools. It's important to use bleached cake flour here; substituting unbleached cake flour or a combination of all-purpose flour and cornstarch will cause the cake to fall. To ensure the proper texture, weigh the flour for the cake. Our favorite bittersweet chocolate is Ghirardelli 60% Cacao Bittersweet Chocolate Premium Baking Bar.

**CAKE**

- 4 large eggs, plus 2 large yolks
- ½ cup buttermilk
- 1 tablespoon vanilla extract
- 2¼ cups (9 ounces) bleached cake flour
- 1¾ cups (12¼ ounces) sugar
- 1¼ teaspoons baking powder
- ¼ teaspoon baking soda
- ½ teaspoon table salt
- 8 tablespoons unsalted butter, softened
- ½ cup vegetable oil

**FROSTING**

- 2¼ cups (9 ounces) confectioners' sugar
- ½ cup (1½ ounces) unsweetened cocoa powder
- 8 tablespoons unsalted butter, softened
- ¼ cup hot water
- ¼ teaspoon table salt
- 2 ounces bittersweet chocolate, melted

**1. FOR THE CAKE:** Adjust oven rack to middle position and heat oven to 350 degrees. Grease and flour 13 by 9-inch baking pan. Combine eggs, yolks, buttermilk, and vanilla in 2-cup liquid measure, and whisk with fork until smooth.

**2.** Combine flour, sugar, baking powder, baking soda, and salt in bowl of stand mixer fitted with paddle. Mix on low speed until combined, about 20 seconds. Add butter and oil and mix on low speed until combined, about 30 seconds. Increase speed to medium, and beat until lightened, about 1 minute. Reduce speed to low and, with mixer running, slowly add egg mixture. When mixture is fully incorporated, stop mixer, and scrape down bowl and paddle thoroughly. Beat on medium-high until batter is pale, smooth, and thick, about 3 minutes. Transfer batter to prepared pan, and smooth top. Rap pan firmly on work surface 5 times to release any large air bubbles.

**3.** Bake until toothpick inserted in center comes out with a few crumbs attached, 28 to 32 minutes. Transfer cake in pan to wire rack to cool completely, about 2 hours.

**4. FOR THE FROSTING:** Combine confectioners' sugar, cocoa, butter, water, and salt in bowl of stand mixer fitted with whisk attachment. Stir on low speed until combined, about 20 seconds. Increase speed to medium and continue to mix until smooth, about 1 minute, scraping down sides as necessary. Add chocolate, and beat on low speed until incorporated. Let sit at room temperature until thickened to spreadable consistency, 30 to 40 minutes.

**5.** Frost cake. Refrigerate for 20 minutes to set frosting before serving.

## Simple Chocolate Sheet Cake

**SERVES** 12

**WHY THIS RECIPE WORKS** For a simple cake that boasted deep chocolate flavor and color, we used a combination of Dutch-processed cocoa and melted bittersweet chocolate; the cocoa offered pure, assertive chocolate flavor while the chocolate contributed complexity as well as fat and sugar. Neutral-tasting oil allowed the chocolate flavor to shine. To minimize cleanup, we mixed the wet and dry ingredients directly into the saucepan where we'd melted the chocolate with cocoa and milk. A milk chocolate ganache frosting contrasted nicely with the deeper flavor of the cake. To make the ganache thick, rich, and creamy, we added plenty of softened butter to the warm chocolate-cream mixture, refrigerated the frosting to cool it quickly so that it would spread nicely, and gave it a quick whisk to smooth it out and lighten its texture. While any high-quality chocolate can be used here, our preferred bittersweet chocolate is Ghirardelli 60% Cacao Bittersweet Chocolate Premium Baking Bar, and our favorite milk chocolate is Endangered Species Chocolate Smooth + Creamy Milk Chocolate. We recommend making this cake with a Dutch-processed cocoa powder; our favorite is from Droste. Using a natural cocoa powder will result in a drier cake.

**CAKE**

- 1½ cups (10½ ounces) granulated sugar
- 1¼ cups (6¼ ounces) all-purpose flour
- ½ teaspoon baking soda
- ½ teaspoon table salt
- 1 cup whole milk
- 8 ounces bittersweet chocolate, chopped fine
- ¾ cup (2¼ ounces) Dutch-processed cocoa powder
- ⅔ cup vegetable oil
- 4 large eggs
- 1 teaspoon vanilla extract

**FROSTING**

- 1 pound milk chocolate, chopped
- ⅔ cup heavy cream
- 16 tablespoons (2 sticks) unsalted butter, cut into 16 pieces and softened

**1. FOR THE CAKE:** Adjust oven rack to middle position and heat oven to 325 degrees. Lightly spray 13 by 9-inch baking pan with vegetable oil spray. Whisk sugar, flour, baking soda, and salt together in medium bowl; set aside.

**2.** Combine milk, chocolate, and cocoa in large saucepan. Place saucepan over low heat and cook, whisking frequently, until chocolate is melted and mixture is smooth. Remove from heat and let cool slightly, about 5 minutes. Whisk oil, eggs, and vanilla into chocolate mixture (mixture may initially look curdled) until smooth and homogeneous. Add sugar mixture and whisk until combined, making sure to scrape corners of saucepan.

**3.** Transfer batter to prepared pan; bake until firm in center when lightly pressed and toothpick inserted in center comes out with few crumbs attached, 30 to 35 minutes, rotating pan halfway through baking. Let cake cool completely in pan on wire rack before frosting, 1 to 2 hours.

**4. FOR THE FROSTING:** While cake is baking, combine chocolate and cream in large heatproof bowl set over saucepan filled with 1 inch barely simmering water, making sure that water does not touch bottom of bowl. Whisk mixture occasionally until chocolate is uniformly smooth and glossy, 10 to 15 minutes. Remove bowl from saucepan. Add butter, whisking once or twice to break up pieces. Let mixture stand for 5 minutes to finish melting butter, then whisk until completely smooth. Refrigerate frosting, without stirring, until cooled and thickened, 30 minutes to 1 hour.

**5.** Once cool, whisk frosting until smooth. (Whisked frosting will lighten in color slightly and should hold its shape on whisk.) Spread frosting evenly over top of cake. Cut cake into squares and serve out of pan. (Leftover cake can be refrigerated in airtight container for up to 2 days.)

## Chocolate Sheet Cake with Milk Chocolate Frosting

**SERVES** 12

**WHY THIS RECIPE WORKS** For a simple cake that boasted deep chocolate flavor and color, we used a combination of Dutch-processed cocoa and melted bittersweet chocolate; the cocoa offered pure, assertive chocolate flavor while the chocolate contributed complexity as well as fat and sugar. Neutral-tasting oil allowed the chocolate flavor to shine. To minimize cleanup, we mixed the wet and dry ingredients directly into the saucepan where we'd melted the chocolate with cocoa and milk. A milk chocolate ganache frosting contrasted nicely with the deeper flavor of the cake. To make the ganache thick, rich, and creamy, we added plenty of softened butter to the warm chocolate-cream mixture, refrigerated the frosting to cool it quickly so that it would spread nicely, and gave it a quick whisk to smooth it out and lighten its texture. While any high-quality chocolate can be used here, our preferred bittersweet chocolate is Ghirardelli 60% Cacao Bittersweet Chocolate Premium Baking Bar, and our favorite milk chocolate is Endangered Species Chocolate Smooth + Creamy Milk Chocolate. We recommend making this cake with a Dutch-processed cocoa powder; our favorite is from Droste. Using a natural cocoa powder will result in a drier cake.

**CAKE**

- 1½ cups (10½ ounces) granulated sugar
- 1¼ cups (6¼ ounces) all-purpose flour
- ½ teaspoon baking soda
- ½ teaspoon table salt
- 1 cup whole milk
- 8 ounces bittersweet chocolate, chopped fine
- ¾ cup (2¼ ounces) Dutch-processed cocoa powder
- ⅔ cup vegetable oil
- 4 large eggs
- 1 teaspoon vanilla extract

**FROSTING**

- 1 pound milk chocolate, chopped
- ⅔ cup heavy cream
- 16 tablespoons unsalted butter, cut into 16 pieces and softened

**1. FOR THE CAKE:** Adjust oven rack to middle position and heat oven to 325 degrees. Lightly spray 13 by 9-inch baking pan with vegetable oil spray. Whisk sugar, flour, baking soda, and salt together in medium bowl; set aside.

**2.** Combine milk, chocolate, and cocoa in large saucepan. Place saucepan over low heat and cook, whisking frequently, until chocolate is melted and mixture is smooth. Remove from heat and let cool slightly, about 5 minutes. Whisk oil, eggs, and vanilla into chocolate mixture (mixture may initially look curdled) until smooth and homogeneous. Add sugar mixture and whisk until combined, making sure to scrape corners of saucepan.

**3.** Transfer batter to prepared pan; bake until firm in center when lightly pressed and toothpick inserted in center comes out with few crumbs attached, 30 to 35 minutes, rotating pan halfway through baking. Let cake cool completely in pan on wire rack before frosting, 1 to 2 hours.

**4. FOR THE FROSTING:** While cake is baking, combine chocolate and cream in large heatproof bowl set over saucepan filled with 1 inch barely simmering water, making sure that water does not touch bottom of bowl. Whisk mixture occasionally until chocolate is uniformly smooth and glossy, 10 to 15 minutes. Remove bowl from saucepan. Add butter, whisking once or twice to break up pieces. Let mixture stand for 5 minutes to finish melting butter, then whisk until completely smooth. Refrigerate frosting, without stirring, until cooled and thickened, 30 minutes to 1 hour.

**5.** Once cool, whisk frosting until smooth. (Whisked frosting will lighten in color slightly and should hold its shape on whisk.) Spread frosting evenly over top of cake. Cut cake into squares and serve out of pan. (Leftover cake can be refrigerated in airtight container for up to 2 days.)

## Dark Chocolate Cupcakes

**MAKES** 12 cupcakes

**WHY THIS RECIPE WORKS** We wanted the consummate chocolate cupcake—one with a rich, buttery flavor, a light, moist, cakey texture, and just the right amount of sugar—but we wanted it to be almost as quick and easy to make as the cupcakes that come from a box. For the mixing method, we found that the melted-butter method often used for mixing muffins, quick breads, and brownies—a method that requires no mixer and no time spent waiting for butter to soften—worked best. That procedure won out over the more conventional creaming method for our cupcakes, delivering a light texture with a tender, fine crumb. Moving on to tackle the chocolate flavor, we found that a combination of cocoa powder and bittersweet chocolate delivered deep chocolate flavor and that mixing the cocoa powder with the butter and chocolate as they melted made the chocolate flavor even stronger and richer.

- 8 tablespoons (1 stick) unsalted butter, cut into 4 pieces
- 2 ounces bittersweet chocolate, chopped
- ½ cup cocoa powder, preferably Dutch-processed
- ¾ cup (3¾ ounces) unbleached all-purpose flour
- ¾ teaspoon baking powder
- ½ teaspoon baking soda
- 2 large eggs, at room temperature
- ¾ cup (5¼ ounces) sugar
- 1 teaspoon vanilla extract
- ½ teaspoon table salt
- ½ cup sour cream
- 1 recipe Easy Vanilla Bean Buttercream

**1.** Adjust an oven rack to the lower-middle position and heat the oven to 350 degrees. Line a standard-size muffin pan with baking cup liners.

**2.** Melt the butter, chocolate, and cocoa in a medium heatproof bowl set over a saucepan filled with 1 inch of barely simmering water, stirring occasionally. Set aside to cool until just warm to the touch.

**3.** Whisk the flour, baking powder, and baking soda in a small bowl to combine.

**4.** Whisk the eggs in a medium bowl to combine; add the sugar, vanilla, and salt and whisk until fully incorporated. Add the cooled chocolate mixture and whisk until combined. Sift about one-third of the flour mixture over the chocolate mixture and whisk until combined; whisk in the sour cream until combined, then sift the remaining flour mixture over the batter and whisk until homogeneous and thick.

**5.** Divide the batter evenly among the muffin cups. Bake until a toothpick or wooden skewer inserted into the center of the cupcakes comes out clean, 18 to 20 minutes, rotating the pan halfway through the baking time.

**6.** Cool the cupcakes in the pan on a wire rack until cool enough to handle, about 15 minutes. Carefully lift each cupcake from the muffin pan and set on a wire rack. Cool to room temperature before icing, about 30 minutes. To frost: Mound about 2 tablespoons of icing on the center of each cupcake. Using a small spatula or butter knife, spread the icing to the edge of the cupcake, leaving a slight mound in the center. (Store leftover cupcakes (frosted or unfrosted) in the refrigerator, but let them come to room temperature before serving.)

### Easy Vanilla Bean Buttercream

**MAKES** about 1½ cups, enough to frost 12 cupcakes

If you prefer to skip the vanilla bean, increase the extract to 1½ teaspoons. The buttercream frostings can be made ahead and refrigerated; if refrigerated, the frosting must stand at room temperature to soften before use. If using a hand-held mixer, increase mixing times significantly (by at least 50 percent).

- 10 tablespoons (1¼ sticks) unsalted butter, softened
- ½ vanilla bean, halved lengthwise
- 1¼ cups (5 ounces) confectioners' sugar
- Pinch table salt
- 1 tablespoon heavy cream
- ½ teaspoon vanilla extract

In a stand mixer fitted with the whisk attachment, beat the butter at medium-high speed until smooth, about 20 seconds. Using a paring knife, scrape the seeds from the vanilla bean into the butter and beat the mixture at medium-high speed to combine, about 15 seconds. Add the confectioners' sugar and salt and beat at medium-low speed until most of the sugar is moistened, about 45 seconds. Scrape down the bowl and beat at medium speed until the mixture is fully combined, about 15 seconds. Scrape down the bowl, add the heavy cream and vanilla extract, and beat at medium speed until incorporated, about 10 seconds, then increase the speed to medium-high and beat until light and fluffy, about 4 minutes, scraping down the bowl once or twice.

## Ultimate Chocolate Cupcakes with Ganache Filling

**MAKES** 12 cupcakes]

**WHY THIS RECIPE WORKS** Chocolate cupcakes pose a unique challenge: If the cupcakes are packed with chocolate flavor they are often too crumbly to be eaten out of hand, but achieving the right structure can mean sacrificing rich chocolate flavor. We wanted a chocolate cupcake that had it all. We started by making cupcakes using our favorite chocolate cake recipe. Tasters liked the chocolate flavor, but their crumbly texture made the cupcakes impossible to eat without a fork. Substituting bread flour—which is specifically engineered for

gluten development—for the all-purpose flour resulted in cupcakes that were markedly less crumbly, but not tough. To intensify the chocolate flavor we mixed the cocoa with hot coffee and also replaced the butter with more neutral-flavored vegetable oil. For a final chocolate burst, we spooned ganache onto the cupcakes before baking, which gave them a truffle-like center. A velvety buttercream with just enough sweetness crowned the cakes perfectly. Use a high-quality bittersweet or semisweet chocolate for this recipe, such as one of the test kitchen's favorite baking chocolates, Ghirardelli 60% Cacao Bittersweet Chocolate. Though we highly recommend the ganache filling, you can omit it for a more traditional cupcake.

**GANACHE FILLING**

- 2 ounces bittersweet chocolate, chopped fine
- ¼ cup heavy cream
- 1 tablespoon confectioners' sugar

**CHOCOLATE CUPCAKES**

- 3 ounces bittersweet chocolate, chopped fine
- ⅓ cup (1 ounce) Dutch-processed cocoa powder
- ¾ cup hot coffee
- ¾ cup (4⅛ ounces) bread flour
- ¾ cup (5¼ ounces) granulated sugar
- ½ teaspoon table salt
- ½ teaspoon baking soda
- 6 tablespoons vegetable oil
- 2 large eggs
- 2 teaspoons distilled white vinegar
- 1 teaspoon vanilla extract
- 1 recipe Creamy Chocolate Frosting (page 892)

**1. FOR THE GANACHE FILLING:** Place chocolate, cream, and confectioners' sugar in medium bowl. Microwave until mixture is warm to touch, 20 to 30 seconds. Whisk mixture until smooth, then refrigerate until just chilled, no longer than 30 minutes.

**2. FOR THE CUPCAKES:** Adjust oven rack to middle position and heat oven to 350 degrees. Line 12-cup muffin tin with baking cup liners. Place chocolate and cocoa in medium bowl. Pour hot coffee over mixture and whisk until smooth. Refrigerate until completely cool, about 20 minutes. Whisk flour, granulated sugar, salt, and baking soda together in medium bowl and set aside.

**3.** Whisk oil, eggs, vinegar, and vanilla into cooled chocolate-cocoa mixture until smooth. Add flour mixture and whisk until smooth.

**4.** Divide batter evenly among muffin tin cups. Place 1 slightly rounded teaspoon of ganache filling on top of each cupcake. Bake until cupcakes are set and just firm to touch, 17 to 19 minutes. Let cupcakes cool in muffin tin on wire rack until cool enough to handle, about 10 minutes. Carefully lift each cupcake from muffin tin and set on wire rack. Let cool completely before frosting, about 1 hour.

**5. TO FROST:** Mound 2 to 3 tablespoons of frosting on center of each cupcake. Use small icing spatula or butter knife to ice each cupcake. (Cupcakes can be made up to 24 hours ahead and stored unfrosted in airtight container.)

## Creamy Chocolate Frosting

**MAKES** 2¼ cups

Cool the chocolate to between 85 and 100 degrees before adding it to the frosting. If the frosting seems too soft after adding the chocolate, chill it briefly in the refrigerator and then rewhip it until creamy.

- ⅓ cup (2⅓ ounces) sugar
- 2 large egg whites
- Pinch table salt
- 12 tablespoons unsalted butter, cut into 12 pieces and softened
- 6 ounces bittersweet chocolate, melted and cooled
- ½ teaspoon vanilla extract

**1.** Combine sugar, egg whites, and salt in bowl of stand mixer, then place bowl over pan of simmering water. Whisking gently but constantly, heat mixture until slightly thickened and foamy and registers 150 degrees, 2 to 3 minutes.

**2.** Using whisk attachment, whip mixture on medium speed in stand mixer until it reaches consistency of shaving cream and is slightly cooled, 1 to 2 minutes. Add butter, 1 piece at a time, until smooth and creamy. (Frosting may look curdled after half of butter has been added; it will smooth with additional butter.) Once all butter is added, add cooled melted chocolate and vanilla and mix until combined. Increase mixer speed to medium-high and beat until light, fluffy, and thoroughly combined, about 30 seconds, scraping beater and sides of bowl with rubber spatula as necessary. (Frosting can be made up to 24 hours ahead and refrigerated in airtight container. When ready to frost, microwave briefly until just slightly softened, 5 to 10 seconds. Once warmed, stir until creamy.)

## Gluten-Free Rainbow Sprinkle Cupcakes

**MAKES** 12 cupcakes

**WHY THIS RECIPE WORKS** In our quest for tender gluten-free cupcakes with a slightly domed top and a light, open crumb, we began by using the easiest mixing method (combining everything in a bowl). We found that we needed baking soda for browning and tenderness but found we could reduce the amount of baking powder substantially. While these adjustments solved the structural problems in these little cakes, the mixing method meant that the butter wasn't getting emulsified into the batter. In the end, we swapped the butter for oil, which fixed the greasiness, but we missed the rich flavor of butter. The addition of sour cream and white chocolate kept the cupcakes rich and moist. To achieve confetti throughout the cakes, we simply mixed rainbow sprinkles into the batter. Mixing more sprinkles into the frosting completed the festive look and added a nice, crunchy texture. After frosting the cupcakes, serve them within a few hours. You can use your favorite frosting recipe or store-bought.

- 4 ounces white chocolate, chopped coarse
- 6 tablespoons vegetable oil
- 6½ ounces (¾ cup plus ⅔ cup) The America's Test Kitchen All-Purpose Gluten-Free Flour Blend (page 811)
- 1 teaspoon baking powder
- ⅛ teaspoon baking soda
- ½ teaspoon xanthan gum
- ½ teaspoon table salt
- 2 large eggs
- 2 teaspoons vanilla extract
- 3½ ounces (½ cup) sugar
- ⅓ cup sour cream
- 2 cups vanilla frosting
- 2 tablespoons rainbow sprinkles

1. Adjust oven rack to middle position and heat oven to 325 degrees. Line 12-cup muffin tin with paper liners. Microwave chocolate and oil together in bowl at 50 percent power, stirring often, until chocolate is melted, about 2 minutes; whisk smooth and let cool slightly. In separate bowl, whisk flour blend, baking powder, baking soda, xanthan gum, and salt together.

2. In large bowl, whisk eggs and vanilla together. Whisk in sugar until well combined. Whisk in cooled chocolate mixture and sour cream until combined. Whisk in flour blend mixture until batter is thoroughly combined and smooth. Gently whisk in sprinkles until thoroughly incorporated.

3. Portion batter evenly into prepared muffin tin. Bake until cupcakes are set on top and toothpick inserted into center of cupcakes comes out clean, 19 to 22 minutes, rotating muffin tin halfway through baking.

4. Let cupcakes cool in muffin tin for 10 minutes, then transfer to wire rack and let cool completely, about 1 hour. Remove cupcakes from tin and let cool completely, about 1 hour. (Unfrosted cupcakes can be stored in airtight container at room temperature for up to 1 day.)

5. Stir sprinkles into frosting. Spread or pipe frosting onto cupcakes before serving.

## Flourless Chocolate Cake

**SERVES** 12 to 16

**WHY THIS RECIPE WORKS** While all flourless chocolate cake recipes share common ingredients (chocolate, butter, and eggs), the techniques used to make them vary, as do the results. You can end up with anything from a fudge brownie to a bittersweet chocolate soufflé. We wanted something dense, moist, and ultra-chocolaty. We started with the type of chocolate. A cake made with unsweetened chocolate was neither smooth nor silky enough for this kind of cake. Bittersweet or semisweet chocolate was ideal, with deep chocolate flavor and a smooth texture. Next we turned to the eggs—we compared cakes made with room temperature eggs and eggs taken straight from the fridge. The batter made with chilled eggs produced a denser foam and the resulting cake boasted a smooth, velvety texture. And the gentle, moist heat of a water bath further preserved the cake's lush texture. This cake is best when baked a day ahead to mellow its flavor. Even though the cake may not look done, pull it from the oven when an instant-read thermometer registers 140 degrees. (Do not let the tip of the thermometer hit the bottom of the pan.) It will continue to firm up as it cools. If you use a 9-inch springform pan instead of the preferred 8-inch pan, reduce the baking time to 18 to 20 minutes. See pages 1046–1047 for our top-rated brands of chocolate.

- 8 large eggs, chilled
- 1 pound bittersweet or semisweet chocolate, chopped
- ½ pound (2 sticks) unsalted butter, cut into ½-inch chunks
- ¼ cup strong coffee
- Confectioners' sugar or cocoa powder, for decoration

1. Adjust an oven rack to the lower-middle position and heat the oven to 325 degrees. Grease an 8-inch springform pan, then line the bottom with parchment paper. Wrap the outside of the pan with two 18-inch-square pieces of heavy-duty foil; set the springform pan in a roasting pan. Bring a kettle of water to a boil.

2. In a stand mixer fitted with the whisk attachment, beat the eggs at medium speed until doubled in volume, about 5 minutes.

3. Meanwhile, melt the chocolate and butter in a large heatproof bowl set over a saucepan filled with 1 inch of barely simmering water until smooth, stirring once or twice; stir in the coffee. Using a large rubber spatula, fold one-third of the egg mixture into the chocolate mixture until only a few streaks of egg are visible; fold the remaining egg mixture, in two additions, until the batter is totally homogeneous.

4. Scrape the batter into the prepared pan and smooth the surface with the spatula. Set the roasting pan on the oven rack and pour in enough boiling water to come about halfway up the sides of the pan. Bake until the cake has risen slightly, the edges are just beginning to set, a thin glazed crust (like a brownie) has formed on the surface, and an instant-read thermometer inserted halfway through the center of the cake registers 140 degrees, 22 to 25 minutes. Remove the pan from the water bath and set on a wire rack; cool to room temperature. Cover and refrigerate overnight to mellow the flavors. (Cake can be covered and refrigerated for up to 4 days.)

5. About 30 minutes before serving, remove the springform pan sides, then flip the cake out onto the wire rack. Peel off the parchment and flip the cake right side up onto a serving platter. Lightly dust the cake with confectioners' sugar or unsweetened cocoa powder, if desired, and serve.

## Torta Caprese

**SERVES** 12 to 14

**WHY THIS RECIPE WORKS** This torte, a classic dessert along the Amalfi Coast, is a showstopper that packs in all the richness and depth of flourless chocolate cake. It features finely ground almonds in the batter that subtly break up the fudgy crumb, making it lighter and less cloying to eat. Our version contains melted butter and bittersweet chocolate as well as vanilla, cocoa powder, and salt to boost the chocolate's complexity. All flourless cakes are aerated with whipped eggs instead of chemical leaveners, and we found that whipping the whites and yolks separately in a stand mixer, each with half the sugar, created strong, stable egg foams that lightened the rich, heavy batter and prevented it from collapsing after baking. For the best results, use a good-quality bittersweet chocolate and Dutch-processed cocoa here. We developed this recipe using our favorite bittersweet chocolate, Ghirardelli 60% Cacao Bittersweet Chocolate Premium Baking Bar, and our favorite Dutch-processed cocoa, Droste Cacao. Either almond flour or almond meal will work in this recipe; we used Bob's Red Mill. Serve with lightly sweetened whipped cream.

- 12 tablespoons unsalted butter, cut into 12 pieces
- 6 ounces bittersweet chocolate, chopped
- 1 teaspoon vanilla extract
- 4 large eggs, separated
- 1 cup (7 ounces) granulated sugar, divided
- 2 cups (7 ounces) almond flour
- 2 tablespoons Dutch-processed cocoa powder
- ½ teaspoon table salt
- Confectioners' sugar (optional)

**1.** Adjust oven rack to middle position and heat oven to 325 degrees. Lightly spray 9-inch springform pan with vegetable oil spray.

**2.** Microwave butter and chocolate in medium bowl at 50 percent power, stirring often, until melted, 1½ to 2 minutes. Stir in vanilla and set aside.

**3.** Using stand mixer fitted with whisk attachment, whip egg whites on medium-low speed until foamy, about 1 minute. Increase speed to medium-high and continue to whip, slowly adding ½ cup granulated sugar, until whites are glossy and thick and hold stiff peaks, about 4 minutes longer. Transfer whites to large bowl.

**4.** Add egg yolks and remaining ½ cup granulated sugar to now-empty mixer bowl and whip on medium-high speed until thick and pale yellow, about 3 minutes, scraping down bowl as necessary. Add chocolate mixture and mix on medium speed until incorporated, about 15 seconds. Add almond flour, cocoa, and salt and mix until incorporated, about 30 seconds.

**5.** Remove bowl from mixer and stir few times with large rubber spatula, scraping bottom of bowl to ensure almond flour is fully incorporated. Add one-third of whipped whites to bowl, return bowl to mixer, and mix on medium speed until no streaks of white remain, about 30 seconds, scraping down bowl halfway through mixing. Transfer batter to bowl with remaining whites. Using large rubber spatula, gently fold whites into batter until no streaks of white remain. Pour batter into prepared pan, smooth top with spatula, and place pan on rimmed baking sheet.

**6.** Bake until toothpick inserted in center comes out with few moist crumbs attached, about 50 minutes, rotating pan halfway through baking. Let cake cool in pan on wire rack for 20 minutes. Remove side of pan and let cake cool completely, about 2 hours. (Cake can be wrapped in plastic wrap and stored at room temperature for up to 3 days.)

**7.** Dust top of cake with confectioners' sugar, if using. Using offset spatula, transfer cake to serving platter. Cut into wedges and serve.

## Chocolate-Raspberry Torte

**SERVES** 12 to 16

**WHY THIS RECIPE WORKS** Sachertorte is a classic Viennese dessert featuring layers of chocolate cake sandwiching apricot jam and enrobed in a rich chocolate glaze. Each element must be perfected. We set out to create a deeply chocolaty dessert using Sachertorte as the inspiration, giving it our own spin by pairing chocolate with raspberries. For a rich, fudgy base, we started by baking our Flourless Chocolate Cake (page 893) in two pans, so we could sandwich two cakes together rather than halving a single delicate cake. But when we tried to stack the layers, the dense cake tore and fell apart. Adding ground nuts gave it the structure it needed, plus a good boost of flavor. The winning approach for our filling was to combine jam with mashed fresh berries for a tangy-sweet mixture that clung to the cake. For a simple glaze, we melted bittersweet chocolate with heavy cream to create a rich-tasting ganache that poured smoothly. For tasty decoration, we dotted fresh raspberries around the top of the torte and pressed sliced, toasted almonds along its sides. Be sure to use cake pans with at least 2-inch-tall sides.

**CAKE**

- 8 ounces bittersweet chocolate, chopped fine
- 12 tablespoons (1½ sticks) unsalted butter, cut into ½-inch pieces
- 2 teaspoons vanilla extract
- ¼ teaspoon instant espresso powder
- 1¾ cups (6⅛ ounces) sliced almonds, toasted
- ¼ cup (1¼ ounces) unbleached all-purpose flour
- ½ teaspoon table salt
- 5 large eggs, at room temperature
- ¾ cup (5¼ ounces) sugar

**FILLING**

- 2½ ounces (½ cup) raspberries, plus 16 individual raspberries
- ¼ cup seedless raspberry jam

**GLAZE**

- 5 ounces bittersweet chocolate, chopped fine
- ½ cup plus 1 tablespoon heavy cream

**1. FOR THE CAKE:** Adjust an oven rack to the middle position and heat the oven to 325 degrees. Grease and flour two 9-inch round cake pans, line the bottoms with parchment paper, then grease and flour the parchment. Melt the chocolate and butter in a large heatproof bowl set over a saucepan filled with 1 inch of simmering water, stirring occasionally until smooth. Remove from the heat and let cool to room temperature, about 30 minutes. Stir in the vanilla and espresso powder.

**2.** Pulse ¾ cup of the almonds in a food processor until coarsely chopped, 6 to 8 pulses, and set aside. Process the remaining 1 cup almonds until very finely ground, about 45 seconds. Add the flour and salt and continue to process until combined, about 15 seconds. Transfer the almond-flour mixture to a medium bowl. Process the eggs until lightened in color and almost doubled in volume, about 3 minutes. With the processor running, slowly add the sugar and process until thoroughly combined, about 15 seconds. Using a whisk, gently fold the egg mixture into the chocolate mixture until some streaks of egg remain. Sprinkle half of the almond-flour mixture over the chocolate mixture and gently whisk until just combined. Sprinkle with the remaining almond-flour mixture and gently whisk until just combined.

**3.** Divide the batter evenly between the prepared pans and smooth the tops with a rubber spatula. Bake until the center is firm and a toothpick inserted in the center comes out with a few moist crumbs attached, 14 to 16 minutes. Transfer the cakes to a wire rack and let cool completely in the pans, about 30 minutes.

**4.** Run a paring knife around the sides of the cakes to loosen and invert the cakes onto cardboard rounds cut the same size as the diameter of the cake; discard the parchment. Using a wire rack, turn 1 cake right side up, then slide from the rack back onto the cardboard round.

### DECORATING CHOCOLATE-RASPBERRY TORTE

**1.** With the fully assembled cake placed on a cardboard round, hold the bottom of the cake in one hand and gently press the chopped nuts onto its side with the other hand.

**2.** Place one raspberry on the cake at 12 o'clock, then another at 6 o'clock. Place a third berry at 9 o'clock and a fourth at 3 o'clock. Continue to place raspberries directly opposite each other until all have been arranged in an evenly spaced circle.

**5. FOR THE FILLING:** Place ½ cup of the raspberries in a medium bowl and coarsely mash with a fork. Stir in the raspberry jam until just combined.

**6. TO ASSEMBLE THE TORTE:** Spread the raspberry mixture onto the cake layer that is right side up. Top with the second cake layer, leaving it upside down. Transfer the assembled cake, still on the cardboard round, to a wire rack set in a rimmed baking sheet.

**7. FOR THE GLAZE:** Melt the chocolate and cream in a medium heatproof bowl set over a saucepan filled with 1 inch of simmering water, stirring occasionally until smooth. Remove from the heat and gently whisk until very smooth. Pour the glaze onto the center of the assembled cake. Using an offset spatula, spread the glaze evenly over the top of the cake, letting it drip down the sides. Spread the glaze along the sides of the cake to coat evenly.

**8.** Using a fine-mesh strainer, sift the reserved chopped almonds to remove any fine bits. Holding the bottom of the cake on the cardboard round with 1 hand, gently press the sifted almonds onto the cake sides with the other hand. Arrange the remaining 16 raspberries around the circumference. Refrigerate the cake on the rack until the glaze is set, at least 1 hour or up to 24 hours (if refrigerating the cake for more than 1 hour, let sit at room temperature for about 30 minutes before serving). Transfer the cake to a platter and serve.

## Chocolate Volcano Cakes with Espresso Ice Cream

**SERVES 8**

**WHY THIS RECIPE WORKS** A common restaurant dessert, volcano cake, or molten chocolate cake, is an intensely chocolate cake that boasts a warm, liquid center. In addition to its great flavor and alluring contrasting textures, the cake can often be made ahead and baked just before serving. The make-ahead appeal of such a cake inspired us to master this dessert for the home cook. The initial recipes we tried revealed a host of problems with this cake—unbalanced chocolate flavor and a soggy or dry texture were just a few issues we faced. After testing various chocolates, we settled on a combination of bittersweet chocolate and unsweetened chocolate—this gave us maximum chocolate flavor. Chocolate alone seemed a little flat, so we added Grand Marnier for another layer of flavor. Whole eggs and egg yolks contributed richness and cornstarch helped make the batter remarkably stable. To help the cakes fall right out of the ramekins without a struggle, we buttered and sugared the ramekins before pouring in the batter. The cakes alone were great, but we felt they were even better when accompanied by a cold, creamy scoop of doctored "espresso" ice cream. Use a bittersweet bar chocolate in this recipe, not chips—the chips include emulsifiers that will alter the cakes' texture.

**ESPRESSO ICE CREAM**

- 2 pints coffee ice cream, softened
- 1½ tablespoons finely ground espresso beans

**CAKES**

- 10 tablespoons (1¼ sticks) unsalted butter, cut into ½-inch pieces, plus extra for the ramekins
- 1½ cups (10½ ounces) granulated sugar, plus extra for the ramekins
- 8 ounces bittersweet chocolate, chopped fine
- 2 ounces unsweetened chocolate, chopped fine
- 2 tablespoons cornstarch
- 3 large eggs plus 4 large egg yolks, at room temperature
- 2 teaspoons Grand Marnier (or other orange-flavored liqueur)
- Confectioners' sugar, for dusting the cakes

**1. FOR THE ICE CREAM:** Transfer the ice cream to a medium bowl and, using a rubber spatula, fold in the ground espresso until incorporated. Press a sheet of plastic wrap directly on the ice cream to prevent freezer burn and return it to the freezer. (The ice cream can be prepared up to 24 hours ahead.)

**2. FOR THE CAKES:** Lightly coat eight 4-ounce ramekins with butter. Dust with sugar, tapping out any excess, and set aside.

**3.** Melt the bittersweet and unsweetened chocolates and the 10 tablespoons butter in a large heatproof bowl set over a pan filled with 1 inch of barely simmering water, stirring occasionally until smooth. In a large bowl, whisk the 1½ cups sugar and cornstarch together. Add the chocolate mixture and stir to combine. Add the whole eggs, egg yolks, and Grand Marnier and whisk until fully combined. Using a ½-cup measure, scoop the batter into each of the prepared ramekins. (The ramekins can be covered tightly with plastic wrap and refrigerated for up to 24 hours. The cold cake batter should be baked straight from the refrigerator.)

**4.** Adjust an oven rack to the upper-middle position and heat the oven to 375 degrees. Place the filled ramekins on a rimmed baking sheet and bake until the tops of the cakes are set, have formed shiny crusts, and are beginning to crack, 16 to 20 minutes.

**5.** Transfer the ramekins to a wire rack and cool slightly, about 2 minutes. Run a small knife around the edge of each cake. Using a towel to protect your hand from the hot ramekins, invert each cake onto a small plate, then immediately invert again right side up onto eight individual plates. Sift confectioners' sugar over each cake. Remove the ice cream from the freezer and scoop a portion next to each cake. Serve immediately.

## Hot Fudge Pudding Cake

**SERVES 8**

---

**WHY THIS RECIPE WORKS** Those who have eaten hot fudge pudding cake know its charms: moist, brownie-like chocolate cake sitting on a pool of thick, chocolate pudding–like sauce, baked together in one dish, as if by magic. We set out to master this homey and humble dessert. Pudding cake is made by sprinkling brownie batter with a mixture of sugar and cocoa, then pouring hot water on top, and baking. To bump up the chocolate flavor, we used a combination of Dutch-processed cocoa and bittersweet chocolate. We also added instant coffee to the water that is poured over the batter to cut the sweetness of the cake. We baked the cake slow and low to promote a good top crust and a silky sauce. And we found that letting the cake rest for 20 to 30 minutes before eating allows the sauce to become pudding-like and the cake brownie-like. If you have cold brewed coffee on hand, it can be used in place of the instant coffee and water, but to make sure it isn't too strong, use 1 cup of cold coffee mixed with ½ cup of water. Serve warm with vanilla or coffee ice cream.

- 2 teaspoons instant coffee powder
- 1½ cups water
- 1 cup (7 ounces) granulated sugar
- ⅔ cup Dutch-processed cocoa powder
- ⅓ cup packed (2⅓ ounces) brown sugar
- 6 tablespoons (¾ stick) unsalted butter
- 2 ounces bittersweet or semisweet chocolate, chopped
- ¾ cup (3¾ ounces) unbleached all-purpose flour
- 2 teaspoons baking powder
- ⅓ cup whole milk
- 1 tablespoon vanilla extract
- ¼ teaspoon table salt
- 1 large egg yolk, at room temperature

**1.** Adjust an oven rack to the lower-middle position and heat the oven to 325 degrees. Lightly grease an 8-inch square glass or ceramic baking dish. Stir the instant coffee into the water; set aside to dissolve. Stir together ⅓ cup of the granulated sugar, ⅓ cup of the cocoa, and the brown sugar in a small bowl, breaking up large clumps with your fingers; set aside. Melt the butter, the remaining ⅓ cup cocoa, and the chocolate in a small bowl set over a saucepan filled with 1 inch of barely simmering water; whisk until smooth and set aside to cool slightly. Whisk the flour and baking powder in a small bowl to combine; set aside. Whisk the remaining ⅔ cup granulated sugar, the milk, vanilla, and salt in a medium bowl until combined; whisk in the egg yolk. Add the chocolate mixture and whisk to combine. Add the flour mixture and whisk until the batter is evenly moistened.

**2.** Pour the batter into the prepared baking dish and spread evenly to the sides and corners. Sprinkle the cocoa-sugar mixture evenly over the batter (the cocoa mixture should cover the entire surface of the batter); pour the coffee mixture gently over the cocoa mixture. Bake until the cake is puffed and bubbling and just beginning to pull away from the sides of the baking dish, about 45 minutes, rotating the pan halfway through the baking time. (Do not overbake.) Cool the cake in the dish on a wire rack for about 25 minutes and serve.

### Individual Hot Fudge Pudding Cakes

Follow the recipe for Hot Fudge Pudding Cake, heating the oven to 400 degrees and lightly greasing eight 6- to 8-ounce ramekins; set the ramekins on a baking sheet. Divide the batter evenly among the ramekins (about ¼ cup per ramekin) and level with the back of a spoon; sprinkle about 2 tablespoons cocoa-sugar mixture over the batter in each ramekin. Pour

3 tablespoons coffee mixture over the cocoa-sugar mixture in each ramekin. Bake until puffed and bubbling, about 20 minutes. (Do not overbake.) Cool the pudding cakes for about 15 minutes before serving (the cakes will fall as they cool).

## Individual Sticky Toffee Pudding Cakes

**SERVES 8**

**WHY THIS RECIPE WORKS** Sticky toffee pudding is a British dessert that's sticky in a good way: It features a moist, date-studded cake soaked in toffee sauce. To bring this dessert stateside, we knew we'd have to find a substitute for treacle, a sweetener similar to molasses that's traditionally used in these cakes. We also wanted to perfect the texture of the cake and showcase the rich, fruity flavor of the dates. Substituting brown sugar for treacle worked, but the dates needed a flavor boost. Typically, sliced dates are soaked in baking soda–laced water to soften their skins. Replacing the water already in our batter with the date soaking liquid improved the flavor significantly, and pulverizing half the dates before mixing them in guaranteed that every bite was laced with date flavor. Baking the cakes in a water bath ensured they remained moist. You will need eight 6-ounce ramekins to make these cakes. Be sure to form a tight seal with the foil before baking the cakes.

**CAKES**

- 8 ounces pitted dates, cut crosswise into ¼-inch-thick slices (1⅓ cups), divided
- ¾ cup warm water (110 degrees)
- ½ teaspoon baking soda
- 1¼ cups (6¼ ounces) all-purpose flour
- ½ teaspoon baking powder
- ½ teaspoon table salt
- ¾ cup packed (5¼ ounces) brown sugar
- 2 large eggs
- 4 tablespoons unsalted butter, melted
- 1½ tablespoons vanilla extract

**SAUCE**

- 4 tablespoons unsalted butter
- 1 tablespoon water
- 1 cup packed (7 ounces) brown sugar
- ¼ teaspoon table salt
- 1 cup heavy cream
- 1 tablespoon rum
- ¼ teaspoon lemon juice

**1. FOR THE CAKES:** Adjust oven rack to middle position and heat oven to 350 degrees. Grease and flour eight 6-ounce ramekins. Fold dish towel in half and place in bottom of large roasting pan. Place prepared ramekins on top of towel; set aside pan. Bring kettle of water to boil.

**2.** Combine half of dates, warm water, and baking soda in 2-cup liquid measuring cup (dates should be submerged beneath water); soak dates for 5 minutes. Meanwhile, whisk flour, baking powder, and salt together in large bowl.

**3.** Process sugar and remaining dates in food processor until no large chunks remain and mixture has texture of damp, coarse sand, about 45 seconds, scraping down sides of bowl as needed. Drain soaked dates and add soaking liquid to processor. Add eggs, melted butter, and vanilla and process until smooth, about 15 seconds. Transfer sugar mixture to bowl with flour mixture and sprinkle soaked dates on top. Using rubber spatula or wooden spoon, gently fold sugar mixture into flour mixture until just combined and date pieces are evenly dispersed.

**4.** Divide batter evenly among prepared ramekins (ramekins should be two-thirds full). Quickly pour enough boiling water into roasting pan to come ¼ inch up sides of ramekins. Cover pan tightly with aluminum foil, crimping edges to seal. Bake until cakes are puffed and surfaces are spongy, firm, and moist to touch, about 40 minutes. Immediately transfer ramekins from water bath to wire rack and let cool for 10 minutes.

**5. FOR THE SAUCE:** While cakes cool, melt butter with water in medium saucepan over medium-high heat. Whisk in sugar and salt until smooth. Continue to cook, stirring occasionally, until sugar is dissolved and slightly darkened, 3 to 4 minutes. Stir in ⅓ cup cream until smooth, about 30 seconds. Slowly pour in rum and remaining ⅔ cup cream, whisking constantly until smooth. Reduce heat to low; simmer until frothy, 3 to 5 minutes. Remove from heat and stir in lemon juice.

**6.** Using toothpick, poke 25 holes in top of each cake and spoon 1 tablespoon toffee sauce over each cake. Let cakes sit until sauce is absorbed, about 5 minutes. Invert each ramekin onto plate or shallow bowl; lift off ramekin. Divide remaining toffee sauce evenly among cakes and serve immediately.

### Large Sticky Toffee Pudding Cake

Substitute 8-inch square baking dish, greased and floured, for ramekins. Bake cake until outer 2 inches develop small holes and center is puffed and firm to touch, about 40 minutes. Cool as directed. Using toothpick, poke about 100 holes in cake and glaze with ½ cup sauce. Let cake sit until sauce is absorbed, about 5 minutes. Cut cake into squares and pour remaining toffee sauce over each square before serving.

## Lemon Pudding Cakes

**SERVES 6**

**WHY THIS RECIPE WORKS** During baking, this dessert's batter separates into two distinct layers magically creating a top-notch cake and a tart lemony pudding. But it takes a little chemistry to create two layers with distinctly different textures. Whipping the egg whites to soft peaks and decreasing the amount of flour gave us the best ratio of pudding to cake. Baking powder gave the cake layer lift, and a golden top. Using a cold water bath in a large roasting pan prevented the pudding from curdling while still allowing the cake to cook through. We infused the milk and cream with lemon zest, which boosted the lemony flavor without marring the smooth texture. To take the temperature of the pudding layer, touch the probe tip to the bottom of the ramekin and pull it up ¼ inch. The batter can also be baked in an 8-inch square glass baking dish. Serve chilled or room temperature.

- 1 cup whole milk
- ½ cup heavy cream
- 3 tablespoons grated lemon zest plus ½ cup juice (3 lemons)
- 1 cup (7 ounces) sugar
- ¼ cup (1¼ ounces) all-purpose flour
- ½ teaspoon baking powder
- ⅛ teaspoon table salt
- 2 large eggs, separated, plus 2 large whites
- ½ teaspoon vanilla extract

**1.** Adjust oven rack to middle position and heat oven to 325 degrees. Bring milk and cream to simmer in medium saucepan over medium-high heat. Remove pan from heat, whisk in lemon zest, cover pan, and let stand for 15 minutes. Meanwhile, fold dish towel in half and place in bottom of large roasting pan. Place six 6-ounce ramekins on top of towel and set aside pan.

**2.** Strain milk mixture through fine-mesh strainer into bowl, pressing on lemon zest to extract liquid; discard lemon zest. Whisk ¾ cup sugar, flour, baking powder, and salt in second bowl until combined. Add egg yolks, vanilla, lemon juice, and milk mixture and whisk until combined. (Batter will have consistency of milk.)

**3.** Using stand mixer fitted with whisk, whip egg whites on medium-low speed until foamy, about 1 minute. Increase speed to medium-high and whip whites to soft, billowy mounds, about 1 minute. Gradually add remaining ¼ cup sugar and whip until glossy, soft peaks form, 1 to 2 minutes.

**4.** Whisk one-quarter of whites into batter to lighten. With rubber spatula, gently fold in remaining whites until no clumps or streaks remain. Ladle batter into ramekins (ramekins should be nearly full). Pour enough cold water into roasting pan to come one-third of way up sides of ramekins. Bake until cake is set and pale golden brown and pudding layer registers 172 to 175 degrees at center, 50 to 55 minutes.

**5.** Remove pan from oven and let ramekins stand in water bath for 10 minutes. Transfer ramekins to wire rack and let cool completely. Serve.

## Triple-Chocolate Mousse Cake

**SERVES 12 to 16**

**WHY THIS RECIPE WORKS** Triple-chocolate mousse cake is a truly decadent dessert. Most times, though, the mousse texture is exactly the same from one layer to the next and the flavor is so overpoweringly rich it's hard to finish more than a few forkfuls. We set out to tweak this showy confection. By finessing one layer at a time, starting with the dark chocolate base and building to the top white chocolate tier, we aimed to create a triple-decker that was incrementally lighter in texture—and richness. For simplicity's sake, we built the dessert, layer by layer, in one springform pan. For a sturdy base layer we chose flourless chocolate cake instead of the typical mousse. For the middle layer, we started with a traditional chocolate mousse, but the texture seemed too heavy when combined with the cake, so we removed the eggs and cut back on the chocolate a bit—this resulted in the lighter, creamier layer we desired. And for the crowning layer, we made an easy white chocolate mousse. This recipe requires a springform pan at least 3 inches high. It is imperative that the layers are made in sequential order. Let the base cool completely before topping it with the middle layer. We recommend Ghirardelli 60% Cacao Bittersweet Chocolate Premium Baking Bar for the base and middle layers. Our preferred brand of white chocolate is Ghirardelli Classic White Baking Chips. For the best results, chill the mixer bowl before whipping the heavy cream. For neater slices, use a cheese wire or dip your knife in hot water before cutting each slice.

**BOTTOM LAYER**

- 6 tablespoons unsalted butter, cut into 6 pieces, plus extra for greasing pan
- 7 ounces bittersweet chocolate, chopped fine
- ¾ teaspoon instant espresso powder
- 4 large eggs, separated
- 1½ teaspoons vanilla extract
- Pinch table salt
- ⅓ cup packed (about 2½ ounces) light brown sugar, crumbled with your fingers to remove lumps, divided

**MIDDLE LAYER**

- 2 tablespoons cocoa powder, preferably Dutch-processed
- 5 tablespoons hot water
- 7 ounces bittersweet chocolate, chopped fine
- 1½ cups heavy cream, chilled
- 1 tablespoon granulated sugar
- ⅛ teaspoon table salt

**TOP LAYER**

- ¾ teaspoon powdered gelatin
- 1 tablespoon water
- 6 ounces white chocolate chips
- 1½ cups heavy cream, chilled, divided
- Shaved chocolate or cocoa powder for serving (optional)

**1. FOR THE BOTTOM LAYER:** Adjust oven rack to middle position and heat oven to 325 degrees. Butter bottom and sides of 9½-inch springform pan. Melt butter, chocolate, and espresso powder in large heatproof bowl set over saucepan filled with 1 inch of barely simmering water, stirring occasionally until smooth. Remove from heat and let mixture cool slightly, about 5 minutes. Whisk in egg yolks and vanilla; set aside.

**2.** Using stand mixer fitted with whisk attachment, beat egg whites and salt at medium speed until frothy, about 30 seconds. Add half of sugar and beat until combined, about 15 seconds. Add remaining sugar and beat at high speed until soft peaks form when whisk is lifted, about 1 minute longer, scraping down sides of bowl halfway through. Using whisk, fold one-third of beaten egg whites into chocolate mixture to lighten. Using rubber spatula, fold in remaining egg whites until no white streaks remain. Carefully transfer batter to prepared springform pan, gently smoothing top with offset spatula.

**3.** Bake until cake has risen, is firm around edges, and center has just set but is still soft (center of cake will spring back after pressing gently with your finger), 13 to 18 minutes. Transfer cake to wire rack and let cool completely, about 1 hour. (Cake will collapse as it cools.) Do not remove cake from pan.

**4. FOR THE MIDDLE LAYER:** Combine cocoa powder and hot water in small bowl; set aside. Melt chocolate in large heatproof bowl set over saucepan filled with 1 inch of barely simmering water, stirring occasionally until smooth. Remove from heat and let cool slightly, 2 to 5 minutes.

**5.** Using clean, dry mixer bowl and whisk attachment, whip cream, granulated sugar, and salt at medium speed until mixture begins to thicken, about 30 seconds. Increase speed to high and whip until soft peaks form when whisk is lifted, 15 to 60 seconds.

**6.** Whisk cocoa powder mixture into melted chocolate until smooth. Using whisk, fold one-third of whipped cream into chocolate mixture to lighten. Using rubber spatula, fold in remaining whipped cream until no white streaks remain. Spoon mousse into springform pan over cooled cake and gently tap pan on counter 3 times to remove any large air bubbles; gently smooth top with offset spatula. Wipe inside edge of pan with damp cloth to remove any drips. Refrigerate cake at least 15 minutes while preparing top layer.

**7. FOR THE TOP LAYER:** In small bowl, sprinkle gelatin over water; let stand for at least 5 minutes. Place white chocolate in medium bowl. Bring ½ cup cream to simmer in small saucepan over medium-high heat. Remove from heat; add gelatin mixture and stir until fully dissolved. Pour cream mixture over white chocolate and whisk until chocolate is melted and mixture is smooth, about 30 seconds. Let cool to room temperature, stirring occasionally, 5 to 8 minutes (mixture will thicken slightly).

**8.** Using clean, dry mixer bowl and whisk attachment, whip remaining 1 cup cream at medium speed until it begins to thicken, about 30 seconds. Increase speed to high and whip until soft peaks form when whisk is lifted, 15 to 60 seconds. Using whisk, fold one-third of whipped cream into white chocolate mixture to lighten. Using rubber spatula, fold remaining whipped cream into white chocolate mixture until no white streaks remain. Spoon white chocolate mousse into pan over middle layer. Smooth top with offset spatula. Return cake to refrigerator and chill until set, at least 2½ hours or up to 24 hours; leave cake in pan at room temperature for 45 minutes before releasing it from the pan and serving.

**9. TO SERVE:** Garnish top of cake with chocolate curls or dust with cocoa. Run thin knife between cake and side of springform pan; remove side of pan. Run cleaned knife along outside of cake to smooth sides. Cut into slices and serve.

## Bittersweet Chocolate Roulade

**SERVES** 8 to 10

**WHY THIS RECIPE WORKS** A chocolate roulade can be a baker's nightmare—a hard-to-roll cake with a dry texture and a filling that won't stay put. We wanted a true showcase roulade, a cake with a velvety texture and deep chocolate flavor; a thick, rich filling; and a decadent icing that covered it all. We used bittersweet chocolate for maximum chocolate flavor. Six eggs gave our cake great support while flour and cocoa provided further structure and extra chocolate flavor. Once the cake was baked, we cooled it briefly, then unmolded it onto a dish towel rubbed with cocoa to prevent sticking. While the cake was still warm, we rolled it up with the towel inside, cooled it briefly, and then unrolled it; this method gave the cake a "memory" so it could be filled and re-rolled. For the filling, we made an espresso-flavored cream using the Italian cream cheese, mascarpone. Mascarpone provided both structural support and rich flavor. For the icing, we chose dark chocolate ganache, with a little cognac for complex flavor. We suggest that you make the filling and ganache first, then make the cake while the ganache is setting up. If serving this cake in the style of a holiday yule log, make wood-grain striations in the ganache with a fork. The roulade is best served at room temperature.

- ¼ cup (1¼ ounces) unbleached all-purpose flour, plus extra for the pan
- 6 ounces bittersweet or semisweet chocolate, chopped fine
- 2 tablespoons cold unsalted butter, cut into 2 pieces
- 2 tablespoons cold water
- ¼ cup Dutch-processed cocoa powder, sifted, plus 1 tablespoon for unmolding
- ⅛ teaspoon table salt
- 6 large eggs, at room temperature and separated
- ⅓ cup (2⅓ ounces) sugar
- 1 teaspoon vanilla extract
- ⅛ teaspoon cream of tartar
- 1 recipe Espresso-Mascarpone Cream
- 1 recipe Dark Chocolate Ganache

**1.** Adjust an oven rack to the upper-middle position and heat the oven to 400 degrees. Spray a 17½ by 12-inch rimmed baking sheet with vegetable oil spray, cover the pan bottom with parchment paper, and spray the parchment with vegetable oil spray; dust with flour and tap out the excess.

**2.** Heat the chocolate, butter, and water in a small heatproof bowl set over a saucepan filled with 1 inch of barely simmering water, stirring occasionally until smooth. Set aside to cool slightly. Sift ¼ cup of the cocoa, the flour, and salt together into a small bowl and set aside.

**3.** In a stand mixer fitted with the whisk attachment, beat the egg yolks at medium-high speed until just combined, about 15 seconds. With the mixer running, add half of the sugar. Continue to beat, scraping down the sides of the bowl as necessary, until the yolks are pale yellow and the mixture falls in a thick ribbon when the whisk is lifted, about 8 minutes. Add the vanilla and beat to combine, scraping down the bowl once, about 30 seconds. Turn the mixture into a medium bowl; wash and dry the mixer bowl and whisk attachment.

**4.** In the clean bowl with the clean whisk attachment, beat the egg whites and cream of tartar at medium speed until foamy, about 30 seconds. With the mixer running, add about 1 teaspoon more sugar; continue beating until soft peaks form, about 40 seconds. Gradually add the remaining sugar and beat until the egg whites are glossy and hold stiff peaks when the whisk is lifted, about 1 minute longer. Do not over beat.

**5.** Stir the chocolate mixture into the egg yolks. With a rubber spatula, stir one-quarter of the egg whites into the chocolate mixture to lighten it. Fold in the remaining egg whites until almost no streaks remain. Sprinkle the cocoa-flour mixture over the top and fold in quickly but gently.

**6.** Pour the batter into the prepared pan; using a spatula and working quickly, even the surface and smooth the batter into the pan corners. Lightly tap the pan against the countertop two or three times to settle the batter. Bake until the center of the cake springs back when touched with a finger, 8 to 10 minutes, rotating the pan halfway through the baking time. Cool the cake in the pan on a wire rack for 5 minutes.

**7.** While the cake is cooling, lay a clean dish towel over the work surface and sift the remaining 1 tablespoon cocoa over the towel; rub the cocoa into the towel. Run a small knife around the baking sheet to loosen the cake. Flip the cake onto the towel and peel off the parchment.

**8.** Roll the cake, towel and all, into a jellyroll shape. Cool for 15 minutes, then unroll the cake and towel. Using a spatula, immediately spread the filling evenly over the cake, almost to the edges. Roll up the cake gently but snugly around the filling. Set a large sheet of parchment paper on an overturned rimmed baking sheet and set the roulade, seam side down, on top. Trim both ends on the diagonal. Spread the ganache evenly over the roulade. Use a fork to make wood-grain striations, if desired, on the surface of the ganache before the icing has set. Refrigerate the cake, on the baking sheet, uncovered, to slightly set the icing, about 20 minutes.

**9.** Carefully slide two wide metal spatulas under the cake and transfer the cake to a serving platter. Cut into slices and serve.

## Espresso-Mascarpone Cream

**MAKES** about 2½ cups

Mascarpone is a fresh Italian cheese. Its flavor is unique—mildly sweet and refreshing. It is sold in small containers in some supermarkets as well as most gourmet stores, cheese shops, and Italian markets.

- ½ cup heavy cream
- 2 teaspoons espresso powder or instant coffee
- 6 tablespoons confectioners' sugar
- 16½ ounces mascarpone cheese (generous 2 cups)

**1.** Bring the cream to a simmer in a small saucepan over high heat. Off the heat, stir in the espresso and confectioners' sugar; cool slightly.

**2.** With a spatula, beat the mascarpone in a medium bowl until softened. Gently whisk in the cooled cream mixture until combined. Cover with plastic wrap and refrigerate until ready to use.

### Dark Chocolate Ganache

**MAKES** about 1½ cups

If your kitchen is cool and the ganache becomes too stiff to spread, set the bowl over a saucepan of simmering water, then stir briefly until it is smooth and icing-like.

- ¾ cup heavy cream
- 2 tablespoons unsalted butter
- 6 ounces high-quality bittersweet or semisweet chocolate, chopped
- 1 tablespoon cognac

Microwave the cream and butter in a microwave-safe measuring cup on high power until bubbling, about 1½ minutes. (Alternatively, bring to a simmer in a small saucepan over medium-high heat.) Place the chocolate in a food processor. With the machine running, gradually add the hot cream mixture and cognac through the feed tube and process until smooth and thickened, about 3 minutes. Transfer the ganache to a medium bowl and let stand at room temperature for 1 hour, until spreadable (the ganache should have the consistency of soft icing).

## Caramel-Espresso Yule Log

**SERVES** 10 to 12

**WHY THIS RECIPE WORKS** Done right, a Yule log is a dessert with a huge "wow" factor: a moist, tender cake rolled around a rich, creamy filling; coated in frosting; and adorned with playful woodsy garnishes. For the cake we picked chiffon for its whipped egg whites, which provided resilience; its oil, which provided moist tenderness; and its baking powder, which provided extra lift. While many recipes involve rolling the warm cake into a sugar-coated towel to "train" it into shape, we found that doing so dried out the surface, making it hard for the ganache to adhere, so we opted for a clean, damp towel instead. For the filling, we started with a classic caramel and added espresso powder, cream, and a stealth ingredient: cream cheese. Its tang was barely detectable, but the cream cheese kept the sweetness in check and also gave the whipped filling enough body to stay put when the cake was rolled, resulting in a graceful spiral every time. A simple ganache made with bittersweet chocolate and cream (plus a bit of corn syrup for added flexibility and cling) made the perfect "bark." In the spirit of authenticity, we developed a recipe for meringue bracket-style mushrooms to adorn the bark and completed our presentation by setting our log on an edible forest floor made from chocolate cookie crumbles and ground pistachios. You will need a pastry bag and a pastry tip with a ¼-inch round opening for this recipe. The chocolate crumbles also make a great topping for ice cream or cupcakes. We developed this recipe using Philadelphia Cream Cheese Brick Original. The filling has to chill for at least 1½ hours before whipping, so make it before organizing the ingredients for the cake and the ganache. A smooth dish towel, not terry cloth, works best for rolling the cake. Some of the cake may cling to the towel, but it washes out easily. Use a high-quality chocolate for the ganache; our favorite is Ghirardelli 60% Cacao Bittersweet Chocolate Premium Baking Bar. We prefer to leave the cut surfaces of the log exposed, but there is enough ganache to cover them.

**MERINGUE BRACKET-STYLE MUSHROOMS**

- 3 large egg whites
- ¼ teaspoon cream of tartar
- Pinch table salt
- ⅔ cup (4⅔ ounces) granulated sugar

**CHOCOLATE CRUMBLES**

- 6 tablespoons unsalted butter, cut into ½-inch pieces
- 2 ounces bittersweet chocolate, chopped
- 1 cup (5 ounces) all-purpose flour
- ½ cup packed (3½ ounces) dark brown sugar
- ½ cup (1 ounce) unsweetened cocoa powder
- ¼ teaspoon table salt
- ¼ cup shelled pistachios, toasted and ground fine (optional)

**FILLING**

- 2 cups heavy cream, divided
- 1 tablespoon instant espresso powder
- ¾ cup (5¼ ounces) granulated sugar
- ¼ cup water
- 1 tablespoon light corn syrup
- 4 ounces cream cheese, cut into 8 pieces and softened

**CAKE**

- 1⅓ cups (5⅓ ounces) cake flour
- ¾ cup (5¼ ounces) granulated sugar
- 1½ teaspoons baking powder
- ¼ teaspoon table salt
- 5 large eggs, separated
- ½ cup vegetable oil
- ¼ cup water
- 2 teaspoons vanilla extract
- ¼ teaspoon cream of tartar

**GANACHE**

- ¾ cup heavy cream
- 6 ounces bittersweet chocolate, chopped fine
- 2 teaspoons light corn syrup
- Confectioners' sugar (optional)

**1. FOR THE MERINGUE BRACKET-STYLE MUSHROOMS:** Adjust oven racks to upper-middle and lower-middle positions and heat oven to 200 degrees. Using pencil, draw 15 half-circles ranging from 1 to 2 inches wide on 1 sheet of parchment paper, leaving at least 1½ inches between half-circles. Repeat with second sheet of parchment. Place parchment pencil side down on 2 rimmed baking sheets.

## ASSEMBLING A YULE LOG

**1.** Lay damp towel over cake on rack. Invert second rack over towel. Invert cake; remove rack.

**2.** Starting from short side, gently roll cake and towel together into jelly roll shape. Let cool for 1 hour.

**3.** Unroll cake. Spread filling evenly over cake, leaving ½-inch margin on each short side.

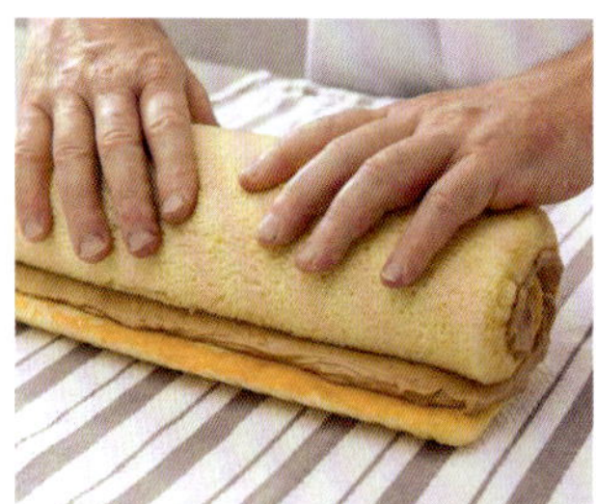

**4.** Reroll cake without towel.

**5.** Trim ½-inch slice from each end of log. To make branch stump, cut 1 end of cake at 45-degree angle, starting 1½ inches from end.

**6.** Transfer cake to platter. Rest stump against log. Spread ganache over log and stump. Use fork to make wood-grain pattern.

**2.** Using stand mixer fitted with whisk attachment, whip egg whites on medium speed until foamy, about 1 minute. Add cream of tartar and salt, increase speed to medium-high, and whip until soft peaks form, about 1 minute. With mixer running, slowly add sugar. Increase speed to high and whip until very thick and stiff peaks form, 3 to 4 minutes.

**3.** Fit pastry bag with ¼-inch round pastry tip and fill with meringue. Using half-circle as guide, pipe concentric arcs of meringue, either smooth or frilly, until half-circle is filled. Repeat with remaining half-circles. Pipe a stem, about ½ inch wide and 1 inch long, onto straight side of each half-circle. Moisten your fingertip with water and smooth any unwanted peaks. Bake meringues for 2 hours, turn off oven, and leave meringues in oven until dry and crisp, about 30 minutes. (Meringues can be stored in airtight container for up to 2 weeks; store directly after cooling. You will have more mushrooms than you need; just select your favorites for the Yule log.)

**4. FOR THE CHOCOLATE CRUMBLES:** Adjust oven rack to middle position and heat oven to 350 degrees. Line rimmed baking sheet with parchment paper. Combine butter and chocolate in medium bowl and microwave until melted, about 1 minute, stirring halfway through microwaving. Add flour, sugar, cocoa, and salt and mix until thoroughly combined and crumbly dough forms.

**5.** Crumble dough over prepared sheet. Bake until crumbles are dry, fragrant, and starting to crisp, about 15 minutes, stirring halfway through baking. Transfer sheet to wire rack and let crumbles cool completely (crumbles will continue to crisp as they cool). Do not turn off oven. (Crumbles can be stored in airtight container at room temperature for up to 2 weeks.)

**6. FOR THE FILLING:** Pour 1 cup cream into wide bowl. Whisk together espresso powder and remaining 1 cup cream in small saucepan and bring to simmer over medium heat. Remove from heat and cover to keep hot. Bring sugar, water, and corn syrup to boil in large heavy-bottomed saucepan over medium-high heat. Cook, without stirring, until mixture is straw-colored, 6 to 8 minutes. Reduce heat to medium-low and continue to cook, swirling saucepan occasionally, until mixture is deep coppery brown and just starting to smoke, 4 to 7 minutes longer. Off heat, carefully whisk in hot cream mixture a little at a time (caramel will bubble and steam). Add cream cheese. Cover and let sit for 5 minutes. Whisk until mostly smooth (some small flecks of cream cheese are OK). Transfer mixture to bowl with cream and stir to combine. Cover and refrigerate until mixture registers 50 degrees or below, at least 1½ hours or up to 4 days.

**7. FOR THE CAKE:** Lightly grease 18 by 13-inch rimmed baking sheet, line with parchment paper, and lightly grease parchment. Whisk flour, sugar, baking powder, and salt together in large, wide bowl. Whisk egg yolks, oil, water, and vanilla into flour mixture until smooth batter forms.

**8.** Using stand mixer fitted with whisk attachment, whip egg whites and cream of tartar on medium-low speed until foamy, about 1 minute. Increase speed to medium-high and whip until stiff peaks form, 1½ to 2 minutes. Transfer one-third of whipped egg whites to batter and whisk gently until mixture is lightened. Using rubber spatula, gently fold remaining egg whites into batter. Pour batter into prepared sheet and spread evenly. Firmly tap sheet on counter 3 times to remove large air bubbles. Bake until cake springs back when pressed lightly in center, 12 to 14 minutes. While cake bakes, soak clean dish towel with water and wring out thoroughly.

**9.** Transfer sheet to wire rack. Immediately run knife around edge of sheet, then carefully invert cake onto second wire rack. Carefully remove parchment. Lay damp towel over cake and invert first wire rack over towel. Invert cake and remove rack. Starting from short side, gently roll cake and towel together into jelly roll shape. Let cake cool on rack, seam side down, for 1 hour.

**10. FOR THE GANACHE:** Bring cream to simmer in small saucepan over medium heat. Place chocolate and corn syrup in bowl, pour over cream, and let stand for 1 minute. Whisk mixture until smooth. Let cool until mixture has consistency of pudding, about 1 hour.

**11.** Transfer chilled filling to bowl of stand mixer fitted with whisk attachment. Whip on high speed until mixture is thick and fluffy and resembles buttercream frosting, 1½ to 2 minutes. Gently unroll cake with short side parallel to counter edge (innermost edge of cake will remain slightly curled; do not flatten). Spread filling evenly over cake, leaving ½-inch margin on each short side. Reroll cake, leaving towel behind as you roll. Wrap in plastic wrap and refrigerate for at least 20 minutes or up to 2 days.

**12.** Arrange two 12 by 4-inch strips of parchment 1 inch apart on serving platter. Unwrap cake and place on cutting board. Using sharp chef's knife, trim ½-inch slice from each end of log, wiping knife clean between cuts; discard trimmings. To make branch stump, cut 1 end of cake at 45-degree angle, starting 1½ inches from end of log (shorter side of stump will be 1½ inches long). Transfer larger cake piece to platter, centering it lengthwise on parchment. To attach stump, rest straight side of smaller piece against side of log. Fill in top of space between pieces with about 1 tablespoon ganache. Using offset spatula, gently spread remaining ganache over log, leaving cut ends exposed. Use tines of fork to make wood-grain pattern on surface of ganache. Carefully slide parchment from beneath cake (hold stump in place with your fingertip while sliding out parchment). Refrigerate cake, uncovered, to slightly set ganache, about 20 minutes. (Cake can be covered loosely and refrigerated for up to 24 hours; let stand at room temperature for 30 minutes before serving.)

**13.** No more than 10 minutes before serving, use paring knife to make small incision in side of log. Gently insert mushroom stem into incision until straight side of mushroom rests against log. Repeat with desired number of mushrooms.

**14.** Scatter chocolate crumbles and pistachios, if using, around cake.

**15.** Dust cake lightly with confectioners' sugar, if using. To slice, dip sharp knife in very hot water and wipe dry between cuts. Serve.

## Chocolate-Espresso Dacquoise

**SERVES** 10 to 12

**WHY THIS RECIPE WORKS** This multilayered showpiece of meringue and buttercream coated in ganache might just be the best dessert you'll ever make—plus you can prepare it the day before. We made this elaborate and impressive-looking dessert more approachable by reworking the meringue and buttercream, making them simpler and more foolproof. We swapped the traditional individually piped layers of meringue for a single sheet that was trimmed into layers after baking, and we shortened the usual 4-plus hours of oven time by increasing the oven temperature. While many recipes call for a Swiss or French buttercream made with a hot sugar syrup, we opted for a German buttercream. With equal parts pastry cream and butter, this option required no hot syrup and it enabled us to use up the egg yolks left over from the meringue. Use a rimless baking sheet or an overturned rimmed baking sheet to bake the meringue. Instant coffee may be substituted for the espresso powder. To skin the hazelnuts, simply place the warm toasted nuts in a clean dish towel and rub gently. We recommend Ghirardelli 60% Cacao Bittersweet Chocolate Baking Bar for this recipe.

**MERINGUE**

- ¾ cup blanched sliced almonds, toasted
- ½ cup hazelnuts, toasted and skinned
- 1 tablespoon cornstarch
- ⅛ teaspoon table salt
- 1 cup (7 ounces) sugar
- 4 large egg whites, room temperature
- ¼ teaspoon cream of tartar

**BUTTERCREAM**

- ¾ cup whole milk
- 4 large egg yolks
- ⅓ cup (2⅓ ounces) sugar
- 1½ teaspoons cornstarch
- ¼ teaspoon table salt
- 2 tablespoons amaretto or water
- 1½ tablespoons instant espresso powder
- 16 tablespoons unsalted butter, softened

**GANACHE**

- 6 ounces bittersweet chocolate, chopped fine
- ¾ cup heavy cream
- 2 teaspoons corn syrup

- 12 whole hazelnuts, toasted and skinned
- 1 cup blanched sliced almonds, toasted

**1. FOR THE MERINGUE:** Adjust oven rack to middle position and heat oven to 250 degrees. Using ruler and pencil, draw 13 by 10½-inch rectangle on piece of parchment paper. Grease baking sheet and place parchment on it, marked side down.

**2.** Process almonds, hazelnuts, cornstarch, and salt in food processor until nuts are finely ground, 15 to 20 seconds. Add ½ cup sugar and pulse to combine, 1 to 2 pulses.

**3.** Using stand mixer fitted with whisk, whip egg whites and cream of tartar on medium-low speed until foamy, about 1 minute. Increase speed to medium-high and whip whites to soft, billowy mounds, about 1 minute. With mixer running at medium-high speed, slowly add remaining ½ cup sugar and continue to whip until glossy, stiff peaks form, 2 to 3 minutes. Fold nut mixture into egg whites in 2 batches. With offset spatula, spread meringue evenly into 13 by 10½-inch rectangle on parchment, using lines on parchment as guide. Using spray bottle, evenly mist surface of meringue with water until glistening. Bake for 1½ hours. Turn off oven and allow meringue to cool in oven for 1½ hours. (Do not open oven during baking and cooling.) Remove from oven and let cool to room temperature, about 10 minutes. (Cooled meringue can be kept at room temperature, wrapped tightly in plastic wrap, for up to 2 days.)

**4. FOR THE BUTTERCREAM:** Heat milk in small saucepan over medium heat until just simmering. Meanwhile, whisk yolks, sugar, cornstarch, and salt in bowl until smooth. Remove milk from heat and, whisking constantly, add half of milk to yolk mixture to temper. Whisking constantly, return tempered yolk mixture to remaining milk in saucepan. Return saucepan to medium heat and cook, whisking constantly, until mixture is bubbling and thickens to consistency of warm pudding, 3 to 5 minutes. Transfer pastry cream to bowl. Cover and refrigerate until set, at least 2 hours or up to 24 hours. Before using, warm gently to room temperature in microwave at 50 percent power, stirring every 10 seconds.

**5.** Stir together amaretto and espresso powder; set aside. Using stand mixer fitted with paddle, beat butter at medium speed until smooth and light, 3 to 4 minutes. Add pastry cream in 3 batches, beating for 30 seconds after each addition. Add amaretto mixture and continue to beat until light and fluffy, about 5 minutes longer, scraping down bowl thoroughly halfway through mixing.

## ASSEMBLING THE DACQUOISE

**1.** Using serrated knife and gentle, repeated scoring motion, trim edges of cooled meringue to form 12 by 10-inch rectangle.

**2.** With long side of meringue parallel to counter, mark top and bottom edges at 3-inch intervals.

**3.** Repeatedly score surface by gently drawing knife from top mark to corresponding bottom mark until cut through. Repeat to make four 10 by 3-inch strips.

**4.** Place 3 strips on wire rack and spread ¼ cup ganache evenly over each. Refrigerate for 15 minutes. Spread remaining strip with ½ cup buttercream.

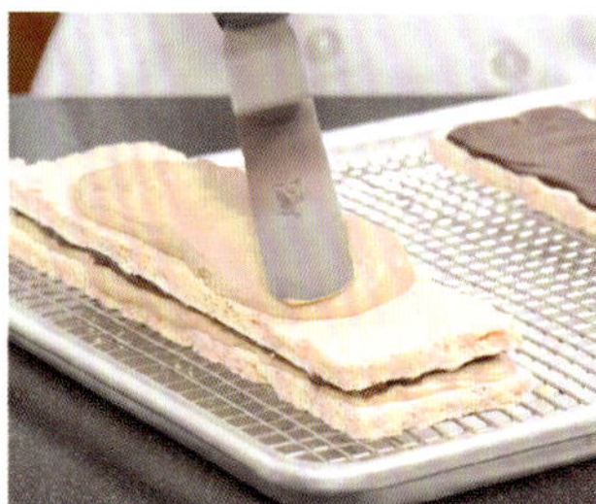

**5.** Invert one ganache-coated strip on top of buttercream-coated strip and press gently. Spread top with buttercream. Repeat twice to form 4 layers.

**6.** Lightly coat sides of cake with half of remaining buttercream; coat top with remaining buttercream. Smooth edges and surfaces; refrigerate until firm.

**7.** Pour ganache over top of cake and spread in thin, even layer, letting excess flow down sides. Spread thinly across sides.

**8.** Place toasted whole hazelnuts in line on top of cake and gently press sliced almonds onto sides.

**6. FOR THE GANACHE:** Place chocolate in heatproof bowl. Bring cream and corn syrup to simmer in small saucepan over medium heat. Pour cream mixture over chocolate and let stand for 1 minute. Stir mixture until smooth. Set aside to cool until chocolate mounds slightly when dripped from spoon, about 5 minutes.

**7.** Carefully invert meringue and peel off parchment. Reinvert meringue and place on cutting board. Using serrated knife and gentle, repeated scoring motion, trim edges of meringue to form 12 by 10-inch rectangle. Discard trimmings. With long side of rectangle parallel to counter, use ruler to mark both long edges of meringue at 3-inch intervals. Using serrated knife, score surface of meringue by drawing knife toward you from mark on top edge to corresponding mark on bottom edge. Repeat scoring until meringue is fully cut through. Repeat until you have four 10 by 3-inch rectangles. (If any rectangles break during cutting, use them as middle layers.)

**8.** Place 3 rectangles on wire rack set in rimmed baking sheet. Using offset spatula, spread ¼ cup ganache evenly over surface of each meringue. Refrigerate until ganache is firm, about 15 minutes. Set aside remaining ganache.

**9.** Using offset spatula, spread top of remaining rectangle with ½ cup buttercream; place on wire rack with ganache-coated meringues. Invert 1 ganache-coated meringue, place on top of buttercream, and press gently to level. Repeat, spreading meringue with ½ cup buttercream and topping with inverted ganache-coated meringue. Spread top with buttercream. Invert final ganache-coated meringue on top of cake. Use 1 hand to steady top of cake and spread half of remaining buttercream to lightly coat sides of cake, then use remaining buttercream to coat top of cake. Smooth until cake resembles box. Refrigerate until buttercream is firm, about 2 hours. (Once buttercream is firm, assembled cake may be wrapped tightly in plastic and refrigerated for up to 2 days.)

**10.** Warm remaining ganache in heatproof bowl set over barely simmering water, stirring occasionally, until mixture is very fluid but not hot. Keeping assembled cake on wire rack, pour ganache over top of cake. Using offset spatula, spread ganache in thin, even layer over top of cake, letting excess flow down sides. Spread ganache over sides in thin layer (top must be completely covered, but some small gaps on sides are OK).

**11.** Garnish top of cake with hazelnuts. Holding bottom of cake with 1 hand, gently press almonds onto sides with other hand. Chill on wire rack, uncovered, for at least 3 hours or up to 12 hours. Transfer to platter. Cut into slices with sharp knife that has been dipped in hot water and wiped dry before each slice. Serve.

## Tiramisu

**SERVES** 10 to 12

---

**WHY THIS RECIPE WORKS** There's a reason restaurant menus (Italian or not) offer tiramisu. Delicate ladyfingers soaked in a spiked coffee mixture layered with a sweet, creamy filling make an irresistible combination. Preparing tiramisu, however, can be labor-intensive. Some versions are overly rich, with ladyfingers that turn soggy. We wanted to avoid these issues and find a streamlined approach—one that highlighted the luxurious combination of flavors and textures that have made this dessert so popular. Instead of hauling out a double boiler to make the fussy custard-based filling (called zabaglione), we simply whipped egg yolks, sugar, salt, rum, and mascarpone together. Salt heightened the filling's subtle flavors. To lighten the filling, we found that whipped cream complemented the mascarpone's flavor better than whipped egg whites. For the coffee soaking mixture, we combined strong brewed coffee and espresso powder (along with more rum). To moisten the ladyfingers so that they were neither too dry nor too saturated, we dropped them one at a time into the spiked coffee mixture and rolled them over to moisten the other side for just a couple of seconds. For the best flavor and texture, we discovered that it was important to allow the tiramisu to chill in the refrigerator for at least 6 hours. Brandy and even whiskey can stand in for the dark rum. The test kitchen prefers a tiramisu with a pronounced rum flavor; for a less potent rum flavor, halve the amount of rum added to the coffee mixture in step 1. Do not allow the mascarpone to warm to room temperature before using it; it has a tendency to break if allowed to do so.

- 2½ cups strong brewed coffee, room temperature
- 9 tablespoons dark rum, divided
- 1½ tablespoons instant espresso powder
- 6 large egg yolks, room temperature
- ⅔ cup (4⅔ ounces) sugar
- ¼ teaspoon table salt
- 1½ pounds mascarpone (generous 3 cups)
- ¾ cup heavy cream, chilled
- 14 ounces (42 to 60, depending on size) dried ladyfingers
- 3½ tablespoons cocoa powder, preferably Dutch-processed, divided
- ¼ cup grated semisweet or bittersweet chocolate (optional)

**1.** Stir together coffee, 5 tablespoons rum, and espresso powder in wide bowl or baking dish until espresso dissolves; set aside.

**2.** Using stand mixer fitted with whisk attachment, beat egg yolks at low speed until just combined. Add sugar and salt and beat at medium-high speed until pale yellow, 1½ to 2 minutes, scraping down sides of bowl with rubber spatula once or twice. Add remaining ¼ cup rum and beat at medium speed until just combined, 20 to 30 seconds; scrape bowl. Add mascarpone and beat at medium speed until no lumps remain, 30 to 45 seconds, scraping down sides of bowl once or twice. Transfer mixture to large bowl and set aside.

**3.** In now-empty mixer bowl, beat cream at medium speed until frothy, 1 to 1½ minutes. Increase speed to high and continue to beat until cream holds stiff peaks, 1 to 1½ minutes longer. Using rubber spatula, fold one-third of whipped cream into mascarpone mixture to lighten, then gently fold in remaining whipped cream until no white streaks remain. Set mascarpone mixture aside.

**4.** Working with one at a time, drop half of ladyfingers into coffee mixture, roll, remove, and transfer to 13 by 9-inch glass or ceramic baking dish. (Do not submerge ladyfingers in coffee mixture; entire process should take no longer than 2 to 3 seconds for each cookie.) Arrange soaked cookies in single layer in baking dish, breaking or trimming ladyfingers as needed to fit neatly into dish.

**5.** Spread half of mascarpone mixture over ladyfingers; use rubber spatula to spread mixture to sides and into corners of dish and smooth the surface. Place 2 tablespoons cocoa in fine-mesh strainer and dust cocoa over mascarpone.

**6.** Repeat dipping and arrangement of ladyfingers; spread remaining mascarpone mixture over ladyfingers and dust with remaining 1½ tablespoons cocoa. Wipe edges of dish with dry paper towel. Cover with plastic wrap and refrigerate for 6 to 24 hours. Sprinkle with grated chocolate, if using; cut into pieces and serve chilled.

### Tiramisu with Cooked Eggs

This recipe involves cooking the yolks in a double boiler, which requires a little more effort and makes for a slightly thicker mascarpone filling, but the results are just as good as with our traditional method. You will need an additional ⅓ cup heavy cream.

After beating egg yolks, sugar, and salt until pale yellow in step 2, add ⅓ cup cream and beat at medium speed until just combined, 20 to 30 seconds; scrape bowl. Set bowl with yolk mixture over medium saucepan containing 1 inch gently simmering water; cook, constantly scraping along bottom and sides of bowl with heat-resistant rubber spatula, until mixture coats back of spoon and registers 160 degrees, 4 to 7 minutes. Remove from heat and stir vigorously to cool slightly, then set aside to cool to room temperature, about 15 minutes. Whisk in remaining ¼ cup rum until combined. Transfer bowl to stand mixer fitted with whisk attachment, add mascarpone, and beat at medium speed until no lumps remain, 30 to 45 seconds. Transfer mixture to large bowl and set aside. Continue with recipe from step 3, using the full ¾ cup cream specified.

## Raspberry Charlotte

**SERVES** 12 to 16

**WHY THIS RECIPE WORKS** The classic Charlotte Russe, a grand dessert consisting of a Bavarian cream encased in sponge cake, has fallen out of favor, partly because it's fussy to make, and partly because lean sponge cake and bouncy gelatinized mousse don't hold much appeal for modern cooks. In our recipe, we swap the sponge for a simple and quick-baking chiffon cake, which is tender and moist but sufficiently sturdy. Instead of basing our filling on a high-moisture crème anglaise, we use a more foolproof homemade raspberry curd lightened with whipped cream with just enough gelatin to give it structure, and we pack in a full pound of berries for bright fruit flavor. Finishing with a swirl of raspberry jam and fresh berries gives our charlotte visual appeal and an extra jolt of flavor. For easy assembly, we baked one round cake and one square cake, using the round as the bottom and slicing the square cake into strips to line the walls of a springform pan. It is fine to use frozen raspberries in the filling. Thaw frozen berries completely before using and use any collected juices, too. It is important to measure the berries for the filling by weight. If you wish to garnish the top of the charlotte with berries, arrange 1 to 1½ cups fresh berries (depending on size) around the edge of the assembled charlotte before refrigerating. For clean, neat slices, dip your knife in hot water and wipe it dry before each slice.

**FILLING**

- 1¼ teaspoons unflavored gelatin
- 2 tablespoons water
- 3 large egg yolks (reserve whites for cake)
- 2 teaspoons cornstarch
- 1 pound (3¼ cups) fresh or thawed frozen raspberries
- ⅔ cup (4⅔ ounces) sugar
- 2 tablespoons unsalted butter
- Pinch table salt
- 1¾ cups heavy cream

**JAM MIXTURE**

- ½ teaspoon unflavored gelatin
- 1 tablespoon lemon juice
- ½ cup seedless raspberry jam

**CAKE**

- ⅔ cup (2⅔ ounces) cake flour
- 6 tablespoons (2⅔ ounces) sugar
- ¾ teaspoon baking powder
- ⅛ teaspoon table salt
- ¼ cup vegetable oil
- 1 large egg plus 3 large egg whites (reserved from filling)
- 2 tablespoons water
- 1 teaspoon vanilla extract
- ¼ teaspoon cream of tartar

**1. FOR THE FILLING:** Sprinkle gelatin over water in large bowl and set aside. Whisk egg yolks and cornstarch together in medium bowl until combined. Combine raspberries, sugar, butter, and salt in medium saucepan. Mash lightly with whisk and stir until no dry sugar remains. Cook over medium heat, whisking frequently, until mixture is simmering and raspberries are almost completely broken down, 4 to 6 minutes.

**2.** Remove raspberry mixture from heat and, whisking constantly, slowly add ½ cup raspberry mixture to yolk mixture to temper. Whisking constantly, return tempered yolk mixture to mixture in saucepan. Return saucepan to medium heat and cook, whisking constantly, until mixture thickens and bubbles, about 1 minute. Pour through fine-mesh strainer set over gelatin mixture and press on solids with back of ladle or rubber spatula until only seeds remain. Discard seeds and stir raspberry mixture until gelatin is dissolved. Set aside, stirring occasionally, until curd is slightly thickened and reaches room temperature, at least 30 minutes or up to 1 hour 15 minutes.

**3. FOR THE JAM MIXTURE:** Sprinkle gelatin over lemon juice in small bowl and let sit until gelatin softens, about 5 minutes. Heat jam in microwave, whisking occasionally, until hot and fluid, 30 to 60 seconds. Add softened gelatin to jam and whisk until dissolved. Set aside.

**4. FOR THE CAKE:** Adjust oven rack to upper-middle position and heat oven to 350 degrees. Lightly grease 8-inch round cake pan and 8-inch square baking pan, line with parchment paper, and lightly grease parchment. Whisk flour, sugar, baking powder, and salt together in medium bowl. Whisk oil, whole egg, water, and vanilla into flour mixture until smooth batter forms.

**5.** Using stand mixer fitted with whisk, whip egg whites and cream of tartar on medium-low speed until foamy, about 1 minute. Increase speed to medium-high and whip until soft peaks form, 2 to 3 minutes. Transfer one-third of egg whites to batter; whisk gently until mixture is lightened. Using rubber spatula, gently fold remaining egg whites into batter.

**6.** Pour 1 cup batter into round pan and spread evenly. Pour remaining batter into square pan and spread evenly. Place pans on rimmed baking sheet and bake until cakes spring back when pressed lightly in center and surface is no longer sticky, 8 to 11 minutes (round cake, which is shallower, will be done before square cake). Cakes should not brown.

**7.** Let cakes cool in pans on wire rack for 5 minutes. Invert round cake onto wire rack. Carefully remove parchment, then reinvert onto second wire rack. Repeat with square cake. Let cool completely, at least 15 minutes.

**8.** Place round cake in center of serving platter. Spread with 2 tablespoons jam mixture. Place ring from 9-inch springform pan around cake, leaving equal space on all sides. Leave clasp of ring slightly loose. Using sharp chef's knife, trim ⅛ inch off all edges of square cake. Spread square cake with 2 tablespoons jam mixture. Cut cake in half. Cut each half lengthwise into two pieces to make four equal-size long strips. Place cake strips vertically around round cake, jam side in, taking care to nestle ends together neatly. Fasten clasp of springform ring.

**9.** Using stand mixer fitted with whisk, whip cream on medium-low speed until foamy, about 1 minute. Increase speed to high and whip until soft peaks form, 1 to 2 minutes. Transfer one-third of whipped cream to curd; whisk gently until mixture is lightened. Using rubber spatula, gently fold in remaining cream until mixture is homogeneous.

**10.** Pour filling into cake ring and spread evenly to edge. (Surface of filling will be above edge of cake.) Drizzle remaining jam mixture over surface of filling. Using knife, swirl jam through surface of filling, making marbled pattern. Refrigerate for at least 5 hours or up to 24 hours.

**11.** To unmold, run thin knife around edge of ring (just ½ inch down). Release ring and lift to remove. Let stand at room temperature for 20 minutes before slicing and serving.

### ASSEMBLING RASPBERRY CHARLOTTE

**1.** Spread round cake with jam mixture and place springform pan ring around cake. Spread square cake with jam mixture, cut into strips, and place strips vertically around round cake. Fasten clasp of ring.

**2.** Whip cream and fold into curd, then pour filling into cake-lined pan.

**3.** Drizzle remaining jam mixture over cake and swirl.

## Paris-Brest

**SERVES** 8 to 10

**WHY THIS RECIPE WORKS** Paris-Brest is an elegant showstopping French dessert that consists of a large ring of pate a choux that is filled with hazelnut praline pastry cream and then sprinkled with chopped almonds and powdered sugar. Its name dates back to 1910 when an enterprising baker whose shop was located along the route of the Paris-Brest-Paris bicycle race—from Paris to the city of Brest, in Brittany, and back again—invented the dessert to honor the cyclists. (His creation was in the shape of a bicycle tire.) For a light cream filling that was firm and sturdy, we started with a flour-thickened pastry cream (more stable than the usual cornstarch-thickened version), added pulverized caramel-coated hazelnuts, and then folded in whipped cream enriched with gelatin. An equal amount of slivered almonds can be substituted for the hazelnuts. To skin the hazelnuts, simply place them in a clean dish towel after toasting, while they are still warm, and rub gently. Use a serrated knife to cut the dessert.

**PRALINE**

- ½ cup (3½ ounces) granulated sugar
- ¼ cup water
- 1 teaspoon lemon juice
- 1 cup hazelnuts, toasted and skinned
- 1 tablespoon vegetable oil
- ½ teaspoon table salt

**PASTRY DOUGH**

- 4 large eggs
- 8 tablespoons unsalted butter, cut into 16 pieces
- ½ cup whole milk
- ⅓ cup water
- 2¾ teaspoons granulated sugar
- ¾ teaspoon table salt
- 1 cup (5 ounces) all-purpose flour
- 2 tablespoons toasted, skinned, and chopped hazelnuts

**CREAM FILLING**

- 2 teaspoons unflavored gelatin
- ¼ cup water
- 1½ cups half-and-half
- 5 large egg yolks
- ⅓ cup (2⅓ ounces) granulated sugar
- 3 tablespoons all-purpose flour
- 3 tablespoons unsalted butter, cut into 3 pieces and chilled
- 1½ teaspoons vanilla extract
- 1 cup heavy cream, chilled
- Confectioners' sugar

**1. FOR THE PRALINE:** Line rimmed baking sheet with parchment paper; spray parchment with vegetable oil spray and set aside. Bring sugar, water, and lemon juice to boil in medium saucepan over medium heat, stirring once or twice to dissolve sugar. Cook, without stirring, until syrup is golden brown, 10 to 15 minutes. Remove saucepan from heat, stir in hazelnuts, and immediately pour mixture onto prepared sheet. Place sheet on wire rack and allow caramel to harden, about 30 minutes.

**2.** Break hardened caramel into 1- to 2-inch pieces; process pieces in food processor until finely ground, about 30 seconds. Add oil and salt and process until uniform paste forms, 1 to 2 minutes. Transfer mixture to bowl, cover with plastic wrap, and set aside.

**3. FOR THE PASTRY DOUGH:** Adjust oven racks to upper-middle and lower-middle positions and heat oven to 400 degrees. Draw or trace 8-inch circle in center of two 12 by 18-inch sheets of parchment paper; flip parchment over. Spray 2 baking sheets with vegetable oil spray and line with parchment (keeping guide rings on underside).

**4.** Beat eggs in measuring cup or small bowl; you should have about 1 cup (discard any excess over 1 cup). Heat butter, milk, water, sugar, and salt in medium saucepan over medium heat, stirring occasionally. When butter mixture reaches full boil (butter should be fully melted), immediately remove saucepan from heat and stir in flour with heat-resistant spatula or wooden spoon until combined and no mixture remains on sides of pan. Return saucepan to low heat and cook, stirring constantly, using smearing motion, until mixture is slightly shiny and tiny beads of fat appear on bottom of saucepan, about 3 minutes.

**5.** Immediately transfer butter mixture to food processor and process with feed tube open for 30 seconds to cool slightly. With processor running, gradually add eggs in steady stream. When all eggs have been added, scrape down sides of bowl, then process for 30 seconds until smooth, thick, sticky paste forms.

**6.** Transfer ¾ cup dough to pastry bag fitted with ⅜-inch round tip. To make narrow inner ring, pipe single ½-inch-wide circle of dough directly on traced guide ring on 1 baking sheet. For large outer ring, squeeze out any excess dough in pastry bag and change pastry bag tip to ½-inch star tip. Put all remaining dough into pastry bag. Pipe ½-inch-wide circle of dough around inside of traced guide ring on remaining baking sheet. Pipe second ½-inch circle of dough around first so they overlap slightly. Pipe third ½-inch circle on top of other 2 circles directly over seam. Discard any excess dough. Sprinkle hazelnuts evenly over surface of ring.

**7.** Place sheet with larger outer ring on upper rack and sheet with narrow inner ring on lower rack and bake until narrow ring is golden brown and firm, 22 to 26 minutes. Remove narrow ring and transfer to wire rack. Reduce oven temperature to 350 degrees and continue to bake larger ring for 10 minutes. Remove sheet from oven and turn off oven. Using paring knife, cut 4 equally spaced ¾-inch-wide slits around edges of larger ring to release steam. Return larger ring to oven and prop oven door open with handle of wooden spoon. Let ring stand in oven until exterior is crisp, about 45 minutes. Transfer ring to wire rack to cool, about 15 minutes.

**8. FOR THE CREAM FILLING:** Sprinkle gelatin over water in small bowl and let sit until gelatin softens, about 5 minutes. Heat half-and-half in medium saucepan over medium heat until just simmering. Meanwhile, whisk egg yolks and sugar in medium bowl until smooth. Add flour to yolk-sugar mixture and whisk until incorporated. Remove half-and-half from heat and, whisking constantly, slowly add ½ cup to yolk-sugar mixture to temper. Whisking constantly, add tempered yolk-sugar mixture back to half-and-half in saucepan.

**9.** Return saucepan to medium heat and cook, whisking constantly, until yolk-sugar mixture thickens slightly, 1 to 2 minutes. Reduce heat to medium-low and continue to cook, whisking constantly, for 8 minutes.

**10.** Increase heat to medium and cook, whisking vigorously, until bubbles burst on surface, 1 to 2 minutes. Remove saucepan from heat; whisk in butter, vanilla, and softened gelatin until butter is melted and incorporated. Strain pastry cream through fine-mesh strainer set over large bowl. Press lightly greased parchment paper directly on surface and refrigerate until chilled but not set, about 45 minutes.

**11.** Using stand mixer fitted with whisk, whip cream on medium-low speed until foamy, about 1 minute. Increase speed to high and whip until soft peaks form, 1 to 3 minutes. Whisk praline paste and half of whipped cream into pastry cream until combined. Gently fold in remaining whipped cream until incorporated. Cover and refrigerate until set, at least 3 hours or up to 24 hours.

**12.** Using serrated knife, slice larger outer ring in half horizontally; place bottom on large serving plate. Fill pastry bag fitted with ½-inch star tip with cream filling. Pipe ½-inch-wide strip of cream filling in narrow zigzag pattern around center of bottom half of ring. Press narrow inner ring gently into cream filling. Pipe cream filling over narrow ring in zigzag pattern to cover. Place top half of larger ring over cream filling, dust with confectioners' sugar, and serve. (Cooled pastry rings can be wrapped tightly in plastic wrap and stored at room temperature for up to 24 hours or frozen for up to 1 month. Before using, recrisp rings in 300-degree oven for 5 to 10 minutes. Praline can be made up to 1 week in advance and refrigerated. Let praline come to room temperature before using. Pastry dough can be transferred to bowl, with surface covered with sheet of lightly greased parchment paper, and stored at room temperature for up to 2 hours. Dessert can be assembled and kept in refrigerator up to 3 hours in advance.)

## PUTTING TOGETHER PARIS-BREST

**1.** As soon as caramel turns golden brown, stir in toasted hazelnuts and pour mixture onto parchment paper–lined baking sheet to set.

**2.** Process broken caramel pieces in food processor until finely ground, about 30 seconds. Add salt and vegetable oil and process again until uniform paste forms, 1 to 2 minutes longer.

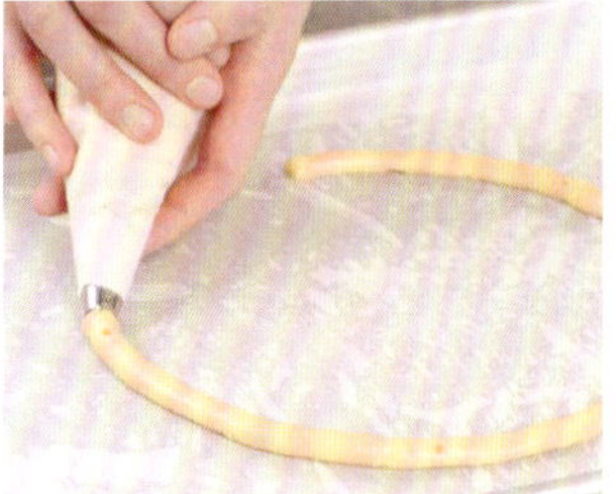

**3.** Using bag fitted with ⅜-inch round tip, pipe narrow circle of pastry dough directly on top of guide ring traced on parchment. Set aside.

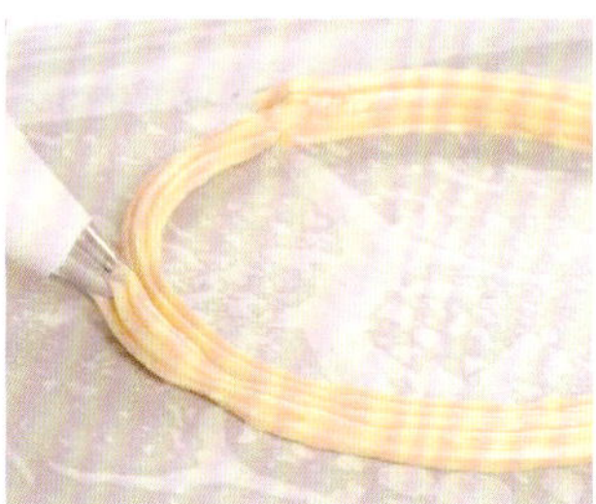

**4.** Use ½-inch star tip to pipe circle of dough around inside of remaining guide ring. Then pipe second circle around first so they overlap slightly.

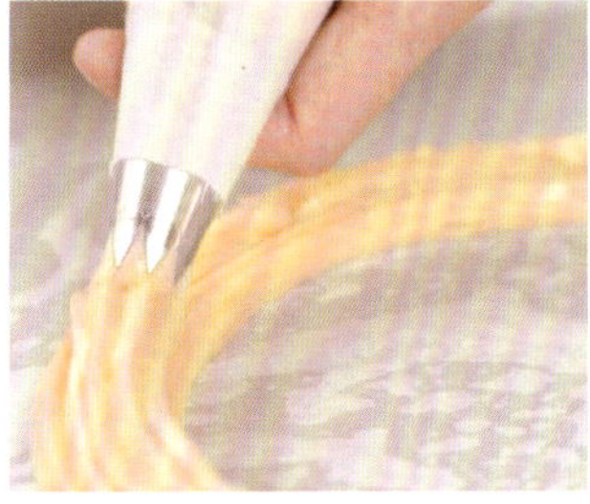

**5.** Finish outer ring by piping third circle on top of other 2 circles, directly over seam. Sprinkle with nuts and bake.

**6.** After letting outer ring cool, halve horizontally using serrated knife.

**7.** Using pastry bag fitted with ½-inch star tip, pipe narrow zigzag of praline cream onto bottom half of outer ring.

**8.** Place inner ring on top of praline cream and press down gently.

**9.** Pipe remaining praline cream over inner ring in zigzag pattern to cover.

**10.** Gently place top half of outer ring over filling and dust with confectioners' sugar.

## Struffoli (Neapolitan Honey Balls)

**SERVES** 6 to 8 (Makes 4½ cups)

**WHY THIS RECIPE WORKS** Struffoli, a classic Neapolitan treat that's traditionally served at Christmas, Easter, and other festive occasions, consists of chickpea-size deep-fried dough balls that have been drenched in warm honey, piled onto a platter, and topped with multicolored nonpareils and sometimes other embellishments. Making the soft, malleable dough with melted (rather than softened) butter meant that it could be quickly mixed together by hand. Portioning hundreds of tiny, uniform dough balls usually involves rolling ropes, cutting them into small pieces, and rolling each one by hand into a chickpea-size ball, but it was much more efficient to flatten hunks of dough into rectangles and make evenly spaced perpendicular cuts like a grid. Even the ball-rolling step was unnecessary, since the tiny dough pieces puffed into rounds when fried. Briefly simmering the cooled fried dough balls in honey married the two components and thickened the honey a bit so that it clung well. Nonpareils were a must for the toppings, but incorporating candied orange peel and cherries and toasted almonds added complex flavor and texture as well as festive appeal. We strongly recommend weighing the flour. Use a Dutch oven that holds 6 quarts or more. Make sure that all your equipment is in place before you start frying. For an impressively tall mound of struffoli, use a serving plate that's 10 to 11 inches across.

- 2 cups (10 ounces) all-purpose flour
- ¼ cup (1¾ ounces) sugar
- ½ teaspoon table salt
- ¼ teaspoon baking powder
- 3 large eggs, lightly beaten
- 4 tablespoons unsalted butter, melted and cooled slightly
- 2 teaspoons vanilla extract
- 2 quarts vegetable oil for frying
- 1 cup honey
- 2 tablespoons multicolored nonpareils, plus extra for garnish
- ¼ cup sliced almonds, toasted (optional)
- 2 tablespoons candied orange peel, chopped fine (optional)
- 8 candied cherries (optional)

**1.** Line 2 rimmed baking sheets with parchment paper. Whisk flour, sugar, salt, and baking powder together in large bowl. Add eggs, melted butter, and vanilla and stir with rubber spatula until soft dough forms. Transfer dough to counter and knead briefly to bring together into ball, about 30 seconds. Dough will be slightly tacky. (Dough can be wrapped in plastic wrap and refrigerated for up to 24 hours.)

**2.** Add oil to large Dutch oven until it measures about 1½ inches deep and heat over medium heat to 350 degrees. While oil heats, divide dough into 6 equal pieces, about 3 ounces each. Flatten 1 piece of dough into 5 by 3-inch rectangle, with shorter side facing you (lightly grease your hands and counter if dough sticks). Using bench scraper or sharp knife, cut dough lengthwise into 6 equal strips. Cut strips crosswise into 10 equal rows to create sixty ½-inch pieces. Separate dough pieces and place on prepared sheets, keeping pieces from touching (pieces needn't be spherical). Repeat with remaining dough.

**3.** Line 13 by 9-inch baking pan with triple layer of paper towels. Place 25 to 30 struffoli in slotted spoon or spider skimmer (it's OK if they touch). Gently submerge spoon in oil to transfer struffoli to pot (oil may foam slightly). Cook, stirring frequently, until struffoli are crisp and golden brown, 2 to 3 minutes.

**4.** Transfer struffoli to prepared pan. Repeat with remaining dough (spoon may be hot), adjusting burner, if necessary, to maintain oil temperature between 350 and 365 degrees. Let struffoli cool completely, about 15 minutes (cooled struffoli can be stored in airtight container at room temperature for up to 3 days or frozen in zipper-lock bag for up to 1 month).

**5.** Heat honey in large saucepan over medium-low heat until small bubbles break constantly and rapidly across surface. Off heat, add struffoli and stir until evenly coated. Return to heat and continue to cook, stirring occasionally, 4 minutes longer. Remove from heat and let struffoli cool in saucepan for 5 minutes. While struffoli cool, spray serving platter lightly with vegetable oil spray and wipe with paper towel, leaving thin film.

**6.** Add nonpareils to saucepan and stir to coat evenly. Stir in almonds and orange peel, if using. Using slotted spoon, lift struffoli from saucepan and transfer to prepared platter, piling into mound. Garnish with candied cherries, if using, and extra nonpareils. Let cool completely, about 20 minutes (Cooled struffoli can be covered with waxed paper or parchment paper and wrapped tightly in plastic wrap for up to 3 days). Use 2 spoons to transfer individual servings to plates or allow guests to pluck pieces from platter.

## Best Angel Food Cake

**SERVES** 10 to 12

**WHY THIS RECIPE WORKS** At its heavenly best, an angel food cake should be tall and perfectly shaped, have a snowy-white, tender crumb, and be encased in a thin, delicate golden crust. The difficulty with making a great angel food cake is that it requires a delicate balance of ingredients and proper cooking techniques. In particular, since this cake is leavened only with beaten egg whites, it is critical that you whip them correctly. Overbeaten egg whites produce a flatter cake. First, we found it key to create a stable egg-white base, starting the whites at medium-low speed just to break them up into a froth and increasing the speed to medium-high speed to form soft, billowy mounds. Next, the sugar should be added, a tablespoon at a time. Once all the sugar is added, the whites become shiny and form soft peaks when the beater is lifted. A delicate touch is required when incorporating the remaining ingredients, such as the flour, which should be sifted over the batter and gently folded in. We like to use a tube pan with a removable bottom but a pan without one can be lined with parchment paper. We avoid greasing the sides of the pan so that the cake can climb up and cling to the sides as it bakes—a greased pan will produce a disappointingly short cake. If your tube pan has a removable bottom, you do not need to line it with parchment. Angel food cake can be served plain or dusted with confectioners' sugar.

- 1½ cups (10½ ounces) sugar
- ¾ cup (3 ounces) cake flour
- 12 large egg whites, at room temperature
- 1 teaspoon cream of tartar
- ¼ teaspoon table salt
- 1½ teaspoons juice from 1 lemon
- 1½ teaspoons vanilla extract
- ½ teaspoon almond extract

**1.** Adjust an oven rack to the lower-middle position and heat the oven to 325 degrees. Line the bottom of a 16-cup tube pan with parchment paper but do not grease. Whisk ¾ cup of the sugar and the flour together in a medium bowl.

**2.** In a stand mixer fitted with the whisk attachment, whip the egg whites and cream of tartar together on medium-low speed until foamy, about 1 minute. Increase the mixer speed to medium-high and whip the whites to soft, billowy mounds, about 1 minute. Gradually whip in the salt and remaining ¾ cup sugar, 1 tablespoon at a time, about 1 minute. Continue to whip the whites until they are shiny and form soft peaks, 1 to 3 minutes.

**3.** Whisk the lemon juice and extracts into the whipped whites by hand. Sift ¼ cup of the flour mixture over the top of the whites, then gently fold to combine with a large rubber spatula until just a few streaks of flour remain. Repeat with the remaining flour mixture, ¼ cup at a time.

**4.** Scrape the batter into the prepared pan and smooth the top. Wipe any drops of batter off the sides of the pan and lightly tap the pan against the countertop two or three times to settle the batter. Bake the cake until golden brown and the top springs back when pressed firmly, 50 to 60 minutes.

**5.** Invert the tube pan over a large metal kitchen funnel or the neck of a sturdy bottle (or, if your pan has "feet" that rise above the top edge of the pan, simply let the cake rest upside down). Cool the cake completely, upside down, 2 to 3 hours.

**6.** Run a small knife around the edge of the cake to loosen. Gently tap the pan upside down on the countertop to release the cake. Peel off the parchment paper, turn the cake right side up onto a serving platter, and serve.

## Foolproof New York Cheesecake

**SERVES** 12 to 16

**WHY THIS RECIPE WORKS** Our original New York Cheesecake had a luxurious texture and brown surface, but some ovens produced inconsistent cakes. To revise our recipe for everyone's ovens, we first created a pastry–graham cracker hybrid crust that wouldn't become soggy. Pulsing graham crackers, sugar, flour, and salt with melted butter coated the starches, making a crisp crust. Straining and resting the filling released bubble-producing air pockets. New York–style cheesecakes usually start in a hot oven so that a burnished outer skin and puffy rim develops before the temperature is dropped, but we found the time it took for the oven temperature to change varied. We flipped the order, baking at a low temperature to set the filling and then removing it before ramping up the oven's heat. Once the oven hit 500 degrees, we put the cheesecake on the upper rack to brown. This cheesecake would now have the same texture, flavor, and appearance no matter what oven was used. This cheesecake takes up to 14 hours to make (including chilling), so we recommend making it the day before serving. An accurate oven thermometer and instant-read thermometer are essential. To ensure proper baking, check that the oven thermometer is holding steady at 200 degrees and refrain from frequently taking the temperature of the cheesecake (unless it is within a few degrees of 165, allow 20 minutes between checking). Keep a close eye on the cheesecake in step 5 to prevent overbrowning.

**CRUST**

- 6 whole graham crackers, broken into pieces
- ⅓ cup packed (2⅓ ounces) dark brown sugar
- ½ cup (2½ ounces) all-purpose flour
- ¼ teaspoon table salt
- 7 tablespoons unsalted butter, melted, divided

**FILLING**

- 2½ pounds cream cheese, softened
- 1½ cups (10½ ounces) granulated sugar, divided
- ⅛ teaspoon table salt
- ⅓ cup sour cream
- 2 teaspoons lemon juice
- 2 teaspoons vanilla extract
- 6 large eggs plus 2 large yolks

**1. FOR THE CRUST:** Adjust oven racks to upper-middle and lower-middle positions and heat oven to 325 degrees. Process cracker pieces and sugar in food processor until finely ground, about 30 seconds. Add flour and salt and pulse to combine, 2 pulses. Add 6 tablespoons melted butter and pulse until crumbs are evenly moistened, about 10 pulses. Brush bottom of 9-inch springform pan with ½ tablespoon melted butter. Using your hands, press crumb mixture evenly into pan bottom. Using flat bottom of measuring cup or ramekin, firmly pack crust into pan. Bake on lower-middle rack until fragrant and beginning to brown around edges, about 13 minutes. Transfer to rimmed baking sheet and set aside to cool completely. Reduce oven temperature to 200 degrees.

**2. FOR THE FILLING:** Using stand mixer fitted with paddle, beat cream cheese, ¾ cup sugar, and salt at medium-low speed until combined, about 1 minute. Beat in remaining ¾ cup sugar until combined, about 1 minute. Scrape beater and bowl well; add sour cream, lemon juice, and vanilla and beat at low speed until combined, about 1 minute. Add egg yolks and beat at medium-low speed until thoroughly combined, about 1 minute. Scrape bowl and beater. Add whole eggs two at a time, beating until thoroughly combined, about 30 seconds after each addition. Pour filling through fine-mesh strainer set in large bowl, pressing against strainer with rubber spatula or back of ladle to help filling pass through strainer.

**3.** Brush sides of springform pan with remaining ½ tablespoon melted butter. Pour filling into crust and set aside for 10 minutes to allow air bubbles to rise to top. Gently draw tines of fork across surface of cake to pop air bubbles that have risen to surface.

**4.** When oven thermometer reads 200 degrees, bake cheesecake on lower rack until center registers 165 degrees, 3 to 3½ hours. Remove cake from oven and increase oven temperature to 500 degrees.

**5.** When oven is at 500 degrees, bake cheesecake on upper rack until top is evenly browned, 4 to 12 minutes. Let cool for 5 minutes; run paring knife between cheesecake and side of springform pan. Let cheesecake cool until barely warm, 2½ to 3 hours. Wrap tightly in plastic wrap and refrigerate until cold and firmly set, at least 6 hours.

**6.** To unmold cheesecake, remove side of pan. Slide thin metal spatula between crust and pan bottom to loosen, then slide cheesecake onto serving plate. Let cheesecake sit at room temperature for about 30 minutes. To slice, dip sharp knife in very hot water and wipe dry between cuts. Serve. (Leftovers, wrapped tightly in plastic wrap, can be refrigerated for up to 4 days.)

## New York Cheesecake

**SERVES 12**

**WHY THIS RECIPE WORKS** The ideal New York cheesecake should be a tall, bronze-skinned, and dense affair. The flavor should be pure and minimalist, sweet and tangy, and rich. But many recipes fall short, with textures that range from fluffy to rubbery and leaden, and flavors that are starchy or overly citrusy. We wanted to perfect New York cheesecake. After trying a variety of crusts, we settled on the classic graham cracker crust—a simple combination of graham crackers, butter, and sugar. For the filling, cream cheese, boosted by the extra tang of a little sour cream, delivered the best flavor. A little lemon juice and vanilla added just the right sweet, bright accents without calling attention to themselves. A combination of eggs and egg yolks yielded a texture that was dense but not heavy. We found that the New York method worked better for this cheesecake than the typical water bath—baking the cake in a hot oven for 10 minutes then in a low oven for a full 90 minutes yielded the satiny texture we were after. For neater slices, clean the knife thoroughly between slices. Serve as is or with Strawberry Topping.

**CRUST**

- 8 whole graham crackers, broken into 1-inch pieces
- 7 tablespoons unsalted butter, melted and cooled
- 3 tablespoons sugar

**FILLING**

- 2½ pounds cream cheese, cut into chunks and softened
- 1½ cups (10½ ounces) sugar
- ⅛ teaspoon table salt
- ⅓ cup sour cream
- 2 teaspoons juice from 1 lemon
- 2 teaspoons vanilla extract
- 6 large eggs plus 2 large egg yolks, at room temperature

**1. FOR THE CRUST:** Adjust an oven rack to the middle position and heat the oven to 325 degrees. Process the graham cracker pieces in a food processor to fine, even crumbs, about 30 seconds. Sprinkle 6 tablespoons of the melted butter and the sugar over the crumbs and pulse to incorporate. Sprinkle the mixture into a 9-inch springform pan. Press the crumbs firmly into an even layer using the bottom of a measuring cup. Bake the crust until fragrant and beginning to brown, 10 to 15 minutes. Cool the crust to room temperature, about 30 minutes.

2. **FOR THE FILLING:** Meanwhile, increase the oven temperature to 500 degrees. In the bowl of a stand mixer fitted with the paddle attachment, beat the cream cheese on medium-low speed until smooth, 1 to 3 minutes. Scrape down the bowl and beaters as needed.

3. Beat in ¾ cup of the sugar and the salt until incorporated, 1 to 3 minutes. Beat in the remaining ¾ cup sugar until incorporated, 1 to 3 minutes. Beat in the sour cream, lemon juice, and vanilla until incorporated, 1 to 3 minutes. Beat in the whole eggs and egg yolks, two at a time, until combined, 1 to 3 minutes.

4. Being careful not to disturb the baked crust, brush the inside of the prepared springform pan with the remaining 1 tablespoon melted butter. Set the pan on a rimmed baking sheet. Carefully pour the filling into the pan. Bake the cheesecake for 10 minutes.

5. Without opening the oven door, reduce the oven temperature to 200 degrees and continue to bake until the center of the cheesecake registers 150 degrees on an instant-read thermometer, about 1½ hours.

6. Transfer the cheesecake to a wire rack and run a knife around the edge of the cake. Cool the cheesecake until just barely warm, 2½ to 3 hours, running a knife around the edge of the cake every hour or so. Wrap the pan tightly in plastic wrap and refrigerate until cold, about 3 hours.

7. To unmold the cheesecake, wrap a wet, hot dish towel around the cake pan and let sit for 1 minute. Remove the sides of the pan and slide the cake onto a cake platter. Let the cheesecake sit at room temperature for 30 minutes before serving. (Leftovers, wrapped tightly in plastic wrap, can be refrigerated for up to 3 days, however, the crust will lose its crispness after 1 day.)

## Strawberry Topping

**MAKES** about 6 cups

This topping is best served the same day it is made.

- 2 pounds fresh strawberries, cleaned, hulled, and cut lengthwise into ⅛- to ¼-inch slices
- ½ cup (3½ ounces) sugar
- Pinch table salt
- 1 cup strawberry jam
- 2 tablespoons juice from 1 lemon

1. Toss the berries, sugar, and salt in a medium bowl; let stand until the berries have released their juices and the sugar has dissolved, about 30 minutes, tossing occasionally to combine.

2. Process the jam in a food processor until smooth, about 8 seconds; transfer to a small saucepan. Bring the jam to a simmer over medium-high heat; simmer, stirring frequently, until dark and no longer frothy, about 3 minutes. Stir in the lemon juice; pour the warm liquid over the strawberries and stir to combine. Let cool, then cover with plastic wrap and refrigerate until cold, at least 2 hours or up to 12 hours. To serve, spoon a portion of topping over each slice of cheesecake.

## Light New York Cheesecake

**SERVES** 12

**WHY THIS RECIPE WORKS** One modest slice of cheesecake boasts nearly 600 calories and about 40 grams of fat. Start removing the fat and sugar in the cake and flavor and texture can suffer terribly, as evidenced by the rubbery and gummy light recipes we tried. Our first step was to replace full-fat cream cheese and sour cream with a combination of light cream cheese, low-fat cottage cheese, and low-fat yogurt cheese. We cut the fat further by using far fewer eggs and no egg yolks. The result? A rich, creamy cheesecake with about half the calories and three-quarters less fat than the original. You can buy low-fat yogurt cheese (also called labneh) or make your own with low-fat yogurt. To make 1 cup yogurt cheese, line a fine-mesh strainer with 3 paper coffee filters or a double layer of cheesecloth. Spoon 2 cups of plain low-fat yogurt into the lined strainer, cover, and refrigerate for 10 to 12 hours (about 1 cup of liquid will have drained out of the yogurt to yield 1 cup yogurt cheese). Serve cake as is, or with Strawberry Topping.

**CRUST**

- 9 whole graham crackers, broken into 1-inch pieces
- 4 tablespoons (½ stick) unsalted butter, melted
- 1 tablespoon sugar

**FILLING**

- 1 pound 1 percent cottage cheese
- 1 pound light cream cheese, cut into chunks and softened
- 8 ounces (1 cup) low-fat yogurt cheese
- 1½ cups (10½ ounces) sugar
- 1 tablespoon vanilla extract
- 1 teaspoon grated zest from 1 lemon
- ¼ teaspoon table salt
- 3 large eggs, at room temperature

1. **FOR THE CRUST:** Adjust an oven rack to the middle position and heat the oven to 325 degrees. Process the graham cracker pieces in a food processor to fine, even crumbs, about 30 seconds. Mix the cracker crumbs, melted butter, and sugar together, then pour into a 9-inch springform pan. Press the crumbs firmly into an even layer using the bottom of a measuring cup. Bake the crust until fragrant, 10 to 15 minutes. Cool on a wire rack, about 30 minutes.

2. **FOR THE FILLING:** Meanwhile, increase the oven temperature to 500 degrees. Line a medium bowl with a clean dish towel or several layers of paper towels. Spoon the cottage cheese into the bowl and let drain for 30 minutes.

3. Process the drained cottage cheese in a food processor until smooth and no visible lumps remain, about 1 minute, scraping down the bowl as needed. Dollop the cream cheese and yogurt cheese into the food processor and continue to process until smooth, 1 to 2 minutes, scraping down the bowl as needed. Add the sugar, vanilla, lemon zest, and salt and continue to process until smooth, about 1 minute. With the processor running, add the eggs one at a time and continue to process until smooth.

**4.** Being careful not to disturb the baked crust, spray the insides of the springform pan with vegetable oil spray. Set the pan on a rimmed baking sheet. Pour the processed cheese mixture into the cooled crust and bake for 10 minutes.

**5.** Without opening the oven door, reduce the oven temperature to 200 degrees and continue to bake until the center of the cheesecake registers 150 degrees on an instant-read thermometer, about 1½ hours.

**6.** Transfer the cake to a wire rack and run a paring knife around the edge of the cake. Cool until barely warm, 2½ to 3 hours, running a paring knife around the edge of the cake every hour or so. Wrap the pan tightly in plastic wrap and refrigerate until cold, about 3 hours.

**7.** To unmold the cheesecake, wrap a wet, hot dish towel around the springform pan and let stand for 1 minute. Remove the sides of the pan. Blot any excess moisture from the top of the cheesecake with paper towels and slide onto a cake platter. Let the cheesecake stand at room temperature for about 30 minutes before slicing.

## New York Cheesecakes for Two

SERVES 2

**WHY THIS RECIPE WORKS** True New York–style cheesecake is a beautiful thing: the dense, velvety, tangy-sweet filling is supported by a crunchy graham-cracker crust. But with a dessert this rich, a full-size cake in a two-person household will mostly go to waste. We wanted to make foolproof individual cheesecakes for two. We started with a simple graham-cracker crust, prebaked to ensure it wouldn't turn soggy once we added the filling. We thinned the cream cheese with just a little tangy sour cream. One whole egg plus an extra yolk gave the cakes a lush texture that was dense but not heavy. A pinch of salt, a small dose of vanilla, and a squeeze of lemon juice perfected the flavors. Finally, we baked the cheesecakes using the classic New York method—first at 500 degrees to get a nicely browned top, then at 200 degrees to cook through gently. You will need two 4½-inch springform pans for this recipe. Serve as is or with fresh berries.

**CRUST**

- 3 whole graham crackers, broken into 1-inch pieces
- 3 tablespoons unsalted butter, melted and cooled, divided
- 1 tablespoon sugar

**FILLING**

- 10 ounces cream cheese, softened
- ⅓ cup (2⅓ ounces) sugar, divided
- Pinch table salt
- 4 teaspoons sour cream
- ½ teaspoon lemon juice
- ½ teaspoon vanilla extract
- 1 large egg plus 1 large yolk

**1. FOR THE CRUST:** Adjust oven rack to middle position and heat oven to 325 degrees. Process graham cracker pieces in food processor to fine, even crumbs, about 30 seconds. Sprinkle 2 tablespoons melted butter and sugar over crumbs and pulse to incorporate, about 5 pulses. Divide mixture evenly between two 4½-inch springform pans. Using bottom of spoon, press crumbs firmly into even layer on bottom of pans, keeping sides as clean as possible. Bake crusts until fragrant and beginning to brown, about 10 minutes. Let crusts cool in pans on wire rack while making filling.

**2. FOR THE FILLING:** Increase oven temperature to 500 degrees. Using hand-held mixer set at medium-low speed, beat cream cheese in large bowl until smooth, 1 to 2 minutes. Scrape down sides of bowl. Add ¼ cup sugar and salt and beat until combined, 30 to 60 seconds. Scrape down bowl, add remaining sugar, and beat until combined, 30 to 60 seconds. Scrape down bowl, add sour cream, lemon juice, and vanilla, and beat until combined, 15 to 30 seconds. Scrape down bowl, add egg and egg yolk, and beat until combined, 30 to 60 seconds.

**3.** Being careful not to disturb baked crusts, brush inside of pans with remaining 1 tablespoon melted butter and place pans on rimmed baking sheet. Pour filling evenly into cooled crusts, smooth tops, and bake cheesecakes for 5 minutes. Without opening oven door, reduce temperature to 200 degrees and continue to bake until cakes register 150 degrees, 10 to 15 minutes, rotating sheet halfway through baking.

**4.** Let cheesecakes cool in pans on wire rack for 5 minutes, then run thin knife around edge of each cake. Let cakes continue to cool to room temperature, about 1 hour. Wrap pans tightly in plastic wrap and refrigerate until cold, at least 2 hours or up to 4 days.

**5.** To unmold cheesecakes, wrap hot dish towel around pans and let sit for 1 minute. Remove sides of pans. Slide thin metal spatula between crusts and pan bottoms to loosen, then slide cakes onto individual serving plates. Let cakes sit at room temperature for 30 minutes before serving. (Cheesecakes can be made up to 3 days in advance; however, crust will begin to lose its crispness after only 1 day.)

## Lemon Cheesecake

SERVES 12

**WHY THIS RECIPE WORKS** Sometimes the fresh flavor of citrus can take cheesecake to a refreshing new level. We aimed to develop a creamy cheesecake with a bracing lemon flavor. Graham crackers, our usual cookie for cheesecakes, were too overpowering for the filling's lemon flavor. Instead, we turned to animal crackers, for a mild-tasting crust that allowed the lemon flavor of the cheesecake to shine. For maximum lemon flavor, we ground lemon zest with a portion of the sugar which released its flavorful oils. Grinding the zest also improved the filling's texture (minced lemon zest baked up into fibrous bits). Heavy cream, in addition to cream cheese, provided richness, and vanilla rounded out the flavors. For ultimate creaminess, we baked the cake in a water bath. And finally, for an additional layer of bright lemon flavor, we topped off the cake with lemon curd. Be sure to zest the lemons before juicing them. For neater slices, clean the knife thoroughly between slices.

**CRUST**

- 5 ounces Nabisco Barnum's Animal Crackers or Social Tea Biscuits
- 7 tablespoons unsalted butter, melted and cooled
- 3 tablespoons sugar

**FILLING**

- 1¼ cups (8¾ ounces) sugar
- 1 tablespoon grated zest from 1 lemon
- 1½ pounds cream cheese, cut into chunks and softened
- ¼ teaspoon table salt
- ¼ cup juice from 2 lemons
- 2 teaspoons vanilla extract
- 4 large eggs, at room temperature
- ½ cup heavy cream

**CURD**

- ⅓ cup juice from 2 lemons
- ½ cup (3½ ounces) sugar
- Pinch table salt
- 2 large whole eggs plus 1 large egg yolk
- 2 tablespoons unsalted butter, cut into ½-inch pieces and frozen
- 1 tablespoon heavy cream
- ¼ teaspoon vanilla extract

**1. FOR THE CRUST:** Adjust an oven rack to the middle position and heat the oven to 325 degrees. Process the cookies in a food processor to fine, even crumbs, about 30 seconds. Sprinkle 6 tablespoons of the melted butter and the sugar over the crumbs and pulse to incorporate. Sprinkle the mixture into a 9-inch springform pan. Press the crumbs firmly into an even layer using the bottom of a measuring cup. Bake the crust until fragrant and beginning to brown, 10 to 15 minutes. Let the crust cool to room temperature, about 30 minutes. Once cool, wrap the outside of the pan with two sheets of heavy-duty foil and set in a large roasting pan lined with a dish towel. Bring a kettle of water to a boil.

**2. FOR THE FILLING:** Process ¼ cup of the sugar and the lemon zest in a food processor until the sugar is yellow and the zest is very fine, about 15 seconds. Pulse in the remaining 1 cup sugar to combine.

**3.** In a stand mixer fitted with the paddle attachment, beat the cream cheese on medium speed until smooth, about 1 minute. Scrape down the bowl and beaters as needed.

**4.** Beat in half of the lemon sugar and the salt until incorporated. Beat in the remaining lemon sugar until incorporated, about 1 minute. Beat in the lemon juice and vanilla until incorporated, about 1 minute. Beat in the eggs, one at a time, until combined, about 1 minute. Beat in the heavy cream until incorporated, about 1 minute.

**5.** Being careful not to disturb the baked crust, brush the inside of the prepared springform pan with the remaining 1 tablespoon melted butter. Carefully pour the filling into the pan. Set the roasting pan, with the cheesecake, on the oven rack and pour the boiling water into the roasting pan until it reaches about halfway up the sides of the springform pan. Bake the cheesecake until the center registers 150 degrees on an instant-read thermometer, about 1½ hours.

**6.** Cool the cheesecake in the roasting pan for 45 minutes, then transfer to a wire rack and cool until barely warm, 2½ to 3 hours, running a knife around the edge of the cake every hour or so. Wrap the pan tightly in plastic wrap and refrigerate until cold, about 3 hours.

**7. FOR THE CURD:** Meanwhile, cook the lemon juice, sugar, and salt together in a small saucepan over medium-high heat until the sugar dissolves and the mixture is hot (do not boil). In a medium bowl, whisk the whole eggs and egg yolk together until combined, then slowly whisk in the hot lemon mixture to temper. Return the mixture to the saucepan and cook over medium-low heat, stirring constantly, until the mixture is thickened and a spatula scraped along the bottom of the pan leaves a trail (170 degrees on an instant-read thermometer), 2 to 4 minutes.

**8.** Off the heat, stir in the frozen butter until melted and incorporated, then stir in the cream and vanilla. Strain the curd through a fine-mesh strainer into a small bowl. Press plastic wrap directly on the surface of the curd and refrigerate until needed.

**9. TO FINISH THE CAKE:** When the cheesecake is cold, spoon the lemon curd over the top of the cake and spread into an even layer. Wrap the pan tightly in plastic wrap and refrigerate until the curd and cake have set, at least 5 hours.

**10.** To unmold the cheesecake, wrap a wet, hot dish towel around the cake pan and let sit for 1 minute. Remove the sides of the pan and carefully slide the cake onto a cake platter. Let the cheesecake sit at room temperature for 30 minutes before serving. (Cheesecake can be made up to a day in advance and refrigerated; leftovers can be refrigerated for up to 4 days, but the crust will be soggy after 1 day.)

## Spiced Pumpkin Cheesecake

**SERVES** 12

**WHY THIS RECIPE WORKS** Pumpkin cheesecake is a welcome alternative to traditional pumpkin pie, but the ideal pumpkin cheesecake is elusive: It's often either too dry and dense or soft and mousse-like, while the flavor veers from too tangy to overspiced to bland. We wanted a pumpkin cheesecake with a velvety texture that balanced the flavor of sweet, earthy pumpkin with tangy cream cheese and just enough spice, and a crisp, buttery, cookie-crumb crust. For a cookie crust that complemented the pumpkin flavor, we spiced up a graham cracker crust with ginger, cinnamon, and cloves. Blotting canned pumpkin puree with paper towels removed its excess moisture, creating a smooth and creamy texture. For dairy, we liked heavy cream, not sour cream, for added richness. We also preferred white sugar to brown, which tended to overpower the pumpkin flavor. Be sure to buy unsweetened canned pumpkin, not pumpkin pie filling, which is preseasoned and sweetened. For neater slices, clean the knife thoroughly between slices.

**CRUST**

- 8 whole graham crackers, broken into 1-inch pieces
- 7 tablespoons unsalted butter, melted, divided
- 3 tablespoons sugar
- ½ teaspoon ground ginger
- ½ teaspoon ground cinnamon
- ¼ teaspoon ground cloves

**FILLING**

- 1 (15-ounce) can pumpkin puree
- 1⅓ cups (9⅓ ounces) sugar
- 1 teaspoon ground cinnamon
- ½ teaspoon ground ginger
- ¼ teaspoon ground nutmeg
- ¼ teaspoon ground cloves
- ¼ teaspoon ground allspice
- ½ teaspoon table salt
- 1½ pounds cream cheese, softened
- 1 tablespoon lemon juice
- 1 tablespoon vanilla extract
- 5 large eggs, room temperature
- 1 cup heavy cream

**1. FOR THE CRUST:** Adjust oven rack to middle position and heat oven to 325 degrees. Process graham cracker pieces in food processor to fine, even crumbs, about 30 seconds. Sprinkle 6 tablespoons melted butter, sugar, and spices over crumbs and pulse to incorporate. Sprinkle mixture into 9-inch springform pan. Press crumbs firmly into even layer using bottom of measuring cup. Bake crust until fragrant and beginning to brown, 10 to 15 minutes. Let crust cool to room temperature, about 30 minutes. Once cool, wrap outside of pan with 2 sheets of heavy-duty aluminum foil and set in large roasting pan lined with dish towel. Bring kettle of water to boil.

**2. FOR THE FILLING:** Line rimmed baking sheet with triple layer of paper towels. Spread pumpkin on paper towels in even layer. Press with second triple layer of paper towels to wick away moisture. Whisk sugar, spices, and salt together in small bowl.

**3.** Using stand mixer fitted with paddle, beat cream cheese on medium-low speed until smooth, about 1 minute. Scrape down bowl and beaters as needed.

**4.** Beat in half of sugar mixture until incorporated, about 1 minute. Beat in remaining sugar mixture until incorporated, about 1 minute. Beat in dried pumpkin, lemon juice, and vanilla until incorporated, about 1 minute. Beat in eggs, one at a time, until combined, about 1 minute. Beat in heavy cream until incorporated, about 1 minute.

**5.** Being careful not to disturb baked crust, brush inside of springform pan with remaining 1 tablespoon melted butter. Carefully pour filling into pan. Set roasting pan, with cheesecake, on oven rack and pour boiling water into roasting pan until it reaches about halfway up sides of pan. Bake cheesecake until center registers 150 degrees, about 1½ hours.

**6.** Let cheesecake cool in roasting pan for 45 minutes, then transfer to wire rack and let cool until barely warm, 2½ to 3 hours, running knife around edge of cake every hour or so. Wrap pan tightly in plastic wrap and refrigerate until cold, about 3 hours or up to 3 days.

**7.** To unmold cheesecake, wrap wet, hot dish towel around cake pan and let sit for 1 minute. Remove side of pan and carefully slide cake onto cake platter. Let cheesecake sit at room temperature for 30 minutes before serving.

## Classic Bread Pudding

**SERVES** 8 to 10

**WHY THIS RECIPE WORKS** Contemporary versions of this humble dish vary in texture, from mushy porridge to chewy, desiccated cousins of overcooked holiday stuffing. We wanted a dessert as refined as any French soufflé. We chose challah for its rich flavor, cut the bread into cubes, toasted them until lightly browned, and soaked them with basic custard. Once the cubes were saturated, we transferred them to a baking dish and slid our pudding into a low-temperature oven to prevent curdling. For a crackly crust, we dotted the top of the pudding with additional toasted bread cubes. Then we brushed it with melted butter and sprinkled it with a flavorful mixture of white and brown sugar before transferring it to the oven. The crunchy, buttery, sugary crust was the perfect partner to the satiny-smooth custard that lay below. If desired, serve this pudding with softly whipped cream or with Bourbon–Brown Sugar Sauce.

- 2 tablespoons light brown sugar
- ¾ cup (5¼ ounces) plus 1 tablespoon granulated sugar
- 1 (14-ounce) loaf challah bread, cut into ¾-inch cubes (about 10 cups)
- 9 large egg yolks
- 4 teaspoons vanilla extract
- ¾ teaspoon table salt
- 2½ cups heavy cream
- 2½ cups milk
- 2 tablespoons unsalted butter, melted

**1.** Adjust the oven racks to the middle and lower-middle positions and heat the oven to 325 degrees. Combine the brown sugar and 1 tablespoon of the granulated sugar in a small bowl; set aside.

**2.** Spread the bread cubes in a single layer on two rimmed baking sheets. Bake, tossing occasionally, until just dry, about 15 minutes, switching the baking sheets halfway through the baking time. Cool the bread cubes for about 15 minutes; set aside 2 cups.

**3.** Whisk the egg yolks, remaining ¾ cup sugar, the vanilla, and salt together in a large bowl. Whisk in the cream and milk until combined. Add the remaining 8 cups cooled bread cubes and toss to coat. Transfer the mixture to a 13 by 9-inch baking dish and let stand, occasionally pressing the bread cubes into the custard, until the cubes are thoroughly saturated, about 30 minutes.

**4.** Spread the reserved bread cubes evenly over the top of the soaked bread mixture and gently press into the custard. Using a pastry brush, dab the melted butter over the top of the unsoaked bread pieces. Sprinkle the brown sugar mixture evenly over the top. Place the bread pudding on a rimmed baking sheet and bake on the middle rack until the custard has just set and pressing the center of the pudding with your finger reveals no runny liquid, 45 to 50 minutes. (An instant-read thermometer inserted into the center of the pudding should read 170 degrees.) Transfer to a wire rack and cool until the pudding is set and just warm, about 45 minutes. Serve. (Leftovers, wrapped tightly with plastic wrap, can be refrigerator for up to 24 hours. To retain a crisp top crust when reheating, cut the bread pudding into squares and heat, uncovered, in a 450-degree oven until warmed through, 6 to 8 minutes.)

### Bourbon–Brown Sugar Sauce

**MAKES** about 1 cup

- ½ cup packed (3½ ounces) light brown sugar
- 7 tablespoons heavy cream
- 2½ tablespoons unsalted butter
- 1½ tablespoons bourbon

Whisk the brown sugar and heavy cream in a small saucepan over medium heat until combined. Continue to cook, whisking frequently, until the mixture comes to a boil, about 5 minutes. Whisk in the butter and bring the mixture back to a boil, about 1 minute. Remove from the heat and whisk in the bourbon. Cool to just warm; serve with the bread pudding.

## Double-Apple Bread Pudding

**SERVES** 6

**WHY THIS RECIPE WORKS** For a bread pudding that was chock-full of apple flavor, we combined the bright Granny Smith apples with cubes of toasted challah and a rich custard laced with autumnal spices. Parcooking the apples in a little water, butter, and sugar prior to combining them with the bread and custard not only helped achieve the perfect texture but also created a fruity apple liquid that we used to boost the flavor of the custard. Toasting the challah bread cubes ensured that they soaked up the maximum amount of custard, giving the pudding a light and fluffy texture. Finally, reserving some of the toasted bread cubes and coating them in melted butter and sugar created a quasi-streusel topping that added crunch to the lush pudding. We like the brightness of Granny Smith apples here, but you can use another firm, tart apple variety. Use a glass or ceramic baking dish. In step 3, you may not need all the milk. Serve with softly whipped cream or vanilla ice cream, if desired.

- 10 ounces challah, cut into ½-inch cubes (6 cups)
- 2 tablespoons unsalted butter, plus 1½ tablespoons melted
- ½ cup packed (3½ ounces) brown sugar, divided, plus 1½ tablespoons
- ⅓ cup water
- 2 large Granny Smith apples (8 ounces each), peeled, cored, and cut into ½-inch pieces
- 1 cup milk
- ¾ teaspoon ground cinnamon
- ½ teaspoon vanilla extract
- ¼ teaspoon ground nutmeg
- ¼ teaspoon table salt
- 2 large eggs
- 1¼ cups heavy cream

**1.** Adjust oven rack to middle position and heat oven to 325 degrees. Spread bread cubes in single layer on rimmed baking sheet. Bake, tossing occasionally, until just dry, about 15 minutes. Let bread cubes cool for about 15 minutes; measure out ¾ cup and set aside.

**2.** Melt 2 tablespoons butter in 10-inch skillet over medium heat. Add ¼ cup sugar and water and whisk until sugar dissolves. Stir in apples, increase heat to medium-high, and bring to simmer. Cover and cook, stirring occasionally, for 4 minutes. Uncover and continue to cook until apples are translucent and just tender, about 4 minutes longer.

**3.** Drain apples in fine-mesh strainer set over 2-cup liquid measuring cup, pressing gently to remove as much juice as possible. Set aside apples. Add enough milk to juice to yield 1¼ cups liquid.

**4.** Combine ¼ cup sugar, cinnamon, vanilla, nutmeg, and salt in large bowl. Whisk in eggs. Whisk in cream and milk-juice mixture until combined. Gently stir in apples. Add remaining 5¼ cups bread cubes and toss to coat. Transfer mixture to 8-inch square baking dish and gently press down with spatula. Let soak for 30 minutes, pressing bread cubes into custard halfway through soaking.

**5.** Toss reserved bread cubes with remaining 1½ tablespoons sugar in separate bowl. Use your fingers to crush bread to create mix of small and large pieces. Add melted butter and toss to combine. Press bread cubes into custard once more and sprinkle bread topping evenly over soaked bread mixture. Place dish on rimmed baking sheet and bake until bread pudding is golden brown and center registers 160 to 165 degrees, 1 hour to 1 hour 5 minutes. Transfer to wire rack and let cool until pudding is set and just warm, about 45 minutes. Serve.

## Chocolate-Hazelnut Slow-Cooker Bread Pudding

**SERVES** 8 to 10

**WHY THIS RECIPE WORKS** Making bread pudding in a slow cooker may seem like a stretch, but we were determined to make a company-worthy version that boasted both decadence and hands-off (and oven-freeing) convenience. After testing various types of bread, we agreed challah, with its rich flavor, had the upper hand. We cut the bread into cubes and toasted it in the oven. This extra step dried out the bread enough to soak up as much custard as possible. Once toasted, we transferred the bread to the slow cooker and added the custard (a combination of egg yolks, milk, heavy cream, sugar, and vanilla). Pressing the bread into the custard ensured every cube soaked up its share. We opted for Nutella as our chief chocolaty component, which took our recipe to the next level. To give our recipe another chocolaty boost, we stirred in chocolate chips, which melted into the pudding and made this dessert that much more decadent.

- 1 (14-ounce) loaf challah bread, cut into 1-inch cubes (about 12 cups)
- ½ cup chocolate chips
- 2 cups heavy cream
- 2 cups whole milk
- 9 large egg yolks
- 1 cup Nutella
- ¾ cup plus 1 tablespoon (5⅔ ounces) granulated sugar
- 4 teaspoons vanilla extract
- ¾ teaspoon table salt
- 2 tablespoons light brown sugar

**1.** Following the photos, line the slow cooker with an aluminum foil collar, then line with a foil sling, and spray with vegetable oil spray. Adjust the oven rack to the middle position and heat the oven to 225 degrees. Spread the bread over a rimmed baking sheet and bake, shaking the pan occasionally, until dry and crisp, about 40 minutes. Let the bread cool slightly, then transfer to a very large bowl.

**2.** Mix the chocolate chips into the dried bread; transfer to the prepared slow cooker. Whisk the cream, milk, egg yolks, Nutella, ¾ cup of the granulated sugar, the vanilla, and salt together in a bowl, then pour the mixture evenly over the bread. Press gently on the bread to submerge.

**3.** Mix the remaining 1 tablespoon granulated sugar with the brown sugar then sprinkle over the top of the casserole. Cover and cook until the center is set, about 4 hours on low. Let cool for 30 minutes before serving.

### PREPARING THE SLOW COOKER

**1. TO MAKE A FOIL COLLAR:** Layer and fold sheets of heavy-duty foil until you have a six-layered foil rectangle that measures roughly 16 inches long by 4 inches wide. Press the collar into the back side of the slow-cooker insert.

**2. TO MAKE A FOIL SLING:** Fit two large sheets of heavy-duty foil into the slow cooker, perpendicular to one another and hanging over the edges of the slow cooker. Use the overhanging foil to lift the pudding out of the slow cooker fully intact.

## Creamy Chocolate Pudding

**SERVES** 6

**WHY THIS RECIPE WORKS** Homemade chocolate pudding often suffers from lackluster chocolate flavor or a grainy texture. We found that using a moderate amount of bittersweet chocolate in combination with unsweetened cocoa and espresso powder helped us achieve maximum chocolate flavor. Using mostly milk, and just half a cup of heavy cream, along with three egg yolks ensured that our pudding had a silky smooth texture. We recommend using one the test kitchen's favorite baking chocolate, Ghirardelli Bittersweet Chocolate, for this recipe, but any high-quality dark, bittersweet, or semisweet chocolate will work. This recipe was developed using a 60 percent cacao chocolate. Using a

chocolate with a higher cacao percentage will result in a thicker pudding. Low-fat milk (1 percent or 2 percent) may be substituted for the whole milk with a small sacrifice in richness. Do not use skim milk as a substitute. Serve the pudding with lightly sweetened whipped cream and chocolate shavings.

- 2 teaspoons vanilla extract
- ½ teaspoon instant espresso powder
- ½ cup (3½ ounces) sugar
- 3 tablespoons Dutch-processed cocoa powder
- 2 tablespoons cornstarch
- ¼ teaspoon table salt
- 3 large egg yolks
- ½ cup heavy cream
- 2½ cups whole milk
- 5 tablespoons unsalted butter, cut into 8 pieces
- 4 ounces bittersweet chocolate, finely chopped

**1.** Stir together the vanilla extract and espresso powder in a bowl; set aside. Whisk the sugar, cocoa, cornstarch, and salt together in a large saucepan. Whisk in the egg yolks and cream until fully incorporated, making sure to scrape the corners of the saucepan. Whisk in the milk until incorporated.

**2.** Place the saucepan over medium heat and cook, whisking constantly, until the mixture is thickened and bubbling over the entire surface, 5 to 8 minutes. Cook for 30 seconds longer, remove from the heat, add the butter and chocolate, and whisk until melted and fully incorporated. Whisk in the vanilla mixture.

**3.** Strain the pudding through a fine-mesh strainer into a bowl. Place lightly greased parchment paper against the surface of the pudding, and place in a refrigerator to cool, at least 4 hours. Serve. (The pudding can be covered with plastic wrap and refrigerated for up to 2 days.)

## Chocolate-Raspberry Trifle

**SERVES** 12 to 16

**WHY THIS RECIPE WORKS** For a showstopper chocolate-raspberry trifle that tasted as good as it looked, we started by making our chocolate custard so that it could chill and set while we prepared the other components. Using a moderate amount of bittersweet chocolate in combination with Dutch-processed cocoa powder and instant espresso powder helped achieve maximum chocolate flavor and a silky-smooth texture. Tender but resilient chiffon cake remained intact in the trifle even after it absorbed the surrounding moisture, and its vegetable oil–enriched crumb stayed softer in this chilled dessert than butter cake would. It baked and cooled quickly in a rimmed baking sheet and was easy to cut into flat, even squares for arranging in the trifle bowl. We mashed half of the raspberries so that their juice—thickened by a brief simmer—helped the trifle components meld. A bit of rum drizzled on each layer of cake added a festive touch. Crowned with billowy whipped cream and (optional) sprinkles, this dessert is fit for the glitziest occasion. To use frozen raspberries, thaw them first and include the juice. Assemble the trifle (except for the top cream layer) at least 6 hours or up to two days before serving. Use at least a 3½ quart glass bowl with straight sides. To dress up the trifle, top it with whole raspberries and decorative chocolate triangles sparkling with luster dust (page 920).

**CUSTARD**

- 2 teaspoons vanilla extract
- ½ teaspoon instant espresso powder
- ½ cup (3½ ounces) sugar
- 3 tablespoons cornstarch
- 2 tablespoons Dutch-processed cocoa powder
- ¼ teaspoon table salt
- 3 cups whole milk, divided
- 3 large egg yolks (reserve whites for cake)
- 4 ounces bittersweet chocolate, chopped fine
- 5 tablespoons unsalted butter, cut into 5 pieces

**RASPBERRY FILLING**

- 1 pound (3¼ cups) raspberries, divided
- 3 tablespoons sugar
- 1 teaspoon cornstarch
- Pinch table salt

**CAKE**

- 1⅓ cups (5⅓ ounces) cake flour
- ¾ cup (5¼ ounces) sugar
- 1½ teaspoons baking powder
- ¼ teaspoon table salt
- ⅓ cup vegetable oil
- ¼ cup water
- 2 large eggs, separated, plus 3 large whites (reserved from custard)
- 2 teaspoons vanilla extract
- ¼ teaspoon cream of tartar

**WHIPPED CREAM**

- 2 cups heavy cream, divided
- 4 teaspoons sugar, divided
- 6 tablespoons rum, divided

Sprinkles (optional)

**1. FOR THE CUSTARD:** Combine vanilla and espresso powder in small bowl and set aside. Whisk sugar, cornstarch, cocoa, and salt together in large saucepan. Whisk in ½ cup milk and egg yolks until fully incorporated, making sure to scrape corners of saucepan. Whisk in remaining 2½ cups milk until incorporated.

**2.** Whisk gently over medium heat until mixture is thickened and bubbling over entire surface, 5 to 8 minutes. Cook 30 seconds longer, remove from heat, add chocolate and butter, and whisk until melted and incorporated. Whisk in vanilla mixture.

**3.** Pour custard through fine-mesh strainer into wide, shallow bowl. Press lightly greased parchment paper against surface of custard and refrigerate until cool, at least 4 hours or up to 2 days.

**4. FOR THE RASPBERRY FILLING:** Place half of raspberries, sugar, cornstarch, and salt in medium saucepan. Place remaining raspberries in large bowl. Using potato masher, thoroughly mash raspberries in saucepan. Cook over medium heat, stirring frequently, until sugar is dissolved and mixture is thick and bubbling, 3 to 5 minutes. Pour over raspberries in bowl and stir to combine. Set aside.

**5. FOR THE CAKE:** Adjust oven rack to middle position and heat oven to 350 degrees. Lightly grease 18 by 13-inch rimmed baking sheet, line with parchment, and lightly grease parchment. Whisk flour, sugar, baking powder, and salt together in medium bowl. Whisk oil, water, egg yolks, and vanilla into flour mixture until smooth batter forms.

**6.** Using stand mixer fitted with whisk attachment, whip 5 egg whites and cream of tartar on medium-low speed until foamy, about 1 minute. Increase speed to medium-high and whip until soft peaks form, 2 to 3 minutes. Transfer one-third of whites to batter; whisk gently until mixture is lightened. Using rubber spatula, gently fold remaining whites into batter.

**7.** Pour batter into prepared sheet; spread evenly. Bake until cake springs back when pressed lightly in center, 10 to 13 minutes.

**8.** Transfer cake to wire rack; let cool for 5 minutes. Run knife around edge of sheet, then invert cake onto rack. Remove parchment, then re-invert cake onto second wire rack. Let cool completely, at least 30 minutes.

**9. FOR THE WHIPPED CREAM:** Using clean, dry mixer bowl and whisk attachment, whip 1 cup cream and 2 teaspoons sugar on medium-low speed until foamy, about 45 seconds. Increase speed to high and whip until soft peaks form, about 1 minute. Trim ¼ inch off each side of cake; discard trimmings. Cut cake into 24 equal pieces (each piece about 2½ inches square). Briefly whisk custard until smooth.

**10.** Spoon ½ cup raspberry mixture into trifle bowl and spread over bottom. Tear 1 cake square into 4 pieces and pile in center of bowl. Shingle 10 cake squares, fallen-domino-style, around bottom of trifle, placing edges against bowl wall. Tear another cake square into 4 pieces and fill in center. Drizzle 3 tablespoons rum evenly over cake. Spoon half of custard over cake and spread evenly. Spoon whipped cream over custard and spread evenly. Spoon remaining raspberry mixture over cream and spread evenly.

**11.** Repeat layering with remaining 12 cake squares, pressing firmly but gently on cake to remove any gaps in layers. Sprinkle with remaining 3 tablespoons rum and spread remaining custard over soaked cake. Cover trifle with plastic wrap and refrigerate for at least 6 hours or up to 2 days.

**12.** Using stand mixer fitted with whisk attachment, whip remaining 1 cup cream and remaining 2 teaspoons sugar on medium-low speed until foamy, about 45 seconds. Increase speed to high and whip until soft peaks form, about 1 minute. Spread or pipe cream over top of trifle. Decorate with sprinkles, if using, and serve.

## DIY Chocolate Decorations

**MAKES** 4 ounces

Our chocolate decorations add height and a touch of elegance to our Chocolate-Raspberry Trifle, but they can also be used on cakes or to adorn plated desserts. We started by melting 3 ounces of finely chopped chocolate, and then we stirred in an additional ounce of finely grated chocolate to seed the chocolate with beta crystals, the ones that give tempered chocolate its snappy texture and attractive sheen. Luster dust is a fine, edible, iridescent powder that gives sweets a little extra finesse. It can be found at cake decorating shops or online.

- 4 ounces bittersweet chocolate (3 ounces chopped fine, 1 ounce grated)
- Gold luster dust (optional)

**1.** Invert rimmed baking sheet and top with sheet of parchment paper. Tape parchment to sheet. Microwave chopped chocolate in bowl at 50 percent power, stirring every 30 seconds, until melted but not much warmer than body temperature (check by holding bowl in palm of your hand), 2 to 3 minutes. Add grated chocolate and stir until smooth, returning to microwave for no more than 5 seconds at a time to finish melting if necessary.

**2.** Spread chocolate thinly and evenly over prepared parchment to form rough 8 by 12-inch rectangle. Refrigerate until surface of chocolate just turns matte, 1 to 2 minutes. Using tip of sharp knife, cut half of chocolate into tall, slim triangles. Refrigerate until fully hardened, about 10 minutes. Brush triangles with luster dust, if using. Break remaining chocolate into 1-inch shards. (Chocolate decorations can be wrapped in plastic wrap and refrigerated for up to 1 week.)

## Stovetop Rice Pudding

**SERVES** 6 to 8

**WHY THIS RECIPE WORKS** At its best, rice pudding is lightly sweet and tastes of its primary component, rice. At its worst, the rice flavor is lost to cloying sweetness, overcooked milk, and a pasty, leaden consistency. We wanted a rice pudding with intact, tender grains bound loosely in a subtly sweet, creamy pudding. For simple, straightforward rice flavor, we avoided aromatic rices like basmati and jasmine. Arborio rice, used for risotto, was stiff and gritty. Overall, medium-grain rice produced the best texture (with long-grain rice a close second). We found that cooking the rice in water rather than milk left its flavor intact. After the rice absorbed the water, we added sugar and equal amounts of milk and half-and-half, which delivered the proper degree of richness; the eggs and butter found in other recipes were just too overpowering. When we cooked the rice in water with the lid on the pan, then removed the lid while the rice simmered in the milk mixture, we got the results we wanted: distinct, tender grains of rice in a milky, subtly sweet sauce. We prefer pudding made with medium-grain rice, but long-grain rice works, too.

- 2 cups water
- 1 cup medium-grain rice
- ¼ teaspoon table salt
- 2½ cups whole milk
- 2½ cups half-and-half
- ⅔ cup (4⅔ ounces) sugar
- ½ cup raisins
- 1½ teaspoons vanilla extract
- 1 teaspoon ground cinnamon

**1.** Bring the water to a boil in a large saucepan. Stir in the rice and salt, cover, and simmer over low heat, stirring once or twice, until the water is almost fully absorbed, 15 to 20 minutes.

**2.** Stir in the milk, half-and-half, and sugar. Increase the heat to medium-high and bring to a simmer, then reduce the heat to maintain a simmer. Cook, uncovered and stirring frequently, until the mixture starts to thicken, about 30 minutes. Reduce the heat to low and continue to cook, stirring every couple of minutes to prevent sticking and scorching, until a spoon is just able to stand up in the pudding, about 15 minutes longer.

**3.** Remove from the heat and stir in the raisins, vanilla, and cinnamon. Serve warm, at room temperature, or chilled. (To store, press plastic wrap directly onto the surface of the pudding and refrigerate for up to 2 days. If serving at room temperature or chilled, stir in up to 1 cup warm milk, 2 tablespoons at a time, as needed to loosen before serving.)

## Best Butterscotch Pudding

**SERVES** 8

**WHY THIS RECIPE WORKS** For butterscotch pudding with rich, bittersweet flavor, we made butterscotch sauce by cooking butter, brown and white sugar, corn syrup, lemon juice, and salt together into a dark caramel. Because making caramel can be finicky—it can go from caramelized to burnt in a matter of seconds—we used a two-step process that gave us a larger window in which to gauge the doneness of the caramel. We first brought the mixture to a rolling boil and then we reduced the heat to a low simmer where it slowly came up to temperature and we could stop the cooking at just the right moment. To turn our butterscotch into pudding, we ditched the classical (yet time-consuming) tempering method in favor of a revolutionary technique that calls for pouring the boiling caramel sauce directly over the thickening agents (egg yolks and cornstarch thinned with a little milk). When taking the temperature of the caramel in step 1, tilt the pan and move the thermometer back and forth to equalize hot and cool spots. Work quickly when pouring the caramel mixture over the egg mixture in step 4 to ensure proper thickening. Serve with lightly sweetened whipped cream.

- 12 tablespoons unsalted butter, cut into ½-inch pieces
- ½ cup (3½ ounces) granulated sugar
- ½ cup packed (3½ ounces) dark brown sugar
- ¼ cup water
- 2 tablespoons light corn syrup
- 1 teaspoon lemon juice
- ¾ teaspoon table salt
- 1 cup heavy cream, divided
- 2¼ cups whole milk, divided
- 4 large egg yolks
- ¼ cup (1 ounce) cornstarch
- 2 teaspoons vanilla extract
- 1 teaspoon dark rum

**1.** Bring butter, granulated sugar, brown sugar, water, corn syrup, lemon juice, and salt to boil in large saucepan over medium heat, stirring occasionally to dissolve sugar and melt butter. Once mixture is at full rolling boil, cook, stirring occasionally, for 5 minutes (caramel will register about 240 degrees). Immediately reduce heat to medium-low and simmer gently (caramel should maintain steady stream of lazy bubbles—if not, adjust heat accordingly), stirring frequently, until mixture is color of dark peanut butter, 12 to 16 minutes longer (caramel will register about 300 degrees and should have slight burnt smell).

**2.** Remove pan from heat; carefully pour ¼ cup cream into caramel mixture and swirl to incorporate (mixture will bubble and steam); let bubbling subside. Whisk vigorously and scrape corners of pan until mixture is completely smooth, at least 30 seconds. Return pan to medium heat and gradually whisk in remaining ¾ cup cream until smooth. Whisk in 2 cups milk until mixture is smooth, making sure to scrape corners and edges of pan to remove any remaining bits of caramel.

**3.** Meanwhile, microwave remaining ¼ cup milk until simmering, 30 to 45 seconds. Whisk egg yolks and cornstarch in large bowl until smooth. Gradually whisk in hot milk until smooth; set aside (do not refrigerate).

**4.** Return saucepan to medium-high heat and bring mixture to full rolling boil, whisking frequently. Once mixture is boiling rapidly and beginning to climb toward top of pan, immediately pour into bowl with yolk mixture in 1 motion (do not add gradually). Whisk thoroughly for 10 to 15 seconds (mixture will thicken after a few seconds). Whisk in vanilla and rum. Spray piece of parchment paper with vegetable oil spray and press on surface of pudding. Refrigerate until cold and set, at least 3 hours. Whisk pudding until smooth before serving.

## Panna Cotta

**SERVES** 8

**WHY THIS RECIPE WORKS** The literal translation of panna cotta, "cooked cream," does nothing to suggest its ethereal qualities. In fact, panna cotta is not cooked at all. Instead, sugar and gelatin are melted in cream and milk and the mixture is then turned into ramekins and chilled. Panna cotta is about nothing if not texture. The cream must be robust enough to unmold but delicate enough to shiver on the plate. After trying several different recipes, we concluded that we needed a higher proportion of cream to milk to achieve the creamiest flavor and texture. The amount of gelatin proved critical—too much turned the panna cotta rubbery; it needs to be just firm enough to unmold, so we used a light hand. And because gelatin sets more quickly at cold temperatures, we minimized the amount of heat by softening the gelatin in cold milk, then heating it very briefly until melted. Chilled until set, our panna cotta was creamy, smooth, and light. A vanilla bean gives the panna cotta the deepest flavor, but 2 teaspoons of vanilla extract can be used instead. Though traditionally unmolded, panna cotta may be chilled and served in wine glasses and sauced on top. Serve with the Raspberry Coulis (recipe follows) or just lightly sweetened berries.

- 1 cup whole milk
- 2¾ teaspoons unflavored gelatin
- 3 cups heavy cream
- 1 vanilla bean, halved lengthwise
- 6 tablespoons sugar
- Pinch table salt
- 1 recipe Raspberry Coulis (recipe follows)

**1.** Pour the milk into a medium saucepan; sprinkle the surface evenly with the gelatin and let stand for 10 minutes. Meanwhile, turn the contents of two ice cube trays (about 32 cubes) into a large bowl; add 4 cups cold water. Pour the cream into a large measuring cup or pitcher. With a paring knife, scrape the vanilla seeds into the cream; place the pod in the cream along with the seeds and set the mixture aside. Set eight 4-ounce ramekins on a rimmed baking sheet.

**2.** Heat the milk and gelatin mixture over high heat, stirring constantly, until the gelatin is dissolved and the mixture registers 135 degrees on an instant-read thermometer, about 1½ minutes. Off the heat, add the sugar and salt; stir until dissolved, about 1 minute.

**3.** Stirring constantly, slowly pour the cream with the vanilla into the saucepan containing the milk, then transfer the mixture to a medium bowl and set the bowl over the ice water bath. Stir frequently until thickened to the consistency of eggnog and the mixture registers 50 degrees on an instant-read thermometer, about 10 minutes. Strain the mixture into a large measuring cup or pitcher, then distribute evenly among the ramekins. Cover the baking sheet with plastic wrap, making sure that the plastic does not mar the surface of the cream; refrigerate until just set (the mixture should wobble when shaken gently), about 4 hours.

**4.** To serve, spoon a portion of the raspberry coulis onto eight individual serving plates. Pour 1 cup boiling water into a small wide-mouthed bowl, dip a ramekin filled with panna cotta into the water for 3 seconds and lift the ramekin out of the water. With a moistened finger, press lightly on the periphery of the panna cotta to loosen the edges. Dip the ramekin back into the hot water for another 3 seconds. Invert the ramekin over your palm and loosen the panna cotta by cupping your fingers between the panna cotta and the edges of the ramekin. Gently lower the panna cotta onto a serving plate with the coulis. Repeat the process with the remaining ramekins of panna cotta. Serve. (To make the panna cotta a day ahead, decrease the amount of gelatin to 2½ teaspoons, and chill the filled wine glasses or ramekins for 18 to 24 hours.)

### Raspberry Coulis

**MAKES** about 1½ cups

- 24 ounces (about 5 cups) frozen raspberries
- ⅓ cup (2⅓ ounces) sugar
- ¼ teaspoon juice from 1 lemon
- Pinch table salt

**1.** Place the frozen raspberries in a 4-quart saucepan. Cover and simmer over medium-high heat, stirring occasionally, for 10 to 12 minutes. Add the sugar and increase the heat to high. Boil for 2 minutes.

**2.** Strain the berries through a fine-mesh strainer into a bowl, using a rubber spatula to push the berries through the strainer; discard the seeds. Stir in the lemon juice and salt. Cover and refrigerate until chilled, at least 2 hours.

## Buttermilk-Vanilla Panna Cotta with Berries and Honey

**SERVES 8**

**WHY THIS RECIPE WORKS** Our silky-smooth, delicately textured buttermilk panna cotta is an elegant dessert that requires some waiting but hardly any work. We made it even simpler by skipping the traditional step of sprinkling gelatin over cold water to bloom it before dissolving it in hot cream. Instead, we whisked together the gelatin, sugar, and salt and then whisked in cold heavy cream. Dispersed by the sugar and salt, the gelatin granules had plenty of space to absorb water from the cream, which readied the gelatin for heating. Bringing the mixture to 150 degrees ensured that the gelatin fully dissolved and the floral notes of the vanilla bean were thoroughly infused into the cream. To prevent curdling, we let the mixture cool to 110 degrees before adding the buttermilk. Finally, we portioned the panna cotta and refrigerated it until it was time to serve. Its tangy richness is the perfect foil for a drizzle of honey and a few ripe summer berries. Make sure to unmold the panna cotta onto cool plates. If you'd rather not unmold the panna cotta, substitute 5- to 6-ounce glasses for the ramekins.

- ½ cup (3½ ounces) sugar
- 2 teaspoons unflavored gelatin
- Pinch table salt
- 2 cups heavy cream
- 1 vanilla bean
- 2 cups buttermilk
- Honey
- Fresh raspberries and/or blackberries

**1.** Whisk sugar, gelatin, and salt in small saucepan until very well combined. Whisk in cream and let sit for 5 minutes. Cut vanilla bean in half lengthwise. Using tip of paring knife, scrape out seeds. Add bean and seeds to cream mixture. Cook over medium heat, stirring occasionally, until mixture registers 150 to 160 degrees, about 5 minutes. Remove from heat and let mixture cool to 105 to 110 degrees, about 15 minutes. Strain cream mixture through fine-mesh strainer into medium bowl, pressing on solids to extract as much liquid as possible. Gently whisk in buttermilk.

**2.** Set eight 5-ounce ramekins on rimmed baking sheet. Divide buttermilk mixture evenly among ramekins. Invert second rimmed baking sheet on top of ramekins and carefully transfer to refrigerator. Chill for at least 6 hours or up to 3 days (if chilling for more than 6 hours, cover each ramekin with plastic wrap).

**3.** Working with 1 panna cotta at a time, insert paring knife between panna cotta and side of ramekin. Gently run knife around edge of ramekin to loosen panna cotta. Cover ramekin with serving plate and invert panna cotta onto plate. (You may need to gently jiggle ramekin.) Drizzle each panna cotta with honey, then top with 3 to 5 berries and serve.

## Classic Crème Brûlée

**SERVES 8**

**WHY THIS RECIPE WORKS** Crème brûlée is all about the contrast between the crisp sugar crust and the silky custard underneath. The texture of the custard should not be firm but rather soft and supple. The secret, we found, is using egg yolks—and lots of them—rather than whole eggs. Heavy cream gave the custard a luxurious richness. Sugar, a vanilla bean, and a pinch of salt were the only other additions. Although many recipes use scalded cream, we found that this was likely to result in overcooked custard. We left the ingredients cold. The downside, however, was that we needed heat to extract flavor from the vanilla bean and dissolve the sugar. Our compromise was to heat only half of the cream with the sugar and vanilla bean and add the remaining cream cold. For the crust, we used crunchy turbinado sugar, which was easy to spread on the baked and chilled custards. A propane or butane torch worked better than the broiler for caramelizing the sugar, and because the blast of heat inevitably warms the custard beneath the crust, we chilled our crèmes brûlées once more before serving. Separate the eggs and whisk the yolks after the cream has finished steeping; if left to sit, the surface of the yolks will dry and form a film. A vanilla bean gives the custard the deepest flavor, but 2 teaspoons of vanilla extract, whisked into the yolks in step 4, can be used instead. The best way to judge doneness is with an instant-read thermometer. While we prefer turbinado or Demerara sugar for the caramelized sugar crust, regular granulated sugar will work, too, but use only 1 scant teaspoon for each ramekin. It's important to use 6-ounce ramekins.

- 1 vanilla bean
- 4 cups heavy cream, divided
- ⅔ cup (4⅔ ounces) granulated sugar
- Pinch table salt
- 12 large egg yolks
- 8 teaspoons turbinado or Demerara sugar

**1.** Adjust oven rack to lower-middle position and heat oven to 300 degrees.

**2.** Cut vanilla bean in half lengthwise. Using tip of paring knife, scrape out seeds. Combine vanilla bean and seeds, 2 cups cream, granulated sugar, and salt in medium saucepan. Bring cream mixture to boil over medium heat, stirring occasionally to dissolve sugar. Off heat, let steep for 15 minutes.

**3.** Meanwhile, place dish towel in bottom of large baking dish or roasting pan; set eight 6-ounce ramekins on towel (they should not touch). Bring kettle of water to boil.

**4.** After cream mixture has steeped, stir in remaining 2 cups cream. Whisk egg yolks in large bowl until uniform. Whisk about 1 cup cream mixture into yolks until combined; repeat with another 1 cup cream mixture. Add remaining cream mixture and whisk until evenly colored and thoroughly combined. Strain mixture through fine-mesh strainer into large bowl; discard solids in strainer. Divide mixture evenly among ramekins.

**5.** Set baking dish on oven rack. Taking care not to splash water into ramekins, pour enough boiling water into dish to reach two-thirds up sides of ramekins. Bake until centers of custards are just barely set and register 170 to 175 degrees, 30 to 35 minutes, checking temperature about 5 minutes before recommended minimum time.

**6.** Transfer ramekins to wire rack and let cool completely, about 2 hours. Set ramekins on baking sheet, cover tightly with plastic wrap, and refrigerate until cold, at least 4 hours.

**7.** Uncover ramekins; if condensation has collected on custards, blot moisture from tops of custards with paper towel. Sprinkle each with about 1 teaspoon turbinado sugar; tilt and tap each ramekin to distribute sugar evenly, dumping out excess sugar. Ignite torch and caramelize sugar, keeping torch flame 2 inches above sugar and slowly sweeping flame across sugar, starting at perimeter and moving toward middle, until sugar is bubbling and deep golden brown. Refrigerate ramekins, uncovered, to rechill, 30 to 45 minutes; serve.

## Sous Vide Crème Brûlée

**SERVES 4**

**WHY THIS RECIPE WORKS** While sous vide is not the answer for most baked desserts, it most definitely is when it comes to custard. Conventional custard recipes require care and attention with temperature-sensitive steps like tempering the eggs with the hot cream to avoid curdling and arranging a water bath in the oven. The precise temperature control of sous vide cooking makes custardy desserts like crème brûlée easier to execute. We whisked the base together, portioned it into Mason jars, and circulated for 1 hour. It was that easy. Once the custards finished cooking, we chilled them before the finale of a torched sugar topping. We found that crunchy turbinado sugar made for a satisfyingly crackly crust. A vanilla bean gives the crème brûlée the deepest flavor, but 1 teaspoon vanilla extract can be substituted. For the caramelized sugar crust, we recommend turbinado or Demerara sugar; regular granulated sugar will work, but use only 1 scant teaspoon (4 grams) for each Mason jar portion. You will need four 8-ounce wide-mouth Mason jars and a kitchen torch for this recipe. Be careful not to overtighten the jars before placing them in the water bath; it can cause the glass to crack.

- ½ vanilla bean
- 2 cups heavy cream
- 5 large egg yolks
- ⅓ cup granulated sugar
- Pinch table salt
- 4 teaspoons turbinado or Demerara sugar

**1.** Using sous vide circulator, bring water to 180 degrees in 7-quart container.

**2.** Cut vanilla bean in half lengthwise. Using tip of paring knife, scrape out seeds. Whisk vanilla bean and seeds, cream, egg yolks, granulated sugar, and salt in bowl until sugar has dissolved. Strain custard through fine-mesh strainer into 4-cup liquid measuring cup, then divide evenly among four 8-ounce wide-mouth Mason jars. Gently tap jars on counter to remove any air bubbles, then seal; do not overtighten lids.

**3.** Gently lower jars into water bath until fully submerged. Cover and cook for at least 1 hour or up to 1¼ hours.

**4.** Transfer jars to wire rack and let cool to room temperature, about 1 hour. Refrigerate until chilled, at least 4 hours. (Custards can be refrigerated for up to 3 days.)

**5.** Gently blot away condensation on top of custards using paper towels. Sprinkle each custard with 1 teaspoon turbinado sugar. Tilt and tap each jar to distribute sugar evenly, then wipe rims of jars clean. Ignite torch and caramelize sugar by sweeping flame of torch from perimeter of custard toward middle, keeping flame about 2 inches above jar, until sugar is bubbling and deep golden brown. Let sit for 5 minutes to allow sugar crust to harden, then serve.

## Classic Crème Caramel

**SERVES 8**

**WHY THIS RECIPE WORKS** This simple, classic French dessert is essentially a baked custard, but what makes it really stand out is the caramel sauce. We found the making of caramel to be relatively simple; what we needed to address was the texture of the custard. We discovered that the proportion of egg whites to yolks in the custard was critical for a custard that was silky smooth and firm but not rubbery. We settled on a formula of three whole eggs and two yolks. Light cream and milk for the dairy component provided the proper amount of richness. For contrast with the sweet caramel, we kept the amount of sugar in the custard to a minimum. The caramel comes together quickly; sugar is dissolved in water and cooked until caramel-colored. Baking the ramekins in a water bath was essential for even cooking and ensured a delicate custard. Most tasters preferred the full ⅔ cup sugar in the custard, but you can reduce that amount to as little as ½ cup to create a greater contrast between the custard and the caramel. Cook the caramel in a pan with a light-colored interior, since a dark surface makes it difficult to judge the color of the syrup. Caramel can leave a real mess in a pan, but it is easy to clean. Simply boil water in the pan for 5 to 10 minutes to loosen the hardened caramel.

**CARAMEL**

- ⅓ cup water
- 2 tablespoons light corn syrup
- ¼ teaspoon juice from 1 lemon
- 1 cup (7 ounces) sugar

**CUSTARD**

- 1½ cups whole milk
- 1½ cups light cream
- 3 large eggs, plus 2 large yolks
- ⅔ cup (4⅔ ounces) sugar
- 1½ teaspoons vanilla extract
- Pinch table salt

**1. FOR THE CARAMEL:** Combine the water, corn syrup, and lemon juice in a 2 to 3-quart saucepan. Pour the sugar into the center of the saucepan, taking care not to let the sugar granules touch the sides of the pan. Gently stir with a clean spatula to moisten the sugar thoroughly. Bring to a boil over medium-high heat and cook, without stirring, until the sugar is completely dissolved and the liquid is clear, 6 to 10 minutes. Reduce the heat to medium-low and continue to cook (swirling occasionally) until the caramel darkens to a honey color, 4 to 5 minutes longer. Remove the pan immediately from the heat and, working quickly but carefully (the caramel is above 300 degrees and will burn if it touches your skin), pour a portion of the caramel into each of eight ungreased 6-ounce ramekins. Allow the caramel to cool and harden, about 15 minutes. (The caramel-coated ramekins can be covered with plastic wrap and refrigerated for up to 2 days; return to room temperature before adding the custard.)

**2. FOR THE CUSTARD:** Adjust an oven rack to the middle position and heat the oven to 350 degrees. Heat the milk and cream in a medium saucepan over medium heat, stirring occasionally, until steam appears and/or the mixture registers 160 degrees on an instant-read thermometer, 6 to 8 minutes; remove from the heat. Meanwhile, gently whisk the whole eggs, egg yolks, and sugar in a large bowl until just combined. Off the heat, gently whisk the warm milk mixture, vanilla, and salt into the eggs until just combined but not at all foamy. Strain the mixture through a fine-mesh strainer into a large measuring cup or pitcher (or clean medium bowl); set aside.

**3.** Bring a kettle or large saucepan of water to a boil. Meanwhile, place a dish towel in the bottom of a large baking dish or roasting pan. Arrange the ramekins on the towel (making sure they do not touch). Divide the reserved custard mixture among the ramekins and carefully place the baking dish on the oven rack. Pour the boiling water into the dish, taking care not to splash water into the ramekins, until the water reaches halfway up the sides of the ramekins; cover the entire pan loosely with aluminum foil. Bake until a paring knife inserted halfway between the center and the edge of the custards comes out clean, 35 to 40 minutes. Transfer the custards to a wire rack and cool to room temperature. (The custards can be covered with plastic wrap and refrigerated for up to 2 days.)

**4.** To unmold, slide a paring knife around the perimeter of each ramekin, pressing the knife against the side of the dish. Hold a serving plate over the top of the ramekin and invert; set the plate on a work surface and shake the ramekin gently to release the custard. Repeat with the remaining ramekins and serve.

## Latin Flan

**SERVES 8 to 10**

**WHY THIS RECIPE WORKS** This cousin to Spanish-style flan and crème caramel boasts a dense sweet profile and rich toffee-like flavor. Latin American flan should be a dense but creamy custard, but the high-protein canned milks that some recipes call for can make its texture stiff and rubbery. Removing one egg from the mix helped, but not enough. To further improve creaminess, we added ½ cup of fresh milk. Wrapping the cake pan in foil before baking prevented a skin from forming on top, and reducing the oven temperature ensured that the custard baked evenly. Switching from a shallow cake pan to a loaf pan produced a gorgeous, tall flan less likely to crack. Adding a bit of water to the warm caramel and letting the baked flan sit overnight helped more of the caramel to come out of the dish, creating a substantial layer of gooey caramel. This recipe should be made at least one day before serving. We recommend an 8½ by 4½-inch loaf pan for this recipe. If your pan is 9 by 5 inches, begin checking for doneness at 1 hour 15 minutes. You may substitute 2 percent milk for the whole milk, but do not use skim milk. Serve the flan on a platter with a raised rim to contain the liquid caramel.

⅔ cup (4⅔ ounces) sugar
¼ cup water plus 2 tablespoons warm tap water, divided
2 large eggs plus 5 large yolks
1 (14-ounce) can sweetened condensed milk
1 (12-ounce) can evaporated milk
½ cup whole milk
1½ tablespoons vanilla extract
½ teaspoon table salt

**1.** Stir together sugar and ¼ cup water in medium heavy saucepan until sugar is completely moistened. Bring to boil over medium-high heat, 3 to 5 minutes, and cook without stirring until mixture begins to turn golden, another 1 to 2 minutes. Gently swirling pan, continue to cook until sugar is the color of peanut butter, 1 to 2 minutes. Remove from heat and swirl pan until sugar is reddish-amber and fragrant, 15 to 20 seconds. Carefully swirl in remaining 2 tablespoons warm tap water until incorporated; mixture will bubble and steam. Pour caramel into 8½ by 4½-inch loaf pan; do not scrape out saucepan. Set loaf pan aside.

**2.** Adjust oven rack to middle position and heat oven to 300 degrees. Line bottom of 13 by 9-inch baking pan with dish towel, folding towel to fit smoothly, and set aside. Bring 2 quarts water to boil.

**3.** Whisk eggs and yolks until combined. Add sweetened condensed milk, evaporated milk, whole milk, vanilla, and salt and whisk until incorporated. Strain mixture through fine-mesh strainer into prepared loaf pan.

**4.** Cover loaf pan tightly with aluminum foil and place in prepared baking pan. Place baking pan in oven and carefully pour boiling water into pan. Bake until center of custard jiggles slightly when shaken and custard registers 180 degrees, 1¼ to 1½ hours. Remove foil and leave custard in water bath until loaf pan has cooled to room temperature. Wrap loaf pan tightly with plastic wrap and chill overnight or up to 4 days.

**5.** To unmold, slide paring knife around edges of pan. Invert serving platter on top of pan and turn pan and platter over. When flan is released, remove loaf pan. Use rubber spatula to scrape residual caramel onto flan. Slice and serve. (Leftover flan may be covered loosely and refrigerated for up to 4 days.)

## Chocolate Pots de Crème

**SERVES 8**

**WHY THIS RECIPE WORKS** Classic pots de crème make a decadent dessert, with a satiny texture and intense chocolate flavor. They can be finicky and laborious, requiring a hot water bath that threatens to splash the custards every time the pan is moved. In addition, the individual custards don't always cook at the same rate. For our user-friendly recipe, we moved the dish out of the oven and onto the stovetop. For richness and body, we chose a combination of heavy cream and half-and-half, along with egg yolks only. For intense chocolate flavor, we focused on bittersweet chocolate—and a lot of it.

Our chocolate content was at least 50 percent more than in any other recipe we had encountered. We prefer pots de crème made with 60 percent bittersweet chocolate (our favorite brand is Ghirardelli Bittersweet Chocolate), but 70 percent bittersweet chocolate can also be used. If using a 70 percent bittersweet chocolate, reduce the amount to 8 ounces.

**POTS DE CRÈME**

10 ounces bittersweet chocolate, chopped fine
5 large egg yolks
5 tablespoons (2¼ ounces) sugar
¼ teaspoon table salt
1½ cups heavy cream
¾ cup half-and-half
1 tablespoon vanilla extract
½ teaspoon instant espresso powder mixed with 1 tablespoon water

**WHIPPED CREAM AND GARNISH**

½ cup heavy cream, chilled
2 teaspoons sugar
½ teaspoon vanilla extract
Cocoa, for dusting (optional)
Chocolate shavings, for sprinkling (optional)

**1. FOR THE POTS DE CRÈME:** Place chocolate in medium heatproof bowl; set fine-mesh strainer over bowl and set aside.

**2.** Whisk egg yolks, sugar, and salt in medium bowl until combined, then whisk in heavy cream and half-and-half. Transfer mixture to medium saucepan. Cook mixture over medium-low heat, stirring constantly and scraping bottom of pot with wooden spoon, until it is thickened and silky and registers 175 to 180 degrees, 8 to 12 minutes. (Do not let custard overcook or simmer.)

**3.** Immediately pour custard through strainer over chocolate. Let mixture stand to melt chocolate, about 5 minutes. Whisk gently until smooth, then whisk in vanilla and dissolved espresso. Divide mixture evenly among eight 5-ounce ramekins. Gently tap ramekins against counter to remove any air bubbles.

**4.** Let pots de crème cool to room temperature, then cover with plastic wrap and refrigerate until chilled, at least 4 hours or up to 3 days. Before serving, let pots de crème stand at room temperature for 20 to 30 minutes.

**5. FOR THE WHIPPED CREAM AND GARNISH:** Using stand mixer fitted with whisk attachment, whip cream, sugar, and vanilla on medium-low speed until small bubbles form, about 30 seconds. Increase speed to medium-high and continue to whip mixture until it thickens and forms stiff peaks, about 1 minute. Dollop each pot de crème with about 2 tablespoons of whipped cream and garnish with cocoa and/or chocolate shavings, if using. Serve.

## Dark Chocolate Mousse

**SERVES** 6 to 8

**WHY THIS RECIPE WORKS** Rich, creamy, and dense, chocolate mousse can be delicious but too filling after a few mouthfuls. On the other hand, light and airy mousse usually lacks deep chocolate flavor. We wanted chocolate mousse with both a light, meltingly smooth texture and a substantial chocolate flavor. To start, we addressed the mousse's dense, heavy texture. Most recipes for chocolate mousse contain butter. Could we do without it? We eliminated the butter and found that our mousse tasted less heavy. We further lightened the mousse's texture by reducing the number of egg whites and yolks. To make up for the lost volume of the eggs, we whipped the cream to soft peaks before adding it to the chocolate. We maximized the chocolate flavor with a combination of bittersweet chocolate and cocoa powder. And to further deepen the chocolate flavor, a small amount of instant espresso powder, salt, and brandy did the trick. When developing this recipe, we used our winning brands of dark chocolate, Callebaut Intense Dark Chocolate and Ghirardelli Bittersweet Chocolate, which each contain about 60 percent cacao. If you choose to make the mousse a day in advance, let it sit at room temperature for 10 minutes before serving. Serve with very lightly sweetened whipped cream and chocolate shavings, if desired.

- 8 ounces bittersweet chocolate, chopped fine
- 5 tablespoons water
- 2 tablespoons Dutch-processed cocoa powder
- 1 teaspoon instant espresso powder
- 2 large eggs, separated
- 1 tablespoon sugar
- ⅛ teaspoon table salt
- 1 cup plus 2 tablespoons heavy cream, chilled

**1.** Melt the chocolate with the water, cocoa powder, brandy, and espresso powder in a medium heatproof bowl set over a saucepan filled with 1 inch of barely simmering water, stirring frequently until smooth. Remove from the heat.

**2.** Whisk the egg yolks, 1½ teaspoons of the sugar, and the salt in a medium bowl until the mixture lightens in color and thickens slightly, about 30 seconds. Pour the melted chocolate into the egg mixture and whisk until combined. Cool until just warmer than room temperature, 3 to 5 minutes.

**3.** Using an electric mixer, whip the egg whites at medium-low speed until frothy, 1 to 2 minutes. Add the remaining 1½ teaspoons sugar, increase the mixer speed to medium-high, and whip until soft peaks form when the whisk is lifted, about 1 minute. Whisk the last few strokes by hand, making sure to scrape any unbeaten whites from the bottom of the bowl. Using the whisk, stir about one-quarter of the whipped egg whites into the chocolate mixture to lighten it; gently fold in the remaining egg whites with a rubber spatula until a few white streaks remain.

**4.** In the now-empty bowl, whip the heavy cream at medium speed until it begins to thicken, about 30 seconds. Increase the speed to high and whip until soft peaks form when the whisk is lifted, about 15 seconds more. Using a rubber spatula, fold the whipped cream into the mousse until no white streaks remain. Spoon the mousse into six to eight individual serving dishes or goblets. Cover with plastic wrap and refrigerate until set and firm, at least 2 hours or up to 24 hours. Serve.

## Low-Fat Chocolate Mousse

**SERVES** 6

**WHY THIS RECIPE WORKS** When presented with the challenge of developing a low-fat chocolate mousse, we admit we were daunted. After all, traditional chocolate mousse gets its lush, creamy texture and decadent richness chiefly from heavy cream—and lots of it. We wanted to ditch the cream but preserve the rich chocolate flavor and silky, fluffy texture. We found the solution in an Italian meringue (egg whites beaten until fluffy, and then cooked in hot sugar syrup). It made a fat-free base that mimicked the volume and texture of a traditional mousse made with heavy cream. Semisweet chocolate and Dutch-processed cocoa added rich chocolate flavor, and a surprise ingredient—melted white chocolate chips—mellowed and rounded out the flavors of each. The meringue and chocolate mixture are combined in two stages so the meringue doesn't collapse. For the best texture, chill the mousse overnight.

- 4 ounces semisweet chocolate, broken into pieces
- ⅓ cup white chocolate chips
- 2 tablespoons Dutch-processed cocoa powder
- 6 tablespoons plus ½ cup water
- 1 teaspoon vanilla extract
- ½ cup (3½ ounces) sugar
- 3 large egg whites
- ¼ teaspoon cream of tartar

1. Melt the semisweet chocolate, white chocolate, cocoa powder, 6 tablespoons of the water, and the vanilla in a medium bowl set over a pot of barely simmering water, stirring until smooth. Set aside to cool slightly.

2. Bring the remaining ½ cup water and the sugar to a vigorous boil in a small saucepan over high heat. Boil until slightly thickened and large bubbles rise to the top, about 4 minutes. Remove from the heat.

3. With an electric mixer on medium-low speed, beat the egg whites in a large bowl until frothy, about 1 minute. Add the cream of tartar and beat, gradually increasing the speed to medium-high, until the whites hold soft peaks, about 2 minutes. With the mixer running, slowly pour the hot syrup into the whites (avoid pouring the syrup onto the beaters or it will splash). Increase the speed to high and beat until the meringue has cooled to just warm and becomes very thick and shiny, 2 to 3 minutes.

4. Whisk one-third of the meringue into the chocolate mixture until combined, then whisk in the remaining meringue. Spoon the mousse into six 6-ounce ramekins or pudding cups. Cover tightly with plastic wrap. Chill overnight. (The mousse can be refrigerated for up to 4 days.)

## Lemon Posset with Berries

SERVES 6

**WHY THIS RECIPE WORKS** This classic English dessert is a lush pudding with a clean citrus flavor that is exceptionally easy to make: There are no temperamental egg yolks or add-ins needed to help the mixture thicken or set or to interfere with the bright taste of citrus. We found that using just the right proportions of sugar and lemon juice—along with a generous amount of lemon zest—was the key to custard with a smooth, silky consistency and a flavor that balanced the richness of the cream. For an optimally dense, firm set, we reduced the cream-sugar mixture to 2 cups before adding the lemon juice, which in turn caused the mixture to solidify. Letting the warm mixture rest for 20 minutes before straining allowed the flavors to meld and ensured a silky-smooth consistency. Reducing the cream mixture to exactly 2 cups creates the best consistency. Transfer the liquid to a 2-cup heatproof liquid measuring cup once or twice during boiling to monitor the amount. Do not leave the cream unattended, as it can boil over easily.

- 2 cups heavy cream
- ⅔ cup (4⅔ ounces) sugar
- 1 tablespoon grated lemon zest plus 6 tablespoons juice (2 lemons)
- 1½ cups (7½ ounces) blueberries or raspberries

1. Combine cream, sugar, and lemon zest in medium saucepan and bring to boil over medium heat. Continue to boil, stirring frequently to dissolve sugar. If mixture begins to boil over, briefly remove from heat. Cook until mixture is reduced to 2 cups, 8 to 12 minutes.

2. Remove saucepan from heat and stir in lemon juice. Let sit until mixture is cooled slightly and skin forms on top, about 20 minutes. Strain through fine-mesh strainer into bowl; discard zest. Divide mixture evenly among 6 individual ramekins or serving glasses.

3. Refrigerate, uncovered, until set, at least 3 hours. (Once chilled, possets can be wrapped in plastic wrap and refrigerated for up to 2 days. Unwrap and let sit at room temperature for 10 minutes before serving.) Garnish with berries and serve.

## Fresh Strawberry Mousse

SERVES 4 to 6

**WHY THIS RECIPE WORKS** There's a good reason that strawberry mousse recipes aren't very prevalent: The berries contain lots of juice that can easily ruin the texture of a mousse. Plus, the fruit flavor produced by most strawberry mousse recipes is too subtle. To achieve a creamy yet firm texture without losing the strawberry flavor, we replaced some of the cream with cream cheese. We processed the berries into small pieces and macerated them with sugar and a little salt to draw out their juice. We then reduced the released liquid to a syrup before adding it to the mousse, which standardized the amount of moisture in the dessert and also concentrated the berry flavor. Fully pureeing the juiced berries contributed bright, fresh berry flavor. This recipe works well with supermarket strawberries and farmers' market strawberries. In step 1, be careful not to overprocess the berries. If you like, substitute 1½ pounds (5¼ cups) of thawed frozen strawberries for fresh strawberries. If using frozen strawberries skip step 1 (do not process berries). Proceed with the recipe, adding the ½ cup of sugar and the salt to the whipped cream in step 4. For more complex berry flavor, replace the 3 tablespoons of raw strawberry juice in step 2 with strawberry or raspberry liqueur. In addition to the diced berries, or if you're using frozen strawberries, you can serve the mousse with Lemon Whipped Cream.

- 2 pounds strawberries, hulled (6½ cups)
- ½ cup (3½ ounces) sugar
- Pinch table salt
- 1¾ teaspoons unflavored gelatin
- 4 ounces cream cheese, cut into 8 pieces and softened
- ½ cup heavy cream, chilled

1. Cut enough strawberries into ¼-inch dice to measure 1 cup; refrigerate until ready to garnish. Pulse remaining strawberries in food processor in 2 batches until most pieces are ¼ to ½ inch thick (some larger pieces are fine), 6 to 10 pulses. Transfer strawberries to bowl and toss with ¼ cup sugar and salt. (Do not clean processor.) Cover bowl and let strawberries stand for 45 minutes, stirring occasionally.

2. Strain processed strawberries through fine-mesh strainer into bowl (you should have about ⅔ cup juice). Measure out 3 tablespoons juice into small bowl, sprinkle gelatin over juice,

and let sit until gelatin softens, about 5 minutes. Place remaining juice in small saucepan and cook over medium-high heat until reduced to 3 tablespoons, about 10 minutes. Remove pan from heat, add softened gelatin mixture, and stir until gelatin has dissolved. Add cream cheese and whisk until smooth. Transfer mixture to large bowl.

**3.** While juice is reducing, return strawberries to now-empty processor and process until smooth, 15 to 20 seconds. Strain puree through fine-mesh strainer into medium bowl, pressing on solids to remove seeds and pulp (you should have about 1⅔ cups puree). Discard any solids in strainer. Add strawberry puree to juice-gelatin mixture and whisk until incorporated.

**4.** Using stand mixer fitted with whisk, whip cream on medium-low speed until foamy, about 1 minute. Increase speed to high and whip until soft peaks form, 1 to 3 minutes. Gradually add remaining ¼ cup sugar and whip until stiff peaks form, 1 to 2 minutes. Whisk whipped cream into strawberry mixture until no white streaks remain. Portion into dessert dishes and chill for at least 4 hours. (Mousse can be made up to 48 hours ahead, wrapped tightly in plastic wrap, and chilled; if chilled longer than 6 hours, let mousse sit at room temperature for 15 minutes before serving.) Garnish with reserved diced strawberries and serve.

## Lemon Whipped Cream

**MAKES** about 1 cup

If preferred, you can replace the lemon with lime.

- ½ cup heavy cream
- 2 tablespoons sugar
- 1 teaspoon finely grated lemon zest plus 1 tablespoon juice

Using stand mixer fitted with whisk, whip cream on medium-low speed until foamy, about 1 minute. Add sugar and lemon zest and juice, increase speed to medium-high, and whip until soft peaks form, 1 to 3 minutes.

## Make-Ahead Chocolate Soufflés

**SERVES** 6 to 8

**WHY THIS RECIPE WORKS** To eliminate the anxiety of making chocolate soufflé, we found a way to make it in advance. We wanted the chocolate to be front and center, so we used a base of egg yolks beaten with sugar, with no flour or milk to mute the chocolate flavor. Instead of an equal number of egg yolks and whites, we found that two extra whites lightened and lifted our chocolaty base. To our amazement, the answer to making these souffle's ahead of time was simple: freezing. Adding a little confectioners' sugar to the egg whites stabilized them so they held up in the freezer, and individual ramekins produced better results than a single large soufflé dish. Now we could make our dinner party dessert in advance, confident that we could pull perfectly risen, rich chocolate soufflés from the oven at the end of the meal. This technique works only for the individual chocolate soufflés, which can be made and frozen for at least 3 hours and up to one month before baking. If you are microwave oriented, melt the chocolate at 50 percent power for 3 minutes, stirring in the butter after 2 minutes.

**RAMEKIN PREPARATION**

- 2 tablespoons unsalted butter, softened
- 2 tablespoons granulated sugar

**SOUFFLÉS**

- 8 ounces bittersweet or semisweet chocolate, chopped coarse
- 4 tablespoons unsalted butter, cut into ½-inch pieces
- 1 tablespoon Grand Marnier
- ½ teaspoon vanilla extract
- ⅛ teaspoon table salt
- 6 large eggs, separated, plus 2 large whites
- ⅓ cup (2⅓ ounces) granulated sugar
- ¼ teaspoon cream of tartar
- 2 tablespoons confectioners' sugar

**1. FOR THE RAMEKINS:** Coat inside of eight 8-ounce ramekins with softened butter, then coat inside of each dish evenly with sugar. Refrigerate until ready to use.

**2. FOR THE SOUFFLÉS:** Melt chocolate and butter in medium heatproof bowl set over saucepan filled with 1 inch of barely simmering water, stirring frequently until smooth. Remove from heat and stir in Grand Marnier, vanilla, and salt; set aside.

**3.** Using stand mixer fitted with whisk attachment, whip egg yolks and granulated sugar at medium speed until mixture triples in volume and is thick and pale yellow, 3 to 8 minutes. Fold yolk mixture into chocolate mixture.

**4.** Using clean, dry mixer bowl and whisk attachment, whip egg whites at medium-low speed until frothy, 1 to 2 minutes. Add cream of tartar, increase mixer speed to medium-high, and whip until soft peaks form, 1 to 2 minutes. Add confectioners' sugar and continue to whip until stiff peaks form, 2 to 4 minutes (do not overwhip). Whisk last few strokes by hand, making sure to scrape any unwhipped whites from bottom of bowl.

**5.** Vigorously stir one-quarter of whipped egg whites into chocolate mixture. Gently fold remaining whites into chocolate mixture until just incorporated. Carefully spoon mixture into prepared ramekins almost to rim, wiping excess filling from rims with wet paper towel. If making foil collar for ramekins, see below. (To serve right away, bake as directed in step 6, reducing baking time to 12 to 15 minutes. To make ahead. Wrap ramekins tightly with plastic wrap and then foil and freeze for at least 3 hours or up to 1 month; do not thaw before baking.)

**6. TO BAKE AND SERVE:** Adjust oven rack to lower-middle position and heat oven to 400 degrees. Unwrap frozen ramekins and spread them out on baking sheet. Bake soufflés until fragrant, fully risen, and exterior is set but interior is still a bit loose and creamy, about 25 minutes. (To check interior, use 2 spoons to pull open top of one and peek inside.) Serve immediately.

### MAKING A FOIL COLLAR

Placing a foil collar around ramekins yields a higher rise and flatter tops. After filling ramekins, secure strip of oiled foil around ramekins so it extends 2 inches above rim. If needed, you can tape collar to dish to prevent it from slipping.

## Grand Marnier Soufflé

**SERVES** 6 to 8

**WHY THIS RECIPE WORKS** Home cooks are wary of attempting soufflés, which have the reputation of being difficult and are best eaten in restaurants. The reality, however, is that they are relatively easy to make. The best soufflés have a crusty top layer above the rim of the dish and a contrasting rich, creamy, almost-fluid center, so we needed to produce height without making the entire dish foamy. Our foolproof soufflé recipe began with a base of bouille (a paste made from flour and milk), enhanced with butter and extra flour for a creamy rather than foamy soufflé. We whipped the egg whites with cream of tartar and granulated sugar, both of which made the whites more stable. Do not open the oven door during the first 15 minutes of baking; as the soufflé nears the end of its baking, you may check its progress by opening the oven door slightly. (If your oven runs hot, the top of the soufflé may burn.) Dust with confectioners' sugar and serve.

**SOUFFLÉ DISH PREPARATION**

- 1 tablespoon unsalted butter, softened
- ¼ cup sugar
- 2 teaspoons sifted cocoa powder

**SOUFFLÉ**

- 5 tablespoons unbleached all-purpose flour
- ½ cup (3½ ounces) sugar
- ¼ teaspoon table salt
- 1 cup whole milk
- 2 tablespoons unsalted butter, at room temperature
- 5 large eggs, separated
- 1 tablespoon grated zest from 1 orange
- 3 tablespoons Grand Marnier
- ⅛ teaspoon cream of tartar

**1. TO PREPARE THE SOUFFLÉ DISH:** Adjust an oven rack to the upper-middle position and heat the oven to 400 degrees. Grease a 1½-quart porcelain soufflé dish with the butter, making sure to coat all of the interior surfaces. Stir the sugar and cocoa together in a small bowl; pour into the buttered soufflé dish and shake to coat the bottom and sides with a thick, even coating. Tap out the excess and set the dish aside.

**2. FOR THE SOUFFLÉ:** Whisk the flour, ¼ cup of the sugar, and the salt in a small saucepan. Gradually whisk in the milk, whisking until smooth and no lumps remain. Bring the mixture to a boil over high heat, whisking constantly, until thickened and the mixture pulls away from the sides of the pan, about 3 minutes. Scrape the mixture into a medium bowl; whisk in the butter until combined. Whisk in the yolks until incorporated; stir in the orange zest and Grand Marnier.

**3.** Using an electric mixer, whip the egg whites, cream of tartar, and 1 teaspoon more sugar at medium-low speed until combined, about 10 seconds. Increase the speed to medium-high and whip until frothy and no longer translucent, about 2 minutes. With the mixer running, sprinkle in half of the remaining sugar; continue whipping until the whites form soft, billowy peaks, about 30 seconds. With the mixer still running, sprinkle in the remaining sugar and whip until just combined, about 10 seconds. The whites should form soft peaks when the beater is lifted but should not appear Styrofoam-like or dry.

**4.** Using a rubber spatula, immediately stir one-quarter of the beaten whites into the soufflé base to lighten until almost no white streaks remain. Scrape the remaining whites into the base and fold in the whites with a balloon whisk until the mixture is just combined, gently flicking the whisk after scraping up the sides of the bowl to free any of the mixture caught in the whisk. Gently pour the mixture into the prepared dish and run your index finger through the mixture, tracing the circumference about ½ inch from the side of the dish, to help the soufflé rise properly. Bake until the surface of the soufflé is deep brown, the center jiggles slightly when shaken, and the soufflé has risen 2 to 2½ inches above the rim of the dish, 20 to 25 minutes. Serve immediately.

## Chilled Lemon Soufflé

**SERVES** 4 to 6

**WHY THIS RECIPE WORKS** The perfect version of a chilled lemon soufflé souffle is a divine marriage of custard and souffle. But the delicate balance of ingredients is hard to get right. Our starting point of egg whites, gelatin, sugar, and lemon juice had none of the creaminess we desired, so we cooked a custard base of milk, egg yolks, and sugar, adding a little cornstarch to prevent the yolks from curdling. Then we added lemon juice and gelatin (to stabilize the mixture so it would set up while chilling). To make this lemon soufflé "soufflé" over the rim of the dish, use a 1-quart soufflé dish and make a foil collar for it before beginning the recipe. For those less concerned about appearance, this dessert can be served from any 1½-quart serving bowl.

- ½ cup juice plus 2½ teaspoons grated zest from 3 lemons
- 1 (¼-ounce) package gelatin
- 1 cup whole milk
- ¾ cup (5¼ ounces) sugar
- 5 large egg whites plus 2 large egg yolks, at room temperature
- ¼ teaspoon cornstarch
- Pinch cream of tartar
- ¾ cup heavy cream
- Mint, raspberries, confectioners' sugar, or finely chopped pistachios, for garnish (optional)

**1.** Place the lemon juice in a small bowl; sprinkle the gelatin over and set aside.

**2.** Heat the milk and ½ cup of the sugar in a medium saucepan over medium-low heat, stirring occasionally, until steaming and the sugar is dissolved, about 5 minutes. Meanwhile, whisk the egg yolks, 2 tablespoons more sugar, and the cornstarch in a medium bowl until pale yellow and thickened. Whisking constantly, gradually add the hot milk to the yolks. Return the milk-egg mixture to the saucepan and cook, stirring constantly, over medium-low heat until the foam has dissipated to a thin layer and the mixture thickens to the consistency of heavy cream and registers 185 degrees on an instant-read thermometer, about 4 minutes. Pour the mixture through a fine-mesh strainer into a medium bowl; stir in the lemon juice mixture and zest. Set the bowl with the custard in a large bowl of ice water; stir occasionally to cool.

**3.** While the custard mixture is chilling, use an electric mixer to whip the egg whites and cream of tartar on medium speed until foamy, about 1 minute. Increase the speed to medium-high; gradually add the remaining 2 tablespoons sugar and continue to whip until glossy and the whites hold soft peaks when the beater is lifted, about 2 minutes longer. Do not over whip. Remove the bowl containing the custard mixture from the ice water bath; gently whisk in about one-third of the egg whites, then fold in the remaining whites with a large rubber spatula until almost no white streaks remain.

**4.** In the same mixer bowl, whip the cream on medium-high speed until soft peaks form when the beater is lifted, 2 to 3 minutes. Fold the cream into the custard and egg-white mixture until no white streaks remain.

**5.** Pour into a 1½ quart soufflé dish or bowl. Chill until set but not stiff, about 1½ hours; remove the foil collar, if using, and serve, garnishing if desired. (The soufflé can be chilled for up to 6 hours though the texture will stiffen slightly; however, it will taste just as good.)

### Individual Chilled Lemon Soufflés

Follow the recipe for Chilled Lemon Soufflé, dividing the batter equally among eight ¾-cup ramekins (filled to the rim) or six 6-ounce ramekins with foil collars.

## Skillet Lemon Soufflé

**SERVES** 6

**WHY THIS RECIPE WORKS** In a break with tradition, we developed an easy technique for making a lemon soufflé in a skillet. First we whipped 5 egg whites with cream of tartar and then gradually added sugar and salt and whipped some more until stiff peaks formed. Adding a little flour to the simple base of whipped egg yolks kept the soufflé creamy rather than foamy. Lemon juice and zest provided flavor that shone through the eggy base. We folded in the beaten egg whites and poured the mixture into a buttered skillet. After a few minutes on the stovetop, the soufflé was just set around the edges and on the bottom, so we moved the skillet to the oven to finish. A few minutes later our soufflé was puffed, golden on top, and creamy in the middle. Don't open the oven door during the first 7 minutes of baking, but do check the soufflé regularly for doneness during the final few minutes in the oven. You will need a 10-inch ovensafe traditional skillet for this recipe. Do not use a nonstick skillet.

- 5 large eggs, separated
- ¼ teaspoon cream of tartar
- ⅔ cup (4⅔ ounces) granulated sugar
- ⅛ teaspoon table salt
- ⅓ cup juice plus 1 teaspoon grated zest from 2 lemons
- 2 tablespoons unbleached all-purpose flour
- 1 tablespoon unsalted butter
- Confectioners' sugar, for dusting

**1.** Adjust an oven rack to the middle position and heat the oven to 375 degrees. Using an electric mixer, whip the egg whites and cream of tartar together on medium-low speed until foamy, about 1 minute. Slowly add ⅓ cup of the granulated sugar and the salt, then increase the mixer speed to medium-high, and continue to whip until stiff peaks form, 3 to 5 minutes. Gently transfer the whites to a clean bowl and set aside.

**2.** Using an electric mixer (no need to wash the mixing bowl), whip the egg yolks and the remaining ⅓ cup granulated sugar together on medium-high speed until pale and thick, about 1 minute. Whip in the lemon juice, zest, and flour until incorporated, about 30 seconds.

**3.** Fold one-quarter of the whipped egg whites into the yolk mixture until almost no white streaks remain. Gently fold in the remaining egg whites until just incorporated.

**4.** Melt the butter in a 10-inch ovensafe skillet over medium-low heat. Swirl the pan to coat it evenly with the melted butter, then gently scrape the soufflé batter into the skillet and cook until the edges begin to set and bubble slightly, about 2 minutes.

**5.** Transfer the skillet to the oven and bake the soufflé until puffed, the center jiggles slightly when shaken, and the surface is golden, 7 to 11 minutes. Using a potholder (the skillet handle will be hot), remove the skillet from the oven. Dust the soufflé with the confectioners' sugar and serve immediately.

## Pavlova with Fruit and Whipped Cream

**SERVES 10**

**WHY THIS RECIPE WORKS** Pavlova is a gorgeous dessert featuring crisp-shelled meringue piled with whipped cream and fresh fruit. For a foolproof pavlova, we switched from the typical French meringue—which requires precise timing when adding sugar to egg whites—to a Swiss meringue, which is made by dissolving the sugar in the egg whites as they are heated over a water bath and then whipping the mixture to stiff peaks. Cornstarch and vinegar produced a meringue that was marshmallowy within, with a slight chew at the edge; plenty of sugar ensured a crisp exterior. We shaped the meringue into a wide disk, baked it, and let it dry in a turned-off oven. Whipped cream and fresh fruit balanced the meringue's sweetness and made for a beautiful presentation. Letting the meringue sit before serving helped soften the crust for neater slices. Because eggs can vary in size, measuring the egg whites by weight or volume is essential to ensure that you are working with the correct ratio of egg whites to sugar. Open the oven door as infrequently as possible while the meringue is inside. Do not worry if the meringue cracks; it is part of the dessert's charm. The inside of the meringue will remain soft.

**MERINGUE**

- 1½ cups (10½ ounces) sugar
- ¾ cup (6 ounces) egg whites (5 to 7 large eggs)
- 1½ teaspoons distilled white vinegar
- 1½ teaspoons cornstarch
- 1 teaspoon vanilla extract

**WHIPPED CREAM**

- 2 cups heavy cream, chilled
- 2 tablespoons sugar

- 1 recipe Orange, Cranberry, and Mint Topping

**1. FOR THE MERINGUE:** Adjust oven rack to middle position and heat oven to 250 degrees. Using pencil, draw 10-inch circle in center of 18 by 13-inch piece of parchment paper.

**2.** Combine sugar and egg whites in bowl of stand mixer; place bowl over saucepan filled with 1 inch simmering water, making sure that water does not touch bottom of bowl. Whisking gently but constantly, heat until sugar is dissolved and mixture registers 160 to 165 degrees, 5 to 8 minutes.

**3.** Fit stand mixer with whisk attachment and whip mixture on high speed until meringue forms stiff peaks, is smooth and creamy, and is bright white with sheen, about 4 minutes (bowl may still be slightly warm to touch). Stop mixer and scrape down bowl with spatula. Add vinegar, cornstarch, and vanilla and whip on high speed until combined, about 10 seconds.

**4.** Spoon about ¼ teaspoon meringue onto each corner of rimmed baking sheet. Press parchment, marked side down, onto sheet to secure. Pile meringue in center of circle on parchment. Using circle as guide, spread and smooth meringue with back of spoon or spatula from center outward, building 10-inch disk that is slightly higher around edges. Finished disk should measure about 1 inch high with ¼-inch depression in center.

**5.** Bake meringue until exterior is dry and crisp and meringue releases cleanly from parchment when gently lifted at edge with thin metal spatula, 1 to 1½ hours. Meringue should be quite pale (a hint of creamy color is OK). Turn off oven, prop door open with wooden spoon, and let meringue cool in oven for 1½ hours. Remove from oven and let cool completely before topping, about 15 minutes. (Cooled meringue can be wrapped tightly in plastic wrap and stored at room temperature for up to 1 week.)

**6. FOR THE WHIPPED CREAM:** Whip cream and sugar in chilled bowl of stand mixer fitted with whisk attachment on low speed until small bubbles form, about 30 seconds. Increase speed to medium and whip until whisk leaves trail, about 30 seconds. Increase speed to high and continue to whip until cream is smooth, thick, and nearly doubled in volume, about 20 seconds longer for soft peaks. If necessary, finish whipping by hand to adjust consistency.

**7.** Carefully peel meringue away from parchment and place on large serving platter. Spoon whipped cream into center of meringue. Top whipped cream with fruit topping. Let stand for at least 5 minutes or up to 1 hour, then slice and serve.

### Individual Pavlovas with Fruit and Whipped Cream

Adjust oven racks to upper-middle and lower-middle positions and heat oven to 250 degrees. In step 4, spoon about ¼ teaspoon meringue onto each corner of 2 rimmed baking sheets. Line sheets with parchment paper. Spoon heaping ½ cup meringue into 5 evenly spaced piles on each sheet. Spread each meringue pile with back of spoon to form 3½-inch disk with slight depression in center. Decrease baking time in step 5 to 50 minutes. Top each meringue with ½ cup whipped cream, followed by ½ cup fruit topping.

### Orange, Cranberry, and Mint Topping

**MAKES** 4½ cups

You can substitute tangelos or Cara Cara oranges for the navel oranges, if desired. Valencia or blood oranges can also be used, but since they are smaller, increase the number of oranges to six.

- 1½ cups (10½ ounces) sugar, divided
- 6 ounces (1½ cups) frozen cranberries
- 5 navel oranges
- ⅓ cup chopped fresh mint, plus 10 small mint leaves

**1.** Bring 1 cup sugar and 1 cup water to boil in medium saucepan over medium heat, stirring to dissolve sugar. Off heat, stir in cranberries. Let cranberries and syrup cool completely, about 30 minutes. (Cranberries in syrup can be refrigerated for up to 24 hours.)

**2.** Place remaining ½ cup sugar in shallow dish. Drain cranberries, discarding syrup. Working in 2 batches, roll ½ cup cranberries in sugar and transfer to large plate or tray. Let stand at room temperature to dry, about 1 hour.

**3.** Cut away peel and pith from oranges. Cut each orange into quarters from pole to pole, then cut crosswise into ¼-inch-thick pieces (you should have 3 cups). Just before serving, toss oranges with non-sugared cranberries and chopped mint in bowl until combined. Using slotted spoon, spoon fruit in even layer over pavlova. Garnish with sugared cranberries and mint leaves. Before serving, drizzle pavlova slices with any juice from bowl.

#### CREATING THE MERINGUE ROUND

**1.** After creating meringue, scoop out of stand mixer onto parchment round as directed and smooth into 10-inch disk. Use back of spoon to create rim around edge.

**2.** Bake for 1 hour, then turn off oven and prop door open for 1½ hours, at which point meringue will be dry and crisp, and lift cleanly from parchment.

## Chocolate Semifreddo

**SERVES** 12

**WHY THIS RECIPE WORKS** Semifreddo is a classic Italian dessert that's often described as a frozen mousse. For a rich, chocolate semifreddo, we prepared a custard base of whole eggs, sugar, cream, and water on the stovetop. Then we melted the chocolate by straining the hot custard directly over it. To ensure a rich, creamy, and sliceable semifreddo we used whole eggs instead of yolks and cut the cream in the custard base with a bit of water. We developed this recipe with our favorite dark chocolate, Ghirardelli 60% Cacao Bittersweet Chocolate Premium Baking Bar. If the semifreddo is difficult to release from the pan, run a thin offset spatula around the edges of the pan or carefully run the sides of the pan under hot water for 5 to 10 seconds. If frozen overnight, the semifreddo should be tempered before serving for the best texture. To temper, place slices on individual plates or a large tray and refrigerate for 30 minutes. If desired, serve with Cherry Sauce (page 934) and a sprinkling of Quick Candied Nuts (page 934).

- 8 ounces bittersweet chocolate, chopped fine
- 1 tablespoon vanilla extract
- ½ teaspoon instant espresso powder
- 3 large eggs
- 5 tablespoons (2¼ ounces) sugar
- ¼ teaspoon table salt
- 2 cups heavy cream, chilled, divided
- ¼ cup water

**1.** Lightly spray loaf pan with vegetable oil spray and line with plastic wrap, leaving 3-inch overhang on all sides. Place chocolate in large heatproof bowl; set fine-mesh strainer over bowl and set aside. Stir vanilla and espresso powder in small bowl until espresso powder is dissolved.

**2.** Whisk eggs, sugar, and salt in medium bowl until combined. Heat ½ cup cream (keep remaining 1½ cups chilled) and water in medium saucepan over medium heat until simmering. Slowly whisk hot cream mixture into egg mixture until combined. Return mixture to saucepan and cook over medium-low heat, stirring constantly and scraping bottom of saucepan with rubber spatula, until mixture is very slightly thickened and registers 160 to 165 degrees, about 5 minutes. Do not let mixture simmer.

**3.** Immediately pour mixture through strainer set over chocolate. Let mixture stand to melt chocolate, about 5 minutes. Whisk until chocolate is melted and smooth, then whisk in vanilla-espresso mixture. Let chocolate mixture cool completely, about 15 minutes.

**4.** Using stand mixer fitted with whisk attachment, beat remaining 1½ cups cream on low speed until bubbles form, about 30 seconds. Increase speed to medium and beat until whisk leaves trail, about 30 seconds. Increase speed to high and continue to beat until nearly doubled in volume and whipped cream forms soft peaks, 30 to 45 seconds longer.

**5.** Whisk one-third of whipped cream into chocolate mixture. Using rubber spatula, gently fold remaining whipped cream into chocolate mixture until incorporated and no streaks of whipped cream remain. Transfer mixture to prepared pan and spread evenly with rubber spatula. Fold overhanging plastic over surface. Freeze until firm, at least 6 hours.

**6.** When ready to serve, remove plastic from surface and invert pan onto serving plate. Remove plastic and smooth surface with spatula as necessary. Dip slicing knife in very hot water and wipe dry. Slice semifreddo ¾ inch thick, transferring slices to individual plates and dipping and wiping knife after each slice. Serve immediately. (Semifreddo can be wrapped tightly in plastic wrap and frozen for up to 2 weeks.)

### Cherry Sauce

**MAKES** 2 cups

Do not thaw the cherries before using. Water can be substituted for the kirsch.

- 12 ounces frozen sweet cherries
- ¼ cup (1¾ ounces) sugar
- 2 tablespoons kirsch
- 1½ teaspoons cornstarch
- 1 tablespoon lemon juice

**1.** Combine cherries and sugar in bowl and microwave for 1½ minutes. Stir, then continue to microwave until sugar is mostly dissolved, about 1 minute longer. Combine kirsch and cornstarch in small bowl.

**2.** Drain cherries in fine-mesh strainer set over small saucepan. Return cherries to bowl and set aside.

**3.** Bring juice in saucepan to simmer over medium-high heat. Stir in kirsch mixture and bring to boil. Boil, stirring occasionally, until mixture has thickened and appears syrupy, 1 to 2 minutes. Remove saucepan from heat and stir in cherries and lemon juice. Let sauce cool completely before serving. (Sauce can be refrigerated for up to 1 week.)

### Quick Candied Nuts

**MAKES** ½ cup

We like this recipe prepared with shelled pistachios, walnut or pecan halves, roasted cashews, salted or unsalted peanuts, and sliced almonds. If you want to make a mixed batch, cook the nuts individually and then toss to combine once you've chopped them.

- ½ cup nuts
- 1 tablespoon sugar
- 1 tablespoon hot water
- ⅛ teaspoon table salt

**1.** Adjust oven rack to middle position and heat oven to 350 degrees. Spread nuts in single layer on rimmed baking sheet and toast until fragrant and slightly darkened, 8 to 12 minutes, shaking sheet halfway through toasting. Transfer nuts to plate and let cool for 10 to 15 minutes. Do not wash sheet.

**2.** Line now-empty sheet with parchment paper. Whisk sugar, hot water, and salt in large bowl until sugar is mostly dissolved. Add nuts and stir to coat. Spread nuts on prepared sheet in single layer and bake until nuts are crisp and dry, 10 to 12 minutes.

**3.** Transfer sheet to wire rack and let nuts cool completely, about 20 minutes. Transfer nuts to cutting board and chop as desired. (Nuts can be stored at room temperature for up to 1 week.)

## Homemade Vanilla Ice Cream

**MAKES** about 1 quart

**WHY THIS RECIPE WORKS** We wanted an incredibly creamy custard-based vanilla ice cream that would rival any pricey artisanal batch. Creating smooth ice cream means reducing the size of the ice crystals; the smaller they are, the less perceptible they are. Our first move was to replace some of the sugar in our custard base with corn syrup, which interferes with crystal formation, making for a super-smooth texture. Instead of freezing the churned ice cream in a tall container, we spread it into a thin layer in a cold metal baking pan and chilled it, which allowed the ice cream to firm up more quickly and delivered a flawlessly smooth texture. Two teaspoons of vanilla extract can be substituted for the vanilla bean; stir the extract into the cold custard in step 3. If using a canister-style ice cream maker, be sure to freeze the empty canister at least 24 hours and preferably 48 hours before churning. For self-refrigerating ice cream makers, prechill the canister by running the machine for 5 to 10 minutes before pouring in the custard.

- 1 vanilla bean
- 1¾ cups heavy cream
- 1¼ cups whole milk
- ½ cup plus 2 tablespoons (4⅖ ounces) sugar

⅓ cup light corn syrup
¼ teaspoon table salt
6 large egg yolks

**1.** Place an 8- or 9-inch-square metal baking pan in the freezer. Cut the vanilla bean in half lengthwise. Using the tip of a paring knife, scrape out the vanilla seeds. Combine the vanilla bean, seeds, cream, milk, ¼ cup plus 2 tablespoons of the sugar, the corn syrup, and salt in a medium saucepan. Heat over medium-high heat, stirring occasionally, until the mixture is steaming steadily and registers 175 degrees on an instant-read thermometer, 5 to 10 minutes. Remove the saucepan from the heat.

**2.** While the cream mixture heats, whisk the egg yolks and the remaining ¼ cup sugar in a bowl until smooth, about 30 seconds. Slowly whisk 1 cup of the heated cream mixture into the egg yolk mixture. Return the mixture to the saucepan and cook over medium-low heat, stirring constantly, until the mixture thickens and registers 180 degrees, 7 to 14 minutes. Immediately pour the custard into a large bowl and let cool until no longer steaming, 10 to 20 minutes. Transfer 1 cup of the custard to a small bowl. Cover both bowls with plastic wrap. Place the large bowl in the refrigerator and the small bowl in the freezer and cool completely, at least 4 hours or up to 24 hours. (The small bowl of custard will freeze solid.)

**3.** Remove the custards from the refrigerator and freezer. Scrape the frozen custard from the small bowl into the large bowl of custard. Stir occasionally until the frozen custard has fully dissolved. Strain the custard through a fine-mesh strainer and transfer to an ice cream maker. Churn until the mixture resembles thick soft-serve ice cream and registers about 21 degrees, 15 to 25 minutes. Transfer the ice cream to the frozen baking pan and press plastic wrap on the surface. Return to the freezer until firm around the edges, about 1 hour.

**4.** Transfer the ice cream to an airtight container, pressing firmly to remove any air pockets, and freeze until firm, at least 2 hours, before serving. (Ice cream can be frozen for up to 5 days.)

## Sweet Cream Ice Cream

**MAKES** 1 quart

**WHY THIS RECIPE WORKS** Sweet cream ice cream doesn't contain vanilla or eggs—just milk, heavy cream, and sugar—so the sweet dairy flavor really shines. The key to a great ice cream is controlling the size of the ice crystals formed during freezing; the smaller the ice crystals, the smoother the ice cream feels on the tongue. To ensure a smooth consistency, we added milk powder, cornstarch, and corn syrup to our sweet cream base. The milk powder replaced a portion of the liquid milk in the mix, decreasing the amount of freezable water, and it also trapped some of the water so that it couldn't freeze. The corn syrup kept a portion of the water from freezing (but without making the ice cream too sweet). If using a canister-style ice cream maker, freeze the empty canister for at least 24 hours or preferably 48 hours before churning. For self-refrigerating ice cream makers, prechill the canister by running the maker for 5 to 10 minutes before pouring in the base. We prefer Carnation Instant Nonfat Dry Milk. Some base may stick to the bottom of the saucepan when pouring it into the strainer in step 3; simply scrape it into the strainer with the rest of the base and press it through with a spatula.

½ cup plus ⅓ cup nonfat dry milk powder
⅓ cup (2⅓ ounces) sugar
¼ teaspoon kosher salt
1½ cups whole milk, divided
1½ cups heavy cream
¼ cup corn syrup
5 teaspoons cornstarch

**1.** Whisk milk powder, sugar, and salt together in small bowl. Whisk 1¼ cups milk, cream, corn syrup, and sugar mixture together in large saucepan. Cook over medium-high heat, whisking frequently to dissolve sugar and break up any clumps, until tiny bubbles form around edge of saucepan and mixture registers 190 degrees, 5 to 7 minutes.

**2.** Meanwhile, whisk cornstarch and remaining ¼ cup milk together in small bowl.

**3.** Reduce heat to medium. Whisk cornstarch mixture to recombine, then whisk into milk mixture in saucepan. Cook, constantly scraping bottom of saucepan with rubber spatula, until mixture thickens, about 30 seconds. Immediately pour ice cream base through fine-mesh strainer into large bowl; let cool until no longer steaming, about 20 minutes. Cover bowl; transfer to refrigerator; and chill until base registers 40 degrees, at least 6 hours. (Base can be chilled overnight. Alternatively, base can be chilled to 40 degrees in about 1½ hours by placing bowl in ice bath of 6 cups ice, ½ cup water, and ⅓ cup table salt.)

**4.** Churn base in ice cream maker until mixture resembles thick soft serve and registers 21 degrees, about 30 minutes. Transfer ice cream to airtight container, pressing firmly to remove air pockets; freeze until firm, at least 2 hours. (Ice cream can be frozen for up to 5 days.)

## Ice Cream Cake

SERVES 10 SEASON 26

**WHY THIS RECIPE WORKS** DIY ice cream cake is a fun, customizable project. It's also the ultimate make-ahead dessert since the components need to freeze after assembly and can be prepared days, if not weeks, in advance. Any ice cream will work here. The fudge sauce will fill in any gaps in the ice cream layer. If you'd like, you can intersperse chopped-up candies, cookies, jam, or more sauce amongst the scoops of ice cream. If your ice cream is too firm to scoop after tempering for 20 minutes in step 6, refrigerate it for another 5 to 10 minutes; do not let it soften on the counter or the ice cream in your cake will be icy.

**FUDGE SAUCE**

- 1¼ cups (8¾ ounces) sugar, divided
- 7 tablespoons unsalted butter, cut into ½-inch pieces
- ⅓ cup milk
- ½ cup (1½ ounces) unsweetened cocoa powder
- ⅓ cup heavy cream
- ¼ teaspoon table salt
- 2½ ounces unsweetened chocolate, chopped fine
- 1 teaspoon vanilla extract

**CHIFFON**

- ⅔ cup (2⅔ ounces) cake flour
- ½ cup (3½ ounces) sugar, divided
- ½ teaspoon baking powder
- ⅛ teaspoon table salt
- 3 large eggs (1 whole, 2 separated)
- 3 tablespoons vegetable oil
- 2 tablespoons water
- 1 teaspoon vanilla extract
- Pinch cream of tartar

**CAKE**

- 3 pints ice cream
- 1½ cups heavy cream
- 2 tablespoons sugar
- 1 teaspoon vanilla extract

**1. FOR THE FUDGE SAUCE:** Combine 1 cup sugar, butter, and milk in small saucepan. Bring to gentle simmer over medium-low heat and simmer, stirring occasionally, for 3 minutes. Meanwhile, stir cocoa, cream, salt, and remaining ¼ cup sugar in bowl until no lumps of cocoa remain. Reduce heat to low and whisk cocoa mixture into sugar-butter mixture in saucepan. Cook, stirring occasionally, until sugar dissolves, about 5 minutes.

**2.** Off heat, add chocolate and stir until well combined. Stir in vanilla. Transfer sauce to bowl and let cool completely, about 1¼ hours. (Sauce can be refrigerated in an airtight container for up to 1 week. Let sit at room temperature for at least 1 hour before using.)

**3. FOR THE CHIFFON:** Adjust oven rack to middle position and heat oven to 300 degrees. Lightly grease bottom only of 9-inch springform pan and line bottom with parchment paper. Secure collar to bottom of pan. Whisk flour, 6 tablespoons sugar, baking powder, and salt in bowl until well combined. Add whole egg and yolks, oil, water, and vanilla and whisk until smooth batter forms.

**4.** Using hand mixer, whip egg whites and cream of tartar on medium-low speed in separate bowl until foamy, 30 to 60 seconds. Sprinkle remaining 2 tablespoons sugar over whites. Increase speed to medium and whip whites until glossy, stiff peaks form, 1 to 2 minutes. Transfer one-third of whites to batter; gently whisk until few streaks of white remain. Using rubber spatula, fold remaining whites into batter.

**5.** Transfer batter to prepared pan and bake until toothpick inserted in center comes out clean, 20 to 25 minutes. Transfer to wire rack and let chiffon cool completely in pan, about 45 minutes. Run thin knife between chiffon and side of pan; remove side of pan. Invert chiffon onto wire rack and remove parchment. Reinvert chiffon. (Cooled chiffon can be stored in airtight container at room temperature for up to 12 hours or frozen for up to 1 month.)

**6. FOR THE CAKE:** Twenty minutes before assembling cake, place ice cream in refrigerator to soften. While ice cream softens, prepare your work station. Lightly grease 9-inch springform pan, line bottom with parchment, line sides with overlapping 3-inch-wide strips of parchment, and place pan in freezer. Measure out ¾ cup fudge sauce and place large spoon, clean dish towel, 12-inch length of plastic wrap, and chiffon nearby.

**7.** Working quickly, use large spoon to transfer ice cream to prepared pan. Place sheet of plastic directly over ice cream. Cover plastic with dish towel. Press firmly with your hands to flatten ice cream into even layer. Remove dish towel and plastic. Spread reserved fudge sauce evenly over ice cream. Invert chiffon on top of fudge and gently press chiffon into fudge. Wrap tightly with plastic wrap and freeze for at least 4 hours or up to 1 week.

**8.** Freeze serving platter for at least 20 minutes. Whip cream, sugar, and vanilla in bowl until stiff peaks form, 3 to 5 minutes. Transfer two-thirds of cream to pastry bag fitted with ½-inch flat petal tip or ½-inch round tip and refrigerate remaining cream. Unwrap cake and remove side of pan. Remove parchment strips. Invert serving platter on top of cake. Invert cake onto platter; remove bottom of pan and parchment.

**9.** Working quickly, pipe whipped cream evenly onto sides and top of cake. (It's OK if there are small gaps between bands of whipped cream.) Using offset spatula, smooth whipped cream into even layer. Freeze cake until whipped cream at bottom edge of cake is firm, about 20 minutes (bottom edge will be last place to harden). Transfer remaining whipped cream to pastry bag. Pipe decorative border along top edge of cake. Freeze until cake is completely hardened, at least 1 hour or up to 24 hours. (Assembled cake can be frozen for up to 1 week.)

**10. TO SERVE:** Thirty minutes before serving, transfer cake to refrigerator. Microwave remaining fudge sauce at 50 percent power until fluid, about 1 minute, stirring halfway through microwaving. Slice cake, wiping blade between cuts, and serve, passing remaining fudge sauce separately.

## Baked Alaska

SERVES 8

---

**WHY THIS RECIPE WORKS** Though making a baked Alaska can be intimidating to some, the dessert is essentially a dressed-up ice cream cake that's no more difficult to make than any other version. Plenty of insulation was the key to a baked Alaska that is toasty on the outside but still firm at the center. Most recipes use cake only as a base, but we used it to encase the ice cream entirely, thereby decreasing the amount of meringue by more than one-third without sacrificing heat resistance. To further improve the balance, we added cocoa to our cake, boosting flavor without adding sweetness. Rather than packing softened ice cream into a mold (refrozen ice cream can be icy, and it can be hard to match cake pans and bowls), we simply cut the cardboard off two pints of firm ice cream and stuck them together to form the core of our dessert. We opted for coffee ice cream, which complements the flavor of the cake and the sweetness of the meringue perfectly. Coffee ice cream provides the best contrast with sweet meringue in this recipe, but other flavors may be substituted, if desired. A high-quality ice cream such as Häagen-Dazs works best because it is slower to melt. To ensure the proper texture when serving, it is necessary to remove the cake from the freezer before making the meringue. This recipe leaves just enough leftover cake and ice cream to make an additional for-two version (page 938).

- 2 (1-pint) containers coffee ice cream

**CAKE**

- 1 cup (4 ounces) cake flour
- ⅓ cup (1 ounce) unsweetened cocoa powder
- ⅔ cup (4⅔ ounces) sugar
- 1½ teaspoons baking powder
- ¼ teaspoon table salt
- ½ cup vegetable oil
- 6 tablespoons water
- 4 large eggs, separated

**MERINGUE**

- ¾ cup (5¼ ounces) sugar
- ⅓ cup light corn syrup
- 3 large egg whites
- 2 tablespoons water
- Pinch table salt
- 1 teaspoon vanilla extract

**1.** Lay 12-inch square sheet of plastic wrap on counter and remove lids from ice cream. Use scissors to cut cardboard tubs from top to bottom. Peel away cardboard and discard. Place ice cream blocks on their sides in center of plastic with wider ends facing each other. Grasp each side of plastic and firmly press blocks together to form barrel shape. Wrap plastic tightly around ice cream and roll briefly on counter to form uniform cylinder. Place cylinder, standing on end, in freezer until completely solid, at least 1 hour.

**2. FOR THE CAKE:** Adjust oven rack to middle position and heat oven to 350 degrees. Lightly grease 18 by 13-inch rimmed baking sheet, line with parchment paper, and lightly grease parchment. Whisk flour, cocoa, ⅓ cup sugar, baking powder, and salt together in large bowl. Whisk oil, water, and egg yolks into flour mixture until smooth batter forms.

**3.** Using stand mixer fitted with whisk attachment, whip egg whites on medium-low speed until foamy, about 1 minute. Increase speed to medium-high and whip whites to soft, billowy mounds, about 1 minute. Gradually add remaining ⅓ cup sugar and whip until glossy, soft peaks form, 1 to 2 minutes. Transfer one-third of egg whites to batter; whisk gently until mixture is lightened. Using rubber spatula, gently fold remaining egg whites into batter.

**4.** Pour batter into prepared sheet; spread evenly. Bake until cake springs back when pressed lightly in center, 10 to 13 minutes. Transfer cake to wire rack and let cool for 5 minutes. Run knife around edge of sheet, then invert cake onto wire rack. Carefully remove parchment, then reinvert cake onto second wire rack. Let cool completely, at least 15 minutes.

**5.** Transfer cake to cutting board with long side of rectangle parallel to edge of counter. Using serrated knife, trim ¼ inch off left side of cake and discard. Using ruler, measure 4½ inches from cut edge and make mark with knife. Using mark as guide, cut 4½-inch rectangle from cake. Trim piece to create 4½ by 11-inch rectangle and set aside. (Depending on pan size and how much cake has shrunk during baking, it may not be necessary to trim piece to measure 11 inches.) Measure 4 inches from new cut edge and make mark. Using mark as guide, cut 4-inch rectangle from cake. Trim piece to create 4 by 10-inch rectangle, wrap rectangle in plastic, and set aside. Cut 3½-inch round from remaining cake and set aside (biscuit cutter works well). Save scraps for Bonus Baked Alaska (page 938).

**6.** Unwrap ice cream. Trim cylinder to 4½ inches in length and return remainder to freezer for Bonus Baked Alaska. Place ice cream cylinder on 4½ by 11-inch cake rectangle and wrap cake around ice cream. (Cake may crack slightly.) Place cake circle on one end of cylinder. Wrap entire cylinder tightly in plastic. Place cylinder, standing on cake-covered end, in freezer until cake is firm, at least 30 minutes.

**BUILDING A NEW BAKED ALASKA**

**1.** Cut ice cream tubs from top to bottom and peel away cardboard. Place blocks on plastic wrap on their sides with wider ends facing each other.

**2.** Wrap plastic tightly around ice cream and roll on counter to form even cylinder. Place in freezer, standing on end, for 1 hour.

**3.** Trim ¼ inch off left side of cake. Cut 4½ by 11-inch rectangle, 4 by 10-inch rectangle, and 3½-inch round. Save scraps for Bonus Baked Alaska.

**4.** Unwrap ice cream and trim cylinder to 4½ inches in length. Return remainder to freezer.

**5.** Place ice cream on 11 by 4½-inch cake rectangle and wrap cake around ice cream. Place cake circle on 1 end of cylinder. Wrap in plastic. Freeze, standing on cake-covered end, for 30 minutes.

**6.** Unwrap cylinder, stand on cake-covered end, and cut in half lengthwise. Place halves on 10 by 4-inch rectangle, ice cream side down, with open ends meeting in middle.

**7.** Unwrap cylinder and place on cutting board, standing on cake-covered end, and cut in half lengthwise. Unwrap reserved 4 by 10-inch cake rectangle and place halves on top, ice cream side down, with open ends meeting in middle. Wrap tightly with plastic and press ends gently to close gap between halves. Return to freezer for at least 2 hours and up to 2 weeks.

**8. FOR THE MERINGUE:** Adjust oven rack to upper-middle position and heat oven to 500 degrees. Spray wire rack set in rimmed baking sheet with vegetable oil spray. Unwrap cake and place on rack. Combine sugar, corn syrup, egg whites, water, and salt in bowl of stand mixer; place bowl over saucepan filled with 1 inch simmering water, making sure that water does not touch bottom of bowl. Whisking gently but constantly, heat until sugar is dissolved and mixture registers 160 degrees, 5 to 8 minutes.

**9.** Place bowl in stand mixer fitted with whisk attachment. Beat mixture on medium speed until bowl is only slightly warm to touch, about 5 minutes. Increase speed to high and beat until mixture begins to lose its gloss and forms stiff peaks, about 5 minutes. Add vanilla and beat until combined.

**10.** Using offset spatula, spread meringue over top and sides of cake, avoiding getting meringue on rack. Use back of spoon to create peaks all over meringue.

**11.** Bake until browned and crisp, about 5 minutes. Run offset spatula or thin knife under dessert to loosen from rack, then use two spatulas to transfer to serving platter. To slice, dip sharp knife in very hot water and wipe dry after each cut. Serve immediately.

### Bonus Baked Alaska

**SERVES** 2

Our Baked Alaska recipe leaves just enough leftover cake and ice cream to make an additional for-two version.

From remaining cake, cut two 3⅓-inch rounds and one 11 by 2-inch strip. Place leftover ice cream disk on top of 1 cake round. Wrap strip of cake around sides of disk. Place remaining cake round on top, wrap tightly in plastic, and freeze. Following step 10, spread meringue over cake and bake as directed.

## Frozen Yogurt

**MAKES** about 1 quart

**WHY THIS RECIPE WORKS** We wanted to make frozen yogurt that put the tart, fresh flavor of yogurt up front and had the texture of a dense, creamy premium ice cream. We found that Greek yogurt produced a chalky frozen yogurt, so instead we used regular plain yogurt that we had strained of excess liquid (the whey) to help minimize the number of ice crystals. Swapping in a few tablespoons of Lyle's Golden Syrup for some of the granulated sugar not only gave us a frozen yogurt with fewer ice crystals but also one that was more scoopable straight from the freezer. This is because about half of Lyle's sugar is invert sugar (the other half is glucose). Unlike

granulated sugar, which is made up of large sucrose molecules, invert sugar is made up of the "small sugars" glucose and fructose, which are much better at depressing the freezing point, which kept more of the water in the frozen yogurt base in liquid form for a smoother, more scoopable final product. The final step in managing the water in our base was to trap some of it using unflavored gelatin. By dissolving and heating just 1 teaspoon of gelatin in a portion of the strained whey, we prevented water molecules from joining together and forming large ice crystals. We prefer the flavor and texture that Lyle's Golden Syrup lends this frozen yogurt, but light corn syrup may be substituted. Any brand of whole-milk yogurt will work in this recipe. Low-fat yogurt can be used, but the results will be less creamy and less flavorful. If more than 1¼ cups of whey drains from the yogurt in step one, simply stir the extra back in.

- 1 quart plain whole-milk yogurt
- 1 teaspoon unflavored gelatin
- ¾ cup sugar
- 3 tablespoons Lyle's Golden Syrup
- ⅛ teaspoon table salt

**1.** Line colander or fine-mesh strainer with triple layer of cheesecloth and place over large bowl or measuring cup. Place yogurt in colander, cover with plastic wrap (plastic should not touch yogurt), and refrigerate until 1¼ cups whey has drained from yogurt, at least 8 hours and up to 12 hours.

**2.** Discard ¾ cup of drained whey. Sprinkle gelatin over remaining ½ cup whey in bowl and let sit until gelatin softens, about 5 minutes. Microwave until mixture is bubbling around edges and gelatin dissolves, about 30 seconds. Let cool for 5 minutes. In large bowl, whisk sugar, Lyle's Golden Syrup, salt, drained yogurt, and cooled gelatin mixture together until sugar is completely dissolved. Cover and refrigerate (or place bowl over ice bath) until yogurt mixture registers 40 degrees or less.

**3.** Churn yogurt mixture in ice cream maker until mixture resembles thick soft-serve frozen yogurt and registers about 21 degrees, 25 to 35 minutes. Transfer frozen yogurt to airtight container and freeze until firm, at least 2 hours. Serve. (Frozen yogurt can be stored for up to 5 days.)

### Ginger Frozen Yogurt

Stir 1 tablespoon grated fresh ginger and 1 teaspoon ground ginger into whey-gelatin mixture as soon as it is removed from microwave. After mixture has cooled for 5 minutes, strain through fine-mesh strainer, pressing on solids to extract all liquid. Proceed with recipe as directed.

## Raspberry Sorbet

**MAKES** 1 quart

**WHY THIS RECIPE WORKS** To make a light, refreshing raspberry sorbet that was beautifully creamy and smooth, we had to avoid both the jagged, unpleasant ice crystals that often develop in homemade sorbets and the tendency toward crumbly, dull results. Finding the right balance of water and sugar was key; corn syrup helped to create a smooth texture without oversweetening. Freezing a small amount of the base separately and adding it back to the rest helped superchill the mix, making it freeze faster and more smoothly. We also added some pectin to bump up the raspberries' natural pectin, which gave the sorbet stability both in the freezer and out and helped to keep it from turning into a puddle too quickly at room temperature. Super-chilling part of the sorbet base before transferring it to the ice cream maker will keep ice crystals to a minimum. If using a canister-style ice cream maker, be sure to freeze the empty canister for at least 24 hours and preferably 48 hours before churning. For self-refrigerating ice cream makers, prechill the canister by running the machine for five to 10 minutes before pouring in the sorbet mixture. Allow the sorbet to sit at room temperature for five minutes to soften before serving. Fresh or frozen berries may be used. If using frozen berries, thaw them before proceeding. Make certain that you use Sure-Jell engineered for low- or no-sugar recipes (packaged in a pink box) and not regular Sure-Jell (in a yellow box).

- 1 cup water
- 1 teaspoon Sure-Jell for Less or No Sugar Needed Recipes
- ⅛ teaspoon table salt
- 1¼ pounds (4 cups) raspberries
- ½ cup (3½ ounces) plus 2 tablespoons sugar
- ¼ cup light corn syrup

**1.** Combine water, Sure-Jell, and salt in medium saucepan. Heat over medium-high heat, stirring occasionally, until Sure-Jell is fully dissolved, about 5 minutes. Remove saucepan from heat and allow mixture to cool slightly, about 10 minutes.

**2.** Process raspberries, sugar, corn syrup, and water mixture in blender or food processor until smooth, about 30 seconds. Strain mixture through fine-mesh strainer, pressing on solids to extract as much liquid as possible. Transfer 1 cup mixture to small bowl and place remaining mixture in large bowl. Cover both bowls with plastic wrap. Place large bowl in refrigerator and small bowl in freezer and cool completely, at least 4 hours or up to 24 hours. (Small bowl of base will freeze solid.)

**3.** Remove mixtures from refrigerator and freezer. Scrape frozen base from small bowl into large bowl of base. Stir occasionally until frozen base has fully dissolved. Transfer mixture to ice cream maker and churn until mixture has consistency of thick milkshake and color lightens, 15 to 25 minutes.

**4.** Transfer sorbet to airtight container, pressing firmly to remove any air pockets, and freeze until firm, at least 2 hours. Serve. (Sorbet can be frozen for up to 5 days.)

### SUPERCHILLING RASPBERRY SORBET

**1.** Transfer 1 cup berry puree to small bowl. Cover bowls; freeze small bowl and refrigerate large bowl for at least 4 hours or up to 1 day.

**2.** Scrape frozen base into large bowl. Stir until completely combined. Transfer to ice cream maker and churn until color lightens.

## Chocolate Sorbet

**MAKES** 1 quart **SEASON 26**

**WHY THIS RECIPE WORKS** A perfect chocolate sorbet isn't a watered-down dairy-free alternative to chocolate ice cream—in fact, without the dairy, chocolate sorbet has the potential to be the most chocolaty, deeply bittersweet of the frozen chocolate desserts. So that our sorbet lived up to that potential, we added a whopping half cup of unsweetened cocoa powder to our water base; we simmered it along with sugar and corn syrup to fully bloom and dissolve the cocoa. But that wasn't all: Off heat, we melted in 8 ounces of bittersweet chocolate. Blending the base ensured we had a grit-free chocolate-packed mixture before churning. Super-chilling a cup of the sorbet base in the freezer before reintroducing it to the rest of the chilled base kept ice crystals to a minimum. How? This small amount of base froze rapidly and formed small "seed" crystals that initiated a chain reaction in the larger base, causing a network of small, imperceptible (rather than large and rough) crystals to form immediately. Pectin, in the form of Sure-Jell, is the secret ingredient that slowed melting and also helped preserve a smooth texture. Make certain that you use Sure-Jell engineered for low- or no-sugar recipes (packaged in a pink box) and not regular Sure-Jell (in a yellow box). We prefer to use Dutch-processed cocoa powder in this recipe, but other cocoa powders will work. If using a canister-style ice cream machine, be sure to freeze the empty canister for at least 24 hours and preferably 48 hours before churning. For self-refrigerating machines, prechill the canister by running the machine for 5 to 10 minutes before pouring in the sorbet mixture. Allow the sorbet to sit at room temperature for 5 minutes to soften before serving.

- 2¼ cups water
- ½ cup (1½ ounces) unsweetened cocoa powder
- ¾ cup (5¼ ounces) sugar
- ¼ cup corn syrup
- 1 teaspoon Sure-Jell for Less or No Sugar Needed Recipes
- ⅛ teaspoon table salt
- 8 ounces bittersweet chocolate, chopped fine
- ½ teaspoon vanilla extract

**1.** Combine water, cocoa, sugar, corn syrup, Sure-Jell, and salt in medium saucepan. Heat over medium-high heat, stirring occasionally, until simmering and sugar and Sure-Jell are fully dissolved, about 5 minutes. Off heat, whisk in chocolate and vanilla until fully combined. Transfer mixture to blender and process until smooth, about 30 seconds.

**2.** Transfer 1 cup mixture to small bowl and place remaining mixture in large bowl. Cover both bowls with plastic wrap. Place large bowl in refrigerator and small bowl in freezer and let cool completely, at least 4 hours or up to 24 hours. (Small bowl of base will freeze solid.)

**3.** Remove mixtures from refrigerator and freezer. Scrape frozen base from small bowl into large bowl of base. Stir until frozen base has fully dissolved. Transfer mixture to ice cream machine and churn until mixture has consistency of thick milkshake and color lightens, 15 to 25 minutes.

**4.** Transfer sorbet to airtight container, pressing firmly to remove any air pockets, and freeze until firm, at least 2 hours. Serve. (Sorbet can be frozen for up to 5 days.)

## Berry Granita

**SERVES** 8

**WHY THIS RECIPE WORKS** During a hot Sicilian summer, a dish of icy granita piled with whipped cream and washed down with a shot of espresso is a traditional breakfast, but this frozen treat can be enjoyed as a refreshing snack or dessert. For a deeply fruity granita with a light, crystalline texture, we blended fresh or frozen berries with enough water to form a silky puree and enough sugar for modest sweetness and to give the puree the proper consistency when frozen. When scraped, this granita yielded light, flaky ice crystals that lingered briefly on the palate for a chilling pause before melting in the mouth in a flood of fruity goodness. Lemon juice contributed acidity that brightened the fruit flavor. This mostly hands-off recipe requires no special equipment: just a blender, baking dish, fork, and freezer. This recipe can be halved; if halving, use an 8-inch glass baking dish. You can use fresh or thawed frozen blueberries, raspberries, blackberries, hulled strawberries, or a combination of berries. If using fresh strawberries, weigh them after hulling. If using any type of thawed berries, do not drain them before adding them to the blender. We think this granita stands well on its own, but if you'd like to add some complexity, you can add one of these: 2 to 3 tablespoons of chopped fresh mint, 1 to 2 teaspoons of grated fresh ginger, or 1 to 2 teaspoons of grated lemon zest to the blender in step 1. Serve granita on its own or garnish it with unsweetened whipped cream (layer it to make a parfait, if desired), fresh berries, or a splash of prosecco or your favorite liqueur.

- 1 pound fresh or thawed frozen berries
- ¾ cup water
- ½ cup sugar
- ¼ cup lemon juice (2 lemons)
- Pinch table salt

### FREEZING GRANITA

When granita is partially frozen, use fork to scrape edges of dish and stir icy crystals into middle of mixture. Return granita to freezer. Repeat scraping and stirring process every 30 minutes to 1 hour until crystals are uniformly light and fluffy.

**1.** Process all ingredients in blender on high speed until very smooth, 1 to 2 minutes. Strain mixture through fine-mesh strainer into 13 by 9-inch glass baking dish. Freeze, uncovered, until edges are frozen and center is slushy, about 1 hour. Using fork, scrape edges to release crystals. Stir crystals into middle of mixture and return dish to freezer. Repeat scraping and stirring, using tines of fork to mash any large chunks, every 30 minutes to 1 hour until granita crystals are uniformly light and fluffy, 2 to 3 hours.

**2.** Immediately before serving, scrape granita with fork to loosen. Spoon into chilled bowls or glasses and serve. (Leftover granita can be transferred to airtight container and frozen for up to 1 week. Scrape granita again to loosen before serving.)

## Dark Chocolate Fudge Sauce

**MAKES** 2 cups

**WHY THIS RECIPE WORKS** Many chocolate fudge sauces are more sweet than chocolaty and are overly thick; we wanted a sauce that was less sugary, boasted a luxurious, pourable consistency, and could be refrigerated and reheated multiple times. So we got to work. Using both cocoa powder and unsweetened chocolate provided a foundation of complex flavor and richness, and choosing milk, rather than cream, allowed the deep chocolate flavor to shine. As far as sweeteners go, we stuck with granulated sugar because it was simplest and we didn't notice enough of a difference when trying other options. To thicken the sauce, we swirled in a few knobs of butter, which gave it body and a glossier appearance. A bit of vanilla extract and salt helped the chocolate flavor pop. We like to serve this sauce over ice cream, but it can also be drizzled over fresh fruit. We prefer to use Dutch-processed cocoa powder in this recipe (our favorite is Droste Cacao), but other cocoa powders will work. Our favorite unsweetened chocolate is Baker's Unsweetened Baking Chocolate Bar 100% Cacao.

- 1¼ cups sugar
- ⅔ cup whole or 2 percent low-fat milk
- ¼ teaspoon table salt
- ⅓ cup unsweetened cocoa powder, sifted
- 3 ounces unsweetened chocolate, chopped fine
- 4 tablespoons unsalted butter, cut into 8 pieces and chilled
- 1 teaspoon vanilla extract

**1.** Heat sugar, milk, and salt in medium saucepan over medium-low heat, whisking gently, until sugar has dissolved and liquid starts to bubble around edges of saucepan, 5 to 6 minutes. Reduce heat to low, add cocoa, and whisk until smooth.

**2.** Remove saucepan from heat, stir in chocolate, and let stand for 3 minutes. Whisk sauce until smooth and chocolate is fully melted. Add butter and whisk until fully incorporated and sauce thickens slightly. Whisk in vanilla and serve. (Sauce can be refrigerated in airtight container for up to 1 month. Gently reheat sauce in microwave [do not let it exceed 110 degrees], stirring every 10 seconds, until just warmed and pourable.)

CHAPTER 15 # Pies and Fruit Desserts

Photos (left to right): Triple Berry Slab Pie with Ginger-Lemon Streusel; Fresh Fruit Tart; Berry Fool; Chocolate-Cherry Pie Pops; Chocolate Cream Pie; Fresh Strawberry Pie; French Apple Tart

## Foolproof All-Butter Dough for Single-Crust Pie

**MAKES** one 9-inch single crust

**WHY THIS RECIPE WORKS** This is now our go-to pie dough: It's supremely supple and extremely easy to roll out. Even better, it bakes up buttery, tender, and flaky. How did we do it? First, we used the food processor to coat two-thirds of the flour with butter, creating a water-resistant paste-like mixture. Next, we broke that dough into pieces, coated the pieces with the remaining flour, and tossed in grated butter. By doing this, we ensured that the water we folded in was absorbed only by the dry flour that coated the butter-flour chunks. Since gluten can develop only when flour is hydrated, the resulting crust was supertender but had enough structure to support flakes. After a 2-hour chill, the dough was completely hydrated and easy to roll out. Be sure to weigh the flour. This dough will be more moist than most pie doughs, but it will absorb a lot of excess moisture as it chills. Roll out the dough on a well-floured counter.

- 10 tablespoons unsalted butter, chilled, divided
- 1¼ cups (6¼ ounces) all-purpose flour, divided
- 1 tablespoon sugar
- ½ teaspoon table salt
- ¼ cup ice water, divided

**1.** Grate 2 tablespoons butter on large holes of box grater and place in freezer. Cut remaining 8 tablespoons butter into ½-inch cubes.

**2.** Pulse ¾ cup flour, sugar, and salt in food processor until combined, 2 pulses. Add cubed butter and process until homogeneous paste forms, about 30 seconds. Using your hands, carefully break paste into 2-inch pieces and redistribute evenly around processor blade. Add remaining ½ cup flour and pulse until mixture is broken into pieces no larger than 1 inch (most pieces will be much smaller), 4 or 5 pulses. Transfer mixture to medium bowl. Add grated butter and toss until butter pieces are separated and coated with flour.

**3.** Sprinkle 2 tablespoons ice water over mixture. Toss with rubber spatula until mixture is evenly moistened. Sprinkle remaining 2 tablespoons ice water over mixture and toss to combine. Press dough with spatula until dough sticks together. Transfer dough to sheet of plastic wrap. Draw edges of plastic over dough and press firmly on sides and top to form compact, fissure-free mass. Wrap in plastic and form into 5-inch disk. Refrigerate dough for at least 2 hours or up to 2 days. Let chilled dough sit on counter to soften slightly, about 10 minutes, before rolling. (Dough, wrapped tightly in plastic, can be frozen for up to 1 month. If frozen, let dough thaw completely on counter before rolling.)

### Foolproof Whole-Wheat Dough for Single-Crust Pie

Substitute ¾ cup (4⅛ ounces) whole-wheat flour for first addition of all-purpose flour, using ½ cup all-purpose flour (2½ ounces) for second addition of flour.

### MIXING ALL-BUTTER PIE DOUGH

**1.** To make flour and butter paste, process most of flour (and sugar and salt) and cubed butter until homogeneous paste forms, about 30 seconds.

**2.** To add more flour, carefully separate paste into 2-inch chunks and redistribute evenly around processor blade, then pulse in remaining flour.

**3.** Transfer mixture to bowl. Add frozen grated butter and toss gently to coat butter shreds with flour.

**4.** Using rubber spatula, mix in ice water in 2 additions to form wet, sticky dough. Transfer to plastic wrap, press into disk, and refrigerate.

## Foolproof All-Butter Dough for Double-Crust Pie

**MAKES** one 9-inch double crust

**WHY THIS RECIPE WORKS** Be sure to weigh the flour for this recipe. This dough will be more moist than most pie doughs, but as it chills it will absorb a lot of excess moisture. Roll the dough on a well-floured counter. If your recipe requires rolling your dough piece(s) to a rectangle after chilling, as when making a lattice top for a pie, form the dough into a 5-inch square instead of a disk.

- 20 tablespoons (2½ sticks) unsalted butter, chilled, divided
- 2½ cups (12½ ounces) all-purpose flour, divided
- 2 tablespoons sugar
- 1 teaspoon table salt
- ½ cup ice water, divided

**1.** Grate 4 tablespoons butter on large holes of box grater and place in freezer. Cut remaining 16 tablespoons butter into ½-inch cubes.

**2.** Pulse 1½ cups flour, sugar, and salt in food processor until combined, 2 pulses. Add cubed butter and process until homogeneous paste forms, 40 to 50 seconds. Using your hands, carefully break paste into 2-inch pieces and redistribute evenly around processor blade. Add remaining 1 cup flour and pulse until mixture is broken into pieces no larger than 1 inch (most pieces will be much smaller), 4 or 5 pulses. Transfer mixture to medium bowl. Add grated butter and toss until butter pieces are separated and coated with flour.

**3.** Sprinkle ¼ cup ice water over mixture. Toss with rubber spatula until mixture is evenly moistened. Sprinkle remaining ¼ cup ice water over mixture and toss to combine. Press dough with spatula until dough sticks together. Use spatula to divide dough into 2 portions. Transfer each portion to sheet of plastic wrap. Working with 1 portion at a time, draw edges of plastic over dough and press firmly on sides and top to form compact, fissure-free mass. Wrap in plastic and form into 5-inch disk (or square). Repeat with remaining portion; refrigerate dough for at least 2 hours or up to 2 days. Let chilled dough sit on counter to soften slightly, about 10 minutes, before rolling. (Dough, wrapped tightly in plastic, can be frozen for up to 1 month. If frozen, let thaw completely on counter before rolling.)

### Foolproof Whole-Wheat Dough for Double-Crust Pie

Substitute 1½ cups (8¼ ounces) whole-wheat flour for first addition of all-purpose flour, using 1 cup all-purpose flour (5 ounces) for second addition of flour.

## Foolproof Dough for Double-Crust Pie

**MAKES** enough for one 9-inch pie

**WHY THIS RECIPE WORKS** This pie dough recipe was a huge breakthrough when we first developed it more than seventeen years ago. We were after a pie dough recipe that rolled out easily every time, even for novice bakers, while producing a tender, flaky crust. A combination of butter and shortening provided the best balance of flavor and tenderness; and the best tool to cut the fat into the flour was the food processor. Rather than starting with all the flour in the processor, we put aside 1 cup of flour and processed the remaining 1½ cups with all of the fat until it formed a unified paste. We added the reserved flour to the bowl and pulsed it until it was just evenly distributed. Finally, we tackled the tenderness issue, which is partially determined by the amount of water added. For the dough to roll easily, it needs a generous amount of water, but more water makes crusts tough. We found the answer in the liquor cabinet: vodka. While gluten (the protein that makes crust tough) forms readily in water, it doesn't form in ethanol, and vodka is 60 percent water and 40 percent ethanol. So adding ¼ cup of vodka produced a moist, easy-to-roll dough that stayed tender. (The alcohol vaporizes in the oven, so you won't taste it in the baked crust.) Vodka is essential to the tender texture of this crust and imparts no flavor—do not substitute water. This dough is moister than most standard pie doughs and will require lots of flour to roll out (up to ¼ cup). The dough, wrapped tightly in plastic wrap, can be refrigerated for up to 2 days or frozen for up to 1 month. If frozen, let the dough thaw completely on the counter before rolling it out.

- 2½ cups (12½ ounces) unbleached all-purpose flour, plus extra for the work surface
- 2 tablespoons sugar
- 1 teaspoon table salt
- 12 tablespoons (1½ sticks) unsalted butter, cut into ¼-inch pieces and chilled
- ½ cup vegetable shortening, cut into 4 pieces and chilled
- ¼ cup vodka, chilled
- ¼ cup ice water

**1.** Process 1½ cups of the flour, the sugar, and salt together in a food processor until combined. Scatter the butter and shortening over the top and continue to process until incorporated and the mixture begins to form uneven clumps with no remaining floury bits, about 15 seconds.

**2.** Scrape down the workbowl and redistribute the dough evenly around the processor blade. Sprinkle the remaining 1 cup flour over the dough and pulse until the mixture has broken up into pieces and is evenly distributed around the bowl, 4 to 6 pulses.

**3.** Transfer the mixture to a medium bowl. Sprinkle the vodka and water over the mixture. Stir and press the dough together, using a stiff rubber spatula, until the dough sticks together.

**4.** Divide the dough into two even pieces. Turn each piece of dough onto a sheet of plastic wrap and flatten each into a 4-inch disk. Wrap each piece tightly in plastic wrap and refrigerate for 1 hour. Before rolling the dough out, let it sit on the counter to soften slightly, about 10 minutes.

### Foolproof Dough for Single-Crust Pie

**MAKES** enough for one 9-inch pie

Vodka is essential to the tender texture of this crust and imparts no flavor—do not substitute water. This dough is moister than most standard pie doughs and will require lots of flour to roll out (up to ¼ cup). The dough, wrapped tightly in plastic wrap, can be refrigerated for up to 2 days or frozen for up to 1 month. Thaw completely on the counter before rolling it out.

- 1¼ cups (6¼ ounces) all-purpose flour
- 1 tablespoon sugar
- ½ teaspoon table salt
- 6 tablespoons unsalted butter, cut into ¼-inch pieces and chilled
- 4 tablespoons vegetable shortening, cut into 2 pieces and chilled
- 2 tablespoons vodka, chilled
- 2 tablespoons ice water

1. Process ¾ cups of the flour, the sugar, and salt together in a food processor until combined. Scatter the butter and shortening over the top and continue to process until incorporated and the mixture begins to form uneven clumps with no remaining floury bits, about 10 seconds.

2. Scrape down the workbowl and redistribute the dough evenly around the processor blade. Sprinkle the remaining ½ cup flour over the dough and pulse until the mixture has broken up into pieces and is evenly distributed around the bowl, 4 to 6 pulses.

3. Transfer the mixture to a medium bowl. Sprinkle the vodka and water over the mixture. Stir and press the dough together, using a stiff rubber spatula, until the dough sticks together.

4. Turn the dough onto a sheet of plastic wrap and flatten into a 4-inch disk. Wrap tightly in plastic wrap and refrigerate for 45 minutes or up to 2 days. Before rolling the dough out, let it sit on the counter to soften slightly, about 10 minutes.

## Graham Cracker Crust

**MAKES** enough for one 9-inch pie

**WHY THIS RECIPE WORKS** Saving time is always a good idea—just as long as you're not sacrificing quality. But while store-bought graham cracker pie crusts are tempting (all you have to do is fill, chill, then serve), they taste stale and bland. We wanted a fresh-tasting homemade crust that wasn't too sweet, with a crisp texture. Turns out, a classic graham cracker crust couldn't be easier to make: We combined crushed crumbs with a little butter and sugar to bind them, then used a measuring cup or flat-bottomed glass to pack the crumbs into the pie plate. Producing a perfect graham cracker crust has a lot to do with the type of graham crackers used. After experimenting with the three leading brands, we discovered subtle but distinct differences among them and found that these differences carried over into crumb crusts made with each kind of cracker. Here in the test kitchen, we prefer Nabisco Original Graham Crackers for their hearty molasses flavor. We don't recommend using store-bought graham cracker crumbs here as they can often be stale. Be sure to note whether the crust needs to be warm or cool before filling (the pie recipes will specify) and plan accordingly.

- 8 whole graham crackers, broken into 1-inch pieces
- 5 tablespoons unsalted butter, melted and cooled
- 3 tablespoons sugar

### MAKING A GRAHAM CRACKER CRUST

Press crumb mixture firmly and evenly across bottom of pie plate, using bottom of dry measuring cup. Tightly pack crumbs against sides of pie plate, using your thumb and measuring cup simultaneously.

1. Adjust oven rack to middle position and heat oven to 325 degrees. Process graham cracker pieces in food processor to fine, even crumbs, about 30 seconds. Sprinkle butter and sugar over crumbs and pulse to incorporate, about 5 pulses.

2. Sprinkle mixture into 9-inch pie plate. Use bottom of dry measuring cup to press crumbs into even layer on bottom and sides of pie plate. Bake until crust is fragrant and beginning to brown, 13 to 18 minutes. Following particular pie recipe, use crust while it is still warm or let it cool completely.

## Classic Tart Dough

**MAKES** enough for one 9-inch tart

**WHY THIS RECIPE WORKS** The problem with most tarts is the crust: It's usually either too tough or too brittle. While regular pie crust is tender and flaky, tart crust should be fine-textured, buttery-rich, crisp, and crumbly—it is often described as shortbread-like. We set out to achieve the perfect tart dough, one that we could use in several of our tart recipes. Using a full stick of butter made tart dough that tasted great and was easy to handle, yet still had a delicate crumb. Instead of using the hard-to-find superfine sugar and pastry flour that many other recipes call for, we used confectioners' sugar and all-purpose flour for a crisp texture. Rolling the dough and fitting it into the tart pan was easy, and we had ample dough to patch any holes. Tart crust is sweeter, crisper, and less flaky than pie crust—it is more similar in texture to a cookie. The dough, wrapped tightly in plastic wrap, can be refrigerated for up to two days or frozen for up to one month. If frozen, let the dough thaw completely on the counter before rolling it out.

- 1 large egg yolk
- 1 tablespoon heavy cream
- ½ teaspoon vanilla extract
- 1¼ cups (6¼ ounces) all-purpose flour
- ⅔ cup (2⅔ ounces) confectioners' sugar
- ¼ teaspoon table salt
- 8 tablespoons unsalted butter, cut into ¼-inch pieces and chilled

1. Whisk egg yolk, cream, and vanilla together in small bowl. Process flour, sugar, and salt in food processor until combined, about 5 seconds. Scatter butter pieces over top and pulse until mixture resembles coarse cornmeal, about 15 pulses.

2. With machine running, add egg mixture through feed tube and continue to process until dough just comes together around processor blade, about 12 seconds.

3. Turn dough onto sheet of plastic wrap and flatten into 6-inch disk. Wrap dough tightly in plastic wrap and refrigerate for 1 hour. Before rolling dough out, let it sit on counter to soften slightly, about 10 minutes.

## MAKING A TART SHELL

**1.** After rolling dough out into 11-inch circle on lightly floured counter, wrap it loosely around rolling pin and unroll dough over 9-inch tart pan with removable bottom.

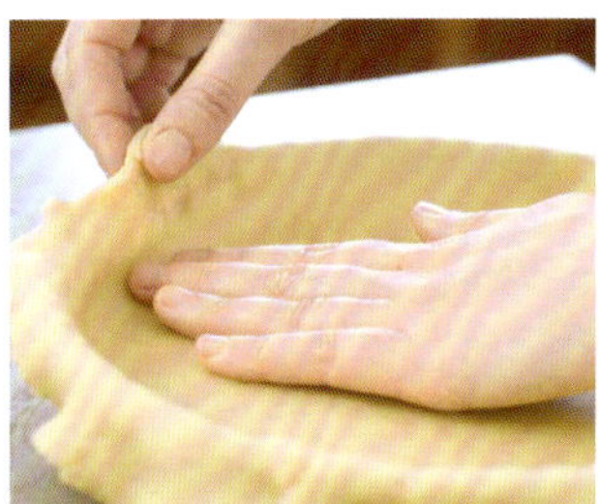

**2.** Lifting edge of dough, gently ease dough into pan. Press dough into corners and fluted sides of pan.

**3.** Run rolling pin over top of tart pan to remove any excess dough and make clean edge.

**4.** If parts of edge are too thin, reinforce them by pressing in some of excess dough. If edge is too thick, press some of dough up over edge of pan and trim it away.

# Classic Apple Pie

**SERVES 8**

**WHY THIS RECIPE WORKS** It is difficult to produce an apple pie with a filling that is tart as well as sweet and juicy. We wanted to develop a classic apple pie recipe—one with the clean, bright taste of apples that could be made year-round, with supermarket apples. To arrive at the tartness and texture we were after, we had to use two kinds of apples in our pie, Granny Smith and McIntosh. The Grannies were tart and kept their shape during cooking; the Macs added flavor, and their tendency to become mushy was a virtue, providing a juicy base for the Grannies. While many bakers add butter to their apple pie fillings, we found that it dulled the fresh taste of the apples, so we did without it. Lemon juice, however, was essential, counterbalancing the sweetness of the apples. This pie is best eaten when cooled to room temperature, or even the next day. Serve with vanilla ice cream or lightly sweetened whipped cream.

- 1 recipe double-crust pie dough (pages 944–945)
- ¾ cup (5¼ ounces) plus 1 tablespoon sugar, divided
- 2 tablespoons all-purpose flour
- 1 teaspoon grated lemon zest plus 1 tablespoon juice
- ¼ teaspoon table salt
- ¼ teaspoon ground nutmeg
- ¼ teaspoon ground cinnamon
- ⅛ teaspoon ground allspice
- 2 pounds firm McIntosh apples, peeled, cored, and sliced ¼ inch thick
- 1½ pounds Granny Smith apples, peeled, cored, and sliced ¼ inch thick
- 1 large egg white, lightly beaten

**1.** Roll 1 disk of dough into 12-inch circle on well-floured counter. Roll dough loosely around rolling pin and gently unroll it onto 9-inch pie plate, leaving at least 1-inch overhang around edge. Ease dough into plate by gently lifting edge of dough with your hand while pressing into plate bottom with your other hand. Wrap dough-lined plate loosely in plastic wrap and refrigerate until dough is firm, about 30 minutes. Roll other disk of dough into 12-inch circle on well-floured counter, then transfer to parchment paper–lined baking sheet; cover with plastic and refrigerate for 30 minutes.

**2.** Adjust oven rack to lowest position and heat oven to 500 degrees. Mix ¾ cup sugar, flour, lemon zest, salt, nutmeg, cinnamon, and allspice together in large bowl. Add lemon juice and apples and toss until combined. Spread apples with their juice into dough-lined pie plate, mounding them slightly in middle.

**3.** Roll remaining dough round loosely around rolling pin and gently unroll it onto filling. Trim overhang to ½ inch beyond lip of plate. Pinch edges of top and bottom crusts firmly together. Tuck overhang under itself; folded edge should be flush with edge of plate. Crimp dough evenly around edge of plate using your fingers. Cut four 2-inch slits in top of dough. Brush surface with beaten egg white and sprinkle with remaining 1 tablespoon sugar.

**4.** Place pie on rimmed baking sheet; reduce oven temperature to 425 degrees; and bake until crust is golden, about 25 minutes. Reduce oven temperature to 375 degrees, rotate sheet, and continue to bake until juices are bubbling and crust is deep golden brown, 35 to 45 minutes longer. Let pie cool on wire rack until filling has set, about 4 hours. Serve.

### ROLLING DOUBLE-CRUST PIE DOUGH

**1.** Roll 1 disk of dough into 12-inch circle on floured counter.

**2.** Loosely roll dough around rolling pin and gently unroll it onto 9-inch pie plate, letting excess dough hang over edge.

**3.** Ease dough into plate by gently lifting edge of dough with your hand while pressing into plate bottom with your other hand. Leave any dough that overhangs plate in place.

**4.** Fill dough-lined plate; loosely roll remaining dough round around rolling pin and gently unroll it onto filling.

## Deep-Dish Apple Pie

**SERVES 8**

**WHY THIS RECIPE WORKS** Deep-dish apple pies can be problematic: unevenly cooked apples and so much juice that the bottom crust is soggy. Then there is the gaping hole left between the apples (which are shrunken from the loss of all that moisture) and the arching top crust, making it impossible to slice and serve a neat piece of pie. We wanted our piece of deep-dish pie to be a towering wedge of tender, juicy apples, fully framed by a buttery, flaky crust. Precooking the apples solved the shrinking problem, helped the apples hold their shape, and prevented juices from collecting in the bottom of the pie plate, giving us a nicely browned bottom crust. You can use All-Butter Double-Crust Pie Dough (page 944) or Foolproof Double-Crust Pie Dough (page 945) for this pie. Use a combination of tart and sweet apples for this pie. Good choices for tart are Granny Smiths, Empires, or Cortlands; for sweet we recommend Golden Delicious, Jonagolds, or Braeburns. Serve with vanilla ice cream or lightly sweetened whipped cream.

- 1 recipe double-crust pie dough (pages 944–945)
- Unbleached all-purpose flour, for the work surface
- 2½ pounds firm tart apples (about 5 large), peeled, cored, and sliced ¼ inch thick
- 2½ pounds firm sweet apples (about 5 large), peeled, cored, and sliced ¼ inch thick
- ½ cup (3½ ounces) plus 1 tablespoon granulated sugar
- ¼ cup packed (1¾ ounces) light brown sugar
- ½ teaspoon grated zest plus 1 tablespoon juice from 1 lemon
- ¼ teaspoon table salt
- ⅛ teaspoon ground cinnamon
- 1 large egg white, lightly beaten

**1.** Roll one disk of dough into a 12-inch circle on a lightly floured work surface, then fit it into a 9-inch pie plate, letting the excess dough hang over the edge; cover with plastic wrap and refrigerate for 30 minutes. Roll the other disk of dough into a 12-inch circle on a lightly floured work surface, then transfer to a parchment-lined baking sheet; cover with plastic wrap and refrigerate for 30 minutes.

**2.** Toss the apples, ½ cup of the granulated sugar, the brown sugar, zest, salt, and cinnamon together in a Dutch oven. Cover and cook over medium heat, stirring frequently, until the apples are tender when poked with a fork but still hold their shape, 15 to 20 minutes. Transfer the apples and their juice to a rimmed baking sheet and cool to room temperature, about 30 minutes.

**3.** Adjust an oven rack to the lowest position and heat the oven to 425 degrees. Drain the cooled apples thoroughly through a colander, reserving ¼ cup of the juice. Stir the lemon juice into the reserved ¼ cup apple juice.

**4.** Spread the apples into the dough-lined pie plate, mounding them slightly in the middle, and drizzle with the lemon juice mixture. Loosely roll the second piece of dough around the rolling pin and gently unroll it over the pie. Trim, fold, and crimp the edges and cut four vent holes in the top. Brush the dough with the egg white and sprinkle with the remaining 1 tablespoon sugar.

**5.** Place the pie on a rimmed baking sheet and bake until the crust is golden, about 25 minutes. Reduce the oven temperature to 375 degrees, rotate the baking sheet, and continue to bake until the juices are bubbling and the crust is deep golden brown, 30 to 40 minutes longer. Cool the pie on a wire rack until the filling has set, about 2 hours; serve slightly warm or at room temperature.

## Salted Caramel Apple Pie

**SERVES 8**

**WHY THIS RECIPE WORKS** This showstopping pie will remind you of caramel apples while looking like an edible bouquet. Rather than stewing the apples beneath a top crust, we used apple slices as a fancy garnish for our caramel custard pie. We made the salted caramel filling by whisking basic custard components into homemade caramel. A surprising ingredient—white miso—deepened the caramel flavor dramatically and kept our filling from being too sweet. To make the apple rosettes for the top of the pie, we softened thin apple slices with sugar and a little lemon juice and microwaved them so they'd become pliable. Carefully tilt the saucepan to pool the caramel to get a more consistent temperature reading. For best results, use a mandoline to slice the apples paper-thin.

- 1 recipe Foolproof All-Butter Dough for Single-Crust Pie (page 944)
- 1½ cups (10½ ounces) plus 2 tablespoons sugar, divided
- 3 large eggs
- ¼ cup (1 ounce) cornstarch
- 2 tablespoons white miso
- ½ teaspoon vanilla extract
- ¼ teaspoon table salt
- 2 tablespoons water
- 1 cup heavy cream, divided
- 1½ cups whole milk
- 3 Fuji, Gala, or Golden Delicious apples, cored, quartered, and sliced very thin lengthwise
- 2 tablespoons lemon juice
- Flake sea salt

**1.** Roll dough into 12-inch circle on well-floured counter. Roll dough loosely around rolling pin and unroll it onto 9-inch pie plate, leaving at least 1-inch overhang around edge. Ease dough into plate by gently lifting edge of dough with your hand while pressing into plate bottom with your other hand.

**2.** Trim overhang to ½ inch beyond lip of plate. Tuck overhang under itself; folded edge should be flush with edge of plate. Crimp dough evenly around edge of plate using your fingers. Refrigerate dough-lined plate until dough is firm, about 30 minutes. Adjust oven rack to middle position and heat oven to 350 degrees.

**3.** Line chilled pie shell with double layer of aluminum foil, covering edges to prevent burning, and fill with pie weights. Bake on foil-lined rimmed baking sheet until pie dough looks dry and is light in color, 25 to 30 minutes, rotating sheet halfway through baking. Remove weights and foil, rotate sheet, and continue to bake crust until deep golden brown, 10 to 15 minutes longer. Transfer sheet to wire rack. (Crust must still be warm when filling is added.)

**4.** While shell is baking, whisk ¾ cup sugar, eggs, cornstarch, miso, vanilla, and table salt together in bowl; set aside. Bring ¾ cup sugar and water to boil in large saucepan over medium-high heat. Cook, without stirring, until mixture is straw-colored, 4 to 6 minutes. Reduce heat to low and continue to cook, swirling saucepan occasionally, until caramel is amber-colored and registers 360 to 370 degrees, 2 to 5 minutes.

**5.** Off heat, carefully stir in ¼ cup cream; mixture will bubble and steam. Whisk vigorously, being sure to scrape corners of saucepan, until mixture is completely smooth, at least 30 seconds. Gradually whisk in remaining ¾ cup cream and milk, then bring to simmer over medium heat. Slowly whisk 1 cup hot caramel mixture into egg mixture to temper, then slowly whisk tempered egg mixture into remaining caramel mixture in saucepan. Cook, whisking constantly, until mixture is thickened and bubbling and registers 180 degrees, 4 to 6 minutes (mixture should have consistency of thick pudding). Strain mixture through fine-mesh strainer into clean bowl.

**6.** With pie still on sheet, pour filling into warm crust, smoothing top with clean spatula into even layer. Bake until center of pie registers 160 degrees, 14 to 18 minutes. Let pie cool completely on wire rack, about 4 hours.

**7.** Before serving, combine apple slices, lemon juice, and remaining 2 tablespoons sugar in bowl. Microwave until apples are pliable, about 2 minutes, stirring halfway through microwaving. Drain apples, then transfer to paper towel–lined sheet and pat dry with paper towels. Shingle 5 apple slices, peel side out, overlapping each slice by about ½ inch on cutting board or counter. Starting at 1 end, roll up slices to form rose shape; place in center of pie. Repeat, arranging apple roses decoratively over top of pie. Sprinkle with sea salt and serve.

## Skillet Apple Pie

**SERVES 6 to 8**

**WHY THIS RECIPE WORKS** Who says a pie needs to bake in a special plate—or even have a bottom crust? We wanted to expand the definition of perfect apple pie: It can come in a skillet, and it can be just about the easiest pie you can make. Unlike the filling for a double-crust pie, the filling for a skillet apple pie can be saucy. Apple cider provided resonant apple flavor and, when thickened with cornstarch, it yielded a juicy filling with just the right body. We used 1/3 cup of maple syrup to further sweeten the filling, and it complemented the natural sweetness of the apples without being cloying. Working in a heavy skillet allowed us to sauté the apples just long enough to caramelize them before we transferred the dough-topped pie to the oven for 20 minutes, where the crust developed a lovely deep-brown hue. Cutting the dough into six pieces prior to baking allowed the crust to develop multiple crisp, flaky edges that contrasted with the saucy, caramelized, and tender apples. If you do not have apple cider, reduced apple juice may be used as a substitute: Simmer 1 cup apple juice in a small saucepan over medium heat until reduced to 1/2 cup (about 10 minutes). You will need a 12-inch ovensafe skillet for this recipe. Use a combination of sweet, crisp apples such as Golden Delicious and firm, tart apples such as Cortland or Empire. Serve the pie warm or at room temperature with vanilla ice cream or whipped cream.

**CRUST**

- 1 cup (5 ounces) all-purpose flour
- 1 tablespoon sugar
- 1/2 teaspoon table salt
- 2 tablespoons vegetable shortening, chilled
- 6 tablespoons unsalted butter, cut into 1/4-inch pieces and chilled
- 3–4 tablespoons ice water

**FILLING**

- 1/2 cup apple cider
- 1/3 cup maple syrup
- 2 tablespoons lemon juice
- 2 teaspoons cornstarch
- 1/8 teaspoon ground cinnamon (optional)
- 2 tablespoons unsalted butter
- 2 1/2 pounds sweet and tart apples, peeled, cored, and cut into 1/2-inch-thick wedges
- 1 large egg white, lightly beaten
- 2 teaspoons sugar

**1. FOR THE CRUST:** Pulse flour, sugar, and salt in food processor until combined, about 4 pulses. Add shortening and pulse until mixture has texture of coarse sand, about 10 pulses. Sprinkle butter pieces over flour mixture and pulse until mixture is pale yellow and resembles coarse crumbs, with butter bits no larger than small peas, about 10 pulses. Transfer mixture to medium bowl.

**2.** Sprinkle 3 tablespoons ice water over mixture. With rubber spatula, use folding motion to mix, pressing down on dough until dough is slightly tacky and sticks together, adding up to 1 tablespoon more ice water if dough does not come together. Flatten dough into 4-inch disk. Wrap disk in plastic wrap and refrigerate for at least 1 hour or up to 2 days. Let dough stand at room temperature for 15 minutes before rolling.

**3. FOR THE FILLING:** Adjust oven rack to upper-middle position (between 7 and 9 inches from the heating element) and heat oven to 500 degrees. Whisk cider; syrup; lemon juice; cornstarch; and cinnamon, if using, in medium bowl until smooth. Melt butter in 12-inch ovensafe skillet over medium-high heat. Add apples and cook, stirring 2 or 3 times, until apples begin to caramelize, about 5 minutes. (Do not fully cook apples.) Remove pan from heat, add cider mixture, and gently stir until apples are well coated. Set aside to cool slightly.

**4. TO ASSEMBLE AND BAKE:** Roll dough out on lightly floured counter to 11-inch circle. Roll dough loosely around rolling pin and unroll over apple filling. Brush dough with egg white and sprinkle with sugar. With sharp knife, gently cut dough into 6 pieces by making 1 vertical cut followed by 2 evenly spaced horizontal cuts (perpendicular to first cut). Bake until apples are tender and crust is deep golden brown, about 20 minutes, rotating skillet halfway through baking. Let pie cool for 15 minutes and serve.

## Blueberry Pie

**SERVES 8**

**WHY THIS RECIPE WORKS** The best blueberry pie has a firm, glistening filling full of fresh, bright flavor and still-plump berries. Since too much thickener can make the filling unappealingly dense, we favored tapioca to thicken our pie because it didn't mute the fresh blueberry flavor as cornstarch and flour did. But too much tapioca produced a stiff, congealed mass. Cooking and reducing half of the berries helped us cut down on the tapioca required, as did adding a peeled and grated Granny Smith apple. Apples are high in pectin, a type of carbohydrate that acts as a thickener when cooked. Combined with a modest 2 tablespoons of tapioca, the apple thickened the filling to a soft, even consistency. The crust posed a much simpler challenge. As with all of our fruit pies, baking on a rimmed baking sheet on the bottom oven rack produced a crisp, golden bottom crust. And we found a fast alternative to a lattice top in a small biscuit cutter, which we used to cut out circles in the top crust before transferring the dough onto the pie. This easy top crust vented the steam from the berries as successfully as a classic lattice top. This recipe was developed using fresh blueberries, but unthawed frozen blueberries will work as well. In step 3, cook half the frozen berries over medium-high heat, without mashing, until reduced to 1 1/4 cups, 12 to 15 minutes. Grind the tapioca to a powder in a spice grinder or mini food processor. If using pearl tapioca, reduce the amount to 5 teaspoons. Serve with vanilla ice cream or lightly sweetened whipped cream.

- 1 recipe Foolproof All-Butter Dough for Double-Crust Pie (page 944)
- 6 cups (30 ounces) blueberries, divided
- 1 Granny Smith apple, peeled, cored, and shredded on large holes of box grater
- 3/4 cup (5 1/4 ounces) sugar
- 2 tablespoons instant tapioca, ground

2 teaspoons grated lemon zest plus 2 teaspoons juice
Pinch table salt
2 tablespoons unsalted butter, cut into ¼-inch pieces
1 large egg white, lightly beaten

**1.** Roll 1 disk of dough into 12-inch circle on well-floured counter. Roll dough loosely around rolling pin and gently unroll it onto 9-inch pie plate, leaving at least 1-inch overhang around edge. Ease dough into plate by gently lifting edge of dough with your hand while pressing into plate bottom with your other hand. Wrap dough-lined plate loosely in plastic and refrigerate until dough is firm, about 30 minutes.

**2.** Roll other disk of dough into 12-inch circle on well-floured counter. Use 1¼-inch round biscuit cutter to cut round from center of dough. Cut 6 more rounds from dough, 1½ inches from edge of center hole and equally spaced around center hole. Transfer dough to parchment-lined baking sheet; cover with plastic wrap and refrigerate for 30 minutes.

**3.** Place 3 cups blueberries in medium saucepan and set over medium heat. Using potato masher, mash berries several times to release juices. Continue to cook, stirring frequently and mashing occasionally, until about half of berries have broken down and mixture is thickened and reduced to 1½ cups, about 8 minutes. Let cool slightly.

**4.** Adjust oven rack to lowest position and heat oven to 400 degrees.

**5.** Place shredded apple in clean dish towel and wring dry. Transfer apple to large bowl and stir in cooked blueberries, remaining 3 cups uncooked blueberries, sugar, tapioca, lemon zest and juice, and salt until combined. Spread mixture into dough-lined pie plate and scatter butter pieces over top.

**6.** Roll remaining dough round loosely around rolling pin and gently unroll it onto filling. Trim overhang to ½ inch beyond lip of plate. Pinch edges of top and bottom crusts firmly together. Tuck overhang under itself; folded edge should be flush with edge of plate. Crimp dough evenly around edge of plate using your fingers. Brush surface with egg white.

**7.** Place pie on aluminum foil–lined rimmed baking sheet and bake until crust is golden, about 25 minutes. Reduce oven temperature to 350 degrees, rotate sheet, and continue to bake until juices are bubbling and crust is deep golden brown, 35 to 50 minutes longer. Let pie cool on wire rack until filling has set, about 4 hours. Serve.

## Summer Berry Pie

**SERVES 8**

**WHY THIS RECIPE WORKS** A fresh berry pie might seem like an easy-to-pull-off summer dessert, but most of the recipes we tried buried the berries in gluey thickeners or embedded them in bouncy gelatin. We wanted a simple pie with great texture and flavor. We started with the test kitchen's quick and easy homemade graham cracker crust. For the filling, we used a combination of raspberries, blackberries, and blueberries. After trying a few different methods, we found a solution that both bound the berries in the graham cracker crust and intensified their bright flavor. We processed a portion of berries in the food processor until they made a smooth puree, then we thickened the puree with cornstarch. Next, we tossed the remaining berries with warm jelly for a glossy coat and a shot of sweetness. Feel free to vary the amount of each berry as desired as long as you have 6 cups of berries total; do not substitute frozen berries here. Serve with lightly sweetened whipped cream.

2 cups (10 ounces) raspberries
2 cups (10 ounces) blackberries
2 cups (10 ounces) blueberries
½ cup (3½ ounces) sugar
3 tablespoons cornstarch
⅛ teaspoon table salt
1 tablespoon juice from 1 lemon
1 recipe Graham Cracker Crust (page 946), baked and cooled
2 tablespoons red currant or apple jelly

**1.** Gently toss the berries together in a large bowl. Process 2½ cups of the berries in a food processor until very smooth, about 1 minute (do not under-process). Strain the puree through a fine-mesh strainer into a small saucepan, pressing on the solids to extract as much puree as possible (you should have about 1½ cups); discard the solids.

**2.** In a small bowl, whisk the sugar, cornstarch, and salt together, then whisk into the strained puree. Bring the puree to a boil over medium heat, stirring constantly, and cook until it is as thick as pudding, about 7 minutes. Off the heat, stir in the lemon juice and set aside to cool slightly.

**3.** Pour the warm berry puree into the baked and cooled pie crust. Melt the jelly in a small saucepan over low heat, then pour over the remaining 3½ cups berries and toss to coat. Spread the berries evenly over the puree and lightly press them into the puree. Cover the pie loosely with plastic wrap and refrigerate until the filling is chilled and set, about 3 hours. Serve chilled or at room temperature.

## Sweet Cherry Pie

SERVES 8

WHY THIS RECIPE WORKS Great cherry pie is typically made with sour cherries because their soft, juicy flesh and bright, punchy flavor isn't dulled by oven heat or sugar. But cherry season is cruelly short and chances are the cherries that are available are the sweet variety; they are great for eating out of hand but don't translate well to baking. We wanted a recipe for sweet cherry pie with all the intense, jammy flavor and softened but still intact fruit texture of the best sour cherry pie. To mimic the bright, tart flavor of a sour cherry pie filling, we supplemented sweet cherries with chopped plums, which are tart and helped tame the cherries' sweet flavor. To fix the texture problem, we cut the cherries in half to expose their sturdy flesh. A splash of bourbon and lemon juice also offset the sweetness and added flavorful depth. To keep the filling juicy, we opted for a traditional top crust which prevented any moisture from evaporating. The tapioca should be measured first, then ground in a coffee grinder or food processor for 30 seconds. If you are using frozen fruit, measure it frozen, but let it thaw before filling the pie. If not, you run the risk of partially cooked fruit and undissolved tapioca.

- 1 recipe Foolproof All-Butter Dough for Double-Crust Pie (page 944)
- 2 red plums, halved and pitted
- 2 pounds pitted sweet cherries or 6 cups pitted frozen cherries, halved, divided
- ½ cup (3½ ounces) sugar
- 2 tablespoons instant tapioca, ground
- 1 tablespoon lemon juice
- 2 teaspoons bourbon (optional)
- ⅛ teaspoon table salt
- ⅛ teaspoon ground cinnamon (optional)
- 2 tablespoons unsalted butter, cut into ¼-inch pieces
- 1 large egg, lightly beaten with 1 teaspoon water

**1.** Roll 1 disk of dough into 12-inch circle on well-floured counter. Roll dough loosely around rolling pin and gently unroll it onto 9-inch pie plate, leaving at least 1-inch overhang around edge. Ease dough into plate by gently lifting edge of dough with your hand while pressing into plate bottom with your other hand. Wrap dough-lined plate loosely in plastic and refrigerate until dough is firm, about 30 minutes. Roll other disk of dough into 12-inch circle on well-floured counter, then transfer to parchment paper–lined baking sheet; cover with plastic and refrigerate for 30 minutes.

**2.** Adjust oven rack to lowest position and heat oven to 400 degrees. Process plums and 1 cup halved cherries in food processor until smooth, about 1 minute, scraping down sides of bowl as necessary. Strain puree through fine-mesh strainer into large bowl, pressing on solids to extract liquid; discard solids. Stir in remaining 5 cups halved cherries; sugar; tapioca; lemon juice; bourbon, if using; salt; and cinnamon, if using, into puree; let stand for 15 minutes.

**3.** Transfer cherry mixture, including juices, to dough-lined plate. Scatter butter pieces over fruit. Roll remaining dough round loosely around rolling pin and gently unroll it onto filling. Trim overhang to ½ inch beyond lip of plate. Pinch edges of top and bottom crusts firmly together. Tuck overhang under itself; folded edge should be flush with edge of plate. Crimp dough evenly around edge of plate using your fingers. Cut eight 1-inch slits in top of dough. Brush dough with egg wash. Freeze pie for 20 minutes.

**4.** Place pie on rimmed baking sheet and bake for 30 minutes. Reduce oven temperature to 350 degrees and continue to bake until juices bubble and crust is deep golden brown, 35 to 50 minutes longer.

**5.** Let pie cool on wire rack until filling has set, about 4 hours, before serving.

## Fresh Peach Pie

SERVES 8

WHY THIS RECIPE WORKS Juicy summer peaches produce the best pies. To control the moisture, we macerated the peaches to draw out some of their juices and then added a measured amount back to the filling. Cornstarch and pectin helped hold the fruit filling together without making it gluey or bouncy, and mashing some of the peaches helped make neat, attractive slices. A buttery, tender lattice-top crust allowed moisture to evaporate and made for an impressive presentation. If your peaches are too soft to withstand the pressure of a peeler, cut a shallow X in the bottom of the fruit, blanch them in a pot of simmering water for 15 seconds, and then shock them in a bowl of ice water before peeling. For fruit pectin we recommend both Sure-Jell for Less or No Sugar Needed Recipes and Ball RealFruit Low or No-Sugar Needed Pectin.

- 3 pounds peaches, peeled, quartered, and pitted, each quarter cut into thirds
- ½ cup (3½ ounces) plus 3 tablespoons sugar, divided
- 1 teaspoon grated lemon zest plus 1 tablespoon juice
- ⅛ teaspoon table salt
- 2 tablespoons low- or no-sugar-needed fruit pectin
- ¼ teaspoon ground cinnamon
- Pinch ground nutmeg
- 1 recipe Pie Dough for Lattice-Top Pie
- 1 tablespoon cornstarch

**1.** Toss peaches, ½ cup sugar, lemon zest and juice, and salt in medium bowl. Let stand at room temperature for at least 30 minutes or up to 1 hour. Combine pectin, cinnamon, nutmeg, and 2 tablespoons sugar in small bowl and set aside.

**2.** Remove dough from refrigerator. Before rolling out dough, let it sit on counter to soften slightly, about 10 minutes. Roll 1 disk of dough into 12-inch circle on lightly floured counter. Transfer to parchment paper–lined baking sheet. With pizza wheel, fluted pastry wheel, or paring knife, cut round into ten 1¼-inch-wide strips. Freeze strips on sheet until firm, about 30 minutes.

**3.** Adjust oven rack to lowest position, place rimmed baking sheet on rack, and heat oven to 425 degrees. Roll other disk of dough into 12-inch circle on lightly floured counter. Loosely roll dough around rolling pin and gently unroll it onto 9-inch pie plate, letting excess dough hang over edge. Ease dough into plate by gently lifting edge of dough with your hand while pressing into plate bottom with your other hand. Leave any dough that overhangs plate in place. Wrap dough-lined pie plate loosely in plastic wrap and refrigerate until dough is firm, about 30 minutes.

**4.** Meanwhile, transfer 1 cup peach mixture to small bowl and mash with fork until coarse paste forms. Drain remaining peach mixture through colander set in large bowl. Transfer peach juice to liquid measuring cup (you should have about ½ cup liquid; if liquid measures more than ½ cup, discard remainder). Return peach pieces to bowl and toss with cornstarch. Transfer peach juice to 12-inch skillet, add pectin mixture, and whisk until combined. Cook over medium heat, stirring occasionally, until slightly thickened and pectin is dissolved (liquid should become less cloudy), 3 to 5 minutes. Remove skillet from heat, add peach pieces and peach paste, and toss to combine.

**5.** Transfer peach mixture to dough-lined pie plate. Remove dough strips from freezer; if too stiff to be workable, let stand at room temperature until malleable and softened slightly but still very cold. Lay 2 longest strips across center of pie perpendicular to each other. Using 4 shortest strips, lay 2 strips across pie parallel to 1 center strip and 2 strips parallel to other center strip, near edges of pie; you should have 6 strips in place. Using remaining 4 strips, lay each one across pie parallel and equidistant from center and edge strips. If dough becomes too soft to work with, refrigerate pie and dough strips until dough firms up.

**6.** Trim overhang to ½ inch beyond lip of pie plate. Press edges of bottom crust and lattice strips together and fold under. Folded edge should be flush with edge of pie plate. Crimp dough evenly around edge of pie using your fingers. Using spray bottle, evenly mist lattice with water and sprinkle with remaining 1 tablespoon sugar.

**7.** Place pie on rimmed baking sheet and bake until crust is set and begins to brown, about 25 minutes. Reduce oven temperature to 375 degrees, rotate sheet, and continue to bake until crust is deep golden brown and filling is bubbly at center, 30 to 40 minutes longer. Let pie cool on wire rack for 3 hours before serving.

## Pie Dough for Lattice-Top Pie

**MAKES** enough for one 9-inch pie

- 3 cups (15 ounces) all-purpose flour
- 2 tablespoons sugar
- 1 teaspoon salt
- 7 tablespoons vegetable shortening, cut into ½-inch pieces and chilled
- 10 tablespoons unsalted butter, cut into ¼-inch pieces and frozen for 30 minutes
- 10–12 tablespoons ice water

**1.** Process flour, sugar, and salt in food processor until combined, about 5 seconds. Scatter shortening over top and process until mixture resembles coarse cornmeal, about 10 seconds. Scatter butter over top and pulse until mixture resembles coarse crumbs, about 10 pulses. Transfer to bowl.

**2.** Sprinkle 5 tablespoons ice water over flour mixture. With rubber spatula, use folding motion to evenly combine water and flour mixture. Sprinkle 5 tablespoons ice water over mixture and continue using folding motion to combine until small portion of dough holds together when squeezed in palm of your hand, adding up to 2 tablespoons remaining ice water if necessary. (Dough should feel quite moist.) Turn out dough onto clean, dry counter and gently press together into cohesive ball. Divide dough into 2 even pieces and flatten each into 4-inch disk. Wrap disks tightly in plastic wrap and refrigerate for 1 hour or up to 2 days.

### BUILDING A "NO-WEAVE" LATTICE TOP

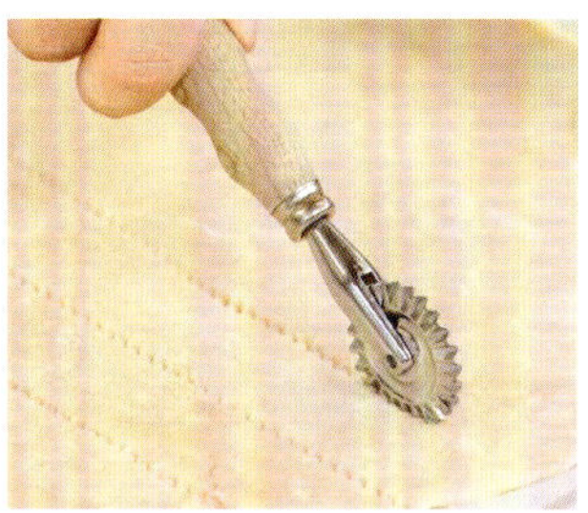

**1.** Roll dough into 12-inch circle, transfer to parchment paper–lined baking sheet, and cut into ten 1¼-inch-wide strips with a fluted pastry wheel, pizza wheel, or paring knife. Freeze for 30 minutes.

**2.** Lay 2 longest strips perpendicular to each other across center of pie to form cross. Place 4 shorter strips along edges of pie, parallel to center strips.

**3.** Lay 4 remaining strips between each edge strip and center strip. Trim off excess lattice ends, press edges of bottom crust and lattice strips together, and fold under.

## Fresh Plum–Ginger Pie with Whole-Wheat Lattice-Top Crust

**SERVES** 8

**WHY THIS RECIPE WORKS** Plum pies are hard to get right: They're either mushy or a dense brick of overcooked fruit. We wanted tender bites of plum in a fresh, jammy filling. Leaving the skins on the plums and cutting them into thin slices resulted in perfectly cooked fruit. A bit of spicy, tangy ginger complemented the sweetness of the plums. You can substitute our Foolproof All-Butter Dough for Double-Crust Pie

## WEAVING A LATTICE TOP

**1.** Evenly space 4 dough strips across top of pie, parallel to counter edge.

**2.** Fold back first and third strips almost completely. Lay 1 strip across pie, perpendicular to counter edge.

**3.** Unfold first and third strips over top of perpendicular strip.

**4.** Fold back second and fourth strips and add second perpendicular strip. Unfold second and fourth strips.

**5.** Repeat, alternating between folding back first and third strips and second and fourth strips and laying remaining strips evenly across pie.

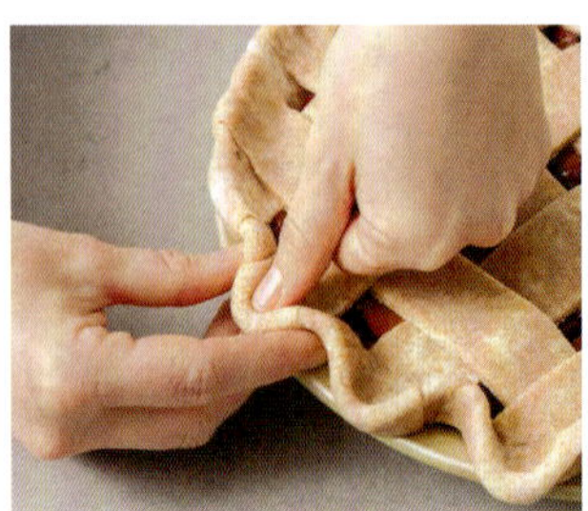

**6.** Trim lattice ends, press edges of bottom crust and lattice strips together, and fold under. Crimp dough evenly around edge of pie.

(page 944) or Foolproof Double Crust Pie Dough (page 945) for the whole-wheat dough recipe if you prefer. If at any point the dough is too stiff to be workable, let it sit at room temperature until slightly softened but still very cold.

- 1 recipe Foolproof Whole-Wheat Dough for Double-Crust Pie (page 945)
- ¾ cup (5¼ ounces) sugar
- 3 tablespoons cornstarch
- 2 teaspoons grated lemon zest plus 1 tablespoon juice
- 1 teaspoon grated fresh ginger
- ¼ teaspoon ground ginger
- ¼ teaspoon table salt
- 2½ pounds plums, pitted and cut into ¼-inch-thick wedges
- 1 large egg, lightly beaten with 1 tablespoon water

**1.** Roll 1 disk of dough into 12-inch circle on well-floured counter. Loosely roll dough around rolling pin and gently unroll it onto 9-inch pie plate, letting excess dough hang over edge. Ease dough into plate by gently lifting edge of dough with your hand while pressing into plate bottom with your other hand. Leave any dough that overhangs plate in place. Wrap dough-lined plate loosely in plastic wrap and refrigerate until firm, about 30 minutes.

**2.** Roll other piece of dough into 13 by 10½-inch rectangle on well-floured counter, then transfer to parchment paper–lined rimmed baking sheet; cover loosely with plastic and refrigerate until firm, about 30 minutes.

**3.** Using pizza wheel, fluted pastry wheel, or paring knife, trim ¼ inch dough from long sides of rectangle, then cut rectangle lengthwise into eight 1¼-inch-wide strips. Cover loosely with plastic and refrigerate until firm, about 30 minutes. Adjust oven rack to middle position and heat oven to 400 degrees.

**4.** Whisk sugar, cornstarch, lemon zest, fresh ginger, ground ginger, and salt together in large bowl. Stir in plums and lemon juice and let sit for 15 minutes. Spread plum mixture into chilled dough-lined plate.

**5.** Remove dough strips from refrigerator; if too stiff to be workable, let sit at room temperature until softened slightly but still very cold. Space 4 strips evenly across top of pie, parallel to counter edge. Fold back first and third strips almost completely. Lay 1 strip across pie, perpendicular to second and fourth strips, keeping it snug to folded edges of dough strips, then unfold first and third strips over top.

**6.** Fold back second and fourth strips and add second perpendicular strip, keeping it snug to folded edge. Unfold second and fourth strips over top. Repeat weaving remaining strips evenly across pie, alternating between folding back first and third strips and second and fourth strips to create lattice pattern. Shift strips as needed so they are evenly spaced over top of pie. (If dough becomes too soft to work with, refrigerate pie and dough strips until firm.)

**7.** Trim overhang to ½ inch beyond lip of plate. Pinch edges of bottom crust and lattice strips together firmly to seal. Tuck overhang under itself; folded edge should be flush with edge of plate. Crimp dough evenly around edge of plate. (If dough is very soft, refrigerate for 10 minutes before baking.) Brush surface with egg wash.

**8.** Place pie on aluminum foil–lined rimmed baking sheet and bake until crust is light golden, 20 to 25 minutes. Reduce oven temperature to 350 degrees, rotate sheet, and continue to bake until juices are bubbling and crust is deep golden brown, 30 to 50 minutes longer. Let pie cool on wire rack until filling has set, about 4 hours. Serve.

## Fresh Strawberry Pie

SERVES 8

WHY THIS RECIPE WORKS We wanted a strawberry pie featuring fresh berries lightly held together by a sheer, glossy glaze in a buttery shell. We knew that the success of our strawberry pie hinged on getting the thickener just right. When none of the thickeners we tried worked on their own, we decided to use a combination of two: pectin (in the form of a homemade strawberry jam) and cornstarch. Together they created just the right supple, lightly clingy glaze. Fresh, flavorful strawberries make this dessert a perfect summery treat. To account for any imperfect strawberries, the ingredient list calls for several more ounces of berries than will be used in the pie. If possible, seek out ripe, farmers' market–quality berries. Make sure to thoroughly dry the strawberries after washing. Make certain that you use fruit pectin engineered for low- or no-sugar recipes (we recommend Sure-Jell Premium Fruit Pectin) and not regular pectin; otherwise, the glaze will not set properly. The pie is at its best after two or three hours of chilling; as it continues to chill, the glaze becomes softer and wetter, though the pie will taste just as good.

- 1 recipe Foolproof Single-Crust Pie Dough (page 945), fitted into a 9-inch pie plate and chilled
- 3 pounds strawberries, hulled (9 cups)
- ¾ cup (5¼ ounces) sugar
- 2 tablespoons cornstarch
- 1½ teaspoons Sure-Jell for low-sugar recipes
- Pinch table salt
- 1 tablespoon juice from 1 lemon
- 1 cup heavy cream, cold
- 1 tablespoon sugar

**1.** Adjust an oven rack to the middle position and heat the oven to 375 degrees. Line the chilled pie shell with a double layer of foil and fill with pie weights.

**2.** Bake until the pie dough looks dry and is light in color, 25 to 30 minutes. Remove the weights and foil and continue to bake the crust until deep golden brown, 10 to 12 minutes longer. Transfer the pie plate to a wire rack and let cool completely, about 1 hour.

**3.** Select 6 ounces misshapen, underripe, or otherwise unattractive berries, halving those that are large; you should have about 1½ cups. Process the berries in a food processor to a smooth puree, 20 to 30 seconds, scraping down the bowl as needed (you should have about ¾ cup puree).

**4.** Whisk the sugar, cornstarch, Sure-Jell, and salt together in a medium saucepan. Stir in the berry puree, making sure to scrape the corners of the pan. Cook over medium-high heat, stirring constantly, and bring to a boil. Boil, scraping the bottom and sides of the pan to prevent scorching, for 2 minutes to ensure that the cornstarch is fully cooked (the mixture will appear frothy when it first reaches a boil, then will darken and thicken with further cooking). Transfer the glaze to a large bowl and stir in the lemon juice; let cool to room temperature.

**5.** Meanwhile, pick over the remaining berries and measure out 2 pounds of the most attractive ones; halve only any extra-large berries. Add the berries to the bowl with the glaze and fold gently with a rubber spatula until the berries are evenly coated. Scoop the berries into the cooled prebaked pie shell, piling into a mound. If any cut sides face up on top, turn them face down. If necessary, rearrange the berries so that holes are filled and the mound looks attractive. Refrigerate the pie until the filling is chilled and has set, about 2 hours. Serve within 5 hours of chilling.

**6.** Just before serving, beat the cream and sugar with an electric mixer on low speed until small bubbles form, about 30 seconds. Increase the speed to medium; continue beating until the beaters leave a trail, about 30 additional seconds. Increase the speed to high; continue beating until the cream is smooth, thick, and nearly doubled in volume and forms soft peaks, 30 to 60 seconds.

**7.** Cut the pie into wedges and serve with whipped cream.

## Strawberry-Rhubarb Pie

SERVES 8

WHY THIS RECIPE WORKS The key to pairing sweet strawberries and tart rhubarb in a pie is to keep their high water content in check. Microwaving rhubarb pieces with sugar allowed them to shed some liquid. We tossed in some of our cut strawberries to macerate among the microwaved rhubarb and used the juices to create a jammy filling. We cooked the rest of the cut strawberries in the liquid, softening them until they were easy to mash into a jam. Adding tapioca to the filling mixture gelatinized the juices, protecting the crust from turning soggy. A sugary crust offered a contrast to the tart rhubarb, and brushing the surface with water before sprinkling it with sugar ensured the granules stayed put during baking. This dough is unusually moist and requires a full ¼ cup of flour when rolling it out to prevent it from sticking. Rhubarb varies in the amount of trimming required. Buy 2 pounds to ensure that you end up with 7 cups of rhubarb pieces. For tips on crimping the dough, see page 960. Serve with whipped cream or ice cream.

CRUST

- 2½ cups (12½ ounces) all-purpose flour
- 2 tablespoons sugar, plus 3 tablespoons for sprinkling
- 1 teaspoon table salt
- 12 tablespoons unsalted butter, cut into ¼-inch slices and chilled
- ½ cup vegetable shortening, cut into 4 pieces and chilled
- ¼ cup vodka, chilled
- ¼ cup cold water, plus extra for brushing

FILLING

- 2 pounds rhubarb, trimmed and cut into ½-inch pieces (7 cups)
- 1¼ cups (8¾ ounces) sugar
- 1 pound strawberries, hulled, halved if less than 1 inch, quartered if more than 1 inch (3 to 4 cups)
- 3 tablespoons instant tapioca

**1. FOR THE CRUST:** Process 1½ cups flour, 2 tablespoons sugar, and salt in food processor until combined, about 5 seconds. Scatter butter and shortening over top and process until incorporated and mixture begins to form uneven clumps with no remaining floury bits, about 15 seconds.

**2.** Scrape down sides of bowl and redistribute dough evenly around processor blade. Sprinkle remaining 1 cup flour over dough and pulse until mixture has broken up into pieces and is evenly distributed around bowl, 4 to 6 pulses.

**3.** Transfer mixture to large bowl. Sprinkle vodka and cold water over mixture. Using rubber spatula, stir and press dough until it sticks together.

**4.** Divide dough in half. Turn each half onto sheet of plastic wrap and form into 4-inch disk. Wrap disks tightly in plastic and refrigerate for 1 hour. Let chilled dough sit on counter to soften slightly, about 10 minutes, before rolling. (Wrapped dough can be refrigerated for up to 2 days or frozen for up to 1 month. If frozen, let dough thaw completely on counter before rolling.)

**5. FOR THE FILLING:** While dough chills, combine rhubarb and sugar in bowl and microwave for 1½ minutes. Stir and continue to microwave until sugar is mostly dissolved, about 1 minute longer. Stir in 1 cup strawberries and set aside for 30 minutes, stirring once halfway through.

**6.** Drain rhubarb mixture through fine-mesh strainer set over large saucepan. Return drained rhubarb mixture to bowl and set aside. Add remaining strawberries to rhubarb liquid and cook over medium-high heat until strawberries are very soft and mixture is reduced to 1½ cups, about 10 to 15 minutes. Mash berries with fork (mixture does not have to be smooth). Add strawberry mixture and tapioca to drained rhubarb mixture and stir to combine. Set aside.

**7.** Roll 1 disk of dough into 12-inch circle on well-floured counter. Loosely roll dough around rolling pin and gently unroll onto 9-inch pie plate, letting excess dough hang over edge. Ease dough into plate by gently lifting edge of dough with your hand while pressing into plate bottom with your other hand. Wrap dough-lined plate loosely in plastic and refrigerate until dough is firm, about 30 minutes.

**8.** Roll other disk of dough into 12-inch circle on well-floured counter, then transfer to parchment paper–lined baking sheet; cover with plastic and refrigerate for 30 minutes. Adjust rack to middle position and heat oven to 425 degrees.

**9.** Transfer filling to chilled dough-lined plate and spread into even layer. Loosely roll remaining dough round around rolling pin and gently unroll it onto filling. Trim overhang to ½ inch beyond lip of plate. Pinch edges of top and bottom crusts firmly together. Tuck overhang under itself; folded edge should be flush with edge of plate. Crimp dough evenly around edge of plate using your fingers or butter knife. Brush surface thoroughly with extra water and sprinkle with 3 tablespoons sugar. Cut eight 2-inch slits in top crust.

**10.** Place pie on parchment-lined rimmed baking sheet and bake until crust is set and begins to brown, about 25 minutes. Rotate pie and reduce oven temperature to 375 degrees; continue to bake until crust is deep golden brown and filling is bubbling, 30 to 40 minutes longer. If edges of pie begin to get too brown before pie is done, cover loosely with aluminum foil. Let cool on wire rack for 2½ hours before serving.

## Triple Berry Slab Pie with Ginger-Lemon Streusel

**SERVES** 18 to 24

**WHY THIS RECIPE WORKS** Our berry slab pie is guaranteed to elicit oohs and aahs before the first slice is even cut. We started by tossing no-prep berries—blueberries, raspberries, and blackberries—with sugar, lemon zest, and tapioca for the filling. Instead of applying a top crust, which would hide the beautiful berries and trap moisture, we sprinkled on a streusel that we flavored with more lemon zest and some crystallized ginger. You will need a 18 by 13-inch rimmed baking sheet for this recipe. You can toss the berry mixture in step 5 in two bowls if it doesn't fit in one.

- 1 recipe Slab Pie Dough

**STREUSEL**

- 1½ cups (7½ ounces) all-purpose flour
- ½ cup packed (3½ ounces) light brown sugar
- ½ cup crystallized ginger, chopped fine
- ¼ cup (1¾ ounces) granulated sugar
- 1 tablespoon ground ginger
- 1 teaspoon grated lemon zest
- ¼ teaspoon table salt
- 10 tablespoons unsalted butter, melted and cooled

**FILLING**

- 1 cup (7 ounces) granulated sugar
- 6 tablespoons instant tapioca, ground
- 1 teaspoon grated lemon zest
- ¼ teaspoon table salt
- 1¼ pounds (4 cups) blackberries
- 1¼ pounds (4 cups) blueberries
- 1¼ pounds (4 cups) raspberries

**1.** Line rimmed baking sheet with parchment paper. Roll each dough square into 16 by 11-inch rectangle on floured counter; stack on prepared sheet, separated by second sheet of parchment. Cover loosely with plastic wrap and refrigerate until dough is firm but still pliable, about 10 minutes.

**2.** Using parchment as sling, transfer chilled dough rectangles to counter; discard parchment. Wipe sheet clean with paper towels and spray with vegetable oil spray. Starting at short side of 1 dough rectangle, loosely roll around rolling pin, then gently unroll over half of long side of prepared sheet, leaving about 2 inches of dough overhanging 3 edges. Repeat with second dough rectangle, unrolling it over empty side of sheet and overlapping first dough piece by ½ inch.

**3.** Ease dough into sheet by gently lifting edges of dough with your hand while pressing into sheet bottom with your other hand. Brush overlapping edge of dough rectangles with water and press to seal. Trim overhang to ½ inch beyond edge of sheet. Tuck overhang under itself; folded edge should rest on edge of sheet. Crimp dough evenly around edge of sheet. Cover loosely with plastic and refrigerate until firm, about 30 minutes.

**4. FOR THE STREUSEL:** Meanwhile, adjust oven racks to lower-middle and lowest positions and heat oven to 375 degrees. Combine flour, brown sugar, crystallized ginger, granulated sugar, ground ginger, lemon zest, and salt in bowl. Stir in melted butter until mixture is completely moistened; let sit for 10 minutes.

**5. FOR THE FILLING:** Whisk sugar, tapioca, lemon zest, and salt together in large bowl. Add blackberries, blueberries, and raspberries and toss gently to combine. Spread berry mixture evenly over chilled dough-lined sheet. Sprinkle streusel evenly over fruit, breaking apart any large chunks. Place large sheet of aluminum foil directly on lower rack (to catch any bubbling juices). Place pie on upper rack and bake until crust and streusel are deep golden brown and juices are bubbling, 45 minutes to 1 hour, rotating sheet halfway through baking. Let pie cool on wire rack until filling has set, about 2 hours. Serve.

### FITTING SLAB PIE DOUGH INTO A BAKING SHEET

**1.** Starting at short side of 1 piece of dough, roll loosely around rolling pin, then gently unroll over half of long side of sheet, leaving about 2 inches of dough overhanging 3 edges of sheet.

**2.** Repeat with second piece of dough, overlapping first piece of dough by ½ inch in center of sheet.

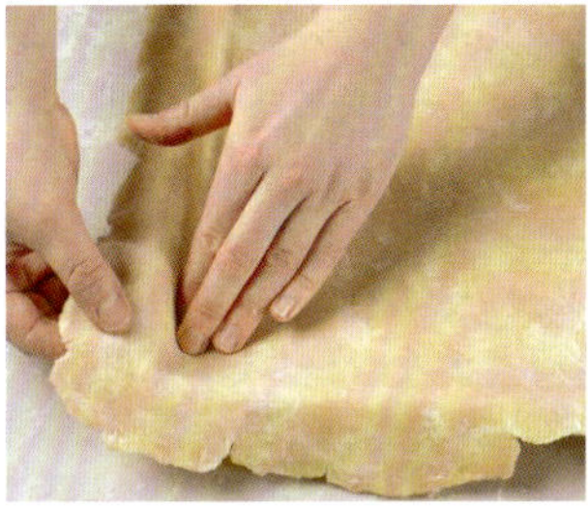

**3.** Ease dough into sheet by gently lifting edges of dough with your hand while pressing into sheet bottom with your other hand.

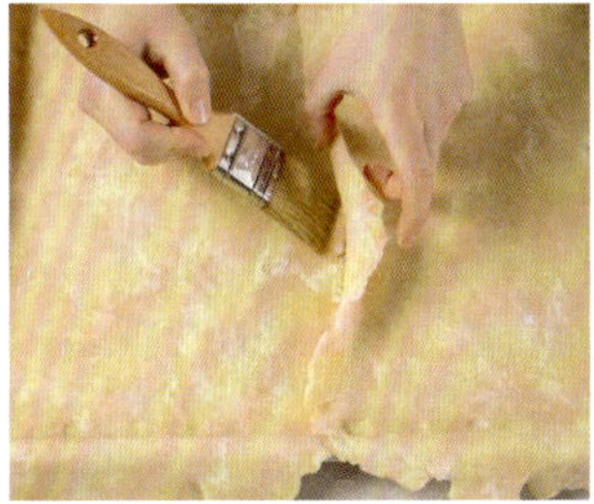

**4.** Brush edge where doughs overlap with water, pressing to seal.

## Slab Pie Dough

**MAKES** one 18 by 13-inch single crust

This dough is very workable, which makes it ideal for rolling into large rectangles that fit into a baking sheet to make this large-scale pie. Be sure to weigh the flour for this recipe. In the mixing stage, this dough will be moister than most pie doughs, but as it chills it will absorb much of the excess moisture. Be sure to roll the dough on a well-floured counter.

- 24 tablespoons (3 sticks) unsalted butter, divided
- 2¾ cups (13¾ ounces) all-purpose flour, divided
- 2 tablespoons sugar
- 1 teaspoon table salt
- ½ cup ice water, divided

**1.** Grate 5 tablespoons butter on large holes of box grater and place in freezer. Cut remaining 19 tablespoons butter into ½-inch cubes.

**2.** Pulse 1¾ cups flour, sugar, and salt in food processor until combined, 2 pulses. Add cubed butter and process until homogeneous paste forms, 40 to 50 seconds. Using your hands, carefully break paste into 2-inch chunks and redistribute evenly around processor blade. Add remaining 1 cup flour and pulse until mixture is broken into pieces no larger than 1 inch (most pieces will be much smaller), 4 to 5 pulses. Transfer mixture to bowl. Add grated butter and toss until butter pieces are separated and coated with flour.

**3.** Sprinkle ¼ cup ice water over mixture. Toss with rubber spatula until mixture is evenly moistened. Sprinkle remaining ¼ cup ice water over mixture and toss to combine. Press dough with spatula until dough sticks together. Using spatula, divide dough into 2 equal portions. Transfer each portion to sheet of plastic wrap. Working with 1 portion at a time, draw edges of plastic over dough and press firmly on sides and top to form compact, fissure-free mass. Wrap in plastic and form into 5 by 6-inch rectangle. Refrigerate dough for at least 2 hours or up to 2 days. Let chilled dough sit on counter to soften slightly, about 10 minutes, before rolling. (Wrapped dough can be wrapped in plastic wrap frozen for up to 1 month. Thaw completely on counter before rolling.)

## Cherry Hand Pies

**MAKES** 8 hand pies

**WHY THIS RECIPE WORKS** Hand pies treat you to the pleasures of sugar-crusted pastry and vibrant, jewel-toned fruit without a plate and fork. The dough needs a little extra structure, so we made rough puff: a type of pastry dough that contains more gluten than most pie pastry and comes together by working cold butter into the flour mixture and then rolling out and folding the dough a few times to create flaky layers. Frozen fruit kept things easy. We briefly chilled the assembled pies to help them maintain their sharp, clean edges. Rolling, filling, and sealing the dough using the same process we use for hand-cut ravioli provided tidy airtight packages. Trimming the pastry edges with a fluted pastry wheel or decorating them with the tines of a fork or a serrated knife added visual appeal. A sprinkle of demerara sugar on the top of each pie added a hint of sweetness and shimmer. Be sure to have the filling ready before you start this recipe. We strongly recommend weighing the flour for this recipe. If you're baking only one sheet of hand pies, adjust the oven rack to the middle position.

- 2½ cups (12½ ounces) all-purpose flour
- 2 tablespoons granulated sugar
- 1 teaspoon plus pinch table salt, divided
- 20 tablespoons (2½ sticks) unsalted butter, halved lengthwise and chilled

- ¾ cup ice water
- 1 large egg
- 1 recipe cherry hand pie filling
- 2 tablespoons demerara or turbinado sugar (optional)

**1.** Place flour, granulated sugar, and 1 teaspoon salt in 1-gallon, heavy-duty zipper-lock bag. Seal and shake well to combine. Add butter to bag and shake to coat with flour mixture. Seal bag, pressing out as much air as possible. Set rolling pin over lowest portion of bag and, using rocking motion, flatten butter beneath pin into large flakes. Working in sections, move pin up bag and flatten remaining butter. Shake bag to mix. Roll over bag with pin, shaking bag occasionally to mix, until flour becomes very pale yellow and almost all of butter is incorporated. Transfer mixture to large bowl (use rubber spatula or bench scraper to scrape any remaining butter and flour mixture from bag). Add ice water and toss with rubber spatula until just combined (mixture will be tacky). Transfer dough to floured counter. With your floured hands, press dough into rough 8-inch square.

**2.** Roll dough into 15 by 10-inch rectangle with short side parallel to edge of counter, flouring counter and dough as needed. Starting at top of dough, fold into thirds like business letter, using bench scraper or metal spatula to release dough from counter. Turn dough 90 degrees and repeat rolling and folding. Divide dough in half crosswise. Wrap each half tightly in plastic wrap and refrigerate for at least 1 hour or up to 2 days.

**3.** Adjust oven racks to upper-middle and lower-middle positions and heat oven to 400 degrees. In small bowl, beat egg and remaining pinch salt until well combined. Line 2 rimmed baking sheets with parchment paper.

**4.** On lightly floured counter, roll 1 piece of dough into 17 by 9-inch rectangle with short side parallel to edge of counter. Roll dough loosely around rolling pin, turn 90 degrees, and arrange on counter so long side is parallel to edge of counter. If dough has contracted, roll again briefly to achieve 17 by 9-inch dimensions. Using pastry brush, apply 1-inch-wide band of egg wash horizontally across center of dough. Apply 1-inch-wide strip of egg wash to edges of lower half of dough. Apply 1-inch-wide bands of egg wash vertically to divide bottom half of dough into 4 equal squares.

**5.** Place 2 tablespoons filling into each square, being careful to keep filling clear of egg wash. Using spoon, shape cherry filling into rough squares. Using pizza cutter or sharp knife, cut dough at center points between filling to create 4 pieces. Leaving pieces in place but working with 1 piece at a time, gently fold dough over, aligning top edge with bottom edge. Use your fingers to gently press dough layers together, working out as much air as possible. Trim ¼ inch of dough from ragged and folded sides of each pie. Arrange pies on prepared sheet, leaving at least ¾ inch between them.

**6.** Repeat steps 4 and 5 with remaining dough and filling. Cut 1-inch vent on top of each pie. Transfer pies to refrigerator to chill for 15 minutes. (Pies can be frozen on baking sheets until solid, at least 4 hours, and then transferred to airtight container and frozen for up to 6 weeks. Transfer to parchment paper–lined rimmed baking sheets and thaw in refrigerator for 2 hours before proceeding with step 7.)

**7.** Brush tops of pies with egg wash and sprinkle with demerara sugar, if using. Bake until dark golden brown, 20 to 25 minutes, switching and rotating sheets halfway through baking. Let cool for 20 minutes; serve warm.

#### ASSEMBLING HAND PIES

**1.** Roll 1 piece of dough into 17 by 9-inch rectangle. Brush 4 squares onto bottom of dough with egg wash. Add 2 tablespoons filling to each square, spreading up to (but not on) grid lines. Cut dough between filling to create 4 even pieces.

**2.** Fold 1 piece of dough over itself, aligning top and bottom edges. Seal edges with your fingers, pressing out as much air as possible. Repeat with remaining 3 pieces.

**3.** Trim ¼ inch from ragged and folded sides of pies.

### Cherry Hand Pie Filling

**MAKES** 1¼ cups

Use your choice of sweet or sour cherries here. You can substitute 10 ounces (2 cups) of fresh pitted cherries for the frozen cherries. Do not use canned cherries.

- 10 ounces frozen cherries, thawed, juice reserved, cut into approximate ½-inch pieces
- ⅓ cup (2⅓ ounces) sugar
- ⅛ teaspoon table salt
- 2 tablespoons lemon juice
- 4 teaspoons cornstarch
- ⅛ teaspoon almond extract

**1.** Combine cherries and reserved juice, sugar, and salt in medium saucepan. Using potato masher, crush one-third of cherries. Cook over medium heat, stirring occasionally, until sugar is dissolved, about 5 minutes.

**2.** Stir lemon juice and cornstarch in small bowl until well combined. Add mixture to saucepan and cook, stirring constantly, until mixture comes to simmer and juice thickens, 30 to 60 seconds. Transfer to bowl and refrigerate until fully cooled, about 1½ hours. Stir in almond extract.

### Peach Hand Pie Filling

Substitute 10 ounces frozen peaches for frozen cherries or use 2 cups fresh peaches, nectarines, plums, or apricots for the frozen peaches; replace almond extract with ¼ teaspoon lemon zest.

### Pineapple Hand Pie Filling

Substitute 10 ounces frozen pineapple for frozen cherries or use 2 cups of fresh pineapple. Use lime juice instead of lemon juice and replace almond extract with ¼ teaspoon ground cinnamon.

## Pumpkin Pie

**SERVES** 8

**WHY THIS RECIPE WORKS** We wanted to create a pumpkin pie recipe destined to be a new classic: velvety smooth, packed with pumpkin flavor, and redolent of just enough fragrant spices. To maximize the flavor of canned pumpkin, we concentrated its liquid by cooking the pumpkin with sugar and spices, then whisked in heavy cream, milk, and eggs. For a sweet but also complex pie, we added canned candied yams to the filling. To keep the custard from curdling, we started the pie at a high temperature for 10 minutes, followed by a reduced temperature for the remainder of the baking time. If candied yams are unavailable, regular canned yams can be substituted. When the pie is properly baked, the center 2 inches of the pie should look firm but jiggle slightly. The pie finishes cooking with residual heat; to ensure that the filling sets, cool it at room temperature and not in the refrigerator. The crust and filling must both be warm when the filling is added. Serve with lightly sweetened whipped cream.

- 1 recipe single-crust pie dough (pages 944 and 945), fitted into a 9-inch pie plate and chilled
- 1 cup heavy cream
- 1 cup whole milk
- 3 large whole eggs plus 2 large egg yolks
- 1 teaspoon vanilla extract
- 1 (15-ounce) can pumpkin puree
- 1 cup candied yams, drained
- ¾ cup (5¼ ounces) sugar
- ¼ cup maple syrup
- 2 teaspoons grated or minced fresh ginger
- 1 teaspoon table salt
- ½ teaspoon ground cinnamon
- ¼ teaspoon ground nutmeg

**1.** Adjust an oven rack to the middle position and heat the oven to 375 degrees. Line the chilled pie shell with a double layer of foil and fill with pie weights.

**2.** Bake until the pie dough looks dry and is light in color, 25 to 30 minutes. Remove the weights and foil and continue to bake the crust until deep golden brown, 10 to 12 minutes longer. Transfer the pie plate to a wire rack. (The crust must still be warm when the filling is added.)

**3.** While the pie shell is baking, whisk the cream, milk, whole eggs, egg yolks, and vanilla together in a medium bowl. Bring the pumpkin puree, yams, sugar, maple syrup, ginger, salt, cinnamon, and nutmeg to a simmer in a large saucepan over medium heat and cook, stirring constantly and mashing the yams against the sides of the pot, until thick and shiny, 15 to 20 minutes.

**4.** Remove the pan from the heat and whisk in the cream mixture until fully incorporated. Strain the mixture through a fine-mesh strainer set over a medium bowl, using the back of a ladle or spatula to press the solids through the strainer. Whisk the mixture, then transfer to the warm prebaked pie crust.

**5.** Bake the pie on a rimmed baking sheet for 10 minutes. Reduce the oven temperature to 300 degrees and continue to bake until the edges of the pie are set and the center registers 175 degrees on an instant-read thermometer, 25 to 45 minutes longer. Cool the pie on a wire rack to room temperature, 2 to 3 hours, before serving.

## Perfect Pecan Pie

SERVES 8

**WHY THIS RECIPE WORKS** Pecan pies can be overwhelmingly sweet, with no real pecan flavor not to mention curdled and separated. Plus, the weepy filling makes the bottom crust soggy. We wanted to create a recipe for a not-too-sweet pie with a smooth-textured filling and a properly baked bottom crust. We tackled this pie's problems by using brown sugar and reducing the amount, which helped bring out the pecan flavor. We also partially baked the crust, which kept it crisp. We found that it's important to add the hot filling to a warm pie crust as this helps keep the crust from getting soggy. In addition, we discovered that simulating a double boiler when you're melting the butter and making the filling is an easy way to maintain gentle heat, which helps ensure that the filling doesn't curdle. To serve the pie warm, cool it thoroughly so that it sets completely, then warm it in a 250-degree oven for about 15 minutes and slice. Serve with vanilla ice cream or lightly sweetened whipped cream.

- 1 recipe Foolproof All-Butter Dough for Single-Crust Pie (page 944)
- 6 tablespoons unsalted butter, cut into 1-inch pieces
- 1 cup packed (7 ounces) dark brown sugar
- ½ teaspoon table salt
- 3 large eggs
- ¾ cup light corn syrup
- 1 tablespoon vanilla extract
- 2 cups whole pecans (8 ounces), toasted and chopped into small pieces

**1.** Roll dough into 12-inch circle on well-floured counter. Roll dough loosely around rolling pin and unroll it onto 9-inch pie plate, leaving at least 1-inch overhang around edge. Ease dough into plate by gently lifting edge of dough with your hand while pressing into plate bottom with your other hand. Trim overhang to ½ inch beyond lip of plate. Tuck overhang under itself; folded edge should be flush with edge of plate. Crimp dough evenly around edge of plate using your fingers. Refrigerate dough-lined plate until dough is firm, about 30 minutes. Adjust oven racks to middle and lower-middle positions and heat oven to 375 degrees.

**2.** Line chilled pie shell with double layer of aluminum foil and fill with pie weights. Bake on upper rack until pie dough looks dry and is light in color, 25 to 30 minutes. Transfer pie plate to wire rack and remove weights and foil. Reduce oven temperature to 275 degrees. (Crust must still be warm when filling is added.)

**3.** Melt butter in heatproof bowl set in skillet of water maintained at just below simmer. Remove bowl from skillet and stir in sugar and salt until butter is absorbed. Whisk in eggs, then corn syrup and vanilla until smooth. Return bowl to hot water and stir until mixture is shiny and hot to touch and registers 130 degrees. Off heat, stir in pecans.

**4.** Pour pecan mixture into warm pie crust. Bake pie on lower rack until filling looks set but yields like Jell-O when gently pressed with back of spoon, 50 minutes to 1 hour. Let pie cool on wire rack until filling has firmed up, at least 4 hours; serve at room temperature or slightly warm.

### CRIMPING A SINGLE-CRUST PIE DOUGH

For fluted edge, use your index finger and your other index finger and thumb to create fluted ridges perpendicular to edge of pie plate.

## Ultimate Lemon Meringue Pie

**SERVES 8**

**WHY THIS RECIPE WORKS** Most everybody loves lemon meringue pie—at least the bottom half of it. On any given day the meringue can shrink, bead, puddle, deflate, burn, sweat, break down, or turn rubbery. We wanted a pie with a crisp, flaky crust and a rich filling that would balance the airy meringue, with clear lemon flavor. The filling should be soft but not runny; firm enough to cut but not stiff and gelatinous. Most important, we wanted a meringue that didn't break down and puddle on the bottom or "bead" on top. The puddling underneath the meringue is from undercooking, while the beading on top of the pie is from overcooking. We discovered that if the filling is piping hot when the meringue is applied, the underside of the meringue will not undercook; if the oven temperature is relatively low, the top of the meringue won't overcook. Baking the pie in a relatively cool oven also produced the best-looking, most evenly baked meringue. To further stabilize the meringue and keep it from weeping (even on hot, humid days), we beat in a small amount of cornstarch. Make the pie crust, let it cool, and then begin work on the filling. As soon as the filling is made, cover it with plastic wrap to keep it hot and then start working on the meringue topping. You want to add hot filling to the pie crust, apply the meringue topping, and then quickly get the pie into the oven.

- 1 recipe Foolproof All-Butter Dough for Single-Crust Pie (page 944)

**FILLING**

- 1½ cups water
- 1 cup (7 ounces) sugar
- ¼ cup (1 ounce) cornstarch
- ⅛ teaspoon table salt
- 6 large egg yolks
- 1 tablespoon grated lemon zest plus ½ cup juice (3 lemons)
- 2 tablespoons unsalted butter, cut into 2 pieces

**MERINGUE**

- ⅓ cup water
- 1 tablespoon cornstarch
- 4 large egg whites
- ½ teaspoon vanilla extract
- ¼ teaspoon cream of tartar
- ½ cup (3½ ounces) sugar

**1.** Roll dough into 12-inch circle on well-floured counter. Roll dough loosely around rolling pin and unroll it onto 9-inch pie plate, leaving at least 1-inch overhang around edge. Ease dough into plate by gently lifting edge of dough with your hand while pressing into plate bottom with your other hand. Trim overhang to ½ inch beyond lip of plate. Tuck overhang under itself; folded edge should be flush with edge of plate. Crimp dough evenly around edge of plate using your fingers. Refrigerate dough-lined plate until dough is firm, about 30 minutes. Adjust oven rack to middle position and heat oven to 375 degrees.

**2.** Line chilled pie shell with double layer of aluminum foil and fill with pie weights. Bake until pie dough looks dry and is light in color, 25 to 30 minutes. Remove weights and foil and continue to bake crust until deep golden brown, 10 to 12 minutes longer. Let crust cool completely. Reduce oven temperature to 325 degrees.

**3. FOR THE FILLING:** Bring water, sugar, cornstarch, and salt to simmer in large saucepan over medium heat, whisking constantly. When mixture starts to turn translucent, whisk in egg yolks, two at a time. Whisk in lemon zest and juice and butter. Return mixture to brief simmer, then remove pan from heat. Lay sheet of plastic wrap directly on surface of filling to keep warm and prevent skin from forming.

**4. FOR THE MERINGUE:** Bring water and cornstarch to simmer in small saucepan and cook, whisking occasionally, until thickened and translucent, 1 to 2 minutes. Set aside off heat to cool slightly.

**5.** Using stand mixer fitted with whisk attachment, whip egg whites, vanilla, and cream of tartar on medium-low speed until foamy, about 1 minute. Increase speed to medium-high and beat in sugar, 1 tablespoon at a time, until incorporated and mixture forms soft, billowy mounds. Add cornstarch mixture, 1 tablespoon at a time, and continue to beat to glossy, stiff peaks, 2 to 3 minutes.

**6.** Meanwhile, remove plastic wrap from filling and return to very low heat during last minute or so of beating meringue (to ensure filling is hot).

**7.** Pour warm filling into pie crust. Using rubber spatula, immediately distribute meringue evenly around edge and then center of pie, attaching meringue to pie crust to prevent shrinking. Use back of spoon to create attractive swirls and peaks in meringue. Bake until meringue is golden brown, about 20 minutes. Let pie cool on wire rack until filling has set, about 2 hours. Serve.

## Lemon Chiffon Pie

SERVES 8 to 10

**WHY THIS RECIPE WORKS** We love the elegant simplicity of lemon chiffon pie but found the gelatin used in most recipes difficult to work with. We used a combination of cornstarch and gelatin to get a creamy pie and add a burst of lemon flavor by tucking a layer of lemon curd beneath the chiffon. Our graham cracker crust added just a hint of flavor and provided a crisp contrast to the soft and fluffy filling. Before cooking the curd mixture, be sure to whisk thoroughly so that no clumps of cornstarch or streaks of egg white remain. Pasteurized egg whites can be substituted for the 3 raw egg whites. Serve with lightly sweetened whipped cream.

CRUST

- 9 whole graham crackers
- 3 tablespoons sugar
- ⅛ teaspoon table salt
- 5 tablespoons unsalted butter, melted

FILLING

- 1 teaspoon unflavored gelatin
- 4 tablespoons water
- 5 large eggs (2 whole, 3 separated)
- 1¼ cups (8¾ ounces) sugar
- 1 tablespoon cornstarch
- ⅛ teaspoon table salt
- 1 tablespoon grated lemon zest plus ¾ cup juice (4 lemons)
- ¼ cup heavy cream
- 4 ounces cream cheese, cut into ½-inch pieces, softened

**1. FOR THE CRUST:** Adjust oven rack to lower-middle position and heat oven to 325 degrees. Process graham crackers in food processor until finely ground, about 30 seconds (you should have about 1¼ cups crumbs). Add sugar and salt and pulse to combine. Add melted butter and pulse until mixture resembles wet sand.

**2.** Transfer crumbs to 9-inch pie plate. Press crumbs evenly into bottom and up sides of plate. Bake until crust is lightly browned, 15 to 18 minutes. Allow crust to cool completely.

**3.** For the Filling: Sprinkle ½ teaspoon gelatin over 2 tablespoons water in small bowl and let sit until gelatin softens, about 5 minutes. Repeat with second small bowl, remaining ½ teaspoon gelatin, and remaining 2 tablespoons water.

**4.** Whisk 2 eggs and 3 yolks together in medium saucepan until thoroughly combined. Whisk in 1 cup sugar, cornstarch, and salt until well combined. Whisk in lemon zest and juice and heavy cream. Cook over medium-low heat, stirring constantly, until thickened and slightly translucent, 4 to 5 minutes (mixture should register 170 degrees). Stir in 1 water-gelatin mixture until dissolved. Remove pan from heat and let stand for 2 minutes.

**5.** Remove 1¼ cups curd from pan and pour through fine-mesh strainer set in bowl. Transfer strained curd to prepared pie shell (do not wash out strainer or bowl). Place filled pie shell in freezer. Add remaining water-gelatin mixture and cream cheese to remaining curd in pan and whisk to combine. (If cream cheese does not melt, briefly return pan to low heat.) Pour through strainer into now-empty bowl.

**6.** Using stand mixer, whip 3 egg whites on medium-low speed until foamy, about 2 minutes. Increase speed to medium-high and slowly add remaining ¼ cup sugar. Continue whipping until whites are stiff and glossy, about 4 minutes. Add curd–cream cheese mixture and whip on medium speed until few streaks remain, about 30 seconds. Remove bowl from mixer and, using spatula, scrape sides of bowl and stir mixture until no streaks remain. Remove pie shell from freezer and carefully pour chiffon over curd, allowing chiffon to mound slightly in center. Refrigerate for at least 4 hours or up to 2 days before serving.

## Key Lime Pie

SERVES 8

**WHY THIS RECIPE WORKS** We wanted to serve classic key lime pie with a fresh flavor and silky filling. Traditional key lime pie is usually not baked; instead, the combination of egg yolks, lime juice, and sweetened condensed milk firms up when chilled because the juice's acidity causes the proteins in the eggs and milk to bind. Although we suspected that the sweetened condensed milk was guilty of giving key lime pies their "off" flavor, we found that the real culprit was the lime juice—bottled, reconstituted lime juice, that is. When we substituted the juice and zest from fresh limes, the pie became a very different experience: pungent and refreshing, cool and yet creamy. We also discovered that while the pie filling will set without baking (most recipes call only for mixing and then chilling), it set more nicely after being baked for only 15 minutes. We tried other, more dramatic departures from the "classic" recipe—folding in egg whites, substituting heavy cream for condensed milk—but they didn't work. Just our two seemingly minor adjustments to the recipe made all the difference. We found that tasters could not tell the difference between pies made with regular supermarket limes (called Persian limes) and true key limes. Since Persian limes are easier to find and juice, we recommend them. You need to make the filling first, then prepare the crust.

PIE

- 4 large egg yolks
- 4 teaspoons grated lime zest plus ½ cup juice (4 limes)
- 1 (14-ounce) can sweetened condensed milk
- 1 recipe Graham Cracker Crust (page 946)

TOPPING (OPTIONAL)

- 1 cup heavy cream, chilled
- ¼ cup (1 ounce) confectioners' sugar

**1. FOR THE PIE:** Whisk egg yolks and lime zest in medium bowl until mixture has light green tint, about 2 minutes. Whisk in condensed milk until smooth, then whisk in lime juice. Cover mixture and set aside at room temperature until thickened, about 30 minutes.

**2.** Meanwhile, prepare and bake crust. Transfer pie plate to wire rack and leave oven at 325 degrees. (Crust must still be warm when filling is added.)

**3.** Pour thickened filling into warm pie crust. Bake pie until center is firm but jiggles slightly when shaken, 15 to 20 minutes. Let pie cool slightly on wire rack, about 1 hour, then cover loosely with plastic wrap and refrigerate until filling is chilled and set, about 3 hours.

**4. FOR THE TOPPING, IF USING:** Before serving, using stand mixer fitted with whisk attachment, whip cream and sugar on medium-low speed until foamy, about 1 minute. Increase speed to high and whip until soft peaks form, 1 to 3 minutes. Spread whipped cream attractively over top of pie and serve.

## Classic Coconut Cream Pie

SERVES 8

**WHY THIS RECIPE WORKS** Most recipes for this diner dessert are nothing more than a redecorated vanilla cream pie. A handful of coconut shreds stirred into the filling or sprinkled on the whipped cream might be enough to give it a new name, but certainly not enough to give it flavor. We wanted a coconut cream pie with the elusive flavor of tropical coconut rather than a thinly disguised vanilla custard. We found that using not-too-sweet graham crackers made a crust with a delicate, cookie-like texture that didn't overshadow the coconut filling. For the filling, we started with a basic custard, using a combination of unsweetened coconut milk and whole milk. For more coconut flavor, we stirred in unsweetened shredded coconut and cooked it so the shreds softened slightly in the hot milk. Lastly, we topped the pie with simple sweetened whipped cream and dusted it with crunchy shreds of toasted coconut. Do not use low-fat coconut milk here because it does not have enough flavor. Also, don't confuse coconut milk with cream of coconut. The filling should be warm—neither piping hot nor room temperature—when poured into the cooled pie crust. To toast the coconut, place it in a small skillet over medium heat and cook, stirring frequently, for 3 to 5 minutes. It burns quite easily, so keep a close eye on it.

**FILLING**

- 1 (14-ounce) can coconut milk
- 1 cup whole milk
- ½ cup (1¼ ounces) unsweetened shredded coconut
- ⅔ cup (4⅔ ounces) sugar
- ¼ teaspoon table salt
- 5 large egg yolks
- ¼ cup (1 ounce) cornstarch
- 2 tablespoons unsalted butter, cut into 2 pieces
- 1½ teaspoons vanilla extract

- 1 recipe Graham Cracker Crust (page 946), baked and cooled

**TOPPING**

- 1½ cups heavy cream, chilled
- 1½ tablespoons sugar
- 1½ teaspoons dark rum (optional)
- ½ teaspoon vanilla extract
- 1 tablespoon unsweetened shredded coconut, toasted

**1. FOR THE FILLING:** Bring the coconut milk, whole milk, shredded coconut, ⅓ cup of the sugar, and the salt to a simmer in a medium saucepan over medium-high heat, stirring occasionally.

**2.** As the milk mixture begins to simmer, whisk the remaining ⅓ cup sugar, the egg yolks, and cornstarch together in a separate bowl. Slowly whisk 1 cup of the simmering coconut milk mixture into the yolk mixture to temper, then slowly whisk the tempered yolks back into the simmering saucepan. Reduce the heat to medium and cook, whisking vigorously, until the mixture is thickened and a few bubbles burst on the surface, about 30 seconds.

**3.** Off the heat, whisk in the butter and vanilla. Cool the mixture until just warm, stirring often, about 5 minutes.

**4.** Pour the warm filling into the baked and cooled pie crust. Lay a sheet of plastic wrap directly on the surface of the filling and refrigerate the pie until the filling is chilled and set, about 4 hours.

**5. FOR THE TOPPING:** Before serving, whip the cream, sugar, rum (if using), and vanilla together with an electric mixer on medium-low speed until frothy, about 1 minute. Increase the mixer speed to high and continue to whip until the cream forms soft peaks, 1 to 3 minutes. Spread the whipped cream attractively over the top of the pie and sprinkle with the toasted coconut.

## Chocolate Cream Pie with Cookie Crust

SERVES 8

**WHY THIS RECIPE WORKS** Chocolate cream pies can look superb but are often gummy, gluey, overly sweet, and impossible to slice. We wanted a voluptuously creamy pie, with a well-balanced chocolate flavor. After testing every type of cookie on the market, we hit on pulverized Oreos and a bit of melted butter for the best crust. We found that the secret to perfect chocolate cream pie filling was to combine two different types of chocolate for a deeper, more complex flavor. Bittersweet or semisweet chocolate provided the main thrust of flavor, and intensely flavored unsweetened chocolate lent depth. One ounce of unsweetened chocolate may not seem like much, but it gives this pie great flavor. For the best chocolate flavor and texture, we recommend Ghirardelli 60% Cacao bittersweet chocolate and Baker's unsweetened chocolate. Other brands of chocolate sandwich cookies may be substituted for the Oreos, but avoid any "double-filled" cookies because the proportion of cookie to filling won't be correct. Do not combine the egg yolks and sugar in advance of making the filling.

**CRUST**

- 16 Oreo cookies, broken into rough pieces
- 4 tablespoons (½ stick) unsalted butter, melted and cooled

**FILLING**

- 2½ cups half-and-half
- ⅓ cup (2⅓ ounces) sugar
- Pinch table salt
- 6 large egg yolks
- 2 tablespoons cornstarch
- 6 tablespoons (¾ stick) unsalted butter, cut into 6 pieces
- 6 ounces semisweet or bittersweet chocolate, chopped fine
- 1 ounce unsweetened chocolate, chopped fine
- 1 teaspoon vanilla extract

**TOPPING**

- 1½ cups heavy cream, chilled
- 2 tablespoons sugar
- ½ teaspoon vanilla extract

**1. FOR THE CRUST:** Adjust an oven rack to the middle position and heat the oven to 350 degrees. Pulse the cookies in a food processor until coarsely ground, about 15 pulses, then continue to process to fine, even crumbs, about 15 seconds. Sprinkle the butter over the crumbs and pulse to incorporate.

**2.** Sprinkle the mixture into a 9-inch pie plate. Use the bottom of a measuring cup to press the crumbs into an even layer on the bottom and sides of the pie plate. Bake until the crust is fragrant and looks set, 10 to 15 minutes. Transfer the crust to a wire rack and cool completely.

**3.** For the filling: Bring the half-and-half, 3 tablespoons of the sugar, and the salt to a simmer in a medium saucepan over medium-high heat, stirring occasionally.

**4.** As the half-and-half mixture begins to simmer, whisk the egg yolks, cornstarch, and remaining sugar together in a medium bowl until smooth. Slowly whisk about 1 cup of the simmering half-and-half mixture into the yolk mixture to temper, then slowly whisk the tempered yolks back into the simmering saucepan. Reduce the heat to medium and cook, whisking vigorously, until the mixture is thickened and a few bubbles burst on the surface, about 30 seconds.

**5.** Off the heat, whisk in the butter and chocolates until completely smooth and melted. Stir in the vanilla. Pour the warm filling into the baked and cooled pie crust. Lay a sheet of plastic wrap directly on the surface of the filling and refrigerate the pie until the filling is chilled and set, about 4 hours.

**6. FOR THE TOPPING:** Before serving, whip the cream, sugar, and vanilla together with an electric mixer on medium-low speed until frothy, about 1 minute. Increase the mixer speed to high and continue to whip until the cream forms soft peaks, 1 to 3 minutes. Spread the whipped cream attractively over the top of the pie.

## Chocolate Cream Pie

SERVES 8 to 10

**WHY THIS RECIPE WORKS** There's no better match for the tender, flaky pie crust made from our moist all-butter pie dough than a luxurious chocolate cream filling. For a deeply chocolaty mixture that wasn't too heavy, we made a milk-based cocoa pudding and then whisked in bittersweet chocolate, along with vanilla for extra depth. A few tablespoons of butter helped the filling set up with a silky consistency once it was poured into the prebaked pie shell and refrigerated. Finally, we finished off the pie with a complementary topping of lightly sweetened whipped cream. We developed this recipe with whole milk, but you can use 2 percent low-fat milk, if desired. Avoid using 1 percent low-fat or skim milk, as the filling will be too thin. Ghirardelli 60% Cacao Bittersweet Chocolate Premium Baking Bar is our favorite dark chocolate.

- 1 recipe Foolproof All-Butter Dough for Single-Crust Pie (page 944)

**FILLING**

- ⅓ cup (2⅓ ounces) sugar
- ¼ cup (1-ounce) cornstarch
- 2 tablespoons unsweetened cocoa powder
- ¼ teaspoon table salt
- 3 cups whole or 2 percent low-fat milk
- 6 ounces bittersweet chocolate, chopped fine
- 3 tablespoons unsalted butter, cut into 3 pieces
- 2 teaspoons vanilla extract

**TOPPING**

1 cup heavy cream
1 tablespoon confectioners' sugar

**1.** Roll dough into 12-inch circle on well-floured counter. Roll dough loosely around rolling pin and unroll it onto 9-inch pie plate, leaving at least 1-inch overhang around edge. Ease dough into plate by gently lifting edge of dough with your hand while pressing into plate bottom with your other hand.

**2.** Trim overhang to ½ inch beyond lip of plate. Tuck overhang under itself; folded edge should be flush with edge of plate. Crimp dough evenly around edge of plate using your fingers. Refrigerate dough-lined plate until firm, about 30 minutes. Adjust oven rack to middle position and heat oven to 350 degrees.

**3.** Line chilled pie shell with aluminum foil, covering edges to prevent burning, and fill with pie weights. Bake until edges are set and just beginning to turn golden, 15 to 20 minutes. Remove foil and weights, rotate plate, and continue to bake until golden brown and crisp, 15 to 20 minutes longer. If crust begins to puff, pierce gently with tip of paring knife. Let crust cool completely in plate on wire rack, about 30 minutes.

**4. FOR THE FILLING:** Whisk sugar, cornstarch, cocoa, and salt together in large saucepan. Whisk in milk until incorporated, making sure to scrape corners of saucepan. Place saucepan over medium heat; cook, whisking constantly, until mixture is thickened and bubbling over entire surface, 8 to 10 minutes. Cook 30 seconds longer; remove from heat. Add chocolate and butter and whisk until melted and fully incorporated. Whisk in vanilla. Pour filling into cooled pie crust. Press lightly greased parchment paper against surface of filling and let cool completely, about 1 hour. Refrigerate until filling is firmly set, at least 2½ hours or up to 24 hours.

**5. FOR THE TOPPING:** Using stand mixer fitted with whisk attachment, whip cream and sugar on medium-low speed until foamy, about 1 minute. Increase speed to high and whip until stiff peaks form, 1 to 2 minutes. Spread whipped cream evenly over chilled pie and serve.

## Chocolate Cream Pie in a Jar

**SERVES** 12 **SEASON 26**

**WHY THIS RECIPE WORKS** While it can be hard to please everyone when it's time for dessert, we're betting that our chocolate cream pies in jars will get you pretty close. We made a rich chocolate pudding with lots of semisweet (and a little bit of unsweetened) chocolate for deep, but not bitter, chocolate flavor that would please both kids and adults alike. We layered our chocolate pudding over crumbled Oreos (for more chocolate flavor and an irresistible crunchy-creamy texture) and topped it with lightly sweetened whipped cream for mini desserts that tasted as good—and as chocolaty—as they looked. We'd call that having your pie and eating it, too. You can either use store-bought whipped cream or whip 1 cup of chilled heavy cream, 1 tablespoon of sugar, 1 teaspoon of vanilla extract, and a pinch of table salt in a stand mixer on medium speed for 1 to 3 minutes, until soft peaks form. You will need twelve 4-ounce wide-mouth Mason jars for this recipe; for larger servings, use eight 6-ounce ramekins.

2½ cups half-and-half
⅓ cup (2⅓ ounces) sugar, divided
Pinch table salt
6 large egg yolks
2 tablespoons cornstarch
6 tablespoons unsalted butter, cut into 6 pieces
6 ounces semisweet chocolate, chopped fine
1 ounce unsweetened chocolate, chopped fine
1 teaspoon vanilla extract
10 Oreo cookies, broken into coarse crumbs, divided
2 cups whipped cream

**1.** Bring half-and-half, 3 tablespoons sugar, and salt to simmer in medium saucepan over medium heat, stirring occasionally. Whisk egg yolks, cornstarch, and remaining sugar in medium bowl until smooth. Slowly whisk 1 cup warm half-and-half mixture into yolk mixture to temper, then slowly whisk tempered yolk mixture into remaining half-and-half mixture in saucepan.

**2.** Cook half-and-half mixture over medium heat, whisking constantly, until mixture is thickened and registers 180 degrees, about 30 seconds. Off heat, whisk in butter, semisweet chocolate, unsweetened chocolate, and vanilla until smooth. Strain pudding through fine-mesh strainer into clean bowl. Spray piece of parchment paper with vegetable oil spray and press directly against surface of pudding. Refrigerate until chilled, at least 1 hour or up to 3 days.

**3.** Just before serving, add 1 tablespoon cookie crumbs to each of twelve 4-ounce wide-mouth Mason jars followed by approximately ½ cup pudding. Top with whipped cream and sprinkle with remaining cookie crumbs. Serve.

## Chocolate-Cherry Pie Pops

**SERVES** 8

**WHY THIS RECIPE WORKS** Pie pops—miniature pies on sticks—are festive, handheld desserts perfect for parties or as a gift for pie lovers, young or old. With their concentrated flavor, fruit preserves made an ideal filling for these two-bite treats. Tasters loved a cherry-chocolate combination, but loosely set cherry preserves leaked out of the pies during baking. Straining the preserves and using only the solids for the filling proved a successful fix. But we didn't let that glossy-pink liquid go to waste; we combined it with confectioners' sugar to create a glaze for drizzling. We found 3-inch circles of dough gave us the best filling-to-crust ratio. Quickly chilling the partially assembled pies set the filling enough to prevent it from squeezing out the sides when we pressed on the top crust. We used Bonne Maman cherry preserves, but you can use any brand. You can find lollipop and ice pop sticks at most craft stores. This recipe can be easily doubled.

- 1 cup cherry preserves
- 1 recipe single-crust pie dough (pages 944–945)
- 2 tablespoons plus 2 teaspoons chocolate chips
- 8 (4- to 6-inch) lollipop or ice pop sticks
- 1 large egg, lightly beaten with 1 tablespoon water
- ½ cup (2 ounces) confectioners' sugar

**1.** Microwave cherry preserves in bowl until fluid, 45 to 60 seconds, stirring halfway through microwaving. Strain preserves through fine-mesh strainer set over bowl, pressing on solids to extract as much liquid as possible; reserve solids (you should have about ⅓ cup) and liquid separately. Set aside to cool.

**2.** Roll dough into 15-inch circle on floured counter. Using 3-inch round biscuit or cookie cutter, cut 16 rounds from dough circle and transfer to parchment paper–lined rimmed baking sheet. Reserve dough scraps for another use. Cover rounds loosely with plastic wrap and refrigerate until firm but still pliable, about 10 minutes.

**3.** Line second rimmed baking sheet with parchment. Transfer 8 dough rounds to second prepared sheet, spaced evenly apart. Working with 1 dough round at a time, lay lollipop stick flat on top of dough with 1 end in center of dough round. Press stick firmly into dough. Mound 2 teaspoons cherry solids and 1 teaspoon chocolate chips in center of each dough round on top of stick. Transfer sheet with filled rounds to freezer and chill for 10 minutes.

**4.** Adjust oven rack to upper-middle position and heat oven to 375 degrees. Brush edges of filled dough rounds with egg wash, then top with remaining chilled dough rounds, pressing edges firmly to seal. Crimp edges of each pie with fork. Cut three ½-inch slits in top of each pie and brush with remaining egg wash. Bake until crusts are golden brown, 22 to 26 minutes, rotating sheet halfway through baking. Transfer sheet to wire rack and let pies cool for 10 minutes. Using spatula, carefully transfer pies to wire rack and let cool completely, about 1 hour.

**FORMING PIE POPS**

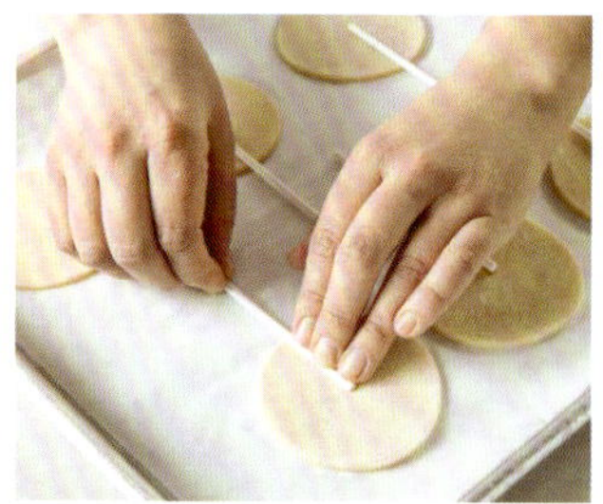

**1.** Working with 1 dough round at a time, lay lollipop stick flat on top of dough with one end in center. Press stick firmly into dough.

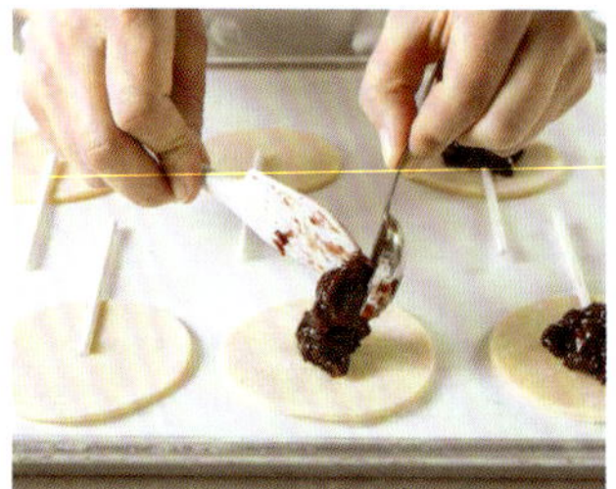

**2.** Mound 1 tablespoon filling in center of each dough round on top of stick. Transfer sheet with filled rounds to freezer and chill for 10 minutes.

**3.** Brush edges of filled dough rounds with egg wash. Top with remaining chilled dough rounds, pressing edges firmly to seal.

**4.** Crimp edges of each pie with fork. Cut three ½-inch slits in top of each pie and brush with remaining egg wash.

**5.** Whisk 2 tablespoons reserved cherry preserve liquid and confectioners' sugar together in small bowl until smooth. Let glaze sit until slightly thickened but still able to be drizzled, about 10 minutes. Adjust thickness with up to 1 teaspoon extra cherry liquid as needed. Drizzle pies with glaze and let sit for 10 minutes. Serve.

## Classic Lemon Tart

**SERVES** 8 to 10

**WHY THIS RECIPE WORKS** Despite its apparent simplicity, there is much that can go wrong with a lemon tart. It can slip over the edge of sweet into cloying; its tartness can grab at your throat; it can be gluey or eggy or, even worse, metallic-tasting. Its crust can be too hard, too soft, too thick, or too sweet. We wanted a proper tart, one in which the filling is baked with the shell. For us, that meant only one thing: lemon curd. For just enough sugar to offset the acid in the lemons,

we used 3 parts sugar to 2 parts lemon juice, plus a ¼ cup of lemon zest. To achieve a curd that was creamy and dense with a vibrant lemony yellow color, we used a combination of whole eggs and egg yolks. We cooked the curd over direct heat, then whisked in cold butter. And for a smooth texture, we strained the curd and stirred in heavy cream just before baking. Once the lemon curd ingredients have been combined, cook the curd immediately; otherwise it will have a grainy finished texture. Dust with confectioners' sugar before serving, or serve with lightly whipped cream.

- 1 recipe Classic Tart Dough (page 946)
- Unbleached all-purpose flour, for the work surface
- 7 large egg yolks plus 2 large whole eggs
- 1 cup (7 ounces) sugar
- ¼ cup grated zest plus ⅔ cup juice from 4 to 5 lemons
- Pinch table salt
- 4 tablespoons (½ stick) unsalted butter, cut into 4 pieces
- 3 tablespoons heavy cream

**1.** Roll the dough out to an 11-inch circle on a lightly floured work surface and fit it into a 9-inch tart pan with a removable bottom. Set the tart pan on a large plate and freeze the tart shell for 30 minutes.

**2.** Adjust an oven rack to the middle position and heat the oven to 375 degrees. Set the tart pan on a large baking sheet. Press a double layer of foil into the frozen tart shell and over the edges of the pan and fill with pie weights. Bake until the tart shell is golden brown and set, about 30 minutes, rotating the baking sheet halfway through.

**3.** Carefully remove the weights and foil and continue to bake the tart shell until it is fully baked and golden, 5 to 10 minutes longer. Transfer the tart crust with the baking sheet to a wire rack and cool the tart shell slightly while making the filling.

**4.** Whisk the egg yolks and whole eggs together in a medium saucepan. Whisk in the sugar until combined, then whisk in the lemon zest and juice and salt. Add the butter and cook over medium-low heat, stirring constantly, until the mixture thickens slightly and registers 170 degrees on an instant-read thermometer, about 5 minutes. Immediately pour the mixture through a fine-mesh strainer into a bowl and stir in the cream.

**5.** Pour the lemon filling into the warm tart shell. Bake the tart on the baking sheet until the filling is shiny and opaque and the center jiggles slightly when shaken, 10 to 15 minutes. Let the tart cool completely on the baking sheet, about 1½ hours. To serve, remove the outer metal ring of the tart pan, slide a thin metal spatula between the tart and the tart pan bottom, and carefully slide the tart onto a serving platter or cutting board.

## Lemon–Olive Oil Tart

SERVES 8

**WHY THIS RECIPE WORKS** A unique ingredient is the key to this simple, elegant, and brightly flavored tart. Most lemon tarts feature butter in the crust and the filling, but here we used extra-virgin olive oil. It made the crust a snap: We just mixed the flour, sugar, and salt with the oil and a little water until a soft dough formed; crumbled it into the tart pan; pressed it into the sides and bottom; and baked it right away—no rolling or chilling required. The filling got plenty of structure from the protein in the eggs, so using olive oil didn't compromise its firmness or sliceability. The olive oil did, however, allow the lemons' acidity to come to the fore in a way that butter doesn't, so we could use a bit less juice and still enjoy plenty of bright lemon flavor. You'll need a 9-inch tart pan with a removable bottom for this recipe. For the best flavor, use a fresh, high-quality extra-virgin olive oil. Make sure that all your metal equipment—saucepan, strainer, and whisk—is nonreactive, or the filling may have a metallic flavor.

**CRUST**

- 1½ cups (7½ ounces) all-purpose flour
- 5 tablespoons (2¼ ounces) sugar
- ½ teaspoon table salt
- ½ cup extra-virgin olive oil
- 2 tablespoons water

**FILLING**

- 1 cup (7 ounces) sugar
- 2 tablespoons all-purpose flour
- ¼ teaspoon table salt
- 3 large eggs plus 3 large yolks
- 1 tablespoon grated lemon zest plus ½ cup juice (3 lemons)
- ¼ cup extra-virgin olive oil

**1. FOR THE CRUST:** Adjust oven rack to middle position and heat oven to 350 degrees. Whisk flour, sugar, and salt together in bowl. Add oil and water and stir until uniform dough forms. Using your hands, crumble three-quarters of dough over bottom of 9-inch tart pan with removable bottom. Press dough to even thickness in bottom of pan. Crumble remaining dough and scatter evenly around edge of pan, then press crumbled dough into fluted sides of pan. Press dough to even thickness.

Bake on rimmed baking sheet until crust is deep golden brown and firm to touch, 30 to 35 minutes, rotating sheet halfway through baking. Transfer sheet to wire rack. (Tart shell must still be warm when filling is added.)

**2. FOR THE FILLING:** About 5 minutes before crust is finished baking, whisk sugar, flour, and salt in medium saucepan until combined. Whisk in eggs and yolks until no streaks of egg remain, then whisk in lemon zest and juice. Cook over medium-low heat, whisking constantly and scraping corners of saucepan, until mixture thickens slightly and registers 160 degrees, 5 to 8 minutes.

**3.** Off heat, whisk in oil until incorporated. Strain curd through fine-mesh strainer into bowl. Pour curd into warm tart shell.

**4.** Bake until filling is set and barely jiggles when pan is shaken, 8 to 12 minutes. Let tart cool completely on sheet on wire rack, about 2 hours. Remove outer ring of tart pan, slide thin metal spatula between tart and tart pan bottom, and carefully slide tart onto serving platter or cutting board. Serve. (Leftovers can be wrapped loosely in plastic wrap and refrigerated for up to 3 days.)

## Cranberry Curd Tart with Almond Crust

SERVES 8

**WHY THIS RECIPE WORKS** Our cranberry curd tart showcases cranberries' bold flavor and brilliant color while making use of their ample pectin content. Quickly simmering the cranberry filling softened the berries and released their acids and pectin, and immediately pureeing the berries with egg yolks and cornstarch allowed the berries' heat to cook the eggs and thicken the cornstarch. The combination of almond flour and cornstarch kept our press-in crust both sturdy and gluten-free. Pureeing butter into the cooled filling, straining it, and pouring the mixture over the baked crust prevented the filling from developing a thick, rubbery skin. We whisked up a whipped cream topping stabilized by a small amount of the pectin-rich puree, which meant that the topping could be piped onto the tart hours in advance without breaking or weeping. You'll need a 9-inch tart pan with a removable bottom for this recipe. We strongly recommend weighing the almond flour and cornstarch for the crust. If preferred, you can use a stand mixer or hand mixer to whip the cream in step 4. The tart crust will be firm if you serve the tart on the day that it's made; if you prefer a more tender crust, make the tart through step 3 up to two days ahead.

**FILLING**

- 1 pound (4 cups) fresh or frozen cranberries
- 1¼ cups (8¾ ounces) plus 1 tablespoon sugar, divided
- ½ cup water
- Pinch table salt
- 3 large egg yolks
- 2 teaspoons cornstarch
- 4 tablespoons unsalted butter, cut into 4 pieces and softened

**CRUST**

- 1 cup (4 ounces) almond flour
- ½ cup (2 ounces) cornstarch
- ⅓ cup (2⅓ ounces) sugar
- ½ teaspoon table salt
- 6 tablespoons unsalted butter, melted and cooled
- ¾ teaspoon almond extract

- 1 cup heavy cream

**1. FOR THE FILLING:** Bring cranberries, 1¼ cups sugar, water, and salt to boil in medium saucepan over medium-high heat, stirring occasionally. Adjust heat to maintain very gentle simmer. Cover and cook until all cranberries have burst and started to shrivel, about 10 minutes. While cranberries cook, whisk egg yolks and cornstarch in bowl until smooth. Transfer hot cranberry mixture to food processor. Immediately add yolk mixture and process until smooth (small flecks of cranberry skin will be visible), about 1 minute, scraping down sides of bowl as necessary. Let mixture cool in processor bowl until skin forms and mixture registers 120 to 125 degrees, 45 minutes to 1 hour. While mixture cools, make crust.

**2. FOR THE CRUST:** Adjust oven rack to middle position and heat oven to 350 degrees. Whisk flour, cornstarch, sugar, and salt in bowl until well combined. Add melted butter and almond extract and stir with wooden spoon until uniform dough forms. Crumble two-thirds of mixture over bottom of 9-inch tart pan with removable bottom. Press dough to even thickness in bottom of pan. Crumble remaining dough and scatter evenly around edge of pan. Press crumbled dough into sides of pan. Press edges to even thickness. Place pan on rimmed baking sheet and bake until crust is golden brown, about 20 minutes, rotating pan halfway through baking.

**3.** Add softened butter to cranberry puree and process until fully combined, about 30 seconds. Strain mixture through fine-mesh strainer set over bowl, pressing on solids with rubber spatula to extract puree. Transfer 2 tablespoons puree to medium bowl, then stir in cream and remaining 1 tablespoon sugar. Cover and refrigerate. Transfer remaining puree to crust (it's OK if crust is still warm) and smooth into even layer. Let tart sit at room temperature for at least 4 hours. (Cover tart with large bowl and refrigerate after 4 hours if making ahead.)

**4.** Whisk cream mixture until stiff peaks form, 1 to 3 minutes. Transfer to pastry bag fitted with pastry tip. Pipe decorative border around edge of tart. Transfer any remaining whipped cream to small serving bowl.

**5. TO SERVE:** Remove outer metal ring of tart pan. Slide thin metal spatula between tart and pan bottom to loosen tart. Carefully slide tart onto serving platter. Slice into wedges, wiping knife clean between cuts if necessary, and serve, passing extra whipped cream separately. (Leftovers can be covered with plastic wrap and refrigerated for up to 3 days.)

### PIPING DECORATIVE DESIGNS

**CONFETTI BORDER:** Squeeze pastry bag fitted with ¾- to 1-inch round tip to create 1-inch dots around perimeter (8 to 12 in total). With each dot, stop squeezing and pull bag straight up to create peak. Fill in empty areas with smaller dots.

**ZIGZAG BORDER:** Squeeze pastry bag fitted with ½- to ¾-inch round tip to pipe 1- to 1½-inch-wide, slightly overlapped zigzag pattern around tart perimeter.

**SIMPLE SWIRLS BORDER:** Squeeze pastry bag fitted with ½- to ¾-inch star tip, moving tip in tight circle. When circle is complete, stop piping and pull bag straight up to create swirl. Repeat at regular intervals around tart perimeter.

## Linzertorte

**SERVES** 10 to 12

**WHY THIS RECIPE WORKS** The components of this old-world tart couldn't be easier to prepare. A buttery, nut-enhanced crust comes together easily in the food processor, and you can simply buy the raspberry jam filling. The beautiful and traditional lattice top is easier than most since you cut the strips out on parchment paper and then follow a simple process of layering them on top of the tart in stages (see page 970). You will have extra dough which may come in handy if any of your strips break. If the dough becomes too soft while forming the lattice, refrigerate it for 15 minutes before continuing. You will need an 11-inch tart pan for this recipe. Linzertorte may be served at room temperature the day it is baked, but it's at its best after a night in the refrigerator.

**TART DOUGH**

- 1 large egg
- 1 teaspoon vanilla extract
- 1 cup hazelnuts, toasted and skinned
- ½ cup plus 2 tablespoons (4⅓ ounces) granulated sugar
- ½ cup blanched almonds
- ½ teaspoon table salt
- 1 teaspoon grated lemon zest
- 1½ cups (7½ ounces) all-purpose flour
- ½ teaspoon ground cinnamon
- ⅛ teaspoon ground allspice
- 12 tablespoons unsalted butter, cut into ½-inch pieces and chilled

**FILLING**

- 1¼ cups raspberry preserves
- 1 tablespoon lemon juice

**GLAZE**

- 1 tablespoon heavy cream
- 1½ teaspoons turbinado or demerara sugar (optional)

**1. FOR THE TART DOUGH:** Whisk egg and vanilla together in bowl. Process hazelnuts, sugar, almonds, and salt in food processor until very finely ground, 45 to 60 seconds. Add lemon zest and pulse to combine, about 5 pulses. Add flour, cinnamon, and allspice and pulse to combine, about 5 pulses. Scatter butter over top and pulse until mixture resembles coarse cornmeal, about 15 pulses. With processor running, add egg mixture and continue to process until dough just comes together, about 12 seconds longer.

**2.** Transfer dough to counter and form into cohesive mound. Divide dough in half and form each half into 5-inch disk. (If not using immediately, wrap disks tightly in plastic wrap and refrigerate for up to 2 days. Let chilled dough sit at room temperature until soft and malleable, about 1 hour, before using.)

**3.** Tear 1 disk into walnut-size pieces, then pat pieces into 11-inch tart pan with removable bottom, pressing dough into corners and ¾ inch up sides of pan. Cover dough with plastic and smooth out any bumps using bottom of measuring cup. Set pan on large plate and freeze until firm, about 30 minutes.

**4.** Roll second disk into 12-inch square between 2 large sheets of floured parchment paper. (If dough sticks to parchment, gently loosen and lift sticky area with bench scraper and dust parchment with additional flour.) Slide dough, still between parchment, onto rimmed baking sheet and refrigerate until firm, about 15 minutes. Remove top layer of parchment and trim edges of dough to form perfect square, then cut ten ¾-inch-wide strips, cutting through underlying parchment. Cover with parchment and freeze until dough is fully chilled and firm, about 20 minutes.

### MAKING A LINZERTORTE LATTICE

**1.** Pick up 1 strip of dough by parchment ends, then flip it over onto tart, positioning it near edge of pan. Remove parchment strip and trim ends of dough strip by pressing down on top edge of pan.

**2.** Place 2 more strips parallel to first, spacing them evenly so that one is across center and other is near opposite edge of pan.

**3.** Rotate pan 90 degrees, then place 3 more strips, spacing as with first three.

**4.** Rotate pan 90 degrees again, then place 2 strips across pan, spaced evenly between first three.

**5.** Rotate pan again and complete lattice by placing last 2 strips between second set of three.

**6.** Use small scraps of dough to fill in crust around edges between lattice strips.

**5.** Meanwhile, adjust oven rack to middle position and heat oven to 350 degrees. Set dough-lined tart pan on rimmed baking sheet. Spray 1 side of double layer of aluminum foil with vegetable oil spray. Press foil, greased side down, into frozen tart shell, covering edges to prevent burning, and fill with pie weights. Bake until tart shell is golden brown and set, about 30 minutes, rotating sheet halfway through baking. Remove foil and weights, transfer sheet to wire rack, and let cool completely, about 1 hour.

**6. FOR THE FILLING:** Stir raspberry preserves and lemon juice together in bowl. Spread filling evenly over bottom of tart shell. Pick up 1 strip of dough by parchment ends, then flip it over onto tart, positioning it near edge of pan. Remove parchment strip and trim ends of dough strip by pressing down on top edge of pan; reserve all dough scraps. Place 2 more strips parallel to first, spacing them evenly so that one is across center and other is near opposite edge of pan. Rotate pan 90 degrees, then place 3 more strips, spacing as with first three. Rotate pan 90 degrees again, then place 2 strips across pan, spaced evenly between first three. Rotate pan again and complete lattice by placing last 2 strips between second set of three. Use small scraps of dough to fill in crust around edges between lattice strips. Top of crust should be just below top of pan.

**7.** Gently brush lattice strips with cream and sprinkle with sugar, if using. Bake on sheet until crust is deep golden brown, 40 to 45 minutes. Let tart cool completely on sheet on wire rack, about 2 hours. Remove outer ring of tart pan, slide thin metal spatula between tart and tart pan bottom, and carefully slide tart onto serving platter or cutting board. Serve or refrigerate overnight.

## Fresh Fruit Tart

**SERVES 8**

**WHY THIS RECIPE WORKS** By trading the traditional rolled pastry and pastry cream filling for easier, faster alternatives, we produced a fresh fruit tart that is as appealing to make as it is to eat. Stirring melted butter into the dry ingredients yielded a malleable dough that could be pressed into the pan; for extra flavor, we browned the butter first and added back water that we lost so that there was enough moisture to help the flour form gluten (the protein network that gives the dough structure). A mix of mascarpone, melted white baking chips, and lime juice and zest gave us a quick filling that was lush and creamy but also tangy and firm enough to slice cleanly. Arranging thin-sliced peaches in lines that radiated from the center of the tart to its outer edge created cutting guides between which we artfully arranged a mix of berries. An apricot preserves and lime juice glaze brightened the fruit. This recipe calls for extra berries to account for any bruising. Ripe, unpeeled nectarines can be substituted for the peaches, if desired. Use white baking chips here, not white chocolate bars, which contain cocoa butter and will result in a loose filling. Be sure to use a light hand when dabbing on the glaze as too much force will dislodge the fruit. If the glaze begins to solidify while dabbing, microwave it for 5 to 10 seconds.

CRUST

- 1 cup (6 ounces) all-purpose flour
- ¼ cup (1¾ ounces) sugar
- ⅛ teaspoon table salt
- 10 tablespoons unsalted butter
- 2 tablespoons water

TART

- ⅓ cup (2 ounces) white baking chips
- ¼ cup heavy cream
- 1 teaspoon grated lime zest plus 7 teaspoons juice (2 limes)
- Pinch table salt
- 6 ounces (¾ cup) mascarpone, room temperature
- 2 ripe peaches, peeled
- 20 ounces (4 cups) raspberries, blackberries, and blueberries
- ⅓ cup apricot preserves

**1. FOR THE CRUST:** Adjust oven rack to middle position and heat oven to 350 degrees. Whisk flour, sugar, and salt together in bowl. Melt butter in small saucepan over medium-high heat, swirling pan occasionally, until foaming subsides. Continue to cook, stirring and scraping bottom of pan with heatproof spatula, until milk solids are dark golden brown and butter has nutty aroma, 1 to 3 minutes. Remove pan from heat and add water. When bubbling subsides, transfer butter to bowl with flour mixture, scraping pan with spatula. Stir until mixture is well combined. Transfer dough to 9-inch tart pan with removable bottom and let dough rest until warm to the touch, about 10 minutes.

**2.** Use hands to evenly press and smooth dough over bottom and up side of pan (using two-thirds of dough for bottom crust and remaining third for side). Place tart pan on wire rack set in rimmed baking sheet. Bake until crust is golden brown, 25 to 30 minutes, rotating pan halfway through baking. Let cool completely, about 1 hour. (Cooled crust can be wrapped loosely in plastic wrap and stored at room temperature for up to 24 hours before filling.)

**3. FOR THE TART:** Microwave baking chips, cream, lime zest, and salt in medium bowl, stirring every 10 seconds, until chips are melted, 30 to 60 seconds. Whisk in one-third of mascarpone to cool mixture, then whisk in 6 teaspoons lime juice and remaining mascarpone until smooth. Transfer filling to cooled tart shell and smooth into even layer.

**4.** Place peach stem side down on cutting board. Placing knife just to side of pit, cut down to remove one side of peach. Turn peach 180 degrees and cut off opposite side. Slice off remaining 2 sides. Arrange pieces cut side down on cutting board and slice into ¼-inch thick half-moon shapes. Repeat with second peach. Select the 24 best slices.

**5.** Arrange 8 berries, evenly spaced, around outer edge of tart. Using berries as guide, arrange 8 sets of 3 peach slices in filling, slightly overlapping them with rounded side up, starting at center and ending on right side of each berry at outer edge of tart. Arrange remaining berries in attractive pattern between peach slices, covering as much of filling as possible and keeping fruit in even layer.

**6.** Microwave preserves and remaining 1 teaspoon lime juice in small bowl until fluid, 20 to 30 seconds. Strain mixture through fine-mesh strainer. Using pastry brush, gently dab mixture over fruit, avoiding crust. Refrigerate tart for 30 minutes.

**7.** Remove outer metal ring of tart pan. Insert thin metal spatula between crust and pan bottom to loosen tart; carefully slide tart onto serving platter. Let tart sit at room temperature for 15 minutes. Using peaches as guide, cut into wedges and serve. (Tart can be covered with plastic wrap and refrigerated for up to 24 hours. If refrigerated for more than 1 hour, let tart sit at room temperature for 1 hour before serving.)

## Classic Fresh Fruit Tart with Pastry Cream

**SERVES** 8 to 10

**WHY THIS RECIPE WORKS** Fresh fruit tarts usually offer dazzling beauty and little else. We set out to create a buttery, crisp crust filled with rich, lightly sweetened pastry cream, topped with fresh, glistening fruit. We started with our classic tart dough and baked it until golden brown. We then filled the crust with pastry cream, made with half-and-half enriched with butter and thickened with just enough cornstarch to keep its shape without becoming gummy. For the fruit, we chose a combination of sliced kiwi, raspberries, and blueberries. We found that it was important not to wash the berries, as washing causes them to bruise and bleed and makes for a less than attractive tart. The finishing touch: a drizzle with a jelly glaze for a glistening presentation. You will need a 9-inch tart pan with a removable bottom for this recipe. The pastry cream can be made a day or two in advance, but do not fill the prebaked tart shell until just before serving. Once filled, the tart should be topped with fruit, glazed, and served within half an hour or so. Don't wash the berries or they will lose their flavor and shape.

PASTRY CREAM

- 2 cups half-and-half
- ½ cup (3½ ounces) sugar, divided
- Pinch table salt
- 5 large egg yolks
- 3 tablespoons cornstarch
- 4 tablespoons unsalted butter, cut into 4 pieces
- 1½ teaspoons vanilla extract

TART SHELL AND FRUIT

- 1 recipe Classic Tart Dough (page 946)
- 2 large kiwis, peeled, halved lengthwise, and sliced ⅜ inch thick
- 10 ounces (2 cups) raspberries
- 5 ounces (1 cup) blueberries
- ½ cup red currant or apple jelly

**1. FOR THE PASTRY CREAM:** Bring half-and-half, 6 tablespoons sugar, and salt to simmer in medium saucepan over medium-high heat, stirring occasionally.

**2.** As half-and-half mixture begins to simmer, whisk egg yolks, cornstarch, and remaining 2 tablespoons sugar in medium bowl until smooth. Slowly whisk 1 cup simmering half-and-half mixture into yolks to temper, then slowly whisk tempered yolks back into simmering saucepan. Reduce heat to medium and cook, whisking vigorously, until mixture is thickened and few bubbles burst on surface, about 30 seconds.

**3.** Off heat, stir in butter and vanilla. Transfer mixture to medium bowl; lay sheet of plastic wrap directly on surface; and refrigerate pastry cream until chilled and firm, about 3 hours.

**4. FOR THE TART SHELL AND FRUIT:** Roll dough out into 11-inch circle on lightly floured counter. Wrap it loosely around rolling pin and unroll dough over 9-inch tart pan with removable bottom. Lifting edge of dough, gently ease dough into pan. Press dough into corners and fluted sides of pan. Run rolling pin over top of tart pan to remove any excess dough and make clean edge. (If parts of edge are too thin, reinforce them by pressing in some of excess dough. If edge is too thick, press some of dough up over edge of pan and trim it away.) Set tart pan on large plate and freeze tart shell for 30 minutes.

**5.** Adjust oven rack to middle position and heat oven to 375 degrees. Set tart pan on rimmed baking sheet. Press double layer of aluminum foil into frozen tart shell and over edges of pan and fill with pie weights. Bake until tart shell is golden brown and set, about 30 minutes, rotating sheet halfway through baking.

**6.** Carefully remove weights and foil and continue to bake tart shell until it is fully baked and golden, 5 to 10 minutes longer. Transfer tart shell on sheet to wire rack and let cool completely, about 1 hour.

**7.** Spread chilled pastry cream evenly over bottom of cooled tart shell. Shingle kiwi slices around edge of tart, then arrange 3 rows of raspberries inside kiwi. Finally, arrange mound of blueberries in center.

**8.** Melt jelly in small saucepan over medium-high heat, stirring occasionally to smooth out any lumps. Using pastry brush, dab melted jelly over fruit. To serve, remove outer metal ring of tart pan, slide thin metal spatula between tart and tart pan bottom, and carefully slide tart onto serving platter or cutting board.

## Free-Form Summer Fruit Tart

SERVES 6

**WHY THIS RECIPE WORKS** Few things are better than a summer fruit pie, but that takes time and skill. This beautiful rustic tart features a free-form tart made with a single layer of pie dough folded up around a center of mixed summer fruit. To make a sturdy crust with enough structure to contain the juicy fruit we used a high proportion of butter to flour, which also provided buttery flavor and tender texture. We then turned to a French technique in pastry making called fraisage. To begin, butter is only partially cut into the dry ingredients. Then, the cook smears the barely mixed dough firmly against the counter multiple times. As a result, the chunks of butter are pressed into long, thin sheets that create lots of flaky layers when the dough is baked. We then rolled the dough into a 12-inch circle for a crust thick enough to contain a lot of fruit but thin enough to bake evenly. We placed the fruit in the middle, then pleated the dough loosely all the way around. The dough, wrapped tightly in plastic wrap, can be refrigerated for up to two days or frozen for up to one month. If frozen, let the dough thaw completely on the counter before rolling it out. Though we prefer a tart made with a mix of stone fruits and berries, you can use only one type of fruit if you prefer. Taste the fruit before adding sugar to it; use the lesser amount if the fruit is very sweet, more if it is tart. Do not add sugar to the fruit until you are ready to fill and form the tart. Serve with vanilla ice cream, whipped cream, or crème fraîche.

RUSTIC TART DOUGH

- 1½ cups (7½ ounces) all-purpose flour
- ½ teaspoon table salt
- 10 tablespoons unsalted butter, cut into ½-inch pieces and chilled
- 4–6 tablespoons ice water

FILLING

- 1 pound peaches, nectarines, apricots, or plums, pitted and sliced into ½-inch-thick wedges
- 5 ounces (1 cup) blueberries, raspberries, or blackberries
- 3–5 tablespoons plus 1 tablespoon sugar, divided

**1. FOR THE RUSTIC TART DOUGH:** Process flour and salt in food processor until combined, about 3 seconds. Scatter butter pieces over top and pulse until mixture resembles coarse bread crumbs and butter pieces are about size of small peas, about 10 pulses. Continue to pulse, adding water through feed tube 1 tablespoon at a time, until dough begins to form small curds that hold together when pinched with your fingers (dough will be crumbly), about 10 pulses.

2. Turn dough crumbs out onto lightly floured counter and gather into rectangular-shaped pile. Starting at farthest end, use heel of your hand to smear small amount of dough against counter. Continue to smear dough until all crumbs have been worked. Gather smeared crumbs together in another rectangular-shaped pile and repeat process. Flatten dough into 6-inch disk, wrap it tightly in plastic wrap, and refrigerate for 1 hour. Before rolling dough out, let it sit on counter to soften slightly, about 10 minutes.

3. Roll dough into 12-inch circle between 2 large sheets of floured parchment paper. Slide dough, still between parchment, onto rimmed baking sheet and refrigerate until firm, about 20 minutes.

4. **FOR THE FILLING:** Adjust oven rack to middle position and heat oven to 375 degrees. Gently toss peaches, blueberries, and sugar together in large bowl. Remove top sheet of parchment from dough. Mound fruit in center of dough, leaving 2½-inch border around edge. Fold 2 inches of dough up over fruit, leaving ½-inch border between fruit and edge of tart shell, pleating it every 2 to 3 inches as needed; gently pinch pleated dough to secure, but do not press dough into fruit. Working quickly, brush dough with water and sprinkle evenly with remaining 1 tablespoon sugar.

5. Bake tart until crust is deep golden brown and fruit is bubbling, about 1 hour, rotating baking sheet halfway through.

6. Let tart cool on baking sheet on wire rack for 10 minutes, then use parchment to gently transfer tart to wire rack. Use metal spatula to loosen tart from parchment and remove parchment. Let tart cool on rack until juices have thickened, about 25 minutes. Serve warm or at room temperature.

### USING FRAISAGE TO MIX DOUGH

**1.** Starting at 1 end of rectangular pile of dough, smear small amount of dough against counter with heel of your hand. Repeat this process (called fraisage) until rest of buttery crumbs have been worked.

**2.** Gather smeared bits into another rectangular pile and repeat smearing process until all of crumbs have been worked again. This second time won't take as long and will result in larger flakes of dough.

## Free-Form Summer Fruit Tartlets for Two

**SERVES 2**

**WHY THIS RECIPE WORKS** For an easy yet elegant take on summer fruit pie, we wanted a recipe for individual free-form fruit tarts. We started with an all-butter crust for the best flavor and tender texture. We turned to the French fraisage method to make the pastry, which calls for smearing the dough with the heel of your hand to spread the butter into long, thin streaks, creating lots of flaky layers when the dough is baked. Then we simply rolled out the chilled dough and pleated it loosely around the fruit filling. Taste the fruit before adding sugar to it; use the lesser amount if the fruit is very sweet, more if it is tart. However much sugar you use, do not add it to the fruit until you are ready to fill and form the tart. Serve with vanilla ice cream or Whipped Cream (page 974), if desired.

**DOUGH**

- ¾ cup (3¾ ounces) all-purpose flour
- ¼ teaspoon table salt
- 5 tablespoons unsalted butter, cut into ½-inch pieces and chilled
- 2–3 tablespoons ice water

**FILLING**

- 8 ounces peaches, nectarines, apricots, or plums, halved, pitted, and cut into ½-inch wedges
- 2½ ounces (½ cup) blackberries, blueberries, or raspberries
- 3–5 tablespoons sugar

1. **FOR THE DOUGH:** Process flour and salt in food processor until combined, about 5 seconds. Scatter butter over top and pulse until mixture resembles coarse crumbs and butter pieces are about size of small peas, 6 to 8 pulses. Continue to pulse, adding 1 tablespoon ice water at a time, until dough begins to form small curds and holds together when pinched with your fingers (dough will be crumbly), about 10 pulses.

2. Turn dough crumbs onto lightly floured counter and gather into rectangular-shaped pile about 8 inches long and 3 inches wide, with short side facing you. Starting at farthest end, use heel of your hand to smear small amount of dough against counter. Continue to smear dough until all crumbs have been worked. Gather smeared crumbs together into

another rectangular-shaped pile and repeat process. Divide dough in half and form each half into 3-inch disk. Wrap disks tightly in plastic wrap and refrigerate for 1 hour. Let chilled dough sit on counter to soften slightly, about 10 minutes, before rolling. (Wrapped dough can be refrigerated for up to 2 days or frozen for up to 2 months. If frozen, let dough thaw completely on counter before rolling.)

**3.** Roll each disk of dough into 7-inch round between 2 small sheets of floured parchment. (If dough sticks to parchment, gently loosen and lift sticky area with bench scraper and dust parchment with additional flour.) Slide dough rounds, still between parchment sheets, onto rimmed baking sheet and refrigerate until firm, 15 to 30 minutes. (If refrigerated longer and dough is hard and brittle, let sit at room temperature until pliant.)

**4. FOR THE FILLING:** Adjust oven rack to lower-middle position and heat oven to 400 degrees. Gently toss peaches, blackberries, and 2 tablespoons sugar together in bowl. (If fruit tastes tart, add up to 2 tablespoons more sugar.) Remove top sheet of parchment from each dough round. Mound half of fruit in center of 1 round, leaving 1½-inch border around edge of fruit. Being careful to leave ½-inch border of dough around edge of fruit, fold outermost 1 inch of dough over fruit, pleating it every 1 to 2 inches as needed; gently pinch pleated dough to secure, but do not press dough into fruit. Repeat with remaining fruit and dough round.

**5.** Working quickly, brush top and sides of dough with water and sprinkle tartlets evenly with remaining 1 tablespoon sugar. Bake until crust is deep golden brown and fruit is bubbling, 40 to 45 minutes, rotating sheet halfway through baking.

**6.** Transfer sheet with tartlets to wire rack and let cool for 10 minutes, then use parchment to gently transfer tartlets to wire rack. Use metal spatula to loosen tartlets from parchment and remove parchment. Let tartlets cool on rack until juices have thickened, about 20 minutes; serve slightly warm or at room temperature.

## Whipped Cream

**MAKES** about ¾ cup

The whipped cream can be refrigerated in a fine-mesh strainer set over a small bowl, wrapped tightly with plastic wrap, for up to 8 hours.

- ⅓ cup heavy cream, chilled
- 1 teaspoon sugar
- ¼ teaspoon vanilla extract

Using hand-held mixer set at medium-low speed, beat cream, sugar, and vanilla in medium bowl until foamy, about 1 minute. Increase speed to high and beat until soft peaks form, 1 to 3 minutes.

## Apple Galette

**SERVES** 10 to 12

**WHY THIS RECIPE WORKS** The French tart known as an apple galette should have a flaky crust and a layer of shingled caramelized apples. But it needs a crust strong enough to hold the apples and still be eaten out of hand. This required using just the right flour. All-purpose flour contained too much gluten; it made the pastry tough. Lower-protein pastry flour created a flaky and sturdy pastry. Since pastry flour is hard to find, we mixed all-purpose flour with instant flour (Wondra). Technique also proved to be important. To create layers of flaky dough, we used the French fraisage method of blending butter into dough (see page 973). We found that any thinly sliced apple would work, although we slightly preferred Granny Smith. The galette can be made without Wondra, using 2 cups unbleached all-purpose flour and 2 tablespoons cornstarch; you might have to increase the amount of ice water. The dough, wrapped tightly in plastic wrap, can be refrigerated for up to two days or frozen for up to one month. If frozen, let the dough thaw on the counter before rolling out. Serve with ice cream, whipped cream, or crème fraîche.

**DOUGH**

- 1½ cups (7½ ounces) all-purpose flour
- ½ cup (2½ ounces) Wondra flour
- ½ teaspoon table salt
- ½ teaspoon sugar
- 12 tablespoons unsalted butter, cut into ¼-inch pieces and chilled
- 7–9 tablespoons ice water

**TOPPING**

- 1½ pounds Granny Smith apples, peeled, cored, and sliced ⅛ inch thick
- 2 tablespoons unsalted butter, cut into ¼-inch pieces
- ¼ cup (1¾ ounces) sugar
- 3 tablespoons apple jelly

**1. FOR THE DOUGH:** Process all-purpose flour, Wondra, salt, and sugar in food processor until combined, about 5 seconds. Scatter butter pieces over top and pulse until mixture resembles coarse cornmeal, about 15 pulses. Continue to pulse, adding water through feed tube 1 tablespoon at a time until dough begins to form small curds that hold together when pinched with your fingers (dough will be crumbly), about 10 pulses.

**2.** Turn dough crumbs onto lightly floured counter and gather into rectangular-shaped pile. Starting at farthest end, use heel of your hand to smear small amount of dough against counter. Continue to smear dough until all crumbs have been worked. Gather smeared crumbs together in another rectangular-shaped pile and repeat process. Press dough into 4-inch square, wrap tightly in plastic wrap, and refrigerate for 1 hour. Before rolling dough out, let it sit on counter to soften slightly, about 10 minutes.

**3.** Adjust oven rack to middle position and heat oven to 400 degrees. Cut piece of parchment to measure exactly 16 by 12 inches. Roll dough out over parchment, dusting with flour as needed, until it just overhangs parchment. Trim edges of dough even with parchment. Roll outer 1 inch of dough up to create ½-inch-thick border. Slide parchment with dough onto rimmed baking sheet.

**4. FOR THE TOPPING:** Starting in 1 corner of tart, shingle apple slices onto crust in tidy diagonal rows, overlapping them by a third. Dot with butter and sprinkle evenly with sugar. Bake tart until bottom is deep golden brown and apples have caramelized, 45 minutes to 1 hour, rotating sheet halfway through baking.

**5.** Melt jelly in small saucepan over medium-high heat, stirring occasionally to smooth out any lumps. Brush glaze over apples and let tart cool slightly on sheet for 10 minutes. Slide tart onto large platter or cutting board and slice tart in half lengthwise, then crosswise into square pieces. Serve warm or at room temperature.

### PREPARING APPLE GALETTE

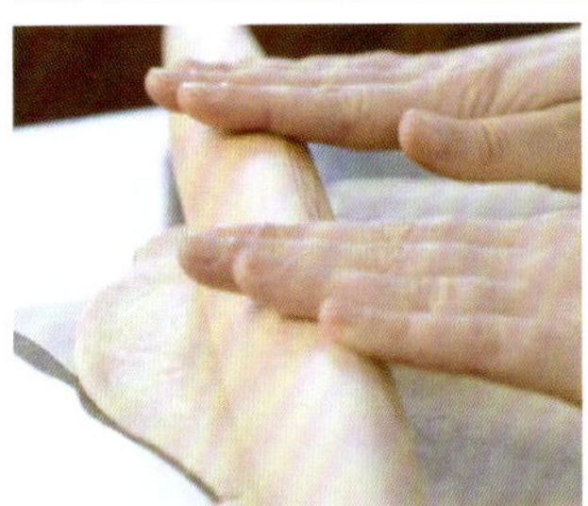

**1.** Cut piece of parchment paper to measure exactly 16 by 12 inches, then roll dough out on top of parchment until it just overhangs edge and is about ⅛ inch thick.

**2.** Trim dough so that edges are even with parchment. (We use parchment as a guide to cut a perfectly even rectangle of dough from which we can make a large thin crust.)

**3.** Roll up 1 inch of each edge to create ½-inch-thick border. (This border is decorative and helps keep the apple slices in place.)

**4.** Slide parchment and dough onto rimmed baking sheet. Starting in 1 corner, shingle apple slices in tidy rows on diagonal over dough, overlapping each row by a third.

## French Apple Tart

**SERVES 8**

**WHY THIS RECIPE WORKS** Classically elegant French apple tart is little more than apples and pastry, but such simplicity means that imperfections like tough or mushy apples, unbalanced flavor, and a sodden crust are hard to hide. We wanted a foolproof way to achieve tender apples and a flavorful, buttery crust. We parbaked our quick pat-in-pan dough for a cookie-like texture that gave the tart a sturdy base. For intense fruit flavor, we packed the tart with a whopping 5 pounds of Golden Delicious apples. We cooked half into a concentrated puree, which we made more luxurious with butter and apricot preserves. Then we sliced and parcooked the remaining apples and used them to adorn the top with concentric circles (see page 976). A thin coat of preserves and a final stint under the broiler provided an attractively caramelized finish. For the best flavor and texture, be sure to bake the crust thoroughly. The tart is best served the day it is assembled. To ensure that the outer ring of the pan releases easily from the tart, avoid getting apple puree and apricot glaze on the crust.

**CRUST**

- 1⅓ cups (6⅔ ounces) all-purpose flour
- 5 tablespoons (2¼ ounces) sugar
- ½ teaspoon table salt
- 10 tablespoons unsalted butter, melted

**FILLING**

- 10 Golden Delicious apples (8 ounces each), peeled and cored
- 3 tablespoons unsalted butter
- 1 tablespoon water
- ½ cup apricot preserves
- ¼ teaspoon table salt

**1. FOR THE CRUST:** Adjust 1 oven rack to lowest position and second rack 5 to 6 inches from broiler element. Heat oven to 350 degrees. Whisk flour, sugar, and salt together in bowl. Add melted butter and stir until dough forms. Using your hands, press two-thirds of dough into bottom of 9-inch tart pan with removable bottom. Press remaining dough into fluted sides of pan. Press and smooth dough with your hands to even thickness. Place pan on wire rack set in rimmed baking sheet and bake on lowest rack, until crust is deep golden brown and firm to touch, 30 to 35 minutes, rotating pan halfway through baking. Set aside until ready to fill.

**2. FOR THE FILLING:** Cut 5 apples lengthwise into quarters and cut each quarter lengthwise into 4 slices. Melt 1 tablespoon butter in 12-inch skillet over medium heat. Add apple slices and water and toss to combine. Cover and cook, stirring occasionally, until apples begin to turn translucent and are slightly pliable, 3 to 5 minutes. Transfer apples to large plate, spread into single layer, and set aside to cool.

**3.** While apples cook, microwave apricot preserves until fluid, about 30 seconds. Strain preserves through fine-mesh strainer into small bowl, reserving solids. Set aside 3 tablespoons strained preserves for brushing tart.

**4.** Cut remaining 5 apples into ½-inch-thick wedges. Melt remaining 2 tablespoons butter in now-empty skillet over medium heat. Add remaining strained apricot preserves, reserved apricot solids, apples, and salt. Cover and cook, stirring occasionally, until apples are very soft, about 10 minutes.

**5.** Mash apples to puree with potato masher. Continue to cook, stirring occasionally, until puree is reduced to 2 cups, about 5 minutes.

**6.** Transfer apple puree to baked tart shell and smooth surface. Select 5 thinnest slices of sautéed apple and set aside. Starting at outer edge of tart, arrange remaining slices, tightly overlapping in concentric circles. Bend reserved slices to fit in center. Bake tart, still on wire rack in sheet, on lowest rack, for 30 minutes. Remove tart from oven and heat broiler.

**7.** While broiler heats, warm reserved preserves in microwave until fluid, about 20 seconds. Brush evenly over surface of apples, avoiding tart crust. Broil tart, checking every 30 seconds and turning as necessary, until apples are attractively caramelized, 1 to 3 minutes. Let tart cool for at least 1½ hours. Remove outer metal ring of tart pan, slide thin metal spatula between tart and pan bottom, and carefully slide tart onto serving platter. Cut into wedges and serve. (The baked crust, apple slices, and apple puree can be made up to 24 hours in advance. Apple slices and puree should be wrapped in plastic wrap and refrigerated separately. Assemble tart with refrigerated apple slices and puree and bake as directed, adding 5 minutes to baking time.)

### MAKING AN APPLE ROSETTE

**1.** Starting at edges and working toward center, arrange most of the cooled sautéed apple slices in tightly overlapping concentric circles.

**2.** Bend remaining slices to fit in center.

## Appeltaart (Dutch Apple Tart)

**SERVES** 8 to 10 **SEASON 26**

**WHY THIS RECIPE WORKS** Dutch appeltaart is a giant among pies: a stately apple dessert featuring densely packed, liberally spiced, lightly sweetened apples (and often raisins) encased in a substantial, cookie-like crust. To make a no-fuss dough, we melted the butter instead of cutting it into the dry mixture and simply stirred it into the dry ingredients. The result was a very malleable dough, easy to press into the bottom and sides of the springform pan. It was also easy to roll out the top portion and cut it into wide strips, which we arranged in a crisscross pattern. The addition of an egg and a generous amount of baking powder gave the crust a fine, crisp texture. Gently parcooking the apples converted their pectin to a more heat-stable form, which kept them from becoming mushy in the oven. Adding a small amount of cornstarch to the parcooked, drained apples and packing them snugly into the formed crust ensured that the filling was compact and appropriately thickened so we could slice it into tidy, towering wedges. Pink Lady apples may be substituted for Golden Delicious but might require a bit more cooking in step 1. Use freshly opened brown sugar to avoid sugar lumps in the crust. If your springform pan is not nonstick, grease it lightly before pressing in the dough. (The tart is best eaten the day it's baked; leftovers can be wrapped in plastic wrap and stored at room temperature for up to 2 days.)

**APPLES**

- 4 pounds Golden Delicious apples, peeled, cored, and cut into ¼-inch-thick wedges
- ¼ cup packed (1¾ ounces) dark brown sugar
- ½ cup golden raisins (optional)
- 1 tablespoon cornstarch
- 1 tablespoon lemon juice
- 1 teaspoon ground cinnamon
- ¼ teaspoon ground ginger
- ¼ teaspoon ground cardamom
- ¼ teaspoon ground coriander
- ⅛ teaspoon ground nutmeg
- Pinch table salt

**CRUST**

- 2½ cups (12½ ounces) all-purpose flour
- ¾ cup packed (5¼ ounces) dark brown sugar
- 1 tablespoon baking powder
- ½ teaspoon table salt
- 1 large egg, beaten
- 14 tablespoons unsalted butter, melted and hot
- 1 tablespoon water
- Whipped cream or vanilla ice cream

**1. FOR THE APPLES:** Combine apples and sugar in Dutch oven. Cook, covered, over medium heat, stirring occasionally, until all apples are slightly softened and about half are just becoming translucent, 8 to 14 minutes (it's OK if a few pieces break). Transfer apples and juices to rimmed baking sheet set on wire rack. Spread apples into even layer and let cool, about 30 minutes. While apples are cooling, prepare crust.

**2. FOR THE CRUST:** Combine flour, sugar, baking powder, and salt in bowl and rub together with your fingers to combine and to break up any lumps of sugar. Set aside 1 tablespoon egg for egg wash. Add remaining egg, melted butter, and water to flour mixture and stir to combine. Transfer mixture to counter (do not wash bowl) and knead until dough is smooth and uniform. Shape into 9-inch cylinder and cut crosswise into 3 equal portions.

3. Place 1 portion of dough on 16 by 12-inch sheet of parchment and press into 8 by 4-inch rectangle. Cover with second piece of parchment and roll into rough 12 by 10-inch rectangle. Transfer to second rimmed baking sheet and refrigerate. Crumble second portion of dough into bottom of 9-inch springform pan. Press to cover bottom of pan. Break off 1-inch chunks of remaining portion of dough and press into sides of pan. Refrigerate.

4. Adjust oven rack to lower-middle position and heat oven to 375 degrees. Using your hands or slotted spoon, transfer apples to now-empty bowl, leaving any juices on sheet. Add raisins, if using; cornstarch; lemon juice; cinnamon; ginger; cardamom; coriander; nutmeg; and salt and stir until combined. Transfer to dough-lined pan. Spread evenly and press gently to compact. Smooth top.

5. Transfer rolled dough, still in parchment, to counter, with long side parallel to edge of counter. Peel parchment from dough and return parchment to baking sheet. Using ruler and sharp knife or pizza cutter, cut dough lengthwise into eight 1¼-inch-wide strips. Using offset spatula to lift dough, place 4 strips equidistant from one another on top of pie (if strips differ in length, place longer strips in middle and shorter strips at sides), letting sides of strips hang over edge of pan. Place remaining 4 strips on top, arranging them at 45-degree angle to first set of strips. Gently press strips down so they rest against filling (it's OK if ends of some strips crack). Trim ends of strips so they are flush with pan edge. Place pie on prepared sheet. (Pie can be wrapped in plastic wrap and refrigerated for up to 24 hours.)

6. Brush top of pie with reserved egg. Bake for 45 minutes. Cover loosely with aluminum foil and continue to bake until skewer can be easily inserted into apples, about 30 minutes longer. Transfer pan to wire rack. Run paring knife around top edge of pie. Carefully release clip and remove ring. Let cool completely, at least 4 hours. Using sharp knife in gentle sawing motion to prevent top crust from crumbling, cut into wedges. Serve with whipped cream or ice cream.

## Rustic Free-Form Apple Tart

**SERVES 6**

**WHY THIS RECIPE WORKS** Apple tarts are easier to make than apple pie, but they have their problems: The filling can dry out owing to the lack of a top crust, and the dough can be limp and tacky. We wanted a simple free-form tart with moist, flavorful apples neatly contained by a flaky, easy-to-handle dough. Off the bat, we decided to borrow the crust from our Free-Form Summer Fruit Tart recipe (page 972)—it's sturdy yet flaky, with a great buttery flavor. As with our Classic Apple Pie (page 947), we favored a combination of Granny Smith and McIntosh apples. To ensure that the apples cooked through in a short amount of time, we sliced them ¼ inch thick. All the apples needed in the way of flavor enhancement was lemon juice, sugar, and cinnamon. Serve with vanilla ice cream or lightly sweetened whipped cream.

- 1 pound Granny Smith apples (about 2 large), peeled, cored, and sliced ¼ inch thick
- 1 pound McIntosh apples (about 2 large), peeled, cored, and sliced ¼ inch thick
- ½ cup (3½ ounces) plus 1 tablespoon sugar
- 1 tablespoon juice from 1 lemon
- ⅛ teaspoon ground cinnamon
- 1 recipe Rustic Tart Dough (page 972), rolled into a 12-inch circle and chilled

1. Adjust an oven rack to the middle position and heat the oven to 375 degrees. Toss the apples, ½ cup of the sugar, the lemon juice, and cinnamon together in a large bowl.

2. Remove the top sheet of parchment paper from the dough. Stack some of the apples into a circular wall, leaving a 2½-inch border around the edge. Fill in the middle of the tart with the remaining apples. Being careful to leave a ½-inch border of dough around the fruit, fold the outermost 2 inches of dough over the fruit, pleating it every 2 to 3 inches as needed; gently

### MAKING A FREE-FORM APPLE TART

1. Discard the top piece of parchment. Stack the apple slices into a circular wall, leaving a 2½-inch border of dough. Fill the center with the remaining apples.

2. Fold 2 inches of the dough up over the fruit, leaving a ½-inch border between the fruit and the edge of the tart shell. This ½-inch space helps prevent the tart juices from leaking through the folds in the shell.

pinch the pleated dough to secure, but do not press the dough into the fruit. Working quickly, brush the dough with water and sprinkle evenly with the remaining 1 tablespoon sugar.

**3.** Bake the tart on a large rimmed baking sheet until the crust is deep golden brown and the apples are tender, about 1 hour, rotating the baking sheet halfway through.

**4.** Cool the tart on the baking sheet on a wire rack for 10 minutes, then use the parchment paper to gently transfer the tart to the wire rack. Use a metal spatula to loosen the tart from the parchment and remove the parchment. Cool the tart on the rack until the juices have thickened, about 25 minutes. Serve warm or at room temperature.

## 30-Minute Tarte Tatin

**SERVES** 6 to 8

**WHY THIS RECIPE WORKS** Making a true tarte Tatin requires an investment of time and a certain amount of skill. Traditionally, the apples are cooked in a skillet until caramelized, then topped with homemade pastry and cooked in the oven. Before serving, the tart is masterfully flipped onto a serving platter. We wanted to simplify this version enough for a weeknight dessert. We first baked a sheet of store-bought puff pastry until it was beautifully golden brown. While the pastry baked, we caramelized the apples in a skillet until they were tender. We then spooned the apples over the pastry, arranging them in three even rows with a border around the outside of the pastry. As a final touch, we created a simple sauce by adding heavy cream and Grand Marnier to the juice left behind in the skillet. To get this dessert on the table in 30 minutes, peel the apples while the oven preheats and the pastry thaws, and then bake the pastry while the apples are caramelizing. This dessert is especially good with Tangy Whipped Cream (page 986).

- 1 (9½ by 9-inch) sheet frozen puff pastry, thawed
- 8 tablespoons (1 stick) unsalted butter
- ¾ cup (5¼ ounces) sugar
- 2 pounds Granny Smith apples (about 4 large), peeled, quartered, and cored
- ¼ cup heavy cream
- 2 tablespoons Grand Marnier, spiced rum, or Calvados (optional)

**1.** Adjust an oven rack to the middle position and heat the oven to 400 degrees. Line a rimmed baking sheet with parchment paper. Unfold the puff pastry, lay it on the prepared baking sheet, and bake until golden brown and puffed, 15 to 20 minutes, rotating the baking sheet halfway through. Transfer the baked pastry sheet to a serving platter and press lightly to flatten if domed.

**2.** Meanwhile, melt the butter in a 12-inch nonstick skillet over high heat. Remove the pan from the heat and sprinkle evenly with the sugar. Lay the apples in the skillet, return the skillet to high heat, and cook until the juice in the pan turns a rich amber color and the apples are caramelized, about 15 minutes, turning the apples halfway through.

**3.** Remove the apples from the pan one at a time and arrange in three overlapping rows on the baked pastry sheet, leaving a ½-inch border. Spoon about half of the pan juice over the apples.

**4.** Whisk the cream and Grand Marnier (if using) into the remaining juice in the pan and bring to a simmer. Pour some sauce over the tart and serve, passing the remaining sauce separately.

## Peach Tarte Tatin

**SERVES** 8

**WHY THIS RECIPE WORKS** We wanted to create a peach version of the classic tartin made with apples, but simply swapping fruits produced a cloying tart that was awash in juice. To make wetter, sweeter, more fragile peaches work, we had to tweak the recipe. We started by layering butter, a small amount of sugar, salt, and peaches in a cool skillet. After cooking the filling on the stovetop until the peach juice was deeply browned, we removed the skillet from the heat, slid a pie pastry disk on top, and baked it. When the crust was browned and crisp, we let the tart cool for 20 minutes before pouring off the excess juice and inverting the tart onto a platter. Reducing the juice with a bit of bourbon and then brushing the mixture back over the peaches gave this tart extra flavor and shine while supporting its cohesiveness. Chill the dough for at least 1 hour before rolling it. We like using firm peaches in this recipe because they are easier to peel and retain their shape when cooked; yellow peaches are also preferable to white peaches. When you're pouring off the liquid in step 4, the peaches may shift in the skillet; shaking the skillet will help redistribute them. Serve the tart with lightly sweetened whipped cream, if desired.

- 1 recipe Foolproof All-Butter Dough for Single-Crust Pie (page 944)
- 3 tablespoons unsalted butter, softened
- ½ cup (3½ ounces) plus 2 tablespoons sugar, divided
- ¼ teaspoon table salt
- 2 pounds ripe but firm peaches, peeled, pitted, and quartered
- 1 tablespoon bourbon (optional)

**1.** Invert rimmed baking sheet and place sheet of parchment paper or waxed paper on top. Roll dough into 10-inch circle on lightly floured counter. Loosely roll dough around rolling pin and gently unroll it onto prepared sheet. Working around circumference, fold ½ inch of dough under itself and pinch to create 9-inch round with raised rim. Cut three 2-inch slits in center of dough and refrigerate until needed.

**2.** Adjust oven rack to middle position and heat oven to 400 degrees. Smear butter over bottom of 10-inch ovensafe skillet. Sprinkle ½ cup sugar over butter and shake skillet to distribute sugar in even layer. Sprinkle salt over sugar. Arrange peaches in circular pattern around edge of skillet, nestling fruit snugly. Tuck remaining peaches into center, squeezing in as much fruit as possible (it is not necessary to maintain circular pattern in center).

**3.** Place skillet over high heat and cook, without stirring fruit, until juice is released and turns from pink to deep amber, 8 to 12 minutes. (If necessary, adjust skillet's placement on burner to even out hot spots and encourage even browning.) Remove skillet from heat. Carefully slide prepared dough over fruit, making sure dough is centered and does not touch edge of skillet. Brush dough lightly with water and sprinkle with remaining 2 tablespoons sugar. Bake until crust is very well browned, 30 to 35 minutes. Transfer skillet to wire rack set in rimmed baking sheet and let cool for 20 minutes.

**4.** Place inverted plate on top of crust. With your hand firmly securing plate, carefully tip skillet over bowl to drain juice (skillet handle may still be hot). When all juice has been transferred to bowl, return skillet to wire rack, remove plate, and shake skillet firmly to redistribute peaches. Carefully invert tart onto plate, then slide tart onto wire rack. (If peaches have shifted during unmolding, gently nudge them back into place with spoon.)

**5.** Pour juice into now-empty skillet (handle may be hot). Stir in bourbon, if using, and cook over high heat, stirring constantly, until mixture is dark and thick and starting to smoke, 2 to 3 minutes. Return mixture to bowl and let cool until mixture is consistency of honey, 2 to 3 minutes. Brush mixture over peaches. Let tart cool for at least 20 minutes. Cut into wedges and serve.

## Rich Chocolate Tart

**SERVES** 12

**WHY THIS RECIPE WORKS** For us, a great chocolate tart should possess deep chocolate flavor, a rich, lush texture, and a sophisticated presentation. First we made a custardy filling by melting intense dark chocolate into hot cream, adding eggs, and baking. To enrich the filling's flavor, we added butter and a little instant espresso to echo the bittersweetness of the chocolate. Because custards tend to curdle under high heat, we baked the tart in a very low 250-degree oven for a smooth and silky texture. To make our tart a showstopper, we topped it with a simple glossy chocolate glaze. A classic sweet pastry dough flavored with ground almonds made the perfect complement to the chocolate filling. Toasted and skinned hazelnuts can be substituted for the almonds. Use good-quality dark chocolate containing a cacao percentage between 60 and 65 percent; our favorites are Ghirardelli 60% Cacao Bittersweet Chocolate and Callebaut Intense Dark Chocolate, L-60-40NV. Let tart sit at room temperature for 30 minutes before glazing in step 6. The tart can be garnished with chocolate curls or with a flaky coarse sea salt. Serve with lightly sweetened whipped cream; if you like, flavor the whipped cream with cognac or vanilla extract.

**CRUST**

- 1 large egg yolk
- 2 tablespoons heavy cream
- ½ cup sliced almonds, toasted
- ¼ cup (1¾ ounces) sugar
- 1 cup (5 ounces) all-purpose flour
- ¼ teaspoon table salt
- 6 tablespoons unsalted butter, cut into ½-inch pieces

**FILLING**

- 1¼ cups heavy cream
- ½ teaspoon instant espresso powder
- ¼ teaspoon table salt
- 9 ounces bittersweet chocolate, chopped fine
- 4 tablespoons unsalted butter, cut into thin slices and softened
- 2 large eggs, lightly beaten, room temperature

**GLAZE**

- 3 tablespoons heavy cream
- 1 tablespoon light corn syrup
- 2 ounces bittersweet chocolate, chopped fine
- 1 tablespoon hot water

**1. FOR THE CRUST:** Beat egg yolk and cream together in small bowl. Process almonds and sugar in food processor until nuts are finely ground, 15 to 20 seconds. Add flour and salt; pulse to combine, about 10 pulses. Scatter butter over flour mixture; pulse to cut butter into flour until mixture resembles coarse meal, about 15 pulses. With processor running, add egg yolk mixture and process until dough forms ball, about 10 seconds. Transfer dough to large sheet of plastic wrap and press into 6-inch disk; wrap dough in plastic and refrigerate until firm but malleable, about 30 minutes. (Dough can be wrapped in plastic wrap and refrigerated for up to 3 days; before using, let stand at room temperature until malleable but still cool.)

**2.** Roll out dough between 2 large sheets of plastic into 11-inch round about ⅜ inch thick. (If dough becomes too soft and sticky to work with, slip it onto baking sheet and refrigerate until workable.) Place dough round (still in plastic) on baking sheet and refrigerate until firm but pliable, about 15 minutes.

3. Adjust oven rack to middle position and heat oven to 375 degrees. Spray 9-inch tart pan with removable bottom with vegetable oil spray. Keeping dough on sheet, remove top layer of plastic. Invert tart pan (with bottom) on top of dough round. Press on tart pan to cut dough. Using both hands, pick up sheet and tart pan and carefully invert both, setting tart pan right side up. Remove sheet and peel off plastic; reserve plastic. Roll over edges of tart pan with rolling pin to cut dough. Gently ease and press dough into bottom of pan, reserving scraps. Roll dough scraps into ¾-inch rope (various lengths are OK). Line edge of tart pan with rope(s) and gently press into fluted sides. Line tart pan with reserved plastic and, using measuring cup, gently press and smooth dough to even thickness (sides should be about ¼ inch thick). Using paring knife, trim any excess dough above rim of tart; discard scraps. Freeze dough-lined pan until dough is firm, 20 to 30 minutes.

4. Set dough-lined pan on baking sheet. Spray 12-inch square of aluminum foil with oil spray and press foil, sprayed side down, into pan; fill with 2 cups pie weights. Bake until dough is dry and light golden brown, about 25 minutes, rotating sheet halfway through baking. Carefully remove foil and weights and continue to bake until pastry is rich golden brown and fragrant, 8 to 10 minutes longer. Let cool completely on baking sheet on wire rack.

5. **FOR THE FILLING:** Heat oven to 250 degrees. Bring cream, espresso powder, and salt to simmer in small saucepan over medium heat, stirring once or twice to dissolve espresso powder and salt. Meanwhile, place chocolate in large heatproof bowl. Pour simmering cream mixture over chocolate, cover, and let stand for 5 minutes to allow chocolate to soften. Using whisk, stir mixture slowly and gently (so as not to incorporate air) until homogeneous. Add butter and continue to whisk gently until fully incorporated. Pour beaten eggs through fine-mesh strainer into chocolate mixture; whisk slowly until mixture is homogeneous and glossy. Pour filling into tart crust and shake gently from side to side to distribute and smooth surface; pop any large bubbles with toothpick or skewer. Bake tart, on baking sheet, until outer edge of filling is just set and very faint cracks appear on surface, 30 to 35 minutes; filling will still be very wobbly. Let cool completely on baking sheet on wire rack. Refrigerate, uncovered, until filling is chilled and set, at least 3 hours or up to 18 hours.

6. **FOR THE GLAZE:** Thirty minutes before glazing, remove tart from refrigerator. Bring cream and corn syrup to simmer in small saucepan over medium heat; stir once or twice to combine. Remove pan from heat, add chocolate, and cover. Let stand for 5 minutes to allow chocolate to soften. Whisk gently (so as not to incorporate air) until mixture is smooth, then whisk in hot water until glaze is homogeneous, shiny, and pourable. Working quickly, pour glaze onto center of tart. To distribute glaze, tilt tart and allow glaze to run to edge. (Spreading glaze with spatula will leave marks on surface.) Pop any large bubbles with toothpick or skewer. Let cool completely, about 1 hour.

7. Remove outer ring from tart pan. Insert thin-bladed metal spatula between crust and pan bottom to loosen tart; slide tart onto serving platter. Cut into wedges and serve.

## Milk Chocolate Crémeux Tart

**SERVES** 8 to 10

**WHY THIS RECIPE WORKS** This decadent French tart features a creamy chocolate filling that is silkier than a ganache but denser than a mousse. Instead of chilling the dough after mixing, we sped up the usual process by rolling out the just-mixed dough between layers of parchment until it was very thin and then freezing it, so it was ready to shape after only 30 minutes. Milk chocolate that we blended with custard instead of cream formed the base of our filling. This recipe was developed using Endangered Species Smooth + Creamy Milk Chocolate, which has a high cacao content. If using another brand, consider adding the optional tablespoon of cocoa powder for a darker milk chocolate flavor. Avoid chocolate chips, which sometimes contain additives to hinder melting. If desired, serve with unsweetened whipped cream or fruit.

**PÂTE SUCRÉE TART SHELL**

- 1 large egg
- 1 teaspoon vanilla extract
- 1½ cups (7½ ounces) all-purpose flour
- ⅔ cup (2⅔ ounces) confectioners' sugar
- ¼ teaspoon table salt
- 8 tablespoons unsalted butter, cut into ½-inch pieces and chilled

**MILK CHOCOLATE FILLING**

- 1 cup half-and-half
- 4 large egg yolks
- 1 tablespoon unsweetened cocoa powder (optional)
- ⅜ teaspoon table salt
- 12 ounces milk chocolate, chopped fine
- 1½ teaspoons vanilla extract
- 10 tablespoons unsalted butter, melted and hot

**1. FOR THE PÂTE SUCRÉE TART SHELL:** Whisk egg and vanilla together in 1-cup liquid measuring cup; set aside. Pulse flour, sugar, and salt in food processor until combined, 2 pulses. Scatter butter over flour mixture; process until mixture looks like very fine crumbs with no pieces of butter visible, about 20 seconds. With processor running, add egg mixture and continue to process until dough just forms mass, about 18 seconds longer.

**2.** Transfer dough to center of 18 by 12-inch piece of parchment paper. Place second sheet of parchment on top of dough and press with your hand to ½-inch thickness. Using rolling pin, roll out dough so it nearly reaches edges of parchment. Using your flat hand on parchment, smooth out wrinkles on both sides. Transfer dough with parchment to baking sheet and freeze until firm, about 30 minutes.

**3.** Place dough and parchment on counter and peel away top layer of parchment. Replace top layer of parchment, flip dough and parchment, and peel away second piece of parchment. Invert 9-inch metal tart ring on left half of dough and press to cut out circle (leave circle on parchment). Using paring knife and ruler, cut right half of dough lengthwise into 1-inch-wide strips. Place removable bottom in tart pan. Lift dough round (if necessary, use thin spatula to loosen) and fit into bottom of tart pan, pressing edges of dough firmly into corners (it's OK if some dough smears up sides of tart pan). Lift strips and fit into sides of pan, overlapping strips only slightly. Trim final strip to fit. If at any point dough becomes too soft to manipulate, freeze for 15 minutes.

**4.** Freeze tart shell until very firm, about 20 minutes. While tart shell chills, adjust oven rack to middle position and heat oven to 350 degrees. Tart shell can be baked up to two days ahead; let it cool, wrap tightly in plastic wrap, and store at room temperature.)

**5.** Hold paring knife parallel to counter and shave off any excess dough to force dough into flutes for clean edge. Spray large sheet of heavy-duty aluminum foil with vegetable oil spray. Place foil sprayed side down in tart shell and smooth gently along bottom and sides. Fill with pie weights. Bake on rimmed baking sheet until tart shell is golden and set, about 30 minutes, rotating sheet halfway through baking. Remove foil and weights and continue to bake tart shell until fully baked and golden brown, about 10 minutes longer. Transfer sheet to wire rack and let cool completely, about 30 minutes.

**6. FOR THE MILK CHOCOLATE FILLING:** Place fine-mesh strainer over medium bowl. Whisk half-and-half; egg yolks; cocoa, if using; and salt in medium saucepan until combined. Cook mixture over medium-low heat, stirring constantly and scraping bottom of saucepan with heatproof spatula, until mixture is thickened and silky and registers 170 to 175 degrees, 5 to 7 minutes. Remove from heat. Working quickly, whisk in chocolate and vanilla until smooth. Add melted butter and whisk gently until incorporated. Pour mixture into prepared strainer and transfer strained mixture to cooled tart shell. Let cool completely, about 20 minutes, then refrigerate until filling is set, at least 2 hours or up to 24 hours.

**7.** Remove outer ring from tart pan. Insert thin metal spatula between crust and pan bottom to loosen tart; slide tart onto serving platter. Cut into wedges and serve. (Leftovers can be wrapped loosely in plastic wrap and refrigerated for up to 3 days.)

### CREATING AN ULTRASLIM TART SHELL

**1.** Using tart pan like giant cookie cutter, cut out fluted base and fit it into bottom of pan.

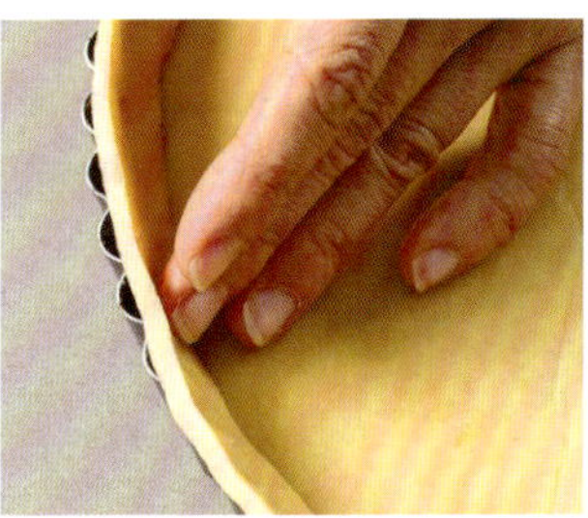

**2.** Fit excess strips of dough along sides of pan to create thin, elegant sides. Trim top to force dough into flutes for pretty and clean edge.

## Nutella Tart

**SERVES** 8 to 10

**WHY THIS RECIPE WORKS** Nutella is the surprise base for this chocolate tart's no-bake filling. For a dense and velvety filling, we included Nutella in a simple ganache made of chocolate and cream. Adding butter to the mixture helped make the filling sliceable once it was chilled. Microwaving was the easiest method for assembling the filling as long as we used a low power and stirred the mixture often as the chocolate and butter melted. If the microwave power is too high, you'll risk breaking the ganache, which then cools into a grainy texture. A layer of chopped toasted hazelnuts beneath the ganache added flavor and crunch. A garnish of whole toasted hazelnuts completed the look; we added them after the filling had firmed slightly to prevent sinking. Serve with whipped cream if desired.

- 1 recipe Classic Tart Dough (page 946)
- 1 cup hazelnuts
- 2 ounces bittersweet chocolate, finely chopped
- 1¼ cups Nutella
- ½ cup heavy cream
- 2 tablespoons unsalted butter
- Whipped cream (optional)

**1.** Roll dough out to 11-inch circle on lightly floured work surface and fit it into 9-inch tart pan with removable bottom. Set tart pan on large plate and freeze tart shell for 30 minutes.

**2.** Adjust oven rack to middle position and heat oven to 375 degrees. Set tart pan on large baking sheet. Press double layer of foil into frozen tart shell and over edges of pan and fill with pie weights. Bake until tart shell is golden brown and set, about 30 minutes, rotating baking sheet halfway through.

3. Carefully remove weights and foil and continue to bake tart shell until it is fully baked and golden, 5 to 10 minutes longer. Transfer tart crust with baking sheet to wire rack and cool tart shell slightly while making filling. (Do not turn off oven.)

4. Toast hazelnuts on rimmed baking sheet until skins begin to blister and crack, 15 to 20 minutes. Wrap warm nuts in dish towel and rub gently to remove skins. Reserve 24 whole nuts for garnish, then chop remaining nuts coarsely. Sprinkle chopped nuts into cooled tart shell.

5. Microwave chocolate, Nutella, cream, and butter in covered bowl at 30 percent power, stirring often, until mixture is smooth and glossy, about 1 minute (do not overheat).

6. Pour warm chocolate mixture evenly into tart shell. Refrigerate tart, uncovered, until filling is just set, about 15 minutes. Arrange reserved whole nuts around edge of tart, cover loosely with plastic wrap, and continue to refrigerate until filling is firm, at least 1½ hours or up to 1 day.

7. To serve, remove outer ring of tart pan, slide thin metal spatula between tart and tart pan bottom, and carefully slide tart onto serving platter or cutting board. Serve with whipped cream if desired.

## Best Baked Apples

SERVES 6

WHY THIS RECIPE WORKS This homey dessert is often plagued with a mushy texture and one-dimensional, cloyingly sweet flavor. After extensive testing, Granny Smith apples, with their firm flesh and tart fruity flavor, proved the best choice. To ensure that our fruit avoided even the occasional collapse, we peeled the apples after cutting off the tops. The skin traps steam from the extra moisture released by the breakdown of the apples' interior cells, and removing it allows the steam to escape and the apple to retain its tender-firm texture. Sautéing our apples cut side down intensified their flavor. Our filling base of dried cranberries, brown sugar, and pecans benefited from some finessing by way of cinnamon, orange zest, and a pat of butter. We intensified the nuttiness with chewy rolled oats, and diced apple. A melon baller helped us to scoop out a spacious cavity that accommodated plenty of filling. We then capped off the filled apples with the tops we had previously lopped off. We basted the apples with an apple cider and maple syrup sauce so they emerged full of flavor. The recipe calls for seven apples; six are left whole and one is diced and added to the filling. You will need a 12-inch ovensafe skillet for this recipe. Serve the apples with vanilla ice cream, if desired.

- 7 large (about 6 ounces each) Granny Smith apples
- 6 tablespoons (¾ stick) unsalted butter, softened
- ⅓ cup dried cranberries, chopped coarse
- ⅓ cup coarsely chopped pecans, toasted
- ¼ cup packed (1¾ ounces) brown sugar
- 3 tablespoons old-fashioned oats
- 1 teaspoon finely grated zest from 1 orange
- ½ teaspoon ground cinnamon
- Pinch table salt
- ⅓ cup maple syrup
- ⅓ cup plus 2 tablespoons apple cider

1. Adjust an oven rack to the middle position and heat the oven to 375 degrees. Peel, core, and cut 1 apple into ¼-inch dice. Combine 5 tablespoons of the butter, the cranberries, pecans, brown sugar, oats, orange zest, cinnamon, salt, and diced apple in a large bowl; set aside.

2. Shave a thin slice off the bottom (blossom end) of the remaining 6 apples to allow them to sit flat. Cut the top ½ inch off the stem end of the apples and reserve. Peel the apples and use a melon baller or small measuring spoon to remove a 1½-inch-diameter core, being careful not to cut through the bottom of the apple.

3. Melt the remaining 1 tablespoon butter in a 12-inch ovensafe nonstick skillet over medium heat. Once the foaming subsides, add the apples, stem side down, and cook until the cut surface is golden brown, about 3 minutes. Flip the apples, reduce the heat to low, and spoon the filling inside, mounding the excess filling over the cavities; top with the reserved apple caps. Add the maple syrup and ⅓ cup of the cider to the skillet. Transfer the skillet to the oven and bake until a skewer inserted into the apples meets little resistance, 35 to 40 minutes, basting every 10 minutes with the maple syrup mixture in the skillet.

4. Transfer the apples to a serving platter. Stir up to 2 tablespoons of the remaining cider into the sauce in the skillet to adjust the consistency. Pour the sauce over the apples and serve.

## Apple Crumble

SERVES 6 to 8

WHY THIS RECIPE WORKS Making an apple crumble that tastes primarily of apples starts with plenty of fruit. We tossed 4 pounds of apples with 2 tablespoons of lemon juice to enhance their bright flavor. Adding just 2 tablespoons of brown sugar to the filling kept the apples from tasting too sweet. We baked the apples in a covered pan before applying the topping, which allowed them to collapse into a thick layer of filling. Adding nuts to the streusel loosened its consistency so that it didn't bake up dense, and a couple of teaspoons of water hydrated the flour so that the mixture clumped nicely. Applying the topping midway through baking minimized its exposure to the juicy fruit, preventing it from becoming soggy. We like Golden Delicious apples here because of their ubiquity and consistent quality, but this recipe also works with Braeburn or Honeycrisp apples or a mix of all three. You should have 4 pounds of apples before peeling and coring. Dark brown sugar gives the topping a deeper color, but light brown sugar will also work. Do not use a glass baking dish here, since it retains heat after baking and may cause the apples to overcook. Serve with ice cream or lightly whipped cream.

- 4 pounds Golden Delicious apples, peeled, cored, and cut into ¾-inch pieces
- ½ cup packed (3½ ounces) plus 2 tablespoons packed dark brown sugar, divided
- 2 tablespoons lemon juice
- 1 teaspoon table salt, divided
- ¾ teaspoon ground cinnamon
- 1 cup (5 ounces) all-purpose flour
- ½ cup sliced almonds, chopped fine
- 6 tablespoons unsalted butter, melted
- 2 teaspoons vanilla extract
- 2 teaspoons water

**1.** Adjust oven racks to upper-middle and lowest positions and heat oven to 400 degrees. Toss apples, 2 tablespoons sugar, lemon juice, ½ teaspoon salt, and cinnamon together in large bowl. Transfer to 8-inch square baking pan with at least 2-inch sides and press into even layer. Cover pan tightly with aluminum foil and place on rimmed baking sheet. Transfer sheet to oven and bake on lower rack for 35 minutes.

**2.** While apples bake, whisk flour, almonds, remaining ½ cup sugar, and remaining ½ teaspoon salt in medium bowl until combined. Add melted butter, vanilla, and water and stir with spatula until clumps form and no dry flour remains.

**3.** Remove sheet from oven and smooth top of apples with spatula. If apples have not collapsed enough to leave at least ¼ inch of space below rim of pan, replace foil, return sheet to oven, and continue to bake 5 to 15 minutes longer.

**4.** Scatter topping evenly over apples, breaking up any clumps larger than a marble. Transfer sheet to upper rack and bake until topping is evenly browned and filling is just bubbling at edges, 25 to 35 minutes. Transfer pan to wire rack and let cool for at least 45 minutes before serving.

## Skillet Apple Crisp

**SERVES** 6 to 8

**WHY THIS RECIPE WORKS** Apple crisp needs to live up to its crisp moniker. We wanted an exemplary apple crisp—a lush (but not mushy) sweet-tart apple filling covered with truly crisp morsels of buttery, sugary topping. For apple crisp, we prefer crisp apples such as Golden Delicious, because they turn tender yet not mushy. But the problem with these apples is that their mellow flesh lacks fruity punch and they tend to cook unevenly. Stirring the fruit helped solve the problem but reaching into a hot oven to stir bubbling fruit was a hassle. Instead, we softened the fruit on the stovetop—in a skillet. The shallow, flared shape of the skillet also encouraged evaporation, browning, and better flavor overall. For even more intense fruity depth we added apple cider, which we first reduced to a syrupy consistency. Rolled oats contributed a pleasant chew to the topping and chopped pecans improved the crunch factor and added rich flavor. We then slid the skillet into the oven for a quick browning and to finish cooking the apples. Top the filling as directed and bake for an additional 5 minutes. We like Golden Delicious apples here, but any sweet, crisp apple such as Honeycrisp or Braeburn can be used. Do not use Granny Smith apples. While old-fashioned oats are preferable, quick-cooking oats can be substituted. You will need a 12-inch ovensafe skillet for this recipe. Serve warm or at room temperature with vanilla ice cream or whipped cream.

**TOPPING**

- ¾ cup (3¾ ounces) all-purpose flour
- ¾ cup pecans, chopped fine
- ¾ cup (2¼ ounces) old-fashioned rolled oats
- ½ cup packed (3½ ounces) light brown sugar
- ¼ cup (1¾ ounces) granulated sugar
- ½ teaspoon ground cinnamon
- ½ teaspoon table salt
- 8 tablespoons unsalted butter, melted

**FILLING**

- 3 pounds Golden Delicious apples, peeled, cored, halved, and cut into ½-inch-thick wedges
- ¼ cup (1¾ ounces) granulated sugar
- ¼ teaspoon ground cinnamon (optional)
- 1 cup apple cider
- 2 teaspoons lemon juice
- 2 tablespoons unsalted butter

**1. FOR THE TOPPING:** Adjust oven rack to middle position and heat oven to 450 degrees. Combine flour, pecans, oats, brown sugar, granulated sugar, cinnamon, and salt in medium bowl. Stir in melted butter until mixture is thoroughly moistened and crumbly. Set aside while preparing fruit filling.

**2. FOR THE FILLING:** Toss apples; sugar; and cinnamon, if using, together in large bowl; set aside. Bring cider to simmer in 12-inch ovensafe skillet over medium heat; cook until reduced to ½ cup, about 5 minutes. Transfer reduced cider to bowl or liquid measuring cup; stir in lemon juice and set aside.

**3.** Melt butter in now-empty skillet over medium heat. Add apple mixture and cook, stirring frequently, until apples are beginning to soften and become translucent, 12 to 14 minutes. (Do not fully cook apples.) Remove pan from heat and gently stir in cider mixture until apples are coated.

**4.** Sprinkle topping evenly over fruit, breaking up any large chunks. Place skillet on rimmed baking sheet and bake until fruit is tender and topping is deep golden brown, 15 to 20 minutes. Let cool on wire rack until warm, at least 15 minutes, and serve.

## Skillet Apple Brown Betty

**SERVES 6 to 8**

**WHY THIS RECIPE WORKS** In its most basic form, apple brown betty contains only four ingredients: apples, bread crumbs, sugar, and butter. It's a classic Colonial dish of tender, lightly spiced chunks of apple topped with toasted bread crumbs. We decided to give "Betty" a serious makeover. For a lightly sweetened, crisp topping, we toasted white sandwich bread crumbs with butter and a bit of sugar. The sweet-tart combination of Granny Smith and Golden Delicious apples made a not-too-sweet apple filling. Instead of baking the dessert, we prepared it in a skillet on the stovetop and cooked the apples in two batches to ensure even cooking. After preparing the bread crumbs, we removed them from the pan and caramelized the apples. Adding brown sugar to the apples along with ginger and cinnamon gave the dessert a deepened, lightly spiced flavor. The addition of apple cider to the fruit brought moisture and a further dimension of apple flavor; a bit of lemon juice brightened the filling. For a thicker filling, we added a portion of the toasted bread crumbs to the apples and reserved the remainder for sprinkling over the top. If your apples are especially tart, omit the lemon juice. If, on the other hand, your apples are exceptionally sweet, use the full amount. Leftovers can be refrigerated in an airtight container; topped with vanilla yogurt, they make an excellent breakfast.

**BREAD CRUMBS**

- 4 slices high-quality white sandwich bread, torn into quarters
- 3 tablespoons unsalted butter, cut into 4 pieces
- 2 tablespoons packed light brown sugar

**FILLING**

- ¼ cup packed (1¾ ounces) light brown sugar
- ¼ teaspoon ground ginger
- ¼ teaspoon ground cinnamon
- Pinch table salt
- 3 tablespoons unsalted butter
- 1½ pounds Granny Smith apples (about 3 large), peeled, cored, and cut into ½-inch cubes (about 4 cups)
- 1½ pounds Golden Delicious apples (about 3 large), peeled, cored, and cut into ½-inch cubes (about 4 cups)
- 1¼ cups apple cider
- 1–3 teaspoons juice from 1 lemon

**1. FOR THE BREAD CRUMBS:** Pulse the bread, butter, and sugar in a food processor until coarsely ground, 5 to 7 pulses. Transfer the bread crumbs to a 12-inch skillet and toast over medium heat, stirring constantly, until they are deep golden brown, 8 to 10 minutes. Transfer to a paper towel–lined plate; wipe out the skillet.

**2. FOR THE FILLING:** Combine the sugar, spices, and salt in a small bowl. Melt 1½ tablespoons of the butter in the now-empty skillet over high heat. Stir in the Granny Smith apples and half of the sugar mixture. Distribute the apples in an even layer and cook, stirring two or three times, until medium brown, about 5 minutes; transfer to a medium bowl. Repeat with the remaining butter, the Golden Delicious apples, and the remaining sugar mixture, returning the first batch of apples to the skillet when the second batch is done.

**3.** Add the apple cider to the skillet and scrape the bottom and sides of the pan with a wooden spoon to loosen the browned bits; cook until the apples are tender but not mushy and the liquid has reduced and is just beginning to thicken, 2 to 4 minutes.

**4.** Remove the skillet from the heat; stir in the lemon juice (if using) and ⅓ cup of the toasted bread crumbs. Using a wooden spoon, lightly flatten the apples into an even layer in the skillet and evenly sprinkle with the remaining toasted bread crumbs. Spoon the warm betty into individual bowls and serve with vanilla ice cream, if desired.

## Apple-Blackberry Betty

**SERVES 6 to 8**

**WHY THIS RECIPE WORKS** An apple Betty is like an apple crisp, but instead of a crumbly butter-sugar-flour topping, it features slightly sweetened bread crumbs both above and below the apples. A combination of Granny Smith and Golden Delicious apples mixed with just ⅓ cup of brown sugar gave our Betty a sweet-tart flavor while blackberries added bursts of wine-like acidity. Two tablespoons of water mixed into the apples created steam in the oven to jump-start the cooking, ensuring that the apples would be luxuriously soft. Bread crumbs made from white sandwich bread, enriched with butter and brown sugar and pressed into the bottom of the baking dish, accommodated any excess moisture shed by the apples as they cooked, while the bread crumbs on the top turned crisp and brown. You can substitute another soft, enriched bread such as challah or brioche for the sandwich bread; be sure to use 10 ounces. We call for a mix of Golden Delicious and Granny Smith apples here, but feel free to substitute any mix of a sweet and tart variety. You can substitute raspberries or blueberries for the blackberries, and it's fine to use frozen berries; alternatively, you can omit the berries.

- 10 ounces hearty white sandwich bread, cut into 1-inch pieces
- ½ cup packed (3½ ounces) plus ⅓ cup packed (2⅓ ounces) light brown sugar, divided
- ¾ teaspoon table salt, divided

- 6 tablespoons unsalted butter, melted
- 1½ pounds Golden Delicious apples, peeled, cored, and cut into ½-inch pieces
- 1 pound Granny Smith apples, peeled, cored, and cut into ½-inch pieces
- 2 tablespoons water
- 1 teaspoon vanilla extract
- ¼ teaspoon ground nutmeg
- 3¾ ounces (¾ cup) blackberries, berries larger than ¾ inch cut in half crosswise
- Vanilla ice cream or sweetened whipped cream

**1.** Adjust oven racks to upper-middle and lower-middle positions and heat oven to 375 degrees. Pulse bread in food processor until coarsely ground, about 15 pulses. Add ½ cup sugar and ½ teaspoon salt and pulse to combine, about 5 pulses. Drizzle with melted butter and pulse until evenly distributed, about 5 pulses. Scatter 2½ cups bread crumb mixture in 8-inch square baking dish. Press gently to create even layer.

**2.** Combine apples, water, vanilla, nutmeg, remaining ⅓ cup sugar, and remaining ¼ teaspoon salt in bowl. Pile apple mixture atop bread crumb mixture in dish and spread and press into even layer. Sprinkle blackberries over apples (dish will be very full). Distribute remaining bread crumb mixture evenly over blackberries and press lightly to form uniform layer. Cover tightly with aluminum foil. (Uncooked Betty can be refrigerated for up to 2 days.) Place on rimmed baking sheet and bake on lower rack until apples are soft, 1 hour to 1 hour 10 minutes.

**3.** Remove foil and transfer dish (still on sheet) to upper rack. Bake until crumbs on top are crisp and well browned, about 15 minutes. Transfer to wire rack and let cool for at least 20 minutes. Serve with ice cream. (This dessert is best served immediately. Leftovers can be covered tightly with foil and refrigerated for up to two days; warm before serving.)

## Easy Apple Strudel

SERVES 6

**WHY THIS RECIPE WORKS** Apple strudel, lightly spiced apples in a thin, flaky pastry, is usually a bit of a project. But we wanted all the flavor and charm of this apple dessert, without all the preparation. Replacing homemade strudel dough with storebought made for a crust with perfect flaky layers in a fraction of the time. We brushed the phyllo sheets with melted butter to keep them crisp and flaky. A combination of Golden Delicious and McIntosh apples, sliced thin, gave us a filling with layered apple flavor and just the right texture. A small amount of bread crumbs thickened the filling, golden raisins, plumped with Calvados (apple brandy), added a sophisticated, fruity dimension to the apple filling. We found that the phyllo on most strudels, including this one, curled and shattered as it cooled; sprinkling sugar between the layers of phyllo "glued" them together in the oven and prevented this. The best ways to thaw the phyllo are in the refrigerator overnight or at room temperature for 3 to 4 hours; do not thaw in a microwave. Make sure that the phyllo sheets you use for the strudel are not badly torn. If they have small cuts or tears in the same location (sometimes an entire package sustains cuts in the same spot), when forming the strudel, flip alternating layers so that the cuts will not line up and cause the strudel to burst during baking. To make the bread crumbs, process one slice of high-quality white sandwich bread in a food processor until fine, 20 to 30 seconds. Serve warm with Tangy Whipped Cream (recipe follows) or regular whipped cream.

- ½ cup golden raisins
- 2 tablespoons Calvados or apple cider
- 8 tablespoons unsalted butter, divided
- ¼ cup fresh bread crumbs
- 1 pound Golden Delicious apples, peeled, cored, and sliced ¼ inch thick
- 1 medium McIntosh apple, peeled, cored, and sliced ¼ inch thick
- 6 tablespoons (2⅔ ounces) granulated sugar, divided
- ⅓ cup finely chopped walnuts, toasted (optional)
- 1 teaspoon lemon juice
- ¼ teaspoon ground cinnamon
- ⅛ teaspoon table salt
- 10 (14 by 9-inch) phyllo sheets, thawed
- 1½ teaspoons confectioners' sugar

**1.** Adjust oven rack to lower-middle position and heat oven to 475 degrees. Line rimmed baking sheet with parchment paper. Bring raisins and Calvados to simmer in small saucepan over medium heat. Cover, remove from heat, and let stand until needed.

**2.** Combine 1 tablespoon butter and bread crumbs in 8-inch skillet and cook over medium heat, stirring frequently, until golden brown, about 2 minutes. Transfer bread crumbs to large bowl.

**3.** Drain off and discard any remaining liquid from raisins. Toss raisins; bread crumbs; apples; ¼ cup granulated sugar; walnuts, if using; lemon juice; cinnamon; and salt in large bowl to combine.

**4.** Melt remaining 7 tablespoons butter in now-empty skillet. Place large sheet of parchment horizontally on counter. Lay 1 sheet phyllo on left side of parchment, then brush with melted butter and sprinkle with ½ teaspoon granulated sugar. Place another sheet of phyllo on right side of parchment, overlapping sheets by 1 inch, then brush with more butter and sprinkle with sugar. Repeat this process with remaining 8 sheets phyllo, butter, and sugar. Mound filling along bottom edge of phyllo, leaving 2½-inch border on bottom and 2-inch border on sides. Fold dough on sides over apples. Fold dough on bottom over apples and continue to roll dough around filling to form strudel.

**5.** Place strudel, seam side down, on prepared sheet; brush with remaining butter and sprinkle with remaining 1 teaspoon sugar. Cut four 1-inch crosswise vents into top of strudel and bake until golden brown, 15 minutes. Transfer sheet to wire rack and let cool until warm, about 40 minutes.

**6.** Dust strudel with confectioners' sugar before serving; slice with serrated knife and serve warm or at room temperature.

### ASSEMBLING EASY APPLE STRUDEL

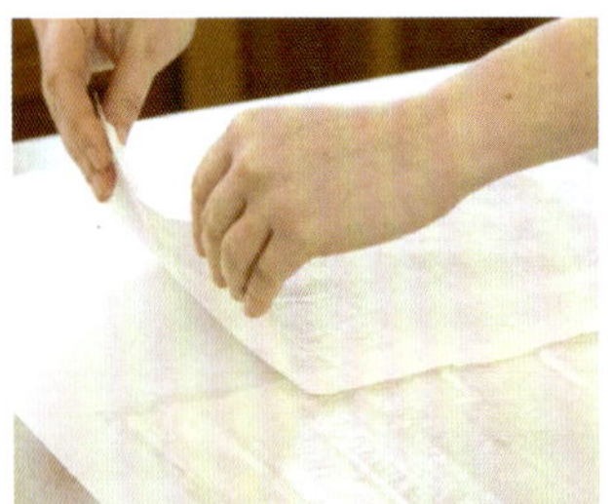

**1.** Brush 1 sheet of phyllo with melted butter and sprinkle with granulated sugar. Place another sheet of phyllo next to it, overlapping sheets. Brush with more butter and sprinkle with sugar. Repeat this process 4 times.

**2.** Mound filling along bottom edge of phyllo, leaving 2½-inch border on bottom and 2-inch border on sides.

**3.** Fold dough on sides over apples. Fold dough on bottom over apples and continue to roll dough around filling to form strudel.

**4.** After strudel has been assembled and rolled, gently lay it seam side down on prepared baking sheet.

## Tangy Whipped Cream

**MAKES** 2 cups

Adding sour cream to whipped cream mimics the pleasantly tart flavor of the rich French-style whipped cream, crème fraîche.

- 1 cup heavy cream
- ½ cup sour cream
- 1 tablespoon sugar
- 1 teaspoon vanilla extract

Using stand mixer fitted with whisk attachment, whip all ingredients on medium-low speed until frothy, about 1 minute. Increase speed to high and whip until soft peaks form, 1 to 3 minutes.

## Apple Strudel

**SERVES** 6

**WHY THIS RECIPE WORKS** Most modern phyllo-based versions of strudel have tough layers of phyllo on the underside, while the sheets on top shatter before you even cut a slice. We parcooked the apples in the microwave to activate an enzyme that sets the pectin in the fruit and allows them to bake without collapsing. We stirred in ultradry panko bread crumbs instead of homemade toasted crumbs since we could use less of them to soak up a comparable amount of liquid (thus avoiding pastiness). To avoid a compressed, tough underside, we used fewer sheets of phyllo and changed the typical wrapping technique so the seam was on the top instead of on the bottom. We were able to minimize the flyaways on top by dusting a small amount of confectioners' sugar between the phyllo layers so that they fused in the oven, and by slicing our strudel while it was warm. Making two smaller strudels simplified assembly. Gala apples can be substituted for Golden Delicious. Phyllo dough is also available in larger 18 by 14-inch sheets; if using, cut them in half to make 14 by 9-inch sheets. Thaw phyllo in the refrigerator overnight or on the counter for 3 to 4 hours; don't thaw it in the microwave.

- 1¾ pounds Golden Delicious apples, peeled, cored, and cut into ½-inch pieces
- 3 tablespoons granulated sugar
- ½ teaspoon grated lemon zest plus 1½ teaspoons juice
- ¼ teaspoon ground cinnamon
- ¼ teaspoon ground ginger
- Table salt
- 3 tablespoons golden raisins
- 1½ tablespoons panko bread crumbs
- 7 tablespoons unsalted butter, melted
- 14 (14 by 9-inch) phyllo sheets, thawed
- 1 tablespoon confectioners' sugar, plus extra for serving

**1.** Toss apples, granulated sugar, lemon zest and juice, cinnamon, ginger, and ⅛ teaspoon salt together in large bowl. Cover and microwave until apples are warm to touch, about

2 minutes, stirring once halfway through microwaving. Let apples stand, covered, for 5 minutes. Transfer apples to colander set in second large bowl and let drain, reserving liquid. Return apples to bowl; stir in raisins and panko.

**2.** Adjust oven rack to upper-middle position and heat oven to 375 degrees. Spray rimmed baking sheet with vegetable oil spray. Stir ⅛ teaspoon salt into melted butter.

**3.** Place 16½ by 12-inch sheet of parchment paper on counter with long side parallel to edge of counter. Place 1 phyllo sheet on parchment with long side parallel to edge of counter. Place 1½ teaspoons confectioners' sugar in fine-mesh strainer (rest strainer in bowl to prevent making mess). Lightly brush sheet with melted butter and dust sparingly with confectioners' sugar. Repeat with 6 more phyllo sheets, melted butter, and confectioners' sugar, stacking sheets one on top of the other as you go.

**4.** Arrange half of apple mixture in 2½ by 10-inch rectangle 2 inches from bottom of phyllo and about 2 inches from each side. Using parchment, fold sides of phyllo over filling, then fold bottom edge of phyllo over filling. Brush folded portions of phyllo with reserved apple liquid. Fold top edge over filling, making sure top and bottom edges overlap by about 1 inch. (If they do not overlap, unfold, rearrange filling into slightly narrower strip, and refold.) Press firmly to seal. Using thin metal spatula, transfer strudel to 1 side of prepared baking sheet, facing seam toward center of sheet. Lightly brush top and sides of strudel with half of remaining apple liquid. Repeat process with remaining phyllo, melted butter, confectioners' sugar, filling, and apple liquid. Place second strudel on other side of prepared sheet, with seam facing center of sheet.

**5.** Bake strudels until golden brown, 27 to 35 minutes, rotating sheet halfway through baking. Using thin metal spatula, immediately transfer strudels to cutting board. Let cool for 3 minutes. Slice each strudel into thirds and let cool for at least 20 minutes. Serve warm or at room temperature.

## Blueberry Cobbler

**SERVES** 6 to 8

**WHY THIS RECIPE WORKS** Too often, blueberry cobbler means a filling that is too sweet, overspiced, and unappealingly thick. We wanted a not-too-thin, not-too-thick filling where the blueberry flavor would be front and center. And we wanted a light, tender biscuit topping that could hold its own against the fruit filling, but allow the blueberries to play a starring role. We prepared a not-too-sweet filling using 6 cups of fresh berries and less than a cup of sugar. Cornstarch worked well as a thickener—it thickened the fruit's juice without leaving a starchy texture behind. A little lemon and cinnamon were all that were needed to enhance the filling. For the topping, ease of preparation was our guiding principle, so we made light, rustic drop biscuits enriched with a little cornmeal. Adding the biscuit topping to the cobbler after the filling had baked on its own allowed the biscuits to brown evenly and cook through. A sprinkling of cinnamon sugar on the dropped biscuit dough added a pleasing sweet crunch. While the

blueberries are baking, prepare the ingredients for the topping, but do not stir the wet ingredients into the dry ingredients until just before the berries come out of the oven. A standard or deep-dish 9-inch pie plate works well; an 8-inch square baking dish can also be used. Serve with vanilla ice cream or lightly sweetened whipped cream. Leftovers can be reheated in a 350-degree oven for 10 to 15 minutes.

**FILLING**

- ½ cup (3½ ounces) sugar
- 1 tablespoon cornstarch
- Pinch ground cinnamon
- Pinch table salt
- 6 cups (30 ounces) fresh blueberries, rinsed and picked over
- 1½ teaspoons grated zest plus 1 tablespoon juice from 1 lemon

**BISCUIT TOPPING**

- 1 cup (5 ounces) unbleached all-purpose flour
- ¼ cup (1¾ ounces) plus 2 teaspoons sugar
- 2 tablespoons stone-ground cornmeal
- 2 teaspoons baking powder
- ¼ teaspoon baking soda
- ¼ teaspoon table salt
- 4 tablespoons (½ stick) unsalted butter, melted
- ⅓ cup buttermilk
- ½ teaspoon vanilla extract
- ⅛ teaspoon ground cinnamon

**1.** Adjust an oven rack to the lower-middle position and heat the oven to 375 degrees.

**2. FOR THE FILLING:** Whisk the sugar, cornstarch, cinnamon, and salt together in a large bowl. Add the berries and mix gently with a rubber spatula until evenly coated; add the lemon zest and juice and mix to combine. Transfer the berry mixture to a 9-inch glass pie plate, place the pie plate on a rimmed baking sheet, and bake until the filling is hot and bubbling around the edges, about 25 minutes.

**3. FOR THE BISCUIT TOPPING:** Meanwhile, whisk the flour, 1/4 cup of the sugar, the cornmeal, baking powder, baking soda, and salt together in a large bowl. Whisk the melted butter, buttermilk, and vanilla together in a small bowl. Mix the remaining 2 teaspoons sugar with the cinnamon in a second small bowl and set aside. One minute before the berries come out of the oven, add the wet ingredients to the dry ingredients; stir with a rubber spatula until just combined and no dry pockets remain.

**4. TO ASSEMBLE AND BAKE:** Remove the berries from the oven; increase the oven temperature to 425 degrees. Divide the biscuit dough into eight equal pieces and place them on the hot berry filling, spacing them at least 1/2 inch apart (they should not touch). Sprinkle each mound of dough evenly with the cinnamon sugar. Bake until the filling is bubbling and the biscuits are golden brown on top and cooked through, 15 to 18 minutes. Transfer the cobbler to a wire rack; cool for 20 minutes and serve.

## Sour Cherry Cobbler

SERVES 12

**WHY THIS RECIPE WORKS** Many cherry cobblers are no more than canned pie filling topped with dry, heavy biscuits. We wanted a filling that highlighted the sweet-tart flavor of sour cherries and a tender, feather-light biscuit crust. Because fresh sour cherries are so hard to find most of the year, we picked jarred Morello cherries—easy to find and available year-round. Embellishing the cherries with cherry juice, cinnamon, and vanilla was a step in the right direction but the filling still tasted a bit flat, so we switched out some of the juice for red wine and replaced the vanilla with almond extract. As for the biscuits, we favored buttermilk biscuits for their fluffy texture. To ensure nicely browned biscuits that didn't become soggy, we parbaked them ahead of time, then slid the biscuits over the warm cherry filling and put it in the oven to finish cooking. Use the smaller amount of sugar in the filling if you prefer your fruit desserts on the tart side and the larger amount if you like them sweet. Serve with vanilla ice cream or lightly sweetened whipped cream.

BISCUIT TOPPING

- 2 cups (10 ounces) all-purpose flour
- ½ cup (3½ ounces) sugar, divided
- ½ teaspoon baking powder
- ½ teaspoon baking soda
- ½ teaspoon table salt
- 6 tablespoons unsalted butter, cut into ½-inch pieces and chilled
- 1 cup buttermilk

FILLING

- 8 cups jarred Morello cherries from 4 (24-ounce) jars, drained, 2 cups juice reserved
- ¾–1 cup (5¼ to 7 ounces) sugar
- 3 tablespoons plus 1 teaspoon cornstarch
- Pinch table salt
- 1 cup dry red wine
- 1 cinnamon stick
- ¼ teaspoon almond extract

**1.** Adjust oven rack to middle position and heat oven to 425 degrees. Line rimmed baking sheet with parchment paper.

**2. FOR THE BISCUIT TOPPING:** Pulse flour, 6 tablespoons sugar, baking powder, baking soda, and salt in food processor until combined, about 3 pulses. Sprinkle butter pieces over top and pulse until mixture resembles coarse meal, about 15 pulses. Transfer mixture to large bowl; add buttermilk and stir with rubber spatula until combined. Using greased 1/4-cup measure, space 12 biscuits 1½ inches apart on prepared sheet. Sprinkle biscuits evenly with remaining 2 tablespoons sugar and bake until lightly browned, about 15 minutes, rotating sheet halfway through baking. (Do not turn oven off.)

**3. FOR THE FILLING:** Meanwhile, arrange drained cherries in even layer in 13 by 9-inch baking dish. Combine sugar, cornstarch, and salt in medium saucepan. Stir in reserved cherry juice and wine and add cinnamon stick; cook over medium-high heat, stirring frequently, until mixture simmers and thickens, about 5 minutes. Discard cinnamon stick, stir in almond extract, and pour hot liquid over cherries in baking dish.

**4. TO BAKE:** Arrange hot biscuits in 3 rows of 4 biscuits over warm filling. Bake cobbler until filling is bubbling and biscuits are deep golden brown, about 10 minutes. Transfer baking dish to wire rack and let cool for 10 minutes; serve.

### Fresh Sour Cherry Cobbler

Morello or Montmorency cherries can be used in this cobbler made with fresh sour cherries. Do not use sweet Bing cherries. If the cherries do not release enough juice after 30 minutes in step 1, add cranberry juice to make up the difference.

- 1¼ cups (8¾ ounces) sugar
- 3 tablespoons plus 1 teaspoon cornstarch
- Pinch table salt
- 4 pounds fresh sour cherries, pitted, juice from pitting reserved
- 1 cup dry red wine
- Cranberry juice, as needed
- 1 recipe Biscuit Topping
- 1 cinnamon stick
- ¼ teaspoon almond extract

**1.** Whisk sugar, cornstarch, and salt together in large bowl; add cherries and toss well to combine. Pour wine over cherries; let stand for 30 minutes. Drain cherries in colander set over medium bowl. Combine drained and reserved juices (from pitting cherries); you should have 3 cups (if not, add cranberry juice to make this amount).

**2.** Meanwhile, prepare and bake biscuit topping.

**3.** Arrange drained cherries in even layer in 13 by 9-inch baking dish. Bring juices and cinnamon stick to simmer in medium saucepan over medium-high heat, stirring frequently, until mixture thickens, about 5 minutes. Discard cinnamon stick, stir in almond extract, and pour hot juices over cherries in baking dish.

4. Arrange hot biscuits in 3 rows of 4 biscuits over warm filling. Bake cobbler until filling is bubbling and biscuits are deep golden brown, about 10 minutes. Transfer baking dish to wire rack and let cool for 10 minutes; serve.

## Cherry Clafouti

**SERVES** 6 to 8

**WHY THIS RECIPE WORKS** This baked French custard studded with fruit is an easy and satisfying dessert. For a clafouti that featured juicy cherries in every bite, we pitted and halved the cherries. To concentrate their flavor and eliminate excess moisture, we roasted them in a hot oven for 15 minutes and then tossed them with a couple of teaspoons of flour. To recover the slightly spicy, floral flavor the pits contributed, we added ⅛ teaspoon of cinnamon to the flour. We found that too much flour made the custard too bready, whereas an excess of dairy made it too loose. Ultimately, we settled on a moderate amount of each for a tender yet slightly resilient custard void of pastiness. Switching from a casserole dish to a preheated ovensafe 12-inch skillet gave us better browning and made the custard easy to slice and serve. We prefer whole milk in this recipe, but 1 or 2 percent low-fat milk may be substituted. Do not substitute frozen cherries for the fresh cherries.

- 1½ pounds fresh sweet cherries, pitted and halved
- 1 teaspoon lemon juice
- 2 teaspoons plus ½ cup (2½ ounces) all-purpose flour, divided
- ⅛ teaspoon ground cinnamon
- 4 large eggs
- ⅔ cup (4⅔ ounces) plus 2 teaspoons sugar, divided
- 2½ teaspoons vanilla extract
- ¼ teaspoon table salt
- 1 cup heavy cream
- ⅔ cup whole milk
- 1 tablespoon unsalted butter

1. Adjust oven racks to upper-middle and lowest positions; place 12-inch ovensafe skillet on lower rack and heat oven to 425 degrees. Line rimmed baking sheet with aluminum foil and place cherries, cut side up, on sheet. Roast cherries on upper rack until just tender and cut sides look dry, about 15 minutes. Transfer cherries to medium bowl, toss with lemon juice, and let cool 5 for minutes. Combine 2 teaspoons flour and cinnamon in small bowl; dust flour mixture evenly over cherries and toss to coat thoroughly.

2. While cherries roast, whisk eggs, ⅔ cup sugar, vanilla, and salt in large bowl until smooth and pale, about 1 minute. Whisk in remaining ½ cup flour until smooth. Whisk in cream and milk until incorporated.

3. Remove skillet (skillet handle will be hot) from oven and set on wire rack. Add butter and swirl to coat bottom and sides of skillet (butter will melt and brown quickly). Pour batter into skillet and place cherries evenly over top (some will sink). Transfer skillet to lower rack and bake until clafouti puffs and surface is golden brown (edges will be dark brown) and center registers 195 degrees, 18 to 22 minutes, rotating skillet halfway through baking. Transfer skillet to wire rack and let cool for 25 minutes. Sprinkle evenly with remaining 2 teaspoons sugar. Slice into wedges and serve.

## Simple Raspberry Gratin

**SERVES** 4 to 6

**WHY THIS RECIPE WORKS** Quicker than a crisp and dressier than a shortcake, a gratin is a layer of fresh fruit piled into a shallow baking dish, dressed up with bread crumbs, and run under a broiler. The topping browns and the fruit is warmed just enough to release a bit of juice. We wanted to find the quickest, easiest route to this pleasing dessert. We started with perfect raspberries: ripe, dry, unbruised, and clean. Tossing the sweet-tart berries with just a bit of sugar and kirsch (a clear cherry brandy; vanilla extract can be substituted) provided enough additional flavor and sweetness. For the topping, we combined soft white bread, brown sugar, cinnamon, and butter in the food processor and topped the berries with the fluffy crumbs. Instead of broiling the gratin, which can produce a crust that's burnt in spots, we simply baked it. We found that a moderately hot oven gave the berries more time to soften and browned the crust more evenly. If you prefer, you can substitute blueberries, blackberries, or strawberries for part or all of the raspberries. If using strawberries, hull them and slice them in half lengthwise if small or into quarters if large. Later in the summer season, ripe, peeled peaches or nectarines, sliced, can be used in combination with the blueberries or raspberries.

- 4 cups (20 ounces) fresh or frozen (not thawed) raspberries
- 1 tablespoon granulated sugar
- 1 tablespoon kirsch or vanilla extract (optional)
- Pinch table salt
- 3 slices high-quality white sandwich bread, torn into quarters
- ¼ cup packed (1¾ ounces) light or dark brown sugar
- 2 tablespoons unsalted butter, softened
- Pinch ground cinnamon

**1.** Adjust an oven rack to the lower-middle position and heat the oven to 400 degrees. Gently toss the raspberries, granulated sugar, kirsch (if using), and salt in a medium bowl. Transfer the mixture to a 9-inch glass pie plate.

**2.** Pulse the bread, brown sugar, butter, and cinnamon in a food processor until the mixture resembles coarse crumbs, about 10 pulses. Sprinkle the crumbs evenly over the fruit and bake until the crumbs are deep golden brown, 15 to 20 minutes. Transfer to a wire rack; cool for 5 minutes and serve.

## Individual Fresh Berry Gratins with Zabaglione

**SERVES 4**

**WHY THIS RECIPE WORKS** Gratins can be very humble or they can be a bit more sophisticated, as when they are topped with the foamy Italian custard called zabaglione. Ideally, the process for making zabaglione transforms egg yolks into a thick, creamy custard. But this tricky topping can be easy to overcook, so we wanted a foolproof method. We chose to make individual gratins—perfect for entertaining—featuring raspberries, strawberries, blueberries, and blackberries. We tossed the berries with sugar and a pinch of salt to draw out their juices and let the mixture sit while we prepared the custard. To prevent scrambled eggs we kept the heat low, and for the right texture we didn't stop whisking when soft peaks formed; instead we waited until the custard became slightly thicker. Zabaglione made with the traditional Marsala wine was a bit sweet on top of the berries. A crisp, dry Sauvignon Blanc allowed the berries to shine; however, with that change our zabaglione was almost runny. Carefully folding a few tablespoons of whipped cream into the cooked and slightly cooled zabaglione base thickened it just enough to spoon over the berries. Finally, we sprinkled the custard with a mixture of brown and white sugar before broiling for a crackly, caramelized crust. When making the zabaglione, make sure to cook the egg mixture in a glass bowl over water that is barely simmering; glass conducts heat more evenly and gently than metal. If the heat is too high, the yolks around the edges of the bowl will start to scramble. Constant whisking is required. Do not use frozen berries for this recipe. You will need four shallow 6-inch gratin dishes, but a broiler-safe pie plate or gratin dish can be used instead. To prevent scorching, pay close attention to the gratins when broiling.

**BERRY MIXTURE**

- 2¼ cups (11 ounces) raspberries, blueberries, and/or blackberries
- ¾ cup (4 ounces) strawberries, hulled and halved lengthwise if small or quartered if large
- 2 teaspoons granulated sugar
- Pinch table salt

**ZABAGLIONE**

- 3 large egg yolks
- 3 tablespoons granulated sugar, divided
- 3 tablespoons dry white wine
- 2 teaspoons packed light brown sugar
- 3 tablespoons heavy cream, chilled

**1. FOR THE BERRY MIXTURE:** Toss berries, strawberries, sugar, and salt together in medium bowl. Divide berry mixture evenly among 4 shallow 6-ounce gratin dishes set on rimmed baking sheet; set aside.

**2. FOR THE ZABAGLIONE:** Whisk egg yolks, 2 tablespoons plus 1 teaspoon granulated sugar, and wine in medium glass bowl until sugar is dissolved, about 1 minute. Set bowl over saucepan of barely simmering water and cook, whisking constantly, until mixture is frothy. Continue to cook, whisking constantly, until mixture is slightly thickened, creamy, and glossy, 5 to 10 minutes (mixture will form loose mounds when dripped from whisk). Remove bowl from saucepan and whisk constantly for 30 seconds to cool slightly. Transfer bowl to refrigerator and chill until egg mixture is completely cool, about 10 minutes.

**3.** Meanwhile, adjust oven rack 6 inches from broiler element and heat broiler. Combine brown sugar and remaining 2 teaspoons granulated sugar in small bowl.

**4.** Whisk heavy cream in large bowl until it holds soft peaks, 30 to 90 seconds. Using rubber spatula, gently fold whipped cream into cooled egg mixture. Spoon zabaglione over berries and sprinkle sugar mixture evenly on top; let stand at room temperature for 10 minutes, until sugar dissolves.

**5.** Broil gratins until sugar is bubbly and caramelized, 1 to 4 minutes. Serve immediately.

### Individual Fresh Berry Gratins with Lemon Zabaglione

Substitute 1 tablespoon lemon juice for 1 tablespoon wine and add 1 teaspoon grated zest to yolk mixture in step 2.

## Easy Strawberry Shortcakes for Two

**SERVES 2**

**WHY THIS RECIPE WORKS** Our ideal strawberry shortcakes are tender, flaky biscuits topped with juicy strawberries and a dollop of whipped cream. And because they're assembled individually, they're an ideal dessert for two. Because the fruit isn't cooked, fresh, ripe berries are essential. Slicing most of the strawberries made for an attractive presentation, while crushing a portion of them helped unify the sliced fruit and prevented it from sliding off the biscuits. We used all-purpose flour for tender, cakey biscuits; an egg and some half-and-half contributed richness. With such a small amount of dough, we found it best to shape the biscuits by hand (rather than stamp them out) to ensure that none went to waste. Fresh blueberries, raspberries, or halved blackberries can be substituted for some or all of the strawberries. Fresh fruit is key to the success of these shortcakes; do not substitute frozen strawberries.

**FRUIT**

- 10 ounces strawberries, hulled (2 cups), divided
- 5 teaspoons sugar

**BISCUITS**

- ⅔ cup (3⅓ ounces) all-purpose flour
- 2 tablespoons sugar, divided
- 1 teaspoon baking powder
- ⅛ teaspoon table salt
- 4 tablespoons unsalted butter, cut into ½-inch pieces and chilled
- 2 tablespoons half-and-half
- 1 large egg, lightly beaten, plus 1 large white, lightly beaten

- 1 recipe Whipped Cream

**1. FOR THE FRUIT:** Crush ¾ cup strawberries in medium bowl with potato masher. Slice remaining 1¼ cups strawberries. Stir sliced strawberries and sugar into crushed strawberries. Set aside until sugar has dissolved and strawberries are juicy, at least 30 minutes or up to 2 hours.

**2. FOR THE BISCUITS:** Meanwhile, adjust oven rack to middle position and heat oven to 425 degrees. Line rimmed baking sheet with parchment paper. Process flour, 5 teaspoons sugar, baking powder, and salt in food processor until combined, about 5 seconds. Scatter butter over top and pulse until mixture resembles coarse cornmeal, about 15 pulses. Transfer mixture to medium bowl.

**3.** In separate bowl, whisk half-and-half and whole egg together, then stir into flour mixture with rubber spatula until large clumps form. Turn dough and any floury bits onto lightly floured counter and knead lightly until dough comes together (do not overwork dough). Divide dough into 2 even pieces, then, with your well-floured hands, shape each into 2½-inch round, about 1 inch thick.

**4.** Arrange biscuits on prepared sheet. Brush tops with egg white and sprinkle evenly with remaining 1 teaspoon sugar. Bake biscuits until golden brown, 10 to 12 minutes, rotating sheet halfway through baking. Transfer biscuits to wire rack and let cool for 15 minutes.

**5.** To assemble, split each biscuit in half and place bottoms on individual serving plates. Spoon strawberries over each bottom, dollop with whipped cream, and cap with biscuit tops. Serve immediately.

### Whipped Cream

**MAKES ¾ cup**

The whipped cream can be refrigerated in a fine-mesh strainer set over a small bowl, wrapped tightly with plastic wrap, for up to 8 hours.

- ⅓ cup heavy cream, chilled
- 1 teaspoon sugar
- ¼ teaspoon vanilla extract

Using hand mixer set at medium-low speed, beat cream, sugar, and vanilla in medium bowl until foamy, about 1 minute. Increase speed to high and beat until soft peaks form, 1 to 3 minutes.

## Strawberry Shortcakes

**SERVES 6**

**WHY THIS RECIPE WORKS** While some cooks like to spoon strawberries over pound cake, sponge cake, and even angel food cake, our idea of strawberry shortcake definitely involves a biscuit. While eggs are not traditional, we found that one whole egg gave our biscuits a light, tender texture. And we used just enough dairy (half-and-half or milk) to bind the dough together. A modest amount of sugar yielded a lightly sweetened biscuit. For the strawberries, we wanted to avoid both a mushy puree and dry chunks of fruit. We found our solution in a compromise—mashing a portion of the berries and slicing the rest for a chunky, juicy mixture that didn't slide off the biscuit. And lightly sweetened whipped cream, flavored with vanilla, provided a cool, creamy contrast to the berries and biscuits. Start the recipe by preparing the fruit, then set the fruit aside while preparing the biscuits to allow the juices to become syrupy.

**FRUIT**

- 8 cups (40 ounces) strawberries, hulled
- 6 tablespoons sugar

SHORTCAKE

- 2 cups (10 ounces) unbleached all-purpose flour, plus extra for the work surface and biscuit cutter
- 5 tablespoons sugar
- 1 tablespoon baking powder
- ½ teaspoon table salt
- 8 tablespoons (1 stick) unsalted butter, cut into ½-inch pieces and chilled
- ½ cup plus 1 tablespoon half-and-half or milk
- 1 large whole egg, lightly beaten
- 1 large egg white, lightly beaten

WHIPPED CREAM

- 1 cup heavy cream, chilled
- 1 tablespoon sugar
- 1 teaspoon vanilla extract

**1. FOR THE FRUIT:** Crush 3 cups of the strawberries in a large bowl with a potato masher. Slice the remaining 5 cups of berries and stir them into the crushed berries along with the sugar. Set aside until the sugar has dissolved and the berries are juicy, at least 30 minutes or up to 2 hours.

**2. FOR THE SHORTCAKE:** Adjust an oven rack to the lower-middle position and heat the oven to 425 degrees. Line a large baking sheet with parchment paper. Pulse the flour, 3 tablespoons of the sugar, the baking powder, and salt in a food processor until combined. Sprinkle the butter pieces over the top and pulse until the mixture resembles coarse meal, about 15 pulses. Transfer the mixture to a large bowl.

**3.** Whisk the half-and-half and lightly beaten whole egg together in a small bowl, then stir into the flour mixture with a rubber spatula until large clumps form. Turn the dough onto a lightly floured work surface and knead lightly until it comes together.

**4.** Pat the dough into a 9 by 6-inch rectangle, about ¾ inch thick. Do not overwork the dough. Using a floured 2¾-inch biscuit cutter, cut out six dough rounds. Arrange the shortcakes on the prepared baking sheet, spaced about 1½ inches apart. Brush the tops with the lightly beaten egg white and sprinkle evenly with the remaining 2 tablespoons sugar. (The unbaked shortcakes can be covered with plastic wrap and refrigerated for up to 2 hours.)

**5.** Bake until the shortcakes are golden brown, 12 to 14 minutes, rotating the sheet halfway through the baking time. Transfer the sheet to a wire rack and cool the shortcakes until warm, about 10 minutes.

**6.** For the whipped cream: In a medium bowl, whip the cream, sugar, and vanilla with an electric mixer on medium-low speed until frothy, about 1 minute. Increase the speed to high and continue to whip until the cream forms soft peaks, 1 to 3 minutes.

**7. TO ASSEMBLE:** When the shortcakes have cooled slightly, split them in half horizontally. Place each shortcake bottom on an individual plate, spoon a portion of the berries over each bottom, dollop with whipped cream, and cap with the shortcake tops. Serve immediately.

## Summer Berry Trifle

**SERVES** 12 to 16

**WHY THIS RECIPE WORKS** Trifles usually look a lot better than they taste because busy cooks simplify the complicated preparation by subbing in shortcut ingredients like store-bought cake and pudding from a box. We wanted to streamline, but not shortchange, the components so that the entire trifle could be made from scratch in just a few hours. We added a little extra flour to a classic chiffon cake so we could bake it in an 18 by 13-inch sheet, which baked and cooled much more quickly than the traditional tall chiffon cake, and we prevented our pastry cream from turning runny during assembly by adding a little extra cornstarch. We mashed one-third of the berries so their juices would provide moisture to the cake. A bit of cream sherry added a sophisticated layer of flavor. For the best texture, this trifle should be assembled at least 6 hours before serving. Use a glass bowl with at least a 3½-quart capacity; straight sides are preferable.

PASTRY CREAM

- 3½ cups whole milk, divided
- 1 cup (7 ounces) sugar
- 6 tablespoons cornstarch
- Pinch table salt
- 5 large egg yolks (reserve whites for cake)
- 4 tablespoons unsalted butter, cut into ½-inch pieces and chilled
- 4 teaspoons vanilla extract

CAKE

- 1⅓ cups (5⅓ ounces) cake flour
- ¾ cup (5¼ ounces) sugar
- 1½ teaspoons baking powder
- ¼ teaspoon table salt
- ⅓ cup vegetable oil
- ¼ cup water
- 1 large egg
- 2 teaspoons vanilla extract
- 5 large egg whites (reserved from pastry cream)
- ¼ teaspoon cream of tartar

FRUIT FILLING

- 1½ pounds strawberries, hulled and cut into ½-inch pieces (4 cups), reserving 3 halved for garnish, divided
- 12 ounces (2⅓ cups) blackberries, large berries halved crosswise, reserving 3 whole for garnish, divided
- 12 ounces (2⅓ cups) raspberries, reserving 3 for garnish, divided
- ¼ cup (1¾ ounces) sugar
- ½ teaspoon cornstarch
- Pinch table salt

WHIPPED CREAM

- 1 cup heavy cream
- 1 tablespoon sugar
- 1 tablespoon plus ½ cup cream sherry, divided

**1. FOR THE PASTRY CREAM:** Heat 3 cups milk in medium saucepan over medium heat until just simmering. Meanwhile, whisk sugar, cornstarch, and salt together in medium bowl. Whisk remaining ½ cup milk and egg yolks into sugar mixture until smooth. Remove milk from heat and, whisking constantly, slowly add 1 cup to sugar mixture to temper. Whisking constantly, return tempered sugar mixture to milk in saucepan.

**2.** Return saucepan to medium heat and cook, whisking constantly, until mixture is very thick and bubbles burst on surface, 4 to 7 minutes. Remove saucepan from heat; whisk in butter and vanilla until butter is melted and incorporated. Strain pastry cream through fine-mesh strainer set over medium bowl. Press lightly greased parchment paper directly on surface and refrigerate until set, at least 2 hours or up to 24 hours.

**3. FOR THE CAKE:** Adjust oven rack to middle position and heat oven to 350 degrees. Lightly grease 18 by 13-inch rimmed baking sheet, line with parchment, and lightly grease parchment. Whisk flour, sugar, baking powder, and salt together in medium bowl. Whisk oil, water, egg, and vanilla into flour mixture until smooth batter forms.

**4.** Using stand mixer fitted with whisk attachment, whip egg whites and cream of tartar on medium-low speed until foamy, about 1 minute. Increase speed to medium-high and whip until soft peaks form, 2 to 3 minutes. Transfer one-third of whipped egg whites to batter; whisk gently until mixture is lightened. Using rubber spatula, gently fold remaining egg whites into batter.

**5.** Pour batter into prepared sheet; spread evenly. Bake until top is golden brown and cake springs back when pressed lightly in center, 13 to 16 minutes.

**6.** Transfer cake to wire rack; let cool for 5 minutes. Run knife around edge of sheet, then invert cake onto wire rack. Carefully remove parchment, then reinvert cake onto second wire rack. Let cool completely, at least 30 minutes.

**7. FOR THE FRUIT FILLING:** Place 1½ cups strawberries, 1 cup blackberries, 1 cup raspberries, sugar, cornstarch, and salt in medium saucepan. Place remaining berries (except those reserved for garnish) in large bowl; set aside. Using potato masher, thoroughly mash berries in saucepan. Cook over medium heat until sugar is dissolved and mixture is thick and bubbling, 4 to 7 minutes. Pour over berries in bowl and stir to combine. Set aside.

**8. FOR THE WHIPPED CREAM:** Using stand mixer fitted with whisk attachment, whip cream, sugar, and 1 tablespoon sherry on medium-low speed until foamy, about 1 minute. Increase speed to high and whip until soft peaks form, 1 to 2 minutes.

**9.** Trim ¼ inch off each side of cake; discard trimmings. Using serrated knife, cut cake into 24 equal pieces (each piece about 2½ inches square).

**10.** Briefly whisk pastry cream until smooth. Spoon ¾ cup pastry cream into trifle bowl; spread over bottom. Shingle 12 cake pieces, fallen-domino-style, around bottom of trifle, placing 10 pieces against dish wall and 2 remaining pieces in center. Drizzle ¼ cup sherry evenly over cake. Spoon half of berry mixture evenly over cake, making sure to use half of liquid. Using back of spoon, spread half of remaining pastry cream over berries, then spread half of whipped cream over pastry cream (whipped cream layer will be thin). Repeat layering with remaining 12 cake pieces, sherry, berries, pastry cream, and whipped cream. Cover bowl with plastic wrap and refrigerate for at least 6 hours or up to 36 hours. Garnish top of trifle with reserved berries and serve.

## Bananas Foster

**SERVES 4**

**WHY THIS RECIPE WORKS** Although the New Orleans dessert bananas Foster is quick and simple, with few ingredients (butter, brown sugar, rum, and bananas), things can go wrong. Sometimes the bananas are overcooked and mushy. Or the sauce can be too thin, overly sweet, or taste too strongly of alcohol. We wanted to fix these issues and come up with a quick, reliable dessert with tender bananas and a flavorful but not boozy sauce. First we kept the amounts of butter and brown sugar in check—most recipes use a high ratio of butter to brown sugar, which makes for a thin, greasy sauce. For the rum, we found that a small amount was just enough to impart a definite rum flavor without turning the dessert into a cocktail. We decided to add some rum to the sauce and use the rest to flambé the bananas. We also enhanced the sauce with cinnamon and lemon zest, which added complexity. As for the bananas, we cooked them in the sauce until soft, flipping them halfway through cooking so they turned out tender, not mushy. While the bananas cook, scoop the ice cream into individual bowls so they are ready to go once the sauce has been flambéed.

- 4 tablespoons (½ stick) unsalted butter
- ½ cup packed (3½ ounces) dark brown sugar
- 1 (3-inch) cinnamon stick
- 1 (2-inch) strip zest from 1 lemon
- 4 tablespoons dark rum
- 2 large, firm, ripe bananas, peeled and quartered
- 1 pint vanilla ice cream, divided among four bowls

**1.** Combine the butter, sugar, cinnamon stick, zest, and 1 tablespoon of the rum in a 12-inch skillet. Cook over medium-high heat, stirring constantly, until the sugar dissolves and the mixture has thickened, about 2 minutes.

**2.** Reduce the heat to medium and add the bananas to the pan, spooning some sauce over each quarter. Cook until the bananas are glossy and golden on the bottom, about 1½ minutes. Flip the bananas; continue to cook until very soft but not mushy or falling apart, about 1½ minutes longer.

**3.** Off the heat, add the remaining 3 tablespoons rum and allow the rum to warm slightly, about 5 seconds. Wave a lit match over the pan until the rum ignites, shaking the pan to distribute the flame over the entire pan. When the flames subside (this will take 15 to 30 seconds), discard the cinnamon stick and zest and divide the bananas and sauce among the four bowls of ice cream. Serve

## Crepes Suzette

**SERVES 6**

**WHY THIS RECIPE WORKS** Classic French restaurants have mastered the fiery theatrics of this tableside treat—a sophisticated combination of crepes, oranges, liqueur, and a showy flambé. We wanted to develop a recipe that would comfortably guide the home cook through the flambé process so this dessert could be prepared for an elegant dinner party. For a foolproof flambé that didn't create a frightening fireball or, conversely, didn't burn at all, we ignited the cognac alone in the skillet before building the sauce. We enriched a reduction of butter, sugar, and fresh orange juice with additional orange juice, fresh orange zest, and triple sec. For tender but sturdy crepes that would stand up to the sauce without turning soggy, we skipped the usual resting of the batter, meant to relax the gluten, before cooking. Then, once the crepes were cooked, we sprinkled them with sugar and ran them under the broiler for a sweet and crunchy coating. Note that it takes a few crepes to get the heat of the pan right; your first two or three will almost inevitably be unusable. (To allow for practice, the recipe yields about 16 crepes; only 12 are needed for the dish.) A dry measuring cup with a ¼-cup capacity is useful for portioning the batter. We prefer crepes made with whole milk, but low-fat or skim milk can also be used.

**CREPES**

- 3 large eggs
- 1½ cups whole milk
- 1½ cups (7½ ounces) unbleached all-purpose flour
- ½ cup water
- 5 tablespoons unsalted butter, melted, plus extra for brushing the pan
- 3 tablespoons sugar
- 2 tablespoons cognac
- ½ teaspoon table salt

**ORANGE SAUCE**

- 4 tablespoons cognac
- 1¼ cups juice plus 1 tablespoon finely grated zest from 3 to 4 large oranges
- 6 tablespoons (¾ stick) unsalted butter, cut into 6 pieces
- ¼ cup (1¾ ounces) sugar
- 2 tablespoons orange-flavored liqueur, preferably triple sec

**1. FOR THE CREPES:** Combine the eggs, milk, flour, water, melted butter, sugar, cognac, and salt in a blender until a smooth batter forms, about 10 seconds. Transfer the batter to a medium bowl.

**2.** Using a pastry brush, brush the bottom and sides of a 10-inch nonstick skillet very lightly with melted butter and heat the skillet over medium heat. When the butter stops sizzling, tilt the pan slightly to the right and begin pouring in a scant ¼ cup batter. Continue to pour the batter in a slow, steady stream, rotating your wrist and twirling the pan slowly counterclockwise until the pan bottom is covered with an even layer of batter. Cook until the crepe starts to lose its opaqueness and turns spotty light golden brown on the bottom, loosening the crepe from the side of the pan with a heatproof rubber spatula, 30 seconds to 1 minute. To flip the crepe, loosen the edge with the spatula and, with your fingertips on the top side, slide the spatula under the crepe and flip. Cook until dry on the second side, about 20 seconds.

**3.** Place the cooked crepe on a plate and repeat the cooking process with the remaining batter, brushing the pan very lightly with butter before making each crepe. As they are done, stack the crepes on a plate (you will need 12 crepes). (The crepes can be double-wrapped in plastic wrap and refrigerated for up to 3 days; bring to room temperature before making the sauce.)

**4. FOR THE ORANGE SAUCE:** Adjust an oven rack to the lower-middle position and heat the broiler. Add 3 tablespoons of the cognac to a broiler-safe 12-inch skillet; heat the pan over medium heat just until the vapors begin to rise from the cognac, about 5 seconds. Remove the pan from the heat and wave a lit match over the pan until the cognac ignites, shaking the pan until the flames subside, about 15 seconds; reignite if the flame dies too soon.

**5.** Add 1 cup of the orange juice, the butter, and 3 tablespoons of the sugar and simmer briskly over high heat, stirring occasionally, until many large bubbles appear and the mixture reduces to a thick syrup, 6 to 8 minutes (you should have just over ½ cup sauce). Transfer the sauce to a small bowl; do not wash the skillet. Stir the remaining ¼ cup orange juice, zest, liqueur, and the remaining 1 tablespoon cognac into the sauce; cover.

**6. TO ASSEMBLE:** Fold each crepe in half, then in half again to form a wedge shape. Arrange nine folded crepes around the edge of the now-empty skillet, with the rounded edges facing inward, overlapping as necessary to fit. Arrange the remaining three crepes in the center of the pan. Sprinkle the crepes evenly with the remaining 1 tablespoon sugar. Broil until the sugar caramelizes and the crepes turn spotty brown, about 5 minutes. (Watch the crepes constantly to prevent scorching; turn the pan as necessary.) Carefully remove the pan from the oven and pour half of the sauce over the crepes, leaving some areas uncovered. Transfer the crepes to individual serving dishes and serve immediately, passing the extra sauce separately.

### MAKING A CREPE

**1.** Pour ¼ cup batter into far side of skillet.

**2.** Tilt and shake skillet gently until batter evenly covers bottom of skillet.

**3.** Gently slide spatula underneath edge of crepe, grasp edge with your fingertips, and flip crepe.

## Crepes with Sugar and Lemon

**SERVES 4**

**WHY THIS RECIPE WORKS** A crepe is nothing but a thin pancake cooked quickly on each side and wrapped around a sweet or savory filling, but it has a reputation for being difficult. We wanted an easy method for crepes that were thin and delicate yet rich and flavorfully browned in spots. Finding the perfect ratio of milk to flour and sugar gave us rich-tasting, lightly sweet pancakes. We were surprised to find that neither the type of flour nor the mixing method seemed to matter, and a plain old 12-inch nonstick skillet worked as well as a specialty crepe pan. What does matter is heating the pan properly (over low heat for at least 10 minutes), using the right amount of batter (we settled on ¼ cup), and flipping the crepe at precisely the right moment, when the edges appear dry, matte, and lacy. To transform our perfectly cooked crepes into decadent desserts, we whipped up a couple of sweet fillings: the simple classic of sugar and lemon, and a banana and Nutella sure to please kids and adults alike. The crepes will give off steam as they cook, but if at any point the skillet begins to smoke, remove it from the heat immediately and turn down the heat. Stacking the crepes on a wire rack allows excess steam to escape so they won't stick together. To allow for practice, the recipe yields 10 crepes; only eight are needed for the filling.

- ½ teaspoon vegetable oil
- 1 cup (5 ounces) unbleached all-purpose flour
- 1 teaspoon sugar, plus 8 teaspoons for sprinkling
- ¼ teaspoon table salt
- 1½ cups whole milk
- 3 large eggs
- 2 tablespoons unsalted butter, melted and cooled
- Lemon wedges, for serving

**1.** Heat the oil in a 12-inch nonstick skillet over low heat for at least 10 minutes.

**2.** While the skillet is heating, whisk the flour, 1 teaspoon of the sugar, and the salt together in a medium bowl. In a separate bowl, whisk together the milk and eggs. Add half of the milk mixture to the dry ingredients and whisk until smooth. Add the butter and whisk until incorporated. Whisk in the remaining milk mixture until smooth.

**3.** Using a paper towel, wipe out the skillet, leaving a thin film of oil on the bottom and sides of the pan. Increase the heat to medium and let the skillet heat for 1 minute. After 1 minute, test the heat of the skillet by placing 1 teaspoon of the batter in the center; cook for 20 seconds. If the mini crepe is golden brown on the bottom, the skillet is properly heated; if it is too light or too dark, adjust the heat accordingly and retest.

**4.** Pour ¼ cup batter into the far side of pan and tilt and shake gently until the batter evenly covers the bottom of the pan. Cook the crepe without moving until the top surface is dry and the edges are starting to brown, loosening the crepe from the side of the pan with a rubber spatula, about 25 seconds. Gently slide the spatula underneath the edge of the crepe, grasp the edge with your fingertips, and flip the crepe. Cook until the second side is lightly spotted, about 20 seconds. Transfer the cooked crepe to a wire rack, inverting so the spotted side is facing up. Return the pan to the heat and heat for 10 seconds before repeating with the remaining batter. As the crepes are done, stack on the wire rack.

**5.** Transfer the stack of crepes to a large plate and invert a second plate over the crepes. Microwave until the crepes are warm, 30 to 45 seconds (45 to 60 seconds if the crepes have cooled completely). Remove the top plate and wipe dry with a paper towel. Sprinkle half of the top crepe with 1 teaspoon sugar. Fold the unsugared bottom half over the sugared half, then fold into quarters. Transfer the sugared crepe to a second plate. Continue with the remaining crepes. Serve immediately, passing the lemon wedges separately.

### Crepes with Bananas and Nutella

Follow the recipe for Crepes with Sugar and Lemon, omitting the 8 teaspoons sugar for sprinkling and the lemon wedges. In step 5, spread 2 teaspoons Nutella over half of each crepe, followed by eight to ten ¼-inch-thick banana slices. Fold the crepes into quarters. Serve immediately.

## Peach Crisp

**SERVES** 4 to 6

**WHY THIS RECIPE WORKS** There is seldom anything crisp about most crisps. This simple fruit dessert usually comes out of the oven with a soggy, mushy topping—quite a letdown from the ideal of a warm, fruity filling covered in a crunchy, sweet topping. We set out to make peach crisp that wouldn't disappoint, one with the perfect balance of nicely thickened filling and a lightly sweetened, crisp topping. We tried everything from Grape-Nuts to cookie crumbs and found the ideal topping mixture to be chopped nuts, butter, and flour. Another issue to tackle was sugar: what kind and how much. White sugar alone was too bland, while brown sugar on its own was too strong tasting. A 50–50 mix of the two proved to be the perfect combination. We decided not to use too much sugar in the fruit filling so there would be some contrast with the topping. And we nixed the idea of a thickener—the filling without one had a nicely bright fresh fruit flavor and the topping remained crisp whether we used one or not. Lightly sweetened whipped cream or vanilla ice cream is the perfect accompaniment, especially if serving the crisp warm. A standard or deep-dish 9-inch pie plate works well; an 8-inch square baking dish can also be used.

**TOPPING**

- 6 tablespoons unbleached all-purpose flour
- ¼ cup packed (1¾ ounces) light brown sugar
- ¼ cup (1¾ ounces) granulated sugar
- ¼ teaspoon ground cinnamon
- ¼ teaspoon ground nutmeg
- ¼ teaspoon table salt
- 5 tablespoons unsalted butter, cut into ½-inch pieces and chilled
- ¾ cup (about 4 ounces) coarsely chopped pecans, walnuts, or almonds

**FILLING**

- 3 pounds peaches (6 to 8 medium), peeled, pitted, and cut into ½-inch slices
- ¼ cup (1¾ ounces) granulated sugar
- ½ teaspoon grated zest plus 1½ tablespoons juice from 1 lemon

**1. FOR THE TOPPING:** Pulse the flour, sugars, cinnamon, nutmeg, and salt in a food processor until combined. Sprinkle the butter pieces over the top and pulse until the mixture resembles coarse meal, about 15 pulses. Add the nuts and pulse until the mixture clumps together and resembles wet sand, about 5 pulses; do not overmix. Transfer the mixture to a bowl and refrigerate while preparing the filling, at least 15 minutes.

**2. FOR THE FILLING:** Adjust an oven rack to the lower-middle position and heat the oven to 375 degrees. Combine the peaches, sugar, zest, and juice in a large bowl and toss gently to combine. Transfer the peach mixture to a 9-inch glass pie plate, place the pie plate on a rimmed baking sheet, and sprinkle the chilled topping evenly over the top.

**3.** Bake for 40 minutes. Increase the oven temperature to 400 degrees and continue to bake until the filling is bubbling and the topping is deep golden brown, about 5 minutes longer. Serve warm.

### Peach Crisp for a Crowd

**SERVES** 10

Follow the recipe for Peach Crisp, doubling all the ingredients and using a 13 by 9-inch baking dish. Increase the baking time to 55 minutes and bake at 375 degrees without increasing the oven temperature.

## Pear Crisp

**SERVES** 6

**WHY THIS RECIPE WORKS** The delicate texture and subtle flavor of pears make this homey dessert a bit more sophisticated and the perfect ending to an elegant fall dinner. But as we learned quickly, simply substituting pears for apples is a recipe for disaster. Our first step was to determine why pears react to baking so differently than apples. It turns out that pears and apples contain the same amount of moisture, but their cell walls are of very different strengths. During the ripening process, the moisture-retaining cell walls in pears break down much faster than apples, and cooking accelerates this process. Using pears that were just becoming ripe helped, as did using less sugar. Also, because pears release more juice than apples do, our pear crisp needed a thickener. A teaspoon of cornstarch mixed into a slurry with lemon juice thickened the juices enough and didn't leave a starchy taste or texture. For a crunchy, sweet topping, the usual combination of cold butter cut into sugar, flour, and nuts didn't work—it simply washed down into the filling. A topping made with melted butter was more cohesive and stayed in place. We prefer a crisp made with Bartlett pears, but Bosc pears can also be used. The pears should be ripe but firm, which means the flesh at the base of the stem should give slightly when gently pressed with your finger. Bartlett pears will turn from green to greenish yellow when ripe. Although almost any unsalted nut may be used in the topping, we prefer almonds or pecans. Serve with vanilla ice cream or lightly sweetened whipped cream, if desired.

**TOPPING**

- ¾ cup nuts, chopped
- ½ cup (2½ ounces) all-purpose flour
- ¼ cup packed (1¾ ounces) light brown sugar
- 2 tablespoons granulated sugar
- ¼ teaspoon ground cinnamon
- ⅛ teaspoon ground nutmeg
- ⅛ teaspoon table salt
- 5 tablespoons unsalted butter, melted and cooled

**FILLING**

- 2 tablespoons granulated sugar
- 2 teaspoons lemon juice
- 1 teaspoon cornstarch
- Pinch table salt
- 3 pounds pears, peeled, halved, cored, each half quartered lengthwise, and each quarter cut in half crosswise

**1.** Adjust oven rack to lower-middle position and heat oven to 425 degrees. Line rimmed baking sheet with aluminum foil.

**2.** For the topping: Pulse nuts, flour, brown sugar, granulated sugar, cinnamon, nutmeg, and salt in food processor until nuts are finely chopped, about 9 pulses. Drizzle melted butter over nut mixture and pulse until mixture resembles crumbly wet sand, about 5 pulses, scraping down sides of bowl halfway through pulsing. Set aside.

**3.** For the filling: Whisk sugar, lemon juice, cornstarch, and salt together in large bowl. Gently toss pears with sugar mixture and transfer to 8-inch square baking dish.

**4.** Sprinkle topping evenly over filling, breaking up any large pieces. Transfer dish to prepared sheet. Bake until fruit is bubbling around edges and topping is deep golden brown, about 30 minutes, rotating sheet halfway through baking. Transfer dish to wire rack and let cool until warm, about 15 minutes. Serve.

## Caramelized Pears with Blue Cheese and Black Pepper–Caramel Sauce

**SERVES 6**

**WHY THIS RECIPE WORKS** Pears and blue cheese are a classic combination, but we upped the flavor ante with another component—caramel. We had encountered this triple play in restaurants, where a caramel sauce is draped over seared pears, and a modest amount of pungent blue cheese provides a nice contrast to the dessert's sweetness. To streamline this classic restaurant recipe, we cooked the pears right in the caramel sauce, instead of separately, saving some time. We brought water and sugar (the basis for caramel sauce) to a boil in a skillet and slid the pears into the hot mixture to cook in the browning caramel. We added cream to the pan to transform the sticky sugar syrup into a smooth sauce that clung lightly to the pears. After removing the pears, we seasoned the sauce left in the skillet with black pepper and salt. For an attractive presentation, we stood the pears upright on a plate and drizzled the caramel sauce around them, then added wedges of strong blue cheese—the perfect foil to the sweet caramel. Any type of pear can be used in this recipe, but the pears must be firm to withstand the heat. If desired, the pears can be served upright on a large platter instead of on individual plates, with the warm caramel sauce and the blue cheese passed separately. Many pepper mills do not have a sufficiently coarse setting; in that case, crush peppercorns with the back of a heavy pan or a rolling pin.

- ⅓ cup water
- ⅔ cup (4⅔ ounces) sugar
- 3 ripe but firm pears (7 to 8 ounces each), halved, cored, and ¼ inch trimmed off bottom
- ⅔ cup heavy cream
- ¼ teaspoon black peppercorns, crushed
- 3 ounces strong blue cheese (such as Stilton), cut into 6 wedges

**1.** Pour water into 12-inch nonstick skillet, then pour sugar into center of pan, being careful not to let it hit sides of pan. Bring to boil over high heat, stirring occasionally, until sugar is fully dissolved and liquid is bubbling. Add pears to skillet, cut side down, cover, reduce heat to medium-high, and cook until pears are almost tender and paring knife inserted into center of pears meets slight resistance, 13 to 15 minutes.

**2.** Uncover, reduce heat to medium, and cook until sauce is golden brown and cut sides of pears are beginning to brown, 3 to 5 minutes. Pour heavy cream around pears and cook, shaking pan until sauce is smooth and deep caramel color and cut sides of pears are golden brown, 3 to 5 minutes.

**3.** Off heat, transfer pears, cut side up, to wire rack set over rimmed baking sheet and let cool slightly. Season sauce left in pan with salt to taste and stir in crushed peppercorns, then transfer it to small bowl.

**4.** Carefully (pears will still be hot) stand each pear half upright on individual plate and place wedge of blue cheese beside it. Drizzle caramel sauce over plate and pear. Serve immediately.

## Roasted Pears with Dried Apricots and Pistachios

**SERVES** 4 to 6

**WHY THIS RECIPE WORKS** Tender, caramelized roasted pears are a delightfully simple dessert, but it took a two-step cooking process to perfect their texture. To eliminate any excess moisture that might weigh down the fruit, we cooked our peeled, halved pears in butter in a hot skillet. Once the pears began to brown, we transferred the skillet to the oven for 30 minutes. We plated the fork-tender fruit and started in on the sauce, deglazing the pan with white wine and adding sweet dried apricots, sugar, cardamom, and salt, plus a pat of butter for a creamy dimension. A touch of lemon juice stirred in once the liquid had thickened contributed citrusy brightness, and a sprinkling of pistachios, added right at serving, gave the dessert some toasty, textural contrast. Select pears that yield slightly when pressed. We prefer Bosc pears in this recipe, but Comice and Bartlett pears also work. The fruit can be served as is or with vanilla ice cream or plain Greek yogurt.

- 2½ tablespoons unsalted butter
- 4 ripe but firm Bosc pears (6 to 7 ounces each), peeled, halved, and cored
- 1¼ cups dry white wine
- ½ cup dried apricots, quartered
- ⅓ cup (2⅓ ounces) sugar
- ¼ teaspoon ground cardamom
- ⅛ teaspoon table salt
- 1 teaspoon lemon juice
- ⅓ cup pistachios, toasted and chopped

**1.** Adjust oven rack to middle position and heat oven to 450 degrees. Melt 1½ tablespoons butter in ovensafe 12-inch skillet over medium-high heat. Place pear halves, cut side down, in skillet. Cook, without moving them, until pears are just beginning to brown, 3 to 5 minutes.

**2.** Transfer skillet to oven and roast pears for 15 minutes. Using tongs, flip pears and continue to roast until fork easily pierces fruit, 10 to 15 minutes longer (skillet handle will be hot).

**3.** Using tongs, transfer pears to platter. Return skillet to medium-high heat and add wine, apricots, sugar, cardamom, salt, and remaining 1 tablespoon butter. Bring to vigorous simmer, whisking to scrape up any browned bits. Cook until sauce is reduced and has consistency of maple syrup, 7 to 10 minutes. Remove pan from heat and stir in lemon juice.

**4.** Pour sauce over pears, sprinkle with pistachios, and serve.

## Eton Mess

**SERVES** 6

**WHY THIS RECIPE WORKS** Eton mess, the iconic English mash-up of macerated strawberries, swoopy cream, and broken meringue, is considered a throw-together dessert, but taking care to balance the components makes their sublime contrast shine. To produce thoroughly, evenly dry and crisp meringue that was easy to break into pieces, we piped the whipped whites into a zigzag "snake" that maximized their exposure to the heat. We also baked the meringue very low and slow—part of the time in the turned-off oven's fading heat. Mashing and briefly simmering a portion of the sweetened berries made them jammy and concentrated; combining that mixture with uncooked chunks created complex strawberry flavor and consistency that rippled through the cream. It was crucial to drastically underwhip the cream because the meringue soaked up moisture from it like a sponge. Stopping well shy of soft peaks—the cream needed to still be pourable—ensured that it would thicken up just enough when the elements were combined. Use a pastry bag with a ½-inch plain round tip or a large zipper-lock bag with a corner snipped off to create a ½-inch opening. Do not open the oven door until it's time to check the meringue; if it isn't done, check again in 20 minutes. Serve promptly after assembling.

**MERINGUE**

- ⅓ cup (2⅓ ounces) sugar
- 1 teaspoon cornstarch
- 2 large egg whites
- ¼ teaspoon vanilla extract
- Pinch table salt

**STRAWBERRIES**

- 1½ pounds strawberries, hulled and quartered (4½ cups), divided
- 3 tablespoons sugar, divided
- 1 tablespoon lemon juice

**WHIPPED CREAM**

- 1½ cups heavy cream, chilled
- 1 tablespoon sugar

**1. FOR THE MERINGUE:** Adjust oven rack to middle position and heat oven to 200 degrees. Line rimmed baking sheet with parchment paper. Combine sugar and cornstarch in small bowl.

**2.** Using stand mixer fitted with whisk attachment, whip egg whites, vanilla, and salt on high speed until frothy, 20 to 30 seconds. Reduce speed to medium and slowly add sugar mixture in steady stream down side of mixer bowl (process should take about 15 seconds). Stop mixer and scrape down sides and bottom of bowl. Return mixer to high speed and beat until glossy, stiff peaks form, 1 to 2 minutes.

**3.** Transfer meringue to pastry bag fitted with ½-inch plain tip. Pipe ½- to ¾-inch-thick strip of meringue in zigzag pattern across width of prepared pan. Bake until exterior is dry, but meringue is still soft, 1½ hours. Meringue should be quite pale (a hint of creamy color is OK). Turn off oven and let meringue cool in oven until dry and crisp, about 1 hour. Remove from oven and let cool to room temperature, about 20 minutes. (Cooled meringue can be wrapped tightly in plastic wrap and stored at room temperature for up to 1 week.)

**4. FOR THE STRAWBERRIES:** Meanwhile, combine half of strawberries, 1 tablespoon sugar, and lemon juice in medium bowl. Combine remaining berries and remaining 2 tablespoons sugar in medium saucepan. Using potato masher, crush strawberries in saucepan. Bring to boil over medium-high heat and cook, stirring frequently, until rubber spatula drawn across bottom of pot leaves distinct trail, 4 to 5 minutes. Remove from heat and let cool slightly. Add to bowl with fresh berries and stir until evenly coated. Set aside 6 coated berry quarters for garnish.

**5. FOR THE WHIPPED CREAM:** Using clean, dry mixer bowl and whisk attachment, whip cream and sugar on medium-low speed until foamy, about 1 minute. Increase speed to medium-high and whip until thickened but still pourable, about 30 seconds (do not overbeat; cream will thicken further when added to meringue).

**6.** Cut meringue into 1-inch pieces, reserving any meringue dust and smaller bits. Set aside ½ cup meringue pieces for garnish and transfer remaining meringue (plus dust and bits) to wide serving bowl. Pour cream over meringue in serving bowl and stir to combine. Dollop strawberry mixture over surface of meringue and cream in 4 places. Lightly fold to just combine (this should take 1 or 2 folds; do not overmix). Garnish with reserved meringue and strawberry pieces. Serve immediately.

## Berry Fool

SERVES 6

**WHY THIS RECIPE WORKS** The secret to a fool that's both creamy and intensely fruity is in how you thicken it. For our recipe, we developed the bold berry flavor with both strawberries and raspberries—although blueberries or blackberries are suitable substitutions for the raspberries. We thickened our fruit puree with the addition of gelatin and incorporated both sour and heavy cream, which added just the right touch of richness with a tangy undertone. To top it all off, we took an unconventional approach with a sprinkling of crushed sweet wheat crackers. The nutty flavor complemented the berries and added a subtle crunch to this sweet dessert. You may substitute frozen fruit for fresh, but there will be a slight compromise in texture. If using frozen fruit, reduce the amount of sugar in the puree by 1 tablespoon. The thickened fruit puree can be made up to 4 hours in advance; just make sure to whisk it well in step 4 to break up any clumps before combining it with the whipped cream. For the best results, chill your beater and bowl before whipping the cream. Graham crackers or gingersnaps may be substituted for the Carr's Crackers.

- 2 pounds strawberries, hulled (6 cups), divided
- 12 ounces (2¼ cups) raspberries, divided
- ¾ cup (5¼ ounces) sugar, divided
- 2 teaspoons unflavored gelatin
- 1 cup heavy cream
- ¼ cup sour cream
- ½ teaspoon vanilla extract
- 4 Carr's Whole Wheat Crackers, crushed fine (about ¼ cup)
- 6 sprigs fresh mint (optional)

**1.** Process 3 cups strawberries, 1 cup raspberries, and ½ cup sugar in food processor until the mixture is completely smooth, about 1 minute. Strain berry puree through fine-mesh strainer into 4-cup liquid measuring cup (you should have about 2½ cups puree; reserve any excess for another use). Transfer ½ cup puree to small bowl and sprinkle gelatin over top; stir until gelatin is incorporated and let stand for at least 5 minutes. Heat remaining 2 cups puree in small saucepan over medium heat until it begins to bubble, 4 to 6 minutes. Off heat, stir in gelatin mixture until dissolved. Transfer gelatin-puree mixture to medium bowl, cover with plastic wrap, and refrigerate until cold, about 2 hours.

**2.** Meanwhile, chop remaining strawberries into rough ¼-inch pieces. Toss strawberries, remaining raspberries, and 2 tablespoons sugar together in medium bowl. Set aside for 1 hour.

3. Place cream, sour cream, vanilla, and remaining 2 tablespoons sugar in chilled bowl of stand mixer. Fit mixer with paddle and beat on low speed until bubbles form, about 30 seconds. Increase mixer speed to medium and continue beating until beaters leave trail, about 30 seconds. Increase mixer speed to high; continue beating until mixture has nearly doubled in volume and holds stiff peaks, about 30 seconds. Transfer ⅓ cup whipped cream mixture to small bowl and set aside.

4. Remove thickened berry puree from refrigerator and whisk until smooth. With mixer running at medium speed, slowly add two-thirds of puree to remaining whipped cream mixture; mix until incorporated, about 15 seconds. Using spatula, gently fold in remaining thickened puree, leaving streaks of puree.

5. Transfer uncooked berries to fine-mesh strainer; shake gently to remove any excess juice. Divide two-thirds of berries evenly among 6 tall parfait or sundae glasses. Divide creamy berry mixture evenly among the glasses, followed by remaining uncooked berries. Top each glass with reserved plain whipped cream mixture. Sprinkle with crushed crackers and garnish with mint sprigs, if using. Serve immediately.

## Rhubarb Fool

**SERVES 8**

**WHY THIS RECIPE WORKS** For a rhubarb fool recipe that would tame the sourness of rhubarb and overcome its tendency to cook into a drab, gray mess, we soaked the rhubarb in water to reduce the acid, simmered it in orange juice and sugar to retain texture and color, and layered the cooked fruit with lightly whipped sweetened cream. For a more elegant presentation, use a pastry bag to pipe the whipped cream into individual glasses. To make one large fool, double the recipe and layer the rhubarb and whipped cream in a 12-cup glass bowl.

- 2¼ pounds rhubarb, trimmed and cut into 6-inch lengths
- ⅓ cup juice from 1 large orange
- 1 cup (7 ounces) plus 2 tablespoons sugar
- Pinch table salt
- 2 cups heavy cream, chilled

1. Soak the rhubarb in cold water for 20 minutes. Drain, pat dry with paper towels, and cut crosswise into ½-inch-thick pieces.

2. Bring the orange juice, ¾ cup of the sugar, and the salt to a boil in a medium saucepan over medium-high heat. Add the rhubarb and return to a boil, then reduce the heat to medium-low and simmer, stirring two or three times, until the rhubarb begins to break down and is tender, 7 to 10 minutes. Transfer the rhubarb to a large bowl, cool to room temperature, cover with plastic wrap, and refrigerate until cold, at least 1 hour or up to 24 hours.

3. Whip the cream and remaining 6 tablespoons sugar in a large bowl with an electric mixer on medium-low speed until frothy, about 1 minute. Increase the speed to high and continue to whip until the cream forms soft peaks, 1 to 3 minutes.

4. To assemble, spoon about ¼ cup rhubarb into each of eight 8-ounce glasses, then layer about ¼ cup whipped cream on top. Repeat, ending with a dollop of cream; serve. The fools can be covered with plastic wrap and refrigerated for up to 6 hours.

## Individual Summer Berry Puddings

**SERVES 6**

**WHY THIS RECIPE WORKS** For these berry puddings, ripe, fragrant, lightly sweetened berries are gently cooked to coax out their juices and then packed into ramekins lined with slices of bread. We set out to master this summertime classic. Instead of lining the ramekins and then filling them with berries, we opted to layer bread (cut out with a biscuit cutter) and berries together in ramekins so that the bread on the inside would melt into the fruit. Fresh bread became too gummy in the pudding, but day-old bread had just the right consistency. We used potato bread; its even, tight-crumbed, tender texture and light sweetness was a perfect match for the berries (challah makes a good substitute). To ensure that the puddings would come together and hold their shape, we weighted and refrigerated them for at least eight hours. The bread should be dry to the touch but not brittle. If working with fresh bread, dry the slices by heating them on an oven rack in a single layer in a 200-degree oven for about 1 hour, flipping them once halfway through the time. For this recipe, you will need six 6-ounce ramekins and a round cookie cutter of a slightly smaller diameter than the ramekins. If you don't have the right size cutter, use a paring knife and the bottom of a ramekin (most ramekins taper toward the bottom) as a guide for trimming the rounds. Challah will need to be cut into slices about ½ inch thick; if both potato bread and challah are unavailable, use high-quality white sandwich bread. Summer pudding can be made up to 24 hours before serving; held any longer, the berries begin to lose their freshness. Serve with lightly sweetened whipped cream.

- 4 cups (20 ounces) strawberries, hulled and sliced
- 2 cups (about 10 ounces) raspberries
- 1 cup (about 5 ounces) blueberries
- 1 cup (about 5 ounces) blackberries
- ¾ cup (5¼ ounces) sugar
- 2 tablespoons juice from 1 lemon
- 12 slices stale potato bread, challah, or high-quality white sandwich bread

**1.** Cook the strawberries, raspberries, blueberries, blackberries, and sugar in a large saucepan over medium heat, stirring occasionally, until the berries begin to release their juice and the sugar has dissolved, about 5 minutes. Off the heat, stir in the lemon juice; cool to room temperature.

**2.** While the berries are cooling, spray six 6-ounce ramekins with vegetable oil spray and place on a rimmed baking sheet. Use a cookie cutter to cut out 12 bread rounds that are slightly smaller in diameter than the ramekins.

**3.** Using a slotted spoon, place ¼ cup of the fruit mixture in each ramekin. Lightly soak one bread round in the fruit juice in the saucepan and place on top of the fruit in a ramekin; repeat with five more bread rounds and the remaining ramekins. Diving the remaining fruit among the ramekins. Lightly soak one bread round in the juice and place on top of the fruit in a ramekin (it should sit above the lip of the ramekin); repeat with the remaining five bread rounds and the remaining ramekins. Pour the remaining fruit juice over the bread and cover the ramekins loosely with plastic wrap. Place a second baking sheet on top of the ramekins and weight it with heavy cans. Refrigerate the puddings for at least 8 hours or up to 24 hours.

**4.** Remove the cans and baking sheet and uncover the puddings. Loosen the puddings by running a paring knife around the edge of each ramekin, unmold into individual bowls, and serve immediately.

### Large Summer Berry Pudding

**SERVES** 6 to 8

You will need a 9 by 5-inch loaf pan for this recipe. Because there is no need to cut out rounds for this version, you will need only about 8 slices bread, depending on their size. Follow the recipe for Individual Summer Berry Puddings through step 1. While the berries are cooling, spray a 9 by 5-inch loaf pan with vegetable oil spray, line it with plastic wrap, and place it on a rimmed baking sheet. Trim the crusts from the bread and trim the slices to fit in a single layer in the loaf pan (you will need about 2½ slices per layer; there will be three layers). Using a slotted spoon, spread about 2 cups of the fruit mixture evenly over the bottom of the prepared pan. Lightly soak enough bread slices for one layer in the fruit juice in the saucepan and place on top of the fruit. Repeat with two more layers of fruit and bread. Pour the remaining fruit juice over the bread and cover loosely with plastic wrap. Place a second baking sheet on top of the loaf pan and weight it with heavy cans. Refrigerate the pudding for at least 8 hours or up to 24 hours. Remove the cans and baking sheet and uncover the pudding. Invert the pudding onto a serving platter, remove the loaf pan and plastic wrap, slice, and serve.

## Khao Niaow Ma Muang (Sticky Rice with Mango)

**SERVES 6**

**WHY THIS RECIPE WORKS** Consisting of thick, golden slices of mango; subtly sweet, coconut-flavored sticky rice; a salty coconut sauce; and crunchy toasted mung beans, this classic Thai dish is a delicate balancing act of flavors and textures. We started with the sticky rice, which needs to be rinsed well to remove excess starch and then soaked for at least 1 hour to hydrate before it is steamed. Wrapping the rice in a wet dish towel prevented it from sticking while it steamed in a bamboo steamer basket. We poured warm, lightly sweetened coconut milk over the hot, tender-chewy rice, which made it glossy and rich. We then made a salted coconut sauce lightly thickened with cornstarch to balance out the rice and the thick slices of very sweet, ripe Ataulfo mango that we served alongside. A topping of toasted mung beans added crunch. Thai sticky rice (also labeled "glutinous" or "sweet") is available online and at Asian markets. Do not substitute other rice such as sushi or arborio. The quality of coconut milk matters here; our favorite brand is Aroy-D. Shake the coconut milk well before opening. Do not use light coconut milk. The mangos are ready to use when their skins have turned yellow, they're a bit wrinkly and spotty, and they yield to gentle pressure. Make the mung beans while the rice soaks. Though they won't offer the same crunch, toasted white or black sesame seeds can be substituted for the mung beans. This dish can be served warm or at room temperature as dessert or a snack.

- 1 cup Thai sticky rice
- 1 (14-ounce) can coconut milk, divided
- ¼ cup (1¾ ounces) sugar
- ¼ teaspoon plus ⅛ teaspoon table salt, divided
- ½ teaspoon cornstarch
- 3 very ripe Ataulfo mangos, peeled, pitted, and sliced crosswise into ½-inch-thick slices
- Toasted Mung Beans (recipe follows)

**1.** Place rice in fine-mesh strainer and rinse under cold running water until water runs clear. Place rinsed rice in medium heatproof bowl and cover with several inches cold water. Let rice stand for at least 1 hour or up to 24 hours. Drain rice well in fine-mesh strainer. Rinse bowl in which rice soaked.

**2.** Bring 4 cups water to boil in 14-inch flat-bottomed wok or 12-inch skillet over high heat. Meanwhile, line steamer basket with clean, damp dish towel. Transfer rice to center of towel and pat rice in even layer. Fold overhang over rice to form bundle and cover with steamer lid. Set steamer in wok and reduce heat to maintain simmer (small wisps of steam should escape from beneath lid). Steam rice until translucent, tender but still chewy, 20 to 25 minutes (check rice by carefully unwrapping bundle; taste rice from center of pile).

**3.** While rice steams, combine 1 cup coconut milk, sugar, and ¼ teaspoon salt in small saucepan over medium heat and cook, stirring frequently, until sugar dissolves. Remove from heat and cover to keep warm.

**4.** Transfer rice to cleaned bowl. Working quickly, pour coconut milk mixture over top (it will look like too much liquid). Stir gently to combine; cover; and let stand until liquid is absorbed, about 15 minutes.

**5.** Meanwhile, rinse saucepan and add remaining coconut milk and remaining ⅛ teaspoon salt. Bring to simmer over medium heat. Combine 1 teaspoon water and cornstarch in small bowl, stirring until cornstarch is dissolved. Stir cornstarch mixture into coconut milk and cook, stirring constantly, until sauce is slightly thickened, 1 to 2 minutes. Remove from heat and set aside. (Cooled sauce may be refrigerated overnight. Bring to room temperature before serving.)

**6.** When ready to serve, divide coconut rice among serving plates. Arrange sliced mango alongside (½ mango per person). Spoon sauce over rice. Sprinkle mung beans over sauce and rice and serve.

### Toasted Mung Beans

**MAKES** ¼ cup

Yellow mung beans are made from whole mung beans that have been hulled and split, resulting in a delicate lentil-like legume. The toasted beans are a classic topping to Khao Niaow Ma Muang. For our recipe, we quickly softened the beans by soaking them in boiling water. After draining and patting them dry, we cooked the beans in an unoiled skillet until they were just starting to brown, which dried them out and gave them a delicate, crunchy texture.

**1.** Bring 1 cup water to boil in small saucepan. Remove from heat; add 2 tablespoons yellow mung beans; cover and set aside until beans have softened, about 10 minutes.

**2.** Drain beans and transfer to paper towel–lined plate, spreading into even layer. Let stand at least 5 minutes to dry. Add beans to small skillet and place over medium-high heat.

**3.** Cook, stirring frequently, until mung beans are just starting to turn lightly golden, 5 to 7 minutes. Transfer to bowl and let cool completely before using. (Toasted mung beans can be stored in airtight container at room temperature for 1 week.)

## Strawberries with Balsamic Vinegar

**SERVES** 6

**WHY THIS RECIPE WORKS** The combination of strawberries and balsamic vinegar dates back hundreds of years to northern Italy. We wanted to pay homage to this time-honored tradition and create our own dessert, with the vinegar enhancing but not overwhelming the flavor of bright summer berries. We didn't want to pay big bucks for a super-pricey balsamic vinegar, so we opted to use an inexpensive vinegar. To coax big flavor out of our bargain balsamic, we simmered it with some sugar to approximate the syrupy texture of an aged vinegar. Next we tried to enhance the flavor with honey or vanilla, but these flavors were too overpowering; a squirt of fresh lemon juice brought just the right amount of brightness. We tossed the berries with light brown sugar—rather than the traditional granulated sugar—for the most complex flavor. Once we mixed the sliced berries and sugar together, it took about 15 minutes for the sugar to dissolve and the berries to release their juice; if the strawberries sat any longer than this, they continued to soften and became quite mushy. If you don't have light brown sugar on hand, sprinkle the berries with an equal amount of granulated sugar. Serve the berries and syrup as is or with vanilla ice cream or lightly sweetened whipped cream.

- ⅓ cup balsamic vinegar
- 2 teaspoons granulated sugar
- ½ teaspoon juice from 1 lemon
- 6 cups (30 ounces) strawberries, hulled, sliced lengthwise ¼ inch thick if large, halved or quartered if small
- ¼ cup packed (1¾ ounces) light brown sugar
- Ground black pepper

**1.** Bring the vinegar, granulated sugar, and lemon juice to a simmer in a small saucepan over medium heat. Simmer until the syrup is reduced by half (about 3 tablespoons), about 3 minutes. Transfer to a small bowl and cool completely.

**2.** Gently toss the berries and brown sugar in a large bowl. Let stand until the sugar dissolves and the berries exude some juice, 10 to 15 minutes. Pour the vinegar syrup over the berries, add pepper to taste, and toss to combine. Serve immediately.

## Honeydew, Mango, and Blueberries with Lime-Ginger Reduction

**MAKES** 6 cups

**WHY THIS RECIPE WORKS** Cut-up fresh fruit is a nice dessert or addition to a brunch, but it can be a little boring. Yogurt-based sauces mask the fresh flavors of the fruit, and sweet syrups make the fruit too dessert-y. Looking for a lighter, more flavorful alternative, we adapted a French dressing called a gastrique, a reduction of an acidic liquid with sugar that usually accompanies savory dishes made with fruit. It's a simple technique, and our experiments with reducing different types of acid—wine, citrus juice, and balsamic vinegar—were an unqualified success. We were able to use additional flavorings in the dressing, such as spices, extracts, and citrus zests, that would complement the flavors of the fruit. Served at room temperature or chilled, fresh fruit bathed in a light dressing is delicious and easy to make. Be sure to zest one of the limes before juicing. Cantaloupe can be used in place of honeydew, although the color contrast with the mango won't be as vivid.

- 1 tablespoon grated lime zest plus 1 cup juice (8 limes)
- ¼ cup (1¾ ounces) sugar
- Pinch table salt
- 1 tablespoon minced fresh ginger
- 1 tablespoon lemon juice
- 2 cups 1-inch honeydew melon pieces
- 1 mango, peeled, pitted, and cut into ½-inch pieces (1½ cups)
- 10 ounces (2 cups) blueberries

**1.** Simmer lime juice, sugar, and salt in small saucepan over high heat until syrupy, honey-colored, and reduced to ¼ cup, about 15 minutes. Off heat, stir in lime zest, ginger, and lemon juice; steep for 1 minute to blend flavors and strain.

**2.** Combine melon, mango, and blueberries in medium bowl; pour warm dressing over fruit and toss to coat. Serve at room temperature, or cover with plastic wrap, refrigerate for up to 4 hours, and serve chilled.

## Strawberries and Grapes with Balsamic and Red Wine Reduction

**MAKES** about 6 cups

**WHY THIS RECIPE WORKS** Cut-up fresh fruit is a nice addition to a brunch, but it can be a little boring. Yogurt-based sauces mask the fresh flavors of the fruit, and sweet syrups make the fruit too much like a dessert. Looking for a lighter, more flavorful alternative, we adapted a French dressing called a gastrique, a reduction of an acidic liquid with sugar that usually accompanies savory dishes made with fruit. It's a simple technique, and our experiments with reducing different types of acid—wine, citrus juice, and balsamic vinegar—were an unqualified success. We were able to use additional flavorings in the dressing, such as spices, extracts, and citrus zests, that would complement the flavors of the fruit. Served at room temperature or chilled, fresh fruit bathed in a light dressing is delicious and easy to make. An inexpensive balsamic vinegar is fine for use in this recipe. Save high-quality vinegar for other preparations in which the vinegar is not cooked.

- ¾ cup balsamic vinegar
- ¼ cup dry red wine
- ¼ cup sugar
- Pinch table salt
- 1 tablespoon grated zest plus 1 tablespoon juice from 1 lemon
- ¼ teaspoon vanilla extract
- 3 whole cloves
- 1 quart strawberries, hulled and halved lengthwise (about 4 cups)
- 9 ounces large seedless red or black grapes, each grape halved pole to pole (about 2 cups)

**1.** Simmer the vinegar, wine, sugar, and salt in a small saucepan over high heat until syrupy and reduced to ¼ cup, about 15 minutes. Off the heat, stir in the lemon zest and juice, vanilla, and cloves; steep for 1 minute to blend the flavors and strain.

**2.** Combine the strawberries and grapes in a medium bowl; pour the warm dressing over the fruit and toss to coat. Serve at room temperature, or cover with plastic wrap, refrigerate for up to 4 hours, and serve chilled.

### Nectarines, Blueberries, and Raspberries with Champagne-Cardamom Reduction

**MAKES** about 6 cups

Dry white wine can be substituted for the champagne.

- 1 cup champagne
- ¼ cup sugar
- Pinch table salt
- 1 tablespoon grated zest plus 1 tablespoon juice from 1 lemon
- 5 cardamom pods, crushed
- 3 medium nectarines (about 18 ounces), cut into ½-inch wedges (about 3 cups)
- 1 pint blueberries
- ½ pint raspberries

**1.** Simmer the champagne, sugar, and salt in a small saucepan over high heat until syrupy, honey-colored, and reduced to ¼ cup, about 15 minutes. Off the heat, stir in the lemon zest and juice and cardamom; steep for 1 minute to blend the flavors and strain.

**2.** Combine the nectarines, blueberries, and raspberries in a medium bowl; pour the warm dressing over the fruit and toss to coat. Serve at room temperature, or cover with plastic wrap, refrigerate for up to 4 hours, and serve chilled.

# The America's Test Kitchen Shopping Guide

DELALLO
Pasta Abruzzese
di semola
di grano duro
DELALLO
DE CECCO

00:49

AMERICA'S
TEST KITCHEN

Live & Probiotic Cultures
karoun
BROWN COW
WHOLE MILK YOGURT

AMERICA'S
TEST KITCHEN

AMERICA'S
TEST KITCHEN

## SHOPPING FOR EQUIPMENT

With a well-stocked kitchen, you'll be able to take on any recipe. But with so much equipment out there on the market, how do you figure out what's what? Price often correlates with design, not performance. Over the years, our test kitchen has evaluated thousands of products. We've gone through copious rounds of testing and have identified the most important attributes in every piece of equipment, so when you go shopping you'll know what to look for. And because our test kitchen accepts no support from product manufacturers, you can trust our ratings. See AmericasTestKitchen.com for updates to these testings.

| KNIVES AND MORE | ITEM | WHAT TO LOOK FOR | TEST KITCHEN FAVORITES |
|---|---|---|---|
| | CHEF'S KNIFE | • High-carbon stainless-steel knife<br>• Thin, curved 8-inch blade<br>• Lightweight<br>• Comfortable grip and nonslip handle | **Victorinox Swiss Army Fibrox Pro 8″ Chef's Knife**<br><br>Great Heavier Option: **Mercer Culinary Renaissance 8-Inch Forged Chef's Knife**<br><br>Best Buy: **Mercer Culinary Milennia 8-Inch Chef's Knife** |
| | SERRATED KNIFE | • 10-inch blade<br>• Fewer broader, deeper, pointed serrations<br>• Thinner blade angle<br>• Comfortable, grippy handle<br>• Medium weight | **Mercer Culinary Millennia 10-Inch Bread Knife** |
| | SLICING/ CARVING KNIFE | • Tapered 12-inch blade for slicing large cuts of meat<br>• Oval scallops (called a granton edge) carved into blade<br>• Fairly rigid blade with rounded tip | **Victorinox Swiss Army 12″ Fibrox Pro Granton Edge Slicing/ Carving Knife** |
| | PARING KNIFE | • Comfortable grip<br>• Thin, flexible blade with pointed tip<br>• 3- to 3½-inch blade | **Victorinox Swiss Army Spear Point Paring Knife** |
| | SERRATED PARING KNIFE | • Thin blade with razor-sharp serrations for safe, precise slicing<br>• Hefty but nimble | **Wüsthof Classic 3.5-Inch Fully Serrated Paring Knife**<br><br>Best Buy: **Victorinox Swiss Army 4″ Serrated Paring Knife** |
| | PETTY AND UTILITY KNIVES | • Lightweight with a medium-size handle<br>• Just-the-right-length blade<br>• Capable of producing near-surgical incisions | Best Overall: **Togiharu PRO Petty 5.9″**<br><br>Best Splurge: **OUL 150mm Wa Petty Ginsanko-Walnut Octagon**<br><br>Best Buy: **MAC PKF-60 Pro Utility 6″** |

| KNIVES AND MORE | ITEM | WHAT TO LOOK FOR | TEST KITCHEN FAVORITES |
| --- | --- | --- | --- |
| | STEAK KNIVES | • Supersharp, straight-edged blade<br>• Sturdy—not wobbly—blade | **Victorinox Swiss Army 6-Piece Rosewood Steak Set**<br><br>Best Buy: **Chicago Cutlery Walnut Tradition 4-Piece Steak Knife Set** |
| | SERRATED UTILITY KNIFE | • Stiff, ultrasharp blade<br>• Long, flexible, tapered blade design<br>• Design and size of handle; textured, comfortable grip | **Zwilling Pro 5.5" Serrated Prep Knife** |
| | SANTOKU KNIFE | • Narrow, curved, and short blade<br>• Comfortable grip | **Misono UX10 Santoku 7.0"** |
| | BONING KNIFE | • Sharp, moderately flexible, 5.5-inch blade that maintains its edge<br>• Slender handle and slim profile for easy grasp | **Zwilling Pro 5.5" Flexible Boning Knife** |
| | MEAT CLEAVER | • Razor-sharp blade<br>• Balanced weight between handle and blade<br>• Comfortable grip | **Masui AUS8 Stainless Meat Cleaver 180mm** |
| | NAKIRI | • Razor-sharp blade capable of both coarser work and fine, precise cuts<br>• Comfortable grip<br>• Lightweight | **Masamoto Sohonten Wa-Nakiri** |
| | HYBRID CHEF'S KNIFE | • High-carbon stainless-steel knife<br>• Lightweight<br>• Thin blade that tapers from spine to cutting edge and from handle to tip | **Masamoto VG-10 Gyutou, 8.2"** |
| | CARBON-STEEL KNIFE | • 8-inch blade<br>• Sloping ergonomic handle<br>• Narrow, razor-sharp blade | **Bob Kramer 8" Carbon Steel Chef's Knife by Zwilling**<br><br>Best Buy: **Togiharu Virgin Carbon Steel Gyutou, 8.2"** |
| | MANDOLINE | • Razor-sharp blades can handle even the toughest produce<br>• Can customize thickness settings broadly (no fixed settings) | Co-Winner: **Super Benriner Mandoline Slicer** |
| | | • Clearly marked, accurate dial allows you to adjust slice thickness in ¹⁄₁₆-inch and 1-millimeter increments<br>• Innovative spring-loaded food pusher | Co-Winner: **OXO Good Grips Chef's Mandoline Slicer 2.0** |
| | CARVING BOARD | • Trenches can contain ½ cup of liquid<br>• Large and stable enough to hold large roasts<br>• Midweight for easy carrying, carving, and cleaning | **J.K. Adams Maple Reversible Carving Board** |

| KNIVES AND MORE | ITEM | WHAT TO LOOK FOR | TEST KITCHEN FAVORITES |
|---|---|---|---|
| | CUTTING BOARDS | • Roomy work surface: at least 20 by 15 inches<br>• Teak wood for minimal maintenance<br>• Durable edge-grain construction (wood grain runs parallel to surface of board)<br>• Two flat surfaces (no feet) so board is reversible<br>• Finger grips on short sides | Heavy Duty: **Teakhaus by Proteak Edge Grain Cutting Board**<br><br>Small: **OXO Good Grips Utility Cutting Board**<br><br>Best Lightweight: **OXO Good Grips Carving & Cutting Board** |
| | BAR BOARDS | • Reversible<br>• Rubbery grips and moderate weight<br>• Easy to clean in the dishwasher<br>• Juice groove on one side | Plastic: **OXO Good Grips Prep Cutting Board**<br><br>Wood: **Teakhaus Square Marine Board with Juice Canal** |
| | FLEXIBLE CUTTING MAT | • Thick and sturdy but still flexible<br>• Textured sides keep mat in place and prevent food from sliding<br>• Textured surface conceals nicks | **Dexas Heavy Duty Grippmats** |
| | KNIFE SHARPENER | • Diamond abrasives and a spring-loaded chamber to precisely guide blade<br>• Quickly removes nicks in blades<br>• Can convert a 20-degree edge to a sharper 15 degrees | Electric: **Chef'sChoice Trizor 15XV Knife Sharpener**<br><br>Electric, Best Buy: **Chef'sChoice 315XV Knife Sharpener**<br><br>Manual: **Chef'sChoice Pronto Diamond Hone Knife Sharpener** |
| | HONING ROD | • Long and thick hone<br>• Alternating textures on rod, lightly ridged and smooth<br>• Easy to use | Winner: **Bob Kramer Double-Cut Sharpening Steel**<br><br>Best Buy: **Idahone Fine Ceramic Sharpening Rod, 12"** |
| | UNIVERSAL KNIFE BLOCK | • Heavy, ultrastable block with rotating base<br>• Durable bamboo exterior for easy cleaning<br>• Well-placed, medium-strength magnets for easy knife attachment | **Design Trifecta 360 Knife Block** |
| | MAGNETIC KNIFE STRIP | • Medium-strength magnets to hold knives with just the right amount of pull<br>• Easy to install and clean<br>• Bamboo surface that is gentle on blades | **Brooklyn Butcher Blocks Knife Rack, 20" Walnut** |
| | CUT-RESISTANT GLOVE | • Fits most hands closely<br>• Thin for better dexterity<br>• Machine-washable | **Mercer Culinary MercerGuard Cut Glove** |

| POTS AND PANS | ITEM | WHAT TO LOOK FOR | TEST KITCHEN FAVORITES |
|---|---|---|---|
| | TRADITIONAL SKILLET | • Stainless-steel interior and fully clad for even heat distribution<br>• 12-inch diameter and flared sides<br>• Comfortable, ovensafe handle<br>• Tight-fitting lid included | **All-Clad D3 Stainless Steel 12" Fry Pan with Lid** |
| | NONSTICK SKILLET | • Dark, nonstick surface<br>• Comfortable, ovensafe handle<br>• Cooking surface of at least 9 inches<br>• Available in 8- and 10-inch sizes | **All-Clad Stainless 12" Nonstick Fry Pan**<br><br>Best Buy: **T-fal Experience Nonstick Fry Pan 12.5 Inch** |
| | CARBON-STEEL SKILLET | • Affordable<br>• Thick, solid construction; ergonomically angled handle<br>• Sides flare up just right for easy access but high enough to contain splashes | **Mauviel M'STEEL Black Carbon Steel Round Frying Pan with Iron Handle, 12.6-In** |
| | CAST-IRON SKILLETS<br>Traditional | • Thick bottom and tall, straight sides<br>• Roomy interior (cooking surface of 10 inches)<br>• Preseasoned | **Smithey Ironware No. 12 Cast Iron Skillet**<br><br>Best Buy: **Lodge 12 Inch Cast Iron Skillet** |
| | Enameled | • Boasts flaring sides, an oversize helper handle, wide pour spouts, satiny interior, and balanced weight | **Le Creuset Signature 11¾" Iron Handle Skillet** |
| | COPPER SKILLETS | • Roomy cooking surface<br>• Open, flared sides with rounded corners<br>• Heats exceptionally evenly across its surface | Steel-Lined: **Mauviel M'Heritage M'200Ci Round Frying Pan, 11.9 In** |
| | | • Remarkably even heating and excellent browning<br>• Induction compatible | Copper Core: **All-Clad Copper Core 5-ply Bonded Cookware, Fry Pan, 12 inch** |
| | CERAMIC NONSTICK SKILLET | • Durable nonstick coating<br>• Broad cooking surface with gently sloped walls<br>• Comfortable handle | **GreenPan Valencia Pro Hard Anodized Nonstick Frypan**<br><br>Best Buy: **Kyocera Ceramic-Coated 12" Nonstick Frypan** |

| POTS AND PANS | ITEM | WHAT TO LOOK FOR | TEST KITCHEN FAVORITES |
|---|---|---|---|
| | WOK | • Carbon steel or lightweight cast iron<br>• 14 inches rim to rim<br>• High walls and rounded shape<br>• Single long handle angled slightly upward<br>• Stay-cool wooden handles | **Taylor and Ng Natural Nonstick Wok Set**<br><br>Co-Winner: **Joyce Chen Classic Series 14-Inch Carbon Steel Wok with Birch Handles**<br><br>Co-Winner: **IMUSA 14" Non-Coated Wok with Wood Handle, Silver** |
| | DUTCH OVEN | • Enameled cast iron or stainless steel<br>• Capacity of at least 6 quarts<br>• Diameter of at least 9 inches<br>• Tight-fitting lid<br>• Wide, sturdy handles | **Le Creuset 7¼ Quart Round Dutch Oven**<br><br>Best Buy: **Cuisinart Chef's Enameled Cast Iron Casserole** |
| | DUTCH OVEN, INNOVATIVE | • Large capacity<br>• Sturdy, thick base<br>• Silicone oil chamber in base spreads heat slowly and evenly<br>• Good heat retention | **Pauli Cookware Never Burn Sauce Pot, 10 Quart** |
| | SAUCEPANS<br>Large | • Steady heating and good visibility to monitor browning<br>• Stay-cool, easy-to-grip handle<br>• Helper handle for extra grabbing point | **All-Clad 4-Quart Stainless Steel Sauce Pan with Loop Helper Handle**<br><br>Best Buy: **Tramontina Gourmet Tri-Ply Clad 4 Qt. Covered Sauce Pan** |
| | Small nonstick | • Heavy, solid, well priced<br>• Easy to control<br>• Shallow shape and generous diameter | **Calphalon Contemporary Nonstick 2½-Quart Shallow Saucepan with Cover** |
| | RIMMED BAKING SHEET | • Light-colored surface (heats and browns evenly)<br>• Thick, sturdy pan<br>• Dimensions of 18 by 13 inches<br>• Good to have at least two | **Nordic Ware Baker's Half Sheet** |
| | SAUTÉ PAN | • Aluminum core surrounded by layers of stainless steel<br>• Relatively lightweight<br>• 9¾-inch diameter<br>• Stay-cool helper handle | **Made In Stainless Clad Saute Pan** |
| | PAELLA PAN | • Shallow, wide shape maximizes the surface area of the paella<br>• Distributes heat evenly | **Matfer Bourgeat Black Steel Paella Pan** |

| POTS AND PANS | ITEM | WHAT TO LOOK FOR | TEST KITCHEN FAVORITES |
|---|---|---|---|
| | CANNING POT | • Comfortable, grippy handles<br>• Clear lid that allows user to easily monitor contents | **Roots and Branches Stainless Steel Multi-Use Canner** |
| | STOCKPOT | • Stainless steel<br>• 12-quart capacity<br>• Thick bottom to prevent scorching<br>• Wide body for easy cleaning and storage<br>• Easy-to-position lid<br>• U-shaped handles with rubbery grips | **Cook N Home Stainless Steel Stockpot with Lid 12 Quart** |
| | ROASTING PAN | • At least 15 by 11 inches<br>• Stainless-steel interior with aluminum core for even heat distribution<br>• Upright handles for easy gripping<br>• Light interior for better food monitoring | **Cuisinart MultiClad Pro Stainless 16" Roasting Pan with Rack** |
| | GRILL PAN | • Cast-iron pan for heat retention and easy cleanup<br>• Tall, well-defined ridges (4- to 5.5-mm high) to keep food above rendered fat<br>• Generous cooking area | Co-Winner: **Lodge Chef Collection 11 inch Cast Iron Square Grill Pan**<br><br>Co-Winner: **Borough Furnace Grill Pan/Braising Lid** |
| | COOKWARE SET | • Fully clad stainless steel with aluminum core for even heat distribution<br>• Moderately heavy, durable construction<br>• Lids included<br>• Good mix of pans includes 10-inch frypan, 8-inch frypan, 3-quart saucepan, 2-quart saucepan, 3-quart sauté pan, 8-quart stockpot | **All-Clad D3 Tri-Ply Bonded Cookware Set, 10 piece**<br><br>Best Buy: **Goldilocks Cookware Set** |

| HANDY TOOLS | ITEM | WHAT TO LOOK FOR | TEST KITCHEN FAVORITES |
|---|---|---|---|
| | KITCHEN SHEARS | • Take-apart scissors (for easy cleaning)<br>• Supersharp blades<br>• Sturdy construction<br>• Work for both right- and left-handed users | **Shun Multi-Purpose Shears**<br><br>Best Buy: **J.A. Henckels International Take-Apart Shears** |
| | TONGS | • Scalloped edges<br>• Slightly concave pincers<br>• Length of 12 inches (to keep your hand far from the heat)<br>• Open and close easily | **OXO Good Grips 12-Inch Locking Tongs** |

| HANDY TOOLS | ITEM | WHAT TO LOOK FOR | TEST KITCHEN FAVORITES |
|---|---|---|---|
| | SLOTTED SPOON | • Lightweight<br>• Wide, shallow bowl<br>• Thin-edged bowl<br>• Long, comfortable handle | **Cuisinart Stainless Steel Slotted Spoon** |
| | SPATULA-SPOON | • Lightweight thanks to lightly textured silicone material and gently rounded handle<br>• Odor-resistant<br>• Vibrant color hides stains | Co-Winner: **Rubbermaid High-Heat Spoon Scraper**<br><br>Co-Winner: **Starpack Premium Silicone Spoonula** |
| | ALL-AROUND SPATULA | • Thin, flexible, gently upward-curving head about 3 inches wide and 5 inches long<br>• Long, vertical slots<br>• Comfortable, easy to control handle<br>• Useful to have a metal spatula to use with traditional cookware and plastic for nonstick cookware | Metal: **Wüsthof Gourmet 7″ Slotted Spatula**<br><br>Best Buy: **MIU France Flexible Fish Turner—Slotted**<br><br>Nonstick-Safe: **Matfer Bourgeat Exoglass Pelton Spatula** |
| | SILICONE SPATULA | • Firm enough for scraping and scooping<br>• Fits neatly into tight corners<br>• Straight sides and wide, flat blade to ensure no food is left unmixed | **Di Oro Living Seamless Silicone Spatula–Large**<br><br>Large: **Rubbermaid 13.5″ High-Heat Scraper** |
| | OFFSET SPATULA | • Flexible blade offset to a roughly 30-degree angle<br>• Enough usable surface area to frost the radius of a 9-inch cake<br>• Comfortable handle | **OXO Good Grips Bent Icing Knife** |
| | COMPACT SPATULA | • High heat resistance<br>• Comfortable grip with 2⅝-inch-wide head | **OXO Good Grips Silicone Cookie Spatula** |
| | JAR SPATULA | • Slim, flexible head maneuvers tight corners and edges<br>• Strong enough to lift heavy food<br>• Seamless silicone for easy cleaning and comfortable feel | **GIR Skinny Spatula**<br><br>Best Buy: **OXO Good Grips Silicone Jar Spatula** |
| | ALL-PURPOSE WHISK | • At least 10 wires<br>• Wires of moderate thickness<br>• Comfortable rubber handle<br>• Balanced, lightweight feel | **OXO Good Grips 11″ Balloon Whisk** |

| HANDY TOOLS | ITEM | WHAT TO LOOK FOR | TEST KITCHEN FAVORITES |
|---|---|---|---|
| | FLAT WHISK | • Comfortable to use for longer periods<br>• Grippy TPE handle<br>• Tines with good rigidity and spacing | **OXO Good Grips Flat Whisk** |
| | MINI WHISK | • Five sturdy wire loops<br>• Relatively broad head<br>• Thick, medium-length handle that is easy to grip and clean | **Tovolo Stainless Steel 6" Mini Whisk** |
| | UTENSIL CROCK | • Large enough to comfortably fit 20 utensils<br>• Removable dividers keeps things organized<br>• Removable silicone mat in the bottom<br>• Dishwasher-safe | **RSVP Oversized Tool Crock** |
| | PEPPER MILL | • Easy-to-adjust, clearly marked grind settings<br>• Efficient, comfortable grinding mechanism<br>• Generous capacity<br>• Easy to fill | **Cole & Mason Derwent Pepper Mill**<br><br>Best Buy: **OXO Good Grips Contoured Mess-Free Pepper Grinder** |
| | LADLE | • Stainless steel or nonstick nylon<br>• Hook handle<br>• Pouring rim to prevent dripping<br>• Handle 9 to 10 inches in length | Co-Winner: **Rösle Hook Ladle with Pouring Rim**<br><br>Co-Winner: **Cuisinart Curve Handle Line Curve Nylon Ladle**<br><br>Best Buy: **Cuisinart Stainless Steel Ladle** |
| | CAN OPENER | • Intuitive and easy to use<br>• Long driving handle<br>• Smooth and effortless opening | **OXO Good Grips Soft Handled Can Opener** |
| | JAR OPENER | • Strong, sturdy clamp grip<br>• Adjusts quickly to any size jar | **Amco Swing-A-Way Jar Opener** |
| | GARLIC PRESS | • Large capacity that holds multiple garlic cloves<br>• Long handle and short distance between pivot point and plunger | **Kuhn Rikon Epicurean Garlic Press** |
| | CHEESE PLANE | • Comfortable handle with relatively long blade<br>• Thin, flexible head produces perfect, clean-edged, even cheese slices | **Wüsthof Gourmet 4¾-inch Cheese Plane** |

| HANDY TOOLS | ITEM | WHAT TO LOOK FOR | TEST KITCHEN FAVORITES |
|---|---|---|---|
| | SERRATED FRUIT PEELER | • Comfortable grip and nonslip handle<br>• Sharp blade | **OXO Good Grips Serrated Peeler** |
| | VEGETABLE PEELER | • Sharp, carbon-steel blade<br>• 1-inch space between blade and peeler to prevent jamming<br>• Lightweight and comfortable | For adults and older kids:<br>**Kuhn Rikon Original Swiss Peeler**<br><br>For younger kids and beginners:<br>**Opinel Le Petit Chef Peeler** |
| | AVOCADO SLICER | • Compact<br>• Relatively comfortable to hold<br>• Double-headed configuration with knife on one end and slicer on the other | **OXO Good Grips 3-in-1 Avocado Slicer** |
| | RASP-STYLE GRATER | • Sharp teeth (require little effort or pressure when grating)<br>• Maneuverable over round shapes<br>• Comfortable handle | **Microplane Premium Classic Zester/Grater** |
| | GRATERS | • Large, long grating surface with stamped holes<br>• Grippy plastic bumper around base for stability<br>• Large comfortable handle | Best Box-Style:<br>**Cuisinart Box Grater**<br><br>Best Paddle-Style:<br>**Rösle Coarse Grater** |
| | GINGER GRATER | • Ample surface area and razor-sharp etched holes<br>• Comfortable grip<br>• Wide paddle shape makes it easy to collect ginger puree and clean | **Microplane Home Series Fine Grater** |
| | ROTARY GRATER | • Compact but with large hopper<br>• Classic turn-crank design with ability to switch handle side to side<br>• Comfortable handle with rubbery grips<br>• Easy to clean | **Zyliss Classic Cheese Grater** |
| | MANUAL CITRUS JUICER | • Handheld squeezer with comfortable handle<br>• Durable, plastic exterior<br>• Large, slat-like holes for efficient draining | **Chef'n FreshForce Citrus Juicer** |
| | ICE CREAM SCOOP | • Comfortable handle<br>• Gently curved bowl for easy releasing<br>• Scoop warms on contact with your hand to slightly melt ice cream | **Zeroll Original Ice Cream Scoop** |
| | MEAT POUNDER | • At least 1½ pounds<br>• Large head<br>• Short, vertical handle for better leverage and control | **Norpro GRIP EZ Meat Pounder** |

| HANDY TOOLS | ITEM | WHAT TO LOOK FOR | TEST KITCHEN FAVORITES |
|---|---|---|---|
| | BENCH SCRAPER | • Sturdy blade<br>• Comfortable handle with plastic, rubber, or nylon grip | **Dexter-Russell Sani-Safe 6" x 3" Dough Cutter/Scraper** |
| | ROLLING PIN | • Moderate weight (1 to 1½ pounds)<br>• 19-inch straight barrel<br>• Slightly textured wooden surface to grip dough for easy rolling | Best Dowel: **JK Adams Plain Rolling Dowel Pin**<br><br>Best Tapered Pin: **JK Adams French Rolling Pin** |
| | MIXING BOWLS<br>Stainless Steel | • Lightweight and easy to handle<br>• Durable<br>• Conducts heat well for double boiler | **Vollrath Economy Stainless Steel Mixing Bowls** |
| | Glass | • Tempered to increase impact and thermal resistance<br>• Can be used in microwave<br>• Durable | **Pyrex Smart Essentials Mixing Bowl Set** |
| | MINI PREP BOWLS | • Wide, shallow bowls are easy to hold, fill, empty, and clean<br>• Can be used in the microwave and oven | **Anchor Hocking Custard Cups** |
| | BOWL STABILIZER | • Firmly attaches bowls to every work surface in the kitchen<br>• Accommodates bowls from 6 to 21 inches in diameter<br>• Forms a tight seal in double boilers | **Staybowlizer** |
| | OVEN MITT | • Form-fitting and not overly bulky for easy maneuvering<br>• Flexible, heat-resistant material<br>• Machine washable | **OXO Silicone Oven Mitt**<br><br>For kids: **Curious Chef Child Chef Mitt Set** |
| | POT HOLDER | • Silicone layer to protect from heat<br>• Flexible to grip comfortably<br>• Machine washable | **OXO Good Grips Silicone Pot Holder** |
| | JAR LIFTER | • Spring-loaded hinge that pops grabbers open when handles are released<br>• Broad, molded handles comfortable and secure<br>• Does not rust | **Ball Secure-Grip Jar Lifter** |
| | COOKIE PRESS | • Produces visually appealing, uniform cookies<br>• Withstands prolonged use with no decline in performance<br>• Consistently produces cookies with intact designs without dough jamming | **MARCATO Biscuit Maker** |

| HANDY TOOLS | ITEM | WHAT TO LOOK FOR | TEST KITCHEN FAVORITES |
|---|---|---|---|
| | PASTRY BRUSHES<br>Wooden Brush | • Bristles of moderate length and density<br>• Loses few bristles<br>• Grippy handle | **Winco Flat Pastry and Basting Brush, 1½ inch** |
| | Silicone Brush | • Flexible bristles<br>• Lightweight handle of grippy plastic | **OXO Good Grips Silicone Pastry Brush** |
| | SPLATTER SCREEN | • 8-, 10-, and 12-inch sizes<br>• Ring design<br>• Dishwasher-safe silicone<br>• Rolls up for storage | **Frywall Stovetop Splatter Guard** |
| | GRILL PRESS | • Cast iron with smooth surface<br>• Surface area of 30 square inches<br>• Coated steel handle | **Lodge Rectangular Cast Iron Grill Press 6.75" x 4.5"** |
| | BOUILLON STRAINER/ CHINOIS | • Conical shape<br>• Depth of 7 to 8 inches<br>• At least one hook on rim for stability | **Winco Reinforced Extra Fine Mesh Bouillon Strainer** |
| | COLANDER | • 4- to 7-quart capacity<br>• Metal ring attached to the bottom for stability<br>• Many holes for quick draining<br>• Small holes so pasta doesn't slip through | **RSVP International Endurance Precision Pierced 5 Qt. Colander** |
| | MINI COLANDER | • Large, comfortable, rubberized grip<br>• Perfectly sized webbed basket<br>• Collapsible | **Progressive Prepworks Collapsible Mini Colander** |
| | FINE-MESH STRAINER | • Roomy, medium-depth basket with fine, stiff mesh<br>• Long, wide hook and rounded steel handle | **Rösle Fine Mesh Strainer, Round Handle, 7.9 inches, 20 cm** |
| | SPIDER SKIMMER | • Long handle for protection from hot water and oil<br>• Well-balanced and easy to maneuver | **Rösle Wire Skimmer** |

| HANDY TOOLS | ITEM | WHAT TO LOOK FOR | TEST KITCHEN FAVORITES |
|---|---|---|---|
| | SMALL STRAINER | • Weight-balanced basket and handle<br>• Wide, rectangular resting hook<br>• Very fine-mesh basket makes quick work of straining | Co-Winner: **Rösle Stainless Steel Fine Mesh Tea Strainer, Wire Handle, 3.2-inch**<br><br>Co-Winner: **Küchenprofi Heavy Duty Fine Mesh Stainless Steel 3-Inch Classic Strainer** |
| | TEA INFUSER | • Large capacity (13.5 tablespoons) allows for good water circulation<br>• Easy to fill and clean<br>• Tightly woven mesh basket keeps even the finest leaves out of finished tea | **Finum Brewing Basket L** |
| | FOOD MILL | • Four interchangeable disks for more processing options<br>• Easy to turn | **Cuisipro Deluxe Food Mill** |
| | FAT SEPARATOR | • Easy-to-read measurement lines<br>• Tightly sealed bottom release valve<br>• Large strainer dotted with many small perforations | **OXO Good Grips Good Gravy Fat Separator–4 Cup**<br><br>Best Buy: **Trudeau Gravy Separator** |
| | FUNNEL | • Spout at least 1½ inches long<br>• Opening at least ⅜ inch in diameter<br>• Dishwasher-safe | **Winco PF-8 Plastic Funnel, 8 oz, 4-inch Diameter** |
| | POTATO MASHER | • Solid mashing disk with small holes<br>• Comfortable grip | **Zyliss Stainless Steel Potato Masher** |
| | SALAD SPINNER | • Large capacity<br>• Easy-to-operate central pump and brake<br>• Wide base for stability<br>• Flat lid for easy cleaning and storage<br>• Dishwasher-safe | **OXO Good Grips Salad Spinner** |
| | STEAMER BASKET | • Stainless-steel basket with feet<br>• Roomy and collapsible | **OXO Good Grips Stainless Steel Steamer with Extendable Handle** |
| | BAMBOO STEAMER | • Steams food efficiently<br>• Durable bamboo slats in base of each tier<br>• Tiers reinforced with steel bands | Co-Winner: **Juvale 10 Inch Bamboo Steamer with Steel Rings for Cooking**<br><br>Co-Winner: **Zest of Moringa Bamboo Steamer Basket Set** |

| HANDY TOOLS | ITEM | WHAT TO LOOK FOR | TEST KITCHEN FAVORITES |
|---|---|---|---|
| | MORTAR AND PESTLE | • Capacity of at least 1.5 cups and interior 3 to 4 inches in diameter<br>• Heavy, stable base with straight walls<br>• Rough interior to help grip and grind ingredients<br>• Heavy, long pestle | **Frieling Goliath Natural Stone Mortar & Pestle** |

| MEASURING EQUIPMENT | ITEM | WHAT TO LOOK FOR | TEST KITCHEN FAVORITES |
|---|---|---|---|
| | DRY MEASURING CUPS | • Accurate measurements<br>• Easy-to-read measurement markings<br>• Stack and store neatly<br>• Durable measurement markings<br>• Stable when empty and filled<br>• Handles perfectly flush with cups | **OXO Good Grips Stainless Steel Measuring Cups** |
| | LIQUID MEASURING CUP (GLASS) | • Crisp, unambiguous markings that include ¼- and ⅓-cup measurements<br>• Heatproof, sturdy cup with handle<br>• Good to have in a variety of sizes (1, 2, and 4 cups) | **Pyrex 2-Cup Liquid Measuring Cup** |
| | ADJUSTABLE MEASURING CUP | • Plunger-like bottom (with a tight seal between plunger and tube) that you can set to correct measurement, then push up to cleanly extract sticky ingredients (such as shortening or peanut butter)<br>• 1- or 2-cup capacity<br>• Dishwasher-safe | **KitchenArt Pro 2 Cup Adjust-A-Cup, Satin** |
| | MEASURING SPOONS | • Long, comfortable handles<br>• Rim of bowl flush with handle (makes it easy to "dip" into a dry ingredient and "sweep" across the top for accurate measuring)<br>• Slim design | **Cuisipro Stainless Steel 5-Piece Measuring Spoons** |
| | KITCHEN RULER | • Stainless steel; easy to clean<br>• 18 inches in length<br>• Large, easy-to-read markings | **Empire 18-inch Stainless Steel Ruler** |
| | DIGITAL SCALE | • Easy-to-read display not blocked by weighing platform<br>• At least 7-pound capacity<br>• Accessible buttons<br>• Gram-to-ounce conversion feature<br>• Roomy platform | **OXO Good Grips 11 lb Food Scale with Pull Out Display**<br><br>Best Buy: **Ozeri Pronto Digital Multifunction Kitchen and Food Scale** |

| THERMOMETERS AND TIMERS | ITEM | WHAT TO LOOK FOR | TEST KITCHEN FAVORITES |
|---|---|---|---|
| | INSTANT-READ THERMOMETER | • Digital model with automatic shut-off<br>• Quick-response readings in 1 second<br>• Wide temperature range (-58 to 572 degrees)<br>• Long stem that can reach interior of large cuts of meat<br>• Water-resistant | **ThermoWorks Thermapen ONE**<br><br>Best Buy: **ThermoWorks ThermoPop**<br><br>Best Midprice: **Lavatools Javelin PRO Duo** |

| THERMOMETERS AND TIMERS | ITEM | WHAT TO LOOK FOR | TEST KITCHEN FAVORITES |
|---|---|---|---|
| | OVEN THERMOMETER | • Clearly marked numbers for easy readability<br>• Large, sturdy base<br>• Large temperature range (up to 600 degrees) | Best Analog: **CDN ProAccurate Oven Thermometer**<br><br>Best Digital: **ThermoWorks Square DOT** |
| | REMOTE-PROBE THERMOMETER | • Easy to set up<br>• Large, bright display<br>• Loud, easy-to-set alarm<br>• Magnetic base and kickstand | **ThermoWorks Smoke 2-Channel Alarm**<br><br>Best Buy: **NutriChef Bluetooth Wireless BBQ Grill Thermometer** |
| | MEAT PROBE/ CANDY/ DEEP-FRY THERMOMETER | • Digital model<br>• Easy-to-read console<br>• Intuitive design and ovensafe probe | **ThermoWorks ChefAlarm**<br><br>Best Buy: **Polder Classic Digital Thermometer/Timer** |
| | REFRIGERATOR/ FREEZER THERMOMETER | • Accurate and customizable<br>• Alerts when temperatures remain outside safe zone for more than 30 minutes | **ThermoWorks Fridge/Freezer Alarm** |
| | KITCHEN TIMERS | • Clearly labeled buttons<br>• Large, readable digits<br>• Entire screen flashes when the timer goes off<br>• Splash-resistant and sturdy<br>• Has magnets and can be positioned on a refrigerator | Best Single-Event Timer **ThermoWorks Extra Big & Loud Timer** |
| | | • Accurate and easy to use<br>• Screen displays all three events at once (no scrolling required)<br>• Each event has its own button and makes a unique sound | Best Multiple-Event Timer **ThermoWorks TimeStack** |

| BAKEWARE | ITEM | WHAT TO LOOK FOR | TEST KITCHEN FAVORITES |
|---|---|---|---|
| | GLASS BAKING DISH | • Large handles<br>• Lightweight<br>• Easy to grip and maneuver | **Pyrex Easy Grab 3-Quart Oblong Baking Dish** |
| | METAL BAKING PAN | • Dimensions of 13 by 9 inches<br>• Straight sides<br>• Nonstick coating for even browning and easy release of cakes and bar cookies | **Williams Sonoma Goldtouch Nonstick Rectangular Cake Pan, 9″ x 13″** |

| BAKEWARE | ITEM | WHAT TO LOOK FOR | TEST KITCHEN FAVORITES |
|---|---|---|---|
| | SQUARE BAKING PAN | • Nonstick coating for easy cleanup<br>• Wide handles makes maneuvering easy<br>• Durable | **All-Clad Pro-Release Nonstick Bakeware 8 inch Square Cake Pan**<br><br>Best Buy: **Wilton Perfect Results Premium Non-Stick Bakeware Square Cake Pan** |
| | ROUND CAKE PANS | • Best for cake<br>• Straight sides<br>• Light finish for tall, evenly baked cakes<br>• Nonstick surface for easy release | Best All Around: **Williams Sonoma Goldtouch Pro Nonstick Round Cake Pan** |
| | | • Dark finish is ideal for pizza and cinnamon buns<br>• Nonstick | Best Buy: **Nordic Ware Naturals Nonstick 9" Round Cake Pan** |
| | PIE PLATE | • Gold-hued metal for even browning and crisping<br>• Nonfluted lip for maximum crust-crimping flexibility<br>• Good to have two | Co-Winner: **Williams Sonoma Goldtouch Pro Nonstick Pie Dish**<br><br>Co-Winner: **USA Pan 9-Inch Pie Pan** |
| | LOAF PAN | • Made of folded metal for baked goods with crisp corners<br>• Good to have both 8½ by 4½-inch and 9 by 5-inch pans | **USA Pan Loaf Pan, 1 lb Volume** |
| | SPRINGFORM PAN | • Wide, ridged base<br>• Tight seal between band and bottom of pan to prevent leakage | Co-Winner and Best Buy: **Nordic Ware 9" Leakproof Springform Pan**<br><br>Co-Winner: **Williams Sonoma Goldtouch Leakproof Springform Cake Pan** |
| | MUFFIN TIN | • Easy to hold and turn<br>• Oversize rim for secure grasping<br>• Gold finish for perfectly browned baked goods | **OXO Good Grips Non-Stick Pro 12-Cup Muffin Pan** |
| | MINI-MUFFIN TIN | • Produces evenly baked and well-browned baked goods<br>• Fairly narrow cups<br>• Foods release easily<br>• Easy and comfortable to maneuver | **Williams Sonoma Goldtouch Pro Mini Muffin Pan**<br><br>Best Buy: **Wilton Perfect Results Premium Non-Stick Mini Muffin and Cupcake Pan, 24-Cup** |
| | WIRE RACK | • Grid-style rack with tightly woven bars<br>• Six feet on three bars for extra stability<br>• Should fit inside standard 18 by 13-inch rimmed baking sheet<br>• Broiler-safe and dishwasher-safe | **Checkered Chef Cooling Rack** |

| BAKEWARE | ITEM | WHAT TO LOOK FOR | TEST KITCHEN FAVORITES |
|---|---|---|---|
| | BISCUIT CUTTERS | • Sharp edges<br>• A set with a variety of sizes | **Ateco 5357 11-Piece Plain Round Cutter Set** |
| | BUNDT PAN | • Thick, easy-to-grip handles<br>• Deep, well-defined ridges that produce perfect cakes | **Nordic Ware Anniversary Bundt Pan** |
| | MINI BUNDT PAN | • Tray-style model with six ¾-cup molds<br>• Silver platinum nonstick surface for even browning and easy release<br>• Clearly defined ridges | **Nordic Ware Platinum Anniversary Bundtlette Pan** |
| | TART PAN | • Nonstick coating for easy transfer<br>• Professional-looking edges<br>• If you bake a lot, it's good to have multiple sizes, though 9 inches is standard | **Matfer Steel Non-stick Fluted Tart Mold with Removable Bottom 9½"** |
| | TUBE PAN | • 16-cup capacity<br>• Leakproof removable bottom<br>• Dark nonstick surface for even browning and easy release<br>• Feet on the rim for sturdy cooling | **Chicago Metallic 2-Piece Angel Food Cake Pan with Feet** |
| | PULLMAN LOAF PAN | • Squared-off pan (4 by 4 inches)<br>• Nonstick aluminized steel for easy cleanup<br>• Light surface for even browning | **USA Pan 13 by 4-Inch Pullman Loaf Pan & Cover** |
| | EDGE PAN | • Attached cutting grid<br>• Dark nonstick surface for easy release | **Baker's Edge Brownie Pan** |
| | SOUFFLÉ DISH | • Round dish with straight sides<br>• Not-too-thick side walls | **HIC 64 Ounce Soufflé** |
| | BAKING STEEL AND STONE | • Dimensions of 16 by 14 inches<br>• Carbon steel for evenly browned crusts | Co-Winner: **The Original Baking Steel**<br><br>Co-Winner: **Nerd Chef Steel Stone, Standard ¼"** |

| BAKEWARE | ITEM | WHAT TO LOOK FOR | TEST KITCHEN FAVORITES |
|---|---|---|---|
| | BAKING PEEL | • Polymer coating guards against moisture<br>• Innovative cloth conveyor belt | Best Overall: **EXO Non-Stick Super Peel Pro Composite**<br><br>Best Wood Peel: **New Star Foodservice 50295 Restaurant-Grade Wooden Pizza Peel**<br><br>Best Buy: **Pizzacraft 14" Wood Pizza Peel** |
| | BAKING MAT | • Fits perfectly inside rimmed baking sheets<br>• Heavy enough to stay put<br>• Dishwasher-safe | **DeMarle Silpat U.S. Half-Size Non-Stick Silicone Baking Mat** |

| SMALL APPLIANCES | ITEM | WHAT TO LOOK FOR | TEST KITCHEN FAVORITES |
|---|---|---|---|
| | AIR FRYER | • Drawer-style model with extra-large capacity<br>• Quick 2-minute preheat<br>• Sturdy handle<br>• Intuitive digital controls | **Instant Vortex Plus 6-Quart Air Fryer** |
| | FOOD PROCESSOR | • 14-cup capacity<br>• Sharp and sturdy blades<br>• Wide feed tube<br>• Should come with basic blades and disks: steel blade, dough blade, shredding/slicing disk | **Cuisinart Custom 14-Cup Food Processor** |
| | STAND MIXER | • Planetary action (stationary bowl and single mixing arm)<br>• Powerful motor<br>• Bowl size of at least 4½ quarts<br>• Slightly squat bowl to keep ingredients in beater's range<br>• Should come with basic attachments: paddle, dough hook, metal whisk | **Ankarsrum Original 6230 Creme and Stainless Steel 7 Liter Stand Mixer**<br><br>Best Midpriced: **KitchenAid Classic Series 4.5 Quart Tilt-Head Stand Mixer** |
|  | SMALL STAND MIXER | • Heavier weight for less vibration<br>• Simple-to-operate controls<br>• Easy-to-use bowls and attachments<br>• Dishwasher-safe bowl | **KitchenAid Artisan Mini 3.5 Quart Tilt-Head Stand Mixer** |

| SMALL APPLIANCES | ITEM | WHAT TO LOOK FOR | TEST KITCHEN FAVORITES |
|---|---|---|---|
| | HAND MIXER | • Silicone-tipped wide beater heads<br>• Well-positioned display screen<br>• Powerful, with a variety of speeds | **Breville Handy Mix Scraper**<br><br>Best Buy: **Cuisinart Power Advantage Plus 9 Speed Hand Mixer** |
| | BLENDER | • Mix of straight and serrated blades at different angles<br>• Jar with curved base<br>• At least 44-ounce capacity<br>• Heavy base for stability | High-End: **Vitamix 5200**<br><br>Midpriced: **Breville Fresh & Furious**<br><br>Less Expensive: **Ninja Professional Plus Blender with Auto-iQ** |
| | PERSONAL BLENDER | • Quick and effective blending thanks to sharp, six-pronged blades angled both up and down<br>• Well-designed travel lid with drinking spout and hinged arm that seals tight | Co-Winner: **Beast Health Blender**<br><br>Co-Winner: **Ninja Nutri-Blender Pro with Auto-iQ**<br><br>Best Buy: **Nutribullet Personal Blender** |
| | IMMERSION BLENDER | • Grippy rubber handle<br>• Easy to change speeds<br>• Lightweight | **Braun Multiquick 5 Hand Blender** |
| | ELECTRIC GRIDDLE | • Large cooking area (about 21 by 12 inches)<br>• Attached pull-out grease trap (won't tip over)<br>• Nonstick surface for easy cleanup | **BroilKing Professional Griddle with Backsplash** |
| | ELECTRIC JUICERS | • Straightforward to assemble, with parts that fit together well<br>• Fast<br>• Easy to clean<br>• Contained debris fairly well | Centrifugal Juicer: **Breville Juice Fountain Cold** |
| | | • Easy to assemble<br>• Helpful auger<br>• Chewed through carrots, kale, and grapes with ease<br>• Relatively easy to clean | Masticating Juicer: **Omega Vsj843 Qs Vertical Square Low Speed Juicer** |

| SMALL APPLIANCES | ITEM | WHAT TO LOOK FOR | TEST KITCHEN FAVORITES |
|---|---|---|---|
| | ELECTRIC KETTLE | • Heats water to a range of different temperatures<br>• Automatic shutoff<br>• Separate base for cordless pouring<br>• Visible water level | **OXO Brew Cordless Glass Electric Kettle**<br><br>Best Buy: **Cosori Original Electric Glass Kettle** |
| | ELECTRIC GOOSENECK KETTLE | • Boils water in under 3 minutes<br>• Accurate custom-select temperatures<br>• Easily visible capacity line and single-knob controls make filling and operating a breeze<br>• Comfortable, grippy handle and lightweight construction | Adjustable: **OXO Brew Adjustable Temperature Pour-Over Kettle** |
| | | • Large on-off switch<br>• Comfortable handle and thin, nimble spout | Boil Only: **Bodum Bistro Gooseneck Electric Water Kettle** |
| | STOVETOP KETTLE | • Lightweight and easy to fill<br>• Generous capacity<br>• Easy-to-clean surface<br>• Comfortable, grippy handle<br>• Spout pours neatly | **Chantal Enamel-on-Steel Anniversary Teakettle Collection (2 QT.)** |
| | COFFEE MAKER | • Thermal carafe that keeps coffee hot and fresh with capacity of at least 10 cups<br>• Short brewing time (6 minutes is ideal)<br>• Copper, not aluminum, heating element<br>• Easy-to-fill water tank<br>• Clear, intuitive controls | **Technivorm Moccamaster KBT**<br><br>Best Buy: **Zojirushi ZUTTO Coffee Maker** |
| | ESPRESSO MACHINE | • Compact, well-made machine<br>• Consistent, excellent espresso<br>• Easy adjustment of flavor, temperature, and shot strength<br>• Simple attached steam wand with silicone grip for easy cleaning<br>• Clear display and well-designed controls | Best Fully Automatic: **Gaggia Anima Automatic Coffee Machine**<br><br>Best for DIY Types: **Breville Barista Express** |
| | PRECISION COFFEE SCALE | • High level of accuracy and sensitivity<br>• Sturdy and user-friendly<br>• Conveniently located power button<br>• Helpful directions | **Timemore Black Mirror Basic Plus Scale** |
| | MANUAL PASTA MACHINE | • Laser-sharp noodle attachment for perfectly shaped pasta<br>• Wide and narrow thickness settings<br>• Easy-to-use dial | **Marcato Atlas 150 Wellness Pasta Machine** |

| SMALL APPLIANCES | ITEM | WHAT TO LOOK FOR | TEST KITCHEN FAVORITES |
|---|---|---|---|
| | WARMING TRAY | • Features a range of heat settings to keep food at a safe serving temperature<br>• Keeps food hot for 4 hours<br>• Stay-cool handles for easy maneuvering<br>• Easily wipes clean and is cool after use in 20 minutes' time | **BroilKing Professional Stainless Warming Tray** |
| | INDUCTION BURNER | • Responsive control panel<br>• Works best with smaller cookware<br>• Easy to clean | Best Buy: **Duxtop Portable Induction Cooktop**<br><br>High End: **Breville/PolyScience Control Freak** |
| | SMART COOKING SYSTEM | • Easy, intuitive Bluetooth system<br>• Sturdy, well-built skillet and pot<br>• Smooth, stainless-steel cooking surface | **Hestan Cue Smart Cooking System: Pan, Burner & Chef's Pot** |
| | ICE CREAM MAKER | • Compact size for easy storage<br>• Simple to use and clean<br>• Produces dense, smooth ice cream | **Cuisinart Frozen Yogurt, Ice Cream, & Sorbet Maker** |
| | ICE CREAM CONE MAKER | • Easy to use<br>• Solidly constructed<br>• Channel around edge to catch excess batter for easy cleanup | **Chef's Choice 838 Waffle Cone Express** |
| | STOVETOP PRESSURE COOKER | • Solidly built<br>• Low sides and wide base for easy access and better browning and heat retention<br>• Easy-to-read pressure indicator | **Fissler Vitaquick 8½-Quart Pressure Cooker**<br><br>Best Buy: **Zavor Duo 8.4 Quart Pressure Cooker** |
| | SLOW COOKER | • At least 6-quart capacity<br>• Insert has handles<br>• Clear lid to see progress of food<br>• Dishwasher-safe insert<br>• Intuitive control panel with programmable timer and warming mode | **KitchenAid 6-Quart Slow Cooker with Solid Glass Lid** |
| | RICE COOKER | • Clearly defined water measurement markings<br>• Convenient cookpot handle placement<br>• Handy "Keep Warm" setting<br>• Makes both small and large batches | **Zojirushi 5.5-Cup Neuro Fuzzy Rice Cooker & Warmer** |

| SMALL APPLIANCES | ITEM | WHAT TO LOOK FOR | TEST KITCHEN FAVORITES |
|---|---|---|---|
| | SMART OVEN | • Easy to use with responsive control panel<br>• Well-designed app that does not lose connectivity with oven<br>• Can also operate as traditional countertop oven<br>• Includes food-temperature probe, wire rack, and baking sheet | **Tovala Smart Oven** |
| | COUNTERTOP STEAM OVEN | • Ability to calibrate the humidity level in small increments<br>• Built-in probe thermometer<br>• Easy-to-navigate control panel<br>• A sous vide mode that "seals" food with humid air | **Anova Precision Oven** |
| | TOASTER OVEN | • Quartz heating elements for steady, controlled heat<br>• Roomy but compact interior<br>• Simple to use | **Breville Smart Oven** |
| | AIR-FRYER TOASTER OVEN | • Clearly displayed settings<br>• Nonstick basket with feet<br>• Easy to clean | Co-Winner: **Breville Smart Oven Air Fryer Pro**<br><br>Co-Winner: **Ninja Foodi 10-in-1 XL Pro Air Fry Oven**<br><br>Best Buy: **Instant Oven 18L Air Fryer Toaster Oven** |
| | WAFFLE MAKER, ELECTRIC | • Indicator lights and audible alert<br>• Makes two waffles at a time<br>• Six-point dial for customizing waffle doneness | Best Belgian Waffle Maker: **Breville Smart Waffle 4 Slice**<br><br>Best Classic Waffle Maker: **Breville No-Mess Waffle Maker** |
| | BREAD MACHINE | • Easy-to-use interface<br>• "Homemade" option lets you customize the kneading, rising, and baking times<br>• Two kneading paddles<br>• Produces traditional, rectangular-shaped loaves | Co-Winner: **Zojirushi Home Bakery Supreme Breadmaker**<br><br>Co-Winner: **Cuisinart Compact Automatic Bread Maker** |

| GRILLING EQUIPMENT | ITEM | WHAT TO LOOK FOR | TEST KITCHEN FAVORITES |
|---|---|---|---|
| | GAS GRILL | • Large main grate<br>• Built-in thermometer<br>• Two burners for varying heat levels (three is even better)<br>• Made of thick, heat-retaining materials such as cast aluminum and enameled steel | **Weber Spirit II E-310 Gas Grill** |
| | CHARCOAL GRILL | • Sturdy construction for maintaining heat<br>• Well-designed cooking grate, handles, lid, and wheels<br>• Generous cooking and charcoal capacity<br>• Well-positioned vents to control air flow<br>• Ash catcher for easy cleanup | **Weber Original Kettle Premium Charcoal Grill, 22-Inch**<br><br>Best Buy: **Weber Original Kettle Charcoal Grill, 22-Inch** |

| GRILLING EQUIPMENT | ITEM | WHAT TO LOOK FOR | TEST KITCHEN FAVORITES |
|---|---|---|---|
| | FLAT-TOP GRILL | • Aluminized steel cookbox<br>• Cooking surface at least 35 inches by 20 inches<br>• Two side tables<br>• Four large, sturdy wheels<br>• Large opening and grease tray for easy cleanup | **Weber Griddle 36"** |
| | SMOKER | • Large cooking area<br>• Water pan<br>• Multiple vents for precise temperature control<br>• Generously sized charcoal basket<br>• Easy to clean | **Weber Smokey Mountain Cooker Smoker 22"**<br><br>No-Frills Model: **18.5" Classic Pit Barrel Cooker** |
| | CHIMNEY STARTER | • 6-quart capacity<br>• Holes in the canister so that air can circulate around the coals<br>• Sturdy construction<br>• Heat-resistant handle<br>• Dual handle for easy control | **Weber Rapidfire Chimney Starter** |
| | GRILL TONGS | • 16 inches in length<br>• Scalloped, not sharp and serrated, edges<br>• Lightweight<br>• Moderate amount of springy tension<br>• Handy loop on end for storage | **OXO Good Grips Grilling Tongs** |
| | GRILL BRUSH | • Short handle for easy leverage<br>• Short metal bristles<br>• Triangular brush head | **Weber 12" Three-Sided Grill Brush** |
| | GRILL GRATE CLEANING BLOCK | • Use for once-per-season grill reconditioning<br>• Pumice scrubber to strip all accumulated gunk even from cold grates | **GrillStone Value Pack Cleaning Kit by Earthstone International** |
| | BARBECUE BASTING BRUSH | • Silicone bristles<br>• Handle 8 to 13 inches in length<br>• Heat-resistant | **OXO Good Grips Grilling Basting Brush** |
| | SKEWERS | • Flat and metal<br>• ³⁄₁₆ inch thick | **Norpro 12-Inch Stainless Steel Skewers** |
| | GRILL GLOVES | • Excellent heat protection<br>• Gloves, rather than mitts, for dexterity<br>• Long sleeves to protect forearms | Best Overall: **WZQH Leather Forge Welding Gloves**<br><br>Best for Easy Cleanup: **Kitchen Perfection Silicone Smoker Oven Gloves** |

| GRILLING EQUIPMENT | ITEM | WHAT TO LOOK FOR | TEST KITCHEN FAVORITES |
|---|---|---|---|
| | GRILL LIGHTER | • Flexible neck<br>• Refillable chamber with large, easy-to-read fuel window<br>• Comfortable grip | **Zippo Flexible Neck Utility Lighter** |
| | OUTDOOR GRILL PAN | • Narrow slits and raised sides, so food can't fall through or off<br>• Sturdy construction with handles | **Weber Professional-Grade Grill Pan** |
| | GRILL GRATE SET | • Stainless-steel grate for 22½-inch charcoal grill<br>• Removable inner circle of grate can be replaced with crosshatched sear grate (shown), griddle, or wok (sold separately) | **Weber 7420 Gourmet BBQ System Sear Grate Set** |
| | PIZZA GRILLING KIT | • Metal collar that elevates the grill's lid<br>• Brings grill heat to over 900 degrees<br>• Cutout that lets you insert pizzas without losing heat | **KettlePizza Pro 22 Kit** |
| | STOVETOP SMOKER | • Sliding snug, flat metal lid<br>• Large drip tray<br>• Rack with parallel wires<br>• Stay-cool handle | **Camerons Stovetop Smoker** |
| | SMOKER BOX | • Cast iron for slow heating and steady smoke<br>• Easy to fill, empty, and clean | **GrillPro Cast Iron Smoker Box Made by Onward Manufacturing Company** |
| | VERTICAL ROASTER | • Helps poultry cook evenly<br>• 8-inch shaft keeps chicken above fat and drippings in pan<br>• Attached basin catches drippings for pan sauce<br>• Sturdy construction | **Vertical Roaster with Infuser by Norpro**<br><br>Best Buy: **Elizabeth Karmel's Grill Friends Porcelain Chicken Sitter** |
| | CHARCOAL STARTER | • Relatively water-resistant<br>• Ignite easily without impacting food flavor | **Weber Lighter Cubes** |
| | PORTABLE OUTDOOR PIZZA OVEN | • Compact design<br>• Propane powered with easy-to-ignite flame<br>• Easy to adjust heat | Co-Winner: **Ooni Koda 12 Gas-Powered Pizza Oven**<br><br>Co-Winner: **Ooni Koda 16 Gas-Powered Pizza Oven** |

| SPECIALTY PIECES | ITEM | WHAT TO LOOK FOR | TEST KITCHEN FAVORITES |
|---|---|---|---|
| | APPLE CORER/ SLICER/ PEELERS | • Peels, cores, slices<br>• Accommodates oddly shaped fruit<br>• Speedy and efficient<br>• Suction base, with a lever to apply it, was easy to use and held very firmly<br>• Adjustable blades<br>• Can also process potatoes | Best Crank-Style: **VKP Brands Johnny Apple Peeler, Suction Base, Stainless Steel Blades, Red** |
| | | • Cores and slices<br>• Plastic base that aids in finalizing cuts<br>• Easy to clean by hand or in the dishwasher | Best Push-Style: **Norpro Grip EZ Fruit Wedger, 16 Slices with Base** |
| | TOMATO CORER | • Good head-handle design<br>• Lightweight<br>• Sharp-edged scoop | **Norpro Tomato Core It** |
| | GRAPEFRUIT KNIFE | • Sturdy, lightweight handle<br>• Gently angled blade for precise cutting | **Messermeister Pro-Touch 4-Inch Grapefruit Knife** |
| | STRAWBERRY HULLER | • Huller with four spring-loaded metal prongs that slice out leaves, stem, and core<br>• Easy and safe to use<br>• Compact for easy storage | **StemGem Strawberry Hull Remover by Chef'n** |
| | PINEAPPLE SLICER | • Corkscrew design<br>• Easy to use<br>• Narrow slicing base for easy storage | **OXO Good Grips Stainless Steel Ratcheting Pineapple Slicer** |
| | CORN STRIPPER | • Prongs to center the corn<br>• Good at containing mess | **RSVP International Deluxe Corn Stripper** |
| | MANUAL NUT CHOPPER | • Sharp, sturdy stainless-steel chopping tines<br>• Dishwasher-safe | **Prepworks from Progressive Nut Chopper with Non-Skid Base** |
| | NUTCRACKER | • Lever-style model<br>• Solidly built<br>• Extra-long handle for good leverage and easy cracking | **Get Crackin' Heavy Duty Steel Lever Nutcracker** |

| SPECIALTY PIECES | ITEM | WHAT TO LOOK FOR | TEST KITCHEN FAVORITES |
|---|---|---|---|
| | SPIRAL SLICER (SPIRALIZER) | • Includes three blades that are stored in the base<br>• Stabilizing suction cups make for safer slicing<br>• Pronged to hold fruit and vegetables against blade for optimal spiralizing<br>• Large rectangular chamber accommodates vegetables up to 10 inches long or 7 inches thick | **OXO Good Grips 3-Blade Tabletop Spiralizer** |
| | TORTILLA PRESS | • Hefty weight<br>• Long handle<br>• Wide plates | **Doña Rosa x Masienda Tortilla Press**<br><br>Best Buy: **Victoria 8" Tortilla Press** |
| | STOVETOP GRIDDLE | • Heats quickly and evenly<br>• Tall sides to contain grease<br>• Upright, sturdy handles<br>• Easy-to-grab handles<br>• Compatible with gas, electric, and induction stoves | **Cuisinart Chef's Classic Nonstick Double Burner Griddle** |
| | HANDHELD MILK FROTHER | • Easy to use and clean<br>• Immersion blender-style wand<br>• Battery operated | **Zulay Kitchen Milk Boss Electric Milk Frother** |
| | OYSTER KNIFE | • Sturdy, flat blade with slightly curved tip for easy penetration<br>• Slim, nonstick handle for secure, comfortable grip | **R. Murphy Knives New Haven Shucker**<br><br>Best Buy: **OXO Good Grips Oyster Knife** |
| | SEAFOOD SCISSORS | • Thin, curved blades to fit into shells<br>• Strong and sturdy | **RSVP International Endurance Seafood Scissors** |
| | SILICONE MICROWAVE LID | • Thin, silicone round to cover splatter-prone food during microwave heating<br>• Easy to clean<br>• Doubles as jar opener | **Piggy Steamer** |
| | RECIPE HOLDER | • Holds pages at perfect angle for viewing<br>• Compact yet sturdy<br>• Strong magnet | **Recipe Rock by Architec** |
| | PORTABLE TABLET STAND | • Small footprint<br>• Neat, foldable design<br>• Well-placed grips | **Arkon Portable Fold-Up Stand for Tablets** |

| SPECIALTY PIECES | ITEM | WHAT TO LOOK FOR | TEST KITCHEN FAVORITES |
|---|---|---|---|
| | SQUEEZE BOTTLE | • Wide mouth of about 2 inches<br>• Flexible plastic body of low-density polyethylene (LDPE)<br>• One-piece bottle top<br>• Dishwasher-safe | **Tablecraft Widemouth Squeeze Bottle** |
| | SALAD DRESSING SHAKER | • Short, wide canister<br>• Screw top with tight seal<br>• Pour spout with even flow<br>• Dishwasher-safe | **OXO Good Grips Salad Dressing Shaker** |
| | MICROWAVE RICE COOKER | • Sturdy and compact<br>• 6-cup capacity<br>• Easy to clean | **Progressive International Microwave Rice Cooker Set** |
| | MICROWAVE CHIP MAKER | • Perforated 11-inch silicone disk that holds 15 to 20 chips<br>• Slicer that produces wafer-thin chips | **Topchips Chips Maker** |
| | PIPING SET | • Large bag (about 18 inches in length) for easier gripping and twisting<br>• Contains all of the essentials: twelve 16-inch pastry bags; four plastic couplers; and the following Wilton tips: #4 round, #12 round, #70 leaf, #103 petal, #2D large closed star, #1M open star | **Test Kitchen Self-Assembled à la Carte Decorating Set** |
| | CHEESE WIRE | • Comfortable plastic handles<br>• Narrow wire | **Fante's Handled Cheese Wire** |
| | PIZZA CUTTER | • Comfortable, soft-grip handle<br>• Thumb guard to protect fingers | **Mercer Culinary Millennia Pizza Cutter 4"** |
| | BANNETON | • Rattan basket<br>• Cotton liner<br>• Sturdy, lightweight, and slightly porous | **Breadtopia Round Bread Proofing Basket and Round Proofing Basket Liner** |
| | COUCHE | • Maintains baguettes' shape and wicks moisture effectively<br>• Fabric easily releases dough | **San Francisco Baking Institute 18" Linen Canvas (Couche)** |

| SPECIALTY PIECES | ITEM | WHAT TO LOOK FOR | TEST KITCHEN FAVORITES |
| --- | --- | --- | --- |
| | LAME | • Scores baguettes cleanly and evenly<br>• Easy to change blades | **Baker of Seville Artisan Bread Lame** |
| | POTATO RICER | • Hopper with many holes, so more food can travel through<br>• Comfortable handles<br>• Easy to assemble and clean | **Chef'n FreshForce Potato Ricer Plus**<br><br>Best Buy: **RSVP International Potato Ricer** |
| | PANCAKE BATTER DISPENSER | • Tall plastic cylinder<br>• Easy to use<br>• Heat-resistant silicone tip | **Tovolo Pancake Pen** |
| | SYRUP/HONEY DISPENSER | • Snug-closing spout cover that allows control of flow and precise pouring<br>• Easy to fill and clean<br>• Dishwasher-safe | **American Metalcraft Beehive Syrup Dispenser, 6 oz.** |
| | ICE POP MOLD | • Easy to fill, transport, and store<br>• Easy to remove and clean molds<br>• Long, grippy, reusable sticks | **Zoku Classic Pop Molds** |
| | CUPCAKE AND CAKE CARRIER | • Fits both round and square cakes and cupcakes<br>• Snap locks<br>• Nonskid base<br>• Collapses for easy storage | **Progressive Collapsible Cupcake and Cake Carrier** |
| | PIE CARRIER | • Collapsible plastic tote expands to accommodate larger pies<br>• Large, nonstick base | **Prepworks Collapsible Party Carrier** |
| | REVOLVING CAKE STAND | • Tall stand with excellent visibility and comfort<br>• Easy to carry<br>• Rotates quickly and smoothly | **Winco Revolving Cake Decorating Stand** |

| SPECIALTY PIECES | ITEM | WHAT TO LOOK FOR | TEST KITCHEN FAVORITES |
|---|---|---|---|
| | CREAM WHIPPER | • Rubber grip<br>• Responsive lever for effortless control | **ISI Gourmet Whip** |
| | BLADE GRINDER | • Relatively even grinding<br>• Wide, clear lid to view the grinding process<br>• Roomy grinding chamber | **Krups Coffee and Spice Grinder** |
| | BURR GRINDER | • Simple design<br>• Clear and intuitive controls<br>• No-fuss and even grinding<br>• Easy to clean grounds container | **Baratza Encore** |
| | MOKA POT | • Classic design that uses steam pressure to force hot water from bottom chamber up through coffee grounds<br>• Stovetop, not electric, model<br>• Easy to use | **Bialetti Moka Express, 3 cups** |
| | FRENCH PRESS | • Fine-mesh filter to eliminate sediment<br>• Insulated pot to keep coffee hot<br>• Smooth, simple, dishwasher-safe parts for easy cleanup | **Bodum Columbia French Press Coffee Maker, 8 Cup**<br><br>Best Buy: **Bodum Chambord French Press, 8 Cup** |
| | COLD-BREW COFFEE MAKER | • Easy to use<br>• Produces smooth, rich-tasting cold-brew concentrate<br>• Enough concentrate to make sixty-four 4-ounce cups of coffee | **Toddy Cold Brew System** |
| | INNOVATIVE TEAPOT | • Contained, ultrafine-mesh strainer keeps tea leaf dregs separate<br>• One-piece design for easy cleaning | **ingenuiTEA by Adagio Teas** |

| SPECIALTY PIECES | ITEM | WHAT TO LOOK FOR | TEST KITCHEN FAVORITES |
|---|---|---|---|
| | TEA MACHINE | • Perforated tea basket for thorough infusion<br>• Programmable temperature and steep times<br>• Fully automated brewing<br>• Dishwasher-safe accessories | **Breville Tea Maker** |
| | TWIST CORKSCREW | • 4.75-inch worm accommodates corks of any length<br>• Nonstick coating ensures smooth, neat piercing<br>• Slim and lightweight, making it easy to handle and store | **Le Creuset Table Model Corkpull** |
| | ELECTRIC WINE OPENER | • Sturdy, quiet corkscrew<br>• Broad base that rests firmly on bottle | **Secura Electric Wine Opener** |
| | WINE AERATOR | • Long, tubelike design that exposes wine to air as it is being poured<br>• Neat, hands-free aerating | **Nuance Wine Finer** |
| | WINE SAVER | • Minimizes amount of contact wine has with air<br>• Easy manual pump<br>• Keeps wine drinkable for at least two weeks | **Vacu Vin Original Wine Saver** |
| | CHAMPAGNE SAVER | • Inexpensive<br>• Attaches with an easy one-handed motion<br>• Fits easily in the fridge | **Cilio Champagne Bottle Sealer** |
| | COCKTAIL SHAKER | • Leakproof and easy to use<br>• Domed top doubles as a 1- and 2-ounce jigger<br>• Comfortable grip<br>• Wide mouth for effortless filling, muddling, and cleaning<br>• Includes reamer attachment | Easiest to Use: **Tovolo Stainless Steel 4-in-1 Cocktail Shaker**<br><br>Best Boston Shaker: **Houdini by Rabbit 24oz Stainless Steel & Glass Boston Cocktail Shaker** |
| | HAWTHORNE STRAINER | • Well-balanced with short, lightweight handle, 3.5 inches or shorter<br>• Long wings or prongs and finger tab on head<br>• Fine strainer | **Cocktail Kingdom Koriko Hawthorne Strainer** |
| | JIGGER | • Single mouth at least 2 inches wide<br>• Tiny spout for a clean pour<br>• Clearly labeled volume lines and numbers<br>• Measurement lines on the interior | **OXO Good Grips Angled Measuring Cup, Clear** |

| SPECIALTY PIECES | ITEM | WHAT TO LOOK FOR | TEST KITCHEN FAVORITES |
|---|---|---|---|
| | MUDDLER | • Easy-to-grip material such as unvarnished wood or bamboo<br>• Length of at least 9.5 inches<br>• Discrete handle<br>• Head at least 1.5 inches in diameter | **Fletcher's Mill Maple Muddler** |
| | LARGE COOLER | • Superior cooling capability<br>• Easy-to-close latches<br>• Durable rope handles | **Yeti Tundra 50**<br><br>Best Buy: **Coleman 50 QT Xtreme Wheeled Cooler** |
| | INSULATED FOOD CARRIER | • Designed to carry two 13 by 9-inch baking dishes<br>• Sturdy, expandable frame<br>• Insulation keeps food above 140 degrees for more than 3 hours | **Rachael Ray Expandable Lasagna Lugger** |
| | WINE CARRIER | • Reusable and washable<br>• Folds up for easy transport<br>• Fits taller and wider bottles | **VinniBag** |
| | INSULATED SHOPPING TOTE | • Shoulder straps for easy toting<br>• Insulation keeps groceries at a food-safe temperature for 2 hours in a 90-degree room | **Rachael Ray ChillOut Thermal Tote** |
| | SODA MAKER | • Can add carbonation along a spectrum from mildly fizzy to very bubbly<br>• Machine is sturdy and fairly compact<br>• Water bottles are a convenient size and dishwasher-safe<br>• Uses SodaStream "quick-connect" $CO_2$ canisters | **SodaStream Terra** |
| | COUNTERTOP ICE MAKER | • Deposits first ice batch in 8 minutes<br>• Convenient handle, lightweight build<br>• Different ice size options<br>• Simple, clear controls<br>• Self-cleaning cycle | Best for Most People: **IGLOO Premium Self-Cleaning Countertop Ice Maker**<br><br>Best Nugget Ice Maker: **GE Profile Opal 2.0 Nugget Ice Maker** |
| | SOUS VIDE MACHINE | • Slim, lightweight machine<br>• Heats water quickly and accurately<br>• Magnetic bottom allows it to stand stably in center of metal pots<br>• Small enough to store in a drawer<br>• Extremely user-friendly app that's compatible with iOS and Android | **Breville Joule Turbo Sous Vide**<br><br>Best Buy: **Yedi Houseware Infinity Sous Vide** |

| SPECIALTY PIECES | ITEM | WHAT TO LOOK FOR | TEST KITCHEN FAVORITES |
|---|---|---|---|
| | ROBOT VACUUM | • Easy to use and program<br>• Periodically docks to recharge and to empty bin<br>• Efficient, grid-pattern cleaning program<br>• Accurately maps multiple rooms | **iRobot Roomba j7+ Robot Vacuum**<br><br>Best Buy: **Shark ION Robot Vacuum** |
| | NEW-GENERATION KITCHEN TRASH CAN | • Sleek, spacious frame<br>• Foot pedal flips lid open completely and allows it to close slowly when released<br>• Fingerprint-proof stainless-steel exterior<br>• Easy bag changes | **Simplehuman 50L Rectangular Step Can**<br><br>Best Buy: **Sterilite Lift-Top Wastebasket** |
| | COMPOST BIN, COUNTERTOP | • Plastic bin with inside bags to collect food scraps<br>• Prevents odors from escaping and allows oxygen to enter<br>• Stay-open lid with wide opening<br>• 1.75-gallon capacity | **OXO Good Grips Easy-Clean Compost Bin-1.75 Gal**<br><br>Best for Larger Households: **Exaco Eco 2000 Compost Pail** |

| KITCHEN SUPPLIES | ITEM | WHAT TO LOOK FOR | TEST KITCHEN FAVORITES |
|---|---|---|---|
| | FIRE EXTINGUISHER | • Fast, effective, and easy to figure out<br>• Manageable size<br>• Powerful spray that quickly puts out fires | **Kidde ABC Multipurpose Home Fire Extinguisher** |
| | PARCHMENT PAPER | • Stores flat<br>• Fits perfectly into a standard rimmed baking sheet<br>• Precut sheets for superior convenience | **King Arthur Baking Company Parchment Paper 100 Half-Sheets** |
| | PLASTIC WRAP | • Clings to vessels of different materials<br>• Dispenses easily<br>• Resilient and strong over long periods of time | **Stretch-Tite Premium Plastic Food Wrap** |
| | PLASTIC WRAP DISPENSER | • Concealed metal teeth for easy, clean cuts<br>• Slightly elevated for easier wrapping | **Stretch-Tite Wrap'n Snap 7500 Dispenser** |
| | VACUUM SEALER (COUNTERTOP) | • Compact, sturdy frame<br>• Clearly labeled buttons and screen<br>• Pulse button<br>• Automatic mode and a manual option<br>• Easily closed lid | **Nesco Deluxe Vacuum Sealer** |

| KITCHEN SUPPLIES | ITEM | WHAT TO LOOK FOR | TEST KITCHEN FAVORITES |
|---|---|---|---|
| | FOOD STORAGE BAGS | • Durable construction, strong and leakproof<br>• Easy to seal securely<br>• Spacious with a wide opening<br>• 1 gallon size | Co-Winner, Single Use: **Ziploc Freezer Bags Gallon**<br><br>Co-Winner, Single Use: **LK 10" x 12" Gallon Heavy Weight Seal Top Freezer Bags (4 mil)** |
| | PARCHMENT COOKING BAGS | • Easy to fill and fold | **PaperChef Culinary Parchment Cooking Bags** |
| | CHEESE STORAGE WRAP | • Two-ply wax-coated paper<br>• Easy to fill and fold | **Formaticum Cheese Bags and Cheese Paper** |
| | SPICE STORAGE | • Expands or collapses to fit wide or narrow cabinets<br>• Impressive capacity<br>• Sturdy | Best Overall Cabinet Option: **Spicy Shelf Deluxe** |
| | | • Expandable design<br>• Impressively large capacity<br>• Durable and stable | Best for Drawers: **Lynk Professional 4 Tier Steel Spice Drawer Organizer** |
| | FOOD STORAGE CONTAINERS<br>Glass | • Large capacity of 8 cups<br>• Airtight, leakproof seal<br>• Plastic lid that attaches easily | **OXO Good Grips 8 Cup Smart Seal Rectangle Container** |
| | Plastic | • Lightweight material that remains stain-free, like glass<br>• Lid with vents for convenient microwaving<br>• Extended rims that stay cool for easy handling<br>• BPA-free | **Rubbermaid Brilliance, Large, 9.6 Cup** |
| | For dry foods | • Sturdy, spacious, and simple to use and clean<br>• Available in a range of sizes<br>• Note: lid sold separately | **Cambro 6-Quart Square Storage Container** |
| | BUTTER STORAGE CONTAINERS | • Made from BPA-free plastic<br>• Flaps that create a tight seal<br>• Lid includes measurement markings and doubles as a flat surface for cutting butter | Best Classic Container: **LocknLock Rectangular Food Container with Tray** |
| | | • Made from bone china<br>• Large, easy-to-grasp lid knob<br>• Spacious container | Best Butter Bell: **Original Butter Bell Crock** |

| KITCHEN SUPPLIES | ITEM | WHAT TO LOOK FOR | TEST KITCHEN FAVORITES |
|---|---|---|---|
| | KITCHEN SPONGE | • Heavily textured scrubbing surface<br>• Midsize, roughly 4.25 by 2.5 inches and 1 inch thick<br>• Dishwasher-safe | **O-Cedar Scrunge Multi-Use Scrubber Sponge** |
| | SPONGE HOLDER | • Spacious and solidly constructed<br>• Attaches firmly to the sink<br>• Airiness helps sponges stay dry between uses | **SunnyPoint NeverRust Kitchen Sink Suction Holder** |
| | LIQUID DISH SOAP | • High concentration of surfactants to wash away oil<br>• Clean scent | **Mrs. Meyer's Clean Day Liquid Dish Soap, Lavender** |
| | ALL-PURPOSE CLEANER | • Natural, green product<br>• Cuts through grease and food splatters quickly and efficiently<br>• Pleasant, not overpowering, scent | **Method All-Purpose Natural Surface Cleaner (French Lavender)** |
| | AUTOMATIC HAND SOAP DISPENSER | • Dispenses soap quickly<br>• Volume dial allows you to adjust amount dispensed<br>• Grippy silicone base<br>• Large soap chamber | **Secura 17oz/500ml Premium Touchless Battery Operated Electric Automatic Soap Dispenser** |
| | CHAIN MAIL POT SCRUBBER | • 5-inch square of chain mail made of 316-grade stainless steel<br>• Ideal for cleaning traditional cast-iron cookware | **Knapp Made Small Ring CM Scrubber** |
| | DISH TOWELS | • Thin cotton for absorbency and flexibility<br>• Dries glassware without streaks<br>• Washes clean with little shrinking | Co-Winner, Cotton: **Williams Sonoma Classic Stripe Towels, Set of 4**<br><br>Co-Winner Cotton: **Now Designs Ripple Kitchen Towel, Set of 2** |
| | PAPER TOWEL HOLDER | • Sturdy, secure, and easy to carry<br>• Angled arm uses spring-loaded tension and tilts to accommodate rolls of all sizes | **Simplehuman Tension Arm Paper Towel Holder**<br><br>Best Buy: **OXO SimplyTear Paper Towel Holder** |

| KITCHEN SUPPLIES | ITEM | WHAT TO LOOK FOR | TEST KITCHEN FAVORITES |
|---|---|---|---|
| | APRON | • Adjustable neck strap and long strings<br>• Full coverage; chest area reinforced with extra layer of fabric<br>• Stains wash out completely | **Bragard Travail Bib Apron** |
| | LAUNDRY STAIN REMOVER | • Clear instructions<br>• Contains enzymes and surfactants to eliminate old and new stains from fabric<br>• Stained fabrics emerged bright as new | **OxiClean Versatile Stain Remover** |
| | UNDER-APPLIANCE DUSTER | • Long, thin duster easily and efficiently picks up dust and flour<br>• Fits under most standard home appliances and long enough to reach into far corners<br>• Microfiber head can be washed in the washing machine | **OXO Good Grips Under Appliance Duster** |
| | MOPS | • Easy to assemble<br>• Incredibly absorbent yet lightweight and nimble<br>• Impressive wringing mechanism<br>• Long handle<br>• Wide, flat head that's machine washable | Best Mop and Bucket Set: **O-Cedar EasyWring Spin Mop & Bucket System** |
| | | • Absorbent microfiber strings that cling to dirt<br>• Long handle<br>• Large head that's machine washable and reusable | Best Self-Wringing Mop: **Rubbermaid Microfiber Twist Mop** |
| | HANDHELD VACUUM CLEANER | • Pivoting nozzle<br>• Built-in brush and crevice tool<br>• Large collection bin | Best Overall: **Black + Decker 20V MAX Cordless Pivot Vac** |

| TABLEWARE | ITEM | WHAT TO LOOK FOR | TEST KITCHEN FAVORITES |
|---|---|---|---|
| | FLATWARE | • Brushed satin finish on gently curved handles<br>• Utensils are well-balanced and feel secure in hand | **Crate and Barrel Caesna Mirror 20-Piece Flatware Place Setting**<br><br>Best Buy: **Oneida Voss 45-Piece Flatware Set** |
| | WINE TUMBLER | • Insulated stainless steel<br>• Grippy surface<br>• Lid creates a tight seal<br>• Sipping port opens smoothly and evenly<br>• Keeps wine chilled for more than 4 hours | **Swig Stemless Wine Cup (12 oz)** |
| | REUSABLE PLASTIC CUPS | • Thin rim that's comfortable to drink from<br>• Textured exterior that ensures a secure grip<br>• Durable | **Amazing Abby 16-Ounce Ice Cube Plastic Tumblers** |

## SHOPPING FOR INGREDIENTS

Using the best ingredients is one way to guarantee success in the kitchen. But how do you know what to buy? Shelves are filled with a dizzying array of choices—and price does not equal quality. Over the years, the test kitchen's blind-tasting panels have evaluated thousands of ingredients, brand by brand, side by side, plain and in prepared applications, to determine which products you can trust and which products to avoid. In the chart that follows, we share the results, revealing our top-rated choices and the attributes that made them stand out among the competition. And because our test kitchen accepts no support from product manufacturers, you can trust our ratings. See AmericasTestKitchen.com for updates to these tastings.

| | ITEM | TEST KITCHEN FAVORITES | WHY WE LIKE IT |
|---|---|---|---|
| | ANCHOVIES | **Merro Flat Fillets in Pure Olive Oil** | • Firm, meaty texture<br>• Savory without being fishy<br>• Packed in olive oil<br>• Moderate saltiness |
| | BACON, SUPERMARKET | **Oscar Mayer Naturally Hardwood Smoked** | • Lightly smoky<br>• Good meaty flavor<br>• Texture has nice balance of crispness and chew |
| | BACON, ARTISANAL | **Vande Rose Applewood Smoked Artisan Dry Cured** | • Thick and chewy, substantial texture<br>• Perfectly balanced salt, sugar, and smoke flavors |
| | BACON, TURKEY | **Wellshire All Natural Uncured** | • Smoky, salty, sweet flavor of bacon<br>• Pleasantly chewy texture that crisped up more than its competitors |
| | BARBECUE SAUCE, HIGH-END | **Pork Barrel Original** | • Generous amounts of vinegar, salt, chili paste, and liquid smoke for bold, spicy flavor<br>• Tangy kick<br>• Good body |
| | BEANS, CANNED BAKED | **B&M Vegetarian** | • Firm and pleasant texture with some bite<br>• Sweetened with molasses for complexity and depth |
| | BEANS, CANNED BLACK | **Bush's Best** | • Clean, mild, and slightly earthy flavor<br>• Firm, almost al dente texture, not mushy or pasty<br>• Good amount of salt |
| | BEANS, CANNED CHICKPEAS | **Goya** | • Nutty flavor<br>• Plump, buttery<br>• Nicely seasoned with just enough salt |

| ITEM | TEST KITCHEN FAVORITES | WHY WE LIKE IT |
|---|---|---|
| BEANS, CANNED WHITE | **Goya Cannellini** | • Clean, earthy flavor<br>• Smooth, creamy interior with tender skins<br>• Not full of broken beans like some competitors |
| BEANS, DRIED WHITE | **Rancho Gordo Classic Cassoulet** | • Creamy and smooth texture<br>• Fresh taste<br>• Nutty and sweet flavors |
| BREAD, WHITE SANDWICH | **Arnold Country White** | • Subtle sweetness, not tasteless or sour<br>• Perfect structure, not too dry or too soft |
| BREAD, WHOLE-WHEAT SANDWICH | **Arnold Whole Grains 100%** | • Mild nuttiness with clean wheat flavor and a touch of sweetness<br>• Tender and chewy with crunchy flecks of bulgur on the crust |
| BREAD CRUMBS | **Progresso Plain** | • Good neutral flavor<br>• Crisp, with a substantial crunch<br>• Not too delicate, stale, sandy, or gritty |
| BROTH, BEEF | **Better Than Bouillon Roasted Beef Base** | • Contains good amount of salt and multiple powerful flavor enhancers<br>• Paste is economical, stores easily, and dissolves quickly in hot water |
| BROTH, BONE | **College Inn Chicken** | • Rich and well seasoned<br>• Meaty umami flavor with a hint of black pepper |
| BROTH, CHICKEN | **Swanson**<br>Best Buy: **Better Than Bouillon Chicken Base** | • Rich chicken flavor<br>• No flavor enhancers<br>• Good balance of salt<br>• Bouillon can last up to two years in the refrigerator |
| BROTH, VEGETABLE | **Orrington Farms Vegan Chicken Flavored Broth Base & Seasoning** | • Savory depth without off-tasting vegetable undertones<br>• Easy to store<br>• Yeast extract adds depth and richness |

| ITEM | TEST KITCHEN FAVORITES | WHY WE LIKE IT |
|---|---|---|
| BROTH, VEGETABLE, LOW-SODIUM | **Edward & Sons Low Sodium Not-Chick'n Natural Bouillon Cubes** | • Mild, chicken-y flavor<br>• Unctuous, meaty body<br>• Lends a clean, fresh flavor to risottos and vegetable soups |
| BROWNIE MIX<br>Supermarket | **Ghirardelli Chocolate Supreme** | • Rich, balanced chocolate flavor from both natural and Dutch-processed cocoa powders<br>• Moist, chewy, and fudgy with perfect texture |
| Mail-Order | **King Arthur All-American** | • Fudgy, moist, and tender<br>• Black cocoa powder provides intense, deep flavor |
| BURGER, VEGGIE<br>Best Bean-Based | **MorningStar Farms Spicy Black Bean** | • Mix of corn and beans has a little kick<br>• Pleasant crisp-chewy texture |
| Best Earthy-Savory | **Dr. Praeger's Mushroom Risotto** | • Soft interior<br>• Cooks up with an ultracrispy crust |
| Most Similar to Homemade | **The Actual Orange Burger** | • A big, substantial burger<br>• Chock-full of big pieces of vegetables and beans so looks homemade<br>• Crispy exterior with slightly coarse interior |
| BUTTER, ALMOND | **Barney Butter Smooth** | • Smooth, creamy texture<br>• Rich, sweet almond flavor<br>• Well seasoned with salt and sugar<br>• Made with almonds that are blanched and roasted |
| BUTTER, UNSALTED | **Challenge** | • Milky sweetness<br>• Fresh dairy flavor |
| CAKE MIX, BOXED CHOCOLATE<br>Best Supermarket | **Ghirardelli Chocolate Dark Chocolate Premium Cake Mix** | • Rich and moist tender crumb<br>• Tiny chocolate chips in the mix |
| Best Mail-Order | **King Arthur Deliciously Simple Chocolate Cake Mix** | • Deep dark and complex chocolate flavor<br>• Moist and tender |

| ITEM | TEST KITCHEN FAVORITES | WHY WE LIKE IT |
|---|---|---|
| CAPERS | **Reese Non Pareil** | • Salty and tangy flavor<br>• Crisp-crunchy texture |
| CHEESE, AMERICAN | **Boar's Head** | • Strong cheesy flavor, unlike some competitors<br>• Higher content of cheese culture contributes to better flavor |
| CHEESE, BRIE, SUPERMARKET | **Fromager d'Affinois** | • Buttery, earthy flavor with gooey, silky texture<br>• Soft, pillowy rind |
| CHEESE, BURRATA, SUPERMARKET | **Lioni** | • Distinct shell with balanced amount of filling<br>• Bright, fresh dairy flavor<br>• Nicely salted<br>• Thick, luscious cream |
| CHEESE, CHEDDAR, ARTISANAL | **Milton Creamery Prairie Breeze** | • Earthy complexity with nutty, buttery, and fruity flavors<br>• Dry and crumbly, not rubbery or overly moist<br>• Aged no more than 12 months to prevent overly sharp flavor |
| CHEESE, CHEDDAR, EXTRA-SHARP | **Cracker Barrel Extra Sharp White** | • Perfect amount of tang<br>• Moderate amounts of fat and moisture ensure toothsome, crumbly texture when eaten plain and melty, creamy texture when cooked |
| CHEESE, CHEDDAR, LOW-FAT | **Cracker Barrel Reduced Fat Sharp** | • Ample creaminess<br>• Strong cheesy flavor<br>• Good for cooking |
| CHEESE, CHEDDAR, SHARP | **Cabot Vermont** | • Nutty, smoky, caramel flavor<br>• Firm, crumbly texture, not moist, rubbery, or springy<br>• Aged a minimum of 9 months for complex flavor |
| CHEESE, COTTAGE | **Daisy 4% Milkfat** | • Large, uniform curds<br>• Thick, creamy consistency<br>• Nice tangy flavor |
| CHEESE, CREAM, ARTISANAL | **Zingerman's Creamery** | • Supercreamy and smooth texture<br>• Impressive depth of flavor |
| CHEESE, CREAM, SUPERMARKET | **Philadelphia Brick Original** | • Rich, tangy, and milky flavor<br>• Thick, creamy texture, not pasty, waxy, or chalky |

| ITEM | TEST KITCHEN FAVORITES | WHY WE LIKE IT |
| --- | --- | --- |
| CHEESE, FETA | **Real Greek Feta P.D.O.** | • Silky, luxurious texture<br>• Savory, complex flavor |
| CHEESE, FONTINA | | |
| For Cheese Plate | **Mitica Fontina Val d'Aosta** | • Earthy, nutty-sweet flavor<br>• Firm and dense but not crumbly<br>• Melts well |
| Supermarket | **Boar's Head** | • Buttery, tangy flavor<br>• Soft, creamy texture<br>• Melts well |
| CHEESE, GRUYÈRE | **1655 Le Gruyère AOP** | • Aged between 12 and 14 months<br>• Crystalline structure with dense, fudgy texture<br>• Deeply aged, caramelized, grassy flavors shine through even when cooked |
| CHEESE, MASCARPONE | **Polenghi** | • Made with all cream and no milk<br>• Soft and creamy but able to hold shape in desserts<br>• Perfect consistency |
| CHEESE, MOZZARELLA, BLOCK | **Polly-O Whole Milk** | • Creamy, rich flavor with hint of salt reminiscent of fresh mozzarella<br>• Elastic but not gooey when melted |
| CHEESE, MOZZARELLA, FRESH | **BelGioioso** | • Plush, pillowy, tender texture<br>• Well seasoned with a balanced tang<br>• Buttery, creamy, fresh flavor |
| CHEESE, PARMESAN, PRESHREDDED | **Sargento Artisan Blends** | • Mix of small and large shreds<br>• Blends 10- and 18-month-aged Parmesan<br>• Rich, nutty flavor |
| CHEESE, PARMESAN, SUPERMARKET | **Boar's Head Parmigiano-Reggiano** | • Rich and complex flavor balances tanginess and nuttiness<br>• Dry, crumbly texture yet creamy with a crystalline crunch, not rubbery or dense<br>• Aged for 24 months for better flavor and texture |
| CHEESE, PECORINO ROMANO | **Boar's Head** | • High sodium content provides supersavory flavor<br>• Pungent, sharp, and creamy in pasta |

| ITEM | TEST KITCHEN FAVORITES | WHY WE LIKE IT |
|---|---|---|
| CHEESE, PEPPER JACK | **Boar's Head Monterey Jack with Jalapeño** | • Buttery, tangy cheese<br>• Clean, balanced flavor with assertive spice |
| CHEESE, AMERICAN PROVOLONE | **Organic Valley—Slices** | • Balanced, mild flavor with subtle sharpness<br>• Hint of savory saltiness adds complexity and richness |
| CHEESE, RICOTTA, WHOLE-MILK | **BelGioioso** | • Rich, dense consistency<br>• Slight sweetness thanks to sweet whey and small amount of milk |
| CHEESE, SWISS<br>For Cheese Plate | **Edelweiss Creamery Emmentaler** | • Subtle flavor with grassy, nutty notes<br>• Firm yet gently giving texture, not rubbery<br>• Mildly pungent yet balanced |
| For Cheese Plate or Cooking | **Emmi Emmentaler Cheese AOC** | • Pleasantly pungent<br>• Creamy texture preferable for grilled cheese sandwiches |
| CHICKEN, BREASTS, BONELESS, SKINLESS | **Bell & Evans Air Chilled** | • Juicy and tender, with clean chicken flavor<br>• Not salted or brined<br>• Air-chilled<br>• Aged on bone for at least 12 hours after slaughter for significantly more tender meat |
| CHICKEN, WHOLE | **Mary's Free Range Air Chilled** (also sold as Pitman's) | • Great, savory chicken flavor<br>• Very tender<br>• Air-chilled for minimum water retention and cleaner flavor |
| CHICKEN NUGGETS, VEGAN | **Impossible Chicken Nuggets Made from Plants** | • Meat-like convincing texture and savory rich flavor<br>• Coating's light crunch |

| ITEM | TEST KITCHEN FAVORITES | WHY WE LIKE IT |
|---|---|---|
| CHILI POWDER | **Morton & Bassett** | • Blend of chile peppers with added seasonings, not assertively hot, overly smoky, or one-dimensional<br>• Balance of sweet and smoky flavors<br>• Potent but not overwhelming |
| CHOCOLATE, DARK | **Ghirardelli 60% Cacao Bittersweet Chocolate Premium Baking Bar** | • Creamy texture<br>• Complex flavor with notes of cherry and wine with slight smokiness<br>• Balance of sweetness and bitterness |
| CHOCOLATE, VERY DARK | **Alter Eco 90% Deepest Dark Super Blackout Organic Chocolate Bar** | • Good balance of bitter and sweet flavors with fruity undertones<br>• Supersmooth texture |
| CHOCOLATE, DARK CHIPS | **Ghirardelli 60% Premium Baking Chips** | • Rich chocolate flavor<br>• Higher cacao and fat percentages |
| CHOCOLATE, MILK | **Endangered Species Chocolate Smooth + Creamy** | • Rich, intense flavor with deep cocoa notes<br>• Balanced sweetness thanks to high cacao percentage<br>• Smooth and snappy texture |
| CHOCOLATE, MILK CHIPS | **Hershey's Kitchens** | • Bold chocolate flavor outshines too-sweet, weak chocolate flavor of other chips<br>• Deep cocoa flavor and creamy texture |
| CHOCOLATE, SINGLE-ORIGIN<br>Ultrachocolaty Bars | **Francois Pralus Ghana 75%** | • Ultrafudgy and cocoa-forward bar<br>• Very creamy with notes of coffee and hazelnut |
| Herbaceous Bars | **9th & Larkin Matasawalevu, Fiji, 74% Cacao** | • Mellow with a delicate snap and grassy, floral notes<br>• Dried-fruit tang |
| Fruity Bars | **Dandelion Anamalai 70 Percent India** | • Notes of guava, berries, and raisins<br>• Nice snap and creamy texture |

| ITEM | TEST KITCHEN FAVORITES | WHY WE LIKE IT |
|---|---|---|
| CHOCOLATE, UNSWEETENED | **Baker's Unsweetened Baking Chocolate Bar 100% Cacao** | • Blend of cacao beans for familiar, classic flavor<br>• Makes a rich and caramelly hot fudge sauce, and brownies with deep cocoa flavor |
| CHOCOLATE, WHITE CHIPS | **Ghirardelli Classic White Baking Chips** | • Milky, sweet, and mild flavor<br>• Creamy texture |
| CINNAMON | **Morton & Bassett** | • Perfect balance of sweet and spicy<br>• Desirable, mellow flavor when baked into cinnamon rolls and on pita chips |
| COCKTAILS, NONALCOHOLIC READY-TO-DRINK | Co-winner: **St. Agrestis Non-Alcoholic Phony Negroni** | • Refreshing light carbonation and bitterness<br>• Right balance of sweetness and slight citrusy finish |
| | Co-winner: **Curious Elixirs No. 2** | • Complex balance of sweet and spice<br>• Thirst-quenching, with a lingering ginger aftertaste |
| COCOA POWDER | **Droste** | • Dark color with earthy flavor<br>• High fat content and less starch<br>• Ensures decadent chocolate desserts with perfectly moist textures and complex, sophisticated flavors |
| COCONUT MILK | **Aroy-D** | • Velvety, luxurious texture that's not too thick<br>• Tastes strongly of coconut but doesn't overwhelm other ingredients |
| COFFEE, COLD-BREW<br>Plain | **La Colombe—Brazilian** | • Smooth and not too acidic<br>• Subtle nutty and chocolaty flavor |
| With Milk | **Starbucks Bottled** | • Bold, with enough intensity to hold up to milk<br>• Notes of vanilla, chocolate, and smoke |
| Concentrate | **Chameleon Organic—Concentrate, Black** | • Fruity and bright<br>• Full-flavored drink that can be enjoyed with or without milk |
| COFFEE, DECAF | **Maxwell House Decaf Original Roast** | • Smooth, mellow flavor without being acidic or harsh<br>• Complex, with a slightly nutty aftertaste<br>• Made with only flavorful Arabica beans |

| ITEM | TEST KITCHEN FAVORITES | WHY WE LIKE IT |
|---|---|---|
| COFFEE, MEDIUM ROAST | **Peet's Coffee Café Domingo** | • Extremely smooth but bold tasting with a strong finish<br>• Rich chocolate and toast flavors<br>• Few defective beans, low acidity, and optimal moisture |
| CORNMEAL | **Anson Mills Fine Yellow** | • Fine grind<br>• Ideal texture<br>• More muted corn flavor |
| COUSCOUS, PEARL | **Roland Israeli** | • Large pearls with a firm, springy texture<br>• Sweet, toasty flavor<br>• Sold in an airtight jar |
| CRABMEAT | **Phillips Premium Crab Jumbo** | • Moist, plump, meaty chunks<br>• Taste comparable to freshly picked crabmeat |
| CRANBERRY SAUCE<br>Best Jellied Sauce | **Ocean Spray Jellied Cranberry Sauce** | • Tangy, tart flavor is the perfect foil for salty, savory, fatty holiday foods<br>• Smooth, melt-in-your-mouth texture |
| Best Whole-Berry Sauce | **New England Cranberry Colonial Cranberry Sauce** | |
| CURRY POWDER | **Penzeys Sweet** | • Balanced, neither too sweet nor too hot<br>• Complex and vivid earthy flavor, not thin, bland, or one-dimensional<br><br>NOTE: Available through amazon.com or mail order (800-741-7787, penzeys.com) |
| DINNER ROLLS, FROZEN | **Pepperidge Farm Stone Baked Artisan French** | • Pleasantly wheaty and yeasty flavor<br>• Chewy, tender insides and crispy crust<br>• Tastes closest to fresh homemade |
| FISH STICKS | Co-winner: **Gorton's Crunchy Breaded** | • Made with whole pollock fillets<br>• Buttery breading with good crunch |
| | Co-winner: **Gorton's Original Crunchy Breaded** | • Made with minced pollock<br>• Mild, sweet fish flavor<br>• Crispy exterior |

| ITEM | TEST KITCHEN FAVORITES | WHY WE LIKE IT |
|---|---|---|
| FIVE-SPICE POWDER | **Frontier Natural Products Co-op** | • Woodsy, sweet, and aromatic taste<br>• Harmonious flavor with a nice spice kick |
| FLOUR, WHOLE-WHEAT | **King Arthur Premium** | • Finely ground for hearty but not overly coarse texture in bread and pancakes<br>• Sweet, nutty flavor |
| GIARDINIERA | **Pastene** | • Sharp, vinegary tang<br>• Crunchy mix of vegetables<br>• Mellow heat that's potent but not overpowering |
| GREEN CHILES, CANNED | **Goya Diced Fire Roasted** | • Full-flavored peppery taste with a hint of sweetness<br>• Soft texture yet maintain their structure |
| HAM, BLACK FOREST DELI | **Dietz & Watson—Smoked Ham with Natural Juices** | • Good texture<br>• Nice ham flavor |
| HAM, SPIRAL-SLICED | **Burgers' Smokehouse—City Ham** | • Smoky flavor with assertive pork taste<br>• Moist and tender |
| HOISIN SAUCE | Co-winner: **Kikkoman**<br><br>Co-winner: **Guangwei Yuan**<br><br>Mail-order favorite: **Koon Chun** | • Balances sweet, salty, pungent, and spicy flavors<br>• Initial burn mellows into harmonious and aromatic blend without bitterness |
| HORSERADISH<br>Refrigerated | Co-winner: **Woeber's Pure** | • Pleasant, slow burn<br>• Looks almost homemade, with distinct shreds of grated horseradish mixed with vinegar |
| Shelf-Stable | Co-winner: **Inglehoffer Cream Style** (also sold as Beaver Brand Grandma Rose's Hot Cream) | • Lots of heat up front with a mustardy burn |
| HOT DOGS, ALL-BEEF | **Nathan's Famous Skinless Beef Franks** | • Meaty, robust, and hearty flavor, not sweet, sour, or too salty<br>• Juicy but not greasy<br>• Firm, craggy texture, not rubbery, mushy, or chewy |

| ITEM | TEST KITCHEN FAVORITES | WHY WE LIKE IT |
|---|---|---|
| HOT FUDGE SAUCE | **Hershey's** | • True fudge flavor, not weak or overly sweet<br>• Thick, smooth, and buttery texture |
| HUMMUS, SUPERMARKET | **Joseph's All Natural Original** | • Pleasantly nutty flavor<br>• Thick, creamy texture<br>• Tahini and lemon flavor with no bitterness |
| ICE CREAM BARS | **Dove Vanilla Ice Cream with Milk Chocolate** | • Rich, prominent chocolate flavor<br>• Thick, crunchy chocolate coating<br>• Dense, creamy ice cream with pure vanilla flavor<br>• Milk chocolate, not coconut oil, listed first in coating ingredients |
| ICE CREAM, CHOCOLATE | **Turkey Hill Premium Dutch** | • Smooth, creamy texture<br>• Well-rounded chocolate flavor<br>• Clean aftertaste with no bitterness |
| ICE CREAM, VEGAN CHOCOLATE | Co-winner: **Jeni's Dairy-Free Texas Sheet Cake Non-Dairy Frozen Dessert**<br><br>Co-winner: **Häagen-Dazs Non-Dairy Chocolate Salted Fudge Truffle Frozen Dessert** | • Coconut cream-based<br>• Lush and very smooth, with a creamy texture that is similar to a traditional dairy ice cream |
| ICE CREAM, VANILLA | **Turkey Hill Original Premium** | • Silky and creamy texture<br>• Rich vanilla flavor<br>• Spoonable and airy but still velvety from the use of viscous corn syrup |
| ICED TEA, BLACK<br>Loose Leaf | **Tazo** | • Distinctive flavor with herbal notes<br>• Balanced level of strength and astringency |
| Bottled, with Lemon | **Lipton PureLeaf** | • Bright, balanced, and natural tea and lemon flavors<br>• Uses concentrated tea leaves to extract flavor |
| KETCHUP | **Heinz Organic** | • Clean, pure sweetness from sugar, not high-fructose corn syrup<br>• Bold, harmonious punch of saltiness, sweetness, tang, and tomato flavor |

| ITEM | TEST KITCHEN FAVORITES | WHY WE LIKE IT |
|---|---|---|
| LEMONADE<br>Best Tart<br><br><br>Best Sweet | <br>**Natalie's Natural**<br><br><br>**Tropicana Lively** | • Natural-tasting lemon flavor without artificial flavors or off notes<br>• Perfect balance of tartness and sweetness, unlike many overly sweet competitors<br>• Contains 20% lemon juice |
| LENTILS | **Eden Organic Green** | • Stayed intact when cooked and hit the perfect balance between firm and tender<br>• Mellow, mildly earthy flavor |
| MACARONI AND CHEESE | **Kraft Velveeta Original Shells & Cheese** | • Strong and rich cheese flavor<br>• Nice, thick liquid, not powdered, sauce<br>• Dry noodles, rather than frozen, for substantial texture and bite |
| MAYONNAISE | **Blue Plate** | • Great balance of taste and texture<br>• Richer, deeper flavor from using egg yolks alone (no egg whites)<br>• Short ingredient list that's close to homemade |
| MAYONNAISE, LOW-FAT | **Hellmann's Light** | • Bright, balanced flavor close to full-fat counterpart, not overly sweet like other light mayos<br>• Not as creamy as full-fat but passable texture<br><br>NOTE: Hellmann's is known as Best Foods west of the Rocky Mountains. |
| MAYONNAISE, VEGAN | Co-winner: **Hellman's Plant Based Mayo Spread and Dressing**<br><br>Co-winner: **Follow Your Heart Original Vegenaise** | • Tangy taste and smooth, supercreamy texture<br>• Tasters liked it as much as Hellmann's Real Mayonnaise when tasted side by side |
| MEAT-FREE BURGERS | **Impossible Foods Impossible Burger** | • Flavor, texture, and appearance are remarkably similar to real ground beef<br>• Browns nicely when cooked<br>• Savory quality that tastes meaty and beefy |
| MEXICAN LAGER | **Tecate** | • Light-bodied and straw-colored<br>• Crisp and clean, with lingering bitterness<br>• Refreshing citrusy flavor |
| MISO PASTE | **Hikari Organic White** | • Intense umami flavor combined with tropical, sweet, and subtly tart flavors<br>• Full-flavored but not overwhelmingly salty |
| MOLASSES | **Brer Rabbit All Natural Unsulphured Mild Flavor** | • Acidic yet balanced<br>• Strong and straightforward raisiny taste<br>• Pleasantly bitter bite |

| ITEM | TEST KITCHEN FAVORITES | WHY WE LIKE IT |
|---|---|---|
| MUSTARD<br>Whole-Grain, Coarse-Ground | **Grey Poupon Harvest** | • Spicy, tangy burst of mustard flavor<br>• High salt content amplifies flavor |
| Whole-Grain, Whole Seeds | **Maille Old Style** | • Excellent texture with good crunch and pop<br>• Bright acidity with pleasant vinegary flavor |
| Dijon | **Three Little Pigs Moutarde de Dijon** | • Strong heat that builds naturally<br>• Tangy, bright flavor evens out the spiciness |
| Yellow | **Heinz** | • Moderate acidity<br>• Mild sweetness<br>• Smooth texture |
| OATS, ROLLED | **Bob's Red Mill Old Fashioned** | • Toasty, nutty flavor<br>• Hearty, tender |
| OATS, STEEL-CUT | **Bob's Red Mill Organic** | • Rich and complex oat flavor with buttery, earthy, nutty, and whole-grain notes<br>• Creamy yet toothsome texture<br>• Moist but not sticky<br><br>NOTE: Not recommended for baking |
| OIL, EXTRA-VIRGIN OLIVE<br>Premium Mild Oil | **Castelines Classic AOP Vallée des Baux de Provence** | • Smooth, buttery, and balanced flavor<br>• Sweet olive fruitiness with peppery aftertaste |
| Premium Medium-Intensity | **Castillo de Canena Reserva Familiar Picual** | • Bold flavor with distinctive aroma<br>• Smooth rich-bodied texture |
| Premium Robust | **McEvoy Ranch Certified Organic** | • Rich, full flavor and aroma<br>• Domestic organic blend |
| Supermarket | **Carapelli Original** | • Fresh-tasting flavor and grassy aroma<br>• Fruity with a peppery finish<br>• Narrow, curving pour spout |

| ITEM | TEST KITCHEN FAVORITES | WHY WE LIKE IT |
| --- | --- | --- |
| OIL, TOASTED SESAME | **Ottogi Premium Roasted** | • Rich, deep toasted sesame flavor<br>• Nutty, tahini-like aroma<br>• Dark-colored, nonreactive bottle protects oil quality and freshness |
| OIL, ALL-PURPOSE VEGETABLE | **Crisco Blends** | • Unobtrusive, mild flavor for stir-frying and sautéing and for use in baked goods and in uncooked applications such as mayonnaise and vinaigrette<br>• Neutral taste and absence of fishy or metallic flavors when used for frying |
| OLIVES, PIMENTO-STUFFED GREEN | **Mezzetta Super Colossal Spanish Queen** | • Meaty and juicy<br>• Bright taste when cooked<br>• Calcium chloride helps to firm flesh |
| ORANGE JUICE | **Natalie's 100% Florida, Gourmet Pasteurized** | • Squeezed within 24 hours of shipping<br>• Superfresh taste with no flavor manipulation<br>• Gentler pasteurization helps retain fresh-squeezed flavor<br>• Pleasantly variable flavor with notes of guava and mango |
| OYSTER CRACKERS | **Sunshine Krispy** | • Wheaty, toasty flavor<br>• Flaky, delicate crackers that retain their crispness in soup |
| PANCAKE MIX | **Hungry Jack Buttermilk** | • Flavorful balance of sweetness and tang, well seasoned with sugar and salt<br>• Light, extra-fluffy texture<br>• Requires vegetable oil (along with milk and egg) to reconstitute the batter |
| PAPRIKA<br>Smoked | **Simply Organic** | • Deep, rich smoky taste<br>• Balanced flavor<br>• Made in Spain according to traditional methods |
| Sweet | **The Spice House Hungarian Sweet** | • Complex flavor with earthy, fruity notes<br>• Bright and bold, not bland and boring<br>• Rich, toasty aroma<br><br>NOTE: Available only through mail order, The Spice House (312-274-0378, thespicehouse.com). |

| ITEM | TEST KITCHEN FAVORITES | WHY WE LIKE IT |
|---|---|---|
| PASTA, CHEESE RAVIOLI, SUPERMARKET | **Rosetto** | • Creamy, plush, and rich blend of ricotta, Romano, and Parmesan cheeses<br>• Pasta with nice springy bite<br>• Perfect dough-to-filling ratio |
| PASTA, CHEESE TORTELLINI, SUPERMARKET | **Barilla Three Cheese** | • Robustly flavored filling from combination of ricotta, Emmentaler, and Grana Padano cheeses<br>• Tender pasta that's sturdy enough to withstand boiling but not so thick that it becomes doughy |
| PASTA, ANGEL HAIR | **Barilla Angel Hair** | • Hearty, chewy strands but still distinctly angel hair<br>• Additional durum flour boosted gluten and made for strands with a springy texture that didn't clump or stick |
| PASTA, EGG NOODLES | **Pennsylvania Dutch Wide** (also sold as Mueller's) | • Balanced, buttery taste with no off-flavors<br>• Light and fluffy texture; not gummy or starchy |
| PASTA, ELBOW MACARONI | **Creamette** | • Distinct buttery flavor<br>• Tender yet slightly firmer texture<br>• Perfectly sized and shaped long tubes |
| PASTA, LASAGNA NOODLES | | |
| No-Boil | **Barilla** | • Taste and texture of fresh pasta<br>• Delicate, flat noodles |
| Whole-Wheat Lasagna Noodles | **Bionaturae Organic 100%** | • Complex nutty, rich wheat flavor<br>• Substantial chewy texture without any grittiness |
| PASTA, PENNE | **Mueller's Penne Rigate** | • Hearty texture; not insubstantial or gummy<br>• Wheaty, slightly sweet flavor, not bland |
| PASTA, SPAGHETTI | **De Cecco No. 12** | • Rich, nutty, wheaty flavor<br>• Firm, ropy strands with good chew; not mushy, gummy, or mealy<br>• Semolina flour for resilient texture<br>• Dried at moderately low temperature for 18 hours to preserve flavor |
| Gluten-Free | **Jovial Organic Brown Rice** | • Springy texture<br>• Clean-tasting flavor<br>• No off-flavors or gumminess |
| Whole-Wheat | **Bionaturae Organic 100%** | • Chewy, firm, and toothsome; not mushy or rubbery<br>• Full and nutty wheat flavor |

| ITEM | TEST KITCHEN FAVORITES | WHY WE LIKE IT |
|---|---|---|
| PASTA, LEGUME | **Modern Table Rotini** | • Smooth texture that holds its shape but still has some chew<br>• Contains rice flour, which gives it a neutral flavor and texture that closely resembles traditional pasta |
| PASTA, SOBA NOODLES | **Shirakiku Soba Japanese Style Buckwheat Noodles** | • Pleasing but mild buckwheat flavor<br>• Firm, bouncy texture |
| PASTA SAUCE, JARRED | **Rao's Homemade Marinara Sauce** | • Vibrant tomato flavor reminiscent of homemade sauce<br>• Bright acidity and gentle aromatic undertones of garlic and basil<br>• Uses whole tomatoes |
| PEANUT BUTTER<br>Creamy | **Skippy** | • Smooth, creamy, and spreadable<br>• Good balance of sweet and salty flavors |
| Crunchy | **Skippy Super Chunk** | • Light, smooth, creamy butter with peanut chunks evenly dispersed<br>• Toasty flavor with a hint of sweetness |
| PEPPERCORNS<br>Black, Supermarket | **Tone's Whole Black** | • Moderate, balanced heat with subtle floral and smoky notes<br>• No overpowering or off-flavors |
| Sichuan | **Savory Spice Shop** | • Strong floral aromas reminiscent of orange zest with a sweet flavor<br>• Balanced, pleasantly strong tingling sensation |
| PEPPERONI, SUPERMARKET | **Margherita Italian Style** | • Nice balance of meatiness and spice<br>• Tangy, fresh flavor with hints of fruity licorice and peppery fennel<br>• Thin slices with the right amount of chew |
| PEPPERS, ROASTED RED | **Dunbars Sweet** | • Balance of smokiness and sweetness<br>• Mild, sweet, and earthy red pepper flavor<br>• Firm texture; not slimy or mushy<br>• Packed in simple yet strong brine of salt and water without distraction of other strongly flavored ingredients |

| ITEM | TEST KITCHEN FAVORITES | WHY WE LIKE IT |
|---|---|---|
| PICKLES<br>Bread-and-Butter | **Bubbies Chips** | • Subtle, briny tang<br>• All-natural solution that uses real sugar, not high-fructose corn syrup |
| Whole Dill | **Boar's Head Kosher** | • Garlic and dill flavor with balanced tanginess<br>• Firm texture with great crunch<br>• Fresh and refrigerated, not processed and shelf-stable |
| PORK, PREMIUM | **Snake River Farms: American Kurobuta Berkshire** | • Deep pink tint, which indicates higher pH level and more flavorful meat<br>• Tender texture and juicy, intensely porky flavor |
| POTATO CHIPS<br>Kettle-Style | **Utz Kettle Classics, Original** | • Perfectly salted, flavorful chips<br>• Slightly thick chips that are crunchy<br>• Not too greasy |
| Regular | **Herr's Crisp 'N Tasty** | • Thin and crispy without being flimsy |
| PRESERVES, APRICOT | **Smucker's** | • Deep, authentic apricot taste<br>• Visible fruit suspended in spreadable jam<br>• Sweetened with sugar and syrup rather than with flavor-muting fruits |
| PRESERVES, RASPBERRY | **Smucker's** | • Clean, strong raspberry flavor, not too tart or sweet<br>• Not overly seedy<br>• Ideal, spreadable texture; not too thick, artificial, or overprocessed |
| SPREADS, STRAWBERRY | **Smucker's Strawberry Preserves** | • Robust, natural strawberry flavor<br>• No added flavoring<br>• Pleasing consistency; neither too runny nor thick |
| PROSCIUTTO, SUPERMARKET | **Volpi Traditional**<br><br>Best Buy: **Del Duca** | • Tender and buttery flavor<br>• Silky and supple texture<br>• Very thin slices |

| | ITEM | TEST KITCHEN FAVORITES | WHY WE LIKE IT |
|---|---|---|---|
| | PUFF PASTRY, STORE-BOUGHT | Co-winners: **Dufour Kitchens Classic** and **Trader Joe's All Butter Sheets** (seasonal product) | • Made with all butter for a rich buttery taste<br>• Sold frozen rather than refrigerated<br>• Easy to thaw and to work with |
| | RICE, ARBORIO | **RiceSelect** | • Creamier than competitors<br>• Smooth grains<br>• Characteristic good bite of arborio rice in risotto, where al dente is ideal |
| | RICE, BASMATI | **Daawat** | • Pleasantly chewy, long, intact, fluffy grains<br>• Fragrant, aromatic flavor<br>• Aged for 18–24 months<br>• Imported from India |
| | RICE, BROWN | **Lundberg Organic Long Grain** | • Firm yet tender grains<br>• Bold, toasty, nutty flavor |
| | RICE, JASMINE | **Dynasty** | • Floral fragrance<br>• Separate, toothsome grains |
| | RICE, LONG-GRAIN WHITE | **Lundberg Organic** | • Nutty, buttery, and toasty flavor<br>• Distinct, smooth grains that offer some chew without being overly chewy |
| | RICE, READY, WHITE | **Minute Ready to Serve** | • Parboiled long-grain white rice that is ready in less than 2 minutes<br>• Toasted, buttery flavor<br>• Firm grains with al dente bite |
| | RICE, WILD | **Reese** (also sold as Gourmet House) | • Plump grains<br>• Firm texture<br>• Faintly wheaty, nutty flavor |
| | SALSA, HOT | **Pace Hot Chunky** | • Good balance of bright tomato, chile, and vegetal flavors<br>• Chunky, almost crunchy texture; not mushy or thin<br>• Spicy and fiery but not overpowering |

| ITEM | TEST KITCHEN FAVORITES | WHY WE LIKE IT |
|---|---|---|
| SALT, KOSHER | **Diamond Crystal** | • Soft, hollow crystals are easy to crush and sprinkle by hand<br>• Grains adhere well to foods and dissolve quickly |
| SAUSAGE, BREAKFAST LINKS | **Jimmy Dean Fully Cooked Original** | • Nice and plump with crisp golden crust<br>• Good balance of sweetness and spiciness with hints of maple<br>• Tender, superjuicy meat; not rubbery, spongy, or greasy |
| SAUSAGE, KIELBASA | **Wellshire Farms Smoked Polska** | • Deeply smoked and distinctive garlicky flavor<br>• Nice coarse texture |
| SMOKED SALMON | **Spence & Co. Traditional Scottish Style** | • Subtle smoky flavor balanced with clean, fresh salmon taste<br>• Thinly sliced for easy eating<br>• Firm and flaky, even when cooked<br>• Uniformly silky and buttery thanks to manufacturer's trimming of pellicle |
| SOUP, CANNED CHICKEN NOODLE | **Progresso Traditional** | • Contained the most chicken (9% of total weight)<br>• Thick, meaty broth |
| SOUP, CANNED TOMATO | **Progresso Vegetable Classics Hearty** | • Includes fresh, unprocessed tomatoes, not just tomato puree like some competitors<br>• Tangy, slightly herbaceous flavor<br>• Balanced seasoning and natural sweetness<br>• Medium body and slightly chunky texture |
| SPIRITS, NONALCOHOLIC | Co-winners: **Wilfred's Non-Alcoholic Aperitif** and **Ritual Zero Proof Tequila Alternative** | • Slightly sweet and slightly medicinal flavor with notes of orange and clove<br>• Notes of smokiness with lime, chili, and black peppercorn |
| SRIRACHA SAUCE | **Kikkoman Sriracha Hot Chili Sauce** | • Thick enough to "zigzag" over food but can still be whisked smoothly into other sauces<br>• Pleasantly garlicky with umami, sweet, spicy flavors |
| STOCK, CHICKEN, SALTED | **Swanson** | • Rich, meaty flavor<br>• More robust and savory than unsalted version |

| ITEM | TEST KITCHEN FAVORITES | WHY WE LIKE IT |
|---|---|---|
| STOCK, CHICKEN, UNSALTED | **Swanson Unsalted** | • Subtle and clean-tasting with mellow chicken flavor<br>• High percentage of meat-based proteins |
| SWEETENED CONDENSED MILK | Co-winners: **Borden Eagle Brand** and **Nestlé Carnation** | • Made with whole milk<br>• Creamy in desserts and balances more-assertive notes with other ingredients |
| TAHINI | **Ziyad** | • Distinct, intense sesame flavor<br>• Smooth, fluid consistency made creamy, buttery hummus |
| TARTAR SAUCE | **McCormick Original** | • Rich, eggy flavor with good acidity<br>• Lots of sweet pickle bits |
| BLACK TEA, SUPERMARKET | | |
| For Plain Tea | **Twinings English Breakfast** | • Bright, bold, and flavorful yet not too strong<br>• Fruity, floral, and fragrant<br>• Smooth, slightly astringent profile preferred for tea without milk |
| For Tea with Milk and Sugar | **Tetley British Blend** | • Clean, strong taste<br>• Caramel notes and pleasant bitterness<br>• Full, deep, smoky flavors<br>• Good balance of flavor and intensity<br>• More astringent profile stands up to milk |
| TERIYAKI SAUCE | **Soy Vay Veri Veri** | • Robust flavor with moderate amounts of sugar and salt<br>• Thin consistency<br>• No thickeners or preservatives |
| TOFU, FIRM | **Nasoya Organic Firm** | • Delicate, clean soy flavor<br>• Consistent, even texture that holds its shape and offers right amount of chew when cooked |
| TOMATOES, CANNED CRUSHED | **San Merican** | • Bright and sweet, full tomato flavor<br>• Added diced tomatoes contribute a firm, tender texture |

| ITEM | TEST KITCHEN FAVORITES | WHY WE LIKE IT |
|---|---|---|
| TOMATOES, CANNED DICED | **San Merican** | • Bright, fresh tomato flavor that balances sweet and tart<br>• Firm yet tender texture |
| TOMATOES, CANNED FIRE-ROASTED | **DeLallo Diced in Juice with Seasonings** | • Intense smoky flavor<br>• Natural tomato texture |
| TOMATOES, CANNED PUREED | **Muir Glen Organic Tomato Puree** | • Full tomato flavor without any bitter, sour, or tinny notes<br>• Pleasantly thick, even consistency; not watery or thin |
| TOMATOES, CANNED WHOLE | **Cento San Marzano Certified Peeled**<br><br>Best Buy:<br>**Red Gold Whole Peeled** | • Pleasing balance of bold acidity and fruity sweetness<br>• Firm yet tender texture, even after hours of simmering |
| TORTILLA CHIPS | **Tostitos Original Restaurant Style** | • Buttery, sweet corn flavor; not bland, artificial, or rancid<br>• Sturdy yet crunchy and crisp texture; not brittle, stale, or cardboard-like |
| TORTILLAS, CORN<br>All-Corn | **Guerrero White Corn** | • Sweet corn flavor<br>• Delicate but not dry texture that makes them easy to fold<br>• Tender with some chew |
| Corn/Wheat Blend | **Maria and Ricardo's Soft Yellow Corn** | • Addition of wheat gluten adds pliability and chewiness<br>• Thicker tortilla with subtle corn flavor |
| TORTILLAS, FLOUR | **Old El Paso—for Soft Tacos and Fajitas** | • Thin, flaky tortilla with tender texture<br>• Made with plenty of fat and salt |

| ITEM | TEST KITCHEN FAVORITES | WHY WE LIKE IT |
|---|---|---|
| TOSTADAS, CORN | **Mission Tostadas Estilo Casero** | • Crisp, crunchy texture<br>• Good corn flavor<br>• Flavor and texture that are substantial enough to stand up to hearty toppings |
| TUNA, CANNED<br>Premium | **Nardin Bonito del Norte Ventresca Fillets**<br><br>Best Buy: **Tonnino Ventresca Yellowfin in Olive Oil** | • Creamy, delicate meat and tender yet firm fillets<br>• Full, rich tuna flavor |
| In Oil | Co-winners: **Tonnino Tuna Fillets** and **Ortiz Bonito del Norte Albacore White Tuna** | • Clean, bright, well-seasoned flavor<br>• Moist, silky texture<br>• Big, smooth, firm, intact flakes |
| In Water | **American Tuna Pole Caught Wild Albacore** | • Moist texture without wateriness, no need to drain<br>• Cooked only once, in the can, so it retains more of its natural moisture<br>• Well-seasoned flavor |
| TURKEY<br>Heritage | **Mary's Free-Range**<br><br>Best Buy: **Heritage Turkey Farm** | • Distinct layer of fat below the skin for moist, flavorful meat<br>• Long-legged with an angular breast and almost bluish-purple dark meat (the sign of a well-exercised bird) |
| Supermarket | **Mary's Free-Range Non-GMO Verified** | • Juicy, moist texture<br>• Rich, colorful turkey taste |
| TURMERIC | **Frontier Co-op Ground** | • Warm, moderate heat<br>• Aromatic and pleasantly earthy |

| ITEM | TEST KITCHEN FAVORITES | WHY WE LIKE IT |
|---|---|---|
| VANILLA BEANS | **McCormick Madagascar** | • Moist, seed-filled pods<br>• Complex, robust flavor with caramel notes |
| VANILLA EXTRACT<br>Pure | **Simply Organic Pure** | • Good vanilla presence<br>• Complex flavor |
| Imitation | **McCormick Premium Vanilla Flavoring** | • Caramelly with notes of cherry cola and tropical fruit<br>• High vanillin level |
| VERMOUTH, DRY | **Dolin Dry Vermouth de Chambéry**<br><br>Best Buy: **Gallo Extra Dry Vermouth** | • Versatile and crisp with notes of fresh fruit, citrus, and mint<br>• Good for cooking and for drinking plain or in cocktails |
| VINEGAR, APPLE CIDER | **Heinz Filtered** | • Good balance of sweet and tart<br>• Distinct apple flavor with a floral aroma and assertive, tangy qualities |
| VINEGAR, BALSAMIC, SUPERMARKET | **Bertolli of Modena** | • Syrupy texture when used in a vinaigrette<br>• Notes of apple, molasses, and dried fruit when served plain |

| | ITEM | TEST KITCHEN FAVORITES | WHY WE LIKE IT |
|---|---|---|---|
| | VINEGAR, RED WINE | **Laurent du Clos** | • Crisp red wine flavor balanced by stronger-than-average acidity and subtle sweetness<br>• Complex yet pleasing taste from multiple varieties of grapes |
| | VINEGAR, SHERRY | **Napa Valley Naturals Reserve** | • Slightly sweet with just the right amount of tang<br>• Boasts flavors ranging from "lemony" to "smoky" |
| | VINEGAR, WHITE WINE | **Napa Valley Naturals Organic** | • High levels of acidity and sweetness<br>• Made from a wine based on crisp-tasting Trebbiano grapes |
| | WATER, SPARKLING | **Polar Original Seltzer** | • Strong but balanced fizz<br>• Crisp, clean flavor |
| | YOGURT, ICELANDIC | **Green Mountain Creamery** | • Rich in flavor and body<br>• Thick without feeling heavy<br>• Subtle yet distinct tangy flavor |
| | YOGURT, WHOLE-MILK | **Brown Cow Cream Top Plain** | • Rich, well-rounded flavor; not sour or bland<br>• Especially creamy, smooth texture; not thin or watery<br>• Higher fat content contributes to flavor and texture |

# CONVERSIONS AND EQUIVALENTS

Some say cooking is a science and an art. We would say that geography has a hand in it, too. Flour milled in the United Kingdom and elsewhere will feel and taste different from flour milled in the United States. So, while we cannot promise that the loaf of bread you bake in Canada or England will taste the same as a loaf baked in the States, we can offer guidelines for converting weights and measures. We also recommend that you rely on your instincts when making our recipes. Refer to the visual cues provided. If the dough hasn't "come together in a ball," as described, you may need to add more flour—even if the recipe doesn't tell you so. You be the judge.

The recipes in this book were developed using standard U.S. measures following U.S. government guidelines. The charts below offer equivalents for U.S. and metric (U.K.) measures. All conversions are approximate and have been rounded up or down to the nearest whole number.

**EXAMPLES:**

1 teaspoon = 4.929 milliliters, rounded up to 5 milliliters

1 ounce = 28.349 grams, rounded down to 28 grams

**VOLUME CONVERSIONS**

| U.S. | METRIC |
|---|---|
| 1 teaspoon | 5 milliliters |
| 2 teaspoons | 10 milliliters |
| 1 tablespoon | 15 milliliters |
| 2 tablespoons | 30 milliliters |
| ¼ cup | 59 milliliters |
| ⅓ cup | 79 milliliters |
| ½ cup | 118 milliliters |
| ¾ cup | 177 milliliters |
| 1 cup | 237 milliliters |
| 1¼ cups | 296 milliliters |
| 1½ cups | 355 milliliters |
| 2 cups (1 pint) | 473 milliliters |
| 2½ cups | 591 milliliters |
| 3 cups | 710 milliliters |
| 4 cups (1 quart) | 0.946 liter |
| 1.06 quarts | 1 liter |
| 4 quarts (1 gallon) | 3.8 liters |

**WEIGHT CONVERSIONS**

| OUNCES | GRAMS |
|---|---|
| ½ | 14 |
| ¾ | 21 |
| 1 | 28 |
| 1½ | 43 |
| 2 | 57 |
| 2½ | 71 |
| 3 | 85 |
| 3½ | 99 |
| 4 | 113 |
| 4½ | 128 |
| 5 | 142 |
| 6 | 170 |
| 7 | 198 |
| 8 | 227 |
| 9 | 255 |
| 10 | 283 |
| 12 | 340 |
| 16 (1 pound) | 454 |

### CONVERSIONS FOR COMMON BAKING INGREDIENTS

Baking is an exacting science. Because measuring by weight is far more accurate than measuring by volume, and thus more likely to achieve reliable results, in our recipes we provide ounce measures in addition to cup measures for many ingredients. Refer to the chart below to convert these measures into grams.

| INGREDIENT | OUNCES | GRAMS |
|---|---|---|
| Flour | | |
| 1 cup all-purpose flour* | 5 | 142 |
| 1 cup cake flour | 4 | 113 |
| 1 cup whole-wheat flour | 5½ | 156 |
| Sugar | | |
| 1 cup granulated (white) sugar | 7 | 198 |
| 1 cup packed brown sugar (light or dark) | 7 | 198 |
| 1 cup confectioners' sugar | 4 | 113 |
| Cocoa Powder | | |
| 1 cup cocoa powder | 3 | 85 |
| Butter† | | |
| 4 tablespoons (½ stick, or ¼ cup) | 2 | 57 |
| 8 tablespoons (1 stick, or ½ cup) | 4 | 113 |
| 16 tablespoons (2 sticks, or 1 cup) | 8 | 227 |

* U.S. all-purpose flour, the most frequently used flour in this book, does not contain leaveners, as some European flours do. These leavened flours are called self-rising or self-raising. If you are using self-rising flour, take this into consideration before adding leavening to a recipe.

† In the United States, butter is sold both salted and unsalted. We generally recommend unsalted butter. If you are using salted butter, take this into consideration before adding salt to a recipe.

### OVEN TEMPERATURES

| FAHRENHEIT | CELSIUS | GAS MARK |
|---|---|---|
| 225 | 105 | ¼ |
| 250 | 120 | ½ |
| 275 | 135 | 1 |
| 300 | 150 | 2 |
| 325 | 165 | 3 |
| 350 | 180 | 4 |
| 375 | 190 | 5 |
| 400 | 200 | 6 |
| 425 | 220 | 7 |
| 450 | 230 | 8 |
| 475 | 245 | 9 |

### CONVERTING TEMPERATURES FROM AN INSTANT-READ THERMOMETER

We include doneness temperatures in many of our recipes, such as those for poultry, meat, and bread. We recommend an instant-read thermometer for the job. Refer to the table above to convert Fahrenheit degrees to Celsius. Or, for temperatures not represented in the chart, use this simple formula:

Subtract 32 degrees from the Fahrenheit reading, then divide the result by 1.8 to find the Celsius reading.

**EXAMPLE:**

"Roast chicken until thighs register 175 degrees."

**TO CONVERT:**

175°F − 32 = 143°

143° ÷ 1.8 = 79.44°C, rounded down to 79°C

# INDEX

Note: Page references in *italics* indicate photographs.

# B

# C

# D

# E

# F

# G

# H

# I



# J



# K

# L

# M

# N



# O

# P

## Q



## R

## S

# T

# W